CHILTON'S TRUCK and VAN REPAIR MANUAL 1977-1984

Pick-Ups, Vans, RV's and 4-Wheel Drives through 1 ton models

Editorial Director	Alan F. Turner
Executive Editor	Kerry A. Freeman, S.A.E.
Senior Editors	Dean F. Morgantini, S.A.E.
	Richard J. Rivele, S.A.E.
Editorial Staff	John M. Baxter
	A. Lindsay Brooke
	Carl W. Canfield
	Martin Gunther
	W. Calvin Settle, Jr.
	Ron Webb
Production Manager	John J. Cantwell
Production Coordinator	Robin S. Miller
Mechanical Artists	Margaret A. Stoner
	Sherry A. Herrlinger
OFFICERS	
President	Lawrence A. Fornasieri
Vice President & General Manager	John P. Kushnerick

 CHILTON BOOK COMPANY
Chilton Way, Radnor, PA 19089

Manufactured in USA
© by 1984 Chilton Book Company
ISBN 0-8019-7357-0 ISSN 0742-0315
Library of Congress Card No. 81-70221

2345678901   4321098765

HOW TO USE THIS MANUAL

This manual is arranged in two sections:

Truck Section

Truck sections are grouped by manufacturer (Chevrolet, Ford, etc.) and arranged in alphabetical order. The text and illustrations that comprise the service procedures in each Truck Section are arranged in the following order of systems and components: Tune-up, Engine Electrical, Engine Mechanical, Engine Lubrication, Engine Cooling, Emission Controls, Fuel System, Manual Transmission, Clutch, Automatic Transmission, Transaxle, Drive Axle, Rear Suspension, Front Suspension, Steering, Brakes, Heater, Radio, Windshield Wiper, Instrument Panel and Fuse Box.

Specification charts are always located at the front of each section. All illustrations are located as close as possible to the pertinent text. Procedures are for all models in the particular section unless specifically noted otherwise.

Unit Repair Section

The Unit Repair Section contains troubleshooting and overhaul procedures for the major components and systems of your truck. This portion of the book is intended to be used in conjunction with the Truck Sections.

For example: If your Truck's engine is misfiring and you do not know the cause, use the "Troubleshooting" portion of the Unit Repair Section to find the cause and its remedy. If the cause should prove to be defective piston rings which are allowing oil to foul the spark plugs, the remedy is to overhaul the engine. Then turn to the proper Truck Section to find the procedure for removing the engine from the Truck. After you have removed the engine, turn to the "Engine Rebuilding" chapter in the Unit Repair Section and follow the steps listed there to overhaul the engine.

Every major Unit Repair Section contains an Identification or Application chart to correlate the information contained in that section. The sections are usually arranged by brands, manufacturers or types of components rather than models of trucks.

All overhaul procedures in the Unit Repair Section begin with the component removed from the Truck. The reason for this division of material is an economic one. The steps involved in overhauling an engine are virtually the same for all engines. However, the operation of removing the engine from the truck varies greatly from model to model. By combining where possible, and separating where necessary, we are able to publish the maximum amount of information.

Locating Information

The Table of Contents, at the front of the book, lists the beginning of each Truck and Unit Repair Section in the manual.

The Index, also at the front of the book, is a comprehensive listing of all major mechanical sections and systems for every section in the book. The Index contains listings for Truck Sections as well as for corresponding Unit Repair Sections. Truck Section pages are prefixed with the letter "T". Unit Repair Sections are prefixed with the letter "U".

To find where a particular Truck Section is located in the book, you need only look in the Table of Contents. Once you have found the proper section, you may wish to find where specific procedures are located in that section. Turn to the Index and read across the top of the page until you reach the appropriate Truck Section. When the proper manufacturer's column has been found, read down the side column to the procedure or system for which you are looking. The intersection of the two columns will provide the page number(s) where the procedure is located.

Safety Notice

Proper service and repair procedures are vital to the safe, reliable operation of all motor vehicles, as well as the personal safety of those performing repairs. This manual outlines procedures for servicing and repairing vehicles using safe effective methods. The procedures contain many NOTES, CAUTIONS and WARNINGS which should be followed along with standard safety procedures to eliminate the possibility of personal injury or improper service which could damage the vehicle or compromise its safety.

It is important to note that repair procedures and techniques, tools and parts for servicing motor vehicles, as well as the skill and experience of the individual performing the work vary widely. It is not possible to anticipate all of the conceivable ways or conditions under which vehicles may be serviced, or to provide cautions as to all of the possible hazards that may result. Standard and accepted safety precautions and equipment should be used when handling toxic or flammable fluids, and safety goggles or other protection should be used during cutting, grinding, chiseling, prying, or any other process that can cause material removal or projectiles.

Some procedures require the use of tools specially designed for a specific purpose. Before substituting another tool or procedure, you must be completely satisfied that neither your personal safety, nor the performance of the vehicle will be endangered.

Part Numbers

Part numbers listed in this book are not recommendations by Chilton for any product by brand name. They are references that can be used with interchange manuals and aftermarket supplier catalogs to locate each brand supplier's discrete part number.

CONTENTS

INDEX

	Chevrolet/GMC	Datsun/Nissan	Dodge/Plymouth	Ford	International Harvester	Isuzu/LUV	Jeep	Mazda/Courier	Mitsubishi/D–50/Arrow	Toyota	Volkswagen
Alternator	U33	T99	U33	U33	U33	T386	U33	T491	T560	T621	T695
Automatic Transmission	T57	T135	T192	T294	T372	T400	T449	T532	T587	T661	T708
Axle Shaft	T64	T138	T198	T312	T375	T402	T453	T535	T589	T667	T710
Ball Joints	T69	T142	T204	T323	T376	T403	T455	T538	T597	T681	T711
Belt Tension	—	T99	T168	T238	—	T386	—	T492	T560	T622	T695
Brake Adjustment	T79	T149	U471	T335	T380	U471	T468	T542	T606	T682	T713
Brakes	U471	U471	U471	U471	U471	U471	U471	U471	U471	U471	U471
Breaker Points/Condenser	—	T93	—	—	—	T384	—	T483	—	T614	T691
Camshaft	T39	T108	T181	T262	T366	T392	T434	T508	T571	T636	T701
Carburetor	U125	T97	U125	U125	U125	T394	U125	T521	T577	T649	—
R & I and Adjustment	T18	T121	T186	T276	T369	T394	T444	T521	T577	T649	—
Overhaul	T18	T122	U125	T276	T369	T394	T444	T521	T577	T649	—
Chassis Electrical	T81	T151	T211	T335	T380	T413	T468	T544	T607	T684	T717
Clutch	T56	T133	T191	T289	T371	T398	T444	T529	T585	T657	T708
Combination Switch	—	T148	T208	T330	—	T409	T462	T539	T602	T673	T711
Cooling System	T46	T110	T184	T273	T368	T394	T438	T500	T574	T640	T702
CV–Joint	U465	U465	U465	U465	U465	U465	U465	U465	U465	U465	U465
Cylinder Head	T26	T102	T174	T251	T364	T389	T428	T502	T564	T629	T698
Diesel Injection	T48	T124	T187	T279	T359	T396	—	T526	T579	T655	T707
Diesel Service	U15	U15	U15	U15	U15	U15	U15	U15	U15	U15	U15
Differential	T68	T139	—	—	T378	—	T461	T536	—	T669	—
Distributor	T20	T97	T168	T237	T362	T386	T422	T489	T559	T620	T694
Drive Axles	U400	U400	U400	U400	U400	U400	U400	U400	U400	U400	U400
Driveshaft	T63	T137	T195	T306	T374	T401	T457	T534	T588	T665	T710
Dwell Angle	—	T94	—	—	—	T384	—	T484	—	T615	T691
Electronic Ignition	U33	T94	U33	U33	U33	T384	U33	T484	T556	T615	T692
Emission Controls	U89	U89	U89	U89	U89	U89	U89	U89	U89	U89	U89
Engine Cooling	T46	T110	T184	T273	T368	T394	T438	T500	T574	T640	T702
Engine Lubrication	T42	T109	T183	T266	—	T393	T436	T499	T572	T637	T702
Engine Mechanical	T23	T101	T172	T239	T363	T388	T424	T495	T564	T627	T697
Engine Rebuilding	U195	U195	U195	U195	U195	U195	U195	U195	U195	U195	U195
Exhaust Manifold	T34	T105	T174	T247	T365	T390	T431	T504	T566	T633	T699
Firing Order	T12	T87	T158	T221	T352	T382	T417	T475	T552	T610	T689
Front Cover	T35	T106	T178	T256	T365	T390	T432	T505	T567	T633	T700
Front End Alignment	U251	U251	U251	U251	U251	U251	U251	U251	U251	U251	U251
Front Suspension	T71	T139	T203	T318	T378	T402	T464	T536	T595	T677	T710
Fuel Filter	T48	T119	T186	T276	—	T394	—	T526	T558	T648	—
Fuel Injection	T48	T124	T187	T279	T359	T396	—	T526	T579	T648	T705
Fuel Injectors	T48	T126	—	T280	T357	—	—	T528	T579	T649	T706
Fuel Pump	T47	T120	T186	T276	T369	T394	T444	T527	T577	T647	T705
Fuel System	T47	T119	T186	T276	T369	T394	T444	T521	T576	T647	T705
Fuse Box	T84	T154	T216	T349	T380	—	T472	T547	T608	T686	—
Heater	T81	T151	T211	T335	T380	T413	T468	T544	T607	T684	T717
Idle Speed and Mixture	T18	T97	T165	T234	T355	T385	T421	T486	T557	T618	T693
Ignition Lock and Switch	T76	T148	—	T349	—	T413	T462	T547	T602	T673	T712
Ignition Timing	T18	T95	T163	T232	T354	T385	T420	T485	T557	T616	T693
Instrument Cluster	T84	T153	T216	T346	T380	T414	T470	T546	T608	T686	T718
Intake Manifold	T31	T105	T173	T244	T365	T390	T429	T504	T566	T632	T699
Lower Control Arm	T73	T142	T204	—	—	T404	T455	T537	T596	T681	—
MacPherson Strut R & I	—	—	T205	—	—	—	—	—	—	—	T711

R & I: Removal and Installation

Chevrolet/GMC	Datsun/Nissan	Dodge/Plymouth	Ford	International Harvester	Isuzu/LUV	Jeep	Mazda/Courier	Mitsubishi/D–50/Arrow	Toyota	Volkswagen	
—	—	T206	—	—	—	—	—	—	—	T711	MacPherson Strut Overhaul
U5	U5	U5	U5	U5	U5	U5	U5	U5	U5	U5	Maintenance
U215	T148	U215	U215	U215	T410	U215	T540	T602	T673	T712	Manual Steering Gear
—	—	T188	—	—	—	—	—	T580	—	T707	Manual Transaxle R & I
—	—	U267	—	—	—	—	—	U267	—	U267	Manual Transaxle Overhaul
T53	T133	T188	T282	T371	T397	T448	T528	T580	T659	T707	Manual Transmission R & I
U267	U267	U267	U267	U267	U267	U267	U267	U267	U267	U267	Manual Trans. Overhaul
T79	—	—	—	—	—	T467	T543	T606	T682	T713	Master Cylinder R & I
U471	U471	U471	U471	U471	U471	U471	U471	U471	U471	U471	Master Cylinder Overhaul
T60	T136	T192	T302	T373	—	T450	T533	T588	T665	T709	Neutral Safety Switch
T42	T109	T183	T266	T366	T393	T436	T499	T572	T637	T702	Oil Pan
T44	T110	T183	T271	T368	T393	T437	T499	T572	T638	T702	Oil Pump
T36	T106	T181	T256	T365	T390	T437	T506	T598	T634	T702	Oil Seal
T80	T151	—	—	T380	—	T468	T544	T607	T683	T717	Parking Brake
T42	T109	T182	T265	T366	T392	T435	T510	—	T636	T703	Piston and Connecting Rod
U215	—	U215	U215	U215	—	U215	T541	T604	T674	T712	Power Steering Gear
T77	—	T210	T330	T379	—	T463	T542	T603	T673	T712	Power Steering Pump
T82	T152	T213	T342	T380	T414	T470	T545	T608	T685	—	Radio
T69	T138	T202	T316	T378	—	T458	T535	T592	T672	—	Rear Axle
T44	T110	T184	T272	T367	T393	T437	T511	T572	T639	T702	Rear Main Oil Seal
T74	T147	T207	T326	T378	T408	T466	T538	T600	T682	T710	Rear Suspension
U33	T100	U33	U33	U33	T387	U33	T492	T562	T622	—	Regulator
T29	T105	T177	T249	T365	T389	T427	T503	—	T632	—	Rocker Shafts
—	T91	—	—	—	—	—	T473	T549	—	T687	Serial Numbers
T71	T140	T204	T321	T379	T402	T466	T536	T596	T680	T710	Shock Absorbers
—	—	—	—	T353	—	T420	—	T555	T614	T691	Spark Plugs
T1	T85	T155	T217	T351	T381	T415	T473	T551	T609	T688	Specifications
T71	T147	T203	T318	T374	T408	T464	T538	T595	T677	T710	Springs
U33	T100	U33	U33	U33	T387	U33	T493	T562	T625	T695	Starter
U215	T147	U215	U215	U215	T408	U215	T539	T601	T672	T711	Steering
T47	T112	T185	T275	—	T394	T438	T500	T574	T640	T703	Thermostat
T37	—	T178	T256	—	T391	—	T506	T568	T635	T700	Timing Belt
T35	T106	T178	T256	—	T390	T432	T505	T567	T633	T700	Timing Belt/Chain Cover
T37	T107	T179	T256	—	T391	T433	T506	T567	T634	—	Timing Chain/Tensioner
—	—	T188	—	—	—	—	—	T580	—	T707	Transaxle
U513	U513	U513	U513	U513	U513	U513	U513	U513	U513	U513	Troubleshooting
T17	T93	T162	T232	T353	T384	T420	T483	T555	T614	T691	Tune–Up
—	—	—	—	—	—	—	—	T566	—	—	Turbocharger R & I
—	—	—	—	—	—	—	—	T567	—	—	Turbocharger Service
—	T148	T208	T329	T379	T409	T462	T539	T602	T673	T711	Turn Signal Switch
U465	U465	U465	U465	U465	U465	U465	U465	U465	U465	U465	U–Joints
T73	T142	T204	—	—	T403	—	T537	T596	T681	—	Upper Control Arm
T28	T96	T164	T237	T355	T385	T421	T488	T557	T617	T693	Valve Adjustment
—	T91	—	—	—	—	—	T473	T549	—	T687	Vehicle Identification
T46	T112	T185	T274	T368	T394	T438	T500	T574	T640	T703	Water Pump
U251	U251	U251	U251	U251	U251	U251	U251	U251	U251	U251	Wheel Alignment
T66	T149	T204	T307	T374	T405	T454	—	T598	—	T716	Wheel Bearings (Front)
T66	T149	T204	T317	—	—	T462	—	T607	—	T717	Wheel Bearings (Rear)
—	T150	U471	U471	T379	—	T468	—	T607	T683	T716	Wheel Cylinders
T83	T152	T214	T343	T380	T414	T470	T545	T608	T686	T718	Windshield Wipers

R & I: Removal and Installation

Chevrolet/GMC

Pickups, Vans, Blazer, Jimmy, Suburban, S-Series

GENERAL ENGINE SPECIFICATIONS

Year	Engine No. Cyl Displace- ment Cu In.	Carburetor Type	Horsepower @ rpm ■	Torque @ rpm (ft lbs) ■	Bore and Stroke (in.)	Compres- sion Ratio	Oil Pressure @ 2000 rpm
'77	6-250	1 bbl	110 @ 3800	195 @ 1600	3.875 × 3.530	8.3:1	40–60
	6-250 HD	1 bbl	100 @ 3600	175 @ 1800	3.875 × 3.530	8.0:1	40–60
	6-292	1 bbl	120 @ 3600	215 @ 2000	3.870 × 4.120	8.0:1	40–60
	8-305 ⑤	2 bbl	145 @ 3800	245 @ 2200	3.740 × 3.480	8.5:1	40
	8-305 HD ⑤	2 bbl	140 @ 3800	235 @ 2000	3.740 × 3.480	8.5:1	40
	8-350	4 bbl	165 @ 3800	260 @ 2400	4.000 × 3.480	8.5:1	40
	8-400	4 bbl	175 @ 3600	290 @ 2800	4,125 × 3.750	8.5:1	40
	8-454	4 bbl	245 @ 3800	365 @ 2800	4.251 × 4.000	8.25:1	40
	8-454 HD	4 bbl	240 @ 3800①	370 @ 2800②	4.251 × 4.000	8.15:1	40
'78	6-250 LD	1 bbl	115 @ 3800	195 @ 1600	3.870 × 3.530	8.0:1	40–60
	6-250 Calif	1 bbl	100 @ 3800	185 @ 1600	3.870 × 3.530	8.1:1	40–60
	6-250 HD	1 bbl	100 @ 3600	175 @ 1800	3.870 × 3.530	8.1:1	40–60
	6-292	1 bbl	120 @ 3600	215 @ 2000	3.870 × 4.120	8.0:1	40–60
	8-305	2 bbl	145 @ 3800	245 @ 2400	3.740 × 3.480	8.4:1	45
	8-350 LD	4 bbl	165 @ 3800	260 @ 2400	4.000 × 3.480	8.2:1	45
	8-350 HD	4 bbl	165 @ 3800	255 @ 2800	4.000 × 3.480	8.3:1	45
	8-350 Diesel	FI	120 @ 3600	220 @ 1600	4.057 × 3.385	22.5:1	35
	8-400	4 bbl	175 @ 3600	290 @ 2800	4.125 × 3.750	8.3:1	40
	8-400 Calif	4 bbl	165 @ 3600	290 @ 2000	4.125 × 3.750	8.2:1	40
	8-454 LD	4 bbl	205 @ 3600	335 @ 2800	4.250 × 4.000	8.0:1	40

GENERAL ENGINE SPECIFICATIONS

Year	Engine No. Cyl Displacement Cu In.	Carburetor Type	Horsepower @ rpm ■	Torque @ rpm (ft lbs) ■	Bore and Stroke (in.)	Compression Ratio	Oil Pressure @ 2000 rpm
	8-454 HD	4 bbl	240 @ 3800	370 @ 2800	4.250 × 4.000	7.9:1	40
	8-454 HD Calif	4 bbl	250 @ 3800	385 @ 2800	4.250 × 4.000	7.9:1	40
'79	6-250 LD	2 bbl	130 @ 3800	210 @ 2400	3.870 × 3.530	8.3:1	40–60
	6-250 Calif	2 bbl	125 @ 4000	205 @ 2000	3.870 × 3.530	8.3:1	40–60
	6-250 HD	2 bbl	130 @ 4000	205 @ 2000	3.870 × 3.530	8.3:1	40–60
	6-292	1 bbl	115 @ 3400	215 @ 1600	3.870 × 4.120	7.8:1	40–60
	8-305	2 bbl	140 @ 4000	240 @ 2000	3.740 × 3.480	8.4:1	45
	8-350 LD	4 bbl	165 @ 3600	270 @ 2000	4.000 × 3.480	8.2:1	45
	8-350 Hi Alt	4 bbl	155 @ 3600	260 @ 2000	4.000 × 3.480	8.2:1	45
	8-350 HD	4 bbl	165 @ 3800	255 @ 2800	4.000 × 3.480	8.3:1	45
	8-350	Diesel	120 @ 3600	220 @ 1600	4.057 × 3.385	22.5:1	35
	8-400 HD	4 bbl	180 @ 3600	310 @ 2400	4.125 × 3.750	8.2:1	40
	8-454 LD	4 bbl	205 @ 3600	335 @ 2800	4.250 × 4.000	8.0:1	40
	8-454 HD	4 bbl	210 @ 3800	340 @ 2800	4.250 × 4.000	7.9:1	40
'80	6-250	2 bbl	130 @ 4000	210 @ 2000	3.870 × 3.530	8.3:1	40–60
	6-250 Calif	2 bbl	130 @ 4000	205 @ 2000	3.870 × 3.530	8.3:1	40–60
	6-292	1 bbl	115 @ 3400	215 @ 1600	3.870 × 4.120	7.8:1	40–60
	8-305	2 bbl	135 @ 4200	235 @ 2400	3.740 × 3.480	8.5:1	45
	8-350 LD	4 bbl	175 @ 4000	275 @ 2400	4.000 × 3.480	8.2:1	45
	8-350 LD Calif	4 bbl	170 @ 4000	275 @ 2000	4.000 × 3.480	8.2:1	45
	8-350 HD	4 bbl	165 @ 3800	255 @ 2800	4.000 × 3.480	8.3:1	45
	8-350	Diesel	125 @ 3600	225 @ 1600	4.057 × 3.385	22.5:1	35
	8-400 HD	4 bbl	180 @ 3600	310 @ 2400	4.125 × 3.750	8.3:1	40
	8-454 HD	4 bbl	210 @ 3800	340 @ 2800	4.250 × 4.000	7.9:1	40
'81	6-250	2 bbl	130 @ 4000	210 @ 2000	3.870 × 3.530	8.3:1	40–60
	6-250 Calif	2 bbl	130 @ 4000	205 @ 2000	3.870 × 3.530	8.3:1	40–60
	6-292	1 bbl	115 @ 3400	215 @ 1600	3.870 × 4.120	7.8:1	40–60
	8-305	2 bbl	135 @ 4200	235 @ 2400	3.740 × 3.480	8.5:1	45
	8-305	4 bbl	155 @ 4400	252 @ 2400	3.740 × 3.480	9.2:1	45
	8-350 LD	4 bbl	175 @ 4000	275 @ 2000	4.000 × 3.480	8.2:1	45
	8-350 HD	4 bbl	165 @ 3800	255 @ 2800	4.000 × 3.480	8.3:1	45
	8-350	Diesel	125 @ 3600	225 @ 1600	4.057 × 3.385	22.5:1	35
	8-454	4 bbl	210 @ 3800	340 @ 2800	4.250 × 4.000	7.9:1	40
'82	4-119	2 bbl	84 @ 4600	101 @ 3000	3.43 × 3.23	8.4:1	57
	4-121	2 bbl	83 @ 4600	108 @ 2400	3.50 × 3.15	9.3:1	45
	4-137	Diesel	58 @ 4300	93 @ 2200	3.46 × 3.62	21.0:1	55

GENERAL ENGINE SPECIFICATIONS

Year	Engine No. Cyl Displacement Cu In.	Carburetor Type	Horsepower @ rpm ■	Torque @ rpm (ft lbs) ■	Bore and Stroke (in.)	Compression Ratio	Oil Pressure @ 2000 rpm
	6-173	2 bbl	110 @ 4800	148 @ 2000	3.50 × 2.99	8.5:1	45
	6-250	2 bbl	130 @ 4000	210 @ 2000	3.870 × 3.530	8.3:1	40–60
	6-292	1 bbl	115 @ 3400	215 @ 1600	3.870 × 4.120	7.8:1	40–60
	8-305	4 bbl	140 @ 4200	240 @ 2400	3.740 × 3.480	8.5:1	45
	8-305	4 bbl	155 @ 4400	252 @ 2100	3.740 × 3.480	9.2:1	45
	8-350 LD	4 bbl	175 @ 4000	275 @ 2000	4.000 × 3.480	8.2:1	45
	8-350 HD	4 bbl	165 @ 3800	255 @ 2800	4.000 × 3.480	8.3:1	45
	8-379	Diesel	130 @ 3600	240 @ 2000	3.980 × 3.800	21.5:1	45
	8-454	4 bbl	210 @ 3800	340 @ 2800	4.250 × 4.000	7.9:1	40
'83	4-119	2 bbl	84 @ 4600	101 @ 3000	3.43 × 3.23	8.4:1	57
	4-121	2 bbl	83 @ 4600	108 @ 2400	3.50 × 3.15	9.3:1	45
	4-137	Diesel	58 @ 4300	93 @ 2200	3.46 × 3.62	21.0:1	55
	6-173	2 bbl	110 @ 4800	148 @ 2000	3.50 × 2.99	8.5:1	45
	6-250	2 bbl	130 @ 4000	210 @ 2000	3.870 × 3.530	8.3:1	40–60
	6-292	1 bbl	115 @ 3400	215 @ 1600	3.870 × 4.120	7.8:1	40–60
	8-305	4 bbl	140 @ 4200	240 @ 2400	3.740 × 3.480	8.5:1	45
	8-305	4 bbl	155 @ 4400	252 @ 2100	3.740 × 3.480	9.2:1	45
	8-350 LD	4 bbl	175 @ 4000	275 @ 2000	4.000 × 3.480	8.2:1	45
	8-350 HD	4 bbl	165 @ 3800	255 @ 2800	4.000 × 3.480	8.3:1	45
	8-379	Diesel	130 @ 3600	240 @ 2000	3.980 × 3.800	21.5:1	45
	8-454 HD	4 bbl	210 @ 3800	340 @ 2800	4.250 × 4.000	7.9:1	40
'84	4-119	2 bbl	84 @ 4600	101 @ 3000	3.43 × 3.23	8.4:1	57
	4-121	2 bbl	83 @ 4600	108 @ 2400	3.50 × 3.15	9.3:1	45
	4-137	Diesel	58 @ 4300	93 @ 2200	3.46 × 3.62	21.0:1	55
	6-173	2 bbl	110 @ 4800	148 @ 2000	3.50 × 2.99	8.5:1	45
	6-250	2 bbl	130 @ 4000	210 @ 2000	3.870 × 3.530	8.3:1	40–60
	6-292	1 bbl	115 @ 3400	215 @ 1600	3.870 × 4.120	7.8:1	40–60
	8-305	4 bbl	140 @ 4200	240 @ 2400	3.740 × 3.480	8.5:1	45
	8-305	4 bbl	155 @ 4400	252 @ 2100	3.740 × 3.480	9.2:1	45
	8-350 LD	4 bbl	175 @ 4000	275 @ 2000	4.000 × 3.480	8.2:1	45
	8-350 HD	4 bbl	165 @ 3800	255 @ 2800	4.000 × 3.480	8.3:1	45
	8-379	Diesel	130 @ 3600	240 @ 2000	3.980 × 3.800	21.5:1	45
	8-454 HD	4 bbl	210 @ 3800	340 @ 2800	4.250 × 4.000	7.9:1	40

■Horsepower and torque are SAE net figures. They are measured at the rear of the transmission with all accessories installed and operating. Since the figures vary when a given engine is installed in different models, some are representative rather than exact.

① 250 @ 3800—Calif.
② 385 @ 2800—Calif.
FI—Fuel Injection

CAPACITIES
Blazer and Jimmy

Year	Engine No. Cyl. Displacement (cu in.)	Engine Crank-case (qts) incl. Filter	Transmission Pts To Refill After Draining			Transfer Case (Pts)	Drive Axle (pts) Front/ Rear	Gasoline Tank (gals) Std/ Opt	Cooling System■ (qts)		
			Manual						With Heater	A/C	With HD Cooling
			3-Speed	4-Speed	Automatic						
'77	6-250	5	3.5	8.3	5	5④	5/3½	25/31	14.8	15.6	14.8
	8-305	5	3.5	8.3	5	5④	5/3½	25/31	17.6	18	18
	8-350	5	3.5	8.3	5	5④	5/3½	25/31	17.6	18	18
	8-400	5	—	—	5	5④	5/3½	25/31	19.6	20.4	20.4
'78	6-250	5	3	8	5	5④	5/3.5⑤	25/31	15	15.6	15.6
	8-305	5	3	8	5	5④	5/3.5⑤	25/31	17.5	18	18.4
	8-350	5	3.0	8.0	5.0	5.0④	5/3.5⑤	25/31	17.6	17.6	17.6
	8-400	5	—	—	5.0	5.0④	5/3.5⑤	25/31	19.7	20.4	20.4
'79	6-250	5	3.0	8.0	5.0	5.0④	5/3.5⑤	25/31	15	15.5	15.5
	8-305	5	3.0	8.0	5.0	5.0④	5/3.5⑤	25/31	17.5	17.5	17.5
	8-350	5	3.0	8.0	5.0	5.0④	5/3.5⑤	25/31	17.5	18	18
	8-400	5	—	—	5.0	5.0④	5/3.5⑤	25/31	18	19	19
'80–'81	6-250	5	3.0	8.0	5.0	5.0	5/3.5⑤	25/31	15	15.5	15.5
	8-305	5	3.0	8.0	5.0	5.0	5/3.5⑤	25/31	17.5	17.5	17.5
	8-350	5	3.0	8.0	5.0	5.0	5/3.5⑤	25/31	17.5	18	18
'82	6-250	5	2.0	8.0	6.0	5.0	5/⑦	25/31	15.0	15.5	—
	8-305	5	2.0	8.0	6.0	5.0	5/⑦	25/31	17.5	18.0	—
	8-350	5	2.0	8.0	6.0⑥	5.0	5/⑦	25/31	17.5	18.0	—
	8-379	7	—	8.0	6.0⑥	5.0	5/⑦	27/32	24.8	24.8	—
'83	6-250	5	3.0	8.0	6.0	5.0	5/⑦	25/31	15.0	15.5	—
	8-305	5	3.0	8.0	6.0	5.0	5/⑦	25/31	17.5	18.0	—
	8-350	5	3.0	8.0	6.0⑥	5.0	5/⑦	25/31	17.5	18.0	—
	8-379	7	—	8.0	6.0⑥	5.0	5/⑦	27/32	24.5	24.5	—
	8-454	7③	—	8.0	6.0⑥	5.0	5/⑦	25/31	23	24.5	—
'84	6-250	5	3.0	8.0	6.0	5.0	5/⑦	25/31	15.0	15.5	—
	8-305	5	3.0	8.0	6.0	5.0	5/⑦	25/31	17.5	18.0	—
	8-350	5	3.0	8.0	6.0⑥	5.0	5/⑦	25/31	17.5	18.0	—
	8-379	7	—	8.0	6.0⑥	5.0	5/⑦	27/32	24.5	24.5	—
	8-454	7③	—	8.0	6.0⑥	5.0	5/⑦	25/31	23	24.5	—

■ Automatic transmission models have either the A/C or HD radiator; capacity may be increased on trucks with 4.11:1 axle ratios; when two figures are separated by a slash, the first is for 2 wheel drive
① Not used
② Not used
③ K-30 Models 5 qts
④ 8¼ with full-time 4 wheel drive
⑤ 8.5 ring gear—4.2
⑥ with TH-M 400: 7.0
   with TH-M 700-R4: 10.0

⑦ 8½" ring gear: 4.25
   8⅞" ring gear: 3.5
   9¾" ring gear (Dana): 6.0
   10½" ring gear (Dana): 7.2
   (Chev.): 6.5

CAPACITIES
Pick-Ups and Suburban

Year	Engine Displacement (cu. in.)	Engine Crankcase (qts) With Filter	Transmission (pts) Manual 3-spd	Manual 4-spd	Auto (Refill)	Drive Axle (pts) Front	Rear	Transfer Case (pts)	Fuel Tank (gals)	Cooling System (qts) w/o A/C	w/A/C	HD
'77–'81	6-250	5	3.2⑦	8.0	②	5⑧	⑥	5⑤	20⑩	15.0	15.6	15.0
	6-292	6	3.2⑦	8.0	②	5⑧	⑥	5⑤	20⑩	14.8	15.4	14.8
	8-305	5	3.2⑦	8.0	②	5⑧	⑥	5⑤	20⑩	17.6	18.0	18.0
	8-350	5	3.2⑦	8.0	②	5⑧	⑥	5⑤	20⑩	17.6	18.0	18.0
	8-350 Diesel	7	—	—	5.0	—	⑥	—	20⑩	18.0	18.0	18.0
	8-400	5	3.2⑦	8.0	②	5⑧	⑥	5⑤	20⑩	20.4	20.4	20.4
	8-454	5⑪	3.2⑦	8.0	②	5⑧	⑥	5⑤	20⑩	24.4⑨	24.7	24.7
'82	6-250	5	3.0	8.0	6.0	5.0	⑯	5.0⑬	⑭	15.0	15.5	—
	6-292	6	3.0	8.0	6.0	5.0	⑯	5.0⑬	⑭	15.0	15.5	—
	8-305	5	3.0	8.0	6.0	5.0	⑯	5.0⑬	⑭	17.5	18.0	—
	8-350	5	3.0	8.0	⑮	5.0	⑯	5.0⑬	⑭	17.5	18.0	—
'83	6-250	5	3.0	8.0	6.0	5.0	⑯	10①	⑭	15	15.5	—
	8-305	5	3.0	8.0	6.0	5.0	⑯	10①	⑭	17.5	18	—
	8-350	5	3.0	8.0	6.0⑥	5.0	⑯	10①	⑭	17.5	18	—
	8-379	7	—	8.0	6.0⑥	5.0	⑯	10①	⑭	23	24.5	—
	8-454	5	—	8.0	6.0⑥	5.0	⑯	10①	⑭	23	24.5	—
'84	6-250	5	3.0	8.0	6.0	5.0	⑯	10①	⑭	15	15.5	
	8-305	5	3.0	8.0	6.0	5.0	⑯	10①	⑭	17.5	18	
	8-350	5	3.0	8.0	6.0⑥	5.0	⑯	10①	⑭	17.5	18	
	8-379	7	—	8.0	6.0⑥	5.0	⑯	10①	⑭	23	24.5	
	8-454	5	—	8.0	6.0⑥	5.0	⑯	10①	⑭	23	24.5	

① Heavy-duty 3-speed—3.5 pts
② Turbo Hydra-Matic 350—5.0 pts
Turbo Hydra-Matic 400—7.5 pts
③ 3,300 and 3,500 lb Chevrolet axles—4.5 pts
5,200 and 7,200 lb Chevrolet axles—6.5 pts
5,500 lb Dana axles—6.0 pts
11,000 lb Chevrolet axles—14.0 pts
④ 20 Series—21.0 gals
⑤ Full-time 4 wd—8.25 pts
⑥ 8½ in. ring gear—4.2 pts
8⅞ in. ring gear (Chevrolet)—4.5 pts (3.5 pts '77–'78)
10½ in. ring gear (Chevrolet)—5.4 pts
10½ in. ring gear (Dana)—7.2 pts
12½ in. ring gear (Chevrolet)—26.8 pts
⑦ Tremec 3-spd—4.0 pts
Muncie 3-spd—3.0 pts
⑧ 8½ in. ring gear—4.25 pts ('77–'81)
⑨ 22.8—'79–'81
⑩ 16.0 gal—short wheelbase models
⑪ 6 qts with filter, 5 qts without filter, '78–'81
⑫ OPT.: 20 gal
⑬ All 1-ton models: 10.0

⑭ Short bed w/single tank: 16 gal.
Short bed w/dual tanks: 32 gal.
Longbed w/single tank: 20 gal.
Long bed gasoline models w/dual tanks, under 8600 lb GVWR: 32 gal
Long bed gasoline models with dual tanks over 8600 lb GVWR, and all diesel models w/dual tanks: 40 gal.
⑮ TH-M 350: 6.0
TH-M 400: 7.0
TH-M 700-R4:10.0
⑯ Ring gear   Capacity

Ring gear	Capacity
8½"	4.25
8⅞"	3.5
9¾" (Dana)	6.0
10½" (Dana)	7.2
10½" (Chev)	6.5
12¼" (Dana)	26.8

CAPACITIES
S10, 15 Pickup, Blazer and Jimmy

Year	Engine Displacement cu. in.	Crankcase (qts.)	Transmission (pts)			Transfer Case (pts)	Rear Drive Axle (pts)	Front Drive Axle (pts)	Gas Tank (gal)	Cooling System (qts)	
			4 sp	5 sp	Auto					Manual	Auto
'82	4-119	4.0	2.7	2.7	7.0②	5.2	3.5	1.7	13.0①	9.6	9.6
	4-121	4.0	2.7	2.7	7.0②	5.2	3.5	1.7	13.0①	9.6	9.6
	4-137 Diesel	5.0	2.7	2.7	7.0②	5.2	3.5	1.7	13.0①	10.0	10.0
	6-173	4.5③	2.7	2.7	7.0②	5.2	3.5	1.7	13.0①	12.4	12.4
'83	4-119	4	2.7	2.7	7	10	3.5	3	13①	9.4	9.5
	4-121	4	2.7	2.7	7	10	3.5	3	13①	9.6	9.7
	4-137 Diesel	4	2.7	2.7	7	10	3.5	3	13①	10	10
	6-173	4.5③	2.7	2.7	7	10	3.5	3	13①	12	12
'84	4-119	4	2.7	2.7	7	10	3.5	3	13①	9.4	9.5
	4-121	4	2.7	2.7	7	10	3.5	3	13①	9.6	9.7
	4-137 Diesel	4	2.7	2.7	7	10	3.5	3	13①	10	10
	6-173	4.5③	2.7	2.7	7	10	3.5	3	13①	12	12

① Optional: 20.0 gal.
② Figure shown is for pan removal only. Total overhaul capacity is 19.0 pts.
③ 4 qts. without filter.

CAPACITIES
Vans

Year	Model	Engine Displacement (cu in.)	Engine Crankcase (qts) With Filter	Transmission (pts)			Drive Axle (pts)	Gasoline Tank (gals)	Cooling System (qts)	
				Manual		Automatic			wo/AC	w/AC
				3-spd	4-spd					
'77–'78	All	6-250	5	3.2	—	5	3.5	22/33	15	16.5
	20, 2500	6-292	6	3.2	—	5	3.5	22/33	14.8	15.7
	30, 3500	6-292	6	3.2	—	5	5.4	22/33	14.8	15.7
	All	8-305	5	3.2	—	5	3.5	22/33	18	19.5
	10, 20, 1500, 2500	8-350	5	4.6①	—	5	3.5	22/33	18	19.5
	30, 3500	8-350	5	4.6①	—	5②	5.4	22/33	18	19.5
	20, 2500	8-400	5	—	—	5	3.5	22/33	19.9	21.0
	30, 3500	8-400	5	—	—	5②	5.4	22/33	19.9	21.0
'79–'82	All	6-250	5	3.2	—	5③	3.5④	22/33	17	18.5
	All	8-305	5	3.2①	—	5③	3.5④	22/33	19.5	21.0
	10, 20, 1500, 2500	8-350	5	3.2①	—	5③	3.5④	22/33	20	21.5
	30, 3500	8-350	5	3.2①	—	5③	3.5④	22/33	20	21.5
	All	8-400	5	3.2①	—	5③	3.5④	22/33	20	21.5
'83	All	6-250	5	3	8	③	④	22/33	17	—
	All	8-305	5	3	8	③	④	22/33	19	20
	All	8-350	5	3	8	③	④	22/33	19	20
	All	8-379	7	3	8	③	④	22/33	24	24

CAPACITIES
Vans

Year	Model	Engine Displacement (cu in.)	Engine Crankcase (qts) With Filter	Transmission (pts) Manual 3-spd	4-spd	Automatic	Drive Axle (pts)	Gasoline Tank (gals)	Cooling System (qts) wo/AC	w/AC
'84	All	6-250	5	3	8	③	④	22/33	17	—
	All	8-305	5	3	8	③	④	22/33	19	20
	All	8-350	5	3	8	③	④	22/33	19	20
	All	8-379	7	3	8	③	④	22/33	24	24

① 4 pts with top-cover Tremec three-speed and Saginaw three-speed
② 7 pts with 10,000 lb or higher GVW.

③ '82 TH-M 350: 6.0
TH-M 400: 7.0
TH-M 700-R4: 10.0

④ 9¾" ring gear: 6.0
10½" ring gear (Dana): 7.2
10½" ring gear (Chev): 6.5
12½" ring gear (Dana): 26.8

TUNE-UP SPECIFICATIONS
Pick-ups and Suburban

Year	Engine Displacement (cu in.)	Spark Plugs Type	Gap (in.)	Distributor	Ignition Timing (deg) MT	AT	Fuel Pump Pressure (psi)	Compression Pressure (psi) ●	Idle Speed (rpm)* MT	AT
'77	6-250	R46TS	0.035	Electronic	8B	12B	3.5–4.5	130	750	550
	6-250 (High Alt)	R46TS	0.035	Electronic	8B	12B	3.5–4.5	130	750	600
	6-250 (Calif)	R46TS	0.035	Electronic	6B	10B	3.5–4.5	130	850	600
	6-250 (HD)	R46T	0.035	Electronic	6B	6B	3.5–4.5	130	600	600(N)
	6-292	R44T	0.035	Electronic	8B	8B	3.5–4.5	130	600	600(N)
	8-305	R45TS	0.045	Electronic	8B	8B	7–8.5	150	600	500
	8-305 (HD)	R44T	0.045	Electronic	6B	6B	7–8.5	150	700	700(N)
	8-350	R45TS	0.045	Electronic	8B	8B	7–8.5	150	700	500
	8-350 (High Alt)	R45TS	0.045	Electronic	—	6B	7–8.5	150	—	600
	8-350 (Calif)	R45TS	0.045	Electronic	6B	6B	7–8.5	150	700	500
	8-350 (HD)	R44T	0.045	Electronic	8B	8B	7–8.5	150	700	700(N)
	8-350 (HD Calif)	R44TX	0.060	Electronic	2B	2B	7–8.5	150	700	700(N)
	8-400 (HD)	R44T	0.045	Electronic	—	4B	7–8.5	150	—	700(N)
	8-400 (HD Calif)	R44T	0.045	Electronic	—	2B	7–8.5	150	—	700(N)
	8-454	R45TS	0.045	Electronic	—	4B	7–8.5	150	—	600
	8-454 (HD)	R44T	0.045	Electronic	8B	8B	7–8.5	150	700	700(N)
'78	6-250 (LD Fed)	R46TS	0.035	Electronic	8B	8B	4.5–6.0	130	750	550
	6-250 (LD Calif)	R46TS	0.035	Electronic	8B	8B	4.5–6.0	130	750	750
	6-250 (LD High Alt)	R46TS	0.035	Electronic	8B	12B	4.5–6.0	130	750	600
	6-250 (HD)	R46T	0.035	Electronic	6B	6B	4.5–6.0	130	600	600(N)
	6-292 (HD)	R44T	0.035	Electronic	8B	8B	4.5–6.0	130	600	600(N)
	8-305 (LD)	R45TS	0.045	Electronic	4B	4B	7.5–9.0	150	600	500
	8-305 (HD)	R44T	0.045	Electronic	6B	6B	7.5–9.0	150	700	700(N)
	8-350 (LD)	R45TS	0.045	Electronic	8B	8B	7.5–9.0	150	600①	500

TUNE-UP SPECIFICATIONS
Pick-ups and Suburban

Year	Engine Displacement (cu in.)	Spark Plugs Type	Gap (in.)	Distributor	Ignition Timing (deg) MT	AT	Fuel Pump Pressure (psi)	Compression Pressure (psi) ●	Idle Speed (rpm)* MT	AT
	8-350 (HD Fed)	R44T	0.045	Electronic	8B	8B	7.5–9.0	150	700	700(N)
	8-350 (HD Calif)	R44TX	0.060	Electronic	2B	2B	7.5–9.0	150	700	700(N)
	8-400 (LD)	R45TS	0.045	Electronic	—	4B	7.5–9.0	150	—	500
	8-400 (HD Fed)	R44T	0.045	Electronic	—	4B	7.5–9.0	150	—	700(N)
	8-400 (HD Calif)	R44T	0.045	Electronic	—	2B	7.5–9.0	150	—	700(N)
	8-454 (LD Fed)	R45TS	0.045	Electronic	—	8B	7.5–9.0②	150	—	550
	8-454 (LD Calif)	R45TS	0.045	Electronic	—	8B	7.5–9.0②	150	—	700(N)
	8-454 (HD)	R44T	0.045	Electronic	8B	8B	7.5–9.0②	150	700	700(N)
'79	6-250 (LD Fed)	R46TS	0.035	Electronic	10B	10B	4.5–6.0	130	750	600
	6-250③	R46TS	0.035	Electronic	6B	8B	4.5–6.0	130	750	600
	6-292	R44T	0.035	Electronic	8B	8B	4.5–6.0	130	700	700
	8-305	R45TS	0.045	Electronic	6B	6B	7.5–9.0	150	600	500
	8-350 (LD)	R45TS	0.045	Electronic	8B	8B	7.5–9.0	150	700	500
	8-350 (HD)	R44T	0.045	Electronic	4B	4B	7.5–9.0	150	700	700(N)
	8-400	R45TS	0.045	Electronic	—	4B	7.5–9.0	150	—	500
	8-454 (LD)	R45TS	0.045	Electronic	8B	8B	7.5–9.0②	150	700	500
	8-454 (HD)	R44T	0.045	Electronic	—	4B	7.5–9.0②	150	—	700(N)
'80	6-250 (LD Fed)	R46TS	0.035	Electronic	10B	10B	4.5–6.0	130	750	650
	6-250 (LD Calif)	R46TS	0.035	Electronic	10B	10B	4.5–6.0	130	750	600
	6-250③	R46TS	0.035	Electronic	—	8B	4.5–6.0	130	—	600
	6-292	R44T	0.035	Electronic	8B	8B	4.5–6.0	130	700	700(N)
	8-305	R45TS	0.045	Electronic	8B	8B	7.5–9.0	150	600	500
	8-350 (LD)	R45TS	0.045	Electronic	8B	8B	7.5–9.0	150	700	500
	8-350 (HD Fed)	R44T	0.045	Electronic	4B	4B	7.5–9.0	150	700	700(N)
	8-350 (HD Calif)	R44T	0.045	Electronic	6B	6B	7.5–9.0	150	700	700(N)
	8-400 (HD Fed)	R44T	0.045	Electronic	—	4B	7.5–9.0	150	—	700(N)
	8-400 (HD Calif)	R44T	0.045	Electronic	—	6B	7.5–9.0	150	—	700(N)
	8-454	R44T	0.045	Electronic	4B	4B	7.5–9.0②	150	700	700(N)
'81	6-250 (Fed)	R45TS	0.035	Electronic	10B	10B	4.5–6.0	130	750	650(D)
	6-250 (Calif)	R46TS	0.035	Electronic	10B	10B	4.5–6.0	130	750	650(D)
	6-292	R44T	0.035	Electronic	8B	8B	4.5–6.0	130	700	700(N)
	8-305 2 bbl	R45TS	0.045	Electronic	8B	8B	7.5–9.0	150	600	500(D)
	8-305 4 bbl	R45TS	0.045	Electronic	4B	4B④	7.5–9.0	150	700	500(D)
	8-350 (LD)	R45TS	0.045	Electronic	8B	8B⑤	7.5–9.0	150	700	500(D)
	8-350 (HD Fed)	R44T	0.045	Electronic	4B	4B	7.5–9.0	150	700	700(N)
	8-350 (HD Calif)	R44T	0.045	Electronic	6B	6B	7.5–9.0	150	700	700(N)
	8-350 Diesel	—	—	Electronic	—	8B⑥		450	—	575(D)⑦
	8-454	R44T	0.045	Electronic	4B	4B	7.5–9.0	150	700	700(N)
'82	6-250	R45TS	⑧	Electronic	⑧		4.5–6	—	⑧	⑧
	6-292	R44T	.035	Electronic	8	8	4–5	—	700	700

TUNE-UP SPECIFICATIONS
Pick-ups and Suburban

Year	Engine Displacement (cu in.)	Spark Plugs Type	Gap (in.)	Distributor	Ignition Timing (deg) MT	AT	Fuel Pump Pressure (psi)	Compression Pressure (psi) ●	Idle Speed (rpm)* MT	AT
	8-305	R45TS	.045	Electronic	⑧		⑧	—	⑧	⑧
	8-350 LD	R45TS	.045	Electronic	⑧		⑧	—	⑧	⑧
	8-350 HD	R44T	.045	Electronic	⑧		⑧	—	⑧	⑧
	8-379	Diesel	—	—	⑧		⑧		⑧	⑧
	8-454	R44T	.045	Electronic	⑧		⑧		⑧	⑧
'83	6-250	R45TS	⑧	Electronic	⑧		4.5–6		⑧	⑧
	6-292	R44T	.035	Electronic	8	8	4–6		700	700
	8-305	R45TS	.045	Electronic	⑧	⑧	⑧		⑧	⑧
	8-350 LD	R45TS	.045	Electronic	⑧	⑧	⑧		⑧	⑧
	8-350 HD	R44T	.045	Electronic	⑧	⑧	⑧		⑧	⑧
	8-379	Diesel	—	—	⑧	⑧	⑧		⑧	⑧
	8-454	R44T	.045	Electronic	⑧	⑧	⑧		⑧	⑧
'84	6-250	R45TS	⑧	Electronic	⑧	⑧	4.5–6		⑧	⑧
	6-292	R44T	.035	Electronic	8	8	4.5–6		700	700
	8-305	R45TS	.045	Electronic	⑧	⑧	⑧		⑧	⑧
	8-350 LD	R45TS	.045	Electronic	⑧	⑧	⑧		⑧	⑧
	8-350 HD	R44T	.045	Electronic	⑧	⑧	⑧		⑧	⑧
	8-379	Diesel	—	—	⑧	⑧	⑧		⑧	⑧
	8-454	R44T	.045	Electronic	⑧	⑧	⑧		⑧	⑧

NOTE: All engines use hydraulic valve lifters
NOTE: Part numbers in this chart are not recommendations by Chilton for any product by brand name.
NOTE: The underhood sticker often reflects tune-up changes made in production. Sticker figures must be used if they disagree with those in this chart.
● Maximum variation among cylinders—20 psi

B Before Top Dead Center
LD Light-duty
HD Heavy-duty
Fed Federal (49 states)
Calif California only
MT Manual transmission
AT Automatic transmission
N Neutral

* Automatic transmission idle speed set in Drive unless otherwise indicated
NA Not available
— Not applicable
Hyd Hydraulic
① 700 rpm—California
② 5.5–7.0 with vapor return line
③ California C-20, C-2500 only

④ Calif.: 8B
  High Alt.: 2B
  Emission Label Code AAN: 6B
⑤ Calif.: 6B
  Calif. w/Emission Label Code AAD: 8B
⑥ Calif.: 5B
⑦ Calif.: 600(D)
⑧ See underhood sticker

TUNE-UP SPECIFICATIONS
Vans

When analyzing compression results, look for uniformity among cylinders rather than specific pressures.

Year	Engine Cu In. Displacement	Spark Plugs Orig Type	Gap (in.)	Distributor	Ignition Timing● (deg)▲ MT	AT	Fuel Pump Pressure (psi)	Curb Idle Speed (rpm)● MT	AT
'77	6-250	R46TS	.035	Electronic	8B(6B)	12B (10B)	3.5–4.5	750(850)②	600②
	6-292	R44T	.035	Electronic	8B	8B	3.5–4.5	600	600 N
	8-305	R45TS	.045	Electronic	8B	8B	7–8.5	600	500

TUNE-UP SPECIFICATIONS
Vans

When analyzing compression results, look for uniformity among cylinders rather than specific pressures.

Year	Engine Cu In. Displacement	Spark Plugs Orig Type	Gap (in.)	Distributor	Ignition Timing● (deg)▲ MT	AT	Fuel Pump Pressure (psi)	Curb Idle Speed (rpm)● MT	AT
	8-350 LD	R45TS	.045	Electronic	8B(6B)	8B(6B)	7–8.5	700	500
	8-350 HD	R44T (R44TX)	.045 (.060)	Electronic	8B(2B)	8B(2B)	7–8.5	700	700N
	8-400	R44T	.045	Electronic	—	4B(2B)	7–8.5	—	700N
'78	6-250	R46TS	.035	Electronic	8B	8B (10B) ④	4.5–6	750	600③
	6-292	R44T	.035	Electronic	8B	8B	4.5–6	600	600
	8-305	R45TS	.045	Electronic	4B	4B	7.5–9	600	500
	8-350 LD	R45TS	.045	Electronic	8B	8B	7.5–9	600(700)	500
	8-350 HD	R44T (R44TX)	.045 (.060)	Electronic	8B(2B)	8B(2B)	7.5–9	700	700
	8-400 LD⑤	R45TS	.045	Electronic	—	4B	7.5–9	—	500
	8-400 HD	R44T	.045	Electronic	—	4B(2B)	7.5–9	—	700
'79	6-250	R46TS	.035	Electronic	10B⑥	10B⑦	4.5–6	750	600
	8-305	R45TS	.045	Electronic	6B	6B	7.5–9	700	600
'79	8–350⑧	R45TS	.045	Electronic	8B	8B	7.5–9	700	500
	8-400⑧	R45TS	.045	Electronic	—	4B	7.5–9	—	500
'80–'81	6-250	R46TS	.035	Electronic	10B	8B⑨	4–6	750	650(D)
	8-305 (2-bbl)	R45TS	.045	Electronic	8B	8B	7–9	700	600(D)
	8-305 (4-bbl)	R45TS	.045	Electronic	6B	4B	7–9	700	500(D)
	8-350	R45TS	.045	Electronic	8B⑩	8B⑪	7–9	700	500(D)⑫
'82	6-250	R45TS	.045	Electronic	①	①	4–6	①	①
	8-305	R45TS	.045	Electronic	①	①	7–9	①	①
	8-350	R45TS	.045	Electronic	①	①	7–9	①	①
'83	6-250	R45TS	.045	Electronic	①	①	4–6	①	①
	8-305	R45TS	.045	Electronic	①	①	7–9	①	①
	8-350	R45TS	.045	Electronic	①	①	7–9	①	①
	8-379	Diesel	—	—	①	①	—	①	①
'84	6-250	R45TS	.045	Electronic	①	①	4–6	①	①
	8-305	R45TS	.045	Electronic	①	①	7–9	①	①
	8-350	R45TS	.045	Electronic	①	①	7–9	①	①
	8-379	Diesel	—	—	①	①	—	①	①

NOTE: The underhood specifications sticker often reflects tune-up specifications changes made in production. Sticker figures must be used if they disagree with those in this chart.

NOTE: Part numbers in this chart are not recommendations by Chilton for any product by brand name.

NOTE: All engines use hydraulic valve lifters.

● Figures in parentheses are for California, and are given only if they differ from the 49 state specification. Automatic transmission idle speeds are set in Drive, unless specified otherwise.

▲ At idle speed with vacuum advance hose disconnected and plugged, unless specified otherwise in the text.
N—Transmission in Neutral
D—Transmission in Drive

HD Heavy Duty
LD Light Duty
① See the underhood specifications sticker
② Not used
③ 49 state without A/C—550

④ High alt.—12B
⑤ California only
⑥ G-20, G-30, 2500, 3500 series in Calif.—6B
⑦ G-20, G-30, 2500, 3500 series in Calif.—8B

⑧ Some G-30/3500 series vans differ. Check the underhood emission sticker.
⑨ High Alt.—10B
⑩ Fed 1 ton models—4B

Calif ¾ and 1 ton models—6B
⑪ 1 ton models—6B
⑫ 1 ton models—700(N)
Calif. ½ and ¾ ton models—550 (D)

TUNE-UP SPECIFICATIONS
Blazer/Jimmy

When analyzing compression test results, look for uniformity among cylinders rather than specific pressures.

Year	Engine No. Cyl Displacement	Spark Plugs Orig Type	Gap (in.)	Distributor	Ignition Timing (deg) Man Trans	Auto Trans	Fuel Pump Pressure (psi)	Idle Speed (rpm) Man Trans	Auto Trans ▲
'77–'78	6-250	R46T	.035	Electronic	6B	6B	3½–4½	600/450	600/450
	8-305	R44T	.045	Electronic	6B	6B	7–8½	700	700
	8-350	R44T (R44TX)	.045 (.060)	Electronic	8B(2B)	8B(2B)	7–8½	700	700
	8-400	R44T	.045	Electronic	—	4B(2B)	7–8½	—	700
'79	6-250	R46TS	.035	Electronic	10B	10B	4½–6	750	600
	8-305	R45TS	.045	Electronic	6B	6B	7–9	600	500
	8-350	R45TS	.045	Electronic	8B	8B	7–9	700	500
	8-400	R45TS	.060	Electronic	—	4B	7–9	—	500
'80–'81	6-250	R46TS	.035	Electronic	10B	10B	3.5–4.5	750	650(D)
	8-305	R45TS	.045	Electronic	4B	2B	7.0–8.5	700	500(D)
	8-350	R45TS	.045	Electronic	8B	8B	7.0–8.5	700	500(D)
'82	6-250	R45TS	.045	Electronic	①	①	4–6	①	①
	8-305	R45TS	.045	Electronic	①	①	7–9	①	①
	8-350	R45TS	.045	Electronic	①	①	7–9	①	①
	8-379	Diesel	—	—	①	①	—	①	①
'83	6-250	R45TS	.045	Electronic	①	①	4–6	①	①
	8-305	R45TS	.045	Electronic	①	①	7–9	①	①
	8-350	R45TS	.045	Electronic	①	①	7–9	①	①
	8-379	Diesel	—	—	①	①	—	①	①
	8-454	R44T	.045	Electronic	①	①	—	①	①
'84	6-250	R45TS	.045	Electronic	①	①	4–6	①	①
	8-305	R45TS	.045	Electronic	①	①	7–9	①	①
	8-350	R45TS	.045	Electronic	①	①	7–9	①	①
	8-379	Diesel	—	—	①	①	—	①	①
	8-454	R44T	.045	Electronic	①	①	—	①	①

NOTE: The underhood specifications sticker often reflects tuneup specification changes made in production. Sticker figures must be used if they disagree with those in this chart. Part numbers in this chart are not recommendations by Chilton for any product name.
NOTE: All engines use hydraulic valve lifters
● Figures in parentheses are for California, and are given only when they differ from the 49 State models. When two idle speeds separated by a slash are given, the lower figure is with the solenoid disconnected.
▲ Automatic transmission idle speed set in Drive unless otherwise indicated

B Before Top Dead Center
N Neutral
TDC Top Dead Center
2WD Two wheel drive
4WD 4 wheel drive
① See under hood sticker

TUNE-UP SPECIFICATIONS
S10, 15 Pickup, Blazer and Jimmy

When analyzing compression results, look for uniformity among cylinders rather than specific pressures.

Year	Engine Cu In. Displacement	Spark Plugs Orig Type	Gap (in.)	Distributor	Ignition Timing (deg)▲ MT	AT	Fuel Pump Pressure (psi)	Idle Speed (rpm) MT	AT
'82	4-119	R-42XLS	.040	Electronic	6B	6B	3.0	800	900
	4-121	R-42CTS	.035	Electronic	12B	12B	5.0	750	700
	6-173	R-42TS	.040	Electronic	6B	10B	7.0	1000	750
'83	4-119	R-42XLS	.040	Electronic	①	①	3.0	①	①
	4-121	R-42CTS	.035	Electronic	①.	①	5.0	①	①
	6-173	R-42TS	.040	Electronic	①	①	7.0	①	①
'84	4-119	R-42XLS	.040	Electronic	①	①	3.0	①	①
	4-121	R-42CTS	.035	Electronic	①	①	5.0	①	①
	6-173	R-42TS	.040	Electronic	①	①	7.0	①	①

Note: The under hood specifications sticker often reflects tune-up specification changes made in production. Sticker figures must be used if they disagree with those in this chart.
① See under hood sticker

DIESEL ENGINE TUNE-UP SPECIFICATIONS

Year	Injector Opening Pressure (psi)	Injection Timing (deg.)	Intake Valve Opens (deg.)	Low Idle (rpm)	Compression Pressure (psi)	Valve Clearance (in.) Intake	Exhaust	Firing Order
'82–'84	1493	15B	16B	750	441*	.016C	.016C	1-3-4-2

*at 200 rpm
Note: The under hood specifications sticker often reflects tune up specification changes made in production. Sticker figures must be used if they disagree with those in this chart.

Firing Orders

To avoid confusion, replace spark plug wires one at a time.

4–119 firing order   4–121 firing order   6–173 firing order

Six cylinder

V8

VALVE SPECIFICATIONS

Engine No. Cyl Displacement (cu in.)	Seat Angle (deg)	Face Angle (deg)	Spring Test Pressure (lbs @ in.)	Spring Installed Height (in.) ①	Stem to Guide Clearance (in.)		Stem Diameter (in.)	
					Intake	Exhaust	Intake	Exhaust
4-119	45	45	35 @ 1.614	20 @ 1.516	.0009–.0022	.0015–.0031	.3102 min.	.3091 min.
4-121	46	45	182 @ 1.330	—	.0011–.0026	.0014–.0031	.3410–.3416	.3410–.3416
4-137	45	45	145 @ 1.535	44 @ 1.457	.0015–.0027	.0025–.0037	.3150	.3150
6-173	46	45	195 @ 1.180	—	.0010–.0027	.0010–.0027	.3410–.3416	.3410–.3416
6-250	46	45	175 @ 1.26	1.66	0.0010–0.0027	0.0015–0.0032	0.3414	0.3414
6-292	46	45⑤	175 @ 1.26	1.66	0.0010–0.0027	0.0015–0.0032	0.3414	0.3414
8-305	46	45	200 @ 1.25	1²³⁄₃₂	0.0010–0.0027	0.0010–0.0027	0.3414	0.3414
8-350	46	45	200 @ 1.25	1²³⁄₃₂	0.0010–0.0027	0.0010–0.0027	0.3414	0.3414
8-379 Diesel	46	45	740 @ 1.40	1¹³⁄₁₆	0.0010–0.0027	0.0010–0.0027	0.3414	0.3414
8-400	46	45	200 @ 1.25	—	0.0010–0.0027	0.0012–0.0029	0.3414	0.3414
8-454	46	45	220 @ 1.40	1⁵¹⁄₆₄	0.0010–0.0027	0.0012–0.0029	0.3719	0.3719
8-350 Diesel	②	③	205 @ 1.30	—	0.0010–0.0027	0.0015–0.0032	0.3429	0.3424

① ± 1/32 in.

② Intake—45°
Exhaust—31°

③ Intake—44°
Exhaust—30°

CRANKSHAFT AND CONNECTING ROD SPECIFICATIONS

(All measurements are given in in.)

Year	Engine No. Cyl Displacement (cu in.)	Crankshaft				Connecting Rod		
		Main Brg Journal Dia	Main Brg Oil Clearance	Shaft End-Play	Thrust on No.	Journal Diameter	Oil Clearance	Side Clearance
'82–'84	4-119	2.2050	0.0008–0.0025	0.0117 max.	3	1.9290	0.0007–0.0030	0.0137 max.
	4-121	⑪	⑫	0.0020–0.0071	3	1.9990	0.0010–0.0031	0.0039–0.0240

CRANKSHAFT AND CONNECTING ROD SPECIFICATIONS

(All measurements are given in in.)

Year	Engine No. Cyl Displacement (cu in.)	Crankshaft				Connecting Rod		
		Main Brg Journal Dia	Main Brg Oil Clearance	Shaft End-Play	Thrust on No.	Journal Diameter	Oil Clearance	Side Clearance
	4-837	2.3590	0.0011–0.0033	0.0018	3	2.0837	0.0016–0.0047	0.0024
	6-173	2.4940	0.0017–0.0030	0.0020–0.0067	3	1.9980	0.0014–0.0032	0.0063–0.0173
'77	6-250	2.2983–2.2993	.0003–.0029	.002–.006	7	1.999–2.000	.0007–.0027	.006–.017
	6-292	2.2983–2.2993	.0008–.0034	.002–.006	7	2.099–2.100	.0007–.0027	.006–.017
	8-305, 307 350, 400	2.4484–2.4493① ⑤	.0008–.0020②	.002–.006	5	2.199–2.200	.0013–.0035	.008–.014
	8-454	③	④	.006–.010	5	2.1985–2.1995	.0009–.0025	.013–.023
'78–'81	6-250	2.2979–2.2994	Nos. 1–6 .0010–.0024 No. 7 .0016–.0035	.002–.006	7	1.999–2.000	.0010–.0026	.006–.017
	6-292	2.2979–2.2994	Nos. 1–6 .0010–.0024 No. 7 .0016–.0035	.002–.006	7	2.099–2.100	.0010–.0026	.006–.017
	8-305, 350, 400	⑤	.0008–.0020②	.002–.006	5	2.199–2.200⑫	.0013–.0035	.008–.014
	8-454	③	④	.006–.010	5	2.1985–2.1995	.0009–.0025	.013–.023
	8-350 Diesel	2.9993–3.0003	Nos. 1–4 .0005–.0021 No. 5 .0015–.0031	.0035–.0135	5	2.1238–2.1248	.0005–.0026	.006–.020
'82–'84	6-250	2.2979–2.2994	Nos. 1–6 0.0010–0.0024 No. 7 0.0016–0.0025⑩	0.002–0.006	7	1.999–2.000	0.0010–0.0026	0.006–0.017
	6-292	2.2979–2.2994	Nos. 1–6 0.0010–0.0024 No. 7 0.0016–0.0025⑩	0.002–0.006	7	2.099–2.100	0.0010–0.0026	0.006–0.017
	8-305	⑤	0.0008–0.0020②	0.002–0.006	5	2.0988–2.0998	0.0013–0.0035	0.008–0.014
	8-350	⑤	0.0008–0.0020②	0.002–0.006	5	2.0988–2.0998	0.0013–0.0035	0.008–0.014
	8-379 Diesel	⑧	⑨	0.002–0.007	5	2.3981–2.3991	0.0018–0.0039	0.007–0.025
	8-454	⑦	④	0.006–0.010	5	2.2000–2.1990	0.0009–0.0025	0.013–0.023

① No. 5—2.4479–2.4488
② Nos. 2–4—.0011–.0023
 No. 5—.0017–.0033
③ No. 1—2.7485–2.7494
 Nos. 2–4—2.7481–2.7490
 No. 5—2.7478–2.7488
④ Nos. 1–4—.0013–.0025
 No. 5—.0024–.0040
⑤ '77–'84 only: 305,

350—No. 1—2.4484–2.4493
 Nos. 2–4—2.4481–2.4490
 No. 5—2.4479–2.4488
 400—Nos. 1–4—2.6484–2.6493
 No. 5—2.6479–2.6488
⑥ '79–'81: 2.0988–2.0998
⑦ Nos. 1–4—2.7481–2.7490
 No. 5—2.7476–2.7486
⑧ Nos. 1–4—2.9495–2.9504

 No. 5—2.9492–2.9502
⑨ Nos. 1–4—0.0018–0.0033
 No. 5—0.0022–0.0037
⑩ '83–'84 .0016–.0035
⑪ Nos. 1–4 2.4940–2.4950
 No. 5 2.4930–2.4950
⑫ Nos. 1–4 .0006–.0019
 No. 5 .0014–.0027

PISTON AND RING SPECIFICATIONS

Engine	Year	Piston to Bore Clearance	Ring Side Clearance			Ring Gap		
			Top Compression	Bottom Compression	Oil Control	Top Compression	Bottom Compression	Oil Control
4-119	'82–'84	.0018–.0026	.0059 Max	.0059 Max	.0059 Max	.012–.020	.008–.016	.008–.035
4-121	'82–'84	.0008–.0018	.0012–.0027	.0012–.0038	.0078 Max	.010–.020	.010–.020	.020–.055
4-137	'82–'84	.0062–.0070	.0018–.0028	.0012–.0021	.0008–.0021	.008–.016	.008–.016	.008–.016
6-173	'82–'84	.0017–.0027	.0012–.0028	.0016–.0037	.0078 Max	.010–.020	.010–.020	.020–.055
6-250	'77–'84	0.0005–0.0015②	0.0012–0.0027	0.0012–0.0032	.005 max	0.010–0.020	0.010–0.020	0.015–0.055
6-292	'77–'84	0.0026–0.0036	0.0020–0.0040	0.0020–0.0040	.005 max	0.010–0.020	0.010–0.020	0.015–0.055
8-305	'77–'84	0.0007–0.0017	0.0012–0.0032	0.0012–0.0032	0.002–0.007	0.010–0.020	0.010–0.025	0.015–0.055
8-350	'77–'84	0.0007–0.0017	0.0012–0.0032	0.0012–0.0032	0.002–0.007	0.010–0.020	0.010–0.025	0.015–0.055
8-350 Diesel	'78–'81	0.0050–0.0060	0.0040–0.0060	0.0018–0.0038	0.001–0.005	0.015–0.025	0.015–0.025	0.015–0.055
8-379 Diesel	'82–'84	0.0040–0.0050	0.0030–0.0070	0.0015–0.0031	0.0016–0.0038	0.012–0.021	0.030–0.039	0.0098–0.020
8-400	'75–'81	0.0014–0.0024	0.0012–0.0032	0.0012–0.0032	0.002–0.007	0.010–0.020	0.010–0.025	0.010–0.055
8-454	'77–'84	0.0014–0.0024③	0.0017–0.0032	0.0017–0.0032	0.002–0.007④	0.010–0.020	0.010–0.020	0.010–0.055

① '78–'82: 0.0010–0.0020
② '83–'84: .0010–.0020
③ '83–'84: .0030–.0040
④ '83–'84: .005–.0065

TORQUE SPECIFICATIONS
(ft. lb.)

Engine	Cylinder Head Bolts	Rod Bearing Bolts	Main Bearing Bolts	Crankshaft Damper Bolt	Flywheel Bolts	Manifold	
						Intake	Exhaust
119	72	43	75	87	76	17	16
121	70	37	70	75	50	23	25
137 Diesel	60	65	116–130	125–150	70	15	15
173	70	37	70	75	50	23	25
6-250	95	35	65	—	60	—	30①
6-292	95	35	65	—	110	35	30
8-305	65	45	70	60	60	30	20
8-350	65	45	70	60	60	30	30①
8-350 Diesel	130②	42	120	200–310	60	40②	25
8-379 Diesel	88–103	44–52	④	140–162	60	25–37	18–25
8-400	65	45	70	60	60	30	30
8-454	80	50③	110	65	65	30	20

① End bolts: 20
② Dip in oil
③ ⁷⁄₁₆ in. bolts: 70
④ inner: 105–117
  outer: 94–105

BATTERY AND STARTER SPECIFICATIONS

	Battery			Starter ③			
						No Load Test	
						Amps	
Year	Amp Hour Capacity	Volts	Ground Terminal	Identification	Volts	①	rpm
'77–'82	60	12	Neg	1108778②	9	50–80	5500–10,500
	80	12	Neg	1187780②	9	50–80	3500–6000
				1109056②	9	50–80	5500–10,500
				1109052②	9	65–95	7500–10,500
				1108776②	9	65–95	7500–10,500
	125	12	Neg	1108776②	9	65–95	7500–10,500
'83–'84	—	12	Neg	1109561	9	50–75	6000—11,900
	—	12	Neg	1109535	9	45–70	7000–11,900
	—	12	Neg	1998241	10	65–95	7500–10,500
	—	12	Neg	1998244	10	60–85	6800–10,500
	—	12	Neg	1998211	10	65–95	7500–10,500
	—	12	Neg	1998396	10	70–110	6500–10,700
	—	12	Neg	1998397	10	70–110	6500–10,700
	—	12	Neg	1109563	10	120–210	9000–13,400

① Solenoid included
② "R" terminal removed
③ Brush spring tension is 35 oz. for all starters. Lock test is not recommended.

ALTERNATOR AND REGULATOR SPECIFICATIONS

	Alternator			
Year	Part No. or Manufacturer	Field Current @ 12 V	Output (amps)	Regulator
'77	1100497	4.4–4.9	37	①
	1100934	4.4–4.5	37	①
	1102394 1102483, 91 1102889	4.0–4.5	37	①
	1102346, 49, 82 1102485 1102841, 87 1100573	4.0–4.5	42	①
	1100560, 75 1102478, 79, 93	4.0–4.5	55	①
	1100597 1102347, 50, 83 1102480, 86, 90 1102886, 88	4.0–4.5	61	①
'78–'82	1102394 1102491 1102889	4.0–4.5	37	①

ALTERNATOR AND REGULATOR SPECIFICATIONS

Year	Alternator Part No. or Manufacturer	Field Current @ 12 V	Output (amps)	Regulator
	1102485 1102841, 87	4.0–4.5	42	①
	1102480, 86 1102886, 88	4.0–4.5	61	①
	1101016, 28	4.0–4.5	80	①
'83–'84	1105185		37	①
	1100227		37	①
	1100204		37	①
	1100203		37	①
	1100207		66	①
	1100249		66	①
	1100275		66	①
	1100242		66	①
	1100208		66	①
	1100241		66	①
	1100209		78	①
	1100273		78	①
	1100276		78	①
	1100217		78	①
	1100259		78	①

—Not available
NA Not applicable
① All alternators use integral regulators

TUNE-UP

High Energy Ignition (HEI) System

The General Motors HEI system is a pulse-triggered, transistored-controlled, inductive discharge ignition system. The entire HEI system is contained within the distributor cap.

The distributor, in addition to housing the mechanical and vacuum advance mechanisms, contains the ignition coil the electronic control module, and the magnetic triggering device. The magnetic pick-up assembly contains a permanent magnet, a pole piece with internal "teeth," and a pick-up coil (not to be confused with the ignition coil).

In the HEI system, as in other electronic ignition systems, the breaker points have been replaced with an electronic switch—a transistor—which is located *within* the control module. This switching transistor performs the same function the points did in a conventional ignition system; it simply turns coil primary current on and off at the correct time. Essentially then, electronic and conventional ignition systems operate on the same principle.

The module which houses the switching transistor is controlled (turned on and off) by a magnetically generated impulse induced in the pick-up coil. When the teeth of the rotating timer align with the teeth of the pole piece, the induced voltage in the pick-up coil signals the electronic module to open the coil primary circuit. The primary current then decreases, and a high voltage is induced in the ignition coil secondary windings which is then directed through the rotor and high voltage leads (spark plug wires) to fire the spark plugs.

In essence then, the pick-up coil module system simply replaces the conventional breaker points and condenser. The condenser found within the distributor is for radio suppression purposes only and has nothing to do with the ignition process. The module automatically controls the dwell period, increasing it with increasing engine speed. Since dwell is automatically controlled, it cannot be adjusted. The module itself is non-adjustable and non-repairable and must be replaced if found defective.

HEI SYSTEM PRECAUTIONS

Before going on to troubleshooting, it might be a good idea to take note of the following precautions.

Timing Light Use

Inductive pick-up timing lights are the best kind to use if your truck is equipped with HEI. Timing lights which connect between the spark plug and the spark plug wire occasionally (not always) give false readings.

Spark Plug Wires

The plug wires used with HEI systems are

V8 HEI wiring

of a different construction than conventional wires. When replacing them, make sure you get the correct wires, since conventional wires won't carry the voltage. Also, handle them carefully to avoid cracking or splitting them and *never* pierce them.

Tachometer Use

Not all tachometers will operate or indicate correctly when used on a HEI system. While some tachometers may give a reading, this does not necessarily mean the reading is correct. In addition, some tachometers hook up differently from others. If you can't figure out whether or not your tachometer will work on your car, check with the tachometer manufacturer. Dwell readings, of course, have no significance at all.

HEI System Testers

Instruments designed specifically for testing HEI systems are available from several tool manufacturers. Some of these will even test the module itself. However, the tests given in the following section will require only an ohmmeter and a voltmeter.

Ignition Timing

Timing should be checked at each tuneup. It isn't likely to change much with HEI. The timing marks consist of a notch on the rim of the crankshaft pulley or vibration damper and a graduated scale attached to the engine front (timing) cover. A stroboscopic flash (dynamic) timing light must be used, as a static light is too inaccurate for emission controlled engines.

There are three basic types of timing light available. The first is a simple neon bulb with two wire connections. One wire connects to the spark plug terminal and the other plugs into the end of the spark plug wire for the no. 1 cylinder, thus connecting the light in series with the spark plug. This type of light is pretty dim and must be held very closely to the timing marks to be seen. Sometimes a dark corner has to be sought out to see the flash at all. This type of light is very inexpensive. The second type operates from the vehicle battery—two alligator clips connect to the battery terminals, while an adapter enables a third clip to be connected between the no. 1 spark plug and

wire. This type is a bit more expensive, but it provides a nice bright flash that you can see even in bright sunlight. It is the type most often seen in professional shops. The third type replaces the battery power source with 110 volt current.

To check and adjust the timing:

1. Warm up the engine to normal operating temperature. Stop the engine and connect the timing light to the no. 1 (left front on V8, front on six) spark plug wire, either at the plug or at the distributor cap. You can also use the No. 6 wire, if it is more convenient. No. 6 is the rear cylinder on a six, and the third cylinder back on the right bank of a V8. Numbering is illustrated in Chapter 3.

NOTE: Do not pierce the plug wire insulation with HEI; it will cause a miss. The best method is an inductive pickup timing light.

Clean off the timing marks and mark the pulley or damper notch and timing scale with white chalk.

2. Disconnect and plug the vacuum line at the distributor. This is done to prevent any distributor vacuum advance. Check the underhood emission sticker for any other hoses or wires which may need to be disconnected.

3. Start the engine and adjust the idle speed to that specified in the "Tune-Up Specifications" chart. With automatic transmission, set the specified idle speed in Park. It will be too high, since it is normally (in most cases) adjusted in Drive. You can disconnect the idle solenoid, if any, to get the speed down. Otherwise, adjust the idle speed screw. This is done to prevent any centrifugal (mechanical) advance. The tachometer connects to the TACH terminal on the distributor or on the coil (sixes through 1977) and to a ground. Some tachometers must connect to the TACH terminal and to

Typical timing marks

the positive battery terminal. Some tachometers won't work with HEI.

CAUTION

Never ground the HEI TACH terminal; serious system damage will result.

4. Aim the timing light at the pointer marks. Be careful not to touch the fan, because it may appear to be standing still. If the pulley or damper notch isn't aligned with the proper timing mark (see the "Tune-Up Specifications" chart), the timing will have to be adjusted.

NOTE: TDC or top dead center corresponds to 0 degrees. B, BTDC or before top dead center may be shown as BEFORE. A, ATDC or after top dead center may be shown as AFTER.

5. Loosen the distributor base clamp locknut. You can buy trick wrenches which make this task a lot easier on V8s. Turn the distributor slowly to adjust the timing, holding it by the body and not the cap. Turn the distributor in the direction of rotor rotation to retard, and against the direction of rotation to advance.

6. Tighten the locknut. Check the timing again, in case the distributor moved slightly as you tightened it.

7. Replace the distributor vacuum line. Correct the idle speed.

8. Stop the engine and disconnect the timing light.

Carburetor

IDLE SPEED AND MIXTURE ADJUSTMENT

These procedures require the use of a tachometer. Tachometer hookup was explained earlier under Ignition Timing, Step 3. In some cases, the degree of accuracy required is greater than that available on a hand-held unit; a shop tachometer would be required to follow the instructions exactly. If the idle speed screws have plastic limiter caps, it is not recommended that they be removed unless a satisfactory idle cannot be obtained with them in place. If the caps are removed, exhaust emissions may go beyond the specified legal limits. This can be checked on an exhaust gas analyzer.

NOTE: Most four barrel carburetors have an internal fuel passage restriction; beyond a certain limited point, turning the idle mixture screws out has no further richening effect.

Idle speed and mixture are set with the engine at normal running temperature. The automatic transmission should be in Drive, except when specified otherwise. The air conditioner should be off for adjusting mixture and off unless otherwise specified in the text or specifications chart for setting idle speed.

— CAUTION —
Block the wheels, set the parking brake, and don't stand in front of the truck.

1977

See the underhood emission sticker for any hoses or wires that may need to be disconnected.

1 bbl: Start the engine and allow it to run until it reaches normal operating temperature. Be sure the choke is fully open and the cam follower is off the steps of the cam. Turn the nut on the end of the solenoid to obtain the specified rpm. See the Tune-Up chart. Disconnect the wire from the solenoid and turn the 1/8 in. allen head screw in the end of the solenoid to set the base idle to specification. Refer to the Tune-Up chart or the underhood emission sticker. Reconnect the wire.

2 and 4 bbl: Be sure the ignition timing is correct. Refer to the underhood emission sticker in order to prepare the vehicle for adjustment.

On carburetors without a solenoid: Be sure the idle speed screw is on the low step of the fast idle cam. Turn the screw to obtain the idle specified in the Tune-Up chart.

On carburetors with a solenoid: Turn the idle screw to obtain the idle speed specified in the Tune-Up chart. Disconnect the electrical lead from between the solenoid and the A/C compressor at the compressor and turn the A/C On. Place the automatic transmission in Drive. Open the throttle momentarily to fully extend the solenoid plunger. Turn the solenoid screw to obtain the base idle speed as specified in the Tune-Up chart or on the emission sticker. Reconnect the electrical lead at the compressor.

1978

1 bbl: The idle speed adjusting procedure is the same as 1977. Refer to the Tune-Up chart for the correct idle speed.

2 bbl: Be sure the ignition timing is correct. Refer to the underhood emission sticker in order to prepare the vehicle for adjustment.

On carburetors without a solenoid: This procedure is the same as 1977. See the Tune-Up chart for the correct idle speed.

On models with a solenoid and without air conditioning: Rev the engine momentarily to fully extend the solenoid plunger. Turn the solenoid screw to obtain the curb idle speed listed in the Tune-Up chart. Disconnect the wire from the solenoid. Turn the idle speed screw to obtain the solenoid idle speed listed on the underhood emission sticker. Reconnect the wire at the solenoid.

On models with air conditioning: Turn the idle speed screw to obtain the idle speed listed in the Tune-Up chart. Disconnect the wire at the A/C compressor and turn the A/C On. Rev the engine momentarily to fully extend the solenoid plunger. Turn the solenoid screw to obtain the solenoid idle speed listed on the underhood emission sticker. Reconnect the wire at the compressor.

Idle Speed adjustment '77–'78 250 and 292 and '79–'82 292 engines

1977 and later 4-bbl and 1979 and later 2-bbl (V8 only) idle speed adjustment with solenoid

1977–78 2-bbl idle speed adjustment with solenoid

4 bbl: Refer to the underhood emission sticker and prepare the vehicle for adjustment as specified on the sticker. On models without a solenoid, turn the idle speed screw to obtain the idle speed listed in the Tune-Up chart. On models with a solenoid, turn the idle speed screw to obtain the idle speed listed in the Tune-Up chart. Disconnect the wire at the A/C compressor and turn the A/C On. Rev the engine momentarily to fully extend the solenoid plunger. Turn the solenoid screw to obtain the solenoid idle speed listed on the underhood emission sticker. Reconnect the A/C wire at the compressor.

1979–82

1 bbl: This procedure is the same as 1977. Refer to the Tune-Up chart for the correct idle speed.

2 bbl (six cylinder): Be sure the ignition timing is correct. Refer to the underhood emission sticker and prepare the engine for adjustment as specified on the sticker. Rev the engine momentarily to fully extend the solenoid plunger. Turn the solenoid screw to obtain the curb idle speed as listed in the Tune-Up chart. Disconnect the wire at the solenoid and turn the idle speed screw to adjust the base idle. Refer to the Tune-Up chart or the underhood emission sticker. Reconnect the wire at the solenoid.

2 bbl (V8): Be sure the engine timing is correct. Refer to the underhood emission label in order to prepare the vehicle for adjustment. Turn the idle speed screw to adjust the curb idle speed. Disconnect the wire from the solenoid to the A/C compressor at the compressor and turn the A/C On. Open the throttle momentarily to fully extend the solenoid plunger .Turn the A/C On. Open the throttle momentarily to fully extend the solenoid plunger. Turn the solenoid screw to obtain the base idle speed. Refer to the Tune-Up chart or the underhood emission sticker for the correct speeds.

4 bbl: This procedure is the same as for 1977.

119 Engine

In order to adjust the idle mixture you must first remove the plug that covers the mixture screw.

1. To remove the plug, first remove the carburetor and turn it upside down.

2. Remove the plug carefully with a hammer and screwdriver, (see illustration).

3. Reinstall the carburetor and adjust as necessary.

4. Turn the mixture screw all the way in, and then back it out 2 turns (Federal) and 1 turn (California).

5. Readjust the idle if necessary.

121, 173 Engines

1. See the underhood sticker for those procedures necessary prior to setting the idle speed.

2. With the truck prepared, turn the idle speed screw to adjust the speed to specifications.

3. On trucks with air conditioning, disconnect the air conditioning compressor lead wire. Turn the air conditioning on and place the transmission in drive (AT) or neutral (MT). Make sure that the handbrake is fully set. Open the throttle slightly to extend the solenoid plunger. Turn the solenoid screw to establish the specified rpm. Reconnect the compressor lead wire.

1983 & Later

No adjustments are possible. All adjustments are to be made only during major overhaul. See the Unit Repair Section.

① PREPARE VEHICLE FOR ADJUSTMENTS –
SEE EMISSION LABEL ON VEHICLE.
NOTE: IGNITION TIMING SET PER LABEL.

② TURN IDLE SPEED SCREW TO
SET CURB IDLE SPEED TO
SPECIFICATIONS – A / C OFF
(SEE EMISSION LABEL)

1977 and later 4-bbl idle speed adjustment without solenoid

① PREPARE VEHICLE FOR ADJUSTMENTS –
SEE EMISSION LABEL ON VEHICLE.
NOTE: IGNITION TIMING SET PER LABEL.

② SOLENOID ENERGIZED - A/T IN DRIVE,
M/T IN NEUTRAL

⑥ RECONNECT SOLENOID ELECTRICAL LEAD AFTER ADJUSTMENT

④ TURN SOLENOID SCREW TO ADJUST CURB IDLE SPEED TO SPECIFIED RPM (SOLENOID ENERGIZED)

⑤ TURN IDLE SPEED SCREW
TO SET BASIC IDLE
SPEED TO SPECIFICATIONS
(SOLENOID DE-ENERGIZED)

③ OPEN THROTTLE SLIGHTLY TO ALLOW SOLENOID PLUNGER TO FULLY EXTEND

1979–82 250 six idle speed adjustment

ENGINE ELECTRICAL

Distributor

REMOVAL & INSTALLATION

1. Disconnect the wiring harness connectors at the side of the distributor cap.

2. Remove the distributor cap and lay it aside.

3. Disconnect the vacuum advance line.

4. Scribe a mark on the engine in line with the rotor and note the approximate position of the vacuum advance unit in relation to the engine.

5. Remove the distributor hold-down clamp and nut.

6. Lift the distributor from the engine.

To install the distributor with the engine undisturbed:

7. Reinsert the distributor into its opening, aligning the previously-made marks on the housing and the engine block.

8. The rotor may have to be turned either way a slight amount to align the rotor-to-housing marks.

9. Install the retaining clamp and bolt. Install the distributor cap, primary wire, and the vacuum hose.

10. Start the engine and check the ignition timing.

To install the distributor with the engine disturbed:

11. Turn the engine so the no. 1 piston is at the top of its compression stroke. This may be determined by covering the no. 1 spark plug hole with your thumb and slowly turning the engine over. When the timing mark on the crankshaft pulley aligns with the 0 on the timing scale and your thumb is pushed out by compression, no. 1 piston is at top-dead-center (TDC).

12. Install the distributor to the engine block so that the vacuum advance unit points in the correct direction.

13. Turn the rotor so that it will point to the no. 1 terminal in the cap.

14. Install the distributor into the engine block. It may be necessary to turn the rotor a little in either direction in order to engage the gears.

15. Tap the starter a few times to ensure that the oil pump shaft is mated to the distributor shaft.

16. Bring the engine to no. 1 TDC again and check to see that the rotor is indeed pointing toward the no. 1 terminal of the cap.

17. After correct positioning is assured, turn the distributor housing so that the points are just opening. Tighten the retaining clamp. Install the cap and hoses. Check the timing.

Alternator

PRECAUTIONS

1. When installing a battery, ensure that the ground polarity of the battery and the ground polarity of the alternator and the regulator are the same.

2. When connecting a jumper battery, be certain that the correct terminals are connected.

3. When charging, connect the correct charger leads to the battery terminals.

4. Never operate the alternator on an open circuit. Be sure that all connections in the charging circuit are tight.

5. Do not short across or ground any of the terminals on the alternator or regulator.

6. Never polarize an AC system.

PRELIMINARY CHARGING SYSTEM TESTS

1. If you suspect a defect in your charging system, first perform these general checks before going on to more specific tests.

2. Check the condition of the alternator belt and tighten it if necessary.

3. Clean the battery cable connections at the battery. Make sure the connections between the battery wires and the battery clamps are good. Reconnect the negative terminal only and proceed to the next step.

4. With the key off, insert a test light between the positive terminal on the battery and the disconnected positive battery terminal clamp. If the test light comes on, there is a short in the electrical system of the van. The short must be repaired before proceeding. If the light does not come on, proceed to the next step.

NOTE: If the truck is equipped with an electric clock, the clock must be disconnected.

5. Check the charging system wiring for any obvious breaks or shorts.

6. Check the battery to make sure it is fully charged and in good condition.

CHARGING SYSTEM OPERATIONAL TEST

NOTE: You will need a current indicator to perform this test. If the current indicator is to give an accurate reading, the battery cables must be the same gauge and length as the original equipment.

1. With the engine running and all electrical systems turned off, place a current indicator over the positive battery cable.

2. If a charge of roughly five amps is recorded, the charging system is working. If a draw of about five amps is recorded, the system is not working. The needle moves toward the battery when a charge condition is indicated, and away from the battery when a draw condition is indicated.

3. If a draw is indicated, proceed with further testing. If an excessive charge (10–15 amps) is indicated, the regulator may be at fault.

OUTPUT TEST

1. You will need an ammeter for this test.

2. Disconnect the battery ground cable.

3. Disconnect the wire from the battery terminal on the alternator.

4. Connect the ammeter negative lead to the battery terminal wire removed in step three, and connect the ammeter positive lead to the battery terminal on the alternator.

5. Reconnect the battery ground cable and turn on all electrical accessories. If the battery is fully charged, disconnect the coil wire and bump the starter a few times to partially discharge it.

6. Start the engine and run it until you obtain a maximum current reading on the ammeter.

7. If the current is within ten amps of the rated output of the alternator, the alternator is working properly. If the current is not within ten amps, insert a screwdriver in the test hole in the end frame of the alternator and ground the tab in the test hole against the side of the hole.

8. If the current is now within ten amps of the rated output, remove the alternator and have the voltage regulator replaced. If it is still below ten amps of rated output, have the alternator repaired.

REMOVAL & INSTALLATION

1. Disconnect the battery ground cable to prevent diode damage.

2. Disconnect and tag all wiring to the alternator.

3. Remove the alternator brace bolt.

4. Remove the drive belt.

5. Support the alternator and remove the mounting bolts. Remove the alternator.

6. Install the unit using the reverse procedure of removal. Adjust the belt to have ½ in. depression under thumb pressure on its longest run.

V 8

6

Typical alternator mounting

Regulator

REMOVAL & INSTALLATION

The regulator on these models is an integral part of the alternator. Alternator disassembly is required to replace it.

VOLTAGE ADJUSTMENT

The 10 SI Delcotron is used which is equipped with an integral regulator that cannot be adjusted.

Typical starter mountings

Starter

REMOVAL & INSTALLATION

The following is a general procedure for all trucks, and may vary slightly depending on model and series.

1. Disconnect the battery ground cable at the battery.
2. Raise and support the vehicle.
3. Disconnect and tag all wires at the solenoid terminal.
4. Reinstall all nuts as soon as they are removed, since the thread sizes are different.
5. Remove the front bracket from the starter and the two mounting bolts. On engines with a solenoid heat shield, remove the front bracket upper bolt and detach the bracket from the starter.

Use a piece of pipe to drive the retainer toward the snap-ring

6. Remove the front bracket bolt or nut. Lower the starter front end first, and then remove the unit from the truck.
7. Reverse the removal procedures to install the starter. Torque the two mounting bolts to 25–35 ft. lbs.

BRUSH REPLACEMENT

1. Disconnect the field coil connectors from the starter motor solenoid terminal.
2. Remove the through bolts.
3. Remove the end frame and the field frame from the drive housing.
4. Disassemble the brush assembly from the field frame by releasing the spring and removing the supporting pin. Pull the brushes and the brush holders out and disconnect the wiring.
5. Install the new brushes into the holders.
6. Assemble the brush holder using the spring and position the unit on the supporting pin.
7. Install the unit in the starter motor and attach the wiring.
8. Position the field frame over the armature.
9. Install the through bolts.
10. Connect the field coil connectors to the solenoid.

STARTER DRIVE REPLACEMENT

1. Remove the starter motor as previously outlined.
2. Disconnect the field coil connections from the solenoid terminal.
3. Remove the through bolts.
4. Remove the commutator end frame, the field frame assembly and the armature assembly from the housing.
5. Remove the armature assembly from the housing. On some models it may be necessary to remove the solenoid and the shift lever assembly from the housing first.
6. Remove the thrust collar from the shaft.
7. Slide a small piece of ½ in. pipe over the end of the shaft so the end of the pipe butts against the edge of the retainer. Carefully tap the end of the pipe with a

Exploded view of the 20MT starter used on the diesel.

Snap-ring installation

hammer, driving the retainer towards the armature end of the snap-ring.

8. Remove the snap-ring from the groove.

9. Slide the retainer and clutch off the shaft.

To assemble the drive mechanism:

10. Slide the drive assembly onto the armature shaft after lubricating it with silicone.

11. Position the retainer on the shaft with the cupped surface facing away from the pinion.

12. Place the snap-ring over the end of the shaft and slide it into the groove.

13. Place the thrust collar on the shaft with its shoulder next to the snap-ring.

14. Using two sets of pliers, one on either side, force the snap-ring into the retainer.

15. Lubricate the drive housing bushing and slide the armature shaft into the housing.

16. Lubricate the commutator bushing with silicone.

17. Place the leather brake washer in position and assemble the commutator end of the starter.

SOLENOID REPLACEMENT

1. Remove the screw and washer from the motor connector strap terminal.

2. Remove the two solenoid retaining screws.

3. Twist the housing clockwise to remove the flange key from the keyway in the housing. Then remove the housing.

4. To install the unit, place the return spring on the plunger and place the solenoid body on the drive housing. Turn counterclockwise to engage the flange key. Place the two retaining screws in position and install the screw and washer which secures the strap terminal. Install the unit on the starter.

ENGINE MECHANICAL

Engine Removal & Installation

VANS

1977–78

1. Scribe matchmarks on the hood hinges for reassembly and remove the hood and the grille. Remove the grille cross brace.

2. Disconnect the negative battery cable, then the positive battery cable, at the battery.

3. Remove the air cleaner.

4. Drain the cooling system and disconnect the heater hoses and radiator hoses at the radiator.

5. Disconnect the A/C compressor mounting bracket and position the compressor out of the way. Also remove the condenser from in front of the radiator. Position it out of the way. DO NOT DISCONNECT ANY OF THE REFRIGERANT LINES.

6. Remove the radiator and the fan shroud.

7. Disconnect and label the wiring at the starter solenoid, alternator, temperature sending switch, oil pressure switch and the coil. Disconnect the engine ground strap.

8. Disconnect:
   a. the accelerator at the intake manifold
   b. the fuel line from the tank at the fuel pump (plug the line)
   c. the hoses at the fuel vapor storage canister (if so equipped)
   d. the vacuum line to the power brake booster at the manifold (if so equipped)

9. Remove the power steering pump mounting bolts and lay the pump aside. Do not disconnect any of the lines.

10. Raise the van on a hoist and drain the crankcase.

11. Disconnect the exhaust pipe at the manifold. If equipped with a catalytic converter, disconnect the converter bracket at the rear transmission mount.

12. Remove the starter motor.

13. Remove the flywheel splash shield or the converter cover, as applicable.

14. On vans with automatic transmissions, remove the converter-to-flywheel attaching bolts.

15. Remove the engine mount through bolts.

16. Remove the bellhousing bolts.

17. Lower the van.

18. Using a floor jack, raise the transmission.

19. Attach a boom hoist to the engine and raise the engine slightly.

20. Remove the engine mount-to-engine brackets.

21. Remove the engine.

22. Reverse the removal procedure to install.

1979 & Later

1. Disconnect the negative battery cable, then the positive battery cable, at the battery.

2. Drain the cooling system.

3. Remove the engine cover.

4. Remove the air cleaner. On the V8 remove the air stove pipe.

5. Remove the grille. On the six cylinder, remove the grille cross brace. On the V8, remove the upper radiator support and the lower grille valance.

6. Disconnect the radiator hoses at the radiator.

7. On the V8, remove the radiator coolant reservoir bottle.

8. If the van is equipped with an automatic transmission, remove the fluid cooler lines from the radiator.

9. Discharge the air conditioning system and remove the A/C vacuum reservoir. On the V8, remove the A/C condenser from in front of the radiator. On the six cylinder, remove the A/C compressor.

10. Remove the windshield washer jar and bracket.

11. Disconnect the accelerator linkage at the carburetor and remove the carburetor.

12. Remove the radiator support bracket and remove the radiator and the shroud.

13. On the six cylinder, remove the A/C compressor mounting bracket and position the compressor out of the way.

14. On the V8, disconnect the engine wiring harness from the firewall connection. On the six cylinder, disconnect the wiring at the alternator, distributor, oil pressure and temperature sending switches and the starter motor.

15. On the V8:
   a. Disconnect the heater hoses at the engine.
   b. Remove the thermostat housing.
   c. Remove the oil filler pipe.
   d. Remove the cruise control servo, servo bracket and transducer.

16. Raise the vehicle and drain the engine oil.

17. Remove the fuel line from the fuel tank at the fuel pump.

18. Disconnect the exhaust pipe at the manifold.

19. Remove the driveshaft and plug the end of the transmission.

20. Disconnect the transmission shift linkage and the speedometer cable.

21. Remove the transmission mounting bolts.

22. On the six cylinder with manual transmission, disconnect the clutch linkage and remove the clutch cross shaft.

23. On the V8, remove the engine mount bracket-to-frame bolts.

24. Remove the engine mount through bolts.

25. On the six cylinder:
   a. Lower the van and attach a lifting device to the engine.
   b. Raise the engine slightly and remove the right hand mount from the engine.

26. On the V8:
   a. Raise the engine slightly and remove the engine mounts. Support the engine with wood between the oil pan and the crossmember.

27. Remove the engine and transmission as one unit.

28. Reverse the removal procedure to install.

PICK-UPS AND SUBURBAN

The factory recommended procedure for engine removal is to remove the engine/transmission as a unit on two wheel drive models, except for the diesel. Only the engine should be removed on diesels and four wheel drive models.

1. Disconnect and remove the battery, negative cable first. On diesels, disconnect the negative cables at the batteries and ground wires at the inner fender panel.

2. Drain the cooling system.

3. Drain the engine oil.

4. Remove the air cleaner and ducts.

5. Scribe alignment marks around the hood hinges, and remove the hood.

6. Remove the radiator and hoses, and the fan shroud if so equipped.

7. Disconnect and label the wires at:

   a. Starter solenoid

   b. Alternator

   c. Temperature switch

   d. Oil pressure switch

   e. Transmission controlled spark solenoid

   f. CEC solenoid

   g. Coil

   h. Neutral safety switch

8. Disconnect:

   a. Accelerator linkage (hairpin at bellcrank, throttle and T.V. cables at intake manifold brackets on diesels. Position away from the engine.)

   b. Choke cable at carburetor (if so equipped)

   c. Fuel line to fuel pump

   d. Heater hoses at engine

   e. Air conditioning compressor with hoses attached. Do not remove the hoses from the air conditioning compressor. Remove it as a unit and set it aside. Its contents are under pressure, and can freeze body tissue on contact.

   f. Transmission dipstick and tube on automatic transmission models, except for diesel. Plug the tube hole.

   g. Oil dipstick and tube. Plug the hole.

   h. Vacuum lines

   i. Oil pressure line to gauge, if so equipped

   j. Parking brake cable

   k. Power steering pump. This can be removed as a unit and set aside, without removing any of the hoses.

   l. Engine ground straps

   m. Exhaust pipe (support if necessary)

9. Loosen and remove the fan belt, remove the fan blades and pulley. If you have the finned aluminum viscous drive fan clutch, keep it upright in its normal position. If the fluid leaks out, the unit will have to be replaced.

10. Remove the clutch cross-shaft.

11. Attach a chain or lifting device to the engine. If your engine doesn't have any lifting eyes, the usual locations are under the intake manifold bolts on V8s, or under the cylinder head bolts at either end on the sixes. You may have to remove the carburetor. Take the engine weight off the engine mounts, and unbolt the mounts. On all models except the gas-engined C-10, 1500, C-20, and 2500, support and disconnect the transmission. With automatic transmission, remove the torque converter underpan and starter, unbolt the converter from the flywheel, detach the throttle linkage and vacuum modulator line, and unbolt the engine from the transmission. Be certain that the converter does not fall out. With manual transmission, unbolt the clutch housing from the engine.

12. On two wheel drive models, remove the driveshaft. Either drain the transmission or plug the driveshaft opening. Disconnect the speedometer cable at the transmission. Disconnect the shift linkage or lever, or the clutch linkage. Disconnect the transmission cooler lines, if so equipped. If you have an automatic or a four speed transmission, the rear crossmember must be removed. With the three speed, unbolt the transmission from the crossmember. Raise the engine/transmission assembly and pull it forward.

13. On diesels, remove the three bolts, transmission, right side; disconnect the wires to the starter and remove the starter.

14. On four wheel drive, raise and pull the engine forward until it is free of the transmission. On diesels, slightly raise the transmission, remove the three left transmission to engine bolts, and remove the engine.

15. On all trucks, lift the engine out slowly, making certain as you go that all lines between the engine and the truck have been disconnected.

Installation is as follows:

1. On four wheel drive and diesels, lower the engine into place and align it with the transmission. Push the engine back gently and turn the crankshaft until the manual transmission shaft and clutch engage. Bolt the transmission to the engine. With automatic transmission, align the converter with the flywheel, bolt the transmission to the engine, bolt the converter to the flywheel, replace the underpan and starter, and connect the throttle linkage and vacuum modulator line.

2. On two wheel drive, lower the engine/transmission unit into place. Replace the rear crossmember if removed. Bolt the three speed transmission back to the crossmember. Replace the driveshaft.

3. Install the engine mounts.

4. Replace all transmission connections and the clutch cross-shaft. Replace the fan, pulley, and belts.

5. Replace all the items removed from the engine earlier. Connect all the wires which were detached.

6. Replace the radiator and fan shroud, air cleaner, and battery or battery cables. Fill the cooling system and check the automatic transmission fuel level. Fill the crankcase with oil. Check for leaks.

BLAZER AND JIMMY

1. Disconnect the negative battery cable, then the positive battery cable.

2. Drain the cooling system.

3. Remove the air cleaner.

4. Scribe matchmarks on the hood hinges for reassembly and remove the hood.

5. Remove the radiator and fan shroud as outlined later in this chapter.

6. Disconnect and label (to avoid confusion) the wires at the following locations:

   a. Starter solenoid

   b. Alternator

   c. Temperature sending switch

   d. Oil pressure sending switch

   e. Coil

   f. Vacuum advance solenoid and/or the CEC solenoid

   g. TCS solenoid (V8, if so equipped)

7. Disconnect the:

   a. Accelerator linkage at the manifold

   b. Fuel line from the tank at the fuel pump

   c. Heater hoses at the engine block

   d. Oil pressure gauge and the vacuum lines at the engine

   e. Evaporative emission system lines at the carburetor (on 1978 and later models, the hose at the fuel vapor storage canister)

   f. Power steering pump at the mounting bracket (lay the pump aside without disconnecting any of the lines)

   g. Ground straps at the engine block

   h. Exhaust pipe at the manifold (hang the pipe from the frame with a wire)

   i. TCS switch at the transmission (V8, if so equipped)

   j. Vacuum line to the power brake unit at the manifold

8. If equipped with air conditioning, unbolt the compressor at the bracket and lay it aside.

CAUTION

Do not disconnect any of the refrigerant lines. Evacuation of the air conditioning system should only be performed by someone who has the proper skill and training to do so, as the refrigerant will instantly freeze anything it contacts, including your eyes.

---

9. Raise the vehicle on a hoist and drain the engine oil.

10. Disconnect the exhaust pipe at the manifold.

11. Remove the flywheel splash shield or the converter housing cover, as applicable.

12. Remove the starter motor as outlined earlier in this chapter.

13. On automatic transmission models remove the converter-to-flywheel attaching bolts.

14. Remove the engine mount through bolts.

15. On 1979 and later four wheel drive models, remove the strut rods at the engine mount.

16. Remove the engine-to-bellhousing attaching bolts.

17. Lower the vehicle from the hoist.

18. Using a floor jack, raise the transmission slightly.

19. Attach a lifting device to the engine and raise it slightly, taking the weight off the engine mounts.

20. Remove the engine mount-to-engine brackets.

21. Remove the engine.

22. Reverse the removal procedure to install.

S-SERIES TRUCKS

Gasoline Engine

1. Raise the hood and disconnect the battery cables.

2. Remove the skid plate and drain both the cooling system and the oil pan.

3. Remove the air cleaner assembly and vacuum hoses. Mark the vacuum hoses for reinstallation.

4. Disconnect all hoses, tubing and electrical leads from the engine and mark them for reinstallation.

5. Remove the radiator and fan blade assembly.

6. Disconnect the exhaust pipe from the exhaust manifold.

7. Raise the vehicle and, if equipped with a manual transmission, remove the clutch return spring and cable.

8. Remove the starter motor and fasten it to the frame rail with a piece of wire.

9. Remove the flywheel cover pan.

10. Remove the bell housing bolts and support the transmission.

11. Lift the engine slightly and remove the engine mount nuts.

12. Make certain that all lines, hoses, wires and cables have been disconnected from the engine and the frame.

13. Remove the engine from the vehicle with the front of the engine raised slightly.

14. Installation is the reverse of removal.

Diesel Engine

2-WHEEL DRIVE

1. Raise engine hood.

2. Disconnect the battery ground cable.

3. Remove the hood.

4. Remove the battery assembly.

5. Remove under cover and drain the cooling system by opening the drain plugs on the radiator and on the cylinder block.

6. Remove the air cleaner assembly as follows:

    a. Remove the intake silencer.

    b. Remove the bolts fixing the air cleaner and loosen the clamp bolt.

    c. Lift the air cleaner slightly and disconnect the breather hose, then remove the air cleaner assembly.

7. Disconnect the upper water hose at the engine side.

8. Loosen the compressor drive belts by moving the power steering oil pump or idler (if so equipped).

9. Remove the cooling fan and fan shroud.

10. Disconnect the lower water hose at the engine side.

11. Remove the radiator grille.

12. Remove the radiator attaching bolts and remove the radiator.

13. Disconnect the accelerator control cable from the injection pump side.

14. Disconnect the air conditioner compressor control cable (if so equipped).

15. Disconnect the fuel hoses from the injection pump.

16. Disconnect the battery cable from the cylinder body.

17. Disconnect the transmission wiring.

18. Disconnect the vacuum hose from the fast idle actuator.

19. Disconnect the connector at fuel cut solenoid.

20. Disconnect the A/C compressor wiring.

21. Disconnect the heater hoses extending from the heater unit from the dash panel side.

22. Disconnect the hose for master-vac from the vacuum pump.

23. Disconnect vacuum hose from the vacuum pump.

24. Disconnect the generator wiring at the connector.

25. Disconnect the exhaust pipe from the exhaust manifold at the flange.

26. Remove the exhaust pipe mounting brake from the engine back plate.

27. Disconnect the starter motor wiring.

28. Disconnect the battery cable from starter motor.

29. Slide the gearshift lever boot upwards on the lever. Remove 2 gearshift lever attaching bolts and remove lever.

30. Place a pan under transmission to receive oil, disconnect speedometer cable at the transmission then disconnect the ground cable.

31. Disconnect the driveshaft at differential side.

32. Remove the driveshaft.

33. Remove return spring from clutch fork.

34. Disconnect clutch cable from hooked portion of clutch fork and pull it out forward through stiffener bracket.

35. Remove two bracket to transmission rear mount bolts and nuts.

36. Raise engine and transmission as required and remove (4) crossmember to frame bracket bolts.

37. Remove the rear mounting nuts from the transmission rear extension.

38. Disconnect electrical connectors at CRS switch and back-up lamp switch.

39. Remove the engine mounting bolt and nuts. Check that the engine is slightly lifted before removing the engine mounting bolt and nuts.

40. Engine removal:

    a. Check to make certain all the parts have been removed or disconnected from the engine that are fastened to the frame side.

    b. Remove the engine toward front of the vehicle by maneuvering the hoist, so that front part of the engine is lifted slightly.

4 WHEEL DRIVE

1. Raise engine hood.

2. Disconnect the battery ground cable.

3. Remove the engine hood.

4. Remove the battery assembly.

5. Remove under cover and drain the cooling system by opening the drain plugs on the radiator and on the cylinder block.

6. Remove the air cleaner as follows:

    a. Remove the intake silencer.

    b. Remove the bolts fixing the air cleaner and loosen the clamp bolt.

    c. Lift the air cleaner slightly and disconnect the breather hose, then remove the air cleaner assembly.

7. Disconnect the upper water hose at the engine side.

8. Loosen the compressor drive belts by moving the power steering oil pump or idler (if so equipped).

9. Remove the cooling fan and fan shroud.

10. Disconnect the lower water hose at the engine side.

11. Remove the radiator grille.

12. Remove the radiator attaching bolts and remove the radiator.

13. Disconnect the accelerator control cable from the injection pump side.

14. Disconnect the air conditioner compressor control cable (if so equipped).

15. Disconnect the fuel hoses from the injection pump.

16. Disconnect the battery cable from the cylinder body.

17. Disconnect the transmission wiring.

18. Disconnect the vacuum hose from the fast idle actuator.

19. Disconnect the connector at fuel cut solenoid.

20. Disconnect the A/C compressor wiring.

21. Disconnect the heater hoses extending from the heater unit from the dash panel side.

22. Disconnect the hose for master-vac from the vacuum pump.

23. Disconnect the vacuum hose from the vacuum pump.

24. Disconnect the generator wiring at the connector.

25. Disconnect the exhaust pipe from the exhaust manifold at the flange.

26. Remove the exhaust pipe mounting brake from the engine back plate.

27. Disconnect the starter motor wiring.

28. Disconnect the battery cable from starter motor.

29. Slide the transmission and transfer gearshift lever boot upwards on each lever, remove gearshift lever attaching bolts.

30. Remove return spring from transfer gear shift lever then remove levers.

31. Remove the transmission.

32. Remove the engine mounting bolts and nuts. Check that the engine is slightly lifted before removing the engine mounting bolts and nuts.

33. Engine removal:

a. Check to make certain all the parts have been removed or disconnected from the engine that are fastened to the frame side.

b. Remove the engine toward front of the vehicle by maneuvering the hoist, so that front part of the engine is lifted slightly.

34. Installation is the reverse of removal.

Cylinder Head

REMOVAL & INSTALLATION

4-119

1. Remove cam cover.
2. Remove EGR pipe clamp bolt at rear of cylinder head.
3. Raise vehicle on hoist.
4. Disconnect exhaust pipe at exhaust manifold.
5. Lower vehicle on hoist.
6. Drain cooling system.
7. Disconnect heater hoses at intake manifold and at front of cylinder head.
8. Remove A/C and/or P/S compressor or pump and lay them aside.
9. Disconnect accelerator linkage at carburetor, fuel line at carburetor, all necessary electrical connections, spark plug wires and necessary vacuum lines.
10. Rotate camshaft until #4 cylinder is in firing position. Remove distributor cap and mark rotor to housing relationship. Remove the distributor.
11. Remove the fuel pump.
12. Lock the shoe on automatic adjuster in fully retracted position by depressing the adjuster lock lever with a screwdriver or equivalent in direction as indicated in the drawing.
13. Remove timing sprocket to camshaft bolt and remove the sprocket and the fuel pump drive cam from the camshaft. Keep the sprocket on the chain damper and tensioner—do not remove the sprocket from the chain.

4–119 head bolt torque sequence

14. Disconnect AIR hose and check valve at air manifold.
15. Remove cylinder head to timing cover bolts.
16. Remove cylinder head bolts using Extension Bar Wrench J-24239-01; remove bolts in progressonal sequence, beginning with the outer bolts.
17. With the aid of an assistant, remove cylinder head, intake and exhaust manifold as an assembly.
18. Clean all gasket material from cylinder head and block surfaces.

NOTE: The gasket surfaces on both the head and block must be clean of any foreign matter and free of nicks or heavy scratches. Cylinder bolt threads in the block and threads on the bolts must be cleaned (dirt will affect bolt torque).

19. Place new gasket over dowel pins with "TOP" side of gasket up.
20. Reverse removal Steps 1–17.

Tighten cylinder head bolts a little at a time in the sequence shown, torque to 60 lb. ft. and then retighten to specified torque of 72 ft. lb.

4-121

NOTE: The engine should be "overnight" cold before removing the cylinder head.

1. Disconnect the negative battery cable.
2. Drain the cooling system into a clean container; the coolant can be reused if it is still good.
3. Remove the air cleaner. Raise and support the front of the vehicle.
4. Remove the exhaust shield. Disconnect the exhaust pipe.
5. Remove the heater hose from the intake manifold and then lower the car.
6. Unscrew the mounting bolts and remove the engine lift bracket (includes air management).

CYLINDER HEAD BOLT
TIGHTENING SEQUENCE

4–121 head bolt torque sequence

7. Remove the distributor. Disconnect the vacuum manifold at the alternator bracket.
8. Tag and disconnect the remaining vacuum lines at the intake manifold and thermostat.
9. Remove the air management pipe at the exhaust check valve.
10. Disconnect the accelerator linkage at the carburetor and then remove the linkage bracket.
11. Tag and disconnect all necessary wires. Remove the upper radiator hose at the thermostat.
12. Remove the bolt attaching the dipstick tube and hot water bracket.
13. Remove the idler pulley. Remove the A.I.R. and power steering pump drive belts.
14. Remove the A.I.R. bracket-to-intake manifold bolt. If equipped with power steering, remove the air pump pulley, The

A.I.R. thru-bolt and the power steering adjusting bracket.
15. Loosen the A.I.R. mounting bracket lower bolt so that the bracket will rotate.
16. Disconnect and plug the fuel line at the carburetor.
17. Remove the alternator. Remove the alternator brace from the head and then remove the upper mounting bracket.
18. Remove the cylinder head cover. Remove the rocker arms and push rods.
19. Remove the cylinder head bolts in the order given in the illustration. Remove the cylinder head with the carburetor, intake and exhaust manifolds still attached. To install, the gasket surfaces on both the head and the block must be clean of any foreign matter and free of any nicks or heavy scratches. Cylinder bolt threads in the block and the bolt must be clean.
20. Place a new cylinder head gasket in position over the dowel pins on the block. Carefully guide the cylinder head into position.
21. Coat the cylinder bolts with sealing compound and install them finger tight.
22. Using a torque wrench, gradually tighten the bolts in the sequence shown in the illustration to the proper specifications.
23. Installation of the remaining components is in the reverse order of removal.

4-137 Diesel

1. Follow the intake and exhaust manifold removal steps.
2. Remove the intake and exhaust manifold gasket.
3. Drain the cooling system by opening the drain plugs on the radiator and on the cylinder block.
4. Disconnect the upper water hose at the engine side.
5. Remove the cooling fan and fan shroud.
6. Remove the sleeve nuts and disconnect the injection pipes.

4–137 diesel head bolt torque sequence

7. Remove the nozzle holder fixing nuts and remove the nozzle holder assembly.
8. Follow the rocker arm, bracket and shaft assembly removal steps.
9. Remove the pushrods.
10. Remove the joint bolt and disconnect the leak-off pipe.
11. Remove the 19 bolts fixing the cyl-

inder head, then remove the cylinder head and gasket.

12. Install the cylinder head gasket with the TOP mark side up on the cylinder body by aligning the holes with the dowels.

13. Install the cylinder head.

14. Install the pushrod in position on the cylinder head.

15. Install the rocker arm assembly on the cylinder head. Tighten the bracket fixing bolts evenly in sequence commencing with the inner ones.

16. Follow the intake and exhaust manifold installation steps.

17. Install the cooling fan and fan shroud.

18. Connect the upper water hose to engine side.

19. Fill the engine cooling system.

6-173
LEFT SIDE

1. Raise and support the truck.

2. Drain the coolant from the block and lower the car.

3. Remove the intake manifold.

4. Remove the crossover.

5. Remove the alternator and AIR pump brackets.

6. Remove the dipstick tube.

7. Loosen the rocker arm bolts and remove the pushrods. Keep the pushrods in the same order as removed.

8. Remove the cylinder head bolts in stages and in the reverse order of the tightening sequence.

9. Remove the cylinder head. Do not pry on the head to loosen it.

10. Installation is the reverse of removal. The words "This side Up" on the new cylinder head gasket should face upward. Coat the cylinder head bolts with sealer and torque to specifications in the sequence shown. Make sure the pushrods seat in the lifter seats and adjust the valves.

RIGHT SIDE

1. Raise the car and drain the coolant from the block.

2. Disconnect the exhaust pipe and lower the car.

3. If equipped, remove the cruise control servo bracket.

4. Remove the air management valve and hose.

6-173 head bolt torque sequence

5. Remove the intake manifold.

6. Remove the exhaust crossover.

7. Loosen the rocker arm nuts and remove the pushrods. Keep the pushrods in the order in which they were removed.

8. Remove the cylinder head bolts in stages and in the reverse order of the tightening sequence.

9. Remove the cylinder head, do not pry on the cylinder head to loosen it.

10. Installation is the reverse of removal. The words "This Side Up" on the new cylinder head gasket should face upwards. Coat the cylinder head bolts with sealer and tighten them to specifications in the sequence shown. Make sure the lower ends of the pushrods seat in the lifter seats and adjust the valves.

Six Cylinder

1. Drain the cooling system and remove the air cleaner. Disconnect the PCV hose. If equipped, disconnect the air injection hose.

2. Disconnect the accelerator pedal rod at the bellcrank on the manifold, and the fuel and vacuum lines at the carburetor.

3. Disconnect the exhaust pipe at the manifold flange, then remove the manifold bolts and clamps and remove the manifolds and carburetor as an assembly.

4. Remove the fuel and vacuum line retaining clip from the water outlet. Then disconnect the wire harness from the heat sending unit and coil, leaving the harness clear of clips on the rocker arm cover.

5. Disconnect the radiator hose at the water outlet housing and the battery ground strap at the cylinder head.

6. Disconnect the wires and remove the spark plugs. Disconnect the coil-to-distributor primary wire lead at the coil and remove the coil on models without HEI.

7. Remove the rocker arm cover. Back off the rocker arm nuts, pivot the rocker arms to clear the pushrods and remove the pushrods.

8. Remove the cylinder head bolts, cylinder head and gasket.

To install:

1. Place a new cylinder head gasket over the dowel pins in the cylinder block with the head up. Do not use sealer on composition steel/asbestos gaskets.

2. Guide and lower the cylinder head into place over the dowels and gasket.

3. Use sealant on the cylinder head bolts, install and tighten them down snugly.

4. Tighten the cylinder head bolts a little at aa time with a torque wrench in the

correct sequence. Final torque should be as specified.

5. Install the valve pushrods down through the cylinder head openings and seat them in their lifter sockets.

6. Install the rocker arms, balls and nuts and tighten the rocker arm nuts until all pushrod play is taken up.

7. Install the thermostat, the thermostat housing and the water outlet using new gaskets. Then connect the radiator hose.

8. Install the temperature sending switch.

9. Install the spark plugs.

10. Use new plug gaskets (if required) and torque to specifications.

11. Install the coil, then connect the heat sending unit and coil primary wires, and the battery ground cable at the cylinder head.

12. Clean the surfaces and install a new gasket over the manifold studs. Install the manifold. Install the bolts and clamps and torque as specified.

13. Connect the throttle linkage.

14. Connect the PCV fuel and vacuum lines and secure the lines in the clip at the water outlet. Connect the air injection line.

15. Fill the cooling system and check for leaks.

16. Adjust the valve lash as explained later.

17. Install the rocker arm cover and position the wiring harness in the clips.

18. Clean and install the air cleaner.

V8 Gasoline Engines

1. Remove the intake manifold as described later.

2. Remove the exhaust manifolds as described later and tie out of the way.

3. If the truck is equipped with air conditioning, remove the A/C compressor and the forward mounting bracket and lay the compressor aside. Do not disconnect any of the refrigerant lines.

4. Back off the rocker arm nuts and pivot the rocker arms out of the way so that the pushrods can be removed. Identify the

Small block V8 head bolt tightening sequence

6-250, 292 head bolt torque sequence

8-454 head bolt torque sequence

pushrods so that they can be installed in their original positions.

5. Remove the cylinder head bolts and remove the heads.

6. Install the cylinder heads using new gaskets. Install the gaskets with the head up.

NOTE: Coat a steel gasket on both sides with sealer. If a composition gasket is used, do not use sealer.

7. Clean the bolts, apply sealer to the threads, and install them hand tight.

8. Tighten the head bolts a little at a time in the sequence shown. Head bolt torque is listed in the Torque Specifications chart.

9. Install the intake and exhaust manifolds.

10. Adjust the rocker arms as explained later.

Diesel

It is strongly recommended that the cylinder heads not be removed on diesels. The procedure requires that the intake manifold and rocker arms be removed, which, in turn, requires removal of the valve lifters, disassembly, and reassembly while submerged in kerosene or diesel fuel. The valve lifters must then be bled down using a specially weighted press. In addition, removal of the intake manifold requires re-timing of the injection pump, which involves grinding off the old timing marks and using a

8-379 (6.2L) diesel head bolt torque sequence

8-350 (5.7L) diesel head bolt torque sequence

special timing tool to scribe new marks while the pump is torqued to specification. It is advised that any work of this nature be performed by a qualified dealer or mechanic, as the tools involved are expensive and not generally available.

However, if the necessary tools are available, the cylinder heads may be removed and installed as follows:

1. Remove the intake manifold, using the procedure outlined later in this chapter.

2. Remove the rocker arm cover(s), after removing any accessory brackets which interfere with cover removal.

3. Disconnect and label the glow plug wiring.

4. If the right cylinder head is being removed, remove the ground strap from the head.

5. Remove the rocker arm bolts, the bridge pivots, the rocker arms, and the pushrods, keeping all the parts in order so that they can be returned to their original positions. It is a good practice to number or mark the parts to avoid interchanging them.

6. Remove the fuel return lines from the nozzles.

7. Remove the exhaust manifold(s), using the procedure outlined later in this chapter.

8. Remove the engine block drain plug on the side of the engine from which the cylinder head is being removed.

9. Remove the head bolts. On the 379 cid (6.2 L), the rear left head bolt may have to remain in the head. Remove the cylinder head.

10. To install, first clean the mating surfaces thoroughly. Install new head gaskets on the engine block. Do NOT coat the gaskets with any sealer. The gaskets have a special coating that eliminates the need for sealer. The use of sealer will interfere with this coating and cause leaks. Install the cylinder head onto the block. On the 379 cid, install the left rear head bolt before installing the head.

11. Clean the head bolts thoroughly. On the 350 (5.7 L), dip the bolts in clean engine oil and install into the cylinder block until the heads of the bolts lightly contact the cylinder head. On the 379 cid, coat the bolt threads with G sealer.

12. Tighten the bolts, in the sequence illustrated, to 100 ft. lbs. for the 350, and 60 ft. lbs. for the 379 (6.2 L). When all bolts have been tightened to this figure, begin the tightening sequence again, and torque all bolts to 130 ft. lbs. for the 350, and 96 ft. lbs. for the 379 (6.2 L).

13. Install the engine block drain plug(s), the exhaust manifold(s), the fuel return lines, the glow plug wiring, and the ground strap for the right cylinder head.

14. After disassembling, cleaning, and reassembling the valve lifters, bleed them down using the appropriate procedure outlined later in this section, and install them into the engine. Install the pushrods, rocker arms, and pivots into their original locations.

15. Install the intake manifold.

16. Install the rocker cover(s). The covers do not use gaskets, but are sealed with a bead of RTV (room temperature vulcanizing) silicone sealer instead. Apply a 3/32 inch bead of RTV sealer, G.M. #1052289 or the equivalent, to the clean and dry mating surface of the rocker arm cover. Run the bead of sealer to the inside of the bolt holes. Install the cover to the head within 10 minutes (while the sealer is still wet).

Rocker Arm Cover

REMOVAL & INSTALLATION

1. Disconnect the negative battery cable.

2. Remove the air cleaner.

3. Disconnect the crankcase ventilation hose at the rocker arm covers.

4. Disconnect the wiring from the rocker arm clips.

5. Remove the carburetor heat stove pipe, on models so equipped. On diesels, remove the injection lines.

6. If the truck is equipped with A/C, remove the compressor rear brace. Do not disconnect any of the refrigerant lines.

7. Remove the rocker arm attaching bolts and remove the cover. If the cover is difficult to remove, gently tap the front of the cover rearward with your hand or a rubber mallet. If this still does not work, CAREFULLY pry the cover off. Be very careful not to distort the sealing surface.

8. On installation, apply a 3/16 in. bead of sealer to the mating surface after removing all the old loose sealer.

9. Reverse the removal procedure to install.

10. Install the fuel lines, and, with the protective covers, J-29664-1 installed, start the engine.

Valve System

VALVE LASH ADJUSTMENT

All engines described in this book use hydraulic lifters, which require no periodic adjustment. In the event of cylinder head removal or any operation that requires disturbing the rocker arms, the rocker arms will have to be adjusted.

4-119 & 4-137 Diesel

NOTE: The valves are adjusted with the engine cold.

1. Make sure that the cylinder head and camshaft retaining bolts are tightened to the proper torque.

2. Remove the camshaft carrier side cover.

3. Turn the crankshaft with a wrench on the front pulley attaching bolt or by bumping the engine with the starter or re-

mote starter button until the no. 1 piston is at TDC of the compression stroke. You can tell when the piston is coming up on the compression stroke by removing the spark plug and placing your thumb over the hole and you will feel air being forced out of the spark plug hole past your thumb. Stop turning the crankshaft when the TDC timing mark on the crankshaft pulley is directly aligned with the timing pointer.

4. With the no. 1 piston at TDC of the compression stroke, check the clearance between the rocker arm an the camshaft with the proper thickness feeler gauge on nos. 1 and 2 intake valves and nos. 1 and 3 exhaust valves.

5. Adjust the clearance by loosening the locknut with an open-end wrench, turning the adjuster screw with a phillips head screwdriver and retightening the locknut. The proper thickness feeler gauge should pass between the camshaft and the rocker with a slight drag when the clearance is correct.

6. Turn the cranshaft one full turn to position the no. 4 piston at TDC of its compression stroke. Adjust the remaining valves: no. 2 and 4 exhaust and nos. 3 and 4 intake in the same manner as outlined in step 5.

7. Install the camshaft carrier sidecover.

Gasoline Engines Except 4-119

1. Remove the rocker covers and gaskets.

2. Adjust the valves on six cylinder engines as follows:

a. Mark the distributor housing with a piece of chalk at No. 1 and 6 plug wire positions. Remove the distributor cap with the plug wires attached.

b. Crank the engine until the distributor rotor points to no. 1 cylinder and the points are open. At this point, adjust the following valves:

No. 1—exhaust and intake
No. 2—intake
No. 3—exhaust
No. 4—intake
No. 5—exhaust

c. Back out the adjusting nut until lash is felt at the pushrod, then turn the adjusting nut in until all lash is removed. This can be determined by checking pushrod end-play while turning the adjusting nut. When all play has been removed, turn the adjusting nut in 1 full turn.

d. Crank the engine until the distributor rotor points to no. 6 cylinder and the points are open. The following valves can be adjusted:

No. 2—exhaust
No. 3—intake
No. 4—exhaust
No. 5—intake
No. 6—intake and exhaust

3. Adjust the valves on V8 engines as follows:

a. Crank the engine until the mark on the damper aligns with the TDC or 0° mark on the timing tab and the engine is in no. 1 firing position. This can be determined by placing the fingers on the no. 1 cylinder valves as the marks align. If the valves do not move, it is in no. 1 firing position. If the valves move, it is in no. 6 firing position and the crankshaft should be rotated one more revolution to the no. 1 firing position.

b. The adjustment is made in the same manner as 6 cylinder engines.

c. With the engine in no. 1 firing position, the following valves can be adjusted:
Exhaust—1,3,4,8
Intake—1,2,5,7

d. Crank the engine 1 full revolution until the marks are again in alignment. This is no. 6 firing position. The following valves can now be adjusted:
Exhaust—2,5,6,7
Intake—3,4,6,8

4. Reinstall the rocker arm covers using new gaskets.

5. Install the distributor cap and wire assembly.

Diesel Except 4-137

Valve lash adjustment in diesel engines is controlled by the valve lifters, rather than through adjustments to the rocker arms. If the intake manifold has been removed, or if the heads have been removed, it will be necessary to remove those valve lifters affected, disassemble, reassemble, and bleed them down under pressure from a specially weighted testing press. It is for this reason that removal of the valve lifters, intake manifold, or cylinder heads is specifically not recommended. The procedure is complicated and requires expensive tools not generally available.

If the intake manifold has not been removed but rocker arms have been loosened or removed, valve lifters can be bled down by the following procedure:

1. For cylinders no. 3,5,7,2,4 and 8, turn the crankshaft so the saw slot on the harmonic balancer is at 0° on the timing indicator. For cylinders no. 1,3,7,2,4 and 6, turn the crankshaft so that the saw slot on the harmonic balancer is at 4 o'clock.

2. Tighten the rocker arm pivot bolts to 25 ft. lbs.

NOTE: It will take up to 45 minutes at each position for the valve lifters to be completely bled down.

— CAUTION —
Do not rotate the engine until the valve lifters have been bled down, or damage to the valve train could occur.

3. If any additional lifters need to be bled, rotate the crankshaft to the second position. Again, you must wait at least 45 minutes before rotating the crankshaft.

4. Finish reassembling the engine as the lifters are being bled.

Six cylinder valve arrangement

V8 valve arrangement

VALVE GUIDES

Valve guides are integral with the cylinder head on all engines. Valve guide bores may be reamed to accommodate oversize valves. If wear permits, valve guides can be knurled to allow the retention of standard valves. Maximum allowable valve stem-to-guide bore clearances are listed under Valve Specifications.

Rocker Arms

REMOVAL & INSTALLATION

4-119

1. Remove the camshaft carrier as outlined under Cylinder Head Removal.

2. Remove the rocker spring from the pivot and lift the rocker from the cylinder head. Be careful not to lose the rocker guide resting on the top of each of the valves.

3. Install in the reverse order of removal.

4-137 Diesel

1. Remove the rocker cover.

2. Remove the 8 bolts fixing the rocker arm brackets in sequence commencing with the outer ones.

3. Remove the rocker arm, bracket and shaft assembly.

4. To install, follow the removal procedure in reverse order.

5. Tighten the bracket fixing bolts evenly in sequence commencing with the inner ones to 15 ft. lbs.

4-121

1. Remove the air cleaner. Remove the cylinder head cover.

2. Remove the rocker arm nut and ball. Lift the rocker arm off the stud. *Always keep the rocker arm assemblies together and install them on the same stud.* Remove the push rods.

To install:

3. Coat the bearing surfaces of the rocker

arms and the rocker arm balls with "Mo-lykote" or its equivalent.

4. Install the push rods making sure that they seat properly in the lifter.

5. Install the rocker arms, balls and nuts. Tighten the rocker arm nuts until all lash is eliminated.

6. Adjust the valves when the lifter is on the base circle of a camshaft lobe:

a. Crank the engine until the mark on the crankshaft pulley lines up with the '0' mark on the timing tab. Make sure that the engine is in the No. 1 firing position. Place your fingers on the No. 1 rocker arms as the mark on the crank pulley comes near the '0' mark. If the valves are not moving, the engine is in the No. 1 firing position. If the valves move, the engine is in the No. 4 firing position; rotate the engine one complete revolution and it will be in the No. 1 position.

b. When the engine is in the No. 1 firing position, adjust the following valves:
Exhaust—1,3
Intake—1,2

c. Back the adjusting nut out until lash can be felt at the push rod, then turn the nut until all lash is removed (this can be determined by rotating the push rod while turning the adjusting nut). When all lash has been removed, turn the nut in 1½ additional turns, this will center the lifter plunger.

d. Crank the engine one complete revolution until the timing tab and the '0' mark are again in alignment. Now the engine is in the No. 4 firing position. Adjust the following valves:
Exhaust—2,4
Intake—3,4

7. Installation of the remaining components is in the reverse order of removal.

LOCKS
CAP
SEAL
SHIELD

Rocker arm components

6-173

NOTE: Some engines are assembled using RTV (Room Temperature Vulcanizing silicone sealant in place of rocker arm cover gasket. If the engine was assembled using RTV, never use a gasket when reassembling. Conversely, if the engine was assembled using a rocker arm cover gasket, never replace it with RTV.

When using RTV, an ⅛ inch bead is sufficient. Always run the bead on the inside of the bolt holes.

Rocker arms are removed by removing the adjusting nut. Be sure to adjust valve lash after replacing rocker arms.

NOTE: When replacing an exhaust rocker, move an old intake rocker arm to the exhaust rocker arm stud and install the new rocker arm on the intake stud.

Cylinder heads use threaded rocker arm studs. If the threads in the head are damaged or stripped, the head can be retapped and a helical type insert installed.

NOTE: If engine is equipped with the A.I.R. exhaust emission control system, the interfering components of the system must be removed. Disconnect the lines at the air injection nozzles in the exhaust manifolds.

Gasoline Engines Except 4-119

Rocker arms are removed by removing the adjusting nut. Be sure to adjust the valve lash after replacing the rocker arms. Coat the replacement rocker arm and ball with engine assembly lube before installation.

Rocker arm studs that have damaged threads or are loose in the cylinder heads may be replaced by reaming the bore and installing oversize studs. Oversizes available are .003 and .013 in. The bores may also be tapped and screw-in studs installed. Several aftermarket companies produce complete rocker arm stud kits with installation tools.

Diesel Engines Except 4-137

1. Remove the air cleaner, high pressure fuel lines to the injectors, and the rocker arm cover.

2. Remove the arm pivot bolts and the pivot(s). Remove the rocker arms. The use of bridged pivots require that the rocker arms be removed in pairs.

3. To install, position the set of rocker arms in the original locations.

4. Lubricate the pivot contact surfaces and install the pivot(s).

5. Install the pivot bolts. Tighten the bolts alternately and evenly to 25 ft. lbs., following the bleed down procedure outlined previously under Valve Lash Adjustment for diesel engines.

6. Install the rocker arm cover as outlined in step 16 of the diesel engine cylinder head removal and installation procedure. Install the fuel lines and the air cleaner.

Valve Lifter Removal, Installation, Disassembly, and Bleed Down

DIESEL ENGINES EXCEPT 4-137

Whenever the rocker arms have been removed and the intake manifold removed, the valve lifters must be removed, disassembled, assembled while submerged in diesel fuel or kerosene, and bled down using a specially-weighted press. The lifters also must be disassembled, reassembled while submerged, and bled down on the press whenever they are removed. Note that if the rocker arms have been removed but the intake manifold has not been disturbed, the lifters can be bled down as outlined in the "Valve Lash Adjustment" procedure for diesel engines. The following procedure is to be used for lifter removal and installation, or whenever both the rocker arms and the intake manifold have been disturbed.

1. Remove the intake manifold.

2. Remove the rocker covers, the rocker arms, and the pushrods. Keep all the parts in order so that they may be installed in their original locations.

3. Remove the valve lifters.

To disassemble the lifters:

4. Remove the retainer ring with a small screwdriver.

5. Remove the pushrod seat. Remove the oil metering valve. Remove the plunger and plunger spring. Remove the check valve retainer from the plunger, and remove the valve and its spring.

6. Clean all parts in a safe solvent. Check for burrs, nicks, scoring, or excessive wear, and replace as necessary.

7. Check for lifter foot for excessive wear:

a. Place a straightedge across the lifter foot.

b. Hold the lifter at eye level. Check for light appearing between the lifter foot and the straightedge.

c. If light is visible, indicating a concave surface, the lifter should be replaced and the camshaft inspected. If the cam lobe is worn across the full width of the cam base circle (opposite the high lobe of the cam), the camshaft should be replaced. Wear at the center of the cam base circle is normal. Wear across the full width of the nose of the lobe is also normal.

8. After the lifter parts have been cleaned, assemble the valve disc spring and retainer into the plunger. Be sure the retainer flange is pressed tightly against the bottom of the recess in the plunger.

9. Install the plunger spring over the check retainer.

10. Hold the plunger with the spring up. Insert into the lifter body. Hold the plunger

vertically while doing this to avoid cocking the spring.

11. Fill the reservoir of G.M. tool no. J-5790 with kerosene to within ½ inch of the top of the reservoir. This tool is a specially weighted press with provision for reservoir rotation.

12. Place the valve lifter assembly into the reservoir. Position the oil control valve and the pushrod seat onto the plunger.

13. Install a ¼ inch steel ball onto the pushrod seat. Lower the tester ram until it contacts the steel ball. Do not press on the ram. Allow the ram to move downward by its own weight, until the air bubbles expelled from the lifter assembly disappear.

14. Raise the ram, then allow it to lower by its own weight. Repeat this operation until all air is expelled from the lifter. Do not attempt to hasten the process by pumping the ram up and down.

15. After all air has been expelled, allow the ram to descend, bleeding the lifter, until the retaining ring groove is exposed. Install the retaining ring.

16. Adjust the ram screw so that it contacts the steel ball in the pushrod seat at the same time as the pointer is at the start line.

17. Raise the arm of the tester, then start the bleed down test by resting the ram on the steel ball and starting a timer. Rotate the reservoir one revolution every two seconds, and time the indicator from the start line to the stop line. Acceptable leak down time is 6 seconds minimum for used lifters, and from 9 to 60 seconds for a new lifter.

18. If the lifter leak down rate falls within the specified limit, the lifter may be reused. If not, new lifters should be installed in the engine.

19. If new lifters are to be installed, they must first be filled with kerosene or diesel fuel. Install the lifter in the tester. Fill the reservoir to within ½ inch of the top, and fill the lifter as outlined i steps 13, 14, and 15 of this procedure.

To install the lifters:

20. Coat the foot of the lifter with G.M. lubricant #562458 or the equivalent.

21. Install the lifters into their original positions. Install the pushrods into their original positions.

22. Install the intake manifold.

23. Install the rocker arms and pivots.

24. Bleed down the lifters as outlined under Valve Lash Adjustment for the diesel engine.

25. Install the rocker covers.

Intake Manifold

REMOVAL & INSTALLATION

4-119

1. Disconnect the battery ground cable and remove the air cleaner assembly.

2. Remove the EGR pipe clamp bolt at the rear of the cylinder head.

3. Raise the vehicle and remove the EGR pipe from the intake and exhaust manifolds.

4. Remove the EGR valve and bracket assembly from the intake manifold.

5. Lower the vehicle and drain the cooling system.

6. Remove the upper coolant hoses from the manifold.

7. Disconnect the accelerator linkage, vacuum lines, electrical wiring and fuel line from the intake manifold.

8. Remove the retaining nuts and remove the manifold from the cylinder head.

9. Remove the lower heater hose while holding the manifold away from the engine. Remove the manifold from the vehicle.

10. Installation is the reverse of removal.

4-137 Diesel

1. Raise engine hood.

2. Remove the bolts fixing the air cleaner and loosen the clamp bolt.

3. Lift the air cleaner slightly and disconnect the breather hose, then remove the air cleaner assembly.

4. Remove the 2 bolts and 4 nuts fixing the intake manifold.

5. Remove the intake manifold.

6. Installation is the reverse of removal. Torque the bolts to 15 ft. lbs.

4-121

1. Disconnect the negative battery cable.

2. Remove the air cleaner. Drain the cooling system.

3. Tag and disconnect all necessary vacuum lines and wires. Remove the idler pulley.

4. Remove the A.I.R. drive belt. If equipped with power steering, remove the drive belt and then remove the pump with the lines attached. Position the pump out of the way.

5. Remove the A.I.R. bracket-to-intake manifold bolt. Remove the air pump pulley.

6. If equipped with power steering, remove the A.I.R. thru-bolt and then the power steering adjusting bracket.

7. Loosen the lower bolt on the air pump mounting bracket so that the bracket will rotate.

8. Disconnect the fuel line at the carburetor. Disconnect the carburetor linkage and then remove the carburetor.

9. Lift off the Early Fuel Evaporation (EFE) heater grid.

10. Remove the distributor.

11. Remove the mounting bolts and nuts and remove the intake manifold. Make sure to disconnect the heater hose and condenser from the bottom of the intake manifold before you lift it all the way out.

12. Using a new gasket, replace the manifold, tightening the nuts and bolts to specification.

13. Installation of the remaining components is in the reverse order of removal. Adjust all necessary drive belts and check the ignition timing.

Exploded view of the 5.7L diesel valve lifter

A specially weighted hand press must be used to assemble the diesel valve lifters

4-119 intake manifold

6-173

1. Remove the rocker covers.

2. Drain the cooling system.

3. If equipped, remove the AIR pump and bracket.

4. Remove the distributor cap. Mark the position of the ignition rotor in relation to the distributor body, and remove the distributor. Do not crank the engine with the distributor removed.

5. Remove the heater and radiator hoses from the intake manifold.

6. Remove the power brake vacuum hose.

7. Disconnect and label the vacuum hoses. Remove the EFE pipe from the rear of the manifold.

8. Remove the carburetor linkage. Disconnect and plug the fuel line.

9. Remove the manifold retaining bolts and nuts.

10. Remove the intake manifold. Remove and discard the gaskets, and scrape off the old silicone seal from the front and rear ridges.

To install:

1. The gaskets are marked for right and left side installation; do not interchange them. Clean the sealing surface of the engine block, and apply a ³⁄₁₆ in. bead of silicone sealer to each ridge.

2. Install the new gaskets onto the heads. The gaskets will have to be cut slightly to fit past the center pushrods. Do not cut any more material than necessary. Hold the gaskets in place by extending the ridge bead of sealer ¼ in. onto the gasket ends.

3. Install the intake manifold. The area

6–173 intake manifold torque sequence

Small block V8 intake manifold torque sequence

8-454 intake manifold torque sequence

between the ridges and the manifold should be completely sealed.

4. Install the retaining bolts and nuts, and tighten in sequence to 23 ft. lbs. Do not overtighten; the manifold is made from aluminum, and can be warped or cracked with excessive force.

5. The rest of installation is the reverse of removal. Adjust the ignition timing after installation, and check the coolant level after the engine has warmed up.

Six Cylinder with Combination Manifold

The intake and exhaust manifolds are removed as an assembly.

1. Remove the air cleaner.

2. Disconnect the throttle rods at the bellcrank and remove the throttle return spring.

3. Disconnect the fuel and vacuum lines at the carburetor. Plug the fuel line. Disconnect the choke cable at the carburetor.

4. Disconnect the crankcase ventilation hose at the carburetor. Disconnect the vapor hose at the evaporativ canister, if so equipped.

5. Disconnect the exhaust pipe at the manifold flange and discard the packing.

6. Disconnect the EGR valve hose (if equipped).

7. Remove the manifold attaching bolts and clamps and remove the manifold assembly. Discard the gaskets.

8. The manifold assembly can be separated by removing 1 bolt and 2 nuts at the center. Don't tighten these down all the way until the manifold assembly is installed on the engine.

9. Check the manifold for straightness along the exhaust port faces. If it is distorted more than 0.015 in. it should be replaced. Clean all mounting faces.

10. Installation is the reverse of removal. Use all new gaskets. Bolt torques are given in the Torque Specifications.

V8 Except Diesel

1. Remove the air cleaner.

2. Drain the radiator.

3. Disconnect:

   a. Battery cables at the battery.

   b. Upper radiator and heater hoses at the manifolds.

   c. Crankcase ventilation hoses as required.

   d. Fuel line and choke cable at the carburetor.

   e. Accelerator linkage at the carburetor.

   f. Vacuum hose at the distributor.

   g. Power brake hose at the carburetor base or manifold, if applicable.

   h. Temperature sending switch wires.

   i. Water pump by-pass at the water pump (Mark IV only).

4. Remove the distributor cap and scribe the rotor position relative to the distributor body.

5. Remove the distributor.

6. As required, remove the oil filler

bracket, air cleaner bracket, air compressor and bracket and accelerator bellcrank.

7. Remove the manifold-to-head attaching bolts then remove the manifold and carburetor as an assembly.

8. If the manifold is to be replaced, transfer the carburetor (and mounting studs), water outlet and thermostat (use a new gasket) heater hose adapter, EGR valve (use new gasket) and, if applicable, TVS switch and the choke coil. All engines use a carburetor heat choke tube which must be transferred to a new manifold.

9. Before installing the manifold, thoroughly clean the gasket and seal surfaces of the cylinder heads and manifold.

10. Install the manifold end seals, folding the tabs if applicable, and the manifold/head gaskets, using a sealing compound around the water passages, 1978 and later models use RTV (Room Temperature Vulcanizing) silicone seal at the front and rear ridges of the cylinder block, instead of seals. On these models, remove any loose RTV from the sealing surfaces. Apply a ³⁄₁₆ inch bead of RTV sealer, G.M. #1052366 or the equivalent, on the front and rear ridges, extending the bead up ½ inch on the cylinder heads to seal and retain the intake manifold side gaskets.

11. When installing the manifold, care should be taken not to dislocate the end seals. It is helpful to use a pilot in the distributor opening. Tighten the manifold bolts to 30 ft. lbs. in the sequence illustrated.

12. Install the distributor with the rotor in its original location as indicated by the scribe line. If the engine has been disturbed, refer to Distributor Removal and Installation.

13. If applicable, install the alternator upper bracket and adjust the belt tension.

14. Connect all components disconnected in steps 3 and 6.

15. Fill the cooling system, start the engine, check for leaks and adjust the ignition timing and carburetor idle speed and mixture.

Diesel

It is not recommended that the intake manifold be removed on diesel engines. The procedure requires re-timing of the injection pump. This involves grinding off the old timing mark and scribing a new mark with a special timing tool while re-torquing the pump to specification. It is strongly advised that any work of this nature be performed only by a qualified mechanic or dealer.

If the necessary tools are available, the intake manifold can be removed and installed using the following procedure.

1. Remove the air cleaner.

2. Drain the radiator. Loosen the upper bypass hose clamp, remove the thermostat housing bolts, and remove the housing and the thermostat from the intake manifold.

3. Remove the breather pipes from the rocker covers and the air crossover. Remove the air crossover. It is a good idea to

cover the air intakes in the manifold to prevent nuts and bolts from falling down into the engine, if dropped. The intake passages can simply be taped over.

4. Disconnect the throttle rod and the return spring. If equipped with cruise control, remove the servo.

5. Remove the hairpin clip at the bellcrank and disconnect the cables. Remove the throttle cable from the bracket on the manifold; position the cable away from the engine. Disconnect and label any wiring as necessary.

6. Remove the alternator bracket as necessary. If the truck is equipped with air conditioning, remove the compressor mounting bolts and move the compressor aside, without disconnecting any of the hoses. Remove the compressor mounting bracket from the intake manifold.

7. Disconnect the fuel line from the pump and the fuel filter. Remove the fuel filter and bracket.

8. Disconnect the fuel return line from the injection pump. Using two wrenches to prevent the lines from being twisted, disconnect the injection pump lines at the nozzles.

━━━━━━ **CAUTION** ━━━━━━
Do not bend the injection pump lines!

9. Remove the three nuts retaining the injection pump, using G.M. special tool no. J-26987 or the equivalent. Remove the pump and cap all open lines and nozzles.

10. Disconnect the vacuum lines at the vacuum pump. Remove the bolt and the bracket holding the pump to the block and remove the pump.

11. Remove the intake manifold drain tube clamp and remove the drain tube.

12. Remove the intake manifold bolts and remove the manifold. Remove the adapter seal. Remove the injection pump adapter.

13. Clean the mating surfaces of the cylinder heads and the intake manifold using a putty knife. Be extremely careful not to scratch or gouge the surfaces. Clean and dry the surfaces with solvent.

To install the manifold:

NOTE: If the rocker arms have been removed, the valve lifters must be removed, disassembled, then reassembled while submerged in kerosene or diesel fuel, then bled down using the specially weighted press. See the procedure earlier in this chapter. Do not install the manifold until the affected lifters have been serviced.

14. Coat both sides of the gasket surface that seal the intake manifold to the cylinder heads with G.M. sealer #1050805 or the equivalent. Position the intake manifold gaskets on the cylinder heads. Install the end seals, making sure that the ends are positioned under the cylinder heads.

15. Carefully lower the intake manifold into place on the engine.

16. Clean the intake manifold bolts thoroughly, then dip them in clean engine oil. Install the bolts and tighten to 15 ft. lbs. in the sequence shown. Next, tighten all the bolts to 30 ft. lbs., in sequence, and finally tighten to 40 ft. lbs. in sequence.

17. Install the intake manifold drain tube and clamp.

18. File the mark from the injection pump adapter.

━━━━━━ **CAUTION** ━━━━━━
Do not file the mark from the injection pump.

19. Place the engine on TDC for the No. 1 cylinder. The mark on the harmonic balancer on the crankshaft will be aligned with the zero mark on the timing tab, and both valves for no. 1 cylinder will be closed. The index mark on the injection pump driven gear should be offset to the right when no. 1 is at TDC. Check that all these conditions are met before continuing.

20. Apply chassis grease to the seal area on the adapter, the tapered edge and the seal area on the intake manifold. Install the adapter but leave the bolts loose.

21. Apply chassis grease to the inside and outside diameters of the adapter seal, and to the seal installing tool, G.M. no J-28425. Install the seal onto the tool.

22. Push the seal onto the injection pump adapter, using the tool (no. J-28425 or the equivalent). Remove the tool and inspect the seal to see if it is properly positioned.

23. Tighten the adapter bolts to 25 ft. lbs.

24. Install a timing tool, G.M. no. J-26896 or the equivalent, into the injection pump adapter. Tighten the tool toward No. 1 cylinder to 50 ft. lbs. While holding the tool and adapter at this torque, mark the injection pump adapter by striking the marking pin with a hammer. Remove the tool.

25. Remove the protective caps from the lines. Line up the offset tang on the injection pump driveshaft with the pump driven gear. Install the pump.

26. Install the three retaining nuts and lockwashers for the injection pump but do not tighten the nuts. Connect the injection pump lines to the nozzles. Use two wrenches to tighten the lines (25 ft. lbs.).

8-350 diesel intake manifold torque sequence

8-379 diesel intake manifold torque sequence

The index mark on the injection pump driven gear will be offset to the right when the no. 1 cylinder is at TDC

Adapter seal installation

Injection pump timing mark application

27. Connect the fuel return lines to the pump.

28. Align the injection pump mark with the adapter mark and tighten the nuts. Use a ¾ inch open end wrench on the boss at the front of the injection pump to aid in rotating the pump to align the marks. Tighten the nuts to 18 ft. lbs.

29. Adjust the throttle rod and return spring.

30. Install the fuel filter and bracket and install the fuel line to the pump and the filter.

31. Install the vacuum pump and the vacuum lines. Do not operate the engine without the vacuum pump installed—it is the drive for the engine oil pump.

32. Connect the wiring.

33. Install the alternator and air conditioning compressor brackets.

34. Install the cable in the bracket and bellcrank, then install the bellcrank.

35. Connect the throttle rod and the return spring.

36. Remove the tape from the air intakes and install the air crossover. Install the breather tubes and the flow control valve at the air crossover. Connect the upper radiator hose and the heater hose, install the thermostat and thermostat housing, fill the cooling system, start the engine and check for leaks.

Exhaust Manifold

REMOVAL & INSTALLATION

4-119

1. Disconnect the battery ground cable and remove the air cleaner assembly.

2. Remove the EGR pipe clamp bolt at the rear of the cylinder head.

3. Raise the vehicle and remove the EGR pipe from the intake and exhaust manifolds.

4. Separate the exhaust pipe from the manifold.

5. Remove the manifold shield and remove the heat stove.

6. Remove the manifold retaining nuts and remove the manifold from the engine.

7. Installation is the reverse of removal.

4-137 Diesel

1. Raise engine hood.

2. Remove the bolts fixing the air cleaner and loosen the clamp bolt.

3. Lift the air cleaner slightly and disconnect the breather hose, then remove the air cleaner assembly.

4. Disconnect the exhaust pipe from the exhaust manifold at the flange.

5. Remove the 3 nuts fixing the exhaust manifold, then remove the engine hanger and exhaust manifold.

6. Installation is the reverse of removal. Torque the bolts to 15 ft. lbs.

4-121

1. Disconnect the negative battery cable.

2. Remove the air cleaner. Remove the exhaust manifold shield. Raise and support the front of the vehicle.

3. Disconnect the exhaust pipe at the manifold and then lower the vehicle.

4. Disconnect the air management-to-check valve hose and remove the bracket. Disconnect the oxygen sensor lead wire.

5. Remove the alternator belt. Remove the alternator adjusting bolts, loosen the pivot bolt and pivot the alternator upward.

6. Remove the alternator brace and the A.I.R. pipes bracket bolt.

7. Unscrew the mounting bolts and remove the exhaust manifold. The manifold should be removed with the A.I.R. plumbing as an assembly. If the manifold is to be replaced, transfer the plumbing to the new one.

8. Clean the mating surface on the manifold and the head, position the manifold and tighten the bolts to the proper specifications.

9. Installation of the remaining components is in the reverse order of removal.

6-173

LEFT SIDE

1. Remove the air cleaner. Remove the carburetor heat stove pipe.

2. Remove the air supply plumbing from the exhaust manifold.

3. Raise and support the car. Unbolt and remove the exhaust pipe at the manifold.

4. Unbolt and remove the manifold.
To install:

1. Clean the mating surfaces of the cylinder head and manifold. Install the manifold onto the head, and install the retaining bolts finger tight.

2. Tighten the manifold bolts in a circular pattern, working from the center to the ends, to 25 ft. lbs. in two stages.

3. Connect the exhaust pipe to the manifold.

4. The remainder of installation is the reverse of removal.

RIGHT SIDE

1. Raise and support the car.

2. Tighten the exhaust pipe-to-manifold flange bolts until they break off. Remove the pipe from the manifold. Later models are equipped with flange bolts.

3. Lower the car. Remove the spark plug wires from the plugs. Number them first if they are not already labeled.

4. Remove the air supply pipes from the manifold. Remove the PULSAIR bracket bolt from the rocker cover, on models so equipped, then remove the pipe assembly.

5. Remove the manifold retaining bolts and remove the manifold.
To install:

1. Clean the mating surfaces of the cyl-inder head and manifold. Position the manifold against the head and install the retaining bolts finger tight.

2. Tighten the bolts in a circular pattern, working from the center to the ends, to 25 ft. lbs. in two stages.

3. Install the air supply system.

4. Install the spark plug wires.

5. Raise and support the car. Connect the exhaust pipe to the manifold and install new flange bolts.

Six Cylinder With Integral Head

1. Remove the air cleaner. Disconnect negative battery terminal.

2. Remove the power steering pump and, if equipped, the AIR pump.

3. Remove the EFE (early fuel evaporation) valve bracket.

4. Disconnect the throttle controls and the throttle return spring.

5. Disconnect the exhaust pipe at the manifold flange. Disconnect the converter bracket at the transmission mount, if so equipped. If equipped with manifold converter, disconnect the exhaust pipe from the converter, and remove the converter.

Six cylinder integral manifold torque sequence

6. Remove the manifold attaching bolts and remove the manifold. Discard the gasket.

7. Check for cracks in the manifold before it is replaced.

8. Install a new gasket on the exhaust manifold.

9. Clean and oil the bolts and install the bolts, torquing them to specifications.

10. Connect the exhaust pipe, throttle controls, and return spring. Install the air cleaner, start the engine, and check for leaks.

V8 Except Diesel

1. If equipped with AIR, remove the air injector assembly. The ¼ in. pipe threads in the manifold are straight cut threads. Do not use a ¼ in. tapered pipe tap to clean the threads.

2. Disconnect the battery.

3. If equipped, remove the carburetor heat stove pipe.

4. Remove the spark plug wire heat shields. On Mark IV, remove spark plugs.

5. On the left exhaust manifold, disconnect and remove the alternator.

6. Disconnect the exhaust pipe from the manifold and hang it from the frame out of the way.

7. Bend the locktabs and remove the end bolts, then the center bolts. Remove the manifold.

NOTE: A ⁹⁄₁₆ in. thin wall 6-point socket, sharpened at the leading edge and tapped onto the head of the bolt, simplifies bending the locktabs.

8. Installation is the reverse of removal. Clean all mating surfaces and use new gaskets. Torque all bolts to specifications from the inside working out.

Diesel
LEFT SIDE

1. Remove the air cleaner.
2. Remove the lower alternator bracket.
3. Raise the truck and remove the exhaust pipe from the manifold flange.
4. Lower the truck. Bend the locktabs away from the manifold mounting bolts. Remove the bolts and remove the manifold from above. Do not lose the locktabs, and do not use the washers for the bolts, which go under the locktabs.
5. Installation is the reverse. Tighten the manifold bolts to 25 ft. lbs. in two stages, working in a circular pattern from the center to the ends. Then tighten the front bolt to 30 ft. lbs.

RIGHT SIDE

1. Raise and support the truck. Remove the bolts retaining the exhaust pipe to the manifold flange.
2. Bend the locktabs away from the manifold mounting bolts. Remove the bolts and remove the manifold. Do not lose the locktabs and the washers for the bolts, which go under the locktabs.
3. Installation is the reverse. Tighten the bolts to 25 ft. lbs. in two progressive steps, working in a circular pattern from the center to the ends.

Timing Gear Cover

REMOVAL & INSTALLATION
4-119

1. Remove cylinder head as outlined previously.
2. Remove oil pan as outlined previously.
3. Remove oil pickup tube from oil pump.
4. Remove harmonic balancer as outlined previously.
5. Remove AIR pump drive belt.
6. Air Conditioned Vehicles—Remove compressor and lay it to one side. Remove compressor mounting brackets. If equipped with power steering, remove pump and bracket and lay aside.
7. Remove distributor cap and then remove distributor.
8. Remove front cover attaching bolts and remove front cover.
9. Remove and discard front cover to block gasket.
10. Install new gasket onto cylinder block.

11. Align the oil pump drive gear punch mark with the oil filter side of cover; then align the center of dowel pin with alignment mark on oil pump case.
12. Rotate crankcase until #1 and #4 cylinders are at top dead center.
13. Install the front cover by engaging the pinion gear with the oil pump drive gear on the crankshaft.
14. Check that the punch mark on the oil pump drive gear is turned to the rear side as viewed through clearance between front cover and cylinder block.
15. Check that the slit at the end of oil pump shaft is parallel with front face of cylinder block and that it is offset forward.
16. With all parts correctly installed, install and tighten front cover bolts.
17. Reverse Steps 1–7 of Removal procedure.
18. Check engine timing.
19. Check for leaks.

4-121

NOTE: The following procedure requires the use of a special tool.

1. Remove the engine drive belts.
2. Although not absolutely necessary, removal of the right front inner fender splash shield will facilitate access to the front cover.
3. Unscrew the center bolt from the crankshaft pulley and slide the pulley and hub from the crankshaft.
4. Remove the alternator lower bracket.
5. Remove the oil pan-to-front cover bolts.
6. Remove the front cover-to-block bolts and then remove the front cover. If the front cover is difficult to remove, use a plastic mallet.
7. The surfaces of the block and front cover must be clean and free of oil. Apply a ⅛ in. bead of RTV sealant to the cover. The sealant must be wet to the touch when the bolts are torqued down.

NOTE: When applying RTV sealant to the front cover, be sure to keep it out of the bolt holes.

8. Position the front cover on the block using a centering tool (J-23042) and tighten the screws.
9. Installation of the remaining components is in the reverse order of removal. The oil seal can be replaced with the cover either on or off the engine. If the cover is on the engine, remove the crankshaft pulley and hub first. Pry out the seal using a large screwdriver, being careful not to distort the seal mating surface. Install the new seal so that the open side or helical side is towards the engine. Press it into place with a seal driver made for the purpose. Install the hub if removed.

4-137 Diesel

1. Remove the radiator.
2. Remove the compressor drive belt by moving the powersteering oil pump or idler (if so equipped).

3. Loosen the generator adjust plate bolt and fixing bolt, then remove the fan belt.
4. Remove the 4 bolts fixing the crankshaft pulley and remove the crankshaft pulley.
5. Remove the bolts fixing the timing pulley housing covers, then remove the covers.
6. Installation is the reverse of removal.

6-173

--- **CAUTION** ---

The engines use a harmonic balancer. Breakage may occur if the balancer is hammered back onto the crankshaft. A press or special installation tool is necessary.

1. Remove the water pump.
2. Remove the compressor without disconnecting any A/C lines and lay it aside.
3. Remove harmonic balancer, using a puller.

NOTE: The outer ring (weight) of the harmonic balancer is bonded to the hub with rubber. The balancer must be removed with a puller which acts on the inner hub only. Pulling on the outer portion of the balancer will break the rubber bond or destroy the tuning of the torsional damper.

4. Disconnect the lower radiator hose and heater hose.
5. Remove timing gear cover attaching screws, and cover and gasket.
6. Clean all the gasket mounting surfaces on the front cover and block. Apply a continuous ³⁄₃₂ in. bead of sealer (1052357 or equivalent) to front cover sealing surface and around coolant passage ports and central bolt holes.
7. Apply a bead of silicone sealer to the oil pan-to-cylinder block joint.
8. Install a centering tool in the crankcase snout hole in the front cover and install the cover.
9. Install the front cover bolts finger tight, remove the centering tool and tighten the cover bolts. Install the harmonic balancer, pulley, water pump, belts, radiator, and all other parts.

Six Cylinder

1. Remove the radiator after draining it.
2. Remove the fan, pulley, and belt. Remove any power steering and/or AIR pump drive belts. Remove any braces for the above pumps which will interfere with cover removal and position the pumps out of the way.
3. Remove the crankshaft pulley and damper. Use a puller to remove the damper. Do not attempt to pry or hammer the damper off, or it will be damaged.
4. On all 1979 and later 250 sixes, pull the cover forward slightly and cut the oil pan front seal off flush with the block. Remove the cover. 1979 and later 292 sixes

Apply sealer to the six cylinder timing cover at the areas shown

have RTV (room temperature vulcanizing) silicone seal at the oil pan to front cover junction; no front rubber seal is used.

5. Cut the tabs from a new oil pan front seal and install the seal to the front cover, pressing the tips into the holes provided in the cover. On 1979 and later models using no rubber seal, apply a ³⁄₁₆ inch bead of RTV silicone seal on the cover sealing surface.

6. On all models, coat the front cover gasket with sealer and use a ⅛ in. bead of silicone sealer at the oil pan to cylinder block joint. Replace the damper before tightening the cover bolts down, so that the cover seal will align. The damper must be drawn into place. Hammering it will destroy it.

7. Replace the oil pan if it was removed, and fill the crankcase with oil.

Small Block V8

1. Drain the oil.
2. Drain and remove the radiator.
3. Remove the fan, pulley and belt. Remove any power steering and/or AIR pump drive belts. Remove any braces for these pumps which will interfere with cover removal and position the pumps out of the way.
4. Remove the water pump.
5. Remove the crankshaft pulley and damper. Use a puller on the damper. Do not attempt to pry or hammer the damper off.
6. Rotate the retaining bolts, and remove the timing cover.
7. Clean the gasket surfaces on the block and the front cover.
8. Use a sharp knife to trim any excess oil pan gasket material which protrudes from the oil pan-to-engine block junction.

Apply sealer to the V8 cover pads at the areas shown

9. Apply a ⅛ inch bead of RTV silicone sealer, G.M. #1052366 or the equivalent, to the joint of the oil pan and cylinder block.

10. Coat the front cover gasket with sealer and install the gasket onto the cover.

11. Install the front cover-to-oil pan seal. Lightly coat the bottom of the seal with clean engine oil and position over the crankshaft end.

12. Loosely install the front cover upper attaching bolts.

13. Press downward on the cover so that the dowels in the block are aligned with the holes in the cover. While holding the cover in position, tighten the upper attaching bolts alternately and evenly.

14. Install the remaining bolts and tighten all the bolts to specification.

15. Install the torsional damper and the water pump.

Mark IV V8

1. Remove the torsional damper and water pump.
2. Remove the two oil pan-to-front cover attaching screws.
3. Remove the front cover-to-block attaching screws.
4. Pull the cover slightly forward to permit cutting the oil pan front seal.
5. Using a sharp knife, cut the oil pan front seal flush with the cylinder block at both sides of the cover.
6. Remove the front cover and the portion of the oil pan front seal. Remove the front cover gasket.
7. Clean the gasket mating surfaces.
8. Cut the tabs from a new oil pan front seal, using a sharp knife to get a clean cut.
9. Install the seal on the front cover pressing the tips into the holes in the front cover.
10. Coat a new gasket with gasket sealer and install the gasket on the cover.
11. Apply a ⅛ in. bead of sealant to the joint formed at the junction of the oil pan and cylinder block.
12. Place the front cover in position.
13. Align the cover over the dowel pins in the block.
14. Further installation is the reverse of removal.

Diesel

1. Drain cooling system. Disconnect radiator hoses and bypass hose.
2. Remove all belts, fan and fan pulley, crankshaft pulley and harmonic balancer, and accessory brackets. The harmonic balancer must be removed with a puller which pulls from the rear center of the balancer. Any other type of puller, such as a universal claw type which pulls on the outside of the hub, can destroy the balancer. The outside ring of the balancer is bonded in rubber to the hub; by pulling on the outside, it is possible to break that bond.
3. Remove cover-to-block attaching

bolts and remove the cover, timing indicator and water pump assembly.

4. Remove the front cover and dowel pins. It may be necessary to grind a flat on the pins to get a rough surface for gripping.
   To install:
5. Grind a chamfer on one end of each dowel pin.
6. Cut excess material from front end of oil pan gasket on each side of engine block.
7. Clean block, oil pan, and front cover mating surfaces with solvent.
8. Trim about ⅛ in. from each end of a new front pan seal, using a sharp knife to insure a straight cut.
9. Install new front cover gasket on engine block and new front seal on front cover. Apply sealer to gasket around coolant holes and place on block.
10. Apply silicone sealer at junction of block, pan, and front cover.
11. Place cover on block and press downward to compress the seal. Rotate cover left and right and guide pan seal into cavity using a small screwdriver.
12. Apply engine oil to bolts (threads and heads). Install two bolts finger tight to hold cover in place.
13. Install two dowel pins chamfered end first.
14. Install timing indicator and water pump assembly. Torque bolts evenly to 13 ft. lbs. for the water pump bolts, and 35 ft. lbs. for cover bolts.
15. Apply lubricant to balancer seal surface. Install balancer, and balancer bolt. Torque to approximately 250 ft. lbs.
16. Install brackets. Connect bypass hose and radiator hoses. Install crankshaft pulley and four attaching bolts. Torque to 20 ft. lbs.
17. Install fan pulley, fan, and four attaching bolts. Torque to 20 ft. lbs. Install belts and adjust tension. Fill radiator. Road test and check for leaks.

Timing Gear Cover Oil Seal

REPLACEMENT

All Engines

The seal may be replaced with the cover either on or off the engine. With the cover removed:

1. Pry the old seal from the cover using a wooden or plastic pick to prevent damage to the sealing lip. A plastic knitting needle makes a good removal tool.
2. Oil the lip of the new seal. Place a support under the cover so that it is not damaged when the seal is installed.
3. Install the seal so that the open side of the seal is toward the inside of the cover. Drive the seal into place with a tool made for the purpose (G.M. tool no. J-23042 or the equivalent).

The seal can also be replaced with the cover in place on the engine:

1. Remove the torsional damper. Pry the old seal from the cover, as outlined in step 1 of the removal procedure with the cover removed.

2. Oil the lip of the new seal and place it into position, with the open side of the seal toward the engine. Drive the seal into position with a tool designed for the purpose (G.M. tool no. J-23042 or the equivalent).

3. Install the damper.

Timing Chain, Gear, or Belt

REMOVAL & INSTALLATION

4-119

1. Remove front cover assembly.
2. Lock the shoe on automatic adjuster in fully retracted position by depressing the adjuster lock lever in direction as shown.
3. Remove timing chain from crankshaft sprocket.
4. Check timing sprockets for wear or damage. If crankshaft sprocket must be replaced, remove sprocket and pinion gear from crankshaft using Puller J-25031.
5. Check timing chain for wear or damage; replace as necessary. Measure distance (L) with chain stretched with a pull of approximately 98 N (22 lbs.). Standard (L) value is 381mm (15.00"); replace chain if (L) is greater than 385mm (15.16").
6. Remove attaching bolt and remove automatic chain adjuster.
7. Check that the shoe becomes locked when shoe is pushed in with the lock lever released.
8. Check that lock is released when the shoe is pushed in. The adjuster assembly must be replaced if rack teeth are found to be worn excessively.
9. Remove "E" clip and remove chain tensioner. Check tensioner for wear or damage; replace as necessary.
10. Inspect tensioner pin for wear or damage. If replacement is necessary, remove pin from cylinder block using locking pliers. Lubricate NEW pin tensioner with clean engine oil. Start new pin in block, place tensioner over appropriate pin. Place "E" clip on pin and then tap pin into block, using a hammer, until clip just clear tensioner. Check tensioner and adjuster for freedom of rotation on pins.
11. Inspect guide for wear or damage and plugged lower oil jet. If replacement or cleaning is necessary, remove guide bolts, guide and oil jet. Install new guide and upper attaching bolt. Install lower oil jet and bolt so that oil port is pointed toward crankshaft as shown.
12. Install timing sprocket and pinion

gear (groove side toward front cover). Align key grooves with key on crankshaft, then drive into position using Installating Tool J-26587.

13. Turn crankshaft so that key is turned toward cylinder head side (#1 and #4 pistons at top dead center).

14. Install the timing chain by aligning mark plate on chain with mark on crankshaft timing sprocket. The side of the chain with the mark plate is on the front side and the side of chain with the most links between mark plates is on the chain guide side. Keep the timing chain engaged with the camshaft timing sprocket until the camshaft timing sprocket is installed on camshaft.

15. Install the camshaft timing sprocket so that marked side of sprocket faces forward and so that the triangular mark aligns with the chain mark plate.

16. Install the automatic chain adjuster.

17. Release lock by depressing the shoe on adjuster by hand, and check to make certain the chain is properly tensioned when lock is released.

18. Install front cover assembly.

4-121

1. Remove the front cover as previously detailed.
2. Place the No. 1 piston at TDC of the compression stroke so that the marks on the camshaft and crankshaft sprockets are in alignment (see illustration).
3. Loosen the timing chain tensioner nut as far as possible without actually removing it.
4. Remove the camshaft sprocket bolts and remove the sprocket and chain together. If the sprocket does not slide from the camshaft easily, a light blow with a soft mallet at the lower edge of the sprocket will dislodge it.
5. Use a gear puller (J-2288-8-20) and remove the crankshaft sprocket.
6. Press the crankshaft sprocket back onto the crankshaft.
7. Install the timing chain over the camshaft sprocket and then around the crankshaft sprocket. Make sure that the marks on the two sprockets are in alignment (see illustration). Lubricate the thrust surface with Molykote or its equivalent.
8. Align the dowel in the camshaft with the dowel hole in the sprocket and then install the sprocket onto the camshaft. Use the mounting bolts to draw the sprocket onto the camshaft and then tighten them to 27–33 ft. lb.
9. Lubricate the timing chain with clean engine oil. Tighten the chain tensioner.
10. Installation of the remaining components is in the reverse order of removal.

4-137 Diesel

1. Follow the timing pulley housing cover removal steps.
2. Remove the bolts fixing the injection pump timing pulley flange, then remove the flange.

Installing the front cover oil seal (cover off)

Installing the front cover oil seal (cover installed)

4–119 checking timing chain for wear

4–121 timing chain alignment

3. When removing tension spring, avoid using excess force, or distortion of spring will result.

4. Remove the fixing nut of the tension pulley, then remove the tension pulley and tension center.

5. Remove the timing belt. Avoid twisting or kinking the belt and keep it free from water, oil, dust and other foreign matter.

Diesel timing mark alignment

Installing the diesel timing belt

1 CYLINDER
AT T.D.C.

4 CYLINDER
AT T.D.C.

6–173 timing chain alignment

TIMING
MARKS

Six cylinder timing gear alignment

No attempt should be made to readjust belt tension. If the belt has been loosened through service of the timing system, it should be replaced with a new one.

1. Check that the setting marks on the crank pulley, injection pump timing pulley, and camshaft timing pulley are in alignment, then install the timing belt in sequence of crankshaft timing pulley, camshaft timing pulley, and injection pump timing pulley.

Make an adjustment, so that slackness of the belt is taken up by the tension pulley.

When installing the belt, care should be taken so as not to damage the belt.

2. Install the tension center and tension pulley, making certain that the end of the tension center is in proper contact with two pins on the timing pulley housing.

3. Hand-tighten the nut, so that tension pulley can slide freely.

4. Install the tension spring correctly and semitighten the tension pulley fixing nut.

5. Turn the crankshaft 2 turns in normal direction of rotation to permit seating of the belt. Further rotate the crankshaft 90 degrees beyond top dead center to settle the injection pump. Never attempt to turn the crankshaft in reverse direction.

6. Loosen the tension pulley fixing nut completely, allowing the pulley to take up looseness of the belt. Then, tighten the nut to 78–95 ft. lbs.

7. Install the flange on the injection pump pulley. The hole in the outer circumference of the flange should be aligned with the timing mark "△" on the injection pump pulley.

8. Turn the crankshaft 2 turns in normal direction of rotation to bring the piston in no. 1 cylinder to top dead center on compression stroke and check that the mark "△" on the timing pulley is in alignment with the hole in the flange.

9. The belt tension should be checked at a point between the injection pump pulley and crankshaft pulley using tool J-29771, to a pull of 33–55 lbs.

10. Adjust valve cleaances.

11. Install remaining parts in the reverse order of removal.

6-173

To replace the chain, remove the crankcase front cover. This will allow access to the timing chain. Crank the engine until the marks punched on both sprockets are closest to one another and in line between the shaft centers. Take out the three bolts that hold the camshaft sprocket to the camshaft. This sprocket is a light press fit on the camshaft and will come off readily. It is located by a dowel. The chain comes off with the camshaft sprocket. A gear puller will be required to remove the camshaft sprocket.

Without disturbing the position of the engine, mount the new crank sprocket on the shaft, then mount the chain over the camshaft sprocket. Arrange the camshaft

sprocket in such a way that the timing marks will line up between the shaft centers and the camshaft locating dowel will enter the dowel hole in the cam sprocket.

Place the cam sprocket, with its chain mounted over it, in position on the front of the camshaft and pull up with the three bolts that hold it to the camshaft.

After the sprockets are in place, turn the engine two full revolutions to make certain that the timing marks are in correct alignment between the shaft centers.

Six Cylinder

The six-cylinder camshaft is gear driven. To remove the camshaft gear, remove the camshaft and press the gear off.

—————— CAUTION ——————

The thrust plate must be positioned so that the Woodruff key in the shaft does not damage it when the shaft is pressed out of the gear. Support the hub of the gear or the gear will be seriously damaged.

The crankshaft gear may be removed with a gear puller while in place in the block.

V8 Except Diesel

V8 models are equipped with a timing chain. To replace the chain, remove the radiator core, water pump harmonic balancer, and the crankcase front cover. This will allow access to the timing chain. Crank the engine until the zero marks punched on both sprockets are closest to one another and in line between the shaft centers. Then, take out the three bolts that hold the camshaft gear to the camshaft. This gear is a light press fit on the camshaft and will come off readily. It is located by a dowel.

The chain comes off with the camshaft gear.

A gear puller will be required to remove the crankshaft gear.

Without disturbing the position of the engine, mount the new crank gear on the shaft, then mount the chain over the camshaft gear. Arrange the camshaft gear in such a way that the timing marks will line up between the shaft centers and the camshaft locating dowel will enter the dowel hole in the cam sprocket.

Place the cam sprocket, with its chain mounted over it, in position on the front of the camshaft and pull up with the three bolts that hold it to the camshaft.

After the gears are in place, turn the engine two full revolutions to make certain that the timing marks are in correct alignment between the shaft centers.

Diesel

It is not recommended that the timing chain and gears be removed or replaced, because this requires that the engine be retimed. Retiming of the engine requires removal of the injection pump and fuel lines, and the injection pump adapter. The timing mark must be filed off the injection pump adapter, and a new mark must be scribed with a special timing tool. It is recommended that all such work be left to a qualified dealer or mechanic who has access to such equipment.

If the necessary tools are available, the timing chain and gears may be replaced as follows:

1. Remove the crankshaft pulley, harmonic balancer and front cover, using the procedure outlined earlier in this section. Be certain to use the correct tool for balancer removal, to avoid damaging the part.

2. Align the timing marks on the crankshaft and camshaft sprockets by rotating the crankshaft in the direction of normal engine rotation. The marks should be closest to one another and in line between the shaft centers, as shown in the accompanying diagram. Do not disturb the position of the engine.

3. Remove the oil slinger from the crankshaft. Remove the camshaft sprocket retaining nut.

4. Remove the crankshaft sprocket. The sprocket-to-crankshaft fit is such that a puller may be necessary. If possible, the crankshaft key should be removed before using the puller. If this is not possible, align the puller so that the fingers of the tool do not overlap the end of the key when the sprocket is removed. The keyway is machined only partway in the crankshaft sprocket, and breakage can occur if the sprocket is improperly removed.

5. Remove the timing chain and camshaft sprocket.

6. The fuel pump eccentric is behind the crankshaft sprocket, and may be removed if necessary.

7. Install the key in the crankshaft, if removed. Install the fuel pump eccentric, if removed.

8. Install the camshaft sprocket, crankshaft sprocket, and the timing chain together, with the timing marks aligned. Tighten the camshaft sprocket retaining bolt to 65 ft. lbs.

NOTE: When the two timing marks are in alignment and closest together, the No. 6 cylinder is at TDC. To obtain TDC for No. 1 cylinder, slowly rotate the crankshaft one full revolution. This will move the camshaft sprocket timing mark to the top. No. 1 cylinder will then be at TDC.

9. Install the oil slinger.

10. The injection pump must be retimed. Follow steps 1, 2, 3, 4, 5, 7, 8 and 9 of the intake manifold removal and installation procedure. Remove the injection pump adapter and the seal from the injection pump adapter.

11. Follow steps 18, 19, 20, 21, 22, 23, 24, 25, 26, 27, 28, 29, 30, 32, 34, 35 and 36 of the intake manifold removal and installation procedure.

12. Install the front cover, harmonic balancer, and the crankshaft pulley.

Camshaft

REMOVAL & INSTALLATION

NOTE: Whenever a new camshaft is installed, it is recommended that all valve lifters be replaced, to insure the durability of the camshaft lobes and the valve lifter feet.

4-119

1. Remove cam cover.

2. Rotate camshaft until #4 cylinder is in firing position. Remove distributor cap and mark rotor to housing position. Remove distributor.

3. Remove the fuel pump.

4. Lock the shoe on automatic adjuster in fully retracted position by depressing the adjuster lock lever with a screwdriver or equivalent in direction as indicated. After locking the automatic adjuster, check that the chain is in free state.

5. Remove the timing sprocket to camshaft bolt and remove the sprocket and fuel pump drive cam from the camshaft. Keep the timing sprocket on the chain damper and tensioner without removing the chain from the sprocket.

6. Remove rocker arm, shaft and bracket assembly as outlined previously.

7. Remove the camshaft assembly.

8. Apply a generous amount of clean engine oil to the camshaft and journals of cylinder head.

9. Install the camshaft assembly.

10. Install the rocker arm, shaft and bracket assembly as outlined previously.

11. Check that the mark on the #1 rocker arm shaft bracket is in alignment with the mark on the camshaft and that the crankshaft pulley groove is aligned with the TDC mark ("0" mark) on the front cover.

12. Assemble the timing sprocket to the camshaft by aligning it with the pin on the camshaft; use care not to remove the chain from the sprocket.

13. Install the fuel pump drive cam and install the sprocket retaining bolt and washer. Remove the half-moon seal in front end of head; then install torque wrench and torque bolt to 60 lb. ft. replace half-moon seal in cylinder head.

14. Install the distributor.

15. Release lock by depressing the shoe on adjuster with a screwdriver or equivalent, check timing chain for proper tension.

16. Check valve timing; rotor and mark on distributor housing should be in alignment when #4 piston is in firing position. Timing mark on crank pulley should align with TDC mark ("O" mark) on front cover.

17. Reinstall distributor cap.

18. Reinstall cam cover as outlined previously.

4-137 Diesel

1. Remove the camshaft carrier as outlined under the "Cylinder Head Removal and Installation" procedure.

V8 timing mark alignment

1979–82 V8 timing sprocket alignment

Diesel V8 timing mark alignment

Injection pump drive gear installation

Depressing the adjusting lock lever

Locking the timing chain adapter

2. Remove the two bolts retaining the thrust plate in position on the front of the camshaft carrier.

3. Remove the thrust plate and carefully slide the camshaft out through the front of the carrier.

4. Install the camshaft in the carrier in the reverse order of removal, coating it liberally with engine oil before sliding it into position. Exercise care not to damage the camshaft bearing journals during the installation.

4-121

1. Remove the engine.
2. Remove the intake manifold.
3. Remove the cylinder head cover, pivot the rocker arms to the sides, and remove the pushrods, keeping them in order. Remove the valve lifters, keeping them in order. There are special tools which make lifter removal easier.
4. Remove the front cover.
5. Remove the distributor.
6. Remove the fuel pump and its pushrod.
7. Remove the timing chain and sprocket as described earlier in this chapter.
8. Carefully pull the camshaft from the block, being sure that the camshaft lobes do not contact the bearings.
9. To install, lubricate the camshaft journals with clean engine oil. Lubricate the lobes with Molykote or the equivalent. Install the camshaft into the engine, being extremely careful not to contact the bearings with the cam lobes.
10. Install the timing chain and sprocket. Install the fuel pump and pushrod. Install the timing cover. Install the distributor.
11. Install the valve lifters. If a new camshaft has been installed, new lifters should be used to ensure durability of the cam lobe.
12. Install the pushrods and rocker arms and the intake manifold. Adjust the valve lash after installing the engine. Install the cylinder head cover.

6-173

Follow the 6-173 engine removal procedure then remove the camshaft as follows:

1. Remove the intake manifold, valve lifters and timing chain cover. If the car is equipped with air conditioning, unbolt the condenser and move it aside *without disconnecting any lines*.

2. Remove fuel pump and pump pushrod.

3. Remove camshaft sprocket bolts, sprocket and timing chain. A light blow to the lower edge of a tight sprocket should free it (use a plastic mallet).

4. Install two bolts in cam bolt holes and pull cam from block.

5. To install, reverse removal procedure aligning the sprocket timing marks.

Six Cylinder

1. In addition to removing the timing gear cover, remove the grille and radiator. If the truck has air conditioning, the condenser must be moved to provide room for camshaft removal. It may be possible to unbolt the condenser and move it aside, far enough for clearance. Otherwise, the air conditioning system must be discharged and the condenser removed. Do not disconnect any of the air conditioning lines unless you are thoroughly familiar with A/C systems and the hazards involved. It is recommended that you have the system discharged by a professional.

CAUTION

Compressed refrigerant expands (boils) into the atmosphere at a temperature of −21°F or less. It will freeze any surface it contacts, including your skin or eyes.

---

2. Remove the valve cover and gasket, loosen all the valve rocker arm nuts and pivot the arms clear of the pushrods.

3. Remove the distributor and fuel pump.

4. Remove the side covers and gaskets. Remove the pushrods and valve lifters.

5. Align the timing gear marks and remove the two camshaft thrust plate retaining screws by working through the holes in the camshaft gear.

6. Remove the camshaft and gear assembly by pulling it out through the front of the block. Be careful not to dislodge the camshaft bearings.

NOTE: If renewing either camshaft or camshaft gear, the gear must be pressed off the camshaft. Install press plates under the camshaft gear and press the camshaft from the gear. The thrust plate must be positioned so that the Woodruff key in the camshaft does not damage the shaft when the camshaft is pressed from the gear. Support the hub of the gear to prevent damage to the part. The replacement parts must be assembled in the same manner (under pressure). In placing the gear on the camshaft, press the gear onto the shaft until it bottoms against the gear spacer ring. The end clearance of the thrust plate should be .001 to .005 in.

7. Install the camshaft assembly in the engine.

NOTE: Pre-lube the cam lobes with E.O.S. or SAE 90 gear lubricant. Do not dislodge the cam bearings when inserting the camshaft.

8. Turn the crankshaft and camshaft to align and bring the timing marks together. Push the camshaft into this aligned position.

9. Runout on either crankshaft or camshaft gear should not exceed .003 in.

10. Backlash between the two gears should be between .004 and .006 in.

11. Install the timing gear cover and gasket.

12. Install the oil pan and gaskets.

13. Install the harmonic balancer.

14. Line up the keyway in the balancer with the key on the crankshaft and drive the balancer onto the shaft until it bottoms against the crankshaft gear.

15. Install the valve lifters and pushrods. Install the side covers with new gaskets. Later models use RTV sealer instead of gaskets. Attach the coil wires; install the fuel pump.

16. Install the distributor and set the timing as described under the Distributor Removal and Installation section at the beginning of the chapter.

17. Pivot the rocker arms over the pushrods and adjust the valves.

18. Add oil to the engine. Install and adjust the fan belt.

19. Install the radiator or shroud.

20. Install the grille assembly.

21. Fill the cooling system, start the engine and check for leaks.

22. Check and adjust the timing.

V8 Except Diesel

1. Remove the intake manifold, valve lifters and timing chain cover as previously described.

2. Remove the grille and radiator. If the truck has air conditioning, the condenser must be moved to provide room for camshaft removal. It may be possible to unbolt the condenser and move it aside, far enough for clearance. Otherwise, the air conditioning system must be discharged and the condenser removed. Do not disconnect any of the air conditioning lines unless you are thoroughly familiar with A/C systems and the hazards involved. It is recommended that you have the system discharged by a professional.

—————— CAUTION ——————

Compressed refrigerant expands (boils) into the atmosphere at a temperature of −21°F or less. It will freeze any surface it contacts, including your skin or eyes.

3. Remove the fuel pump and pump pushrod.

4. Remove the camshaft sprocket bolts, sprocket and timing chain. A light blow to the lower edge of a tight sprocket should free it (use a plastic mallet).

5. Install two 1/16-18 × 14 in. bolts in the cam bolt holes and pull the cam from the block.

6. To install, reverse the removal procedure aligning the timing marks.

NOTE: Pre-lube the cam lobes with E.O.S. or SAE 90 gear lubricant. Do not dislodge the cam bearings when installing the camshaft.

350 (5.7L) Diesel

Removal of the camshaft also requires removal of the injection pump drive and driven gears, removal of the intake manifold, disassembly of the valve lifters, and re-timing of the injection pump.

1. Disconnect the negative battery cables. Drain the coolant. Remove the radiator.

2. Remove the intake manifold and gasket and the front and rear intake manifold seals. Refer to the intake manifold removal and installation procedure.

3. Remove the balancer pulley and the balancer. Refer to the procedure earlier in this chapter. Remove the engine front cover using the appropriate procedure.

4. Remove the valve covers. Remove the rocker arms, pushrods and valve lifters; see the procedures earlier in this chapter. Be sure to keep the parts in order so that they may be returned to their original positions.

5. If the truck has air conditioning, the condenser must be moved to provide room for camshaft removal. It may be possible

to unbolt the condenser and move it aside far enough for clearance. Otherwise, the air conditioning system must be discharged and the condenser removed. Do not disconnect any of the air conditioning lines unless you are thoroughly familiar with A/C systems and the hazards involved. It is recommended that you have the system discharged by a professional.

—————— CAUTION ——————

Compressed refrigerant expands (boils) into the atmosphere at a temperature of −21°F or less. It will freeze any surface it contacts, including your skin or eyes.

6. Remove the camshaft sprocket retaining bolt, and remove the timing chain and sprockets, using the procedure outlined earlier in this chapter.

7. Position the camshaft dowel pin at the 3 o'clock position.

8. Push the camshaft rearward and hold it there, being careful not to dislodge the oil gallery plug at the rear of the engine. Remove the pump drive gear by sliding it from the camshaft while rocking the pump driven gear.

9. To remove the pump driven gear, remove the injection pump adapter, remove the snap-ring, and remove the selective washer. Remove the driven gear and spring.

10. Remove the camshaft by sliding it out the front of the engine. Be extremely careful not to allow the cam lobes to contact any of the bearings, or the journals to dislodge the bearings during camshaft removal. Do not force the camshaft, or bearing damage will result.

11. Coat the camshaft and the cam bearings with G.M. lubricant #562458 or the equivalent.

12. Carefully slide the camshaft into position in the engine.

13. Install the timing chain and sprockets, aligning the marks as shown in the procedure earlier in the section.

14. Check the injection pump driven gear bushing and replace as necessary.

15. Install the injection pump driven gear, spring, shim, and snap-ring. Check the gear end-play. If the end-play is not within 0.002–0.005 in., replace the shim to obtain the specified clearance. Shims are available in 0.003 in. increments, from 0.080 to 0.115 in.

16. Position the camshaft dowel pin at the 3 o'clock position. Align the zero marks on the pump drive gear and pump driven gear. Hold the camshaft in the rearward position and slide the pump drive gear onto the camshaft.

17. Disassemble, assemble, and bleed the valve lifters as outlined earlier. Install the lifters, pushrods, rocker arms, and pivots. Install the injection pump adapter and injection pump, re-timing the engine as outlined in the intake manifold removal and installation procedure.

18. Install the intake manifold, as outlined earlier. Install the rocker covers.

19. Install the engine front cover, balancer and pulley.

20. Install the radiator. Install the air conditioning condenser, if equipped. Fill the cooling system. Check the automatic transmission fluid level. Connect the negative battery cables.

379 (6.2L) Diesel

1. Disconnect the battery.

2. Raise the vehicle.

3. Drain the radiator and block.

4. Disconnect the exhaust pipe at the exhaust manifolds.

5. Remove the fan shroud lower attaching bolts.

6. Lower the vehicle.

7. Remove the fan shroud upper attaching bolts.

8. Remove the radiator.

9. Remove the fan.

10. Remove the vacuum pump.

11. Remove the intake manifold as previously outlined.

12. Remove the injection pump lines at the pump and nozzles. Cap the injection nozzles to prevent dirt from entering fuel. (Tag injection lines for reinstallation).

13. Remove the water pump.

14. Remove the injection pump gear.

15. Scribe a mark on the front cover aligning the line on the injection pump flange to the front cover.

16. Remove the power steering pump and the generator and lay aside.

18. If equipped with A/C remove the compressor and lay aside.

19. Remove the rocker arm covers as previously outlined.

20. Remove the rocker arm shaft assembly and pushrods. Place the parts in a rack so they may be reinstalled in the same location.

21. Remove the thermostat housing/crossover from the cylinder heads.

22. Remove the cylinder head as previously outlined with the exhaust manifolds attached.

23. Remove the valve lifter clamps, guide plates and valve lifters. Place the parts in a rack so they may be reinstalled in the same location.

24. Remove the front cover.

26. Remove the timing chain.

26. Remove the fuel pump.

27. Remove the cam retainer plate.

28. If equipped with A/C remove the A/C condensor mounting bolts, and with the aid of an assistant, lift the condenser.

29. Remove the camshaft.

NOTE: Whenever a new camshaft is installed, replacement of all valve lifters, oil filter, and new oil is recommended to insure durability of the camshaft lobes and lifters. Whenever a new camshaft is installed coat the camshaft lobes with Molycote or its equivalent.

30. Lubricate the camshaft journals with engine oil and install the camshaft.

31. Install the retainer plate (20 ft. lbs.).

6-250 and 292 piston/rod assembly

NOTCH TO FRONT OF ENGINE

"F" TOWARD FRONT OF ENGINE

OIL SPURT HOLE TOWARD CAMSHAFT SIDE OF ENGINE

HEAVY SIDE OF ROD BEARING TO FRONT OF ENGINE

TANGS

Small block V8 piston/rod assembly

NOTCH TO FRONT OF ENGINE

"F" TOWARD FRONT OF ENGINE

HEAVY SIDE BEARING END OF ROD TO REAR

OIL SPURT HOLES

HEAVY SIDE BEARING END OF ROD TO FRONT

RIGHT BANK 2-4-6-8

LEFT BANK 1-3-5-7

8-454 piston/rod assembly

VALVE CLEARANCE DEPRESSION TO CENTER OF CYLINDER BLOCK

OIL SPURT HOLES

RIGHT BANK 2-4-6-8

LEFT BANK 1-3-5-7

BEARING TANG OPPOSITE CAMSHAFT

BEARING TANG OPPOSITE CAMSHAFT

Diesel piston assembly

TOP COMPRESSION RING

SECOND COMPRESSION RING

EXPANDER

OIL RINGS

SNAP RING

PISTON PIN

SNAP RING

32. Install the fuel pump.
33. Install the timing chain.
34. Install the front cover.
35. Install the valve lifters, guide plates and clamps, rotate the crankshaft as outlined in Valve Lifter Installation to insure the valve lifters are free to travel.
36. Install the cylinder head as previously outlined.
37. Install the rocker arm shaft assembly and pushrods as outlined. Care must be taken to insure the pushrods are installed properly.
38. Install the rocker arm covers.
39. Install the injection pump to the front cover, making sure the lines on the pump and the scribe line on the front cover are aligned.
40. Install the injection pump driven gear, making sure the gears are aligned. Any time the timing chain, gears, or sprockets are replaced, it will be necessary to retime the engine.
41. Install the water pump.
42. Install the injection lines.
43. Install the generator, power steering and A/C.
44. Install the crank pulley.
45. Install the fan.
46. Install the drive belts and adjust as necessary.
47. Install the fan shroud.
48. Install the radiator, and fill with coolant.
49. Connect the necessary wires and hoses.
50. Raise the vehicle.
51. Connect the exhaust pipes to the exhaust manifold.
52. Lower the vehicle.
53. Install the vacuum pump.
54. Connect the secondary fuel filter lines (with adapter).
55. Install the cylinder head covers J-29664-1.
56. Connect the battery.
57. Start the engine and check for leaks.
58. Stop the engine.
59. Remove the protective covers.
60. Loosen the vacuum pump hold-down and disconnect the secondary filter (with adapter) from the fuel lines.
61. Install the intake manifold as previously outlined.

Piston and Connecting Rods

Piston and connecting rod removal, installation and piston ring removal/installation are detailed in the Engine Rebuilding section.

Crankshaft & Main Bearings

REMOVAL & INSTALLATION

NOTE: Refer to the Unit Repair Section.

Flywheel

REMOVAL & INSTALLATION

All Engines

1. Remove the transmission and clutch, or torque converter.
2. Unbolt and remove the flywheel.
3. If the ring gear is to be replaced, split it with a cold chisel or electric drill and remove it.
4. Heat the new ring gear in an oven at about 450°F for 20 minutes. Using protective gloves, hammer the hot ring gear into position and allow it to cool.
5. Installation is the reverse of removal.

ENGINE LUBRICATION

Oil Pan

PICK-UPS AND SUBURBAN

Removal & Installation
SIX CYLINDER

1. Disconnect the battery ground cable.
2. Raise and support the vehicle. Disconnect the starter leaving the wires attached and swing it out of the way.
3. If there is not enough clearance, remove the bolts securing the engine mounts to the crossmember and raise the engine high enough to insert a 2 in. × 4 in. piece of wood between the engine mounts and the crossmember brackets.
4. Drain the engine oil.
5. Remove the flywheel or converter cover.
6. Remove the oil pan.
7. Clean all gasket surfaces and install a new seal in the rear main bearing groove and a new seal in the crankcase front cover. Installation is the reverse of removal. Install new side gaskets on the block, but do not use sealer. Fill the engine with oil and run the engine, checking for leaks.

V8 EXCEPT DIESEL

1. Drain the engine oil.
2. Remove the oil dipstick and tube.
3. If necessary, remove the exhaust crossover. On 454s, remove the air cleaner, fan shroud, and distributor cap.
4. Remove the flywheel or converter cover. Remove the starter. On 454s, remove the oil pressure line from the block. On four wheel drive models with automatic transmission, remove the strut rods at the motor mounts.
5. On 454s only, remove the engine mount through bolts and raise the engine.
6. Remove the oil pan and discard the gaskets.

7. Installation is the reverse of removal. Clean all gasket surfaces and use new gaskets to assemble. Use gasket sealer to retain the side gaskets to the cylinder block. Install a new oil pan rear seal in the rear main bearing cap slot with the ends butting the side gaskets. Install a new front seal in the crankcase front cover with the ends butting the side gaskets. Fill the engine with oil and check for leaks.

DIESEL

1. Remove the drive and vacuum pump.
2. Disconnect the battery cables.
3. Remove the fan shroud attaching screws and pull the shroud up from the clips.
4. Block the rear wheels and jack up the front of the truck. Drain the oil.
5. Remove the flywheel cover.
6. Remove the starter and solenoid.
7. Remove both of the engine mount through bolts and raise the engine. Loosen the right hand mount and remove the left hand mount.
8. Unbolt and remove the oil pan.

NOTE: If extended work is to be done, the mounts should be reinstalled and the engine lowered to the frame brackets.

To install:
1. After cleaning the mounting surfaces thoroughly, apply sealer to both sides of the pan gaskets and install the gaskets on the block.
2. Install the front and rear rubber seals.
3. Apply a thin coat of all purpose grease on the seals, and install the oil pan. Torque the bolts to 10 ft. lbs. in a circular sequence, starting in the middle and working out.
4. Further installation is the reverse of removal. Fill the engine with oil and check for leaks.

VANS

Removal and Installation
1977 SIX CYLINDER

1. Disconnect the battery ground cable.
2. Drain the oil.
3. Remove the starter.
4. Remove the manual transmission flywheel splash shield or the automatic transmission converter housing underpan.
5. Support the front of the engine. Remove the engine mount through-bolts.
6. Raise the front of the engine enough to replace the through-bolts in the engine half of the mounts.
7. Lower the engine and remove the pan bolts.
8. Clean all gasket surfaces and install a new seal in the rear main bearing cap and on the crankcase front cover. Install new side gaskets to the block, using sealer.
9. Replace the pan.
10. Raise the engine and replace the mount through-bolts. Fill the engine with oil and run it, watching for leaks.

1978 AND LATER SIX CYLINDER

1. Disconnect the negative battery cable and remove the engine cover.
2. Remove the air cleaner and studs.
3. Remove the fan finger guard.
4. Remove the radiator upper supporting brackets.
5. Raise the van on a hoist.
6. On vans with manual transmissions:
   a. Disconnect the clutch cross shaft from the left front mounting bracket.
   b. Remove the transmission-to-bellhousing upper bolt.
   c. Remove the transmission rear mounting bolts and install two $7/16 \times 3$ in. bolts.
   d. Raise the transmission and place a small piece of 2×4 wood in between the mount and the crossmember.
7. Remove the starter motor.
8. Drain the engine oil.
9. Remove the engine mount through bolts.
10. Raise the engine slightly and place small 2×4 wooden blocks in between the mount and the block.
11. Remove the flywheel splash shield or the converter cover, as applicable.
12. Remove the oil pan attaching bolts and remove the oil pan.
13. Clean the gasket surface thoroughly and use a new gasket on installation.
14. Reverse to install.

V8

1. Drain the engine oil.
2. Remove the oil dipstick and tube.
3. If necessary, remove the exhaust pipe crossover.
4. If equipped with automatic transmission, remove the converter housing pan.
5. Remove the starter brace and bolt and swing the starter aside.
6. Remove the oil pan and discard the gaskets.
7. Installation is the reverse of removal. Clean all gasket surfaces and use new gaskets to assemble. Use gasket sealer to retain the side gaskets to the cylinder block. Install a new oil pan rear seal in the rear main bearing cap slot with the ends butting the side gaskets. Install a new front seal in the crankcase front cover with the ends butting the side gaskets. Fill the engine with oil and check for leaks.

BLAZER AND JIMMY

Removal & Installation
SIX CYLINDER

1. Disconnect the battery ground cable.
2. Raise and support the vehicle. Disconnect the starter leaving the wires attached and swing it out of the way.
3. Remove the flywheel or converter cover.
4. Drain the engine oil.
5. On some models, there may be enough clearance to remove the oil pan without raising the engine. If there isn't,

remove the bolts securing the engine mounts to the crossmember and raise the engine high enough to insert a 2 in. × 4 in. piece of wood between the engine mounts and the crossmember brackets.
6. On 1977 and later models:
   a. Remove the front engine mount through bolts.
   b. Using a floor jack, raise the engine about three inches.
   c. Install the through bolts and tighten them just enough to hold them in place.
   d. Lower the engine so it rests on the engine mounts, in a slightly raised position. This should provide enough clearance.
7. Remove the oil pan attaching screws.
8. Remove the oil pan.
9. Clean all gasket surfaces and install a new seal in the rear main bearing groove and a new seal in the crankcase front cover. Installation is the reverse of removal. Install new side gaskets on the block, but do not use sealer. Fill the engine with oil and run the engine, checking for leaks.

V8 EXCEPT DIESEL

NOTE: For diesel engine pan removal and installation, see the Pick-up instructions above.

1. Drain the engine oil.
2. On models through 1978, remove the oil dipstick and tube.
3. If necessary, remove the exhaust pipe crossover.
4. If equipped with automatic transmission, remove the converter housing pan.
5. On models through 1978, remove the starter brace and bolt and swing the starter aside.
6. On 1979 and later four wheel drive models equipped with automatic transmission, remove the strut rods at the engine mounts.
7. Remove the oil pan and discard the gaskets.
8. Installation is the reverse of removal. Clean all gasket surfaces and use new gaskets to assemble. Use gasket sealer to retain the side gaskets to the cylinder block. Install a new oil pan rear seal in the rear main bearing cap slot with the ends butting the side gaskets. Install a new front seal in the crankcase front cover with the ends butting the side gaskets. Reassemble, fill the engine with oil and check for leaks.

S-SERIES TRUCKS

Removal & Installation
4-119

NOTE: On 4-wheel drive the engine must be removed before removing the oil pan.

1. Disconnect the negative battery terminal.
2. Jack up your vehicle and support it with jack stands.

3. Drain the oil.

4. Remove the front splash shield.

5. Remove the front crossmember, if necessary.

6. Disconnect the relay rod at the idler arm and lower the relay rod.

7. Remove the left side bellhousing bracket.

8. Remove the vacuum line at the oil pan.

9. Remove the oil pan bolts and the pan.

NOTE: It may be necessary to remove the motor mounts and jack up the engine in order to remove the oil pan.

10. Installation is the reverse of removal. Tighten the retaining bolts to 43 in. lbs.

4-121

1. Disconnect the negative battery cable.

2. Drain the crankcase. Raise and support the front of the vehicle.

3. Remove the A/C brace if so equipped.

4. Remove the exhaust shield and disconnect the exhaust pipe at the manifold.

5. Remove the starter motor and position it out of the way.

6. Remove the flywheel cover. Remove the oil pan.

NOTE: Prior to oil pan installation, check that the sealing surfaces on the pan, cylinder block and front cover are clean and free of oil. If installing the old pan, be sure that all old RTV has been removed.

7. Apply a ⅛ in. bead of RTV sealant to the oil pan sealing surface. Use a new oil pan rear seal and install the pan in place. Tighten the bolts to 9–13 ft. lbs.

8. Installation of the remaining components is in the reverse order of removal.

4-137 Diesel

The engine must be removed from the truck.

1. With the engine on a work stand, unbolt and remove the oil pan from the crankcase.

2. Discard the gasket and clean the gasket surfaces.

3. At this time, the crankcase may also be removed from the block. Discard the gasket and seals and clean the gasket surfaces.

4. Install the oil pan and/or crankcase using new gaskets coated with sealer. Torque the oil pan bolts to 5–9 ft. lb.; the crankcase bolts to 15 ft. lb.

6-173

The engine must be removed from the truck.

1. With the engine on a work stand, unbolt and remove the pan.

2. Discard the gasket and clean the gasket surfaces.

3. The oil pan does not use a preformed gasket. Rather it is sealed with RTV gasket

material. Make sure that the sealing surfaces are free of oil and old RTV material.

4. Run a ⅛ in. bead of sealer along the entire sealing surface of the pan.

5. Place the pan on the engine and finger tighten the bolts. Torque the smaller bolts to 6–9 ft. lb.; the larger bolts to 15–22 ft. lb.

Oil Pump

REMOVAL & INSTALLATION

4-119

1. Drain and remove the oil pan.

2. Disconnect the oil feed pipe.

3. Remove the two bolts securing the oil pump to the cylinder block and remove the oil pump.

4. Install in the reverse order of removal.

4-121

1. Remove the engine oil pan.

2. Remove the pump attaching bolts and carefully lower the pump.

3. Install in reverse order. To ensure immediate oil pressure on start-up, the oil pump gear cavity should be packed with petroleum jelly. Installation torque is 26–35 ft. lbs.

4-137 Diesel

1. Follow the engine assembly removal steps.

2. Remove the 20 bolts fixing the crankcase and remove the crankcase together with the oil pan.

NOTE: Pry off the crankcase by fitting a screwdriver into the slots in the crankcase.

3. Remove the oil pipe sleeve nut.

4. Remove the 2 bolts fixing the oil pump and remove the oil pump with oil pipe.

5. Install the oil pipe and leave the joints semi-tight.

6. Fully tighten the oil pump fixing screws, then tighten the oil pipe joints.

7. Reverse the removal procedure for the remaining parts.

6-173

1. Remove the oil pan as described earlier.

2. Unbolt and remove the oil pump and pickup.

3. Installation is the reverse of removal. Torque the pump bolts to 26–35 ft. lb.

NOTE: Before installing an oil pump, fill it with clean oil.

Six Cylinder

1. Drain the oil and remove the oil pan.

2. Remove the 2 flanged mounting bolts and remove the pickup pipe bolt.

3. Remove the pump and screen as an assembly.

4. To install, align the oil pump driveshafts with the distributor tang and install the oil pump. Position the flange over the distributor lower bushing, using no gasket. The oil pump should slide easily into place. If not, remove it and reposition the slot to align with the distributor tang.

5. Reinstall the oil pan and fill the engine with oil.

V8 and Diesel

1. Drain the oil and remove the oil pan.

2. Remove the bolt (two bolts on diesels) holding the pump to the rear main bearing cap. Remove the pump and extension shaft.

3. To install, assemble the pump and extension shaft to the rear main bearing cap aligning the slot on the top of the extension shaft with the drive tang on the distributor driveshaft. The installed position of the oil pump screen is with the bottom edge parallel to the oil pan rails. Further installation is the reverse of removal.

Oil Cooler

REMOVAL & INSTALLATION

4-137 Diesel

1. Place a suitable size tray under the oil filter to receive oil and water flowing out from the filter.

2. Drain the cooling system by opening the drain plugs on the radiator and on the cylinder block.

3. Remove the oil cooler water drain plug and drain the water.

4. Disconnect the oil cooler hoses at the cooler side.

5. Remove the oil filter cartridge using filter wrench.

6. Remove the nut fixing the oil cooler, then remove the oil cooler assembly.

7. Install the cooler using a new O-ring. Torque to 55–60 ft. lbs.

Rear Main Oil Seal

REPLACEMENT

All Engines Except Diesel

Both halves of the rear main oil seal can be replaced without removing the crankshaft. Always replace the upper and lower seal together. The lip should face the front of the engine. Be very careful that you do not break the sealing bead in the channel on the outside portion of the seal while installing it. An installation tool can be fabricated to protect the seal bead.

1. Remove the oil pan, oil pump and rear main bearing cap.

2. Remove the oil seal from the bearing cap by prying it out with a small screwdriver.

3. Remove the upper half of the seal with a small punch. Drive it around far enough to be gripped with pliers.

4. Clean the crankshaft and bearing cap.

5. Coat the lips and bead of the seal with light engine oil, keeping oil from the ends of the seal.

6. Position the fabricated tool between the crankshaft and seal seat.

7. Position the seal between the crankshaft and tip of the tool so that the seal bead contacts the tip of the tool. The oil seal lip should face forward.

8. Roll the seal around the crankshaft using the tool to protect the seal bead from the sharp corners of the crankcase.

9. The installation tool should be left installed until the seal is properly positioned with both ends flush with the block.

10. Remove the tool.

11. Install the other half of the seal in the bearing cap using the tool in the same manner as before. Light thumb pressure should install the seal.

12. Install the bearing cap with sealant applied to the mating areas of the cap and block. Keep sealant from the ends of the seal.

13. Torque the main bearing cap retaining bolts to 10–12 ft. lbs. Tap the end of the crankshaft first rearward, then forward with a lead hammer. This will line up the rear main bearing and the crankshaft thrust surfaces. Tighten the main bearing cap to specification.

14. Further installation is the reverse of removal.

Diesel

It is not necessary to remove the crankshaft to correct seal leaks at the rear main bearing.

1. Drain oil and remove oil pan as previously outlined. Remove rear main bearing cap.

2. Insert a packing tool such as a screwdriver or a punch against one end of the seal in the cylinder block and drive the old seal gently into the groove until it is packed tight. This varies from ¼ in. to ¾ in., depending on the pack required. Be careful not to nick the main bearing when packing the seal.

3. Repeat this procedure on the other end of the cylinder block seal.

4. Measure the amount the seal was driven up on one side. Add ¹⁄₁₆ in., then use a razor blade to cut this length from the old seal removed from the bearing cap. Repeat for the other side.

5. Place a drop of sealer on each end of the cut pieces of seal.

6. Work these two pieces of seal into the cylinder block with two small screwdrivers. Pack them into the block firmly. Trim the ends of the seal flush with the block.

NOTE: Place a piece of shim stock or strip of metal between the seal and the crankshaft to protect the bearing surface before trimming.

7. Clean the bearing cap and seal grooves.

8. Install a new seal into the bearing cap, packing by hand.

9. Using a seal installer, pack the seal firmly into the groove. These tools are generally available in automotive parts stores.

10. Cut the seal flush with the mating surface of the bearing cap. Pack the seal end fibers away from the edges, toward the center with a screwdriver.

11. Clean the bearing insert and install in the bearing cap.

12. Clean the crankshaft bearing journal, and the mating surface of the bearing cap. Place a dab of sealer, such as Loctite® 496, on the mating surface of the cap. Lay a piece of Plastigage® on the bearing surface.

13. Install the bearing cap, lubricate the bolt threads with engine oil, and install. Torque the bolts to 120 ft. lbs. on the 350 and 70 ft. lbs. on the 379. Check the bearing clearance. If clearance is excessive, check for frayed seal edges. When the clearance is correct, retorque the cap.

14. Install the oil pan as previously outlined.

4-119

1. Disconnect the negative battery terminal.

2. Remove the oil pan as previously described.

3. Remove the transmission.

NOTE: On manual transmissions, remove the clutch assembly.

4. Unbolt the starter and tie it out of the way.

5. Remove the flywheel.

6. Remove the rear main seal retainer.

7. Remove the oil seal and discard it.

8. Install the new oil seal.

9. Installation is the reverse of removal. Fill the space between the seal lips with grease and lubricate the seal lips with engine oil.

Fabricated oil seal installation tool

Pack the old seal into the groove

Use the bearing cap as a holding fixture for cutting the old rope seal

Removing the upper half of the oil seal

4–119 rear main seal

4–119 rear main seal installation

4-121

1. Remove the oil pan and pump.
2. Remove the rear main bearing cap.
3. Gently pack the upper seal into the groove approximately ¼ inch on each side.
4. Measure the amount the seal was driven in on one side and add ¹⁄₁₆ in. Cut this length from the old lower cap seal. Be sure to get a sharp cut. Repeat for the other side.
5. Place the piece of cut seal into the groove and pack the seal into the block. Do this for each side.
6. Install a piece of Plastigage or the equivalent on the bearing journal. Install the rear cap and tighten to 75 ft. lbs. Remove the cap and check the gauge for bearing clearance. If out of specification, the ends of the seal may be frayed or not flush, preventing the cap from proper seating. Correct as required.
7. Clean the journal, and apply a thin film of sealer to the mating surfaces of the cap and tighten to 70 ft. lbs. Install the pan and pump.

4-137 Diesel

1. Follow the engine removal steps.
2. Remove the 6 bolts mounting the flywheel and remove the flywheel assembly.

When loosening the flywheel bolts, hold the crankshaft front bolt with a wrench to prevent turning of the crankshaft.

3. Remove the crankshaft rear seal.
4. Install the new seal with seal installer, J-22928 or equivalent. Reverse removal procedures for all other parts.

4–137 diesel rear main seal installation

6-173

1. Remove the oil pan and pump.
2. Remove the rear main bearing cap.
3. Gently pack the upper seal into the groove approximately ¼ inch on each side.
4. Measure the amount the seal was driven in on one side and add ¹⁄₁₆ in. Cut this length from the old lower cap seal. Be sure to get a sharp cut. Repeat for the other side.
5. Place the piece of cut seal into the groove and pack the seal into the block. Do this for each side.

NOTE: G.M. makes a guide tool (J-29114-1) which bolts to the block via on oil pan bolt hole, and a packing tool (J-29114-2) which are machined to provide a built-in stop for the installation of the short cut pieces. Using the packing tool, work the short pieces of seal onto the guide tool, then pack them into the block with the packing tool.

6. Install a new lower seal in the rear main cap.
7. Install a piece of Plastigage or the equivalent on the bearing journal. Install the rear cap and tighten to 70 ft. lbs. Remove the cap and check the gauge for bearing clearance. If out of specification, the ends of the seal may be frayed or not flush, preventing the cap from proper sealing. Correct as required.
8. Clean the journal, and apply a thin film of sealer to the mating surfaces of cap and block. Do not allow any sealer to get onto the journal or bearing. Install the bearing cap and tighten to 70 ft. lbs. Install the pan and pump.

NOTE: This procedure uses the same tools as the V8 gasoline engines.

ENGINE COOLING

Radiator

REMOVAL & INSTALLATION

1. Drain the radiator.

CAUTION

Do not attempt to start the siphoning process with your mouth. The coolant is poisonous and can cause death.

---

2. Disconnect the hoses and automatic transmission cooler line (if equipped). Plug the cooler lines. Diesels have transmission cooler and oil cooler lines.
3. Disconnect the coolant recovery system hose.
4. If the vehicle is equipped with a fan shroud, detach the shroud and hang it over the fan to provide clearance.
5. On six cylinder engines, remove the finger guard.
6. Remove the mounting panel from the radiator support and remove the upper mounting pads.
7. Lift the radiator up and out of the truck. Lift the shroud out if necessary.
8. Installation is the reverse of removal. Fill the cooling system and check the automatic transmission fluid level, and run the engine, checking for leaks.

Water Pump

REMOVAL & INSTALLATION

Except 4-119, 4-121, 4-137, 6-173

1. Drain the radiator and loosen the fan pulley bolts.
2. Disconnect the heater hose and radiator. Disconnect the lower radiator hose at the water pump.
3. Loosen the alternator swivel bolt and remove the fan belt. Remove the fan bolts, fan and pulley.
4. Remove the water pump attaching bolts and remove the pump and gasket from the engine. On inline engines, remove the water pump straight out of the block to avoid damaging the impeller.

NOTE: Do not store viscous drive (thermostatic) fan clutches in any other position than the normal installed position. They should be supported so that the clutch disc remains vertical; otherwise, silicone fluid may leak out.

5. Installation is the reverse of removal. Clean the gasket surfaces and install new gaskets. Coat the gasket with sealer. A ⁵⁄₁₆ in. × 24 × 1 in. guide stud installed in one hole of the fan will make installing the fan onto the hub easier. It can be removed after the other 3 bolts are started. Fill the cooling system and adjust the fan belt tension.

4-119 and 4-137 Diesel

1. Disconnect the battery ground. Drain the cooling system.
2. Remove the front cover. Disconnect the hoses at the pump.
3. On models without air conditioning, remove the fan.
4. On models with air conditioning, re-

move the fan belt, fan pulley, fan, air pump pulley and fan set plate.

5. Unbolt and remove the pump.

6. Clean the gasket surfaces thoroughly.

7. Installation is the reverse of removal. Always use a new gasket.

4-121

1. Disconnect the battery ground.

2. Drain the cooling system.

3. Remove all drive belts. Disconnect the hoses at the pump.

4. Remove the alternator.

5. Unbolt and remove the pump.

6. Thoroughly clean the gasket surfaces. Discard the old gasket.

7. Using a new gasket, install the pump and assemble all other components in reverse order of removal.

6-173

1. Disconnect the battery ground.

2. Drain the cooling system.

3. Disconnect the hoses at the pump.

4. Unbolt and remove the pump.

5. Thoroughly clean the sealing surfaces of old gasket material. This engine uses RTV sealant in place of a gasket.

6. Place a ³⁄₃₂ in. bead of sealer on the water pump mating surface. Coat the bolt threads with pipe compound and mount the pump on the engine.

7. Assemble all other components in reverse order of removal.

Thermostat

The factory installed thermostat is a 195°F unit.

NOTE: Poor heater output and slow warmup is often caused by a thermostat stuck in the open position; occasionally one sticks shut causing immediate overheating. Do not attempt to correct a chronic overheating condition by permanently removing the thermostat. Thermostat flow restriction is designed into the system; without it, localized overheating due to turbulence may occur.

REMOVAL & INSTALLATION

1. Drain approximately ⅓ of the coolant. This will reduce the coolant level to below the level of the thermostat housing.

2. It is not necessary to remove the upper radiator hose from the thermostat housing. Remove the 2 retaining bolts from the thermostat housing (located on the front top of V8 intake manifolds and directly in front of the valve cover on six cylinder engines) and remove the thermostat.

3. To test the thermostat, place it in hot water or a solution of 33% glycol, 25° above the temperature stamped on the valve. Submerge the valve and agitate the solution. The valve should open fully. Remove the thermostat and place it in the same solution 10° below the temperature stamped

on the valve. The valve should close completely.

4. Installation is the reverse of removal. Use a new gasket and sealer. Refill the cooling system and run the engine, checking for leaks.

EMISSION CONTROLS

NOTE: Refer to the Unit Repair Section.

GASOLINE FUEL SYSTEM

Fuel Pump

The fuel pump is a single action AC diaphragm type. All fuel pumps are diaphragm type and because of design are serviced by replacement only. No adjustments or repairs are possible.

The pump is operated by an eccentric on the camshaft. On six cylinder engines, the eccentric acts directly on the pump rocker arm. On V8 engines, a pushrod between the camshaft eccentric and the fuel pump operates the pump rocker arm.

TESTING THE FUEL PUMP

Fuel pumps should always be tested on the vehicle. The larger line between the pump and tank is the suction side of the system and the smaller line, between the pump and carburetor, is the pressure side. A leak in the pressure side would be apparent because of dripping fuel. A leak in the suction side is usually only apparent because of a reduced volume of fuel delivered to the pressure side.

1. Tighten any loose line connections and look for any kinks or restrictions.

2. Disconnect the fuel line at the carburetor. Disconnect the distributor-to-coil primary wire. Place a container at the end of the fuel line and crank the engine a few revolutions. If little or no gasoline flows from the line, either the fuel pump is inoperative or the line is plugged. Disconnect the line at the pump and the tank; blow through the line with compressed air and try again. Reconnect the line. If the problem is traced to the tank, the tank and gauge unit must be removed to check the condition of the inlet filter screen.

3. If fuel flows in good volume, check the fuel pump pressure to be sure.

4. Attach a pressure gauge to the pressure side of the fuel line.

FUEL PIPE ASSEMBLY

ROD

GASKET

PLUG

FUEL PUMP

Typical gasoline fuel pump

5. Run the engine and note the reading on the gauge. Stop the engine and compare the reading with the specifications listed in the Tune-Up Specifications. If the pump is operating properly, the pressure will be as specified and will be constant at idle speed. If pressure varies or is too high or low, the pump should be replaced.

6. Remove the pressure gauge.

REMOVAL & INSTALLATION

Except 4-119, 4-121, 4-137, 6-173

NOTE: When you connect the fuel pump outlet fitting, always use 2 wrenches to avoid damaging the pump.

1. Disconnect the fuel intake and outlet lines at the pump and plug the pump intake line.

2. On V8 engines, you can remove the upper bolt from the right front engine mounting boss (on the front of the block) and insert a long bolt ³⁄₈-16 × 2 in.) to hold the fuel pump pushrod.

3. Remove the two pump mounting bolts and lockwashers; remove the pump and its gasket.

4. If the rocker arm pushrod is to be removed from V8s, remove the two adapter bolts and lockwashers and remove the adapter and its gasket.

5. Install the fuel pump with a new gasket reversing the removal procedure. Heavy grease can be used to hold the fuel pump pushrod up while installing the pump, if you didn't install the long bolt in step 2. Coat the mating surfaces with sealer.

6. Connect the fuel lines and check for leaks.

4-119

1. Disconnect the battery ground.

2. Remove the distributor.

3. Disconnect the fuel hoses at the pump.

4. Remove the engine lifting hook.

5. Unbolt and remove the fuel pump. Discard the gasket.

6. Installation is the reverse of removal. It will be easier if you rotate the engine so the cam lobe is on a down stroke. Use sealer on the new gasket. Set the timing.

4-121

The fuel pump is located at the center rear of the engine.

1. Disconnect the negative cable at the battery. Raise and support the car.

2. Disconnect the inlet hose from the pump. Disconnect the vapor return hose, if equipped.

3. Loosen the fuel line at the carburetor, then disconnect the outlet pipe from the pump.

4. Remove the two mounting bolts and remove the pump from the engine.

5. To install, place a new gasket on the pump and install the pump on the engine. Tighten the two mounting bolts alternately and evenly.

6. Install the pump outlet pipe. This is easier if the pipe is disconnected from the carburetor. Tighten the fitting while backing up the pump nut with another wrench. Install the pipe at the carburetor.

7. Install the inlet and vapor hoses. Lower the car, connect the negative battery cable, start the engine, and check for leaks.

6-173

1. Disconnect the battery ground.

2. Disconnect the fuel hoses at the pump.

3. Unbolt and remove the pump. Discard the gasket.

4. Installation is the reverse of removal. Use sealer on the new gasket. It will be easier if you rotate the engine so that the cam lobe is on a down stroke.

Carburetor

REMOVAL & INSTALLATION

NOTE: This procedure is a general one that covers all models. Remember that each carburetor application may differ slightly.

1. Remove the air cleaner and its gasket.

2. Disconnect the fuel and vacuum lines from the carburetor.

3. Disconnect the choke coil rod or heated air line tube.

4. Disconnect the throttle linkage.

5. On automatic transmission trucks, disconnect the throttle valve linkage.

6. Remove the CEC valve vacuum hose and electrical connector.

7. Remove the idle stop electrical wiring from the idle stop solenoid, if so equipped.

8. Remove the carburetor attaching nuts and/or bolts, gasket or insulator, and remove the carburetor.

9. Install the carburetor using a reverse of the removal procedure. Use a new gasket and fill the float bowl with gasoline to ease starting the engine.

For carburetor overhaul and adjustments, see the Unit Repair Section of this book.

Fuel Tank
REMOVAL & INSTALLATION

1. Drain the tank.

2. Raise and support the truck on jackstands.

3. Disconnect the wiring and ground strap at the tank.

4. Disconnect the filler neck hose and vent hose at the tank.

5. Disconnect the fuel feed line and vapor line at the tank.

6. Place a floor jack under the tank to take up its weight.

7. Remove the fuel tank support bolts and lower the tank.

8. Installation is the reverse of removal.

DIESEL FUEL SYSTEM

Fuel Supply Pump

REMOVAL & INSTALLATION

The fuel supply pump is serviced in the same manner as the fuel pump on the gasoline engine.

Fuel Filter

REMOVAL & INSTALLATION

The fuel filter is a square assembly located at the back of the engine above the intake manifold. Disconnect the fuel lines and remove the filter. Install the lines to the new filter. Start the engine and check for leaks.

Fuel Injection Pump and Lines

REMOVAL & INSTALLATION

Except 4-137

NOTE: This procedure contains throttle rod and transmission cable adjustments.

1. Remove the air cleaner.

2. Remove the filters and pipes from the valve covers and air crossover.

3. Remove the air crossover and cap the intake manifold with screened covers (tool J-26996-1) or tape.

4. Disconnect the throttle rod and return spring.

5. Remove the ballcrank.

6. Remove the throttle and transmission cables from the intake manifold brackets.

7. Disconnect the fuel lines from the filter and remove the filter.

8. Disconnect the fuel inlet line at the pump.

9. Remove the rear A/C compressor brace and remove the fuel line.

10. Disconnect the fuel return line from the injection pump.

11. Remove the clamps and pull the fuel return lines from each injection nozzle.

12. Using two wrenches, disconnect the high pressure lines at the nozzles.

13. Remove the three injection pump retaining nuts with tool J-26987 or its equivalent.

14. Remove the pump and cap all lines and nozzles.

To install:

15. Remove the protective caps from all lines and nozzles. Place the engine on TDC for the no. 1 cylinder. The mark on the harmonic balancer on the crankshaft will be aligned with the zero mark on the timing tab, and both valves for no. 1 cylinder will be closed. The index mark on the injection pump driven gear should be offset to the right when no. 1 is at TDC. Check that all of these conditions are met before continuing.

16. Line up the offset tang on the pump driveshaft with the pump driven gear and install the pump.

17. Install, but do not tighten the pump retaining nuts.

18. Connect the high pressure lines at the nozzles.

19. Using two wrenches, torque the high pressure line nuts to 25 ft. lbs.

20. Connect the fuel return lines to the nozzles and pump.

21. Align the timing mark on the injection pump with the line on the timing mark adapter and torque the mounting nuts to 35 ft. lbs.

NOTE: A ¾ in. open end wrench on the boss at the front of the injection pump will aid in rotating the pump to align the marks.

22. Adjust the throttle rod:

a. Remove the clip from the cruise control rod and remove the rod from the bellcrank.

b. Loosen the locknut on the throttle rod a few turns, then shorten the rod several turns.

c. Rotate the bellcrank to the full throttle stop, then lengthen the throttle rod until the injection pump lever contacts the injection pump full throttle stop, then release the bellcrank.

d. Tighten the throttle rod locknut.

23. Install the fuel inlet line between the transfer pump and the filter.

24. Install the rear A/C compressor brace.
25. Install the bellcrank and clip.
26. Connect the throttle rod and return spring.
27. Adjust the transmission cable:
   a. Push the snap-lock to the disengaged position.
   b. Rotate the injection pump lever to the full throttle stop and hold it there.
   c. Push in the snap-lock until it is flush.
   d. Release the injection pump lever.
28. Start the engine and check for fuel leaks.
29. Remove the screened covers or tape and install the air crossover.
30. Install the tubes in the air flow control valve in the air crossover and install the ventilation filters in the valve covers.
31. Install the air cleaner.
32. Start the engine and allow it to run for two minutes. Stop the engine, let it stand for two minutes, then restart. This permits the air to bleed off within the pump.

4-137

1. Raise engine hood.
2. Disconnect the battery ground cable.
3. Remove the battery.
4. Remove the under cover.
5. Drain the cooling system by opening the drain plugs on the radiator and on the cylinder block.
6. Disconnect the upper water hose at the engine side.
7. Loosen the compressor drive belt by moving the power steering oil pump or idler. (If so equipped.)
8. Remove the cooling fan and fan shroud.
9. Disconnect the lower water hose at the engine side.
10. Remove the air conditioner compressor. (If so equipped.)
11. Remove the fan belt.
12. Remove the crankshaft pulley.
13. Remove the timing pulley housing coers.
14. Remove the tension spring and fixing bolt, then remove the tension center and pulley.
15. Remove the timing belt.
16. Remove the engine control cable and wiring harness of the fuel cut solenoid.
17. Remove the fuel hoses and injection pipes. Use a wrench to hold the delivery holder when loosening the sleeve nuts on the injection pump side.
18. Install a 6 mm bolt (with pitch of 1.25) into threaded hole in the timing pulley housing through the hole in pulley to prevent turning of the pulley.
   Remove the bolts fixing the injection pump timing pulley, then remove the pulley using pulley puller.
19. Remove injection pump flange fixing nuts and rear bracket bolts, then remove the injection pump.
   The following steps are required when reinstalling the fuel pump.
   1. Install the injection pump by align-

ing notched line on the flange with the line on the front bracket.
2. Install the injection pump timing pulley by aligning it with the key groove. Torque to 42–52 ft. lbs.
3. Bring the piston in no. 1 cylinder to top dead center on compression stroke and align marks on the timing pulleys.
4. Follow the timing belt installation steps.
5. Check the injection timing.
6. To install remaining parts, follow the removal steps in reverse order.

SLOW IDLE SPEED ADJUSTMENT

Except 4-137 and 8-379

1. Run the engine to normal operating temperature.
2. Insert the probe of a magnetic pickup tachometer into the timing indicator hole.
3. Set the parking brake and block the drive wheels.
4. Place the transmission in Drive and turn the A/C Off.
5. Turn the slow idle screw on the injection pump to obtain the idle specification on the emission control label.

4-137

1. Set parking brake and block drive wheels.
2. Place transmission in neutral.
3. Start and normalize the engine. Engine coolant temperature: above 80°C (176°F).
4. Set the engine tachometer.
5. If the idle speed deviates from the specified range of 700–800 rpm, loosen the idle speed adjusting screw lock nut.
6. Turn the adjusting screw in or out until the idle speed is in the correct range. After tightening the lock nut lock it in place.

Idle Speed Adjustment

379

1. All idle speeds are to be set within 25 RPM of specified value.
2. Set parking brake and block drive wheels.
3. Engine must be at normal operating temperature. Air cleaner should be on and all accessories should be turned off.
4. Install, tool J-26925, diesel tachometer or equivalent per manufacturers instructions.
5. Adjust low idle speed screw on fuel injection pump to an engine speed of 650 RPM in neutral or park for automatic transmission and for manual transmissions.
6. Adjust fast idle speed as follows:
   a. Remove connector from fast idle solenoid. Use an insulated jumper wire from battery positive terminal to solenoid terminal to energize solenoid.
   b. Open throttle momentarily to en-

Loosening tension pulley

Removing timing pulley

4–137 diesel idle speed adjustment points

sure that the fast idle solenoid plunger is energized and fully extended.
   c. Adjust the extended plunger by turning the hex head to an engine fast idle speed of 800 RPM in neutral.
   d. Remove jumper wire and reinstall connector to fast idle solenoid.
7. Remove tachometer.

FAST IDLE SOLENOID ADJUSTMENT

1978–79 Except 4-137

1. Set the parking brake and block the drive wheels.
2. Run the engine to normal operating temperature.
3. Place the transmission in Drive and disconnect the compressor clutch wire. Turn the A/C On. On trucks without A/C, disconnect the solenoid wire, and connect jumper wires to the solenoid terminals. Ground one of the wires and connect the other to a 12 volt battery to activate the solenoid.

4-137 diesel fast idle speed adjustment points

#1 piston at TDC

Static timing gauge installed

#1 piston 45-60 degrees before TDC

#1 piston 15 degrees before TDC

4. Adjust the fast idle solenoid plunger to obtain 650 rpm.

1980 and Later, Except 4-137 and 8-379

1. With the ignition off, disconnect the single green wire from the fast idle relay located on the front of the firewall.
2. Set the parking brake and block the drive wheels.
3. Start the engine and adjust the solenoid (energized) to the specifications on the underhood emission control label.
4. Turn off the engine and reconnect the green wire.

4-137

1. Start and normalize the engine. Engine coolant temperature: above 80°C (176°F).
2. Set the engine tachometer.
3. Disconnect the hoses from the vacuum switch valve, then connect a pipe (4 mm dia.) in position between the hoses.
4. Loosen adjust nut and adjust engine idle speed by moving the nut. Fast idle should be 900–950 rpm.
5. Tighten the nut.
6. Remove engine tachometer.

CRUISE CONTROL SERVO RELAY ROD ADJUSTMENT

1. Turn the engine Off.
2. Adjust the rod to minimum slack then put the clip in the first free hole closest to the bellcrank, but within the servo ball.

INJECTION TIMING ADJUSTMENT

Except 4-137, 8-379

For the engine to be properly timed, the lines on the top of the injection pump adapter and the flange of the injection pump must be aligned.

1. The engine must be off for resetting the timing.
2. Loosen the three pump retaining nuts with J-26987, an injection pump intake manifold wrench, or its equivalent.
3. Align the timing marks and torque the pump retaining nuts to 35 ft. lbs.

NOTE: The use of a ¾ in. open end wrench on the boss at the front of the pump will aid in rotating the pump to align the marks.

4. Adjust the throttle rod. (See Fuel Injection Pump Removal and Installation, step 22.)

4-137

1. Check that notched line on the injection pump flange is in alignment with notched line on the injection pump front bracket.
2. Bring the piston in no. 1 cylinder to

top dead center on compression stroke by turning the crankshaft as necessary.
3. With the timing pulley housing cover removed, check that timing belt is properly tensioned, and that timing marks are aligned.
4. Disconnect the injection pipe from the injection pump and remove the distributor head screw, then install static timing gauge. Set the lift approximately 1 mm (0.04 in.) from the plunger.
5. Use a wrench to hold the delivery holder when loosening the sleeve nuts on the injection pump side.
6. Bring the piston in no. 1 cylinder to a point 45–60 degrees before top dead center by turning the crankshaft, then calibrate the dial indicator to zero.
7. Turn the crankshaft pulley slightly in both directions and check that gauge indication is stable.
8. Turn the crankshaft in normal direction of rotation, and take the reading of the dial indicator when the timing mark (15 degrees) on the crankshaft pulley is in alignment with the pointer. Reading should be 0.020 in.
9. If the reading of dial indicator deviates from the specified range, hold crankshaft in position 15 degrees before top dead center and loosen two nuts on injection pump flange.
10. Move the injection pump to a point where dial indicator gives reading of 0.020 in., then tighten the pump flange nuts.

8-379

For the engine to be properly timed, the marks on the top of the engine front cover and the injection pump flange must be aligned. The engine must be off when the timing is reset. On Federal models, align scribe marks. On California models, align half circles.

Adjusting

If the marks are not aligned, adjustment is necessary.

1. Loosen the three pump retaining nuts.
2. Align mark on injection pump with mark on front cover and tighten nuts to 40 N·m (30 ft. lbs.).
3. Adjust throttle rod.

NOTE: In order to mark the front housing the following must be completed:

1. Set engine to TDC #1 cylinder (firing).
2. Install timing fixing J-33042 or equivalent in F.I. pump location. Do not use gasket.
3. Slot of F.I. pump gear to be in vertical 6 o'clock position—(If not, remove fixture and rotate engine crankshaft 360°). The timing marks on gears will be aligned.
4. Fasten gear to fixture, and tighten.
5. Install on 10mm nut to housing upper stud to hold fixture flange nut to be "finger" tight.
6. Torque large bolt (18mm head)

counterclockwise (toward left bank) to 50 ft. lbs. Tighten 10mm nut.

7. Insure crankshaft has not rotated (and fixture did not bind on 10mm nut).

8. Strike scriber with mallet to mark "TDC" on front housing.

9. Remove timing fixture.

10. Install fuel injection pump with gasket.

11. Install one 8mm bolt to attach gear to pump hub and tighten to specification.

12. Align timing marks on F.I. pump to front housing mark. Tighten to specification (3) 10mm attachment nuts.

13. Rotate engine and install remaining (2) pump gear attaching bolts and tighten to specification.

Injection Nozzle

REMOVAL & INSTALLATION

1978–79 8-350 Diesel

1. Remove the fuel return line from the nozzle.

2. Remove the nozzle hold-down clamp and spacer using tool J-26952.

3. Cap the high pressure line and nozzle tip.

NOTE: The nozzle tip is highly susceptible to damage and must be protected at all times.

4. If an old nozzle is to be reinstalled, a new compression seal and carbon stop seal must be installed after removal of the used seals.

5. Remove the caps and install the nozzle, spacer and clamp. Torque to 25 ft. lbs.

6. Replace return line, start the engine and check for leaks.

1980–81 8-350 Diesel

The injection nozzles on these engines are simply unbolted from the cylinder head, after the fuel lines are removed, in similar fashion to a spark plug. Be careful not to damage the nozzle end and make sure you remove the copper nozzle gasket from the cylinder head if it does not come off with the nozzle.

Clean the carbon off the tip of the nozzle with a soft brass wire brush and install the nozzles, with gaskets.

NOTE: 1981 and later models use two type of injectors, CAV Lucas and Diesel Equipment. When installing the inlet fittings, torque the Diesel Equipment injector fitting to 45 ft. lbs. and the CAV Lucas to 25 ft. lbs.

8-379

NOTE: Nozzles used in Pickups and Blazers are different than those used in Vans and are not interchangeable.

1. Disconnect batteries.
2. Disconnect fuel line clip.
3. Remove fuel return hose.

4. Remove fuel injection line as previously outlined.

5. Remove injection nozzle using tool J-29873 or equivalent whenever possible.

NOTE: When removing an injection nozzle, use tool J-29873 or equivalent. Be sure to remove the nozzle using the 30mm hex. Failure to do so will result in damage to the injection nozzle. Always cap the nozzle and lines to prevent damage and contamination.

Injection Pump Adapter, Adapter Seal, and New Adapter Timing Mark

REMOVAL & INSTALLATION

NOTE: Skip steps 4 and 9 if a new adapter is not being installed.

1. Remove injection pump and lines as described earlier.

2. Remove the injection pump adapter.

3. Remove the seal from the adapter.

4. File the timing mark from the adapter. Do not file the mark off the pump.

5. Position the engine at TDC of No. 1 cylinder. Align the mark on the balancer with the zero mark on the indicator. The index is offset to the right when No. 1 is at TDC.

6. Apply chassis lube to the seal areas. Install, but do not tighten the injection pump.

7. Install the new seal on the adapter using tool J-28425, or its equivalent.

8. Torque the adapter bolts to 25 ft. lbs.

9. Install timing tool J-26896 into the injection pump adapter. Torque the tool, toward No. 1 cylinder, to 50 ft. lbs. Mark the injection pump adapter. Remove the tool.

10. Install the injection pump.

Injection Pump

REMOVAL & INSTALLATION

8-379 Pickup-Blazer

1. Disconnect batteries.
2. Remove fan.
3. Remove fan shroud.
4. Remove intake manifold.
5. Remove fuel lines as previously outlined.
6. Disconnect accelerator cable at injection pump, and detent cable where applicable.
7. Disconnect necessary wires and hoses at injection pump.
8. Disconnect fuel return line at top of injection pump.
9. Disconnect fuel feed line at injection pump.

DIESEL EQUIPMENT   **C.A.V. LUCAS**

Diesel injector identification—1980 and later

DO NOT INTERCHANGE

FAST GLOW TYPE GLOW PLUGS (6 VOLT)   5/16"

1/4"   **SLOW GLOW TYPE GLOW PLUGS (12 VOLT)**

Glow plug identification

FUEL RETURN

REMOVE HERE

8–379 injection nozzle

Marking the injection pump adapter

Offset on the diesel fuel pump driven gear

Injection pump adapter bolts

Injection pump

NOTE: LUBRICATE SEAL, TOOL, ADAPTER & MANIFOLD

Installing the adapter seal

10. Remove A/C hose retainer bracket if equipped with A/C.

11. Remove oil fill tube, includes C.D.R.V. vent hose assembly.

12. Remove grommet.

13. Scribe or paint a mark on front cover and injection pump flange.

14. It will be necessary to rotate engine in order to gain access to driven gear to injection pump retaining bolts through the oil filler neck hole.

15. Remove injection pump to front cover attaching nuts.

Diesel injection pump timing marks

16. Remove pump and cap all open lines and nozzles.

NOTE: Install pump per the following:

1. Replace gasket.

2. Align locating pin on pump hub with slot in injection pump driven gear. At the same time, align timing marks.

3. Attach injection pump to front cover, torque nuts to 40 N·m (30 ft. lbs.). Align timing marks before fully torquing nuts.

4. Install drive gear to injection pump bolts, torque bolts to 25 N·m (20 ft. lbs.).

5. Install oil fill tube, includes C.D.R.V. vent hose assembly.

6. Install grommet.

7. Install A/C hose retainer bracket if equipped.

8. Install fuel feed line at injection pump, torque to 25 N·m (20 ft. lbs.).

9. Install fuel return line at top of injection pump.

10. Connect necessary wires and hoses.

11. Connect accelerator cable.

12. Connect injection lines.

13. Install intake manifold.

14. Install fan shroud.

15. Install fan.

16. Connect batteries.

17. Start engine and check for leaks.

Vans

1. Remove intake manifold as previously outlined.

2. Remove air cleaner inlet hose (rotate snorkel up).

3. Remove hood latch, disconnect cable and move aside.

4. Remove windshield washer bottle.

5. Remove fan shroud bolts.

6. Remove upper shroud.

7. Disconnect rubber hose from oil fill tube.

8. Disconnect oil fill tube attaching nuts and remove oil fill tube.

9. Remove oil fill tube grommet.

10. Rotate engine as necessary and remove drive gear to pump bolts.

11. Remove fuel filter and bracket—includes line to injection pump.

12. Disconnect wire looms from injection lines.

13. Disconnect injection lines at brackets. Also disconnect oil pan dipstick tube at left cylinder head.

14. Disconnect electrical connections at injection pump.

15. If equipped with automatic transmission, disconnect T.V. cable.

16. Disconnect accelerator cable.

17. Disconnect injection lines at nozzles Numbers 2, 4, 5, 6, 7, 8.

18. Raise vehicle.

19. Disconnect Number 1 and 3 injection lines at nozzles.

20. Cover nozzles Numbers 1, 3, 5, 7.

21. Lower vehicle.

22. Cover nozzles Number 2, 4, 6, 8.

23. Disconnect injection lines at pump and remove lines. Tag lines for reinstallation.

24. Cap all lines.

25. Disconnect fuel return line.

26. Scribe a mark on front cover and pump flange for reinstallation.

27. Remove pump to front cover attaching nuts.

28. Remove injection pump and cap all open discharge fittings.

NOTE: Install using the following sequence.

1. Replace gasket.

2. Align locating pin on pump hub with slot in injection pump gear. At the same time, align timing marks.

3. Attach injection pump to front cover, torque nuts to 40 N·m (30 ft. lbs.). Align timing marks before fully torquing nuts.

4. Attach pump to drive gear, torque bolts to 25 N·m (20 ft. lbs.).

5. For the remainder of installation procedures, reverse removal steps.

Fuel Injection Line

REMOVAL & INSTALLATION

Pickup & Blazer

1. Disconnect batteries.

2. Disconnect air cleaner bracket at valve cover.

3. Remove crankcase ventilator bracket and move aside.

4. Disconnect secondary filter lines.

5. Remove secondary filter adapter.

6. Loosen vacuum pump hold-down clamp and rotate pump in order to gain access to intake manifold bolt.

7. Remove intake manifold bolts. Injection line clips are retained by the same bolts.

8. Remove intake manifold.

9. Install protective covers J-29664-1 or equivalent.

10. Remove injection line clips at loom brackets.

11. Remove injection lines at nozzles and cover nozzles with protective caps.

12. Remove injection lines at pump and tag lines for reinstallation.

13. Remove fuel line from injection pump.

14. Installation is the reverse of removal.

Vans

1. Disconnect batteries.

2. Remove engine cover.

3. Remove intake manifold.

4. Install protective covers J-29664-1 or equivalent.

5. Remove injection line clips at loom brackets.

6. Raise vehicle (left bank only).

7. Remove injection lines at nozzles and cover nozzles with protective caps.

8. Lower vehicle (left bank only).

9. Remove injection lines at pump and tag lines for reinstallation.

10. Installation is the reverse of removal.

GLOW PLUGS

There are two types of glow plugs used on General Motors Corp. diesels: the "fast glow" type and the "slow glow" type. The fast glow type use pulsing current applied to 6 volt glow plugs while the slow glow type use continuous current applied to 12 volt glow plugs.

An easy way to tell the plugs apart is that the fast glow (6 volt) plugs have a 5/16 in. wide electrical connector plug while the slow glow (12 volt) connector plug is 1/4 in. wide. Do not attempt to interchange any parts of these two glow plug systems.

MANUAL TRANSMISSION

2-Wheel Drive except Vans

REMOVAL & INSTALLATION

1. Raise the vehicle and support on jack stands.

2. Drain the transmission.

3. Disconnect the speedometer cable, TCS switch and back-up lamp wire at the transmission.

4. Disconnect the shift control levers or shift control from the transmission. On 4-speeds, remove the gearshift lever by pressing down firmly on the slotted collar plate with a pair of channel lock pliers and rotating counterclockwise. Plug the opening to keep out dirt.

5. Disconnect the parking brake lever and controls (if used).

6. Remove the driveshaft after marking the position of shaft to flange.

7. Position a jack under the transmission to support the weight of the transmission.

8. Remove the crossmember. Visually inspect to see if other equipment, brackets or lines, must be removed to permit removal of transmission.

NOTE: Mark the position of the crossmember when removing to prevent incorrect installation. The tapered surface should face the rear.

9. Remove the flywheel housing underpan.

10. Remove the top two transmission-to-housing bolts and insert two guide pins.

NOTE: The use of guide pins will not only support the transmission but will prevent damage to the clutch disc. Guide pins can be made by taking two bolts, the same as those just removed, only longer, and cutting off the heads. Slot them for a screwdriver. Be sure to sup-port the clutch release bearing and support assembly during removal of the transmission. This will prevent the release bearing from falling out of the flywheel housing.

11. Remove the two remaining bolts and slide transmission straight back from engine. Use care to keep the transmission drive gear straight in line with clutch disc hub.

NOTE: Be sure to support release bearing when removing transmission to avoid having bearing fall into flywheel housing.

12. When the transmission is free from the engine, move from under the vehicle. To install the transmission:

13. Place the transmission on guide pins, slide forward starting the main drive gear into the clutch disc's splines.

NOTE: Place the transmission in gear and rotate transmission flange or output yoke to aid the entry of the main drive gear into the disc's splines. Make sure the clutch release bearing is in position.

———— CAUTION ————

Avoid springing the clutch when the transmission is being installed on the engine. Do not force the transmission into the clutch disc hub. Do not let the transmission hang unsupported in the splined portion of the clutch disc.

14. Install the two lower transmission mounting bolts, and flywheel lower pan (if equipped).

15. Remove the guide pins and install upper mounting bolts. Torque to 75 ft. lbs.

16. Install the driveshaft, watch alignment marks. Install the crossmember according to the alignment marks.

17. Connect the parking brake, back-up lamp and TCS switch (if used).

18. Connect the shift levers, or install the shifter, and adjust if needed.

19. Connect the speedometer cable and refill transmission.

20. Lower the vehicle and road test.

Vans

REMOVAL & INSTALLATION

1. Raise and support the van.

2. Drain the transmission. The Tremec top-cover transmission is drained by removing the lower case to extension housing bolt.

3. Disconnect the speedometer cable, back-up light and TCS switch.

4. Remove the shift controls from the transmission.

5. Disconnect the driveshaft and remove it from the vehicle.

6. Support the transmission with a floor jack.

7. Inspect the transmission to be sure that all necessary components have been removed or disconnected.

8. Mark the front of the crossmember to be sure that it is installed correctly.

9. Support the clutch release bearing to prevent it from falling out of the flywheel housing when the transmission is removed.

10. Remove the flywheel housing under pan and transmission mounting bolts.

11. Move the transmission slowly away from the engine, keeping the mainshaft in alignment with the clutch disc hub. Be sure that the transmission is supported.

12. Remove the transmission from under the vehicle.

13. Installation is the reverse of removal. Lightly coat the mainshaft with high temperature grease. Do not use much grease, since, under normal operation, the grease will be thrown onto the clutch, causing it to fail.

14. Tighten the transmission to flywheel housing bolts to 75 ft. lbs. Fill the transmission with lubricant. Road test the vehicle.

Four Wheel Drive

REMOVAL & INSTALLATION

3-Speed

1. Jack up the vehicle and support it safely on stands. Remove the skid plate, if any.

2. Drain the transmission and transfer case. Remove the speedometer cable and the TCS switch from the side of the transmission.

3. Disconnect the driveshafts and secure them out of the way.

4. Remove the shifter lever by removing the pivot bolt to the adapter assembly. You can then push the shifter up out of the way.

5. On 1978 and later models, remove the bolts attaching the strut to the right side of the transfer case and to the rear of the engine, and remove the strut.

6. While supporting the transfer case securely, remove the attaching bolts to the adapter.

7. Remove the transfer case securing bolts from the frame and lower and remove the transfer case. (The case is attached to the right side of the frame.)

8. Disconnect the shift rods from the transmission.

9. While holding the rear of the engine with a jack, remove the adapter mounting bolts.

10. Remove the upper transmission bolts and insert two guide pins to keep the assembly aligned. See the two wheel drive procedure (step 10) for details on making these.

11. Remove the flywheel pan and the lower transmission bolts.

12. Pull the transmission and the adapter straight back on the guide pins until the input shaft is free of the clutch disc.

13. The transmission and the adapter are removed as on assembly. The adapter can be separated once the assembly is out.

14. Installation is the reverse of removal. Place the transmission in gear and turn the output shaft to align the clutch splines. Transmission bolt torque is 75 ft. lbs. See Transfer Case Removal and Installation for adapter bolt torques.

4-Speed

1. Remove the shifter boots and the floor mat or carpeting from the front passenger compartment.

2. Remove the transmission shift lever. See Step 4 of the two wheel drive procedure for details on removing the lever. It may be necessary to remove the center floor outlet from the heater to complete the next step. Remove the center console, if so equipped.

3. Remove the transmission cover after releasing the attaching screws. It will be necessary to rotate the cover 90° to clear the transfer case shift lever.

4. Disconnect the transfer case shift lever link assembly and the lever from the adapter. Remove the skid plate, if any.

5. Remove the back-up light, the TCS switch, and the speedometer cable from the side of the transmission.

6. Raise and support the truck. Support the engine. Drain the transmission and the transfer case. Detach both driveshafts and secure them out of the way.

7. Remove the transmission-to-frame bolts. To do this, it will be necessary to open the locking tabs. Remove the transfer case-to-frame bracket bolts.

8. While supporting the transmission and transfer case, remove the crossmember bolts and the crossmember. It will be necessary to rotate the crossmember to remove it from the frame.

9. Remove the lower clutch housing cover.

NOTE: On V8 engines it is necessary to remove the exhaust crossover pipe.

10. Remove the transmission-to-clutch-housing bolts. Remove the upper bolts first and install guide pins. See step 10 of the two wheel drive procedure for details.

11. Slide the transmission back until the main drive gear clears the clutch assembly and then lower the unit.

12. Install the transfer case on the transmission as an assembly. Attach the assembly to the clutch housing. Put the transmission in gear and turn the output shaft to align the clutch splines. Torque the transmission bolts to 75 ft. lbs.

13. Install the clutch housing cover and, on V8 models, the exhaust pipe.

14. Install the frame crossmember, the retaining adapter, and the transfer case.

15. The front and rear transfer case yoke locknuts must be torqued to 150 ft. lbs.

16. Install the front and rear driveshafts.

17. Connect the speedometer cable, back-up lights, and TCS switches.

18. Fill the transmission and the transfer case to the proper level.

19. Position the transfer case shift lever and the shift lever link on the shift rail bar.

20. Install the transmission floor cover and the center heating duct.

21. Install the center console, if so equipped.

22. Install the transmission shift lever.

S-Series Trucks

REMOVAL & INSTALLATION

4-Speed 77.5mm

NOTE: On 4-wheel drive models, see Transfer Case Removal and Installation.

1. Disconnect the battery ground.

2. Remove the upper starter retaining nut.

3. Remove the shift lever boot attaching screws and slide the boot up the shift lever.

4. Disconnect the shift lever at the transmission.

5. Disconnect the electrical connector at the transmission.

6. Raise and support the truck on jackstands.

7. Remove the driveshaft.

8. Disconnect the exhaust pipe at the manifold.

9. Disconnect the speedometer cable and electrical connector at the transmission.

10. Disconnect the clutch cable at the transmission.

11. Place a floor jack under the transmission to take up its weight.

12. Remove the transmission mount bolts.

13. Remove the catalytic converter hanger.

14. Remove the crossmember.

15. Remove the lower dust cover bolts.

16. Remove the lower starter bolt.

17. Unbolt the transmission from the engine and lower it on the jack.

18. Installation is the reverse of removal. Torque the transmission-to-engine bolts to 25 ft. lb. on the 4 cylinder and 55 ft. lb. on the 6 cylinder. Torque the transmission mount-to-transmission bolts to 35 ft. lb.; the crossmember-to-frame bolts to 25 ft. lb.; the dust cover bolts to 7 ft. lb.

4-Speed 77mm and 5-Speed 77mm

NOTE: On 4-wheel drive models, see Transfer Case Removal and Installation.

1. Disconnect the battery ground.

2. Remove the shift lever boot screws and slide the boot up the lever.

3. Shift the transmission into neutral and remove the shift lever.

4. Raise and support the track on jackstands.

5. Remove the driveshaft.

6. Disconnect the speedometer cable and wiring at the transmission.

7. Disconnect the clutch cable at the transmission.

8. Place a floor jack under the transmission and take up its weight. Remove the transmission mount bolts.

9. Remove the catalytic converter hanger.

10. Remove the crossmember.

11. Remove the dust cover bolts.

12. Unbolt the transmission from the bell housing and lower the jack. It will be necessary to pull the transmission back a ways to clear the clutch. Installation is the reverse of removal. Lightly grease the input shaft splines with chassis lube. Torque the transmission mount bolts to 35 ft. lb.; the mount-to-crossmember bolts to 25 ft. lb.; the crossmember-to-frame bolts to 25 ft. lb.; the transmission to-bell housing bolts to 55 ft. lb.

Linkage Adjustments

EXCEPT VANS

3-Speed Column Shift

1. Place the column lever in the neutral position.

2. Under the truck, loosen the shift rod clamps. These are at the transmission end.

3. Make sure that the two levers on the transmission are in their center, neutral positions.

4. Install a 3/16 to 7/32 in. pin or drill bit through the alignment holes in the levers at the bottom of the steering column. This holds these levers in the neutral position.

5. Tighten the shift rod clamps.

6. Remove the pin and check the shifting operation.

VANS

The gearshift linkage should be adjusted each time it is disturbed or removed.

1. Install the control rods to both of the levers and set both shifter levers in the Neutral position.

2. Align both shifter tube levers on the mast jacket in Neutral. Install a 3/16–7/16 in. gauge to hold them in place. The gauge is inserted in the holes of the levers.

3. Connect the control rods to the tube levers, making sure that the clamps and tube levers are properly positioned in Neutral.

4. Remove the gauge and move the gearshift lever through all positions to be sure that the adjustment is correct in all positions.

S-Series Trucks

NOTE: No linkage adjustments are necessary or possible on these vehicles.

Three speed column shift controls, except vans

Van 3-speed column shift details

Clutch linkage adjustment

COAT THIS GROOVE

PACK THIS RECESS

Throwout bearing lube points

CLUTCH

LINKAGE ADJUSTMENT

Except S-Series

This adjustment is for the amount of clutch pedal free travel before the throwout bearing contacts the clutch release fingers. It is required periodically to compensate for clutch lining wear. Incorrect adjustment will cause gear grinding and clutch slippage or wear.

NOTE: If you have a problem with grinding when shifting into gear, shorten the pedal stop bumper to ⅜ in. and readjust the linkage.

1. Disconnect the clutch fork return spring at the fork on the clutch housing.
2. Loosen the outer adjusting nut (A) and back it off approximately ½ in. from the swivel.
3. Hold the clutch fork pushrod against the fork to move the throwout bearing against the clutch fingers. The pushrod will slide through the swivel at the cross-shaft.
4. Adjust the inner adjusting nut (B) to obtain ¼ in. clearance between nut (B) and the swivel.
5. Release the pushrod, connect the re-

turn spring and tighten the outer nut (A) to lock the swivel against the inner nut (B).
6. Check the free travel at the pedal and readjust as necessary. It should be 1¼–1½ in.

REMOVAL & INSTALLATION

Except S-Series

There are two types of clutch pressure plates used, diaphragm and coil spring. In general, the larger heavy duty clutches are usually of the coil spring pressure plate type. Most removal and installation details are similar for both types.

Diaphragm Spring Pressure Plate

1. Remove the transmission as previously outlined.
2. Disconnect the fork pushrod and remove the flywheel housing. Remove the clutch throwout bearing from the fork.
3. Remove the clutch fork by pressing it away from the ball mounting with a screwdriver until the fork snaps loose from the ball or remove the ball stud from the clutch housing.
4. Install a pilot tool (an old mainshaft makes a good pilot tool) to hold the clutch while you are removing it.

NOTE: Before removing the clutch from the flywheel, matchmark the flywheel, the clutch cover and one of the pressure plate lugs. These parts must be reassembled in their original positions as they are a balanced assembly.

5. Loosen the clutch attaching bolts one turn at a time to prevent distortion of the clutch cover until the tension is released.
6. Remove the clutch pilot tool and the clutch from the vehicle.
   Inspect the flywheel and pressure plate for discoloration, scoring or wear marks. The flywheel can be refaced if necessary, otherwise replace the parts. Also inspect the clutch fork and throwout bearing for looseness or wear. Replace if either is evident.
   To install:
7. Install the pressure plate in the cover assembly, aligning the notch in the pressure plate with the notch in the cover flange.
8. Install the pressure plate retracting springs, lockwashers and the drive strap to the pressure plate bolts. Torque to 11 ft. lbs.
9. Turn the flywheel until the X mark is at the bottom.
10. Install the clutch disc, pressure plate and cover, using an old mainshaft as an aligning tool.
11. Turn the clutch until the X mark on the clutch cover aligns with the X mark on the flywheel.
12. Install the attaching bolts and tighten them a little at a time in a crisscross pattern until the spring pressure is taken up.
13. Remove the aligning tool.

14. Pack the clutch ball fork seat with a small amount of high temperature grease. Too much grease will cause slippage.. Install a new retainer in the groove of the clutch fork, if necessary. Install the retainer with the high side up and the open end on the horizontal.
15. If the clutch fork ball was removed, reinstall it in the clutch housing and snap the clutch fork onto the ball.
16. Lubricate the inside of the throwout bearing collar and the throwout fork groove with a small amount of graphite grease.
17. Install the throwout bearing.
18. Install the flywheel housing and transmission.
19. Further installation is the reverse of removal. Adjust the clutch linkage.

Coil Spring Pressure Plate

Basically, the same procedures apply to diaphragm clutch removal as to coil spring clutch removal.
   When loosening the clutch holding bolts, loosen them only a turn or two at a time in order to avoid bending the rim of the cover. It will be helpful to place wood or metal spacers, about ⅜ in. thick, between the clutch levers and the cover to hold the levers down as the holding bolts are being removed or when the clutch is being removed from the engine.

S-Series Trucks

ADJUSTMENT

1. Lift up on the pedal to allow the self adjuster to adjust the cable length.
2. Depress the pedal several times to set the pawl into mesh with the detent teeth.
3. Check the linkage for lost motion caused by loose or worn swivels, mounting brackets or a damaged cable.

REMOVAL & INSTALLATION

1. Remove the transmission.
2. Remove the flywheel housing.
3. Remove the clutch fork.
4. Insert a clutch alignment tool in the clutch hub and into the crankshaft pilot bearing.
5. Check for an X or other painted mark on the pressure plate and flywheel. If there isn't any mark, mark the assembly for installation purposes.
6. Loosen the pressure plate bolts, evenly and alternately, a little at a time until spring tension is released. Remove the pressure plate and driven plate.
7. Check the flywheel for cracks, wear, scoring or other damage. Check the pilot bearing for wear. Replace it by yanking it out with a slide hammer and driving in a new one with a wood or plastic hammer.
8. Installation is the reverse of removal. Use the alignment tool to aid installation. The raised hub of the driven plate

VIEW B

VIEW A

S-Series self-adjusting clutch mechanism

faces the transmission. Align the mating marks and tighten the bolts evenly and alternately to 20 ft. lb.

AUTOMATIC TRANSMISSION

Adjustments

SHIFT LINKAGE ADJUSTMENT

Except Vans

1. The shift tube and lever assembly must be free in the mast jacket.
2. Lift the selector lever toward the steering wheel and allow the selector lever to be positioned in Drive by the detent. Do not use the selector lever pointer as a reference.
3. Release the selector lever. The lever should not be able to go into Low unless the lever is lifted.
4. Lift the selector lever toward the steering wheel and allow the lever to be positioned in Neutral by the transmission detent.
5. Release the selector lever. The lever should not be able to engage reverse unless the lever is lifted. A properly adjusted linkage will prevent the lever from moving beyond both the Neutral and Drive detents unless the lever is lifted.
6. If adjustment is required, remove the screw (A) and spring washer from the swivel clamp (B).

7. Set the transmission lever (C) in Neutral by moving it to L_1 and then three detents clockwise.
8. Put the transmission selector lever in Neutral as determined by the mechanical stop in the steering column. Do not use the indicator pointer as a reference. The pointer is the last thing to be adjusted.
9. Assemble the swivel spring and washer to the lever (D) and tighten.
10. Readjust the Neutral safety switch if necessary.
11. To adjust the shift position indicator, remove the column cover at the bottom of the instrument panel and loosen the screw to move the pointer.
12. Check the operation. With the switch in RUN, and the transmission in Reverse, be sure that the key cannot be removed and that the steering wheel is locked.
    With the key in LOCK and the shift lever in PARK, be sure that the key can be removed, the steering wheel is locked, and that the transmission remains in PARK when the steering column is locked.

Vans
1977 AND LATER

———— CAUTION ————
Any inaccuracies in this procedure may lead to premature transmission failure due to operation without the controls in the full detent position. Such operation will result in reduced oil pressure, and therefore only partial engagement of the drive clutches. Partial engagement of the clutches with sufficient pressure to cause apparent normal operation will result in transmission failure after only a few miles of operation.

Automatic transmission shift linkage adjustment—except vans

The adjustment point for the transmission shift position indicator is accessible after removing the lower column cover

1. Remove the nut (F) and slide off the washers, grommet, bushing, and clamp (E). Remove swivel (D).
2. Remove the retainer, grommets and the transmission lever (C) from the shaft assembly.

1977 and later shift linkage adjustment—vans

3. Set the transmission lever (C) in the Neutral position either by moving the lever (C) counterclockwise to the L1 position, then clockwise three steps to the Neutral position, or by moving the lever (C) clockwise to the Park position, then counterclockwise two steps to the Neutral position.

4. Set the column shift lever in the Neutral position by rotating the shift lever until it locks into the stop in the column. Do not use the gear select pointer as a reference to position the column shift lever.

5. Attach rod (A) to the shaft assembly (B) as shown.

6. Slide the swivel (D) and the clamp (E) onto rod (A). Align the column shift lever and loosely attach the assembly.

7. Hold the column shift lever against the Neutral stop, on the Park position side.

8. Tighten the nut (F) to 18 ft. lbs.

9. Adjust the indicator needle if necessary. It may also be necessary to adjust the neutral start switch.

THROTTLE VALVE LINKAGE ADJUSTMENT

Six Cylinder Engines

1. With the accelerator depressed, the bellcrank on the engine must be in the wide-open throttle position.

2. The dash lever must be $1/64$–$1/16$ in. off the lever stop and the transmission lever must be against the transmission internal stop.

V8 Engines

1. Remove the air cleaner.

2. Disconnect the accelerator linkage at the carburetor.

3. Disconnect the accelerator return spring and throttle valve rod return springs.

4. Pull the throttle valve rod forward until the transmission is through the detent. Open the carburetor to the wide-open throttle position. The carburetor must reach the wide-open throttle position at the same time that the ball stud contacts the end of the slot in the upper throttle valve rod.

5. Adjust the swivel on the end of the upper throttle valve rod as per Step 4. The allowable tolerance is approximately $1/32$ in.

6. Connect and adjust the accelerator linkage.

7. Check for freedom of operation. Install the air cleaner.

NEUTRAL START SWITCH ADJUSTMENT

This switch prevents the engine from being started unless the transmission is in Neutral or Park. It is located on the shift linkage on the left side of the transmission. The switch is also used for the backup lights.

NOTE: The manual transmission backup light switch is on the rear of the transmission.

1. Loosen the switch mounting screws.

2. Make sure the transmission is in Neutral.

3. Insert a pin through the hole in the switch actuating arm into the switch body to hold the switch in the Neutral position. Adjust as necessary to make the pin fit.

4. Tighten the adjustment. Remove the pin.

5. Check that the engine can be started only in Park and Neutral and that the backup lights go on only in Reverse. Adjust as necessary.

DOWNSHIFT ADJUSTMENT

Turbo Hydra-Matic 350

This cable runs from the carburetor linkage to the transmission. It regulates the throttle position at which a downshift occurs. With the snap-lock disengaged from the bracket, position the carburetor at the wide open throttle position. Push the snap-lock downward until the top is flush with the rest of the cable.

Turbo Hydra-Matic 400 and 700-R4

When installing a new downshift switch, press the plunger as far forward as possible. The switch will adjust itself the first time the accelerator is floorboarded.

S-Series Trucks

LINKAGE

With the selector lever in Park, the parking pawl should engage and immobilize the transmission. The pointer on the indicator quadrant should line up properly with the indicated gear position in all ranges. To adjust the linkage, raise and support the truck on jackstands. Place the selector in Park. Loosen the locknut on the linkage arm at the transmission and make sure that the transmission lever is fully in the Park position. Tighten the locknut.

Detent cable adjustment—except diesel

Transmission linkage adjustment

Throttle valve cable adjustment point

THROTTLE VALVE CABLE

1. With the engine off, depress the readjusting tab.

2. Move the slider back through the fitting in the direction away from the throttle body until the slider stops against the fitting. Release the readjusting tab.

3. Open the carburetor throttle plate to the wide open position. This will automatically adjust the cable. Release the throttle plate.

Transmission Removal & Installation

NOTE: It would be best to drain the transmission before starting.

It may be necessary to disconnect and remove the exhaust crossover pipe on V8s, and to disconnect the catalytic converter and remove its support bracket, on models so equipped.

TWO WHEEL DRIVE

1. Disconnect the battery ground cable. Disconnect the detent cable at the carburetor.

2. Raise and support the truck.

3. Remove the driveshaft, after matchmarking its flanges.

4. Disconnect the speedometer cable, downshift cable, vacuum modulator line, shift linkage, and fluid cooler lines at the transmission. Remove the filler tube.

5. Support the transmission and unbolt the rear mount from the crossmember. Remove the crossmember.

6. Remove the torque converter un-

derpan, matchmark the flywheel and converter, and remove the converter bolts.

7. Support the engine and lower the transmission slightly for access to the upper transmission to engine bolts.

8. Remove the transmission to engine bolts and pull the transmission back. Rig up a strap or keep the front of the transmission up so the converter doesn't fall out.

9. Reverse the procedure for installation. Bolt the transmission to the engine first (30 ft. lbs.), then the converter to the flywheel (35 ft. lbs.). Make sure that the converter attaching lugs are flush and that the converter can turn freely before installing the bolts. Tighten the bolts finger tight, then torque to specification, to insure proper converter alignment.

NOTE: Lubricate the internal yoke splines at the transmission end of the driveshaft with lithium base grease. The grease should seep out through the vent hole.

FOUR WHEEL DRIVE

1. Disconnect the battery ground cable and remove the transmission dipstick. Detach the downshift cable at the carburetor. Remove the transfer case shift lever knob and boot.

2. Raise and support the truck.

3. Remove the skid plate, if any. Remove the flywheel cover.

4. Matchmark the flywheel and torque converter, remove the bolts, and secure the

converter so it doesn't fall out of the transmission.

5. Detach the shift linkage, speedometer cable, vacuum modulator line, downshift cable, and cooler lines at the transmission. Remove the filler tube.

6. Remove the exhaust crossover pipe to manifold bolts.

7. Unbolt the transfer case adapter from the crossmember. Support the transmission and transfer case. Remove the crossmember.

8. Move the exhaust system aside. Detach the driveshafts after matchmarking their flanges. Disconnect the parking brake cable.

9. Unbolt the transfer case from the frame bracket. Support the engine. Unbolt the transmission from the engine, pull the assembly back, and remove.

Neutral start switch adjustment

Throttle valve/detent cable adjustment—diesel

10. Reverse the procedure for installation. Bolt the transmission to the engine first (30 ft. lbs.), then the converter to the flywheel (35 ft. lbs.). Make sure that the converter attaching lugs are flush and that the converter can turn freely before installing the bolts. See Transfer Case Removal and Installation for adapter bolt torques.

Pan & Filter

REMOVAL & INSTALLATION

1. Jack up your truck and support it with jack stands.
2. Loosen the pan bolts on the transmission.
3. Remove all pan bolts except for 2 or 3 at one corner.
4. Gently tap the pan using a rubber mallet and drain the oil into an appropriate container.
5. Remove the pan and remove the filter. Clean the pan with a lint free rag.
6. Install a new filter and pan gasket.
7. Add new transmission fluid to the proper level. Start your truck and check for leaks.

S-Series Trucks

NOTE: On 4-wheel drive models, see Transfer Case Removal and Installation.

1. Remove the air cleaner assembly.
2. Disconnect the throttle valve cable at the carburetor.
3. On the 4-119c engine, remove the upper starter bolt.
4. Raise and support the truck on jackstands.
5. Remove the driveshaft.
6. Disconnect the speedometer cable, linkage and wiring at the transmission.
7. Remove any other components attached to the transmission case.
8. Remove the exhaust system from the truck.
9. Remove the torque converter cover and match-mark the converter and flywheel.
10. Remove the converter-to-flywheel bolts.
11. Place a floor jack under the transmission to take up its weight.
12. Unbolt the transmission from its mounts. Unbolt and remove the mounts.
13. Lower the transmission slightly to gain access to the fluid cooler lines. Disconnect and cap these lines.
14. Disconnect the throttle valve cable.
15. Place a jack or jackstand under the engine for support.
16. Unbolt the transmission from the engine.
17. Pull the transmission rearward to disengage it and lower it from the truck.

NOTE: Take care to avoid dropping the converter.

18. Installation is the reverse of removal. Match up the mating marks on the converter. Torque the transmission-to-engine bolts to 25 ft. lb. on 4-cylinder models and 55 ft. lb. on the 6-cylinder; torque the converter-to-flywheel bolts to 35 ft. lb.; torque the transmission-to-mount bolts to 35 ft. lb.; the mount-to-frame bolts to 25 ft. lb.

TRANSFER CASE

There are three transfer cases used. The New Process 205 is used in part time systems with all transmissions in 1980, and with manual transmissions only 1977–79. It has a large New Process emblem on the back of the case. The full time New Process 203 is used with automatics from mid-1977 to 1979. It can be identified by the H LOC and L LOC positions on the shifter.

The aluminum case New Process 208 was introduced in 1981 on K-10 and 20 models. S-Series trucks use the New Process 207. This unit is an aluminum case model with

chain drive. Proper fluid for this unit is Dexron II automatic transmission fluid.

NOTE: Models with the New Process 203 full time four wheel drive transfer case, especially with manual transmissions, may give a front wheel "chatter" or vibration on sharp turns. This is a normal characteristic of this drivetrain combination. If it occurs shortly after

NP 203 linkage adjustment

NP 203 shift linkage

shifting out of a LOC position, the transfer case is probably still locked up. This should correct itself after about a mile of driving, or can be alleviated by backing up for a short distance.

———— CAUTION ————

Owners of full time four wheel drive trucks (New Process 203 transfer case) often consider either removing the front driveshaft, or installing locking front hubs and operating in a LOC position, as a means of improving gas mileage. This practice will submit the transfer case to stresses beyond its design limits and will void all warranties. Use of any lubricant additive in the transfer case is also not recommended.

NEW PROCESS 203 SHIFT LINKAGE ADJUSTMENT

The full time four wheel drive transfer case is the only one on which linkage adjustment is possible.

1. Place the selector lever in the cab in the Neutral position.
2. Detach the adjustable rod ends from the transfer case levers.
3. Insert an 11/64 in. drill bit through the alignment holes in the shifter levers. This will lock the shifter in the neutral position with both levers vertical.
4. Place the range shift lever (the outer lever) on the transfer case in the Neutral position.
5. Place the lockout shift lever (the inner lever) on the transfer case in the unlocked position. Both levers should now be vertical.
6. Adjust the rods so that the linkage fits together. The indicator plate can be moved to align with the correct symbol.
7. Remove the drill bit.

NEW PROCESS 208 SHIFT LINKAGE ADJUSTMENT

1. Put transfer case lever in 4HI detent.
2. Push lower shifter lever forward to 4HI stop.
3. Install rod swivel in shift lever hole.
4. Hang .200 thick gauge cover rod behind swivel.
5. Run rear rod nut A against gauge with shifter against 4HI stop.
6. Remove gauge and push swivel rearward against nut A.
7. Run front rod nut B against swivel and tighten.

New Process 207 Linkage Adjustment

1. Loosen the transfer case switch bolt and the case shift lever pivot bolt.
2. Shift the transfer case to the 4H position.

3. Remove the console and slide the boot up the lever.
4. Install a 5/16 in. drill bit through the shifter and into the switch bracket.
5. Install a bolt at the case lever to lock it in position.
6. Tighten the switch bracket bolt to 30 ft. lb. and the shifter pivot bolt to 100 ft. lb.
7. Remove the bolt you installed to lock the lever.
8. Remove the drill bit. Check the drill bit. Check the linkage action.

REMOVAL & INSTALLATION

NP 203 and 205

1. Raise and support the truck.
2. Drain the transfer case.
3. Disconnect the speedometer cable, back-up light switch, and the TCS switch.
4. If necessary, remove the skid plate and crossmember support.
5. Disconnect the front and rear driveshafts and support them out of the way.
On New Process 205 models, disconnect the shift lever rod from the shift rail link.
On New Process 203 models, disconnect the shift levers at the transfer case.

Adapter to Transfer Case Bolt Torque

Model	Year	Torque (ft. lbs.)
NP 205	'75–'82	25
NP 203	'75–'79	38

NP 208 linkage adjustment

4-SPEED TRANSMISSION WITH MODEL 205 TRANSFER CASE

AUTOMATIC TRANSMISSION WITH MODEL 203 TRANSFER CASE

AUTOMATIC TRANSMISSION WITH MODEL 205 TRANSFER CASE

SUPPORT AND BRACKET ASSEMBLY (ALL MODELS)
1975–81 transfer case installation

Adapter to Transmission Bolt Torque

Model	Torque (ft. lbs.)
NP 205	22 manual
	35 automatic
NP 203	40

Adapter to Frame Bolt Torque

Model	Torque (ft. lbs.)
NP 205	130
NP 203 (bracket to frame)	50 upper
	65 lower

6. Remove the transfer case-to-frame mounting bolts.

7. Support the transfer case and remove the bolts attaching the transfer case to transmission adaptor.

8. Move the transfer case to the rear until the input shaft clears the adaptor and lower the transfer case from the truck.

To install the transfer case:

9. Lifting the transfer case on a transmission jack, attach the case to the adapter using through bolts. Torque to specification.

10. Remove the transmission jack and install the transfer case-to-frame rail bolts.

Make certain to bend the locking tabs after installation.

11. Connect the shift linkage.

12. Connect the front driveshaft to the front transfer case output shaft and the rear drive shaft to the rear output shaft.

13. Install the crossmember and skid plate, if equipped.

14. Connect the speedometer cable, back-up light, and TCS switches.

15. Fill the transfer case to the proper level with lubricant.

16. Lower the vehicle.

NOTE: Recheck all bolt torques. When attaching the driveshafts, make sure that the flange locknuts are torqued to specifications.

REMOVAL & INSTALLATION
NP 207

1. Shift transfer case into 4 Hi.
2. Disconnect negative cable at battery.
3. Raise vehicle and remove skid plate.
4. Drain lubricant from transfer case.
5. Mark transfer case front output shaft yoke and propeller shaft for assembly reference. Disconnect front propeller shaft from transfer case.
6. Mark rear axle yoke and propeller shaft for assembly reference. Remove rear propeller shaft.
7. Disconnect speedometer cable and vacuum harness at transfer case. Remove shift lever from transfer case.
8. Remove catalytic converter hanger bolts at converter.

9. Raise transmission and transfer case and remove transmission mount attaching bolts. Remove mount and catalytic converter hanger and lower transmission and transfer case.

10. Support transfer case and remove transfer case attaching bolts.

On vehicles equipped with an automatic transmission, it will be necessary to remove the shift lever bracket mounting bolts from the transfer case adapter in order to remove the upper left transfer case attaching bolt.

11. Separate transfer case from adapter (auto) or extension housing (man.) and remove from vehicle.

NOTE: Install the transfer case using the following recommendations:

1. Position new gasket on the transfer case.

2. Install transfer case, aligning splines of input shaft with transmission and slide transfer case forward until seated against transmission.

3. Install transfer case attaching bolts and torque to specification. On vehicles equipped with automatic transmission, reinstall shift lever bracket bolts.

4. Raise transmission and transfer case and install mount and hanger bracket. Install attaching bolts and torque to specification.

5. Install catalytic converter hanger bolts at converter and torque to specification.

6. Attach shift lever at transfer case. Connect speedometer cable and vacuum harness at transfer case.

7. Connect the front and install the rear propeller shaft. Be sure to align reference marks made during removal.

8. Fill transfer case with Dexron II.

9. Install skid plate and lower vehicle.

10. Connect negative cable at battery.

11. Road test vehicle, check to make sure vehicle shifts and operates into all ranges.

NP 208

1. Place the transfer case in 4H.
2. Raise the vehicle.
3. Drain the lubricant from the transfer case.
4. Remove the cotter pin from the shift lever swivel.
5. Mark the transfer case front and rear output shaft yokes and propeller shafts for assembly alignment reference.
6. Disconnect the speedometer cable and indicator switch wires.
7. Disconnect the front propeller shaft at the transfer case yoke.
8. Disconnect the parking brake cable guide from the pivot located on right frame rail, if necessary.
9. Remove the engine strut rod from the transfer case on automatic transmission models.
10. Place a support under the transfer case and remove the transfer case-to-transmission adapter bolts.

INDICATOR TO BE LOCATED AT DEPRESSION

SHIFT PATTERN SHOULD BE IN HORIZONTAL POSITION TO DRIVER

FWD

NO INSULATION TO BE INSTALLED UNDER RETAINER

WITH TRANS CASE IN 2 WHEEL "HI" POSITION, ALIGN INDICATOR PLATE TO CENTER OF INDICATOR

VIEW A

VIEW B

DO NOT LUBRICATE BOLT THREADS ONLY SHANK GROOVE

NP 205 linkage

11. Move the transfer case assembly rearward until free of the transmission output shaft and remove the assembly.

12. Remove all gasket material from the rear of the transmission adapter housing.

13. Install the transmission-to-transfer case gasket on the transmission.

14. Shift the transfer case to 4H position if not done previously.

15. Rotate the transfer case output shaft (by turning yoke) until the transmission output shaft gear engages the transfer case input shaft. Move the transfer case forward until the case seats against the transmission. Be sure the transfer case is flush against the transmission. Severe damage to the transfer case will result if the attaching bolts are tightened while the transfer case is cocked or in a bind.

16. Install the transfer case attaching bolts. Tighten the bolts to 30 ft. lbs.

17. Connect the speedometer driven gear to the transfer case.

18. Connect the front and rear propeller shafts to the transfer case. Be sure to align the shafts-to-yokes using the reference marks made during removal. Tighten the shaft-to-yoke clamp strap nuts to 15 ft. lbs.

19. Remove the support stand from under the transfer case.

20. Connect the parking brake cable if disconnected.

21. Attach the cotter pin to the shift lever swivel.

22. Connect the engine strut to the transfer case on automatic models.

23. Fill the transfer case with Dexron® II.

24. Lower the vehicle.

DRIVELINE

Front Driveshaft (4 WD Only)

REMOVAL & INSTALLATION

Chevrolet and GMC use U-bolts or straps to secure the driveshaft to the pinion flange. Use the following procedure to remove the driveshaft.

1. Jack the front of the vehicle so that the front wheels are off the ground. Block

4-SPEED TRANSMISSION WITH MODEL 205 TRANSFER CASE

AUTOMATIC TRANSMISSION WITH MODEL 203 TRANSFER CASE

AUTOMATIC TRANSMISSION WITH MODEL 205 TRANSFER CASE

SUPPORT AND BRACKET ASSEMBLY (ALL MODELS)

Transfer case adapters

WITH AUTOMATIC TRANSMISSION

WITH MANUAL TRANSMISSION

NP 208 installation

Rear driveshaft U-bolt attachment

Rear driveshaft strap attachment

32 splined shaft U-joint alignment keyway

Injection molded retainer U-joint repair kit

the rear wheels and safely support the truck on stands.

2. Scribe aligning marks on the driveshaft and the pinion flange to aid in reassembly.

3. Remove the U-bolts or straps at the axle end of the shaft. Compress the shaft slightly and tape the bearings into place to avoid losing them.

4. Remove the U-bolts or straps at the transfer case end of the shaft. Tape the bearings into place.

5. Remove the driveshaft.

6. Reverse the procedure for installation. Make certain that the marks made earlier line up correctly to prevent possible imbalances. Be sure that the constant velocity joint (the big double one) is at the transfer case end.

Rear Driveshaft (All Models)

REMOVAL & INSTALLATION

1. Raise and safely support the rear of the truck as necessary. There is less chance of lubricant leakage from the rear of the transmission on two wheel drive models if the rear is raised. Block the front wheels.

2. Scribe alignment marks on the driveshaft and flange of the rear axle, and transfer case or transmission. If the truck is equipped with a two piece driveshaft, be certain to also scribe marks at the center joint near the splined connection. When reinstalling driveshafts, it is necessary to place the shafts into the same position from which they were removed. This is called phasing. Failure to reinstall the driveshaft properly will cause driveline vibrations and reduced component life.

3. Disconnect the rear universal joint by removing U-bolts or straps. Tape the bearings into place to avoid losing them.

4. If there are U-bolts or straps at the front end of the shaft, remove them. Tape the bearings into place. For trucks with two piece shafts, remove the bolts retaining the bearing support to the frame crossmember. Compress the shaft slightly and remove it. All four wheel drive trucks are of this type.

5. If there are no fasteners at the front end of the transmission, there will only be a splined fitting. Slide the shaft forward slightly to disengage the axle flange, lower the rear end of the shaft, then pull it back out of the transmission. Most two wheel drive trucks are of this type. For trucks with two piece driveshafts, remove the bolts retaining the bearing support to the frame crossmember.

6. Reverse the procedure for installation. It may be tricky to get the scribed alignment marks to match up on trucks with two piece driveshafts. For those models only, the following instructions may be of some help. First, slide the grease cap and gasket onto the rear splines. Then:

1977–and later 4-wheel drive models with 16 splines, after installing the front shaft to the transmission and bolting the support to the crossmember, arrange the front trunnion vertically and the second trunnion horizontally.

Models with 32 splines have an alignment key. The driveshaft cannot be replaced incorrectly. Simply match up the key with the keyway.

7. On two-wheel drive automatic transmission models, lubricate the internal yoke splines at the transmission end of the shaft with lithium base grease. The grease should seep out through the vent hole.

NOTE: A thump in the rear driveshaft sometimes occurs when releasing the brakes after braking to a stop, especially on a downgrade. This is most common with automatic transmission. It is often caused by the driveshaft splines binding and can be cured by removing the driveshaft, inspecting the splines for rough edges, and carefully lubricating. A similar thump may be caused by the clutch plates in Positraction limited slip rear axles binding. If this isn't caused by wear, it can be cured by draining and refilling the rear axle with the special lubricant and adding Positraction additive, both of which are available from dealers.

DRIVESHAFT ATTACHMENT TORQUE SPECIFICATIONS

To rear axle (strap)	12–17 ft. lbs.
To rear axle (U-bolt)	18–22 ft. lbs.
Bearing support to hanger	20–30 ft. lbs.
Hanger to frame	40–50 ft. lbs.
To transfer case	70–80 ft. lbs.

UNIVERSAL JOINT ATTACHMENT TORQUE SPECIFICATIONS

Strap attachments	15 ft. lbs.
U-bolt attachments	20 ft. lbs.

FRONT DRIVE AXLE

Locking Hub

REMOVAL & INSTALLATION

NOTE: Locking hubs may not be used with full time four wheel drive. Locking hubs should be run in the lock position for at least 10 miles each month to assure proper differential lubrication.

This procedure requires snap-ring pliers and a special hub nut wrench. It isn't very easy without them. You will have to modify this procedure if you have non-factory installed hubs.

1. Set the hub in the Lock position.
2. Remove the outer retaining plate allen head bolts and take off the plate, O-ring, and knob.
3. Take out the large snap-ring inside the hub and remove the outer clutch retaining ring and actuating cam body.
4. Relieve pressure on the axle shaft snap-ring and remove it.
5. Take out the axle shaft sleeve and clutch ring assembly and the inner clutch ring and bushing assembly. Remove the spring and retainer plate.
6. Clean all the hub components in a safe solvent and dry them. Lubricate everything with a high temperature grease.
7. Install the spring retainer plate with the flange side to the bearing and seat it against the outer bearing cup.
8. Install the spring with the large end against the retainer plate.

NOTE: When the spring is properly installed and seated it will extend past the spindle nuts about ⅞ in.

9. Place the inner clutch ring and bushing assembly into the axle shaft sleeve and clutch ring assembly. Install these components, push in, and install the axle shaft snap-ring. If there are two axle shaft snap-ring grooves, use the inner one.

NOTE: You can install a ⁷⁄₁₆ in. bolt in the axle and pull outward on it to aid in seating the snap-ring.

10. Install the actuating cam body with the cams out. Replace the outer clutch retaining ring and then the internal snap-ring.
11. Install a new O-ring, then install the actuating knob and retaining plate in the lock position. The grooves in the knob must fit into the actuator cam body. Install the cover bolts and seals.

Axle Shaft

REMOVAL & INSTALLATION

NOTE: This procedure requires snap-ring pliers and a special hub nut wrench. It is not very easy without them.

1. Remove the wheel and tire.
2. For K-10 or K-1500 models and K-20 or K-2500 models 1977–and later with locking front hubs: Lock the hubs. Remove the outer retaining plate Allen head bolts and take off the plate, O-ring, and knob. Take out the large snap-ring inside the hub and remove the outer clutch retaining ring and actuating cam body. This is a lot easier with snap-ring pliers. Relieve pressure on the axle shaft snap-ring and remove it. Take out the axle shaft sleeve and clutch ring assembly and the inner clutch ring and

bushing assembly. Remove the spring and retainer plate.

NOTE: You will have to modify this procedure for either of the models mentioned above if you have non-factory installed locking hubs.

3. If you don't have locking front hubs, remove the hub cap and snap-ring. Next, remove the drive gear and pressure spring. To prevent the spring from popping out, place a hand over the drive gear and use a screwdriver to pry the gear out. Remove the spring.
4. Remove the wheel bearing outer lock nut, lock ring, and wheel bearing inner adjusting nut. A special wrench is required.
5. Remove the brake disc assembly and outer wheel bearing. Remove the spring retainer plate if you don't have locking hubs. Pull out the axle shaft and universal assembly. When installing the shaft, turn it slowly to mesh the splines.
6. Remove the oil seal and inner bearing cone from the hub using a brass drift and hammer. Discard the oil seal. Use the drift to remove the inner and outer bearing cups.
7. Check the condition of the spindle bearing. If you have drum brakes, remove the grease retainer, gasket, and backing plate after removing the bolts. Unbolt the spindle and tap it with a soft hammer to break it loose. Remove the spindle and check the condition of the thrust washer, replacing it if worn. Now you can remove the oil seal and spindle roller bearing.

NOTE: The spindle bearings must be greased each time the wheel bearings are serviced.

8. Clean all parts in solvent, dry, and check for wear or damage.
9. Pack both wheel bearings (and the

spindle bearing) using wheel bearing grease. Place a healthy glob of grease in the palm of one hand and force the edge of the bearing into it so that grease fills the bearing. Do this until the whole bearing is packed.

Exploded view of a constant velocity joint

Correct C-lock positioning on locking differentials

Details of the locking hubs used on all K-10 and 1500 models and 1977 and later K-20 and 2500 models

Grease packing tools are available to make this job a lot less messy.

10. To reassemble the spindle: drive the repacked bearing into the spindle and install the grease seal onto the slinger with the lip toward the spindle. It would be best to replace the axle shaft slinger when the spindle seal is replaced. If you are using the improved seals, fill the seal end of the spindle with grease. If not, apply grease only to the lip of the seal. Install the thrust washer over the axle shaft. The chamfered side of the thrust washer should be toward the slinger. Replace the spindle and torque the nuts to 25 ft. lbs., 1977–78, and 33 ft. lbs., 1979–and later.

11. To reassemble the wheel bearings: drive the outer bearing cup into the hub, replace the inner bearing cup, and insert the repacked bearing.

12. Install the disc or drum and outer wheel bearing to the spindle.

13. Adjust the bearings by rotating the hub and torquing the inner adjusting nut to 50 ft. lbs. then loosening it and retorquing to 35 ft. lb. Next, back the nut off ⅜ turn or less. Turn the nut to the nearest hole in the lockwasher. Install the outer locknut and torque to a minimum of 50 ft. lbs. through 1978, or 80 ft. lbs., 1979–and later. There should be 0.001–0.010 in. bearing end-play. This can be measured with a dial indicator.

14. Replace the brake components.

15. Lubricate the locking hub components with high temperature grease. Lubrication must be applied to prevent component failure. For K-10 or K-1500 models, and K-20 and K-2500 models, 1977–and later, install the spring retainer plate with the flange side facing the bearing over the spindle nuts and seat it against the bearing outer cup. Install the pressure spring with the large end against the spring retaining plate. The spring is an interference fit; when seated, its end extends past the spindle nuts by approximately ⅞ in. Place the inner clutch ring and bushing assembly into the axle shaft sleeve and clutch ring assembly and install that as an assembly onto the axle shaft. Press in on this assembly and install the axle shaft ring. If there are two axle shaft snap-ring grooves (1977–79), use the inner one.

NOTE: You can install a ⁷⁄₁₆ in. bolt in the axle shaft end and pull outward on it to aid in seating the snap-ring.

Install the actuating cam body in the cams facing outward, the outer clutch retaining ring, and the internal snap-ring. Install a new O-ring on the retaining plate, and then install the actuating knob in the Lock position. Install the retaining plate. The grooves in the knob must fit into the actuator cam body. Install the seals and six cover bolts and torque them to 30 ft. lbs. Turn the knob to the Free position and check for proper operation.

NOTE: Remove the head from a 5 in.

long ¾ in. bolt and use this to align the hub assembly.

Install the headless bolt into one of the hub housing bolt holes. Install a new exterior sleeve extension housing gasket, the housing, and a new hub retainer cap assembly gasket, and the cap assembly. Install the six Allen head bolts and their washers, and torque them to 30 ft. lbs. Turn the knob to Lock and check engagement.

16. Without locking hubs, replace the snap-ring and hub cap. If there are two axle shaft snap-ring grooves (1977–79), use the inner one.

Wheel Bearings

REMOVAL, PACKING, INSTALLATION

NOTE: This procedure requires snap ring pliers and a special hub nut wrench. It is not very easy without them. Note: This procedure does not apply to S-Series Trucks.

1. Remove the wheel and tire.

2. For ½ and ¾ ton trucks with lock front hubs: lock the hubs. Remove the outer retaining plate Allen head bolts and take off the plate, O-ring, and knob. Take out the large snap ring inside the hub and remove the outer clutch retaining ring and actuating cam body. This is a lot easier with snap ring pliers. Relieve pressure on the axle shaft snap ring and remove it. Take out the axle shaft sleeve and clutch ring assembly and the innerclutch ring and bushing assembly and the inner clutch ring and bushing assembly. Remove the spring and retainer plate.

3. If you don't have locking front hubs, remove the hub cap and snap ring. Next, remove the drive gear and pressure spring. To prevent the spring from popping out, place a hand over the drive gear and use a screwdriver to pry the gear out. Remove the spring.

4. Remove the wheel bearing outer lock nut, lock ring, and wheel bearing inner adjusting nut. A special wrench is required.

5. Remove the brake disc assembly and outer wheel bearing. Remove the spring retainer plate if you don't have locking hubs.

6. Remove the oil seal and inner bearing cone from the hub using a brass drift and hammer. Discard the oil seal. Use the drift to remove the inner and outer bearing cups.

7. Check the condition of the spindle bearing. Unbolt the spindle and tap it with a soft hammer to break it loose. Remove the spindle and check the condition of the thrust washer, replacing it if worn. Now you can remove the oil seal and spindle roller bearing.

NOTE: The spindle bearings must be greased each time the wheel bearings are serviced.

8. Clean all parts in solvent, dry, and check for wear or damage.

9. Pack both wheel bearings (and the spindle bearing) using wheel bearing grease. Place a healthy glob of grease in the palm of one hand and force the edge of the bearing into it so that grease fills the bearing. Do this until the whole bearing is packed Grease packing tools are available to make this job easier.

10. To reassemble the spindle: drive the repacked bearing into the spindle and install the grease seal onto the slinger with the lip toward the spindle. It would be best to replace the axle shaft slinger when the spindle seal is replaced.

If you are using the improved seals, fill the seal end of the spindle with grease. If not, apply grease only to the lip of the seal. Install the thrust washer over the axle shaft. On late 1982 models, the chamfered side of the thrust washer should be toward the slinger. Replace the spindle and torque the nuts to 25 ft. lbs., 1977–78, 33 ft. lbs., 1979–80, 65 ft. lbs. 1981 and later.

11. To reassemble the sheel bearings: drive the outer bearing cup into the hub, replace the inner bearing cup, and insert the repacked bearing.

12. Install the disc or drum and outer wheel bearing to the spindle.

13. Adjust the bearings by rotating the hub and torquing the inner adjusting nut to 50 ft. lbs., then loosening it and retorquing to 35 ft. lbs. Next, back the nut off ⅜ turn or less. Turn the nut to the nearest hole in the lock-washer. Install the outer locknut and torque to minimum of 50 ft. lbs. through 1978, or 80 ft. lbs., 1979–80, 160–205 ft. lbs. 1981 and later ½ and ¾ ton, and 65 ft. lbs. on 1 ton vehicles. There should be 0.001–0.010 in. bearing end play. This can be measured with a dial indicator.

14. Replace the brake components.

15. Lubricate the locking hub components with high temperature grease. Lubrication must be applied to prevent component failure. For ½ ton 1977 and later ¾ and 1 ton models, install the spring retainer plate with the flange side facing the bearing over the spindle nuts and seat it against the bearing outer cup. Install the pressure spring with the large end against the spring retaining plate. The spring is an interference fit; when seated, its end extends past the spindle nuts by approximately ⅞ in. Place the inner clutch ring and bushing assembly into the axle shaft sleeve and clutch ring assembly and install that as an assembly onto the axle shaft. Press in on this assembly and install the axle shaft ring. If there are two axle shaft snap ring grooves (1977–79), use the inner one.

S-Series Trucks

REMOVAL & INSTALLATION

NOTE: Your can install a ⁷⁄₁₆ in. bolt

in the axle shaft end and pull outward on it to aid in seating the snap ring.

Install the actuating cam body in the cams facing outward, the outer clutch retaining ring, and the internal snap ring. Install a new O-ring on the retaining plate, and then install the actuating knob in the Lock position. Install the retaining plate. The grooves in the knob must fit into the actuator cam body. Install the seals and six cover bolts and torque them to 30 ft. lbs. Turn the knob to the Free position and check for proper operation.

NOTE: Remove the head from a 5 in. long ⅜ in. bolt and use this to align the hub assembly.

Install the headless bolt into one of the hub housing bolt holes. Install a new exterior sleeve extension housing gasket, the housing, and a new hub retainer cap assembly gasket, and the cap assembly. Install the six Allen head bolts and their washers, and torque them to 30 ft. lbs. Turn the knob to Lock and check engagement.

16. Without locking hubs, replace the snap ring and hub cap. If there are two axle shaft snap ring grooves (1977–79), use the inner one.

S-Series Trucks

TUBE/SHAFT ASSEMBLY REMOVAL

1. Disconnect negative battery cable.
2. Disconnect shift cable from vacuum actuator by disengaging locking spring. Then push actuator diaphragm in to release cable.

3. Unlock steering wheel at steering column so linkage is free to move.
4. Raise vehicle. If twin post hoist is used, place jack stands under frame and lower front post hoist.
5. Remove front wheels.
6. Remove engine drive belt shield.
7. Remove front axle skid plate (if equipped).
8. Place support under right hand lower control arm and disconnect right hand upper, ball joint, then remove support so control arm will hang free.
9. Disconnect right hand drive axle shaft from tube assembly by removing six bolts.
Keep axle from turning by inserting a drift through opening in top of brake caliper into corresponding vane of brake rotor.
10. Disconnect four wheel drive indicator light electrical connection from switch.
11. Remove three bolts securing cable and switch housing to carrier and pull housing away to gain access to cable locking spring. Do not unscrew cable coupling nut unless cable is being replaced.
12. Disconnect cable from shift fork shaft by lifting spring over slot in shift fork.
13. Remove two bolts securing tube bracket to frame.
14. Remove remaining two upper bolts securing tube assembly to carrier.
15. Remove tube assembly by working around drive axle. Be careful not to allow sleeve, thrust washers, connector, and output shaft to fall out of carrier or be damaged when removing tube.

INSTALLATION

1. Install sleeve, thrust washers, connector and output shaft in carrier. Apply

sealer #1052357, Locktite 514 or equivalent on tube to carrier surface.

Be sure to install thrust washer. Apply grease to washer to hold it in place during assembly.

2. Install tube and shaft assembly to carrier and install bolt at one o'clock po-

Drive axle bolts

Thrust washer

Vacuum actuator

Tube–to–frame attachment

NUT
60-80 N·m
(45-60 FT. LBS.)

Cable–to–vacuum actuator attachment

Right side output shaft and tube

CV joint disassembly sequence

sition but do not torque. Pull assembly down and install cable and switch housing, and remaining four bolts. Torque all bolts to 45–60 ft. lb.

3. Install two bolts securing tube to frame and torque.

4. Check operation of four wheel drive mechanism using Tool J-33799. Insert tool into shift fork and check for rotation of axle shaft.

5. Remove tool and install shift cable switch housing by pushing cable through into fork shaft hole. Cable will automatically snap in place.

6. Connect four wheel drive indicator light electrical connection to switch.

7. Install support under right hand lower control arm to raise arm and connect upper ball joint.

8. Install right-hand drive axle to axle tube by installing one bolt first, then, rotate axle to install remaining five bolts. Hold axle from turning by inserting a drift through opening in top of brake caliper into corresponding vane of brake rotor. Tighten bolts to 53–63 ft lb.

9. Install front axle skid plate, if equipped.

10. Install engine drive belt shield.

11. Install front wheels.

12. Lower vehicle.

13. Connect shift cable to vacuum actuator by pushing cable end into vacuum actuator shaft hole. Cable will snap in place automatically.

14. Connect negative battery cable.

S-Series Trucks

SHIFT CABLE REPLACEMENT

1. Disengage shift cable from vacuum actuator by disengaging locking spring, then, push actuator diaphragm in to release cable. Squeeze the two locking fingers of the cable with pliers, then pull cable out of bracket hole.

2. Raise vehicle and remove three bolts securing cable and switch housing to carrier and pull housing away to gain access to cable locking spring. Disconnect cable from shaft fork shaft by lifting spring over slot in shift fork.

3. Unscrew cable from housing.

4. Remove cable from vehicle.

5. Install cable observing proper routing.

6. Install cable and switch housing to carrier using three attaching bolts. Torque mounting bolts to 30–40 ft. lbs.

7. Guide cable through switch housing into fork shaft hole and push cable in. Cable will automatically snap in place. Start turning coupling nut by hand, to avoid cross threading, then torque nut to 71–106 in. lbs. Do not overtorque nut as this will cause thread damage to plastic housing.

8. Lower vehicle.

9. Connect shift cable to vacuum actuator by pressing cable into bracket hole.

Cable and housing will snap in place automatically.

10. Check cable operation.

Differential Carrier Right Half Output Shaft and Tube

DISASSEMBLY

1. Remove right-hand output shaft from tube by striking inside of flange with a soft face hammer while holding tube.

2. Remove output shaft tube seal by prying out of tube.

3. Remove output shaft tube bearing using J-29369-2.

4. Remove differential shift cable housing seal by driving out with a punch or similar tool.

ASSEMBLY

1. Install output shaft tube bearing using tool J-33844. Tool must be flush with tube when bearing is correctly installed.

2. Install output shaft tube seal using tool J-33893. Flange of seal must be flush with tube outer surface when seal is installed.

3. Install output shaft into tube and seat by striking flange with a soft face hammer.

4. Install differential shift cable housing seal using J-33799.

Axle Shaft U-Joint

OVERHAUL

1. Remove the axle shaft.

2. Squeeze the ends of the trunnion bearings in a vise to relieve the load on the snap-rings. Remove the snap-rings.

3. Support the yoke in a vise and drive on one end of the trunnion bearing with a brass drift enough to drive the opposite bearing from the yoke.

4. Support the other side of the yoke and drive the other bearing out.

5. Remove the trunnion.

6. Clean and check all parts. You can buy U-joint repair kits to replace all the wearing parts.

7. Lubricate the bearings with wheel bearing grease.

8. Replace the trunnion and press the bearings into the yoke and over the trunnion hubs far enough to install the lock rings.

9. Hold the trunnion in one hand and tap the yoke lightly to seat the bearings against the lock rings.

10. The axle slingers can be pressed off the shafts.

NOTE: Always replace the slingers if the spindle seals are replaced.

You can use the spindle to start the slinger on the shaft.

11. Replace the shaft.

Ball Joint

REPLACEMENT

The steering knuckle pivot ball joints may need replacement when there is excessive steering play, hard steering, irregular tire wear (especially on the inner edge), or persistent tie rod loosening.

This procedure requires a shop press. Your best bet would be to remove the steering knuckle and take it to the machine shop with the new parts.

1. Remove the hub assembly as previously outlined.
2. Remove the spindle attaching bolts.
3. Tap on the end of the spindle lightly with a wooden mallet (not a metal hammer) to break it loose from the steering knuckle.
4. Remove the spindle and the bronze washer. Replace the washer if it was distorted during removal or if it appears worn.
5. Remove the cotter pin from the tie rod nut.
6. Loosen the tie rod nut and tap on the nut with a wooden mallet in order to break the studs loose from the knuckle arm.
7. Remove the nuts and disconnect the tie rod.
8. Remove the steering arm attaching nuts. Use new, self-locking nuts on installation.
9. Remove the cotter pin from the upper ball joint socket nut.
10. Remove the retaining nuts from the upper and lower ball joint sockets.
11. Remove the knuckle by forcing a wedge between the lower ball stud and the yoke, then between the upper ball stud and the yoke.

NOTE: If you have to loosen the upper ball stud adjusting sleeve to remove the knuckle, don't loosen it more than two turns. The soft threads on the yoke are easily damaged.

12. Remove the lower ball joint snap ring.
13. Remove the lower ball joint as illustrated using special tool no. J-9519-10 (or a similar C-clamp), J-23454-1 (a solid metal punch), and J-6382-3 (or a piece of 2½ in. outer diameter steel pipe with a ³⁄₁₆ in. wall thickness cut to a length of 2½ ins.). The lower ball joint must be removed before the upper ball joint can be serviced.
14. Press the new lower ball joint into the knuckle and install the snap-ring. The lower joint doesn't have a cotter pin hole.
15. Press the upper ball joint into the knuckle.
16. Position the knuckle to the yoke. Install new stud nuts finger tight.
17. Push up on the knuckle and tighten the lower nut to 70 ft. lbs.
18. Using a spanner wrench, install and torque the upper ball stud adjusting sleeve to 50 ft. lbs. Torque the upper stud nut to 100 ft. lbs. and install the cotter pin. Don't loosen the nut, but make it tighter to line up the cotter pin hole.

19. Replace the steering arm, using new nuts and torquing to 90 ft. lbs.
20. Attach the tie rod to the steering arm. Tighten the nuts to 45 ft. lbs.
21. Check the knuckle turning torque with a spring scale hooked to the tie rod hole in the steering arm. With the knuckle straight ahead, measure the right angle pull to keep the knuckle turning after initial breakaway, in both directions. The pull should be 25 lbs. or less for axles assembled after Feb. 10, 1976.
22. Replace the axle shaft and other components. Tighten the steering linkage nuts to 45 ft. lbs.

Pinion Seal

REPLACEMENT

1. Mark the drive shaft and pinion flange so they can be reassembled in the same position.
2. Disconnect drive shaft from rear axle pinion flange and support shaft up in body tunnel by wiring drive shaft to the exhaust pipe. If joint bearings are not retained by a retainer strap, use a piece of tape to hold bearings on their journals.
3. Mark the position of the pinion flange, pinion shaft and nut so the proper pinion bearing pre-load can be maintained.
4. Remove pinion flange nut and washer.
5. With suitable container in place to hold any fluid that may drain from rear axle, remove pinion flange.
6. Remove oil seal by driving it out of carrier with a blunt chisel. Do not damage carrier.
7. Examine seal surface of pinion flange for tool marks, nicks, or damage, such as a groove worn by the seal. If damaged, replace flange as outlined under PINION FLANGE REPLACEMENT.
8. Examine carrier bore and remove any burrs that might cause leaks around the O.D. of the seal.
9. Installation is the reverse of removal. Apply Special Seal Lubricant No. 1050169 or equivalent to the O.D. of the pinion flange and sealing lip of new seal.

REAR AXLE

Some models are equipped with a locking differential rear axle. If you're not sure which one is in your truck, block the front wheels and jack up the rear of the truck. With the transmission in Neutral, spin one of the rear wheels in a forward motion with your hands. If the other wheel travels in the same direction, it is a locking differential.

Axle Shaft, Bearing, and Seal

REMOVAL & INSTALLATION

All Axles Except Floating and Locking Differentials

This procedure applies to all standard rear axles.

1. Support the axle on jackstands.
2. Remove the wheels and brake drums.
3. Clean off the differential cover area, loosen the cover to drain the lubricant, and remove the cover.
4. Turn the differential until you can reach the differential pinion shaft lockscrew. Remove the lockscrew and the pinion shaft.
5. Push in on the axle end. Remove the C-lock from the inner (button) end of the shaft.
6. Remove the shaft, being careful of the oil seal.
7. You can pry the oil seal out of the housing by placing the inner end of the axle shaft behind the steel case of the seal, then prying it out carefully.
8. A puller or a slide hammer is required to remove the bearing from the housing.
9. Pack the new or reused bearing with wheel bearing grease and lubricate the cavity between the seal lips with the same grease.
10. The bearing has to be driven into the housing. Don't use a drift, you might cock the bearing in its bore. Use a piece of pipe or a large socket instead. Drive only on the outer bearing race. In a similar manner, drive the seal in flush with the end of the tube.
11. Slide the shaft into place, turning it slowly until the splines are engaged with the differential. Be careful of the oil seal.
12. Install the C-lock on the inner axle end. Pull the shaft out so that the C-lock seats in the counterbore of the differential side gear.
13. Position the differential pinion shaft through the case and the pinion gears, aligning the lockscrew hole. Install the lockscrew.
14. Install the cover with a new gasket and tighten the bolts evenly in a criss-cross pattern.
15. Fill the axle with lubricant.
16. Replace the brake drums and wheels.

Locking Differential Axles

This axle uses a thrust block on the differentia pinion shaft.

1. Follow Steps 1-3 of the preceding procedure.
2. Rotate the differential case so that you can remove the lockscrew and support thepinion shaft so it can't fall into the housing. Remove the differential pinion shaft lockscrew.
3. Carefully pull thepinion shaft part-

way out and rotate the differential case until the shaft touches the housing at the top.

4. Use a screwdriver to position the C-lock with its open end directly inward. You can't push in the axle shaft till you do this. Do not force the axle shaft in.

5. Push the axle shaft in and remove the C-lock. Remove the axle shaft and repeat steps 4 and 5 for the other shaft.

6. Follow Steps 7-11 of the preceding procedure.

7. Keep the pinion shaft partway out of the differential case while installing the C-lock on the axle shaft. Put the C-lock on the axle shaft and carefully pull out on the axle shaft until the C-lock is clear of the thrust block.

8. Follow Steps 13-16 of the previous procedure.

Floating Differentials

Some 20,2500 and all 30 and 3500 models use axles of full floating design. The procedures are the same for locking and non-locking axles. The best way to remove the bearings from the wheel hub is with an arbor press. Use of a press reduces the chances of damaging the bearing races, cocking the bearing in its bore, or scoring the hub walls. A local maching shop is probably equipped with the tools to remove and install bearings and seals. However, if one is not available, the hammer and drift method outlined can be used.

1. Support the axle on jackstands.
2. Remove the wheels.
3. Remove the bolts and lock washers that attach the axle shaft flange to the hub.

4. Rap on the flange with a soft faced hammer to loosen the shaft. Grip the rib on the end of the flange with a pair of locking pliers and twist to start shaft remova. Remove the shaft from the axle tube.

5. The hub and drum assembly must be removed to remove the bearings and oil seals. You will need a large socket to remove and later adjust the bearing adjustment nut. There are also tools available which resemble the four wheel drive front wheel bearing adjusting tool.

6. Disengage the tang of the locknut retainer from the slot or flat of the locknut, then remove the locknut from the housing tube, using the earlier mentioned tool.

7. Disengage the tang of the retainer from the slot or flat of the adjusting nut and remove the retainer from the housing tube.

8. Remove the adjusting nut from the housing tube with the tool mentioned earlier.

9. Remove the thrust waser from the housing tube.

10. Pull the hub and drum straight off the axle housing.

11. Remove the oil seal and discard.

12. Use a hammer and a long drift to knock the inner bearing cup, and oil seal from the hub assembly.

13. Remove the outer bearing snap-ring with a pair of pliers. It may be necessary to tap the bearing outer race away from the retaining ring slightly by tapping on the ring to remove the ring.

14. Drive the outer bearing from the hub with a hammer and drift.

15. To reinstall the bearings, place the outer bearing into the hub. The larger outside diameter of the bearing should face the outer end of the hub. Drive the bearing into the hub using a washer that will cover both the inner and outer races of the bearing. Place a socket on the top of this washer, then drive the bearing into place with a series of light taps. If available, an arbor press should be used for this job.

16. Drive the bearing past the snap-ring groove, and install the snap-ring. Then, turning the hub assembly over, drive the bearing back against the snap-ring. Again, protect the bearing by placing a washer on top of it. You can use the thrust washer that fits between the bearing and the adjusting nut for this job.

17. Place the inner bearing into the hub. The thick edge should be toward the shoulder in the hub. Press the bearing into the hub until it seats against the shoulder, using a washer and socket as outlined earlier. Make certain that the bearing is not cocked and that it is fully seated on the shoulder.

18. Pack the cavity between the oil seal lips wit front wheel bearing grease, and position it in the hub bore. Carefully press it into place on top of the inner bearing.

19. Pack the wheel bearings with the grease, and lightly coat the inside diameter of the hub bearing contact surface and the outside diameter of the axle housing tube.

20. Make sure that the inner bearing, oil seal, axle housing oil deflector, and outer bearing are properly positioned. Install the hub and drum assembly on the axle housing, exercising case so as not to damage the oil seal or dislocate other internal components.

21. Install the thrust washer so that the tang on the inside diameter of the washer is in the keyway on the axle housing.

22 Install the adjusting nut. Tighten to 50 ft. lbs., at the same time rotating the hub to make sure that all the bearing surfaces are in contact. Back off the nut and retighten to 35 ft. lbs., then back off ¼ of a turn.

23. Install the tanged retainer against the inner adjusting nut. Align the adjusting nut so that the short tang of the retainer will engage the nearest slot on the adjusting nut.

24. Install the outer locknut and tighten to 65 ft. lbs. Bend the long tang of the retainer into the slot of the outer nut. This method of adjustment should provide .001 to .010 in. of end play.

25. Place a new gasket over the axle shaft and position the axle shaft in the housing so that the shaft splines enter the differential side gear. Position the gasket so that the holes are in alignment, and install the flange-to-hub attaching bolts. Torque to 155 ft. lbs. 1977 and later

NOTE: To prevent lubricant from leaking through the flange holes, apply a non-hardening sealer to the bolt threads. Use the sealer sparingly.

27. Replace the wheels.

FRONT SUSPENSION

Two wheel drive models use coil spring independent front suspension. A stabilizer (sway) bar is optional to minimize body lean and sway in curves. Four wheel drive models have a non-independent leaf spring front suspension. A stabilizer bar is standard. A steering linkage damper is standard on late models. Heavy duty shock absorbers, springs, and stabilizer bars have been optional for most models. 5-Series Trucks (2WD) front suspension is similar to standard size pickups. Four wheel drive vehicle use a torsion bar-type front suspension.

Springs

REMOVAL & INSTALLATION

NOTE: Springs, particularly coil springs, are under considerable tension. Be very careful when removing and installing them; they can exert enough force to cause very serious injuries.

Two Wheel Drive

1. Raise the vehicle and support it under the frame so that the control arms will hang free.

2. Remove the lower shock absorber mounting bolt. Detach the stabilizer bar from the lower control arm.

3. Place a floor jack under the lower control arm crosshaft.

NOTE: As a safety precaution, install a chain through the spring and the lower control arm.

4. Raise the jack. This will remove the tension on the lower control arm so that the two U-bolts which secure the cross-shaft can be removed.

5. Lower the control arm *slowly* by releasing the floor jack to the point where the spring can be removed.

6. Remove the spring.

7. Place the spring on the control arm and then, using a jack, slowly raise the control arm. Use the safety chain as described in Step 3.

8. Place the control arm cross-shaft onto the crossmember and then install the U-bolts and the attaching nuts. Make certain that the indexing hole in the cross-shaft is lined up with the crossmember stud.

9. Torque the U-bolt nuts to 85 ft. lbs. for 1977 and later models. Remove the safety chain.

10. Install the lower part of the shock absorber and the stabilizer bar.

11. Lower the vehicle.

Four Wheel Drive

1. Raise and support the truck under the front axle and frame so that the tension on the springs is relieved.

2. Remove the shackle upper retaining bolt and the front spring eye bolt.

3. Remove the spring-to-axle U-bolt nuts. Pull off the spring, the lowerplate, and the spring pads.

4. Remove the shackle-to-spring bolt, bushings, and shackle.

To replace the bushing, place the spring onto a press or vise and press out the bushing. Press in the new bushing. The new bushing should protrude evenly on both sides of the spring.

5. Install the spring shackle bushings into the spring and then attach the shackle. Do not tighten the bolt.

6. Place the upper spring cushion onto the spring.

7. Place the front of the spring into the frame and install the bolt but do not tighten it.

8. Position the shackle bushing into the frame and attach the rear shackle but do not tighten it.

9. Install the lower spring pad and the spring retainer plate. Tighten the U-bolts to 150 ft. lbs.

10. Torque the rear spring shackle bolts and the rear eye bolts to 50 ft. lbs. and the front eye bolts to 90 ft. lbs.

11. Lower the vehicle.

Torsion Bar (S-Series 4WD)

REMOVAL & INSTALLATION

1. Raise vehicle on a hoist.
2. Remove torsion bar adjusting screw.
3. Remove support retainer attaching nuts and bolts.
4. Slide torsion bar forward in lower control arm until torsion bar clears support. Pull down on bar and remove from control arm.
5. Installation is the reverse of removal.

NOTE: Count the number of turns when removing the torsion bar for easy reinstallation.

NOTE: Apply lubricant to top of adjusting arm and adjusting bolt for easy reinstallation. Also apply lubricant to hex ends of torsion bar.

Shock Absorbers

The usual procedure for testing shock absorbers is to stand on the bumper at the end

nearest the shock being tested and start the vehicle bouncing up and down. Step off; the vehicle should come to rest within one bounce cycle. Another good test is to drive the vehicle over a bumpy road. Bouncing over bumps is normal, but the shock absorbers should stop the bouncing, after the bump is passed, within one or two cycles.

REMOVAL & INSTALLATION

The usual procedure is to replace shock absorbers in axle pairs, to provide equal damping. Heavy duty replacements are available for firmer control.

1. Raise and support the front axle as necessary.

2. Remove the bolt and nut from the lower shock end.

3. On two wheel drive original equipment shocks, remove the upper stud nut from inside the frame. On four wheel drive shocks, remove the upper bolt and nut.

4. Purge the new shock of air by extending it in its normal position and compressing it while inverted. Do this several times. It is normal for there to be more resistance to extension than to compression.

5. Install the shock absorber. Tighten the two wheel drive upper stud nut (inside the frame) to 8 ft. lbs. and the four wheel drive upper bolt to 65 ft. lbs. Tighten the two wheel drive lower bolt to 60 ft. lbs. Tighten the four wheel drive lower bolt to 65 ft. lbs.

Steering Knuckle S-Series

REMOVAL

1. Raise front of vehicle and support with floor stands under front lift points. Remove wheel.

Spring tension is needed to assist in breaking ball joint studs loose from steering knuckle. Do not place stands under lower control arm.

2. Remove caliper.
3. Remove hub and rotor assembly.
4. Remove the three bolts attaching shield to knuckle.
5. Remove tie-rod end from knuckle using Tool J-6627 or equivalent.
6. Carefully remove knuckle seal if knuckle is to be replaced.
7. Remove ball studs from steering knuckle using tool J-23742 or equivalent.

──── **CAUTION** ────

Floor jack must remain under control arm spring seat during removal and installation to retain spring and control arm in position.

8. Position a floor jack under lower control arm near spring seat and raise jack until it just supports lower control arm.

9. Raise upper control arm to disengage ball joint stud from knuckle.

10. Raise knuckle from lower ball joint stud and remove knuckle.

INSPECTION

Inspect the tapered hole in the steering knuckle. Remove any dirt. If out-of-roundness, deformation, or damage is noted, the knuckle MUST be replaced.

Two wheel drive coil spring and stabilizer

Four wheel drive front leaf spring

Two wheel drive front shock absorber

Four wheel drive front shock absorber

DO NOT BACK OFF NUT TO INSTALL NEW COTTER PIN.

68 N·m (50 ft. lbs.)

KNUCKLE

KNUCKLE SEAL

235 N·m (174 FT. LBS.)

HUB AND
BEARING ASSEMBLY

105 N·m (78 FT. LBS.)   48 N·m (35 ft. lbs.)   113 N·m (83 ft. lbs.)

Removal and installation of hub, bearing assembly, knuckle and seal

INSTALLATION

1. Insert upper and lower ball joint studs into knuckle and install nuts.

2. Install shield to knuckle seal and splash shield. Torque attaching bolts to 14 N·m (10 ft. lbs.).

3. Install tie rod end into knuckle. Install tool J-29193 or equivalent and torque to 20 N·m (15 ft. lbs.). Remove tool and install nut to 54 N·m (40 ft. lbs.).

4. Replace wheel bearings. Install hub and disc assembly.

5. Adjust wheel bearings. Install caliper.

6. Install remaining parts in reverse order of removal.

Steering Knuckle

2 WHEEL DRIVE

REMOVAL

1. Raise vehicle on hoist and support lower control arms as noted above.

2. Remove wheel and tire assembly.

3. Remove caliper.

4. Remove disc splash shield bolts securing the shield to the steering knuckle. Remove Shield.

6. Remove upper and lower ball stud cotter pins and lossen ball stud nuts. Free steering knuckle from ball studs by installing Special Tool J-23742 or equivalent. Remove ball stud nuts and withdraw steering knuckle.

INSTALLATION

1. Place steering knuckle in position and insert upper and lower ball studs into knuckle bosses.

Steering knuckle hole, ball stud and nut should be free of dirt and grease before tightening nut.

2. Install ball stud nuts and tighten nut to 80-100 ft. lbs.

If necessary, tighten one more notch to insert cotter pins. Do not loosen nut to insert cotter pin.

3. Reverse remaining removal procedure, and tighten splash shield mounting bolt. Tighten two caliper assembly mounting bolts to 48 N·m (35 ft. lbs.) torque.

4. Adjust wheel bearings.

5. Tighten wheel nuts to 100 N·m (75 ft. lbs.).

Steering Knuckle

4WD WITH BALL JOINTS

REMOVAL

1. Remove the automatic locking hub, hub-and-disc assembly, and spindle components.

2. If the steering arm is to be removed, disconnect the tie rod.

   a. Remove cotter pin.

   b. Loosen tie rod nuts and tap on nut with a soft hammer to break the studs loose from the knuckle arm.

   c. Remove nuts and disconnect the tie rod. If it is necessary to remove the steering arm, discard the self-locking nuts and replace with new nuts at assembly.

3. Remove the cotter pin from the upper ball socket nut.

4. Remove the retaining nuts from the upper and lower ball sockets.

5. Remove the knuckle assembly from the yoke by inserting a suitable wedge-shaped tool between the lower ball stud and the yoke and tapping on the tool to release the knuckle assembly. Repeat as required at the upper ball stud location.

6. Installation is the reverse of removal.

NOTE: Do not remove the yoke upper ball stud adjusting sleeve unless new ball studs are being installed. If it is necessary to loosen the sleeve to remove the knuckle, do not loosen it more than two threads. The non-hardened threads in the yoke can be easily damaged by the hardened threads in the adjusting sleeve if caution is not used.

INSTALLATION

1. Position the knuckle and sockets to the yoke. Install new nuts finger tight to the upper (the nut with the cotter pin slot) and lower ball socket studs.

2. Push up on the knuckle (to keep the ball socket from turning in the knuckle) while tightening the lower socket retaining nut. PARTIALLY torque lower nut to 40 N·m (30 ft. lbs.).

3. Torque the yoke upper ball stud adjusting sleeve to 70 N·m (50 ft. lbs.).

4. Torque the upper ball socket nut to 100 ft. lbs. After torquing the nut, do not loosen to install cotter pin, apply additional torque, if necessary, to line up hole in stud with slot in nut.

5. Apply FINAL torque to lower nut, 95 N·m (70 ft. lbs.).

6. If the tie rod and steering arm were removed:

   a. Assemble the steering arm using the three stud adapters and three new self-locking nuts. Torque the nuts to 120 N·m (90 ft. lbs.).

   b. Assemble the tie rod to the knuckle arm. Torque the tie rod nuts to 60 N·m (45 ft. lbs.) and install cotter pin.

Steering Knuckle

WITH KING PINS

REMOVAL

1. Remove the hub and spindle as outlined earlier. If necessary, tap lightly with a rawhide hammer to free it from the knuckle. Check bronze spacer located between axle shaft joint assembly and bearing. If wear is evident, replace with a new one.

2. Remove four nuts from upper king pin cap. Remove nuts alternately as compression spring will force cap up.

3. Remove cap, compression spring, and gasket. Discard gasket, replace with new one at time of assembly.

4. From the underside of the knuckle, remove four cap screws from the lower king pin bearing cap. Remove the bearing cap-and-lower king pin.

5. Remove upper king pin tapered bushing and knuckle from yoke. Remove king-pin felt seal. Remove knuckle.

6. Remove upper king-pin from yoke with large breaker bar and J-26871 or equivalent.

Torque specification is 677-813 N·m (500-600 ft. lbs.).

7. Remove lower king pin bearing cup, cone, grease retainer, and seal all at the same time. Discard seal and replace with new one at time of assembly. If grease retainer is damaged, replace with new one at time of assembly.

INSTALLATION

1. Assemble new grease retainer and lower king pin bearing cup, using J-7817 or equivalent.

2. Fill the area in grease retainer with specified grease, then grease the bearing cone and install. Install new lower king pin bearing oil seal, using J-22281 or equivalent.

Do not distort oil seal. It will protrude slightly from the surface of yoke flange when fully installed.

3. Install upper king-pin, using J-28871 or equivalent. Torque to 677.50-813.00 N·m (500-600 ft. lbs.).

4. Assemble felt seal to king pin, assemble knuckle, assemble tapered bushing over king pin.

5. Assemble lower bearing cap-and-king pin with four cap screws. Tighten cap screws alternately and evenly. Torque cap screws to 95-120 N·m (70–90 ft. lbs.).

6. Assemble compression spring on upper king pin bushing. Assemble bearing cap, with new gasket, over four studs. Tighten nuts alternately and evenly. Torque nuts to 95-120 N·m (70–90 lb. ft.).

NOTE: Do not distort the rubber shock grommets when tightening shock bolts or nuts.

Ball Joints

Service procedures for the four wheel drive front drive axle are found earlier.

INSPECTION

Excessive ball joint wear will usually show up as wear on the inside of the front tires. Don't jump to conclusions; front end misalignment can give the same symptom.

Upper Ball Joint

1. Raise and support the truck; let the control arms hang freely.

2. The upper ball joint is spring-loaded in its socket. If it has any perceptible lateral shake or can be twisted in its socket, it should be replaced.

Lower Ball Joint

The lower ball joint gets the most wear due to the distribution of suspension load.

1. Support the weight of the control arm at the bottom of the tire.

2. Measure the distance between the tip of the ball joint stud and the tip of the grease fitting below the ball joint.

3. Move the support to the control arm and allow the wheel and tire to hang free. Measure the distance again. If the vibration between the two measurements exceed 3/32 in the ball joint should be replaced.

NOTE: This is the manufacturer's recommended wear limit. Your state inspection regulations may disagree.

REMOVAL & INSTALLATION

NOTE: Observe the Caution under Front Spring Removal and Installation when working with ball joints.

Lower Ball Joint

1. Raise and support the truck. Support the lower control arm with a floor jack.

2. Remove the tire and wheel.

3. Remove the lower stud cotter pin and loosen, but do not remove, the stud nut.

4. Loosen the ball joint stud with a ball joint stud removal tool. It may be necessary to remove the brake caliper and wire it to the frame to gain enough clearance. Do not let the caliper hang by the hose.

5. When the stud is loose, remove the tool and ball stud nut.

6. Pull the brake disc and knuckle assembly up and off the ball stud and support the upper arm with a block of wood.

7. Remove the ball joint from the control arm with a ball joint removal tool. It must be pressed out.

To install:

8. Start the new ball joint into the control arm. Position the bleed vent in the rubber boot facing inward.

9. Seat the ball joint in the control arm. It must be pressed in.

10. Lower the upper arm and match the steering knuckle to the lower ball stud.

11. Install the brake caliper, if removed.

12. Install the ball stud nut and torque it to 90 ft. lbs. plus the additional torque necessary to align the cotter pin hole. Do not exceed 130 ft. lbs. or back the nut off to align the holes with the pin.

13. Install a new lube fitting and lubricate the new joint.

14. Install the tire and wheel.

15. Lower the truck.

Upper Ball Joint

1. Raise and support the truck.

2. Support the lower control arm with a floor jack.

3. Remove the cotter pin from the upper ball stud and loosen, but do not remove the stud nut.

4. Using a ball joint stud removal tool, loosen the ball stud in the steering knuckle. When the stud is loose, remove the tool and the stud nut. It will be necessary to remove the brake caliper and wire it to the frame to gain clearance. Do not allow the caliper to hang by the hose.

5. Drill out the rivets. Remove the ball joint assembly.

To install:

6. Install the service ball joint, using the nuts supplied. Tighten the nuts to 45 ft. lbs.

7. Torque the ball stud nut to 50 ft. lbs. plus the additional torque required to align the cotter pin. Do not exceed 90 ft. lbs. and never back the nut off to align the pin.

8. Install a new cotter pin.

Lower ball joint inspection

9. Install a new lube fitting and lubricate the new joint.

10. If removed, install the brake caliper.

11. Install the wheel and tire and lower the truck.

Upper Control Arm

REMOVAL & INSTALLATION

1. Raise and support the truck on jackstands.

2. Support the lower control arm with a floor jack.

3. Remove the wheel and tire.

4. Remove the cotter pin from the upper control arm ball stud and loosen the stud nut one turn.

5. Loosen the upper control arm ball stud in the steering knuckle using a ball joint stud removal tool. Remove the nut from the ball stud and raise the upper arm to clear the steering knuckle. It will be necessary to remove the brake caliper and wire it to the frame to gain clearance.

6. Remove the nuts securing the control arm shaft to the frame and remove the control arm. Tape the shims and spacers together and tag for proper reassembly.

7. Installation is the reverse of removal. Place the control arm in position and install the nuts. Before tightening the nuts to 70 ft. lbs., insert the caster and camber shims in the same order as when removed. Have the front end alignment checked, and as necessary, adjusted.

Lower Control Arm

REMOVAL & INSTALLATION

1. Raise and support the truck on jackstands.

2. Remove the spring. See Spring Removal and Installation.

3. Support the inboard end of the control arm after spring removal.

4. Remove the cotter pin from the lower ball stud and loosen the nut one turn.

5. Loosen the lower ball stud in the steering knuckle using a ball joint stud removal tool. When the stud is loose, remove

UPPER
CONTROL
ARM

BUMPER

SHIMS

KNUCKLE
ASSY.

Upper control arm

BOLT/SCREW
MUST BE INSTALLED
IN DIRECTION SHOWN.

FRT

BOLT/SCREW
MUST BE INSTALLED
IN DIRECTION SHOWN.

SUGGESTED ASSEMBLY SEQUENCE
INSTALL THE FRONT LEG OF THE LOWER CONTROL
ARM INTO THE CROSSMEMBER PRIOR TO
INSTALLING THE REAR LEG IN THE FRAME
BRACKET.

Lower control arm attachment

the nut from the stud. It will be necessary to remove the brake caliper and wire it to the frame to gain clearance.

6. Remove the lower control arm.
7. Installation is the reverse of removal.

Upper Control Arm S-Series

REMOVAL

1. Note the location of the shims. Alignment shims are to be installed in the same position from which they were removed. Remove nuts and shims. Raise front of vehicle and support lower control arm with floor stands.

——— CAUTION ———

Floor jack must remain under control arm spring seat during removal and installation to retain spring and control arm in position.

Since the weight of the vehicle is used to relieve spring tension on the upper control arm, the floor stands must be positioned between the spring seats and ball joints of the lower control arms for maximum leverage.

2. Remove wheel, then loosen the upper ball joint from the steering knuckle as previously outlined.
3. Support hub assembly to prevent weight from damaging brake hose.
4. It is necessary to remove the upper control arm attaching bolts to allow clearance to remove upper control arm assembly.
5. Remove upper control arm.

INSTALLATION

1. Position upper control arm attaching bolts loosely in the frame and install pivot shaft on the attaching bolts.

The inner pivot bolts must be installed with the bolt heads to the front (on the front bushing) and to the rear (on the rear bushing).

2. Install alignment shims in their original position between the pivot shaft and frame on their respective bolts. Torque nuts to 45 ft. lbs.
3. Remove the temporary support from the hub assembly, then connect ball joint to steering knuckle as previously outlined.
4. Install wheel, then check wheel alignment, and adjust if necessary.

Lower Control Arm

REMOVAL

1. Remove coil spring as described earlier in this section.
2. Remove lower ball joint stud as previously outlined.
3. After stud breaks loose, hold up on lower control arm. Remove control arm.
4. Guide lower control arm out of opening in splash shield with a putty knife or similar tool.

INSTALLATION

1. Install lower ball joint stud into knuckle. Install nut as previously outlined.
2. Install spring.
3. Check front alignment. Reset as required.

Stabilizer Bar

REMOVAL & INSTALLATION

1. Hoist vehicle.
2. Disconnect each side of stabilizer linkage by removing nut from link bolt, pull bolt from linkage and remove retainers, grommets and spacer.

3. Remove bracket to frame or body bolts and remove stabilizer shaft, rubber bushings and brackets.
4. To replace, reverse sequence of operations, being sure to install with the identification forming on the right side of the vehicle. The rubber bushings should be positioned squarely in the brackets with the slit in the bushings facing the front car. Torque stabilizer link nut to 13 ft. lbs. and bracket bolts to 24 ft. lbs.

REAR SUSPENSION

Springs

REMOVAL & INSTALLATION

1. Raise the vehicle and support it so that there is no tension on the left spring assembly.
2. Loosen the spring-to-shackle retaining bolts. (Do not remove these bolts).
3. Remove the securing bolts which attach the shackle to the spring hanger.
4. Remove the nut and bolt which attach the spring to the front hanger.
5. Remove the U-bolt nuts and remove the spring plate.
6. Pull the spring from the vehicle.
7. If the bushings need to be replaced, they must be pressed in and out.
8. Place the spring assembly onto the axle housing.

NOTE: The shackle assembly must be attached to the rear spring eye before the rear shackle is installed.

9. Position the spring retaining plate and the U-bolts (loosely).
10. Install the rear shackle bolt and nut,

then the front eye bolt and nut. Tighten the bolts to 110 ft. lbs.

S-Series Trucks

REMOVAL

1. Raise vehicle on hoist, then support the body-chassis and axle separately, so that the load on the spring is relieved.
2. Loosen, but do not remove, spring-to-shackle retaining nut.
3. Remove the U-bolt retaining nuts, withdraw the U-bolts, and rotate the spring anchor plate, on the shock absorber, to clear the spring.
4. Remove the nut and bolt securing the shackle to the frame. Be careful to restrain the spring, since the spring is now free to rotate about the front hanger bolt.
5. Remove the nut and bolt at the front hanger, then remove the spring from the vehicle.

INSTALLATION

1. Clean axle spring pad.
2. Attach spring to vehicle at the front hanger by installing the nut and bolt. Do not apply final torque at this time.
3. Install the shackle-to-frame attaching nut and bolt, but do not apply final torque at this time. Be sure that:
   a. The shackle is loosely attached to the rear spring eye before attaching the shackle to the frame, and
   b. the shackle must be positioned with its open end toward the front of the vehicle, and
   c. the axle must be in position above the spring before attaching the shackle to the frame.
4. Position axle spring pad onto the spring so that the center bolt head is seated in the pilot hole of the spring pad seat.
5. Rotate the anchor plate, on shock absorber, underneath the spring assembly and install the U-bolts. Align the anchor plate, install the retaining nuts evenly (handtight), then tighten diagonally opposite nuts to 34 ft. lb.
6. Lower the vehicle so that the weight of the vehicle is supported by the suspension components. Torque the U-bolt nuts, spring eye bolt nuts (front and rear), and shackle-to-frame bolt nuts to 85 ft. lb.
7. Lower the vehicle and remove from the hoist.

Shock Absorbers

REMOVAL & INSTALLATION

The usual procedure is to replace shock absorbers in axle pairs, to provide equal damping. Heavy duty replacements are available for firmer control. Air adjustable shock absorbers can be used to maintain a level ride with heavy loads or when towing.

1. Raise and support the rear axle as necessary.
2. If air shocks are installed, bleed the air and detach the lines.
3. Remove the nut and washer at the top.
4. Remove the nut, washer, and bolt at the bottom.
5. Purge the new shock of air by extending it in its normal position and compressing it while inverted. Do this several times. It is normal for there to be more resistance to extension than to compression.
6. Install the shock absorber. Tighten the upper nuts to 140 ft. lbs for 1977-78 models and 150 ft. lbs. for 1979 and later models. Tighten the lower nuts to 115 ft. lbs. for all models. Tighten S-Series top nuts 15 ft. lbs., lower nuts 50 ft. lbs.

Typical leaf spring installation

Staggered rear shock absorber details

STEERING

A common cause of excessive steering play on these trucks is the steering gear box coming loose from the frame. The torque for these bolts is 65 ft. lbs.

Steering Wheel

REMOVAL & INSTALLATION

1. Disconnect the battery ground cable.
2. Remove the horn button. Remove the receiving cup, belleville washer, and bushing (if equipped).
3. Mark the steering wheel-to-steering shaft relationship.
4. Remove the snap-ring from the steering shaft.

Steering wheel—typical

Leaf spring attachment

5. Remove the nut and washer from the steering shaft.

6. Remove the steering wheel with a puller.

———— CAUTION ————
Don't hammer on the steering shaft.

7. Installation is the reverse of removal. The turn signal control assembly must be in the neutral position to prevent damaging the cancelling cam and control assembly. Tighten the nut to 30 ft. lbs.

NOTE: A steering wheel puller can be made by drilling two holes in a piece of steel the same distance apart as the two threaded holes in the steering wheel. Sometimes an old spring shackle will have the right dimensions. Drill another hole in the center. Place a center bolt with the head against the steering shaft and a nut against the bottom of the homemade puller bar. Thread the two outer bolts into the holes in the wheel. Unscrew the nut on the center bolt to draw the wheel off the shaft.

S-Series Trucks

REMOVAL & INSTALLATION

1. Disconnect battery ground cable.
2. Remove steering wheel shroud screws on underside of steering wheel.
3. Lift steering wheel shroud and horn contact lead assembly from the steering wheel.
4. Remove snap ring.
5. Remove steering wheel nut.
6. Using Tool J-2927, thread puller anchor screws into threaded holes provided in steering wheel. Turn center bolt of tool clockwise (butting against the steering shaft) to remove steering wheel.

Do not hammer on puller while turning. The tool centering adapters need not be installed.

7. Installation is the reverse of removal. Torque steering wheel nut 30 ft. lbs.

NOTE: Do not over-torque shaft nut or steering wheel rub may result.

Turn Signal Switch

REPLACEMENT

1. Remove the steering wheel as previously outlined.
2. Remove the column to instrument panel trim cover. Loosen the three cover screws and lift the cover off the shaft. On 1977 and later models, place a screwdriver in the cover slot and pry out to free the cover.
3. The round lockplate must be pushed down to remove the wire snap-ring from the shaft. A special tool is available to do this. The tool is an inverted U-shape with

a hole for the shaft. The shaft nut is used to force it down. Pry the wire snap-ring out of the shaft groove.

4. Remove the tool and lift the lockplate off the shaft.
5. Slip the cancelling cam, upper bearing preload spring, and thrust washer off the shaft.
6. Remove the turn signal lever screw and the lever. Push the flasher knob in and unscrew it.
7. Pull the switch connector out of the mast jacket and tape the upper part to facilitate switch removal. On tilt wheels, place the turn signal and shifter housing in the low position and remove the harness cover.
8. Remove the three switch mounting screws. Remove the switch by pulling it straight up while guiding the wiring harness cover through the column.
9. Install the replacement switch by working the connector and cover down through the housing and under the bracket. On tilt models, the connector is worked down through the housing, under the bracket, and then the cover is installed on the harness.
10. Install the switch mounting screws and the connector on the mast jacket bracket. Install the column to instrument panel trim plate.
11. Install the flasher knob and the turn signal lever.
12. With the turn signal lever in neutral and the flasher knob out, slide the thrust washer, upper bearing pre-load spring, and cancelling cam onto the shaft.
13. Position the lockplate on the shaft and press it down until a new snap-ring can be inserted in the shaft groove.
14. Install the cover and the steering wheel.

S-Series Trucks

REMOVAL & INSTALLATION

1. Remove the steering wheel.
2. Pry out the steering shaft lock cover.
3. Remove the retaining ring and shaft lock.
4. Remove the cancelling cam and spring.
5. Remove the switch actuator arm, unscrew and remove the switch and unplug the wire connector.
6. Installation is the reverse of removal.

Ignition Switch and Lock Cylinder

1977–78 LOCK CYLINDER REMOVAL & INSTALLATION

The key and lock code numbers are kept in the records of the original selling dealer. This number enables a dealer to supply a new lock cylinder that will operate with the old key.

1. Remove steering wheel and turn signal switch as previously outlined.

NOTE: It is not necessary to completely remove the turn signal switch. Pull the switch over the end of the shaft—no farther.

2. Place lock cylinder in the Run position.
3. Insert a small screwdriver into the rectangular column housing slot. Keeping the screwdriver to the right-side of the slot, break the housing flash loose and depress the spring latch at the lower end of the lock cylinder. Remove the lock cylinder.

NOTE: When ordering a new lock cylinder, specify a cylinder assembly. This will save assembling the cylinder, washer, sleeve and adapter.

4. To install, hold the lock cylinder sleeve and rotate the knob clockwise against the stop. Insert the cylinder into the housing, aligning the key and keyway. Hold a 0.070 in. drill bit between the lock bezel and housing. Rotate the cylinder counterclockwise, maintaining a light pressure until the drive section of the cylinder mates with the sector. Push in until the snap-ring pops into the grooves. Remove the bit. Check cylinder operation.

———— CAUTION ————
The drill prevents forcing the lock cylinder inward beyond its normal position. The buzzer switch and spring latch can hold the lock cylinder in too far. Complete disassembly of the upper bearing housing is necessary to release an improperly installed lock cylinder.

1979 AND LATER LOCK CYLINDER REMOVAL & INSTALLATION

1. Remove the steering wheel and the turn signal switch as previously outlined. It is not necessary to completely remove the turn signal switch. Just pull the switch out far enough so it can hang out of the steering column shaft. Do not disconnect the wiring harness.
2. With the lock cylinder in the Run position, remove the lock cylinder attaching screw and the cylinder.
3. To install, align the cylinder key with the keyway in the housing and rotate the key all the way clockwise while holding the cylinder body.
4. Insert the cylinder into the housing and install the attaching screw.
5. Install the turn signal switch and the steering wheel as previously outlined.

S-Series Trucks

REMOVAL & INSTALLATION

1. Disconnect the battery ground.

2. Turn the lock to the RUN position.

3. Remove the turn signal switch.

4. Remove the cylinder retaining screw.

5. Pull out the cylinder.

6. Installation is the reverse of removal. Turn the cylinder to the STOP position while installing.

IGNITION SWITCH REMOVAL & INSTALLATION

Except S-Series

The switch is on the steering column, behind the instrument panel.

1. Lower the steering column, making sure that it is supported.

——————— CAUTION ———————

Extreme care is necessary to prevent damage to the collapsible column.

2. Make sure the switch is in the Lock position. If the lock cylinder is out, pull the switch rod up to the stop, then go down one detent.

3. Remove the two screws and the switch.

4. Before installation, make sure the switch is in the lock position. The switch can be moved to the Lock position using a screwdriver inserted into the locking rod slot.

5. Install the switch using the original screws.

——————— CAUTION ———————

Use of screws that are too long could prevent the column from collapsing on impact.

6. Replace the column.

S-Series

1. Remove the steering wheel, lock cylinder, turn signal switch, shift lever, shift lever bowl, shift bowl shroud and bowl lower bearing.

2. Unbolt and remove the ignition switch and dimmer switch from the column.

3. For installation, on all columns except key-release type, move the switch slider to the extreme left position, then two detents right. This is the OFF-UNLOCK position. On key-release columns, leave the slider in the extreme left postion. This is ACCESSORIES. To adjust the dimmer switch, depress the switch slightly to allow insertion of a 3/32 in. drill bit into the hole above the acuator rod. Force the switch upward to take up any lash, then tighten the screw.

NOTE: On tilt columns, the ACC position on the ignition switch is the extreme right position. On these columns, move the slider two detents left to the OFF-UNLOCK position.

Power Steering Pump

REMOVAL & INSTALLATION

1. Disconnect the hoses at the pump. When the hoses are disconnected, secure the ends in a raised position to prevent leakage. Cap the ends of the hoses to prevent the entrance of dirt.

2. Cap the pump fittings.

3. Loosen the bracket-to-pump mounting nuts.

4. Remove the pump drive belt.

5. Remove the bracket-to-pump bolts and remove the pump from the truck.

6. Installation is the reverse of removal. Fill the reservoir and bleed the pump by turning the pulley counterclockwise (as viewed from the front) until bubbles stop forming. Bleed the system. Adjust the belt tension.

BLEEDING THE SYSTEM

1. Fill the reservoir to the proper level and let the fluid remain undisturbed for at least 2 minutes.

2. Start the engine and run it for only about 2 seconds.

3. Add fluid as necessary.

4. Repeat steps 1–3 until the level remains constant.

5. Raise the front of the vehicle so that the front wheels are off the ground. Set the parking brake and block both rear wheels front and rear. Manual transmissions should be in Neutral; automatic transmissions should be in Park.

6. Start the engine and run it at approximately 1,500 rpm.

7. Turn the wheels (off the ground) to the right and left, lightly contacting the stops.

8. Add fluid as necessary.

Removing the lockplate retaining ring

1975–78 ignition lock cylinder removal

Ignition switch details

1979–82 ignition lock cylinder removal

9. Lower the vehicle and turn the wheels right and left on the ground.

10. Check the level and refill as necessary.

6-250 power steering pump mounting

SECTOR LASH
ADJUSTMENT SCREW

LOCK
NUT

WORM BEARING
ADJUSTMENT

Steering gear adjustment points

```
CLAMPING INSTRUCTIONS FOR
ALL LIGHT TRUCKS.

A. All bolts must be installed in
   direction shown.
B. Rotate both inner and outer tie
   rod sockets rearward to limit of
   ball stud travel.
C. Position clamps within angles shown.
D. Tighten clamps.
E. With this same rearward rotation,
   all bolt centerlines must be
   between angles shown.

   CAUTION: CLAMPS MUST BE
   BETWEEN AND CLEAR OF DIMPLES
   BEFORE TORQUING NUT.
```

ADJUSTER SLEEVE

FWD

VERTICAL LINE

ADJUSTER
SLEEVE

CLAMP

45°

```
NOTE: IMPORTANT - SLOT
IN ADJUSTER SLEEVE
MUST NOT BE WITHIN
OPEN AREA OF CLAMP
JAWS OR CLOSER THAN
.10 TO THE EDGE OF
CLAMP JAW OPENING.
ROTATE CLAMP TO MEET
REQUIREMENTS WITHIN
PROPER POSITION AS SHOWN.
```

CAUTION: CENTERLINE OF SLOT
IN CLAMP MUST BE IN THIS
RANGE OF ADJUSTMENT.

Tie rod sleeve clamp installation

11. If the fluid is extremely foamy, let the truck stand for a few minutes with the engine off and repeat the above procedure. Check the belt tension and check for a bent or loose pulley. The pulley should not wobble with the engine running.

12. Check that no hoses are contacting any parts of the truck, particularly sheet metal.

13. Check the level and refill as necessary. This step and the next are very important. When filling, follow steps 1–10.

14. Check for air in the fluid. Aerated fluid appears milky. If air is present, repeat the above operations. If it is obvious that the pump will not respond to bleeding after several attempts, a pressure test may be required.

Power Steering Gear

ADJUSTMENTS

Refer to the Unit Repair Section.

REMOVAL & INSTALLATION

1. Disconnect hoses at gear. When hoses are disconnected, secure ends in raised position to prevent drainage of oil. Cap or tape the ends of the hoses to prevent entrance of dirt.

2. Install two plugs in gear fittings to prevent entrance of dirt.

3. Remove the flexible coupling to steering shaft flange bolts. Mark the relationship of the universal yoke to the stub shaft.

4. Mark the relationship of the Pitman arm to the Pitman shaft. Remove the Pitman shaft nut or Pitman arm from the Pitman shaft using puller J-6632.

5. Remove the steering gear to frame bolts and remove the gear assembly.

6. On G, C and K models, remove the flexible coupling pinch bolt and remove the coupling from the steering gear stub shaft.

7. Install the flexible coupling onto the steering gear stub shaft, aligning the flat in the coupling with the flat on the shaft. Push the coupling onto the shaft until the stub shaft bottoms on the coupling reinforcement. Install the pinch bolt.

NOTE: The coupling bolt must pass through the shaft undercut, or damage to the components could occur.

8. Place the steering gear in position, guiding the coupling bolt into the steering shaft flange.

9. Install the steering gear to frame bolts.

10. If flexible coupling alignment pin plastic spacers were used, make sure they are buttoned on the pins, tighten the flange bolt nuts and then remove the plastic spacers.

11. If flexible coupling alignment pin plastic spacers were not used, center the pins in the slots in the steering shaft flange and then install and torque the flange bolt nuts.

12. Install the Pitman arm onto the Pitman shaft, lining up the marks made at removal. Install the Pitman shaft nut.

13. Remove the plugs and caps from the steering gear and hoses and connect the hoses to the gear. Tighten the hose fittings.

Manual Steering Gear

ADJUSTMENTS

Refer to the Unit Repair Section.

REMOVAL & INSTALLATION

1. Set the front wheels in straight ahead position by driving vehicle a short distance on a flat surface.

2. Remove the flexible coupling to steering shaft flange bolts. Mark the relationship of the universal yoke to the wormshaft.

3. Mark the relationship of the Pitman arm to the Pitman shaft. Remove the Pitman shaft nut or Pitman arm pinch bolt and then remove the Pitman arm from the Pitman shaft, using puller J-6632.

4. Remove the steering gear to frame bolts and remove the gear assembly.

5. Remove the flexible coupling pinch bolt and remove the coupling from the steering gear wormshaft.

6. Install the flexible coupling onto the steering gear wormshaft, aligning the flat

in the coupling with the flat on the shaft. Push the coupling onto the shaft until the wormshaft bottoms on the coupling reinforcement. Install the pinch bolt and torque to 25 ft. lbs. The coupling bolt must pass through the shaft undercut.

7. Place the steering gear in position, guiding the coupling bolt into the steering shaft flange.

8. Install the steering gear to frame bolts and torque to 70 ft. lbs. 55 ft. lbs. S-Series trucks.

9. If flexible coupling alignment pin plastic spacers were used, make sure they are bottomed on the pins, torque the flange bolt nuts to 25 ft. lbs. and then remove the plastic spacers.

10. If flexible coupling alignment pin plastic spacers were not used, center the pins in the slots in the steering shaft flange and then install and torque the flange bolt nuts to 25 ft. lbs.

11. Install the Pitman arm onto the Pitman shaft, lining up the marks made at removal. Install the Pitman shaft nut torque to 185 ft. lb.

Tie Rod Ends

REMOVAL & INSTALLATION

1. Raise the front of the truck and support it safely on jack stands.

2. Remove the tie rod end stud cotter pin and nut.

3. You can use a tie rod end ball joint removal too to loosen the stud, or you can loosen it by tapping on the steering arm with a hammer while using a heavy hammer as a backup.

4. Remove the inner stud in the same way.

5. Loosen the tie rod adjuster sleeve clamp nuts.

6. Unscrew the tie rod end from the threaded sleeve. The threads may be left or right hand threads. Count the number of turns required to remove it.

7. To install, grease the threads and turn the new tie rod end in as many turns as were needed to remove it. This will give approximately correct toe-in. Tighten the clamp bolts.

8. Tighten the stud nuts to 45 ft. lbs. and install new cotter pins. You may tighten the nut to align the cotter pin, but don't loosen it.

9. Adjust the toe-in.

Relay Rod

REMOVAL & INSTALLATION

1. Raise vehicle on hoist.

2. Disconnect inner ends of tie rods from relay rod.

3. Remove nut from relay rod ball stud attachment at pitman arm.

4. Detach relay rod from pitman arm by using tool such as J-24319-01. Shift steering linkage as required to free pitman arm from relay rod.

5. Remove nut from idler arm and remove relay rod from idler arm.

6. Installation is the reverse of removal. Torque the nuts to 40 ft. lbs. Adjust Toe-in if necessary.

Idler Arm

REMOVAL & INSTALLATION

1. Raise vehicle on hoist.

2. Remove idler arm to frame nuts, washers, and bolts.

3. Remove nut from idler arm to relay rod ball stud.

4. Disconnect relay rod from idler arm by using J-24319-01 or similar puller.

5. Remove idler arm.

6. Installation is the reverse of removal. Torque nuts to 30 ft. lbs.

BRAKE SYSTEM

Adjustment

REAR DRUM BRAKES

These brakes are equipped with self-adjusters and no manual adjustment is necessary, except when brake linings are replaced.

FRONT DISC BRAKES

These brakes are inherently self-adjusting and no adjustment is ever necessary or possible.

Master Cylinder

REMOVAL & INSTALLATION

NOTE: Clean any master cylinder parts in alcohol or brake fluid. Never use mineral-based cleaning solvents such as gasoline, kerosene, carbon-tetrachloride, acetone, or paint thinner as these will destroy rubber parts.

1. Using a clean cloth, wipe the master cylinder and its lines to remove excess dirt and then place cloths under the unit to absorb spilled fluid.

2. Remove the hydraulic lines from the master cylinder and plug the outlets to prevent the entrance of foreign material.

3. Disconnect the brake pushrod from the brake pedal on non-power brakes.

4. Remove the attaching bolts and remove the master cylinder from the firewall or the brake booster.

To install:

5. Connect the pushrod to the brake pedal with the pin and retainer.

6. Connect the brake lines and fill the

Freeing the tie rod end

Four wheel drive steering linkage

Typical master cylinder installations

Exploded view of a master cylinder

master cylinder reservoirs to the proper levels.

7. Bleed the brake system as outlined in the Unit Repair Section.

NOTE: For additional brake service information refer to the Unit Repair Section.

Brake Light Switch

ADJUSTMENT

With pedal in fully released position, the stop light switch plunger should be fully depressed against the pedal shank. Adjust switch by moving in or out as necessary.

1. Make certain that the tubular clip is in brake pedal mounting bracket.

2. With brake pedal depressed, insert switch into tubular clip until switch body seats on clip. Audible clicks can be heard as the threaded portion of the switch is pushed through the clip toward the brake pedal.

3. Pull brake pedal fully rearward against pedal stop until audible clicking sounds can no longer be heard. Switch will be moved in tubular clip providing adjustment.

4. Release brake pedal and then repeat step 3, to assure that no audible clicking sounds remain.

Wheel Bearing

LUBRICATION AND ADJUSTMENT

Only front wheel bearings require periodic service. A premium high melting point grease meeting GM specification 6031-M must be used. Long fiber type greases must not be used. This service is recommended at 20,000 mile intervals or whenever the truck has been driven in water up to the hubs.

1. Remove the wheel and tire assembly, and the brake drum or brake caliper.

2. Remove the hub and disc as an assembly. Remove the caliper mounting bolts and insert a block between the brake pads as the caliper is removed. Remove the caliper and wire it out of the way. Do not allow the caliper to hang by the brake hose.

3. Pry out the grease cap, cotter pin, spindle nut, and washer, then remove the hub. Do not drop the wheel bearings.

4. Remove the outer roller bearing assembly from the hub. The inner bearing assembly will remain in the hub and may be removed after prying out the inner seal. Discard the seal.

5. Clean all parts in solvent (air dry) and check for excessive wear or damage.

6. Using a hammer and drift, remove the bearing caps from the hub. When installing new cups, make sure that they are not cocked and that they are fully seated against the hub shoulder.

7. Pack both wheel bearings using high melting point wheel bearing grease made for disc brakes. Ordinary grease will melt and ooze out, ruining the pads. Place a healthy globe of grease in the palm of one hand and force the edge of the bearing into it so that the grease fills the bearing. Do this until the whole bearing is packed. Grease packing tools are available to make this job a lot less messy. There are also tools which make it possible to grease the inner bearing without removing it or the disc from the spindle.

8. Place the inner bearing in the hub and install a new inner seal, making sure that the seal flange faces the bearing cup.

9. Carefully install the wheel hub over the spindle.

10. Using your hands, firmly press the outer bearing into the hub. Install the spindle washer and nut.

11. To adjust the bearings, spin the wheel hub by hand and tighten the nut till it is just snug (12 ft. lbs.). Back off the nut till it is loose, then tighten it finger tight. Loosen the nut until either hole in the spindle lines up with a slot in the nut and insert a new cotter pin. There should be 0.001–0.005 in, end-play. This can be measured with a dial indicator, if you wish.

12. Replace the dust cap, wheel and tire.

Parking Brakes

ADJUSTMENT

Before attempting parking brake adjustment, make sure that the rear brakes are fully adjusted by making several stops in reverse.

1. Raise and support the rear axle. Release the parking brake.

2. On 1977 and later models, apply the pedal four clicks.

3. Adjust the cable equilizer nut under the truck until a moderate drag can be felt when the rear wheels are turned forward.

4. Release the parking brake and check that there is no drag when the wheels are turned forward.

NOTE: If the parking brake cable is replaced, prestretch it by applying the parking brake hard about three times before attempting adjustment.

S-Series Trucks

Adjustment of parking brake system is necessary whenever the parking brake cables have been disconnected.

1. Set parking brake pedal at specified number of clicks:
—2 wheel drive pickups = 8 clicks
—4 wheel drive pickups = 10 clicks
—All Blazers = 10 clicks

2. Raise and suitably support vehicle

3. Place a properly calibrated cable tension gage on the designated rear cable as close to the equilizer as practical.
-LH cable on 2 wheel drive pickups
-RH cable on 4 wheel drive pickup
-RH cable on all Blazers

4. Drive adjusting nut until specified tension is indicated on gage.
—890 to 979N (200 to 220 lbs.) 2 wheel drive pickups
—623 to 667N (140 to 150 lbs.) 4 wheel drive pickups
—623 to 667N (140 to 150 lbs.) Blazers

5. Cables are not to be adjusted too tightly, as this will result in brake drag.

6. Remove support and lower vehicle.

CABLE REPLACEMENT

Except S-Series Trucks
FRONT CABLE

1. Raise vehicle on hoist
2. Remove adjusting nut from equalizer.
3. Remove retainer clip from rear portion of front cable at frame and from lever arm.
4. Disconnect front brake cable from parking brake pedal or lever assemblies. Remove front brake cable. On some models, it may assist installation of new cable if a heavy cord is tied to other end of cable in order to guide new cable through proper routing.
5. Install cable by reversing removal procedure.
6. Adjust parking brake.

CENTER CABLE

1. Raise vehicle on hoist.
2. Remove adjusting nut from equalizer.
3. Unhook connector at each end and disengage hooks and guides.
4. Install new cable by reversing removal procedure.
5. Adjust parking brake.
6. Apply parking brake 3 times with heavy pressure and repeat adjustment.

REAR CABLE

1. Raise vehicle on hoist.
2. Remove rear wheel and brake drum.
3. Loosen adjusting nut at equalizer.
4. Disengage rear cable at connector.
5. Bend retainer fingers.
6. Disengage cable at brake shoe operating lever.
7. Install new cable by reversing removal procedure.
8. Adjust parking brake.

S-SERIES TRUCKS

Front Cable

1. Raise and suitably support vehicle.
2. Loosen adjuster nut and disconnect front cable from connector. Compress retainer fingers and loosen at frame.
3. Remove support and lower vehicle.
4. Remove windshield washer bottle.
5. Disconnect cable from parking brake pedal assembly, compress retainer fingers and remove cable.
6. Install cable by reversing procedure.
7. Adjust parking brake.

CENTER CABLE

1. Raise and suitably support vehicle.
2. Remove adjuster nut at equalizer and pull cable from equalizer.
3. Disconnect cable at retainers.
4. Install cable by reversing procedure and adjust parking brake.

LEFT/RIGHT REAR

1. Raise and suitably support vehicle.
2. Mark relationship of tire and wheel assembly to axle flange and remove.
3. Remove brake drum.
4. Loosen equalizer and disconnect cable at center retainer.
5. Compress plastic retainer fingers and remove retainer from frame bracket.
6. Remove rear brake shoe and disconnect cable.
7. Remove cable at frame and from brake backing plate.
8. Install cable by reversing procedure. Make sure cable is routed properly and securely retained.
9. Adjust parking brake cable and lower vehicle.

CHASSIS ELECTRICAL

Blower—Except Vans

REMOVAL & INSTALLATION

1. Disconnect the battery leads, open the hood, and securely support it.
2. Mark the position of the blower motor in relation to its case. Remove the electrical connection at the motor.
3. Remove the blower attaching screws and remove the assembly. Pry gently on the flange if the sealer sticks.
4. The blower wheel can be removed from the motor shaft by removing the nut at the center.
To assemble the unit:
5. Assemble the blower wheel to the motor with the open end of the wheel away from the motor and install the unit into the blower case. Connect the ground strap and the electrical connection.
6. Position the hood hinge using the scribe marks and check the hood alignment.
7. Connect the battery.

Core—Except Vans

REMOVAL & INSTALLATION

Without Air Conditioning

1. Disconnect the battery ground cable.
2. Disconnect the heater hoses at the core tubes and drain the engine coolant. Plug the core tubes to prevent spillage.

3. Remove the nuts from the distributor air ducts in the engine compartment.
4. Remove the glove compartment and door.
5. Disconnect the "Air-Defrost" and "Temperature" door cables.
6. Remove the floor outlet and remove the defroster duct-to-heater distributor screw.
7. Remove the heater distributor-to-instrument panel screws. Pull the assembly rearward to gain access to the wiring harness and disconnect the wires attached to the unit.
8. Remove the heater distributor from the truck.
9. Remove the heater core retaining straps and remove the core from the truck.
10. Installation is the reverse of removal. Be sure that the core-to-case and case-to-dash panel sealer is intact. Fill the cooling system and check for leaks.

With Air Conditioning

1. Disconnect the battery ground cable.
2. Drain the coolant.
3. Remove the heater hoses from the core tubes. Plug the tubes to prevent spillage.
4. Remove the glove box and door.
5. Remove the screws holding the center duct to the selector duct and to the instrument panel. Remove the center upper and lower ducts.
6. Disconnect the control cable at the temperature door.
7. Remove the three stud nuts from the firewall. Remove the selector duct to firewall screw inside the truck.
8. Pull the selector duct assembly back until the core tubes clear the firewall, then lower it to disconnect the vacuum and electrical connections.
9. Remove the selector duct assembly and remove the core from the truck.
10. Reverse the procedure for installation.

Blower—Vans

REMOVAL & INSTALLATION

1. 1. Disconnect the battery cables. Remove the battery.
2. Unclip the blower motor lead wire.
3. Remove the blower attaching screws.
4. Remove the blower assembly. It may

be necessary to pry gently on the blower flange. Sometimes the sealer acts as an adhesive.
5. If the motor is being replaced, remove the nut attaching the blower wheel to the blower motor shaft and separate the two.
6. Assemble the blower wheel to the motor with the open end away from the motor.

Heater blower assembly—except vans

Heater distributor—except vans

Van blower motor

Van heater hose routing

7. If the sealer has hardened or is otherwise useless, apply a new bead of sealer to the mounting flange.

8. Installation of the blower motor and wheel is the reverse of removal. Connect the lead wires and the battery cables and check the operation of the motor.

Core—Vans

REMOVAL & INSTALLATION

1977 Without Air Conditioning

This procedure applies to models without air conditioning and to those with the floor mounted air conditioner.

1. Disconnect the battery ground cable.
2. Place a pan under the van and disconnect the heater intake and outlet hoses. Quickly, remove the plug the heater hoses and support them in an upright position. Drain the coolant from the heater core into the pan.
3. Disconnect the right-hand air distributor hose from the heater case and put it aside.
4. Pry the eyelet clip from the temperature door cable and remove the Bowden cable attaching screw.
5. Remove the distributor duct and pull it rearward from the retainer.
6. Remove the heater case and core as an assembly.
7. Remove the core from the case. To install a new core, reverse the above steps.

1978 Without Air Conditioning

1. Disconnect the negative battery cable.
2. Place a pan under the van and disconnect the heater intake and outlet hoses. Quickly, remove and plug the hoses and support them in an upright position. Drain the coolant from the heater core into the pan.
3. Remove the heater distributor duct-to-case attaching screws and the duct-to-engine cover screw. Remove the duct.
4. Remove the screw attaching the defroster duct to the distributor case.
5. Disconnect the temperature door cable. Carefully fold the cable back and out of the way.
6. Remove the three nuts from the engine compartment side of the distributor case and the screw from the passenger compartment side.
7. Remove the heater case and core assembly.
8. Remove the core retaining straps and remove the core.
9. Reverse to install.

1979 and Later Without Air Conditioning

1. Refer to steps 1–3 of the 1978 procedure.
2. Remove the engine cover.
3. Remove all the instrument panel attaching screws.

4. Carefully lower the steering column. Raise and support the right side of the instrument panel.
5. Remove the defroster duct-to-case attaching screws and the two screws attaching the distributor to the heater case.
6. Refer to steps 5–9 of the 1978 procedure.

1977 With Air Conditioning

These models have the air conditioning equipment mounted under the right side of the instrument panel.

1. Remove the battery.
2. Remove the engine cover.
3. Remove the evaporator-blower shield and bracket.
5. Loosen the steering column to instrument panel reinforcement screws. Remove one screw.
6. Disconnect the speedometer cable at the instrument.
7. Remove the instrument panel to lower reinforcement screws. Move the instrument panel back and detach the radio antenna and wires. Disconnect the brake switch electrical connector.
8. Detach the blower-evaporator support bracket from the door pillar and the engine housing. Move it back for access.
9. Detach the heater hoses at the core (from under the hood). Plug the hoses to prevent spillage.
10. Remove the air inlet valve assembly from the kick panel. Remove the temperature door control cable at the heater case.
11. Remove the heater assembly. Remove the core from the assembly.
12. Reverse the procedure for installation. Tighten the column screws to 22 ft. lbs. Refill the cooling system as necessary.

1978 and later With Air Conditioning

1. Disconnect the battery ground cable.
2. Remove the engine cover.
3. Remove the steering column to instrument panel bolts. Lower the column carefully.
4. Remove the upper and lower instrument panel attaching screws. Remove the radio support bracket screw.
5. Raise and support the right side of the instrument panel.
6. Remove the lower right instrument panel bracket.
7. Remove the vacuum actuator from the kick panel.
8. Disconnect the temperature cable and vacuum hoses at the case. Remove the heater distributor duct from over the engine hump.
9. Remove the two defroster duct to firewall attaching screws below the windshield.
10. Under the hood, disconnect and plug the heater hoses at the firewall.
11. Remove the three nuts and one screw (inside) holding the heater case to the firewall.
12. Remove the case from the truck. Re-

move the gasket for access to the screws holding the case together. Remove the temperature cable support bracket. Remove the screws and separate the case. Remove the heater core.
13. Reverse the procedure for installation. Refill the cooling system as necessary.

S - Series Blower

REMOVAL & INSTALLATION

1. Disconnect the battery ground.
2. Disconnect all wires at the blower.
3. Remove the vacuum tank if so equipped.
4. Remove the blower motor mounting screws and lift out the blower.
5. Installation is the reverse of removal.

Heater Core

REMOVAL & INSTALLATION

1. Disconnect the battery ground.
2. Drain the cooling system.
3. Remove the heater hoses at the core tubes.
4. Remove the core over retaining screws.
5. Remove the retainers at each end of the core.
6. Lift out the core.
7. Installation is the reverse of removal.

Radio

REMOVAL & INSTALLATION

Except Vans

1. Remove the negative battery cable and the control knobs and the bezels from the radio control shafts.
2. On AM radios, remove the support bracket stud nut and its lockwasher.
3. On AM/FM radios, remove the support bracket-to-instrument panel screws.
4. Lifting the rear edge of the radio, push the radio forward until the control shafts clear the instrument panel. Then lower the radio far enough so that the electrical connections can be disconnected.
5. Remove the power lead, and antenna wires and then pull out the unit.
6. To install the radio, reverse the above procedure.

Vans

1. Disconnect the ground cable from the battery.
2. Remove the engine cover.
3. Remove the air cleaner from the carburetor.
4. On models through 1977, remove

the stud in the carburetor which holds the air cleaner.

5. Cover the carburetor with a clean rag.

6. Remove the knobs, washers and nuts from the front of the radio.

7. Remove the rear bracket screw and bracket from the radio.

8. Remove the radio through the engine access area. Lower the radio far enough to detach the wiring.

9. Remove the radio.

Installation is the reverse of removal.

S-Series Trucks

1. Disconnect the battery ground.

2. Remove the instrument panel center bezel.

3. Remove the four screws from the radio bracket and pull the radio forward.

4. Disconnect the antenna and electrical wires. Pull the radio out.

5. Installation is the reverse of removal.

Windshield Wiper Motor

REMOVAL & INSTALLATION

Except Vans

1. Make sure the wipers are in the park position.

2. Disconnect the battery ground cable.

3. Disconnect the wiring and hoses at the windshield washer pump.

4. Remove the plastic air intake cover screen and reach in to loosen the wiper drive rod attaching screws. There is a small access hole provided. Remove the drive rod from the motor crank arm.

5. Unbolt and remove the motor.

6. Reverse the procedure for installation, making sure to lubricate the motor crank arm pivot.

NOTE: Failure of the washers to operate or to shut off is often caused by grease or dirt on the electromagnetic contacts. Simply unplug the wire and pull off the plastic cover for access. Likewise, failure of the wipers to park is often caused by grease or dirt on the park switch contacts. The park switch is under the cove behind the pump.

Vans

1. Be sure that the wiper motor is in PARK position. The wiper arms should be in their normal OFF position.

2. Open the hood and disconnect the battery ground cable.

3. Remove the exposed cowl cover screws with the hood up.

4. Remove the wiper arms. This can be done by pulling the wiper arms away from the glass to release the clip under-

neath. The wiper arms are splined to the shafts and can be pulled off.

5. Remove the remaining screws securing the cowl panel and remove it.

6. Loosen the nuts holding the transmission linkage to the wiper motor crank arm.

7. Disconnect the power feed to the wiper arm at the connector next to the radio.

8. Remove the flex hose from the left defroster outlet to gain access to the wiper motor screws.

9. Remove the one screw holding the left-hand heater duct to the engine shroud and move the heater duct down and out.

10. Remove the windshield washer hoses from the pump.

11. Remove the 3 screws holding the wiper motor to the cowl and lift the wiper motor out from under the dash.

12. Installation is the reverse of removal. Install the wiper motor in the PARK position.

S-Series Trucks

1. Disconnect the battery ground.

2. Remove the wiper arms.

3. Remove the cowl, vent and grille.

4. Loosen, but do not remove, the nuts

which hold the drive link to the motor crank arm.

5. Detach the drive link from the crank arm.

6. Disconnect the wiring at the motor.

7. Remove the motor mounting screws. Turn the motor upward and outward and remove it.

8. Installation is the reverse of removal. Torque the attaching screws to 50–75 in. lb.

Wiper Linkage

REMOVAL & INSTALLATION

S-Series

1. Disconnect the battery ground.

2. Remove the wiper arms.

3. Remove the cowl vent and grille.

4. Remove the nut securing the linkage to the motor.

5. Remove the screw securing the linkage to the cowl panel.

6. Installation is the reverse of removal. Torque the screws and nuts to 50–80 in. lb.

1. Arm, windshield wiper	7. Lever	15. Strap
2. Blade	8. Module	16. Connector
insert	9. Lens, pulse switch	17. Motor assembly
3. Nozzle	10. Knob, pulse switch	18. Bolt (M5 × .8 × 28)
4. Spacer, nozzle	11. Nut, pulse module retaining	19. Screw, (M6.3 × 1.69 × 20)
5. Nut, type R stamped (M16)	12. Reserovir	20. Pump
6. Transmission, left hand	13. Bolt, (M6 × 1 × 25)	
transmission, right hand	14. Hose, (5/32" ID)	

S–Series windshield wiper system

Instrument Cluster

REMOVAL & INSTALLATION

Except Vans

1977 and Later

1. Disconnect battery ground cable.
2. Remove headlamp switch control knob and radio control knobs.
3. Remove eight screws and remove instrument bezel.
4. Reach up under instrument cluster and disconnect speedometer by first depressing the tang on the rear of the speedometer head, then pulling cable free from head as tang is depressed.

Wiper motor installation—except vans

Van wiper motor installation

Instrument cluster—except vans

5. Disconnect oil pressure gauge line at fitting in engine compartment.
6. Pull instrument cluster out just far enough to disconnect line from oil pressure gauge.
7. Remove cluster.
8. Install cluster in reverse order of removal.

Vans

1. Open the hood and disconnect the battery ground cable.
2. Reach up under the dash and disconnect the speedometer cable by first depressing the tang on the rear of the speedometer head and detaching the cable as the tang is depressed.
3. Unplug the instrument panel harness connector.
4. Disconnect and plug the oil pressure gauge line (if equipped).
5. Remove the two nuts from the instrument cluster studs.
6. Pull the top of the cluster away from instrument panel and lift out the bottom of the cluster.
7. Remove the cluster.
8. Installation is the reverse of removal. The clips at the top of the cluster slip into the openings in the instrument panel after the bottom of the cluster is installed.

S-Series Trucks

1. Disconnect the battery ground.
2. Remove the five screws retaining, the cluster trim plate and carefully lift off the plate.
3. Remove the instrument panel face plate.
4. Remove the cluster lens.
5. Disconnect the speedometer cable.
6. Disconnect the cluster electrical connector.
7. Lift out the cluster.
8. Installation is the reverse of removal.

Speedometer Cable

REMOVAL & INSTALLATION

1. Disconnect the speedometer cable from the rear of the speedometer head.
2. Remove the old cable by pulling it out from the speedometer end of the cable housing. If the old cable is broken, the speedometer cable will have to be disconnected from the transmission and the cable removed from the other end.
3. Lubricate the lower ¾ of the new cable with speedometer cable lubricant and feed the cable into the cable housing.

Lighting

HEADLIGHT REMOVAL & INSTALLATION

NOTE: Some 1978 and later models

have rectangular headlights. Otherwise the following removal and installation procedures apply.

1. Remove the headlight bezel by releasing the attaching screws.
2. Remove the spring (if any) from the retaining ring and turn the unit to disengage it from the headlamp adjusting screws.
3. Disconnect the wiring harness connector.

NOTE: Do not disturb the adjusting screws.

4. Remove the retaining ring and the headlamp.
5. Position the new sealed beam unit in the retaining ring.

NOTE: The number which is moulded into the lens must be at the top.

6. Attach the wiring connector.
7. Install the headlamp assembly, twisting the ring slightly to engage the adjusting screws.
8. Install the retaining ring spring and check the operation of the unit. Install the bezel.

Fusible Links

Fusible links are sections of wire, with special insulation, designed to melt under electrical overload. Replacements are simply spliced into the wire in most cases. Circuits protected by fusible links are: high beam indicator, air conditioning hi-blower, horn, and ignition.

Circuit Breakers

A circuit breaker is an electrical switch which breaks the circuit in case of an overload. All models have a circuit breaker in the headlight switch to protect the headlight and parking light systems. An overload may cause the lights to flash on and off. 1975 wiper motors have a circuit breaker at the motor. 1975-82 rear mounted air conditioners have a circuit breaker at the firewall.

Fuses and Flashers

The fuse block is mounted to the firewall, inside the truck, to the left of the steering column. The turn signal flasher and hazard warning flasher plug into the fuse block. Each fuse receptacle is marked as to the circuits it protects and the correct amperage. In-line fuses are also used to protect some circuits. These are: ammeter, and auxiliary heater.

NOTE: A special heavy duty turn signal flasher is required to properly operate the turn signals when a trailer's lights are connected to the system.

Datsun/Nissan

GENERAL ENGINE SPECIFICATIONS

Year	Engine Displacement cc (cu. in.)	Carb Type	Advertised Horsepower @ rpm	Advertised Torque @ rpm (ft. lbs.)	Bore and Stroke (in.)	Advertised Compression Ratio	Oil Pressure (psi/idle)
'77–'80	1952 (119)	2 bbl	97 @ 5600	102 @ 3200	3.35 × 3.39	8.5:1	50–57
'81	2164 (132)	Diesel	61 @ 4000	102 @ 1800	3.27 × 3.94	21.6:1	60
	2187 (133.5)	2 bbl	98 @ 4000	117 @ 1800	3.43 × 3.62	8.5:1	60
'82–'83	2187 (133.5)	2 bbl	98 @ 4000	117 @ 1800	3.43 × 3.62	8.5:1	60
	2164 (132)	Diesel	61 @ 4000	102 @ 1800	3.27 × 3.94	21.6:1	60
'84	1952 (119)	2 bbl	97 @ 5600	102 @ 3200	3.35 × 3.39	9.0:1	60
	2389 (146)	2 bbl	103 @ 4800	134 @ 2800	3.50 × 3.78	8.3:1	60
	2488 (152)	Diesel	70 @ 4000	115 @ 2000	3.50 × 3.94	21.4:1	60

CAPACITIES

Year	Engine Displacement cc (cu in.)	Crankcase L (qts)		Transmission L (pts)			Transfer Case L (pts)	Rear Drive Axle L (pts)	Front Drive Axle L (pts)	Gas Tank L (gal)	Cooling System L (qts)	
		w/filter	wo/filter	4sp	5sp	Auto					Manual	Auto
'77	1952 (119.1)	4.3(4.5)	3.8(4.0)	1.7(3.6)	2.0(4.2)	5.5 (11.7)	—	1.0 (2.1)	—	45(11.8)	8.0 (8.5)	7.8 (8.2)
'78	1952 (119.1)	4.3(4.5)	3.8(4.0)	1.7(3.6)	2.0(4.2)	5.5 (11.7)	—	1.0 (2.1)	—	45(11.8)	8.9 (9.3)	8.7 (9.2)

CAPACITIES

Year	Engine Displacement cc (cu in.)	Crankcase L (qts)		Transmission L (pts)			Transfer Case L (pts)	Rear Drive Axle L (pts)	Front Drive Axle L (pts)	Gas Tank L (gal)	Cooling System L (qts)	
		w/filter	wo/filter	4sp	5sp	Auto					Manual	Auto
'79	1952 (119.1)	4.3(4.5)	3.8(4.0)	1.7(3.6)	2.0(4.2)	5.5 (11.7)	—	1.0 (2.1)	—	50(13.2)①	8.9 (9.3)	8.7 (9.2)
'80	1952 (119.1)	4.3(4.5)	3.8(4.0)	1.7(3.6)	2.0(4.2)	5.5 (11.7)	1.4(3.0)	1.25(2.6)	1.0(2.1)	50(13.2)①	8.9 (9.3)	8.7 (9.2)
'81 2-WD	2187 (133.5)	4.4(4.6)	3.9(4.12)	1.7(3.6)	2.0(4.2)	5.5 (11.7)	—	1.25(2.6)	—	50(13.2)①	10.2(10.75)	10.1(10.6)
4-WD	2187 (133.5)	4.2(4.5)	3.7(3.8)	1.7(3.6)	2.0(4.2)	5.5 (11.7)	1.4(3.0)	1.25(2.6)	1.0(2.1)	60(15.8)②	10.2(10.75)	10.1(10.6)
Diesel	2164 (132)	5.5(5.8)	—	—	2.0(4.2)	—	—	1.25(2.6)	—	60(15.8)②	—	—
'82–'83 2-WD	2187 (133.5)	4.4(4.6)	3.9(4.12)	1.7(3.6)	2.0(4.2)	5.5 (11.7)	—	1.25(2.6)	—	50(13.25)①	10.2(10.75)	10.1(10.6)
4-WD	2187 (133.5)	4.2(4.5)	3.7(3.8)	1.7(3.6)	2.0(4.2)	5.5 (11.7)	1.4(3.0)	1.25(2.6)	1.0(2.12)	60(15.8)②	10.2(10.75)	10.1(10.6)
Diesel	2164 (132)	6.0(6.4)③	—	—	2.0(4.2)	—	—	1.25(2.6)	—	50(13.25)①	9.9(10.5)	—
'84 2-WD	1952(119) 2389(146)	4.1(4.3)	3.6(3.9)	—	2.0(4.2)	5.5 (11.7)	—	1.25(2.6)④	—	50(13.25)①	10.2(10.75)	9.4 (10)
4-WD	1952(119) 2389(146)	4.3(4.5)	3.8(4.0)	—	2.0(4.2)	—	1.4(3.0)	1.25(2.6)	1.0(2.12)	60(15.8)②	10.2(10.75)	—
Diesel	2488(152)	5.1(5.3)	4.6(4.8)	—	2.0(4.2)	—	—	1.25(2.6)	—	50(13.25)①	10.5(11.1)	—

① Long bed: 64(16.8)
② Longbed w/4-WD: 75(19.8)
③ '83:5.2(5.5)
④ With dual rear wheels:1.30(2.7)
—Not applicable

DIESEL ENGINE TUNE-UP SPECIFICATIONS

Year	Injector Opening Pressure (psi)	Low Idle (rpm)	Dashpot Speed (rpm)	Valve Clearance (in.) Intake	Valve Clearance (in.) Exhaust	Intake Valve Opens (deg.)	Injection Timing rpm	Firing Order
'81–'83	1422.5	550–700	1280–1350	.014	.014	28	20 BTDC	1-3-4-2
'84	1422.5	650–800	1280–1350	.014	.014	28	18 BTDC	1-3-4-2

GASOLINE ENGINE TUNE-UP SPECIFICATIONS

Year	Engine Displacement cu in. (cc)	Spark Plug Type	Spark Plug Gap (in.)	Distributor Point Dwell (deg)	Distributor Point Gap (in.)	Ignition Timing (deg) MT	Ignition Timing (deg) AT	Intake Valve Opens (deg)	Fuel Pump Pressure (psi)	Compression Pressure (psi)▲	Idle Speed (rpm) MT	Idle Speed (rpm) AT	Valve Clearance (in.)● In	Valve Clearance (in.)● Ex
'77	4-119 (1952)	BP6ES④	0.033⑤	52	0.020⑥	12B③	12B	16B	3.0–3.8	171②	750	650①	0.010	0.012
'78	4-119 (1952)	BP6ES-11	0.041	—	⑥	12B	12B	16B	3.0–3.9⑦	171②	600	600①	0.010	0.012
'79	4-119 (1952)	BP6ES-11	0.041	—	⑧	12B	12B	16B	3.0–3.9⑦	171②	650	630①	0.010	0.012
'80	4-119 (1952)	BP6ES-11	0.041	—	⑧	12B⑨	12B⑨	16B	3.0–3.9⑦	171②	600	600	0.010	0.012
'81	4-133.5 (2187)	BP6ES⑩	0.033	—	⑧	5B	5B	16B	3.0–3.9	171②	650⑪	650	0.012	0.012
'82–'83	4-133.5 (2187)	⑫	0.033	—	⑧	3B	3B	16B	3.0–3.9	171②	650⑪	650	0.012	0.012

GASOLINE ENGINE TUNE-UP SPECIFICATIONS

Year	Engine Displacement cu in. (cc)	Spark Plug Type	Spark Plug Gap (in.)	Distributor Point Dwell (deg)	Distributor Point Gap (in.)	Ignition Timing (deg) MT	Ignition Timing (deg) AT	Intake Valve Opens (deg)	Fuel Pump Pressure (psi)	Compression Pressure (psi)▲	Idle Speed (rpm) MT	Idle Speed (rpm) AT	Valve Clearance (in.)● In	Valve Clearance (in.)● Ex
'84	4-119 (1952)	⑫	0.033	—	⑧	5B	—	16B	2.7–3.4	171②	600	—	0.012	0.012
	4-146 (2389)	⑫	0.033	—	⑧	3B	3B	16B	2.7–3.4	171②	650⑪	650	0.012	0.012

NOTE: Part numbers in this chart are not recommendations by Chilton for any product by brand name.

● Measured with engine hot
▲ Lowest reading must be at least 80% of the highest
B Before top dead center
① Transmission in Drive
② 128 psi minimum
③ 10° B in California

④ BP6ES-11, Transistor ignition; BPR6ES, Canada, 1977 and later with conventional ignition
⑤ 0.041, Transistor ignition
⑥ 0.008–0.016, Transistor ignition air gap
⑦ 4.6 or less with electric fuel pump (air conditioned models)

⑧ 0.012—0.020, Transistor ignition air gap
⑨ Calif. Heavy Duty models: 10B
⑩ Canada: BPR6ES
⑪ 4-WD: 800
⑫ Intake side: BPR6ES
   Exhaust side: BPR5ES

FIRING ORDERS

NOTE: To avoid confusion, always replace spark plug wires one at a time.

L20B firing order: 1-3-4-2

SD22,SD25 firing order: 1-3-4-2

Z20, Z22, Z24 firing order: 1-3-4-2

CRANKSHAFT AND CONNECTING ROD SPECIFICATIONS

(All measurements given in in.)

Year	Engine Displacement cc (cu in.)	Crankshaft Main Brg Journal Dia	Crankshaft Main Brg Oil Clearance	Crankshaft Shaft End-Play	Thrust on No.	Connecting Rod Journal Dia	Connecting Rod Oil Clearance	Connecting Rod Side Clearance
'77–'78	1952 (119)	2.3599–2.3604	0.0008–0.0024	0.0020–0.0071	3	1.9670–1.9675	0.0010–0.0020	0.008–0.012
'79–'80	1952 (119)	2.3599–2.3604	0.0008–0.0026	0.0020–0.0071	3	1.9670–1.9675	0.0009–0.0026	0.008–0.012
'81	2164 (132)	2.7918–2.7988	0.0013–0.0038	0.0024–0.0094	3	2.0840–2.0906	0.0013–0.0038	0.0039–0.0079
	2187 (133.5)	2.1631–2.1636	0.0008–0.0024	0.0021–0.0070	3	1.9670–1.9675	0.0010–0.0022	0.008–0.012

CRANKSHAFT AND CONNECTING ROD SPECIFICATIONS

(All measurements given in in.)

Year	Engine Displacement cc (cu in.)	Crankshaft Main Brg Journal Dia	Main Brg Oil Clearance	Shaft End-Play	Thrust on No.	Connecting Rod Journal Dia	Oil Clearance	Side Clearance
'82–'83	2164 (132)	2.7916–2.7921	0.0014–0.0037	0.0024–0.0055	3	2.0832–2.0837	0.0014–0.0034	0.004–0.008
	2187 (133.5)	2.1631–2.1636	0.0008–0.0024	0.0020–0.0071	3	1.9670–1.9675	0.0010–0.0022	0.008–0.012
'84	1952 (119)	2.1631–2.1636	0.0008–0.0024	0.0020–0.0071	3	1.9670–1.9675	0.0005–0.0021	0.008–0.012
	2389 (146)	2.1631–2.1636	0.0008–0.0024	0.0020–0.0071	3	1.9670–1.9675	0.0005–0.0021	0.008–0.012
	2488 (152)	2.7916–2.7921	0.0014–0.0034	0.0024–0.0055	3	2.0832–2.0837	0.0014–0.0032	0.004–0.008

VALVE SPECIFICATIONS

Year	Engine Displacement cc (cu in.)	Seat Angle (deg)	Face Angle (deg)	Spring Test Pressure (lbs. @ in.) Outer	Inner	Free Length (in.) Outer	Inner	Stem-to-Guide Clearance (in.) Intake	Exhaust	Stem Diameter (in.) Intake	Exhaust
'77–'80	1952 (119)	45	45①	47 @ 1.58	27 @ 1.38	1.97	1.77	0.0008–0.0021	0.0016–0.0029	0.3139	0.3131
'81	2164 (132)	45.5	44.5	33 @ 1.634	—	1.929	—	0.0006–0.0018	0.0016–0.0028	0.3137–0.3143	0.3137–0.3143
	2187 (133.5)	45.5	44.5	51 @ 1.575	24 @ 1.378	1.959	1.736	0.0008–0.0021	0.0016–0.0029	0.3136–0.3142	0.3128–0.3134
'82–'83	2164 (132)	45.5	44.5	134.7 @ 1.197	—	1.9764	—	0.0006–0.0018	0.0016–0.0028	0.3138–0.3144	0.3128–0.3134
	2187 (133.5)	45.5	44.5	115.3 @ 1.180	57 @ 0.98	1.9594	1.7362	0.0008–0.0021	0.0016–0.0029	0.3136–0.3142	0.3128–0.3134
'84	1952 (119)	45.5	44.5	115.3 @ 1.180	57 @ 0.98	1.959	1.7362	0.0008–0.0021	0.0016–0.0029	0.3136–0.3142	
	2389 (146)	45.5	44.5	115.3 @ 1.180	57 @ 0.98	1.959	1.7362	0.0008–0.0021	0.0016–0.0029	0.3136–0.3142	
	2488 (152)	45.5	44.5	148 @ 1.224	—	1.982	—	0.0006–0.0018	0.0016–0.0028	0.3138–0.3144	

① 45°30 '78–'79

PISTON AND RING SPECIFICATIONS

All measurements are given in inches.

Year	Engine Disp. (cu in.)	Piston-to-Bore Clearance	Ring Gap Top Compression	Bottom Compression	Oil Control	Ring Side Clearance Top Compression	Bottom Compression	Oil Control
'77–'80	1952 (119)	0.0010–0.0018	0.0098–0.0157	0.0118–0.0197	0.0118–0.0354	0.0016–0.0029	0.0012–0.0028	Snug
'81	2187 (133.5)	0.0010–0.0018	0.0098–0.0157	0.0059–0.0118	0.0118–0.0354	0.0016–0.0029	0.0012–0.0025	Snug
	2164 (132)	0.0047–0.0075	0.0118–0.0197	0.0118–0.0197	0.0118–0.0197	0.0024–0.0039	0.0016–0.0031①	0.0008–0.0024

PISTON AND RING SPECIFICATIONS

All measurements are given in inches.

| Year | Engine Disp. (cu in.) | Piston-to-Bore Clearance | Ring Gap | | | Ring Side Clearance | | |
			Top Compression	Bottom Compression	Oil Control	Top Compression	Bottom Compression	Oil Control
'82–'83	2187 (133.5)	0.0010–0.0018	0.0098–0.0157	0.0059–0.0118	0.0118–0.0354	0.0016–0.0029	0.0012–0.0025	Snug
	2164 (132)	0.0016–0.0043	0.0118–0.0177	0.0079–0.0138	0.0059–0.0118	0.0024–0.0039	0.0016–0.0031①	0.0008–0.0024
'84	1952 (119)	0.0010–0.0018	0.0098–0.0157	0.0059–0.0118	0.0118–0.0354	0.0016–0.0029	0.0012–0.0025	Snug
	2389 (146)	0.0010–0.0018	0.0098–0.0157	0.0059–0.0118	0.0118–0.0354	0.0016–0.0029	0.0012–0.0025	Snug
	2488 (152)	0.0031–0.0041	0.0118–0.0177	0.0079–0.0138	0.0059–0.0118	0.0024–0.0039	0.0016–0.0031①	0.0008–0.0024

① Diesel: 2nd and 3rd rings

TORQUE SPECIFICATIONS

(All readings in ft. lbs. unless noted)

| Year | Engine Displacement cc (cu in.) | Cylinder Head Bolts | Rod Bearing Bolts | Main Bearing Bolts | Crankshaft Pulley Bolts | Flywheel to Crankshaft Bolts | Manifolds | |
							Intake	Exhaust
'77–'80	1952 (119)	61	37	37	102	109	11	11
'81–'83	2187 (133.5)	51–58	33–40	33–40	87–116	101–116	12–15	12–16
	2164 (132)	94 large 40 small	36–40	109–116①	217–239	33–36	11–13	11–13
'84	1952 (119)	②	33–40	33–40	87–116	101–116	12–15	12–15
	2389 (146)	②	33–40	33–40	87–116	101–116	12–15	12–15
	2488 (152)	94 large 40 small	49–52	123–127	217–239	108–123	11–13	11–13

① 1982–'83: 123–127
② Five step torque procedure: Step 1; 22 ft. lbs., Step 2; 58 ft. lbs., Step 3; loosen all bolts completely, Step 4; 22 ft. lbs., Step 5; 54 to 61 ft. lbs.

BATTERY AND STARTER SPECIFICATIONS

| Year | Engine Displacement cc (cu in.) | Battery | | | Starter | | | | | | Brush Spring Tension (oz) |
| | | | | | Lock Test | | | No Load Test | | | |
		Amp Hour Capacity	Volts	Ground	Amps	Volts	Torque (ft. lbs.)	Amps	Volts	RPM	
'77–'80	1952 (119)	①	12	Neg	Not Recommended			60—	12	7000+②	56
'81–'83	2187 (133.5)	①	12	Neg	Not Recommended			60③	11.5④	6000–7000⑤	56
	2164 (132)	①	12	Neg	800	5.0	21.0	150	12	3500	123.2
'84	1952 (119)	①	12	Neg	Not Recommended			60③	11.5	6000–7000⑤	56
	2389 (146)	①	12	Neg	Not Recommended			60③	11.5	6000–7000⑤	56

BATTERY AND STARTER SPECIFICATIONS

Year	Engine Displacement cc (cu in.)	Battery			Starter						Brush Spring Tension (oz)
		Amp Hour Capacity	Volts	Ground	Lock Test			No Load Test			
					Amps	Volts	Torque (ft. lbs.)	Amps	Volts	RPM	
	2488 (152)	①	12	Neg	Not Recommended			150	12	3500	123.2

① 60 and 80 amp hour batteries were available
② 6000+ if equipped with automatic transmission
③ Canada: 100
④ Canada: 11.0
⑤ Canada: 3900

ALTERNATOR AND REGULATOR SPECIFICATIONS

Year	Alternator Manufacturer and/or Part Number	Output @ Alternator rpm	Charge Indicator Relay			Voltage Regulator			Regulated Voltage
			Back Gap (in.)	Air Gap (in.)	Point Gap (in.)	Back Gap (in.)	Air Gap (in.)	Point Gap (in.)	
'77	Hitachi LT135-36B	28 @ 2500	—	0.035	0.020	—	0.032	0.016	14.3–15.3
	LT138-01B①	30 @ 2500							
'78–'80	Hitachi LT135-44	27.5 @ 2500	—Transistorized Non-Adjustable Relay—						14.4–15.0
	LR138-01①	30.0 @ 2500							
'81	Hitachi LR150-98	50 @ 5000	—Transistorized Non-Adjustable Relay—						14.4–15.0
	LR160-78	60 @ 5000							
	LR150-52	50 @ 5000							
	LR160-78	60 @ 5000							
'82	Hitachi LR150-98B	40 @ 2500	—Transistorized Non-Adjustable Relay—						14.4–15.0
	LR160-78 & 78B	50 @ 2500							
	LR160-97B	52 @ 2500							
'83	Hitachi LR150-98B	40 @ 2500	—Transistorized Non-Adjustable Relay—						14.4–15.0
	LR160-78 & 78B	50 @ 2500							
	LR160-97B	42 @ 2500							
	LR150-133E	42 @ 2500							
'84	Hitachi LR150-98B	40 @ 2500	—Transistorized Non-Adjustable Relay—						14.4–15.0
	LR160-78B	50 @ 2500							
	LR150-177	50 @ 2500							
	LR160-120	50 @ 2500							
	LR150-403	42 @ 2500							
	LR155-401	50 @ 2500							

① With air conditioning
—Not applicable

BRAKE SPECIFICATIONS

(All measurements are given in in.)

Year	Master Cylinder Bore	Wheel Cylinder or Caliper Bore		Piston-to-Bore Clearance	Brake Drum or Rotor Diameter		Minimum Lining Thickness	Brake Disc	
		Front	Rear		Front	Rear		Minimum Thickness	Maximum Run-out
'77	0.750	0.750	0.750	0.006	10.00	10.00	0.0394	—	—
'78–'79	0.813	2.125	0.625	0.006	10.67	10.00	0.08 (disc) 0.06 (drum)	0.413	0.0059
'80–'83	0.875	2.125	0.625	0.006	10.67	10.00	0.08 (disc) 0.06 (drum)	0.413	0.0059
'84	0.9375	2.386	0.687①	—	9.84②	10.00③	0.08 (disc) 0.06 (drum)	0.787	0.0028

① 4WD: 0.625   ② 4WD: 10.50   ③ With dual rear wheels: 8.66

IDENTIFICATION

Vehicle

The vehicle identification plate is located on the hood ledge in the engine compartment. The plate gives the vehicle type, engine capacity, maximum engine horsepower, wheelbase, engine number, and truck serial numbers.

The chassis serial number is stamped on the upper face of the right-side frame member.

The vehicle identification model codes may be interpreted as follows:

• 1977–79: Four prefix and four suffix letters are used. The first letter is a K or a

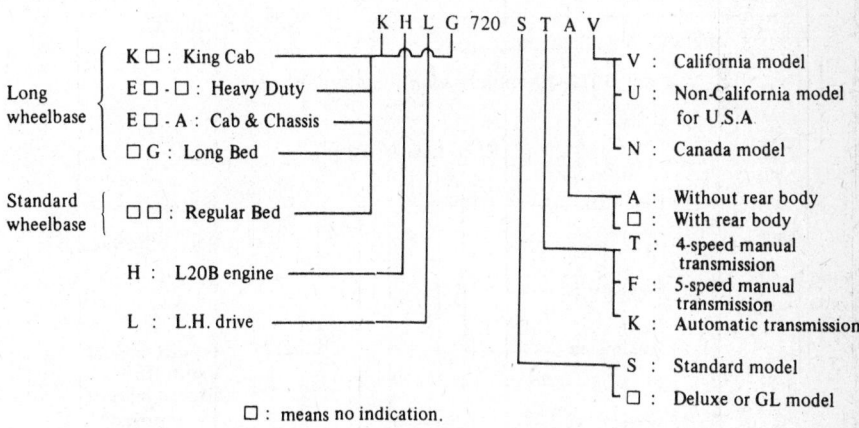

□ : means no indication.

1980–81 2-wd vehicle identification number

Vehicle identification plate locations

K H L G 620 K T U V

V : California model
N : Canada model
U : Destined for U.S.A. and Canada
T : Floor shift vehicle
K : Automatic transmission
F : 5-speed manual transmission
☐ : 4-speed manual transmission
G : Long wheelbase model
☐ : Except long wheelbase model
L : Left-hand drive
H : Equipped with L20B engine
K : Deluxe Cab model

Note: ☐ means no indication.

1977–79 vehicle identification number

K H L G Y 720 T V

Long wheelbase
{
  K☐ : King Cab
  ☐G : Long Bed
}

Standard wheelbase
{
  ☐☐ : Regular Bed
}

H : L20B engine
L : L.H. drive
Y : 4-wheel drive

V : California model
U : Non-California model for U.S.A.
N : Canada model

T : 4-speed manual transmission
F : 5-speed manual transmission

☐ : means no indication.

1981 4-wd vehicle identification number

blank; K indicates a king cab model. The second letter is an H, for the L20B engine. The third letter is L, for left hand drive. The fourth letter is either a G or a blank; G is for long-wheelbase (long bed) trucks. The next three numbers are the model number, 620. The first suffix letter is either a K, an F, or a blank; K indicates automatic transmission, F indicates a 5-speed, a blank indicates a 4-speed. The second and third suffix letters, T and U, have the same meaning as in earlier years. The last letter is either a V, an N, or a blank; V indicates a California model, N indicates a Canada model, a blank indicates a 49 States model.

1980–84: A four letter prefix for 2-wheel drive models and a five letter prefix for 4-wheel drive models followed by a three digit code denoting the truck series is used. The suffix for these years is either four letters for 2-wheel drive or two letters for 4-wheel drive. See the illustrations for an explanation of these serial numbers.

Engine

The gasoline engine serial number is stamped on the right-side of the cylinder block, just below the number four spark plug. The diesel engine serial number is stamped on the

Manual transmission serial number location

Prefix and suffix destinations

K N L G Y 720 S T V V/S

Long wheelbase
{
  K☐ : King Cab
  E☐-☐ : Heavy Duty
  E☐-A : Cab & Chassis
  ☐G : Long Bed
}

Standard wheelbase
{
  ☐☐ : Regular Bed
}

F : Z20 engine
N : Z24 engine
J : SD25 engine

L : L.H. drive

Y : 4WD (4-wheel drive)
☐ : 2WD (2-wheel drive)

A : Cab & Chassis (Combined with E prefix and W suffix)
F : 5-speed manual transmission (Combined with T suffix)
V : California model
U : Non-California model for U.S.A.
N : Canada model

T : Manual transmission
K : Automatic transmission

S : Standard model
J : GL model
☐ : DX model
W : Dual wheel (Combined with E prefix)

☐: means no indications.

1982–84 vehicle identification number

left side of the block, just in front of the starter.

Gasoline engine

Diesel engine

Engine serial number location

Automatic transmission serial number location

Transfer case identification number location

Transmission

The transmission serial number is stamped on the front upper face of the transmission case on manual transmissions, or on the right-side of the transmission case on automatic transmissions.

TUNE-UP

NOTE: 1977 and later Datsun trucks sold in California, and all 1978 and later models sold in the U.S. use a fully transistorized ignition system. 1977 49 States and Canada models use the single breaker points system.

Breaker Points and Condenser

INSPECTION

1. Disconnect the high-tension wire from the top of the distributor and the coil.

2. The distributor cap is retained by two spring clips. Insert a screwdriver under their ends and release them. Lift off the cap with the spark plug wires attached. Inspect the inside of the cap. Wipe it clean with a rag and check for burned contacts, cracks and carbon tracks. A carbon track shows as a dark line running from one terminal to another. It cannot be successfully removed, so replace the cap if it has one of these. Generally, a cap and rotor will last 36,000 miles.

3. Remove the rotor from the distributor shaft by pulling it straight up. Examine the condition of the rotor. If it is cracked or the metal tip is excessively worn or burned, it should be replaced. Clean the metal tip with a clean cloth, but don't file it.

4. Pry open the contacts of the points with a screwdriver and check the condition of the contacts. If they are excessively worn, burned or pitted, they should be replaced.

5. If the points are in good condition, adjust them and replace the rotor and the distributor cap. If the points need to be replaced, follow the replacement procedure given next.

REPLACEMENT

1. Remove the cap and rotor as outlined in steps 1–3 of the preceding section.

2. Loosen the two screws securing the points. Use a magnetic screwdriver to avoid losing a screw down the distributor. Loosen the screw in the side of the distributor and slip the points wire out. Remove the point set.

To remove the distributor, first note and mark the position of the distributor on the

Arrow indicates the feeler gauge used to measure point gap

small timing scale on the front of the distributor. Then mark the position of the rotor in relation to the distributor body. Do this by simply replacing the rotor on the distributor shaft and marking the spot on the distributor body where the rotor is pointing. Remove the small bolt at the rear of the distributor, and lift the distributor out of the block. DO NOT CRANK THE ENGINE WITH THE DISTRIBUTOR REMOVED.

3. The condenser is held in place by the same screw as the points mounting screw, and its lead is attached at the same place as the points wire. Simply remove the condenser.

4. Before installing the new points and condenser, place a matchhead-sized dab of grease on the distributor shaft cam and smear it evenly around the cam. Do not use oil, because it will lead to rapid point burning.

5. Install the new points set and condenser. Tighten the condenser mounting screws, but leave the points screws slightly loose.

6. Check that the faces of the points meet squarely. If not, the *fixed* mount can be bent slightly with gentle force and a set of needlenose pliers. Do not bend the movable contact.

7. The point gap must be adjusted next. The gap is adjusted with the rubbing block of the points resting on one of the four high spots of the distributor cam. To get it there, the engine can be rotated by bumping the starter with the ignition key, or the crankshaft can be turned with a wrench on the crankshaft pulley bolt; this is easier to do with the spark plugs removed.

If the distributor shaft can be rotated until the points blocks are resting on the high spots of the cam. It won't matter if you move the distributor shaft; it can only go back into the engine one way. Just note the position from which it is moved, and move it back there prior to replacing the distributor in the engine.

8. Insert a 0.020 in. thick flat feeler gauge between the points. A slight drag should be felt. If no drag can be felt, or if the gauge cannot be inserted at all, insert a screwdriver into the eccentric adjusting screw, or into the notch provided for adjustment, and use it to open or close the

gap between the points until it is correct.

9. When the gap is set, tighten the points screws, and then recheck the gap. Sometimes it takes three or four tries to get it correct, so don't feel frustrated if they seem to move around on you a little. It is not easy to feel the correct gap, either. Use gauges 0.002 in. larger and smaller than 0.020 as a test. If the points are spread slightly by a 0.022 in. gauge, and not touched at all by a 0.018 in. gauge, the setting should be right.

10. After all the adjustments are complete, pull a clean piece of tissue or a white business card between the points to clear any bits of grit.

11. Replace the rotor and distributor cap, and snap on the clips. If you have a dwell meter (recommended) you should next set the dwell. Otherwise, go on to the ignition timing.

ADJUSTMENT WITH A DWELL METER

The dwell angle is the number of degrees of distributor cam rotation through which the points remain closed (conducting electricity). Increasing the point gap decreases dwell, while decreasing the gap increases dwell.

The dwell angle may be checked with the distributor cap and rotor installed and the engine running, or with the cap and rotor removed and the engine cranking at starter speed. The meter gives a constant reading with the engine running. With the engine cranking, the meter will fluctuate between zero degrees dwell and the maximum figure for that setting. Never attempt to adjust the points when the ignition is on, or you may receive a shock.

1. Connect a meter as per the manufacturer's instructions (usually one lead to the distributor terminal of the coil and the other lead to a ground). Zero the meter, if necessary.

NOTE: If the dwell meter does not have a four cylinder scale, multiply the eight cylinder reading by two.

2. Check the dwell by either the cranking method, or with the engine running. If the setting is incorrect, the points must be adjusted.

─── CAUTION ───
Keep your hands, hair and clothing clear of the engine fan and pulleys. Be sure the wires from the dwell meter are routed out of the way. If the engine is running, block the front wheels, put the transmission in Neutral, and set the parking brake.

3. To change the dwell angle, turn the ignition off, loosen the points hold down screw and adjust the point gap; increase the gap to decrease dwell, and vice versa. Tighten the hold down screw and check the dwell angle with the engine cranking. If it seems to be correct, replace the cap and

rotor and check dwell with the engine running. Readjust as necessary.

4. Run the engine speed up to about 2,500 rpm, and then let the speed drop abruptly; the dwell reading should not change. If it does, a worn distributor shaft, bushing or cam, or a worn breaker plate is indicated. The parts must be inspected and replaced, if necessary.

5. After adjusting dwell angle, go on to the Ignition Timing section following. Ignition timing must be checked after adjusting the point gap, as a 1° increase in dwell results in an ignition timing retard of 2°, and vice versa.

Electronic Ignition

Datsun pick-ups sold in California beginning in 1977 were equipped with electronic ignition, and all 1978 and later trucks are equipped with the system. The 1978 system differs somewhat from the earlier system; the 1979 and later system is markedly different.

The electronic ignition differs from its conventional counterpart only in the distributor component area. The secondary side of the ignition system is the same as a conventional breaker points system.

Located in the distributor, in addition to the normal ignition rotor, is a four spoke rotor (reluctor) which rests on the distributor shaft where the breaker points cam is found on earlier systems. A pick-up coil, consisting of a magnet, coil, and wiring, rests on the "breaker plate" next to the reluctor. The system also uses a transistor ignition unit, located on the right side of the firewall in the passenger compartment, through 1978, 1979 and later models have an integrated circuit (IC) ignition unit, which is mounted on the side of the distributor. In addition, 1979 and later models use a ring-type pick-up coil, which surrounds the reluctor, rather than the arm-type coil used through 1978.

When a reluctor spoke is not aligned with the pick-up coil, it generates large lines of flux between itself, the magnet, and the pick-up coil. This large flux variation results in a high generated voltage in the pick-up coil, preventing current from flowing to the pick-up coil. When a reluctor spoke

1977 air gap adjustment

lines up with the pick-up coil, the flux variation is low—thus, zero voltage is generated, allowing current to flow to the pick-up coil. Ignition primary current is then cut off by the electronic unit, allowing the field in the ignition coil to collapse, inducing high secondary voltage in the conventional manner. The high voltage then flows through the distributor to the spark plug, as usual.

Because no points or condenser are used, and because dwell is determined by the electronic unit, no adjustments are necessary. Ignition timing is checked in the usual way, but unless the distributor is disturbed it is not likely to ever change very much.

Service consists of inspection of the distributor cap, rotor, and ignition wires, replacing when necessary. These parts can be expected to last for at least 40,000 miles. In addition, the reluctor air gap should be checked periodically.

1. The distributor cap is held on by two clips. Release them with a screwdriver and lift the cap straight up and off, with the wires attached. Inspect the cap for cracks, carbon tracks, or a worn center contact. Replace it if necessary, transferring the wires one at a time from the old cap to the new.

COLOR CODE

B :BLACK
BW :BLACK WITH WHITE STRIPE
R :RED
G :GREEN
L :BLUE

Electronic control unit connection: upper 1977, lower 1978 and later

2. Pull the ignition rotor (not the spoked reluctor) straight up to remove. Replace it if its contacts are worn, burned, or pitted. Do not file the contacts. To replace, press it firmly onto the shaft. It only goes on one way, so be sure it is fully seated.

3. Before replacing the ignition rotor, check the reluctor air gap. Use a non-magnetic feeler gauge. Rotate the engine until a reluctor spoke is aligned with the pick-up coil (either bump the engine around with

the starter, or turn it with a wrench on the crankshaft pulley bolt). The gap should measure 0.008–0.016 in. through 1978, or 0.012–0.020 in. for 1979 and later. Adjustment, if necessary, is made by loosening the pick-up coil mounting screws and shifting its position on the "breaker plate" either closer to or farther from the reluctor. On 1979 and later models, center the pick-up coil (ring) around the reluctor. Tighten the screws and recheck the gap.

4. Inspect the wires for cracks or brittleness. Replace them one at a time to prevent crosswiring, carefully pressing the replacement wires into place. The cores of electronic wires are more susceptible to breakage than those of standard wires, so treat them gently.

TROUBLESHOOTING

1977–78

The main differences between the 1977 and 1978 systems are: (1) the 1977 system uses an external ballast resistor located next to the ignition coil, and (2) the earlier system uses a wiring harness with individual eyelet connectors to the electronic unit, while the later system uses a multiple plug connector. You will need an accurate voltmeter and ohmmeter for these tests, which must be performed in the order given.

1. Check all connections for corrosion, looseness, breaks, etc., and correct if necessary. Clean and gap the spark plugs.

2a. Disconnect the harness (connector or plug) from the electronic unit. Turn the ignition switch On. Set the voltmeter to the DC 50V range. Connect the positive (+) voltmeter lead to the black/white wire terminal, and the negative (−) lead to the black wire terminal. Battery voltage should be obtained. If not, check the black/white and black wires for continuity; check the battery terminals for corrosion; check the battery state of charge.

2b. Next, connect the voltmeter + lead to the blue wire and the − lead to the black wire. Battery voltage should be obtained. If not, check the blue wire for continuity; check the ignition coil terminals for corrosion or looseness; check the coil for continuity. On 1977 models, also check the external ballast resistor.

3. Disconnect the distributor harness wires from the ignition coil ballast resistor on 1977 models, leaving the ballast resistor-to-coil wires attached. On 1978 models, disconnect the ignition coil wires. Connect the leads of an ohmmeter to the ballast resistor outside terminals (at each end) through 1977; resistance should be 1.6–2.0 ohms. In 1978, connect the ohmmeter to the coil terminals: resistance should be 0 ohms. If more than 2.0 ohms, 1977, or 1.8 ohms, 1978, replace the coil.

4. Disconnect the harness from the electronic control unit. Connect an ohmmeter to the red and green wire terminals. Resistance should be 720 ohms. If far more

or far less, replace the distributor pick-up coil.

5. Disconnect the anti-dieseling solenoid connector. Connect a voltmeter to the red and green terminals of the electronic control harness. When the starter is cranked, the needle should deflect slightly. If not, replace the distributor pick-up coil.

6. Reconnect the ignition coil and the electronic control unit. Leave the anti-dieseling solenoid wire disconnected. Unplug the high ension lead (coil to distributor) from the distributor and hold it ⅛–¼ in. from the cylinder head with a pair of insulated pliers and a heavy glove. When the engine is cranked, a spark should be observed. If not, check the lead, and replace the electronic control unit.

7. Reconnect all wires:

1977: connect the voltmeter + lead to the blue electronic control harness connector and the − lead to the black wire. The harness should be attached to the control unit.

1978: connect the voltmeter + lead to the − terminal of the ignition coil and the − lead to ground.

As soon as the ignition switch is turned ON, the meter should indicate battery voltage. If not, replace the electronic control unit.

1979 and Later

1. Make a check of the power supply circuit. Turn the ignition OFF. Disconnect the connector from the top of the IC unit. Turn the ignition ON. Measure the voltage at each terminal of the connector in turn by touching the probe of the positive lead of the voltmeter to one of the terminals, and touching the probe of the negative lead of the voltmeter to a ground, such as the engine. In each case, battery voltage should be indicated. If not, check all wiring, the ignition switch, and all connectors for breaks, corrosion, discontinuity, etc., and repair as necessary.

2. Check the primary windings off the ignition coil. Turn the ignition OFF. Disconnect the harness connector from the negative coil terminals. Use an ohmmeter to measure the resistance between the positive and negative coil terminals. If resistance is 0.84–1.02 ohms, the coil is OK. Replace if far from this range.

If the power supply, circuits, wiring, and coil are in good shape, check the IC unit and pick-up coil, as follows:

3. Turn the ignition OFF. Remove the distributor cap and ignition rotor. Use an ohmmeter to measure the resistance between the two terminals of the pick-up coil, where they attach to the IC unit. Measure the resistance by reversing the polarity of the probes. If approximately 400 ohms are indicated, the pick-up coil is OK, but the IC unit is bad and must be replaced. If other than 400 ohms are measured, go to the next step.

4. Be certain the two pin connector to the IC unit is secure. Turn the ignition ON.

Measure the voltage at the ignition coil negative terminal. Turn the ignition OFF.

—————— CAUTION ——————

Remove the tester probe from the coil negative terminal before switching the ignition OFF, to prevent burning out the tester.

If zero voltage is indicated, the IC unit is bad and must be replaced. If battery voltage is indicated, proceed.

5. Remove the IC unit from the distributor:

a. Disconnect the battery ground (negative) cable.

b. Remove the distributor cap and ignition rotor.

c. Disconnect the harness connector at the top of the IC unit.

d. Remove the two screws securing the IC unit to the distributor.

e. Disconnect the two pick-up coil wires from the IC unit.

—————— CAUTION ——————

Pull the connectors free with a pair of needlenosed pliers. Do not pull on the wires to detach the connectors.

f. Remove the IC unit.

6. Measure the resistance between the terminals of the pick-up coil. It should be approximately 400 ohms. If so, the pick-up coil is OK, and the IC unit is bad. If not approximately 400 ohms, the pick-up coil is bad and must be replaced.

7. With a new pick-up coil installed, install the IC unit. Check for a spark at one of the spark plugs. If a good spark is obtained, the IC unit is OK. If not, replace the IC unit.

Ignition Timing

NOTE: For diesel engine injection pump timing, see the fuel system section.

Ignition timing is the measurement, in degrees of crankshaft rotation, of the point at which the spark plugs fire in each of the cylinders. It is measured in degrees before or after Top Dead Center (TDC) of the compression stroke.

Because it takes a fraction of a second for the spark plug to ignite the mixture in the cylinder, the spark plug must fire a little before the piston reaches TDC. Otherwise, the mixture will not be completely ignited as the piston passes TDC and the full power of the explosion will not be used by the engine.

The timing measurement is given in degrees of crankshaft rotation before the piston reaches TDC (BTDC). If the setting for the ignition timing is 5° BTDC, the spark plug must fire 5° before each piston reaches TDC. This only holds true, however, when the engine is at idle speed.

As the engine speed increases, the pistons go faster. The spark plugs have to ignite the fuel even sooner if it is to be completely ignited when the piston reaches TDC.

T95

Ignition timing marks on the distributor

To do this, the distributor has a means to advance the timing of the spark as the engine speed increases. This is accomplished by centrifugal weights within the distributor and a vacuum diaphragm, mounted on the side of the distributor. On Datsun pick-ups, it is not necessary to disconnect the vacuum line from the diaphragm when the ignition timing is being set.

If the ignition is set too far advanced (BTDC), the ignition and expansion of the fuel in the cylinder will occur too soon and tend to force the piston down while it is still traveling up. This causes engine ping. If the ignition spark is set too far retarded, after TDC (ATDC), the piston will have already passed TDC and started on its way down when the fuel is ignited. This will cause the piston to be forced down for only a portion of its travel. This will result in poor engine performance and lack of power.

Timing marks consist of a notch on the rim of the crankshaft pulley and a scale of degrees attached to the front of the engine. The notch correpsonds to the position of the piston in the no. 1 cylinder. A stroboscopic (dynamic) timing light is used, which is hooked into the circuit of the no. 1 cylinder spark plug. Every time the spark plug fires, the timing light flashes. By aiming the timing light at the timing marks, the exact position of the piston within the cylinder can be read, since the stroboscopic flash makes the mark on the pulley appear to be standing still. Proper timing is indicated when the notch is aligned with the correct number on the scale. There are three basic types of timing light available. The first is a simple neon bulb with two wire connections (one for the spark plug and one for the plug wire, connecting the light in a series). This type of light is quite dim, and must be held closely to the marks to be seen, but it is quite inexpensive. The second type of light operates from the truck battery. Two alligator clips connect to the battery terminals, while a third wire connects to the spark plug with an adapter. This type of light is more expensive, but the xenon bulb provides a nice bright flash which can even be seen in sunlight. The third type replaces the battery source with 110 volt

house current. Some timing lights have other functions built into them, such as dwell meters, tachometers, or remote starting switches. These are convenient, in that they reduce the tangle of wires under the hood, but may duplicate the functions of tools you already have.

If your Datsun has electronic ignition, you should use a timing light with an inductive pickup. This pickup simply clamps onto the no. 1 plug wire, eliminating the adapter. It is not susceptible to crossfiring or false triggering, which may occur with a conventional light, due to the greater voltages produced by electronic ignition.

IGNITION TIMING ADJUSTMENT

NOTE: Refer to Fuel System for the procedure to time diesel engines

1. Set the dwell of the breaker points to the proper specification.
2. Locate the timing marks on the crankshaft pulley and the front of the engine.
3. Clean off the timing marks, so that you can see them.
4. Use chalk or white paint to color the mark on the crankshaft pulley and the mark on the scale which will indicate the correct timing when aligned with the notch on the crankshaft pulley.
5. Attach a tachometer to the engine.
6. Attach a timing light to the engine, according to the manufacturer's instructions. If the timing light has three wires, one, usually green or blue, is attached to the no. 1 spark plug with an adapter. The other wires are connected to the battery. The red wire goes to the positive side of the battery and the black wire is connected to the negative terminal of the battery.
7. Leave the vacuum line connected to the distributor vacuum diaphragm.
8. Check to make sure that all of the wires clear the fan and then start the engine. Allow the engine to reach normal operating temperature.

——————— CAUTION ———————
Block the front wheels and set the parking brake. Shift the manual transmission to Neutral or the automatic to Drive. Do not stand in front of the truck when making adjustments!

9. Adjust the idle to the correct setting.
10. Aim the timing light at the timing marks. If the marks which you put on the pulley and the engine are aligned when the light flashes, the timing is correct. Turn off the engine and remove the tachometer and the timing light. If the marks are not in alignment, proceed with the following steps.
11. Turn off the engine.
12. Loosen the distributor lockbolt just enough so that the distributor can be turned with a little effort.
13. Start the engine. Keep the wires of the timing light clear of the fan.

14. With the timing light aimed at the pulley and the marks on the engine, turn the distributor in the direction of rotor rotation to retard the spark, and in the opposite direction of rotor rotation to advance the spark. Align the marks on the pulley and the engine with the flashes of the timing light.
15. Tighten the distributor lockbolt and recheck the timing.

Valve Lash

Valve adjustment determines how far the valves enter the cylinder and how long they stay open and closed.

If the valve clearance is too large, part of the lift of the camshaft will be used in removing the excessive clearance. Consequently, the valve will not be opening for as long as it should. This condition has two effects; the valve train components will emit a tapping sound as they take up the excessive clearance and the engine will perform poorly because the valves don't open fully and allow the proper amount of gases to flow into and out of the engine.

If the valve clearance is too small, the intake valves and the exhaust valves will open too far and they will not fully seat on the cylinder head when they close. When a valve seats itself on the cylinder head, it does two things: it seals the combustion chamber so that none of the gases in the cylinder escape and it cools itself by transferring some of the heat it absorbs from the combustion in the cylinder to the cylinder head and to the engine's cooling system. If the valve clearance is too small, the engine will run poorly because of the gases escaping from the combustion chamber. The valves will also become overheated and will warp, since they cannot transfer heat unless they are touching the valve seat in the cylinder head.

NOTE: While all valve adjustments must be made as accurately as possible, it is better to have the valve adjustment slightly loose than slightly tight, as a burned valve may result from overly tight adjustments.

ADJUSTMENT

1. The valves are adjusted with the engine at normal operating temperature. Oil temperature, and the resultant parts expansion, is much more important than water temperature. Run the engine for at least fifteen minutes to ensure that all the parts have reached their full expansion. After the engine is warmed up, shut it off.
2. Purchase either a new gasket or some silicone gasket seal before removing the camshaft cover. Note the location of any wires and hoses which may interfere with cam cover removal, disconnect them and move them aside. Then remove the bolts which hold the cam cover in place and remove the cam cover.

3. Place a wrench on the crankshaft pulley bolt and turn the engine over until the valves for no. 1 cylinder are closed. If you have not done this before, it is a good idea to turn the engine over slowly several times and watch the valve action until you have a clear idea of just when the valve is closed.

NOTE: On all engine except the Z series, the valves are closed when both cam lobes are pointing up. On the Z series engines the valves are closed when the cam lobe points straight down.

4. Check the clearance of the intake and exhaust valves. You can differentiate between them by lining them up with the tubes of the intake and exhaust manifolds. The correct size feeler gauge should pass between the base circle of the cam and the rocker arm with just a slight drag. Be sure the feeler gauge is inserted *straight* and not on an angle.

5. If the valves need adjustment, loosen the locking nut and then adjust the clearance with the adjusting screw. You will probably find it necessary to hold the locking nut while you turn the adjuster. After you have the correct clearance, tighten the locking nut and recheck the clearance. Remember, it's better to have them too loose than too tight, especially exhaust valves.

NO. 1 CAM LOBE

Cam lobe pointing straight down—Z series engines

6. Repeat this procedure until you have checked and/or adjusted all the valves. Keep in mind that all that is necessary is to have the valves closed and the camshaft lobes pointing up. It is not particularly important what stroke the engine is on.

7. Install the cam cover gasket, the cam cover, and any wires and hoses which were removed.

Carburetor

This section contains only tune-up adjustment procedures for carburetors. Descriptions, adjustments, and overhaul procedures for carburetors can be found in the Fuel System section.

When the engine in your Datsun is running, the air-fuel mixture from the carburetor is being drawn into the engine by a partial vacuum which is created by the movement of the pistons downward on the intake stroke. The amount of air-fuel mixture that enters into the engine is controlled by the throttle plates in the bottom of the carburetor. When the engine is not running the throttle plates are closed, completely blocking off the bottom of the carburetor from the inside of the engine. The throttle plates are connected by the throttle linkage to the accelerator pedal in the passenger compartment of the Datsun. When you depress the pedal, you open the throttle plates in the carburetor to admit more air-fuel mixture to the engine.

When the engine is not running, the throttle plates are closed. When the engine is idling, it is necessary to have the throttle plates open slightly. To prevent having to hold your foot on the pedal when the engine is idling, an idle speed adjusting screw is added to the carburetor linkage.

The idle adjusting screw contacts a lever (throttle lever) on the outside of the carburetor. When the screw is turned, it either opens or closes the throttle plates of the carburetor, raising or lowering the idle speed of the engine. This screw is called the curb idle adjusting screw.

A special mixture circuit is incorporated into the carburetor to enable the engine to run smoothly at idle. This circuit is controlled by the mixture screw, which determines the amount of fuel admitted at idle.

IDLE SPEED AND MIXTURE ADJUSTMENT

1. Start the engine and run it until it reaches operating temperature.
2. Allow the engine idle speed to stabilize by running the engine at idle for at least one minute.
3. If it hasn't already been done, check and adjust the ignition timing to the proper setting.
4. Turn off the engine and connect a tachometer to the engine.
5. Disconnect and plug the air hose between the three way connector and the check valve, if equipped. Start the engine. With the transmission in Neutral, check the idle speed on the tachometer. If the reading on the tachometer is correct, turn the idle adjusting screw clockwise with a screwdriver to increase the idle speed and counterclockwise to decrease it.
6. With an automatic transmission in

1. Idle speed adjusting screw
2. Air/fuel mixture adjusting screw

Idle speed and mixture adjustments

Drive (wheels chocked and parking brake applied) or a manual transmission in Neutral, turn the mixture screw out until the engine rpm starts to drop due to an overly rich mixture.

7. Turn the screw in past the starting point until the engine rpm start to drop because of a too lean mixture. On 1977 models, turn the mixture screw in until the idle speed drops 60–70 rpm with manual transmission, or 15–25 rpm with automatic transmission (in Drive). On 1978 models, the rpm drop should be 45–55 rpm for all trucks. For 1979 and later the rpm drop should be 45–55 rpm with manual transmission, or 25–35 rpm with automatic transmission (in Drive). If the mixture limiter cap will not allow this adjustment, remove it, make the adjustment, and reinstall it.

8. Install the air hose. If the engine speed increases, reduce it with the idle speed screw.

NOTE: To be sure that the vehicle is complying with emission laws, have the exhaust checked with a "CO" meter. The percentages of CO should be 2% 1977, and 1% 1978–84 at idle speed.

NOTE: Idle limiter caps are installed on the mixture adjusting screws so that an incorrect adjustment cannot be made. If a satisfactory idle cannot be obtained within the range of the limiter caps or if the limiter caps prevent access to the mixture screws, remove them and make the adjustment as outlined above. Reinstall the limiter caps so that the cap can be turned only $\frac{1}{8}$ of a turn counterclockwise before it reaches the stop. Have the engine checked with a CO meter after making the adjustment.

ENGINE ELECTRICAL

Distributor

REMOVAL

1. Remove the high-tension wires from the distributor cap terminal towers, noting their positions to assure correct reassembly. Number the wires with pieces of adhesive tape if they are not already numbered.
2. Disconnect the distributor wiring harness.
3. Disconnect the vacuum line(s).
4. Unlatch the two distributor cap retaining clips and remove the distributor cap.
5. Note the position of the rotor in relation to the base. Scribe a mark on the base of the distributor and on the engine block to facilitate reinstallation. Align the marks with the direction the metal tip of the rotor is pointing.
6. Remove the bolt which holds the

1. Cap assembly
2. Rotor head assembly
3. Roll pin
4. Reluctor
5. Pick-up coil
6. Contactor
7. Breaker plate assembly
8. Packing
9. Rotor shaft
10. Governor spring
11. Governor weight
12. Shaft assembly
13. Cap setter
14. Vacuum controller
15. Housing
16. Fixing plate
17. O-ring
18. Collar

Exploded view of the electronic ignition distributor

Z series engine distributor

distributor to the engine.

7. Lift the distributor assembly from the engine.

INSTALLATION

1. Insert the distributor shaft and assembly into the engine. Line up the mark on the distributor and the one on the engine with the metal tip of the rotor. Make sure that the vacuum advance diaphragm is pointed in the same direction as it was pointed originally. This will be done automatically if the marks on the engine and the distributor are lined up with the rotor.

2. Install the distributor hold-down bolt and clamp. Leave the screw loose enough so that you can move the distributor with heavy hand pressure.

3. Connect the distributor wiring harness. Install the distributor cap on the distributor housing. Secure the distributor cap with the spring clips.

4. Install the spark plug wires. Make sure that the wires are pressed all the way into the top of the distributor cap and firmly onto the spark plug.

5. Adjust the point dwell and set the ignition timing.

NOTE: If the crankshaft has been turned or the engine disturbed in any manner (i.e., disassembled and rebuilt) while the distributor was removed, or if the marks were not drawn, it will be necessary to initially time the engine. Follow the procedure given below.

1. It is necessary to place the no. 1 cylinder in the firing position to correctly install the distributor. To locate this position, the ignition timing marks on the crankshaft front pulley are used.

2. Remove the no. 1 cylinder spark plug. Turn the crankshaft until the piston in the no. 1 cylinder is moving up on the compression stroke. This can be determined by placing your thumb over the spark plug hole and feeling the air being forced out of the cylinder. Stop turning the crankshaft when the timing marks that are used to time the engine are aligned.

3. Oil the distributor housing lightly where the distributor bears on the cylinder block.

4. Install the distributor so that the rotor, which is mounted on the shaft, points toward the no. 1 spark plug terminal tower position when the cap is installed. Of course you won't be able to see the direction in which the rotor is pointing if the cap is on the distributor. Lay the cap on the top of the distributor and make a mark on the side of the distributor housing just below the no. 1 spark plug terminal. Make sure that the rotor points toward that mark when you install the distributor.

5. When the distributor shaft has reached the bottom of the hole, move the rotor back and forth slightly until the driving lug on the end of the shaft enters the slots cut in the end of the oil pump shaft and the distributor assembly slides down into place.

6. When the distributor is correctly installed, the breaker points should be in such a position that they are just ready to break contact with each other. This is accomplished by rotating the distributor body after it has been installed in the engine. Once again, line up the marks that you made before the distributor was removed from the engine.

7. Install the distributor hold-down bolt.

8. Install the spark plug into the no. 1 spark plug hole and continue from step 3 of the distributor installation procedure.

Alternator

Datsun pick-ups are equipped with a 35 amp alternator with electromechanical, adjustable voltage regulators through 1977. Trucks with factory air conditioning have 38 amp alternators. 1978–80 models use 35 amp alternators (38 amp with A/C), but have a transistorized, non-adjustable regulator integral with the alternator. 1981–84 models have a 40, 50, or 60 amp unit, with the diesel featuring a 70 or 80 amp unit.

PRECAUTIONS

To prevent damage to the alternator and regulator, the following precautionary measures must be taken when working with the electrical system.

1. Never reverse battery connections. Always check the battery polarity visually. This is to be done before any connections are made to be sure that all of the connections correspond to the battery ground polarity of the truck.

2. Booster batteries for starting must be connected properly. Make sure that the positive cable of the booster battery is connected to the positive terminal of the battery which is getting the boost.

3. Disconnect the battery cables before using a fast charger; the charger has a tendency to force current through the diodes

1. Pulley assembly
2. Front cover
3. Front bearing
4. Rotor
5. Rear bearing
6. Brush assembly
7. Rear cover
8. Diode assembly
9. Diode cover
10. Through-bolts

Typical alternator used on 1977 models

in the opposite direction for which they were designed. This burns out the diodes.

4. Never use a fast charger as a booster for starting the vehicle.

5. Never disconnect the voltage regulator while the engine is running.

6. Do not ground the alternator output terminal.

7. Do not operate the alternator on an open circuit with the field energized.

8. Do not attempt to polarize an alternator.

9. Disconnect the battery cables before using an electric arc welder on the truck.

BELT TENSION ADJUSTMENTS

Belt tension should be checked with a gauge made for the purpose. If a tension gauge is not available, tension can be checked with

moderate thumb pressure applied to the belt at its longest span midway between pulleys. If the belt has a free span less than twelve inches, it should deflect approximately 1/8–1/4 inch. If the span is longer than twelve inches, deflection can range between 1/8 and 3/8 inches.

To adjust or replace belts:

1. Loosen the driven accessory's pivot and mounting bolts.

2. Move the accessory toward or away from the engine until the tension is correct. You can use a wooden hammer handle, or broomstick, as a lever, but do not use anything metallic, such as a prybar.

3. Tighten the bolts and recheck the tension. If new belts have been installed, run the engine for a few minutes, then recheck and readjust as necessary.

It is better to have belts too loose than too tight, because overtight belts will lead to bearing failure, particularly in the water pump and alternator. However, loose belts place an extremely high impact load on the driven component due to the whipping action of the belt.

REMOVAL & INSTALLATION

1. Disconnect the negative battery terminal.

2. Disconnect the two lead wires and connector from the alternator.

3. Loosen the drive belt adjusting bolt and remove the belt.

4. Unscrew the alternator attaching bolts and remove the alternator from the vehicle.

5. Install the alternator in the reverse order of removal.

TESTING AND OVERHAUL

NOTE: For alternator testing and overhaul procedures, please refer to the

1. Pulley and fan assembly
2. Front cover
3. Front bearing
4. Rotor
5. Rear bearing
6. Stator
7. Diode plate
8. Brush assembly
9. Regulator
10. Rear cover
11. Through-bolts

Typical alternator used on 1978 and later models

Unit Repair section.

Regulator

REMOVAL & INSTALLATION

1977

1. Disconnect the negative battery terminal.

2. Disconnect the electrical lead connector of the regulator.

3. Remove the two mounting screws and remove the regulator from the vehicle.

4. Install the regulator in the reverse order of removal.

1978–84

The transistorized regulator is soldered to the brush assembly inside the alternator. It

1. Contact set
2. Thickness gauge
3. 4 mm (0.1575 in.) dia. screw
4. Crosshead screwdriver

1977 voltage regulator core gap adjustment

1. Thickness gauge
2. 3 mm (0.1181 in.) dia. screw
3. Crosshead screwdriver
4. Upper contact

1977 voltage regulator coil point adjustment

1. Wrench   3. Adjusting screw
2. Phillips screwdriver 4. Locknut

1977 regulated voltage adjustment

is non-adjustable, and must be replaced together with the brush assembly if faulty.

1. Remove the alternator.

2. Remove the through bolts and separate the front cover from the stator housing.

3. Unsolder the wire connecting the diode plate to the brush at the brush terminal.

4. Remove the bolt retaining the diode plate to the rear cover.

5. Remove the nut securing the battery terminal bolt.

6. Lift the stator slightly, together with the diode plate, to gain access to the diode plate screw. Remove the screw.

7. Separate the stator and diode, and remove the brush and regulator assembly.

8. Assembly is the reverse. Apply soldering heat sparingly, carrying out the operation as quickly as possible, to avoid heat damage to the transistors and diodes. Before assembling the alternator halves, bend a piece of wire in an "L" and slip it through the rear cover next to the brushes. Use the wire to hold the brushes in a retracted position until the case halves are assembled. Remove the wire carefully, to prevent damage to the slip rings.

ADJUSTMENT

1977

1. Adjust the voltage regulator core gap by loosening the screw which is used to secure the contact set on the yoke, and move the contact up or down as necessary. Retighten the screw. The gap should be 0.024–0.039 in.

2. Adjust the point gap of the voltage regulator coil by loosening the screw used to secure the upper contact and move the upper contact up or down. The gap should be 0.014–0.018 1977.

3. The core gap and point gap on the charge relay coil is or are adjusted in the same manner as previously outlined for the voltage regulator coil. The core gap is to be set at 0.032–0.039 in. and the point gap

adjusted to 0.016–0.024in.

4. The regulated voltage is adjusted by loosening the locknut and turning the adjusting screw clockwise to increase, or counterclockwise to decrease the regulated voltage. The voltage should be between 14.3–15.3 volts at 68°F.

Starter

A standard non-reduction gear starting motor is used on all models in 1977, and most 1978–79 models. This motor has its brushes located within the rear cover. A reduction gear starting motor is installed in all 1978–79 Canadian models, and is optional for 1979–84 U.S. trucks. The reduction gear motor brushes are on a plate located just behind the starter drive housing.

REMOVAL & INSTALLATION

1. Disconnect the negative battery cable from the battery.

2. Disconnect the starter wiring at the starter, taking note of the positions for correct reinstallation.

3. Remove the bolts attaching the starter to the engine and remove the starter from the vehicle.

4. Install the starter in the reverse order of removal.

BRUSH REPLACEMENT

Non-Reduction Gear Type

1. With the starter out of the vehicle, remove the bolts holding the solenoid to the top of the starter and remove the solenoid.

2. To remove the brushes, remove the two thru-bolts, and the two rear cover attaching screws and remove the rear cover.

3. Disconnect the electrical leads and remove the brushes.

4. Install the brushes in the reverse order of removal.

1. Solenoid
2. Adjusting washer
3. Spring
4. Shift lever
5. Throughbolt
6. Rear cover
7. O-ring
8. Starter housing
9. Field coil
10. Brush
11. Armature
12. Center bearing
13. Brush spring
14. Brush holder
15. Dust cover
16. Center (drive) housing
17. Reduction gear
18. Pinion gear
19. Gasket
20. Front cover

Typical reduction gear starter

1. Magnetic switch assembly
2. Dust cover (adjusting washer)
3. Torsion spring
4. Shift lever
5. Dust cover
6. Thrust washer
7. E-ring
8. Rear cover metal
9. Through bolt
10. Rear cover
11. Brush holder assembly
12. Brush (−)
13. Brush spring
14. Brush (+)

15. Yoke
16. Field coil assembly
17. Armature assembly
18. Center plate (S114-180 only)
19. Pinion assembly
20. Dust cover
21. Pinion stopper
22. Stopper clip
23. Gear case
24. Gear case metal

Typical non reduction type starter

Reduction Gear Type

1. Remove the starter. Remove the solenoid.

2. Remove the through bolts and the rear cover. The rear cover can be pried off with a screwdriver, but be careful not to damage the O-ring.

3. Remove the starter housing, armature, and brush holder from the center housing. They can be removed as an assembly.

4. Remove the positive side brush from its holder. The positive brush is insulated from the brush holder, and its lead wire is connected to the field coil.

5. Carefully lift the negative brush from the commutator and remove it from the holder.

6. Installation is the reverse.

STARTER DRIVE REPLACEMENT

Non-Reduction Gear Type

1. With the starter motor removed from the vehicle, remove the solenoid from the starter.

2. Remove the two thru-bolts and separate the gear from the yoke housing.

3. Remove the pinion stopper clip and the pinion stopper.

4. Slide the starter drive off the armature shaft.

5. Install the starter drive and reassemble the starter in the reverse order of removal.

Reduction Gear Type

1. Remove the starter.

2. Remove the solenoid and the shift lever.

3. Remove the bolts securing the center housing to the front cover and separate the parts.

4. Remove the gears and starter drive.

5. Installation is the reverse.

TESTING AND OVERHAUL

NOTE: For starter testing and overhaul procedures, please refer to the Unit Repair section.

ENGINE MECHANICAL

Engine

REMOVAL & INSTALLATION

It is much easier to remove the engine and the transmission together as an assembly than to remove only the engine from the engine compartment. After the engine and transmission are removed from the vehicle, the two can be separated.

1. Disconnect the battery ground cable. Remove the battery.

2. Mark the location of the hood hinges on the body in order to facilitate installation and remove the hood.

3. Remove the air cleaner after disconnecting the PCV hose from the rocker cover.

4. Drain the radiator of coolant and the engine crankcase of oil.

5. Disconnect the upper and lower radiator hoses from the engine. Disconnect and plug the automatic transmission cooler lines at the radiator, if so equipped. Use a flare nut wrench if one is available.

6. Remove the four bolts securing the radiator and remove the radiator from the vehicle.

7. Disconnect the engine ground cable at the cylinder head.

8. Disconnect the electrical leads at the starter, alternator, distributor, the high-tension ignition coil cable, and the oil pressure and temperature sending units' wires.

9. Disconnect the fuel pump (or filter on electric pump models), the heater hose at the engine side, and the choke wire and

Remove the C-clip and pin on later models for shift lever removal

accelerator cable at the carburetor. Disconnect the emission hoses or wires to the carbon canister, air pump, B.C.D.D. solenoid, and fuel cut solenoid; the vacuum hose to the brake booster (on models so equipped), and any other wires or hoses running to the engine. Tag all wires as they are disconnected for assembly.

10. Remove the transmission control linkage from the transmission; in the case of an automatic transmission, remove the cross-shaft assembly from the transmission. Remove the selector rod from the selector lever on the automatic transmission. On manual transmissions, lift the rubber boot and remove the nut or C-clip from the shift lever and detach the shift lever from the transmission.

11. Remove the two bolts securing the clutch slave cylinder. Disconnect the clutch slave cylinder and flexible tubing as an assembly.

12. Disconnect the speedometer cable and the back-up light wiring (and neutral switch, if equipped) from the rear section of the transmission.

13. Disconnect the exhaust pipe from the exhaust manifold.

14. Disconnect the driveshaft center bearing bracket from the third crossmember of the frame. Disconnect the driveshaft at the differential housing. Remove the driveshaft assembly from the vehicle and plug the rear end of the transmission extension housing to prevent loss of transmission lubricant.

1. Engine mount bolts
2. Exhaust pipe bolts
3. Crossmember bolts

Engine and transmission cross member removal

15. Attach a suitable lifting device to the engine and lift the engine slightly.

16. Remove the front engine mount bolts on both sides of the engine.

17. Place a jack under the transmission and lift it slightly.

18. Loosen the two combination engine rear mounting/transmission mounting bolts. On models with a catalytic converter, loosen the two exhaust pipe hanger bolts.

19. Remove the bolts securing the idler arm to the frame, and push down the tie-rod.

20. Pull the engine toward the front as far as possible and carefully raise the engine

Idler arm removal

with the transmission up and out of the vehicle.

21. Install the engine in the reverse order of removal, taking note of the following:

Do not connect any parts to the engine or transmission until the engine and transmission are in place on the engine/transmission mounts and secured by the mounting bolts. Secure the rear support first and then the front engine mounts, using the upper bolt hole as a guide.

Cylinder Head

REMOVAL & INSTALLATION

L20B Engines

1. Crank the engine until the no. 1 piston is at TDC of the compression stroke and disconnect the negative battery cable, drain the cooling system, and remove the air cleaner and attending hoses.

2. Remove the alternator.

3. If equipped with air conditioning, unbolt the compressor and move it aside onto the fender. Do not detach any of the compressor lines; the escaping refrigerant will freeze any surface it contacts, including your skin.

4. Disconnect the carburetor throttle linkage, the fuel line and any other vacuum lines or electrical leads, and remove the carburetor.

5. Disconnect the exhaust pipe from the exhaust manifold.

6. Remove the fan and fan pulley.

7. Remove the spark plugs to protect them from damage. Lay the spark plugs aside and out of the way.

8. Remove the rocker cover.

9. Remove the water pump.

10. Remove the fuel pump from the head, on models without the electric pump.

11. Remove the fuel pump drive cam.

12. Mark the relationship of the camshaft sprocket to the timing chain with paint or chalk. If this is done, it will not be necessary to locate the factory timing marks. Before removing the camshaft sprocket, it will be necessary to wedge the chain in place so that it will not fall down into the front cover. The factory procedure is to wedge the timing chain in place with the wooden wedge shown here. The problem with this is that it may allow the chain tensioner to move out far enough to cock itself

Dimensions for fabricating the wooden wedge used to support the timing chain

against the chain. If this happens, you'll find that the chain won't go back over the sprocket after you've put the sprocket back on. In this case, you'll have to remove the front cover and push the tensioner back.

After installing the wedge, unbolt and remove the camshaft sprocket.

13. Loosen and remove the cylinder head bolts. You will need a 10 mm Allen wrench to remove the head bolts. Keep the bolts in order, because they are different sizes. Lift

Removing the camshaft sprocket and chain

Support the timing chain with a wedge

Installing the camshaft sprocket

the cylinder head assembly from the engine. Remove the intake and exhaust manifolds as necessary.

14. Thoroughly clean the cylinder block and head mating surfaces. Check the block and head for flatness before installing the head. Install a new cylinder head gasket. Do not use sealer on the cylinder head gasket.

15. With the crankshaft turned so that the no. 1 piston is at TDC of the compression stroke (if not already done so as mentioned in step 1), make sure that the camshaft sprocket timing mark and the oblong groove in the camshaft retaining plate are aligned.

16. Place the cylinder head in position on the cylinder block, being careful not to allow any of the valves to come in contact with any of the pistons. Do not rotate the crankshaft or camshaft separately because of possible damage which might occur to the valves.

17. Temporarily tighten the two center right and left cylinder head bolts to 14.5 ft. lbs.

18. Install the camshaft sprocket together with the timing chain to the camshaft. Make sure that the marks you made earlier line up. If the chain will not stretch over the sprocket, the problem lies in the tensioner. See "Timing Chain Removal and Installation" for timing procedure, if necessary.

19. Install the cylinder head bolts. Note that there are two sizes of bolts used; the longer bolts are installed on the driver side of the engine with a smaller bolt in the center position. The remaining small bolts are installed on the opposite side of the cylinder head.

20. Tighten the cylinder head bolts in three stages: first to 29 ft. lbs, second to 43 ft. lbs, and lastly to 47–62 ft. lbs.

Different size cylinder head bolts

L20B head bolt tightening sequence

Tighten the cylinder head bolts on all models in the proper sequence.

21. Install and assemble the remaining components of the engine in the reverse order of removal.

Z20, Z22 and Z24 Engine

1. Complete steps 1 through 5 under L20 Overhead Camshaft Engine. Observe the following note for step 5.

NOTE: The spark plug leads should be marked, however it would be wise to mark them yourself.

2. Disconnect the throttle linkage, the air cleaner or its intake hose assembly (fuel injection). Disconnect the fuel line, the return fuel line and any other vacuum lines or electrical leads. Remove the carburetor to avoid damaging it while removing the head.

NOTE: A good rule of thumb when disconnecting the rather complex engine wiring of today's automobiles is to put a piece of masking tape on the wire or hose and on the connection you removed the wire or hose from, then mark both pieces of tape 1, 2, 3, etc. When replacing wiring, simply match the pieces of tape.

Z series engine head bolt loosening sequence

3. Remove the EGR tube from around the rear of the engine.

4. Remove the exhaust air induction tubes from around the front of the engine.

5. Unbolt the exhaust manifold from the exhaust pipe. Remove the fuel pump.

6. Remove the PCV valve from around the rear of the engine if necessary.

7. Remove the spark plugs to protect them from damage. Remove the valve cover.

8. Mark the relationship of the camshaft sprocket to the timing chain with paint or chalk. If this is done, it will not be necessary to locate the factory timing marks. Before removing the camshaft sprocket, it will be necessary to wedge the chain in place so that it will not fall down into the front cover. The factory procedure is to wedge the timing chain in place with the wooden wedge shown here. The problem with this procedure is that it may allow the chain tensioner to move out far enough to cock itself against the chain. If this happens, you'll find that the chain won't go back on. In this case, you'll have to remove the front cover and push the tensioner back.

After you've wedged the chain, unbolt the camshaft sprocket and remove it.

9. Working from both ends in, loosen the cylinder head bolts and remove them. Remove the bolts securing the cylinder head to the front cover assembly.

10. Lift the cylinder head off the engine block. It may be necessary to tap the head lightly with a copper or brass mallet to loosen it.

To install the cylinder head:

11. Thoroughly clean the cylinder block and head surfaces and check both for warpage.

12. Fit the new head gasket. Don't use sealant. Make sure that no open valves are in the way of raised pistons, and do not rotate the crankshaft or camshaft separately because of possible damage which might occur to the valves.

Z series engine head bolt tightening sequence

13. Temporarily tighten the two center right and left cylinder head bolts to 14 ft. lbs.

14. Install the camshaft sprocket together with the timing chain to the camshaft. Make sure the marks you made earlier line up with each other. If you get into trouble, see "Timing Chain Removal and Installation" for timing procedures.

15. Install the cylinder head bolts and torque them to 20 ft. lbs., then 40 ft. lbs., then 58 ft. lbs. in the order shown in the illustration.

16. Assemble the rest of the components in the reverse order of disassembly.

NOTE: It is always wise to drain the crankcase oil after the cylinder head has been installed to avoid coolant contamination.

Overhaul

Cylinder head overhaul should be referred to a competent automotive machine shop. Valve guides and seats are removable and oversizes are available from Datsun. See overhaul section of Unit Repair.

SD22 and SD25 Diesel

1. Remove the air cleaner.

2. Remove the crankcase vent hose and remove the intake and exhaust manifolds. These are bolted together.

3. Remove the alternator, bracket and belts.

SD22, SD25 head bolt loosening sequence

4. Disconnect the coolant hose between the head and the oil cooler.

5. Remove the fuel filter assembly.

6. Disconnect the injection lines from the pump and the injectors. Cap all openings at once.

7. Remove the bypass hoses between the coolant pump and the thermostat housing.

8. Remove the fan.

9. Remove the rocker arm cover.

10. Remove the rocker arm shaft assembly.

11. Remove the pushrods and keep them in order.

12. Remove the fuel return lines.

13. Remove the nozzles from the head.

14. Remove the cylinder head bolts in the sequence shown.

15. Attach a hoist to the head and lift it clear of the block. On occasion, the pre-combustion chambers may fall out, especially if the head is bumped or handled roughly. Take care that they are returned to their original positions if this occurs.

16. Remove the head gasket and O-rings.

17. Clean and inspect all parts.

18. Check the head with a straight-edge. Maximum warpage is .0079″. Do not remove more than .011″ from the head.

SD22, SD25 head bolt tightening sequence

19. Place a new cylinder head gasket on the block with the stainless steel inset side facing up.

20. Install the O-rings around the water and oil passages.

21. Position the head on the block.

22. Coat the head bolts with clean engine oil and torque them in sequence, in stages as follows:
    Large: 43, 94
    Small: 21, 36

23. Install the pushrods, pressing down and turning them to be sure of proper seating.

24. Install the rocker arm shaft assembly, torquing the bolts to 18 ft. lbs. in sequence from the center to each end.

25. Install the injection nozzles.

26. Install all other parts in reverse order of removal.

VALVE GUIDE REMOVAL AND INSTALLATION

Gasoline Engines

1. With the cylinder head removed from the engine, and the valves removed from the head, use a drift and a hammer or press. Drive the valve guides out from the combustion chamber side toward the rocker cover side. A heated cylinder head will facilitate the operation.

2. Ream the cylinder head side guide hole at room temperature. The guide hole should be 0.4719–0.4723 in. for standard valves and 0.4797–0.4802 in. for 0.0079 in. oversize valves which are available for service.

3. After heating the cylinder head to 302–392°F, press the new valve guide carefully into the cylinder head. The top of the

Gasoline engine valve guide installation

Valve guide dimensions

Measuring the valve stem-to-guide clearance

valve guide should protrude out the top of the guide hole 0.4173 in.

4. Ream the bore of the valve guide with the valve guide pressed into the cylinder head. The standard valve guide bore size is 0.3150–0.3157 in.

5. Assemble the cylinder head and install it on the engine in the reverse order of removal.

Diesel Engine

The guides are not replaceable.

VALVE SEAT REMOVAL AND INSTALLATION

Gasoline Engines

1. With the cylinder head removed from the engine and the valves removed from the cylinder head, old valve seat inserts can be removed by boring them out until they collapse. Be careful that the boring doesn't continue beyond the bottom face of the insert recess in the cylinder head.

2. Select the suitable valve seat insert and check its outside diameter.

3. Machine the cylinder head recess using the center of the valve guide as the center of the valve seat insert so that the insert will have the correct fit.

4. Ream the cylinder head recess at room temperature.

5. Heat the cylinder head to 302–392°F.

6. Fit the insert, making sure that it seats fully in the recess in the cylinder head. Peen the insert with a punch in at least four places equally spaced around its circumference.

7. Grind the valve seats to the proper angle.

8. Lap the valves with lapping compound to each seat to which they are to be mated. Thoroughly clean both the valve and the seat of all lapping compound before installing the valves.

Diesel Engines

1. The seats may be removed by cracking with a cold chisel.

2. Immerse the head in water at 175°F while at the same time cool the valve seats in dry ice. The processes should take about 5–10 minutes.

3. Install the seats and reface and lap according to specifications.

Valve Rockers and Rocker Pivots

REMOVAL & INSTALLATION

L20B

1. Loosen the rocker pivot locknut, lower the pivot by screwing it down into the cylinder head, and remove the rocker arm by pressing down on the valve spring.

2. To remove the rocker pivots, loosen

L20B rocker arm removal

Z series engine rocker arm assembly

Intake manifold and gasket

the locknut, then unscrew the pivot from the cylinder head.

3. Install the pivots and rockers and assemble the engine in the reverse order of removal.

Rocker Shaft Assembly

REMOVAL & INSTALLATION

Z20, Z22 and Z24

1. The rocker shaft assembly is removed by simply removing the retaining bolts.

NOTE: When removing the bolts, DO NOT REMOVE THE NO. 1 AND NO. 5 BRACKET BOLTS SINCE THE ROCKER SHAFT BRACKET AND ROCKER ARM WILL SPRING OUT!

2. Installation is the reverse of removal. Torque the bolts evenly from the ends toward the center to 11–18 ft. lbs.

SD22 and SD25 Diesel

1. Remove the shaft retaining bolts evenly, from the center towards the ends.

2. Lift the shaft assembly off the head.

3. If you are disassembling the shaft and rocker arms, it may be necessary to immerse the assembly in water heated to 160°F for a few minutes to free the rocker arms. NEVER HAMMER THEM OFF!

4. Installation is the reverse of removal. Torque the retaining bolts evenly from the ends toward the center to 14–18 ft. lbs.

Intake Manifold

REMOVAL & INSTALLATION

All Engines

1. Remove the air cleaner assembly together with all of the attending hoses. Remove the EGR tube.

NOTE: It is important to replace the gasket whenever the intake manifold is

removed. **Because the intake and exhaust manifolds share a common gasket, whenever the intake manifold is removed, the exhaust manifold must also be removed, so that the gasket can be replaced.**

2. Disconnect the throttle linkage, fuel, and vacuum lines from the carburetor. Label all wires and hoses as they are removed to simplify installation.

3. The carburetor can be removed from the manifold at this point or can be removed as an assembly with the intake manifold.

4. Loosen the intake manifold attaching nuts, working from the two ends toward the center, and then remove them.

5. Remove the intake manifold from the engine.

6. Install the intake manifold in the reverse order of removal. Always use a new gasket when installing the manifold; air leaks will cause burnt valves. Tighten the manifold bolts from the center outwards, in two progressive steps, to 9–12 ft. lbs.

Exhaust Manifold

REMOVAL & INSTALLATION

All Engines

1. Remove the air cleaner assembly.

2. Disconnect the exhaust pipe from the exhaust manifold.

NOTE: It is not absolutely necessary to replace the gasket when only the exhaust manifold is removed, unless the gasket is damaged, or leaks develop.

3. Loosen and remove the exhaust manifold attaching nuts and remove the manifold from the engine.

4. Install the exhaust manifold in the reverse order of removal. Use new gaskets at the cylinder head (if necessary) and exhaust pipe. Tighten the mounting bolts in

1. Bolt
2. Lock washer
3. Flat washer
4. Lock nut
5. Valve rocker A
6. Rocker shaft bracket
7. Valve rocker B
8. Inside spring
9. Valve rocker C
10. Rocker shaft bracket
11. Valve rocker D
12. Inside spring
13. Adjusting screw
14. Valve rocker A
15. Rocker shaft bracket
16. Valve rocker B
17. Inside spring
18. Valve rocker C
19. Rocker shaft bracket

20. Valve rocker D
21. Cotter pin
22. Washer
23. Outside spring
24. Plug
25. Rocker shaft
26. Plug
27. Outside spring
28. Washer
29. Cotter pin
30. Split collar
31. Spring seat
32. Valve stem seal
33. Push rod
34. Valve spring
35. Valve lifter
36. Valve

SD22, SD25 rocker arm assembly

Exhaust manifold and heat stove

a circular pattern, working from the center to the ends, in two progressive steps to the figures in the torque chart.

NOTE: On 1978–84 gasoline models, install the stud bolt into the center of the outermost guide hole (no. 4 cylinder) of the manifold.

Timing Gear Cover

REMOVAL & INSTALLATION

Gasoline Engines

1. Disconnect the negative battery cable from the battery, drain the cooling system, and remove the radiator together with the upper and lower radiator hoses.

2. Loosen the alternator drive belt adjusting screw and remove the drive belt. Remove the bolts which attach the alternator bracket to the engine and set the alternator aside out of the way.

3. Remove the distributor.

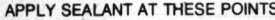
APPLY SEALANT AT THESE POINTS

Gasoline engine front cover installation

4. Remove the oil pump attaching screws, and take out the pump and its drive spindle.

5. Remove the cooling fan and the fan pulley together with the drive belt.

6. Remove the water pump.

7. Remove the crankshaft pulley bolt and remove the crankshaft pulley.

8. Remove the bolts holding the front cover to the front of the cylinder block, the four bolts which retain the front of the oil pan to the bottom of the front cover and the two bolts which are screwed down through the front of the cylinder head and into the top of the front cover.

9. Carefully pry the front cover off the front of the engine.

10. Cut the exposed front section of the oil pan gasket away from the oil pan. Do the same to the gasket at the top of the front cover. Remove the two side gaskets and clean all of the mating surfaces.

11. Cut the portions needed from a new oil pan gasket and top front cover gasket.

12. Apply sealer to all of the gaskets and position them on the engine in their proper places.

13. Apply a light coating of oil to the crankshaft oil seal and carefully mount the front cover to the front of the engine and

Gasoline engine front cover bolts

install all of the mounting bolts.

Tighten the 8 mm bolts to 7–12 ft. lbs. and the 6 mm bolts to 3–6 ft. lbs. Tighten the oil pan attaching bolts to 4–7 ft. lbs.

14. Before installing the oil pump, place the gasket over the shaft and make sure that the mark on the drive spindle faces (aligned with) the oil pump hole. Install the oil pump so that the projection on the top of the shaft is located in the exact position as when it was removed in the 11:25 o'clock position with the piston in the no. 1 cylinder is placed at TDC on the compression stroke, if the engine was disturbed since disassembly. Tighten the oil pump attaching screws to 8–10 ft. lbs. See Oil Pump Removal and Installation.

Diesel Engines

NOTE: A 41mm (1.614 in.) socket is needed for this procedure.

Crankshaft pulley nut removal

Lifting the pulley assembly

1. Remove the fan and pulley.

2. Remove the water pump bypass hose and allow the cooling system to drain below the level of the water pump.

3. Remove the three bolts and lift the water pump and gasket off the block. Discard the gasket.

4. Remove the crankshaft pulley nut with a 41mm socket.

5. Drive the pulley from the crankshaft with a wooden or plastic mallet.

6. Remove the five bolts and lift the timing gear cover from the case.

7. Installation is the reverse of removal. Always replace the cover oil seal and use a new cover gasket. Torque the cover bolts to 8 ft. lbs., the crankshaft pulley nut to 238 ft. lbs., and the water pump bolts to 8 ft. lbs. for the 8mm bolt and 16 ft. lbs. for the 10mm bolts.

NOTE: Do not tighten the water pump bolts until the belt adjuster is installed when installing the alternator.

Timing Gear Cover Oil Seal

REMOVAL & INSTALLATION

1. Remove the front cover.

2. Pry the old seal from the cover with a pointed piece of plastic or wood. Do not use a screwdriver to avoid scratching the seal surface.

3. Oil the lip of the new seal. Do not use grease. Press it into place, making sure the flat side faces forward and the lip faces the engine.

4. Install the front cover.

Timing Gears and Case

The following requires use of special tools.

REMOVAL & INSTALLATION

SD22 and SD25 Diesel

1. Remove the timing gear cover.

Measuring backlash

Timing gear case removal

Timing mark alignment

Timer removal

Oil slinger installation

2. Remove the timing gear round nut.

3. Using timer extractor 57926-581, thread the tool into the timer weight holder. Remove the timing gear assembly by threading in the extractor tool bolt.

4. Unbolt and remove the camshaft gear set.

1. Crankshaft gear   3. Camshaft gear
2. Idler   4. Oil jet

Oil jet orientation

5. Remove the oil slinger. Unbolt the crankshaft gear and remove it with a gear puller.

6. Install the camshaft gear.

7. Install the crankshaft gear and oil slinger while carefully aligning the timing marks as shown. Measure the gear backlash. Backlash should be 0.0028–0.0079 in.

8. With the no. 1 piston at TDC, mesh the timing gear and idler gear at the "Y" marks. After aligning the gear with the keyway, secure the timer assembly with a lock washer and the round nut. Torque the nut to 50–58 ft. lbs.

9. Install the cover.

NOTE: If the gear case oil jet was removed, install in the relationship as shown.

Timing Chain and Tensioner

REMOVAL & INSTALLATION

Gasoline Engines

1. Before beginning any disassembly

procedures, position the no. 1 piston at TDC on the compression stroke.

2. Remove the front cover. Remove the camshaft cover.

3. With the no. 1 piston at TDC, the timing marks on the camshaft sprocket and the timing chain should be visible. Mark both of them with paint. Also mark the relationship of the camshaft sprocket to the camshaft. At this point you will see that there are three sets of timing marks and locating holes in the sprocket. They are for making adjustments to compensate for timing chain stretch. See the "Timing Chain Adjustment" section following for details.

Gasoline engine crankshaft sprocket removal

4. With the timing marks on the cam sprocket clearly marked, locate and mark the timing marks on the crankshaft sprocket. Also mark the chain timing mark. Of course, if the chain is not to be reused, marking it is useless.

5. Unbolt the camshaft sprocket and remove the sprocket along with the chain. As you remove the chain, hold it where the chain tensioner contacts it. When the chain is removed, the tensioner is going to come apart. Hold on to it and you won't lose any of the parts.

The crankshaft sprocket can be removed with a puller, if necessary. There is no need to remove the chain guide unless it is being replaced.

6. Install the timing chain and the camshaft sprocket together after first positioning the chain over the crankshaft sprocket. Position the sprocket so that the marks made earlier line up. This is assuming that the engine has not been disturbed. The camshaft and the crankshaft keys should both be pointing upward. If a new chain and/or gear is being installed, position the sprocket so that the timing marks on the chain align with the marks on the sprocket (with both keys pointing up). The marks are on the right-hand side of the sprockets as you face the engine. Engines have 44 pins between the mating marks of the chain and sprockets when the chain is installed correctly. The factory refers to the pins as links, but in American terminology this is incorrect. Count the pins. There are two pins per chain link. This is an important step. If you do not get the exact number of pins between the timing marks, valve timing will be incorrect, and the engine will either not run at all or run very badly.

7. Install the chain tensioner. Adjust the protrusion of the chain tensioner spindle to zero clearance.

8. With a new seal installed in the front cover and a light coat of oil applied to the seal, assemble the remaining components of the engine in the reverse order of disassembly.

TIMING CHAIN ADJUSTMENT

When the timing chain stretches excessively, the valve timing will be adversely affected. There are two camshaft sprocket locating holes provided to correct the valve timing. Actually there are three sets of holes and timing marks on the camshaft sprocket; the third hole and timing mark are for 6 cylinder Datsun engines and in the case of the Datsun pick-up 4 cylinder engines, are obviously ignored.

If the stretch of the chain roller links is excessive, adjust the camshaft sprocket location by transferring the camshaft set position of the camshaft sprocket from the factory position of no. 1 to no. 2 as follows:

1. Turn the crankshaft until the no. 1 piston is at TDC on its compression stroke.

Installing the timing chain tensioner

Examine whether the camshaft sprocket location notch is to the left of the oblong groove on the camshaft retaining plate. If the notch in the sprocket is to the left of the groove in the retaining plate, then the chain is stretched and needs adjusting.

2. Remove the camshaft sprocket together with the chain and reinstall the sprocket and chain with the locating dowel on the camshaft inserted into the no. 2 hole of the sprocket and the timing mark on the timing chain aligned with the no. 2 mark on the sprocket. The amount of modification is 4° of the crankshaft rotation.

3. Recheck the valve timing as outlined in step 1. The notch in the sprocket should be to the right of the groove in the camshaft retaining plate.

4. If and when the notch cannot be brought to the right of the groove with the sprocket installed in the no. 2 hole, the timing chain must be replaced to gain the proper valve timing.

Camshaft

REMOVAL & INSTALLATION

Gasoline Engines

1. Removal of the cylinder head from the engine is optional. Remove the camshaft sprocket from the camshaft together with the timing chain.

2. Loosen the valve rocker pivot locknut and remove the rocker arm by pressing down on the valve spring. Remove all of

The camshaft retaining plate

the rocker arms in this manner.

3. Remove the two retaining nuts on the camshaft retainer plate at the front of the cylinder head and carefully slide the camshaft out of the camshaft carrier.

4. Lightly coat the camshaft bearings with clean motor oil and carefully slide the camshaft in place in the camshaft carrier.

5. Install the camshaft retainer plate with the oblong groove in the face of the plate facing toward the front of the engine.

6. Check the valve timing as outlined under "Timing Chain Removal and Installation" and install the timing sprocket on the camshaft, tightening the bolt together with the fuel pump cam to 86–116 ft. lbs.

7. Install the rocker arms by pressing down the valve springs with a screwdriver and install the valve rocker springs.

8. Install the cylinder head, if it was removed, and assemble the rest of the engine in the reverse order of removal.

Diesel Engines

1. Remove the head.
2. Remove the lifters and mark them for reassembly.
3. Remove the front case and cover.
4. Remove the tachometer drive support nuts.
5. Remove the timer round nut.
6. Thread the timer extractor, ST 57926-581, into the timer weight holder. Remove the timer assembly by tightening the extractor bolt.

Adjusting the camshaft sprocket to obtain proper valve timing due to a worn timing chain

Removing the SD22, SD25 camshaft retaining bolts

7. Remove the oil pump drive spindle.

8. Remove the camshaft locating plate bolts and carefully slide the camshaft from the engine.

9. Coat the camshaft with clean engine oil and carefully slide it into the block. Install the locating plate.

10. Install the oil pump drive spindle by aligning the oil pump drive shaft groove and the camshaft oil pump drive gear with the spindle.

11. Install all other parts in reverse order.

Pistons and Connecting Rods

REMOVAL & INSTALLATION

See the "Engine Rebuilding" section for general procedures.

1. Remove the cylinder head.

2. Remove the oil pan.

3. Remove any carbon buildup from the cylinder wall at the top end of the piston travel with a ridge reamer tool.

4. Position the piston to be removed at the bottom of its stroke so that the connecting rod bearing cap can be reached easily from under the engine.

5. Unscrew the connecting rod bearing cap and remove the cap and lower half of the bearing.

6. Push the piston and connecting rod up and out of the cylinder block with a length of wood. Use care not to scratch the cylinder wall with the connecting rod or the wooden tool.

Removing the piston and connecting rod assemblies from the block

7. Keep all of the components from each cylinder together and install them in the cylinder from which they were removed.

8. Coat the bearing face of the connecting rod and the outer face of the pistons with engine oil.

9. Turn the top compression ring to bring its gap to about the 1:30 o'clock position. Set the remaining rings so that their gaps are positioned 180° apart around the piston. The oil ring gap will be directly under the top compression ring gap.

10. Turn the crankshaft until the rod journal of the particular cylinder you are working on is brought to the TDC position.

11. With the piston and rings clamped in a ring compressor, the notched mark on the head of the piston toward the front of the engine, and the oil hole side of the connecting rod toward the right side of the engine, push the piston and connecting rod assembly into the cylinder bore until the big bearing end of the connecting rod contacts and is seated on the rod journal of the crankshaft. Use care not to scratch the cylinder wall with the connecting rod.

12. Push down farther on the piston and turn the crankshaft while the connecting rod rides around on the crankshaft rod journal. Turn the crankshaft until the crankshaft rod journal is at BDC (bottom dead center).

13. Align the mark on the connecting rod bearing cap with that on the connecting rod and tighten the bearing cap bolts to the specified torque.

14. Install all of the piston/connecting rod assemblies in the manner outlined above and assemble the oil pan and cylinder head to the engine in the reverse order of removal.

Arrangement of the piston ring gaps around the piston

Piston ring installation

Installing the piston and connecting rod

PISTON AND CONNECTING ROD IDENTIFICATION AND POSITIONING

The pistons are marked with a notch in the piston head. When installed in the engine, the notch markings are to be facing toward the front of the engine.

The connecting rods are installed in the engine with the oil hole facing toward the fuel pump side (right) of the engine.

NOTE: It is advisable to number the pistons, connecting rods, and bearing caps in some manner so that they can be reinstalled in the same cylinder, facing the same direction from which they are removed.

Crankshaft and Main Bearings

REMOVAL & INSTALLATION

NOTE: For crankshaft and main bearing removal and installation, please refer to the Unit Repair section.

ENGINE LUBRICATION

Oil Pan

REMOVAL & INSTALLATION

To remove the oil pan it will be necessary

to unbolt the motor mounts and jack the engine to gain clearance. Drain the oil and remove the attaching screws and remove the oil pan and gasket. Install the oil pan in the reverse order with a new gasket. Apply a thin bead of silicone seal to the engine block at the junction of the block and front cover, and the junction of the block and main bearing cap. Then apply a thin coat of silicone seal to the new oil pan gasket, install the gasket to the block, and install the pan. Tighten the pan bolts in a circular pattern from the center to the ends, to 4–7 ft. lbs. Overtightening will distort the pan lip, causing leakage.

Rear Main Oil Seal

REPLACEMENT

In order to replace the rear main oil seal, the rear main bearing cap must be removed. Removal of the rear main bearing cap requires the use of a special rear main bearing cap puller. Also, the oil seal is installed with a special crankshaft rear oil seal drift. Unless these or similar tools are available to you, it is recommended that the oil seal be replaced by a Datsun service center.

1. Remove the engine and transmission assembly from the vehicle.
2. Remove the transmission from the engine.
3. Remove the clutch from the flywheel.

APPLY SEALANT AT THESE POINTS

Apply a thin bead of silicone sealer to these areas before installation

Removing the rear main bearing cap with a puller

4. Remove the flywheel from the crankshaft.
5. Remove the rear main bearing cap together with the bearing cap side seals.
6. Remove the rear main oil seal from around the crankshaft.

CYLINDER BLOCK   REAR MAIN BEARING CAP

20 TO 25 MM (0.79 TO 0.98)

25 TO 30 MM (0.98 TO 1.18)

Application of sealer to the rear main bearing cap

Removing the rear main seal

Installing the rear main seal

Installing the rear main bearing cap side seals

7. Apply oil to the sealing lip of the oil seal and install the seal around the crankshaft using a suitable tool.
8. Apply sealer to the rear main bearing cap as indicated and install the rear main bearing cap and tighten the cap bolts to 33–40 ft. lbs.
9. Apply sealant to the rear main bearing cap side seals and install the side seals, driving the seals into place with a suitable drift.
10. Assemble the engine and install it in the vehicle in the reverse order of removal.

Oil Pump

REMOVAL & INSTALLATION

Gasoline Engines

The oil pump is mounted externally on the engine, eliminating the need to remove the oil pan in order to remove the oil pump.

1. Remove the distributor.
2. Drain the engine oil.
3. Remove the front stabilizer.
4. Remove the splash shield board.
5. Remove the oil pump body with the drive spindle assembly.
6. Before installing the oil pump in the engine, turn the crankshaft so that the no. 1 piston is at TDC of the compression stroke.
7. Fill the pump housing with engine oil, then align the punch mark on the spindle with the hole in the oil pump.

PUNCH MARK

OIL HOLE

Aligning the punch mark on the spindle with the hole in the oil pump on gasoline engines

Removing the gasoline engine oil pump

The projection on the top of the oil pump drive spindle located at the 11:25 o'clock position. The smaller crescent formed by the notch faces forward.

1. Oil pump body
2. Inner rotor and shaft
3. Outer rotor
4. Oil pump cover
5. Regulator valve
6. Regulator spring
7. Washer
8. Regulator cap
9. Cover gasket

Gasoline engine oil pump

8. With a new gasket placed over the drive spindle, install the oil pump and drive spindle assembly so that the projection on the top of the drive spindle is located in the 11:25 o'clock position.

9. Install the distributor with the metal tip of the rotor pointing toward the no. 1 spark plug tower of the distributor.

Diesel Engines

1. Remove the oil pump drive spindle.
2. Remove the oil pan.
3. Unbolt and remove the oil pump. Discard the gasket.

Diesel engine oil pump drive spindle removal

Removing the diesel engine oil pump

4. Using a new gasket, install the oil pump. Torque the bolts to 7–9 ft. lbs.

5. Install the drive spindle by aligning it with the oil pump drive shaft groove in the cylinder block and the camshaft oil pump drive gear.

6. Place a new O-ring on the spindle support and bolt it to the block.

Oil Filter Canister Assembly

REMOVAL & INSTALLATION

SD22 and SD25 Diesel

1. Remove the bolts at the oil filter end of the oil inlet and outlet lines.

2. Remove the four filter assembly mounting bolts and separate the filter from the block.

NOTE: Have a drip pan ready, since some oil will drain out.

3. Installation is the reverse of removal. Torque the bolts to 14–18 ft. lbs.

Oil filter showing the four mounting bolts

Oil cooler removal

Oil Cooler

REMOVAL & INSTALLATION

SD22 and SD25 Diesel

1. Remove the water hose from the cooler.

2. Remove the eight mounting bolts and lift the cooler from the block.

NOTE: Have a drip pan ready, since some oil will drain out.

3. Installation is the reverse of removal. Torque bolts to 14–18 ft. lbs

ENGINE COOLING

Radiator

REMOVAL & INSTALLATION

1. Drain the engine coolant into a clean container.

2. Remove the front grille.

3. Disconnect the upper and lower radiator hoses. On a truck with an automatic transmission, disconnect the fluid cooler inlet and outlet lines from the radiator. Plug the lines to prevent the loss of transmission fluid and the entrance of dirt. Remove the fan shroud, if equipped.

4. Remove the bolts retaining the radiator from the radiator side supports and

Removing the radiator securing bolts

remove the radiator upward.

5. Install the radiator in the reverse order of removal.

Water Pump

REMOVAL & INSTALLATION

1. Drain the engine coolant into a clean container. On the diesel engine, remove the bypass hose from the pump.

2. Loosen the four bolts retaining the fan shroud to the radiator and remove the shroud.

3. Loosen the belt, then remove the fan and pulley from the water pump hub.

Removing the water pump

4. Remove the bolts (3 on the diesel engine and 5 on the gasoline engine) retaining the pump and remove the pump together with the gasket from the front cover.

5. Remove all traces of gasket material and install the water pump in the reverse order with a new gasket and sealer. Tighten the bolts uniformly.

Thermostat

The factory-installed thermostat opening temperature is 180°F for trucks sold in the U.S., 190°F for trucks sold in Canada.

REMOVAL & INSTALLATION

1. Drain the engine coolant into a clean container so that the level is below the thermostat housing.

Removing the thermostat

2. Disconnect the upper radiator hose at the water outlet.

3. Loosen the two securing nuts and remove the water outlet, gasket, and the thermostat from the thermostat housing.

4. Install the thermostat in the reverse order of removal, using a new gasket with sealer and with the thermostat spring toward the inside of the engine.

EMISSION CONTROLS

There are three sources of automotive pollutants: crankcase fumes, exhaust gases and gasoline evaporation. The pollutants formed from these substances fall into three categories: unburnt hydrocarbons (HC), carbon monoxide (CO), and oxides of nitrogen (NO_x). The equipment that is used to limit these pollutants is commonly called emission control equipment.

For information on emission controls not detailed below, please refer to "Emissions" in the Unit Repair section.

Crankcase Emission Controls

The crankcase emission control equipment consists of a positive crankcase ventilation valve (PCV), a closed or open oil filler cap and hoses to connect this equipment.

When the engine is running, a small portion of the gases which are formed in the combustion chamber during combustion leak by the piston rings and enter the crankcase. Since these gases are under pressure they tend to escape from the crankcase and enter into the atmosphere. If these gases were

1. Crankcase ventilation control valve
2. Flame arrester
3. Sealed filler cap
4. Baffle plate
5. Oil level gauge
6. O-ring
7. Oil separator
8. Baffle plate
9. Flame arrester

Positive crankcase ventilation system

allowed to remain in the crankcase for any length of time, they would contaminate the engine oil and cause sludge to build up. If the gases were allowed to escape into the atmosphere, they would pollute the air, as they contain unburned hydrocarbons. The crankcase emission control equipment recycles these gases back into the engine combustion chamber where they are burned.

Crankcase gases are recycled in the following manner: while the engine is running, clean filtered air is drawn into the crankcase through the carburetor air filter and then through a hose leading to the rocker cover. As the air passes through the crankcase it picks up the combustion gases and carries them out of the crankcase, up through the PCV valve and into the intake manifold. After they enter the intake manifold they are drawn into the combustion chamber and burned.

The most critical component in the system is the PCV valve. This vacuum controlled valve regulates the amount of gases which are recycled into the combustion chamber. At low engine speeds the valve is partially closed, limiting the flow of gases into the intake manifold. As engine speed increases, the valve opens to admit greater quantities of the gases into the intake manifold. If the valve should become blocked or plugged, the gases will be prevented from escaping from the crankcase by the normal route. Since these gases are under pressure, they will find their own way out of the crankcase. This alternate route is usually a weak oil seal or gasket in the engine. As the gas escapes by the gasket, it also creates an oil leak. Besides causing oil leaks, a clogged PCV valve also allows these gases to remain in the crankcase for an extended period of time, promoting the formation of sludge in the engine.

The above explanation and the troubleshooting procedure which follows applies to all engines with PCV systems.

TESTING

Check the PCV system hoses and connections, to see that there are no leaks; then replace or tighten, as necessary.

To check the valve, remove it and blow through both of its ends. When blowing from the side which goes toward the intake manifold, very little air should pass through it. When blowing from the crankcase side, air should pass through freely.

NOTE: Do not attempt to clean or adjust the valve; replace it with a new one.

REMOVAL & INSTALLATION

To remove the PCV valve, simply loosen the hose clamp and remove the valve from the manifold-to-crankcase hose and intake manifold. Install the PCV valve in the reverse order of removal.

Evaporative Emission Control System

When raw fuel evaporates, the vapors contain hydrocarbons. To prevent these nasties from escaping into the atmosphere, the fuel evaporative emission control system was developed.

The system consists of a sealed fuel tank, vapor-liquid separator, vapor vent line, and a canister purge line.

In operation, fuel vapors and/or liquid are routed to the liquid/vapor separator where liquid fuel is directed back into the fuel tank as fuel vapors flow into the charcoal-filled canister. The charcoal absorbs and stores the fuel vapors when the engine is not running or is at idle. When the throttle valves in the carburetor are opened, vacuum from above the throttle valves is routed through a vacuum signal line to the purge control valve on the canister. The control valve opens and allows the fuel vapors to be drawn from the canister through a purge line and into the intake manifold and combustion chambers.

INSPECTION AND SERVICE

Check the hoses for proper connections and damage. Replace as necessary. Check the vapor separator tank for fuel leaks, distortion and dents, and replace as necessary.

Carbon Canister and Purge Control Valve

To check the operation of the carbon canister purge control valve, disconnect the rubber hose between the canister control valve and the T-fitting, at the T-fitting. Apply vacuum to the hose leading to the control valve. The vacuum condition should be maintained indefinitely. If the control valve leaks, remove the top cover of the valve and check for a dislocated or cracked diaphragm. If the diaphragm is damaged, a repair kit containing a new diaphragm, retainer, and spring is available and should be installed.

The carbon canister has an air filter in the bottom of the canister. The filter element should be checked once a year or every 12,000 miles; more frequently if the truck is operated in dusty areas. Replace the filter by pulling it out of the bottom of the canister and installing a new one.

Removal & Installation

Removal and installation of the various evaporative emission control system components consists of disconnecting the hoses, loosening retaining screws, and removing the part which is to be replaced or checked. Install in the reverse order. When replacing hose, make sure that it is fuel and vapor resistant.

Evaporative emission control system

The evaporative emission control system running above idle

Exhaust Emission Control

Air Injection System (AIS)

In gasoline engines, it is difficult to burn the air/fuel mixture completely through normal combustion in the combustion chambers. Under certain operating conditions, unburned fuel is exhausted into the atmosphere.

The air injection reactor system is designed so that ambient air, pressurized by an air pump, is injected through the injection nozzles into exhaust ports near each exhaust valve. The exhaust gases are at high temperatures and ignite when brought into contact with the oxygen of the ambient air. Thus, the unburned fuel is burned in the exhaust ports and manifold.

A check valve is installed in the air pump discharge line to prevent the airflow from reversing due to a broken drive belt, relief valve spring failure, or backfire in the exhaust manifold. Reversed airflow could damage the air pump.

The air pump relief valve bleeds off excess air from the pump at high speeds. The valve is mounted on the carburetor air cleaner.

Trucks with a catalytic converter (1977 and later pick-ups sold in California) have protection devices to prevent converter overheating due to large quantities of injected air. 1977 models use an emergency air relief valve and an air control valve. The emergency valve has a diaphragm operated by engine vacuum. When intake manifold vacuum reaches a predetermined level, the valve opens, diverting air from the pump into the atmosphere. When vacuum drops, the valve closes allowing normal AIS operation.

The air control valve is also controlled by engine vacuum. High vacuum and high pressure from the air pump open the control valve, venting air from the pump into the air cleaner.

1978–79 models have a combined air control valve instead of the relief valve, emergency valve, and air control valve. The combined air control valve regulates the amount of injected air according to intake manifold and air pump discharge pressure, to prevent the converter from overheating.

Anti-backfire valve operation

An anti-backfire valve is installed in an air delivery hose. The purpose of the valve is to prevent backfiring in the exhaust manifold during deceleration. When the throttle closes suddenly, an overly rich air/fuel mixture exists in the intake manifold due to the lack of air getting past the throttle valves. This rich mixture will not completely burn in the combustion chamber. If the unburned gases were to come in contact with the oxygen pumped into the exhaust ports by the air pump, they would ignite and cause backfiring and possible damage.

The anti-backfire valve is connected to the intake manifold by a vacuum line and when the vacuum rises, the valve opens a port in the intake manifold, allowing extra filtered air from the air cleaner to be admitted into the combustion chambers, leaning out the overly rich mixture.

1979–84 cab and chassis models have a transistorized programmed control unit, a vacuum switching valve, and an air control switch which govern air flow through the AIS. The air control switch, located between the intake manifold and the control unit, turns off when manifold vacuum is high, and on when vacuum is low. This provides a signal to the control unit, which determines when to turn the vacuum switching valve on or off accordingly. The vacuum switching valve controls the upper chamber of the CAC valve diaphragm, opening or closing the CAC valve according to signals received from the control unit.

Thus, the amount of air injected into the AIS is monitored and adjusted as conditions warrant.

Air Induction System

Description

The air induction system is designed to send secondary air to the exhaust manifold, utilizing a vacuum caused by exhaust pulsation in the exhaust manifold.

The exhaust pressure in the exhaust manifold usually pulsates in response to the opening and closing of the exhaust valve and it decreases below atmospheric pressure periodically.

If a secondary air intake pipe is opened to the atmosphere under vacuum conditions, secondary air can be drawn into the exhaust manifold in proportion to the vacuum.

Therefore, the air induction system reduces CO and HC emissions in exhaust gases. The system consists of two air induction valves, a filter, hoses and E.A.I tube(s).

California type air induction case

49 states air induction case

Air Induction Valve Case

The air induction valve case consists of two reed valves, a rubber seal and a filter and is attached to the air cleaner. There are two types of air induction valve cases. Type-A is equipped with two hose connectors and is installed on California models, while Type-B is equipped with one connector and is installed on non-California models.

Air Induction Valve

Two reed valve type check valves are installed in the air cleaner. When the exhaust

Air induction valve

pressure is below atmospheric pressure (negative pressure), secondary air is sent to the exhaust manifold.

When the exhaust pressure is above atmospheric pressure, the reed valves prevent secondary air from being sent back to the air cleaner.

Air Induction Valve Filter

The air induction valve filter is installed at the dust side of the air cleaner. It purifies secondary air to be sent to the exhaust manifold.

Air induction filter

Air Induction Pipe

The secondary air fed from the air induction valve goes through the E.A.I. pipe to the exhaust manifold.

Air induction pipes on California trucks

Air induction pipe on non-California trucks

Anti-Backfire (A.B.) Valve

This valve is actuated by intake manifold vacuum to prevent backfire in the exhaust system at the initial period of deceleration.

At this period, the mixture in the intake manifold becomes too rich to ignite and burn in the combustion chamber and burns easily in the exhaust system with injected air in the exhaust manifold.

The A.B. valve provides air to the intake manifold to make the air-fuel mixture leaner and prevents backfire.

The correct function of this valve reduces hydrocarbon emission during deceleration.

Boost Control Deceleration Device (BCDD)

The BCDD reduces hydrocarbon emissions

1. Diaphragm I
2. Vacuum control valve
3. Diaphragm II
4. Mixture control valve
5. Coasting air bleed II

6. Coasting air bleed I
7. Coasting jet
8. Air jet
9. Secondary main jet
10. Mixture air passage
11. Boost passage
12. Secondary barrel
13. Mixture outlet
14. Intake manifold
15. Vacuum control solenoid valve

Boost Control Deceleration Device

during coasting conditions.

High manifold vacuum during coasting prevents the complete combustion of the air/fuel mixture because of the reduced amount of air. This condition will result in large HC emissions. Enriching the air/fuel mixture for a short time (during the high vacuum condition) will reduce the emission of HC in conjunction with the AIR system.

However, enriching the air/fuel mixture with only the mixture adjusting screw will cause poor engine idle, or invite an increase in the carbon monoxide (CO) content of the exhaust gases.

The BCDD consists of an independently operated auxiliary fuel system. This system functions when the engine is coasting to enrich the air-fuel mixture which minimizes the hydrocarbon content of the exhaust gases through more efficient combustion. This is accomplished without adversely affecting engine idle and the carbon monoxide content of the exhaust gases.

When intake manifold vacuum exceeds a predetermined value, a vacuum-actuated diaphragm opens an air passage allowing additional air to enter the intake manifold. When the additional air passage is opened, vacuum is brought to bear on another diaphragm which opens a fuel passage allowing additional fuel to enter the intake manifold.

When the engine changes from a coasting condition to that of idling, the transmission speed sensor closes an electrical circuit, energizing the vacuum control solenoid valve. When energized, the vacuum control solenoid valve vents the intake manifold vacuum to the atmosphere, thus causing the two diaphragms to return to their normal positions, closing off the additional air and fuel mixture. The transmission switch is not used on 1978–79 models.

Automatic Temperature Controlled (ATC) Air Cleaner

The rate of fuel atomization varies with the temperature of the air with which the fuel is being mixed. The air/fuel ratio cannot be held constant for efficient fuel combustion with a wide range of air temperatures. Cold air being drawn into the engine causes a denser and richer air/fuel mixture, inefficient fuel atomization, and thus, more hydrocarbons in the exhaust gas. Hot air being drawn into the engine causes a leaner air/fuel mixture and more efficient atomization and combustion for less hydrocarbons in the exhaust gases.

1. Air inlet pipe
2. Air control valve
3. Diaphragm spring
4. Diaphragm
5. Vacuum hoses
6. Air bleed valve (fully open)
7. Hot air pipe
8. Temperature sensor assembly

Automatic temperature control air cleaner open to underhood, warm air

The automatic temperature controlled air cleaner is designed so that the temperature of the ambient air being drawn into the engine is automatically controlled, to hold the temperature of the air and, consequently, the fuel/air ratio at a constant rate for efficient fuel combustion.

A temperature sensing vacuum switch controls vacuum applied to a vacuum motor operating a valve in the intake snorkle of the air cleaner. When the engine is cold or the air being drawn into the engine is cold, the vacuum motor opens the valve, allowing air heated by the exhaust manifold to be drawn into the engine. As the engine warms up, the temperature sensing unit shuts off the vacuum applied to the vacuum motor which allows the valve to close, shutting off the heated air and allowing cooler, outside (underhood) air to be drawn into the engine.

Installation of the EGR thermal vacuum valve

Exhaust Gas Recirculation System (EGR)

Exhaust gas recirculation is used to reduce combustion temperatures in the engine, thereby reducing the oxides of nitrogen emissions.

An EGR valve is mounted on the center of the center of the intake manifold. The recycled exhaust gas is drawn into the bottom of the intake manifold riser portion through the exhaust manifold heat stove and EGR valve. A vacuum diaphragm is connected to a timed signal port at the carburetor flange.

As the throttle valve is opened, vacuum is applied to the EGR valve vacuum diaphragm. When the vacuum reaches about 2 in. Hg, the diaphragm moves against spring pressure and is in a fully up position at 8 in. Hg of vacuum. As the diaphragm moves up, it opens the exhaust gas metering valve which allows exhaust gas to be pulled into the engine intake manifold. The system does not operate when the engine is idling because the exhaust gas recirculation would cause a rough idle.

A thermal vacuum valve inserted in the engine thermostat housing controls the application of vacuum to the EGR valve. When the engine coolant reaches a predetermined temperature, the thermal vacuum valve opens and allows vacuum to be routed to the EGR valve. Below the predetermined temperature, the thermal vacuum valve closes and blocks vacuum to the EGR valve.

1978–79 models have a B.P.T. valve installed between the EGR and the thermal vacuum valve. The B.P.T. valve has a diaphragm raised or lowered by exhaust back pressure. The diaphragm opens or closes an air bleed, which is connected into the EGR vacuum line. High pressure results in higher levels of EGR, because the diaphragm is raised, closing off the air bleed, which allows more vacuum to reach and open the EGR valve. Thus, the amount of recirculated exhaust gas varies with exhaust pressure.

1978–79 California models have a vacuum delay valve installed in the line between the thermal vacuum valve and the EGR valve. This valve delays rapid drops in vacuum in the EGR line, thus effecting a longer EGR time.

On all 1977 49 States model trucks, the EGR system is equipped with a warning system which monitors the distance the pickup has traveled and activates a warning light when the EGR system must be checked and possibly serviced. The EGR warning light, mounted on top of the dash, comes on when a predetermined number of miles has been traveled and every time the starter is engaged as a check for a burned-out bulb.

To reset the counter, which is mounted on the right fender apron under the hood, remove the grommet installed in the side of the counter and insert the tip of a small screwdriver into the hole. Press down on the knob inside the hole. Reinstall the grommet.

1. EGR vacuum hose
2. EGR control valve
3. EGR solenoid valve
4. EGR tube

1977 EGR system

1. Thermal vacuum valve
2. Vacuum delay valve (California only)
3. B.P.T. valve
4. EGR valve

1978 and later EGR system components. The hose at top runs to the carburetor; the hose at the bottom runs to the exhaust manifold

Electric Choke

The purpose of the electric choke installed on the Datsun pick-up is to shorten the time that the choke is in operation after the engine is started, thus shortening the time of high HC output.

An electric heater warms the bimetal

spring which controls the opening and closing of the choke valve. The heater starts to heat as soon as the engine starts.

Catalytic Converter

1977 and later trucks sold in California have a catalytic converter, which is a muffler-shaped device installed into the exhaust system. The converter is filled with a monolithic substrate coated with small amounts of platinum and palladium. Through catalytic action, a chemical change converts carbon monoxide and hydrocarbons into carbon dioxide and water. The catalytic process is aided by the injection of air from the air pump system, which oxidizes the HC and CO before they reach the converter.

1977–78 catalyst-equipped trucks have a floor temperature warning system, consisting of a temperature sensor, installed onto the floor of the cab above the converter; a relay, located with the other relays on the right fender of the engine compartment, and a light installed on the instrument panel. The lamp turns on when floor temperatures become abnormally high, due to converter or engine malfunction. The light also comes on when the ignition switch is turned to Start, to check its operation. 1979 and later models do not have the warning system.

Trucks with the catalytic converter also have a combined air control valve in 1978 and later, which controls the amount of secondary air injected into the exhaust manifold. It is regulated by engine vacuum and air pump pressure, and works to keep the converter temperatures within proper limits. The combined air control valve replaces the air pump relief valve, found in the air pump system of trucks not equipped with a catalytic converter. 1977 models have an emergency air relief valve for catalyst protection. See the AIS section for a description.

Spark Timing Control System

A spark timing control system is added to manual transmission models sold in the U.S. in 1979. The system controls distributor vacuum advance, giving full vacuum advance when the transmission is in 4th or 5th, and partial advance in the first three gears. This provides better control of the combustion process, lowering emissions of HC and NO.

The system components include a top detecting switch, installed into the transmission, and a vacuum switching valve spliced into the distributor vacuum advance hose by means of a three way connector. When the transmission is shifted into either of the two top gears, the transmission switch goes on, thus activating the vacuum switching valve which closes its air bleed, giving full advance. Shifting into any gear but 4th or 5th turns the transmission switch off,

deactivating the vacuum switching valve. The valve opens a vacuum leak, providing only partial vacuum advance to the distributor.

Inspection and Adjustments

AIR INJECTION SYSTEM

Air Pump

If the air pump makes an abnormal noise and cannot be corrected without removing the pump from the vehicle, check the following in sequence:

1. Turn the pulley ¾ of a turn in the clockwise direction and ¼ of a turn in the counterclockwise direction. If the pulley is binding and if rotation is not smooth, a defective bearing is indicated.

2. Check the inner wall of the pump body, vanes, and rotor for wear. If the rotor has abnormal wear, replace the air pump.

3. Check the needle roller bearing for wear and damage. If the bearings are defective, the air pump should be replaced.

4. Check and replace the rear side seal if abnormal wear or damage is noticed.

5. Check and replace the carbon shoes holding the vanes if they are found to be worn or damaged.

6. A deposit of carbon particles on the inner wall of the pump body and vanes is normal, but should be removed with compressed air before reassembling the air pump.

The AIR check valve

Check Valve

Remove the check valve from the air pump discharge line. Test it for leakage by blowing air into the valve from the air pump side and from the air manifold side. Air should only pass through the valve from the air pump side if the valve is functioning normally. A small amount of air leakage from the manifold side can be overlooked. Replace the check valve if it is found to be defective.

The air injection system

The AIR anti-backfire valve

Anti-Backfire Valve

To check the valve, disconnect the hose from the air cleaner and place a finger on the end. Run the engine up to about 3,000 rpm, then quickly release the throttle. If the valve is performing correctly, suction should be felt at the end of the hose. If no suction is felt, replace the anti-backfire valve.

Air Pump Relief Valve

1. Disconnect the hoses leading to the check valve (on the air injection manifold) and the air control valve from the air hose connector. Plug the connector.

2. Start the engine and increase the engine speed to about 3,000 rpm. Place your finger on the outlet of the relief valve (inside the air cleaner housing) and check for air discharge. If you do not feel any air coming out, the relief valve is faulty, and must be replaced.

Air Injection Nozzles

Check around the air manifold for air leakage with the engine running at 2,000 rpm. If air is leaking from the eye joint bolt, retighten or replace the gasket. Check the air nozzles for restrictions by blowing air into the nozzles.

Hoses

Check and replace hoses if they are found to be weakened or cracked. Check all hose connections and clips. Be sure that the hoses are not in contact with other parts of the engine.

Emergency Air Relief Valve

1. Warm up the engine.
2. Check all hoses for leaks, kinks, improper connections, etc.
3. Run the engine up to 2,000 rpm under no load. No air should be discharged

from the valve.

4. Disconnect the vacuum hose from the valve. This is the hose which runs to the intake manifold. Run the engine up to 2,000 rpm. Air should be discharged from the valve. If not, replace it.

Combined Air Control Valve

1. Check all hoses for leaks, kinks, and improper connections.
2. Thoroughly warm up the engine.
3. With the engine idling, check for air discharge from the relief opening in the air cleaner case.
4. Disconnect and plug the vacuum hose from the valve. Air should be discharged from the valve with the engine idling. If the disconnected vacuum hose is not plugged, the engine will stumble.
5. Connect a hand-operated vacuum pump to the vacuum fitting on the valve and apply 7.8–9.8 in. Hg of vacuum. Run the engine speed up to 3,000 rpm. No air should be discharged from the valve.
6. Disconnect and plug the air hose at the check valve, with the conditions as in the preceding step. This should cause the valve to discharge air. If not, or if any of

the conditions in this procedure are not met, replace the valve.

AIR INDUCTION SYSTEM

Air Induction Valve and Filter

Remove the valve and filter on the air cleaner. The air induction valve and valve filter can then be taken out easily. Installation is in the reverse sequence of removal.

Air Induction Pipe

Remove nut securing the pipe to the exhaust manifold. At the same time, remove the screws securing the bracket and rubber hose clamp.

The air induction pipe can then be taken out. Installation is in the reverse sequence of removal.

A.B. Valve

1. Remove air cleaner.
2. Remove air hoses and vacuum tube. Then the A.B. valve can be taken out.

BOOST CONTROLLED DECELERATION DEVICE (BCDD)

Normally, the BCDD never needs adjustment. However, if the need should arise because of suspected malfunction of the system, proceed as follows:

1. Connect a tachometer to the engine.
2. Connect a quick-response vacuum gauge to the intake manifold.
3. Disconnect the BCDD solenoid valve electrical leads.
4. Start and warm up the engine until it reaches normal operating temperature.
5. Adjust the idle speed to the proper specification.
6. Raise the engine speed to 3,000–3,500 rpm under no-load (transmission in Neutral or Park), then allow the throttle to close quickly. Take notice as to whether or not the engine rpm returns to idle speed and if it does, how long the fall in rpm is interrupted before it reaches idle speed.

At the moment the throttle is snapped closed at high engine rpm, the vacuum in the intake manifold reaches −23.6 in. Hg on 1975 models, and then gradually falls

AIR CLEANER

AIR INDUCTION VALVE CASE

RUBBER HOSE

Air induction filter location

1. Adjusting screw "S"
2. Cover "C"

The BCDD operating pressure adjusting screw

to about −16.5 in. Hg at idle speed. The process of the fall of intake manifold vacuum and engine rpm will take one of the following three forms:

a. When the operating pressure of the BCDD is too high, the system remains inoperative, and the vacuum in the intake manifold decreases without interruption just like that of an engine without a BCDD;

b. When the operating pressure is lower than that of the case given, but still higher than the properly set pressure, the fall of vacuum in the intake manifold is interrupted and kept constant at a certain level (operating pressure) for about one second and then gradually falls down to the normal vacuum at idle speed;

c. When the set operating pressure of the BCDD is lower than the intake manifold vacuum when the throttle is suddenly released, the engine speed will not lower to idle speed.

To adjust the set operating pressure of the BCDD, remove the adjusting screw cover from the BCDD mechanism mounted on the side of the carburetor.

The adjusting screw is a left-hand threaded screw. Turning the screw ⅛ of a turn in either direction will change the operation pressure about 0.79 in. Hg. Turning the screw counterclockwise will increase the amount of vacuum needed to operate the mechanism and turning the screw clockwise will decrease the amount of vacuum needed to operate the mechanism.

The operating pressure for the BCDD is listed below. The decrease in intake manifold vacuum should be interrupted at these levels for about one second when the BCDD is operating correctly.

1977:
−20.1 to −21.7, manual transmission;
−19.3 to −20.9, automatic transmission;
1978:
−22.05±0.79, all models;
1979
−21.65±0.75, all models.

Don't forget to install the adjusting screw cover when the system is adjusted.

AUTOMATIC TEMPERATURE CONTROLLED AIR CLEANER

When the air around the temperature sensor of the unit mounted inside the air cleaner housing reaches 100°F, the sensor should block the flow of vacuum to the air control valve vacuum motor. When the temperature around the temperature sensor is below 100°F, the sensor should allow vacuum to pass onto the air valve vacuum motor, thus blocking off the air cleaner snorkle to underhood (unheated) air.

When the temperature around the sensor is about 118°F, the air control valve should be completely open to underhood air.

When the engine is operating under a heavy load (wide open throttle acceleration), the air control valve fully opens to underhood air to obtain full power no matter what the temperature is around the temperature sensor.

EXHAUST GAS RECIRCULATION

1. Remove the EGR valve and apply enough vacuum to the diaphragm to open the valve.

2. The valve should remain open for over 30 seconds after the vacuum is removed.

3. Check the valve for damage, such as warpage, cracks, and excessive wear around the valve and seat.

4. Clean the seat with a brush and compressed air and remove any deposits from around the valve and port (seat).

5. To check the operation of the thermal vacuum valve, remove the valve from the engine and apply vacuum to the ports of the valve. The valve should not allow vacuum to pass.

The EGR water temperature sensing switch

1. Spring
2. Bi-metal
3. O-ring

Cutaway view of the EGR thermal vacuum valve

6. Place the valve in a container of water with a thermometer and heat the water. When the temperature of the water reaches 134°–145°F, remove the valve and apply vacuum to the ports; the valve should allow vacuum to pass through it.

7. To test the B.P.T. valve installed on 1978 and later models, disconnect the two vacuum hoses from the valve. Plug one of the ports. While applying pressure to the bottom of the valve, apply vacuum to the unplugged port and check for leakage. If

any exists, replace the valve.

8. To test the check valve installed in some 1978 and later models, remove the valve and blow into the side which connects to the EGR valve. Air should flow. When air is applied to the other side, air flow resistance should be greater. If not, replace the valve.

SPARK TIMING CONTROL SYSTEM

1. Check all hoses and electrical wires for proper connections, leaks or corrosion, and so on.

2. Check the distributor vacuum advance unit for proper operation. This can be checked by hooking up a timing light, starting the engine, then increasing engine speed and observing whether or not the timing marks advance. If not, the advance unit must be checked for binding or leaks.

3. With the timing light installed, increase the engine speed to 2,000 rpm. Have an assistant disengage the clutch, then shift between 3, 4, and 5, then back down and into neutral. Spark timing should vary when the transmission is in 4 or 5 (advance should be greater). If this is not the case, check the vacuum switching valve.

Vacuum Switching Valve

1. Disconnect the valve's electrical connectors. With the timing light installed, run the engine up to about 2,000 rpm and keep it there. Check the timing.

2. Connect the valve's electrical connectors directly to the battery with a pair of jumper wires. Be sure to observe correct polarity. If spark timing varies, the valve is ok. If not, replace it.

Transmission Switch

The switch can be checked easily with an ohmmeter. Connect the ohmmeter leads to the switch leads on the transmission. Shift back and forth between either 4 or 5 and one of the other gears. If the resistance does not change, replace the switch.

GASOLINE ENGINE FUEL SYSTEM

If the fuel pump is suspected as being faulty, tests for both pressure and volume should be performed. Never replace the pump without performing these simple tests first. Always check all hoses for leaks or clogs before testing the pump.

Fuel Filter

The gasoline fuel filter is located on the

right inner fender in the engine compartment. It is a disposable cartridge type, and should be replaced every 24,000 miles.

To replace the filter, loosen the clamps on the fuel lines and slide the clamps down the hoses past the point to which the filter pipes extend. Gently twist and pull on the hoses to remove them from the filter. Be careful, because some gas will spill from the bottom fuel line. Remove the old filter from the clip, install a new filter, and replace the hoses and clamps. Be certain that the line from the fuel tank connects to the fuel inlet, and that the carburetor line connects to the outlet. Start the engine and check for leaks.

Mechanical Fuel Pump

The fuel pump is a mechanically-operated, diaphragm-type driven by the fuel pump eccentric cam on the front of the camshaft.

Design of the fuel pump permits disassembly, cleaning, and repair or replacement of defective parts.

TESTING

1. Disconnect the line between the carburetor and the pump at the carburetor.
2. Connect a fuel pump pressure gauge into the line.
3. Start the engine. The pressure should be between 3.0 and 3.9 psi. There is usually enough gas in the float bowl to perform this test.
4. If the pressure is ok, perform a capacity test. Remove the gauge from the line.

1. End cover
2. Magnet
3. Gasket
4. Filter
5. Gasket
6. Retainer
7. Washer
8. O-ring
9. Inlet valve
10. Return spring
11. Plunger
12. Plunger cylinder
13. Body

The electric fuel pump

Use a graduated container to catch the gas from the fuel line. Fill the carburetor float bowl with gas. Run the engine for one minute at about 1,000 rpm. The pump should deliver 1,000cc in one minute or less.

REMOVAL & INSTALLATION

1. Disconnect the two fuel lines from the fuel pump. Be sure to keep the line leading from the fuel tank up high to prevent the excessive loss of fuel.
2. Remove the two fuel pump mounting nuts and remove the fuel pump assembly from the side of the engine.
3. Install the fuel pump in the reverse order of removal, using a new gasket and sealer on the mating surface.

Electric Fuel Pump

An electric fuel pump is used on 1977 and

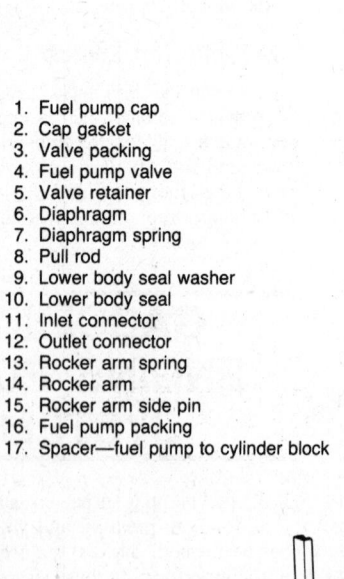

1. Fuel pump cap
2. Cap gasket
3. Valve packing
4. Fuel pump valve
5. Valve retainer
6. Diaphragm
7. Diaphragm spring
8. Pull rod
9. Lower body seal washer
10. Lower body seal
11. Inlet connector
12. Outlet connector
13. Rocker arm spring
14. Rocker arm
15. Rocker arm side pin
16. Fuel pump packing
17. Spacer—fuel pump to cylinder block

The mechanical fuel pump

later models with factory-installed air conditioning, and also on 1979 and later cab and chassis models. The pump is mounted on a bracket located on the right frame rail next to the fuel tank. There is a filter mounted in the body of the pump, which does not normally require service. The pump can be disassembled, if necessary, but all electronic parts within the body (one transistor, two diodes, and three resistors) must be replaced as an assembly.

TESTING

1. Disconnect the hose from the pump outlet at the pump.
2. Connect a length of hose to the outlet. The hose should have an inside diameter of ¼ in. (6mm.). The diameter of the hose is important for accurate measurements.
3. Raise the end of the hose above the level of the pump. Turn the ignition switch on and catch the gasoline in a graduated container. Pump output should be 1,400cc in one minute or less.
4. Fuel pump pressure should be 4.6 psi through 1978, and between 3.1 and 3.8 psi in 1979 and later.

REMOVAL & INSTALLATION

1. Remove the inlet and outlet hoses, catching the fuel that drains in a metal container.
2. Disconnect the wiring at the connector.
3. Remove the two bolts securing the pump to the bracket and remove the pump.
4. Installation is the reverse. Replace the hose clamps if their condition warrants.

Carburetor

The carburetor used on the Datsun pick-up is a two-barrel, downdraft-type with a low-speed (primary) side and a high-speed (secondary) side.

The carburetor has an electrically-operated anti-dieseling solenoid. As the ignition switch is turned off, the valve is energized and shuts off the supply of fuel to the idle circuit of the carburetor.

REMOVAL & INSTALLATION

1. Remove the air cleaner.
2. Disconnect and label the fuel and vacuum lines from the carburetor.
3. Remove the throttle linkage.
4. Remove the four nuts and washers retaining the carburetor to the manifold.
5. Lift the carburetor from the manifold.
6. Remove and discard the gasket used between the carburetor and the manifold.
7. Install the carburetor in the reverse order of removal using a new carburetor base gasket.

AUTOMATIC CHOKE ADJUSTMENT

1. With the engine cold, make sure the choke is fully closed (press the gas pedal all the way to the floor and release, or pull the choke knob out on early models with that system).
2. Check the choke linkage for binding. The choke plate should be easily opened and closed with your finger. If the choke sticks or binds, it can usually be freed with a liberal application of a carburetor cleaner made for the purpose. A couple of quick shots from a spray can of this stuff normally does the trick. If not, the carburetor will have to be disassembled for repairs.

Align the choke cover mark with the center notch on the carburetor

3. The choke is correctly adjusted when the index mark on the choke housing (notch) aligns with the center mark on the carburetor body. If the setting is incorrect, loosen the three screws clamping the choke body in place and rotate the choke cover left or right until the marks align. Tighten the screws carefully to avoid cracking the housing.

THROTTLE LINKAGE ADJUSTMENT

When the primary throttle valve is opened to an angle of 50° from its closed position, the adjust plate which is integral with the primary throttle valve, is brought into contact with portion A (see illustration) of the return plate. When the primary throttle valve is opened farther, the return plate is pulled

SECONDARY   PRIMARY

1. Roller
2. Connecting lever
3. Return plate
4. Adjust plate
5. Throttle chamber
6. Throttle valve

Throttle linkage adjustment

apart from the stopper (B in the illustration), allowing the secondary throttle valve to open.

To adjust the linkage:
1. Measure the clearance between the primary throttle valve and the wall of the throttle chamber at the center of the throttle valve when the adjust plate is brought into contact with portion A of the return plate. Standard clearance is 0.26–0.32 in.
2. If necessary, make the adjustment by bending the portion A of the return plate.

FLOAT LEVEL ADJUSTMENT

The fuel level is normal if it is within the lines on the window glass of the float chamber when the vehicle is resting on level ground and the engine is off.

If the fuel level is outside the lines, remove the float housing cover. Have an absorbent cloth under the cover to catch the fuel from the fuel bowl. Adjust the float level by bending the needle seat on the float.

The needle valve should have an effective stroke of about 0.0591 in. When necessary, the needle valve stroke can be adjusted by bending the float stopper.

NOTE: Be careful not to bend the

EFFECTIVE STROKE OF
NEEDLE VALVE: H

1. Float seat
2. Float
3. Float chamber
4. Needle valve

Float level adjustment

needle valve rod when installing the float and baffle plate, if removed.

FAST IDLE ADJUSTMENT

1. With the carburetor removed from the vehicle, place the upper side of the fast idle screw on the second step of the fast idle cam and measure the clearance between the throttle valve and the wall of the throttle valve chamber at the center of the throttle valve (A in the illustration).

The fast idle screw should be placed on the first step of the fast idle cam. This is the highest of the four. Clearance A should be 0.052–0.058 in., manual transmission, or 0.062–0.068 in., automatic.

1. Fast idle cam
2. Nut
3. Fast idle screw
4. Choke valve
5. Choke connecting rod
6. Throttle valve

Fast idle screw

2. Install the carburetor on the engine. Place the fast idle screw on the second step of the cam.
3. Start the engine and measure the fast idle rpm with the engine at operating temperature. The rpm should be between 1,900 and 2,800 for manual transmission, 2,200–3,200 for automatic. There is a "reference" value given for distance A, with the carburetor mounted on the engine and the fast idle screw on the *second* step of the cam: 0.037–0.046 in., manual transmission, 0.046–0.055 in., automatic transmission.
4. To adjust the fast idle speed, loosen the locknut and turn the fast idle adjusting screw.

NOTE: The first step of the fast idle adjustment procedure is not absolutely necessary; it should be used as a guide to correct adjustment at overhaul.

CHOKE UNLOADER ADJUSTMENT

1. Close the choke valve completely.
2. Hold the choke valve closed by stretching a rubber band between the choke piston lever and a stationary part of the carburetor.

3. Open the throttle lever fully.

4. With the throttle lever fully open, adjust the clearance between the choke valve and the carburetor body to 0.096 in., by bending the unloader tongue.

NOTE: Make sure that the throttle valve opens completely when the carburetor is mounted on the engine.

DASHPOT ADJUSTMENT

The purpose of this device is to prevent the throttle from suddenly snapping shut. The dashpot has a plunger which extends when the throttle is closed suddenly. The plunger contacts a tab on the throttle lever and holds the throttle open slightly for a second, then closes the throttle slowly over the period of another second or so.

1. Adjust the idle speed and mixture before making adjustments to the dashpot. Warm the engine to operating temperature, and connect a tachometer to the engine.

2. Move the throttle lever by hand, and note the engine speed when the dashpot

Dashpot adjustment on all non-air conditioned models

Dashpot adjustment on air conditioned models

plunger just touches the throttle lever.

3. The engine speed should be 1,650–1,850 rpm with automatic transmission, or 1,900–2,100 rpm with manual transmission through 1980. On 1981–84 models the speed is 1,600 rpm.

4. If not, loosen the locknut and turn the adjusting screw until the engine speed is in the proper range. Tighten the locknut. On 1978–79 models with air conditioning, a different dashpot is used. Adjustment is made by turning the screw on the throttle lever which contacts the plunger.

5. Open the throttle and allow it to close by itself. The dashpot should smoothly reduce the idling speed from 2,000 to 1,000 rpm in about three seconds.

OVERHAUL

Efficient carburetion depends greatly on careful cleaning and inspection during overhaul, since dirt, gum, water, or varnish in or on the carburetor parts are often responsible for poor performance.

Overhaul your carburetor in a clean, dustfree area. Carefully disassemble the carburetor, referring often to the exploded views. Keep all similar and look-alike parts segregated during disassembly and cleaning to avoid accidental interchange during assembly. Make a note of all jet sizes.

When the carburetor is disassembled, wash all parts (except diaphragms, electric choke units, pump plunger, and any other plastic, leather, fiber, or rubber parts) in clean carburetor solvent. Do not leave parts in the solvent any longer than is necessary to sufficiently loosen the deposits. Excessive cleaning may remove the special finish from the float bowl and choke valve bodies, leaving these parts unfit for service. Rinse all parts in clean solvent and blow them dry with compressed air or allow them to air dry. Wipe clean all cork, plastic, leather, and fiber parts with a clean, lint-free cloth.

Blow out all passages and jets with compressed air and be sure that there are no restrictions or blockages. Never use wire or similar tools to clean jets, fuel passages, or air bleeds. Clean all jets and valves separately to avoid accidental interchange.

Check all parts for wear or damage. If wear or damage is found, replace the defective parts. Especially check the following:

1. Check the float needle and seat for

wear. If wear is found, replace the complete assembly.

2. Check the float hinge pin for wear and the float(s) for dents or distortion. Replace the float if fuel has leaked into it.

3. Check the throttle and choke shaft bores for wear or an out-of-round condition. Damage or wear to the throttle arm, shaft, or shaft bore will often require replacements of the throttle body. These parts require a close tolerance of fit; wear may allow air leakage, which could affect starting and idling.

NOTE: Throttle shafts and bushings are not included in overhaul kits. They can be purchased separately.

4. Inspect the idle mixture adjusting needles for burrs or grooves. Any such condition requires replacement of the needle, since you will not be able to obtain a satisfactory idle.

5. Test the accelerator pump check valves. They should pass air one way but not the other. Test for proper seating by blowing and sucking on the valve. Replace the valve if necessary. If the valve is satisfactory, wash the valve again to remove breath moisture.

6. Check the bowl cover for warped surfaces with a straightedge.

7. Closely inspect the valves and seats for wear and damage, replacing as necessary.

8. After the carburetor is assembled, check the choke valve for freedom of operation

Carburetor overhaul kits are recommended for each overhaul. These kits contain all gaskets and new parts to replace those that deteriorate most rapidly. Failure to replace all parts supplied with the kit (especially gaskets) can result in poor performance later.

Some carburetor manufacturers supply overhaul kits of three basic types: minor repair; major repair; and gasket kits.

After cleaning and checking all components, reassemble the carburetor, using new parts and referring to the exploded view. When reassembling, make sure that all screws and jets are tight in their seats, but do not overtighten as the tips will be distorted. Tighten all screws gradually, in rotation. Do not tighten needle valves into their seats; uneven jetting will result. Always use new gaskets. Be sure to adjust the float level when reassembling.

CARBURETOR SPECIFICATIONS

Year	Engine Displacement cc (cu in.)	Model Number	Main Jet Primary	Main Jet Secondary	Main Air Bleed Primary	Main Air Bleed Secondary	Slow Jet Primary	Slow Jet Secondary	Slow Jet Air Bleed Primary	Slow Jet Air Bleed Secondary	Float Level (in.)	Power Jet
'77	1952(119)	①	#99	#160	#70	#60	#48	#100	NA	NA	0.906	#43
		②	#101	#160	#70	#60	#48	#100	NA	NA	0.906	#40
		③	#101	#160	#70	#60	#48	#80	NA	NA	0.906	#40

CARBURETOR SPECIFICATIONS

Year	Engine Displacement cc (cu in.)	Model Number	Main Jet		Main Air Bleed		Slow Jet		Slow Jet Air Bleed		Float Level (in.)	Power Jet
			Primary	Secondary	Primary	Secondary	Primary	Secondary	Primary	Secondary		
'78	1952(119)	④	#101	#158	#70	#60	#48	#70	NA	NA	0.910	#40
		⑤	#103	#160	#60	#60	#48	#70	NA	NA	0.910	#43
'79	1952(119)	⑥	#103⑦	#158	#70	#60	#48	#70⑧	NA	NA	0.901	#43
		⑨	#103⑩	#160	#60	#60	#48	#70	NA	NA	0.910	#35
		⑪	#103	#150	#60	#60	#48	#50	NA	NA	0.910	#35
'80	1952(119)	DCH340–111,112	#104	#158	#70	#60	#48	#70	—	—	0.910	#35
		DCH340–115	#103	#140	#70	#60	#48	#60	—	—	0.910	#35
		DCH340–113	#105	#158	#60	#60	#48	#70	—	—	0.910	#35
		DCH340–116	#103	#140	#60	#60	#48	#50	—	—	0.910	#35
		DCH340–114	#105	#158	#60	#60	#48	#70	—	—	0.910	#35
		DCH340–117,118	#106	#160	#60	#60	#48	#70	—	—	0.910	#35
'81	2187 (133.5)	DCR342–11, DCR342–12, DCR342–13	#112	#155	#90	#60	#47	#100	—	—	0.910	#35
		DCR342–21 DCR342–22	#110	#145	#90	#60	#47	#80	—	—	0.910	#35
		DCR342–17, DCR342–18	#110	#155	#90	#60	#47	#100	—	—	0.910	#35
		DCR342–14, DCR342–15	#105	#155	#80	#60	#47	#100	—	—	0.910	#40
		DCR342–23, DCR342–24	#105	#155	#80	#60	#47	#100	—	—	0.910	#40
'82	2187 (133.5)	DCR342-11A DCR342-13A	#113	#155	#80	#60	#47	#100	—	—	0.910	#35
		DCR342-21A	#112	#145	#80	#60	#47	#80	—	—	0.910	#35
		DCR342-17A	#112	#155	#80	#60	#47	#100	—	—	0.910	#35
		DCR342-14A DCR342-16A	#105	#155	#80	#60	#47	#100	—	—	0.910	#40
		DCR342-23A	#105	#155	#80	#60	#47	#100	—	—	0.910	#40
'83	2187 (133.5)	DCR342-11A DCR342-13A	#113	#155	#80	#60	#47	#100	—	—	0.910	#35
		DCR342-21A	#112	#145	#80	#60	#47	#80	—	—	0.910	#35
		DCR342-17B	#113	#155	#80	#60	#47	#100	—	—	0.910	#35
		DCR342-14B DCR342-16B	#107	#155	#80	#60	#47	#100	—	—	0.910	#40
		DCR342-23B	#107	#155	#80	#60	#47	#100	—	—	0.910	#40
		DCR342-19	#110	#155	#80	#60	#47	#100	—	—	0.910	#40
'84	1952 (119)	DCR342-8	#107	#155	#80	#60	#47	#100	—	—	0.910	#40
	2389 (146)	DCR384-3 DCR384-4	#109	#170	#75	#60	#50	#100	—	—	0.910	#45
		DCR384-5 DCR384-6	#107	#170	#75	#60	#50	#100	—	—	0.910	#50
		DCR384-11A DCR384-15	#110	#170	#75	#60	#50	#100	—	—	0.910	#40
		DCR384-21A DCR384-25	#111	#170	#75	#60	#50	#100	—	—	0.910	#40

CARBURETOR SPECIFICATIONS

Year	Engine Displacement cc (cu in.)	Model Number	Main Jet		Main Air Bleed		Slow Jet		Slow Jet Air Bleed		Float Level (in.)	Power Jet
			Primary	Secondary	Primary	Secondary	Primary	Secondary	Primary	Secondary		
'84	2389 (146)	DFP384-3 DFP384-4	#94	#170	#75	#60	#50	#100	—	—	0.910	—
		DFP384-12	#94	#165	#75	#60	#50	#60	—	—	0.910	—

① DCH340-47—49 States and Canada, manual transmission
DCH340-48—49 States and Canada, automatic transmission
DCH340-45A—California, manual transmission
② DCH340-46—California, automatic transmission
③ DCH340-47A—49 States and Canada, manual transmission
DCH340-48A—49 States and Canada, automatic transmission
④ DCH340-45B—California, manual transmission

⑤ DCH340-46A—California, automatic transmission
⑥ DCH340-95—California, manual transmission
DCH340-96—California, automatic transmission
⑦ DCH340-97—49 States and Canada, manual transmission
DCH340-98—49 States and Canada, automatic transmission
⑧ DCH340-95C—California, manual transmission except cab and chassis
DCH340-65A—California, manual transmission, cab and chassis

DCH340-96C—California, automatic transmission
⑨ #101, DCH340-65A
⑩ #60, DCH340-65A
⑪ DCH340-97C—49 States, manual transmission
DCH340-57A—Canada, manual transmission
DCH340-98B—49 States, automatic transmission
DCH340-58A—Canada, automatic transmission
NA Not available
—Not used

DIESEL ENGINE FUEL SYSTEM

For additional information on diesel engines, please refer to "Diesel service" in the Unit Repair section.

Fuel Filter

The diesel fuel filter is located on the upper right front of the engine. It is the canister type with a paper cartridge inside. To replace the filter, unbolt the top of the canister and lift out the old filter. Insert the new filter using new gaskets and O-rings. Replace the top. The filter should be replaced every 6,000 miles.

Injection Pump

REMOVAL & INSTALLATION

The following procedure requires the use of special tools.

Fuel line removal

Fuel filter removal

Injection line removal

Water passage removal

Timing cover removal

Oil seal removal

Removing the timer round nut

Injection pump and end plate assembly

Timer installation

Tachometer drive coupling installation

NOTE: In some applications, this procedure is best done with the engine removed from the vehicle.

1. Remove the inlet and outlet lines from the oil cooler.

2. Remove the bolts (4) and separate the oil filter and lines from the cooler.

3. Remove the coolant hose between the oil cooler and the head.

4. Remove the bolts (10) and separate the cooler from the block.

5. Disconnect the fuel lines and remove the fuel filter from the bracket.

6. Remove the injection lines from the nozzles and pump. Cover all openings immediately.

7. Remove the fan, spacer and pulley from the water pump.

8. Remove the bypass hose from the pump and thermostat housing.

9. Remove the three bolts and lift off the water pump and gasket.

10. Remove the inspection cover and pointer from the flywheel housing and lock the flywheel in place with a locking tool.

11. Flatten the lockwasher and remove the crankshaft pulley nut.

12. Tap evenly around the edge of the pulley using a brass drift, until the cone protrudes from the pulley. Remove the cone.

13. Drive the pulley and damper from the crankshaft with a soft mallet.

14. Remove the inner cover from the timing gear case.

15. Pry out the oil seal.

16. Remove the mounting bolts and tap the case loose with a soft mallet.

17. Remove the tachometer drive support nuts.

18. Remove the timer round nut.

19. Thread the timer extractor, special tool #57926-581 into the timer weight holder. Remove the timer assembly by tightening the extractor bolt.

20. Unbolt and separate the injection pump from the front end plate.

21. Temporarily install the injection pump and gasket on the front plate.

22. Check the timing marks and bring the #1 piston to TDC.

23. Mesh the injection pump drive gear and idler gear at the timing marks.

24. After aligning the injection pump keyway, install the lockwasher and round nut and torque to 50–58 ft. lbs.

25. Install the tachometer drive coupling.

26. Check the backlash between the pump drive gear and the idler gear. Backlash should be .0028–0079″. Adjust if necessary.

27. Remove the no.1 cylinder holder clamp, loosen the delivery valve and pull out the delivery spring. Tighten the valve holder to 22–25 ft. lbs.

28. Connect the fuel supply lines.

Connecting the injection lines

#1 piston at BTDC

Delivery valve spring removal

Lock the pump at this point which is the beginning of injection

29. Bring the no. 1 piston to 20° BTDC. This can be done by aligning the first mark, in normal rotation, on the crankshaft pulley with the raised line on the gear case.

30. Hand prime the pump. Push the pump in all the way toward the block. Move the pump slowly away from the block until the fuel just stops flowing from the valve holder.

Lock the pump in place.

31. Remove the delivery holder and assemble the spring. Torque the holder to 22–25 ft. lbs.

32. Install remaining parts in reverse order of removal.

NOTE: Oil filter bolt torque is 15–18 ft. lbs.

Injection Nozzle

REMOVAL, OVERHAUL & INSTALLATION

1. Loosen the injection lines at the pump and nozzles and remove the lines. Cap the openings immediately.

2. Unscrew the injector and holder from the head.

3. Secure the nozzle holder in a vise and remove the lock nut.

4. Remove the nipple.

5. Remove the nozzle holder body from the nozzle nut.

6. Remove the spacer collar and pushrod.

7. Remove the nozzle holder body from the vise and remove the nozzle spring and adjusting shims.

NOTE: The adjusting shims may be removed with a piece of wire, but great care must be taken to avoid damage to the nozzle tip.

8. Clean fuel oil may be used to clean all parts. Inspect all parts for damage and good fit.

9. Assemble the nozzle in reverse order of disassembly.

10. Install the nozzle in a tester.

11. Operate the tester lever at 1 stroke per second and read the pressure at injection. The pointer will oscillate slightly during injection.

12. Increase or decrease the thickness of the nozzle spring adjusting shims until opening pressure is 1,422.3 psi. A total of 31 different shims are available. A shim thickness of .05 mm equals a difference of 85.338 psi.

13. Install the nozzles and lines. Torque the nozzles to 50–65 ft. lbs.

Governor
RSV AND RAD MECHANICAL TYPE REMOVAL

1. Remove the injection pump and place

Feed pump removal

Removing the idle spring from RAD type governors

Removing the cam cover

Removing the idling spring from RSV type governors

Removing the idling sub spring

Timer removal

it in a holding fixture.

   2. Install the timer.

   3. Drain the cam and governor chambers.

   4. Remove the supply pump.

   5. Remove the cam cover.

   6. Using a special wrench, ST-57916-432, on the timer, turn the camshaft until all the tappets are raised to TDC. Place a tappet holder, 57931-210, between the tappet adjusting bolt and nut for each cylinder.

   7. Remove the rear cover and dipstick.

   8. Loosen the balance idler spring and the auxiliary idler spring lock nut.

   9. Loosen the governor cover lock screw.

   10. Unbolt and remove the governor cover from the governor body. Remove the link from the control rack.

Removing the governor cover and link

Removing the governor body

Counterweight removal

11. Remove the start spring from the spring eye.

12. Remove the counterweights from the camshaft.

13. Hold the timer and remove the slotted nuts and lockwashers.

14. Using a puller, ST57926-512, remove the flyweight assembly.

15. Remove the timer.

16. Unbolt and remove the governor body.

MZ PNEUMATIC TYPE REMOVAL

1. Follow steps 1 through 6 of RSV Type Removal.

2. Unbolt and remove the diaphragm housing and main spring.

3. Remove the diaphragm ring with a screwdriver.

4. Remove the cotter pin from the connecting rod bolt with a needle-nosed pliers.

5. Remove the diaphragm assembly from the control rack.

6. Remove the five set screws and remove the governor body by applying force with a screwdriver blade in the slit between the governor and pump housings.

7. Remove the timer.

RSV TYPE INSTALLATION

1. Apply RTV silicone gasket material

to the governor body and install the governor on the injection pump.

2. Tighten the upper spring eye screw holding the starting spring.

3. Install the timer.

4. Install the flyweight assembly.

5. Apply RTV silicone gasket material to the governor cover and install the starting spring on the housing side of the spring eye.

6. Install the link leaf spring in the hole in the end of the control rack.

7. Install the cover and set screws.

MZ TYPE INSTALLATION

1. Apply RTV silicone gasket material to the governor body, position it on the

Removing the delivery valve holder lock plate

Removing the delivery valve holder and spring

Loosening the delivery valve holder

Removing the delivery valve with tool 57930-032

Plunger barrel removal with delivery valves removed

Setscrew removal and installation

Inserting the plunger spring holder

Measuring end-play

pump body and tap it into position with a plastic mallet. Install the set screw.

2. Install the diaphragm and balance spring on the control rack connecting bolt and lock with a new cotter pin. Apply chassis lube to the diaphragm ring.

3. Insert the main spring and install diaphragm housing with the four bolts.

Injection Pump Service

REPLACING THE DELIVERY VALVE

1. Thoroughly clean the area around the nozzle tube and delivery valve.

2. Remove the nozzle tube.

3. Remove the delivery valve holder lock plate.

4. Remove the delivery valve holder and spring.

5. Using ST57930-032, remove the delivery valve.

6. Position the delivery valve in the pump housing making sure no dirt gets between the top of the plunger barrel and the delivery valve.

7. Install a new delivery valve gasket. The gasket is installed with the larger face downward and may be tapped into place through the extractor.

8. Install the delivery valve spring.

9. Install the delivery valve holder and torque it to 22–25 ft. lbs.

10. Loosen the holder and retorque it.

11. Install the lock plate, nozzle tube and nozzle clamp.

REPLACING THE PLUNGER

1. Remove the delivery valve.

2. Push the plunger spring up with two screwdrivers and remove the lower spring seat from the plunger.

3. Insert a hooked wire through the top of the pump housing, down through the plunger opening and hook it on the lead unit of the plunger. Pull up to remove the plunger and barrel.

4. Immerse a new plunger in clean fuel

Removing tappet with tappet clamp

oil and thoroughly wash off the rust preventive.

NOTE: The plunger was lapped at the factory. Do not hold it by the lapped section.

5. Operate the plunger in clean fuel oil to check its operation.

6. Slowly insert the plunger and barrel into the pump with the barrel groove and plunger notch facing forward. Make certain the plunger piston pin is properly seated in the groove in the control sleeve.

7. Push the plunger spring up with two screwdrivers and insert the lower spring seat.

8. Install the remaining parts in reverse of disassembly.

CAMSHAFT REMOVAL & INSTALLATION

1. Remove the key from the camshaft and remove the four setscrews on the drive side of the pump housing. Remove the bearing cover.

2. Lay the pump on its side and remove the screw plugs from the bottom of the housing with tool 57910-112 or a ratchet handle.

3. Remove the set screws from the center bearing.

Screw plug removal and installation

Camshaft removal

4. Remove the camshaft from the housing.

5. Install the bearing cover on the timer side of the housing.

6. Install the camshaft so that alignment mark ''A'' is toward the timer.

7. Check end play as illustrated. End play is 0-.0012 in.

TAPPET REMOVAL & INSTALLATION

1. Remove the camshaft.

2. Install a tappet insert tool 57912-012 and remove the tappet holder, at the same time, removing the tappet from the holder. Be careful to avoid damaging the housing plug hole threads.

3. Lossen the tappet insert tool, withdraw the tappet assembly into the camshaft chamber and remove the tappet from the housing with a tappet clamp.

4. Installation is the reverse of removal. Make sure that the mechanism works smoothly.

Inserting tappet holder and insert tool

Removing plungers with tool 57921-412

PLUNGER REMOVAL & INSTALLATION

1. Remove the tappets.

2. Remove the plungers using plunger pinchers 57921-412 or equivalent, together with the lower spring seat.

3. Place any reusable plungers in the corresponding plunger barrels and immerse them in kerosene or safe solvent.

4. Remove the plunger springs, upper

Removing plunger springs, control sleeves and upper spring seats

spring seats and control sleeves.

5. Lay the housing on its side and position the control rack so that the punch marks on both sides are the same distance from each end of the housing.

6. Install the control sleeve with the gap in the sleeve facing straight upward.

Control rack: punch mark is indicated by arrow

Control sleeves installed

At the same time install the spring seats.

7. Install the plunger spring in the housing.

8. Install the plunger in the barrel using

Feed pump removal

Checking tappet clearance

Installing the tester lock screw

tool 57921-412, along with the lower spring seat.

9. Make sure the mechanism functions smoothly.

TESTING AND ADJUSTING THE FUEL INJECTION PUMP

NOTE: It is necessary to inspect and adjust the pump, using a pump tester, whenever it has been disassembled and assembled, when the plunger or plunger barrel have been replaced or when any of the component parts have been replaced. Use nozzle tube 57805-002 and test nozzle 5000-101, starting pressure 1422.3 psi. Clean no. 2 fuel should be used. Rotating direction, from drive side, is clockwise. Sequence is 1-4-3-2.

Starting Timing

1. Remove the fuel feed pump and cover plate from the injection pump.

2. Install the injection pump on the tester and holding fixture.

Checking injection start timing with a lift gauge

Turning the adjusting bolt

3. Connect the test coupling to the tester drive shaft with the coupling disc.

4. Remove the cap and position the tester dial to measure the camshaft rotating angle.

5. Install a tappet lift gauge on the #1 tappet.

6. Bottom the tappet and set the dial gauge to 0.

7. Bleed the pump at the bleeder screw.

8. Loosen the nozzle holder ball valve.

9. Feed fuel to the pump inlet while slowly turning the pump tester by hand in the normal engine rotation direction. Fuel will flow from the test nozzle. When the fuel stops flowing the injection point has been reached. The tappet, at this precise point, must be .08858–.09251″ above BDC.

10. If the fuel does not stop flowing after .0926″, turn the adjusting bolt counterclockwise to raise the position of the plunger.

11. If the fuel stops flowing before .0886″, turn the adjusting bolt clockwise to lower the plunger position.

12. When adjustment is made, torque the locknut to 43–50 ft. lbs.

13. With the pump set at initial injection, set the angle scale mark on the tester flywheel at 0 or 180°.

14. If adjustment is correct, fuel should stop flowing at no. 4 cylinder when the tester has been turned 60° in normal rotation. If fuel does not stop flowing at the correct time, adjust as above.

15. Check and adjust each cylinder in turn.

16. When timing for each cylinder is correct, position the cam at TDC, check the plunger piston pin-to-plunger barrel clearance and make sure that the tappet vertical clearance is at least .0118″ for each tappet.

Attaching a measuring device to the pump

Standard Fuel Injection Volume Adjustment

1. Determine the zero position of the control by attaching the measuring device to the pump and pushing the index all the way to governor side. Match the scale on the left end of the index and set the 0(zero) position of the scale at the position at which the measuring device index stops. On RSV mechanical governors, loosen the stop bolt to align this index.

2. Remove the rack guide screw from the rear of the pump housing and apply the lock screw attached to the tester. Secure the control rack in the standard position for adjustment.

NOTE: The lock screw should be tightened by hand; overtightening will bend the rack.

3. Start the tester and run the pump at rated speed.

4. Set the pump feed pressure at 21.3–22.75 psi and measure the injection volume at the rated stroke of the female cylinder.

5. In the same manner, measure the injection volume at rated speed and standard rack position. Compute the rate of unevenness of the injection.

Loosening the pinion setscrew

Installing the appropriate sized pin

Adjusting the RAD full load stopper bolt

6. If the results show that the mean injection volume and rate of unevenness are not within the limits, adjust by changing the relative position of the control pinion and control sleeve. This may be done as follows:

a. Loosen the pinion set screw.

b. Place a pin in the hole in the control sleeve and adjust by moving the control sleeve along the control rack a little at a time.

c. When adjustment is completed, secure the pinion set screw.

d. Remove the lock screw from the control rack and reinstall the guide screw.

Testing and Adjusting the Governor

RSV AND RAD MECHANICAL GOVERNOR

1. Match the adjusting device index to the zero point on the scale and set the control rack to the zero position.

2. Operate the control lever and make certain the full stroke of the rack is .827″.

3. Make certain that the rack moves freely in the direction for maximum fuel injection by the spring force of the starting spring.

4. Set the stop bolt to remove any significant load on the governor linkage.

5. Set the stop bolt to give a control rack setting of .0197–.03937dp.

Maximum speed stopper adjustment

High Speed Adjustment

6. Remove the governor rear cover.

7. Loosen the full load stop lock nut and adjust the full load stop so that its setting corresponds to an A rack position between "K" rotation and BC. See the accompanying chart for the uneveness formula:

$$\frac{\text{Max. or min. injection volume for each plunger} - \text{Main injection volume}}{\text{Mean injection volume}} \times 100$$

8. To increase the volume, turn the stop to the right; left to decrease.

Maximum Speed Adjustment

9. Operate the pump at speed G and adjust the maximum speed stop so that the control rack position is G mm.

Speed Fluctuation Adjustment

10. Speed fluctuation can be controlled by varying the spring rate on RSV governors.

1. Speed control lever
2. Speed adjusting bolt (stopper bolt)

Adjusting the RSV speed adjustment bolt

Balance Spring Adjustment

11. Set the control lever to the point where it contacts the maximum speed stop and operate the pump at a rate of F, between A and B.

12. Install the balance spring assembly under the tension lever.

13. Tighten the balance spring assembly with tool 57916-212 until the control rack position G is H mm. and secure with the lock nut.

14. Gradually accelerate the engine from speed D and make certain that the control rack is at G mm when the action of the spring ends at speed E.

Auxiliary idle spring adjustment

Adjusting the idling spring

Idle Speed Adjustment

15. Set the control lever at the stop position so that the control rack is at point B.

16. Set the speed to D and tighten the idle auxiliary spring so that the position of the rack is C mm. Secure with the lock nut.

NOTE: Do not tighten the auxiliary idle spring too much or overspeeding will result.

Testing and Adjusting the Timer

1. Install a timing light, such as tool 5783-001 on the tester using the cover plate attaching bolts, so that the synchronizer lever attachment is applied to the tappet.

2. Start the pump and turn on the timing light.

3. Direct the light at the angle scale on the flywheel and measure the angular change based on variations in pump speed.

4. If the tester does not have an angle scale:

a. Attach an angle scale to the timer coupling and mount a pointer on the tester drive shaft.

b. Operate the pump and direct the light on the scale.

Pump installed on a tester with synchronizer and strobe light

5. If the angular change is not within limits, disassemble the timer and adjust the spring force by increasing or decreasing the shims, or if necessary, replace the spring.

FUEL TANK

The fuel tank is located under the floor of the bed on the right side, directly behind the cab.

REMOVAL & INSTALLATION

1. Disconnect the negative cable from the battery.

2. Remove the drain plug at the bottom of the tank and drain the fuel into a suitable container.

3. Disconnect the filler tube from the filler hose.

4. Disconnect the ventilation hoses, the fuel return hose and fuel outlet hose from the tank. Disconnect the gauge unit wires at the electrical connector.

5. Remove the mounting bolts and remove the fuel tank.

6. Installation is the reverse. Install the clamps securely, but do not crimp any of the lines. Install the clips holding the fuel tube to the underbody securely. Do not attach the filler hose to the tube until the tank is in place. Failure to do this will cause leaks around the connection.

GAUGE UNIT

The fuel tank must be removed for access

to the gauge unit. The unit is installed into the tank with a bayonet-type of mount. Turn it counterclockwise with a screwdriver to remove. Use a new O-ring when installing, aligning the tab in the unit with the notch in the tank.

MANUAL TRANSMISSION

The Datsun pick-up uses an F4W71B four speed or an optional FS5W71B five speed transmission. The two models have a one piece case, an adapter plate which supports the mainshaft and countershaft, and an extension housing. All units have internal shift rails; no linkage adjustments are necessary.

REMOVAL & INSTALLATION

1. Disconnect the battery ground cable from the battery.

2. Remove the shift lever from inside the cab. It is retained to the shift rail by a C-clip, accessible under the boot. Remove the C-clip and retaining pin, and remove the lever.

3. Jack up the vehicle and support it with jackstands.

4. Disconnect the exhaust pipe from the exhaust manifold. On trucks with a catalytic converter, also remove the exhaust pipe bracket next to the speedometer cable by unscrewing the two mounting bolts.

5. Remove the clutch slave cylinder from the transmission case.

6. Disconnect the speedometer cable from the transmission extension housing, and the back-up light and transmission switch wires at the switch(es).

7. Remove the bracket holding the center bearing of the driveshaft on the third crossmember of the frame.

8. Remove the driveshaft(s).

NOTE: On 4-wheel drive models, this requires removal of the transfer case, which should be performed at this time.

9. Support the engine with a jack located under the oil pan. Place a block of wood between the jack and the oil pan to prevent damage to the oil pan. Support the transmission with a jack.

10. Remove the rear engine mount securing bolts and the crossmember mounting bolts. Only the rear engine/transmission extension housing mount is removable from the crossmember.

11. Remove the starter motor.

12. Remove the bolts securing the transmission to the engine, pull the transmission toward the rear until the transmission mainshaft is free of the back of the engine. Separate the transmission from the engine, then lower the transmission out from under the truck.

14. Install the transmission in the reverse order of removal. Before installing, clean the mating surfaces of the engine and transmission thoroughly. Lightly coat the input shaft splines with grease. Tighten the engine-to-transmission bolts to 32–43 ft. lbs., 1977 and later. Tighten the crossmember to chassis bolts to 20–27 ft. lbs. and the clutch slave cylinder mounting bolts to 18–22 ft. lbs. Be sure to align the marks made earlier on the U-joint and differential flange when installing the driveshaft, to maintain driveline balance.

OVERHAUL

For all overhaul procedures, please refer to "Manual Transmission Overhaul" in the Unit Repair section.

CLUTCH

The clutch is a hydraulically-operated single-plate, dry friction disc, diaphragm spring type.

The clutch is operated by a clutch pedal which is mechanically connected to a clutch master cylinder. When the pedal is depressed, the piston in the master cylinder is moved in the master cylinder bore. This movement compresses the fluid in the master cylinder causing hydraulic pressure which is transferred through a tube to the slave cylinder. The slave cylinder is mounted to the clutch housing with its piston connected to the clutch release lever. The hydraulic pressure in the slave cylinder forces the

1. Fuel tank
2. Drain plug
3. Filler tube
4. Reservoir tank
5. Protection plate
6. Bracket
7. Bracket
8. Ventilation hose
9. Filler hose

Fuel tank and lines

slave cylinder piston to travel out the cylinder bore and move the clutch release lever, disengaging the clutch.

PEDAL HEIGHT AND FREE-PLAY ADJUSTMENT

1. Disconnect the pushrod clevis from the clutch pedal and adjust the clutch pedal height to 6.02 in. 1977; 6.42 in., 1978–84, by loosening the locknut on the pedal stopper. Turn the pedal stopper in or out as necessary and retighten the locknut.

1. Clevis pin
2. Cotter pin
3. Return spring
4. Pedal boss
5. Pedal assembly
6. Bush
7. Nut
8. Clevis
9. Fulcrum pin

Clutch pedal assembly

1. Release (throwout) bearing
2. Bearing sleeve
3. Sleeve spring
4. Boot
5. Release lever
6. Retaining spring

Clutch release mechanism

PACK THIS RECESS

Coat the area indicated in the bearing sleeve with grease

(MG) = Multi-purpose grease

1. Lock nut "A"
2. Lock nut "B"

Clutch pedal adjustment: "a" is pedal height, "b" is pedal stroke

2. Loosen the locknut on the pushrod and adjust the position of the clevis so that 0.039–0.118 in. 1977 or 0.04–0.20 in. 1978–84 of free-play exists between the clevis and the clutch pedal. Retighten the locknut and install the clevis pin and cotter pin.

3. After making the adjustments, make sure that the clutch pedal travels its full stroke of: 4.61–4.84 in., 1977; 4.69–4.92 in., 1978–84. The clutch linkage should operate smoothly and completely disengage and engage the clutch.

REMOVAL & INSTALLATION

1. Raise the vehicle on a hoist.
2. Remove the transmission.
3. Mark the clutch assembly-to-flywheel relationship with paint or a center punch so that the clutch assembly can be reassembled in the same position from which it is removed. Insert a clutch aligning tool (dummy shaft) into the hub. This tool is available from your dealer or an auto parts store. It is important to support the weight of the clutch while the retaining bolts are being removed.
4. Loosen the six clutch cover-to-flywheel attaching bolts, one turn at a time in an alternating sequence, until the spring tension is relieved to avoid distorting or bending the clutch cover. Remove the clutch assembly.
5. Inspect the flywheel for scoring, roughness, or signs of overheating. Light scoring may be cleaned up with emery cloth, but any deep grooves or scoring warrant replacement or refacing (if possible) of the flywheel. If the clutch facings or flywheel are oily, inspect the transmission front cover oil seal, the pilot bushing, and engine rear seals, etc. for leakage, and correct before replacing the clutch. If the pilot bushing in the crankshaft is worn, replace it. Install it using a soft hammer. The factory-supplied part does not have to be oiled, but check

the procedure if you are using an aftermarket part. Inspect the clutch cover for wear or scoring, and replace as necessary. The pressure plate and spring cannot be disassembled; you must replace the clutch cover as an assembly.

6. Inspect the clutch release bearing. If it is rough or noisy, it should be replaced. The bearing can be removed from the sleeve with a puller; this requires a press to install the new bearing. After installation, coat the groove in the sleeve, the contact surfaces of the release lever, pivot pin and sleeve, and the release bearing contact surfaces on the transmission front cover with a light coat of grease. Be careful not to use too much grease, which will run at high temperatures and get onto the clutch facings. Reinstall the release bearing on the lever.

7. Apply a thin coat of grease to the pressure plate wire ring, diaphragm spring, clutch cover grooves and the drive bosses on the pressure plate.

8. Apply a thin coat of Lubriplate to the splines in the driven plate. Slide the clutch disc onto the splines, and move it back and forth several times. Remove the disc and wipe off the excess lubricant. Be very careful not to get any grease on the clutch facings.

9. Assemble the clutch cover and the clutch plate on the clutch alignment arbor.

10. Align the marks made on the clutch cover and the flywheel (if the old cover is being used) and install the six clutch cover-to-flywheel attaching bolts. Three dowels are used to locate the clutch cover on the flywheel properly. Tighten the bolts in an alternating sequence one turn at a time to 12-15 ft. lbs. Remove the aligning arbor.

11. Install the transmission.

Clutch Master Cylinder

REMOVAL & INSTALLATION

1. Disconnect the clutch pedal arm from the pushrod clevis. Remove the dust cover (boot) from the master cylinder body and pushrod. It will not go through the firewall without tearing.

2. Disconnect the clutch hydraulic line from the master cylinder.

1. Valve spring
2. Spring seat
3. Valve assembly
4. Return spring
5. Piston cup
6. Piston

Cutaway view of the clutch master cylinder piston

NOTE: Take precautions to keep brake fluid from coming in contact with any painted surfaces.

3. Remove the nuts attaching the master cylinder and remove the master cylinder and pushrod toward the engine compartment side.

4. Install the master cylinder in the reverse order of removal and bleed the clutch hydraulic system.

OVERHAUL

NOTE: Datsun obtains its clutch master cylinder parts from two suppliers: Nabco and Tokico. There is no interchangeability between the parts. Be absolutely certain that you get the correct parts for the master cylinder installed on your truck. The manufacturer's name is clearly written on the cylinder.

1. Remove the master cylinder.

2. Drain the clutch fluid from the master cylinder reservoir.

3. Remove the circlip and remove the pushrod.

4. Remove the stopper, piston, cup, and return spring.

5. Clean all of the parts in clean brake fluid.

6. Check the master cylinder and piston for wear, corrosion and scores, and replace the parts as necessary. Light scoring and glaze can be removed with crocus cloth soaked in brake fluid. Move the crocus cloth in a circular motion; not in and out.

7. Generally, the cup seal should be replaced each time the master cylinder is disassembled. Check the cup and replace it if it is worn, fatigued, or damaged.

8. Check the clutch fluid reservoir, filler cap, dust cover, and the pipe for distortion and damage and replace the parts as necessary.

9. Lubricate all new parts with clean brake fluid.

10. Reassemble the master cylinder parts in the reverse order of disassembly, taking note of the following:

a. Reinstall the cup seal carefully to prevent damaging the lipped portions;

b. Adjust the height of the clutch pedal after installing the master cylinder in position on the vehicle;

c. Fill the master cylinder and clutch fluid reservoir and then bleed the clutch hydraulic system.

Clutch Slave Cylinder

REMOVAL & INSTALLATION

1. Remove the slave cylinder attaching bolts and the pushrod from the shift fork.

2. Disconnect the flexible fluid hose from the slave cylinder and remove the unit from the vehicle.

3. Install the slave cylinder in the reverse order of removal and bleed the clutch

1. Push rod
2. Dust cover
3. Piston spring
4. Piston
5. Operating cylinder
6. Bleeder screw

Clutch slave cylinder

hydraulic system. Tighten the attaching bolts to 18–25 ft. lbs.

OVERHAUL

NOTE: Datsun obtains its slave cylinders from two manufacturers: Nabco and Tokico. Parts are not interchangeable. Be sure you get the correct rebuilding parts for the model on your truck.

1. Remove the slave cylinder from the vehicle.

2. Remove the pushrod and boot.

3. Force out the piston by blowing compressed air into the slave cylinder at the hose connection.

NOTE: Be careful not to apply excess air pressure to avoid possible injury.

4. Clean all of the parts in clean brake fluid.

5. Check and replace the slave cylinder bore and piston if wear or severe scoring exists. Light scoring and glaze can be removed with crocus cloth soaked in brake fluid. Move the crocus cloth in a circular motion; not in and out.

6. Normally the piston cup should be replaced when the slave cylinder is disassembled. Check the piston cup and replace it if it is found to be worn, fatigued or scored.

7. Replace the rubber boot if it is cracked or broken.

8. Lubricate all of the new parts in clean brake fluid and reassemble in the reverse order of disassembly, taking note of the following:

a. Use care when reassembling the piston cup to prevent damaging the lipped portion of the piston cup;

b. Fill the master cylinder with brake fluid and bleed the clutch hydraulic system;

Bleeding the Clutch Hydraulic System

1. Check and fill the clutch fluid reservoir to the full mark if necessary. During the bleeding process, continue to check and replenish the reservoir to prevent the fluid level from getting lower than ½ full.

2. Connect a clear vinyl hose to the bleeder screw on the slave cylinder. Immerse the other end of the hose in a clear jar half filled with brake fluid.

NOTE: Don't drip brake fluid on any painted surfaces.

3. Have an assistant pump the clutch pedal several times and hold it down. Loosen the bleeder screw slowly.

4. Tighten the bleeder screw and release the clutch pedal gradually. Repeat this operation until air bubbles disappear from the brake fluid being expelled out through the bleeder screw.

5. When the air is completely removed, securely tighten the bleeder screw and replace the dust cap.

6. Check and refill the master cylinder reservoir as necessary.

7. Depress the clutch pedal several times to check the operation of the clutch and check for leaks.

AUTOMATIC TRANSMISSION

The optional automatic transmission is a JATCO (Japan Automatic Transmission Co., Ltd.) model 3N71B. It is a fully automatic unit, with a three element torque converter and two planetary gear sets. The transmission shifts gears in response to signals of both engine speed and manifold vacuum.

PAN REMOVAL

Loosen the automatic transmission pan attaching bolts more at one corner than the other three corners. Allow the fluid to drain out the one corner. Remove all of the pan attaching bolts and remove the pan. Install the pan in the reverse order of removal. Always use a new gasket.

Adjustments

SHIFT LINKAGE ADJUSTMENT

Adjustment of the shift linkage is a critical operation. If the adjustment is made sloppily, the result will be partial application of the band or clutches, and will eventually burn up the transmission.

1. If the control knob is removed, prior to installation set dimension "A" in the illustration to 0.43–0.47 in.

2. Install the control knob, adjusting dimension "B" to 0.004–0.043 in. by turning the pushing rod (2).

3. Loosen the adjusting nuts ("H"). Set both the shift lever (3) and the transmission selector lever (4) into the neutral positions. Set clearance "C" to 0.04 in. (1

1. Control lever knob
2. Pusher
3. Control lever assembly
4. Selector range lever
5. Control lever bracket
6. Selector rod

Tightening torque (T) of nuts and screws—ft. lbs.

(D) T = 0.5 to 0.9
(E) T = 12 to 16
(F) T = 22 to 29
(G) T = 2.5 to 3.3
(H) T = 5.8 to 8.0

Automatic transmission shift linkage

mm) by turning the adjusting nuts which connect to the selector rod (6).

After making the adjustments, check for proper engagement in each gear, and that the mechanism operates without binding. Readjust as necessary.

KICK-DOWN SWITCH AND DOWNSHIFT SOLENOID

With the ignition switch in the ON position and the engine off, when the accelerator pedal is depressed fully, the kick-down switch contacts should be closed and the downshift solenoid activated, emitting a clicking sound. If the components fail to operate in this manner, check for continuity first at the switch and then at the solenoid if the switch checks out as being satisfactory. Replace either of the components as necessary.

Downshift solenoid

NEUTRAL SAFETY SWITCH

The neutral safety switch is located on the transmission range selector lever. The switch operates the back-up lights and controls the operation of the starter. The starter should only operate when the transmission is in Park or Neutral.

To adjust the neutral safety switch, unscrew the securing nut of the range selector lever and the two bolts securing the switch

1. Inhibitor switch
2. Manual shaft
3. Washer
4. Nut
5. Manual plate
6. Washer
7. Nut
8. Inhibitor switch
9. Selector lever

Neutral safety switch

body. Remove the machine screw under the switch body. Adjust the shift selector to the Neutral position (in vertical position and detent clicks).

Move the switch slightly aside so that the screw hole will be aligned with the pin hole of the internal rotor combined with the manual shaft and check their alignment by inserting a 0.0591 in. (1.5 mm) diameter pin into the holes. A #53 drill bit will work for this. Fasten the switch body with the bolts, pull out the pin, and tighten the screw into the hole. Connect the selector lever.

If the neutral safety switch does not perform satisfactorily after adjustment, replace it with a new one.

Transmission

REMOVAL & INSTALLATION

1. Disconnect the negative battery cable.
2. Disconnect the shaft from the accelerator linkage.
3. Raise and support the truck.
4. Matchmark the U-joint and differential flange and disconnect them. Remove the center bearing mounting bolts and remove the driveshaft. Plug the transmission

extension housing.

5. Disconnect the exhaust pipe from the manifold and discard the gasket. Use a new gasket upon assembly. On trucks with a catalytic converter, disconnect the exhaust pipe bracket.
6. Disconnect the shift linkage at the transmission.
7. Disconnect the neutral switch wires. Disconnect the vacuum hose from the diaphragm, and the wire from the downshift solenoid. Disconnect the speedometer cable from the extension housing.
8. Remove the fluid filler tube.
9. Disconnect the fluid cooler lines at the transmission. Use a flare nut wrench if one is available.
10. Support the engine with a jack under the oil pan, placing a wooden block between the pan and the jack as a buffer. Also support the transmission with a jack.
11. Remove the torque converter cover. Matchmark the converter and the drive plate for reassembly; they were balanced as a unit at the factory. Remove the bolts attaching the converter to the drive plate (flywheel). You will have to rotate the engine to do this, using a wrench on the crankshaft pulley bolt.
12. Remove the bolts for the rear engine mount and the crossmember. Remove the crossmember.
13. Remove the starter.
14. Remove the transmission-to-engine bolts. Lower the transmission back and down, out from under the truck.
15. Before installing the transmission, check the drive plate runout with a dial indicator. Turn the crankshaft one full turn. Maximum allowable runout is 0.012 in. (0.3 mm). Replace the drive plate if runout exceeds 0.020 in. (0.5 mm); otherwise, reface it.
16. When installing the torque converter, be sure to line up the notch in the converter with the projection on the oil pump. Align the marks made during removal and bolt the converter to the drive plate, tightening the bolts to 29–36 ft. lbs. Then rotate the engine a few turns to make sure the transmission rotates freely without binding. The engine-to-transmission bolt torque is 29–36 ft. lbs. Adjust the shift linkage and neutral switch after installation.

TRANSFER CASE

REMOVAL & INSTALLATION

1. Disconnect the battery ground.
2. Raise the vehicle and support it on stands.
3. Remove the transfer case shield.
4. Remove the primary driveshaft securing nuts.
5. Remove the front and rear driveshafts.
6. Disconnect the 4-wd switch wire.

Transfer case shield bolts

Transfer case mounting bolts

Transfer case insulator bolts

7. Disconnect the speedometer cable.
8. Remove the exhaust pipe.
9. Support the transfer case with a jack.
10. Temporarily loosen the transfer case insulator bolts.
11. Remove the shift lever rubber boot from the floor.
12. Unbolt and remove the transfer case and primary driveshaft from the vehicle.
13. Installation is the reverse of removal. Torque all mounting bolts to 20–26 ft. lbs.

OVERHAUL

For all transfer case overhaul procedures, please refer to "Transfer Cases" in the Unit Repair section.

Front axle propellor shaft: the left insert shows the primary driveshaft which connects the transfer case with the transmission

DRIVELINE

2-Wheel Drive

REMOVAL & INSTALLATION

Driveshaft and U-Joints

1. Raise the truck on a hoist. Mark the relationship of the driveshaft to the companion flange at the differential housing so that the driveshaft can be reinstalled in the same position.
2. Remove the bolts retaining the center bearing bracket.
3. Remove the bolts connecting the driveshaft to the companion flange at the differential housing (and at the front flange on early models).
4. Move the driveshaft assembly toward the rear of the truck, passing it under the rear axle, removing the sleeve yoke from the transmission. Watch for oil leaking out the end of the transmission. Plug if necessary.
5. Install the driveshaft in the reverse order of removal. Be careful not to bang the sleeve yoke into the seal inside the transmission extension housing, which will damage the seal, causing leakage. Align the driveshaft with the differential housing companion flange in their original position. Tighten the U-joint nuts to 17–24 ft. lbs., and the nuts retaining the center bearing bracket to 12–16 ft. lbs.

4-Wheel Drive 1981–84

REMOVAL & INSTALLATION

Primary Driveshaft

1. Match-mark the flanges and separate the primary driveshaft from the transfer case.
2. Remove the transfer case.
3. Pull the primary shaft from the

transmission and plug the opening.
4. Installation is the reverse of removal. Align your match-marks.

Front Driveshaft

1. Match-mark the flanges and unbolt the front shaft from the front differential.
2. Pull the shaft from the transfer case and plug the opening.
3. Installation is the reverse of removal. Align your match-marks.

Rear Driveshaft

1. Match-mark the flanges and unbolt the shaft from the rear differential.
2. Remove the center bearing bracket.
3. Pull the shaft from the transmission and plug the opening.
4. Installation is the reverse of removal. Align your match-marks.

U-Joint Overhaul

For all overhaul procedures, please refer to "U-Joint/CV-Joint Overhaul" in the Unit Repair section.

CENTER BEARING REPLACEMENT

The center bearing is a sealed unit which must be replaced as an assembly if defective.
1. Remove the driveshaft.
2. Matchmark the flange yoke and the companion flange which connect the front half of the driveshaft to the rear. Also matchmark the companion flange and the front driveshaft. Remove the bolts and separate the shafts.
3. You must devise a way to hold the driveshaft while unbolting the companion flange from the front driveshaft. Do not place the front driveshaft tube in a vise, because the chances are it will get crushed. The best way is to grip the flange somehow

while loosening the nut. It is going to require some strength to remove.

4. Slide the companion flange off the front driveshaft and remove the center bearing from its mount.

5. The new bearing is already lubricated. Install it into the mount, making sure that the seals and so on are facing the same way as when removed.

6. Slide the companion flange onto the front driveshaft, aligning the marks made during removal. Install the washer and locknut. Tighten the nut to 145–175 ft. lbs. Check that the bearing rotates freely around the driveshaft.

7. Connect the companion flange to the flange yoke, aligning the marks made during disassembly. Torque to 18–23 ft. lbs.

8. Install the driveshaft, aligning the marks made at the axle flange during removal.

REAR AXLE

Axle Shaft, Bearing and Seal

REMOVAL & INSTALLATION

1. Raise the rear of the vehicle and support it. Remove the rear wheel and tire.

2. Disconnect the rear parking brake cable by removing the adjusting nut and clamps.

Disconnecting the brake backing plate from the axle housing

Removing the axle shaft with a slide hammer

3. Disconnect the brake tube at the rear brake backing plate. Plug the end of the brake tube to prevent loss of brake fluid.

4. Remove the brake drum.

5. Remove the nuts securing the wheel bearing retainer to the brake backing plate.

6. Pull out the axle shaft assembly together with the brake backing plate using a slide hammer.

7. Remove the oil seal in the axle housing if necessary. It can be pried out with a screwdriver. Oil the lips of the new seal and install it carefully to avoid damage to the lip.

Unbend the lockwasher to remove the bearing locknut; use a new nut at installation

8. To replace the bearing, unbend and discard the lockwasher. Remove the locknut with a soft drift and a hammer.

9. Press the old bearing and cage off the shaft.

10. Remove the oil seal in the cage. Use a brass drift to remove the bearing cup after the seal has been removed.

11. Install the new cup with a brass drift. Install a new oil seal over the bearing cup. Lubricate the area between the seal lips with grease after installation.

12. Place the bearing cage and spacer on the axle shaft, then fit the bearing, tapping it into place with a soft drift and light hammer blows.

13. Place the flat bearing lockwasher over the bearing, then the new nut lockwasher. Install the locknut, tightening to 108 ft. lbs. Continue to tighten after that until the grooves

Axle shaft end play is adjusted by the addition or subtraction of shims behind the brake backing plate

Measure the axial end-play with a dial indicator

line up with the lockwasher tabs. The nut can be tightened up to 145 ft. lbs. Bend the lockwasher tabs into place.

14. Lubricate the bearing and the recess in the axle housing with wheel bearing grease. Coat the axle splines with gear oil. Coat the seal surface of the shaft with grease.

15. Install the axle shaft in the reverse order of removal. The axle end-play should be 0.012–0.035 in. The end-play is adjusted by adding or removing shims behind the brake backing plate. Tighten the backing plate attaching nuts to 39–46 ft. lbs.

OVERHAUL

For rear axle overhaul procedures, please refer to "Drive Axles" in the Unit Repair section.

FRONT AXLE

Free Running Hub

REMOVAL & INSTALLATION

1. Raise and support the front axle on stands.

2. Set the hub in the lock position.

3. Remove the driven clutch by turning it clockwise.

DRIVE SHAFT FIXING BOLT

Axle shaft-to-carrier bolts

◀ : GREASING POINT

Copper wheel bearing support greasing locations

NOTE: A pin is located inside the hub case to lock the driven clutch. Pull and turn the clutch while attracting the pin with a magnet.

4. Remove the lock pin.
5. Set the hub at the free position.
6. Screw the driven clutch into place by turning it counterclockwise until it bottoms.
7. Turn it clockwise until it aligns with the bolt hole.
8. Install the lock pin.

Axle Shaft

REMOVAL & INSTALLATION

1. Remove the free running hub.
2. Remove the snap-ring and remove the driven clutch.

3. Remove the rebound bumper.
4. Disconnect the stabilizer bar at the lower link.
5. Remove the bolts attaching the axle shaft to the carrier. DO NOT REMOVE THE RUBBER BOOTS!
6. Pull the axle shaft from the suspension.
7. Installation is the reverse of removal. Observe the following points:

a. Apply multi-purpose wheel bearing grease to the copper portion of the wheel bearing support.

b. Adjust the axle shaft axial end play by installing the proper thickness of snaprings on the end of the shaft.

c. Torque the axle shaft flange bolts to 20–27 ft. lbs.; the free running hub bolts to 18–25 ft. lbs.; the stabilizer bar-to-frame bolts to 12–16 ft. lbs.; the stabilizer bar-to-lower link bolts to 12–16 ft. lbs. and the wheel nuts to 87–108 ft. lbs.

Free-running hub snap-ring and driven clutch location

Hub removal sequence

DIFFERENTIAL

Differential service is best left to those extremely familiar with their vagaries and idiosyncrasies. A great many specialized tools are required as well as a good deal of experience.

2-WHEEL DRIVE FRONT SUSPENSION

The front suspension on Datsum pick-ups is of an independent, unequal length control arm type with torsion bar springs.

The control arms are attached to a bracket which is welded to the frame at their inner pivot points and to the steering knuckle/spindle support at their outer points.

The torsion bar has splines on each end; the front end is installed to the torque arm which is attached to the lower control arm and the rear end is installed to the torsion bar anchor which is secured to the chassis frame.

Fore-and-aft movement of the front suspension is controlled by strut bars connected to the lower control arms at one end and mounted to the chassis frame at the forward end.

An optional torsion bar type stabilizer is connected to the lower control arms through vertical stabilizer links.

The steering knuckle/spindle is attached to the steering knuckle/spindle support by

Front drive axle

a kingpin through 1977. Ball joints are used from 1978.

Torsion Bars

REMOVAL & INSTALLATION

1. Jack up the front of the vehicle and support it with jackstands. Remove the wheel. On trucks with a catalytic converter, the converter must be removed if the left torsion bar is being removed.

2. Loosen the ride height adjusting nuts at the anchor (rear) end of the torsion bar, allowing the anchor arm to hang down.

3. Remove the dust cover at the rear end of the torsion bar and remove the snapring.

Installing the torsion bar anchor end on 2-wheel drive models

1. Lock nut
2. Adjusting nut
3. Anchor arm
4. Dust cover

2-wheel drive torsion bar anchor

4. Pull the anchor arm rearward and off the torsion bar. Withdraw the torsion bar from the lower control arm and remove it from under the vehicle.

5. Before installing the torsion bar, apply a light coat of grease to the splines. Install the torsion bar to the lower control arm.

NOTE: The torsion bars are marked on the end with an "L" (left) or an "R" (right). The torsion bars must be installed on the same side from which they are removed.

6. Install the anchor arm on the rear end of the torsion bar. Dimension "A" must be:

1977: 0.59–0.98 in. all models;
1978–84: 0.28–0.67 in., all models.

Note that there are two different methods used for measuring this distance. Be sure you are using the correct illustration for your truck.

7. Install a new retaining snap-ring and dust boot to the anchor arm end of the torsion bar.

NOTE: Always use a new snap-ring. Never reinstall the old one.

8. Tighten the adjusting nut until the link protrudes above the support bracket 2.36–2.76 in. on all models (dimension "B").

9. Install the wheel and lower the vehicle.

10. Adjust the vehicle ride height with the truck at curb weight (full tank of gas and no passengers). Refer to "Ride Height Adjustment." Tighten the locknut to 23–30 ft. lbs.

Shock Absorbers

TESTING

Visually inspect the shock absorber. If there is evidence of leakage and the shock absorber is covered with oil, the shock is defective and must be replaced.

Front shock absorber attaching bolts

If there is no sign of excessive leakage (a small amount of weeping is natural) bounce the truck at one corner by pressing up and down on the fender or bumper. When you have the truck bouncing as much as you can, stop bouncing it, and release the fender or bumper. The truck should stop bouncing after the first rebound. If the bouncing continues past the center point of the bounce more than once, the shock absorbers are worn and should be replaced.

REMOVAL & INSTALLATION

1. Jack up the vehicle and support it. Remove the wheel.

2. Hold the upper stem of the shock absorber and remove the nuts, washer, and rubber bushing.

3. Remove the bolt from the lower end of the shock absorber and remove the shock absorber from the vehicle.

4. Install the shock absorber in the reverse order of removal. Replace all of the rubber bushings with new ones if a new shock absorber is being installed. Install the lower retaining bolt from the front of the truck. Tighten the upper attaching nut to 12–16 ft. lbs. and the lower nut to 23–30 ft. lbs.

Kingpins

INSPECTION

1. Jack the vehicle so that the tire on the side to be checked is off the ground. Adjust wheel bearing preload to the proper specification.

2. Grasp the top and bottom of the tire and try to move the top and bottom of the tire alternately in and out. If there is noticeable play between the steering knuckle/spindle and the spindle support then it can be assumed that the kingpins or bushings are worn and should be replaced.

NOTE: Before performing this test make sure that the wheel bearings are properly adjusted.

The kingpin lock bolt with the steering arm disconnected

REMOVAL & INSTALLATION

1. Jack up the front of the vehicle and support it by placing jackstands under the frame.

2. Remove the front wheel.

3. Remove the brake hose and connector from the wheel cylinder.

NOTE: It is not absolutely necessary to remove the drum, hub, brake, and backing plate from the spindle, although it will make working with the spindle a great deal easier. If you choose to leave the parts in place, skip down to step 8.

4. Remove the brake drum.

5. Remove the hub dust cap, cotter pin, adjusting cap, and spindle nut from the spindle.

6. Remove the wheel hub, inner and outer wheel bearings, bearing washer, and grease seal from the spindle.

Removing the steering knuckle/spindle

Installing the kingpin bushings flush with the plug counterbores

7. Remove the brake backing plate from the knuckle/spindle flange.

8. Remove the knuckle/spindle steering arm from the knuckle/spindle.

9. Remove the kingpin lockbolt.

10. Remove the plug from the top of the kingpin by drilling a small hole in the plug, screwing a sheet metal screw into the hole, and pulling out the plug.

11. Drive out the kingpin together with the lower plug with a suitable drift and a hammer.

12. Tap the steering knuckle/spindle lightly with a hammer and detach it from knuckle/spindle support. Be careful not to drop the thrust bearing.

The kingpin bushings should be aligned with the grease nipple hole in the spindle

13. Drive the steering knuckle/spindle bushing and grease seal out of the kingpin bore with a kingpin bushing driver. Do not try to use a drift, because it will probably score the inner wall of the knuckle spindle.

14. After cleaning the pin bores thoroughly, install the new bushing carefully by using a bushing driver. Position the bushings in the spindle so that they are flush with the counterbores for the plugs. The bushings in the factory rebuilding kit have a grease gallery which should align with the grease nipple hole in the spindle (see the illustration).

15. Remove the grease nipples and drill grease holes through the bushings, placing the drill through the threaded grease nipple hole. The grease hole should be ⅛ in. or less. Remove *all* metal filings and burrs after drilling the grease holes. This step is not necessary if you have used the factory bushings and installed them as outlined in step 14.

16. Ream the inside of the kingpin bushings, if necessary, to 0.7878–0.7888 in. The fit should be such that the kingpin, when greased, can be turned or pushed in or out with thumb pressure. Use the lower bore as a guide for reaming the upper bore, and vice versa, to keep the bores aligned.

17. Press fit the grease seal on the upper bushing. Take care not to damage the grease seal lip.

18. Install the steering knuckle/spindle to the steering knuckle/spindle support in the reverse order of removal as follows:

19. Insert the O-ring in the lower end of the knuckle/spindle support. Install the thrust bearing and shim together with the steering knuckle/spindle to the knuckle/spindle support.

Select the spindle shims which will obtain 0.004 in. or less clearance between the

1. Upper arm pivot shaft	19. Wheel hub	lbs.)
2. Camber adjusting shim	20. Rotor	A. 8.0 to 10.0 (58 to 72)
3. Rebound bumper	21. Backing plate	B. 3.9 to 5.3 (28 to 38)
4. Bushing	22. Inner wheel bearing	C. 3.1 to 4.1 (22 to 30)
5. Upper arm	23. Grease seal	D. 7.7 to 10.5 (56 to 76)
6. Upper ball joint	24. Spacer	E. 8.0 to 10.0 (58 to 72)
7. Knuckle spindle	25. Lower ball joint	F. 17.2 to 19.5 (124 to 141)
8. Torsion bar	26. Lower arm	G. 3.9 to 5.3 (28 to 38)
9. Boot	27. Tension rod (strut)	H. 3.0 to 4.2 (22 to 30)
10. Anchor arm	28. Shock absorber	I. 1.6 to 2.2 (12 to 16)
11. Anchor arm adjusting bolt	29. Torque arm	J. 11.1 to 15.0 (90 to 108)
12. Adjusting nut	30. Lower arm pivot shaft	K. 3.1 to 4.1 (22 to 30)
13. Cotter pin	31. Bumper stop	L. 1.6 to 2.2 (12 to 16)
14. O-ring	32. Stabilizer (optional)	M. 2.7 to 3.7 (20 to 27)
15. Hub cap	33. Stabilizer connecting bolt	N. 1.7 to 2.2 (12 to 16)
16. Spindle nut	34. Lower arm bushing	O. 11.1 to 15.0 (80 to 108)
17. Washer	35. Stabilizer collar	P. 3.6 to 4.6 (26 to 33)
18. Outer wheel bearing	Tightening torque kg-m (ft.	Q. 3.9 to 5.3 (28 to 38)

1978 and later front suspension

steering knuckle/spindle and the support. To measure this clearance with a feeler gauge, jack up the bottom of the spindle slightly.

NOTE: The thrust bearing is installed so that the covered side faces upward. You will probably be able to use the same shims that were originally installed.

20. Drive the new kingpin into the kingpin bores, securing the steering knuckle/spindle to the support.

21. Align the locking bolt hole of the knuckle/spindle support with the notch in the kingpin and install the lockbolt.

22. Install the upper and lower kingpin plugs.

23. Install the steering knuckle/spindle arm to the steering knuckle/spindle together with a new lockplate. Tighten the steering knuckle arm attaching bolts to 75–88 ft. lbs. Bend the tabs of the lockplate to engage the flats on the bolt head.

24. Install the brake backing plate, hub and wheel bearings, brake drum, and wheel. Bleed the brake hydraulic system and grease the newly installed bushings until grease is visible around the upper and lower grease seals.

Ball Joints

Ball joints are used on 1978 and later trucks, replacing the kingpins used previously.

INSPECTION

The ball joint should be replaced when play becomes excessive. Datsun does not publish specifications on just what constitutes excessive play, relying instead on a method of determining the force (in inch pounds) required to keep the ball joint turning. This method is not very helpful to the backyard mechanic since it involves removing the ball joint, which is what we are trying to avoid in the first place. An effective way to determine ball joint play is to jack up the truck until the wheel is just a couple of inches off the ground and the ball joint is unloaded, which means that you can't jack directly under the ball joint. Place a long bar under the tire and move the wheel and tire assembly up and down. Keep one hand on top of the tire while you are doing this. If there is over ¼ inch of play at the top of the tire, the ball joint is probably bad. This assuming that the wheel bearings are in good shape and properly adjusted. As a double check, have someone watch the ball joint while you move the tire up and down with the bar. If considerable play is seen, besides feeling play at the top of the wheel, the ball joints need to be replaced.

REMOVAL & INSTALLATION

Upper

1. Raise and support the truck on stands placed on the frame rails.

2. Remove the wheels.

3. Loosen the torsion bar anchor lock and adjusting nuts to relieve spring tension.

4. Remove and discard the cotter pin from the ball joint stud and remove the nut. Separate the stud from the knuckle spindle with a ball joint removal tool.

5. Loosen the bolts retaining the ball joint to the control arm, and remove the joint.

6. Install the new ball joint into the control arm, tightening the bolts to 12–16 ft. lbs. Install the ball joint stud into the knuckle spindle and install the nut. Tighten the nut to 60 ft. lbs., then continue to tighten until the holes align (limit: 72 ft. lbs.). Install a new cotter pin. Install the wheel, lower the truck, and adjust the ride height. Have the alignment checked.

Lower

1. Perform steps 1 and 2 of the upper ball joint removal procedure. Remove the lower shock absorber mounting bolt.

2. Loosen the torsion bar spring anchor lock and adjusting nuts, and remove the anchor arm bolt from the anchor arm.

3. Remove the snap-ring, then move the anchor arm and torsion bar fully rearward.

4. Disconnect the stabilizer bar from the lower arm, if equipped.

5. Disconnect the strut (tension rod) from the lower arm.

6. Remove and discard the cotter pin from the ball joint stud, and remove the nut. Separate the ball joint from the knuckle spindle with a ball joint removal tool.

7. Remove the attaching bolts, and remove the ball joint from the lower arm.

8. Install the new ball joint in the arm, tightening the bolts to 28–38 ft. lbs. Install the ball joint stud into the knuckle spindle and tighten the nut to 127 ft. lbs. Continue to tighten until the holes align, then install the new cotter pin (limit: 141 ft. lbs.). The torsion bar ride height must be adjusted after assembly.

Upper and Lower Control Arms

REMOVAL & INSTALLATION

1977

1. Raise the truck on a hoist or jack up the front end and support it with jackstands placed under the frame.

2. Remove the wheel and brake drum.

3. Remove the hub.

4. Remove the brake backing plate from the steering knuckle/spindle support.

5. Remove the steering knuckle/spindle arm, torsion bar, stabilizer bar, shock absorber, and strut rod, in this order.

6. Remove the upper fulcrum bolt securing the knuckle/spindle support to the upper control arm assembly and detach the two.

Driving the fulcrum pin out of the lower control arm in order to remove the steering knuckle support

7. Remove the upper control arm bushings from the knuckle/spindle support.

8. Remove the screw bushings from both ends of the lower control arm fulcrum pin.

9. Loosen the nut at the lower end of the knuckle/spindle support from the inside

The upper control arm pivot shaft

ST36070000

Removing the lower control arm pivot shaft bushing

UNIT: MM (IN)

9.05 TO 11.05 (0.3563 TO 0.4350) 36.5 (1.437) 9.05 TO 11.05 (0.3563 TO 0.4350)

Installation of the lower control arm-to-knuckle screw bushing

and pull out the cotter pin retaining the fulcrum.

10. Drive the fulcrum pin out of the lower control arm and remove the knuckle/spindle support and steering knuckle/spindle from the lower control arm.

11. Remove the bolts retaining the upper control arm pivot shaft and remove the upper control arm pivot shaft with the camber adjusting shims from the body bracket.

12. Remove the nut retaining the lower control arm pivot shaft and remove the lower control arm pivot shaft. Remove the lower control arm with the torque arm from the mounting bracket.

13. The lower control arm bushing is removed with a drift and hammer.

14. Install the upper and lower control arms in the reverse order of removal. Tighten the lower control arm attaching nut to 54–58 ft. lbs. Tighten the upper control arm and camber adjusting shim bolts to 51–65 ft. lbs.

15. Coat the threads of the fulcrum pin with grease and line up the notch of the fulcrum pin with the knuckle/spindle support for the insertion of the cotter pin. Install the fulcrum pin to the knuckle/spindle support with a soft hammer, attaching the support to the upper control arm. Install the cotter pin and tighten the locknut to 5.8–8.0 ft. lbs.

16. Coat the threaded portion inside of the screw bushing liberally with grease. Position the support at the center of the lower control arm and install the screw bushings. Check the dimensions of the installed screw bushing against those in the illustration, then tighten the bushing to 145–216 ft. lbs.

17. Replace the grease filler plug with a grease fitting and pump grease in until grease comes out around the dust cover. Reinstall the filler plug.

18. Install the upper control arm bushing to the knuckle/spindle support and then connect the knuckle/spindle support to the upper control arm. Insert the connecting bolt from the rear and tighten the nut to 28–38 ft. lbs.

19. Install the strut rod, shock absorber, stabilizer rod, torsion bar, and steering knuckle arm.

20. Install the brake backing plate to the steering knuckle/spindle and tighten the attaching bolts to 30–36 ft. lbs.

21. Install the brake drum and wheel and adjust the wheel bearing preload.

1978–84
UPPER

1. Perform steps 1–4 of the upper ball joint removal procedure.

2. Remove the bolts retaining the upper arm pivot shaft and remove the shaft, arm, and camber adjusting shims from the body. Note the location of the shims so that they may be installed in their original positions during assembly.

3. To remove the upper arm shaft and bushings from the arm, remove the nuts and

DIMENSION
C = 4.5 MM (0.177 IN)
D = 144.6 to 146.6 MM (5.69 TO 5.77 IN)
E = 28.3 MM (1.114 IN)

1. Outer collar
2. Inner collar

Upper arm pivot shaft and bushing installation dimensions, 1978 and later

Upper arm pivot shaft installation before tightening the shaft nuts, 1978 and later

washers from the shaft. Use a press, first on one end of the shaft and then the other, to press out the bushings. Remove the shaft.

4. To install, coat the bushing with soapy water and press it into the upper arm. Install the washers onto the shaft and install the shaft into the arm. Be sure the chamfered side of the washer is against the shaft flange. Measure the distance between the outer collar on the bushing and the washer on the shaft (dimension "C" in the illustration); it should exceed 4.5 mm (0.177 in.).

5. Press the other bushing into the arm, and check dimension "C." Also check the distance between the outer collars of both bushings (dimension "D") and the distance between the end of the bushing and the centerline of the shaft mounting bolt bore (dimension "E"). D should be 144.6–146.6 mm (5.69–5.77 in.); E should be 28.3 mm (1.114 in.).

6. Rotate the pivot shaft in the arm until the angle is as specified in the illustration. Install the nuts and washers on the shaft. Tighten the bushings to 56–76 ft. lbs.

7. Install the upper arm and shaft assembly to the body, replacing the camber shims in their original locations. Tighten the bolts to 80–108 ft. lbs.

8. Follow step 6 of the upper ball joint removal procedure.

LOWER

1. Perform steps 1–6 of the lower ball joint removal procedure.

2. Remove the lower arm pivot shaft bolt and washer. Tap the pivot shaft out of the bushing. Push down on the torsion bar and remove the lower arm.

3. Use a bushing driver to tap the lower arm bushing from the frame.

4. Drive the new bushing into the frame.

5. Install the arm and pivot shaft, tightening the nut to 80–108 ft. lbs.

6. Follow step 8 of the lower ball joint removal procedure.

4-WHEEL DRIVE FRONT SUSPENSION

Hub and Knuckle

REMOVAL & INSTALLATION

1. Block the rear wheels, raise and support the front of the vehicle on jackstands.

2. Remove the wheels.

3. Remove the brake caliper and suspend it out of the way. DO NOT DISCONNECT THE BRAKE HOSE!

4. Remove the axle shaft.

Knuckle arm attaching bolt

Upper and lower ball joint nuts

5. Remove the bolt securing the knuckle arm to the knuckle.

6. Loosen, but do not remove the upper and lower ball joint tightening nuts.

7. Separate the ball joints from the knuckle with a ball joint removing tool.

—————— CAUTION ——————
NEVER REMOVE THE BALLJOINT NUT IN THE PREVIOUS STEP!

8. Jack up the lower link and remove the ball joint tightening nut.

9. Remove the knuckle.

10. Unbend the lockwasher with a screwdriver and remove the front hub locknut.

11. Remove the lockwasher and special washer.

12. Push the wheel bearing support out of the hub.

13. Separate the knuckle from the hub with a puller.

14. Remove the bearing collar.

15. Remove the inside bearing and seal.

ST29020001

Removing the ball joint using a ball joint tool

JACK UP

Removing the ball joint tightening nuts

Unbending the lockwasher

Drive the race out with a brass driver.

16. Separate the hub from the rotor.

17. Knock the hub on a wood block to move the outer bearing away from the hub surface, then pull it the rest of the way with a bearing puller. Remove the grease seal.

18. Remove the axle shaft bearing from the bearing support with a brass driver.

19. Clean and thoroughly repack the bearings.

20. Assembly is the reverse of removal. Note the following points:

a. Install the bearing outer race into each side of the knuckle with a brass driver.

b. Install the outer grease seal and bearing with a brass driver.

c. Pack the seal lip with wheel bearing grease. Be sure that the seal faces the right direction.

d. The wheel bearing collar thickness determines end-play. Determine what thickness to use as follows:

Determining Bearing Collar Thickness

1. Install the collar which was removed.

2. Install the inside bearing with a brass driver.

KV40102500

SPECIAL WASHER

LOCK WASHER

Removing the special washer and lock-washer

WHEEL BEARING SUPPORT

Wheel bearing support greasing location

Using a puller to separate the hub from the knuckle

Driving out the inner bearing and seal

Removing the outer bearing with a puller

Installing the outer bearing into the knuckle

Bearing collars are stamped with a number to indicate thickness

Proper positioning of the lockwasher and special washer

WHEEL BEARING PRELOAD
(AS MEASURED AT WHEEL HUB BOLT):
9.8 - 42.2N (1.0 - 4.3 KG, 2.2 - 9.5 LB)

Measuring preload with a spring scale

3. Install the special washer and lockwasher.

4. Tighten the locknut to 108–145 ft. lbs.

5. Turn the hub several times in both directions to seat the bearings.

6. Using a spring scale as shown, check the preload to see that it falls between 2.2 and 9.5 ft. lbs.

7. If not, adjust by replacing the collar with one of a different thickness, as shown by the number stamped on the collar. The larger the number, the thicker the collar.

8. When preload has been correctly set, secure the nut by bending the lockwasher tip.

Observe the following torques:

Item	ft. lbs.
Upper ball joint-to-knuckle	36–65
Lower ball joint-to-knuckle	43–72
Knuckle arm-to-knuckle	53–72
Caliper-to-knuckle	53–72
Axle shaft-to-carrier	20–27
Free running hub	18–25
Stabilizer bar	12–16
Wheel nut	87–108

Hit the hub on a block of wood to break the outer bearing loose from the hub face

Shock Absorbers

See the 2-wheel drive section.

Torsion Bars

REMOVAL & INSTALLATION

1. Raise and support the front end on jack stands.

2. Remove the torsion bar spring anchor bolt.

3. Pull the anchor arm out rearward.

4. Pull the torsion bar spring rearward.

5. Remove the torsion bar.

6. Install the torsion arm to the lower link. Torque the outer bolt to 20–27 ft. lbs. and the inner to 26–33 ft. lbs.

7. Place a coating of grease on the torsion bar spring serrated end and install it in the torsion arm.

8. Install the anchor arm to the serrated end of the torsion bar spring and install the anchor arm adjusting bolt. Turn the bolt until the bottom of the nut is about ½ (Dimension A) inch from the end of the bolt.

9. Install the dust cover.

10. Adjust the anchor arm position until the distance between the end of the dust cover and the bottom of the nut (Dimension B) is about 2½ inches.

11. Lower the vehicle.

12. Turn the anchor bolt adjusting nut until the center line of the lower link spindle is 5.28–5.47 inches above the tension rod attaching bolts. This is dimension H in the accompanying figure.

Torsion bar spring anchor bolt

Torque arm-to-torsion bar attachment

B: 60 - 70 mm (2.36 - 2.76 in)

Anchor arm position adjustment

Four wheel drive front suspension

Attaching the tension rod and stabilizer bar to the lower control arm

Torque arm-to-lower control arm attachment

A: 7 - 17 mm (0.28 - 0.67 in)

Anchor arm adjusting bolt measurement

Torsion bar anchor arm

Tension Bar and Stabilizer Link

See the 2-wheel drive section.

Ball Joints and Control Arms

See the 2-wheel drive section with the following exceptions:

INSTALLATION

1. Install the lower ball joint to the con-

trol arm. Torque the attaching bolts to 28–38 ft. lbs.

2. Install the lower control arm spindle bushing to the frame.

Torsion bar spring serrated ends. Note that they are marked and not interchangeable

Ride height adjustment

Torsion arm-to-link bolts

Ball joint-to-control arm bolts

3. Attach the torque arm to the torsion bar.

4. Install the lower control arm.

5. Install the torque arm on the lower control arm. Torque the inner side to 26–33 ft. lbs. and the outer side to 20–27 ft. lbs.

6. Jack up the lower link.

7. Install the lower ball joint in the spindle and torque the nut to 43–72 ft. lbs.

8. Install the shock absorber lower end to the control arm and torque to 22–30 ft. lbs.

9. Install the tension rod and stabilizer connecting rod to the control arm.

10. Lower the vehicle.

11. Turn the anchor bolt adjusting nut to obtain the dimension specified in step 12 of Torsion Bar Removal and Installation.

12. After installation, check wheel alignment.

REAR SUSPENSION

The rear suspension consists of semielliptic leaf springs and telescopic hydraulic shock absorbers. There are rubber bushings at either end of the leaf springs and shock absorbers to absorb vibration and noise.

Springs

REMOVAL & INSTALLATION

———— CAUTION ————

The leaf springs are under a considerable amount of tension. Be very careful when removing or installing them; they can exert enough force to cause serious injuries.

1. Jack up the rear of the truck and support it with jackstands placed under the frame.

2. Disconnect the shock absorbers at their lower end.

3. Remove the nuts securing the U-bolts around the axle housing.

4. Place a jack under the rear axle housing and raise the housing to remove the weight off the spring.

1. Shock absorber lower attaching nut
2. U-bolt attaching nut

Shock absorber lower end and U-bolt attaching nuts

Spring shackle

Spring pin

5. Remove the nuts from the spring shackles, drive out the shackle pins and remove the spring from the vehicle.

6. Install the spring in the reverse order of removal. The weight of the truck must be on the rear wheels before tightening the front pin, shackle, and shock absorber attaching nuts. Tighten the front pin and shackle nuts to 83–94 ft. lbs. (37–50 ft. lbs. for the spring shackle nuts, 1978–82), the U-bolt nuts to 53–72 ft. lbs., and the shock absorber lower end nut to 12–16 ft. lbs.

Shock Absorbers

INSPECTION AND TESTING

Inspect and test the rear shock absorbers in the same manner as outlined for the front shock absorbers.

REMOVAL & INSTALLATION

The rear shock absorbers are removed simply by removing the upper and lower attaching nuts, and removing the component from the vehicle. They are installed in the reverse order. The weight of the vehicle must be on the rear wheels before tightening the shock absorber attaching nuts to 12–16 ft. lbs.

STEERING

Steering Wheel

REMOVAL & INSTALLATION

1. Position the wheels in the straight-ahead position.

2. Disconnect the battery ground cable from the battery.

3. Remove the horn pad by unscrewing the two screws from the rear side of the steering wheel crossbar.

4. Punch mark the top of the steering column shaft and the steering wheel flange.

Removing the horn pad from the steering wheel

Removing the steering wheel with a puller

5. Remove the attaching nut and remove the steering wheel with a puller.

CAUTION

Do not strike the shaft with a hammer, which may cause the column to collapse.

---

6. Install the steering wheel in the reverse order of removal aligning the punch marks. Tighten the steering wheel attaching nut to 51–54 ft. lbs.

Turn Signal and Dimmer Switch

REMOVAL & INSTALLATION

1. Disconnect the negative cable from the battery.
2. Remove the steering wheel.
3. Disconnect the wiring harness from the clip which retains it to the lower instrument panel.
4. Disconnect the multiple connector and lead wire from the instrument panel wiring harness.
5. Remove the steering column shell covers (upper and lower).
6. Loosen the two screws attaching the switch assembly to the steering column jacket and remove the switch assembly.
7. Install the turn signal and dimmer switch and the steering wheel in the reverse order of removal.

Ignition Switch

REMOVAL & INSTALLATION

1. Disconnect the negative cable from the battery.
2. Unscrew and remove the escutcheon from the front of the ignition switch.
3. Remove the ignition switch and wiring harness with spacer from the steering shell cover.
4. Disconnect the wiring connector from the back of the ignition switch.
5. Install the ignition switch in the reverse order of removal.

NOTE: On models with the optional steering lock cylinder, remove the switch by removing the two retaining screws from the back of the steering lock cylinder.

Steering Lock

REMOVAL & INSTALLATION

1. Remove the ignition switch.
2. Drill out the two shear screws.
3. Remove the two other normal type screws and dismount the steering lock from the steering jacket tube.
4. Install a new steering lock in the reverse order, being sure to tighten the two shear screws until they shear.

1. Steering wheel
2. Column clamp
3. Post grommet
4. Steering column jacket
5. Steering column shaft
6. Knuckle arm
7. Idler arm assembly
8. Cross rod socket
9. Cross rod
10. Steering gear assembly
11. Steering gear arm
12. Side rod
13. Knuckle arm

1977–79 steering linkage

Steering Linkage

REMOVAL & INSTALLATION

1. Jack up the front of the truck and support it with jackstands placed under the frame.
2. Remove the cotter pins and nuts securing the side rod ball studs to the steering knuckle/spindle arms.
3. Use a puller to disconnect the side rod ball studs from the steering knuckle arms. If a puller is not available, strike the side of the steering knuckle arm boss with

The idler arm attaching nuts

1980–84 steering linkage

1. Cross rod (tie rod)
2. Side rod
3. Ball socket
4. Idler arm assembly
5. Steering gear assembly

← 516 mm (20.31 in) →

*After adjustment of toe-in, be sure that dimension "A" at both ends of cross rod is not less than 20 mm (0.79 in).

Steering linkage installation dimensions, all models

a hammer, backing it up with a heavy hammer on the opposite side, and at the same time having an assistant pull the ball stud out of the steering knuckle arm.

NOTE: Do not strike the ball stud head, the ball socket on the side rod, or the side rod with the hammer.

4. Remove the nut securing the steering gear arm on the sector shaft and remove the gear arm with a puller. If a puller is not available, and the steering gear arm need not be removed, disconnect the side arm and tie-rod ball studs from the steering gear arm in the same manner as outlined in Step 3.

5. Remove the idler arm assembly from the frame by unscrewing the two attaching nuts.

6. Install the steering linkage in the reverse order of removal. Tighten the ball stud nuts to 40–55 ft. lbs. idler arm assembly attaching nuts to 23–27 ft. lbs., and the tie-rod adjustment locknuts to 58–72 ft. lbs. Adjust the toe-in and steering angle.

Steering Gear

REMOVAL & INSTALLATION

1. Raise and support the truck on jack stands.
2. Unbolt the wormshaft at the rubber coupling.

3. Matchmark the idler arm and sector shaft, and with the wheels in a straight ahead position, remove the idler arm-to-sector shaft nut and remove the idler arm with a puller.

4. Unbolt and remove the gear from the frame.

5. Installation is the reverse of removal. Torque the wormshaft coupling bolt to 29–36 ft. lbs.; the idle arm nut to 94–108 ft. lbs. and the gear-to-frame bolts to 62–71 ft. lbs.

BRAKE SYSTEM

For all brake system service and repair procedures not detailed below, please refer to "Brakes" in the Unit Repair section.

Worm shaft to rubber coupling
Ⓣ 39 - 49 (4.0 - 5.0, 29 - 36)
Align the groove in worm shaft with the bolt hole in rubber coupling flange yoke, and press coupling bolt through the undercut section of worm shaft.

Ⓣ: N·m (kg-m, ft-lb)

Undercut section

Sector shaft to idler arm
Ⓣ 127 - 147 (13 - 15, 94 - 108)
● Remove gear arm

ST29020001

● Install gear arm
Align four grooves of gear arm serrations with four projections of sector shaft serrations, and install and tighten lock washer and nut.

Gear housing to frame
Ⓣ 84 - 96 (8.6 - 9.8, 62 - 71)

Steering gear removal and installation

Adjustment

DISC BRAKES

The front disc brakes are inherently self-adjusting. No adjustments are either necessary or possible.

DRUM BRAKES

1. Jack up the wheel to be adjusted until it completely clears the ground.
2. Make sure that the parking brake is completely released if the rear brakes are being adjusted.
3. Remove the rubber boot from the rear of the brake backing plate.
4. Lightly tap the adjuster housing forward with a hammer and screwdriver.
5. Turn the adjuster wheel downward with a screwdriver to spread the brake shoes. Stop turning the adjuster wheel when the brake drum is locked and the wheel cannot be turned by hand.
6. Turn the adjuster wheel upward, backing off the shoes from the brake drum 12 notches, to obtain the correct clearance between the brake shoes and drum. Turn the wheel to make sure that the brake drum turns without dragging.
7. Install the rubber boot.

BRAKE PEDAL ADJUSTMENT

The trucks are equipped with an adjustable master cylinder pushrod for setting free-play.

1. Adjust the height of the stop light switch so that the top surface of the brake pedal is off the surface of the floor board (without rugs): 5.8 in., 1977, 6.06 in., 1978–79, and 6.7 in. for 1980–84. Tighten the stop light switch locknut.
2. Adjust the length of the master cylinder pushrod (booster pushrod on vehicles so equipped) clevis so that the specified free-play exists between the brake pedal and the pushrod. Free-play should be 0.024–0.047 in., 1977, or 0.04–0.20 in., 1978–84.
3. Operate the brake pedal to make sure that it operates freely with no noise or interference.

Wheel Bearings

The following is for 2-wheel drive only. For 4-wheel drive vehicles, see the Front Drive Axle section.

Only the front wheel bearings require periodic service. The lubricant to use is high temperature disc brake wheel bearing grease meeting NLGI No. 2 specifications. (This grease should be used even if your Datsun is equipped with drum brakes; it has superior protection characteristics.)

You will not need any special tools for this job, although the use of a torque wrench

Drive worn bearing cups from the hub with a soft drift and hammer

1. Spacer
2. Grease seal
3. Inner bearing
4. Hub bolt
5. Backing plate
6. Disc (rotor)
7. Hub
8. Lug nut
9. Outer bearing
10. Washer
11. Adjusting nut
12. Lock (castle) nut
13. Cotter pin
14. O-ring
15. Grease cap

2-wheel drive hub and bearings with disc brakes. Drum brakes are similar

is strongly recommended for accurate measurement of bearing preload. Procedures are basically the same for either drum or disc brakes.

The most important thing to remember when working with the wheel bearings is that although they are basically durable, in some ways they are remarkably fragile. Mishandling, grit, misalignment, scratches, improper preload, etc. will quickly destroy any roller bearing, no matter how well hardened during manufacture.

REMOVAL & INSTALLATION

1. Loosen the wheel nuts, raise the truck, and remove the wheel and tire. Remove the brake drum or brake caliper.

2. It is not necessary to remove the drum or disc from the hub. The outer wheel bearing will come off with the hub. Simply pull the hub and disc or drum assembly toward you off the spindle. Be sure to catch the bearing before it falls to the ground.

3. From the inner side of the hub, remove the inner grease seal, and lift the inner bearing from the hub. Discard the grease seal.

4. Clean the bearings in solvent and allow them to air dry. You risk leaving bits of lint in the races if you dry them with a

Fill the shaded portion of the hub and grease cap with wheel bearing grease. Also coat the cups with grease

rag. Clean the grease cap, nuts, spindle, and the races in the hub thoroughly, and allow the parts to dry.

5. Inspect the bearing carefully. If they are worn, cracked, brinelled, pitted, burned, scored, etc., they should be replaced, along with the bearing cups in which they run in the hub. Do not mix old and new parts.

6. If the cups are worn, remove them from the hub, by using a brass rod as a drift.

To install:

7. If the old cups were removed, install the new inner and outer cups into the hub, using either a tool made for the purpose, or a socket or piece of pipe of a large enough diameter to press on the outside rim of the cup only.

CAUTION

Use care not to cock the bearing cups in the hub. If they are not fully seated, the bearings will be impossible to adjust properly.

8. Pack the inside area of the hub and cups with grease, according to the illustration given. Pack the inside of the grease cap while you're at it, but do not install the cap into the hub.

9. Pack the inner bearing with grease. Place a large glob of grease into the palm of one hand and push the inner bearing through it with a sliding motion. The grease must be forced through the side of the bearing and in between each roller. Continue until the grease begins to ooze out the other side through the gaps between the rollers; the bearing must be completely packed with grease. Install the inner bearing into its cup in the hub, then press a new grease seal into place over it.

10. Install the hub and rotor or drum assembly onto the spindle. Pack the outer bearing with grease in the same manner as the inner bearing, then install the outer bearing into place in the hub.

11. Apply a thin coat of grease to the washer and the threaded portion of the spindle, then loosely install the washer and adjusting nut. Go on to the bearing preload adjustment following.

BEARING PRELOAD ADJUSTMENT

1. While turning the hub forward, tighten the adjusting nut to 22–29 ft. lbs.

2. Rotate the hub a few more times to snug down the bearings.

3. Retighten the nut to 22–29 ft. lbs. Unscrew the adjusting nut ⅛ of a turn (45 degrees). Install the lock nut (castellated nut) and snug it down against the adjusting nut until one of its grooves lines up with the hole in the spindle. It is okay to tighten the adjusting nut up to 15 degrees to allow the lock nut holes to align. Install a new cotter pin, bending its ends around the lock nut.

4. Install the wheel and a couple of lug nuts. Check the axial play of the wheel by shaking it back and forth. The bearing free play should feel close to zero, but the wheel should spin freely. Be sure the brake shoes are not dragging against the drum, if your truck has drum brakes.

5. If the bearing play is correct, with drum brakes you can install the grease cap and the rest of the lug nuts. With disc brakes, remove the wheel, replace the caliper, then install the wheel and grease cap.

Rear Wheel Cylinders

REMOVAL & INSTALLATION

1. Jack up the vehicle, remove the wheel, brake drum, and brake shoes.

2. Disconnect the brake tube from the rear of the wheel cylinder.

3. Remove the wheel cylinder retaining nuts and remove the wheel cylinder from the backing plate.

4. Install the wheel cylinder and assemble the brake in the reverse order of removal and disassembly.

5. Bleed the brake hydraulic system.

OVERHAUL

The rear wheel cylinders are overhauled in the same manner as is outlined for the front wheel cylinders. The only difference is that the rear wheel cylinder bores are open at both ends and contain two pistons, piston heads, and dust boots.

Parking brake adjusting nut

Parking Brake Cable

ADJUSTMENT

1. Jack up the rear of the vehicle until the rear wheels clear the ground.
2. Adjust the rear brakes as outlined under "Brake System Adjustment."
3. Loosen the locknut at the parking cable lever assembly mounted on the driveshaft center bearing crossmember.
4. Turn the adjusting nut until the parking brake control lever operating stroke is between 3 in. and 4 in.
5. Release the parking brake and make sure that the rear wheels turn freely with no drag.
6. Lower the vehicle.

REMOVAL & INSTALLATION

1. Fully release the parking brake control lever.
2. Loosen the adjusting nut at the cable lever mounted to the frame crossmember.
3. Disconnect the cable from the control lever.
4. Remove the rear brake drums, and disconnect the parking brake cables from the parking brake toggle levers of the rear service brake assemblies.
5. Remove lockplate, spring and clip, and pull the parking brake cable out toward the cable lever.
6. Remove the cotter pin at the cable lever and disconnect the cable.
7. Install the cables in the reverse order of removal. Apply a light coat of grease to the cables to make sure that they slide properly. Adjust the parking brake cables.

CHASSIS ELECTRICAL

Heater Assembly

REMOVAL & INSTALLATION
1977–79

1. Disconnect the battery ground cable.

1. Defroster nozzle (LH)	5. Heater motor	9. Control cable clip
2. Defroster duct (LH)	6. Heater case	10. Heater cock
3. Heater control	7. Ventilator knob	11. Defroster duct (RH)
4. Resistor	8. Heater core	12. Defroster nozzle (RH)

1977–79 heater assembly

Removing the heater assembly front cover

Control cable positioning

VENTILATION DOOR

HEATER CORE

AIR MIX DOOR

FLOOR/ROSTER DOOR

WATER COCK

1980–84 heater assembly

2. Drain the engine coolant.

3. Remove the defroster hoses.

4. Remove the three cable retaining clips and disconnect the control cables from the valves and water cock.

5. Disconnect the two fan motor leads from each connector.

6. Disconnect the two resistor lead wires from each connector.

7. Disconnect the water hoses from the heater core and water cock.

8. Remove the three heater housing mounting bolts and remove the heater assembly from the vehicle.

9. Install the heater assembly in the reverse order of removal.

1980–84

1. Disconnect the battery ground cable.

2. Drain the cooling system.

3. On models with air conditioning, disconnect the heater hose from the engine.

4. On models without air conditioning, remove the heater duct and disconnect the heater hose at the heater.

5. Remove the console box and instrument panel assembly.

6. Disconnect the air intake control cable from the blower.

7. On models equipped with A/C, remove the blower. Remove the evaporator unit nuts and bolts, but do not remove the evaporator unit.

8. Remove the heater assembly.

9. Installation is the reverse of removal. Adjust the control cable for proper operation.

Blower

REMOVAL & INSTALLATION

1977–79

1. Remove the heater assembly from the vehicle as previously outlined.

2. Remove the nine spring clips and disassemble the heater housing.

3. Remove the fan from the electric motor.

4. Remove the fan motor retaining screws and remove the motor.

5. Install the blower motor and heater assembly in the reverse order.

1980–84

1. Disconnect the battery ground.

2. Remove the package tray.

3. Remove the heater duct on models without air conditioning.

4. Remove the resistor connector and disconnect the control cable.

5. Remove the blower.

6. Installation is the reverse of removal. Adjust the control cable for proper operation.

Heater Core

REMOVAL & INSTALLATION

1. Drain the engine coolant.

2. Remove the defroster hoses.

3. Disconnect the water hoses from the inlet and outlet pipes of the heater core.

4. Remove the four clips and front cover.

5. Remove the heater core from the heater housing.

6. Install the heater core in the reverse order of removal.

Removing the heater core

Radio

Observe the following cautions when working on the radio:

1. Always observe the proper polarity of the connections (positive to positive and negative to negative).

2. Never operate the radio without a speaker, to prevent damage to the output transistors. If a new speaker is installed, make sure it has the correct impedance (ohms) for the radio.

1977–79 radio removal

If a new antenna or antenna cable is used, or if poor AM reception is noted, the antenna trimmer can be adjusted. Tune the radio to a weak station around 1400kc. Adjust the trimmer screw until best reception and maximum volume are obtained. The trimmer screw for the factory-installed radio is located in the lower left corner of the rear of the radio case 1977–78 and above the left knob on the front of the radio in 1979. For best FM reception, raise the antenna to 31 inches. For best AM reception, raise the antenna to its full height.

REMOVAL & INSTALLATION

1977–79

1. Pull the knobs off the radio control shafts.

2. Remove the radio retaining nuts and washer from the radio control shafts.

3. Remove the bezel plate from the front of the radio.

4. Disconnect the antenna cable and the power and speaker wires from under the instrument panel.

5. Remove the radio from the instrument panel.

6. Install the radio in the reverse order of removal.

1980–84

1. Disconnect the battery ground.

2. Remove the ash tray and heater/air conditioner control panel.

3. Disconnect the wiring plug at the back of the radio.

4. Remove the plug covering the mounting screws, remove the screws and pull the radio from the dash.

5. Disconnect the wiring harness and the antenna.

6. Installation is the reverse of removal.

1980–84 radio removal

Windshield Wiper Motor

REMOVAL & INSTALLATION

1. Remove the wiper blades and arms as an assembly from the pivots. The arms are retained to the pivots by nuts. Remove the nuts and pull the arms straight off.

2. Remove the cowl top grille. It is retained by four screws at its front edge. Remove the screws and pull the grille forward to disengage the tabs at the rear.

3. Remove the stop ring which connects the wiper motor arm to the connecting rod.

4. Disconnect the wiper motor harness at the connector on the wiper motor body

Windshield wiper motor

from under the instrument panel.

5. Remove the three retaining screws and pull the wiper motor outward and remove the motor from the vehicle.

6. Install the wiper motor in the reverse order of removal. The wiper arms should be installed so that the blades are .98 in. (25 mm) above, and parallel to, the windshield molding. If the motor has been run, be sure the motor and linkage is in its parked position before installing the wiper arms. To do this, turn the ignition switch on, and cycle the motor three or four times. Shut off the motor with the wiper switch (not the ignition switch), and allow the motor to return to the park position.

Wiper Linkage

REMOVAL & INSTALLATION

1. Remove the wiper blade and arm from the pivot.

2. Remove the cowl top grille.

25 MM (0.98 IN)

Wiper arm installation

3. Remove the two flange nuts retaining the wiper linkage pivot to the cowl top.

4. Remove the stop ring which retains the connecting rod to the wiper motor arm.

5. Remove the wiper motor linkage assembly from the truck.

6. Install the linkage in the reverse order of removal.

Instrument Cluster

REMOVAL & INSTALLATION

1977–79

1. Disconnect the battery ground (negative) cable.

1977–79 cluster cover removal

2. Working through the openings of the instrument cluster cover, remove the three screws retaining the cluster cover to the instrument panel and remove cover.

3. From underneath the instrument panel, remove the one screw retaining the cluster assembly to the lower instrument panel.

4. Withdraw the cluster lid slightly. Press the windshield wiper control knob in, turn it counterclockwise and pull it off the switch. Remove the headlight/parking light switch knob in the same manner.

5. From behind the instrument cluster, disconnect the speedometer cable at the speedometer head and the multiple connector from the printed circuit.

6. On vehicles with a clock, disconnect the wires at each connection on the instrument panel printed circuit.

7. Remove the four screws retaining the cluster assembly to the cluster lid.

8. Remove the instrument cluster assembly from under the instrument panel.

9. Install the instrument cluster in the reverse order of removal.

1980–84

1. Disconnect the battery ground.

2. Remove the cluster lid.

1980–83 cluster lid removal

1980–83 cluster removal

3. Remove the cluster assembly.

4. Remove the gauges from the cluster, individually.

5. Installation is the reverse of removal.

Speedometer Cable

REPLACEMENT

1. Reach up under the instrument panel

1984 cluster removal

and disconnect the cable housing from the back of the speedometer. It is attached by a knurled knob which simply unscrews.

2. Pull the cable from the cable housing. If the cable is broken, the other half of the cable will have to be removed from the transmission end. Unscrew the retaining knob and remove the cable from the transmission extension housing.

3. Lubricate the cable with graphite powder (sold as speedometer cable lubricant, curiously enough) and feed the cable into the housing. It is best to start at the speedometer end and feed the cable down towards the transmission. It is also usually necessary to unscrew the transmission connection and install the cable end to the gear, then reconnect the housing to the transmission. Slip the cable end into the speedometer, and reconnect the cable housing.

Headlights

REMOVAL & INSTALLATION

1. Remove the radiator grille retaining screws and remove the radiator grille.

2. Loosen and remove, if necessary, the three retaining ring screws. Do not disturb the aiming adjusting screws.

3. Remove the retaining ring by rotating it clockwise.

4. Remove the headlight from the mounting ring and disconnect the electrical connector from behind the light.

5. Change the headlight and connect the wiring connector to the new light.

6. Place the headlight in position so that the three locating tabs behind the light fit in the three holes on the mounting ring.

7. Install the headlight retaining ring and tighten the retaining screws.

8. Install the radiator grille.

Fusible Links

A fusible link is a protective device used in an electrical circuit. When current increases beyond a certain amperage, the fusible metal wire of the link melts, thus breaking the electrical circuit and preventing further damage to other components and wiring. Whenever a fusible link is melted because of a short circuit, correct the cause before installing a new fusible link.

There is only one fusible link in Datsun pick-ups installed in the thinner of the two wires connected to the positive battery terminal. Replacements are simply plugged into the connectors in this wire.

———— CAUTION ————
Use only replacements of the same electrical capacity as the original, available from your dealer. Replacements of a different electrical value will not provide adequate system protection.

Fuses

Fuses protect all the major electrical systems in the truck. In case of an electrical overload, the fuse melts, breaking the circuit and stopping the flow of electricity.

If a fuse blows, the cause should be investigated and corrected before the installation of a new fuse. This, however, is easier to say than to do. Because each fuse protects a limited number of components, your job is narrowed down somewhat. Begin your investigation by looking for obvious fraying, loose connections, breaks in

Fusible link

insulation, etc. Electrical problems are almost always a real headache to solve, but patience and persistence, coupled with logic, usually provide a solution.

The amperage of each fuse and the circuit it protects are marked on the cover of the fusebox, which is located under the instrument panel next to the steering column.

Flashers and Relays

The turn signal and four-way hazard flashers are located under the instrument panel on opposite sides of the steering column. The turn signal flasher is the larger of the two. Replacement is made by unplugging the old flasher and plugging in the new one.

Relays are used for the horn, headlights, wiper, heater, choke heater, catalyst floor sensor, air conditioner compressor, and transmission switches, although obviously not all relays are used on all models. All relays used are grouped together, and mounted on the right fender in the engine compartment.

Dodge/Plymouth
Pickups, Vans, Ramcharger, Trail Duster, Rampage

GENERAL ENGINE SPECIFICATIONS

Year	Engine Displacement (cu in.)	Estimated Horsepower (@ rpm)	Estimated Torque@ rpm (ft lbs)	Bore and Stroke (in.)	Compression Ratio	Oil Pressure (psi @ rpm)
'77	6-225	95 @ 3600①	170 @ 1600	3.40 × 4.12	8.4 : 1	30–70 @ 2000
	8-318	150 @ 4000	225 @ 1600	3.91 × 3.31	8.6 : 1	30–80 @ 2000
	8-360	170 @ 4000	285 @ 2400	4.00 × 3.58	8.4 : 1	30–80 @ 2000
	8-400	180 @ 3600	315 @ 2400	4.34 × 3.38	8.2 : 1	30–80 @ 2000
	8-440	195 @ 3600	320 @ 2000	4.32 × 3.75	8.2 : 1	30–80 @ 2000
'78	6-225	90 @ 3600①	160 @ 1600	3.40 × 4.12	8.4 : 1	30–70 @ 2000
	6-243 Diesel	100 @ 3700	163 @ 2200	3.62 × 3.94	20 : 1	43 @ 1000
	8-318	140 @ 4000	245 @ 1600	3.91 × 3.31	8.5 : 1	30–80 @ 2000
	8-360	155 @ 3600	270 @ 2400	4.00 × 3.58	8.4 : 1	30–80 @ 2000
	8-400	190 @ 3600	305 @ 3200	4.34 × 3.38	8.2 : 1	30–80 @ 2000
	8-440	225 @ 4400	360 @ 3200	4.32 × 3.75	8.2 : 1	30–80 @ 2000
'79	6-225	90 @ 3600	160 @ 1600	3.40 × 4.12	8.4 : 1	30–70 @ 2000
	6-243 Diesel	100 @ 3700	163 @ 2200	3.62 × 3.94	20 : 1	43 @ 1000
	8-318	140 @ 4000	245 @ 1600	3.91 × 3.31	8.6 : 1	30–80 @ 2000
	8-360	155 @ 3600	270 @ 2400	4.00 × 3.58	8.5 : 1	30–80 @ 2000
'80–'81④	6-225	90 @ 3600	160 @ 1600	3.40 × 4.12	8.4 : 1	35–65 @ 2000
	8-318②	120 @ 3600	245 @ 1600	3.91 × 3.31	8.5 : 1	35–65 @ 2000
	8-318③	155 @ 4000	240 @ 2000	3.91 × 3.31	8.5 : 1	35–65 @ 2000
	8-360②	130 @ 3200	255 @ 2000	4.00 × 3.58	8.4 : 1	35–65 @ 2000
	8-360③	185 @ 4000	275 @ 2000	4.00 × 3.58	8.0 : 1	35–65 @ 2000

GENERAL ENGINE SPECIFICATIONS

Year	Engine Displacement (cu in.)	Estimated Horsepower (@ rpm)	Estimated Torque@ rpm (ft lbs)	Bore and Stroke (in.)	Compression Ratio	Oil Pressure (psi @ rpm)
'82–'84④	4-135	84 @ 4800	111 @ 2400	3.44 × 3.62	8.5 : 1	50 @ 2000
	4-155.9	92 @ 4500	131 @ 2500	3.59 × 3.86	8.2 : 1	56 @ 2000
	6-225	90 @ 3600	160 @ 1600	3.40 × 4.12	8.4 : 1	35–65 @ 2000
	8-318②	120 @ 3600	245 @ 1600	3.91 × 3.31	8.5 : 1	35–65 @ 2000
	8-318③	155 @ 4000	240 @ 2000	3.91 × 3.31	8.5 : 1	35–65 @ 2000
	8-360②	130 @ 3200	255 @ 2000	4.00 × 3.58	8.4 : 1	35–65 @ 2000
	8-360③	185 @ 4000	275 @ 2000	4.00 × 3.58	8.0 : 1	35–65 @ 2000

①10 more hp with two barrel carburetor
②2 barrel carb
③4 barrel carb
④Horsepower and torque are SAE net figures. They are measured at the rear of the transmission with all accessories installed and operating. Since the figures vary when a given engine is installed in different models, some ratings are representative rather than exact

TUNE-UP SPECIFICATIONS

Year	Engine No. Cyl. Displacement (cu in.)	Spark Plugs Original Type	Gap (in.)	Distributor Point Dwell (deg)	Point Gap (in.)	Ignition Timing (±2°) (deg)▲ MT	AT	Intake Valve Opens (deg)	Fuel Pump Pressure (psi)	Compression Pressure (psi)	Idle Speed (rpm) MT	●AT	Valve Clearance (in.) In	Ex
'77	6-225 LD	RBL15Y	.035	Elec.	Elec.	2B	2B	16B	3.5–5.0	100 (Min.)	750	750	.010	.020
	6-225 LD Calif.	RBL15Y	.035	Elec.	Elec.	TDC	2A	16B	3.5–5.0	100 (Min.)	750	750	.010	.020
	6-225 HD	RBL15Y	.035	Elec.	Elec.	TDC	TDC	16B	3.5–5.0	100 (Min.)	700	700	.010	.020
	V8-318 LD	RN11Y	.035	Elec.	Elec.	2B⑮	2B⑮	10B	5.0–7.0	100 (Min.)	750	750	Hyd.	Hyd.
	V8-318 LD Calif.	RN11Y	.035	Elec.	Elec.	2B	2B	10B	5.0–7.0	100 (Min.)	750	750	Hyd.	Hyd.
	V8-318 HD	RN11Y	.035	Elec.	Elec.	2A	2A	10B	5.0–7.0	100 (Min.)	750	750	Hyd.	Hyd.
	V8-318 HD Calif.	RN11Y	.035	Elec.	Elec.	TDC	TDC	10B	5.0–7.0	100 (Min.)	700	700	Hyd.	Hyd.
	V8-360 LD	RN12Y	.035	Elec.	Elec.	—	6B	18B	5.0–7.0	100 (Min.)	—	700	Hyd.	Hyd.
	V8-360 HD	RN12Y	.035	Elec.	Elec.	2A	TDC	18B	5.0–7.0	100 (Min.)	750	750	Hyd.	Hyd.
	V8-360 HD Calif.	RN12Y	.035	Elec.	Elec.	4B	4B	18B	5.0–7.0	100 (Min.)	700	700	Hyd.	Hyd.
	V8-400 HD	RJ11Y	.035	Elec.	Elec.	2B	2B	18B	5.0–7.0	100 (Min.)	700	700	Hyd.	Hyd.
	V8-440 HD	RJ11Y	.035	Elec.	Elec.	8B	8B	18B	5.0–7.0	100 (Min.)	700	700	Hyd.	Hyd.
	V8-440 HD Calif.	RJ11Y	.035	Elec.	Elec.	8B	8B	18B	5.0–7.0	100 (Min.)	700	700	Hyd.	Hyd.
'78	6-225 LD	RBL16Y	.035	Elec.	Elec.	12B	12B	16B	3.5–5.0	100 (Min.)	750	750	.010	.020
	6-225 LD Calif.	RBL16Y	.035	Elec.	Elec.	8B	8B	16B	3.5–5.0	100 (Min.)	750	750	.010	.020
	6-225 HD	RBL11Y	.035	Elec.	Elec.	TDC	TDC	16B	3.5–5.0	100 (Min.)	700	700	.010	.020
	6-225 HD Calif.	RBL16Y	.035	Elec.	Elec.	8B	8B	16B	3.5–5.0	100 (Min.)	750	750	.010	.020
	6-243 Diesel	—	—	—	—	—	18B㉒	32B	1800㉑	426	—	650	.012	.012
	V8-318 LD	RN11Y	.035	Elec.	Elec.	12B	12B	10B	5.0–7.0	100 (Min.)	750	750	Hyd.	Hyd.
	V8-318 LD Calif.	RN11Y	.035	Elec.	Elec.	12B	12B	10B	5.0–7.0	100 (Min.)	750	750	Hyd.	Hyd.
	V8-318 HD	RN11Y	.035	Elec.	Elec.	2A	2A	10B	5.0–7.0	100 (Min.)	750	750	Hyd.	Hyd.
	V8-318 HD Calif.	RN11Y	.035	Elec.	Elec.	12B	12B	10B	5.0–7.0	100 (Min.)	750	750	Hyd.	Hyd.
	V8-360 LD	RN12Y	.035	Elec.	Elec.	—	6B	18B	5.0–7.0	100 (Min.)	—	750	Hyd.	Hyd.
	V8-360 LD Calif.	RN12Y	.035	Elec.	Elec.	6B	6B	18B	5.0–7.0	100 (Min.)	750	750	Hyd.	Hyd.
	V8-360 HD	RN12Y	.035	Elec.	Elec.	4B	4B	18B	5.0–7.0	100 (Min.)	750	750	Hyd.	Hyd.
	V8-360 HD Calif.	RN12Y	.035	Elec.	Elec.	6B⑯	6B⑯	18B	5.0–7.0	100 (Min.)	750⑯	750⑯	Hyd.	Hyd.
	V8-400 LD	OJ11Y	.035	Elec.	Elec.	—	10B	18B	5.0–7.0	100 (Min.)	—	700	Hyd.	Hyd.
	V8-400 HD	OJ11Y	.035	Elec.	Elec.	2B	2B	18B	5.0–7.0	100 (Min.)	700	700	Hyd.	Hyd.
	V8-440 HD	OJ11Y	.035	Elec.	Elec.	—	8B	18B	5.0–7.0	100 (Min.)	—	700	Hyd.	Hyd.
	V8-440 HD Calif.	OJ11Y	.035	Elec.	Elec.	—	8B	18B	5.0–7.0	100 (Min.)	—	750⑰	Hyd.	Hyd.

TUNE-UP SPECIFICATIONS

Year	Engine No. Cyl. Displacement (cu in.)	Spark Plugs Original Type	Gap (in.)	Distributor Point Dwell (deg)	Point Gap (in.)	Ignition Timing (±2°)▲ MT	AT	Intake Valve Opens (deg)	Fuel Pump Pressure (psi)	Compression Pressure (psi)	Idle Speed (rpm) MT	●AT	Valve Clearance (in.) In	Ex
'79	6-225 LD	P-560PR	.035	Elec.	Elec.	12B	12B	16B	3.5–5.0	100 (Min.)	675	675	.010	.020
	6-225 LD Calif.	P-560PR	.035	Elec.	Elec.	8B	8B	16B	3.5–5.0	100 (Min.)	800	800	.010	.020
	6-225 HD	P-560PR	.035	Elec.	Elec.	12B	12B	16B	3.5–5.0	100 (Min.)	675	675	.010	.020
	6-243 Diesel	—	—	—	—	—	18B[22]	32B	1800[21]	426	—	650	.012	.012
	V8-318 LD	P-64PR	.035	Elec.	Elec.	12B	12B	10B	5.0–7.0	100 (Min.)	680	680	Hyd.	Hyd.
	V8-318 LD Calif.	P-64PR	.035	Elec.	Elec.	6B	6B[19]	10B	5.0–7.0	100 (Min.)	750	750	Hyd.	Hyd.
	V8-318 HD	P-64PR	.035	Elec.	Elec.	2A	2A[18]	10B	5.0–7.0	100 (Min.)	750	750	Hyd.	Hyd.
	V8-360 LD	P-65PR	.035	Elec.	Elec.	10B[20]	10B[20]	18B	5.0–7.0	100 (Min.)	750[20]	750[20]	Hyd.	Hyd.
	V8-360 LD Calif.	P-65PR	.035	Elec.	Elec.	10B	10B	18B	5.0–7.0	100 (Min.)	750	750	Hyd.	Hyd.
	V8-360 HD	P-65PR	.035	Elec.	Elec.	4B	4B	18B	5.0–7.0	100 (Min.)	750	750	Hyd.	Hyd.
	V8-360 HD Calif.	P-65PR	.035	Elec.	Elec.	—	4B	18B	5.0–7.0	—	750	750	Hyd.	Hyd.
'80	6-225 LD	560PR	.035	Elec.	Elec.	12B	12B	16B	3.5–5.0	100 (Min.)	600[23]	600[23]	.010	.020
	6-225 MD Calif.	560PR	.035	Elec.	Elec.	12B	12B	16B	3.5–5.0	100 (Min.)	800	800	.010	.020
	6-225 HD Canada	560PR	.035	Elec.	Elec.	12B	12B	16B	3.5–5.0	100 (Min.)	675	675	.010	.020
	V8-318 LD[24]	64PR	.035	Elec.	Elec.	12B	12B	10B	5.0–7.0	100 (Min.)	600	600	Hyd.	Hyd.
	V8-318 LD[25]	64PR	.035	Elec.	Elec.	10B	10B	10B	5.0–7.0	100 (Min.)	750	750	Hyd.	Hyd.
	V8-318 MD Calif.	64PR	.035	Elec.	Elec.	10B	10B	10B	5.0–7.0	100 (Min.)	750	750	Hyd.	Hyd.
	V8-318 HD	64PR	.035	Elec.	Elec.	8B[26]	8B[26]	10B	5.0–7.0	100 (Min.)	750	750	Hyd.	Hyd.
	V8-360 Canada	65PR	.035	Elec.	Elec.	—	4B[24]	18B	5.0–7.0	100 (Min.)	—	750	Hyd.	Hyd.
	V8-360 Canada	65PR	.035	Elec.	Elec.	12B	12B[27]	18B	5.0–7.0	100 (Min.)	650	650	Hyd.	Hyd.
	V8-360 LD[28]	65PR	.035	Elec.	Elec.	12B	12B	18B	5.0–7.0	100 (Min.)	650	650	Hyd.	Hyd.
	V8-360 LD[29]	65PR	.035	Elec.	Elec.	—	10B	18B	5.0–7.0	100 (Min.)	—	750	Hyd.	Hyd.
	V8-360 MD[30]	65PR	.035	Elec.	Elec.	10B	10B	18B	5.0–7.0	100 (Min.)	750	750	Hyd.	Hyd.
	V8-360 HD[30]	65PR	.035	Elec.	Elec.	10B	10B	18B	5.0–7.0	100 (Min.)	750	750	Hyd.	Hyd.
	V8-360 HD	65PR	.035	Elec.	Elec.	4B	4B	18B	5.0–7.0	100 (Min.)	700	700	Hyd.	Hyd.
'81	6-225 LD	560PR	.035	Elec.	Elec.	12B	16B	6B	3.5–5.0	100 (Min.)	[31]	[31]	Hyd.	Hyd.
	6-225 HD	560PR	.035	Elec.	Elec.	12B	16B	6B	3.5–5.0	100 (Min.)	725	750	Hyd.	Hyd.
	V8-318 LD[24]	64PR	.035	Elec.	Elec.	10B	16B	10B	5.0–7.0	100 (Min.)	650	650	Hyd.	Hyd.
	V8-318 HD Canada[24]	64PR	.035	Elec.	Elec.	2A	2A	10B	5.0–7.0	100 (Min.)	750	750	Hyd.	Hyd.
	V8-318 LD[25]	64PR	.035	Elec.	Elec.	12B	16B	10B	5.0–7.0	100 (Min.)	750	750	Hyd.	Hyd.
	V8-318 HD[25]	64PR	.035	Elec.	Elec.	12B	12B	10B	5.0–7.0	100 (Min.)	750	750	Hyd.	Hyd.
	V8-360-1 LD[25]	64PR	.035	Elec.	Elec.	12B	16B	18B	5.0–7.0	100 (Min.)	600[34]	625[34]	Hyd.	Hyd.
	V8-360-1 HD[24]	64PR	.035	Elec.	Elec.	—	4B	18B	5.0–7.0	100 (Min.)	—	750	Hyd.	Hyd.
	V8-360-1 HD[25]	64PR	.035	Elec.	Elec.	—	4B	18B	5.0–7.0	100 (Min.)	—	700	Hyd.	Hyd.
	V8-360-3 HD	73SR	.035	Elec.	Elec.	—	4B[35]	18B	5.0–7.0	100 (Min.)	—	700	Hyd.	Hyd.
	V8-360-3 HD	73SR	.035	Elec.	Elec.	—	10B	18B	5.0–7.0	100 (Min.)	—	750	Hyd.	Hyd.
'82	4-135	65PR	.035	Elec.	Elec.	12B	12B	14B	4.5–6.0	100 (Min.)	850	900	Hyd.	Hyd.
	6-225-1	560PR	.035	Elec.	Elec.	12B	16B	6B	3.5–5.0	100 (Min.)	600[37]	600[38]	Hyd.	Hyd.
	V8-318[24]	64PR	.035	Elec.	Elec.	12B	12B	10B	4.75–6.25	100 (Min.)	750	750	Hyd.	Hyd.
	V8-318[25]	64PR	.035	Elec.	Elec.	12B	16B	10B	4.75–6.25	100 (Min.)	750	750	Hyd.	Hyd.
	V8-360[24]	65PR	.035	Elec.	Elec.	4B	4B	18B	5.0–7.0	100 (Min.)	—	700	Hyd.	Hyd.
	V8-360[25]	65PR	.035	Elec.	Elec.	—	4B[39]	18B	5.0–7.0	100 (Min.)	—	700[40]	Hyd.	Hyd.
'83	4-135	65PR	.035	Elec.	Elec.	12B	12B	14B	4.5–6.0	100(Min.)	800[45]	800[45]	Hyd.	Hyd.
	6-225	560PR	.035	Elec.	Elec.	12B	16B	6B	3.5–5.0	100(Min.)	[42]	[42]	Hyd.	Hyd.
	8-318[24]	64PR	.035	Elec.	Elec.	12B[41]	12B[41]	10B	4.75–6.25	100(Min.)	[43]	[43]	Hyd.	Hyd.
	8-318[25]	64PR	.035	Elec.	Elec.	12B[44]	12B[44]	10B	4.75–6.25	100(Min.)	750	750	Hyd.	Hyd.
	8-360[24]	65PR	.035	Elec.	Elec.	—	4B	18B	5.0–7.0	100(Min.)	—	750	Hyd.	Hyd.
	8-360[25]	RF10	.035	Elec.	Elec.	4B[39]	4B[39]	18B	5.0–7.0	100(Min.)	700[40]	700[40]	Hyd.	Hyd.
'84					Refer to Underhood Specifications Sticker									

NOTE: The underhood specifications sticker often reflects tune-up specifications changes made in production. Sticker figures must be used if they disagree with those in this chart.

NOTE: All Canadian specifications are the same as Federal specifications unless noted otherwise.

● Manual in neutral, automatic in park.

—Not Applicable

▲ With vacuum advance disconnected and plugged.

B Before Top Dead Center

A After Top Dead Center

TUNE-UP SPECIFICATIONS

TDC Top Dead Center
CAP Cleaner Air Package
Fed. All states except California
(Min.) Minimum
Hyd. Hydraulic valve lifters; no service adjustment
LD Light Duty emissions
MD Medium Duty emissions
HD Heavy Duty emissions
Elec. Electronic ignition
① Without CAP—5B
② Without CAP—5B
③ Without CAP—10B
④ Automatic transmission—110–140
⑤ Without CAP—700 rpm
⑥ 800 for Canada
⑦ With ECS (Electronically Controlled Spark)—700 rpm
⑧ Can be advanced or retarded 2.5° if conditions warrant
⑨ California vehicles only—700 rpm
⑩ California vehicles only—TDC

⑪ 15 Passenger only—800 rpm
⑫ TDC for Canada
⑬ 750 for Canada
⑭ 2B for Canada
⑮ 6B for High Altitude w/auto trans.
⑯ Over 8501 GVWR—TDC @ 700 rpm
⑰ Over 8501 GVWR—700
⑱ 4 bbl for Canada—8B
⑲ For GVWR under 6,000 lbs.—8B
⑳ With 4 bbl for Canada—4B @ 700
㉑ Injector pressure
㉒ Static
㉓ Canada: MT & AT: 675
㉔ 2 barrel carb.
㉕ 4 barrel carb.
㉖ Canada HD engine w/2 bbl.: 2A
㉗ Canada w/4 bbl. and distributor 4111487: 10B
㉘ Distributor 4111947
㉙ Distributor 4111487
㉚ California

㉛ Federal: 600
   California: 800
   Canada: 725
㉜ Canada: 750
㉝ Canada: 10B
㉞ California: 750
㉟ Distributor 4091661
㊱ Distributor 4111950
㊲ Canada: M/T 725
㊳ Canada: A/T 750
㊴ California: 10B
㊵ California: 750
㊶ High Alt: 16B
   Calif: 16B
㊷ Fed 1-bbl: 600 MT, 650 AT
   Calif: 750 All
   Canada 1-bbl: 725 MT, 750 AT
   All 2-bbl: 700
㊸ Fed & Canada: 750
   High Alt. & Calif: 700
㊹ H.D. Engines: 8B
㊺ High Alt: 900

FIRING ORDERS

NOTE: To avoid confusion, always replace spark plug wires one at a time.

400, 440 V8 engines

318, 360 V8 engines

6 cylinder engines

4 cylinder engines

VALVE SPECIFICATIONS

Year	Engine Displacement (cu in.)	Seat Angle (deg)	Face Angle (deg)	Spring Test Pressure (lbs @ in.)	Spring Installed Height (in.)	Stem to Guide Clearance (in.)		Stem Diameter (in.)	
						Intake	Exhaust	Intake	Exhaust
'82–'84	4-135	45	45	175 @ 1.22	1.65	.001–.003	.002–.004	.312–.313	.311–.312
'84	4-155.9	45	45	61 @ 1.59	1.59	.0012–.0024	.0020–.0035	.315	.315
'77–'84	6-225	45	④	137–150 @ 1⁵⁄₁₆	1¹¹⁄₁₆	.001–.003	.002–.004	.372–.373	.371–.372
'78–'79	6-243 Diesel	45	45	NA	1⁴⁹⁄₆₄	.002–.003	.003–.004	.314	.314
'77–'78	8-318	45	④	170–184 @1⁵⁄₁₆	1¹¹⁄₁₆	.001–.003	.002–.004	.372–.373	.371–.372
'79–'81	8-318	45	45	⑤	⑥	.001–.003	.002–.004	.372–.373	.371–.372
'82–'84	8-318	45	45	⑨	⑨	.001–.003	.002–.004	.372–.373	.371–.372
'77	8-360	45	④	177–188 @1⁵⁄₁₆	1¹¹⁄₁₆	.001–.003	.002–.004	.372–.373	.371–.372
'78–'81	8-360	45	45	⑤	⑥	.001–.003	.002–.004	.372–.373	.371–.372
'82–'84	8-360	45	45	⑤	⑤	.001–.003	.002–.004	.372–.373	.371–.372
'77–'78	8-400 8-440	45	45	192–208 @ 1⅞	1⁵⁵⁄₆₄	.001–.003	.002–.004⑦	.372–.373	.371–.372⑧

NA—Not available
① Intake; 45°33′
 Exhaust; 43°33′
② Outer; 101 @ .878
 Inner; 49 @ .720
③ Outer; 1.28
 Inner; 1.13

④ Intake; 45°
 Exhaust; 43°
⑤ Intake; 170–184 @ 1⁵⁄₁₆
 Exhaust; 181–197 @ 1¹⁄₁₆
⑥ Intake; 1¹¹⁄₁₆
 Exhaust; 1³³⁄₆₄

⑦ At hot end; .001–.003 at cold end
⑧ At hot end; .372–.373 at cold end
⑨ Intake; 170–184 @ 1⁵⁄₁₆
 Exhaust: 180–194 @ 1¹⁄₁₆

CRANKSHAFT AND CONNECTING ROD SPECIFICATIONS

(All measurements given in in.)

Year	Engine Displacement (cu in.)	Crankshaft				Connecting Rod		
		Main Brg Journal Dia	Main Brg Oil Clearance	Shaft End Play	Thrust on No.	Journal Dia	Oil Clearance	Side Clearance
'82–'84	4-135	2.362–2.363	.0004–.0026	.002–.007	3	1.968–1.969	.0004–.0026	.005–.015
'84	4-155.9	2.3622	.0008–.0028	.002–.007	3	2.0866	.0008–.0028	.004–.010
'77–'78	6-225	2.7495–2.7505	.0005–.0020	.002–.009	3	2.1865–2.1875	.0005–.0020	.006–.025
'79–'80	6-225	2.7495–2.7505	.0002–.0022	.002–.009	3	2.1865–2.1875	.0002–.0022	.006–.025
'81–'84	6-225	2.7495–2.7505	.0010–.0025	.0035–.0095	3	2.1865–2.1875	.0010–.0022	.007–.013
'78–'79	6-243 Diesel	2.754–2.755	.0012–.0035	.0012–.0035	7	2.281–2.282	.0015–.0044	.006–.018
'77–'80	8-318	2.4995–2.5005	.0005–.0020	.002–.007	3	2.124–2.125	.0005–.0025	.006–.014
'81–'84	8-318	2.4995–2.5005	.0005–.0020	.002–.007	3	2.124–2.125	.0005–.0022	.006–.014
'77–'80	8-360	2.8095–2.8105	.0005–.0020	.002–.009	3	2.124–2.125	.0005–.0025	.006–.014
'81–'84	8-360	2.8095–2.8105	.0005–.0020	.002–.009	3	2.124–2.125	.0005–.0022	.006–.014

CRANKSHAFT AND CONNECTING ROD SPECIFICATIONS

(All measurements given in in.)

| Year | Engine Displacement (cu in.) | Crankshaft | | | | Connecting Rod | | |
		Main Brg Journal Dia	Main Brg Oil Clearance	Shaft End Play	Thrust on No.	Journal Dia	Oil Clearance	Side Clearance
'77–'78	8-400	2.6245–2.6255	.0005–.0020	.002–.009	3	2.3750–2.3760	.0005–.0025	.009–.017
'77–'78	8-440	2.7495–2.7505	.0005–.0020	.002–.009	3	2.3750–2.3760	.0005–.0030	.009–.017

CAMSHAFT SPECIFICATIONS

| Engine | Year | Journal Diameter | | | | | Bearing Oil Clearance | Camshaft End Play |
		#1	#2	#3	#4	#5		
4-135	'82–'84	1.375	1.375	1.375	1.375	1.375	.002–.004	.005–.013
4-155.9	'84	—	—	—	—	—	.002–.004	.004–.008
6-225	'77–'84	1.998	1.982	1.967	1.951	—	.001–.003	0
6-243	'78–'79	2.145	2.145	2.125	2.086	—	.0016–.0035	.002–.008
8-318	'77–'84	1.998	1.982	1.967	1.951	1.561	.001–.003	.002–.010
8-360	'77–'84	1.998	1.982	1.967	1.951	1.561	.001–.003	.002–.010
8-400	'77–'78	2.000	1.984	1.969	1.953	1.750	.001–.003	0
8-440	'77–'78	2.000	1.984	1.969	1.953	1.750	.001–.003	0

TORQUE SPECIFICATIONS

| Year | Engine Displacement (cu in.) | Cylinder Head Bolts | Rod Bearing Bolts | Main Bearing Bolts | Crankshaft Bolt | Flywheel-to-Crankshaft Bolts | Manifold | |
							Intake	Exhaust
'82–'84	4-135⑨	30⑤	40⑤	30⑤	50	55	15	15
'84	4-155.9⑩	69⑦	34	58	87	—	⑧	⑧
'77–'84	6-225	70	45	85	Press fit	55	20②	10
'78–'79	Diesel	90③	65③	69③④	289	80	—	—
'77	8-318 8-360	95	45	85	100	55	40	20①
'78–'84	8-318 8-360	105	45	85	100	55	40	20①
'77–'78	8-400 8-440	70	45	85	135	55	45	30

① 15 ft lbs for nuts
② Stud-30; Nut-20
③ Bolts must be oiled
④ 80 ft lbs with "H" mark
⑤ Tighten in 3 steps-30, 45, 45, plus ¼ turn more
⑥ 50 with auto. trans.
⑦ 2 Front Bolts to Timing Case: 160 in. lbs.
⑧ 150 in. lbs.
⑨ Cam Cap Bolts: 165 in. lbs.
⑩ Cam Cap Bolts: 160 in. lbs.

PISTON AND RING SPECIFICATIONS

Engine	Year	Piston–to–Bore Clearance	Ring Gap			Ring Side Clearance		
			Top Compression	Bottom Compression	Oil Control	Top Compression	Bottom Compression	Oil Control
4–135	'83–'84	.0005–.0240	.011–.021	.011–.021	.015–.055	.0015–.0031	.0015–.0037	.00024–.00075
4–155.9	'83–'84	.0008–.0016	.01–.018	.01–.018	.0078–.035	.0024–.0039	.0008–.0024	.00020–.00035
6–225	'77–'84	.0005–.0015	.010–.020	.010–.020	.015–.055	.0015–.0030	.0015–.0030	.0002–.0050
6–243	'78–'79	.0008–.0020	.012–.020	.010–.020	.010–.020	.0010–.0020	.0010–.0020	.0010–.0020
8–318	'77–'84	.0005–.0015	.010–.020	.010–.020	.015–.055	.0015–.0030	.0015–.0030	.0002–.0050
8–360	'77–'84	.0005–.0015	.010–.020	.010–.020	.015–.055	.0015–.0030	.0015–.0030	.0002–.0050
8–400	'77–'78	.0003–.0013	.013–.023	.013–.023	.015–.055	.0015–.0030	.0015–.0030	.0000–.0050
8–440	'77–'78	.0003–.0013	.013–.023	.013–.023	.015–.055	.0015–.0030	.0015–.0030	.0000–.0050

CAPACITIES

Year	Engine Displacement Cu In. No. of Cyls	Engine Crankcase (qts)		Transmission (pts)		Drive Axle (pts)	Transfer Case (pts)	Cooling System (qts)
		With Filter	Without Filter	Manual	Automatic			
'77	6-225	6	5	⑥	19⑦	⑤	9	13②
	V8-318	6	5	⑥	19⑦	⑤	9	17
	V8-360	6	5	⑥	19⑦	⑤	9	16②
	V8-400,440	6	5	⑥	19⑦	⑤	9	15½②
'78	6-225	6	5	⑥	19	⑤	9	13
	243 Diesel	8	7	⑥	19	⑤	9	13
	V8-318	6	5	⑥	19	⑤	9	17
	V8-360	6	5	⑥	19	⑤	9	16
	V8-400,440	6	5	⑥	19	⑤	9	14½
'79–'80	6-225	6	5	⑥	16⅔	⑤	9⑫	12⑧
	V8-318	6	5	⑥	16⅔	⑤	9⑫	16⑧
	V8-360	6	5	⑥	16⅔	⑤	9⑫	14½⑧
'81	6-225	6	5	⑥	⑩	⑤	⑫	12②
	V8-318	6	5	⑥	⑩	⑤	⑫	16②
	V8-360	6	5	⑥	⑩	⑤	⑫	14½②
'82	4-135	4	3.5	4	15⑪	⑪	⑫	7
	6-225	6	5	⑥	⑩	⑤	⑫	12②
	V8-318	6	5	⑥	⑩	⑤	⑫	16②
	V8-360	6	5	⑥	⑩	⑤	⑫	14½②

CAPACITIES

Year	Engine Displacement Cu In. No. of Cyls	Engine Crankcase (qts)		Transmission (pts)		Drive Axle (pts)	Transfer Case (pts)	Cooling System (qts)
		With Filter	Without Filter	Manual	Automatic			
'83–'84	4-135	4	3.5	⑬	⑭	⑮	⑫	9
	4-155.9	5	4.5	⑬	⑭	⑮	⑫	9
	6-225	6	5	7	⑩	⑤	⑫	12⑮
	8-318	6	5	7	⑩	⑤	⑫	16⑯
	8-360	6	5	7	⑩	⑤	⑫	14.5⑰

① A-903 3 spd (Std)—6 pts
A-745 3 spd (Opt)—3¼ pts
② Add 1 qt for auxiliary rear heater, air conditioning, or Heavy Duty cooling; add 2 qts for A/C with 400 or 440 V8
③ 100 and 200 (Chrysler)—4¼ pts
300 (Spicer)—6 pts
④ 100 and 200 (Chrysler)—4¼ pts
300 (Spicer)—5½ pts
⑤ See Rear Axle Identification Chart
⑥ 4¼ with A-230 heavy duty three speed, 3½ with A-390 top-cover three speed, 7 with

1976 Overdrive-4, 7.5 with 1977 and later Overdrive-4: NP435, 4 speed, 7.5
⑦ 1977—16⅔ pts
⑧ Add 2 qts. with A/C or increased cooling
⑨ Models vary: 1981 Sports models: 35
⑩ A904T/A999: 17.1—A727:7.7 without converter drain
⑪ Auto Transaxle differential; 2.4 pts. 1982 only
⑫ '79: 9 pts, '80: NP208-6.0 pts, NP205:4.5 pts

⑬ 4 speed: 4
5 speed: 4.6
⑭ 8.9 qts. w/converter total. 4.0 qts: drain and refill w/o converter
⑮ Models from 1983 share common sump between transmission and differential.
⑯ 13 w/AC
⑰ 17 w/AC
⑱ 15.5 w/AC

TUNE UP

Electronic Ignition

NOTE: For testing and troubleshooting procedures refer to the "Electrical" Section of Unit Repair.

An electronic ignition system is installed as standard equipment. The distributor housing, cap, rotor and advance unit are the same used on point type systems. A magnetic pickup and control (reluctor) have replaced the points and distributor cam. A condenser is no longer necessary. The only maintenance required with electronic ignition is inspection of the wiring, cap, rotor and periodic cleaning and changing of the spark plugs.

In later model years, depending on the model, the distributor might have two pickups. One controls the start mode; the other, the run mode. If the distributor needs parts replacement or servicing, maintaining the proper air gap between the pickup and reluctor is necessary.

The electronic ignition system eliminates the contact points and the need to set dwell. Hence, the dwell is non-adjustable and cannot be altered in any way.

Air Gap

Except 4 Cylinder Engines

The air gap adjustment is not a regular maintenance item. However, if the gap is too wide a no start condition can exist.

NOTE: When checking the pickup air gap use a non-magnetic feeler gauge. If a non-magnetic feeler-gauge is not available, use brass shim stock of the proper thickness.

NOTE: The reluctor teeth may appear ragged at the edges, but no attempt should be made to clean them. A sharp edge is necessary to quickly decrease the magnetic field and induce negative voltage in the pickup coil. If the teeth are rounded, the voltage signal to the control unit may be erratic.

——— CAUTION ———
Do not touch the round transistor mounted on the control unit when the ignition switch is "On", it can produce a nasty electrical shock.

ADJUSTMENT

Models with a single pickup require .006 inch adjustment. Dual pickup equipped distributors require; Start pickup (identified by a two male prong distributor connector) .006 inch; Run pickup (identified by a male and female connector) .012 inch.

Single Pickup Distributor

1. Align a reluctor tooth with the pickup coil tooth. Loosen the pickup coil hold-down screw.

2. Insert a non-magnetic feeler gauge of the proper size between the reluctor tooth and the pickup coil tooth. Adjust the air gap so that contact is made between the reluctor tooth, feeler gauge and pickup coil tooth. Tighten the holddown screw.

135 (2.2L) timing mark location

155.9 (2.6L) timing mark location

Air gap adjustment

3. Remove the feeler gauge. No force should be required to remove the feeler gauge.

4. Check the air gap with a larger size (about .002 inch larger) feeler gauge. It should not fit into the air gap so do not try to force it.

Dual Pickup Distributor

The procedure is the same as for the single pickup distributor. Adjust the start pickup first and then the run pickup. Test each adjustment with a larger feeler gauge as mentioned in the single pickup distributor air gap adjustment.

Ignition Timing

NOTE: On engines with electronic ignition, your timing light may or may not work, depending on the construction of the light. Consult the manufacturer of the light if in doubt.

ADJUSTMENT

135 (2.2L) 4 Cylinder

1. Connect a timing light according to the manufacturer's instructions.

2. Run the engine to normal operating temperature.

3. Make sure the idle speed is correct.

4. Loosen the distributor holddown screw just enough so that the distributor can be rotated.

5. Ground the carburetor switch (if equipped). Disconnect and plug the vacuum line(s) to the distributor control.

6. Remove the timing hole access cover and aim the timing light at the hole in the clutch housing. Carefully rotate the distributor until the timing marks are aligned.

7. Tighten the distributor and recheck the timing.

8. Check, and if necessary adjust, the idle speed.

155.9 (2.6L) 4 Cylinder

1. Locate, clean and mark the timing scale and pointer on the crank pulley and front cover.

Dual pickup distributor

2. Connect a timing light and tachometer to the engine (follow the equipment manufacturer's instructions). Start the engine and run at idle until normal operating temperature is reached.

3. Momentarily open the throttle and release to check for binding in the linkage. Be sure the throttle linkage idle screw is against the stop and carburetor is off fast idle.

4. Disconnect and plug the vacuum line at the distributor. Check idle RPM and adjust if necessary.

5. Aim the timing light at the crankshaft pulley and check the timing. Loosen the distributor locknut and rotate the distributor in the direction necessary to align the timing marks. Tighten the locknut and recheck timing. Check idle RPM, readjust idle and timing as necessary.

6. Reconnect the distributor vacuum line. Shut off engine and disconnect the tachometer and timing light.

6 and 8 Cylinder Engines

1. Connect a timing light and a tachometer. Never puncture the spark plug wires or boots with a probe. Always use the proper adapters.

2. Start the engine and allow it to reach normal operating temperature.

3. Set the idle speed.

4. Put the transmission in Neutral; Park for automatic.

5. Disconnect and plug the vacuum line(s) at the distributor. **1981 and later models;** disconnect and plug lines to distributor and EGR valve. Disconnect the PCV valve and vapor canister purge hose at the carburetor end. Leave both open to underhood air.

Typical ignition timing marks—6 cylinder engine

Typical timing marks—V8 engine

6. Loosen the distributor hold-down screw just enough to permit the distributor to be turned.

7. Aim the timing light at the timing marks on the case cover. Slowly turn the distributor to align the marks to the proper setting.

8. Turn the engine off and tighten the distributor hold-down bolt. Be careful not to move the distributor while you are tightening.

9. Start the engine and recheck the timing.

10. When the timing is correct, reconnect the vacuum line to the distributor.

11. If the engine idle speed has changed, readjust the carburetor. Do not reset the timing.

12. Remove the timing light from the engine.

Motor Home Chassis

On some models there is a hole in the torque converter housing to see the timing marks that are located on the converter. The corresponding timing marks are located on the housing. Timing light hook up is the same as on crankshaft pulley timing.

Valve Adjustment
GASOLINE ENGINES

Valve lash adjustment is necessary on the 6 cylinder 225 engine through 1980 and the optional 155.9 (2.6L) engine used in the Mini-Van from 1984.

The 6 cylinder 225 engine (through 1980) requires adjustment at least every 20,000 miles, or when there is excessive valve train noise.

No valve lash adjustment is necessary or possible on any other Chrysler-built engine. Hydraulic valve lifters or lash adjusters automatically maintain zero clearance. After engine reassembly these lifters adjust themselves as soon as engine oil pressure builds up.

— CAUTION —
Do not set the valve lash closer than specified in an attempt to quiet the valve mechanism. This will result in burned valves.

Hydraulic valve adjuster used on (2.2) 4 cylinder engine

155.9 (2.6L) 4 Cylinder

NOTE: A jet valve is added on USA models. The jet valve adjuster is located on the intake valve rocker arm and must be adjusted before the intake valve.

1. Start the engine and allow it to reach normal operating temperature.

NOTE: Do not run the engine with the rocker arm cover removed, oil will be sprayed on to the hot exhaust manifold.

2. Shut off engine and remove the rocker arm cover.

3. Watch the valve operation on No. 1 cylinder (No. 1 cylinder on transverse mounted engines is on the driver's side) while turning the crankshaft to close the exhaust valve and have the intake valve just begin to open. This places the No. 4 cylinder on TDC of its firing stroke and permites the adjustment of the valves.

Adjusting the jet valve on 155.9 (2.6L) engines

Exhaust Valve Closing	Adjust
No. 1 cylinder	No. 4 cylinder valves
No. 2 cylinder	No. 3 cylinder valves
No. 3 cylinder	No. 2 cylinder valves
No. 4 cylinder	No. 1 cylinder valves

4. Jet valves must be adjusted before the intake valve.

To adjust the jet valves:

a. Loosen the intake valve lock nut and back off the adjustment screw two or more turns.

b. Loosen the lock nut on the jet valve adjusting screw. Turn the jet valve adjusting screw counterclockwise and insert a .006 in. feeler gauge between the valve stem and the adjusting screw.

c. Tighten the adjusting screw until it touches the feeler gauge.

NOTE: The jet valve spring is weak, be careful not to force the jet valve in.

d. After adjustment is made, hold the adjusting screw with a screwdriver and tighten the lock nut.

5. Proceed to adjust the intake and the exhaust valves on the same cylinder as the jet valve you finished adjusting. Adjust by

loosening the locknut and passing a feeler gauge of the correct thickness between the bottom of the rocker arm and top of the valve stem. If the clearance is too great or too small, turn the adjusting screw until the gauge will pass through with a slight drag. Tighten the locknut and proceed to the next valve. Refer to the chart in Step 3 for the adjusting sequence.

6-225—thru 1980

1. The engine must be at normal operating temperature. Mark the crankshaft pulley into three equal 120° segments, starting at the TDC mark.

2. Remove the valve (rocker) cover and the distributor cap.

3. Set the engine at TDC on the No. 1 cylinder by aligning the mark on the crankshaft pulley with the "0" mark on the timing cover pointer. The distributor rotor should point at the position of the No. 1 spark plug wire in the distributor cap. Both rocker arms on the No. 1 cylinder should be free to move slightly.

4. The cylinders are numbered from the front to rear.

5. The lash is measured between the rocker arm and the end of the valve. To check the lash, insert the correct size feeler gauge between the rocker arm and the valve. Press down lightly on the other end of the rocker arm. If the gauge cannot be inserted, loosen the self-locking adjustment nut on the top of the rocker arm. Tighten the nut until the gauge can just be inserted and withdrawn without buckling.

FRONT OF ENGINE

E = EXHAUST
I = INTAKE

Valve location—6 cylinder engine

6. After both valves for the No. 1 cylinder are adjusted, turn the engine so that the pulley turns 120° in the normal direction of rotation (clockwise). The distributor rotor will turn 60°, since it turns at half engine speed.

7. Check that the rocker arms are free and adjust the valves for the next cylinder in the firing order, 5. The firing order is 1-5-3-6-2-4.

8. Turn the engine 120° to adjust each of the remaining cylinders in the firing order. When you are done the crankshaft will have made two complete revolutions (720°) and the distributor rotor one complete revolution (360°).

9. Replace the rocker cover with a new gasket. Replace the distributor cap. Start the engine and check for leaks.

DIESEL ENGINE

6-243

Valve adjustment is required on the diesel engine every 36,000 miles.

─────── CAUTION ───────

Do not set the valve lash closer than specified in an attempt to quiet the lifters. This will only result in burned valves.

─────────────────────────

1. The engine must be cold for this adjustment. Mark the crankshaft pulley into three equal 120° sections, starting at the TDC or "0" mark.

2. Remove the valve cover.

3. Disconnect the fuel line from the injector on cylinder No. 1. Be very careful not to kink the line.

4. Using a socket and a breaker bar on the crankshaft bolt, turn the engine in the same direction as it normally runs until the "0" mark on the crankshaft damper rear face is aligned with the pointer on the bottom of the timing gear case. As you are turning, keep an eye on the fuel line that was disconnected. Fuel will squirt out of the line a few degrees before you reach the "0" mark. If it doesn't squirt out, you've got the wrong cylinder at TDC. Turn the engine another 360° (one revolution) and you will have No. 1 at TDC.

5. The cylinders are numbered from front to rear.

6. The lash is measured between the rocker arm and the end of the valve. To check the lash, insert a .012 in. feeler gauge between the rocker arm and the valve. Adjust the proper clearance by loosening the locknut on the rocker arm and turning the adjusting screw. After the adjustment is made, tighten the locknut and recheck the clearance to be sure it did not change as the locknut was being tightened.

7. After both valves for the No. 1 cylinder are adjusted, turn the engine so that the pulley turns 120° in the normal direction of rotation (clockwise). The distributor rotor will turn 60°, since it turns at half engine speed.

8. Check that the rocker arms are free and adjust the valves for the next cylinder in the firing order, 5. The firing order is 1-5-3-6-2-4.

9. Turn the engine 120° to adjust each of the remaining cylinders in the firing order. When you are done the crankshaft will have made two complete revolutions (720°).

10. Replace the rocker cover with a new gasket. Attach the fuel line to the injector. Start the engine and check for leaks.

Carburetor

IDLE SPEED AND MIXTURE ADJUSTMENT

NOTE: Various calibrations are used, refer to the emissions decal under the hood for procedures when adjusting idle or mixture.

Before suspecting the carburetor as the cause of poor performance or rough idle, check the ignition system thoroughly, including the distributor, timing, spark plugs and wires. Also check the air cleaner, evaporative emission system, PCV system, EGR valve and engine compression. Check the intake manifold, vacuum hoses and other vacuum connections for leaks and cracks.

Mixture, on today's carburetors, is preset at the factory and tampering with the mixture screw will produce little change. Some carburetors have hidden mixture screws which makes adjustment impossible unless special equipment is used.

When performing a tune-up, adjust the idle speed to the specified rpm (tachometer connected), using the idle speed screw or the solenoid adjustment.

6 & 8 Cylinder Engines

NOTE: Adjust with the air cleaner installed.

1. Run the engine at fast idle to stabilize engine temperature.

2. Make sure that the choke plate is fully released.

3. Attach a tachometer to the engine. With electronic ignition, connect the meter to the negative primary coil terminal and to a ground.

NOTE: Not all tachometers or dwell/tachometers will work with electronic ignition; some may be damaged. Check the manufacturer's instructions carefully.

4. Connect an exhaust analyzer to the engine and insert the probe as far into the tailpipe as possible. On vehicles with dual exhaust, insert the probe into the left tailpipe as this is the side without the heat riser valve.

5. Check ignition timing and adjust it as required.

6. If the truck has air conditioning, turn the air conditioner off. On six-cylinder engines, turn the headlights on high beam.

7. Place the manual transmission in neutral; put the automatic in Park. Make sure the hot idle compensator valve (if any) on the carburetor is fully seated in the closed position.

8. Turn the engine idle speed adjustment screw in or out to adjust idle speed to specification. If the carburetor has an electric solenoid, turn the solenoid adjusting screw in or out to obtain the specified rpm. Then, adjust the curb idle speed screw until it just touches the stop on the carburetor body. Now, back the curb idle speed adjusting screw out one full turn.

9. Turn each idle mixture adjustment screw 1/16 turn richer (counterclockwise). Wait 30 seconds and observe the reading on the exhaust gas analyzer. Continue this procedure until the meter indicates a definite increase in the richness of the mixture.

NOTE: This step is very important. A carburetor that is set too lean will cause the exhaust gas analyzer to give a false reading indicating a rich mixture. Because of this, the carburetor must be known to have a rich mixture to verify the reading on the exhaust gas analyzer.

10. After verifying the reading obtained on the meter, adjust the mixture screws to get the air/fuel ratio and percentage of CO indicated on the engine compartment sticker. Turn the mixture screws clockwise (leaner) to raise the meter reading or counterclockwise (richer) to lower the meter reading.

135 (2.2L) 4 Cylinder

1. Set the parking brake and place the transmission in neutral.

2. Turn off all the lights and accessories.

3. Connect a tachometer to the engine following the manufacturer's instructions.

4. Start the engine and allow it to reach normal operating temperature.

5. Disconnect and plug the vacuum hoses to the EGR valve and the distributor.

6. Unplug the connector at the radiator fan and install a jumper so it will run continuously.

7. On models equipped with the fuel control computer, connect a jumper wire between the carburetor switch and ground.

8. Remove the PCV from the rubber molded connector and disconnect the purge hose to the vapor canister at the carburetor end. Leave the PCV valve open to underhood air. Plug the 3/16 inch diameter control hose at the canister.

9. Read the RPM indicated on the tachometer. If the RPM is not the same as the idle set rpm specified on the emissions label, turn the idle speed screw (on top of the solenoid) to correct it.

10. Unplug and connect all hoses and replace all wires.

155.9 (2.6L) 4 Cylinder

1. Set the parking brake and place the transmission in neutral.

2. Turn off all the lights and accessories and disconnect the cooling fan.

3. Connect a tachometer to the engine following the manufacturer's instructions.

4. Start the engine and allow it to reach normal operating temperature.

5. Check the timing and adjust if necessary.

6. Remove the timing light and read the rpm indicated on the tachometer. It is not the same as the curb idle specified on the emission label adjust the idle speed adjusting screw. The screw is accessible through the hole in the choke cover plate using a long narrow screwdriver at a 45° angle inwards.

Idle speed adjusting—155.9 (2.6L) engines

7. After adjusting the curb idle speed, press the A/C button on. With the compressor running, set the engine speed to 900 rpm by turning the idle up adjusting screw. The idle up adjusting screw is accessible through a hole in the choke cover plate using a long narrow shaft screwdriver at a 45° angle downwards.

8. Turn the engine off, disconnect the tachometer and reconnect the cooling fan.

IDLE SPEED SOLENOID

Adjustment

This solenoid is energized whenever the ignition circuit is on. Its function is to allow the throttle plates to close farther when the ignition is switched off, thereby preventing engine over-running.

1. Bring the engine to operating temperature and attach a tachometer.

2. With the engine running, adjust the solenoid screw to the proper rpm.

3. Adjust the slow curb idle screw until the screw end just contacts the stop on the carburetor body. Back the screw off one full turn.

4. Test the above procedure by disconnecting the solenoid wire at the connector. Be sure not to let the lead short to the engine. The solenoid should de-energize and idle speed should drop down below normal. Now reconnect the wire. After you reconnect the solenoid, move the throttle linkage by hand since the solenoid isn't strong enough to move it.

ELECTRONIC THROTTLE CONTROL

Carter Electronic Throttle Control

1. Energize ETC solenoid (separate electrical connector and apply 12 volt current to BLUE wire spade).

2. Momentarily open throttle to allow plunger to extend from solenoid (plunger will extend and hold position but will not "push").

3. Adjust to obtain 850 Engine RPM.

Holly Electronic Throttle Control

1. Remove screw from ETC solenoid. Energize solenoid, by separating electrical connector and applying 12 volts current to

Idle speed adjusting location—135 (2.2L) engine

BLUE wire spade.

2. Momentarily open throttle to allow plunger to extend.

3. Position ⅛ inch allen wrench into adjusting nut (through screw hole). Adjust engine idle speed to 850 RPM.

4. Reinstall screw with solenoid **de-energized** reset curb idle speed using **only** the screw.

5. Remove tachometer and any jumper wires. Check for the proper installation of all hoses and electrical connections.

DASHPOT ADJUSTMENT

With the curb idle speed and mixture properly set and a tachometer installed, start the engine and position the throttle lever so that the actuating tab on the lever is contacting the stem of the dashpot but not depressing it. Allow 30 seconds for engine to stabilize. The tachometer should read 2300 RPM with throttle lever in this position.

To adjust setting, loosen the lock nut and screw the dashpot in or out as required. When the desired setting is obtained, tighten the lock nut on the dashpot against the bracket. Check to make sure curb idle returns to specified speed.

Procedure—Adjusting Engine Fast Idle

1. Adjust engine fast idle to conform with Emission Control Label. Disconnect and plug both distributor and EGR valve vacuum hoses. Place transmission in neutral and set parking brake.

2. Remove air cleaner top.

3. Adjust engine fast idle speed to the specified RPM (shown on Emission Control Label) on Step 2 (second highest) of the fast idle cam.

4. Reconnect all hoses, as the engine has been correctly adjusted for proper Emission Control.

IDLE MIXTURE PLUGS

Removal—6 and 8 Cylinder

NOTE: Tampering with the carburetor is a violation of Federal Law. Adjustment of the idle air fuel mixture can only be done under certain circumstances. The idle mixture adjusting screws are covered with tamper-proof plugs. If the plugs are removed and the mixture adjusted, then new plugs and roll pins must be installed.

The mixture should be adjusted only if an idle defect remains after a complete diagnosis reveals that no other fault exists, such as a bad spark plug wire or a vacuum leak. Also, the computer controlled fuel

Typical Holley 2 barrel carburetor

system must be operating properly. Adjustment to the idle mixture should be performed after a major carburetor overhaul.

1. Remove the carburetor from the engine.

2. Hold the carburetor in a suitable fixture for removing the roll pin and concealment plug.

3. Drill a small pilot hole in the casting into the base gasket surface and at a 45° angle toward the concealment plug. Redrill the hole to a larger size.

4. Insert a blunt punch into the hole and drive out the plug.

5. Insert a sharp punch through the idle mixture adjusting hole and slide out the roll pin.

6. Install the carburetor on the engine and perform the idle mixture adjustments using the propane enrichment method.

7. Remove the carburetor and install the roll pin and concealment plug in the carburetor.

8. Install the carburetor.

PROPANE ENRICHMENT

Adjustment—6 and 8 Cylinder

1. Place the transmission in neutral position and set the parking brake. Turn all lights and accessories off. Connect a tachometer and a timing light to the engine. Start the engine and allow it to warm up on the second stop of the fast idle cam. Do this until normal operation temperature is reached, then return the engine to idle.

2. Disconnect and plug the EGR vacuum hose and the distributor vacuum hose. Check the engine timing and adjust if necessary. Disconnect the heated air door vacuum hose at the carburetor nipple and in it's place, install the propane supply hose. On 440 Cu. In. engines without the heated air system, insert the propane supply hose 12 in. into the air cleaner snorkel. Make

sure that the propane bottle is in an upright and safe position. Remove the PCV valve from the cylinder head cover and disconnect the purge hose to the vapor canister at the carburetor end. Leave both open to underhood air.

3. Open the propane main flow valve. With the air cleaner in place, slowly open the propane metering valve until the maximum engine rpm is reached. When too much propane is added, the engine rpm will decrease. Fine tune the metering valve to obtain the highest engine rpm.

4. With the propane still flowing, adjust the idle speed screw to attain the propane rpm specified on the emissions label. If there has been a change in the maximum rpm, readjust the idle speed screw to the specified propane rpm.

5. Turn off the propane main valve and allow the engine speed to stabilize. With the air cleaner in place, slowly adjust the idle air mixture screws to achieve the smoothest idle at the specified idle set rpm. Pause between adjustments to allow the engine speed to stabilize. If it appears necessary to remove the limiter caps to reach the idle set rpm, first check for engine malfunctions and vacuum leaks. If idle limiter caps are removed, service caps must be installed with the tang against the maximum rich stop.

6. Turn the propane main valve on. If the maximum speed is more than 25 rpm different than the specified propane rpm, repeat steps 3 through 6.

7. Turn both the propane main valve and the metering valve off. Remove the tachometer. Remove the propane supply hose and reinstall the heated air door vacuum hose (except models without heated air). Unplug and reinstall the vacuum hose to the EGR valve and to the distributor.

8. Replace the PCV valve. Reconnect the canister purge hose to its proper place. A variation in the engine RPM may occur, but do not readjust.

ENGINE ELECTRICAL

Distributor
REMOVAL & INSTALLATION

1. Remove splash shield (if equipped). Disconnect the vacuum line(s) at the distributor.

2. Disconnect the pickup lead wire connector or connectors from the wiring harness.

3. Unfasten the clips or screws that retain the distributor cap and lift off the cap.

NOTE: The spark plug and coil wires used on the 2.2L engine are equipped with forked type distributor cap connectors. The cap must be removed from the distributor and the forked clip compressed before the wire can be removed from the cap.

Typical single pickup distributor

case and crank pulley are aligned. Disconnect the negative battery cable from the battery.

4. Bump the engine around until the rotor is pointing at No. 1 cylinder firing position and the timing marks on the front

5. Mark the distributor body and the engine block to indicate the position of the distributor in the block. Mark the distributor body to indicate the rotor position. These marks are used as guides when installing the distributor.

6. Remove the distributor holddown bolt and bracket. Carefully lift the distributor from the engine. The shaft may rotate slightly as the distributor is removed. Make a note of where the movement stops. That point is where the rotor must point when the distributor is reinstalled into the block.

7. If the crankshaft has not been rotated while the distributor was removed from the engine, installation is the reverse of the removal procedure. Use the reference marks made before removal to correctly position the distributor in the block. The shaft may have to be rotated slightly to engage the cam gear (4 and 6 cyl.) or intermediate shaft gear (V-8).

8. If the crankshaft was rotated or otherwise distributed (e.g., during engine rebuilding) after the distributor was removed, proceed as follows.

Installation—Engine Disturbed
4 AND 6 CYLINDER ENGINES

1. Remove No. 1 spark plug and, with your thumb plugging the hole, rotate the engine until No. 1 piston is up on compression at top dead center. You'll feel the pressure of the compression stroke with your thumb and the "0" mark on the crankshaft pulley hub will be aligned with the timing pointer.

2. Turn the rotor to a position just ahead of the No. 1 distributor cap terminal.

3. Lower the distributor into the opening, engaging the distributor gear with the drive gear on camshaft. With the distributor fully seated in the engine, the rotor should be under the cap No. 1 tower.

4. Install the cap, tighten the hold-down bracket bolt. Connect the wiring and the vacuum hose. Check the timing with a timing light. Adjust if necessary.

V8 ENGINES

1. Rotate the crankshaft until No. 1 cylinder is at top dead center (TDC) of the compression stroke. To do this, remove the spark plug from cylinder No. 1 and place your thumb over the hole. Slowly turn the engine by hand in the normal direction of rotation until compression is felt at the hole. The "0" mark on the crankshaft pulley should be aligned with the pointer on the timing case cover.

2. Hold the distributor over the mounting pad on the cylinder block so that the distributor body flange coincides with the mounting pad and the rotor points to the No. 1 cylinder firing position.

Typical distributor—4 cylinder engine

3. Install the distributor while holding the rotor in position, allowing it to move only enough to engage the slot in the drive gear.

4. Install the cap, tighten the hold-down bracket bolt. Connect the wiring and vacuum hose. Check the timing with a timing light. Adjust if necessary.

Alternator

PRECAUTIONS

The following are a few precautions to observe when servicing the alternator.

1. Never switch battery polarity.

2. When installing a battery, always connect the non-grounded (positive) terminal first.

3. Never disconnect the battery while the engine is running.

4. If the molded connector is disconnected from the alternator, do not ground the hot wire.

5. Never run the alternator with the main output cable disconnected.

6. Never electric weld around the truck without disconnecting the alternator.

7. Never apply any voltage in excess of battery voltage during testing.

8. Never "jump" a battery for starting purposes with more than 12 volts.

BELT TENSION ADJUSTMENT

NOTE: On some models it may be necessary to remove the lower splash shield to gain clearance when installing a new drive belt.

Belt tension should be checked with a gauge made for the purpose. If a gauge is not available, tension can be checked with moderate thumb pressure applied to the belt at its longest span midway between pulleys. If the belt has a free span less than twelve inches, it should deflect approximately ¼

NEGATIVE RECTIFIER
AND HEAT SINK ASSEMBLY

RECTIFIER END SHIELD

NEEDLE BEARING

INSERT

NUT AND WASHER

INSULATOR

INSULATOR

TERMINAL
BLOCK

STATOR
LEAD TERMINALS

SCREW

INSULATOR
WASHER

BRUSH

BRUSH HOLDER

CAPACITOR

INSULATOR

POSITIVE RECTIFIER
AND HEAT SINK ASSEMBLY

BRUSH HOLDER

SCREW

INSULATOR WASHER

BRUSH

ROTOR

GREASE
RETAINER

STATOR

DRIVE END SHIELD

BALL BEARING

BEARING RETAINER

PULLEY

THROUGH BOLT 3 LOCATIONS

Exploded view of conventional alternator

inch. If the span is longer than twelve inches, deflection can range between ¼ and ⅜ inches.

To adjust or replace belts:

1. Loosen the driven accessory's pivot and mounting bolts.

2. Move the accessory toward or away from the engine until the tension is correct. You can use a wooden hammer handle or broomstick as a lever, but do not use anything metallic.

3. Tighten the bolts and recheck the tension. If new belts have been installed, run the engine for a few minutes, then recheck and readjust as necessary.

NOTE: If the driven component has two drive belts, the belts should be replaced in pairs to maintain proper tension.

It is better to have belts too loose than too tight, because overtight belts will lead to bearing failure, particularly in the water

pump and alternator. However, loose belts place an extremely high impact load on the driven component due to the whipping action of the belt.

7" TO 10"
1/4" DEFLECTION

13" TO 16"
1/2" DEFLECTION

Checking drive belt deflection

REMOVAL & INSTALLATION

1. Disconnect the battery ground cable at the battery.

2. Disconnect and label the alternator output (BATT) and field (FLD) leads and disconnect the ground wire.

3. Loosen the alternator adjusting bolt and swing the alternator in toward the engine. Disengage the alternator drive belt.

4. Remove the alternator mounting bolts and remove the alternator from the vehicle.

5. Installation is the reverse of removal. Be sure to connect all ground wires and leads securely.

6. Adjust the belt tension.

Regulator

ADJUSTMENTS

The electronic voltage regulator has no moving parts and requires no adjustment after it leaves the factory. Any repairs are accomplished by replacement with a new regulator.

NOTE: Some 2.6 engines may use a Chrysler built external regulator with the Chrysler built alternator. If so, refer to the above procedures for regulator removal.

Most 2.6 engines are equipped with a Mitsubishi-built alternator that contains a built-in regulator. See the alternator replacement procedures for removal and installation.

REMOVAL & INSTALLATION

1. Release the spring clips and pull off the regulator wiring plug.

2. Unbolt and remove the regulator.

3. Installation is the reverse of removal. Be sure that the spring clips engage the wiring plug.

Starter

NOTE: Starter motor testing and troubleshooting procedures are found in the Electrical section of Unit Repair.

REMOVAL & INSTALLATION

1. Disconnect the ground cable at the battery.

2. Remove the cable from the starter.

3. Disconnect the solenoid leads at their solenoid terminals.

4. Remove the starter attachment bolts and withdraw the starter from the engine flywheel housing. On some models with automatic transmissions, the oil cooler tube bracket will interfere with the starter removal. In this case, remove the starter attachment bolts, slide the cooler tube bracket off the stud, and then withdraw the starter.

Conventional gear reduction starter

5. Installation is the reverse of the above. Be sure that the starter and flywheel housing mating surfaces are free of dirt and oil to make a good electrical contact.

STARTER SERVICING

Reduction-Gear Type

Three different reduction-gear starters are used. Two of them, the 1.5 hp and 1.8 hp motors are basically the same design, the chief difference being the 1.8 hp model is ½ an inch longer and larger than the 1.5 hp model.

Mini-vans equipped with the optional 2.6 L engine have a Nippondenso reduction gear starter.

Removal, installation, disassembly and assembly procedures are the same for these two starters. Disassembly procedures for the Nippondenso starter are given separately.

DISASSEMBLY-EXCEPT NIPPONDENSO STARTERS

1. Support assembly in a vise equipped with soft jaws. Do not clamp. Care must be used not to distort or damage the die cast aluminum.

2. Remove the thru-bolts and the end housing.

3. Carefully pull the armature up and out of the gear housing, and the starter frame and field assembly.

4. Pull the field frame assembly out enough to get at the terminal screw. Remove the screw.

5. Remove the field frame assembly.

6. Remove the nuts holding the solenoid and brush holder plate to the gear housing. Remove the solenoid and brush plate.

7. Remove the nut, washer, and sealing washer from the solenoid brush terminal.

8. Unwind the solenoid lead wire from the brush terminal. Remove the screws and remove the solenoid from the brush plate. Remove the nut and battery terminal from the brush plate.

9. Remove the solenoid contact and plunger assembly, and the return spring.

10. Remove the gear housing dust cover. Remove the driven gear retainer clip.

NOTE: The retainer is under tension; cover it with a cloth before removal to prevent loss.

11. Remove the pinion shaft C-clip at the end of the housing. Push the pinion shaft in and remove the clutch assembly. Remove the driven gear and the washer.

12. Remove the retainer pin to remove the shifting fork.

NIPPONDENSO STARTER

1. Disconnect wire from terminal "M".

2. Remove the two through bolts from the end frame.

3. Remove the two screws from the end of the frame cap.

4. Remov the upper left solenoid screw and remove the wire retainer.

5. Remove the end shield.

6. Remove the two field frame brushes from the brush plate.

7. Remove the brush plate, slide the armature out of the field frame, and remove the field frame.

8. Remove the two screws from the gear housing and remove the gear housing from the solenoid.

9. Remove the clutch rollers and retainer and remove the pinion and clutch.

10. Remove the steel ball and spring.

11. Remove the solenoid cover screws, remove the solenoid cover and remove the solenoid plunger.

Replacement of Brushes

NOTE: The brushes in the Nippondenso gear reduction starter motors are not replaced individually. Field brushes are serviced as part of the field and frame assembly. Ground brushes and all springs come as part of the brush plate assembly.

1. Brushes that are worn more than one-half the length of new brushes, or are oil-soaked, should be replaced.
2. When resoldering the shunt field and solenoid lead, make a strong, low-resistance connection using a high-temperature solder and resin flux. Do not use acid or acid-core solder. Do not break the shunt field wire units when removing and installing the brushes.
3. Brush spring tension should be 32–36 ounces.

Starter Clutch and Pinion Gear Inspection

1. Do not immerse the starter clutch unit in a cleaning solvent. The outside of the clutch and pinion must be cleaned with a cloth so as not to wash the lubricant from the inside of the clutch.
2. Rotate the pinion. The pinion gear should rotate smoothly (although it may require some force) and in one direction only. If the starter clutch unit does not function properly, or if the pinion is worn, chipped, or burred, replace the starter clutch unit.

ASSEMBLY—EXCEPT NIPPONDENSO STARTER

1. The shifter fork consists of two spring steel plates held together by two rivets. Before assembling the starter, check the plates for side movement. After lubricating between the plates with a small amount of SAE 10 engine oil, they should have about 1/16 in. side movement to insure proper pinion gear engagement.
2. Position the shift fork in the drive housing and install the shifting fork retainer pin. One tip of the pin should be straight and the other bent at a 15 degree angle away from the housing. The fork and retainer pin should operate freely after bending the tip of the pin.
3. Install the solenoid moving core and engage the shifting fork.
4. Place the pinion shaft into the drive housing and install the friction washer and drive gear.
5. Install the clutch and pinion assembly, thrust washer, and retaining washer.
6. Engage the shifting fork with the clutch actuators.

CAUTION

The fraction washer must be positioned on the shoulder of the splines of the pinion shaft before the driven gear is positioned.

7. Install the driven gear snap ring.
8. Install the pinion shaft retaining ring.
9. The starter solenoid return spring can now be inserted in the movable core.
10. Check the condition of the starter solenoid switch washer; if burned, disassemble the plunger assembly and reverse the washer. Install the solenoid contact plunger assembly into the solenoid.
11. Assemble the battery terminal stud in the brush holder.
12. Position the seal on the brush holder plate.
13. Run the solenoid lead wire through the hole in the brush holder and attach the solenoid stud, insulating washer, flat washer, and nut.
14. Wrap the solenoid lead wire tightly around the brush terminal post and solder it (resin core solder only).
15. Fix the brush holder to the solenoid attaching screws.
16. Gently lower the solenoid coil and brush plate into the gear housing.
17. Position the brush plate assembly into the starter gear housing, install the nuts, and tighten.
18. Position the brushes with the armature thrust washer.
19. Install the brush terminal screw.
20. Position the field frame on the gear housing and start the armature into the housing, carefully engaging the splines on the shaft with the reduction gear by rotating the armature.
21. Install the thrust washer on the armature shaft.
22. Replace the starter end housing and starter thru-bolts; tighten securely.

NIPPONDENSO STARTER

Assemble in the reverse order of disassembly. Lubricate all bearings and gears with high temperature grease. Grease the ball before inserting in the clutch shaft bore. Align the tab on the brush holder with the notch on the field frame. Make sure the brush leads are not grounded.

Nippondenso or Bosch Direct Drive Starter Motor

Either a Nippondenso or Bosch direct drive starter may be used on models equipped with the 2.2L engine.

DISASSEMBLY

1. Disconnect the field coil wire from the solenoid terminal.
2. Remove the solenoid mounting screws (and the solenoid—Bosch auto. trans. models) and work the solenoid (plunger—Bosch auto. trans. models) off the shift fork.
3. On Nippondenso units, remove the bearing cover, armature shaft lock, washer, spring, and seal.
4. On Bosch units, remove the two screws holding down the end shield bearing cap and remove the cap and washers.

5. Remove the two thru-bolts and the commutator end frame cover.
6. Remove the two brushes and the brush plate.
7. Slide the field frame off over the armature.
8. Take out the shift lever pivot bolt.
9. Take off the rubber gasket and metal plate.
10. For the Bosch auto. trans. starter and all Nippondenso starters, remove the armature assembly and shift lever from the drive end housing. For the Bosch man. trans. starter, press the stop collar off the snap ring, remove the snap ring, remove the clutch assembly and remove the drive end housing from the armature.
11. For all except the Bosch man. trans. starter, press the stop collar off the snap ring, then remove the snap ring, stop collar and clutch.

INSPECTION AND SERVICE

1. Brushes that are worn more than one-half the length of new brushes, or are oil-soaked, should be replaced. New brushes are 11/16 in. long.
2. Do not immerse the starter clutch unit in cleaning solvent. Solvent will wash the lubricant from the clutch.
3. Plate the drive unit on the armature shaft and, while holding the armature, rotate the pinion. The drive pinion should rotate smoothly in one direction only. The pinion may not rotate easily but as long as it rotates smoothly it is in good condition. If the clutch unit does not function properly, or if the pinion is worn, chipped, or burred, replace the unit.

ASSEMBLY

1. Lubricate the armature shaft and splines with SAE 10 or 30 W oil.
2. On all except the Bosch man. trans. starter, install the clutch, stop collar, lock ring and shift fork on the armature. On the Bosch man. trans. starter, fit the drive end housing on the armature, then install the clutch, stop collar and snap ring on the armature.
3. On all except the Bosch man. trans. starter, install the armature assembly and shift fork in the drive end housing.
4. Install the shift fork pivot bolt. Install the rubber gasket and metal plate.
5. Slide the field frame into position. Install the brush holder and brushes.
6. Position the commutator end frame cover and install the thru-bolts.
7. On Nippondenso units, install the seal, spring, washer, armature shaft lock and bearing cover.
8. On Bosch units, install the shim and armature shaft lock. Check the end play (0.002–0.012 in.). Install the bearing cover.
9. Assemble the solenoid (or plunger—Bosch auto. trans. models) to the shift fork and install the solenoid with its mounting bolts. Connect the field wire to the solenoid.

ENGINE MECHANICAL

Engine

REMOVAL & INSTALLATION

4 Cylinder With Manual Transaxle

1. Scribe the hood hinge outlines on the hood and remove the hood.
2. Drain the cooling system. Disconnect the battery cables and remove the battery.
3. Remove all water hoses from the radiator and engine. Remove the radiator and cooling fan assembly.
4. Remove the air cleaner, duct and hose assembly. Label vacuum hoses for reinstallation identification.
5. Remove the A/C compressor and mounting brackets. Leave the hoses attached and position the compressor out of the way.
6. Remove the power steering pump and brackets. Leave the hoses attached and position the pump out of the way.
7. Position a suitable container under the oil filter to catch any spilled oil and remove the oil filter.
8. Disconnect and identify all electrical connectors that will interfere with engine removal. Disconnect the fuel lines, accelerator linkage, heater hoses and air pump hoses.
9. Remove the alternator. Disconnect the clutch cable from the throwout bearing arm.
10. Remove the lower transaxle case lower cover. Disconnect the exhaust pipe from the exhaust manifold.
11. Remove the starter motor. Install a suitable jack under the transaxle assembly.
12. Install an engine lifting sling and attach to a chain hoist. Take slack out of the lifting chain. Raise transmission jack until contact is made with the transaxle.
13. Remove the inner right side splash shield. Remove the engine ground to chassis bonding strap.
14. Remove the transaxle to engine mounting bolts.
15. Remove the "through" nut(s) and bolt(s) from the front engine mount and anti-roll struts. Remove the left mount through bolt or insulator mounting bolts. Raise or lower the engine slightly with the chain hoist to relieve pressure on the through bolts.
16. Raise engine, separate from the transaxle and remove from vehicle.
17. To install the engine; lower into position with chain hoist and engage transaxle in drive.
18. Position engine against the transaxle and install mounting "through bolts". Do not tighten until all mount bolts have been

installed. Tighten to 40 ft. lbs.
19. Install the transaxle to engine mounting bolts and tighten to 70 ft. lbs.
20. Remove the engine lifting sling and transaxle support jack.
21. Install remaining components in the reverse order of removal.
22. Fill the cooling system, add oil (if necessary), connect the battery. Start the engine and allow to reach normal operating temperature. Check for leaks. Check and reset timing and idle speed if necessary.

4 Cylinder With Automatic Transaxle

1. Follow Steps 1-10 of the Manual Transaxle procedure.
2. Remove the lower transaxle case lower cover, mark converter and flywheel for installation reference. Remove the converter to flywheel mounting bolts. Attach a "C" clamp on the front of the converter housing to prevent the torque converter from falling out when the engine is removed.
3. Proceed with the following steps of manual transaxle procedure. When installing the engine, converter and flywheel mounting holes and reference marks must line up.

VANS AND WAGONS

Except Diesel and 4 Cylinder Engine

NOTE: Engine removal is a complicated operation. A floor jack is a necessity and you will probably have to fabricate several stands and attaching apparatus. On vehicles equipped with air conditioning, before removing the engine, have an air conditioning expert evacuate the system.

1. Disconnect the battery and drain the coolant from the radiator and engine block. Drain the engine oil. On V8s, remove the oil filter.
2. Remove the engine cover, air cleaner, and starter.
3. Remove the front bumper, grille, and support brace. Disconnect both radiator hoses and remove the radiator and support brace as a unit.
4. Remove the power steering and air pumps with the hoses attached and lay them aside.
5. Disconnect the throttle linkage, heater and vacuum hoses and all electrical connections to the ignition, alternator, and all other electrical connections.
6. Remove the alternator, fan, pulley, and drive belts.
7. Remove the heater blower motor.
8. Remove and plug the inlet line to the fuel pump.
9. Remove the oil dipstick tube. On V8s, remove the intake manifold and left exhaust manifold. If equipped with air conditioning, remove the right side valve cover.

Dimensions for building an engine lift for vans

10. To provide clearance for engine removal, the oil pan and transmission must be removed.
11. Raise the engine slightly in preparation for transmission removal. Support it with an engine lifting fixture. This tool can be fabricated from galvanized pipe fittings obtained locally. Use only galvanized parts with an inside diameter of 1½ in. or larger. Be sure they are firmly threaded together to assure maximum strength.
12. Raise the vehicle and support it on jackstands. Remove the starter and distributor.
13. Remove the driveshaft and engine rear support. Remove the rear support by removing the rear mount through-bolt and the U-shaped bracket from the crossmember. Remove the insulator from the bottom face of the transmission housing.
14. If equipped with an automatic transmission, remove the transmission intact with the filler tube and the torque converter separated from the drive plate.
15. Raise the rear of the engine approximately 2 in. and remove the clutch or drive plate and the flywheel.

  a. On V8s, position the cut-out in the crankshaft flange at 3 o'clock. Remove the oil pan screws and lower the oil pan far enough to reach inside and turn the oil pump pick-up tube slightly to the right to clear the pan. Remove the oil pan.

16. Lower the vehicle.
17. Using a boom hoist attached to the engine with the shortest hook-up possible, take up all tension and support the engine. The boom hoist is the ideal tool to use. If one is not available, it may be possible to support the engine on a stationary hoist and roll the vehicle out from under the engine.
18. Remove the engine front mounts and insulators.
19. Carefully remove the engine from the vehicle.
20. Installation is the reverse of removal. Check all fluid levels and perform all tune-up adjustments if the engine was rebuilt.

NOTE: If the engine was rebuilt or new camshaft or lifters installed, add 1 quart of engine oil supplement to aid break-in. This should be left in the engine for at least 500 miles.

DIESEL ENGINE

NOTE: If the truck is equipped with air conditioning, have the system evacuated by a qualified technician. Refer to the air conditioning caution note at the beginning of this section.

1. Disconnect the battery cables and remove the battery.
2. Remove the air cleaner.
3. Scribe matchmarks on the hood hinges and remove the hood.
4. Drain the cooling system.
5. Remove the upper and lower radiator hoses.
6. Remove the coolant reserve tank.
7. Raise the truck and safely support on jackstands. Disconnect and remove the transmission oil cooler lines from the radiator. Remove the lower radiator and fan shroud mounting screws.
8. Lower the truck and remove the upper radiator and fan shroud mounting screws and remove the radiator and the fan shroud.
9. Disconnect the heater hoses from the engine and push them aside.
10. Disconnect the speedometer cable housing from the engine.
11. Disconnect the electrical connections at the alternator, temperature sending unit, starter relay-to-solenoid wires, the oil gauge sending unit and the injection pump control motor. Set the wiring harness aside.
12. Disconnect and plug the fuel line at the transfer pump inlet. Disconnect and cap return line at the injector lines bleed-back connection.
13. Disconnect and remove the injection pump linkage. Disconnect and remove the accelerator and throttle cable linkage.
14. Disconnect the starter motor wire from the solenoid. Remove the starter motor.
15. Remove the battery ground cable from the engine block.
16. Disconnect and plug the power steering hoses at the power steering gear.
17. Raise the truck and disconnect the exhaust pipe from the exhaust manifold.
18. Drain the engine oil and remove the dipstick tube from the oil pan. Remove the transmission cooler line and road draft tube bracket from the oil pan.
19. Remove the oil pan bolts from the oil pan.
20. Remove the transmission inspection plate. Remove the oil pan on vans to gain clearance if necessary. Use a new gasket on installation.
21. Remove the four flex plate-to-torque converter cover bolts.
22. Remove the exhaust pipe bracket and the lower bell housing bolts.
23. Remove any other brackets that can interfere with removal.
24. Support the transmission with a floor jack.
25. Remove the cylinder head (valve) cover and the gasket.

26. Attach a boom hoist to the engine, wrapping the chain as tight and close as possible.
27. Remove the four bolts and six nuts from the engine mounts.
28. Remove the two upper bell housing bolts.
29. Roll the boom hoist back, removing the engine from the van or truck.
30. Installation is the reverse of removal.

PICKUPS, RAMCHARGER & TRAILDUSTER

1. Drain the coolant from the radiator and cylinder block.
2. Disconnect the battery ground cable. Remove the battery on V8 models.
3. Scribe the outline of the hood hinges and remove the hood.
4. If equipped with air conditioning, remove the compressor with lines attached and lay it aside.

—————— CAUTION ——————
Do not disconnect any refrigerant lines. Bodily injury could result.

5. Disconnect the electrical connections at the alternator, ignition coil, temperature and oil pressure sending units, starter-to-solenoid, and engine/body ground.
6. Remove the air cleaner. Disconnect throttle and transmission linkage at the carburetor.
7. Remove the distributor cap, wires and rotor.
8. Disconnect and plug the fuel pump line.
9. Disconnect the radiator and heater hoses. Disconnect and plug the oil cooler lines.
10. Remove the fan, spacer, fluid drive, and radiator. Do not store the fan drive unit with the shaft pointing downward. Fluid will leak out.
11. Raise the truck and support the rear of the engine.
12. Disconnect the exhaust pipes at the manifolds.
13. Remove the starter on V8 models.
14. Remove the automatic transmission dust cover and attach a C-clamp to the front bottom of the torque converter housing to prevent the converter from falling out. Remove the drive plate bolts from the torque converter. On manual transmission models, remove the rear crossmember, transmission, transfer case and adapter. You can leave the transfer case in place on six-cylinder models.
15. Support the transmission and remove the transmission attaching bolts.
16. Lower the truck and attach a lifting sling and hoist to the engine.
17. Remove the front motor mount bolt stud nuts and washers.
18. Carefully remove the engine.
19. Installation is the reverse of removal. Fill the engine with coolant and fresh

oil. Adjust the transmission linkage, carburetor, and ignition timing.

Intake Manifold

REMOVAL & INSTALLATION
155.9 (2.6L) 4 Cylinder

1. Disconnect the negative battery cable.
2. Drain the cooling system and disconnect the hoses from the water pump to the intake manifold.
3. Disconnect the carburetor air horn adapter and move to one side.
4. Disconnect the vacuum hoses and throttle linkage from the carburetor.
5. Disconnect the fuel inlet line at the fuel filter.
6. Remove the fuel filter and fuel pump and move to one side.
7. Remove the intake manifold retaining nuts and washers and remove the manifold.
8. Installation is the reverse of removal. Tighten the retaining nuts to 150 in. lbs.

243 (3.9L) Diesel

1. Disconnect the negative battery cable.
2. Remove the air cleaner assembly and mounting brackets from the intake manifold.
3. Disconnect or remove any linkage, controls or hoses that will interfere with manifold removal.
4. Disconnect the hoses from the fuel filter at the transfer pump and injection pump. Drain the fuel filter and remove (with mounting brackets) from the intake manifold.
5. Disconnect the injector lines for cylinders 3 and 6 from the injector pump if necessary for clearance. Disconnect the clamps that attach the fuel lines to the manifold and push the lines up and out of the way.
6. Remove the manifold to cylinder head attaching fasteners and remove the manifold. Clean all gasket mounting surfaces.
7. Install a new intake manifold gasket and the manifold in the reverse order of removal.

V8 Engines

1. Drain cooling system and disconnect battery, negative cable first.
2. Remove alternator, carburetor air cleaner, and fuel line.
3. Disconnect accelerator linkage.
4. Remove vacuum control between carburetor and distributor.
5. Remove the distributor cap and wires.
6. Disconnect coil wires, temperature sending unit wire, heater hoses and bypass hose.
7. Remove intake manifold, ignition coil and carburetor as an assembly.
8. Installation is the reverse of the above procedure. Tighten the intake manifold to head bolts in the sequence illustrated, from center alternating out.

V8 intake manifold tightening sequence

Combination Manifold

REMOVAL & INSTALLATION

135 (2.2L) 4 Cylinder

1. Disconnect the battery and drain the cooling system.
2. Remove the air cleaner and disconnect all vacuum lines, electrical wiring and fuel lines from the carburetor. Remove the throttle linkage.
3. Loosen the power steering pump and remove the drive belt. Remove the power brake vacuum hose from the intake manifold.
4. On vehicles equipped with A.I.R.—remove the coupling hose from the diverter valve to exhaust manifold air injection tube assembly.
5. Remove the water hoses from the water crossover and raise the vehicle. Remove the exhaust pipe from the manifold.
6. Remove the intake manifold support bracket and the EGR tube.
7. On vehicles equipped with A.I.R.—remove the four air injection tube bolts and remove the air injection tube assembly from the exhaust manifold.
8. Remove the intake manifold and then remove the exhaust manifold.
9. If necessary remove the water crossover cover from the intake manifold.
10. Installation is the reverse of removal. Use new manifold gaskets. Tighten the exhaust manifold from the center and progress outward to both ends. Torque the manifold nuts to 16.7 ft. lbs. and repeat the sequence until all bolts are torqued to specification.
11. Tighten the intake manifold bolts from the center of the head, progressing outward to both ends. Torque the bolts to 16.7 ft. lbs. and repeat the sequence until all bolts are torqued to specification.

6 Cylinder Except Diesel

1. Remove the air cleaner, lines and tubes to the carburetor.
2. Disconnect all the linkages to the carburetor and remove the carburetor from the manifold.

---

3. Disconnect the exhaust pipe from the manifold, remove the manifold attaching washers and retaining nuts, and remove the manifold from the cylinder head.
4. Separate the exhaust manifold from the intake manifold, if necessary, and install a new gasket between the two upon reassembly.

NOTE: Do not tighten the three securing bolts until the manifold assembly has been installed on the cylinder head.

5. Position the manifold on the cylinder head using a new gasket, and install the conical and triangular washers, the retaining nuts, and torque the retaining nuts and the three securing bolts to the specified torque.
6. Attach the exhaust pipe to the exhaust manifold flange.
7. Install the carburetor and attach all the lines, tubes, and linkages. Install the air cleaner assembly.

Exhaust Manifold

REMOVAL & INSTALLATION

155.9 (2.6L) 4 Cylinder

1. Disconnect the battery.
2. Remove the air cleaner.
3. Remove the belt from the power steering pump.
4. Raise the vehicle and make sure it is supported safely.
5. Remove the exhaust pipe from the manifold or converter.
6. Disconnect the air injection tube assembly from the exhaust manifold and lower the vehicle.
7. Remove the power steering pump assembly and move to one side.
8. Remove the heat cowl from the exhaust manifold.
9. Remove the exhaust manifold retaining nuts and remove the assembly from the vehicle.
10. Remove the carburetor air heater from the manifold.
11. Separate the exhaust manifold from the catalytic converter by removing the retaining screws.
12. Installation is the reverse of removal. Use a new gasket between the exhaust manifold and the front catalytic converter and torque the mounting screws to 24 ft. lbs. Use a new manifold gasket and coat the cylinder head side lightly with sealer. Torque the manifold center mounting nuts to 150 in. lbs. then torque the outer mounting nuts to 150 in. lbs.

243 (3.9L) Diesel

NOTE: Refer to "Cylinder Head" section for procedures.

V8 Engines

1. Disconnect the exhaust manifold at the flange where it mates to the exhaust pipe.

---

2. If the vehicle is equipped with air injection and/or a carburetor-heated air stove, remove them.
3. Remove the exhaust manifold by removing the securing bolts and washers. To reach these bolts, it may be necessary to jack the engine slightly off its front mounts. When the exhaust manifold is removed, sometimes the securing studs will screw out with the nuts. If this occurs, the studs must be replaced with the aid of sealing compound on the coarse thread ends. If this is not done, water leaks may develop at the studs.
4. To install, reverse the removal procedures. On the center branch of the 318 and the 360 exhaust manifold, no conical washers are used.

Cylinder Head

REMOVAL & INSTALLATION

135 (2.2L) 4 Cylinder

--- **CAUTION** ---

Do not perform this operation on a warm engine. Remove the head bolts in reverse of installation sequence shown. Loosen evenly in several steps. Do not attempt to slide the cylinder head off of the block. Lift the head straight up an off of the engine block.

1. Disconnect the negative battery cable. Drain the cooling system.
2. Remove the air cleaner assembly. Mark the various hoses for installation identification.
3. Disconnect all lines, hoses, wiring harnesses, etc. from the manifold, carburetor and cylinder head.
4. Disconnect the accelerator linkage. Remove the carburetor. Disconnect the converter and exhaust pipe. Remove the intake and exhaust manifolds.
5. Remove the upper part of the timing case (front cover).
6. Turn the engine by hand until all gear timing marks line up (engine at TDC, No. 1 piston).
7. Loosen the drive belt tensioner and slip the timing belt off of the camshaft gear.

Cylinder head torque sequence—155.9 (2.6L) engine

8. If the car is equipped with air conditioning, remove the compressor and mounting brackets, place out of the way. Do not disconnect any of the compressor lines unless the system is safely bled of freon.

9. Remove the valve cover, gaskets and seals. Remove the head bolts in the reverse order of the tightening sequence.

10. Lift off the cylinder head, clean all gasket surfaces.

11. Installation is in the reverse order of removal. Refer to the timing belt replacement section to check camshaft timing. Make sure all gasket surfaces are cleaned and free of deep nicks or scratches. Always install new gaskets and seals. Tighten bolts in the order shown in illustrations. Make sure all timing marks are aligned before installing the drive belt. The drive belt is correctly tensioned when possible to twist 90° with the thumb and index finger midway between the cam and intermediate shafts.

155.9 (2.6L) 4 Cylinder

Cylinder head torque sequence—135 (2.2L) engine

1. Disconnect the battery and drain the cooling system. Disconnect the upper radiator hose.

2. Remove the breather hoses and purge hose.

3. Remove the air cleaner and fuel line.

4. Remove the vacuum hose at the distributor and purge control valve. Remove alternator belt. Remove power steering pump and A/C compressor with brackets and lines attached. DO NOT DISCONNECT COMPRESSOR LINES.

5. Disconnect the spark plug wires after marking them for reinstallation.

6. Turn engine to No. 1 piston on TDC (top dead center) on the compression stroke. Remove the distributor cap, and distributor by removing the retainer nut and pulling the unit out.

7. Disconnect the heater hose at the intake manifold.

8. Disconnect the water temperature gauge unit wire.

9. Disconnect the fuel hoses and plug the line leading to the gas tank to prevent fuel leakage.

10. Remove the fuel pump mounting nuts or bolts and remove the pump assembly. Remove the insulator and gaskets.

11. Disconnect the exhaust pipe at the exhaust manifold flange.

12. Remove the rocker cover.

13. Remove its breather and semi-circular seal.

14. After slightly loosening the camshaft sprocket bolt confirm that No. 1 piston is at TDC on compression stroke (both valves closed).

NOTE: Never turn the engine over using the camshaft bolt; it puts undue strain on the chain and other components.

15. Mark the timing chain and sprocket with white paint for alignment reference. Remove the camshaft sprocket bolt and distributor drive gear. Remove the camshaft sprocket and allow it to rest in the chain on the holder below.

16. Remove the cylinder head bolts in reverse of the sequence shown. Head bolts should be loosened in two or three stages to prevent head warpage.

17. Remove the cylinder head and cylinder head gasket.

Installation is performed in the following manner.

6-Cylinder Except Diesel

1. Drain the cooling system and disconnect the battery.

2. Remove the air cleaner and the fuel line from the carburetor.

3. Disconnect the accelerator linkage.

4. Remove the vacuum advance line from between the carburetor and the distributor.

5. Disconnect the cables from the spark plugs.

6. Disconnect the heater hose and the clamp which secures the by-pass hose.

7. Disconnect the water temperature sending unit.

8. Disconnect the exhaust pipe at the exhaust manifold flange. Disconnect the diverter valve line (if equipped) from the intake manifold and remove the air tube assembly from the cylinder head.

9. Remove the intake and exhaust manifolds and the carburetor as an assembly.

10. Remove the closed ventilation system, the evaporative control system (if so equipped), and the valve cover.

11. Remove the rocker arm and shaft assembly.

12. Remove the pushrods and keep them in order to ensure installation in their original locations.

13. Remove the head bolts and remove the cylinder head.

14. Clean all of the gasket surfaces of the engine block and the cylinder head, and install the spark plugs.

Cylinder head torque sequence—6 cylinder

15. Inspect all surfaces with a straight-edge. If warpage is indicated, measure the amount. This amount must not exceed 0.00075 times the span length in any direction. For example, if a 12 in. span is 0.004 warped, the maximum allowable is $12 \times 0.00075 = 0.009$ in. In this case, the head is within limits. If warpage exceeds the specified limits, either replace the head or lightly machine the head gasket surface.

16. Coat a new cylinder head gasket with sealer, install the gasket, and install the cylinder head.

17. Install the cylinder head bolts. Torque the cylinder head bolts to 50 ft lbs. in the sequence indicated in the illustration. Repeat this sequence to retorque all the head bolts to specifications.

18. Reverse the removal procedure. Steps 1-12, to complete the installation. When installing the intake and exhaust manifold assembly, loosen the 3 bolts which secure the intake manifold to the exhaust manifold to maintain proper alignment. After installation, torque the 3 bolts in this sequence: inner bolts, then outer bolts. Refer to the manifold section, later in this chapter, for the proper tightening sequence. Check the valve adjustment.

V8

1. Drain the cooling system and disconnect the battery ground cable.

2. Remove the alternator, air cleaner, and fuel line.

3. Disconnect the accelerator linkage.

4. Remove the vacuum advance line from between the carburetor and the distributor.

Cylinder head torque sequence—318, 360-V8

5. Remove the distributor cap and wires as an assembly.

6. Disconnect the coil wires, water temperature sending unit, heater hoses, and by-pass hose.

7. Remove the closed ventilation system, the evaporative control system (if so equipped), and the valve covers.

8. Remove the intake manifold, ignition coil, and the carburetor as an assembly.

9. Remove the exhaust manifolds.

10. Remove the rocker and shaft assemblies.

11. Remove the pushrods and keep them in order to ensure installation in their original locations.

12. Remove the head bolts from each cylinder head and remove the cylinder heads.

Cylinder head torque sequence—400, 440-V8

13. Clean all the gasket surfaces of the engine block and the cylinder heads. Install the spark plugs.

14. Inspect all surfaces with a straightedge. If warpage is indicated, measure the amount. This amount must not exceed 0.00075 times the span length in any direction. For example, if a 12 in. span is 0.004 in. warped, the maximum allowable difference is $12 \times 0.00075 = 0.009$ in. In this case, the head is within limits. If the warpage exceeds the specified limits, either replace the head or lightly machine the head gasket surface.

15. Coat new cylinder head gaskets with sealer, install the gaskets, and install the cylinder heads.

16. Install the cylinder head bolts. Torque the cylinder head bolts to 50 ft. lbs. in the sequence indicated. Repeat this sequence to retorque all the cylinder head bolts to specifications.

17. Reverse the removal procedure Steps 1-12 to complete the installation.

Diesel Engine

1. Drain the cooling system.
2. Disconnect the negative battery cable.
3. Remove the air cleaner.
4. Disconnect the hoses from the fuel filter at the transfer pump and the injection pump. Drain the filter and remove it from the manifold.
5. Remove the manifold nuts and air cleaner mounting bracket attaching nuts.
6. Disconnect the injection lines for cylinders 3 and 6 from the injection pump.
7. Remove the intake manifold and gaskets from the head.
8. Push the exhaust manifold shield to one side.
9. Remove the heater hose and the bypass hose.
10. Remove the thermostat housing and the upper radiator hose from the water manifold. Remove the spray gasket.

11. Disconnect the temperature sending unit wire.
12. Disconnect the fuel line mounting brackets from the cylinder head and push the fuel lines aside.
13. Remove the three exhaust manifold bridges.
14. Remove the water manifold and gasket from the cylinder head.
15. Raise the truck and support with jackstands.
16. Disconnect the exhaust pipe from the exhaust manifold.
17. Lower the truck. Remove the exhaust manifold, heat shield and gasket.
18. Disconnect and remove the wire from the glow plug buss bar.
19. Remove the injection lines from the injection pump.
20. Disconnect the fuel injection line from the head. Remove the bracket and the ground strap.
21. Disconnect the alternator bracket and the engine lifting fixture. Push them aside.
22. Remove the cylinder head cover and the gasket.
23. Loosen and remove the cylinder head bolts in the sequence illustrated.
24. Lift out the rocker arm and shaft assembly.
25. Remove the push rods, keeping them in order. The push rods MUST be installed in their original location.
26. Remove the injector tubes, injector holders and the injectors.
27. Disconnect and remove the glow plug buss bar.
28. Remove the six glow plugs from the cylinder head.
29. Remove the cylinder head. Check the head for cracks, damage or evidence of water leaks. Clean all the oil, grease, scale, sealant and carbon from the head. Thoroughly clean the gasket surfaces. Also check each combustion chamber jet for cracks or melting. If a jet is cracked or melted, remove it with a push rod inserted through a glow plug bore.

Inspect all cylinder head surfaces with a straightedge. Out-of-flatness must not exceed .010 in. If it does, a surface grinder must be used to bring the head to an out-of-flatness of less than .006 in.

30. Install the glow plugs in the head. Tighten them firmly.
31. Install the glow plug buss bar. Be sure the connections are good.

32. Install the injectors, injector tubes and the injector holders in the head. Tighten the nozzle holder attaching nuts to 37 ft. lbs.

33. Coat the new gasket lightly with sealer. Place the gasket on the block and place the cylinder head over the dowels.

34. Install the cylinder head bolts and tighten them in the sequence illustrated to 90.4 ft lbs. Do not install the head bolts which retain the rocker shaft assembly.

35. Install the push rods in their original locations.

36. Install the rocker arm and shaft assembly. Tighten the mounting bolts, the same as the cylinder head bolts, to 90.4 ft. lbs.

37. Adjust the valve clearance to .012 in. at top dead center of each compression stroke.

38. Install the cylinder head cover and gasket.

39. Install the alternator bracket and engine lifting fixture.

40. Connect the fuel lines to the injection pump (except Nos. 3 and 6). Install the bracket and the ground strap.

41. Install the fuel line to the transfer pump.

42. Install the exhaust manifold and the heat shield assembly, using a new gasket.

43. Raise the truck and support it safely. Attach the exhaust pipe to the exhaust manifold.

44. Lower the truck and install the water manifold on the head using a new gasket.

45. Install the three exhaust manifold bridges.

46. Install the fuel lines in the bracket.

47. Connect the temperature sending unit wire.

48. Using a new gasket, install the thermostat housing. Attach the upper radiator hose to the thermostat housing.

49. Install the bypass and heater hoses.

50. Install the exhaust manifold heat shield and the exhaust manifold.

51. Using a new gasket and spray shield, install the air intake manifold.

52. Connect the injection lines from cylinders 3 and 6 to the injection pump.

53. Install the fuel filter to the back of the manifold.

54. Connect the fuel hoses.

55. Install the air cleaner bracket and install the air cleaner.

56. Fill the cooling system and connect the battery cables.

Diesel cylinder head bolt loosening sequence

*BOLTS TO BE TIGHTENED TOGETHER WITH THE ROCKER SHAFT BRACKETS.

Diesel cylinder head bolt tightening sequence

Rocker Arms and Shafts

REMOVAL & INSTALLATION

135 (2.2L) 4 Cylinder

—— **CAUTION** ——

When depressing the valve spring with Chrysler tool 4682, or the equivalent, the valve locks can become dislocated. Check and make sure both locks are fully seated in the valve grooves and retainer.

1. Remove the valve cover.
2. Rotate the camshaft until the lobe base is on the rocker arm that is to be removed.
3. Slightly depress the valve spring using Chrysler tool 4682 or equivalent. Slide the rocker off the lash adjuster and valve tip and remove. Label the rocker arms for position identification. Proceed to next rocker arm and repeat step 2 and 3.
4. Install in reserve order. Check the valve keys, be sure they are not dislocated.

155.9 (2.6L) 4 Cylinder

1. Turn the engine until No. 1 piston is at TDC (top dead center) of the compression stroke. Remove the distributor cap and confirm that the rotor tip is pointed at the No. 1 plug wire location. Disconnect the negative battery cable. Remove the distributor.
2. Remove the water pump cover (upper shield) and valve cover.
3. Confirm that No. 1 piston is at TDC of the compression stroke. Take white paint and mark the timing chain in line with the camshaft sprocket timing mark.
4. Remove the camshaft sprocket bolt, distributor drive gear and sprocket with chain meshed. Secure sprocket and chain in holder.

5. Loosen the camshaft bearing bracket and rocker arm assembly mounting bolts. Start at each end and work toward the center. Do not remove the retaining bolts. When all retaining bolts are loose, lift assembly from the cylinder head.
6. Remove the bolts from the camshaft bearing caps and remove the rocker shafts and arms. Keep all parts in order. Note the way the rocker shafts, rocker arms, springs and wave washers are mounted, the left shaft has 12 oil holes which face down. The right shaft has 4 oil holes that face down.
7. Lubricate all parts and assemble in reverse order. Secure the assembled shafts in position with retaining bolts through the cam bearing caps and install on head.

6-Cylinder (Except Diesel)

The rocker arm shaft has 12 straight steel rocker arms arranged on it with hardened steel spacers fitted between each pair of rocker arms. The shaft is secured by bolts and steel retainers which are attached to the 7 cylinder head brackets. To remove the rocker arm and shaft:
1. Remove the closed ventilation system.
2. Remove the evaporative control system (if so equipped).
3. Remove the valve cover and its gasket.
4. Remove the rocker shaft bolts and retainers.
5. Remove the rocker arm and shaft assembly.
6. Reverse the above for installation. The oil hole on the end of the shaft must be on top and point toward the front of the engine to provide proper lubrication to the rocker arms. The special bolt goes to the rear.

Inspect the rocker-arm-to-rocker shaft contact area

7. Torque all bolts to 25 ft. lbs.
8. Temporarily set the intake valve tappet at .015 in. and the exhaust valve at .025 in.
9. Run the engine at 550 rpm until it is fully warmed up and adjust the valves.

V8

The stamped steel rocker arms are arranged on one rocker arm shaft per cylinder head. Because the angle of the pushrods tends to force the rocker arm pairs toward each other, oilite spacers are fitted to absorb the side thrust of each rocker arm. The shaft is secured by bolts and steel retainers attached to the brackets on the cylinder head. To remove the arm and shaft from each cylinder head:
1. Disconnect the spark plug wires.
2. Disconnect the closed ventilation system and evaporative control system (if so equipped) from the valve cover.
3. Remove each valve cover and gasket.
4. Remove the rocker shaft bolts and retainer.
5. Remove each rocker arm and shaft assembly. Keep everything in order for installation in the original position.

155.9 (2.6L) engine—rocker arm and shaft assembly

6. Reverse the above for installation. The notch on the end of both 318 and 360 rocker shafts should point to the engine centerline and toward the front of the engine on the left cylinder head and toward the rear on the right side. On the 400 and 440, the rocker arm lubrication holes must point down and toward the valves. Torque the rocker shaft bolts to 17 ft. lbs. on the 318 and 360, and 25 ft. lbs. on the others.

Diesel Engine

1. Remove the valve cover and the gasket.

2. Remove the nozzle holders and the glow plugs.

3. Remove the rocker shaft retaining bolts.

4. Remove the rocker arm and shaft assembly. Keep everything in order so the rocker assembly can be installed in the original position.

5. To install, position the rocker arm and shaft assembly so the bracket with the oil hole is at the front of the engine.

6. Install the rocker shaft retaining bolts and tighten them to 90.4 ft. lbs.

7. Install the nozzle holders and the glow plugs.

8. Install and tighten the injection lines. Tighten the nozzle holder retaining nuts to between 43.4 and 57.9 ft. lbs.

9. Adjust the valves.

Valve Stem Oil Seal

REPLACEMENT

If valve stem oil seals are found to be the cause of excessive oil consumption, they may be replaced without removing the cylinder heads.

1. Remove the air cleaner.

2. Remove the rocker arm covers and spark plugs.

3. Detach the coil wire from the distributor.

4. Turn the engine so that No. 1 cylinder is at Top Dead Center on the compression stroke. Both valves for No. 1 cylinder should be fully closed and the crankshaft damper timing mark at TDC. The distributor rotor will point at the No. 1 spark plug wire location in the cap.

5. Remove the rocker shaft and install a dummy shaft for spring compressor use.

6. Apply 90-100 psi air pressure to No. 1 cylinder, using a spark plug hole air hose adaptor.

7. Use a valve spring compressor to compress each No. 1 cylinder valve spring and remove the retainer locks and the spring. Remove the old seals.

8. Install a cup shield on the exhaust valve stem. Position it down against the valve guide.

9. Push the intake valve stem seal firmly and squarely over the valve guide.

10. Compress the valve spring only enough to install the lock.

11. Repeat the operation on each successive cylinder in the firing order, making sure that the crankshaft is exactly on TDC for each cylinder. See the Firing Order and Distributor Rotation illustrations in the Specifications section of this chapter for cylinder numbering.

12. Replace the rocker arms, covers, spark plugs, and coil wire.

Timing Cover, Belt and Sprockets

REMOVAL & INSTALLATION

135 (2.2L) 4 Cylinder

TIMING COVER

1. Loosen the alternator lock screw and adjusting screw. Remove the drive belt.

2. Remove the power steering pump lock screw. Remove the pivot bolt and nut. Remove the drive belt. Remove the power steering pump and mounting bracket. The hoses need not be disconnected, locate the pump out of the way.

3. Loosen and remove the water pump pulley mounting screws and remove the pulley.

4. From under the vehicle remove the right inner splash shield.

5. Remove the crankshaft pulley.

6. The upper part of the timing cover is retained by nuts, the lower part is retained with screws. Remove the fasteners and the two halves of the timing cover.

7. Reverse the removal order for installation.

TIMING BELT

1. Follow steps 1-6 of the Timing Cover Removal and Installation section.

2. Place a jack under the engine with a piece of wood separating it from the jacking point.

3. Remove the right engine mounting bolt and raise the engine slightly. Be sure the engine is supported securely.

4. Loosen the belt tensioner and remove the timing belt.

Timing belt and components—135 (2.2L) engine

Camshaft timing—135 (2.2L) engine

5. Turn the crankshaft until the dot mark on the sprocket is at about two o'clock. Turn the intermediate shaft sprocket until the dot mark is at about eight o'clock. Line up the crankshaft and intermediate sprocket marks.

6. Turn the camshaft until the arrows on the mounting hub are in line with the front (no. 1) camshaft retaining cap flat spots. The small hole in the camshaft sprocket must be at the top and be in a vertical center line with the engine.

7. Install the timing belt. Adjust and tighten the belt tensioner.

8. Adjust the tensioner by turning the large tensioner hex to the right. Tension should be correct when the belt can be twisted 90° with the thumb and the forefinger, midway between the camshaft and the intermediate sprocket.

9. Complete the belt installation by reversing the removal steps.

NOTE: After applying the belt tensioner, rotate the engine two complete revolutions and recheck the timing marks for alignment.

TIMING SPROCKETS

The camshaft, intermediate shaft, and crankshaft sprockets are located by keys on their respective shafts and each is retained by a bolt. To remove any or all of the pulleys, first remove the timing belt cover and belt and then use the following procedure.

NOTE: When removing the crankshaft pulley, don't remove the four socket head bolts which retain the outer belt pulley to the timing belt pulley.

1. Remove the center bolt.
2. Gently pry the pulley off the shaft.
3. If the pulley is stubborn in coming off, use a gear puller. Don't hammer on the pulley.
4. Remove the pulley and key.
5. Install the pulley in the reverse order of removal.
6. Tighten the center bolt to 58 ft. lbs.
7. Install the timing belt, check valve timing, tension belt, and install the cover.

Timing Chain, Cover, "Silent Shafts" and Tensioner

REMOVAL & INSTALLATION

155.9 (2.6L) 4 Cylinder

1. Bring the engine to No. 1 piston at TDC (top dead center) of the compression stroke.
2. Disconnect the negative battery cable. Remove the air cleaner assembly.
3. Remove the alternator drive belt. Disconnect the spark plug wires from the plugs, free wires from supports. Remove the distributor with cap and wires attached.

Crankshaft and intermediate shaft timing alignment—135 (2.2L) engine

4. Remove the air conditioner compressor drive belt. Remove the compressor and mounting brackets, with lines attached; and position out of the way.
5. Remove the power steering drive belt. Remove the power steering pump and brackets, with lines attached, and position out of the way.
6. Raise and support the front of the vehicle on jackstands.
7. Remove the right front inner splash shield. Drain the engine oil. Remove the crankshaft pulley.
8. Place a floor jack under the engine with a piece of wood mounted between jack and lifting point.
9. Raise the jack until contact is made with the engine. Relieve pressure by jacking slightly and remove the center bolt from the right engine mount.
10. Remove the engine oil dipstick. Disconnect all vacuum hoses that run across the valve cover. Remove the valve cover.
11. Remove the two front cylinder head to timing case cover bolts (bolts in front of the cam sprocket). DO NOT LOOSEN ANY OTHER CYLINDER HEAD BOLTS.
12. Remove the oil pan retaining bolts and lower the oil pan. Remove the timing indicator and engine mounting plate from the timing chain case cover. Remove the remaining bolts retaining the chain cover and remove the cover.
13. Remove the three "silent shaft" drive chain guides. Remove the left side silent shaft and right side oil pump drive sprocket retaining bolts.
14. Remove the silent shaft drive chain, crankshaft sprocket and silent shaft sprockets.

"Silent Shaft" balance system timing mark alignment—155.9 (2.6L) engine

15. Remove the camshaft sprocket retaining bolt. Remove the distributor drive gear. Remove the sprocket holder bracket and right and left timing chain guides.

16. Depress the timing chain tensioner and remove the timing chain, camshaft sprocket and crankshaft sprocket. Remove tensioner, spring and washer from the oil pump.

17. If the silent shafts require service, remove the thrust plate or oil pump retaining screws, remove plate or pump and shaft.

18. Clean all parts, especially gasket mounting surfaces. Inspect all parts for cracks, damage or wear. Replace worn parts.

19. Install the left side silent shaft and thrust plate with a new O-ring. Tighten the retaining bolts to 71 in. lbs.

20. Install the right side silent shaft, prime the oil pump with fresh oil and install. Tighten the retaining bolts to 71 in. lbs.

NOTE: Use a part of bolts without heads to act as guides when installing the silent shaft thrust plate or oil pump. When plate or pump is installed, remove the guide bolts and install regular bolts.

21. Verify that No. 1 piston is at TDC on the compression stroke (keyway at approx. 3 o'clock). Make sure the dowel pin hole on the front of the camshaft is in the vertical position at 12 o'clock.

22. Install the cam sprocket holder. Install the right and left chain guides. Install the tensioner spring, washer and shoe on the oil pump body.

23. Position the crankshaft and camshaft sprockets on the timing chain with timing marks aligned. The crank and camshaft sprockets have a punch mark on one gear tooth. The timing chain is equipped with two plated links. The marked tooth on each gear should be installed in the plated link.

24. Using both hands, lift the gears and chain with marks aligned, slide the gears

CAMSHAFT SPROCKET — PLATED LINK — MATING MARK — TIMING CHAIN — MATING MARK — PLATED LINK — CRANKSHAFT SPROCKET

Timing gears and chain alignment—155.9 (2.6L) engine

onto their respective shafts with dowel hole and keyway in proper position. Verify gear marks and plated links are aligned.

25. Install the dowel pin, distributor drive gear and sprocket bolt on the camshaft. Torque bolt to 40 ft. lbs.

26. Install the silent shaft chain drive sprocket on the crankshaft.

27. Install the oil pump and silent shaft drive sprockets in the silent drive chain with the punch marked tooth on each sprocket inserted into the plated links on the timing chain.

28. Hold the sprockets and chain with both hands, lift and align the remaining plated link with the punch marked tooth on the crankshaft sprocket.

29. Install plated link over the punch marked tooth on the crank sprocket. Install the silent shaft and oil pump sprocket with plated links and marked tooth aligned.

30. Tighten oil pump and silent shaft sprocket bolts to 25 ft. lbs.

31. Install the silent shaft chain guides. Do not tighten the mounting bolts at this time.

DOWEL PIN

Camshaft alignment—155.9 (2.6L) engine

32. After the guides are installed loosely, tighten the mounting bolts on chain Guide A.

33. Tighten the mounting bolts on chain Guide C. Shake the chain on all of the sprockets to ensure snug seating. Make sure chain slack is collected at point (P) as shown in illustration.

34. Adjust chain Guide B so that slack is pulled in the direction of arrow F in the illustration. The clearance between the chain guide and links should be between .04 and .14 inches. Tighten the chain Guide B mounting bolts.

35. Fit new cover case gaskets to the chain case. Trim gaskets as required for snug fit at the top and bottom. Coat the gaskets with sealer and install case cover.

36. Installation from this point is in the reverse order of removal.

Timing Cover and Chain
REMOVAL & INSTALLATION
6-Cylinder Engines—Except Diesel

1. Drain the cooling system and disconnect the battery.

2. Remove the radiator and fan.

3. With a puller, remove the vibration damper.

4. Loosen the oil pan bolts to allow clearance, and remove the timing case cover and gasket.

5. Slide the crankshaft oil slinger off the front of the crankshaft.

6. Remove the camshaft sprocket bolt.

7. Remove the timing chain with the camshaft sprocket.

8. On installation: Turn the crankshaft to line up the timing mark on the crankshaft sprocket with the centerline of the camshaft (without the chain).

9. Install the camshaft sprocket and chain. Align the timing marks.

10. Torque the camshaft sprocket bolt to 35 ft. lbs.

11. Replace the oil slinger.

12. Reinstall the timing case cover with a new gasket and torque the bolts to 17 ft. lbs. Retighten the engine oil pan to 17 ft. lbs.

13. Press the vibration damper back on.

14. Replace the radiator and hoses.

15. Refill the cooling system.

V8 Engines

1. Disconnect the battery and drain the cooling system. Remove the radiator.

2. Remove the vibration damper pulley. Unbolt and remove the vibration damper with a puller. On 318 and 360 engines, remove the fuel lines and fuel pump, then loosen the oil pan bolts and remove the front bolt on each side.

3. Remove the timing gear cover and the crankshaft oil slinger.

4. On 318 and 360 engines, remove the camshaft sprocket lockbolt, securing cup washer, and fuel pump eccentric. Remove the timing chain with both sprockets. On 400 and 440 engines, remove the camshaft sprocket lockbolt and remove the timing chain with the camshaft and crankshaft sprockets.

TIMING MARKS

Timing mark alignment—6 cylinder engine

5. To begin the installation procedure, place the camshaft and crankshaft sprockets on a flat surface with the timing indicators on an imaginary centerline through both sprocket bores. Place the timing chain around both sprockets. Be sure that the timing marks are in alignment.

——————— **CAUTION** ———————

When installing the timing chain, have an assistant support the camshaft with a suitable tool to prevent it from contacting the plug in the rear of the engine block. Remove the distributor and the oil pump/distributor drive gear. Position the suitable tool against the rear side of the cam gear and be careful not to damage the cam lobes.

Timing mark alignment—V8 engine

6. Turn the crankshaft and camshaft to align them with the keyway location in the crankshaft sprocket and the keyway or dowel hole in the camshaft sprocket.

7. Lift the sprockets and timing chain while keeping the sprockets tight against the chain in the correct position. Slide both sprockets evenly onto their respective shafts.

8. Use a straightedge to measure the alignment of the sprocket timing marks. They must be perfectly aligned.

9. On 318 and 360 engines, install the fuel pump eccentric, cup washer, and camshaft sprocket lockbolt and torque to 35 ft. lbs. If camshaft end play exceeds 0.010 in., install a new thrust plate. It should be 0.002–0.006 in. with the new plate.

On 400 and 440 V8s, install the washer and camshaft sprocket lockbolt(s) and then torque the lockbolt to 35–40 ft. lbs. Check to make sure that the rear face of the camshaft sprocket is flush with the camshaft end.

CHECKING TIMING CHAIN SLACK

1. Position a scale (ruler or straightedge) next to the timing chain to detect any

movement in the chain.

2. Place a torque wrench and socket on the camshaft sprocket attaching bolt. Apply either 30 ft. lbs. (if the cylinder heads are installed on the engine) or 15 ft. lbs. (cylinder heads removed) of force to the bolt and rotate the bolt in the direction of crankshaft rotation in order to remove all slack from the chain.

3. While applying torque to the camshaft sprocket bolt, the crankshaft should not be allowed to rotate. It may be necessary to block the crankshaft to prevent rotation.

4. Position the scale over the edge of a timing chain link and apply an equal amount of torque in the opposite direction. If the movement of the chain exceeds ⅛ in., replace the chain.

Timing Cover Seal

REPLACEMENT

NOTE: A seal remover and installer tool is required to prevent seal damage.

1. Using a seal puller, separate the seal from the retainer.
2. Pull the seal from the case.
3. To install the seal place it face down in the case with the seal lips downward.
4. Seat the seal tightly against the cover face. There should be a maximum clearance of .0014 in. between the seal and the cover. Be careful not to over-compress the seal.

Timing Gear (Diesel)

REMOVAL & INSTALLATION

1. Remove the timing gear cover, the gasket and the front oil seal. Remove the idler pulley bracket.
2. Align the timing marks.
3. Using a puller, remove the camshaft drive gear.
4. Turn the injection pump to allow the notch in the drive gear to pass by the idler gear teeth.
5. Loosen the idler gear mounting bolt. Remove the thrust plate and remove the idler gear.
To install:
1. Be sure that the crankshaft is set with No. 1 cylinder at TDC.
2. Install the idler gear on the shaft so the marks on the camshaft drive gear match up with the marks on the idler gear.
3. Install the thrust plate and the hold down bolt.
4. Install the camshaft gear and the thrust plate on the camshaft. Be sure all the marks line up with the marks on the idler gear. Tighten the hold down bolt.
5. Put the injection pump in position and mesh the pump drive gear with the idler gear so the marks on the drive gear match up properly with the marks on the idler gear. Be sure the pump mounting flange

Timing gear alignment—diesel engine

scale is set at the proper injection point.
6. Install the mounting nuts to the timing gear case and tighten them.
7. Connect the fuel feed line and the filter hoses to the pump.
8. Bleed the air from the fuel system.
9. Connect the injector pipes.
10. Check the idler gear for end play using a feeler gauge between the gear and the thrust plate. It should be between .002 and .006 in. If it exceeds .014 in., replace the thrust plate.
11. Install a new front oil seal (using a new gasket), the timing gear cover and the crankshaft drive pulley.

Camshaft

REMOVAL & INSTALLATION

135 (2.2L) 4 Cylinder

1. Remove the timing belt cover.
2. Remove the timing belt.
3. Remove the air cleaner assembly.
4. Remove the valve cover.
5. Remove the Nos. 1, 3, and 5 camshaft bearing caps.
6. Loosen caps 2 and 4 diagonally and in increments.
7. Lift the camshaft out.
8. Lubricate the camshaft journals and lobes with engine assembly lubricant and position it in the head.
9. Install new oil seal.
10. Install the Nos. 1, 3, 5 bearing caps and torque the nuts to 14 ft. lbs.
11. Install the Nos. 2 and 4 caps and diagonally torque the nuts to 14 ft. lbs.

——————— **CAUTION** ———————

All bearing caps are slightly offset. They should be installed so the numbers on the cap read right side up from the driver's seat.

12. Position a dial indicator so that the feeler touches the front end of the camshaft. Check for end play. Play should not exceed .006 in.

13. Place a new seal on the No. 1 bearing cap. If necessary, replace the end plug in the head.

14. Follow the procedures under Timing Belt Removal and Installation for belt installation and timing.

15. Check the valve clearance and ignition timing.

155.9 (2.6L) 4 Cylinder

1. Remove the breather hoses and purge hose.

2. Remove the air cleaner and fuel line.

3. Remove the fuel pump. Remove the distributor.

4. Disconnect the spark plug cables.

5. Remove the rocker cover.

6. Remove the breather and semi-circular seal.

7. After slightly loosening the camshaft sprocket bolt, turn the crankshaft until No. 1 piston is at Top Dead Center on compression stroke (both valves closed).

8. Remove the camshaft sprocket bolt and distributor drive gear.

9. Remove the camshaft sprocket with chain and allow it to rest on the camshaft sprocket holder.

10. Remove the camshaft bearing cap tightening bolts. Do not remove the front and rear bearing cap bolts altogether, but keep them inserted in the bearing caps so that the rocker assembly can be removed as a unit.

11. Remove the rocker arms, rocker shafts and bearing caps as an assembly.

12. Remove the camshaft.

13. Installation is the reverse of removal. Lubricate the camshaft lobes and bearings and fit camshaft into head. Install the assembled rocker arm shaft assembly.

6-Cylinder Engines

1. Remove the cylinder head, timing gear cover, camshaft sprocket, and timing chain.

2. Remove the valve tappets, keeping them in order to ensure installation in their original locations.

3. Remove the crankshaft sprocket.

4. Remove the distributor and oil pump.

5. Remove the fuel pump.

6. Install a long bolt into the front of the camshaft to facilitate its removal.

7. Remove the camshaft, being careful not to damage the cam bearings with the cam lobes.

8. Prior to installation, lubricate the camshaft lobes and bearing journals. It is recommended that 1 pt. of crankcase conditioner be added to the initial crankcase oil fill.

9. Install the camshaft in the engine block. From this point, reverse the removal procedure.

V8 Engines

1. Remove the intake manifold, cylinder head covers, rocker arm assemblies, push rods, and valve tappets, keeping them in order to insure the installation in their original locations.

2. Remove the timing gear cover, the camshaft and crankshaft sprockets, and timing chain.

3. Remove the distributor and lift out the oil pump and distributor driveshaft. On 400 and 440 cu. in. engines, remove the fuel pump to allow the push rod to drop away from the cam eccentric.

4. Remove the camshaft thrust plate (on 318 and 360).

5. Install a long bolt into the front of the camshaft and remove the camshaft, being careful not to damage the cam bearings with the cam lobes.

6. Prior to installation, lubricate the camshaft lobes and bearing journals. It is recommended that 1 pt. of Crankcase Conditioner be added to the initial crankcase oil fill. Insert the camshaft into the engine block within 2 in. of its final position in the block.

7. Have an assistant support the camshaft with a suitable tool to prevent the camshaft from contacting the plug in the rear of the engine block. Position the suitable tool against the rear side of the cam gear and be careful not to damage the cam lobes.

8. Replace the camshaft thrust plate. If camshaft end play exceeds 0.010 in., install a new thrust plate. It should be 0.002–0.006 in. with the new plate.

9. Install the timing chain and sprockets, timing gear cover, and pulley.

10. Install the tappets, pushrods, rocker arms, and cylinder head covers. Install fuel pump, if removed.

11. Install the distributor and oil pump driveshaft. Install the distributor.

12. After starting the engine, adjust the ignition timing.

Pistons and Connecting Rods

REMOVAL & INSTALLATION

NOTE: Refer to the "Engine Rebuilding" section in Unit Repair for procedures.

4 Cylinder

The piston crown is marked with an arrow which must point toward the drive belt end of the engine when installed. The connecting rod and cap are marked with rectangular forge marks which must be mated when assembled and which must be on the intermediate shaft side of the engine when installed.

6 and 8 Cylinder

The notch on the top of each piston must face the front of the engine.

To position the connecting rod correctly, the oil squirt hole should point to the right-side on all six-cylinder engines. On all V8 engines, the larger chamfer of the lower connecting rod bore must face to the rear on the right bank and to the front on the left bank.

135 (2.2L) engine piston installation

155.9 (2.6L) engine piston installation (mark faces front)

Relation of the piston and connecting rod—V8

Relation of the piston and connecting rod—6 cylinder

Crankshaft & Main Bearings

REMOVAL & INSTALLATION

NOTE: Refer to the "Engine Rebuilding" section in Unit Repair for procedures.

ENGINE LUBRICATION

Oil Pan

REMOVAL & INSTALLATION

4 Cylinder

1. Raise and safely support the truck on jackstands. Drain the oil pan.
2. Support the pan and remove the attaching bolts.
3. Lower the pan and discard the gaskets.
4. Clean all gasket surfaces thoroughly and install the pan using gasket sealer and a new gasket.
5. Torque the pan bolts to 7 ft. lbs.
6. Refill the pan, start the engine, and check for leaks.

6 Cylinder Vans and Pick-ups

1. Disconnect the battery and remove the dipstick.
2. Remove the engine cover and remove the starter and air cleaner.
3. Raise the van on a hoist or support on jackstands and drain the crankcase oil.
4. Install an engine support as described under "Engine Removal."
5. Disconnect and tie out of the way: driveshaft, transmission linkage, and exhaust pipe at the manifold.
6. Remove the clutch torque shaft (if equipped) and the oil cooler lines (if equipped).
7. Disconnect the speedometer cable and electrical connections to the transmission.
8. Remove the support bracket, inspection plate, and drive plate-to-converter attaching screws if equipped.
9. Remove the bolts which attach the transmission to the clutch housing. Carefully work the transmission and converter rearward off the engine dowels and disengage the converter hub from the end of the crankshaft. Remove the transmission.
10. Support the rear of the engine and raise it two inches.
11. Remove the oil pan attaching bolts. Positioning the crankshaft so that the counterweights will clear the pan, rotate the pan to the steering gear side and remove it. You

may have to turn the pump pickup tube for clearance.
12. Installation is the reverse of removal. Make sure that the pickup screen contacts the bottom of the pan. Fill the engine with oil and check for leaks.
13. Remove the oil pan attaching screws and position the crankshaft so that the pan will clear the counterweights. Remove the pan.
14. Installation is the reverse of removal. Check all fluid levels and be sure that there are no leaks.

318 and 360 V8 Vans and Pick-ups

1. Disconnect the battery ground cable. Remove the dipstick and tube, engine cover, and air cleaner.
2. Disconnect the throttle linkage at the rear of the engine and the clutch or automatic transmission linkage.
3. Raise the engine slightly and support it with the device described under "Engine Removal."
4. Raise and support the vehicle and drain the oil. Remove the starter.
5. Remove the driveshaft and engine rear support.
6. Remove the transmission from the van. Remove the automatic transmission with the filler tube installed and the torque converter separated from the drive plate.
7. Remove the clutch assembly and flywheel (or driveplate) from the crankshaft.
8. Raise the engine about 2 in.
9. Rotate the crankshaft so that the counterweights will clear the oil pan. Maximum clearance is with the notch in the crankshaft flange at the 3 o'clock position. Remove the oil pan. It will be necessary to reach inside the oil pan and turn the oil pick-up tube and strainer slightly to the right to clear the pan.
10. Installation is the reverse of removal. Be sure to check all fluid levels and be sure that there are no leaks.

Two-Wheel Drive Ramcharger and Trail Duster

1. Disconnect the battery cable and remove the dipstick.
2. Raise and support the truck.
3. Drain the oil.
4. Remove the torque converter or clutch housing brace.
5. If necessary, remove the exhaust pipe.
6. Remove the oil pan bolts and remove the pan.
7. Installation is the reverse of removal.

Four-Wheel Drive Ramcharger and Trail Duster

1. Raise vehicle and support the truck.
2. Remove the two front engine mounting bolts.
3. Remove the left-side support, connecting the converter housing and cylinder block.
4. Raise the engine approximately 2 in.

Apply ⅛ inch beads of silicone sealer to the corners of the oil pan—6 cylinder shown

5. Drain oil.
6. Remove the oil pan bolts, lower pan down and to the rear. (Do not turn oil pickup out of position)

Oil Pump

REMOVAL & INSTALLATION

135 (2.2L) 4 Cylinder

1. Raise and safely support the truck. Drain oil. Remove the oil pan.
2. Remove the two pump mounting bolts.
3. Pull the pump down and out of the engine.
4. Prime, by filling pump with fresh oil. Installation is the reverse. Torque the pump mounting bolts to 14 ft. lbs.

155.9 (2.6L) 4 Cylinder

Refer to the "Timing Chain, Cover; Silent Shaft" section for oil pump removal and installation procedures.

6 Cylinder—Except Diesel

The rotor type oil pump is externally mounted on the rear right-hand (camshaft) side of the engine and is gear driven (helical) from the camshaft. The oil filter screws into the pump body.

1. Remove the oil pump mounting bolts and remove pump and filter assembly from engine.
2. Remove the oil filter, service pump or replace as required.
3. Prime, by filling pump with fresh oil. Install pump and new mounting gasket in the reverse order of removal after cleaning all gasket surfaces.

Diesel Engine

1. Raise and safely support the vehicle. Drain engine oil. Remove the oil pan, oil pickup tube, strainer and all old gaskets.
2. Remove the oil pump joint bolt, filter assembly to pump tube and the oil pump.
3. Clean all gasket surfaces. Prime by filling pump with fresh oil.

4. Installation is in the reverse order of removal. Always use new gaskets.

318, 360 V8 Engines

NOTE: **It is necessary to remove the oil pan, and to remove the oil pump from the rear main bearing cap to service the oil pump.**

1. Raise and safely support the vehicle. Drain the engine oil and remove the oil pan.
2. Remove the oil pump mounting bolts and remove the oil pump from the rear main bearing cap. Service or replace pump as necessary.
3. Prime the oil pump before installation by filling the rotor cavity with engine oil. Install the oil pump on the engine and tighten attaching bolts to 30 ft. lbs.
4. Continue the installation in the reverse order of the removal.
5. Fill the engine with the proper grade motor oil. Start the engine and check for leaks.

400, 440 V8 Engines

The rotor type oil pump is externally mounted and gear driven from the camshaft. The oil filter screws into the pumpbody.

1. Raise and safely support the vehicle. Drain engine oil.
2. Remove oil pump and filter assembly. Remove the oil filter from the pump. Service or replace pump as necessary. Clean mounting surfaces.
3. Fill pump with fresh oil. Install oil pump on engine using new gasket and tightening bolts to 30 ft. lbs. The distributor drive gear slot should parallel the crankshaft with No. 1 cylinder on TDC.
4. Install oil filter and fill crankcase with oil.

Rear Main Bearing Oil Seal

REMOVAL & INSTALLATION

135 (2.2L) 4 Cylinder

The rear main seal is located in a housing on the rear of the block. To replace the seal it is necessary to remove the engine.

1. Remove the transaxle and flywheel.

——— **CAUTION** ———

Before removing the transaxle, align the dimple on the flywheel with the pointer on the flywheel housing. The transaxle will not mate with the engine during installation unless this alignment is observed.

2. Very carefully, pry the old seal out of the support ring.
3. Coat the new seal with clean engine oil and press it into place with a flat piece of metal. Take great care not to scratch the seal or crankshaft.
4. Install the flywheel and transaxle.

155.9 (2.6L) 4 Cylinder

The rear main oil seal is located in a housing on the rear of the block. To replace the seal, remove the transaxle and do the work from underneath the vehicle or remove the engine and do the work on the bench.

1. Remove the housing from the block.
2. Remove the separator from the housing.
3. Pry out the old seal.
4. Lightly oil the replacement seal. The oil seal should be installed so that the seal plate fits into the inner contact surface of the seal case. Install the separator with the oil holes facing down.

6 and 8 Cylinder Engines (Except Diesel)

Service replacement seals are of the split rubber type composition. This type of seal makes it possible to replace the upper rear seal without removing the crankshaft. The seal must be used as an upper and lower set and cannot be used with the rope type seal.

NOTE: **Rope type seals are included in overhaul gasket sets, for use when the crankshaft has been removed, on all engines, except the 360 which uses only the composition seal.**

The following procedure is for removing the rope type rear main seal and replacing it with the rubber type seal.

1. Remove the oil pan, and both the rear seal retainer and the rear main bearing cap, if separate.
2. Remove the lower rope seal from the cap or retainer by prying the seal out of the groove.
3. With the use of suitable tools, either pull or push the seal from its seat, while rotating the crankshaft, being careful not to damage the surface of the journal. If necessary, loosen all the main bearing caps slightly, to lower the crankshaft, which will aid in the removal and replacement of the seal.
4. Clean and lubricate the crankshaft journal. Hold the seal tight against the crankshaft with the painted stripe to the rear, and install the seal into the block groove.
5. Rotate the crankshaft while pushing the seal into the groove. Be careful that the sharp edges of the block groove, *do not cut or nick the rear of the seal*.
6. Install the lower half of the seal into the lower seal retainer or the main bearing cap, if separate, with the paint stripe facing to the rear.
7. Install the lower seal retainer and/or the rear main bearing cap. Torque all main bearing caps to specifications.
8. Install the oil pan, add oil and check for oil leaks.

Diesel Engine

The rear main oil seal is a one piece design mounted with a sleeve. Two side seals are also used in grooves located on No. 7 main bearing cap.

1. Oil pan and flywheel are removed.
2. Rear seal retainer bolts, retainer and No. 7 main bearing cap are removed.
3. The two side seals are installed after No. 7 main bearing cap has been mounted and torqued to specs. Apply gasket sealer to the seals. Slide the seals into place, do not "drive" them in. When properly installed, the seal should conform to the corners of the mounting grooves.
4. The rear main seal is retained by a sleeve and plate. Remove the old seal from the retainer, clean the retainer, mount a new seal, lubricate the lips of the seal and install seal sleeve and retainer. Torque the mounting bolts to 2.2 ft. lbs. Install the flywheel, oil pan etc.

ENGINE COOLING

Radiator

REMOVAL & INSTALLATION

4 Cylinder

1. Disconnect negative battery cable. Open the radiator drain cock.
2. Remove the upper and lower hoses and coolant recovery tank.
3. Disconnect wiring harness from fan motor. Remove the upper shroud mounting bolts.
4. Remove the shroud and fan assembly.
5. Disconnect and plug automatic transmission fluid cooling lines, if equipped. Remove the top radiator attaching bolts.
6. Remove the bottom radiator attaching bolts, if equipped.
7. Lift radiator from engine compartment.
8. Installation is the reverse of removal.

6 and 8 Cylinder Engines

1. Drain the cooling system.
2. Disconnect the battery ground cable.
3. Detach the upper hose from the radiator.
4. Remove the shroud mounting nuts and position it out of the way.
5. Remove the radiator top mounting screws. If equipped with air conditioning, remove the condenser attaching screws, accessible through the grille. Do not disconnect any air conditioning lines.
6. Raise the vehicle and support it. Disconnect and plug the automatic transmission cooler lines and cap the openings in the cooler.

Typical 4 cylinder engine cooling system components

7. Hold the radiator in place and remove the lower mounting screws. Carefully lower the radiator out of the van or lift it up and out if a pickup truck.

8. Installation is the reverse of removal. Check all fluid levels and run the engine, making sure that there are no leaks.

Typical radiator and fan shroud mounting—6 and V8 engines

Water Pump

REMOVAL & INSTALLATION

135 (2.2L) 4 Cylinder

1. Drain the cooling system.
2. Remove the upper radiator hose.
3. Without discharging the system, remove the air conditioning compressor from the engine brackets and set to one side.
4. Remove the alternator and move to one side.
5. Disconnect the lower radiator hose and the bypass hose and remove the water pump by removing the pump to engine retaining screws.

6. Installation is the reverse of removal. Tighten the top three retaining screws to 250 in. lbs. and the lower screw to 50 ft. lbs.

155.9 (2.6L) 4 Cylinder

1. Drain the cooling system.
2. Remove the radiator hose, by-pass hose and heater hose from the water pump.
3. Remove the drive pulley shield.
4. Remove the locking screw and pivot screws.
5. Remove the drive belt and water pump from the engine.
6. Install new mounting gasket and pump. Installation is the reverse of removal. Tighten mounting bolts to 80 in. lbs. After adjusting the belt tension tighten the locking screw and pivot screws to 204 in. lbs. Tighten the drive pulley shield to 105 in. lbs.

6 Cylinder—Except Diesel

NOTE: This job can sometimes be done without removing the radiator on models without air-conditioning, if there is enough room to get at the water pump bolts.

1. Remove the radiator.
2. Remove all drive belts.
3. Remove the fan, spacer, pulley, and bolts as an assembly.
4. If equipped with an air pump, remove the pump brackets with the hoses attached and tie it out of the way.
5. Disconnect the heater hose and all other hoses from the pump.
6. Remove the pump from the block.
7. Installation is the reverse of removal. Fill the cooling system and adjust the tension of the drive belts.

Diesel Engine

1. Drain the cooling system and remove the heater hoses and the bypass hose.
2. Loosen the alternator mounting bolts and remove the belt.
3. Remove the cooling fan, the spacer and the drive pulley.
4. Remove the water pump mounting bolts and remove the pump.
5. Reverse to install.

318 and 360 V8

1. Remove the radiator.
2. Loosen all accessories that are belt driven and remove all the drive belts.
3. On engines without air conditioning, remove the alternator bracket attaching bolts and tie the alternator and bracket out of the way.
4. On engines with air conditioning, remove the idler pulley assembly, alternator, and adjusting bracket.
5. Remove the fan blade, spacer (or fluid unit), pulley, and bolts as an assembly.

NOTE: To prevent silicone fluid from draining into the drive bearing and ruining the lubricant, do not place the thermostatic fan drive unit with the shaft pointing downward.

6. Disconnect all hoses from the water pump.
7. Remove the air conditioning compressor front mounting bolts.
8. Remove the water pump-to-compressor front bracket bolts and the bracket.

NOTE: Do not disconnect any refrigerant lines from the compressor.

9. Remove the water pump.
10. Installation is the reverse of removal. Fill with coolant and check for leaks.

400 and 440 V8

1. Disconnect the negative battery cable and drain the cooling system.
2. Loosen all of the drive belts.
3. Remove the lower crankshaft pulley.
4. Remove the fan shroud screws and set the shroud back out of the way.
5. Remove the fluid fan drive bolts and set the fluid fan and the fan assembly aside.
6. Remove the water pump and the gasket.
7. Reverse to install. Rotate the pump by hand before attaching any of the drive belts to be sure it rotates freely.

Thermostat

REMOVAL & INSTALLATION

4 Cylinder Engines

The thermostat is located in the bottom radiator hose neck in the water pump on 2.2 engines or in the intake manifold under the upper radiator hose, on 2.6 engines.

1. Drain the cooling system to a level below the thermostat.

2. Remove the hoses from the thermostat housing.

3. Remove the thermostat housing.

4. Remove the thermostat and discard the gasket. Clean the gasket surfaces thoroughly.

5. Using a new gasket, position the thermostat and install the housing and bolts. Make sure that the thermostat is seated properly.

6. Refill the cooling system.

6 and 8 Cylinder Engines

1. Drain the cooling system to below the level of the thermostat.

2. Remove the upper radiator hose from the thermostat housing. Note the positioning of the thermostat. It is important that the thermostat is correctly installed.

3. Withdraw the housing bolts and remove the housing and the thermostat.

4. Check to make sure that the thermostat valve closes tightly. If the valve does not close completely due to foreign material, carefully clean the sealing edge of the valve while being careful not to damage the sealing edge. If the valve does not close tightly after it has been cleaned, a new thermostat must be installed.

5. Immerse the thermostat in a container of warm water so that its pellet is completely covered and does not touch the bottom or sides of the container.

6. Heat the water and, while stirring the water continuously (to ensure uniform temperature), check the water temperature with a thermometer at the point when a 0.001 in. feeler gauge can be inserted in the valve opening at a water temperature with ± 5 degrees of the standard thermostat opening temperature. If the thermostat does not open within the temperature range, replace it with a new thermostat.

7. Continue heating the water to a temperature of approximately 20 degrees higher than the standard thermostat opening temperature. At this point, the thermostat should be fully open. If it is not, install a new thermostat.

8. To install, use a new gasket and position the thermostat so that its pellet end (the part with the spring) is toward the engine block. On the six, the vent hole must be up. Refit the thermostat housing and tighten its securing bolts.

9. Refit the upper radiator hose.

10. Fill the cooling system to 1.25 in. below the filler neck with the correct water and antifreeze mixture. Warm the engine and inspect the upper radiator hose and the thermostat housing for leaks.

NOTE: Poor heater output and slow engine warm-up is often caused by a thermostat stuck in the open position; occasionally one sticks shut causing immediate overheating. Do not attempt to correct an overheating condition by permanently removing the thermostat.

Thermostat flow restriction is designed into the system; without it, localized overheating due to turbulence may occur.

EMISSION CONTROLS

Description

Two basic approaches to emission control have been used on Dodge engines. The first is engine design modifications, which apply to some extent to all engines. The second is a group of specific emission control systems, the application of which varies with model and power train. Those models rated under a specific GVW are subject to stricter light-duty emission regulations, and therefore use more of these systems.

NOTE: Refer to the "Emissions" section of Unit Repair for servicing procedures.

GASOLINE FUEL SYSTEM

Carburetor

REMOVAL & INSTALLATION

The following is a general removal procedure for all carburetors.

1. Disconnect the battery ground cable.

2. Remove the air cleaner.

3. Remove the fuel tank pressure-vacuum filler cap. The tank could be under a small amount of pressure.

4. Disconnect and plug the fuel lines. Use two wrenches to avoid twisting the fuel line. A container is also useful to catch any fuel which spills from the lines.

5. Disconnect the throttle and choke linkage.

6. Disconnect any vacuum lines.

7. Remove the mounting bolts.

8. Carefully remove the carburetor from the engine and carry it in a level position to a clean work place.

9. Installation is the reverse of removal. Adjust the curb idle speed.

ADJUSTMENTS

NOTE: Carburetor specifications, exploded views, and basic adjustments are found in the General Repair section under Carburetor Repairs.

Fuel Filter

REMOVAL & INSTALLATION

4 Cylinder Engines

Two filters are used. One is part of the fuel pickup in the fuel tank. The other is a sealed paper unit located in the carburetor inlet (2.2 engines) or an in-line filter (2.6 engines). The tank unit does not usually need replacing, but can be replaced if necessary. The carburetor filter should be replaced periodically. To replace the inlet filter, place a rag or container under the inlet and disconnect the fuel line. Unscrew the inlet fitting. The filter has a spring behind it so take care not to lose it. Replacement is the reverse of removal.

The inline filter can be removed by placing a rag under the filter and removing the clamps. Pull the filter out of the lines and discard it. Install a new filter, noting the direction of fuel flow, usually indicated by an arrow.

6 and 8 Cylinder Engines

Locate the filter in the fuel line between the fuel pump and the carburetor. Using hose-clamp pliers, remove the attaching clamps and pull the filter off. Reverse this procedure for installation. Be sure that the arrow on the filter is pointing toward the carburetor (direction of fuel flow). Replace the filter every 30,000 miles.

NOTE: Some filters have a third line, the purpose of which is to prevent vapor lock by allowing fuel vapors to return to the tank.

Fuel Pump

REMOVAL & INSTALLATION

1. Disconnect the fuel lines from the inlet, output a return (if equipped) sides of the fuel pump.

2. Plug these lines to prevent gasoline from leaking out.

3. Unbolt the retaining bolts from the fuel pump and remove the fuel pump from the engine.

4. Remove the old gasket from the engine and/or fuel pump.

5. Clean all mounting surfaces.

6. Using a new gasket, install the fuel pump. Installation is the reverse of removal.

Fuel Tank

REMOVAL & INSTALLATION

Vans and Pickups

1. Disconnect the battery ground cable.

2. Remove the fuel tank filler cap.

3. Raise the vehicle on a lift. Pump all fuel from the tank into an approved holding tank, and raise the vehicle.

318 and 360 V8 engine fuel pump details

Fuel pump—6 cylinder

4. Disconnect the fuel line and wire lead to the gauge unit. Remove the ground strap.

5. Remove the vent hose shield and the hose clamps from the hoses running to the vapor vent tube.

6. Remove the filler tube hose clamps and disconnect the hose from the tank.

7. Place a transmission jack under the center of the tank and apply sufficient pressure to support the tank.

8. Disconnect the two J-bolts and remove the retaining straps at the rear of the tank. Lower the tank from the vehicle. Feed the two vent tube hoses and filler tube vent hose through the grommets in the frame as the tank is being lowered. Remove the tank gauge unit.

9. Inspect the fuel filter, and if it is clogged or damaged, replace it.

10. Insert a new gasket in the recess of the fuel gauge opening and slide the gauge into the tank. Align the positioning tangs on the gauge with those on the tank. Install the lock ring, and tighten securely.

11. Position the tank on a transmission jack and hoist it into place, feeding the vent hoses through the grommets on the way up.

12. Connect the J-bolts and retaining straps, and tighten. Remove the jack.

13. Connect the filler tube and all vent hoses.

14. Connect the fuel supply line, ground strap, and gauge unit wire lead.

15. Refill the tank and inspect it for leaks. Connect the battery ground cable.

Ramcharger and Trail Duster

1. If there is a tank skid plate, remove it.

2. Disconnect the battery ground cable.

3. Remove the tank filler cap.

4. Pump or siphon the contents of the tank into a safe container.

— CAUTION —

Siphoning should not be started by mouth. Only fuel-safe pumps should be used.

---

5. Raise the vehicle on a hoist and disconnect the fuel line and tank sending unit wire. Remove the ground strap or wire.

6. Remove the hose clamps from the vent dome hose.

7. Remove the filler tube hose clamps. Detach the hoses from the tank.

8. Support the tank with a padded transmission jack.

9. Disconnect the two J-bolts and remove the straps at the rear of the tank.

10. Remove the tank gauge sending unit.

11. Use a new tank gauge sending unit gasket. Check the filter on the end of the fuel suction tube.

12. Use a new or undamaged tank to frame insulator. Raise the tank into position.

13. Connect the J-bolts and retaining straps and tighten.

14. Connect the filler tube and all hoses. Tighten the clamps.

15. Connect the fuel line, ground strap or wire, and tank sending unit wire. Make sure that all fuel line heat shields are in place.

16. Reconnect the battery ground cable.

DIESEL FUEL SYSTEM

Diesel Injection Pump

TESTING (ON THE VEHICLE)

1. With the engine running, loosen the cap on the fuel injection line at the injection pump outlet. This will relieve pressure and prevent fuel injection into the cylinder.

2. If a cylinder is misfiring, uneven combustion will stop when the fuel is cut off.

3. Proceed from cylinder to cylinder until the faulty cylinder is located.

4. Perform a compression test on the cylinder in question. If the cylinder in question meets the compression specifications, replace the injection pump.

REMOVAL & INSTALLATION

1. Disconnect the batteries.

2. Disconnect the fuel shutoff rod at the stop lever.

3. Remove the power steering pump and the mounting bracket from the engine and set it aside.

4. Thoroughly clean the area around the hose fittings and the injection pipes.

5. Drain the engine oil and remove the dipstick and the dipstick tube.

6. Disconnect the throttle cable and the linkage from the injection pump control lever.

Diesel injection pump details

7. Remove the throttle control bracket assembly from the crankcase, injection pump and the control bracket and set it aside.

8. Disconnect the fuel supply line to the fuel feed pump and set it aside, loosening the anchoring clamps as necessary.

9. Disconnect the fuel hoses leading to the filter from the feed pump and the injection pump. Replace the screws and seals to prevent dirt from getting into the pump.

10. Rotate the engine so piston No. 1 is approximately 7° before top dead center on the compression stroke.

11. Disconnect the injection pipes from the delivery valves and set them aside. Cap the ends of the valves to prevent the entry of dirt.

12. Disconnect the injection pump lube lines.

13. Remove the five screws and one bolt attaching the pump.

14. Pull the pump to the rear and disengage it from the front plate and timing gear case. Rotate the pump toward the crankcase and continue pulling it to the rear until the automatic timer is freed.
To install.

Diesel injection pump linkage components

1. Loosen the four nuts attaching the pump to the mounting flange plate and align the center timing mark on the pump flange with the pointer on the plate. Tighten the four nuts.

2. Be sure that the O-ring is in place on the forward face of the pump mounting flange.

3. Remove the threaded timing port plug on the governor housing behind the control lever to expose the camshaft bushing timing mark. Rotate the pump drive gear to align the timing mark on the camshaft bushing with the pointer on the governor. The guide plate notch will be at approximately the 8 o'clock position as viewed from the front. Be sure the engine is positioned as described in Step 10 of the removal procedure.

4. Insert the automatic timer into the timing gear case and with the injection pump rotated against the crankshaft, rotate the pump driver gear to mesh the drive and idler gears. *Do not force the pump into position.*

5. Push the pump forward into the case. Rotate it away from the crankcase to align the attachment holes.

6. Attach the pump to the timing gear case.

7. Rotate the engine crankshaft in the opposite direction of normal operation until the crankshaft reaches the 18° before TDC mark on the crankshaft pulley. The governor pointer and the injection pump camshaft bushing timing marks should now be aligned. If they are not aligned, the pump has been installed incorrectly and must be removed and reinstalled.

8. Install the governor housing timing port plug and proceed with the pump installation by reversing the remainder of the removal procedure. Do not connect the No. 1 injecting pipe, fuel control rod or the batteries.

9. Bleed the air from the fuel filter and the injection pump by removing the air bleeder screws.

10. Time the injection pump.

INJECTION PUMP TIMING

1. Disconnect the batteries and the fuel shut off rod at the stop lever.

2. Rotate the crankshaft in the direction of normal operation until No. 1 cylinder reaches top dead center of the compression stroke. This is done by aligning the lines on the crankshaft pulley rear face with the pointer on the bottom of the case.

3. Remove the forward oil filler cap on the rocker cover and check the No. 1 cylinder valves for looseness. If they are loose, you are at TDC.

4. Rotate the crankshaft in the normal direction of engine operation 1¾ turns.

5. Disconnect No. 1 injection pipe from the delivery valve holder.

6. Turn the crankshaft in the normal direction of engine operation in small steps. Stop when fuel begins to flow from the delivery valve holder. Injection begins at this point. The control lever must be in the idle position.

7. Read the injection timing point from the scale on the back of the crankshaft damper. If the timing is correct, the timing mark should be at the value shown on the Vehicle Emission Control Information label on the rocker cover minus 2 degrees.

Injection pump timing marks

8. If the timing point determined differs from the standard value, minus 2 degrees, loosen the four pump-to-flange plate nuts and rotate the pump (toward the crankcase to advance the timing, away from the crankcase to retard it) to correct the difference. Each mark on the injection pump timing scale represents 6 degrees. Tighten the flange plate nuts and repeat the timing procedure to be sure the timing is correct.

MANUAL TRANSMISSION/ TRANSAXLE

NOTE: Refer to the "Transmission or Transfer Case" section of the Unit Repair for repair and service procedures.

REMOVAL & INSTALLATION

Manual Transaxle

1. Disconnect the battery cable and install a lifting eye on number 4 cylinder exhaust manifold bolt. Install a locally fabricated engine support fixture across the shock towers in the engine compartment.

2. Disconnect the gearshift linkage and clutch cable from the transaxle.

3. Remove the left front splash shield.

4. Remove the right and left drive shafts from the transaxle and support them. Do not let the drive axles hang free.

5. Remove the anti-rotational link from the transaxle and support the transmission with a suitable jack. Install a chain around the jack and transmission for safety.

6. Remove the speedometer adaptor and pinion from the transaxle.

7. Remove the engine mount from the front crossmember and the front mount insulator through bolt. Remove the upper bell housing bolts.

8. Remove the left engine mount and remove the lower bell housing bolts.

9. Pry the transaxle away from the engine and lower the assembly from the vehicle.

NOTE: When installing the transaxle use two bolts with the heads removed to act as locating guides. Place guides in the top two transaxle to engine block mounting location. When transaxle is in place, remove guides and install mounting bolts.

Fabricated engine support fixture

10. Installation is the reverse of removal. Refill the transaxle with Dexron® II or equivalent automatic transmission fluid. Adjust the clutch free play and transmission linkage.

11. Torque the engine mounting bolts to 40 ft. lbs. Torque the transmission to cylinder block bolts to 70 ft. lbs. Torque the hub nut to 180 ft. lbs. and torque the lug nuts to 80 ft. lbs.

3-Speed 2WD Models

1. Raise and safely support. Drain lubricant.

2. Disconnect and match-mark the driveshaft. On the sliding spline type, disconnect driveshaft at the rear universal joint, then carefully pull the shaft yoke out of the transmission extension housing. Do not nick or scratch the splines.

3. Disconnect gearshift control rods and speedometer cable.

4. Remove backup light switch if so equipped.

5. Support engine.

6. Remove crossmember and rubber insulator on models with A-390 transmission. On all other models, unbolt the insulator or mount from the crossmember. Support the transmission with a jack.

7. Remove transmission to clutch housing bolts.

8. Slide transmission rearward until pinion shaft clears clutch completely, then lower transmission from vehicle.

9. Installation is the reverse order of the above procedure. Before inserting transmission drive shaft into clutch, make sure clutch housing bore, disc and face are aligned. Tighten clutch housing to transmission bolts to 50 ft. lbs. torque.

10. Fill with lubricant.

11. Adjust shift linkage.

12. Road test.

4-Speed 2WD Models

1. Raise and support the truck. Shift transmission into any gear. Drain lubricant.

2. Disconnect universal joint and loosen yoke retaining nut.

3. Disconnect parking brake (if so equipped) and speedometer cables at transmission.

4. Remove lever retainer by pressing down, rotating retainer counterclockwise slightly, then releasing.

5. Remove lever and its springs and washers.

6. Support the rear of the engine and remove the crossmember. Remove transmission to clutch bell housing retaining bolts and pull transmission rearward until drive pinion clears clutch, then remove transmission.

7. To install, place ½ teaspoon of short fibre grease in pinion shaft pilot bushing, taking care not to get any grease on fly-

wheel face.

8. Align clutch disc and backing plate with a spare drive pinion shaft or clutch aligning tool, then carefully install transmission.

9. Install transmission to bell housing bolts, tightening to 50 ft. lbs. torque. Replace the crossmember.

10. Install gear shift lever, shift into any gear and tighten yoke nut to 95–105 ft. lbs. torque.

11. Install universal joint, speedometer cable and brake cable.

12. Adjust clutch.

13. Install transmission drain plug and fill transmission with lubricant.

14. Road test.

3 and 4-Speed-4WD Models

1. Raise and support the truck. Drain lubricant.

2. Remove the skid plate, if any.

3. Disconnect the speedometer cable.

4. Disconnect and match-mark the front and rear driveshafts. Suspend each shaft from a convenient place; do not allow them to hang free.

5. Disconnect the shift rods at the transfer case. On 4-speed transmissions, remove the shift lever retainer by pressing down and turning it counterclockwise. Remove the shift lever springs and washers.

6. Remove the rear driveshaft. Match-mark the driveshaft and rear U-joints before removing the driveshaft.

7. Support the transfer case.

8. Remove the extension-to-transfer case mounting bolts.

9. Move the transfer case rearward to disengage the front input shaft spline.

10. Lower and remove the transfer case.

11. Disconnect the back-up light switch.

12. Support the engine.

13. Support the transmission.

14. Remove the transmission crossmember.

15. Remove the transmission-to-clutch housing bolts.

16. Slide the transmission rearward until the mainshaft clears the clutch disc.

17. Lower and remove the transmission.

18. Installation is the reverse of removal. The transmission pilot bushing in the end of the crankshaft requires high-temperature grease. Multipurpose grease should be used. Do not lubricate the end of the mainshaft, clutch splines, or clutch release levers. Adjust the gearshift linkage on 3-speed transmissions.

Overdrive 4–Four Speed

1. Disconnect the negative battery cable. Raise and support truck. Drain lubricant.

2. Remove the retaining screws from the floor pan boot and slide the boot up and off the shift lever.

3. Remove the shift lever, retaining

clips, washers, and control rods from the shift unit.

4. Remove the two bolts and washers which secure the shift unit to mounting plate on the extension housing and remove the unit.

5. Drain the fluid from the transmission.

6. Disconnect the propeller shaft at the rear universal joint, marking the parts for re-installation in the same position. Carefully pull the shaft yoke out of the transmission extension housing.

7. Disconnect the speedometer cable and backup light switch leads.

8. Install engine support fixture C-3487-A or equivalent. Be sure that the support points are tight against the oil pan flange.

9. Raise engine slightly with the support fixture. Disconnect the extension housing from the center crossmember.

10. Support the transmission with a suitable jack and remove the center crossmember.

11. Remove the transmission to clutch housing bolts. Slide the transmission toward the rear until drive pinion shaft clears the clutch disc, before lowering the transmission. Remove the transmission.

12. Installation is the reverse of removal. Use high temperature multi-purpose grease on the pilot bushing in the end of the crankshaft, around the inner end of the pinion shaft pilot bushing in the flywheel and on the pinion bearing retainer release bearing area. Do not lubricate the end of the pinion shaft, clutch disc splines or clutch release levers.

13. Torque the clutch housing bolts to 50 ft. lbs. Tighten the crossmember bolts to 30 ft. lbs. Torque engine and transmission mounts to 50 ft. lbs.

14. Fill the transmission with 7.5 pints of Dexron II® (or equivalent) automatic transmission fluid.

15. Road test the vehicle.

Transfer Case

REMOVAL & INSTALLATION

1. Raise and support the truck.

2. Remove the skid plate, if any.

3. Drain the transfer case by removing the bottom bolt from the front output rear cover.

4. Disconnect the speedometer cable.

5. Disconnect the front and rear output shafts. Suspend these from a convenient location; do not allow them to hang free.

6. Disconnect the shift rods at the transfer case.

7. Support the transfer case.

8. Remove the adaptor-to-transfer case mounting bolts and move the transfer case rearward to disengage the front input splines.

9. Lower and remove the transfer case.

10. Installation is the reverse of removal. Adjust the linkage.

Shift Linkage Adjustment

VANS AND PICKUPS

A230, A250

1. Adjust the length of the 2-3 shift rod so the position of the shift lever on the steering column will be correct.

2. Assemble the 1st-reverse and 2-3 shift rods, and place each in its normal position, secured with a clip. Loosen both swivel clamp bolts.

3. Move the 2-3 shift lever into 3rd position (this means moving the forward lever forward). Move the steering column lever until it is about five degrees above the horizontal. Tighten the shift rod swivel clamp bolt.

4. Shift the transmission to neutral. Place a suitable tool between the crossover blade and the 2-3 lever at the steering column so that both lever pins are engaged by the crossover blade.

5. Set the 1st-reverse lever in neutral. Tighten the swivel clamp bolt.

6. Remove the tool from the cross over blade, and check all shifts for smoothness.

RAMCHARGER AND TRAIL DUSTER

A230

1. Remove both shift rod swivels from the transmission shift levers. Make sure that the transmission shift levers are in the neutral position (middle detent).

2. Move the shift lever to line up the locating slots in the bottom of the steering column shift housing and bearing housing.

3. Place a suitable tool between the crossover blade and the 2nd and 3rd lever at the steering column, so that both lever pins are engaged by the crossover blade.

4. Set the 1st-reverse lever on the transmission to the reverse position (rotate clockwise).

5. Adjust the 1st-reverse rod swivel by loosening the clamp bolt and sliding the swivel along the rod so it will enter the 1st-reverse lever at the transmission. Install the washers and the clip. Tighten the swivel bolt.

6. Remove the gearshift housing locating tool, and shift the transmission into the neutral position.

7. Adjust the 2nd-3rd rod swivel by loosening the clamp bolt and sliding the swivel along the rod so it will enter the 2nd-3rd lever at the transmission. Install the washers and the clip. Tighten the swivel bolt.

8. Remove the tool from the cross-over blade at the steering column and shift the transmission through all the gears to check the adjustment and the crossover smoothness.

Shift linkage A250 transmission

Shift linkage A230 transmission

ALL MODELS

A-390

1. Loosen both shift rod swivels. Make sure that the transmission shift levers are in the neutral position (middle detent).

2. Move the shift lever to line up the locating slots in the bottom of the steering column shift housing and bearing housing. Install a suitable tool in the slot.

3. Place a suitable tool between the crossover blade and the 2nd-3rd lever at the steering column so that both lever pins are engaged by the crossover blade.

4. Tighten both rod swivel bolts. Remove the gearshift housing locating tool.

5. Remove the tool from the crossover blade at the steering column and shift the transmission through all gears to check adjustment and crossover smoothness.

6. Check for proper operation of the steering column lock in reverse. With the proper linkage adjustment, the ignition should lock in reverse only, with hands off the gearshift lever.

Overdrive-4

1. Place the floorshift lever in Neutral. Insert a ¼ in. drill bit through the bottom of the shifter to hold the levers in place.

2. Detach the shift rods. Make sure that the three transmission levers are in their Neutral detents.

Shift linkage A390 transmission

3. Adjust the shift rods to make the length exactly right to fit into the transmission levers. Start with the 1st-2nd shift rod. It may be necessary to remove the clip at the shifter end of the rod to rotate this rod.

4. Replace the washers and the clips.

5. Remove the drill bit and check the shifting action.

TRANSAXLE SHIFT ADJUSTMENT

A double ended pin that is used to lock the linkage in place prior to adjustment.

1. Remove the screw from the top and reinsert the other end, locking the linkage in place.

2. The linkage is locked in the Neutral detent between 1st and 2nd gears.

3. Align the marks on the linkage.

4. Remove the pin and replace it in its original location. Check the operation of the shift linkage.

Shift linkage Overdrive 4 adjustment

Clutch Interlock

ADJUSTMENT

A-250 3-Speed

This adjustment is required only on the A-250 3-speed transmission. This is a top cover unit used only as base equipment on light duty six cylinder models. It has synchromesh only on second and third gears.

1. Disconnect the clutch rod swivel from the interlock pawl. Adjust the clutch pedal free play.

2. Shift the transmission to neutral. Loosen swivel clamp bolt and slide the swivel onto the rod until the pawl is positioned fully within the slot in the first-reverse lever. Install the washers and clip.

3. Hold the interlock pawl forward and tighten the swivel clamp bolt. The clutch pedal must be in fully returned position during the adjustment.

NOTE: Do not pull the clutch rod rearward to engage the swivel in the pawl.

4. Shift the transmission into first and reverse and release the clutch pedal while in either gear to check for normal clutch action. Then, shift halfway between neutral and either gear and release clutch. The interlock should hold it to within one or two inches of the floor.

CLUTCH

ADJUSTMENT

4 Cylinder Engines

Models with the A460, A465 and A525 transaxles are equipped with self-adjusting clutches. The clutch cable cannot be adjusted.

6 and 8 Cylinder Engines

The only adjustment required is pedal free-play. Adjust the clutch actuating fork rod by turning the self-locking adjusting nut to provide 1/8 in. (3/32 in. on vans and wagons) free movement at the end of the fork. This will provide the recommended 1 1/2 in. (1 in. on Vans, Wagons, Ramcharger, and Trailduster) freeplay at the pedal.

REMOVAL & INSTALLATION

4 Cylinder Engines

1. Remove the transaxle.

2. Mark the clutch cover and flywheel for reinstallation position if reused.

3. Install a clutch aligning tool for support purposes.

4. Loosen the attaching bolts one or two turns at a time in succession to avoid bending the cover flange.

5. Remove the pressure plate and clutch disc.

6. Service the throwout bearing and fork if necessary.

7. Inspect for oil leakage from the rear main oil seal. Service if necessary. Examine the flywheel surface, replace the flywheel if badly scored.

8. Position the clutch disc and pressure plate assembly on the flywheel. Install clutch aligning tool and install the clutch in the reverse order of removal. Tighten the mounting bolts in stages. Torque bolts to 250 in. lbs.

6 and 8 Cylinder Engines

1. Raise and support truck. Support the engine on a suitable jack.

2. Remove crossmember.

3. Remove transfer case, if equipped. Remove transmission.

4. Remove clutch housing pan if so equipped.

5. Remove clutch fork, clutch bearing and sleeve assembly if not removed with transmission.

6. Mark clutch cover and flywheel, with a suitable tool to assure correct reassembly. Install clutch aligning tool for support.

7. Remove clutch cover retaining bolts, loosening them evenly so clutch cover will not be distorted.

8. Pull pressure plate assembly clear of flywheel and, while supporting pressure plate, slide clutch disc from between flywheel and pressure plate.

9. To install, thoroughly clean all working surfaces of the flywheel and the pressure plate.

10. Grease radius at back of bushing.

Clutch release fork, bearing and sleeve

11. Rotate clutch cover and pressure plate assembly for maximum clearance between flywheel and frame crossmember if crossmember was not removed during clutch removal.

12. Tilt top edge of clutch cover and pressure plate assembly back and move it up into the clutch housing. Support clutch cover and pressure plate assembly and slide clutch disc into position.

13. Position clutch disc and plate against flywheel and insert spare transmission main drive gear shaft or clutch installing tool through clutch disc hub and into main drive pilot bearing.

14. Rotate clutch cover until the punch marks on cover and flywheel line up.

15. Bolt cover loosely to flywheel. Tighten cover bolts a few turns at a time, in progression, until tight. Then tighten bolts to 20 ft. lbs. torque.

16. Install transmission.

17. Install frame crossmembers and insulator, tighten all bolts.

AUTOMATIC TRANSAXLE

REMOVAL & INSTALLATION

The automatic transaxle can be removed by itself with the engine still mounted in the truck, but the transaxle and converter must be removed as an assembly. The drive plate, oil pump seal and pump bushing will not support weight such as the converter. If the converter is not removed with the transaxle, damage may occur.

1. Disconnect the negative battery cable.

2. Disconnect the throttle and shift linkage from the transaxle.

3. Raise and support the truck safely on jackstands.

4. Remove the front wheels. Remove the inner fender splash shields.

5. Drain the fluid from the transaxle. Remove the speedometer adapter, cable and drive pinion as an assembly.

6. Remove the sway bar. Remove the lower ball joint to steering knuckle bolts. Pry the lower ball joint from the steering knuckle.

7. Remove the drive axles from the front wheel hubs. See shaft removal in following section.

8. Matchmark the torque converter and drive plate. Remove the torque converter mounting bolts. On some models, the right front splash shield may be removed to provide access to rotate the engine.

9. Remove the lower oil cooler tube, if equipped. Disconnect any wire harness (neutral safety switch, etc.)

10. Install a portable engine support, or devise a method of supporting the engine from the top.

11. Remove the upper bell housing bolts. Remove the engine mount bracket from the front crossmember. Support the transmission.

12. Remove the front mount insulator "through" bolts and the bell housing mount.

13. Remove the long "through" bolt from the left hand engine mount.

14. Raise the transaxle, remove any remaining mounting bolts and separate from the engine. Slowly lower the transaxle to the ground.

15. Installation is in the reverse order of removal. Fill the transaxle with the correct amount of Dexron II. Check for leaks.

NOTE: Pan gaskets are formed with RTV sealant, follow the directions on the tube when applying.

SHIFT LINKAGE

Adjustment

NOTE: When it is necessary to disconnect the linkage cable from the lever, which uses plastic grommets as retainers, the grommets should be replaced.

1. Make sure that the adjustable swivel block is free to slide on the shift cable.

2. Place the shift lever in Park.

3. With the linkage assembled, and the swivel lock bolt loose, move the shift on the transaxle all the way to the rear detent.

4. Tighten the adjuster swivel lock bolt to 8 ft. lb.

5. Check the linkage action.

NOTE: The automatic transmission gear selector release button may pop up in the knob when shifting from PARK to DRIVE. This is caused by inadequate retention of the selector release knob retaining tab. The release button will always work but the loose button can be annoying. A sleeve and washers are available to cure this condition. If these are unavailable, do the following:

1. Remove the release button.

2. Cut and fold a standard paper match stem as shown.

3. Using tweezers, insert the folded match as far as possible into the clearance slot as shown. The match should be below the knob surface.

4. Insert the button, taking care not to break the button stem.

THROTTLE CABLE

Adjustment

1. Adjust the idle speed as previously described.

2. Run the engine to normal operating temperature.

3. Loosen the adjustment bracket lock scre.

4. Make sure the adjustment bracket is free to slide in its slot.

5. Hold the transmission lever firmly rearward against its internal stop and tighten

the adjustment bracket lock screw to 105 in. lbs.

6. Test the cable operation.

BAND ADJUSTMENTS

Front (Kickdown) Band

Chrysler recommends that the band be adjusted at each fluid change. The adjustment screw is located on the left side of the case.

1. Loosen the locknut and back off the nut about five full turns.

2. Tighten the band adjusting screw to 72 in. lbs.

3. Back off the adjusting screw exactly 2.5 turns.

4. Hold the adjusting screw and tighten the locknut to 35 ft. lbs.

Rear (Low and Reverse) Band

1. Drain fluid and remove transaxle oil pan.

2. Loosen and back off lock nut approximately 5 turns. Using an inch-pound torque wrench, tighten adjusting screw to 41 in. lbs.

3. Back off adjusting screw 3.5 turns.

4. Tighten lock nut to 10 ft. lbs.

5. Reinstall oil pan and fill with proper fluid.

NEUTRAL START SWITCH

Adjustment

The neutral start circuit is the center contact of the three-terminal switch located in the transmission case.

1. Remove the wiring connector and test for continuity between the center pin and the case. Continuity should exist only in Park and Neutral.

2. Remove the switch and check that the operating lever fingers are centered in the switch opening.

3. Install the switch and a new seal and tighten to 24 ft. lbs. Retest with a lamp.

4. Replace the lost transmission fluid.

5. If shift linkage adjustment is correct and the switch still malfunctions, replace the switch.

PAN REMOVAL AND INSTALLATION, FLUID AND FILTER CHANGE

NOTE: RTV silicone sealer is used in place of a pan gasket.

Chrysler recommends no fluid or filter changes during the normal service life. Severe usage requires a fluid and filter change every 15,000 miles. Severe usage is defined as:

1. More than 50% heavy city traffic during 90°F weather.

2. Commercial operation or trailer towing.

When changing the fluid, only Dexron® II fluid should be used. A filter change should be performed at every fluid change.

1. Raise the vehicle and support it on jackstands.

2. Place a large container under the pan, loosen the pan bolts and tap at one corner to break it loose. Drain the fluid.

3. When the fluid is drained remove the pan bolts.

4. Remove the retaining screws and replace the filter. Tighten the screws to 35 in. lbs.

5. Clean the fluid pan, peel off the old RTV silicone sealer and install the pan, using a 1/8 inch bead of new RTV sealer. Always run the sealer bead inside the bolt holes. Tighten the pan bolts to 165 in. lbs.

6. Pour four quarts of Dexron® II fluid through the filler tube.

7. Start the engine and idle it for at least 2 minutes. Set the parking brake and move the selector through each position, ending in Park.

8. Add sufficient fluid to bring the level to the FULL mark on the dipstick. The level should be checked in Park, with the engine idling at normal operating temperatures.

AUTOMATIC TRANSMISSION

REMOVAL & INSTALLATION

1. Remove the transmission and converter as an assembly; otherwise the converter drive plate pump bushing, and oil seal will be damaged. The drive plate will not support a load. Therefore, none of the weight of transmission should be allowed to rest on the plate during removal. Remove the transfer case, as necessary.

2. Attach a remote control starter switch to the starter solenoid so the engine can be rotated from under the vehicle.

3. Disconnect high tension cable from the ignition coil.

4. Remove cover plate from in front of converter assembly to provide access to the converter drain plug and mounting bolts.

5. Rotate engine to bring drain plug to the 6 o'clock position. Drain the converter and transmission.

NOTE: A running production change was made in January 1977 which eliminated the converter drain plug. This means that the transmission must be removed in order to drain the converter on models manufactured after this date.

6. Mark converter and drive plate to aid in reassembly.

7. Rotate the engine with the remote control switch to locate two converter to drive plate bolts at 5 and 7 o'clock positions. Remove the two bolts, rotate engine again and remove the other two bolts.

CAUTION

Do not rotate converter on drive plate by prying with a screwdriver or similar tool as drive plate might become distorted. Also the starter should never be engaged if drive plate is not attached to converter with at least one bolt or if transmission case to engine block bolts have been loosened.

---

8. Disconnect battery ground cable. Remove engine to transmission struts, if necessary. You may have to drop the exhaust system on some models.

9. Remove the starter.

10. Remove wire from the neutral starting switch.

11. Remove gearshift cable or rod from the transmission and the lever.

12. Disconnect the throttle rod from left side of transmission.

13. Disconnect the oil cooler lines at transmission and remove the oil filler tube. Disconnect the speedometer cable.

14. Disconnect the driveshaft.

15. Install engine support fixture to hold up the rear of the engine.

16. Raise transmission slightly with jack to relieve load and remove support bracket or crossmember. Remove all bell housing bolts and carefully work transmission and converter rearward off engine dowels and disengage converter hub from end of crankshaft.

CAUTION

Attach a small C-clamp to edge of bell housing to hold converter in place during transmission removal; otherwise the front pump bushing might be damaged.

NOTE: Install transmission and converter as an assembly. The drive plate will not support a load. Do not allow weight of transmission to rest on the plate during installation.

17. Rotate pump rotors until the rotor lugs are vertical.

18. Carefully slide converter assembly over input shaft and reaction shaft. Make sure converter impeller shaft slots are also vertical and fully engage front pump inner rotor lugs.

19. Use a "C" clamp on edge of converter housing to hold converter in place during transmission installation.

20. Converter drive plate should be free of distortion and drive plate to crankshaft bolts tightened to 55 ft. lbs. torque.

21. Using a jack, position transmission and converter assembly in alignment with engine.

22. Rotate converter so mark on converter (made during removal) will align with mark on drive plate. The offset holes in plate are located next to the 1/8" hole in inner circle of the plate. A stamped "V" mark identifies the offset hole in converter front

cover. Carefully work transmission assembly forward over engine block dowels with converter hub entering the crankshaft opening.

23. Install converter housing to engine bolts and tighten to 28 ft. lbs.

24. Install the two lower drive plate to converter bolts and tighten to 270 in. lbs. torque.

25. Install engine to transmission struts, if required. Install starting motor and connect battery ground cable.

26. Rotate engine and install two remaining drive plate to converter bolts.

27. Install crossmember and tighten attaching bolts to 90 ft. lbs. torque. Lower transmission so that extension housing is aligned and rests on the rear mount. Install bolts and tighten to 40 ft. lbs. torque.

28. Remove transmission jack and engine support fixture, then install tie-bars under the transmission.

29. Replace the driveshaft.

30. Connect oil cooler lines, install oil filler tube and connect the speedometer cable.

31. Connect gearshift cable or rod and torqueshaft assembly to the transmission case and to the lever.

32. Connect throttle rod to the lever at left side of transmission bell housing.

33. Connect wire to back-up and neutral starting switch.

34. Install cover plate in front of the converter assembly.

35. Refill transmission with fluid.

36. Adjust throttle and shift linkage.

PAN AND FILTER SERVICE

NOTE: A running production change was made in January, 1977, which eliminated the converter drain plug. This means that the transmission must be removed in order to drain the converter on models manufactured after this date.

With Converter Drain Plug

NOTE: To drain only the transmission (not the converter), use steps 1, 2, 4, 6, 7, 8, 9 and 11–15.

1. Jack up the front of the vehicle and support it on jackstands.

2. Remove the converter access plate and turn the converter using the starter, until the converter drain plug is accessible.

3. Remove the converter drain plug and allow the converter to drain completely. 1977 models use a 5/16 in. hex head bolt. A six-point socket must be used on the 5/16 in. head.

4. Remove the bolts securing transmission pan and carefully remove the pan to drain the fluid.

5. Reinstall the drain plug.

6. Clean the transmission pan thoroughly.

Removing the transmission oil pan bolts

Clean pan with safe solvent and a rag

Remove filter attaching screws

Install a new gasket

7. Remove the three screws from the fluid filter in the bottom of the valve body; remove the filter and discard it.

8. Install a new filter using three screws.

9. Install the pan using a new gasket. Tighten the pan screws to 150 in. lbs. of torque in a criss-cross pattern.

10. Install the torque converter access plate.

11. Pour 6 quarts of Dexron® automatic transmission fluid through the filter tube. If the converter was not drained, use 4 quarts.

12. Start the engine.

13. Let the engine idle for 2 minutes and move the gear selector through all the drive positions, pausing momentarily in each position.

14. Leave the gear selector in Neutral and check the fluid level. If necessary, add enough fluid to bring the level to the "ADD ONE PINT" mark on the dipstick.

— CAUTION —

Do not overfill the transmission.

15. Make sure the dipstick is fully seated and lower the vehicle.

Without Drain Plug

1. Raise the front of the truck and support it on jackstands. Place a large drain pan under the transmission.

2. Loosen the pan attaching bolts and tap the pan at one corner to break it loose.

3. Allow the fluid to drain into the drain pan.

4. After most of the fluid has drained, carefully remove the attaching bolts, lower the pan and drain the rest of the fluid.

5. Remove the filter attaching screws and remove the filter.

6. Install a new filter. Tighten the screws to 35 in. lbs.

7. Thoroughly clean the fluid pan with safe solvent and allow it to dry.

8. Using a new gasket, install the pan to the transmission. Tighten the attaching bolts to 150 in. lbs.

9. Pour four quarts of Dexron® automatic transmission fluid in through the dipstick tube.

10. Start the engine and allow it to run for a few minutes. With the parking brake set, slowly move the gear selector to each position. Return it to the Neutral position.

11. Check the fluid level. Add more fluid as necessary to bring it up to the "ADD ONE PINT" level.

12. Drive the truck to bring the transmission up to normal operating temperature. Check the level again. It should be between the "ADD" and "FULL" marks.

BAND ADJUSTMENTS

Kickdown Band

The kickdown band adjusting screw is located on the left-hand side of the transmission case near the throttle lever shaft.

1. Loosen the locknut and back it off about five turns. Be sure that the adjusting screw turns freely in the case.

2. Torque the adjusting screw to 72 in. lbs.

3. Back off the adjusting screw as follows: 1977-84 V8—2½ turns, 1977-84 6 cyl.—2 turns, Diesel—2 turns. Tighten the locknut to 30 ft. lb.

Low and Reverse Band

The pan must be removed from the transmission to gain access to the low and reverse band adjusting screw.

1. Remove the skid plate, if any. Drain the transmission fluid and remove the pan.

2. Loosen the band adjusting screw locknut and back if off about five turns. Be sure that the adjusting screw turns freely in the lever.

1979 and later gearshift linkage—typical

3. Torque the adjusting screw to 72 in. lbs.

4. Back off the adjusting screw: All LoadFlite through 1980; 2 turns. 1981 and later A904T and A999 (wide ratio); 4 turns. 1981 and later A727; 2 turns. Keep the adjusting screw from turning, tighten and torque the locknut to 30 ft. lbs.

5. Use a new gasket and install the transmission pan. Torque the pan bolts to 150 in. lbs. Refill the transmission with Dexron® II fluid.

SHIFT LINKAGE ADJUSTMENT

NOTE: To insure proper adjustment, it is suggested that new linkage grommets be installed.

1. Place the gearshift lever in the Park position.

2. Move the shift control lever on the transmission all the way to the rear (in the Park detent).

3. Set the adjustable rod to the proper length and install it with no load in either direction. Tighten the swivel bolt.

4. The shift linkage must be free of binding and be positive in all positions. Make sure that the engine can start only when the gearshift lever is in the Park or Neutral position. Be sure that the gearshift lever will not jump into an unwanted gear.

Loadflite adjusting points

To remove the switch, disconnect the electrical leads and unscrew the switch. Use a drain pan to catch the transmission fluid. Using a new seal, install the new switch and torque it to 24 ft. lbs. Refill the transmission.

DRIVESHAFT & U-JOINTS

Driveshaft-Rear Wheel Drive

REMOVAL & INSTALLATION

Single Section Type

This driveshaft has a universal joint at either end and no external supports.

1. Raise and support the truck with the rear higher.
2. Matchmark the shaft and pinion flange to assure proper balance at installation.
3. Remove both rear U-joint roller and bushing clamps from the rear axle pinion flange. Do not disturb the retaining strap which holds the bushing assemblies on the U-joint cross.

NOTE: Do not allow the driveshaft to hang during removal. Suspend it from the frame with a piece of wire. Before removing the driveshaft, raise the rear end of the truck to prevent loss of transmission fluid.

4. Slide the driveshaft, with the front sliding yoke, off the transmission output shaft.
5. Installation is the reverse of removal. Align the matchmarks made during removal.

Two-Section Type

This driveshaft has a universal joint at either end, with a third universal joint and a support bearing at the center.

1. Matchmark the shaft and the rear axle pinion hub yoke. Matchmark the center bearing spline and slip yoke.

THROTTLE KICKDOWN ROD ADJUSTMENT

1977–78

1. Warm the engine to operating temperature.
2. Block the choke plate fully open.
3. Remove the throttle return spring from the carburetor.
4. Remove the clip, washer and slotted throttle rod from the carburetor pin.
5. Rotate the threaded end of the rod so that the rear edge of the slot in the rod contacts the carburetor pin when the transmission throttle lever is held forward against its stop.
6. Install the washer and clip to retain the throttle rod to the carburetor.
7. Install the throttle rod return spring.
8. Check the transmission linkage for freedom of operation and unblock the choke plate.

1979 and Later

1. Warm the engine up to normal operating temperature. Turn the engine Off.
2. Block the choke plate fully open.
3. Raise the van on a hoist.
4. Loosen the adjusting swivel lock screw.
5. To insure the proper alignment, the swivel must be free to slide along the flat end of the throttle rod so the preload spring action is not restricted. Clean the parts if necessary.
6. Hold the transmission lever firmly forward against the internal stop and tighten the swivel lock screw to 100 in. lbs. Linkage backlash will automatically be taken up by the preload spring.

NEUTRAL START SWITCH ADJUSTMENT

The neutral safety switch is thread mounted into the transmission case. When the gearshift lever is placed in either the Park or Neutral position, a cam, which is attached to the transmission throttle lever inside the transmission, contacts the neutral safety switch and provides a ground to complete the starter solenoid circuit.

The back-up light switch is incorporated into the neutral safety switch. The center terminal is for the neutral safety switch and the two outer terminals are for the backup lamps.

There is no adjustment for the switch. If a malfunction occurs, the switch must be removed and replaced.

Low and reverse band adjusting screw location

Typical gearshift linkage—through 1978

Single shaft-yoke alignment

YOKES MUST BE PARALLEL

Two-piece shaft-yoke vertical alignment

NOTE: Do not allow the driveshaft to hang down during removal. Suspend it from the frame. Raise the rear of the truck to prevent loss of transmission fluid.

2. Remove both rear U-joint roller and bushing assembly clamps from the rear axle pinion yoke. Do not disturb the retaining strap used to hold the bushing assemblies on the U-joint cross.

3. Slide the rear half of the shaft off the front shaft splines at the center bearing. Remove the rear half.

4. At the transmission end of the front half, remove the bushing retaining bolts and clamps, after matchmarking. If there is a driveshaft brake, there will be flange nuts.

5. Unbolt the center bearing mounting nuts and bolts and remove the front half of the shaft.

6. On installation, align the matchmarks at the transmission and start all the bolts and nuts at the front U-joint and the center support bearing.

7. Tighten ¼ in. clamp bolts to 170 in. lbs, and ⁵⁄₁₆ in. bolts to 300 in. lbs. Tighten driveshaft brake flange nuts to 35 ft. lbs. Leave the center bearing bolts just snug.

8. Align the rear shaft matchmarks and slide the yoke onto the front shaft splines.

9. Align the rear U-joint matchmarks and install the bushing clamps and bolts. Tighten the bolts to the torque given in Step 7. Grease the joints and splines.

10. Jack up the rear wheels and let the engine drive the shaft. The center support bearing will align itself.

11. Tighten the center bearing bolts to 50 ft. lbs.

Four-Wheel Drive Front Driveshaft

1. Remove the four flange retaining bolts and lockwashers from the constant velocity U-joint at the transfer case. Mark the parts to reinstall them in the same position. To prevent the constant velocity joint from turning while removing the nuts, use a press bar.

2. Remove the nuts and lockwashers from the U-bolts at the differential flange and remove the U-bolts.

3. Support the driveshaft and separate the U-joint at the front of the driveshaft yoke, pulling backward to clear the flange. The driveshaft should never be allowed to hang by either universal joint.

4. Remove the driveshaft.

5. Installation is the reverse of removal.

Universal Joint

REMOVAL & INSTALLATION

Lock Ring and Snap Ring Types

1. Hammer the bushings (roller cups) slightly inward to relieve pressure on the retainers. Remove the retainers.

2. Place the yoke in a vise with a socket bigger than the bushing on one side and one smaller than the bushing on the other side.

3. Apply pressure, forcing one bushing out into the larger socket.

4. Reverse the vise and socket arrangement to remove the other bushing and the cross.

5. On installation, press the new bushings in just far enough to install the retainers.

Strap Clamp Type (Rear Axle Yoke)

Unbolt strap bolts and remove straps, bushings, seals and washer retainers. Install new components as required. When assembling, grease bearings. Install with grease fitting

parallel to other fittings in drive train. Tighten strap bolts to 20 ft. lbs. torque.

Constant Velocity U-Joint

This is the double universal joint used in the front driveshaft on four-wheel drive models. These are disassembled in the same way as the snap-ring type U-Joint. Original equipment U-joints are held together by plastic retainers which shear when pressed out. The bearing cups in the center part of the joint should be pressed out before those in the yoke. Original equipment constant velocity joints cannot be reassembled. Replacement part kits have bearing cups with grooves for retaining rings.

Slip Joints

When reassembling slip joints make sure that arrows stamped on each side are matched. This will assure proper universal joint alignment.

Center Bearing

When two or more driveshafts are used in tandem, a rubber mounted center bearing supports the center portion of the drive line. The center bearing is mounted in rubber in a bracket which is bolted to the frame crossmember.

REMOVAL & INSTALLATION

1. Mark parts for reassembly and remove driveshafts as described earlier.

2. Place the front shaft in a vise and pull the bearing support and insulator away from the bearing.

3. Bend the slinger away from the bearing with a hammer to obtain clearance to install a bearing puller.

4. Remove the bearing with a puller. Remove the slinger. Discard all parts. A replacement kit contains all necessary repair parts.

5. Place the new slinger, bearing assembly and retainer on the driveshaft. Each part is a press fit.

6. Use a strong tube or pipe which clears the shaft spline. Press or drive the parts forward into position.

7. Connect the two piece driveshaft and install in the reverse order of removal.

FRONT DRIVE AXLE—4WD

Warn Front Locking Hubs

REMOVAL & INSTALLATION

1. Straighten the lock tabs and remove the six hub mounting bolts.

Sliding yoke type universal joint

2. Tap the hub gently with a mallet to remove.

3. Separate the clutch assembly from the body assembly.

4. Remove the snap ring from the rear of the body assembly, using snap-ring pliers. Slip the axle shaft hub out of the body from the front.

5. Remove the Allen screw from the inner side of the clutch, and remove the bronze dial assembly from the front side of the clutch housing assembly.

6. Remove the clutch assembly from the rear of the housing, complete with the twelve roller pins.

7. Coat the moving parts with a waterproof grease.

8. Slide the axle shaft hub into the body from the front, and replace the snap-ring.

9. Replace the bronze dial assembly and the inner clutch. Tighten the Allen screw and stake the edge of the screw with a center punch to prevent loosening.

10. With the dial in the free position, rotate the outer clutch body into the inner assembly until it bottoms in the housing. Back it up to the nearest hole and install the roller pins.

11. Position the hub and clutch assembly together with a new gasket in between.

Hub yoke type universal joint

Slip yoke center bearing

Dana and "Dualmatic" Front Locking Hubs

REMOVAL & INSTALLATION

1. Place hub in lock position. Remove Allen head mounting bolts and washers.

2. Carefully remove retainer, O-ring seal and knob. Separate knob from retainer.

3. Remove large internal snap-ring. Slide retainer ring and cam from hub.

4. While pressing against sleeve and ring assembly, remove axle shaft snap-ring.

12. Position the hub assembly over the end of the axle and replace the six hub mounting bolts and lock tabs.

13. Torque the bolts to 35 ft. lbs. and bend the lock tabs to anchor the bolts.

14. Verify the operation by road testing.

Relieve pressure and remove sleeve and ring, ring and bushing, spring and plate.

5. Inspect all parts for wear, nicks and burrs. Replace all parts which appear questionable.

6. Slide plate and spring (large coils first) into wheel hub housing.

7. Assemble ring and bushing, sleeve and bushing. Slide complete assembly into housing.

8. Compress spring and install axle shaft snap-ring.

9. Position cam and retainer in housing and install large internal snap-ring.

10. Place small O-ring seal on knob, lubricate with waterproof grease and install in retainer at lock position.

11. Place large O-ring seal on retainer. Align retainer and retainer ring and install washers and Allen head mounting screws.

12. Check operation.

Axle Shaft, Bearing and Seal

REMOVAL & INSTALLATION

Enclosed U-Joint

1. Raise and support the truck. Remove wheel assembly and locking hubs, remove grease cap from drive flange.

2. Remove drive flange bolts and snap-ring. Then, using a suitable puller, remove drive flange.

3. Remove locknut, lockwasher and adjusting nut.

4. Remove wheel hub and brake drum assembly, being careful not to damage oil seal.

Locking hub component parts

5. Remove brake assembly and wire to frame, leaving hydraulic line connected.

6. Tap end of spindle with a soft hammer and remove spindle.

7. Inspect spindle and bushing for wear. Bushing is pressed on and requires no reaming for proper fit.

8. Remove axle shaft assembly. Inspect universal joint. Disassemble and replace any worn components.

9. Install axle assemly, being careful not to damage inner oil seal.

10. Lubricate flanged bushing and install spindle and brake support assembly.

11. Remove, clean, inspect and repack inner and outer wheel bearings.

12. Install inner wheel bearing, position hub, drum and wheel assembly on spindle, then install outer bearing, washer and adjusting nut.

13. Adjust bearing by tightening adjusting nut to 50 ft. lbs. torque, then back off ¼ to ⅓ turn. Tighten locknut and bend tab of lockwasher.

14. Install drive flange, retaining nuts, snap-ring and grease cup.

Exposed U-Joint

1. Raise and support the truck. Remove the locking hubs. Remove the cotter key and loosen the axle shaft nut.

2. Block the brake pedal up. Remove the wheel.

3. Remove and hang the caliper out of the way. Remove the inner pad.

4. Working through the hole in the disc hub, remove the socket head capscrews.

5. Remove the axle shaft nut and use a hub puller to remove the disc and hub.

6. Remove the O-ring from the steering knuckle. Remove the disc brake adapter from the knuckle. Punch out the inner oil seal from the rear of the knuckle.

7. Slide the axle shaft from the housing.

8. On replacement, first slide the shaft into place, then drive a new seal into the steering knuckle.

9. Install the disc brake adapter and torque the mounting bolts to 85 ft. lbs.

10. Install a new O-ring on the steering knuckle.

11. Slide the disc and hub, retainer and bearing assembly over the shaft and start it into the housing. Install the axle shaft nut.

12. Install the capscrews holding the retainer to the steering knuckle flange. Tighten them to 30 ft. lbs. in a criss-cross pattern.

13. Torque the axle shaft nut to 100 ft. lbs. and tighten further until the cotter key can be installed.

14. Locate the inner pad on the adapter with the shoe flanges in the adapter ways. Slide the caliper into position, being careful not to pull the dust boot from its grooves.

15. Install the anti-rattle springs, making sure that the inner one is on top of the retainer spring plate. Tighten the retaining clips to 200 in. lbs.

16. Install the wheel and lower the vehicle.

Automatic locking hub—disassembled

Steering Knuckle Service—4WD

REMOVAL & INSTALLATION

Enclosed U-Joint

1. Remove wheel, hub, brake drum assembly, brake support assembly, spindle and axle shaft.

2. Disconnect tie rod ends from steering knuckles and drag link from steering knuckle arm.

3. Remove steering knuckle felt and oil seal retainers.

4. Remove lower bearing cap and shims.

5. Remove upper bearing cap or knuckle arm and shims.

6. Remove knuckle housing, felt and oil seal.

7. Remove upper and lower bearing cones, then clean and inspect bearings.

8. Check bearing cups for wear and remove with drift if required.

9. To assemble, place felt and oil seal over end of axle housing.

10. Install steering knuckle arm or upper bearing cap and shim pack and tighten retaining bolts or nuts. If a new shim pack is used, use *only* one which is .060″ thick.

11. Lubricate and install cone (press in) on upper bearing pivot, making sure serration or key and slot are properly located, if so equipped.

12. Seat bearing cups in yokes of axle housing. Slide knuckle assembly over yoke and enter bronze cone in its cup.

Late model wheel bearing adjusting nut, lock nut and ring—4WD

13. Lubricate and insert lower bearing cone, tilting knuckle to provide access. Install lower bearing cap and shim pack. If a new pack is required, use *only* .025" thick pack for 44-3F axle or .055" thick pack for 44-3HF or 70F axle.

14. Using a torque wrench on a top outer knuckle bearing cap retaining bolt or nut, measure bearing preload as knuckle is turning. It must read 5-15 ft. lbs. for 44-3F axle and 15-35 ft. lbs. for the 44-3HDF or 70-F axles. Remove or add shims to adjust preload.

15. Attach oiled felt and oil seal to knuckle housing with retainers and screws.

16. Install axle shaft, spindle and brake support assembly, tightening spindle to steering knuckle flange bolts.

17. Install hub, brake drum and wheel assembly.

18. Fill steering knuckle housing with SAE 140 oil to level of filler plug opening.

19. Check and adjust toe-in and turning radius.

Exposed U-Joint

The ball joints should be replaced if there is any looseness or end-play. The steering knuckle and ball joint must be removed to replace the ball joint.

1. Refer to the Front Drive Axle Removal and Replacement, on Exposed U-Joint, Ball Joint Type, Steps 1 through 6.

2. Remove and discard the O-ring from the steering knuckle.

3. Remove the capscrews from the brake splash shield and remove the splash shield. Remove the brake disc adapter from the steering knuckle.

4. Disconnect the tie-rod from the steering knuckle. On the left side, disconnect the drag link from the steering knuckle arm.

5. Using a punch and hammer, remove the inner oil seal from the rear of the steering knuckle.

6. Carefully, slide the outer and inner axle shaft complete with U-joint from the axle housing.

7. On the left-side, remove the steering knuckle arm by tapping it to loosen the tapered dowels.

8. Remove the cotter pin from the upper ball joint nut. Remove the upper and lower ball joint nuts and discard the lower nut.

9. Separate the steering knuckle from the axle housing yoke with a brass drift and hammer. Remove and discard the sleeve from the upper ball joint yoke on the axle housing.

10. Position the steering knuckle upside down in a vise with soft jaws and remove the snap-ring from the lower ball joint.

11. Press the lower and upper ball joints from the steering knuckle individually.

1. Position the steering knuckle right side up in a vise with soft jaws. Press the lower ball joint into position and install the snap-ring.

2. Press the upper ball joint into position. Install new boots on both ball joints.

3. Screw a new sleeve into the upper ball joint yoke on the axle housing, leaving about two threads showing at the top.

4. Install the steering knuckle on the axle housing yoke and install a new lower ball joint nut, tightening it to 80 ft. lbs.

5. Tighten the sleeve in the upper ball joint yoke to 40 ft. lbs. Install the upper ball joint nut and tighten it to 100 ft. lbs. Align the cotter key hole in the stud with the slot in the castellated nut and install the cotter pin. Do not loosen the nut to align the holes.

6. On the left-side, position the steering knuckle arm over the studs on the steering knuckle. Install the tapered dowels and nuts. Tighten the nuts to 90 ft. lbs. Install the drag link on the steering arm. Install the nut and tighten it to 60 ft. lbs. Install the cotter pin.

7. Install the tie-rod end on the steering knuckle. Tighten the nut to 45 ft. lbs. and install the cotter pin.

8. Install the axle shaft. Install the brake splash shield and tighten the screws to 13 ft. lbs. Install the brake disc adapter and tighten the bolts to 85 ft. lbs.

9. Install a new O-ring in the steering knuckle.

10. Clean any rust from the axle shaft splines.

11. Carefully, slide the hub, rotor and retainer, and bearing onto the axle shaft and start it into the housing. Install the axle shaft nut.

12. Align the retainer with the steering knuckle flange. Install the retainer screws and tighten them in a criss-cross pattern to 30 ft. lbs.

13. Tighten the axle shaft nut to 100 ft. lbs. Tighten the nut until the next slot in the nut aligns with the hole in the axle shaft. Install the cotter pin.

14. Install the inboard brake shoe on the adapter with the shoe flanges in the adapter ways. Install the caliper in the adapter and over the disc. Align the caliper on the machined ways of the adapter. Be careful not to pull the dust boot from its grooves as the piston and boot slide over the inboard shoe.

15. Install the anti-rattle springs and retaining clips. Torque to 16–17 ft. lbs. The inboard shoe anti-rattle spring must always be installed on top of the retainer spring plate.

16. Install the wheel, tire, and locking hub and lower the truck. Lubricate all fittings.

ELECTRONIC THROTTLE CONTROL

Carter Electronic Throttle Control

1. Energize ETC solenoid (separate electrical connector and apply 12 volt current to BLUE wire spade).

2. Momentarily open throttle to allow plunger to extend from solenoid (plunger will extend and hold position but will not "push").

3. Adjust to obtain 850 Engine RPM.

Holly Electronic Throttle Control

1. Remove screw from ETC solenoid. Energize solenoid, by separating electrical connector and applying 12 volts current to BLUE wire spade.

2. Momentarily open throttle to allow plunger to extend.

3. Position ⅛ inch allen wrench into adjusting nut (through screw hole). Adjust engine idle speed to 850 RPM.

4. Reinstall screw with solenoid de-energized reset curb idle speed using only the screw.

5. Remove tachometer and any jumper wires. Check for the proper installation of all hoses and electrical connections.

DASHPOT ADJUSTMENT

With the curb idle speed and mixture properly set and a tachometer installed, start the engine and position the throttle lever so that the actuating tab on the lever is contacting the stem of the dashpot but not depressing it. Allow 30 seconds for engine to stabilize. The tachometer should read 2300 RPM with throttle lever in this position.

To adjust setting, loosen the lock nut and screw the dashpot in or out as required. When the desired setting is obtained, tighten the lock nut on the dashpot against the bracket. Check to make sure curb idle returns to specified speed.

Procedure—Adjusting Engine Fast Idle

1. Adjust engine fast idle to conform with Emission Control Label. Disconnect and plug both distributor and EGR valve vacuum hoses. Place transmission in neutral and set parking brake.

2. Remove air cleaner top.

3. Adjust engine fast idle speed to the specified RPM (shown on Emission Control Label) on Step 2 (second highest) of the fast idle cam.

4. Reconnect all hoses, as the engine has been correctly adjusted for proper Emission Control.

SERVICING 44 FBJ DRIVE AXLE

Removal and Disassembly

1. Raise vehicle to a comfortable working height and install jack stands. Remove wheel.

2. Remove caliper retainer and anti-rattle spring assemblies. Remove caliper from disc by sliding out and away from disc. Hang caliper out of the way. Do not allow caliper to hang or be supported by hydraulic brake hose. Remove inboard shoe.

3. Remove outer axle shaft nut and washer. Position a wheel puller and remover hub and rotor assembly.

4. Using Modified Bearing Press, Tool C-293-PA, Extension Tool C-293-3 and Adapters, Tool C-293-49 or equivalent, positioned in a vise, pull the outer bearing cone from the hub and rotor assembly. Discard outer seal. Remove the six retainer bolts and retainer.

5. Remove the brake caliper adapter from the knuckle (if required).

6. Position a pry bar behind the inner axle shaft yoke and push the bearings out of the knuckle.

7. Remove the "O" ring from the knuckle (if so equipped) and discard.

8. Carefully remove the axle shaft assembly.

Inspection

1. Examine the knuckle bore and inner seal surface for evidence of severe wear or damage. Replace the knuckle, if required.

2. Inspect the outer axle shaft seal surface for grooving. If the surface is grooved, repair as follows:

(a) Measure in from the yoke shoulder of the axle approximately ⅜ inch (9.5mm). Using a center punch, stake at ¼ inch (6 mm) intervals around the circumference of the shaft. This will size the shaft to insure a tight fit of the inner seal slinger.

3. Check for proper bearing clamp as follows:

(a) Install the bearing cups and spacer into the knuckle bore.

(b) Position the bearing retainer onto the steering knuckle. Install retainer bolts and tighten to 30 foot-pounds.

(c) Insert a .004 inch (.101mm) feeler gauge between the knuckle and the retainer at a point approximately midway between the retainer mounting ears (six places).

NOTE: The brake dust shield may have to be removed to complete this check. If .004 (.101mm) clearance cannot be obtained at each measuring point, the knuckle must be replaced.

(d) Remove retainer plate, bearing cups and spacer. Install brake dust shield (if removed), tighten mounting bolts to 160 inch-pounds (18 N·m).

Assembly and Installation

1. Apply RTV sealer (Silicone Rubber Adhesive or equivalent) to the seal surface of the axle shaft.

2. Using Driver, Tool C-4398-1 or equivalent, install the seal slinger onto the outer axle shaft.

3. Install lip seal on the slinger with the lip toward the axle shaft spline.

4. Carefully insert axle shaft into the housing so as not to damage the differential seal at the side gears.

5. Insert a pry bar through the axle shaft "U" joint and wedge so that the axle shaft is in all the way and cannot be moved out.

6. Using Adapter, Tool C-4398-2 and Driver, Tool C-4398-1 or equivalent, carefully install the seal cup until bottomed in the knuckle.

NOTE: A small amount of wheel bearing grease on the Adapter face will aid in holding the cup in position. Do not remove the tool at this time.

7. Using Tool C-4250 or its equivalent install new outer seal in retainer plate. Locate retainer plate over hub of rotor assembly.

8. Thoroughly pack wheel bearings with Multi-Purpose Grease.

9. Using Tool C-4246-A and Adapters or its equivalent positioned as shown in illustration, carefully press outer bearing onto hub. Remove tool.

10. Place grease coated outer bearing cup over outer bearing cone followed by spacer, grease coated inner bearing cup and inner bearing cone. Again using Tool C-4246-A and Adapters or its equivalent positioned as before, carefully press into position. Remove tool.

11. Apply a ¼ inch (6 mm) bead of RTV sealer (Silicone Rubber Adhesive or equivalent) to the retainer face on the chamfer, (this takes the place of the "O" ring discarded at disassembly).

12. Carefully remove seal installing tool from the knuckle bore so that the outer axle shaft remains centered.

NOTE: If the shaft is disturbed, check to make sure that the lip seal is still riding inside the cup. Correct if necessary.

13. Position the bearing retainer in the hub and rotor so that the lube fitting is facing directly forward. **This is extremely important.**

14. Assemble the hub and rotor to the knuckle and tighten retainer plate bolts to 30 foot-pounds (41 N·m) using a criss-cross method to position it evenly.

15. Install brake adapter and tighten mounting bolts to 85 foot-pounds (115 N·m).

16. Remove pry bar from "U" joint and install axle shaft washer and nut. Tighten nut to 100 foot-pounds (136 N·m), continue to tighten nut until next slot in nut aligns with cotter key hole in axle shaft. Install cotter key.

Front Drive Axle—4WD

REMOVAL & INSTALLATION

1. Raise the truck and install stands under the frame rails, behind the front springs.

2. Disconnect front driveshaft at drive pinion yoke.

3. Disconnect steering linkage at drag link.

4. Disconnect front shock absorbers and brake line at frame. Disconnect the sway bar link assembly from the spring clip plate.

5. Remove nuts from the spring hold down bolts and remove axle assembly from under vehicle.

6. To install, place axle assembly under vehicle and line up spring center bolts with locating hole in axle housing pad.

7. Install spring clips or spring U-bolts, new lock washer and nuts.

8. Connect the shock absorbers, and the brake line at the frame.

9. Connect the steering linkage to the drag link, and the driveshaft to the pinion yoke. Check lubricants and bleed the brakes.

10. Lower the vehicle and test the operation.

NOTE: Refer to the "Front Drive Axle" section of Unit Repair for service procedures.

FRONT WHEEL DRIVE

NOTE: Refer to the "Transaxle" section of Unit Repair for service procedures.

Drive Axles

REMOVAL & INSTALLATION

The inboard CV joints on early production models may be retained by circlips in the differential side gears. On later production models, the shafts incorporate the use of a spring within the right and left inboard tripod joint assemblies and do not use a circlip.

To determine whether a spring loaded shaft is installed, place a pry bar between the transaxle extension housing (right shaft) and the face of the tripod joint housing, pry towards the outside of the vehicle taking care not to damage the seal in the extension housing. If the joint can be moved at least ½ inch from the extension housing, the driveshaft is spring loaded and does not have a circlip retainer.

If complete removal of these driveshafts is required, the splines on the transaxle ends of both shafts can be easily pulled out without having to enter the transaxle.

NOTE: On models equipped with spring loaded shafts, exclude steps 2, 4 and 5.

1. With the vehicle on the ground, loosen the hub nut.

2. Drain the transaxle differential and remove the cover if axles are retained with circlips.

NOTE: Anytime the transaxle differential cover is removed, a new gasket should be formed from RTV sealant.

3. To remove the right-hand driveshaft, disconnect the speedometer cable and remove the cable and gear before removing the driveshaft.

Rotate the driveshaft (axle) to expose the circlip tangs

4. Rotate the driveshaft to expose the circlip tangs.

5. Compress the circlip with needle nose pliers and push the shaft into the side gear cavity.

6. Remove the clamp bolt from the ball stud and steering knuckle.

7. Separate the ball joint stud from the steering knuckle, by prying against the knuckle leg and control arm.

8. Separate the outer CV (constant velocity) joint splined shaft from the hub by holding the CV housing and moving the hub away. Do not pry on the slinger or outer CV joint.

9. Support the shaft at the CV joints, remove the six allen head screws (if equipped) from the transaxle drive flange and remove the shaft. Do not pull on the shaft.

NOTE: Removal of the left shaft may be made easier by inserting the blade of a thin prybar between the differential pinion shaft and prying against the end face of the shaft.

10. Installation is the reverse of removal. Be sure the circlip tangs are positioned against the flattened end of the shaft before installing the shaft. A quick thrust will lock the circlip in the groove. Tighten the hub nut with the wheels on the ground to 180–200 ft. lbs.

Steering Knuckle—FWD

REMOVAL & INSTALLATION

Service or repair to the bearing, hub, brake dust shield or the steering knuckle itself will require removal of the knuckle. Before attempting this operation, be aware that to reassemble the components it is necessary to torque the front hub nut to at least 200 ft. lbs. You will need a large torque wrench to read that high and a great deal of strength to attain that much torque on the nut.

1. Remove the cotter pin and nut-lock.

2. Loosen the hub nut while the car is resting on the wheels with the brakes applied.

NOTE: The hub and driveshaft are splined together through the knuckle and retained by the hub nut:

3. Raise and support the car.

4. Remove the wheel and tire.

5. Remove the hub nut. Be sure the splined driveshaft is free to separate from the spline in hub when the knuckle is removed.

6. Disconnect the tie rod end from the steering arm.

7. Disconnect the brake hose retainer from the strut.

8. Remove the clamp bolt holding the ball joint stud in the steering knuckle.

9. Remove the brake caliper adapter screw and washers.

10. Support the caliper on a wire hook.

11. Remove the brake disc.

12. Matchmark the camber adjusting cams and loosen both bolts.

13. Support the steering knuckle and remove the cam adjusting and through-bolts. Remove the upper knuckle leg out of the strut bracket and lift the knuckle from the ball joint stud.

NOTE: Do not allow the driveshaft to hang during this procedure.

14. Service procedures requiring hub removal also require that a new bearing be installed.

15. Installation is the reverse of removal. A new hub nut is required. When the car is resting on the wheels, with the brakes applied, tighten the hub nut to 180–200 ft. lbs.

REAR AXLE

NOTE: Refer to the ''Drive Axle'' section in unit repair for service procedures.

Axle Shaft and Bearing

REMOVAL & INSTALLATION

8³⁄₈ and 9¹⁄₄ Inch Rear

NOTE: There is no provision for axle shaft end-play adjustment on these axles.

1. Jack up the vehicle and remove the rear wheels.

2. Clean all dirt from the housing cover and remove the housing cover to drain the lubricant.

3. Remove the brake drum.

4. Rotate the differential case until the differential pinion shaft lockscrew can be removed. Remove the lockscrew and pinion shaft.

5. Push the axle shafts toward the center of the vehicle and remove the C-locks from the grooves on the axle shafts.

6. Pull the axle shafts from the housing, being careful not to damage the bearing

which remains in the housing.

7. Inspect the axle shaft bearings and replace any doubtful parts. Whenever the axle shaft is replaced, the bearings should also be replaced.

8. Remove the axle shaft seal from the bore in the housing, using the button end of the axle shaft.

9. Remove the axle shaft bearing from the housing. Do not reuse the bearing or the seal.

10. Check the bearing shoulder in the axle housing for imperfections. These should be corrected with a file.

11. Clean the axle shaft bearing cavity.

12. Grease and install the axle shaft bearing in the cavity. Be sure that the bearing is not cocked and that it is seated firmly against the shoulder.

13. Install the axle shaft bearing seal. It should be seated beyond the end of the flange face.

14. Insert the axle shaft, making sure that the splines do not damage the seal. Be sure that the splines are properly engaged with the differential side gear splines.

15. Install the C-locks in the grooves on the axles shafts. Pull the shafts outward so that the C-locks seat in the counterbore of the differential side gears.

16. Install the differential pinion shaft through the case and pinions. Install the lockscrew and secure it in position.

17. Clean the housing and gasket surfaces. Install the cover and a new gasket. Refill the axle with the specified lubricant.

NOTE: Replacement differential cover gaskets may not be available. The use of gel type nonsticking sealant is recommended.

18. Install the brake drum and wheel.

9³⁄₄ and 10¹⁄₂ Inch Rear

1. Remove the axle shaft flange nuts and washers.

2. Rap the axle shafts sharply in the center of the flange with a hammer to free the dowels.

3. Remove the tapered dowels and axle shafts. Some models are equipped with bolts rather than dowels.

Rear axle cover sealant application

REAR AXLE IDENTIFICATION CHART

Identification	Ring Gear Size (in.)	Maker and Model	Approximately Capacity (pts) ①
10 bolt cover, front filler plug	8⅜	Chrysler	4.4
12 bolt cover, filler plug in cover	9¼	Chrysler	4.5
10 bolt cover, filler plug in cover	9¾	Spicer 60	6.0
10 bolt cover, filler plug in cover	10½	Spicer 70	7.0 thru 1976, 6.5 for 1977 and later

① These are design capacities and may differ slightly from those given in the Capacities Chart.

4. Clean the gasket area with solvent and install a new flange gasket.

5. Install the axle shaft into the housing.

6. If the axle has an outer wheel bearing seal, install new gaskets on each side of the seal mounting flange.

7. Install the tapered dowels, lockwashers, and nuts. Torque the nuts to 40–70 ft. lbs. with ⁷⁄₁₆ in. studs and 65–105 with ½ in. Some axles have bolts instead of studs and tapered dowels. Bolt torque is 45–75 ft. lbs.

BEARING ADJUSTMENT

1. Raise and support the rear axle.

2. Remove the axle shaft, outer nut, and lockring.

3. Rotate the wheel and tire and tighten the adjusting nut until a slight binding is felt. Back the nut off ⅙ turn.

4. Install the lockring and jamnut. Don't overtighten the jamnut or you will change the adjustment.

5. Install a new gasket and the axle shaft. Lower the vehicle.

FRONT WHEEL DRIVE MODELS

Rear Wheel Bearings

The rear wheel bearings should be inspected and relubricated whenever the rear brakes are serviced or at least every 30,000 miles. Repack the bearings with high temperature multi-purpose grease.

Check the lubricant to see if it is contaminated. If it contains dirt or has a milky appearance indicating the presence of water, the bearings should be cleaned and repacked.

Clean the bearings in kerosene, mineral spirits or other suitable cleaning fluid. Do not dry them by spinning the bearings. Allow them to air dry.

1. Raise and support the truck with the rear wheels off the floor.

2. Remove the wheel grease cap, cotter pin, nut-lock and bearing adjusting nut.

3. Remove the thrust washer and bearing.

4. Remove the drum from the spindle.

5. Thoroughly clean the old lubricant from the bearings and hub cavity. Inspect the bearing rollers for pitting or other signs of wear. Light discoloration is normal.

6. Repack the bearings with high temperature multi-purpose EP grease and add a small amount of new grease to the hub cavity. Be sure to force the lubricant between all rollers in the bearing.

7. Install the drum on the spindle after coating the polished spindle surfaces with wheel bearing lubricant.

8. Install the outer bearing cone, thrust washer and adjusting nut.

9. Tighten the adjusting nut to 20–25 ft. lbs. while rotating the wheel.

10. Back off the adjusting nut to completely release the preload from the bearing.

11. Tighten the adjusting nut fingertight.

12. Position the nut-lock with one pair of slots in line with the cotter pin hole. Install the cotter pin.

13. Clean and install the grease cap and wheel.

14. Lower the truck.

FRONT SUSPENSION

NOTE: Front end alignment procedures and specifications are found in the "Alignment" section of Unit Repair.

I-Beam Axle

KINGPINS

Removal & Installation

1. Raise the front of the vehicle and safely support it on stands. Remove the wheels, calipers, and rotors.

2. Remove the brake support plate attaching bolts, and remove the support plate from the steering knuckle. Secure the plate to the frame so that it does not hang by the brake hose. If equipped with air brakes, disconnect the push rod and remove the air chamber.

3. Remove the steering arm from the steering knuckle.

4. Remove the pivot pin locking screw or pin from the knuckle. Some models may have two locking screws.

5. Remove the upper pivot pin oil seal plug from the knuckle and drive the pivot pin down, forcing the lower oil seal plug from its seat.

NOTE: On some models, a lock ring is used to hold the oil seal plug in place. Others have caps with hold-down screws.

6. Remove the knuckle from the axle and if equipped with bronze bushings, press the old ones out and press the new ones in and line ream them to fit the new pin. If equipped with Delrin or Zytel type bushings, bronze bushings must be used as service replacements. Upon installation of the bushings, align the grease hole in the bushing to that of the grease fitting hole in the knuckle.

7. Install the knuckle on the axle. Position the thrust bearing, and install the pivot pin through the knuckle and axle, securing it with the locking pins or screws.

8. Install the oil seal plugs and secure them by staking in four locations.

9. Lubricate to assure grease channels are open. Complete the assembly by reversing step 1 through 3.

FRONT LEAF SPRING

Removal & Installation

1. Raise truck until weight is removed from springs.

2. Install stands under side frame members as a safety precaution.

3. Disconnect the sway bar at the spring plate. Remove nuts, lockwashers and U-bolts securing spring to axle.

4. Remove spring shackle bolts, shackles and spring front eye bolt.

5. Remove spring.

6. Install in reverse order.

Independent Front Suspension

NOTE: These procedures apply to all vans, wagons, and conventional trucks with independent front suspension.

COIL SPRING

Removal & Installation

1. Raise the vehicle and support it with jackstands under the front ends of the frame rails.

2. Remove the wheel.

3. Remove the shock absorber and upper shock absorber bushing and sleeve.

1. Cam and bolt assembly
2. Cam
3. Lock washer
4. Nut
6. Ball joint assembly
7. Bushing assembly
8. Lock nut
9. Upper control arm
10. Upper ball joint assembly
11. Bumper assembly

1979 and later coil spring and control arm components

Typical upper control arm—through 1978

4. If equipped, remove the sway bar.

5. Remove the strut.

6. Install a spring compressor and tighten finger-tight.

7. Remove the cotter pins and ball joint nuts.

8. Install a ball joint breaker tool and turn the threaded portion of the tool to lock it against the lower stud.

9. Spread the tool to place the lower stud under pressure, then strike the steering knuckle sharply with a hammer to free the stud. Do not attempt to force the stud out of the steering knuckle with the tool.

10. Remove the tool. Slowly release the spring compressor until all tension is relieved from the spring.

11. Remove the spring compressor and spring.

12. Installation is the reverse of removal. Compress the spring until the ball joint can be properly positioned in the steering knuckle.

SHOCK ABSORBER

Removal & Installation

1. Raise and support the vehicle with jackstands positioned at the extreme front ends of the frame rails.

2. Remove the wheel.

3. Remove the upper nut and retainer.

4. Remove the two lower mounting bolts.

5. Remove the shock absorber.

6. Installation is the reverse of removal.

UPPER CONTROL ARM

Removal & Installation

NOTE: Any time the control arm is removed, it is necessary to align the front end.

1. Raise and support the vehicle with jackstands under the frame rails.

2. Remove the wheel.

3. Remove the shock absorber and shock absorber upper bushing and sleeve.

4. Install a spring compressor and tighten it finger-tight.

5. Remove the cotter pins and ball joint nuts.

6. Install a ball joint breaker and turn the threaded portion of the tool, locking it securely against the upper stud. Spread the tool enough to place the upper ball joint under pressure and strike the steering knuckle sharply to loosen the stud. Do not attempt to remove the stud from the steering knuckle with the tool.

7. Remove the tool.

8. Remove the eccentric pivot bolts, after making their relative positions in the control arm.

9. Remove the upper control arm.

10. Installation is the reverse of removal. Tighten the ball joint nuts to 135 ft. lbs. Tighten the eccentric pivot bolts to 70 ft. lbs.

11. Adjust the caster and camber.

LOWER CONTROL ARM

Removal & Installation

1. Follow the procedure outlined under "Coil Spring Removal and Installation."

2. Remove the mounting bolt from the crossmember.

3. Remove the lower control arm from the vehicle.

4. Installation is the reverse of removal. After the vehicle has been lowered to the ground, tighten the mounting bolt to 210 ft. lbs.

LOWER BALL JOINT

Removal & Installation

1. Remove the lower control arm.

2. Remove the ball joint seal.

3. Using an arbor press and a sleeve, press the ball joint from the control arm.

4. Installation is the reverse of removal. Be sure that the ball joint is fully seated. Install a new ball joint seal.

5. Install the lower control arm. Be sure to install the ball joint cotter pins.

UPPER BALL JOINT

Removal & Installation

1. Install a jack under the outer end of the lower control arm and raise the vehicle.

2. Remove the wheel.

3. Remove the ball joint nuts. Using a ball joint breaker, loosen the upper ball joint.

4. Unscrew the ball joint from the control arm.

5. Screw a new ball joint into the control arm and tighten 125 ft. lbs.

6. Install the new ball joint seal, using a 2 in. socket. Be sure that the seal is seated on the ball joint housing.

7. Insert the ball joint into the steering knuckle and install the ball joint nuts. Tighten the nuts to 135 ft. lbs. and install the cotter pins.

8. Install the wheel and lower the truck to the ground.

Wheel Bearings

It is recommended that the front wheel bearings be cleaned, inspected and repacked periodically and as soon as possible after the front hubs have been submerged in water.

NOTE: Sodium based grease is not compatible with lithium based grease. Be careful not to mix the two types. The best way to prevent this is to completely clean all of the old grease from the hub assembly before installing any new grease.

Before handling the bearings there are a few things that you should remember to do and try to avoid.

DO the following:

1. Remove all outside dirt from the housing before exposing the bearing.

2. Treat a used bearing as gently as you would a new one.

3. Work with clean tools in clean surroundings.

4. Use clean, dry canvas gloves, or at least clean, dry hands.

5. Clean solvents and flushing fluids are a must.

6. Use clean paper when laying out the bearings to dry.

7. Protect disassembled bearings from rust and dirt. Cover them up.

8. Use clean rags to wipe bearings.

9. Keep the bearings in oil-proof paper when they are to be stored or are not in use.

10. Clean the inside of the housing before replacing the bearing.

Do NOT do the following:

1. Don't work in dirty surroundings.

2. Don't use dirty, chipped, or damaged tools.

3. Try not to work on wooden work benches or use wooden mallets.

4. Don't handle bearings with dirty or moist hands.

5. Do not use gasoline for cleaning; use a safe solvent.

6. Do not spin-dry bearings with compressed air. They will be damaged.

7. Do not spin unclean bearings.

8. Avoid using cotton waste or dirty cloths to wipe bearings.

9. Try not to scratch or nick bearing surfaces.

10. Do not allow the bearing to come in contact with dirt or rust at any time.

REPACKING

NOTE: Sodium based grease is not compatible with lithium based grease. Be careful not to mix the two types. The best way to prevent this is to completely clean all of the old grease from the hub assembly before installing any new grease.

1. Raise the front of the vehicle and place jackstands under the vehicle. Remove the wheel.

2. Remove the front hub grease cap and driving hub snap-ring.

3. Remove the splined driving hub and the pressure spring. This may require slight prying with a pry bar.

4. Remove the wheel bearing locknut, lockring, and adjusting nut.

5. Removal brake caliper suspend on wire out of the way.

6. Carefully drive out the inner bearing cone and grease seal from the hub.

7. Inspect the bearing cups (races) for cracks and pits. If the cups are excessively worn or there are pits or cracks visible, replace them along with the cones. The cups are removed from the hub by driving them

out with a drift pin. They are installed in the same manner.

8. If it is determined that the cups are in satisfactory condition and are to remain in the hub, clean and inspect the cones (bearings). Refer to the bearing diagnosis chart. Replace the bearings if necessary. If it is necessary to replace either the cone or the cup, both parts should be replaced as a unit.

9. Thoroughly clean all components in a suitable solvent and blow them dry with compressed air or allow them to dry while resting on clean paper.

NOTE: Do not spin the bearings with compressed air while drying them.

10. Cover the spindle with a cloth and brush all loose dust and dirt from the brake assembly. Remove the cloth and thoroughly clean the inside of the hub and the spindle.

11. Pack the inside of the hub with wheel bearing grease. Add grease to the hub until the grease is flush with the inside diameter of the bearing cup.

12. Pack the bearing cone and roller assemblies with wheel bearing grease. A bearing packer is desirable for this operation. If a packer is not available, place a large portion of grease in the palm of your hand and sliding the edge of the roller cage through the grease with your other hand, work as much grease in between the rollers as possible.

13. Position the inner bearing into the inner bearing cup and install the new grease seal.

14. Carefully position the hub assembly onto the spindle. Be careful not to damage the new seal. Install the rotor or caliper.

15. Place the outer bearing into position on the spindle and into the bearing cup.

16. Install the bearing adjusting nut and tighten it while rotating the hub back and forth to seat the bearings.

17. Back off the adjusting nut about ¼ turn.

18. Assemble the lockring by turning the nut to the nearest notch where the dowel pin will enter. Install the outer locknut.

19. Install the pressure spring retainer, spring, the driving hub and driving hub snapring. This is for vehicles without freerunning hubs.

20. Install the grease cap and adjust the brakes, if they were backed off to remove the hub assembly. Remove the jackstands and lower the vehicle.

Front Wheel Drive

STRUT ASSEMBLY

Removal & Installation

1. Loosen the wheel lug nuts.

2. Raise the vehicle and remove the wheel assembly.

3. Mark the camber cam to damper bracket position before removing the cam adjusting bolt.

4. Remove the cam adjusting bolt, the through bolt and the brake hose to damper bracket retaining screw.

5. Remove the strut damper to fender shield (strut tower) mounting nut and washer assembly.

6. Install strut assembly into fender (strut tower) and install nut and washer assemblies. Torque the retaining nuts to 20 ft. lbs.

7. Position the steering knuckle neck into the strut damper bracket, install the cam adjusting and through bolts.

8. Attach the brake hose retainer to the damper bracket, torque the screws to 10 ft. lbs. (13 Nm).

9. Adjust the camber to the original marked position.

10. Place a 4 inch or larger "C" clamp on the strut and knuckle. Tighten the clamp just enough to eliminate any looseness between the knuckle and the strut. Recheck the alignment marks and tighten the bolts to 45 ft. lbs. Turn the bolts an additional

Exploded view front suspension—Rampage

¼ turn (90°) beyond the specified torque.

11. Install the wheel and tire assembly. Torque the wheel nuts to 80 ft. lbs.

STRUT TYPE COIL SPRING

Removal & Installation

1. Use a coil spring compressor (strut type) to compress the coil spring.

2. Hold the strut rod while removing the strut rod.

3. Remove the strut damper mount assembly and the coil spring.

NOTE: If both strut springs are to be removed and reinstalled, mark them so they can be returned to their original position.

—————— CAUTION ——————

If Chrysler special tool spring compressor tool L-4514 is used, do not open the tool jaws beyond 9¼ inches (230 mm).

4. Reinstall the strut rod nut and torque it to 60 ft. lbs. before releasing the spring compressor.

LOWER CONTROL ARM

Removal & Installation

1. Raise the vehicle.

2. Remove the front inner pivot through bolt, rear stub strut nut, retainer and bushing.

3. Remove the ball joint to steering knuckle clamp bolt.

4. Separate the ball joint stud from steering knuckle.

—————— CAUTION ——————

Do not pull the steering knuckle away from the vehicle, while the ball joint is disconnected, it can separate the inner C/V joint.

5. Remove the sway bar to control arm end bushing retainer nuts and rotate the control arm over the sway bar. Remove rear stub strut bushing, sleeve and retainer.

6. Install retainer, bushing and sleeve on stub strut.

7. Position control arm over sway bar and install rear stub strut and front pivot into crossmember.

8. Install front pivot bolt and loosely assemble the nut.

9. Install the stub strut bushing and retainer and loosely assemble the nut.

10. Install ball joint stud into steering knuckle and install the clamp bolt. Tighten the clamp bolt to 50 ft. lbs.

11. Position sway bar end bushing retainer to control arm. Install retainer bolts and tighten nuts to 22 ft. lbs.

12. Lower the vehicle and support the control arm to design height. Tighten the front pivot bolt to 105 ft. lbs. and the stub strut nut to 70 ft. lbs.

LOWER BALL JOINT

Inspection

1. With the weight of the vehicle resting on the road wheels, grasp the grease

Mini-Van front suspension

fitting and attempt to move it.

2. No mechanical force is necessary. If the ball joint is worn the grease fitting will move easily. Replace worn ball joints.

Removal & Installation

The lower front ball joints are pressed into the lower control arm and an arbor press will be needed to remove and install them.

1. Pry the seal from the ball joint.

2. Position special tool C-4699-2 or equivalent to support the lower control arm while receiving ball joint assembly.

3. Use a 1¹/₁₆ inch deep well socket in the arbor press to remove the ball joint.

4. Position the ball joint into the control arm cavity.

5. Position the control arm assembly in the press with special tool C-4699-1 or equivalent supporting the control arm.

6. Align the assembly and press until the ball joint housing ledge stops against control arm cavity down flange.

7. Support the ball joint housing with special tool C-4699-2 or equivalent and position a new seal over the ball joint stud.

8. Using a 1½ inch socket in an arbor press force the seal to seat against the control arm.

WHEEL BEARING

Adjustment

1. Remove the wheel and tire assembly.

2. Remove the hub lock nut cotter pin and lock nut.

3. Loosen the hub nut and apply the brakes.

4. With brakes applied, tighten hub nut to 180–200 ft. lbs.

5. Install nut lock and new cotter pin. Wrap cotter pin tightly against nut lock.

6. Install wheel and tire assembly and tighten wheel nuts to 80 ft. lbs.

REAR SUSPENSION

Leaf Springs

REMOVAL & INSTALLATION

1. Raise the truck and support the rear with jackstands under the bumper brackets. Be sure that the front wheels are chocked and that the parking brake is set. Support the axle with a jack.

2. Remove the U-bolts and the U-bolt plate that holds the axle to the springs.

3. Remove the front pivot bolt.

4. Remove the rear shackle bolt nuts and the rear shackle plate.

5. Remove the outer shackle and bolt assembly from the hanger and remove the spring.

LET	TORQUE	
A	35 FT. LBS.	47 N·m
B	70 IN. LBS.	7 N·m
C	95 FT. LBS.	129 N·m
D	80. FT. LBS.	108 N·m
E	60 FT. LBS.	81 N·m
F	45 FT. LBS.	61 N·m
G	50 FT. LBS.	68 N·m

Mini-Van rear suspension

6. Installation is the reverse of removal. Be sure that the shackled end of the spring is above the shackle bracket pivot.

Rampage

The use of a coil spring compressor is necessary.

1. Remove the strut and spring assembly.

NOTE: Refer to the Shock Absorber Strut removal and installation procedure which follows.

2. Install the spring compressor on the spring and place it in a vise.

——————— CAUTION ———————
Always grip 4 or 5 coils and never extend the retractors beyond 9¼ inches.

3. Tighten the retractors evenly until pressure is removed from the upper spring seat.

4. Loosen the retaining nut.

——————— CAUTION ———————
Be very careful when loosening the retaining nut. If the spring is not properly compressed, serious injury could result.

5. Remove the lower isolator, pushrod sleeve, and upper spring seat.

6. Carefully slip the strut from the spring.

7. Remove the rebound bumper and dust shield from the strut.

8. Remove the lower spring seat.

9. Carefully and evenly, remove the compressor from the spring.

10. Install the compressor on the spring, gripping four or five coils.

11. Compress the spring.

12. Install the lower spring seat, dust shield and rebound bumper on the strut.

13. Slip the unit inside the coil spring and install the upper spring seat.

14. Make sure that the level surfaces on the seats are in position with the spring.

15. Install the sleeve on the pushrod and install the retaining nut. Torque the nut to 20 ft. lbs.

16. Install the lower isolator.

17. Install the strut and spring assembly.

Shock Absorber Strut

REMOVAL & INSTALLATION

Rampage

1. Remove the protective cap from the upper mounting nut.

2. Remove the upper mounting nut, isolator retainer and isolator.

3. Raise and support the vehicle.

4. Remove the lower strut mounting bolt.

5. Remove the strut and spring assembly.

6. Installation is the reverse of removal. Torque the lower mounting bolt to 40 ft. lbs. and the upper nut to 20 ft. lbs.

Shock Absorbers

REMOVAL & INSTALLATION

1. Jack and support the truck. Remove the wheel.

2. Remove the nut from the stud or bolt at the upper end. Remove the stud or bolt from the upper end.

3. Remove the lower nut at the bushing end.

4. Pivot the shock absorber and washers from the lower stud.

5. Remove the shock absorber and washers from the lower stud.

6. Installation is the reverse of removal. Purge the new shock of air by extending it in its normal position and compressing it while inverted. Do this several times. It is normal for there to be more resistance to extension than to compression.

REAR WHEEL ALIGNMENT

Front Wheel Drive

Due to the design of the rear suspension, it is possible to adjust both the camber and toe-in of the rear wheels. Alignment is controlled by inserting shim stock between the spindle mounting surface and the spindle mounting plate. Each shim stock changes wheel alignment by approximately 0°18′ on Rampage and .3° on other models. Be sure to adjust the rear wheel bearings.

STEERING

Steering Wheel

REMOVAL & INSTALLATION

Except Front Wheel Drive

1. Remove the horn button from the retainer by rotating it to the left, or remove the horn pad from the retainer by removing the two screws from underneath.
2. Disconnect the horn wire from the horn switch terminal.
3. Remove three screws and lift out the horn switch and button or pad retainer assembly.
4. Back the steering wheel retaining nut off to the top of the shaft.
5. Install a steering wheel puller and draw the steering wheel from the steering shaft splines.
6. Remove the steering wheel nut and pull the steering wheel off of the steering shaft.
7. Installation is the reverse of removal. Tighten the nut to 24 ft. lbs. through 1977, 60 ft. lbs. for 1978 and later models.

Front Wheel Drive

1. Remove the horn button or pad and horn switch. See Step 1 in previous section.
2. Remove the steering wheel nut.
3. Using a steering wheel puller, remove the steering wheel.
4. Align the master serration in the wheel hub with the missing tooth on the shaft. Torque the shaft nut to 60 ft. lbs.

───── CAUTION ─────

Do not torque the nut against the steering column lock or damage will occur.

5. Replace the horn switch and button.

1978 and later steering wheel—typical

Turn Signal/Hazard Warning Flasher Switch

REMOVAL & INSTALLATION

Except Front Wheel Drive

1. Disconnect the battery ground cable. Remove the steering wheel.
2. Remove the turn signal lever screw and the lever. Don't remove the speed control, just let it hang.
3. Remove the switch retainer screws.
4. Lift the automatic transmission selector light out.

Steering column switch components—Rampage

5. Remove the retainer plate.
6. Remove the wire cover extension, if any, below the column clamp. Remove the steering column mounting clamp. Remove the column wire cover.
7. Detach the switch wiring connector under the instrument panel.
8. Remove the switch.
9. Reverse the procedure for installation. Tighten the column clamp bolts to 30 ft. lbs.

Turn Signal Switch

REMOVAL & INSTALLATION

Front Wheel Drive
WITHOUT TILT WHEEL

1. Disconnect the negative battery cable.

2. Remove the steering wheel as described earlier.
3. On vehicles equipped with intermittent wipe or intermittent wipe with speed control, remove the two screws that attach the turn signal lever cover to the lock housing and remove the turn signal lever cover.
4. Remove the wash/wipe switch assembly.
5. Pull the hider up the control stalk and remove the two screws that attach the control stalk sleeve to the wash/wipe switch.
6. Rotate the control stalk shaft to the full clockwise position and remove the shaft from the switch by pulling straight out of the switch.
7. Remove the turn signal switch and upper bearing retainer screws. Remove the retainer and lift the switch up and out.
8. Installation is the reverse of removal.

WITH TILT WHEEL

1. Disconnect the negative battery cable.
2. Remove the steering wheel as previously described.
3. Remove the tilt lever and push the hazard warning knob in and unscrew it to remove it.
4. Remove the ignition key lamp assembly.
5. Pull the knob off the wash/wipe switch assembly.
6. Pull the hider up the stalk and remove the two screws that attach the sleeve to the wash/wipe switch and remove the sleeve.
7. Rotate the shaft in the wiper switch to the full clockwise position and remove the shaft by pulling straight out of the wash/wipe switch.
8. Remove the plastic cover from the lock plate. Depress the lock plate with tool C-4156, or suitable substitute. Pry the retaining ring out of the groove. Remove the lock plate, canceling cam and upper bearing spring.
9. Remove the switch actuator screw and arm.
10. Remove the three turn signal switch attaching screws and place the shift bowl in low position. Wrap a piece of tape around the connector and wires to prevent snagging then remove the switch and wires.
11. Installation is the reverse of removal.

Manual Steering Gear

REMOVAL & INSTALLATION

Except Front Wheel Drive
RAMCHARGER AND TRAIL DUSTER

1. Remove the two bolts from the wormshaft coupling.
2. Remove the steering arm from the steering gear using a suitable tool.
3. Remove the steering gear-to-frame bolts and remove the unit from the vehicle.

4. To install, position the steering gear to the frame and install the mounting bolts.

5. Install the steering arm and place the front wheels in the straight ahead position.

6. Place the steering wheel in the straight ahead position.

7. Install the wormshaft-to-column coupling bolts.

VANS AND PICK-UPS

1. Disconnect the battery.

2. Raise the vehicle on a hoist and disconnect "rubber and fabric" coupling (leaving the lower half of the coupling on the wormshaft).

3. Disconnect the shift linkage at the steering column.

4. Remove the steering arm retaining nut and washer. With a suitable tool remove the steering arm from the sector shaft.

5. Remove the three gear mounting bolts. Lower the vehicle from the hoist and remove the toe plate and column support bolts.

6. Disconnect the wiring and remove the column assembly.

7. Raise the vehicle on the hoist and remove the steering gear through the opening on the inboard side of the frame. (It may be helpful to remove the three bolts from the left idle arm bracket and move the bracket out of the way to provide additional clearance.)

NOTE: If the lower half of the steering coupling was removed from the gear, reinstall it on the wormshaft and secure it with a roll pin before installing the gear into the vehicle.

8. From underneath the vehicle, place the steering gear in position and install the three mounting bolts.

9. Reinstall the idler arm bracket, if it was removed.

10. Install the steering arm on the sector shaft. Install the washer and retaining nut.

11. Install the steering column assembly. Connect the steering column wiring. Install the shift linkage at the steering column.

12. Connect the steering shaft coupling at the wormshaft.

13. Connect the battery.

ADJUSTMENTS

Worm Bearing Preload

1. Detach the steering gear arm from the cross-shaft with a suitable puller, after removing the nut.

2. Remove the horn button, ring, or pad from the steering wheel.

3. Loosen the sector shaft screw locknut several turns. Then loosen the adjusting screw two turns. This will remove any friction load present between the ball nut rack and the sector gear teeth.

4. Rotate the steering wheel two *full* turns from straight-ahead. Attach a torque wrench on the steering shaft nut.

Manual steering gear adjustment points—typical

5. Turn the steering shaft at least one full turn toward straight-ahead. As the shaft is being rotated, check the torque reading on the wrench. The torque necessary to keep the wheel moving should fall between 1 and 1½ in. lbs. for 1977 and later. If the reading does not fall within specifications, adjustment is required. The adjuster is threaded into the housing on the upper end of the wormshaft.

6. To adjust, loosen the adjuster locknut. Turn the adjuster clockwise to increase the preload, or counterclockwise to decrease the preload.

7. Tighten the locknut while keeping the adjuster from turning. Retest the preload to see if it falls within specifications.

Ball Nut Rack & Sector Mesh

1. Complete the worm bearing preload adjustment first.

2. Turn the steering wheel gently from one lock to the other. Count the number of turns. Turn the wheel back *exactly* to the midpoint of its travel.

3. Turn the sector shaft adjusting screw, which is located on the housing cover, clockwise until there is no lash present between ball nut and sector teeth. Tighten the locknut to 35 ft. lbs.

4. Rotate the steering wheel one-quarter turn away from the center "high spot." Use a torque wrench, attached to the steering wheel nut, to measure the torque force required to turn the wheel through the "high spot." The reading should fall between 8–11 in. lbs. Rotate the sector shaft adjustment screw, if required, to obtain the correct preload.

5. Once the adjustments are completed, straighten the front wheels and install the steering arm on the cross-shaft.

NOTE: Not only should the front wheels be straight-ahead, but both the steering gear and the steering wheel should be centered as well.

6. Tighten the steering arm securing nut to 175 ft. lbs.

7. Install the horn button, ring, or trim pad on the steering wheel.

Power Steering Gear

REMOVAL & INSTALLATION

Except Front Wheel Drive

1. Raise the hood and remove the battery.

2. Disconnect the wires from the windshield washer pump. Remove the windshield washer reservoir mounting screws and position the reservoir out of the way.

3. Disconnect the power steering hoses at the steering gear. Cap the fittings at the steering gear and tie the hoses above the fluid level in the pump reservoir to prevent oil leakage.

4. Raise the vehicle on a hoist and disconnect the "rubber and fabric" coupling at the steering gear (leaving the lower half of the coupling on the wormshaft).

5. Disconnect the shift linkage at the steering column.

6. Remove the steering arm shield if so equipped. Remove the nut and washer, then with a suitable tool, remove the steering arm from the sector shaft.

7. Remove the mounting bolt on the left side of the gear.

Turn signal switch—typical of Rampage

8. Lower the vehicle and remove one of the two remaining steering gear mounting bolts.

9. Remove the toe plate and column support bolts.

10. Disconnect the steering column wiring and remove the assembly.

11. Raise the vehicle on the hoist. Remove the three bolts from the left idler arm bracket and swing the bracket out of the way.

12. Remove the remaining bolt and the steering gear from underneath of the vehicle, through the opening on the inboard side of the frame.

NOTE: Before installing the steering gear into the vehicle, install the coupling half of the wormshaft and secure it with the roll pin.

13. From the underside of the vehicle, place the steering gear into position on the mounting bracket and install the three mounting bolts.

14. Continue the installation in the reverse order of the removal.

15. Lower the vehicle, start the engine and turn the steering wheel several times from stop to stop to bleed the system of air.

16. Stop the engine and check the fluid level, correct if necessary. Inspect for leaks.

ADJUSTMENT

Sector

1. Disconnect the center link from the steering gear arm.

2. Start the engine and allow it to run at normal idle speed.

3. Rotate the steering wheel from lock to lock. Carefully count the number of turns required, then rotate the wheel back, exactly to the midpoint of its travel.

4. Loosen the adjusting screw until backlash in the steering gear arm becomes apparent.

NOTE: Backlash is felt by holding the end of the steering gear arm lightly between your thumb and forefinger.

5. Tighten the adjusting screw just enough so that the backlash disappears. Continue to tighten the screw for another ⅜ to ½ turn from this point. Tighten the locknut to 28 ft. lbs.

6. Attach the center link to the steering gear arm.

Manual or Power Steering Gear

REMOVAL & INSTALLATION

Front Wheel Drive

1. Raise and support truck. Remove the front wheels.

2. Remove the tie rod ends, using a suitable puller.

3. Drive out the lower roll pin attaching the pinion shaft to the lower universal joint.

Typical steering assembly mounting—Mini-Van

LET	TORQUE	
	NEWTON METERS	POUNDS
△	28	250 INCH
△	47	35 FOOT
△	75	55 FOOT

Use a back up counter weight, to protect the universal joint, while driving the roll pin.

4. Support the front suspension crossmember with a hydraulic jack. Remove the two rear nuts attaching the crossmember to the frame. Loosen the two front bolts attaching the crossmember to frame and lower the crossmember slightly for access to the boot seal shields.

5. Remove the splash shields and boot seal shields.

6. On power steering models remove the hoses from the steering gear box.

7. Disconnect the tie rod ends from the steering knuckles and remove the bolts attaching the gear to the front suspension crossmember.

8. Remove the gear from driver's side of vehicle.

9. Installation is the reverse of removal.

10. Torque the steering gear to crossmember bolts to 20.8 ft. lbs.

Power Steering Pump

REMOVAL & INSTALLATION

Except Front Wheel Drive

1. Loosen the pump mounting and locking bolts and remove the drive belt.

2. Disconnect and plug both hoses.

3. Remove the mounting and locking bolts and remove the pump.

4. Install the pump on the engine and install the mounting and locking bolts.

5. Install and adjust the drive belt. Tighten the mounting bolts to 30 ft. lbs.

6. Connect the pressure and return hoses. Route the hoses in the same manner as they were prior to removal. They should be routed smoothly with no sharp bends. Tighten the pump end hose fitting to 30 ft. lbs. (35 ft. lbs. for 1975 and later) and the gear end fitting to 19 ft. lbs. (25 ft. lbs. for 1975 and later). The hoses should remain at least 1 in. away from pulleys, battery case, and brake lines and at least 2 in. away from exhaust manifolds. If equipped, the protective sponge sleeves should be used to protect the hoses from contact with other parts.

7. Fill the pump with the specified power steering fluid or the equivalent.

8. Start the engine and turn the steering wheel lock-to-lock several times to bleed the system. Check for leaks and recheck the fluid level.

Front Wheel Drive

1. Disconnect the power steering hoses from the pump.

2. Remove the adjusting bolt and slip off the belt.

3. Support the pump, remove the mounting bolts and lift out the pump.

4. Installation is the reverse of removal. Adjust the belt to specifications.

Tie Rod Ends

REMOVAL & INSTALLATION

Except Front Wheel Drive

1. Raise the front of the truck and support it safely on jackstands.

2. Remove the cotter pin and the nut from the end of the tie rod.

3. Install a puller and apply sufficient pressure to release the tie rod end from the knuckle. Measure or count the number of exposed threads.

4. Loosen the tie rod sleeve clamping bolt and unscrew the tie rod end.

To install:

1. Screw the new tie rod end into the sleeve.

2. Connect the tie rod end to the knuckle and tighten the nut as follows: ½ in. nut—45 ft. lbs.; ⁹⁄₁₆ in. nut—55 ft. lbs.; ⅝ in. nut—75 ft. lbs. Install the cotter pin.

3. Lower the truck and adjust the toe-in.

4. Tighten the clamping bolts.

Front Wheel Drive

1. Raise the front of the truck and safely support it on jackstands.

2. Remove the cotter pin and the nut from the end of the tie rod.

3. Install a puller and apply sufficient pressure to release the tie rod from the knuckle arm.

4. Loosen the jam nut and unscrew the tie rod end.

5. Installation is in the reverse order of removal. Have the toe adjustment checked.

BRAKES

NOTE: Refer to the ''Brakes'' section of Unit Repair for service procedures.

CHASSIS ELECTRICAL

Heater Core

REMOVAL & INSTALLATION

Without Air Conditioning— Except Front Wheel Drive

1. Disconnect the battery ground cable.
2. Drain the radiator.

NOTE: Remove the radiator and grille for clearance, if necessary.

3. Cover the alternator with a waterproof cover.

4. Disconnect the blower motor resistor and ground wires from the heater.

5. Disconnect and plug the heater core hoses.

6. Disconnect the control cables and underdash braces.

7. Remove the retaining screws from the water valve. Do not disconnect the hoses from the water valve; place the water valve with hoses attached to one side.

8. Remove the blower motor cooler tube.

9. Remove the nuts holding the housing to the mounting studs and tip the complete unit for removal.

To remove the heater core:

10. Remove the retaining nuts and lift the blower assembly out of the housing.

11. Remove the cover retaining nuts and lift the cover off the housing.

12. Remove the core retaining screws and lift the core out of the housing.

13. Installation is the reverse of removal. Fill the cooling system.

14. Let the engine warm up with the heater on, then check the coolant level.

With Air Conditioning—Vans and Pick-ups Except Front Wheel Drive

——————— CAUTION ———————
The air conditioning system must be discharged to remove the heater core. Do not attempt if you are not familiar with air conditioning service, have a professional discharge the system.

1. Disconnect the battery ground cable and drain the coolant.

2. Remove the grille, condenser, and radiator, if necessary.

3. Place a waterproof cover over the alternator.

4. Disconnect the heater hoses at the water valve and remove the valve and bracket. Disconnect and cap the refrigerant lines.

5. Remove the glovebox, spot cooler bezel, and appearance shield.

6. Working through the glovebox opening, remove the evaporator housing to firewall screws and nuts.

7. Remove the wiper motor. Detach all evaporator housing vacuum and electrical connections. Detach the blower motor cooling hose and the drain hoses.

8. Remove the two 2¼ in. bolts from the crossbar and the four screws from the sealplate on the front of the housing. Separate the evaporator and blower motor housings, remove the evaporator housing.

9. Remove the receiver drier and cap all the openings. Carefully pry the heater core out, leaving the air seal at the front intact.

10. On installation, connect the hoses to the core. Position the evaporator housing on top of the blower housing. Install the mounting screws and nuts.

11. Position the crossbar under the lip on the blower housing opening and install the two 2¼ in. bolts. Install the four seal plate screws at the front of the housing.

12. Replace the wiper motor and connect the vacuum and electrical lines. Connect the blower motor cooler hose and the drain hoses.

13. Connect the heater hoses to the water valve.

14. Install the receiver drier and connect the refrigerant lines.

15. Install the radiator, condenser, and grille.

16. Replace the glove box, spot cooler bezel, and appearance shield.

17. Install the battery ground cable and fill the cooling system. Let the engine warm up with the *heater on*, then check the coolant. Have the air conditioner charged.

Heater Assembly

REMOVAL & INSTALLATION

Rampage—Without Air Conditioning

1. Disconnect the battery and drain the cooling system.

2. Remove the center outside air floor vent housing.

3. Remove the ash tray.

4. Remove the two defroster duct adapter screws. The left one is reached through the ash tray opening.

5. Remove the defrost duct adapter and push the flexible hose up out of the way.

6. Disconnect the temperature control cable.

7. Disconnect the blower motor wiring connector.

8. Disconnect the hoses from the heater core and plug the core openings.

9. Remove the two nuts retaining the heater unit to the firewall.

10. Remove the glove compartment and door.

11. Remove the screw attaching the heater brace bracket to the instrument panel.

12. Remove the heater assembly support strap nut. Disconnect the strap from the plenum stud and lower the heater from the instrument panel.

13. Disconnect the control cable and remove the unit from the car.

14. Connect the control cable and raise the unit into position so that the core tubes and mounting studs fit through their holes in the firewall.

15. Install the support strap and hand tighten the nut.

16. Install and tighten the two heater-to-firewall nuts.

17. Unplug and connect the core tubes.

18. Install the defroster duct adaptor.

19. Install the ash tray.

20. Install the center outside air floor vent housing.

21. Install the glove compartment.

22. Refill the cooling system.

Blower Motor

REMOVAL & INSTALLATION

Rampage—Without Air Conditioning

The blower motor is located under the instrument panel on the left side of the heater assembly.

1. Disconnect the motor wiring.

2. Remove the left outlet duct.

3. Remove the four motor retaining screws and remove the motor.

4. Installation is the reverse of removal.

Rampage—With Air Conditioning

1. Disconnect the battery ground.
2. Remove the three screws securing the glovebox to the instrument panel.
3. Disconnect the wiring from the blower and case.
4. Remove the blower vent tube from the case.
5. Loosen the recirculating door from its bracket and remove the actuator from the housing. Leave the vacuum lines attached.
6. Remove the seven screws attaching the recirculating housing to the A/C unit and remove the housing.
7. Remove the three mounting flange nuts and washers.
8. Remove the blower motor from the unit.
9. Installation is the reverse of removal. Replace any damaged sealer.

Heater Core

REMOVAL & INSTALLATION

NOTE: Removal of the Heater-Evaporator Unit is required for core removal. Two people will be required to perform the operation. Discharge, evacuation and recharge and leak testing of the refrigerant system is necessary.

———— CAUTION ————

This work should be performed only by a trained technician. Have the system discharged before attempting removal.

Rampage—Without Air Conditioning

1. Remove the heater assembly.
2. Remove the left outlet duct.
3. Remove the blower motor.
4. Remove the defroster duct adapter.
5. Remove the outside air and defroster door cover.
6. Remove the defroster door.
7. Remove the defroster door control rod.
8. Remove the core cover.
9. Lift the core from the unit.
10. Installation is the reverse of removal.

Rampage—With Air Conditioning

NOTE: During installation, a small can of refrigerant oil will be necessary.

1. Disconnect the battery ground.
2. Drain the coolant.
3. Disconnect the temperature door cable from the heater-evaporator unit.
4. Disconnect the temperature door cable from the retaining clips.
5. Remove the glovebox.

6. Disconnect the vacuum harness from the control head.
7. Disconnect the blower motor lead and anti-diesel relay wire.
8. Remove the seven screws fastening the right trim bezel to the instrument panel. Starting at the right side, swing the bezel clear and remove it.
9. Remove the three screws on the bottom of the center distribution duct cover and slide the cover rearward and remove it.
10. Remove the center distribution duct.
11. Remove the defroster duct adaptor.
12. Remove the H-type expansion valve, located on the right side of the firewall:
    a. Remove the 5/16 in. bolt in the center of the plumbing sealing plate.
    b. Carefully pull the refrigerant lines toward the front of the car, taking care to avoid scratching the valve sealing surfaces.
    c. Remove the two 1/4-20 Allen head cap screws and remove the valve.
13. Cap the pipe openings at once. Wrap the valve in a plastic bag.
14. Disconnect the hoses from the core tubes.
15. Disconnect the vacuum lines at the intake manifold and water valve.
16. Remove the unit-to-firewall retaining nuts.
17. Remove the panel support bracket.
18. Remove the right cowl lower panel.
19. Remove the instrument panel pivot bracket screw from the right side.
20. Remove the screws securing the lower instrument panel at the steering column.
21. Pull back the carpet from under the unit as far as possible.
22. Remove the nut from the evaporator-heater unit-to-plenum mounting brace and blower motor ground cable. While supporting the unit, remove the brace from its stud.
23. Lift the unit, pulling it rearward to allow clearance. These operations may require two people.
24. Slowly lower the unit taking care to keep the studs from hanging-up on the insulation.
25. When the unit reaches the floor, slide it rearward until it is out from under the instrument panel.
26. Remove the unit.
27. Place the unit on a workbench. On the inside side, remove the 1/4-20 nut from the mode door actuator on the top cover and the two retaining clips from the front edge of the cover. To remove the mode door actuator, remove the two screws securing it to the cover.
28. Remove the fifteen screws attaching the cover to the assembly and lift off the cover. Lift the mode door out of the unit.
29. Remove the screw from the core retaining bracket and lift out the core.
To install:
30. Place the core in the unit and install the bracket.
31. Install the actuator arm.

———— CAUTION ————

When installing the unit, care must be taken that the vacuum lines to the engine compartment do not hang-up on the accelerator or become trapped between the unit and the firewall. If this happens, kinked lines will result and the unit will have to be removed to free them. Proper routing of these lines will require two people. The portion of the vacuum harness which is routed through the steering column support MUST be positioned BEFORE the distribution housing is installed. The harness MUST be routed ABOVE the temperature control cable.

32. Place the unit on the floor as far under the panel as possible.
33. Raise the unit carefully, at the same time pull the lower instrument panel rearward as far as possible.
34. Position the unit in place and attach the brace to the stud.
35. Install the lower ground cable and attach the nut.
36. Install and tighten the unit-to-firewall nuts.
37. Reposition the carpet and install, but do not tighten the right instrument panel pivot bracket screw.
38. Place a piece of sheet metal or thin cardboard against the evaporator-heater assembly to center the assembly duct seal.
39. Position the center distributor duct in place making sure that the upper left tab comes in through the left center A/C outlet opening and that each air take-off is properly inserted in its respective outlet.

NOTE: Make sure that the radio wiring connector does not interfere with the duct.

40. Install and tighten the screw securing the upper left tab of the center air distribution duct to the instrument panel.
41. Remove the sheet metal or cardboard from between the unit and the duct.

NOTE: Make sure that the unit seal is properly aligned with the duct opening.

42. Install and tighten the two lower screws fastening the center distribution duct to the instrument panel.
43. Install and tighten the screws securing the lower instrument panel at the steering column.
44. Install and tighten the nut securing the instrument panel to the support bracket.
45. Make sure that the seal on the unit is properly aligned and seated against the distribution duct assembly.
46. Tighten the instrument panel pivot bracket screw and install the right cowl lower trim.
47. Slide the distributor duct cover assembly onto the center distribution duct so that the notches lock into the tabs and the tabs slide over the rear and side ledges of the center duct assembly.
48. Install the three screws securing the ducting.

49. Install the right trim bezel.

50. Connect the vacuum harness to the control head.

51. Connect the blower lead and the anti-diesel wire.

52. Install the glovebox.

53. Connect the temperature door cable.

54. Install new O-rings on the evaporator plate and the plumbing plate. Coat the new O-rings with clean refrigerant oil.

55. Place the H-valve against the evaporator sealing plate surface and install the two ¼-20NC throughbolts. Torque to 6–10 ft. lbs.

56. Carefully hold the refrigerant line connector against the valve and install the 5/16-18-NC bolt. Torque to 14–20 ft. lbs.

57. Install the heater hoses at the core tubes.

58. Connect the vacuum lines at the manifold and water valve.

59. Install the condensate drain tube.

60. Have the system evacuated, charged and leak tested by a trained technician.

Heater Assembly and Core

REMOVAL & INSTALLATION

Front Wheel Drive with Air Conditioning—Except Rampage

NOTE: Removal of the Heater-Evaporator Unit is required for core removal. Two people will be required to perform the operation. Discharge, evacuation and recharge and leak testing of the refrigerant system is necessary.

——————— CAUTION ———————

This work should be performed only by a trained technician. Have the system discharged before attempting removal.

1. Discharge system before opening any lines and drain engine coolant. Disconnect negative battery cable.

2. Disconnect heater hoses at heater core. Plug heater core tube openings to prevent coolant from spilling out when assembly is removed.

3. Disconnect vacuum lines at brake booster and at water valve.

4. Remove "H" valve.

5. Remove condensate drain tube.

6. Remove evaporator heater assembly to dash retaining nuts.

7. Remove wire connector from resistor block, push out dash grommet, feed wire through grommet hole into passenger compartment.

8. Remove the steering wheel and lower the steering column to the drivers seat.

9. Remove lower instrument panel. The lower instrument panel must be disconnected to the point that the right side can be moved rearward and rested on the passenger seat. The left side of the instrument panel can remain electrically connected. This

will disconnect the blower motor and resistor block wiring, the temperature control cable and vacuum harness from the instrument panel control.

10. Remove the evaporator heater unit hangar strap and swing out of the way.

11. Pull the unit rearward and out of vehicle.

12. Place evaporator heater assembly on work bench in position as would be viewed by front seat passenger.

13. Remove one (1) screw retaining the vacuum harness. Feed harness through hole in cover.

14. Remove thirteen (13) screws from cover, remove cover. Temperature control door will come out with the cover. Remove the nut and lever from the door shaft to remove the temperature door from the cover.

15. Remove screw from heater core tube retaining bracket and lift core out of unit.

16. Blower assembly, sound helmet, motor and wheel. Remove five (5) screws from the sound helmet.

17. To remove blower wheel remove retaining clamp from blower wheel hub and slide blower wheel from blower motor shaft.

18. Remove motor by taking out three (3) screws in helmet. Remove motor with wires and grommet.

19. Place heater core into unit and fasten with screws.

20. Reinstall blower wheel onto blower motor shaft and secure with retaining clamp.

21. Feed blower motor wires through hole in sound helmet. Lower blower assembly (rubber seal in place) into helmet. Pull wiring grommet into place and install three (3) mounting screws. Entire blower assembly and helmet can be installed into fan scroll with five (5) screws.

22. Install cover: Line up to housing using pilot pin, temperature door and screw holes for alignment. Drive thirteen (13) screws.

23. Vacuum Harness—Route through holes in cover. Drive one (1) screw to retain vacuum harness. Make all vacuum hose attachments to actuators.

——————— CAUTION ———————

Care must be taken that the vacuum lines to the engine compartment do not hang up on the accelerator, or become trapped between the assembly and dash. Such a situation will result in kinked lines and the necessity of a second unit removal to free them. Proper routing of these lines as the unit is positioned to the dash may require two people.

24. Place unit on the floor as far forward under the instrument panel as possible.

25. Raise unit taking care not to catch studs in dashliner. Route vacuum lines through opening.

26. Position assembly in place and attach hanger strap.

27. Reinstall assembly to dash retaining nuts and tighten.

28. Install condensate drain tube.

29. Remove plugs from heater core tube openings and install heater hoses.

30. Install vacuum lines (Black line to brake booster and grey line to water valve).

31. Install "H" valve. See "H" valve installation.

32. Make sure that the evaporator heater assembly seal is properly aligned with top of center distribution duct opening.

33. Reinstall lower instrument panel. See Group 8 Electrical.

34. Route resistor block wires through dash and install remaining parts in reverse order of removal. Recharge system.

Auxiliary Heater, Core and Blower

The auxiliary heater, in some vans, is a rear mounted recirculating heater, temperature controlled by a Bowden cable.

REMOVAL & INSTALLATION

1. Drain the radiator.

2. Disconnect the negative battery cable.

3. From under the vehicle, disconnect the intake and outlet hoses from the heater. On 1970 and later models, or if so equipped, remove the water valve with hoses attached.

4. Remove the screws that mount the heater to the floor pan and disconnect the wiring to the heater.

To remove the auxiliary heater core:

5. Remove the heater cover attaching screws. The heater core is attached to the heater cover and will come out with the cover.

6. Remove the core from the cover.

To remove the auxiliary heater blower:

7. Remove the screws attaching the blower motor to the heater and remove the blower motor.

8. Installation is the reverse of removal. Be sure to fill the cooling system and check for leaks. Check the operation of the auxiliary heater.

Radio

REMOVAL & INSTALLATION

1977

1. Disconnect the negative battery cable.

2. Remove the mounting strap on the glove box door.

3. Remove the hinge screws and remove the glove box door.

4. Remove the glove box mounting screws and pull the box out of the instrument panel.

5. Remove the radio bezel mounting nuts and remove the bezel.

6. Remove the radio-to-instrument panel attaching bolts and push the radio in to release the mounting tabs.

7. Working through the glove box opening, disconnect the antenna wire from the

radio. Remove the right defroster distribution duct on trucks equipped with A/C. Remove the radio rear support bracket nut, tilt the unit up and pull it out to release it from the support bracket. Disconnect the electrical and speaker wires.

8. Remove the radio through the glove box door. If the truck is equipped with A/C, remove the radio through the duct opening.

9. Reverse to install.

1978 and Later—Except Front Wheel Drive

1. Disconnect the negative battery cable.
2. Remove the seven instrument panel and bezel attaching screws. Pull the bezel off the retaining clip.
3. Remove the five instrument cluster screws.
4. Pull the cluster out far enough to gain access to the speedometer cable. Push the cable spring clip toward the cluster and disconnect the cable.
5. Remove the right and left printed circuit board multiple connectors.
6. Remove the instrument cluster.
7. Remove the radio mounting screws.
8. Remove the ground strap screw.
9. Pull the radio out of the instrument panel and disconnect the wiring.
10. Reverse to install.

Front Wheel Drive

1. Remove the seven bezel attaching screws and open the glove compartment.
2. Remove the bezel, guiding the right end around the glove compartment and away from the panel.
3. Disconnect the radio ground strap and remove the two radio mounting screws.
4. Pull the radio from the panel and disconnect the wiring and antenna lead.
5. Installation is the reverse of removal.

TRIMMING THE ANTENNA

All radios are trimmed at the factory and should require no further trimmer adjustment unless the radio is being installed after repair, or if trimmer adjustment is desired because of poor performance.

1. Extend the antenna to full length or to 31–33 in. for best FM reception.
2. Tune the radio to a weak signal between 1400 and 1600 kilocycles on the AM band.
3. Increase the radio volume and set the tone control to maximum treble.
4. The trimmer screw on most radios is located lower rear right-hand corner of the radio and can be reached by inserting a screwdriver into the recess hole.
5. Adjust the trimmer by turning it back and forth until the peak response in volume is obtained.

Wiper Motor

REMOVAL & INSTALLATION

Except Front Wheel Drive

The wiper motor is removed from under the hood. It is not necessary to remove the cowl grille.

1. Unplug the electrical wiring at the motor.
2. Remove the 3 mounting bolts from the wiper motor flange.
3. Lower the motor down far enough to gain access to the crank arm to drive link bushing. Pry the bushing from the crank arm.
4. Remove the motor.
5. Hold the drive crank with a wrench while removing the crank nut. Remove the drive crank from the motor.
6. Installation is the reverse of removal. Check and adjust (if necessary) the wiper arm park position.

Typical fuse block-1981 shown

Rampage

1. Disconnect the linkage from the motor crank arm.
2. Remove the wiper motor plastic cover.
3. Disconnect the wiring harness from the motor.
4. Remove the three mounting bolts from the motor bracket and remove the motor.
5. Installation is the reverse of removal.

Front Wheel Drive—Except Rampage

1. Park system.
2. Remove wiper arms and blades, disconnect hoses from connectors.
3. Open the hood assembly.
4. Remove cowl top plenum grill and disconnect washer hose from connector.
5. Remove cowl plenum chamber plastic screen.
6. Remove the wiper pivot screws.
7. Disengage the pivots from the cowl top mounting positions.

8. Push pivots down into plenum chamber.
9. Disconnect wiper motor wiring harness from suppressor.
10. Remove three (3) mounting nuts from wiper motor.
11. Remove wiper motor assembly and linkage.
12. Clamp motor crank in a vise and remove nut from end of motor shaft. **Do not rotate motor output shaft from park position.** Remove crank from motor.
13. Do the necessary service needed on the motor, pivots, links and cranks.

Linkage

DRIVE LINK

Except Rampage

1. Remove the wiper arms.
2. Remove the cowl grille cover.
3. Reach through the access hole and remove the drive link from the connecting arm and the crank arm. Remove the connecting link pins by prying.
4. Remove the drive link through the access hole.
5. Reverse to install. Use slip joint pliers to snap the links and pins together.

CONNECTING LINK

Except Front Wheel Drive

1. Remove the cowl grille cover.
2. Reach through the access hole and remove the connecting link from the drive link and the pivot pins by prying the bushings apart.
3. Remove the connecting link through the access hole.
4. Reverse to install. Use slip joint pliers to snap the links and pins together.

Adjusting wiper arms

WIPER ARM ADJUSTMENT

Except Front Wheel Drive

To determine if an adjustment is required, apply a downward force of 25 oz parallel to the windshield glass at the tip of the wiper arm (where the blade is attached to the arm). With this force applied, pull the

HEATER BLOWER MOTOR AND CONTROL SYSTEM DIAGNOSIS (ELECTRICAL)

BLOWER MOTOR INOPERATIVE

FUSE BLOWN ← INSPECT FUSE → FUSE GOOD

CHECK FOR SHORT ← CHECK FOR STALLED MOTOR

CHECK FOR BATTERY VOLTAGE AT BOTH ENDS OF FUSE

CORRECT SHORT

MOTOR STALLED

VOLTAGE AT BOTH ENDS OF FUSE

VOLTAGE AT BATTERY SIDE OF FUSE ONLY

REPLACE FUSE AND RESISTOR BLOCK IF MICRO-TEMP CLOSED ← REPLACE MOTOR

CHECK BLOWER MOTOR GROUND

REPLACE FUSE

LOCATE OPEN CONNECTION AND CORRECT ← MOTOR RUNS ←

ATTACH JUMPER WIRE BETWEEN MOTOR GROUND WIRE AND BODY OR ENGINE (MOTOR IN PASSENGER COMPARTMENT) OR CHECK ATTACHMENT OF GROUND LEAD OF MOTOR IN ENGINE COMPARTMENT

CHECK MOTOR CONTINUITY ← MOTOR DOES NOT RUN ←

MAKE SURE FEED WIRE TERMINALS ARE NOT BACKED OUT OF INSULATOR OR OFF CENTER. REASSEMBLE MOTOR WIRE CONNECTOR

ATTACH JUMPER WIRE FROM THE MOTOR FEEDWIRE TO THE POSITIVE POST OF THE BATTERY. MAKE SURE THAT GROUND WIRE IS PROPERLY GROUNDED FOR THIS TEST

MOTOR DOES NOT RUN

REPLACE MOTOR

LOCATE OPEN CONNECTION AND CORRECT ←

NO VOLTAGE IN ANY SWITCH POSITION

MOTOR RUNS

REPLACE PUSHBUTTON SWITCH ←

CHECK RESISTOR CONTINUITY AND RESISTOR CONNECTIONS

VOLTAGE IN ALL SWITCH POSITIONS ←

REMOVE WIRING CONNECTORS FROM RESISTOR TERMINALS. MAKE SURE THAT TERMINALS ARE NOT BACKED OUT OF INSULATOR. CHECK FOR BATTERY VOLTAGE IN EACH FAN SWITCH POSITION.

NO VOLTAGE IN ONE OR MORE LEADS

REPLACE RESISTOR

VOLTAGE AT BATTERY TERMINAL ←

REMOVE WIRING CONNECTOR FROM SWITCH TERMINALS. MAKE SURE TERMINALS ARE PROPERLY LOCKED IN SOCKET OF INSULATOR. CHECK FOR BATTERY VOLTAGE AT BATTERY TERMINAL IN INSULATOR.

CHECK BLOWER SWITCH AND CONNECTIONS

REPLACE BLOWER SWITCH*

*IF BLOWER SWITCH HAS FAILED DUE TO BURNING OR CHARRING CHECK CURRENT DRAW OF THE BLOWER MOTOR

BLOWER MOTOR OPERATES AT HIGH SPEED ONLY → OPERATE BLOWER SWITCH IN ALL MODES → FUSE BLOWS, INDICATING PRESENCE OF A SHORT → CORRECT SHORT → CHECK AND REPLACE RESISTOR BLOCK IF DEFECTIVE → REPLACE FUSE

RESISTOR BLOCK DEFECTIVE → REPLACE RESISTOR BLOCK

FUSE DOES NOT BLOW → INSPECT RESISTOR BLOCK → RESISTOR BLOCK O.K. → INSPECT BLOWER SWITCH → BLOWER SWITCH DEFECTIVE → REPLACE BLOWER SWITCH wiper blade away from the glass several times to prevent glass friction from affecting downward movement. The clearance between the tip of the wiper blade and the windshield molding should be as specified in the illustration. If the clearance is not as specified, reposition the wiper arm.

To remove the arm, lift it and look for a spring retainer at the bottom. Hold the retainer out of the way, wiggle the arm, and pull it off. To replace it, just push it on, making sure that the latch is out of the way.

Instrument Cluster

REMOVAL & INSTALLATION

Except Front Wheel Drive

For instrument cluster removal and installation procedures, refer to steps 1–6 of the 1978 and Later Radio Removal and Installation procedure.

Rampage

1. Remove the two lens assembly lower attaching retaining springs by pulling rearward with a pliers.
2. Allow the lens assembly to drop as it is pulled rearward.
3. Remove the speedometer assembly (two screws).
4. Remove the two wiring harness connectors.

5. Remove the two cluster attaching screws.
6. Pull the two upper spring retainers away from the panel.
7. If equipped with a clock, reach behind the panel and disconnect the wires.
8. Remove the cluster assembly.
9. Installation is the reverse of removal.

Front Wheel Drive—Except Rampage

1. Open ash tray, remove tray and disconnect lighter.
2. From underneath panel, remove the mounting screw that attach upper and lower panels.
3. Push housing forward and lower rear to remove.
4. Reverse procedure for installation.

Headlights

REMOVAL & INSTALLATION

1. Remove the headlight bezel attaching screws and remove the bezel. On some models it may not be necessary to remove the bezel, depending on whether the headlight retaining ring is accessible.
2. Remove the headlight ring attaching screws and remove the ring. Do not touch the headlight aiming screws.
3. Pull the sealed beam out slightly and unplug the connector.

4. Reverse to install. As long as the adjusting screws were not moved, the headlight will be held in proper adjustment by the retaining ring.

Fuses and Fusible Links

The fuse panel is usually located on the left side of the steering column, either on the kick panel, steering colum or firewall.

Always replace a blown fuse with one of the same rating. If the same fuse continues to blow out, check the circuit for overload or short circuit.

When a fusible link blows it is very important to find out why it blew. They are placed in vehicles electrical system for protection against dead shorts to ground which can be caused by electrical component failure or various wiring failure. Do not just replace a fusible link to correct a problem, find out what caused the problem. For fusible link repair, refer to the Electrical Unit Repair Section.

Ford
Pickups, Vans, Bronco, Bronco II, Ranger

GENERAL ENGINE SPECIFICATIONS

Year	Engine Displacement Cu In. (cc)	Carburetor Type	Horsepower (@ rpm)	Torque @ rpm (ft. lbs.)	Bore x Stroke (in.)	Compression Ratio	Oil Pressure @ rpm (psi)
'77	6–300 (3934)	1 bbl	120 @ 3400①	229 @ 1400②	4.00 × 3.98	8.0 : 1③	40–60
	8–302 (4950)	2 bbl	134 @ 3600	242 @ 2000	4.000 × 3.000	8.0 : 1	40–60
	8–351M (5753)	2 bbl	132 @ 3600	242 @ 1600	4.00 × 3.50	8.0 : 1	50–75
	8–351W (5753)	2 bbl	147 @ 3400④	276 @ 1800⑤	4.00 × 3.50	8.3 : 1	40–60
	8–400 (6600)	2 bbl	149 @ 3200	300 @ 1400	4.00 × 4.00	8.0 : 1	50–75
	8–460 (7539)	4 bbl	237 @ 4000⑥	365 @ 2600⑦	4.36 × 3.85	8.0 : 1	40–60
'78	6–300 (3934)	1 bbl	132 @ 3600	241 @ 1800	4.00 × 3.98	8.0 : 1③	40–60
	8–302 (4950)	2 bbl	134 @ 3600	242 @ 2000	4.00 × 3.00	8.0 : 1	40–60
	8–351W (5753)	2 bbl	147 @ 3400④	276 @ 1800⑤	4.00 × 3.50	8.3 : 1	40–60
	8–351M (5753)	2 bbl	132 @ 3600①	242 @ 1600②	4.00 × 3.50	8.0 : 1	50–75
	8–400 (6600)	2 bbl	149 @ 3200	300 @ 1400	4.00 × 4.00	8.0 : 1	50–75
	8–460 (7539)	4 bbl	237 @ 4000⑥	365 @ 2600⑦	4.36 × 3.85	8.0 : 1	40–60

GENERAL ENGINE SPECIFICATIONS

Year	Engine Displacement Cu In. (cc)	Carburetor Type	Horsepower (@ rpm)	Torque @ rpm (ft. lbs.)	Bore x Stroke (in.)	Compression Ratio	Oil Pressure @ rpm (psi)
'79	6–300 (3934)	1 bbl	⑧	⑨	4.00 × 3.98	⑩	40–60
	8–302 (4950)	2 bbl	⑪	⑫	4.00 × 3.00	8.4 : 1	40–60
	8–351W (5753)	2 bbl	⑬	⑭	4.00 × 3.50	8.3 : 1	40–60
	8–351M (5753)	2 bbl	132 @ 3600①	242 @ 1600②	4.00 × 3.50	8.0 : 1	50–75
	8–400 (6600)	2 bbl	149 @ 3200	300 @ 1400	4.00 × 4.00	8.0 : 1	50–75
	8–460 (7539)	4 bbl	⑮	⑯	4.36 × 3.85	8.0 : 1	40–60
'80	6–300 (3934)	1 bbl	⑱	⑲	4.00 × 3.98	⑩	40–60
	8–302 (4950)	2 bbl	⑳	㉑	4.00 × 3.98	8.4 : 1	40–60
	8–351W (5753)	2 bbl	㉒	㉓	4.00 × 3.50	8.3 : 1	40–60
	8–400 (6600)	2 bbl	㉔	㉕	4.00 × 4.00	8.0 : 1	55–75
	8–460 (7539)	4 bbl	212 @ 4000	339 @ 2400	4.36 × 3.85	8.0 : 1	40–65
'81	6–300 (4917)	1 bbl	⑱	⑲	4.00 × 3.98	8.9 : 1	40–60
	8–302 (4950)	2 bbl	⑳	㉑	4.00 × 3.00	8.4 : 1	40–60
	8–351W (5753)	2 bbl	㉒	㉓	4.00 × 3.50	8.0 : 1	40–65
	8–400 (6600)	2 bbl	㉔	㉕	4.00 × 4.00	8.0 : 1	50–75
	8–460 (7539)	4 bbl	212 @ 4000	339 @ 2400	4.36 × 3.85	8.0 : 1	40–65
'82	6-232 (3802)	2 bbl	112 @ 4000	175 @ 2600	3.81 × 3.39	8.65:1	40–60
	6–300 (4917)	1 bbl	⑳	㉑	4.00 × 3.98	8.9 : 1⑰	40–60
	8–255 (4179)	2 bbl	115 @ 3400	195 @ 2200	3.68 × 3.00	8.2 : 1	40–60
	8–302 (4950)	2 bbl	130 @ 3400	247 @ 2400	4.00 × 3.00	8.4 : 1	40–60
	8–351W (5753)	2 bbl	145 @ 3400	265 @ 2000	4.00 × 3.50	8.3 : 1	40–65
	8–400 (6600)	2 bbl	㉔	㉕	4.00 × 4.00	8.0 : 1	50–75

GENERAL ENGINE SPECIFICATIONS

Year	Engine Displacement Cu In. (cc)	Carburetor Type	Horsepower (@ rpm)	Torque @ rpm (ft. lbs.)	Bore x Stroke (in.)	Compression Ratio	Oil Pressure @ rpm (psi)
	8–460 (7539)	4 bbl	212 @ 4000	339 @ 2400	4.36 × 3.85	8.0 : 1	40–60
'83–'84	4–122 (1999)	1 bbl	73 @ 4000	107 @ 2400	3.52 × 3.13	9.0 : 1	40–60
	4–134 (2196)	diesel	59 @ 4000	90 @ 2500	3.50 × 3.50	22.0 : 1	51 @ 3600
	4–140 (2294)	1 bbl	79 @ 3800 ㉖	124 @ 2400 ㉖	3.78 × 3.13	9.0 : 1	40–60
	6–173 (2835)	2 bbl	115 @ 4600	150 @ 2600	3.66 × 2.70	8.7 : 1	40–60
	6–232 (3802)	2 bbl	109 @ 3600	184 @ 1600	3.81 × 3.39	8.7 : 1	40–60
	6–300 (4917)	1 bbl	137 @ 3600	239 @ 1800	4.00 × 3.98	8.0 : 1	40–60
	8–302 (4950)	2 bbl	139 @ 3400	250 @ 2000	4.00 × 3.00	8.4 : 1	40–60
	8–351W (5753)	2 bbl	139 @ 3200 ㉗	278 @ 1400 ㉗	4.00 × 3.50	8.4 : 1	40–60
	8–351 (5753)	4 bbl	210 @ 4000	305 @ 2800	4.00 × 3.50	8.3 : 1	40–65
	8–420 (6883)	diesel	161 @ 3300	307 @ 1800	4.00 × 4.18	20.7 : 1	40–60
	8–460 (7539)	4 bbl	202 @ 4000	331 @ 2200	4.36 × 3.85	8.0 : 1	40–65

① F & E-100 49 states: 122 @ 3200
F & E-100 Calif.: 123 @ 3200
② F & E-100 49 states: 252 @ 1600
F & E-100 Calif.: 253 @ 1600
③ F & E-100 8.9 : 1
④ F & E-100 49 states: 141 @ 3200
F&E-100 Calif.:
Man Trans., 152 @ 3200
Auto Trans., 143 @ 3200
⑤ Engines subject to noise legislation:
275 @ 1800
F & E-100 49 states: 286 @ 1400
F & E-100 Calif.,
with Man Trans.: 286 @ 2000
with Auto Trans.: 287 @ 1600
⑥ Engines subject to noise legislation:
230 @ 4000
⑦ Engines subject to noise legislation:
359 @ 2600
⑧ F & E-100 exc Calif.; all E-150: 117
@ 3000
F & E-250 Manual trans.: 114 @
3000
F & E-250 Automatic trans.: 116 @
3200
F & E-350: 114 @ 3000

⑨ F & E-100, 150: 243 @ 1600
F & E-250 Manual trans.: 234 @
1600
F & E-250 Automatic trans.: 247 @
1000
F & E-350: 247 @ 1000
⑩ F & E-100, 150, 250: 8.9:1
F & E-350: 8.0:1
⑪ F & E-100, 150 exc Calif.: 135 @
3400
F & E-100 Calif.: 129 @ 3200
F & E-150 Calif.: 137 @ 3400
F & E-250: 136 @ 3400
⑫ F & E-100, 150 exc Calif.: 243 @
2000
F & E-100 Calif.: 238 @ 2400
F & E-150 Calif.: 245 @ 2000
F & E-250: 235 @ 2400
⑬ F & E-100: 135 @ 2800
F & E-150 Manual trans.: 130 @
3000
F & E-150 Automatic trans, except
Calif.: 135 @ 2800
F & E-150 Automatic trans, Calif.:
139 @ 3200
F & E-250 Manual trans.: 130 @
3000

F & E-250 Automatic trans.: 126 @
2800
F & E-350: 143 @ 3200
⑭ F & E-100: 274 @ 1400
F & E-150 Manual trans, except
Calif.: 267 @ 1800
F & E-150 Automatic trans, except
Calif.: 274 @ 1400
F & E-150 Automatic trans, Calif.:
269 @ 1200
F & E-250 Manual trans, 267 @
1800
F & E-250 Automatic trans, 270 @
1400
F & E-350: 272 @ 2000
⑮ F & E-250: 214 @ 3600
F & E-350: 217 @ 4000
⑯ F & E-250: 362 @ 1800
F & E-350: 358 @ 2600
⑰ F-250 over 8500 lb GVWR and
E&F-350: 8.0:1
⑱ Bronco, F-100, 250 49 states: 119
@ 3200
E-100, 250 49 states: 115 @ 3200
All Calif.: 116 @ 3200

GENERAL ENGINE SPECIFICATIONS

⑲Bronco, F-100, 250 49 states: 243 @ 1200
E-100, 250 49 states: 241 @ 1200
All Calif.: 244 @ 1200
⑳Bronco, F-100, 250 49 states: 137 @ 3600
E-100, 250 49 states: 138 @ 3600
Bronco, F-150 (4×4), 250, E-100, 250 Calif.: 136 @ 3600
F-100, 150 (4×2) Calif.: 133 @ 3400
㉑Bronco, F-100, 250 49 states: 239 @ 1800

E-100, 250 49 states: 242 @ 1800
Bronco, F-150 (4×4), 250, E-100, 250 Calif.: 235 @ 1800
F-100, 150 (4×2) Calif.: 235 @ 2000
㉒Bronco, F-150, 250 49 states: 138 @ 3400
E-250: 133 @ 3200
Bronco, F-150, E-250 Calif.: 135 @ 3200
F-350, E-350: 142 @ 3400
㉓Bronco, F-150, 250 49 states: 263 @ 2000

E-250: 265 @ 1600
Bronco, F-150, E-250 Calif.: 259 @ 1600
F-350, E-350: 251 @ 2400
㉔F-250 (4×4): 136 @ 2800
E-250: 133 @ 2600
F-350, E-350: 153 @ 3200
㉕F-250 (4×4): 310 @ 1200
E-250: 309 @ 1200
F-350, E-350: 296 @ 1600
㉖Auto trans: 82 @ 4200, 126 @ 2200
㉗F250 and Vans: 145 @ 3200, 270 @ 1400

TUNE UP SPECIFICATIONS
Pick-Ups

When analyzing compression test results, look for uniformity among cylinders rather than specific pressures.

Year	Engine No. Cyl. Displacement (cu In.)	Spark Plugs Orig Type	Gap (in.)	Distributor Point Dwell (deg)	Point Gap (in.)	Ignition Timing (deg) Man	Auto	Intake Valve Opens (deg)	Fuel Pump Pressure (psi)	Idle Speed (rpm) ▲ Man	Auto
'77	6—300	BSF-42B	0.044②	Electronic		①	①	12B	5–7	①	①
	8—302	ASF-42B	0.044	Electronic		①	①	16B	6–8	①	①
	8—351	ASF-42B	0.044	Electronic		①	①	—	6–8	①	①
	8—400	ASF-42B	0.044	Electronic		①	①	—	6–8	①	①
	8—460	ASF-42B	0.044	Electronic		①	①	—	5–7	①	①
'78–'84	All	See Underhood Specifications Sticker (See NOTE)									

NOTE: Specifications vary according to calibration, always use "Specs" on emissions decal.
①See underhood specifications sticker
②Engines built after 11/15/76: 0.054

▲Where two figures are separated by a slash, the lower of the two is the rpm with the idle solenoid disconnected.

TUNE-UP SPECIFICATIONS
Bronco & Bronco II

Year	Engine No. Cyl Displacement	Spark Plugs Type	Gap (in.)	Distributor Point Dwell (deg)	Point Gap (in.)	Ignition Timing (deg) Manual Trans	Auto Trans	Intake Valve Opens (deg)	Fuel Pump Pressure (psi)	Compression Pressure (psi)	Idle Speed Manual Trans	Auto Trans	Clearance (in) Intake	Exhaust
'77	8–302	ARF42	.044	Electronic		②	②	20	5–6	①	②	②	Hyd.	Hyd.
'78	8–351M	ASF42	.042–.046	Electronic		6B	14B	—	6–8	①	650	500	Hyd.	Hyd.
	8–400	ASF42	.042–.046	Electronic		12B	12B	—	6–8	①	650	500	Hyd.	Hyd.
'79	8–351M	ASF42	.042–.046	Electronic		②	②	—	6–8	①	②	②	Hyd.	Hyd.
	8–400	ASF42	.042–.046	Electronic		②	②	—	6–8	①	②	②	Hyd.	Hyd.
'80–'82	6–300	BSF42	.042–.046	Electronic		②	②	—	6–8	①	②	②	Hyd.	Hyd.
	8–302	ASF42	.042–.046	Electronic		②	②	—	6–8	①	②	②	Hyd.	Hyd.
	8–351W	ASF42	.042–.046	Electronic		②	②	—	6–8	①	②	②	Hyd.	Hyd.
'83–'84	All	See Underhood Specification Sticker (See NOTE)												

NOTE: Specifications vary according to calibration, always use "Specs" on emissions decal.
①Lowest compression ratio should be within 75% of the highest
②See underhood specifications sticker Should the figures given on the underhood

specifications sticker disagree with those given above, use the sticker figures.

TUNE-UP SPECIFICATIONS
Vans

When analyzing compression test results, look for uniformity among cylinders, rather than specific pressures.

Year	Engine Displacement (Cu In.)	Spark Plugs Type	Gap (in.)	Distributor Point Dwell (deg)	Distributor Point Gap (in.)	Ignition Timing (deg) MT	Ignition Timing (deg) AT	Intake Valve Opens (deg)	Fuel Pump Pressure (psi)	Idle Speed (rpm) MT/AT●	Valve Clear (in.) In	Valve Clear (in.) Ex
'77	300	BSF-42	.044	Electronic		10B⑤	10B⑤	12B	4–6	600/600⑥	Hyd.	Hyd.
	351W	ASF-34④	.044	Electronic		8B⑦	8B⑦	16B	5–7	650/550⑧	Hyd.	Hyd.
	460	ASF-42	.044	Electronic		—	12B	8B	5–7	—/650	Hyd.	Hyd.
'78	300	BSF-42	.054⑨	Electronic		⑩	⑩	12B	4–6	⑩	Hyd.	Hyd.
	351W	ASF-42	.044	Electronic		—	⑩	16B	5–7	⑩	Hyd.	Hyd.
	460	ASF-42	.044	Electronic		—	⑩	8B	5–7	⑩	Hyd.	Hyd.
'79	300	BSF-42	.044	Electronic		⑩	⑩	12B	4–6	⑩	Hyd.	Hyd.
	302	ASF-42	.044	Electronic		⑩	⑩	16B	5–7	⑩	Hyd.	Hyd.
	351W	ASF-42	.044	Electronic		—	⑩	16B	5–7	⑩	Hyd.	Hyd.
	460	ASF-42	.044	Electronic		—	⑩	8B	5–7	⑩	Hyd.	Hyd.
'80–'84	See Underhood Specifications Sticker (See NOTE)											

NOTE: Specifications vary according to calibration, always use "Specs" on emission decal. Part numbers in this chart are not recommendations by Chilton for any product by brand name.

① Calif.: 6B
② E-100: ARF-42
③ Calif.: 12B
④ E-100: ASF-42
⑤ E-100: 6B
⑥ E-100: MT 700, AT 550

⑦ E-100 High Altitude: 12B
   E-100 Calif.: MT 8B, AT 14B
   All other E-100: see underhood sticker
⑧ E-100 High Altitude: 550
   E-100 Calif.: MT 900, AT 700
   E-100 49 states: MT 800, AT 650

⑨ Calif., and all E-100: .044
⑩ See underhood sticker
● AT in Drive; brake on

FIRING ORDER

NOTE: To avoid confusion, always replace spark plug wires one at a time.

122 (2.0L), 140 (2.3L) 4 cylinder

173 (2.8L) V6

232 (3.8L) V6

FIRING ORDERS

NOTE: To avoid confusion, always replace spark plug wires one at a time.

300 6-cylinder

255, 302, 460 V8

351M & 400 w/Frigidaire A/C only: timing pointer is viewed from left; all others viewed from right.

351W, 351M, 400 V8

CAPACITIES
Bronco & Bronco II

Year	Engine	Crankcase With Filter (qts)	Transmission (pts) Manual	Transmission (pts) Auto-matic ③	Transfer Case (pts)	Axle (pts) Front	Axle (pts) Rear	Gasoline Tank (gals) Main	Gasoline Tank (gals) Auxilliary	Cooling System (qts)
'77	8-302	6	3.5	22.0	2.75	3.5	9.0	14.0	7.50	16.0①
'78–'79	8-351M	6	7.0	26.4	4.0②	5.8	6.5③	25.0④	—	20.0⑤
	8-400	6	7.0	26.4	4.0②	5.8	6.5③	25.0④	—	22.0⑥
'80–'82	6-300	6	7.0⑩	26.8	6.5	4.0	6.5③	25.0④	—	13.0⑦
	8-302	6	7.0⑩	26.8	6.5	4.0	6.5③	25.0④	—	13.0⑧
	8-351W	6	7.0⑩	26.8	6.5	4.0	6.5③	25.0④	—	15.0⑨
'83–'84	6-173	5	⑬	15.8	3.0	1.0	5.5	17.0⑪	—	7.2⑫
	6-300	6	7.0⑩	26.8	7.0	4.0	6.5③	25.0④	—	13.0⑦
	8-302	6	7.0⑩	26.8	7.0	4.0	6.5③	25.0④	—	13.0⑧
	8-351	6	7.0⑩	26.8	7.0	4.0	6.5③	25.0④	—	15.0⑨

① With autotrans; 17.0 qts.
② Full-time unit; 9.0 pts.
③ With locking differential use Special Lubricant Ford ESW-MC119A or equivalent

④ Optional tank; 32 gal.
⑤ Heavy duty; 22.0 qts.
⑥ Heavy duty; 24.0 qts.
⑦ A/C or heavy duty; 14.0 qts.
⑧ Heavy duty; 14.0 qts.

⑨ Heavy duty or A/C; 16.0 qts.
⑩ 4 speed overdrive 4.5 pts.
⑪ Optional; 21.0 gal.
⑫ With A/C; 7.8 qts.
⑬ 4 Speed; 3 pts.　　5 Speed; 3.6 pts.

CAPACITIES
Vans

Year	Engine Displacement Cu In.	Engine Crankcase (qts)		Transmission (pts)			Drive Axle▲ (pts)	Gasoline Tank (gals)	Cooling System (qts)		
		With Filter	Without Filter	Manual 3-spd	4-spd	Automatic■			W/AC	W/O	W/Extra Cooling
'77	300	6.0	5.0	3.5	—	20.0	⑥	③	—	14.5	—
	351W	6.0	5.0	3.5	—	20.0②	⑥	③	20.0	17.0	20.0
	460	6.0	5.0	—	—	20.0②	⑥	③	28.0	28.0	—
'78	300	6.0	5.0	3.5	5.0	20.5	⑥	③	—	14.5	—
	351W	6.0	5.0	—	—	20.0②	⑥	③	20.0	17.0	20.0
	460	6.0	5.0	—	—	20.0②	⑥	③	28.0	28.0	—
'79–'84	300	6.0	5.0	3.5	5.0	20.0②	⑥	⑦	20.0	15.0	—
	302	6.0	5.0	3.5	5.0	20.0②	⑥	⑦	17.5	15.0⑧	17.5
	351W	6.0	5.0	—	—	23.5	⑥	⑦	20.0	20.0	21.0
	420 diesel	10.0	9.0	—	—	23.5	⑥	⑦	31.0⑨	31.0⑨	—
	460	6.0	5.0	—	—	23.5	⑥	⑦	28.0	28.0	—

① Ford axles: 5.0
　Dana axles: 6.0
② C-6: 24.5
③ E-100 van and club wagon with evaporative emission controls: 18.0
　E-150: 18.0
　All others: 22.1
　Optional auxiliary: 18.0

④ With auto trans.: 16.6
⑤ Ford axles: 6.5
　Dana axles: 6.0
⑥ Ford Axles: 6.5
　Dana model 61-1:5.0
　Dana model 70:5.5
⑦ E-100, 150 with 124 inch wheel base: 18.0
　All others: 22.1

　Optional auxiliary: 18.0 except E-350 cutaway
　chassis: 40.0
⑧ With auto trans.: 17.5
⑨ Includes 5 qts. in the reservoir bottle
▲For limited slip units, add 1 oz of limited slip additive
■ Includes torque converter

CRANKCASE AND COOLING SYSTEM (QTS) CAPACITIES
Pick-Up

Year	Engine and Model	Crankcase Oil and Filter Change	Cooling System					
			Standard System		Extra Cooling		With A/C	Super Cooling
			Man Trans	Auto Trans	Man Trans	Auto Trans		
'77	300 eng., F-100/150/250 4 × 2	6.0	12.5	14.5	14.5	14.5	—	—
	F-150/250 4 × 4	6.0	14.5	14.5	14.5	14.5	—	—
	F-350	6.0	14.5	14.5	14.5	14.5	—	—
	302 eng., F-100 4 × 2	6.0	15.5	17.5	15.5	17.5	17.5	—
	351 eng., F-100 4 × 2	6.0	19.5	22.0	19.5	19.5	22.0	24.0
	F-150/250 4 × 2	6.0	19.5	19.5	19.5	19.5	22.0	24.0
	F-150/250 4 × 4	6.0	22.0	22.0	22.0	22.0	22.0	24.0
	F-350	6.0	22.0	22.0	22.0	22.0	22.0	—
	400 eng., F-100/150/250/350	6.0	22.0	22.0	22.0	22.0	22.0	24.0
	460 eng., F-150/250/350	6.0	22.5	22.5	22.5	22.5	22.5	—

CRANKCASE AND COOLING SYSTEM (QTS) CAPACITIES
Pick-Up

| Year | Engine and Model | Crankcase Oil and Filter Change | Cooling System | | | | | |
| | | | Standard System | | Extra Cooling | | | |
			Man Trans	Auto Trans	Man Trans	Auto Trans	With A/C	Super Cooling
'78–'84	122(2.0L)	5.0	6.5	6.5	—	—	7.2	—
	140(2.3L)	6.0	6.5	6.5	—	—	7.2	—
	300 eng., F-100/250/350	7.0	13.0	14.0	13.0	14.0	17.0	—
	232, 255, 302 eng., F-100/150	6.0	15.0①	15.0①	15.0①	18.0①	18.0①	—
	351 eng., F-100/150/350	6.0	17.0	—	17.0	—	—	24.0
	400 eng., F/250/350	6.0	18.0	—	18.0	—	18.0	24.0
	420 diesel All	10.0	29.0	29.0	29.0	29.0	29.0	29.0
	460 eng., 150/250/350	6.0	24.0②	24.0②	24.0②	24.0②	24.0②	24.0②

SRW—Single rear wheels
DRW—Dual rear wheels
① 10 qts—1983 and later
② 18 qts—1983 and later

TRANSMISSION AND TRANSFER CASE CAPACITIES
Pick-up

Year	Model	Type	Capacity (pints)
'77–'78	F-100/150/250	Ford 3.03, 3-sp	3.5
	F-100/150/250 4 × 2 F-250 4 × 4 F-350	Warner T-18 4-sp	6.5
	F-100/150/250/350	New process 435, 4-sp with extension without extension	7.0 6.5
	F-100/150/250	C-4 w/300 cid eng w/302 cid eng	20.0 17.5
	F-100/150/250/350	C-6 4 × 2 4 × 4	24.5 27.5
	F-150/250 4 × 4	New Process 205, 2-sp Transfer Case	4.0
	F-150/250 4 × 4	New Process 203 Full Time Transfer Case	9.0

TRANSMISSION AND TRANSFER CASE CAPACITIES
Pick-up

Year	Model	Type	Capacity (pints)
'79–'84	F-100/250	Ford 3.03, 3-sp	3.5
	F-150/250/350	Warner T-18 4-sp	7.0
	F-100/150/250/350	New Process 435 4-sp with extension without extension	7.0 6.5
	All F Series	Clark 4-sp Overdrive	5.0
	F-100/150 F-150/350	C-4 Automatic	20.0
	F-250 4 × 4	C-6 Automatic 351, 400, 460 engs. All others	26.75 23.5
	F-150/250 4 × 4	New Process, 205, 2-sp Transfer Case	4.5
	F-150/250/350 4 × 4	New Process, 203 Full Time Transfer Case	9.0
	F-150/250 F-250/350	New Process, 208 Transfer Case Borg Warner, 1345 Transfer Case	6.0 6.0
	F-100/150 F-250/350	C-5 Automatic	22.0
	All Models, exc Ranger	Automatic Overdrive (AOD)	24.0
	Ranger	4 and 5 speed C-3 C-5 (4 × 2) C-5 (4 × 4)	3.0 15.4 15.0 15.6
	Ranger	Warner 1350	3.0

DRIVE AXLES CAPACITIES
Pick-up

Year	Model	Type	Capacity (pints)
'77–'78	F-100/150	Ford 3300, 3750	6.5
	F-250	Dana 60, 61	6.0
	F-250	Dana 61-2	5.0
	F-350	Dana-70	6.0
	F-150	Dana 44-7F Front axle	4.75
	F-250	Dana 44-6CF HD Front axle	4.0
	F-250	Dana 60F Front axle	5.5

FORD

DRIVE AXLES CAPACITIES
Pick-up

Year	Model	Type	Capacity (pints)
'79–'84	F-100/150	Ford	6.0
	F-250, 4×2, F-250/350 4×4	Dana 60-2	7.0
	F-250	Dana 61-2	6.0
	F-350	Dana 70	7.0
	F-150/250 4×4	Dana 44-9F Front axle	3.5*
	F-250/350 4×4	Dana 60-7F Front axle	6.0
	F-250/350 4×4 HD	Dana 50-IFS	4.1
	F-250/350 SRW	Dana 61-1 (Rear)	6.0
	F-350 DRW	Dana 70 HD (Rear)	7.4
	F-250 4×2 F-250 4×4	Dana 44 IFS (Front Axle)	3.8
	Ranger 4×4	Dana 28 (Front Axle) 6-¾ RG (Rear Axle) 7.5 RG (Rear Axle)	1.0 3.0 4.0

*4.0—with New Process 205 2-sp Transfer Case   SEW-Single Rear Wheels   DRW-Dual Rear Wheels

FUEL TANK CAPACITIES
Pick-up

Year	Model	Standard	Optional
'77–'78	F-100	19.2	20.2 frame mount
	F-150 4×2, 4×4, F-250 4×2	19.2 exc. Calif. 20.2 Calif.	22.5 frame mount 19.3 in-cab 17.5 in-cab
	F-250 4×4 and Crew Cab	22.5 exc. Calif. 20.2 Calif.	—
	F-350	20.2	21.0 Aft./Axle
	All Supercab	19.5 frame mount	—
'79–'82	F-100/250/350 4×2 (Reg Cab)	19.2	20.2
	F-250 4×4 (Reg Cab)	19.2	—
	F-250/350 4×2, (Crew Cab)	20.2	—
	Super Cab	19.2	19.5
	F-350 4×2 (Reg Cab)	20.2	19.0
	F-250/350 4×4, (Reg Cab)	26.0	19.2

FUEL TANK CAPACITIES
Pick-up

Year	Model	Standard	Optional
'83–'84	F-100 4 × 2 (Reg Cab)	16.5	19.0 Aft./Axle
	F-150 4 × 2 (Crew Cab)	16.5	19.0 Aft./Axle
	F-150 4 × 4 (Reg Cab)	16.5	19.0 Aft./Axle
	F-250 4 × 2 (Crew Cab)	16.5	19.0 Aft./Axle
	F-150 4 × 2 (Reg Cab)	19.0	19.0 Aft./Axle
	F-150 4 × 4 (Reg Cab)	19.0	19.0 Aft./Axle
	F-150 4 × 2 (Crew Cab)	19.0	19.0 Aft./Axle
	F-150 4 × 4 (Crew Cab)	19.0	19.0 Aft./Axle
	F-250 4 × 2 (Reg Cab)	19.0	19.0 Aft./Axle
	F-250 4 × 2 (Crew Cab)	19.0	19.0 Aft./Axle
	F-250 4 × 4 (All)	19.0	19.0 Aft./Axle
	F-350 4 × 2 (Reg Cab)	19.0	19.0 Aft./Axle
	F-350 4 × 2 (Super Cab)	19.0	19.0 Aft./Axle
	F-350 4 × 2 (Cab Chassis)	19.0①	19.0① Aft./Axle
	Ranger 15.2 (SWB) 17.0 (LWB)	—	13.0 Aft./Axle

Aft./Axle—After Rear Axle

VALVE SPECIFICATIONS

Year	Engine Displacement Cu In.	Seat Angle (deg)	Face Angle (deg)	Spring Test Pressure (lbs @ in.)	Spring Installed Height (in.)	Steam to Guide Clearance (in.)		Stem Diameter (in.)	
						Intake	Exhaust	Intake	Exhaust
'83–'84	4-122 (2.0L)	45	44	⑪	1.49–1.55	.0010–.0032	.0015–.0032	.3416–.3423	.3411–.3418
'83–84	4-134 (2.2L)	I:45 E:30	I:45 E:30	⑬	O:1.587 I:1.488	.0015–.0046	.002–.0051	.3150	.3150
'83–'84	4-140 (2.3L)	45	44	⑫	1.53–1.59	.0010–.0027	.0015–.0032	.3416–.3423	.3411–.3418
'83–'84	6-173 (2.8L)	45	44	152 @ 1.22	1.59	.0008–.0025	.0008–.0035	.3159–.3167	.3149–.3156
'82–'84	6-232	45	44	202 @ 1.28 ⑭	1.70	.0010–.0025	.0015–.0032	.3422	.3415
'77–'84	6-300	45	44	①	②	.0010–.0027	.0010–.0027	.3420	.3420
'82	8-255	45	46	③	④	.0010–.0027	.0010–.0027	.3420	.3415
'77–'78	8-302	45	44	200 @ 1.31 ⑤	1.70	.0010–.0027	.0015–.0032	.3420	.3415
'79–'84	8-302	45	44	⑥	④	.0010–.0027	.0015–.0032	.3420	.3415
'77–'80	8-351M	45	44	226 @ 1.39	1.81	.0010–.0027	.0015–.0032	.3420	.3415

VALVE SPECIFICATIONS

Year	Engine Displacement Cu In.	Seat Angle (deg)	Face Angle (deg)	Spring Test Pressure (lbs @ in.)	Spring Installed Height (in.)	Steam to Guide Clearance (in.)		Stem Diameter (in.)	
						Intake	Exhaust	Intake	Exhaust
'77–'84	8-351W	45	44	⑦	1.80	.0010–.0027	.0015–.0032	.3420	.3415⑧
'77–'82	8-400	45	44	229 @ 1.39⑨	1.82	.0010–.0027	.0015–.0032	.3420	.3415⑩
'83–'84	8-420	⑮	⑮	60 @ 1.798	2.040	.0012–.0029	.0012–.0029	.3716–.3723	.3716–.3723
'77–'84	8-460	45	44	229 @ 1.33	1.82	.0010–.0027	.0010–.0027	.3420	.3420

① 1977–81 intake: 190 @ 1.30
  1982–84 intake: 197 @ 1.30
  All exhaust: 192 @ 1.18
② All intake: 1.70
  1977–81 exhaust: 1.69
  1982–84 exhaust: 1.58
③ Intake: 204 @ 1.36
  Exhaust: 200 @ 1.20

④ Intake: 1.78
  Exhaust: 1.60
⑤ 1977 exhaust: 1.20
⑥ Intake: 202 @ 1.36
  Exhaust: 200 @ 1.20
⑦ Intake: 200 @ 1.36
  Exhaust: 200 @ 1.20
⑧ 1982–84: .3420
⑨ 1982: 226 @ 1.39
⑩ 1982: .3420

⑪ Intake: 71–79 @ 1.52
  Exhaust: 142–156 @ 1.12
⑫ Intake: 71–79 @ 1.56
  Exhaust: 159–175 @ 1.16
⑬ Outer: 32 @ 1.587
  Inner: 22.7 @ 1.488
⑭ '83–'84: 152 @ 1.22
⑮ Intake: 30°
  Exhaust: 37.5°

CRANKSHAFT AND CONNECTING ROD SPECIFICATIONS

Year	Engine No. Cyl Displacement (cu in.)	Crankshaft				Connecting Rod		
		Main Brg Jounal Dia	Main Brg Oil Clearance	Shaft End-Play	Thrust on No.	Journal Diameter	Oil Clearance	Side Clearance
'83–'84	4-122	2.3982	.0008–.0015	.004–.008	3	2.0472	.0008–.0015	.0035–.0105
'83–'84	4-134	2.5591	.0016–.0036	.0055–.0154	3	2.0866	.0014–.0030	.0094–.0134
'83–'84	4-140	2.3982	.0008–.0015	.004–.008	3	2.0472	.0008–.0015	.0035–.0105
'83–'84	6-173	2.2441	.0008–.0015	.012	3	2.1260	.0006–.0016	.004–.011
'82–'84	6-232	2.5190	.0009–.0027	.004–.008	3	2.3107	.0009–.0027	.004–.011
'77–'84	6-300	2.3986	.0008–.0015	.004–.008	5	2.1230	.0008–.0015	.0060–.0130
'82	8-255	2.2490	.0005–.0024③	.004–.008	3	2.1232	.0008–.0025	.010–.020
'77	8-302	2.2486	.0005–.0024②	.004–.008	3	2.1232	.0008–.0026	.010–.020
'78–'84	8-302	2.2486	.0005–.0015①	.004–.008	3	2.1232	.0008–.0026	.010–.020
'77–'80	8-351M	2.9998	.0008–.0015	.004–.008	3	2.3107	.0008–.0015	.010–.020
'77–'84	8-351W	2.9998	.0008–.0015	.004–.008	3	2.3107	.0008–.0015	.010–.020
'77–'82	8-400	2.9998	.0008–.0015	.004–.008	3	2.3107	.0008–.0015	.010–.020
'83–'84	8-420	3.1228–3.1236	.0018–.0036	.0010–.0090	3	2.4980–2.4990	.0011–.0026	.0080–.0200
'77–'84	8-460	2.9998	.0008–.0015	.004–.008	3	2.4995	.0008–.0015	.010–.020

① # 1: .0001–.0015
② # 1: .0001–.0015
③ # 1: .0001–.0020

PISTON AND RING SPECIFICATIONS
All measurements given in inches

Year	Engine	Piston to Bore Clearance	Ring Side Clearance			Ring Gap		
			Top Compression	Bottom Compression	Oil Control	Top Compression	Bottom Compression	Oil Control③
'83–'84	4-122	.0014–.0022	.0020–.0040	.0020–.0040	snug	.0100–.0200	.0100–.0200	.015–.055
'83–'84	4-134	.0021–.0031	.0020–.0035	.0016–.0031	.0012–.0028	.0157–.0217	.0118–.0157	.0138–.0217
'83–'84	4-140	.0014–.0022	.0020–.0040	.0020–.0040	snug	.0100–.0200	.0100–.0200	.015–.055
'83–'84	6-173	.0011–.0019	.0020–.0033	.0020–.0033	snug	.0150–.0230	.0150–.0230	.015–.055
'82–'84	6-232	.0014–.0022	.0020–.0040	.0020–.0040	snug	.0100–.0200	.0100–.0200	.015–.055
'77	6-300	.0014–.0022	.0019–.0036	.0020–.0040	snug	.0100–.0200	.0100–.0200	.010–.035
'78	6-300	.0002–.0004①	.0019–.0036	.0020–.0040	snug	.0100–.0200	.0100–.0200	.015–.055
'79–'84	6-300	.0014–.0022	.0019–.0036	.0020–.0040	snug	.0100–.0200	.0100–.0200	.010–.035
'82	8-255	.0014–.0024	.0020–.0040	.0020–.0040	snug	.0100–.0200	.0100–.0200	.015–.055
'75–'77	8-302	.0018–.0026	.0020–.0040	.0020–.0040	snug	.010–.020	.0100–.0200	.015–.055
'78–'84	8-302	.0018–.0026	.0020–.0040	.0020–.0040	snug	.010–.020	.0100–.0200	.015–.035
'77–'80	8-351M	.0014–.0022	.0019–.0036	.0020–.0040	snug	.010–.020	.0100–.0200	.010–.035
'77–'84	8-351W	.0022–.0030	.0019–.0036	.0020–.0040	snug	.010–.020	.0100–.0200	.015–.035②
'77–'82	8-400	.0014–.0022	.0019–.0036	.0020–.0040	snug	.0100–.0200	.0100–.0200	.015–.035
'77	8-460	.0014–.0022	.0025–.0045	.0025–.0045	snug	.0100–.0200	.0100–.0200	.010–.030
'78	8-460	.0022–.0030	.0025–.0045	.0025–.0045	snug	.0100–.0200	.0100–.0200	.010–.030
'79–'84	8-460	.0022–.0300	.0019–.0036	.0020–.0040	snug	.0100–.0200	.0100–.0200	.010–.035
'83–'84	8-420	.0055–.0075	.0020–.0040	.0020–.0040	.0010–.0030	.0140–.0240	.0100–.0240	.0600–.0700

① over 6,000 lb GVW: .0003–.0005
② 1978: .015–.055
③ Steel rails

TORQUE SPECIFICATIONS
(All readings in ft. lbs.)

Year	Engine	Cylinder Head Bolts	Rod Bearing Bolts	Main Bearing Bolts	Crank-shaft Pulley Bolt	Flywheel-to-Crankshaft Bolts	Manifold	
							Intake	Exhaust
'83–'84	4-122	⑩	⑪	⑫	100–120	56–64	14–21⑭	16–23⑭
'83–'84	4-134	80–85	50–54	80–85	253–289	95–137	12–17⑭	17–20⑭
'83–'84	4-140	⑩	⑪	⑫	100–120	56–64	14–21⑭	16–23⑭
'83–'84	6-173	⑬	19–24	65–75	85–96	47–52	15–18⑭	20–30⑭
'82–'84	6-232	⑮	30–36	62–81	85–100	75–85	18	15–22
'77–'84	6-300	70–75	40–45	60–70	130–150	75–85	22–32	28–33
'82	8-255	65–72	19–24	60–70	70–90	75–85	18–20	18–24
'77–'84	8-302	65–70	19–24	60–70	70–90①	75–85	②	12–16③
'77–'80	8-351M	95–105	40–45	④	70–90	75–85	⑤	18–24
'77–'84	8-351W	105–112	40–45	95–105	70–90	75–85	23–25	18–24
'77	8-400	95–105	40–45	35–45	70–90	75–85	⑤	18–24
'78–'80	8-400	95–105	40–45	95–105	70–90	75–85	⑤	18–24

TORQUE SPECIFICATIONS
(All readings in ft. lbs.)

Year	Engine	Cylinder Head Bolts	Rod Bearing Bolts	Main Bearing Bolts	Crank-shaft Pulley Bolt	Flywheel-to-Crankshaft Bolts	Manifold Intake	Manifold Exhaust
'83–'84	420 (diesel)	⑥	46–51 ⑦	95 ⑧	90	44–50 ⑨	24	30
'75–'84	8-460	130–140	40–45	95–105	70–90	75–85	25–30	28–33

① '77: 35–50
② '77: 19–27
   '78–'84: 23–25
③ '80–'84: 18–24
④ '77: 35–45
   '78–'80: 95–105
⑤ ³⁄₈": 22–32
   ⁵⁄₁₆": 17–25
⑥ First pull 40 ft. lbs., Second pull 65 ft. lbs., Final 75 ft. lbs.

⑦ First tighten to 38 ft. lbs. then to 46–51 ft. lbs.
⑧ First tighten to 75 ft. lbs. then to 95 ft. lbs.
⑨ Apply thread locking Sealant before installation
⑩ Torque bolts in two steps: Step 1-50–60 ft. lbs: Step 2-80–90 ft. lbs.
⑪ Torque nuts in two steps: Step 1-25–30 ft. lbs: Step 2-30–36 ft. lbs.

⑫ Torque bolts in two steps: Step 1-50–60 ft. lbs. Step 2-80–90 ft. lbs.
⑬ Torque bolts in 3 steps: Step 1-29–40 ft. lbs. Step 2-40–51 ft. lbs. Step 3-70–85 ft. lbs.
⑭ Torque in stages, recheck after engine is warmed.
⑮ Tighten in four steps; Step 1-47 ft. lbs; Step 2-55 ft. lbs: Step 3-63 ft. lbs: Step 4-74 ft. lbs. Back off all bolts 2-3 turns and retorque in four steps.

ALTERNATOR SPECIFICATIONS

Year	Color Code	Output Amps	Output Watts	Field Current Amps	Cut-In rpm	Brush Length Inches New	Brush Length Inches Limit
'77–'81	Orange	40	600	2.9	400	½	⁵⁄₁₆
	Green	60	900	2.9	400	½	⁵⁄₁₆
	Green ①	60	900	4.0	400	½	³⁄₁₆
'82–84'	Orange	40	600	2.9	900	½	⁵⁄₁₆
	Green	60	900	6.0	1025	½	⁵⁄₁₆
	Black	70	1050	6.0	780	½	¼
	Red	100	1500	6.0	930	½	¼

① Blue ink on pulley face

BATTERY AND STARTER SPECIFICATIONS

Year	Engine	Battery Ampere/Hour Capacity	Battery Volts	Battery Ground	Starter Lock Test Amps	Starter Lock Test Volts	Starter Lock Test Torque (ft lbs)	Starter No Load Test Amps	Starter No Load Test Volts	Starter No Load Test rpm	Brush Spring Tension (oz)
'77	All	45	12	Neg	670	5	15.5	70	12	9500	40
		55	12	Neg	670	5	15.5	70	12	9500	40
		70	12	Neg	670	5	15.5	70	12	9500	40
		80	12	Neg	670	5	15.5	70	12	9500	40
'78	All	41	12	Neg	460	5	9.0	70	12	9500	40
		68	12	Neg	670	5	15.5	80	12	9500	80
					525 ①	5	17.2	80	11	10,000	50

BATTERY AND STARTER SPECIFICATIONS

| | | Battery | | | Starter | | | | | | Brush Spring Tension (oz) |
| | | | | | Lock Test | | | No Load Test | | | |
Year	Engine	Ampere/ Hour Capacity	Volts	Ground	Amps	Volts	Torque (ft lbs)	Amps	Volts	rpm	
'79	All	41	12	Neg	460	5	9.0	70	12	9500	40
		53	12	Neg	670	5	15.5	80	12	9500	80
		68	12	Neg							
'80–'84	All	36	12	Neg	460	5	9.0	70	12	9500	40
		45	12	Neg	670	5	15.5	80	12	9500	80
		63	12	Neg							
		81	12	Neg							

① Prestolite model with 400 cid engine

BRAKE SPECIFICATIONS
Pickups and Vans

Year	Model	Master Cylinder Bore	Caliper Bore	Wheel Cylinder Bore Front	Wheel Cylinder Bore Rear	Rotor Diameter	Rotor Minimum Thickness	Rotor Maximum Run-out	Brake Drum Diameter Front	Brake Drum Diameter Rear	Machined Oversize Front	Machined Oversize Rear
'77	F&E-100, 150	1.00	2.875	—	.9375	11.54	1.180	.003	—	11.03	—	11.09
	F&E-250	1.062	2.180	—	1.000	12.50	1.120	.003	—	12.0	—	12.06
	F&E-350	1.062	2.180	—	1.062	12.50	1.120	.003	—	12.0	—	12.06
'78	F&E-100, 150	1.00	2.875	—	.9375	11.54	1.180	.003	—	11.03	—	11.09
	F&E-250	1.062	2.180	—	1.000	12.50	1.120	.003	—	12.0	—	12.06
	F&E-350	1.062	2.180	—	1.062	12.50	1.120	.003	—	12.0	—	12.06
'79–'80	F&E-100, 150	1.00	2.875	—	.9375	11.54	1.180	.003	—	11.03	—	11.09
	F&E-250	1.062	2.180	—	1.000	12.50	1.120	.003	—	12.0	—	12.06
	F&E-350	1.062	2.180	—	1.062	12.50	1.120	.003	—	12.0	—	12.06
'81	F-100①	1.00	2.599	—	.9375	10.97	1.120⑧	.003	—	10.0	—	10.09
'82–84	Ranger 4×2	.9375	2.597	—	.750	10.28	.81	.002	—	9.0	—	9.06
	Ranger 4×4	.9375	2.597	—	.750	10.86	.81	.002	—	9.0	—	9.06
	F-100②, F-150 4×2, E-100, E-150③	1.00④	2.875	—	.9375	11.65	1.120	.003	—	11.03	—	11.09
	F-150 4×4, E-150⑤	1.00④	2.875	—	.9375	11.65	1.120	.003	—	11.03	—	11.09
	F-250 4×2⑥	1.00	2.875	—	.9375	12.59	1.120	.003	—	12.0	—	12.06
	F-250 Super cab, F-200⑦ 4×2, E-250, E-350	1.062	2.180	—	1.062⑨	12.56	1.180	.003	—	12.0	—	12.06
	F-350 4×4, F-350 4×4	1.062	2.180	—	1.062⑨	12.48	1.180	.003	—	12.0	—	12.06

① w/std payload package
② exc. std payload package
③ w/GVWR under 6350 lb.
④ E-150: 1.062
⑤ w/GVWR over 6350 lb.
⑥ Regular cab w/payload under 8500 lb.
⑦ Regular cab w/payload over 8500 lb.
⑧ 1982: .810 or LD models
⑨ '83–'84 1.00

BRAKE SPECIFICATIONS
Bronco and Bronco II
(All measurements in inches)

Year	Master Cylinder Bore	Caliper Bore	Wheel Cylinder Bore		Rotor Diameter	Rotor Minimum Thickness	Rotor Maximum Run-out	Brake Drum Diameter		Machined Oversize	
			Front	Rear				Front	Rear	Front	Rear
'77	1.00	2.875	—	.9375	11.54	1.180	.003	—	11.03	—	11.09
'78–'81	1.00	2.875	—	.9375	11.72	1.120	.003	—	11.03	—	11.09
'82–'84	1.00	2.875	—	.9375	11.65	1.120	.003	—	11.03	—	11.09
'83–'84 Bronco II (4 × 2)	.9375	2.597	—	.750	10.28	.81	.002	—	9.0	—	9.06
Bronco II (4 × 4)	.9375	2.597	—	.750	10.86	.81	.002	—	9.0	—	9.06

TUNE UP

Electronic Ignition

Ford truck engines are equipped with one of the following systems; Dura Spark II, Dura Spark III or Thick Film Integrated (TFI) Universal Distributor (Hall Effect) which is controlled by the EEC IV (electronic engine control) system.

NOTE: Procedures for diagnosis and repair of the ignition system are found in the Electrical Chapter of the Unit Repair Section.

On Dura Spark distributors, the contact breaker points and condenser in the distributor are replaced by a permanent magnet low-voltage generator. The generator consists of an armature with four, six or eight teeth mounted on the top of the distributor shaft, and a permanent magnet inside a small coil. The coil is riveted in place to provide a preset air gap with the armature. The distributor base, cap, rotor and vacuum and centrifugal spark advance are about the same as the conventional system.

The distributor is wired to a solid state module in the engine compartment. Inside the module is an electronic circuit board which consists of inner connecting resistors, capacitors, transistors and diodes. The module senses a signal from the magnetic generator to perform the switching function of conventional points and it senses and controls dwell.

Unless a malfunction occurs, or the distributor is moved or replaced, the initial ignition timing remains constant. Because the low voltage coil in the distributor is riveted in position, gap adjustment is not possible.

The 2.0L and 2.3L engines, found in light trucks, are equipped with Dura Spark II. However, depending on engine calibration, the Dura Spark II system may use a standard module or a "Universal Ignition Module". The Universal Ignition Module

(UIM) is capable of providing spark timing retard in response to barometric or engine sensors, or MCU signal.

Light trucks equipped with the 2.8L V6 engine use a universal distributor design which incorporates an integrally mounted TFI-IV module. The distributor uses a "Hall Effect" vane switch stator assembly and has provision for fixed octane adjustment. A new cap, adapter and rotor are designed for use on the Universal Distributor. The Thick Film Integrated (TFI) module is contained in moulded thermo-plastic and is mounted on the distributor base. The TFI-IV features a "push start" mode which allows push starting of the vehicle, if necessary. The TFI-IV system uses an "E-Core" ignition coil, which replaces the oil-filled coil found on other systems.

Either the Dura Spark II, or Dura Spark III system is used on other truck models. The system used depends on engine calibration and truck size.

EEC BI-LEVEL ROTOR & DISTRIBUTOR CAP

Conventional distributors are restricted to approximately 20 degrees of centrifugal distributor advance. In order to permit a flexibility in choosing engine calibrations, based totally on engine need, the EEC system was designed to allow up to 50 degrees distributor advance.

The distributor rotor and cap electrodes have been re-designed to handle the additional spark advance capability. The technique involves using two separate levels of secondary voltage distribution. Both the rotor and cap have an upper and lower electrode levels.

As the rotor turns, one of the high voltage electrode pick-up arms is aligned with one arm of the distributor cap center electrode plate, allowing high voltage to be transmitted from the plate through the rotor, distributor cap, and plug wire to the appropriate spark plug.

The numbers in the top of the distributor

cap are spark plug wire/cylinder identification numbers only.

— CAUTION —
The engine firing order cannot be read off the top of the distributor cap.

In a conventional distributor, the firing order follows the circular path of the rotor. In an EEC distributor, however, the upper and lower level electrodes fire alternately in a pattern that jumps from one side of the cap to the other.

NOTE: Refer to Distributor Removal and Installation for rotor alignment instructions.

Ignition Timing

Ignition timing is the measurement, in degrees of crankshaft rotation, of the point at which the spark plugs fire in each of the cylinders. It is measured in degrees before or after Top Dead Center (TDC) of the compression stroke. Ignition timing is controlled by turning the distributor body in the engine.

Ideally, the air/fuel mixture in the cylinder will be ignited by the spark plug just as the piston passes TDC of the compression stroke. If this happens, the piston will

Typical timing marks: left, block mounted; right, pulley mounted

be beginning the power stroke just as the compressed and ignited air/fuel mixture starts to expand. The expansion of the air/fuel mixture then forces the piston down on the power stroke and turns the crankshaft.

Because it takes a fraction of a second for the spark plug to ignite the mixture in the cylinder, the spark plug must fire a little before the piston reaches TDC. Otherwise, the mixture will not be completely ignited as the piston passes TDC and the full power of the explosion will not be used by the engine.

The timing measurement is given in degrees of crankshaft rotation before the piston reaches TDC (BTDC). If the setting for the ignition timing is 5° BTDC, each spark plug must fire 5° before each piston reaches TDC. This only holds true, however, when the engine is at idle speed.

As the engine speed increases, the pistons go faster. The spark plugs have to ignite the fuel even sooner if it is to be completely ignited when the piston reaches TDC. To do this, the distributor has a means to advance the timing of the spark as the engine speed increases. This is accomplished by centrifugal weights within the distributor and a vacuum diaphragm mounted on the side of the distributor. It is usually necessary to disconnect the vacuum lines from the diaphragm when the ignition timing is being set, however this is not true in all cases. Always refer to the emission decal in the engine compartment to determine if the lines should be disconnected and plugged.

If the ignition is set too far advanced (BTDC), the ignition and expansion of the fuel in the cylinder will occur too soon and tend to force the piston down while it is still traveling up. This causes engine ping. If the ignition spark is set too far retarded after TDC (ATDC), the piston will have already passed TDC and started on its way down when the fuel is ignited. This will cause the piston to be forced down for only a portion of its travel. This will result in poor engine performance and lack of power.

The timing is best checked with an inductive type timing light. This device is connected in series with the No. 1 spark plug. The current that fires the spark plug also causes the timing light to flash.

Timing marks are located at the front of the engine and consist of a pointer or scale on the timing case or belt cover and reference mark or marks on the crankshaft pulley. A scale of degrees is either on the pointer plate or pulley, depending on year, model and engine. When the engine is running, and curb idle adjusted, the timing light is aimed at the mark on the crankshaft pulley and the scale.

TACHOMETER HOOKUP

Models equipped with a "conventional" type coil have an adapter on the top of the coil that provides a clip marked "Tach Test". On models (TFI) equipped with an "E"

Attaching a tachometer lead to the coil connector

type coil, the tach connection is made at the back of the wire harness connector. A cut-out is provided and the tachometer lead wire alligator clip can be connected to the dark green/yellow dotted wire of the electrical harness plug.

ADJUSTMENT

NOTE: On models equipped with EEC III, all ignition timing is controlled by the EEC III module. Initial ignition timing is not adjustable and no attempt at adjustment should be made. For a description of EEC systems, refer to the Unit Repair sections on "Electronic Ignition Systems" and on "Emission Controls."

NOTE: Models equipped with TFI-IV ignition system require special procedures, refer to next paragraph for instructions then follow steps below.

1. Locate the timing marks on the crankshaft pulley and the front of the engine or at the "window" in the flywheel housing.
2. Clean the timing marks so that you can see them.
3. Mark the timing marks with a piece of chalk or with paint. Color the mark on the scale that will indicate the correct timing when it is aligned with the mark on the pulley or the pointer. It is also helpful to mark the notch in the pulley or the tip of the pointer with a small dab of color.
4. Attach a tachometer to the engine. (See tachometer hook-up instructions).
5. Attach a timing light according to the manufacturer's instructions. If the timing light has three wires, one is attached to the No. 1 spark plug with an adapter. The other wires are connected to the battery. The red wire goes to the positive side of the battery and the black wire is connected to the negative terminal of the battery.

NOTE: Refer to emissions decal in the engine compartment to determine if the vacuum line(s) should be disconnected.

6. Disconnect the vacuum line to the distributor at the distributor and plug the vacuum line. A golf tee does a fine job.
7. Check to make sure that all of the

wires clear the fan and then start the engine.
8. Adjust the idle to the correct setting.
9. Aim the timing light at the timing marks. If the marks that you put on the flywheel or pulley and the engine are aligned when the light flashes, the timing is correct. Turn off the engine and remove the tachometer and the timing light. If the marks are not in alignment, proceed with the following steps.
10. Turn off the engine.
11. Loosen the distributor lockbolt just enough so that the distributor can be turned with a little effort.
12. Start the engine. Keep the wires of the timing light clear of the fan.
13. With the timing light aimed at the pulley and the marks on the engine, turn the distributor in the direction of rotor rotation to retard the spark, and in the opposite direction of rotor rotation to advance the spark. Align the marks on the pulley and the engine with the flashes of the timing light.
14. When the marks are aligned, tighten the distributor lockbolt and recheck the timing with the timing light to make sure that the distributor did not move when you tightened the lockbolt.
15. Turn off the engine and remove the timing light.

MODELS EQUIPPED WITH EEC-IV AND TFI

The connection between the EEC-IV microprocessor and the Thick Film Integrated (TFI) ignition module is called the SPOUT circuit. SPOUT simply means "spark out" since a signal carried to the TFI shuts off the coil and produces a spark for firing the spark plugs. A description of the system operation to control spark and advance follows:

1. The TFI-IV module sends a voltage signal to the PIP (Profile Ignition Pickup) sensor, part of the Hall Effect assembly inside the distributor.
2. The PIP sensor then provides crankshaft position information and sends this signal back to the TFI module.
3. The TFI module sends the information to the EEC-IV module and the required spark timing need is calculated.
4. The required timing information goes back to the TFI module through electrical circuitry (the SPOUT) and the coil turns off the primary circuit to fire the spark plugs at the precise time.
5. The TFI module also determines dwell and limits primary circuit to a safe value. If there is an open in the SPOUT signal wire, the TFI module will use the PIP sensor to provide spark; but the engine will only run at basic timing setting.
6. To set basic timing the SPOUT wire must be disconnected. An inline connector is provided on the "yellow with green dot" SPOUT wire. The wire is located between the distributor and engine harness.

With the wire disconnected the TFI module is locked into no advance and basic timing may be checked and adjusted if necessary. See proceeding paragraph.

Idle Mixture Adjustment

CARBURETORS

NOTE: For this procedure, Ford recommends a propane enrichment procedure. This requires special equipment not available to the general public. In lieu of this equipment the following procedure may be followed to obtain a satisfactory idle mixture.

1. Block the wheels, set the parking brake and run the engine to bring it to normal operating temperature.
2. Disconnect the hose between the emission canister and the air cleaner.
3. On engines equipped with the Thermactor air injection system, the routing of the vacuum lines connected to the dump valve will have to be temporarily changed. Mark them for reconnection before switching them.
4. For valves with one or two vacuum lines at the side, disconnect and plug the lines.
5. For valves with one vacuum line at the top, check the line to see if it is connected to the intake manifold or an intake manifold source such as the carburetor or distributor vacuum line. If not, remove and plug the line at the dump valve and connect a temporary length of vacuum hose from the dump valve fitting to a source of intake manifold vacuum.
6. Remove the limiter caps from the mixture screws by CAREFULLY cutting them with a sharp knife.
7. Place the transmission in neutral and run the engine at 2500 rpm for 15 seconds.
8. Place the automatic transmission in Drive; the manual in neutral.
9. Adjust the idle speed to the higher of the two figures given on the underhood sticker.
10. Turn the idle mixture screw(s) to obtain the highest possible rpm, leaving the screw(s) in the leanest position that will maintain this rpm.
11. Repeat steps 7 thru 10 until further adjustment of the mixture screw(s) does not increase the rpm.
12. Turn the screw(s) in until the lower of the two idle speed figures is reached. Turn the screw(s) in ¼ turn increments each to insure a balance.
13. Turn the engine off and remove the tachometer. Reinstall all equipment.

NOTE: Rough idle, that cannot be corrected by normal service procedures may be caused by leakage between the EGR valve body and diaphragm. To determine if this is the cause:

Some 1980 and later models have 2-piece metal plugs in place of the plastic limiter caps on the idle mixture adjusting screws. These caps should be carefully removed before attempting any adjustments.

1. Tighten the EGR bolts to 15 ft. lbs. Connect a vacuum gauge to the intake manifold.
2. Lift to exert a sideways pressure on the diaphragm housing. If the idle changes or the reading on the vacuum gauge varies, replace the EGR valve.

Motorcraft 2150 carburetor with solenoid

Motocraft 7200VV carburetor

Idle Speed Adjustment

CARBURETORS

Through 1982

1. Remove the air cleaner and disconnect and plug the vacuum lines.

2. Block the wheels, apply the parking brake, turn off all accessories, start the engine and run it to normalize underhood temperatures.

3. Check that the choke plate is fully open and connect a tachometer according to the manufacturer's instructions.

4. Check the throttle stop positioner (TSP)-off speed as follows:

a. Collapse the plunger by forcing the throttle lever against it.

b. Place the transmission in neutral and check the engine speed. If necessary, adjust to specified TSP-Off speed with the throttle adjusting screw. See the underhood sticker.

5. Place the manual transmission in neutral; the automatic in Drive and make certain the TSP plunger is extended.

6. Turn the TSP until the specified idle speed is obtained.

7. Install the air cleaner and connect the vacuum lines. Check the idle speed. Adjust, if necessary, with the air cleaner on.

Throttle solenoid (TSP) adjustment-typical

1983 and Later
122 (2.0L) AND 140 (2.3L)
YFA-IV & YFA IV-FB (FEEDBACK)

1. Block the wheels and apply parking brake. Place the transmission in Neutral or Park.

2. Bring engine to normal operating temperature.

3. Place A/C selector in the Off position.

4. Place transmission in specified position as refered to on emissions decal.

5. Check/adjust curb idle RPM. If adjustment is required, turn the hex head adjustment at the rear of the TSP (throttle solenoid positioner) housing.

6. Place the transmission in Neutral or Park. Rev the engine momentarily. Place transmission in specified position and recheck curb idle RPM. Readjust if required.

7. Turn the ignition key to the Off position.

8. If a curb idle RPM adjustment was required and the carburetor is equipped with a dashpot, adjust the dashpot clearance to specification as follows:

a. Turn key to On position. Open throttle to allow TSP solenoid plunger to extend to the curb idle position.

b. Collapse dashpot plunger to maximum extent. Measure clearance between tip of plunger and extension pad on throttle vent lever. If required, adjust to specification. Tighten dashpot locknut. Recheck clearance. Turn key to Off position.

9. If curb idle adjustment was required: Check/adjust the bowl vent setting as follows:

a. Turn ignition key to the On position to activate the TSP (engine not running). Open throttle to allow the TSP solenoid plunger to extend to the curb idle position.

b. Secure the choke plate in the wide open position.

c. Open throttle so that the throttle vent lever does not touch the bowl vent

rod. Close the throttle to the idle set position and measure the travel of the fuel bowl vent rod from the open throttle position.

d. Travel of the bowl vent rod should be within specification (.100 to .150 inches).

e. If out of specification, bend the throttle vent lever at notch to obtain required travel.

10. Remove all test equipment and reinstall air cleaner assembly. Tighten the hold-down bolt to specification.

300 (4.9L)
YFA-IV & YFA-IV-FB

1. Block the wheels and apply the parking brake. Place the transmission in Neutral or Park.

2. Bring engine to normal operating temperature.

3. Place A/C Heat Selector to Off position.

4. Place transmission in specified gear.

5. Check/adjust curb idle RPM:

a. TSP-dashpot. Insure that TSP is activated using a ⅜-inch open end wrench, adjust curb idle RPM by rotating the nut directly behind the dashpot housing.

b. Adjust curb idle RPM by turning the idle RPM speed screw.

c. Front mounted TSP—(Note same as A/C kicker on all other calibrations) insure that TSP is activated. After loosening lock nut, adjust curb idle RPM by rotating TSP solenoid until specified RPM is obtained. Tighten locknut.

6. Check/adjust anti-diesel (TSP-Off). Manually collapse the TSP by rotating the carb throttle shaft lever until the TSP-Off adjusting screw contacts the carburetor body. If adjustment is required, turn the TSP-Off adjusting screw while holding the lever adjustment screw against the stop.

7. Place the transmission in Neutral or Park. Rev the engine momentarily. Place the transmission in specified position and recheck curb idle rpm. Readjust if required.

8. Check/adjust dashpot clearance to .120 ± .030.

9. If a final curb idle speed adjustment is required, the bowl vent setting must be checked as follows:

a. Stop the engine and turn the ignition key to the On position, so that the TSP dashpot or TSP is activated but the engine is not running (where applicable). Secure the choke plate in the wide-open position.

b. Open the throttle, so that the throttle vent lever does not touch the fuel bowl vent rod.

c. Close the throttle, and measure the travel of the fuel bowl vent rod from the open throttle position. Travel of the fuel bowl vent rod should be within .100 to .150 in.

d. If out of specification, bend the throttle vent lever to obtain the required travel.

e. Remove all test equipment, and

tighten the air cleaner holddown bolt to specification.

10. Whenever it is required to adjust engine idle speed by more than 50 rpm, the adjustment screw on the AOD linkage lever at the carburetor should also be readjusted.

173 (2.8L), 232 (3.8L) & 302 (5.0L) 2150-2V FB (FEEDBACK)

1. Set parking brake and block wheels.
2. Place the transmission in Park.
3. Bring the engine to normal operating temperature.
4. Disconnect the electric connector on the EVAP purge solenoid.
5. Disconnect and plug the vacuum hose to the VOTM kicker.
6. Place the transmission in Drive position.
7. Check/adjust curb idle rpm—if adjustment is required:
   - Use the curb idle speed screw.
   - Use the saddle bracket adjusting screw.
8. Place the transmission in Neutral or Park. Rev the engine momentarily. Place the transmission in Drive position and recheck curb idle rpm. Readjust if required.
9. Remove the plug from the vacuum hose to the VOTM kicker and reconnect.
10. Reconnect the electrical connector on the EVAP purge solenoid.

302 (5.0L) 2150-2V (NON-FEEDBACK)

1. Set parking brake and block wheels.
2. Place the transmission in Neutral or Park.
3. Bring engine to normal operating temperature.
4. Place A/C Heat selector to Off position.
5. Disconnect and plug vacuum hose to thermactor air bypass valve.
6. Place the transmission in specified gear.
7. Check curb idle rpm. Adjust to specification:
   - Using the curb idle rpm speed screw.
   - Using the saddle bracket adjusting screw.
8. Place the transmission in Neutral or Park. Rev the engine momentarily. Place the transmission in specified position, and recheck curb idle rpm. Readjust if required.
9. Remove plug from vacuum hose to thermactor air bypass valve and reconnect.
10. Whenever it is required to adjust engine idle speed by more than 50 rpm, the adjustment screw on the AOD linkage lever at the carburetor should also be readjusted.

351 (5.8L) 2150-2V OR 7200 VV

1. Block the wheels and apply parking brake. Place the transmission in Neutral or Park.
2. Bring the engine to normal operating temperature.
3. Disconnect purge hose on canister

side of evaporator purge solenoid. Check to ensure that purge vacuum is present (solenoid has opened—will require 3- to 5-minute wait after starting engine followed by a short time at part-throttle). Reconnect purge hose.

4. Disconnect and plug the vacuum hose to the VOTM kicker.
5. Place the transmission in specified position.
6. Check/adjust curb idle rpm—if adjustment is required:
   - Use the curb idle speed screw.
   - Use the saddle bracket adjusting screw (ensure curb idle speed screw is not touching throttle shaft lever).
7. Place the transmission in Neutral or Park. Rev the engine momentarily. Place the transmission in specified position and recheck curb idle rpm. Readjust if required.
8. Check/adjust throttle position sensor (TPS).
9. Remove the plug from the vacuum hose to the VOTM kicker and reconnect.
10. Apply a slight pressure on top of the nylon nut located on the accelerator pump to take up the linkage clearance.
11. Turn the nylon nut on the accelerator pump rod clockwise until a .010 ± .005 clearance is obtained between the top of the accelerator pump and the pump lever.
12. Turn the accelerator pump rod nut one turn counterclockwise to set the lever lash preload.
13. If curb idle adjustment exceeds 50 rpm, adjust automatic transmission TV linkage.

302 (5.0L) & 351 (5.8L) CANADA 2150-2V

1. Place the transmission in Neutral or Park.
2. Bring engine to normal operating temperature.
3. Place A/C Heat Selector to Off position.
4. Place the transmission in specified gear.
5. Check curb idle rpm. Adjust to specification:
   - Using the curb idle speed screw.
   - Using the hex head on the rear of the solenoid or the saddle bracket adjustment screw.
6. Place the transmission in Neutral or Park. Rev the engine momentarily. Place the transmission in specified position and recheck curb idle rpm. Readjust if required.
7. TSP-Off: With transmission in specified gear, collapse the solenoid plunger, and set specified TSP-Off speed on the speed screw.
8. Disconnect vacuum hose to decel throttle control modulator and plug (if so equipped).
9. Connect a slave vacuum from manifold vacuum to the decel throttle control modulator (if so equipped).
10. Check/adjust decel throttle control rpm. Adjust if necessary.

11. Remove slave vacuum hose.
12. Remove plug from decel throttle control modulator hose and reconnect.

460 (7.5L)

1. Block the wheels and apply parking brake.
2. Run engine until normal operating temperature is reached.
3. Place the vehicle in Park or Neutral, A/C in Off position, and set parking brake.
4. Remove air cleaner.
5. Disconnect and plug decel throttle control kicker diaphragm vacuum hose.
6. Connect a slave vacuum hose from an engine manifold vacuum source to the decel throttle control kicker.
7. Run engine at approximately 2500 rpm for 15-seconds, then release the throttle.
8. If decel throttle control rpm is not within ± 50 rpm of specification, adjust the kicker.
9. Disconnect the slave vacuum hose and allow engine to return to curb idle.
10. Adjust curb idle, if necessary, using the curb idle adjusting screw.
11. Rev the engine momentarily, recheck curb idle and adjust if necessary.
12. Reconnect the decel throttle control vacuum hose to the diaphragm.
13. Reinstall the air cleaner.

DIESEL

NOTE: A special tachometer is required to check engine RPM on a diesel engine.

134 (2.2L)

1. Block the wheels and apply the parking brake.
2. Start and run engine until the normal operating temperature is reached. Shut off engine.
3. Connect diesel engine tachometer.
4. Start engine and check RPM. Refer to emissions decal for latest specifications. RPM is usually adjusted in Neutral for manual transmissions and Drive for automatic models.
5. The adjustment bolt is located on the bell crank at the top of the injector pump. The upper bolt is for curb idle, the lower for max speed.
6. Loosen the locknut. Turn the adjustment screw clockwise to increase RPM, counter-clockwise to lower the RPM.
7. Tighten the locknut. Increase engine speed several times and recheck idle. Readjust if necessary.

420 (6.9L)

1. Block the wheels and apply the parking brake.
2. Bring the engine to normal operating temperature. Shut off engine.
3. Connect diesel engine tachometer.
4. Start the engine and check RPM. Refer to the emissions decal for latest specifications. RPM is usually adjusted in Neutral for manual transmissions and Drive for automatic models.

5. Turn the idle speed adjusting screw in the required direction to increase or decrease RPM. The adjusting screw is located on the top of the injector pump above the cold start valve.

6. Place the gear selector in neutral, if automatic, and speed up engine several times. Recheck idle RPM, readjust if necessary.

Valve Adjustment

GASOLINE ENGINES

NOTE: Refer to the "Rocker Arm/Rocker Shaft and Stud Section" for valve adjustment procedures for the 173 (2.8L) V6 engine.

All gasoline engines used, except the 2.8L V6, are equipped with hydraulic valve lifters or lash adjusters. Hydraulic valve lifters or lash adjusters operate with zero clearance in the valve train, and because of this the rocker arms are non-adjustable. The only means by which valve system clearances can be altered is by installing over or undersize pushrods except on OHC (overhead cam) models; but, because of the hydraulic lifter's natural ability to compensate for slack in the valve train, all components of all the valve system should be checked for wear if there is excessive play in the system. Refer to Rocker Arm section.

DIESEL ENGINES

134 (2.2L)

1. Warm the engine until normal operating temperature is reached.
2. Remove the valve cover. Check the head bolt torque in sequence.

WHEN NO. 1 CYLINDER IS AT TOP DEAD ENTER

WHEN NO. 4 CYLINDER IS AT TOP DEAD ENTER

Valve adjusting sequence 134 (2.2L) diesel

3. Turn the engine to bring the No. 1 piston to TDC (top dead center) of the compression stroke.
4. Adjust the following valves:
   No. 1 Intake
   No. 1 Exhaust
   No. 2 Intake
   No. 3 Exhaust
5. Rotate the crankshaft 360° and bring No. 4 piston to TDC of the compression stroke.

6. Adjust the following valves:
   No. 2 Exhaust
   No. 3 Intake
   No. 4 Intake
   No. 4 Exhaust
7. To adjust the valves, loosen the locknut on the rocker arm. Rotate the adjusting screw clockwise to reduce clearance, counter-clockwise to increase clearance. Clearance is checked with a flat feeler gauge that is passed between the rocker arm and valve stem.
8. After adjustments are made, be sure the locknuts are tight. Be sure mounting surfaces are clean. Install the valve cover and new valve cover gasket.

420 (6.9L)

The 6.9L diesel engine is equipped with hydraulic lifters that minimize engine noise and maintain zero lash or tappet clearance. This eliminates the need for periodic adjustment. The hydraulic tappets also incorporate camshaft roller followers for improved camshaft wear characteristics.

IGNITION SYSTEM

NOTE: Complete service and troubleshooting information on "Dura Spark" systems can be found in the "Electronic Ignition" section of Unit Repair.

Distributor

REMOVAL & INSTALLATION

—————— CAUTION ——————
Certain models are equipped with EEC III

TOOTH MUST BE PERFECTLY ALIGNED WITH TIMING MARKS

Align armature and stator (4 cylinder shown)

or IV. The distributor is locked into position and all timing control is handled by the EEC module. No timing adjustment is required or possible. Rotor alignment is critical, and any required servicing should be done only by mechanics familiar with the system. See the Emissions Section in Unit Repair for rotor alignment information.

1. Remove the air cleaner on V6 and V8 engines. On 4 and 6 cylinder in-line engines, removal of a thermactor (air) pump mounting bolt and drive belt will allow the pump to be moved to the side and permit access to the distributor. If necessary, disconnect the thermactor air filter and lines as well.
2. Remove the distributor cap and position the cap and ignition wires to the side.
3. Disconnect the wire harness plug from the distributor connector. Disconnect and plug the vacuum hoses from the vacuum diaphragm assembly. (DuraSpark III systems are not equipped with a vacuum diaphragm).

DuraSpark III rotor alignment

4. Rotate the engine (in normal direction of rotation) until No. 1 piston is on TDC (Top Dead Center) of the compression stroke. The TDC mark on the crankshaft pulley and the pointer should align. Rotor tip pointing at No. 1 position on distributor cap.

5. On DuraSpark II, turn the engine a slight bit more (if required) to align the stator (pick-up coil) assembly pole with an (the closest) armature pole. On DuraSpark III, the distributor sleeve groove (when looking down from the top) and the cap adaptor alignment slot should align.

6. On DuraSpark II, scribe a mark on the distributor body and engine block to indicate the position of the rotor tip and position of the distributor in the engine. DuraSpark III distributors are equipped with a notched base and will only locate at one position on the engine.

7. Remove the holddown bolt and clamp located at the base of the distributor. (Some DuraSpark distributors are equipped with a special holddown bolt that requires a Torx head wrench for removal). Remove the distributor from the engine. Pay attention to the direction the rotor turns and the position to which the rotor tip points when the drive gear disengages. For reinstallation purposes, the rotor should be at this position to insure proper gear mesh and timing.

8. Avoid turning the engine, if possible, while the distributor is removed. If the engine is turned from TDC position, TDC timing marks will have to be reset before the distributor is installed; Steps 4 and 5.

9. On DuraSpark II systems; position the distributor in the engine with the rotor aligned to the marks made on the distributor, or to the place the rotor pointed when the distributor was removed. The stator and armature or vane and vane switch should also be aligned. Engage the oil pump intermediate shaft and insert the distributor until fully seated on the engine, if the distributor does not fully seat, turn the engine slightly to fully engage the intermediate shaft.

10. On DuraSpark III systems, follow the above procedures. Make sure when positioning the distributor that the slot in the distributor base will engage the block tab and the sleeve/adaptor slots are aligned.

11. After the distributor has been fully seated on the block install the hold down bracket and bolt. On DuraSpark III, tighten the mounting bolt. On DuraSpark II, snug the mounting bolt so the distributor can be turned for ignition timing purposes.

12. The rest of the installation is in the reverse order of removal. Check and reset the ignition timing (if necessary) on DuraSpark II systems.

NOTE: A silicone compound is used on rotor tips, distributor cap contacts and on the inside of the connectors on the spark plugs cable and module couplers. Always apply Silicone Dielectric Compound after servicing any component of the ignition system. Various models use a multi-point rotor which do not require the application of dielectric compound.

Alternator

PRECAUTIONS

To prevent damage to the alternator and regulator, the following precautions should be taken when working with the electrical system.

1. Never reverse the battery connections.
2. Booster batteries for starting must be connected properly—positive-to-positive and negative-to-negative.

Typical alternator connections and mounting (color codes may differ)

3. Disconnect the battery cables before using a fast charger; the charger has a tendency to force current through the diodes in the opposite direction for which they were designed. This burns out the diodes.

4. Never use a fast charger as a booster for starting the vehicle.

5. Never disconnect the voltage regulator while the engine is running.

6. Avoid long soldering times when replacing diodes or transistors. Prolonged heat is damaging to AC generators.

7. Do not use test lamps of more than 12 volts (V) for checking diode continuity.

8. Do not short across or ground any of the terminals on the AC generator.

9. The polarity of the battery, generator, and regulator must be matched and considered before making any electrical connections within the system.

10. Never operate the alternator on an open circuit. Make sure that all connections within the circuit are clean and tight.

11. Disconnect the battery terminals when performing any service on the electrical system. This will eliminate the possibility of accidental reversal of polarity.

12. Disconnect the battery ground cable if arc welding is to be done on any part of the car.

REMOVAL & INSTALLATION

While internal alternator repairs are possible, they require specialized tools and training. Therefore, it is advisable to replace a defective alternator, or have it repaired by a qualified shop.

1. Open the hood and disconnect the battery ground cable.
2. Remove the adjusting arm bolt.
3. Remove the alternator through-bolt. Remove the drive belt from the alternator pulley and lower the alternator.
4. Label all of the leads to the alternator so that you can install them correctly and disconnect the leads from the alternator.
5. Remove the alternator from the vehicle.
6. To install, reverse the above procedure.

Belt Tension Adjustment

The fan belt drives the alternator and water pump. If the belt is too loose, it will slip and the alternator will not be able to produce its rated current. Also, the water pump will not operate efficiently and the engine could overheat.

Check the tension of the belt by pushing your thumb down on the longest span of the belt, midway between the pulleys. Belt deflection should be approximately ½ in.

To adjust belt tension, proceed as follows:

1. Loosen the alternator mounting bolt and the adjusting arm bolts.
2. Apply pressure on the alternator front housing only, moving the alternator away from the engine to tighten the belt. Do not apply pressure to the rear of the cast aluminum housing of an alternator; damage to the housing could result.
3. Tighten the alternator mounting bolt and the adjusting arm bolts when the correct tension is reached.

Regulator

The alternator regular has been designed to control the charging system's rate of charge. The electromechanical regulator is calibrated at the factory and is not adjustable.

REMOVAL & INSTALLATION

1. Disconnect the negative terminal of the battery. On some models it may be necessary to move the battery.
2. Disconnect all of the electrical leads at the regulator. Label them as removed, so that you can replace them in the correct order on the replacement unit.
3. Remove all of the hold-down screws, then remove the unit from the vehicle.
4. Install the new voltage regulator using the hold-down screws from the old one, or new ones if they are provided with the replacement unit. Tighten the hold-down screws.
5. Connect all the leads to the new regulator.

Starter Motor

REMOVAL & INSTALLATION

Positive Engagement Type

1. Disconnect the positive battery terminal.
2. Raise the vehicle and disconnect the starter cable at the starter terminal.
3. Remove all of the starter attaching bolts that attach the starter to the bellhousing.
4. Remove the starter from the engine.
5. Install the starter in the reverse order of removal.

Solenoid Actuated Type

1. Disconnect the battery ground cable.
2. Raise the vehicle and disconnect the cables and wires at the starter solenoid.
3. Turn the front wheels to the right and remove the two bolts attaching the steering idler arm to the frame.
4. Remove the starter mounting bolts and remove the starter.
5. Install in the reverse order of removal.

STARTER DRIVE REPLACEMENT

1. Remove the cover of the starter drive's plunger lever arm, and the brush cover band. Remove the through-bolts, starter drive gear housing, and the return spring of the driver gear's actuating lever.
2. Remove the pivot pin which retains the starter gear plunger lever and remove the lever.
3. Remove the stop-ring retainer. Remove and discard the stop-ring which holds the drive gear to the armature shaft and then remove the drive gear assembly.
To install the drive gear assembly:
4. Lightly Lubriplate® the armature shaft splines and install the starter drive gear assembly on the shaft. Install a new stop-ring and stop-ring retainer.
5. Position the starter drive gear plunger lever to the frame and starter drive assembly.
6. Install the pivot pin.
7. Position the drive plunger lever return spring and the drive gear housing to the frame, then install and tighten the through-bolts. Be sure that the stop-ring retainer is properly seated in the drive housing.
8. Position the starter drive plunger lever cover and the brush cover band on the starter. Tighten the brush cover band retaining screw.

BRUSH REPLACEMENT

Replace the starter brushes when they are worn to ¼ in. Always install a complete set of new brushes.
1. Remove the starter from the truck.
2. Loosen and remove the brush cover band, gasket, and starter drive plunger lever

cover. Remove the commutator brushes from their holders.
3. Remove the two through-bolts from the starter frame.
4. Remove the drive end housing and the plunger lever return spring.
5. Remove the starter drive plunger lever pivot pin and lever, and remove the armature.
6. Remove the brush end plate.
7. Remove the ground brush attaching screws from the frame and remove the brushes.
8. Cut the insulated brush leads from the field coils as close to the field connection as possible.
9. Clean and inspect the starter motor. Use a brush or air to clean the field coils, armature, commutator, armature shaft, brush end plate, and drive end housing. Wash all of the other parts in solvent and dry them.
Inspect the armature windings for broken or burned insulation and unsoldered connections.
10. Replace the brush end plate if the insulator between the field brush holder and the end plate is cracked or broken.
11. Position the new insulated field brushes lead on the field coil connection. Position and crimp the clip provided with the brushes to hold the brush lead to the connection. Solder the lead, clip, and connection together.
12. Install the ground brush leads to the frame with the attaching screws.
13. Clean the commutator with 00 to 000 sandpaper.
14. Position the brush end plate to the starter frame, with the end plate boss in the frame slot.
15. Install the armature in the starter frame.
16. Install the starter drive gear plunger lever to the frame and starter drive assembly, and install the pivot pin.
17. Fill and drive end housing bearing bore about ¼ full with grease. Position the return spring on the plunger lever, and the drive end housing to the starter frame. Install the through-bolts and tighten them to 55–75 in. lbs. Be sure that the stop ring retainer is seated properly in the drive end housing.
18. Install the commutator brushes in the brush holders. Center the brush springs on the brushes.
19. Position the plunger lever cover and the brush cover band, with its gasket on the starter. Tighten the band attaching screw.
20. Connect the starter to the battery to check its operation. If it works, install it in the engine.

STARTER RELAY REPLACEMENT

The starter relay is mounted on the inside of the right wheel well. To replace it, disconnect the negative battery cable from the battery, disconnect all of the electrical leads

from the relay and remove the relay from the fender wall. Replace in the reverse order of removal.

ENGINE MECHANICAL

Engine

REMOVAL & INSTALLATION

Pickups and Bronco, Bronco II

122 (2.0L) & 140 (2.3L)

1. Raise the hood and install protective fender covers. Drain the coolant from the radiator. Remove the air cleaner and duct assembly.
2. Disconnect the battery ground cable at the engine and disconnect the battery positive cable at the battery and set aside.
3. Mark the location of the hood hinges and remove the hood.
4. Disconnect the upper and lower radiator hoses from the engine. Remove the radiator shroud screws. Remove the radiator upper supports.
5. Remove engine fan and shroud assembly. Then remove the radiator. Remove the oil fill cap.
6. Disconnect the coil primary wire at the coil. Disconnect the oil pressure and the water temperature sending unit wires from the sending units.
7. Disconnect the alternator wire from the alternator, the starter cable from the starter and the accelerator cable from the carburetor. If so equipped, disconnect the transmission kickdown rod.
8. If so equipped, remove the A/C compressor from the mounting bracket and position it out of the way, leaving the refrigerant lines attached.
9. Disconnect the power brake vacuum hose. Disconnect the chassis fuel line from the fuel pump. Disconnect the heater hoses from the engine.
10. Remove the engine mount nuts. Raise the vehicle and safely support on jackstands.
11. Drain engine oil from the crankcase. Remove the starter motor.
12. Disconnect the muffler exhaust inlet pipe at the exhaust manifold.
13. Remove the dust cover (manual transmission) or converter inspection plate (automatic transmission).
14. On vehicles with a manual transmission, remove the flywheel housing cover lower attaching bolts. On vehicles with automatic transmissions, remove the converter-to-flywheel bolts, then remove the converter housing lower attaching bolts.
15. Remove clutch slave cylinder (manual transmission). Lower the vehicle.
16. Support the transmission and flywheel or converter housing with a jack.

17. Remove the flywheel housing or converter housing upper attaching bolts.

18. Attach the engine lifting hooks to the existing lifting brackets. Carefully, so as not to damage any components, lift the engine out of the vehicle.

19. To install the engine: If clutch was removed, reinstall. Carefully lower the engine into the engine compartment. On a vehicle with automatic transmission, start the converter pilot into the crankshaft. On a vehicle with a manual transmission, start the transmission main drive gear into the clutch disc. It may be necessary to adjust the position of the transmission in relation to the engine if the input shaft will not enter the clutch disc. If the engine hangs up after the shaft enters, turn the crankshaft in the clockwise direction slowly (transmission in gear), until the shaft splines mesh with the clutch disc splines.

20. Install the flywheel or converter housing upper attaching bolts. Remove the engine lifting hooks from the lifting brackets.

21. Remove the jack from under the transmission. Raise the vehicle and safely support on jackstands.

22. On a vehicle with a manual transmission, install the flywheel lower housing bolts and tighten to specifications. On a vehicle with an automatic transmission, attach the converter to the flywheel bolts and tighten to specifications. Install the converter housing-to-engine bolts and tighten to specifications.

23. Install clutch slave cylinder.

24. Install the dust cover (manual transmission) or converter inspection plate (automatic transmission). Connect the exhaust inlet pipe to the exhaust manifold.

25. Install the starter motor and connect the starter cables.

26. Lower the vehicle. Install the engine mount nuts and tighten to 65–85 ft. lbs. (88–115 N·m).

27. Connect the heater hoses to the engine. Connect the chassis fuel line to the fuel pump. Connect the power brake vacuum hose.

28. Connect the alternator wire to the alternator, connect the accelerator cable to the carburetor. If so equipped, connect the transmission kickdown rod. If so equipped, install the A/C compressor to the mounting bracket.

29. Connect the coil primary wire at the coil. Connect the oil pressure and water temperature sending unit wires. Install oil fill cap.

30. Install the radiator and secure with upper support brackets. Install the fan and shroud assembly. Connect upper and lower radiator hoses.

31. Install the hood and align.

32. Install the air cleaner assembly. Fill and bleed the cooling system.

33. Fill the crankcase with specified oil. Connect battery ground cable to engine and battery positive cable to battery.

34. Start the engine and check for leaks.

134 (2.2L) Diesel

1. Open hood and install protective fender covers. Mark location of hood hinges and remove hood.

2. Disconnect battery ground cables from both batteries. Disconnect battery ground cables at engine.

3. Drain coolant from radiator.

4. Disconnect air intake hose from air cleaner and intake manifold.

5. Disconnect upper and lower radiator hoses from engine. Remove engine cooling fan. Remove radiator shroud screws. Remove radiator upper supports and remove radiator and shroud.

6. Disconnect radio ground strap, if so equipped.

7. Remove No. 2 glow plug relay from firewall, with harness attached, and lay on engine.

8. Disconnect engine wiring harness at main connector located on left fender apron. Disconnect starter cable from starter.

9. Disconnect accelerator cable and speed control cable, if so equipped, from injection pump.

10. Remove cold start cable from injection pump.

---------------- CAUTION ----------------
Do not disconnect air conditioning lines or discharge the system unless the proper equipment is on hand and you are familiar with the procedure. Have the system discharged by a qualified mechanic prior to start of engine removal.
----

11. Discharge A/C system and remove A/C refrigerant lines and position out of the way.

12. Remove pressure and return hoses from power steering pump, if so equipped.

13. Disconnect vacuum fitting from vacuum pump and position fitting and vacuum hoses out of the way.

14. Disconnect and cap fuel inlet line at fuel line heater and fuel return line at injection pump.

15. Disconnect heater hoses from engine.

16. Loosen engine insulator nuts. Raise vehicle and safely support on jackstands.

17. Drain engine oil from oil pan and remove primary oil filter.

18. Disconnect oil pressure sender hose from oil filter mounting adapter.

19. Disconnect muffler inlet pipe at exhaust manifold.

20. Remove bottom engine insulator nuts. Remove transmission bolts. Lower vehicle. Attach engine lifting sling and chain hoist.

21. Carefully lift engine out of vehicle to avoid damage to components.

22. Install engine on work stand, if necessary.

23. When installing the engine: Carefully lower engine into engine compartment to avoid damage to components.

24. Install two top transmission-to-engine attaching bolts. Remove engine lifting sling.

25. Raise vehicle and safely support on jackstands.

26. Install engine insulator nuts and tighten to specification.

27. Install remaining transmission-to-engine attaching bolts and tighten all bolts to specification.

28. Connect muffler inlet pipe to exhaust manifold and tighten to specification.

29. Install oil pressure sender hose and install new oil filter as described in this Section.

30. Lower vehicle.

31. Tighten upper engine insulator nuts to specification.

32. Connect heater hoses to engine. Connect fuel inlet line to fuel line heater and fuel return line to injection pump. Connect vacuum fitting and hoses to vacuum pump. Connect pressure and return hoses to power steering pump, if so equipped. Check and add power steering fluid.

33. Install A/C refrigerant lines and charge system, if so equipped.

NOTE: System can be charged after engine installation is completed.

34. Connect cold start cable to injection pump. Connect accelerator cable and speed control cable, if so equipped, to injection pump.

35. Connect engine wiring harness to main wiring harness at left fender apron. Connect radio ground strap, if so equipped.

36. Position radiator in vehicle, install radiator upper support brackets and tighten to specification. Install radiator fan shroud and tighten to specification. Install radiator fan and tighten to specification.

37. Connect upper and lower radiator hoses to engine and tighten clamps to specification. Connect air intake hose to air cleaner and intake manifold.

38. Fill and bleed cooling system.

39. Fill crankcase with specified quantity and quality of oil.

40. Connect battery ground cables to engine. Connect battery ground cables to both batteries.

41. Run engine and check for oil, fuel and coolant leaks. Close hood.

173 (2.8L) V6

1. Disconnect the battery ground cable and drain the cooling system.

2. Remove the hood after scribing hinge positions. Remove the air cleaner and intake duct assembly.

3. Remove or disconnect thermactor system parts that will interfere with removal or installation of the engine.

4. Disconnect the radiator upper and lower hoses at the radiator. Remove the fan shroud attaching bolts and position the shroud over the fan. Remove the radiator and shroud.

5. Remove the alternator and bracket. Position the alternator out of the way. Disconnect the alternator ground wire from the cylinder block.

6. Remove A/C compressor and power

steering and position out of way, if so equipped.

CAUTION

Do not disconnect air conditioning lines or discharge the system unless the proper equipment is on hand and you are familiar with the procedure. Have the system discharged by a qualified mechanic prior to start of engine removal.

7. Disconnect the heater hoses at the block and water pump.

8. Remove the ground wires from the cylinder block.

9. Disconnect the fuel tank to fuel pump fuel line at the fuel pump. Plug the fuel tank line.

10. Disconnect the throttle cable linkage at the carburetor and intake manifold.

11. Disconnect the primary wires from the ignition coil. Disconnect the brake booster vacuum hose. Disconnect the wiring from the oil pressure and engine coolant temperature senders.

12. Raise the vehicle and secure with safety stands. Disconnect the muffler inlet pipes at the exhaust manifolds.

13. Disconnect the starter cable and remove the starter.

14. Remove the engine front support to crossmember attaching nuts or through bolts.

15. If equipped with automatic transmission, remove the converter inspection cover and disconnect the flywheel from the converter.

16. Remove the kickdown rod. Remove the converter housing-to-cylinder block bolts and the adapter plate-to-converter housing bolt.

17. On vehicles equipped with a manual transmission, remove the clutch linkage and mounting bolts. Lower the vehicle.

18. Attach engine lifting sling and hoist to lifting brackets at exhaust manifolds.

19. Position a jack under the transmission. Raise the engine slightly and carefully pull it from the transmission. Carefully lift the engine out of the engine compartment so that the rear cover plate is not bent or components damaged.

20. When installing the engine: Attach engine lifting sling and hoist to lifting brackets at exhaust manifolds.

21. Lower the engine carefully into the engine compartment. Make sure the exhaust manifolds are properly aligned with the muffler inlet pipes.

22. On a vehicle with a manual transmission, start the transmission main shaft into the clutch disc. It may be necessary to adjust the position of the transmission in relation to the engine if the input shaft will not enter the clutch disc. **If the engine hangs up after the shaft enters, turn the crankshaft slowly (transmission in gear) until the shaft splines mesh with the clutch disc splines.** On a vehicle with an automatic transmission, start the converter pilot into the crankshaft.

Install the clutch housing or converter

housing upper bolts, making sure that the dowels in the cylinder block engage the flywheel housing. Remove the jack from under the transmission.

Remove the lifting sling.

23. On a vehicle with an automatic transmission, position the kickdown rod on the transmission and engine. Raise the vehicle and secure with safety stands. On a vehicle with an automatic transmission, position the transmission linkage bracket and install the remaining converter housing bolts. Install the adapter plate-to-converter housing bolt. Install the converter-to-flywheel nuts and install the inspection cover. Connect the kickdown rod on the transmission.

24. Install the starter and connect the cable.

25. Connect the muffler inlet pipes at the exhaust manifolds.

26. Install the engine front support nuts and washer attaching it to the crossmember or through bolts. Lower the vehicle.

27. Install the battery ground cable. Connect the ignition coil primary wires, then connect the coolant temperature sending unit and oil pressure sending unit. Connect brake booster vacuum hose.

Install the throttle linkage.

28. Connect the fuel tank line at the fuel pump. Connect the ground cable at the cylinder block. Connect the heater hoses to the water pump and cylinder block.

29. Install the alternator and bracket. Connect the alternator ground wire to the cylinder block. Install the drive belt and adjust the belt tension to specifications.

30. Install A/C compressor and power steering pump, if so equipped.

31. Position the fan shroud over the fan. Install the radiator and connect the radiator upper and lower hoses. Install the fan shroud attaching bolts. Fill and bleed the cooling system. Fill the crankcase with the proper grade and quantity of oil. Install thermactor parts removed or disconnected. Reconnect battery ground cable.

32. Charge A/C system if so equipped.

NOTE: System can be charged after engine installation is completed.

33. Operate the engine at fast idle until it reaches normal operating temperature and check all gaskets and hose connections for leaks. Adjust ignition timing and idle speed. Install the air cleaner and intake duct. Install and adjust the hood.

300 (4.9L)

1. Drain the cooling system and the crankcase. Remove the hood and the air cleaner. Disconnect the negative battery cable.

2. Disconnect the heater hose from the water pump and coolant outlet housing. Disconnect the flexible fuel line from the fuel pump.

3. Remove the radiator.

4. Remove the fan, water pump pulley, and fan belt.

5. Disconnect the accelerator cable at

the carburetor. Remove the throttle return spring. On trucks equipped with power brakes, disconnect the brake booster vacuum hose at the intake manifold. On trucks with automatic transmissions, disconnect the transmission kickdown rod at the bellcrank assembly.

6. Disconnect the exhaust pipe from the exhaust manifold.

7. Disconnect the body ground strap and the battery ground cable from the engine.

8. Disconnect the engine wiring harness at the ignition coil, the coolant temperature sending unit, and the oil pressure sending unit. Position the wiring harness out of the way.

9. Remove the alternator mounting bolts and position the alternator out of the way.

10. On a truck equipped with power steering, remove the power steering pump from the mounting brackets and move it to one side, leaving the lines attached.

11. Raise the truck on a hoist and remove the starter and automatic transmission filler tube bracket, if so equipped. Also, remove the rear engine plate upper right bolt.

12. On manual transmission equipped trucks, remove the flywheel housing lower attaching bolts and disconnect the clutch return spring.

13. On automatic transmission equipped trucks, remove the converter housing access cover assembly and remove the flywheel-to-converter attaching nuts. Secure the converter in the housing. Remove the transmission oil cooler lines from the retaining clip at the engine. Remove the lower converter housing-to-engine attaching bolts.

14. Remove the nut from each of the two front engine mounts.

15. Lower the vehicle and position a jack under the transmission and support it. Remove the remaining bellhousing-to-engine attaching bolts.

16. Attach the engine lifting device and raise the engine slightly and carefully pull it from the transmission. Lift the engine out of the vehicle.

To install the engine:

17. Place a new gasket on the muffler inlet pipe.

18. Carefully lower the engine into the truck. Make sure that the dowels in the engine block engage the holes in the bellhousing.

19. On manual transmission equipped trucks, start the transmission input shaft into the clutch disc. It may be necessary to adjust the position of the engine or transmission in order for the input shaft to enter the clutch disc. If necessary, turn the crankshaft until the input shaft splines mesh with the clutch disc splines.

20. On automatic transmission equipped trucks, start the converter pilot into the crankshaft. Unsecure the converter in the housing.

21. Install the bellhousing upper attaching bolts. Remove the jack supporting the transmission.

22. Lower the engine until it rests on the engine mounts. Remove the lifting device.

23. Install the engine mount nuts and tighten them to 45–55 ft. lbs.

24. Install the automatic transmission coil cooler lines bracket, if so equipped.

25. Install the remaining bellhousing attaching bolts.

26. Connect the clutch return spring, if so equipped.

27. Install the starter and connect the starter cable. Attach the automatic transmission fluid filler tube bracket, if so equipped.

28. On trucks with automatic transmissions, install the transmission oil cooler lines in the bracket at the cylinder block.

29. Connect the exhaust pipe to the exhaust manifold. Tighten the nuts to 25–35 ft. lbs.

30. Connect the engine ground strap and negative battery cable.

31. On a truck with an automatic transmission, connect the kick-down rod to the bellcrank assembly on the intake manifold.

32. Connect the accelerator linkage to the carburetor and install the return spring.

33. On a truck with power brakes, connect the brake booster vacuum line to the intake manifold.

34. Connect the coil primary wire, oil pressure and coolant temperature sending unit wires, fuel line, heater hoses, and the battery positive cable.

35. Install the alternator to its mounting bracket. Install the power steering pump to its bracket, if so equipped.

36. Install the water pump pulley, spacer, fan, and fan belt. Adjust the belt tension.

37. Install the radiator and connect the upper and lower radiator hoses to the radiator and engine. Connect the automatic transmission oil cooler lines, if so equipped.

38. Install and adjust the hood.

39. Fill the cooling system. Fill the crankcase.

40. Start the engine and check for leaks. Bleed the cooling system. Adjust the clutch pedal free-play or the automatic transmission control linkage. Install the air cleaner.

232(3.8L)V6 and V8 Except 420(6.9L) Diesel and 460(7.5L)V8

1. Drain the cooling system and crankcase. Remove the hood.

2. Disconnect the battery, negative cable first, and alternator cables from the cylinder block.

3. Remove the air cleaner and intake duct assembly, plus the crankcase ventilation hose.

4. Disconnect the upper and lower radiator hoses, and, if so equipped, the automatic transmission oil cooler lines.

5. Remove the fan shroud and lay it over the fan. Remove the radiator and fan, shroud, fan, spacer, pulley, and belt.

6. Disconnect the alternator leads and the alternator adjusting bolts. Allow the alternator to swing down out of the way.

7. Disconnect the oil pressure sending unit lead from the sending unit.

8. Disconnect the fuel tank-to-pump fuel line at the fuel pump and plug the line.

9. Disconnect the accelerator linkage at the carburetor. Disconnect the automatic transmission kick-down rod and remove the return spring, if so equipped.

10. Disconnect the heater hoses from the water pump and intake manifold. Disconnect the temperature sending unit wire from the sending unit.

11. Remove the upper bellhousing-to-engine attaching bolts.

12. Disconnect the primary wire from the coil. Remove the wiring harness from the left rocker arm cover and position the wires out of the way. Disconnect the ground strap from the cylinder block.

13. Raise the front of the truck and disconnect the starter cable from the starter. Remove the starter.

14. Disconnect the exhaust pipe from the exhaust manifolds.

15. Disconnect the engine mounts from the brackets on the frame.

16. On trucks with automatic transmissions, remove the converter inspection plate and remove the torque converter-to-flywheel attaching bolts.

17. Remove the remaining bellhousing-to-engine attaching bolts.

18. Lower the vehicle and support the transmission with a jack.

19. Install an engine lifting device.

NOTE: On the V6, the intake manifold is aluminum. If a lifting device is attached to the manifold, all manifold bolts must be installed.

20. Raise the engine slightly and carefully pull it out from the transmission. Lift the engine out of the engine compartment.

21. Install the engine in the reverse order of removal. Make sure that the dowels in the engine block engage the holes in the bellhousing through the rear cover plate. If the engine hangs up after the transmission input shaft enters the clutch disc (manual transmission only), turn the crankshaft with the transmission in gear until the input shaft splines mesh with the clutch disc splines.

Tighten the exhaust pipe-to-exhaust manifold nuts to 25–35 ft. lbs., and all others as follows:

¼ in. 20—6–9 ft. lbs.
⁵⁄₁₆ in. 18—12–18 ft. lbs.
⅜ in. 16—22–32 ft. lbs.
⁷⁄₁₆ in. 14—45–57 ft. lbs.
½ in. 13—55–80 ft. lbs.
⁹⁄₁₆ in.—85–120 ft. lbs

460 (7.5L)V8

1. Remove the hood.

2. Drain the cooling system, the radiator and the cylinder block.

3. Disconnect the negative battery cable and remove the air cleaner assembly.

4. Disconnect the upper and lower radiator hoses and the transmission oil cooler lines from the radiator.

5. Remove the fan shroud from the radiator and remove the fan from the water pump. Remove the fan and shroud from the engine compartment.

6. Remove the upper support and remove the radiator.

7. If the truck is equipped with air conditioning, remove the compressor from the engine and position it out of the way. If the compressor must be removed completely, loosen the air conditioning service valves (disconnect) carefully to discharge the air conditioning system. Remove the compressor.

8. Remove the power steering pump from the engine, if so equipped, and position it to one side. Do not disconnect the fluid lines.

9. Disconnect the fuel pump inlet line from the pump and plug the line.

10. Remove the alternator drive belts and disconnect the alternator from the engine, positioning it aside.

11. Disconnect the ground cable from the right front corner of the engine.

12. Disconnect the heater hoses.

13. Remove the transmission fluid filler tube attaching bolt from the right-side valve cover and position the tube out of the way.

14. Disconnect all vacuum lines at the rear of the intake manifold.

15. Disconnect the speed control cable at the carburetor, if so equipped. Disconnect the accelerator rod and the transmission kickdown rod and secure them out of the way.

16. Disconnect the engine wiring harness at the connector on the fire wall.

17. Raise the vehicle and disconnect the exhaust pipes at the exhaust manifolds.

18. Disconnect the starter cable and remove the starter. Bring the starter forward and rotate the solenoid outward to remove the assembly.

19. Remove the access cover from the converter housing and remove the flywheel-to-converter attaching nuts. Remove the lower converter housing-to-engine attaching bolts.

20. Remove the engine mount through-bolts attaching the rubber insulators to the frame brackets.

21. Lower the vehicle and place a jack under the transmission to support it.

22. Remove the converter housing-to-engine block attaching bolts (left-side).

23. Disconnect the coil wire and remove the coil and bracket assembly from the intake manifold.

24. Attach the engine lifting device and carefully lift the engine from the engine compartment.

25. Install the engine in the reverse order of removal.

Tighten the alternator pivot bolt to 45–57 ft. lbs. and all the rest of the nuts and bolts as is outlined in step 21 of the preceding "V8 except 460 Removal and Installation" procedure.

420 (6.9L) Diesel

1. Open hood. Disconnect battery ground cables from both batteries.

2. Scribe alignment marks at hood hinges and remove hood.

3. Drain cooling system.

4. Remove air cleaner and intake duct assembly. Install intake manifold cover over air intake opening.

5. Remove radiator fan shroud halves.

6. Remove fan and clutch assembly.

--- CAUTION ---

Left-hand thread. Remove by turning nut clockwise.

7. Disconnect radiator upper and lower hoses from radiator.

8. Disconnect automatic transmission oil cooler lines at radiator, if so equipped.

9. Remove radiator.

10. Loosen A/C compressor, if so equipped, and remove drive belt.

11. Remove A/C compressor, if so equipped, and position it on radiator upper support.

--- CAUTION ---

If compressor cannot be secured with lines connected, do not disconnect the lines unless you are familiar with discharging the system and have the proper tools. Have the system discharged by a qualified mechanic prior to the start of engine removal.

12. Loosen power steering pump and remove drive belt. Remove power steering pump and position out of the way on left side of engine compartment.

13. Disconnect fuel supply line heater and alternator wires at alternator. Disconnect oil pressure sending unit wire at sending unit. Remove oil pressure sender from dash panel and lay on engine.

14. Disconnect accelerator cable from injection pump. Disconnect speed control cable from injection pump, if so equipped. Remove accelerator cable bracket with cables attached, from intake manifold and position out of the way.

15. Disconnect transmission kick down rod from injection pump, if so equipped. Disconnect main wiring harness connector from right side of engine. Disconnect engine ground strap from rear of engine. Disconnect fuel return hose from left rear of engine.

16. Remove two upper transmission-to-engine attaching bolts.

17. Disconnect heater hoses from water pump and right cylinder head. Disconnect water temperature sender wire from sender on left front of engine block. Disconnect water temperature overheat light switch wire from switch on top front of left cylinder head. Position wires out of the way.

18. Raise vehicle and safely support on jackstands.

19. Disconnect both battery ground cables from lower front of engine.

20. Disconnect and cap fuel inlet line at fuel supply pump.

21. Disconnect starter cables at starter motor.

22. Disconnect muffler inlet pipe at exhaust manifold.

23. Disconnect engine insulators from No. 1 crossmember. Remove flywheel inspection plate. Remove four converter-to-flywheel attaching nuts, if so equipped. Lower vehicle.

24. Support transmission with a floorjack. Remove four lower transmission to engine attaching bolts.

25. Attach engine lifting sling and chain hoist. Raise engine high enough to clear number one crossmember and pull forward.

26. Rotate the front of the engine approximately 45 degrees to the left and lift it out of the engine compartment.

27. When installing the engine; lower engine into engine compartment.

--- CAUTION ---

Use care not to damage windshield wiper motor when installing engine in vehicle.

28. Start transmission main shaft into clutch disc. It may be necessary to adjust position of transmission in relation to engine if main shaft binds or will not enter clutch disc. If engine hangs up after main shaft enters clutch disc, rotate crankshaft slowly (transmission in gear) until mainshaft splines mesh with clutch disc splines. Align convertor to flywheel studs, if so equipped.

29. Lower into engine insulator brackets on number one crossmember.

30. Install four lower transmission to engine attaching bolts and tighten. Remove engine lifting sling. Raise vehicle and safely support on jackstands.

31. Install four convertor to flywheel attaching nuts, if so equipped. Install flywheel inspection plate.

32. Install engine insulator support to crossmember bracket attaching nuts and washers. Connect muffler inlet pipes to exhaust manifolds. Connect both battery ground cables to the lower front of the engine. Connect starter cables to starter. Install fuel pump inlet line on fuel pump. Lower vehicle.

33. Connect water temperature sender wire to sender on left front of engine block. Connect wire to water temperature overheat light switch on top of left cylinder head. Install heater hoses on right cylinder head and water pump and tighten clamps.

34. Connect engine ground strap at rear of engine. Connect fuel return hose at left rear of engine. Connect transmission kickdown rod, if so equipped.

35. Install accelerator cable bracket on intake manifold. Connect accelerator cable to injection pump. Connect speed control cable, if so equipped, to injection pump.

36. Install oil pressure sender on dash panel. Connect oil pressure gauge sender wire to oil pressure sender.

37. Connect fuel supply line heater and alternator wires to alternator.

38. Install power steering pump and drive belt. Do not adjust belt at this time.

39. Install A/C compressor and drive belt.

NOTE: A/C system can be recharged after engine installation is completed.

Adjust A/C compressor and power steer-steering pump drive belts.

40. Install radiator. Connect automatic transmission oil cooler lines at radiator, if so equipped. Connect upper and lower radiator hoses to radiator and tighten hose clamps. Fill and bleed the cooling system.

41. Install fan and clutch assembly.

--- CAUTION ---

Left hand thread. Turn nut counterclockwise to tighten.

42. Install radiator fan shroud halves.

42. Remove intake manifold cover, and install air cleaner. Install intake duct assembly.

43. Install hood using scribe marks drawn on hood at removal.

44. Connect battery ground cables at both batteries. Check the engine oil level and fill as needed with the specified type and grade of oil. Run engine and check for fuel, oil and coolant leaks.

VANS

300 (4.9L)

1. Take off the engine cover, drain the coolant, remove the air cleaner, and disconnect the battery.

2. Remove the bumper, grille, and gravel deflector.

3. Detach the upper radiator hose at the engine. Remove the alternator splash shield and detach the lower hose at the radiator. Remove the radiator and shroud, if any.

4. Disconnect the engine heater hoses and the alternator wires. Remove the power steering pump and support.

5. Disconnect and plug the fuel line at the pump.

6. Detach from the engine: distributor and gauge sending unit wires, brake booster hose, accelerator cable and bracket.

7. Disconnect the automatic transmission kickdown linkage at the bellcrank.

8. Remove the exhaust manifold heat deflector and unbolt the pipe from the manifold.

9. Disconnect the automatic transmission vacuum line from the intake manifold and from the junction. Remove the transmission dipstick tube support bolt at the intake manifold.

10. Remove the upper engine-to-transmission bolts.

11. Remove the starter. Remove the flywheel inspection cover. Remove the four automatic transmission torque converter nuts, then remove to front engine support nuts. Take off the oil filter.

12. Remove the rest of the transmission-to-engine fasteners, then lift the engine out from the engine compartment with a floor crane.

13. To replace the engine, lower it into place and start the mounting bolts. Install the upper transmission bolts, the converter nuts, and the lower transmission bolts. Tighten the mounting bolts. Replace all the items removed in the previous steps.

V8 Engines

—————— **CAUTION** ——————
Refer to the proceeding pickup truck section for unit disconnection details on the 6.9L diesel engine.
————————————————————

1. Take off the engine cover, drain the coolant, remove the air cleaner, and disconnect the battery. Remove the bumper, grille, and gravel deflector. Remove the upper grille support bracket, hood lock support, and air conditioning condenser upper mounting brackets.

2. With air conditioning, the system must be discharged to remove the condenser. Do not attempt to do this yourself, unless you are trained in air conditioning. Disconnect the lines at the compressor.

3. Remove the accelerator cable bracket and the heater hoses. Detach the radiator hoses and the automatic transmission cooler lines, if any. Remove the fan shroud, fan, and radiator.

4. Pivot the alternator in and detach the wires.

5. Remove the air cleaner, duct and valve, exhaust manifold shroud, and flex tube.

6. Disconnect the automatic transmission shift rod.

7. Disconnect the fuel and choke lines, detach the vacuum lines, and remove the carburetor and spacer.

8. Remove the oil filter. Detach the exhaust pipe from the manifold. Unbolt the automatic transmission tube bracket from the cylinder head. Remove the starter.

9. Remove the engine mount bolts. With automatic, remove the converter inspection cover and unbolt the converter from the flex plate.

10. Unbolt the engine ground cable and support the transmission.

11. Remove the power steering front bracket. Detach only one vacuum line at the rear of the intake manifold. Disconnect the engine wiring loom. Remove the speed control servo from the manifold. Detach the compressor clutch wire.

12. Install a lifting bracket and attach a floor crane. Remove the transmission-to-engine bolts, making sure the transmission is supported. Remove the engine.

13. To install the engine, align the converter to the flex plate and the engine dowels to the transmission. With manual transmission, start the transmission shaft into the clutch disc. You may have to turn the crankshaft slowly with the transmission in gear. Install the transmission bolts, then the mounting bolts. Replace all the items removed in the previous steps.

122 (2.0L), 140 (2.3L) intake manifold bolt tightening sequence

Intake Manifold

REMOVAL & INSTALLATION

122 (2.0L) and 140 (2.3L)

1. Drain the cooling system. Remove the air cleaner and duct assembly. Disconnect the negative battery cable.

2. Disconnect the accelerator cable, vacuum hoses (as required) and the hot water hose at the manifold fitting. Be sure to identify all vacuum hoses for proper reinstallation.

3. Remove the engine oil dipstick. Disconnect the heat tube at the EGR (exhaust gas recirculation) valve. Disconnect the fuel line at the carburetor fuel fitting.

4. Remove the dipstick retaining bolt from the intake manifold.

5. Disconnect and remove the PCV at the engine and intake manifold.

6. Remove the distributor cap and position the cap and wires out of the way, after removing the plastic plug connector from the valve cover.

7. Remove the intake manifold retaining bolts. Remove the manifold from the engine.

8. Clean all gasket mounting surfaces.

9. Install a new mounting gasket and intake manifold on the engine. Torque the bolts in proper sequence. The rest of the installation is in the reverse order of removal.

134 (2.2L) Diesel

1. Disconnect the battery ground cables from both batteries.

2. Disconnect the air inlet hose from the air cleaner and intake manifold. Disconnect and remove the fuel injection lines

from the nozzles and injection pump. Cap all lines and fittings to prevent dirt pickup.

3. Remove the nut that attaching the lower fuel return line brace to the intake manifold.

4. Disconnect and remove the lower fuel line from the injector pump and upper fuel return line.

5. Remove the air conditioner compressor with the lines attached and position out of the way. Remove the power steering pump and rear support with the lines still attached and position out of the way.

6. Remove the air inlet adapter, dropping resistor (electrical measuring device) and the gaskets.

7. Disconnect the fuel filter inlet line, remove the fuel filter mounting bracket from the cylinder head and position the filter assembly out of the way.

8. Remove the mounting nuts for the fuel line heater assembly to intake manifold and position the heater out of the way.

9. Remove the nuts that attach the intake manifold to the cylinder head. Remove the intake manifold and gasket.

10. Clean all gasket mounting surfaces.

11. Use a new intake manifold mounting gasket. Install the intake manifold in the reverse order of removal.

12. Do not tighten the mounting nuts until No. 3 lower nut that holds the fuel return line bracket is installed. After installation of the No. 3 nut, tighten all of the mounting nuts.

173 (2.8L) V6

1. Drain the cooling system. Remove the air cleaner and duct assembly.

2. Disconnect the negative battery cable. Disconnect the accelerator cable from

173 (2.8L) V6 intake manifold bolt tightening sequence

the carburetor linkage.

3. Disconnect and remove the upper radiator hose. Disconnect and remove the bypass hose from the intake manifold and thermostat housing.

4. Remove the distributor cap and spark plug wires as an assembly. Turn the engine till No. 1 piston is at TDC (top dead center) on the compression stroke. Remove the distributor.

5. Remove any vacuum lines and controls that will interfere with the intake manifold removal. Label all hoses for identification.

6. Remove both valve covers. Remove the manifold mounting nuts and bolts. Remove the manifold. Tap the manifold lightly with a plastic mallet (if necessary) to break the gasket seal.

7. Remove all old gasket material and sealing compound from the mounting surfaces.

8. Apply sealing compound to the joining surfaces. Place the intake mounting gasket into position. Make sure that the tab on the right bank head gasket fits into the cutout of the manifold gasket. Apply sealing compound to the intake manifold bolt bosses and install the intake manifold. Tighten the mounting nuts and bolts in the proper torque sequence.

9. Install the distributor and the rest of the removed components in reverse order.

10. Refill the cooling system, start the engine and check for coolant or oil leaks.

11. Check idle RPM and ignition timing. Adjust if necessary.

300 (4.9L)

The intake and exhaust manifolds on these engines are known as combination manifolds and are serviced as a unit.

1. Remove the air cleaner. Disconnect the choke cable at the carburetor. Disconnect the accelerator cable or rod at the carburetor. Remove the accelerator retracting spring.

2. On a vehicle with automatic transmission, remove the kick-down rod-retracting spring. Remove the accelerator rod bellcrank assembly.

3. Disconnect the fuel inlet line and the distributor vacuum line from the carburetor.

4. Disconnect the muffler inlet pipe from the exhaust manifold.

5. Disconnect the power brake vacuum line, if so equipped.

6. Remove the bolts and nuts attaching the manifolds to the cylinder head. Lift the manifold assemblies from the engine. Remove and discard the gaskets.

7. To separate the manifolds, remove the nuts joining the intake and exhaust manifolds.

8. Clean the mating surfaces of the cylinder head and the manifolds.

9. If the intake and exhaust manifolds have been separated, coat the mating surfaces lightly with graphite grease and place the exhaust manifold over the studs on the intake manifold. Install the lockwashers and nuts. Tighten them finger tight.

10. Install a new intake manifold gasket.

11. Coat the mating surfaces lightly with graphite grease. Place the manifold assemblies in position against the cylinder head. Make sure that the gaskets have not become dislodged. Install the attaching washers, bolts and nuts. Tighten the attaching nuts and bolts in the proper sequence to 26 ft. lbs. If the intake and exhaust manifolds were separated, tighten the nuts joining them.

12. Position a new gasket on the muffler inlet pipe and connect the inlet pipe to the exhaust manifold.

13. Connect the crankcase vent hose to the intake manifold inlet tube and position the hose clamp.

14. Connect the fuel inlet line and the distributor vacuum line to the carburetor.

15. Connect the accelerator cable to the carburetor and install the retracting spring. Connect the choke cable to the carburetor.

16. On a vehicle with an automatic transmission, install the bellcrank assembly and the kick-down rod retracting spring. Adjust the transmission control linkage.

17. Install the air cleaner.

232 (3.8L) V6 and V8's except 420 (6.9L) Diesel, 460 (7.5L)

1. Drain the cooling system, remove

8-255, 302, 351W intake manifold bolt tightening sequence

6-300 manifold bolt tightening sequence

8-351M, 400 intake manifold bolt tightening sequence

Sealer application area for the intake manifold on V6 and V8's except the 460

the air cleaner and the intake duct assembly.

2. Disconnect the accelerator rod from the carburetor and remove the accelerator retracting spring. Disconnect the automatic transmission kick-down rod at the carburetor, if so equipped.

3. Disconnect the high-tension lead and all other wires from the ignition coil.

NOTE: Distributor removal is not necessary on 3.8L V6 engines, disregard steps pretaining to its removal.

4. Disconnect the spark plug wires from the spark plugs by grasping the rubber boots and twisting and pulling at the same time. Remove the wires from the brackets on the rocker covers. Remove the distributor cap and spark plug wire assembly.

5. Remove the carburetor fuel inlet line and the distributor vacuum line from the carburetor. (See Note above Step 4).

6. Remove the distributor lockbolt and remove the distributor and vacuum line. See "Distributor Removal and Installation."

7. Disconnect the upper radiator hose from the coolant outlet housing and the water temperature sending unit wire at the sending unit. Remove the heater hose from the intake manifold.

8. Loosen the clamp on the water pump bypass hose at the coolant outlet housing and slide the hose off the outlet housing.

9. Disconnect the PCV hose at the rocker cover.

10. If the engine is equipped with the Thermactor exhaust emission control system, remove the air pump to cylinder head air hose at the air pump and position it out of the way. Also remove the air hose at the backfire suppressor valve. Remove the air hose bracket from the valve rocker arm cover and position the air hose out of the way. Remove EGR valve tube on V6 models.

11. Remove the intake manifold and carburetor as an assembly. It may be necessary to pry the intake manifold from the cylinder head. Remove all traces of the intake manifold-to-cylinder head gaskets and the two end seals from both the manifold and the other mating surfaces of the engine.

Installation is as follows:

12. Clean the mating surfaces of the intake manifold, cylinder heads and block with laquer thinner or similar solvent. On V8 engines: Apply a ⅛ in. bead of silicone-rubber RTV sealant at the points shown in the accompanying diagram.

NOTE: The 3.8L V6 engine does not use end seals. RTV sealant is used. Apply ⅛ inch bead of sealant to each end of the engine block at the points where the intake manifold rests. Assembly must occur within 15 minutes of sealant application.

—— **CAUTION** ——

Do not apply sealer to the waffle portions of the seals as the sealer will rupture the end seal material.

13. On V8 engines: Position new seals on the block and press the seal locating extensions into the holes in the mating surfaces.

232 (3.8L) V6 intake manifold bolt tightening sequence

14. Apply a ⅟₁₆ in. bead of sealer to the outer end of each manifold seal for the full length of the seal (4 places). As before, do not apply sealer to the waffle portion of the end seals.

NOTE: This sealer sets in about 15 minutes, depending on brand, so work quickly but carefully. DO NOT DROP ANY SEALER INTO THE MANIFOLD CAVITY. IT WILL FORM AND SET AND PLUG THE OIL GALLERY.

15. Position the manifold gasket onto the block and heads with the alignment notches under the dowels in the heads. Be sure gasket holes align with head holes.
16. Install the manifold and related equipment in reverse order of removal.

460 (7.5)L

1. Drain the cooling system and remove the air cleaner assembly.
2. Disconnect the upper radiator hose at the engine.
3. Disconnect the heater hoses at the intake manifold and the water pump. Position them out of the way. Loosen the water pump by-pass hose clamp at the intake manifold.

8-460 intake manifold bolt tightening sequence

4. Disconnect the PCV valve and hose at right valve cover. Disconnect all of the vacuum lines at the rear of the intake manifold and tag them for proper reinstallation.
5. Disconnect the wires at the spark plugs, and remove the wires from the brackets on the valve covers. Disconnect the high-tension wire from the coil and remove the distributor cap and wires as an assembly.
6. Disconnect all of the distributor vacuum lines at the carburetor and vacuum

RTV sealer application area for the intake manifold on the 8-460

control valve and tag them for proper installation. Remove the distributor and vacuum lines as an assembly.
7. Disconnect the accelerator linkage at the carburetor. Remove the speed control linkage bracket, if so equipped, from the manifold and carburetor.
8. Remove the bolts holding the accelerator linkage bellcrank and position the linkage and return springs out of the way.
9. Disconnect the fuel line at the carburetor.
10. Disconnect the wiring harness at the coil battery terminal, engine temperature sending unit, oil pressure sending unit, and other connections as necessary. Disconnect the wiring harness from the clips at the left valve cover and position the harness out of the way.
11. Remove the coil and bracket assembly.
12. Remove the intake manifold attaching bolts and lift the manifold and carburetor from the engine as an assembly. It may be necessary to pry the manifold away from the cylinder heads. Do not damage the gasket sealing surfaces.
Installation is as follows:
13. Clean the mating surfaces of the intake manifold, cylinder heads and block with laquer, thinner or similar solvent. Apply a ⅛ in. bead of silicone-rubber RTV sealant at the points shown in the accompanying diagram.

CAUTION
Do not apply sealer to the waffle portions of the seals as the sealer will rupture the end seal material.

14. Position new seals on the block and press the seal locating extensions into the holes in the mating surfaces.
15. Apply a ⅟₁₆ in. bead of sealer to the outer end of each manifold seal for the full length of the seal (4 places). As before, do not apply sealer to the waffle portion of the end seals.

NOTE: This sealer sets in about 15 minutes, depending on brand, so work quickly but carefully. DO NOT DROP ANY SEALER INTO THE MANIFOLD CAVITY. IT WILL FORM AND SET AND PLUG THE OIL GALLERY.

16. Position the manifold gasket onto the block and heads with the alignment notches under the dowels in the heads. Be sure gasket holes align with head holes.
17. Install the manifold and related equipment in reverse order of removal.

420 (6.9L) Diesel

1. Disconnect the battery ground cables from both batteries.
2. Remove the air cleaner and duct hose assembly. Cover the air inlet on the intake manifold.
3. Remove the injection pump. Disconnect and remove the fuel return hoses and block from the No. 7 and 8 (rear) nozzles. Remove the fuel return to tank line.

420 (6.9L) diesel intake manifold bolt tightening sequence. Torque in 2 steps;
1. **Torque bolts to 24 ft. lbs. in numbered sequence.**
2. **Torque bolts to 24 ft. lbs. in line sequence.**

4. Disconnect and remove the engine wiring harness. Be sure to remove the harness ground cable from the rear of the cylinder head.
5. Remove the bolts that retain the intake manifold and remove the manifold.
6. If the lifter valley pan is to be removed; remove the CDR valve tube and mounting grommet from the valley pan.
7. Remove the valley pan drain plug and remove the valley pan.
8. Clean all mounting surfaces. Apply a ⅛ inch bead of RTV sealant to each end of the engine block.
9. Install the valley pan and intake manifold in the reverse order of removal.

Exhaust Manifolds

REMOVAL & INSTALLATION

122 (2.0L) and 140 (2.3L)

1. Remove the air cleaner and duct assembly. Disconnect the negative battery cable.

122 (2.0L), 140 (2.3L) exhaust manifold bolt tightening sequence

2. Remove the EGR line at the exhaust manifold. Loosen the EGR tube. Remove the check valve at the exhaust manifold and disconnect the hose at the end of the air by-pass valve.

3. Remove the bracket attaching the heater hoses to the valve cover. Disconnect the exhaust pipe from the exhaust manifold.

4. Remove the exhaust manifold mounting bolts/nuts and remove the manifold.

5. Install the exhaust manifold in the reverse order.

134 (2.2L) Diesel

1. Disconnect the ground cables from both batteries.

2. Disconnect the exhaust pipe from the manifold.

3. Remove the heater hose bracket from the valve cover and exhaust manifold studs.

4. Remove the vacuum pump support brace and bracket. Remove the bolt that attaches the engine oil dipstick tube support bracket to the exhaust manifold.

5. Remove the nuts that attach the exhaust manifold to the engine and remove the manifold.

6. Clean all gasket mounting surfaces. Install a new mounting gasket and install the exhaust manifold and components in the reverse order of removal.

173 (2.8L) V6

1. Disconnect the negative battery cable. Remove the air cleaner and duct assembly.

2. Remove the left side heat shroud from the exhaust manifold. Remove any thermactor system parts that will interfere with manifold removal. Disconnect the choke heat tube at the carburetor.

3. Disconnect the exhaust pipes from the exhaust manifolds. Remove the mounting nuts from exhaust manifold studs. Remove the exhaust manifolds.

4. Install in the reverse order using new exhaust pipe to manifold gaskets.

300 (4.9L)

The intake and exhaust manifold on these engines are known as combination manifolds and are serviced as a unit. See "Intake Manifold Removal and Installation."

232 (3.8L) V6 and V8 Except 420 (6.9L) Diesel

1. Remove the air cleaner if the manifold being removed has the carburetor heat

232 (3.8L) V6 exhaust manifold bolt tightening sequence

173 (2.8L) V6 exhaust manifold bolt tightening sequence

LINE SEQUENCE
START HERE
(STEPS 2 AND 3)

FRONT

V8 exhaust manifold bolt tightening sequence. Torque in 2 steps;
1. **Torque to required specification in numbered sequence.**
2. **Torque to required specification in line sequence.**

stove attached to it. On 351 and 400 remove the oil filter.

2. Remove the dipstick tube bracket bolt/nut on the 302 V8. On 351 and 400 V8 vehicles with a column mounted automatic transmission lever, disconnect the selector lever cross-shaft for clearance. On 1981 and later models, disconnect the EGO sensor, if equipped.

3. Remove any thermactor parts that will interfere with manifold removal.

4. Disconnect the exhaust pipe or catalytic converter from the exhaust manifold. Remove and discard the donut gasket.

5. Disconnect the EGR downtube. Remove the exhaust manifold attaching screws and remove the manifold from the cylinder head.

6. Install the exhaust manifold in the reverse order of removal. Apply a light coat of graphite grease to the mating surface of the manifold. Install and tighten the attaching bolts, starting from the center and working to both ends alternately. Tighten to the proper specifications.

420 (6.9L) Diesel

1. Disconnect the ground cables from both batteries.

2. Raise and safely support the front of the vehicle on jackstands.

3. Disconnect the exhaust pipes from the manifolds.

4. If the right side manifold is to be removed, lower the vehicle. Remove the left side manifold from underneath while vehicle is raised.

5. The manifold attaching bolts are retained by lock tabs. Use a suitable tool to bend the tabs away from the bolt heads.

6. Clean all mounting surfaces. Apply anti-seize compound to the mounting bolts. Use new gaskets. Reverse the removal procedure for installation.

Rocker Arm/Rocker Shaft and Studs

REMOVAL & INSTALLATION

NOTE: Refer to the 300 (4.9L) paragraph for rocker stud replacement procedures.

122 (2.0L) and 140 (2.3L)

NOTE: A special tool is required to compress the lash adjuster.

1. Remove the valve cover and associated parts as required.

2. Rotate the camshaft so that the base circle of the cam is against the cam follower you intend to remove.

3. Remove the retaining spring from the cam follower, if so equipped.

4. Using special tool T74P-6565-B or a valve spring compressor tool, collapse the lash adjuster and/or depress the valve spring, as necessary, and slide the cam follower over the lash adjuster and out from under the camshaft.

5. Install the cam follower in the reverse order of removal. Make sure that the lash adjuster is collapsed and released before rotating the cam shaft.

134 (2.2L) Diesel

1. Remove the rocker arm (valve) cover.

2. Remove the rocker arm shaft mounting bolts, two turns at a time for each bolt. Start at the ends of the rocker shaft and work toward the middle.

3. Lift the rocker arm shaft assembly from the engine. Remove the pin and washer from each end of the shaft. Slide the rocker arms, springs and supports off the shaft. Keep all parts in order or label them for position.

4. Clean and inspect all parts, replace as necessary.

5. Assemble the rocke shaft parts in reverse order of removal. Be sure the oil holes in the shaft are pointed downward. Reinstall the rocker shaft assembly on the engine.

NOTE: Lubricate all parts with motor oil before installation.

Clean all mounting surfaces, use a new valve cover gasket and valve cover.

T79T-6527-A

VIEW A

STUD REMOVER
T79T-6527-A

VIEW B

Typical rocker arm stud removal

300 (4.9L)

1. Disconnect the inlet air hose at the oil fill cap. Remove the air cleaner.

2. Disconnect the accelerator cable at the carburetor. Remove the cable retracting spring. Remove the accelerator cable bracket from the cylinder head and position the cable and bracket assembly out of the way.

3. Remove the PCV valve from the valve rocker arm cover. Remove the cover bolts and remove the valve rocker arm cover.

4. Remove the valve rocker arm stud nut, fulcrum seat and rocker arm. Inspect the rocker arm cover bolts for worn or damaged seals under the bolt heads and replace as necessary. If it is necessary to remove a rocker arm stud, Tool T79T-6527-A is available. A 0.006 oversize reamer T62F-6527-B3 or equivalent and a 0.015 inch

oversize reamer T62F-6527-B5 or equivalent are available. For 0.010 inch oversize studs, use reamer T66P-6527-B or equivalent. To press in replacement studs, use stud replacer T79T-6527-B or equivalent for 6-300.

Rocker arm studs that are broken or have damaged threads may be replaced with standard studs. Loose studs in the head may be replaced with 0.006, 0.010 or 0.015 inch oversize studs which area available for service.

Standard and oversize studs can be identified by measuring the stud diameter within 1⅛ inch from the pilot end of the stud. The stud diameters are:

- 0.006 oversize . . . 0.3774–0.7781
- 0.010 oversize . . . 0.3814–0.3821
- 0.015 oversize . . . 0.3864–0.3871

When going from a standard size rocker arm stud to a 0.010 or 0.015 inch oversize stud, always use the 0.006 inch oversize reamer before finish reaming with the 0.010 or 0.015 inch oversize reamer.

5. Position the sleeve of the rocker arm stud remover over the stud with the bearing end down. Thread the puller into the sleeve and over the stud until it is fully bottomed. Hold the sleeve with a wrench; then, rotate the puller clockwise to remove the stud.

If the rocker arm stud was broken off flush with the stud boss, use an easy-out to remove the broken stud following the instructions of the tool manufacturer.

6. If a loose rocker arm stud is being replaced, ream the stud bore using the proper reamer (or reamers in sequence) for the selected oversize stud. Make sure the metal particles do not enter the valve area.

7. Coat the end of the stud with Lubriplate® or it's equivalent. Align the stud with the stud bore; then, tap the sliding driver until it bottoms. When the driver contacts the stud boss, the stud is installed to its correct height.

8. Apply Lubriplate® or equivalent to the top of the valve stem and at the push rod guide in the cylinder head.

9. Apply Lubriplate® or equivalent to the rocker arm fulcrum seat and the fulcrum seat socket in the rocker arm. Install the valve rocker arm, fulcrum seat and stud nut.

10. Clean the valve rocker arm cover and the cylinder head gasket surface. Place the new gasket in the cover making sure that the tabs of the gasket engage in the notches provided in the cover.

11. Install the cover on the cylinder head. Make sure the gasket seats evenly all around the head. Partially tighten the cover bolts in sequence, starting at the middle bolts. Then tighten the bolts to 3–5 ft. lb.

12. Install the PCV valve in the rocker arm cover. Install the accelerator cable bracket on the cylinder head and connect the cable to the carburetor.

13. Connect the the inlet air hose to the oil fill cap.

14. Install air cleaner.

VALVE ADJUSTMENT

1. Crank the engine until the TDC mark on the crankshaft damper is aligned with timing pointer on the cylinder front cover.

2. Scribe a mark on the damper at this point.

3. Scribe two more marks on the damper, each equally spaced from the first mark (see illustration).

4. With the engine on TDC of the compression stroke (mark A aligned with the pointer), back off the rocker arm adjusting nut until there is end-play in the pushrod. Tighten the adjusting nut until all clearance is removed, then tighten the adjusting nut one additional turn. To determine when all clearance is removed from the rocker arm, turn the pushrod with the fingers. When the pushrod can no longer be turned, all clearance has been removed.

5. Repeat this procedure for each valve, turning the crankshaft ⅓ turn to the next mark each time and following the engine firing order of 1-5-3-6-2-4.

173 (2.8L) V6

Remove emission control equipment as necessary to remove the cover.

1. Remove spark plug wires from spark plugs and rocker arm cover, using the proper plier-type tool to remove the boots from the plugs.

2. Remove throttle linkage to carburetor if it interferes with removal operation.

3. Remove rocker arm cover attaching screws. Tap rocker arm cover lightly to break gasket seal. Lift off rocker arm cover.

4. Remove rocker arm shaft stand retaining bolts by loosening the bolt two turns at a time, in sequence. Lift off rocker arm and shaft assembly and oil baffle.

5. Loosen the valve lash adjusting screws a few turns.

6. Apply engine oil to the assembly to provide initial lubrication.

7. Install oil baffle and rocker arm shaft assembly to the cylinder block and guide adjusting screws on to push rods.

8. Install and tighten rocker arm stand attaching bolts to specifications, two turns at a time, in sequence.

9. Adjust valve lash to cold specified setting.

10. Clean the valve rocker arm cover and cylinder head gasket surfaces. Coat one side of a new gasket with an oil-resistant sealer and lay cemented side of gasket on the cover. Install the cover, making sure the gasket seats evenly around the head. Tighten the cover attaching bolts.

11. Install all parts removed to gain access to rocker arm and shaft assemblies.

12. Run the engine at fast idle and check for oil leaks.

VALVE ADJUSTMENT

1. With engine cold and valve covers removed, place a finger on the adjusting screw of the intake valve rocker arm for cylinder No. 5. Valve arrangement, from

front to rear, on the left bank is I(intake)-E(exhaust)-E-I-E-I; on the right it is I-E-I-E-E-I.

2. Use a remote starter switch to bump the engine over until you can just feel the valve begin to open. Now the cam is in position to adjust the intake and exhaust valves on the No. 1 cylinder.

3. Adjust the No. 1 intake valve so that a 0.014 in. feeler gauge has a slight drag, while a 0.015 in. feeler gauge is a tight fit. To decrease lash, turn the adjusting screw clockwise; to increase lash, turn the adjusting screw counterclockwise. There are no lockbolts to tighten as the adjusting screws are self-tightening.

Adjusting the valves-173 (2.8L) V6 engine

Intake Valve Just Opening	Adjust both Valves for this Cylinder (Intake—0.014 in.; Exhaust—0.016 in.)
5	1
3	4
6	2
1	5
4	3
2	6

CAUTION

Do not use a step-type, "go-no go" feeler gauge. When checking lash, you must insert the feeler gauge and move it parallel with the crankshaft. Do not move it in and out perpendicular with the crankshaft as this will give an erroneous feel which will result in overtightened valves.

11. Adjust the exhaust valve the same way so that an 0.016 in. feeler gauge has a slight drag, while a 0.017 in. gauge is a tight fit.

12. The rest of the valves are adjusted in the same way, in their firing order (1–4–2–5–3–6), by positioning the cam according to the chart:

13. Remove all the old gasket material from the cylinder heads and rocker cover gasket surfaces, and disconnect the negative cable from the battery.

14. Remove the spark plug wires and reinstall the rocker arm covers.

15. Reinstall any hoses and wires which were removed previously.

16. Reinstall the spark plug wires, the alternator drive belt, and the thermactor air by-pass valve and its mounting bracket.

17. Reconnect the battery cable, replace the air cleaner assembly, start the engine, and check for leaks.

232 (3.8L) V6 and V8s Except 420 (6.9L) Diesel

These engines are equipped with individually mounted rocker arms. Use the following procedure to remove the rocker arms:

1. Disconnect the choke heat chamber air hose, the air cleaner and inlet duct assembly, the choke heat tube, PCV valve and hose, and the EGR hoses (if so equipped).

2. On models so equipped, disconnect the Thermactor by-pass valve and air supply hoses.

3. Label and disconnect the spark plug wires at the plugs. Remove the plug wires from the looms.

4. Remove the valve cover attaching bolts and remove the cover(s).

5. Remove the valve rocker arm stud nut.

VALVE ADJUSTMENT

This adjustment is actually part of the installation procedure for the individually mounted rocker arms found on the V6 and V8 engines, and is necessary to achieve an accurate torque value for each rocker arm nut.

By its nature, an hydraulic valve lifter will expand when it is not under load. Thus, when the rocker arms are removed and the pressure via the pushrod is taken off the lifter, the lifter expands to its maximum. If the lifter happens to be at the top of the camshaft lobe when the rocker arm is being reinstalled, a large amount of torque would

be necessary when tightening the rocker arm nut just to overcome the pressure of the expanded lifter. This makes it very difficult to get an accurate torque setting with individually mounted rocker arms. For this reason, the rocker arms are installed in a certain sequence which corresponds to the low points of the camshaft lobes.

1. Crank the engine until No. 1 cylinder is at TDC of the compression stroke and the timing pointer is aligned with the mark on the crankshaft damper.

2. Scribe a mark on the damper at this point.

3. Scribe two additional marks on the damper (see illustration).

4. With the timing pointer aligned with mark 1 on the damper, tighten the following valves to the specified torque:

- *V6-232* No. 1 intake and exhaust; No. 3 intake and exhaust; No. 4 exhaust and No. 6 intake.
- *255, 302, and 460* No. 1, 7 and 8 Intake; No. 1, 5, and 4 Exhaust
- *351 and 400* No. 1, 4 and 8 Intake; No. 1, 3 and 7 Exhaust.

5. Rotate the crankshaft 180° to point 2 and tighten the following valves:

- *V6-232* No. 2 intake; No. 3 exhaust; No. 4 intake; No. 5 intake and exhaust; No. 6 exhaust.
- *255, 302, and 460* No. 5 and 4 Intake; No. 2 and 6 Exhaust
- *351 and 400* No. 3 and 7 Intake; No. 2 and 6 Exhaust

6. Rotate the crankshaft 270° to point 3 and tighten the following valves:

- *302 and 460* No. 2, 3, and 6 Intake; No. 7, 3 and 8 Exhaust
- *351 and 400* No. 2, 5 and 6 Intake; No. 4, 5 and 8 Exhaust

7. Rocker arm tighten specifications are 232, 255, 302 and 351W—tighten nut until it contacts the rocker shoulder, then torque to 18–20 ft. lbs.; 351C and 400—tighten bolt to 18–25 ft. lbs.; 460—tighten nut until it contacts rocker shoulder, then torque to 18–22 ft. lbs.

420 (6.9L) Diesel

1. Disconnect the ground cables from both batteries.

2. Remove the valve cover retaining bolts and the valve covers.

3. Remove the rocker arm retaining bolts and posts. Keep the rockers and posts in order and identify for reinstallation to original positions.

4. Turn the engine until the timing mark is at the 11 o'clock position as viewed from the front of the engine.

5. Install all rocker arms, posts and retaining bolts and tighten.

6. Clean all gasket mounting surfaces, install new valve cover gaskets and reinstall the valve covers to the engine. Reconnect the battery cables, start the engine and check for oil leaks.

VALVE ARRANGEMENT

122/140 (2.0L/2.3L) Four:
E-I-E-I-E-I

134 (2.2L) Diesel Four:
I-E-I-E-I-E

173 (2.8L) V6:
Right: I-E-E-E-I
Left: I-E-E-I-E-I

232 (3.8L) V6:
Right: I-E-I-E-I-E
Left: E-I-E-I-E-I

420 (6.9L) Diesel V8:
Right: I-E-I-E-I-E-I-E
Left: E-I-E-I-E-I-E-I

255, 302, 351, 400, 460 V8:
(4.2L, 5.0L, 5.8L, 6.6L, 7.5L)
Right: I-E-I-E-I-E-I-E
Left: E-I-E-I-E-I-E-I

HYDRAULIC VALVE LIFTER INSPECTION

NOTE: The lifters used on diesel engines require a special test fluid, kerosene is not satisfactory.

Remove the lifters from their bores and remove any gum and varnish with safe solvent. Check the lifters for concave wear. If the bottom of the lifter is worn concave or flat, replace the lifter. Lifters are built with a convex bottom, flatness indicates wear. If a worn lifter is detected, carefully check the camshaft for wear.

To test lifter leak down, submerge the lifter in a container of kerosene. Chuck a used pushrod or its equivalent into a drill press. Position the container of kerosene so the pushrod acts on the lifter plunger. Pump the lifter with the drill press until resistance increases. Pump several more times to bleed any air from the lifter. Apply very firm, constant pressure to the lifter and observe the rate which fluid bleeds out of the lifter. If the lifter bleeds down very quickly (less than 15 seconds), the lifter should be replaced. If the time exceeds 60 seconds, the lifter is sticking and should be cleaned or replaced. If the lifter is operating properly (leak down time 15–60 seconds) and not worn, lubricate and reinstall in engine.

NOTE: Always inspect the valve pushrods for wear, straightness and oil blockage. Damaged pushrods will cause erratic valve operation.

Cylinder Head
REMOVAL & INSTALLATION
122 (2.0L) and 140 (2.3L)

1. Drain the cooling system. Disconnect the negative battery cable.

2. Remove the air cleaner.

3. Remove the valve cover.

NOTE: On models with air conditioning, remove the mounting bolts and the

TIMING POINTER

POSITION 1 – No. 1 at TDC at end of compression stroke.

POSITION 2 – Rotate the crankshaft 180 degrees (one half revolution) clockwise from POSITION 1.

POSITION 3 – Rotate the crankshaft 270 degrees (three quarter revolution) clockwise from POSITION 2.

Crankshaft pulley marking instructions for rocker arm installation on V8 engines

122 (2.0L), 140 (2.3L) 4 cylinder head bolt tightening sequence

134 (2.2L) diesel head bolt tightening sequence

drive belt, and position the compressor out of the way. Remove the compressor upper mounting bracket from the cylinder head.

— CAUTION —

If the compressor refrigerant lines do not have enough slack to permit repositioning of the compressor without first disconnecting the refrigerant lines, the air conditioning system will have to be evacuated by a trained air conditioning serviceman. Under no circumstances should an untrained person attempt to disconnect the air conditioning refrigerant lines.

---

4. Remove the intake and exhaust manifolds from the head.

5. Remove the camshaft drive belt cover. Note the location of the belt cover attaching screws that have rubber grommets.

6. Loosen the drive belt tensioner and remove the bolt.

7. Remove the water outlet elbow from the cylinder head with the hose attached.

8. Remove the cylinder head attaching bolts.

9. Remove the cylinder head from the engine.

10. Clean all gasket material and carbon from the top of the cylinder block and pistons and from the bottom of the cylinder head.

11. Position a new cylinder head gasket on the engine and place the head on the engine.

NOTE: If you encounter difficulty in positioning the cylinder head on the engine block, it may be necessary to install guide studs in the block to correctly align the head and the block. To fabricate guide studs, obtain two new cylinder head bolts and cut their heads off with a hack saw. Install the bolts in the holes in the engine block which correspond with cylinder head bolt holes nos. 3 and 4, as identified in the cylinder head bolt tightening sequence illustration. Then, install the head gasket and head over the bolts. Install the cylinder head attaching bolts, replacing the studs with the original head bolts.

12. Using a torque wrench, tighten the head bolts in the sequence.

13. Install the camshaft drive belt.

14. Install the camshaft drive belt cover and its attaching bolts. Make sure the rubber grommets are installed on the bolts.

Tighten the bolts to 6–13 ft. lbs.

15. Install the water outlet elbow and a new gasket on the engine and tighten the attaching bolts to 12–15 ft. lbs.

16. Install the intake and exhaust manifolds.

17. Assemble the rest of the components in reverse order of removal.

134 (2.2L) Diesel

1. Disconnect the ground cables from both batteries.

2. Mark the hood hinges for realignment on installation and remove the hood. Drain the cooling system.

3. Disconnect the breather hose from the valve cover and remove the intake hose and breather hose from the air cleaner and intake manifold.

4. Remove the heater hose bracket from the valve cover and exhaust manifold. Disconnect the heater hoses from the water pump and thermostat housing and position tube assembly out of the way.

5. Remove the vacuum pump support brace from the pump bracket and cylinder head.

6. Loosen and remove the alternator and vacuum pump drive belts. Loosen and remove the A/C compressor and/or power steering drive belt.

7. Disconnect the brake booster vacuum hose and remove the vacuum pump.

8. Disconnect the exhaust pipe from the exhaust manifold. Disconnect the coolant thermoswitch and coolant temperature sender wiring harness.

9. Disconnect and remove the fuel injection lines from the injector nozzles and pump. Cap all lines and fittings to prevent dirt from entering the system.

10. Disconnect the engine wire harness from the alternator, the glow plug harness and dropping resistor and position the harness out of the way.

11. Disconnect the fuel lines from both sides of the fuel heater. Remove the fuel filter assembly from the mounting bracket and position out of the way with the fuel line attached.

12. Loosen the lower No. 3 intake port nut and the bolt on the injection pump; disconnect the lower fuel return line from the intake manifold stud and the upper fuel return line.

13. If equipped with power steering, remove the bolt that attaches the pump rear support bracket to the cylinder head.

14. Remove the upper radiator hose. Disconnect the by-pass hose from the thermostat housing.

15. Remove the A/C compressor and position out of the way with the lines still attached.

— CAUTION —

Do not disconnect the compressor lines unless the proper tools are on hand to discharge the system and you are familiar with the procedure.

---

16. Remove the valve cover, rocker arm shaft assembly and the pushrods. Identify the pushrods and keep them in order for return to their original position.

17. Remove the cylinder head attaching bolts, starting at the ends of the head, working alternately toward the center. Remove the cylinder head from the truck.

18. Clean all gasket mounting surfaces. Install the cylinder head in the reverse order of removal. Torque the cylinder head bolts in the proper sequence.

173 (2.8L) V6 head bolt tightening sequence

173 (2.8L) V6

1. Remove the air cleaner assembly and disconnect the negative battery cable, and accelerator linkage. Drain the cooling system.

2. Remove the distributor cap with the spark plug wires attached. Remove the distributor vacuum line and distributor. Remove the hose from the water pump to the water outlet which is on the carburetor.

3. Remove the valve covers, fuel line and filter, carburetor, and the intake manifold.

4. Remove the rocker arm shaft and oil baffles. Remove the pushrods, keeping them in the proper sequence for installation.

5. Remove the exhaust manifold, referring to the appropriate procedures.

6. Remove the cylinder head retaining bolts and remove the cylinder heads and gaskets.

7. Remove all gasket material and carbon from the engine block and cylinder heads.

8. Place the head gaskets on the engine block.

NOTE: The left and right gaskets are not interchangeable.

9. Install guide studs in the engine block. Install the cylinder head assembles on the engine block one at a time. Tighten the cylinder head bolts in sequence.

10. Install the intake and exhaust manifolds.

11. Install the pushrods in the proper sequence. Install the oil baffles and the rocker arm shaft assemblies. Adjust the valve clearances.

12. Install the valve covers with new gaskets.

13. Install the distributor and set the ignition timing.

14. Install the carburetor and the distributor cap with the spark plug wires.

15. Connect the accelerator linkage, fuel line, with fuel filter installed, and distributor vacuum line to the carburetor. Fill the cooling system.

6-300 cylinder head bolt torque sequence

300(4.9L)

1. Drain the cooling system. Remove the air cleaner. Remove the oil filler tube. Disconnect the negative battery cable.

2. Disconnect the muffler inlet pipe at the exhaust manifold. Pull the muffler inlet pipe down. Remove the gasket.

3. Disconnect the accelerator rod or cable retracting spring. Disconnect the choke control cable if applicable and the accelerator rod at the carburetor.

4. Disconnect the transmission kickdown rod. Disconnect the accelerator linkage at the bellcrank assembly.

5. Disconnect the fuel inlet line at the fuel filter hose, and the distributor vacuum line at the carburetor. Disconnect other vacuum lines as necessary for accessibility and identify them for proper connection.

6. Remove the radiator upper hose at the coolant outlet housing.

7. Disconnect the distributor vacuum

line at the distributor. Disconnect the carburetor fuel inlet line at the fuel pump. Remove the lines as an assembly.

8. Disconnect the spark plug wires at the spark plugs and the temperature sending unit wire at the sending unit.

9. Grasp the PCV vent hose near the PCV valve and pull the valve out of the grommet in the valve rocker arm cover. Disconnect the PCV vent hose at the hose fitting in the intake manifold spacer and remove the vent hose and PCV valve.

10. Disconnect the carburetor air vent tube and remove the valve rocker arm cover.

11. Remove the valve rocker arm shaft assembly. Remove the pushrods in sequence so that they can be identified and reinstalled in their original positions.

12. Remove the cylinder head bolts and remove the cylinder head. Do not pry between the cylinder head and the block as the gasket surfaces may be damaged.

13. To install the cylinder head: Clean the head and block gasket surfaces. If the cylinder head was removed for a gasket change, check the flatness of the cylinder head and block.

14. Apply sealer to both sides of the new cylinder head gasket. Position the gasket on the cylinder block.

15. Install a new gasket on the flange of the muffler inlet pipe.

16. Lift the cylinder head above the cylinder block and lower it into position using two head bolts installed through the head as guides.

17. Coat the threads of the No. 1 and 6 bolts for the right-side of the cylinder head with a small amount of water-resistant sealer. Oil the threads of the remaining bolts. Install, but do not tighten, two bolts at the opposite ends of the head to hold the head and gasket in position.

18. The cylinder head bolts are tightened in 3 progressive steps. Torque them (in the proper sequence) to 55 ft. lbs., then 65 ft. lbs., and finally to 75 ft. lbs.

19. Apply Lubriplate® to both ends of the pushrods and install them in their original positions.

20. Install the valve rocker arm shaft assembly.

21. Adjust the valves, as necessary.

22. Install the muffler inlet pipe lockwashers and attaching nuts.

23. Connect the radiator upper hose at the coolant outlet housing.

24. Position the distributor vacuum line and the carburetor fuel inlet line on the engine. Connect the fuel line at the fuel filter hose and install a new clamp. Install the distributor vacuum line at the carburetor. Connect the accelerator linkage at the bellcrank assembly. Connect the transmission kickdown rod.

25. Connect the accelerator rod retracting spring. Connect the choke control cable (if applicable) and the accelerator rod at the carburetor.

26. Connect the distributor vacuum line at the distributor. Connect the carburetor

fuel inlet line at the fuel pump. Connect all the vacuum lines using their previous identification for proper connection.

27. Connect the temperature sending unit wire at the sending unit. Connect the spark plug wires. Connect the battery cable at the cylinder head.

28. Fill the cooling system.

29. Install the valve rocker cover. Connect the carburetor air vent tube.

30. Connect the PCV vent hose at the carburetor spacer fitting. Insert the PCV valve with the vent hose attached, into the valve rocker arm cover grommet. Install the air cleaner, start the engine and check for leaks.

232(3.8L)V6

1. Drain the cooling system.

2. Disconnect the cable from the battery negative terminal.

3. Remove the air cleaner assembly including air intake duct and heat tube.

4. Loosen the accessory drive belt idler. Remove the drive belt.

5. If the left cylinder head is being removed:

   a. If equipped with power steering, remove the pump mounting brackets' attaching bolts, leaving the hoses connected, place the pump/bracket assembly aside in a position to prevent the fluid from leaking out.

232 (3.8L) V6 head bolt tightening sequence

   b. If equipped with air conditioning, remove the mounting brackets' attaching bolts, leaving the hoses connected, position the compressor aside.

6. If the right cylinder head is being removed:

   a. Disconnect the thermactor diverter valve and hose assembly at the by-pass valve and downstream air tube.

   b. Remove the assembly.

   c. Remove the accessory drive idler.

   d. Remove the alternator.

   e. Remove the thermactor pump pulley. Remove the thermactor pump.

   f. Remove the alternator bracket.

   g. Remove the PCV valve.

7. Remove the intake manifold.

8. Remove the valve rocker arm cover

attaching screws. Loosen the silicone rubber gasketing material by inserting a putty knife under the cover flange. Work the cover loose and remove.

— **CAUTION** —

The plastic rocker arm covers will break if excessive prying is applied.

9. Remove the exhaust manifold(s).

10. Loosen the rocker arm fulcrum attaching bolts enough to allow the rocker arm to be lifted off the pushrod and rotated to one side.

11. Remove the pushrods. The position of each rod should be installed in the original position during assembly.

12. Remove the cylinder head attaching bolts. Remove the cylinder head(s).

13. Remove and discard the old cylinder head gasket(s). Discard the cylinder head bolts.

14. Lightly oil all bolt and stud bolt threads before installation except those specifying special sealant.

15. Clean the cylinder head, intake manifold, valve rocker arm cover and cylinder head gasket surfaces. If the cylinder head was removed for a cylinder head gasket replacement, check the flatness of the cylinder head and block gasket surfaces.

16. Position new head gasket(s) on the cylinder block using the dowels for alignment.

17. Position the cylinder heads to the block.

18. Apply a thin coating of pipe sealant or equivalent to the threads of the short cylinder head bolts (nearest to the exhaust manifold). Do not apply sealant to the long bolts. Lightly oil the cylinder head bolt flat washers. Install the flat washers and cylinder head bolts (Eight each side).

— **CAUTION** —

Always use new cylinder head bolts to assure a leak tight assembly. Torque retention with used bolts can vary, which may result in coolant or compression leakage at the cylinder head mating surface area.

19. Tighten the bolts in four steps following sequence:
Step 1, 47 ft. lbs.
Step 2, 55 ft. lbs.
Step 3, 63 ft. lbs.
Step 4, 74 ft. lbs.
Back-off the attaching bolts 2–3 turns. Repeat tightening sequence.

NOTE: When the cylinder head attaching bolts have been tightened using the above sequential procedure, it is not necessary to retighten the bolts after extended engine operation. However, the bolts can be checked for tightness if desired.

20. Dip each pushrod end in heavy engine oil. Install the pushrods in their original position. For each valve rotate the crankshaft until the tappet rests on the heel (base circle) of the camshaft lobe.

21. Position the rocker arms over the pushrods, install the fulcrums, and tighten the fulcrum attaching bolts to 61–132 in. lbs.

— **CAUTION** —

Fulcrums must be fully seated in cylinder head and pushrods must be seated in rocker arm sockets prior to final tightening.

22. Lubricate all rocker arm assemblies with heavy engine oil. Finally tighten the fulcrum bolts to 19–25 ft. lbs. For final tightening, the camshaft may be in any position.

NOTE: If the original valve train components are being installed, a valve clearance check is not required. If a component has been replaced, perform a valve clearance check.

23. Install the exhaust manifold(s).

24. Apply a ⅛–³⁄₁₆ inch bead of RTV silicone sealant to the rocker arm cover flange. Make sure the sealer fills the channel in the cover flange. The rocker arm cover must be installed within 15 minutes after the silicone sealer application. After this time, the sealer may start to set-up, and its sealing effectiveness may be reduced.

25. Position the cover on the cylinder head and install the attaching bolts. Note the location of the wiring harness routing clips and spark plug wire routing clip stud bolts. Tighten the attaching bolts to 36–60 in. lbs. torque.

26. Install the intake manifold.

27. Install the spark plugs, if necessary.

28. Connect the secondary wires to the spark plugs.

29. Install the oil fill cap. If equipped with air conditioning, install the compressor mounting and support brackets.

30. On the right cylinder head:
a. Install the PCV valve.
b. Install the alternator bracket. Tighten attaching nuts to 30–40 ft. lbs.
c. Install the thermactor pump and pump pulley.
d. Install the alternator.
e. Install the accessory drive idler.
f. Install the thermactor diverter valve and hose assembly. Tighten the clamps securely.

31. Install the accessory drive belt and tighten to the specified tension.

32. Connect the cable to the battery negative terminal.

33. Fill the cooling system with the specified coolant.

— **CAUTION** —

This engine has an aluminum cylinder head and requires a special unique corrosion inhibited coolant formulation to avoid radiator damage.

34. Start the engine and check for coolant, fuel, and oil leaks.

35. Check and, if necessary, adjust the curb idle speed.

36. Install the air cleaner assembly including the air intake duct and heat tube.

Cylinder head bolt torque sequence, all V8's

V8 Except 420(6.9L) Diesel & 460(7.5L)

1. Remove the intake manifolds and the carburetor as an assembly.

2. Remove the rocker arm cover(s).

3. If the right cylinder head is to be removed, loosen the alternator adjusting arm bolt and remove the alternator mounting bracket bolt and spacer. Swing the alternator down and out of the way. Remove the air cleaner inlet duct from the right cylinder head assembly. On 351 and 400 remove the ground strap at the rear of the head.

If the left cylinder head is being removed, remove the bolts fastening the accelerator shaft assembly at the front of the cylinder head. On vehicles equipped with air conditioning, the system must be discharged and the compressor removed. The procedure is best left to an air conditioning specialist. Persons not familiar with A/C systems can be easily injured when working on the systems.

4. Disconnect the exhaust manifold(s) from the muffler inlet pipe(s).

5. Loosen the rocker arm stud nuts so that the rocker arms can be rotated to the side. Remove the pushrods and identify them so that they can be reinstalled in their original positions.

6. Remove the cylinder head bolts and lift the cylinder head from the block.

To install the cylinder head(s):

1. Clean the cylinder head, intake manifold, and the valve cover and head gasket surfaces.

2. A specially treated composition head gasket is used. Do not apply sealer to a composition gasket. Position the new gasket over the locating dowels on the cylinder block. Then, position the cylinder head on the block and install the attaching bolts.

3. The cylinder head bolts are tightened in 3 progressive steps. Tighten all the bolts in the proper sequence to 50 ft. lbs., 60 ft. lbs., and finally to 70 ft. lbs. of torque on the 255, 302 and 351W. On 351M and 400 V8s, tighten to 70, 80 then 95–105 ft. lbs.

4. Clean the pushrods. Blow out the oil passage in the rods with compressed air. Check the pushrods for straightness. Never try to straighten a pushrod; always replace it.

5. Apply Lubriplate® to the ends of the pushrods and install them in their original positions.

6. Apply Lubriplate® to the rocker arms and their fulcrum seats and install the rocker arms. Adjust the valves.

7. Position a new gasket(s) on the muffler inlet pipe(s) as necessary. Connect the exhaust manifold(s) at the muffler inlet pipe(s).

8. If the right cylinder head was removed, install the alternator, ignition coil and air cleaner duct on the right cylinder head. Adjust the drive belt.

If the left cylinder head was removed, install the accelerator shaft assembly at the front of the cylinder head.

9. Clean the valve rocker arm cover and the cylinder head gasket surfaces. Place the new gaskets in the covers, making sure that the tabs of the gasket engage the notches provided in the cover. Install the compressor, evacuate, charge and leak test the system. Let an expert do this.

10. Install the intake manifold and related parts.

460 (7.5L)V8

1. Disconnect the negative battery cable. Remove the intake manifold and carburetor as an assembly.

2. Disconnect the exhaust pipe from the exhaust manifold.

3. Loosen the air conditioning compressor drive belt, if so equipped.

4. Loosen the alternator attaching bolts and remove the bolt attaching the alternator bracket to the right cylinder head.

5. Disconnect the air conditioning compressor from the engine and move it aside, out of the way.

--- CAUTION ---

Do not disconnect the compressor lines unless the proper tools are on hand to discharge the system and you are familiar with the procedure.

6. Remove the bolts securing the power steering reservoir bracket to the left cylinder head. Position the reservoir and bracket out of the way.

7. Remove the valve rocker arm covers. Remove the rocker arm bolts, rocker arms, oil deflectors, fulcrums and pushrods in sequence so that they can be reinstalled in their original positions.

8. Remove the cylinder head bolts and lift the head and exhaust manifold off the engine. If necessary, pry at the forward corners of the cylinder head against the casting bosses provided on the cylinder block. Do not damage the gasket mating surfaces of the cylinder head and block by prying against them.

9. Remove all gasket material from the cylinder head and block. Clean all gasket material from the mating surfaces of the intake manifold. If the exhaust manifold was removed, clean the mating surfaces of the cylinder head and exhaust manifold. Apply a thin coat of graphite grease to the cylinder head exhaust port areas and install the exhaust manifold.

10. Position two long cylinder head bolts in the two rear lower bolt holes of the left cylinder head. Place a long cylinder head bolt in the rear lower bolt hole of the right cylinder head. Use rubber bands to keep the bolts in position until the cylinder heads are installed on the cylinder block.

11. Position new cylinder head gaskets on the cylinder block dowels. Do not apply sealer to the gaskets, heads, or block.

12. Place the cylinder heads on the block, guiding the exhaust manifold studs into the exhaust pipe connections. Install the remaining cylinder head bolts. The longer bolts go in the lower row of holes.

13. Tighten all the cylinder head attaching bolts in the proper sequence in three stages: 75 ft. lbs., 105 ft. lbs., and finally, to 135 ft. lbs. When this procedure is used, it is not necessary to retorque the heads after extended use.

14. Make sure that the oil holes in the pushrods are open and install the pushrods in their original positions. Place a dab of Lubriplate® to the ends of the pushrods before installing them.

15. Lubricate and install the valve rockers. Make sure that the pushrods remain seated in their lifters.

16. Connect the exhaust pipes to the exhaust manifolds.

17. Install the intake manifold and carburetor assembly. Tighten the intake manifold attaching bolts in the proper sequence to 25–30 ft. lbs.

18. Install the air conditioning compressor to the engine.

19. Install the power steering reservoir to the engine.

20. Apply oil-resistant sealer to one side of the new valve cover gaskets and lay the cemented side in place in the valve covers. Install the covers.

21. Install the alternator on the right cylinder head and adjust the alternator drive belt tension.

22. Adjust the air conditioning compressor drive belt tension.

23. Fill the radiator with coolant.

24. Start the engine and check for leaks.

420 (6.9L) V8 Diesel

1. Disconnect the ground cables from both batteries. Drain the cooling system.

2. Remove the radiator shroud halves. Remove the fan and clutch assembly using Ford special tool T83T6312A and B or the equivalent. The attaching nut is equipped with a left hand thread, remove by turning clockwise.

3. Disconnect the alternator and fuel heater wiring harness from the alternator. Remove the alternator. Remove the vacuum pump.

4. Remove the fuel filter, cap all lines and fittings to prevent dirt from entering the system. Remove the alternator, vacuum pump and fuel filter mounting brackets, leave the fuel filter attached.

5. Remove the heater hose from the

420 (6.9L) diesel head bolt tightening sequence. Torque in 4 steps;

1. Torque bolts to 40 ft. lbs. in numbered sequence.
2. Torque bolts to 65 ft. lbs. in numbered sequence.
3. Torque bolts to 75 ft. lbs. in line sequence.
4. Repeat step 3.

cylinder head. Remove the injector pump, cap all lines and fittings.

6. Remove the intake manifold and valley cover.

7. Raise and safely support the front of the vehicle with jackstands.

8. Disconnect the exhaust pipes from the exhaust manifolds.

9. Remove the clamp holding the engine oil dipstick tube in position on the right side cylinder head. Remove the bolt securing the transmission fluid dipstick tube to the rear of the cylinder head.

10. Lower the vehicle. Remove the engine oil dipstick and tube from the right side.

11. Remove the valve covers, rocker arms and pushrods. Identify all parts and keep in order for installation in the original positions.

12. Remove the injector nozzles and glow plugs.

13. Remove the cylinder head attaching bolts. Remove the cylinder heads from the engine.

--- CAUTION ---

The prechambers may fall out of the cylinder head on removal. Prevent damage to the prechambers.

14. Prechambers can be removed using a brass drift and suitable hammer.

15. Clean all gasket mounting surfaces. Clean and inspect the prechambers and ports for cracks. Apply a light coating of extra heavy duty grease to the mounting edge of the prechambers and install the prechambers in the cylinder head. Lightly tap with a plastic headed hammer if necessary.

16. Install the cylinder head in the reverse order of removal. Use care to prevent the prechambers from fall into the cylinder bores when installing the heads. Torque the mounting bolts in sequence.

17. If necessary, purge the high pressure fuel lines of air by loosening the connector one half to one turn. Crank the engine until a solid flow of air free fuel comes out.

Timing Cover and Belt

REMOVAL & INSTALLATION

122 (2.0L) and 140 (2.3L)

The correct installation and adjustment of the camshaft drive belt is mandatory if the engine is to run properly. The camshaft controls the opening of the engine valves through coordination of the movement of the camshaft and the crankshaft. When any given piston is on the intake stroke the corresponding intake valve must be open to admit air/fuel mixture into the cylinder. When the same piston is on the compression and power strokes, both valves in that cylinder must be closed. When the piston is on the exhaust stroke, the exhaust valve for that cylinder must be open. If the opening and closing of the valves is not coordinated with the movements of the pistons, the engine will run very poorly, if at all.

The camshaft drive belt also turns the engine auxiliary shaft. The distributor is driven by the engine auxiliary shaft. Since the distributor controls ignition timing, the auxiliary shaft must be coordinated with the camshaft and the crankshaft, because both valves in any given cylinder must be closed and the piston in that cylinder near the top of the compression stroke when the spark plug fires.

Due to this complex interrelationship between the camshaft, the crankshaft and the auxiliary shaft, the cogged pulleys on each component must be aligned when the camshaft drive belt is installed.

122 (2.0L), 140 (2.3L) timing mark alignment

Should the camshaft drive belt jump timing by a tooth or two, the engine could still run; but very poorly. To visually check for correct timing of the crankshaft, auxiliary shaft, and the camshaft:

There is an access plug provided in the cam drive belt cover so that the camshaft timing can be checked without removing the drive belt cover.

1. Remove the access plug.
2. Turn the crankshaft until the timing marks on the crankshaft indicate TDC.
3. Make sure that the timing mark on the camshaft drive sprocket is aligned with the pointer on the inner belt cover. Also, the rotor of the distributor must align with the No. 1 cylinder firing position.

NOTE: Never turn the crankshaft of any of the overhead cam engines in the opposite direction of normal rotation. Backward rotation of the crankshaft may cause the timing belt to slip and alter the timing.

4. To replace the timing belt, set the engine to TDC with No. 1 piston on the compression stroke. The crankshaft and camshaft timing marks should align with their respective pointers and the distributor rotor should point to the no. 1 plug tower.
5. Loosen the adjustment bolts on the alternator and accessories and remove the drive belts. To provide clearance for removing the camshaft belt, remove the fan and pulley.
6. Remove the belt outer cover.
7. Remove the distributor cap from the distributor and position it out of the way.
8. Loosen the belt tensioner adjustment and pivot bolts. Lever the tensioner away from the belt and retighten the adjustment bolt to hold it away.
9. Remove the crankshaft bolt and pulley. Remove the belt guide behind the pulley.
10. Remove the camshaft drive belt.
11. Install the new belt over the crankshaft pulley first, then counterclockwise over the auxiliary shaft sprocket and the camshaft sprocket. Adjust the belt fore and aft so that it is centered on the sprockets.
12. Loosen the tensioner adjustment bolt, allowing it to spring back against the belt.
13. Remove the spark plugs and rotate the crankshaft two complete turns in the normal rotation direction to remove any belt slack. Turn the crankshaft until the timing check marks are lined up. If the timing has slipped, remove the belt and repeat the procedure.
14. Tighten the tensioner adjustment bolt to 14–21 ft. lbs., and the pivot bolt to 28–40 ft. lbs.
15. Replace the belt guide and crankshaft pulley, distributor cap, belt outer cover, fan and pulley, drive belts and accessories. Adjust the accessory drive belt tension. Start the engine and check the ignition timing.

Timing Cover/Seal and Timing Chain/Gears

REMOVAL & INSTALLATION

134 (2.2L) Diesel

1. Bring the engine to No. 1 piston at TDC on the compression stroke.
2. Disconnect the ground cables from the batteries. Drain the cooling system.

3. Remove the radiator fan shroud and cooling fan. Drain the engine oil from the crankcase.
4. Loosen the idler pulley and remove the A/C compressor belt. Remove the power steering belt. Remove the power steering pump and mounting bracket, position out of the way with the hoses attached.
5. Loosen and remove the alternator and vacuum pump drive belts.
6. Remove the water pump. Using a suitable puller, remove the crankshaft pulley.
7. Remove the nuts and bolts retaining the timing case cover to the engine block. Remove the timing case cover.
8. Remove the engine oil pan.
9. Verify that all timing marks are aligned. Rotate the engine, if necessary, to align marks.
10. Remove the bolt attaching the camshaft gear and remove the washer and friction gear.

134 (2.2L) diesel timing mark alignment

134 (2.2L) diesel injection pump gear removal

11. Remove the bolt attaching the injection pump gear and remove the washer and friction gear.
12. Install Ford tool T83T6306A or equivalent on to the camshaft drive gear and remove the gear. Attach the puller to the injection pump drive gear and remove the gear.
13. Remove the nuts attaching the idler gears after marking reference points on the idler gears for reinstallation position. Remove the idler gear assemblies.

14. Remove the nuts attaching the injection pump to the timing gear case. Support the injection pump in position.

15. Remove the bolts that attaching the timing gear case to the engine block and remove the case if necessary.

16. Clean all gasket mounting surfaces. Clean all parts, replace as necessary.

17. Remove the old oil seal from the front cover and replace.

18. Position the timing gear cover case with a new mounting gasket and install.

19. Install the timing gears as follows:

a. Verify that the crankshaft and the right idler pulley timing marks align and install the right idler gear assembly.

b. Install the camshaft gear so that the timing marks align with the timing mark on the right idler gear.

c. Install the left idler gear assembly so that the timing marks align with the timing mark on the right idler gear.

d. Install the injection pump gear so that the timing marks align with the timing mark on the left idler gear.

e. Install all friction gears, washers, nuts and bolts on the gears.

20. Install the timing case covers using a new mounting gasket.

21. Install the remaining components in the reverse order of removal.

173 (2.8L) V6
FRONT COVER

1. Disconnect negative battery cable. Remove the oil pan.

2. Drain the coolant. Remove the radiator and any other parts to provide necessary clearance.

3. If equipped with air conditioning, unbolt the compressor and bracket and move them aside; *do not* disconnect the A/C lines.

4. Remove alternator, thermactor, and drive belt(s).

5. Remove the fan.

6. Remove the drive pulley from the crankshaft.

7. Remove the front cover retaining bolts. If necessary, tap cover lightly with a plastic hammer to break gasket seal. Remove front cover. If front cover plate gasket needs replacement, remove two screws and remove plate. If necessary, remove guide sleeves from cylinder block.

8. Clean the mating surfaces of gasket material. Apply sealing compound to the gasket surfaces on the cylinder block and back side of the front cover plate. Position the gasket and front cover plate on cylinder block. Temporarily install four front cover screws to position the gasket and cover plate in place. Install and tighten two cover plate attaching bolts, then remove four screws that were temporarily installed.

9. If removed, fit new seal rings to the guide sleeves and, with no sealer used, insert the sleeves in the cylinder block with the chamfered side of the sleeve toward the front cover.

10. Apply sealing compound to front

cover gasket surface. Place the gasket in position on front cover.

11. Place the front cover on the engine and start all retaining screws two or three turns. Center the cover by inserting tool in the oil seal.

12. Tighten the front cover attaching screws to specifications.

13. Install the belt drive pulley and tighten the attaching bolt to specifications.

14. Install the oil pan.

15. Install the water pump, water hose, A/C compressor, alternator and drive belt(s). Adjust the drive belt tension to specifications.

16. Fill the cooling system to the proper level with the specified coolant.

17. Operate the engine at fast idle speed and check for coolant and oil leaks.

NOTE: If the guide sleeves were removed, install them with new seal rings but do not use sealing compound.

FRONT COVER SEAL

1. Support the front cover to prevent damage while driving out the seal.

2. Drive out the seal from the front cover.

173 (2.3L) V6 timing mark alignment

3. Support the front cover to prevent damage while installing the seal.

4. Coat the new front cover oil seal with a light grease. Install the new seal in the front cover.

GEARS

1. Drain the cooling system and the crankcase. Remove the oil pan and the radiator.

2. Remove the cylinder front cover and water pump, drive belt, and camshaft following the procedures in this section.

3. Using a gear puller, remove the crankshaft gear. Remove the key from the crankshaft.

4. Place the spacer and thrust plate on the camshaft.

5. Install the key in the camshaft. Align

the keyway in the gear with the key, then slide the gear onto the shaft, making sure that it seats tight against the spacer.

6. Check the camshaft end play. If not within specifications, replace the thrust plate.

7. Position the key in the crankshaft. Align the keyway and install the gear.

8. Install the cylinder front cover following the procedures in this section. Replace the oil pan and the radiator.

9. Fill the cooling system and crankcase.

10. Start the engine and adjust the ignition timing. Operate the engine at fast idle and check all hose connections and gaskets for leaks.

300 (4.9L)

1. Bring the engine to No. 1 piston at TDC (top dead center) on the compression stroke. Drain the cooling system. Disconnect negative battery cable.

2. Remove the radiator and shroud.

3. Remove the alternator adjusting arm bolt, loosen the drive belt and swing the alternator arm aside. Remove the fan, drive belts and pulleys.

6-300 valve timing mark alignment

4. Remove the screw and washer from the end of the crankshaft, remove the crankshaft damper.

5. Remove the front oil pan and front cover attaching screws.

NOTE: Be careful not to get foreign material in the crankcase during service work, or the crankcase oil will have to be changed.

6. Remove the cylinder front cover and discard the gasket. It is a good idea to replace the crankshaft oil seal when the cylinder front cover is removed.

7. Drive out the crankshaft oil seal with a pin punch. Clean the seal bore in the cover.

8. Remove the camshaft and crankshaft gears using a suitable puller. Install the new gears, camshaft first using Ford tool T65L6306A or the equivalent. Do not hammer on the gears. Install the crankshaft

gear over the drive key and install with tool. Verify that the timing marks on both gears are aligned. Install the crankshaft oil slinger.

9. Coat a new crankshaft oil seal with grease and install the seal in the cover. Drive the seal in until it is fully seated in the seal bore.

10. Cut the old front oil pan seal flush at the cylinder block/pan junction and remove the old seal material.

11. Clean all gasket surfaces.

12. Cut and fit a new pan seal flush to the cylinder block pan junction. Use the old seal as a pattern.

13. Coat the gasket surfaces of the block and cover with a resistant sealer. Position a new front cover gasket on the cylinder block.

14. Align the pan seal locating tabs with the pan holes. Pull the seal tabs through until the seal is completely seated. Apply a silicone sealer to the block/pan junction.

15. Position the front cover assembly over the end of the crankshaft and against the cylinder block. Start the cover and pan attaching screw. Slide the cover alignment tool over the crank stub and into the seal bore of the cover. Install the alternator adjusting arm, tighten all attaching screws to specification.

NOTE: Tighten the oil pan screws first (compressing the pan seal) to obtain the proper alignment of the cover.

16. Lubricate the crank stub, damper hub I.D. and the seal rubbing surface with Lubriplate. Align the damper keyway with the key on the crankshaft and install the damper.

17. Install the washer and capscrew into the damper and tighten specification.

18. Install the pulleys, drive belts, and fan. Adjust all drive belts to correct tension.

19. Install the radiator and shroud. Connect all cooling system hoses.

20. Fill and bleed the cooling system. If no foreign material has entered the crankcase during service work, it is not necessary to change the engine oil.

21. Operate the engine at fast idle and check for coolant and oil leaks.

232 (3.8L) V6

1. Bring No. 1 piston to T.D.C. (top dead center) of the compression stroke. Drain the cooling system. Disconnect the negative battery cable.

2. Remove the air cleaner and duct assembly.

3. Remove the fan shroud attaching bolts, position the shroud back and remove the cooling fan and clutch assembly.

4. Remove all drive belts. If equipped with power steering, remove pump and mounting brackets as an assembly. Position out of the way with the hoses attached.

5. Remove the front A/C compressor support bracket. Leave the compressor in place.

6. Disconnect the coolant by-pass hose at the water pump. Disconnect the heater hose at the water pump. Disconnect the

upper radiator hose at the thermostat housing.

7. Disconnect the coil wire from the distributor cap and remove the distributor cap with plug wires attached. Remove the distributor.

8. Raise and safely support the front of the car on jackstands.

9. Remove the crankshaft belt drive and damper using the suitable puller.

10. Remove the fuel pump shield (if equipped). Disconnect and plug all lines to and from the fuel pump. Remove the fuel pump.

11. Remove the oil filter and disconnect the lower radiator hose at the water pump.

12. Remove the oil pan after draining the engine oil. The front cover cannot be removed without removing the oil pan.

13. Lower the car. Remove the front cover attaching bolts (the water pump need not be removed).

CAUTION

A front cover attaching bolt is located behind the oil filter mounting adapter, be sure the bolt is removed before attempting cover removal.

Camshaft thrust button and spring 232 (3.8L) V6 engine

14. Remove the timing indicator and remove the front cover and water pump as an assembly.

15. Remove the camshaft thrust button and spring from the end of the camshaft.

16. Remove the camshaft gear retaining bolts.

17. Remove the camshaft gear, crankshaft gear and timing chain. If the crankshaft gear is difficult to remove, evenly pry on the sides of the gear with two small pry bars.

18. Clean all gasket mounting surfaces on the front cover, engine block and fuel pump mountings. Install a new crankshaft oil seal in the front cover.

19. Verify that the No. 1 piston is at TDC on the compression stroke. The keyway on the crankshaft should be at 12 o'clock.

20. Lubricate the timing chain with engine oil. Install the two gears and chain as an assembly.

21. Make sure the timing marks on the gears are positioned across from each other. Install the camshaft retaining bolts.

22. Install the camshaft thrust button and spring. Lubricate the thrust button with Polyethylene Grease before installation. The thrust button and spring must be bottomed out in the camshaft seat and must not be allowed to fall out during cover installation.

23. Apply sealer to the gasket mounting surfaces, install a new front cover mounting gasket and the front cover using the two dowels for alignment. Position the timing indicator in place.

24. Apply pipe sealer to the cover mounting bolts before installation. Install bolts and tighten.

25. Install the remaining components in the reverse order of removal.

NOTE: When installing the fuel pump, turn the engine until the least resistance is encountered on the pump lever. Evenly tighten the mounting bolts, the cover is aluminum and the treads can be damaged.

255 (4.2L), 302 (5.0L) and 351 (5.8L) V8—Except Econoline

1. Bring the engine to No. 1 cylinder at TDC (top dead center) on the compression stroke. Disconnect the negative battery cable at the battery. Drain the cooling system.

2. Remove the fan shroud to radiator attaching bolts. Position shroud over the fan.

V6 and V8 valve timing mark alignment

3. Disconnect the radiator lower hose, heater hose and by-pass hose at the water pump. Remove the drive belts, fan, fan spacer, and pulley.

4. Remove the fan shroud.

5. Loosen the alternator pivot bolt and bolt attaching the alternator adjusting arm to the water pump.

6. Remove the crankshaft pulley from the crankshaft vibration damper. Remove

the damper attaching bolt and washer. Install a pulley, the vibration damper and remove the damper.

7. Disconnect the fuel pump outlet line from the fuel pump. Remove the fuel pump to one side with the flexible fuel line still attached.

8. Remove the oil dipstick and the bolt attaching the dipstick to the exhaust manifold.

9. Remove the oil pan to cylinder front cover attaching bolts. Use a knife with a thin blade to cut the oil pan gasket flush with the cylinder block face prior to separating the cover from the cylinder block. Remove the cylinder front cover and water pump as an assembly.

10. Discard the cylinder front cover gasket. Remove the crankshaft front oil slinger.

Front end of the camshaft and related components

11. Check the timing chain deflection. The method for checking timing chain deflection is outlined at the end of this section. If the deflection exceeds specification, replace the chain and sprockets as follows:

a. Crank the engine until the timing marks on the sprockets are correctly aligned.

b. Remove the camshaft sprocket capscrew, washers, and fuel pump eccentric. Slide both sprockets and the timing chain forward and remove the chain and sprockets as an assembly.

c. Position the sprockets and timing chain on the camshaft. Be sure that the timing marks are properly aligned.

d. Install the fuel pump, eccentric, washers, and camshaft sprocket capscrew. Tighten the capscrew to specification.

12. Install the crankshaft front oil slinger.

13. Clean the cylinder front cover, oil pan and block gasket surfaces. Clean the oil pan gasket surface where the oil pan and front cover fasten.

14. Install a new crankshaft front oil seal.

15. Lubricate the timing chain and fuel pump eccentric with a heavy engine oil.

16. Coat the gasket surface of the oil pan with sealer, then cut and position the required sections of a new gasket on the oil

pan and apply sealer at the corners. Install the pan seal as required. Coat the gasket surfaces of the block and cover with sealer, and position a new gasket on the block.

17. Position the cylinder front cover on the cylinder block. Use care when installing the cover to avoid seal damage or possible gasket dislocation.

18. Install the cylinder front cover to seal alignment tool.

19. It may be necessary to force the cover downward to slightly compress the pan gasket. This operation can be facilitated by using a suitable tool at the front cover attaching hole locations.

20. Coat the threads of the attaching bolts with a oil-resistant sealer and install the bolts. While pushing in on the alignment tool, tighten the oil pan to cover attaching bolts to specification. Tighten the cover to block attaching bolts to specification. Remove the alignment tool.

21. Apply Lubriplate or equivalent to the oil seal rubbing surface of the vibration damper inner hub to prevent damage to the seal. Apply a white lead and oil mixture to the front of the crankshaft for damper installation.

22. Line up the crankshaft vibration damper keyway with the key in the crankshaft. Install the vibration damper on the crankshaft. Install the capscrew and washer and tighten to specification. Install the crankshaft pulley.

23. Lubricate the fuel pump lever with heavy engine oil and install the pump using a new gasket. Connect the fuel pump outlet pipe.

24. Install the alternator pivot bolt and bolt attaching the alternator adjusting arm to the water pump.

25. Position the fan shroud over the water pump. Install the pulley, spacer and fan. Install and adjust the drive belts and adjust to specified tension. Connect the radiator, heater, and by-pass hoses. Position the fan shroud on the radiator and install the attaching bolts.

26. Fill and bleed the cooling system.

27. Run the engine at fast idle and check for coolant and oil leaks. Check the coolant level. Check and adjust the ignition timing.

28. Install the air cleaner and intake duct assembly including the crankcase ventilation hose.

302 (5.0L) and 351W (5.8L) V8— Econoline

1. Bring engine to No. 1 cylinder at TDC (top dead center) on the compression stroke. Disconnect the negative battery cable at the battery. Drain the radiator.

2. Remove the air conditioning idler pulley, bracket and drive belt if equipped.

3. Remove the upper radiator hose. Remove the fan and shroud as an assembly. Raise the vehicle on a hoist.

4. Loosen the thermactor and alternator drive belts.

5. Disconnect the lower radiator hose

at the water pump. Disconnect the fuel line at the fuel pump and remove the pump. Lower the vehicle.

6. Remove the by-pass hose. Remove the power steering pump drive belt if equipped. Remove the water pump pulley and disconnect the heater hose at the water pump.

7. Remove the air condition compressor upper bracket and the power steering pump mount.

8. Remove the crankshaft pulley. Remove the oil pan to front cover bolts. Remove the front cover.

9. Check timing chain deflection, as outlined at the end of this section. If the deflection exceeds specification, replace the chain and sprockets as follows:

a. Crank the engine until the timing marks on the sprockets are correctly aligned.

b. Remove the camshaft sprocket capscrew, washers, and fuel pump eccentric. Slide both sprockets and the timing chain forward and remove the chain and sprockets as an assembly.

c. Position the sprockets and timing chain on the camshaft. Be sure that the timing marks are properly aligned.

d. Install the fuel pump, eccentric, washers, and camshaft sprocket capscrew. Tighten the capscrew to specification.

10. Clean the front cover, fuel pump, and damper. Lubricate the crankshaft front seal. Clean the gasket surface at the pan and trim the gasket. Clean the front cover gasket surface at the block.

11. Replace the oil seal in the front cover. Position the gasket on the front cylinder cover. Apply a silicone sealer to the oil pan and cylinder block junction. Cut the pan gasket and position on pan and front cover.

12. Install the front cover, fuel pump, and crankshaft pulley.

13. Install the power steering pump and water pump by-pass hose. Connect the heater hose at the water pump.

14. Install the air conditioning compressor upper bracket, water pump pulley and power steering drive belt.

15. Install the alternator belt, thermactor belt, and fan/shroud assembly.

16. Adjust the power steering pump drive belt tension to specification.

17. Install the air conditioning drive belt idler pulley and bracket. Install the air conditioning drive belt and tighten to specification.

18. Install the upper radiator hose.

19. Raise the vehicle on a hoist. Install the fuel pump with a new gasket and connect the fuel line.

20. Install the lower radiator hose. Adjust the alternator and air injection pump drive belts to specified tension.

21. Drain the crankcase and replace the oil filter. Lower the vehicle.

22. Fill the crankcase and cooling system. Check and adjust ignition timing.

23. Start the engine and run at a fast idle,

check for oil and coolant leaks.

351M (5.8L) and 400 (6.6L) V8

1. Bring the engine to No. 1 piston at TDC (top dead center) on the compression stroke. Drain the cooling system and disconnect the battery.

2. Remove the fan shroud attaching bolts and move the shroud to the rear.

3. Remove the fan and spacer from the water pump shaft.

4. Remove the air conditioner compressor drive belt lower idler pulley and the compressor mount to water pump bracket.

5. Loosen the alternator and power steering pump and remove the drive belts.

6. Remove the water pump pulley.

7. Remove the alternator and power steering pump brackets from the water pump and position them out of the way.

8. Disconnect the lower radiator and heater hose from the water pump.

9. Remove the crankshaft pulley from the crankshaft vibration damper. Remove the vibration damper attaching screw. Install a puller and remove the damper.

10. Remove the timing pointer.

11. Remove the bolts attaching the front cylinder cover to the cylinder block. Remove the front cover and water pump assembly.

12. Disconnect the fuel pump outlet line from the pump. Remove the fuel pump attaching bolts and lay the pump to one side with the flexible line still attached.

13. Discard the cylinder front cover gasket and oil pan seal.

14. Check the timing chain deflection, as outlined at the end of this section.

15. If the timing chain deflection exceeds specification, proceed as follows:

  a. Crank the engine until the timing marks on the sprockets are aligned.

  b. Remove the camshaft sprocket capscrew, washer, and two piece fuel pump eccentric. Slide both sprockets and the timing chain forward, and remove them as an assembly.

  c. Position the sprockets and timing chain on the camshaft and crankshaft. Be certain that the timing marks on the sprockets are correctly aligned.

  d. Install the two piece fuel pump eccentric, washers, and camshaft sprocket capscrew. Tighten the camshaft capscrew to specification. Make sure that the outer fuel pump eccentric sleeve rotates freely.

16. Coat a new fuel pump gasket with oil resistant sealer and position the fuel pump and gasket on the cylinder block with the fuel pump arm resting on the eccentric outer sleeve. Install the pump attaching bolt and nut and tighten to specification. Connect the fuel pump outlet line.

17. Remove the front crankshaft seal from the front cover. Clean the cylinder front cover and the engine block gasket surfaces.

18. Coat the gasket surfaces of the block and cover with sealer, and position a new gasket on the cylinder block alignment dowels.

19. Position the cylinder front cover and water pump assembly on the cylinder block alignment dowels.

20. Coat the threads of the attaching bolts with an oil resistant sealer and install the timing pointer and attaching bolts. Tighten the bolts to specifications.

21. Install the front cover oil seal into the cylinder front cover.

22. Apply Lubriplate® or its equivalent to the oil seal rubbing surface of the vibration damper inner hub to prevent damage to the seal. Apply a white lead and oil mixture to the front of the crankshaft for damper installation.

23. Line up the crankshaft vibration damper keyway with the key on the crankshaft. Install the vibration damper on the crankshaft by pressing on with appropriate tool. Install the capscrew and washer, tighten to specification. Install the crankshaft pulley.

24. Connect the heater hose and the lower radiator hose to the water pump.

25. Install the air conditioner compressor to water pump bracket and lower idler pulley.

26. Position the alternator bracket and power steering pump bracket on the water pump and install the bolts.

27. Position the water pump pulley on the water pump shaft and install the drive belts.

28. Place the fan shroud over the pulley, and install the fan and spacer.

29. Position the fan shroud over the radiator and install the attaching bolts.

30. Adjust the drive belts to specification.

31. Raise the vehicle and remove the oil pan and install new gasket and seals as described in "Oil Pan Removal and Installation."

32. Lower the vehicle. Fill the crankcase. Fill and bleed the cooling system. Connect the battery cable.

33. Operate the engine until normal operating temperature has been reached and check for oil or coolant leaks.

460 (7.5L) V8

1. Bring the engine to No. 1 piston at TDC (top dead center) on the compression stroke. Drain the cooling system and crankcase.

2. Remove the radiator shroud and fan.

3. Disconnect the upper and lower radiator hoses, and the automatic transmission oil cooler lines from the radiator.

4. Remove the radiator upper support and remove the radiator.

5. Loosen the alternator attaching bolts and air conditioning compressor idler pulley and remove the drive belts with the water pump pulley. Remove the bolts attaching the compressor support to the water pump and remove the bracket (support), if so equipped.

6. Remove the crankshaft pulley from the vibration damper. Remove the bolt and washer attaching the crankshaft damper and remove the damper with a puller. Remove the Woodruff key from the crankshaft.

7. Loosen the by-pass hose at the water pump, and disconnect the heater return tube at the water pump.

8. Disconnect and plug the fuel inlet and outlet lines at the fuel pump, and remove the fuel pump.

9. Remove the bolts attaching the front cover to the cylinder block. Cut the oil pan seal flush with the cylinder block face with a thin knife blade prior to separating the cover from the cylinder block. Remove the cover and water pump as an assembly. Discard the front cover gasket and oil pan seal.

10. Tranfer the water pump if a new cover is going to be installed. Clean all of the gasket sealing surfaces on both the front cover and the cylinder block.

11. Check the timing chain deflection, as outlined at the end of this section. If timing chain deflection exceeds specification, proceed as follows:

  a. Crank the engine until the timing marks on the sprockets are aligned.

  b. Remove the camshaft sprocket capscrew, washer, and two piece fuel pump eccentric. Slide both sprockets and the timing chain forward, and remove them as an assembly.

  c. Position the sprockets and timing chain on the camshaft and crankshaft. Be certain that the timing marks on the sprockets are correctly aligned.

  d. Install the two piece fuel pump eccentric, washers, and camshaft sprocket capscrew. Tighten the camshaft capscrew to specification.

12. Coat the gasket surface of the oil pan with sealer. Cut and position the required sections of a new seal on the oil pan. Apply sealer to the corners.

13. Coat the gasket surfaces of the cylinder block and cover with sealer and position the new gasket on the block.

14. Position the front cover on the cylinder block. Use care not to damage the seal and gasket or mislocate them.

15. Coat the front cover attaching screws with sealer and install them.

NOTE: It may be necessary to force the front cover downward to compress the oil pan seal in order to install the front cover attaching bolts. Use a drift to engage the cover screw holes through the cover and pry downward.

16. Assemble and install the remaining components in the reverse order of removal. Tighten the front cover bolts to 15–20 ft. lbs., the water pump attaching screws to 12–15 ft. lbs., the crankshaft damper to 70–90 ft. lbs., the crankshaft pulley to 35–50 ft. lbs., fuel pump to 19–27 ft. lbs., the oil pan bolts to 9–11 ft. lbs. for the ⁵⁄₁₆″ screws to 7–9 ft. lbs. for the ¼″ screws, and the alternator pivot bolt to 45–50 ft. lbs.

420 (6.9L) Diesel
FRONT COVER AND OIL SEAL

1. Disconnect the battery ground cables from both batteries. Drain cooling system. Remove the air cleaner and install intake air opening.

Fan clutch removal

2. Remove the radiator fan shroud halves. Remove the fan and clutch assembly using Tool T83T-6312-A and B.

— **CAUTION** —

Left hand thread. Remove by turning nut clockwise.

3. Remove the injection pump and adapter. Remove the water pump. Remove power steering pump and bracket, place out of the way with hoses attached. Remove A/C compressor front mounting bracket. Remove alternator, if necessary.

NOTE: If A/C compressor is in the way, remove with hoses attached and position out of the way.

4. Raise vehicle and safely support on jackstands.
5. Remove crankshaft pulley and vibration damper. Remove ground cables at front of engine.
6. Remove five bolts attaching front cover to engine block and oil pan.
7. Lower vehicle.
8. Remove the bolts attaching engine front cover to engine block, and remove front cover.
9. Support engine front cover, and using an arbor press and suitable driver, drive crankshaft seal out of front cover.
10. Remove old gasket material and clean engine block, engine front cover, and oil pan sealing surfaces with a suitable solvent and dry throughly.
11. Clean water pump sealing surface.
12. Coat new front crankshaft oil seal with Polyethylene grease. Install new oil seal using front crankshaft seal replacer, a suitable spacer, and an arbor press.

— **CAUTION** —

Support engine front cover.

Front cover installation on the 420 (6.9L) diesel

13. Bottom out tool on front cover surface. Seal is automatically installed at proper depth.
14. Install fabricated alignment dowels, on engine block to align front cover and gaskets. Apply gasket sealer on engine block sealing surfaces. Install gaskets on engine block.

NOTE: RTV Sealant should be applied immediately prior to front cover installation.

15. Apply a 1/8″ bead of RTV sealant on front of engine block.
16. Apply a 1/4″ bead of RTV sealant on oil pan mounting surface. Install engine front cover in position and install three attaching bolts. Remove alignment dowels from engine and oil pan and install and hand tighten remaining front cover bolts.
17. Install fabricated alignment dowels in engine block, if necessary. Install water pump gasket on engine front cover alignment dowels. Install water pump and hand tighten bolts.

NOTE: Apply RTV sealant to the four bolts. Remove alignment dowels and install two remaining attaching bolts.

Front cover sealant application 420 (6.9L) diesel

— **CAUTION** —

Top two water pump bolts must be no more than 31.75mm (1¼ inches) long, in order to avoid contact with engine drive gears.

Tighten all water pump bolts to specification.

18. Tighten engine front cover bolts to specification. Install injection pump adaptor and pump.
19. Install heater hose fitting in pump using pipe sealant. Connect heater hose to water pump and tighten clamp to specification.
20. Raise vehicle and safely support on jackstands. Lubricate damper seal nose with clean engine oil and install crankshaft vibration damper.

NOTE: Add RTV sealant to the engine side of retaining bolt washer to prevent oil leakage past keyway.

21. Install vibration damper-to-crankshaft attaching bolt and tighten to specification. Install crankshaft pulley and tighten to specification.
22. Install both battery ground cables on front of engine. Lower vehicle.
23. Install alternator adjusting arm bracket and tighten to specification.
24. Install water pump pulley and tighten to specification.
25. Install power steering pump bracket and tighten to specification. Install power steering pump and drive belt.
26. Install A/C compressor bracket and tighten to specification. Install A/C compressor and drive belt.
27. Install alternator adjusting arm and install alternator and vacuum pump drive belts.
28. Adjust alternator, vacuum pump, power steering pump and A/C compressor drive belts.
29. Refill and bleed cooling system.
30. Connect battery ground cables to both batteries.
31. Remove intake manifold cover, install air cleaner and tighten to specification.
32. Run engine and check for coolant and oil leaks.
33. Install fan and clutch assembly. Install radiator fan shroud halves.

CRANKSHAFT DRIVE GEAR

1. Complete front cover removal procedures.
2. Install crankshaft drive gear remover Tool T83T-6316-A, and using a breaker bar to prevent crankshaft rotation, or flywheel holding Tool T74R-6375-A, remove crankshaft gear.
3. Install crankshaft gear using Tool T83T-6316-B aligning crankshaft drive gear timing mark with crankshaft drive gear timing mark.

NOTE: Gear may be heated to 167–194°C (300–350°F) for ease of installation. Heat in oven. Do not use torch.

4. Complete front cover installation procedures.

Timing mark alignment 420 (6.9L) diesel

INJECTION PUMP DRIVE GEAR AND ADAPTER

1. Disconnect battery ground cables from both batteries. Remove air cleaner and install intake opening cover.
2. Remove injection pump. Remove bolts attaching injection pump adapter to engine block, and remove adapter.
3. Remove engine front cover. Remove drive gear.
4. Clean all gasket and sealant surfaces of components removed with a suitable solvent and dry thoroughly.
5. Install drive gear in position, aligning all drive gear timing marks.

NOTE: To determine that No. 1 piston is at TDC of compression stroke, position injection pump drive gear dowel at four o'clock position. The scribe line in vibration damper should be at TDC.

— CAUTION —
Use extreme care to avoid disturbing injection pump drive gear, once it is in position.

6. Install engine front cover. Apply a 3.16mm (⅛ inch) bead of RTV Sealant along bottom surface or injection pump adapter.

NOTE: RTV should be applied immediately prior to adapter installation.

7. Install injection pump adaptor. Apply sealer to bolt threads before assembly.

NOTE: With injection pump adapter installed the injection pump drive gear cannot "jump" timing.

8. Install all removed components. Run engine and check for leaks.

NOTE: If necessary, purge the high pressure fuel lines of air by loosening the connector one half to one turn and crank the engine until a solid flow of fuel, free of air bubbles flow from the connection.

CAMSHAFT DRIVE GEAR, FUEL PUMP CAM, SPACER AND THRUST PLATE

1. Complete front cover removal procedures.

2. Remove camshaft allen screw.
3. Install gear puller, Tool T83T-6316-A and remove gear. Remove fuel supply pump, if necessary.
4. Install gear puller, Tool T77E-4220-B and shaft protector T83T-6316-A and remove fuel pump cam and spacer, if necessary.
5. Remove bolts attaching thrust plate, and remove thrust plate, if necessary.
6. Install new thrust plate, if removed.
7. Install spacer and fuel pump cam against camshaft thrust flange, using installation sleeve and replacer Tool T83T-6316-B, if removed.
8. Install camshaft drive gear against fuel pump cam, aligning timing mark with timing mark on crankshaft drive gear, using installation sleeve and replacer Tool T83T-6316-B.
9. Install camshaft allen screw and tighten to specification.
10. Install fuel pump as described in this Section, if removed.
11. Install front cover, following previous procedure.

CHECKING TIMING CHAIN DEFLECTION, EXCEPT 232 (3.8L) V6 ENGINE

To measure timing chain deflection, rotate crankshaft clockwise to take up slack on the left side of chain. Choose a reference point and measure distance from this point and the chain. Rotate crankshaft in the opposite direction to take up slack on the right side of chain. Force the left (slack) side of the chain out and measure the distance to the reference point chosen earlier. The difference between the two measurements is the deflection.

Timing chain should be replaced if deflection measurement exceed specified limit. The deflection measurement should not exceed ½ in.

TIMING CHAIN DEFLECTION—232 (3.8L) V6 ENGINE

1. Remove the right valve rocker arm cover.
2. Loosen the No. 3 exhaust valve rocker arm and rotate it to one side.
3. Install a dial indicator on the end of the push rod, using proper adapter tools.
4. Turn the crankshaft clockwise until the No. 1 piston is at TDC. The damper mark should point to TDC on the timing degree indicator. This will also take up the slack on the right side of the chain.
5. Zero the dial indicator needle.
6. Turn the crankshaft slowly counterclockwise until the slightest movement is seen on the dial indicator. Stop and observe the damper timing mark for the number of degrees of travel from TDC.
7. If the reading on the timing degree

indicator exceeds 6°, replace the timing chain and sprockets.

CAMSHAFT ENDPLAY MEASUREMENT

The camshaft gears used on some engines are easily damaged if pried upon while the valve train load is on the camshaft. Loosen rocker arm nuts or rocker arm shaft support bolts before checking camshaft endplay.

Push camshaft toward rear of engine, install and zero a dial indicator, then pry between camshaft gear and block to pull the camshaft forward. If endplay is excessive, check for correct installation of spacer. If spacer is installed correctly, then replace thrust plate.

MEASURING TIMING GEAR BACKLASH

Use a dial indicator installed on block to measure timing gear backlash. Hold gear firmly against the block while making measurement. If excessive backlash exists, replace both gears.

Camshaft

REMOVAL & INSTALLATION

NOTE: When installing the camshaft refer to the proceeding section for gear alignment.

122 (2.0L) and 140 (2.3L)

NOTE: The following procedure covers camshaft removal and installation with the cylinder head on or off the engine. If the cylinder head has been removed start at Step 9.

1. Drain the cooling system. Remove the air cleaner assembly and disconnect the negative battery cable.
2. Remove the spark plug wires from the plugs, disconnect the retainer from the valve cover and position the wires out of the way. Disconnect rubber vacuum lines as necessary.
3. Remove all drive belts. Remove the alternator mounting bracket-to-cylinder head mounting bolts, position bracket and alternator out of the way.
4. Disconnect and remove the upper radiator hose. Disconnect the radiator shroud.
5. Remove the fan blades and water pump pulley and fan shroud. Remove cam belt and valve covers.
6. Align engine timing marks at TDC for No. 1 cylinder. Remove cam drive belt.
7. Jack up the front of the vehicle and support on jackstands. Remove the front motor mount bolts. Disconnect the lower radiator hose from the radiator. Disconnect and plug the automatic transmission cooler lines.
8. Position a piece of wood on a floor

Camshaft removal/installation 122 (2.0L), 140 (2.3L) 4 cylinder

Camshaft retainer plate-122 (2.0L), 140 (2.3L) 4 cylinder

jack and raise the engine carefully as far as it will go. Place blocks of wood between the engine mounts and crossmember pedestals.

9. Remove the rocker arms.

10. Remove the camshaft drive gear and belt guide using a suitable puller. Remove the front oil seal with a sheet metal screw and slide hammer.

11. Remove the camshaft retainer located on the rear mounting stand by unbolting the two bolts.

12. Remove the camshaft by carefully withdrawing toward the front of the engine. Caution should be used to prevent damage to cam bearings, lobes and journals.

13. Check the camshaft journals and lobes for wear. Inspect the cam bearings, if worn (unless the proper bearing installing tool is on hand), the cylinder head must be removed for new bearings to be installed by a machine shop.

14. Cam installation is in the reverse order of removal. See following notes.

NOTE: Coat the camshaft with heavy SF oil before sliding it into the cylinder head. Install a new front seal. Apply a coat of sealer or teflon tape to the cam drive gear bolt before installation.

NOTE: After any procedure requiring removal of the rocker arms, each lash adjuster must be fully collapsed after assembly, then released. This must be done before the camshaft is turned.

Auxiliary Shaft

1. Remove the camshaft drive belt cover.

2. Remove the drive belt. Remove the auxiliary shaft sprocket. A puller may be necessary to remove the sprocket.

3. Remove the distributor and fuel pump.

4. Remove the auxiliary shaft cover and thrust plate.

5. Withdraw the auxiliary shaft from the block.

NOTE: The distributor drive gear and

the fuel pump eccentric on the auxiliary shaft must not be allowed to touch the auxiliary shaft bearings during removal and installation. Completely coat the shaft with oil before sliding it into place.

6. Slide the auxiliary shaft into the housing and insert the thrust plate to hold the shaft.

7. Install a new gasket and auxiliary shaft cover.

NOTE: The auxiliary shaft cover and cylinder front cover share a gasket. Cut off the old gasket around the cylinder cover and use half of the new gasket on the auxiliary shaft cover.

8. Fit a new gasket into the fuel pump and install the pump.

9. Insert the distributor and install the auxiliary shaft sprocket.

10. Align the timing marks and install the drive belt.

11. Install the drive belt cover.

12. Check the ignition timing.

134 (2.2L) Diesel

1. Ford recommends that the engine be removed from the vehicle when camshaft replacement is necessary.

2. With the engine removed; remove the valve cover, rocker arms and shaft assembly and the pushrods. Remove the lifters, identify and keep in order if they are to be reused.

3. Remove the front timing case cover and camshaft gear.

4. Remove the engine oil pan and oil pump.

5. Remove the camshaft thrust plate and the camshaft. Take care when removing the camshaft not to damage lobes or bearings.

6. Apply oil to the camshaft bearings and bearing journals. Apply Polyethylene grease to the camshaft lobes and install the camshaft into the engine.

7. Reinstall components in the reverse order of removal.

173 (2.8L) V6

1. Disconnect the negative battery cable from the battery. Bring engine to No. 1 cylinder at TDC (top dead center) on the compression stroke. Drain the coolant and remove the radiator, fan, spacer, water pump pulley and the drive belt.

2. Remove the distributor cap with spark plug wires as an assembly. Remove the distributor vacuum line, distributor, alternator, thermactor, rocker arm covers, fuel line and filter, carburetor, EGR tube, and intake manifold. Remove the spark plug wire boots.

3. Drain the crankcase. Remove the rocker arm and the shaft assemblies. Lift out the pushrods and place in a marked rack so they can be reinstalled in the same location.

4. Remove the oil pan.

5. Remove the drive sprocket attaching

bolt and slide the sprocket off the end of the shaft.

6. Remove the engine front cover and water pump as an assembly.

7. Remove the camshaft gear retaining bolt and slide the gear off the camshaft.

8. Remove the camshaft thrust plate and the screws.

9. Using a magnet, remove the valve lifters.

10. Carefully pull the camshaft from the block, avoiding any damage to the camshaft bearings. Remove the camshaft gear key and spacer ring.

11. Oil the camshaft journals with gear oil or assembly lube and apply it to the cam lobes.

12. Install the camshaft in the block, carefully avoiding damage to the bearing surfaces.

13. Install the spacer ring with the chamfered side toward the camshaft. Insert the camshaft key and install the thrust plate so that it covers the main oil gallery. Torque the attaching screws to specifications.

14. Check the camshaft for the specified end-play. The spacer ring and thrust plate are available in two thicknesses to permit adjusting the end-play.

15. Turn the camshaft and the crankshaft as necessary to align the timing marks and install the camshaft gear. Install the retaining washer and bolt and tighten to specifications.

16. Install the valve lifters to their original locations.

17. Install the engine front cover and water pump as an assembly.

18. Install the belt drive pulley and secure with washer and retaining bolt. Tighten the bolt to specifications.

19. Install the oil pan.

20. Apply a light grease to both ends of the pushrods. Install the valve pushrods in their original locations.

21. Install the intake manifold.

22. Install the oil baffles and the rocker arm and shaft assemblies. Tighten the rocker arm stand bolts to specifications. Adjust the valves to specified cold setting.

23. Install the water pump pulley, fan spacer, fan, and the drive belt. Adjust the belt tension to specifications. Install the carburetor, EGR tube, fuel line and filter, alternator, thermactor, distributor, distributor vacuum line, and distributor cap and wires. Install the radiator. Fill the cooling system to the proper level with the specified coolant. Adjust the ignition timing.

24. Install the rocker arm covers.

25. Run the engine and check the idle speed.

26. Run the engine at fast idle speed and check for coolant and oil leaks.

300 (4.9L)

1. Drain the cooling system. Disconnect the negative battery cable. Remove the radiator shroud and radiator. On some models it may be necessary to remove the

6-300 camshaft removal

grille and radiator support for necessary clearance.

2. Remove the front cover following procedure described in Front Cover Removal and Installation.

3. Remove air cleaner and crankcase vent tube at the rocker cover.

4. Disconnect accelerator cable, choke cable and hand throttle cable (if so equipped). Remove accelerator cable retracting spring.

5. If applicable, remove air compressor and power steering belts.

6. Disconnect oil filler hose from rocker cover.

7. Remove distributor cap and wiring as an assembly, then disconnect vacuum line and primary wire and remove distributor.

8. Remove fuel pump.

9. Remove valve rocker cover, loosen rocker arm stud nuts and move rocker arms to one side. Remove push rods, identifying each so that they may be installed in their original locations.

10. Remove push rod cover and valve lifters, identifying the position of each.

11. Turn crankshaft to align timing marks, remove camshaft thrust plate bolts and carefully pull camshaft and gear from block. Metal camshaft gear (300 HD) is bolted onto camshaft and fiber gear (300 LD) is pressed on and must be removed with an arbor press.

6-300 camshaft sprocket installation

12. To install camshaft, oil journals and apply Lubriplate to lobes, then carefully install camshaft, spacer, thrustplate and gear as an assembly, making sure timing marks are aligned, then tightening thrustplate bolts to 19–20 ft. lbs. Do not rotate crankshaft

until distributor is installed.

13. Install front cover, referring to Front Cover Removal and Installation for correct procedure.

14. Install valve lifters, then the pushrods in their original locations. Apply heavy engine oil to the lifters and Lubriplate to the pushrods.

15. Install in order the following components, referring to appropriate sections by topic for detailed instructions if necessary and using new gaskets with sealer: pushrod cover, valve rocker cover (adjust valve lash first), distributor (rotor in No. 1 cylinder firing position), fuel pump, distributor cap and wiring assembly, crankcase ventilation valve (in rocker cover), oil filler hose, accelerator cable and retracting spring, choke cable, hand throttle cable, front cylinder cover, water pump pulley, fan, belt, air compressor and power steering belts, radiator, hood latch, grill and air cleaner.

16. Fill crankcase if drained.

17. Install grille, support, radiator, hoses, etc. Fill and bleed cooling system, checking for leaks.

18. Set the ignition timing, then connect distributor vacuum line.

19. Adjust carburetor idle speed and idle fuel mixture.

232 (3.8L) V6 and V8's Except 420 (6.9L) Diesel

1. Disconnect the negative battery cable. Drain cooling system. Bring engine to No. 1 piston at TDC. Remove the intake manifold and valley pan, if so equipped.

2. Remove the rocker covers, loosen the rockers on their pivots and remove the pushrod. The pushrods must be reinstalled in their original positions.

3. Remove the valve lifters in sequence with a magnet. They must be replaced in their original positions.

4. Remove the timing gear cover and timing chain and sprockets.

5. In addition to the radiator and air conditioning condenser, if so equipped, it may be necessary to remove the front grille assembly and the hood lock assembly to gain the necessary clearance to slide the camshaft out the front of the engine.

6. Remove the camshaft thrust plate attaching screws and carefully slide the camshaft out of its bearing bores. Use extra caution not to scratch the bearing journals with the camshaft lobes.

7. Install the camshaft in the reverse order of removal. Coat the camshaft with engine oil liberally before installing it. Slide the camshaft into the engine very carefully so as not to scratch the bearing bores with the camshaft lobes. Install the camshaft thrust plate and tighten the attaching screws to 9–12 ft. lbs. Measure the camshaft end-play. If the end-play is more than 0.009 in., replace the thrust plate. Assemble the remaining components in the reverse order of removal.

V8 camshaft and related parts

173 (2.8L) V6 piston installation

134 (2.2L) diesel piston installation

420 (6.9L) Diesel

1. Remove engine from vehicle. Attach engine to stand or suitable device. Remove injection pump and adapter, intake manifold and tappets, engine front cover and fuel supply pump.

2. Remove camshaft drive gear, fuel supply pump cam, spacer and thrust plate from the camshaft.

3. Carefully remove camshaft with Ford Tool T65L-6250-A and adapter, 14-0314, by pulling toward front of engine.

— CAUTION —
Use care to avoid damaging camshaft bearings.

4. Camshaft lobes are to be coated with Polyethylene Grease and journals lubricated with recommended quality engine oil before installation.

5. Oil camshaft journal and apply Polyethylene Grease to lobes. Carefully slide camshaft through bearings. Install new camshaft thrust plate onto cylinder block and tighten to specification.

6. Install spacer and fuel pump cam against camshaft thrust flange using installation sleeve and replacer Ford Tool T83T-6316-B.

7. Install camshaft drive gear against fuel pump cam, aligning timing mark with timing mark on crankshaft drivegear using installation sleeve and replacer Ford Tool T83T-6316-B.

8. Install camshaft allen screw and tighten.

9. Install fuel supply pump, as described in this Section.

10. Install new crankshaft oil seal in engine front cover. Install engine front cover.

11. Install water pump. Install injection pump adapter.

12. Lubricate tappets and bores with recommended quality engine oil and install

tappets in their original positions. Install tappet guides. Install tappet guide retainer.

13. Position pushrods, copper colored ends toward rocker arms, into their respective tappets making sure they are seated fully in pushrod seats. Install rocker arms and valve covers with new gaskets.

14. Install intake manifold.

15. Install injection pump.

16. Install engine in vehicle.

Pistons and Connecting Rods

REMOVAL & INSTALLATION

Refer to the Engine Rebuilding Chapter in the Unit Repair Section for instructions.

122 (2.0L), 140 (2.3L) engines-the piston is installed with the notches toward the front of the engine and the oil squirt hole in the connecting rod as shown

420 (6.9L) diesel piston installation

Piston ring positioning on 420 (6.9L) diesel

T265

Proper spacing of the piston ring gaps around the piston

Connecting rod and piston positioning on the 6-300

Connecting rod and piston position for 232 V6, 255, 302, 351, 400, 460 V8 engines

RING POSITIONING

An illustration is provided for proper ring end gap location. Position the rings as shown prior to piston installation. If the instruction sheet that generally comes with a set of new piston rings differs, install as per instruction sheet.

Crankshaft and Main Bearings

REMOVAL & INSTALLATION

Refer to the Engine Rebuilding Chapter in the Unit Repair Section for instructions.

Flywheel

REMOVAL & INSTALLATION

1. If the vehicle is equipped with a manual transmission, remove the transmission and flywheel housing, clutch pressure and disc.

2. If the vehicle is equipped with an automatic transmission, remove the transmission and converter housing with converter mounted. Remove the converter to flywheel mounting bolts first, make sure the converter does not come off of the transmission shaft when removing the transmission.

3. Remove the flywheel mounting bolts and the flywheel. Inspect and replace the pilot bearing if necessary.

4. Installation is in the reverse order of removal.

ENGINE LUBRICATION

Oil Pan

REMOVAL & INSTALLATION

122 (2.0) and 140 (2.3L)

1. Disconnect the negative battery cable.
2. Remove air cleaner assembly. Remove oil dipstick. Remove engine mount retaining nuts.
3. Remove oil cooler lines at the radiator, if so equipped. Remove (2) bolts retaining the fan shroud to the radiator and remove shroud.
4. Remove radiator retaining bolts (automatic only). Position radiator upward and wire to the hood (automatic only).
5. Raise the vehicle and safely support on jackstands.
6. Drain oil from crankcase.
7. Remove starter cable from starter and remove starter.
8. Disconnect the exhaust manifold tube to the inlet pipe bracket at the thermactor check valve.
9. Remove transmission mount retaining nuts to the crossmember.
10. Remove bellcrank from converter housing (automatic only).
11. Remove oil cooler lines from retainer at the block (automatic only).

12. Remove front crossmember (automatic only).
13. Disconnect right front lower shock absorber mount (manual only).
14. Position jack under engine, raise and block with a piece of wood approximately 2-½" high. Remove jack.
15. Position jack under the transmission and raise slightly (automatic only).
16. Remove oil pan retaining bolts, lower pan to the chassis. Remove oil pump drive and pick-up tube assembly.
17. Remove oil pan (out the front—automatic only) (out the rear—manual only).
18. Clean oil pan and inspect for damage. Clean oil pan gasket surface at the cylinder block. Clean oil pump exterior and oil pump pick-up tube screen.
19. Position oil pan gasket and end seals to the cylinder block (use contact cement to retain).
20. Position oil pan to the crossmember.
21. Install oil pump and pick-up tube assembly. Install oil pan to cylinder block with retaining bolts.
22. Lower jack under transmission (automatic only).
23. Position jack under engine, raise slightly, and remove wood spacer block.
24. Replace oil filter.
25. Connect the exhaust manifold tube to the inlet pipe bracket at the thermactor check valve.
26. Install transmission mount to the crossmember.
27. Install oil cooler lines to the retainer at the block (automatic only).
28. Install bellcrank to converter housing (automatic only.)
29. Install right front lower shock absorber mount (manual only). Install front crossmember (automatic only).
30. Install starter and connect cable. Lower vehicle.
31. Install engine mount bolts.
32. Locate the radiator to the supports and install the (2) retaining bracket bolts (automatic only). Install fan shroud on the radiator.
33. Connect oil cooler lines to the radiator (automatic only).
34. Install air cleaner assembly.
35. Install oil dipstick. Fill crankcase with oil.
36. Start engine and check for leaks.

134 (2.2L) Diesel

1. Disconnect the ground cables from both batteries.
2. Remove engine oil dipstick. Disconnect air intake hose from air cleaner and intake manifold.
3. Drain coolant. Remove engine fan. Remove engine fan shroud.
4. Disconnect radiator hoses. Remove radiator upper support brackets and remove radiator and fan shroud.
5. Disconnect and cap fuel inlet and outlet lines at fuel filter and return line at injection pump.
6. Remove fuel filter assembly from

DRAIN PLUG
TIGHTEN TO 20 0-34.0 N·m
(15-25 FT·LBS)

SCREW & WASHER
TIGHTEN TO 9.0-11.5 N·m
(80-102 IN·LBS)

SCREW & WASHER
TIGHTEN TO 12.0-15.0 N·m
(106-133 IN·LBS)

HOLE "A"

OIL PAN—

GASKET LH—

GASKET RH

ESE-M4G195-A SEALER ·
APPLY A 3.0mm (.12 IN) DIA X 6.4mm
(.25 IN) LONG BEAD ON EACH
CORNER OF THE FRONT AND REAR
OIL PAN SEALS AFTER SEALS
ARE INSTALLED (4) PLACES

SEE BONDING
NOTE BELOW

SEAL · REAR

HOLE "A" REF.

SEAL · FRONT—

GASKET

ESE-M4G195-A SEALER APPROX. 3.0mm
(.12 IN) WIDE BEAD TO JOINT OF BLOCK &
FRONT COVER (2) PLACES PRIOR
TO STEPS BELOW

FRONT COVER
OR REAR CAP

CYLINDER BLOCK

FRONT OF ENGINE

SEAL TAB

VIEW TYPICAL

THERMAL BONDING INSTRUCTIONS · OIL PAN GASKETS TO BE BONDED SECURELY TO OIL PAN
USING A THERMAL PROCESS MEETING THE REQUIREMENTS OF THE (ES-DOAE-6584-A OR EQUIVALENT)
ADHESIVE COATING SPECIFICATION · IF NECESSARY IN PLACE OF THERMAL BONDING USE ADHESIVE
(ESE-M2G52-A OR B OR EQUIVALENT) APPLY EVENLY TO OIL PAN FLANGE & TO PAN SIDE OF GASKETS
ALLOW ADHESIVE TO DRY PAST "WET" STAGE THEN INSTALL GASKETS TO OIL PAN.

1. APPLY SEALER AS NOTED ABOVE
2. INSTALL SEALS TO FRONT COVER & REAR BEARING CAP · PRESS SEAL TABS FIRMLY INTO BLOCK
3. INSTALL (2) GUIDE PINS
4. INSTALL OIL PAN OVER GUIDE PINS & SECURE WITH (4) BOLTS
5. INSTALL (18) BOLTS
6. TORQUE ALL BOLTS IN SEQUENCE CLOCKWISE FROM HOLE "A" AS NOTED ABOVE

Oil pan and gasket installation 122 (2.0L), 140 (2.3L) engines

mounting bracket. Remove the fuel filter mounting bracket from cylinder head.

7. Remove nuts and washers attaching engine brackets to insulators.

8. Raise vehicle and safely support on jackstands.

9. Loosen transmission insulator bolts at rear of transmission. Remove bottom engine insulator bolts.

10. Drain engine oil from crankcase. Remove primary oil filter from left side of engine.

11. Remove by-pass filter mounting bracket and hoses.

12. Lower vehicle.

13. Attach engine lifting sling and hoist. Raise engine until insulator studs clear insulators. Slide engine forward, then raise engine approximately 3 inches.

14. Install a wooden block 3 inches high between left mount and bracket. Install a wooden block 4-¼ inches high between right mount and bracket. Lower engine.

15. Remove lifting sling and raise vehicle.

16. Remove oil pan attaching bolts, and lower oil pan onto cross member.

17. Disconnect oil pickup from oil pump and bearing cap, and lay in oil pan.

18. Move oil pan forward and up between front of engine and front body sheet metal.

NOTE: If additional clearance is needed, move A/C condensor forward.

19. Clean gasket mating surfaces of oil pan and engine block with a suitable solvent and dry thoroughly. Apply ⅛ inch bead of Silicone Sealer on split line between engine block and engine front cover and along side rails.

20. Locate oil pan gaskets in position with Gasket Cement and make sure that gasket tabs are seated in seal cap grooves.

21. Press front and rear oil pan seals in seal cap grooves with both ends of seals contacting oil pan gaskets.

22. Apply ⅛ inch bead of sealer at ends of oil pan seals where they meet oil pan gaskets.

23. Position oil pan with pickup tube on No. 1 crossmember.

24. Install oil pickup tube, with a new gasket, and tighten bolts to specification. Install oil pan with attaching bolt and plates. Tighten bolts to specification.

25. Lower vehicle.

26. Install lifting sling, raise engine and remove wooden blocks.

27. Lower engine onto insulators and install and tighten nuts and washers to specification.

28. Raise vehicle and safely support on jackstands.

29. Install transmission mount nuts.

30. Install by-pass filter bracket and hoses. Install new by-pass oil filter.

31. Install oil pan drain plug. Install new primary oil filter.

32. Lower vehicle.

33. Install fuel filter bracket on engine.

34. Install fuel filter and adaptor on mounting bracket.

35. Install fuel return line on injection pump and fuel lines on fuel filter.

36. Position radiator in vehicle, install

radiator hoses and upper support brackets.

37. Install radiator fan shroud. Install radiator fan and tighten to specification.

38. Fill and bleed cooling system.

39. Fill crankcase with specified quantity and quality of oil.

40. Install engine oil dipstick.

41. Install air intake hose on air cleaner and intake manifold.

42. Connect battery ground cables to both batteries.

43. Run engine and check for oil, fuel and coolant leaks.

173 (2.8L) V6

1. Disconnect negative battery cable. Remove carburetor air cleaner assembly.

2. Remove fan shroud and position over fan.

3. Remove distributor cap, position forward of dash panel. Remove distributor and cover bore opening.

4. Remove nuts attaching engine front insulators to cross member. Remove engine oil dipstick tube.

5. Raise vehicle and safely support on jackstands.

6. Drain engine crankcase. Remove transmission fluid filler tube and plug pan hole (auto trans. only).

7. Remove engine oil filter element. Disconnect muffler inlet pipe(s).

8. Disconnect oil cooler bracket and lower (if so equipped). Remove starter motor.

9. Position out of way, transmission oil cooler lines (if so equipped). Disconnect front stabilizer bar and position forward.

10. Position jack under engine and raise engine maximum height (until it touches dash panel) and install wooden blocks between front insulator mounts and No. 2 crossmember.

11. Lower engine onto blocks and remove jack.

12. Remove oil pan attaching bolts. Lower oil pan assembly.

13. Remove oil pump and pickup tube assembly (attached to bearing cap) and lower into oil pan. Remove oil pan assembly.

14. Clean gasket surfaces on engine and oil pan. Apply adhesive to gasket mating surfaces and install oil pan gaskets.

15. With oil pump and pickup tube assembly positioned in oil pan, install oil pump and then install oil pan. Be sure gasket forms an air tight seal. Tighten pan bolts to specification.

16. Position jack under engine and raise engine to remove wooden blocks.

17. Lower engine and remove jack. Install starter motor.

18. Connect muffler inlet pipe(s).

19. Connect front stabilizer bar. Reposition transmission oil cooler lines. Connect cooler bracket (if so equipped).

20. Install new engine oil filter element.

21. Unplug transmission oil pan and install oil filler tube (auto trans. only). Lower vehicle.

22. Install engine oil dipstick tube.

23. Install nuts attaching engine front insulators to crossmember and torque to specification.

24. Install distributor assembly and cap.

25. Position fan shroud in place and install and torque attaching screws to specification.

26. Fill engine crankcase with specified amount of oil and transmission with specified amount of fluid.

27. Connect battery negative cable.

28. Start engine, allow to run until normal operating temperature and check for oil or fluid leaks.

29. Verify ignition timing is set to specification.

30. Turn engine off. Install carburetor air cleaner assembly.

300 (4.9L)-F100 through F350

1. Drain the crankcase.

2. On the F-100—250, also drain the cooling system.

3. Remove radiator from F-100—250 vehicles.

4. Raise vehicle on a hoist. On F-100—250 trucks disconnect and remove the starter.

APPLY SEALER IN CAVITIES PRIOR TO INSTALLING SHIELD

REAR MAIN BEARING CAP

APPLY BEAD OF SEALER AS SHOWN

OIL SEAL

6-300 oil pan rear seal installation

5. On F-100—250, remove engine front support insulator to support bracket nuts and washers. Use a transmission jack to raise the front of the engine, then install blocks (1" thick) between the front support insulators and support brackets. Lower engine onto blocks and remove jack.

6. Remove the attaching bolts and oil pan. It may be necessary to remove the oil pump inlet tube and screen assembly in order to free the pan.

7. Remove the rear main bearing cap

SEAL SURFACE

FRONT

GASKET

FRONT SEAL TABS

6-300 oil pan front seal installation

and front cover seals. Clean out the seal grooves and all gasket surfaces.

8. Apply oil-resistant sealer in the spaces between the rear main bearing cap and the block as illustrated. Install new rear cap seal, then apply a bead of sealer to the tapered ends of the seal.

9. Install new oil pan side gaskets with sealer and position the front cover seal.

10. Clean oil pump pick-up assembly and place it in the pan.

11. Position pan under the engine and install pick-up assembly.

12. Install pan and attaching bolts, tightening to 10—12 ft. lbs.

13. Raise engine enough with a jack and remove wood blocks. Lower engine and install washers and nuts on the support insulator studs, tightening to 40—60 ft. lbs.

14. Install starter and starter cable on F-100—250 trucks.

15. Lower vehicle and install radiator if it was removed.

16. Fill crankcase and cooling system and start engine to check for leaks.

300 (4.9L)—E100 through 350, 1977–78

1. Remove the engine cover. Remove the air cleaner and carburetor.

2. Remove retaining bolts and position the radiator shroud on the fan.

3. Remove exhaust inlet pipe to manifold nuts.

4. Raise the vehicle on a hoist and remove the fuel line from the frame retainer.

5. Remove the alternator splash shield, front engine support nuts, and the starter.

6. Hoist the engine and place blocks under the engine support. Remove the oil pan dipstick tube. Remove the oil pan.

7. Clean the oil pan, tube and screen assembly and the gasket surfaces of the block and oil pan.

8. If removed, install the oil pump screen and tube assembly. Cement a new oil pan gasket on the oil pan. Position a new oil pan to cylinder front cover seal on the oil pan. Position the rear seal to the rear bearing cap and apply sealer. Install the oil pan.

9. Install the dipstick tube and lower the engine. Install the support nuts, starter and position the fuel line in the retainer.

10. Install the alternator splash shield and remove the hoist. Install the carburetor. Connect the exhaust and install the radiator.

11. Fill the cooling system. Replace the oil filter and fill the crankcase with the proper grade oil. Start the engine and check for leaks. Adjust the carburetor curb idle speed. Install the air cleaner.

300 (4.9L)—E100 through 350, 1979 and Later

1. Remove the engine cover. Remove the air cleaner and the carburetor.

2. If equipped with air conditioning, discharge the system and remove the compressor.

3. If the vehicle is an E-350, disconnect the thermactor check valve inlet hose and remove the check valve. Remove the EGR valve.

4. Remove the radiator hoses. Unbolt the fan shroud and position on the fan. If equipped with automatic transmission, disconnect the cooler lines and remove the oil filler tube.

5. Remove exhaust inlet pipe to manifold nuts. Raise the vehicle on a hoist and disconnect and plug fuel pump inlet line. Remove the starter. Remove alternator splash shield and front engine support nuts.

6. Remove the power steering return line clip which is located in front of the No. 1 crossmember.

7. Raise the engine and place 3 in. blocks under the engine mounts. Remove the oil pan dipstick tube.

8. Remove the oil pan bolts and remove the oil pan. Remove the pickup tube and screen from the oil pump.

9. Clean the oil pan, tube and screen assembly and the gasket surfaces of the block and oil pan.

10. Install the oil pump and screen assembly, if removed. Cement a new oil pan gasket on the oil pan. Position a new oil pan to cylinder front cover seal on the oil pan. Position the rear seal to the rear bearing cap and apply sealer. Install the oil pan.

11. Install the dipstick tube and lower the engine. Install the support nuts, starter, and connect the fuel line.

12. Install the lower radiator hose. Connect the transmission cooler lines and the transmission fill tube, if equipped.

13. Install the power steering return line clip and position the line.

14. Install the alternator splash shield and lower the hoist. Install the EGR valve and the carburetor. Connect the exhaust.

15. On E-350 models, install the thermactor check valve and connect the inlet hose.

16. Install the fan shroud and the upper radiator hose. Fill the coolin system.

17. Install the air conditioning compressor and charge the system.

18. Replace the oil filter and fill the crankcase. Start the engine and check for leaks. Adjust the carburetor curb idle speed. Install the air cleaner.

232 (3.8L) V6

1. Disconnect the cable from the battery negative cable.

2. Remove the air cleaner and duct assembly.

3. Remove the bolts attaching the fan shroud to the radiator and position the shroud over the fan.

4. Remove the engine oil dipstick.

5. Raise the vehicle and safely support on jackstands. Drain the engine oil and replace the drain plug.

6. Remove the oil filter.

7. Disconnect the muffler inlet pipes from the exhaust manifolds. Remove the

clamp attaching inlet pipe to converter pipe and remove inlet pipe from vehicle.

8. Disconnect the transmission shift linkage at the transmission.

9. Disconnect the transmission cooler lines at the radiator if so equipped.

10. Remove the nuts attaching the engine supports to the chassis brackets.

11. Raise the engine as high as possible, and place wood blocks between the engine supports and the chassis brackets. Remove the jack.

12. Remove the oil pan attaching bolts and drop the oil pan. Remove the oil pickup and tube assembly and let them lay in the oil pan. Remove the oil pan from the vehicle.

13. Clean oil pan and sealing surfaces. Inspect the gasket sealing surfaces for damages and distortion due to overtightening of the bolts. Repair and straighten as required.

14. Trial fit the oil pan to the cylinder block. Make sure enough clearance has been provided to allow the oil pan to be installed without the sealant being scraped off when the pan is positioned under the engine.

15. Remove the oil pan.

16. Lay the oil pick-up and tube assembly and place them in the oil pan.

17. Place the oil pan in position on No. 1 crossmember.

18. Install the oil pick-up and tube assembly using a new gasket. Make sure the support bracket engages the stud on the No. 2 main bearing cap attaching bolt.

19. Tighten the attaching bolts to 15–22 lb–ft and the attaching nut to 15–22 lb–ft.

20. Install a new oil pan rear seal. Using a small screwdriver, work the tabs on each end of the seal into the gap between the rear main cap and cylinder block. With the tabs positioned work the edge of the seal into the seal groove in the rear main cap.

21. Install the oil pan as follows:

a. Apply a ⅛ inch bead of RTV Sealer to the seam where the front cover and cylinder block join.

b. Apply a ⅛ inch bead of RTV Sealer to each end of the rear seal where the rear main cap and cylinder block join.

c. Apply a ⅛-inch bead of RTV Sealer along the oil pan rails on the cylinder block. As the bead crosses the front cover increase the bead width to ¼ inch.

d. Position oil pan to bottom of engine and secure with bolts. Tighten bolts to 7–8 ft–lbs.

22. Raise the engine and remove the wood blocks. Lower the engine and install the insulator-to-chassis bracket nuts and washers. Tighten the nuts to 50–70 ft–lbs.

23. Position the inlet pipe to the converter pipe and secure with attaching clamp. Connect inlet pipe to exhaust manifolds and secure with attaching nuts. Tighten to 25–38 ft–lbs.

24. Connect the transmission shift linkage at the transmission.

25. Connect the transmission cooler lines at the radiator if so equipped.

26. Install a new oil filter.

27. Lower the vehicle. Install the air cleaner assembly. Position fan shroud to radiator brace and secure with bolts.

28. Connect the battery negative cable to the battery.

29. Install the engine oil dipstick.

30. Fill crankcase with oil. Run the engine and check for possible leaks.

8-302 oil pan gasket and seals

302 (5.0L) & 351W (5.8L) V8

BRONCO

1. Remove the air cleaner and duct assembly. Remove the oil dipstick tube. Drain the engine oil.

2. Remove the oil pan bolts and remove the oil pan.

3. To install, clean the oil pan and the cylinder block of all old gasket material. Position a new oil pan gasket and end seals to the cylinder block.

4. Clean and install the oil pump pickup tube and screen assembly, if removed.

5. Install the oil pan to the cylinder block. Install the oil dipstick tube, air cleaner and duct assembly.

6. Fill the crankcase with the proper oil. Start the engine and check for leaks.

F-SERIES

1. Remove the oil dipstick. Remove the bolts attaching the fan shroud to the radiator and position the shroud over the fan.

2. Remove the nuts and lockwashers attaching the engine support insulators to the chassis bracket.

3. Disconnect the oil cooler line at the left side of the radiator, if equipped with automatic transmission.

4. Raise the engine and place wood

blocks under the engine supports. Drain the crankcase.

5. Remove the oil pan bolts and lower the oil pan onto the crossmember.

6. Remove the oil pump pick-up tube and screen. Lower this assembly, into the oil pan. Remove the oil pan.

7. To install, clean the oil pan, inlet tube and gasket surfaces. Position a new oil pan gasket and seals to the cylinder block.

8. Install the oil pick-up tube and screen to the oil pump, and install the lower attaching bolt and gasket loosely. Place the oil pan on the crossmember. Install the upper pick-up tube bolt. Tighten both pick-up tube bolts.

9. Install the oil pan. Remove the wood blocks and lower the engine.

10. Install the insulator-to-chassis bracket nuts and washers.

11. Connect the automatic transmission cooler line, if equipped. Install the fan shroud attaching bolts.

12. Fill the crankcase with oil. Install the oil dipstick. Start the engine and check for leaks.

ECONOLINE

1. Disconnect the battery and remove engine cover. Remove the air cleaner. Drain the cooling system.

2. If equipped with power steering remove the pump and position it out of the way. If so equipped, remove the air conditioning compressor retainer and position the compressor out of the way.

3. Disconnect the radiator hoses. Remove the fan shroud bolts and oil filler tube. Remove the oil dipstick bolt. Raise the vehicle on a hoist.

4. Remove the alternator splash shield. If equipped, disconnect the automatic transmission cooler lines at the radiator.

5. Disconnect and plug the fuel line at the fuel pump. Remove the engine mount nuts. Drain the engine oil. Remove the dipstick tube. Disconnect the muffler inlet pipe from the exhaust manifolds.

6. If equipped, remove the automatic transmission dipstick and tube. Disconnect the manual linkage at the transmission. Remove the center driveshaft support and remove the driveshaft from the transmission.

7. Place a transmission jack under the oil pan and insert a wooden block between the pan and jack.

─────── **CAUTION** ───────

The engine and transmission assembly will pivot around the rear engine mount. The engine assembly must be raised four inches (measured from the front motor mounts). The engine must remain centered in the engine compartment to obtain this much lift.

8. Raise the engine and transmission assembly. Insert wooden blocks to support the engine in its uppermost position.

9. Remove the oil pan bolts and lower the oil pan. Unbolt the oil pump and the oil pick-up tube and lay them in the oil pan.

Remove the oil pan from the vehicle.

NOTE: The oil pump must be removed along with the removal of the oil pan. When installing the oil pump refer to the procedure for Oil Pump Removal and Installation.

10. To install, clean the oil pan, oil pick-up tube, oil pump and gasket surfaces. Position new gasket and seals to the engine block.

11. Position the oil pan with the oil pump to vehicle and install the oil pump. Install the oil pan.

12. Continue the installation in the reverse order of removal.

13. Install a new oil filter and fill the crankcase with the proper grade oil. Fill the cooling system. Start the engine and check for oil and water.

351M (5.8L) & 400 (6.6L) V8

1. Remove the oil dipstick. Remove the fan shroud bolts and position the shroud over the fan.

2. Raise the vehicle. Drain the crankcase. Disconnect the starter cable and remove the starter.

3. Place a jack and a wood block under the oil pan and support the engine. Remove the engine front support through bolts.

4. Raise the engine and place wood blocks between the engine supports and the chassis brackets. Remove the jack.

5. If equipped with an automatic transmission, position the oil cooler lines out of the way.

6. Remove the oil pan attaching bolts and remove the oil pan.

7. To install, clean the gasket surfaces of the block, oil pan, oil pick-up tube, and screen. Coat the block surface and the oil pan gasket with sealer. Position the oil pan gasket to the cylinder block.

8. Position the oil pan front seal on the cylinder front cover plate. Position the oil pan rear seal on the rear main bearing cap. Be sure that the tabs on both the front and rear seals are over the oil pan gasket.

9. Position and install the oil pan. Continue the installation in the reverse order of removal.

10. Fill the crankcase. Start the engine and check for oil leaks.

460 (7.5L) V8
EXCEPT ECONOLINE

1. Disconnect the battery ground cable. Disconnect the radiator shroud and position it over the fan.

2. Raise the vehicle on a hoist and drain the crankcase. Remove the oil filter.

3. Remove the through bolt from each engine support. Place a floor jack under the front edge of the oil pan, with a block of wood between the jack and the oil pan. Raise the engine just high enough to insert 1¼″ blocks of wood between the insulators and the brackets. Remove the floor jack.

4. Remove the oil pan bolts and remove the oil pan. It may be necessary to rotate the crankshaft to provide clearance between the pan and the crankshaft counterweights.

5. To install, clean the gasket surfaces of the block and the oil pan. Coat both surfaces with sealer. Position the oil pan gasket on the cylinder block. Position the oil pan front seal on the cylinder front cover. Position the oil pan rear seal on the rear main bearing cap. Be sure that the tabs on both the front and rear seals are over the oil pan gasket.

6. Position and install the oil pan. Continue the installation in the reverse order of removal.

7. Replace the oil filter and fill the crankcase. Start the engine and check for oil leaks.

ECONOLINE

1. Remove the engine cover, disconnect the battery and drain the cooling system.

2. Remove the air cleaner assembly. Disconnect the throttle and transmission linkage at the carburetor. Disconnect the power brake vacuum lines.

3. Disconnect the fuel line, choke lines and remove the carburetor air cleaner adaptor from the carburetor.

4. Disconnect the radiator hoses. If equipped, disconnect the oil cooler lines. Remove the fan assembly and remove the radiator. If equipped, remove the power steering pump and position it aside.

5. Remove the front engine mount attaching bolts. Remove the engine oil dipstick tube from the exhaust manifold. Remove the oil filler tube and bracket.

6. If so equipped, rotate the air conditioning lines (at the rear of the compressor) down to clear the dash (or remove them).

7. Raise the vehicle on a hoist, drain the crankcase and remove the oil filter.

8. Remove the muffler inlet pipe assembly. Disconnect the manual and kickdown linkage from the transmission. Remove the driveshaft and coupling shaft assembly. Remove the transmission tube assembly.

9. Remove the dipstick and tube from the oil pan. Place a transmission jack under the engine oil pan. Insert a wood block between the jack surface and the oil pan. Jack the engine upward, pivoting on the rear mount until the transmission contacts the floor. Block the engine in position.

NOTE: The engine must remain centralized to obtain the maximum height. The engine must be raised four inches at the mounts to remove the oil pan.

10. Remove the oil pan bolts and lower the oil pan. Remove the oil pump and pick-up tube attachments and drop them into the oil pan. Remove the oil pan rearward from the vehicle.

NOTE: The oil pump must be removed when removing the oil pan. When installing refer to the procedure for Oil

Pump Removal and Installation.

11. To install, clean the oil pan gasket surface at the cylinder block, the oil pan assembly, the oil pump pick-up tube, and the screen.

12. *Position the oil pan gaskets and end seals to the cylinder block using sealer*. Position the oil pan with the oil pump and pick-up tube assembly to the chassis and install the oil pump assembly. Position and install the oil pan. Continue the installation in the reverse order of the removal.

13. Fill the cooling system, replace the oil filter, fill the crankcase and connect the battery. Start the engine and check for oil and water leaks.

420 (6.9L) Diesel

1. Disconnect battery ground cable from both batteries.

2. Remove engine oil level dipstick. Remove transmission oil level dipstick, if so equipped.

3. Remove air cleaner and install intake opening cover.

4. Remove fan and clutch assembly using Ford Tool T83T-6312-A and B or equivalent.

— **CAUTION** —

Left hand thread. Remove by turning nut counterclockwise.

5. Drain cooling system. Disconnect lower radiator hose.

6. Disconnect power steering return hose from pump. Plug hose and pump to prevent contamination of the system.

7. Disconnect alternator wiring harness and fuel line heater connector from alternator.

8. Raise vehicle and safely support on jackstands.

9. Disconnect and plug transmission oil cooler lines from radiator, if so equipped.

10. Disconnect and plug fuel pump inlet fuel line.

11. Drain crankcase and remove oil filter. Remove bolt attaching transmission oil filler tube to engine block and remove tube.

12. Disconnect muffler inlet pipe from exhaust manifolds.

13. Disconnect muffler inlet pipe at muffler flange and remove inlet pipe.

14. Remove upper inlet pipe mounting stud from right exhaust manifold.

15. Remove nuts and washers attaching engine insulators to No. 1 crossmember. Lower vehicle.

16. Install lifting sling and raise engine until transmission housing contacts body.

17. Install wood blocks (2¾ inch LH side, 2 inch RH side) between engine insulators and crossmember.

18. Lower engine so that blocks support engine.

19. Raise vehicle and safely support.

20. Remove flywheel inspection plate.

21. Position fuel pump inlet line at rear of No. 1 crossmember and transmission oil

cooler lines, if so equipped, out of the way.

22. Remove oil pan attaching bolts.

23. Remove oil pump and pick-up tube from engine and lay in oil pan.

24. Remove oil pan by pulling down and toward rear of vehicle.

NOTE: Crankshaft may have to be turned to reposition counterweights to aid in removal of oil pan.

25. Remove oil pump pickup tube from oil pump, if required.

26. Remove old gasket material and clean mating surfaces of oil pan, engine block and front and rear covers with a suitable solvent and dry thoroughly.

27. Clean mating surfaces of oil pickup tube. Inspect for cracks, and assemble to oil pump with new gasket, if removed. Tighten nuts to specification.

28. Prime oil pump with recommended engine oil. Rotate pump drive gear to distribute oil within pump body. Place oil pump and pick-up tube in oil pan.

29. Place oil pan in position on No. 1 crossmember.

30. Install oil pump and pick-up tube and tighten to specifications.

31. Apply ⅛ inch bead of RTV Sealant on side rails of engine block oil pan mating surface, and a ¼ inch bead of RTV Sealant on ends of engine oil pan mating surface on front and rear covers, and in mating corners.

32. Install locally fabricated oil pan installation dowels in position.

33. Position oil pan on engine and install attaching bolts. Remove oil pan locating dowels and install two remaining oil pan bolts. Tighten all oil pan bolts.

34. Install flywheel inspection plate and tighten to specifications. Lower vehicle.

35. Raise engine and remove wooden engine support blocks.

36. Lower engine onto No. 1 crossmember and remove lifting sling. Raise vehicle and safely support.

37. Install nuts and washers attaching engine insulators to No. 1 crossmember and tighten.

38. Install upper muffler inlet pipe mounting stud on right exhaust manifold.

39. Position muffler inlet pipe in vehicle and connect muffler inlet pipe to muffler flange, using a new gasket and tighten. Connect muffler inlet pipe to exhaust manifolds and tighten.

40. Install transmission oil filler tube, using a new O-ring and tighten attaching bolt. Install oil pan drain plug and new oil filter and tighten.

41. Connect fuel pump inlet line to fuel pump and tighten to specification.

NOTE: Make sure fuel line clip is reinstalled in No. 1 crossmember.

42. Connect transmission oil cooler lines and tighten to specification, if so equipped. Lower vehicle.

43. Connect alternator wiring harness and fuel line heater connector to alternator.

44. Connect power steering return hose to power steering pump.

45. Connect lower radiator hose clamp and tighten. Install radiator fan and clutch assembly using suitable tools.

— **CAUTION** —

Left hand thread. Install by turning nut counterclockwise.

46. Remove intake manifold cover, and install air cleaner and tighten.

47. Install engine oil and transmission oil dipsticks.

48. Refill cooling system.

49. Fill Crankcase with specified quantity, quality, and viscosity of engine oil.

50. Connect battery ground cables to both batteries.

51. Run engine and check for oil, fuel and coolant leaks.

52. Check power steering fluid and add, if necessary.

Typical oil pump installation

Oil Pump

REMOVAL & INSTALLATION

NOTE: Refer to the proceeding Oil Pan removal and installation section for details.

Except 232 (3.8L) V6

1. Remove the oil pan.

2. Remove the oil pump inlet tube and screen assembly.

3. Remove the oil pump attaching bolts and remove the oil pump gasket and intermediate driveshaft.

4. Before installing the oil pump, prime it by filling the inlet and outlet port with engine oil and rotating the shaft of the pump to distribute it.

5. Position the intermediate driveshaft

into the distributor socket.

6. Position the new gasket on the pump body and insert the intermediate driveshaft into the pump body.

7. Install the pump and intermediate driveshaft as an assembly. Do not force the pump if it does not seal readily. The driveshaft may be misaligned with the distributor shaft. To align it, rotate the intermediate driveshaft into a new position.

8. Install the oil pump attaching bolts and torque them to 12–15 ft. lbs. on the 6 cylinder engines and to 20–25 ft. lbs. on the V8 engines.

9. Install the oil pan.

232 (3.8L) V6

1. If necessary remove the oil filter.
2. Remove the oil pump cover attaching bolts and remove the cover.
3. Lift the pump gears of the pocket in the front cover.
4. Remove the cover gasket. Discard the gasket.
5. If necessary, remove the pump gears from the cover.
6. Pack the gear pocket with petroleum jelly.

DO NOT USE CHASSIS LUBRICANTS.

7. Install the gears in the cover pocket making sure the petroleum jelly fills all voids between the gears and the pocket.

——————— CAUTION ———————
Failure to properly pack the oil pump gears with petroleum jelly may result in failure of the pump to prime when the engine is started.

8. Position the cover gasket and install the pump cover.
9. Tighten the pump cover attaching bolts to 18–22 ft. lbs.

Rear Main Oil Seal

REMOVAL & INSTALLATION

122 (2.0L), 140 (2.3L), 134 (2.2L), 173 (2.8L), 300 (4.9L) and 420 (6.9L)

1. Remove the transmission, clutch assembly or converter and flywheel.
2. The rear main oil seal on the 2.0L,

Install sheet metal screws to help in removal of a one piece rear main oil seal

REAR OIL SEAL–2.0 AND 2.3L ENGINES

CYLINDER BLOCK

FRONT OF ENGINE

LUBRICATE SEAL AND SEAL MATING SURFACE WITH OIL, (ESE-M2C39-F) OR EQUIVALENT.

SEAL INSTALLER TOOL–T82L-6701-A

SEAL (INSTALL WITH SPRING SIDE TOWARD ENGINE).

NOTE: REAR FACE OF SEAL MUST BE WITHIN 0.127mm (0.005-INCH) OF THE REAR FACE OF THE BLOCK.

Rear main oil seal installation, typical of models using a one piece seal

2.3L, 2.8L and 4.9L is one piece. (See Step 7 for diesel engines). Lower the oil pan if necessary for working room.

3. On engines except 2.2L and 6.9L diesels, use an awl to punch two small holes on opposite sides of the seal just above the split between the main bearing cap and engine block. Install a sheet metal screw in each hole. Use two small pry bars and pry evenly on both screws using two small blocks of wood as a fulcrum point for the pry bars. Use caution throughout to avoid scratching or damage to the oil seal mounting surfaces.

4. When the seal has been removed, clean the mounting recess.

5. Coat the seal and block mounting surfaces with oil. Apply white lube to the contact surface of the seal and crankshaft. Start the seal into the mounting recess and install with seal mounting tool Ford number T82L6701A or equivalent.

6. Install the remaining components in the reverse.

7. On the 2.2L and 6.9L diesel engines; the oil seal is one piece but mounted on a retaining plate. Remove the mounting plate from the rear of the engine and replace the seal. Reinstall in reverse order of removal.

INSTALL SEAL WITH LIP TOWARDS FRONT OF ENGINE

FRONT OF ENGINE

3/8"

SEAL HALVES TO PROTRUDE BEYOND PARTING FACES THIS DISTANCE TO ALLOW FOR CAP TO BLOCK ALIGNMENT

3/8"

REAR FACE OF REAR MAIN BEARING CAP AND CYLINDER BLOCK

VIEW LOOKING AT PARTING FACE OF SPLIT, LIP TYPE CRANKSHAFT SEAL

V8 rear main oil seal positioning

All Other Engines

On all models, remove the oil pan as described below. In some cases it may be necessary to remove the oil pump pick-up and screen or the whole pump assembly.

Use only the split-lip type crankshaft rear oil seal as a replacement.

1. Loosen all main bearing caps, lowering the crankshaft slightly, but not more than 1/32".

2. Remove the rear main bearing cap.

3. Remove the seal halves from cap and block. Use a seal removing tool on the block half or install a small metal screw in one end so that the seal may be pulled out.

CAUTION
Do not damage or scratch the crankshaft seal surfaces.

4. If so equipped (not used on split-lip type), remove the oil seal retaining pin from the bearing cap.

5. Thoroughly clean seal grooves in block and cap with brush and solvent.

6. Dip seal halves in engine oil.

7. Carefully install upper half of seal with the lip facing toward the front of the engine until 3/8" is left protruding below parting surface. Be careful not to scrape seal.

8. Tighten all but the rear main bearing caps to specified torque.

9. Install lower seal half in the rear main bearing cap with the lip facing toward the front of the engine. Apply a light coat of oil-resistant sealer to the rear of the top mating surface of the cap. Do not apply sealer to the area forward of the side seal groove.

10. Install rear main bearing cap and tighten bolts to specified torque.

11. Install oil pump and oil pan.

12. Fill crankcase and operate engine to check for leaks.

COOLING SYSTEM

The satisfactory performance of any engine is controlled to a great extent by the proper operation of the cooling system. The engine block is fully waterjacketed to prevent distortion of the cylinder walls. Directed cooling and water holes in the cylinder head causes water to flow past the valve seats, which are one of the hottest parts of any engine, to carry heat away from the valves and seats.

The minimum temperature of the coolant is controlled by the thermostat, mounted in the coolant outlet passage of the engine. When the coolant temperature is below the temperature rating of the thermostat, the thermostat remains closed and the coolant is directed through the radiator by-pass hose to the water pump and back into the engine. When the coolant temperature reaches the temperature rating of the thermostat, the thermostat opens and allows coolant to flow past it and into the top of the radiator. The radiator dissipates the excess engine heat before the coolant is recirculated through the engine.

The cooling system is pressurized and operating pressure is regulated by the rating of the radiator cap which contains a relief valve. The reason for a pressurized cooling system is to allow for higher engine operating temperatures with a higher coolant boiling point.

Radiator

REMOVAL & INSTALLATION

1. Drain the cooling system.
2. Disconnect the transmission cooling

Typical 6-300 radiator installation

Applying RTV sealant to the main bearing cap on all V8's

8-400 radiator installation in 1978–79 Bronco

V8 radiator installation typical of Bronco and pick-ups

Typical coolant recovery system

Typical V8 van radiator installation

lines from the bottom of the radiator, if so equipped.

3. Remove the bolts mounting the shroud or shroud halves if so equipped, and position the shroud over the fan, clear the radiator.

4. Disconnect the upper and lower hoses from the radiator.

5. Remove the radiator retaining bolts or the upper supports and lift the radiator from the vehicle. On some 300 cu in. sixes only, remove the right hood lock bracket and bolts from the radiator grille before removing the radiator.

6. Install the radiator in the reverse order of removal. Fill the cooling system and check for leaks.

Water Pump

REMOVAL & INSTALLATION

122 (2.0L) and 140 (2.3L)

1. Disconnect the negative battery cable. Drain the cooling system. Loosen and remove the drive belt.

2. Remove the two bolts that retain the fan shroud and position the shroud back over the fan.

3. Remove the four bolts that retain the cooling fan. Remove the fan and shroud.

4. Loosen and remove the power steering and A/C compressor drive belts.

5. Remove the water pump pulley and

the vent hose to the emissions canister.

6. Remove the heater hose at the water pump.

7. Remove the cam belt cover. Remove the lower radiator hose from the water pump.

8. Remove the water pump mounting bolts and the water pump. Clean all gasket mounting surfaces.

9. Install the water pump in the reverse order of removal. Coat the threads of the mounting bolts with sealer before installation.

2.2L Diesel

1. Disconnect the ground cables from both batteries. Drain the cooling system.

2. Remove all drive belts.

3. Remove the radiator fan shroud and cooling fan and pump pulley. Disconnect the heater hose, by-pass hose and radiator hose from the water pump.

4. Remove the nuts and bolts that mount the water pump to the engine.

5. Clean all gasket mounting surfaces.

6. Install water pump in the reverse order of removal.

173 (2.8L) V6

1. Disconnect the negative battery cable. Drain the cooling system.

2. Loosen and remove drive belts. Remove pump pulley. Disconnect all the water hoses from the water pump and thermostat housing.

3. Remove the radiator shroud (if necessary) and cooling fan and clutch assembly. The fan clutch assembly mounting nut is equipped with a left hand thread, remove by turning clockwise.

4. Remove the mounting bolts and water pump, water inlet and thermostat housing as an assembly.

5. Clean all gasket mounting surfaces. Transfer parts to the new pump.

6. Install the water pump in the reverse order of removal.

232 (3.8L) V6

1. Disconnect the negative battery cable. Drain the cooling system.
2. Remove the air cleaner and duct assembly.
3. Remove drive belts and pump pulley. Remove the fan shroud and cooling fan/clutch assembly.
4. Remove the power steering pump with mounting brackets and hoses attached. Position out of the way.
5. Remove the A/C compressor front mounting bracket. Leave the compressor in place.
6. Disconnect the by-pass hose from the water pump. Disconnect the heater and radiator hose at the water pump.
7. Remove the mounting bolts and the water pump.
8. Clean all gasket mounting surfaces. Installation is in the reverse order of removal.

300 (4.9L)

1. Disconnect the negative battery cable. Drain the cooling system.
2. Disconnect the lower radiator hose from the water pump.
3. Remove the drive belt, fan and water pump pulley. Remove the alternator and air pump belts.
4. Disconnect the heater hose at the water pump.
5. Remove the water pump.
6. Before installing the old water pump, clean the gasket mounting surfaces on the pump and on the cylinder block. If a new water pump is being installed, remove the heater hose fitting from the old pump and install it on the new one. Coat the new gaskets with sealer on both sides and install the water pump in the reverse order of removal.

255 (4.2L), 302 (5.0L), 351W (5.8L) V8

1. Drain the cooling system.
2. Remove the bolts securing the fan shroud to the radiator, if so equipped, and position the shroud over the fan.
3. Disconnect the lower radiator hose, heater hose and by-pass hose at the water pump. Remove the drive belts, fan, fan spacer and pulley. Remove the fan shroud, if so equipped.
4. Loosen the alternator pivot bolt and the bolt attaching the alternator adjusting arm to the water pump.
5. Remove the bolts securing the water pump to the timing chain cover and remove the water pump.
6. Install the water pump in the reverse order of removal, using a new gasket.

351M (5.8L), 400 (6.6L), 460 (7.5L) V8

1. Drain the cooling system and remove the fan shroud attaching bolts.
2. Remove the fan assembly attaching screws and remove the shroud and fan.

3. Loosen the power steering pump attaching bolts.
4. If the truck is equipped with air conditioning, loosen the compressor attaching bolts, and remove the air conditioning compressor and power steering pump drive belts.
5. Loosen the alternator pivot bolt. Remove the two attaching bolts and spacer. Remove the drive belt, then rotate the bracket out of the way.
6. Remove the three air conditioning compressor attaching bolts and secure the compressor out of the way.
7. Remove the power steering pump attaching bolts and position the pump to one side.
8. Remove the air conditioner bracket attaching bolts and remove the bracket.
9. Disconnect the lower radiator hose and heater hose from the water pump.
10. Loosen the by-pass hose clamp at the water pump.
11. Remove the remaining water pump attaching bolts and remove the pump from the front cover. Remove the separator plate from the pump. Discard the gaskets.
12. Remove all gasket material from all of the mating surfaces.
13. Install the water pump in the reverse order of removal, using a new gasket and waterproof sealer. When the water pump is first positioned to the front cover of the engine, install only those bolts not used to secure the air conditioner and alternator brackets.

420 (6.9L) Diesel

1. Disconnect battery ground cables from both batteries. Drain cooling system.
2. Remove radiator fan shroud halves.
3. Remove fan and clutch assembly using suitable tools.

─────── CAUTION ───────
Left hand thread: Remove by turning nut clockwise.

4. Loosen power steering pump and A/C compressor and remove drive belts.
5. Loosen vacuum pump and remove drive belt. Loosen alternator and remove drive belt.
6. Remove water pump pulley.
7. Disconnect heater hose from water pump. Remove heater hose fitting from water pump.
8. Remove alternator adjusting arm and adjusting arm bracket. Remove A/C compressor with hoses attached, and position out of the way. Remove A/C compressor brackets.
9. Remove power steering pump and bracket and position out of the way.
10. Remove bolts attaching water pump to front cover and remove pump.
11. Clean water pump and engine front cover mating surfaces with solvent.
12. Install fabricated dowel pins for water pump alignment.
13. Install water pump with new gasket and tighten to specifications.

NOTE: Coat two bolts and two bottom bolts with RTV Sealer before installation.

14. Install alternator adjusting arm bracket.
15. Install water pump pulley.
16. Coat heater hose fitting with pipe sealant and install in water pump.
17. Connect heater hose to water pump and tighten clamp to specifications.
18. Install power steering pump bracket. Install power steering pump and drive belt. Install A/C compressor bracket. Install A/C compressor and drive belt.
19. Install alternator adjusting arm and alternator drive belt. Install vacuum pump drive belt.
20. Adjust accessory drive belts.
21. Install fan and clutch assembly.

─────── CAUTION ───────
Left hand thread. Turn nut counterclockwise to tighten.

22. Install radiator fan shroud halves. Fill and bleed cooling system.
23. Connect battery ground cables to both batteries. Run engine and check for coolant leaks.

Thermostat
REMOVAL & INSTALLATION

1. Drain the cooling system to a level below the coolant outlet housing. Use the petcock valve at the bottom of the radiator to drain the system, or disconnect the lower hose at the radiator.
2. Disconnect the by-pass hose, if equipped. Remove the coolant outlet housing retaining bolts and slide the housing with the hose attached to one side.
3. Turn the thermostat counterclockwise to unlock it from the outlet.
4. Remove the gasket from the engine block and clean both mating surfaces.
5. To install the thermostat, coat a new gasket with water-resistant sealer and position it on the outlet of the engine. The gasket must be in place before the thermostat is installed.
6. Install the thermostat with the bridge (opposite end from the spring) inside the elbow connection and turn it clockwise to lock it in position with the bridge against the flats cast into the elbow connection.
7. Position the elbow connection onto the mounting surface of the outlet so that the thermostat flange is resting on the gasket and install the retaining bolts.
8. Fill the radiator and operate the engine until it reaches operating temperature. Check the coolant level and adjust as necessary.

NOTE: It is a good practice to check the operation of a new thermostat before it is installed in an engine. Place the thermostat in a pan of boiling water. If it does not open more than ¼ in., do not install it in the engine.

EMISSION CONTROLS

Refer to Emission Controls in the Unit Repair section for a description and service procedures for the various systems.

GASOLINE FUEL SYSTEM

Carburetor

REMOVAL & INSTALLATION

1. Disconnect the negative battery cable. Remove the air cleaner and duct assembly.
2. Remove the throttle cable or rod from the throttle lever. Disconnect the distributor vacuum line EGR vacuum line, if so equipped, the inline fuel filter, and the choke heat tube at the carburetor.
3. Disconnect the choke clean air tube from the air horn. Disconnect the choke actuating cable, if so equipped.
4. Remove the carburetor retaining nuts then remove the carburetor. Remove the carburetor mounting gasket, spacer (if so equipped), and the lower gasket from the intake manifold.
5. Before installing the carburetor, clean the gasket mounting surfaces of the spacer and carburetor. Place the spacer between two new gaskets and position the spacer and gaskets on the intake manifold. Position the carburetor body flange, snug the nuts, then alternately tighten each nut in a criss-cross pattern.
6. Connect the inline fuel filter, throttle cable, choke heat tube, distributor vacuum line, EGR vacuum line, and choke cable.
7. Connect the choke clean air line to the air horn.
8. Adjust the engine idle speed, the idle fuel mixture and anti-stall dashpot (if so equipped). Install the air cleaner.

REBUILDING

Refer to the Carburetor/Fuel System chapter in the Unit Repair Section for service and rebuilding information.

Fuel Filter

REMOVAL & INSTALLATION

Two types of fuel filters are used; an inline (screwed into the carburetor inlet fitting) and a internally mounted (located behind the carburetor inlet fitting). Carburetors except the Variable Venturi and Holley 4180/4190 4 barrel, use the in-line type.

In-line/Screw-in Fuel Filter

1. Remove the air cleaner and duct assembly.
2. If the connection between the filter and inlet is rubber, release the two clamps and slide the line away from the filter.
3. Unscrew the fuel filter from the carburetor inlet fitting using the proper size openend wrench, usually $^{11}/_{16}$ inch.
4. Screw in the new filter and install the gas line using the new hose and clamps contained in the filter kit. Start the engine and and check for leaks. Install the air cleaner and duct assembly.
5. If the filter is connected with a steel line and fitting, use the proper size wrench on the filter hex fitting to hold the filter, and the proper size flare fitting or openend wrench to loosen the gas line. Disconnect the gas line and remove the fuel filter.
6. Install the new filter into the carburetor inlet fitting. Install gas line into the filter while holding the filter with a wrench. Start the engine and check for fuel leaks. Install the air cleaner and duct assembly.

Inlet Fitting Fuel Filter Variable Venturi and Holley 4 Barrel Carburetors.

1. Remove the air cleaner and duct assembly.
2. Hold the carburetor inlet fitting with the proper size openend wrench and disconnect the gas line.
3. Unscrew the inlet fitting from the carburetor. Position a rag underneath the fitting to absorb any spill. Dispose of the rag safely after the fitting has been removed.
4. Unscrew the fitting and remove with gasket, filter and spring.
5. Install the spring, new filter and gasket into the fuel inlet of the carburetor.
6. Hand start the inlet fitting into the carburetor and tighten with a wrench.
7. Hand start the fuel line fitting, hold the filter with the proper size wrench and tighten the fuel line.
8. Start the engine and check for fuel leaks.
9. Install the remainder of the parts.

Mechanical Fuel Pump

The mechanical fuel pump is bolted to the side of the engine block or front cover, and is driven by an eccentric, either built-in or mounted on the camshaft or auxiliary shaft.

REMOVAL & INSTALLATION

1. Loosen the threaded fittings to the fuel pump (use the proper size flare wrench), do not remove the lines at this time.
2. Loosen the fuel pump mounting bolts one or two turns. Loosen the pump and gasket from the engine or front cover. Rotate the engine, in the proper direction, while checking the tension on the fuel pump. When

the cam or eccentric lobe is near the low point pressure on the fuel pump arm will be greatly reduced. This is especially important on engines using an aluminum front cover to help prevent thread stripping.
3. Have a rag handy to catch fuel spill and disconnect all lines from the fuel pump. Dispose of the rag safely.
4. Remove the fuel pump mounting bolts, the fuel pump and mounting gasket.
5. Clean all mounting surfaces. Apply oil resistant sealer to mounting surfaces. Install the fuel pump and new gasket in the reverse order of removal. Start the engine and check for leaks.

TESTING

Incorrect fuel pump pressure and low volume (flow rate) are the two most likely fuel pump troubles that will affect engine performance. Low pressure will cause a lean mixture and fuel starvation at high speeds and excessive pressure will cause high fuel consumption and carburetor flooding.

To determine that the fuel pump is in satisfactory operating condition, tests for both fuel pump pressure and volume should be performed.

The tests are performed with the fuel pump installed on the engine and the engine at normal operating temperature and at idle speed.

Before the test, make sure that the replaceable fuel filter has been changed at the proper mileage interval. If in doubt, install a new filter.

Pressure Test

1. Remove the air cleaner assembly. Disconnect the fuel inlet line of the fuel filter at the carburetor. Use care to prevent fire, due to fuel spillage. Place an absorbent cloth under the connection before removing the line to catch any fuel that might flow out of the line.
2. Connect a pressure gauge, a restrictor and a flexible hose between the fuel filter and the carburetor.
3. Position the flexible hose and the restrictor so that the fuel can be discharged into a suitable, graduated container.
4. Before taking a pressure reading, operate the engine at the specified idle rpm and vent the system into the container by opening the hose restrictor momentarily.
5. Close the hose restrictor, allow the pressure to stabilize and note the reading. The pressure should be 5 psi.

If the pump pressure is not within 4–6 psi and the fuel lines and filter are in satisfactory condition, the pump is defective and should be replaced.

If the pump pressure is within the proper range, perform the test for fuel volume.

Volume Test

1. Operate the engine at the specified idle rpm.
2. Open the hose restrictor and catch

the fuel in the container while observing the time it takes to pump 1 pint. 1 pint should be pumped in 20 seconds. If the pump does not pump to specifications, check for proper fuel tank venting or a restriction in the fuel line leading from the fuel tank to the carburetor before replacing the fuel pump.

Fuel Tank

REMOVAL & INSTALLATION

In-Cab Fuel Tank

1. Siphon the fuel from the tank into a suitable container through the filler neck.
2. Move the seat to the full forward position and tilt the seat forward.
3. Disconnect the fuel gauge sending unit wire and fuel line from the tank. Disconnect the vapor vent chamber and vapor lines of the fuel evaporative emission control system.
4. Loosen the filler neck hose clamp at the tank end of the hose, and pull the filler neck away from the tank.
5. Remove the fuel tank retaining nuts and bolts and lift the tank out of the cab. If the tank is being replaced, remove the fuel gauge sending unit and install it in the new tank.
6. Install the fuel tank in the reverse order of removal.

In-Frame Fuel Tank

1. Drain the fuel from the tank into a suitable container by either removing the drain plug, if so equipped, or siphoning through the filler cap opening.
2. Disconnect the fuel gauge sending unit wire and fuel outlet line.
3. Disconnect the air relief tube from the filler neck and fuel tank.
4. Loosen the filler neck hose clamp at the fuel tank and pull the filler neck away from the tank.
5. Remove the retaining strap mounting nuts and bolts and lower the tank to the floor.
6. If a new tank is being installed, change over the fuel gauge sending unit to the new tank.
7. Install the fuel tank in the reverse order of removal.

Behind-The-Axle Fuel Tank

1. Raise the rear of the truck.
2. Disconnect the negative battery cable.
3. Disconnect the fuel gauge sending unit wire at the fuel tank.
4. Remove the fuel drain plug or siphon the fuel from the tank into a suitable container.
5. Loosen the fuel line hose clamps, slide the clamps forward and disconnect the fuel line at the fuel gauge sending unit.
6. If the sending unit is to be removed, turn the unit retaining ring counterclockwise and remove the sending unit, retaining

ring and gasket. Discard the gasket.
7. Loosen the clamps on the fuel filler pipe and vent hose as necessary and disconnect the filler pipe hose and vent hose from the tank.
8. If the tank is the metal type, support the tank and remove the bolts attaching the tank supports to the frame. Carefully lower the tank and disconnect the vent tube from the vapor emission control valve in the top of the tank. Finish removing the filler pipe and filler pipe vent hose if not possible previously. Remove the tank from under the vehicle.
9. If the tank is the plastic type, support the tank and remove the bolts attaching the combination skid plate and tank support to the frame. Carefully lower the tank and disconnect the vent tube from the vapor emission control valve in the top of the tank. Finish removing the filler pipe and filler pipe vent hose if it was not possible previously. Remove the skid plate and tank from under the vehicle. Remove the skid plate from the tank.

DIESEL FUEL SYSTEM

Adjustments

INJECTOR TIMING

134 (2.2L)

NOTE: Special Tools Ford 14-0303,

Idle speed adjustment 134 (2.2L) diesel

Injection timing gauge installation on the 134 (2.2L) diesel

Static Timing Gauge Adapter and D82L4201A, Metric Dial Indicator, or the equivalents are necessary to set or check the injector timing.

1. Disconnect both battery ground cables. Remove the air inlet hose from the air cleaner and intake manifold.
2. Remove the distributor head plug bolt and washer from the injection pump.
3. Install the Timing Gauge Adapter and Metric Dial Indicator so that the indicator pointer is in contact with the injector pump plunger and gauge reads approximately 2.0mm (0.08 inch).
4. Align the 2° ATDC (after top dead center) on the crankshaft pulley with the indicator on the timing case cover.

ALIGN WHITE TIMING MARK WITH INDICATOR PIN

Aligning the 134 (2.2L) diesel timing marks

5. Slowly turn the engine counterclockwise until the dial indicator pointer stops moving (approximately 30°–50°).
6. Adjust the dial indicator to 0 (Zero). Confirm that the dial indicator does not move from Zero, by rotating the crankshaft slightly right and left.
7. Turn the crankshaft clockwise until the timing mark aligns with the cover indicator. The dial indicator should read 1, plus or minus 0.02mm (0.04, plus or minus 0.0008 inch). If the reading is not within specifications, adjust the timing as follows;

  a. Loosen the injection pump mounting nuts and bolts.

  b. Rotate the injection pump counterclockwise (reverse direction of engine rotation) past the correct timing position, then clockwise until the timing is correct. This procedure will eliminate gear backlash.

  c. Repeat Steps 5, 6, and 7 to check that the timing is properly adjusted.

MOVE WHITE TIMING MARK FROM 2ᵈ ATDC TO POSITION A

Moving the crankshaft pulley timing mark on the 134 (2.2L) diesel

8. Remove the dial indicator and adapter. Install the injector head gasket and plug. Install all removed parts.

9. Run engine, check and adjust idle RPM. Check for fuel leaks.

420 (6.9L)

NOTE: Special equipment, a Dynamic Timing Meter, Ford D83T6002A or the equivalent is necessary to set or check the "dynamic" injection timing. Both static and dynamic methods follow.

STATIC TIMING

1. Loosen the injection pump to mounting nuts.

2. Rotate the injection pump to bring the mark on the pump into alignment with the mark on pump mounting adapter.

3. Visually recheck the alignment of the timing marks and tighten injection pump mounting nuts.

DYNAMIC TIMING

1. Bring the engine up to normal operating temperature.

2. Stop the engine and install a dynamic timing meter, Rotunda® 78-0100 or equivalent, by placing the magnetic probe pick-up into the probe hole.

3. Remove the No. 1 glow plug wire and remove the glow plug, install luminosity probe and tighten to 12 ft. lbs. (16 Nm). Install the photocell over the probe.

4. Connect a dynamic timing meter to the battery and adjust the offset of the meter.

5. Set the transmission in neutral and raise the rear wheels off the ground. Using Rotunda® 14-0302, throttle control, set the engine speed to 1400 rpm with no accessory load. Observe the injection timing on the dynamic timing meter.

6. If dynamic timing is not within ± 2° of specification, then injection pump timing will require adjustment.

7. Turn the engine off. Note the timing mark alignment. Loosen the injection pump-to-adapter nuts.

8. Rotate the injection pump clockwise (when viewed from the front of engine) to retard and counter-clockwise to advance timing. Two degrees of dynamic timing is approximately .030 in. (.75 mm) of timing mark movement.

9. Start the engine and recheck the timing. If the timing is not within ± 1° of specification, repeat steps 7 through 9.

10. Turn off the engine. Remove the dynamic timing equipment. Lightly coat the glow plug threads with anti-seize compound, install the glow plug and tighten to 12 ft. lbs. (16 Nm). Connect the glow plug wires.

Fuel Supply Pump

REMOVAL & INSTALLATION

134 (2.2L)

1. Disconnect both ground cables from the batteries.

2. Disconnect and cap the fuel inlet and outlet lines. Remove the nuts and bolts mounting the pump to mounting bracket and remove the pump.

3. Install in the reverse order of removal.

420 (6.9L)

The pump used on the 6.9L Diesel Engine is mounted on the front cover. Refer to the Gasoline Engines fuel pump section for procedures.

Fuel Filter

REMOVAL & INSTALLATION

1. Remove the spin-on filter by turning counterclockwise as viewed from the bottom of the filter.

2. Clean the filter mounting flange. Coat the new filter sealing lip with diesel fuel.

3. Install and tighten filter until the gasket touches the mounting flange. Tighten an additional one-half turn. Refer to the instructions with the new filter, if they call for more than one-half turn tightening-follow the instructions.

Water Separator

SERVICING

134 (2.2L)

Water should be drained from the fuel sedimenter whenever the warning light comes on or every 5,000 miles. More frequent drain intervals may be required depending on fuel quality and vehicle usage.

The instrument panel warning lamp (WATER IN FUEL) will glow when approximately 0.5 liters (0.53 quarts) of water has accumulated in the sedimenter. When the warning lamp glows, shut off the engine as soon as safely possible. A suitable drain pan or container should be placed under the sedimenter, which is mounted inside the frame rail, underneath the driver's side of the cab. To drain the fuel sedimenter, pull up on the T-handle (located on the cab floor behind the driver's seat) until resistance is felt. Turn the ignition switch to the On position, so the warning lamp glows and hold T-handle up for approximately 45 seconds after lamp goes out.

To stop draining fuel, release T-handle and inspect sedimenter to verify that draining has stopped. Discard drained fluid suitably.

420 (6.9L)

The 6.9 Liter diesel engine is equipped with a fuel/water separator in the fuel supply line. A "Water in Fuel" indicator light is provided on the instrument panel to alert the operator. The light should glow when the ignition switch is in the START position to indicate proper light and water sensor function. If the light glows continuously while the engine is running, the water must be drained from the separator as soon as practical to prevent damage to the fuel injection system.

F-SERIES

1. Stop the vehicle and shut off the engine.

NOTE: Failure to shut off engine prior to draining separator will cause air to enter the fuel system.

2. Unscrew the vent 2-½ to 3 turns. The vent is located on the top center of the fuel/water separator unit.

3. Unscrew the water drain located on the bottom of the fuel/water separator 1-½ to 2 turns and drain water. Use an appropriate container.

4. After water is completely drained, close the water drain fingertight.

5. Tighten the vent until snug, then turn it an additional ¼ turn.

6. Restart the engine and check "Water in Fuel" indicator light. The light should not glow. If it continues to glow, have fuel system checked and repaired.

E-SERIES

1. Stop the vehicle and shut Off the engine.

2. Locate the water/fuel separator drain cable knob, attached to the upper cowl flange on the left side of the vehicle, under the hood.

3. Place an approved container under the separator; which is accessible behind the left front wheel.

4. Pull the knob out and hold for 45 seconds.

5. Release knob and remove container.

6. Restart the engine and check "Water in Fuel" indicator lamp. The lamp should not be lit. If it continues to stay lit, have fuel system checked and repaired.

The electrical sensor is the only replaceable item on the water/fuel separator. This assembly is threaded into the top of the separator. The remainder of the water/fuel separator is serviced as a complete unit.

—— **CAUTION** ——
When draining the water/fuel separator, the water must be drained into an approved container.

Fuel Injector Lines

REMOVAL & INSTALLATION

420 (6.9L)

NOTE: Before removing any fuel lines, clean exterior with clean fuel oil, or solvent to prevent entry of dirt into fuel system when fuel lines are removed. Blow dry with compressed air.

1. Disconnect battery ground cables from both batteries.

2. Remove air cleaner and cap intake manifold opening with Ford Tool T831-9424-A or equivalent.

3. Disconnect accelerator cable and speed control cable, if so equipped, from injection pump.

4. Remove accelerator cable bracket from intake manifold and position out of the way with cable(s) attached.

NOTE: To prevent fuel system contamination, cap all fuel lines and fittings with protective cap set.

5. Disconnect fuel line from fuel filter to injection pump and cap all fittings.

6. Disconnect and cap nozzle fuel lines at nozzles.

7. Remove the fuel line clamps from fuel lines to be removed.

8. Remove and cap injection pump inlet elbow.

9. Remove and cap inlet fitting adapter.

10. Remove injection nozzle lines, one at a time, from injection pump.

NOTE: Fuel lines must be removed following this sequence; 5-6-4-8-3-1-7-2. Install caps on each end of each fuel line and pump fitting as it is removed and identify each fuel line accordingly.

Injector pump cylinder numbering on the 420 (6.9L) diesel

11. Install fuel lines on injection pump, one at a time and tighten to 22 ft. lbs. (30 Nm).

NOTE: Fuel lines must be installed in the sequence; 2-7-1-3-8-4-6-5.

12. Clean old sealant from injection pump elbow, using clean solvent, and dry thoroughly.

13. Apply a light coating of pipe sealant on elbow threads.

14. Install elbow in injection pump adapter and tighten to a minimum of 6 ft. lbs. (8 Nm) then tighten further, if necessary, to align elbow with injection pump fuel inlet lines, but do not exceed 360° of rotation or 10 ft. lbs. (13 Nm).

15. Remove caps from fuel lines and connect lines to nozzles and tighten to 22 ft. lbs. (30 Nm).

16. Uncap and connect fuel line from

fuel filler to injection pump and tighten.

17. Install fuel line retaining clamps and tighten.

18. Install accelerator cable bracket on intake manifold.

19. Connect accelerator and speed control cable, if so equipped, to injection pump throttle lever.

20. Remove intake manifold cover, and install air cleaner.

21. Connect battery ground cables to both batteries.

22. Run engine and check for fuel leaks.

23. If necessary, purge high pressure fuel lines of air by loosening connector one half to one turn and cranking engine until solid fuel, free from bubbles, flows from connection.

── **CAUTION** ──

Keep eyes and hands away from nozzle spray. Fuel spraying from the nozzle under high pressure can penetrate the skin.

Injection Pump

REMOVAL & INSTALLATION

134 (2.2L)

1. Disconnect battery ground cables from both batteries.

2. Remove radiator fan and shroud. Loosen and remove A/C compressor/power steering pump drive belt and idler pulley, if so equipped. Remove injection pump drive gear cover and gasket.

3. Rotate engine until injection pump drive gear keyway is at TDC.

4. Remove large nut and washer attaching drive gear to injection pump.

NOTE: Care should be taken not to drop washer into timing gear case.

5. Disconnect intake hose from air cleaner and intake manifold.

6. Disconnect throttle cable and speed control cable, if so equipped.

7. Disconnect and cap fuel inlet line at injection pump.

8. Disconnect fuel shut-off solenoid lead at injection pump.

9. Disconnect and remove fuel injection lines from nozzles and injection pump. Cap all fuel lines and fittings.

10. Disconnect lower fuel return line from injection pump and fuel hoses. Loosen lower No. 3 intake port nut and remove fuel return line.

11. Remove two nuts attaching injection pump to front timing gear cover and one bolt attaching pump to rear support bracket.

12. Install Gear and Hub Remover, Tool T83T-6306-A or equivalent, in drive gear cover and attach to injection pump drive gear. Rotate screw clockwise until injection pump disengages from drive gear. Remove the injection pump.

NOTE: Carefully remove injection pump to avoid dropping key into timing

gear case. Disconnect cold start cable before removing injection pump from vehicle.

NOTE: Connect cold start cable to pump before positioning injection pump in timing gear case.

13. Install injection pump in position in timing gear case aligning key with keyway in drive gear in TDC position.

NOTE: Use care to avoid dropping key in timing gear case.

14. Install nuts and washers attaching injection pump to timing gear case and tighten to draw injection pump into position.

NOTE: Do not tighten to specification at this time.

15. Install bolt attaching injection pump to rear support. Install washer and nut attaching injection drive gear to injection pump and tighten.

16. Install injection pump drive gear cover, with new gasket, on timing gear case cover and tighten.

17. Adjust injection timing at this time.

18. Install lower fuel return line to injection pump and intake manifold stud. Tighten Banjo bolt on injection pump and nut on intake manifold. Install connecting fuel hoses and clamps. Install fuel injection lines to injection pump and nozzles and tighten.

19. Connect lead to fuel shut-off solenoid on injection pump. Connect fuel inlet line to injection pump and install hose clamp.

20. Install throttle cable and speed control cable, if so equipped.

21. Air bleed fuel system.

22. Install intake hose on air cleaner and intake manifold.

23. Install A/C compressor/power steering pump drive belt and idler pulley, if so equipped and tighten.

24. Install radiator shroud and radiator fan.

25. Connect battery ground cables to both batteries.

26. Run engine and check for oil and fuel leaks.

420 (6.9L)

NOTE: Before removing any fuel lines, clean exterior with clean fuel oil or solvent to prevent entry of dirt into engine when fuel lines are removed.

── **CAUTION** ──

Do not wash or steam clean engine while engine is running. Serious damage to injection pump could occur.

1. Disconnect battery ground cables from both batteries.

2. Remove engine oil filter neck.

3. Remove bolts attaching injection pump to drive gear.

4. Disconnect electrical connectors to injection pump.

5. Disconnect accelerator cable and

speed control cable from throttle lever, if so equipped.

6. Remove air cleaner and install intake opening cover.

7. Remove accelerator cable bracket, with cables attached, from intake manifold and position out of the way.

NOTE: All fuel lines and fittings must be capped, to prevent fuel contamination.

8. Remove fuel filter-to-injection pump fuel line and cap fittings.

9. Remove and cap injection pump inlet elbow.

10. Remove and cap injection pump fitting adapter.

11. Remove fuel return line on injection pump, rotate out of the way, and cap all fittings.

NOTE: It is not necessary to remove injection lines from injection pump to remove injection pump. If lines are to be removed, loosen injection line fittings at injection pump before removing it from engine.

12. Remove fuel injection lines from nozzles and cap lines and nozzles.

13. Remove three nuts attaching injection pump to injection pump adapter.

14. If injection pump is to be replaced, loosen injection line retaining clips and injection nozzle fuel lines and cap all fittings. Do not install injection nozzle fuel lines until new pump is installed in engine.

15. Lift injection pump, with nozzle lines attached, up and out of engine compartment.

—— CAUTION ——
Do not carry injection pump by injection nozzle fuel lines as this could cause lines to bend or crimp.

16. Install new O-ring on drive gear end of injection pump.

17. Move injection pump down and into position.

18. Position alignment dowel on injection pump into alignment hole on drive gear.

19. Install bolts attaching injection pump to drive gear and tighten.

20. Install nuts attaching injection pump to adapter. Align scribe lines on injection pump flange and injection pump adapter and tighten to 14 ft. lbs. (19 Nm).

21. If injection nozzle fuel lines were removed from injection pump install at this time.

22. Remove caps from nozzles and fuel lines and install fuel line nuts on nozzles and tighten to 22 ft. lbs. (30 Nm).

23. Connect fuel return line to injection pump.

24. Install injection pump fitting adapter with a new O-ring.

25. Clean old sealant from injection pump elbow threads, using clean solvent, and dry thoroughly. Apply a light coating of pipe sealant on elbow threads.

26. Install elbow in injection pump adapter and tighten to a minimum of 6 ft.

lbs. (8 Nm). Then tighten further, if necessary, to align elbow with injection pump fuel inlet line, but do not exceed 360° of rotation or 10 ft. lbs. (13 Nm).

27. Remove caps and connect fuel filter-to-injection pump fuel line.

28. Install accelerator cable bracket to intake manifold.

29. Remove intake manifold cover and install air cleaner.

30. Connect accelerator and speed control cable, if so equipped, to throttle lever.

31. Install electrical connectors on injection pump.

32. Clean injection pump adapter and oil filler neck sealing surfaces.

33. Apply a ⅛ inch bead of RTV Sealant on adapter housing.

34. Install oil filter neck and tighten.

35. Connect battery ground cables to both batteries. Run engine and check for fuel leaks.

36. If necessary, purge high pressure fuel lines of air by loosening connector one half to one turn and cranking engine until solid fuel, free from bubbles flows from connection.

—— CAUTION ——
Keep eyes and hands away from nozzle spray. Fuel spraying from the nozzle under high pressure can penetrate the skin and cause infection. Medical attention should be provided immediately in the event of skin penetration.

37. Check and adjust injection pump timing.

Injectors

REMOVAL & INSTALLATION

134 (2.2L)

1. Disconnect battery ground cables from both batteries.

2. Disconnect and remove injection lines from nozzles and injection pump. Cap all lines and fittings.

3. Remove fuel return line and gaskets.

4. Remove bolts attaching fuel line heater clamp to cylinder head and position heater out of the way.

5. Remove nozzles, using a 27mm deepwell socket.

6. Remove nozzle washer (copper) and nozzle gasket (steel), using Tool T71-P-19703-C or equivalent.

7. Clean nozzle assemblies with Nozzle Cleaning Kit, Rotunda 14-0301 or equivalent, and a suitable solvent, and dry thoroughly. Clean nozzle seats in cylinder head with Nozzle Seat Cleaner, T83T-9527-B or equivalant.

8. Position new nozzle washers and gaskets in nozzle seats, install nozzles and tighten.

NOTE: Install nozzle gaskets with blue side face up (toward nozzle).

9. Position fuel line heater clamps, install attaching bolts, and tighten to specification.

10. Install fuel return line with new gaskets on nozzles.

11. Install injection lines on nozzles and injection pump and tighten line nuts.

12. Connect battery ground cables to both batteries. Run engine and check for fuel leaks.

421 (6.9L)

NOTE: Before removing nozzle assemblies, clean exterior of each nozzle assembly and the surrounding area with clean fuel oil or solvent to prevent entry of dirt into engine when nozzle assemblies are removed. Also, clean fuel inlet and fuel leak-off piping connections. Blow dry with compressed air.

1. Remove fuel line retaining clamp(s) from effected nozzle line(s).

2. Disconnect nozzle fuel inlet (high pressure) and fuel leak-off tees from each nozzle assembly and position out of the way. **Cover open ends of fuel inlet lines and nozzles to prevent entry of dirt.**

3. Remove injection nozzles by turning counterclockwise. Pull nozzle assembly with copper washer from engine. **Be careful not to strike nozzle tip against any hard surface during removal. Cover nozzle assembly fuel inlet opening and nozzle tip with plastic cap to prevent entry of dirt.**

NOTE: Remove copper injector nozzle gasket from nozzle bore with Tool T71P-19703-C, or equivalent, if not attached to nozzle tip.

4. Place nozzle assemblies in a fabricated holder as they are removed from the heads. The holder should be marked with numbers corresponding to the cylinder numbering of the engine. Use of this holder permits replacing nozzles in their respective ports in the cylinder heads.

5. Thoroughly clean nozzle bore in cylinder head before reinserting nozzle assembly with nozzle seat cleaner, Tool T83T-9527-A or equivalent. Pay particular attention to seating surface, in order that no small particles of metal or carbon will cause assembly to be cocked or permit blow-by of combustion gases. Blow out particles with compressed air.

6. Remove protective cap and install a new copper gasket on nozzle assembly, with a small dab of grease.

NOTE: Anti-Seize Compound or equivalent should be used on nozzle threads to aid installation and future removal.

7. Install nozzle assembly into cylinder head nozzle bore.

—— CAUTION ——
Be careful that nozzle tip does not strike against recess wall.

8. Tighten nozzle assembly.

9. Remove protective caps from nozzle assemblies and fuel lines. Install leak-off tees to nozzle assembly.

NOTE: Install two new O-ring seals for each fuel return tee.

10. Connect high pressure fuel line and tighten using a fuel line flare wrench.

11. Install fuel line retainer clamp(s), and tighten.

12. Start engine.

13. If necessary, purge high pressure fuel lines of air by loosening connector one half to one turn and cranking engine until solid fuel, free from bubbles flows from connection.

──────── CAUTION ────────
Keep eyes and hands away from nozzle spray. Fuel spraying from the nozzle under high pressure can penetrate the skin and cause infection. Medical attention should be provided immediately in the event of skin penetration.
────────────────────────────

14. Check for fuel leakage at high pressure connections.

TESTING

Where ideal conditions of good combustion, specified engine temperature control and absolutely clean fuel prevail, nozzles require little attention.

Nozzle trouble is usually indicated by one or more of the following symptoms:

1. Smoky exhaust (black)
2. Loss of power
3. Misfiring
4. Increased fuel consumption
5. Combustion knock
6. Engine overheating

Where faulty nozzle operation is suspected on an engine that is misfiring or puffing black smoke, a simple test can be made to determine which cylinder is causing the difficulty.

With the engine running at a speed that makes the problem most pronounced, momentarily loosen the high pressure fuel inlet line connection on one nozzle assembly sufficiently to "cut-out" the cylinder (one half to one turn) to leak off the fuel charge to the cylinder. Then tighten to specifications.

Check each cylinder in the same manner. If one is found where loosening makes no difference in the irregular operation or causes puffing black smoke to stop, the injection nozzle for the cylinder should be serviced or replaced.

──────── CAUTION ────────
Keep eyes and hands away from nozzle spray. Fuel spraying from the nozzle under high pressure can penetrate the skin and cause infection. Medical attention should be provided immediately in the event of skin penetration.
────────────────────────────

Fuel Control

On-off fuel control is provided by an electric solenoid located in the diesel injection pump housing cover. Current is supplied to the solenoid when the ignition switch is turned on. If no fuel is supplied with the ignition switch in the on position, check for current at the solenoid terminal before condemning the solenoid.

Fuel Cut-Off Solenoid

REMOVAL & INSTALLATION

1. Disconnect battery ground cables from both batteries.

2. Remove connector from fuel cut-off solenoid.

3. Remove fuel cut-off solenoid assembly.

4. Install fuel cut-off solenoid, with new O-ring, and tighten.

5. Install connector on fuel cut-off solenoid.

6. Connect battery ground cables to both batteries. Run engine and check for fuel leaks.

Glow Plug System

134 (2.2L)

The "quick start; afterglow" system is used to enable the engine to start more quickly when the engine is cold. It consists of the flour glow plugs, the control module, two relays, a glow plug resistor assembly, coolant temperature switch, clutch and neutral switches and connecting wiring. Relay power and feedback circuits are protected by fuse links in the wiring harness. The control module is protected by a separate 10A fuse in the fuse panel.

When the ignition switch is turned to the ON position, a Wait-to-Start signal appears near the cold-start knob on the panel. When the signal appears, relay No. 1 also closes and full system voltage is applied to the glow plugs. If engine coolant temperature is below 30°C (86°F), relay No. 2 also closes at this time. After three seconds, the control module turns off the Wait-to-Start light indicating that the engine is ready for starting. If the ignition switch is left in the ON position about three seconds more without cranking, the control opens relay No. 1 and current to the plugs stops to prevent overheating. However, if coolant temperature is below 30°C (86°F) when relay No. 1 opens, relay No. 2 remains closed to apply reduced voltage to the plugs through the glow plug resistor until the ignition switch is turned off.

When the engine is cranked, the control module cycles relay No. 1 intermittently. Thus, glow plug voltage will alternate between 12 and four volts, during cranking, with relay No. 2 closed, or between 12 and zero volts with relay No. 2 open. After the engine starts, alternator output signals the control module to stop the No. 1 relay cycling and the afterglow function takes over.

If the engine coolant temperature is below 30°C (86°F), the No. 2 relay remains closed. This applies reduced (4.2 to 5.3) voltage to the glow plugs through the glow plug resistor. When the vehicle is under way (clutch and neutral switches closed), or coolant temperature is above 30°C (86°F), the control module opens relay No. 2, cutting off all current to the glow plugs.

TESTING THE GLOW PLUGS

1. Disconnect the leads from each glow plug. Connect one lead of the ohmmeter to the glow plug terminal and the other lead to a good ground. Set the ohmmeter on the X1 scale. Test each glow plug in the like manner.

2. If the meter indicates less than one ohm, the problem is not with the glow plug.

3. If the ohmmeter indicates one or more ohms, replace the glow plug and retest.

REMOVAL & INSTALLATION

1. Disconnect battery ground cables from both batteries.

2. Disconnect glow plug harness from glow plugs.

3. Using a 12mm deepwell socket, remove glow plugs.

4. Install glow plugs, using a 12mm deepwell socket, and tighten.

5. Install glow plug harness on glow plugs and tighten.

6. Connect battery ground cables to both batteries.

420 (6.9L)

The 6.9L diesel engine utilizes an electric glow plug system to aid in the start of the engine. The function of this system is to pre-heat the combustion chamber to aid ignition of the fuel.

The system consists of eight glow plugs (one for each cylinder), control switch, power relay, after glow relay, wait lamp latching relay, wait lamp and the eight fusible links located between the harness and the glow plug terminal.

On initial start with cold engine, the glow plug system operates as follows: The glow plug control switch energizes the power relay (which is a magnetic switch) and the power relay contacts close. Battery current energizes the glow plugs. Current to the glow plugs and a wait lamp will be shut off when the glow plugs are hot enough. This takes from 2 to 10 seconds after the key is first turned on. When the wait lamp goes off, the engine is ready to start. After the engine is started the glow plugs begin an on-off cycle for about 40 to 90 seconds. This cycle helps to clear start-up smoke.

The control switch (the brain of the operation) is threaded into the left cylinder head coolant jacket. The control unit senses engine coolant temperature. Since the control unit senses temperature and glow plug operation the glow plug system will not be activated unless needed. On a restart (warm engine) the glow plug system will not be activated unless the coolant temperature drops below 165°F (91°C).

The fast start system utilizes 6 volt glow plugs in a 12 volt system to achieve rapid heating of the glow plug, a cycling device is required in the circuit.

―――――― CAUTION ――――――
Never bypass the power relay of the glow plug system. Constant battery current (12 volts) to glow plugs will cause them to overheat and fail.

TESTING THE GLOW PLUG

1. Disconnect the leads from the glow plug. Connect one lead of an ohmmeter to the glow plug terminal and the other lead to the metal case of the glow plug. Set the ohmmeter to the X1 scale. Test each glow plug.

2. If the meter indicates less than 2 ohms the problem is not with the glow plug.

3. If the meter indicates 2 ohms or more replace the glow plug and retest.

MANUAL TRANSMISSION

NOTE: For overhaul procedures refer to the Unit Repair Section

Linkage

ADJUSTMENT—EXCEPT VANS

Ford 3.03, Warner T85N, T87, T89

1. Place the shifter in the Neutral position and insert a gauge pin (3/16 in. diameter) through the steering column shift levers and the locating hole in the spacer.

2. If the shift rods at the transmission are equipped with threaded sleeves, adjust the sleeves so that they enter the shift levers on the transmission easily with the shift levers in the Neutral position. Now lengthen the rods seven turns of the sleeves and insert them into the shift levers.

3. If the shift rods are slotted, loosen the attaching nut, make sure that the transmission shift levers are in the Neutral position, then retighten the attaching nuts.

4. Remove the gauge pin and check the operation of the shift linkage.

Four-Speed Overdrive— w/External Linkage

1. Attach the shift rods to the levers.
2. Rotate the output shaft to determine that the transmission is in neutral.
3. Insert an alignment pin into the shift control assembly alignment hole.
4. Attach the slotted end of the shift rods over the flats of the studs in the shift control assembly.
5. Install the locknuts and remove the alignment pin.

ADJUSTMENT—VANS

3-Speed

1. Place the gearshift lever in the Neutral position.
2. Loosen the adjustment nuts on the transmission shift levers sufficiently to allow the shift rods to slide freely on the transmission shift levers.
3. Insert a 3/16 in. rod through the pilot hole in the shift tube mounting bracket until it enters the adjustment hole of both the upper and lower shift lever.
4. Place the transmission shift levers in the Neutral position and tighten the adjustment nuts on the transmission shift levers.
5. Remove the 1/4 in. rod from the pilot hole, and check the operation of the gearshift lever in all gear positions.

4-Speed Overdrive—w/External Linkage

1. Disconnect the 3 shift rods from the shifter assembly.
2. Insert a .25" diameter pin through the alignment hole in the shifter assembly. Make sure the levers are in the neutral position.
3. Align the 3 transmission levers as follows: forward lever (3rd–4th lever) in the mid-position (neutral), rearward lever (1st–2nd lever) in the mid-position (neutral), and middle lever (reverse lever) rotate counterclockwise to the neutral position.
4. Rotate the output shaft to assure that the transmission is in neutral.
5. Attach the slotted end of the shift rods over the slots of the studs in the shifter assembly. Install and tighten the locknuts to 15–20 ft. lbs.
6. Remove the alignment pin. Check for proper operation.

Pick-Up Trucks

REMOVAL AND INSTALLATION

Ford 3.03, Warner T85N, T87, T89

1. Raise the vehicle and support it with jackstands. Support the engine with a jack and a block of wood placed under the oil pan.

2. Drain the lubricant out of the transmission by removing the drain plug if so equipped, or removing the lower extension housing-to-transmission bolt.

3. Position a transmission jack under the transmission.

4. Disconnect the gearshift linkage at the transmission.

5. On the Warner T-85N model, disconnect the solenoid and governor wires at the connectors near the solenoid. Remove the overdrive wiring harness from its clip on the transmission. Disconnect the overdrive cable.

6. If the vehicle has 4WD, remove the transfer case shift lever bracket from the transmission.

7. Disconnect the speedometer cable.

8. Disconnect the driveshaft from the differential and transmission and remove it from the vehicle.

9. Raise the transmission if necessary and remove the rear support.

10. Remove the transmission-to-flywheel housing attaching bolts.

11. Move the transmission to the rear until the input shaft clears the flywheel housing and lower the transmission out and from under the vehicle.

NOTE: Do not depress the clutch pedal while the transmission is removed.

12. Before installing the transmission, apply a light film of grease to the release bearing inner hub surface, the release lever fulcrum and fork, and the front bearing retainer of the transmission. Do not apply excessive grease because it will fly off due to centrifugal force and contaminate the clutch disc.

13. Install the transmission in the reverse order of removal. It may be necessary to turn the output shaft with the transmission in gear to align the input shaft splines with the splines in the clutch disc. Fill the transmission with lubricant and adjust the shift linkage.

Warner T-18 4-Speed

1. Disconnect the back-up light switch at the rear of the gearshift housing cover.

2. Remove the rubber boot, floor mat, and the body floor pan cover. Remove the gearshift lever. Remove the weatherpad.

3. Raise the vehicle and support it with jackstands. Position a transmission jack under the transmission and disconnect the speedometer cable.

4. Disconnect the driveshaft from the transmission and wire it up to one side.

5. Remove the rear transmission support.

6. Remove the transmission attaching bolts.

7. Move the transmission to the rear until the input shaft clears the flywheel housing and lower the transmission.

8. Before installing the transmission, apply a light film of grease to the inner hub surface of the clutch release bearing, the

release lever fulcrum and the front bearing retainer of the transmission. Do not apply excessive grease because it will fly off onto the clutch disc.

9. Install the transmission in the reverse order of removal. It may be necessary to turn the output shaft with the transmission in gear to align the input shaft splines with the splines in the clutch disc. Fill the transmission with lubricant if it was drained.

Warner T19B 4 Speed

4×2

1. Remove the floor mat, and the body floor pan cover, and remove the gearshift lever shift ball and boot as an assembly. Remove the weather pad.

2. Raise the vehicle and position safety stands. Position a suitable jack under the transmission, and disconnect the speedometer cable.

3. Disconnect the back-up lamp switch located at the rear of the gear shift housing cover.

4. Disconnect the drive shaft or coupling shaft and clutch linkage from the transmission and wire it to one side.

5. Remove the transmission rear insulator and lower retainer. Remove the crossmember. Remove the transmission attaching bolts.

6. Move the transmission to the rear until the in shaft clears the clutch housing. Lower transmission.

7. Place the transmission on a suitable jack install guide studs in the clutch housing and raise the transmission until the input shaft splines are aligned with the clutch disc splines. The clutch release bearing and hub must be properly positioned in the release lever fork.

8. Slide the transmission forward on the guide stud until it is in position on the clutch housing. Install the attaching bolts and tighten them to 45–50 ft. lbs. Remove the guide studs and install the lower attaching bolts.

9. Install the crossmember. Position the insulator and retainer between the transmission and crossmember. Install bolts and tighten to 45–60 ft. lbs. Install the nut retaining the insulator and retainer to crossmember. Tighten to 50–70 ft. lbs. Remove the transmission jack.

10. Connect the speedometer cable and driven gear and clutch linkage.

11. Install the bolts attaching the front U-joint of the coupling shaft to the transmission output shaft flange. Install the transmission rear support and upper and lower absorbers. Connect the back-up lamp switch.

12. Install the shift lever, boot and shift ball as an assembly and lubricate the spherical ball seat with Multi-Purpose Long-Life Lubricant C1AZ-1959 (ESA-M1C75-B) or equivalent.

13. Install the weather pad. Install the floor pan cover and floor mat.

4×4

1. Open door and cover seat. Remove the screws holding the floor mat.

2. Remove the screws holding the access cover to the floor pan. Place the shift lever in the reverse position and remove the cover.

3. Remove the insulator and dust cover.

4. Remove the transfer case shift lever, shift ball and boot as an assembly.

5. Remove transmission shift lever, shift ball and boot as an assembly.

6. Raise and safely support the vehicle.

7. Remove the drain plug and drain the transmission. Disconnect the rear driveshaft from the transfer case and wire it out of the way.

8. Disconnect the front driveshaft from the transfer case and wire it out of the way.

9. Remove the retainer ring that holds the shift link in place and remove the shift link from transfer case.

10. Remove the speedometer cable from the transfer case.

11. Position a suitable jack under the transfer case. Remove the six bolts holding the transfer case to the transmission and lower the transfer case from the vehicle.

12. Remove the eight bolts that hold the rear support bracket to the transmission.

13. Position a suitable jack under the transmission and remove the rear support bracket and brace.

14. Remove the four bolts that hold the transmission to the bell housing. Remove

the transmission from the vehicle.

15. Place the transmission on a transmission jack and install it in the vehicle installing two guide studs in the bell housing top holes, to guide the transmission into position.

16. Install the two lower bolts. Remove the guide studs and install the upper bolts.

17. Place the rear support bracket in position and install the eight retaining bolts.

18. Install the two bolts at the rear support insulator bracket. Remove the transmission jack.

19. Position the transfer case on a suitable jack and install the six retaining bolts and gasket. Position the transfer case on the transmission and tighten the bolts.

20. Install the transfer case shift link and retaining ring. Position and install the speedometer cable. Remove wire and connect front driveshaft. Remove wire and connect rear driveshaft.

21. Fill transfer case with Dexron®-II, automatic transmission fluid. The manual transmission with Standard Transmission Lubricant (SAE 80W) lubricant. Lower vehicle.

22. Remove fabricated dirt shield and prepare gasket area.

23. Position gasket and shift cover.

24. Install two pilot bolts, then install remaining shift cover retaining bolts.

25. Install transfer case shift lever, shift ball and boot as an assembly and transmission shift lever, shift ball and boot as an assembly.

26. Install dust cover and insulator. Install access cover to floor pan screws. Install the floor mat screws. Install the boot area screws.

New Process 435 4-Speed

1. Remove the rubber boot and floor mat.

2. Remove the floor pan, transmission cover plate, and weather pad. It may be

1978 and later NP435 transmission-to-transfer case mounting

REVERSE SWITCH

ASSEMBLE CLIP TO GEAR WITH
TABS ON BACK SIDE OF CLIP
TOWARD TEETH ON SPEEDOMETER GEAR

1978 and later NP435 4-speed installation

necessary to remove the seat assembly.

3. Disconnect the back-up light switch located in the rear of the gearshift housing cover.

4. Raise the vehicle and place jackstands under the frame to support it. Place a transmission jack under the transmission and disconnect the speedometer cable.

5. Disconnect the parking brake lever from its linkage and remove the gearshift housing.

6. Disconnect the driveshaft.

7. Remove the transmission rear support.

8. Remove the transmission-to-flywheel housing attaching bolts, slide the transmission rearward until the input shaft clears the flywheel housing and lower it out from under the truck.

9. Before installing the transmission, apply a light film of grease to the inner hub surface of the clutch release bearing, release lever fulcrum and fork, and the front bearing retainer of the transmission. Do not apply excessive grease because it will fly off and contaminate the clutch disc.

10. Install the transmission in the reverse order of removal. It may be necessary to turn the output shaft with the transmission in gear to align the input shaft splines with the splines in the clutch disc. The front bearing retainer is installed through the clutch release bearing.

Ford Four-Speed Overdrive

1. Raise the truck and support it on jackstands.

2. Mark the driveshaft so that it can be installed in the same position.

3. Disconnect the driveshaft at the rear U-joint and slide it off the transmission output shaft.

4. Disconnect the speedometer cable from the transmission.

5. Remove the shift rods from the levers and the shift control from the extension housing.

6. Support the engine and remove the extension housing-to-crossmember bolts.

7. Support the transmission on a jack and unbolt it from the engine.

8. Move the transmission and jack rearward until clear. If necessary, lower the engine enough for clearance.

9. Installation is the reverse of removal. It is a good idea to install and snug-down the upper transmission-to-engine bolts first, then the lower. For linkage adjustment, see the beginning of this chapter. Check the fluid level.

Single Rail Four-Speed Overdrive

1. Raise the vehicle on a hoist and remove the lubricant.

2. Mark the driveshaft so that it can be

installed in the same position then disconnect the driveshaft from the rear U-joint flange. Slide the driveshaft off the transmission output shaft.

3. Disconnect the speedometer cable from the extension housing.

4. Remove the three screws securing the shift tower to the turret assembly.

5. Remove the shift tower from the turret assembly.

6. Support the engine with a transmission jack and remove the bolts which attach the rear extension housing to the engine.

7. Raise the rear of the engine high enough to remove the weight from the crossmember.

8. Remove the bolts retaining the crossmember to the frame side supports and remove the crossmember.

9. Support the transmission on a jack and remove the bolts that attach the transmission to the flywheel housing.

10. Move the transmission and jack rearward until the transmission input shaft clears the flywheel housing.

NOTE: If necessary, lower the engine enough to obtain clearance for transmission removal. Do not depress the clutch pedal while the transmission is removed.

11. Before installing the transmission install two guide pins in the flywheel housing lower mounting bolt holes.

12. Move the transmission forward on the guide pins until the input shaft splines enter the clutch hub splines and the case is positioned against the flywheel housing.

13. Install the two upper transmission to flywheel housing mounting bolts snug, and then remove the two guide pins. Install the two lower mounting bolts.

14. Raise the rear of the engine and install the crossmember and attaching bolts then lower the engine.

15. With the transmission extension housing resting on the engine rear support, install the transmission extension housing attaching bolts.

16. Position the shift tower to the extension housing and secure with the three screws.

17. Reconnect the speedometer cable to the extension housing.

18. Slide the forward end of the driveshaft over the transmission output shaft. Connect the driveshaft to the rear U-joint flange.

19. Fill with transmission lubricant and lower the vehicle.

Ranger and Bronco II

REMOVAL & INSTALLATION

Five Speed Overdrive—Diesel Engine

1. Place the gearshift lever in neutral. Remove the boot retainer screws. Remove the bolts attaching the retainer cover to the gearshift lever retainer. Disconnect the clutch master cylinder push rod from the clutch pedal.

2. Pull the gearshift lever assembly, shim and bushing straight up and away from the gearshift lever retainer. Cover the shift tower opening in the extension housing with a cloth.

3. Disconnect the clutch hydraulic system master cylinder push rod from the clutch pedal.

4. Open the hood and disconnect the negative battery cable from the battery terminal.

5. Raise and safely support the vehicle on jackstands. Disconnect the driveshaft at the rear. Pull the driveshaft rearward and disconnect from the transmission. Install a suitable plug in the extension housing to prevent lubricant leakage.

6. Remove the clutch housing dust shield and slave cylinder and secure it at one side.

7. Remove the speedometer cable from the extension housing.

8. Disconnect the starter motor and back-up lamp switch wires.

9. Place a jack under the engine, protecting the oil pan with a wood block.

10. Remove the starter motor. Position a suitable jack under the transmission.

11. Remove the bolts, lockwashers and flat washers attaching the transmission to the engine rear plate.

12. Remove the nuts and bolts attaching the transmission mount and damper to the crossmember.

13. Remove the nuts attaching the crossmember to the frame side rails and remove the crossmember.

14. Lower the engine jack. Work the clutch housing off the locating dowels and slide the transmission rearward until the input shaft spline clears the clutch disc. Remove the transmission from the vehicle.

15. Make sure that the machined mating surfaces and the locating dowels on the engine rear plate are free of burrs, dirt or paint. Check the mating face of the clutch housing and the locating dowel holes for burrs, dirt or paint.

16. Support the transmission on a suitable jack. Position it under the vehicle and start the input shaft into the clutch disc. Align the splines on the input shaft with the splines in the clutch disc. Move the transmission forward and carefully seat the clutch housing on the locating dowels of the engine rear plate. The engine plate dowels must not shave or burr the clutch housing dowel holes.

17. Install the bolts and flat washers that attach the clutch housing to the engine rear plate and tighten to specifications. Remove the transmission jack.

18. Install the starter motor. Tighten the attaching nuts.

19. Raise the engine and install the rear crossmember, insulator and damper, and attaching nuts and washers. Tighten the nuts.

20. Install the bolts, nuts and washers attaching the transmission mount to the crossmember. Tighten the nuts. Remove the engine jack.

21. Insert the driveshaft into the transmission extension housing and install the center bearing attaching nuts, washers and lockwashers. Tighten the nuts.

22. Connect the driveshaft to the rear axle drive flange. Tighten the attaching nuts.

23. Connect the starter and back-up lamp switch wires.

24. Install the clutch slave cylinder and dust shield on the clutch housing. Install the speedometer cable.

25. Check the transmission fluid level at both fill plugs. Fill with lubricant if necessary.

26. Lower the vehicle.

27. Open the hood and connect the negative battery cable to the battery terminal.

Five Speed Transmission—Gas Engine

1. Place the gearshift lever in neutral. Remove the boot retainer screws. Remove the bolts attaching the retainer cover to the gearshift lever retainer. Disconnect the clutch master cylinder push rod from the clutch pedal.

2. Pull the gearshift lever assembly, shim and bushing straight up and away from the gearshift lever retainer.

3. Cover the shift tower opening in the extension housing with a cloth.

4. Disconnect the clutch hydraulic system master cylinder push rod from the clutch pedal.

5. Open the hood and disconnect the negative battery cable from the battery terminal.

6. Raise and safely support the vehicle on jackstands. Disconnect the driveshaft at the rear axle.

7. Pull the driveshaft rearward and disconnect from the tranmission. Install a suitable plug in the extension housing to prevent lubricant leakage.

8. Remove the clutch housing dust shield and slave cylinder and secure it at one side. Remove the speedometer cable from the extension housing.

9. Disconnect the starter motor and back-up lamp switch wires.

10. Place a jack under the engine, protecting the oil pan with a wood block.

11. On 4 × 4 vehicles, remove the transfer case.

12. Remove the starter motor. Position a suitable jack under the transmission.

13. Remove the bolts, lockwashers and flat washers attaching the transmission to the engine rear plate.

14. Remove the nuts and bolts attaching the transmission mount and damper to the crossmember.

15. Remove the nuts attaching the crossmember to the frame side rails and remove the crossmember.

16. Lower the engine jack. Work the clutch housing off the locating dowels and slide the transmission rearward until the input shaft spline clears the clutch disc. Remove the transmission from the vehicle.

17. Make sure that the machined mating surfaces and the locating dowels on the engine rear plate are free of burrs, dirt or paint. Check the mating face of the clutch housing and the locating dowel holes for burrs, dirt or paint.

18. Mount the transmission on a suitable jack. Position it under the vehicle and start the input shaft into the clutch disc. Align the splines on the input shaft with the splines in the clutch disc. Move the transmission forward and carefully seat the clutch housing on the locating dowels of the engine rear plate. The engine plate dowels must not shave or burr the clutch housing dowel holes. Install the bolts and flat washers that attach the clutch housing to the engine rear plate and tighten to specifications. Remove the transmission jack.

19. Install the starter motor. Tighten the attaching nuts.

20. Raise the engine and install the rear crossmember, insulator and damper, and attaching nuts and washers.

21. Install the bolts, nuts and washers attaching the transmission mount to the crossmember. Remove the engine jack.

22. On 4 × 4 vehicles, install the transfer case.

23. Insert the driveshaft into the transmission extension housing and install the

center bearing attaching nuts, washers and lockwashers.

24. Connect the driveshaft to the rear axle drive flange.

25. Connect the starter and back-up lamp switch wires. Install the clutch slave cylinder and dust shield on the clutch housing. Install the speedometer cable.

26. Check the transmission fluid level at both fill plugs. Fill with specified lubricant if necessary.

27. Lower the vehicle.

28. Open the hood and connect the negative battery cable to the battery terminal.

29. Re-connect the clutch master cylinder push rod to the clutch pedal.

30. Remove the cloth from the shift tower opening in the extension housing. Avoid getting dirt inside the transmission.

31. Position the gearshift lever assembly straight up above the gearshift lever retainer, then insert the gearshift in the retainer. Install the bolts attaching the retainer cover to the gearshift lever retainer and tighten them to specifications. Install the cover boot with the retainer screws.

Four-Speed Transmission— Diesel Engine

1. Place the gearshift lever in Neutral. Remove the boot retainer screws. Remove the bolts attaching the retainer cover to the gearshift lever retainer. Disconnect the clutch master cylinder push rod from the clutch pedal.

2. Pull the gearshift lever assembly, shim and bushing straight up and away from the gearshift lever retainer. Cover the shift tower opening in the extension housing with a cloth.

3. Disconnect the clutch hydraulic system master cylinder push rod from the clutch pedal.

4. Open the hood and disconnect the negative battery cable from the battery terminal.

5. Raise and safely support the vehicle on jackstands. Disconnect the driveshaft at the rear axle. Pull the driveshaft rearward and disconnect from the transmission. Install a suitable plug in the extension housing to prevent lubricant leakage.

6. Remove the clutch housing dust shield and slave cylinder and secure it at one side.

7. Remove the speedometer cable from the extension housing or from the speed control sensor, if so equipped.

8. Disconnect the starter motor and back-up lamp switch wires.

Place a jack under the engine, protecting the oil pan with a wood block. Remove the starter motor. Position a suitable jack under the transmission.

9. Remove the bolts attaching the transmission to the engine rear plate.

Remove the nuts and bolts attaching the transmission mount and damper to the crossmember.

10. Remove the nuts attaching the crossmember to the frame side rails and remove the crossmember.

11. Lower the engine jack. Work the clutch housing off the locating dowels and slide the transmission rearward until the input shaft spline clears the clutch disc. Remove the transmission from the vehicle.

13. Make sure that the machined mating surfaces and the locating dowels on the engine rear plate are free of burrs, dirt or paint. Check the mating face of the clutch housing and the locating dowel holes for burrs, dirt or paint.

Mount the transmission on a suitable jack. Position it under the vehicle and start the input shaft into the clutch disc. Align the splines on the input shaft with the splines in the clutch disc. Move the transmission forward and carefully seat the clutch housing on the locating dowels of the engine rear plate. The engine plate dowels must not shave or burr the clutch housing dowel holes.

14. Install the bolts that attach the clutch housing to the engine rear plate. Remove the transmission jack.

15. Install the starter motor.

16. Raise the engine and install the rear crossmember and attaching nuts and washers.

17. Install the bolts, nuts and washers attaching the transmission mount and damper to the crossmember. Remove the engine jack.

18. Insert the driveshaft into the transmission extension housing and install the center bearing attaching nuts, washers and lockwashers.

19. Connect the driveshaft to the rear axle drive flange.

20. Connect the starter and back-up lamp switch wires. Install the clutch slave cylinder and dust shield on the clutch housing. Install the speedometer cable.

21. Check the transmission fluid level at the fill plug. Fill with specified lubricant if necessary. Lower the vehicle.

22. Open the hood and connect the negative battery cable to the battery terminal.

23. Re-connect the clutch master cylinder push rod to the clutch pedal.

24. Remove the cloth from the shift tower opening in the extension housing. Avoid getting dirt inside the transmission.

25. Position the gearshift lever assembly straight up above the gearshift lever retainer, then insert the gearshift in the retainer. Install the bolts attaching the retainer cover to the gearshift lever retainer.

26. Install the cover boot with the retainer screws.

Transfer Case

REMOVAL & INSTALLATION

1. Raise and safely support the vehicle. Remove the skid plate from frame.

2. Place a drain pan under transfer case, remove the drain plug and drain fluid from the transfer case.

3. Disconnect the four-wheel drive indicator switch wire connector at the transfer case.

4. Disconnect the front driveshaft from the axle input yoke.

5. Loosen the clamp retaining the front driveshaft boot to the transfer case, and pull the driveshaft and front boot assembly out of the transfer case front output shaft.

6. Disconnect the rear driveshaft from the transfer case output shaft yoke.

7. Disconnect the speedometer driven gear from the transfer case rear cover. Disconnect the vent hose from the control lever.

8. Loosen or remove the large bolt and the small bolt retaining the shifter to the extension housing. Pull on the control lever until the bushing slides off the transfer case shift lever pin. If necessary, unscrew the shift lever from the control lever. Remove the heat shield from the transfer case.

——————— **CAUTION** ———————

The catalytic converter is located beside the heat shield. Be careful when working around the catalytic converter because of the extremely high temperatures generated by the converter.

9. Support the transfer case with a suitable jack. Remove the five bolts retaining the transfer case to the transmission and the extension housing.

10. Slide the transfer case rearward off the transmission output shaft and lower the transfer case from the vehicle. Remove the gasket from between the transfer case and extension housing.

11. Place a new gasket between the transfer case and the extension housing.

12. Raise the transfer case with a suitable jack so that the transmission output shaft aligns with the splined transfer case input shaft. Slide the transfer case forward onto the transmission output shafts and onto the dowel pin. Install the five bolts retaining the transfer case to the extension housing. Tighten bolts to 25–35 ft. lbs.

13. Remove the transmission jack from the transfer case.

14. Install the heat shield on the transfer case. Tighten the bolts to 27–37 ft. lbs.

15. Move the control lever until the bushing is in position over the transfer case shift lever pin. Install and hand start the attaching bolts. First, tighten the large bolt retaining the shifter to the extension housing to 70–90 ft. lbs., then the small bolt to 31–42 ft. lbs.

NOTE: Always tighten the large bolt retaining the shifter to the extension housing before tightening the small bolt.

16. Install the vent assembly so the white marking on the hose is in position in the notch in the shifter.

NOTE: The upper end of the vent hose should be two inches above the top of the shifter and positioned inside of the shift lever boot.

17. Connect the speedometer driven gear to the transfer case rear cover. Tighten the screw to 20–25 in. lbs.

18. Connect the rear driveshaft to the

transfer case output shaft yoke. Tighten the bolts to 12–15 ft. lbs.

19. Clean the transfer case front output shaft female splines. Apply 5–8 grams of Multi-Purpose Long-Life Lubricant, C1AZ-19590-B(ESA-M1C175-B) or equivalent to the splines. Insert the front driveshaft male spline.

20. Connect the front driveshaft to the axle input yoke. Tighten the bolts to 12–15 ft. lbs.

21. Push the driveshaft boot to engage the external groove on the transfer case front output shaft. Secure with a clamp.

22. Connect the four-wheel drive indicator switch wire connector at the transfer case.

Install the drain plug and tighten to 14–22 ft. lbs. Remove the fill plug and install 3 pints of DEXRON®-II, automatic transmission fluid. Install fill plug and tighten to 14–22 ft. lbs.

23. Install the skid plate to frame. Tighten nuts and bolts to 22–30 ft. lbs. Lower the vehicle.

Bronco

REMOVAL & INSTALLATION

3.03 3-Speed

1. Shift the transfer case into Neutral.
2. Remove the bolts attaching the fan shroud to the radiator support, if so equipped.
3. Raise the vehicle on a hoist.
4. Support the transfer case shield with a jack and remove the bolts that attach the shield to the frame side rails. Remove the shield.
5. Drain the transmission and transfer case lubricant. To drain the transmission lubricant, remove the lower extension housing-to-transmission bolt.
6. Disconnect the front and rear driveshafts at the transfer case.
7. Disconnect the speedometer cable at the transfer case.
8. Disconnect the T.R.S. switch, if so equipped.
9. Disconnect the shift rods from the transmission shift levers. Place the First-Reverse gear shift lever into the First gear position and insert the fabricated tool. The tool consists of a length of rod, the same diameter as the holes in the shift levers, which is bent in such a way to fit in the holes in the two shift levers and hold them in the position stated above. More important, this tool will prevent the input shaft roller bearings from dropping into the transmission and output shaft. THIS TOOL IS A MUST.
10. Support the engine with a jack.
11. Remove the two cotter pins, bolts, washers, plate and insulators that secure the crossmember to the transfer case adapter.
12. Remove the crossmember-to-frame side support attaching bolts.
13. Position a transmission jack under

the transfer case and remove the upper insulators from the crossmember. Remove the crossmember.

14. Roll back the boot enclosing the transfer case shift linkage. Remove the threaded cap holding the shift lever assembly to the shift bracket. Remove the shift lever assembly.

15. Remove the two lower bolts attaching the transmission to the flywheel housing.

16. Reposition the transmission jack under the transmission and secure it with a chain.

17. Remove the two upper bolts securing the transmission to the flywheel housing. Move the transmission and transfer case rearward and downward out of the vehicle.

18. Move the assembly to a bench and remove the transfer case-to-transmission attaching bolts.

19. Slide the transmission assembly off the transfer case.

To install the transmission:

20. Position the transfer case to the transmission. Apply an oil-resistant sealer to the bolt threads and install the attaching bolts. Tighten to 42–50 ft. lbs.

21. Position the transmission and transfer case on a transmission jack and secure them with a chain.

22. Raise the transmission and transfer case assembly into position and install the transmission case to the flywheel housing.

23. Install the two upper and two lower transmission attaching bolts and torque them to 37–42 ft. lbs.

24. Position the transfer case shift lever and install the threaded cap to the shift bracket. Reposition the rubber boot.

25. Raise the transmission and transfer case high enough to provide clearance for installing the crossmember. Position the upper insulators to the crossmember and install the crossmember-to-frame side support attaching bolts.

26. Align the bolt holes in the transfer case adapter with those in the crossmember, then lower the transmission and remove the jack.

27. Install the crossmember-to-transfer case adapter bolts, nuts, insulators, plates and washers. Tighten the nuts and secure them with cotter pins.

28. Remove the engine jack.

29. Remove the fabricated tool and connect each shift rod to its respective lever on the transmission. Adjust the linkage.

30. Connect the speedometer cable.

31. Connect the T.R.S. switch, if so equipped.

32. Install the front and rear driveshafts to the transfer case.

33. Fill the transmission and transfer case to the bottom of the filler hole with the recommended lubricant.

34. Position the transfer case shield to the frame side rails and install the attaching bolts.

35. Lower the vehicle.

36. Install the fan shroud, if so equipped.

37. Check the operation of the transfer

case and the transmission shift linkage.

NP435

1. Remove the rubber boot and floor mat.
2. Remove the weather pad. It may be necessary first to remove the seat assembly.
3. Disconnect the back-up light switch located in the rear of the gearshift housing cover.
4. Raise the vehicle and position safety stands. Position a transmission jack under the transmission, and disconnect the speedometer cable.
5. Disconnect the parking brake lever from its linkage, and remove the gearshift housing.
6. Disconnect the driveshaft or coupling shaft. Remove the bolts that attach the coupling shaft center support to the crossmember and wire the coupling shaft and driveshaft to one side. Remove the transfer case.
7. Remove the transmission attaching bolts at the clutch housing, and remove the transmission.
8. Before installing the transmission apply a light film of chassis lubricant to the release lever fulcrum and fork. Do not apply a thick coat of grease to these parts, as it will work out and contaminate the clutch disc.
9. Place the transmission on a transmission jack, and raise the transmission until the input shaft splines are aligned with the clutch disc splines. The clutch release bearing and hub must be properly positioned in the release lever fork.
10. Install guide studs in the clutch housing and slide the transmission forward on the guide studs until it is in position on the clutch housing. Install the attaching bolts or nuts, and tighten them to the following torques:

$\frac{7}{16}$–14: 40–50 ft. lbs.
$\frac{5}{8}$–11: 120–150 ft. lbs.
$\frac{9}{16}$–12: 90–115 ft. lbs.
$\frac{5}{8}$–18C: 120–150 ft. lbs.
$\frac{9}{16}$–18C: 90–115 ft. lbs.

Remove the guide studs and install the two lower attaching bolts.

11. Install the bolts attaching the coupling shaft center support to the crossmember. Tighten the bolts to 40–50 ft. lbs.

12. Connect the driveshaft or coupling shaft and the speedometer cable. Tighten the U-joint nuts.

13. Connect the back-up light switch wire.

14. Install the transmission cover plate. Install the seat assembly if it was removed.

15. Install weather pad, pad retainer, floor mat, and rubber boot.

T-18 through 1979

1. Open door cover seat.
2. Remove shift knobs.
3. Remove the four screws attaching the transmission shift lever boot assembly.

4. Remove the four screws holding the floor mat.

5. Remove the eleven screws holding the access cover to the floor pan. Place the shift lever in the reverse position and remove the cover.

6. Remove the insulator and dust cover.

7. Remove the transfer case shift lever.

8. Remove the eight bolts holding the shift cover and gasket.

9. Use cardboard or heavy paper to fabricate a suitable cover for the shift cover opening to protect the transmission from dirt during removal.

10. Raise the vehicle on a hoist.

11. Remove the drain pan and drain the transmission.

12. Disconnect the rear driveshaft from the transfer case and wire it out of the way.

13. Disconnect the front driveshaft from the transfer case and wire it out of the way.

14. Remove the cotter key that holds the shift link in place and remove the shift link.

15. Remove the speedometer cable from the transfer case.

16. Position a transmission jack under the transfer case. Remove the six bolts holding the transfer case to the transmission and lower the transfer case from the vehicle.

17. Remove the eight bolts that hold the rear support bracket to the transmission.

18. Position a transmission jack under the transmission and remove the rear support bracket and brace.

19. Remove the four bolts that hold the transmission to the bell housing.

20. Remove the transmission from the vehicle.

21. Place the transmission on a transmission jack and install it in the vehicle installing two guide studs in the bell housing top holes, to guide the transmission into position.

22. Install the two lower bolts. Remove the guide studs and install the upper bolts.

23. Place the rear support bracket in position and install the eight retaining bolts.

24. Install the two bolts at the rear support insulator bracket. Remove the transmission jack.

25. Position the transfer case on the transmission jack and install the six retaining bolts and gasket. Position the transfer case on the transmission and tighten the bolts to 50–60 ft. lbs.

26. Install the transfer case shift link and cotter pin.

27. Position and install the speedometer cable.

28. Remove wire and connect front driveshaft.

29. Remove wire and connect rear driveshaft.

30. Fill transfer case and manual transmission with lubricant.

31. Lower vehicle.

32. Remove fabricated dirt shield and prepare gasket area.

33. Position gasket and shift cover.

34. Install two pilot bolts, then install remaining shift cover retaining bolts.

35. Install transfer case shift handle.

36. Install dust cover and insulator.

37. Install access cover to floor pan screws.

38. Install the four floor mat screws.

39. Install the four boot area screws.

40. Install the shift knobs.

T-18 from 1980

1. Open door cover seat.

2. Remove shift knobs.

3. Remove the four screws attaching the transmission shift lever boot assembly.

4. Remove the four screws holding the floor mat.

5. Remove the eleven screws holding the access cover to the floor pan. Place the shift lever in the reverse position and remove the cover.

6. Remove the insulator and dust cover.

7. Remove the transfer case shift lever.

8. Remove transmission shift lever.

9. Raise the vehicle on a hoist.

10. Remove the drain plug and drain the transmission.

11. Disconnect the rear driveshaft from the transfer case and wire it out of the way.

12. Disconnect the front driveshaft from the transfer case and wire it out of the way.

13. Remove the retainer ring that holds the shift link in place and remove the shift link from transfer case.

14. Remove the speedometer cable from the transfer case.

15. Position a transmission jack under the transfer case. Remove the six bolts holding the transfer case to the transmission and lower the transfer case from the vehicle.

16. Remove the eight bolts that hold the rear support bracket to the transmission.

17. Position a transmission jack under the transmission and remove the rear support bracket and brace.

18. Remove the four bolts that hold the transmission to the bell housing.

19. Remove the transmission from the vehicle.

20. Place the transmission on a transmission jack and install it in the vehicle installing two guide studs in the bell housing top holes, to guide the transmission into position.

22. Install the two lower bolts. Remove the guide studs and install the upper bolts.

23. Place the rear support bracket in position and install the eight retaining bolts. Torque to 35–50 ft. lbs.

24. Install the two bolts at the rear support insulator bracket. Remove the transmission jack.

25. Position the transfer case on the transmission jack and install the six retaining bolts and gasket. Position the transfer case on the transmission and tighten the bolts to 28–33 ft. lbs.

26. Install the transfer case shift link and retainer ring.

27. Position and install the speedometer cable.

28. Remove wire and connect front driveshaft.

29. Remove wire and connect rear driveshaft.

30. Fill transfer case and transmission.

31. Lower vehicle.

32. Remove fabricated dirt shield and prepare gasket area.

33. Position gasket and shift cover.

34. Install two pilot bolts, then install remaining shift cover retaining bolts.

35. Install transfer case shift handle and transmission shift lever.

36. Install dust cover and insulator.

37. Install access cover to floor pan screws.

38. Install the four floor mat screws.

39. Install the four boot area screws.

40. Install the shift knobs.

Single Rail Overdrive

1. Raise the vehicle and support it on jackstands.

2. Mark the driveshaft so that it may be installed in the same relative position. Disconnect the driveshaft from the rear U-joint flange. Slide the driveshaft off the transmission output shaft and install an extension housing seal installation tool, or rags into the extension housing to prevent lubricant leakage.

3. Disconnect the speedometer cable from the extension housing.

4. Remove three screws securing shift lever to turret assembly.

5. Remove shift lever from turret assembly.

6. Support the engine with a transmission jack and remove the extension housing-to-engine rear support attaching bolts.

7. Raise the rear of the engine high enough to remove the weight from the crossmember. Remove the bolts retaining the crossmember to the frame side supports and remove the crossmember.

8. Support the transmission on a jack and remove the bolts that attach the transmission to the flywheel housing.

9. Move the transmission and jack rearward until the transmission input shaft clears the flywheel housing. If necessary, lower the engine enough to obtain clearance for transmission removal.

— CAUTION —

Do not depress the clutch pedal while the transmission is removed.

---

10. Make sure that the mounting surface of the transmission and the flywheel housing are free of dirt, paint, and burrs. Install two guide pins in the flywheel housing lower mounting bolt holes. Move the transmission forward on the guide pins until the input shaft splines enter the clutch hub splines and the case is positioned against the flywheel housing.

11. Install the two upper transmission to flywheel housing mounting bolts snug, and then remove the two guide pins. Install the two lower mounting bolts. Torque all mounting bolts to specifications.

12. Raise the rear of the engine and install the crossmember. Install and torque the crossmember attaching bolts to specifications, then lower the engine.

13. With the transmission extension housing resting on the engine rear support, install the transmission extension housing attaching bolts. Torque the bolts to specifications.

14. Position shift tower to extension housing and secure with three screws.

15. Connect the speedometer cable to the extension housing.

16. Remove the extension housing installation tool and slide the forward end of the driveshaft over the transmission output shaft. Connect the driveshaft to the rear U-joint flange.

17. Fill the transmission to the proper level with the specified lubricant.

18. Lower the truck. Check the shift and crossover motion for full shift engagement and smooth crossover operation.

Vans

REMOVAL & INSTALLATION

3-Speed

1. Raise the vehicle on a hoist and drain the lubricant from the transmission by removing the lower extension housing-to-transmission bolt.

2. Disconnect the driveshaft from the flange at the transmission. Secure the front end of the driveshaft out of the way by tying it up with a length of wire.

3. Disconnect the speedometer cable from the extension housing and disconnect the gearshift rods from the transmission. Disconnect the transmission regulated spark switch, if so equipped.

4. Position a transmission jack under the transmission. Chain the transmission to the jack.

5. Raise the transmission slightly and remove the 4 bolts which retain the transmission support crossmember to the frame side rails. Remove the bolt which retains the transmission extension housing to the crossmember.

6. Remove the 4 transmission-to-flywheel housing bolts.

7. Position a bar under the rear of the engine to support it.

8. Remove the transmission from the vehicle by lowering the jack.

To install the transmission:

9. Make sure that the machined surfaces of the transmission case and the flywheel housing are free of dirt, paint, and burrs.

10. Install a guide pin in each lower mounting bolt hole.

11. Start the input shaft through the release bearing. Align the splines on the input shaft with the splines in the clutch disc. Move the transmission forward on the guide pins until the input shaft pilot enters the bearing or bushing in the crankshaft. If the transmission front bearing retainer binds up on the clutch release bearing hub, work the release bearing lever until the hub slides onto the transmission front bearing retainer. Install the two upper mounting bolts and lockwashers which attach the flywheel housing to the transmission. Remove the two guide pins and install the lower mounting bolts and lockwashers.

12. Raise the jack slightly and remove the engine support bar. Position the support crossmember on the frame side rails and install the retaining bolts. Install the extension housing-to-crossmember retaining bolt.

13. Connect the gearshift rods and the speedometer cable. Connect the transmission regulated spark switch lead, if so equipped.

14. Install the driveshaft.

15. Fill the transmission to the bottom of the filler hole with the proper lubricant.

16. Adjust the clutch pedal free-play and the shift linkage as required.

4-Speed Overdrive

1. Raise the vehicle on a hoist.

2. Mark the driveshaft so that it may be installed in the same relative position. Disconnect the driveshaft from the rear U-joint flange. Slide the driveshaft off the transmission output shaft and install the extension housing seal installation tool into the extension housing to prevent lubricant leakage.

3. Disconnect the speedometer cable from the extension housing.

4. Remove the retaining clips, flat washers, and spring washers that secure the shift rods to the shift levers. Remove the bolts connecting the shift control to the transmission extension housing. Remove the nut connecting the shift control to the transmission case.

NOTE: A '6' and '8' is stamped on transmission extension housing by the shift control plate bolt holes. The '6' and '8' refer to either a 6 or 8 cylinder engine application. The shift control plate bolts must be placed in the right holes for proper plate positioning dependent upon engine application.

5. Remove the rear transmission support connecting bolts attaching the support on the crossmember to the transmission extension housing.

6. Support the engine with a transmission jack and remove the extension housing-to-engine rear support attaching bolts.

7. Raise the rear of the engine high enough to remove the weight from the crossmember. Remove the bolts retaining the crossmember to the frame side supports and remove the crossmember.

8. Support the transmission on a jack and remove the bolts that attach the transmission to the flywheel housing.

9. Move the transmission and jack rearward until the transmission input shaft clears the flywheel housing. If necessary, lower the engine enough to obtain clearance for transmission removal. **Do not depress the clutch pedal while the transmission is removed.**

10. Make sure that the mounting surfaces of the transmission and the flywheel housing are free of dirt, paint, and burrs. Install two guide pins in the flywheel housing lower mounting bolt holes. Move the transmission forward on the guide pins until the input shaft splines enter the clutch hub splines and the case is positioned against the flywheel housing.

11. Install the two upper transmission to flywheel housing mounting bolts snug, and then remove the two guide pins. Install the two lower mounting bolts. Tighten all mounting bolts to 40–45 ft. lbs.

12. Raise the rear of the engine and install the crossmember. Install and torque the crossmember attaching bolts to 20–30 ft. lbs. then lower the engine.

13. With the transmission extension housing resting on the engine rear support, install the transmission extension housing attaching bolts. Tighten the bolts to 42–50 ft. lbs.

14. Install the transmission support bolts and tighten to 40–50 ft. lbs.

15. Position the shift control bracket on the stud on the transmission case and on the bolt attaching holes (holes marked either '6' or '8' dependent upon 6 or 8 cylinder engine application) on the transmission extension housing. Install and hand tighten connecting bolts.

NOTE: The bracket must be placed in the proper position for correct shift control operation.

Tighten the nut connecting the bracket to the transmission case to 22–30 ft. lbs. Tighten the bolts to 22–30 ft. lbs.

16. Secure each shift rod to its respective lever with the spring washer, flat washer, and retaining pin.

17. Connect the speedometer cable to the extension housing.

18. Remove the extension housing installation tool and slide the forward end of the driveshaft over the transmission output shaft. Connect the driveshaft to the rear U-joint flange. Adjust the linkage.

19. Fill the transmission to the proper level with the specified lubricant.

20. Lower the vehicle. Check the shift and crossover motion for full shift engagement and smooth crossover operation.

CLUTCH

Pick-up

NOTE: Refer to following Ranger/Bronco II Section for instructions on those vehicles.

8-351, 400 clutch installation

FREEPLAY ADJUSTMENT
MANUAL LINKAGE

1. Measure the clutch pedal free-play by depressing the pedal slowly until the free-play between the release bearing assembly and the pressure plate is removed. Note this measurement. The difference between this measurement and when the pedal is not depressed is the free-play measurement.

2. If the free-play measurement is less than ½–¾ inch, the clutch linkage must be adjusted.

3. Loosen the two jam nuts on the release rod under the truck and back off both nuts several turns.

4. Loosen or tighten the first jam nut (nearest the release lever) against the bullet (rod extension) until a free-play measurement of ¾–1½ in. is obtained. A free-play measurement closer to 1½ in. is more desirable.

5. When the correct free-play measurement is obtained, hold the first jam nut in position and securely tighten the other nut against the first.

6. Recheck the free-play adjustment.

NOTE: Total pedal travel is fixed and is not adjustable.

HYDRAULIC CLUTCH

The Hydraulic clutch system consists of a combination clutch and master cylinder assembly, a slave cylinder and connecting tubing. The slave cylinder is mounted on the bell housing. The hydraulic clutch system provides automatic clutch adjustment. No adjustment of the clutch linkage or pedal position is required.

REMOVAL & INSTALLATION

1. Disconnect the release lever retracting spring and pushrod assembly. If equipped

with an hydraulic clutch, remove the slave cylinder with line connected.

2. Remove the transmission.

3. If the clutch housing does not have a dust cover, remove the starter. Remove the flywheel housing attaching bolts and remove the housing.

4. If the flywheel housing does have a dust cover, remove the cover and then remove the release lever and bearing from the clutch housing.

5. Mark the pressure plate and cover assembly and the flywheel so that they can be reinstalled in the same relative position.

6. Loosen the pressure plate and cover attaching bolts evenly in a staggered sequence a turn at a time until the pressure plate springs are relieved of their tension. Remove the attaching bolts.

7. Remove the pressure plate and cover assembly and the clutch disc from the flywheel.

8. Position the clutch disc on the flywheel so that an aligning tool or spare transmission mainshaft can enter the clutch pilot bearing and align the disc.

9. When reinstalling the original pressure plate and cover assembly, align the assembly and flywheel according to the marks made during removal. Position the pressure plate and cover assembly on the flywheel, align the pressure plate and disc, and install the retaining bolts. Tighten the bolts in an alternating sequence a few turns at a time until 15–20 ft. lbs. is reached.

10. Remove the tool used to align the clutch disc.

11. With the clutch fully released, apply a light coat of grease on the sides of the driving lugs.

12. Position the clutch release bearing and the bearing hub on the release lever. Install the release lever on the fulcrum in the flywheel housing. Apply a light coating of grease to the release lever fingers and the fulcrum. Fill the groove of the release bearing hub with grease.

13. If the flywheel housing has been removed, position it against the rear engine cover plate and install the attaching bolts and tighten them to 40–50 ft. lbs.

14. Install the starter motor.

15. Install the transmission.

16. Connect the release lever retracting spring and install the dust cover, if so equipped.

17. Adjust the clutch linkage.

Bronco

PEDAL HEIGHT ADJUSTMENT

1977

1. Measure the total travel of the pedal. If the total travel is less than 6¾ in. or more than 6¼ in., move the clutch pedal bumper and bracket up or down until the travel is within these limits.

2. To check and adjust the pedal free travel, slowly apply the clutch pedal until the clutch fingers contact the clutch release bearing. The distance the clutch pedal moves is the free travel dimension. The free travel should be 1¼ to 1⅞₁₆ in. If it is not within these limits, loosen the nut at the bullet on the clutch release rod and adjust the bullet until the free travel is within the specified range.

3. Tighten the nut at the turnbuckle.

1978–79

1. Measure the clutch pedal free travel using a steel tape. Measure the distance from the clutch pedal pad to the steering

1978 and later Bronco and pick-up clutch pedal free play measurement

1977 clutch linkage

wheel rim. Depress the pedal slowly until the free travel between the release bearing assembly and the pressure plate assembly is taken up. Note this measurement. The difference between the two measurements is the free travel.

2. If the free-travel measurement is less than ½ in. 1978; ¾ in. 1979 or greater than 2 inches 1978; 1½ inches 1979, the clutch linkage must be adjusted.

3. With retracting spring removed, hold the release rod firmly against release lever, eliminating lever free play.

4. Position first jam nut .062 inches from the bar while holding needle firmly against release lever.

5. Position second jam nut finger tight against the first nut, while holding second nut. Lock the first nut with 15–20 ft. lbs. torque. This gives ¾ to 1½ inch at pedal pad with 1½ inches prefered.

6. Check adjustment with retracting spring in place.

1980 and Later

1. Measure the clutch pedal free travel using a steel tape. Measure the distance from the clutch pedal pad to the steering wheel rim. Depress the pedal slowly until the free travel between the release bearing assembly and the pressure plate assembly is taken up. Note this measurement. The difference between the two measurements is the free travel.

2. If the free travel measurement is less than ½ inch or more than 2 inches, the clutch linkage must be adjusted.

3. Remove the retracting spring.

4. Loosen the two jam nuts on the release rod assembly and back off both nuts several turns.

5. Slide the release rod extension (bullet) firmly against the release lever. Push the release rod forward against the equalizer bar lever to eliminate all freeplay from the linkage system.

6. Insert 0.135 inch thick gauge between the jam nut and bullet. Tighten the first jam nut finger tight against the gauge with all freeplay eliminated.

7. Tighten the second jam nut finger tight against the first jam nut. Hold the first nut and tighten the second jam nut to 15–20 ft. lbs. Freeplay should measure ¾–1½ inches at the pedal.

8. With the recommended free travel obtained, and holding the first jam nut, position and securely tighten the second jam nut against the first jam nut.

9. Re-check the pedal free travel.

REMOVAL & INSTALLATION

1977

1. Disconnect the cable from the starter and remove the starter.

2. Remove the transmission and transfer case.

3. Disconnect the release lever retracting spring and the release rod.

4. Remove the hub and release bearing assembly.

5. Remove the flywheel housing-to-engine bolts and lower the flywheel housing.

6. Remove the pressure plate and disc from the flywheel. Unscrew the attaching bolts a few turns at a time, in a staggered sequence to prevent distortion of the pressure plate.

To install the clutch:

7. Wash the flywheel surface with alcohol. Do not use an oil-base cleaner, carbon tetrachloride or gasoline.

8. Place the clutch disc and the pressure plate and cover assembly in position on the flywheel. Start the retaining bolts until finger-tight.

9. Align the clutch disc on aligning tool (an old mainshaft works well), and then evenly torque the bolts to 23–28 ft. lbs.

10. Lightly lubricate the release lever

fulcrum and ends with lithium base grease and position the release lever in the flywheel housing. Crimp the dust seal tabs flush against the flywheel housing. Attach the springs of the release bearing hub to the ends of the release fork. Be careful not to distort the springs.

11. Fill the groove in the clutch release bearing hub with lithium base grease. Wipe the excess grease from the hub.

12. Position the flywheel housing and release lever assembly, and install the mounting bolts. Make sure that the muffler front hanger is in place on the flywheel housing. Install the dust cover, and tighten the attaching bolts.

13. Remove any dirt, paint or burrs from the mounting surfaces of the flywheel housing and the transmission.

14. Install the transmission and transfer case.

15. Install the starter and connect the starter cable.

16. Adjust the clutch pedal free travel and check the operation of the clutch.

1978–79

1. Disconnect the release lever retracting spring and push rod assembly at the lever.

2. Refer to the appropriate transmission part of this chapter for instructions and remove the transmission from the vehicle.

3. If the clutch housing is not provided with a dust cover, remove the starting motor. Remove the flywheel housing attaching bolts and remove the housing.

4. If the flywheel housing is provided with a dust cover, remove it from the housing. Remove the release lever and release bearing from the clutch housing.

5. Mark the pressure plate and cover assembly and the flywheel, so that the parts can be reinstalled in the same relative position.

6. Loosen the pressure plate and cover attaching bolts evenly until the pressure plate springs are expanded, and remove the bolts.

7. Remove the pressure plate and cover assembly and the clutch disc from the flywheel or through the opening in the bottom of the clutch housing. Remove the pilot bearing only for replacement.

8. Position the clutch disc on the flywheel so that the pilot tool can enter the clutch pilot bearing and align the disc.

9. When re-installing the original pressure plate and cover assembly, align the assembly and flywheel according to the marks made during the removal operations. Position the pressure plate and cover assembly on the flywheel, align the pressure plate and disc, and install the retaining bolts that fasten the assembly to the flywheel. Tighten the bolts to 20–30 ft. lbs., and remove the clutch disc pilot tool.

10. With the clutch fully released, apply a light film of lithium-base grease ESA-M1C75-B or equivalent on the sides of the driving lugs.

11. Position the clutch release bearing

and the bearing hub on the release lever. Install the release lever on the trunnion in the flywheel housing. Apply a light film of lithium-base grease ESA-M1C75-B or equivalent to the release lever fingers and to the lever trunnion or fulcrum. Fill the annular groove of the release bearing hub with grease.

12. If the flywheel housing has been removed, position it against the engine rear cover plate and install the attaching bolts. Tighten the bolts to 40–50 ft. lbs.

13. Install the starter motor. Install the transmission assembly on the clutch housing. Tighten the bolts to 50–60 ft. lbs.

14. Install the slave cylinder on vehicles so equipped, and tighten the bolts.

15. Adjust the release lever push rod assembly. Connect the release lever retracting spring.

16. Install the clutch housing dust cover if so equipped.

1980 and Later

1. Disconnect the release lever retracting spring and push rod assembly at the lever. Remove starter.

2. Refer to the appropriate transmission part of this chapter for instructions and remove the transmission from the vehicle.

3. If the clutch housing is not provided with a dust cover, remove the starting motor. Remove the flywheel housing attaching bolts and remove the housing.

4. If the flywheel housing is provided

with a dust cover, remove it from the housing. Remove the release lever and release bearing from the clutch housing.

5. Loosen the pressure plate and cover attaching bolts evenly until the pressure plate springs are expanded, and remove the bolts.

6. Remove the pressure plate and cover assembly and the clutch disc from the flywheel or through the opening in the bottom of the clutch housing. Remove the pilot bearing only for replacement.

7. Position the clutch disc on the flywheel so that the pilot tool can enter the clutch pilot bearing and align the disc.

8. When re-installing the original pressure plate and cover assembly, align the assembly and flywheel according to the marks made during the removal operations. Position the pressure plate and cover assembly on the flywheel, align the pressure plate and disc, and install the retaining bolts that fasten the assembly to the flywheel. Tighten the bolts to 20–30 ft. lbs., and remove the clutch disc pilot tool.

9. Position the clutch release bearing and the bearing hub on the release lever. Install the release lever on the pivot bar pedestal in the flywheel housing. Apply a light film of lithium-base grease ESA-M1C75-B or equivalent to the release lever fingers and to the lever pivot ball. Fill the annular groove of the release bearing hub with grease.

10. If the flywheel housing has been removed, position it against the engine rear cover plate and install the attaching bolts.

Tighten the bolts to 40–50 ft. lbs.

11. Install the starter motor. Install the transmission assembly on the clutch housing. Tighten the bolts.

12. Adjust the release lever push rod assembly. Connect the release lever retracting spring.

13. Install the clutch housing dust cover if so equipped.

Ranger and Bronco II

REMOVAL & INSTALLATION

1. Disconnect the clutch hydraulic system master cylinder from the clutch pedal.

2. Raise the vehicle and safely support on jack stands. Remove the dust shield from the clutch housing.

3. Disconnect the hydraulic clutch linkage from the housing and release lever. Remove the starter.

4. Remove the bolts attaching the clutch housing to the engine block. Note the direction in which the bolts are installed.

5. Index the driveshaft to the companion flange and remove the driveshaft.

6. Remove the nuts attaching the transmission and insulator to the #2 crossmember support. Raise the transmission with a suitable jack. Remove the #2 crossmember support. Lower the transmission and clutch housing.

7. Remove the release lever, and hub

Clutch installation-134 (2.2L) diesel

FLYWHEEL

CLUTCH PLATE AND COVER

ENGINE END PLATE

DOWEL PIN

CLUTCH DISC

BOLT AND WASHER

21-32 N·m
(15-24 FT-LB)

CLUTCH HOUSING

and bearing. Mark the assembled position of the pressure plate and cover to the flywheel (for re-assembly).

8. Loosen the pressure plate and cover attaching bolts evenly until the pressure plate springs are expanded, and remove the bolts.

9. Remove the pressure plate and cover assembly and the clutch disc from the flywheel. These parts can be removed through the opening in the bottom of the clutch housing on models where the housing is fitted with a dust cover. Remove the pilot bearing only for replacement.

10. Position the clutch disc on the flywheel so that the Clutch Alignment Shaft D79T-7550-A or equivalent can enter the clutch pilot bearing and align the disc.

11. When re-installing the original pressure plate and cover assembly, align the assembly and flywheel according to the marks made during the removal operations. Position the pressure plate and cover assembly on the flywheel, align the pressure plate and disc, and install the retaining bolts that fasten the assembly to the flywheel. Tighten the bolts to 15-24 ft-lbs, and remove the clutch disc pilot tool.

12. Position the clutch release bearing and the bearing hub on the release lever. Install the release lever on the release lever seat in the flywheel housing. Apply a light film of lithium-base grease C1AZ-19590-B (ESA-M1C75-B) or equivalent to the release lever fingers and to the lever pivot ball. Fill the annular groove of the release bearing hub with grease.

13. Raise the transmission and clutch housing into position. Install the No. 2 crossmember support to the frame. Install connecting nuts, bolts and washers.

14. Lower the transmission and insulator into the support. Install and tighten nuts. Remove the transmission jack.

15. Install the driveshaft, making sure the index marks on the driveshaft are aligned with the marks on the companion flange.

16. Install the bolts attaching the housing to the engine block in the correct position as removed. Tighten to 28-38 ft-lbs.

17. Install the hydraulic clutch linkage on the housing in position with the release lever. Install dust shield. Install starter.

18. Lower the vehicle and connect the clutch hydraulic system master cylinder to the clutch pedal. Check clutch for proper operation.

Vans

FREEPLAY ADJUSTMENT

To check and adjust the pedal free travel measure and note the distance from the floor pan to the top of the pedal: then depress the pedal slowly until the clutch release fingers contact the clutch release bearing. Measure and record the distance. The difference between the reading with the pedal in the depressed position and the reading

1978–79 van clutch pedal free travel adjustment

1980 and later van clutch pedal free travel adjustment

with the pedal in the fully released postion is the pedal free travel. The free travel should be as specified.

The pedal height is not adjustable. Pedal height is adjusted by loosening the nut securing the clutch pedal eccentric bumper and rotating the bumper until the clutch pedal height is within 1¼–1½ in.

REMOVAL & INSTALLATION

1. Disconnect the cable from the starter and remove the starter.
2. Remove the transmission.
3. Disconnect the release lever retracting spring and release the rod.
4. Remove the hub and release bearing assembly.
5. Remove the flywheel housing-to-engine bolts, and lower the flywheel housing.
6. Remove the pressure plate and the

disc from the flywheel. Unscrew the attaching bolts a few turns at a time, in a staggered sequence to prevent distortion of the pressure plate.

7. Wash the flywheel surface with alcohol. Do not use an oil-base cleaner, carbon tetrachloride or gasoline.

To install the clutch:

8. Place the clutch disc and the pressure plate and cover assembly in position on the flywheel. Start the retaining bolts until finger-tight.

9. Align the clutch disc with a clutch arbor (an old mainshaft works well) and then evenly torque the bolts to 23–28 ft. lbs.

10. Do not grease the release lever pivot assembly. Crimp the dust seal tabs flush against the flywheel housing. Attach the springs of the release bearing hub to the ends of the release fork. Be careful not to distort the springs.

11. Fill the groove in the clutch release bearing hub with lithium-base grease. Wipe the excess grease from the hub.

12. Position the flywheel housing and release lever assembly, and install the mounting bolts. Make sure that the muffler front hanger is in place on the flywheel housing. Install the dust cover, and tighten the attaching bolts.

13. Remove any dirt, paint, or burrs from the mounting surfaces of the flywheel housing and the transmission.

14. Install the transmission.

15. Install the starter and connect the starter cable.

16. Adjust the clutch pedal free-play and check the operation of the clutch.

CLUTCH PEDAL ADJUSTMENT

To check and adjust the pedal free travel, measure and note the distance from the floor pan to the top of the pedal; then depress the pedal slowly until the clutch release fingers contact the clutch release bearing. Measure and record the distance. The difference between the reading with the pedal in the depressed position and the reading with the pedal in the fully released position is the pedal free travel. The free travel should be as specified.

The pedal height is not adjustable. Pedal height is adjusted by loosening the nut securing the clutch pedal eccentric bumper and rotating the bumper until the clutch pedal height is within 1¼–1½ in.

AUTOMATIC TRANSMISSION

REMOVAL & INSTALLATION

C4, C5

F-100 THRU 250, 1977 E-100 THRU 250

1. Raise the vehicle on a hoist.
2. Place the drain pan under the transmission fluid pan. Remove the fluid filler tube from the pan and drain the transmission fluid.
3. Remove the converter drain plug access cover from the lower end of the converter housing.
4. Remove the converter-to-flywheel attaching nuts. Place a wrench on the crankshaft pulley attaching bolt to turn the converter to gain access to the nuts.
5. With the wrench on the crankshaft pulley attaching bolt, turn the converter to gain access to the converter drain plug and remove the plug. Place a drain pan under the converter to catch the fluid. With fluid drained, reinstall the plug.
6. Remove the driveshaft.
7. Disconnect the oil cooler lines from the transmission.
8. Disconnect the manual and downshift linkage rods from the transmission control levers.
9. Remove the speedometer gear from the extension housing.
10. Disconnect the back-up switch wires from the retaining clips and retainer.
11. Disconnect the starter cable. Remove the three starter-to-converter housing attaching bolts and remove the starter.
12. Remove the vacuum line hose from the transmission vacuum unit. Disconnect the vacuum line from the retaining clip.
13. Position the transmission jack to support the transmission. Install the safety chain to hold the transmission on the jack.

14. Remove the two engine rear support crossmember-to-frame attaching bolts.
15. Remove the two engine rear support-to-extension housing attaching bolts.
16. Raise the transmission and remove the rear support. Remove the six converter housing-to-engine attaching bolts.
17. Move the converter and transmission assembly away from the engine. Lower the transmission and remove it from under the vehicle.
18. Tighten the converter drain plug to 15-28 ft. lbs.
19. Position the converter on the transmission making sure the converter drive flats are fully engaged in the pump gear.
20. With the converter properly installed, place the transmission on the jack. Secure the transmission to the jack with the safety chain.
21. Rotate the converter until the studs and drain plug are in alignment with their holes in the flywheel.
22. Move the converter and transmission assembly forward into position, using care not to damage the flywheel and the converter pilot. **The converter must rest squarely against the flywheel. This indicates that the converter pilot is not binding in the engine crankshaft.**
23. Install the six converter housing-to-engine attaching bolts. Tighten the bolts to 40–50 ft. lbs.
24. Install the converter-to-flywheel attaching nuts. Tighten the nuts to 20–34 ft. lbs. Remove the safety chain from the transmission.
25. Install the rear support. Install the rear support-to-extension housing attaching bolts. Tighten the bolts.
26. Position the starter into the converter housing and install the three attaching bolts. Tighten the bolts to 20–30 ft. lbs. Install the starter cable.
26. Remove the transmission jack.
27. Connect the transmission filler tube to the transmission pan. Connect the oil cooler lines to the transmission.
28. Attach the back-up switch wires to the connector clip.
29. Install the speedometer driven gear in the extension housing. Tighten the attaching bolt.
30. Connect the transmission linkage rods to the transmission control levers.

NOTE: When making transmission control attachments, new retaining rings and grommets should always be used.

Attach the shift rod to the steering column shift lever. Align the flats of the adjusting stud with the flats of the rod slot and insert the stud through the rod. Assemble the adjusting stud nut and washer to a loose fit. Perform a linkage adjustment.
32. Install the driveshaft.
33. Install the vacuum line in the retaining clip. Connect the vacuum line to the diaphragm unit.
34. At the front lower area of the converter housing, install the lower cover and

the control lever dust shield. Install the attaching bolts. Tighten the bolts.
35. Secure the fluid filler tube to the pan. Tighten the fitting to 32–42 ft. lbs.
36. Lower the vehicle.
37. Fill the transmission to the proper level.
38. Raise the vehicle and check for transmission fluid leakage. Lower the vehicle and adjust the throttle and manual linkage.

Bronco 1977

1. Disconnect the fan shroud from the radiator.
2. Raise and support the vehicle on jack stands.
3. Remove the transfer case skid plate.
4. Remove the transmission filler tube and drain the fluid.
5. Drain the transfer case.
6. Remove the converter drain plug access cover from the lower end of the converter housing.
7. Remove the converter-to-flywheel attaching nuts. Place a wrench on the crankshaft pulley attaching bolt to turn the converter, thereby giving access to the nuts.
8. Turn the converter to gain access to the drain plug and remove it.
9. When the fluid has drained, replace the plug.
10. Disconnect the rear driveshaft.
11. Remove the front driveshaft.
12. Remove the complete exhaust system.
13. Remove the speedometer cable.
14. Disconnect the transmission oil cooler lines.
15. Disconnect the transmission linkage.
16. Remove the starter.
17. Disconnect the vacuum lines from the transmission.
18. Disconnect the transfer case adapter from the crossmember.
19. Remove the crossmember-to-frame side support attaching bolts.
20. Support the transmisson and transfer case on a jack.
21. Raise the jack slightly, to take up the weight and remove the four bolts securing the left side support bracket, crossmember and upper crossmember insulators.
22. Disconnect the shift rod from the transfer case shift lever bracket.
23. Remove the bolts that attach the shift lever bracket to the transfer case adapter and allow the assembly to hang by the shift lever.
24. Make sure the transmission is secure on the jack and remove the six converter housing-to-engine bolts.
25. Remove the transmission assembly from the engine by rolling the jack backwards and letting it down slowly.
26. When installing the transmisson, turn the converter so that the studs and drain plug are aligned with their holes in the flywheel.
27. Roll the assembly forward into position.

——————— **CAUTION** ———————

Make certain that the converter rests squarely against the flywheel. This ensures that the converter pilot is not binding in the engine crankshaft.

28. Install the six mounting bolts and torque to 30 ft. lbs.

29. Install the shift lever bracket.

30. Install the shift rod, spring washer, flat washer and cotter pin.

31. Install the crossmember and insulators.

32. Lower the transmission assembly onto the crossmember and remove the jack.

33. Bolt the transfer case to the crossmember.

34. Install the flywheel-to-converter nuts and torque to 30 ft. lbs.

35. Install the starter and torque the bolts to 30 ft. lbs.

36. Connect the filler tube and oil cooler lines.

37. Install the vacuum lines.

38. Install the speedometer cable.

39. Connect the transmission linkage rods to the levers.

40. Adjust the linkage.

41. Install the exhaust system.

42. Connect the rear driveshaft.

43. Connect the front axle driveshaft.

44. Install the converter drain plug access cover.

45. Fill the transfer case with lubricant as outlined in the first chapter and install the skid plate.

46. Lower the vehicle, install the fan shroud and fill the transmission with type "F" fluid.

47. Adjust the manual and downshift linkage.

C6 and FMX
BRONCO, F-150-350

1. Drive the vehicle on a hoist, but do not raise at this time.

2. Remove the two upper converter housing-to-engine bolts.

3. Remove the bolt securing the fluid filler tube to the engine cylinder head.

4. Raise the vehicle on a hoist or stands.

5. Place the drain pan under the transmission fluid pan. Starting at the rear of the pan and working toward the front, loosen the attaching bolts and allow the fluid to drain. Finally remove all of the pan attaching bolts except two at the front, to allow the fluid to further drain. With fluid drained, install two bolts on the rear side of the pan to temporarily hold it in place.

6. Remove the converter drain plug access cover from the lower end of the converter housing.

7. Remove the converter-to-flywheel attaching nuts. Place a wrench on the crankshaft pulley attaching bolt to turn the converter to gain access to the nuts.

8. With the wrench on the crankshaft pulley attaching bolt, turn the converter to gain access to the converter drain plug. Place

a drain pan under the converter to catch the fluid and remove the plug. After the fluid has been drained, re-install the plug.

9. Disconnect the driveshaft from the rear axle and slide shaft rearward from the transmission. Install a seal installation tool in the extension housing to prevent fluid leakage.

10. Disconnect the speedometer cable from the extension housing.

11. Disconnect the downshift and manual linkage rods from the levers at the transmission.

12. Disconnect the oil cooler lines from the transmission.

13. Remove the vacuum hose from the vacuum diaphragm unit. Remove the vacuum line retaining clip.

14. Disconnect the cable from the terminal on the starter motor. Remove the three attaching bolts and remove the starter motor.

15. On F-150—F-350 (4 × 4) and Bronco vehicles, remove the transfer case.

16. Remove the two engine rear support and insulator assembly-to-attaching bolts.

17. Remove the two engine rear support and insulator assembly-to-extension housing attaching bolts.

18. Remove the six bolts securing the No. 2 crossmember to the frame side rails.

19. Raise the transmission with a transmission jack and remove both crossmembers.

20. Secure the transmission to the jack with the safety chain.

21. Remove the remaining converter housing-to-engine attaching bolts.

22. Move the transmission away from the engine. Lower the jack and remove the converter and transmission assembly from under the vehicle.

23. Tighten the converter drain plug.

24. Position the converter on the transmission making sure the converter drive flats are fully engaged in the pump gear.

25. With the converter properly installed, place the transmission on the jack. Secure the transmission to the jack with the chain.

26. Rotate the converter until the studs and drain plug are in alignment with their holes in the flywheel.

27. Move the converter and transmission assembly forward into position, using care not to damage the flywheel and the converter pilot. **The converter must rest squarely against the flywheel. This indicates that the converter pilot is not binding in the engine crankshaft.**

28. Install and tighten the converter housing-to-engine attaching bolts.

29. Remove the transmission jack safety chain from around the transmission.

30. Position the No. 2 crossmember to the frame side rails. Install and tighten the attaching bolts.

31. Install transfer case on F-150–F-350 (4 × 4) and Bronco.

32. Positon the engine rear support and insulator assembly above the crossmember. Install the rear suport and insulator assembly-to-extension housing mounting bolts and

tighten the bolts.

33. Lower the transmission and remove the jack.

34. Secure the engine rear support and insulator assembly to the crossmember with the attaching bolts and tighten them.

35. Connect the vacuum line to the vacuum diaphragm making sure that the line is in the retaining clip.

36. Connect the oil cooler lines to the transmission.

37. Connect the downshift and manual linkage rods to their respective levers on the transmission.

38. Connect the speedometer cable to the extension housing.

39. Secure the starter motor in place with the attaching bolts. Connect the cable to the terminal on the starter.

40. Install a new O-ring on the lower end of the transmission filler tube and insert the tube in the case.

41. Secure the converter-to-flywheel attaching nuts and tighten them.

42. Install the converter housing access cover and secure it with the attaching bolts.

43. Connect the drive shaft.

44. Adjust the shift linkage as required.

45. Lower the vehicle. Then install the two upper converter housing-to-engine bolts and tighten them.

46. Position the transmission fluid filler tube to the cylinder head and secure with the attaching bolt.

47. Make sure the drain pan is securely attached, and fill the transmission to the correct level with the specified fluid.

E-100—E-350

1. Working from inside the vehicle, remove the engine compartment cover.

2. Disconnect the neutral start switch wires at the plug connector.

3. If the vehicle is equipped with a V-8 engine, remove the flexhose from the air cleaner heat tube.

4. Remove the upper converter housing-to-engine attaching bolts (three bolts on 6-cylinder engines; four bolts on 8-cylinder engines).

5. Raise the vehicle on a hoist.

6. Place the drain pan under the transmission fluid pan. Starting at the rear of the pan and working toward the front, loosen the attaching bolts and allow the fluid to drain. Finally remove all of the pan attaching bolts except two at the front, to allow the fluid to further drain. With fluid drained, install two bolts on the rear side of the pan to temporarily hold it in place.

7. Remove the converter drain plug access cover from the lower end of the converter housing.

8. Remove the converter-to-flywheel attaching nuts. Place a wrench on the crankshaft pulley attaching bolt to turn the converter to gain access to the nuts.

9. With the wrench on the crankshaft pulley attaching bolt, turn the converter to gain access to the converter drain plug. Place a drain pan under the converter to catch the

fluid. Then, remove the plug. With fluid drained, re-install the plug.

10. Disconnect the drive shaft.

11. Remove fluid filler tube.

12. Disconnect the starter cable at the starter. Remove the starter-to-converter housing attaching bolts and remove the starter.

13. Position the engine support bar (tool T65E-6000-JO) to the frame and engine oil pan flanges.

14. Disconnect the cooler lines from the transmission. Disconnect the vacuum line from the vacuum diaphragm unit. Remove the vacuum line from the retaining clip at the transmission.

15. Remove the speedometer driven gear from the extension housing.

16. Disconnect the manual and downshift linkage rods from the transmission control levers.

17. Position a transmission jack to support the transmission. Install the safety chain to hold the transmission.

18. Remove the bolts and nuts securing the rear support and insulator assembly to the crossmember. Remove the six bolts retaining the crossmember to the side rails and remove the two support gussets. Raise the transmission with the jack and remove the crossmember.

19. Remove the bolt that retains the transmission filler tube to the cylinder block. Lift the filler tube and dipstick from the transmission.

20. Remove the remaining converter housing-to-engine attaching bolts. Lower the jack and remove the converter and transmission assembly from under the vehicle.

21. Remove the converter and mount the transmission in a holding fixture.

22. Tighten the converter drain plug.

23. Position the converter on the transmission making sure the converter drive flats are fully engaged in the pump gear.

24. With the converter properly installed, place the transmission on the jack. Secure the transmission to the jack with the safety chain.

25. Rotate the converter until the studs and drain plug are in alignment with their holes in the flywheel.

26. Move the converter and transmission assembly forward into position, using care not to damage the flywheel and the converter pilot.

The converter must rest squarely against the flywheel. This indicates that the converter pilot is not binding in the engine crankshaft.

27. Install the lower converter housing-to-engine attaching bolts. Tighten the bolts. Install the converter-to-flywheel attaching nuts. Tighten the nuts.

28. Install the crossmember. Install the rear support and insulator assembly-to-crossmember attaching bolts and nuts. Tighten the bolts.

29. Remove the safety chain and remove the jack from under the vehicle. Remove

the engine support bar.

30. Install a new O-ring on the lower end of the transmission filler tube and insert the tube and dipstick in the case.

31. Connect the vacuum line to the vacuum diaphragm making sure the line is secured in the retaining clip.

32. Connect the cooler lines to the transmission.

33. Install the speedometer driven gear into the extension housing. Tighten the attaching bolt.

34. Connect the transmission linkage rods to the transmission control levers. When making transmission control attachments new retaining ring and grommet should always be used. Attach the shift rod to the steering column shift lever. Align the flats of the adjusting stud with the flats of the rod slot and insert the stud through the rod. Assemble the adjusting stud nut and washer to a loose fit. Perform a linkage adjustment.

35. Install the converter housing access cover and tighten the attaching bolts.

36. Position the starter into the converter housing and install the attaching bolts. Tighten the bolts. Install the starter cable.

37. Install the driveshaft.

38. Lower the vehicle.

39. Install the upper converter housing-to-engine attaching bolts. Tighten the bolts.

40. On V8 engines, install the flex hose to the air cleaner heat tube. Install the bolt that retains the filler tube to the cylinder block.

41. Connect the neutral start switch wires at the plug connector.

42. Make sure the transmission fluid pan is securely attached, and fill the transmission to the proper level with the specified fluid.

43. Raise the vehicle and check for transmission fluid leakage. Lower the vehicle and adjust the downshift and manual linkage.

44. Install the engine compartment cover.

Automatic Overdrive

1. Raise the vehicle on a hoist or stands.

2. Place the drain pan under the transmission fluid pan. Starting at the rear of the pan and working toward the front, loosen the attaching bolts and allow the fluid to drain. Finally remove all of the pan attaching bolts except two at the front, to allow the fluid to further drain. With fluid drained, install two bolts on the rear side of the pan to temporarily hold it in place.

3. Remove the converter drain plug access cover from the lower end of the converter housing.

4. Remove the converter-to-flywheel attaching nuts. Place a wrench on the crankshaft pulley attaching bolt to turn the converter to gain access to the nuts.

5. Place a drain pan under the converter to catch the fluid. With the wrench on the crankshaft pulley attaching bolt, turn the converter to gain access to the converter drain plug and remove the plug. After the fluid has been drained, reinstall the plug.

6. Disconnect the driveshaft from the rear axle and slide shaft rearward from the transmission. Install a seal installation tool in the extension housing to prevent fluid leakage.

7. Disconnect the cable from the terminal on the starter motor. Remove the three attaching bolts and remove the starter motor. Disconnect the neutral start switch wires at the plug connector.

8. Remove the rear mount-to-crossmember attaching bolts and the two crossmember-to-frame attaching bolts.

9. Remove the two engine rear support-to-extension housing attaching bolts.

10. Disconnect the TV linkage rod from the transmission TV lever. Disconnect the manual rod from the transmission manual lever at the transmission.

11. Remove the two bolts securing the bellcrank bracket to the converter housing.

12. Raise the transmission with a transmission jack to provide clearance to remove the crossmember. Remove the rear mount from the crossmember and remove the crossmember from the side supports.

13. Lower the transmission to gain access to the oil cooler lines.

14. Disconnect each oil line from the fittings on the transmission.

15. Disconnect the speedometer cable from the extension housing.

16. Remove the bolt that secures the transmission fluid filler tube to the cylinder block. Lift the filler tube and the dipstick from the transmission.

17. Secure the transmission to the jack with the chain.

18. Remove the converter housing-to-cylinder block attaching bolts.

19. Carefully move the transmission and converter assembly away from the engine and, at the same time, lower the jack to clear the underside of the vehicle.

20. Remove the converter and mount the transmission in a holding fixture.

21. Tighten the converter drain plug.

22. Position the converter on the transmission, making sure the converter drive flats are fully engaged in the pump gear by rotating the converter.

23. With the converter properly installed, place the transmission on the jack. Secure the transmission to the jack with a chain.

24. Rotate the converter until the studs and drain plug are in alignment with the holes in the flywheel.

25. Move the converter and transmission assembly forward into position, using care not to damage the flywheel and the converter pilot. The converter must rest squarely against the flywheel. This indicates that the converter pilot is not binding in the engine crankshaft.

26. Install and tighten the converter housing-to-engine attaching bolts to 40–50 ft. lbs.

27. Remove the safety chain from around the transmission.

28. Install a new O-ring on the lower

end of the transmission filler tube. Insert the tube in the transmission case and secure the tube to the engine with the attaching bolt.

29. Connect the speedometer cable to the extension housing.

30. Connect the oil cooler lines to the right side of transmission case.

31. Position the crossmember on the side supports. Position the rear mount on the crossmember and install the attaching bolt and nut.

32. Secure the engine rear support to the extension housing and tighten the bolts to 16–20 ft. lbs.

33. Lower the transmission and remove the jack.

C3

RANGER/BRONCO II

1. Raise the vehicle and safely support on jackstands. Place a drain pan under the transmission fluid pan. Starting at the rear of the pan and working toward the front, loosen the attaching bolts and allow the fluid to drain. Then remove all of the pan attaching bolts except two at the front, to allow the fluid to further drain. After all the fluid has drained, install two bolts on the rear side of the pan to temporarily hold it in place.

2. Remove the converter drain plug access cover and adapter plate bolts from the lower end of the converter housing.

3. Remove the four flywheel to converter attaching nuts. Crank the engine to turn the converter to gain access to the nuts, using a wrench on the crankshaft pulley attaching bolt. *On belt driven overhead camshaft engines, never turn the engine backwards.*

4. Crank the engine until the converter drain plug is accessible and remove the plug. Place a drain pan under the converter to catch the fluid. After all the fluid has been drained from the converter, reinstall the plug and tighten to 20–30 ft. lbs. Remove the driveshaft. Install cover, plastic bag etc. over end of extension housing.

5. Remove the speedometer cable from the extension housing. Disconnect the shift rod at the transmission manual lever. Disconnect the downshift rod at the transmission downshift lever.

6. Remove the starter-to-converter housing attaching bolts and position the starter out of the way.

7. Disconnect the neutral start switch wires from the switch. Remove the vacuum line from the transmission vacuum modulator.

8. Position a suitable jack under the transmission and raise it slightly.

9. Remove the engine rear support-to-crossmember bolts. Remove the crossmember-to-frame side support attaching bolts and remove the crossmember insulator and support and damper.

10. Lower the jack under the transmission and allow the transmission to hang.

11. Position a jack to the front of the engine and raise the engine to gain access to the two upper converter housing-to-engine attaching bolts.

12. Disconnect the oil cooler lines at the transmission. Plug all openings to keep out dirt.

13. Remove the lower converter housing-to-engine attaching bolts. Remove the transmission filler tube.

14. Secure the transmission to the jack with a safety chain.

15. Remove the two upper converter housing-to-engine attaching bolts. Move the transmission to the rear and down to remove it from under the vehicle.

16. Position the converter to the transmission making sure the converter hub is fully engaged in the pump. With the converter properly installed, place the transmission on the jack and secure with safety chain.

17. Rotate the converter so the drive studs and drain plug are in alignment with their holes in the flywheel. With the transmission mounted on a transmission jack, move the converter and transmission assembly forward into position being careful not to damage the flywheel and the converter pilot.

—————— CAUTION ——————

During this move, to avoid damage, do not allow the transmission to get into a nosed down position as this will cause the converter to move forward and disengage from the pump gear. The converter must rest squarely against the flywheel. This indicates that the converter pilot is not binding in the engine crankshaft.

18. Install the two upper converter housing-to-engine attaching bolts and tighten to 28–38 ft. lbs.

19. Remove the safety chain from the transmission. Insert the filler tube in the stub tube and secure it to th cylinder block with the attaching bolt. Tighten the bolt to 28–38 ft. lbs. If the stub tube is loosened or dislodged, it should be replaced. Install the oil cooler lines in the retaining clip at the cylinder block. Connect the lines to the transmission case.

20. Remove the jack supporting the front of the engine. Raise the transmission. Position the crossmember, insulator and support and damper to the frame side supports and install the attaching bolts. Tighten the bolts to 20–30 ft. lbs.

21. Lower the transmission and install the rear engine support-to-crossmember nut. Tighten the bolt to 60–80 ft. lbs.

22. Remove the transmission jack. Install the vacuum hose on the transmission vacuum unit. Install the vacuum line into the retaining clip.

23. Connect the neutral start switch plug to the switch. Install the starter and tighten the attaching bolts to 15–20 ft. lbs.

24. Install the four flywheel-to-converter attaching nuts.

When assembling the flywheel to the converter, first install the attaching nuts and tighten to 20–34 ft. lbs.

25. Install the converter drain plug access cover and adaptor plate bolts. Tighten the bolts to 12–16 ft. lbs.

26. Connect the muffler inlet pipe to the exhaust manifold.

27. Connect the transmission shift rod to the manual lever. Connect the downshift rod to the downshift lever.

28. Connect the speedometer cable to the extension housing. Install the driveshaft. Tighten the companion flange U-bolt attaching nuts to 70–95 ft. lbs.

29. Adjust the manual and downshift linkage as required.

30. Lower the vehicle. Fill the transmission to the proper level with the specified fluid.

Pour in five quarts of fluid; then run the engine and add fluid as required.

Check the transmission, converter assembly and oil cooler lines for leaks.

C5—4×2

1. Raise the vehicle and safely support on jackstands. Place the drain pan under the transmission fluid pan. Starting at the rear of the pan and working toward the front, loosen the attaching bolts and allow the fluid to drain. Finally remove all of the pan attaching bolts except two at the front, to allow the fluid to further drain. Finally remove all of the pan attaching bolts except two at the front, to allow the fluid to further drain. With fluid drained, install two bolts on the rear side of the pan to temporarily hold it in place.

2. Remove the converter drain plug access cover from the lower end of the converter housing.

3. Remove the converter-to-flywheel attaching nuts. Place a wrench on the crankshaft pulley attaching bolt to turn the converter to gain access to the nuts.

4. Place a drain pan under the converter to catch the fluid. With the wrench on the crankshaft pulley attaching bolt, turn the converter to gain access to the converter drain plug and remove the plug. After the fluid has been drained, reinstall the plug.

5. Disconnect the driveshaft from the rear axle and slide shaft rearward from the transmission. Install a suitable cover in the extension housing to prevent fluid leakage. Mark the rear driveshaft yoke and axle flange so they can be installed in their original position.

6. Disconnect the cable from the terminal on the starter motor. Remove the three attaching bolts and remove the starter motor. Disconnect the neutral start switch wires at the plug connector.

7. Remove the rear mount-to-crossmember attaching nuts and the two crossmember-to-frame attaching bolts. Remove the right and left gusset.

8. Remove the two engine rear insulator-to-extension housing attaching bolts.

9. Disconnect the TV linkage rod from

the transmission TV lever. Disconnect the manual rod from the transmission manual lever at the transmission.

10. Remove the two bolts securing the bellcrank bracket to the converter housing.

11. Raise the transmission with a suitable jack to provide clearance to remove the crossmember. Remove the rear mount from the crossmember and remove the crossmember from the side supports. Lower the transmission to gain access to the oil cooler lines. Disconnect each oil line from the fittings on the transmission.

12. Disconnect the speedometer cable from the extension housing.

13. Remove the bolt that secures the transmission fluid filler tube to the cylinder block. Lift the filler tube and the dipstick from the transmission.

14. Secure the transmission to the jack with the chain. Remove the converter housing-to-cylinder block attaching bolts.

15. Carefully move the transmission and converter assembly away from the engine and, at the same time, lower the jack to clear the underside of the vehicle.

16. Tighten the converter drain plug to specifications. Position the converter on the transmission, making sure the converter drive flats are fully engaged in the pump gear by rotating the converter.

17. With the converter properly installed, place the transmission on the jack. Secure the transmission to the jack with a chain.

18. Rotate the converter until the studs and drain plug are in alignment with the holes in the flywheel. Move the converter and transmission assembly forward into position, using care not to damage the flywheel and the converter pilot. The converter must rest squarely against the flywheel. This indicates that the converter pilot is not binding in the engine crankshaft.

19. Install and tighten the converter housing-to-engine attaching bolts to specification.

20. Remove the safety chain from around the transmission.

21. Install the new O-ring on the lower end of the transmission filler tube. Insert the tube in the transmission case and secure the tube to the engine with the attaching bolt.

22. Connect the speedometer cable to the extension housing.

23. Connect the oil cooler lines to the right side of transmission case.

24. Secure the engine rear support to the extension housing and tighten the bolts to specification.

25. Position the crossmember on the side supports. Lower the transmission and remove the jack. Secure the crossmember to the side supports with the attaching bolts.

26. Position the damper assembly over the engine rear support studs. (The painted face of the damper is facing forward when installed in the vehicle.) Secure the rear engine support to the crossmember.

27. Position the bellcrank to the con-

verter housing and install the two attaching bolts.

28. Connect the TV linkage rod to the transmission TV lever. Connect the manual linkage rod to the manual lever at the transmission.

29. Secure the converter-to-flywheel attaching nuts and tighten them to specification.

30. Install the converter housing access cover and secure it with the attaching bolts.

31. Secure the starter motor in place with the attaching bolts. Connect the cable to the terminal on the starter. Connect the neutral start switch wires at the plug connector.

32. Connect the driveshaft to the rear axle so the index marks on the companion flange and the rear yoke are aligned. Lubricate the slip yoke with grease. Adjust the shift linkage as required.

33. Adjust throttle linkage.

34. Lower the vehicle. Fill the transmission to the correct level with the specified fluid. Start the engine and shift the transmission to all ranges, then recheck the fluid level.

C5-4 × 4

1. Remove the bolt securing the fluid filler tube to the engine valve cover bracket.

2. Place a drain pan under the transmission fluid pan. Starting at the rear of the pan and working towards the front, loosen the attaching bolts and allow the fluid to drain. Finally, remove all of the pan attaching bolts except two at the front, to allow the fluid to drain further. With fluid drained, install two bolts on the rear side of the pan to temporarily hold it in place.

3. Remove the converter drain plug access cover from the lower end of the converter housing. Remove the converter-to-flywheel attaching nuts. Place a wrench on the crankshaft pulley attaching bolt to turn the converter to gain access to the nuts.

4. Place a drain pan under the converter to catch the fluid. With the wrench on the crankshaft pulley attaching bolt, turn the converter to gain access to th converter drain plug and remove the plug. After the fluid has been drained, reinstall the plug.

5. Disconnect the cable from the terminal at the starter motor. Remove the three attaching bolts and remove the starter motor. Disconnect the neutral start switch wires at the plug connector.

6. Remove the rear mount-to-crossmember attaching nuts and the two crossmember-to-frame attaching bolts. Remove the right and left gusset.

7. Remove the two engine rear insulator-to-extension housing attaching bolts.

8. Disconnect the TV linkage rod from the transmission TV lever. Disconnect the manual rod from the transmission manual lever at the transmission. Disconnect the downshift and manual linkage rods from the levers on the transmission.

9. Remove the vacuum hose from the vacuum diaphragm unit. Remove the vacuum line from the retaining clip.

10. Remove the two bolts securing the bellcrank bracket to the converter housing.

11. Remove the transfer case. Refer to the Transfer Case section behind Manual Transmissions.

12. Raise the transmission with a transmission jack to provide clearance to remove the crossmember. Remove the rear mount from the crossmember and remove the crossmember from the side supports.

13. Lower the transmission to gain access to the oil cooler lines.

14. Disconnect each oil line from the fittings on the transmission.

15. Disconnect the speedometer cable from the extension housing.

16. Secure the transmission to the jack with the chain. Remove the converter housing-to-cylinder block attaching bolts.

17. Carefully move the transmission and converter assembly away from the engine and, at the same time, lower the jack to clear the underside of the vehicle.

18. Position the converter on the transmission, making sure the converter drive flats are fully engaged in the pump gear by rotating the converter.

19. With the converter properly installed, place the transmission on the jack. Secure the transmission to the jack with a chain.

20. Rotate the converter until the studs and drain plug are in alignment with the holes in the flywheel.

21. Move the converter and transmission assembly forward into position, using care not to damage the flywheel and the converter pilot. The converter must rest squarely against the flywheel. This indicates that the converter pilot is not binding in the engine crankshaft.

22. Install and tighten the converter housing-to-engine attaching bolts.

23. Remove the safety chain from around the transmission.

24. Install a new O-ring on the lower end of the transmission filler tube. Insert the tube in the transmission case.

25. Connect the speedometer cable to the extension housing.

26. Connect the oil cooler lines to the right of the transmission case.

27. Position the crossmember on the side supports. Position the rear mount insulator on the crossmember and install the attaching bolts and nuts.

28. Install the transfer case.

29. Secure the engine rear support to the extension housing. Lower the transmission and remove the jack.

30. Secure the crossmember to the side supports with the attaching bolts and tighten to specification.

31. Position the bellcrank to the converter housing and install the two attaching bolts.

32. Connect the downshift and manual linkage rods to their respective levers on the transmission.

33. Connect the vacuum line to the vacuum diaphragm making sure that the line

is in the retaining clip.

34. Secure the converter-to-flywheel attaching nuts. Install the converter housing access cover and secure it with the attaching bolts.

35. Secure the starter motor in place with the attaching bolts. Connect the cable to the terminal on the starter. Connect the neutral start switch wires at the plug connector.

36. Adjust the shift linkage as required. Lower the vehicle.

37. Position the transmission fluid filler tube to the valve cover bracket and secure with the attaching bolt. Fill the transmission to the correct level. Start the engine and shift the transmission to all ranges, then recheck the fluid level.

Pan

REMOVAL & INSTALLATION

1. Raise the truck on a hoist or jackstands.

2. Place a drain pan under the transmission.

3. Loosen the pan attaching bolts and drain the fluid from the transmission.

4. When the fluid has drained to the level of the pan flange, remove the remaining pan bolts working from the rear and both sides of the pan to allow it to drop and drain slowly.

5. When all of the fluid has drained, remove the pan and clean it thoroughly. Discard the pan gasket.

6. Clean the transmission oil pan and transmission mating surfaces.

7. Install the transmission oil pan in the reverse order of removal, torquing the attaching bolts to 12–16 ft. lbs. and using a new gasket. Fill the transmission with 3 qts. of the correct type fluid, check the operation of the transmission and check for leakage.

NOTE: When starting the engine after the transmission fluid has been drained,

do not race the engine. Move the gearshift selector through all of the ranges before moving the vehicle.

View showing the filter screen which is attached to the lower valve body. Bolts indicated by arrows hold the valve body. If the screen only is being serviced, do not remove these bolts

FILTER SERVICE

1. Remove the transmission oil pan and gasket.

2. Remove the screws holding the fine mesh screen to the lower valve body.

NOTE: Be careful not to lose the throttle pressure limit valve and spring when separating the oil screen from the valve body on a C4.

3. Install the new filter screen and transmission oil pan gasket in the reverse order of removal.

FRONT BAND ADJUSTMENT

FMX

1. Remove the transmission oil pan.

2. Loosen the front servo adjusting screw locknut.

3. Pull back on the actuating rod, and insert a ¼ in. spacer between the adjusting screw and the servo piston stem.

4. Tighten the adjusting screw to 10 in. lbs.

5. Remove the spacer and tighten the adjusting screw an additional ¾ turn.

6. Hold the adjusting screw stationary and tighten the locknut. Tighten the locknut to 20–25 ft. lbs.

7. Install the oil pan and a new gasket in the reverse order of removal.

C3

1. Remove the downshift rod from the transmission downshift lever. Clean all of the dirt away from the bank adjusting nut and screw area. Remove and discard the locknut.

2. Tighten the adjusting screw to 10 ft. lbs. Back off the adjusting screw exactly two turns.

3. Install a new locknut, hold the adjusting screw in position and tighten the locknut to 35–45 ft. lbs. Install the downshift rod.

INTERMEDIATE BAND ADJUSTMENT

C4, C5 and C6

1. Raise the truck on a hoist or jackstands.

2. Clean all dirt away from the band adjusting screw. Remove and discard the locknut.

3. Install a new locknut and tighten the adjusting screw to 10 ft. lbs.

4. On the C4 transmission, back off the adjusting screw *exactly 1¾ turns*. On the C5 back off the adjusting screw exactly 4¼ turns. On a C6 transmission, back off the adjusting screw *exactly 1½ turns*.

5. Hold the adjusting screw from turning and tighten the locknut to 35–45 ft. lbs.

C4 throttle pressure limiter valve which is held in place in the valve body by the filter. The valve is installed with the larger end toward the valve body. The spring fits over the valve stem.

FMX front band adjustment

C4 intermediate band adjustment

C6 intermediate band adjustment

6. Remove the jackstands and lower the vehicle.

LOW-REVERSE BAND ADJUSTMENT

C4, C5

1. Clean all dirt from around the band adjusting screw and remove and discard the locknut.

2. Install a new locknut on the adjusting screw. Using a torque wrench, tighten the adjusting screw to 10 ft. lbs.

3. Back off the adjusting screw *exactly 3 full turns*.

Low-reverse band adjustment

4. Hold the adjusting screw steady and tighten the locknut to 35–45 ft. lbs.

REAR BAND ADJUSTMENT

FMX

1. Remove all dirt away from the adjusting screw threads then oil the threads.

2. Loosen the rear band adjusting screw locknut.

3. Tighten the adjusting screw to 10 ft. lbs.

4. Back off the adjusting screw *exactly 1½ turns*.

5. Hold the adjusting screw stationary and tighten the adjusting screw locknut to 35–40 ft. lbs.

6. Reinstall the oil pan and a new gasket.

FMX rear band adjustment

SHIFT LINKAGE ADJUSTMENT

1. With the engine stopped, place the transmission selector lever at the steering column in the D position against the D stop.

2. Loosen the shift rod adjusting nut at the transmission lever.

3. Shift the manual lever at the transmission to the D position, two detents from the rear. On an F-100 with 4WD, move the bellcrank lever.

4. With the selector lever and transmission manual lever in the D position, tighten the adjusting nut to 12–18 ft. lbs. Do not allow the rod or shift lever to move while tightening the nut.

5. Check the operation of the shift linkage.

THROTTLE VALVE LINKAGE ADJUSTMENT

Automatic Overdrive
ADJUSTMENT AT THE CARBURETOR-W/ROD

The TV control linkage may be adjusted at the carburetor using the following procedure:

1. Check that engine idle speed is set at specification.

2. De-cam the fast idle cam on the carburetor so that the throttle lever is at its idle stop. Place shift lever in N (neutral), set park brake (engine off).

3. Backout linkage lever adjusting screw all the way (screw end is flush with lever face).

4. Turn in adjusting screw until a thin shim (.005 inch max.) or piece of writing paper fits snugly between end of screw and Throttle Lever. **To eliminate effect of friction, push linkage lever forward (tending to close gap) and release before checking clearance between end of screw and throttle lever. Do not apply any load on levers with tools or hands while checking gap.**

5. Turn in adjusting screw an additional four turns. (Four turns are preferred. Two turns minimum is permissible if screw travel is limited).

6. If it is not possible to turn in adjusting screw at least two additional turns

C5 floor shift controls

SHIFT QUADRANT
SHIFT LEVER
SELECTOR LEVER
GROMMET
SHIFT ROD
SHIFT ROD
NEUTRAL START SWITCH

P R N D 2 1

0.091 INCH DIAMETER GAUGE PIN

TRANSMISSION MANUAL LEVER
SHIFT ROD
STUD
POINT A
P R N D
RETAINER (INSTALL WITH CONCAVE SIDE AGAINST LEVER)

C6 shift linkage adjustment

or if there was insufficient screw adjusting capacity to obtain an initial gap in Step 2 above, refer to Linkage Adjustment at Transmission.

Whenever it is required to adjust idle speed by more than 50 rpm, the adjustment screw on the linkage lever at the carburetor should also be readjusted as shown in following chart:

Idle Speed Change	Turns on Linkage Lever Adjustment Screw
Less than 50 rpm	No change required
50 to 100 rpm increase	1½ turns out
50 to 100 rpm decrease	1½ turns in
100 to 150 rpm increase	2½ turns out
100 to 150 rpm decrease	2½ turns in

After making any idle speed adjustments, always verify the linkage lever and

throttle lever are in contact with the throttle lever at its idle stop and the shift lever is in N (neutral).

ADJUSTMENT AT TRANSMISSION

The linkage lever adjustment screw has limited adjustment capability. If it is not possible to adjust the TV linkage using this screw, the length of the TV control rod assembly must be readjusted using the following procedure. This procedure must also be followed whenever a new TV control rod asssembly is installed.

This procedure requires placing the vehicle on jackstands to give access to the linkage components at the transmission TV control lever.

1. Set the engine curb idle speed to specification.

2. With engine off, de-cam the fast idle cam on the carburetor so that the throttle lever is against the idle stop. Place shift lever in Neutral and set park brake (engine off).

3. Set the linkage lever adjustment screw at its approximately mid-range.

4. If a new TV control rod assembly is

being installed, connect the rod to the linkage lever at the carburetor.

— CAUTION —
The following steps involve working in proximity to the exhaust system. Allow the exhaust system to cool before proceeding.

5. Raise the vehicle on the hoist.

6. Using a 13 mm box end wrench, loosen the bolt on the sliding trunnion block on the TV control rod assembly. Remove any corrosion from the control rod and free-up the trunnion block so that it slides freely on the control rod. Insert pin into transmission lever grommet.

7. Push up on the lower end of the control rod to insure that the linkage lever at carburetor is firmly against the throttle lever. Release force on rod. Rod must stay up.

8. Push the TV control lever on the transmission up against its internal stop with a firm force (approximately 5 pounds) and tighten the bolt on the trunnion block. Do not relax force on lever until nut is tightened.

9. Lower the vehicle and verify that the throttle lever is still against the idle stop. If not, repeat steps 2 through 9.

ADJUSTMENT-W/CABLE

Whenever it is required to adjust the idle speed by more than 150 RPM, the TV control cable should be readjusted. Failure to do so may result in the symptoms due to a "too short" cable if the idle speed was increased or a "too long" cable if the idle speed was reduced.

1. Check and set, if necessary, engine idle speed to specification with and without TSP activated.

2. Shut engine off. Remove air cleaner. Set parking brake block wheels, and put selector in "N". (Do not put selector in "P").

3. Verify that the cable routing is free of sharp bends or pressure points and that the cable operates freely. Lubricate the TV lever ball stud. Check for damage to cable or rubber boot.

4. Unlock the locking tab at the carburetor end by pushing up from below, and prying up the rest of the way to free the cable.

5. A retention spring must be installed on the TV control lever, to hold it in the idle position (as far to rear as the lever will travel) with about ten pounds of force. If a suitable spring is not available, two V8 TV return springs may be used. Attach retention spring(s) to the transmission TV lever and hook rear end of spring to the transmission case.

6. De-cam the carburetor. The carburetor throttle lever must be in the anti-diesel position. Verify that the take-up spring (carburetor end of the cable) properly tensions the cable. If the spring is loose or bottomed out, check for bent brackets.

7. Push down the locking tab until flush.

8. Remove the detent springs from the transmission lever.

Neutral safety switch adjustment (C5 shown)

NEUTRAL SAFETY SWITCH ADJUSTMENT

1. Hold the steering column transmission selector lever against the Neutral stop.

2. Move the sliding block assembly on the neutral switch to the neutral position and insert a 0.091 in. gauge pin or 3/32 inch drill in the alignment hole on the terminal side of the switch.

3. Move the switch assembly housing so that the sliding block contacts the actuating pin lever. Secure the switch to the

outer tube of the steering column and remove the gauge pin.

4. Check the operation of the switch. The engine should only start in Neutral and Park.

THROTTLE KICK-DOWN LINKAGE ADJUSTMENT

1. Move the carburetor throttle linkage to the wide open position.

2. Insert a 0.060 in. thick spacer between the throttle lever and the kickdown adjusting screw.

3. Rotate the transmission kick-down lever until the lever engages the transmission internal stop. Do not use the kick-down rod to turn the transmission lever.

4. Turn the adjusting screw until it contacts the 0.060 in. spacer.

5. Remove the spacer.

TRANSFER CASE

Pick-up

NOTE: For Bronco II and Ranger refer to Manual Transmission section.

REMOVAL &INSTALLATION
Dana Model 21

1. Raise the vehicle on a hoist.

2. Disconnect the front and rear driveshafts at the transfer case.

3. Disconnect the shift rod from the transfer case shift lever arm.

4. Remove the bolts and nuts which attach the transfer case to the transmission extension housing and remove the transfer case from under the truck.

5. Install the transfer case in the reverse order of removal, using a new gasket between the transfer case and the transmission extension housing.

New Process Model 205

1. Drain the transfer case and disconnect the rear axle driveshaft from the flange at the transfer case.

2. Disconnect the front wheel driveshaft and the transmission output shaft at the transfer case if on an F-250. On an F-100, disconnect the front wheel driveshaft and remove the bolts attaching the transmission adapter to the transfer case.

3. Disconnect the shift selector rod and the speedometer cable at the transfer case.

4. Place a transmission jack under the transfer case and secure it with a chain.

NP203 transfer case installation on 1978 and later F-150, 250

5. Remove the transfer case mounting bolts and remove the unit from under the vehicle.

6. Install the transfer case in the reverse order of removal.

New Process Model 203
1977

1. Drain the transfer case by removing the power take-off lower bolts and the front output rear cover lower bolts.

2. Disconnect the front axle driveshaft from the flange at the transfer case.

3. Disconnect the shift rods from the transfer case.

4. Disconnect the speedometer cable and lockout light switch wire from the transfer case rear output shaft housing.

5. On F-250 pick-ups, disconnect the front input and output shafts from the transfer case flanges. On F-100, 150 trucks, remove the transfer case-to-transmission adapter attaching bolts. Disconnect the rear axle driveshaft at the transfer case flange.

6. Position a transmission jack under the transfer case and secure it with a chain.

7. Remove the transfer case mounting

bolts and remove the unit from the vehicle. On F-250 models, remove the stabilizer bar-to-transfer case attaching bolt before lowering the case.

8. Install the transfer case in the reverse order of removal.

1978–79

1. Drain the transfer case by removing the power take-off lower bolts and the front output rear cover lower bolts.

2. Disconnect the front axle drive shaft from the flange of the transfer case.

3. Disconnect the shift rods from the transfer case.

4. Disconnect the speedometer cable and lockout lamp switch wire from the transfer case rear output shaft housing.

5. Remove the bolts which attach the transfer case to the transmission adapter. Disconnect the rear axle drive shaft at the transfer case flange.

6. Position a transmission jack under the transfer case and secure it to the jack.

7. Remove the transfer case mounting bolts and remove the transfer case.

8. Install the transfer case in the reverse order of removal.

New Process Model 208

1. Raise the vehicle on a hoist and drain the fluid from the transfer case.

2. Disconnect the four wheel drive indicator switch wire connector at the transfer case.

3. Disconnect the speedometer driven gear from the transfer case rear bearing retainer.

4. Remove the nut retaining the transmission shift lever assembly to the transfer case.

5. Remove the skid plate from the frame, if so equipped.

6. Remove the heat shield from the frame.

7. Support the transfer case with a transmission jack or equivalent.

8. Disconnect the front driveshaft from the front output shaft yoke.

9. Disconnect the rear driveshaft from the rear output shaft yoke.

10. Remove the bolts retaining the transfer case to the transmission adapter.

11. Lower the transfer case from the vehicle.

12. When installing place a new gasket

NP205 transfer case installation

between the transfer case and the adapter.

13. Raise the transfer case with a transmission jack so the transmission output shaft aligns with the splined transfer case input shaft.

14. Install the bolts retaining the case to the adapter.

15. Connect the rear driveshaft to the rear output shaft yoke.

16. Connect the front driveshaft to the front output yoke.

17. Remove the transmission jack from the transfer case.

18. Position the heat shield to the frame crossmember and mounting lug to the transfer case and install and tighten the bolts and screw.

19. Install the skid plate to the frame.

20. Install the shift lever to the transfer case and tighten the retaining nut.

21. Install the speedometer driven gear to the transfer case.

22. Connect the four wheel drive indicator switch wire to the transfer case.

23. Install the drain plug. Remove the filler plug and install six pints of Dexron® II or equivalent type transmission fluid.

24. Lower the vehicle.

Borg-Warner Model 1345

1. Raise the vehicle on a hoist.
2. Drain the fluid from the transfer case.
3. Disconnect the four wheel drive indicator switch wire connector at the transfer case.
4. Remove the skid plate from the frame, if so equipped.
5. Disconnect the front driveshaft from the front output yoke.
6. Disconnect the rear driveshaft from the rear output shaft yoke.
7. Disconnect the speedometer driven gear from the transfer case rear bearing retainer.
8. Remove the retaining rings and shift rod from the transfer case shift lever.
9. Disconnect the vent hose from the transfer case.
10. Remove the heat shield from the frame.
11. Support the transfer case with a transmission jack.
12. Remove the bolts retaining the transfer case to the transmission adapter.
13. Lower the transfer case from the vehicle.
14. When installing place a new gasket between the transfer case and the adapter.
15. Raise the transfer case with the transmission jack so that the transmission output shaft aligns with the splined transfer case input shaft. Install the bolts retaining the transfer case to the adapter.
16. Remove the transmission jack from the transfer case.
17. Connect the rear driveshaft to the rear output shaft yoke.
18. Install the shift lever to the transfer case and install the retaining nut.
19. Connect the speedometer driven gear to the transfer case.

20. Connect the four wheel drive indicator switch wire connector at the transfer case.

21. Connect the front driveshaft to the front output yoke.

22. Position the heat shield to the frame crossmember and the mounting lug on the transfer case. Install and tighten the retaining bolts.

23. Install the skid plate to the frame.

24. Install the drain plug. Remove the filler plug and install six pints of Dexron® II type transmission fluid or equivalent.

25. Lower the vehicle.

TRANSFER CASE SHIFT LINKAGE ADJUSTMENT

New Process Model 205
MANUAL TRANSMISSION

Adjust the length of the shift rod between the transfer case and the shift lever with the lever in 4WD-Low so that the distance between the rear face of the transmission and the shift lever-to-rod clevis pin is 3.94 to 3.82 in.

AUTOMATIC TRANSMISSION
EXTENSION HOUSING

ROD

VIEW IN DIRECTION OF ARROW

ADJUSTMENT (AUTOMATIC TRANSMISSION)
TRANSFER CASE MUST BE IN 4 WHEEL LOW
(CROSS LINK ASSEMBLY ALL THE WAY IN)
DIMENSION "B" MUST BE .64
.60
ADJUST ROD (78051) TO CORRECT LENGTH
AND TIGHTEN LOCK NUT AT CLEVIS

NP205 transfer case installation showing the adjustment of the shift linkage with automatic transmission

AUTOMATIC TRANSMISSION

Adjust the length of the shift rod between the transfer case and the shift lever with the lever in 4WD-Low so that the distance between the upper surface of the automatic transmission extension housing and the upper horizontal edge of the shift lever is 0.640 to 0.600 in.

New Process 203 Full-Time 4WD

1977–82

1. Place the shift in the neutral position.
2. Remove the two adjusting stud nuts.

3. Install a 0.025 inch diameter alignment pin (1.25 inches long through the shifter assembly.

4. Align the bottom transfer case lever (Lock lever) by rotating clockwise to the forward position.

5. Align the top transfer case lever (range lever) by placing in the middle or neutral position.

6. Re-position the two shift rods and tighten the adjusting stud nuts to 15–20 ft. lbs.

7. Remove the alignment pin from the shifter assembly.

Bronco

NOTE: For Bronco II, refer to the Manual Transmission Section

REMOVAL & INSTALLATION

Dana 20

1. Shift the transfer case into Neutral.
2. Remove the bolts attaching the fan shroud to the radiator support.
3. Raise the vehicle on a hoist.
4. Support the transfer case shield with a jack and remove the bolts that attach the shield to the frame side rails. Remove the shield.
5. Drain the transmission and transfer case lubricant.
6. Disconnect the front and rear driveshafts at the transfer case.
7. Disconnect the speedometer cable at the transfer case.
8. If equipped with a manual transmission, disconnect the shift rods from the transmission shift levers. Then, place the First-Reverse gear shift lever in to the First gear position and insert the fabricated tool. (See transmission removal and installation). This tool will prevent the input shaft roller bearings from dropping into the transmission case when separating the transfer case from the transmission and output shaft.
9. Support the engine with a jack.
10. Remove the two cotter pins, bolts, washers, plates and insulators that secure the crossmember to the transfer case adapter.
11. Remove the crossmember to frame side support attaching bolts.
12. Raise the transmission and remove the upper insulators from the crossmember. Remove the crossmember.
13. Remove the carpet from around the shift levers. Remove the bolts holding the shifter to the transmission adapter. Remove the lower spring from the shifter. Remove the boot from the bottom of the shifter. Bend up the left side of the floor opening as required to remove the shifter assembly.
14. Secure the transfer case to a transmission jack and remove the transfer case adapter-to-transmission attaching bolts.
15. Move the transfer case and jack rearward until it clears the transmission output shaft. Lower the transfer case.

Removal or installation of the Dana 20 transfer case and the dimensions of the holding tool which must be used

16. Installation is the reverse of the removal procedure.

New Process 205

1. Drain the transfer case. Disconnect the rear axle driveshaft and front driveshaft from the flange at the transfer case.

2. Disconnect the shift selector rod steady rest and the speedometer cable at the transfer case.

3. Secure the transfer case to a transmission jack, and remove the mounting bolts.

4. Remove transfer case, and place it on a floor stand or work bench.

5. Remove the transfer case from the floor stand or bench and place it on the transmission jack.

6. Raise the transfer case into position and attach the mounting bolts. Tighten the bolts and nuts to 20–40 ft. lbs.

7. Connect the shift selector rod, the speedometer cable, and steady rest.

8. Connect the front and rear axle drive shafts and tighten the universal joint U-bolt nuts.

9. Fill the transfer case to filler plug level with SAE 80W/90 oil. Tighten drain plug to 25–35 ft. lbs.

New Process 203

1. Drain the transfer case by removing the power take-off lower bolts and the front output rear cover lower bolts.

2. Disconnect the front axle drive shaft from the flange at the transfer case.

3. Disconnect the shift rods from the transfer case.

4. Disconnect the speedometer cable and lockout lamp switch wire from the transfer case rear output shaft housing.

5. Remove the transfer case-to-transmission adapter attaching bolts. Disconnect

the rear axle driveshaft at the transfer case flange.

6. Position a transmission jack under the transfer case and secure it to the jack.

7. Remove the transfer case mounting bracket support to frame crossmember nuts, bolts, spacers and upper absorbers and remove the transfer case.

8. Using a chain fall, place the transfer case on a suitable work bench.

9. Using a chain fall, secure the transfer case on a transmission jack.

10. Position the transfer case in the truck, aligning the mounting bracket supports with the lower absorbers. Align the transfer case-to-transmission attaching bolts.

11. Install the transfer case mounting bracket support to frame crossmember bolts with upper absorbers and spacers. Tighten all mounting bolts to 40–50 ft. lbs.

12. Remove the transmission jack.

13. Connect the speedometer cable and the lockout switch wire to the transfer case.

14. Connect the rear axle driveshaft to the transfer case rear output flange.

15. Install the shift rods on the transfer case and adjust the shift linkage.

16. Connect the front axle driveshaft to the transfer case flange.

17. Fill the transfer case with SAE 80W/90 oil. Tighten the filler plug to 25–35 ft. lbs.

New Process 208

1. Raise vehicle on a hoist.

2. Place a drain pan under transfer case, remove drain plug and drain fluid from transfer case.

3. Disconnect four wheel drive indicator switch wire connector at transfer case.

4. Disconnect speedometer driven gear from transfer case rear bearing retainer.

5. Remove nut retaining transmission shift lever assembly to transfer case.

6. If so equipped, remove skid plate from frame.

7. Remove heat shield from frame.

CAUTION
Catalytic converter is located beside the heat shield. Be careful when working around catalytic converter because of the extremely high temperatures generated by the converter.

8. Support transfer case with transmission jack.

9. Disconnect front driveshaft from front output shaft yoke.

10. Disconnect rear driveshaft from rear output shaft yoke.

11. Remove the bolts retaining transfer case to transmission adapter. Remove gasket between transfer case and adapter.

12. Lower transfer case from vehicle.

13. Place a new gasket between transfer case and adapter.

14. Raise transfer case with transmission jack so transmission output shaft aligns with splined transfer case input shaft. Install bolts retaining transfer case to adapter. Tighten bolts to 30–40 ft. lbs.

15. Connect rear driveshaft to rear output shaft yoke.

16. Connect front driveshaft to front output yoke.

17. Remove transmission jack from transfer case.

18. Position heat shield to frame crossmember and mounting lug on transfer case. Install and tighten bolts and screw to 11–16 ft. lbs.

19. Install skid plate to frame. Tighten nuts and bolts.

20. Install shift lever to transfer case. Install retaining nut.

21. Connect speedometer driven gear to transfer case.

22. Connect four-wheel drive indicator switch wire connector at transfer case.

23. Install drain plug. Remove filler plug and install 2.8 liters (six pints) of automatic transmission fluid Ford type CJ or Dexron® II, Series D or equivalent. Install filler plug.

24. Lower vehicle.

Shift Lever Adjustment

NOTE: The NP 205 and 208 do not require adjustment.

NP 203

1. Place shift lever in neutral position.

2. Remove two adjusting stud nuts.

3. Install 0.25 inch diameter alignment pin (1.25 inches long) through shifter assembly.

4. Align the two transfer case levers as follows:

a. Bottom lever, (lock lever)—Rotate clockwise to the forward position.

b. Top lever, (range lever)—Place in the Mid-position or Neutral position.

5. Re-position the two shift rods and tighten new adjusting stud nuts to 15–20 ft. lbs.

6. Remove alignment pin from shifter assembly.

DRIVELINE

Driveshaft

REMOVAL & INSTALLATION
4WD

1. Mark shaft and flange for installation in same position. To remove the rear driveshaft, disconnect the double Cardan joint from the flange at the transfer case and the single U-joint from the flange at the rear axle. Remove the driveshaft.

2. To remove the front driveshaft, disconnect the double Cardan joint from the flange at the transfer case and the single U-joint from the front axle. Remove the driveshaft.

3. Installation is the reverse of removal. Torque driveshaft-to-transfer case bolts to 20–25 ft. lbs.; driveshaft to axle bolts to 8–15 ft. lbs.

2WD

1. Mark shaft and flange for installation in same position. Unscrew the nuts attaching the U-bolts to the flange at the rear axle, or remove the bolts and clips. Remove the U-bolts or bolts and clips and allow the rear of the driveshaft to drop down. Slide the front of the driveshaft out of the rear of the transmission, transfer case, or the center support bearing. Remove the driveshaft from the vehicle.

2. On those vehicles equipped with two driveshafts and a center support bearing, unscrew the attaching bolts holding the center support bearing to the frame. If equipped with a sliding yoke at the transmission, slide the coupling shaft out of the rear of the extension housing. Otherwise, remove the nuts from the U-bolts or bolts and clips holding the front of the coupling shaft to the flange on the rear of the transmission while supporting the center bearing. Remove the U-bolts or bolts and clips from the front flange and remove the coupling shaft assembly together with the center support bearing.

3. Install the driveshaft(s) in the reverse order of removal.

NOTE: All U-joints on two-piece driveshafts must be on the same horizontal plane when installed.

U-JOINT OVERHAUL

1. Remove the driveshaft from the vehicle and place it in a vise, being careful not to damage it.

2. Remove the snap-rings which retain the bearings in the flange and in the driveshaft.

3. Remove the driveshaft tube from the vise and position the U-joint in the vise with a socket smaller than the bearing cap on one side and a socket larger than the bearing cap on the other side.

4. Slowly tighten the jaws of the vise so that the smaller socket forces the U-joint spider and the opposite bearing into the larger socket.

5. Remove the other side of the spider in the same manner (if applicable) and remove the spider assembly from the driveshaft. Discard the spider assemblies.

6. Clean all foreign matter from the yoke areas at the end of the driveshaft(s).

7. Start the new spider and one of the bearing cap assemblies into a yoke by positioning the yoke in a vise with the spider positioned in place with one of the bearing cap assemblies positioned over one of the holes in the yoke. Slowly close the vise, pressing the bearing cap assembly in the yoke. Press the cap in far enough so that the retaining snap-ring can be installed. Use the smaller socket to recess the bearing cap.

8. Open the vise and position the opposite bearing cap assembly over the proper hole in the yoke with the socket that is smaller than the diameter of the bearing cap located on the cap. Slowly close the vise, pressing the bearing cap into the hole in the yoke with the socket. Make sure that the spider assembly is in line with the bearing cap as it is pressed in. Press the bearing

One-piece driveshaft with a slip yoke

SHAFTS MUST BE ASSEMBLED WITH THESE YOKES IN (PHASE) LINE AS SHOWN
Two-piece driveshaft with a slip yoke at the transmission end

REAR SHAFT SLIP YOKE AND SPLINE END OF FRONT SHAFT TO BE INDEXED WITH ARROWS IN ALIGMENT AT ASSEMBLY
Two-piece driveshaft with a fixed yoke at the transmission end

cap in far enough so that the retaining snap-ring can be installed.

9. Install all remaining U-joints in the same manner.

10. Install the driveshaft and grease the new U-joints.

Center Bearing

REMOVAL & INSTALLATION

1. Remove the driveshafts.

2. Remove the two center support bearing attaching bolts and remove the assembly from the vehicle.

3. Do not immerse the sealed bearing in any type of cleaning fluid. Wipe the bearing and cushion clean with a cloth dampened with cleaning fluid.

4. Check the bearing for wear or rough action by rotating the inner race while holding the outer race. If wear or roughness is evident, replace the bearing.

Examine the rubber cushion for evidence of hardening, cracking, or deterioration. Replace it if it is damaged in any way.

5. Place the bearing in the rubber support and the rubber support in the U-shaped support and install the bearing in the reverse order of removal.

Wheel Bearings

The wheel bearings should be serviced (cleaned, inspected, repacked or replaced) every 20,000 miles, or whenever operated in deep water.

Before handling the bearings there are a few things that you should remember to do and try to avoid.

DO the following:

1. Remove all outside dirt from the housing before exposing the bearing.

2. Treat a used bearing as gently as you would a new one.

3. Work with clean tools in clean surroundings.

4. Use clean, dry canvas gloves, or at least clean, dry hands.

5. Clean solvents and flushing fluids are a must.

6. Use clean paper when laying out the bearings to dry.

GREASE

Hand-packing the wheel bearings

7. Protect disassembled bearings from rust and dirt. Cover them up.

8. Use clean rags to wipe bearings.

9. Keep the bearings in oil-proof paper when they are to be stored or are not in use.

10. Clean the inside of the housing before replacing the bearing.

Do NOT do the following:

1. Don't work in dirty surroundings.

2. Don't use dirty, chipped, or damaged tools.

3. Try not to work on wooden work benches or use wooden mallets.

4. Don't handle bearings with dirty or moist hands.

5. Do not use gasoline for cleaning; use a safe solvent.

6. Do not spin-dry bearings with compressed air. They will be damaged.

7. Do not spin unclean bearings.

8. Avoid using cotton waste or dirty cloths to wipe bearings.

9. Try not to scratch or nick bearing surfaces.

10. Do not allow the bearing to come in contact with dirt or rust at any time.

SERVICE

2WD Front

1. Jack the truck up until the wheel to be serviced is off the ground and can spin freely. It is easier to check all the bearings at the same time. If the equipment needed is available, raise the front end of the truck so that both front wheels are off the ground. Use jackstands to support the vehicle. Make sure that the truck is completely stable before proceeding any further.

2. Remove the lug nuts and remove the wheel/tire assembly from the hub. It is necessary to remove the caliper assembly from the rotor and caliper support. Do not disconnect the brake line from the caliper. Simply hang the caliper with a length of heavy wire above the hub. Be careful not to strain the flexible brake tube.

3. Remove the grease cap with a screwdriver or pliers.

4. Remove the cotter pin and discard it. Cotter pins should never be reused.

5. Remove the nut lock, adjusting nut, and washer from the spindle.

6. Wiggle the hub so that the outer wheel bearing comes loose and can be removed. Remove the outer bearing.

7. Remove the hub from the spindle and place it on a work surface, supported by two blocks of wood under the hub.

8. Place a block of wood or drift pin through the spindle hole and tap out the inner grease seal. Tap lightly so not to damage the bearing. When the seal falls out, so will the inner bearing. Discard the seal.

9. Place all of the bearings, nuts, nut locks, washers and grease caps in a container of solvent. Use a light soft brush to thoroughly clean each part. Make sure that every bit of dirt and grease is rinsed off,

then place each cleaned part on an absorbent cloth or paper and allow them to dry completely.

10. Clean the inside of the hub, including the bearing races, and the spindle. Remove all traces of old lubricant from these components.

11. Inspect the bearings for pitting, flat spots, rust, and rough areas. Check the races in the hub and the spindle for the same defects and rub them clean with a cloth that has been soaked in solvent. If the races show hair line cracks or worn shiny areas, they must be replaced. The races are installed in the hub with a press fit and are removed by driving them out with a suitable punch or drift. Place the new races squarely onto the hub and place a block of wood over them. Drive the race into place with a hammer, striking the block of wood. Never hit the race with any metal object.

Replacement seals, bearings, and other required parts can be bought at an auto parts store. The old parts should be taken along to be compared with the replacement parts to ensure a perfect match.

12. Pack the wheel bearings with grease. There are special devices made for the specific purpose of greasing bearings, but if one is not available, pack the wheel bearings by hand. Put a large dab of grease in the palm of your hand and push the bearing through it with a sliding motion. The grease must be forced through the side of the bearing and in between each roller. Continue until the grease begins to ooze out the other side and through the gaps between the rollers; the bearing must be completely packed with grease.

NOTE: Sodium based grease is not compatible with lithium based grease. Be careful not to mix the two types. The best way to prevent this is to completely clean all of the old grease from the hub and spindle before installing any new grease.

13. Turn the hub assembly over so that the inner side faces up, making sure that the race and inner area are clean, and drop the inner wheel bearing into place. Using a hammer and a block of wood, tap the new grease seal in place. Never hit the seal with the hammer directly. Move the block of wood around the circumference until it is properly seated.

14. Slide the hub assembly onto the spindle and push it as far as it will go, making sure that it has completely covered the brake shoes. Keep the hub centered on the spindle to prevent damage to the grease seal and the spindle threads.

15. Place the outer wheel bearing in place over the spindle. Press it in until it is snug. Place the washer on the spindle after the bearing. Screw on the spindle nut and turn it down until a slight binding is felt.

16. With a torque wrench, tighten the nut to 17–25 ft. lbs. to seat the bearings. Install the nut lock over the nut so that the cotter pin hole in the spindle is aligned with a slot in the nut lock. Back off the adjusting

nut and the nut lock two slots of the nut lock and install the cotter pin.

17. Bend the longer of the two ends opposite the looped end out and over the end of the spindle. Trim both ends of the cotter pin just enough so that the grease cap will fit, leaving the bent end shaped over the end of the spindle.

18. Install the grease cap, brake caliper if so equipped, and the wheel/tire assembly. The wheel should rotate freely with no noise or noticeable end-play.

4WD Front Without Free-Running Hubs
EXCEPT RANGER & BRONCO II

NOTE: Sodium based grease is not compatible with lithium based grease. Be careful not to mix the two types. The best way to prevent this is to completely clean all of the old grease from the hub assembly before installing any new grease.

1. Raise the front of the vehicle and place jackstands under the vehicle. Remove the wheel.

2. Remove the front hub grease cap and driving hub snap-ring.

3. Remove the splined driving hub and the pressure spring. This may require slight prying with an appropriate tool.

4. Remove the wheel bearing locknut, lockring, and adjusting nut.

5. Suspend the caliper out of the way and remove the hub and rotor assembly.

6. Carefully drive out the inner bearing cone and grease seal from the hub.

7. Inspect the bearing cups (races) for cracks and pits. If the cups are excessively worn or there are pits or cracks visible, replace them along with the cones. The cups are removed from the hub by driving them out with a drift pin. They are installed in the same manner.

8. If it is determined that the cups are in satisfactory condition and are to remain in the hub, clean and inspect the cones (bearings). Refer to the bearing diagnosis

Typical front hub without free-wheeling (locking hubs)

chart. Replace the bearings if necessary. If it is necessary to replace either the cone or the cup, both parts should be replaced as a unit.

9. Thoroughly clean all components in a suitable solvent and blow them dry with compressed air or allow them to dry while resting on clean paper.

NOTE: Do not spin the bearings with compressed air while drying them.

10. Cover the spindle with a cloth and brush all loose dust and dirt from the brake assembly. Remove the cloth and thoroughly clean the inside of the hub and the spindle.

11. Pack the inside of the hub with wheel bearing grease. Add grease to the hub until the grease is flush with the inside diameter of the bearing cup.

12. Pack the bearing cone and roller assemblies with wheel bearing grease. A bearing packer is desirable for this operation. If a packer is not available, place a large portion of grease into the palm of your hand and sliding the edge of the roller cage through the grease with your other hand,

work as much grease in between the rollers as possible.

13. Position the inner bearing into the inner bearing cup and install the new grease seal.

14. Carefully position the hub assembly onto the spindle. Be careful not to damage the new seal. Install the caliper.

15. Place the outer bearing into position on the spindle and into the bearing cup.

16. Install the bearing adjusting nut and tighten it to 50 ft. lbs. while rotating the hub back and forth to seat the bearings.

17. Back off the adjusting nut about 90°.

18. Assemble the lockring by turning the nut to the nearest notch where the dowel pin will enter.

19. Install the outer locknut and torque to 80–100 ft. lbs. The final end-play of the wheel on the spindle should be 0.001–0.010 in.

20. Install the pressure spring retainer, spring, the driving hub and driving hub snap-ring.

21. Install the grease cap and adjust the brakes, if they were backed off to remove the hub assembly. Remove the jackstands and lower the vehicle.

4WD Front With Free-Running Hub
EXCEPT RANGER & BRONCO II
1977–79

1. Remove the free-running hub bolts and washers.

2. Remove the hub ring and the knob. Wipe the parts clean.

3. Remove the internal snap-ring from the groove in the hub.

4. Remove the cam body ring and clutch retainer (as an assembly) from the hub. Disassemble the parts.

5. Remove the axle shaft snap-ring. For easier snap-ring removal, push inward on the axle shaft sleeve ring and, at the same time, pull out on the axle with a bolt.

6. Remove the axle shaft sleeve ring and inner clutch ring. A slight rocking of

Typical internal locking hub used on 1977–79 models

Grease application

Spring retainer ring installation

Coil spring installation

Axle shaft sleeve and ring, and inner clutch ring installation

Installing the axle shaft snap-ring

Installing the cam body ring into the clutch retaining ring

the hub may make them slide out easier.

7. Remove the pressure spring.

8. Remove the spring retainer ring.

9. Grease the hub inner spline with Moly grease or equivalent.

10. Install the spring retainer ring, positioned as shown with recessed undercut area going in first. Be sure ring seats against the bearing.

11. Install the coil spring with large end entering first.

12. Grease with Moly grease or equivalent and install the axle shaft sleeve and ring and the inner clutch ring. Be sure that the teeth are meshed together in a locked position for easy assembly. It may be necessary to rock the hub back and forth for spline alignment. Keep the two gears in locked position.

13. Install the axle shaft snap-ring. Push inward on gear and, if necessary, pull out axle shaft with bolt to allow groove clearance on shaft for the snap-ring. Be sure snap-ring is fully seated in the snap-ring groove on the shaft.

14. Install the actuating cam body ring into the outer clutch retaining ring. Assemble into hub.

15. Install the internal snap-ring. Be sure snap-ring is fully seated in the snap-ring groove of the hub.

16. Apply a small amount of Moly grease or equivalent on the ears of the cam.

17. Apply a small amount of Parker O-ring lube or an equivalent lube in groove of actuating knob before assembling outer O-ring.

18. Assemble knob in hub ring and assemble to axle with knob in locked position. Assemble screws and washers alternately and evenly, making sure the retainer ring is not cocked in the hub.

19. Tighten the six lock-out hub bolts to 30 to 35 in. lbs. Be sure the washers are under each retaining screw. Each free-running hub will fit either wheel. Do not drive vehicle until you are sure that both free-running hubs are functioning properly.

FROM 1980

Manual Hubs—Except Ranger & Bronco II

1. To remove hub, first separate cap

Installing the internal snap-ring

Applying a small amount of grease on the ears of the cam

assembly from body assembly by removing the six (6) socket head capscrews from the cap assembly and slip apart.

2. Remove snap-ring (retainer ring) from the end of the axle shaft.

3. Remove the lock ring seated in the groove of the wheel hub. The body assembly will now slide out of the wheel hub. If necessary, use an appropriate puller to remove the body assembly.

4. Install hub in reverse order of removal. Torque socket head capscrews to 30–35 in. lbs.

Automatic Locking Hubs—Except Ranger & Bronco II

1. Remove capscrews and remove hub cap assembly from spindle.

2. Remove capscrew from end of axle shaft.

3. Remove lock ring seated in the groove of the wheel hub with a knife blade or with a small sharp awl with the tip bent in a hook.

4. Remove body assembly from spindle. If body assembly does not slide out easily, use an appropriate puller.

5. Unscrew all three sets in the spindle

Lubricating the selector knob

locknut until the heads are flush with the edge of the locknut. Remove outer spindle locknut with tool T80T-4000-V, automatic hub lock nut wrench.

6. Reinstall in reverse order of removal. Tighten the outer spindle locknut to 15–20 ft. lbs. with special tool T80T-4000-V, automatic hub lock nut wrench. Tighten down all three set screws. Firmly push in body assembly until the friction shoes are on top of the spindle outer locknut.

7. Install capscrew into the axle shaft and tighten to 35–50 ft. lbs.

8. Place cap on spindle and install capscrews. Tighten to 35–50 in. lbs. Turn dial firmly from stop to stop, causing the dialing mechanism to engage the body spline.

NOTE: Be sure both hub dials are in the same position; "AUTO" or "LOCK."

BEARING REPLACEMENT OR REPACKING

1. Raise the vehicle and install safety stands.

2. If equipped with free-running hubs refer to Free-Running Hub Removal and Installation.

3. Remove the front hub grease cap and driving hub snap-ring.

4. Remove the splined driving hub and the pressure spring. This may require a slight prying assist.

5. Remove the wheel bearing lock nut, lock ring, and adjusting nut using tool T59T-1197-B, or equivalent.

6. Remove the hub and disc assembly. The outer wheel bearing and spring retainer will slide out as the hub is removed.

7. Remove the spindle retaining nuts, then carefully remove the spindle from the knuckle studs and axle shaft.

8. Clean all old grease from the needle bearings and wipe clean the spindle face that mates with the spindle bore seal.

9. Remove the spindle bore seal, V-seal, and thrust washer from the outer axle shaft. Clean any old grease or dirt from these parts and replace those that show signs of excessive wear.

10. Using Multi-Purpose Lubricant, Ford Specification ESA-M1C75-B or equivalent, thoroughly lubricate the needle bearing and pack the spindle face that mates with the spindle bore seal.

11. Assemble the V-seal in the spindle bore next to the needle bearing. Assemble the spindle bore seal on the axle shaft.

12. Assemble the spindle with the axle shaft on the knuckle studs. Adjust the retaining nuts to 50–60 ft. lbs.

13. Carefully drive the inner bearing cone and grease seal out of the hub using Tool T69L-1102-A.

14. Inspect the bearing cups for pits or cracks. If necessary, remove them with a drift. If new cups are installed, install new bearings.

15. Lubricate the bearings with Multi-Purpose Lubricant Ford Specification, ESA-M1C7-B or equivalent. Clean all old grease from the hub. Pack the cones and rollers. If a bearing packer is not available, work as much lubricant as possible between the rollers and the cages.

16. Position the inner bearing cone and roller in the inner cup and install the grease retainer.

17. Carefully position the hub and disc assembly on the spindle.

18. Install the outer bearing cone and roller, and the adjusting nut.

19. Using a torque wrench, tighten the bearing adjusting nut to 50 ft. lbs., while rotating the wheel back and forth to seat the bearings.

20. Back off the adjusting nut approximately 90 degrees.

21. Assemble the lock ring by turning the nut to the nearest hole and inserting the dowel pin. Note: The dowel pin must seat in a lock ring hole for proper bearing adjustment and wheel retention.

22. Install the outer lock nut and tighten to 50–80 ft. lbs. Final end play of the wheel on the spindle should be 0.001 to 0.010 inch.

23. Install the pressure spring and driving hub snap-ring.

24. Apply non-hardening sealer to the seating edge of the grease cap, and install the grease cap.

25. Adjust the brake if it was backed off.

26. Remove the safety stands and lower the vehicle.

Bronco II and Ranger

MANUAL HUB

1. Raise the vehicle and install safety stands.

2. Remove the wheel lug nuts and remove the wheel and tire assembly.

3. Remove the retainer washers from the lug nut studs and remove the manual locking hub assembly. To remove the internal hub lock assembly from the outer body assembly, remove the outer lock ring seated in the hub body groove.

The internal assembly, spring and clutch gear will now slide out of the hub body.

--- **CAUTION** ---
Do not remove the screw from the plastic dial.

4. Rebuild the hub assembly in the reverse order of disassembly.

5. Install the manual locking hub assembly over the spindle and place the retainer washers on the lug nut studs.

1980 and later manual locking hubs

1980 and later automatic locking hubs

6. Install the wheel and tire assembly. Install the lug nuts and tighten to 85–115 ft. lbs.

ADJUSTMENT

1. Raise the vehicle and install safety stands. Remove the wheel lug nuts and remove the wheel and tire assembly.
2. Remove the retainer washers from the lug nut studs and remove the manual locking hub assembly from the spindle.
3. Remove the snap ring from the end of the spindle shaft.
4. Remove the axle shaft spacer, needle thrust bearing and the bearing spacer.
5. Remove the outer wheel bearing locknut from the spindle, using Four-Prong Spindle Nut Spanner Wrench, T83T-1197-A or the equivalent. Make sure the tabs on the tool engage the slots in the locknut. Remove the locknut washer from the spindle.
6. Loosen the inner wheel bearing locknut using Four Prong Spindle Nut Spanner Wrench or equivalent. Make sure that the tabs on the tool engage the slots in the locknut and that the slot in the tool is over the pin on the locknut.
7. Tighten the inner locknut to 35 ft. lbs. to seat the bearings.

Spin the rotor and back off the inner locknut ¼ turn. Install the lockwasher on the spindle. It may be necessary to turn the inner locknut slightly so that the pin on the locknut aligns with the closest hole in the lockwasher.
8. Install the outer wheel bearing locknut using Four-Prong Spindle Nut Spanner Wrench or equivalent.
9. Tighten locknut to 150 ft. lbs.
10. Install the bearing thrust spacer, needle thrust bearing and axle shaft spacer.
11. Clip the snap ring onto the end of the spindle.
12. Install the manual hub assembly over the spindle. Install the retainer washers.
13. Install the wheel and tire assembly.

Install and tighten lugnuts to 85–115 ft. lbs.
14. Check the end play of the wheel and tire assembly on the spindle. End play should be 0.001–0.003 inch.

AUTOMATIC LOCKING HUBS

1. Raise the vehicle and install safety stands. Remove the wheel lug nuts and remove the wheel and tire assembly.
2. Remove the retainer washers from the lug nut studs and remove the automatic locking hub assembly from the spindle.
3. Remove the snap ring from the end of the spindle shaft.
4. Remove the axle shaft spacer, needle thrust bearing and the bearing spacer. Being careful not to damage the plastic moving cam, pull the cam assembly off the wheel bearing adjusting nut and remove the thrust washer and needle thrust bearing from the adjusting nut.
5. Loosen the wheel bearing adjusting

Axle shaft spacer, thrust bearing and bearing spacer on Ranger/Bronco II with automatic locking hubs- 4x4

Wheel bearing adjusting nut assembly-Ranger/Bronco II 4x4

nut from the spindle using a 2¾ inch hex socket tool.
6. While rotating the hub and rotor assembly, tighten the wheel bearing adjusting nut to 35 ft. lbs. to seat the bearings, then back off the nut ¼ turn (90°).
7. Retighten the adjusting nut to 16 in. lb. using a torque wrench. Align the closest hole in the wheel bearing adjusting nut with the center of the spindle keyway slot. Advance the nut to the next hole if required.
8. Install the locknut needle bearing and thrust washer in the order of removal and push or press the cam assembly onto the locknut by lining up the key in the fixed cam with the spindle keyway.
9. Install the bearing thrust washer, needle thrust bearing and axle shaft spacer. Clip the snap ring onto the end of the spindle.
10. Install the automatic locking hub assembly over the spindle by lining up the three legs in the hub assembly with three pockets in the cam assembly. Install the retainer washers.
11. Install the wheel and tire assembly. Install and tighten lugnuts to 85–115 ft. lbs.
12. Final end play of the wheel on the spindle should be 0.02–0.08mm (0.001–0.003 inch).

Automatic locking hubs used on the Ranger/Bronco II 4x4

FRONT DRIVE AXLE

Axle Shaft

REMOVAL & INSTALLATION

F-100, 150—Through 1979

1. Raise and support the vehicle on jackstands.

2. Remove the grease cap. Remove the driving hub retaining snap-ring, then slide splined driving hub from between axle shaft and wheel hub.

3. Remove driving hub spring.

NOTE: If equipped with free-wheeling hubs, see hub removal.

4. Remove lock nut, washer, and wheel

Typical removal/installation of an axle shaft on 1977–79 models

Removing the steering knuckle nut on the Dana 44-IFS

bearing adjusting nut from spindle. Remove wheel, hub and drum as an assembly. The wheel outer bearing will be forced off the spindle at the same time. Remove wheel inner bearing cone.

5. Remove capscrews that attach brake backing plate and spindle to steering knuckle. Remove brake backing plate and secure it to one side. Carefully remove the spindle.

6. Pull shaft assembly from axle housing, working universal joint through bore in steering knuckle.

7. To install reverse the removal procedure.

F-250-350 Through 1979

1. Raise and support the front of the truck.

2. Remove the wheel.

3. Remove the caliper from the rotor and suspend it from the frame.

4. Remove the dust cap, cotter pin, nut, washer and outer bearing and remove the

Removing the camber bushing on the Dana 44-IFS

rotor from the spindle.

5. Remove the inner bearing cone and seal.

6. Remove the axle shaft, working the U-joint through the bore of the steering knuckle. Be careful not to damage the seal.

7. Installation is the reverse of removal.

F-150, F-250, F-350 From 1980

1. Remove the axle shaft assembly. Remove the axle bearing as follows:

2. Remove the stub assembly by removing the three bolts attaching the retainer plate to the carrier housing.

3. Place the axle shaft in a vise and drill a ½″ hole in the outside of the bearing retaining ring to a depth of ¾ of the thickness of the ring.

4. Place a chisel across the hole and strike sharply with a hammer to remove the retaining ring. Replace the bearing retaining ring upon assembly.

5. Press the bearing from the axle shaft using special tools axle bearing remover no. T80T-4000M and sleeve no. T80T-4000L.

6. Remove the steal and retainer plate from the stub shaft.

7. To install place the new seal and retainer plate on the shaft.

8. Place the bearing on the shaft with the large radius on the inner race facing the yoke end of the shaft.

9. Press the bearing onto the shaft using an axle bearing replacer no. T80T-4000-N and a pinion bearing cone remover no. T71P-4621-B. A 0.0015 inch feeler gauge should not fit between the bearing seat and the bearing.

10. Using the same special tools in step 9 press the bearing retainer ring onto the stub shaft. A 0.0015 inch feeler gauge should not fit between the ring and the bearing. There must be one point between the bearing and the ring where the feeler gauge cannot enter. If the feeler gauge enters completely around the circumference press the retainer further onto the shaft.

11. Push the seal and retainer plate away from the bearing to form a space between the seal and the bearing. Fill the space with the proper bearing grease and wrap tape around the space.

12. Pull the seal towards the bearing until it contacts the inner race and forces the grease between the rollers and cup. Remove the tape.

13. Install the stub shaft in the carrier and install the three retainer bolts. Tighten to 35 ft. lbs.

14. Install the right hand axle shaft assembly into the slip yoke.

15. Install the spindle.

Bronco—Through 1979

1. Raise the vehicle and support it on jack stands.

2. Remove the front wheels.

3. On drum brake models, remove the hub, brake drum, backing plate and spindle. Tie the backing plate up to avoid damage to the hose.

4. On disc brake models, remove the hubs, calipers and rotors. Tie up the calipers to avoid damage to the hoses. Remove the nuts that attach the brake support bracket, dust shield and spindle.

5. Pull the axle shaft from the housing, carefully working the U-joint through the steering knuckle.

6. Install the shaft in reverse order of removal.

Bronco—From 1980

NOTE: This procedure requires the use of special tools.

1. Remove spindle nuts and remove spindle. It may be necessary to tap the spindle with a rawhide or plastic hammer to break the spindle loose. Remove spindle, splash shield and axle shaft assembly.

2. Place the spindle in a vise with a shop towel around the spindle to protect the

spindle from damage. Using a slide hammer T50-T-100-A and seal remover, tool 1175-AC remove the axle shaft seal and then the needle bearing from the spindle bar.

3. If the tie rod has not been removed, then remove cotter key from the tie rod nut and then remove nut. Tap on the tie rod stud to free it from the steering arm.

4. Remove the cotter pin from the top ball joint stud. Loosen the nut on the top stud and the bottom nut inside the knuckle. Remove the top nut.

5. Sharply hit the top stud with a plastic or rawhide hammer to free the knuckle from the tube yoke. Remove and discard bottom nut. Use new nut upon assembly.

6. Remove camber adjuster with Pitman arm puller T64P-3590-F.

7. Place knuckle in vise and remove snap ring from bottom ball joint socket if so equipped.

8. Press the bottom ball joint socket from the knuckle with the special tools receiver cup tool (P79P-3010-AG) and C1 clamp tool (D79T-3010-A)-B. Remove the top ball joint in the same manner.

NOTE: Always remove bottom ball joint first.

9. Pull out the seal with the appropriate puller tool. Remove and discard seal.

10. Install a new seal on the differential seal replacer tool T80T-4000-H.

11. Slide the seal and tool into the carrier housing bore. Seat the seal with a plastic or rawhide hammer.

12. Place lower ball joint (stud does not have a cotter key hole in stud) in knuckle and press into position using ball joint installation set T80T-3010-A.

13. Install uper ball joint (stud has cotter key hole) in knuckle with ball joint installation set T80T-3010-A.

14. Assemble knuckle to tube and yoke assembly. Install camber adjuster on top ball joint stud with the arrow pointing outboard for "positive" camber, pointed inboard for "negative" camber.

15. Install new nut on bottom socket finger tight. Install and tighten nut on top socket finger tight. Tighten bottom nut to 90–110 ft. lbs.

16. Tighten top nut to 100 ft. lbs., then advance nut until castellation aligns with cotter pin hole. Install cotter pin.

NOTE: Do not loosen top nut to install cotter pin.

17. Remove and install a new needle to bearing in the spindle bare with T80T-4000-R or S spindle bearing replacer and driver handle, T80T-4000-W. Install a new seal with tool T80T-4000-W. Install a new seal with tool T80T-400-T or U, seal replacer and T80T-4000-W driven handle.

18. Install the axle shaft assembly into the housing. Install the splash shield and spindle. Install and tighten the spindle attaching nuts.

Ranger and Bronco II

REMOVAL & INSTALLATION

Dana 28

AXLE SHAFT AND BEARINGS

1. Raise the vehicle and install safety stands. Remove the wheel and tire assembly. Remove the caliper.

2. Remove hub locks, wheel bearings, and lock nuts.

3. Remove the hub and rotor. Remove the outer wheel bearing cone. Remove the grease seal from the rotor. Remove the inner wheel bearing.

4. Remove the inner and outer bearing cups from the rotor. Remove the nuts retaining the spindle to the steering knuckle. Tap the spindle with a plastic hammer to jar the spindle from the knuckle. Remove the splash shield.

5. Remove the shaft and joint assembly by pulling the assembly out of the carrier.

6. On the right side of the carrier, remove and discard the keystone clamp from the shaft and joint assembly and the stub shaft. Slide the rubber boot onto the stub shaft and pull the shaft and joint assembly from the splines of the stub shaft.

7. Place the spindle in a vise on the second step of the spindle. Wrap a shop towel around the spindle or use a brass-jawed vise to protect the spindle. Remove the oil seal and needle bearing from the spindle with slide hammer and seal remover. If required, remove the seal from the shaft, by driving off with a hammer.

8. Clean all dirt and grease from the spindle bearing bore. Bearing bores must be free from nicks and burrs.

Place the bearing in the bore with the manufacturer's identification facing outward. Drive the bearing into the bore using Spindle Bearing Replacer, T83T-3123-A and Driver Handle T80T-4000-W or equivalents.

9. Install the grease seal in the bearing bore with the lip side of the seal facing towards the tool. Drive the seal in the bore with Spindle Bearing Replacer, T83T-3123-A and Driver Handle T80-4000-W or equivalents. Coat the bearing seal lip with Multi-Purpose Long Life Lubricant, C1AZ-19590-B (ESA-M1C75-B) or equivalent.

10. If removed, install a new shaft seal. Place the shaft in a press, and install the seal with Spindle/Axle Seal Installer, T83T-3132-A, or equivalent.

11. On the right side of the carrier, install the rubber boot and new keystone clamps on the stub shaft slip yoke. Since the splines on the shaft are phased, there is only one way to assemble the right shaft and joint assembly into the slip yoke. Align the missing spline in the slip yoke barrel with the gapless male spline on the shaft and joint assembly. Slide the right shaft and joint assembly into the slip yoke making sure the splines are fully engaged. Slide the boot over the assembly and crimp the keystone clamp using Clamp Pliers.

12. On the left side of the carrier slide the shaft and joint assembly through the knuckle and engage the splines on the shaft in the carrier.

13. Install the splash shield and spindle onto the steering knuckle. Install and tighten the spindle nuts to 35–45 ft. lbs.

14. Drive the bearing cups into the rotor using bearing cup replacer T73T-4222-B

Carrier, slip yoke and stub axle- Ranger/Bronco II 4x4

and Driver Handle, T80T-4000-W or equivalents.

15. Pack the inner and outer wheel bearings and the lip of the oil seal with Multi-Purpose Long-Life Lubricant, C1AZ-19590-B (ESA-M1C75-B) or equivalent.

16. Place the inner wheel bearing in the inner cup. Drive the grease seal into the bore with Hub Seal Replacer, T83T-1175-B and Driver Handle, T80T-4000-W or equivalents. Coat the bearing seal lip with multipurpose long life lubricant, C1AZ-19590-B (ESA-M1C75-B) or equivalent.

17. Install the rotor on the spindle. Install the outer wheel bearing into cup.

NOTE: Verify that the grease seal lip totally encircles the spindle.

Right axle and joint assembly Ranger/Bronco II 4x4

Dana 44-IFS front axle

18. Install the wheel bearing, locknut, thrust bearing, snap ring, and locking hubs.

RIGHT SIDE STUB AXLE AND CARRIER

1. Remove the nuts and U-bolts connecting the driveshaft to the yoke. Disconnect the driveshaft from the yoke. Wire the driveshaft out of the way, so it will not interfere in the carrier removal process.

2. Remove both spindles and the Left and Right Shaft and U-joint assemblies as described previously.

3. Support the carrier with a suitable jack and remove the bolts retaining the carrier to the support arm. Separate the carrier from the support arm and drain the lubricant from the carrier. Remove the carrier from the vehicle.

4. Place the carrier in a holding fixture.

5. Rotate the slip yoke and shaft assembly so the open side of the snap ring is exposed.

6. Remove the snap ring from the shaft. Remove the slip yoke and shaft assembly from the carrier.

7. Remove the oil seal and caged needle bearings at the same time, using Slide Hammer, T50T-100-A and Collet, D80L-100-A or equivalents. Discard the seal and needle bearing.

8. Make sure the bearing bore is free from nicks and burrs. Install a new caged needle bearing on Needle Bearing Replacer, T83T-1244-A or equivalent, with the manufacturer name and part number facing outward towards the tool. Drive the needle bearing until it is seated in the bore.

9. Coat the seal with Long-Life Multi-Purpose Lubricant, C1AZ-19590-B (ESA-M1C75-B) or equivalent. Drive the seal into the carrier using Needle Bearing Replacer T83T-1244-A or equivalent.

10. Install the slip yoke and shaft assembly into the carrier so the groove in the shaft is visible in the differential case.

11. Install the snap ring in the groove in the shaft. Force the snap ring into position with a suitable tool. Remove the carrier from the holding fixture.

NOTE: Do not tap on the center of the snap ring. This may damage the snap ring.

12. Clean all traces of gasket RTV sealant from the surfaces of the carrier and support arm and make sure the surfaces are free from dirt and oil. Apply a bead of RTV sealant, D6AZ-19562-A (clear) or -B (black) (ESB-M4G92-A and ESE-M4G195-A) or equivalent, in a bead between 6.35–9.53mm (¼–⅜ inch) wide. The bead should be continuous and should not pass through or outside the holes.

NOTE: The carrier must be installed on the support arm within five minutes after applying the RTV sealant.

13. Position the carrier on a suitable jack and install it in position on the support arm using guide pins to align. Install the attaching bolts and hand tighten. Tighten the bolts in a clockwise or counter-clockwise pattern to 40–50 ft. lbs.

14. Install the shear bolt retaining the carrier to the axle arm and tighten to 75–95 ft. lbs.

15. Install both spindles and the left and right shaft and joint assemblies as described in the removal and installation portion of this section.

Connect the driveshaft to the yoke. Install the nuts and U-bolts and tighten to 8–15 ft. lbs.

Drilling the stub shaft bearing retaining ring on the Dana 44-IFS

Axle Shaft Bearing

1980–81 MODELS WITH DANA 44IFS, 44IFS-HD OR 50IFS AXLES

This procedure requires the use of special tools.

REMOVAL & INSTALLATION

1. Remove the axle shaft assembly as

Removing the bearing retainer ring on the Dana 44-IFS

described in this part under Axle Shaft and Steering Knuckle.

2. Remove the stub assembly by removing 3 bolts attaching retainer plate to carrier housing.

3. Place the axle shaft in a vise and drill a 6.35mm (¼ inch) hole in the outside of the bearing retaining ring to a depth ¾ the thickness of the ring.

NOTE: Do not drill through the ring because this will damage the axle shaft.

4. With a chisel placed across the hole, strike sharply with a hammer to remove the retaining ring. Replace bearing retaining ring upon assembly.

5. Press the bearing from the axle shaft with the special tools T80 axle bearing remover T80T-4000-M and sleeve T80T-4000-L.

NOTE: Do not use a torch to aid in bearing removal or the stub shaft will be damaged.

6. Remove the seal and retainer plate from the stub shaft. Discard seal and replace with new seal upon assembly.

Lubricating the axle bearing on the Dana 44-IFS

7. Inspect the retainer plate and stub shaft for distortion, nicks or burns. Replace if necessary.

8. Install retainer plate and new seal on shaft. Coat oil seal with ESA-M175B or equivalent.

9. Place the bearing on the shaft. The large radius on the inner race must face the yoke end of the shaft.

10. Use axle bearing replacer T80T-4000-N and pinion bearing cone remover T71P-4621-B to press the bearing onto the shaft until completely seated. A 0.038mm (0.0015 inch) feeler gauge should not fit between the bearing seat and bearing.

11. Use axle bearing replacer T80T-4000-N and pinion bearing cone remover T71P-4621-B to press the bearing retainer ring onto the stub shaft. Press the bearing retainer ring until completely seated. A 0.038mm (0.0015 inch) feeler gauge should not fit between the ring and bearing. There must be one point between the bearing and ring where the feeler gauge cannot enter. If feeler gauge enters completely around the circumference press the retainer further onto the shaft.

12. Push the seal and retainer plate away from the bearing to form a space between the seal and bearing. Fill the space with wheel bearing grease meeting Ford specification ESA-M1C75B or equivalent.

13. With the space filled with grease, wrap tape around the space.

14. Pull the seal towards the bearing until it contacts the inner race. This will force grease between the rollers and cup. Remove tape.

NOTE: If grease is not visible on the small end of the rollers, repeat steps 6 through 8 until grease is visible. Install the slip yoke and U-joint to stub shaft.

15. Install the stub shaft in the carrier and install 3 retainer bolts. Torque to 30–40 ft. lbs. Install right hand axle shaft assembly into slip yoke.

16. Install splash shield and spindle.

Axle Shaft U-Joint Overhaul

Follow the procedures outlined under Axle Shaft Removal and Installation to gain access to the U-joints. Overhaul them as described under U-joints.

Pinion Seal

REMOVAL & INSTALLATION

NOTE: A torque wrench capable of at least 225 ft. lbs. is required for pinion seal installation.

——————— CAUTION ———————
Ranger and Bronco II models use a collapsible spacer to set pinion depth and preload. When replacing the pinion seal always install a new spacer. Never tighten the pinion nut more than 225 ft. lbs. or the spacer will be compressed too far.

1. Raise and safely support the vehicle with jackstands under the frame rails. Allow the axle to drop to rebound position for working clearance.

2. Mark the companion flanges and U-joints for correct reinstallation position.

3. Remove the drive shaft. Use a suitable tool to hold the companion flange. Remove the pinion nut and companion flange.

4. Use a slide hammer and hook or sheet metal screw to remove the oil seal.

5. If the vehicle uses a collapsible spacer, install new spacer. Install a new pinion seal after lubricating the sealing surfaces. Use a suitable seal driver. Install the companion flange and pinion nut. On models using a spacer, tighten the nut to 225 ft. lbs. On other models, pinion nut torque is 200–220 ft. lbs.

REAR AXLE

NOTE: Refer to Rear Axles in the Unit Repair Section for overhaul procedures.

Axle Shaft and Bearing

REMOVAL & INSTALLATION

Removable Carrier Type

NOTE: The following procedure requires the use of special tools, including a shop press.

1. Raise and support the vehicle and remove the wheel/tire assembly from the brake drum.

2. Remove the clips which secure the brake drum to the axle flange, then remove the drum from the flange.

3. Working through the hole provided

Tapered roller bearings used on some E-100, 150 and 200 axle shafts

in each axle shaft flange, remove the nuts which secure the wheel bearing retainer plate.

4. Pull the axle shaft assembly out of the axle housing. You may need a slide hammer.

NOTE: The brake backing plate must not be dislodged. Install one nut to hold the plate in place after the axle shaft is removed.

5. If the axle has ball bearings:
Loosen the bearing retainer ring by nicking it in several places with a cold chisel, then slide it off the axle shaft. On models equipped with a thick retaining ring drill a ¼ to ½ in. hole part way through the ring, then break it with a cold chisel. A hydraulic press is needed to press the bearing off and to press the new one on. Press the new bearing and the new retainer ring on separately. Use a slide hammer to pull the old seal out of the axle housing. Carefully drive the new seal evenly into the axle housing, preferably with a seal drive tool.

6. If the axle has tapered roller bearings. Use a slide hammer to remove the bearing cup from the axle housing. Drill a ¼ to ½ in. hole part way through the bearing retainer ring, then break it with a cold chisel. A hydraulic press is needed to press the bearing off and remove the seal. Press on the new seal and bearing, then the new retainer ring. Do not press the bearing and ring on together. Put the cup on the bearing, not in the housing, and lubricate the outer diameter of the cup and seal.

7. With ball bearings:
Place a new gasket between the housing flange and backing plate. Carefully slide the axle shaft into place. Turn the shaft to start the splines into the side gear and push it in.

8. With tapered roller bearings:
Move the seal out toward the axle shaft flange so there is at least ³⁄₃₂ between the edge of the outer seal and the bearing cup, to prevent snagging on installation. Carefully slide the axle shaft into place. Turn the shaft to start the splines into the side gear and push it in.

9. Install the bearing retainer plate.

10. Replace the brake drum and the wheel and tire.

Full Floating Axle Type

1. Remove the lockbolts and lockwashers which hold the axle flange to the hub and drum assembly.

NOTE: It is not necessary to raise the vehicle to remove the axle shafts.

2. Carefully slide the axle shaft out of the axle housing.

3. Clean the mating surfaces of the axle flange and the hub and drum assembly.

4. Position a new gasket on the axle flange and carefully slide the axle shaft into the axle housing. When the splined end of the axle shaft reaches the side gear, gently rotate the shaft until it is inserted into the side gear.

5. Position the gasket between the axle flange and the hub and drum and install the lockbolts and lockwashers.

REAR WHEEL BEARINGS

F-250, 350, E-250, E-300, E-350 Rear

The wheel bearings on the full floating rear axle are packed with wheel bearing grease. Axle lubricant can also flow into the wheel hubs and bearings, however, wheel bearing grease is the primary lubricant. The wheel bearing grease provides lubrication until the axle lubricant reaches the bearings during normal operation.

1. Set the parking brake and loosen the axle shaft bolts.

2. Raise the rear wheels off the floor and place jackstands under the rear axle housing so that the axle is parallel with the floor.

3. Remove the axle shaft bolts.

4. Remove the axle shaft and gaskets.

5. With the axle shaft removed, remove the gasket from the axle shaft flange studs.

6. Bend the lockwasher tab away from the locknut, and then remove the locknut, lockwasher, and the adjusting nut.

7. Remove the outer bearing cone and pull the wheel straight off the axle.

8. With a piece of hardwood which will just clear the outer bearing cup, drive the inner bearing cone and inner seal out of the wheel hub.

9. Wash all the old grease or axle lubricant out of the wheel hub, using a suitable solvent.

10. Wash the bearing cups and rollers and inspect them for pitting, galling, and uneven wear patterns. Inspect the roller for end wear.

Lock nut, lock ring and adjusting nut removal

11. If the bearing cups are to be replaced, drive them out with a drift. Install the new cups with a block of wood and hammer or press them in.

12. If the bearing cups are properly seated, a 0.0015 in. feeler gauge will not fit between the cup and the wheel hub.

13. Pack each bearing cone and roller with a bearing packer or in the manner previously outlined for the front wheel bearings on 2WD trucks.

14. Place the inner bearing cone and roller assembly in the wheel hub. Install a new inner seal in the hub.

15. Install the wheel.

16. Install and tighten the bearing adjusting nut to 50–80 ft. lbs. while rotating the wheel.

17. Back off (loosen) the adjusting nut ⅜ of a turn.

18. Apply axle lube to a new lockwasher and install it with the smooth side out.

19. Install the locknut and tighten it to 90–110 ft. lbs. The wheel must rotate freely after the locknut is tightened. The wheel end-play should be within 0.001–0.010 in.

20. Bend two lockwasher tabs inward

over an adjusting nut flat and two lockwasher tabs outward over the locknut flat.

21. Install the axle shaft, gasket, lockbolts, and washers. Tighten the bolts to 40–50 ft. lbs.

22. Adjust the brakes, if necessary.

6¾ Inch-Integral Carrier Type

NOTE: The 6¾ inch, integral Carrier is used on some Ranger and Bronco II models. Refer to the Removable Carrier section for procedures.

Integral Carrier—"C"-Lock Type

1. Raise and safely support the vehicle on jackstands.

2. Remove the wheels and tires from the brake drums.

3. Place a drain pan under the housing and drain the lubricant by loosening the housing cover.

4. Remove the locks securing the brake drums to the axle shaft flanges and remove the drums.

5. Remove the housing cover and gasket, if used.

6. Working through the opening in the differential case, remove the side gear pinion shaft lockbolt and the side gear pinion shaft.

7. Working through the opening in the differential case, remove the side gear pinion shaft lockbolt and the side gear pinion shaft.

8. Push the axle shafts inward and remove the C-locks from the inner end of the axle shafts. Temporarily replace the shaft and lockbolt to retain the differential gears in position.

9. Remove the axle shafts with a slide

Integral rear with "C-locks"-pinion shaft and lock bolt location

"C-lock" removal/installation

F-250, 350 rear wheel hub assembly with full-floating axles

hammer. Be sure the seal is not damaged by the splines on the axle shaft.

10. Remove the bearing and oil seal from the housing. Both the seal and bearing can be removed with a slide hammer. Two types of bearings are used on some axles, one requiring a press fit and the other a loose fit. A loose fitting bearing does not necessarily indicate excessive wear.

11. Inspect the axle shaft housing and axle shafts for burrs or other irregularities. Replace any work or damaged parts. A light yellow color on the bearing journal of the axle shaft is normal, and does not require replacement of the axle shaft. Slight pitting and wear is also normal.

12. Lightly coat the wheel bearing rollers with axle lubricant. Install the bearings in the axle housing until the bearing seats firmly against the shoulder.

13. Wipe all lubricant from the oil seal bore, before installing the seal.

14. Inspect the original seals for wear. If necessary, these may be replaced with new seals, which are prepacked with lubricant and do not require soaking.

15. Install the oil seal.

16. Remove the lockbolt and pinion shaft. Carefully slide the axle shafts into place. Be careful that you do not damage the seal with the splined end of the axle shaft. Engage the splined end of the shaft with the differential side gears.

17. Install the axle shaft C-locks on the inner end of the axle shafts and seat the C-locks in the counterbore of the differential side gears.

18. Rotate the differential pinion gears until the differential pinion shaft can be installed. Install the differential pinion shaft lockbolt. Tighten to 15–22 ft. lbs.

19. Install the brake drum on the axle shaft flange.

20. Install the wheel and tire on the brake drum and tighten the attaching nuts.

21. Clean the gasket surface of the rear housing and install a new cover gasket and the housing cover. Some covers do not use a gasket. On these models, apply a bead of silicone sealer on the gasket surface. The bead should run inside of the bolt holes.

22. Raise the rear axle so that it is in the running position. Add the amount of specified lubricant to bring the lubricant level to ½ in. below the filler hole.

FRONT SUSPENSION

Springs

REMOVAL & INSTALLATION
2WD

1. Raise the front of the vehicle and

place jackstands under the frame and a jack under the axle. Remove wheel and tire assemblies. Remove caliper and suspend with wire so that there is no tension on the brake hose.

2. Disconnect the shock absorber from the lower bracket.

3. Remove the rebound bracket on Ranger and Bronco II, remove the lower spring retainer.

4. On models except Ranger and Bronco II: Remove the two spring upper retainer attaching bolts from the top of the spring upper seat and remove the retainer.

5. Remove the nut attaching the spring lower retainer to the lower seat and axle and remove the retainer.

6. Lower the axle and remove the spring. Some downward pressure using a prybar may be required.

7. Place the spring in position and raise the front axle.

8. Position the spring lower retainer over the stud and lower seat, and install the two attaching bolts.

9. Position the upper retainer over the spring coil and against the spring upper seat,

Exploded view of the front spring assembly and shock absorber on 2WD pick-ups

2WD twin I-beam front suspension

and install the two attaching bolts.

10. Tighten the upper and lower retainer attaching nuts and bolts to 15–25 ft. lbs.

11. Connect the shock absorber to the lower bracket and install the rebound bracket.

12. Remove the jack and safety stands.

4WD—1977 Bronco; F-100, F-150 Through 1979

1. Raise the vehicle until the tires are a few inches off the ground and place jackstands under the frame side rails. Position a hydraulic floor jack under the center of the front axle housing.

2. Remove the shock absorber-to-lower bracket attaching bolt and nut.

3. Remove the spring lower retainer attaching bolts from the inside of the spring coil.

4. Lower the axle enough to relieve tension from the spring.

5. Remove the spring upper retainer attaching bolts and nuts and remove the upper retainer.

6. Remove the spring, lower retainer and the lower seat from the front spring:

7. Position the upper retainer over the spring coil and loosely install the attaching bolts and nuts.

8. Position the spring lower seat, and the lower retainer to the frame spring pocket and the radius arm.

9. Raise the axle up into position and install the two lower retainer attaching bolts and tighten them.

10. Tighten the upper retainer attaching bolts.

11. Position the shock absorber to the lower bracket and install the attaching bolt and nut.

12. Remove the jack stands and lower the vehicle.

1978–1979 Bronco

1. Raise the vehicle and support on jackstands. Remove wheels and calipers. Support the calipers with wire, do not allow tension on the brake hose. Remove the shock absorber-to-lower bracket attaching bolt and nut.

2. Remove two spring lower retainer attaching bolts from inside of the spring coil.

3. Remove two spring upper retainer attaching bolts and nuts and remove the upper retainer.

4. Position safety stands under the frame side rails and lower the axle enough to relieve tension from the spring. Remove the spring, lower retainer, and lower the spring from the vehicle.

5. Position the spring, spring lower seat, and lower retainer to the frame spring pocket and the radius arm. Position the spring seat and the lower retainer.

6. Position the upper retainer over the spring coil and loosely install the two attaching bolts and nuts.

7. Install the two lower retainer attaching bolts and tighten to 80–120 ft. lbs.

F-100, 150 4WD front suspension

1977 Bronco front suspension

8. Tighten the upper retainer attaching bolts to 20–30 ft. lbs.

9. Position the shock absorber to the lower bracket and install the attaching bolt and nut. Tighten the bolt and nut to 40–60 ft. lbs. Remove safety stands and lower the vehicle.

4WD—F-250–F-350 Through 1979

1. Raise the vehicle until the weight is off the front spring with the wheels still touching the floor.

2. Disconnect the lower end of the shock absorber from the axle. Remove the U-bolts and spacer.

3. Remove the nut from the shackle bolt retaining spring at the front and drive the shackle bolt out with a drift.

4. Remove the nuts and shackle bar at the rear shackle bracket. Drive out the two shackle bolts and remove the spring.

5. Position the spring on the spring seat cap and install the shackle bolts through the shackle bracket and spring.

6. Install the shackle bar and nuts on the shackle bolts and tighten them to 90–130 ft. lbs.

7. Position the front of the spring to allow the front shackle bolts to be installed. Tighten the nut to 90–130 ft. lbs.

8. Position the U-bolt spacer and place the U-bolts in position through the holes in the spring seat cap. Install the U-bolt nuts, but do not tighten them yet.

9. Connect the lower end of the shock absorber to the axle.

10. Lower the vehicle and tighten the U-bolt nuts to 100–135 ft. lbs.

4WD—Bronco, F-150- From 1980

1. Raise the vehicle and remove the shock absorber lower attaching bolt and nut.

2. Remove the spring lower retainer nuts from inside of the spring coil.

3. Remove the upper spring retainer by removing the attaching screw.

4. Position safety stands under the frame side rails and lower the axle enough to relieve tension from the spring.

NOTE: The axle must be supported on the jack throughout spring removal, and must not be permitted to hang from the brake hose. If the length of the brake hose does not provide sufficient clearance it may be necessary to remove and support the brake caliper.

5. Remove the spring lower retainer and lower the spring from the vehicle.

6. To install place the spring in position and slowly raise the front axle. Make sure the springs are positioned correctly in the upper spring seats.

7. Install the lower spring retainer and torque the nut to 50 ft. lbs.

8. Position the upper retainer over the spring coil and install the attaching screws.

9. Position the shock absorber to the lower bracket and torque the attaching bolt and nut to 53 ft. lbs.

10. Remove the safety stands and lower the vehicle.

4WD—F-250, F-350—From 1980

1. Raise the vehicle frame until the weight is off the front spring with the wheels still touching the floor. Support the axle to prevent rotation.

2. Disconnect the lower end of the shock absorber from the U-bolt spacer. Remove the U-bolts. U-bolt cap and spacer.

3. Remove the nut from the hanger bolt retaining the spring at the rear and drive out the hanger bolt.

4. Remove the nut connecting the front shackle and spring eye and drive out the shackle bolt and remove the spring.

5. To install position the spring on the spring seat. Install the shackle bolt through the shackle and spring. Torque the nuts to 135 ft. lbs.

6. Position the rear of the spring and install the hanger bolt. Torque the nut to 175 ft. lbs.

7. Position the U-bolt spacer and place the U-bolts in position through the holes in the spring seat cap. Install but do not tighten the U-bolt nuts.

8. Connect the lower end of the shock absorber to the U-bolt spacer.

9. Lower the vehicle and tighten the U-bolt nuts to 100 ft. lbs.

4WD-Ranger and Bronco II

1. Raise the vehicle and install safety stands. Position a jack beneath the spring under the axle. Raise the jack and compress the spring.

2. Remove the bolt and nut retaining the shock absorber to the radius arm. Slide the shock out from the bracket.

3. Remove the nut that retains the spring to the axle and radius arm. Remove retainer.

4. Slowly lower the axle until all spring tension is released and adequate clearance exists to remove the spring. Remove the

COIL SPRINGS MUST BE INSTALLED IN MATCHED SETS (EITHER BOTH MEAN TO HIGH LOAD RANGE OR BOTH LOW TO MEAN LOAD RANGE)

FRONT OF VEHICLE

STEERING LINKAGE MUST BE INSTALLED WITH STEERING GEAR FIXTURED ON CENTER (±45° AT INPUT SHAFT) BALL STUDS MUST BE SEATED IN TAPERS TO PREVENT ROTATION WHILE TIGHTENING.

CLAMPS MUST BE INSTALLED IN POSITION SHOWN WITHIN ± 45° TIGHTEN NUTS 40 57 N·m (30-42 FT-LB) LH AND RH SIDE.

MAIN VIEW FRONT SUSPENSION

Ranger/Bronco II 4x4 front suspension

spring by rotating upper coil out of tabs in upper spring seat. Remove the spacer and seat.

NOTE: The axle must be supported on the jack throughout spring removal and installation, and must not be permitted to hang by the brake hose. If the length of the brake hose is not sufficient to provide adequate clearance for removal and installation of the spring, the disc brake caliper must be removed from the spindle. After removal, the caliper must be placed on the frame or otherwise supported to prevent suspending the caliper from the caliper hose. These precautions are absolutely necessary to prevent serious damage to the tube portion of the caliper hose assembly.

5. If required, remove the stud from the axle assembly.

6. If removed, install the stud in the axle. Tighten to 160–220 ft. lbs.

7. Install the lower seat and spacer over the stud/bolt. Position upper end of spring so end of coil fits into spring stop in upper spring seat and top coil fits over upper spring retainer.

8. Rotate spring into position. Slowly raise axle until lower end of spring is in position on the lower insulator.

9. Install the retainer and nut on the stud. Tighten nut to 70–100 ft. lbs.

10. Position the shock in the lower bracket. Install nut and bolt and tighten to 42–72 ft. lbs.

11. Remove the jack.

Shock Absorbers

REMOVAL & INSTALLATION

2WD

1. Insert a wrench from the rear side of the upper spring seat to hold the upper shock retaining nut. Loosen the stud by using another wrench on the hex on the shaft.

2. Remove the bolt and nut at the lower end.

3. On installation, make sure to get the washers and insulators in the right place. Tighten the upper nut by turning the hex on the shaft Replace the lower bolt. It is recommended that new rubber insulators be used.

4WD

1. Remove the bolt and nut attaching the shock absorber to the lower bracket on the radius arm.

2. Remove the nut, washer and insulator from the shock absorber at the frame bracket and remove the shock absorber.

To install the front shock absorber:

3. Position the washer and insulator on the shock absorber rod and position the shock absorber to the frame bracket.

4. Position the insulator and washer on the shock absorber rod and install the attaching nut loosely.

5. Position the shock absorber to the lower bracket and install the attaching bolt and nut loosely.

6. Tighten the lower attaching bolts to 40–70 ft. lbs., and the upper attaching bolts to 25–30 ft. lbs.

Front Wheel Spindle and King Pin 2WD

REMOVAL & INSTALLATION

1. Raise the front of the truck until the front wheel clears the ground and place jackstands under the frame.

2. Remove the wheel and tire.

3. Remove the caliper key retaining screw. Drive out the caliper support key and spring with brass drift and hammer. Remove the caliper from the spindle by pushing the caliper downward against the spindle assembly and rotating the upper end of the caliper upward and out of the spindle assembly. It is not necessary to disconnect the brake fluid hose. Wire the caliper to a suspension part to remove the weight of the caliper from the hose. Disconnect the steering linkage from the spindle arm.

4. Disconnect the steering linkage from the integral spindle and spindle arm.

5. Remove the nut and lockwasher from the locking pin, and remove the locking pin.

6. Remove the upper and lower spindle bolt plugs, and drive the spindle bolt out from the top of the axle. Remove the spindle and bearing. Knock out the seal.

7. Make sure that the spindle bolt hole

Ranger/Bronco II 2x4 front suspension

1980 F-150 4WD front suspension

1981–82 4WD pick-up and Bronco front suspension

in the axle is free of nicks, burrs, and dirt. Install a new seal and coat the spindle bolt bushings and bolt hole with oil.

8. Place the spindle in position on the axle.

9. Pack the spindle thrust bearing with chassis lubricant and insert the bearing into the spindle with the open end of the bearing seal facing down into the spindle.

10. Install the spindle pin in the spindle with the locking pin notch in the spindle bolt aligned with the locking pin hole in the axle. Drive the spindle bolt through the axle from the top side until the spindle bolt locking pin notch is aligned with the locking pin hole.

11. Install a new locking pin. Install the locking pin lockwasher and nut. Tighten the nut to 40–55 ft. lbs. Install the spindle bolt plugs at the top and bottom of the spindle bolt.

12. Position the caliper on the spindle assembly. Be careful to prevent tearing or cutting of the piston boot as the caliper is slipped over the inner brake pad. Use a screwdriver or brake adjusting tool to hold the upper machined surface of the caliper against the surface of the spindle. Install the caliper support spring and key. Drive the key and spring into position with a soft hammer. Install the key retaining screw and tighten it to 12–18 ft. lbs. Connect the steering linkage to the spindle and tighten the nut to 50–70 ft. lbs. advancing the nut as necessary to install the cotter pin.

13. Install the wheel.

14. Grease the spindle assembly with a grease gun.

Spindle installation on light duty 2WD pick-ups

Spindle installation on heavy duty 2WD pick-ups

15. Check and adjust, if necessary, the toe-in adjustment.

Front Wheel Spindle— Stamped I-Beam with Balljoints

REMOVAL & INSTALLATION

Spindle

1. Raise the front of the vehicle and install safety stands. Remove the wheel and tire assembly.

2. Remove the caliper assembly from the rotor and hold it out of the way with wire.

3. Remove the dust cap, cotter pin, nut retainer, nut, washer, and outer bearing, and remove the rotor from the spindle.

4. Remove inner bearing cone and seal. Discard the seal. Remove brake dust shield.

Spindle, camber adaptor and ball joints-Ranger/Bronco II

5. Disconnect the steering linkage from the integral spindle and spindle arm by removing the cotter pin and nut and then removing the tie rod end from the spindle arm.

6. Remove the cotter pins from the upper and lower ball joint studs. Remove the nuts from the upper and lower ball joint stud.

7. Strike the inside area of the spindle to pop the ball joints loose from the spindle.

— CAUTION —
Do not use a pickle fork to separate the ball joint from the spindle as this will damage the seal and the ball joint socket.

8. Remove the spindle.

1. Prior to assembly, make sure the upper and lower ball joint seals are in place. Place the spindle over the ball joints.

2. Install the nut on the lower ball joint stud and partially tighten to 30 ft. lbs. Advance the castellated nut as required and install the cotter pin. If the lower ball stud turns while the nut is being tightened, push the spindle up against the ball stud.

NOTE: The lower nut must be tightened first.

3. Install the camber adapter in the upper spindle over the upper ball joint stud. Be sure the adapter is aligned properly.

4. Install the nut on the upper ball joint stud. Hold the camber adaptor with a wrench to keep the ball stud from turning. If the ball stud turns, tap the adaptor deeper into the spindle. Tighten the nut to 85–110 ft. lbs. and continue tightening the castellated nut until it lines up with the hole in the stud. Install the cotter pin.

5. Retighten lower nut to 140–180 ft. lbs. Install the dust shield.

6. Pack the inner and outer bearing cone with C1AZ-19590-B (ESA-M1C75-B) or equivalent bearing grease. Use a bearing packer. If a bearing packer is unavailable, pack the bearing cone by hand working the grease through the cage behind the rollers.

7. Install the inner bearing cone and seal. Install the hub and rotor on the spindle.

8. Install the outer bearing cone, washer, and nut. Adjust bearing end play and install the nut retainer, cotter pin and dust cap.

9. Install the caliper.

10. Connect the steering linkage to the spindle. Tighten the nut to 52–73 ft. lbs. and advance the nut as required for installation of the cotter pin.

11. Install the wheel and tire assembly. Lower the vehicle.

12. Check and, if necessary adjust the toe setting.

Camber Adjuster

1. Remove the cotter pin and nut from the upper ball joint stud.

2. Strike the inside of the spindle to pop the upper ball joint from the spindle.

3. If the upper ball joint does not pop loose, remove the cotter pin and back the lower ball joint nut about half way down the lower ball joint stud, and strike the side of the lower spindle.

4. Remove the camber adapter (camber adjustment sleeve) using Ball Joint Removing Tool (D81T-3010-B) or equivalent.

Coil spring removal/installation Ranger/Bronco II 4x4

5. Install the correct adaptor in the spindle. On the right spindle the adaptor slot must point forward to make a positive camber change or rearward for a negative camber change. On the left spindle, the adaptor slot must point rearward for a positive camber change and forward for a negative change.

6. If both nuts were loosened, completely remove the spindle, and reinstall. Be sure the lower ball joint stud is always tightened before the upper nut. Apply Locktite No. 242 (D5AZ 19554-A) or equivalent to stud threads before installing nut.

7. If only the upper ball joint stud nut was removed, install the nut and tighten to 85–110 ft. lbs. and continue tightening the castellated nut until it lines up with the hole in the upper stud. Install the cotter pin.

Ball Joints

1. Remove the spindle as described previously.

2. Remove snap ring from ball joints. Assemble C-Frame puller and adapters on upper ball joint. Turn forcing screw clockwise until ball joint is removed from axle.

3. Assemble C-Frame assembly and receiver cup on lower ball joint and turn forcing screw clockwise until ball joint is removed.

NOTE: Always remove upper ball joint first.

—————— CAUTION ——————
Do not heat the ball joint or the axle to aid in removal.

4. To install the lower ball joint, assemble C-Frame puller and adaptors. Turn forcing screw clockwise until ball joint is seated.

NOTE: Lower ball joint must be installed first.

—————— CAUTION ——————
Do not heat the ball joint or axle to aid in installation.

5. Install the snap ring onto the ball joint.

To install the upper ball joint, assemble the C-frame and repeat Steps 1 and 2.

6. Install the spindle.

Front Wheel Spindle 4WD

REMOVAL & INSTALLATION

NOTE: This procedure also includes bearing and seal replacement and repacking.

1. Raise the vehicle and install safety stands.

2. If equipped with manual locking hubs remove the hubs as follows:

   a. Remove the six socket heat bolts from the cap assembly and separate the cap assembly from the body.

   b. Remove the snap-ring from the end of the axle shaft.

   c. Remove the lock ring seated in the groove of the wheel hub and slide the body assembly out of the wheel hub.

3. If equipped with automatic locking hubs remove the hubs as follows:

   a. Remove the bolts and remove the hub cap assembly from the spindle.

   b. Remove the bolt from the end of the shaft.

   c. Remove the lock ring seated in the groove of the wheel hub.

   d. Remove the body assembly from the spindle. Use a puller if necessary.

   e. Unscrew all three set screws in the spindle locknut until the heads are flush with the edge of the locknut.

f. Remove the outer spindle locknut with tool T80T-4000-V, automatic hub locknut wrench.

4. Remove the front hub grease cap and driving hub snap-ring.

5. Remove the splined driving hub and the pressure spring. Slightly pry off if necessary.

6. Remove the wheel bearing locknut, lock ring and adjusting nut using special tool T59T-1197-B or equivalent.

7. Remove the hub and disc assembly. The outer wheel bearing and spring retainer will slide out as the hub is removed.

8. Remove the spindle nuts and remove the spindle, splash shield and axle shaft assembly.

NOTE: It may be necessary to break the spindle loose with a plastic hammer.

9. Clean all old grease from the needle bearings and wipe clean the spindle face that mates with the spindle bore seal.

10. Remove the spindle bore seal, V-seal, and thrust washer from the outer axle shaft. Clean and replace if necessary.

11. Using Multi-Purpose Lubricant Ford ESA-M1C75-B or equivalent, thoroughly lubricate the needle bearing and pack the spindle face that mates with the spindle bore seal.

12. Position the V-seal in the spindle bore next to the needle bearing. Assemble the spindle bore seal on the axle shaft.

13. Assemble the spindle with the axle shaft on the knuckle studs and tighten the retaining nuts to 75 ft. lbs.

14. Carefully drive the inner bearing cone and grease seal out of the hub using tool T77F-1102-A or equivalent.

15. Inspect the inner bearing cups and if necessary remove with a drift.

NOTE: If new cups are installed, install new bearings.

16. Lubricate the bearings with the lubricant specified earlier and clean all old grease from the hub. Pack the cones and rollers with lubricant. Try to pack as much as possible between the rollers and the cages.

17. Position the inner bearing cone and

roller in the inner cup and install the grease retainer.

18. Install the hub and disc assembly on the spindle.

19. Install the outer bearing cone and roller, and the adjusting nut.

20. Using tool T59T-1197-B or equivalent and a torque wrench tighten the bearing adjusting nut to 50 ft. lbs. while rotating the wheel back and forth. Back off the adjusting nut no more than 90 degrees.

21. Assemble the lock ring by turning the nut to the nearest hole and inserting the dowel pin.

NOTE: The dowel pin must seat in the lock ring hole for proper bearing adjustment and wheel retention.

22. Install the outer lock nut and tighten to 65 ft. lbs. Final end play on the wheel and spindle should be 0.001–0.006 inch.

23. Adjust the brake if necessary and lower the vehicle.

Knuckle and Ball Joint—4-WD

REPLACEMENT

NOTE: A combination ball joint puller/press and a special spanner wrench are needed for this job. If these aren't available the job should not be attempted.

1. Follow the procedures under Axle Shaft Removal.

2. Disconnect the connecting rod end from the knuckle.

3. Remove the cotter pin from the upper ball socket and loosen the upper and lower ball socket nuts. Discard the nut from the lower ball socket after the knuckle breaks loose from the yoke.

4. Remove the knuckle from the yoke. If the upper socket remains in the yoke, remove it by hitting the top of the stud with a soft-faced hammer. Discard the socket and adjusting sleeve.

5. Remove the bottom socket with a ball joint puller (available at most auto parts

1980 and later knuckle and spindle assembly on 4WD vehicles

stores) after first removing the snap ring.
For installation:

6. Place the knuckle in a vise and assemble the bottom socket. Place the new socket into the knuckle making sure it isn't cocked, place the driver over the socket, place the forcing screw into the socket and force the socket into the knuckle.

7. Make sure that the socket shoulder is seated against the knuckle. Use a .0015 in. feeler gauge between the socket seat and the knuckle.

8. The gauge should not enter the area of minimum contact. Install the snap ring.

9. Assemble the top socket into the knuckle. Assemble the holding plate onto the backing plate screw. Tighten the nuts snugly. Place a new socket in the knuckle. Be sure it is not cocked. Place a driver over the socket and force the socket assembly into the knuckle. Using a .0015 in. gauge, check the fit at the shoulder. The gauge should not enter the area of minimum wrench.

10. Install a new adjusting sleeve into the top of the yoke leaving about two threads exposed.

11. Assemble the knuckle and yoke. Install a new nut on the bottom socket and make it finger tight.

12. Place a wrench and step plate over the adjusting sleeve and install the puller so that it grasps the step plate. Tighten the forcing screw to pull the knuckle assembly into the yoke. With torque still applied, tighten the nut to 70–90 ft. lbs. If the bottom stud should turn with the nut, add more torque to the puller forcing screw. Remove the puller, step plate and holding plate.

13. Tighten the adjusting sleeve to 40 ft. lbs. and remove the wrench.

14. Install the top socket nut and torque it to 100 ft. lbs. Line up the cotter pin hole by tightening, *not loosening*, the nut. Install the cotter pin and test the steering effort with a spring scale attached to the knuckle. Pull should not exceed 26 ft. lbs. If it does, the ball joints will have to be replaced.

15. Connect the steering linkage to the knuckle. Torque it to 40 ft. lbs.

16. Install the axle shaft as described in the Axle Shaft Removal and Installation procedure.

Radius Arm

REMOVAL & INSTALLATION

All Except Bronco, 1980 and Later F-150 with 4WD Ranger and Bronco II

1. Raise the front of the vehicle and place safety stands under the frame and a jack under the wheel or axle.

2. Disconnect the shock absorber from the radius arm bracket.

3. Remove the two spring upper retainer attaching bolts from the top of the spring upper seat and remove the retainer.

4. Remove the nut which attaches the spring lower retainer to the lower seat and axle and remove the retainer.

5. Lower the axle and remove the spring.

6. Disconnect the steering rod from the spindle arm.

7. Remove the spring lower seat and shim from the radius arm. Then, remove the bolt and nut which attach the radius arm to the axle.

8. Remove the cotter pin, nut and washer from the radius arm rear attachment.

9. Remove the bushing from the radius arm and remove the radius arm from the vehicle.

10. Remove the inner bushing from the radius arm.

11. Position the radius arm to the axle and install the bolt and nut finger-tight.

12. Install the inner bushing on the radius arm and position the arm to the frame bracket.

13. Install the bushing, washer, and attaching nut. Tighten the nut and install the cotter pin.

14. Connect the steering rod to the spindle arm and install the attaching nut. Tighten the radius arm-to-axle attaching bolt and nut.

F-150 4WD—From 1980

1. Raise the vehicle and position safety stands under the frame side rails.

2. Remove the shock absorber lower attaching bolt and nut and pull the shock abosrber free of the radius arm.

3. Remove the lower spring retaining bolt from the inside of the spring coil.

4. Remove the nut attaching the radius arm to the frame bracket and remove the radius arm rear insulator. Lower the axle and allow the axle to move forward.

NOTE: The axle must be supported on the jack throughout spring removal, and must not be permitted to hang from the brake hose. If the length of the brake hose does not provide sufficient clearance it may be necessary to remove and support the brake caliper.

5. Remove the bolt and stud attaching the radius arm to the axle.

6. Move the axle forward and remove the radius arm from the axle. Then, pull the radius arm from the frame bracket.

7. Installation is the reverse of removal. Install new bolts and the stud type bolt which attach the radius arm to the axle and tighten to 210 ft. lbs. Tighten the radius arm rear attaching nut to 100 ft. lbs.

1977 Bronco

1. Raise the vehicle and position safety stands under the frame side rails.

2. Remove the shock absorber-to-lower bracket attaching bolt and nut and pull the shock absorber free of the radius arm.

3. Remove the two spring lower retainer attaching bolts from inside of the spring coil.

4. Remove the cotter pin and nut attaching the radius arm to the frame bracket and remove the radius arm rear insulator.

5. Remove the four bolts attaching the radius arm cap to the radius arm and remove the cap and insulator. **The cap and radius arm are a matched set with identical numbers on each part and should not be mixed.**

6. Move the axle forward and remove the radius arm and insulator from the axle. Then, pull the radius arm from the frame bracket.

The radius arm and cap must be identified by a T on each piece in addition to a number (1 through 100).

7. Position the washer and insulator on the rear of the radius arm and insert the radius arm and insulator into the frame bracket.

8. Position the rear insulator and washer on the radius arm and loosely install the attaching nut.

9. Position the insulator on the axle and position the radius arm to the insulator and axle.

10. Position the front insulator to the axle and install the radius arm cap with the numbers on the radius arm and cap together. Torque the attaching bolts diagonally in pairs to 90–10 ft. lbs.

11. Position the spring lower seat and retainer to the spring and axle. Install the two attaching bolts. Torque the bolts to 45–55 ft. lbs.

12. Torque the radius rod rear attaching nut to 80–120 ft. lbs. Advance the nut as required and install the cotter pin.

13. Position the shock absorber to the lower bracket and install the attaching bolt and nut. Torque the nut to 40–60 ft. lbs. Remove safety stands and lower the vehicle.

1978–79 Bronco

1. Raise the vehicle and position safety stands under the frame side rails.

2. Remove the shock absorber-to-lower bracket attaching bolt and nut and pull the shock absorber free of the radius arm.

3. Remove two spring lower retainer attaching bolts from inside of the spring coil.

4. Remove the nut attaching the radius arm to the frame bracket and remove the radius arm rear insulator.

5. Remove four bolts attaching the radius arm cap to the radius arm and remove the cap and insulator. **The cap and radius arm are a matched set with identical numbers on each part and should not be mixed.**

6. Move the axle forward and remove the radius arm and insulator from the axle. Then, pull the radius arm from the frame bracket.

The radius arm and cap must be identified by a T on each piece in addition to a number (1 through 100).

7. Position the washer and insulator on the rear of the radius arm and insert the

radius arm and insulator into the frame bracket.

8. Position the rear insulator and washer on the radius arm and loosely install the attaching nut.

9. Position the insulator on the axle and position the radius arm to the insulator and axle.

10. Position the front insulator to the axle and install the radius arm cap with the numbers on the radius arm and cap together. Tighten the attaching bolts diagonally in pairs to 90–110 ft. lbs.

11. Position the spring lower seat and retainer to the spring and axle. Install the two attaching bolts. Tighten the bolts to 45–55 ft. lbs.

12. Tighten the radius rod rear attaching nut to 80–120 ft. lbs.

13. Position the shock absorber to the lower bracket and install the attaching bolt and nut. Tighten the nut to 40–60 ft. lbs. Remove safety stands and lower the vehicle.

1980 and Later Bronco

1. Raise the vehicle and position safety stands under the frame side rails.

2. Remove the shock absorber-to-lower bracket attaching bolt and nut and pull the shock absorber free of the radius arm.

3. Remove spring lower retainer attaching bolt from inside of the spring coil.

4. Remove the nut attaching the radius arm to the frame bracket and remove the radius arm rear insulator. Lower the axle and allow axle to move forward.

NOTE: The axle must be supported on the jack throughout spring removal and installation, and must not be permitted to hang by the brake hose. If the length of the brake hose is not sufficient to provide adequate clearance for removal and installation of the spring, the disc brake caliper must be removed from the spindle. After removal, the caliper must be placed on the frame or otherwise supported to prevent suspending the caliper from the caliper hose. These precautions are absolutely necessary to prevent serious damage to the tube portion of the caliper hose assembly.

5. Remove the bolt and stud attaching radius arm to axle.

6. Move the axle forward and remove the radius arm from the axle. Then, pull the radius arm from the frame bracket.

7. Position the washer and insulator on the rear of the radius arm and insert the radius arm into the frame bracket.

8. Position the rear insulator and washer on the radius arm and loosely install the attaching nut.

9. Position the radius arm to the axle.

10. Install new bolts and study-type bolt attaching radius arm to axle. Tighten to 180–240 ft. lbs.

11. Position the spring lower seat, spring insulator and retainer to the spring and axle. Install the two attaching bolts. Tighten the nuts to 30–70 ft. lbs.

12. Tighten the radius rod rear attaching nut to 80–120 ft. lbs.

13. Position the shock absorber to the lower bracket and install the attaching bolt and nut. Tighten the nut to 40–60 ft. lbs. Remove safety stands and lower the vehicle.

Ranger and Bronco II

1. Raise the front of the vehicle and place safety stands under the frame. Place a jack under the axle.

NOTE: The axle must be supported on the jack throughout spring removal and installation, and must not be permitted to hang by the brake hose. If the length of the brake hose is not sufficient to provide adequate clearance for removal and installation of the spring, the disc brake caliper must be removed from the spindle. After removal, the caliper must be placed on the frame or otherwise supported to prevent suspending the caliper from the caliper hose. These precautions are absolutely necessary to prevent serious damage to the tube portion of the caliper hose assembly.

2. Disconnect the lower end of the shock absorber from the shock lower bracket (bolt and nut).

3. Remove the front spring. Loosen the axle pivot bolt.

4. Remove the spring lower seat and stud from the radius arm, and then remove the bolts that attach the radius arm to the axle and front bracket.

5. Remove the nut, rear washer and insulator from the rear side of the radius arm rear bracket.

6. Remove the radius arm from the vehicle, and remove the inner insulator and retainer from the radius arm stud.

7. Install in reverse order.

Stabilizer Bar

REMOVAL & INSTALLATION
Bronco and 4-WD Pickups
1978–79

1. Remove locknut, washers, and insulator to remove link assemblies from stabilizer bar. Remove nuts, bolts, and washers connecting link assemblies to frame.

2. Remove nuts on U-bolts to remove stabilizer bar from retainers. Remove stabilizer bar. Remove U-bolts, brackets and retainers.

3. Place bracket assemblies on axle aligning holes in brackets with alignment pins on axles.

4. Install U-bolts through bracket assembly. Position stabilizer bar on brackets. Install retainer and tighten nuts to 35–55 ft. lbs.

5. Install link assemblies on frame. Connect link assemblies to stabilizer bar. Tighten link to stabilizer bar nuts to 18–25 ft. lbs. Tighten link to frame nuts to 40–60 ft. lbs.

FROM 1980

1. Remove nuts, bolts and washers connecting the stabilizer bar to connecting links. Remove nuts and bolts of the stabilizer bar retainer.

2. Remove stabilizer bar insulator assembly.

3. To remove the stabilizer bar mounting bracket, the coil spring must be removed as described above under spring removal. Remove the lower spring seat. The bracket attaching stud and bracket can now be removed.

4. To install the stabilizer bar mounting brackets, locate the brackets so that the locating tang is positioned in the radius arm notch (or quad shock bracket notch if vehicle has quad shocks). Install a new stud. Torque to 180–220 ft. lbs.

NOTE: A new stud is required because of the adhesive on the threads.

Reposition the spring lower seat and reinstall the spring and retainers.

5. To reinstall the stabilizer bar insulator assembly, assemble all nuts, bolts and washers to the bar, brackets, retainers and links loosely. With the bar positioned correctly, torque retainer nuts to 32–35 ft. lbs. with retainer around the insulator. Then torque all remaining nuts at the link assemblies to 41–50 ft. lbs.

RANGER AND BRONCO II

1. Remove the nuts and U-bolts retaining the lower shock bracket/stabilizer bar bushing to radius arm.

2. Remove retainers and remove the stabilizer bar and bushing.

3. Place stabilizer bar in position on the radius arm and bracket.

4. Install retainers and U-bolts. Tighten retainer bolts to 35-50 ft-lbs. Tighten U-bolt nuts to 48-64 ft-lbs.

REAR SUSPENSION

Springs

REMOVAL & INSTALLATION

2WD Pick-Ups and Ranger/ Bronco II

1. Raise the vehicle by the frame until the weight is off the rear spring with the tires still on the floor.

2. Remove the nuts from the spring U-bolts and drive the U-bolts from the U-bolt plate. Remove the auxiliary spring and spacer, if so equipped.

3. Remove the spring-to-bracket nut and bolt at the front of the spring.

Rear spring installation, F-100, 150 2WD and 4WD, and F-250 2WD

8. Align the shackle pin lockbolt groove with the lockbolt hole in the shackle, and install the lockbolt, washer, and nut.

9. Position the spring on the axle with the spring center bolt in the hole provided in the axle spring seat or spacer. Install the spacer between the spring seat and the spring. Make sure that the spacer dowel is positioned in the pilot hole of the axle spring seat.

10. Install the shackle pin through the shackle and rear bracket. The lubrication fitting on the shackle pin faces outboard. Align the pin groove with the lock bolt hole in the bracket and install the lockbolt, washer, and nut.

11. Install the shackle pin at the front bracket and spring eye in the same manner as above.

12. Install the auxiliary spring and spacer, if so equipped. Place the spring cap on top of the spring at the center bolt and place the spring U-bolts over the spring assembly and axle.

13. Position the spring seat cap, and install the nuts on the spring U-bolts.

14. Lower the truck to the ground and tighten the attaching hardware.

Bronco

1. Raise the vehicle and install jackstands under the frame. The vehicle must be supported in such a way that the rear axle hangs free with the tire a few inches off the ground. Place a hydraulic floor jack under the center of the axle housing.

2. Disconnect the shock absorber from the axle.

3. Remove the U-bolt attaching nuts and remove the two U-bolts and the spring clip plate.

4. Remove the upper and lower shackle nuts and bolts at the rear of the spring and remove the spring and shackle assembly from the rear shackle bracket.

5. Remove the bushings in the spring or shackle, if they are worn or damaged, and install new ones.

6. Position the spring in the shackle and install the upper shackle-to-spring nut and bolt with the bolt head facing outward.

7. Position the front end of the spring in the bracket and install the nut and bolt.

8. Position the shackle in the rear bracket and install the nut and bolt.

9. Position the spring on top of the axle with the spring center bolt centered in the hole provided in the seat. Install the auxiliary spring and spacer, if so equipped.

10. Install the spring U-bolts, plate, and nuts.

11. Lower the vehicle and tighten the attaching hardware as follows: U-bolt nuts, ½ in.—45–70 ft. lbs.; ⁹⁄₁₆ in.—85–115 ft. lbs.; front spring hanger, ⁹⁄₁₆ in.—75–105 ft. lbs.; ⅝ in.—150–190 ft. lbs.; rear spring hanger—75–105 ft. lbs.

4WD Pick-ups

1. Raise the truck by the frame until the weight is off the rear springs and the wheels are still touching the ground.

2. Remove the nuts from the spring U-bolts and drive the U-bolts out of the spring seat cap. Remove the spring cap. Remove the auxiliary spring and spacer, if so equipped.

3. Remove the shackle pin lockbolts from each end of the spring. Insert a drift in the hole provided in the frame from the inner side and drive the shackle pin out of each spring bracket.

4. Remove the spring and shackle from the truck. Remove the spring-to-axle spacer.

5. Drive the remaining shackle pin out of the rear spring eye and remove the shackle from the spring.

6. After checking and replacing worn or damaged bushings, nuts and bolts, and broken or weak springs, position the shackle to the rear spring eye.

7. Install the shackle pin through the shackle and spring eye with the lubrication fitting on the shackle pin facing outboard.

Rear spring installation, F-350

4. Lower the axle to relieve the spring tension and remove the nut from the spring front attaching bolt.

5. Remove the spring front attaching bolt from the spring and hanger with a drift.

6. Remove the nut from the shackle-to-hanger attaching bolt and drive the bolt from the shackle and hanger with a drift and remove the spring from the vehicle.

7. Remove the nut from the spring rear attaching bolt. Drive the bolt out of the spring and shackle with a drift.

To install the rear spring:

8. Position the shackle (closed section facing toward the front of the vehicle) to the spring rear eye and install the bolt and nut.

9. Position the spring front eye and bushing to the spring front hanger, and install the attaching bolt and nut.

10. Position the spring rear eye and bushing to the shackle, and install the attaching bolt and nut.

11. Raise the axle to the spring and install the U-bolts and spring clip plate.

12. Torque the U-bolt nuts and spring front and rear attaching bolt nuts to 45–60 ft. lbs.

13. Remove the jackstands and lower the vehicle.

NOTE: Squeaky rear springs can be corrected by tightening the front and rear eye bolts to 150–204 ft. lbs., then raising and supporting the rear of the vehicle so that the rear springs hang, spreading the leaves. Apply a silicone based lubricant for a distance of three inches in from each leaf tip.

E-100, E-150, and E-200

1. Raise the rear of the vehicle and support the chassis with jackstands. Support the rear axle with a floor jack or hoist.

2. Disconnect the lower end of the shock absorber from the bracket on the axle housing.

3. Remove the two U-bolts and plate.

4. Lower the axle and remove the upper and lower rear shackle bolts.

5. Pull the rear shackle assembly and rubber bushings from the bracket and spring.

6. Remove the nut and mounting bolt which secure the front end of the spring. Remove the spring assembly from the front shackle bracket.

7. Install new rubber bushings in the rear shackle bracket and in the rear eye of the replacement spring.

8. Assemble the front eye of the spring to the front shackle bracket with the front mounting bolt and nut. Do not tighten the nut.

9. Mount the rear end of the spring with the upper bolt of the rear shackle assembly passing through the eye of the spring. Insert the lower bolt through the rear spring hanger.

10. Assemble the spring center bolt in the pilot hole in the axle and install the plate. Install the U-bolts through the plate.

Rear spring installation, F-250 4WD

Do not tighten the attaching nuts at this time.

11. Raise the axle with a floor jack or hoist until the vehicle is free of the jack-stands. Connect the lower end of the shock absorber to the bracket on the axle housing.

12. Tighten the spring front mounting bolt and nut, the rear shackle nuts and the U-bolt nuts.

13. Remove the jackstands and lower the vehicle.

E-250, E-300, and E-350

1. Raise the rear of the vehicle and support the chassis with jackstands. Support the rear axle with a floor jack or hoist.

2. Disconnect the lower end of the shock absorber from the bracket on the axle housing.

3. Remove the two spring U-bolts and the spring cap.

4. Lower the axle and remove the spring front bolt from the hanger.

5. Remove the two attaching bolts from the rear of the spring. Remove the spring and shackle.

6. Assemble the upper end of the shackle to the spring with the attaching bolt.

7. Connect the front of the spring to the front bracket with the attaching bolt.

8. Assemble the spring and shackle to the rear bracket with the attaching bolt.

9. Place the spring plate over the head of the center bolt.

10. Raise the axle with a jack. Install the center bolt through the pilot hole in the pad on the axle housing.

11. Install the spring U-bolts, cap and attaching nuts. Tighten the nuts snugly.

12. Connect the lower end of the shock absorber to the lower bracket.

13. Tighten the spring front mounting bolt and nut, the rear shackle nuts and the

Rear spring installation, E-100, 150 and 200

Rear spring installation, E-250, 300 and 350

spring U-bolt nuts.

14. Remove the jackstands and lower the vehicle.

Shock Absorbers

REMOVAL & INSTALLATION

1. Raise the vehicle and place jackstands under the frame.

2. Remove the shock absorber-to-upper bracket attaching nut and washers, and bushing from the shock absorber rod or if mounted with nut and bolt, remove as lower.

3. Remove the shock absorber-to-axle attaching bolt. Drive the bolts from the axle bracket and shock absorber with a brass drift and remove the shock absorber.

4. Position the washers and bushing on the shock absorber rod and position the shock absorber at the upper bracket.

5. Position the bushing and washers on the shock absorber rod and install the attaching nut loosely.

6. Position the shock absorber at the axle housing bracket and install the attaching bolt and nut. Tighten the lower nut to 40–60 ft. lbs. and the upper nut to 15–25 ft. lbs. If attached at top with similar mounting, torque is same.

FRONT END ALIGNMENT

Caster

1977 F-250 (4WD)

The caster angle is controlled by the angle of the front spring pads. The caster angle can be adjusted by installing tapered wedges between the springs and the spring pads. Only one wedge per side should be used.

1977 All Models Exc. F-250 (4WD)
1978 and Later All Models

The caster angles are designed into the front axle and cannot be adjusted.

CAMBER

The camber angles are designed into the front axle and cannot be adjusted except on 1983 and later 2WD vehicles.

1983 and Later—2WD

Camber is adjusted by replacing the camber adapter on the upper ball joint stud. Adapters are available in 0°, ½°, 1° and 1-½° increments.

If camber needs adjustment, replace the camber adapter as described in this Section under camber adapter—Removal and Installation. On the right spindle, the slot in the camber adapter must point forward for a positive camber change and rearward for a negative camber change. On the left spindle, the slot in the adapter must point rearward for a positive camber change and forward for a negative camber change.

TOE-IN ADJUSTMENT

All Models

Toe-in can be measured by either a front end alignment machine or by the following method:

With the front wheels in the straight-ahead position, measure the distance between the extreme front and the extreme rear of the front wheels. In other words, measure the distance across the undercarriage of the vehicle between the two front edges and the two rear edges of the two front wheels. Both of these measurements (front and rear of the two wheels) must be taken at an equal distance from the floor and at the approximate centerline of the spindle. The difference between these two distances is the amount that the wheels toe-in or toe-out. The wheels should always be adjusted to toe-in according to specifications.

1. Loosen the clamp bolts at each end of the left tie-rod, seen from the front of the vehicle. Rotate the connecting rod tube until the correct toe-in is obtained, then tighten the clamp bolts.

2. Recheck the toe-in to make sure that no changes occurred when the bolts were tightened.

NOTE: The clamps should be positioned ³⁄₁₆ in. fron the end of the rod with the clamp bolts in a vertical position in front of the tube, with the nut down.

STEERING

Steering Wheel

REMOVAL & INSTALLATION

1977–82

1. Disconnect the battery ground and mark the steering wheel-to-column alignment.

2. Remove one screw from the underside of each spoke and lift the horn assembly from the wheel. On vehicles with a sport wheel option, pry or unscrew (try unscrewing first) the button cover off with a screwdriver.

3. Disconnect the horn switch wires by pulling the spade terminal from the blade connector. Squeeze or pinch the J-clip ground wire terminal fully and pull it out of the hole in the steering wheel. Do not pull the ground terminal out of the threaded hole without squeezing the clip to remove the spring tension.

4. Remove the horn switch assembly.

5. Remove the steering wheel retaining nut.

6. Using a steering wheel puller, remove the wheel.

To install:

7. Position the steering wheel in alignment with the marks.

8. Tighten the retaining nut to 50 ft. lbs.

9. Connect the wires, install the horn assembly and connect the battery ground.

Turn Signal Switch

REPLACEMENT

1977

1. Disconnect the horn and turn signal wires at the connectors located behind the

1978 and later turn signal switch wiring connector

1978 and later turn signal switch terminal removal

instrument panel. Remove the steering column wires and terminals from the connectors by inserting a small screwdriver or similar tool in the opposite end from which the wire is inserted and depress the tang on the wire. The wire can then be removed from the connector.

NOTE: Be sure to record the color code and location of each wire before removing it from the connector plug. Tape a pull-through wire or cord to one of the wire ends.

2. Remove the steering wheel.
3. Turn the signal switch lever counterclockwise to remove it. Remove the screws and retainer which hold the turn signal switch and wire assembly to the steering column, and pull the assembly from the column. Disconnect the pull-through wire or cord from the end of the wire to which it was taped.
To install the switch:
4. Tape the loose ends of the new turn signal switch wires to the pull-through wire or cord. Carefully pull the wires through the steering column, while guiding the turn signal switch into position. Install the switch retainer screws.
5. Assemble the rest of the steering column in the reverse order of disassembly.

From 1978 Except Ranger and Bronco II

1. Disconnect the battery ground cable.
2. Remove the horn switch.
3. Remove the steering wheel retaining nut and using tool 3600AA or equivalent, remove the steering wheel from the shaft.
4. Remove the turn signal switch lever by unscrewing it from the steering column.
5. Disconnect the turn indicator switch wiring connector plug by lifting up on the tabs and separating and remove the screws that secure the switch assembly to the column.
6. Remove the wires and terminals from the steering column wiring connector plug. Record the color code and location of each

wire before removing it from the connector plug.
7. Connect pull through wire to end of wiring harness with tape.
8. Remove the protective wire cover from the wiring harness and remove the switch and wires through the top of the column.
9. Tape the loose ends of the new turn signal switch wires to the pull-through wire or cord. Carefully pull the wires through the steering column while guiding the turn signal switch into position.
10. Install switch assembly retaining screws to column.
11. Install wires into steering column wire connector terminal and connect terminals.
12. Install turn signal lever. Hand-tighten the lever (on flat side) to 10–20 in. lbs. Test turn signal operation, hazard signal operation and PRND21 dial-lamp (if so equipped).
13. Install steering wheel.
14. Install horn switch.
15. Connect battery ground cable.

RANGER AND BRONCO II

1. For tilt column only, remove upper extension shroud by squeezing it at the six and twelve o'clock positions and popping it free of the retaining plate at the three o'clock position.
2. On standard and tilt, remove the two trim shroud halves by removing the two attaching screws.
3. Remove the turn signal switch lever by grasping the lever and by using a pulling and twisting motion of the hand while pulling the lever straight out from the switch.
4. Peel back the foam sight shield from the turn signal switch.
5. Disconnect the two turn signal switch electrical connectors.
6. Remove the two self-tapping screws attaching the turn signal switch to the lock cylinder housing. Disengage the switch from the housing.
7. Align the turn signal switch mounting holes with the corresponding holes in

the lock cylinder housing, and install two self-tapping screws 18–26 in-lbs.
8. Stick the foam sight shield to the turn signal switch. Install the turn signal switch lever into the switch manually, by aligning the key on the lever with the keyway in the switch and by pushing the lever toward the switch to full engagement.
9. Install the two turn signal switch electrical connectors to full engagement.
10. Install the steering column trim shrouds.

Power Steering Pump

REMOVAL & INSTALLATION
Except CII Pump

1. Disconnect the pressure and return lines from the pump and plug them to prevent loss of fluid or entrance of dirt into the system.
2. Loosen the belt tension adjusting bolt all the way.
3. Remove the bolts attaching the pump mounting bracket to the air conditioning bracket (if equipped).
4. Remove the pump, mounting bracket, and pulley assembly.
5. Install the pump, bracket and pulley assembly and loosely attach the bolts that secure the pump mounting bracket to the air conditioning bracket (if equipped).
6. Install the drive belts on the pulley.
7. Loosely install the belt tension adjusting nut.
8. Pry between the pump adjustment bracket and the engine block until correct tension is achieved. While still holding this tension, tighten the adjusting bolt.
9. Tighten all attaching bolts.
10. Connect the pressure and return lines to the pump.
11. Fill the reservoir with power steering fluid. Bleed the air from the sytem by turning the steering wheel from left to right several times. Inspect for leaks.

Quick Connect Power Steering Fitting Service

The quick connect power steering fitting, under certain conditions may leak and/or result in improper engagement. The leak can be caused by a cut O-ring, imperfections in the outlet fitting inside diameter, or improperly machined O-ring groove. Improper engagement can be caused by an improperly machined tube end, tube nut, snap ring, outlet fitting, or gear port.

If a leak occurs, the O-ring should be replaced with quick connect O-rings (⅜ tube end: 388749-S; ⁵⁄₁₆ tube end: 388748-S). The O-rings that are used on the tube-O power steering fitting should not be used on the quick connect fitting because of dimensional and material changes. If O-ring replacement does not solve the leak problem, outlet fitting replacement and, lastly, hose replacement should be made.

If improper engagement occurs due to a missing or bent snap ring, or improperly machined tube nut, it may be repaired with a service snap ring kit (kit includes a new tube nut). The system should then be properly filled, the engine started, and the steering wheel cycled from lock-to-lock to test for positive engagement. If the hose assembly still does not engage, replace the entire hose assembly.

Quick connect hose assemblies for service have tube nuts, snap rings, and O-rings already attached.

When the quick connect tube nut is tightened or loosened, a tube nut wrench, not an open end wrench, is recommended. An open end wrench may result in tube nut deformation under excessive torque conditions. Care must be taken not to overtighten the tube nut. Tighten to 10–15 ft-lbs. Swivel and/or end play of the quick connect fittings is normal, and does not indicate an undertightened fitting.

CII Pump

NOTE: The CII pump is equipped with a fiberglas reservoir and can be identified by the reservoir. Never pry against the fiberglas, as damage will occur.

NOTE: The 3.8L V-6 with a serpentine belt driving the power steering pump uses a separate idler pulley on a slider-type bracket for belt tension adjustment. To adjust or remove the belt tension, loosen the bolts in the slider slots and tighten the adjusting belt as required to obtain the correct belt tension.

1. To remove the power steering fluid from the pump reservoir, disconnect the fluid return hose at the reservoir and drain the fluid into a container. Remove the pressure hose from the pump.

2. Remove the bolts from the pump adjustment bracket. Loosen the pump sufficiently to remove the belt off the pulley. Remove the pump (still attached to the adjustment bracket) from the support bracket.

3. Remove the pulley from the pump if required.

4. Remove the bolts attaching the adjustment bracket to the pump and remove the pump.

5. Place the adjustment bracket on the pump. Install and tighten the bolts to specification listed at the end of this Section.

6. Install the pulley on the pump if removed.

7. Place the pump with adjustment bracket and pulley on the support bracket. Install the bolts connecting the support bracket to the adjustment bracket.

8. Place the belt on the pulley and adjust belt tension. Tighten bolts on adjustment bracket.

9. Install the pressure hose to the pump fitting.

10. Connect the return hose to the pump, and tighten the clamp.

11. Fill the reservoir with specified power steering fluid, start the engine and turn the steering wheel from stop to stop to remove air from the system.

11. Check for leaks and recheck the fluid level. Add fluid if necessary.

Manual Steering Gear

REMOVAL & INSTALLATION

1977–79

1. Raise the vehicle on a hoist and remove the Pitman arm attaching nut and lockwasher.

2. Remove the Pitman arm from the sector shaft using tool T64P-3590-F.

3. Remove bolts, nuts and flat washers that attach the steering gear to the frame side rail, and lower the vehicle.

4. Remove the flex coupling bolt and nut from the coupling clamp. Loosen the clamp from the coupling at the end of the steering column and separate the coupling from the steering gear input shaft by pushing the steering shaft toward the steering column. Discard the clamp, bolt, and nut.

5. Remove and discard the flex coupling clamp from the steering gear input shaft, and remove the steering gear from the frame side rail.

6. Place the steering gear on the frame side rail and install the attaching bolts, nuts, and flat washers.

7. Place the flex coupling and a new clamp on the steering gear input shaft and install the clamp bolt and nut. Tighten the bolt and nut to 28–35 ft. lbs.

8. Install a new steering shaft clamp at the end of the steering column and tighten the bolt and nut to 20–30 ft. lbs.

9. Raise the vehicle and tighten the steering gear attaching bolts and nuts to 60–80 ft. lbs.

10. Place the Pitman arm on the sector shaft and install the washer and attaching nut. Tighten the nut to 170–230 ft. lbs. lower the vehicle, and fill the gear with lubricant SAE-90EP oil.

From 1980

1. Raise the vehicle on a hoist.

Typical steering gear installation-from 1980

Typical steering gear installation-thru 1979

2. Disconnect the flex coupling from the steering shaft flange by removing the two attaching nuts.

3. Disconnect the drag link from the sector shaft (Pitman) arm, using a suitable puller.

4. Remove the Pitman arm-to-sector shaft attaching nut and washer. Remove the Pitman arm from the gear sector shaft using a suitable puller. (Do not hammer on end of sector shaft.)

5. While supporting the steering gear, remove the bolts and washers that attach the steering gear assembly to the frame side rail. Lower the steering gear assembly from the vehicle.

6. Remove the coupling to gear attaching bolt from the lower half of the flex coupling and remove the coupling from the steering gear assembly.

7. Install the flex coupling on the worm (input) shaft of the gear assembly. Install a new coupling-to-gear attaching bolt and tighten to 11–21 ft. lbs.

8. Center the input shaft (the center position is approximately three turns from either stop).

9. Position the steering gear assembly so that the stud bolts on the flex coupling enter the bolt holes in the steering shaft flange, and the holes in the mounting bosses of the gear match the bolt holes in the frame side rail.

10. While supporting the gear in proper position, install the gear-to-frame side rail attaching bolts and washers and tighten to 70 ft. lbs.

If new gear-to-frame bolts and washers are required, use only Grade 9 bolts.

11. Connect the drag link to the Pitman arm, install the drag link ball stud nut, and tighten to 50–75 ft. lbs. Then install the cotter pin.

12. Assemble the Pitman arm on the sector shaft pointing downward. Install the attaching nut and washer, and tighten to 170–230 ft. lbs.

13. Secure the flex coupling to the steering shaft flange with the two attaching nuts and tighten to 28–35 ft. lbs.

ADJUSTMENTS

1. Be sure that the steering column is properly aligned and is not causing excessive turning effort.

2. The steering gear must be removed from the truck.

3. Be sure that the ball nut assembly and the sector gear are properly adjusted as follows to maintain minimum steering shaft endplay and backlash between the sector gear and ball nut (preload adjustment). Make sure sector shaft cover bolts are torqued to 30 ft. lbs., or 40 ft. lbs. on Ranger and Bronco II.

4. Loosen the sector shaft adjusting screw locknut and tighten worm bearing adjuster screw until all end-play is removed.

5. Measure the worm bearing preload by attaching an in. lbs. torque wrench to the input shaft. Measure the torque required to rotate the input shaft all the way to the right and then turn back about one half turn. The worm bearing preload should be 10–16 in. lbs., 9–10 in. lbs. for Ranger and Bronco II.

6. Turn the sector shaft adjusting screw clockwise until the specified pull is obtained to rotate the worm past its center.

With the steering gear in the center position, hold the sector shaft to prevent rotation and check the lash between the ball nuts, balls and worm shaft by applying a 15 in. lbs. torque on the steering gear input shaft, in both right and left turn directions. Total travel of the wrench should not exceed 1¼ in. when applying a 15 in. lbs. torque on the steering shaft.

7. Tighten the sector shaft adjusting screw locknut, and recheck the backlash adjustment.

Power Steering Gear

REMOVAL & INSTALLATION

1977

When servicing the steering gear, label hoses before disconnecting them so they can be easily identified for reassembly.

Service the steering gear as follows:

1. Position a drain pan under the steering gear. Disconnect the pressure and the return lines from the steering gear and plug the lines and ports in the gear to prevent entry of dirt.

2. Raise the vehicle on a hoist and remove the Pitman arm attaching nut and lock washer.

3. Remove the Pitman arm from the sector shaft using tool T64P-3590-F.

4. Remove the bolts and nuts that attach the steering gear to the frame side rail. Lower the vehicle.

5. Remove the pinch bolt from the flange and insulator assembly.

6. Loosen the nut holding the horn and turn the horn outward.

7. Remove the steering gear attaching bolts and remove the steering gear, shaft, and joint assemblies as a unit.

8. Remove the pinch bolt and nut from the shaft and joint assembly.

9. Remove the shaft and joint assembly from the steering gear.

10. Before installing the gear in the vehicle, attach the shaft and joint assembly to the steering gear. Install the pinch bolt and torque the nut to 45 to 60 ft. lbs.

11. Raise the vehicle on a hoist. Place the steering gear on the frame side rail and loosely attach the forward attaching bolt and nut.

12. Center the steering gear input shaft.

13. Insert the shaft end of the shaft and joint assembly into the flange and insulator assembly while supporting the rear of the steering gear.

14. Install the remaining steering gear attaching bolts through the steering gear flange, through the frame side rail.

15. Install the remaining steering gear attaching nuts and torque all three attaching nuts to 52 to 90 ft. lbs.

16. Make sure the wheels are in the straight ahead position and install the Pitman arm, lock washer and nut. Torque the nut to 170–230 ft. lbs. Lower the vehicle.

17. Install the pinch bolt in the flange and insulator assembly, and torque to 28 to 35 ft. lbs.

18. Remove the plugs from the pressure and return lines and ports to the steering

Power steering gear installation-thru 1979

gear. Connect the lines to gear and torque to 16 to 25 ft. lbs.

19. Turn the horn inward and tighten the retaining nut. Disconnect the coil wire. Fill the power steering pump reservoir. Turn on the ignition and turn the steering wheel to distribute the fluid. Check the fluid level and add fluid, if necessary. Connect the coil wire, start the engine and turn the steering wheel from side to side. Check for fluid leaks.

From 1978

Service the steering gear as follows:

1. Disconnect the pressure and return lines from the steering gear. Plug the lines and the ports in the gear to prevent entry of dirt. Disconnect brake lines from the steering gear bracket.

2. Remove the bolts that secure the flex coupling to the steering gear and to the column steering shaft assembly.

3. Raise the vehicle and remove the Pitman arm attaching nut, and washer.

4. Remove the Pitman arm from the sector shaft using tool T64P-3590-F. Remove the tool from the Pitman arm. Do not damage the seals.

5. On vehicles with standard transmission remove the clutch release lever retracting spring to provide clearance for removing the steering gear.

6. Support the steering gear, and remove the steering gear attaching bolts.

7. Work the steering gear free of the flex coupling. Remove the steering gear from the vehicle.

8. Slide the flex coupling into place on the steering shaft assembly. Turn the steering wheel so the spokes are in the horizontal position.

9. Center the steering gear input shaft.

10. Slide the steering gear input shaft into the flex coupling and into place on the frame side rail. Install the attaching bolts and tighten to 60–80 ft. lbs.

11. Be sure the wheels are in the straight ahead position, then install the Pitman arm on the sector shaft. Install the Pitman arm attaching washer and nut. Tighten nut to 170–230 ft. lbs.

12. Connect and tighten the pressure and the return lines to the steering gear. Reinstall the brake lines on the steering gear bracket.

13. Disconnect the coil wire. Fill the reservoir. Turn on the ignition and turn the steering wheel from left to right to distribute the fluid.

14. Re-check fluid level and add fluid, if necessary. Connect the coil wire, start the engine and turn the steering wheel from side to side. Inspect for fluid leaks.

ADJUSTMENTS

Steering Gear Meshload

1. Make sure that the steering column is correctly aligned.

2. Disconnect the steering linkage

from the Pitman arm on the steering gear. Remove the horn pad as explained under Steering Wheel Removal and Installation.

3. Disconnect the fluid reservoir return line and cap the reservoir return line tube. Place the end of the return line in a clean container and turn the steering wheel back and forth several times to empty the steering gear.

4. Turn the steering wheel nut with an inch pound torque wrench slowly. Find the torque required at ½ turn off right and left stops, ½ turn off center both right and left, and over-center (full turn). The over-center torque should be 4–6 in. lbs. more than the end readings, but the total over-center torque must not exceed 14 in. lbs.

5. To correct, back off the Pitman shaft adjuster all the way, then back in ½ turn. Recheck the over-center torque. Loosen the locknut and tighten the sector shaft adjusting screw until the over-center torque reads 4–6 in. lbs. higher, but doesn't exceed 14 in. lbs. Tighten the adjusting screw locknut and recheck.

6. Refill the system with the fluid specified. Bleed the system of air by turning the steering wheel all the way to the right and left several times with the engine warmed up. Do not hold the steering against the stops or pump damage will result.

Steering Linkage Connecting Rods

Replace the drag link if a ball stud is excessively loose or if the drag link is bent.

Do not attempt to straighten a drag link.

Replace the connecting rod if the ball stud is excessively loose, if the connecting rod is bent or if the threads are stripped. Do not attempt to straighten connecting rod. Always check to insure that the adjustment sleeve and clamp stops are correctly installed on the Bronco.

REMOVAL & INSTALLATION

Vans and 2-WD Pick-ups

Replace the drag link if a ball stud is excessively loose or if the drag link is bent. **Do not attempt to straighten a drag link.**

Replace the connecting rod if the ball stud is excessively loose, if the connecting rod is bent or if the threads are stripped. Do not attempt to straighten connecting rod.

After installing a connecting rod or adjusting toe-in check to insure that the adjustment sleeve clamps are correctly positioned on the F and E-100 and F and E-150 and to insure that the clamp stop is correctly installed on the F and E-250 and F and E-350.

1. Remove the cotter pins and nuts from the drag link, ball studs and from the right connecting rod ball stud.

2. Remove the right connecting rod ball stud from the drag link.

3. Remove the drag link ball studs from the spindle and the Pitman arm.

4. Position the new drag link, ball studs in the spindle, and Pitman arm and install nuts.

5. Position the right connecting rod ball stud in the drag link and install nut.

1978–79 Bronco steering linkage

1980 and later Bronco steering linkage

6. Tighten the nuts to 50–75 ft. lbs. and install the cotter pins.

7. Remove the cotter pin and nut from the connecting rod.

8. Remove the ball stud from the mating part.

9. Loosen the clamp bolt and turn the rod out of the adjustment sleeve. Count the number of turns for approximate position when installing.

10. Lubricate the threads of the new connecting rod, and turn it into the adjustment sleeve to about the same distance the old rods were installed. This will provide an approximate toe-in setting. Position the connecting rod ball studs in the spindle arms.

11. Install the nuts on to the connecting rod ball studs, tighten the nut to 50–75 ft. lbs. and install the cotter pin.

12. Check the toe-in and adjust, if necessary. After checking or adjusting toe-in, center the adjustment sleeve clamps between the locating nibs, position the clamps and tighten the nuts to 29–41 ft. lbs.

4-WD Pick-ups

1. Raise the vehicle and support on jackstands. Disconnect the drag link from the spindle connecting rod end.

2. Disconnect the right spindle connecting rod end from the right spindle arm.

3. Disconnect the left spindle connecting rod ends from the left spindle arm and remove the spindle connecting rod ends from the truck.

4. Place the connecting rod ends in a vise and loosen the connecting rod tube clamps.

5. Remove the short (right) rod end from the connecting rod tube and remove the tube from the long (left) connecting rod end.

6. Clean and oil the threads on all the parts to be reused.

7. Install the connecting rod tube and clamps on the left spindle connecting rod

end. Don't tighten the clamps yet.

8. Install the right connecting rod end in the tube and remove the assembly from the vise.

9. Install new dust seals on the left spindle connecting rod end and position the end on the left spindle arm.

10. Install the connecting rod end attaching nut, tighten it, and install the cotter pin.

11. Install new dust seals on the right spindle connecting rod end and position the end on the right spindle arm. Install the attaching nut, tighten it, and install the cotter pin.

12. Install new seals on the drag link ball stud and position the drag link on the spindle connecting rod end. Install the attaching nut, tighten it, and install the cotter pin.

13. Lubricate the spindle connecting rod ends and drag link.

14. Lower the vehicle and check and adjust the toe-in setting. Tighten the connecting rod clamps after adjusting the toe-in.

1977 Bronco

1. Raise vehicle and support on jackstands.

2. Disconnect connecting rod ends from spindles.

3. Remove U-bolts securing left connecting rod to brace.

4. Disconnect right connecting rod end from steering arm.

5. Mount the assembly in a vise and disconnect the right and left rod assemblies.

6. Mark the position of the clamp on the left connecting halves.

7. Clean and oil all threaded parts.

8. Assemble left connecting rod halves in clamp at about the same position marked.

9. Attach right and left connecting rods, but do not tighten nut.

10. Attach connecting rods to the spindles. Torque the nuts to 40 ft. lbs.

11. Check and adjust toe-in by turning the left connecting rod halves. Tighten clamp bolts.

12. Attach the left connecting rod to the brace by tightening the two U-bolts evenly to 20 ft. lbs.

1978–79 Bronco

1. Remove the cotter pins and nuts from

1977 Bronco steering linkage

the drag link, ball studs and from the right connecting rod ball stud.

2. Remove the right connecting rod ball stud from the drag link.

3. Remove the drag link ball studs from the spindle and the Pitman arm.

4. Position the new drag link, ball studs in the spindle, and Pitman arm and install nuts.

5. Position the right connecting rod ball stud in the drag link and install nut.

6. Tighten the nuts as follows and install the cotter pins: Drag link studs, 50–75 ft. lbs. Ball studs, 50–60 ft. lbs. Connecting rod studs, 35–45 ft. lbs.

7. Remove the cotter pin and nut from the connecting rod.

8. Remove the ball stud from the mating part.

9. Loosen the clamp bolt and turn the rod out of the adjustment sleeve.

10. Lubricate the threads of the new connecting rod, and turn it into the adjustment sleeve to about the same distance the old rods were installed. This will provide an approximate toe-in setting. Position the connecting rod ball studs in the spindle arms.

11. Install the nuts on to the connecting rod ball studs, tighten the nut to specification and install the cotter pins.

12. Check the toe-in and adjust, if necessary. After checking or adjusting toe-in, center the adjustment sleeve clamps between the locating nibbs, position the clamps and tighten the nuts to 35–45 ft. lbs.

1980 and Later Bronco

1. Remove the cotter pins and nuts from the drag link, ball studs and from the right connecting rod ball studs.

2. Remove the right connecting rod ball stud from the right spindle assembly and Pitman arm.

3. Remove the drag link ball studs from the spindle and the connecting rod assembly.

4. Loosen the clamp bolt and turn the rod out of the adjustment sleeve.

5. Lubricate the threads of the new connecting rod, and turn it into the adjustment sleeve to about the same distance the old rods were installed. This will provide an approximate toe-in setting. Position the connecting rod ball studs in the spindle arms.

6. Position the new drag link, ball studs in the spindle, and connecting rod assembly and install nuts.

7. Position the right connecting rod ball stud in the drag link and install nut.

8. Tighten all the nuts to 50–75 ft. lbs. and install the cotter pins.

9. Remove the cotter pin and nut from the left connecting rod.

10. Install the nuts on the connecting rod ball studs, tighten the nut to 50–75 ft. lbs. and install the cotter pin.

11. Check the toe-in and adjust, if necessary. After checking or adjusting toe-in, center the adjustment sleeve clamps between the locating nibbs, position the clamps and tighten the nuts to 29–41 ft. lbs.

BRAKES

NOTE: Refer to the Brake Unit Repair Section for servicing procedures

ADJUSTMENT

The drum brakes are self-adjusting and require a manual adjustment only after the brake shoes have been relined, replaced, or when the length of the adjusting screw has been changed while performing some other service operation, as i.e., taking off the self-adjusters and putting on manual ones.

To adjust the brakes, follow the procedure given below:

1. Raise the vehicle and support it with safety stands.

2. Remove the rubber plug from the adjusting slot on the backing plate.

3. Insert a brake adjusting spoon into the slot and engage the lowest possible tooth on the starwheel. Move the end of the brake spoon downward to move the starwheel upward and expand the adjusting screw. Repeat this operation until the brakes lock the wheel.

NOTE: Step 4 applies only to vehicles equipped with self-adjusters.

4. Insert a small screwdriver or piece of firm wire (coathanger wire) into the adjusting slot and push the automatic adjusting lever out and free of the starwheel on the adjusting screw and hold it there.

5. Engage the topmost tooth possible on the starwheel with the brake adjusting spoon. Move the end of the adjusting spoon upward to move the adjusting screw starwheel downward and contract the adjusting screw. Back off the adjusting screw starwheel until the wheel spins freely with a minimum of drag. Keep track of the number of turns that the starwheel is backed off, or the number of strokes taken with the brake adjusting spoon.

6. Repeat this operation for the other side. When backing off the brakes on the other side, the starwheel adjuster must be backed off the same number of turns to prevent side-to-side brake pull.

7. Repeat this operation on the other set of brakes (front or rear).

8. When all 4 brakes are adjusted, on vehicles equipped with self-adjusting brakes, make several stops while backing the vehicle, to equalize the brakes at all of the wheels. On vehicles not equipped with self-adjusters, make a few low-speed stops while going forward to check for brake pull. If the front end of the car has a tendency to pull to one side when the brakes are applied, back off the adjustment of the brake assembly on the side the vehicle pulls to.

9. Remove the safety stands and lower the vehicle. Road test the vehicle.

NOTE: Disc brakes are not adjustable.

Brake Drums

REMOVAL & INSTALLATION

Front—1977 Bronco

1. Raise the vehicle and install jackstands.

2. Back off the brake shoe adjustment. Remove the hub dust cap. Remove the hub retaining snap-ring, and slide the splined driving hub from between the axle shaft and the wheel hub. Remove the driving hub spacer and spring.

3. Remove the locknut, nut lock, and the wheel bearing adjusting nut from the spindle. Remove the wheel, hub and drum as an assembly. The wheel outer bearing will be forced off the spindle at the same time, so be prepared to catch it to prevent it from becoming dirty. Remove the wheel inner bearing cone.

NOTE: If the Bronco is equipped with locking-type hubs, refer to "Front Hub Assembly—Wheel Bearings" for the removal and installation procedure.

4. Remove the front wheel-to-hub retaining nuts. Remove the wheel and tire from the hub and drum.

5. Remove the brake drum retaining bolts and nuts.

6. Remove the brake drum from the hub.

To install the brake drum on the vehicle:

7. Place the brake drum to the hub and install the retaining bolts and nuts.

8. Install the wheel and tire to the hub and start the retaining nuts.

9. Install the wheel hub and drum assembly on the spindle. Install the driving hub spacer and then the wheel outer bearing cone and the adjusting nut with the dowel outboard.

10. Rotate the wheel in either direction and, at the same time, tighten the inner locknut to 50 ft. lbs. with a torque wrench.

11. Adjust the front wheel bearings.

12. Slide the driving hub onto the axle shaft and install the snap-ring.

13. Adjust the brake and then tighten the wheel nuts.

14. Install the hub dust cap.

15. Remove the jackstands and lower the vehicle.

CHASSIS ELECTRICAL

NOTE: Always disconnect the battery ground cable before working on electrical equipment.

Blower Motor
REMOVAL & INSTALLATION

Vans, w/o Air Conditioning

1. Disconnect the orange (orange with

FORD

VIEW A
INSTRUMENT PANEL

DEFROSTER NOZZLE ASSEMBLY — SEE VIEW A — SCREW (6 REQD.) — CONNECTOR (SEAL)

DEFROSTER NOZZLE

HEATER REGISTER — HEATER ASSEMBLY — SCREW (5 REQD.) — AIR INLET DUCT

Heater installation-thru 1979

SEE VIEW-A — SEE VIEW-A

SCREW (TORQUE TO 13-20 IN. LBS.) 55923-S2

PART OF DASH PANEL

PART OF WIRING ASSY 14401

DEFROSTER DUCT ASSY 18490

VIEW -A

CLIP

PART OF WIRING ASSY 19A885

VIEW -B

PART OF WIRING ASSY 14401

PART OF WIRING ASSY 19A885

BLOWER MOTOR RESISTOR

DEFROSTER DUCT ASSY 18490

VACUUM HARNESS 19D699

SCREW 42134-S2 (TIGHTEN TO 30-35 IN. LBS.)

SEE VIEW-B

YELLOW VACUUM HOSE

RED VACUUM HOSE

PLENUM CHAMBER

BLUE VACUUM HOSE

ORANGE VACUUM HOSE

1978–79 plenum chamber and nozzle

black strips) motor lead wire. Remove the ground wire screw from the firewall.

2. Disconnect the blower motor cooling tube.

3. Remove the four mounting plate screws and the motor assembly.

4. Reverse the procedure for installation.

Vans, w/Air Conditioning

1. Disconnect the resistor electrical leads on the front of the blower cover inside the truck.

2. Remove the blower cover.

3. Push the wiring grommet forward out of the housing hole.

4. Remove the blower motor mounting plate. Remove the blower motor.

5. Reverse the procedure for installation.

1977 Bronco

1. Disconnect the electrical connectors and the ground wire from the top of the heater.

2. Remove the screws retaining the motor to the plenum chamber and remove the motor assembly.

3. Loosen the blower wheel allen screw and remove the wheel.

4. Remove the motor from the mounting plate.

5. Install the motor to the mounting plate.

6. Install the blower wheel.

7. Position the motor to the plenum chamber. Install the retaining screws.

8. Connect the electrical lead and the ground wire.

9. Check the operation of the blower motor.

1978–79 Bronco and 1977–79 Pick-ups, Standard Heater, Without Air Conditioning

1. Disconnect the temperature and function control Bowden cables from the

heater housing. This must be done to prevent damage to the cables.

2. Disconnect the wires from the blower resistor.

3. Remove five screws attaching the air inlet (vent) duct to the heater housing.

4. Disconnect the blower wires.

5. Drain the radiator and remove the heater hoses from the heater core.

6. Remove three heater stud retaining nuts and remove heater.

7. Remove gasket between the heater hose ends and the dash panel at core tubes.

8. Remove two screws and two nuts attaching blower to heater.

9. Remove blower fan from motor shaft, and remove motor from mounting plate.

10. Install new motor on mounting plate and install blower fan on motor shaft.

11. Install blower and motor in heater.

12. Position heater assembly in vehicle and install three stud retaining nuts.

13. Connect heater hoses to heater core and fill radiator.

14. Connect blower motor wires.

15. Place defroster nozzle on heater so that the defroster and heater openings are in the up position and there is no air leak around the seal.

16. Install air inlet (vent) duct to heater. Push duct firmly against seal on side cowl and tighten five attaching screws.

17. Connect wires to blower motor resistor.

18. Connect temperature and function control cables to heater, and adjust the cables.

19. Re-install gasket between the heater hose ends and the dash panel at core ends.

20. Fill cooling system.

1978–79 Bronco and 1977–79 Pick-ups, Deluxe Hi-Lo Heater, Without Air Conditioning

1. Disconnect the battery cable, remove the carburetor air cleaner and partially drain the coolant system.

2. Remove the heater hoses from the heater core.

3. Remove the glove box liner and remove the register duct by pulling from the instrument panel register and releasing the clip at the plenum.

4. Disconnect the right cowl outside air inlet vacuum hose from the outside-recirculating door vacuum motor.

5. Remove the rear housing from under the instrument panel. Remove the outside air inlet duct from the rear housing (4 nuts and 1 bolt) and install one upper nut to retain heater housing-to-dash after rear housing is removed.

6. Remove two screws retaining plenum-to-dash (above transmission tunnel) and two screws to heater housing and remove the plenum.

7. Install a piece of protective tape on "A" pillar inner cowl panel, at lower right corner of instrument panel.

8. Remove the lower right instrument panel-to-"A" pillar bolt and lower the center instrument panel brace, bolt and nut.

1978–79 evaporator rear housing

Typical heater case and plenum-from 1980

9. Position the instrument panel rearward and install the "A" pillar bolt to hold the panel in the rearward position.

10. Remove the heater core (3 screws retaining 2 plates).

11. Remove the temperature blend door (snaps off).

12. Remove the temperature blend door arm support (2 screws) and pivot arm retainer (1 screw).

13. Remove blower motor (2 screws) and remove blower wheel.

14. Transfer blower to blower motor and panel assembly.

15. Install door arm pivot retainer (1 screw) and door arm support (2 screws).

16. Install the temperature blend door (snaps on).

17. Install heater core.

18. Install the plenum (4 screws).

19. Connect blower wires.

20. Remove heater housing upper retaining nut and install the heater outlet (4

nuts and 1 bolt). Position the air inlet duct.

21. Connect the white vacuum hose to the outside-recirculating door vacuum motor.

22. Reposition the instrument panel, install the retaining bolts and remove the protective tape at the "A" pillar inner cowl panel, lower right corner of instrument panel.

23. Install the right register duct assembly and install the glove box liner.

24. Connect heater hoses to the heater core assembly.

25. Fill cooling system, install the air cleaner and connect the battery cable to the battery.

26. Check blower motor operation.

1978–79 Bronco and 1977–79 Pick-ups With Air Conditioning
REMOVAL (WITHOUT DISCHARGING THE A/C SYSTEM)

1. Disconnect the battery cable, remove the carburetor air cleaner and par-

tially drain the coolant system.

2. Remove the heater hoses from the heater core.

3. From under the hood, remove A/C hose support bracket from the cowl (one screw).

4. Remove the insulation tape from the expansion valve and sensing bulb. Then remove the cover plate and seal from the evaporator housing at the expansion valve (two screws).

5. Remove the glove box liner and remove the A/C duct by pulling from the instrument panel register and releasing the clip at the plenum.

6. Disconnect the right cowl fresh air inlet vacuum hose from the fresh air door vacuum motor.

7. Remove the evaporator rear housing from under the instrument panel. Then, remove the fresh air inlet tube from the evaporator rear housing (4 nuts and 1 bolt) and install one upper nut to retain evaporator housing-to-dash after rear housing is removed.

8. Disconnect wires from the de-icing switch and pull capillary tube out of evaporator core. Remove the de-icing switch mounting plate (four screws).

9. Remove two screws retaining plenum-to-dash (above transmission tunnel) and two screws to evaporator case and remove the plenum.

10. Install a piece of protective tape on "A" pillar inner cowl panel, at lower right corner of instrument panel.

11. Then, remove the lower right instrument panel-to-"A" pillar bolt and lower the center instrument panel brace, bolt and nut.

12. Position the instrument panel rearward and install the "A" pillar bolt to hold the panel in the rearward position.

13. Remove four evaporator retaining screws.

14. Position the evaporator away from the case and secure it rearward and upward. Remove evaporator sealing grommet.

15. Remove heater core (3 screws retaining 2 plates).

16. Remove A/C-heat door (snaps off).

17. Remove A/C-heat door arm support (2 screws) and pivot arm retainer (1 screw).

18. Remove blower motor (2 screws) and remove blower wheel.

INSTALLATION

1. Transfer blower wheel to blower motor and panel assembly.

2. Install door arm pivot retainer (1 screw) and door arm support (2 screws).

3. Install A/C-heat door (snaps on).

4. Install heater core.

5. Remove the retainer that held the evaporator away from the case, install evaporator and tube sealing grommet.

6. Install the plenum (4 screws).

7. Install the de-icing switch mounting plate, install de-icing switch capillary tube back into evaporator core and position blower wire grommet.

8. Connect blower and de-icing switch wires.

9. Remove upper evaporator case retaining nut and install the evaporator outlet (4 nuts and 1 bolt). Then, position the air inlet bellows.

10. Connect the right cowl fresh air inlet vacuum hose to the fresh air door vacuum motor.

11. Reposition the instrument panel, install the retaining bolts and remove the protective tape at the "A" pillar inner cowl panel, lower right corner of instrument panel.

12. Install the right A/C duct assembly and install the glove box liner.

13. Install seal and cover plate to the evaporator case at the expansion valve.

14. Install insulation tape over the expansion valve and sensing bulb.

15. Install the A/C hose support bracket-to-cowl.

16. Connect heater hoses to the heater core assembly.

17. Fill cooling system, install the carburetor air cleaner and connect the battery cable to the battery.

18. Check blower motor operation.

1980 and Later, Bronco and Pick-ups, Comfort Vent Heaters, Without Air Conditioning

1. Disconnect the motor wires at the hard shell connectors.

2. Disconnect the blower motor air cooling tube from the motor.

3. Remove four blower motor mounting plate attaching screws and remove the motor and wheel assembly from the blower housing.

4. Remove the hub clamp spring from the blower wheel hub and the retainer from the motor shaft. Then, remove the blower wheel from the motor shaft.

5. Position the blower wheel on the blower motor shaft. Then, install a new hub clamp spring on the blower hub as shown. The hub clamp spring is included with a new blower wheel but not with the blower motor.

6. Install a new flange gasket on the blower motor flange.

Typical blower motor and wheel with A/C-from 1980

7. Position the blower motor and wheel assembly in the blower housing and install the four attaching screws.

NOTE: The wire clamp should be installed under the screw closest to the resistor assembly.

8. Cement the blower motor air tube on the nipple of the blower housing with RTV silicone adhesive.

9. Connect the blower motor wires at the hard shell connectors.

10. Check the blower motor for proper operation.

1980 and Later Bronco and Pick-ups Standard & High Output Heaters, Without Air Conditioning

1. Disconnect the motor wire at the hard shell connector and the ground wire at the ground screw.

2. Remove four screws attaching the blower motor and wheel to the heater case.

3. Remove the blower motor and wheel from the heater case.

4. Remove the blower wheel hub clamp

spring and the tab lock washer from the motor shaft. Then, pull the blower wheel from the motor shaft.

5. Install the blower wheel on the blower motor shaft.

6. Install the hub clamp spring on the blower hub.

7. Position the blower motor and wheel to the heater case, and install the four attaching screws.

8. Connect the blower motor wires and check the blower motor for proper operation.

1980 and Later Bronco and Pick-ups With Air Conditioning
REMOVAL (WITHOUT DISCHARGING THE A/C SYSTEM)

1. Disconnect the motor wires at the hard shell connectors.

2. Disconnect the blower motor air cooling tube from the motor.

3. Remove four blower motor mounting plate attaching screws and remove the motor and wheel assembly from the blower housing.

4. Remove the hub clamp spring from the blower wheel hub and the retainer from the motor shaft. Then, remove the blower wheel from the motor shaft.

INSTALLATION

1. Position the blower wheel on the blower motor shaft to the dimension shown. Then, install a new hub clamp spring on the blower hub as shown. The hub clamp spring is included with a new blower wheel but not with the blower motor.

2. Install a new flange gasket on the blower motor flange.

3. Position the blower motor and wheel assembly in the blower housing and install the four attaching screws.

NOTE: The wire clamp should be installed under the screw closest to the resistor assembly.

Typical blower motor and wheel without A/C-from 1980

4. Cement the blower motor air tube on the nipple of the blower housing with RTV silicone adhesive.

5. Connect the blower motor wires at the hard shell connectors.

6. Check the blower motor for proper operation.

Ranger and Bronco II w/o A/C

1. Remove the nut from the bottom of the plenum assembly just to the right of the heater core access cover.

2. Open the hood and disconnect the electrical harness from the blower motor by pushing on the connector tab and pulling off the connector.

3. Remove the mounting bolt from the upper right side of firewall. Remove the mounting nuts from the heater case assembly.

4. Pull the blower motor assembly from the firewall case.

5. Install in the reverse order.

Ranger and Bronco II with A/C

1. Open the hood and disconnect the heater blower wiring harness from the blower by pushing down on the locking tab and pulling the connector from the motor.

2. Remove the emission control, if equipped, from the front of the blower case. Three bolts hold the "box" in position.

3. Disconnect the blower motor cooling tube. Remove the blower plate mounting screws and remove the blower motor from the case on the firewall.

4. Install in the reverse order.

Heater Core

REMOVAL & INSTALLATION

1977 Bronco

1. Drain the cooling system.

2. Disconnect the two heater hoses at the heater and remove the rubber pads from the core.

3. Remove the nuts and star washers retaining the heater assembly to the dash panel.

4. Disconnect the right and left defroster hoses at the plenum.

5. Disconnect the fresh air inlet at the cowl. Rest the heater on the floor.

6. Disconnect the heat/defrost door cable at the door crank arm.

7. Disconnect the outside air door cable at the crank arm.

8. Disconnect the electrical wires at the connector.

9. Remove the heater assembly from the vehicle.

10. Remove the screws retaining the rear cover. Remove the clip retaining the core in the case and remove the core.

11. Transfer the seals from the old heater core to the new heater core.

12. Position the core in the case. Install the retaining clip. Position the cover and install the retaining screws.

13. Position the heater assembly on the floor in the vehicle. Connect the wire connectors.

14. Connect and adjust the outside air door control cable.

15. Connect and adjust the heat/defrost door control cable.

16. Position the heater assembly to the dash and install the nuts and washers.

17. Position the heater core pads over the core and connect both hoses.

18. Connect the defroster hoses and fresh air intake.

19. Fill the cooling system with the proper coolant mixture.

20. Check the heater operation and check for leaks.

1978–79 A/C-heater control connections

Vans Without Air Conditioning

1. Drain the coolant; remove the battery.

2. Disconnect the resistor wiring harness and the orange blower motor lead. Remove the ground wire screw from the firewall.

3. Detach the heater hoses and the plastic hose retaining strap.

4. Remove the five mounting screws inside the truck.

5. Remove the heater assembly.

6. Cut the seal at the top and bottom edge of the core retainer. Remove the two screws and the retainer. Slide the core and seal out of the case.

7. Reverse the procedure for installation.

1977 Bronco heater

Vans With Air Conditioning

1. Disconnect the resistor electrical leads on the front of the blower cover inside the truck. Detach the vacuum line from the vacuum motor. Remove the blower cover.

2. Remove the nut and push washer from the air door shaft. Remove the control cable from the bracket and the air door shaft.

3. Remove the blower motor housing and the air door housing.

4. Drain the coolant and detach the heater hoses.

5. Remove the heater core retaining brackets. Remove the core and seal assembly.

6. Reverse the procedure for installation.

1978–79 Bronco and 1977–79 Pick-ups Without Air Conditioning

1. Disconnect the temperature and function control Bowden cables from the heater housing. This must be done to prevent damage to the cables.

2. Disconnect the wires from the blower resistor.

3. Remove five screws attaching the air inlet (vent) duct to the heater housing.

4. Disconnect the blower wires.

5. Drain the radiator and remove the heater hoses from the heater core.

6. Remove three heater stud retaining nuts and remove heater.

7. Remove gasket between the heater hose ends and the dash panel at core tubes.

8. Remove heater core cover and gasket (four screws).

9. Pull heater core and lower support from heater.

10. Install foam gaskets on heater core and install in heater assembly.

11. Install the core seal and cover plate.

12. Position heater assembly in vehicle and install three stud retaining nuts.

13. Connect heater hoses to heater core and fill radiator.

14. Connect blower motor wires.

15. Place defroster nozzle on heater so that the defroster and heater openings are in the up position and there is no air leak around the seal.

16. Install air inlet (vent) duct to heater. Push duct firmly against seal on side cowl and tighten five attaching screws.

17. Connect wires to blower motor resistor.

18. Connect temperature and function control cables to heater, and adjust the cables.

19. Re-install gasket between the heater hose ends and the dash panel at core ends.

20. Fill Cooling System.

1978–79 Bronco and 1977–79 Pick-Ups, Deluxe Hi-Lo Heater, Without Air Conditioning

1. Disconnect the battery cable, remove the carburetor air cleaner and partially drain the coolant system.

2. Remove the heater hoses from the heater core.

3. Remove the glove box liner and remove the register duct by pulling from the instrument panel register and releasing the clip at the plenum.

4. Disconnect the right cowl outside air inlet vacuum hose from the outside-recirculating door vacuum motor.

5. Remove the rear housing from under the instrument panel. Remove the outside air inlet duct from the rear housing (4 nuts and 1 bolt) and install one upper nut to retain heater housing-to-dash after rear housing is removed.

6. Remove two screws retaining plenum-to-dash (above transmission tunnel) and two screws to heater housing and remove the plenum.

7. Install a piece of protective tape on "A" pillar inner cowl panel, at lower right corner of instrument panel.

8. Remove the lower right instrument panel-to-"A" pillar bolt and lower the center instrument panel brace, bolt and nut.

9. Position the instrument panel rearward and install the "A" pillar bolt to hold the panel in the rearward position.

10. Remove heater core (3 screws retaining 2 plates).

11. Remove the temperature blend door (snaps off).

12. Remove the temperature blend door arm support (2 screws) and pivot arm retainer (1 screw).

13. Remove blower motor (2 screws) and remove blower wheel.

14. Transfer blower wheel to blower motor and panel assembly.

15. Install door arm pivot retainer (1 screw) and door arm support (2 screws).

16. Install the temperature blend door (snaps on).

17. Install heater core.

18. Install the plenum (4 screws).

19. Connect blower wires.

20. Remove heater housing upper retaining nut and install the heater outlet (4 nuts and 1 bolt). Position the air inlet duct.

21. Connect the white vacuum hose to the outside-recirculating door vacuum motor.

22. Reposition the instrument panel, install the retaining bolts and remove the protective tape at the "A" pillar inner cowl panel, lower right corner of instrument panel.

Typical comfort heater plenum-from 1980

23. Install the right register duct assembly and install the glove box liner.

24. Connect heater hoses to the heater core assembly.

25. Fill cooling system, install the air cleaner and connect the battery cable to the battery.

26. Check bower motor operation.

1978–79 Bronco and 1977–79 Pick-ups With Air Conditioning
REMOVAL (WITHOUT DISCHARGING A/C SYSTEM)

1. Disconnect the battery cable, remove the carburetor air cleaner and partially drain the coolant system.

2. Remove the heater hoses from the heater core.

3. From under the hood, remove A/C hose support bracket from the cowl (one screw).

4. Remove the insulation tape from the expansion valve and sensing bulb. Then remove the cover plate and seal from the evaporator housing at the expansion valve (two screws).

5. Remove the glove box liner and remove the A/C duct by pulling from the instrument panel register and releasing the clip at the plenum.

6. Disconnect the right cowl fresh air inlet vacuum hose from the fresh air door vacuum motor.

7. Remove the evaporator rear housing from under the instrument panel. Then, remove the fresh air inlet tube from the evaporator rear housing (4 nuts and 1 bolt) and install one upper nut to retain evaporator housing-to-dash after rear housing is removed.

8. Disconnect wires from the de-icing switch and pull capillary tube out of evaporator core. Remove the de-icing switch mounting plate (four screws).

9. Remove two screws retaining plenum-to-dash (above transmission tunnel) and two screws to evaporator case and remove the plenum.

10. Install a piece of protective tape on "A" pillar inner cowl panel, at lower right corner of instrument panel.

11. Then, remove the lower right instrument panel-to-"A" pillar bolt and lower the center instrument panel brace, bolt and nut.

12. Position the instrument panel and rearward and install the "A" pillar bolt to hold the panel in the rearward position.

13. Remove four evaporator retaining screws.

14. Position the evaporator away from the case and secure it rearward and upward. Remove evaporator sealing grommet.

15. Remove heater core (3 screws retaining 2 plates).

16. Remove A/C-heat door (snaps off).

17. Remove A/C-heat door arm support (2 screws) and pivot arm retainer (1 screw).

INSTALLATION

1. Install door arm pivot retainer (1 screw) and door arm support (2 screws).

2. Install A/C-heat door (snaps on).

3. Install heater core.

4. Remove the retainer that held the evaporator away from the case, install evaporator and tube sealing grommet.

5. Install the plenum (4 screws).

6. Install the de-icing switch mounting plate, install de-icing switch capillary tube back into evaporator core and position blower wire grommet.

7. Connect blower and de-icing switch wires.

8. Remove upper evaporator case retaining nut and install the evaporator outlet (4 nuts and 1 bolt). Then, position the air inlet bellows.

9. Connect the right cowl fresh air inlet vacuum hose to the fresh air door vacuum motor.

10. Reposition the instrument panel, install the retaining bolts and remove the protective tape at the "A" pillar inner cowl panel, lower right corner of instrument panel.

11. Install the right A/C duct assembly and install the glove box liner.

12. Install seal and cover plate to the evaporator case at the expansion valve.

13. Install insulation tape over the expansion valve and sensing bulb.

14. Install the A/C hose support bracket-to-cowl.

15. Connect heater hoses to the heater core assembly.

16. Fill cooling system, install the carburetor air cleaner and connect the battery cable to the battery.

17. Check blower motor operation.

1980 and Later Bronco and Pick-ups, Comfort Vent Heaters, Without Air Conditioning

1. Disconnect the heater hoses from the heater core tubes and plug the hoses with suitable ⅝ inch plugs.

2. Remove the glove compartment liner.

3. Remove two spring clips attaching the heater core cover to the plenum along the top edge of the heater core cover.

4. Remove eight screws attaching the heater core cover to the penum and remove the cover.

5. Remove the heater core from the plenum taking care not to spill coolant from the core.

6. Install the heater core in the planum.

7. Install the heater core cover (eight (8) screws and two spring clips along the top edge of the cover).

8. Install the glove compartment liner.

9. Connect the heater hoses to the heater core. Tighten the hose clamps.

10. Add coolant to raise the coolant level to specification.

11. Check the system for proper operation and for coolant leaks.

1980 and Later Bronco and Pick-ups, Standard & High Output Heaters, Without Air Conditioning

1. Disconnect the temperature cable from the temperature blend door and the mounting bracket on top of the heater case.

2. Disconnect the wires from the blower motor resistor and the blower motor.

3. Disconnect the heater hoses from the heater core and plug the hoses with suitable ⅝ inch plugs.

4. Working under the instrument panel, remove two nuts retaining the left end of the heater case and the right end of the plenum to the dash panel.

5. In the engine compartment, remove one screw attaching the top center of the heater case to the dash panel.

6. Remove two screws attaching the right end of the heater case to the dash panel, and remove the heater case from the vehicle.

Heater case and plenum assemblies on 1980 and later standard and high output units without A/C

7. Remove nine screws and one (1) bolt and nut attaching the heater housing plate to the heater case, and remove the heater housing plate.

8. Remove three screws attaching the heater core frame to the heater case and remove the frame.

9. Remove the heater core and seal from the heater case.

10. Position the heater core and seal in the heater case.

11. Install the heater core frame (3 screws).

12. Position the heater housing plate on the heater case and install the nine screws and one bolt and nut.

13. Position the heater case to the dash panel and install the three attaching screws.

14. Working in the passenger compartment, install two nuts to retain the heater case and plenum right end to the dash panel.

15. Connect the heater hoses to the heater core. Tighten the hose clamps.

16. Connect the wires to the blower motor resistor assembly.

17. Connect the blower motor wires.

18. Position (slide) the self-adjusting clip on the temperature cable to a position approximately one inch from the cable end loop.

19. Snap the temperature cable on the cable mounting bracket of the heater case. Then, position the self-adjusting clip on the door crank arm.

20. Adjust the temperature cable.

21. Check the system for proper operation.

1980 and Later Bronco and Pick-ups With Air Conditioning

REMOVAL (WITHOUT DISCHARGING THE A/C SYSTEM)

1. Disconnect the heater hoses from the heater core tubes and plug the hoses with suitable ⅝ inch plugs.

2. Remove the glove compartment liner.

3. Remove eight screws attaching heater core cover to the plenum and remove the cover.

4. Remove the heater core from the plenum taking care not to spill coolant from the core.

INSTALLATION

1. Install the heater core in the plenum.

2. Install the heater core cover (eight screws).

3. Install the glove compartment liner.

4. Connect the heater hoses to the heater core. Tighten the hose clamps.

5. Add coolant to raise the coolant level to specification.

Ranger and Bronco II w/o A/C

1. Allow the engine to cool down completely. Drain the cooling system to a point that is below the heater hoses.

2. Disconnect the heater hoses from the heater core tubes. Plug the core tubes.

3. From under the dash, remove the

screws that attach the access cover to the plenum assembly. Remove the access cover.

4. Pull the core down and out of the plenum assembly.

5. Install in the reverse order. Fill cooling system, start the engine and check for leaks.

Ranger and Bronco II with A/C

1. Refer to the without A/C section. Procedure is the same.

Auxiliary Heater Case (With or Without A/C)

VANS

Removal and Installation

1. Remove the first bench seat (if so equipped).

2. Remove the auxiliary heater and/or air conditioning cover assembly attaching screws and remove the cover.

3. Position the cover assembly to the body side panel and install the attaching screws.

4. Install the bench seat (if removed) and tighten the retaining bolts 25–45 ft. lbs.

Auxiliary Heater Core and Seal Assembly

VANS

Removal and Installation

1. Remove the first bench seat (if so equipped).

2. Remove auxiliary heater and/or air conditioning cover attaching screws (15) and remove the cover.

3. Partially drain the engine coolant from the coolant system.

4. Remove the heater hoses from the auxiliary heater core assembly (2 clamps).

5. Pull the wiring assembly away from the heater core seal.

6. Slide the heater core and seal assembly out of the housing slot.

7. Slide the heater core and seal assembly into the housing slot (position the wiring to one side).

8. Install the heater hoses to the heater core assembly (2 clamps).

9. Fill the cooling system to specification.

10. Position the cover assembly to the body side panel and install the attaching screws (15).

11. Install the bench seat (if removed) and tighten the retaining bolts 25–45 ft. lbs.

RADIO

REMOVAL & INSTALLATION

1977 Bronco

1. Disconnect the radio lead wire at the receptacle on the fuse panel.

2. Disconnect the speaker leads at the receptacle on the underside of the radio chassis.

3. Disconnect the antenna lead at the receptacle on the right side of the radio chassis.

4. Remove (pull) the volume control

1977 Bronco radio installation

and the manual tuning control knobs from the shafts.

5. Remove the screws that retain the dial assembly to the instrument panel and remove the dial assembly.

6. Remove the retaining nuts and the retaining plate that secure the radio to the instrument panel.

7. Remove the radio bottom support bracket retaining screw and remove the radio assembly from the instrument panel.

To install the radio:

8. Position the radio to the inner side of the instrument panel, and install the right and left support bracket to the radio retaining nuts.

9. Position the retaining plate to the outer side of the instrument panel over the pilot light and control shafts, and install the retaining nuts.

10. Position the dial assembly, install the retaining screw and seat the knobs on the control shafts.

11. Connect the speaker leads, the antenna lead, and the radio power lead wire at the fuse panel.

12. Calibrate the dial pointer with the tuner by rotating the tuning knob until the dial pointer reaches the end of its travel at the right side of the dial.

13. Check the operation of the radio and adjust the antenna trimmer.

Vans

1. Detach the battery ground cable.

2. Remove the heater and A/C control knobs. Remove the lighter.

3. Remove the radio knobs and discs.

4. If the truck has a lighter, snap out the name plate at the right side to remove the panel attaching screw.

5. Remove the five finish panel screws.

6. Very carefully pry out the cluster panel in two places.

7. Detach the antenna lead and speaker wires.

8. Remove the two nuts and washers and the mounting plate.

9. Remove the four front radio attaching screws. Remove the rear support nut and washer, and remove the radio.

10. Reverse the procedure for installation.

1978 and Later Bronco, Pick-ups

1. Disconnect the battery ground cable.

2. On 1975–79 models, remove the ash tray and bracket.

3. Disconnect the antenna, speakers and radio lead.

4. Remove the bolt attaching the radio rear support to the lower edge of the instrument panel.

5. On 1975–78 models equipped with air conditioning, disconnect the left A/C duct hose from the A/C plenum.

6. Remove the knobs and discs from the radio control shafts.

7. Remove the retaining nuts from the control shafts and remove the bezel.

8. Remove the nuts and washers from the control shafts and remove the radio from the panel.

9. Installation is the reverse of removal.

Ranger and Bronco II

1. Disconnect the negative battery cable.

2. Remove the knobs and discs from the radio control shafts. Remove the front finish panel assembly.

3. Remove the screws that attach the mounting plate assembly to the instrument panel and remove the radio with mounting plate and rear bracket.

4. Disconnect the antenna, speaker wires and power lead.

5. Install in the reverse order.

Typical van radio installation

Typical pick-up, 1978 and later Bronco radio installation

WINDSHIELD WIPERS

Motor

REMOVAL & INSTALLATION
1977 Bronco

1. The motor is mounted on the left side of the windshield header. To remove the motor it will be necessary to first remove the cover and disconnect the linkage arm and pivot shaft assembly from the motor driving arm by removing the retaining clip.

2. Disconnect the motor electrical leads at the multiple connector. Remove the two bolts and nuts that attach the motor mounting bracket to the windshield header, and remove the bracket and motor assembly.

3. Install the windshield wiper motor

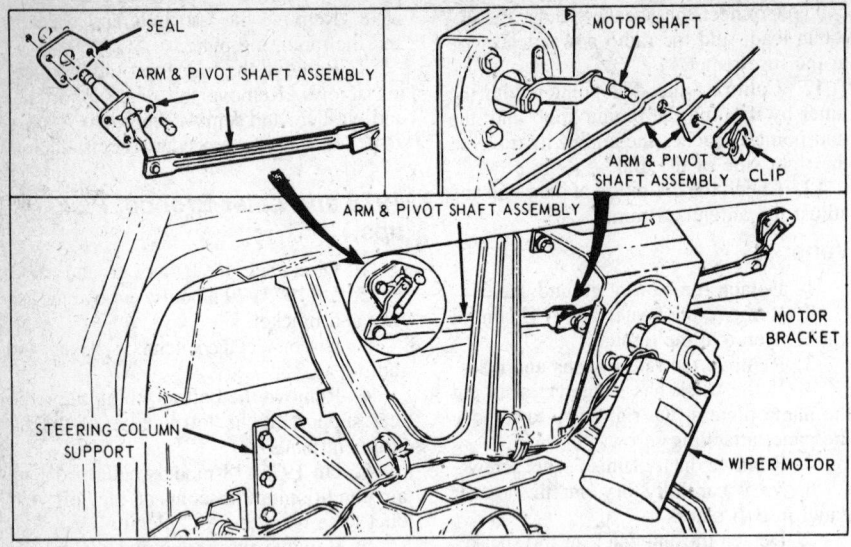

Typical 1977–79 wiper motor installation except 1977 Bronco

in the reverse order of removal. When installing the motor, tighten the motor bracket-to-windshield header bolts to 48–72 in. lbs. and the nuts to 20–30 in. lbs.

1978–79 Bronco, 1977–79 Pick-ups

1. Disconnect the battery ground cable.
2. Remove the radio.
3. Remove the engine components attached to the lower wiper bracket bolt, if so equipped.
4. Remove the wiper motor bracket attaching bolts.
5. Disconnect the wiper motor wires. Then, disconnect the wiper arm linkage from

Typical 1980 and later wiper motor installation

the motor shaft.
6. Connect the linkage to motor and install motor bracket attaching bolts. Tighten bolts to 8–12 ft. lbs. and install engine components to lower bracket bolts.
7. Connect wiper motor wires.
8. Install radio.
9. Connect battery cable and check wiper motor operation.

1980 and Later Bronco, Pick-ups

1. Disconnect the battery ground cable.
2. Remove the cowl grille attaching screws and lift the cowl grille slightly.
3. Disconnect the washer nozzle hose

and remove the cowl grille assembly.
4. Remove the wiper linkage clip from the motor output arm.
5. Disconnect the wiper motor's wiring connector.
6. Remove the wiper motor's three attaching screws and remove the motor.
7. Install the motor and attach the three attaching screws. Tighten to 60–85 in. lbs.
8. Connect wiper motor's wiring connector.
9. Install wiper linkage clip to the motor's output arm.
10. Connect the washer nozzle hose and install the cowl assembly and attaching screws.
11. Install both wiper arm assemblies.
12. Connect battery ground cable.

Vans

1. Disconnect the battery ground cable. Remove the fuse panel and bracket.
2. Disconnect the motor wires.
3. Remove the arms and blades.
4. Remove the outer air inlet cowl. Take off the motor linkage clip.
5. Unbolt and remove the motor.
6. Reverse the procedure for installation.

Ranger and Bronco II

1. Turn on the ignition and wiper switches. When the wiper blades are straight up and down on the windshield, turn off the ignition switch so that the wiper arms and blades remain in position.
2. Disconnect the negative battery cable.
3. Remove the wiper arm and blade from the right side. Remove the pivot nut from the wiper arm drive and allow the pivot to drop into the cowl.
4. Remove the access cover from the right side of the firewall. Reach in and disconnect the linkage from the wiper motor drive arm.
5. Disconnect the wiring at the wiper motor. Remove the wiper motor mounting bolts and remove the motor.
6. Install in the reverse order. Make sure the linkage lock clips are snapped in position.

Linkage

REMOVAL & INSTALLATION

1977 Bronco

1. Remove the windshield wiper arm and blade assemblies from their pivot shafts.
2. Disconnect the linkage arm from the motor drive arm by removing the retaining clip.
3. The right and left pivot shaft assemblies are each retained to the windshield header by two mounting screws and a nut. Remove these mounting screws and the nut, and remove the pivot shafts and linkage as an assembly.
4. Install the linkage in the reverse order of removal.

Wiper linkage and motor removal/installation- Ranger/Bronco II

Vans

1. Disconnect the battery ground cable.
2. Remove the wiper blades and arms. Detach the washer hoses.
3. Remove the cowl grille.
4. Remove the linkage clips. Remove the pivot to cowl screws and remove the assembly.

1978–79 Bronco, 1977–79 Pickups

1. Open the hood and disconnect the battery ground cable. Remove the arm and blade assemblies from the pivot shafts.
2. Reach under the instrument panel and disconnect the speedometer cable from the rear of the instrument cluster.
3. Remove the instrument cluster bezel.
4. Loosen the three bolts retaining the wiper motor bracket to the cowl. This will allow access between the cowl panel and the link assembly.
5. Remove the clip retaining the motor drive arm to the link assemblies.
6. Through the cluster bezel opening, remove the retaining bolts from the left pivot assembly. Remove the left pivot and link assembly from under the instrument panel.
7. Remove the glove box assembly.
8. Remove the three bolts retaining the right pivot and link assembly to the cowl panel.
9. Disconnect the right link assembly from the drive arm and remove the right pivot and link assembly.

10. Place gaskets on the pivot shafts and position the shafts to the cowl panel and install the retaining bolts.
11. Install the glove box assembly.
12. Position the link assemblies to the motor drive arm and install the retaining clip.
13. Tighten the bolts retaining the motor bracket to the cowl and then re-install engine components to lower bracket bolt.
14. Install the wiper arm and blade assemblies.
15. Position and install the instrument cluster bezel.
16. Connect the speedometer cable.
17. Connect the battery ground cable and close the hood and check the operation of the wipers.

1980 and Later Bronco, Pickups

1. Disconnect the battery ground cable.
2. Remove both wiper arm assemblies.
3. Remove the cowl grille attaching screws and lift the cowl grille slightly.
4. Disconnect the washer nozzle hose and remove the cowl grille assembly.
5. Remove the wiper linkage clip from the motor output arm and pull the linkage from the output arm.
6. Remove the pivot body to cowl screws and remove the linkage and pivot shaft assembly (three screws on each side). The left and right pivots and linkage are independent and can be serviced separately.

7. Attach the linkage and pivot shaft assembly to cowl with attaching screws.
8. Replace the linkage to the output arm and attach the linkage clip.
9. Connect the washer nozzle hose and cowl grills assembly.
10. Attach cowl grille attaching screws.
11. Replace both wiper arm assemblies.
12. Connect battery ground cable.

Ranger and Bronco II

1. Refer to the wiper motor removal section and follow procedure until the linkage has been disconnected from the wiper motor.
2. Slide the right side linkage and pivot out through the access hole.
3. Remove the left side wiper arm and blade assembly.
4. Remove the left side access cover. Remove the pivot nut and slide the linkage and pivot through the access hole.
5. Install in the reverse order.

Wiper Arm Assembly

REPLACEMENT

1977–79

Bend the arm backwards at the joint next to the pivot. Now, pull the arm straight off the splined pivot shaft. To replace the arm, hold it in the bent position and slide it on the pivot.

1980 and Later

Raise the blade end of the arm off of the windshield and move the slide latch away from the pivot shaft. This will unlock the wiper arm from the pivot shaft and hold the blade end of the arm off of the glass at the same time. The wiper arm can now be pulled off of the pivot shaft without the aid of any tools.

Blade Assembly to Wiper Arm

REPLACEMENT

1977-79

Wiper blades are used from two different manufacturers.

Trico and Anco blades come in two types. With a bayonet type, the blade saddle slides over the end of the arm and is engaged by a locking stud. With the bottom type, a screw and nut is used to retain the blade on the arm.

BAYONET TYPE

To remove a Trico type blade, press down on the arm to unlatch the top stud. Depress the tab on the saddle and pull the blade from the arm.

To remove an Anco type blade, press inward on the tab and pull the blade from the arm.

To install a new blade assembly, slide the blade saddle over the end of the wiper arm so that the locking stud snaps into place.

SIDE SADDLE PIN TYPE

To remove a pin type Trico-type blade, insert an appropriate tool into the spring release opening of the blade saddle, depress the spring clip and pull the blade from the arm.

To install, push the blade saddle on to the pin, so that the spring clip engages the pin. Be sure the blade is securely attached to the arm.

From 1980

1. Cycle arm and blade assembly to a position on the windshield where removal of blade assembly can be performed without difficulty. Turn ignition key off at desired position.

2. With blade assembly resting on windshield, grasp either end of the wiper blade frame and pull away from windshield, then pull blade assembly from pin.

NOTE: Rubber element extends past frame. To prevent damage to the blade element, be sure to grasp blade frame and not the end of the blade element.

3. To install, push blade assembly onto pin until fully seated. Be sure blade is securely attached to the wiper arm.

INSTRUMENT CLUSTER

REMOVAL & INSTALLATION

1977 Bronco

1. Disconnect the battery ground cable and disconnect the speedometer cable from the speedometer head.

2. Remove the screws retaining the instrument cluster assembly to the instrument panel.

3. Remove the cluster from behind the instrument panel.

4. Disconnect the feed wires to the instruments and the instrument voltage regulator and remove the light sockets from the cluster back, noting their positions. Remove the two clips that retain the wiring harness to the cluster back and pull the harness away from the cluster. Remove the instrument cluster assembly.

To install the instrument cluster:

5. Mount the wiring harness to the lower edge of the cluster back by installing the two retaining clips.

6. Connect the instrument voltage regulator and the instrument wires to the cluster assembly and install the light sockets. Be sure that the ammeter wire is routed through the ammeter loop of the charge indicator correctly to prevent reverse gauge indications.

7. Connect the speedometer cable and tighten the nut.

8. Carefully move the instrument cluster into position from behind the instrument panel, guiding all wiring and cables into position to prevent damage. Be careful not to kink the speedometer cable.

9. Install the screws retaining the instrument cluster to the instrument panel.

10. Connect the battery ground cable and check the operation of all gauges, lights and signals.

1978-79 Bronco, 1977-79 Pick-ups

1. Disconnect the battery ground cable.

2. Remove the radio knobs from the radio shafts (if so equipped).

3. Remove the fuel gauge switch knob (if so equipped), heater control knobs and wiper-washer knob. Use a hook-shaped tool to release each knob lock tab.

4. Remove the knob and shaft from the light switch.

5. Remove one nut and washer from each radio control shaft, and remove the radio bezel.

6. Remove the cluster trim cover. The attaching screws are located as follows: four screws along top of bezel; one screw between the lights and wiper-washer switch, and two screws below the radio. Then, disconnect the A/C duct (if so equipped), and illumination light from the bezel. The illumination light is located between the lights and wiper-washer switches. Remove four cluster attaching screws, disconnect the speedometer cable and wire connector from the printed circuit, and remove the cluster.

7. Position cluster to opening and connect the multiple connector and the speedometer cable. Connect the A/C duct and A/C illumination light (if so equipped) and install the four cluster retaining screws.

8. Install the trim cover.

9. Install the radio bezel (if so equipped).

10. Install the light switch knob and shaft.

11. Install the heater control knobs and the wiper-washer control knobs.

12. Install the radio knobs, (if so equipped).

13. Connect the battery cable, and check the operation of all gauges, lights and signals.

1980 and Later Bronco, Pick-ups

1. Disconnect the battery ground cable.

2. Remove the fuel gauge switch knob (if so equipped), and wiper-washer knob.

CLUSTER ASSEMBLY

SCREW

1977 Bronco instrument cluster

1977–79 pick-up, 1978–79 Bronco instrument panel-rear view

Use a hook tool to release each knob lock tab.

3. Remove the knob from the head-lamp and windshield wiper switch. Remove the fog lamp switch knob, if so equipped.

4. Remove steering column shroud. Care must be taken not to damage trans-mission control selector indicator (PRNDL) cable on vehicles equipped with automatic transmission.

5. On vehicles equipped with auto-matic transmission, remove loop on indi-cator cable assembly from retainer pin. Re-move bracket screw from cable bracket and

slide bracket out of slot in tube.

6. Remove the cluster trim cover. Re-move four cluster attaching screws, dis-connect the speedometer cable, wire con-nector from the printed circuit, 4 × 4 indicator light and remove the cluster.

7. Position cluster to opening and con-nect the multiple connector, the speedom-eter cable and 4 × 4 indicator light. Install the four cluster retaining screws.

8. If so equipped, place loop on trans-mission indicator cable assembly over re-tainer on column.

9. Position the tab on steering column

bracket into slot on column. Align and at-tach screw.

10. Place transmission selector lever on steering column into "D" position.

11. Adjust slotted bracket so the pin is within the letter band.

12. Install the trim cover.

13. Install the headlamp switch knob. If so equipped, install the fog lamp switch.

14. Install the wiper-washer control knobs.

15. Connect the battery cable, and check the operation of all gauges, lights and signals.

1977 Vans

1. Disconnect the battery ground cable.

2. Remove seven instrument cluster-to-panel retaining screws.

3. Position cluster part away from the panel for access to the back of the cluster to disconnect the speedometer cable.

If there is not sufficient access to dis-engage the speedometer cable from the speedometer, it may be necessary to re-move the speedometer cable at the trans-mission and pull cable through cowl, to allow room to reach the speedometer quick disconnect.

4. Disconnect the harness connector plug from the printed circuit board and re-move the cluster assembly from the instru-ment panel.

5. Remove the cluster.

6. Apply approximately 3/16 inch di-ameter ball of silicone lubricant or equiv-alent in the drive hole of the speedometer head.

7. Position the cluster near its opening in the instrument panel.

8. Connect the harness connector plug

Typical pick-up and Bronco instrument cluster rear view-from 1980

to the printed circuit board.

9. Connect the speedometer cable (quick disconnect) to the speedometer head.

Connect the speedometer cable and housing assembly to the transmission (if removed).

10. Install the seven instrument cluster-to-panel retaining screws and connect the battery ground cable.

11. Check operation of all gauges, lights, and signals.

1978 and Later Vans

1. Disconnect the battery ground cable.

2. Remove two steering column shroud to panel retaining screws and remove shroud.

3. Loosen bolts which attach the column to the B and C Support to provide sufficient clearance for cluster removal. (Required for tilt steering column vehicles only).

4. Remove seven instrument cluster to panel retaining screws.

5. Position cluster part away from the panel for access to the back of the cluster to disconnect the speedometer.

If there is not sufficient access to disengage the speedometer cable from the speedometer, it may be necessary to remove the speedometer cable at the transmission and pull cable through cowl, to allow room to reach the speedometer quick disconnect.

6. Disconnect the harness connector plug from the printed circuit board and remove the cluster assembly from the instrument panel.

7. Apply approximately 3/16 inch diameter ball of silicone lubricant or equivalent in the drive hole of the speedometer head.

8. Position the cluster near its opening in the instrument panel.

9. Connect the harness connector plug to the printed circuit board.

10. Connect the speedometer cable (quick disconnect) to the speedometer head.

Connect the speedometer cable and housing assembly to the transmission (if removed).

11. Install the seven instrument cluster-to-panel retaining screws and connect the battery ground cable.

12. Check operation of all gauges, lights, and signals.

13. Reinstall the steering column.

14. Position steering column shroud to instrument panel and install two screws.

Ranger and Bronco II

1. Disconnect the negative battery cable.

2. Remove the two steering column shroud-to-panel retaining screws and remove the shroud.

3. Remove the lower instrument panel trim. Detach the trim cover from the panel by removing the retaining screws.

4. Remove the four instrument cluster to panel retaining screws.

5. Pull the cluster slightly away from the panel and disconnect the speedometer cable. If there is not enough room to disconnect the cable, disconnect from transmission and gently pull through the firewall until enough slack is gained.

6. Disconnect the wiring harness connector from the back of the cluster. Disconnect any bulb and socket assemblies from the cluster. Remove the cluster.

7. Install in the reverse order of removal.

Speedometer Cable Core

REMOVAL & INSTALLATION

1. Reach up behind the cluster and disconnect the cable by depressing the quick disconnect tab and pulling the cable away.

2. Remove the cable from the casing.

Speedometer cable installation, typical

If the cable is broken, raise the vehicle on a hoist and disconnect the cable from the transmission.

3. Remove the cable from the casing.

4. To remove the casing from the vehicle, pull it through the floor pan.

5. To replace the cable, slide the new cable into the casing and connect it at the transmission.

6. Route the cable through the floor pan and position the grommet in its groove in the floor.

7. Push the cable onto the speedometer head.

Ignition Switch

NOTE: Refer to the steering section for Ranger/Bronco II procedures.

REMOVAL & INSTALLATION

1977–79

1. Disconnect the battery ground cable.

2. Turn the ignition key to Accessories and slightly depress the release pin in the face of the lock cylinder.

3. Turn the key counterclockwise and pull the key and lock assembly out of the switch.

4. From under the instrument panel, press in on the rear of the switch ⅛ turn counterclockwise.

5. Remove the bezel and switch. Remove the retainer and spring.

6. Remove the nut from the back of the switch.

7. Remove the accessory and gauge feed wires from the accessory terminal of the switch. Pull the insulated plug from the rear of the switch.

8. To install: insert a screwdriver into the lock opening of the switch and turn the slot in the switch to the full counterclockwise position.

9. Connect the insulated plug and wires to the back of the switch. Connect the accessory and gauge wires to the switch and install the retaining nut.

10. Place the bezel and switch in the switch opening, press the switch toward the instrument panel and rotate it ⅛ turn to lock it.

11. Position the spring and retainer on the switch with the open face of the retainer away from the switch. Place the switch in the opening.

12. Press the switch toward the instrument panel and install the bezel.

13. Place the key in the cylinder and turn the key to the accessory position. Place the lock and key in the switch, depress the release pin slightly, and turn the key counterclockwise. Push the new lock cylinder into the switch. Turn the key to check the operation.

14. Connect the battery.

From 1980

1. Disconnect the battery ground cable.

2. Remove steering column shroud and lower the steering column.

3. Disconnect the switch wiring at the multiple plug.

4. Remove the two nuts that retain the switch to the steering column.

5. Lift the switch vertically upward to disengage the actuator rod from the switch and remove switch.

6. When installing the ignition switch, both the locking mechanism at the top of the column and the switch itself must be in LOCK position for correct adjustment.

To hold the mechanical parts of the column in LOCK position, move the shift lever into PARK (with automatic transmissions) or REVERSE (with manual transmissions), turn the key to LOCK position, and remove the key. New replacement switches, when received, are already pinned in LOCK position by a metal shipping pin inserted in a locking hole on the side of the switch.

7. Engage the actuator rod in the switch.

8. Position the switch on the column and install the retaining nuts, but do not tighten them.

9. Move the switch up and down along the column to locate the mid-position of rod lash, and then tighten the retaining nuts.

10. Remove the locking pin, connect the battery cable, and check for proper start in PARK or NEUTRAL.

Also check to make certain that the start circuit cannot be actuated in the DRIVE and REVERSE position.

11. Raise the steering column into position at instrument panel. Install steering column shroud.

HEADLIGHTS

REMOVAL & INSTALLATION

Vans, 1977 Bronco, 1977 Pickups, 1978 Pick-ups and Bronco Except Ranger and XLT Options

1. Remove the screws retaining the headlight trim ring and remove the trim ring.

2. Loosen the headlight retaining ring screws, rotate the ring counterclockwise and remove it. Do not disturb the adjusting screw settings.

3. Pull the headlight bulb forward and disconnect the wiring assembly plug from the hub.

4. Connect the wiring assembly plug to the new bulb. Place the bulb in position, making sure that the locating tabs of the bulb are fitted in the positioning slots.

5. Install the headlight retaining ring, slipping the ring tabs over the screws and rotating the ring clockwise as far as possible. Tighten the screws.

6. Place the headlight trim ring into position, and install the retaining screws.

7. Check the operation of the headlight.

1978 Pick-ups and Bronco with Ranger and XLT Option and All 1979 and Later Pick-up, Bronco, Ranger and Bronco II Models

1. Remove the attaching screws and remove the headlamp door attaching screws and remove the headlamp door.

2. Remove the headlight retaining ring screws, and remove the retaining ring. Do not disturb the adjusting screw settings.

3. Pull the headlight bulb forward and disconnect the wiring assembly plug from the bulb.

4. Connect the wiring assembly plug to the new bulb. Place the bulb in position, making sure that the locating tabs of the bulb are fitted in the positioning slots.

5. Install the headlight retaining ring.

6. Place the headlight trim ring or door into position, and install the retaining screws.

Headlight Switch

REMOVAL & INSTALLATION

1. Disconnect the battery ground cable.

2. Depending on the year and model remove the wiper-washer and fog lamp switch knob if they will interfere with the headlight switch knob removal. Check the switch body (behind dash, see Step 3) for a release button. Press in on the button and remove the knob and shaft assembly. If not equipped with a release button, a hook tool may be necessary for knob removal.

3. Remove the steering column shrouds and cluster panel finish panel if they interfere with the required clearance for working behind the dash.

4. Unscrew the switch mounting nut from the front of the dash. Remove the switch from the back of the dash and disconnect the wiring harness.

5. Install in reverse order.

FUSE LINK

The fuse link is a short length of special, Hypalon (high temperature) insulated wire, integral with the engine compartment wiring harness and should not be confused with standard wire. It is several wire gauges smaller than the circuit which it protects. Under no circumstances should a fuse link replacement repair be made using a length of standard wire cut from bulk stock or from another wiring harness.

To repair any blown fuse link use the following procedure:

1. Determine which circuit is damaged, its location and the cause of the open fuse link. If the damaged fuse link is one of three fed by a common No. 10 or 12

REMOVE EXISTING VINYL TUBE SHIELDING
REINSTALL OVER FUSE LINK BEFORE CRIMPING
FUSE LINK TO WIRE ENDS

TAPE

TAPE OR STRAP

TYPICAL REPAIR USING THE SPECIAL #17 GA. (9.00" LONG-YELLOW) FUSE LINK REQUIRED FOR THE AIR/COND.
CIRCUITS (2) #687E and #261A LOCATED IN THE ENGINE COMPARTMENT

FUSE LINK

TAPE OR STRAP

TYPICAL REPAIR FOR ANY IN-LINE FUSE LINK USING THE SPECIFIED GAUGE FUSE LINK FOR THE SPECIFIC CIRCUIT

TAPE

TYPICAL REPAIR USING THE EYELET TERMINAL FUSE LINK OF THE SPECIFIED GAUGE FOR ATTACHMENT TO A CIRCUIT WIRE END

TAPE

(3) FUSE LINKS

TYPICAL REPAIR ATTACHING THREE LIGHT GAUGE
FUSE LINKS TO A SINGLE HEAVY GAUGE FEED WIRE

TAPE

TAPE

D3AZ-14488-Y BUTT CONNECTOR
FOR 10 OR 12 GA. WIRE

DOUBLED WIRE CRIMPED

#10 OR 12 GA. WIRE

LIGHT GAUGE WIRE

D3AZ-14488-Z BUTT CONNECTOR
FOR #14 OR 16 WIRE

FUSIBLE LINK REPAIR PROCEDURE

General fuse link repair procedure

gauge feed wire, determine the specific affected circuit.

2. Disconnect the negative battery cable.

3. Cut the damaged fuse link from the wiring harness and discard it. If the fuse link is one of three circuits fed by a single feed wire, cut it out of the harness at each splice end and discard it.

4. Identify and procure the proper fuse link and butt connectors for attaching the fuse link to the harness.

5. To repair any fuse link in a 3-link group with one feed:

a. After cutting the open link out of the harness, cut each of the remaining undamaged fuse links close to the feed wire weld.

b. Strip approximately ½ inch of insulation from the detached ends of the two good fuse links. Then insert two wire ends into one end of a butt connector and carefully push one stripped end of the replacement fuse link into the same end of the butt connector and crimp all three

firmly together.

NOTE: Care must be taken when fitting the three fuse links into the butt connector as the internal diameter is a snug fit for three wires. Make sure to use a proper crimping tool. Pliers, side cutters, etc. will not apply the proper crimp to retain the wires and withstand a pull test.

c. After crimping the butt connector to the three fuse links, cut the weld portion from the feed wire and strip approximately ½ inch of insulation from the cut end. Insert the stripped end into the open end of the butt connector and crimp very firmly.

d. To attach the remaining end of the replacement fuse link, strip approximately ½ inch of insulation from the wire end of the circuit from which the blown fuse link was removed, and firmly crimp a butt connector or equivalent to the stripped wire. Then, insert the end of the replacement link into the other end of the butt connector and crimp firmly.

e. Using rosin core solder with a consistency of 60 percent tin and 40 percent lead, solder the connectors and the wires at the repairs and insulate with electrical tape.

6. To replace any fuse link on a single circuit in a harness, cut out the damaged portion, strip approximately ½ inch of insulation from the two wire ends and attach the appropriate replacement fuse link to the stripped wire ends with two proper size butt connectors. Solder the connectors and wires and insulate with tape.

7. To repair any fuse link which has an eyelet terminal on one end such as the charging circuit, cut off the open fuse link behind the weld, strip approximately ½ inch of insulation from the cut end and attach the appropriate new eyelet fuse link to the cut stripped wire with an appropriate size butt connector. Solder the connectors and wires at the repair and insulate with tape.

8. Connect the negative battery cable to the battery and test the system for proper operation.

NOTE: Do not mistake a resistor wire for a fuse link. The resistor wire is generally longer and has print stating, "Resistor-don't cut or splice."

NOTE: When attaching a single No. 16, 17, 18 or 20 gauge fuse link to a heavy gauge wire, always double the stripped wire end of the fuse link before inserting and crimping it into the butt connector for positive wire retention.

International Harvester

Pickups, Scout, Traveler, Travelette

GENERAL ENGINE SPECIFICATIONS

Year	Engine No. Cyl Displacement (cu. in.)	Carburetor Type	Horsepower @ rpm	Torque @rpm (ft lbs)	Bore × Stroke (in.)	Compression Ratio	Oil Pressure @2000 rpm (psi)
'77–80	4–196	1V	111 @ 4400	180 @ 2000	4.125 × 3.656	8.1:1	50
'80	6–198 (Turbo)	Diesel	101 @ 3800	175 @ 2200	3.27 × 3.94	20.8:1	—
'77–79	6–198	Diesel	73 @ 3200	133 @ 1600	3.27 × 3.94	22.0:1	—
'77–80	8–304	2V	147 @ 3900	240 @ 2400	3.875 × 3.218	8.2:1	45
'77–80	8–345	2V	157 @ 3800	266 @ 2400	3.875 × 3.656	8.1:1	45

VALVE SPECIFICATIONS

Year	Engine No. Cyl Displacement (cu in.)	Seat Angle (deg)	Face Angle (deg)	Spring Test Pressure (lbs @ in.)	Spring Free Height	Stem-to-Guide Clearance (in.) Intake	Stem-to-Guide Clearance (in.) Exhaust	Stem Diameter (in.) Intake	Stem Diameter (in.) Exhaust
'77–80	4–196	①	①	188 @ 1.428	2.065	.001–.0035	.0015–.004	.372	.415
'80	6–198	45	45	57 @ 1.57	1.89	.0006–.0018	.0016–.0028	.314	.314
'77–79	6–198	45	45	33 @ 1.634	1.929	.0006–.0018	.0016–.0028	.314	.314
'77–80	8–304	45	45	180–195 @ 1.429	2.065	.001–.0035	.0015–.004	.372	.371
'77–80	8–345	45	45	180–195 @ 1.429	2.065	.001–.0035	.0015–.004	.372	.371

① Intake 30°; Exhaust 45°

FIRING ORDER

NOTE: To avoid confusion, always replace spark plug wires one at a time.

4 cylinder: 1-3-4-2

8 cylinder: 1-8-4-3-6-5-7-2

TUNE-UP SPECIFICATIONS

Year	Engine No. Cyl Displacement (cu. in.)	Spark Plugs Gap (in.)	Distributor	Ignition Timing (deg) Man	Ignition Timing (deg) Auto	Fuel Pump Pressure (psi)	Idle Speed (rpm) Man	Idle Speed (rpm) Auto
'77–80	4-196	.035	Electronic	TDC	5B	5	575	600
'77–80	8-304	.030	Electronic	TDC	TDC	5	575	600
'77–80	8-345	.035	Electronic	TDC	5B	5	650	700

CRANKSHAFT AND CONNECTING ROD SPECIFICATIONS

(All measurements given in inches)

Year	Engine No Cyl Displacement (cu in.)	Crankshaft Main Brg Journal Dia	Crankshaft Main Brg Oil Clearance	Crankshaft Shaft End-play	Crankshaft Thrust on No	Connecting Rod Journal Diameter	Connecting Rod Oil Clearance	Connecting Rod Side Clearance
'77–80	4–196	2.7484–2.7494	.001–.004	.003–.008	3	2.373–2.374	.0011–.0036	.004–.011
'80	6–198	2.795	.0016–.0036	.0024–.0055	3	2.087	.0012–.0036	.0039–.0079
'77–79	6–198	2.7918–2.7988	.0013–.0038	.0024–.0094	3	2.0840–2.0906	.0013–.0038	.0039–.0079
'77–80	8–304	2.7484–2.7494	.001–.004	.003–.008	3	2.373–2.374	.0011–.0036	.008–.0016
'77–80	8–345	2.7484–2.7494	.001–.004	.003–.008	3	2.373–2.374	.0011–.0036	.008–.0016

CAMSHAFT SPECIFICATIONS

(All measurements in inches)

Engine	Journal Diameter 1	2	3	4	5	Bearing Clearance	Valve Lift Intake	Valve Lift Exhaust	Camshaft End Play
4–196	2.099–2.100	2.089–2.090	2.079–2.080	2.069–2.070	2.059–2.060	.0015–.0035	.440	.395	.006–.014
6–198①	2.024	2.016	2.008	2.000	—	.0063–.0079	.358	.358	.0032–.0111
6–198②	1.774–1.789	1.714–1.729	1.714–1.729	1.608–1.624	—	.0059–.0079③	.248	.248	.0032–.0102
8–304	2.099–2.100	2.089–2.090	2.079–2.080	2.069–2.070	2.059–2.060	.0015–.0035	.440	.395	.006–.014
8–345	2.099–2.100	2.089–2.090	2.079–2.080	2.069–2.070	2.059–2.060	.0015–.0035	.440	.395	.006–.014

①1980   ②1977–79   ③No. 4 bearing

PISTON AND RING SPECIFICATIONS
(All measurements given in inches)

Year	Engine	Piston to Bore Clearance	Ring Side Clearance			Ring Gap		
			Top Compression	Bottom Compression	Oil Control	Top Compression	Bottom Compression	Oil Control
'75–80	4–196	.0035	.0015–.003	.0015–.003	.002–.0035	.013–.023	.013–.023	.013–.028
'80	6–198	.0047–.0075	.0024–.0039	.0016–.0032①	.0008–.0024	.0059–.0197	.0059–.0197①	.0059–.0197
'77–79	6–198	.0047–.0067	.0024–.0039	.0016–.0032①	.0008–.0024	.0118–.0197	.0118–.0197①	.0118–.0197
'77–80	8–304	.0035	.0015–.003	.0015–.003	.000–.0084	.010–.020	.010–.020	.015–.055
'77–80	8–345	.0035	.0015–.003	.0015–.003	.000–.0084	.010–.020	.010–.020	.015–.055

① 2nd and 3rd compression rings

TORQUE SPECIFICATIONS
(All readings in ft. lbs.)

Year	Engine	Cylinder Head Bolts	Rod Bearing Bolts	Main Bearing Bolts	In.-Ex. Manifold Bolts	Crankshaft Damper Bolt	Flywheel	Injector Nozzle Holder	Injection Pump
'80	6–198	94 large 36 small	37–41	108–116	11–13	217–239	33–36	50–65	15–18
'77–'79	6–198	94 large 36 small	36–40	109–116	11–13	217–239	33–36	50–65	15–18

TORQUE SPECIFICATIONS
(All readings in ft. lbs.)

Year	Engine	Cylinder Head Bolts	Rod Bearing Bolts	Main Bearing Bolts	Crankshaft Pulley Bolt	Flywheel-to-Crankshaft Bolts	Manifold	
							Intake	Exhaust
'77–'80	4–196	90–100	40–45	75–80	100–110	45–55	40–45	40–45
'77–'80	8–304	90–100	45–55	75–85	100–110	45–55	40–45	40–45
	8–345	90–100	45–55	75–85	100–110	45–55	40–45	40–45

TUNE-UP

Periodic tune-ups are necessary to keep a vehicle in good running condition. Some owners disregard service until something breaks or until the vehicle will not run. It is important to keep some type of service schedule which lists the date and mileage when the vehicle was last tuned.

Spark Plugs

Before servicing the spark plugs (about every 12,000 miles is suggested), clean any foreign material away from the spark plug ports. This material could fall into the combustion chamber when the plug is removed. Remove the spark plug wires from the plugs, one at a time, by pulling the slip-on connector from the top of the plug. Do not handle or pull on the wire itself. The inner portion breaks easily or could get kinked. This will cause the plug to misfire or not fire at all.

Remove the spark plug with a spark plug socket and examine the condition of the plug electrode. (See the Unit Repair Section for examples of sparkplug wear and problems.) Although sand blasting and cleaning is an acceptable means of servicing spark plugs, it will not provide the benefits of installing new ones.

Install the plugs and replace the plug wires making certain that they fit snugly over the top of the plug. If there is a loose fit, apply light pressure to the end of the wire with a pair of spark plug pliers. Run the wires through the looms making certain that none are touching the exhaust manifolds.

Electronic Ignition System

1977 THROUGH EARLY 1978

The electronic ignition system consists of three major component units: a distributor, an ignition coil and an electronic control unit.

The distributor is conventional except that a sensor and trigger wheel replace the usual contact points, condenser and distributor cam. A standard type ignition coil is used. The electronic ignition control is a completely solid state unit designed for trouble-free service. The control unit electronically makes and breaks the ignition primary circuit in response to triggering signals from

Electronic ignition with external control unit

To make compression tests; disconnect the harness plug at the control box or disconnect the lead at the negative terminal of the coil.

NOTE: Further ignition testing can be found in the Electrical Unit Section.

1978 AND LATER

The electronic control unit is built into the distributor body instead of being a separate unit. Distributor wiring has been changed and a new design distributor cap is used. The red wire from the distributor connects to the coil positive terminal. The brown wire from the distributor connects to the coil negative terminal and the third wire from the distributor, white in color, connects to the deceleration throttle modulator when used. Because primary voltage (low voltage) current is regulated within the electronic control unit, a ballast resistor or resistance wire is not required in the primary circuit.

NOTE: Refer to the 1977 section for air gap adjustment instructions.

the sensor in the distributor. The high voltage is directed in the conventional way, to the rotor, distributor cap, spark plug cables, and to the spark plugs.

Dwell angle is determined by the angle between the adjacent teeth of the trigger wheel and by the air gap between the ends of the wheel teeth and the center line of the sensor. Since no wearing surfaces exist on the trigger wheel and sensor, dwell remains constant and no adjustment is required after the initial sensor air gap is made.

Adjusting Air Gap

The air gap should be adjusted with the use of a brass (non-metallic) feeler gauge, placed between the center line of the sensor and a aligned tooth of the trigger wheel. Loosen

the sensor hold down screw and move the sensor until the gauge will pass through with a slight drag. Tighten the hold down screw.

Engine Misfiring/No Start Condition

In the event of engine misfire or surging, other possible sources of trouble should be checked first, such as carburetion and the fuel supply, before checking the ignition. Check for breaks in the wiring and for corroded or loose connections.

If the engine will not run at all, remove a lead from one of the spark plugs and hold it ½ inch from the engine block while cranking the engine. If there is no spark, check wiring and connections.

––––––––– CAUTION –––––––––
Never disconnect the high voltage lead between the coil and the distributor and never disconnect more than three spark plugs at a time unless the ignition switch is off.

Ignition Timing

NOTE: The timing light is connected to the No. 1 spark plug wire on 4 cylinder engines: No. 8 plug wire on V8 engines (304 and 345).

Ignition timing is the measurement in degrees of crankshaft rotation at the instant the spark plugs in the cylinders fire, in relation to the location of the piston, while the piston is on the compression stroke.

1. Remove and plug the vacuum line(s) from the distributor advance/retard mechanism. Be sure there is no vacuum leak at the line(s).
2. Connect the timing light.
3. Mark the crank pulley and timing quadrant lines with chalk or paint to make them easier to see.

Air gap—4 cylinder

Air gap—V8

1. Battery
2. Ignition switch
3. Ignition coil
4. Spark plug
5. Trigger wheel
6. Electronic control
7. Sensor
8. Air gap

Electronic ignition with built-in control unit

4. Start the engine and aim the timing light at the timing quadrant.

5. The timing is adjusted by loosening the distributor hold-down nut and turning the distributor either clockwise or counterclockwise as required until the mark on the pulley aligns with the correct degree marking on the quadrant.

6. Tighten the hold-down nut and recheck the timing, readjust if necessary.

7. Stop the engine, remove the timing light and reconnect the vacuum line(s).

Valve Lash

ADJUSTMENT (GASOLINE ENGINES)

The valve lash is not adjustable since hydraulic valve lifters are employed. If a lifter should become noisy; dirt, grit or metal chips may have becomed lodged in the lifter body. This problem may be alleviated by frequently changing the engine oil and filter. Remove the lifter, clean or replace it if the noise persists. Check the other valve train components for wear, replace as necessary.

Idle Speed and Mixture Adjustment

To comply with the mandated emission control requirements, certain procedures must be followed when adjusting the air/fuel mixture and speed. The engine must be at normal operating temperature, choke open, air cleaner installed, dwell and ignition timing correct, and the parking brake applied. The following procedures apply to all carburetors, with minor deviations possible, depending upon the carburetor used.

Observe the following precautions when adjusting the idle mixture and speed.

1. Do not idle the engine for longer than three minutes at a time.

2. After each three minute interval, increase the engine speed to 2,000 rpm for one minute.

3. Continue with the idle adjustment and repeat step 2 as necessary.

PRELIMINARY IDLE SETTING (AFTER CARBURETOR OVERHAUL)

1. Connect a calibrated tachometer to the engine.

2. Connect a test vacuum gauge to the engine intake manifold.

3. Operate the engine at a fast idle speed to bring the operating temperature to normal.

4. Adjust the carburetor to the specified idle speed. Refer to the chart at the beginning of this section.

1. Ignition coil
2. Trigger wheel
3. Electronic control
4. Distributor

Components of ignition system

5. Adjust the idle mixture screw(s) and idle speed screw to obtain "Lean best idle" at the specified speed.

NOTE: "Lean best idle" is the point at which intake manifold vacuum starts to drop due to leanness.

6. Install the colored (service) plastic cap(s) with the tab fully turned counterclockwise against the stop.

7. Adjust the idle speed to specifications.

8. Make final idle adjustments to obtain the recommended idle setting.

IDLE ADJUSTMENT—LEAN DROP METHOD

1. Connect a calibrated tachometer to the engine.

2. Rotate the idle adjusting screw(s) counterclockwise against the stops.

Typical timing marks

Fuel filter removal

Injection line removal

Water passage removal

3. Adjust the idle speed to give an engine speed 25 rpm higher than the specified idle speed.

4. Rotate the idle mixture screw(s) clockwise slowly and equally (if two) until the specified speed is obtained.

5. If the engine is rough or the specified idle speed cannot be attained, remove the limiter cap(s) and continue the adjustment as outlined in step 4, until the specified rpm is attained and the engine is smooth.

6. Install new plastic limiter cap(s) with the tab fully counterclockwise against the stop.

7. Readjust as necessary to maintain the specified rpm.

IDLE ADJUSTMENT— EXHAUST ANALYZER METHOD

When exhaust analyzer equipment is used, the following procedure is recommended to be used to adjust the idle mixture and speed. The test equipment must give accurate readings in the 0–5% carbon monoxide (CO) range.

1. Connect a calibrated tachometer to the engine and insert the exhaust analyzer into the exhaust pipe.

NOTE: Refer to the manufacturers instructions for complete connection procedures.

2. Operate the engine for fifteen minutes at fast idle speed (approximately 1000–1200 rpm), to bring engine to normal operating temperature and to stabilize the temperature of the exhaust analyzer.

3. Calibrate the test equipment as per the manufacturers instructions.

NOTE: If the combustion analyzer does not respond to changes in the mixture quality, check for leaks or restrictions in the sample lines. The thermal conductivity instruments used in the analyzer are both temperature and pressure sensitive, and require a definite sample flow. Refer to the manufacturer's instructions as necessary.

4. Adjust the idle mixture screw(s) counterclockwise against the tab stop.

5. Adjust the idle speed screw to obtain the specified idle speed.

6. Observe the analyzer dial and adjust the idle mixture screw(s) clockwise by 1/16 turn increments to obtain the specified idle mixture setting and readjust the idle speed as necessary.

7. If the idle speed and mixture cannot be obtained, remove the idle limiter cap(s).

NOTE: To prevent damage to the mixture screw(s) or seat, file or grind the side of the plastic cap. Do not pry cap off.

8. With the engine operating, adjust the mixture screw(s) to obtain the "lean best idle" at the specified idle speed.

NOTE: "Lean best idle" is the point at which maximum manifold vacuum begins to drop due to leanness.

9. Install new plastic limiter cap(s) with the tab fully counterclockwise against the stop.

10. Readjust the idle mixture screw(s) to obtain the recommended CO setting.

NOTE: After completing the idle adjustment procedure, if unsatisfactory idle operation still exists, a recheck of the ignition system, crankcase ventilation system, timing advance system, air induction system, exhaust gas recirculation system, or hot idle compensation system should be made.

Diesel Fuel Systems

NOTE: This section contains procedures requiring many special tools. For reference purposes, International Harvester factory numbers are included in the text. These tools may be available from a number of different sources. We encourage you to shop competitively for price and quality and to cross-reference these numbers as necessary in purchasing your tools.

1. Remove the inlet and outlet lines from the oil cooler.

2. Remove the bolts (4) and separate the oil filter and lines from the cooler.

3. Remove the coolant hose between the oil cooler and the head.

4. Remove the bolts (10) and separate the cooler from the block.

5. Disconnect the fuel lines and remove the fuel filter from the bracket.

6. Remove the injection lines from the nozzles and pump. Cover all openings immediately.

7. Remove the fan, spacer and pulley from the water pump.

8. Remove the bypass hose from the pump and thermostat housing.

9. Remove the three bolts and lift off the water pump and gasket.

10. Remove the inspection cover and pointer from the flywheel housing and lock the flywheel in place with a locking tool.

11. Flatten the lockwasher and remove the crankshaft pulley nut.

12. Tap evenly around the edge of the pulley using a brass drift, until the cone protrudes from the pulley. Remove the cone.

13. Drive the pulley and damper from the crankshaft with a soft mallet.

14. Remove the inner cover from the timing gear case.

15. Pry out the oil seal.

16. Remove the mounting bolts and tap the case loose with a soft mallet.

17. Remove the tachometer drive support nuts.

18. Remove the timer round nut.

19. Thread the timer extractor, special tool #57926-581 into the timer weight holder. Remove the timer assembly by tightening the extractor bolt.

20. Unbolt and separate the injection pump from the front end plate.

21. Temporarily install the injection pump and gasket on the front plate.

22. Check the timing marks and bring the #1 piston to TDC.

23. Mesh the injection pump drive gear and idler gear at the timing marks.

24. After aligning the injection pump keyway, install the lockwasher and round nut and torque to 50–58 ft. lbs.

25. Install the tachometer drive coupling.

26. Check the backlash between the pump drive gear and the idler gear. Backlash should be .0028–.0079". Adjust if necessary.

27. Remove the #1 cylinder holder clamp, loosen the delivery valve and pull out the delivery spring. Tighten the valve holder to 22–25 ft. lbs.

28. Connect the fuel supply lines.

29. Bring the #1 piston to 20° BTDC. This can be done by aligning the first mark, in normal rotation, on the crankshaft pulley with the raised line on the gear case.

30. Hand prime the pump. Push the pump in all the way toward the block. Move the pump slowly away from the block until the fuel just stops flowing from the valve holder. Lock the pump in place.

31. Remove the delivery holder and assemble the spring. Torque the holder to 22–25 ft. lbs.

32. Install remaining parts in reverse order of removal.

NOTE: Oil filter bolt torque is 15–18 ft. lbs.

Injection Nozzle

REMOVAL, OVERHAUL & INSTALLATION

1. Loosen the injection lines at the pump and nozzles and remove the lines. Cap the openings immediately.

2. Unscrew the injector and holder from the head.

3. Secure the nozzle holder in a vise and remove the lock nut.

4. Remove the nipple.

5. Remove the nozzle holder body from the nozzle nut.

6. Remove the spacer collar and pushrod.

7. Remove the nozzle holder body from the vise and remove the nozzle spring and adjusting shims.

NOTE: The adjusting shims may be removed with a piece of wire, but great care must be taken to avoid damage to the nozzle tip.

8. Clean fuel oil may be used to clean all parts. Inspect all parts for damage and good fit.

9. Assemble the nozzle in reverse order of disassembly.

Timing cover removal

Tachometer drive coupling installation

Connecting injection lines

Oil seal removal

Delivery valve spring removal

Removing the cam cover

Removing timer round nut

#1 piston at 20° BTDC

Feed pump removal

Injection pump and endplate assembly

Removing the idling spring, type RAD

Timer installation

Lock the pump at this point, which is the beginning of injection

Removing the idling spring, type RSV

Removing the idling sub spring

Removing the timer

Removing the governor cover and link

Removing delivery valve holder lock plate

Loosening the delivery valve holder

Removing the counterweights

Removing the delivery valve holder and spring

Removing the governor body

Removing the delivery valve with tool 57930-032

10. Install the nozzle in a tester.

11. Operate the tester lever at 1 stroke per second and read the pressure at injection. The pointer will oscillate slightly during injection.

12. Increase or decrease the thickness of the nozzle spring adjusting shims until opening pressure is 1,422.3 psi. A total of 31 different shims are available. A shim thickness of .05mm equals a difference of 85.338 psi.

13. Install the nozzles and lines. Torque the nozzles to 50–65 ft. lbs.

Governor

RSV MECHANICAL TYPE REMOVAL

1. Remove the injection pump and place it in a holding fixture.
2. Install the timer.
3. Drain the cam and governor chambers.
4. Remove the supply pump.
5. Remove the cam cover.
6. Using a special wrench, ST-57916-432, on the timer, turn the camshaft until all the tappets are raised to TDC. Place a tappet holder, 57931-210, between the tappet adjusting bolt and nut for each cylinder.
7. Remove the rear cover and dipstick.
8. Loosen the balance idler spring and the auxiliary idler spring lock nut.
9. Loosen the governor cover lock screw.
10. Unbolt and remove the governor cover from the governor body. Remove the link from the control rack.
11. Remove the start spring from the spring eye.
12. Remove the counterweights from the camshaft.
13. Hold the timer and remove the slotted nuts and lockwashers.
14. Using a puller, ST57926-512, remove the flyweight assembly.
15. Remove the timer.
16. Unbolt and remove the governor body.

MZ PNEUMATIC TYPE REMOVAL

1. Follow steps 1 through 6 of RSV Type Removal.
2. Unbolt and remove the diaphragm housing and main spring.
3. Remove the diaphragm ring with a screwdriver.
4. Remove the cotter pin from the connecting rod bolt with a needle-nosed pliers.
5. Remove the diaphragm assembly from the control rack.
6. Remove the five set screws and remove the governor body by applying force with a screwdriver blade in the slit between the governor and pump housings.
7. Remove the timer.

RSV TYPE INSTALLATION

1. Apply RTV silicone gasket material to the governor body and install the governor on the injection pump.
2. Tighten the upper spring eye screw holding the starting spring.
3. Install the timer.
4. Install the flyweight assembly.
5. Apply RTV silicone gasket material to the governor cover and install the starting spring on the housing side of the spring eye.
6. Install the link leaf spring in the hole in the end of the control rack.
7. Install the cover and set screws.

MZ TYPE INSTALLATION

1. Apply RTV silicone gasket material to the governor body, position it on the pump body and tap it into position with a plastic mallet. Install the set screws.
2. Install the diaphragm and balance spring on the control rack connecting bolt and lock with a new cotter pin. Apply chassis lube to the diaphragm ring.
3. Insert the main spring and install diaphragm housing with the four bolts.

Injection Pump Service

REPLACING THE DELIVERY VALVE

1. Thoroughly clean the area around the nozzle tube and delivery valve.
2. Remove the nozzle tube.
3. Remove the delivery valve holder lock plate.
4. Remove the delivery valve holder and spring.
5. Using ST57930-032, remove the delivery valve.
6. Position the delivery valve in the pump housing making sure no dirt gets between the top of the plunger barrel and the delivery valve.
7. Install a new delivery valve gasket. The gasket is installed with the larger face downward and may be tapped into place through the extractor.
8. Install the delivery valve spring.
9. Install the delivery valve holder and torque it to 22–25 ft. lbs.
10. Loosen the holder and retorque it.
11. Install the lock plate, nozzle tube and nozzle clamp.

REPLACING THE PLUNGER

1. Remove the delivery valve.
2. Push the plunger spring up with two screwdrivers and remove the lower spring seat from the plunger.
3. Insert a hooked wire through the top of the pump housing, down through the plunger opening and hook it on the lead unit of the plunger. Pull up to remove the plunger and barrel.

4. Immerse a new plunger in clean fuel oil and thoroughly wash off the rust preventive.

NOTE: The plunger was lapped at the factory. Do not hold it by the lapped section.

5. Operate the plunger in clean fuel oil to check its operation.
6. Slowly insert the plunger and barrel into the pump with the barrel groove and plunger notch facing forward. Make certain

Plunger barrel removal, with delivery valves removed

Inserting the plunger spring holder

Inserting tappet holder and insert tool

Removing tappet with tappet clamp

Removing plunger springs, control sleeves and upper spring seats

Control rack; punch mark is indicated by arrow

Control sleeves installed

Removing plungers with tool 57921-412

Fuel feed pump removal

Checking injection start timing with a lift gauge

Turning the adjusting bolt

Loosening the pinion set screw

Installing the appropriate sized pin

the plunger piston pin is properly seated in the groove in the control sleeve.

7. Push the plunger spring up with two screwdrivers and insert the lower spring seat.

8. Install the remaining parts in reverse of disassembly.

REPLACING THE TAPPETS

1. Remove the delivery valve, plunger and plunger barrel.
2. Remove the plunger spring.
3. Remove the tappet.
4. Installation is the reverse of removal.

TESTING AND ADJUSTING THE FUEL INJECTION PUMP

NOTE: It is necessary to inspect and adjust the pump, using a pump tester, whenever it has been disassembled and assembled, when the plunger or plunger barrel have been replaced or when any of the component parts have been re-

Checking tappet clearance

Attaching a measuring device to the pump

Installing the tester lock screw

placed. Use nozzle tube 57805-002 and test nozzle 5000-101, starting pressure 1422.3 psi. Clean No. 2 fuel should be used. Rotating direction, from drive side, is clockwise. Sequence is 1-4-2-6-3-5.

1. Remove the fuel feed pump and cover plate from the injection pump.
2. Install the injection pump on the tester and holding fixture.
3. Connect the test coupling to the tester drive shaft with the coupling disc.
4. Remove the cap and position the tester dial to measure the camshaft rotating angle.
5. Install a tappet lift gauge on the No. 1 tappet.
6. Bottom the tappet and set the dial gauge to 0.
7. Bleed the pump at the bleeder screw.
8. Loosen the nozzle holder ball valve.
9. Feed fuel to the pump inlet while slowly turning the pump tester by hand in the normal engine rotation direction. Fuel will flow from the test nozzle. When the fuel stops flowing the injection point has been reached. The tappet, at this precise point, must be .08858–.09251″ above BDC.
10. If the fuel does not stop flowing after .0926″, turn the adjusting bolt counterclockwise to raise the position of the plunger.
11. If the fuel stops flowing before .0886″, turn the adjusting bolt clockwise to lower the plunger position.
12. When adjustment is made, torque the locknut to 43–50 ft. lbs.
13. With the pump set at initial injection, set the angle scale mark on the tester flywheel at 0 or 180°.
14. If adjustment is correct, fuel should stop flowing at No. 4 cylinder when the tester has been turned 60° in normal rotation. If fuel does not stop flowing at the correct time, adjust as above.
15. Check and adjust each cylinder in turn.
16. When timing for each cylinder is correct, position the cam at TDC, check the plunger piston pin-to-plunger barrel clearance and make sure that the tappet vertical clearance is at least .0118″ for each tappet.

STANDARD FUEL INJECTION VOLUME ADJUSTMENT

1. Determine the zero position of the control by attaching the measuring device to the pump and pushing the index all the way to governor side. Match the scale on the left end of the index and set the 0 (zero) position of the scale at the position at which the measuring device index stops. On RSV mechanical governors, loosen the stop bolt to align this index.
2. Remove the rack guide screw from the rear of the pump housing and apply the lock screw attached to the tester. Secure the control rack in the standard position for adjustment.

NOTE: The lock screw should be tightened by hand; overtightening will bend the rack.

3. Start the tester and run the pump at rated speed.

4. Set the pump feed pressure at 21.3–22.75 psi and measure the injection volume at the rated stroke of the female cylinder.

5. In the same manner, measure the injection volume at rated speed and standard rack position. Compute the rate of unevenness of the injection.

6. If the results show that the mean injection volume and rate of unevenness are not within the limits, adjust by changing the relative position of the control pinion and control sleeve. This may be done by:

a. Loosen the pinion set screw.

b. Place a pin in the hole in the control sleeve and adjust by moving the control sleeve along the control rack a little at a time.

c. When adjustment is completed, secure the pinion set screw.

d. Remove the lock screw from the control rack and reinstall the guide screw.

Testing and Adjusting the Governor

RSV MECHANICAL GOVERNOR

1. Match the adjusting device index to the zero point on the scale and set the control rack to the zero position.

2. Operate the control lever and make certain the full stroke of the rack is .827".

3. Make certain that the rack moves freely in the direction for maximum fuel injection by the spring force of the starting spring.

4. Set the stop bolt to remove any significant load on the governor linkage.

5. Set the stop bolt to give a control rack setting of .0197–.03937".

HIGH SPEED ADJUSTMENT

6. Remove the governor rear cover.

7. Loosen the full load stop lock nut and adjust the full load stop so that its setting corresponds to an A rack position between rotation and BC. See the accompanying chart.

8. To increase the volume, turn the stop to the right; left to decrease.

$$\text{Unevenness} = \frac{\text{Max or min injection volume for each plunger} - \text{Main injection volume}}{\text{Mean injection volume}} \times 100$$

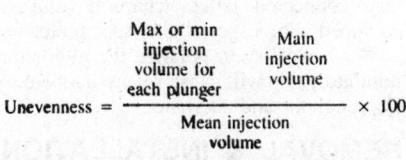

MAXIMUM SPEED ADJUSTMENT

9. Operate the pump at speed G and adjust the maximum speed stop so that the control rack position is G mm.

SPEED FLUCTUATION ADJUSTMENT

10. Speed fluctuation can be controlled by varying the spring rate on RSV governors.

BALANCE SPRING ADJUSTMENT

11. Set the control lever to the point where it contacts the maximum speed stop and operate the pump at a rate of F, between A and B.

12. Install the balance spring assembly under the tension lever.

13. Tighten the balance spring assembly with tool 57916-212 until the control rack position G is H mm. and secure with the lock nut.

14. Gradually accelerate the engine from speed D and make certain that the control rack is at G mm when the action of the spring ends at speed E.

Adjusting the idling spring

Auxiliary idle spring adjustment

Pump installed on tester, with synchronizer and strobe light

Adjusting the full load stopper bolt (RAD shown)

Schematic diagram of the governor

1. Speed control lever
2. Speed adjusting bolt (stopper bolt)

Adjusting the speed adjustment bolt (RSV shown)

Maximum speed stopper adjustment

IDLE SPEED ADJUSTMENT

15. Set the control lever at the stop position so that the control rack is at point B.

16. Set the speed to D and tighten the idle auxiliary spring so that the position of the rack is C mm. Secure with the lock nut.

NOTE: Do not tighten the auxiliary idle spring too much or overspeeding will result.

MZ PNEUMATIC GOVERNOR

1. Set the measuring device index at the zero point on the scale and set the control rack at the zero position.

2. Operate the control lever and make certain the full stroke of the control rack is .827".

3. Connect a hose between the vacuum pump of the tester and the negative pressure chamber of the governor. Apply negative pressure equal to engine operation.

4. Operate the pump at 500 rpm and adjust the governor.

5. Tighten the stroke set screw so that the control rack is set at a position equal to zero.

6. Adjust the stroke of the balance spring to .236".

7. If movement of the control rack deviates considerably from the performance curve, adjust by increasing or decreasing the thickness of the adjusting shims.

8. Operate the tester vacuum pump and check the control rack position and movement in relation to the pressure shown on the gauge. If the movement of the control rack for pressure variations does not conform to the performance curve, the idle speed is either too high or too low. Turn the auxiliary idle spring right to increase and left to decrease speed.

TESTING AND ADJUSTING THE TIMER

1. Install a timing light, such as tool 5783-001 on the tester using the cover plate attaching bolts, so that the synchronizer lever attachment is applied to the tappet.

2. Start the pump and turn on the timing light.

3. Direct the light at the angle scale on the flywheel and measure the angular change based on variations in pump speed.

4. If the tester does not have an angle scale:
   a. Attach an angle scale to the timer coupling and mount a pointer on the tester drive shaft.
   b. Operate the pump and direct the light on the scale.

5. If the angular change is not within limits, disassemble the timer and adjust the spring force by increasing or decreasing the shims, or if necessary, replace the spring.

ENGINE ELECTRICAL

Distributor

REMOVAL

1. Remove the distributor wire harness connected to the coil.

2. Remove the distributor cap by either unsnapping the retaining clips or twisting the retaining clamps with a screwdriver. Bump the engine until the top dead center marks on the timing case and pointer are aligned on the compression stroke.

3. Using chalk or paint, carefully mark the position of the distributor rotor in relation to the distributor housing, and the position of the distributor housing in relation to the engine block. When this is done, you should have a line on the distributor housing directly in line with the tip of the rotor and another line on the engine block directly in line with the mark on the distributor housing. These markings are important because the distributor must be installed in the *exact* same position to avoid having to retime the engine.

4. Remove the vacuum line(s) from the advance diaphragm.

5. Remove the bolt that attaches the distributor to the engine block and pull the unit straight up and out of the engine.

INSTALLATION—ENGINE NOT DISTURBED

1. Before installing the distributor, replace the distributor mounting gasket in the engine counterbore.

2. Turn the rotor so the tip is aligned with the mark made on the housing during removal. Then turn the rotor about ⅛ turn in the opposite direction of distributor rotation past the mark.

3. Lower the distributor into the mounting hole and align the mark on the distributor housing with the one on the engine block.

NOTE: It may be necessary to move the rotor slightly to start the gear into mesh with the camshaft gear, but the rotor should align with the mark on the distributor housing when the distributor is down in place.

4. Install the distributor hold-down bolt and lockwasher but do not fully tighten.

5. Connect the distributor wire to the negative pole of the coil.

6. Install the distributor cap making certain that all the leads are all the way into the cap. Secure the cap.

NOTE: If the distributor cap is misaligned on its locating slots, the rotor and the cap will be damaged.

7. Start the engine and set the timing.

INSTALLATION WHEN THE ENGINE HAS BEEN DISTURBED

If the engine was turned over with the distributor removed or if you have installed the distributor incorrectly and the engine will not start, it will be necessary to time the engine from scratch.

1. Remove No. 1 spark plug. Have an assistant rotate the engine while you hold your finger over the plug port. Continue rotating slowly until you feel pressure and the timing mark on the crankshaft pulley lines up with the mark on the timing tab.

2. Install a new distributor mounting gasket in the counterbore of the engine.

3. Locate the No. 1 spark plug wire tower on the distributor cap.

4. Scribe a locating mark on the body of the distributor directly below the No. 1 spark plug wire tower with the cap installed.

5. Remove the cap, install the distributor, and align the rotor with the mark on the housing.

6. It may be necessary to turn the rotor slightly to get the distributor and the camshaft gears to mesh but the rotor should still align when the distributor is bottomed.

7. Install the distributor hold-down bolt and hand tighten.

8. Install the No. 1 spark plug, the distributor lead to the coil, and any plug wires which were removed.

9. Install the distributor cap making certain that the tang on the distributor body aligns with the slot in the distributor cap.

10. Start the engine and check the timing.

Alternator

PRECAUTIONS

Rectifiers and regulators in alternator systems are easily damaged by incorrect polarity. Observe the following precautions when wiring and testing circuits:

1. Always be certain of battery polarity.

2. Always connect booster battery negative to negative and positive to positive.

3. Never ground alternator output terminal.

4. When adjusting voltage regulator, be careful not to short adjusting tool.

5. Before making any tests, turn off ignition switch and disconnect battery ground.

6. Never use a fast charge with the battery connected unless charging unit is equipped with a special alternator protector.

7. Never try to polarize the alternator regulator, this will cause severe damage to the regulator and alternator.

REMOVAL & INSTALLATION

1. Disconnect the negative battery cable.

2. Remove the wire terminals from the rear of the alternator.

3. Loosen the adjusting strap and pivot bolts. Push inward on the alternator to loosen the belt and slip it off the pulley.

4. Remove the adjusting strap and pivot bolts, and remove the alternator from the engine.

5. Installation is in the reverse of the removal. Adjust the belt to have no more than ½ inch deflection on the longest span of the belt.

Voltage Regulators

Two types of voltage regulators are used to control the output of the alternators. One type is the internal unit, mounted with-in the alternator, and the second is an external type, normally mounted on the inner fender panel or the firewall.

VOLTAGE REGULATOR REMOVAL

External Type

1. Disconnect clamp lead at the negative terminal of battery.

2. Disconnect the wiring harness connector at regulator terminals.

3. Remove mounting screws and regulator unit from vehicle.

4. To install, reverse the above procedure.

5. Reconnect cable clamp to battery terminal, checking polarity first.

Internal Type

1. Remove the alternator as outlined.

2. Mark and separate the front housing from the rear housing.

3. Remove the diode trio screws and nuts, and remove the trio assembly.

4. Remove the two remaining screws in the regulator, and remove the brush holder and the regulator from the rear housing.

5. Installation is the reverse order of the removal, assuring that the insulated sleeves are installed on the proper screws, during installation.

NOTE: Refer to the General Repair Section for more repair information.

Starter

For servicing and overhauling starter motors, see General Repair Section.

REMOVAL & INSTALLATION

1. Disconnect cable clamp from negative terminal of battery.

2. Disconnect cable and wire leads from terminals of solenoid assembly, identifying leads with tags. If the solenoid is not mounted directly on the starter motor, disconnect the cable from the solenoid to the motor at the motor terminal.

3. Remove starter motor mounting bolts or stud nuts.

4. Pull starter assembly forward to clear housing and remove starter.

5. To install, reverse the above procedure, installing new tang lockwashers where removed.

ENGINE MECHANICAL

Design

4 CYLINDER

The 196 cubic inch engine is a slant model with overhead valves and hydraulic lifters. The cylinder block and head are cast iron. The crankshaft is supported by five main bearings.

6 CYLINDER DIESEL

The six cylinder diesel engine is built for IHC by Nissan. Between 1976 and 1979, the engine was normally aspirated. In 1980, it was offered in a turbocharged mode.

V8 ENGINES

The V8 engines are overhead valve, 90° engines, all using a cast iron block and heads. The crankshaft is forged steel and is supported by five main bearings. Pistons are aluminum alloy and use cast iron connecting rods. Piston pins are press fit with the lower end of the connecting rod and cap containing a locking type bearing insert.

Hydraulic lifters are used in all V8s and maintain a zero valve lash.

The cylinder heads use positive valve rotators on the exhaust valves. This device is called a "rotocap" and is located at the base of each valve spring.

The distributor, which is located at the front of the engine, is driven directly by the camshaft.

ENGINE REMOVAL & INSTALLATION

The following is an outline of general engine removal. Removal procedure will vary from truck to truck due to the variety of body models and accessory equipment. Before lifting out engine be certain that everything has been disconnected. Remove anything that might be in the way of the actual lifting.

1. Drain water from radiator and engine block.

2. Drain crankcase oil.

3. Disconnect negative battery ground cable and remove cable clamp from hot terminal of battery.

4. Remove all water hoses to radiator and heater.

5. Remove fan blades and fan shroud.

6. Remove any radiator cross-brace rods or brackets.

7. Remove radiator mounting bolts and lift out radiator.

8. Remove hood hinge bracket mounting bolts and remove hood assembly.

9. Disconnect and remove air filter from engine. Remove breather hose from air cleaner, if applicable.

10. Disconnect fuel pump inlet line.

11. Remove vacuum lines from manifold and all other components, and lines from air compressor, and air pump, if applicable.

12. Disconnect throttle linkage, choke control wire and hand throttle control wire, if applicable. On V8 engines remove the carburetor, if necessary, for the fitting of the lifting fixture.

13. If so equipped, disconnect wire from heater control valve.

14. Disconnect all wiring from engine:
   a. Water temperature gauge sender.
   b. Oil pressure gauge sender.
   c. Generator wires.
   d. Primary ignition wire to resistor.
   e. Starter solenoid wires and battery cable.

15. If so equipped, remove tachometer drive at the distributor on the small V8— or at the rear of the block on the big V8.

16. Disconnect exhaust pipes at manifolds.

—— CAUTION ——
Have the air conditioning system "bled" by a professional using the proper tools and safe procedures.

17. If so equipped, remove automatic transmission filler tube, freon compressor lines and disconnect power steering pump line and hose.

18. Install lifting fixtures and suitable sling. On V-8 models the lifting fixture is mounted on the intake manifold where the carburetor was removed.

19. Connect hoisting equipment to lifting fixture and hoist enough to support engine.

20. Remove bell housing mounting bolts. On V8 engines the flywheel housing front cover is removed before the flywheel housing is removed from crankcase.

21. Disconnect clutch linkage.

22. Remove front engine mounting bolts. On some models it is easier to unbolt the mount from the frame crossmember.

23. Remove side engine mount bolts.

24. In hoisting out engine, first pull engine forward to clear clutch assembly from transmission, then tilt front up and carefully out of the chassis.

—— CAUTION ——
Avoid damaging clutch driven disc.

25. Installation of the engine is in general the reverse of the above described pro-

Diesel engine—cylinder head tightening sequence

Gas engine—6 cyl head tightening sequence

Rotator used under the exhaust valve spring

CAUTION

Do not use a power wrench on heads of engines with hydraulic lifters. Torque head bolts slowly so that the leakdown of the lifters may relieve strain from the valve train.

12. On all engines, tighten the head bolts in the sequence illustrated to 90–100 ft. lbs.

13. Retorque head bolts to the specified torque after 1000 miles of operation.

14. Install rocker covers and any other equipment removed for head work. Replace rocker cover gasket if necessary.

Diesel Engine

1. Remove the air cleaner.

2. Remove the crankcase vent hose and remove the intake and exhaust manifolds. These are bolted together.

3. Remove the alternator, bracket and belts.

4. Disconnect the coolant hose between the head and the oil cooler.

5. Remove the fuel filter assembly.

6. Disconnect the injection lines from the pump and the injectors. Cap all openings at once.

7. Remove the bypass hoses between the coolant pump and the thermostat housing.

8. Remove the fan.

9. Remove the rocker arm cover.

10. Remove the rocker arm shaft assembly.

11. Remove the pushrods and keep them in order.

12. Remove the fuel return lines.

13. Remove the nozzles from the head.

14. Remove the cylinder head bolts in the sequence shown.

15. Attach a hoist to the head and lift it clear of the block. On occasion, the precombustion chambers may fall out, especially if the head is bumped or handled roughly. Take care that they are returned to their original positions if this occurs.

16. Remove the head gasket and O-rings.

NOTE: Before disassembling the head, make all necessary valve train measurements.

17. Place the head in a holding fixture.

18. Disassemble the valves. Mark all parts for assembly in their original positions.

19. Remove the retaining wire and lift off the valve stem seals.

20. Unscrew the glow plugs.

21. Disassemble the rocker arm shaft by removing the cotter pins at either end. Keep all parts in order. If rocker arm brackets prove to be difficult to remove, immerse the assembly in water heated to about 160°F. Immersion for a few minutes will loosen the parts.

22. Clean and inspect all parts.

23. Check the head with a straightedge. Maximum warpage is .0079″. Do not remove more than .011″ from the head.

---

cedure. Be careful when installing that wires are not pinched between engine and frame. Lower the engine until transmission main drive gear spline can be aligned with the clutch driven disc. The weight of the engine must remain supported until the bell housing is secured to flywheel housing. After engine has been secured to chassis, remove hoisting equipment and lifting fixtures.

Reconnect all air conditioning lines. Have the system evacuated and recharged.

Cylinder Head

CYLINDER HEAD REMOVAL AND INSTALLATION

V8 and 4 Cylinder Engines

1. Disconnect negative battery cable. Remove spark plug wires and spark plugs. Remove intake and exhaust manifolds as described in the following section. On V8's, this may entail removal of the air compressor and air compressor mounting bracket.

2. Remove valve covers and gaskets.

3. Loosen rocker arm shaft bracket bolts and remove the rocker arm assembly.

NOTE: Be sure to remove and keep track of the two dowel sleeves on the end brackets of the rocker arm assembly.

4. Remove pushrods, marking them so that they may be installed in their same locations.

5. Remove cylinder head bolts.

6. When lifting off cylinder, do not lose the two locating dowel sleeves.

7. Installation is basically the reverse of the above procedure, with the exception of the following additional steps.

8. Be sure to use a new head gasket and to reinstall dowel sleeves when positioning the head and mounting the rocker assembly. Reinstall pushrods in their original locations.

9. On all engines, turn engine crankshaft until leading edge of balance weight on crankshaft pulley is aligned with the zero degree mark on the timing indicator before installing rocker arm assembly.

10. On 4-196 engines, be sure to install rocker assembly so that the oil feed shaft bracket is third from the rear.

11. On V8 engines, install rocker arm assembly so that the notches at the end of the shaft are facing upward. Oil feed brackets are third from the rear on the right (even numbers) bank and third from the front on the left (odd numbers) bank.

24. Check the valve springs for free length and tilt. Free length must not be less than 1.850″ and tilt must not exceed .03937″ (1mm).

25. Valve seats may be removed by cracking with a cold chisel or with a valve seat remover. New valve seats should be put in dry ice for five minutes prior to installation, at the same time the head should be immersed in 175°F water.

26. Assemble the head in reverse order of disassembly.

27. Place a new cylinder head gasket on the block with the stainless steel inset side facing up.

28. Install the O-rings around the water and oil passages.

29. Position the head on the block.

30. Coat the head bolts with clean engine oil and torque them in sequence, in stages as follows:
   a. Large: 43, 94
   b. Small: 21, 36

31. Install the pushrods, pressing down and turning them to be sure of proper seating.

32. Install the rocker arm shaft assembly, torquing the bolts to 18 ft. lbs. in sequence from the center to each end.

33. Install the injection nozzles.

34. Install all other parts in reverse order of removal.

Gasoline Engines

VALVE ROTATORS

4 Cylinder and V8 Engines

On the 4-196, V-304, V-345 engines, rotators are used between the valve spring and the cylinder head on the exhaust valve only.

NOTE: Keep the valves and their related parts together so they may be reinstalled in their respective positions.

Valve Train Service

The 4-196 and V-8 engines utilized hydraulic lifters for which there is no lash adjustment. Excess noise in the valve train of these engines indicates that service is required. Instructions for servicing hydraulic lifters may be found in the General Repair Section.

Valve removal, service, and installation procedures may be found in the Engine Rebuilding section. See specifications table at the beginning of this section for valve spring and valve seat angle specifications.

ROCKER ARM

Removal and Installation

1. Remove rocker cover and gasket.
2. Remove rocker arm assembly mounting bolts and flat washers.
3. Remove rocker assembly.
4. If applicable, remove clip-ring and

retainer to disassemble rocker components. Be sure to keep all parts in order so that they may be replaced in their original positions.

5. Clean all parts thoroughly, making sure that oil passages are clear. If necessary to remove plugs from ends of shaft, drill a hole in one plug, knock out the other with a steel rod, then knock out the drilled plug.

6. Inspect shaft for wear and warpage. Replace bent or worn shaft.

Intake Manifold

REMOVAL & INSTALLATION

4 Cylinder and V8 Engines

1. If engine is in vehicle, remove air cleaner and, if applicable, governor vacuum line.

2. Disconnect throttle linkage, choke cable and fuel line.

3. Remove carburetor.

4. On V-304, 345 engines, disconnect hose from thermostat housing and bracket for spark plug wires.

5. On 4 cylinder models, remove coil, coil mounting bracket and ignition resistor from intake manifold.

6. Remove positive crankcase ventilation pipe and vacuum line.

7. Remove mounting bolts, manifold and gasket.

8. Installation is the reverse of the above procedure. Install new gaskets and tighten the mounting bolts from the center out, torquing to 40–45 ft. lbs.

Exhaust Manifold

REMOVAL & INSTALLATION

4 Cylinder and V8 Engines

1. Disconnect exhaust pipe from manifold.

2. Unbolt exhaust manifold from head.

3. Remove manifold.

4. Installation is the reverse of the above procedure. Install new manifold-to-head gasket and new manifold-to-pipe gasket.

5. Torque manifold-to-head bolts to 25–30 ft. lbs.

6. Inspect rocker arm shaft bushings for wear, the bushing is integral with the rocker arm, and if the bushing is worn, the whole rocker arm must be replaced.

7. Inspect valve stem contact pad surfaces of rocker arm and resurface if wear is excessive. Do not remove more than .010″ of material when resurfacing.

8. If applicable, replace any defective tension springs.

9. Remove and inspect push rods one by one (to insure original position). Roll them on a flat surface to check for straightness. Replace any pushrods that are bent, have loose ends or are worn.

11. Reassemble all rocker arm assembly components in their original order.

12. Install rocker arm assembly, making sure that the oil feed bracket is in the proper position and that dowel sleeves are in place. On 4-196 and V-304, 345 engines turn the crankshaft until leading edge of balance weight on crankshaft pulley is aligned with the zero degree mark on the timing indicator before installing rocker arm assembly.

13. Tighten mounting bolts.

14. Adjust rocker arm to valve stem clearance as described above.

15. Install rocker cover, replacing gasket if necessary.

Timing Case & Gears

4-196 AND V8 ENGINES CRANKSHAFT PULLEY REMOVAL

Accessibility of the crankcase pulley and front (timing) cover will vary according to the model. On some vehicles the timing case will be accessible only if the engine is completely removed. The following instructions are general and apply to most front cover repairs and service.

1. Drain cooling system.

2. Disconnect radiator hoses and remove radiator. In some cases the radiator shroud and truck hood must be removed.

3. Loosen front engine mounts and jack up engine enough to provide access to the crankshaft pulley with a puller.

4. Loosen and remove fan belts and remove fan blades.

5. Remove crankshaft pulley retaining bolt. The vibration damper behind the pulley must be removed with a puller.

6. Using a suitable puller, remove the pulley from the crankshaft. On some models the pulley is in two pieces and the pulley must be unbolted from its hub before the hub is removed with a puller.

Front Oil Seal

REMOVAL & INSTALLATION

1. Remove crankshaft pulley as described in the preceding procedure, steps 1 through 6.

2. Remove seal. It is preferable to use an appropriate seal puller. Use a new gasket when installing front cover and be sure to align cover before tightening.

3. Install a new seal using a suitable seal installing tool if possible. Lubricate first and be careful not to damage seal or seating surface of cover.

4. Install crankshaft pulley, fan belt and fan blades.

5. Lower engine and tighten mounting bolts.

6. Install radiator, shroud, hoses and whatever else was removed.

7. Fill cooling system.

TIMING GEAR REMOVAL

Timing gears can be removed without disassembling the engine. In some cases, however, the engine must be removed.

1. Remove crankcase pulley as described in steps 1 through 6 of Crankshaft Pulley Removal.

2. Remove engine front cover.

3. Rotate engine to align timing marks on crankshaft gear and camshaft gear.

4. To remove either gear, remove bolt and washer. Use a suitable puller.

NOTE: Replace both the cam gear and crankshaft gear, due to being serviced in matched sets.

5. Use a suitable installing tool to install gears. Lubricate with engine oil and insert key in shaft to align gear. Align timing marks as illustrated. Be careful not to damage threads on shaft. Install and tighten retaining bolt.

6. Rotate engine to check that gears are not binding.

7. Check gear backlash with a dial indicator. It should be within .0005–.0045" on OHV4 and V8 engines.

8. Use a new gasket when installing front cover and be sure to align cover before tightening. On some models there is an oil slinger on the crankshaft.

9. Install crankshaft pulley, belt and fan blades. Tighten retaining bolt.

10. Lower engine and tighten engine mounting bolts.

11. Install radiator and hoses.

12. Fill cooling system.

CAMSHAFT REMOVAL AND INSTALLATION

On most models, it is possible to remove the camshaft with the engine remaining in

Timing gear alignment

the vehicle. However, the body grille work, radiator, A/C condensor (if equipped), hood, bumper, and braces must be removed to allow clearance for the camshaft to be withdrawn from the engine block. In some cases, it would be more advantageous to remove the engine from the vehicle to replace the camshaft. The decision would depend upon the individual and his shop facilities.

1. Remove the intake manifolds on the V8 engines, and the rocker covers on all engines.

2. Remove the rocker arms or assemblies, pushrods and tappets.

3. Remove the distributor and mechanical fuel pump.

4. Remove the oil pan and oil pump, if necessary.

5. Remove the crankshaft pulley as previously described.

6. Remove the front timing cover, gasket and seal.

7. Remove the two screws securing the camshaft thrust flange to the block.

8. Remove the camshaft and gear. To prevent nicking and damaging the camshaft or bearings, use a camshaft removal and installation tool, which is an extension on the front of the camshaft to act as a handle.

9. When installing the camshaft and gear, coat the bearing surfaces and lobes with lubricant and use the installing tool if possible, to aid in the installation of the camshaft. Make sure the gear timing marks align properly.

10. Working through the two large holes in the camshaft gear, install the two thrust flange screws and tighten to proper torque specifications.

11. Check timing gear backlash. If the end play exceeds the allowable limits, replace the thrust flange.

12. Place the oil slinger over the end of the crankshaft.

13. Install the front cover, using a new seal and gasket. Align the cover before tightening the bolts to the specified torque.

14. Install the crankshaft pulley, tightening to the proper torque.

15. Install the cylinder head, if removed, the intake manifold, tappets, pushrods, and rocker arms. Torque all bolts to the specified torque.

16. Install the fan pulley, blades and belts.

17. Install the distributor and fuel pump.

18. Install the oil pump and oil pan.

19. If the engine was raised, lower and tighten the engine mounts.

20. Complete the assembly as necessary for the removed body parts.

21. Start the engine, time it to specifications, and check for proper operation.

Pistons and Connecting Rods

For piston and connecting rod overhaul procedures see Engine Rebuilding General Sections.

PISTON REMOVAL AND INSTALLATION

1. Remove the cylinder head, the oil pan and the oil pump.

2. It may be necessary, on some models, to raise and block the front of the engine in order to gain enough room to drop the oil pan.

3. Use a ridge reamer and remove the ridge from the top of each cylinder.

4. Rotate the crankshaft until a connecting rod is to the bottom of its travel. Remove the connecting rod bearing cap. Place a piece of rubber tubing on each rod bolt to protect the crankshaft and cylinder wall. Push the connecting rod and piston assembly up and out of the cylinder. Remove all pistons in a like manner.

5. Place the crank journal at the bottom of its travel. Correctly seat rod bearing insert in rod then dip piston assembly in clean oil to lubricate rings. Using a ring compressor, install piston and rod in cylinder. Push piston in, do not strike. On 4-196 and all V8 engines, the piston assembly is installed with the word "UP" toward the top (camshaft) side of the engine block.

6. Place lower half of bearing insert in rod cap and lubricate with oil. Assemble bearing cap to connecting rod with the number side of cap on the same side as the number on the connecting rod. Lubricate threads of bolts with engine oil and install bolts, tightening to the correct torque (see Specifications at the beginning of this section).

7. Rotate crankshaft and repeat installation procedure with the rest of the pistons and connecting rods.

8. Install oil pump and oil pan, using a new pan gasket.

9. Install cylinder head as described in Cylinder Head Removal and Installation.

10. If engine was raised, remove spacers and lower engine. Tighten engine mount bolts.

Piston Ring Replacement

1. Remove pistons as described above.

2. Remove both compression rings and three-piece oil ring.

3. Using rings which correspond to the piston size (standard or oversize), check rings for gap clearance and ring-to-groove side clearance.

4. Install rings on piston with a suitable ring expander tool.

5. Install piston assembly as described above.

Oil Pan

REMOVAL & INSTALLATION

The engine and mounts may have to be loosened from the crossmember and lifted, and spacer blocks installed between the mounts and crossmember, to gain clearance to remove the oil pan from the engine. Other engine applications may only require the removal of steering linkage to gain sufficient clearance. Be sure to clean all old gasket material from the oil pan and the block before installing the oil pan and new gasket.

Main Bearing Replacement

On most models it is possible to replace main bearings without removing the engine from the vehicle. However, it is easier to do a better job with the engine removed and, if facilities are available for pulling the engine, this is the preferable method. See Engine Removal and Installation. For detailed procedures on main bearing, rod bearing and crankshaft servicing see General Repair Section.

1. Remove crankshaft pulley and front (timing) cover.

2. Remove cylinder head(s) and piston assemblies.

3. If the bell housing and transmission were not removed during engine removal, remove them now.

4. On many engines the clutch plate may be compressed by installing three cap screws ⅜"–16 × 2" for V-304, 345, 392 engines). If the clutch plate cannot be compressed in this way, cut three ½" × 1" × 3" wood blocks and insert them between the clutch fingers and back plate. Loosen

backing plate mounting bolts slightly if it is difficult to insert wood blocks. A third alternative procedure for compressing the clutch plate is to insert three retaining clips. The clutch plate is compressed during removal and installation of the clutch to prevent warpage.

5. Remove the backing plate mounting bolts and clutch assembly.

6. Remove flywheel bolts and pull off flywheel.

7. Remove main bearing caps. On OHV4, V-304, 345 engines use a rear main bearing cap puller to remove rear main bearing cap. Note that the caps are numbered and should be reinstalled in their original positions.

8. When installing new main bearings make sure that the oil holes are properly aligned and that bearing tangs are fitted into tang recesses. Thoroughly clean all surfaces and coat lightly with oil. Be sure to align timing marks when positioning crankshaft. On the OHV4 and V-304, 345 engines the numbered sides of the main bearing caps face the left side of the engine. When tightening main bearing caps, first tap them lightly into place, then tighten bolts in an alternating manner until the specified torque is reached. See Specifications for correct torque.

9. Install a new rear main bearing oil seal. On OHV4 and V-304, 345, 392 engines the round seal is pressed in after the rear main bearing cap is installed. Rear main bearing cap side oil seals are installed on these engines with an installer tool made from a piece of ⅛" welding rod. Puddle a ball on the end of the rod and file the ball to approximately 5.32" diameter.

V8 engine—piston and rod assembly

10. Check main bearing clearance and crankshaft endplay and compare to clearance limits listed in Specifications at the beginning of this section. See Engine Rebuilding General Section for clearance measurement and service procedures.

11. Reassemble engine following Steps 1 through 7 in reverse order. Be sure to align clutch driven disc with transmission shaft or clutch aligning tool before tightening clutch plate mounting bolts.

Rear Main Bearing Seal Replacement

4-196 AND V8 ENGINES

The rear main bearing cap seal can be replaced with the engine in the chassis, but the transmission, clutch assembly, and flywheel must be removed to gain access to the seal.

Installation of connecting rod to crankshaft

1. Remove the transmission, clutch assembly, and the flywheel.

2. Remove the engine oil pan.

3. With a slide hammer with a screw end adapter pierce the seal and remove it from the recess in the cap and block.

4. Lubricate the new seal, seat it squarely with a seal installer tool .085 inch from the rear face of the block.

NOTE: Production installed seals are seated flush with the rear of the block.

5. Install the bearing cap side seals with the use of a 1/8 inch welding rod, 8 inches long, with a 5/32 inch puddled ball on the end. Cut off any excess side seal, flush with the oil pan block surface.

6. Install the oil pan, flywheel, clutch assembly, and transmission.

Oil Filter Replacement

The oil filter unit is on the left side of the engine block. All engines use a spin-on type oil filter, which is replaced as a complete unit, using a strap wrench to remove it from the engine. Follow the instructions printed on the filter assembly to install.

Oil Pump

REMOVAL & INSTALLATION

1. Drain crankcase and remove oil pan.
2. Remove oil pump mounting bolts and pull straight down on pump to remove.

3. When installing oil pump, guide pump shaft into position and rotate shaft until tang of drive gear is engaged.

4. Tighten oil pump mounting bolts to: 25–30 ft. lbs.

5. Install oil pan and fill crankcase.

OIL PUMP SERVICE

1. Thoroughly clean oil pump. Do not disturb or remove pickup tube unless absolutely necessary.

2. Remove pump cover bolts and pump cover.

3. Check gear to body clearance. If it is not within .0007–.0027″ on the OHV4 and V8 engines, obtain new parts.

4. Check gear backlash. If it exceeds .011″ on OHV4 and V8 engines replace gears.

5. Check pump shaft clearance in bore. If it exceeds .003″ on V8 and OHV4 engines, replace the whole pump assembly.

6. Remove relief valve and spring. Remove any burrs and clean. Be sure to install with bevelled or pointed end in seat. Check that valve moves freely in bore.

7. Check body and gear clearance. This is the distance between the pump gears and the pump cover. Adjustment of this clearance is made by the addition or removal of cover gaskets. On the OHV4 and V-304, 345, 392 engines the clearance is .0015–.006″.

8. When installing drive gears on pump shaft be sure that the correct drive gear to pump body clearance is obtained. On OHV4 and V-304, 345 engines the oil pump shaft

sleeve is crimped onto the shaft. On the OHV4 the assembly dimension is .200″ and on the V-304, 345 engines the assembly dimension is .375″.

Lubrication System Priming

The recommended procedure to prime the internal parts and the oil pump is to attach a bearing leak detector or similar tool to a suitable fitting on the oil gallery, located on the left side of the engine block. Inject enough oil into the engine to fill the oil filter and the various passage ways for the lubrication system. Disconnect the primary coil wire and turn the engine over, while the priming operation is in process. Do not overfill the crankcase when this method is used. This type of priming will minimize the possibility of scuffing or heat build-up in the areas of friction, which could cause premature engine failure.

ENGINE COOLING

The cooling system is a closed type, utilizing a two valve pressure cap. One valve is used to relieve excessive pressure from the system, and the second valve is used to allow atmospheric air to enter the system during the cooling down period. The engine temperature is controlled by a thermostat, located on the front of the engine block or cylinder head. The coolant is forced through the engine and radiator by the water pump, located on the front of the engine, which is belt driven by the crankshaft pulley.

— CAUTION —

To avoid personal injury, remove the pressure cap from the radiator in two steps. Loosen the cap to its first notch and allow the pressure to escape through the overflow pipe. After the pressure has been released, press on the cap and continue to turn until the prongs on the cap disengage from the radiator neck.

Water Pump

REMOVAL & INSTALLATION

1. Drain cooling system.
2. If radiator shrouds hinder access they must be removed before proceeding.
3. Loosen alternator pivot bolts and adjusting bolt on bracket to relieve tension on the fan belt and remove belt from water pump pulley.
4. Remove all pipes and hoses connected to the water pump.

Lubrication system—V8 engine

5. Remove mounting bolts or stud nuts and water pump.

6. Installation is the reverse of the above procedure. Be sure to install new gaskets and, if applicable, new O-rings on pipe end fittings.

EMISSION CONTROLS

NOTE: Refer to the Emission Control Unit Repair Section.

FUEL SYSTEM

Fuel Pump

REMOVAL

1. Remove the fuel inlet pipe or hose and the outlet fuel pipe to the carburetor from the fuel pump fittings.

2. Remove the attaching bolts from the fuel pump housing to engine block and remove the fuel pump.

3. Clean the gasket surfaces of all gasket particles.

INSTALLATION

1. Install new gasket on the fuel pump mounting flange and install the fuel pump operating arm into the hole in the block, and into contact with the eccentric lobe on the camshaft.

2. Install the attaching bolts and tighten the pump to the block securely.

3. Install the inlet hose or pipe, and the outlet pipe to the fuel pump and tighten securely to avoid air leaks.

FUEL PUMP PRESSURE TEST

1. Disconnect fuel line at carburetor inlet and attach pressure gauge between the inlet and disconnected line.

2. Start engine and take reading. Consult Tune-up Specifications at the beginning of this section for correct pump pressure.

3. When engine is stopped, the pressure should remain constant or very slowly return to zero.

FUEL PUMP CAPACITY TEST

1. Disconnect fuel line from the fuel pump.

2. Connect a piece of hose to the line

so that fuel can be directed into a measuring container.

3. Start engine and note time it takes to fill a pint container. Pump should fill one pint within 20–30 seconds.

Carburetor

REMOVAL

Single-Barrel Holley Model 1940

1. Remove the air cleaner, fuel lines, vacuum lines and any other lines or linkage attached to the carburetor.

2. Remove the attaching bolts from the base of the carburetor and remove the carburetor from the manifold. Remove and discard the old gasket from under the carburetor.

3. To install reverse the removal procedure making sure to install a new gasket under the carburetor base.

Two-Barrel Models

1. Remove air cleaner, throttle linkage and choke cable.

2. Disconnect fuel line and distributor vacuum lines.

3. Remove bolts from mounting studs and lift off carburetor.

4. To install, clean manifold mating surface and install a new flange gasket.

5. Install carburetor but do not tighten down stud nuts.

6. Connect fuel line and vacuum lines.

7. Tighten nuts on mounting studs in an alternating fashion so that flange gasket compresses evenly for a good seal.

1. Lever, cam
2. Spring, cam lever return
3. Plug
4. Pin
5. Diaphragm assembly
6. Screw and lockwasher
7. Housing, valve assembly
8. Screw and lockwasher
9. Diaphragm, air dome
10. Air dome and filter assembly
11. Gasket, filter bowl
12. Filter
13. Elbow
14. Spring
15. Filter bowl
16. Retainer
17. Washer
18. Bolt
19. Lockwasher
20. Pump body
21. Pin, cam lever
22. Gasket, mounting

8. Connect throttle linkage and choke cable, making sure that choke plates are fully open when the choke knob is pushed in.

9. Check throttle for complete travel.
10. Install air cleaner.
11. Adjust carburetor.

4-Barrel Models

1. Remove the air cleaner, throttle linkage, vacuum hoses, fuel lines, and any other hoses and linkages attached to the carburetor.

2. Remove the bolts or nuts holding the carburetor to the manifold, and remove the carburetor from the intake manifold.

3. Discard the base gasket and clean the base and manifold surface of gasket particles.

4. To install the carburetor, reverse the removal procedure, using a new base gasket.

5. Adjust the idle speed and air mixture.

NOTE: Refer to the Unit Repair Section for more repair information.

OVERHAUL NOTES

All Types

Efficient carburetion depends greatly on careful cleaning and inspection during overhaul since dirt, gum, water, or varnish in or on the carburetor parts are often responsible for poor performance.

Overhaul in a clean, dust-free area. Carefully disassemble the carburetor, referring often to the exploded views. Keep all similar and look-alike parts segregated during disassembly and cleaning to avoid acciden-

Exploded view of a typical fuel pump

tal interchange during assembly. Make a note of all jet sizes.

When the carburetor is disassembled, wash all parts (except diaphragms, electric choke units, pump plunger, and any other plastic, leather, fiber, or rubber parts) in clean carburetor solvent. Do not leave parts in the solvent any long than is necessary to sufficiently loosen the deposits. Excessive cleaning may remove the special finish from the float bowl and choke valve bodies, leaving these parts unfit for service. Rinse all parts in clean solvent and blow them dry with compressed air or allow to air dry. Wipe clean all cork, plastic, leather, and fiber parts with a clean, lint-free cloth.

Blow out all passages and jets with compressed air and be sure that there are no restrictions or blockages. Never use wire or similar tools to clean jets, fuel passages, or air bleeds. Clean all jets and valves separately to avoid accidental interchange.

Check all parts for wear or damage. If wear or damage is found, replace the defective parts. Especially check the following:

1. Check the float needle and seat for wear. If wear is found, replace the complete assembly.

2. Check the float hinge pin for wear and the float(s) for dents or distortion. Replace the float if fuel has leaked into it.

3. Check the throttle and choke shaft bores for wear or an out-of-round condition. Damage or wear to the throttle arm, shaft, or shaft bore will often require replacement of the throttle body. These parts require a close tolerance fit, wear may allow air leakage, which could effect starting and idling.

NOTE: Throttle shafts and bushings are not included in overhaul kits. They can be purchased separately.

4. Inspect the idle mixture adjusting needles for burrs or grooves. Any such condition requires replacement of the needle, since you will not be able to obtain a satisfactory idle.

5. Test the accelerator pump check valves. They should pass air one way but not the other. Test for proper seating by blowing and sucking on the valve. Replace the valve if necessary. If the valve is satisfactory, wash the valve again to remove breath moisture.

6. Check the bowl cover for warped surfaces with a straight edge.

7. Closely inspect the valves and seats for wear and damage, replacing as necessary.

8. After the carburetor is assembled, check the choke valve for freedom of operation.

Carburetor overhaul kits are recommended for each overhaul. These kits contain all gaskets and new parts to replace those that deteriorate most rapidly. Failure to replace all parts supplied with the kit (especially gaskets) can result in poor performance later.

Some carburetor manufacturers supply overhaul kits of three basic types: minor

repair; major repair; and gasket kits. Basically, they contain the following:
1. Minor Repair Kits:
   a. All gaskets
   b. Float needle valve
   c. Volume control screw
   d. All diaphragms
   e. Spring for the pump diaphragm
2. Major Repair Kits:
   a. All jets and gaskets
   b. All diaphragms
   c. Float needle valve
   d. Volume control screw
   e. Pump ball valve
   f. Main jet carrier
   g. Float
   h. Complete intermediate rod
   i. Intermediate pump lever
   j. Complete injector tube
   k. Some cover hold-down screws and washers
3. Gasket Kits: All gaskets

After cleaning and checking all components, reassemble the carburetor, using new parts and referring to the exploded view. When reassembling, make sure all screws and jets are tight in their seats, but do not overtighten as the tips will be distorted. Tighten all screws gradually, in rotation. Do not tighten needle valves into their seats; uneven jetting will result. Always use new gaskets. Be sure to adjust the float level when reassembling.

Carburetor Diagnostic Service

The following diagnostic and troubleshooting information can be used as a general guide to determine the cause of carburetor related problems. When the problem has been isolated to a particular component and more information is needed, refer to the related chapter within this section or to the Unit Repair Section.

ROUGH IDLE OR STALLING—ENGINE HOT OR COLD

1. Binding linkage, choke valve, or choke piston
2. Disconnected or broken choke control cable
3. Incorrect choke thermostat adjustment
4. Fast idle linkage and cam not properly adjusted
5. Idle mixture screw(s) out of adjustment
6. Idle speed screw out of adjustment
7. Air cleaner air flow restricted
8. Hot idle compensator valve stuck
9. Secondary throttle plates open (4V carburetors)
10. Clogged air bleed or idle passages
11. Vacuum leakage
12. Improper float level
13. Electrical or emission control systems malfunction

POOR LOW SPEED OPERATION

1. Clogged idle transfer slots
2. Clogged air bleed or idle passages
3. Air cleaner air flow restricted
4. Improper float level
5. Faulty automatic choke operation
6. Improper use of hand controlled choke
7. Vacuum leakage
8. Electrical or emission control system malfunction

POOR ENGINE ACCELERATION

1. Improper acceleration pump stroke
2. Inoperative or missing pump discharge check valve, ball, or needle
3. Damaged or worn pump diaphragm or piston
4. Leaking gaskets
5. Defective fuel pump
6. Clogged discharge jets
7. Electrical or emission control systems malfunction

POOR HIGH SPEED OPERATION

1. Defective fuel pump or clogged fuel filter
2. Clogged vacuum passages
3. Power valve stuck
4. Metering rods stuck
5. Improper size or obstructions in the main jets
6. Restricted air supply to air cleaner
7. Improper float level
8. Electrical or emission control system malfunction

SURGING—CRUISING SPEEDS

1. Clogged main jets
2. Undersize main jets
3. Low fuel level
4. Defective fuel pump or clogged fuel filter
5. Blocked air bleeds
6. Restricted air supply to air cleaner
7. Vacuum leakage
8. Metering rods out of adjustment
9. Power valve sticking
10. Electrical or emission control system malfunction

STALLING WHEN THE ACCELERATOR IS CLOSED QUICKLY

1. Improperly adjusted or defective throttle modulator or dash pot
2. Clogged air bleed or idle passages
3. Vacuum leakage
4. Throttle plates not closing

CLUTCH

REMOVAL & INSTALLATION

1. Remove transmission. Extreme care should be taken to support the transmission until it is completely removed so that the main shaft splines will clear the driven member. For transmission removal procedures see Transmission Removal and Installation.

2. Remove flywheel housing cover.

3. Disconnect clevis yoke from clutch release lever.

4. Compress clutch assembly. On 9 spring clutches, the pressure plate is drilled and tapped so that three retaining cap screws and flat washers may be installed. Tighten the cap screws until flat washers and cap screw heads are seated on the back plate. On the 11″, 12″ and 10″ (6 spring, open back plate type) clutches, three retaining spacers are used to hold the clutch assembly compressed during removal. Slightly loosen the back plate to flywheel mounting screws to wedge the retaining spacers into place. On the 10″ six spring (full back plate type) clutch, three ⅝″ × 3″ × ¼″ hardwood blocks are used to compress the clutch during removal. Loosen back plate to flywheel retaining screws enough to wedge the blocks between the back plate inner flange and release fingers.

5. Remove back plate to flywheel screws and remove back plate assembly and driven disc.

6. When removing the clutch assembly, observe that the balance mark (spot of white paint) on the back plate flange is located as near as possible to the balance mark (''L'') stamped on the flywheel face. These balance marks should be located in the same relative position at clutch installation. If there are no marks, scribe a line to indicate correct position.

7. To install clutch, position the clutch driven member so that the long portion of the hub is toward the rear (all except the 10″ 6 spring open back plate type, which may be fitted either way). Clutch must be compressed for correct installation.

8. Place clutch assembly over the driven member on the flywheel so that the balance mark (spot of white paint) is as near as possible to the flywheel balance mark (''L''). Loosely install two or three back plate to flywheel mounting screws.

9. Using a clutch aligning arbor or transmission main drive gear shaft to hold the driven member in place, complete installation of the remaining back plate to flywheel mounting screws and lockwashers. Tighten capscrews alternately and evenly.

10. Remove retaining capscrews, wood blocks or retaining spacers which were used to hold the clutch compressed.

11. Install transmission as described in Transmission Removal and Installation.

12. Connect linkage to clutch release lever.

13. Install flywheel housing cover. Adjust linkage or cable as described.

Clutch Adjustment

1. Measure and correct the clutch pedal height to approximately 9 inches.

NOTE: On some models it may be necessary to increase the clutch pedal height setting slightly over the amount specified, in order to obtain complete clutch release.

2. Disconnect the return spring on release fork.

3. Loosen the nut on the cable or linkage rod.

4. Hold the pedal assembly against the pedal stop and lengthen or shorten the rod or cable to obtain zero clearance at the release bearing face and the pressure plate fingers.

5. After obtaining zero clearance, lengthen or shorten cable or linkage to obtain ³⁄₃₂ inch between the bearing face and the fingers of the pressure plate.

6. Tighten nut on the cable or linkage rod.

7. Reconnect the return spring.

MANUAL TRANSMISSION

NOTE: For all overhaul procedures, refer to ''Manual Transmission Overhaul'' in the Unit Repair section.

REMOVAL & INSTALLATION

Removal and installation of manual transmissions will vary in detail, depending on which vehicle is being serviced. The following general procedure includes the basic steps common to all models.

1. Access to the transmission may be improved by removing cab floor panels if vehicle is equipped.

2. Raise vehicle on a hoist or jack up and support with jack stands.

3. Drain the transmission lubricant.

4. Disconnect drive shaft at the transmission. If the vehicle is equipped with a transfer case which is not mounted directly to the transmission, disconnect the shaft between the transfer case and transmission at the yoke. If the vehicle is equipped with a transfer case which is mounted directly to the transmission, it must be removed with the transmission as a unit and the forward and rear drive shafts must be discon-

nected. Secure shaft out of the way with wire.

5. Disconnect shift linkage from transmission shift levers. If the vehicle is equipped with a transfer case which is mounted directly to the transmission, disconnect the shift linkage from the transfer case shift levers.

6. If the vehicle is equipped with a transmission mounted handbrake, disconnect the handbrake cable at the relay lever.

7. Disconnect speedometer cable from the transmission.

8. On some models it may be necessary to remove the starter motor.

9. Support the rear of engine by means of a hydraulic jack.

10. Remove the transmission mounting bolts and insulators at the engine rear crossmember. If possible, remove the rear engine crossmember. Remove gear shift lever and housing from top of transmission if applicable.

11. Attach suitable hoisting equipment or jack to transmission and raise enough to support the transmission assembly.

12. Remove top transmission to clutch housing bolts and install transmission guide pins.

13. Remove remaining transmission to clutch housing bolts.

14. Carefully pull transmission rearward, keeping it in line until the main drive gear shaft is clear of the clutch.

CAUTION

Extreme care must be exercised to insure that the weight of the transmission does not rest on the hub of the clutch driven disc.

15. Depending on vehicle model, either lift the transmission up through the floorboard and out the right door or lower it with a jack.

16. Installation is the reverse of the above procedure.

17. Fill transmission with fluid.

Shift Linkage

Different types of transmissions are used which may require the shift linkage to be either mounted in the transmission and controlled by a shift lever, or to have a slight lever mounted remotely with linkage rods connecting the lever to the transmission. No adjustment is provided when the linkage is mounted in the transmission. When the shift lever is remotely mounted, the connecting rods have adjustment provisions. The adjustments are made with the shift control and the transmission arms in the neutral position, and the control rods adjusted to enter either the transmission arms or the shift lever arms with a free fit. Normally the control rods are threaded and trunnions and jam nuts are used to position the rods.

LINKAGE AND CABLE ADJUSTMENT

Shifter rods connect the shift arms of the transfer case to the shift lever arms. Non-adjustable and adjustable links are used on the various models of vehicles. To insure the proper alignment of the rods to the arms, use the following procedure.

Linkage Adjustment

1. Place the shift lever in the neutral position.
2. Remove the shift control rod at the transfer case.
3. Assure that the shift arm of the transfer case is in the center or neutral position.
4. If the control rod is adjustable, position the trunnion or clevis to align with the hole in the shift arm of the transfer case.
5. If the control rod is non-adjustable and the rod does not line up with the hole in the shift arm of the transfer case, replacement or bending will be necessary for the control rod.
6. Reconnect the control rod to the transfer case shift arm and check for proper operation.

Clutch linkage

Cable Adjustment

A pull on the cable will engage the gears. To disengage, merely push the control cable in. To adjust, follow this procedure.

1. Pull the control cable knob out approximately two inches and block in this position.
2. Loosen the cable mounting housing jam nut.
3. Remove the two cable mounting housing bolts.
4. Unscrew the cable mounting housing away from the transfer case housing.
5. Confirm the inner clevis is positioned in the engaged position.
6. Turn the cable housing down the cable jacket to a snug fit against the gasket

on the transfer case mounting boss. Install the two retaining screws.
7. Turn the jam nut down the cable jacket and secure against the cable mounting housing.
8. Remove the control cable knob block and operate the cable assembly to check the shifter operation.

CABLE

Removal

1. Leave the control knob pushed in.
2. Loosen the cable jam nut at the cable mounting housing on the transfer case and turn it back to the end of the threads.
3. Remove the two bolts holding the cable mounting housing to the transfer case.
4. Unscrew the housing all the way to the jam nut.
5. Pull the cable mounting housing forward until the inner cable jam nut is clear.
6. Loosen the inner cable jam nut at the shift clevis and unhook the cable end pin from the clevis.
7. Position the shift cable to obtain working clearance.

Installation

1. Turn the jam nut and the cable mounting housing to the bottom of the thread end.
2. With the transfer case shifter assembly in the fully engaged position, install the cable mounting housing gasket to the case.

NOTE: The clevis is pulled out to engage.

3. Connect the cable end pin to the shifter assembly and secure with the jam nut.

NOTE: Confirm that the pin is installed flush with the cable end.

4. Block the control knob out approximately two inches.
5. Turn the cable mounting housing down the cable jacket to a snug fit against the gasket on the transfer case mounting boss.
6. Secure the cable mounting housing with the two mounting bolts to the transfer case.
7. Turn the jam nut down the cable jacket and lock against the cable mounting housing.
8. Remove the block from the shift control cable knob and operate the cable to check the shifter operation.

TRANSFER CASE

REMOVAL & INSTALLATION

Frame Mounted

1. Drain the transfer case and disconnect the rear axle drive shaft at the transfer case.
2. Disconnect the front drive shaft at the transfer case.
3. Disconnect the speedometer cable, and indicator light switch wire, if equipped.
4. Disconnect the shift linkage. If equipped with a shift cable, refer to the cable removal and installation outlined previously.
5. Place a transmission jack under the transfer case and remove the mounting bolts from the frame to case.
6. Remove the transfer case from the vehicle.
7. The installation of the transfer case is the reverse of removal.

Transmission Mounted

1. Disconnect the rear driveshaft at the transfer case and drain the case assembly.
2. Disconnect the front driveshaft at the transfer case.
3. Disconnect the speedometer cable and the indicator light switch wire, if equipped.
4. Disconnect the shift linkage or cable.
5. Place a transmission jack under the transfer case and remove the flange bolts holding the transfer case to the transmission.
6. Pull the transfer case rearward to disengage the transmission output shaft from the coupler.
7. Lower the transfer case and remove from the vehicle.
8. The installation of the transfer case is the reverse of removal.

AUTOMATIC TRANSMISSION

Model T-407

REMOVAL

NOTE: The transmission and converter must be removed as a unit assembly. Damage can result to the converter drive plate, pump bushing, or to the pump seal, if the converter is allowed to remain on the converter drive plate.

1. Connect a remote switch to the starter solenoid so that the engine can be rotated from under the vehicle.
2. Disconnect the coil high tension cable.
3. Raise the vehicle and support safely.
4. Remove the engine rear crossmember on 4 × 4 vehicles, if necessary.
5. Remove the cover plate from the front of the converter housing to provide access to the converter drain plug and mounting bolts.
6. Rotate the engine to bring the drain

plug to the six o'clock position. Drain the converter and loosen the pan bolts to drain the transmission.

7. Mark the converter and drive plate to aid in the assembly. Rotate the engine to locate the converter-to-drive plate bolts and remove the bolts.

8. Disconnect the negative battery cable and remove the starter motor assembly.

9. Disconnect the wires from the back-up light and neutral start switch.

10. Disconnect the gearshift cable or rod and bellcrank from the transmission.

11. Disconnect the throttle rod from the left side of the transmission.

12. Disconnect the cooler lines at the transmission and remove the filler tube.

13. Disconnect the speedometer cable, and move cable away from the transmission.

14. Disconnect the front universal joint and secure the shaft out of the way.

15. On vehicles equipped with parking brake mounted on the rear extension, remove the parking brake cable.

16. On vehicles equipped with dual exhaust, the left exhaust system may have to be removed.

17. Install an engine support fixture to hold the rear of the engine.

18. Raise the transmission slightly, and remove the support crossmember holding the rear mount assembly.

19. Remove all bell housing bolts.

20. Carefully move the transmission assembly rearward off the block dowels and disengage the converter hub from the end of the crankshaft. Place a converter holding tool on the bell housing to hold the converter in place.

21. Lower the transmission assembly and remove the transmission from the vehicle.

22. To remove the converter assembly from the transmission, remove the holding tool and carefully slide the converter out of the transmission.

INSTALLATION

1. Rotate the pump rotors with tool SE-2402 or its equivalent, so that the lugs on the pump inner rotor are vertical.

2. Position the converter so that the impeller shaft slots are vertical and carefully slide the converter assembly over the input shaft and reaction shaft. Make sure that the converter slots fully engage the pump inner rotor lugs.

NOTE: The surface of the converter front cover lug should be at least ½ inch to the rear of a straightedge, placed on the face of the bell housing, when the converter is pushed all the way into the transmission.

3. Install the converter holding tool to hold the converter in place.

4. Position the transmission on a jack assembly and move the unit under the vehicle.

5. Rotate the converter to align the pre-

viously made marks on the drive plate and converter.

6. Raise the transmission and align with the engine. Install a pilot stud to aid in the alignment of the converter to the drive plate. Carefully work the transmission assembly forward over the engine block dowels with the converter hub entering the crankshaft opening.

7. Install the converter housing bolts and tighten to specified torque.

8. Install the crossmember and mount at the rear of the transmission. Remove the engine support fixture.

9. Install the oil filler tube and speedometer cable.

10. Connect the throttle rod and the gear shift rod to the transmission levers.

11. Connect the wires to the neutral start and back-up light switch.

12. Install the drive shaft and front universal joint.

13. Install the starter motor assembly.

14. Remove the pilot stud from the converter and install the bolts to the converter-drive plate assembly.

15. Install the cooler lines to the transmission.

16. Install the converter access plate on the front of the converter housing.

17. If the left exhaust system was removed, replace the pipes and brackets.

18. Install the parking brake cable and adjust, if equipped with the extension housing parking brake assembly.

19. Adjust the shift and throttle linkage.

20. Fill the transmission and connect the negative battery cable, if not done, and start the engine. Recheck the fluid level and refill as necessary.

TRANSMISSION FLUID DRAIN AND REFILL

1. Raise the vehicle on a jack or hoist. Support safely.

2. Place a large drain container under the transmission oil pan.

3. Loosen the pan bolts and tap one corner of the pan to break it loose, allowing the fluid to drain.

4. Remove the access plate from the front of the converter housing. Remove the converter drain plug and allow the fluid to drain.

5. Remove and clean the pan, remove the fluid filter and discard.

6. Install a new filter assembly on the valve body and tighten the screws securely.

7. Using a new pan gasket, install the pan and tighten the bolts securely.

8. Install and tighten the converter drain plug.

9. Install the converter housing access plate.

10. Install six quarts of transmission fluid into the transmission. Start the engine and allow to run for two minutes. Check the fluid level and add enough oil to bring the level to the "ADD ONE PINT" mark.

11. Recheck the level after moving the selector lever through all the gear positions and after the transmission has reached normal operating temperature. The level should be between the "FULL" mark and the "ADD ONE PINT" mark.

KICKDOWN BAND ADJUSTMENT

NOTE: The kickdown band is located on the left side of the transmission case near the throttle lever shaft.

1. Loosen the locknut and back off approximately five turns.

2. Tighten the adjusting screw to 10 ft. lbs.

3. Back off the adjusting screw 2¼ turns with the 6 and 8 cylinder engines. Hold the adjusting screw in position and tighten the lock nut to 29 ft. lbs.

LOW AND REVERSE BAND ADJUSTMENT

1. Raise the vehicle, support safely, drain the transmission fluid, and remove the pan.

2. Loosen the lock nut on the adjusting screw.

3. Tighten the adjusting screw to 10 ft. lbs.

4. Tighten the lock nut to 30 ft. lbs.

5. Install the pan using a new pan gasket.

6. Fill the transmission with fluid, start the engine and recheck the level. Add as necessary.

BACK-UP LIGHT AND NEUTRAL START SWITCH

No provisions are made for any adjustments of the back-up light and neutral start switch. The neutral start circuit is controlled by the inner terminal and the back-up light circuits are controlled by the two outside terminals.

The replacement of the switch is accomplished by unscrewing the switch from the transmission case, and screwing a new switch into the case. Since fluid leakage will occur when removing the switch, fluid must be added after the new switch is installed.

SHIFT LINKAGE

Adjustable Cable Control

1. Install cable conduit anchor clamps at both ends.

2. Install swivel on the control lever so that a distance of .55 inch exists from the end of the cable to the opposite side of the trunnion. Tighten the jam nut securely.

3. With the control in PARK position and transmission lever in the full rearward position (PARK detent), adjust the yoke so that the rod end pin installs freely and secure the yoke nut and install the cotter pin.

Column Shift

1. Assemble all linkage parts, but leave the upper control rod bolt loose.
2. Place the selector lever in DRIVE position.
3. Move the shift control lever on the transmission to the DRIVE position.
4. Tighten the upper bolt on the control rod to 14–16 ft. lbs.
5. Check the adjustment as follows.
    a. Shift effort must be free and detents feel crisp. All gate stops must be positive.
    b. Key start must only occur in the PARK or NEUTRAL positions.
    c. Detent positions must be in proper relationship to the transmission lever positions.

THROTTLE VALVE LINKAGE ADJUSTMENT

1. With the engine off and an assistant holding the accelerator pedal to the floor, check for full carburetor throttle plate opening.
2. If necessary, adjust the throttle cable and pedal floor stop to obtain wide open throttle.
3. If necessary, adjust the idle speed of the engine with the use of a tachometer and with the engine at normal operating temperature and the carburetor off the fast idle cam. Adjust the curb idle speed, (throttle stop solenoid activated) with the transmission in neutral and the air conditioning in the OFF position.

NOTE: Be sure that carburetor is not being held open by a deceleration valve dashpot, solenoid valve, or a vacuum throttle modulator valve.

—— CAUTION ——
All components in the throttle control and transmission linkage system must operate freely with absolutely no sticking, excessive friction, or interference from other chassis components.

DRIVETRAIN

Front Driveshaft

The front driveshaft connects from the transfer case to the front axle companion flange. The U-joints are attached to the differential by bearing flanges on older models and U-bolts on newer ones.

REMOVAL & INSTALLATION

1. Raise the front of the vehicle and place it on jackstands.
2. Place the transfer case in gear.
3. Remove the attaching bolts from the flange on the transfer case. Lower the driveshaft slowly to the ground.
4. Remove the attaching bolts from the flange on the front axle and pull the shaft from the vehicle.
    To install:
5. Attach the front and rear universal joints.
6. Lower the vehicle.

Rear Driveshaft

REMOVAL & INSTALLATION

2WD

1. Raise the vehicle and support it securely.
2. Remove the attaching bolts from the companion flange and lower the end of the driveshaft to the floor.
3. Partially drain the transmission lubricant.
4. Pull the yoke from the rear of the transmission.
    To install:
5. Insert the yoke onto the transmission output shaft.

—— CAUTION ——
Be careful not to damage the rear transmission seal.

6. Attach the rear U-joint to the companion flange.
7. Fill the transmission to the proper level.
8. Lower the vehicle.

4WD

1. Raise and securely support the vehicle.
2. Disconnect the rear driveshaft bolts from the companion flange.
3. Remove the driveshaft-to-transfer case flange attaching bolts.
4. Remove the driveshaft.
    To install:
5. Attach the front U-joint to the transfer case flange.
6. Connect the rear end of the driveshaft to the companion flange of the rear axle.
7. Lower the vehicle.

U-Joints (Driveshaft)

NOTE: Refer to the Unit Repair Section.

FRONT DRIVE AXLE

Leaf Spring

REMOVAL & INSTALLATION

1. Raise the vehicle and support on the frame rails behind the front springs with floor stands.
2. Remove the shock absorber from the spring.
3. Remove the U-bolts, spring bumpers and retainer, or the U-bolt seat.
4. Remove the lubricators, if used.
5. Remove the nuts from the shackles and bracket pins.
6. Slide the spring off the bracket and shackle pins.
7. Remove the spring from the vehicle.
8. Installation is the reverse of removal. Tighten all nuts and bolts securely.

Front Drive Axle Removal

1. Jack up truck until load is removed from springs and block up frame to safely hold weight.
2. Drain lubricant from main housing and, if applicable, from wheel end housings.
3. Disconnect brakes.
4. Disconnect drag link from ball stud bracket.
5. Disconnect drive shaft from pinion shaft yoke.
6. Supporting axle with a portable floor jack, remove spring U-bolts.
7. Roll axle assembly out from under truck.
8. To install, reverse the above procedure.

Front Drive Axle Adjustments

Preload on the knuckle bearings of these front axles must be maintained at all times. Check for looseness each time knuckle is lubricated.

1. Jack up front end of truck until off-center weight of the wheel is relieved (wheel just barely touching ground).
2. Remove wheel and wheel adapter from hub.
3. Disconnect tie rod and drag link.
4. Remove axle shaft.
5. To remove play (check for play by pushing and pulling on top and bottom of knuckle) and increase preload drag, turn adjusting bolt into back of knuckle. Preload should read (spring scale hooked into end of steering arm) 12 lbs.

Front Wheel Bearing Adjustment

1. While continuously rotating the front wheel, gently tighten the wheel bearing adjusting nut until it places tension on the bearing or thrust washer. If you notice possible brake drag, adjust the brakes to make sure brake shoe drag does not interfere with the adjustment.

2. Continue rotating the wheel while torquing the adjusting nut to 30 lb-ft.

3. Then, back off the adjusting nut 1/4 to 1/3 of a turn. Install the wheel bearing nut lockwasher and jam nut. Torque the jam nut to 125–150 lb-ft.

4. Bend the lockwasher over the jam nut and/or locknut.

NOTE: For overhaul procedures, see Unit Repair Section.

Front Axle Shaft

REMOVAL

Axles Having Drive Flange

1. Raise vehicle, support with floor stands and remove wheel from vehicle.

2. Remove grease cap and snap-ring from end of axle shaft.

3. Remove drive flange cap screws, lock-washer, flange and gasket. If equipped with locking hubs, bend up locking tab, take out capscrews and remove clutch body.

NOTE: Lift off clutch body holding it erect so as not to let drive pins fall out of body. If they do fall out, be certain to install them during reassembly.

Remove hub body. Loosen setscrew and unscrew drag shoe from spindle.

4. Remove brake drum countersunk setscrews, where applicable and remove drum.

5. Bend the lip on the wheel bearing lockwasher away from the outer wheel bearing nut and remove the nut and lock-washer. Remove wheel bearing adjusting nut (inner) and bearing lockwasher.

6. Remove the wheel hub with wheel bearing.

7. Remove backing plate and wheel spindle retaining bolts and lockwashers. Support backing plate to prevent damage to brake hose if hose is not disconnected.

8. Remove wheel bearing spindle with bushing. If spindle bushing requires replacing, press out bushing using an adapter of correct size. An alternate method of bushing removal is the use of a cape chisel or punch to collapse the bushing.

9. Pull axle shaft and universal joint assembly out of axle housing.

Typical front drive mounting

Front spring mounting

INSTALLATION

1. Insert axle shaft and universal joint assembly into axle housing. Position splined end of axle shaft into differential pinion gear and push into place.

2. If wheel bearing spindle bushing was removed, press new bushing into spindle using an installer tool or adapter of proper size. Lubricate ID of bushing with chassis lube when installed to provide initial lubrication. Bushing should be pressed in until bushing flange is seated against shoulder in spindle. Assemble wheel spindle and backing plate to steering knuckle. Secure with six (6) bolts and lockwashers and tighten to specifications. Connect hydraulic brake fluid line if disconnected.

3. Pack wheel bearings using a pressure lubricator or by carefully working lubricant into bearing cones by hand. Slide lubricated inner wheel bearing on spindle until it stops against spindle shoulder.

4. Apply thin coating of lubricant specified for wheel bearings to seal lip and install seal into wheel hub using an adapter of correct diameter. Lip of seal should extend towards wheel (away from backing plate assembly).

5. Assemble wheel hub on spindle. Install lubricated outer wheel bearing cone on spindle. Push cone on spindle until it rests against bearing cup.

6. Install wheel bearing lockwasher and adjusting (inner) nut. Tighten adjusting nut until there is a slight drag on the bearings when the hub is turned; then back-off approximately one-sixth turn.

7. Install tang-type lockwasher and lock nut (outer). Tighten nut and bend lockwasher tang over lock nut. If axle is equipped with locking hubs, install drag shoe on spindle and tighten setscrew.

8. Align splines of drive flange with those of axle shaft and secure drive flange and new gasket to wheel hub with capscrews and lockwashers. Tighten capscrews securely. If equipped with locking hubs, lightly lubricate hub body and clutch using a light grade chassis lubricant an install new gasket, hub body, snap ring and hub clutch. Be certain that all drive pins are positioned in locking hub clutch when clutch is installed. Secure hub clutch to wheel hub with capscrews and lock. Tighten to specifications and bend tang over head of capscrew.

9. Install snap-ring and grease cup if not equipped with locking hubs.

10. Assemble brake drum and wheels to wheel hub. Bleed and adjust brakes.

—————— CAUTION ——————
Be certain that master cylinder is full of brake fluid after completing bleeding operation.

REMOVAL

Axles Having Drive Gear

1. Raise and support vehicle with floor stands placed under frame rails. Remove wheel from vehicle.

2. Lightly tap alternately around edge of hub cap with hammer and screwdriver or similar tool until hub cap is removed.

3. If axle is equipped with locking hubs, remove the eight (8) socket-head setscrews securing hub clutch assembly to wheel hub assembly.

NOTE: Drive pins may fall out of hub clutch when separated from wheel hub assembly. Be certain to replace them during installation.

4. Remove retaining ring from wheel hub if equipped with locking hubs.

5. Remove snap-ring from axle shaft.

6. Pull drive gear out of wheel hub. If difficulty is encountered in removing drive gear, obtain a screwdriver or similar tool having the end bent approximately 90° with the handle. Insert end of tool into groove in drive gear and withdraw gear. If necessary, move wheel alternately backward and forward to aid removal of gear.

7. Remove retaining ring and locking hub body, if so equipped.

8. Using Wheel Bearing Adjusting Nut Wrench, remove wheel bearing outer nut and slide lock ring off of axle shaft. Again using wrench, remove wheel bearing inner nut.

9. Pull drive gear spacer out of wheel hub.

10. Remove brake drum or disc brake assembly from wheel hub and slide wheel hub assembly off of spindle.

NOTE: Do not allow tapered roller bearings to drop on floor as bearings may be damaged.

11. Remove screws retaining grease guard to backing plate. Take off grease guard and gasket.

12. Remove the six (6) bolts securing wheel spindle and backing plate to steering knuckle. Pull spindle with bushing off of axle shaft. If spindle bushing requires replacing, press or drive out bushing using an adapter of correct size. An alternate method of bushing removal is the use of a cape chisel or punch to collapse the bushing.

13. Pull axle shaft and universal joint assembly out of axle housing.

INSTALLATION

1. Proceed with steps 1 through 5 of Axle Shaft and Universal Joint Installation (Axles having drive flange).

2. Insert drive gear spacer over spindle and against outer wheel bearing cup.

3. Position wheel bearing inner adjusting nut Wheel Bearing Adjusting Nut wrench with pin in nut extending toward handlle end of wrench. Install nut on spindle and tighten until it is snug against outer wheel bearing; then loosen adjusting nut ¼ turn. Align tang on adjusting nut lock ring with groove in wheel spindle. Slide ring on spindle and index pin on adjusting nut with hole in lock ring. If pin will not index with hole in lock ring, turn adjusting nut to the left (Loosen) until it will index.

NOTE: When attempting to index pin with hole in lock ring, turn nut very slightly since adjusting nut should be locked with first hole in lock ring past ¼ turn lose.

Position wheel bearing out nut in adjusting nut wrench and install on spindle. Tighten nut securely.

4. Align splines on axle shaft and splines in wheel hub with those of drive gear. Insert drive gear on axle shaft. Push gear into hub until it rests again drive gear spacer.

NOTE: Groove on side of gear must be toward hub cap.

5. If axle is equipped with locking hubs, lightly lubricate locking hub body using a light grade chassis lubricant. Align splines and insert hub body into wheel hub.

6. Install snap-ring on end of axle shaft.

7. Place retaining groove in wheel hub, if equipped with locking hub.

8. If applicable, lightly grease hub clutch assembly using a light grade chassis lubricant. Be sure that all eight (8) drive pins are positioned in the locking hub clutch. Assemble hub clutch to hub body and secure with eight (8) socket head setscrews.

9. Position hub cap on wheel hub and lightly tap alternately around cap until flange is against edge of hub.

10. Assemble brake or disc brake assembly and wheel to wheel hub. Bleed and adjust brakes.

—————— CAUTION ——————
Be certain that the master cylinder is full of brake fluid after bleeding operation.

Steering Knuckle
(Ball Joint)

REMOVAL

1. With the vehicle safely supported, remove the wheel, caliper and rotor.

2. Remove the backing plate and the spindle from the knuckle.

NOTE: If necessary, tap the spindle lightly with a soft hammer to loosen it from the knuckle bolts. The spindle oil seal, needle bearings, and bronze spacer can be removed and replaced at this time.

3. Remove the axle from the housing.

NOTE: The slingers can be removed from the axle by using pullers or tapping the axle through the slingers.

4. Disconnect and remove the tie rod from the steering arm.

5. Remove the cotter pin from the upper ball socket stud and remove the nut.

6. Remove the nut from the lowerball socket stud and discard.

NOTE: This nut is of a special torque design and should only be used one time.

7. Remove the lower ball socket snapring (used on 4 × 4 applications only), and unseat the upper and lower ball socket studs with a lead hammer or with a puller tool arrangement, to separate the knuckle from the yoke.

NOTE: If the upper ball socket stud remains in the yoke flange, remove it by striking it on the stud with a soft hammer.

8. With the aid of puller tools or a press and ram, remove the bottom ball socket.

9. Reverse the knuckle and remove the upper ball socket.

10. With the aid of a special socket, remove the threaded sleeve in the top flange of the yoke.

INSTALLATION

1. Assemble the lower ball socket into the knuckle with a press and ram or a puller tool arrangements, making sure that the ball socket is firmly seated against the knuckle. Install the snap-ring on the 4 × 4 application.

2. Assemble the upper ball socket into the knuckle with a press and ram or a puller type tool arrangement, making sure that the ball socket is firmly seated against the knuckle.

NOTE: Use a .0015 inch feeler gauge blade between the socket and knuckle. The blade should not enter at the minimum area of contact.

3. Install new threaded sleeve into the top flange of the yoke, leaving approximately two threads exposed.

4. Install the knuckle assembly to the yoke, using a new nut on the lower ball socket stud. Torque the lower nut to 80 ft. lbs.

5. With the use of a special socket, torque the threaded sleeve to 50 ft. lbs. in the upper yoke flange.

6. Install the top ball socket stud nut and torque to 100 ft. lbs. Align the cotterpin holes between the stud and the castellated nut. Do not loosen nut to align the holes. Install the cotter pin.

7. Assemble the tie rod to the steering arm.

8. Assure that slingers are properly installed on the axle shaft and install the shaft into the housing.

9. Position the spindle over the axle end with the bronze bushing in place.

10. Install the backing plate.

11. Install the hub rotor, caliper and wheel assembly, and lower the vehicle.

Checking Ball Sockets For Looseness

To check the ball sockets for excessive looseness, raise the vehicle and attach a dial indicator to the lower yoke or axle tube and set the indicator against the knuckle or lower ball socket, with a loaded pressure so as to read in both directions. Grasp the wheel at the top and bottom and move the wheel inward and outward. If the total indicator reading exceeds .020 inch, both the upper and lower ball sockets should be replaced.

Front Drive Locking Hubs

Three types of locking hubs are used: Manual, Lock-O-Matic and Warn. Manual locking hubs are either engaged or disengaged, depending on how they are set. Lock-O-Matic hubs, when in "free" position, automatically engage axle and wheel when forward torque is applied by the axle shaft. Thus, whenever front wheel drive is disengaged at the transmission, the wheels free wheel. "Lock" position is required only when engine braking control on the front wheel is desired.

1. Clutch assembly
2. Body assembly

Components of a Dualmatic locking hub

1. Clutch and bearing assembly	5. Washer	10. Dial screw	15. Washer
2. Cap assembly	6. Hub	11. O-ring seal	16. Detent dial
3. Retaining ring	7. Compression spring	12. Clutch cup	17. Control dial
4. Bearing hub	8. Clutch ring	13. Compression spring	18. Screw
	9. Clutch nut	14. Hub cap	19. Label

Components of a manual locking hub

SPINDLE NUT KIT   **HUB BODY ASSEMBLY**   **CLUTCH ASSEMBLY**

1. Lockwasher	8. Centering spring	15. Retaining ring	22. Lockwasher tab
2. Spindle nut	9. Shaft axle hub	16. Clutch nut	23. O-ring
3. Set screw	10. Centering spring	17. Clutch, ring and cup	24. U-ring
4. Garter spring	11. Gasket	18. Compression ring	25. Cap screw
5. Friction shoe	12. Hub body	19. Retaining ring	26. Control dial
6. Roller	13. Washer, bearing	20. Gasket	27. Groove pin
7. Cage	14. Retaining ring	21. Cap	

Components of an automatic locking hub

FRONT LOCKING HUBS
REMOVAL

1. Bend up tabs on mounting bolt lock washers.
2. Remove mounting bolts using a thin-walled socket or appropriate hex wrench (externally splined type).
3. When clutch body is lifted off, immediately tilt it up so that the drive pins do not fall out.
4. Remove lock ring holding hub body onto axle shaft and pull off hub body.
5. Remove drag shoe (Lock-O-Matic only) from axle spindle by loosening hex-head set screw and unscrew drag shoe.
6. To install, reverse the above procedure.

REAR AXLE

BEARING AND SEAL REPLACEMENT

Adjustable Bearing Ring Type

1. Raise and support the vehicle securely using jackstands.
2. Remove the rear wheels.
3. Remove the metal retaining clips from the wheel lugs and pull off the brake drum.

CAUTION

It may be necessary to back off the brake shoe adjuster to prevent binding between the shoes and the drum.

---

4. Remove the backing plate retaining bolts. These bolts also run through the axle retaining plate.
5. Pull the axle from the housing with a puller or similar tool.

CAUTION

Never strike the axle shaft during removal as permanent damage will result.

---

6. The bearing assembly, retainer, and adjusting ring are removed with the assembly.
To install:
7. Clean the mating surfaces of the backing plate, axle housing flange, and wheel bearing retainer.
8. Install a new gasket between the backing plate and the axle housing flange.
9. Place a new gasket on the front face of the backing plate so that when the axle is installed the gasket will be between backing plate and the wheel bearing retainer.
10. Turn the adjusting ring into the bearing retainer approximately two turns. This is to prevent excessive pressure on the wheel bearings or movement of the bearing cone or the clinch ring on the axle shaft.

NOTE: Do not thread the adjusting ring completely into the bearing retainer until the retainer and the backing plate

have been bolted to the axle housing flange and tightened to the correct torque.

11. Install the axle shaft assembly.

CAUTION

Do not damage the axle seal when inserting the shaft.

---

12. Install the adjuster ring lock and secure the lock.
13. Secure the bearing retainer and the backing plate to the axle housing flange and torque to 40–45 ft. lbs.

NOTE: There is a fifth hole in the axle housing flange. This is for lubricant drain in case of axle seal leakage.

14. Coat the threads on the adjuster with a good waterproof sealer and install the adjusting ring into the wheel bearing retainer.
15. Adjust the axle shaft end-play.
16. Install the brake drums and retaining clips.

Unit Bearing Type

1. Raise the rear of the vehicle and support securely.
2. Remove the tires and wheels.
3. Remove the brake drums.

NOTE: It might be necessary to back off the brake adjusting mechanism to avoid contact between the brake shoes and the drum. Make certain to hold the automatic self-adjuster away before turning the adjuster screw.

4. Turn the axle shaft until the access hole in the axle flange is aligned with the backing plate retaining bolts. Remove the bolts and nuts.
5. Using a puller or other tool, pull the axle assembly from the axle housing. If a puller is not available, install the brake drum backwards and tighten two lug nuts. Exert outward pressure to remove the outside seal from the housing bore.
6. Remove the wheel bearing cup and the inside oil seal from the axle housing.

NOTE: The bearing cup is a loose fit in the housing but the clearance may not be sufficient to permit removal with your fingers.

7. Install the new oil seal with the closed side of the seal toward the housing flange. The seal should fit squarely against the seat in the housing bore. Lubricate the lip of the seal with rear axle lube.
8. Install the wheel bearing cup in the axle housing bore. The cup is installed with the thin side toward the housing flange. It may be necessary to lightly tap around the cup to ensure that the cup is tight around its seat.

NOTE: If a new wheel bearing is used, the bearing cup will be bonded to the rib ring and the cup will be installed with the axle shaft. Do not break the bond or install the cup separately.

9. Install the splined end of the axle

shaft into the housing and start the splines into the differential pinion gears.

CAUTION

Be careful when inserting the axle shaft that the splines do not cut the inside oil seal.

---

10. Align the retaining plate and the backing plate mounting holes with those in the axle housing flange and push the axle shaft into the housing as far as possible.
11. Install the backing plate mounting bolts and tighten the nuts finger tight. Tighten the nuts alternately to approximately 15 ft. lbs. working through the hole in the axle shaft flange.

NOTE: The nuts should be tightened so that the seal and the wheel bearing are drawn tight against their seats.

12. Torque the backing plate mounting bolts to 50–60 ft. lbs.
13. Adjust the brakes until the brake drum will just slip over the shoes. Install the drum.
14. Install the rear wheels and tighten the lug nuts. Back the vehicle up and apply the brakes. This will activate the automatic brake adjusters.

Locking Differentials

For overhaul procedures of differentials with "NoSPIN" and "PowrLok" locking units, see Rear Axle in the General Repair Section.

STEERING AND SUSPENSION

Steering Wheel

REMOVAL & INSTALLATION

1. Raise the hood and disconnect the battery cables.
2. Remove the horn cap, spring, and horn button baseplate.
3. Remove the retaining bolt and washer from the center shaft.

NOTE: Note the position of the long screw.

4. Using a puller, remove the wheel from the steering column.
5. To install, reverse the removal procedure.

Turn Signal Switch

REPLACEMENT

1. Disconnect the battery cables.
2. Remove the horn button and spring.

3. Remove the three screws which hold the horn button retaining plate.

4. Remove the steering wheel.

5. Remove the horn button contact ring located at the upper end of the column assembly.

6. Remove the turn signal switch retaining screws and pull out the switch assembly.

7. Installation is in the reverse of removal.

Steering Gear

For manual steering gear overhaul, see the General Repair Section.

STEERING GEAR REMOVAL

1. Loosen collar clamp at bottom of steering wheel column. Disconnect any wiring.

2. Remove nut or loosen clamp bolt which secures steering arm to lever shaft, removing steering arm from lever shaft using a suitable puller if necessary.

3. Remove mounting bolts and steering gear assembly.

4. To install, reverse the above procedure, taking special care not to bind steering column if there is no universal joint.

DRAG LINK ADJUSTMENT

To adjust the drag link, remove the cotter pin and turn the adjusting plug in the desired direction. If excess play is present in the link, turn the adjusting plug inward until it is tight and then back off to the first cotter pin hole. Install a new cotter pin of the correct size.

Power Steering Pump

REMOVAL & INSTALLATION

1. Disconnect the reservoir hoses at the pump. Fasten the hoses with the ends raised upward to prevent fluid leakage.

2. Plug the pump fittings to prevent leakage of oil from the pump.

3. Loosen the pump-to-bracket mounting bolts, lean the pump to one side, and remove the drive belt.

4. Remove the bolts which hold the pump to the mounting bracket and remove the pump assembly.

5. Installation is the reverse of removal.

Tie Rod End

REMOVAL & INSTALLATION

1. Remove the cotter pins and retaining nuts at both ends of the tie rod and from the end of the connecting rod where it attaches to the tie rod.

2. Remove the nut attaching the steering damper push rod to the tie rod bracket and move the damper aside.

3. Remove the tie rod ends from the steering arms and connecting rod with a puller.

4. Count the number of threads showing on the tie rod before removing the ends, as a guide to installation.

5. Loosen the adjusting tube clamp bolts and unthread the ends.

6. Installation is the reverse of removal. Adjust toe-in, if necessary.

Shock Absorbers

REMOVAL & INSTALLATION

NOTE: Before installing new shocks, they should be purged of air. To do this, hold the shock upright and fully extend it, then invert and compress it. Do this several times.

1. Remove the locknuts and washers.

2. Pull the shock absorber eyes and rubber bushings from the mounting pins.

3. Install the shocks in the reverse order of the removal procedure.

NOTE: Squeaking usually occurs when movement takes place between the rubber bushings and the metal parts. The squeaking may be eliminated by placing the bushings under greater pressure. This is accomplished either by adding additional washers or by tightening the locknuts. Do not use mineral lubricant to stop the squeaking as it will deteriorate the rubber.

Front End Alignment

NOTE: Refer to the Unit Repair Section.

BRAKES

Late model trucks are equipped with a dual hydraulic brake system in which there are separate hydraulic systems for the front and rear brakes. In this dual system a warning light switch operates a warning light on the dashboard when there is a pressure failure in either the front or rear system. A power system may be employed to reduce the effort applied to the brake pedal.

NOTE: For all brake system service procedures not detailed below, refer to "Brakes" in the Unit Repair section.

RESETTING THE WARNING LIGHT SWITCH

Once a difference of 85–150 psi pressure between the front and rear systems has activated the warning light switch, it will not go off by itself and must be manually reset.

1. Clean switch and disconnect wire from terminal.

2. Unscrew and completely remove switch from body. This will allow the pistons to center and hold the switch in "off" position.

3. Screw switch back into body and reconnect wire to terminal.

4. **NOTE: If fluid is in the switch cavity, press brake pedal to see if pistol O-ring seals are leaking. If there is leakage, the O-rings must be replaced.**

5. Warning light switch should be checked periodically for proper function and the presence of foreign matter and dirt.

Wheel Cylinder (Rear Wheel)

REMOVAL

1. Raise the rear of the vehicle and support it safely.

2. Remove the drum.

3. Remove the brake lining from the brake support plate.

4. Remove the hydraulic line from the wheel cylinder.

5. Remove the wheel cylinder attaching bolts and remove the cylinder.

INSTALLATION

1. Install the wheel cylinder on the brake support plate.

2. Install the hydraulic line to the wheel cylinder.

3. Install the brake shoes on the brake support plate.

4. Install the drum.

5. Install the wheel assembly.

6. Bleed the system and refill the master cylinder.

Warning light switch circuit closed

MOVE TOOL UPWARDS TO RELEASE

Backing off adjustment—self-adjusting brakes

Brake Pedal Adjustment

There are no provisions available for the adjustment of the brake pedal height. However, it should be checked to determine if sufficient height exists. Corrections can only be made by replacement of parts, alignment, or straightening of the affected parts. To determine if sufficient pedal height exists, open a wheel cylinder bleed valve to simulate a failed system, and depress the brake pedal. The pedal should not contact the floor board during this test.

NOTE: Close the bleeder valve before releasing the brake pedal. The brake warning light switch will have to be reset after the test is completed.

Stoplight Switch Adjustment

No stoplight switch adjustments are provided. If the stop lamps are inoperative, a defective switch, defective bulbs, loose or broken connections, or an improper positioned switch would be indicated. A mechanical type switch is located on the brake pedal, at the pushrod bolt location, while the hydraulic type switch is located on or near the master cylinder, and operated by hydraulic pressure.

Parking Brake Adjustment

1. Loosen locknut on the equalizer rod and turn front nut forward several turns.
2. Turn the locknut (rear) forward just enough to remove any slack but not so much that the brake shoes lift of their anchors.
3. Tighten both nuts against the equalizer.

CHASSIS ELECTRICAL

Heater

The Scout heater core and blower motor assembly are located in the right rear corner of the engine compartment.

Heater Core

REMOVAL & INSTALLATION

1. Drain the cooling system and remove the negative battery cable.
2. Remove the heater hoses from the heater core outlets.
3. Remove the windshield washer bottle from the firewall.
4. Remove the cover plate from the heater box and remove the heater core from the housing.
5. Remove the core end cover.

NOTE: Do not damage the core fins during the removal and installation procedure.

6. Installation is the reverse of removal. Fill the cooling system and check the operation of the heater system.

Heater Blower

REMOVAL & INSTALLATION

1. Disconnect the negative battery cable.
2. Disconnect the wire harness to the blower motor.
3. Remove the six sheet metal screws securing motor to the blower housing. Remove the motor with the blower.
4. Loosen and remove the bolt from the end of the motor shaft and detach the squirrel cage.
5. To install reverse the removal procedure.

Radio

REMOVAL & INSTALLATION

1. Disconnect the negative battery cable.
2. Remove the bolts which hold the radio to the radio support.
3. Remove the attaching screws which hold the radio cover bezel to the instrument panel.
4. Pull the radio from the instrument panel and disconnect the radio lead wires.
5. Remove the radio from the car.
6. Installation is in reverse order of removal.

Wiper Motor and Linkage

REMOVAL & INSTALLATION

1. Raise the hood and disconnect the windshield washer hose from the cowl.
2. Remove the attaching screws and pull off the cowl.
3. Remove the bolts from the wiper mounting bracket.
4. Release the attaching link from the motor to the wiper arm linkage.
5. Disconnect the motor wiring.
6. Remove the motor with the link assembly from the vehicle.
   To install:
7. Position the wiper motor on the mounting bracket and connect the wiring.
8. Connect the wiper linkage to the motor.
9. Install the cowl and the windshield washer hose.

Instrument Cluster

REMOVAL & INSTALLATION

Scouts use eight securing screws to mount the dash. Remove the screws and pull the panel out. It will be necessary to remove the speedometer cable and the electrical connections from the gauges if the cluster is to be totally removed. If an oil pressure gauge is used, plug the capillary tube to prevent leakage. To install, reverse the removal procedure.

Turn Signal and Hazard Flasher Locations

The turn signal indicator is located on the left side of the steering column below the steering wheel.

On some Scout models the turn signal indicator has two positions, one for lane change and the other for full turn. Moving the indicator one stop, either upward or downward, will activate the signal. The indicator must be held in position for the signal to work. Moving the indicator two stops to the lock position will activate the signal for a turn. The indicator will stay in a lock position until the turn is completed.

Headlights

REMOVAL & INSTALLATION

1. Remove the screws retaining the headlight door and remove the door.
2. Remove the screws retaining the retaining ring and remove the ring.
3. Pull the headlight out, disconnect the wire harness and remove the headlight from the vehicle.
4. Install the headlight in the reverse order of removal.

Isuzu/LUV

GENERAL ENGINE SPECIFICATIONS

Engine Displacement cc (cu. in.)	Carb Type	Horsepower @ rpm	Torque @ rpm (ft. lbs.)	Bore and Stroke (in.)	Compression Ratio	Oil Pressure psi @ 1400 rpm
1800 (110.8)	2-bbl	80 @ 4800	95 @ 3000	3.31 × 3.23	8.5:1	57
1900 (116.0)	2-bbl	82 @ 4600	101 @ 3000	3.42 × 3.23	8.4:1	56
2238 (136.6)	Diesel	58 @ 4300	93 @ 2200	3.46 × 3.62	21.0:1	55

CAPACITIES

Engine Displacement cc (cu in.)	Crankcase L (qts)	Transmission L (pts) 4 sp	Transmission L (pts) 5sp	Transmission L (pts) Auto	Transfer Case L (pts)	Rear Drive Axle L (pts)	Front Drive Axle L (pts)	Gas Tank L (gal)	Cooling System L (qts) Manual	Cooling System L (qts) Auto
1800 (110.8)	5.4 (5.72)①	1.3 (2.7)	1.3 (2.7)	6.6 (14)	2.5 (5.2)	1.3 (2.7)	0.8 (1.7)	56 (13)	6.4 (6.7)	6.1 (6.4)
1900 (116.0)	3.9 (4.1)	1.3 (2.7)	1.3 (2.7)	6.3 (13.3)	2.5 (5.2)	1.3 (2.7)	0.8 (1.7)	56.5 (13.2)②	8.0 (8.6)	7.8 (8.3)
2238 (136.6)	4.8 (5.1)	1.3 (2.7)	1.3 (2.7)	6.6 (14)	2.5 (5.2)	1.3 (2.7)	0.8 (1.7)	56 (13)	6.4 (6.7)	6.1 (6.4)

① 1981 and 82: 4.2 qts ② Optional 19.1 gal (Long WB)

GASOLINE ENGINE TUNE-UP SPECIFICATIONS

Engine Displacement cc (cu in.)	Spark Plug Type	Spark Plug Gap (in.)	Distributor Point Dwell (deg)	Distributor Point Gap (in.)	Ignition Timing (deg) MT	Ignition Timing (deg) AT	Intake Valve Opens (deg)	Fuel Pump Pressure (psi)	Idle Speed (rpm) MT	Idle Speed (rpm) AT	Valve Clearance (in.) In	Valve Clearance (in.) Ex
1800 (110.8)	BPR-6ES11	0.040①	Electronic②		6B	6B	21B	3.0	800	900	0.006	0.010
1900 (116.0)	BPR-6ES11	0.040	Electronic		6B	6B	21B	3.0	800	900	0.006	0.010

① Models with point ignition:
Plugs: BPR-6ES
Gap: 0.030

② Models with point ignition:
Gap: 0.016–0.020
Dwell: 47–57

FIRING ORDER

NOTE: To avoid confusion, always replace spark plug wires one at a time.

FIRING ORDER   1-3-4-2

Gasoline engine firing order

DIESEL ENGINE TUNE-UP SPECIFICATIONS

Injector Opening Pressure (psi)	Low Idle (rpm)	Valve Clearance (in.)		Intake Valve Opens (deg)	Injection Timing (deg)	Firing Order
		Intake	Exhaust			
2133①	750	0.016C	0.016C	16B	15B	1-3-4-2

① ISUZU: 1493

CRANKSHAFT AND CONNECTING ROD SPECIFICATIONS

(All measurements given in in.)

Engine Displacement cc (cu in.)	Crankshaft				Connecting Rod		
	Main Brg Journal Dia	Main Brg Oil Clearance	Shaft End-Play	Thrust on No.	Journal Dia	Oil Clearance	Side Clearance
1800 (110.8)	2.2050	0.0008–0.0025	0.0117	3	1.9290	0.0007–0.0030	0.0137
1900 (116.0)	2.2050	0.0008–0.0025	0.0117	3	1.9290	0.0007–0.0030	0.0137
2238 (136.6)	2.3593	0.0011–0.0033	0.0018	3	2.0837	0.0016–0.0047	0.0024

VALVE SPECIFICATIONS

Engine Displacement cc (cu in.)	Seat Angle (deg)	Face Angle (deg)	Spring Test Pressure (lbs. @ in.)		Stem-to-Guide Clearance (in.)		Stem Diameter (in.)	
			Outer	Inner	Intake	Exhaust	Intake	Exhaust
1800 (110.8)	45	45	35 @ 1.614	20 @ 1.516	0.0009–0.0022	0.0015–0.0031	0.3102	0.3091
1900 (116.0)	45	45	35 @ 1.614	20 @ 1.516	0.0009–0.0022	0.0015–0.0031	0.3102	0.3091
2238 (136.6)	45	45	145 @ 1.535	44 @ 1.457	0.0015–0.0027	0.0025–0.0037	0.3150	0.3150

PISTON AND RING SPECIFICATIONS

(All measurements in inches)

Engine Displacement cu. in. (cc)	Piston Clearance	Ring Gap			Ring Side Clearance		
		Top Compression	Bottom Compression	Oil Control	Top Compression	Bottom Compression	Oil Control
110.8 (1817)	0.0018–0.0026	0.008–0.016	0.008–0.016	0.008–0.035	0.0059	0.0059	0.0059
116.0 (1900)	0.0018–0.0026	0.014–0.020	0.014–0.020	0.008–0.035	0.0059	0.0059	0.0059
136.6 (2238)	0.0062–0.0070	0.0079–0.0158	0.0079–0.0158	0.0079–0.0158	0.0018–0.0028	0.0012–0.0021	0.0008–0.0021

TORQUE SPECIFICATIONS

(All readings in ft. lbs. unless noted)

Engine Displacement cc (cu in.)	Cylinder Head Bolts	Rod Bearing Bolts	Main Bearing Bolts	Crankshaft Pulley Bolts	Flywheel to Crankshaft Bolts	Manifolds	
						Intake	Exhaust
1800 (110.8)	72①	43	72	87	69	13	15
1900 (116.0)	72①	43	72	87	69	13	15
2238 (136.6)	65②	61	123	136	68	15	15

① Tighten to 61 ft. lbs. first. Retighten to 72 ft. lbs.
② Tighten in 2 steps: 44 ft. lbs. first, then 65 ft. lbs. final torque.

ALTERNATOR AND REGULATOR SPECIFICATIONS

Alternator		Voltage Regulator					
Manufacturer and/or Part Number	Output Amps @ Generator rpm	Charge Indicator Relay		Voltage Regulator			Regulated Voltage
		Back Gap (in.)	Point Gap (in.)	Back Gap (in.)	Air Gap (in.)	Point Gap (in.)	
LT140-126	40	0.036	0.020	0.015	0.014	0.012	13.8–14.8
LT150-144	50	0.036	0.020	0.015	0.014	0.012	13.8–14.8
LT150-131B	50	0.036	0.020	0.015	0.014	0.012	13.8–14.8

BATTERY AND STARTER SPECIFICATIONS

Engine Displacement cc (cu in.)	Battery			Starter							Brush Spring Tension (oz)
	Amp Hour Capacity	Volts	Ground	Lock Test			No Load Test				
				Amps	Volts	Torque (ft. lbs.)	Amps	Volts	RPM		
1800–1900 (110.8) (116.0)	50	12	N	Not Recommended							56
2238 (136.6)	80	12	N	Not Recommended							56

TUNE-UP

Breaker Points and Condenser

When replacing the points, always install a new condenser.

Remember that a change in the point gap or dwell also changes the ignition timing. Therefore, if the points are adjusted, you must also correct the ignition timing.

INSPECTION

1. Disconnect the high-tension wire from the top of the distributor.
2. Remove the distributor cap by prying off the spring clips on the sides of the cap.
3. Remove the rotor from the distributor shaft by pulling it straight up. Examine the condition of the rotor. If it is cracked or the brass tip is excessively worn or burned, the rotor should be replaced. If not excessively worn, clean the brass tip with fine emery paper until shiny.
4. Pry open the contacts of the points with a screwdriver and check the condition of the contacts. If they are excessively worn, burned or pitted, they should be replaced.
5. If the points are in good condition, adjust them and replace the rotor and the distributor cap. If the points need to be replaced, follow the replacement procedure given below.

REMOVAL & INSTALLATION

1. Remove the coil high-tension wire from top of the distributor cap. Remove the distributor cap from the distributor and place it out of the way. Remove the rotor from the distributor shaft.
2. Loosen the screw that holds the condenser lead to the body of the breaker points and remove the condenser lead from the points.
3. Remove the screw that holds and grounds the condenser to the distributor body. Remove the condenser from the distributor and discard it.
4. Remove the points assembly attaching screws and adjustment lockscrews. A screwdriver with a holding mechanism will come in handy here, so that you don't drop a screw into the distributor and have to remove the entire distributor to retrieve it.
5. Remove the points by lifting them straight up and off the locating dowel on the plate. Wipe off the cam and apply new cam lubricant. Discard the old set of points.
6. Slip the new set of points onto the locating dowel and install the screws that hold the assembly onto the plate. Do not tighten them all the way.
7. Attach the new condenser to the plate with the ground screw.
8. Attach the condenser lead to the points at the proper place.

9. Apply a small amount of cam lubricant to the shaft where the rubbing block of the points touches.

ADJUSTMENT WITH A FEELER GAUGE

1. If the contact points of the assembly are not parallel, bend the stationary contact so that they make contact across the entire surface of the contacts. Bend only the stationary bracket part of the point assembly; not the moveable contact.
2. With the vehicle in neutral and parking brake on, turn the engine until the rubbing block of the points is on the crest of one of the high points of the distributor cam. You can do this by either having an assistant turn the ignition switch "on" and then releasing it quickly ("bumping" the engine) or by turning the crankshaft pulley bolt with a wrench or socket wrench.
3. Place the correct size feeler gauge between the contacts. Make sure it is parallel with the contact surfaces.
4. With your free hand, insert a screwdriver into the notch provided for adjustment or into the eccentric adjusting screw, then twist the screwdriver to either increase or decrease the gap to the proper setting.
5. Tighten the adjustment lockscrew, and turn the engine until the rubbing block of the points rests on the next crest of the distributor cam.

Recheck the contact gap to make sure that it didn't change when the lockscrew was tightened.
6. Replace the rotor and distributor cap, and the high-tension wire that connects the top of the distributor and the coil. Make sure that the rotor is firmly seated all the way onto the distributor shaft and that the tab of the rotor is aligned with the notch in the shaft. Align the tab in the base of the distributor cap with the notch in the distributor body. Make sure that the cap is firmly seated on the distributor and that the retainer springs are in place. Make sure that the end of the high-tension wire is firmly placed in the top of the distributor and the coil.

ADJUSTMENT WITH A DWELL METER

1. Adjust the points with a feeler gauge as previously described.
2. Connect the dwell meter to the ignition circuit according to the manufacturer's instructions. One lead of the meter is connected to a ground and the other lead is connected to the distributor post on the coil. An adapter is usually provided for this purpose.
3. If the dwell meter has a set line on it, adjust the meter to zero the indicator.
4. Start the engine.

NOTE: Be careful when working on any vehicle while the engine is running.

Make sure that the transmission is in Neutral and that the parking brake is applied. Keep hands, clothing, tools and the wires of the test instruments clear of the rotating fan blades.

5. Observe the reading on the dwell meter. If the reading is within the specified range, turn off the engine and remove the dwell meter.

NOTE: If the meter does not have a scale for 4 cylinder engines, multiply the 8 cylinder reading by two.

6. If the reading is above the specified range, the breaker point gap is too small. If the reading is below the specified range, the gap is too large. In either case, the engine must be stopped and the gap adjusted in the manner previously covered. After making the adjustment, start the engine and check the reading on the dwell meter. When the correct reading is obtained, disconnect the dwell meter.
7. Check the adjustment of the ignition timing.

Electronic Ignition

AIR GAP SETTING

All 1981 and later models have electronic ignition. The only adjustment possible on this ignition is setting of the air gap.

1. Remove the distributor cap and O-ring.
2. Remove the rotor.
3. Use a feeler gauge to measure the air gap at the pick up coil projection. The gap should be 0.008–0.016 in. Adjust if necessary.

AIR GAP

PICK-UP COIL

Adjusting the air gap

4. Loosen the screws and move the signal generator until the gap is correct. Tighten the screws and recheck the gap.

NOTE: The electrical parts in this system are not repairable. If found to be defective they must be replaced.

You can also check the signal generator by using an ohmmeter to determine its resistance. It should be 140–180 ohms. If the resistance is not correct, it must be replaced.

Ignition timing marks

Ignition Timing

NOTE: For diesel injection timing, see Diesel Fuel System section.

The timing marks are located at the front crankshaft pulley and consist of a pointer attached to the engine block and graduations on the crankshaft pulley.

1. Set the dwell angle to the proper specification.
2. Locate the timing marks on the crankshaft pulley and the front of the engine.
3. Clean off the timing marks, so that you can see them.
4. Use chalk or white paint to color the mark on the crankshaft pulley that will indicate the correct timing, when aligned with the pointer. It is also helpful to mark the tip of the pointer with a small dab of color.
5. Attach a tachometer to the engine.
6. Attach a timing light to the engine according to the manufacturer's instructions. If the timing light has three wires, one, usually green or blue, is attached to the No. 1 spark plug with an adapter. The other wires are connected to the battery. The red wire goes to the positive side of the battery and the black wire is connected to the negative terminal of the battery.
7. Disconnect the vacuum line to the distributor at the distributor and plug the vacuum line. A golf tee does a good job.
8. Make sure that all wires from the timing light and tachometer are clear of the fan and belts. Start the engine.
9. Adjust the idle to the correct setting and rpm.
10. Aim the timing light at the timing marks. If the marks that you put on the pulley and the engine are aligned when the light flashes, the timing is correct. Turn off the engine and remove the tachometer and the timing light. If the marks are not in alignment, proceed with the following steps.
11. Turn off the engine.
12. Loosen the distributor lockbolt just enough so that the distributor can be turned with a little effort.
13. Start the engine. Keep the wires of the timing light clear of the fan.
14. With the timing light aimed at the pulley and the marks on the engine, turn the distributor in the direction of rotor rotation to retard the spark, and in the op-

posite direction of the rotor rotation to advance the spark. Align the marks on the pulley and the engine with the flashes of the timing light.
15. Tighten distributor lockbolt, unplug vacuum line and test instruments, and reconnect.

Valve Lash

NOTE: The valves are adjusted with the engine COLD. It is best to allow an engine to sit overnight before beginning a valve adjustment.

NOTE: While all valve adjustments must be made as accurately as possible, it is better to have the valve adjustment slightly loose than slightly tight, as a burned valve may result from overly tight adjustments.

1. Make sure that both the cylinder head and camshaft retaining bolts are tightened to the proper torque.
2. Remove the camshaft carrier side-cover, and discard the gasket if it is torn, cracked, or worn in any way.
3. Turn the crankshaft with a wrench on the front pulley attaching bolt or by "bumping" the engine with the starter until the No. 1 piston is at TDC of the compression stroke. You can tell when the piston is coming up on the compression stroke by removing the spark plug and placing your thumb over the hole; you will feel air being forced out of the spark plug hole past your thumb. Both valves on No. 1 cylinder will be closed. Stop turning the crankshaft when the TDC timing mark on the crankshaft pulley is directly aligned with the timing mark pointer.
4. With the No. 1 piston at TDC of the compression stroke, check the clearance between the rocker arm and valve stem with the proper thickness feeler gauge on Nos. 1 and 2, intake valves and Nos. 1 and 3 exhaust valves.
5. Adjust the clearance by loosening the locknut with an open-end wrench, turning the adjusting screw with a phillips head screwdriver and retightening the locknut. The proper thickness feeler gauge should pass between the camshaft or valve stem and the rocker with a slight drag when the clearance is corrected.
6. Turn the crankshaft one full turn to position the No. 4 piston at TDC of its compression stroke. Adjust the remaining valves: Nos. 2 and 4 exhaust and Nos. 3 and 4 intake in the same manner as outlined in Step 5.
7. Install the camshaft carrier side-cover with a new gasket and sealer.

Carburetor

This section contains only tune-up adjustment procedures for carburetors. Descriptions, adjustments, and overhaul procedures for carburetors can be found in the

Valve clearance adjustment

Number of Cylinders	1		2		3		4	
Valve Arrangement	Exh.	In.	In.	Exh.	Exh.	In.	In.	Exh.
When piston in No. 1 cylinder is held at T.D.C.	0	0	0		0			
When piston in No. 4 cylinder is held at T.D.C.				0		0	0	0

Valve adjusting sequence

Fuel System section.

IDLE SPEED AND MIXTURE ADJUSTMENT

Through 1980

1. Start the engine and run it until it reaches operating temperature.
2. If it hasn't already been done, check and adjust the ignition timing. After you have set the timing, turn off the engine.
3. Attach tachometer to the engine.
4. Remove the air cleaner.
5. Start the engine and, with transmission in Neutral, check the idle speed on the tachometer. If the reading is correct, turn off the engine and remove the tachometer. If it is not correct, proceed to the following steps.
6. Turn the idle adjusting screw with a screwdriver—clockwise to increase idle speed and counterclockwise to decrease it.
7. If the vehicle is equipped with air conditioning:
   a. Turn on the AC to maximum cold and high blower. Disconnect the vacuum line to the air cleaner housing air compensator and plug the inlet manifold;
   b. Open the throttle approximately ⅓ and allow the throttle to close. This will allow the speed-up solenoid to reach full travel;
   c. Adjust the fast-idle screw to set the idle speed to 900 rpm;
   d. Open the throttle about ⅓ and allow it to close. Read the idle rpm. Repeat Step C until the correct reading is obtained. Shut off the engine.
8. Turn the mixture adjusting screw all the way. Seat the needle tip *lightly* to avoid damaging the tip. Back the screw out 3½ turns.

9. Start the engine. Turn the mixture screw until the maximum engine rpm is achieved.

10. Reset the engine idle speed.

11. Turn the idle mixture screw clockwise (lean) until the engine speed drops 50 rpm.

12. Reset the idle mixture screw ½ turn counter-clockwise (rich) from Step 11 position.

13. Rest the throttle adjusting screw to required idle speed.

14. Unplug and reconnect any vacuum lines that may have been disconnected.

1981 and Later Models

The idle mixture adjustment is the same as previously described with the following exceptions:

1. Make the idle speed adjustment with the engine at normal operating temperature. Be sure the choke is fully opened, air conditioning off and the air cleaner installed.

2. Disconnect and plug the distributor vacuum, the canister purge and EGR vacuum lines. Shut off the vacuum to the idle compensator by bending the rubber hose.

3. Adjust to required idle speed with throttle adjusting screw.

4. If equipped with air conditioning, turn AC to max cold and high blower.

5. Open throttle to approx. ⅓ and allow throttle to close, the speed up solenoid should activate. Adjust speed up solenoid screw until 900 rpm is reached.

In order to adjust the idle mixture you must first remove the plug that covers the mixture screw.

1. To remove the plug, first remove the carburetor and turn it upside down.

2. Remove the plug carefully with a hammer and screwdriver (see illustration).

3. Reinstall the carburetor.

4. Turn the mixture screw all the way in, and then back it out 2 turns (Federal) and 1 turn (California).

5. Readjust the idle if necessary.

PLUG: IDLE
MIXTURE SCREW

Removing the idle mixture plugs

ENGINE ELECTRICAL

Distributor

REMOVAL & INSTALLATION

1. Remove the high-tension wires from the distributor cap terminal towers, noting their positions to assure correct reassembly.

2. Remove the primary lead from the coil terminal.

3. Disconnect the vacuum line.

4. Unlatch the two distributor cap retaining clips and remove the distributor cap.

5. Note the position of the rotor in relation to the base. Scribe a mark on the base of the distributor and on the engine block to facilitate reinstallation. Align the marks with the direction the metal tip of the rotor is pointing.

6. Remove the bolt which holds the distributor to the engine.

7. Lift the distributor assembly from the engine.

To install:

8. Insert the distributor into the engine. Line up the mark on the engine with the metal tip of the rotor. Make sure that the vacuum advance diaphragm is pointed in the same direction as it was pointed originally. This will be done automatically if the marks on the engine and the distributor are lined up with the rotor.

9. Install the distributor hold-down bolt and clamp. Leave the screw loose enough so that you can move the distributor with heavy hand pressure.

10. Connect the primary wire to the coil. Install the distributor cap on the distributor housing. Secure the distributor cap with the spring clips.

11. Install the spark plug wires, checking the wire placement with the firing order diagram in the front of this section. Make sure the wires are pressed all the way into the top of the distributor cap and firmly onto the spark plugs.

12. Adjust the point dwell and set the ignition timing.

NOTE: If the crankshaft has been turned or the engine disturbed in any manner while the distributor was removed, or if the marks were not drawn, it will be necessary to initially time the engine. Follow the procedure given below:

1. It is necessary to place the No. 1 cylinder in the firing position to correctly install the distributor. To locate this position, the ignition timing marks on the crankshaft front pulley are used.

2. Remove the No. 1 cylinder spark plug. Turn the crankshaft until the piston in the No. 1 cylinder is moving up on the compression stroke. This can be determined by placing your thumb over the spark plug hole and feeling the air being forced out of the cylinder. Stop turning the crankshaft when the timing marks that are used to time the engine are aligned.

3. Oil the distributor housing lightly where the distributor bears on the cylinder block.

4. Install the distributor so that the rotor, which is mounted on the shaft, points toward the No. 1 spark plug terminal tower position when the cap is installed. Of course you won't be able to see the direction in which the rotor is pointing if the cap is on the distributor. Lay the cap on the top of the distributor and make a mark on the side of the distributor housing just below the No. 1 spark plug terminal. Make sure that the rotor points toward the mark when you install the distributor.

5. When the distributor shaft has reached the bottom of the hole, move the rotor back and forth slightly until the driving lug on the end of the shaft enters the slots cut in the end of the oil pump shaft and the distributor assembly slides down into place.

6. When the distributor is correctly installed, the breaker points should be in such a position that they are just ready to break contact with each other. This is accomplished by rotating the distributor body after it has been installed in the engine. Once again, line up the marks that you made before the distributor was removed from the engine.

7. Install the distributor hold-down bolt.

8. Install the spark plug into the No. 1 spark plug hole and continue from Step 9 of the distributor installation procedure.

Alternator

PRECAUTIONS

To prevent damage to the alternator and regulator, the following precautionary measures must be taken when working with the electrical system.

1. Never reverse battery connections. Always check the battery polarity visually. This is to be done before any connections are made to be sure that all of the connections correspond to the battery ground polarity.

2. Booster batteries for starting must be connected properly. Make sure that the positive cable of the booster battery is connected to the positive terminal of the battery that is getting the boost. Connect the negative boost cable from booster battery to a good chassis ground on the vehicle with the dead battery.

3. Disconnect the battery cables before using a fast charger; the charger has a tendency to force current through the diodes in the opposite direction for which they were designed. This burns out the diodes.

4. Never use a fast charger as a booster for starting the vehicle.

5. Never disconnect the voltage regulator while the engine is running.

6. Do not ground the alternator output terminal.

7. Do not operate the alternator on an open circuit with the field energized.

8. Do not attempt to polarize an alternator.

REMOVAL & INSTALLATION

1. Remove the air pump.

2. Disconnect the battery ground cable before disconnecting the cable from the alternator "A" terminal. This is a hot cable connected directly to the battery.

3. Disconnect the alternator circuit at the connector and disconnect the cable from the "A" terminal.

4. Remove the mounting bolts on the lower part of the alternator and the fan belt adjusting bolt. Pull belt clear of alternator pulley and remove alternator.

5. Install the alternator in the reverse order of removal and tighten the fan belt and air pump belt tension.

BELT TENSION ADJUSTMENT

Any engine V-belt is correctly tensioned when the longest span of belt between pulleys can be depressed about ¼ in. in the middle by moderate thumb pressure. To adjust, loosen the accessory's slotted adjusting bracket bolt. If the hinge bolt is very tight, it may be necessary to loosen it slightly to move the item.

─── CAUTION ───

Be careful not to overtighten belts, as this will damage the bearings, particularly in air or water pumps and alternators.

Voltage relay adjustment

Regulator

REMOVAL & INSTALLATION

1. Remove the negative battery cable from the battery.

2. Disconnect the electrical leads at the

regulator, taking note to the positions in order to facilitate correct reconnection.

3. Remove the two mounting screws and remove the regulator.

4. Install the regulator in the reverse order of removal.

ADJUSTMENT

1. Remove the regulator from the vehicle and remove the regulator cover.

2. If the contact points are rough, carefully dress them with fine emery paper (a 600-grit autobody paper works fine).

3. Check and adjust the core gap first, and then the point gap. Adjustment of the yoke gap is unnecessary.

4. Adjust the core gap by loosening the screws attaching the contact set to the yoke.

Voltage regulator adjustment

Move the contact set up or down as required. The standard core gap is 0.024–0.039 in. Tighten the attaching screw.

5. Adjust the point gap by loosening the screw attaching the upper contact. Move the upper contact up or down as required. The standard point gap is 0.012–0.016 in.

6. Adjust the regulated voltage by means of the adjusting screw. Turn the adjusting screw in to increase voltage and out to reduce voltage. When the correct adjustment is obtained, secure the adjusting screw by tightening the locknut. The regulated voltage is 13.8–14.8 volts.

7. Install the regulator cover, reconnect the electrical leads and install the regulator.

Starter

REMOVAL & INSTALLATION

1. Disconnect the negative battery cable from the battery. Disconnect and remove the EGR pipe, if equipped.

2. Disconnect the starter wiring at the starter, taking note of the positions for correct reinstallation.

3. Remove the bolts attaching the starter to the engine and remove the starter from the vehicle.

4. Install the starter in the reverse order of removal.

BRUSH REPLACEMENT

1. With the starter out of the vehicle,

1. Thrust washer	11. Brush holder
2. Spacer	12. Brush (field coil)
3. Washer	13. Brush (ground)
4. Stopper washer	14. Brush tension spring
5. Armature	15. Rear cover
6. Pinion stopper	16. Rear armature bearing
7. Snap-ring	17. Clutch drive
8. Field coil retaining screw	18. Front armature bearing
9. Yoke housing	19. Gear case
10. Field coils	20. Shift lever

21. Shift lever pivot bolt	
22. Solenoid switch	
23. Through-bolts	
24. Solenoid-to-gear case attaching bolts	
25. Washer	
26. Dust cover	
27. Insulator	
28. Brush holder-to-rear cover attaching screw	

Starter motor

remove the bolts holding the solenoid to the top of the starter and remove the solenoid.

2. To remove the brushes, remove the two through-bolts and the two rear cover attaching screws and remove the rear cover.

3. Disconnect the brushes, electrical leads and remove the brushes.

4. Install the brushes in the reverse order of removal.

STARTER DRIVE REPLACEMENT

1. With the starter motor removed from the vehicle, remove the solenoid from the starter.

2. Remove the two through-bolts and separate the gear case from the yoke housing.

3. Remove the pinion stopper clip and the pinion stopper.

4. Slide the starter drive off the armature shaft.

5. Install the starter drive and reassemble the starter in the reverse order of removal.

ENGINE MECHANICAL

Engine

REMOVAL & INSTALLATION

Gasoline Engine

NOTE: On models with 2 wheel drive, the engine and transmission may be removed as an assembly. 4 wheel drive models require transmission separation prior to engine removal.

1. Raise and remove hood and disconnect the battery cables.

2. Remove the skid plate and drain both the cooling system and the oil pan.

3. Remove the air cleaner assembly and the many vacuum hoses. Mark all vacuum hoses and the places they connect for installation.

4. Disconnect all hoses, tubing and electrical leads from the engine and mark them where they connect for reinstallation.

5. Remove the radiator and fan blade assembly.

6. Using penetrating oil where necessary, disconnect the exhaust pipe from the exhaust manifold.

7. Raise the vehicle and remove the clutch return spring and slave cylinder, if equipped with a manual transmission. Fasten the cylinder to the frame with a piece of wire or duct tape.

8. Remove the starter motor. On 2 WD, remove driveshaft. Remove transmission mount bolts. Remove gearshift lever assembly.

9. On 4WD; remove the flywheel cover pan.

10. On 4WD; remove the bell housing bolts and support the transmission with a floor jack or suitable stand.

11. Lift the engine slightly and remove the engine mount nuts.

12. Make certain that all lines, hoses, cables and wires have been disconnected from the engine and frame.

13. Lift the engine from the vehicle with the front of the engine raised slightly to clear the transmission input shaft.

14. Installation is the reverse of removal.

Diesel Engine
2-WHEEL DRIVE

1. Raise engine hood.
2. Disconnect the battery ground cable.
3. Remove the engine hood.
4. Remove the battery assembly.
5. Remove under cover and drain the cooling system by opening the drain plugs on the radiator and on the cylinder block.
6. Remove the air cleaner assembly as follows:
   a. Remove the intake silencer.
   b. Remove the bolts fixing the air cleaner and loosen the clamp bolt.
   c. Lift the air cleaner slightly and disconnect the breather hose, then remove the air cleaner assembly.
7. Disconnect the upper water hose at the engine side.
8. Loosen the compressor drive belts by moving the power steering oil pump or idler if so equipped.
9. Remove the cooling fan and fan shroud.
10. Disconnect the lower water hose at the engine side.
11. Remove the radiator grille.
12. Remove the radiator attaching bolts and remove the radiator.
13. Disconnect the accelerator control cable from the injection pump side.
14. Disconnect the air conditioner compressor control cable. (If so equipped).
15. Disconnect the fuel hoses from the injection pump.
16. Disconnect the battery cable from the cylinder body.
17. Disconnect the transmission wiring.
18. Disconnect the vacuum hose from the fast idle actuator.
19. Disconnect the connector at fuel cut solenoid.
20. Disconnect the A/C compressor wiring.
21. Disconnect the heater hoses extending from the heater unit from the dash panel side.
22. Disconnect the hose for master-vac from the vacuum pump.
23. Disconnect vacuum hose from the vacuum pump.
24. Disconnect the generator wiring at the connector.
25. Disconnect the exhaust pipe from the exhaust manifold at the flange.
26. Remove the exhaust pipe mounting brake from the engine back plate.

27. Disconnect the starter motor wiring.
28. Disconnect the battery cable from starter motor.
29. Slide the gearshift lever boot upwards on the lever. Remove 2 gearshift lever attaching bolts and remove lever.
30. Place a pan under transmission to receive oil, disconnect speedometer cable at the transmission then disconnect the ground cable.
31. Disconnect the propeller shaft at differential side.
32. Remove the propeller shaft.
33. Remove return spring from clutch fork.
34. Disconnect clutch cable from hooked portion of clutch fork and pull it out forward through stiffener bracket.
35. Remove two bracket to transmission rear mount bolts and nuts.
36. Raise engine and transmission as required and remove (4) crossmember to frame bracket bolts.
37. Remove the rear mounting nuts from the transmission rear extension.
38. Disconnect electrical connectors at CRS switch and back-up lamp switch.
39. Remove the engine mounting bolt and nuts. Check that the engine is slightly lifted before removing the engine mounting bolt and nuts.
40. Engine removal:
   a. Check to make certain all the parts have been removed or disconnected from the engine that are fastened to the frame side.
   b. Remove the engine toward front of the vehicle by maneuvering the hoist, so that front part of the engine is lifted slightly.

4 WHEEL DRIVE

1. Raise engine hood.
2. Disconnect the battery ground cable.
3. Remove the engine hood.
4. Remove the battery assembly.
5. Remove under cover and drain the cooling system by opening the drain plugs on the radiator and on the cylinder block.
6. Remove the air cleaner as follows:
   a. Remove the intake silencer.
   b. Remove the bolts fixing the air cleaner and loosen the clamp bolt.
   c. Lift the air cleaner slightly and disconnect the breather hose, then remove the air cleaner assembly.
7. Disconnect the upper water hose at the engine side.
8. Loosen the compressor drive belts by moving the power steering oil pump or idler. (If so equipped).
9. Remove the cooling fan and fan shroud.
10. Disconnect the lower water hose at the engine side.
11. Remove the radiator grille.
12. Remove the radiator attaching bolts and remove the radiator.
13. Disconnect the accelerator control cable from the injection pump side.

14. Disconnect the air conditioner compressor control cable. (If so equipped).

15. Disconnect the fuel hose from the injection pump.

16. Disconnect the battery cable from the cylinder body.

17. Disconnect the transmission wiring.

18. Disconnect the vacuum hose from the fast idle actuator.

19. Disconnect the connector at fuel cut solenoid.

20. Disconnect the A/C compressor wiring.

21. Disconnect the heater hoses extending from the heater unit from the dash panel side.

22. Disconnect the hose for master-vac from the vacuum pump.

23. Disconnect the vacuum hose from the vacuum pump.

24. Disconnect the generator wiring at the connector.

25. Disconnect the exhaust pipe from the exhaust manifold at the flange.

26. Remove the exhaust pipe mounting brake from the engine back plate.

27. Disconnect the starter motor wiring.

28. Disconnect the battery cable from starter motor.

29. Slide the transmission and transfer gearshift lever boot upwards on each lever, remove gearshift lever attaching bolts.

30. Remove return spring from transfer gear shift lever then remove levers.

31. Remove the transmission.

32. Remove the engine mounting bolts and nuts. Check that the engine is slightly lifted before removing the engine mounting bolts and nuts.

33. Engine removal:

    a. Check to make certain all the parts have been removed or disconnected from the engine that are fastened to the frame side.

    b. Remove the engine toward front of the vehicle by maneuvering the hoist, so that front part of the engine is lifted slightly above the level.

Cylinder Head

REMOVAL & INSTALLATION

Gasoline Engine

1. Remove the cam cover.

2. Remove the EGR pipe clamp bolt at the rear of the cylinder head.

3. Jack up the vehicle and safely support it. Disconnect the exhaust pipe at the exhaust manifold.

4. Lower the vehicle and drain the cooling system.

5. Disconnect the heater hoses at the inlet manifold and at the rear of the cylinder head. Remove the A/C compressor and/or power steering pump with hoses attached, and position out of the way. Do not loosen the compressor lines unless familiar with the proper safe procedure.

Gasoline engine head bolt torque sequence

6. Disconnect the accelerator linkage and fuel line at the carburetor, all necessary electrical connections, spark plug wires and vacuum lines.

7. Rotate the camshaft until the No. 4 cylinder is in the firing position. Remove the distributor cap and mark the rotor to housing relationship. Remove distributor and the fuel pump.

8. Lock the timing chain adjuster by depressing and turning the automatic adjuster side pin 90° clockwise.

9. Remove the timing sprocket to camshaft bolt and remove the sprocket from the camshaft.

NOTE: Keep the sprocket on the chain damper and chain.

10. Disconnect the AIR hose and the check valve at the exhaust manifold.

11. Remove the cylinder head to timing cover bolts.

12. Remove the cylinder head bolts in a progressional sequence, starting with the outer bolts.

13. Remove the cylinder head, intake and exhaust manifold as a unit.

14. To install, reverse the removal procedure and tighten the bolts in the sequence and torque shown in the specifications table in the front of the section.

Diesel Engine

1. Follow the intake and exhaust manifold removal steps.

2. Remove the intake and exhaust manifold gasket.

3. Drain the cooling system by opening the drain plugs on the radiator and on the cylinder block.

4. Disconnect the upper water hose at the engine side.

5. Remove the cooling fan and fan shroud.

Diesel engine head bolt torque sequence

6. Remove the sleeve nuts and disconnect the injection pipes.

7. Remove the nozzle holder fixing nuts and remove the nozzle holder assembly.

8. Follow the rocker arm, bracket and shaft assembly removal steps.

9. Remove the pushrods.

10. Remove the joint bolt and disconnect the leak-off pipe.

11. Remove the 19 bolts fixing the cylinder head then remove the cylinder head and gasket.

12. Install the cylinder head gasket with the TOP mark side up on the cylinder body by aligning the holes with the dowels.

13. Install the cylinder head.

14. Install the pushrod in position on the cylinder head.

15. Install the rocker arm assembly on the cylinder head. Tighten the bracket fixing bolts evenly in sequence commencing with the inner ones.

16. Follow the intake and exhaust manifold installation steps.

17. Install the cooling fan and fan shroud.

18. Connect the upper water hose to engine side.

19. Fill the engine cooling system.

VALVE GUIDE REPLACEMENT

1. With the cylinder head removed from the vehicle and the valves removed from the head, drive the guides out toward the upper face of the cylinder head with a suitable driver. The valve guides cannot be driven out downward because they are secured in place with a snap-ring.

2. Lubricate the outside of the new valve guide with oil. Press it all the way into position, from the upper face of the cylinder head, until it is brought in contact with the snap-ring. Allowable interference between the cylinder head and the valve guide is 0.0016 in.

Valve Rockers

REMOVAL & INSTALLATION

Gasoline Engine

1. Remove the cam cover.

2. Loosen the rocker arm shaft bracket nuts a little at a time, in sequence, starting with the outer brackets.

3. Remove the nuts from the rocker arm shaft brackets. Remove shaft assembly.

4. To disassembly rocker and shafts: Remove the spring from the rocker arm shaft and remove the rocker brackets and arms. Keep parts in order for reassembly.

5. Before installing apply a generous amount of clean engine oil to the rocker arm shaft, rocker arms and valve stems.

6. Install the longer shaft on the exhaust valve side and the shorter shaft on the intake side so that the aligning marks on the shafts are turned on the front (timing)

Rocker arm spring installation

side of the engine.

7. Assemble the rocker arm shaft brackets and rocker arms to the shafts so that the cylinder number that is on the upper face of the brackets is pointed toward the front of the engine.

8. Align the mark on the No. 1 rocker arm shaft bracket with the mark on the intake and exhaust valve side rocker arm shaft.

9. Make certain the amount of projection of the rocker arm shaft beyond the face of the No. 1 rocker arm shaft bracket is longer on the exhaust side shaft than on the intake shaft when the rocker arm shaft stud holes are aligned with the rocker arm shaft bracket stud holes.

10. Place the rocker arm shaft springs in position between the shaft bracket and rocker arm.

11. Check that the punch mark on the rocker arm shaft is turned upward, then install the rocker arm shaft bracket assembly onto the cylinder head studs. Align the mark on the camshaft with the mark on the No. 1 rocker arm shaft bracket.

12. Tighten the rocker arm shaft brackets stud nuts to 16 ft. lbs.

NOTE: Hold the rocker arm springs with an adjustable wrench while torquing nuts to prevent damage to the spring. Start with the center nut and work outward.

13. Adjust the valves and install the camshaft cover, with a new gasket and sealer.

Diesel Engine

1. Remove the rocker cover.
2. Remove the 8 bolts fixing the rocker arm brackets in sequence commencing with the outer ones.
3. Remove the rocker arm, bracket and shaft assembly.
4. To install, follow the removal procedure in reverse order.
5. Tighten the bracket fixing bolts evenly in sequence commencing with the inner ones to 15 ft. lbs.

Intake Manifold

REMOVAL & INSTALLATION

Gasoline Engine

1. Disconnect the battery ground cable

and remove the air cleaner assembly.

2. Remove the EGR pipe clamp bolt at the rear of the cylinder head.
3. Raise the vehicle and remove the EGR pipe from the intake and exhaust manifolds.
4. Remove the EGR valve and bracket assembly from the intake manifold.
5. Lower the vehicle and drain the cooling system.
6. Remove the upper coolant hoses from the manifold.
7. Disconnect the accelerator linkage, vacuum lines, electrical wiring and fuel line from the intake manifold.
8. Remove the retaining nuts and remove the manifold from the cylinder head.
9. Remove the lower heater hose while holding the manifold away from the engine. Remove the manifold from the vehicle.
10. Installation is reverse of removal.

Diesel Engine

1. Raise engine hood.
2. Remove the bolts fixing the air cleaner and loosen the clamp bolt.
3. Lift the air cleaner slightly and disconnect the breather hose, then remove the air cleaner assembly.
4. Remove the 2 bolts and 4 nuts fixing the intake manifold.
5. Remove the intake manifold.
6. Installation is the reverse of removal. Torque the bolts to 15 ft. lbs.

Exhaust Manifold

REMOVAL & INSTALLATION

Gasoline Engine

1. Disconnect the battery ground cable and remove the air cleaner assembly.
2. Remove the EGR pipe clamp bolt at the rear of the cylinder head.
3. Raise the vehicle and remove the EGR pipe from the intake and exhaust manifolds.
4. Separate the exhaust pipe from the manifold.
5. Remove the manifold shield and remove the heat stove.
6. Remove the manifold retaining nuts and remove the manifold from the engine.
7. Installation is the reverse of removal.

Diesel Engine

1. Raise engine hood.
2. Remove the bolts fixing the air cleaner and loosen the clamp bolt.
3. Lift the air cleaner slightly and disconnect the breather hose, then remove the air cleaner assembly.
4. Disconnect the exhaust pipe from the exhaust manifold at the flange.
5. Remove the 3 nuts fixing the exhaust manifold, then remove the engine hanger and exhaust manifold.
6. Installation is the reverse of removal. Torque the bolts to 15 ft. lbs.

Timing Gear Cover

REMOVAL & INSTALLATION

Gasoline Engine

1. Remove the cylinder head.
2. Remove the oil pan.
3. Remove the oil pickup tube from the oil pump.
4. Remove the harmonic balancer. (See Timing Cover Seal—Removal and Installation).
5. Remove the air pump drive belt.
6. If equipped with air conditioning, remove the compressor and lay it to one side. Then remove the mounting brackets.
7. Remove the distributor cap and the distributor.
8. Remove the front cover attaching bolts then the cover.
9. Install a new gasket onto the cylinder block.
10. Align the oil pump drive gear punch mark with the oil filter side of the cover; then align the center of the dowel pin with the alignment mark on the oil pump case.
11. Rotate the crankshaft until the No. 1 and the No. 4 cylinders are at TDC.
12. Install the front cover by engaging the pinion gear with the oil pump drive gear on the crankshaft.
13. Check that the punch mark on the oil pump drive gear is turned to the rear side as viewed through the clearance between the front cover and the cylinder block.
14. Check that the slit at the end of the oil pump shaft is parallel with the front face of the cylinder block and is offset forward.
15. Reverse Steps 1–7 for assembly, using new gaskets and sealer on the oil pan, and a new head gasket.

Diesel Engine

1. Remove the radiator.
2. Remove the compressor drive belt by moving the power steering oil pump or idler. (If so equipped.)
3. Loosen the generator adjust plate bolt and fixing bolt, then remove the fan belt.
4. Remove the 4 bolts fixing the crankshaft pulley and remove the crankshaft pulley.
5. Remove the bolts fixing the timing pulley housing covers, then remove the covers.
6. Installation is the reverse of removal.

Timing Cover Seal

REMOVAL & INSTALLATION

Gasoline Engine

1. Disconnect the negative battery cable.
2. Drain the cooling system.
3. Disconnect the radiator inlet and outlet hoses.
4. Remove the radiator assembly.
5. Remove the alternator and compressor drive belts.

6. Remove the engine fan.

7. Remove the crankshaft pulley center bolt and remove the pulley and balancer assembly.

8. Carefully pry out the timing cover seal using a small pry bar. (A brake adjusting spoon makes a good tool here).

9. Using the butt-end of a wooden-handled screwdriver or block of wood and hammer, carefully tap the new seal into place on the cover.

10. Reverse Steps 1 through 7 for reassembly, using a new gasket and sealer between the timing cover and engine block.

Diesel Engine

1. Refer to the appropriate sections and remove the timing case cover and timing belt.

2. Remove the crankshaft timing belt pulley.

3. Remove the seal cover retaining bolts and cover. Remove the seal.

4. Apply clean engine oil to a new seal and install.

5. Install seal cover and crank pulley. Tighten pulley nut to 124–151 ft. lbs.

6. Install timing belt and remaining parts in reverse order of removal.

Timing Chain, Sprockets and Tensioner

REMOVAL & INSTALLATION

Gasoline Engine

1. Bring engine to No. 1 piston at TDC

(top dead center) on the compression stroke. Remove the front cover assembly as previously described. Depress or lock the shoe of the automatic chain adjuster in the retracted position.

2. Remove the timing chain from the crankshaft sprocket.

3. Remove the sprocket and the pinion gear from the crankshaft using a puller.

4. Remove the bolt or E-clip and remove the automatic chain adjuster.

5. Inspect adjuster pin, arm, wedge and rack teeth. Replace assembly if worn. Remove the chain tensioner.

6. Check the timing chain for wear. Stretch chain with a pull of approximately 22 lbs., the standard length is 15.00"; replace the chain if it is greater than 15.16".

7. Check tensioner pins for wear or damage, and replace if necessary.

8. Replace the chain tensioner and adjuster using the E-clips or bolt.

9. Install the timing sprocket and pinion gear with the groove side toward the front cover. Align the key grooves with the key on the crankshaft, then drive into position using the appropriate tool.

10. Confirm No. 1 piston at TDC, if not—turn the crankshaft so that the key is turned toward the cylinder head side (No. 1 and No. 4 pistons at top dead center).

11. Install the timing chain by aligning the mark plate on the chain with the mark on the crankshaft timing sprocket. The side of the chain with the mark plate is on the front side and the side of the chain with the most links between the mark plates is on the chain guide side.

12. Install the camshaft timing sprocket so that the mark side of the sprocket faces forward and so that the triangular mark aligns with the chain mark plate.

NOTE: Keep the timing chain engaged with the camshaft timing sprocket until the sprocket is installed on the camshaft.

13. Install the front cover assembly, using a new gasket and sealer.

Timing Belt

REMOVAL & INSTALLATION

Diesel Engine

1. Follow the timing cover removal steps.

2. Remove the bolts fixing the injection pump timing pulley flange, then remove the flange.

3. When removing tension spring, avoid using excess force, or distortion of spring will result.

4. Remove the fixing nut of the tension pulley, then remove the tension pulley and tension center.

5. Remove the timing belt. Avoid twisting or kinking the belt and keep it free from water, oil, dust and other foreign matter.

Removing the tension spring

Removing the tension pulley

NOTE: No attempt should be made to readjust belt tension. If the belt has been loosened through service of the timing system, it should be replaced with a new one.

6. Check that the setting marks on the crank pulley, injection pump timing pulley, and camshaft timing pulley are in alignment, then install the timing belt in sequence of crankshaft timing pulley, camshaft timing pulley, and injection pump

Timing chain adjuster

Timing marks aligned on the diesel

Installing belt

The tension pulley making proper contact with the two pins on the housing

Torquing the tension pulley

Bringing the #1 cylinder to TDC

timing pulley.

Make an adjustment so that slackness of the belt is taken up by the tension pulley.

When installing the belt, care should be taken so as not to damage the belt.

7. Install the tension center and tension pulley, making certain the end of the tension center is in proper contact with two pins on the timing pulley housing.

8. Hand-tighten the nut so that tension pulley can slide freely.

9. Install the tension spring correctly and semitighten the tension pulley fixing nut. Tighten to 22–36 ft. lbs.

10. Turn the crankshaft 2 turns in normal direction of rotation to permit seating of the belt. Further rotate the crankshaft 90 degrees beyond top dead center to settle the injection pump. Never attempt to turn the crankshaft in reverse direction.

11. Loosen the tension pulley fixing nut completely, allowing the pulley to take up looseness of the belt. Then, tighten the nut to 78–95 ft. lbs.

12. Install the flange on the injection pump pulley. The hole in the outer circumference of the flange should be aligned with the timing mark "△" on the injection pump pulley.

13. Turn the crankshaft 2 turns in normal direction of rotation to bring the piston in No. 1 cylinder to top dead center on compression stroke and check that the mark "△" on the timing pulley is in alignment with the hole in the flange.

14. The belt tension should be checked at a point between the injection pump pulley and crankshaft pulley using tool J-29771, to a pull of 33–55 lbs.

15. Adjust valve clearances.

16. Install remaining parts in the reverse order of removal.

Removing camshaft pulley

Checking belt tension

Camshaft

REMOVAL & INSTALLATION

Gasoline Engine

1. Remove the cam cover.
2. Rotate the engine until the No. 4 cylinder is at TDC (top dead center) on the compression stroke. Remove the distributor cap and mark the rotor to housing position.
3. Lock the timing chain adjuster by depressing and turning the automatic adjuster slide pin 90° in a clockwise position.

NOTE: Make sure that the chain is in a free state, after locking the chain adjuster.

4. Remove the bolt retaining the sprocket to the camshaft and remove the sprocket.

NOTE: Keep the timing sprocket on the chain damper and tensioner without removing the chain from the sprocket.

5. Remove the rocker arm, shaft and bracket assembly.
6. Remove the camshaft assembly.
7. To install reverse the removal procedure.

Pistons & Connecting Rods

NOTE: Refer to "Engine Rebuilding" in the Unit Repair Section for removal, installation and servicing procedures.

IDENTIFICATION & POSITIONING

The pistons are marked with the word "Front" and/or a notch in the piston head. When installed in the engine the "Front" and notch markings are to be facing the front of the engine. The connecting rods are numbered corresponding to the cylinders in which they are to be installed. Install the connecting rods in their correct cylinders with the marking to the right of the notch in the piston (looking from the rear of the engine).

Piston ring positioning

ENGINE LUBRICATION

Oil Pan

REMOVAL & INSTALLATION

All models have a one-piece stamped steel oil pan attached to the crankcase.

NOTE: On 4-wheel drive and diesel models, the engine must be removed before removing the oil pan.

1. Raise the hood and disconnect the battery ground cable.
2. Jack up the vehicle and safely support it.
3. Drain the oil.
4. Remove the front splash shield.
5. Remove the front crossmember, if necessary.
6. Disconnect the relay rod at the idler arm and lower the relay rod.
7. Remove the left side bellhousing bracket.
8. Disconnect the vacuum line at the oil pan.
9. Remove the oil pan bolts and the pan.
10. Installation is the reverse of removal. Tighten the retaining bolts to 43 in. lbs. On models with a separate crankcase tighten the bolts 15 ft. lbs. (180 in. lbs.). Use a new gasket and sealer.

Rear Main Oil Seal

REMOVAL & INSTALLATION

Gasoline Engine

1. Disconnect the negative battery terminal.
2. Remove the oil pan as previously described.
3. Remove the transmission.

NOTE: On manual transmissions, remove the clutch assembly.

Installing the crankshaft rear seal on gasoline engines

Correct tightening of the oil pan bolts

Use sealer at the points indicated when installing the pan gasket

Installing the rear main seal on diesel engines

4. Unbolt the starter and secure out of the way.
5. Remove the flywheel.
6. Remove the rear main seal retainer.
7. Remove the oil seal, using a pin punch. Work the punch around the diameter of the seal with a hammer until the seal begins to lift out, using care not to damage the seat and area around the seal.
8. Install the new oil seal.
9. Installation is the reverse of removal. Fill the space between the seal lips with grease and lubricate the seal lips with clean engine oil.
10. Install the oil pan with a new gasket and sealer.

Diesel Engine

1. Follow the engine assembly removal steps.

2. Remove the 6 bolts mounting the flywheel and remove the flywheel assembly.

When loosening the flywheel bolts, hold the crankshaft front bolt with a wrench to prevent turning of the crankshaft.

3. Remove the crankshaft rear seal.
4. Install the new seal with seal installer J-22928 or equivalent. Reverse removal procedures for all other parts.

Oil Pump

REMOVAL & INSTALLATION

Gasoline Engine

1. Drain and remove the oil pan.
2. Disconnect the oil feed pipe.
3. Remove the two bolts securing the oil pump to the cylinder block and remove the oil pump.
4. Install in the reverse order of removal.

Diesel Engine

1. Follow the engine assembly removal steps.
2. Remove the 20 bolts fixing the crankcase and remove the crankcase together with the oil pan.

NOTE: Pry off the crankcase by fitting a screwdriver into the slots in the crankcase.

3. Remove the oil pipe sleeve nut.
4. Remove the 3 bolts fixing the oil pump and remove the oil pump with oil pipe.
5. Install the oil pipe and leave the joints semi-tight.
6. Fully tighten the oil pump fixing screws, then tighten the oil pipe joints.
7. Reverse the removal procedure for the remaining parts.

Oil Cooler

REMOVAL & INSTALLATION

Diesel Engine

1. Place a suitable size tray under the oil filter to receive oil and water flowing out from the filter.

Diesel oil pan

Diesel oil cooler

2. Drain the cooling system by opening the drain plugs on the radiator and on the cylinder block.

3. Remove the oil cooler water drain plug and drain the water.

4. Disconnect the oil cooler hoses at the cooler side.

5. Remove the oil filter cartridge using filter wrench.

6. Remove the nut fixing the oil cooler, then remove the oil cooler assembly.

7. Install the cooler using a new O-ring. Torque to 55–60 ft. lbs.

ENGINE COOLING

Radiator

REMOVAL & INSTALLATION

1. Drain the radiator by opening the drain cock on the lower part of the radiator.

2. Disconnect the radiator upper, lower and expansion tank hoses.

3. Remove the four bolts retaining the radiator and remove the radiator assembly.

4. Install the radiator in the reverse order of removal.

Water Pump

REMOVAL & INSTALLATION

1. Disconnect the battery ground cable.

2. Remove the lower cover and drain the cooling system. Remove the coolant hoses from the pump body.

3. On non-air conditioned gasoline models, remove the fan blades and pulleys from the hub.

4. On air conditioned gasoline models, remove the air pump and alternator belts, fan blades and pulleys.

5. On diesel models, remove drive belts and crankshaft drive pulley. Remove fan pulley.

6. Remove the water pump assembly.

7. Installation is the reverse of removal.

Thermostat

REMOVAL & INSTALLATION

1. Drain the radiator by opening the petcock on the bottom of the radiator.

2. Remove the air cleaner assembly. Disconnect the upper and/or lower radiator hoses for necessary clearance.

3. Disconnect the water outlet from the engine.

4. Remove the thermostat.

5. Replace the thermostat in the reverse

order of removal, using a new gasket under the new outlet housing and making sure that the thermostat is placed so that the spring end is inside the engine.

EMISSION CONTROLS

There are three types of automative pollutants; crankcase fumes, exhaust gases, and gasoline evaporation. The equipment that is used to limit these pollutants is commonly called emission control equipment.

NOTE: Refer to the ''Emissions'' section in Unit Repair for description and service procedures.

GASOLINE FUEL SYSTEM

Fuel Filter

REMOVAL & INSTALLATION

A fuel filter is located in the fuel line leading from the fuel tank to the fuel pump. It is of the cartridge type with a replaceable paper filter element. If the fuel line is suspected of being clogged (rough running, hesitation, uneven throttle response), check the fuel filter. The fuel filter element should be checked once a year and replaced if excessively dirty.

NOTE: 1977–80 models require filter element replacement every 15,000 miles, 1981 and later models at 30,000 mile intervals.

Mechanical Fuel Pump

REMOVAL & INSTALLATION

The fuel pump is a mechanically-operated, diaphragm-type driven by the fuel pump eccentric cam on the jackshaft.

Design of the fuel pump permits disassembly, cleaning, and repair or replacement of defective parts.

1. Disconnect the rubber hose at the side of the fuel pump.

2. Remove the joint bolt and disconnect the fuel at the side of the fuel pump. Be careful not to lose the joint bolt gaskets when removing the joint bolt.

3. Remove the two fuel pump mounting nuts and remove the fuel pump assembly from the side of the engine.

4. Install the fuel pump in the reverse

Fuel pump

order of removal, using a new gasket and sealer on the mating surface.

Electric Fuel Pump

The fuel pump is of the electro-magnetic type and is installed on the inner face of the third crossmember at the left hand side. This fuel pump is a totally enclosed type and cannot be disassembled.

REMOVAL & INSTALLATION

1. Disconnect the negative battery cable and wiring connection to the fuel pump. Disconnect the hoses at the fuel pump.

2. Remove the two bolts and one nut mounting the fuel pump and remove the fuel pump assembly.

Carburetor

The carburetor used on gas-engined trucks is a two-barrel, down-draft type with a low-speed (primary) side and a high-speed (secondary) side.

REMOVAL & INSTALLATION

1. Remove the air cleaner wing nut and disconnect the rubber hoses from the clips on the air cleaner cover and the vacuum hose from the vacuum motor.

2. Remove the bracket bolts at the air cleaner and remove the air cleaner cover and filter element.

3. Disconnect the hot air hose (to the hot air duct), the air hose to the air pump at the air cleaner, and the vacuum hose at the joint nipple side of the intake manifold.

4. Loosen the bolt clamping the air cleaner to the carburetor. Separate the air cleaner body from the carburetor but do not remove it completely as the hoses remain connected.

5. Disconnect the PCV hose (to the camshaft cover), the rubber hoses to the check and relief valve and remove the air cleaner body.

6. Disconnect the vacuum hoses from the EGR valve.

7. Disconnect the choke control wire.

8. Disconnect the lead from the throttle solenoid.

9. Disconnect the throttle linkage return spring.

10. Disconnect the accelerator linkage wire.

11. Disconnect the fuel line at the carburetor.

12. Remove the four retaining nuts and lockwashers securing the carburetor to the manifold and remove the carburetor.

13. Install the carburetor in the reverse order of removal.

OVERHAUL

NOTE: Refer to the "Carburetor" section of the Unit Repair for servicing procedures.

THROTTLE LINKAGE ADJUSTMENT

When the primary throttle valve is opened to an angle of 50° from its closed position, the adjust plate which is interlocked with the primary throttle valve, is brought into contact with the return plate. When the primary throttle valve is opened farther, the return plate is pulled apart from the stopper allowing the secondary throtttle valve to open.

Throttle linkage adjustment

To adjust the linkage:

1. Measure the clearance between the primary throttle valve and the wall of the throttle chamber at the center of the throttle valve when the adjust plate is brought into contact with the return plate. Standard clearance is 0.26–0.32 in.

2. If necessary, make the adjustment by bending the tab of the return plate.

FLOAT LEVEL ADJUSTMENT

The fuel level is normal if it is within the lines on the window glass of the float chamber when the vehicle is resting on level ground and the engine is off.

Float level adjustment

If the fuel level is outside the lines, remove the float housing cover. Have an absorbent cloth under the cover to catch the fuel from the fuel bowl. Adjust the float level by bending the needle seat on the float.

The needle valve should have an effective stroke of about 0.059 in. When necessary, the needle valve stroke can be adjusted by bending the float stopper.

NOTE: Be careful not to bend the needle valve rod when installing the float and baffle plate, if removed.

KICK LEVER ADJUSTMENT

1. Bring the primary side throttle valve into the complete closed position, by turning the throttle adjustment screw.

2. On manual transmission models, with the throttle valve completely closed, loosen the lock nut on the kick lever screw and turn the screw until it is in contact with the return plate and tighten the lock nut.

3. On automatic transmission models with the throttle valve completely closed, bend the end of the kick lever until it is in contact with the return plate.

Kickdown lever

ELECTRIC AUTOMATIC CHOKE

1. Install the thermostat cover by fitting the end of the choke lever into the bimetal hook.

2. Align the thermostat housing line (thickest one) with the line on the thermostat cover.

3. Measure the clearance (between the choke valve edge and the choke chamber wall) when the choke is fully closed. The standard clearance should be (0.11–0.29 in.). This clearance is equal to a bimetal lever angle of 30°.

4. If the measured value is not correct adjust it by bending the bimetal lever as necessary.

ELECTRIC CHOKE ADJUSTMENT

Align the thickest line on the thermostat

Choke thermostat housing alignment

Electric choke

Stopper clearance

housing with the line on the thermostat cover. Measure clearance between the cover side stopper and the bimetal level side stopper when the diaphragm is fully stroked with negative pressure or finger pressure. If the measured value deviates from the standard clearance of 0.28–0.29 in. or the equivalent bimetal lever angle of 20 degrees adjust with the adjusting screw.

DIESEL FUEL SYSTEM

Fuel Filter

REMOVAL & INSTALLATION

1. Disconnect water separator sensor wiring at the connector and water drain hose.
2. Remove the filter using a filter wrench. Use care so as not to spill fuel within the cartridge.
3. Drain the cartridge into a suitable pan, then remove the sensor from the filter cartridge.
4. Install the sensor on a new filter cartridge, applying clean diesel fuel to the O-ring before installation.
5. Turn in the filter until sealing face is brought into contact with the O-ring. Further tighten ⅔ of a turn. Connect the connector to the sensor and install the water drain hose.
6. Fill the cartridge with fuel by operating the priming pump handle 30 to 40 times.

NOTE: The force needed to operate the priming pump increases when the filter becomes filled.

7. Start the engine and check for fuel leaks.

WATER SEPARATOR DRAINING PROCEDURE

1. Place a container (approx. ½ gal. capacity) at the end of the vinyl hose beneath the drain plug of the separator.
2. Loosen the drain plug approximately four turns.
3. Continue to operate the priming pump ten times by hand.

4. Tighten the drain plug, and continue to operate the priming pump again several strokes.
5. Start the engine and check for fuel leakage from around the sealing portions. Also check to see that the "FILTER" indicator light has turned off.

Injection Timing

1. Check that notched line on the injection pump flange is in alignment with notched line on the injection pump front bracket.
2. Bring the piston in No. 1 cylinder to top dead center on compression stroke by turning the crankshaft as necessary.
3. With the timing pulley housing cover removed, check that timing belt is properly tensioned and that timing marks are aligned.
4. Disconnect the injection pipe from the injection pump and remove the distributor head screw, then install static timing gauge. Set the lift approximately 1 mm (0.04 in.) from the plunger.

Injection pump and flange alignment

#1 piston 45–60 degrees before TDC

#1 piston 15 degrees before TDC

5. Use a wrench to hold the delivery holder when loosening the sleeve nuts on the injection pump side.
6. Bring the piston in No. 1 cylinder to a point 45–60 degrees before top dead center by turning the crankshaft, then calibrate the dial indicator to zero.

Static timing gauge installed

#1 piston at TDC

Idle speed adjustment points

Diesel tachometer

Fast idle adjusting points

Loosening tension pulley

Timing marks aligned

Removing timing pulley

7. Turn the crankshaft pulley slightly in both directions and check that gauge indication is stable.

8. Turn the crankshaft in normal direction of rotation, and take the reading of the dial indicator when the timing mark (15 degrees) on the crankshaft pulley is in alignment with the pointer. Reading should be 0.020 in.

9. If the reading of dial indicator deviates from the specified range, hold crankshaft in position 15 degrees before to dead center and loosen two nuts on injection pump flange.

10. Move the injection pump to a point where dial indicator gives reading of 0.020 in., then tighten pump flange nuts.

IDLE SPEED ADJUSTMENT

1. Set parking brake and block drive wheels.

2. Place transmission in neutral.

3. Start and normalize the engine. Engine coolant temperature: above 80°C (176°F).

4. Set the engine tachometer.

5. If the idle speed deviates from the specified range of 700–800 rpm, loosen the idle speed adjusting screw lock nut.

6. Turn the adjusting screw in or out until the idle speed is in the correct range. After tightening the lock nut, lock it in place

FAST IDLE SPEED

1. Start and normalize the engine. Engine coolant temperature above 80°C (176°F).

2. Set the engine tachometer.

3. Disconnect the hoses from the vacuum switch valve, then connect a pipe (4mm dia.) in position between the hoses.

4. Loosen adjust nut and adjust engine idle speed by moving the nut. Fast idle should be 900–950 rpm.

5. Tighten the nut.

6. Remove engine tachometer.

Injection Pump

REMOVAL & INSTALLATION

1. Raise engine hood.

2. Disconnect the battery ground cable.

3. Remove the battery assembly.

4. Remove the under cover.

5. Drain the cooling system by opening the drain plugs on the radiator and on the cylinder block.

6. Disconnect the upper water hose at the engine side.

7. Loosen the compressor drive belt by moving the power-steering oil pump or idler. (If so equipped.)

8. Remove the cooling fan and fan shroud.

9. Disconnect the lower water hose at the engine side.

10. Remove the air conditioner compressor. (If so equipped.)

11. Remove the fan belt.

12. Remove the crankshaft pulley.

13. Remove the timing pulley housing covers.

14. Remove the tension spring and fixing bolt, then remove the tension center and pulley.

15. Remove the timing belt.

16. Remove the engine control cable and wiring harness of the fuel cut solenoid.

17. Remove the fuel hoses and injection pipes. Use a wrench to hold the delivery holder when loosening the sleeve nuts on the injection pump side.

18. Install a 6 mm bolt (with pitch of 1.25) into threaded hole in the timing pulley housing through the hole in pulley to prevent turning of the pulley.

Remove the bolts fixing the injection pump timing pulley, then remove the pulley using pulley puller.

19. Remove injection pump flange fixing nuts and rear bracket bolts, then remove the injection pump.

20. Install the injection pump by aligning notched line on the flange with the line

on the front bracket.

21. Install the injection pump timing pulley by aligning it with the key groove. Torque to 42–52 ft. lbs.

22. Bring the piston in No. 1 cylinder to top dead center on compression stroke and align marks on the timing pulleys.

23. Follow the timing belt installation steps.

24. Check the injection timing.

25. To install remaining parts, follow the removal steps in reverse order. flange.

Fuel Tank

REMOVAL & INSTALLATION

— CAUTION —

Before attempting to remove the fuel tank, the following suggestions are recommended: Remove the negative battery terminal; Empty the fuel tank.

1. Remove the filler neck bolts, the hose clamps, the filler neck and the vent hose

2. Disconnect the sending unit from the electrical terminal.

3. Disconnect the four rubber hoses on the left side of the tank.

4. Disconnect the feed and return lines.

NOTE: Plug the fuel lines to prevent fuel from leaking.

5. Remove the tank mounting bolts and remove the tank.

6. Installation is the reverse of removal.

MANUAL TRANSMISSION

2-Wheel Drive Models

REMOVAL & INSTALLATION

4-Speed

1. Disconnect the negative battery cable.

2. Remove the air cleaner assembly, and disconnect the accelerator linkage at the carburetor throttle lever.

3. Slide the gearshift lever boot upward on the lever, remove the two gearshift lever attaching bolts and remove the lever.

4. Remove the starter attaching bolts and lay the starter assembly aside.

5. Jack up the vehicle and safely support it with jackstands. Disconnect the exhaust pipe at the flange and disconnect the exhaust pipe hanger at the transmission.

6. Disconnect the speedometer cable at the transmission and disconnect the driveshaft at the differential. Either drain the transmission oil or have a rag ready to plug the output shaft opening (at rear of trans) to prevent spillage. Remove the driveshaft.

7. On 1977 models, disconnect the clutch slave cylinder and pushrod from the transmission case and wire the slave cylinder to the frame. On 1978 and later models, disconnect the clutch cable from the bell housing and clutch fork.

8. Remove the bolts attaching the stiffeners, then remove the skid plate (all models).

9. Remove the three frame bracket-to-transmission rear mounting bolts.

10. Raise the engine and transmission as required and remove the four crossmember-to-frame bracket bolts.

11. Lower the engine and transmission assembly and support the rear of the engine. Make sure all jacks, jackstands and support devices are clear of the oil pan when supporting the engine.

12. Disconnect the electrical connectors at the TCS or CRS switch and the back-up light switch.

13. Remove the transmission-to-engine attaching bolts and slide the transmission straight back until the input shaft is clear of the clutch.

Tip the front of the transmission downward and remove the transmission from the vehicle.

14. Install the transmission in the reverse order of removal, using a clutch aligning arbor or discarded transmission input shaft to align the clutch disc and pilot bearing, if the clutch was also removed. Coat the input shaft lightly with Lubriplate® or similar grease before installation.

5 Speed

1. Disconnect battery ground cable.

2. Slide the gearshift lever boot upwards on the lever, remove two gearshift lever attaching bolts and remove lever.

3. Remove starter attaching bolts and lay starter assembly aside.

4. Raise vehicle on hoist and disconnect exhaust pipe hanger at transmission.

5. Place pan under transmission to catch the oil and drain transmission. Disconnect the speedometer cable at the transmission, disconnect ground cable and disconnect propeller shaft at differential. Remove propeller shaft.

6. Remove return spring from clutch fork.

7. Take out two bolts (lower bolts) mounting the flywheel stone guard.

8. Remove two frame bracket to transmission rear mount bolts and nuts.

9. Raise engine and transmission as required and remove four crossmember to frame bracket bolts.

10. Remove the rear mounting (2 nuts) from the transmission rear extension.

11. Lower engine and transmission assembly and support rear of engine.

12. Disconnect electrical connector at back-up lamp switch.

13. Remove transmission to engine attaching bolts.

14. Pull transmission straight back until disengaged from clutch. Tip front of transmission downward and remove.

1. Position transmission in vehicle and slide forward guiding clutch gear into pilot bearing.

Installation is as follows:

2. Install transmission to engine attaching bolts.

3. Raise and lower engine and transmission as required and install crossmember frame bracket and rear mount.

4. Install the two bolts (lower bolts) mounting the flywheel stone guard.

5. Remove plug (if used) from rear extension and install propeller shaft.

6. Connect speedometer cable, ground cable and exhaust pipe hanger.

7. Connect clutch cable and adjust shift fork as outlined in Clutch Section.

8. Connect electrical connector at back-up lamp switch. Fill transmission with lubricant.

9. Lower vehicle and install starter assembly.

10. Connect battery negative cable.

11. Install gearshift lever and adjust clutch pedal height as outlined in Clutch Section.

12. Check transmission operation.

4-Wheel Drive Models
REMOVAL & INSTALLATION

Transmission and Transfer Case

1. Disconnect the negative battery terminal.

2. Drain the transmission oil.

3. Slide the shift lever boots upward and unbolt each lever.

4. Remove the return spring from the transfer case shift lever and remove both levers.

5. Remove the starter attaching bolts and remove the starter assembly.

6. Jack up your vehicle and support it with jackstands. Disconnect the exhaust pipe from the manifold and disconnect the pipe support from the transmission.

7. Disconnect the speedometer cable at the transmission. Disconnect the rear driveshaft at the differential. Disconnect the ground strap.

8. Remove the rear driveshaft from the transfer case. Remove the front driveshaft.

9. Disconnect the clutch return spring.

10. Disconnect the clutch cable at the fork.

11. Remove the flywheel stoneguard.

12. Remove the transmission rear crossmember bolts.

13. Raise the engine and transmission, and remove the rear crossmember-to-frame bolts.

14. Remove the rear mounting bolts from the transfer case.

15. Unbolt and remove the side case from the transmission.

16. Remove the stud bolt from the transfer case.

17. Lower the engine and transmission assembly and support the rear of the engine.

18. Disconnect the CRS switch and backup light switch.

19. Remove the shifter cover and gasket from the transfer case.

20. Remove the transmission-to-engine bolts. When removing the transmission, turn the side case fitting face of the case downward and pull the case straight back until free from the clutch. Tip the front of the transmission downward and remove it.

21. Installation is the reverse of removal. Torque shifter cover bolts to 14 ft. lbs.

OVERHAUL

NOTE: Refer to the "Transmission" section of Unit Repair for service procedures.

CLUTCH

1977

The clutch is operated by a clutch pedal which is mechanically connected to a clutch master cylinder. When the pedal is depressed, the piston in the master cylinder.

1978 and Later

The clutch is operated by a steel cable connecting the pedal with the throw-out arm.

REMOVAL & INSTALLATION

1. Jack up the vehicle and safely support it using jackstands.

Clutch components

2. Remove the transmission.

3. Mark the clutch assembly-to-fly-wheel relationship with a center punch or scribe so that the clutch assembly can be reassembled in the same position from which it is removed.

4. Loosen the six clutch cover-to-fly-wheel attaching bolts, one turn at a time in an alternating sequence, until the spring tension is relieved to avoid distorting or bending the clutch cover.

5. Support the clutch pressure plate and cover assembly with a clutch aligning arbor, then remove the bolts and the clutch assembly.

6. Apply a thin coat of grease to the pressure plate wire ring, diaphragm spring, clutch cover grooves and the drive bosses on the pressure plate.

7. Apply a thin coat of Lubriplate® to the splines in the driven plate.

8. Assemble the clutch cover and pressure plate and the driven plate on a clutch alignment arbor.

9. Align the marks made on the clutch cover and flywheel and install the six clutch cover-to-flywheel attaching bolts. Tighten the bolts to 50 in. lbs. Remove the aligning arbor.

PEDAL HEIGHT ADJUSTMENT

1977

1. Disconnect the battery ground cable.
2. Measure the clutch pedal height after making sure that the pedal is fully returned by the pedal return spring. The pedal height should be between 5.9 and 6.3 in.
3. To adjust the height, disconnect the clutch switch and remove it from its mounting bracket.
4. Loosen the locknut on the master cylinder pushrod.
5. Adjust the clutch pedal to the specified height by rotating the pushrod in the appropriate direction. Tighten the locknut when finished with the adjustment.
6. Install the clutch switch. Adjust the clearance between the switch housing (not the switch actuating pin) and the clutch pedal tab to 0.02–0.04 in. Tighten the switch locknut.
7. Connect the electrical leads to the clutch switch and connect the negative battery cable.

1978 and Later

Adjust the pedal stop so that the clutch and brake pedals are the same height. Make sure that the clutch switch is in contact with the clutch pedal bracket.

CLUTCH RELEASE FORK ADJUSTMENT

1977

1. Remove the clutch release fork re-

turn spring and move the release fork slightly rearward.
2. Loosen the adjusting nut and adjust the pushrod until it contacts the release fork.
3. Back off the pushrod about 1¾ turns and tighten the locknut.

NOTE: Excess clearance between the release (throwout) bearing and the diaphragm spring fingers will cause the clutch to drag while too little clearance can cause the clutch to slip.

Clutch Master Cylinder
REMOVAL & INSTALLATION

1. Disconnect the clutch pedal arm from the pushrod.
2. Disconnect the clutch hydraulic line from the master cylinder.

NOTE: Brake fluid can act like paint remover when it comes in contact with a painted surface. Use care in keeping brake fluid away from finish paint on the vehicle.

3. Remove the nuts attaching the master cylinder and remove the master cylinder and pushrod toward the engine compartment side.
4. Install the master cylinder in the reverse order of removal and bleed the clutch hydraulic system.

OVERHAUL

1. Remove the master cylinder from the vehicle.
2. Drain the clutch fluid from the master cylinder reservoir.
3. Remove the boot and circlip and remove the pushrod.
4. Remove the stopper, piston, cup and return spring.
5. Clean all of the parts in clean brake fluid.
6. Check the master cylinder and piston for wear corrosion, and scoring and replace the parts if wear is more than minimal. Light scoring and glaze can be removed with crocus cloth soaked in brake fluid.

Clutch Slave Cylinder
REMOVAL & INSTALLATION

1. Remove the slave cylinder attaching bolts and the pushrod from the shift fork.
2. Disconnect the flexible fluid hose from the slave cylinder and remove the unit from the vehicle.
3. Install the slave cylinder in the reverse order of removal and bleed the clutch hydraulic system.

OVERHAUL

1. Remove the slave cylinder from the vehicle.

2. Remove the pushrod and boot.
3. Force out the piston by blowing compressed air into the slave cylinder at the hose connection.

NOTE: Be careful not to apply excess air pressure to avoid possible injury.

4. Clean all of the parts in brake fluid.
5. Check and replace the slave cylinder bore and piston if wear or severe scoring exists. Light scoring and glaze can be removed with crocus clotch soaked in brake fluid.
6. Normally the piston cup should be replaced when the slave cylinder is disassembled. Check the piston cup and replace it if it is found to be worn, fatigued or scored.
7. Replace the rubber boot if it is cracked or broken.
8. Lubricate all of the new parts in clean brake fluid and reassemble in the reverse order of disassembly, taking note of the following:
   a. Use care when reassembling the piston cup to the piston and when inserting the piston assembly into the cylinder, to prevent damage to the lipped portion of the cup;
   b. Fill the master cylinder with brake fluid and bleed the clutch hydraulic system;
   c. Adjust the clearance between the pushrod and the shift fork to ⁵⁄₆₄ in.
7. Generally, the cup seal should be replaced each time the master cylinder is disassembled. Check the cup and replace it if it is worn, fatigued, or damaged.
8. Check the clutch fluid reservoir, filler cap, dust cover and the pipe for distortion and damage and replace the parts as necessary.
9. Lubricate all new parts with clean brake fluid.
10. Reassemble the master cylinder parts in the reverse order of disassembly, taking note of the following:
   a. Reinstall the cup seal carefully to prevent damaging the lipped portions;
   b. Adjust the height of the clutch pedal after installing the master cylinder in position on the vehicle;
   c. Fill the master cylinder and clutch fluid reservoir and then bleed the clutch hydraulic system.

HYDRAULIC SYSTEM BLEEDING

1. Bleed the clutch master cylinder by pumping the clutch pedal several times, to push the air out of the system. While holding the pedal down, slowly open the bleeder screw.
2. Repeat step one until all signs of air bubbles disappear in the release fluid.

———— CAUTION ————
Don't let the master cylinder fluid level get too low.

3. Connect a tube to the clutch slave

cylinder bleeder screw and insert the other end into a clean glass container, ¼ to ½ filled with brake fluid.

4. Bleed the slave cylinder in the same manner as the master cylinder until the air bubbles disappear.

5. Refill the system reservoir and depress the clutch pedal several times.

6. Check for leaks and smooth operation.

Clutch Cable

REMOVAL & INSTALLATION

1. Loosen the clutch cable lock and adjusting nuts. Remove the clutch cable clip at the engine compartment location.

2. Raise the vehicle and remove the spring from the shift fork end.

3. Disconnect the cable end from the shift fork and pull the cable assembly through the bracket.

4. Lower the vehicle enough to disengage the hooked part of the clutch pedal from the cable eye. Pull the cable assembly towards the engine compartment and remove the cable from the vehicle.

5. Installation is the reverse of removal.

Clutch cable adjustment

ADJUSTMENT

1. Pull the outer cable forward and turn the adjusting nut inward until the rubber lip on the washer damper touches the firewall.

2. Depress and release the clutch pedal a few times.

3. Pull the outer cable forward again and fully tighten the adjusting nut. Back the nut off to provide a 0.20 clearance.

4. Release the outer cable and tighten the nut.

AUTOMATIC TRANSMISSION

A Turbo Hydra-Matic 200 transmission is used. The transmission is a fully automatic unit having three speeds forward and one in reverse. It is coupled to the engine by a torque converter which supplies hydraulic torque multiplication when required.

REMOVAL & INSTALLATION

1. Disconnect the negative battery cable and remove the throttle valve cable from the carburetor.

2. Remove the transmission dipstick assembly.

3. Raise the vehicle and remove the pan from the converter housing. Drain the transmission fluid.

4. Remove the starter assembly.

5. Have a clean rag ready to use as a plug for the end of the transmission. Disconnect the driveshaft and remove it from the vehicle. Plug the rear of the transmission to avoid oil leakage.

6. Disconnect the shift lever control rod from the transmission shift lever.

7. Remove the exhaust pipe bracket. Remove the speedometer cable from the transmission.

8. Remove the oil cooler lines and position them along the vehicle frame to prevent damage.

9. Remove the bolts and nuts coupling the drive plate to the converter.

10. Remove the bolts holding the frame bracket to the transmission rear mount.

11. Raise the engine and transmission assembly and remove the frame bracket from the cross member. Remove the rear mount from the transmission.

12. Remove the bell housing bolts and move the transmission and converter assembly.

— **CAUTION** —
Do not allow the torque converter to drop from the transmission during removal.

13. Install in reverse order.

Shift Linkage
ADJUSTMENT

1. Loosen the control rod lock nuts so that trunnion will slide on the control rod.

2. Turn the manual shaft of the transmission counterclockwise, viewed from the left side of the transmission, as far as it will go.

3. Back off the manual shaft three stops to the neutral position.

4. Holding the shaft in this position, move the shift lever to the neutral position and push the shift control lower lever rearward to remove play. Tighten the lock nuts.

5. Check for proper operation of the transmission in all transmission ranges.

Throttle Valve Control Cable

REMOVAL & INSTALLATION

1. Loosen the throttle valve control cable adjusting nuts and disconnect the cable

Throttle valve cable removal

from the carburetor throttle lever by removing the pin.

2. Remove the throttle valve cable clip from the right side of the cylinder body.

3. Remove the bolt holding the throttle cable to the transmission and pull the cable upward. Disconnect the end of the inner cable from the throttle lever link on the transmission side.

4. Remove the cable assembly from the vehicle.

5. Installation is the reverse of removal.

Throttle valve cable adjustment

ADJUSTMENT

1. Loosen the throttle valve control cable adjusting nuts.

2. Open the carburetor throttle lever to the wide open position and adjust the inner cable by turning the adjustment nut (lower) on the outer cable by hand so that the inner cable has a free play of approximately 0.040 in.

3. Tighten the lock nut (upper) securely.

4. Make sure that the stroke of the inner cable from the wide open position to the closed position is within the range of 1.37 to 1.41 inches.

Inhibitor switch adjustment

Inhibitor Switch

ADJUSTMENT

1. Loosen the screws holding the switch. Move the switch body so that the center of the moveable part of the switch, aligns with the neutral position indicator line on the steel case when the shift lever is in the neutral position.

2. Tighten the holding screws, and make sure that the engine does not start in gear.

Intermediate Band

The bands are not adjustable. A selective band apply pin is installed at time of assembly or overhaul that compensates for normal band wear.

Transmission Fluid

DRAIN AND REFILL

1. Jack up the vehicle and support it with jackstands. Support the transmission at the vibration damper, and remove the oil pan retaining bolts from the front and sides of the fluid pan.

2. Loosen the rear fluid pan bolts approximately four (4) turns.

───────── CAUTION ─────────

If the vehicle has been running, the transmission fluid will be HOT, exceeding 350°F.

3. Carefully pry the front of the fluid pan loose from the transmission case using a small pry bar or brake adjusting spoon. Allow the fluid to drain into a waste container.

4. Remove and clean the pan.

5. Remove the two retaining screen-to-valve body bolts, screen and gasket and clean the screen thoroughly.

6. Install screen and new gasket in place on valve body. Tighten retaining bolts to 6–10 ft. lbs.

7. Install the fluid pan with a new gasket and torque the pan retaining bolts to 10–13 ft. lbs.

8. Lower the vehicle and install six pints of Dexron® II in the transmission. Start the engine and move the selector lever through each gear position.

9. Recheck the fluid level and fill to the following levels.

   a. Fluid at room temperature: Level should be ⅛ to ⅜ in. below the add mark on the dip stick.

   b. Fluid at normal operating temperature:

Fluid level should be at the full mark on the dip stick.

NOTE: Normal operating temperature is reached after approximately 15 miles of highway type driving or equivalent.

DRIVELINE

Rear Driveshaft and U-Joints

REMOVAL & INSTALLATION

Standard Wheel Base Models

NOTE: Match-mark all parts for installation.

1. Disconnect the driveshaft rear flange from the differential pinion flange.

2. Pull the one piece driveshaft from the end of the transmission housing cover.

3. Plug or cover the transmission housing cover end to prevent lubricant leakage.

4. Installation is the reverse of removal.

Long Wheel Base Models

NOTE: Match-mark all parts for installation.

1. Disconnect the flanged yokes between the front and rear driveshafts.

2. Disconnect the rear driveshaft flange from the differential pinion flange and remove the rear shaft.

3. Remove the center bearing support bracket from the fourth crossmember and pull the front driveshaft from the rear of the transmission housing cover.

4. Install a plug or cover the transmission housing cover end to prevent lubricant loss.

5. Installation is the reverse of removal.

Front Drive Shaft

REMOVAL & INSTALLATION

1. Jack up your vehicle and support it with jack stands.

NOTE: You must raise the vehicle enough for the front wheels to turn freely.

2. Place the transmission and transfer case in the neutral position.

3. Match-mark each end of the driveshaft and the flanges on the rear and transfer case.

4. Remove the U-bolts from the rear and the transfer case flanges.

5. Remove the driveshaft.

6. Installation is the reverse of removal.

U-JOINT OVERHAUL

1. Remove the driveshaft from the vehicle.

2. Punch mating marks on both the yokes at either end of the driveshaft and the driveshaft itself so that the driveshaft assembly can be reassembled in the same position.

3. Remove the snap-rings from the bearing hole of the yokes.

4. Place the yoke in a vise with a small socket positioned against one of the bearing cups and a larger socket placed against the yoke on the opposite side. The larger socket must be able to receive the bearing cap when it is pressed out of the yoke.

5. Tighten the vise until the bearing caps are free of the yoke.

6. Remove the two remaining bearings from the opposite yoke in the same manner and remove the spider bearing journal.

7. Make sure that the new spiders and needle bearings in the bearing caps are well lubricated.

8. Assemble the universal joint spider and bearing caps to the yoke in the reverse manner of removal, using the smaller socket to press the bearing caps into the yoke and the larger socket to bear against the yoke bearing cap hole at the opposite end. Use a vise to press the bearing caps in place.

9. Install the hole snap-ring to secure the bearing caps.

10. Assemble the slide yoke to the

1. Driveshaft
2. Spline yoke
3. Cover
4. Plate plug
5. Flange yoke
6. Bearing caps
7. Snap-rings

Driveshaft

1. Differetial carrier and case assembly
2. Mounting bolt
3. Gasket
4. Drain plug
5. Filler plug
6. Vent
7. Through-bolt
8. Oil seal
9. Shims
10. Locknut
11. Lockwasher
12. Axle shaft bearing
13. Bearing holder
14. Grease seal
15. Axle shaft
16. Wheel stud
17. Brake drum
18. Wheel nut
19. Drum-to-flange screw

Axle shaft and housing

driveshaft, aligning the marks made prior to disassembly.

11. Install the driveshaft assembly on the vehicle.

Rear Axle Shaft

REMOVAL & INSTALLATION

1. Raise and safely support the truck.
2. Remove the rear wheel cover and the wheel and tire.
3. Remove the brake drum, brake shoes and disconnect the parking brake inner cable.
4. Disconnect the brake line at the wheel cylinder and plug the end of the line.
5. Remove the four nuts from the bearing holder through-bolts from the inside of the brake backing plate.
6. Using an axle puller, pull out the axle shaft assembly. Never strike the brake backing plate with a hammer in an attempt to remove the axle shaft.
7. Install the axle shaft in the reverse order of removal, tightening the bearing holding plate attaching nuts to 55 ft. lbs., bleeding the brake hydraulic system after installing the brakes and adjusting the parking brake cable as necessary.

Front Axle and Axle Shaft

REMOVAL & INSTALLATION

1. Raise and support the vehicle.
2. Disconnect the front driveshaft at the differential.
3. Remove the wheels and skid plate.
4. Loosen the torsion bar completely

with the height control adjusting bolts.
5. Remove the strut bars.
6. Disconnect the stabilizer bars at the lower control arms.
7. Remove the caliper assemblies and wire them to the frame. It is not necessary to disconnect the brake lines.
8. Remove the ball joints from the tie rods.
9. Disconnect the upper control arms at the frame. Make sure to note the number and positions of the shims.
10. Remove the steering link ends from the lower control arms.
11. Disconnect the shock absorbers from the lower control arms.
12. Disconnect the lower control arms from the frame.
13. Remove the free wheeling hub. See Front Bearing Removal.
14. Remove the rotors and upper links.
15. Remove the pitman arm and idler arm along with the steering linkage assembly.
16. Support the differential housing with a jack, lower it clear of the vehicle and roll it out. Take care to avoid damaging the birfield joints.
17. Drain the differential case and remove the four bolts attaching the axle mounting bracket to the case.
18. Pull the shaft assemblies from the case on both sides.
19. Installation is the reverse of removal. Observe the following torque values:

Item	Ft. Lbs.
Axle shaft-to-case	43
Differential case-to-frame	15
Pitman arm-to-sector shaft	160
Idler arm-to-pivot shaft	87
Lower control arm-to-frame	94
Ball joint castellated nut	100

2-WHEEL DRIVE FRONT SUSPENSION

Torsion Bars

REMOVAL & INSTALLATION

1. Jack up the front of the vehicle and support it with jackstands.
2. Remove the adjusting bolt from the height control arm.
3. Mark the location and remove the height control arm from the torsion bar and the third crossmember.
4. Mark the location and withdraw the torsion bar from the lower control arm.
5. For installation, apply a generous amount of grease to the serrated ends of the torsion bar.
6. Hold the rubber bumpers in contact with the lower control arm. Jack the vehicle up under the lower control arm to accomplish this.
7. Insert the front end of the torsion bar into the control arm.
8. Install the height control arm in position so that its end is reaching the adjusting bolt. Be sure to lubricate the part of the height control arm that fits into the chassis with grease.
9. Install a new cotter pin in the control arm.
10. Turn the adjusting bolt to the location marked before removal.
11. Lower the vehicle and check the vehicle height.

Shock Absorbers

REMOVAL & INSTALLATION

1. Raise the vehicle and support it with jackstands.
2. Hold the upper stem of the shock absorber from turning with an open-end wrench, and then, remove the upper stem retaining nut, retainer and rubber grommet.
3. Remove the bolt retaining the lower shock absorber pivot to the power control arm and remove the shock absorber from the vehicle.
4. Install the shock absorber by first installing the lower retainer and rubber grommet over the upper stem and then, installing the shock fully extended up through the upper control arm so that the upper stem passes through the mounting hole in the frame bracket.
5. Install the upper rubber grommet, retainer and attaching nut over the shock absorber upper stem.
6. Hold the upper stem of the shock absorber from turning with an open-end wrench and tighten the retaining nut.

5. To remove the pivot shaft and bushings from the upper control arm assembly, remove the bushing nuts from the pivot shaft by loosening them alternately, then remove the pivot shaft.

6. To install the upper control arm and ball joint assembly, first install the pivot shaft boots to the pivot shaft.

7. Fill the internal part of the bushings with grease (molybdenum disulfide) and screw the bushings into the pivot shaft. Be sure to screw the right-side and the left-side bushings alternately into the pivot shafts carefully avoiding getting grease on the outer face of the bushings. Tighten the nuts to 250 ft. lbs. for 2-wheel drive and 220 ft. lbs. for 4-wheel drive.

NOTE: Be sure that the control arm and bushings are centered properly and that the control arm rotates with resistance but not binding on the pivot shaft when tightened to the proper torque.

8. Install the grease fittings and lubricate the parts with grease through the grease fittings.

9. Install the ball joint stud through the steering knuckle. Install the castellated nut and tighten it to 75 ft. lbs. and just enough additional torque to install the cotter pin. Use a new cotter pin.

10. Mount the upper control arm to the chassis frame and install the shims in their original positions between the pivot shaft and bracket. Tighten the pivot shaft attaching nuts to 55 ft. lbs.

NOTE: Tighten the thinner shim pack's nut first for improved shaft-to-frame clamping force and torque retention.

11. Install the dust cover.

12. Install the wheel and tire assembly and lower the vehicle to the floor.

Lower Ball Joint

REMOVAL & INSTALLATION

1. Raise the front of the vehicle and support it with jackstands.

2. Remove the wheel and tire assembly.

3. Remove the cotter pin and castellated nut which retains the ball joint to the steering knuckle.

4. Remove the two bolts retaining the lower ball joint and strut rod.

5. Remove the remaining two bolts.

6. Remove the ball joint.

7. Install the lower ball joint by mounting the joint to the lower control arm and tightening the four bolts to 45 ft. lbs.

8. Install the ball joint stud into the steering knuckle and install the castellated nut and torque it to 75 ft. lbs. and just enough additional torque to align the cotter pin hole with one of the castellations on the nut. Install a new cotter pin.

9. Lubricate the lower ball joint through the grease fitting.

10. Install the wheel and tire assembly and lower the vehicle to the ground.

1. Upper control arm
2. Washer
3. Bolt
4. Pivot shaft
5. Bushing
6. Upper ball joint
7. Boot
8. Grease fitting
9. Bolt
10. Nut
11. Nut
12. Cotter pin
13. Lowering control arm
14. Bushing
15. Snap-ring
16. Seal
17. Lower ball joint
18. Boot
19. Grease fitting
20. Nut
21. Cotter pin
22. Bolt
23. Bolt
24. Nut
25. Bolt
26. Plate
27. Bolt
28. Nut

2-wheel drive front suspension

7. Install the retainers attaching the shock absorber lower pivot to the lower control arm and tighten them.

8. Lower the vehicle.

Upper Control Arm and Ball Joint

REMOVAL & INSTALLATION

NOTE: The upper control arm and ball joint are replaced as an assembly.

1. Raise the vehicle and support it on jackstands placed under the lower control arms.

2. Remove the wheel and tire assembly.

3. Remove the cotter pin nut fastening the upper control arm and upper ball joint assembly and disconnect the upper control arm from the steering knuckle.

NOTE: Do not allow the steering knuckle to hang by the flexible brake line. Wire the steering knuckle up to the frame temporarily.

4. Remove the two bolts from the upper pivot shaft and remove the upper control arm from the bracket. Be sure to note the position and number of shims used for adjusting the camber and caster angles when removing the upper control arm. This is to ensure that the shims are reinstalled in their original positions.

1. Torsion bar
2. Height control arm
3. Upper pivot nut
4. Lower pivot nut
5. Height control bolt
6. Stopper plate
7. Bolt
8. Strut rod
9. Strut rod bushing
10. Strut rod washer
11. Tube
12. Nut
13. Bolt
14. Bolt
15. Shock absorber
16. Shock absorber bushing
17. Bushing retainer
18. Nut
19. Bolt
20. Nut
21. Dust cover
22. Screw
23. Lower control arm bumper
24. Upper control arm bumper
25. Stabilizer bar
26. Bolt
27. Stabilizer bar bushing
28. Stabilizer bar upper clamp
29. Stabilizer bar lower clamp
30. Bolt
31. Nut
32. Bolt
33. Nut
34. Bracket, stabilizer bar to frame
35. Bolt
36. Bushing
37. Washer
38. Nut
39. Nut
40. Nut

2-wheel drive torsion, strut and stabilizer bars

Lower Control Arm

REMOVAL & INSTALLATION

1. Jack up the vehicle and support it with jackstands.

2. Remove the wheel and tire.

3. Remove the strut bar by removing the frame side bracket and the double nuts, washer and the rubber bushing from the front side of the strut bar. Next, remove the two bolts fastening the strut bar to lower control arm and remove the bar.

4. Disconnect the stabilizer bar from the lower control arm.

5. Remove the torsion bar.

6. Disconnect the shock absorber from the lower control arm.

7. If you so desire, remove the lower ball joint from the lower control arm joint at this time.

8. Remove the retaining nut and drive out the bolt holding the lower control arm to the chassis with a soft metal drift. Remove the lower control arm from the vehicle.

9. To install the lower control arm, first, install the lower ball joint to the lower control arm. Tighten the retaining nuts to 45 ft. lbs.

10. Mount the lower control arm to the frame. Drive the bolt into position carefully with a soft metal drift. Use care not to damage the serrated portions. Tighten the nut on the end of the pivot bolt to 135 ft. lbs.

11. Install the stabilizer bar to the lower control arm.

12. Place the washers and bushings on the strut rod and install it through the frame bracket. Install the second set of washers and bushings on the strut rod together with the lockwashers and nut. Leave the nut loose temporarily.

13. Install the strut rod to the lower control arm and tighten the bolts to 45 ft. lbs.

14. Assemble the lower ball joint to the steering knuckle.

15. Assemble the wheel and tire and lower the vehicle.

16. Tighten the first strut bar-to-chassis frame attaching nut to 175 ft. lbs., and the second locknut to 55 ft. lbs.

Front Wheel Bearings

REMOVAL & INSTALLATION

2 Wheel Drive

1. Remove the hub assembly.
2. Remove the outer roller bearing assembly from the hub. Pry out the inner bearing lip seal and remove the inner bearing assembly.
3. Wash all parts in a cleaning solvent and dry with compressed air.
4. Check the bearings for pitting or scoring. Also check for smooth rotation and lack of noise.
5. Thoroughly lubricate the bearings with new wheel bearing lubricant.
6. Apply a light coat of lubricant to the spindle and inside surface of the hub.
7. Place the inner bearing in the race of the hub and install a new grease seal.
8. Install the hub assembly on the spindle.
9. Install the outer wheel bearing, washer and adjust nut.
10. Adjust the wheel bearings as outlined below.
11. Install the dust cap on the hub.
12. Install the brake caliper and support assembly.
13. Install the wheel and tighten the nuts.

ADJUSTMENT

1. With the wheel raised, remove the hub cap and dust cap and then remove the cotter pin and nut retainer from the end of the spindle.
2. While rotating the wheel, tighten the spindle nut to 22 ft. lbs.
3. Turn the hub 2–3 turns and loosen the nut just enough so that it can be turned with your fingers.
4. Turn the nut all the way in with your fingers and check to be sure the hub has no free play.
5. Measure the starting torque by pulling one of the wheel hub studs with a pull scale. Tighten the spindle nut so that the pull scale reads 1.1–2.6 lbs. when the hub begins to rotate.

NOTE: Make sure that the brake pads are not in contact with the drum when measuring rotating torque.

6. Install the nut retainer, new cotter pin, dust cap and hub cap.

4-WHEEL DRIVE FRONT SUSPENSION

Locking Hub

REMOVAL & INSTALLATION

1. Jack up your vehicle and support it

1. Upper control arm
2. Washer
3. Bolt
4. Pivot shaft
5. Collar
6. Bushing
7. Upper ball joint
8. Boot
9. Grease fitting
10. Bolt
11. Nut
12. Nut
13. Cotter pin
14. Lower control arm
15. Lower control arm shaft
16. Bushing
17. Nut
18. Lower ball joint
19. Grease fitting
20. Boot
21. Nut
22. Cotter pin
23. Bolt
24. Nut
25. Bolt
26. Plate
27. Plate
28. Shim
29. Nut

4-wheel drive front suspension

with jackstands.

2. Place the transfer case in the 2H position.
3. Set the hubs in the free position.
4. Remove the hub cover bolts and remove the hub cover.

Cover Assembly

1. While pushing the follower toward the knob, turn the clutch assembly clockwise, and then remove the clutch assembly from the knob.
2. Remove the snap-ring and remove the knob from the cover.

NOTE: Do not lose the detent ball.

3. Remove the ball and spring from the knob.
4. Remove the X-ring from the knob

by pressing it off with your fingers.

NOTE: Do not use a screwdriver to remove this ring because it may scratch the ring.

Front hub cover removal

SNAP RING

Hub snap-ring

X-RING

Removing X-ring

FOLLOWER **RETAINING SPRING**

CLUTCH

Removing clutch follower

1. Knuckle
2. Oil seal
3. Washer
4. Bearing
5. Adaptor
6. Shield
7. Retainer ring
8. Oil seal
9. Hub bearing inner
10. Dust shield
11. Bolt
12. Wheel pin
13. Bolt
14. Hub and disc
15. Wheel bearing outer
16. Hub nut
17. Lock washer
18. Shim
19. Snap-ring
20. Ring
21. Spacer
22. Inner
23. Body
24. Clutch
25. Retaining spring
26. Follower
27. Compression spring
28. Snap-ring
29. Detent ball and spring
30. Knob
31. X–Ring
32. Cover
33. Bolt

4-wheel drive front hub

5. Remove the compression spring, retaining spring, and the follower from the clutch assembly.

6. Remove the retaining spring from the clutch assembly by turning it counterclockwise.

Body Assembly

1. Remove the snap-ring and then remove the inner assembly from the body.

2. Separate the ring, inner, and spacer by removing the snap-ring.

3. Installation is the reverse of removal with the following suggestions.

Apply grease to the X-ring, the inner cover and the outside cicumference of the knob.

Front Wheel Hub

REMOVAL & INSTALLATION

1. Jack up your vehicle and support it with jackstands.

2. Remove the front wheel.

3. Remove the free wheeling hub as previously outlined.

4. Remove the brake caliper and tie it out of the way.

5. Remove the lockwasher and hub nut.

6. Remove the hub and rotor assembly.

NOTE: Do not drop any of the wheel bearings as damage could result.

7. Installation is the reverse of removal.

BODY

SNAP RING **RING** **SPACER** **INNER**

Hub body components

1. Torsion bar
2. Rubber seat
3. Height control arm
4. Pivot Nut
5. Height control seat and bolt
6. Strut bar
7. Strut bar bushing
8. Strut bar washer
9. Nut
10. Bolt
11. Bolt
12. Nut
13. Shock absorber
14. Bushing
15. Retainer
16. Nut
17. Bolt
18. Nut
19. Lower control arm bumper
20. Bolt
21. Upper control arm bumper
22. Stabilizer bar
23. Stabilizer bar bushing
24. Stabilizer bar support
25. Stabilizer bar bracket
26. Bolt
27. Bushing
28. Washer
29. Nut
30. Bolt
31. Bushing
32. Washer
33. Nut

4-wheel drive torsion, strut and stabilizer bars

Front End Alignment

NOTE: Refer to the "Alignment" section of the Unit Repair for specifications and procedures.

Proper alignment of the front wheels must be maintained in order to ensure ease of steering and satisfactory tire life.

The most important factors of front wheel alignment are wheel camber, axle caster, and wheel toe-in.

Wheel toe-in is the distance by which the wheels are closer together at the front than at the rear.

Wheel camber is the amount in which the top of the wheels incline outward from the vertical.

Front axle caster is the amount in degrees which the steering knuckle pivot axis is tilted toward the rear of the vehicle. Positive caster is the inclination of the top of the steering knuckle toward the rear of the vehicle.

These points should be checked at regular intervals, particularly when the front suspension has been subjected to severe impact. When checking the wheel alignment, it is important that the wheel bearings be properly adjusted and the ball joints have no free-play.

FREE POSITION

Front hub knob

T407

RIDE HEIGHT ADJUSTMENT

NOTE: The ride height should be measured with a full tank of gas, spare tire, jack, no passengers, and with the tires inflated to the correct pressure.

1. Place the vehicle on a smooth level floor and bounce the front end several times. Raise the vehicle and then allow it to settle to a normal height.

Ride height measurement, front

2. Measure the distance between the bottom of the lower ball joint stud which fits through the steering knuckle and the ground and the distance between the frame crossmember that the lower control arm attaches to and the ground.

The difference between these two measurements should be 2.52 in. (1.54 in. with the vehicle loaded to GVW).

3. Adjust the vehicle height by first loosening the nuts on the front end of the strut bar and then turning the vehicle height adjusting bolt. Turn the bolt clockwise to raise the vehicle. As an additional check, measure the clearance between the rubber bumper and the lower control arm. The clearance should be ⅞ in.

Ride height measurement, front

Ride height measurement, rear

4. Check the ride height at the front of the vehicle as outlined in step 2 above and the ride height at the rear axle by measuring the clearance between the top of the axle and the bottom of the frame where the frame rises to clear the axle. The clearance between the frame and axle at this point should be 7.90 in. (6.26 in. with the vehicle loaded to GVW).

5. After obtaining the correct clearances, securely tighten the strut bar attaching nuts to the proper torque.

Front Wheel Bearings

REMOVAL, INSTALLATION & ADJUSTMENT

4 Wheel Drive

1. Raise and support the front end. Place the hub in 2H.

2. Remove the free wheeling hub cover assembly.

3. Remove the snap-ring and shims from the spindle.

4. Remove the free wheeling hub body and lock washer.

5. Remove the outer roller bearing assembly from the hub with your fingers.

6. Using a brass or wood drift, drive out the inner bearing assembly along with the oil seal. Replace the seal.

7. Wash all parts in a non-flammable solvent.

8. Check all parts for cracks or wear. Thoroughly lubricate all bearing parts with a high-temperature (molybdenum-disulfide) wheel bearing grease. Remove any excess. Apply about 2 ounces of the grease to the hub.

9. Lightly coat the spindle with the same grease.

10. Place the inner bearing into the hub race and install a new seal and retaining ring.

11. Carefully install the hub on the spindle and install the outer bearing.

12. Install the spindle nut.

13. While rotating the hub, tighten the hub so that the wheel can just be turned by hand.

14. Turn the hub 2–3 turns and back off the nut just enough so that it can be loosened with the fingers.

15. Finger-tighten the nut so that all play is taken up at the bearing.

16. Attach a pull scale to one of the lugs and check the amount of pull needed to start the wheel turning. Initial pull should be 2.6–4.0 lbs. When performing this test, make sure the brake pads are not touching the rotor. If the rotating torque is not correct, tighten the spindle nut until it is.

17. Install the snap-ring and shims, gasket and cover. Torque the cover bolts to 14 ft. lbs.

REAR SUSPENSION

Springs

REMOVAL & INSTALLATION

1. Jack up the rear of the vehicle and place jackstands under the frame near the

rear end of the rear spring brackets.

2. Remove the rear shock absorbers.

3. Remove the parking brake cable clips.

4. Remove the nuts from the U-bolts holding the springs to the axle housing.

5. Jack the rear axle up to remove the weight of the axle housing from the springs.

6. Remove the front and rear shackle pin nuts.

7. Drive out the rear shackle pin by using a hammer and drift and lower the rear end of the leaf spring assembly to the floor.

8. Drive out the front shackle pin and remove the leaf spring assembly rearward.

9. Remove the shackle pin from the rear spring bracket and remove the shackle.

10. Check the leaf springs for cracks, wear and broken leaves. Replace any leaves found to be cracked, broken, fatigued or seriously worn.

11. Check the shackles for bending and the pins for wear.

12. Check the U-bolts for distortion or other damage.

13. Mount the shackle to the bracket.

14. Align the front end of the leaf spring assembly with the front bracket and install the shackle pin.

15. Align the rear end of the leaf spring assembly with the shackle and install the shackle pin.

16. Loosely install the shackle pin nuts and install the U-bolts. Tighten the U-bolt nuts to 40 ft. lbs.

17. Install the shock absorbers.

18. Clip the parking brake cable to the bracket.

19. Remove the jackstands and lower the vehicle so that the vehicle weight is on the leaf springs.

20. Tighten the shackle pin nuts to 130 ft. lbs.

Shock Absorbers

REMOVAL & INSTALLATION

Remove the rear shock absorbers by loosening and removing the upper and lower attaching nuts and pulling the shock absorber ends off the mounting studs, together with the washers and rubber bushings. Install the shock absorbers in the reverse order of removal, making sure that you use new rubber bushings and that they are installed correctly in the bevel shaped mounting holes in the end of the shock absorbers.

STEERING

Steering Wheel

REMOVAL & INSTALLATION

1. Disconnect the battery ground cable.

2. Remove the horn shroud and spring

VIEW C

4 X 4

VIEW B

VIEW A

1. Shock absorber
2. Bushing
3. Washer
4. Washer
5. Washer
6. Nut
7. Rubber
8. Bolt
9. Rubber
10. Spring pin
11. Bushing
12. Bushing
13. Nut
14. Washer
15. Spring pin
16. Bolt
17. Washer
18. U-bolt
19. Plate
20. Washer
21. Nut
22. Seat
23. Spring assy.

Rear suspension

by pushing and turning it counterclockwise. Remove the horn contact ring and wire.

3. Remove the steering wheel-to-steering shaft retaining nut, washer and lockwasher.

4. Mark the relative position of the steering wheel and shaft to each other.

5. Remove the steering column cowling by removing the four attaching screws and washers.

6. Remove the steering wheel from the shaft with a puller.

NOTE: Under no circumstances is the steering shaft to be hammered upon, jarred, or leaned upon. The steering column is a collapsible, energy-absorbing type and can be easily damaged through mistreatment.

7. Install the steering wheel in the reverse order of removal, aligning the marks made on the steering wheel and the shaft. Draw the steering wheel onto the shaft with the attaching nut.

Turn Signal and Dimmer Switch

REMOVAL & INSTALLATION

1. Disconnect the battery ground cable.
2. Remove the five screws retaining the steering column cowling and remove the cowling.
3. Remove the wire connectors from the switch.
4. Remove the switch by removing the two screws which retain the switch clamp to the steering column mast jacket.

5. Replace the switch in the reverse order of removal.

Tie Rod Ends

REMOVAL & INSTALLATION

1. Jack up your vehicle and support it with jackstands.
2. Match-mark the tie rod ends and the sleeves for installation.
3. Remove the cotter pin and nut from the tie rod end, and loosen the clamping bolts on the sleeve.
4. Use a puller to remove the tie rod from the steering knuckle.
5. Unscrew the tie rod and remove it.
6. Check it for damage and replace it if necessary.

1. Coupling
2. Flange, upper coupling
3. Flange, lower coupling
4. Cross-strap
5. Cross-strap
6. Thrust washer
7. Spring
8. Through-bolt
9. Lock nut
10. Pinch bolt, lock washer
11. Steering unit assembly
12. Bolt
13. Nut
14. Shaft nut and washer
15. Bolt
16. Capsule
17. Bezel, starter switch
18. Bolt
19. Nut
20. Bracket, RH
21. Bracket, LH
22. Bolt
23. Bracket
24. Gasket
25. Grommet
26. Steering shaft assembly
27. Wheel assembly
28. Emblem
29. Button
30. Screw
31. Contact plate
32. Screw
33. Contact ring
34. Screw
35. Screw
36. Cowling screws and washer
37. Column cowling

Steering column

7. Installation is the reverse of removal.

NOTE: Make sure to use a new cotter pin when installing the tie rod.

Steering Gear

ADJUSTMENTS

NOTE: These adjustments must be performed in the following sequence.

1. Disconnect the battery ground cable. Raise vehicle.

Pitman arm removal

2. Remove the Pitman arm nut and lockwasher. Remove the Pitman arm.

3. Remove the horn shroud and spring.

4. Turn the steering wheel gently in one direction until stopped by the gear; then turn back half way.

NOTE: Do not turn the steering wheel hard against the stops when the steering linkage is disconnected from the gear as damage to the ball guides could result.

5. Measure and record "bearing drag"

Steering gear adjustment

by applying a torque wrench with a socket on the steering wheel nut and rotating through a 90° arc.

Do not use a torque wrench having a maximum torque reading of more than 0.5 kg-m (50 in. lbs.).

6. Adjust "over-center preload" as follows:

a. Turn the steering wheel gently from one stop all the way to the other carefully counting the total number of turns. Turn the wheel back exactly half-way, to center position.

b. Loosen the lock nut and turn the lash adjuster screw clockwise to take out all lash between the ball nut and Pitman shaft sector teeth and then tighten the locknut.

c. Check the torque at the steering wheel, taking the highest reading as the wheel is turned through center position. Preload should be 4.3–10.5 in. lbs.

d. If necessary, loosen locknut and readjust lash adjuster screw to obtain proper torque. Tighten the locknut to 20 ft. lbs. and again check torque reading

1. Steering gear housing
2. Sector shaft bushing
3. Sector (Pitman) shaft seal
4. Wormshaft seal
5. Worm and ball nut assembly
6. O-ring
7. End cover
8. Lock nut
9. Worm shaft seal
10. Sector shaft
11. Sector adjuster screw
12. Adusting shim
13. Gasket
14. Top cover
15. Filler plug
16. Lock nut
17. Bolt
18. Pitman shaft nut
19. Lock washer

Steering gear

9. Install Pitman arm to shaft. Install washer and torque nut to 160 ft. lbs.
10. Lower engine stone shield.
11. Lower vehicle to floor.

Pitman Shaft Seal

REPLACEMENT

A defective seal may be replaced without removing the steering gear from the vehicle. If it has been diagnosed that the seal should be replaced proceed as follows:
1. Raise and safely support the vehicle.
2. Remove Pitman arm as previously described.
3. Wipe clean the area around the seal.
4. Using an awl, screwdriver or similar tool, pry out the old seal being careful not to damage the housing bore.

NOTE: Inspect the lubricant in the gear for contamination. If the lubricant is contaminated in any way, the gear must be removed from the vehicle and completely overhauled.

5. Coat the new Pitman shaft seal with steering gear lubricant (or equivalent). Position the seal in the Pitman shaft bore and tap into position using a suitable size socket.
6. Install Pitman arm as previously described.
7. Lower vehicle to floor.
8. Check lubricant level in gear box; total capacity 0.2L (7 oz.). Do not overfill.

Idler Arm, Idler Arm Pivot Shaft and/or Bracket

REMOVAL & INSTALLATION

1. Raise and safely support the vehicle.
2. Remove lockwasher and nut that retain the intermediate rod to the idle arm.
3. The ball studs for the above may be removed using tool J-21687-02 or equivalent.
4. Remove the four bolts, nuts and washers retaining the bracket to the frame, and remove the idler arm pivot shaft and bracket with idler arm.
5. If the idler arm is being replaced proceed as follows:
   a. Remove idler arm to idler arm pivot shaft nut and lockwashers.
   b. Remove the idler arm from the pivot shaft.
6. Install bracket and shaft assembly to frame and torque to 29 ft. lbs.
7. Install the idler arm to the shaft and torque nut to 87 ft. lbs.
8. Install the ball studs and intermediate rod to the idler arm. Torque the castellated nuts to 50 ft. lbs. and just enough additional to line up cotter pin holes. Install new cotter pins.
9. Lubricate idler arm pivot shaft.

through center of travel. If maximum specification is exceeded, turn lash adjuster screw counterclockwise, then come up on adjustment by turning the adjuster locknut in a clockwise motion.
7. Reassemble the Pitman arm to the Pitman shaft. Tighten the Pitman shaft nut to 160 ft. lbs.
8. Install the horn spring and connect the battery ground cable.
9. Lower vehicle to floor.

REMOVAL & INSTALLATION

1. Raise and safely support the vehicle.
2. Remove Pitman arm nut and washer and use a suitable puller to remove Pitman arm from Pitman shaft.
3. Remove engine stone shield.
4. Remove lower clamp to flexible coupling bolts.
5. Remove steering gear to frame bolts

and remove steering gear from vehicle.
6. Place gear in position and start mounting bolts; temporarily leave loose.
7. Install steering gear flexible coupling bolts and torque to 22 ft. lbs.
8. Torque steering column mounting bolts to 13 ft. lbs.

Steering gear mounting

10. Lower vehicle to floor.

Intermediate Rod and Tie Rods

REMOVAL & INSTALLATION

1. Raise and safely support the vehicle.
2. Remove cotter pin from the ball studs connecting tie rods to intermediate rod and steering damper. Remove the castellated nuts and disconnect the parts using special tool J-21687-02 or equivalent.

Tie-rod end removal

3. Remove the nut and lockwasher on ball stud connecting the intermediate rod to idler arm. Disconnect the parts using special tool J-21687-02 or equivalent.
4. Remove the intermediate rod together with tie rods.
5. If the tie rod is replaced, disconnect the intermediate rod from tie rod.
6. If the tie rod has been removed, proceed as follows:
   a. Apply liquid gasket (Felcobond 401) to portion B. Install and tighten tie rod end to specified torque of 9.0 kg-m (65 ft. lbs.).
   b. Caulk two portions (upper and lower portions) of A.
7. Make sure threads on ball studs and nuts are clean and smooth.
8. Install intermediate rod to idler arm, install lockwasher, nut, and torque nut to 50 ft. lbs.
9. Raise end of rod and install on Pitman arm. Torque nut to 44 ft. lbs., then advance nut just enough to insert cotter pin and install new cotter pin.

Installing tie rod to intermediate rod

10. Install intermediate rod to steering damper end. Torque nut to 87 ft. lbs., then advance nut just enough to insert cotter pin and install new cotter pin.
11. Install the tie rods to adapter, torque nut to 44 ft. lbs., then advance nut just enough to insert cotter pin and install new cotter pin, and lubricate tie rod ball studs.

Steering Damper

REPLACEMENT

1. Raise vehicle on hoist.
2. Remove cotter pin and castellated nut on stud connecting the damper end with intermediate rod.
3. Remove the cotter pin and castellated nut on the stud connecting the damper end to second crossmember (on 4 × 2 model) or to idler arm bracket (on 4 × 4 model).
4. Remove the steering damper.
5. To install, reverse steps 1–4.

Pitman Arm

REMOVAL & INSTALLATION

1. Raise and safely support the vehicle.
2. Remove nut and lockwasher retaining Pitman arm to Pitman shaft.
3. Using tool J-29107 or equivalent remove Pitman arm from pitman shaft.
4. Remove cotter pins and castellated nuts retaining the Pitman arm to the tie rod and intermediate rod.
5. The ball studs may be removed from the Pitman arm using tool J-21687-02.
6. Remove the Pitman arm.
7. Install Pitman arm to intermediate rod and tie rod ball studs. Install castellated nuts (do not torque yet).
8. Install Pitman arm to Pitman shaft.
9. Install Pitman shaft lockwashers and nut, and torque to 160 ft. lbs.
10. Torque ball stud nuts to 44 ft. lbs. and just enough additional to align cotter pin hole. Install new cotter pin.
11. Lower vehicle to floor.

Steering Column and Shaft Assembly

REMOVAL & INSTALLATION

1. Disconnect the battery ground cable.
2. Remove upper coupling clamp pinch bolt from the steering shaft flexible coupling in the engine compartment.

NOTE: Apply a setting mark across the steering shaft and coupling clamp.

3. Disconnect the combination switch and ignition switch wiring at the harness connector.

Steering column flexible coupling

4. Remove the two column to instrument panel bolts.
5. Remove the steering column toward the cab being careful not to damage or jar the shaft as it is an energy absorbing unit.
6. Remove the five screws that retain the steering column cowling.
7. Remove the steering wheel as outlined previously.
8. Remove two screws that retain the combination switch to column on flange.
9. Remove the combination switch assembly.
10. Remove bolt that retains the ignition switch bracket.
11. Install the combination switch on the column flange using 2 screws.
12. Install the ignition switch to the column as previously described.
13. Install the steering wheel lockwasher and nut and torque the nut to 29 ft. lbs.
14. Install the horn shroud.
15. Install the steering column cowling.
16. Place column through cowl and move into position.
17. Install end of steering shaft into flexible coupling clamp. Install coupling to worm gear shaft. Torque pinch bolts to 22 ft. lbs.

NOTE: Align setting marks applied at disassembly when connecting steering shaft end to coupling clamp.

18. Install column to instrument panel unless vehicle is setting on its wheels or suspension.
19. Tighten the column to instrument panel bolts. Tightening torque 1.5 kg-m (11 ft. lbs.).
20. Make connections of combination switch and ignition switch wiring at the connector.
21. Check operation of horn and combination switch.
22. Check for interference between steering column cowling and steering wheel.
23. Check alignment between front wheels and steering wheel.
24. Check steering wheel free-play when the steering unit assembly is installed in position on the vehicle. The standard steering wheel play is about 10 mm (0.4 in.) when measured at the outside diameter of the steering wheel.

Steering Shaft Flexible Coupling

REMOVAL & INSTALLATION

1. Jack up front of vehicle until wheels are just off the ground.
2. Remove coupling through-bolts and lock nut. Only two bolts can be removed.
3. Remove the pinch bolts on the upper and lower flanges of the coupling.
4. Remove two bolts fixing the column bracket.
5. Pull the steering column and shaft approximately 50 mm (1.968 in.) in toward the cab.
6. Remove the upper coupling flange and coupling, then remove the lower coupling flange.
7. Install the lower coupling flange, then install the coupling and upper coupling flange.
8. Install the coupling assembly and torque the through bolts to 22 ft. lbs.
9. Install pinch bolts and torque to 22 ft. lbs.
10. Lower vehicle to floor.
11. Install and torque the column bracket bolts to 13 ft. lbs.

BRAKE SYSTEM

NOTE: Refer to the "Brake" section of Unit Repair for service procedures.

CHASSIS ELECTRICAL

Blower

REMOVAL & INSTALLATION

1. Disconnect the battery ground cable.
2. Disconnect the blower motor electrical leads.
3. Remove the blower-to-heater core screws and remove the blower motor assembly.
4. Install in the reverse order.

Heater Core

REMOVAL & INSTALLATION

1. Disconnect the battery ground cable.
2. Place a drain pan under the heater hoses at the heater and remove the heater hoses from the core tubes, securing the heater hoses in a raised position to prevent further

Heater

Heater-air conditioner

loss of coolant. Plug or tape the heater core tubes to prevent spillage of coolant in the passenger compartment when removing.
3. Remove the five parcel shelf attaching screws and remove the shelf.
4. Loosen the air diverter and defroster door bowden cable clamps at the heater case and disconnect the cables from the doors.
5. Disconnect the blower resistor leads.
6. Remove the control assembly-to-instrument panel screws and swing the control to the left and lay it on the floor. Be careful not to kink the water valve bowden cable.
7. Remove the four heater-to-firewall screws. Pull the heater rearward until the core tubes clear the dash opening, then remove the heater by moving it to the right and down.

8. Remove the core tube clamp screw and remove the clamp.
9. Remove the seven screws and separate the heater case halves.
10. Remove the core from the case.
11. Install and assemble the heater core and heater case in the reverse order of removal, using new seals around the heater core.

Ignition Switch

REMOVAL & INSTALLATION

1. Disconnect the negative battery terminal.
2. Remove the multi-connector from the rear of the ignition switch.
3. Remove the lock nut from the front

of the switch. Remove the switch from the rear of the instrument panel.

4. Installation is the reverse of removal.

NOTE: Align the locating lug on the switch body with the slot in the instrument panel mounting hole during installation.

Radio

REMOVAL & INSTALLATION

1. Disconnect the battery ground cable.
2. Remove the ash tray and ash tray plate.
3. Remove the tuner and volume control knobs, jam nuts, washers and face panel.

Radio installation

4. Remove the screws from the front and rear mounting brackets.
5. Disconnect the electrical connections, antenna lead and remove the radio. Remove the front mounting brackets from the radio.
6. Install the radio in the reverse order of removal.

Windshield Wiper Motor and Linkage

REMOVAL & INSTALLATION

1. Remove the wiper blades and arms.
2. Remove the two bolts attaching the pivot.
3. Remove the four wiper motor mounting bolts and remove the wiper motor and linkage.
4. To remove the motor independently, take out the motor shaft nut and three bolts and then pull off the connector and disconnect the ground cable.
order of removal. Make sure to install the

Windshield wiper motor and linkage

wiper motor linkage so that it is not twisted or touching any adjacent parts.

WIPER REFILL REPLACEMENT

Normally, if the wipers are not cleaning the windshield properly, only the refill has to be replaced. The blade and arm usually require replacement only in the event of damage. It is not necessary (except on new Tridon refills) to remove the arm or the blade to replace the refill (rubber part), though you may have to position the arm higher on the glass. You can do this turning the ignition switch on and operating the wipers. When they are positioned where they are accessible, turn the ignition switch off.

There are several types of refills and your vehicle could have any kind, since aftermarket blades and arms may not use exactly the same refill as the original equipment.

Most Trico styles use a release button that is pushed down to allow the refill to slide out of the yoke jaws. The new refill slides in and locks in place. Some Trico refills are removed by locating where the metal backing strip or the refill is wider. Insert a small screwdriver blade between the frame and metal backing strip. Press down to release the refill from the retaining tab.

The Anco style is unlocked at one end by squeezing 2 metal tabs, and the refill is slid out of the frame jaws. When the new refill is installed, the tabs will click into place, locking the refill.

The polycarbonate type is held in place by a locking lever that is pushed downward out of the groove in the aim to fill the refill. When the new refill is installed, it will lock in place automatically.

The Tridon refill has a plastic backing

strip with a notch about an inch from the end. Hold the blade (frame) on a hard surface so that the frame is tightly bowed. Grip the tip of the backing strip and pull up while twisting counterclockwise. The backing strip will snap out of the retaining tab. Do this for the remaining tabs until the refill is free of the arm. The length of these refills is molded into the end and they should be replaced with identical types.

No matter which type of refill you use, be sure that all of the frame claws engage the refill. Before operating the wipers, be sure that no part of the metal frame is contacting the windshield.

Instrument Cluster

REMOVAL & INSTALLATION

1. Disconnect the speedometer cable.
2. Remove the wing nuts on the rear side of the instrument panel and pull the assembly part way out.
3. Disconnect the wiring harness at the connector and remove the instrument panel.
4. Install the instrument panel in the reverse order of removal.

Headlights

REMOVAL & INSTALLATION

1. Remove the headlight trim rim.
2. Loosen and remove screws attaching the retaining ring. Remove lamp.
3. Install the headlight by fitting the bosses on the headlight lens into the grooves so that the "TOP" mark is up.
4. Install retainer and tighten the attaching screws. Install the headlight trim rim.

Jeep

GENERAL ENGINE SPECIFICATIONS

Engine Year	Carburetor Type	Horsepower @ rpm	Torque (ft. lb.) @ rpm	Bore × Stroke	Compression Ratio	Cranking Compression Pressure	Oil Pressure (psi) @ 2000 rpm
4-150, '83–'84	1 bbl	83 @ 4200	116 @ 2600	3.876 × 3.188	9.2:1	150	40
4-151, '80–'84	2 bbl	90 @ 4400	128 @ 2400	4.000 × 3.000	8.24:1	140	38
6-173, '83–'84	2 bbl	110 @ 4800	148 @ 2000	3.50 × 2.99	8.5:1	140	45
6-232, '77–'78	1 bbl	90 @ 3050	170 @ 2000	3.750 × 3.500	8.0:1	140 Minimum	50
6-258, '77–'78	1 bbl	95 @ 3050	180 @ 2100	3.750 × 3.895	8.0:1	120–150	50
6-258, '79–'84	2 bbl	114 @ 3600	196 @ 2000	3.750 × 3.895	8.0:1	120–150	50
V8-304, '77–'81	2 bbl	120 @ 3200	220 @ 2200	3.750 × 3.440	8.4:1	120–150	50
V8-360, '77–'84	2 bbl	175 @ 4000	285 @ 2900	4.080 × 3.440	8.25:1	120–150	50
V8-401, '77–'78	4 bbl	215 @ 4400	320 @ 2800	4.165 × 3.680	8.25:1	120–150	50

TUNE-UP SPECIFICATIONS

(When analyzing compression test results, look for uniformity among cylinders rather than specific pressures.)

Year	Engine No. Cyl Displacement (cu. in.)	hp	Spark Plugs Type	Gap (in.)	Distributor	Ignition Timing (deg) ▲	Intake Valve Opens (deg)■	Fuel Pump Pressure (psi)	Idle Speed (rpm)● Man Trans	Idle Speed (rpm)● Auto Trans
'77	6-232	90	N-12Y	.035	Electronic	8B	12	4–5	600	—
	6-258	95	N-12Y	.035	Electronic	6B②	12	4–5	600	550(700)
	8-304	120	N-12Y	.035	Electronic	5B③	14¾	5–6½	750	700
	8-360	175	N-12Y	.035	Electronic	5B④	14¾	5–6½	750	700
	8-401	215	N-12Y	.035	Electronic	5B④	25½	5–6½	750	700
'78	6-232	90	N-13L	.035	Electronic	5B⑤	12	4–5	850⑥	—
	6-258	100	N-13L	.035	Electronic	6B⑦ ⑧	14½	4–5	850⑨ ⑩	550
	8-304	130	N-12Y	.035	Electronic	5B⑪	14¾	5–6½	750	700
	8-360	140	N-12Y	.035	Electronic	5B	14¾	5–6½	750	700
	8-401	215	N-12Y	.035	Electronic	8B	25½	5–6½	—	700
'79	6-258	110	N-13L	.035	Electronic	8B⑫	14½	4–5	700	600
	8-304	125	N-12Y	.035	Electronic	8B⑬	14¾	5–6½	700(750)	600
	8-360	175	N-12Y	.035	Electronic	8B	14¾	5–6½	800	600
'80–'82	4-151	80	R44TSX	.060	Electronic	10B⑰	33B	6½–8	900	700
	6-258	110	N-14L	.035	Electronic	8B⑭	14½	4–5	700	600⑮
	8-304	125	N-12Y	.035	Electronic	⑯	14¾	5–6	700	600
	8-360	175	N-12Y	.035	Electronic	8B	14¾	5–6	800	600
'83–'84	4-150	93	RFN14LY	.033-.038	Electronic	12B	27B	6½–8	750	750
	4-151	80	R44TSX	.060	Electronic	10B⑰	33B	6½–8	900	700
	6-173	110	RN12YC	.041	Electronic	10B	21B	5–7	750	750
	6-258	110	N-14L	.035	Electronic	8B⑭	14½	4–5	700	600⑮
	8-360	175	N-12Y	.035	Electronic	8B	14¾	5–6	800	600

NOTE: If the information given in this chart disagrees with the information on the engine tune-up decal, use the specifications on the decal—they are current for the engine in your car.

NOTE: Figures in parentheses are for California engines

▲ With vacuum advance disconnected
■ All figures before TDC (BTDC)
● With manual transmission in Neutral and automatic transmission in Drive
B Before top dead center (BTDC)
① Not used
② 8B w/Automatic transmission
③ 10B w/Automatic transmission; 5B in California
④ 8B w/Automatic transmission; 5B in California
⑤ 10B for altitude
⑥ 600 rpm for altitude
⑦ w/Manual transmission; 10B altitude, 8B Calif.
⑧ w/Auto transmission; 8B 49 states and Calif., 10B altitude

⑨ w/Manual transmission and 1 bbl. carb 600 rpm for altitude
⑩ w/Manual transmission and 2 bbl. carb 650 rpm
⑪ w/Auto transmission; 10B 49 states and Calif.
⑫ w/Manual transmission; 4B w/Auto transmission; 6B, CJ model only
⑬ w/Manual transmission; 5B, CJ model only
⑭ California CJ with manual transmission, 6B
⑮ Not used
⑯ Manual transmission, except Calif. and hilly terrain; 8B @ 700 rpm
⑰ w/Automatic transmission; 12B

FIRING ORDER

NOTE: To avoid confusion, always replace spark plug wires one at a time.

V6–173 firing order

4–150 firing order

6 cylinder firing order: 1-5-3-6-2-4

4 cylinder firing order: 1-3-4-2

V8 firing order: 1-8-4-3-6-5-7-2

VALVE SPECIFICATIONS

Year	Engine No. Cyl. Displacement (cu in.)	Seat Angle (deg)①	Face Angle (deg)②	Spring Test Pressure (lbs. @ in.)	Spring Installed Height (in.)	Stem to Guide Clearance (in.)		Stem Diameter (in.)	
						Intake	Exhaust	Intake	Exhaust
'81–'82	4-151	46	45	176 @ 1¼	1²¹⁄₃₂	.0010–.0030	.0010–.0027	.3422	.3422
'77–'82	6-232	44½	44	100 @ 1¹³⁄₁₆	2¹⁵⁄₆₄③	.0010–.0030	.0010–.0030	.3720	.3720
	6-258	44½	44	100 @ 1¹³⁄₁₆	2¹⁵⁄₆₄③	.0010–.0030	.0010–.0030	.3720	.3720
	8-304	44½	44	84 @ 1¹³⁄₁₆	2⁷⁄₃₂③	.0010–.0030	.0010–.0030	.3720	.3720
	8-360	44½	44	84 @ 1¹³⁄₁₆	2⁷⁄₃₂③	.0010–.0030	.0010–.0030	.3720	.3720
'77–'78	8-401	44½	44	84 @ 1¹³⁄₁₆	2⁷⁄₃₂③	.0010–.0030	.0010–.0030	.3720	.3720
'83–'84	4-150	—	44	212 @ 1¹³⁄₆₄	1¹³⁄₁₆	.0010–.0030	.0010–.0030	.311–.312	.311–.312
	4-151	46	45	176 @ 1¼	1²¹⁄₃₂	.0010–.0030	.0010–.0027	.3422	.3422
	6-173	46④	45④	195 @ 1³⁄₁₆	1³⁷⁄₆₄	.0010–.0027	.0010–.0027	.3410–.3416	.3410–.3416
	6-232	44½	44	100 @ 1¹³⁄₁₆	2¹⁵⁄₆₄③	.0010–.0030	.0010–.0030	.3720	.3720
	6-258	44½	44	100 @ 1¹³⁄₁₆	2¹⁵⁄₆₄③	.0010–.0030	.0010–.0030	.3720	.3720
	8-360	44½	44	212 @ 1¹¹⁄₃₂	2⁷⁄₃₂③	.0010–.0030	.0010–.0030	.3720	.3720

① Exhaust valve seat angle given; all intake valve seat angles are 30° unless otherwise noted
② Exhaust valve face angle given; all intake valve face angles are 29° unless otherwise noted
③ '78–'82—2"; except 1978—304, 360, 401—2⅛
④ Intake or exhaust V6 only

CRANKSHAFT AND CONNECTING ROD SPECIFICATIONS

(All measurements given in inches)

Engine	Crankshaft				Connecting Rod		
	Main Bearing Journal Dia	Main Bearing Oil Clearance	Shaft End Play	Thrust on No.	Journal Dia	Oil Clearance	Side Clearance
4-150	2.4996–2.5001	.0001–.0025	.0015–.0065		2.0934–2.0955	.001–.003	.010–.019
4-151	2.2988	.0005–.0022	.0035–.0085	5	1.8690	.0007–.0027	.006–.022
6-173	2.4940	.0017–.0030	.0020–.0067	3	1.9980	.0014–.0032	.0063–.0173
6-232	2.4986–2.5001	.0010–.0020	.0015–.0065	3	2.0934–2.0955	.0010–.0020	.005–.014
6-258	2.4986–2.5001	.0010–.0020①	.0015–.0065⑤	3	2.0934–2.0955	.0010–.0020②	.005–.014
V8-304	2.7474–2.7489③	.0010–.0020④	.003–.008⑥	3	2.0934–2.0955	.0010–.0020	.006–.018
V8-360	2.7474–2.7489③	.0010–.0020④	.003–.008	3	2.0934–2.0955	.0010–.0030	.006–.018

① '77–'79: .0010–.0030 (.0025 preferred)
② '77–'82: .0010–.0025 (.0015–.0020 preferred)
③ #5: 2.7464–2.7479
④ #5: .0020–.0030
⑤ '81–'82: #1: .005–.0026
  2, 3, 4, 5, 6: .0005–.0030
  7: .0011–.0035
⑥ '81–'82: .0010–.0030 #5: .0020–.0040

PISTON RING SPECIFICATIONS

		Ring Gap			Ring Side Clearance			Piston to Bore Clearance
	Engine	Top Compression	Bottom Compression	Oil Control	Top Compression	Bottom Compression	Oil Control	
'84	4-150	.010–.020	.010–.020	.010–.025	.0017–.0032	.0017–.0032	.001–.008	.0009–.0017
'81–'83	4-151	.0027–.0033	.009–.019	.015–.055	.0025–.0033	.0025–.0033	.0025–.0033	.0025–.0033
'77–'82	6-232	.010–.020	.010–.020	.010–.025	.0015–.003	.0015–.003	.001–.008	.0009–.0017
	6-258	.010–.020	.010–.020	.010–.025	.0015–.003	.0015–.003	.001–.008	.0009–.0017
	8-304	.010–.020	.010–.020	.010–.025	.0015–.0035	.0015–.003	.0011–.008	.0010–.0018
	8-360	.010–.020	.010–.020	.015–.045	.0015–.0035	.0015–.0035	.000–.007	.0012–.0020
	8-401	.010–.020	.010–.020	.0015–.055	.0015–.003	.0015–.0035	.000–.007	.0010–.0018
'83–'84	6-173	.010–.020	.010–.020	.020–.055	.0012–.0028	.0016–.0037	.0078 Max.	.0017–.0027
	6-258	.010–.020	.010–.020	.010–.025	.0015–.003	.0015–.003	.001–.008	.0009–.0017
	8-360	.010–.020	.010–.020	.015–.045	.0015–.0035	.0015–.0035	.000–.007	.0012–.0020

TORQUE SPECIFICATIONS

(All readings in ft. lbs.)

Engine No. Cyl. Displacement (cu. in.)	Cylinder Head Bolts	Rod Bearing Bolts	Main Bearing Bolts	Crankshaft Balancer Bolt	Flywheel to Crankshaft Bolts	Manifold	
						Intake	Exhaust
4-150	85	33	80	20	65	23	23
4-151	95	30	65	160	35	Bolt: 40 Nut: 30	Bolt: 40 Nut: 30
6-173	70	37	70	75	50	23	25
6-232, 258	95–115	26–30①	75–85	50–64	95–120	37–47②	20–30②
8-304, 360	100–120	26–30①	90–105	48–64	95–120	37–47	20–30③
8-401	100–120	35–40	90–105	48–64	95–120	37–47	20–30

① 30–35 for '78–'80
② 18–20 for '77–'80
③ 20–30, center two bolts; 12–18, outer four bolts for '79–'80

TUNE-UP

Spark Plugs

Spark plugs ignite the air and fuel mixture in the cylinder as the piston reaches the top of the compression stroke. The controlled explosion that results forces the piston down, turning the crankshaft and the rest of the drive train.

The average life of a spark plug is dependent on a number of factors: the mechanical condition of the engine; the type of fuel; driving conditions; and the driver.

When you remove the spark plugs, check their condition. They are a good indicator of the condition of the engine.

A small deposit of light tan or gray material on a spark plug that has been used for any period of time is to be considered normal. Additives in unleaded fuels may give a number of unusual color indications; for instance, MMT (a manganese anti-knock compound) will cause rust red deposits.

The gap between the center electrode and the side or ground electrode can be expected to increase not more than 0.001 in. every 1,000 miles under normal conditions.

When a spark plug is functioning normally or, more accurately, when the plug is installed in an engine that is functioning properly, the plugs can be taken out, cleaned, regapped, and reinstalled in the engine without doing the engine any harm.

When, and if, a plug fouls and begins to misfire, you will have to investigate, correct the cause of the fouling, and either clean or replace the plug.

There are several reasons why a spark plug will foul and you can learn which reason by just looking at the plug. A few of the most common reasons for plug fouling, and a description of the fouled plug's appearance, is listed in the electrical unit repair section which also offers solutions to the problems.

REMOVAL

1. Number the wires so you won't cross them when you replace them.
2. Remove the wire from the end of the spark plug by grasping the wire by the rubber boot. If the boot sticks to the plug, remove it by twisting and pulling at the same time. Do not pull the wire itself or you will most certainly damage the delicate carbon core.
3. Use a spark plug plug socket to loosen all of the plugs about two turns.
4. If compressed air is available, blow off the area around the spark plug holes. Otherwise, use a rag or a brush to clean the area. Be careful not to allow any foreign material to drop into the spark plug holes.
5. Remove the plugs by unscrewing them the rest of the way from the engine.

INSPECTION

Check the plugs for deposits and wear. If they are not going to be replaced, clean the plugs thoroughly. Remember that any kind of deposit will decrease the efficiency of the plug. Plugs can be cleaned on a spark plug cleaning machine, which can sometimes be found in service stations, or you can do an acceptable job of cleaning with a stiff brush.

Check spark plug gap before installation. The ground electrode must be parallel to the center electrode and the specified size wire gauge should pass theough the gap with a slight drag. If the electrodes are worn, it is possible to file them level.

INSTALLATION

1. Insert the plugs in the spark plug hole and tighten them hand-tight. Take care not to cross-thread them.
2. Tighten the plugs firmly. The correct torque for all engines is 28 ft. lbs.
3. Install the spark plugs wires on their plugs. Make sure that each wire is firmly connected to each plug.

Electronic Ignition

All later models are equipped with an electronic ignition system.

NOTE: Refer to the "Electrical" Unit Repair section for detailed procedures on troubleshooting and repairing the electronic ignition.

The HEI (high energy ignition) system used on 6.173 engines uses an externally mounted coil. There are two different methods for controlling spark timing. 49 state vehicles use a conventional type distributor with vacuum advance. California vehicles do not use a vacuum advance. Advance is controlled by the ECM (Electronic Control Module).

Ignition Timing

ALL ENGINES

1. Locate the timing marks on the crankshaft pulley and the front of the timing case cover.
2. Clean off the timing marks, so that you can see them.
3. Use chalk or white paint to color the mark on the scale that will indicate the correct timing, when aligned with the mark on the pulley or the pointer. It is also helpful to mark the notch in the pulley or the tip of the pointer with a small dab of color.
4. Attach a tachometer to the engine.
5. Attach a timing light to the engine.
6. Disconnect the vacuum lines to the distributor at the distributor and plug the vacuum lines. Loosen the distributor lockbolt just enough so that the distributor can

1. Distributor cap
2. Rotor
3. Dust shield
4. Trigger wheel
5. Felt wick
6. Sensor assembly
7. Shaft assembly
8. Housing
9. Vacuum control
10. Shim
11. Drive gear
12. Pin

Exploded view of typical 6 cylinder distributor

be turned with a little resistance.

7. Check to make sure that all of the wires clear the fan and then start the engine.
8. Adjust the idle to the correct specification.
9. With the timing light aimed at the pulley and the marks on the engine, turn the distributor in the direction of rotor rotation to retard the spark, and in the opposite direction of rotor rotation to advance the spark. Align the marks on the pulley and the engine with the flushes of the timing light.
10. When the marks are aligned, tighten the distributor locknut and recheck the timing with the timing light to make sure that the distributor did not move when you tightened the locknut.
11. Turn off the engine and disconnect the test equipment.

MAGNETIC TIMING PROBE

A bracket and hole are cast into the timing case cover for the use of a magnetic timing probe, connected to a special electronic timing meter for precise ignition timing. The probe is inserted into the hole of the bracket until the vibration damper is touched. When the engine is started, the probe is automatically spaced away from the damper by the damper's eccentricity, or being slightly out of center. The probe senses a milled slot on the damper and compensating

1. PIN
2. GEAR
3. WASHER
4. DISTRIBUTOR BODY
5. VACUUM ADVANCE MECHANISM
6. WICK
7. WASHERS
8. PICK-UP COIL
9. RETAINER
10. TRIGGER WHEEL
11. PIN
12. ROTOR
13. CAP.

4–150 distributor

for the bracket's 9.5° ATDC position, registers the reading on the timing meter. Any necessary corrections can then be made to the ignition timing.

NOTE: Do not use the probe bracket and hole the check the ignition timing, using a conventional timing light.

Valve Lash Adjustment

Manual valve lash adjustment is not necessary nor possible since hydraulic valve lifters are used.

Idle Speed

ADJUSTMENT

1977–80

The procedure for adjusting the idle speed

and mixture is called the lean drop procedure and is made with the engine operating at normal operating temperature and the air cleaner in place as follows:

1. Turn the mixture screws to the full rich position with the tabs on limiters against stops. Note position of screw head slot inside limiter cap slots.
2. Remove idle limiter caps.
3. Remove limiter caps by threading a sheet metal screw in center of cap and turning clockwise. Discard limiter caps.
4. Reset adjustment screws to same position noted before limiter caps were removed.
5. Start engine and allow it to reach normal operating temperature.
6. Adjust idle speed to 30 rpm above the specified rpm. See "Tune-Up Specifications" chart.
   a. On 6 cylinder engines with throttle stop solenoid, turn solenoid in or out to obtain specified rpm;

b. On V8 engines with throttle stop solenoid, turn hex screw on throttle stop solenoid carriage to obtain specified rpm. This is done with solenoid wire connected;
   c. Tighten solenoid locknut, if so equipped.
   d. Disconnect solenoid wire and adjust curb idle speed screw to obtain idle speed of 500 rpm;
   e. Reconnect solenoid wire.
7. Starting from full rich stop position, as was determined before limiter caps were removed, turn mixture adjusting screws clockwise (leaner) until a loss of engine speed is noticed.
8. Turn screws counterclockwise (richer) until the highest rpm reading is obtained at lean best idle setting. The lean best idle setting is on the lean side of the highest rpm setting without changing rpm.
9. If the idle speed changed more than 30 rpm during the mixture adjustment procedure, reset the idle speed to 30 rpm above the specified rpm with idle speed adjusting screw or the throttle stop solenoid and repeat the mixture adjustment.
10. Install new limiter caps over mixture adjusting screws with tabs positioned against full rich stops. Be careful not to disturb idle mixture setting while installing caps.

1981 and Later

Idle mixture screws on these carburetors are sealed with plugs or dowel pins. A mixture adjustment must be undertaken ONLY when the carburetor is overhauled, the throttle body replaced, or the engine does not meet required emission standards. Since expensive testing equipment is needed to properly set the mixture, only the idle speed adjusting procedure is given below.

NOTE: The adjustment is made with the manual transmission in neutral and the automatic in drive. Therefore, make certain that the vehicles parking brake is set firmly, and that the wheels are blocked. It may be a good idea to have someone in the vehicle with their foot on the brake.

1. Connect tachometer, start engine and warm to normal operating temperature. Choke and intake manifold heater (six-cylinder engine only) must be off.
2. If not within OK range, turn curb idle adjustment screw to obtain specified curb idle rpm.
3. For six cylinder engine (BBD carburetor):
   a. Disconnect vacuum hose from vacuum actuator and holding solenoid wire connector. Adjust curb (slow) idle speed adjustment screw to obtain specified curb (slow) idle rpm if not within OK range. Refer to Emission Control Information label, and Tune-Up Specifications.
   b. Apply direct source of vacuum to vacuum actuator.
   c. Turn vacuum actuator adjustment screw on throttle lever until specified rpm

4–151 distributor

is obtained (900 rpm for manual transmissions, and 800 rpm for automatic transmissions).

d. Disconnect manifold vacuum source from vacuum actuator.

e. With jumper wire apply battery voltage (12V) to energize holding solenoid. Turn A/C on, if equipped.

NOTE: Throttle must be opened manually to allow Sol-Vac throttle positioner to be extended.

f. With Sol-Vac throttle positioner extended, idle speed should be 650 rpm for automatic transmission equipped vehicles and 750 rpm for manual transmission equipped vehicles.

g. If idle speed is not within tolerance, adjust Sol-Vac (hex-head adjustment screw) to obtain specified rpm.

h. Remove jumper wire from Sol-Vac holding solenoid wire connector.

i. Connect Sol-Vac holding solenoid wire connector.

j. Connect original hose to vacuum actuator.

4. For four and eight cylinder engines (2SE, E2SE or 2150 carburetor, turn nut on solenoid plunger or hex screw on solenoid carriage to obtain specified idle rpm:

a. Tighten locknut, if equipped.

b. Disconnect solenoid wire connector and adjust curb idle screw to obtain 500 rpm idle speed.

c. Connect solenoid wire connector.

d. If model 2150 carburetor (eight-cylinder engine, is equipped with dashpot. With throttle at curb idle position, fully depress dashpot stem and measure clearance between stem and throttle lever. Clearance should be 0.032 inch (0.813 mm). Adjust by loosening locknut and turning dashpot.

ENGINE ELECTRICAL

Distributor

REMOVAL

1. Remove the air cleaner assembly and any other component that will interfere with distributor removal.

2. Disconnect the distributor wiring connector at the harness plug.

NOTE: The wire connector (from 1978) will contain special conductive grease. Do not remove the grease. The same grease will also be found on the metal parts of the rotor. Do not remove it even if it looks charred.

3. If the distributor is equipped with a vacuum diaphragm, disconnect the vacuum hose(s).

4. Release the distributor cap retainers, remove the cap and position it out of the way. If it is necessary to disconnect any plug wires, be sure to mark them for proper location.

5. Use chalk or paint and carefully mark the distributor body that the center of the rotor tip points to. Mark the engine block in relation to the mark on the distributor body. When this is done, the tip of the rotor, the line on the distributor and the engine block mark should match. When the distributor is reinstalled in the engine the distributor must be in the same position if

V8 engine timing marks

4–151 timing marks

6 cylinder timing marks

correct ignition timing is to be maintained.

6. Remove the distributor hold-down bolt(s), lockwasher and clamp. Lift the distributor from the engine.

NOTE: The shaft and rotor will move slightly (about an ⅛ of a turn) away from the mark on the distributor body when the distributor (lifted for removal. When reinstalling the distributor, the rotor must be keyed to the same position, to insure gear mesh.

INSTALLATION

1. Align the rotor with the mark on the distributor body. Turn the rotor about an ⅛ turn counterclockwise and install the distributor into the engine. The rotor should turn back to align with the mark if the distributor body has not rotated and is fully seated. Install the hold-down clamp, lockwasher and bolt(s) but do not tighten fully.

2. Connect the wiring harness and install the distributor cap. If any plug wires were removed from the cap reinstall them.

3. Start the engine, allow it to reach normal operating temperature and check/reset the ignition timing.

NOTE: If the engine has been turned with the distributor removed, or if marks were not drawn, it will be necessary to initially time the engine. Follow the next procedure.

INSTALLATION, ENGINE DISTURBED

1. It is necessary to place the no. 1 cylinder in the firing position to correctly install the distributor.

2. Remove the no. 1 cylinder spark plug. Turn the engine until the piston in no. 1 cylinder is moving up on the compression stroke. This can be determined by placing your thumb over the spark plug hole and feeling the air being forced out of the cylinder. Stop turning the engine when the marks on the crankshaft pulley and the timing gear cover are in alignment at TDC ("O" mark).

3. Install the rotor and align the rotor tip with no. 1 spark plug terminal tower position when the cap is installed. To locate no. 1 position, temporarily install the distributor cap and mark the side of the distributor body just below the cap terminal tower.

4. Remove the cap. Align the rotor with the no. 1 mark on the distributor body.

5. Refer to Steps 1–3 of proceeding distributor installation.

Alternator

Refer to the Electrical section of the Unit Repair for detailed alternator test and overhaul procedures.

CAUTION

Since the AC generator and regulator are designed for use on only one polarity system, the following precautions must be observed.

1. The polarity of the battery, generator and regulator must be matched and considered before making any electrical connections in the system.

2. When connecting a booster battery, be sure to connect the negative battery terminal to ground and the positive battery terminals together.

3. When connecting a charger to the battery, connect the charger positive lead to the battery positive terminal. Connect the charger negative lead to the battery negative terminal.

4. Never operate the AC generator on open circuit. Be sure that all connections in the circuit are clean and tight.

5. Do not short across or ground any of the terminals on the AC generator.

6. Do not attempt to polarize the AC generator.

7. Do not use test lamps of more than 12V for checking diode continuity.

8. Avoid long soldering times when replacing diodes or transistors. Prolonged heat is damaging to these units.

1. Rotor
2. Front bearing retainer
3. Collar (inner)
4. Bearing
5. Washer
6. Front housing
7. Collar (outer)
8. Fan
9. Pulley
10. Lockwasher
11. Pulley nut
12. Terminal assembly
13. Rectifier bridge
14. Regulator
15. Brush assembly
16. Screw
17. Stator
18. Insulating washer
19. Capacitor
20. Diode trio
21. Rear housing
22. Throughbolt
23. Bearing and seal assembly

Exploded view of an alternator

9. Disconnect the battery ground terminal when servicing any AC system. This will prevent the possibility of accidentally reversing polarity.

REMOVAL & INSTALLATION

1. Remove the negative battery cable from the battery.
2. Remove the wire terminals attached to the rear of the alternator.
3. Loosen the bolt holding the adjusting bar and the pivot bolt at the opposite side of the alternator.
4. Move the alternator inward to relieve the belt tension and remove the belt.
5. Remove the adjusting bar and pivot bolts and remove the alternator from the engine.
6. Install the alternator in the reverse procedure of the disassembly.
7. When installing the belt, adjust to allow ½ inch play on the longest run between the pulleys.

Voltage Regulator

The voltage regulator is an integral part of the Delco alternator. Refer to the Unit Repair Section for the integral voltage regulator removal and installation procedures.

Starter

REFERENCE

Refer to the Electrical section of the Unit Repair for detailed starter test and overhaul procedures.

REMOVAL & INSTALLATION

1. Disconnect the battery ground cable.
2. If necessary, raise the vehicle to gain working clearance.
3. Remove the positive battery lead from the starter or solenoid. Remove remaining wires as necessary.
4. Remove the starter retaining bolts and remove the starter from the vehicle.
5. The installation is in the reverse order of the removal procedure.

On some models, the transmission oil filler tube may have to be removed.

ENGINE MECHANICAL

Engine

REMOVAL & INSTALLATION

4–150

1. Disconnect the battery cables.

2. Remove the air cleaner.
3. Remove the hood.

CAUTION

If the engine has been recently operated, use care to prevent scalding by hot coolant. The system is pressurized.

4. Drain the radiator.
5. Remove the lower radiator hose.
6. Remove the upper radiator hose and coolant recovery hose.
7. Remove the fan shroud and disconnect the transmission fluid cooler tubing (automatic transmission).
8. Remove the radiator/condenser (if equipped with A/C).
9. Remove the fan assembly and install a 5/16 × 1/2-inch SAE capscrew through the fan pulley into the water pump flange to maintain the pulley and water pump in alignment when the crankshaft is rotated.
10. Disconnect the heater hoses.
11. Disconnect the throttle linkages, cruise control cable (if equipped) and throttle valve rod.
12. Disconnect the wires from the starter motor solenoid and disconnect CEC System wire harness connector.
13. Disconnect the fuel pipe from the fuel pump.
14. If equipped with air conditioning, remove the service valves and cap the compressor ports.
15. Disconnect the fuel return hose from the fuel filter.
16. Remove the power brake vacuum check valve from the booster, if equipped.
17. If equipped with power steering:
   a. disconnect the power steering hoses from the fittings at the steering gear
   b. drain the pump reservoir
   c. cap the fittings on the hoses and steering gear to prevent foreign objects from entering the system
18. Identify, tag and disconnect all necessary wire connectors and vacuum hoses.
19. Raise the vehicle.
20. Remove the starter motor.
21. Disconnect the exhaust pipe from the manifold.
22. Remove the flywheel/converter housing access cover. On models with automatic transmission, mark the converter and drive plate location and remove the converter-to-drive plate bolts.
23. Remove the upper flywheel/converter housing bolts and loosen the bottom bolts.
24. Remove the engine mount cushion-to-engine compartment bracket bolts.
25. Attach a lifting device to the engine.
26. Raise the engine off the front supports.
27. Place a support stand under the converter (or flywheel) housing.
28. Remove the remaining converter (or flywheel) housing bolts.
29. Lift the engine out of the engine compartment.
30. Installation is the reverse of removal.

Item	Ft. lbs.
Exhaust pipe to manifold	17
Torque converter drive plate to crankshaft bolts	60
Clutch housing spacer–to–block	27
Clutch housing–to–block	43
Engine mounts	35

4–151

1. Disconnect the battery.
2. Remove the air cleaner.
3. Jack up the vehicle and support it on jackstands.

4. Disconnect the exhaust pipe from the manifold.
5. Disconnect the oxygen sensor.
6. Disconnect the wires from the starter.
7. Unbolt the starter and remove it from the vehicle.
8. Disconnect the wires from the distributor and oil pressure sending unit.
9. Remove the engine mount nuts.
10. On vehicles with manual transmission, remove the clutch slave cylinder and flywheel inspection plate.
11. Remove the clutch or converter housing-to-engine bolts.
12. On vehicle with automatic transmission, disconnect the converter from the drive plate.
13. Lower the vehicle.
14. Support the transmission with a jack.
15. Tag all hoses at the carburetor and remove them.
16. Disconnect the mixture control solenoid wire from the carburetor. (not all vehicles have these)
17. Disconnect the wires from the alternator.
18. Disconnect the throttle cable from the bracket and the carburetor.
19. Disconnect the choke and solenoid wires at the carburetor.
20. Disconnect the temperature sender wire.
21. Drain the radiator at the drain cock, then remove the lower hose.
22. Remove the upper radiator hose and the heater hoses.
23. Remove the fan shroud, and radiator.
24. Disconnect the power steering hoses at the pump.
25. Attach a shop crane to the engine and lift it out of the vehicle.

NOTE: The manual transmission may have to be raised slightly to allow a smooth separation.

26. Installation is the reverse of removal.
Observe the following torque values:

Item	Ft. Lbs.
Clutch/converter housing-to-engine	35

Item	Ft. Lbs.
Clutch slave cylinder	18
Engine mount nuts	34
Starter mounting bolts	27
Starter bracket nut	40 in. lbs.
Exhaust pipe-to-manifold nuts	35

4–173

1. Disconnect the battery cables.
2. Remove the air cleaner.
3. Remove the hood.

───── **CAUTION** ─────

DO NOT remove the block drain plugs or loosen radiator draincock with the system hot and under pressure because serious burns from coolant can occur.

NOTE: DO NOT WASTE reusable coolant. If the solution is clean and is being drained only for service, drain coolant into a clean container for reuse.

4. Drain the radiator.
5. Remove the lower radiator hose.
6. Remove the upper radiator hose and coolant recovery hose.
7. Remove the fan shroud.
8. Disconnect the transmission fluid cooler tube fittings.
9. Remove the radiator/condenser (if equipped with A/C).
10. Remove the fan assembly.
11. Remove the heater hoses.
12. Disconnect the throttle linkage, including the cruise control cable and automatic transmission throttle valve cable.
13. Remove the power brake booster hose.
14. Identify, mark and disconnect the necessary wire connectors and vacuum hoses.
15. Remove the power steering pump assembly and lay aside.
16. Disconnect the fuel tubing fittings at the fuel pump.
17. Disconnect the hoses from the A/C compressor.
18. Raise and support the vehicle.
19. Remove the exhaust pipes from the exhaust manifold.
20. Disconnect the exhaust pipe at the catalytic converter flange and allow the exhaust pipe to drop out of the way.
21. Remove the flywheel/converter housing access cover.
22. Remove the torque converter bolts.
23. Disconnect the wires at the starter motor.
24. Remove the flywheel/converter housing bolts.
25. Lower the vehicle.
26. Place a support under the transmission.
27. Remove the air pump and hose from the bracket.
28. Attach an engine lifting device to the engine.
29. Remove the engine mount through bolts.
30. Disconnect the ground strap at the rear of the left cylinder head.
31. Remove the engine from the engine compartment.
32. Installation is the reverse of removal, observe the following torques:

Item	Ft. lb.
Engine mounting bracket	70–92
Engine torque strut	30–40
Drive plate-to-torque converter	25–35
Transmission-to-block	48–63

232 and 258 Sixes

NOTE: This operation requires discharging the air conditioning system. This requires special tools and skills for safety reasons. It should not be attempted by untrained persons.

1. Remove the hood after marking the hinge locations. The hood need not be removed on most CJ series.
2. Remove the air cleaner.
3. Drain the coolant. Disconnect the radiator hoses. Disconnect automatic transmission cooler lines from the radiator. If there is a radiator shroud, remove it, then remove the radiator.

Exploded view of a starter motor

4. Remove the fan.

5. Remove and set aside the power steering pump and belt. Do not disconnect the hydralic lines.

6. Bleed the compressor refrigerant charge. See the note at the start of this procedure. Remove the condenser and receiver assembly.

7. Disconnect all wires, lines, linkage, and hoses from the engine.

8. Drain the oil and remove the filter.

9. Remove both engine front support cushion-to-frame retaining nuts.

10. Disconnect the exhaust pipe at the support bracket and the manifold.

11. Support the engine with the lifting equipment.

12. Remove the front support cushion and bracket assemblies from the engine.

13. Remove the transfer case lever boot, the floor mat, and the transmission access cover.

14. On automatic transmissions, remove the upper bolts holding the bellhousing to the engine adapter plate. On manual transmissions, remove the upper bolts holding the clutch housing to the engine.

15. Remove the starter.

16. On automatics, remove the two adapter plate inspection covers. Mark the relationship of the converter to the flex plate and remove the converter-to-flex plate bolts. Remove the rest of the bolts holding the bellhousing to the adapter plate. On manual transmissions, remove the clutch housing lower cover and the rest of the bolts holding the clutch housing to the engine.

17. Support the transmission with a floor jack and remove the engine by pulling it forward and upward.

To install the engines:

1. Lower the engine into place and align it with the bellhousing or clutch housing. Make sure the manual transmission clutch shaft aligns with the splines of the clutch driven plate.

2. On automatics, install the bellhousing-to-engine adapter plate bolts. On manuals, install the clutch housing-to-engine bolts. Torque the bolts to 25–28 ft. lbs. at the top and 40–45 ft. lbs. at the bottom.

3. Remove the floor jack.

4. Align the marks made in step 16 and install the converter-to-flex plate bolts, torquing them to 21–23 ft. lbs.

5. Install the two engine adapter plate inspection covers or the clutch housing lower cover.

6. Replace the starter.

7. Install the front support cushion and bracket assemblies to the engine, torquing the bolts to 25–30 ft. lbs. Lower the engine onto the frame supports. Install the front support cushion retaining nuts, torquing them to 25–30 ft. lbs.

8. Connect the exhaust pipe at the support bracket and manifold. A new manifold seal is advisable.

9. Install the oil filter.

10. Replace all the items removed in step seven.

11. Replace the air conditioning condenser and receiver assembly and recharge the system.

12. Replace the power steering pump and belt. Install the fan and tighten the bolts to 15–25 ft. lbs.

13. Replace and reconnect the radiator. Replace the oil cooler lines. Fill the cooling system.

14. Fill the crankcase and replace the air cleaner. Install the transmission access cover, floor mat, and transfer case lever boot. Replace the hood.

V8's

NOTE: This operation requires discharging the air conditioning system. This requires special tools and skills. For safety reasons, it should not be attempted by untrained persons.

The engine is removed without the transmission and bellhousing.

1. On the Commando, Cherokee, Truck, and Wagoneer, the hood must be removed. Mark the hinge locations at the hood panel for alignment during installation. Remove the hood from the hinges.

2. Remove the air cleaner assembly.

3. Drain the cooling system and disconnect the upper and lower radiator hoses. If equipped with automatic transmission, disconnect the cooler lines from the radiator.

NOTE: If the vehicle is equipped with a radiator shroud, it is necessary to separate the shroud from the radiator to facilitate removal and installation of the radiator and engine fan.

4. Remove the radiator.

5. Remove the engine fan.

6. If equipped with power steering, remove the pump from the engine and lay it aside. Do not disconnect the hoses.

7. If equipped with air conditioning, turn both service valves clockwise to the front seated position. Bleed the compressor refrigerant charge by slowly loosening the service valve fittings. Disconnect the condenser and evaporator lines from the compressor. Disconnect the receiver outlet at the disconnect coupling. Remove the condenser and receiver assembly.

8. Remove the battery and tray.

9. If equipped, remove cruise command vacuum servo bellows and mounting bracket as a complete assembly.

10. On CJ models, (1977–82) remove left cushion front support cushion and bracket from cylinder block.

11. Disconnect all wires, lines linkage, and hoses which are connected to the engine.

12. If equipped with automatic transmission, disconnect the transmission filler tube bracket from the right cylinder head. Do not remove the filler tube from the transmission.

13. Remove both engine front support cushion-to-frame retaining nuts.

14. Support the weight of the engine with a lifting device.

15. On CJ and Commando models, remove the transfer case shift lever boot, floor (if so equipped), and transmission access cover.

16. Remove the upper bolts which secure the transmission bellhousing to the engine adapter plate on vehicles equipped with automatic transmission. If equipped with manual transmission, remove the upper bolts which secure the clutch housing to the engine.

17. Disconnect the exhaust pipes at the exhaust manifolds and support bracket.

18. Remove the starter motor.

19. Support the transmission with a floor jack.

20. If equipped with automatic transmission, remove the two engine adapter plate inspection covers. Mark the assembled position of the converter and flex plate and remove the converter-to-flex plate cap screws. Remove the remaining bolts which secure the transmission bellhousing to the engine adapter plate.

21. If equipped with manual transmission, remove the clutch housing lower cover and the remaining bolts which secure the clutch housing to the engine.

22. Remove the engine by pulling upward and forward.

NOTE: If equipped with power brakes, care must be taken to avoid damaging the power unit while removing the engine.

To install the engine:

1. Lower the engine slowly into the engine compartment and align with the transmission bellhousing (automatic transmission) or clutch housing (manual transmission). On manual transmissions, make certain the clutch shaft is aligned properly with the splines of the clutch driven plate.

2. Install the transmission bellhousing-to-engine adapter plate bolts (automatic transmission) or the clutch housing to engine bolts (manual transmission). Tighten the bolts to the specified torque. Remove the floor jack which was used to support the transmission.

3. If equipped with automatic transmission, align the marks previously made on the converter and flex plate, install the converter-to-flex plate cap screws and tighten to the specified torque.

4. Install the two engine adapter plate inspection covers (automatic transmission) or the clutch housing lower cover (manual transmission).

5. Install the starter motor.

6. Lower the engine onto the frame supports, remove the lifting device and install the front support cushion retaining nuts. Tighten the nuts to the specified torque.

7. Connect the exhaust pipes at the exhaust manifolds and support bracket.

8. If equipped with automatic transmission, connect the transmission filler tube bracket to the right cylinder head.

9. On Wagoneers and Cherokees, install the heater core housing and charcoal canister to the firewall.

10. If removed, install the battery and tray.

11. Connect all wires, lines linkage and hoses which were previously disconnected from the engine.

12. If removed, install the air conditioning condenser and receiver assembly. Connect the receiver outlet to the disconnect coupling. Connect the condenser and evaporator lines to the compressor. Purge the compressor of air.

NOTE: Both service valves must be open before the air conditioning system is operated.

13. If equipped with power steering, connect the power steering, pump to the engine.

14. Install the engine fan and tighten the retaining bolts to the specified torque.

15. Install the radiator and connect the upper and lower hoses. If equipped with automatic transmission, connect the cooler lines.

16. Fill the cooling system to the specified level.

17. Install the air cleaner assembly. Install cruise command vacuum servo bellows and mounting bracket.

18. Start the engine. Check all connections for leaks. Stop the engine.

19. If removed, install the transmission access cover, floor mat and transfer case shift lever boot.

20. If removed, install the transmission access cover, floor mat and transfer case shift level boot.

Rocker Shafts and Rocker Studs

REMOVAL & INSTALLATION

4-150

1. Remove the valve cover.
2. Remove the capscrews at each bridge and pivot assembly.
3. Alternately loosen the capscrews one turn at a time to avoid damaging the bridge.
4. Remove the bridges, pivots and corresponding pair of rocker arms.
5. Installation is the reverse of removal. Tighten capscrews to 19 ft. lbs.

4-151

1. Remove the rocker arm cover.
2. Remove the rocker arm capscrew and ball.
3. Remove the rocker arm.
4. Installation is the reverse of removal. Torque the capscrew to 20 ft. lbs. DO NOT OVERTORQUE!

6-173

NOTE: Some engines are assembled using RTV (Room Temperature Vulcanizing silicone sealant in place of rocker

arm cover gasket. If the engine was assembled using RTV, never use a gasket when reassembling. Conversely, if the engine was assembled using a rocker arm cover gasket, never replace it with RTV.

When using RTV, an ⅛ inch bead is sufficient. Always run the bead on the inside of the bolt holes.

Rocker arms are removed by removing the adjusting nut. Be sure to adjust valve lash after replacing rocker arms.

NOTE: When replacing an exhaust rocker, move an old intake rocker arm to the exhaust rocker arm stud and install the new rocker arm on the intake stud.

Cylinder heads use threaded rocker arm studs. If the threads in the head are damaged or stripped, the head can be retapped and a helical type insert installed.

4-151 rocker arm and pushrod removal

6-232 and 258

On these engines the rocker arms pivot on a bridged pivot that is secured with two capscrews. The bridged pivots maintain proper rocker arm-to-valve tip alignment.

1. Remove the rocker cover and gasket.
2. Remove the two capscrews at each bridged pivot, backing off each capscrew one turn at a time to avoid breaking the bridge.
3. Remove each bridged pivot and corresponding pair of rocker arms and place them on a clean surface in the same order as they are removed.

NOTE: Bridged pivots, capscrews, rockers, and pushrods must all be reinstalled in their original positions.

4. Clean all the parts in a suitable solvent and use compressed air to blow out the oil passages in the pushrods and the

rocker arms. Replace any excessively worn parts.

5. Install rocker arms, pushrods and bridged pivots in the same positions from which they were removed.

NOTE: Be sure that the bottom end of each pushrod is centered in the plunger cap of each hydraulic valve tappet.

6. Install the capscrews and tighten them one turn at a time, alternating between the two screws on each bridge. Tighten the capscrews to 21 ft. lbs.
7. Install the rocker cover with new gasket.

V8 Engines

1. Remove the cylinder head cover and gasket.
2. Loosen the bridged pivot capscrews a turn at a time, so as not to break the bridge.
3. Remove the rocker arm and bridge assembly from the cylinder head.

To install:
1. Install the rocker arms and bridge assembly on the cylinder head, and align the push rods.
2. Install the capscrews and tighten each one a turn at a time to avoid breaking the bridge. Tighten the capscrews to 19 ft. lbs. torque.
3. Install the cylinder head cover with a new gasket and torque the cover bolts to 50 in. lbs.

Valve Arrangement

4 Cylinder Engines:
I E I E E I E I → Front
6 Cylinder Engines:
E I I E E I I E E I I E → Front
V8 Engines:
E I I E E I I E
E I I E E I I E → Front

Bridged pivot type rocker arms found on 6 and V8 engines

Crankshaft Pulley Assembly (Vibration Damper)

REMOVAL & INSTALLATION

1. Remove drive belts from pulley.
2. Remove the retaining bolts and separate the pulley from the vibration damper.
3. Remove the vibration damper retaining bolt from the crankshaft end.
4. Using a vibration damper puller, remove the damper from the crankshaft.
5. Upon installation, align the key slot of the pulley hub to the crankshaft key. Complete the assembly in the reverse order of removal. Torque the retaining bolts to specifications.

Cylinder Head

REMOVAL & INSTALLATION

4-150

1. Disconnect the battery cables.

―――――― CAUTION ――――――
Do not perform this procedure on a hot engine.

2. Drain the coolant and disconnect the hoses at the thermostat housing.
3. Remove the air cleaner.
4. Remove the valve cover.
5. Remove the rocker arms, bridge and pivot assemblies. Remove the push rods.

NOTE: Retain the push rods, bridge, pivot and rocker arms in the same order as removed to facilitate installation in the original positions.

6. Disconnect the power steering pump bracket. Set the pump and bracket aside. Do not disconnect the hoses.
7. Remove the intake and exhaust manifolds from the cylinder head.
8. If equipped with air conditioning, perform the following:
   a. remove the air conditioner compressor drive belt
   b. loosen the alternator drive belt
   c. remove the A/C compressor/alternator bracket-to-cylinder head mounting screw

NOTE: The serpentine drive belt tension is released by loosening the alternator.

   d. remove the bolts from the A/C compressor (if equipped) and alternator mounting bracket and set the compressor aside
9. Disconnect the ignition wires and remove the spark plugs.
10. Disconnect the temperature sending unit wire connector.
11. Remove the cylinder head bolts, cylinder head and gasket.

12. Thoroughly clean the machined surfaces of the cylinder head and block. Remove all gasket material and cement.
13. Installation is the reverse of removal, with the following recommendations.

―――――― CAUTION ――――――
Do not apply sealing compound to the cylinder head and block machined surfaces. Do not allow the sealing compound to enter the cylinder bores.

14. Apply an even coat of Perfect Seal sealing compound, or equivalent, to both sides of the replacement cylinder head gasket and position the gasket on the cylinder block with word TOP facing upward.
15. Torque the head bolts to 85 ft. lbs. in the sequence illustrated.

4-151 and 232 and 258 Sixes

NOTE: The 151 rocker cover is sealed with RTV silicone gasket material. Do not use a conventional Gasket.

1. Drain the cooling system and disconnect the hoses at the thermostat housing.
2. Remove the cylinder head cover (valve cover), the gasket, the rocker arm assembly, and the pushrods.

NOTE: The push rods must be replaced in their original positions.

3. Remove the intake and exhaust manifold from the cylinder head.
4. Disconnect the spark plug wires and remove the spark plugs to avoid damaging them.
5. Disconnect the temperature sending unit wire, ignition coil and bracket assembly and battery ground cable from the engine.
6. Remove the cylinder head bolts, cylinder head and gasket from the block.
7. To install reverse the procedure. Tighten the headbolts to the specified torque, in the proper sequence.

6-173

LEFT SIDE

1. Raise and support the truck.
2. Drain the coolant from the block and lower the car.

3. Remove the intake manifold.
4. Remove the crossover.
5. Remove the alternator and AIR pump brackets, if so equipped.
6. Remove the dipstick tube.
7. Loosen the rocker arm bolts and remove the pushrods. Keep the pushrods in the same order as removed.
8. Remove the cylinder head bolts in stages and in the reverse order of the tightening sequence.
9. Remove the cylinder head. Do not pry on the head to loosen it.
10. Installation is the reverse of removal. The words ''This side Up'' on the new cylinder head gasket should face upward. Coat the cylinder head bolts with sealer and torque to specifications in the sequence shown. Make sure the pushrods seat in the lifter seats and adjust the valves.

RIGHT SIDE

1. Raise the car and drain the coolant from the block.
2. Disconnect the exhaust pipe and lower the car.
3. If equipped, remove the cruise control servo bracket.
4. Remove the air management valve and hose.
5. Remove the intake manifold.
6. Remove the exhaust crossover.
7. Loosen the rocker arm nuts and remove the pushrods. Keep the pushrods in the order in which they were removed.
8. Remove the cylinder head bolts in stages and in the reverse order of the tightening sequence.
9. Remove the cylinder head. Do not pry on the cylinder head to loosen it.
10. Installation is the reverse of removal. The words ''This Side Up'' on the new cylinder head gasket should face upwards. Coat the cylinder head bolts with sealer and tighten them to specifications in the sequence shown. Make sure the lower ends of the pushrods seat in the lifter seats and adjust the valves.

V8 Engines

1. Drain the cooling system and cylinder block.

4-150 cylinder head torque sequence

6 cylinder engine cylinder head bolt tightening sequence

2. When removing the right cylinder head, it may be necessary to remove the heater core housing from the firewall.

3. Remove the valve cover(s) and gasket(s).

4. Remove the rocker arm assemblies and the push rods.

NOTE: The valve train components must be replaced in their original positions.

5. Remove the spark plugs to avoid damaging them.

6. Remove the intake manifold with the carburetor still attached.

7. Remove the exhaust pipes at the flange of the exhaust manifold. When replacing the exhaust pipes it is advisable to install new gaskets at the flange.

8. Loosen all of the drive belts.

9. Disconnect the battery ground cable and alternator bracket from the right cylinder head.

10. Disconnect the air pump and power steering pump brackets from the left cylinder head.

4-151 cylinder head bolt torque sequence

11. Remove the cylinder head bolts and lift the head(s) from the cylinder block.

12. Remove the cylinder head gasket from the head or the block.

13. To install, reverse the above procedure.

NOTE: Apply an even coat of sealing compound to both sides of the new head gasket only. Wire brush the cylinder head bolts, then lightly oil them prior to installation. First, tighten all bolts to 80 ft.

lbs. then tighten to the specified torque. Follow the correct sequence.

Intake Manifold

REMOVAL & INSTALLATION

4-150

NOTE: It is necessary to remove the carburetor from the intake manifold before the manifold is removed. After removing the carburetor from the intake manifold, it may be set to one side with vacuum hoses still attached.

---- **CAUTION** ----
If the engine has been recently operated, use care to prevent scalding by hot coolant. The system is pressurized.

1. Remove the radiator cap and draincock to drain the coolant.

NOTE: Do not waste reusable coolant. If the coolant is acceptable for reuse, drain into a clean container.

2. Remove the air cleaner. Disconnect the fuel pipe, carburetor air horn vent hose, idle speed control vacuum hose and wire connector.

3. Disconnect the coolant hoses from the intake manifold.

4. Disconnect the throttle cable from the bellcrank.

5. Disconnect the PCV valve vacuum hose from the intake manifold.

6. Remove the vacuum advance CTO valve vacuum hoses.

7. Disconnect the feedback system coolant temperature sender wire connector (located on the intake manifold).

8. Disconnect the vacuum hose from the EGR valve.

9. Disconnect the intake manifold electric heater wire connector.

10. Remove the power steering mounting bracket, if equipped.

11. Detach the power steering pump and set aside, if equipped.

12. Do not remove the hoses.

13. Disconnect the throttle valve linkage, if equipped with automatic transmission.

14. Disconnect the EGR valve tube from the intake manifold.

15. Remove the intake manifold attaching screws, nuts and clamps. Remove the intake manifold. Discard the gasket.

16. Clean the mating surfaces of the manifold and cylinder head.

NOTE: If the manifold is being replaced, ensure all fittings, etc. are transferred to the replacement manifold.

17. Installation is the reverse of removal. Torque manifold bolts to 23 ft. lbs.

4-151

1. Remove battery negative cable.

2. Remove air cleaner and PCV valve hose.

---- **CAUTION** ----
Do not remove block drain plugs or loosen radiator draincock with system hot and under pressure because serious burns from coolant can occur.

3. Drain cooling system.

NOTE: Do not waste reusable coolant. If solution is clean, drain into a clean container for reuse.

4. Tag and remove vacuum hoses (ensure distributor vacuum advance hose is removed).

5. Disconnect fuel pipe and electrical wire connections from carburetor.

6. Disconnect carburetor throttle linkage. Remove carburetor and carburetor spacer.

7. Remove bellcrank and throttle linkage brackets and move to one side for clearance.

8. Remove heater hose at intake manifold.

9. Remove alternator. Note position of spacers for installation.

10. Remove manifold-to-cylinder head bolts and remove manifold.

11. Position replacement gasket and install replacement manifold on cylinder head. Start all bolts.

12. Tighten all bolts with 37 ft. lbs. torque.

13. Connect heater hose to intake manifold.

14. Install bellcrank and throttle linkage brackets.

15. Connect carburetor throttle linkage to brackets and bellcrank.

16. Install carburetor spacer and tighten bolts with 15 ft. lbs. torque.

17. Install carburetor and gasket. Tighten nuts with 15 ft. lbs. torque.

18. Install fuel pipe and electrical wire connections. Install vacuum hoses.

19. Install battery negative cable.

V8 engine cylinder head bolt tightening sequence

4–150 intake manifold

6–173 head bolt torque sequence

6–173 intake manifold

CAUTION

Use extreme caution when engine is operating. Do not stand in direct line with fan. Do not put hands near pulleys, belts or fan. Do not wear loose clothing.

20. Refill cooling system. Start engine and inspect for leaks.

21. Install air cleaner and PCV valve hose.

232 and 258 Sixes

The intake manifold and exhaust manifold are mounted externally on the left side of the engine and are attached to the cylinder head. The intake and exhaust manifolds are removed as a unit. On some engines, an exhaust gas recirculation valve is mounted on the side of the intake manifold.

1. Disconnect negative battery cable. Remove the air cleaner and carburetor.

2. Disconnect the accelerator cable from the accelerator bellcrank.

3. Disconnect the PCV vacuum hose from the intake manifold.

4. Disconnect the distributor vacuum hose and electrical wires at the TCS solenoid vacuum valve.

5. Remove the TCS solenoid vacuum valve and bracket from the intake manifold. In some cases it might not be necessary to remove the TCS unit.

6. If so equipped, disconnect the EGR valve vacuum hoses.

7. Remove the power steering mounting bracket and pump and set it aside without disconnecting the hoses.

8. Remove the EGR valve, if so equipped.

9. Disconnect the exhaust pipe from the manifold flange. Disconnect the spark CTO hoses and remove the oxygen sensor.

10. Remove the manifold attaching bolts, nuts and clamps.

11. Separate the intake manifold and exhaust manifold from the engine as an assembly. Discard the gasket.

12. If either manifold is to be replaced, they should be separated at the heat riser area.

13. Clean the mating surfaces of the manifolds and the cylinder head before replacing the manifolds. Replace them in reverse order of the above procedure with a new gasket. Tighten the bolts and nuts to the specified torque in the proper sequence.

6–173

1. Remove the rocker covers.

2. Drain the cooling system.

3. If equipped, remove the AIR pump and bracket.

4. Remove the distributor cap. Mark the position of the ignition rotor in relation to the distributor body, and remove the distributor. Do not crank the engine with the distributor removed.

5. Remove the heater and radiator hoses from the intake manifold.

6. Remove the power brake vacuum hose.

7. Disconnect and label the vacuum hoses. Remove the EFE pipe from the rear of the manifold.

8. Remove the carburetor linkage. Disconnect and plug the fuel line.

9. Remove the manifold retaining bolts and nuts.

10. Remove the intake manifold. Remove and discard the gaskets, and scrape off the old silicone seal from the front and rear ridges.

To install:

1. The gaskets are marked for right and left side installation; do not interchange them. Clean the sealing surface of the engine block, and apply a $3/16$ in. bead of silicone sealer to each ridge.

2. Install the new gaskets onto the heads. The gaskets will have to be cut slightly to fit past the center pushrods. Do not cut any more material than necessary. Hold the gaskets in place by extending the ridge bead of sealer $1/4$ in. onto the gasket ends.

3. Install the intake manifold. The area

between the ridges and the manifold should be completely sealed.

4. Install the retaining bolts and nuts, and tighten in sequence to 23 ft. lbs. Do not overtighten; the manifold is made from aluminum, and can be warped or cracked with excessive force.

5. The rest of installation is the reverse of removal. Adjust the ignition timing after installation, and check the coolant level after the engine has warmed up.

4–151 intake manifold bolt torque sequence

V8 Engines

1. Disconnect negative battery cable. Drain the coolant from the radiator.

2. Remove the air cleaner assembly.

3. Disconnect the spark plug wires. Remove the spark plug wire brackets from the valve covers, and the bypass valve bracket.

4. Disconnect the upper radiator hose and the by-pass hose from the intake manifold. Disconnect the heater hose from the rear of the manifold.

5. Disconnect the ignition coil bracket and lay the coil aside.

6. Disconnect the TCS solenoid vacuum valve from the right side valve cover.

7. Disconnect all lines, hoses, linkages and wires from the carburetor and intake manifold and TCS components as required.

8. Disconnect the air delivery hoses at the air distribution manifolds.

9. Disconnect the air pump diverter valve and lay the valve and the bracket assembly, including the hoses, forward of the engine.

10. Remove the intake manifold after removing the cap bolts that hold it in place. Remove and discard the side gaskets and the end seals.

11. Clean the mating surfaces of the intake manifold and the cylinder head before replacing the intake manifold. Use new gaskets and tighten the cap bolts to the correct torque. Install in reverse order of the above procedure.

NOTE: There is no specified tightening sequence for this intake manifold. Start at the center bolts and work outward.

Exhaust Manifolds

REMOVAL & INSTALLATION

4–150

1. Remove the intake manifold.
2. Disconnect the EGR valve tube.
3. Disconnect the exhaust pipe from the exhaust manifold.
4. Disconnect the oxygen sensor wire connector.
5. Remove the sensor from the manifold if a replacement manifold is to be installed.
6. Remove the nuts from the end studs. Remove the exhaust manifold.
7. Installation is the reverse of removal. Torque manifold nuts 23 ft. lbs., oxygen sensor 35 ft. lbs.

4–151

1. Remove air cleaner and heated air tube.
2. Remove engine oil dipstick tube attaching bolt.
3. Remove oxygen sensor, if equipped.
4. Raise vehicle and disconnect exhaust pipe from manifold. Lower vehicle.
5. Remove exhaust manifold bolts and remove manifold and gasket.
6. Install replacement gasket and exhaust manifold on cylinder head. Tighten all bolts to 39 foot-pounds torque.
7. Install dipstick tube attaching bolt.

232 and 258 Sixes

The intake and exhaust manifolds of the 232 and 258 cu. in. Sixes must be removed together. See the procedure for removing and installing the intake manifold.

6–173

LEFT SIDE

1. Remove the air cleaner. Remove the carburetor heat stove pipe.
2. Remove the air supply plumbing from the exhaust manifold.
3. Raise and support the car. Unbolt and remove the exhaust pipe at the manifold.
4. Unbolt and remove the manifold.

To install:

1. Clean the mating surfaces of the cylinder head and manifold. Install the manifold onto the head, and install the retaining bolts finger tight.
2. Tighten the manifold bolts in a circular pattern, working from the center to the ends, to 25 ft. lbs. in two stages.
3. Connect the exhaust pipe to the manifold.
4. The remainder of installation is the reverse of removal.

RIGHT SIDE

1. Raise and support the car.
2. Tighten the exhaust pipe-to-manifold flange bolts until they break off. Remove the pipe from the manifold. Later models are equipped with flange bolts.

Intake and exhaust manifolds on 6 cylinder engine with oxygen sensor

4–151 exhaust manifold bolt torque sequence

6 cylinder engine intake manifold bolt tightening sequence

3. Lower the car. Remove the spark plug wires from the plugs. Number them first if they are not already labeled.

4. Remove the air supply pipes from the manifold. Remove the PULSAIR bracket bolts from the rocker cover, on models so equipped, then remove the pipe assembly.

5. Remove the manifold retaining bolts and remove the manifold.

To install:

1. Clean the mating surfaces of the cylinder head and manifold. Position the manifold against the head and install the retaining bolts finger tight.

2. Tighten the bolts in a circular pattern, working from the center to the ends, to 25 ft. lbs. in two stages.

3. Install the air supply system.

4. Install the spark plug wires.

5. Raise and support the truck. Connect the exhaust pipe to the manifold and install new flange bolts.

LH

RH

6–173 exhaust manifold

V8 Engines

1. Disconnect the spark plug wires.

2. Disconnect the air delivery hose at the distribution manifold.

3. Remove the air distribution manifold and the injection trubes.

4. Disconnect the exhaust pipe at the manifold.

5. Remove the exhaust manifold attaching bolts and washers along with the spark plug shields.

6. Separate the exhaust manifold from the cylinder head.

7. Install in reverse order of the above procedure. Clean the mating surfaces and tighten the attaching bolts to the correct torque.

Timing Gear Cover

TIMING GEAR COVER & OIL SEAL REPLACEMENT

4–151

1. Disconnect the battery ground.

2. Remove the crankshaft pulley hub.

3. Remove the alternator bracket.

4. Remove the fan and radiator shroud.

5. Remove the oil pan-to-timing case cover bolts.

6. Pull the cover forward just enough to allow cutting the oil pan front seal flush with the block on both sides of the cover. Use a sharp knife or razor.

7. Remove the front cover.

8. Clean the gasket surface on the block and cover.

9. Cut the tabs from the new oil pan front seal.

10. Install the seal on the cover, pressing the tips into the holes provided in the cover.

11. Coat a new gasket with sealer and place on the cover.

12. Apply a ⅛ inch bead of RTV sealant to the joint formed at the oil pan and block.

13. Install an aligning tool such as tool J-23042 in the timing case cover seal.

NOTE: It is important that an aligning tool is used to avoid seal damage and to ensure a tight, even seal fit.

14. Position the cover on the block and partially tighten the two oil pan-to-cover bolts.

15. Install the remaining bolts, and tighten all bolts to 45 in. lbs.

16. Install all other parts in reverse order of removal. Torque the fan assembly bolts to 18 ft. lbs.

4–150, 6–232 and 258

1. Remove the drive belts, engine fan and hub assembly, the accessory pulley, and vibration damper.

2. Remove the oil pan to timing chain cover screws and the screws that attach the cover to the block.

3. Raise the timing chain cover just high enough to detach the retaining nibs of the oil pan neoprene seal from the bottom side of the cover. This must be done to prevent pulling the seal end tabs away from the tongues of the oil pan gaskets which would cause a leak.

4. Remove the timing chain cover and gasket from the engine.

5. Use a razor blade to cut off the oil pan seal end tabs flush with the front face of the cylinder block and remove the seal. Clean the timing chain cover, oil pan, and cylinder block surfaces.

6. Apply seal compound (Perfect Seal, or equivalent) to both sides of replacement timing case cover gasket and position gasket on cylinder block.

7. Cut end tabs off replacement oil pan gasket corresponding to pieces cut off original gasket. Cement these pieces on oil pan.

8. Coat oil pan seal end tabs generously with Permatex No. 2, or equivalent, and position seal on timing case cover.

9. Position timing case cover on engine. Place timing case cover alignment tool and seal installer J-22248 in crankshaft opening of cover.

10. Install cover-to-block screws and oil pan-to-cover screws. Tighten cover-to-block screws with 5 ft. lbs. torque and oil pan-to-cover screws with 11 ft. lbs. torque.

11. Remove cover aligning tool and position replacement oil seal on tool with seal lip facing outward. Apply light film of Perfect Seal, or equivalent, on outside diameter of seal.

12. Insert draw screw from tool J-9163 into seal installing tool. Tighten nut against tool until tool contacts cover.

13. Remove tools and apply light film of engine oil to seal lip.

Cutting the pan gasket on the 4 cylinder engine

Applying sealant on the 4–151

ALIGNMENT TOOL INSTALLED

4–151 timing case cover alignment tool in place

SCREW-PART OF J-9163

TOOL J-22248

Timing case cover seal installation 6 cylinder engine

14. Install vibration damper and tighten retaining screw with 80 ft. lbs. torque.

15. Install damper pulley. Tighten cap-screws with 20 ft. lbs. torque.

16. Install engine fan and hub assembly.

17. Install drive belt(s).

Cover on Engine

1. Remove drive belts.

2. Remove vibration damper pulley.

3. Remove vibration damper.

4. Remove oil seal with tool J-9256.

5. Position replacement oil seal on timing case cover alignment tool and seal installer J-22248 with seal lip facing outward. Apply light film of Perfect Seal, or equivalent, to outside diameter of seal.

6. Insert draw screw from tool J-9163 into seal installing tool. Tighten nut against tool until tool contacts cover.

7. Remove tools. Apply light film of engine oil to seal lip.

8. Install vibration damper and tighten retaining bolt with 80 ft. lbs. torque.

9. Install damper pulley. Tighten cap-screws with 20 ft. lbs. torque.

10. Install drive belt(s).

6–173

———— CAUTION ————

The engines use a harmonic balancer. Breakage may occur if the balancer is hammered back onto the crankshaft. A press or special installation tool is necessary.

1. Remove the water pump.

2. Remove the compressor without disconnecting any A/C lines and lay it aside.

3. Remove harmonic balancer, using a puller.

NOTE: The outer ring (weight) of the harmonic balancer is bonded to the hub with rubber. The balancer must be removed with a puller which acts on the inner hub only. Pulling on the outer portion of the balancer will break the rubber bond or destroy the tuning of the torsional damper.

4. Disconnect the lower radiator hose and heater hose.

5. Remove timing gear cover attaching screws, and cover and gasket.

6. Clean all the gasket mounting surfaces on the front cover and block. Apply a continous $\frac{3}{32}$ in. bead of sealer (1052357

6 cylinder engine timing case cover seal removal

or equivalent) to front cover sealing surface and around coolant passage ports and central bolt holes.

7. Apply a bead of silicone sealer to the oil pan-to-cylinder block joint.

8. Install a centering tool in the crankcase snout hole in the front cover and install the cover.

9. Install the front cover bolts finger tight, remove the centering tool and tighten the cover bolts. Install the harmonic balancer, pulley, water pump, belts, radiator, and all other parts.

V8 Engines

1. Remove the negative battery cable.

2. Drain the cooling system and disconnect the radiator hoses and by-pass hose.

3. Remove all of the drive belts and the fan and spacer assembly.

4. Remove the alternator and the front portion of the alternator bracket as an assembly.

5. Disconnect the heater hose.

6. Remove the power steering pump, and/or the air pump, and the mounting bracket as an assembly. Do not disconnect the power steering hoses.

7. Remove the distributor cap and note the position of the rotor. Remove the distributor. (See the Engine Electrical Section.)

8. Remove the fuel pump.

9. Remove the vibration damper and pulley.

10. Remove the two front oil pan bolts and the bolts which secure the timing chain cover to the engine block.

NOTE: The timing gear cover retaining bolts vary in length and must be installed in the same locations from which they were removed.

11. Remove the cover by pulling forward until it is free of the locating dowel pins.

12. Clean the gasket surface of the cover and the engine block.

13. Pry out the original seal from inside the timing chain cover and clean the seal bore.

14. Drive the new seal into place from the inside with a block of wood until it contacts the outer flange of the cover.

15. Apply a light film of motor oil to the lips of the new seal.

16. Before reinstalling the timing gear cover, remove the lower locating dowel pin from the engine block. The pin is required for correct alignment of the cover and must either be reused or a replacement dowel pin installed after the cover is in position.

17. Cut both sides of the oil pan gasket flush with the engine block with a razor blade.

18. Trim a new gasket to correspond to the amount cut off at the oil pan.

19. Apply sealer to both sides of the new gasket and install the gasket on the timing case cover.

20. Install the new front oil pan seal.

21. Align the tongues of the new oil pan

Trim the timing gear cover gasket as indicated before installing on V8 engine

gasket pieces with the oil pan seal and cement them into place on the cover.

22. Apply a bead of sealer to the cutoff edges of the original oil pan gaskets.

23. Place the timing case cover into position and install the front oil pan bolts. Tighten the bolts slowly and evenly until the cover aligns with the upper locating dowel.

24. Install the lower dowel through the cover and drive it into the corresponding hole in the engine block.

25. Install the cover retaining bolts in the same locations from which they were removed. Tighten to 25 ft. lbs.

26. Assemble the remaining components in the reverse order of removal.

Timing Chain or Gears

REMOVAL & INSTALLATION

4–150

1. Remove the timing case cover as previously outlined.

2. Rotate the crankshaft until the zero timing mark on the crankshaft sprocket is closest to and on center line with the mark on the cam sprocket.

3. Remove the oil slinger from the crankshaft.

4. Remove the camshaft retaining bolt and remove the sprockets and chain as an assembly.

5. Installation is the reverse of removal, with the following recommendations:

   a. Turn the tensioner lever to the unlock (down) position.

   b. Pull the tensioner block toward the tensioner lever to compress the spring. Hold the block and turn the tensioner lever to the lock (up) position.

4–151

Refer to Camshaft removal and installation.

232 and 258 Sixes

1. Remove the drive belts, engine fan and hub assembly, accessory pulley, vibration damper and timing chain cover.

4–150 timing chain tensioner

4–150 timing mark alignment

2. Remove the oil seal from the timing chain cover.

3. Remove the camshaft sprocket retaining bolt and washer.

4. Rotate the crankshaft until the timing mark on the crankshaft sprocket is closest to and in a center line with the timing pointer of the camshaft sprocket.

5. Remove the crankshaft sprocket, camshaft sprocket and timing chain as an assembly. Disassemble the chain and sprockets.

Installation is as follows:

1. Assemble the timing chain, crankshaft sprocket and camshaft sprocket with the timing marks aligned.

2. Install the assembly to the crankshaft and the camshaft.

3. Install the camshaft sprocket retaining bolt and washer and tighten to 45–55 ft. lbs.

4. Install the timing chain cover and install a new oil seal.

5. Install the vibration damper, accessory pulley, engine fan and hub assembly and drive belts. Tighten the belts to the proper tension.

6–173

To replace the chain, remove the crankcase

front cover. This will allow access to the timing chain. Crank the engine until the marks punched on both sprockets are closest to one another and in line between the shaft centers. Take out the three bolts that hold the camshaft sprocket to the camshaft. This sprocket is a light press fit on the camshaft and will come off readily. It is located by a dowel. The chain comes off with the camshaft sprocket. A gear puller will be required to remove the camshaft sprocket.

Without disturbing the position of the engine, mount the new crank sprocket on the shaft, then mount the chain over the camshaft sprocket. Arrange the camshaft sprocket in such a way that the timing marks will line up between the shaft centers and the camshaft locating dowel will enter the dowel hole in the cam sprocket.

Place the cam sprocket, with its chain mounted over it, in position on the front of the camshaft and pull up with the three bolts that hold it to the camshaft.

After the sprockets are in place, turn the engine two full revolutions to make certain that the timing marks are in correct alignment between the shaft centers.

V8 Engines

1. Remove the timing chain cover and gasket.

2. Remove the crankshaft oil slinger.

3. Remove the camshaft sprocket retaining bolt and washer, distributor drive gear and fuel pump eccentric.

4. Rotate the crankshaft until the timing mark on the crankshaft sprocket is adjacent to, and on a center line with, the timing mark on the camshaft sprocket.

5. Remove the crankshaft sprocket, camshaft sprocket and timing chain as an assembly. Disassemble the chain and sprockets.

Installation is as follows:

1. Assemble the timing chain, crankshaft sprocket and camshaft sprocket with the timing marks on both sprockets aligned.

2. Install the assembly to the crankshaft and the camshaft.

3. Install the fuel pump eccentric, distributor drive gear, washer and retaining bolt. Tighten the bolt to 25–35 ft. lbs.

1 CYLINDER AT T.D.C.

4 CYLINDER AT T.D.C.

6–173 timing mark alignment

6 cylinder 232 and 258 timing gear alignment

Timing gear alignment—V8 engines

NOTE: The fuel pump eccentric must be installed with the stamped word "REAR" facing the camshaft sprocket.

4. Install the crankshaft oil slinger.

5. Install the timing chain cover using a new gasket and oil seal.

Camshaft

REMOVAL & INSTALLATION

4–151

NOTE: Replacement of the cam gear requires the removal of the camshaft.

1. Disconnect the negative battery cable.

2. Drain the coolant. Disconnect the radiator hoses at the radiator. Remove fan, shroud and radiator.

3. Remove the timing case cover. Refer to previous section.

NOTE: Keep all valve train components in order to position and cylinder. They must be returned to their original positions.

4. Remove valve cover, rocker arms and push rods. Remove side cover and lifters.

5. Remove distributor, oil pump drive and fuel pump.

6. Remove the camshaft thrust plate screws. Remove the camshaft and gear assembly by pulling them from the engine block.

NOTE: Removal of the camshaft gear requires a special adapter and the use of a press. Camshaft removal is necessary.

7. Place the adapter on the press and place the camshaft through the opening.

8. Press the shaft out of the gear using a socket or other suitable tool.

———— **CAUTION** ————

The thrust plate must be in position so that the Woodruff key does not damage the gear when the shaft is pressed out.

9. To install the gear firmly support the shaft at the back of the front journal in an arbor press using press plate adapters.

10. Place the gear spacer ring and thrust plate over the end of the shaft, and install the Woodruff key in the shaft keyway.

11. Install the camshaft gear and press it onto the shaft until it bottoms against the gear spacer ring. The end clearance of the thrust plate should be .0015″ to .0050″. If less than .0015″, the spacer ring should be replaced. If more than .0050″, the thrust plate should be replaced.

12. Thoroughly coat camshaft journals with high quality engine oil supplement.

13. Install camshaft assembly in engine block. Use care to prevent damaging bearings or camshaft.

14. Turn crankshaft and camshaft so that valve timing marks on gear teeth are aligned. Engine is now in number four cylinder firing position. Install camshaft thrust plate-to-block screws and tighten with 75 inch-pounds torque.

15. Install timing gear cover and gasket.

16. Line up keyway in hub with key on crankshaft and slide hub onto shaft. Install center bolt and tighten with 160 ft. lbs. torque.

17. Install valve tappets, push rods, push rod cover, oil pump shaft and gear assembly and fuel pump. Install distributor according to following procedure.

    a. Turn crankshaft 360 degrees to firing position of number one cylinder (number one exhaust and intake valve tappets both on base circle (heel) of camshaft and timing notch on vibration damper indexed with top dead center mark [TDC] on timing degree scale).

    b. Install distributor and align shaft so that rotor arm points toward number one cylinder spark plug contact.

18. Install rocker arms and pivot balls over push rods. With tappets on base circle (heel) of camshaft, tighten rocker arm capscrews with 20 ft. lbs. torque. Do not overtighten.

19. Install cylinder head cover.

20. Install intake manifold.

Installing 4-151 camshaft timing gear and measuring thrust plate end clearance

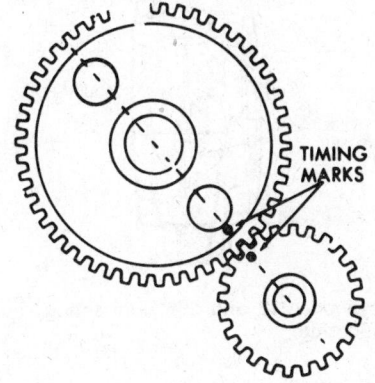

Timing gear alignment—4-151 engine

21. Install radiator and lower radiator hose.

22. Install belt, fan and shroud. Tighten fan bolts with 18 ft. lbs. torque. Install upper radiator hose. Tighten belts.

4–150, 6–232, 258

1. Drain and remove radiator.

2. If equipped, remove air conditioning condenser and receiver assembly as a charged unit.

3. Remove fuel pump, distributor and ignition wires.

4. Remove cylinder head cover and gasket.

5. Remove rocker arms, bridged pivot assemblies and pushrods. Be sure to replace these parts in the same order as removed.

6. Remove cylinder head and gasket and lifters.

7. Remove timing case cover.

8. Remove timing chain and sprockets as one assembly, being careful to rotate the crankshaft until the timing mark on the crankshaft sprocket is lined up with the timing pointer on the camshaft sprocket.

9. Remove the front bumper or grill as required.

10. Carefully remove the camshaft from the engine.

11. Installation is the reverse of removal.

6–173

1. Remove the intake manifold, valve lifters and timing chain cover as described in this section. If the truck is equipped with air conditioning, unbolt the condenser and move it aside *without disconnecting any lines.*

2. Remove fuel pump and pump pushrod.

3. Remove camshaft sprocket bolts, sprocket and timing chain. A light blow to the lower edge of a tight sprocket should free it (use a plastic mallet).

4. Install two bolts in cam bolt holes and pull cam from block.

5. To install, reverse removal procedure aligning the sprocket timing marks.

V8 Engines

1. Drain and remove radiator.

2. If equipped, remove air conditioning condenser and receiver assembly as a charged unit.

3. Remove fuel pump, distributor and ignition wires.

4. Remove cylinder head cover and gasket.

5. Remove drive belts, fan, and hub assembly.

6. Remove intake manifold.

7. Remove rocker arms, bridged pivot assemblies and pushrods. Be sure to replace these parts in the same order as removed.

8. Remove cylinder head and gasket and lifters.

9. Remove timing case cover.

10. Remove distributor drive gear and fuel pump eccentric from the camshaft.

NOTE: The fuel pump eccentric must be installed with the word "REAR" facing the camshaft sprocket.

11. Remove timing chain and sprocket as assembly, being careful to rotate the crankshaft until the timing mark on the crankshaft sprocket is lined up with the timing pointer on the camshaft sprocket.

12. Remove the front bumper or grill, and hood latch support bracket as required.

13. Carefully remove the camshaft from the engine.

14. Installation is the reverse of removal.

Pistons and Connecting Rods

REMOVAL & INSTALLATION

1. Remove the cylinder head. (See previous section).

2. Raise the vehicle and safely support on jackstands. Drain the engine oil. Remove the oil pan. (See following section).

3. Position the pistons, one at a time, near the bottom of their stroke and use a ridge reamer to remove any ridge from the top of the cylinder walls.

4. Inspect the connecting rod and cap for cylinder number identification, if not

identified mark them.

5. Remove the connecting rod bearing caps and bearing inserts, retain them in the same order they were removed.

6. Remove the connecting rod and piston assembly through the top of the cylinder.

NOTE: When removing the pistons and connecting rods, have the crank at the bottom of its stroke on the cylinder you are removing the piston from. After the rod cap has been removed, place two pieces of rubber tubing on the rod bolts to prevent damage to the crankshaft when removing the piston.

7. Use a cylinder hone and break the glaze on the cylinder walls. Refer to the instruction sheet that comes with the new piston rings for the necessary hone pattern.

8. After thoroughly cleaning the cylinder bores, apply a light film of clean engine oil to the bores with a clean cloth.

9. Arrange the piston ring gaps around the piston as follows:

   a. Oil spacer gap on centerline of either skirt face.

   b. Oil rail gaps 180° apart and in line with piston pin centerline.

   c. Second compression ring gap 180° from top oil rail gap.

   d. First compression ring gap 180° from second compression ring gap.

10. Lubricate piston and ring surfaces with clean engine oil.

11. With the notch or other front mark on the top of the pistons forward use a ring compressor to install the piston assemblies through the top of the cylinder bores. Place the lengths of rubber hose over the connecting rod bolts so to protect the cylinder bores and crankshaft bearing journals.

12. Install the connecting rod bearing caps and inserts in the same order as removed. Tighten the nuts to the proper torque.

13. Install the oil pan with new gaskets and tighten the drain plug.

14. Install the cylinder heads and gaskets.

15. Install the push rods and rocker assemblies.

16. Install the intake manifold assembly.

17. Install the cylinder head covers with new gaskets.

18. Fill the crankshaft with new oil.

Piston Identification

NOTE: If there is a notch on top of the piston or an F mark anywhere on the piston, it must face to the front of the engine.

4–151

The letter F, or the notches in the edge of the piston, goes toward the front of the engine.

On the 151 4 cylinder engine the notch on the connecting rod should be opposite the notch on the piston.

4-151 connecting rod numbers and squirt hole

6 cylinder 232 and 258 connecting rod numbering

4–150, 232, 258 SIXES AND V8 ENGINES

The connecting rods and caps are stamped with the number of the cylinder to which they belong. Replace them in their original positions.

The numbered sides and squirt hole must face the camshaft when assembled in the Sixes. The numbered sides must face out on the V8s.

Crankshaft

REMOVAL & INSTALLATION

4–151

1. Remove the engine and mount it on a work stand.

2. Remove the spark plugs.

3. Remove the fan and pulley.

4. Remove the vibration damper and hub.

5. Remove the oil pan and oil pump.

6. Remove the timing case cover.

7. Remove the crankshaft timing gear.

8. Remove the connecting rod bearing caps. Mark each for reassembly.

9. Remove the main bearing caps, marking each for reassembly.

10. Remove the crankshaft.

11. Installation is the reverse of removal. Note the following points:

a. Oil all parts with clean engine oil.

b. After installing the crankshaft, install the main and rod bearing caps loosely and strike both ends of the crankshaft with a rubber mallet, first the front, then the rear, to center the thrust bearing.

c. Tighten all bearing caps to the values shown in the torque chart. If new bearings are used, check the clearances with Plastigage.

d. Make sure timing marks are aligned in timing gears.

4–150, V6–173, 6–232, 258 and V8 Engines

1. Remove the engine from the vehicle and mount it on a work stand.

2. Drain the oil.

3. Remove the flywheel or torque converter, match marking the pieces for installation.

4. Remove all drive belts.

5. Remove the fan and hub assembly.

6. Remove the crankshaft pulley and vibration damper.

7. Remove the timing case cover.

8. Remove the oil pan.

9. Remove the oil pump and pickup.

10. Remove the rod bearing caps, marking them for installation.

11. Remove the main bearing caps, marking them for installation.

12. Lift out the crankshaft.

13. Installation is the reverse of removal. Coat all moving parts with clean engine oil. Observe all torque values listed in the torque chart.

NOTE: A replacement oil pickup tube must be used. Do not attempt to install the original. Make sure the plastic button is inserted in the bottom of the pickup screen. Always use a new rear main seal. If new bearings are installed, check clearances with Plastigage.

ENGINE LUBRICATION

Oil Pan

REMOVAL & INSTALLATION

4–151

1. Disconnect the battery ground.

2. Raise the vehicle and support it on jackstands.

3. Drain the oil.

4. Remove the starter.

5. Unbolt and remove the oil pan.

6. Clean all gasket surfaces, and remove all sludge and deposits from the pan.

7. Install the rear pan gasket in the main bearing cap and apply a small amount of RTV sealant in the depressions where the pan gasket contacts the block.

8. Position the gasket on the pan. Apply a 1/8 × 1/4 inch bead of RTV sealant at the split lines of the front and side gaskets.

9. Position the pan on the block carefully to avoid gasket misalignment. Install the bolts and tighten them to 45 in. lbs.

10. Install the starter. Tighten the bolts to 17 ft. lbs.; the nut to 40 in. lbs.

11. Connect the starter cables, lower the vehicle, fill the crankcase and run the engine to operating temperature, checking for leaks.

V6–173

1. Disconnect the battery grand.

2. Disconnect the right exhaust pipe at the manifold.

3. Raise and support the truck on jackstands.

4. Disconnect the left exhaust pipe at the manifold.

5. Remove the starter.

6. Remove the flywheel access cover.

7. Disconnect the exhaust pipe at the converter and lower it so that the Y portion rests on the upper control arms.

8. Unbolt and remove the oil pan.

9. Clean all RTV gasket material from the mating surfaces.

10. Installation is the reverse of removal. Apply RTV in a 1/8" bead on the pan lip. Torque the 6 mm bolts to 6–9 ft. lb.; the 8 mm bolts to 14–22 ft. lb.

4–150, 6–232, 258

1. Raise the vehicle and safely support it on jackstands. Disconnect the negative battery cable. Drain the engine oil.

2. Remove the starter motor.

3. If clearance is insufficient, place a jack under the transmission bell housing. Disconnect the engine right support cushion bracket from the block and raise the engine to allow sufficient clearance for oil pan removal. On the 4–150, remove the flywheel access cover.

4. Remove the oil pan attaching bolts and remove the oil pan.

5. Remove the oil pan front and rear neoprene oil seals and the side gaskets. Thoroughly clean the gasket surfaces of the oil pan and the engine block. Remove all of the sludge and dirt from the oil pan sump.

Rear main bearing oil seal installation—6 and V8 engines

6. Apply a generous amount of RTV silicone to the end tabs of a new oil pan front seal and install the seal to the timing case cover.

7. Cement new oil pan side gaskets into position on the engine block and apply a generous amount of RTV silicone to the side gasket contacting surface of the seal end tabs.

8. Install the seal in the recess of the rear main bearing cap, making sure that it is fully seated.

9. Coat the oil pan contacting surface of the front and rear oil pan seals with engine oil.

10. Install the oil pan and assemble the engine mount in the reverse order of removal.

Rear Main Oil Seal

REPLACEMENT

4–151

NOTE: The seal is a one piece unit that can be removed and installed without removing the oil pan or crankshaft.

1. Raise and support the vehicle on jackstands.

2. Remove the transmission and transfer case as an assembly.

3. Disconnect and remove the starter.

4. On manual transmission vehicles, remove the flywheel inspection plate, and clutch slave cylinder.

5. Pry out the old seal, being careful to avoid scratching the bearing.

6. Coat the new seal with clean engine oil and tap it gently into place with a rubber mallet.

7. Installation of the remaining parts is the reverse of removal.

232, 258 Sixes, V6, and V8 Engines

This seal is a two-piece neoprene type with a single lip.

1. Raise and support the vehicle on jackstands.

2. Remove the oil pan.

3. Remove the rear main bearing cap and discard the lower seal.

4. Loosen all remaining main bearing caps.

5. Using a center punch, carefully drive the upper half of the seal out of the block just far enough to grasp with a pliers and pull out.

6. Remove the oil pan front and rear seals and the side gaskets.

7. Clean all gasket surfaces.

8. Wipe clean the sealing surface of the crankshaft and coat it lightly with engine oil.

9. Coat the lip of the upper seal with engine oil and install it in the block. The lip faces forward.

10. Coat both end tabs of the lower seal with RTV silicone sealer. Do not get any RTV sealer on the seal lip.

11. Coat the outer curved surface of the seal with liquid soap. Coat the seal lip with engine oil.

12. Install the seal into the cap, pressing firmly.

13. Coat both chamfered edges of the cap with RTV sealer.

--- **CAUTION** ---

Do not allow any RTV sealer to get on the mating surfaces of the cap or block as this will affect bearing clearance.

---

14. Install the rear main cap.

15. Tighten all main bearing cap bolts gradually to 80 ft. lbs.

16. Replace the oil pan.

Oil Pump

REMOVAL & INSTALLATION

4–150, 4–151, V6–173, 6–232, 258

1. Drain the oil and remove the oil pan.

2. Remove the oil pump retaining screws and separate the oil pump and gasket from the engine block.

NOTE: On 6-cyl. engines, do not disturb the position of the oil pick-up tube and screen assembly in the pump body. If the tube is moved within the pump body, a new assembly must be installed to assure an airtight seal.

3. Install in reverse order of the above procedure.

V8 Engines
Removal

1. Remove the oil pump cover from the timing chain cover and remove the oil pump gears and shaft.

2. Remove the oil pressure relief valve from the body.

3. Inspect the gears for abnormal wear, chips, looseness on the shafts, galling, and scoring.

4. Inspect the cover and cavity for breaks, cracks, distortion, and abnormal wear.

5. Install the gears into the pump cavity, and with the use of a straight edge and feeler gauge, check the gear to housing clearance.

6. If the clearances measure out of the allowable span, the timing chain cover and gears should be replaced.

Installation

1. Install the pressure relief valve if previously removed.

2. Install the gears into the gear cavity, and pack the cavity with petroleum jelly to insure the self priming of the pump.

NOTE: Never use chassis or wheel bearing grease to pack the gear cavity.

4-151 oil pump

Inline six oil pump

3. Install the gear cover, using a new gasket.

OIL PUMP CLEARANCES— CHECKING 6 CYL. AND V8 ENGINES

1. Remove cover and gasket from pump body.

2. Place a strip of plastigage across the full width of each gear.

3. Install pump cover with gasket and tighten.

4. Remove pump cover and determine the amount of clearance by measuring the width of the compressed plastigage. Clearance should be .002–.006 inch for 1975–76 and .002–.008 inch for 1977–82.

5. Measure gear-to-body clearance by inserting a feeler gauge between gear tooth and pump body inner wall directly opposite the point of gear mesh. The reading should be .0005–.0025 inch.

NOTE: On the 6 cylinder engine, if gear-to-body clearance is more than specified, replace idler gear, idler shaft, and drive gear assembly. On V8 engines, if gear-to-body clearance is more than specified, measure gear diameter with micrometer. If gear diameter is correct, check gear end clearance and correct. If gear clearance is acceptable and relief

valve is functioning properly, replace timing case cover. If gear diameter is incorrect, replace gears and idler shaft.

ENGINE COOLING

Radiator

REMOVAL & INSTALLATION

NOTE: On 1984 Wagoneer and Cherokee models the A/C condenser must be removed with the radiator. This involves purging the refrigerant. This operation can be dangerous and is best left to a qualified technician.

1. Drain the radiator by opening the drain cock and removing the radiator pressure cap.

2. Remove the upper and lower hose clamps and hoses at the radiator.

3. Disconnect the automatic transmission oil cooler lines at the radiator, if so equipped. Remove the radiator shroud from the radiator, if so equipped.

4. Remove all attaching screws that secure the radiator to the radiator body support.

5. Remove the radiator.

6. Replace in reverse order of the above procedure.

Thermostat

REMOVAL & INSTALLATION

The thermostat is located in the water outlet housing at the front or on top of the engine. On the V8 the water outlet housing is located in the front of the intake manifold.

To remove the thermostats from all of these engines, first drain the cooling system. It is not necessary to disconnect or remove any of the hoses. Remove the two attaching screws and lift the housing from the engine. Remove the thermostat and the gasket. To install, place the thermostat in the housing with the spring inside the engine. Install a new gasket with a small amount of sealing compound applied to both sides. Install the water outlet and tighten the attaching bolts to 30 ft. lbs. Refill the cooling system.

Water Pump

REMOVAL & INSTALLATION
4–151

1. Remove the fan belt.
2. Remove the fan and hub assembly.
3. Disconnect the hoses at the pump.

Typical V8 oil pump

4. Unbolt and remove the pump.

5. Installation is the reverse of removal. Always use a new gasket coated with sealer. Torque the water pump bolts to 25 ft. lbs. Tighten the fan and hub bolts to 18 ft. lbs.

4–150, 6–232, 258

1. Disconnect all hoses at the pump.
2. Remove the drive belts.
3. Remove the fan shroud attaching screws.
4. Unbolt the fan and fan drive assembly and remove along with the shroud. On some models it may be easier to turn the shroud ½ turn.
5. Unbolt and remove the pump.

CAUTION

Engines built for sale in California having a single, serpentine drive belt and viscous fan drive, have a reverse rotating pump and drive. These components are identified by the word REVERSE stamped on the drive cover and inner side of the fan, and REV cast into the water pump body. Never interchange standard rotating parts with these.

---

6. Installation is the reverse of removal. Always use a new gasket coated with sealer. Torque the water pump bolts to 13 ft. lbs.; the fan bolts to 18 ft. lbs.

V6 and V8 Engines

1. Disconnect all hoses at the pump.
2. Loosen all drive belts.
3. Remove the shroud, but reinsert one bolt to hold the radiator.
4. Remove the fan and hub.
5. If the vehicle is equipped with A/C install a double nut on the compressor bracket-to-water pump stud and remove the stud.

6. Remove, but do not disconnect the alternator and bracket.

7. If so equipped, remove the nuts that attach the power steering pump to the rear half of the pump bracket.

8. Remove the two bolts that attach the front half to the rear half of the bracket.

9. Remove the remaining upper screw from the inner air pump support bracket, loosen the lower bolt and drop the bracket away from the power steering front bracket.

10. Remove the front half of the power steering bracket from the water pump mounting stud.

11. Unbolt and remove the water pump.

12. Installation is the reverse of removal. Always use a new gasket coated with sealer. Torque the pump-to timing case bolts to 48 in. lbs. and the pump-to-block bolts to 25 ft. lbs. Torque the power steering pulley nut to 60 ft. lbs.

EMISSION CONTROLS

There are three types of automotive pollutants; crankcase fumes, exhaust gases and gasoline evaporation. The equipment that is used to limit these pollutants is commonly called emission control equipment.

PCV System

The crankcase emission control equipment consists of a positive crankcase ventilation valve (PCV), a closed or open oil filler cap and hoses to connect this equipment.

When the engine is running, a small portion of the gases which are formed in the combustion chamber during combustion leak by the piston rings and enter the crankcase. Since these gases are under pressure they tend to escape from the crankcase and enter into the atmosphere. If these gases were allowed to remain in the crankcase for any length of time, they would contaminate the engine oil and cause sludge to build up. If the gases are allowed to escape into the atmosphere, they would pollute the air, as they contain unburned hydrocarbons. The crankcase emission control equipment recycles these gases back into the engine combustion chamber where they are burned.

Crankcase gases are recycled in the following manner: while the engine is running, clean filtered air is drawn into the crankcase either directly through the oil filler cap, or through the carburetor air filter and then through a hose leading to the oil filler cap. As the air passes through the crankcase it picks up the combustion gases and carries them out of the crankcase, up through the PCV valve and into the intake manifold. After they enter the intake manifold they are drawn into the combustion chamber where they are burned.

4-151 water pump and related parts

The most critical component in the system is the PCV valve. This vacuum controlled valve regulates the amount of gases which are recycled into the combustion chamber. At low engine speeds the valve is partially closed, limiting the flow of gases into the intake manifold. As engine speed increases, the valve opens to admit greater quantities of the gases into the intake manifold. If the valve should become blocked or plugged, the gases will be prevented from escaping from the crankcases by the normal route. Since these gases are under pressure, they will find their own way out of the crankcase. This alternate route is usually a weak oil seal or gasket in the engine. As the gas escapes by the gasket, it also creates an oil leak. Besides causing oil leaks, a clogged PCV valve also allows these gases to remain in the crankcase for an extended period of time, promoting the formation of sludge in the engine.

The above explanation and the troubleshooting procedure which follows applies to all engines equipped with PCV systems.

Typical PCV system

TROUBLESHOOTING

With the engine running, pull the PCV valve and hose from the engine. Block off the end of the valve with your finger. The engine speed should drop at least 50 rpm when the end of the valve is blocked. If the engine speed does not drop at least 50 rpm, then the valve is defective and should be replaced. Shake the valve; if it rattles it probably isn't clogged.

REMOVAL & INSTALLATION

1. Pull the PCV valve and hose from the engine.
2. Remove the PCV valve from the hose. Inspect the inside of the PCV valve hose. If it is dirty, disconnect it from the intake manifold and clean it.

To install, proceed as follows:
1. If the PCV valve hose was removed, connect it to the intake manifold.
2. Connect the PCV valve to its hose.
3. Install the PCV valve on the engine.

Air Injection System

All of the engines used except the 4–151 at some point incorporated the air injection system for controlling the emission of exhaust gases into the atmosphere.

The exhaust emission control air injection system consists of a belt driven air pump which directs compressed air through connecting hoses to a steel distribution manifold into stainless steel injection tubes in the exhaust port adjacent to each exhaust valve. The air, with its normal oxygen content, reacts with the hot, but incompletely burned exhaust gases and permits further combustion in the exhaust port or manifold.

Air Pump

The air injection pump is a positive displacement vane type which is permanently lubricated and requires little periodic maintenance. The only serviceable parts on the air pump are the filter, exhaust tube, and relief valve. The relief valve relieves the air flow when the pump pressure reaches a preset level. This occurs at high engine rpm. This serves to prevent damage to the pump and to limit maximum exhaust manifold temperatures.

NOTE: On some models the relief valve assembly is incorporated in the diverter valve. If the relief valve is believed to be defective, the diverter valve assembly must be replaced.

Air Delivery Manifold

The air delivery manifold distributes the air from the pump to each of the air delivery tubes in a uniform manner. A check valve is integral with the air delivery manifold. Its function is to prevent the reverse flow of exhaust gases to the pump should the pump fail. The reverse flow would damage the air pump and connecting hose.

Air Injection Tubes

The air injection tubes are inserted into the exhaust ports. The tubes project into the exhaust ports, directing air into the vicinity of the exhaust valve.

Anti-Backfire Valve

The anti-backfire diverter valve prevents engine backfire by briefly interrupting the air being injected into the exhaust manifold during periods of deceleration or rapid throttle closure. The valve opens when a sudden increase in manifold vacuum overcomes the diaphragm spring tension. With the valve in the open position the air flow is directed to the atmosphere.

The valve prevents backfiring in the exhaust manifold and also prevents an over rich fuel mixture from being burned in the exhaust manifold, which would cause backfiring and possible damage to the engine.

Thermostatically Controlled Air Cleaner System (TAC)

232 AND 258 SIXES THROUGH 1977

The TAC system consists of a two-piece heat shroud positioned on the exhaust manifold, a hot air hose, and an air duct and valve assembly located in the air cleaner snorkel.

The air duct and valve assembly incorporates an air valve, a thermostat mechanism, and a spring.

The temperature of the air entering the air cleaner is thermostatically regulated by the air duct and valve assembly. Cold air is supplied from the engine compartment and hot air from the shrouded exhaust manifold.

The thermostat unit in the air duct is exposed to incoming air on the air filter side of the air valve. The spring-loaded air valve is connected to the thermostat unit through linkage. The spring holds the valve in the closed (heat on) position until the thermostat overcomes the spring tension.

While the engine is warming up and the air temperature entering the air duct is less than 105°F, the thermostat is in the retracted position and the air valve is held in the closed (heat on) position.

As the temperature of the air passing over the thermostat unit rises, the thermostat starts to open and pulls the air valve down, closing off the heated air intake and opening the cool air intake, allowing cooler engine compartment air to enter the air cleaner.

When the temperature of the air reaches 130°F, the air valve is completely open to engine compartment air.

4–151, 1978–82 SIXES AND V8 ENGINES

This system consists of a heat shroud which is integral with the right side exhaust manifold, a hot air hose and a special air cleaner assembly equipped with a thermal sensor and a vacuum motor and air valve assembly.

The thermal sensor incorporates an air bleed valve which regulates the amount of vacuum applied to the vacuum motor, controlling the air valve position to supply either heated air from the exhaust manifold or air from the engine compartment.

During the warm-up period when underhood temperatures are low, the air bleed valve is closed and sufficient vacuum is applied to the vacuum motor to hold the air valve in the closed (heat on) position.

As the temperature of the air entering the air cleaner approaches approximately 115°F, the air bled valve opens to decrease the amount of vacuum applied to the vacuum motor. The diaphragm spring in the vacuum motor then moves the air valve into the open (heat off) position, allowing only underhood air to enter the air cleaner.

The air valve in the air cleaner will also open, regardless of air temperature, during heavy acceleration to obtain maximum air flow through the air cleaner.

Solenoid Vacuum Valve

This valve is attached to the right rear intake manifold (V8), or to a bracket at the rear of the intake manifold (Sixes). When the valve is energized, carburetor vacuum is blocked off and the distributor vacuum line is vented to the atmosphere through a port in the valve, resulting in no vacuum advance. When the valve is de-energized, vacuum is applied to the distributor resulting in normal vacuum advance.

Solenoid Control Switch

This switch is located on the transmission on vehicles with manual transmissions. It opens or closes in relation to speed and gear range. When the transmission is in high gear, the switch opens and breaks the ground circuit to the solenoid vacuum valve. In lower gear ranges the switch closes and completes the ground circuit to the solenoid vacuum valve. The switch is operated by the transmission shifter shaft.

On vehicles equipped with an automatic transmission, the switch is located along the speedometer cable on the firewall. The switch is operated by speedometer cable rpm. At about 32 to 36 mph the switch will open the electrical ground circuit to the solenoid vacuum valve.

NOTE: From 1976, the switch closes at a lower speed (22–28 mph) on deceleration.

Coolant Temperature Override Switch

The switch reacts to coolant temperatures to route either intake manifold or carburetor vacuum to the distributor vacuum advance diaphragm.

When the coolant temperature is below 160°F, intake manifold vacuum is applied through a hose connection to the distributor advance diaphragm, resulting in full vacuum advance.

When the coolant temperature is above 160°F, intake manifold vacuum is blocked off and carburetor vacuum is then applied through the solenoid vacuum valve to the distributor advance diaphragm, resulting in decreased vacuum advance.

NOTE: On some vehicles made for California, intake manifold vacuum (routed through the TCS solenoid) is applied to the distributor when the coolant temperature is above 160°F.

The relationship between distributor vacuum advance and the operation of the TCS system and coolant temperature override switch can be determined by referring to the Emission Control Distributor Vacuum Application Chart.

Exhaust Gas Recirculation (EGR) System

The EGR system consists of a diaphragm actuated flow control valve (EGR valve), coolant temperature override switch (EGR CTO) and connecting hoses. In 1980, a Thermal Vacuum Switch, located in the air cleaner, was added to control the vacuum signal between the EGR and CTO.

The purpose of the EGR system is to limit the formation of oxides of nitrogen by

Typical V8 air pump system

diluting the fresh air intake charge with a metered amount of exhaust gas, thereby reducing the peak temperatures of the burning gases in the combustion chambers.

EGR Valve

The EGR valve is mounted on a machined surface at the rear of the intake manifold on V8 engines and on the side of the intake manifold on the Sixes. When a backpressure sensor is used, the EGR valve is mounted on a spacer which is an integral part of the backpressure sensor.

The valve is held in a normally closed position by a coil spring located above the diaphragm. A special fitting is provided at the carburetor to route ported (above the throttle plates) vacuum through the CTO and a TVS or BPS (when used) and hose connections to a fitting located above the diaphragm on the valve. A passage in the intake manifold directs exhaust gas from the exhaust crossover passage on V8s and from near the heat riser on the Sixes, to the EGR valve. When the diaphragm is actuated by vacuum, the valve opens and meters exhaust gas through special passages into the intake manifold below the carburetor.

Coolant Temperature Override Switch

This switch is located in the intake manifold at the coolant passage adjacent to the oil filler tube on V8s and on the left-side of the cylinder block on the Sixes. The outer port of the switch is connected to either the EGR valve or BPS (when used). The inner port is connected by a hose to the EGR fitting at the carburetor. When the coolant temperature reaches 115°F the inner port of the switch opens and a vacuum signal is applied to the EGR valve. This vacuum signal is subject to regulation by the BPS when used.

Thermal Vacuum Switch (TVS)

The TVS is located in the air cleaner on all 1980 and later engines, and functions as an on/off switch controlled by air cleaner air temperature. The TVS controls the vacuum passage between the EGR CTO valve and the EGR valve. Air temperature in the 40–50°F range cause the TVS to limit the vacuum applied to the EGR valve, thus improving cold engine driveability.

EMISSION CONTROL DISTRIBUTOR VACUUM APPLICATION CHART

Transmission Gear			Coolant Temperature	Vacuum Source
3 Speed	4 Speed	Automatic		
1–2	1–2–3	Below 32–36 mph	Below 160°F	Manifold
1–2	1–2–3	Below 32–36 mph	Above 160°F	Through the Solenoid Vacuum Valve
3	4	Above 32–36 mph	Below 160°F	Manifold
3	4	Above 32–36 mph	Above 160°F	No Vacuum

Exhaust Backpressure Sensor (BPS)

This device is used on 1975 California vehicles, on all 1976 models, and on some 1977–81 models in conjunction with the EGR system.

The BPS monitors exhaust backpressure and permits EGR operation only when engine operating conditions are favorable. The BPR units are variously calibrated, are not serviceable, and must be replaced with the identical part as a unit when necessary.

The BPS consists of a diaphragm valve and a spacer connected by a metal tube projecting into an exhaust port in the spacer body. The EGR valve mounts directly on the spacer. On some 1977–81 sixes, the sensor is integral with the EGR valve.

In operation, the metal tube connecting the diaphragm valve to the spacer routes exhaust backpressure from the particular exhaust port to the sensor. When the backpressure reaches a certain level the diaphragm valve spring pressure is overcome, permitting a vacuum signal to the EGR valve, providing that the CTO switch is open.

Thus, EGR operations is only permitted when the engine is warmed up sufficiently and exhaust backpressure relatively high, such as during acceleration and at some cruising speeds. When temperature or backpressure conditions are not met, the vacuum signal is vented to the atmosphere from a vent at the diaphragm valve.

Feedback Systems

Two different feedback systems are used with 1981 and later Jeep vehicles. One, the C4 system is used with 4-151 engines built for sale in California; the other, the Computerized Emission Control (CEC) System is used on 6-258 engines built for sale in California. Each system is designed for the same purpose, to reduce exhaust emission using a Three-Way Catalytic Converter (TWC).

Each system is computerized, utilizing microprocessors, and each is highly complex, requiring professional service. Therefore, no service procedures are given in this book for the diagnosis or repair of these systems.

Catalytic Converter

The catalytic converter is a muffler-like device inserted in the exhaust system. Exhaust gases flow through the converter where a chemical change takes place, reducing carbon monoxide and hydrocarbons to carbon dioxide and water; the latter two elements being harmless. The catalysts promoting this reaction are platinum and palladium-coated beads of alumina.

Because of the chemical reaction which

does take place in the converter, the temperature of the converter during operation is higher than the exhaust gases when they leave the engine. However, insulation keeps the outside skin of the converter about the same temperature as the muffler.

An improperly adjusted carburetor or ignition problem which would permit unburned fuel to enter the converter could produce excessive heat. Excessive heat in the converter could result in bulging or other distortion of the converter's shape. If the converter is heat-damaged and must be replaced, the ignition or carburetor problem must be corrected also.

Fuel Tank Vapor Emission Control System

On 1975–76 models, the fuel vapor is routed from the fuel tank through vapor vent hoses to the liquid check valve. From the liquid check valve, the fuel vapor is routed to the vapor storage canister which is filled with charcoal. When the engine is not operating the charcoal retains the vapors. When the engine is started vacuum from the air cleaner snorkle routed through a hose leading to the top of the vapor storage canister sucks the vapors from the storage canister. There are three nipples on the top of the canister; one for vapors coming from the fuel tank, one for vapors going to the air cleaner snorkle, and the other nipple is plugged (for use with 4 bbl carburetors on other AMC engines). Fresh air is drawn up through the canister from the bottom through a replaceable filter during operation.

Limit Fill Valve

This valve is essentially a combination vapor flow regulator and pressure relief valve. It regulates vapor flow from the fuel tank vent line into the valve cover. The valve consists of a housing, a spring loaded diaphragm and a diaphragm cover. As tank vent pressure increases, the diaphragm lifts permitting vapor to flow through. The pressure at which this occurs is 4–6 in. of water column. This action regulates the flow of vapors under severe conditions but generally prohibits the flow of vapor during normal temperature operation, thus minimizing driveability problems.

LIQUID CHECK VALVE

The liquid check valve prevents liquid fuel from entering the vapor lines leading to the storage canister. The check valve incorporates a float and needle valve assembly. If liquid fuel should enter the check valve, the float will rise and force the needle upward to close the vent passage. With no liquid fuel present in the check valve, fuel vapors pass freely from the tank, through

the check valve, and on to the storage canister.

Choke Heat By-Pass Valve (CHBPV) 1976 and later V8

When the engine is first started and begins to warm up, heated air from the exhaust crossover passage in the intake manifold is routed through a heat tube to the choke housing containing the thermostatic spring for regulating the choke flap. A thermostatic by-pass valve, which is integral with the choke heat tube, helps prevent premature choke valve opening during the early part of the warmup period. This is important when ambient temperatures are relatively low and adverse drivability could occur if the choke was opened too soon.

The thermostatic by-pass valve regulates the temperature of the hot airflow to the choke housing by allowing outside unheated air to enter the heat tube. A thermostatic disc in the valve is calibrated to close the valve at 75°F and open it at 55°F.

Fuel Return System

The purpose of the fuel return system is to reduce high temperature fuel vapor problems. The system consists of a fuel return line to the fuel tank and a special fuel filter with an extra outlet nipple to which the return line is connected. During normal operation, a small amount of fuel is returned to the fuel tank. During periods of high underhood temperatures, vaporized fuel in the fuel line is returned to the fuel tank and not passed through the carburetor.

NOTE: The extra nipple on the special fuel filter should be positioned upward to ensure proper operation of the system.

Emission Control Checks

ANTI-BACKFIRE DIVERTER VALVE

To check the diverter valve start the engine and let it idle. With the engine idling, there should be little or no air coming out the vents. When the engine is accelerated to 2,000–3,000 rpm, a strong flow of air should be felt at the vents. If the flow of air from the air pump is not diverted through the diverter valve vents when the engine is accelerated to the above mentioned rpm, check and make sure that the vacuum sensing line leading to the valve has vacuum and is not leaking or disconnected. The diverter valve should bleed air when 20 in. Hg or more vacuum is applied to the vacuum sensing line or when the output of the air pump exceeds 5 psi. When the engine is slowly accelerated, the diverter valve should begin to bleed off air between 2,500 and 3,500 rpm.

CHECK VALVE

The check valve in the air distribution manifold prevents the reverse flow of exhaust gases to the pump in the event the pump should become inoperative or should exhaust pressure ever exceed the pump pressure.

To check this valve for proper operation, remove the air supply hose from the pump at the distribution manifold. With the engine running, listen for exhaust leakage where the check valve is connected to the distribution manifold. If leakage is audible, the valve is not operating correctly. A small amount of leakage is normal.

AIR PUMP

Check for the proper drive belt tension and adjust as necessary. Do not pry on the die cast pump housing. Check to see if the pump is discharging air. Remove the air outlet hose at the pump. With the engine running, air should be felt at the pump outlet opening.

EGR VALVE

With the engine idling and at normal operating temperature, manually depress the EGR valve diaphragm. This should cause engine speed to drop about 200 rpm. This indicates that the EGR valve had been properly cutting off the flow of exhaust gas at idle and is operating properly.

If the engine speed did not change and the idle is smooth, exhaust gases are not reaching the combustion chambers. The probable cause of this is a plugged passage between the EGR valve and the intake manifold.

If the engine idle is rough and rpm is not affected by depressing the EGR valve diaphragm, the EGR valve is not closing off the flow of exhaust at idle like it's supposed to and there is most likely a fault in the hoses, hose routing, or the EGR valve itself.

NOTE: The EGR valve can be removed and cleaned with a wire brush and a 9/16 in. drill bit coated with grease (to hold dirt particles) inserted in discharge passage. The drill should be held with a pair of pliers only.

EGR CTO SWITCH

Before checking the operating of the EGR CTO switch, make sure that the engine coolant is below 100°F.

1. Check the vacuum lines for leaks and proper routing.
2. Disconnect the vacuum line at the backpressure sensor, if so equipped, or at the EGR valve, and connect the line to a vacuum gauge.

3. Operate the engine at 1,500 rpm. No vacuum should be indicated at the gauge. If vacuum is indicated, replace the EGR CTO switch.
4. Allow the engine to idle until the coolant temperature exceeds 115°F.
5. Accelerate the engine to 1,500 rpm. Vacuum should be present at the gauge. If not, replace the EGR CTO switch.

EXHAUST BPS UNIT

1. Make sure that all the EGR vacuum lines are routed correctly and are not leaking.
2. Install a "T" in the vacuum line between the EGR valve and BPS, and attach a vacuum gauge to the "T".
3. Start the engine and allow it to idle. No vacuum should be present.

If vacuum is indicated at idle speed, make sure of correct line connections. Also, be sure that manifold vacuum is not the source. If the carburetor is providing the vacuum, look for a partially open throttle plate which could cause premature ported vacuum to the BPS unit.
4. Accelerate the engine to 2,000 rpm and observe the vacuum gauge for the following:

   a. If the coolant is below 115°F, no vacuum should be present;

   b. With coolant temperature above 115°F, ported vacuum should be indicated;

   c. If no vacuum is indicated at any time, make sure that vacuum is being applied to the inlet side of the BPS. If correct, remove the BPS and either clean it with a wire brush (if blocked) or replace it.

SPARK CTO SWITCH

Before testing the spark CTO switch, make sure that the engine coolant temperature is below 160°F.

1. Remove all the hoses from the CTO switch and plug those which will create a vacuum leak.
2. Connect a vacuum line from a manifold vacuum source to the top port of the CTO switch.
3. Connect a vacuum gauge to the center port.
4. Start the engine. Manifold vacuum should be indicated on the gauge. If not, replace the switch.
5. With the engine still running and the coolant temperature still below 160°F, disconnect the vacuum line from the top port and connect it to the bottom port.
6. No vacuum should be indicated. Replace the switch if there is vacuum.
7. Allow the engine to run until the coolant temperature exceeds 160°F. Manifold vacuum should be indicated. If not, replace the CTO switch.
8. Disconnect the hose from the bottom port and connect it to the top port again. With the coolant temperature above 160°F, no vacuum should be indicated. If there is, replace the CTO switch.

EGR system 4-151 (typical)

Typical 6-258 EGR system

Typical V8 EGR system

TVS FUNCTIONAL TEST

1. Allow the air cleaner to cool to between 40 and 50°F.
2. Disconnect the vacuum hoses from the TVS and connect an external vacuum source to one nipple and a vacuum gauge to the other.
3. Apply vacuum to the TVS. Vacuum should not be present when the air temperature is 40–50°F. If vacuum is present, replace the switch.

T443

4. Start the engine and allow the air cleaner to warm above 50°F. Vacuum should be present.

FUEL SYSTEM

Fuel Pump

REMOVAL & INSTALLATION

All Engines

1. Disconnect the inlet and outlet fuel lines, and any vacuum lines.
2. Remove the two fuel pump body attaching nuts and lockwashers.
3. Pull the pump and gasket free of the engine. Make sure that the mating surfaces of the fuel pump and the engine are clean.
4. Cement a new gasket to the mounting flange of the fuel pump.
5. Position the fuel pump on the engine block so that the lever of the fuel pump rests on the fuel pump cam of the camshaft.
6. Secure the fuel pump to the block with the two cap screws and lock washers.
7. Connect the intake and outlet fuel lines to the fuel pump, and any vacuum lines.

FUEL PUMP TESTING

Volume Check

Disconnect the fuel line from the carburetor. Place the open end in a suitable container. Start the engine and operate it at normal idle speed. The pump should deliver at least one pin in 30 seconds.

Pressure Check

Disconnect the fuel line at the carburetor. Disconnect the fuel return line from the fuel filter if so equipped, and plug the nipple on the filter. Install a T-fitting on the open end of the fuel line and refit the line to the carburetor. Plug a pressure gauge into the remaining opening of the T-fitting. The hose leading to the pressure gauge should not be any longer than 6 inches. Start the engine and let it run at idle speed. Bleed any air out of the hose between the gauge and the T-fitting. Pressure readings are given in the Tune-up Specifications Chart.

Carburetors

NOTE: For detailed rebuilding and settings refer to the Unit Repair Section on carburetors.

REMOVAL & INSTALLATION

All Engines

To remove the carburetor from any engine, first remove the air cleaner from the top of the carburetor. Remove all lines and hoses, noting their positions to facilitate installation. Remove all throttle and choke linkage at the carburetor. Remove the carburetor attaching nuts which hold it to the intake manifold. Lift the carburetor from the engine along with the carburetor base gasket. Discard the gasket. Install the carburetor in the reverse order of removal, using a new base gasket.

OVERHAUL

Efficient carburetion depends greatly on careful cleaning and inspection during overhaul since dirt, gum, water, or varnish in or on the carburetor parts are often responsible for poor performance.

Overhaul your carburetor in a clean, dust-free area. Carefully disassemble the carburetor, referring often to the exploded views. Keep all similar and look-alike parts segregated during disassembly and cleaning to avoid accidental interchange during assembly. Make a note of all jet sizes.

When the carburetor is disassembled, wash all parts (except diaphragms, electric choke units, pump plunger, and any other plastic, leather, fiber, or rubber parts) in clean carburetor solvent. Do not leave parts in the solvent any longer than is necessary to sufficiently loosen the deposits. Excessive cleaning may remove the special finish from the float bowl and choke valve bodies, leaving these parts unfit for service. Rinse all parts in clean solvent and blow them dry with compressed air or allow them to air dry. Wipe clean all cork, plastic, leather, and fiber parts with a clean, lint-free cloth.

Blow out all passages and jets with compressed air and be sure that there are no restrictions or blockages. Never use wire or similar tools to clean jets, fuel passages, or air bleeds. Clean all jets and valves separately to avoid accidental interchange.

Check all parts for wear or damage. If wear or damage is found, replace the defective parts. Especially check the following:

1. Check the float needle and seat for wear. If wear is found, replace the complete assembly.
2. Check the float hinge pin for wear and the float(s) for dents or distortion. Replace the float if fuel has leaked into it.
3. Check the throttle and choke shaft bores for wear or an out-of-round condition. Damage or wear to the throttle arm, shaft, or shaft bore will often require replacement of the throttle body. These parts require a close tolerance of fit; wear may allow air leakage, which could affect starting and idling.

NOTE: Throttle shafts and bushings are not included in overhaul kits. They can be purchased separately.

4. Inspect the idle mixture adjusting needles for burrs or grooves. Any such condition requires replacement of the needle, since you will not be able to obtain a satisfactory idle.

5. Test the accelerator pump check valves. They should pass air one way but not the other. Test for proper seating by blowing and sucking on the valve. Replace the valve if necessary. If the valve is satisfactory, wash the valve again to remove breath moisture.
6. Check the bowl cover for warped surfaces with a straightedge.
7. Closely inspect the valves and seats for wear and damage, replacing as necessary.
8. After the carburetor is assembled, check the choke valve for freedom of operation.

Carburetor overhaul kits are recommended for each overhaul. These kits contain all gaskets and new parts to replace those that deteriorate most rapidly. Failure to replace all parts supplied with the kit (especially gaskets) can result in poor performance later.

After cleaning and checking all components, reassemble the carburetor, using new parts and referring to the exploded view. When reassembling, make sure that all screws and jets are tight in their seats, but do not overtighten, as the tips will be distorted. Tighten all screws gradually, in rotation. Do not tighten needle valves into their seats, uneven jetting will result. Always use new gaskets. Be sure to adjust the float level when reassembling.

Fuel Tank

REMOVAL & INSTALLATION

All exc. 1984 Wagoneer/ Cherokee

The fuel tank is attached to the frame by brackets and bolts. The brackets are attached to the tank at the seam flange or the skid plate.

Before removing the fuel tank, make sure that the level of the fuel inside the tank is at least below any of the various hoses connected. It is best to either drain or siphon the majority of fuel out of the tank to make it easier to handle while removing it.

1984 Wagoneer and Cherokee

1. Place a jack under the skid plate and remove the strap nuts.
2. Disconnect all hoses and wires connected to the tank.
3. Partially lower the tank and disconnect the tank vapor vent hoses.
4. Remove the tank.

CLUTCH

REMOVAL & INSTALLATION

4-151

1. Remove the shift lever boot.
2. Remove the shift lever assembly.

3. Raise the vehicle and support it on jack stands.

4. Remove the transmission and transfer case.

5. Remove the slave cylinder-to-clutch housing bolts.

6. Disengage the slave cylinder pushrod from the throwout lever and move the cylinder out of the way.

7. Remove the starter.

8. Remove the throwout bearing.

9. Unbolt and remove the clutch housing.

10. Mark the position of the clutch pressure plate and remove the pressure plate bolts evenly, a little at a time in rotation.

11. Remove the pilot bushing lubricating wick from its bore in the crankshaft and soak the wick in clean engine oil.

12. Installation is the reverse of removal. Torque the pressure plate bolts to 23 ft. lbs., tightening them evenly, a little at a time in rotation. Torque the clutch housing to 54 ft. lbs.; the transmission-to-clutch housing bolts to 54 ft. lbs.; the transfer case-to-transmission bolts to 30 ft. lbs. See Note below.

4–150, V6–173

1. Remove the transmission/transfer case assembly as described later in this section.

2. Mark the position of the clutch pressure plate in relation to the flywheel for installation.

3. Loosen the pressure plate bolts evenly, a little at a time each! Failure to loosen the bolts evenly, in rotation, will cause warping of the pressure plate.

4. When all spring tension is relieved from the pressure plate, back out the bolts and remove the pressure plate and driven plate.

5. If the pilot bushing is equipped with a lubricating wick, remove it and soak it in clean engine oil.

6. Installation is the reverse of removal. Tighten the pressure plate bolts evenly, in rotation in three or four different steps, to:
4–150: 23 ft. lb.
6–173: 16 ft. lb.

6–232, 258, V8

1. Remove the transmission.

2. Remove the starter.

3. Remove the throwout bearing and sleeve assembly.

4. Remove the bell housing.

5. Mark the clutch cover, pressure plate and the flywheel with a center punch so that these parts can be later installed in the same position.

6. Remove the clutch cover-to-flywheel attaching bolts. When removing these bolts, loosen them in rotation, one or two turns at a time, until the spring tension is released. The clutch cover is a steel stamping which could be warped by improper removal procedures, resulting in clutch

4-151, exploded view clutch assembly

Typical 6 and V8 clutch assembly

chatter when reused.

7. Remove the clutch assembly from the flywheel. Install in reverse order of removal. Torque pressure plate bolts to 40 ft. lb. See Note below.

NOTE: Use extreme care at all times not to get the clutch driven plate dirty in any way. Lightly lubricate the inside of the clutch driven plate's spline with a coat of wheel bearing grease. Do the same to the input shaft of the transmission. Wipe off all excess grease so that none will fly off and get onto the driven plate. Lubricate the throwout bearing collar, the ball stud and the clutch fork with wheel bearing grease. Use a pilot shaft or a spare transmission main shaft to align the driven shaft and the clutch pressure plate when attaching the assembly to the flywheel. Tighten down on the clutch-to-flywheel attaching bolts alternately so that the clutch is drawn squarely

into position on the flywheel. Each bolt must be tightened one turn at a time to avoid bending the clutch cover flange.

CLUTCH PEDAL FREE-PLAY ADJUSTMENT

NOTE: 4–151 equipped vehicles and all 1984 vehicles with the 4–150 and V6 are equipped with a non-adjustable hydraulic clutch.

1. Lift the pedal up against the stop.

2. Loosen the release rod adjuster jam nut, under the vehicle. On Cherokee and Truck models, adjust clutch push rod lower ball pivot assembly in-or-out on push rod until bellcrank inner lever is parallel to front face of clutch housing. Lever should be slightly forward from vertical.

3. Adjust the pedal free-play to about one inch.

4. Tighten the jam nut.

Clutch Master Cylinder

REMOVAL & INSTALLATION

CJ and Scrambler with 4–151 Engine and All 1984 Models with the 4–150 and V6 Engines

1. Disconnect the hydraulic line at the cylinder. A flarenut wrench is recommended, since an open end wrench may damage the nut.

2. Cap the hydraulic line to prevent dirt from entering.

3. Remove the cotter pin and washer securing the clutch pushrod to the pedal arm.

4. Unbolt the master cylinder from the firewall.

5. Installation is the reverse of removal. Torque the mounting nuts to 11 ft. lb. on 4–151 models and 19 ft. lb on 4–150 and V6 models. Fill the reservoir with clean brake fluid.

Clutch Slave Cylinder

REMOVAL & INSTALLATION

CJ and Scrambler with 4–151 Engine and All 1984 Models with the 4–150 and V6 Engines

1. Disconnect the hydraulic line at the cylinder.

2. Remove the bolts attaching the cylinder to the clutch cover housing. On 4–151s, remove the throwout lever-to-pushrod retaining spring.

3. Remove the cylinder and cap the hydraulic line.

4. Installation is the reverse of removal. Torque the attaching bolts to 16 ft. lb.

TRANSFER CASE

Refer to "Transfer Case" in the Unit Repair section for troubleshooting and overhaul procedures.

Removal & Installation

SPICER 20

1. Remove shift lever knob, boot, and shift lever.

2. Remove floor covering and remove transmission access cover from floorpan.

3. Drain lubricant from transfer case. On CJ models drain the transmission also.

4. If equipped, disconnect torque reaction bracket from crossmember. Disconnect speedometer at transfer case.

Clutch master cylinder

5. On CJ models, place support stand under clutch housing to support engine and transmission, and remove rear crossmember.

6. Disconnect front and rear driveshafts at transfer case, making sure to mark shaft yokes for assembly.

7. On Cherokee and Truck models, disconnect parking brake cable at equalizer and exhaust pipe support bracket at transfer case.

8. Remove bolts attaching transfer case to transmission and remove transfer case.

NOTE: One transfer case attaching bolt must be removed from front end of the case. This bolt is located at the bottom right corner of the transmission.

9. Install a new gasket on the transmission.

10. Shift the transfer case into 4WD low and install the case assembly on the guide bolts.

11. Rotate the transfer case output shaft until the transmission main shaft gear engages the rear output shaft gear of the transfer case.

12. Slide the transfer case forward until the two units mate flush.

13. Install one upper bolt, remove the dowel guide bolts and install the remaining bolts. Torque to 30 ft. lbs.

14. Connect the speedometer cable and parking brake cable.

15. Install the propeller shafts after aligning the indexing marks.

16. Fill the unit with gear lube, and lower the vehicle.

17. Install the transfer case shift lever, boot, and knob.

MODELS 208 AND 300

1980 and Later
CHEROKEE, WAGONEER AND TRUCK MODELS

1. Raise and safely support the vehicle on jackstands.

2. Drain the lubricant from the transfer case.

3. Disconnect the speedometer cable and indicator switch wires. Disconnect the transfer case shift lever link at the operating lever.

4. Support the rear of the transmission and remove the rear crossmember.

5. Mark the transfer case front and rear output shaft yokes and driveshafts for assembly alignment reference.

6. Disconnect the front and rear driveshafts at the transfer case yokes. Secure the shafts to the frame rails with wires to keep them out of the way.

7. Disconnect the parking brake cable guide from the pivot located on the right frame rail, if necessary.

8. Remove the bolts that attach the exhaust pipe support bracket to transfer case, if necessary.

9. Remove the bolts that attach the transfer case to the transmission.

10. Move the transfer case assembly rearward until it is free of the transmission

output shaft. Remove and lower the transfer case.

11. Installation is in the reverse order of removal. Torque the transfer case mounting bolts to 40 ft. lbs.

CJ AND SCRAMBLER MODELS

1. On models with an automatic transmission; remove the shift lever knob, trim ring and boot from the transfer case shift lever.

2. On models with a manual transmission; remove the shift lever knob, trim ring and boot from the transmission and transfer case shift levers.

3. Remove the floor covering and remove the transmission access cover from the floorpan.

4. Raise and safely support the vehicle on jackstands. Drain the lubricant from the transfer case.

5. Support the engine and transmission under the clutch bell housing and remove the rear crossmember.

6. Mark the transfer case front and rear yokes and driveshafts for assembly alignment reference.

7. Disconnect the front and rear driveshafts at the transfer case. Secure the shafts out of the way.

8. Disconnect the speedometer cable at the transfer case. Disconnect the parking brake cable at the equalizer and the exhaust pipe support bracket at the transfer case to gain any needed clearance.

9. Remove the bolts mounting the transfer case to the transmission. Remove the transfer case.

10. Installation is in the reverse order of removal. The transfer case should be shifted into the 4L position before installation. Rotate the output shaft yoke until the transmission output shaft gear engages the transfer case input shaft. Torque the mounting bolts to 30 ft. lbs.

219 QUADRA-TRAC®

1. Lift and support the vehicle safely.

2. Remove reduction unit on Cherokee, Wagoneer, and Truck models, if equipped.

3. Index the marks on the front and rear yokes and propeller shafts for proper alignment during assembly.

4. Disconnect both the front and rear propeller shafts. On CJ-7 models, place support stand under transmission and remove crossmember.

5. Mark the vacuum diaphragm control for identification during the assembly, and then disconnect the vacuum hoses, wiring, and speedometer cable.

6. Disconnect the parking brake cable guide from the pivot on the right frame side.

7. Remove the two front side transfer case to transmission bolts, and install a guide bolt into the upper hole.

8. Remove the two rear side bolts, holding the transfer case to the transmission, and install a guide bolt into the upper hole.

9. Move the transfer case rearward until the unit is free of the transmission output shaft and guide pins. Lower the assembly to the floor.

10. Remove all gasket material from the rear of the transmission.

11. Install a new gasket on the rear of the transmission.

12. Install the guide bolts in the upper transmission adapter and transfer case, if they were removed.

13. Raise the transfer case, engage the guide bolts, and move the case assembly forward to the transmission. Make sure a flush fit is achieved.

14. If necessary, rotate the transfer case rear output shaft yoke until the drive hub splines align with the transmission output shaft.

15. Install front and rear attaching bolts, and remove the guide bolts during this operation.

16. Attach the exhaust pipe bracket support, if removed.

17. Align the propeller shaft and indexing marks on the yokes and attach the propeller shafts.

18. Connect the speedometer cable, wiring, and vacuum hoses.

19. Connect the parking brake cable guide to the pivot bracket on the right frame side.

20. Install the specified lubricant, and lower the vehicle.

207 Command-Trac®

1. Shift the unit into 4-High.

2. Raise and support the vehicle on jackstands.

3. Drain the lubricant from the case.

4. Mark the rear axle yoke and drive shaft for reference.

5. Remove the rear driveshaft.

6. Disconnect the speedometer cable, vacuum hoses and vent hose from the case.

7. Using a floor jack, raise the transmission and transfer case slightly, and remove the crossmember attaching bolts.

8. Remove the crossmember and lower the jack.

9. Mark the front driveshaft and transfer case flange for reference.

10. Disconnect the front driveshaft from the transfer case.

11. Disconnect the shift lever linkage at the case.

12. Remove the shift lever bracket bolts.

13. Support the transfer case on a jack, remove the attaching bolts and lower the case from the vehicle.

14. Installation is the reverse of removal. Observe the following torques:
Shift lever nut: 18 ft. lb.
Transfer case-to-Transmission adapter nut: 26 ft. lb.
Transfer case mounting bolt: 22 ft. lb.

229 Selec-Trac®

1. Raise and support the vehicle.

2. Drain the lubricant from the transfer case.

3. Disconnect the speedometer cable and vent hose. Disconnect the transfer case shift lever link at the operating lever.

4. Support the weight of the transmission with a jack. Remove the rear crossmember.

5. Mark the relation of the front and rear driveshafts with their yokes for reference.

6. Disconnect the front and rear driveshafts at the yokes.

7. Disconnect the shift motor vacuum hoses.

8. Disconnect the transfer case shift linkage.

9. Support the transfer case with a jack and remove the transfer case-to-transmission bolts.

10. Move the transfer case rearward and lower it from the truck.

11. Installation is the reverse of removal. Don't install any mounting bolts until all parts are aligned. Make sure that all splined shafts mesh properly before tightening bolts. Torque the transfer case-to-transmission bolts to 40 ft. lb. and the driveshaft yoke nuts to 10 ft. lb. (120 in. lb.)

Linkage Adjustments

The Shifter rails of the transfer case lever assembly connect to the shifter rails of the transfer case either directly or through non-adjustable links on vehicles with manual transmissions. An adjustable trunnion is provided on the lower shift rod to provide desired adjustment on automatic transmission equipped models. The linkage should be lubricated periodically.

QUADRA-TRAC®

Since the Quadra-Trac® system is a "full time 4WD" system, and is constantly engaged in 4WD, there is no "shift linkage" as such. There are two features which can be operated manually concerning the transfer case: the "Lock-Out" feature and the engagement of the optional "Low Range Reduction Unit."

Since the "Lock-Out" feature is a vacuum actuated unit, there are no external adjustments that can be made other than making sure that all vacuum lines are in place, connected and not damaged in any way.

The reduction unit is actuated by a shift cable and can be adjusted in the following manner:

1. Loosen the nut which clamps the cable to the shift lever pivot. Be sure that the cable can move freely in the pivot.

2. Move the reduction shift lever to the most rearward detent position (Hi-Range position).

3. Push the Low Range lever inward until it stops. Pull the Low Range lever out slightly, no more than 1/16 in.

4. Tighten the cable clamp nut at the reduction unit shift lever.

NOTE: This procedure only applies to the Quadra-Trac transfer case equipped with a reduction unit.

207 COMMAND-TRAC® AND 229 SELEC-TRAC® RANGE CONTROL LINKAGE ADJUSTMENT

1. Place the range control lever in the 2WD position.
2. Insert a ⅛ inch spacer between the shift gate and the lever.
3. Hold the lever in this position and place the transfer case lever in 2WD.
4. Adjust the link at the block, A (207) or B (229), to provide a free pin at the case outer lever.

A is the adjusting point on the 207

MANUAL TRANSMISSION

Refer to "Manual Transmission Overhaul" in the Unit Repair section for application, troubleshooting and overhaul.

Transmission

REMOVAL & INSTALLATION

1977–83 All Models and 1984 J10, 20

The transmission and transfer case can be removed as a unit. These instructions apply to both three and four-speed transmission.

1. Remove the shift lever knobs, trim rings, and bolts.
2. On three-speed floorshift models, remove the floor covering. Remove the floor pan section from above the transmission. Remove the shift control and lever assembly. On some four-speed models, remove the shift control housing cap, washer, spring, shift lever, and pin. Other four-speed models (SR4, T4 and T5) require the removal of the shift lever housing assembly.
3. Remove the transfer case shift lever and bracket.
4. Raise the vehicle on a lift.
5. Disconnect the column shift rods.
6. Remove the front driveshaft and disconnect the front of the rear driveshaft. Disconnect the vacuum line and electrical lead on a Quadra-Trac unit.
7. Disconnect the clutch cable, if so equipped and remove the cable mounting bracket from the transfer case.
8. Disconnect the speedometer cable, TCS switch, and back-up light switch. Disconnect the parking brake cable if it is connected to the crossmember.
9. On models equipped with V8 engines, disconnect and lower the exhaust pipes

B is the adjusting point on the 229

from the exhaust manifolds, and catalytic converter, if equipped.
10. Support the transmission with a floor jack.
11. Unbolt the crossmember from the frame. Unbolt the transmission from the clutch housing.
12. Lower the transmission slightly and move it to the rear to disengage the clutch shaft. Remove the unit.

To replace the transmission:

13. Place the wave washer and throw-out bearing and sleeve assembly in the fork. Center the bearing over the release levers.
14. Slide the transmission into place, being careful to align the transmission splines with those on the clutch plate. Bolt the transmission to the clutch housing and torque the bolts.
15. Bolt the crossmember to the frame. Remove the jack.
16. On models equipped with V8 engines, connect the exhaust pipes to the exhaust manifolds, and catalytic converter, if equipped.
17. Connect the speedometer cable, backup light switch, TCS switch, parking brake cable, clutch cable and cable mounting bracket.
18. Install the driveshafts. Flange bolts should be torqued to 25–45 ft. lbs.
19. Replace the column shift linkage.
20. Lower the vehicle.

21. Replace the transfer case shift lever and bracket.
22. On four-speeds, install the lever pivot pin, shift lever, spring, washer, and control housing cap or shift lever and housing. On three-speeds, install the shift control and lever assembly. Set the gears and the cover in the neutral position. Install the cover, placing the shift forks into the sleeves.
23. Replace the floor covering, boots, trim rings, and shift lever knobs.

1984 exc. J-10, 20

1. Raise the shift lever boot and remove the upper part of the console.
2. Remove the lower part of the console.
3. Remove the inner boot.
4. Remove the shift lever using tool J-34635, illustrated.
5. Raise and support the truck. Drain the transmission and transfer case. Mark the relation between the rear driveshaft and the transmission output yoke. Remove the driveshaft.
6. Position a jackstand under the transfer case.
7. Remove the rear crossmember.
8. Disconnect the speedometer cable, backup light switch and transfer case vent hose.
9. Disconnect the transfer case vacuum hoses and linkage. Remove the clutch slave cylinder.
10. Mark the relation between the front driveshaft and yoke and remove the driveshaft.
11. Place a floor jack under the transmission and secure the transmission/transfer case to the jack with a chain.
12. Remove the transmission-to-engine mounting bolts, move the assembly rearward and lower it from the truck.
13. Installation is the reverse of removal. Make sure that the shaft splines mesh before tightening the mounting bolts. Observe the following torques:
Crossmember-to-transmission: 33 ft. lb.
Transmission-to-engine: 28 ft. lb.
Transfer case-to-transmission adapter: 26 ft. lb.
U-joints-to-yokes: 170 in. lb.

Shifter removing tool

LINKAGE ADJUSTMENTS

The shift lever is connected to the transfer case shift rails through rods and nonadjustable links, therefore external adjustments are not possible.

AUTOMATIC TRANSMISSION

The General Motors Turbo-Hydramatic 400 transmission was used through 1979. From 1980, depending on the engine and model, either a Chrysler Loadflite 727, 904 or 999 transmission was installed. The 904 was discontinued in 1982. A lockup torque converter is used on some models.

REMOVAL & INSTALLATION

1977–79

1. Remove transmission dipstick.
2. If vehicle is equipped with radiator shroud, remove bolts attaching shroud to core support. Raise vehicle and support safety.
3. Mark front and rear universal joints and axle yokes.
4. On Cherokee, Wagoneer, and Truck models, remove parking brake cable jamnut and adjuster nut, remove clip attaching parking brake cable to crossmember and pull out of crossmember.
5. On CJ, and Truck models, with low range reduction unit, disconnect shift rod at reduction unit shift lever and remove reduction unit. On all other models, remove reduction unit shift lever from shift shaft and remove reduction unit.
6. Disconnect speedometer cable. Disconnect and mark emergency drive control vacuum lines and indicator lamp wire. Remove bolt attaching vacuum line routing bracket to rear of transfer case.
7. Disconnect detent solenoid wire at transmission case connector. Remove starter. Remove converter housing inspection cover and mark the torque converter. Remove converter-to-drive plate attaching bolts.
8. Support the transmission and remove the rear crossmember. Disconnect exhaust system components where necessary.
9. Remove spring clip and flat washer attaching transmission gearshift rod trunion to outer range selector lever. Do not loosen trunnion locknut. Disengage gearshift rod and trunnion from outer range selector lever. Remove spring clip and spring attaching outer range selector lever to transmission selector lever. Remove bolts attaching outer range selector lever bracket and bushing to frame and remove bracket, lever, and bushing as an assembly.

Shift lever removal for T-18A and all 3-speed units

10. Disconnect front propeller shaft at transfer case yoke and secure shaft. Disconnect transmission oil cooler lines. Disconnect engine-to-modulator vacuum hose, and remove transmission filler tube.
11. Position a support stand under the engine. Remove the transmission filler tube.
12. Remove the converter housing to engine attaching bolts and move the transmission assembly rearward with a supporting jack until it clears the crankshaft.
13. Hold the converter in place and lower the transmission from the vehicle.
14. The installation of the transmission is in the reverse of the removal procedure. Be sure the converter is properly aligned to the drive plate during installation.

T-176 shift lever removal

SR-4 shift lever removal

1980 and Later

1. Disconnect the negative battery cable.
2. Disconnect the fan shroud, if equipped.
3. Disconnect the transmission oil fill tube top bracket.
4. Raise the vehicle and safely support it on jackstands.
5. Remove the inspection cover from the lower part of the converter housing.
6. Remove the oil filler tube and dipstick.
7. Remove the starter motor.
8. Mark the driveshafts and yokes for position. Disconnect the driveshafts from the transfer case yokes. Secure the shafts to the frame with wire so they are out of the way.
9. On eight cylinder models, disconnect the exhaust pipes at the exhaust manifolds and remove, if necessary, to gain clearance.
10. Drain the transfer case lubricant and transmission fluid.
11. Disconnect the speedometer cable, gearshift linkage, throttle linkage and the wires to the neutral safety switch.
12. Mark the converter drive plate and converter for location reference.
13. Remove the bolts that attach the converter to the drive plate. Use a ratchet and socket on the crankshaft pulley bolt to turn the engine when removing the converter mounting bolts.
14. Support the transmission-transfer case assembly on a suitable jack (transmission type jack if possible). Be sure the transmission assembly is firmly chained or secured on the jack for removal.
15. Remove the rear crossmember. Lower the transmission slightly and disconnect the oil coller lines.
16. Remove the bolts that mount the transmission to the engine.
17. Move the transmission and converter back and away from the engine. Make sure the converter breaks loose from the drive plate and is firmly mounted on the transmission.
18. Hold the converter in position and lower the transmission assembly until the converter housing clears the engine.

19. Remove the transmission and transfer case assembly from under the vehicle.

20. Remove the transfer case.

21. Installation is in the reverse order of removal. Be sure to line up the marks on the converter and drive plate when reinstalling. Transmission mounting bolts are torqued to 28 ft. lbs.

GEARSHIFT LINKAGE ADJUSTMENT

Through 1979

1. Place the steering column gearshift lever in the Neutral position.

2. Raise the vehicle on a hoist.

3. Loosen the locknut on the gearshift rod trunnion just enough to permit movement of the gearshift rod in the trunnion.

4. Place the outer range selector lever at the transmission, fully into the Neutral detent position and tighten the locknut at the trunnion to 9 ft. lbs.

5. Lower the car and operate the steering column gearshift in all ranges. The car should start in Park and Neutral only and the column gearshift lever engage properly in all detent positions.

1980 and Later

1. Raise and safely support the vehicle on jackstands.

2. Loosen the shift rod trunnion jamnuts.

3. Remove the lockpin that retains the shift rod trunnion to the bell crank. Disengage the trunnion and shift rod at the bell crank.

4. Place the gear shift lever in the Park position and lock the steering column.

5. Move the transmission lever rearward into the Park detent. Be sure the lever is as far rearward as it will go.

6. Check the engagement of the Park detent by trying to rotate the driveshaft (rear wheels must be off of the ground). The shaft will not rotate if the Park detent is engaged.

7. Adjust the trunnion until it will fit in the bell crank arm freely. Tighten the jamnuts. Install the lock pin.

8. Check engine starting in Park and Neutral, be sure it will not start in any other gear.

9. Lower vehicle from stands.

BAND ADJUSTMENT

Through 1979

No provisions are made for the external band adjustments of this transmission. Only during the assembly, can a different sized pin be installed in the rear band apply system, to compensate for lining wear.

FRONT BAND

1980 and Later

The front band adjusting screw is located

Turbo Hydra-Matic 400 shift linkage and neutral start switch

on the left side of the transmission case just above the manual valve and throttle control levers.

1. Raise and safely support the vehicle on jackstands.

2. Loosen the adjusting screw locknut and back if off five turns.

3. Check the adjusting screw to make sure it turns freely, lubricate it if necessary.

4. Tighten the adjusting screw to 36 in. lbs.

5. Back of the adjusting screw two turns. Tighten the locknut. Do not allow the adjusting screw to turn when tightening the locknut.

REAR BAND ADJUSTMENT

1980 and Later

NOTE: The transmission oil pan must be removed to gain access to the adjusting screw. See Pan and Filter Removal Section.

1. Raise and safely support the vehicle on jackstands.

2. Remove the oil pan and drain the fluid.

3. The adjusting screw is located on the right rear side above the rear side edge of the filter.

4. Loosen the locknut. Tighten the adjusting screw to 41 in. lbs. Back off the adjusting screw four turns on models 904 through 1983 and 7 turns on 904 in 1984, four turns on 999, and two turns on model 727.

5. Hold the adjusting screw so that it will not turn and tighten the locknut.

6. Install the oil pan and new gasket.

7. Lower the vehicle and fill the transmission to the correct level.

NEUTRAL SWITCH ADJUSTMENT

Through 1979

1. Apply the parking brake.

2. Check and adjust the manual linkage, if necessary.

3. Remove the Neutral switch from the steering column.

4. Place the selector lever in Park and lock the steering column.

5. Move the switch actuating lever until it is aligned with the letter "P" stamped on the back of the switch.

6. Insert a $\frac{3}{32}$ in. drill in the hole located below the letter "N" stamped on the back of the switch.

7. Move the switch actuating lever until it stops against the drill.

8. Position the switch on the steering column, install the attaching screws and remove the drill.

9. Check the operation of the switch. The engine should start in Park and Neutral only. The backup light should glow only in the Reverse position.

1980 and later

The neutral safety switch is located on the

side of the transmission by the manual linkage. It is an electrical switch that is thread mounted. The neutral starting section of the switch is contained in the center terminal of the three terminal switch. The other terminals control the backup lights.

TEST AND REPLACEMENT

1. Remove the wiring connector from the switch. Test for continuity between the center terminal pin and the transmission case. Continuity should exist only when the transmission control is in Park or Neutral.
2. If test shows that the switch is defective, check the gearshift linkage adjustment before replacing the switch.
3. Remove the switch from the transmission. A certain amount of fluid will leak out when the switch is removed, have a container ready to catch the fluid.
4. Move the gearshift lever to Park and neutral positions. Inspect the switch operating lever fingers and manual lever and shaft for proper alignment with the switch opening in the transmission case.
5. Install a new switch and seal into the transmission case. Tighten to 24 ft. lbs. Test for continuity.
6. Correct the transmission fluid level. Lower vehicle from stands.

Transmission Oil Pan and Filter

REMOVAL & INSTALLATION

1. Raise the vehicle and support safely.
2. Position a drain pan under the transmission and remove the oil pan bolts, except the four corner ones.
3. Loosen the corner bolts and pry the oil pan loose from the transmission case.
4. Allow the oil to drain from the corners of the oil pan, while tilting the pan to remove as much oil as possible.
5. Carefully remove the corner bolts and the oil pan from the transmission case.
6. Remove the oil filter, oil pan gasket, and through 1979, the intake tube O-ring seal.
7. Place a new O-ring on the intake tube and install the tube in place through 1979.
8. Install a new filter and retain it to the control valve assembly with the attaching bolt.
9. Install the oil pan and gasket. Torque the pan bolts to 10 ft. lbs.
10. Lower the vehicle and fill the transmission with the specified fluid. (Dexron® II equivalent).

THROTTLE LINKAGE ADJUSTMENT—1980–81

4–151

1. Remove the air cleaner.

2. Remove the spark plug wire holder from the throttle cable bracket and move the holder and wires aside.
3. Raise and support the vehicle on jackstands.
4. Hold the throttle control lever rearward against its stop. Hook one end of a spare spring to the lever and hook the opposite end to any convenient point. This will hold the lever in position.
5. Lower the vehicle.
6. Block the choke open and move the carburetor linkage completely off the fast idle cam.
7. On vehicles without air conditioning, turn the ignition to ON to energize the solenoid.
8. Unlock the throttle control cable by releasing the T shaped adjuster clamp on the cable by lifting it upward with a small screwdriver.
9. Grasp the outer sheath of the cable and move the cable and sheath forward to remove any load on the cable bell crank.
10. Adjust the cable by removing the cable and sheath rearward until there is no play at all between the plastic cable and the bell crank ball.
11. When play has been eliminated, lock the cable by pressing the T shaped clamp downward until it snaps into place.
12. Turn the ignition off. Install all parts and remove the spare spring.

6–173, 258

1. Disconnect the throttle control rod spring at the carburetor.
2. Raise and support the vehicle on jackstands.
3. Use the throttle control rod spring to hold the throttle control lever forward against its stop, by hooking one end of the spring on the throttle control lever and the other end on the throttle linkage bell crank bracket which is attached to the transmission housing.
4. Block the choke plate open and move the throttle linkage off the fast idle cam.
5. On carburetors equipped with a throttle operated solenoid valve, turn the ignition ON to energize the solenoid, then open the throttle halfway to allow the solenoid to lock and return the carburetor to the idle position.
6. Loosen the retaining bolt on the throttle control adjusting link. DO NOT REMOVE THE SPRING CLIP AND NYLON WASHER!
7. Pull on the end of the link to eliminate play and tighten the retaining bolt.
8. Remove the throttle control rod spring and install it on the control rod from where it came.
9. Lower the vehicle.

V8 Engines

1. Disconnect the throttle control rod spring at the carburetor.
2. Raise and support the vehicle on jackstands.

Front band adjustment-TorqueFlite

Rear band adjustment-TorqueFlite

Torqueflite neutral start and backup light switch

3. Use the throttle control rod spring to hold the transmission throttle valve control lever against its stop.
4. Block the choke plate open and make sure the throttle linkage is off the fast idle cam.

NOTE: On carburetors equipped with a throttle operated solenoid valve, turn the ignition to ON to energize the solenoid. Then turn the throttle halfway to allow the solenoid to lock and return the carburetor to idle.

5. Loosen the retaining bolt on the throttle control rod adjuster link. Remove the spring clip and move the nylon washer to the rear of the link.

6. Push on the end of the link to eliminate play and tighten the link retaining bolt.

7. Install the nylon washer and spring clip.

8. Remove the throttle control rod spring and install it in its intended position.

9. Lower the vehicle.

FRONT DRIVE AXLE

Front Locking Hubs

Selective drive hubs are used to disengage the front axles from the drive train when the vehicle is used in two-wheel drive. When Quadra-Trac®, Selec-Trac® or Command-Trac® is used, the selector hubs are not used. Two different types are used, automatic and manual.

CJ MODELS, AUTOMATIC HUBS

Removal

1. Remove the allen screws from the clutch assembly and remove the assembly from the hub body assembly.

2. Remove the retaining ring from the axle shaft end.

3. Straighten lock tabs and remove the screws attaching the hub body assembly to the front hub. Remove the hub body assembly.

CLUTCH ASSEMBLY OVERHAUL—AUTOMATIC HUBS

1. Push out the control dial, turn the unit over and remove the cluster ring and disc.

2. Clean and inspect all parts for damage. Replace U-ring and O-ring seals on the control dial.

3. Install the control dial assembly and install the disc.

NOTE: Lubricate O-ring and inside of cap.

4. Rotate the control dial to "FREE" position. Install the clutch ring and thread to the bottom.

5. Turn back the clutch ring until the holes align and install in the body assembly.

6. Turn the control from "FREE" to "LOCK" and check the operation.

BODY ASSEMBLY

Overhaul

1. Remove the friction shoe spring, retaining ring, and separate the hub body from the roller clutch.

2. Remove the centering spring, and spirolock ring. Separate the cage and axle shaft hub.

3. Clean and inspect all parts, coat lightly with grease.

4. Install the friction shoe on the cage, (avoid stretching the shoe) and lubricate the friction shoes liberally, and install.

Installation

1. Position the gasket and body assembly on the wheel hub.

2. Install the tab lock washer and screws. Torque the screws to 40–45 ft. lbs. and secure with the lock washer tabs.

3. Install the retaining ring on the axle shaft end.

4. Place the gasket and cap assembly on the body assembly and torque the allen headed screws to 6–8 ft. lbs.

CHEROKEE AND TRUCK

Removal

1. Remove the six allen screws and remove the clutch assembly.

2. Remove the capscrews, lock washers, and stop-ring on the axle shaft end.

3. Remove the retaining ring(s) and slide the hub body off the axle end.

Clutch Assembly— Automatic Hubs

OVERHAUL

1. Remove the taper headed screw from the clutch screw unit.

2. Push out the control dial, turn the assembly over and push out the clutch and clutch screw.

3. Clean and inspect all parts. Replace the U-ring and O-ring seals on the control dial.

4. Lubricate the clutch ring and thread the clutch screw into the clutch ring until the ring raises slightly.

5. Install the taper headed screw and stake it in place.

NOTE: If new parts are used, drill a ³⁄₁₆ inch hole through the clutch screw into the thick webbing on the control dial ⅝ inch deep. Install a pin and stake into place.

6. Turn the dial from "FREE" to "LOCK" and check the operation.

Hub Body—Automatic Hubs

OVERHAUL

1. Remove the friction shoe spring and the retaining ring.

2. Clean and inspect all parts.

3. Lubricate the bearing race lightly.

4. Place the cage into the body and pack rollers with chassis lub.

5. Place the body over the axle shaft hub, carefully, and install the retaining ring.

Installation

1. Carefully install the friction shoe spring and lubricate the shoes with chassis lube, and slide the body assembly into the hub.

NOTE: The body assembly will stop about ¼ inch from full position. Allow the body to slide to full position by pushing the assembly to expand the friction shoes over the drag shoe nut.

2. Install the retaining ring to hold the body assembly to the hub.

3. Install the screw, lock washer, and stop ring in the axle end and torque to 35–40 ft. lbs.

4. Install the clutch assembly to the body assembly with the allen headed screws, and torque to 4–6 ft. lbs.

5. Rotate the wheel and check for freedom of movement.

Typical front hub and rotor assembly

Manual Hubs

REMOVAL

1. Remove the allen screws from the clutch hub.
2. Remove the hub body bolts from the front hub.
3. Remove the retaining ring and pull the clutch ring assembly and axle shaft hub body from the axle.

NOTE: The clutch ring assembly cannot be disassembled. The control assembly and the clutch screw cannot be separated.

DISASSEMBLY

1. Remove the snap-ring from the hub bore.
2. Remove the needle bearing and thrust washer from the clutch hub body and the axle shaft hub, noting the side of the hub body from which the axle shaft hub is removed.

ASSEMBLY

1. Install the axle shaft hub into the hub body from the same side as it was removed.
2. Install the needle bearings in the hub and install the snap ring.

INSTALLATION

1. With a new gasket, install the hub body assembly onto the wheel hub and over the axle shaft, and install the attaching bolts.
2. Install the retaining ring in the groove at the end of the axle shaft hub.
3. Lubricate the bearing side and the grooves of the control assembly and install the new O-rings.
4. Insert the clutch ring assembly into the hub body and retain it with the snap-ring.

NOTE: Try the clutch ring for a free sliding fit on the drive pins. If a binding

occurs, lift the unit out and reposition it. If the binding still exists, remove and examine for damage.

5. Position the control assembly with the dowel pin into the face of the clutch body, so that the arrow stops on the dot marked "FREE".
6. Install the control assembly over the axle end and retain it to the hub body with the allen headed screws. Use a new gasket.
7. Move the control from the "FREE" position to the "LOCK" position and assure that the unit is operating satisfactorily.

Axle Shaft

REMOVAL & INSTALLATION

All except 1984 CJ–7, Scrambler, Wagoneer and Cherokee

1. Raise and support the vehicle.
2. Remove the wheel and dust cover.
3. Remove the axle shaft snap-ring, drive flange, pressure spring and spring retainer. If the drive flange is stuck to the shaft, use a pry bar to pry it out.
4. Use the special nut wrench to remove the wheel bearing locknut, lockring, and wheel bearing adjusting nut.
5. Remove the two bolts securing the brake caliper assembly to the disc brake shield and move the caliper assembly aside.
6. Remove the rotor and hub assembly. The spring retainer and outer wheel bearing will slide out as the hub assembly is removed.
7. Remove the nuts and bolts attaching the spindle and disc brake shield.
8. Remove the spindle and disc brake shield. It may be necessary to tap the spindle lightly to free it.
9. Remove the axle shaft.
10. Install the new axle shaft, spindle, and bearing assembly.
11. Install the hub, brake shield, rotor, and the brake caliper assembly.
12. Install the inner wheel bearing adjusting nut. This is the nut with the peg on

the side. Tighten the nut to 50 ft. lbs. with the special wheel bearing nut wrench. Rotate the hub and back off the adjusting nut ¼ turn maximum.

13. Install the lockwasher with the inner tab lined up with the keyway spindle. Turn the inner adjusting nut until the peg engages the nearest hole in the lockwasher. Install the outer locknut and tighten it to 50 ft. lbs. Install the spring retainer, pressure spring and drive flange.
14. Push the drive flange inward to provide clearance and install the axle shaft snap-ring.
15. Install the wheel and dust cover and lower the vehicle.

1984 CJ–7, Scrambler, Wagoneer, Cherokee

1. Raise and support the front end on jackstands.
2. Remove the wheels, calipers and rotors.
3. Remove the cotter pin, locknut and axle hub nut.
4. Remove the hub-to-knuckle attaching bolts.
5. Remove the hub and splash shield from the steering knuckle.
To remove the left shaft:
6. Remove the axle shaft from the housing.
To remove the right shaft:
7. Disconnect the vacuum harness from the shift motor.
8. Remove the shift motor from the housing.
9. Remove the axle shaft from the housing.
To install the right shaft:
10. Be sure that the shift collar is in position on the intermediate shaft and that the axle shaft is fully engaged in the intermediate shaft end.
11. Install the shift motor, making sure that the fork engages with the collar. Tighten the bolts to 8 ft. lb.
12. On the left side, install the axle shaft in the housing.
13. Partially fill the hub cavity of the knuckle with chassis lube and install the hub and splash shield.
14. Tighten the hub bolts to 75 ft. lb.
15. Install the hub washer and nut. Torque the nut to 175 ft. lb. Install the locknut. Install a new cotter pin.
16. Install the rotor, caliper and wheel.

Axle Shaft Seal

REMOVAL & INSTALLATION

1. Remove axle shaft.
2. Remove seal and bronze thrust washer. If washer is worn it must be replaced.
3. Install seal and washer with washer chamfered side toward the axle shaft seal.
4. Installation is the reverse of removal

Exploded view of a manual front hub

NOTE: Pack wheel bearing grease around thrust face of shaft and seal and fill seal area of spindle with wheel bearing grease.

Wheel Bearing Adjustment

CJ MODELS

1. With the front of the vehicle raised, remove the hubcaps, snapsprings, capscrews, and washers attaching the drive flange to the hub.
2. Remove the drive flange from the front hub.

NOTE: A puller may be needed for this operation.

3. Straighten the edge of the lock washer, so that the lock nut and lock washer can be removed.
4. With a special wrench or equivalent, tighten the adjusting nut until the wheel binds, and back off approximately ⅙ turn, so that the wheel turns freely without any lateral shake.
5. Install the lock washer and lock nut on the housing end, tighten the lock nut and crimp the lock washer edge over the lock nut.
6. Assemble the drive flange, bolts, and the hub cap. Assure that the gasket is properly installed between the hub and the flange.

1977–83 CHEROKEE, WAGONEER, AND 1977–84 TRUCKS

1. Remove the hub caps, snap-ring, drive gear pressure spring, outer lock nut, and lock washer.
2. Loosen the inner wheel bearing nut, and then retighten to 50 ft. lbs. torque (inner nut has peg on outer side).
3. Rotate the hub, back off the adjusting nut ¼ turn maximum.
4. Install the lock washer to have the tab engage the key way in the spindle and move the adjusting nut until the peg engages the nearest hole in the lock washer.
5. Install the outer lock washer and tighten to 50 ft. lbs.

1984 CJ–7, Scrambler, Wagoneer, Cherokee

1. Raise and support the front end on jackstands.
2. Remove the wheel, caliper and rotor.
3. Remove the cotter pin, locknut and hub nut.
4. Remove the hub-to-knuckle attaching bolts and remove the hub assembly from the vehicle.
5. Press the hub out of the carrier and remove the seals and bearings.
6. Inspect and replace any worn or damaged parts.

7. Bearings and cups must be replaced as a set. If the hub carrier bearings are to be replaced, remove the existing cups and install the replacement cups in the carrier using a brass drift.
8. Fill the cavities in the knuckle, hub and carrier and the lip type seals with an EP-lithium based grease.
9. Install the bearings in the hub carrier. Install the seal.
10. Press the hub through the bearings in the carrier.
11. Install the splash shield.
12. Install the hub on the knuckle.
13. Tighten the hub mounting bolts to 75 ft. lb.
14. Install the hub washer and nut. Torque the nut to 175 ft. lb. Install the locknut and cotter pin.
15. Install the rotor, caliper and wheel.

Steering Knuckle Service

REMOVAL & INSTALLATION

All except 1984 CJ-7, Scrambler, Wagoneer, Cherokee

1. Follow the Axle Removal procedure as outlined previously.
2. Remove the steering rods from the steering arm.
3. Remove the lower ball stud nut.

NOTE: This nut is a self-locking nut and should be discarded and replaced with a new nut upon assembly.

4. Remove the cotter pin from the upper ball stud nut and loosen it to the top of the stud in a flush manner. With the aid of a lead hammer, unseat the upper and lower ball studs from the yoke.
5. Remove the knuckle assembly from the axle.
6. With the use of a suitable tool remove the upper ball stud seat from the axle yoke.
7. Securely clamp the knuckle assembly in a vise with the upper ball stud pointed down.
8. Using a large socket or drift, of approximately the same size as the ball stud, and a mallet, drive the lower stud out of the knuckle.
9. Place the socket on the bottom surface of the upper ball stud. Place the drift through the hole where the lower ball stud was and place it on the socket. Drive the upper ball stud out of the knuckle with a mallet.
10. Before installing the lower ball stud, run the lower ball stud nut onto the stud just far enough so the head of the stud is flush with the top edge of the nut.
11. Invert the knuckle in the vise. Position the lower ball stud in the knuckle with the nut in place. Place the same size socket over the nut and drive the ball stud into place with the drift and mallet.

12. Use the same procedure for installing the upper ball stud. The drift will not be needed to install the upper ball stud.
13. Install the upper ball stud seat into the axle yoke. Use a new one if the old one shows evidence of wear. The top of the seat should be flush with the top of the yoke.
14. Install the knuckle assembly onto the axle yoke. Install the lower stud nut. Tighten it to 70–90 ft. lbs.
15. Install the upper stud nut and tighten it to 100 ft. lbs. Install the cotter pin. If the cotter pin holes do not align, tighten the nut until the pin can be installed. Do not loosen the nut to align the holes.
16. Install the axle shaft, spindle and bearing assembly, and brake assembly. Connect the steering rods. Install the drum and hub, and wheel assembly. Adjust the wheel bearings. Check the turning angle. Adjust the stop screw to permit the proper turning angle of 31°.

1984 CJ-7, Scrambler, Wagoneer, Cherokee

1. Remove the outer axle shaft.
2. Remove the caliper anchor plate from the knuckle.
3. Remove the knuckle-to-ball joint cotter pins and nuts.
4. Drive the knuckle out with a brass hammer.

NOTE: A split ring seat (3) is located in the bottom of the knuckle. During installation, this ring seat must be set to a depth of 5.23mm (.206). Measure the depth to the top of the ring seat (4).

5. Installation is the reverse of removal. Tighten the knuckle retaining nuts to 75 ft. lb. and the caliper anchor bolts to 77 ft. lb.

Split retaining ring

Steering knuckle components-typical

Ball Joints

REMOVAL & INSTALLATION

All except 1984 CJ-7, Scrambler, Wagoneer, Cherokee

1. Replacement of the ball joints, or ball stud, as they will be called from here on, requires the removal of the steering knuckle. To remove the steering knuckle, first remove the wheel, brake drum or disc, and hub as an assembly. Remove the brake assembly from the spindle. Position the brake assembly on the front axle in a convenient place. Remove the snap ring from the axle shaft.

2. Remove the spindle and bearing assembly. It may be necessary to tap the spindle with a soft mallet to disengage it from the steering knuckle.

3. Slide the axle shaft out through the steering knuckle.

4. Disconnect the steering tie-rods from the knuckle arm.

5. Remove and discard the lower ball stud nut.

6. Remove the cotter pin from the upper stud. Loosen the upper stud until the top edge of the nut is flush with the top end of the stud.

7. Use a lead hammer to unseat the upper and lower studs from the yoke. Remove the upper nut and the knuckle assembly.

8. Remove the ball stud seat from the upper hole in the axle yoke. It is threaded in the hole. There are special wrenches available for removing the seat. Remove the lower ball stud snap ring.

9. Securely clamp the knuckle assembly in a vise with the upper ball stud pointed down.

10. Using a large socket or drift, of approximately the same size as the ball stud, and a mallet, drive the lower stud out of the knuckle.

NOTE: Throughout this procedure, where a ball stud is either removed or installed, a hydraulic press or a two jawed gear puller can be used and, if at all possible, should be used to make the job easier. However it is possible to complete the job using a mallet, drift and a large socket the same size as the ball studs.

11. Place the socket on the bottom surface of the upper ball stud. Place the drift through the hole where the lower ball stud was and place it on the socket. Drive the upper ball stud out of the knuckle with a mallet.

12. Before installing the lower ball stud, run the lower ball stud nut onto the stud just far enough so the head of the stud is flush with the top edge of the nut.

13. Invert the knuckle in the vise. Position the lower ball stud in the knuckle with the nut in place. Place the same size socket over the nut and drive the ball stud into place with the drift and mallet.

14. Tighten the upper ball stud to 10–20 ft. lb. to draw the lower ball stud into the tapered hold in the yoke. Install the upper stud in the same manner as the lower. The drift will not be needed to install the upper ball stud.

15. Install the upper ball stud seat into the axle yoke. Use a new one if the old one shows evidence of wear. Torque the seat to 50 ft. lb.

16. Install the knuckle assembly onto the axle yoke. Install the lower stud nut. Tighten it to 70–90 ft. lbs.

17. Install the upper stud nut and tighten it to 100 ft. lbs. Install the cotter pin. If the cotter pin holes do not align, tighten the nut until the pin can be installed. Do not loosen the nut to align the holes.

18. Install the axle shaft, spindle and bearing assembly, and braake assembly. Connect the steering rods. Install the drum and hub, and wheel assembly. Adjust the wheel bearings.

1984 CJ-7, Scrambler, Wagoneer, Cherokee
UPPER BALL JOINT

1. Remove the steering knuckle as previously outlined.

2. Position the receiver, tool J-34503, (1) over the top of the ball joint. Set the adapter, tool J-34503-3, (2) in a C-clamp (3) and position the clamp so that tightening the clamp screw will remove the ball joint.

3. To install, use the same C-clamp, with tool J-34503-5, (4) as illustrated.

LOWER BALL JOINT

1. With the knuckle removed, as previously outlined, use a C-clamp, with tool J-34503 (6) and tool J-34503-3 (7) as illustrated, to force out the ball joint.

2. To install, use the same C-clamp, with tool J-34503-4 (8) and tool J-34503-2 (9), as illustrated.

Lower ball stud jamnut removal

Upper Ball Joint Adjustment

ALL EXCEPT 1984 CJ-7, SCRAMBLER, WAGONEER, CHEROKEE

Adjustment of the upper ball joint is necessary only when there is excessive play in the steering, persistent loosening of the steering linkage, or abnormal wear of the tires.

ADJUSTMENT PROCEDURE

1. Raise the vehicle on a hoist or jack and support with stands if necessary.
2. Disconnect the steering linkage from the left and right knuckle assemblies.
3. Attach a torque wrench and socket to a steering arm stud and check the torque needed to move the knuckle through its arc.
4. Maximum torque is 12–16 lbs. on model 30 axle, and 15–20 lbs. on model 44 axle.

NOTE: The knuckle should turn smoothly through the turning arc and have no vertical end play.

Lower ball stud removal

Upper ball stud removal

Lower ball stud installation

Upper ball stud installation

Steering knuckle installation

Tightening the upper ball stud seat

5. If the torque is too low, perform the following procedures.

   a. Remove the upper ball stud cotter pin.

   b. Torque the stud adjusting sleeve to 50 ft. lbs.

   c. Install the lock nut and a new cotter pin.

   d. Recheck the torque necessary to turn the knuckle through its arc, and if the torque is still too low, retorque the sleeve to 60 ft. lbs. and recheck.

   e. If the torque specifications can not be obtained, it will be necessary to replace parts in the knuckle assembly.

NOTE: Temperature will affect the turning torque, therefore, allowances in the torque reading should be made.

Front Axle Assembly

REMOVAL & INSTALLATION

All exc. 1984 CJ-7, Scrambler, Wagoneer, Cherokee

1. Raise and support the front of the vehicle, supporting the weight at the rear of the front spring.

2. Remove the wheel covers and wheels.

3. Index the propeller shaft to the differential yoke for the proper alignment upon installation.

4. Disconnect the steering linkage from the steering knuckles.

5. On vehicles equipped with sway bar, remove nuts attaching sway bar connecting links to spring tie plates.

6. Disconnect the shock absorbers and breather tube from the axle housing.

7. Remove the brake calipers, hub and rotor, and the brake shield.

8. Remove the spring clips and the spring clip plates.

9. Support the assembly on a jack and loosen the nuts securing the rear shackles, but do not remove the bolts.

10. Remove the front spring shackle bolts and rest the front of the spring on the floor.

11. Pull the jack and axle housing from underneath the vehicle.

12. Support the axle on a jack and slide the assembly under the vehicle, and position it over the springs.

13. Raise the front of the springs and install the front shackle bolts, but do not tighten.

14. Position the axle on the springs and install the spring clips and spring clip plates.

15. Tighten the front and rear shackle bolts.

16. Install the brake shield, hub and rotor, and brake calipers.

17. Connect the breather tube and shock absorbers.

18. Connect the steering linkage at the steering knuckles.

19. Align the indexing marks and install the propeller shaft.

20. Install the wheels and tighten. Install the wheel covers.

21. Lower the vehicle and check the wheel alignment and turning angle.

1984 CJ-7, Scrambler, Wagoneer, Cherokee

1. Raise and support the truck on jackstands.

2. Remove the wheels, calipers and rotors.

3. Disconnect all vacuum hoses at the axle.

4. Mark the relation between the front driveshaft and yoke.

5. Disconnect the stabilizer bar, rod and center link, front driveshaft, shock absorbers, steering damper, track bar.

6. Place a floor jack under the axle to take up the weight.

7. Disconnect the upper and lower control arms at the axle and lower the axle from the truck.

8. Installation is the reverse of removal. Observe the following torques:
  Center link-to-knuckle: 35 ft. lb.
  Upper control arm-to-axle: 37 ft. lb.
  Lower control arm-to-axle: 133 ft. lb.
  Shock absorber-to-axle: 14 ft. lb.
  Track bar-to-axle: 55 ft. lb.
  Stabilizer bar-to-axle: 70 ft. lb.
  Steering damper-to-axle: 55 ft. lb.

Driveshaft

REMOVAL & INSTALLATION

In order to remove the front and rear driveshafts, first match-mark the driveshaft and yoke for reference, unscrew the attaching nuts from the universal joint's U-bolts, remove the U-bolts and slide the shaft forward or backward toward the slip-joint. The shaft can then be removed from the end yokes and removed from under the vehicle. Install the driveshaft in the reverse order.

NOTE: Some driveshafts are marked at the slip-joints with arrows on the spline and sleeve yoke. When installing the driveshaft, align the arrows to have the yokes at the front and rear of the shaft in the same parallel plane.

Upper ball joint removal

Lower ball joint removal

Lower ball joint installation

U-Joint Overhaul

SNAP-RING TYPE DISASSEMBLY AND REPAIR

1. Remove the snap-rings.
2. Press on the end of one bearing until the opposite bearing is pushed from the yoke arm.
3. Turn the joint over. Press the first bearing back out of the arm by pressing on the exposed end of the journal shaft. Repeat this operation for the other two bearings, then lift out the journal assembly by sliding it to one side.
4. Wash all parts in solvent and inspect for wear. Replace all worn parts.
5. Install new gaskets on the journal assembly. Make certain that the grease channel in each journal trunnion is open.
6. Pack the bearing cones one-third full of grease and install the rollers.
7. Assemble in the reverse order of disassembly. If the joint binds when assembled, tap the arms lightly to relieve any pressure on the bearings at the end of the journal.

U-BOLT TYPE DISASSEMBLY AND REPAIR

Remove the attaching U-bolts to release one set of bearing races. Slide the driveshaft into the yoke flange to remove the races. The rest of the disassembly and repair procedure is the same as that given above for the snap-ring type of cross and roller joint. The correct U-bolt torque is 15–20 ft. lbs.

REAR AXLE

Refer to the Drive Axle General Repair Section for application, troubleshooting, and overhaul procedures.

Rear Axle Assembly

REMOVAL & INSTALLATION

Exc. 1984 Wagoneer and Cherokee

1. Raise the vehicle and place jack stands forward of the rear springs.
2. Remove the rear wheels.
3. Place an indexing mark on the rear yoke and propeller shaft, and disconnect the shaft.
4. Disconnect the shock absorbers from the axle tubes.
5. Disconnect the brake hose from the tee fitting on the axle housing.
6. Disconnect the parking brake cable at the frame mounting.

Exploded view of typical U-joint

7. Remove U-Bolts. On vehicles with spring mounted above axle, disconnect spring at rear shackle.
8. Support the axle on a Jack, remove the spring clips, and remove the axle assembly from under the vehicle.
9. Installation is the reverse of removal.

NOTE: Bleed and adjust brakes accordingly.

1984 Wagoneer, Cherokee

1. Raise and support the truck on jackstands.
2. Remove the wheels and brake drums.
3. Disconnect the shock absorbers.
4. Disconnect the brake hose at the frame rail.
5. Disconnect the parking brake cables at the equalizer.
6. Mark the relation between the driveshaft and yoke, and disconnect the driveshaft.
7. Place a floor jack under the axle to take up the weight.
8. Remove the axle-to-spring U-bolts and lower the axle.
9. Installation is the reverse of removal. Observe the following torques:
   U-joint strap bolts: 170 in. lb.
   Shock absorber-to-axle: 44 ft. lb.
   Spring-to-axle U-bolts: 52 ft. lb.
10. Bleed the brakes. Road test the truck.

Axle Shaft

REMOVAL & INSTALLATION

All exc. 1984 Wagoneer and Cherokee

TAPERED SHAFT

1. Jack up the vehicle and remove the hub cap.
2. Remove the wheel.
3. Remove the axle nut dust cap.
4. Remove the axle shaft cotter pin, castle nut and flat washer.
5. Back-off the brake adjustment.
6. Use a puller to remove the wheel hub.
7. Remove the screws attaching the brake dust protector, grease and bearing retainers, brake assembly and shim to the housing.

8. Remove the hydraulic line from the brake assembly.
9. Remove the dust shield and oil seal.
10. Use a puller to remove the axle shaft.
11. Install the axle shaft in the reverse order of removal, using a new grease seal and installing the hub assembly before the woodruff key.

NOTE: Should the axle shaft be broken, the inner end can usually be drawn out of the housing with a wire loop after the outer oil seal is removed. However, if the broken end is less than 8 in. long, it usually is necessary to remove the differential assembly.

FLANGED SHAFT

1. Raise the vehicle and support safely. Remove the wheel.
2. Remove the brake drum spring lock nuts and remove the drum.
3. Remove the axle shaft flange cup plug by piercing the center with a sharp tool and prying it out.
4. Using the access hole in the axle shaft flange, remove the nuts which attach the brake support plate and retainer to the axle tube flange.
5. Remove the axle shaft from the housing with an axle puller.
6. Remove the inner oil seal from the axle housing tube. Install a new seal in the tube.

NOTE: Lip of seal must be facing towards the center of the differential.

7. Mount the axle in a vise, and with a chisel, cut the bearing retaining ring and drive the ring off the axle shaft.
8. Using a hacksaw, cut through the oil seal and remove from the axle shaft. Do not damage the seal contact surface while cutting.
9. With the aid of a puller or its equivalent, remove the bearing from the shaft.
10. Install the retainer plate on the axle shaft.
11. Apply wheel bearing grease to the oil seal cavity and between the seal lips and install seal on the axle shaft seal seat.

NOTE: Outer face of seal must face the axle flange.

12. Pack wheel bearing with grease and install on the axle shaft.

NOTE: Cup rib ring should be facing the axle flange.

13. Install the retainer ring on the axle shaft, and press both the retainer and the bearing on the shaft at the same time, until both are seated against the shaft shoulder.
14. Install the axle shaft into the housing bore, being careful not to damage the inner seal.
15. Lubricate the outer surface of the bearing cup before installing into the bearing bore.
16. Tap the flanged end of the axle to position it into the bearing bore.

17. Attach the axle shaft retainer and brake support plate to the axle tube flange, and secure with the nuts and lockwashers.

18. Install the brake drum, spring type locknuts, and rear wheels.

19. Remove the safety stands and lower the vehicle.

FULL-FLOATING AXLE SHAFT

It is not necessary to raise the rear wheels in order to remove the rear axle shaft on full-floating rear axles.

1. Remove the axle flange nuts, lock washers, and split washers retaining the axle shaft flange.

2. Remove the axle shaft from the axle housing.

3. Clean the axle flange mating area on the hub and axle, removing all old gasket material.

4. Install a new flange gasket onto the hub studs.

5. Insert the axle shaft into the housing. It may be necessary to rotate the axle shaft to align the shaft splines with the differential gear splines and the flange attaching holes with the hub studs.

6. Install the split washers, lockwashers, and flange nuts. Tighten the nuts securely.

1984 Wagoneer and Cherokee

1. Raise and support the truck on jackstands.

2. Remove the wheel, brake drum and brake support retaining nuts.

3. Pull the axle with a slide hammer.

4. Installation is the reverse of removal. Clean the bore in the axle housing and apply a thin coat of grease to the outer diameter of the bearing cup. Tighten the brake support nuts alternately and evenly to seat the bearing cup rib ring.

Axle Shaft Bearing

REMOVAL & INSTALLATION

All exc. 1984 Wagoneer and Cherokee

1. With the aid of a combination puller, remove the bearing from the axle shaft.

NOTE: If a puller is not available, place the threaded end of the axle on a heavy block of wood and with the aid of an assistant, drive the bearing from the axle shaft with a punch and hammer. Contact the inner race only with the punch.

2. The new bearing can be installed with the use of a combination puller, or with the use of a length of pipe, fitted to the diameter of the inner bearing race, and slipped over the axle end to contact and drive the bearing to its seat on the axle shaft.

3. Lubricate the bearing with wheel bearing grease, making sure the grease fills the cavities between the bearing rollers.

Typical CJ rear axle components

1984 Wagoneer and Cherokee

1. Position the axle shaft in a vise as shown.

2. Remove the retaining ring by drilling a ¼ inch hole about ¾ of the way through the ring, then using a cold chisel over the hole, split the ring.

3. Remove the bearing with an arbor press, discard the seal and remove the retainer plate.

4. Installation is the reverse of removal. The new bearing must be pressed on. Make sure it is squarely seated.

Inner Oil Seal

REMOVAL & INSTALLATION (AXLE OUT)

Exc. CJ Models

1. Insert the splined end of the axle shaft into the inner seal, hooking the axle end to the seal, and prying downward. The seal will move outward from the housing tube.

2. Install a new seal into the housing tube with the aid of a seal installer or its equivalent.

4. Seat the seal and lubricate the lip.

NOTE: The lip of the seal should point towards the center of the axle housing.

5. The outer seal is installed during the assembly of the brake support plate.

CJ Models

1. With the wheel on the ground, remove the axle shaft cotter pin and nut. Loosen the wheel nuts.

2. Raise and support the rear of the car, preferably with jackstands under the axle housing.

3. Remove the wheel.

4. Remove the drum retaining screws, 3 per drum

5. Remove the drum from the hub. If the brake shoes hold the drum, the brake adjustment will have to be backed off slightly.

6. Attach a puller to the wheel bolts and pull off the hub.

— **CAUTION** —
Don't use a knockout type puller. It could damage the rear wheel bearings or the differential.

7. Disconnect the parking brake cable at the equalizer. The equalizer is where the single cable from the parking brake pedal joins the double cable from the rear wheels.

8. Disconnect the brake tube at the wheel cylinder and remove the brake support plate assembly (backing plate), oil seal, and shims (left-side only).

9. Use a puller to remove the axle shaft and bearing.

10. Remove and discard the axle shaft inner oil seal.

11. The bearing cone is pressed onto the shaft. A hydraulic press must be used to remove it.

12. Before installation, pack the axle shaft bearings with high quality grease. Place a healthy glob of grease in the palm of one hand and force the edge of the bearing into it so that grease fills the bearing. Do this until the whole bearing is packed. Grease packing tools are available which make this task much easier.

13. Press the axle shaft bearings onto the axle shafts with the small diameter of the cone toward the outer end of the shaft.

— **CAUTION** —
Always press on the inner bearing race.

Full-floating rear axle assembly

14. Coat the inner axle shaft seal with light oil.

15. Coat the outer surface of the metal seal retainer with sealant.

16. Use a seal driver to install the inner oil seal in the axle housing.

17. Install the axle shaft(s), turning them as necessary to fit the splines into the differential.

18. Install the outer bearing cup.

19. Apply sealant to the axle housing flange and brake support plate mounting areas. Install the original shims in their original locations, oil seal assembly, and brake support plate. Tighten the retaining bolts to 35 ft. lbs.

NOTE: The oil seal and retainer go on the outside of the brake support plate.

20. Axle shaft end-play can be measured by installing the hub retaining nut on the shaft so it can be pushed and pulled with relative ease. Strike the end of each axle shaft with a lead hammer to seat the bearing cups against the support plate. Mount a dial indicator on the left side support plate with the stylus resting on the end of the axle shaft. Check the end-play while pushing and pulling on the axle shaft. End play should be within 0.004–0.008 in., with 0.006 in. ideal. Add shims to increase end play and subtract whims to decrease endplay. Remove the hub retaining nut when finished

checking endplay.

NOTE: When a new axle shaft is installed, a new hub must also be installed. However, a new hub can be installed on an original axle shaft if the serrations on the shaft are not worn or damaged. The procedures for installing an original hub and a new hub are different.

21. Install an original hub in the following manner:

   a. Align the keyway in the hub with the axle shaft key.

   b. Slide the hub onto the axle shaft as far as possible.

   c. Install the axle shaft nut and washer.

Semi-floating rear axle assembly

d. Install the drum, drum retaining screws, and wheel.

e. Lower the vehicle onto its wheels and tighten the axle shaft nut to 250 ft. lbs. If the cotter pin hole is not aligned, tighten the nut to the next castellation and install the pin. Do not loosen the nut to align the cotter pin hole.

22. Install a new hub in the following manner:

a. Align the keyway in the hub with the axle shaft key.

b. Slide the hub onto the axle shaft as far as possible.

c. Install two well-lubricated thrust washers and the axle shaft nut.

d. Install the brake drum, drum retaining screws, and wheel.

e. Lower the vehicle onto its wheels.

f. Tighten the axle shaft nut until the distance from the outer face of the hub eto to the outer end of the axle shaft is 1 ⁵/₁₆ in. Pressing the hub onto the axle to the specified distance is necessary to form the hub serrations properly.

g. Remove the axle shaft nut and one thrust washer.

h. Install the axle shaft nut and tighten it to 250 ft. lbs. If the cotter pin hole is not aligned, tighten the nut to the next castellation and install the pin. Do not loosen the nut to install the cotter pin.

Splitting the rear axle bearing retainer on 1984 Wagoneer and Cherokee

Removing the rear axle bearing with a press on 1984 Wagoneer and Cherokee

23. Connect the brake line to the wheel cylinder and bleed the brake hydraulic system and adjust the brake shoes.

Differential Assembly

REMOVAL & INSTALLATION

1. Raise the vehicle and support safely. Remove the wheels, drums and axle shafts.

2. Drain the axle housing lubricant and remove the axle housing cover.

3. Mark the differential bearing caps for alignment during the assembly.

4. Loosen the bearing cap bolts, but do not remove.

5. Install an axle housing spreader tool on the axle housing and secure with the hold-down clamps.

6. Mount a dial indicator on the axle housing to measure the amount of spread. Zero the indicator dial.

7. Spread the axle housing no more than 0.020 inch.

8. Remove the differential bearing caps and the dial indicator from the housing.

9. Using two pry bars, remove the differential carrier from the axle housing.

10. Remove the spreader tool from the housing as soon as the differential carrier is removed to avoid the possibility of the axle housing taking a set.

11. The differential housing can now be overhauled or replaced.

To install:

1. Install the axle housing spreader tool on the axle housing and secure with the hold down clamps. Install a dial indicator and center the dial.

2. Spread the axle housing to a maximum of 0.020 inch. Remove the dial indicator.

3. Lubricate the differential side bearings and install the differential carrier in the axle housing.

NOTE: Prior shim fitting and bearing preload should be accomplished before differential carrier installation.

4. Tap the unit in place with a soft faced hammer. Remove the axle housing spreader tool.

5. Install the bearing caps in their proper place and torque to 40 ft. lbs. on model 30 rear axle and to 80 ft. lbs. on models 44 and 60.

6. Install a dial indicator and recheck the ring gear backlash at two points. Correct as necessary.

7. Complete the assembly in the reverse of the removal, add lubricant and road test.

Pinion Oil Seal

REMOVAL & INSTALLATION

Semi-Floating Axle With Tapered Shaft

1. Raise and support the vehicle and

remove the rear wheels and brake drums.

2. Mark the driveshaft and yoke for reassembly and disconnect the driveshaft from the rear yoke.

3. With a socket on the pinion nut and an in. lb. torque wrench, rotate the drive pinion several revolutions. Check and record the torque required to turn the drive pinion.

4. Remove the pinion nut. Use a flange holding tool to hold the flange while removing the pinion nut. Discard the pinion nut.

5. Mark the yoke and the drive pinion shaft for reassembly reference.

6. Remove the rear yoke with a puller.

7. Inspect the seal surface of the yoke and replace it with a new one if the seal surface is pitted, grooved, or otherwise damaged.

8. Remove the pinion oil seal.

9. Before installing the new seal, coat the lip of the seal with rear axle lubricant.

10. Install the seal, driving it into place with the proper driving tool.

11. Install the yoke on the pinion shaft. Align the marks made on the pinion shaft and yoke during disassembly.

12. Install a new pinion nut. Tighten nut until end play is removed from the pinion bearing. Do not overtighten.

13. Check the torque required to turn the drive pinion. The pinion must be turned several revolutions to obtain an accurate reading.

14. Tighten the pinion nut to obtain the torque reading observed during disassembly (step 3) plus 5 in. lbs. Tighten the nut minutely each time, to avoid overtightening. Do not loosen and then retighten the nut.

NOTE: If the desired torque is exceeded a new collapsible pinion spacer sleeve must be installed and the pinion gear preload reset. Refer to the General Repair Section and Overhaul procedures for this operation.

15. Install the driveshaft, aligning the index marks made during disassembly. Install the rear brake drums and wheels.

Semi-Floating and Full-Floating Axles With Flange Shaft

1. Raise and support the vehicle.

2. Mark the driveshaft and yoke for reference during assembly and disconnect the driveshaft at the yoke.

3. Remove the pinion shaft nut and washer.

4. Remove the yoke from the pinion shaft, using a puller.

5. Remove the pinion shaft oil seal.

6. Install the new seal with a suitable driver.

7. Install the pinion shaft washer and nut. Tighten the nut to 210 ft. lbs. on the semi-floating axles and 260 ft. lbs. on the full-floating axles.

8. Align the index marks on the driveshaft and yoke and install the driveshaft.

Tighten the attaching bolts or nuts to 16 ft. lbs.

9. Remove the supports and lower the vehicle.

Wheel Bearing

ADJUSTMENT
Full Floating Axle

1. Raise the vehicle so that the wheel can be rotated. Support the vehicle safely.
2. Remove the axle shaft.
3. Straighten the lip of the lock washer and remove the lock washer and lock nut.
4. Tighten the adjusting nut and rotate the wheel until binding exists. Back off the adjusting nut 1/16 turn until the wheel rotates freely without any lateral shake.
5. Replace the lock washer and tighten the lock nut, bending the lip of the lock washer over the lock nut.
6. Install the axle with a new gasket and tighten the axle nuts securely.

STEERING

Steering Wheel

REMOVAL & INSTALLATION

1. Disconnect the negative battery cable.
2. Place the front wheels in the straight-ahead position.
3. Remove the horn button from the steering wheel. Turn the botton until the locktabe on the button align with the notches in the contact cup and pull upward to remove it. With the sport wheel, just pull the button up.
4. Remove the steering wheel nut and washer.
5. If the Jeep is equipped with a sport style steering wheel, remove the horn button, nut and washer, bottom retaining ring, and horn contact ring.
6. Remove the plastic horn contact cup retainer and remove the cup and contact plate from the steering wheel.
7. Remove the horn contact pin and bushing from the steering wheel.
8. Paint or scribe alignment marks on the steering wheel and shaft for reference during assembly.
9. Remove the steering wheel using a puller.
10. Install the steering wheel in the reverse order, tightening the nut to 20 ft. lbs. for 1977, 30 ft. lbs. for 1978–83, and 25 ft. lb. for 1984.

Turn Signal Switch

REPLACEMENT

1977–79

1. Disconnect the negative battery cable.

2. Remove the steering wheel.
3. Loosen the anti-theft cover retaining screws on 1976 models and lift the cover from the steering column. It is not necessary to completely remove these screws.
4. Depress the lockplate and pry the round wire snap-ring from the steering shaft groove. A lockplate compressor tool is available for compressing the lockplate.
5. Remove the lockplate, directional signal canceling cam, upper bearing pre-load spring, and thrust washer from the steering shaft.
6. Move the directional signal actuating lever to the right turn position and remove the lever.
7. Depress the hazard warning light switch and remove the button by turning it counterclockwise.
8. Remove the directional signal wiring harness connector block from its mounting bracket on the right-side of the lower column.
9. On vehicles equipped with an automatic transmission, use a stiff wire, such as a paper clip, to depress the lock tab which retains the shift quadrant light wire in the connector block.
10. Remove the directional signal switch retaining screws and pull the switch and wiring harness from the steering column.
11. Guide the wiring harness of the new switch into position and carefully align the switch assembly. Make sure that the actuating lever pivot is correctly aligned and seated in the upper housing pivot boss prior to installing the retaining screws.
12. Install the directional signal lever and actuate the directional signal switch to assure correct operation.
13. Place the thrust washer, spring, and directional signal canceling cam on the upper end of the steering shaft.
14. Align the lockplate splines with the steering shaft splines and place the lockplate in position with the directional signal canceling cam shaft protruding through the dogleg opening in the lockplate.
15. Install the snap-ring.
16. Install the anti-theft cover.
17. Install the steering wheel and connect the negative battery cable.
18. Check the operation of the turn signal switch.

1980 and Later

1. Disconnect the battery ground.
2. Cover the painted areas of the column.

Steering wheel removal

3. Remove the column-to-dash bezel.
4. Loosen the toe plate screws.
5. With tilt columns, place the column in the non-tilt position.
6. Remove the steering wheel.
7. Remove the lockplate cover.
8. Compress the lockplate and unseat the steering shaft snap-ring as follows:
   a. Check the steering shaft nut threads. Metric threads have an identifying groove in the steering wheel splines. SAE threads do not.
   b. With SAE threads use a compressor tool such as tool J-23653 to compress the lockplate and remove the snap-ring.
   c. If the shaft has metric threads, replace the forcing screw in the compressor with metric forcing screw J-23653-4 before using.
9. Remove the compressor and snap-ring.
10. Remove the lockplate, canceling cam and upper bearing preload spring.
11. Place the turn signal lever in the right turn position and remove the lever.
12. Remove the hazard warning knob. Press the knob inward and turn counterclockwise to remove it.
13. Remove the wiring harness protectors.
14. Disconnect the wiring harness connectors.
15. Remove the turn signal switch attaching screws and lift out the switch.

Ignition Switch

REPLACEMENT

The ignition switch is on top of the lower part of the steering column, inside the vehicle.

1. Put the key in the lock and turn to the Off-unlocked position.

Using a slide hammer to pull the rear axle shaft

2. Disconnect the battery ground cable.
3. Detach the wire connectors at the switch.
4. Remove the switch screws.
5. Disconnect the actuating rod from the switch and remove the switch.
6. Move the switch slider all the way down the column. Move it back toward the steering wheel two clicks to the center Off-unlocked position.
7. Engage the column actuating rod in the switch slider and fasten the switch down.
8. Connect the wire connectors, then the battery ground cable.

Ignition Lock Cylinder

REPLACEMENT

1. Disconnect the battery ground cable.
2. Remove the turn signal switch as described earlier in this chapter. You don't have to remove the switch completely, just set it aside.
3. Insert the key. With manual transmission, put it in the On position: with automatic, put it in Off-Lock.
4. Working through the slot next to the turn signal switch mounting boss, use a thin screwdriver to release the lock cylinder.
5. To install, insert the key in the new lock cylinder. Hold the sleeve and turn the key clockwise until it stops. Align the cylinder retaining tab with the housing slot and insert the cylinder. Push the cylinder in, rotate to engage, then push in until the retaining tab engages the housing groove.
6. The rest of the procedure is the reverse of removal.

Power Steering Pump

REMOVAL & INSTALLATION

If the power steering pump has to be removed to service another component, it is not necessary to remove the hoses from the pump. Just disconnect the mounting fixtures and lift the pump away from the engine and lay it out of the way. The only time the power steering hoses have to be removed from the pump is when the pump has to be removed from the vehicle for service or replacement.
1. Remove the pump drive belt tension adjusting bolt. Disconnect the belt from the pump.
2. Disconnect the return and pressure hoses from the pump. Cover the hose connector and union on the pump and open ends of the hoses to avoid the entrance of dirt.
3. On the 304 v8, remove the front bracket from the engine.
4. Remove the two nuts which secure the rear of the pump to the bracket, and the two bolts which secure the front of the pump to the bracket and remove the pump.

5. To install, position the pump in the bracket and install the rear attaching screws. On the 304 V8, install the front bracket.
6. Connect the hydraulic hoses. Adjust the drive belt tension.
7. Fill the pump reservoir to the correct level.
8. Start the engine and wait for at least three minutes before turning the steering wheel. Check the level frequently during this time.
9. Slowly turn the steering wheel through its entire range a few times with the engine running. Recheck the level and inspect for possible leaks.

NOTE: If air becomes trapped in the fluid, the pump may become noisy until all of the air is out. This may take some time since trapped air does not bleed out rapidly.

Manual Steering Gear

REMOVAL & INSTALLATION

Exc. 1984 Wagoneer and Cherokee

1. Remove the intermediate shaft-to-wormshaft coupling clamp bolt and disconnect the intermediate shaft.
2. Remove the pitman arm nut and lockwasher.
3. Using a puller, remove the Pitman arm from the shaft.
4. Raise the left side of the vehicle slightly to relieve tension on the left front spring and rest the frame on a jackstand.
5. Remove the steering gear lower bracket-to-frame bolts.
6. Remove the bolts attaching the steering gear upper bracket to the crossmember. Beginning in 1979, one of these bolts is a Torx® head bolt. This bolt, and some others may be removed with the aid of a 9 inch extension. Remove the gear.

NOTE: Loctite 271® or similar material must be applied to all attaching bolt threads prior to installation.

7. Position the tie plate upper and lower mounting brackets on the gear and install the bolts. Torque the bracket-to-gear bolts to 70 ft. lbs. and the bracket-to-tie plate bolt to 55 ft. lbs.
8. Align and engage the intermediate shaft coupling with the steering gear wormshaft splines.
9. Position the steering gear on the frame and install the mounting bolts. Torque the bolts to 55 ft. lbs. Install the Pitman arm and torque the nut to 185 ft. lbs.

NOTE: The steering gear may produce a slight roughness, this can be eliminated by turning the steering wheel full left and right 10–15 times.

1984 Wagoneer and Cherokee

1. Disconnnect the steering shaft from the gear.

2. Raise and support the truck.
3. Disconnect the center link from the pitman arm.
4. Remove the front stabilizer bar.
5. Remove the pitman arm nut, mark the relation between the arm and shaft, and using a puller, pull the pitman arm from the shaft.
6. Remove the gear attaching bolts and remove the gear.
7. Installation is the reverse of removal. Observe the following torques:
   Center link-to-pitman arm: 35 ft. lb.
   Stabilizer bar-to-link: 27 ft. lb.
   Pitman arm-to-gear: 185 ft. lb.
   Steering gear-to-frame: 65 ft. lb.

STEERING GEAR CLEARANCE ADJUSTMENT

1. Loosen the locknut and turn the adjusting screw on the side cover, counterclockwise until the worm gear shaft turns freely through its entire range of travel.
2. Count the number of turns necessary to rotate the worm gear shaft through its travel.
3. Turn the shaft to center point.
4. Rotate the shaft back and forth over center, and tighten the adjusting screw until the shaft binds slightly at the center point.
5. Adjust the screw to obtain a rolling torque of 7–12 in. lbs. through the center.
6. Hold the adjusting screw and tighten the locknut to 16–20 ft. lbs.

WORM BEARING PRELOAD ADJUSTMENT

1. Tighten the worm bearing adjuster until it bottoms, then back it off ¼ turn.
2. Install a torque wrench and socket J-7754 or its equivalent on the splined end of the wormshaft.
3. Rotate the wormshaft clockwise until it hits the stop, then back it off ½ turn.
4. Tighten the wormshaft bearing adjuster until the torque required to rotate the shaft is 5–8 in. lbs.

NOTE: The adjustment must be made with the wormshaft no more than ½ turn from the stop.

5. Tighten the worm bearing adjuster locknut to 23 ft. lbs.; 50 ft. lb. on 1984 Wagoneer and Cherokee. Check rotating torque. Check and record the worm bearing preload reading.

PITMAN SHAFT OVERCENTER ADJUSTMENT

All exc. 1984 Wagoneer and Cherokee

1. Rotate the wormshaft from stop-to-stop and count the number of turns.
2. Rotate the wormshaft back from the stop, ½ the total number of turns.

3. Install a torque wrench and socket J-7754 on the splined end of the wormshaft.

4. Tighten the pitman shaft adjuster screw, while rotating the shaft back and forth over center, until the torque equals the worm bearing preload setting of 5–8 in. lbs. previously recorded.

5. Rotate the shaft over center and continue tightening the adjuster until the drag torque is increased by an additional 4–10 in. lbs., but do not exceed 16 in. lbs. combined total.

6. Hold the adjuster screw and tighten the locknut to 23 ft. lbs. Do not allow the adjuster to turn, or the adjustment will have to be made over again!

Power Steering Gear

REMOVAL & INSTALLATION

Exc. 1984 Wagoneer and Cherokee

1. Disconnect the hoses at the gear and raise them above the pump to prevent fluid loss.

2. Remove the clamp bolt and nut attaching the intermediate shaft coupling to the steering gear stub shaft and disconnect the intermediate shaft.

3. Mark the Pitman shaft and arm for alignment. Remove the Pitman nut and lockwasher and remove the Pitman arm with a puller.

4. Raise the left side of the vehicle slightly to relieve tension from the spring. Support with a jack stand under the frame.

5. Remove the three lower steering gear mounting bracket-to-frame bolts.

6. Remove the two steering gear-to-crossmember upper bolts. Remove the gear and brackets as an assembly.

7. Remove the brackets from the gear.

NOTE: Prior to installation, all bolts must be coated with Loctite 271® or its equivalent.

8. Position the mounting brackets on the gear and torque the bolts to 70 ft. lbs.

9. Align and connect the intermediate shaft coupling to the steering gear stub shaft.

10. Position the steering gear on the frame and crossmember. Install and tighten the bolts to 55 ft. lbs.

11. Lower the vehicle.

12. Install the intermediate shaft coupling-to-steering gear stub shaft clamp bolt and nut. Tighten the nut to 45 ft. lbs.

13. Align and install the Pitman arm, nut and lockwasher. Torque the nut to 185 ft. lbs. Stake the nut in two places.

14. Connect the hoses. Torque the hose connections to 25 ft. lbs.

1984 Wagoneer and Cherokee

1. Place the wheels in a straight ahead position.

2. Position a drain pan under the gear.

3. Disconnect the hoses at the gear and raise and secure the hose ends to prevent draining. Cap the hose ends.

4. Disconnect the intermediate shaft from the stub shaft.

5. Raise and support the front end on jackstands. Mark the relation between the pitman arm and shaft.

6. Disconnect the center link from the pitman arm and remove the stabilizer bar.

7. Using a puller, remove the pitman arm.

8. Unbolt and remove the gear.

9. Installation is the reverse of removal. Observe the following torques:
Steering gear-to-frame: 65 ft. lb.
Pitman arm-to-shaft: 185 ft. lb.
Stabilizer bar-to-frame: 55 ft. lb.
Stabilizer bar-to-link: 27 ft. lb.
Center link-to-pitman arm: 35 ft. lb.

ADJUSTMENTS

NOTE: The gear must be adjusted off the vehicle. All adjustments must be made in the sequence described below. Worm bearing preload is always adjusted first!

WORM BEARING PRELOAD ADJUSTMENT

1. Mount the gear assembly in a vise.

2. Torque the adjuster plug to 20 ft. lbs.

3. Mark the gear housing in line with one of the adjuster plug holes.

4. Measure counterclockwise $3/16$–$1/4$ in from the first mark on models through 1979 and $1/2$ inch from the first mark on 1980–81 models, and make another mark.

5. Turn the adjuster plug counterclockwise to align the hole with the second mark.

6. Hold the adjuster plug and torque the locknut to 85 ft. lbs. Do not allow the adjuster to turn.

7. Turn the stubshaft clockwise to its stop, then back $1/4$ turn.

8. Using a torque wrench of no more than 50 in. lb. capacity and a 12 point deep socket, check the rotating torque at the splined end of the stub shaft at or near a vertical position. Torque should be 4–10 in. lbs.

9. If the torque cannot be adjusted within these limits, the gear will have to be rebuilt.

PITMAN SHAFT OVERCENTER ADJUSTMENT

1. Loosen the adjuster screw locknut.

2. Turn the adjuster screw counterclockwise until the screw is fully extended. Turn the screw back in one full turn.

3. Count the number of turns to rotate the stubshaft from stop-to-stop.

4. Turn the shaft back $1/2$ the number of turns. At this point the flat surface of the stubshaft should be upward and the master spline on the Pitman shaft should be aligned with the adjuster screw.

5. Install a 50 in. lbs. torque wrench and deep 12 point socket on the splined end of the stub shaft. Place the torque wrench in a vertical position.

6. Rotate the torque wrench 45° to each side and record the highest torque at or near center. Record this reading.

7. Adjust the torque by turning the adjuster screw clockwise. Adjustment is: the recorded reading plus 4–8 in. lbs. for new gears, but not exceeding 14 in. lbs. total; the previously recorded reading plus 4–5 in. lbs. for used gears, but not exceeding 14 in. lbs. combined total.

8. Tighten the adjuster screw locknut to 20 ft. lbs. while holding the adjuster screw.

9. Install the gear.

Tie Rod End

REMOVAL & INSTALLATION

1. Remove the cotter pins and retaining nuts at both ends of the tie rod and from the end of the connecting rod where it attaches to the tie rod.

2. Remove the nut attaching the steering damper push rod to the tie rod bracket and move the damper aside.

3. Remove the tie rod ends from the steering arms and connecting rod with a puller.

4. Count the number of threads showing on the tie rod before removing the ends, as a guide to installation.

5. Loosen the adjusting tube clamp bolts and unthread the ends.

6. Installation is the reverse of removal. Torque the connecting rod-to-tie rod nut to 70 ft. lbs.

7. Adjust toe-in, if necessary.

FRONT SUSPENSION

Front Leaf Spring

REMOVAL & INSTALLATION

1. Raise the vehicle with a jack under the axle. Place a jackstand under the frame side rail. Then lower the axle jack so the load is relieved from the spring and the wheels just touch the floor.

2. Disconnect the shock absorber from the spring clip plate. Disconnect the front stabilizer bar, if any.

3. Remove the nuts which secure the spring clips (U-bolts). Remove the spring plate and spring clips. Free the spring from the axle by raising the axle.

4. Remove the pivot bolt nut and drive out the pivot bolt. Disconnect the shackle.

5. With the spring removed, the spring shackle and/or shackle plate may be removed from the spring.

6. Inspect the bushings in the eye of the main spring leaf and the bushings of the spring shackle for excessive wear. Replace if necessary.

7. The spring can be disassembled for replacing an individual spring leaf by removing the clips and the center bolts.

8. To install the spring on the vehicle, with the bushings in place and the spring shackle attached to the springs, position the spring in the pivot hanger and install the pivot bolt and lock nut. Only tighten the lock nut enough to hold the bushings in position until the vehicle is lowered from the jack.

9. Position the spring and install the shackle, shackle bolts, shackle plate if applicable, lockwasher, and nut. Only finger tighten the nuts at this time.

10. Move the axle into position on the spring by lowering the axle jack. Place the spring center bolt in the axle saddle hole. Install the spring clips, spring plate, lockwashers and nuts. Torque the 7/16 in. nuts to 36–42 ft. lbs and the 1/2 in. nuts to 45–65 ft. lbs. and the 9/16 nuts to 100 ft. lbs.

NOTE: Be sure that the center bolt is properly centered in the axle saddle.

11. Connect the shock absorber.

12. Remove the axle and allow the weight of the vehicle to seat the bushings in their operating positions. Then torque the 7/16 in. spring pivot bolt nuts and spring shackle nuts.

Front Coil Spring

REMOVAL & INSTALLATION

1. Raise the vehicle and place jackstands under the axle.

2. Remove the wheels.

3. Match-mark and disconnect the front driveshaft.

4. Disconnect the lower control arm at the axle.

5. Disconnect the track bar at the frame. Place a floor jack under the axle.

6. Disconnect the stabilizer bar and shock absorbers.

7. Disconnect the center link at the pitman arm.

FRONT OF VEHICLE

Typical tie-rod assembly

RUBBER SEAL
UPPER BALL STUD
TURNING ANGLE STOP SCREW
OIL SEAL
LOCK NUT
DUST COVER (DJ ONLY)
SPACERS
BEARING ROLLERS
SPINDLE
STEERING KNUCKLE
TIE ROD END
LUBE FITTING
TIE ROD END
COTTER PIN
UPPER BALL STUD NUT
UPPER BALL STUD SEAT
AXLE YOKE
COTTER PIN
CASTLE NUT
LOWER BALL STUD NUT
RUBBER SEAL
LOWER BALL STUD
CLAMP
PITMAN ARM
LOCKWASHER
NUT

Typical steering linkage

8. Lower the axle with a floor jack, loosen the spring retainer and remove the spring.

9. Installation is the reverse of removal. Observe the following torques:
Lower control arms-to-axle: 133 ft. lb.
Shock absorbers-to-axle: 14 ft. lb.
Stabilizer bar links-to-axle: 70 ft. lb.
U-joint strap nuts: 14 ft. lb.
Center link-to-pitman arm: 35 ft. lb.
Track bar-to-frame: 35 ft. lb.

TOE-IN ADJUSTMENT

First raise the front of the vehicle to free the front wheels. Turn the wheels to the straight ahead position. Use a steadyrest to scribe a pencil line in the center of each tire tread as the wheel is turned by hand. A good way to do this is to first coat a strip with chalk around the circumference of the tread at the center to form a base for a fine pencil line.

SHOCK ABSORBER BUSHINGS
SPRING HANGER
SHACKLE PLATE
SPRING SHACKLE BUSHINGS
SHOCK BRACKET
SHOCK ABSORBER
SPRING HANGER
CENTER BOLT
REBOUND CLIP
INSULATOR
SPRING SHACKLE
SPRING EYE BUSHING
MAIN LEAF
INSULATOR
SPRING LEAVES
U-BOLT
SHOCK ABSORBER BUSHINGS
TIE PLATE
U-BOLT NUT

Typical front spring and shock absorber

Measure the distance between the scribed lines at the front and rear of the wheels using care that both measurements are made at an equal distance from the floor. The distance between the lines should be greater at the rear than at the front by 3/64 in. to 3/32 in. To adjust, loosen the clamp bolts and turn the tie rod with a small pipe wrench. The tie rod is threaded with right and left hand threads to provide equal adjustment at both wheels. Do not overlook retightening the clamp bolts.

It is common practice to measure between the wheel rims. This is satisfactory providing the wheels run true. By scribing a line on the tire tread, measurement is taken between the road contact points reducing error caused by wheel run-out.

Shock Absorbers

REMOVAL & INSTALLATION

1. Remove the locknuts and washers.
2. Pull the shock absorber eyes and rubber bushings from the mounting pins.
3. Install the shocks in reverse order of the removal procedure. Torque the upper bolt to 35 ft. lbs. on all except 1984 Wagoneer and Cherokee; 8 ft. lb. on 1984 Wagoneer and Cherokee and the lower bolt to 45 ft. lbs. on all except 1984 Wagoneer and Cherokee; 14 ft. lb. on 1984 Wagoneer and Cherokee.

NOTE: Squeaking usually occurs when movement takes place between the rubber bushings and the metal parts. The squeaking may be eliminated by placing the bushings under great pressure. This is accomplished either by adding additional washers where the cotter pins are used or by tightening the locknuts. Do not use mineral lubricant to stop the squeaking as it will deteriorate the rubber.

REAR SUSPENSION

Spring

REMOVAL & INSTALLATION

Mounted Below the Axle

1. Raise the vehicle and support the axle.
2. Disconnect the shock absorber and stabilizer bar, if so equipped.
3. Remove the U-bolts and tie plates.
4. Disconnect the front and rear ends of the spring and remove the spring.
5. The spring can be disassembled by removing the spring rebound clips and the center bolt.
6. Mount the spring in the vehicle, but do not tighten the pivot bolts.

7. Align the spring center bolt and install the tie plate and U-bolts.
8. Connect the shock absorber and stabilizer bar, if so equipped.
9. Remove the axle support and lower the vehicle.
10. Tighten the pivot bolts with the weight of the vehicle on the springs to 45 ft. lbs. on CJ models and 75 ft. lbs. on all other models. Tighten 9/16 in. U-bolt nuts to 100 ft. lbs., 1/2 in. nuts to 55 ft. lbs. and 7/16 in. U-bolt nuts to 40 ft. lbs.

NOTE: If left-side spring is to be serviced, remove fuel tank skid plate.

Mounted Above the Axle

1. Raise the vehicle and support the frame ahead of the axle.
2. Remove the U-bolts.
3. Unclip the axle vent hose from the frame.
4. Disconnect the shock absorber.
5. Remove the spring pivot bolts.
6. Lower the axle enough so the spring can be turned over and remove the spring. The spring can be disassembled by removing the rebound clips and center bolt.
7. Mount the spring in the vehicle and install the pivot bolts and nuts.
8. Raise the axle, align the spring center bolt, and install the U-bolts.

9. Connect the shock absorber, vent hose, and remove the supports and lower the vehicle.
10. Tighten the spring pivot bolts with the weight of the vehicle on the springs. Tighten the pivot bolts to 75 ft. lbs. Tighten 9/16 in. U-bolt nuts to 100 ft. lbs., 1/2 in. nuts to 55 ft. lbs., and 7/16 in. U-bolt nuts to 40 ft. lbs.

Spring Bushing

REMOVAL & INSTALLATION

Small Bushing

1. Install an 8 in. length of threaded rod halfway through the bushing and place a 1 1/8 in. socket with the open end toward the bushing, one 1/2 in. flat washer, and one 3/8 in. hex nut on one end of the rod.
2. Place a 2 in. section of 1 5/8 in. or 1 3/8 in. ID pipe, one 3/4 in. flat washer, or 1/2 in. flat washer and on 3/8 in. hex nut on the opposite end of the threaded rod.
3. Tighten both of the 3/8 in. nuts finger-tight and align all of the components. Make sure the socket is positioned in the eye of the spring and aligns with the bushing. The pipe section must butt against the spring eye so the bushing can pass through it. The socket will act as a press and will

Typical rear spring and shock absorber assembly

press the bushing out of the spring eye.

4. Tighten the nut at the socket end of the rod until the bushing is pressed out of the spring eye. Remove the tools and the bushing.

5. Install the replacement bushing on the threaded rod and assemble the bushing tools as outlined in steps 1 and 2, and press the bushing into the spring eye. Make sure the bushing is centered in the spring eye.

Large Bushing

1. Place ½ × 11 in. length of threaded rod half-way through the bushing and install 1 ¹⁄₁₆ in. deep socket with the open end toward the bushing, one ½ in. flat washer, and one ½ in. nut on the end of the rod.

2. Install a 3 in. length of 1 ½ in. ID pipe, one ½ in. flat washer and one ½ in. nut on the opposite end of the threaded rod.

3. Tighten both nuts finger tight and align all of the components. Make sure the socket is positioned in the eye of the spring and aligns with the bushing. The pipe section must butt against the spring eye so the bushing can pass through it. The socket will act as a press ram and press the bushing out of the spring eye.

4. Tighten the nut at the socket and press the bushing out of the spring eye.

5. Install the new bushing on the threaded rod and assemble the tushing tools as outlined in steps 1 and 2. Press the bushing into the spring eye until it is centered in the eye.

Shock Absorber

REMOVAL & INSTALLATION

1. Raise the vehicle for working clearance and support safely.

2. Place a jack under the axle assembly and raise to relieve the springs of axle weight and to place the shock absorber in its mid stroke.

3. Remove the retaining nuts or bolts and remove the shock absorber from the vehicle.

4. Install the new shock absorber and tighten the attaching nuts or bolts. (upper bolts: 15 ft. lb. lower nut: 44 ft. lb.)

5. Lower the vehicle to the ground.

BRAKES

Refer to "Brakes" in the Unit Repair section for detail troubleshooting and brake hydraulic system repair procedures.

Master Cylinder

REMOVAL & INSTALLATION

1. Disconnect and plug the brake lines at the master cylinder.

2. Disconnect the wires from the stoplight switch.

3. Disconnect the master cylinder push rod at the brake pedal on vehicles with manual brakes.

4. Remove all attaching bolts and nuts and lift the master cylinder from the vehicle.

5. Install the master cylinder in the reverse order of removal. Torque the mounting nuts to 10–12 ft. lb. Bleed the hydraulic system.

Power Unit

REMOVAL & INSTALLATION

1977

1. Clean the master cylinder and booster unit.

2. Remove the cotter and clevis pins securing the booster pushrod to the pedal linkage.

3. Disconnect the vacuum hose from the booster check valve.

4. Disconnect the fluid lines from the master cylinder. Plug the ends and catch any escaping fluid. Do not reuse brake fluid.

5. Disconnect the stoplight wires from the switch.

6. Remove the attaching nuts, booster unit assembly, and block spacers.

7. Remove the attaching nuts and separate the master cylinder from the booster.

To install the booster unit, reverse the removal procedure and bleed the brakes.

— CAUTION —
Do not pressure-bleed power-assisted brake systems.

1978 and later

1. Disconnect brake pedal pushrod rod at brake pedal.

2. Disconnect vacuum hose from booster check valve.

3. Remove attaching nuts and separate master cylinder from brake booster. Do not disconnect brake lines at master cylinder.

4. On CJ models, remove bolts holding power unit bellcrank to dash panel and remove power unit and bellcrank as one assembly. Remove the bellcrank from the original power unit and lubricate the pivot pins with chassis lubricant before installing it on the replacement unit.

5. On all other models, remove bolts attaching power unit to dash panel and remove the unit.

6. Installation is the reverse of removal. Torque the booster-to-firewall nuts to 30 ft. lb.; the master cylinder-to-booster nuts to 10–12 ft. lb.

NOTE: When replacing the power brake unit, use the push rod that is supplied with the new unit, as it has been correctly gauged and preset to the new unit. Torque the booster-to-firewall nuts to 30 ft. lb.; the master cylinder-to-booster nuts to 10–12 ft. lb.

Exploded view of a typical master cylinder

Wheel Cylinder

REMOVAL & INSTALLATION

1. Raise and support the vehicle and remove the brake drums and brake shoes.

2. Disconnect the brake line. Do not bend the line away from the wheel cylinder. When the cylinder is removed from the support plate, the line will separate from the wheel cylinder easily.

3. Remove the wheel cylinder mounting bolts and remove the wheel cylinder from the brake backing plate.

4. Clean the wheel cylinder mounting surface on the brake support plate. Clean the brake line fitting and threads.

5. Start the brake line fitting into the wheel cylinder and attach the wheel cylinder to the support plate and tighten the brake line fitting. Tighten the wheel cylinder mounting bolts to 18 ft. lbs.

Stop Light Switch

Two types of switches are used on the Jeep vehicles. One type is attached to the brake pedal rod end of the push rod, and cannot be adjusted. The second type is mounted on a flange attached to the brake pedal support bracket and is held in the off position by the brake pedal being in its released position. Upon depressing the brake pedal, the switch plunger is allowed to move outward and contact is made within the switch to allow current to pass the operate the stop lights.

SWITCH ADJUSTMENT

NOTE: CJ models with air conditioning, remove screws attaching the evaporator housing to the instrument panel and move housing away from the panel.

1. Hold the brake pedal in the applied position.

2. Push the stop light switch through the mounting bracket until it stops against the brake pedal bracket. Release the pedal to set the switch in the proper position.

3. Check the position of the switch. The switch plunger should be in the ON position and activate the brake lights after a brake pedal travel of 3/8 to 5/8 inch.

Parking Brakes

ADJUSTMENTS—TYPICAL

1. Make sure that the hydraulic brakes are in satisfactory adjustment.

2. Raise the rear wheels off the ground and disengage the parking brake pedal.

3. Loosen the locknut on the brake cable adjusting rod, located directly behind the frame center crossmember.

4. Spin the wheels and tighten the adjustment until the rear wheels drag slightly.

Power brake booster—typical

Parking brake components—typical

Loosen the adjustment until there is no drag and the wheels spin freely.

5. Tighten the locknut to lock the adjusting nut.

CHASSIS ELECTRICAL

Heater Core

NOTE: (All models) If equipped with air conditioning, the unit must be removed from the dash and lowered to gain access to the heater control box for the removal of the heater core.

CJ MODELS

Removal

1. Remove the battery, drain the cooling system, and disconnect the heater hoses.

2. Disconnect the damper door control cable.

3. Disconnect the blower motor wire harness and ground wire at the switch and instrument panel.

4. Remove the glove box; water drain hose and defroster duct hose.

5. Disconnect the heater to air deflector duct at the heater housing.

6. Remove the nuts from the heater housing studs, protruding into the engine compartment.

7. Remove the heater housing assembly from the vehicle and remove the core from the housing.

Installation

1. The assembly is in the reverse of the disassembly.
2. When the assembly is completed, test the heater for proper operation.

1977–83 CHEROKEE-WAGONEER
1977–84 TRUCK AND GRAND WAGONEER

Removal

1. Remove the negative battery cable and drain the cooling system.
2. Disconnect the temperature control cable from the blend air door.
3. Remove the heater hoses and blower motor resistor wires.
4. Remove the heater core housing to dash panel attaching screws or nuts, projecting into the engine compartment.
5. Remove the heater housing assembly from the vehicle.
6. Separate the halves of the housing, after scribing a mark on the two halves, remove the core retaining screws and remove the heater core.

Typical 1977–83 Wagoneer and Cherokee, and 1977–84 Grand Wagoneer and Truck heater/defroster

Installation

1. The assembly is in the reverse of the disassembly.
2. When the assembly is completed, test the heater for proper operation.

1984 WAGONEER AND CHEROKEE

Removal & Installation

1. Drain the cooling system.

2. Disconnect the hoses at the core tubes.
3. Disconnect the battery ground cable.
4. Discharge the refrigerant from the A/C system.
5. Disconnect the refrigerant lines at the expansion valve.
6. Disconnect the blower motor wires and vent tube.
7. Remove the console.
8. Remove the lower instrument panel section.
9. Disconnect all wires and hoses at the case.

Typical CJ heater/defroster assembly

10. Cut the plastic retaining strap which holds the evaporator/blower housing to the heater core housing.

11. Disconnect the heater control cables.

12. Remove the clip at the rear of the blower housing flange and remove the retaining screws.

13. Remove the housing attaching nuts from the studs on the engine compartment side of the firewall. Remove the evaporator drain tube.

14. Remove the right kick panel and the instrument panel support bolt.

15. From the right side, gently pull the housing down and toward the rear. Remove the housing from the truck.

16. Remove the left kick panel and remove the instrument panel retaining bolt. Remove the right and left A pillar trim.

17. Remove the defroster bezel attaching screws. Remove the bezel and panel screws.

18. Lower the steering column.

19. Pull the instrument panel about 3 inches outward.

20. Unscrew and remove the defroster ducts. Disconnect the hoses.

21. Disconnect the vacuum hoses at the core housing.

22. Remove the two heater housing retaining nuts in the engine compartment and remove the core housing.

23. Installation is the reverse of removal. Observe the following torques:
Steering column retaining nuts: 28 ft. lb.

24. Evacuate, charge and leak test the A/C system.

Blower Motor

REMOVAL & INSTALLATION

CJ Models

The heater housing assembly has to be removed to get out the blower motor.

1. Drain about two quarts of coolant.

2. Disconnect the heater hoses at the engine side of the firewall.

3. Detach the heater control cables.

4. Disconnect the motor wiring.

5. Detach the water drain hose and the defroster hose.

6. Remove the nuts from the studs in the engine compartment.

Cherokee-Wagoneer-Truck

1. Disconnect the blower motor wiring connector.

2. Remove the blower motor to blower housing mounting screws. Remove the blower motor and fan assembly.

3. Installation is in the reverse order of removal.

Radio

REMOVAL & INSTALLATION

NOTE: On Wagoneer and Cherokee models the glove box door, liner and lock striker must be removed. The radio is removed through the glove box.

1. Disconnect the battery ground cable.

2. Remove the control knobs, nuts, and bezel.

3. On early 1977 models, you may have to detach the defroster hose. With air conditioning, remove the screws and lower the assembly.

4. Disconnect the radio bracket from the instrument panel.

5. Tilt the radio down and remove it toward the steering wheel.

6. Detach the antenna, speaker and power wires.

7. Reverse the procedure for installation.

Wiper Blades and Arms

REMOVAL & INSTALLATION

To remove the blade, pull it away from the windshield. Push against the tip of the wiper arm to compress the locking spring and disengage the retaining pin. Pivot the blade clockwise to unhook it from the arm. To install the blade, just snap it into position.

To remove the arm, simply pry it straight off carefully. When you reinstall it, make sure that it doesn't hit the rubber moulding at either edge of the windshield while running. Install in the reverse order.

Wiper Motor

REMOVAL & INSTALLATION

CJ Models

1. If your Jeep has crash padding, you have to fold the windshield down for access. Even if you don't have the padding, you can't get the wires out to remove the motor from the vehicle, unless the windshield is down.

2. Remove the wiper motor cover.

3. Remove the left access plug from the bottom of the windshield.

4. Disconnect the drive link from the left wiper pivot by sliding the clip off.

5. Detach the wiring from the switch.

6. Remove the mounting screws and the wiper motor.

7. Reverse the procedure for installation.

1977–83 Wagoneer and Cherokee
1977–84 Grand Wagoneer, Truck

1. Disconnect the wiper drive link from the crank under the instrument panel.

2. Mark the locations of the wires at the motor to facilitate proper assembly under the hood.

3. Disconnect the motor and washer pump wires at the motor under the hood.

4. Remove the motor-to-dash mounting screws and remove the motor from the vehicle.

5. Install the windshield wiper motor in the reverse order of removal.

Commando

1. Disconnect the wire harness plug and speedometer cable from the instrument cluster.

2. Remove the instrument cluster from the instrument panel by depressing the retainer springs at each corner.

3. Remove the 3 motor-to-brake and clutch pedal mounting bracket screws.

4. Disconnect the wiper drive link from the motor crank.

5. Disconnect the washer hoses from the washer pump. Pivot the motor assembly to the right and drop it below the instrument panel.

6. Mark the wire locations for proper assembly.

7. Disconnect the wire harness from the motor and washer pump and remove the motor.

8. Install the windshield wiper motor in the reverse order of removal.

Wiper Motor and Linkage

REMOVAL & INSTALLATION

1984 Wagoneer and Cherokee

1. Remove the wiper arms.

2. Remove the cowl trim panel.

3. Disconnect the washer hose. Remove the cowl mounting bracket attaching nuts and pivot pin attaching screws.

Typical windshield wiper components

4. Disconnect the wiring connector and remove the motor.

5. Installation is the reverse of removal. Torque the mounting nuts to 50 in. lb.

Wiper Linkage

REMOVAL & INSTALLATION

CJ Models

1. Remove the wiper arms.

2. Remove the nuts attaching the pivots to the windshield frame.

3. Remove the necessary components from the top of the windshield frame.

4. Remove the windshield hold-down knobs and fold the windshield forward.

5. Remove the access hole covers on both sides of the windshield.

6. Disconnect the wiper motor drive link from the left wiper pivot.

7. Remove the wiper pivot shafts and linkage from the access hole.

8. Install the linkage in the reverse order.

Wagoneer, Cherokee and Commando, Truck

1. Remove the wiper arms and pivot shaft nuts, washers, escutcheons and gaskets.

2. Disconnect the drive arm from the motor crank.

3. Remove individual links where necessary, to remove the pivot shaft bodies without excessive interference.

4. Install in the reverse order of removal.

Instrument Cluster

REMOVAL & INSTALLATION

CJ Models

1. Disconnect the negative battery cable.

2. Disconnect the speedometer cable from the back of the speedometer.

3. Remove the instrument cluster attaching screws/nuts and remove the cluster.

4. Disconnect the instrument cluster electrical connectors and remove the cluster from the vehicle.

5. Install in the reverse order.

1977–83 Wagoneer, Cherokee and Commando
1977–84 Grand Wagoneer, Truck

1. Disconnect the battery ground.

2. Disconnect the speedometer cable.

3. Cover the steering column.

4. Remove the cluster attaching screws and tilt the top toward the interior of the vehicle.

5. Mark the electrical connectors and hoses, disconnect them and the blend door air cable.

6. Remove the cluster.

7. Installation is the reverse of removal.

1984 Wagoneer and Cherokee

1. Disconnect the battery ground.

2. Remove the four instrument panel bezel screws and lift off the bezel. The bezel unsnaps.

3. Remove the cigar lighter housing screws.

4. Remove the rocker switch housing screws.

5. Remove the cluster screws.

6. Disconnect the speedometer cable, pull the cluster out slowly and disconnect two multi-connectors at the cluster back. Remove the cluster.

7. Installation is the reverse of removal.

Speedometer Cable

REPLACEMENT

1. Reach up behind the center of the speedometer head. The cable is connected by a threaded ring. Unscrew the ring and pull the cable sheath from the head.

2. The cable core can be pulled from the sheath.

3. If the core is broken, detach the other end of the sheath from the transmission. Pull out the broken end.

4. When installing the cable, apply a very small amount of speedometer cable graphite lubricant.

Headlight

REMOVAL & INSTALLATION

1. Remove the attaching screws from the headlight trim ring. Pull out slightly at the bottom and push up to disengage the upper retaining tab.

Typical front end lighting arrangement

2. Remove the trim ring.

3. Remove the three retaining screws from the retaining ring.

4. Pull the headlamp out and disconnect the wire harness.

5. Install in reverse order of the above procedure. Check for proper seating of the lamp in its mounting ring and check for proper alignment.

Fusible Links

Fusible links are sections of wire, with special insulation, designed to melt under electrical overload. There is usually one in the main wire from the battery, and near the alternator output side. If one melts, it must be replaced with a new link of the correct amperage rating. Never replace a melted link with ordinary wire; you run the risk of melting your entire wiring harness.

Mazda/Courier

IDENTIFICATION

Vehicle

COURIER

The Courier vehicle identification number is located on a metal tag fastened to the top of the cowl on the driver's side and visible through the windshield. The identification number also appears on the Safety Compliance Certification Label, located on the driver's door rear pillar. This label includes additional information as shown.

Courier serial number location—top of cowl

COURIER	
MODEL	PAINT
1981 MODEL	DE
VEHICLE I.D. NO.	
JC2UA122-B0000000	
2.3L DISPLACEMENT	3.64 REAR AXLE RATIO
TOYO KOGYO CO., LTD.	MADE IN JAPAN

Courier Safety Compliance Certification Label, located on the driver's door rear pillar

MAZDA

The Mazda vehicle identification number plate is located on top of the cowl on the driver's side, and can be read through the windshield. There is also a model identification plate attached to the cowl at the right/rear of the engine compartment. The chassis number is stamped on the front portion of the left frame member.

Engine

MAZDA B2000 GAS ENGINE

The engine number is stamped on the machined surface on the right side of the engine block.

MAZDA B2200 DIESEL

The engine number is stamped on the left side of the block on a machined surface.

Vehicle identification number (VIN) plate
Mazda serial number location—top of cowl

GENERAL ENGINE SPECIFICATIONS—COURIER

Year	Engine Displacement cu. in. (ltrs.)	Carb. Type	Horsepower @ rpm	Torque @ rpm	Bore × Stroke (in.)	Compression Ratio	Oil Pressure psi @ rpm
'77–'78	109.6 (1.8)	2 bbl.	67 @ 5000	88 @ 3000	3.07 × 3.70	8.6:1	50–64 @ 3000
'77–'82	140.3 (2.3)	2 bbl.	92 @ 5000	121 @ 3000	3.78 × 3.126	9.0:1	40–60 @ 2000
'79–'82	120.2 (2.0)	2 bbl.	NA	NA	3.15 × 3.86	8.6:1	50–64 @ 3000

NA: Not available

GENERAL ENGINE SPECIFICATIONS—MAZDA
Piston Engine

Year	Engine Displacement Cu in.	(cc)	Carb Type	Net Horsepower (@ rpm)	Net Torque @ rpm (ft lbs)	Bore and Stroke (in.)	Compression Ratio	Oil Pressure (@ rpm)
'77–'78	109.6	(1796)	2-bbl	66 @ 4500	92 @ 3000	3.07 × 3.07	8.6:1	48–64 @ 3000
'79–'84	120.2	(2000)	2-bbl	NA	NA	3.15 × 3.86	8.6:1	50–64 @ 3000
'82–'84	134.8	(2209)	①	58 @ 4000	88 @ 2500	3.50 × 3.50	2.1:1	57 @ 3600

NA—Not available
① Distributor pump type diesel injection system

GENERAL ENGINE SPECIFICATIONS—MAZDA
Rotary

Model	Engine Displacement Cu in.	(cc)	Carburetor Type	Net Horsepower	Net Torque	Rotor Displacement (cu in.)	Compression Ratio	Oil Pressure @ rpm (psi)
Pick-up	80	(1,308)	4-bbl	110	117	40	9.2:1	71.1 @ 3,000

TUNE-UP SPECIFICATIONS—COURIER

Year	Engine Displacement cu. in. (liters)	Spark Plugs Type	Gap (in.)	Distributor Point Dwell (deg.)	Point Gap (in.)	Ignition Timing (BTDC)	Intake Valve Opens (BTDC)	Fuel Pump Pressure (psi)	Compression Pressure (psi)	Idle Speed② MT (rpm)	AT (rpm)	Valve Clearance③ Intake (in.)	Exhaust (in.)
'77	109.6 (1.8)	AG32	0.032	49–55	0.020	5°	13°	2.8–3.6	①	700	700	0.012	0.012
	140.3 (2.3)	AGRF52	0.034	Electronic		6°	NA	2.8–3.6	①	825	700	⑤	⑤
'78	109.6 (1.8)	AG32	0.032	49–55	0.020	8°	18°	2.8–3.6	①	700	700	0.012	0.012
	140.3 (2.3)	AGRF52	0.034	Electronic		6°	NA	2.8–3.6	①	825	700	⑤	⑤
'79–'80	120.2 (2.0)	AGR32	0.031	Electronic		8°	14°	2.8–3.6	①	650	650	0.012	0.012
	140.3 (2.3)	AGRF52	0.043	Electronic		6°	NA	2.8–3.6	①	800	700	⑤	⑤
'81–'82	120.2 (2.0)	AGR32	0.031	Electronic		8°	14°	2.8–3.6	①	650⑥	650⑥	0.012	0.012
	140.3 (2.3)	AGRF52	0.034	Electronic		6°	NA	2.8–3.6	①	850	700	⑤	⑤

NOTE: If the specifications on the engine decal differs from the above information, use the specifications as listed on the engine decal.
BTDC: Before top dead center
① The lowest reading cylinder should be within 75% of the highest.
② MT: Manual transmission (adjusted in NEUTRAL)
   AT: Automatic transmission (adjusted in DRIVE)
③ Adjusted with the engine of normal operating temperature.
④ For 1975 models. Use type AG32 for 1976 models.
⑤ Adjustment is not required.
⑥ 600 for California vehicles.

TUNE-UP SPECIFICATIONS—MAZDA
Piston Engine

Year	Engine Displacement Cu in.	(cc)	Spark Plugs Type	Gap (in.)	Distributor Point Dwell (deg)	Point Gap (in.)	Ignition Timing (deg) MT	AT	Intake Valve Opens (deg)	Fuel Pump Pressure (psi)	Idle Speed (rpm) MT	AT	Valve Clearance (in.)▲ In	Ex
'77–'78	109.6	(1796)	BP-6ES	.031	49–55	0.020	8B	8B	18B	2.8–3.6	700–750	—	.012–	.012
'79–'84	120.2	(2000)	BPR-6ES	.031	Elec.	Elec.	8B	—	14B	2.8–3.6	600–700	—	.012–③	.012 ③
'82–'84	134.8	(2209)	—	—	—	—	2A④	—	14B	—	700	—		.012

▲ At the valve (warm engine)
—Not applicable

③ 0.009 on the cam side
④ Diesel injection timing at pump, cam lift of .039"

CO—% at idle: '73–'75—1.5–2.5%
B—BTDC (before top dead center)

TUNE-UP SPECIFICATIONS—MAZDA
Rotary

Year	Engine Cu in.	Spark Plugs Type	Gap	Distributors (both) Point Gap (in.)	Point Dwell (deg)	Ignition Timing (deg) Leading Normal	Retarded	Trailing Normal	Idle Speed (rpm) MT	AT
'77	80	RN 278B	0.039–0.043	0.018	58 ± 3	5A	—	25A	725–775	725–775

① Transmission in drive (D)
TDC—Top dead center

A—After top dead center
deg—degrees

FIRING ORDER

NOTE: To avoid confusion, always replace spark plug wires one at a time.

Firing Order—Courier 1.8L and 2.0L engines

Firing Order—2.3L liter engine

Mazda piston engine firing order—gas and diesel

Rotary engine firing order

DISTRIBUTOR POSITION

CLOCKWISE

CAPACITIES—COURIER

Year	Engine Crankcase		Transmission			Rear Axle pts. (L)	Gas Tank gals. (L)	Cooling System qts. (L)
	With Filter qts. (L)	Without Filter qts. (L)	4-Speed pts. (L)	5-Speed pts. (L)	Auto-matic qts. (L)			
'77–'82	5 (4.7)	4 (3.8)	3 (1.4)	3.6 (1.7)	6.6 (6.3)	2.8 (1.3)	①	②

① Short bed truck—15 (57)
  Long bed truck—17.5 (66)
② With 1.8 or 2.0 liter engines—7.5 (7.2)
  With 2.3 liter engine—8.8 (8.3)

CAPACITIES—MAZDA

Year	Model	Engine Displacement		Engine Crankcase (qts)		Transmission (pts)			Drive Axle (pts)	Gasoline Tank (gals)	Cooling System (qts)	
		Cu in.	(cc)	With Filter	Without Filter	Manual		Automatic			W/ AC	W/O AC
						4-spd	5-spd					
'77	Rotary Pick-up	80	(1308)	6.80	5.30	3.60	4.60	13.20	2.80	20.8	—	10.30
'77–'78	B-1800	109.6	(1796)	3.8	—	3.00	3.8	—	3.0	14.8②	—	7.6
'79–'84	B-2000	120.2	(2000)	4.1	—	3.2	3.6	—	2.8	14.8②	—	7.6③
'82–'84	B-2200	134.8	(2209)	5.3	—	—	3.6	—	2.8	14.6④	—	11.1⑤

① After #49825—3.20
② Long body—17.4 gal.
③ 7.0 without heater
④ Long body—17.2
⑤ Without heater—10.0

VALVE SPECIFICATIONS—COURIER

Year	Engine Displacement cu in. (liters)	Seat Angle (deg)	Face Angle (deg)	Spring Test Pressure (lbs. @ in.)	Spring Free Length (in.)	Stem to Guide Clearance (in.)		Stem Diameter (in.)	
						Intake	Exhaust	Intake	Exhaust
'77–'78	109.6 (1.8)	45	45	16.3 @ 1.30① 26.8 @ 1.36②	1.438① 1.469②	.0007–.0021③	.0007–.0023③	.3161–.3167	.3159–.3167
'79–'81	120.2 (2.0)	45	45	20.9 @ 1.26① 31.4 @ 1.34②	1.438① 1.469②	.0007–.0021③	.0007–.0023③	.3162–.3168	.3160–.3168
'77–'81	140.3 (2.3)	45	44	71–79 @ 1.56	1.820	.0010–.0027④	.0015–.0032④	.3416–.3423	.3411–.3418
'82	120.2 (2.0)	45	45	56.8 @ 1.35	1.598	.0007–.0021③	.0007–.0023③	.3162–.3168	.3160–.3168
	140.3 (2.3)	45	44	71–79 @ 1.56	1.890	.0010–.0027④	.0015–.0032④	.3416–.3423	.3411–.3418

① Inner spring only
② Outer spring only
③ Wear limit: 0.008 in.
④ Service clearance 0.0055 in.

VALVE SPECIFICATIONS—MAZDA
Piston Engine

Year	Engine Displacement Cu In.	(cc)	Seat Angle (deg)	Face Angle (deg)	Spring Test Pressure (lbs @ in.)	Spring Installed Height (in.)	Stem-to-Guide Clearance (in.) Intake	Exhaust	Stem Diameter (in.) Intake	Exhaust
'77–'78	109.6	(1796)	45	45	③	②	.0007–.0021	.0007–.0023	.3150	.3150
'79–'82	120.2	(2000)	45	45	①	②	.0007–.0021	.0007–.0023	.3150	.3150
'82–'84	134.8	(2209)	45④	45④	⑤	1.587⑥	.0015–.0046	.002–.0051	.3170–.3180	.3175–.3185

① Outer: 31.4 @ 1.339
   Inner: 20.9 @ 1.260
② Outer: 1.339
   Inner: 1.260
③ Outer: 31.4 @ 1.339
   Inner: 20.9 @ 1.260
④ Refers to intake. Exhaust—30°
⑤ Outer: 32.1 @ Installed height
   Inner: 28 @ Installed height
⑥ Refers to outer. Inner—1.488

CAMSHAFT SPECIFICATIONS—COURIER
(All measurements in inches)

Engine Displacement cu. in. (liters)	Journal Diameter #1	#2	#3	#4	Bearing Clearance #1	#2	#3	#4	Maximum Journal Run-out	Lobe Lift① Int.	Exh.	End-Play Pref.	Max.
109.6 & 120.2 (1.8) (2.0)	1.7695–1.7701	1.7691–1.7697	1.7695–1.7701	—	.0007–.0027	.0011–.0031	.0007–.0027	—	.0012	NA	NA	.0010–.0070	.0080
140.3 (2.3)	1.7713–1.7720	1.7713–1.7720	1.7713–1.7720	1.7713–1.7720	.0010–.0030②	.0010–.0030②	.0010–.0030②	.0010–.0030②	.0005	.2437③	.2437③	.0010–.0070	.0090

① Subtract the small diameter (base circle) of the cam lobe from the large diameter (total lobe height) of the cam lobe to determine the lobe lift.
② Maximum allowable bearing clearance—.006 in.
③ Maximum allowable lift loss—.005 in.

CAMSHAFT SPECIFICATIONS—MAZDA
Gasoline Engine
(All measurements in inches)

Engine Displacement Cu. in. (liters)	Journal Diameter #1, #3	Center	Bearing Clearance #1, #3	Center	Maximum Journal Runout	Lobe Lift In.	Exh.	End Play
109.6 (1796) 120.2 (1970)	1.7695–1.7733	1.7691–1.7737	.0087–.0027	.0021–.0031	.0012	1.7731	1.7784	.001–.007

CAMSHAFT SPECIFICATIONS—MAZDA
Diesel Engine
(All measurements in inches)

Engine Displacement Cu. in. Liters	Journal Diameter			Bearing Clearance			Maximum Journal Runout	Lobe Lift		End Play
	#1	#2	#3	#1	#2	#3		Int.	Exh.	
134.8 (2209)	2.0438–2.0497	2.0439–2.0498	1.9827–2.0201	.0024–.0047	.0024–.0047	.0024–.0047	.0031	1.6767	1.6727	.0008–.0071

CRANKSHAFT AND CONNECTING ROD SPECIFICATIONS—COURIER
(All measurements in inches)

Year	Engine Displacement cu in. (liters)	Crankshaft				Connecting Rod		
		Main Brg Journal Dia	Main Brg Oil Clearance	Shaft End-Play	Thrust on No	Journal Dia	Oil Clearance	Side Clearance
'78	109.6 (1.8)	2.4779–2.4785	0.0005–0.0015①	0.003–0.010	4	2.0842–2.0848	0.001–0.0011③	0.004–0.008②
'79–'82	120.2 (2.0)	2.4780–2.4786	0.0005–0.0015①	0.003–0.009	4	2.0842–2.0848	0.001–0.0026③	0.004–0.008②
'77–'82	140.3 (2.3)	2.3990–2.3982	0.0008–0.0015④	0.004–0.008	4	2.0464–2.0472	0.0008–0.0015④	0.0035–0.0105⑤

① Wear limit: 0.0012–0.0024 in.
② Wear limit: 0.014
③ Wear limit: 0.001–0.003 in.
④ Wear limit: 0.0008–0.0026 in.
⑤ Wear limit: 0.0150

CRANKSHAFT AND CONNECTING ROD SPECIFICATIONS—MAZDA
Gasoline Piston Engine
(All measurements are given in inches)

Year	Engine Displacement		Crankshaft				Connecting Rod		
	Cu in.	(cc)	Main Brg Journal Dia	Main Brg Oil Clearance	Shaft End-Play	Thrust on No.	Journal Dia	Oil Clearance	Side Clearance
'77–'78	109.6	(1796)	2.4804	.0012–.0019	.003–.009	5	2.0866	.0011–.0030	.004–.008
'79–'84	120.2	(2000)	2.4804	.0012–.0020	.003–.009	5	.7874①	.0011–.0030	.004–.008

① Small end, inner diameter

CRANKSHAFT AND CONNECTING ROD SPECIFICATIONS—MAZDA
Diesel Engine
(All measurements in inches)

Year	Engine Displacement cu in. (liters)	Crankshaft				Connecting Rod		
		Main Brg Journal Dia	Main Brg Oil Clearance	Shaft End-Play	Thrust on No	Journal Dia	Oil Clearance	Side Clearance
'82–'84	134.8 (2209)	2.5591	.0016–.0036	.055–.0153	3	2.0866	.0014–.0030	.0044–.0134

PISTON AND RING SPECIFICATIONS—COURIER

(All measurements in inches)

Engine Displacement cu. in. (liters)	Piston to-bore Clearance	Ring Gap			Ring Side Clearance		
		First	Second	Oil Control	First	Second	Oil Control
109.6 (1.8)	0.0022–0.0028	0.008–0.016	0.008–0.016	0.008–0.016	0.0014–0.0028	0.0012–0.0025	0.0012–0.0024
120.2 (2.0)	0.0014–0.0030	0.008–0.016	0.008–0.016	0.012–0.035	0.0011–0.0027	0.0011–0.0025	Snug
140.3 (2.3)	0.0014–0.0022	0.010–0.020	0.010–0.020	0.015–0.055	0.002–0.004①	0.002–0.004①	Snug

① Service Limit—0.006 in.

PISTON AND RING SPECIFICATIONS—MAZDA
Gasoline Piston Engine

(All measurements are given in inches)

Year	Engine Displacement		Piston Clearance	Ring Gap			Ring Side Clearance		
	Cu in.	(cc)		Top Compression	Bottom Compression	Oil Control	Top Compression	Bottom Compression	Oil Control
'77–'78	109.6	(1796)	.0022–.0028	.008–.016	.008–.016	.012–.035	.0014–.0028	.0012–.0025	—
'79–'81	120.2	(2000)	.0014–.0030	.008–.016	.008–.016	.012–.035	.0012–.0028	.0012–.0025	—
'82–'84	120.2	2000	.0019–.0025	.008–.016	.008–.016	.012–.035	.0012–.0028	.0012–.0025	—

PISTON AND RING SPECIFICATIONS—MAZDA
Diesel Engine

(All measurements are given in inches)

Year	Engine Displacement		Piston Clearance	Ring Gap			Ring Side Clearance		
	Cu in.	(cc)		Top Compression	Bottom Compression	Oil Control	Top Compression	Bottom Compression	Oil Control
'82–'84	139.8	(2209)	.0021–.0031	.0157–.0217	.0118–.0157	.0138–.0217	.0020–.0035	.0016–.0031	.0012–.0028

TORQUE SPECIFICATIONS—COURIER

(All readings in ft. lbs. unless noted)

Engine Displacement cu in. (liters)	Cylinder Head Bolts	Rod Bearing Bolts	Main Bearing Bolts	Camshaft Sprocket-to-Cam	Flywheel-to Crankshaft Bolts	Manifolds	
						Intake	Exhaust
109.6 (1.8)	①	29–33	60–65	50–64	112–118	14–19	16–21
120.2 (2.0)	②	36–40	61–65	51–58	112–118	14–20	16–21
140.3 (2.3)	④	30–36	80–90	⑤	54–64	14–21③	27–38

① Torque to 63–68 ft. lbs. cold; re-torque to 69–73 ft. lbs. hot.

② Torque to 59–64 ft. lbs. cold; re-torque to 69–72 ft. lbs. hot.

③ Torque in two steps: 1st—5–7 ft. lbs.; 2nd—14–21 ft. lbs.

④ Torque in two steps: 1st—50–60 ft. lbs.; 2nd—80–90 ft. lbs.

⑤ '75–'81 models: 80–90 ft. lbs. '82 models: 50–71 ft. lbs.

TORQUE SPECIFICATIONS—MAZDA
Gasoline Piston Engine
(All figures given in ft. lbs.)

Year	Cylinder Head Bolts	Rod Bearing Bolts	Main Bearing Bolts	Crankshaft Pulley Bolt	Flywheel-to Crankshaft Bolts	Manifold Intake	Manifold Exhaust
'75–'78	②	36–40	61–65	101–108	112–118	14–19	12–17①
'79–'82	③	30–33	61–65	101–108	112–118	14–19	16–21
'83–'84	④	30–33	61–65	101–108	112–118	14–19	18–21

① B1800—16–21
② Cold—56–60
   Hot—69–72
③ Cold—59–64
   Hot—69–72
④ Cold—65–69
   Hot—69–72

TORQUE SPECIFICATIONS—MAZDA
Diesel Engine
(All figures given in ft. lbs.)

Year	Cylinder Head Bolts	Rod Bearing Bolts	Main Bearing Bolts	Crankshaft Pulley Bolt	Flywheel-to-Crankshaft Bolts	Manifold Intake	Manifold Exhaust
'82–'84	80–85	50–54	80–85	145–181	95–137	11.6–17.4	11.6–17.4

TORQUE SPECIFICATIONS—MAZDA
Rotary
(All figures in ft. lbs.)

Engine Displacement Cu In.	(cc)	Front Cover	Bearing Housing	Rear Stationary Gear	Eccentric Shaft Pulley Bolt	Flywheel to Eccentric Shaft Nut	Manifold Intake	Manifold Exhaust	Oil Pan	Tension Bolts
80	(1,308)	—	—	—	54–69	289–362	15	32–43	5–7	23–27

ROTOR AND HOUSING SPECIFICATIONS—MAZDA
Rotary
(All measurements are given in inches)

Model	Rotor Side Clearance	Rotor Standard Protrusion of Land	Rotor Limit of Protrusion of Land	Rotor Front and Rear Distortion Limit	Rotor Front and Rear Wear Limit	Housing Rotor Width	Housing Rotor Distortion Limit	Housing Intermediate Distortion Limit	Housing Intermediate Wear Limit
Pick-up	.0047–.0083	.004–.006	.003	.002	.004	3.1438	.002	.002	.004

ECCENTRIC SHAFT SPECIFICATIONS—MAZDA
Rotary
(All measurements are given in inches)

Model	Journal Diameter		Oil Clearance		Eccentric Shaft End-Play		Min. Shaft Runout
	Main Bearing	Rotor Bearing	Main Bearing	Rotor Bearing	Normal	Limit	
Pick-up	1.6929	2.9134	.0016–.0028	.0016–.0031	.0016–.0028	.0035	.0024

SEAL SPECIFICATIONS—MAZDA
Rotary
(All measurements are given in inches)

Model	Apex Seal		Corner Seal Width (OD)	Side Seal		Oil Seal Contact Width of Lip	
	Normal Height	Height Limit		Thickness	Width	Normal	Limit
Pick-up	.33500	.27600	.4331	.0394	.1378	.008	.031

SEAL CLEARANCES—MAZDA
Rotary
(All measurements are given in inches)

Model	Apex Seals				Corner Seal to Rotor Groove		Side Seal			
	To Side Housing		To Rotor Groove				To Rotor Groove		To Corner Seal	
	Normal	Limit	Normal	Limit	Normal	Limit	Normal	Limit	Normal	Limit
Pick-up	.0051–.0067	.012	.0020–.0035	.006	.0008–.0019	.0031	.0016–.0028	.0040	.0020–.0059	.016

ALTERNATOR AND REGULATOR SPECIFICATIONS—MAZDA

Year	Model	Alternator		Regulator			
		Field Current @ 14V	Output (amps)	Air Gap (in.)	Point Gap (in.)	Back Gap (in.)	Volts @ 75°
'77	Rotary Pick-up	56	63	0.028–0.051	0.012–0.018	0.028–0.059	1.40
'77–'78	B1800	—	—	0.028–0.051	0.012–0.018	0.028–0.059	14–15①
'79–'82	B2000	—	—	0.028–0.051	0.012–0.018	0.028–0.059	14–15①
'82–'84	B2000	—	23	—	—	—	14.1–14.7
	B2200	—	28	—	—	—	14.1–14.7

① Alternator @ 4,000 rpm and battery fully charged.

BATTERY AND STARTER SPECIFICATIONS—COURIER

Year	Engine	Battery Amp Hour Capacity	Volts	Ground	Lock Test Amps	Lock Test Volts	Torque (ft. lbs.)	No Load Test Amps	No Load Test Volts	No Load Test RPM	Brush Spring Tension (oz)
'77–'82	All	①	12	Neg	Not Recommended			50 (or less)	11	5000 (or more)	38

① '77–'78 models: 60 amp standard; 70 amp optional
'79–'82 models: 45 amp standard: 70 amp optional

BATTERY AND STARTER SPECIFICATIONS—MAZDA

(All trucks use 12 volt, negative ground electrical systems)

Year	Model	Battery Amp Hour Capacity	Lock Test Amps	Lock Test Volts	Torque (ft/lbs)	No Load Test Amps	No Load Test Volts	No Load Test rpm	Brush Spring Tension (oz)	Min. Brush Length (in.)
'77	Rotary Pick-up	60MT 70AT	780MT 1100AT	5.0	8.0MT 17.4AT	75MT 100AT	11.5	4900MT 7800AT	49–63	0.45
'75–'76	B1600	60	560	7.5	9.4	60	11.5	6000	35–46	0.45
'77–'78	B1800	45	310	5.0	5.4	53	11.5	6800	49–63	0.45
'79–'84	B2000	45①	310	5.0	5.4	53	11.5	6800	49–63	0.45
'82–'84	B2200	80	1050	2.0	21.6	180	11.0	3800	49–63	.45

① Heavy duty—70

BRAKE SPECIFICATIONS—COURIER

(All measurements in inches)

Year	Model	Master Cylinder Bore	Caliper Piston Bore	Wheel Cylinder Bore Front	Wheel Cylinder Bore Rear	Front Disc Thickness	Drum Diameter Front	Drum Diameter Rear	Minimum Lining Thickness Disc	Minimum Lining Thickness Drum①
'77–'78	All	0.875	2.1248	—	0.750	0.4724②	—	10.24③	0.315	1/32
'79–'82	All	0.875	2.1248	—	0.875	0.4724②	—	10.24③	0.276	1/32

① Measured from the brake shoe to the outermost portion of the lining.

② Minimum thickness—0.4331 in.; maximum run-out—0.004

③ Exact dimension—10.2362–10.2445; wear limit—10.2756

BRAKE SPECIFICATIONS—MAZDA

(All measurements are in. unless noted)

Model	Lug Nut Torque (ft. lbs.)	Brake Disc Master Cylinder Bore	Brake Disc Minimum Thickness	Brake Disc Maximum Run-Out	Brake Drum Diameter	Brake Drum Max. Machine O/S	Brake Drum Max. Wear Limit	Minimum Lining Thickness Front	Minimum Lining Thickness Rear
B1600	65–72	0.750	—	—	10.236	10.276	—	0.039	0.039
Rotary Pick-up	65–72	0.875	0.433	0.004	10.236	10.275	—	0.276	0.039
B1800	58–65	0.750	0.433	0.004	10.236	—	10.276	0.276	0.039

BRAKE SPECIFICATIONS—MAZDA

(All measurements are in. unless noted)

| Model | Lug Nut Torque (ft. lbs.) | Brake Disc | | | Brake Drum | | | Minimum Lining Thickness | |
		Master Cylinder Bore	Minimum Thick-ness	Maximum Run-Out	Diam-eter	Max. Machine O/S	Max. Wear Limit	Front	Rear
B2000	58–65	0.875	0.433	0.0039	10.236	—	10.276	0.039	0.039
B2200	58–65	0.8125	0.7480	0.0039	10.236	—	10.276	0.039	0.039

NOTE: Minimum lining thickness is as recommended by the manufacturer. Due to variations in state inspection regulations, the minimum allowable thickness may be different than recommended by the manufacturer.

TUNE-UP

Breaker Points and Condenser

NOTE: California and Canada Mazda gasoline engines have breaker points through 1978. Courier 1977–78 1.8 liter engines have breaker points. All other gasoline engines have electronic ignition, eliminating breaker points and condenser service.

1. Release the clips on the distributor cap with a screwdriver. Lift off the cap and move it aside, leaving the wires attached. Pull the rotor from the shaft.

2. Inspect the points. If they are badly pitted or burned, they must be replaced. If they are only slightly burned, they may be filed flat and reused. In either case, they must be removed from the distributor. If the points are in good shape and only require adjustment, proceed to Step 9.

3. Disconnect the primary and condenser wires from the breaker point terminal.

4. Remove the screws securing the points to the distributor breaker plate. Use a magnetic screwdriver to avoid dropping the screws. Remove the points.

5. If the points are slightly burned and are to be reused, clean them with a few strokes of a flat points file. Do this with the points removed from the distributor to avoid getting filings and grit in the works. Do not use an emery board, sandpaper, or the like for this job.

LATERAL MISALIGNMENT   PROPER LATERAL ALIGNMENT

CORRECT LATERAL MISALIGNMENT BY BENDING FIXED CONTACT SUPPORT *NEVER BEND BREAKER LEVER*

Breaker point alignment—1.8 engines

Adjusting the points with the rubbing block on the high point of the cam lobe

6. Install the new or cleaned points onto the breaker plate, but leave the mounting screws slightly loose. Apply a small dab of grease onto the distributor cam. Do not use oil, which will get onto the points, causing them to burn.

7. The condenser should be replaced whenever the points are replaced. Disconnect the condenser leads and remove the condenser mounting screws. Dual points models have a condenser for each set of points. A smaller condenser, used for radio noise suppression, is mounted next to the other condenser; it need only be replaced if ignition noise (clicking or popping) is heard over the radio. Install and connect the new condenser.

8. Check the breaker point alignment. If the points do not meet squarely, gently bend the fixed point slightly. Do not bend the movable point arm to adjust.

9. Rotate the engine until the rubbing block of the points arm is on one of the four high spots (lobes) of the distributor cam. The cam must open the points fully before the gap can be adjusted. The engine can be rotated by cranking it around in short bursts with the starter. You can also rotate the engine by hand with a wrench on the crankshaft (or eccentric shaft) pulley bolt; this is easier with the spark plugs removed. Move the engine only in the direction of normal rotation, to avoid damage to the apex seals (rotary engines).

10. Check the point gap with a flat feeler gauge of the proper thickness (see the Tune-Up Specifications). The feeler gauge should move through the points with only a light drag. If there is no drag, or if the gauge cannot be inserted at all, the gap is incorrect.

11. If the gap is incorrect, loosen the point set mounting screws slightly, if they are not already loose. Insert a screwdriver into the adjusting slot and lever the points open or closed until the gap is correct. Tighten the mounting screws and recheck the adjustment.

12. Install the rotor onto the distributor shaft (if the tip is burned or pitted, a new rotor should be used; similarly, if the distributor cap contacts are burned, a new cap should be installed). Install the distributor cap. If a new cap is being installed, hold the new cap next to the old and transfer the wires one at a time to avoid cross-wiring.

ADJUSTMENT

There are two methods used to adjust breaker point gap. The first uses flat feeler gauges of a specified size which are inserted between the points. The movable point is adjusted until the proper clearance is obtained. The second method of adjustment is made after the first, and while not mandatory, is much more accurate, especially with worn points. In this method, a dwell meter is used to fine tune the point gap, so that the points remain open for only an exact number of degrees of distributor cam rotation.

If you do not have a dwell meter, the feeler blade method is adequate. If a dwell meter is available, perform the dwell meter adjustment after the initial feeler gauge setting is made.

Feeler Blade Method

1. Check the breaker point alignment and adjust if necessary, as outlined earlier.

2. Turn the engine until the rubbing block of the points rests on a high spot of the distributor cam. You can rotate the engine by putting the truck into high gear and pushing it forward, if you have a manual

T483

transmission. Otherwise, use the starter to bump the engine around in short bursts. The important thing here is to get the point block on one of the four corners of the cam, so that the points are at the widest possible opening. The object is to set the points correctly to the specified gap when wide open.

3. Insert a flat feeler blade of the correct size (found in the "Tune-Up Specifications" chart) between the points. The blades can be stacked to obtain the correct width, if necessary. The point gap setting is correct if the blade slips through with a slight drag. To adjust, slightly loosen the screw holding the movable point. There is a slot at the end of this point. By levering the slot with a screwdriver, the points can be adjusted. It isn't easy to get the correct setting right away. Try gauges 0.001–0.002 in. larger and smaller than the setting size. The larger should spread the points slightly, while the smaller should not drag at all. When correct, tighten the hold down screw.

4. The gap often changes during the tightening process, so check it afterward and readjust if necessary.

5. If you have a dwell meter, go on to the following operation. If not, replace the rotor and distributor cap, and go on to the "Ignition Timing" section. The ignition timing must be checked, as a 1° increase in dwell results in an ignition timing retard of 2°, and vice versa.

Dwell Meter Method

The dwell angle is the number of degrees of distributor cam rotation through which the points remain closed (conducting electricity). Increasing the point gap decreases dwell, while decreasing the gap increases dwell.

Dwell as a function of point gap

The dwell angle may be checked with the distributor cap and rotor installed and the engine running or with the cap and rotor removed and the engine cranking at starter speed. The meter gives a constant reading with the engine running. With the engine cranking, the meter will fluctuate between zero degrees dwell and the maximum figure for that setting. Never attempt to adjust the points when the ignition is on, or you may receive a shock.

1. Connect the meter as per the manufacturer's instructions (usually red lead to the positive (+) primary terminal of the coil and black wire to a ground). Zero the meter if necessary.

2. Check the dwell by either the cranking method, or with the engine running. If the setting is incorrect, the points must be adjusted.

3. To change the dwell angle, loosen the point hold down screw and insert a screwdriver into the adjustment slot. Increase point gap to decrease dwell, and vice versa. Tighten the hold down screw and check the dwell angle with the engine cranking. If it seems to be correct, replace the cap and rotor and check dwell with the engine running. Readjust as necessary.

4. Run the engine speed up to about 2,500 rpm and then let the speed drop abruptly; the dwell reading should not fluctuate. If it does, a worn distributor shaft, bushing or cam, or a worn breaker plate is indicated. The parts should be inspected and replaced if necessary.

5. After adjusting dwell angle, go on to the Ignition Timing section.

Electronic Ignition

COURIER

The 2.0 and 2.3 liter engines use an electronic ignition system which eliminates the points and condenser. Located in the distributor, in addition to the normal ignition rotor, is a four spoke signal rotor which turns on the shaft in the same manner as the points cam found in conventional systems. A magnetic pickup coil is the only other component in the distributor. The system also includes an ignition module, mounted on the left fender apron on 2.3 liter engines or right fender apron on 1979 2.0 liter engines; the module is mounted on the distributor on the 1980 and later 2.0 liter engines. A conventional ignition coil is also used.

When a rotor spoke is not lined up with the pickup coil, it generates large lines of flux between itself, the magnet, and the pickup coil. This large flux variation results in a high generated voltage in the pickup coil, preventing battery current from flowing to the pickup coil. When a rotor spoke lines up with the coil, the flux variation is low—thus, zero voltage is generated in the pickup coil, allowing current to flow to it. Ignition primary current is then cut off by the ignition module, causing high voltage to be induced in the ignition coil secondary windings. The high voltage flows through the distributor to the spark plug.

Because no points or condenser are used, and because dwell is determined by the module, no adjustments are necessary. Ignition timing is checked in the usual way, but unless the distributor is disturbed it is not likely to change.

Service for the electronic ignition consists of inspection of the distributor cap, rotor, and ignition wires, replacing when necessary. These parts can be expected to last for at least 40,000 miles.

1. The cap is held on by two screws. After unscrewing them, lift the cap straight up and off, with the wires attached. Inspect the cap for cracks, carbon paths, or a worn center contact. Replace it if necessary, transferring the wires one at a time from the old cap to the new.

2. On all models except 1980 and later 2.0 liter engines, pull the ignition rotor (not the spoked timing rotor) straight up to remove. The ignition rotor on 1980 and later 2.0 liter engines is retained by two screws. Use a magnetic screwdriver to remove the screws, and remove the rotor from the distributor shaft. Inspect the rotor, and replace it if the contacts are worn, burned or pitted. Do not file the contacts. Replace the rotor: on 2.3 liter and 1979 2.0 liter engines, press the rotor onto the shaft, and check to see that it is fully seated; on 1980 and later 2.0 liter models, replace the retaining screws and washers.

3. Inspect the wires for cracks or brittleness. Replace them one at a time to prevent crosswiring, carefully pressing the replacement wires into place. The cores of electronic ignition wires are more susceptible to breakage than those of standard wires, so handle them carefully.

Troubleshooting

Troubleshooting the electronic ignition is easy, but you will need an accurate ohmmeter, a jumper wire, and a 3.4 watt test light. Before suspecting the module or pickup coil, inspect all connections for breaks, improper hookups, shorts, or corrosion. Repair any faults before proceeding.

1. Check for a spark at the coil high tension lead: remove the coil high tension lead from the distributor and position it approximately ¼ inch from the engine block or other suitable ground. Hold the lead with a pair of insulated pliers and a heavy glove. Crank the engine and check for a spark. If the spark is good and consistent, inspect the cap and rotor. If the spark is weak or nonexistent, replace the high tension lead, clean and tighten all connections, and retest. If the spark is still weak, go to the next step.

2. Check the coil primary resistance: connect an ohmmeter across the coil primary terminals and read the resistance on the low scale. Resistance should measure approximately .9 ± .09 ohms @ 68°F. If the reading is far different, replace the coil.

3. Check the coil secondary resistance: connect an ohmmeter across the distributor side of the coil and the coil center tower. Read the resistance on the high scale of the meter. Resistance should measure 6,800–9,200 ohms @ 70°F. If the resistance is much higher (30,000–40,000 ohms), replace the coil.

4. Next, remove the distributor cap and ignition rotor. Crank the engine around until a rotor spoke of the armature is aligned with the pickup coil. Use a flat feeler gauge to check the armature gap. It should measure 0.008–0.024 in. (0.20–0.60 mm). If it does not, gently bend the pickup coil to adjust.

Electronic ignition troubleshooting

Ignition Timing

ADJUSTMENT

Courier

Timing should be checked at each tune-up and any time the points are adjusted or replaced. It is not likely to change very much on engines with electronic ignition.

If the ignition is set too far advanced (BTDC), the ignition and expansion of the fuel in the cylinder will occur too soon and tend to force the piston down while it is still traveling up. This causes engine ping.

VIEWED FROM RIGHT SIDE OF ENGINE

1. Denotes 5° BTDC on 1975–77 and 1980 models; denotes 8° BTDC on 1978–79 and 1981–82 models.
2. Denotes TDC—all models

Timing mark identification. The ATDC mark is to the right of top dead center (above it in the illustration).

If the ignition spark is set too far retarded, after TDC (ATDC), the piston will have already passed TDC and started on its way down when the fuel is ignited. This will cause the piston to be forced down for only a portion of its travel, resulting in poor engine performance and lack of power.

To check and adjust the timing:

1. Warm the engine to normal operating temperature. Stop the engine and clean off the notches in the crankshaft pulley. Use some paint or chalk to make the marks more

NOTE: This does not apply to 1980 and later 2.0 liter engines. The armature gap is not adjustable on these models.

5. Using the ohmmeter, measure the pickup coil resistance. Disconnect the 2 wire (red and green) connector at the distributor. The ignition switch should be OFF. Insert the probes of the ohmmeter into the pickup coil side of the connector. Resistance should be 760–840 ohms for the 2.3 liter and 1979 2.0 liter models. Resistance should be 1,050 ± 10% ohms @ 68°F for 1980 and later 2.0 liter models. If resistance is not within specifications, replace the pickup coil.

6. Finally, test the ignition module. On 2.3 liter and 1979 2.0 liter models, connect the test light between the positive and negative terminals of the ignition coil. Connect a jumper wire between the positive coil terminal and the red wire of the pickup coil (at the connector unplugged in the preceding pickup coil test). Be sure you are attaching the wire to the pickup coil side of the connector. Turn the ignition switch ON. The test light should come on. Disconnect the jumper wire from the red wire at the electrical connector. The test light should go out. If the module does not test out correctly, replace it.

On 1980 and later 2.0 liter models, the only way to test the ignition module is through a substitution test. If all other systems have been checked and are working correctly, remove the ignition module and install a new module known to be good. If the ignition system operates properly with the new module installed, the original one can be considered to be defective.

MAZDA

The only checks that can be made on this system are pick-up coil resistance and coil primary resistance. To check the pick-up coil resistance, connect an ohmmeter as shown (the pick-up may be checked in the distributor). Resistance must be 945–1155 ohms. Otherwise, replace the pick-up.

To check the coil primary resistance, the coil must be brought to normal operating temperature. If the vehicle is outside in cold weather, bring the coil into a room which is heated to about 68°F and allow it to warm up to room temperature. Resistance must be .81–.99 ohms, as measured between the two primary terminals with an ohmmeter. Otherwise, replace the coil.

Checking Pick-up coil resistance—Mazda

visible, if necessary. You will probably have to "bump" the engine around with the starter to get the notches into an accessible position.

2. There are two notches cut into the crankshaft pulley. Looking down at the marks, the Top Dead Center (TDC) mark is on the exhaust system side of the engine. The one on the carburetor side indicates the proper number of degrees before TDC (BTDC) at which the spark plug is to fire. On 1975–78 models, TDC is marked with white paint and the BTDC timing mark is colored with yellow paint. On 1979 and later models, TDC is not colored at all, and the BTDC timing mark is colored white.

3. Disconnect and plug the vacuum hose at the distributor. The line must be plugged to prevent a vacuum leak.

4. Connect the timing light according to the manufacturer's instructions to the Number 1 spark plug (at the front of the engine). Connect a tachometer according to the manufacturer's instructions.

5. Set the parking brake, block the front wheels, put the transmission in Neutral, and start the engine.

CAUTION

Keep your hands, hair, clothes, and the various wires clear of the fan, belts and pulleys.

Reduce the idle speed by means of the idle speed screw. Adjust the idle to 700–750 rpm (800–850 rpm with the 2.3 and manual transmission). This prevents the centrifugal advance mechanism from affecting the timing.

6. Aim the timing light at the timing marks. If the BTDC mark on the pulley and the pointer are lined up, the timing is okay.

7. If the timing marks are not aligned, adjust by loosening the distributor hold-down clamp bolt at the base of the distributor

1600 engine timing marks—except California

1600 engine timing marks—California

1800 engine timing marks

shaft and turning the distributor slightly in one direction or the other until the marks coincide. Hold the distributor body, not the cap. When the marks are aligned, tighten the bolt.

8. Check the timing again to be sure it didn't change during the tightening process.

9. Check the centrifugal advance mechanism by acclerating the engine to 2000 rpm. The timing should advance (the marks should move away from the pointer, towards the carburetor side of the engine). Note the speed at which the advance begins.

10. Unplug and reattach the vacuum hose. Accelerate the engine to 2000 rpm. The engine speed at which advance begins should be sooner (and the advance should be greater) than with only the centrifugal advance operating. If this does not occur, the vacuum advance unit should be inspected for free operation, and the hose checked for vacuum. Reset the idle to specification.

11. Shut off the engine, and disconnect the timing light and tachometer.

Mazda
1977 ROTARY

1. Check the point gap for both leading and trailing sets. Adjust if necessary.

2. Warm-up engine and run it at specified idle speed.

3. Connect a timing light to the leading spark plug and aim it at the pointer on the front cover. If timing mark and pointer do not align as specified, adjust by loosening and rotating distributor body.

4. Tighten distributor body and switch timing light to trailing plug.

2000 engine timing marks

5. Check trailing timing by pointing timing light at pointer on front cover. If not within specifications, adjust by loosening and rotating distributor body.

6. Adjust leading timing by loosening the breaker base set screws in the distributor body and rotating the breaker base. Then, tighten the base, replace the cap and rotor. Start the engine and check the timing. Adjust the timing to specifications by loosening and rotating the distributor body.

7. Recheck the trailing timing and adjust as above, if necessary.

PISTON ENGINE

1. Raise the hood and clean and mark

the timing marks. Chalk or fluorescent paint makes a good, visible mark.

2. Disconnect the vacuum line at the distributor and plug the disconnected line.

3. Connect a timing light to the front (no. 1) cylinder, a power source and ground. Follow the manufacturer's instructions.

4. Connect a tachometer to the engine.

5. Start the engine and reduce the idle to 700–750 rpm to be sure that the centrifugal advance mechanism is not working.

6. With the engine running, shine the timing light at the timing pointer and observe the position of the pointer in relation to the timing mark on the crankshaft pulley.

7. If the timing is not as specified, adjust the timing by loosening the distributor hold-down bolt and rotating the distributor in the proper direction. When the proper ignition timing is obtained, tighten the hold-down bolt on the distributor.

8. Check the centrifugal advance mechanism by accelerating the engine to about 2,000 rpm. If the ignition timing advances, the mechanism is working properly.

9. Stop the engine and remove the timing light.

10. Reset the idle to specifications.

11. Remove the tachometer.

Idle Speed & Mixture Adjustments

COURIER

1. Put the transmission in Neutral.

2. Connect a tachometer to the engine.

3. Start the engine and allow it to reach normal operating temperature. The choke should be fully open and the air cleaner on.

4. On 1978 and later models, run the engine for 3 minutes at 2000 rpm. Disconnect the canister purge hose between the canister and the air cleaner case.

5. Set the curb idle speed to specifications, using the curb idle speed adjusting screw. The correct idle speed can be found in the "Tune-Up Specifications" chart located at the beginning of this section, or on the emission control information label in the engine compartment.

6. The carburetor is probably equipped with idle limiter caps, which are small caps designed to provide a limited range of mixture adjustment.

7. The mixture can be checked only with the truck hooked up to an exhaust emission HC/CO analyzer. Your dealer, state inspection center, or service station may have one of these. The mixture is adjusted after the idle speed. The engine should be warm, choke open, and air cleaner on.

8. Disconnect the air hose between the air pump and the check valve, and plug the port of the check valve. See the Emission Control chapter for the location of these parts.

9. Turn the idle mixture adjusting screw in or out to obtain the specified idle/CO

CURB IDLE ADJUSTING
SCREW

IDLE MIXTURE ADJUSTING
SCREW

Carburetor adjusting screws

Gasoline Piston Engines
1977–80

1. Connect a tachometer to the engine. Warm the engine to normal operating temperature.

2. Run the engine (in neutral) to 2,000 rpm for a minute or two.

3. Allow the engine to return to idle. Adjust the idle to specifications by means of the idle speed screw.

4. The mixture can only be adjusted with the air of an exhaust gas analyzer. Connect the CO meter to the exhaust and note the reading.

5. On models sold in California, disconnect the air hose between the air pump and the check valve, and plug the port of the check valve. On 49 States vehicles, disconnect the air hose between the air cleaner and reed valve and plug the port of the reed valve.

6. Adjust the mixture by means of the mixture screw until the CO concentration is 2%–4%.

7. If the limiter cap was removed from the mixture screw, reinstall it.

1981–84

1. Remove the mixture screw by pulling out the entire shell while turning it counterclockwise. Install a new mixture screw.

2. Turn the new screw very slowly until it seats *very lightly*. Then, reverse rotation and turn three turns.

3. Connect an exhaust gas analyzer to the vehicle. (You should be able to have an analyzer connected to your vehicle at an automotive diagnostic center.)

4. On California vehicles, disconnect the air hose between the air bypass valve and check valve and plug the check valve port. On 49 States vehicles, disconnect the air hose connecting the air cleaner and reed valve and plug the port in the reed valve.

5. Turn the throttle adjusting screw until idle speed (engine hot) is 620 rpm in Neutral for California vehicles and 670 rpm for 49 States vehicles. Then, turn the mixture screw to get the highest idle rpm. Repeat these two procedures until the idle speed meets spec's at the mixture giving the highest rpm.

---

setting. The proper figure is given on the emission control information label in the engine compartment.

10. Unplug the check valve port and reconnect the hose. On 1978 and later models, connect the canister purge hose.

Supplemental Checks

If a satisfactory idle speed cannot be obtained after the normal idle adjustments, check the following:

1. Vacuum leaks;
2. Ignition system wiring;
3. Spark plugs;
4. Dwell angle;
5. Distributor point condition, and;
6. Ignition timing.

If the idle condition does not improve, check these items, and correct, if necessary:

1. Fuel level;
2. Crankcase ventilation system;
3. Valve clearance; and,
4. Engine compression.

If a satisfactory idle still cannot be obtained, have someone with an exhaust gas analyzer look into the problem for a possible too lean mixture or over-rich mixture.

1977 Rotary

Idle speed changes with air temperature. It is suggested by Mazda that the idle adjustment be made indoors with a floor fan blowing through the radiator to assist in cooling. Whenever operating an engine indoors, make certain that provision is made for removal of exhaust gases. Idle speed should be adjusted with the engine at normal operating temperature, all accessories off and fuel tank cap removed.

1. Connect a tachometer to the engine.

2. Set the idle speed to specification by turning the adjusting screw.

3. Disconnect the idle compensator tube at the air cleaner.

4. Run the engine at normal operating temperature and make sure that the choke is wide open.

5. Check the float level as described in the Fuel System Section.

6. Connect an exhaust gas analyzer and tachometer to the engine.

7. With engine at idle, check the CO density.

8. Adjust the idle speed to specification by turning the idle adjusting screw.

9. Turn the mixture adjusting screw clockwise until the engine lopes severely.

10. Turn the screw slowly counterclockwise until the CO density reaches 0.1%, then turn it an additional one quarter turn in the same direction.

Idle Mixture
Screw

Idle Speed

Idle Limiter

Idle adjustments—rotary engine

Mixture adjust screw

Mixture adjusting screw location on 81-84 engines

6. Turn the mixture screw clockwise until rpm is 600 rpm for California vehicles and 650 rpm for 49 States vehicles.

7. Check CO concentration. If it is less than 1%, turn the mixture screw counterclockwise ¼ turn.

8. Reconnect the disconnected air hose (with plugs you installed removed) and then recheck and, if necessary, readjust idle speed.

9. Install a blind plug into the mixture adjusting screw shell.

Diesel Engine

1. Run the engine until it reaches normal operating temperature. Check idle speed with a special diesel tachometer at the injection pump. If idle speed is not 700 rpm, check the play in the accelerator cable (next step) and then adjust the idle speed adjusting bolt.

2. Check the play in the accelerator linkage—it should be .04–.12 in. If the play has to be adjusted, loosen the locknut (1), and then turn the adjusting nut (2) clockwise to increase the play or counterclockwise to decrease it. Tighten the locknut.

3. Then, loosen the locknut (3) for the idle adjusting bolt, and turn the adjusting bolt clockwise to increase the idle speed or counterclockwise to decrease it. Tighten the locknut.

4. Open the throttle slightly and then release it to check that the throttle linkage

Mazda diesel idle speed adjustment

Mazda 2200 diesel throttle linkage adjustment

permits the injection pump to return to idle. Adjust the throttle linkage to provide free operation, if necessary.

Valve Adjustment

COURIER

NOTE: While all valve adjustments must be made as accurately as possible, it is better to have the valve adjustment slightly loose than slightly tight, as burned valves may result from overly tight adjustments.

1.8 and 2.0 Liter Engines

1. Start the engine and allow it to reach normal operating temperature.

2. Turn the engine off.

3. Note the location of any wires and hoses which may interfere with cam cover removal, disconnect them and move them aside. Then remove the bolts which hold the cam cover in place and remove the cam cover.

Checking the valve clearances at the valve

Checking the valve clearances at the camshaft

4. Torque the cylinder head bolts to 70 ft. lbs. in sequence. The pattern is shown in the beginning of this section. When tightening the bolts, the proper procedure is to slightly loosen each bolt in turn, then tighten the bolt to the proper torque specification.

5. Place a wrench on the crankshaft pulley bolt and turn the engine over until the valves for no. 1 cylinder are closed. This is easier to do if the spark plugs are removed. When both camshaft lobes are pointing up, the valves are closed. If you have not done this before, it is a good idea to turn the engine over slowly several times and watch the valve action until you have a clear idea of just when the valves are closed.

6. Check the clearance of the valves. The correct size flat feeler gauge should pass between the base circle of the cam and the valve rocker arm with just a slight drag. Be sure the feeler gauge is inserted straight and not on an angle. You can also measure the clearance at the valve, if it is easier.

7. If the valves need adjustment, loosen the locking nut and then adjust the clearance with the adjusting screw. You will probably find it necessary to hold the locking nut while you turn the adjuster. After you have the correct clearance, tighten the locking nut and recheck the clearance. Remember, it's better to have them too loose than too tight, especially exhaust valves.

8. Repeat this procedure until you have checked and/or adjusted all the valves. Keep in mind that all that is necessary is to have the valves closed and the camshaft lobes pointing up. It is not particularly important what stroke the engine is on.

9. Install the cam cover gasket, the cam cover, and any wires and hoses which were removed.

2.3 Liter Engine

Valve clearance in the 2.3 liter engine are automatically adjusted by hydraulic valve lash adjusters, which resemble hydraulic valve lifters both in appearance and in function. Adjustments are not necessary.

MAZDA

All Piston Engines

1. Run the engine to warm it to normal operating temperature. Remove the valve cover.

2. Torque gas engine head bolts to 69–72 ft. lbs. and diesel head bolts to 80–85 ft. lbs. Follow the sequence illustrated in the specifications section above.

3. Turn the engine until timing marks indicate it's at Top Dead Center. Depending on whether the engine is on TDC number one compression stroke or TDC number one exhaust stroke, you will find four valves loose and ready for adjustment. Check the sequence below and see the illustration.

Intake: No. 1 and 2
Exhaust: No. 1 and 3

① ··· When No. I cylinder is at top dead center
② ··· When No.4 cylinder is at top dead center

Mazda gasoline piston engine valve adjusting sequence

When No.I cylinder is at top dead enter

Front ◄

When No.4 cylinder is at top dead center

Mazda diesel valve adjusting sequence

Intake: No. 3 and 4
Exhaust: No. 2 and 4

When you've determined which four valves are loose by rocking the rocker arms, adjust those four as follows:

Slip the feeler gauge (.012 in. on all engines) between the top of the valve stem and the rocker. The gauge should fit in and slide with very little resistance between the surfaces. If the clearance requires adjustment, loosen the locknut and turn the adjusting screw with a screwdriver until the clearance is *just* taken up. Make sure not to tighten the screw—resistance to sliding the gauge must be very slight. Hold the adjusting screw in position while tightening the locknut. Recheck the adjustment to make sure the adjusting screw has not tightened up, and readjust if necessary.

4. Turn the engine one full turn until it is again at Top Center and adjust the other four valves.

ENGINE ELECTRICAL

Distributor

REMOVAL & INSTALLATION

Courier

1. Matchmark the distributor cap and the body of the distributor. Remove the distributor cap.

2. Disconnect the vacuum hose from the diaphragm.

3. On 2.3 liter engines, remove the rubber plug from the timing belt cover. On all engines, scribe matchmarks on the distributor body and the cylinder block to indicate their relative positions.

4. Scribe another mark on the distributor body indicating the position of the rotor. On 2.3 liter engines, also scribe a mark on the cam pulley and on the indicator inside the timing belt cover to mark the position of the pulley relative to the indicator.

5. Disconnect the primary wires from the distributor.

6. Remove the distributor hold-down nut, lockwasher and flat washer.

7. Remove the distributor from the engine.

NOTE: Do not crank the engine while the distributor is removed. All distributors have a helical drive gear, which will cause the rotor to turn slightly when the distributor is removed. If the amount of movement is noted during removal, the rotor can be adjusted slightly before installation to compensate. Lubricate the drive gear and distributor shaft with engine oil before installation.

To install the distributor:

8. If the engine was cranked while the distributor was removed, turn the crankshaft until no. 1 cylinder is at the top of the compression stroke. This can be determined by feeling compression with your thumb through the spark plug port. The TDC mark on the crankshaft pulley should also be aligned with the timing pointer. On

Exploded view of the point type distributor

1. Distributor cap
2. Rotor
3. Cover
4. Pickup set
5. Cam
6. Spring
7. Shaft
8. Governor weight
9. Gear
10. Housing
11. Bale clamp

Exploded view of the electronic distributor used on 2.3 engines (1979 and earlier 2.0 engines similar)

Exploded view of the electronic distributor used on 1980 and later 2.0 engines

12. Install the distributor cap and connect the primary wires.

13. Set the ignition timing.

14. Connect the vacuum tube to the vacuum unit on the distributor.

PISTON ENGINE

1. Matchmark the distributor cap and the body of the distributor. Remove the distributor cap.

2. Disconnect the vacuum hose from the diaphragm. Disconnect the electrical wire at the distributor, if so equipped.

3. Scribe matchmarks on the distributor and the cylinder block to indicate the relative positions.

4. Scribe another mark on the distributor body indicating the position of the rotor.

5. Disconnect the primary wires from the distributor.

6. Remove the distributor hold-down nut, lockwasher and flat washer.

7. Remove the distributor from the engine.

NOTE: Do not crank the engine while the distributor is removed.

To install the distributor:

8. Align the matchmarks on the distributor gear and body.

9. If the engine was cranked while the distributor was removed, turn the crankshaft until the no. 1 cylinder is at the top of the compression stroke. This can be determined by feeling compression with your thumb over the spark plug port. The timing mark on the crankshaft pulley should also be aligned with the timing pointer. Slide the distributor into the engine with the rotor

2.3 liter engines, match the mark on the cam pulley and the TDC mark on the crankshaft pulley. Slide the distributor into the engine with the rotor pointing to no. 1 firing position.

9. If the engine has not been cranked while the distributor was removed, slide the distributor (with the O-ring) into the engine, aligning the matchmarks made during removal.

10. Install the flat washer, lockwasher and hold-down nut, but do not tighten the nut.

11. Install the distributor cap and connect the primary wires.

12. Set the ignition timing as previously outlined and tighten the hold-down nut.

13. Connect the vacuum line.

Mazda

ROTARY ENGINE—1977–78

The distributor is located on the right front side of the engine.

1. Open the hood and locate the distributor.

2. Remove the distributor cap.

3. Disconnect the vacuum tube from the advance unit.

4. Disconnect the primary wires from the distributor.

5. Matchmark the distributor body in relation to the engine front housing.

6. Remove the distributor hold-down bolt.

7. Pull the distributor from the front cover.

To install the distributor:

8. Turn the eccentric shaft until the TDC mark on the drive pulley aligns with the indicator pin on the front cover.

9. Align the matchmarks on the distributor housing and drive gear.

10. Install the distributor so that the distributor lockbolt is located in the center of the slot. Engage the gears.

11. Rotate the distributor clockwise until the leading contact point set starts to separate, and tighten the distributor lockbolt.

1. Cap	8. Point set	14. Governor
2. Rotor	9. Felt	15. Governor spring
3. Point set	10. Ignition condenser	16. Shaft
4. Breaker plate	11. Terminal	17. Oil seal
5. Cam	12. Radio supression condenser	18. Distributor housing
6. Spring		19. Vacuum advance unit
7. Ground wire	13. Vacuum switch—trailing distributor only	20. Ignition condenser

Rotary engine distributor components

1. Rotor
2. Rubber seal
3. Screw
4. Pick-up coil
5. Clip
6. Screw and washer
7. Vacuum advance unit
8. Cap retaining clip
9. Cap retaining clip and screw
10. Pick-up coil plate
11. Screw and washer

12. Cam
13. Advance weights and springs
14. Retaining pin
15. Drive gear and washer
16. Thrust washer
17. Shaft
18. Oil seal

1. Rotor	7. Vacuum advance unit	13. Advance weights and springs
2. Rubber seal	8. Cap retaining clip	14. Retaining pin
3. Screw	9. Cap retaining clip and screw	15. Drive gear and washer
4. Pick-up coil	10. Pick-up coil plate	16. Thrust washer
5. Clip	11. Screw and washer	17. Shaft
6. Screw and washer	12. Cam	18. Oil seal

Exploded view of the electronic ignition distributor

pointing to the no. 1 cylinder firing position (see Firing Order).

10. If the engine has not been cranked while the distributor was removed, slide the distributor (with the O-ring) into the engine, aligning the matchmarks made during removal.

11. Install the flat washer, lockwasher and hold-down nut, but do not tighten the nut.

12. Install the distributor cap and connect the primary wires.

13. Set the ignition timing, and tighten the hold-down nut.

14. Connect the vacuum line wire, if so equipped.

FIRING ORDER

The firing order for the Mazda rotary engine is 1-2, with the trailing spark plugs firing ten degrees after the leading.

The firing order for the piston engine is 1-3-4-2.

Alternator

PRECAUTIONS

Because of the nature of alternator design, special care must be taken when servicing the charging system.

1. Battery polarity should be checked before making any connections such as jumper cables or battery charger leads. Reversed battery connections will damage the diode rectifiers.

2. The battery must never be disconnected while the alternator is running because the regulator will be ruined.

3. Always disconnect the battery ground cable before replacing the alternator.

4. Do not attempt to polarize an alternator.

5. Do not short across or ground any alternator terminals.

6. Always disconnect the battery ground cable before removing the alternator output cable.

7. If electric arc welding equipment is to be used on the car, first disconnect the battery and alternator cables. Never operate the car with the electric arc welding equipment attached.

8. If the battery is to be "quick charged", disconnect the negative cable from the battery.

REMOVAL & INSTALLATION

Courier

1. Open the hood and remove the battery. Disconnect the negative (ground) cable first.

2. Remove the nut holding the alternator wire to the terminal at the rear of the alternator.

3. Pull the multiple connector from the rear of the alternator.

4. Remove the alternator adjusting arm bolt. Swing the alternator in and disengage the fan belt.

5. Remove the distributor cap and rotor from the distributor on 1.8s only to provide clearance.

6. Remove the alternator pivot bolt and remove the alternator from the truck.

7. Installation is the reverse of removal. Be sure to adjust the drive belt tension and to connect the battery properly.

Mazda

1. Disconnect the negative battery terminal.

2. Label and disconnect all wiring.

3. Remove the alternator adjusting bolt.

4. Remove the V-belt.

5. On the diesel, remove the vacuum and oil hoses.

6. Remove the remaining attaching bolts and remove the alternator.

Exploded view of the alternator

Mazda alternator removal · **Mazda alternator removal**

1. End cover
2. IC regulator/Brush holder
3. Front bracket assembly
4. Rear bracket assembly
5. Nut set
6. Pulley/Fan assembly
7. Front bracket
8. Rotor assembly
9. Rear bracket
10. Stator

Mazda diesel alternator exploded view

7. Install in exact reverse order, adjusting belt tension as described below.

BELT TENSION ADJUSTMENT

Courier

1. Check the alternator drive belt tension by applying thumb pressure to the belt midway between the fan pulley and the alternator. It should deflect $3/8–1/2$ in. with a new belt or $1/2–5/8$ in. with a used belt.
2. If it does not have the correct tension, loosen the alternator mounting bolts slightly and loosen the adjusting arm bolt.
3. Apply pressure on the alternator front

housing until the correct tension is obtained. Tighten the adjusting arm bolt securely.
4. Tighten the alternator mounting bolts securely.
5. Recheck the tension.

Mazda

1. Check the drivebelt tension by applying about 22 lbs. of thumb pressure to the belt, at the midpoint of the longest span between pulleys. The belt should deflect to the following specifications:
Old belt—0.59–0.67 in.
New belt—0.47–0.55 in.
2. If belt deflection is not within specifications loosen but do not remove the bolt on the adjusting link.
3. Push the alternator in the direction required to obtain proper belt deflection.

— CAUTION ———
Do not pry or pound the alternator housing.

4. Tighten the adjusting link bolt to 20 ft. lbs.

Regulator

REMOVAL & INSTALLATION

Courier

External regulators have been used on the courier from 1975–81. The external regulator is mounted on the fender splash shield.

Beginning with the 1982 model year, internal voltage regulators are used. The internal regulator is mounted inside the alternator assembly. The alternator must be removed and disassembled in order to gain access to the internal regulator.
1. Raise the hood and disconnect the negative battery cable.
2. Disconnect the regulator wires at the multiple connector.
3. Remove the two regulator attaching screws and remove the regulator from the splash shield.
To install the regulator:
4. Position the regulator on the fender splash shield and install the two attaching screws.

5. Connect the regulator wires at the multiple connector.
6. Connect the negative battery cable.
7. Start the engine and be sure that the charging system indicator light goes out.

Mazda

1. Disconnect the battery ground cable at the negative (–) battery terminal.
2. Disconnect the wiring from the regulator.
3. Remove the regulator mounting screws.
4. Remove the regulator.

Installation is performed in the reverse order of removal.

TESTING

Courier

The alternator regulator is not adjustable, but if it is suspected to be malfunctioning, the following test can be performed.
1. Connect a tachometer to the engine. Follow the manufacturer's hook-up instructions.
2. Connect the positive lead of a voltmeter to the alternator B terminal.
3. Connect the negative lead of a voltmeter to the regulator body (ground).
4. Set the voltmeter on the 20 volt scale.
5. Put the transmission in Neutral and set the parking brake.
6. Start the engine and run it at 1,800 rpm. The voltmeter should read 14–15 volts. If not the regulator should be replaced.

Mazda

MODELS WITH WARNING LIGHT

The alternator regulator is composed of two control units: a constant voltage relay and a pilot lamp relay.

CONSTANT VOLTAGE RELAY

1. Use an almost fully charged battery and connect a voltmeter between the "A" and "E" terminals of the regulator.
2. Run the engine at 2,000 rpm and read the voltmeter. It should read from 14–15 volts.
3. If not, adjust the voltage relay.

PILOT LAMP RELAY

1. Using a voltmeter and variable resistor, construct a circuit as shown.
2. Light the pilot lamp.
3. Slide the knob of the variable resistor so that the voltage gradually increases.
4. Read the voltage between the "N" and "E" terminals of the regulator. If the voltage is 3.7–5.7 (4.2–5.2 for 1977 and later) volts, it is operating properly.
5. Slide the knob of the variable resistor to decrease the voltage. Note the point on the voltmeter where the light will light again. If the reading is less than 3.5 volts through 1976 or 3.0 volts for 1977–80, the unit is working properly.
6. Disconnect the test instruments.

MODELS WITH INTEGRAL REGULATOR (1982–84)

1. Connect an ammeter and voltmeter as shown in the accompanying wiring diagram. Turn the ignition switch off.
2. Read the voltmeter (connected between "L" terminal and ground). Voltage should be zero, or the alternator may be defective.
3. Turn the ignition switch on and read the voltmeter again. Voltage should be 1–3 volts; if voltage is still zero, the alternator or associated wiring is defective.
4. If the voltage in the above step is nearly battery voltage, connect the "F" terminal to ground with the voltmeter and read it. If the voltage now drops to less than battery voltage, the regulator may be at fault.
5. Disconnect the wiring connected to alternator terminal "B". Connect an ammeter of more than 40 amps capacity between "B" and the battery positive terminal. Connect a voltmeter between the "L" terminal of the alternator and ground.

Connecting voltmeter and ammeter for test of 1982–84 Mazda charging system

6. Start the engine and run it at about 2,000 rpm. Turn off all accessories.
7. Read the ammeter. When amperage drops under five amps, read the regulated voltage (terminal "L"). It should be 14.1–14.7 volts.
8. Turn on all accessories, and then accelerate the engine to 2,500 rpm. The ammeter will read 90% or more of the alternator rating if the alternator output is satisfactory.

ADJUSTMENT

Mazda Models with Ammeters only

1. Remove the cover from the regulator.
2. Check the air gap, the point gap, and the back gap with a feeler gauge (see illustration).
3. If they do not fall within the specifications given in the "Alternator and Regulator" chart, adjust the gaps by bending the stationary contact bracket.
4. Connect a voltmeter between the "A" and "E" terminal of the regulator.

NOTE: Be sure that the battery is fully charged before proceeding with this test.

5. Start the engine and run it at 2,000 rpm (4,000 alternator rpm). The voltmeter reading should be 13.5–14.5 V.
6. Stop the engine.
7. Bend the upper plate *down* to decrease the voltage setting or *up* to increase the setting, as required.
8. If the regulator cannot be brought within specifications, replace it.
9. When the test is completed, disconnect the voltmeter and replace the regulator cover.

Mazda Models with a Warning Light (Up to 1982)

1. Check the air gap, back gap and point gap with a wire gauge. If they are not within specification, adjust the gap by bending the stationary bracket.
2. After the gaps are correctly set, adjust the voltage setting. Bend the upper plate down to decrease the voltage setting, or bend it up to increase the voltage setting.

Location of "F" terminal on Mazda 1982–84 alternator

Regulator mechanical adjustments

CONSTANT VOLTAGE RELAY
Air Gap .028–.051 in.
Point Gap .012–.018 in.
Back Gap .028–.059 in.

PILOT LAMP RELAY
Air Gap .039–.059 from 1977
Point Gap .028–.043 in. .020–.035 in. from 1977
Back Gap .028–.059 in.

Starter

REMOVAL & INSTALLATION

Rotary Engine

NOTE: There are two possible locations for the starter motor; one is on the lower right-hand side of the engine and the other is on the upper right-hand side.

1. Remove the ground cable from the negative (−) battery terminal.
2. If the car is equipped with the lower mounted starter, remove the gravel shield from underneath the engine.

— **CAUTION** —
Be extremely careful not to contact the hot exhaust pipe while working underneath the car.

3. Remove the battery cable from the starter terminal.
4. Disconnect the solenoid leads from the solenoid terminals.
5. Remove the starter securing bolts and withdraw the starter assembly.
Installation is the reverse.

Piston Engines

1. Raise the hood and disconnect the battery ground cable.
2. Remove the carburetor air cleaner and air intake tube to provide clearance, if necessary.
3. Disconnect the battery cable from the starter solenoid battery terminal.
4. Pull the ignition switch wire from the solenoid terminal. (On Couriers, this is identified as "50").
5. Raise and support the truck on jackstands.

Courier starter exploded view

Starter drive end clearance

6. Working under the truck, remove the starter attaching bolts, washers and nuts.

7. Tilt the drive end of the starter and remove the starter by working it out below the emission system hoses.

To install the starter:

8. Install the starter and bolts, washers and nuts.

9. Connect the ignition switch wire to the solenoid terminal.

10. Connect the battery cable to the solenoid battery terminal.

11. Install the carburetor air cleaner and air intake tube, if removed.

12. Connect the ground cable to the battery.

13. Lower the truck to the ground and check the operation of the starter.

OVERHAUL

Brush Replacement
COURIER

1. Remove the starter. Remove the two screws attaching the brush end bearing cover and remove the bearing cover.

2. Remove the through-bolts.

3. Remove the C-washer, washer and spring from the brush end of the armature shaft.

4. Pull the brush end cover from the starter frame.

5. Unsolder the two brushes from the field terminals and slide the brush holder from the armature shaft.

6. Cut the two brush wires at the brush holder and solder two new brushes to the brush holder. Solder two new brushes to the field coil terminals.

7. Install the brush holder on the armature shaft and install the brushes in the brush holder.

8. Install the brush end cover on the starter frame and be sure that the ear tabs of the brush holder are aligned with the through-bolt holes.

9. Install the through-bolts.

10. Install the rubber gasket, spring, washer and C-washer on the armature shaft.

11. Install the brush end bearing cover on the brush end cover and install the two screws. If the brush holder tabs are not aligned with the through-bolts, the bearing cover screws cannot be installed.

Drive Replacement
COURIER

1. Remove the starter from the truck.

2. Disconnect the field strap from the solenoid MT terminal.

3. Remove the screws attaching the solenoid to the drive end housing. Disengage the solenoid plunger hook from the shift fork and remove the solenoid.

Starter solenoid plunger adjustment—adjust to 0.8 in.

Starter solenoid terminals

4. Remove the shift fork pivot bolt, nut and lockwasher. Later models don't have the nut and washer.

5. Remove the through-bolts and separate the drive end housing from the starter frame. At the same time, disengage the shift fork from the drive assembly.

6. Slide the drive stop-ring retainer toward the armature and remove the stopring. Slide the retainer and drive assembly off the armature shaft.

To assemble:

7. Position the drive assembly on the armature shaft.

8. Position the drive stop-ring retainer on the armature shaft and install the drive stop-ring. Slide the stop-ring retainer over the stop-ring to secure the stop-ring on the shaft.

9. Install the drive end housing on the armature shaft and starter housing. Engage the shift fork with the starter drive assembly as you move the drive end housing toward the starter frame.

10. Install the through-bolts.

11. Align the shift fork with the pivot bolt hole and install the pivot bolt, lockwasher and nut. Tighten the nut securely. On 1977 and later models, install the pivot bolt through the shift fork to locate it in place.

12. Check the solenoid plunger length. The tip of the solenoid plunger should be 0.8 in. from the front edge of the solenoid body. If the dimension is not correct, loosen the locknut and adjust the plunger length as necessary. Tighten the locknut.

13. Position the solenoid on the drive end housing. Be sure that the solenoid plunger hook is engaged with the shift fork.

14. Install the two solenoid retaining screws and washers.

15. Apply a minimum of 8 volts to the solenoid 50 terminal and check the clearance between the starter drive and the stopring retainer. The clearance should be 0.080–0.160 in. If not, the solenoid plunger is not properly adjusted. To increase the clearance, lengthen the solenoid plunger and shorten the plunger to decrease the clearance.

16. Install the field strap on the solenoid MT terminal and tighten the nut.

17. Install the starter. Check the operation of the starter.

Solenoid Replacement
COURIER

Follow steps 1, 2, 3, 12, 13, 14, 15, 16, and 17 of the Starter Drive Replacement procedure.

OVERHAUL

Gasoline Engines—1977–81
SOLENOID REPLACEMENT
Mazda

Perform solenoid replacement with the starter motor removed from the car.

1. Detach the field strap from the solenoid terminals.
2. Remove the solenoid securing screws.
3. Withdraw the solenoid spring and washers from the starter drive housing.

Solenoid installation is performed in the reverse order of removal.

STARTER DRIVE REPLACEMENT
Mazda

1. Perform the solenoid removal procedure as above.
2. Remove the plunger from the drive engagement fork.
3. Unfasten the nuts from the thru-bolts.

NOTE: Unless further disassembly of the starter is desired, do not remove the thru bolts.

4. Remove the drive housing from the front of the starter.
5. Remove the engagement fork, spring, and spring seat.
6. Withdraw the over-running clutch from the armature shaft.

Assembly is performed in the reverse order of disassembly. Check the clearance between the pinion and the stop collar with the solenoid engaged. It should be 0.02–0.08 in.

Mazda Gas and Diesel Engines— 1982–84

See the illustrations and disassemble in numbered order. Assemble in reverse order.

ENGINE MECHANICAL— ROTARY

Engine

REMOVAL & INSTALLATION

NOTE: Because of the unique design of the Mazda rotary engine, some procedures require the use of special factory tools. The text notes where these tools are necessary. If the tools are not available, the job should not be undertaken.

1. Front housing
2. Overrunning clutch
3. Engagement fork
4. Center frame
5. Solenoid
6. Stop
7. Idler gear
8. Armature
9. Field coil
10. Brush holder
11. End frame

Mazda gas piston engine starter—exploded view

1. Starter Solenoid
2. Bolts
3. Rear cover
4. Brush holder assembly
5. Yoke assembly
6. Lever assembly
7. Front cover assembly
8. Drive pinion
9. Armature set

Exploded view of Mazda B2000 gas engine starter

4. Brush holder
   assembly
5. Yoke assembly
6. Armatuer &
   bearing
7. Cover

1. Glow switch
2. Starter solenoid
3. Rear housing

8. Center bracket
9. Drive pinion
10. Pinion shaft
11. Gear
12. Lever & spring

13. Over running
    clutch
14. Front housing
    assembly

Exploded view of Mazda B2200 diesel starter

—————— CAUTION ——————

Be sure that the engine has completely cooled before attempting to remove it.

1. Scribe matchmarks on the hood and hinges. Remove the hood from the hinges.
2. Working from underneath the car, remove the gravel shield; then drain the cooling system and the engine oil.
3. Disconnect the cable from the negative (−) battery terminal.
4. Remove the air cleaner, its bracket, and its attendant hoses.
5. Detach the accelerator cable, choke cable, and fuel lines from the carburetor.
6. Remove the nuts which secure the thermostat housing. Disconnect the ground cable from the housing and install the housing again after the cable is removed.
7. Disconnect the power brake vacuum line from the intake manifold.
8. Remove the fan shroud securing bolts and then the shroud itself.
9. Remove the bolts which secure the fan clutch to the eccentric shaft pulley.
Withdraw the fan and clutch as a single unit.

NOTE: Keep the fan clutch in an upright position, so that its fluid does not leak out.

10. Unfasten the clamps and remove both of the radiator hoses.
11. Note their respective positions and remove the spark plug cables. Disconnect the primary leads from the distributors and remove both of the distributor caps.
12. Detach all of the leads from the alternator, the water temperature sender, the oil pressure sender, and the starter motor.
13. Disconnect all of the wiring from the emission control system components.
14. Detach the heater hoses at the engine.
15. Detach the oil lines from the front and the rear of the engine.
16. Disconnect the battery cable from the (+) battery terminal and from the engine.

17. Unfasten the nuts which secure the clutch slave cylinder and tie the cylinder up out of the way.

NOTE: Do not remove the hydraulic line from the slave cylinder.

18. Remove the exhaust pipe and the thermal reactor.

—————— CAUTION ——————

Be sure that the thermal reactor has completely cooled; severe burns could result if it has not.

19. Evenly and in two or three stages, remove the nuts and bolts which secure the clutch housing to the engine.
20. Support the transmission with a jack.
21. Remove the nuts from each of the engine mounts.
22. Attach a lifting sling to the lifting bracket on the rear of the engine housing.
23. Use a hoist to take up the slack on the sling.

—————— CAUTION ——————

Be sure that the hoist is secure to prevent possible personal injury or damage to the engine.

24. Pull the engine forward until it clears the transmission input shaft. Lift the engine straight up and out of the car.

NOTE: Be careful not to damage any of the components which remain in the car.

25. Remove the heat stove from exhaust manifold.
26. Remove the thermal reactor.
Engine installation is performed in the reverse order of removal.

Engine Overhaul

DISASSEMBLY

1. Mount the engine on a stand.

2. Remove the oil hose support bracket from the front housing.
3. Disconnect the vacuum hoses, air hoses and remove the decel valve.
4. Remove the air pump and drive belt. Remove the air pump adjusting bar.
5. Remove the alternator and drive belt.
6. Disconnect the metering oil pump connecting rod, oil tubes and vacuum sensing tube from the carburetor.
7. Remove the carburetor and intake manifold as an assembly.
8. Remove the gasket and two rubber rings.
9. Remove the thermal reactor and gaskets.
10. Remove the distributor from the front cover.
11. Remove the water pump and gasket.
12. Invert the engine on the stand.
13. Remove the oil pan and gasket.
14. Remove the oil pump screen and gasket.
15. Identify the front and rear rotor housings with a felt tip pen. These are common parts and must be identified to be reassembled in their respective locations.
16. Turn the engine on the stand so that the top of the engine is up.
17. Remove the engine mounting bracket from the front cover.
18. Hold the flywheel with a flywheel holder and remove the eccentric shaft pulley.
19. Turn the engine on a stand so that the front end of the engine is up.
20. Remove the front cover and gasket.
21. Remove the O-ring from the oil passage on the front housing.
22. Remove the oil slinger and distributor drive gear from the shaft.
23. Unbolt and remove the chain adjuster.
24. Remove the locknut and washer from the oil pump driven sprocket.
25. Slide the oil pump drive sprocket and driven sprocket together with the drive chain off the eccentric shaft and oil pump simultaneously.
26. Remove the keys from the eccentric and oil pump shafts.
27. Slide the balance weight, thrust washer and needle bearing from the shaft.
28. Unbolt the bearing housing and slide the bearing housing, needle bearing, spacer and thrust plate off the shaft.
29. Turn the engine on the stand so that the top of the engine is up.
30. If equipped with a manual transmission, remove the clutch pressure plate and clutch disc. Loosen the pressure plate bolts evenly in small stages to prevent distortion and possible injury from the pressure plate flying off. Straighten the tab of the lockwasher and remove the flywheel nut. Remove the flywheel with a puller.
31. If equipped with an automatic transmission, remove the drive plate. Straighten the tab on the lockwasher and remove the counterweight nut, while holding the flywheel with a flywheel holder. Remove the counterweight using a puller.
32. Working at the rear of the engine,

Rotary engine tension bolt *loosening* sequence

loosen the tension bolts in the sequence shown, and remove the tension bolts.

NOTE: Do not loosen the tension bolts one at a time. Loosen the bolts evenly in small stages to prevent distortion.

33. Lift the rear housing off the shaft.

34. Remove any seals that are stuck to the rotor sliding surface of the rear housing and reinstall them in their original locations.

35. Remove all the corner seals, corner seal springs, side seal and side seal springs from the rear side of the rotor. Mazda has a special tray which holds all the seals and keeps them segregated to prevent mistakes during reassembly. Each seal groove is marked to prevent confusion.

36. Remove the two rubber seals and two O-rings from the rear rotor housing.

37. Remove the dowels from the rear rotor housing.

38. Lift the rear rotor housing away from the rear rotor, being very careful not to drop the apex seals on the rear rotor.

39. Remove each apex seal, side piece and spring from the rear rotor and segregate them.

40. Remove the rear rotor from the eccentric shaft and place it upside down on a clean rag.

41. Remove each seal and spring from the other side of the rotor and segregate these.

42. If some of the seals fall off the rotor, be careful not to change the original position of each seal.

43. Identify the rear rotor with a felt tip pen.

44. Remove the oil seals and the springs. Do not exert heavy pressure at only one place on the seal, since it could be deformed. Replace the O-rings in the oil seal when the engine is overhauled.

45. Hold the intermediate housing down and remove the dowels from it.

46. Lift off the intermediate housing being careful not to damage the eccentric shaft. It should be removed by sliding it beyond the rear rotor journal on the eccentric shaft

while holding the intermediate housing up and, at the same time, pushing the eccentric shaft up.

47. Lift out the eccentric shaft.

48. Repeat the above procedures to remove the front rotor housing and front rotor.

ASSEMBLY

1. Place the rotor on a rubber pad or cloth.

2. Install the oil seal rings in their respective grooves in the rotors with the edge of the spring in the stopper hole. The oil seal springs are painted cream or blue in color. The cream colored springs must be installed on the front faces of both rotors. The blue colored springs must be installed on the rear faces of both rotors. When installing each oil seal spring, the painted side (square side) of the spring must face upward (toward the oil seal.)

3. Install a new O-ring in each groove. Place each oil seal in the groove so that the square edge of the spring fits in the stopper hole of the oil seal. Push the head of the

oil seal slowly with the fingers, being careful that the seal is not deformed. Be sure that the oil seal moves smoothly in the groove before installing the O-ring.

4. Lubricate each oil seal and groove with engine oil and check the movement of the seal. It should move freely when the head of the seal is pressed.

5. Check the oil seal protrusion and install the seals on the other side of each rotor.

6. Install the apex seals without springs and side pieces into their respective grooves so that each side piece positions on the side of each rotor.

7. Install the corner seal springs and corner seals into their respective grooves.

8. Install the side seal springs and side seals into their respective grooves.

9. Apply engine oil to each spring and check each spring for smooth movement.

10. Check each seal protrusion.

11. Invert the rotor being careful that the seals do not fall out, and install the oil seals on the other side in the same manner.

12. Mount the front housing on a workstand so that the top of the housing is up.

13. Lubricate the internal gear of the rotor with engine oil.

14. Hold the apex seals with used O-rings to keep the apex seals installed and place the rotor on the front housing. Be careful not to drop the seals. Turn the front housing so that the sliding surface faces upward.

15. Mesh the internal and stationary gears and remove the old O-ring which is holding the apex seals in position.

16. Lubricate the front rotor journal of the eccentric shaft with engine oil and lubricate the eccentric shaft main journal.

17. Insert the eccentric shaft. Be careful that you do not damage the rotor bearing and main bearing.

18. Apply sealing agent to the front side of the front rotor housing.

19. Apply a light coat of petroleum jelly onto new O-rings and rubber seals (to prevent them from coming off) and install the

Rotary engine tension bolt *tightening* sequence

O-rings and rubber seals on the front side of the rotor housing.

NOTE: The inner rubber seal is of the square type. The wider white line of the rubber seal should face the combustion chamber and the rubber seal should be positioned as shown. Do not stretch the rubber seal.

20. If the engine is being overhauled, install the seal protector to only the inner rubber seal to improve durability.

21. Invert the front rotor housing, being careful not to let the rubber seals and O-rings fall from their grooves, and mount it on the front housing.

22. Lubricate the dowels with engine oil and insert them through the front rotor housing holes and into the front housing.

23. Apply sealer to the front side of the rotor housing.

24. Install new O-rings and rubber seals on the front rotor housing in the same manner as for the other side.

25. Insert each apex spring seal, making sure that the seal is installed in the proper direction.

26. Install each side piece in its original position and be sure that the springs seat on the side piece.

27. Lubricate the side pieces with engine oil. Make sure that the front rotor housing is free of foreign matter and lubricate the sliding surface of the front housing with engine oil.

28. Turn the front housing assembly with the rotor, so that the top of the housing is up. Pull the eccentric shaft about 1 in.

29. Position the eccentric portion of the eccentric shaft diagonally, to the upper right.

30. Install the intermediate housing over the eccentric shaft onto the front rotor housing. Turn the engine so that the rear of the engine is up.

31. Install the rear rotor and rear rotor housing following the same steps as for the front rotor and the front housing.

32. Turn the engine so that the rear of the engine is up.

33. Lubricate the stationary gear and main bearing.

34. Install the rear housing onto the rear rotor housing. If necessary, turn the rear rotor slightly to mesh the rear housing stationary gear with the rear rotor internal gear.

35. Install a new washer on each tension bolt, and lubricate each bolt with engine oil.

36. Install the tension bolts and tighten them evenly, in several stages in sequence. The specified torque is 23–27 ft. lbs.

37. After tightening the bolts, turn the eccentric shaft to be sure that the shaft and rotors turn smoothly and easily.

38. Lubricate the oil seal in the rear housing.

39. On vehicles with manual transmission, install the flywheel on the rear of the eccentric shaft so that the keyway of the flywheel fits the key on the shaft.

40. Apply sealer to both sides of the flywheel lockwasher and install the lockwasher.

41. Install the flywheel locknut. Hold the flywheel *securely* and tighten the nut to *three hundred and fifty ft. lbs*. (350 ft. lbs.) of torque.

NOTE: 350 ft. lbs. is a great deal of torque. In actual practice, it is practically impossible to accurately measure that much torque on the nut. At least a 3 ft. bar will be required to generate sufficient torque. Tighten it as tight as possible, with no longer than 3 ft. of leverage. Be sure the engine is held SECURELY.

42. On vehicles with automatic transmission, install the key, counterweight, lockwasher and nut. Tighten the nut to 350 ft. lbs. *See step 41 and the note following step 41*. Install the drive plate on the counterweight and tighten the attaching nuts.

43. Turn the engine so that the front faces up.

44. Install the thrust plate with the tapered face down, and install the needle bearing on the eccentric shaft. Lubricate with engine oil.

45. Install the bearing housing on the front housing. Tighten the bolts and bend up the lockwasher tabs.

The spacer should be installed so that the center of the needle bearing comes to the center of the eccentric shaft and the spacer should be seated on the thrust plate.

46. Install the needle bearing on the shaft and lubricate it with engine oil.

47. Install the balancer and thrust washer on the eccentric shaft.

48. Install the oil pump drive chain over both of the sprockets. Install the sprocket and chain assembly over the eccentric shaft and oil pump shafts simultaneously. Install the key on the eccentric shaft.

NOTE: Be sure that both of the sprockets are engaged with the chain before installing them over the shafts.

49. Install the distributor drive gear onto the eccentric shaft with the "F" mark on the gear facing the front of the engine. Slide the spacer and oil slinger onto the eccentric shaft.

50. Align the keyway and install the eccentric shaft pulley. Tighten the pulley bolt to 60 ft. lbs.

51. Turn the engine top so the engine faces up.

52. Check eccentric shaft end-play in the following manner:

   a. Attach a dial indicator to the flywheel. Move the flywheel forward and backward.

   b. Note the reading on the dial indicator; it should be 0.0016–0.0028 in.

   c. If the end-play is not within specifications, adjust it by replacing the front spacer. Spacers come in four sizes, ranging from 0.3150–0.3181 in. If necessary, a spacer can be ground on a surface plate with emery paper.

   d. Check the end-play again and, if it is now within specifications, proceed with the next step.

ECCENTRIC SHAFT SPACER THICKNESS CHART

Marking	Thickness
X	8.08 ± 0.01 mm (0.3181 ± 0.0004 in)
Y	8.04 ± 0.01 mm (0.3165 ± 0.0004 in)
V	8.02 ± 0.01 mm (0.3158 ± 0.0004 in)
Z	.800 ± 0.01 mm (0.3150 ± 0.0004 in)

53. Remove the pulley from the front of the eccentric shaft. Tighten the oil pump drive sprocket nut and bend the locktabs on the lockwasher.

54. Fit a new O-ring over the front cover oil passage.

55. Install the chain tensioner and tighten its securing bolts.

56. Position the front cover gasket and the front cover on the front housing, then secure the front cover with its attachment bolts.

57. Install the eccentric shaft pulley again. Tighten its bolt to 60 ft. lbs.

58. Turn the engine so that the bottom faces up.

59. Cut off the excess gasket on the front cover along the mounting surface of the oil pan.

60. Install the oil strainer gasket and strainer on the front housing and tighten the attaching bolts.

61. Apply sealer to the joint surfaces of each housing.

62. Install the gasket and oil pan. Tighten the bolts evenly in two stages to 3.5 ft. lbs.

63. Turn the engine so that the top is up.

64. Install the water pump gasket on the front housing. Tighten the attaching bolts.

65. Rotate the eccentric shaft until the yellow mark (leading side mark) aligns with the pointer on the front cover.

66. Align the marks on the distributor gear and housing and install the distributor so that the lockbolt is in the center of the slot.

67. Rotate the distributor until the leading points start to separate and tighten the distributor locknut.

68. Install the gaskets and thermal reactor and tighten the attaching nuts.

69. Install the hot air duct.

70. Install the carburetor and intake manifold assembly with a new gasket. Tighten the attaching nuts.

71. Connect the oil tubes, vacuum tube and metering oil pump connecting rod to the carburetor.

72. Install the decel valve and connect the vacuum lines, air hoses and wires.

73. Install the alternator bracket, alternator and bolt and check the clearance. If the clearance is more than 0.006 in., adjust the clearance using a shim. Shims are available in three sizes: 0.0059 in., 0.0118 in., and 0.0197 in.

74. Install the alternator drive belt. Attach the alternator to the adjusting brace and adjust the belt tension to specification.

75. Install the air pump with the adjusting brace and install the air pump drive belt. Adjust the air pump drive belt to specifications.

76. Install the engine hanger bracket to the front cover.

77. Remove the engine from the stand.

78. Install the engine in the vehicle.

79. Fill the engine with fresh engine oil and install a new filter. Fill the engine with coolant. Start the engine, check the oil pressure, and warm it to normal operating temperature. Adjust the idle speed, timing and dwell. Recheck all capacities and refill if necessary. Check for leaks.

Intake Manifold

REMOVAL & INSTALLATION

To remove the intake manifold and carburetor assembly with the engine remaining in the automobile, proceed in the following manner:

1. Perform steps 2, 3, 4, 5, 7, and 13 of Engine Removal and Installation, above. Do not remove the engine. Do not drain the engine oil; merely remove the metering oil pump hose from the carburetor.

2. Perform steps 6 and 7 of the Engine Disassembly procedure.

Install the intake manifold and carburetor assembly in the reverse order of removal. Tighten the manifold securing nuts, working from the inside out, and in two or three stages, to the torque specifications found in the Torque Specifications. Refill the cooling system.

Thermal Reactor

REMOVAL & INSTALLATION

─────── CAUTION ───────
The thermal reactor operates at extremely high temperatures. Allow the engine to cool completely before attempting to remove it.

To remove the thermal reactor, which replaces the exhaust manifold, proceed in the following manner:

1. Remove the air cleaner assembly from the carburetor.

2. Unbolt and remove the air injection pump as outlined in Emission Controls.

3. Remove the intake manifold assembly, complete with carburetor.

4. Remove the heat stove from the thermal reactor.

5. Unfasten the thermal reactor securing nuts, including those on the exhaust pipe flange.

NOTE: The bottom nut is difficult to reach. Mazda makes a special wrench (part number 49 213 001) to remove it. If the wrench is unavailable, a flexible drive metric socket wrench may be substituted.

6. Lift the thermal reactor away from the engine.

Installation of the thermal reactor is performed in the reverse order of removal.

LUBRICATION SYSTEM— ROTARY

A conventional pump, which is chain driven, circulates oil through the rotary engine. A full-flow filter is mounted on the top of the rear housing and an oil cooler is used to reduce the temperature of the engine oil.

An unusual feature of the rotary engine lubrication system is a metering oil pump which injects oil into the float chamber of the carburetor. Once there, it is mixed with the fuel which is to be burned, thus providing extra lubrication for the seals. The metering oil pump is designed to work only when the engine is working under a load.

Oil Pan

REMOVAL & INSTALLATION

1. Raise the front of the car and support it with jackstands.

─────── CAUTION ───────
Be sure that the car is supported securely.

2. Remove the drain plug and drain the engine oil.

3. Remove the nuts and bolts which secure the gravel shield and withdraw it from underneath the car.

4. Unfasten the retaining bolts and remove the oil pan with its gasket.

Oil pan installation is performed in the reverse order of removal. Coat both the oil pan flange and its mounting flange with sealer, prior to assembly.

tained in the engine overhaul section above. Perform only those steps needed to remove the oil pump.

CHECKING CLEARANCES

1. Separate the halves of the oil pump housing.

Measure the clearance between the rotors with a feeler gauge

Measure the gap between the straight edge and the housing

2. Measure the clearance between the lobes of the rotors with a feeler gauge. The clearance should be 0.004–0.0035 in. Replace both of the rotors if the clearance exceeds 0.006 in.

3. Check the clearance between the outer rotor and the housing with a feeler gauge. The clearance should be 0.008–0.010 in. If the clearance is greater than 0.012 in., replace both of the rotors.

4. Place a straightedge across the pump housing. Measure the gap between the straightedge and the housing with a feeler gauge. The gap should be 0.001–0.005 in. If the gap exceeds 0.012 in., replace the rotors or the pump housing.

Metering Oil Pump

OPERATION

A metering oil pump, mounted on the top of the engine, is used to provide additional lubrication to the engine when it is operating under a load. The pump provides oil to the carburetor, where it is mixed in the float chamber with the fuel to be burned.

The metering pump is a plunger type and is controlled by throttle opening. A cam arrangement, connected to the carburetor throttle lever, operates a plunger. The plunger, in turn, acts on a differential plunger, the stroke of which determines the amount of oil flow.

When the throttle opening is small, the

amount of the plunger stroke is small; as the throttle opening increases, so does the amount of the plunger stroke.

TESTING

1. At the carburetor, disconnect the oil lines which run from the metering oil pump to the carburetor.

2. Use a container which has a scale calibrated in cubic centimeters (cc) on its side to catch the pump discharge from the oil lines.

3. Run the engine at 2,000 rpm for six minutes.

4. At the end of this time, 2.0–2.5cc's should be collected in the container. If not, adjust the pump as explained below.

ADJUSTMENTS

Rotate the adjusting screw on the metering oil pump to obtain the proper oil flow. Clockwise rotation of the screw *increases* the flow; counterclockwise rotation *decreases* the flow.

If necessary, the oil discharge rate may be further adjusted by changing the position of the cam in the pump connecting rod. The shorter the rod throw, the more oil will be pumped. Adjust the throw by means of the three holes provided.

Arrow (right) indicates the metering oil pump adjusting screw. The three arrows (left) indicate the connecting rod adjusting holes.

① : 248cc / 6,000rpm / Hr
② : 174cc / 6,000rpm / Hr
③ : 104cc / 6,000rpm / Hr

Connecting rod adjusting holes

Oil Cooler

REMOVAL & INSTALLATION

1. Raise the car and support it with jackstands.

Rotary engine cooling system

―――――― CAUTION ――――――
Be sure that the car is securely supported.

2. Drain the engine oil.

3. Unfasten the screws which retain the gravel shield and remove the shield.

4. Unfasten the oil lines from the oil cooler.

5. Unfasten the nuts which secure the oil cooler to the radiator.

6. Remove the oil cooler.

Examine the oil cooler for signs of leakage. Blow the cooler fins clean with compressed air. Later models coolers are made from aluminum; they must be repaired by aluminum welding.

Installation is performed in the reverse order of removal.

COOLING SYSTEM— ROTARY

Radiator

REMOVAL & INSTALLATION

―――――― CAUTION ――――――
Perform this operation when the engine has cooled completely.

1. Drain the engine coolant into a large, clean container so that it may be reused.

2. Remove the nuts and bolts which attach the shroud to the radiator. Withdraw the shroud.

3. Remove the upper, lower, and expansion tank hoses from the radiator.

4. Unfasten the bolts which attach the radiator to its mounting bracket. Remove the oil cooler nuts and bolts.

5. Withdraw the radiator from the car. Install the radiator in the reverse order of removal.

Water Pump

REMOVAL & INSTALLATION

1. Drain the cooling system.

2. Remove the air cleaner.

3. Remove the bolts attaching the rear of the fan drive and remove the fan drive.

4. If necessary to disassemble the water pump, loosen the bolts attaching the water pump pulley to the water pump boss.

5. Remove the air pump and drive belt.

6. Remove the alternator and disconnect the drive belt.

7. If necessary, remove the water pump pulley and bolts.

8. Unbolt and remove the water pump.

9. Installation is the reverse of removal.

Thermostat

REMOVAL & INSTALLATION

1. Drain the engine coolant into a large, clean container for reuse.

2. Remove the nuts which secure the thermostat housing to the water pump.

Thermostat installation and by-pass circuit

3. Lift the thermostat.

Thermostat installation is performed in the reverse order of removal.

CAUTION

The thermostat is equipped with a plunger which covers and uncovers a by-pass hole at its bottom. Because of this unusual construction, only the specified Mazda thermostat should be used for replacement. A standard thermostat will cause the engine to overheat.

ENGINE MECHANICAL— GASOLINE PISTON ENGINES

Engine

REMOVAL & INSTALLATION

Courier

The engine is removed through the engine compartment leaving the transmission in place. When installing nuts or bolts, lubricate the threads with light engine oil, but do not oil threads which require oil-resistant or water-resistant sealer.

NOTE: Always label all disconnected hoses as they are removed, as an aid to correct installation.

1. Scribe the locations of the hood hinges and remove the hood.
2. Drain the coolant.
3. Remove the air cleaner and, on the 2.3, the heat stove.
4. Disconnect the upper radiator hose at the engine and the lower radiator hose at the radiator on the 1.8 and 2.0. With the 2.3, disconnect both at the radiator. If you have an automatic transmission, also disconnect and plug the two fluid cooler lines at the radiator.
5. Unbolt and remove the radiator. With the 2.3, you will first have to loosen the shroud mounting bolts and slide the shroud rearward.
6. Disconnect the accelerator linkage at the carburetor.
7. Disconnect and plug the fuel line at the carburetor.
8. Remove the linkage attaching nuts at the intake manifold and remove the linkage.
9. Disconnect the cable at the air by-pass valve (if equipped).
10. Disconnect the choke cable.
11. Disconnect the battery cables, negative cable first.
12. Disconnect the coil high tension wire at the distributor. Disconnect the coil lead wire.

13. Remove the fan.
14. Loosen the alternator retaining bolts and remove the alternator drive belt.
15. If equipped, remove the Thermactor air pump drive belt.
16. Remove the alternator bracket and adjusting arm bolts. Position the alternator out of the way. If your Courier has air conditioning, unbolt the compressor and set it aside without detaching any lines.

CAUTION

Never open any air conditioning lines. Escaping compressed refrigerant can freeze any body surface, including the eyes, that it contacts. It also decomposes into a poisonous gas in the presence of flame.

17. If equipped, disconnect the Thermactor hoses at the pump. Remove the Thermactor bracket and adjusting arm bolt and lay the Thermactor pump aside. On the 2.3, disconnect the brake vacuum booster hose at the engine, and the vacuum lines at the vacuum amplifier.
18. Remove the heater hoses from the front and rear of the intake manifold on the 1.8 and 2.0. On the 2.3, remove the heater hoses altogether.
19. If equipped, disconnect the Thermactor air filter hose at the air by-pass valve.
20. Disconnect the oil pressure gauge lead wire and boot from the sending unit.
21. Disconnect the battery ground cable from the block.
22. Disconnect the wires from the starter solenoid.
23. Raise and support the vehicle and drain the oil from the engine.
24. Remove the engine front lower skid plate, 1.8 and 2.0 only.
25. Disconnect the exhaust pipe at the exhaust manifold. With the 2.3 also unbolt the exhaust pipe hanger from the transmission.
26. With manual transmission, on the 1.8 and 2.0 remove the flywheel housing bolt and the lower starter nuts and one lower bolt. On the 2.3, just remove the lower transmission-to-engine bolts at this time. With automatic transmission, first disconnect the vacuum hose from the diaphragm. Unbolt the access cover from the lower end of the torque converter housing. Match-mark the driveplate (flywheel) and the torque converter for later alignment, then remove the four bolts connecting the driveplate to the torque converter. Disconnect the throttle linkage from the transmission.
27. Remove the lower exhaust pipe bolt and let the pipe hang on the 1.8 and 2.0. Remove the engine support bolts and remove the right engine mount bracket, with the 2.3.
28. Lower the truck.
29. Remove the starter upper bolts and remove the starter on the 1.8 and 2.0.
30. Support the transmission with a jack. Remove the remaining transmission-to-engine bolts on the 2.3.
31. Install a lifting sling on the engine at the engine hanger brackets. Remove the

clutch slave cylinder from the transmission on the 2.3.
32. Attach a sling to the hoist and pull the engine forward until it clears the transmission shaft. Be sure that the transmission is not dislodged from the jack. Unbolt the engine from the mounts.
33. Lift the engine from the truck. If your truck has an automatic transmission, be careful not to let the torque converter fall out of its housing.

To install the engine:

34. Lower the engine into the chassis. Loosely install several clutch housing bolts.
35. Install the engine mount bolts. Install the 2.3s right engine mount and the clutch slave cylinder.
36. Remove the lifting sling and transmission jack. Be sure that the mainshaft is engaged with the engine.
37. Install the starter and upper attaching bolt on the 1.8 and 2.0.
38. Raise and support the truck.
39. Install the flywheel housing bolts with manual transmission. With automatic, line up the marks made earlier on the driveplate and the torque converter, and install the four bolts. Torque them to 25–36 ft. lbs. Install the torque converter housing-to-engine bolts, and torque to 23–34 ft. lbs. Replace the access cover on the torque converter housing.
40. Connect the exhaust pipe to the exhaust manifold. Install the bracket bolt. Install the exhaust pipe hanger to the transmission on 2.3s.
41. Install the lower starter bolts on the 1.8 and 2.0.
42. Install the 1.8 and 2.0 engine front skid plate.
43. Connect the starter wires and lower the vehicle.
44. Install the accelerator linkage. Connect the fuel line and choke cable. With automatics, also connect the throttle linkage and the vacuum hose.
45. Connect the heater hoses. If equipped, connect the Thermactor air filter hose. Connect the 2.3s brake vacuum booster hose and the vacuum line at the amplifier.
46. Install the battery ground cable to the block. Install the coil wires.
47. Install the alternator on the bracket and install the bolts. Install the air conditioning compressor, if removed.
48. If equipped, install the Thermactor air pump.
49. Install the fan.
50. Install the drive belts and adjust the tension.
51. Install the radiator. Connect the upper and lower hoses. Connect the automatic transmission cooler lines, if equipped.
52. Connect the oil pressure sending unit.
53. Fill the cooling system and crankcase with the specified type and amount of fluid. Install the air cleaner (and heat stove on 2.3s).
54. Install the hood. Connect the battery cables. Start the engine and check for leaks and proper operation.

Mazda

The engine is removed through the engine compartment, leaving the transmission in place.

1. Scribe the locations of the hood hinges and remove the hood.
2. Remove the engine splash shield.
3. Drain the coolant.
4. Drain the engine oil.
5. Disconnect and remove the battery.
6. Disconnect the primary wire and coil wire from the distributor.
7. Disconnect the wire at the "B" terminal of the alternator and disconnect the plug from the rear of the alternator.
8. Disconnect the wire from the oil pressure switch.
9. Disconnect the engine ground wire.
10. Remove the air cleaner and heat insulator.
11. Disconnect the breather hose from the rocker cover.
12. Disconnect the water temperature gauge wire and solenoid valve wire.
13. Disconnect the coupler for the backup light switch.
14. Disconnect the vacuum tubes at the intake manifold and the carburetor.
15. Disconnect the starter wires.
16. Remove the upper and lower radiator hoses.
17. Remove the bolts attaching the radiator cowling. The cowling can only be removed after the radiator has been removed.
18. Remove the radiator.
19. Disconnect the heater hoses from the intake manifold.
20. Disconnect the throttle cable from the carburetor and remove the throttle linkage from the rocker cover.
21. Disconnect the choke cable from the carburetor.
22. Disconnect the fuel ventilation hose from the oil separator.
23. Disconnect the fuel line at the carburetor and plug the fuel line.
24. Remove the starter.
25. Disconnect the exhaust pipe from the manifold.
26. Remove the clutch or torque converter cover plate.
27. Support the transmission with a jack and remove the bolts attaching the engine to the transmission.
28. Unbolt the engine mounts.
29. Attach a lifting sling to the engine and pull the engine forward until it clears the transmission shaft.
30. Lift the engine from the vehicle.
31. Installation is the reverse of removal. Be sure to check all fluid levels.

Cylinder Head

REMOVAL & INSTALLATION

All Except 2.3L

Be sure that the cylinder head is cold before removal. This will prevent warpage.

1. Drain the cooling system.
2. On 1977 and earlier models, scribe alignment marks around the hood hinges and remove the hood.
3. Remove the air cleaner.
4. Disconnect the coil wire and vacuum line from the distributor.
5. Rotate the crankshaft to place no. 1 cylinder at TDC, on the compression stroke.
6. Remove the plug wires and distributor cap as a unit. Number wires.
7. Remove the distributor.
8. Remove the rocker arm cover.
9. Raise and support the truck. Disconnect the exhaust pipe from the manifold.
10. Remove the accelerator linkage. Disconnect the wire from the water thermo switch, under the intake manifold and behind the carburetor, which should be disconnected. Disconnect the throttle cable at the air by-pass valve, and the choke cable and fuel line at the carburetor.
11. If your Courier has an air pump, remove the hoses from the pump. Disconnect the heater return hose at the intake manifold, the coolant by-pass hose, the water pump hose, and the upper radiator hose (at the engine).
12. Disconnect the wire from the slow fuel valve (throttle solenoid on the carburetor). Remove the intake manifold bracket.
13. Remove the water pump.
14. Remove the nut, washer, and the distributor gear from the camshaft.

Cylinder head bolt torque sequence—1.8L and 2.0L engines

15. Remove the nut and washer from the camshaft gear. You will have to lock up the engine to do this. The best way is with a tool which locks onto the flywheel teeth. These tools are available in auto parts stores or from your dealer. Support the timing chain in such a way that it cannot fall into the timing chain case. Do not remove the cam gear from the timing chain. The relationship between the chain and the gear teeth should not be disturbed, since cam timing is dependent on this relationship. You can wire the chain and gear together to keep them in position.
16. Loosen the cylinder head bolts a little at a time in the reverse order of the tightening sequence, and remove them. Also remove the cylinder head-to-front cover bolt.
17. Remove the rocker arm assembly.
18. Remove the camshaft from the camshaft gear. See the "Camshaft Removal" section.
19. Lift off the cylinder head being careful not to let the timing chain and gear fall into the timing case.
20. Remove all tension from the timing

chain. See the Timing Chain Tensioner Adjustment procedure.

To install the cylinder head:

1. Clean the rocker cover gasket surface at the head and the cover. Clean the head gasket surface at the head and the block. Clean the water pump gasket surface at the head gasket surface and the front cover. Be careful not to scratch the flat surfaces. Vacuum out any bits that fall into the cylinders or passages, being careful not to nick the cylinder walls.
2. Check the cylinder head flatness with a straightedge and feeler blades. It should not exceed 0.003 in. in any 6 in. span or 0.006 in. overall.
3. Clean the cylinder head bolt holes of oil and dirt.
4. Position a new head gasket on the cylinder block.
5. Install the cylinder head on the block using the guides at either end of the block.
6. Coat the camshaft bearings and camshaft with engine oil, and install the camshaft to the camshaft gear. See the Camshaft Installation procedure.
7. Install the rocker arm assembly.
8. Install the head bolts. Torque the bolts to specifications in three passes.
9. Install the camshaft gear washer and nut. Torque to specifications.
10. Install the distributor gear, washer and nut.
11. Time the engine. Follow the instructions under "Timing Chain and Sprocket Installation."
12. Adjust the timing chain tension. See "Timing Chain Tensioner Adjustment."
13. Connect the exhaust pipe to the exhaust manifold. Lower the truck.
14. Install the distributor, distributor cap and plug wires.
15. Install the water pump.
16. Install the lower intake bracket bolt.
17. Install the accelerator linkage.
18. Connect the vacuum line and coil wire. Connect all the hoses and wires disconnected earlier.
19. Adjust the valve clearance cold.
20. Install the rocker arm cover. Fill the cooling system.
21. Run the engine until normal operating temperature is reached, and check for leaks. Adjust the valve clearance hot.
22. Adjust the carburetor and ignition timing. Install the air cleaner and install the hood.

2.3L Engine

It is easier to remove the cylinder head if the intake and exhaust manifolds are removed first. It is not necessary to remove the camshaft. The engine should be cold to reduce the chance of warpage when the cylinder head bolts are removed.

1. Drain the cooling system.
2. Remove the air cleaner. Remove the spark plug wires from the plugs. Remove the spark plugs.
3. Remove the valve cover. It is held on by eight bolts.

TORQUE THE CYLINDER HEAD BOLTS TO SPECIFICATIONS
IN TWO PROGRESSIVE STEPS IN THE SEQUENCE SHOWN.

FRONT OF
ENGINE

WHEN INSTALLING CYLINDER
HEAD, POSITION THE CAMSHAFT
AS SHOWN TO AVOID DAMAGE
TO PROTRUDING VALVES.

PIN

Cylinder head removal and installation—2.3 engines

4. Remove the intake and exhaust manifolds from the head. See the appropriate procedures for each.

5. Remove the camshaft drive belt cover. There are tubular spacers underneath the two bolts directly above the crankshaft pulley.

6. Loosen the drive belt tensioner and slip the belt off of the cam sprocket and tensioner. See the "Belt Tensioner Adjustment" section. It is not necessary to remove the tensioner from the head.

7. Remove the coolant outlet elbow, with the hose attached, from the cylinder head.

8. Loosen the cylinder head bolts a little at a time in the reverse order of the torque sequence shown for tightening.

9. Remove the cylinder head.
To install:

1. Clean all the gasket material and sealer from the cylinder head, engine block, valve cover, and water outlet. Be careful not to scratch the surfaces. Vacuum out any particles which fall into the cylinders or passages, being careful not to nick the cylinder walls.

2. Check the cylinder head for flatness. It should not exceed 0.003 in. in any 6 in. span, or 0.006 in. overall. If the head must

be machined, do not remove more than 0.010 in. from the original surface. Remove any burrs or scratches with an oil stone.

3. Clean the cylinder head and block bolt holes of any oil or dirt.

4. Place a new gasket on the cylinder block.

5. Position the cam with the pin in the position shown in the illustration.

6. Lower the head carefully onto the block and gasket.

7. Lightly oil the threads of the cylinder head bolts before installation. Torque the bolts to specification in at least three passes, increasing the amount of torque used each time. Torque the bolts in the sequence shown.

8. Slip the camshaft drive belt back over the cam sprocket and tensioner, then time the camshaft. See the "Camshaft Timing Belt" removal and installation procedure for instructions.

9. Install the camshaft drive belt cover and its attaching bolts. Make sure the two spacers are installed correctly. Tighten the bolts to 6–13 ft. lbs.

10. Install the water outlet elbow and a new gasket onto the head. Tighten the bolts to 12–15 ft. lbs.

11. Install the intake and exhaust manifolds. See the appropriate section for each.

12. Install the valve cover, using a new gasket. Use an oil resistant sealer, such as silicone, on both sides of the gasket. Install the air cleaner. Install the spark plugs and wires.

13. Fill the cooling system.

Rocker Arms and Shafts

REMOVAL & INSTALLATION

1.8L and 2.0L Engines

This operation should only be performed on a cold engine; the bolts which hold the

Cylinder head bolt torque sequence—2.3L engines

1. Locks	9. Rocker arm
2. Spring retainer	10. Rocker shaft spring
3. Outer valve spring	11. Rocker shaft support
4. Inner valve spring	12. Adjusting screw
5. Lower spring seat	13. Rocker shaft
6. Valve seal	14. Lubrication tube
7. Exhaust valve	15. Seal
8. Intake valve	

Rocker arms, shafts and valves—1.8 and 2.0 engines

rocker shafts in place also hold the cylinder head to the block.

1. Raise the hood and cover the fenders.
2. Disconnect the choke cable.
3. If equipped, disconnect the air by-pass valve cable.
4. Label the spark plug wires to prevent crosswiring upon installation and disconnect them from the spark plugs. Remove the wires from the clips on the rocker cover and position them out of the way.
5. Remove the rocker cover and discard the gasket.
6. Remove the rocker arm shaft attaching bolts evenly and remove the rocker arm shafts.

To install the rocker shafts:

7. Install the rocker arm assemblies on the cylinder head. Torque the bolts to specifications in sequence.
8. Adjust the valves cold.
9. Clean the mating surfaces of the cylinder head and rocker cover.
10. Install the rocker cover with a new gasket.
11. Install the spark plug wires on the plugs. Place the wires in the clips on the rocker cover. Connect the choke and air by-pass valve cable.
12. Start the engine and check for leaks.
13. Allow the engine to reach operating temperature, torque the head bolts to specifications and adjust the valves hot.

Intake Manifold

REMOVAL & INSTALLATION

1.8L and 2.0L Engines

1. Drain the cooling system and remove the air cleaner assembly.

2. Disconnect the following items at the carburetor:
   a. Accelerator linkage
   b. Choke cable
   c. Fuel line
3. Disconnect the heater return hose and by-pass hose.
4. Disconnect the electrical connectors from both the carburetor solenoid and the water temperature sender.
5. Disconnect all of the vacuum hoses from the carburetor and the intake manifold. Tag the hoses so that they may be reinstalled correctly.
6. Disconnect the air injection system hoses at the air by-pass valve (or the anti-afterburn valve for Calif.) and remove the valve.
7. Disconnect and remove the EGR control valve and pipe assembly.
8. Remove the PCV valve.
9. Disconnect the servo diaphragm (for the throttle positioner system) and remove the diaphragm.
10. Remove the intake manifold-to-cylinder head fasteners and remove the manifold and carburetor as an assembly.
11. Clean the gasket mating surfaces.
12. Installation is the reverse of the previous steps. Replenish the cooling system with coolant and check the system for leaks after the engine is started.

NOTE: Torque the manifold fasteners starting from the center and work outward in a circular pattern.

2.3L Engine

1. Drain the cooling system and remove the air cleaner assembly.
2. Disconnect the accelerator cable at the carburetor.
3. Disconnect all of the vacuum hoses

from the carburetor and the intake manifold. Tag the hoses so that they may be reinstalled correctly.

4. Disconnect the heat tube at the EGR valve.
5. Remove the engine oil dipstick and tube assembly.
6. Disconnect the fuel lines at the carburetor.
7. Remove the PCV valve.
8. Remove the two distributor cap screws and move the distributor cap aside.
9. Remove the intake manifold retaining bolts and remove the manifold and carburetor as an assembly.
10. Clean the gasket mating surfaces.
11. Installation is the reverse of the previous steps. Replenish the cooling system with coolant and check the system for leaks after the engine is started.

NOTE: Torque the manifold fasteners according to the accompanying illustration.

Intake manifold torque sequence for the 2.3 engine

Exhaust Manifold

REMOVAL & INSTALLATION

Courier

1. Remove the hot air duct which runs to the air cleaner case, if equipped. Remove the air injection nozzles or air pipe assembly, if equipped, on the 1.8 and 2.0. If the engine has a hot air duct, remove the upper and lower heat insulators. If the engine has an EGR valve, remove it.
2. Raise and support the truck.
3. Remove the two attaching nuts from the exhaust pipe at the manifold. Discard the gold gasket.
4. Remove the manifold attaching nuts. On 2.3s, disconnect the air pump check valve hose.
5. Remove the manifold.

To install the manifold:

6. Apply a light film of graphite grease to the exhaust manifold mating surfaces before installation.
7. Install the manifold on the studs and install the attaching nuts. Tighten the nuts to 16–21 ft. lbs. on the 1.8 and 2.0. Final torque for the 2.3 is 16–23 ft. lbs., 1977–78, or 27–38 ft. lbs., 1979 and later. Tighten

Exhaust manifold torque sequence for the 2.3 engine

the nuts in a circular pattern, working from the center out towards the ends, on the 1.8 and 2.0. On the 2.3, follow the pattern illustrated.

8. Install a new exhaust pipe gasket. Connect the exhaust pipe and torque the nuts to 15 ft. lbs.

9. On 2.3s, connect the hose to the air pump check valve. Install the EGR valve, heat insulators, air injection nozzles or air pipe, and hot air duct, as applicable.

Mazda

1. Raise and support the vehicle.

2. Remove the two attaching nuts from the exhaust pipe at the manifold.

3. Remove the air pump air injection hose from the check valve or air injection manifold, if equipped. Remove the heat stove and hot air to the air cleaner, if equipped.

4. Disconnect the EGR pipe, if so equipped.

5. Remove the exhaust pipe hanger from the bracket on the transmission, if so equipped.

6. Remove the manifold attaching nuts.

7. Remove the manifold.

8. Installation is the reverse of removal.

Front Cover

REMOVAL & INSTALLATION

1.8L and 2.0L Engines

1. On 1977 models, scribe alignment marks on the hood hinges and remove the hood.

2. Drain the cooling system.

3. Disconnect the upper and lower radiator hoses. Remove the radiator.

4. Remove the accessory drive belts.

5. Remove the crankshaft pulley, water pump, and engine cooling fan.

6. Remove the cylinder head-to-front cover bolt.

7. Raise and support the truck.

8. Remove the engine skid plate.

9. Disconnect the emission line from the oil pan, if equipped. Drain the oil from the engine.

10. Remove the oil pan.

11. Remove the alternator and bracket and lay the alternator aside.

12. Remove the Thermactor pump (if equipped) and lay the pump aside.

13. Remove the steel tube from the front of the engine.

14. Unbolt and remove the front cover. To install the front cover:

15. Clean all the gasket mating surfaces.

16. Clean the crankshaft pulley.

17. Use contact cement and cement a new front cover gasket on the block.

18. Install the front cover and torque the attaching bolts to specifications.

19. Install the Thermactor pump (if equipped).

20. Install the alternator and bracket.

21. Install the water pump and a new gasket. Torque the bolts to specifications.

22. Connect the by-pass hose and heater hose to the water pump.

23. Install the crankshaft pulley and attaching bolt. Torque the bolt to specifications.

24. Install the Thermactor (if equipped), and alternator belts. Install the water pump pulley and the engine cooling fan.

25. Install the fan. Adjust the tension of the belt(s).

26. Install the radiator and the upper and lower hoses.

27. Install the air cleaner.

28. Install the oil pan and the emission line.

29. Install the engine skid plate.

30. Lower the truck to the ground.

31. Fill the engine with oil and fill the cooling system. Run the engine and check for leaks.

32. Install the hood on 1977 and earlier models.

2.3L Engine

There are actually two front covers on the 2.3 liter engine, which share a common gasket. You will need either the special Ford tool or a stepped socket (or pipe) to align the crankshaft cover upon reinstallation, and a thin-fingered gear puller to remove the crankshaft sprocket.

1. Drain the cooling system. Remove the upper and lower radiator hoses at the radiator. If your Courier has an automatic transmission, remove and plug the fluid cooler lines from the bottom of the radiator. Remove the radiator.

2. Remove the drive belts to the alternator, air pump and air conditioning compressor, if so equipped, and move the components out of the way. Do NOT disconnect any air conditioning lines. Unbolt and remove the fan and its pulley from the water pump shaft.

3. Remove the camshaft belt outer cover. There are tubular spacers underneath the two bolts directly above the crankshaft pulley.

4. Remove the crankshaft pulley. It is held on with a single center bolt. Remove the belt guide underneath the pulley. It is pressed onto the crankshaft over the locating key.

5. Loosen the cam belt tensioner and remove the belt. See the Timing Belt and Tensioner procedure section.

6. Remove the belt inner cover.

7. Use a puller to remove the crankshaft cam belt sprocket. Be sure that the puller does not cock the sprocket on the shaft.

8. Drain the engine oil and remove the oil pan. See the appropriate section in this chapter-

9. Unbolt and remove the cylinder front cover and the auxiliary shaft cover, and the common gasket.

If only one cover is to be removed, cut the gasket around the remaining cover, then

Cylinder head-to-front cover bolt on the 1.8 and the 2.0 engines

View of the 2.3 engine front cover showing the stepped front cover alignment tool which must be used during installation of the front cover. The cylinder block is shown inverted for clarity.

use the necessary half of a new gasket when the cover is replaced.

Before reinstalling the cover(s), clean all the gasket surfaces thoroughly. Pry out the old seals from the covers, but do not install new shaft seals until the covers are in place. Position a new gasket on the front of the engine, install the covers and bolts, but do not tighten them. Using either the Ford tool (illustrated) or a stepped pipe, align the cylinder cover and the crankshaft, so that the timing belt will not interfere with the front cover. Torque the bolts to 6–9 ft. lbs. with the tool in place.

Install new shaft seals after the covers have been installed. Oil the lips of the seals before installation. The rest of the installation process is the reverse of removal. Be sure to use sealer on the oil pan gasket, front cover and rear main bearing cap seals. No special tool is necessary to replace the crankshaft sprocket; just align it with the key and press it into place. After assembly, fill the crankcase with oil, the cooling system with coolant, and adjust the belt tension. Start the engine, check for leaks, and adjust the initial ignition and engine (belt) timing.

Front Cover Oil Seal
REMOVAL & INSTALLATION
1.8L and 2.0L Engines

The front cover oil seal can be removed and a new one installed without removing the front cover.

1. On 1977 and earlier models, scribe alignment marks on the hood hinges and remove the hood.
2. Drain the cooling system.
3. Disconnect the upper and lower radiator hoses and remove the radiator.
4. Remove the drive belt(s).
5. Remove the crankshaft pulley.
6. Pry the front oil seal from the front cover.

To install a new oil seal:

7. Clean the pulley and seal area.
8. Press a new front seal into position (flush).
9. Install the crankshaft pulley and torque the bolt to specifications.
10. Install the drive belt(s) and adjust the tension.
11. Install the radiator and connect the upper and lower hoses. Fill the cooling system.
12. Start the engine and check for leaks.
13. Install the hood on 1977 and earlier models.

2.3L Engine

The cylinder and auxiliary shaft front cover seals can be replaced without removing the covers. Follow steps 1, 2, 3, 4, 5, and 7 of the 2.3 Engine Front Cover procedure. Ford recommends the use of a puller to remove the old seal; you can also use a sharp pointed piece of plastic or wood to pry it out. Do not use a screwdriver, though,

because you may damage the seal seat. Coat the lips of the new seal with engine oil and press it into place. Ford has a threaded arbor press available for this job. You should also be able to press it home using a socket with a diameter slightly smaller than that of the seal (the socket should just clear the seal seat in the front cover). Place a block of wood on the socket, and tap the seal into place with light hammer blows on the wood.

After installing the new seals, replace the crankshaft sprocket, cam belt, belt guide, crankshaft pulley, belt outer cover, fan drive belts, and radiator. Replace the coolant, adjust the tension of the various belts, and check the initial ignition timing and the engine (belt) timing.

Timing Chain/Belt
REMOVAL & INSTALLATION
1.8L and 2.0L Engines

1. Remove the cylinder head and front cover. It is not necessary to remove the intake and exhaust manifolds from the head.
2. On the Mazda engine, remove the oil pump and chain. Remove the timing chain tensioner.
3. Remove the timing chain tensioner.
4. Loosen the timing chain guide strip screws.
5. Remove the oil slinger.
6. On Mazda engines, remove the oil pump gear and chain as an assembly. On Courier engines, first straighten the locktab on the oil pump gear nut washer, and remove the nut. Then remove the oil pump gear and chain.
7. Remove the timing chain, crankshaft gear, and camshaft gears from the engine.

To install,

8. Position the crankshaft gear in the timing chain. On Courier engines, the two bright links must align with the timing mark.
9. Position the oil pump chain and gear on the crankshaft and oil pump. On Mazda engines, check the oil pump drive chain slack. It should be .015 in. Adjusting shims

KEYWAY STRAIGHT UP

NUMBER ONE CYLINDER ON TDC

CHAIN GUIDE STRIP

CHAIN TENSIONER

NICKEL PLATED LINK

TIMING MARK AND NICKEL PLATED LINK ALIGNED

VIBRATION DAMPER

KEYWAY STRAIGHT UP

TWO NICKEL PLATED LINKS AT BDC OF THE CRANKSHAFT SPROCKET WITH A TIMING MARK IN-BETWEEN

Positions of timing chain and related components for the 1.8L and 2.0L engines. Align all marks as illustrated during installation of the chain

(between the oil pump body and cylinder block) are available in thicknesses of .006 in.

10. Install the oil slinger.

11. Install the oil pump washer and nut. Bend the washer over the nut.

12. Install the timing chain tensioner. Fully compress the snubber spring and wedge a screwdriver into the tensioner release mechanism. Without removing the screwdriver, install the tensioner.

13. Install the cylinder head and camshaft. Be sure that the valve timing is as illustrated. It must be exact. You may have to move the cam gear one or two teeth to obtain the correct alignment.

Installing timing chain—Mazda 1800 and 2000 engines

14. Install the rocker arm shafts and cam bearing caps.

15. Install and torque the cylinder head bolts.

16. Adjust the timing chain tension. Press in on the chain guide strip. Tighten the guide strip attaching screws. Remove the screwdriver from the tensioner, allowing the snubber to take up the chain slack.

17. Replace the front cover.

18. Adjust the valve clearance cold. Run the engine. Torque the cylinder head bolts and adjust the valve clearance hot.

2.3L Engines

1. Remove the access plug from the front of the belt cover.

2. Turn the crankshaft until the engine is at TDC, indicated when the timing pointer is aligned with the TDC notch on the crankshaft pulley. You can turn the crankshaft with a wrench on the pulley bolt; it is also easier with the spark plugs removed.

— **CAUTION** —
Always turn the engine in the direction of normal rotation (clockwise as you face it). Backward rotation will cause the belt to jump time or lose teeth.

Timing belt outer cover on the 2.3 engine

3. Remove the distributor cap. The rotor should point to the no. 1 cylinder plug wire tower.

4. Look through the access hole in the belt cover. The cam sprocket timing mark should be aligned with the timing pointer attached to the inner belt cover.

5. Loosen the adjustment bolts on the alternator, air pump, and a/c compressor (if equipped), and remove their drive belts. To provide clearance for removing the camshaft belt, remove the fan and its pulley from the water pump shaft.

6. Remove the belt outer cover. Note that there are tubular spacers underneath the two lower bolts.

7. Loosen the belt tensioner adjustment and pivot bolts. Lever the belt tensioner away from the belt and retighten the adjustment bolt to hold it away.

8. Remove the crankshaft pulley. It is held on by a single center bolt. Remove the belt guide behind it also.

9. Remove the camshaft drive belt. If it is not to be replaced, inspect it carefully for wear, cracks, or broken or missing teeth.

Proper timing belt alignment during belt installation on the 2.3 engine

Timing chain tensioner adjustment with the front cover installed—1.8 and 2.0 engines

If it shows any signs of wear, replace it.

10. With the belt still removed, turn the crankshaft until the key is vertical. Remove the distributor cap and set the distributor rotor to the no. 1 firing position by turning the auxiliary shaft sprocket. Turn the camshaft sprocket until its timing mark is aligned with the pointer attached to the inner belt cover. (This step is not necessary if the engine is in time and set to TDC).

11. Install the timing belt, first over the crankshaft sprocket. Then push it on counterclockwise over the auxiliary sprocket and cam sprocket (from the bottom up on the auxiliary sprocket and from the intake to exhaust side on the cam sprocket). Adjust the belt fore and aft so it is centered on the sprockets.

12. Loosen the tensioner adjustment bolt, allowing it to spring back against the belt.

13. With the spark plugs removed, rotate the crankshaft two complete turns in the direction of normal rotation (clockwise as you face it). This will remove any slack from the belt. Torque the tensioner adjustment bolt to 14–21 ft. lbs., and pivot bolt to 28–40 ft. lbs.

14. Replace the belt guide and crankshaft pulley.

15. Replace the spark plugs, distributor cap, outer cover, fan and pulley, and drive belts for the alternator and accessories. Adjust the drive belt tension. Start the engine and check the ignition timing; adjusting as necessary.

Timing Chain Tensioner

REMOVAL & INSTALLATION

1.8L and 2.0L Engines

1. Remove the water pump.
2. Remove the tensioner cover.
3. Remove the attaching bolts from the tensioner. Remove the tensioner.
To install the tensioner:
4. Fully compress the snubber spring.

Insert a screwdriver into the tensioner release mechanism.

5. Without removing the screwdriver, insert the tensioner and align the bolt holes. Install and torque the bolts.

6. Adjust the chain tension as follows:
   a. Remove the two blind plugs and aluminum washers from the front cover.
   b. Loosen the guide strip attaching screws.
   c. Press the top of the chain guide strip through the adjusting hole in the cylinder head.
   d. Tighten the guide strip attaching screws.
   e. Remove the screwdriver from the tensioner and let the snubber take up the slack in the chain.
   f. Install the blind plugs and aluminum washers.
   g. Install the tensioner cover and gasket.
   h. Install a new gasket and water pump. Install the crankshaft pulley and drive belt and adjust the tension. Check the coolant system level.

Camshaft

REMOVAL & INSTALLATION

1.8L and 2.0L Engines

Perform this operation on a cold engine only.

1. On 1977 and earlier Courier models, scribe alignment marks on the hood hinges and remove the hood.
2. Drain the cooling system and remove the water pump.
3. Disconnect the coil wire and vacuum line from the distributor.
4. Rotate the crankshaft to place no. 1 cylinder on TDC of the compression stroke.

This can be determined by removing the spark plug and feeling compression with your thumb. When compression is felt, rotate the crankshaft until the pointer aligns with the TDC mark on the pulley.

5. Remove the plug wires and distributor cap. Remove the distributor.
6. Remove the valve cover.
7. Release the tension on the timing chain.
8. Remove the cylinder head bolts. Only do this on a cold engine.
9. Remove the rocker arm assembly.
10. Remove the nut, washer and distributor gear from the camshaft.
11. Remove the nut and washer holding the camshaft gear.
12. Remove the camshaft. Do not remove the camshaft gear from the timing chain. Be sure that the gear teeth and chain relationship is not disturbed. Wire the chain and cam gear in place so that they will not fall into the front cover.

To install the camshaft:
13. Clean all the gasket surfaces.
14. Clean the cylinder head bolt holes.
15. Coat the camshaft and bearings thoroughly with engine oil. Install the camshaft on the head and install the camshaft gear.
16. Check the valve timing.
17. Install the rocker arm assembly.
18. Install and torque the head bolts.
19. Install the cam gear washer and nut.
20. Install the distributor gear, washer, and nut.
21. Adjust the timing chain tension.
22. Check the camshaft end-play. It should be 0.001–0.007 in. If it exceeds 0.008 in., replace the thrust plate with a new one.
23. Install the distributor, distributor cap and plug wires.
24. Connect the vacuum line and coil wire.

Camshaft and related components—1.8 and 2.0 engines

25. Adjust the valve clearance cold. Install the valve cover and water pump. Fill the cooling system.

26. Run the engine and check for leaks. When normal operating temperature is reached, adjust the hot valve clearance.

27. Adjust the carburetor and ignition timing.

28. Install the air cleaner.

29. On 1977 and earlier models, install the hood.

2.3L Engines

You will need a special forked tool for this job. The forked tool is used to compress the hydraulic lash adjusters so that the cam followers may be removed and installed. You will also need a puller to remove the cam sprocket and a strip of teflon sealing tape (available at plumbing supply houses) for the cam sprocket bolt.

1. Turn the engine to TDC.

2. Remove the air cleaner. Number and remove the spark plug wires from the plugs. Remove the hose from the oil filler cap on the valve cover. Remove any other wires or hoses crossing the valve cover, and remove the valve cover.

3. Remove the camshaft belt outer cover.

You will need a forked compressing tool like this to remove the 2.3 cam followers

Camshaft follower depressing tool used on the 2.3 engine—see text

4. Loosen the belt tensioner adjuster and pivot bolts, and lever the tensioner away from the belt. Retighten the adjuster bolt to hold it away.

5. Slip the cam belt off the cam sprocket.

6. Remove the cam sprocket bolt and washer. Use a puller to remove the cam sprocket. Remove the belt guide.

7. Position the camshaft so that the base circle (low point) of the cam lobe is on the cam follower of the rearmost valve (#4 intake). Compress the lash adjuster with the forked tool, and withdraw the cam follower over the lash adjuster and out. It may also be necessary to compress the valve spring.

8. Repeat this procedure with all eight cam followers, working from the rear of the head to the front. Keep the followers in order; they must be returned to their original positions.

9. When all the followers have been removed, remove the two phillips head screws and washers and the retaining plate from the rear of the rear cam bearing tower.

10. Using a puller or a pointed piece of wood or plastic, pry the seal from the front of the camshaft. Slide the camshaft out through the front of the head.

Camshaft installation—2.3 engine

To install:

1. Coat the camshaft and bearings thoroughly with engine oil. Slide the cam into the head.

2. Replace the retaining plate, screws and washers. Press a new front cam seal into place. Oil the lips of the seal before installation.

3. Coat the valve tips with Lubriplate® or its equivalent. Coat each cam follower with engine oil.

4. Working from the front to the rear, replace the cam followers. Rotate the cam so that the base circle of the cam lobe for the appropriate valve is facing the head. Use the forked tool to compress the lash adjuster, and install the follower over the lash adjuster and valve stem. It may also be necessary to compress the valve spring, using the same tool. Be sure the cam followers are returned to their original valves.

Before rotating the camshaft to the proper position for the next valve, fully compress and release the lash adjuster of the cam follower just installed. It is imperative that this is done to prevent the adjusters from pumping up and providing incorrect clearance.

5. Slide the cam belt guide into place over the key. Install the cam sprocket over the key. Wrap the sprocket bolt threads with teflon tape, and install the bolt and washer.

6. Measure the camshaft end play. Push the cam to the rear of the head. Install a dial indicator so that the point is on the cam sprocket. By inserting a large screwdriver between the cam sprocket and head, lever the cam forward and release it. If the end play measures more than 0.009 in., the retaining plate must be replaced.

7. Turn the cam until its sprocket timing mark lines up with the indicator on the belt sprocket, pushing it on from the intake side to the exhaust side. Adjust the belt fore and aft on the sprocket so that it is centered.

8. Release the cam belt tensioner so that it springs back against the belt. Remove the spark plugs. Using a wrench on the crankshaft pulley, rotate the engine two complete turns to remove slack from the belt. Rotate the engine in the normal direction of rotation (clockwise as you face it).

9. Tighten the belt tensioner adjuster bolt to 14–21 ft. lbs., the pivot bolt to 28–40 ft. lbs. Check the belt timing.

10. Replace the belt outer cover.

11. Install a new gasket on the valve cover with sealer, and install the valve cover. Replace the spark plugs, spark plug wires, oil filler cap hose, air cleaner, and any other hoses or wires disconnected.

Auxiliary Shaft

REMOVAL & INSTALLATION

2.3L Engine Only

1. Set the engine to TDC.
2. Remove the camshaft drive (timing) belt as previously outlined.
3. Remove the auxiliary shaft sprocket. It is held on by a single center bolt and washer. You will probably need a puller to get the sprocket off the shaft.
4. Remove the distributor as previously outlined.
5. Remove the auxiliary shaft cover and retaining plate.
6. Remove the shaft through the front of the block.

NOTE: Do not allow the distributor drive gear to touch the bearing surfaces in the block.

To install:

1. Because the auxiliary shaft cover gasket is shared with the cylinder front (timing) cover, you will have to carefully cut off the old gasket around the marks left by the cover, if it did not tear and pull off when you removed the cover. Scrape off any traces of the old gasket, and cut a new gasket to fit. Do not install the new gasket yet.
2. Coat the auxiliary shaft, bearings, and gear with engine oil.
3. Slide the shaft into place, being careful not to bang the gear into the bearings.
4. Replace the retaining plate. Coat the new gasket with a thin layer of sealer and install onto the front of the block. Install the cover.
5. Install the distributor.
6. Install the auxiliary shaft sprocket, washer, and bolt.
7. Remove the distributor cap. Turn the auxiliary shaft sprocket until the distributor rotor points to the no. 1 spark plug tower position. The camshaft and crankshaft should still be at the TDC position.
8. Install the camshaft drive belt, outer cover, belts, fan and pulley as previously outlined.

Pistons and Connecting Rods

REMOVAL & INSTALLATION

Piston, connecting rod, and piston ring removal and installation are detailed in the Engine Rebuilding section. Removal and installation are outlined with the engine out of the truck, but the same procedures may be used with the block in the chassis.

Apply a light coat of oil to all parts before reassembly. You may need to start the piston pin back into place with a few taps of a soft mallet. Always check the fit of new rings in the cylinder in which they are to

Piston and connecting rod relationship—1.8 and 2.0 engines

Piston and connecting rod relationship—2.3 engine

Piston ring positioning on the piston—2.3 engine

be used before installing. Press them square in the bore with a piston before measuring.

Piston installation position is shown in the illustrations. On the 1.8 and 2.0 space the piston rings 120° apart, so that the gaps are not located on the thrust side or piston pin side.

On the 2.3, install the rings as shown. Be very careful when reinstalling pistons not to nick the crankshaft journals with the connecting rod bolts. Cover the bolts with a length of hose for protection.

Crankshaft

REMOVAL & INSTALLATION

Main bearings may be replaced without removing the crankshaft. If the crankshaft

must be removed, it is recommended that the engine be removed from the vehicle and mounted in a work stand. Refer to the Engine Rebuilding section.

LUBRICATION— GASOLINE PISTON ENGINES

Oil Pan

REMOVAL & INSTALLATION

1. Raise and support the truck.
2. Remove the engine skid plate (1.8 and 2.0).
3. Drain the engine oil.
4. Remove the clutch release cylinder attaching nuts. Let the cylinder hang.
5. Remove the engine rear brace attaching bolts and loosen the bolts on the left side.
6. Disconnect the emission line from the oil pan (some 1.8s).
7. Remove the oil pan nuts and bolts and let the oil pan rest on the crossmember. The 2.3 oil pan is held on by 18 16 mm long bolts and washers around the perimeter, and 4 20mm long bolts and washers. These must be returned to their original positions.
8. Remove the oil pump pickup tube from the pump (1.8 and 2.0).
9. Remove the oil pan.
To install the oil pan:
10. Clean all the gasket surfaces.
11. Clean the oil pan, oil pump pickup tube and oil pump screen.
12. Install a new oil pan gasket with oil-resistant sealer. There are two side gaskets and a front and rear seal on the 2.3. The seals go on to the engine block, and the side pan gaskets go onto the pan. Refer to the illustration.
13. Install the oil pump pickup tube and screen (1.8 and 2.0).
14. Install the oil pan on the block. Torque the bolts to 5–8 ft. lbs.
15. Connect the emission line to the oil pan, if applicable.
16. Attach the rear engine bracket. Torque the bolts to specification.
17. Install the clutch release cylinder.
18. Replace the engine skid plate.
19. Lower the truck. Fill the crankcase, and run the engine. Check for leaks and oil pressure.

Oil Pump

REMOVAL & INSTALLATION

1.8L and 2.0L Engines

1. Remove the oil pan.

DRAIN PLUG – 6730

OIL PAN 6675

M6X 16.0 MM LONG SCREW AND WASHER-18 PLACES

M8X 20.0 LONG SCREW AND WASHER 4 PLACES

PAN GASKET (R) 6710

PAN GASKET (L) 6711

SEAL-6723

SEAL-6722

GUIDE PINS

HOLE

OIL-RESISTANT SEALER APPROX. 0.125" WIDE BEAD TO JOINT OF BLOCK AND FRONT COVER

OIL PAN GASKET (REF.)

FRONT COVER OR REAR CAP

BLOCK

SEAL TAB

FRONT

Oil pan gasket installation—2.3 engine

2. Remove the oil pump gear attaching nut.

3. Remove the bolts attaching the oil pump to the block. Loosen the gear on the pump.

4. Remove the oil pump and gear.

To install the oil pump:

5. Install the oil pump gear in the chain.

6. Prime the oil pump and install it on the gear and cylinder block. Install the bolts and torque them to 13–20 ft. lbs.

7. Install the washer, gear and nut. Bend the locktab on the washer.

8. Install the oil pan. Fill the engine with oil. Start the engine and check for oil pressure. Check for leaks.

2.3L Engines

The oil pump is mounted on the bottom of the engine block and is enclosed by the oil pan. To remove the pump, remove the oil pan, attaching bolts, and the pump. When installing, use a new gasket, and fill the pump with oil to prime it.

OIL PUMP INSPECTION

Courier

1. Thoroughly wash the pump with cleaning solvent.

2. Visually inspect the pump rotor and race for damage.

3. Visually check the mating surface of the pump cover for excessive wear and/or

damage. Replace the pump cover if necessary.

4. Using a feeler gauge, measure the clearance between the pump (outer) race and the pump body. The measurement should be within the following range: .001–.013 in. for 2.3 liter engines; .006–.010 in. for 1.8 and 2.0 liter engines.

5. Place a straightedge across the pump housing and measure the distance between the pump housing and the pump rotor/race, using a feeler gauge. The total clearance (rotor end-play) should be within the following range: .002–.004.

6. Measure the outer diameter of the pump shaft and the inner diameter of the corresponding housing bearing bore. The difference between these two measurements should be within the following range: .0015–.0030.

The pump cover is the only part of the pump which is serviced separately from the pump assembly. If any of the previous measurements exceed the specification limits, or if damage to the pump is apparent, the entire pump assembly must be replaced.

Mazda

1. Measure the clearance between the lobes of the rotors with a feeler gauge. If the clearance exceeds 0.010 in., replace both rotors.

2. Check the clearance between the outer rotor and the pump body with a feeler gauge.

Clearance should be 0.006–0.010 in. If it exceeds 0.012 in., replace the pump.

3. Place a straight-edge across the pump body and measure the clearance between the rotor and the straight-edge with a feeler gauge. Then, place a straight-edge across the pump cover and measure the clearance between the straight-edge and the cover. The combined clearances is the rotor end float. If it is 0.006 in. or more, correct it by grinding the cover. End float should be 0.002–0.004 in.

Oil Pump Chain

TENSION CHECK AND ADJUSTMENT

1.8L and 2.0L Engines

Oil pump chain tension can be checked with a straightedge and a ruler. Lay the straightedge against the oil pump and crankshaft gears, alongside the chain. Depress the chain and measure the slack with a ruler. If slack exceeds 0.157 inches, the chain tension will have to be adjusted. Chain slack is reduced by the addition of shims between the oil pump and the cylinder block. The shims should be of equal thickness on each side of the pump.

Rear Main Oil Seal

REMOVAL & INSTALLATION

1.8L and 2.0L Engines

If the rear main oil seal is being replaced independently of any other parts, it can be done with the engine in place. If the rear main oil seal and the rear main bearing are being replaced together, the engine must be removed from the truck.

1. Remove the transmission.

2. Remove the clutch disc, pressure plate and flywheel.

3. Using an awl, punch two holes in the crankshaft rear oil seal. They should be punched on opposite sides of the crankshaft, just above the bearing cap-to-cylinder block split line.

4. Install a sheet metal screw in each hole. Pry against both screws at the same time to remove the oil seal. Do not scratch the oil seal surface on the crankshaft.

5. Clean the oil recess in the cylinder block and bearing cap. Clean the oil seal surface on the crankshaft.

6. Coat the oil seal surfaces with oil. Coat the oil seal surface and the seal surface on the crankshaft with Lubriplate®. Install the oil seal and be sure that it is not cocked. Be sure that the seal surface was not damaged.

7. Install the flywheel. Coat the threads of the flywheel attaching bolts with oil-resistant sealer. Torque the bolts to specification, in sequence, across from each other.

Rear main seal installation—2.3 engine

DIP SEALS IN ENGINE OIL BEFORE INSTALLING

REAR BEARING CAP

REAR OIL SEAL

TAB

UPPER AND LOWER SEAL ENDS TO BE FLUSH IN BLOCK AND CAP

APPLY SEALER AS SHOWN SEE NOTE BELOW

SEALER NOTE: CLEAN THE AREA WHERE SEALER IS TO BE APPLIED BEFORE INSTALLING THE SEALS. USE FORD SPOT REMOVER B7A-19521-A OR EQUIVALENT. AFTER THE SEALS ARE IN PLACE, APPLY A 1/16 INCH BEAD OF C3AZ-19562-A OR -B SEALER AS SHOWN. SEALER MUST NOT CONTACT SEALS.

FRONT OF ENGINE

LOCATING TAB

8. Install the clutch, pressure plate, and transmission.

2.3L Engines

1. Remove the oil pan. It may also be necessary to remove the oil pump to provide access to the main bearing cap bolts.

2. Loosen all the main bearing cap bolts, thereby lowering the crankshaft slightly, but not more than 1/32 in.

3. Remove the rear main bearing cap, and remove the oil seal from the bearing cap and cylinder block. Install a small sheet metal screw in one end of the cylinder block half of the seal, and pull on the screw to remove the seal. Be careful not to scratch the seal surfaces.

4. Clean the seal grooves in the cap and block with solvent (such as lacquer thinner). Use a brush to get behind the groove lip. Dry the area thoroughly. No solvent should remain to come in contact with the seal.

5. Dip the new seal halves in clean engine oil.

6. Carefully install the upper seal (block half) into its groove with the undercut side of the seal toward the front of the engine, by rotating it on the seal journal of the crankshaft until the ends are flush with the parting surface. Be sure that no rubber has been shaved off. Wipe the oil from the mating surface of the bearing cap and cylinder block.

7. Tighten the bearing cap bolts to 80–90 ft. lbs.

8. Install the lower seal in the rear main bearing cap with the undercut side of the seal toward the front of the engine. Be sure that the seal ends are flush with the parting surface to mate with the upper seal when the cap is installed.

NOTE: Install the seals so that the locating tab faces the rear of the engine.

9. Apply a *small* amount of silicone sealer to the mating surface of the bearing cap. No sealer should come in contact with the rubber seals when the bearing cap is installed and tightened.

10. Install the rear main bearing cap and torque to 80–90 ft. lbs.

11. Install the oil pump (if removed) and oil pan. Fill the crankcase with oil, and operate the engine, checking for leaks.

COOLING SYSTEM— GASOLINE PISTON ENGINES

Water Pump

REMOVAL & INSTALLATION

1.8L and 2.0L Engines

1. Drain the cooling system. Remove the fan shroud, if so equipped.

2. Remove the lower hose from the water pump.

3. Disconnect the upper radiator hose from the engine and the lower radiator hose at the radiator.

4. Remove the radiator.

5. Remove the drive belts.

6. Remove the fan and pulley. Remove the crankshaft pulley.

7. Disconnect the coolant bypass hoses from the water pump.

8. Unbolt and remove the water pump. To install the water pump:

9. Clean the gasket surfaces of the water pump and cylinder block.

10. Install the water pump and new gasket on the block. Torque the bolts to specification.

11. Install the lower hose on the water pump. Install the bypass hoses.

12. Install the fan and pulley. Install the crankshaft pulley.

13. Install the drive-belts and adjust the crankshaft pulley.

14. Install the radiator.

15. Refill the cooling system with the specified amount and type of coolant. Install the radiator cap and start the engine. Check for leaks.

2.3L Engine

1. Drain the cooling system.

2. Disconnect the lower radiator hose and heater hose from the water pump.

3. Remove the alternator, air pump, and air conditioner drive belts. Remove the fan shroud, if your truck has one.

4. Remove the fan and pulley.

5. Remove the camshaft drive belt outer cover.

6. Remove the water pump attaching bolts and the water pump. It is not necessary to remove the belt inner cover. To install:

1. Clean all gasket material from the mating surfaces.

2. Transfer the heater hose fitting to the new water pump.

3. Coat the new gasket with sealer and position the pump and gasket on the engine.

4. Install the pump mounting bolts.

5. Install the belt outer cover, fan and pulley, and accessory drive belts. Install the fan shroud, if equipped.

6. Connect the radiator hose.

7. Fill the cooling system. Turn the heater on, install the radiator and coolant recovery tank caps, and run the engine. Check for leaks. When the engine has cooled, check the coolant level, and add as necessary.

Radiator

REMOVAL & INSTALLATION

1. Drain the cooling system.

2. If equipped, remove the fan shroud.

3. Remove the fan. On California models, remove the fan clutch.

4. Disconnect the upper and lower radiator hoses. If your truck has automatic transmission, disconnect and plug the fluid cooler lines at the bottom of the radiator.

5. Unbolt and remove the radiator.

OUTLET CONNECTION

THERMOSTAT—OUTLET
SIDE TO RADIATOR
GASKET

GASKET

FRONT OF
ENGINE

SEALS TO
BE FLUSH WITH
TOP OF COVER

STUD AND WASHER
SEALING TYPE

WATER PUMP

BOLT-SEALING TYPE

BELT
COVER INNER

Water pump and thermostat—2.3 engine. It is not necessary to remove the inner timing belt cover to replace the pump.

To install the radiator:

6. Install the radiator against the supports and tighten the mounting bolts.

7. Install the hoses on the radiator. Tighten the clamps. Install the automatic transmission cooler lines, if removed.

8. Install the fan and fan clutch (California models).

9. If equipped, install the fan shroud.

10. Refill the cooling system with the specified amount and type of coolant. Run the engine and check for leaks.

Thermostat

REMOVAL & INSTALLATION

1.8L and 2.0L Engines

1. Drain enough coolant to bring the coolant level down below the thermostat housing. The thermostat housing is located on the left front side of the cylinder block. Disconnect the temperature sending unit wire.

2. Remove the coolant outlet elbow. If so equipped, position the vacuum control valve out of the way. The vacuum control valve is not used on California models.

3. Disconnect the coolant by-pass hose from the thermostat housing on Couriers only.

4. Remove the thermostat and housing from the engine.

5. Remove the thermostat from the housing and note the position of the jiggle pin.

To install the thermostat:

6. Remove all gasket material from the parts.

7. Install the thermostat housing using a new gasket with water-resistant sealer.

8. Position the thermostat in the housing with the jiggle pin up. Coat a new gasket with sealer and install it on the thermostat housing.

9. Install the coolant outlet elbow and vacuum control valve (if equipped).

10. Connect the by-pass and radiator hoses.

11. Connect the temperature sending unit wire.

12. Fill the cooling system with the proper coolant. Operate the engine and check the coolant level. Check for leaks.

2.3L Engine

1. Drain the coolant so that the level is below the thermostat.

2. It is not necessary to remove the hose from the outlet connection, if you're careful. Remove the two bolts holding the outlet to the block and pull it away enough to provide access to the thermostat.

3. Remove the thermostat and gasket. To install:

1. Clean the mounting surface and outlet housing of all old gasket material.

2. Coat a new gasket with silicone sealer. The gasket must go on before the thermostat.

3. Position the gasket against the engine, then place the thermostat on top of it with the outlet side towards the radiator.

4. Install the coolant outlet and the two retaining bolts. Torque the bolts to 14–21 ft. lbs. Refill the cooling system, start the engine, and check for leaks and proper thermostat operation.

ENGINE MECHANICAL— DIESEL

REMOVAL & INSTALLATION

1. Remove the hood.

2. Disconnect the negative battery cable. Remove the air cleaner.

3. Drain the engine oil. Drain the cooling system by removing drain plugs in both the block and radiator.

4. Disconnect wiring in the order shown:

   a. B terminal wire at the alternator.

   b. Engine ground wire at the mount.

   c. Oil pressure sending unit wire.

   d. Water temperature sending unit wire.

   e. Bullet connector at fuel solenoid valve.

   f. B terminal cable and S terminal wire on the starter.

   g. Glow plug connector

   h. Temperature switch connector

   i. QSS relay connector

5. Disconnect the following linkages, hoses, etc. from the engine

   a. The accelerator cable at the injection pump.

   b. Fuel line

   c. Overflow line

   d. Heater hoses

   e. Upper and lower radiator hoses. Disconnect these also at the radiator and remove them.

   f. Exhaust pipe at the manifold

   g. Clutch slave cylinder

5. Remove the following items for clearance:

   a. Cooling fan and shroud.

   b. Radiator and oil cooler.

   c. Exhaust pipe hanger

6. Support the transmission with a floorjack.

7. Remove the transmission-to-engine supporting bolts.

8. Install a suitable lifting sling and connect it to all engine lifting hooks. Put tension on the sling until all slack is removed.

9. Remove the engine mounting bolts arrowed in the illustration.

Remove arrowed engine mount bolts

Disconnecting wiring for 2200 diesel engine removal

9. Bleed the fuel system as described in the fuel system section.

Exhaust Manifold

REMOVAL & INSTALLATION

1. Unbolt the exhaust pipe from the manifold at the flange and disconnect it.

2. Remove exhaust manifold bolts and remove the manifold.

3. Clean all gasket surfaces and replace gaskets. Then, position gasket and manifold and install bolts. Torque in an alternating pattern to 12–17 ft. lbs.

4. Reconnect exhaust pipe and torque nuts to 20–22 ft. lbs.

Rocker Arms and Shaft

REMOVAL & INSTALLATION

1. Drain the cooling system. Disconnect the breather hose and remove the valve cover.

2. Loosen all head bolts in reverse of torque sequence. (See valve adjustment procedure, above). Remove the four bolts that hold the rocker shaft assembly onto the head. Remove the assembly.

Rocker arms and shafts

10. Pull the engine forward until it clears the clutch shaft, and then remove it from the vehicle.

11. Installation is the reverse of removal.

Intake Manifold

REMOVAL & INSTALLATION

1. Remove the air cleaner and intake piping.

2. Disconnect the temperature switch connector at the front of the block. Following the same part of the harness over to a connector leading to the alternator on the exhaust side of the block and disconnect the multi-prong connector there. Now, remove this branch of the harness away from the intake manifold for clearance.

3. Disconnect the fuel return line going into the injection pump from the top. Disconnect the vacuum line going to the 3-way vacuum valve mounted on the manifold.

4. Disconnect the vacuum sensing tube where it is mounted to the intake tube. Unbolt the injection line clamp from the manifold, and remove the clamp. Remove the injection lines by unbolting them at the pump and injectors and remove them (see injection line removal and installation under fuel

system service below). Remove the crankcase ventilation breather hose.

5. Unbolt and remove the manifold. Clean all gasket surfaces.

6. Install the manifold over a new gasket and torque bolts in an alternating pattern to 12–17 ft. lbs.

7. Refer to fuel system service and reinstall injection lines. Use torque figures specified there.

8. Install remaining items in reverse of the removal procedure.

Removing vacuum hose from 3-way valve. Note the injection line clamp on the right

3. Inspect all surfaces for excessive, uneven wear or cracks. Make sure all oil passages are clear. You can replace worn rockers by removing snap rings, washers and springs as shown.

4. To install, position the rocker shaft assembly on the head and install mounting bolts. Then, retorque all head bolts in the order shown in the valve adjusting procedure. If new rockers or associated parts have been installed, adjust as described in the valve adjusting procedure.

5. Reinstall the valve cover with a new gasket and refill the engine with coolant. Run the engine until hot.

6. Remove valve cover, retorque the head, and adjust all valves. Re-install the valve cover. Run the engine and check for leaks.

VALVE ARRANGEMENT

For a diagram of valve arrangement, see the valve adjustment procedure, above.

Cylinder Head

REMOVAL & INSTALLATION

1. Disconnect the battery and remove the air cleaner. Remove the hood.

2. Drain the cooling system.

3. If equipped with air conditioning, remove the compressor drive belt and unbolt the compressor from its mounting bracket. Tie the compressor out of the way. Do not remove any refrigerant lines.

4. Remove the alternator, drive belt and bracket.

5. Disconnect and move aside all hoses and cables above the valve cover.

6. Remove the injection nozzles, fuel lines, and glow plugs (see fuel system service, below).

7. Remove the thermostat housing and valve cover.

8. Remove the intake and exhaust manifolds as described above.

9. Loosen all head bolts in reverse of the torque sequence shown in the valve adjustment procedure.

10. Remove the rocker arm assembly. Remove the pushrods, keeping them in exact order and marking for reassembly in the same position.

11. With a suitable hoist and sling, using the hooks bolted to the head, remove it.

12. Use a straightedge and feeler gauges to check the head for distortion. Maximums are .004 in. along lines A and B, and .010 in. along C, D, E and F.

13. Reinstall the head, with a new gasket, generally in reverse order. Note the following points in reassembly:
Make sure pushrods are arranged in order.
Torque head bolts to 80–85 ft. lbs. in the order shown in the valve adjustment procedure. Then, adjust the valves.
Complete the reinstallation, including refilling the cooling system. Run the engine

Cylinder Head bolt torque sequence— Mazda 2200 diesel engine

until it reaches operating temperature. Then, remove the valve cover, retorque the head and readjust the valves. Replace the valve cover, run the engine and check for leaks. Check coolant level and refill as necessary.

Timing Cover

REMOVAL & INSTALLATION

1. Remove the radiator, hoses, fan, and belts as described below in the cooling system service section for this engine.

2. Remove the crankshaft bolt and, with a puller, remove the crankshaft pulley.

3. Remove the attaching bolts, and remove the cover and gasket.

4. Clean all gasket surfaces. Use a new gasket coated with sealer. Position the cover over the crankshaft carefully, being careful not to damage the seal. The cover will end up over the locating dowels.

5. Install the cover bolts, torquing to 12–17 ft. lbs. in several stages.

6. Reverse the remaining removal steps. Torque the crankshaft pulley to 145–180 ft. lbs.

Timing Cover Oil Seal

REMOVAL & INSTALLATION

NOTE: This procedure requires a special tool, a specially designed oil seal puller and installer, Mazda 49 0559 205 or equivalent.

1. Perform Steps 1 and 2 of the procedure above.

2. Screw the puller bolt into the crankshaft bolt threads, and then, when the puller seats, reverse rotation to draw out the old seal.

Oil seal puller and installer for front cover oil seal

3. To install the new seal, coat the outside of the new seal with oil. Remove retracting fingers from the tool. Start the seal into the timing cover hole. Install the installer and start its bolt into the crankshaft threads. Then, turn the bolt clockwise until the installer just seats on the timing cover. Then, remove the installer.

4. Reinstall the crankshaft pulley and bolt, torquing the bolt to 145–180 ft. lbs. Reverse the procedures of Step 1 in the procedure above.

Timing Gear

REMOVAL & INSTALLATION

NOTE: This procedure requires a special puller set Mazda part 49 0839 425c or equivalent.

1. Remove the timing cover as de-

Checking the cylinder head for warping

Make sure to assemble timing gears so match marks align as shown

scribed in the "Timing Cover Removal & Installation" procedure above.

2. To remove the cam gear, bite a clean cloth between camshaft gear and its idler gear. Then, install the puller via bolts as shown, and turn the puller handle clockwise to remove the gear.

3. Remove the crankshaft timing gear by utilizing the puller with fingers installed as shown.

4. To install, reverse above procedures, making sure each gear's single match mark is between double matchmarks on the adjacent idler gear and aligning keys and keyways. Torque the camshaft gear bolt to 45–51 ft. lbs.

Use the puller illustrated or the equivalent, in the manner shown, to pull cam gear and crankshaft timing gear

Camshaft

REMOVAL

NOTE: To perform this procedure, you must have an engine stand capable of safely supporting the engine and turning it to an upside-down position.

Checking cam height with a micrometer

NOTE: Refer to appropriate procedures above and below as necessary.

1. Remove the engine from the vehicle.
2. Remove the crankshaft pulley, alternator, water pump, and timing gear cover.
3. Remove the oil pan and oil pump.
4. Remove the camshaft and crankshaft gears.
5. Disconnect all injection pump fuel lines.
6. Remove the timing case and injection pump as a unit. Carefully store this assembly so the pump remains in an upright position.
7. Remove the valve cover, loosen headbolts, and remove the rocker assembly. Remove pushrods and mark them for installation in the same position.
8. Invert the engine so all the lifters move to the tops of their bores.
9. Remove the bolts retaining the thrust plate. Slide the camshaft out very carefully to avoid damage to the bearings.

INSPECTION

1. Check camshaft for cracks, cuts and damage to lobes or journals. Repair minor damage with fine wet stone.
2. Check cam height and replace camshaft if lift is less than 42.49 mm (1.67 in.).
3. Measure camshaft bearing journal diameter and replace if wear exceeds limits.

4. Check camshaft runout. It should not exceed 0.08 mm (0.0003 in.).
5. Measure the camshaft end play and replace the thrust plate if the value exceeds 0.3 mm (0.0118 in.). Measure by inserting a feeler gauge between the thrust plate and side of the cam gear.
6. Check the oil clearances by measuring the inner diameter of the camshaft bearing in the cylinder block and the outer diameter of the cam journal. If the oil clearance exceeds 0.145 mm (0.0057 in.) replace the camshaft or cylinder block.

INSTALLATION

1. Install in exact reverse order, noting the following points:
   a. Oil the camshaft bearing surfaces with engine oil before inserting it into the bearing bores. Insert carefully to avoid nicking cam or bearing surfaces.
   b. Torque the camshaft thrust plate to 12–17 ft. lbs.
   c. When reinstalling gears, see the procedure above, "Timing Gear Removal & Installation" for proper timing of gearteeth and torque figures.
   d. After the camshaft is in position, turn the engine right side up. When installing pushrods, make sure they are in their original positions. Push downward lightly on each to make sure each cam follower is riding on its cam.

Checking runout with V-blocks and a dial indicator. Rotate the cam after zeroing the indicator and look for a reading of less than .0003 in.

Checking end play

e. When installing the rocker shaft assembly, make sure to locate each pushrod in its rocker socket before attempting to put the assembly in its final position. Install rocker assembly mounting bolts and then torque all head bolts in the proper sequence to 80–85 ft. lbs. Make sure that after oil and water have been installed you run the engine until hot, retorque the head bolts to specification, and then readjust the valves.

f. Make sure to torque the injection line flare nuts to 18.1–21.7 ft. lbs. and bleed the fuel system.

Pistons and Connecting Rods

REMOVAL & INSTALLATION

NOTE: Refer to the Unit Repair Section on Engine rebuilding for general information. Refer to procedures above and below for engine removal and major disassembly operations.

1. Remove the engine from the vehicle. Remove the oil pan and cylinder head. Remove the oil pump and supply lines.

2. Mark the connecting rod caps and rods. Then, remove the rod caps. Wipe oil from the journal and bearing. Insert a Plastigage® insert in the axial direction along the journal of No. 1 cylinder. Reinstall the connecting rod cap and torque nuts to 50–54 ft. lbs. Remove the cap and measure the width of the mark on the Plastigage®. Standard oil clearance is .0014–.0030 in. with a wear limit of .0039 in. If the crankpins are worn past the limit, the shaft must be machined for use of undersize bearings which are available for .010, .020, .030 in. under the standard dimension. Repeat the clearance measuring procedure for each of the four connecting rod bearings.

3. Measure the end-play of each connecting rod big end with a dial indicator. Push the rod away from the indicator as far as it will go. Mount the indicator with the pin directly against the side of the rod. Push the rod as far as it will go away from the indicator. Zero the indicator, and then pull the rod as far as it will go toward the indicator. The clearance must be .0157 in. or less, or the rod must be replaced.

Checking rod bearing clearance with Plastigauge®

4. Now remove all the rod caps. Check the condition of cylinder bores. If there is a substantial ridge above the stroke of the top ring in the cylinder bore, remove it with a ridge reamer. Do this for every cylinder. The pistons and rods may now be removed by pushing upward on rods from underneath. Make sure you measure crankpin diameter as described in the procedure below.

5. Matchmark all parts. Then, remove circlips and push the piston pins out of the pistons. Mark the pins, too.

INSPECTION

1. Inspect side surfaces of the rod at big and small ends. Replace the rod if there are excessive cracking or other damage.

2. Check the rod for a bent or twisted condition with a connecting rod aligner. The limit is .0020 in. per 3.9371 in. of length.

3. Assemble each pin into the rod bush, mount the assembly into a vise, and check the clearance between the pin and bush with a dial indicator. If the limit of .0020 in. is exceeded, replace the pin or have the small end of the rod re-bushed (or both) as necessary to bring within specified limits.

4. Inspect the wear surfaces of the piston for cracking or damage. This includes both the thrust surfaces on the side of the piston and ring grooves. Also inspect rings for breakage, thermal damage, or excessive wear, and replace as necessary. With rings installed on the pistons, force a feeler gauge between the top of the ring and top of ring groove. The limit is .012 in.

5. Ring end-gap must also be measured. On rings you're re-using, slip the ring into the most worn part of the cylinder, make sure it is square, and measure the end gap. It must not exceed .059 in. for any ring. New rings must also be checked, but at the least worn part of the cylinder (the very bottom). Make sure new rings meet the specifications in the chart at the beginning of this section.

6. Measure the piston dimension "H" (.62 in.) above the bottom of the skirt. Diameter must be 3.4984–3.4994 in.

7. Measure each of the cylinder liners top middle and bottom and at 90 degrees—that is, lengthwise and crosswise. Maximum dimension is 3.50080 in. Also, if the smallest dimension is as much as .0079 in.

Measuring piston diameter. Measure distance H above the skirt

less than the maximum dimension top-to-bottom, the liner must be replaced.

8. Compare these dimensions to verify that piston-to-liner clearance is .0021–.0031 in. If piston and liner each pass specifications, but clearance between the two is excessive, you may be able to bring the cylinder within spec by replacing the piston only. If cylinder liner replacement is required, you'll have to send the block to a machine shop for replacement with special tools and a large press.

REASSEMBLY

1. When assembling rods to pistons, make sure the locking groove for the upper part of the big-end bearing is opposite the combustion chamber in the piston.

2. Make sure stamped marks on the rings face upward when assembling them onto pistons.

Measure cylinder liners at locations and in directions shown

Install rings with stamped marks facing upward

Identify and install top, second, and oil rings by cross-sections shown. Stagger ring gaps as shown

3. Identify top, second, and oil rings by their cross-sections as shown, and stagger ring gaps as shown, also. This means that the gaps of top and second rings should be positioned opposite the combustion chamber in the piston, that no ring gap should

Assemble pistons and rods in the relationship shown. Install in the engine with the side of the piston indicated facing forward

be aligned with either thrust side of the piston, and that the top ring gap should be 180 degrees away from the oil control ring gap.

4. When installing the pistons, make sure to follow the positioning shown in the illustration relating rod and piston position. That is, the combustion chamber that is in the piston should end up on intake manifold side of the engine.

5. Reassemble the engine in reverse order, coating all wear surfaces with clean engine oil. Pay careful attention to all torque figures, and use new gaskets and seals wherever they are required. Make sure that after the cooling system and oil pan are refilled, the engine is run until hot and the head is retorqued and valves are adjusted. Check for leaks.

Crankshaft and Main Bearings

REMOVAL & INSTALLATION

1. Refer to appropriate procedures above and below. Remove the engine. Remove the flywheel and rear end-plate. Remove the rear main seal.

2. Remove the crankshaft pulley, fan, and fan pulley. Then, remove the timing gear cover and with a puller pull the crankshaft timing gear off the front of the crankshaft. Remove the oil pan, oil pump lines, and oil pump. Remove the rear main oil seal. Invert the engine on a stand.

3. Matchmark all main and connecting rod caps, and then remove. Check connecting rod big-end bearing clearances as described in the procedure above.

4. Check main bearing clearances with Plastigauge®. This involves placing a Plastigauge® strip along the diameter of the crankpin, and then reinstalling and torquing the cap to 80–85 ft. lbs.

NOTE: Make sure bearings are free of oil. Remove each cap and read the width of the mark that's left with the ruler supplied by Plastigauge®. Oil clearance is .0016–.0036 in., with a wear limit of .0047 in. If the wear limit is exceeded, the crankshaft will have to be machined

undersize and undersize bearings (.010, .020, or .030 in.) will have to be fitted.

NOTE: Throughout disassembly and inspection, make sure all main bearings and thrust washers (at center main) stay in their original positions.

Check end-play with a dial indicator. If it exceeds .0157 in., use a .007 oversize thrust washer set when reassembling.

5. Now remove the crank. It's best to use a hoist. Be careful not to allow crankpins or bearing journals to be damaged. Measure crank pin and main journal diameters at at least two locations across the width and at 90 degree angles. Wear limit for main journals is 2.571 in., and for crankpins it is 2.0846 in. Again, if the wear limit is exceeded, the crankshaft must be machined undersize and undersize bearings installed.

6. Inspect the crankshaft for cracks. If there is excessive cracking, the assembly must be replaced. Check all oil passages and clean them if necessary.

Measure main journal and crankpin diameters at locations shown

7. Support both ends of the crank on V-blocks. Locate the pin of a dial indicator against the center main journal and zero it. Then, rotate the crank slowly and read the gauge. The limit for runout is .0019 in.

8. If you can re-use main bearings because of wear that's still within limits, you must still inspect them for peeling, thermal damage, or evidence of melting. Replace any bearings that are damaged.

INSTALLATION

1. In reinstallation, make sure all wear surfaces are lubricated with clean engine

oil but that outside bearing surfaces remain dry. Make sure all bearings being re-used are in the same position. Make sure all bearing caps are installed with the arrow facing forward. Make sure the thrust washers at the center bearing are installed with oil grooves outward. Observe all torque figures.

2. Reverse all remaining assembly procedures, consulting applicable procedures above and below. Use new gaskets and seals wherever they have been disturbed and pay attention to all torque requirements.

Make sure all bearings are re-installed in original positions. Make sure all thrust washers are installed as shown

LUBRICATION SYSTEM—DIESEL

Oil Pans

REMOVAL & INSTALLATION

1. Raise the vehicle and support it securely.

2. Remove attaching bolts and remove the underengine cover.

3. Drain the oil pan. Then, remove the oil pan attaching bolts from either side, and remove the pan.

4. To install, first apply sealer as shown.

5. Using new gaskets on either side and either end, install the pan and start the bolts. Then, torque them evenly around the pan to 5–8 ft. lbs.

6. Replace the under-engine cover, drain plug, and oil. Run the engine to check for leaks.

Apply sealer as shown

Oil pan removal

Oil pump removal

Oil Pump

REMOVAL & INSTALLATION

1. Remove the oil pan as described above. Remove the oil pump set screw (1).

2. Remove the oil pipe attaching bolts (2) and remove the pump.

3. To install, reverse the removal procedure, torquing the oil pipe attaching bolts to 5.8–8.7 ft. lbs.

4. Apply sealing tape to the setscrew before installation. Then, replace the oil pan, refill, and run the engine to check for leaks.

Rear Main Oil Seal

REMOVAL & INSTALLATION

1. Remove the engine as described above.

2. Remove the clutch cover by slowly turning all clutch cover mounting bolts out in rotation to slowly release the tension on the clutch springs. Then, remove bolts, clutch cover, and disc.

3. Support the flywheel. Then remove the mounting bolts and washer, and remove the flywheel.

4. Remove the seal housing and seal.

5. Force the seal out of the housing with a mandrel, as shown. Then, coat the new seal's outer diameter with clean engine oil. Press the seal into the housing by tapping all around the outer diameter, using a flat plate and hammer, as shown.

NOTE: If the crankshaft surface where the seal rode is worn, put the seal into a position .12 in. away from its original position so it will not ride against the worn portion of the crank.

6. Install the seal housing and bolts, torquing bolts to 11–14 ft. lbs.

7. Install the flywheel, washer, and bolts, torquing bolts to 95–135 ft. lbs.

8. Put the clutch disc in position and hold with a clutch centering tool that inserts into the pilot bearing. Then, put the clutch

cover in position, start bolts, and turn them evenly in rotation until the clutch cover seats. Torque the cover bolts to 14–20 ft. lbs. Remove the centering tool.

9. Install the engine. Make sure to run the engine and check for leaks.

COOLING SYSTEM—DIESEL

Water Pump

REMOVAL & INSTALLATION

1. Drain the cooling system. Loosen the alternator mounts and take the tension off the V-belt.

2. Remove the four fan shroud mounting bolts, but leave the shroud in position.

3. Remove the nuts from the front of the fan hub. Then, slide the fan off the studs attaching it and the hub to the water pump shaft. Now, remove the fan and shroud together. Do not lay the fan down, but leave it propped in an upright position so that silicone fluid in the fan clutch will not migrate to the wrong part of the unit.

4. Pull the hub off the studs. Move the belt out of the way.

5. Loosen clamps and disconnect inlet and discharge hoses at the pump. Then, remove pump mounting bolts and remove the pump.

6. To install, coat a new gasket and pump and block surfaces with sealer. Put the pump in position and install bolts loosely. Then, tighten in several stages, going around the pump, to 12–17 ft. lbs.

7. Reconnect hoses and tighten clamps.

8. Put the fan hub in position on the mounting studs. Insert the fan into the fan shroud, and then put them into position in front of the engine.

Parts to be removed in water pump removal include the fan (1), drive belt (2) and fan hub (3)

Removal

Removal and installation of rear main seal from its housing

9. Install the fan clutch over the studs, and install nuts, tightening finger tight.

10. Install and tighten V-belt at alternator adjusting points. Now, tighten fan and hub mounting nuts.

11. Install and tighten fan shroud mounting screws.

12. Fill the system with antifreeze/water mix. Run the engine to check for leaks and refill radiator as necessary.

Radiator

REMOVAL & INSTALLATION

1. Allow the engine to cool. Then, remove the radiator cap and the drain plug that's at bottom center of the lower radiator tank.

2. Disconnect upper and lower hoses by loosening clamps and sliding them back, and then pulling hoses off the radiator piping.

3. Remove the four attaching bolts and remove the fan shroud from the rear of the radiator.

4. Remove the four radiator mounting bolts by removing the four mounting bolts at the sides, and remove the radiator.

5. Installation is the reverse of the removal procedure. Make sure to fill the cooling system completely and then recheck coolant level after the engine has purged itself of air. Check for leaks and retighten or reposition hose clamps as necessary.

Thermostat

REMOVAL & INSTALLATION

1. Allow the engine to cool and then remove the radiator cap. Drain coolant until the level is below the level of the cooling tubes in the top tank.

2. Loosen the hose clamp that's on the thermostat housing, and pull the upper radiator hose (2) off the housing.

3. Remove thermostat housing bolts (3) and then pull the housing (4) straight upward to remove it.

4. Remove the thermostat (5) and then remove the gasket.

Termostat installation—B2200

5. Coat both sides of a new gasket with sealer and then position the gasket on the thermostat housing.

6. Install a new thermostat with the bellows downward (see illustration).

7. Reverse the remaining removal procedures, tight-engine thermostat housing bolts evenly in several stages. Make sure the cooling system is full by rechecking radiator level after the engine has run at operating temperature.

EMISSION CONTROLS

NOTE: Basic diagnosis and repair of emissions systems (including the rotary engine) are covered in the Emission Control Unit Repair Section. A few items unique to Courier/Mazda vehicles are covered here.

Mazda/Courier 3-Way Solenoid Valve Testing

GASOLINE PISTON ENGINES

1. Disconnect the wiring to the water thermo switch and connect a jumper wire to the two connectors of the switch.

2. Disconnect the vacuum sensing tube from the EGR valve.

3. Disconnect the vacuum sensing tube which runs to the vacuum amplifier from the three way solenoid valve.

4. Turn the ignition switch on.

5. Blow through the solenoid valve from the tube disconnected from the EGR valve. Air should pass through the valve to the valve air filter.

6. Disconnect the jumper wire from the thermo switch.

7. Blow through the tube disconnected from the EGR valve and make sure the air passes through the opening to the vacuum amplifier tube.

8. If the solenoid valve does not operate properly, replace.

Diesel Engine Emissions

The B2200 has only 2 basic emission control systems—a crankcase ventilation system, and a system which maintains a slight vacuum in the intake manifold, known as the "Intake Shutter Valve System". The only maintenance required of the crankcase ventilation system is to occasionally check the cleanliness of the inside of the hose (see photo caption).

1. Baffle plate
2. Oil baffle plate
3. Bolt
4. Breather hose

The Mazda B2200 diesel crankcase ventilation system has no PCV valve and requires no periodic maintenance. Check the inside of the breather hose occasionally and clean with solvent, if necessary

INTAKE SHUTTER VALVE SYSTEM

The intake shutter valve system may require checking of the vacuum it generates and adjustment of the diaphragm that operates the air shutter. To check, remove the plug in the intake manifold. Install an adapter with metric threads in place of the plug, and connect a vacuum gauge. Disconnect the electrical connector at the 3-way valve. Then, start the engine and run it at idle. Now, read the vacuum gauge—it should read approx. 16.92 in.

If the reading is not correct, adjust the adjusting screw on the shutter valve (located just to the right of the vacuum gauge in the illustration, on the air intake). Then, stop the engine, reconnect the electrical connector, and replace the plug in the intake manifold.

3-WAY SOLENOID VALVE

1. Disconnect the vacuum line leading to the intake shutter valve diaphragm. Plug a vacuum gauge into the open end of the vacuum tube. Disconnect the electrical connector at the 3-way valve.
2. Run the engine at idle and check for vacuum. If vacuum is present, the 3-way valve is ok. If not, replace it.
3. Remove the vacuum gauge and reconnect the vacuum line and electrical connector.

GASOLINE FUEL SYSTEM

Carburetor

REMOVAL & INSTALLATION

Rotary Engine

1. Remove the air cleaner assembly complete with its hoses and mounting bracket.
2. Detach the choke and accelerator cables from the carburetor.
3. Disconnect the fuel and vacuum lines from the carburetor.
4. Remove the oil line which runs to the metering oil pump, at the carburetor.
5. Remove all electrical wiring from carburetor.
6. Remove the carburetor attaching nuts and/or bolts, gasket or head insulator, and remove the carburetor.

Installation is performed in the reverse order of removal. Use a new gasket.

Piston Engines

1. Remove the air cleaner and duct.

2. Disconnect the accelerator shaft from the throttle lever.
3. Disconnect and plug the fuel supply and fuel return lines.
4. Disconnect the leads from the throttle solenoid and decelleration valve at the quick-disconnects.
5. Disconnect the carburetor-to-distributor vacuum line.
6. Disconnect the throttle return spring.
7. Disconnect the choke cable.
8. Remove the carburetor attaching nuts from the intake manifold studs and remove the carburetor. The attaching nuts are tucked underneath the carburetor body and are difficult to reach; a small socket with an "L" shaped hex drive, or a short, thin wrench sold for work on ignition systems will make removal easier.

To install the carburetor:
9. Install a new carburetor gasket on the manifold.
10. Install the carburetor and tighten the carburetor attaching nuts.

11. Connect the various wires and hoses to the carburetor, adjust the choke and accelerator linkage, start the engine, and check for fuel or vacuum leaks.

FAST IDLE ADJUSTMENT

Courier

1977–78

1. Remove the air cleaner.
2. With the choke plate fully closed, measure the clearance between the primary throttle plate and the wall of the throttle bore. The clearance should measure 0.071 in 1977–78, or 0.067 in. for 1977–78 California models.
3. If the clearance is not as specified, bend the fast idle lever where it contacts the throttle lever tang until the proper clearance is obtained.
4. Install the air cleaner.

Exploded view of piston engine carburetor

1. Air horn
2. Choke valve lever
3. Clip
4. Choke lever shaft
5. Screw
6. Setscrew
7. Spring
8. Choke valve
9. Connector
10. Connecting rod
11. Spring
12. Fuel return valve
13. Hanger
14. Screw
15. Ring
16. Bolt
17. Carburetor body
18. Bolt
19. Diaphragm cover
20. Screw
21. Diaphragm
22. Accelerator pump arm
23. Float
24. Gasket
25. Connecting rod
26. Spring
27. Spring
28. Small venturi
29. Small venturi
30. Bolt
31. Check ball plug
32. Steel ball
33. Flange
34. Throttle shaft
35. Throttle shaft
36. Throttle lever
37. Spring washer
38. Nut
39. Lock
40. Adjusting arm
41. Starting lever
42. Arm
43. Screw
44. Gasket
45. Valve
46. Screw
47. Throttle valve
48. Throttle lever link
49. Ring
50. Throttle return spring
51. Arm
52. Retainer
53. Metering pump lever
54. Metering pump arm
55. Screw
56. Pin
57. Union bolt
58. Cover
59. Diaphragm spring
60. Diaphragm lever
61. Diaphragm pin
62. Diaphragm chamber
63. Screw
64. Diaphragm
65. Gasket
66. Connecting rod
67. Pin
68. Ring
69. Washer
70. Diaphragm stop ring
71. Diaphragm stop ring
72. Screw
73. Level gauge screw
74. Gasket
75. Gasket
76. Stop ring
77. Float pin
78. Needle valve seat
79. Gasket
80. Collar
81. Throttle adjusting screw
82. Idle adjusting screw
83. Spring
84. Main jet
85. Main jet
86. Gasket
87. Plug
88. Gasket
89. Air bleed
90. Air bleed
91. Slow jet
92. Step jet
93. Air bleed screw
94. Air bleed step
95. Cover
96. Diaphragm
97. Spring
98. Gasket
99. Washer
100. Shim
101. Jet
102. Bleed plug
103. Retainer
104. Pin
105. Screw
106. Gasket
107. Plug
108. Gasket
109. Gasket
110. Bolt
111. Nut
113. Cover
114. Gasket
115. Sight glass
116. Gasket
117. Filter
118. Accelerator
119. Gasket
120. Plug
121. Cover
122. Coasting valve bracket
123. Clip
124. Screw
125. Spring
126. Screw
127. Spring
128. Shim
129. Throttle positioner
130. Nut
131. Rod
132. Collar
133. Shim
134. Collar
135. Arm
136. Plate
137. Retaining spring
138. Lever
139. Setscrew
140. Ring

Exploded view of carburetor from a rotary engine

1979–82

1. Close the choke fully.
2. Place the fast idle adjusting screw on the first step of the fast idle cam.
3. Check the clearance between the throttle plate and the inside of the throttle wall with a wire feeler gauge. It should measure 0.051–0.059 in. for the 2.0 liter engine, or 0.058–0.066 in. for the 2.3 liter. (0.061–0.071 in. for 1981–82 2.3 engine Calif. models)
4. If the clearance is incorrect, adjust by means of the fast idle screw, clockwise to increase or counterclockwise to decrease.

1979 and later fast idle adjustment

FLOAT AND FUEL LEVEL ADJUSTMENT—COURIER

1. With the engine running, check the fuel level in the sight glass (in the fuel bowl).
2. If the fuel level is not at the specified mark on the sight glass, remove the carburetor from the truck.

Float level adjustment—measure the distance indicated by the opposed arrows

Bend this tang to adjust the float level

3. Remove the fuel bowl cover.
4. Invert the carburetor and lower the float until the tang on the float just contacts the needle valve.
5. Measure the clearance between the float and the edge of the bowl. It should be:

Year		In
1977–78		0.047
1979–82	2.0	0.335
	2.3	0.236

6. If the clearance is not as specified, bend the float tang until the proper clearance is obtained.
7. Install the fuel bowl cover.
8. Reinstall the carburetor on the truck.
9. Recheck the fuel level at the sight glass.

VACUUM PULLDOWN ADJUSTMENT—COURIER

1977–78 Only

1. On California Couriers, unplug the electrical connectors from the water thermo switch and connect a jumper wire between the connectors. Turn the ignition switch on.
2. Pull the choke knob out to fully close the choke.
3. Disconnect the vacuum hose from the pulldown diaphragm.
4. Connect an external vacuum source to the pulldown diaphragm. Gradually apply vacuum. The pulldown should start to operate (open the choke) at 5.9–7.5 in. Hg.
5. Increase the vacuum to 9.8–12.0 in. Hg. Check the clearance between the carburetor air horn wall and the choke plate using a wire gauge. The clearance should measure 0.066–0.075 in. all 1977–78 1.8 and 49 states and Canada 2.3 models, and 0.075–0.084 in. 1977–78 2.3 California trucks.
6. Adjust the clearance if necessary by bending the pulldown connecting rod.

CHOKE ADJUSTMENT— COURIER

1977–78

1. Push the choke knob all the way in.
2. Loosen the choke cable attaching screws at the choke lever and the choke cable bracket.
3. Be sure that the choke plate is fully open.
4. Insert the choke cable into the choke lever. Tighten the attaching screw.
5. Pull the cable outward to remove all slack between the choke lever and choke cable bracket and tighten the attaching screw at the choke cable bracket.
6. Operate the choke to be sure that there is no binding and that it is operating properly.

1979–80

There are four adjustments to be made to the choke in these years; choke/throttle valve opening adjustment; choke diaphragm adjustment; choke unloader adjustment; and choke thermostat (bi-metal) adjustment.

CHOKE/THROTTLE VALVE OPENING ANGLE

1. Adjust the fast idle cam as previously outlined before making this adjustment.
2. Place the fast idle screw on the second step of the fast idle cam.
3. Measure the clearance between the edge of the choke plate and the throttle bore with a wire gauge. Clearances should be as follows:

Year/Engine	In.
1979–80	
2.0	0.047–0.067
2.3	0.051–0.071
1981–82	
2.0 exc. Calif.	0.016–0.028
2.0 Calif.	0.024–0.036
2.3 exc. Calif.	0.039–0.051
2.3 Calif.	0.041–0.067

4. If the clearance is incorrect, adjust by bending the starting arm. If a large adjustment is required, the choke rod can be bent slightly.

CHOKE DIAPHRAGM

1. Remove the vacuum hose from the choke diaphragm. Attach a vacuum pump to the diaphragm fitting and apply approximately 15.6 inches of mercury vacuum to the diaphragm.
2. Check to see that the fast idle screw is on the first step of the fast idle cam.
3. Press on the choke plate slightly to settle it. Measure the clearance between the edge of the choke plate and the throttle bore. Clearances should be as follows:

Year/Engine	In.
Except 1981–82	
California models	
2.0	0.047–0.067
2.3	0.051–0.071
1981–82	
California models	
2.0	0.065–0.085
2.3	0.063–0.079

4. If the clearance is incorrect, adjust by bending the choke lever.

CHOKE UNLOADER

1. Close the choke plate fully. Open the throttle plate fully.

Vacuum pulldown adjustment—Courier

Adjusting the accelerator linkage on piston engine models—Mazda

1979 and later choke/throttle valve opening adjustment—Courier

2. Measure the clearance between the edge of the choke plate and the throttle bore with a wire gauge. Clearances should be as follows:

Year/Engine	In.
Models through 1981 exc. 1981 Calif.	
2.0	0.079–0.099
2.3	0.090–0.110
1981 California models	
2.0	0.079–0.099
2.3	0.094–0.126
1982 models exc. California	
2.0	0.075–0.107
2.3	0.090–0.110
1982 California models	
2.0	0.075–0.107
2.3	0.094–0.126

3. If the clearance is incorrect, bend the choke unloader adjusting nail (tang).

THERMOSTAT

1. The index mark on the thermostat cover should be aligned with the center mark on the choke housing.

2. Adjust by loosening the thermostat cover retaining screws slightly and shifting the position of the cover. Tighten the screws after adjustment.

Throttle Linkage Adjustment—Courier

1. Loosen the locknuts on the longer linkage rod and rotate both ends in the sockets until the proper accelerator travel from idle to wide-open throttle is obtained.

2. Tighten the locknuts to set the adjustment.

ACCELERATOR LINKAGE ADJUSTMENT—MAZDA

Rotary, B1800 and B2000

1. Check the pedal position. The accelerator pedal should be lower than the brake pedal by 2.3″ on the rotary pickup and 1.75 inches on the piston engine pick up.

2. If necessary, adjust the nut on the linkage above the pedal to obtain the proper height.

3. Check the free-play of the cable at the carburetor. It should be 0.04–0.12″. If not, adjust by turning the clevis nut.

1979 and later choke diaphragm adjustment—Courier

FLOAT AND FUEL LEVEL ADJUSTMENTS—ROTARY ENGINE

1. With the engine running, check the fuel level in the sight glass, using a mirror.

2. If the fuel levels are not within the specified marks on the sight glass, remove the air horn with the floats.

3. Invert the air horn and let the float hang so that it just contacts the needle valve.

4. Measure the clearance between the float and the air horn gasket, which should be 0.10 in. for 1977–1978 models. Bend the float seat lip to adjust the clearance if necessary.

Float level adjustment—float bowl inverted and gasket installed

5. Install the air horn and recheck the fuel levels in the sight glass.

Float Drop
ROTARY PICK-UP

1. Remove the air horn with the floats and allow the floats to hang free.

2. Measure the clearance between the bottom of the float and the air horn gasket. The clearance should be 2.03–2.07 in.

3. If not, adjust the distance by bending the float stop.

4. Install the air horn and recheck the fuel level in the sight glass.

B-1800 AND B-2000

1. Check the fuel level within the float bowl through the sight glass, with the engine running. If the float is not aligned with the level mark, adjustment is necessary.

2. For adjustment, remove the carburetor. Remove the sight glass and invert the carburetor.

Fuel level mark on the sight glass—piston engine

3. Measure the distance between the float and the top of the bowl. It should be 0.236 in. on the B1800, and 0.335 in. on the B2000.

4. Adjust by bending the float seat lip.

5. Turn the carburetor upright and allow the float to drip by its own weight.

6. Measure the clearance between the bottom of the float and the bowl. It should be 0.047 in. on the B1800 and 0.039 in. on the B2000. Bend the float stopper to adjust.

Piston engine float adjustment: bend tab "A" to adjust float drop and bend tab "B" to adjust float level

FAST IDLE ADJUSTMENT— MAZDA

1. Remove the carburetor.

2. With the choke plate fully closed, adjust the clearance between the primary throttle plate and the wall of the throat by bending the connecting rod between the choke plate linkage and the throttle plate. Clearances are as follows:

B1800—0.071 ± 0.008 inch
Rotary Pick-up—0.060 ± 0.008 inch
(Calif. 0.080 ± 0.006 inch)

Fuel Pump

REMOVAL & INSTALLATION

An external electric fuel pump is mounted on the left frame rail adjacent to the fuel

Fast idle adjustments; measure the angle "A" and clearance "B"

tank. Current is supplied to the pump through the ignition circuit and the pump will operate with the key in the RUN position.

1. Remove the fuel pump shield from the frame. Disconnect the electrical leads from the pump.

2. Disconnect the inlet and outlet lines from the pump. Plug the lines.

3. Unbolt and remove the pump from its mounting bracket.

To install the fuel pump:

4. Position the fuel pump on the mounting bracket and install the bolts. Be sure that both mounting surfaces are clean.

5. Connect the inlet and outlet hoses.

6. Connect the electrical leads to the pump.

7. Install the fuel pump shield.

TESTING

To determine that the fuel pump is in good operating condition, tests for both volume and pressure should be performed. The tests are performed with the fuel pump installed, and the engine at normal operating temperature and idle speed.

NOTE: Steps 1 through 6 test the fuel pump for proper pressure; steps 7 and 8 test the pump for proper output volume.

1. Remove the air cleaner.

2. Disconnect the fuel inlet line at the carburetor.

3. Connect a pressure gauge, a restrictor and a flexible hose between the fuel filter and the carburetor. Position the flexible hose and restrictor so that the fuel can be discharged into a suitable graduated container.

4. Before taking a pressure reading, operate the engine at idle speed and vent the system into the container by momentarily opening the hose restrictor.

5. Close the hose restrictor and allow the pressure to stabilize and note the reading. It should be 2.8–3.6 psi.

6. If the pump pressure is not within specifications, and the fuel filter and fuel lines are not blocked, the pump is malfunctioning and should be replaced. If the pressure is within specifications, perform the volume test.

7. Open the hose restrictor and expel the fuel into the container, while observing the time required to discharge 1 pint. Close the restrictor. Fuel pump volume should be approximately 2 pints/minute.

8. If the pump volume is below specifications, repeat the test using an auxiliary fuel supply and a new filter. If the pump volume meets specifications while using the auxiliary fuel supply, check for a restriction in the fuel lines or vent.

Fuel pump testing

Fuel Tank

REMOVAL & INSTALLATION

NOTE: It is best to run the fuel tank as low as possible before removing the tank.

1. Raise and support the rear of the truck.
2. Remove the fuel tank drain plug and drain the gasoline into a metal container.
3. Install the drain plug.

NOTE: On models not equipped with a drain plug, disconnect the line which runs to the fuel pump at the tank and allow the tank to drain. Plug the line connection at the tank before proceeding.

4. Disconnect and plug the fuel pump line at the tank.
5. Disconnect the line from the condenser tank or vapor valve at the fuel tank.
6. If so equipped, disconnect the fuel return line.
7. Disconnect the fuel sending unit lead and the electrical connector.
8. Remove the fuel tank attaching bolts at the mounting bracket and lower the tank.

To install:
1. Raise the tank into position and install the attaching bolts securely.
2. Connect the fuel sending unit lead.
3. Connect the fuel return line if equipped.
4. Connect the condenser tank or vapor valve line.
5. Connect the fuel pump line.

DIESEL FUEL SYSTEM

Fuel Filter

REMOVAL & INSTALLATION

1. Remove the filter with a strap wrench, just as you would remove an ordinary screw-on type oil filter.

The fuel filter canister may be removed with a strap wrench, just as you would remove an oil filter. The air vent plug is on the right side, at the top. The priming pump is actuated by repeatedly pressing down on the disc at the top of the unit

2. Coat the O-ring at the top of the replacement filter with clean diesel fuel. Then, start the filter on the threads, and turn it until it is tight *by hand only*.
3. You must now bleed the system by first loosening the vent plug, and then operating the priming pump until fuel without air bubbles is discharged from the vent. Tighten the vent plug back up and then run the engine to check for leaks.

Water Separator

REMOVAL & INSTALLATION

1. Disconnect the wiring connectors (1) and fuel lines (2).
2. Remove the bolts on either side, and remove the protective cover (3).
3. Remove the bolts on the bracket above the water separator, and remove the unit.

To remove the water separator, first disconnect the wiring electrical connectors (1), fuel lines (2) and shield (3). The separator itself is indicated by (4)

4. Bleed the system as described above at the end of the Fuel Filter Removal & Installation procedure.

Fuel Injection Lines

REMOVAL & INSTALLATION

1. Remove the bracket that fastens the four injection lines to the intake manifold.

2. Keeping track of which cylinder each line serves (lines are not interchangeable) and where each connects on the injection pump, unscrew injection line flare nuts at both ends and remove injection lines.
3. To install reverse the removal procedure torquing flare nuts to 18.1–21.7 ft. lbs.
4. Start the engine and check for leaks. Note that until air is expelled from the system, the engine may run roughly.

Injection Timing

CHECKING & ADJUSTING

NOTE: Precise adjustment of injection timing is necessary for proper functioning of the B2200 diesel. Such problems as hard starting, poor performance, engine knock or smoke may be due to improper timing. As your engine accumulates substantial mileage, a check and adjustment of timing may prove advisable. You *must* have a special tool—a form of dial indicator, Mazda part No. 49 9140 076 or equivalent to perform this job.

1. Bar the engine over until the pointer on the timing cover aligns with the 2° ATDC timing mark.

Location of 2° ATDC timing mark

2. Disconnect the four injection lines and remove them for access, as described in the procedure above. Remove the head plug from the pump—it's in the middle of the four injection line connections.
3. Install the special dial indicator as shown. Adjust the position of the tool so that tip of the dial gauge pointer touches

Install the special dial indicator as shown

the plunger in the end of the pump and the gauge reads .08 in.

4. Turn the crankshaft so the pulley turns counter-clockwise (opposite the direction of engine rotation) until the timing mark on the pulley moves counter-clockwise 30–50 degrees while watching the dial gauge. The gauge should stop moving before you stop rotating the engine. Zero the dial indicator gauge, and then rock the engine back and forth slightly to confirm that the gauge does not move.

Turn the crankshaft pulley counterclockwise, as shown

5. Now, turn the engine back in the clockwise direction until the pointer on the cover again aligns with the 2° ATDC mark on the pulley.

Then, return the pulley to its original position, turning it clockwise

6. Read the gauge. It should read .04 plus or minus .0008 in. If the reading is within this range, timing is ok. If not, proceed with the adjustment, below.

7. Loosen the pump attaching nuts and bolt.

8. The pump must now be rotated until the cam lift meets specifications. Mark the pump's location. If the gauge reading is *more than* .0408 in., the timing is advanced and you'll have to turn the pump counter-clockwise, or in reverse of the direction of engine rotation. If the reading is outside spec' in the minus direction, timing is retarded and you must turn the pump clockwise, or in the direction of engine rotation. To make the adjustment, first turn the pump counter-clockwise to cancel timing gear backlash, and then turn the pump clockwise

until it is slightly to one side or the other of its original position. Use the marks you made at the beginning of this step to estimate where the pump should end up. Rotate the pump slowly using your mark and reading the gauge until the reading meets specification.

9. Then, tighten injection pump attaching nuts and bolt. Make sure the gauge reading meets specification, and repeat step 8 if it does not.

10. Install injection lines (see the procedure above) and then pump the priming pump mounted on the filter about 15 times—until there is a maximum of resistance.

Items to be disconnected in injection pump removal (see text)

Injection pump drive gear lock nut and spring washer (8) and lock plate (9)

Arrows show locations of pump attaching nuts and bolt. Loosen them just slightly—so it's just possible to turn the pump

Injection Pump

REMOVAL & INSTALLATION

NOTE: This procedure requires a special puller Mazda part No. 49 SEO1 157 or equivalent.

1. Scribe the relationship between injection pump flange and the timing gear case for reinstallation. Otherwise, the pump will have to be retimed.

2. Disconnect: the battery negative cable, accelerator control cable (2), cold start device control cable (3), fuel cut solenoid

connector (4), fuel injection lines (5), fuel supply hoses (6), and the injection pump drive gear cover, which is located on the timing gear cover.

3. During the next step, *be careful not to drop the spring washer into the timing gear case. Use a wire to remove it.* Remove the injection pump drive gear locknut and spring washer.

4. Remove the injection pump attaching nuts and bolt.

5. In accomplishing this step, avoid dropping the key which drives the injection pump into the gear case. Do this by sliding the drive gear against the wall of the gear case and maintaining contact while pulling

Using the special puller to slide the drive gear off the injection pump driveshaft

it off the pump. Now, have someone hold the pump, install the puller Mazda part No. 49 SEO1 157 or equivalent, and turn the puller bolt to force the drive gear off the pump shaft. Then, pull the key out of the key groove in the pump driveshaft.

6. To install, first insert the key into the key groove in the injection pump and tap it lightly with a hammer to make sure it's securely in place.

7. Have someone hold the injection pump in position while you install and tighten the injection pump drive gear locknut and washer. Make sure the key and keyway are aligned before starting to tighten the locknut. Torque it to 29–51 ft. lbs.

8. Precisely align the matchmarks you made and then install and tighten the injection pump attaching nuts and bolt.

9. Reconnect items disconnected during removal in reverse order. Torque injection lines to 18.1–21.7 ft. lbs.

10. Bleed the fuel system as described under fuel filter removal & installation above.

Injectors

REMOVAL & INSTALLATION

NOTE: Injector testing, disassembly and repair require specialized test equipment and training as a diesel mechanic. However, you may want to remove the injectors and take them to a diesel specialist to have them checked and rebuilt.

Removing injection nozzles (see text)

Get new copper washers before removing them.

1. Disconnect fuel injection lines (1), and fuel return lines (2 and 3).

2. Install a suitable socket wrench and unscrew injection nozzles. Remove nozzles and copper washers underneath.

3. Install the nozzle with a new copper washer and torque to 43–51 ft. lbs.

4. Reverse the remaining steps of the removal procedure, torquing injection line nuts to 18.1–21.7 ft. lbs.

Glow Plugs

TESTING

1. Remove the glow plug connector attaching nut and the connector.

Checking glow plug continuity

In removing the glow plug, first remove the connector attaching nut (1) and then remove the connector (2)

2. Connect an ohmmeter between the electrical connector at the top of each glow plug (+) and a ground on the cylinder head (−) as shown, and check it for continuity. Replace each glow plug that shows no continuity.

NOTE: Since all glow plugs are subjected to the same operating conditions, if one glow plug fails it's a good idea to replace them all.

REMOVAL & INSTALLATION

1. Remove the connector and attaching nut, and the electrical connector. Then, remove the glow-plug with a suitable socket wrench.

2. To install, reverse the removal procedure, torquing the glow plug to 7.2–10.8 ft. lbs.

MANUAL TRANSMISSION

REMOVAL & INSTALLATION

Courier

1. Put the gearshift in Neutral.

2. Lift up the boot covering the shift lever and detach the gearshift tower from the extension housing. Remove the shift lever, tower and gasket as an assembly.

3. Cover the opening in the case with a heavy rag to keep dirt out.

4. Remove the negative battery cable. Raise and support the truck.

5. Disconnect the driveshaft at the rear axle.

6. Remove the driveshaft center bearing support and pull the driveshaft rearward to disconnect the driveshaft from the transmission. Install a plug in the extension housing to prevent lubricant from leaking out.

7. Remove the exhaust pipe brackets from the transmission case.

8. Disconnect the exhaust pipe hanger from the clutch housing.

9. Disconnect the exhaust pipe at the manifold and muffler and remove the exhaust pipe-resonator assembly or catalytic converter.

10. Unhook the clutch release lever return spring. Remove the clutch release cylinder and secure it out of the way.

11. Remove the speedometer cable from the extension housing.

12. Disconnect the starter motor and back-up light wires.

13. Protect the oil pan with a block of wood and support the engine with a jack. Support the transmission with a separate jack.

14. Remove the starter.

15. Unbolt the transmission from the engine rear plate.

16. Unbolt the transmission mount from the crossmember.

17. Remove the crossmember.

18. Work the clutch housing off the locating dowels. Slide the transmission rearward until the input shaft spline clears the clutch disc.

19. Remove the transmission from the truck. Refer to the Unit Repair Section for overhaul procedures.

To install the transmission:

20. Be sure that all mating surfaces are free of dirt, burrs and paint.

21. Lift the transmission into place and start the input shaft into the clutch disc. Be sure that the splines align and move the transmission forward until the clutch housing seats on the locating dowels of the engine rear plate.

22. Bolt the clutch housing to the rear plate.

23. Install the starter motor.

24. Raise the engine and install the rear crossmember.

25. Install the rear transmission mount on the crossmember. Bolt the transmission to the rear mount.

26. Remove the jacks.

27. Install the driveshaft in the transmission extension housing. Install the center bearing.

28. Connect the driveshaft to the rear axle flange.

29. Install the exhaust pipe and resonator.

30. Connect the exhaust pipe to the flywheel housing and transmission brackets.

31. Connect the starter and back-up light wires.

32. Install the clutch release cylinder.

33. Adjust the clutch release lever free travel. Connect the return spring.

34. Connect the speedometer cable.

35. Fill the transmission with lubricant.

36. Lower the truck.

37. Install the shift tower and gasket. Install the boot.

38. Road test the truck and check for leaks.

Mazda B-1800, B-2000, and B-2200 4 and 5-Speed

1. Raise and support the truck. Drain the lubricant from the transmission.

2. Disconnect the ground wire from the battery.

3. Remove the gearshift lever boot.

4. Unbolt the cover plate from the gearshift lever retainer.

5. Pull the gearshift lever, shim and bushing straight up and away from the gearshift lever retainer.

6. Disconnect the wires from the starter motor and back-up light switch.

7. Disconnect the speedometer cable from the extension housing.

8. Remove the driveshaft.

9. Unbolt the exhaust pipe from the bracket on the transmission case.

10. Disconnect the exhaust pipe at the exhaust manifold.

11. Unhook the clutch release fork return spring and remove the clutch release cylinder from the clutch housing.

12. Remove the starter.

13. Support the transmission with a jack.

14. Unbolt the transmission from the rear of the engine.

15. Place a jack under the engine, protecting the oil pan with a block of wood.

16. Unbolt the transmission from the crossmember.

17. Unbolt and remove the crossmember.

18. Lower the jack and slide the transmission rearward until the mainshaft clears the clutch disc.

19. Remove the transmission from under the truck.

20. Installation is the reverse of removal.

Rotary Pick-Up 4 Speed or 5 Speed

1. Remove the knob from the gearshift lever.

2. Remove the gearshift lever boot.

3. Unbolt the retainer cover from the gearshift lever retainer.

4. Pull the gearshift lever, shim and bushing straight up and away from the gearshift lever retainer.

5. Disconnect the battery ground wire.

6. Remove the belt attaching the power brake vacuum pipe to the clutch housing.

7. Disconnect the ground strap from the transmission case.

8. Remove the clutch release cylinder.

9. Remove the one upper bolt holding the starter and the three bolts and nuts securing the transmission to the engine.

10. Raise and support the truck.

11. Disconnect the wires from the starter motor and the back-up light switch wires.

12. Unbolt and remove the heat insulator from the front exhaust pipe.

13. Disconnect the exhaust pipe from the brackets.

14. Disconnect the exhaust pipe front flange from the exhaust manifold. Remove the front exhaust pipe.

15. Remove the driveshaft.

16. Insert a transmission oil plug into the extension housing.

17. Remove the starter.

18. Install a jack under the engine and support the engine.

19. Unbolt the transmission support from the body.

20. Remove the two lower bolts holding the transmission to the engine.

21. Slide the transmission rearward until the mainshaft clears the clutch disc and remove the transmission from under the truck.

22. Installation is the reverse of removal.

LINKAGE ADJUSTMENT

The shifting mechanism of either Courier or Mazda manual transmissions is built into the transmission extension housing, therefore adjustments are not required.

NOTE: For overhaul procedures, refer to the Import Trucks portion of the Transmission Unit Repair Section.

CLUTCH

PEDAL HEIGHT ADJUSTMENT (FREE-PLAY)

Courier

1. The clutch pedal free-play is adjusted by loosening the locknut on the pushrod and adjusting the pushrod length by rotating the rod. Free travel should measure 0.025–0.121 in., 1977–80; 0.80–1.18 in. for 1981–82 models. Tighten the locknut when the adjustment is complete.

PEDAL HEIGHT ADJUSTMENT

Mazda

1. Loosen the locknut on the adjusting bolt.

2. Turn the adjusting bolt until the clearance between the pedal pad and the floormat is 8.46 in.

3. Carefully tighten the locknut.

PEDAL FREE-PLAY ADJUSTMENT

Mazda

The free-play of the clutch pedal before the

1. Master cylinder	4. Adjusting bolt
2. Rod	5. Locknut
3. Locknut	6. Clutch pedal

Clutch pedal height adjustment—Mazda

Clutch pedal adjustment

pushrod contacts the piston in the master cylinder should be 0.02–0.12 in.

To adjust the free-play, loosen the locknut and turn the pushrod until the proper adjustment is obtained. Tighten the locknut after the adjustment is complete.

REMOVAL & INSTALLATION

Courier

1. Remove the transmission as outlined earlier in this section.

Clutch components—typical of Courier

2. Remove the four attaching and two pilot bolts holding the clutch cover to the flywheel. Loosen the bolts evenly and a turn or two at a time. If the clutch cover is to be reinstalled, mark the flywheel and clutch cover to show the location of the two pilot holes.

3. Remove the clutch disc.

Inspect the old clutch for signs of oil or grease contamination. If present, correct the cause before installing a new clutch. Probable sources of leakage would include the transmission input shaft seal and the engine rear main bearing seal. Inspect the flywheel and pressure plate for signs of scoring, wear, or overheating. Light scoring can be cleaned up with crocus cloth, or by refacing the flywheel; however, heavy wear warrants replacement of the part. Overheated parts will usually be discolored (dark blue or black) and should be replaced. Check the fit of the clutch pilot bearing in the bore of the crankshaft. If it is loose or rough, it should be replaced.

To install the clutch:

4. Install the clutch disc on the flywheel. Do not touch the facing or allow the facing to come in contact with grease or oil. The clutch disc can be aligned using a tool made for that purpose, or with an old input shaft.

5. Install the clutch cover on the flywheel aligning the marks made during removal, and install the four standard bolts and the two pilot bolts.

6. To avoid distorting the pressure plate, tighten the bolts evenly a few turns at a time until they are all tight.

7. Torque the bolts to 13–20 ft. lbs. using a crossing pattern.

8. Remove the aligning tool.

9. Apply a light film of lubricant to the release bearing, release lever contact area on the release bearing hub and to the input shaft bearing retainer. Check the release lever for free operation.

10. Install the transmission.

11. Check the operation of the clutch and if necessary, adjust the pedal free-play and the release lever.

Mazda

1. Remove the transmission.

2. Attach a locking tool to the flywheel.

3. Install a clutch arbor to hold the clutch in place. An old input shaft makes an excellent arbor. Matchmark the pressure plate and flywheel for installation.

4. Unfasten the bolts (4 securing and 2 pilot) which secure the clutch cover, one turn at a time in sequence, until the clutch spring tension is released. Remove the bolts evenly.

5. Remove the clutch disc.

--- **CAUTION** ---

Be careful not to get grease or oil on the surface of the clutch disc.

6. Unfasten the nut which secures the

COURIER CLUTCH INSTALLATION TORQUES

Item	Ft. Lbs.
Clutch housing to engine	34–45 (1.8 and 2.0)
	28–40 (2.3)
Crossmember to frame	23–34
Trans. mount to crossmember	23–34
Transmission to mount	12–17
Driveshaft to flange	40–47
Exhaust to transmission	12–17
Release cylinder to case	12–17
Lever retainer to tower	5–8
Tower to extension	12–17

flywheel to the eccentric shaft, using a suitably large wrench.

7. Remove the flywheel with a puller.

8. Unhook the return spring from the throwout bearing and remove the bearing.

9. Pull out the release fork until the retaining spring frees itself from the ball stud. Withdraw the fork from the housing. Clutch installation is performed in the following order:

1. Clean the flywheel and pressure plate surfaces with fine sandpaper. Check the flywheel and pressure plate for warpage, scoring, or signs of heat distortion. If scoring damage is minor, it can usually be cleaned up. Heavy wear or damage warrants replacement of the parts. Be sure there is no oil or grease on them. Grease the eccentric shaft needle bearing.

2. Install the flywheel with its keyway over the key on the eccentric shaft.

3. Apply sealer to both sides of the flywheel lockwasher and position the lockwasher on the eccentric shaft.

4. Install the flywheel locknut(s) and tighten it to 350 ft. lbs. (rotary engines) or 112–118 ft. lbs. (piston engines); then bend the tabs of the lockwasher up around it.

5. Use an arbor to center the clutch disc during installation. Install the clutch disc with the long end of its hub facing the transmission.

NOTE: Use an old input shaft to center the clutch disc, if an arbor is not available.

6. Align the O-mark on the clutch cover with the reamed hole or the O-mark on the flywheel or align the matchmarks made during removal.

7. Tighten the clutch cover bolts evenly, and in two or three stages, to 13 20 ft. lbs.

--- **CAUTION** ---
Do not tighten the bolts one at a time.

8. Grease the pivot pin. Insert the release fork through its boot so that its retaining spring contacts the pivot pin.

9. Lightly grease the face of the throwout bearing and its clutch housing retainer.

10. Install the throwout bearing and return spring. Check the operation of the release fork and throwout bearing for smoothness.

11. Install the transmission.

Clutch Master Cylinder

REMOVAL & INSTALLATION

1. Disconnect and plug the fluid outlet line at the outlet fitting on the master cylinder one-way valve.

2. Remove the nuts and bolts attaching the master cylinder to the firewall.

3. Remove the cylinder straight out away from the firewall.

To install the master cylinder:

4. Start the pedal pushrod into the master cylinder and position the master cylinder on the firewall.

5. Install the attaching nuts and bolts. Torque the nuts to 12–17 ft. lbs.

6. Connect the fluid outlet line to the master cylinder fitting.

7. Bleed the hydraulic system.

8. Check the clutch pedal free-travel and adjust as necessary.

Clutch Slave Cylinder

REMOVAL & INSTALLATION

Courier

1. Disconnect and plug the slave cylinder inlet line at the slave cylinder.

2. Unhook the lever from the pushrod.

3. Remove the nuts and washers attaching the slave cylinder to the clutch housing.

To install the slave cylinder:

4. Install the slave cylinder on the clutch housing, torquing the nuts to 12–17 ft. lbs.

5. Connect the slave cylinder inlet line to the slave cylinder.

6. Fill the master cylinder and bleed the hydraulic system.

7. Check and adjust the release lever, (1975).

8. Hook the release lever onto the pushrod.

9. Check the system for proper operation.

1. Clutch disc
2. Bolt
3. Clutch cover and pressure plate assembly
4. Service hole cover
5. Release fork
6. Oil seal
7. Dust boot
8. Reamer bolt
9. Release bearing
10. Spring
11. Clutch housing

Clutch components—typical of Mazda

Mazda

1. Unscrew the hydraulic line from the release cylinder and plug it.

2. Unhook the release fork return spring from the cylinder.

3. Unfasten the nuts which secure the release cylinder to the transmission.

Installation is performed in the reverse order of removal. Bleed the hydraulic system, as detailed below, and adjust the release fork free-play, as detailed above.

SYSTEM BLEEDING

1. Remove the rubber cap from the bleeder screw on the release cylinder.

2. Place a bleeder tube over the end of the bleeder screw.

3. Submerge the other end of the tube in a jar half-filled with hydraulic (brake) fluid.

4. Depress the clutch pedal fully and allow it to return slowly.

5. Keep repeating step 4, while watching the hydraulic fluid in the jar. As soon as the air bubbles disappear, close the bleeder screw.

NOTE: During the bleeding procedure the reservoir must be kept at least ¾ full.

6. Remove the tube and refit the rubber cap. Fill the reservoir with fresh hydraulic fluid.

Clutch Release Lever and Bearing

REMOVAL & INSTALLATION

Courier

1. The release lever is retained by a spring clip. Remove the spring and pull the fork from the pivot pin.

2. Remove the lever, dust cover boot and the release (throwout) bearing.

3. Inspect the parts carefully. Wipe off all the oil and dirt from the bearing, but do not soak it in solvent; it is prelubricated. Any burrs should be smoothed with crocus cloth. If burrs are present, inspect the transmission input shaft bearing retainer, and smooth any scoring with crocus cloth.

4. Coat the bearing retainer with a thin film of lithium base grease (Ford specification C3VY-19586 A or equivalent). Apply a thin film of this grease to both sides of the fork at contact points. Also lightly coat the release bearing surface where it contacts the pressure plate fingers.

5. Fill the grease groove inside the bearing hub with the lithium grease. Do not use polyethylene grease. Clean any excess grease from the bore of the hub, because excess grease will eventually work its way onto the clutch disc.

6. Before installing the bearing, hold the inner race and rotate the outer race, applying pressure. If the rotation is noisy or rough, replace the bearing. Bearing failure is generally caused by improper free play settings at the release cylinder or pedal. Riding the pedal can reduce clearance, causing the bearing to constantly spin, increasing wear. The bearing can also fail due to release lever misalignment (bent out of plane or not centered on the housing bracket) or misalignment between the engine and transmission.

To install:

7. Apply a thin film of lithium grease to the input shaft bearing retainer portion of the clutch housing.

8. Dab the end of the pivot pin with grease, and drive the release lever onto it. Apply a thin film of grease to the contact points of the release lever, and install the release bearing. Hook the release collar spring back into place (if applicable).

9. Check the operation of the release bearing hub. It should slide freely on the input shaft bearing retainer.

10. Install the dust boot.

AUTOMATIC TRANSMISSION

Pan & Filter

REMOVAL & INSTALLATION

1. Raise and support the vehicle.

2. Place a drain pan under the transmission pan.

3. Remove the pan attaching bolts (except the two at the front). Loosen the two at the front slightly. Allow the fluid to drain.

4. Remove the pan.

5. Remove and discard the gasket.

6. Install a new pan gasket and install the pan on the transmission.

7. Lower the vehicle and fill the transmission with fluid. Check the transmission operation.

SHIFT LINKAGE ADJUSTMENT

Courier and Mazda Rotary

1. Put the gearshift lever in Neutral.

2. Raise and support the truck.

3. Disconnect the clevis from the lower end of the selector lever operating arm.

4. Move the transmission manual lever to Neutral, the 3rd detent position from the rear of the transmission.

5. Loosen the two clevis retaining nuts and adjust the clevis so that it freely enters the hole of the lever. Tighten the retaining nuts to secure the adjustment.

6. Connect the clevis to the lever and attach it with the spring washer, flat washer and retaining clip.

7. Lower the truck and check the operation of the linkage. Be sure that all gears engage properly.

KICK-DOWN SWITCH ADJUSTMENT

Courier

1. Turn the ignition switch to the ON position.

2. Loosen the kick-down switch attaching nut and adjust the switch to engage when the accelerator pedal is depressed about ⅞ of the way. The down-shift solenoid will click when the switch engages.

3. Tighten the attaching nut and check the switch for proper operation.

KICKDOWN SWITCH AND DOWNSHIFT SOLENOID ADJUSTMENT

Mazda Rotary Pickup

1. Check the accelerator linkage for smooth operation.

2. Turn the ignition on but do not start the engine.

Automatic transmission shift linkage—Courier & Mazda Rotary

3. Depress the accelerator pedal fully to the floor. As the pedal nears the end of its travel, a light "click" should be heard from the downshift solenoid.

4. If if kickdown switch operates too soon, loosen the locknut on the switch shaft. Adjust the shaft so that the accelerator linkage makes contact with it when the pedal is depressed 7/8–15/16 of the way to the floor. Tighten the locknut.

5. If no noise comes from the solenoid at all, then check the wiring for the solenoid and the switch.

6. If the wiring is in good condition, then remove the wire from the solenoid and connect it to a 12V power source. If the solenoid does not click when connected, it is defective and should be replaced.

Kickdown switch and downshift solenoid circuit—Mazda Rotary Pickup

NOTE: When the solenoid is removed, about two pints of transmission fluid will leak out; have a container ready to catch it. Remember to add more fluid to the transmission after installing the new solenoid.

NEUTRAL SAFETY SWITCH ADJUSTMENT

Courier

1. Adjust the manual linkage.
2. Place the transmission manual lever in Neutral (3rd detent from the rear of the transmission).
3. Remove the transmission manual lever retaining nut and lever.
4. Loosen the inhibitor switch attaching bolts. Remove the screw from the alignment pin hole at the bottom of the switch.
4. Rotate the switch and insert an alignment pin (0.079 in. diameter) into the alignment pin hole and internal rotor.

Neutral safety switch adjustment—Courier

6. Tighten the two switch attaching bolts and remove the alignment pin.
7. Reinstall the alignment pin hole screw in the switch body.
8. Install the manual lever.
9. Check the operation of the switch. The engine should only start with the transmission selector lever in Neutral or Park.

Rotary Pick-Up

1. Remove the housing from the shift lever.
2. Adjust the shift lever so that there is 0.–0.12 in. clearance between the pin and the guide plate, when the lever is in neutral.

Rotary pickup neutral safety switch

3. Adjust the neutral safety switch so that the pin hole in the switch body is aligned with the pin hole of the sliding plate when the shift lever is in Neutral.
4. Check the adjustment by trying to start the engine in all gears. It should only start in Park or Neutral.
5. Reinstall the housing on the shift lever.

BAND ADJUSTMENT

JATCO Model 3N71B

1. Raise and support the vehicle.
2. Drain the transmission fluid and remove the pan.
3. Loosen the locknut and tighten the servo adjusting bolt to 9–11 ft. lbs.

Intermediate band adjustment—JATCO 3N71B

4. Back off the servo bolt exactly two full turns. Hold the bolt in this position and tighten the locknut securely.
5. Install the pan and refill the transmission.

JATCO Model R3A

1. Raise and support the vehicle.
2. The servo is located on the right side of the transmission case. Remove the servo cover.
3. Loosen the locknut and tighten the servo adjusting bolt to 9–11 ft. lbs.
4. Loosen the servo bolt exactly two full turns. Hold the bolt in this position and tighten the locknut securely.
5. Install the servo cover.

Automatic transmission intermediate band adjustment—JATCO R3A

Transmission

REMOVAL & INSTALLATION

Courier

1. Disconnect the negative cable from the battery.
2. Raise and support the truck.
3. Drain the transmission fluid, but do not remove the pan. After the fluid has drained, install a few bolts to hold the pan in place, temporarily.
4. Remove the exhaust pipe bracket bolt from the right side of the converter housing.
5. Remove the exhaust pipe flange bolts from the rear of the resonator or catalytic converter, and disconnect the pipe.
6. Disconnect the driveshaft from the rear axle flange.
7. Remove the driveshaft center bearing support nuts, washers, and lockwashers. Lower the driveshaft and remove it from the transmission.
8. Disconnect the speedometer cable.
9. Disconnect the shift rod from the manual lever.
10. Remove the vacuum hose from the diaphragm. Disconnect the electrical connectors from the downshift solenoid and inhibitor switch, and remove their wires from the clip.

11. Disconnect and plug the cooler lines from the radiator at the transmission. Use a flare nut wrench if one is available.

12. Remove the access cover from the lower front of the converter housing.

13. Matchmark the drive plate (flywheel) and torque converter for reassembly. Remove the four bolts holding the torque converter to the drive plate.

14. Remove the bolts connecting the crossmember to the transmission.

15. Support the transmission with a jack. Remove the crossmember-to-frame bolts, and remove the crossmember.

16. Make sure that the transmission is securely supported. Secure it to the jack with a safety chain, if necessary.

17. Lower the transmission to provide working clearance, and remove the starter.

18. Remove the converter housing-to-engine bolts.

19. Remove the fluid filler tube.

20. With a pry bar, exert light pressure between the converter and the drive plate to prevent the converter from disengaging from the transmission as it is removed.

21. Lower the transmission and converter as an assembly. Be careful not to let the converter fall out.

To install:

22. Place the transmission on the jack. Be sure that the converter is properly installed.

23. Raise the transmission into place. Install the converter housing-to-engine bolts, and torque in two stages to 23–34 ft. lbs.

24. Lower the transmission on the jack and install the starter.

25. Install the fluid filler tube with a new O-ring.

26. Raise the transmission slightly, and install the crossmember to the frame. Tighten the bolts to 23–34 ft. lbs.

27. Lower the transmission and install the transmission-to-crossmember bolts. Tighten to 23–34 ft. lbs.

28. Align the matchmarks made earlier on the torque converter and drive plate. Install the four attaching bolts and torque to 25–36 ft. lbs. in three stages.

29. Install the access cover. Remove the jack.

30. Connect the cooler lines.

31. Install the electrical connectors to the switch and solenoid, and replace the wires in the clip. Install the diaphragm vacuum hose.

32. Connect the shift rod to the lever.

33. Reconnect the speedometer cable.

34. Insert the driveshaft into the transmission. Install the center bearing support. Bolt the driveshaft to the rear axle flange.

35. Connect the exhaust pipe to the resonator or catalytic converter, using a new gasket. Reinstall the exhaust pipe clamp onto the converter housing, and torque the bolt to 10–15 ft. lbs.

36. Install a new pan gasket and the fluid pan, if this has not already been done.

37. Lower the truck. Connect the battery cable. Fill the transmission through the dipstick tube with the specified fluid, being careful not to overfill, and check for leaks.

Mazda Rotary Pickup

1. Disconnect the cable from the negative (−) battery terminal.

2. Remove the power brake vacuum line bracket from the converter housing.

3. Remove the converter access hole cover. Lock the flex-plate by holding the drive pulley lockbolt with a wrench.

4. Matchmark the converter and flexplate. Unfasten the four converter-to-flexplate securing bolts.

5. Jack up the vehicle and securely support it with jackstands.

———— CAUTION ————

The exhaust system on rotary engine-equipped Mazdas gets considerably hotter than a conventional system; be sure to allow enough time for it to cool before performing steps 6 and 7.

6. Remove the heat shroud. Unfasten the exhaust pipe bracket on the right-hand side of the torque converter housing.

7. Unfasten the bolts which secure the exhaust pipe to the rear side of the front muffler. Detach the exhaust pipe.

8. Unfasten the bolts from the driveshaft flange and center bearing. Push the driveshaft out of the extension housing. Plug the hole in the extension housing, so that fluid doesn't leak out.

9. Detach the speedometer cable at the extension housing.

10. Remove the control rod.

11. Disconnect the starter wiring. Remove the starter from the converter housing.

12. Remove the bottom cover from the converter housing.

13. Support the transmission with a jack.

14. Unfasten the nuts which secure the transmission support member and remove the member.

15. Lower the transmission jack to increase the gap between the transmission and the underbody of the truck.

16. Remove the vacuum fitting from the intake manifold. Unfasten the vacuum line from the converter housing, transmission case, and extension housing. Disconnect the hose from the vacuum modulator and remove the vacuum line.

17. Disconnect the downshift solenoid wiring and separate the wires from the clip.

18. Disconnect the lines which run to the cooler at the left-hand side of the transmission. Remove the clips for these lines from the converter housing and transmission case.

19. Unfasten evenly, and in several stages, the bolts which secure the torque converter housing to the top of the engine.

20. Raise the transmission so that it is level again.

21. Use a small pry bar to carefully apply pressure between the torque converter and the flex-plate.

22. Slide the transmission rearward and lower it from the truck.

———— CAUTION ————

Do not rest the weight of the transmission on the torque converter splines.

To install:

Automatic transmission installation is performed in almost the reverse order of removal. There are several points which should be noted, however:

1. Before installing the transmission, use a dial indicator to measure flex-plate runout. Runout should be about 0.012 in. If runout exceeds 0.020 in., the flexplate must be replaced.

2. Hand-tighten the four torque converter installation bolts and then lock the flex-plate with a locking tool. Next, tighten the four bolts evenly, and in several stages, to 27–40 ft. lbs.

3. After completing transmission installation, rotate the eccentric shaft to be sure that there is no interference in the transmission.

4. Fill the transmission with type F transmission fluid. Converter capacity is 6.6 qts.

5. Check and adjust the following items, after completing installation:
   a. Shift linkage.
   b. Neutral safety switch.
   c. Engine idle speed.
   d. Kickdown switch and downshift solenoid.

6. Check the fluid level again and road test the truck.

DRIVELINE

Driveshaft

REMOVAL & INSTALLATION

Courier

The two piece driveshaft is removed as an assembly. It is not necessary to disassemble the center bearing.

1. Raise and support the rear of the truck.

2. Paint or scribe a matchmark across the universal joint yoke and the axle flange. The driveshaft was balanced at the factory as an assembly, and should be replaced in its original position to avoid driveline vibrations or imbalances.

3. On two piece driveshafts only, remove the two nuts and their washers securing the center bearing support bracket to the frame, and remove the bracket.

4. Remove the four bolts from the universal joint yoke and axle flange. On some earlier models, the axle flange has studs, and the universal joint yoke is retained by nuts, instead of bolts.

5. Drop the rear end of the driveshaft down, and slide the splined sliding yoke out of the transmission.

Disassembled view of the two-piece Courier Driveshaft

NOTE: Plug the end of the transmission to avoid the loss of gear oil.

To install:

6. Apply a lithium grease to the interior splines of the sliding yoke.

7. Unplug the transmission end. Slide the yoke into the extension housing. Be careful not to damage the extension housing seal.

8. Align the mating marks on the rear flange. Install the bolts and tighten to 40–47 ft. lbs.

9. On two piece driveshafts only, install the center support bracket, and tighten the nuts to 27–38 ft. lbs.

10. Lower the truck.

Mazda

1. Raise the rear end of the truck and support it using jackstands.

————— CAUTION —————

Be sure that the truck is securely supported. Remember, you will be working underneath it.

2. Matchmark the flanges on the driveshaft and pinion so that they may be installed in their original position.

3. Remove the four bolts which secure the driveshaft to the pinion flange. Unbolt the center bearing.

4. Lower the back end of the driveshaft and slide the front end out of the transmission.

5. Plug up the hole in the transmission to prevent it from leaking.

NOTE: Use an old U-joint yoke; or, if none is available, place a plastic bag, secured with rubber bands, over the hole.

NOTE: Do not remove the oil seals and the center bearing from the support unless they are defective.

Installation is performed in the reverse order of removal. Tighten the center bearing support bolts to 14–21 ft. lbs. and the driveshaft-to-pinion flange bolts to 40–47 ft. lbs.

U-Joint

OVERHAUL

For all information on U-Joint overhaul, please refer to "U-Joint/CV-Joint Overhaul" in the Unit Repair section.

Center Bearing

REMOVAL & INSTALLATION

Courier

The center support bearing is a sealed unit which requires no periodic maintenance. The following procedure should be used if it becomes necessary to replace the bearing.

You will need a pair of snap-ring pliers for this job.

1. Remove the driveshaft assembly.

2. To maintain driveline balance, matchmark the rear driveshaft, the center yoke and the front driveshaft so that they may be installed in their original positions.

3. Remove the center universal joint from the center yoke, leaving it attached to the rear driveshaft. See the following section for the correct procedure.

4. Remove the nut and washer securing the center yoke to the front driveshaft.

5. Slide the center yoke off the splines. The rear oil seal should slide off with it.

6. If the oil seal has remained on top of the snap-ring, remove and discard the seal. Remove the snap-ring from its groove. Remove the bearing.

7. Slide the center support and front oil seal from the front driveshaft. Discard the seal.

To assemble:

8. Install the new bearing into the center support. Secure it with the snap-ring.

9. Apply a coat of grease to the lips of the new oil seals, and install them into the center support on either side of the bearing.

10. Coat the splines of the front driveshaft with grease. Install the center support assembly and the center yoke onto the front driveshaft, being sure to match up the marks made during disassembly.

11. Install the washer and nut. Torque the nut to 116–130 ft. lbs.

12. Check that the center support assembly rotates smoothly around the driveshaft.

13. Align the mating marks on the center yoke and the rear driveshaft, and assemble the center universal joint.

14. Install the driveshaft. Be sure that the rear yoke and the axle flange are aligned properly.

REAR AXLE

NOTE: For rear axle overhaul, refer to the Import Truck portion of the Drive Axle Unit Repair Section.

Axle Shafts

REMOVAL & INSTALLATION

1. Raise and support the truck.

2. Remove the rear wheel and brake drum.

3. Remove the brake shoes.

4. Remove the parking brake cable retainer.

5. Disconnect and plug the hydraulic brake lines at the wheel cylinders.

6. Unbolt the backing plate and bearing housing.

7. Slide the complete axle shaft from the housing. If necessary, remove the oil seal from the housing.

1. Shims
2. Bearing housing
3. Outer oil seal
4. Gasket
5. Rivet

6. Baffle seal
7. Axle shaft
8. Inner oil seal
9. Lock nut

10. Lock washer
11. Bearing
12. Spacer
13. Hub bolt and lug nut

Rear axle shaft exploded view

To install the axle shaft:

8. Install a new axle oil seal in the housing if the old one was removed.

9. Install the axle shaft assembly.

10. Using two bolts and nuts, temporarily install the bearing housing and backing plate to the housing flange.

11. Check the axle shaft end-play with a dial indicator mounted on the backing plate.

12. If only one axle shaft has been removed, the end-play should be 0.002–0.006 in. If both axle shafts have been removed, check the end-play after the first shaft is installed. It should be 0.026–0.033 in. The end-play of the second shaft should then be 0.002–0.006 in. Shims are available to adjust the end-play.

13. After adjusting the end-play, install all bolts and torque them to 40–50 ft. lbs. on Couriers and 12–16 ft. lbs. on Mazdas.

14. Install the brake shoes.

15. Install the brake drum and wheel.

16. Connect the brake lines.

17. Bleed the brakes.

18. Lower the truck and road-test it.

BEARING AND SEAL REPLACEMENT

Mazda

1. Remove the axle shaft.

2. Using a suitable press, press the axle shaft out of the collar and bearing.

NOTE: If the pressure needed to press out the shaft exceeds 10 tons, grind off part of the bearing retaining collar and cut it with a cold chisel, taking care not to damage the shaft surface.

3. Remove the bearing retainer from the shaft.

4. Clean all parts and inspect the condition of the collar, spacer and shaft.

5. Install the retainer and spacer on the shaft.

6. Position the bearing on the shaft with the sealed side toward the shaft flange. Press it on until the spacer comes in contact with the shoulder of the shaft.

Courier

1. Remove the axle shaft as described above. Remove the bearing housing assembly and shims.

2. Remove the inner oil seal from the bearing housing.

3. Loosen the locknut and remove the locknut and lockwasher. There are special wrenches available to fit the locknut, but you can remove it with a hammer and a flat-nosed punch, if you work carefully.

4. Remove the bearing and housing assembly from the axle shaft, using either a puller on the housing, or a press on the axle shaft while supporting the housing.

5. Remove the bearing, spacer, and outer oil seal.

6. Oil the lips of a new oil seal, and press it into place in the housing.

7. Install the spacer and a new bearing into the housing.

8. Press the bearing housing assembly onto the axle shaft. Install a new lockwasher and the locknut.

9. Oil the lips of a new inner seal, and press it into place. Check that the bearing and housing assembly rotate smoothly on the axle shaft.

10. Replace the bearing housing assembly, shims, and axle shaft as described above.

Differential
REMOVAL & INSTALLATION

1. Raise the vehicle and support it safely with jackstands.

2. Remove the differential drain plug and drain the lubricant from the differential. Install the plug after all of the fluid has drained.

3. Remove the axle shafts as previously outlined.

4. Remove the driveshaft(s) as previously outlined.

5. Remove the carrier-to-differential housing retaining fasteners and remove the carrier assembly from the housing.

Installation is performed in the following manner:

6. Clean the carrier and axle housing mating surfaces.

7. If the differential originally used a gasket between the carrier and the differential housing, replace the gasket. If the unit had no gasket, apply a thin film of oil-resistant silicone sealer to the mating surfaces of both the carrier and the housing and allow the sealer to set according to the manufacturer's instructions.

8. Place the carrier assembly onto the housing and install the carrier-to-housing fasteners. Torque the fasteners to 12–17 ft. lbs.

9. Install the driveshaft(s) and axle shafts as previously outlined.

10. Install the brake drums and wheels.

11. Fill the differential with the proper amount of fluid (see the Capacities Chart). Couriers must be filled with fluid meeting Ford specifications ESW-MC2C105-A. Mazdas require HP SAE 90 above 0° F. or HP SAE 80 for colder temperatures.

FRONT SUSPENSION

Shock Absorbers
REMOVAL & INSTALLATION

Courier

1. Remove the nuts attaching the upper end of the shock absorber to the crossmember.

2. Remove the rubber bushings and washers.

3. Remove the bolts attaching the lower end of the shock absorber to the lower control arm.

4. Remove the shock from under the lower control arm.

To install the shock absorber:

5. Replace any worn or damaged bushings.

FRONT UPPER

Shock absorber upper mount installation—Courier

6. From under the lower control arm, install the shock with bushings and attach the shock to the lower control arm. Torque the lower mount to 12–17 ft. lbs.

7. Attach the upper end of the shock to the crossmember and tighten the nuts so that there is 0.256 in. between the top of the shock absorber rod and the top of the upper nut.

Mazda

1. Raise and support the truck.
2. Remove the nuts attaching the upper end of the shock absorber to the crossmember.
3. Remove the rubber bushings and washers.
4. Remove the bolts attaching the lower end of the shock absorber to the lower control arm.

Tightening front shock absorber nuts—Mazda

5. Remove the shock from under the lower control arm.

6. Installation is the reverse of removal. Tighten the lower mount to 12–17 ft. lbs. Attach the upper end of the shock to the crossmember and tighten the nuts so that there is 0.256 in. between the top of the shock absorber rod and the top of the upper nut.

7. Lower the truck.

Upper Control Arm

REMOVAL & INSTALLATION

1. Raise the front of the vehicle.
2. Place jackstands under the lower

control arms and lower the vehicle onto the jackstands until the upper arm is off of the frame bumper.

3. Remove the wheel. Install a chain around the coil spring as a safety measure.
4. Remove the cotter pin and nut retaining the upper ball joint.
5. Break the tapered fit loose by striking it with a hammer and separate the ball joint from the spindle.
6. From under the hood, remove the two upper arm retaining bolts and remove the arm from the vehicle. Keep track of the shims under the bolts.
7. Remove the three ball joint retaining bolts and remove the ball joint from the upper arm.

To install the upper control arm:

8. Install the ball joint in the upper control arm and torque the retaining bolts to 15–20 ft. lbs.
9. Position the upper control arm in the truck and install the alignment shims from where they were removed. Install the retaining nuts and bolts on the shaft and torque them to 62–76 ft. lbs.

10. Position the spindle on the ball joint and install the retaining nut and cotter pin. The nut should be torqued to 40–55 ft. lbs.
11. Remove the safety chain.
12. Install the wheel.
13. Remove the jackstands and lower the truck. Have the front end alignment checked.

Lower Control Arm

REMOVAL & INSTALLATION

— CAUTION —
Be extremely careful while working with coil springs. Failure to follow safety measures could result in personal injury.

1. Raise the front of the truck and position jackstands under both sides of the frame just behind the lower control arms.
2. Remove the wheel.
3. Remove the lower shock absorber retaining bolts and push the shock up into the spring.

1. Plug
2. Threaded bushing
3. Dust seal
4. Retainer
5. Bushing
6. Retainer
7. Adjusting shim
8. Upper arm shaft
9. Upper control arm
10. Plug
11. Set-ring
12. Dust seal
13. Ball joint assembly
14. Stop
15. Coil spring
16. Seat
17. Adjusting plate
18. Shock absorber
19. Washer
20. Bushing
21. Stop
22. Lower arm shaft
23. Stop
24. Set-ring
25. Dust seal
26. Ball joint
27. Bracket
28. Lower control arm

Front suspension

4. Remove the front stabilizer bar retaining bolt, nut and bushings and disconnect the stabilizer bar from the lower control arm.

5. Position a floor jack under the lower control arm and raise the arm to take the spring pressure off. Install a safety chain on the spring.

6. Unbolt the ball joint from the lower control arm.

7. Pull the spindle and ball joint away from the lower arm.

8. If necessary, the lower ball joint can be removed by removing the cotter pin and nut and loosening the ball joint with a hammer.

9. Carefully lower the control arm on the jack, being careful that the spring does not fly out.

10. Remove the three lower control arm retaining bolts and remove the lower control arm.

To install the lower control arm:

11. Position the lower control arm in place and install the three retaining bolts and nuts.

Do not tighten. If removed, install the ball joint in the spindle. Tighten to 60–70 ft. lbs.

12. Position the spring on the lower control arm and in the upper frame retaining pocket.

13. Use a C-clamp to clamp the spring to the lower control arm.

14. Raise the lower control arm with a floor jack and position the ball joint and spindle in the lower arm.

15. Loosely install the three lower arm-to-ball joint bolts. Remove the safety chain from the spring, and remove the floor jack and C-clamp.

16. Torque the three ball joint retaining nuts to 60–70 ft. lbs.

17. Pull the shock absorber down and install the bolts and nuts. Torque to 12–17 ft. lbs.

18. Install the stabilizer bar on the lower control arm.

19. Install the front wheel. Lower the truck and have the front wheel alignment checked.

Ball Joints

INSPECTION

1. Check the ball joint dust seals and replace them if they are defective.

2. Check ball joint end play. If it exceeds specifications, replace. Spec's are: Courier—.031 in.; Mazda—.039 in.

REAR SUSPENSION

Leaf Springs

REMOVAL & INSTALLATION

1. Raise and support the truck, allowing the spring to hang freely.

— CAUTION —
The rear leaf springs are under considerable tension. Be very careful when removing and installing them; they can exert enough force to cause serious injuries.

2. Support the rear axle with jackstands.

3. Disconnect the rear shock absorber at the lower mount.

4. Remove the spring clip nuts and the spring plate.

5. Remove the spring pin nut and remove the two bolts and nuts attaching the spring pin to the frame bracket.

6. Remove the spring pin and remove the front end of the spring from the truck.

7. Remove the shackle plate nuts and the shackle plate.

8. Remove the spring from the truck.

To install the spring:

9. Install the rubber bushings in the front eye of the spring and position it in the frame bracket. Align the holes of the bushings with the hole of the frame bracket.

10. Insert the spring pin from the outside through the rubber bushing.

11. Install the spring pin plate to the frame bracket and torque the nuts to 15–18 ft. lbs.

12. Install the rubber bushings in the rear spring eye and shackle plate. Install the spring and shackle plate to the frame bracket. Do not tighten the nuts.

13. Lower the rear axle and place the center hole of the axle spring clip plate over the head of the spring center bolt.

14. Install the spring plate under the spring and install the spring clips. Torque the nuts to 46–58 ft. lbs.

15. Connect the shock absorber at the lower mount and torque the mount to 18–26 ft. lbs.

16. Lower the vehicle and bounce it several times to seat the springs.

17. Tighten the spring pin nuts to 62–76

1. Rear spring
2. Spring pin assembly
3. Nut
4. Bolt
5. Spacer
6. Bushing
7. Shackle plate assembly
8. Shackle plate
9. Nut and washer
10. Bushing
11. Spring clamp
12. Pach
13. U-bolt
14. Nut and washer
15. Rubber stop
16. Shock absorber
17. Bushing
18. Retainer
19. Centering washer
20. Nut

Rear suspension

ft. lbs. and the shackle plate nuts to 44–58 ft. lbs.

Shock Absorbers

REMOVAL & INSTALLATION

1. Remove the nuts, washers and bushings from the upper and lower shock mounts.
2. Compress the shock absorber and remove it.
   To install the shock absorber:
3. If the rubber bushings are worn or damaged, use new ones.
4. Compress the shock absorber and install it in the truck.
5. Install the rubber bushings, washers and nuts on both the upper and lower mounts. Both the lower and upper mounts must be tightened to provide outside nut and the end of the shock rod in 1975, and 0.217 in. between the outside nut and the end of the shock rod. See the front shock absorber installation section for an illustration of this measurement.

STEERING

Steering Wheel

REMOVAL & INSTALLATION

Courier

1. Disconnect the negative battery cable.
2. Remove the horn button by turning it counterclockwise. Remove the horn contact spring.
3. Matchmark the steering wheel and shaft.
4. Remove the wheel attaching nut and remove the steering wheel with a puller.

NOTE: Do not use a hammer for removal, and under no circumstances hammer on the steering shaft.

5. Installation is the reverse of removal. Use the matchmarks to assemble properly. Torque the steering wheel nut to 22–29 ft. lbs.

Mazda

1. Remove the screws which secure the crash pad/horn button assembly to the steering wheel. Remove the assembly. On four-spoke steering wheels, pull the center cap toward the wheel top.
2. Punch matchmarks on the steering wheel and steering shaft.
3. Unfasten the steering wheel hub nut and remove the steering wheel with a puller.

———— CAUTION ————
The steering column is collapsible; pounding on it or applying excessive pressure to it may cause it to deform, in which case, the entire column will have to be replaced.

Combination switch installed. Some models also have a LIGHTS-HAZARD indicator at the top of the shroud.

Installation of the steering wheel is performed in the reverse order of removal. Tighten the steering wheel nut to 25 ft. lbs.

Turn Signal (Combination) Switch

REMOVAL & INSTALLATION

Courier

1. Disconnect the negative battery cable.
2. Remove the steering wheel.
3. Remove the "Lights-Hazard" Indicator and the steering column shroud.
4. Unplug the electrical multiple connectors at the base of the steering column.
5. Pull the headlight knob from its shaft.
6. Remove the snap-ring, which retains the switch, from the steering shaft. Pull the turn indicator canceling cam from the shaft.
7. Remove the single retaining bolt near the bottom of the switch. Remove the complete switch from the column.
   Installation is the reverse of removal. Check the operation of the switch before installing the steering wheel.

Removing Mazda steering column shroud

Mazda

1. Disconnect the ground cable from the battery.
2. Remove the steering wheel, as detailed above.
3. Unfasten the left-hand column shroud securing screws and remove the shroud.
4. Remove the retaining ring from the combination (turn signal) switch.
5. Withdraw the switch over the steer-

Turn signal arm and related components—Courier

ing column, after unfastening its multiconnector from underneath the dash panel.

Installation is performed in the reverse order of removal.

Steering Linkage

REMOVAL & INSTALLATION

Courier

The center link can be removed from both tie-rods, Pitman arm and idler arm by removing the ball socket nuts and using a ball socket puller to remove the ball socket. After removing the center link, the Pitman arm can be removed from the sector shaft by removing the nut and using the puller. Tie rods can also be removed by use of a puller. Toe-in must be reset when tie rods or ball sockets are replaced.

Mazda

1. Turn the steering wheel so that the front wheels are pointing straight ahead. Then raise the front end of the vehicle and support it with jackstands.
2. Remove the cotter pins and the castellated nuts which secure the ends of the tie-rods to the center link and the steering knuckle.
3. Use a ball joint puller to disconnect the tie rods from the center link and steering knuckle. Remove the tie-rods.
4. Remove the cotter pin and the castellated nut which secure the idler arm to the center link.
5. Use the ball joint puller to detach the idler arm from the center link.
6. Unfasten the nuts at the other end of the idler arm and remove the arm from its bracket.
7. Perform steps 4–5 for the Pitman arm. Remove the center link.
8. Unfasten the nut which secures the Pitman arm to the sector shaft and use a puller to separate them.

Installation is performed in the reverse order of removal. Align the marks on the pitman arm and the sector shaft to ensure proper steering linkage alignment. Torque the removed nuts and bolts to the specifications given in appropriate procedures below. Check and adjust the toe-in.

Tie Rod Ends

REMOVAL & INSTALLATION

Courier

1. Loosen the tie rod clamp nuts (jam nuts, 1977 and later).
2. Remove and discard the cotter pin from the ball socket end, and remove the nut.
3. Use a ball joint puller to loosen the ball socket stud from the center link. Remove the stud from the kingpin steering arm in the same way.

Exploded view of Courier steering linkage

4. Unscrew the tie rod end from the threaded sleeve. The threads may be left or right hand threads. Count the number of threads required to remove it.
5. To install, lightly coat the threads with grease, and turn the new end in as many turns as were required to remove it. This will give approximately correct toe-in.
6. Install the ball socket studs into center link and kingpin steering arm. Tighten the nuts to 22–29 ft. lbs. Install a new cotter pin. You may tighten the nut to fit the cotter pin, but don't loosen it.
7. Check and adjust the toe-in, and tighten the tie rod clamps or jam nuts.

Tie Rod

REMOVAL & INSTALLATION

Mazda

1. Raise and support the front end.
2. Disconnect the tie-rod from the center link and knuckle arm. A puller will be necessary.
3. Install the tie-rod to the center link and knuckle arm. Tighten the nuts to 22–28 ft. lbs. and install new cotter pins.

Idler Arm

REMOVAL & INSTALLATION

Mazda

1. Remove the cotter pin and nut from the idler arm. Disconnect the center link from the idler arm with a puller.
2. Unbolt and remove the idler arm from the frame.
3. Remove the cotter pin, nut and washer, and remove the idler arm from the bracket.
4. To install, assemble the arm to the bracket, first lubricating the arm and bushings with lithium grease. Install all parts in the reverse order of removal, using new cotter pins.

Correct positioning of tie rod clamps—Mazda

Pitman Arm

REMOVAL & INSTALLATION

Mazda

1. Raise and support the front end.
2. Remove the wheels.
3. Disconnect the center link at the pitman arm.
4. Remove the nut attaching the pitman arm to the sector shaft and remove the arm with a puller.
5. Install the Pitman arm onto the sector shaft, aligning the identification marks. Tighten the nut to 108–130 ft. lbs.
6. Connect the center link to the pitman arm and torque the nut to 22–29 ft. lbs. Install a new cotter pin.

Center Link

REMOVAL & INSTALLATION

Mazda

1. Raise and support the front end.
2. Remove the center link from both tie-rods, pitman arm and idler arm by removing the cotter pins and nuts. A puller will also be necessary.
3. Install the center link and tighten the nuts as follows: center link to pitman arm—22–29 ft. lbs.; center link to idler arm—36–58 ft. lbs. Install new cotter pins.

Steering Column & Gear

REMOVAL & INSTALLATION

Courier

1977–78

1. Disconnect the negative battery cable at the battery.
2. Rotate the horn button counterclockwise and remove the horn button and horn button contact spring.
3. Remove the steering wheel as previously outlined.
4. Remove the turn signal cancelling cam snap-ring and the cancelling cam from the top of the steering shaft.
5. Disconnect the steering column wiring by disconnecting the snap connectors.
6. Remove the steering column support bracket.
7. Move the floor covering and insulation away from the bottom of the steering column. Remove the four screws and two bolts which secure the toe plate and boot to the dash panel.
8. Loosen the bolt which secures the bottom of the steering column jacket and remove the jacket from the shaft.
9. Remove the air cleaner assembly.
10. Dismount the heater (coolant) hoses from their brackets and move the hoses out of the way.

11. Remove and plug the hydraulic lines from both the brake and clutch master cylinders.
12. Remove the brake and clutch master cylinders from the vehicle.
13. Raise the vehicle and support it safely with jackstands.
14. Disconnect the Pitman arm from the steering gear shaft using a puller.
15. Remove the steering gear-to-frame fasteners and remove the steering gear from the vehicle. Note the position of the shim(s) located between the gear and the frame, if so equipped. During installation, place the shim(s) in its original position.
16. Installation of the gear and column is the reverse of the previous steps. Note the following points during installation:

   a. Align the steering wheel and steering column shaft markings made during step 3.

   b. Bleed the hydraulic clutch system as previously outlined.

   c. Bleed the brake system. Refer to the Brake Section for the appropriate procedure.

1979–81

1. Follow steps 1–11 of the previous 1977–78 procedure.

NOTE: After performing step 3, remove the light switch knob, then proceed.

2. Remove the intake manifold and carburetor assembly. Refer to the appropriate sections (Fuel and Engine).
3. Remove the dust cover from the tire apron panel.

4. Raise the front of the vehicle and support it safely with jackstands.
5. Remove the left side wheel and tire assembly.
6. Disconnect the steering center link from the Pitman arm using a puller.
7. Remove the Pitman arm nut and the Pitman arm.
8. Jack up the left side lower control arm.
9. Remove the left upper control arm. Note the position and number of alignment shims so that proper front end alignment is retained after installation.
10. Remove the steering gear-to-frame fasteners and remove the steering gear from the vehicle.
11. Installation of the components is the reverse of the previous steps. Refer to step 16 of the 1975–78 procedure for points which should be noted during installation.

1982

1. Disconnect the negative battery cable at the battery.
2. Remove the horn cap from the steering wheel and remove the steering wheel as previously outlined.
3. Remove the screws which retain the steering column cover and remove the cover.
4. Remove the stop ring, cancelling cam and spring from the top of the steering column shaft.
5. Disconnect the wiring couplings for the combination switch.
6. Remove the combination switch retaining screws and remove the combination switch.

Exploded view of typical Courier steering column and gear

7. Remove the steering column mounting bracket-to-dash panel bolts.

8. Move the floor covering and insulation out of the way and remove the bolts which attach the steering column set plate to the dash panel.

9. Pull the steering column jacket off of the steering shaft.

10. Remove the yoke joint-to-worm shaft bolts and remove the steering shaft.

11. Remove the air cleaner assembly.

12. Disconnect and plug the hydraulic lines from both the brake and clutch master cylinders.

13. Remove both the brake and clutch master cylinders from the vehicle.

14. Raise the front of the vehicle and support it safely with jackstands.

15. Remove the left side wheel and tire assembly.

16. Disconnect the center steering link from the Pitman arm using a puller.

17. Remove the steering gear-to-frame fasteners and remove the steering gear from the vehicle.

18. Installation of the components is the reverse of the previous steps. Refer to step 16 of the 1977–78 procedure for points which should be noted during installation.

NOTE: To secure the steering column jacket, insert U-pins into the holes of the steering column jacket to centralize the jacket as shown in the accompanying illustration. Tighten the steering column jacket bolts and remove the U-pins from the jacket.

Power Steering Pump

REMOVAL & INSTALLATION

Mazda

1. Disconnect the fluid hoses from the pump.

2. Loosen the pump belt adjusting bolt, slide the pump to one side and remove the belt.

3. Support the pump, remove the mounting bolts and lift out the pump.

Installation is the reverse of removal. Adjust belt to give a ½" deflection at the mid-point of its longest straight stretch. Fill the reservoir and bleed the system.

WORM BEARING PRELOAD ADJUSTMENT

Courier

1. It is necessary to drain the steering gear to make this adjustment. Refill the steering gear after adjustment.

2. Disconnect the Pitman arm from the gear.

3. Loosen the sector adjusting screw locknut and turn the adjusting screw counterclockwise.

4. Rotate the worm shaft with a torque wrench. The preload should be 5.2–7.8 in.

lbs. If it is not, unscrew the end cover bolts and remove the end cover with the shim pack. If the preload is less than specified, replace the shim size. If it is more than specified, increase the shim size. Shims are available in 0.002, 0.003, 0.004 and 0.008 in.

5. Reconnect the Pitman arm.

Mazda

1. Remove the gear from the vehicle.

2. Rotate the worm shaft with a torque wrench and check the torque. Rotating torque should be 8–10 in. lbs. for rotary pickup; 5–7 in. lbs. for B–1600, 5–8 in. lbs. for the B–1800, B–2000 and B–2200. If not adjust as follows on all models:

3. Remove the end cover and shims.

4. If the preload was too light, remove shims; if too heavy, add shims.

5. Install the end cover.

SECTOR GEAR AND BALL NUT BACKLASH

Mazda

The sector shaft adjusting screw, located in the cover, raises or lowers the sector shaft to provide proper mesh with the sector gear and rack. Adjust as follows:

1. Turn the wormshaft gently and stop it at the center position.

2. Loosen the locknut and turn the adjuster in or out. The standard backlash is zero.

3. Tighten the adjusting screw.

Adjusting backlash on the Mazda steering gear

BRAKES

For all brake system service and repair procedures not detailed below, please refer to "Brakes" in the Unit Repair section.

Adjustments

BRAKE PEDAL

Courier

There should be 0.12–0.34 in. of brake pedal free-travel before the brakes are ap-

plied on 1975–76 trucks. 1977 and later vacuum boosted models should have 0.33–0.39 in. of play.

1. Loosen the locknut on the master cylinder pushrod at the clevis, which attaches the pushrod to the pedal.

2. Turn the master cylinder pushrod either in or out to obtain the specified clearance.

3. When the adjustment is complete, tighten the locknut to 8–13 ft. lbs.

Mazda
ROTARY PICK-UP

1. Detach the wiring from the brake light switch terminals.

2. Loosen the locknut on the switch.

3. Turn the switch until the distance between the pedal and the floor is 7.3 in.

4. Tighten the locknut on switch.

5. Loosen the locknut located on the pushrod.

6. Rotate the pushrod, until a pedal free travel of 0.2–0.6 in. is obtained.

7. Tighten the pushrod locknut.

PISTON ENGINE MODELS

There should be 0.28–0.35 in on the B–1800 and B–2000 brake pedal free-travel before the push-rod contacts the piston.

1. Loosen the locknut on the master cylinder pushrod at the clevis, which attaches the pushrod to the pedal.

2. Turn the master cylinder pushrod either in or out to obtain the specified clearance.

3. When the adjustment is complete, tighten the locknut to 8–13 ft. lbs.

DRUM BRAKES

Courier Front Brakes

The brake shoes should be at normal room temperature. Adjust each front brake shoe as follows:

1. Raise and support the truck. The wheels must be able to turn freely.

2. Remove the adjusting slot covers from the brake backing plate.

3. Insert a brake adjusting spoon (a screwdriver will do in a pinch) to grab the starwheel of the wheel cylinder.

4. Rotate the starwheel of one wheel cylinder toward the inside of the brake drum until the wheel is locked. Then back off the starwheel five notches.

5. Repeat step 4 for all the wheel cylinders.

6. Install the adjusting slot covers.

7. Check the brake adjustment by spinning the wheel by hand. There should be no drag.

8. Lower the truck.

Courier Rear Brakes
1977–78

The brake shoes should be at normal room temperature. Make the adjustment as follows:

1. Be sure that the parking brake is fully

released. Disconnect the equalizer clevis pin.

2. Raise and support the truck so that the wheels are free to turn.

3. Remove the adjusting slot covers from the brake backing plate.

4. Insert a brake spoon (or screwdriver) into the lower adjusting slot to contact the starwheel of the lower wheel cylinder.

5. Turn the lower wheel cylinder star wheel to expand the brake shoe until it locks against the drum. Back the starwheel off five notches. Check the wheel; by rotating it, to be sure that there is no drag.

6. Repeat step 5 for all the wheel cylinders.

7. Connect the parking brake equalizer clevis pin and check the parking brake adjustment.

8. Install the adjusting hole covers.

9. Lower the truck and road-test the brakes. Readjust if necessary.

1979 AND LATER MODELS

The rear drum brakes are self-adjusting on these models. Manual adjustment is required only when the brake shoes have been replaced, or when the length of the self-adjusting rod has been changed for some reason. The brakes should be cold (room temperature).

1. If the shoe retaining spring has been removed, first retract the pushrod fully (drum removed).

2. Raise and support the rear of the truck. The wheels must be free to turn.

3. Make sure the parking brake is fully released.

4. Remove the two adjusting hole plugs from the brake backing plate.

5. An arrow stamped on the backing plate indicates the direction to turn the adjuster starwheel to expand the shoes. Insert a screwdriver through the adjuster hole and turn the starwheel until the brakes are locked.

6. Insert a drift through the other adjuster hole. Use the drift to hold the pole lever of the self-adjuster firmly. Back off the starwheel three or four notches; the wheel should rotate freely (no drag).

7. Repeat the adjustment on the other wheel. Make sure the adjustment is exactly the same. Road test for equal brake action and readjust as necessary.

Mazda Rear Brakes

1. Block the front wheels, raise the car, and support it with jackstands.

2. Release the parking brake completely. Disconnect the equalizer clevis pin.

3. Remove the adjusting hole plugs from the backing plate.

4. Engage the adjuster with a screwdriver. Turn the adjuster in the direction of the arrow stamped on the backing plate until the brake shoes are fully expanded, i.e., the wheel will not turn.

5. Pump the brake pedal several times to be sure that the brake shoe contracts the drum evenly.

NOTE: If the wheel turns after you remove your foot from the brake pedal, continue turning the adjuster until the wheel will no longer rotate.

6. Back off on the adjuster about five notches. The wheel should rotate freely, without dragging. If it does not, turn the adjuster an additional notch.

7. Pump the brake pedal several times and check wheel rotation again.

8. Fit the plug into the adjusting procedure for the three other rear brake shoes.

Master Cylinder

REMOVAL & INSTALLATION

Courier

1. Wipe off the master cylinder and lines, then place cloths under it to absorb spilled fluid. Disconnect and plug the brake lines from the master cylinder outlets. The 1977 and later models have a remote reservoir, so the two inlet hoses should be disconnected at the master cylinder and plugged. If you pinch the reservoir hoses while removing them, and then raise their ends above the level of the reservoir, spillage will be reduced.

NOTE: Brake fluid destroys paint. Be careful not to spill fluid on painted surfaces.

2. Remove the two nuts and lockwashers which secure the master cylinder to the firewall or vacuum booster.

3. Lift the master cylinder outward and upward away from the firewall and brake pushrod.

To install the master cylinder:

4. Install the master cylinder (and boot if equipped) on the firewall or booster, while carefully guiding the brake pushrod into contact with the master cylinder piston.

5. Install the two nuts and lockwashers and tighten the nuts to 11–17 ft. lbs.

6. Connect the brake lines to the master cylinder ports.

7. Bleed the brake system.

8. Check the brake pedal free-travel adjustment.

Mazda

1. Detach all of the hydraulic lines from the master cylinder. Detach the fluid level sensor lead if equipped.

NOTE: On models which have a fluid reservoir located separately from the master cylinder, remove the lines which run between the two and plug the lines to prevent leakage.

2. Unfasten the nuts which secure the master cylinder to the power brake unit or firewall.

3. Withdraw the master cylinder assembly straight out and away from the power brake unit or the firewall and pushrod.

─── CAUTION ───
Be careful not to spill brake fluid on the painted surfaces of the car, as it makes an excellent paint remover.

Installation of the master cylinder is performed in the reverse order of its removal. Fill up its reservoir and bleed the brake system, as detailed below.

Courier Pressure Differential Valve

REMOVAL & INSTALLATION

1. Disconnect the warning light switch connector from the warning light switch.

2. Disconnect the brake inlet and outlet lines. Plug the lines.

3. Remove the valve assembly-to-cowl attaching bolt and remove the valve and switch assembly.

To install the valve and switch:

4. Position the valve and switch on the cowl. Install the retaining bolt.

5. Connect the brake lines to the valve.

6. Connect the warning light to the switch wiring connector.

7. Depress the brake pedal several times, then bleed the brake system.

8. Fill the master cylinder and check for proper operation.

CENTRALIZING THE PRESSURE DIFFERENTIAL VALVE

Normally, the brake warning light will remain ON after any repairs to the brake system, or after bleeding the brakes. This is caused by the pressure differential valve remaining in the off center position.

To centralize the pressure differential valve and turn the warning light OFF:

1. Turn the ignition switch to ON.

2. Check the fluid levels in the master cylinder reservoirs and fill them to within ¼ in. of the top, if necessary.

3. Depress the brake pedal and the piston will center itself, causing the warning light to go out.

4. Turn the ignition switch OFF.

5. Before driving the truck, check the operation of the brakes to be sure that a firm pedal has been obtained.

Mazda Brake Failure Warning Valve

CENTRALIZING

1. Turn the ignition switch to the ON position.

2. Make sure that the fluid level in the master cylinder is at the ¾ mark.

3. Depress the brake pedal and the pis-

ton will center itself causing the light to go off.

4. Turn the switch to OFF and check the fluid level. Check for a firm pedal.

Parking Brake

ADJUSTMENT

Courier

1. Adjust the service brakes before attempting to adjust the parking brake.

2. Use the adjusting nut to adjust the length of the front cable so that the rear brakes are locked when the parking brake lever is pulled out 5–10 notches.

3. After adjustment, apply the parking brake several times. Release the parking brake and make sure that the rear wheels rotate without dragging. If they drag, repeat the adjustment.

NOTE: If the parking brake cable is replaced, prestretch it by applying the parking brake hard three or four times before attempting adjustment.

Mazda

1. Adjust the service brakes before attempting to adjust the parking brake.

2. Use the adjusting nut to adjust the length of the front cable so that the rear brakes are locked when the parking brake lever is pulled out 5–10 notches.

3. After adjustment, apply the parking brake several times. Release the parking brake and make sure that the rear wheels rotate without dragging. If they drag, repeat the adjustment.

Parking Brake Warning Light Switch

REMOVAL & INSTALLATION

Courier

1. Apply the parking brake to provide clearance between the switch assembly and the switch stop tab on the parking brake lever shaft.

2. Disconnect the switch wiring connector.

3. Remove the switch from its mounting bracket.

To install the switch:

4. Install the switch on the mounting bracket.

5. Install the attaching screws.

6. Connect the switch wire connector.

7. Turn the ignition switch ON and check the operation of the switch. No adjustment to the switch is possible. If it is defective, replace the switch.

CHASSIS ELECTRICAL

Heater Assembly

REMOVAL & INSTALLATION

Courier

1. Disconnect the battery ground cable.

2. Drain the cooling system.

3. Remove the water valve shield at the left side of the heater.

4. Disconnect the two hoses from the left side of the heater.

5. At the heat-defroster door, at the water valve and at the outside recirculation door, disengage the control cable housing from the mounting clip on the heater. Disconnect each of the three cable wires from the crank arms.

6. Disconnect the fan motor electrical lead.

7. On 1977 models, remove the glove compartment for clearance.

8. Working inside the engine compartment, remove the two retaining nuts and the single bolt and washer which hold the heater to the firewall. 1978 and later models also have a retaining bolt inside the passenger compartment which must be removed.

9. Disconnect the two defroster ducts from the heater and remove the heater.

To install the heater:

10. Install the heater on the dash so that the heater duct indexes with the air intake duct and the two mounting studs enter their respective holes.

11. From the engine side of the firewall, install the nuts on the mounting studs. While an assistant holds the heater in position, install the mounting bolt.

12. Connect the defroster ducts.

13. Connect the heat-defrost door control cable to the door crank arm. Set the control lever (upper) in the HEAT position and turn the crank arm toward the mounting clip as far as it will go. Engage the cable housing in the clip and install the screw in the clip.

14. Connect the water valve control cable wire to the crank arm on the water valve lever. Locate the cable housing in the mounting clip. Set the control lever in the HOT position and pull the valve plunger and lever to the full outward position. This will move the lever crank arm toward the cable mounting clip as far as it will go. Tighten the clip and screw.

15. Insert the outside-recirculation door control cable into the hole in the door crank arm. Bend the wire over and tighten the screw. Set the center control lever in the REC position and turn the door crank arm toward the mounting clip as far as it will go. Engage the cable housing in the clip and install the screw in the clip.

16. Connect the fan motor electrical lead.

17. Connect the two hoses to the heater core tubes, at the left side of the heater, and tighten the clamp.

18. Install the water valve shield and tighten the three screws (left side of the heater).

19. Refill the cooling system and connect the battery ground cable.

20. Run the engine and check for leaks. Check the operation of the heater.

21. On 1977 models replace the glove compartment.

Heater Motor and Blower Fan

REMOVAL & INSTALLATION

Courier

1. Remove the heater assembly.

2. Remove the five screws and separate the halves of the heater assembly.

3. Loosen the fan retaining nut. Lightly tap on the nut to loosen the fan. Remove the fan and nut from the motor shaft.

4. Remove the three motor-to-case retaining screws and disconnect the bullet connector to the resistor and ground screw.

5. Rotate the motor and remove it from the case.

To install the motor and fan:

6. Install the motor in the case, rotating it slightly.

7. Install the retaining screws and connect the bullet connector and ground wire.

8. Install the fan on the shaft and install the nut.

9. Assemble the halves together and install the five retaining screws.

10. Install the heater in the truck. Check the operation of the heater.

Heater Core

REMOVAL & INSTALLATION

Courier

1. Remove the heater from the truck.

2. Remove the five screws and separate the halves of the case.

3. Loosen the hose clamps and slide the heater core from the case.

4. Slide the replacement core into the case. At the same time, connect the core tube to the water valve tube with the short hose and clamps.

5. Assemble the halves of the heater and install the five screws.

6. Install the heater in the truck. Check the operation of the heater.

VIEW A

VIEW B

MOTOR RETAINING SCREWS

RESISTOR

GROUND SCREW

FAN

RETAINING NUT

RETAINING SCREWS

VIEW C

Courier heater system components

Radio

REMOVAL & INSTALLATION

Courier

— CAUTION —

Never operate the radio with the speaker lead or antenna disconnected. Operation of the radio without a load will damage the amplifier's output transistors. If a replacement speaker is installed, be sure it is of the same impedance (resistance in ohms) as the original.

1977–78

1. Remove the ash tray, ash tray retainer and rear retainer support. Remove the heater control knobs, heater control bezel and right-hand defroster hose.
2. Remove the heater control and position it to the left.
3. Remove the radio chassis rear support bracket.
4. Bend the bracket down 90°.
5. Remove the radio knobs, attaching nuts and bezel.
6. Pull the chassis forward until the control shafts clear the holes in the instrument panel. Disconnect the speaker wires, power lead and antenna lead. Rotate the chassis so that the control shafts point upward and lower the radio.

To install the radio:

7. Install the radio vertically, with the control shafts pointed upward.
8. Connect the speaker wires, power lead and antenna cable.
9. Slide the chassis upward and posi-

tion it with the control shafts in the holes in the instrument panel.

10. Install the radio attaching nuts, and control knobs.
11. Bend the bracket on the dash panel back into position.
12. Install the radio rear support nut to the ash tray retainer rear support.
13. Install the ash tray retainer, heater control bezel and knobs, ash tray, and right-hand defroster hose.

1979 AND LATER

1. Disconnect the negative battery cable.
2. Pull off the heater control knobs, the instrument light brightness control knob, and the radio knobs.
3. Remove the ring nut and fiber washer for the brightness control. Remove the radio attaching nuts (shaft nuts). Remove the four screws for the meter hood (instrument trim panel) and remove the hood.
4. Slide the radio to the left until the rear support pin clears the support bracket. Pull the radio out from the instrument panel far enough to gain access to the wires at the rear of the radio chassis.
5. Disconnect the power lead, speaker leads and the antenna cable. Remove the radio.
6. To install, connect the wires to the radio.
7. Slide the radio into place. Move the radio to the left, engage the support pin with its bracket, then slide the radio to the right.
8. Install the meter hood, inserting the radio shafts and heater knobs through it as it is fitted into place. Install the four retaining screws but do not tighten them yet.
9. Install the washer and ring nut for the brightness control. Install the radio shaft

nuts loosely. Tighten the meter hood screws, then tighten the radio shaft nuts.

10. Install the knobs. Connect the negative battery cable.

Wiper Motor Linkage and Bracket

REMOVAL & INSTALLATION

Courier

1. Disconnect the battery ground cable.
2. Remove the wiper arms and blades by removing the retaining nuts.
3. Remove the rubber cap, nut, tapered spacer and rubber grommet from each pivot shaft.
4. Remove the two motor and bracket retaining bolts and washers.
5. Disconnect the wiper motor leads at the multiple connector.
6. Remove the motor and bracket assembly. Note the position of the ground washer and the rubber washer at the bracket mounting holes. Remove the plastic water shield.
7. To disconnect the motor from the bracket, remove the retaining clip that holds the linkage to the motor output arm. Note the position of the washers before removing the motor from the bracket.
8. Remove the four motor-to-bracket retaining bolts and remove the motor.

To install the motor linkage and bracket:

9. Install the wiper motor on the bracket and install the four retaining bolts.
10. Install the washers and position the linkage on the motor output arm. Install the retaining clip.

RUBBER GROMMET

BRACKET

ARM RETAINING NUT

PIVOT SHAFT

LINKAGE

RUBBER GROMMET

RUBBER CAP

NUT

MOTOR

WATER SHIELD

GROMMET

MOUNTING BOLTS

SPACER

GROUND WASHER

RUBBER WASHER

CONNECTOR

Courier windshield wiper components

11. Install the plastic water shield.

12. Install the motor and bracket assembly in the truck.

13. Connect the multiple connector.

14. Install the washers, spacers and nuts on the pivot shafts.

15. Install the wiper arms and blades. Be sure the motor is in the Park position. This can be determined by cycling the motor several times. Adjust the position of the wipers.

16. Connect the battery cable and check the operation of the wipers.

Wiper Motor

REMOVAL & INSTALLATION

Mazda

1. Remove the wiper arm attaching screws and remove the wiper arms.

2. Remove the cowl plate screws, move the cowl plate up at the front and disconnect the washer hose. Remove the cowl plate.

3. Disconnect the wires from the wiper motor.

4. Unbolt and remove the motor.

5. Installation is the reverse of removal.

Instrument Cluster

REMOVAL & INSTALLATION

Courier

1. Disconnect the battery ground cable.

2. On 1979 and later models only, the meter hood (instrument cluster trim panel) must be removed for access to the cluster. See steps 1–3 of the 1979 and later radio removal and installation procedure for details on meter hood removal.

Radio removal & installation—1979 and later Courier

3. Remove the screws holding the cluster to the instrument panel.

4. Pull the cluster rearward enough to gain access to the cluster assembly.

5. Reach behind the cluster and disconnect the speedometer cable.

6. Pull the multiple connector from the printed circuit.

7. Note the position of the two ammeter leads and disconnect them.

8. Remove the screw attaching the ground wire to the rear of the cluster. On trucks equipped with a coasting richer valve, remove the two connectors at the speedometer sensor switch.

9. Remove the instrument cluster.

To install the instrument cluster:

10. Position the cluster assembly near the opening and connect the ground lead.

11. Connect the two ammeter leads to the ammeter.

12. Install the multiple connector at the rear of the cluster. On trucks equipped with a coasting richer valve, connect the two wires to the speedometer speed sensor.

13. Connect the speedometer cable to the speedometer head.

14. Install the four attaching screws.

15. On 1979 and later models, replace the meter hood.

16. Connect the battery cable.

17. Run the engine and check the operation of all gauges.

Mazda
ROTARY PICK-UP

1. Remove the two bolts which secure the steering column bracket to the instrument panel.

2. Unfasten the four instrument cluster securing screws.

3. To disconnect the speedometer cable, reach up under the dash and depress the flat plastic connector tab while pulling the cable away from the head.

4. Unfasten the wiring harness from the instrument cluster.

5. Lift the cluster out.

Installation is performed in the reverse order of removal.

B-1800, B-2000 AND B-2200

1. Disconnect the cable from the negative (−) battery terminal.

2. Remove the four instrument cluster securing screws.

3. Move the cluster rearward, so that you can gain access to the back of it.

4. To disconnect the speedometer cable, reach up under the dash and depress the flat plastic connector tab while pulling the cable away from the head.

5. Disconnect the cluster wiring harness from the printed circuit. Note the position of the ammeter leads and disconnect them as well.

6. Remove the screw which secures the

ground lead to the cluster. On models with air injection, unfasten the two speedometer sensor lead connectors.

7. Remove the cluster.

Installation is the reverse of removal.

Speedometer Cable

REMOVAL & INSTALLATION
Courier

1. Remove the instrument cluster.

2. Remove the old cable by pulling it out from the speedometer end of the cable housing. If the old cable is broken, the speedometer cable will have to be disconnected from the transmission and the broken piece removed from the transmission end.

3. Lubricate the lower ¾ of the new cable with graphite speedometer cable lubricant, and feed the cable into the housing.

4. Connect the speedometer cable to the speedometer, and to the transmission if disconnected there.

5. Replace the instrument cluster.

Mazda

Speedometer cable removal—Mazda

Ignition Switch

REMOVAL & INSTALLATION
Courier

1. Disconnect the battery ground cable.

2. Reach under the instrument panel and pull the wire connector from the rear of the switch.

3. Hold the switch body from behind the instrument panel and remove the black retaining nut by turning it counterclockwise.

4. Remove the switch from the rear of the instrument panel.

To install the switch:

5. Position the switch in the instrument panel.

6. Hold the switch from behind the instrument panel. Install the retaining nut by turning it clockwise.

7. Plug the multiple connector into the back of the switch.

8. Connect the battery ground cable and check the operation of the switch.

Headlights

REMOVAL & INSTALLATION
Courier

1. Remove the six radiator grille attaching screws and remove the grille.

2. Remove the headlight bulb trim ring, by removing the three screws and rotating the ring clockwise. Support the headlight bulb and remove the trim ring.

NOTE: Do not disturb the headlight aim screws, which are installed in the housing next to the retaining ring screws.

3. Pull the plug connector from the rear of the bulb and remove the bulb.

To install a new bulb:

4. Connect the plug connector to the rear of a new headlight.

5. Install the headlight in the housing, and locate the bulb tabs in the slots and the housing.

6. Position the trim ring over the bulb and loosely install the retaining screws. Rotate the ring counterclockwise to lock it in position. Tighten the three attaching screws. Check the headlight operation.

7. Install the grille.

8. Have the headlight aim checked.

Fuses and Fusible Links

LOCATION AND REPAIR
Courier

The fuse box is located on the left side of the engine compartment near the windshield.

Couriers built after 1977 have a fusible link instead of the master fuse. The fusible link is a length of wire specially designed to melt under excessive electrical loads. It protects the entire electrical system. Replacements are made by splicing a new section into place. To replace the fusible link, first disconnect the battery negative cable. Then remove the old link and replace it with a link of similar capacity, available at your dealer.

Fuses

FUSE BOX LOCATION

Rotary Pick-Up

The main fuse block is mounted behind the seat at the right side of the cab. Another fuse box is attached to the firewall at the left, rear corner of the engine compartment. Fuse amperage and location are printed on the inside of the fuse box cover.

B-1800

The main fuse is located behind the battery. The fuse box is located at the left, rear corner of the engine compartment. Fuse amperage and location are printed on the inside of the cover.

Mazda B-2000 fusible link location

B-2000 and B-2200

The fuse box is located in the engine compartment at the rear left corner.

Fusible Links

LOCATION AND REPAIR

On all models except the B-2000 and B-2200, these are located in either one or two boxes next to the battery in the engine compartment. On the B-2000, the fusible link is located on the right fender apron. If these links blow, they must be replaced with the specified parts by disconnecting the battery, disconnecting wiring to each link requiring replacement, removing the

attaching screws and the link, and installing the new links or links in the reverse of the removal procedure.

Mazda B-2200 fusible link location

Mitsubishi/D-50/Arrow

VEHICLE IDENTIFICATION THROUGH 1980

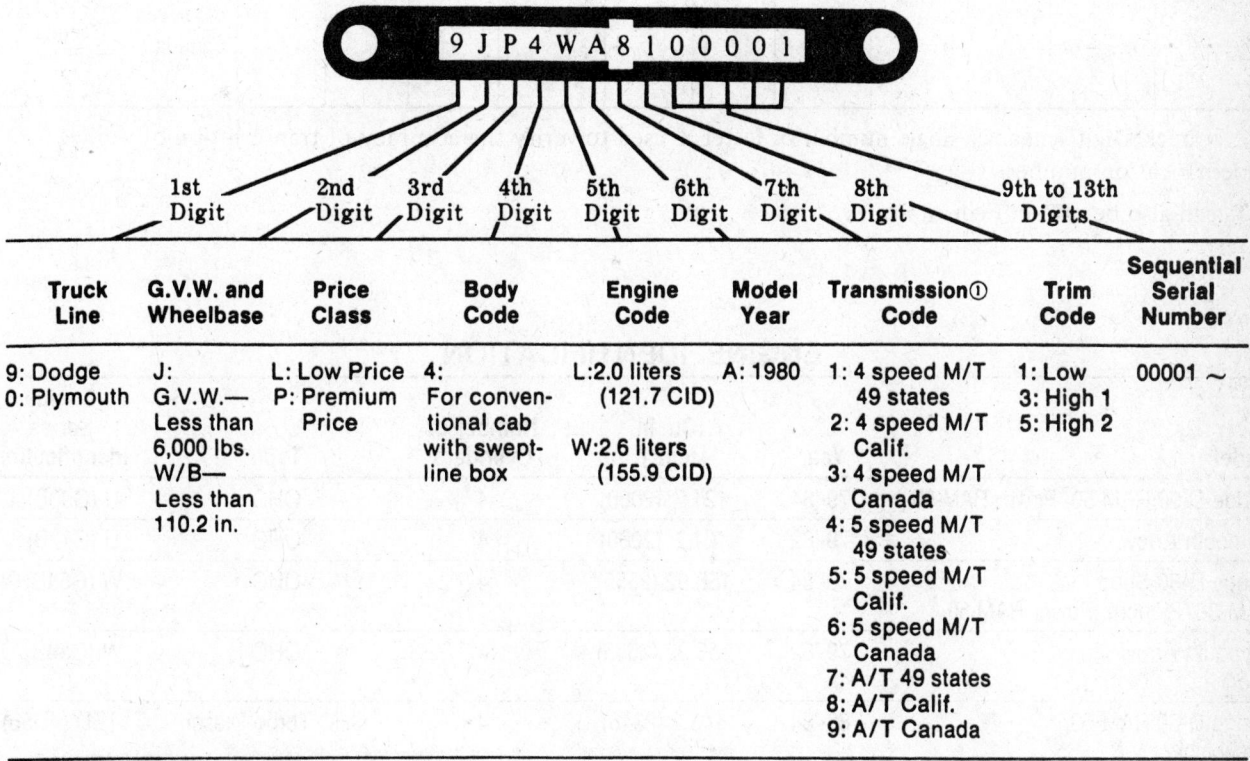

Truck Line	G.V.W. and Wheelbase	Price Class	Body Code	Engine Code	Model Year	Transmission① Code	Trim Code	Sequential Serial Number
9: Dodge 0: Plymouth	J: G.V.W.— Less than 6,000 lbs. W/B— Less than 110.2 in.	L: Low Price P: Premium Price	4: For conventional cab with sweptline box	L: 2.0 liters (121.7 CID) W: 2.6 liters (155.9 CID)	A: 1980	1: 4 speed M/T 49 states 2: 4 speed M/T Calif. 3: 4 speed M/T Canada 4: 5 speed M/T 49 states 5: 5 speed M/T Calif. 6: 5 speed M/T Canada 7: A/T 49 states 8: A/T Calif. 9: A/T Canada	1: Low 3: High 1 5: High 2	00001 ~

① M/T: Manual transmission,
A/T: Automatic transmission
G.V.W. Gross Vehicle Weight
W/B: Wheel Base

VEHICLE IDENTIFICATION FROM 1981

All vehicle identification number contains 17 digits. The vehicle number is a code which tells destination, brand, sales code, price class, engine displacement, type of body, etc.

J B 7 F P 2 4 D 1 E Y 1 0 0 1 0 1

1st Digit	2nd Digit	3rd Digit	4th Digit	5th Digit	6th Digit	7th Digit	8th Digit	9th Digit	10th Digit	11th Digit	12th Digit	13th to 17th Digit
Country	Make	Vehicle type	Other	Line	Series	Body	Engine	*Check digits	Model year	Plant	Transmission	Serial number
J- Japan	B- Dodge	7- Truck	F- 4001lbs. more and with hydraulic brake	P- RAM50 rear-wheel drive models K- POWER RAM50 4-wheel drive models	2- Low 4- High 5- Premium	4- Conventional cab	D- 2.0 liters (121.9 CID) E- 2.6 liters (155.9 CID) J- 2.3 liters (143.2 CID)	0 1 2 . . 9 X	E- 1984 year	Y- OYE plant	1-4 speed 49 States 2-4 speed **California or 50 States 3-4 speed Canada 4-5 speed 49 States 5-5 speed **California or 50 States 6-5 speed Canada	00101~ 7-A/T 49 States 8-A/T **California or 50 States 9-A/T Canada

* "Check Digit" means a single number or letter X used to verify the accuracy of transcription of vehicle identification number.

** can also be sold in Federal States.

ENGINE IDENTIFICATION

Model	Year	Cu. in. (cm³)	Number of Cylinders	Type	Engine Series Identification
Dodge D-50/RAM-50, Power RAM-50	'79-'84	121.7 (2000)	4	OHC	U (G63B)①
Plymouth Arrow	'79-'82	121.7 (2000)	4	OHC	U (G63B)①
Dodge D-50 Sport, RAM-50, Bighorn, Power RAM-50	'79-'84	155.92 (2555)	4	OHC	W (G54B)②
Plymouth Arrow Sport	'79-'82	155.92 (2555)	4	OHC	W (G54B)②
Dodge D-50/RAM 50, Mitsubishi	'83-'84	143.2 (2346)	4	OHC-Turbo Diesel	TBD (4D55)
Mitsubishi	'83-'84	121.7 (2000)	4	OHC	U (G63B)①
Mitsubishi, Mitsubishi Montero	'83-'84	155.92 (2555)	4	OHC	W (G54B)②

OHC: overhead cam
① 4G63 in Canada
② 4G54 in Canada

Engine I.D. location—2.0L (U-Series) engine

Engine I.D. location—2.6L (W-Series) engine

Engine I.D. location—turbo diesel

GENERAL ENGINE SPECIFICATIONS

Year	Engine Displacement cu in. (cc)	Carburetor Type	Horsepower @ rpm	Torque @ rpm (ft-lbs)	Bore X Stroke (in.)	Compression Ratio	Oil Pressure (psi)
'79-'84	121.7 (1995)	1 × 2 bbl	93 @ 5200① ⑤	108 @ 3000②	3.31 × 3.54	8.5:1	50-64
	155.92 (2555)	1 × 2 bbl	105 @ 5000③ ⑥	139 @ 2500④	3.59 × 3.86	8.2:1	50-64
'83-'84	143.2 (2346)	Turbo Diesel	84 @ 4200	136 @ 2500	3.59 × 3.54	21.0:1	56 @ 2000 rpm

① Canada: 96 @ 5500 HP
② Canada: 109 @ 3500 torque
③ Canada: 108 @ 5000 HP (thru '80)
④ Canada: 140 @ 2500 torque (thru '80)
⑤ '82-'84 California 88 @ 5000
⑥ '82-'84 California 103 @ 5000

ENGINE TUNE-UP SPECIFICATIONS
U.S.A. Gasoline Engines

Engine	Transmission	Curb Idle Speed	Curb Idle CO	Enriched Idle Speed	Enriched Idle CO	Ignition Timing
49-state U-engine	Manual	650 ± 50 rpm	Below 0.1%	730 ± 10	1.0 ± 0.1%	5° BTDC ± 1°②
	Automatic	700 ± 50 rpm	Below 0.1%	780 ± 10	1.0 ± 0.1%	5° BTDC ± 1°②
W-engine	Manual	750 ± 50 rpm③	1.0 ± 0.5%①	—	—	7° BTDC ± 1°②
	Automatic	750 ± 50 rpm④	1.0 ± 0.5%①	—	—	7° BTDC ± 1°②
California U-engine	Manual	650 ± 50 rpm	1.0 ± 0.5%①	—	—	5° BTDC ± 1°②
	Automatic	700 ± 50 rpm	1.0 ± 0.5%①	—	—	5° BTDC ± 1°②
W-engine	Manual	750 ± 50 rpm③	1.0 ± 0.5%①	—	—	7° BTDC ± 1°②
	Automatic	750 ± 50 rpm④	1.0 ± 0.5%①	—	—	7° BTDC ± 1°②

Canadian Gasoline Engines

Engine	Transmission	Curb Idle Speed	Curb Idle CO	Enriched Idle Speed	Enriched Idle CO	Ignition Timing
U-engine	Manual	850 ± 50 rpm	1.0 ± 0.5%①	—	—	13° BTDC ± 2°
	Automatic			—	—	
W-engine	Manual	850 ± 50 rpm	1.0 ± 0.5%①	—	—	7° BTDC ± 2°
	Automatic			—	—	

① With air injection system disconnected
② ± 2° 1983-84
③ 1983-84: 675 ± 150 rpm
④ 1983-84: 725 ± 150 rpm

GASOLINE ENGINE TUNE-UP SPECIFICATIONS

(When analyzing compression test results, look for uniformity among cylinders, rather than specific pressures)

Year	Engine Displacement cu in. (cc)	Spark Plug Gap (in.)	Ignition Timing (deg)		Intake Valve Opens (deg) BTDC	Fuel Pump Pressure (psi)	Idle Speed (rpm)	Valve Clearance (in.)	
			MT	AT				In	Ex
'79–'84	121.7 (2000)	0.039–0.043①④	5B⑥	5B⑥	25	4.6–6.0	650±50③⑤	0.006② Hot	0.010 Hot
	155.92 (2555)	0.039–0.043①④	7B⑥	7B⑥	25	4.6–6.0	750±50⑤	0.006② Hot	0.010 Hot

NOTE: The underhood specification sticker sometimes reflects tune-up specification changes made in production. Sticker figures must be used if they disagree with this chart.

① Canada: 0.028–0.031 in.
② Jet valve clearance: 0.006 (Hot) to 1982; 1983 and later jet valve 0.010 in.
③ Automatic transmission: 700±50 rpm.

④ For 1983-84 models, see underhood specifications sticker
⑤ See preceding specifications chart for 1983-84 models

⑥ See preceding specifications chart for Canadian timing specs.
MT: manual transmission
AT: automatic transmission

DIESEL ENGINE TUNE–UP SPECIFICATIONS

Year	Engine Displacement cu. in. (cc)	Transmission	Curb Idle Speed (rpm)	Initial Injection Timing	Valve Clearnace (hot) in
1983-84	143.2 (2346)	Manual	750±100	2° ATDC @ 1mm (.0394 in.) plunger stroke	.010 intake .010 exhaust

FIRING ORDER

NOTE: To avoid confusion, always replace spark plug wires one at a time.

Gasoline engines

CAPACITIES

Year	Model	Engine Displacement (cc)	Crankcase (qts) With Filter	Crankcase (qts) Without Filter	Transmission (qts) Manual 4-spd	Transmission (qts) Manual 5-spd	Transmission (qts) Automatic	Drive Axle (pts)	Gasoline Tank (gals)	Cooling System (qts) With AC	Cooling System (qts) Without AC
'79–'82	Pickups	2000	4.5	4.0	2.2	—	6.8①	2.8④	15.8②	9.5	9.5
		2555	4.5	4.0	—	2.4	6.8①	2.8④	15.8②	9.7	9.7
		2346③	5.9	5.3	2.2	2.4	—	2.3④	15.1②	8.5	8.5
'83–'84	Montero	2555	6.1	5.5	—	2.3	—	2.3	15.9	8.45	8.45

① '80–'82: 7.2 U.S. quarts
② '81 (2000) 15.1 gal
   (2555) 18.0 gal. also optional with 2000
   '82 and later: 18.0 optional on all
   pickup models
③ Turbo Diesel
④ Front axle; rear axle 3.8 pts.

VALVE SPECIFICATIONS

Year	Engine Displacement cu in. (cc)	Seat Angle (deg)	Face Angle (deg)	Spring Test Pressure (lbs @ in.)	Spring Installed Height (in.)	Stem to Guide Clearance (in.) Intake	Stem to Guide Clearance (in.) Exhaust	Stem Diameter (in.) Intake	Stem Diameter (in.) Exhaust
'79–'84	121.7 (2000)	45	45	61 @ 1.59	1.590	0.0012–0.0024	0.002–0.0035	0.315	0.315
	155.92 (2555)	45	45	61 @ 1.59	1.590	0.0012–0.0024	0.002–0.0035	0.315	0.315
	All (Jet valve)	45	45	5.5 @ .846	—	—	—	0.1693	0.1693
'83–'84	143.2 Turbo Diesel	45	45	61 @ 1.59		0.0012–0.0024	0.0020–0.0035	0.3150	0.3150

NOTE: Jet valve is found in both 2.0L and 2.6L engines.

CRANKSHAFT AND CONNECTING ROD SPECIFICATIONS

(All measurements given in inches)

Year	Engine cu. in.	Crankshaft Main Brg. Journal Dia.	Crankshaft Main Brg. Oil Clearance	Crankshaft Shaft End Play	Crankshaft Thrust on No.	Connecting Rod Journal Diameter	Connecting Rod Oil Clearance	Connecting Rod Side Clearance
'79–'84	121.7 155.9	2.3622	0.0008–0.0028	0.002–0.007	3	2.0866	0.0008–0.0028	0.004–0.010
'83–'84	143.2 Turbo Diesel	2.598	0.008–0.0020	0.0008–0.0020	3	2.087	0.0008–0.0024	0.004–0.010

PISTON AND RING SPECIFICATIONS

(All measurements given in inches)

Year	Engine (cu in.)	Piston to Bore Clearance	Ring Side Clearance			Ring Gap		
			Top Compression	Bottom Compression	Oil Control	Top Compression	Bottom Compression	Oil Control
'79–'84	121.7 155.92	0.0008– 0.0016	0.0024– 0.0039	0.0008– 0.0024	—	0.010– 0.018	0.010– 0.018①	0.0078– 0.035② ③
'83–'84	143.2 Turbo Diesel	.0016– .0024	0.001– 0.002	0.001– 0.003	0.001– 0.003	0.010– 0.016	0.010– 0.016	0.010– 0.018

① .010–.015 in. on 1983 and later 2.6L engine (155 cu. in.)
② .012–.024 in. on 1983 and later 2.6L engine (155 cu. in.)
③ .008–.020 in. on 1983 and later 2.0L engine (121 cu. in.)

TORQUE SPECIFICATIONS

(All readings in ft. lbs.)

Year	Engine Displacement cu in. (cc)	Cylinder Head Bolts	Rod Bearing Bolts	Main Bearing Bolts	Crankshaft Pulley Bolt	Flywheel to Crankshaft Bolts	Manifolds	
							Intake	Exhaust
'79–'84	All Gasoline	65–72①	33–34	55–61④	80–94⑤	94–101	11–14	11–14
'83–'84	143 (2346)②	76–83③	33–34	55–61	123–137	94–101	11–14	11–14

① Cold engine; hot engine—73–79 ft. lbs.
② Turbo Diesel
③ Cold engine; hot engine—84–90 ft. lbs
④ "W" (2.6L) engine; 2.0L 37–39 ft. lbs.
⑤ "W" (2.6L) engine; 2.0L 11–15 ft. lbs. each bolt

ALTERNATOR AND REGULATOR SPECIFICATIONS

Model	Year	Alternator Identification Number	Rated Output @ 5000	Rated Output @ 2500	Brush Length (in.)	Brush Spring Tension (lbs.)	Regulated Voltage
All	'79	AQ2245G	41 amps	34 amps	0.669①	2.9–3.7②	14.1–14.7
	'80–'82	A2T16471	44 amps	37 amps	0.709	0.7–1	14.1–14.7
	'83–'84	A5T15470	—	45 amps	③	—	13.9–14.9
	'83–'84	A5T15370	—	45 amps	③	—	13.9–14.9

① Built-in type brush: 0.709 in.
② Built-in type spring: 0.71–1 lbs.
③ Replace brushes when worn down to wear limit line

BATTERY AND STARTER SPECIFICATIONS

Year	Engine Model	Battery Amp Hour Capacity	Amps	Starter No Load Test Volts	RPM	Brush Spring Tension (lbs)	Min. Brush Length (in.)	Type of Starter
'79–'82	U, W w/MT	45, 60①	60	11.5	6,600	2.9–3.7	0.453	Direct Drive
	U, W w/AT	45, 60①	90④	11.5③	②3,300	2.9–3.7	0.453	Gear Reduction
'83–'84	U, W	45	100	11.5	3,000	2.9–3.7	0.453	Gear Reduction
	U, W	65	100	11.5	3,000	2.9–3.7	0.453	Gear Reduction
	W 4 × 4	80	60	11.5	6,500	2.9–3.7	0.453	Direct Drive
	TBD	110	130	11.0	4,000	2.9–3.7	0.453	Gear Reduction

MT: Manual Transmission
AT: Automatic Transmission
TBD: Turbo Diesel
① 60 amp for Canada
② 1979: 4,500 rpm
③ 1979: 11 volts
④ 1979: 62 amps

BRAKE SPECIFICATIONS
(All measurements are given in inches unless noted)

Model	Year	Lug Nut Torque Ft-lb	Master Cylinder Bore	Brake Disc Thickness Std.	Min.	Runout	Brake Drum Diameter	Maximum Wear	Lining Thickness Front Min.	Rear Min.
All	'79	51–58	7/8	0.79	0.72	0.006	9.5	9.579	0.04①	0.04①
	'80–'84	51–58	7/8	0.79	0.72	0.006	9.5	9.579	0.04①	0.04①

① Due to the variations in state inspection regulations, the minimum allowable lining thickness may be different from that recommended by the manufacturer.

TUNE-UP

NOTE: The procedures outlined below are the specific procedures for the Dodge, Plymouth and Mitsubishi pickup and Montero. General tune-up procedures may be found in the section at the end of this book.

Spark Plugs

Check, clean and adjust the spark plugs every 12,000 miles. Replace them every 30,000 miles.

Clean any foreign material from around the spark plugs before removing them. When removing plug cables, grasp them at the cable caps.

Inspect the plugs for cracked or damaged threads or insulators, worn electrodes and damaged or worn plug gaskets. Always replace all four plugs as a set, it will be cheaper and more effective in the long run.

Set the plug gap to 0.039–0.043 in. (USA), 0.028–0.031 in. (Canada) using a wire feeler gauge.

NOTE: Do not use a flat gauge; an inaccurate reading will result. Hand start, then torque each plug into its hole at 18–21 ft. lbs.

—— CAUTION ——
Don't over-torque plugs or thread stripping could result.

Electronic ignition to 1980

Testing ignition through 1980

Electronic Ignition System (EIS)

All pick-ups are equipped with electronic ignition systems which replace the contact points and condenser with a transistorized integrated circuit. No adjustments can be done on this type of ignition system.

IGNITION SYSTEM TEST

NOTE: If engine will not start, go to test 1 or test 2, depending on the year of your truck.

If the engine will run:

1. Start the engine, allow to idle until the normal operating temperature is reached.
2. Check the ignition timing, adjust if necessary.
3. Visually check electrical connections for frayed insulation or bare wires. Make sure all plug-in connectors are clean and tight. Check the spark plug and coil wires for cracking, crossfiring, corroded terminals, continuity and resistance.

Check the distributor cap for cracks or carbon tracking. Check any suspect parts. Check the spark plugs for foiling, nonfiring and correct gap.

4. If none of the checks have solved the problem, or the car fails to start, proceed to the following tests.

1979–80 TEST 1

1. Remove the distributor cap by inserting a screwdriver in the ends of the two retaining screws, pushing in and turning the screws clockwise.
2. Remove the screws holding the rotor assembly and lift out the rotor.
3. Turn the ignition switch to the ON position.
4. Disconnect the high tension cable (coil wire) from the center terminal of the distributor cap and hold its end about a quarter of an inch away from a ground (cylinder block etc.).

NOTE: Use insulated pliers to hold the cable.

Insert a flatblade screwdriver between the reluctor and the stator. A spark should jump from the high tension wire to the ground.

If a spark is not produced, a defective control unit, pick-up coil, ignition coil or faulty wiring may be the problem. Further service should be left to a qualified service technician. However, in the paragraphs that follow further tests are described.

FROM 1981 TEST 2

Remove the coil wire from the distributor cap tower. Hold the end of the wire with insulated pliers (prevents you from getting a shock). Locate the end of the wire about a quarter of an inch away from the cylinder head and have a friend crank the engine with the starter. Observe the spark or no spark condition. If a spark is produced, the IC igniter and ignition coil may be considered in good condition. Remove the distributor cap and check it for cracks, carbon tracking or dirt. Check the rotor for wear. Replace as necessary. If no sparks are produced a defective control unit (internal), pick-up coil, ignition coil or faulty wiring may be the problem.

IGNITION COIL

If either test 1 or test 2 produces no spark, the ignition coil could be at fault. The fastest way to check is by substituting a known good coil. If a coil is not on hand, proceed with one or more of the following tests.

1. With the ignition switch in the ON position measure the voltage at the negative terminal of the ignition coil. If zero volts are shown, there is an open circuit in the coil.
2. Check the ignition coil resistance. If the engine will run allow it to reach normal operating temperature (the ignition coil should be hot). Shut off the engine and disconnect the high tension lead (coil wire) from the coil tower.

2a. Measure primary resistance with an ohmmeter, connecting the coil minus and plus primary terminals. Resistance should be; 0.7–0.85 ohms.

2b. Measure the secondary resistance by connecting the ohmmeter between the contacts in the coil tower and the plus primary terminal. Resistance should be; 9–11 k ohms.

3. Replace the coil if the voltage tests show zero volts or the resistances are not within specifications.

TESTING THE EXTERNAL RESISTOR

1. With the ignition switch off: connect an ohmmeter between the terminals of the external resistor.
2. Obtain a reading from the ohmmeter. Resistance should be 1.22–1.49 ohms.
3. If the reading on the ohmmeter is zero or not within specs, replace the resistor.

TESTING THE PICK-UP COIL

The pick-up coil may be tested while mounted in the distributor. Remove the cap and rotor and connect an ohmmeter between the two terminals of the pick-up coil. If the resistance is not within the limits; (1980) 1,050 plus or minus 50 ohms: (from 1981) 920–1.120 ohms; replace the pick-up coil.

PICK-UP COIL REPLACEMENT

Distributor must be removed from the engine. (see distributor removal procedure).

1. Remove the distributor cap and rotor.
2. Remove the center mounting bolt (screw) and remove the governor assembly. Take care not to mix up the governor springs they must be installed in the same position. Remove the reluctor.
3. Remove the two mounting screws and take out the pick-up coil (79–80) or the pick-up coil and IC Igniter (81–82). Carefully pull the Igniter from the pick-up coil (81–82).

Distributor locknut location

Timing marks

Jet valve adjustment

4. Installation of the new pick-up coil is the reverse of the removal.

Ignition Timing

1. Warm up the engine. Connect a tachometer and check the engine idle speed. Adjust it as outlined if not within specifications.

If the timing mark on the front pulley is difficult to see, use chalk or a dab of paint to make it more visible.

2. Connect a timing light to the engine, as outlined in the instructions supplied by the manufacturer of the light.

3. Allow the engine to run at the specified idle speed with the gear shift in Neutral (Park, if automatic) and the air conditioning compressor and lights off.

Valve adjustment

— **CAUTION** —
Be sure the parking brake is firmly set and that the wheels are chocked.

4. Point the timing light at the timing marks indicated on the front timing chain cover. With engine at idle, timing should be at the specifications given in the tune-up chart at the beginning of this section. If it is not, loosen the attaching nut at the base

of the distributor and rotate the distributor until the correct timing is achieved.

5. Stop the engine and retighten the attaching nut. Start the engine and recheck the timing.

6. Stop the engine and disconnect the timing light and tachometer.

Valve Lash

ADJUSTMENT

Gasoline Engines

Both the U engine (1995 c.c.) and the W engine (2555 c.c.) have a jet valve located beside the intake valve of each cylinder. The jet valve works off the intake valve rocker arm and injects a swirl of air into the combustion chamber to promote more complete burning of fuel.

NOTE: When adjusting valve clearances, the jet valve must be adjusted before the intake valve.

1. Start the engine and allow it to reach normal operating temperature (170–190°F).

2. Stop the engine and remove the air cleaner and its hoses. Remove any other cables, hoses, wires, etc., which are attached to the valve cover, and remove the valve cover.

3. Disconnect the high tension coil-to-distributor wire at the coil.

4. Watch the rocker arms for no. 1 cylinder and rotate the crankshaft until the exhaust valve is closing and the intake valve has just started to open. At this point, no. 4 cylinder will be at top dead center (TDC) commencing its firing stroke.

5. Loosen the lock nut on cylinder no. 4 intake valve and back off the intake valve adjusting screw 2 or more turns.

6. Loosen the lock nut on the jet valve adjusting screw.

7. Turn the jet valve adjusting screw counter-clockwise and insert a 0.006 in. feeler gauge between the jet valve stem and the adjusting screw.

8. Tighten the adjusting screw until it touches the feeler gauge.

Take care not to press in the valve while adjusting because the jet valve spring is very weak.

NOTE: If the adjusting screw is tight, special care must be taken to avoid pressing down on the jet valve when adjusting the clearance or a false reading will result.

9. Tighten the lock nut securely while holding the rocker arm adjusting screw with a screwdriver to prevent it from turning.

10. Make sure that a 0.006 in. feeler gauge can be easily inserted between the jet valve and the rocker arm.

11. Adjust no. 4 cylinder's intake valve to 0.006 in. and its exhaust valve to 0.010 in. Tighten the adjusting screw locknuts and re-check each clearance.

12. Perform step 4 in conjunction with the chart below to set up the remaining three

cylinders for valve adjustments.

13. Replace the valve cover and all other components. Run the engine and check for oil leaks at the valve cover.

Exhaust Valve Closing	Adjust
No. 1 cylinder	No. 4 cylinder valves
No. 2 cylinder	No. 3 cylinder valves
No. 3 cylinder	No. 2 cylinder valves
No. 4 cylinder	No. 1 cylinder valves

Diesel Engines

1. Make sure the engine is at normal operating temperature.

2. Place the No. 1 piston at top dead center (TDC) on the compression stroke.

Diesel valve adjustment order

3. Loosen the locknuts on the rocker arms marked "A" in the illustration, and adjust the clearances to .010 in. with a feeler gauge. Retighten the locknuts.

4. After retightening the nuts, recheck clearances.

5. Place the No. 4 piston at TDC on the compression stroke.

6. Adjust valve clearances on the valves marked "B" in the illustration by following step 3 above. Recheck clearances after tightening the locknuts.

7. Check the idle speed and readjust if necessary.

Idle Speed And Mixture

ADJUSTMENT

Gasoline Engine

NOTE: See Fuel System for other carburetor adjustments.

1. Start and run the engine at idle until normal operating temperature is reached.

2. Check the tune-up specifications chart or the underhood decal for the correct curb idle speed.

3. Connect a tachometer (follow the instructions that came with the meter) and adjust the idle speed screw until the correct rpm is reached.

4. *Idle mixture adjustments should be*

made by an authorized garage using a CO meter. However, a small amount of adjustment is possible (within the limits of the idle mixture screw limiter cap—which must not be removed).

NOTE: Some late model carburetors have a tamperproof, sealed idle mixture screw—these cannot be adjusted, except by an authorized garage.

5. To adjust the idle mixture; first, adjust carb to correct curb idle speed. Next, watch the tachometer scale, listen to the engine and slowly turn the idle mixture screw clockwise. A drop in engine rpm or engine roughness will tell you when to stop. Then, slowly turn the mixture screw counterclockwise until once again you encounter rpm drop or engine roughness. A point, in between the clockwise or counterclockwise positions that gives you the highest rpm or smoothest running engine, is the best setting.

6. Check and readjust the curb idle speed, if necessary.

7. Have your adjustment checked with a CO meter as soon as possible.

Carburetor idle adjustments

Diesel Engine

1. Make sure all accessories and lights are off, and the transmission is in Neutral.

2. Run the engine until the engine is at normal operating temperature.

3. Run the engine for more than 5 seconds at an engine speed of 2,000–3,000 rpm.

Turbo diesel idle speed adjustment

4. Run the engine at idle for 2 minutes.

5. Using a tachometer suitable for diesel engines, read the idle speed. If outside specified limits, readjust to specs using the idle speed adjusting screw on the injection pump.

NOTE: Do not disturb the other screws on the injection pump.

Fuel Filter Element

REPLACEMENT

Diesel Engines Only

The fuel filter (and its maintenance) is crucial to the protection of the turbodiesel engine, keeping water and dirt out of the injection pump. The fuel filter also has a built-in fuel heater, which prevents the waxing of diesel fuel in cold weather.

To remove the fuel filter element, the fuel filter must be removed. The fuel system must be bled after the new filter has been installed.

Diesel fuel filter hose and sensor connections

1. Disconnect the water level sensor connector, fuel heater connector, fuel temperature sensor connector (all electrical connections) and main fuel hoses at the fuel filter.

2. Remove the two bolts attaching the fuel filter to the vehicle, and remove the filter. Remove the protector and bracket.

3. Screw the filter cartridge out of the fuel filter pump body by hand. Remove the water level sensor and the drain plug from the cartridge.

4. Check the filter for dirt deposits, and clean with kerosene if necessary.

5. Install the drain plug and water level sensor on the new cartridge. Torque the drain plug to 3-4 ft. lbs.; torque the water level sonsor to 9-10 ft. lbs.

6. Whenever the fuel supply has run out, or the filter has been replaced, or the fuel lines have been disconnected, the fuel system must be bled of air. Loosen the air plug on the filter body; this is the plug protruding out the top of the filter body on an angle.

7. Pull out the hand pump knob on the filter (on the side of the filter body) by turning it to the left. Pump the hand pump until the fuel coming out of the air plug hole has no air bubbles in it. Tighten the air plug.

DRAINING WATER FROM THE FUEL FILTER

Diesel Engines Only

When water accumulates in the fuel filter, the fuel water separator light will come on. Follow the procedure below as soon as possible.

1. Loosen the drain plug on the bottom of the fuel filter.

2. Drain the water by pumping the hand pump on the side of the filter body, then tighten the drain plug.

Distributor mounting

ENGINE ELECTRICAL

Distributor

REMOVAL

1. Disconnect the battery ground cable.
2. Disconnect the wiring harness from the distributor control unit.
3. Mark the spark plug cables and pull them off the spark plugs.

NOTE: Always pull spark plug and coil cables at their boots to avoid breaking the wires inside the cables.

4. Remove the distributor cap by inserting a screwdriver into the two retaining screws, pushing in and turning clockwise.
5. Match-mark the distributor housing and the engine block; mark the rotor position in the distributor as well. This will aid in correct positioning of the distributor during installation.
6. Disconnect the vacuum hose from the vacuum control unit.
7. Remove the distributor mounting nut and lift off the distributor assembly.

INSTALLATION—ENGINE DISTURBED

1. Turn the engine crankshaft until the No. 1 cylinder is at top dead center on compression stroke. To find No. 1 cylinder, compression stroke, take off the distributor cap and turn the rotor and shaft until the rotor assembly is pointing toward the No. 1 cylinder lead in the distributor cap. Verify top dead center on the crankshaft pulley.
2. Align the mating mark (line) on the distributor housing with the mating mark (punch mark) on the distributor driven gear.
3. Install the distributor with the mating mark on the distributor attaching flange even with the center of the distributor retaining stud. Tighten the nut and replace the distributor cap, wires, and plug wires.
4. Set ignition timing as described above.

INSTALLATION—ENGINE NOT DISTURBED

1. Insert the distributor in the engine and align the marks made during removal.
2. Install the mounting nut, distributor cap, wires and plug wires, and vacuum line.
3. Start engine and check ignition timing.

Align mark on flange with stud

Mating mark alignment

9. Pickup coil
10. Breaker
11. Plate
12. Vacuum control unit
13. E-ring
14. Washer
15. Shaft
16. Ball bearing
17. Oil seal
18. Housing
19. Control unit
20. O-ring
21. Spring pin
22. Driven gear

1. Cap
2. Contact carbon
3. Rotor assembly
4. Governor spring
5. Governor plate
6. Governor weight
7. Governor base
8. Reluctor

Exploded view of distributor—typical

Exploded view of a gasoline engine alternator

Alternator

PRECAUTIONS

1. Always observe proper polarity of the battery connections; be especially careful when jump-starting the car.

2. Never ground or short out any alternator or alternator regulator terminals.

3. Never operate the alternator with any of its or the battery's leads disconnected.

4. Always remove the battery or disconnect the cables while charging it.

5. Always disconnect the ground cable when replacing any electrical components.

6. Never subject the alternator to excessive heat or dampness if the engine is being steam-cleaned.

7. Never use arc-welding equipment with the alternator connected.

REMOVAL & INSTALLATION

1. Disconnect the battery ground cable.

2. Disconnect the cable from terminal "B" on the back of the alternator. Disconnect the other cables.

3. Remove the alternator brace bolt and the support bolt nut. Remove the drive belt.

4. Pull out the support bolt and remove the alternator assembly.

To install alternator:

1. Align the hole in the alternator leg with the hole in the front case and insert the alternator support bolt from the front bracket side.

2. Install the brace bolt.

3. Install drive belt.

4. Push the alternator toward the front of the engine and check the clearance between the alternator leg and the front case. If the clearance is more than 0.008 in., insert spacers as required. 0.0078 in. thick spacers are available.

5. Adjust the belt tension as described below.

6. Tighten the alternator support bolt nut to 15–18 ft. lbs. and the brace bolt to 9–11 ft. lbs.

BELT ADJUSTMENT

Inspection and adjustment to the alternator drive belt should be performed every 15,000 miles. The belt should be replaced every 30,000 miles.

1. Inspect the drive belt to see that it is not cracked or worn. Be sure that its surfaces are free of grease or oil.

Drive belt tension adjustment

2. Pull the belt with a force of about 22 lbs. at a point halfway between the alternator pulley and the water pump pulley. The belt deflection should be 1/4 to 3/8 in.

3. If the belt requires adjustment, loosen the alternator support bolt and alternator brace bolt and move the alternator to obtain specified deflection at 22 lbs. pressure.

4. After adjustment, tighten the alternator support bolt to 14–18 ft. lbs., and the alternator brace bolt to 9 to 11 ft. lbs.

Unsolder the three wires to remove the stator assembly

— **CAUTION** —
Do not overtighten the belt, or damage to the alternator bearings might result.

CHARGING SYSTEM TEST (ON-VEHICLE)

1. Place the ignition switch at off.

2. Disconnect the battery ground cable.

3. Disconnect the cable from terminal "B" of the alternator and connect an ammeter between the terminal "B" and the cable.

4. Connect a voltmeter between terminal "B" (+) and ground (−).

5. Set the engine tachometer.

6. Connect the battery ground cable to the battery. The voltmeter should indicate the battery voltage.

7. Start the engine.

8. Turn on the lamps, accelerate the engine to the speed specified in the chart at the beginning of this section and measure the output current. Check it against the chart.

OVERHAUL

Gasoline Engine Models

1. Remove alternator from vehicle.

2. Remove the three through bolts from the alternator body.

3. Insert a screwdriver between the front bracket and stator (see illustration). Pry the front bracket away from the stator. Remove the front bracket along with the rotor.

NOTE: If the screwdriver is inserted too deeply, the stator coil might be damaged.

4. Hold the rotor in a vise and remove the pulley nut. Then remove the pulley, fan, spacer and seal. Remove the rotor from the front bracket and remove the seal.

Location of rectifier and brush holder

Insert a wire to hold the brushes

5. Unsolder the rectifier from the stator coil lead wires and remove the stator assembly.

NOTE: Make sure the solder is removed quickly (in less than five seconds). If a diode is heated to more than 150°C, it might be damaged.

6. Remove the condenser from the terminal "B".

7. Unsolder the plates "B" and "L" from the rectifier assembly.

8. Remove the mounting screw and terminal "B" bolt and remove the electronic voltage regulator and brush holder. The regulator and brush holder cannot be separated.

9. Remove the rectifier assembly.

10. Brush and brush spring replacement; When only a brush or brush spring is to be replaced, it is not necessary to remove the stator, etc. Raise the brush holder assembly and unsolder the wire pigtail of the brush and remove the brush.

NOTE: Be very careful when bending the plates "B" and "L" so as not to disturb the rectifier moulding.

11. Check the outside circumference of the slip ring for dirtiness and roughness. Clean or polish with armature paper, if required. A badly damaged slip ring or a slip ring worn down beyond the service limit should also be replaced. The service limit for the slip ring outside diameter is 1.268 in.

12. Check for continuity between the field coil and slip ring. If there is not continuity, the field coil is defective and the rotor must be replaced.

13. Check for continuity between the slip ring and the shaft (or core). If there is continuity, the rotor assembly must be replaced.

14. Check for continuity between the leads of the stator coil. If there is no continuity, the stator coil is defective.

15. Check for an open circuit between the stator coil leads and the stator core. If there is continuity between the stator core and the coil leads, the stator assembly must be replaced.

16. Check for continuity between the (+) heat sink and the stator coil lead connection terminal with a circuit tester. If there is continuity in both directions, the diode is short-circuited and the rectifier assembly must be replaced.

17. Perform step 16 between the (−) heat sink and the stator coil lead connection.

18. Using a circuit tester, check the three diodes for continuity in both directions. If there is either continuity or an open circuit in both directions, the diode is defective and must be replaced.

19. Measure the length of the brush. If it is worn below 0.315 in., it must be replaced.

Assembly is the reverse of disassembly with the following notes:

1. Be sure to install both the front and rear seals on the front bearing.

2. To install the rotor assembly in the rear bracket, push the brushes into the brush holder, insert a wire to hold them in the raised position and install the rotor. Remove the wire.

Diesel Engine Models

The alternator on the turbo-diesel models

1 Bolt (3)	3 O-ring	11 Front bracket and rotor
2 Vacuum housing	4 Vane	assembly
assembly	5 Vacuum pump rotor	1 Nut
1 Check valve	6 Screw (2)	2 Spring washer
2 Gasket (2)	7 Cover	3 Pulley
3 Nipple	8 Brush holder	4 Fan
4 Joint	9 Electronic voltage	5 Collar
5 Gasket	regulator	6 Rotor
6 Vacuum pump	10 Throught bolt (3)	7 Rear ball bearing
housing		

8 Screw (3)
9 Bearing retainer
10 Front ball bearing
11 Front bracket
12 Stator and rear
bracket
1 Stator
2 Nut (2)
3 Insulator (2)
4 Rectifier
5 Oil seal set
6 Rear bracket

Turbo diesel alternator showing vacuum pump

is the same as on the 2.6L gasoline engine, except that the rear end of the rotor shaft is longer. Mounted on the end of the rotor shaft is a small vacuum pump, which generates vacuum for the brake booster. The vacuum pump is a vane-type. Oil for lubricating the pump passes through an oil hose from the oil filter bracket, and is supplied to the vacuum pump. After lubricating the pump, the oil passes through a return hose back to the oil pan.

Follow the "Overhaul" procedure above for gasoline engine alternators. The vacuum pump housing unbolts from the rear of the alternator housing. Always replace the O-ring; grease the O-ring groove before installing the ring. Follow the following

Installing vacuum pump housing—turbo diesel alternator

precautions below when assembling the vacuum pump.

1. Install the pump vanes with the rounded end outward. Any vane with worn or chipped ends should be replaced.

2. Make sure no foreign material is present when installing the pump. Any dirt can cause the pump to seize.

3. When the pump housing is installed, push it lightly in the direction of the arrow (illustration) to minimize clearance at point "A". Tighten the three bolts evenly. Pump performance is affected by the way the housing is installed.

4. Fill the pump with clean engine oil before bench testing or running the alternator. Do not operate the alternator without first lubing the pump.

Regulator

REMOVAL & INSTALLATION

Both the 2.0L and 2.6L engines use an integrated circuit-type regulator which is contained in the alternator. See Alternator Removal and Installation removal procedures. Adjustments of the regulator are confined to replacement.

Starter

REMOVAL & INSTALLATION

1. Disconnect the battery ground cable.
2. Disconnect the starter motor wiring.
3. Loosen and remove the two starter

motor mounting bolts and remove the starter motor.

4. Installation is the reverse of removal.

STARTER DRIVE, SOLENOID AND BRUSH REPLACEMENT

NOTE: Starter must be removed from vehicle for this operation.

Direct Drive Type

1. Remove the wire connecting the starter solenoid to the starter.

2. Remove the two screws holding the starter solenoid on the starter-drive housing and remove the solenoid.

3. Remove the two long through bolts at the rear of the starter and separate the armature yoke from the armature.

4. Carefully remove the armature and the starter drive engagement lever from the front bracket, after making a mental note of the way they are positioned along with the attendant spring and spring retainer.

5. Loosen the two screws and remove the rear bracket.

6. Tap the stopper ring at the end of the drive gear engagement shaft in towards the drive gear to expose the snap-ring. Remove the snap-ring.

7. Pull the stopper, drive gear and overrunning clutch from the end of the shaft. For 1979 models with automatic transmissions, remove the center bracket, spring and spring retainer.

Inspect the pinion and spline teeth for wear or damage. If the engagement teeth are damaged, visually check the flywheel

1. Front bearing	7. Lever
2. Front bracket	8. Lever spring
3. Washer	9. Spring retainer
4. Snap ring	10. Armature
5. Stopper	
6. Overrunning clutch and pinion	

11. Washer set
12. Yoke
13. Brush
14. Brush
15. Brush holder
16. Brush spring
17. Rear bearing
18. Rear bracket
19. Brush holder tightening screw
20. Through bolt
21. Washer set
22. Magnetic switch
23. Magnetic switch tightening screw

Exploded view of direct drive starter

1. Lever spring	4. Front bracket	7. Ring	10. Center bracket	13. Field coil	16. Through bolt	19. Terminal "M"
2. Packing	5. Pinion	8. Pinion shaft assy	11. Pole	14. Brush	17. Rear bracket	20. Terminal "S"
3. Lever	6. Stopper	9. Gear	12. Yoke	15. Brush holder	18. Magnetic switch	21. Terminal "B"

Gear reduction starter

ring gear through the starter hole to insure that it is not damaged. It will be necessary to turn the engine over by hand to completely inspect the ring gear.

Check the brushes for wear. Their service limit length is 0.453 in. Replace if necessary.

Assembly is performed in the following manner. For 1979 models with automatic transmissions, fit the spring retainer, spring and center bracket on the shaft.

Removing snap-ring

8. Install the spring retainer and spring on the armature shaft.

9. Install the overrunning clutch assembly on the armature shaft.

10. Fit the stopper ring with its open side facing out on the shaft.

11. Install a new snap-ring and, using a gear puller, pull the stopper ring into place over the snap-ring.

12. Fit the small washer on the front end of the armature shaft.

13. Fit the engagement lever into the overrunning clutch and refit the armature into the front housing.

14. Fit the engagement lever spring and spring retainer into place and slide the armature yoke over the armature. Make sure you position the yoke with the spring retainer cut-out space in line with the spring retainer.

NOTE: Make sure the brushes are seated on the commutator.

15. Replace the rear bracket and two retainer screws.

16. Install the two through bolts in the end of the yoke.

17. Refit the starter solenoid, making sure you fit the plunger over the engagement lever. Install the screws and connect the wire running from the starter yoke to the starter solenoid.

Gear Reduction Type

1. Remove the wire connecting the starter solenoid to the starter.

2. Remove the two screws holding the solenoid and, pulling out, unhook it from the engagement lever.

3. Remove the two through bolts in the

end of the starter and remove the two bracket screws. Pull off the rear bracket.

NOTE: Since the conical spring washer is contained in the rear bracket, be sure to take it out.

4. Remove the yoke and brush holder assembly while pulling the brush upward.

5. Pull the armature assembly out of the mounting bracket.

6. In the side of the mounting bracket that the armature fits into, there is a small dust cap held by two screws. Remove it and remove the snap-ring and washer under it.

7. Remove the remaining bolts in the mounting bracket and split the reduction case.

NOTE: Several washers will come out when the case is split. These adjust the end play for the pinion shaft. Do not lose them.

8. Remove the reduction gear, lever and lever spring from the front bracket.

9. Using a brass drift or deep socket, knock the stopper ring on the end of the shaft in toward the pinion. Remove the snap-ring. Remove the stopper, pinion and pinion shaft assembly.

10. Remove the ball bearings at both ends of the armature.

NOTE: The ball bearings are pressed in the front bracket and are not replaceable. Replace them together with the bracket.

Inspect the pinion and spline teeth for wear or damage. If the engagement teeth are damaged, visually check the flywheel ring gear through the starter hole to insure that it is not damaged also. It will be necessary to turn the engine over by hand to completely inspect the ring gear.

Check the brushes for wear. Their service limit length is 0.0453 in. Replace if necessary.

Assembly is the reverse of disassembly. Be sure to replace all adjusting and thrust washers. When replacing the rear bracket, fit the conical spring pinion washer with its convex side facing out. Make sure that the brushes seat themselves on the commutator.

ENGINE MECHANICAL

REMOVAL & INSTALLATION

Gasoline Engines

———— **CAUTION** ————
Be sure the car is supported securely during engine removal.

NOTE: The engine and transmission are removed as a unit.

1. Working inside the engine compartment, remove the splash shield below the engine. Drain the coolant from the radiator and the engine by opening the drain plug at the bottom of the radiator and the drain cock located at the right rear of the cylinder block. Use a suitable container to catch coolant.

NOTE: It would be wise to drain the radiator in an area other than the one in which the engine is to be removed so that you will not be in contact with coolant when working under the vehicle.

2. Disconnect and remove the battery.
3. Disconnect the ground strap and the wiring of the ignition coil, fuel cut-off solenoid valve, alternator, starter motor, water temperature gauge unit and oil pressure gauge unit.
4. Disconnect the air cleaner breather hose. Remove the air cleaner and disconnect the hot air duct and the vacuum hose.
5. Disconnect the accelerator control cable. For automatic transmissions, disconnect the transmission control rod.
6. Disconnect the radiator hoses by loosening their clips.
7. Disconnect the heater hose.
8. Disconnect the exhaust pipe from the exhaust manifold. The muffler pipe bracket should be detached at the transmission.
9. Disconnect the fuel hoses and vapor hose.
10. Remove the radiator and radiator cowl. Four bolts hold the radiator in place. On vehicles with automatic transmissions, remove and plug the two oil cooling pipes in the bottom of the radiator.

11. For trucks with four and five speed transmissions:
   a. Remove the lock screws and lift up the console box, inside the driver's compartment. In trucks without a console box, remove the carpet.
   b. Remove the attaching screws and lift out the dust cover retainer plate.
   c. Pull up the dust cover and remove the four attaching bolts holding the shift lever to the transmission extension housing. Remove the shift lever control assembly.

NOTE: On four speed transmissions, remove the gear shift lever with the lever in 2nd speed position. On five speed transmissions, place the lever in 1st speed position.

12. Mark the position of the hood retaining bolts in relation to the hood and remove the hood.
13. Jack up the vehicle and support it on stands.
14. Disconnect the speedometer cable and backup light switch wiring from the transmission.
15. For trucks with manual transmissions, disconnect the clutch cable from the transmission by removing the cotter key and sliding it off the arm. Disconnect the cable from the cable bracket. For automatic transmissions, remove shift linkage between transmission and shift lever.
16. Drain the transmission.
17. Remove the bolts holding the rear of the driveshaft to the rear axle. Remove the two nuts holding the center bearing assembly of the driveshaft to the frame and pull the driveshaft out of the rear of the transmission.
18. On two-wheel drive models, support the transmission on a jack and remove the bolts holding the front motor mounts. For four-wheel drive models, support the transfer case with a jack, and, after removing the transfer case mounting bracket and support insulator, remove the plate from the side frame. Detach the transfer case mounting bracket from the transfer case.
19. Unbolt the rear transmission mount crossmember and remove the two bolts holding it to the transmission. Remove the crossmember.
20. Attach steel lifting cables to the engine front and rear hangers and attach the cables to a suitable hoist.
21. Have an assistant slowly lower the jack under the transmission and pull the engine/transmission out of the vehicle by tilting it upwards and pulling forward.

NOTE: If the transmission will not clear the steering relay rod, raise it until the bell housing is above the rod, then remove the engine/transmission from the truck.

Installation is the reverse of removal. Adjust all transmission and carburetor linkages as detailed in the appropriate sections. Install and adjust the hood. Refill the engine, transmission and radiator to capacity.

Diesel Engine

1. Disconnect the negative battery cable.
2. Drain the engine oil.
3. Remove the hood.
4. Remove the air cleaner duct. Remove the heater hoses.
5. Disconnect the throttle cable.
6. Disconnect the fuel lines. Disconnect the water level sensor connector (see illustration) and remove the fuel filter.
7. Remove the power steering pump, if equipped.
8. Disconnect the glow system cable, and the gauge unit harness connectors.
9. Disconnect the engine ground cable.
10. Disconnect the starter motor wiring harness.
11. Separate the clutch release cylinder from the transmission.
12. Disconnect the engine oil cooler hoses.
13. Disconnect the brake booster vacuum hose.
14. Disconnect the alternator wiring harness. Disconnect the oil pressure switch harness or the oil pressure gauge unit harness.
15. Remove the radiator assembly.
16. Remove the front exhaust pipe.
17. On 4 × 4 models, remove the engine and transfer case skid plates and under cover. On 2WD models, remove the under cover.
18. Disconnect the speedometer cable.
19. For 2WD models, disconnect the back-up light switch harness; on 4 × 4 models, disconnect the backup light switch harness and 4WD indicator light switch harness.
20. Remove the drive shafts.
21. Remove the gearshift lever assembly.
22. Support the transmission with a jack.
23. Detach the rear insulator from the transmission. Remove the No. 2 crossmember.
24. On 4 × 4 models, support the transfer case with a jack and, after removing the transfer case mounting bracket and support insulator, remove the plate from the side frame. Detach the transfer case mounting bracket from the transfer case.
25. Remove the engine mounting nuts from the front insulators. Using a chain block-and-tackle, raise and remove the engine and transmission assembly diagonally from the engine compartment.
26. Reverse the removal procedure for installation. Adjust the clutch and accelerator controls, align the hood and add coolant, engine oil and transmission lubricant. Check all controls for proper function before road testing.

Cylinder Head

REMOVAL & INSTALLATION

Gasoline Engine

———— **CAUTION** ————
Do not perform this operation on a warm

Cross-section of gasoline engine cylinder head

engine. Remove the head bolts in the sequence shown at the front of this section and in several steps. Loosen the head bolts evenly, not one at a time. Do not attempt to slide the cylinder head off the block, as it is located with dowel pins. Lift the head straight up and off the block.

1. Disconnect the battery and drain the cooling system. Disconnect the upper radiator hose.
2. Remove the breather hoses and purge hose.
3. Remove the air cleaner and fuel line.
4. Remove the vacuum hose at the distributor and purge control valve.
5. Disconnect the spark plug wires after marking them for reinstallation.
6. Remove the distributor cap, and distributor by removing the retainer nut and pulling the unit out.
7. Disconnect the heater hose at the intake manifold.
8. Disconnect the water temperature gauge unit wire.
9. Place no. 1 piston in the Top Dead Center position to take pressure off the fuel pump rocker arm. Disconnect the fuel hoses and plug the line leading to the gas tank to prevent fuel leakage.
10. Remove the fuel pump mounting nuts or bolts and remove the fuel assembly. Remove the insulator and gaskets.

11. Disconnect the exhaust pipe at the exhaust manifold flange.
12. Remove the rocker cover.
13. Remove its breather and semi-circular seal.
14. After slightly loosening the camshaft sprocket bolt, turn the crankshaft until no. 1 piston is at top dead center on compression stroke (both valves closed).

NOTE: Never turn the engine over using the camshaft bolt: it puts undue strain on the chain and other components.

15. Remove the camshaft sprocket bolt and distributor drive gear. Remove the camshaft sprocket and allow it to rest in the chain on the holder below.
16. Remove the cylinder head bolts in the sequence shown in the illustration. Head bolts should be loosened in two or three stages to prevent head warpage.

NOTE: The cylinder head assembly is located with two dowel pins, front and rear, on the cylinder block. When removing, be careful not to slide it, or twist the camshaft sprocket and chain.

17. Remove the cylinder head assembly and cylinder head gasket.
Installation is performed in the following manner.
18. Clean all gasket surfaces of cylinder block and cylinder head.
19. Install a new cylinder head gasket. Install the cylinder head assembly.

NOTE: Do not apply sealant to the head gasket and do not reuse an old head gasket.

20. Install the ten cylinder head bolts. Starting at top center, tighten all cylinder head bolts to 35 ft. lbs. in the sequence shown in the illustration. Repeat the tightening procedure, this time torque the bolts to 65–72 ft. lbs. (cold engine), (72–80 ft. lbs. hot engine).
21. Tighten the two front bolts (number 11 in illustration) to 11–15 ft. lbs.

22. Verify that no. 1 cylinder is at top dead center. Align the dowel pin in the end of the camshaft sprocket with the groove in the top of the front camshaft bearing cap and install the camshaft sprocket and chain while pulling up on the sprocket.
23. Install the distributor drive gear and the sprocket bolt.
24. Turn the crankshaft about 90° back, and tighten the camshaft sprocket bolt to 37–43 ft. lbs.
Very slowly turn the engine over two times to make sure the valve timing is correct. If the engine locks at a certain point in these two revolutions, the valve timing is not correct. Repeat steps 22–24.

— CAUTION —
At this point, do not turn the engine over using the starter. If the valve timing is off, several of the valves could be bent.

25. Install the breather and semicircular seal to the cylinder head after applying sealant to surface contact points. Install the rocker cover with a new gasket.
26. Connect the exhaust pipe to the exhaust manifold flange. Tighten the bolts to 11–18 ft. lbs.
27. Put no. 1 cylinder at top dead center and install the fuel pump with a new gasket and insulator. Connect all hoses.
28. Connect the water temperature gauge unit wire. Connect the heater hose to the intake manifold.
Install the distributor and spark plug cables. See distributor section, above, for procedure.
29. Connect the vacuum hose to the distributor and purge control valve. Connect the upper radiator hose and fill the cooling system with coolant.
Many mechanics recommend that the engine oil be replaced after the head is removed to avoid water contamination from the coolant.

Diesel Engine

1. Observe the "Caution" at the beginning of the Gasoline Engine cylinder head removal procedure.
2. Disconnect the battery and drain the cooling system. Disconnect the upper radiator hose.
3. Label and disconnect any breather hoses which run over the cylinder head.
4. Disconnect the heater hose at the intake manifold. Disconnect the temperature sensor lead.
5. Unbolt the inlet piping and oil lines to the turbocharger. *Make sure you cover the turbo intake with a clean rag, as no foreign material must enter any part of the turbo or turbo intake system.*
6. Remove the fuel injection lines and glow plug connections. Remove the intake and exhaust manifolds.
7. Remove the timing belt front upper and lower covers. Set the No. 1 cylinder at TDC on the compression stroke. The timing marks should be lined up as shown

Gasoline engine head removal

Gasoline engine head installation

Diesel cylinder head gasket—top side

in the illustration under "Timing Belt". Remove the timing belt and remove injection pump.

NOTE: DO NOT disturb the crankshaft (if possible) while the timing belt is removed.

8. Remove the rocker cover. Loosen the cylinder head bolts in the reverse order of the tightening sequence. Loosen the bolts gradually, making two or three passes.

9. Remove the cylinder head and gasket. Installation is performed in the following manner:

10. Clean all gasket surfaces of the cylinder block and head. *Always install a new gasket.*

11. Install the cylinder head gasket very carefully, as it has no identification marks. The accompanying illustration shows the top surface of the gasket.

12. Install the cylinder head to the block. Starting at No. 1 bolt, tighten all bolts to ½ of their specified torque in the sequence shown. Finally, tighten all bolts to full specification in the same sequence. Proper bolt torque is 76–83 ft. lbs.

13. Install the injection pump.

14. Move the timing belt tensioner fully toward the water pump and temporarily secure the tensioner.

14. Install the timing belt onto the injection pump sprocket and camshaft sprockets, making sure you don't turn the crankshaft sprocket while doing so. Make sure the tension side of the belt (the "top" side that runs between the camshaft sprocket and the injection pump sprocket) is *not slack*.

NOTE: When aligning the timing marks, the injection pump sprocket tends to rotate itself. Hold the sprocket while fitting the timing belt to prevent rotation.

16. With the belt fitted, check the timing

Diesel head torque sequence—removal

Diesel head torque sequence—installation

mark alignment on both sprockets. Loosen the tensioner mounting bolts, which will apply tension to the belt.

NOTE: Check that the "A" portion of the belt (illustration) is not floating up.

17. Tighten the belt tensioner mounting nut and bolt. Tighten the slot side bolt before tightening the fulcrum side bolt. If the fulcrum side bolt is tightened first, the tension bracket will be turned together and the belt will be too tight.

18. Check again to make sure the timing marks on all sprockets are aligned with their respective timing marks.

19. Turn the crankshaft in the normal (clockwise) direction through two camshaft sprocket teeth and hold. Reverse the crankshaft to align the timing marks, and push down the belt with your finger at a point halfway, to check that the belt has about .16 to .20 in. deflection.

20. Install the rocker cover, along with a new gasket if necessary. Install the timing belt front upper and lower cover.

21. Install the intake and exhaust manifolds.

22. Reconnect the glow plugs and fuel injection lines.

23. Connect the turbocharger oil lines and inlet ducting.

NOTE: Be sure to prime the turbocharger with oil before installing the oil feed pipe.

24. Connect the heater hose and temperature sensor lead. Connect all breather hoses to their proper locations. Install the upper radiator hose and fill the cooling system. Connect the battery, start the engine and check timing. Check for water leaks.

Intake Manifold
REMOVAL & INSTALLATION
Gasoline Engines

1. Drain the cooling system.
2. Remove the air cleaner assembly with its hoses from the engine.
3. Disconnect the fuel line and EGR lines.
4. Disconnect the accelerator linkage and, if so equipped, the automatic transmission shift cables at the carburetor.
5. Remove the water hose at the intake manifold. Remove the water hose at the carburetor.
6. Disconnect the water temperature sending unit.
7. Remove the manifold with the carburetor as a unit.

Installation is the reverse of removal. Tighten manifold nuts to 11–14 ft. lbs.

Exhaust Manifold
REMOVAL & INSTALLATION
Gasoline Engines

1. Remove air cleaner.

2. Remove the heat shield from the exhaust manifold. Remove the EGR lines and reed valve, if equipped.
3. Unbolt the exhaust flange connection.
4. Remove nuts holding manifold to cylinder head.
5. Remove manifold.

Installation is the reverse of removal. Tighten flange connection bolts to 11–18 ft. lbs. Tighten manifold bolts to 11–14 ft. lbs.

Intake And Exhaust Manifolds
REMOVAL & INSTALLATION
Diesel Engines

NOTE: Although they are individual pieces, the intake and exhaust manifolds share the same gasket. Whenever one is removed, the other must be also, to replace the gasket.

1. Remove the turbocharger.
2. Remove the manifold connection from the intake manifold to the injection pump.
3. Loosen the attaching bolts and remove the intake manifold.
4. Loosen the attaching bolts and remove the exhaust manifold. Remove the gasket.
5. Installation is the reverse of removal. Clean all gasket mating surfaces before replacing the gasket. Torque the intake and exhaust manifold attaching bolts to 11–14 ft. lbs.

NOTE: Be sure to prime the turbocharger with oil before installing the oil feed pipe.

Turbocharger
REMOVAL & INSTALLATION
Diesel Engines

1. Remove the exhaust pipe and gasket from the turbocharger. Remove the heat shield.
2. Remove the attaching bolts from the inlet fitting to the intake manifold. Loosen the hose clamps and remove the inlet fitting. Discard the gasket. Remove the rubber connecting hose.
3. Loosen the fitting and remove the oil feed pipe from the turbocharger assembly.
4. Loosen the hose clamps from the oil return line and remove the oil return line and flanged pipe from the turbocharger.
5. Remove the attaching bolts to the exhaust manifold flange and remove the turbocharger. Discard the mounting gasket; a new one should be fitted during assembly.
6. Installation is the reverse of removal. Clean all mounting surfaces before

Turbocharger fittings and installation

assembly, *and make sure no foreign material is allowed to enter the turbo manifolding or the turbo unit itself.*

NOTE: Before installing the oil feed pipe, pour clean engine oil into the turbocharger oil inlet. Make sure oil connections are tight and free from leaks. Replace all old gaskets with new ones.

Timing Chain, Cover, "Silent Shafts" and Tensioner

REMOVAL & INSTALLATION
Gasoline Engines

NOTE: All pick-ups are equipped with two "Silent Shafts" which cancel the vertical vibrating force of the engine and the secondary vibrating forces, which include the sideways rocking of the engine due to the turning direction of the crankshaft and other rolling parts. The secondary vibrating forces can be cancelled if forces equivalent in magnitude but opposite in direction are produced. In these engines, the opposite force is produced by silent shafts located in the upper left and lower right sides in the front of the cylinder block. The shafts are driven by a duplex chain and are turned by the crankshaft. The silent shaft chain assembly is mounted in front of the timing chain assembly and must be removed to service the timing chain.

1. Remove the battery cables.
2. Drain the radiator and remove it from the vehicle.
3. Remove the cylinder head (refer to cylinder head section for procedures).
4. Remove the cooling fan, spacer, water pump pulley and belt.

5. Remove the alternator. Remove the water pump.
6. Raise the front of the vehicle and support it on jack stands.
7. Remove the oil pan and screen. Remove the crankshaft pulley.
8. Remove the timing case cover.
9. Remove the chain guides, side (A), top (B), bottom (C), from the "B" chain (outer).
10. Remove the locking bolts from the "B" chain sprockets.
11. Remove the crankshaft sprocket, silent shaft sprocket and the outer chain.
12. Remove the crankshaft and camshaft sprockets and the timing chain.
13. Remove the camshaft sprocket holder and the chain guides, both left and right.
14. Remove the tensioner.
15. Remove the sleeve from the oil pump. Remove the oil pump by first removing the bolt locking the oil pump driven gear and the right silent shaft, then remove the oil pump mounting bolts. Remove the silent shaft from the engine block.

NOTE: If the bolt locking the oil pump and the silent shaft is hard to loosen, remove the oil pump and the shaft as a unit.

16. Remove the left silent shaft thrust

Front view of gasoline engine showing timing and silent shaft chains

washer and take the shaft from the engine block.

Installation is performed in the following manner:

1. Install the right silent shaft into the engine block.

2. Install the oil pump assembly. Do not lose the woodruff key from the end of the silent shaft. Torque the oil pump mounting bolts to 6 to 7 ft. lbs.

3. Tighten the silent shaft and the oil pump driven gear mounting bolt.

NOTE: The silent shaft and the oil pump can be installed as a unit, if necessary.

4. Install the left silent shaft into the engine block.

5. Install a new O-ring on the thrust plate and install the unit into the engine block, using a pair of bolts without heads, as alignment guides.

---------- **CAUTION** ----------
If the thrust plate is turned to align the bolt holes, the O-ring may be damaged.

---

6. Remove the guide bolts and install the regular bolts into the thrust plate and tighten securely.

7. Rotate the crankshaft to bring no. 1 piston to TDC.

8. Install the cylinder head.

9. Install the sprocket holder and the right and left chain guides.

10. Install the tensioner spring and sleeve on the oil pump body.

11. Install the camshaft and crankshaft sprockets on the timing chain, aligning the sprocket punch marks to the plated chain links.

Timing chain installation: align the plated links with the punch-marks on the cam sprocket and the crankshaft sprocket

"Silent Shaft" balancing system—gasoline engine shown

12. While holding the sprocket and chain as a unit, install the crankshaft sprocket over the crankshaft and align it with the keyway.

13. Keeping the dowel pin hole on the camshaft in a vertical position, install the camshaft sprocket and chain on the camshaft.

NOTE: The sprocket timing mark and the plated chain link should be at the 2 to 3 O'clock position when correctly installed.

---------- **CAUTION** ----------
The chain must be aligned in the right and left chain guides with the tensioner pushing against the chain. The tension for the inner chain is predetermined by spring tension.

---

14. Install the crankshaft sprocket for the outer or "B" chain.

15. Install the two silent shaft sprockets and align the punched mating marks with the plated links of the chain.

16. Holding the two shaft sprockets and chain, install the outer chain in alignment with the mark on the crankshaft sprocket. Install the shaft sprockets on the silent shaft and the oil pump driver gear. Install the lock bolts and recheck the alignment of the punch marks and the plated links.

17. Temporarily install the chain guides, side (A), top (B), and bottom (C).

18. Tighten side (A) chain guide securely.

19. Tighten bottom (B) chain guide securely.

20. Adjust the position of the top (B) chain guide, after shaking the right and left sprockets to collect any chain slack, so that when the chain is moved toward the center, the clearance between the chain guide and the chain links will be approximately ⁹⁄₆₄ inch. Tighten the top (B) chain guide bolts.

21. Install the timing chain cover using a new gasket, being careful not to damage the front seal.

22. Install the oil screen and the oil pan, using a new gasket. Torque the bolts to 4.5–5.5 ft. lbs.

23. Install the crankshaft pulley, alternator and accessory belts, and the distributor.

24. Install the oil pressure switch, if removed, and install the battery ground cable.

25. Install the fan blades, radiator, fill the system with coolant and start the engine.

Timing Belts

REMOVAL & INSTALLATION

Diesel Engines

1. Set the No. 1 cylinder at TDC on the compression stroke. Make sure all timing marks align.

2. If you will be reusing the belts, mark them both (the valve timing belt and the silent shaft belt) with an arrow indicating the direction of rotation before removal.

3. Remove the crankshaft pulley and both timing belt covers.

4. Slightly loosen both belt tensioner bolts, move the tensioners toward the water pump, then secure the tensioners by tightening the tensioner bolt temporarily.

5. Remove the camshaft sprocket and injection pump sprocket. *It is not necessary to remove the silent shaft sprockets or loosen the tensioner if the silent shaft timing belt is not being replaced.*

6. If the silent shaft belt is to be replaced, loosen the silent shaft sprockets after first locking the shafts in place with a small pry bar.

Diesel timing belt train

allow the spring tension to take up any belt slack. *Do not attempt to move the tensioner to obtain more tension.* Tighten the tensioner bolt to 25-28 ft. lbs.

11. Make sure to install the belt so it rotates in the same direction as marked (if reusing the old belt). Standard belt deflection ("Play") when properly tensioned is 4-5 mm (.16-.20 in.) as measured at midpoint between the upper silent shaft and crankshaft sprockets.

12. Align the timing marks for the camshaft, injection pump and crankshaft sprockets and install the timing belt. Install the timing belt first on the crankshaft sprocket, then on the injection pump and camshaft sprockets.

NOTE: With the tension side kept taut, engage the timing belt teeth with each sprocket. The injection pump sprocket tends to to rotate itself, so it must be held while installing the belt.

13. Loosen the tensioner belt and allow the spring tension to take up the slack in the timing belt. *Do not attempt to apply more tension by manually moving the tensioner.* Once the belt is tensioned, tighten the tensioner bolt to 16-21 ft.lbs.

NOTE: Tighten the slot side bolt before tightening the fulcrum side bolt. If the fulcrum side is tightened earlier, the tension bracket will be turned together and the belt will be too tight.

14. Make sure the timing marks on all sprockets are still in correct alignment.

15. Turn the crankshaft in the normal direction of rotation through two camshaft

Preventing rotation of silent shafts

7. Remove the timing belt(s) and inspect for damage, wear or deterioration. *Do not use solvents or detergent to clean the timing belts, sprockets or tensioners.* Replace any component that is excessively contaminated with dirt, oil or grease.

8. Installation is the reverse of removal. Install the spacer to the left silent shaft with its chamfered edge toward the oil seal.

— CAUTION —
Installing this spacer incorrectly will result in damage to the oil seal.

9. Align the timing marks of the crankshaft and silent shaft drive sprockets when installing the silent shaft belt.

10. Loosen the silent belt tensioner and

Check timing belt for wear

Adjusting timing belt tension

Loosening timing belt tensioner

T569

Checking timing belt alignment

PISTON AND PISTON RING APPLICATION

Description	Engine	Identification Mark
Piston	U (for U.S.A.)	52J①
	U (for Canada)	52①
	W (for U.S.A.)	54J①
	W (for Canada)	54①
	TBD	TC①
Piston ring No. 1	U	N1②
	W	T②
	TBD	TT③
No. 2	U	N②
	W	2T②
	TBD	
Oil ring		None
	TBD	TT

① Stamped on top of piston
② Stamped on ring end
③ Stamped on top edge of ring

sprocket teeth and hold it there. Reverse direction to align the timing marks, and push down on the belt at a point halfway between the camshaft and injection pump sprocket to check belt deflection. Normal deflection is 4-5 mm (.16-.20 in.).

16. Reset the timing belt switch by depressing its knob until it is flush with the base and mount the timing belt covers.

Silent Shafts

REMOVAL & INSTALLATION

Diesel Engine

NOTE: This procedure is normally performed during a complete engine overhaul since it requires disassembly of most major engine components.

1. Remove the engine. Drain and remove the oil pan.
2. Remove the timing belts.
3. Remove the front case and oil pump assembly. When loosening the silent shaft driven gear attaching bolts, remove the plug on the right side of the cylinder block and insert a pry bar to prevent rotation of the shaft while loosening the bolt.
4. Before removing the oil pump gears, make alignment marks on the gears as a reference for reassembly.

5. Once the front case (upper and lower) has been removed, the silent shafts may be removed from the front of the engine.

6. Check the journals of the silent shaft for wear, damage and seizure. Check the bearing oil clearance and shaft end play. Make sure all oil passages are clear. Silent shaft bearings require special tools for replacement, if necessary.

7. Installation is the reverse of removal. Torque all attaching bolts evenly. The silent shaft sprocket bolts are torqued to 25-28 ft, lbs.; silent shaft chamber cover bolts to 3-4 ft. lbs.; the timing belt tensioner nut to 16-21 ft.lbs.; and the front case bolts to 9-10 ft. lbs. Align the drive gear marks on the oil pump and silent shaft gears during assembly. Replace all gaskets and oil seals on the upper and lower front case.

NOTE: See the "Engine Lubrication" section of this chapter for procedures on checking the oil pump gear clearances and installing the oil pump.

PISTON RING SERVICE SIZE

Size mm (in.)	Size Mark
STD	None
0.25 (.010) O.S.	25
0.50 (.020) O.S.	50
0.75 (.030) O.S.	75
1.00 (.039) O.S.	100

Piston ring end gap positioning—gasoline engines

Gasoline engine piston ring installation

Installing the piston pin. Front marks on piston and connecting rod also shown

Piston ring end gap positioning—diesels

Piston crown I.D. marking—diesels

Diesel piston ring installation

Camshaft

REMOVAL & INSTALLATION

Gasoline Engines

1. Remove the breather hoses and purge hose.

2. Remove the air cleaner and fuel line.

3. Remove the fuel pump. Remove the distributor.

4. Disconnect the spark plug cables.

5. Remove the rocker cover.

6. Remove the breather and semi-circular seal.

7. After slightly loosening the camshaft sprocket bolt, turn the crankshaft until no. 1 piston is at top dead center on compression stroke (both valves closed).

8. Remove the camshaft sprocket bolt and distributor drive gear.

9. Remove the camshaft sprocket with chain and allow it to rest on the camshaft sprocket holder.

10. Remove the camshaft bearing cap tightening bolts. Do not remove the front and rear bearing cap bolts altogether, but

Installing the camshaft: align the dowel pin with the notch in the top of the front bearing cap

keep them inserted in the bearing caps so that the rocker assembly can be removed as a unit.

11. Remove the rocker arms, rocker shafts and bearing caps as an assembly.

12. Remove the camshaft.

Installation is performed in the following manner.

13. Lubricate the camshaft lobes and bearings and fit camshaft into head.

14. Install the assembled rocker arm shaft assembly. The camshaft should be positioned so that the dowel pin on the front end of the cam is in the 12 o'clock position and in line with the notch in the top of the front bearing cap.

15. Install the bearing cap bolts. Starting at the center and working out, tighten the bolts to 7 ft. lbs. Repeat the procedure, this time tightening them to 14–15 ft. lbs.

16. Install the camshaft sprocket and distributor drive gear onto the camshaft while pulling it upward. Temporarily tighten the locking bolt.

17. Turn the crankshaft about 90° back and tighten the camshaft sprocket bolt to 37–43 ft. lbs.

18. Temporarily set the valve clearance to cold engine specifications (see Valve Lash section).

19. Temporarily install the breather, semicircular seal and rocker cover and start

1 Breather hose
2 Bolt (2)
3 Washer (2)
4 Oil seal
5 Rocker cover
6 Rocker cover gasket
7 Semi-circular packing
8 Flange bolt (5)
9 Washer (5)
10 Rocker arm and shaft assembly
  1 Exhaust rocker arm (4)
  2 Rocker shaft spring (4)
  3 Inlet rocker arm (4)
  4 Rocker arm adjusting screw (8)
  5 Nut (8)
  6 Rocker arm shaft
11 Cylinder head

Diesel rocker assembly; torque specs in parentheses are ft. lbs.

the engine and run it at idle speed.

20. After the engine is at normal operational temperature, adjust the valves to hot engine specifications (see Valve Lash section).

21. Install breather and seal and apply sealant to the contact surfaces.

22. Install the rocker cover and tighten to 4–5 ft. lbs.

23. Install distributor, fuel pump, air cleaner, fuel line, plug leads and other assemblies.

Diesel Engines

1. Label and disconnect all breather hoses that are in the way of removing the valve rocker cover.

2. Remove the rocker cover.

3. Loosen, very slightly, the camshaft sprocket bolt. Turn the engine so that No. 1 cylinder is at Top Dead Center on the compression stroke. Both valves are now closed on No. 1 cylinder.

4. Remove the camshaft sprocket bolt. Remove the camshaft sprocket with the timing belt and allow it to rest aside.

5. Remove the camshaft bearing caps, keeping them in order. If you intend to check camshaft bearing clearances, now is the time to do it. Use Plastigage® or equivalent. If beyond specifications, you must replace either the camshaft or cylinder head, as the engine has no camshaft bearings per se (the cam runs directly on the cylinder head).

Camshaft timing sprocket installation showing timing marks

6. Remove the rocker assembly.

7. Remove the camshaft.

8. Before installation, check the camshaft for wear and/or damage. Check the faces of all lobes for unusual wear, and check cam lobe height and runout. Check the camshaft oil seal lip and replace if evidence of leakage.

9. Lubricate the camshaft saddles liberally with clean engine oil. Fit the cam-

Camshaft oil seal installation—diesels

shaft into the head and lubricate the entire camshaft with clean engine oil. Install the rocker assembly. Make sure that when the rocker shaft is installed to the front bearing cap, the oil hole side is *down* and that the end of the rocker shaft with the one oil hole is the *front end*. See the illustration for details.

10. Install the camshaft bearing cap bolts in numerical order, after lubricating each with clean engine oil. Torque the cap bolts to 14-15 ft. lbs., starting at the center and working out.

Apply sealant here—diesel camshaft installation

Diesel rocker shaft orientation

NOTE: No. 1 and No. 5 bearing caps are not stamped with an identification number.

11. Install the camshaft sprocket and belt, and torque the sprocket bolt to 47-54 ft. lbs.

12. Install the rocker cover and apply sealer to the areas indicated in the illustration. Install the breather hoses.

ENGINE LUBRICATION

Oil Pan

REMOVAL & INSTALLATION

The engine must be raised off its mounts and safely blocked, for the pan to clear the suspension crossmember.

1. Remove the underbody splash shield.

2. Unbolt the left and right engine mounts.

3. Jack up the engine under the bell housing.

4. Remove the oil pan.

5. Installation is the reverse of removal.

Rear Main Oil Seal

REPLACEMENT

The rear main oil seal is located in a housing on the rear of the block. To replace the seal, remove the transmission and do the work from underneath the vehicle or remove the engine and do the work on the bench.

Rear main oil seal

1. Remove the housing from the block.

2. Remove the separator from the housing.

3. Pry out the old seal.

4. Lightly oil the replacement seal. The oil seal should be installed so that the seal plate fits into the inner contact surface of the seal case. Install the separator with the oil holes facing down.

NOTE: To install the rear oil seal in the 2.3L diesel engine, you must use a special oil seal installation tool, Mitsubishi part #MD 998376. The tool ensures that the seal is driven in evenly.

Oil Pump

REMOVAL & INSTALLATION

Gasoline Engines

See Timing Chain, Cover, "Silent Shaft" and Tensioner Removal and Installation procedure.

GASOLINE ENGINE OIL PUMP SPECIFICATIONS

Engine	Type	Drive Gear Rear End Clearance With Bearing	Tip Clearance: Gear to Cover (in.)	Maximum Oil Pressure (psi)	Relief Valve Spring Free Length (in.)	Relief Valve Opening Pressure (psi)
U. W	Gear	0.0016-0.0028	0.0043-0.0059	64.0	1.850	49.8-64

DIESEL ENGINE OIL PUMP SPECIFICATIONS

Engine	Type	Outer gear –to– Pump Housing (in.)	Inner gear –to– Outer gear (in.)	Inner gear –to–cover clearance (in.)	Side clearance (in.)
TBD	Gear	.005–.009	.009–.014	.001–.004	.002–.004

OVERHAUL

Gasoline Engines

1. Remove the two screws at the rear of the oil pump and remove the cover and gear.

2. Remove the relief valve plug and withdraw the relief spring and plunger.

3. Check the pump for cracks and wear. Check all oil holes for clogging.

4. Clearance between the gears and the pump assembly (tip clearance) should be 0.0043-0.0059 in.

5. Both gears front bearing clearance should be within 0.0008 and 0.0020 in.

6. The rear bearing clearance of the drive gear should be 0.0016-0.0028 in.

1 Oil drain plug
2 Gasket
3 Bolt (24)
4 Oil pan gasket
5 Oil pan
6 Bolt (2)
7 Bolt (2)
8 Oil screen
9 Flange bolt (3)
10 Front upper case
11 Front upper case gasket
12 Oil seal
13 Left silent shaft
14 Plug cap
15 O-ring
16 Flange bolt
17 Flange bolt (7)
18 Front lower case assembly
1 Flange bolt (3)
2 Silent shaft gear cover
3 Silent shaft driven gear
4 Silent shaft drive gear
5 Machine screw (5)
6 Oil pump cover
7 Oil pump outer gear
8 Oil pump inner gear
9 Plug
10 Gasket
11 Relief valve spring
12 Relief valve
13 Oil seal
14 Front lower case
19 Front lower case gasket
20 Front oil seal
21 Oil pump gear drive shaft
22 Right silent shaft
23 Oil filter

Installing diesel front cover oil seal

Apply oil pan sealant here—diesels

Diesel engine front cover assembly showing oil pump and silent shafts

Gasoline engine oil pump layout. Notice mating marks on gears

NOTE: When bearing replacement is necessary, replace the oil pump body assembly.

7. Insert the relief plunger into the pump body and make sure it operates smoothly. Check the relief spring for breakage or sagging.

When reassembling, observe the following:

8. Coat all parts in oil before reassembling.

9. Match the two punch marks on the gears so that they mate where the gears meet.

10. Check for smooth rotation after assembly.

———— CAUTION ————
Make sure the mating marks meet, or the silent shaft will be out of time and cause vibration.

Before installing the pump, fill the delivery port with clean oil to prime it.

Diesel Engines

The oil pump on the 2.3L diesel is located behind the front lower case assembly and is driven directly by the crankshaft. Removal requires disassembly of the lower front case, and this is best done with the engine removed.

1. Drain the crankcase oil and remove the oil pan.

2. Remove the crankcase oil strainer.

3. Remove the timing belt assembly. Remove the belt drive gears.

4. Unbolt and remove the front upper case. The oil seal in the case can now be pried out carefully.

5. Remove the lower front case.

6. Before the oil pump inner and outer gears are removed, make alignment marks on both gears for reference during reassembly. Remove the oil pump.

7. Measure oil pump gear clearances. If side clearances are excessively large, or if the case or cover has evidence of step wear, replace the front case assembly.

8. Install the oil pump gears in the same direction as before disassembly, making sure the alignment marks made earlier line up. Lightly oil the gears with engine oil before installing the pump into the front case.

9. A special oil seal guide, Mitsubishi part #MD998385 or equivalent, is needed to install the oil seals into the front case. *New oil seals should always be installed.* A crankshaft seal installation tool and guide, Mitsubishi parts #MD998382 and MD998383 or equivalent are also needed.

10. Reverse the removal procedure for reassembly. You will need the above mentioned oil seal tools and guide to install the lower front case over the shafts. Also, use a new gasket behind the front case. Apply sealer to the oil pan flange.

ENGINE COOLING

Radiator

REMOVAL & INSTALLATION

Pickup Trucks

1. Remove the splash panel from the bottom of the vehicle. Drain the radiator by opening the petcock. Remove the shroud on models so equipped.

2. Disconnect the radiator hoses at the engine. On automatic transmission vehicles, disconnect and plug the transmission lines to the bottom of the radiator.

3. Remove the two retaining bolts from either side of the radiator. Lift out the radiator.

4. Install the radiator in the reverse order of removal. Tighten the retaining bolts gradually in a criss-cross pattern.

Montero

1. Set the warm water flow control lever to the "hot" position.

2. Loosen the radiator drain plug to drain the coolant.

3. Disconnect the upper and lower hoses.

4. Remove the upper and lower radiator fan shrouds. Remove the radiator mounting bolts and remove the radiator.

Water Pump

REMOVAL & INSTALLATION

All Models

1. Drain the cooling system.

2. Remove the fan shroud and radiator if necessary for working room.

3. Remove the alternator and accessory belts.

4. Remove the fan blades and/or automatic hub, if equipped.

5. Remove the water pump assembly from the timing chain case or the cylinder block.

6. Install the water pump to the timing chain case or the engine block and tighten the bolts securely.

7. Install the fan blades and/or the automatic clutch fan hub.

8. Install the alternator and accessory belts and adjust as necessary.

9. Install the fan shroud and the radiator, if removed.

10. Fill the cooling system, start the engine, and check for coolant leakage.

Thermostat

REMOVAL & INSTALLATION

Gasoline Engines

The thermostat is located in the intake manifold under the upper radiator hose.

1. Drain the coolant below the level of the thermostat.

2. Remove the two retaining bolts and lift the thermostat housing off the intake manifold with the hose still attached.

NOTE: If you are careful, it is not necessary to remove the upper radiator hose.

3. Lift the thermostat out of the manifold.

4. Install the thermostat in the reverse order of removal. Use a new gasket and coat the mating surfaces with sealer.

Diesel Engines

The diesel thermostat is located in the right side of the water pump, underneath the hose inlet elbow.

1. Drain the coolant below the level of the thermostat housing. Remove the lower radiator hose from the water inlet fitting on the water pump. Remove the inlet fitting and remove the thermostat.

2. To install, insert the thermostat in the inlet fitting and make sure the thermostat flange is well seated in the spot-faced area of the inlet fitting.

3. Apply sealant to both sides of the new water inlet gasket and install the gasket on the water pump. Install the fitting and tighten the two bolts.

4. Connect the lower radiator hose to the water inlet fitting.

5. Fill the cooling system.

GASOLINE ENGINE EMISSIONS SYSTEMS

Crankcase Emission Control System

A closed-type crankcase ventilation system is used to prevent engine blow-by gases from escaping into the atmosphere.

A small fixed orifice, located in the intake manifold, is connected to the rear section of the rocker arm cover by a hose.

A larger hose is connected from the front of the rocker arm cover to the air cleaner assembly. Under light to medium carburetor throttle opening, the blow-by gases are drawn through the fixed orifice. Under heavy acceleration, both the fixed orifice and the large hose route the gases into the engine.

The only maintenance required is to regularly check the breather hose condition, clean the orifice in the intake manifold, and clean the steel wool filter, in the air cleaner.

A PCV valve is not used in the system.

Fuel Evaporation Control System

This system is designed to prevent hydrocarbons from escaping into the atmosphere from the fuel tank, due to normal evaporation.

The parts of the system are as follow:

1. **Separator tank:** Located near the gasoline tank, used to accommodate expansion, and to allow maximum condensation of the fuel vapors.

2. **Canister:** Located in the engine compartment to trap and retain gasoline vapors while the engine is not operating. When the engine is started, fresh air is drawn into the canister, removing the stored vapors, and is directed to the air cleaner.

3. **Two-way Valve:** Because of different methods of tank venting and the use of sealed gasoline tank cap, the two-way valve is used in the vapor lines. The valve relieves either pressure or vacuum in the tank.

4. **Purge Control Valve:** The purge control valve replaces the check valve used in previous years. During idle, the valve closes off the vapor passage to the air cleaner.

5. **Fuel Check Valve:** This valve is used to prevent fuel leakage in case of roll

over. It is installed in the vapor line between the separator and the two-way valve.

MAINTENANCE

Be sure that all hoses are clamped and not dry-rotted or broken. Check the valves for cracks, signs of gasoline leakage, and proper operating condition. The canister air filter should be inspected and changed at least every 24,000 miles.

Heated Air Intake System

All models are equipped with a temperature regulated air control valve in the air cleaner snorkel.

When the underhood air temperature is 41 degrees or lower, the air control valve allows preheated air to flow through the heat cowl of the exhaust manifold, via a flexible hose, to the air cleaner and into the carburetor.

When the underhood temperature is 108 degrees or above, the air flow is directed through the air cleaner snorkel.

At intermediate temperature, the carburetor intake air is a blend of the direct underhood and preheated air.

MAINTENANCE

Visually check the control valve assembly when the engine is cold, to be sure that the valve is closed.

Warm up the engine and check that the control valve opens to the outside air.

Secondary Air Supply System

This system supplies air for the further

1. Purge control valve
2. Canister
3. Fuel pipe, vapor
4. Fuel check valve
5. Two-way valve
6. Separator tank
7. Fuel tank cap

Evaporation control system

combustion of unburned gases in the thermal reactor (California only) or exhaust manifold and consists of a reed valve, air hoses, and air passages built into the cylinder head.

The reed valve is operated by exhaust pulsations in the exhaust manifold. It draws fresh air through the air cleaner and supplies it to the exhaust ports.

MAINTENANCE

Check for damage to the air hoses and air pipes. Make sure the air passages are open in the head.

Exhaust Gas Recirculation System

The EGR system recirculates part of the exhaust gases into the combustion chambers. This dilutes the air/fuel mixture, reducing formation of oxides of nitrogen in the exhaust gases by lowering the peak combustion temperatures.

The parts of the EGR system are:

1. **EGR Valve:** Operated by vacuum drawn from a point above the carburetor throttle plate. The vacuum controls the raising and lowering of the valve pintle to allow exhaust gases to pass from the exhaust system to the intake manifold.

2. **Thermo Valve:** Used to stop EGR valve operation below approximately 131 degrees, in order to improve cold driveability and starting.

Dual EGR Control Valve

The EGR vacuum flow is suspended during idle and wide open throttle operation.

The primary valve controls EGR flow when the throttle valve opening is relatively narrow, while the secondary control valve operates at wider openings.
Sub-EGR control valve is linked to the throttle valve to closely modulate the EGR gas flow.

EGR Maintenance Warning Light

A light in the speedometer assembly to alert the driver to the need for EGR system maintenance.

This device has a mileage sensor to light the visual signal at 15,000 mile intervals.

Upon completion of the required EGR system maintenance, the warning light can be turned off by resetting the switch. It is in the speedometer cable, under the instrument panel.

MAINTENANCE

1. Check all vacuum hoses for cracks, breakage and correct installation.
2. Check EGR valve operation by applying vacuum to the EGR valve vacuum nipple with the engine idling. The idle should become rough.
3. Check the passages in the cylinder head and intake manifold for clogging. Clean as necessary.
4. Cold start the engine. The EGR port nipple should be open. When the coolant is warmed to over 131 degrees, the port should be closed.

Catalytic Converter

This unit replaces the thermal reactor. It is filled with catalyst to oxidize hydrocarbons and carbon monoxide in the exhaust gases.

MAINTENANCE

1. Check the core for cracks and damages.
2. If the idle carbon monoxide and hydrocarbon content exceeds specifications and the ignition timing and idle mixture are correct, the converter must be replaced.

Jet Air System

A jet air passage is provided in the carburetor, intake manifold, and cylinder head to direct air to a jet valve, operated simultaneously with the intake valve.

On the intake stroke, jet air is forced into the combustion chamber because of the pressure difference between the ends of the air jet passage.

This jet of air produces a strong swirl in the combustion chamber scavenging the residual gases around the spark plug.

The jet air volume lessens with increased throttle opening. It is at a maximum at idle.

MAINTENANCE

NOTE: Refer to Valve Lash Adjustment for adjusting jet valve clearance.

No maintenance is required other than clearance adjustment during valve adjustment. The valve can be removed from the cylinder head for service or replacement.

Ignition Timing Control System

When the engine is idling or operating at low speeds under light load or deceleration, the exhaust gas temperature is low, resulting in incomplete combustion of the air/fuel mixture. To prevent this, ignition timing is retarded under these conditions to maintain high exhaust gas temperature.

The units in the Ignition Timing Control system are as follow:

1. **Thermo Valve:** This valve is used to protect the engine from overheating. When coolant temperature reaches 203 degrees, the advance unit is allowed to operate, causing an increase in engine speed and a decrease in coolant temperature.

2. **Single Diaphragm Distributor:** This distributor has a single diaphragm vacuum advance unit, which advances the ignition timing as engine vacuum dictates. The single diaphragm distributor must not be interchanged with the dual diaphragm distributor. The distributor operating curves are different and would cause increased emissions. A thermo valve is not used with this type of distributor.

Deceleration Device

Closing of the throttle valve on deceleration is delayed in order to burn the air/fuel mixture more thoroughly. A vacuum controlled dashpot, attached to the carburetor linkage is used.

Cross-section of cylinder head showing Jet Valve

A servo valve detects intake manifold vacuum and closes if vacuum exceeds a preset valve. Since the air in the dash pot diaphragm chamber can not escape, the throttle linkage opening is temporarily retained. If the vacuum is below the preset value, the servo valve opens and the dashpot works normally.

MAINTENANCE

Inspect the hoses for breaks and damage, and the valve body for cracks.

ADJUSTMENT

1. Have the engine running, brakes locked, and a tachometer attached.
2. Push the dashpot rod, connected to the carburetor arm, upward and into the dashpot until it stops.
3. Note the rpm at the dashpot stop and adjust to specifications. Note the time required between suddenly releasing the dashpot rod and the return to normal curb idle.

Mixture Control Valve

This control valve is used to supply additional air into the intake manifold to decrease manifold vacuum during deceleration, and is activated by the intake manifold vacuum level.

Manual Altitude Compensation System

An off-on valve is used to increase the air supply to the carburetor to lean the mixture and decrease the EGR flow for high altitude operation.

MAINTENANCE

The required maintenance is to inspect any vacuum hoses and routing for kinks, breakage and cracks. The off-on valve should be on for high altitude and off for driving under 4000 ft.

FUEL SYSTEM—GASOLINE ENGINES

Fuel Filter

REPLACEMENT

All models use an in-line filter which should be replaced every 12,000 miles.

Fuel Pump

REMOVAL & INSTALLATION

1. Remove the fuel lines.
2. Unbolt the pump mounting bolts, and remove the pump, insulator, and gasket.
3. Coat both sides of a new insulator and gasket with sealer, and install the pump in the reverse order of removal.

TESTING

Disconnect the fuel line from the carburetor and attach a pressure tester to the end of the line. Crank the engine. The tester should show 4.6–6 psi.

Carburetors

REMOVAL & INSTALLATION

1. Remove the solenoid valve wiring.
2. Disconnect the air cleaner breather hose, air duct and vacuum tube.
3. Remove the air cleaner.
4. Remove the air cleaner case.
5. Disconnect the accelerator and shift cables (automatic transmission) at the carburetor.
6. Disconnect the purge valve hose; remove the vacuum compensator, and fuel lines.

Removing springs

7. Drain the coolant.
8. Remove the water hose between the carburetor and the cylinder head.
9. Remove the carburetor.
10. Installation is the reverse of removal.

OVERHAUL—THROUGH 1980

1. Disconnect the water hose.
2. Remove the throttle return spring and damper spring.
3. Remove the throttle adjuster lever spring and the secondary return spring.
4. Remove the choke unloader link retaining clip and disconnect the choke unloader link.
5. Disconnect the vacuum hose.

Removing the air switching valve (ASV)

6. Disconnect the lower end of the diaphragm chamber link and remove the diaphragm chamber. *Do not immerse the diaphragm chamber assembly in cleaner.*
7. Remove the two screws and remove the air switching valve (ASV).
8. Remove the six float chamber cover screws. Separate the float chamber cover from the carburetor main body by tapping with a plastic hammer. Do not pry it off.
9. Remove the float chamber cover gasket.
10. Remove the float lever pin and the float.
11. Remove the needle valve assembly, gasket and filter.
12. Do not remove the automatic choke system because the factory setting will be disturbed.
13. Turn the main body upside down and remove the pump discharge check ball and weight.
14. Remove the fuel cut-off solenoid.
15. Remove the main jets and pilot jets. Do not tamper with the screws with white paint on heads.
16. Remove the enrichment assembly.
17. Disconnect the pump rod from the throttle shaft lever and remove the accelerator pump assembly.

Location of jets

Do not touch these screws (painted white) when disassembling the carburetor

18. Remove the sub-EGR valve link retaining clip and remove the washer and spring, then disconnect the link. Do not touch the EGR adjusting screw because it was preset at the factory. Do not distort the sub-EGR valve link.

19. Remove the two main body-to-throttle body screws. Separate the throttle body from the main body and remove the gasket.

20. Remove the idle speed adjusting screw, spring washer and packing from the throttle body.

Assembly is the reverse of disassembly.

OVERHAUL—FROM 1981

NOTE: A thorough test and check of minor carburetor adjustments should precede any major carburetor overhauls. Sometimes poor performance can be the result of loose, misadjusted or malfunctioning engine or electrical components.

Disassembly

1. Pull the water hose off the nipple of throttle body and off the nipple of wax element portion.

2. Grind down the head of choke cover lock screws (in 2 positions) by using a hand grinder or other instruments.

3. Disconnect the ground line of the fuel cut-off solenoid at the float chamber cover.

4. Remove the throttle return spring and the damper spring.

5. Pull off the vacuum hose connecting the depression chamber and the throttle body.

6. Remove the accelerator pump rod from the throttle lever.

7. Remove the dashpot rod (manual transmission) or throttle opener rod (automatic transmission) from the free lever.

8. Remove the depression chamber rod from the secondary throttle lever.

9. Remove the float chamber cover screws (6). Four screws connect the float chamber cover to the main body. Two screws connect the cover to the throttle body.

10. Remove only the main body by lifting the float chamber cover (the cover can not be removed because the choke unloader

rod is connected to the throttle shaft.) Don't turn the carburetor up side down, during the procedure. Turning the carburetor causes accelerator pump check weight, ball, and steel ball of anti-overfill device to drop.

NOTE: When lifting the chamber cover, the venturi retaining spring may drop down.

11. Remove the E-ring at the lower end of the choke unloader rod, and disconnect the rod from the lever.

12. Do not remove any device from the float chamber unless necessary, especially the autochoke system.

13. The float can be removed by pulling the pin off.

14. The needle valve can be removed by removing the screw and retainer.

15. Remove the accelerator pump and fuel cut off solenoid.

16. Don't remove parts without necessity. Don't remove the throttle valves and don't touch SAS and dashpot adjusting screws.

17. Assembly is the reverse of disassembly.

OVERHAUL TIPS

When the carburetor is disassembled, wash all parts (except diaphragms, electric choke units, pump plunger, and any other plastic, leather, fiber, or rubber parts) in clean carburetor solvent. Do not leave parts in the solvent any longer than is necessary to sufficiently loosen the deposits. Excessive cleaning may remove the special finish from the float bowl and choke valve bodies, leaving these parts unfit for service. Rinse all parts in clean solvent and blow them dry with compressed air or allow them to air dry. Wipe clean all cork, plastic, leather, and fiber parts with a clean, lint-free cloth.

Blow out all passages and jets with compressed air and be sure that there are no restrictions or blockages. Never use wire or similar tools to clean jets, fuel passages, or air bleeds. Clean all jets and valves separately to avoid accidental interchange.

Check all parts for wear or damage. If wear or damage is found, replace the defective parts. Especially check the following:

1. Check the float needle and seat for wear. If wear is found; replace the complete assembly.

2. Check the float hinge pin for wear and the float(s) for dents or distortion. Replace the float if fuel has leaked into it.

3. Check the throttle and choke shaft bores for wear or an out-of-round condition. Damage or wear to the throttle arm, shaft, or shaft bore will often require replacement of the throttle body. These parts require a close tolerance of fit; wear may allow air leakage, which could affect starting and idling.

NOTE: Throttle shafts and bushings are not included in overhaul kits. They can be purchased separately.

4. Inspect the idle mixture adjusting

needles for burrs or grooves. Any such condition requires replacement of the needle, since you will not be able to obtain a satisfactory idle.

5. Test the accelerator pump check valves. They should pass air one way but not the other. Test for proper seating by blowing and sucking on the valve. Replace the valve if necessary. If the valve is satisfactory, wash the valve again to remove breath moisture.

6. Check the bowl cover for warped surfaces with a straight edge.

7. Closely inspect the valves and seats for wear and damage, replacing as necessary.

8. After the carburetor is assembled, check the choke valve for freedom of operation.

Carburetor overhaul kits are recommended for each overhaul. These kits contain all gaskets and new parts to replace those that deteriorate most rapidly. Failure to replace all parts supplied with the kit (especially gaskets) can result in poor performance later.

After cleaning and checking all components, reassemble the carburetor, using new parts and referring to the exploded view. When reassembling, make sure that all screws and jets are tight in their seats, but do not overtighten as the tips will be distorted. Tighten all screws gradually, in rotation. Do not tighten needle valves into their seats; uneven jetting will result. Always use new gaskets. Be sure to adjust the float level, following the instructions contained in the rebuilding kit, when reassembling.

Fast Idle Adjustment

1. Start the engine and open the throttle valve about 45 degrees. Manually close the choke valve and slowly return the throttle valve to the stop position.

2. With a tachometer, check that the fast idle speed is 2,000 rpm or lower (not less than 1700 rpm). Adjust the speed as necessary with the fast idle speed screw.

3. Cold start the engine and check the automatic choke and fast idle operation.

Automatic Choke Adjustment

The choke case has five small projections. Align the center projection with the yellow punch mark of the bimetal case.

Removing injectors

FUEL SYSTEM— DIESEL ENGINES

Injection Pump

REMOVAL & INSTALLATION

1. Remove the timing belt upper cover.
2. Remove the nut and washer securing the injection pump sprocket.

NOTE: Be careful not to drop the nut and washer into the lower cover.

3. Turn the crankshaft to bring No. 1 piston to TDC on its compression stroke.
4. Use a suitable puller to loosen the sprocket from the taper section of the pump drive shaft. Do not remove the sprocket; carefully set it in the timing belt lower cover with the belt engaged.
5. Remove the two water hoses from the wax element. Keep the end of the removed hose higher than the cylinder head to prevent coolant drainage.
6. Disconnect the boost compensator hose at the injection pump.
7. Remove the fuel injection pump. Make sure the delivery valves do not turn when loosening the pipe connections at the pump.
8. Remove the injection pump support bracket bolts.

Diesel injection pump fittings

1 Hose
2 Vacuum regulating valve
3 Accel lever
4 Idle speed adjusting screw
5 Fast idle lever
6 Hose (to constant pressure valve)
7 Fuel inlet nipple
8 Connector (for timing control solenoid valve, fuel cut-off solenoid valve and accel switch)
9 Fuel injection pipe assembly
10 Connector

Tightening torque: Nm (ft-lbs.)

Timing marks set up for injection pump removal

9. Remove the injection pump mounting nuts and remove the injection pump from the engine.

CAUTION

DO NOT rotate the crankshaft with the injection pump removed.

---

10. Installation is the reverse of removal. Make sure the timing marks on the camshaft sprocket and crankshaft pulley are aligned with their respective timing marks.
11. After mounting the injection pump, carefully install the injection pump sprocket and belt. Make sure that the injection pump drive shaft key is not misplaced or dropped.
12. Adjust the injection timing and bleed the fuel system.

Fuel Injectors

REMOVAL & INSTALLATION

1. Remove the fuel delivery lines from the injectors and injection pump. Remove the lines as an assembly and cap all open fuel fittings on the injection pump immediately to prevent contamination with dirt or grease. *This is very important.*

2. Remove the fuel return pipe nuts, then remove the fuel return line.
3. Remove the injection nozzle assembly from the cylinder head with special tool (Mitsubishi part # MD998387 or a long, deepset socket).
4. Installation is the reverse of removal. Clean the area around each injector on the cylinder head before installing injectors, and fit a new nozzle tip gasket to each injector. Torque each injector to 44-50 ft. lbs. Replace the heat shields.

NOTE: Exercise care when handling the fuel injector. It is a high-precision part that is easily damaged by dirt or dropping.

Fuel Filter

See Diesel Engine Tune-Up.

Diesel Fuel Injection Specifications

	Injection Pump				Fuel Injectors	
Turning Direction	Injection Order	Injection Timing	Delivery Valve Opening Pressure		Injection Pressure	Injector Installation Torque
Clockwise, viewed from drive side	1–3–4–2	5°ATDC@ 1mm plunger stroke	306 psi		1,707 psi	44–50 ft. lbs.

MANUAL TRANSMISSION

Four and Five Speed

REMOVAL & INSTALLATION

2WD Pickup Trucks

1. Disconnect the battery ground cable, remove the air cleaner and the starter.
2. Remove the top transmission mounting bolts from the bell housing.
3. From inside the vehicle, raise the console assembly, if equipped, or the carpet and remove the dust cover retaining plate at the shift lever.
4. Place the four speed transmission in second gear and the five speed transmission in first gear. Remove the control lever assembly.
5. Raise the vehicle and support it safely. Drain the transmission. Disconnect the speedometer and the back up light switch.
6. Remove the drive shaft, exhaust pipe, and the clutch cable. On diesel trucks, remove the clutch release cylinder.
7. Support the transmission and remove the engine rear support bracket.
8. Remove the bell housing cover and bolts, move the transmission rearward, and lower it carefully to the floor. Remove the transmission from under the vehicle.
9. To install the transmission, reverse the removal procedure. Make sure the transmission is in the proper gear before installing the gear shift lever.

4WD Pickup Trucks

1. Disconnect the battery ground (negative) terminal.
2. Remove the air cleaner and starting motor.
3. Remove the transmission mounting bolts (two bolts on the upper side) from the bell housing.
4. In the cab, remove the lock screws and lift up the console box. In trucks without a console box, remove the back bone carpet.
5. Remove the attaching screws and lift out the dust cover retaining plate.
6. Turn up the dust cover, and remove the control housing attaching bolts from the extension housing, and remove the control lever assembly.
7. Jack up the truck and support it with jackstands.
8. Drain the gearbox.
9. Remove the propeller shafts. Disconnect the speedometer cable at the transmission.
10. Disconnect the back-up light switch harness and the 4WD indicator light switch harness, which is resting on the upper middle section of the transfer case.
11. Disconnect the front exhaust pipe.
12. On gasoline-engined trucks, disconnect the clutch cable from the clutch control lever. On diesel models, remove the clutch release cylinder.

13. Support the rear of the engine with a jack.
14. Disconnect and remove the transfer case mounting bracket.
15. Place a floor jack or transmission jack underneath the transmission. Remove the no. 2 crossmember.

_____ **CAUTION** _____
When the transmission is supported on a service jack the supporting area should be as wide as possible.
_____

16. After removing the bell housing cover, remove the remaining transmission bolts from the bell housing.
17. Remove the transmission from the truck. Use care not to twist the front end of the main drive gear.
18. Reverse the above procedure for installation. Torque the transmission mounting bolts to 31-40 ft. lbs.; the transmission-to-rear insulator bolts to 14-18 ft.lbs.; the transfer case support insulator-to-transfer case mounting bracket bolts to 14-18 ft. lbs.; and the transfer case mounting bracket bolts to 14-18 ft. lbs. Set the transmission

1. Transmission case
2. Main drive pinion
3. Synchronizer assy (3-4 speed)
4. 3rd speed gear
5. 2nd speed gear
6. Synchronizer assy (1-2 speed)
7. 1st speed gear
8. Rear bearing retainer
9. Reverse gear
10. Control finger
11. Control shaft
12. Control lever cover
13. Control level assy
14. Stopper plate
15. Control housing
16. Change shifter
17. Mainshaft
18. Extension housing
19. Counter reverse gear
20. Reverse idler gear
21. Reverse idler gear shaft
22. Under cover
23. Counter gear
24. Front bearing retainer
25. Clutch shift arm
26. Release bearing carrier
27. Clutch control shaft
28. Return spring

Cross section of four speed transmission

shift lever to the "neutral" position and the transfer case shift lever to the "4H" position when installing the gear shift lever assembly. Adjust the clutch and fill the KM130 transmission with 2.2 qts. of hypoid gear oil; the KM132 with 2.4 qts.; the KM144 and KM145 transmission and transfer case with 2.3 qts., respectively.

Montero

1. Disconnect the negative cable from the battery.
2. Place the transmission lever in neutral, and the transfer case lever in 4H. Remove the gearshift lever assembly. Cover the opening with a shop rag to prevent any dirt from entering.
3. Jack up the truck and safely support it with jackstands. Remove the transfer case skid plate.
4. Drain the transfer case and transmission gearbox.
5. Remove the front and rear propeller shafts.
6. Disconnect the speedometer cable, back-up light switch harness, and the 4WD indicator light harness, which rests on the top center of the transfer case.
7. Detach the clutch release cylinder from the transmission.
8. Remove the bell housing cover.
9. Detach the starter motor from the bell housing.

NOTE: On air conditioned Monteros, remove the front propeller shaft, then lower the starting motor downward from underneath the vehicle to remove it.

10. Remove the front exhaust pipe mounting bracket.
11. Detach the engine support rear insulator from the no. 2 crossmember, and remove the no. 2 crossmember.
12. Support the transmission and transfer case assembly with a transmission jack or floor jack.
13. Unbolt the transfer case from the transfer case mounting bracket.
14. Remove the transmission mounting bolts from the engine.
15. Remove the transmission mounting bolts from the engine. With the jack still underneath the assembly and securely positioned, pull the transfer case and transmission assembly away from the engine.
16. Tilt the front of the transmission and transfer case assembly downward. Slowly lower the assembly with the jack, being careful that the rear of the transmission does not hit the no. 3 crossmember.

Transfer Case

REMOVAL & INSTALLATION

4WD Pickup Trucks and Montero

The transfer case is removed from the transmission while the transmission/transfer case assembly is out of the vehicle.

1. Remove the backup light switch from the lower right of the adapter. Take out the steel ball (manual transmission models only).
2. Remove the plug from the right side of the transfer case and take out the select spring and the select plunger.
3. Remove the six bolts securing the control lever assembly and remove the control lever assembly and gasket.
4. On the four-speed only, remove the plug from the top of the adaptor and take out the neutral return spring and plunger.
5. On five-speed models, remove the plugs from the top of the adaptor and take out the resistance spring, steel ball, neutral springs and plungers.

4WD switch location on manual transmissions

6. On the four-speed and automatic transmission transfer case, remove the bolts securing the transfer case adapter to the transmission.
7. On the four-speed model only, with the change shifter tilted to the left, remove the control finger from the shift lug groove. Take out the transfer case assembly.
8. On the five-speed model, drive out the lock pin from the change shifter using a ³⁄₁₆ in. punch. Remove the four bolts and two nuts securing the transfer case to the adapter, and remove the transfer case assembly from the adapter. Remove the change shifter from the control shaft.
9. Reverse the above procedure for installation. Make sure you mount the neutral return plungers and the springs in the hole on top of the adapter and tighten the plug until it is flush with the adapter surface.

OVERHAUL

NOTE: Proper transmission overhaul requires the use of certain special tools. If these are not available, the job should not be undertaken.

4-Speed

1. Remove the undercover.
2. Remove the backup light switch. Be careful not to lose the steel ball.
3. Remove the speedometer gear sleeve clamp and remove the speedometer driven gear and sleeve assembly from the extension housing assembly.

4. Remove the extension housing bolts. Turn the shift lever to the left and pull off the extension housing.
5. Loosen the three poppet plugs, then remove the three poppet springs and the three steel balls.
6. Place the 1st–2nd speed shift rod in Neutral position.
7. Remove the reverse shift rail and fork assembly together with the reverse idler gear.
8. Using a ³⁄₁₆ in. punch, drive off the 3rd–4th and 1st–2nd speed shift fork spring pins. Push each shift rod toward the rear of the transmission case and remove the shift forks. Remember to remove the interlock plunger.
9. Remove the snap-ring from the rear end of the counter gear and then remove the reverse counter gear.
10. Unlock the main shaft lock nut and remove the lock nut. The lock nut can be loosened by double-engaging the 3rd speed gear and the 1st speed gear.
11. Remove the reverse gear from the main shaft.
12. Remove the five attaching screws and then remove the rear bearing retainer.
13. Remove the front bearing retainer.
14. With the counter gear pressed to the rear, remove the rear bearing snap-ring. Then using a bearing puller remove the rear counter bearing.
15. Remove the snap-ring from the front counter bearing. Pull off the bearing with a bearing puller.
16. Pull the counter gear out of the case.
17. Remove the main drive pinion from the front of the case. To remove the bearing from the main drive pinion, remove the two snap-rings and then remove the bearing with a bearing puller.
18. Remove the mainshaft bearing snap-ring and remove the bearing using a dual post bearing puller (D-50/Plymouth Arrow special tool MD998056-10 and MD998056).
19. Remove the main shaft assembly by lifting it up through the case.
20. Disassemble the mainshaft assembly in the following order.

    a. Pull off the 1st speed gear, the 1st–2nd speed synchronizer and the 2nd speed gear toward the rear of the mainshaft.

    b. Remove the snap-ring from the forward end of the mainshaft, then remove the 3rd–4th speed synchronizer and the 3rd speed gear.

21. If removing the shift control shaft assembly, remove the pin locking the gear shifter using a ³⁄₁₆ in. punch. To remove the lock pin, press the gear shifter forward and drive the lock pin off, being careful not to bend the control shaft.

Inspect the parts after cleaning. Replace any worn, damaged or defective.

Assembly is as follows.

22. If the main drive pinion bearing has been removed, replace it using a pipe fit over the end of the pinion shaft.

1. 3rd speed gear
2. 2nd speed gear
3. 1st speed gear
4. Mainshaft
5. Snap ring
6. Synchronizer ring (3-4 speed)
7. Synchronizer piece
8. Synchronizer sleeve (3-4 speed)
9. Synchronizer spring (3-4 speed)
10. Synchronizer hub (3-4 speed)
11. Needle bearing (3rd speed gear)
12. Needle bearing (2nd speed gear)
13. Synchronizer ring (1-2 speed)
14. Synchronizer piece
15. Synchronizer sleeve (1-2 speed)
16. Synchronizer spring (1-2 speed)
17. Synchronizer hub (1-2 speed)
18. Needle bearing (1st speed gear)
19. 1st gear bearing sleeve
20. Bearing spacer

Mainshaft assembly—four and five speed transmissions

──────── **CAUTION** ────────

Make sure the pipe does not apply pressure on the ball bearings but only on the bearing race, or bearing damage could result.

23. Fit a snap-ring which gives a clearance of no more than 0–0.002 in. and install it on the drive pinion.

24. Assemble the main shaft in the following order.
  a. Assemble the 3rd–4th speed and the 1st–2nd speed synchronizers. The front and rear ends of the synchronizer sleeve and hub can be identified as shown in the illustration. The synchronizer spring is installed as shown.
  b. Install the needle bearing, 3rd speed gear, synchronizer ring and the 3rd–4th speed synchronizer assembly onto the mainshaft from the front end. Be careful not to confuse the front and the rear of the synchronizer assembly.

25. Select and install a snap-ring that will give the 3rd–4th speed synchronizer hub an end-play from 0.0 to 0.003 in.

26. Third speed gear end-play should be from 0.002 to 0.008 in.

27. Install the needle bearing, the 2nd speed gear, the synchronizer assembly, the bearing sleeve, the needle bearing, the 1st speed gear, and the bearing spacer onto the mainshaft from the rear end.

28. Push the bearing spacer forward and check the 1st and 2nd speed gear end play.

Clearance should be within 0.002–0.008 in.

29. Insert the mainshaft assembly into the transmission case and fit the mainshaft center bearing using a bearing driver. Hold the forward end of the mainshaft by hand at the front of the case.

30. Install the needle bearing and the synchronizer ring, then insert the main drive pinion assembly into the case from the front.

31. Insert the countershaft gear into the case. With a snap-ring fitted to the countershaft front needle bearing, drive the bearing into the case by hammering on the outer race of the bearing.

32. Fit a snap-ring to the countershaft rear ball bearing and then install the bearing with a bearing installer.

33. Install the front bearing retainer. When installing the retainer, install a spacer that will give a clearance (C) of 0.0–0.004 in. (see illustration). Apply sealant to both sides of the front bearing retainer packing and apply gear oil to the oil seal lip. Install packing and oil seal.

34. Install the rear bearing retainer and its five screws. It is suggested that each screw head be staked with a pointed punch to prevent them from coming loose.

35. Install the reverse gear on the mainshaft and tighten the lock nut to 73–94 ft. lbs. Lock the nut at the notch of the mainshaft.

36. Install the spacer and counter re-

verse gear to the counter gear rear end.

37. Install a snap-ring of the proper size so that the reverse counter gear and play will be from 0.0 to 0.003 in.

38. Install the 3rd–4th and 1st–2nd speed shift forks into their respective synchronizer sleeves. Insert each shift rod from the rear of the case. Lock the shift forks and rod with spring pins, install the interlock plunger between the shift rods.

NOTE: The spring pins should be installed with the slits parallel to the shift rod.

Retainer-to-bearing clearance adjustment

39. Install the reverse shift rod and fork assembly together with the reverse idler gear.

40. Insert the ball and poppet spring with the small end of the ball side into each shift rod. Tighten the plugs to the specified positions. After installation, seal each plug head with sealant.

41. Apply sealant to both sides of the extension housing packing and fit the packing into the housing.

42. Turn the gear shift control down to the left and install the extension to the transmission case.

43. Make sure the forward end of the

Installing reverse idler gear—four speed transmission

45. Rotate the speedometer driven gear and sleeve assembly so that the number on the sleeve, which is the same as the number of teeth on the gear, is in the "U" mark position as the assembly is installed.

46. Install the speedometer gear clamp with its tongs in the sleeve positioning slots.

47. Install the backup light switch with its steel ball.

48. Refit the under cover and torque the bolts to 6–7 ft. lbs.

49. Install the transmission control lever assembly and fill the gear shifter area with grease. Fill the transmission with lubricant.

5 Speed

1. Drain the oil and remove the case cover.

2. Remove the backup light switch and ball.

3. Remove the extension housing attaching bolts, back off the plug of the neutral return plunger, turn the shift lever down

1 High-low shift rail	7 4WD lamp switch (H-L)	12 2WD-4WD shift lug	17 Transmission control shaft (M/T)	22 3-4 shift rail (M/T-4 speed) OD-R shift rail (M/T-5 speed)
2 Poppet spring	8 4WD lamp switch (2WD-4WD)	13 Select plunger	18 Neutral return plunger B (M/T-5 speed)	23 1-2 shift rail (M/T-4 speed) 3-4 shift rail (M/T-5 speed)
3 Poppet ball	9 Spring	14 Select spring	19 Resistance ball (M/T-5 speed)	24 Reverse shift rail M/T-4 speed)
4 Interlock plunger	10 2WD-4WD shift fork	15 2WD-4WD shift fork	20 Neutral return plunger A (M/T)	1-2 shift rail (M/T-5 speed)
5 High-low shift fork	11 Distance callor	16 Transmission control lever (M/T)	21 Control finger (M/T)	
6 Transfer case control lever				

Transfer case control assembly

control finger is snug in the slot of the shift lug and fit the extension housing bolts after coating their threads with sealant.

44. Apply gear oil to the speedometer driven gear and install the gear and sleeve assembly in the extension housing. Make sure the sleeve flange and its mating areas on the extension housing are free of dirt, or it will cause the gears to be misaligned and could damage them.

1. Transmission case	9. Synchronizer assy (overdrive)	17. Control housing	25. Reverse idler gear shaft
2. Main drive pinion	10. Overdrive gear	18. Change shifter	26. Under cover
3. Synchronizer assy (3-4 speed)	11. Control finger	19. Mainshaft	27. Counter gear
4. 3rd speed gear	12. Neutral return finger	20. Speedometer drive gear	28. Front bearing retainer
5. 2nd speed gear	13. Control shaft	21. Extension housing	29. Clutch shift arm
6. Synchronizer assy (1-2 speed)	14. Control lever cover	22. Counter overdrive gear	30. Release bearing carrier
7. 1st speed gear	15. Control lever assy	23. Counter reverse gear	31. Clutch control shaft
8. Rear bearing retainer	16. Stopper plate	24. Reverse idler gear	32. Return spring

Cross section of five speed transmission

to the left and pull off the extension housing.

4. Remove the snap-ring and speed-ometer drive gear.

5. Remove the snap-ring and mainshaft rear bearing.

6. Remove the three plugs and remove the poppet springs and balls.

7. Remove the 1–2 and 3–4 shift fork pins with a ³⁄₁₆" punch. Pull each rail toward the rear of the case and remove the forks and interlock plunger.

8. In the same manner, remove the 5th-reverse forks.

9. Engage the reverse and 2nd gears and remove the mainshaft and countershaft rear locknuts.

10. Remove the 5th counter gear and bearing with a puller. Remove the spacer and reverse counter gear.

11. Remove the 5th gear and sleeve from the mainshaft. Remove the 5th synchro-nizer and spacer.

12. Remove the cotter pin, nut and re-verse idler gear.

13. Remove the rear bearing retainer.

14. Drive the reverse idler gear shaft from the case.

15. Remove the front bearing retainer.

16. Press the countergear to the rear and remove the rear bearing snap-ring.

17. Using a puller, remove the counter rear bearing.

18. Remove the snap-ring and pull the counter front bearing. Remove the coun-tergear from the case.

19. Remove the main drive pinion from the case.

20. Remove the two snap-rings and pull the bearing.

21. Remove the snap-ring and pull the mainshaft bearing.

22. Remove the mainshaft from the case.

23. Disassemble the mainshaft.

24. Disassemble the extension housing. To assemble:

25. Install the bearing on the main drive pinion and select a snap-ring which will give a clearance of 0–0.0024 in. between the snap-ring and the bearing.

26. Assemble the mainshaft. Use a spacer which will give a 3–4 synchronizer end play of 0–0.003". Use a snap-ring which will give a 1–2 gear end play of 0.002–0.008".

27. Insert the mainshaft into the case and drive in the center bearing.

28. Install the needle bearing and syn-chronizer ring, then insert the main drive pinion into the case from the front.

29. Insert the countershaft gear into the case.

30. Install the snap-ring on the counter-shaft front needle bearing and drive the bearing into the case by hammering the outer race.

31. Install the snap-ring on the counter-shaft rear bearing and install it in place.

32. Install the front bearing retainer us-ing a spacer which will give clearance of 0–0.004" between the bearing and retainer.

33. Install the front retainer oil seal.

34. Install the rear retainer.

35. Install the reverse idler gear shaft.

36. Install the needle bearing, reverse idler gear and thrust washer. Tighten the locknut and install the cotter pin. Idler gear end play should be 0.0047–0.0110". If not, replace the thrust washer.

37. Assemble the 5th synchronizer.

38. Install the spacer, stop plate and 5th

Driving out transfer case lock pin from change shifter

synchronizer assembly, the 5th gear bear-ing sleeve and needle bearing, the syn-chronizer ring and 5th gear, in that order, to the mainshaft from the rear. 5th gear end play should be 0.004–0.010".

39. Install the spacer, counter reverse

Fifth speed (overdrive) synchronizer hub installation direction

Installing poppet spring and plug assem-bly—four and five speed transmissions

Synchronizer ring to gear clearance: "A" equals 0.032 in. on both four and five speed transmissions

Synchronizer hub assemblies and spring installation. Note direction of hubs in relation to arrow

gear spacer, counter 5th gear and the ball bearing onto the countershaft gear from the rear. Tighten and lock the nut.

40. Insert the 3–4 and 1–2 forks into their synchronizer sleeves. Insert each shift rail from the rear of the case. Install the spring pins and interlock plunger.

NOTE: The slit in the pins should be parallel with the rail.

41. Insert the ball and poppet spring into each shift rail. Tighten the plugs flush with the case.

42. Install the ball bearing on the rear of the mainshaft.

43. Install the speedometer drive gear.

44. Turn the shifter down and to the left and install the extension housing.

45. Install the neutral return plungers, spring, and resistance spring and ball. Tighten the plugs flush with the case.

46. Install the speedometer driven gear sleeve and lock plate.

47. Install the backup light switch and ball.

48. Install the bottom cover and torque the bolts to 6–7 ft. lbs.

49. Install the control lever assembly.

CLUTCH

Clutch Cable

REMOVAL & INSTALLATION

All Gasoline Engined Pickup Trucks

1. Loosen the cable adjusting wheel inside the engine compartment while pulling the cable.

2. Loosen the clutch pedal adjusting bolt locknut and loosen the adjusting bolt.

3. Remove the cable end from the clutch throwout lever.

4. Remove the cable end from the clutch pedal.

5. Installation is the reverse of removal.

NOTE: Apply engine oil to the cable before replacing. Make sure the isolating pad is fitted on the cable after installation to keep the cable from rubbing the motor mount during operation.

Adjustment

PEDAL HEIGHT

1. Adjust the pedal height to the standard value with the adjusting bolt (see illustration), and check the pedal stroke and distance "A".

— **CAUTION** —
Insufficient pedal stroke results in only partial clutch release, causing hard gear

PEDAL HEIGHT ADJUSTMENT
GASOLINE ENGINED PICKUP TRUCKS

Description	Standard valve mm (in.)	
	2.0L	**2.6L**
Distance A	22 (.9)	20 (.8)
Pedal height	166 (6.5)	176 (6.9)
Pedal stroke	140 (5.5)	150 (5.9)

Pedal Height Adjustments
Diesel Pickups and Montero

Description	Standard value mm (in.)	
	Diesel pickups	**Montero**
Pedal height A	174 (6.8)	186–191 (7.3–7.5)
Pedal free play B	10 to 15 (.4 to .5)	5–10 (.2–.4)
Pedal to floorboard C	22 (.9) or more	—

shifting and gear grinding when shifting.

2. In the engine compartment, at the fire wall, pull out the clutch cable a little and adjust the cable by turning the adjusting wheel until it is 0.12–0.16 in from the insulator.

3. Clutch pedal free play should be within 0.8–1.4 in.

Adjusting clutch pedal height

Adjusting the clutch cable

Hydraulic Clutch

All Turbo Diesel Models and Montero utilize a hydraulic clutch system. Clutch pedal pressure is converted, through the master cylinder, into fluid pressure, which operates a slave cylinder at the clutch. The slave cylinder operates the clutch control lever and shift arm, which moves the clutch release bearing and operates the clutch.

The master cylinder can be disassembled and rebuilt if worn and/or leaking. The slave cylinder should be replaced as a unit if defective.

1. Clutch control shaft
2. Return spring
3. Clutch shift arm
4. Return clip
5. Release bearing carrier
6. Release bearing
7. Pressure plate assembly
8. Clutch disc

Exploded view of clutch assembly

13 to 16 (10 to 12)
10 to 14 (8 to 10)
25 to 29 (19 to 21)

1 Piston assembly
2 Piston stop ring
3 Damper and push rod assembly
4 Fluid reservoir
5 Master cylinder
6 Clutch tube
7 Clutch hose
8 Gasket and banjo
9 Eye bolt

Tightening torque: Nm (ft.lbs.)

Hydraulic clutch assembly—diesel trucks and Montero

Master Cylinder

REMOVAL

1. Disconnect the clutch fluid tube from the master cylinder. Slowly depress the clutch pedal to drain the fluid.
2. Remove the cotter pin connecting the master cylinder pushrod to the clutch pedal.

Montero and diesel pickup clutch release lever

Removing master cylinder piston stop ring, hydraulic clutches

3. Remove the two retaining nuts and remove the master cylinder.

DISASSEMBLY

1. Using snap-ring pliers, remove the piston stop ring. Pull out the piston assembly.
2. Wash the master cylinder, piston and cup in clean brake fluid. Never use solvents. Use care not to damage the cylinder, piston and piston cup.

—— CAUTION ——
Do not disassemble the piston assembly.

INSPECTION

1. Check the inner surface of the master cylinder and the outer surface of the piston. Replace the piston if damaged or scored.
2. Check the master cylinder-to-piston clearance. If clearance exceeds the service limit (.0059 in.), replace either the piston or master cylinder unit. Standard piston diameter is .6231-.6248 in.; standard master cylinder inside diameter is .6248 to .6265 in.
3. Check the piston cup for damage, deformation and wear. Replace the cup if at all defective. Also check the return springs for loss of tension and damage. Replace any part that is defective.

—— CAUTION ——
When any related parts such as the return spring, piston cup and piston require replacement, it is necessary to replace the piston assembly.

ASSEMBLY

After checking clearances, assemble the master cylinder in the reverse order of disassembly. Always apply clean brake fluid to the master cylinder bore and piston cup prior to assembly.

INSTALLATION

1. Reverse the order of removal for installation. Tighten the master cylinder and clutch tube flare nut to 8-10 ft.lbs. and 10-12 ft. lbs., respectively.
2. Adjust the clutch pedal free play and bleed the hydraulic system.

Clutch Release Cylinder (Slave Cylinder)

REMOVAL & DISASSEMBLY

1. Remove the eye bolt and gaskets and disconnect the clutch hose from the clutch slave cylinder.
2. Remove the two bolts securing the clutch slave cylinder and clutch housing, and remove the slave cylinder assembly.
3. Remove the rubber boot and push rod and take out the piston and spring.

Slave cylinder assembly

INSPECTION

1. Check inside the slave cylinder body for scoring, rust or unusual wear.
2. Check the piston cup for wear or deformation.
3. Check the piston for rust or scoring.

REASSEMBLY & INSTALLATION

1. Insert the spring into the slave cylinder.
2. Liberally apply clean brake fluid to the outer surface of the piston, piston cup and cylinder bore.
3. Install the piston and piston cup into the release cylinder.
4. Install the push rod and boot.
5. Install the slave cylinder to the clutch housing and tighten the two bolts to 22-30 ft. lbs.
6. Connect the clutch fluid line to the cylinder and tighten the eye bolt.
7. Bleed the clutch system.

HYDRAULIC CLUTCH BLEEDING

Whenever the clutch fluid line, clutch hose and/or the clutch master cylinder have been removed, or if the clutch pedal feels spongy (indicating air in the system), bleed the system. This is much the same as bleeding an hydraulic brake system.

1. Loosen the bleeder screw on the clutch slave cylinder. You'll have to jack up the truck and safely support it with jackstands for this.

2. Connect a length of rubber tubing to the bleeder nipple, with the other end of the tube submerged in a clear glass jar filled with clean brake fluid. Make sure the clutch master cylinder is topped up with fluid; keep it topped up throughout the procedure.

3. Have an assistant push the clutch pedal down slowly until air bubbles stop coming out of the rubber hose in the jar. All air is now expelled from the system.

4. Have the assistant hold the clutch pedal down until you retighten the bleeder screw.

5. Refill the clutch master cylinder with DOT 3 brake fluid.

─────── **CAUTION** ───────
Never mix brake fluids. Use only approved DOT 3 fluid.

CLUTCH PEDAL ADJUSTMENT

If clutch pedal height from floor or free play is not within the standard value, adjust as follows:

1. Turn the pedal adjusting bolt back to a position where it does not contact the pedal arm.

2. Loosen the push rod lock nut and adjust the pedal height to the standard value by turning the push rod.

3. Turn the pedal adjusting bolt until it comes into contact with the pedal arm, and then tighten the lock nut.

4. After making the adjustment depress the clutch pedal several times and check the clutch pedal-to-floorboard clearance. The pedal on diesel pickups should be within 22 mm (.9 in.) or more when the clutch is fully disengaged. The Montero pedal should be close to this same distance. If the pedal-to-floor clearance is less then this, air may be in the hydraulic system; if so, the system should be bled. Also, the clutch plates could be worn.

Clutch Disc Replacement

1. Remove the transmission as outlined in Manual Transmission Removal and Installation.

NOTE: It is recommended that a clutch aligning tool be inserted in the clutch hub

Installing the clutch disc—use clutch disc guide as shown

to prevent dropping of the clutch disc during disassembly.

2. Remove pressure plate bolts, pressure plate and clutch disc.

3. From inside the transmission bell housing, remove the return spring clip and remove the release bearing assembly.

4. If necessary, remove the release control lever and spring pin with a 3/16 inch punch. Remove the control lever shaft assembly and clutch shift arm, two felt packings and two return springs.

5. Installation is the reverse of removal.

AUTOMATIC TRANSMISSION

REMOVAL & INSTALLATION

The transmission and converter must be removed as an assembly; otherwise, the converter drive plate, pump bushing, or oil seal may be damaged. The drive plate will not support a load; therefore, none of the weight of the transmission should be allowed to rest on the plate during removal.

1. Disconnect battery ground cable, drain the transmission, and remove cooler lines at transmission.

2. Remove starter and cooler line bracket.

3. Rotate crankshaft clockwise and remove bolts attaching torque converter to

1. Selector handle
2. Push button
3. Set screw
4. Rod adjusting cam
5. Selector lever rod
6. Selector lever

7. Detent plate
8. Position indicator cover (for sports)
9. Inhibitor switch
10. Position indicator cover
11. Lever bracket cover
12. Control cover
13. Control rod

Exploded view of automatic transmission shift control

drive plate.

4. Remove the driveshaft(s).

5. Disconnect gearshift rod and torque shaft.

6. Disconnect throttle rod from lever at the left side of transmission. Remove linkage bellcrank from transmission if so equipped.

7. Remove the oil filler tube and speedometer cable.

8. On 2WD models, disconnect the back-up light switch harness. On 4WD models, disconnect the back-up light switch harness and 4WD indicator light switch harness which are located near the upper middle of the transfer case.

9. Support the rear of the engine with jack.

10. Raise transmission slightly.

11. Remove crossmember.

12. Remove all bell housing bolts.

13. Carefully work transmission converter assembly rearward off engine block dowels and disengage converter hub from end of crankshaft. Attach a small C-clamp to edge of bell housing to hold converter in place during transmission removal.

14. Remove transmission.

15. Installation is the reverse of removal.

Pan and Filter

REMOVAL & INSTALLATION

1. Raise and support vehicle.

2. Loosen the pan bolts from one end to the other allowing the fluid to drain out.

T587

3. Unbolt the old filter from the pan.

4. Clean the pan and install a new filter. Tighten filter bolts to 35 in. lbs.

5. Install the pan and new gasket. Torque pan bolts to 6–9 ft. lbs.

6. Add four quarts of Dexron fluid, start the engine and move the lever through all positions, pausing momentarily in each. Add enough fluid to bring the level to the full mark on the dipstick.

Adjustments

THROTTLE LINKAGE

The throttle rod adjustment is very important to proper transmission operation. This adjustment positions a valve which controls shift speed, shift quality and part throttle-down shift sensitivity. If the setting is too short, early shifts and slippage between shifts may occur. If the setting is too long, shifts may be delayed and part throttle-down shifts may be very sensitive.

To adjust the throttle rod:

1. Warm up the engine until it reaches the normal operating temperature. With the carburetor automatic choke disengaged from the fast idle cam, adjust the engine idle speed by rotating speed adjusting screw (SAS). See "Tune-up Procedures" at the beginning of this section.

2. Loosen the bolts on the linkage so that both rod "B" and "C" can slide properly.

Throttle rod adjustment—automatic transmission

3. Lightly push rod "A" or the transmission throttle lever and rod "C" toward the idle stopper, and set the rods to the idle position. Tighten the bolt securely that connects rods "B" and "C".

4. Make sure that when the carburetor throttle valve is wide-open, the transmission throttle lever smoothly moves from the IDLE to the WIDE OPEN position (from 47.5° to 54°), and that there is some range in the lever stroke.

5. Also make sure that when the throttle linkage alone is slowly returned from the fully closed position, the transmission throttle lever completely returns to *idle* by return spring force.

KICKDOWN BAND

The kickdown band adjusting screw is located on the left side of the transmission case.

1. Loosen locknut and back off approximately 5 turns. Test adjusting screw for free turning in the transmission case.

2. Tighten the adjusting screw to 72 in. lbs.

3. Back off adjusting screw 3 turns from step 2. Tighten the locknut to 35 ft. lbs.

LOW & REVERSE BAND

1. Raise vehicle, drain transmission fluid and remove the pan.

2. This transmission has an allen socket adjustment screw at the servo end of lever. After removing the locknut this screw is tightened to 41 in. lbs. torque then backed off 7½ turns. Tighten locknut to 30 ft. lbs.

3. Reinstall the pan.

NEUTRAL SAFETY SWITCH

1. When testing the safety switch, check to see if the switch has been properly installed. Move the selector lever into N position and adjust the switch by moving it so that the pin on the forward end of the rod assembly will be in the position near the lobe of detent plate and that this position will be at the front end of the range of N connection of the switch. Temporarily

tighten the attaching screws. After adjusting the selection lever clearance to 0.059 in. securely tighten the screws.

2. Test the continuity of the switch circuit by using a test light with switch connector disconnected.

SHIFT LINKAGE ADJUSTMENT

To adjust the shift linkage, the control cover must be removed.

Removal and Installation

1. Remove the shift handle assembly from the lever.

2. Take the position indicator assembly out upward.

Remove the position indicator lamp.

3. Disconnect the control rod from the arm.

Remove the lever bracket assembly.

4. Installation is the reverse of removal. If the proper turning effort (13–29 in. lbs.) is not obtained, adjust it by using a selective wave-washer of proper size.

--- **CAUTION** ---

When the turning effort at the pivot A is checked, the pin at the forward end of the rod assembly must not slide with the detent plate. If the arm is loose, the bushing should be replaced.

DRIVELINE

Driveshaft

REMOVAL & INSTALLATION

2WD Pickup Trucks

1. Make mating marks on the flange

1. Sleeve yoke
2. Snap ring
3. Needle bearing
4. Universal joint journal
5. Front propeller shaft
6. Center bearing assembly
7. Center yoke
8. Center yoke attaching nut
9. Rear propeller shaft
10. Propeller shaft flange yoke
11. Universal joint journal kit

Exploded view of driveshaft

yoke and the differential companion flange.

2. Remove the bolts connecting the flange yoke to the differential companion flange, and remove the nuts attaching the center bearing assembly.

3. Remove the propeller shaft by drawing it out. Installation is reverse of removal.

NOTE: When the sleeve yoke end of the propeller shaft is pulled out from the transmission extension housing, transmission oil will flow out it if the front of the truck is raised higher, than the rear.

— **CAUTION** —
When removing the propeller shaft, be careful not to damage the oil seal lip and see that no foreign substance is present in the lip area.

4WD Pickups and Montero

1. Set the free-wheeling hubs to "unlocked", and also set the transfer case gear shift lever to the 2H position.

2. Make mating marks on the U-joint flange yoke and the companion flange on the differential and/or transfer case.

3. Remove the bolts connecting the flange yoke to the differential and/or transfer case companion flange.

4. Remove the propeller shaft by pulling it out. Be careful not to damage the oil seal lip.

NOTE: When the propeller shaft is pulled out of the transmission extension housing or the transfer case, transmission or transfer case oil may leak out depending on the angle of the vehicle. Be ready to catch any spills.

U-Joint Overhaul

1. Remove the bearing retainer snap-rings from the flange yoke.

U-joint overhaul

Checking U-joint snap-ring clearance

When installing center bearing align three mating marks

2. With a vise and suitable sockets, force one needle bearing cup outward from the yoke, using the cross as a ram.

3. Grasp the protruding bearing with pliers or vise grips and remove it from the yoke.

4. Reverse the sockets and again using the cross as a ram, force the opposite bearing outward from the yoke and remove it with pliers or vise grips.

5. Follow the same procedure to remove the remaining bearing in the yoke.

6. To install, place the cross in the yoke and start a bearing cup into the yoke collar, engaging the cross arm.

7. With the aid of a vise, force the bearing cup into the yoke collar until it bottoms. Install the opposite bearing cup in the same manner.

NOTE: Sockets may be used to force the bearing cup inward so that the retaining snap-rings can be installed.

8. Different thickness snap-rings are used to control the clearance between the bearing and the snap-ring.

9. Install a snap-ring and measure the clearance with a feeler gauge. Replace the snap-ring with one of the proper thickness to have a total clearance tolerance of .000 to .001 inch.

Snap-ring selection range:
No color—0.0504 inch
Yellow—0.0561 inch
Blue—0.0528 inch
Purple—0.0539 inch

NOTE: When snap-rings are installed, press each bearing towards the opposite side to measure the maximum clearance.

Center Bearing

REMOVAL & INSTALLATION

2WD Models

1. Remove driveshaft.

2. Disconnect the center universal joint.

3. Remove the nut holding the center yoke and remove the yoke. Remove the center bearing bracket from the bearing by prying on it.

4. Remove the center bearing using a gear puller.

NOTE: The center bracket and the

mounting rubber are welded together and must be replaced as a unit.

To assemble:

5. Fill the bearing grease cavity with multipurpose grease.

6. Partially insert the center bearing into the shaft and install the bracket to the bearing.

7. Verify that the bracket mounting rubber is properly fitted in the bearing groove.

8. Refit the center yoke, making sure you align the notch on the yoke with the notch on the front propeller shaft. Replace the attaching nut and tighten to 116–159 ft. lbs.

9. Replace the center universal joint, making sure you align the notch on the rear propeller shaft with the notch on the yoke.

10. Install the driveshaft.

NOTE: The manufacturer suggests that a new center yoke locking nut be used when the center bearing is removed.

DRIVE AXLE

Axle Shaft, Bearing and Seal

REMOVAL & INSTALLATION

All Rear Axles

1. Jack up the vehicle and support it on stands.

2. Remove the rear wheels and brake drums.

3. Disconnect the brake line from the wheel cylinder and plug it to prevent fluid loss.

Removing the oil seal

4. Remove the four nuts behind the brake backing plate holding the bearing case to the axle housing assembly.

5. Remove the braking plate, bearing case and the axle shaft as an assembly.

NOTE: It may be necessary to use a slide hammer to remove the assembly.

6. Remove the O-ring and the bearing preload shims. Save the preload shims, as you will need them for reassembly.

7. Remove the oil seal with a hooked slide hammer.

8. To remove the axle shaft bearing, remove the notched locknut. This calls for a special tool, but you should be able to use a brass drift to knock it loose.

9. Remove the lock washer and plain washer.

10. Screw the lock nut back on to the axle shaft about three turns.

11. It will be necessary to fabricate a metal plate that fits over the axle shaft and butts the lock nut. Drill four holes in the plate that align with the four bearing case studs and fit the plate. Refit two nuts and washers to the bearing case studs diagonally across from each other and tighten them evenly to free the bearing case and the bearing.

12. Use a hammer and drift to remove the bearing outer race from the bearing case.

13. Remove the outer oil seal from the bearing case.

To assemble:

NOTE: Always use new O-rings and check the condition of all oil seals and dust covers.

14. Apply grease to the outer surface on the bearing outer race and to the lip of the outer oil seal, and drive them into the bearing case from each side.

15. Slide the bearing case and bearing

Removing axle shaft locknut

METAL PLATE

Removing axle bearing-fabricate metal plate indicated in picture

over the rear axle shaft. Apply grease on the bearing rollers and fit the inner race by pressing it into place.

——— CAUTION ———
Be careful not to damage or deform the dust cover.

16. Pack the bearing with grease.

17. Install the washer, the crowned lock washer and the lock nut in the order just given and tighten the lock nut to 130–159 ft. lbs. if possible.

18. Bend the tab on the lock washer into the groove on the lock nut. If the tab and the groove do not line up, slightly tighten the lock nut until they do.

19. Drive the new inner oil seal into place after greasing it and refit the assembly. Be sure to fit the O-ring and shim and apply silicone rubber sealant to the bearing case face.

NOTE: Be sure to bleed the brakes before road testing!

To adjust preload:

1. Begin with the left side rear axle assembly and insert a 0.04 in. shim between the bearing case and the axle shaft housing. Tighten the four nuts to 36–43 ft. lbs.

NOTE: Be sure to fit the O-ring and apply sealant.

2. Install the right side axle assembly into the right side housing without its shim and O-ring. Tighten the four nuts to 0.4 ft. lbs.

3. Using a flat blade feeler gauge, measure the gap between the bearing case and the axle housing face. It should range between 0.002–0.008 in. Record the measurement.

4. Remove the axle shaft and select a shim that is the same thickness as the gap between the faces just measured, plus a shim with a thickness from 0.002–0.0079 in. and install them on the housing. Fit the O-ring and apply sealant. Fit the axle assembly and tighten the four nuts to 36–43 ft. lbs.

5. Assemble remaining components. Be sure to bleed the brakes.

Free-Wheeling Hubs

REMOVAL & INSTALLATION

4WD Truck and Montero Front Axles

MANUAL LOCKING HUBS

1. Set the control handle to the "free" position. Unbolt the six cover bolts and remove the hub cover.

2. Using snap-ring pliers, remove the snap-ring from the driveshaft.

Sticker indicating the gear ratio

1. Differential carrier assembly
2. Packing
3. Rear axle housing
4. Rear axle shaft oil seal (Inner)
5. Shim
6. O-ring
7. Lock nut
8. Lock washer
9. Washer
10. Rear axle shaft bearing
11. Collar
12. Bearing case
13. Rear axle shaft oil seal (Outer)
14. Dust cover
15. Rear axle shaft
16. Air breather

Exploded view of drive axle assembly

Removing snap-ring from front hub—4WD models

Free-wheeling hub installation. Notice keyway

3. Remove the hub assembly from the front wheel.

4. To install, apply a semi-drying sealant to the front hub mounting surface of the hub body assembly, then torque the bolts to 36–43 ft. lbs.

5. Measure drive shaft end-play using a dial indicator as shown in the illustration. If end-play exceeds .008–.020 in., install a spacer on the shaft end so that the measurement will be within specifications. These are available from Dodge or Mitsubishi dealers.

6. Install the snap-ring. Install the hub cover.

Use a dial indicator to measure axial drive shaft play—4WD models

AUTOMATIC LOCKING HUBS

1. Remove the hub cover. If the cover cannot be loosened by hand, protect the cover with a shop towel to avoid damaging it and use an oil filter strap wrench to loosen it.

2. Remove the O-ring from the hub cover.

3. Using snap-ring pliers, remove the snap-ring and spacer.

4. Remove the hub.

5. To install, apply a semi-drying sealer to the hub surface.

NOTE: Make sure there is no excess sealer on the outside of the hub.

6. Align the key of brake "B" in the illustration with the slot in the knuckle spindle. Loosely install the automatic hub assembly.

7. Make sure that the hub and the free-wheeling hub assembly are in close contact when the assembly is forced lightly against the hub. If not, turn the hub until close contact is obtained.

8. Tighten the free-wheeling hub mounting bolts to 37–43 ft. lbs.

9. Apply a suitable grease to the O-ring before mounting it into the cover.

10. Install the cover securely.

Driveshafts (Axle Shafts)

REMOVAL

4WD Pickups and Montero

1. Remove the wheel and tire.

2. Remove the front brake caliper assembly; do not disconnect the brake hose. Hang the caliper close by with a wire hook.

3. Remove the free-wheeling hub cover assembly and remove the snap-ring from the drive shaft.

4. Remove the knuckle and the front hub together as a unit.

5. Remove the drive shaft as follows: for the left drive shaft on all 4WD pickups and Monteros, pull the drive shaft out of the differential carrier assembly.

——— CAUTION ———
When pulling the left drive shaft from the differential carrier assembly, be careful that the drive shaft spline does not damage the oil seal.

6. On 4WD pickups jack up the right lower suspension arm. Remove the right shock absorber.

——— CAUTION ———
Do not lower the jack while disconnecting the shock absorber or after it is disconnected. The jack should not be removed until the upper part of the shock has been reconnected to the arm post of the side frame.

7. On 4WD pickups, detach the right drive shaft from the inner shaft assembly and remove the drive shaft.

8. On Monteros, the right side shock absorber doesn't have to be removed. Detach the drive shaft from the differential carrier inner shaft, and remove the drive shaft.

JOINT INSPECTION AND REPACKING

1. Pry off the boot bands from around the rubber joint boots. Discard the bands; new ones must be fitted upon reassembly. Carefully inspect the boots; replace if there are any cracks, splits, or evidence of dry rot in the rubber.

2. Pull back the rubber boots and closely inspect the inner and outer ball races and the balls for wear, bluing, damage or rust. Bluing is evidence that the joints are low on or out of grease; any rust is evidence that water has penetrated the rubber joint boot. Pitting or scoring of the balls indicates one or both of the above, and can also indicate dirt or foreign material has entered the joint.

3. When you are satisfied that the internals of the CV joint are in good condition, repack the joint with about five ounces of high-temperature CV joint grease. The grease can be packed by hand; a needle fitting on the end of a grease gun also works in getting the grease deep into the joint. Make sure the joint is completely and thoroughly packed.

4. Replace the rubber joint boot if necessary. Always replace the boot bands with new ones.

DISASSEMBLY

For all CV–Joints removal, installation and overhaul procedures, please refer to "U–Joint/CV–Joint Overhaul" in the Unit Repair section.

INSTALLATION

1. On all models, drive the left drive shaft into the differential carrier assembly with a plastic hammer. Be careful not to damage the lip of the oil seal. Replace the circlip on the spline with a new one.

2. Mount the knuckle together with the front hub assembly. Adjust the drive shaft end-play using a dial indicator; play should be within .008–.020 in. Install a spacer (available in .012 in. increments from Dodge

Use a plastic mallet to drive in left drive shaft

and Mitsubishi dealers) if end-play exceeds the above limits.

3. Install the right drive shaft to the inner shaft, and torque to 37–43 ft. lbs. On 4WD pickup trucks, install the right shock absorber.

For left side

50 to 58 (37 to 43)

Axle shaft and CV-joint assemblies—4WD models and Montero

For right side

4. Install the knuckle and front hub assembly.

Inner Shaft

REMOVAL & INSTALLATION

1. Slightly raise the lower suspension arm on a jack.

2. Remove the mounting nut from the top of the shock absorber and then detach the shock absorber from the crossmember. The shock must be removed when working on either side.

> ### — CAUTION —
> *When removing the shock absorber, do not lower the jack. Do not remove the jack until the top of the shock absorber is reattached to the crossmember.*

1 Dust cover
2 Drive shaft and B.J.
3 Boot band (A)
4 B.J. boot
5 Boot band (C)
6 D.O.J. boot
7 Boot band (B)
8 Circlip
9 D.O.J. cage
10 D.O.J. inner race
11 Ball
12 Snap ring
13 D.O.J. outer race
14 End plate
15 Inner shaft
16 Bearing

Abbreviation:
D.O.J.–Double offset joint
B.J.–Birfield joint

Tightening torque:
Nm (ft-lbs.)

3. Remove the drive shaft.

4. Attach a special drive shaft puller, Mitsubishi part #MB990906 or equivalent, to the inner shaft flange. Pull the inner shaft from the front differential carrier.

> ### — CAUTION —
> *When pulling the inner shaft from the carrier, be careful that the spline part of the inner shaft does not damage the oil seal.*

5. If necessary, remove the housing tube.

6. Check for unusual wear or discoloration on the inner shaft.

7. Install the housing tube onto the front differential carrier and differential mounting bracket.

8. Drive the inner shaft into the front differential with the same special tool used to remove the shaft.

NOTE: Replace the circlip on the spline part of the inner shaft with a new one. Use care not to damage the lip of the oil seal.

9. Install the right drive shaft.

Measuring clearance between bearing case and axle housing face

Removing side bearing nuts with special spanner

Rear Axle Assembly

REMOVAL & INSTALLATION

1. Loosen the rear wheel hub nuts and jack up the truck. Support the truck on jack stands placed forward of the rear spring front brackets.

2. Remove the rear wheels and remove the propeller shaft.

NOTE: Support the differential housing with a jack to keep a slight amount of pressure on the springs.

3. Loosen the joint between the brake hose and the brake line and remove the stops to disconnect the brake hose. Plug the lines to prevent fluid loss.

4. Disconnect the rear cable of the parking brake at the balancer (refer to Brake section for procedure.)

5. Remove the shock absorbers, and the spring seats after removing the spring U-bolts.

6. Remove the spring shackle pin nuts and the shackle plate.

— CAUTION —

The axle assembly will be supported solely by the jack under the differential case. Be careful not to allow it to drop.

7. With an assistant holding the axle assembly, slowly lower it to the ground.

Installation is the reverse of removal. Bleed the brakes after assembly.

OVERHAUL

Differential overhaul requires many special tools and access to a range of preload shims and other dealer equipment. If you have never overhauled a rear axle assembly before, it would be wise to let a specialist perform this operation.

1. Remove the lock bolts and plates holding the side bearing nut in place.

2. Remove the side bearing nuts with the special adjusting spanner no. MB990201.

3. Remove the carrier caps and pry out the differential.

4. Pull off the differential side bearings.

AXLE SHAFT ASSEMBLY PRELOAD SHIMS

Part No.	Thickness of shim	
	mm	in.
MB092491	0.05 ± 0.005	.0020 ± .0002
MB092492	0.10 ± 0.010	.0040 ± .0004
MB092493	0.20 ± 0.015	.0079 ± .0006
MB092494	0.30 ± 0.020	.0118 ± .0008
MB092495	0.50 ± 0.025	.0197 ± .0010
MB092496	1.00 ± 0.040	.0394 ± .0016
MB092497	1.50 ± 0.050	.0591 ± .0020
MB092498	2.00 ± 0.055	.0787 ± .0022

NOTE: Be sure to keep the right and left bearings and shims separated.

5. Loosen the ring gear mounting bolts in diagonal sequence. Remove the ring gear.

6. Drive the pinion shaft lock pin out from the rear of the ring gear using a punch, and remove the pinion shaft.

7. Remove the side gears with their spacers. Keep left and right side gears and spacers separate.

8. Hold the end yoke and remove the pinion lock nut.

9. Remove the end yoke.

10. Tap the end of the drive pinion shaft with a plastic hammer and force out the drive pinion along with its adjusting shim, the rear inner race, the drive pinion spacer and the preload adjusting shim. The rear bearing inner race can be pressed off the pinion shaft.

11. Remove the front and rear pinion bearing outer races. The front race should be removed with its oil seal.

NOTE: Do not reuse the old oil seal. If the unit is to be assembled using no replacement parts except oil seals, the same spacers and shims can generally be used. If either pinion bearing or ring gear and drive pinion are being replaced, new shims should be used. Only replace the drive pinion and ring gear in matched sets.

Assemble the side gears in the differential case. Install the spacers in the same positions they were in when removed.

12. With the washers, insert both differential gears at the same time to mesh with the side gears. Insert the pinion shaft.

13. Measure the backlash of the differential pinion gears and the side gears. Backlash should be within 0.002–0.005 in. If not, replace the side gear spacers with the appropriate ones listed below.

14. Align the differential drive pinion shaft with the lock pin hole in the differential case and drive the pin in from the

1. Self-locking nut
2. Washer
3. End yoke (companion flange)
4. Dust cover
5. Oil seal
6. Drive pinion bearing, front
7. Preload adjusting shim
8. Gear carrier
9. Carrier cap
10. Drive pinion spacer
11. Drive pinion bearing, rear
12. Drive pinion height adjusting shim
13. Side bearing nut
14. Side bearing
15. Side gear thrust spacer
16. Side gear
17. Center block
18. Pinion shaft
19. Pinion gear
20. Pinion washer
21. Lock pin
22. Packing
23. Final gear set
24. Differential case
25. Lock bolt
26. Lock plate

Exploded view of rear end drive gears

Pinion and ring gear markings

Measuring pinion height (clearance)

rear of the case. Stake the pin with a small pointed punch to secure it.

15. Remove the old adhesive from the ring gear mounting bolts and apply new adhesive. Snug up all bolts then tighten them on a criss-cross pattern of 58–65 ft. lbs.

NOTE: To allow the adhesive to set on the bolt threads, keep the unit stationary for about an hour.

16. Press the front and rear bearing outer races into the gear carrier.

—————— **CAUTION** ——————
Make sure that the races do not tilt and that they sit fully in the case.

Look at the top face of the drive pinion (gear side). If there is an etched number, such as −0, −1, −2, +1, +2, etc., complete step 17. If not, skip step 17 and go on to step 18.

17. Insert a shim between the drive pinion and rear bearing. If the original gear set is being replaced, the original shims may be used. If a new gear set is being installed, calculate the shim dimension in the following manner. Assuming the pinion height before disassembly is correct, subtract the new pinion variation marking (on the pinion head) from the old pinion variation marking. If the answer is positive, add shims in the corresponding amount. If the answer is negative, subtract shims in the corresponding amount. This will produce a reasonable starting point for assembly. If the shim choice is proved incorrect, the entire pinion must be disassembled, and the shim changed accordingly. The etched marking on the face of the pinion represents a positive or negative variation from the standard in millimeters.

Measuring pinion preload

NOTE: If the original gear set is being reused in the differential case, the original shims may be used.

18. If the drive pinion has no marking on its gear-side face, it will be necessary to obtain two D-50/Plymouth Arrow dealer special tools; MB990819 and MB990552. Install parts marked 1,6,2,7,3,4, and 5 in the illustration labeled "Measuring pinion height (clearance)" with special tool MB990819 into the carrier case. Gradually tighten the nut to produce 6–9 in. lbs. without the oil seal. Fit special tool MB990552

in the differential caps and replace the caps on the case. Measure the clearance between the two special tools (see illustration) and select a shim of an equivalent thickness to the clearance to make the pinion height within tolerance of ±0.0012 in.

NOTE: If the pinion height has to be adjusted by more than 0.0650 in. use two shims including one 0.0118 in. thick.

19. Install the selected shim between the drive pinion and the rear bearing. Press the bearing onto the drive pinion shaft.

20. Assemble the drive pinion in the case and torque the pinion nut gradually to 137–180 ft. lbs. Check the pinion preload.

Installing the packing

SIDE GEAR SPACERS

Part No.	Thickness of spacer			
	mm		in.	
MB092034	0.8	-0.08 / -0.17	.0315	$-.0031$ / $-.0067$
MB092035	0.8	-0.18 / -0.27	.0315	$-.0071$ / $-.0106$
MB092036	0.8	0 / -0.07	.0315	0 / $-.0028$

DRIVE PINION HEIGHT SHIMS

Part No.	Thickness of shim	
	Mm	In.
MB092160	1.38 ± 0.01	.0543 ± .0004
MB092161	1.41 ± 0.01	.0555 ± .0004
MB092162	1.44 ± 0.01	.0567 ± .0004
MB092163	1.47 ± 0.01	.0579 ± .0004
MB092164	1.50 ± 0.01	.0591 ± .0004
MB092165	1.53 ± 0.01	.0603 ± .0004
MB092166	1.56 ± 0.01	.0614 ± .0004
MB092167	1.59 ± 0.01	.0626 ± .0004
MB092168	1.62 ± 0.01	.0638 ± .0004
MB092169	1.65 ± 0.01	.0650 ± .0004
MB092170	0.30 ± 0.013	.0118 ± .0005

PINION BEARING PRELOAD SHIMS

Part No.	Thickness of shim	
	Mm	In.
MB092130	0.30 ± 0.01	.0118 ± .0004
MB092131	2.00 ± 0.01	.0787 ± .0004
MB092132	2.03 ± 0.01	.0799 ± .0004
MB092133	2.06 ± 0.01	.0811 ± .0004
MB092134	2.09 ± 0.01	.0823 ± .0004
MB092135	2.12 ± 0.01	.0835 ± .0004
MB092136	2.15 ± 0.01	.0846 ± .0004
MB092137	2.18 ± 0.01	.0858 ± .0004
MB092138	2.21 ± 0.01	.0870 ± .0004
MB092139	2.24 ± 0.01	.0882 ± .0004
MB092140	2.27 ± 0.01	.0894 ± .0004
MB092141	2.30 ± 0.01	.0906 ± .0004
MB092142	2.33 ± 0.01	.0917 ± .0004

Proper tooth contact

Face contact

Heel contact

Toe contact

Flank contact

With oil seal, it should be between 9–11 in. lbs. Without the oil seal, it should be 6–9 in. lbs. The preload shim selection ranges from 0.0118 to 0.0917 in.

21. If you have not already done so, apply a thin coat of grease to the drive pinion oil seal and insert it in the case. Refit the yoke and tighten to 137–180 ft. lbs.

22. Press the side bearings into the differential case and fit the case into the carrier.

23. Install the carrier caps with their mating marks in line with the marks on the carriers and finger tighten the four set bolts.

24. Install the side bearing nuts, and tighten the carrier cap bolts to 40–47 ft. lbs.

25. Screw in the side bearing nuts to adjust the standard backlash value. Each nut should be tightened to 11 lbs. Repeatedly loosen and tighten the bearing nuts to insure smooth operation, then tighten them until they become hard to turn.

26. Attach a dial indicator to the ring gear teeth and make certain the backlash is between 0.005–0.007 in.

Backlash adjustment

NOTE: If the backlash is less than the limit, loosen the bearing nut on the back side of the ring gear and tighten the bearing nut on the teeth side by the same amount.

27. After adjusting backlash, tighten the bearing nuts ½ pitch.

NOTE: One pitch is the space between two adjacent holes on the side of the bearing nut.

28. Again measure the backlash and install a one or two pronged lock plate whichever lines up with the bearing nut holes. Tighten the lock plate bolts to 11–16 ft. lbs.

29. Measure the ring gear runout in four or more spots. Runout should be 0.002 in. or less.

30. Make a ring gear tooth pattern check.

31. Apply gear oil to all moving parts and use sealant when assembling. Install the packing with the embossed portion at about 3 o'clock position on the axle housing.

32. Fit the differential and tighten the mounting nuts to 18–22 ft. lbs.

33. Be sure to fill the rear axle with about 3 pints of gear oil before testing.

FRONT SUSPENSION— 2WD PICKUP TRUCKS

Coil Spring

REMOVAL & INSTALLATION

1. Raise the front of the vehicle and support it on jack stands.
2. Remove the wheel.
3. Remove the shock absorber (see below for procedures).
4. Remove stabilizer and strut bar (see below for procedures).
5. Compress the coil spring with a spring compressor.
6. Remove the relay rod from the steering arm.
7. Remove the upper and lower ball joints using a ball joint remover.
8. Remove the coil spring.

Installation is the reverse of removal.

NOTE: The coil springs are color coded. The left side spring has a green band on it and the right side spring has a pink band on it. Do not mix the left and right springs.

9. Tighten the ball joint castle nuts to: upper, 43–65 ft. lbs.; lower, 87–130 ft. lbs.

Shock Absorbers

REMOVAL & INSTALLATION

1. Raise the vehicle and support it on jack stands.
2. Remove the wheel.
3. Remove the double lock nuts at the top of the shock absorber along with the rubber washer and its metal caps.

4. Remove the two bolts at the bottom of the shock absorber and withdraw the shock absorber through the bottom arm.

Installation is the reverse of removal.

5. Be sure to refit all of the rubber cushion washers and their metal caps in the correct order. Tighten the upper shock absorber nut to 9–13 ft. lbs. and install the lock nut. Tighten the two lower shock absorber bolts to 6–9 ft. lbs.

Steering Knuckle

REMOVAL & INSTALLATION

1. Raise the vehicle and support it on jack stands.
2. Remove the wheel.
3. Remove the brake caliper assembly and the front hub assembly (see brake caliper and hub removal section, below).
4. Disconnect the stabilizer and strut bar from the lower arm (see stabilizer and strut bar removal section, below).
5. Remove the shock absorber and compress the coil spring (see above for shock absorber removal).
6. Remove the relay rod from the steering arm using a ball joint remover.
7. Remove the cotter pins and castle nuts from the steering knuckle ball joints, and using either a gear puller or a ball joint remover, free the ball joints from the knuckle. Remove the knuckle.

When installing, tighten the upper ball joint castle nut to 43–65 ft. lbs. and the lower ball joint nut to 87–130 ft. lbs. Tighten the tie rod end ball joint nut to 25–33 ft. lbs. Fit new cotter keys. Installation is the reverse of removal.

Upper Control Arm

REMOVAL & INSTALLATION

1. Jack up the front of the truck and support it on stands.
2. Remove the wheel.
3. Remove the shock absorber and compress the coil spring.
4. Remove the cotter pin and castle nut from the upper ball joint.
5. Using a gear puller or ball joint remover, free the ball joint from the steering knuckle.
6. Remove the bolts holding the upper control arm to the crossmember and remove the control arm as an assembly.

NOTE: Save all of the adjustment shims from the upper control arm for reassembly.

Installation is the reverse of removal. Replace all camber adjustment shims behind the upper control arm. Observe the following torques: upper control arm to crossmember bolts, 40–54 ft. lbs., ball joint to knuckle, 43–65 ft. lbs.

Lower Control Arm

REMOVAL & INSTALLATION

1. Raise the front of the truck and support it on jackstands.

1. Crossmember
2. Pivot bushing
3. Dust seal
4. Upper arm shaft
5. Upper arm
6. Upper ball joint
7. Rebound stop
8. Front coil spring
9. Lower arm bushing
10. Lower arm shaft
11. Lower arm
12. Bump stop
13. Shock absorber
14. Lower ball joint
15. Stabilizer
16. Strut bar

Exploded view of front suspension

1. Oil seal
2. Wheel bearing (inner)
3. Brake disc
4. Wheel hub
5. Wheel bearing (outer)
6. Washer
7. Hub nut
8. Cotter pin
9. Hub cap

Steering knuckle and hub assembly

2. Remove the wheel.

3. Remove the shock absorber and compress the coil spring (see above for procedure).

4. Remove the stabilizer and strut bar (see below for procedures).

5. Remove the cotter pin and castle nut from the lower ball joint and separate the ball joint from the steering knuckle using a ball joint remover.

6. Remove the coil spring.

7. Remove the nut in the front of the lower control arm mounting shaft. Remove the nuts at the rear of the shaft. Remove the shaft and remove the lower arm.

8. Installation is the reverse of removal. Tighten the front mounting shaft nut to 40–54 ft. lbs. Tighten the rear nut to 6–9 ft. lbs. Tighten the ball joint castle nut to 87–130 ft. lbs. Tighten control arm shaft only after truck is on the ground.

Stabilizer and Strut Bar

REMOVAL & INSTALLATION

1. Raise the vehicle and support it on jack stands.

2. Remove the wheels.

3. Disconnect the stabilizer and the strut bars from the lower control arms.

—————— **CAUTION** ——————

When removing the strut bar, loosen the adjusting nut at the other end of the bar before loosening the bolts at the control arm.

NOTE: Before removing stabilizer bar, note the order and direction of the rubber cushion washers and their metal caps for reassembly.

4. Remove the nut and spacers at the threaded end of the strut bar and remove the bar.

5. Remove the two stabilizer brackets and remove the stabilizer.

Installation is the reverse of removal. Observe the following.

There is a letter "L" on the left side strut bar, do not confuse it with the right side bar. The rubber cushions on the front of the strut bar are different; the cushion with a protruded lip is mounted at the front and the regular cushion is mounted at the back.

When installing the strut bar, set the standard distance of 3.8 in. from the tip of the threaded end of the bar to the rear face of the rear double nut. Lower the vehicle to the ground and tighten all nuts and bolts.

—————— **CAUTION** ——————

Make sure you check the front wheel alignment after installing the strut bar in order to obtain the correct caster, and then re-adjust the distance as required.

When installing both ends of the stabilizer, tighten the first nut (adjustment nut)

to obtain length 0.87–0.94 in., then tighten the lock nut to 18–25 ft. lbs.

Upper Ball Joint

REMOVAL & INSTALLATION

1. Remove the upper control arm from the vehicle (see above for procedure).

2. Remove the ball joint dust seal by prying up the dust seal ring evenly.

3. Remove the snap ring using snap ring pliers.

4. Using a ball joint remover and installer tool, press off the ball joint.

NOTE: A minimum of 2200 lb. pressure will be required to remove the upper ball joint from the control arm.

5. To install the ball joint, press it into the burred hole, with the ball joint and upper arm mating marks aligned.

6. Make sure the ball joint snap-ring is a tight fit and install the dust cover.

Lower Ball Joint

REMOVAL & INSTALLATION

1. Jack up and safely support the vehicle. Remove the wheel.

2. Remove the coil spring (see above for procedures).

3. If you have not already done so, free the lower ball joint from the steering knuckle using a ball joint remover. Remove the dust cover from the ball joint.

4. Unbolt and remove the ball joint.

5. Installation is the reverse of removal. Install the ball joint with its tab side pointing to the rear of the vehicle. Tighten the ball joint to lower control arm bolts to 22–30 ft. lbs.

FRONT SUSPENSION— 4WD PICKUPS AND MONTERO

Torsion Bars

REMOVAL & INSTALLATION

1. Jack up the front end of the vehicle and safely support it with jackstands.

2. Remove the front wheel, brake caliper assembly (but don't disconnect the brake hose) and the front hub assembly.

3. Support the lower arm from which the torsion bar is to be removed with a jack.

4. Detach the torsion bar dust covers

Torsion bar installation—4WD pickups and Montero

from the torsion bar anchor arm assembly, and slide the covers a few inches down the torsion bar and out of the way.

5. Match mark the torsion bar to the anchor arm. This is important for later assembly. It is best to make scratch marks, as punching could damage the bar.

6. Loosen the adjusting nut and remove the torsion bar from the anchor arm.

NOTE: Remove the anchor arm assembly as necessary to make torsion bar removal easier.

7. To install, apply a multi-purpose grease to the torsion bar splines, the anchor arm splines and the inside of the dust boot and the anchor boot thread.

8. Make sure that the torsion bars are replaced on their proper sides respectively, if both bars were removed. Face the end of the bar with the identification mark forward, and align the mark on the anchor arm with the mating mark on the torsion bar when the bar is inserted in the anchor arm.

NOTE: When installing a new torsion bar, align the spline painted white with the mark on the anchor arm.

9. Select the relative position of the torsion bar splines and the anchor arm splines so that the dimension illustrated is as specified below, when the torsion bar and anchor arm are assembled, and with the rebound stop in contact with the side frame. Dimension "A": left side Montero: 5.43–5.73 in.; left side pickup truck: 5.52–5.82 in. Right side Montero: 5.04–5.35 in.; right side pickup truck: 5.32–5.62 in.

10. Tighten the adjusting nut so that the anchor bolt protrusion will become the dimensions shown in the illustration. Pickup truck dimensions are illustrated; Montero dimensions are 2.17 in. left side; 2.68 in. right side.

	Left side	Right side
U-engine	72 (2.8)	68 (2.7)
W-engine	76.5 (3.0)	68 (2.7)
TBD-engine	81 (3.2)	78 (3.1)

mm (in.)

Torsion bar installation showing anchor arm and bolt adjustment

11. Install the stabilizer bar to the lower arm. Tighten the nut so that the dimension from the bottom of the nut to the top of the bolt end is about 17 mm.

12. Install the front hub assembly and brake caliper. Install the front wheel. Torque the lower arm-to-side frame bracket bolt to 108 ft. lbs.

13. Measure the distance between the suspension bump stop bumper and bump stop bracket on the side frame with the vehicle unloaded. Distance should be 2.8 in. Tighten the adjusting nut on the anchor bolt if out of specification.

Shock Absorber

REMOVAL & INSTALLATION

This procedure for 4WD pickup trucks and Montero is similar to that for 2WD pickups.

Steering Knuckle

REMOVAL & INSTALLATION

1. Remove the tire and wheel assembly.

99 to 117 (73 to 86)

1 Upper arm shaft
2 Camber adjusting shim
3 Upper arm
4 Upper ball joint
5 Rebound stop
6 Snap ring
7 Ring
8 Dust cover
9 Joint cup (A)
10 Bushing
11 Shock absorber
12 Bushing (B)
13 Lower arm
14 Bushing (A)
15 Bump stop
16 Lower arm shaft
17 Anchor arm (B)
18 Lower ball joint
19 Torsion bar
20 Anchor bolt
21 Adjusting nut
22 Anchor arm assembly
23 Oil seal
24 Spacer
25 Needle bearing
26 Knuckle

8 to 11 (6 to 8)

12 to 17 (9 to 13)

59 to 88 (44 to 65)

69 to 98 (51 to 72)

8 to 11 (6 to 8)

118 to 176 (87 to 130)

94 to 117 (69 to 86)

138 to 156 (102 to 115)

138 to 156 (102 to 115)

20 to 29 (15 to 21)

53 to 73 (40 to 54)

40 to 49 (29 to 36)

Tightening torque : Nm (ft-lbs.)

4WD pickup and Montero front suspension and knuckle assemblies

2. Remove the front hub assembly, including the brake rotor.

3. Using a tie-rod tool, disconnect the tie-rod from the steering knuckle.

4. Using ball joint tools, remove the upper and lower ball joints.

5. Remove the knuckle from the drive shaft.

6. If you intend to replace either the oil seal or needle bearing, refer to procedure below.

7. Reverse the removal procedure for installation.

Oil Seal and Needle Bearing

REMOVAL & INSTALLATION

1. Remove the steering knuckle.

2. Remove the oil seal then remove the spacer. Remove the needle bearing by tapping the needles uniformly.

NOTE: Once removed, the needle bearing cannot be reused and must be replaced.

3. To install, apply an SAE no. 2 EP grease to the roller surface of the new needle bearing. Press in the needle bearing using a bearing installation tool until it is flush with the knuckle end face. Be careful not to drive the bearing in too far.

4. Apply the SAE no. 2 EP grease to the knuckle contacting surface of the spacer. Install the spacer onto the knuckle with chamfered side toward the center of the vehicle.

C-4171

MB990985

Press fitting oil seal into steering knuckle

5. Press the new oil seal with the bearing tools until it is flush with the knuckle end face. Apply the grease to the inside and lip of the oil seal.

6. Install the steering knuckle.

Front Axle Hub and Bearings

REMOVAL & INSTALLATION

1. Remove the front tire assembly. Remove the front brake caliper, but do not

disconnect the brake hose. Suspend the caliper with a wire out of the way.

2. Remove the free-wheeling hub.

3. Remove the lock washer, then remove the lock nut with special tool MB990954 or equivalent.

4. Remove the front hub assembly from the knuckle, together with the inner and outer bearings.

5. Remove the outer bearing inner race from the brake rotor. Remove the oil seal and the inner bearing race.

6. If necessary, make match-marks on the brake rotor and front hub and separate them.

BEARING REPLACEMENT

1. Carefully wipe all old grease from inside the front hub.

2. Using a brass drift, carefully tap out the inner and outer bearing races. Tap around each bearing uniformly.

3. Apply an SAE no. 2 EP grease to the outside surface of the new inner and outer bearing outer races.

NOTE: The bearing inner and outer race should be replaced as an assembly.

4. You'll need a special bearing installation tool to replace the inner and outer bearing outer races; the tools are Mitsubishi part no. MB990938 and MB990933 or equivalent.

HUB INSTALLATION

1. Apply an SAE no. 2 EP multipurpose grease to the outer bearing outer race, oil seal lip and inside surface of the front hub.

2. Apply the grease to the inner bearing inner race and fit the inner race into the front hub.

3. Press the new oil seal into the front hub with the special tools until it is flush with the front hub end face.

4. Fit the knuckle into the front hub assembly. Using a special tool, part no. MB990954 or equivalent, which fits standard torque wrenches, torque the lock nut to 95–145 ft. lbs. Loosen the lock nut to 0 ft. lbs. (just loose), then torque to 18 ft. lbs. Finally, loosen the nut 30°.

5. Install the lock washer. If the lock washer and lock nut holes do not align, align the holes by loosening the nut by not more than 20°.

6. Before installing the free-wheeling hub assembly, measure the turning force of the front hub using a spring scale. If the measured value does not meet specifications (1–4 lbs.) retighten the lock nut to the specified torque given earlier.

7. Apply a semi-drying sealant to the free-wheeling hub surface of the front hub and then tighten the front hub to the specified torque, 36–43 ft. lbs.

8. Measure front drive shaft end play as described elsewhere in this chapter.

1 Oil seal
2 Wheel bearing (Inner)
3 Brake disc
4 Front hub
5 Wheel bearing (Outer)
6 Lock nut
7 Lock washer
8 Thrust washer
9 Spacers
10 Snap rings
11 Automatic free wheeling hub

50 to 58 (37 to 43)

50 to 58 (37 to 43)

Front hub assembly including brake rotor—4WD trucks and Montero

MB990954

Removing front hub lock nut

9. Assemble the remaining components in the reverse order of removal.

Upper Control Arm

REMOVAL & INSTALLATION

1. Jack up the front of the vehicle and safely support it with jackstands.

2. Loosen the anchor bolt of the torsion bar all the way.

3. Remove the shock absorber.

4. Discharge the brake fluid and disconnect the brake hose.

5. Loosen the nut holding the upper ball joint to the steering knuckle. Do not remove the nut; just loosen it.

6. Using a ball joint tool, disconnect the upper ball joint from the knuckle. Do not tear the rubber ball joint boot.

7. Remove the bolts connecting the upper arm shaft to the arm post of the side frame. Remove the upper control arm.

NOTE: The camber adjusting shims should be marked for later assembly.

8. Replace the upper ball joint if necessary.

9. Reassemble the upper control arm in the reverse order of disassembly, while noting the following:

a. When installing the upper arm assembly into the crossmember insert the

1 Upper arm shaft
2 Adjusting shim
3 Upper arm
4 Upper ball joint
5 Rebound stopper

	Nm	ft. lbs.
A	100-120	72-87
B	8-12	6-9
C	60-90	43-65

4WD and Montero upper control arm showing camber adjustment shim(s)

upper arm shaft mounting bolts from the outside of the crossmember and put adjusting shims between the crossmember and the upper arm shaft in the order in which they were removed.

b. Tighten the torsion bar anchor bolts to the specs given under ''Torsion Bar Removal.''

c. Tighten the upper arm shaft-to-crossmember bolts to 72–87 ft. lbs. Tighten the upper ball joint-to-knuckle nut to 43–65 ft. lbs.

d. Check front wheel alignment.

Lower Control Arm

REMOVAL & INSTALLATION

1. Remove the front skid plate and under cover if equipped.
2. Remove the torsion bar.
3. Remove the stabilizer bar.
4. Remove the shock absorber.
5. Remove the nut which retains the lower ball joint to the knuckle. Using a ball joint tool, carefully disconnect the lower ball joint from the knuckle.
6. Remove the front mounting bolts for the lower arm, and remove the lower arm assembly.
7. Replace the lower ball joint if necessary.
8. To install, temporarily mount the lower arm shaft to the crossmember.

NOTE: Assembly is easier if a solution of soapy water is applied to the lower arm shaft and to the rubber bushing.

9. Install the shock absorber and torsion bar.
10. Tighten the lower arm shaft to 101–116 ft. lbs. with the vehicle lowered to the ground and unloaded.
11. Install the stabilizer bar.
12. Reinstall the remaining parts in the

reverse order of removal.

Upper Ball Joint

REPLACEMENT

1. Jack up the front of the vehicle and safely support it with jackstands. Remove the tire.
2. Separate the upper ball joint from the steering knuckle.
3. Remove the rubber dust boot together with the ring.

Press fitting upper ball joint—4WD and Montero

4. Remove the snap-ring from the ball joint.
5. The upper ball joint must be pressed out of the arm. Depending on the type of press available, the control arm may or may not have to be removed.
6. The ball joint must be pressed into position when installing. Make sure the mating mark on the ball joint and the mark center of the control arm are aligned.

NOTE: Check to make sure there is no play between the ball joint groove and the snap-ring. If play exists, replace the snap-ring with a new one.

7. Apply an SAE no. 2 EP multipurpose grease to both the interior of the rubber boot (fill the boot up) and the upper ball joint.
8. Apply a semi-drying sealant to the grooves in the upper ball joint. Secure the boot to the ball joint with the ring.
9. Install the remaining components in the reverse order of removal. Check front end alignment. Torque the ball joint-to-knuckle nut to 43–65 ft. lbs.

Lower Ball Joint

REMOVAL & INSTALLATION

1. Remove the tire, after jacking up the front of the vehicle and supporting it with jackstands.
2. Unbolt the bottom of the shock absorber from the control arm.
3. Remove the nut which retains the lower ball joint to the steering knuckle.
4. Using a ball joint tool, disconnect the lower ball joint from the knuckle.

Removing lower ball joint

5. Unbolt the lower ball joint from the control arm.
6. Reverse the above procedure for installation. Fill the rubber ball joint boot with an SAE no. 2 multipurpose grease, and also apply the grease to the ball joint. Apply a semi-drying sealant to the grooves in the lower ball joint. Secure the boot to the joint with the ring.

Front Stabilizer Bar

REMOVAL & INSTALLATION

1. Jack up the front of the vehicle and safely support it with jackstands.
2. Remove the front skid plate.
3. Unbolt the stabilizer bar from its front support bushings on the stabilizer link, and from the control arm. Remove the stabilizer bar.
4. When mounting the stabilizer link to the no. 1 crossmember, tighten the nut so as to obtain a 0.63–0.71 in. dimension between the bottom of the nut and the top of the threaded bolt end. Tighten the stabilizer bar-to-control arm nut so that the bottom of nut-to-top of threaded bolt end dimension is 0.63–0.71 in.

REAR SUSPENSION

Leaf Springs

REMOVAL & INSTALLATION

1. Loosen the wheel nuts and jack up the vehicle. Support the frame on jack stands and lower the jack under the rear axle housing.

— **CAUTION** —
Do not put jack stands under axle housing shafts.

2. Remove the parking brake cable clamp from the leaf spring.
3. Disconnect the upper end of the shock

1. Shock absorber
2. Bump stop
3. Spring U-bolt
4. Spring shackle assembly
5. Rear eye bushing
6. Shackle plate
7. Front eye bushing
8. Spring pin assembly
9. Leaf spring assembly
10. Silencer
11. U-bolt seat

Rear suspension

absorber and the lower end at the spring U-bolt seat.

NOTE: If the shock absorber is not going to be replaced or serviced, leave the lower end on the spring U-bolt seat.

4. Loosen the U-bolt nuts and jack up the rear axle housing until it clears the spring seat. Remove the spring seat.

5. Remove the front spring pin and the rear shackle pin and remove the spring.

Installation is the reverse of removal. Observe the following:

6. Install the spring front eye bushings from both sides of the eye with the bushing flanges facing out. Insert the spring pin assembly from the wheel side and secure it to the hanger bracket with its bolt. Temporarily tighten the spring pin nut.

7. Repeat step 6 on the rear spring mount.

8. Align the center of the U-bolt seat with the center bolt hole in the spring. Tighten the U-bolts to 47–54 ft. lbs.

NOTE: Tighten the nuts on the U-bolts until all of the U-bolt threads protrude evenly.

Tighten the spring pins and shackle pins to 22–33 ft. lbs.

Shock Absorbers

REMOVAL & INSTALLATION

1. Jack up the vehicle and remove the wheel.

2. Unbolt the top and bottom of the shock absorber and remove.

Installation is the reverse of removal. Tighten the shock absorber upper and lower mounting nuts to 13–18 ft. lbs.

STEERING

Steering Wheel

REMOVAL & INSTALLATION

1. Pry off the steering wheel center foam pad.

2. Remove the steering wheel retaining nut.

3. Using a steering wheel puller, remove the wheel.

4. Be sure the front wheels are in a straight ahead position. Reverse the removal procedure for installation.

Steering Column

REMOVAL & INSTALLATION

1. Remove the air cleaner. Match mark the column shaft on the steering gear shaft.

2. Remove the clamp bolt which holds the steering column shaft on the steering gear shaft.

NOTE: On vehicles with air conditioning, step 2 must be done from under the truck.

3. Remove the horn pad and steering wheel retaining nut, then remove the steering wheel using a puller.

4. Loosen the tilt lock knob and lower the steering column fully.

5. Remove the steering column cover and disconnect the column wiring under the dashboard.

6. Remove the five bolts holding the base of the column at the fire wall.

7. Remove the four bolts holding the tilt column and remove the steering column from the vehicle.

Installation is the reverse of removal. Align the match marks on the steering column shaft and the steering gear shaft and couple the shafts before installing any bolts. Tighten the clamp bolt to 15–18 ft. lbs.

1. Steering wheel
2. Tilt bracket
3. Steering column assembly
4. Dust cover
5. Steering coupling
6. Gear box
7. Pitman arm
8. Tie rod assembly (right)
9. Relay rod
10. Idler arm
11. Tie rod assembly (left)

Manual steering column and gear assembly

1. Steering wheel
2. Tilt bracket
3. Gear box
4. Oil reservoir
5. Oil pump
6. Relay rod
7. Tie rod
8. Idler arm

Power steering column and assembly

MANUAL STEERING MAINSHAFT SHIMS

Part No.	Thickness	
	Mm	In.
MB005890	0.05	.0020
MB005891	0.06	.0024
MB005892	0.07	.0030
MB005893	0.10	.0040
MB005894	0.20	.0080
MB005895	0.30	.0120
MB005896	0.50	.0200

Manual Steering

REMOVAL & INSTALLATION

1. Remove the clamp bolt connecting the steering shaft with the steering gear housing mainshaft.

2. Disconnect the tie rod and Pitman arm from the relay rod using a ball joint remover or gear puller.

3. Remove the three bolts holding the

Ignition Switch/Lock

REMOVAL & INSTALLATION

1. Remove the column cover.

2. Cut a notch in the lock bracket bolt head with a hack saw.

3. Remove the lock bolts.

4. Disconnect the ignition harness and remove the switch/lock as a unit.

5. To remove the ignition switch, remove the screw holding it on the harness side and pull out the switch.

Installation is the reverse of removal.

NOTE: The steering wheel upper lock bracket and bolts should be replaced with new parts when the unit is installed.

Before fully tightening the screw in the back of the ignition switch, insert the key and make sure the switch works smoothly.

Turn Signal Switch

REMOVAL & INSTALLATION

1. Remove the steering wheel (see above for procedure).

2. Put the tilt handle in its lowest position.

3. Remove the upper and lower column covers.

4. Remove the wiring harness band clip

and disconnect the harness.

5. Remove the switch.

Installation is the reverse of removal with the following notes.

6. Make sure the column switch aligns with the steering shaft center.

7. Place the wiring harness along the column tube as close as possible to the center line. Be sure to replace the adjustable wiring harness bands.

Steering Linkage

REMOVAL & INSTALLATION

1. Jack up the vehicle and support it on stands.

2. Remove the cotter pins and castle nuts holding the tie rod ends to the steering arms and the relay rod, and free the tie rods using either a suitable gear puller or a ball joint remover.

3. Unbolt and remove the relay rod in the same manner.

4. To remove the idler arm, remove the two bolts holding it to the frame and pull it out.

NOTE: The outer tie rod end has a left hand thread and the inner tie rod has a right handed thread on the driver's side.

Installation is the reverse of removal. Tighten all tie rod end nuts and relay rod nuts to 25–33 ft. lbs.

1. Gear housing upper cover
2. Packing
3. Gear housing
4. Gear housing end cover
5. Mainshaft adjusting shim
6. Mainshaft bearing
7. Mainshaft assembly
8. Mainshaft bearing
9. Mainshaft oil seal
10. Gear adjusting spacer
11. Gear adjusting bolt
12. Cross shaft
13. Cross shaft oil seal
14. Pitman arm

Exploded view of manual steering gear

gear box to the frame and remove the gear box from under the vehicle.

Installation is the reverse of removal. Tighten the Pitman arm to relay rod nut to 94–109 ft. lbs. and the tie rod socket to relay rod to 29–33 ft. lbs.

OVERHAUL AND ADJUSTMENTS

1. Remove the gear box from the vehicle.

2. Remove the nut holding the Pitman arm on the cross shaft and using a gear puller, pull the arm from the shaft.

3. Before disassembling any further, record the starting preload of the mainshaft as a guide for reassembly.

4. Loosen the lock nut on the cross shaft adjusting bolt and turn the bolt slightly counterclockwise. Remove the cover bolts.

5. Lift the cover up slightly and turn the adjusting bolt in until it unfastens from the cover and remove the cover.

6. Turn the cross shaft until its teeth will fit through the cover hole and pull it out of the gear housing.

NOTE: Use care not to damage the cross shaft splines and the oil seal when removing the cross shaft.

7. Measure the main shaft starting preload with the cross shaft removed.

8. Loosen the end cover attaching bolts and remove the end cover and shim.

NOTE: Keep the shim for reassembly.

9. Gently pull out the main shaft, ball nut assembly and the bearings.

——————— CAUTION ———————
Never attempt to disassemble the main shaft and ball nut assembly.

Check the component parts for wear or damage. Make sure the ball nut slides easily on the mainshaft. There should not be excessive free play.

——————— CAUTION ———————
Never allow the ball not to run entirely to the end of its travel, or it could be damaged.

To assemble:
10. Insert the main shaft assembly into the gear housing. Hold the main shaft horizontally.

11. Install the oil seal after applying a small amount of grease to its lip.

12. Install the gasket, shim and gasket end cover to the housing. Tighten the four end cover bolts to 11–45 ft. lbs. Use sealant on both the cover gasket and the bolt threads.

13. Measure the main shaft preload. It should be between 3–4.8 ft. lbs. If not, adjust it replacing the shim with a thicker or thinner shim. Shims come in thicknesses from 0.0020 to 0.0200 in.

14. Fit the adjusting bolt and shim in the top of the cross shaft and, using a feeler gauge, check the clearance between the adjusting bolt head and the cross shaft. Clear-

ance should be 0–0.002. If not, replace the shim.

15. Insert the cross shaft into the gear housing. Be sure to align the teeth on both shafts in the center of their travel.

16. Install the cover and torque the bolts to 11–14 ft. lbs. Apply sealant to the cover gasket and the threads of the bolts.

17. Verify that the unit works smoothly, then screw the adjusting bolt in and out of the cover two or three times to adjust the cross shaft into proper mesh with the main shaft.

18. Then loosen the adjusting bolt, making sure there is no free play at the mainshaft center position. Back lash should be 0–0.002 in.

19. Test the main shaft preload. Starting torque should be 5.7–7.4 ft. lbs.

20. Fill the unit with multipurpose gear oil and install the pitman arm. Its two match marks should align with the match mark on the cross shaft. Tighten the nut to 94–109 ft. lbs.

Power Steering Pump

REMOVAL & INSTALLATION

1. Remove the drive belt. If the pulley is to be removed, do so now.

2. Disconnect the pressure and return lines. Catch any leaking fluid.

3. Remove the pump attaching bolts and lift the pump from the brackets.

4. Make sure the bracket bolts are tight and install the pump to the brackets.

5. If pulley had been removed, install

it and tighten the nut securely. Bend the lock tab over the nut.

6. Install the drive belt and adjust to a tension of 22 lbs. at a deflection of .28 to .39 inches at the top center of the belt. Tighten the pump bolts securely to hold the tension.

7. Connect the pressure and return lines and fill the reservoir with approved fluid. (Dexron® I).

8. Bleed the system (refer to the bleeding procedure).

OVERHAUL

Separate Reservoir Type

1. Remove the pulley bracket with a gear puller.

2. Loosen and remove the suction port assembly.

3. Remove the pressure hose fitting assembly.

4. Remove the end plate retaining ring by inserting a small punch in the 0.13 in. diameter hole in the housing opposite the flow control valve hole. Compress the retaining ring with the punch and remove it by inserting a screwdriver under the ring and twisting.

5. Remove the end plate and the end plate O-ring. The end plate is spring loaded and should pop out. If it sticks, rocking it from side to side should free it.

6. Turn the pump over and allow the flow control valve and the valve spring to fall out.

7. With the end cover O-ring removed, tap lightly on the end of the drive shaft to free the pressure plate.

1. Oil reservoir cap	9. Fitting pipe	17. Thrust plate
2. Oil filter	10. Fitting connector	18. Pump ring & rotor
3. Oil reservoir	11. Flow control spring	19. Drive shaft retaining ring
4. Oil reservoir bracket	12. Flow control plunger	20. Dowel
5. Drive belt	13. Connector & fitting assembly	21. Pressure plate
6. Oil pump pulley	14. Drive shaft seal	22. End plate spring
7. Pulley bracket	15. Oil pump body	23. End plate
8. Drive shaft	16. O-ring	24. Retaining ring

Separate reservoir power steering pump assembly—others similar

8. Remove the pressure plate, drive shaft, pump ring, vanes and rotor.

--- CAUTION ---

Do not remove the welch plug. If it is cracked or otherwise damaged, replace the whole housing body.

9. Remove the drive shaft retaining ring.

10. Remove the rotor and thrust plate from the drive shaft and both dowel pins from the housing.

11. Pry the drive shaft seal out of the housing, being careful not to damage the housing, discard the shaft seal.

Clean all parts and inspect them for wear or damage.

To assemble, proceed as follows.

12. Install new drive shaft seal using a seal installer with a press or hammer.

NOTE: Only use as much force as necessary to seat the seal.

13. Lubricate the pressure plate O-ring with Dexron® II or its equivalent, and install it in the third groove from the rear of the housing.

14. Insert both dowel pins in the housing.

15. Assemble the drive shaft, thrust plate and rotor, then fit a new snap-ring on the drive shaft. The rotor must have its countersunk side toward the thrust plate.

16. Lubricate the oil seal and drive shaft with Dexron® II or its equivalent, and insert the drive shaft in the housing. Be sure to align the dowel pins with the thrust plate so as not to damage the oil seal lip.

17. Install the pump ring on the dowel pins with the arrow in the pump ring facing the rear of the housing.

18. Insert all ten vanes in the rotor slots with their rounded edges outward. They should slide freely in the rotor.

19. Lubricate the pressure plate and install with O-ring on the dowel pins with the circular depression which holds the spring toward the rear of the housing. The pressure plate must be pressed about 0.06 in. over the O-ring to seat properly.

20. Fit the end plate O-ring in the second groove from the rear of the housing.

21. Install the end plate spring in the groove provided in the pressure plate.

22. Lubricate the end plate to avoid damage to the O-ring and press it into the housing. Fit the end plate retaining ring.

23. Be sure to bleed the system (refer to bleeding procedure).

Reservoir in Unit Type

1. Remove the oil reservoir.

2. Hold the pump in a vise, loosen the pump cover bolts and remove the cover.

3. Remove the following parts from the pump body: cam ring, vanes, O-ring, side plate assembly, and the shaft assembly which includes the shaft, rotor, side plate, collar and snap-ring.

4. Remove the shaft assembly snap-ring and remove the collar, rotor side plate.

5. Remove the oil seal with a screw driver. Remove the suction connector.

6. Remove the connector at the top of the pump body and remove the flow control valve assembly and flow control spring.

7. Clean and check all parts for wear. Always use new gaskets and lubricate all parts with Dexron® II before assembling.

Assembly is the reverse of disassembly with the following notes.

8. Pay close attention to the illustrations for the installing direction of the side plate, rotor and collar.

9. When installing the cam ring, the counter-sunk holes at the end of the vanes face toward the cover.

10. Fit the vanes with their rounded sides pointed out.

11. Bleed the system (see bleeding procedures).

Power Steering Gear

REMOVAL & INSTALLATION

1. Disconnect the steering shaft from the gear box mainshaft.

2. Disconnect the tie rod from the relay rod, and the Pitman arm from the relay rod using a gear puller.

3. Remove the air cleaner and disconnect the pressure hose and the return hose from the gear box using a pipe wrench, then remove the undercover.

4. Loosen the gear box mounting bolts. On vehicles with automatic transmissions, remove the throttle linkage with the throttle linkage splash shield. On vehicles with manual transmissions, remove the starter

1. Side cover	15. O-ring	29. Cross shaft
2. O-ring	16. Seal ring	30. Adjusting plate
3. O-ring	17. O-ring	31. Adjusting bolt
4. Seal ring	18. Seal ring	32. Needle bearing, upper
5. Needle bearing	19. Rack piston	33. Snap ring
6. Gear box	20. O-ring	34. Needle bearing, lower
7. Bleeder plug	21. O-ring	35. O-ring
8. Circulator holder	22. Input worm shaft	36. Seal housing
8. Circulator	23. Thrust needle bearing	37. Seal ring
10. Ball	24. O-ring	38. O-ring
11. Valve housing	25. Ball bearing	39. Oil seal
12. Seal ring	26. Oil seal	40. Backup ring
13. O-ring	27. Top cover	41. Snap ring
14. Thrust needle bearing	28. Nut	42. Pitman arm

Exploded view of power steering gear assembly

on the transmission.

5. Remove the gear box from under the vehicle.

6. Remove the Pitman arm with a gear puller.

Installation is the reverse of removal. Observe the following torques: gear box to frame, 40–47 ft. lbs.; tie rod socket and relay rod connection, 25–33 ft. lbs.; pressure hose connection, 22–29 ft. lbs.; return hose connection 29–36 ft. lbs.

OVERHAUL

1. Loosen the adjusting lock nut and remove it.

2. With the gear in neutral position, tap the bottom of the cross shaft with a plastic hammer to remove the cross shaft.

3. Remove the side cover bolts, and screw in the adjusting bolt two or three turns.

4. Remove the valve housing nut.

5. Remove the valve housing bolts and take out the valve housing and rack piston, holding the rack piston to avoid turning it.

NOTE: Be careful not to let the rack piston fall off of the shaft.

6. Hold the valve housing in a vise and move the rack piston up and down to check the backlash between the groove of the rack piston and the balls. Measure the backlash after fully tightening the rack piston on the shaft and then loosening it two turns. Service limit is 0.008 in. If backlash exceeds the service limit, replace the ball screw unit and the rack piston as an assembly.

7. To remove the rack piston, turn it counter-clockwise.

--------- CAUTION ---------
There are twenty-six steel balls in the rack piston which will probably fall out when you remove it from the shaft. Do not lose them.

8. To disassemble the rack piston, remove the circular holder, the circulator, the steel balls, the seal ring and the O-ring. Do not disassemble the rack piston end cap.

9. Loosen the top cover and remove it and the input worm shaft from the valve housing.

10. Remove worm shaft thrust plate, thrust needle roller bearing, two seal rings and two O-rings.

11. Screw in the adjusting bolt at the tip of the cross shaft and remove the side cover.

--------- CAUTION ---------
There are thirty-three needle bearing rollers which may fall out when you remove the cross shaft. Do not lose them.

12. Remove the following parts from the side cover: O-ring, needle bearings, adjusting bolt and adjusting plate.

NOTE: If no oil leaks through the threads of the adjusting bolt, do not remove the sealing at the rear of the needle bearing seat.

13. Remove the seal ring and O-ring from the valve housing.

14. To remove the ball bearing and oil seal in the top cover, use a brass drift.

15. Remove the oil seal and seal ring from the gear box using a screwdriver.

Clean and inspect all parts for wear or damage. Always use new gaskets and oil seals and coat indicated parts with Dexron® II before installing.

To assemble, proceed as follows.

16. Apply a thin coat of multipurpose grease to the bearing race in the side cover and insert the thirty-three roller bearings. Apply a dab of grease to bottom of the side cover. Be careful not to disturb the needle bearings.

17. Install the side cover O-ring.

18. With the adjusting bolt and adjusting plate inserted in the top of the cross shaft, measure the clearance between the bolt head and the cross shaft. It should be from 0 to 0.002 in. Adjust clearance by replacing shim plate.

NOTE: Install the adjusting plate with its chamfered side in contact with the surface of the cross shaft.

19. Align the cross shaft with the side cover and install. Attach them by tightening the adjusting bolt. Take care not to disturb the needle bearings while installing the cross shaft. Make sure you don't damage the oil seal. Tighten the adjusting bolt lock nut temporarily.

20. To assemble the top cover, apply a thin coat of multipurpose grease to the lip of the oil seal and press fit it in the cover.

21. Press fit the ball bearing.

22. Apply a thin coat of multipurpose grease on the gear box oil seal and install it.

23. Install the O-ring first and then the seal ring on the input worm shaft. Lubricate with Dexron.

24. Install the thrust plate, thrust needle bearing and the thrust plate in the order given on the input worm shaft.

25. Install the O-rings and the seal ring into their seats in the valve housing without using undue force. The seal ring should be compressed into a heart shape when fit.

26. Install the input worm shaft in the valve housing.

27. Install the thrust plate, needle roller bearing and the thrust plate in the given order in the top cover.

NOTE: Install the thinner thrust plate on the top cover side.

28. Temporarily tighten the top cover to the valve housing.

NOTE: Take care not to disturb the thrust plate and needle roller bearing in the top cover.

29. Tighten the top cover bolts to 12–16 in. lbs.

NOTE: Turn the input worm shaft and check for smooth rotation and noise.

30. Tighten the valve housing nut to 130–166 ft. lbs.

NOTE: Do not allow the top cover to rotate while tightening the nut.

31. Measure the starting preload of the input worm shaft. It should be from 3–5 in. lbs. If not, adjust by tightening or loosening the valve housing nut in accordance with steps 30 and 31.

POWER STEERING CROSS SHAFT SHIM PLATES

Part No.	Thickness	
	Mm	In.
MB076596	1.95	.077
MB076196	2.00	.079
MB076597	2.05	.081
MB076598	2.10	.083
MB076599	2.15	.085

32. Install the O-ring and seal ring on the rack piston in the given order.

33. Insert the rack piston in the input worm shaft until the piston reaches the end of its travel. Rotate the input shaft and align the ball running surface on the worm with the ball insertion holes. Insert nineteen balls into the hole, pushing them lightly with a brass rod.

--------- CAUTION ---------
Do not rotate the worm shaft on rack piston at this point or the balls might enter other grooves.

After installing all nineteen of the balls, make sure the last ball is about half an inch below the end of the rack piston. If there is more than a half inch clearance, it probably means one or more of the balls has fallen into a different worm groove. Remove the assembly and begin again.

34. Insert the remaining seven balls in the circulator, holding them in place with grease. Fit the circulator in place and tighten the screws.

35. Hold the gear box in a vise and install the ball screw unit. Tighten the valve housing to 33–40 ft. lbs. After installation, rotate the input worm shaft to move the rack piston to the neutral (center) position.

NOTE: Be careful not to damage the seal ring when installing the rack piston.

36. Install the cross shaft assembly (with side cover) in to the gear box and tighten the side cover to 33–40 ft. lbs. When installing the cross shaft, apply a thin coat of ATF to the teeth and shaft of the rack piston and multipurpose grease to the oil seal lip. Do not rotate the side cover during installation or risk damage to the O-ring. It might be a good idea to wrap tape around the splined end of the cross shaft to prevent

damage to the seals.

37. Measure the total starting torque of the input worm shaft to neutral position (center). Make sure the ball screw operates smoothly through its entire travel. Starting torque should be between 4–6 in. lbs. Tighten the valve housing nut to 130–166 ft. lbs. Measure the preload after tightening.

38. Install the Pitman arm on the cross shaft aligning the slit in the end of the shaft with the two slits on the Pitman arm. Tighten the Pitman nut to 94–109 ft. lbs.

39. After tightening the Pitman arm, measure the distance between the center of the frame mounting bolt hole closest to the Pitman arm and the inner surface of the Pitman arm. This length should be about 0.77 in.

BLEEDING THE SYSTEM

1. The reservoir should be full of Dexron® II.
2. Jack up the front wheels and support the vehicle safely.
3. Turn the steering wheel fully to the right and left until no air bubbles appear in the fluid. Maintain the reservoir level.
4. Lower the vehicle and with the engine idling, turn the wheels fully to the right and left. Stop the engine.
5. Install a tube from the bleeder screw on the steering gear box to the reservoir.
6. Start the engine, turn the steering wheel fully to the left and loosen the bleeder screw.
7. Repeat the procedure until no air bubbles pass through the tube.
8. Tighten the bleeder screw and remove the tube. Refill the reservoir as needed, and check that no further bubbles are present in the fluid.

--- **CAUTION** ---
An abrupt rise in the fluid level after stopping the engine is a sign of incomplete bleeding. This will cause noise from the pump or control valve.

Front End Alignment

CASTER AND CAMBER

To adjust caster, adjust the tightening of the upper arm shaft. A half turn of the upper arm shaft will cause 0.049 in. play in the upper arm shaft resulting in a ¼ degree caster adjustment. The standard caster value and other wheel alignment specifications can be found at the beginning of this chapter.

To adjust the camber, it is necessary to adjust the number and thickness of the shims under the upper arm shaft. A total of 0.16 in. shim thickness between the upper arm shaft and the crossmember is normally required for standard camber. A 0.024 in. adjustment in thickness of shims will provide about 8 minutes adjustment of camber.

TOE-IN

Toe-in can be adjusted by screwing the left tie rod turnbuckle in or out. One revolution of the turnbuckle will vary in about 0.3 in. of toe-in adjustment. The toe-in may be increased or decreased by turning the tie rod turnbuckle toward the front or the rear of the vehicle respectively. After completion of the toe-in adjustment, check the difference in the length of the left and the right tie rods. If the difference exceeds 0.2 in., remove the right tie rod and adjust the length until the difference is reduced to 0.2 in. or less. An "L" stamped on the outer surface of the tie rod stands for left-hand thread end.

BRAKES

Master Cylinder

REMOVAL & INSTALLATION

1. Remove all lines connected to the master cylinder. Slowly depress the brake pedal to remove the fluid.

2. Remove the master cylinder from the booster assembly.

3. Installation is the reverse of removal. Bleed the brakes.

OVERHAUL

1. Remove the stop ring, piston stop, primary piston assembly, secondary piston assembly and the secondary return spring in the given order.

2. Loosen the valve case and remove the check valve and the check valve spring.

3. Wash the master cylinder, pistons and cups in brake fluid. Use care not to damage the cylinder, piston or cups.

--- **CAUTION** ---
Do not attempt to disassemble the primary piston assembly; its length is factory adjusted.

NOTE: When any related parts such as the return spring, piston cup and piston require replacement, you must replace the entire piston assembly.

To assemble:

4. Hone the master cylinder slightly. The cylinder bore inside diameter should be between 0.8748–0.8768 in. If not, replace cylinder. Coat the cylinder with brake fluid.

1. Reservoir cap	7. Valve case	13. Stop ring
2. Fluid reservoir	8. Master cylinder	14. Reservoir hose
3. Check valve cap	9. Secondary piston stop	15. Bracket
4. Outer pipe seat	10. Secondary piston assembly	16. Nipple
5. Check valve	11. Primary piston assembly	17. Master cylinder kit
6. Check valve spring	12. Piston stop	

Typical master cylinder

5. Measure the piston outside diameter. It should be between 0.8719–0.8732. If not replace.

6. Assemble the master cylinder components in the master cylinder after coating the rubber seals with brake fluid. Bleed the brakes after installation.

NOTE: Prime the cylinder by pouring a little fluid in the reservoirs and working the piston until fluid squirts out of the two brake line ports.

SYSTEM BLEEDING

1. Check the master cylinder fluid level.
2. Remove the cap from the bleeder screw of the wheel farthest from the master cylinder.
3. Connect a length of rubber tubing to the screw and place the other end in a jar half full of clean brake fluid.
4. Pump the brake pedal until no bubbles are visible in the container.
5. Hold the pedal in the depressed position and tighten the screw. Replace the cap and proceed to each wheel in turn.

NOTE: Periodically check the master cylinder during the bleeding operation to check the fluid level does not go too low. If it does, air will enter the master cylinder and it will have to be bled as well.

Brake Disc and Wheel Bearing

REMOVAL & INSTALLATION

1. Remove the caliper.
2. Pry off the dust cap. Tap out and discard the cotter pin. Remove the locknut.
3. Remove the brake disc and wheel hub.
4. Using a brass drift, carefully drive the outer bearing race out of the hub.
5. Remove the inner bearing seal and bearing.
6. Check the bearings for wear or damage and replace them if necessary. Drift the bearing race into place in the hub.
7. Pack the inner and outer wheel bearings with grease.
8. Install the inner bearing in the hub. Drive the seal on until its outer edge is even with the edge of the hub.
9. Install the hub/disc assembly on the spindle, being careful not to damage the oil seal.
10. Install the outer bearing, washer, and spindle nut. Adjust the bearing.

ADJUSTMENT

1. Tighten the spindle nut to 22 ft. lbs. and then loosen it.
2. Tighten the nut to 6 ft. lbs.
3. Install the cap on the nut. Do not back off the nut more than 30° for cotter

pin hole-to-slot alignment.

Wheel Cylinder

REMOVAL & INSTALLATION

1. Remove brake shoes.
2. Disconnect the brake pipe from the rear of the wheel cylinder and plug it to prevent it from leaking fluid.
3. Remove the wheel cylinder from the brake backing plate.
Installation is the reverse of removal.

OVERHAUL

1. Remove dust caps from both ends of the wheel cylinder.
2. Pull out the plungers, rubber seals and piston cups.
Clean and lightly hone the wheel cylinder.
Assembly is the reverse of disassembly. Lubricate all parts with brake fluid before assembly.

Power Brake Unit

REMOVAL & INSTALLATION

1. Remove the master cylinder.
2. Disconnect the vacuum hose from the power brake.
3. Remove the pin connecting the power brake operating rod to the pedal.
4. Loosen the nuts attaching the power brake to the fire wall and remove the power brake.
Installation is the reverse of removal. Apply sealer to all mounting surfaces before assembling.

Parking Brake

ADJUSTMENT

1. Release the parking brake.
2. Jack up the vehicle and support it on jack stands.
3. Make sure the balancer that the front of the cable rides in is parallel with the center line of the truck. The clearance between the balancer and the crossmember should be about 8 in.
4. Adjust the parking brake by turning the turnbuckle on the cable. The brake is properly adjusted when the parking brake handle can be pulled 16 to 17 notches (approx. 4.3 in.).
5. After adjusting the parking brake, make sure there is slack in the cable when the brake is in the off position.
If the brake will not adjust correctly or fails on a hill, the rear brake shoes should be inspected for wear, oil or grease covered surfaces or malfunction.

CHASSIS ELECTRICAL

Blower Motor Without Air Conditioning

REMOVAL & INSTALLATION

1. Remove the cluster panel.
2. Disconnect the cable between the motor and the heater unit.
3. Remove the three bolts holding the motor in the heater unit and pull out the fan.

NOTE: It may be necessary to unfasten the fan from the motor to remove them from under the dashboard.

Installation is the reverse of removal.

Blower Motor With Air Conditioning

REMOVAL & INSTALLATION

The air conditioning system used on Dodge and Plymouth pick-up trucks utilizes the blower motor assembly of the heater unit. However, it may be necessary to remove some of the air conditioning components to gain access to the motor. If this is the case, never attempt to loosen any of the air conditioning hoses during your work. They contain refrigerant under pressure, which could severely damage your eyes or skin on contact.

Heater Unit Without Air Conditioning

REMOVAL & INSTALLATION

1. Drain the cooling system.
2. Place the hot water flow control lever in the off position.
3. Remove the glove box, the center ventilation grille and duct, and the defroster duct.
4. Disconnect all control cables at the heater side.
5. Disconnect the water hoses.
6. Disconnect the harness from the heater fan motor.
7. Remove the top mounting bolts and the center mounting nuts, and remove the heater assembly.

Heater Unit With Air Conditioning

REMOVAL & INSTALLATION

Removing the heater unit with air conditioning attached is similar to procedures used on units without air conditioning. It may be necessary to loosen or remove certain components of the air conditioning system to facilitate heater unit removal, however, *never* loosen the refrigerant pipes that lead into the air conditioning evaporator assembly. They are filled with a noxious fluid which, under certain conditions, could cause severe damage to your face or skin. Always leave all air conditioning work to skilled professionals.

Heater Core

REPLACEMENT

Montero

1. Remove the heater control lever arm and remove the water valve cover on the heater.
2. Remove the heater pipe and water valve.
3. Disconnect the control arm linkage.
4. Remove the control arm.
5. Remove the heater core by moving it sideways.

NOTE: To prevent foreign material from getting in between the heater core and case, be careful not to remove the heater core felt when removing the heater core.

6. To install, after the center ventilator open/close damper has been placed in the fully closed position, turn the arm fully clockwise, then connect it to the link.
7. With the defroster/changeover damper in the fully closed defroster position, turn the arm fully counterclockwise, then connect it to the link.
8. With the water valve fully closed and the air intake damper fully closed, connect the arm to the link.
9. Connect each heater hose up to the proper inlet/outlet.
10. When installing the water hoses, apply a non-drying adhesive to the engine compartment side of the grommet. Tighten the clamps so that the bolt heads are accessible.

Heater Blower Assembly

REMOVAL & INSTALLATION

Montero

1. Disconnect the front wiring harness

and blower motor coupling connectors.
2. Remove the lower mounting bolts of the blower assembly.
3. Remove the lap heater duct.
4. Remove the stopper of the glove box and push the glove box down.
5. Remove the "Recirc-Fresh" control wire and blower assembly mounting bolts.
6. Remove the blower assembly.
7. Reverse the above procedure for installation.

Radio

REMOVAL & INSTALLATION

1. Remove the instrument cluster bezel.
2. Remove the radio bracket attaching screws from the instrument panel, and remove the radio bracket.
3. Pull the radio out slightly, disconnect the antenna lead-in, speaker connector and the power supply connector.
4. Take out the radio.
Installation is the reverse of removal.

Windshield Wipers Motor and Linkage

REMOVAL & INSTALLATION

1. Remove the wiper arms. Remove the arm shaft lock nuts and push in the shafts. Disconnect the electrical wiring.
2. Remove the bolts holding the motor bracket to the body and pull the wiper assembly outward and away from the body.
3. Hold the motor shaft and the linkage at right angles to each other and disconnect them. Remove the motor.
4. The linkages can be pulled from the opening in the front deck.
5. The installation is in the reverse of the removal, being sure to insert the linkage shaft bracket positioning boss positively in the hole provided in the body before tightening the wiper shaft nut.
6. Locate the wiper blades in the stopped position approximately ½ to ¾ inch above the bottom moulding or sealer of the windshield.

Instrument Panel

REMOVAL & INSTALLATION

Pickup Trucks

1. Disconnect the negative battery cable.

2. Remove the heater fan control knob, heater control knobs and the radio knobs.
3. Remove the ash tray and remove the two screws behind it holding the instrument panel bezel. Remove the two screws at the top of the bezel and remove the bezel.
4. Remove the four screws in the corners of the meter case.
5. Disconnect the speedometer cable and connectors from the back of the meter, and remove the meter assembly.
Installation is the reverse of removal.

Speedometer Cable

REMOVAL & INSTALLATION

1. Unfasten the speedometer cable from the rear of the speedometer. The instrument panel may have to be removed.

NOTE: The cable is fastened to the speedometer via a snap clip, which must be pressed down while the cable is being unfastened.

2. Unfasten the speedometer cable from the transmission.
3. Remove the bands holding the cable with the wiring harness and withdraw the cable through the engine compartment.
Installation is the reverse of removal.

—— CAUTION ——
Always install the speedometer cable with the largest radius possible to prevent cable binding and noise.

Circuit Protection

FUSE BOX LOCATION

The fuse box is located below the hood release handle on the driver's side of the vehicle.

FUSIBLE LINK

The fusible link is located on the battery running from the positive (+) battery terminal. It is necessary to test the link for continuity with a circuit tester, since visual inspection is not enough to detect a melted fusible link. When the fusible link is melted, a dead short may be the cause.

Toyota

GENERAL ENGINE SPECIFICATIONS

Year	Engine Type	Engine Displacement Cu. In. (cc)	Carburetor Type	Horsepower (@ rpm)	Torque @ rpm (ft lbs)	Bore × Stroke (in.)	Compression Ratio	Oil Pressure @ rpm (psi)
'77–'80	20R	133.6 (2189)	2-bbl	95 @ 4800①	122 @ 2400	3.48 × 3.50	8.4:1	64 @ 2500
'81–'84	22R	144.4 (2366)	2-bbl	96 @ 4800②	93 @ 2800③	3.62 × 3.50	9.0:1	64 @ 2500
'84	22R-E	144.4 (2366)	E.F.I.	106 @ 4800	137 @ 2800	3.62 × 3.50	9.0:1	64 @ 2500
'77–'84	2F	258 (4230)	2-bbl	125 @ 3600	200 @ 1800	4.02 × 4.13	7.8:1	50–70 @ 2000
'81–'83	L	133.5 (2188)	D.F.I.	62 @ 4200④	93 @ 2400	3.54 × 3.39	21.5:1	60 @ 2000
'84	L	149.2 (2446)	D.F.I.	75 @ 4000	114 @ 2400	3.62 × 3.62	20.0:1	60 @ 2000

E.F.I. Electronic Fuel Injection
D.F.I. Diesel Fuel Injection
① '79–'80: 90 @ 4800
② '83 Federal and '84 all: 100 @ 4800
③ '84: 130 @ 2800
④ '83: 59 @ 4200

TUNE-UP SPECIFICATIONS

Year	Engine Type	Spark Plugs Type	Spark Plugs Gap (in.)	Distributor Point Dwell (deg)	Distributor Point Gap (in.)	Ignition Timing (deg)▲ MT	Ignition Timing (deg)▲ AT	Fuel Pump Pressure (psi)	Manifold Vacuum at Idle* in. Hg	Compression Pressure (psi) @ 250 rpm**	Idle Speed (rpm) MT	Idle Speed (rpm) AT	Valve Clearance (in.) In	Valve Clearance (in.) Ex
'77	2F	W14 EX	0.037	41	0.018	7B	—	3.4–4.7	16.5	149	650	—	0.008	0.014
'77–'78	20R	W16 EP	0.031	52	0.018②	8B①	8B①	2.1–4.3	16.5	156	800	850	0.008	0.012
'78–'84	2F	④	⑤	Electronic		7B	—	3.4–4.7	16.5	149	⑥	—	0.008	0.014
'79–'80	20R	W16 EX-U	0.031	52	0.018	8B	8B	2.1–4.3	15.75	156	850	850	0.008	0.012③

TOYOTA

TUNE-UP SPECIFICATIONS

Year	Engine Type	Spark Plugs Type	Spark Plugs Gap (in.)	Distributor Point Dwell (deg)	Distributor Point Gap (in.)	Ignition Timing (deg)▲ MT	Ignition Timing (deg)▲ AT	Fuel Pump Pressure (psi)	Manifold Vacuum at Idle* in. Hg	Compression Pressure (psi) @ 250 rpm**	Idle Speed (rpm) MT	Idle Speed (rpm) AT	Valve Clearance (in.) In	Valve Clearance (in.) Ex
'81–'82	22R	W16 EXR-U	0.031	Electronic		8B	8B	2.1–4.3	15.8	156	700	750	0.008	0.012
'83–'84	22R	W16 EXR-U	0.031	Electronic		5B	5B	2.1–4.3	15.8	156	700	750	0.008	0.012
'84	22R-E	W16 EXR-U	0.031	Electronic		5B	—	36–38	15.8	156	750	—	0.008	0.012

NOTE: If these figures do not correspond to information given on the engine compartment decal, use the figures on the decal. They are current for the engine in your truck.

▲ With automatic transmission in D (drive) and manual transmission in Neutral
*These are the minimum readings you must obtain
**Look for uniformity among cylinders rather than specific pressure
① 13B with High Altitude Compensation— see text
② Distributor air gap 0.008–0.016 in.—'78
③ 1979 20R exhaust valve 0.010 in.
④ '78–'79—W14EX '80—W14EX-U '81– '82—W14EXR-U
⑤ '78–'79—0.039 '80–'82—0.031
⑥ '78–'80—800 '81–'82—650

DIESEL ENGINE TUNE-UP SPECIFICATIONS

Injector Opening Pressure (psi)	Idle Speed (rpm)	Valve Clearance (in.) Intake	Valve Clearance (in.) Exhaust	Cranking Compression Pressure @ 250 rpm	Maximum Compression Variance ③	Firing Order
1636–1778① 1493–1777②	700	.010	.014	④	71 psi	1-3-4-2

① New
② Used
③ Between highest and lowest cylinder readings

④ '84–'83: min. 284; max 427 psi
'84: min. 284; max 455 psi

FIRING ORDERS

NOTE: To avoid confusion, always replace spark plug wires one at a time.

Firing order—20R and 22R engines

Firing order—2F engines

CAPACITIES

Year	Model	Engine Type	Crankcase▲ w/filter	Crankcase▲ wo/filter	Transmission▲ Manual	Transmission▲ Automatic	Trans. Case▲	Differential▲ Front	Differential▲ Rear	Fuel Tank■	Cooling System▲
'77–'79	Pickup 2WD	20R	5.0	4.0	2.0①	7.0④	—	—	1.6	12.1②	8.5③
'79½	Pickup 4WD	20R	5.0	4.0	2.0	6.7	1.7	2.0	2.1	—	7.4
'80	Pickup (all)	20R	5.0	4.0	2.0⑥	6.7④	1.7	2.4	2.3	—	8.9
'81–'82	Pickup (Gasoline)	22R	5.0	4.0	2.1	6.7	1.7	2.4	1.8⑦	13.7⑤	8.9
'81–'83	Pickup (Diesel)	L	6.1	5.1	1.9	—	—	—	1.8	16.0	11.1
'83	Pickup (Gasoline)	22R	5.0	4.0	⑪	6.9	1.7	2.3	1.8⑫	13.7⑤	8.9
'84	Pickup (Gasoline)	22R 22R-E	5.0	4.0	⑬	6.9	1.7	2.4	1.8⑫	13.7⑤	8.9
'84	Pickup (Diesel)	L	6.0⑭	5.0⑭	⑮	—	1.7	2.3	1.8⑫	16.0	12.0
'75–'84	Land Cruiser	2F	8.4	7.4	⑧	—	3.6	5.2	5.2	22.2⑨	17.5⑩

▲Measurements in quarts
■ Measurements in gallons
① 5 speed trans.—2.8
② Long bed '77–'78—16.1
③ '78 only—7.4
④ '78 only—6.7
⑤ Long bed—16.1
⑥ 5 speed trans.—2.7
⑦ ¾ Ton—1.9; 4 × 4—2.3
⑧ 3 speed trans.—1.8; 4 speed trans.—3.3
⑨ Station Wagon—21.7
⑩ '78–'82 2-Door—19.9
   '78–'82 Wagon—18.3
⑪ 4 sp.: 2.9; 5 sp: 2.3
⑫ 4 × 4: 2.3

⑬ W52: 2.7
   W42: 2.9
   G52 2WD: 2.3
   G52 4WD: 4.1
⑭ Calif.: 7 w/filter; 6 w/o filter
⑮ 2WD: 2.5
   4WD: 4.1

VALVE SPECIFICATIONS

Year	Engine Type	Seat Angle (deg)	Face Angle (deg)	Spring Test Pressure (lbs)	Spring Installed Height (in.)	Stem-to-Guide Clearance (in.)▲ Intake	Stem-to-Guide Clearance (in.)▲ Exhaust	Stem Diameter (in.) Intake	Stem Diameter (in.) Exhaust
'77–'84	2F	45	44.5	71.6	1.693	0.0012–0.0024	0.0016–0.0028	0.3140	0.3137
'77	20R	45	45	60①	1.594	0.0006–0.0024	0.0012–0.0026	0.3138–0.3144	0.3136–0.3142
'78–'80	20R	45	44.5	55.1	1.594	0.0008–0.0024	0.0012–0.0026	0.3138–0.3144	0.3136–0.3142
'81–'84	22R	45③	44.5	55.1	1.594	0.0008–0.0024	0.0012–0.0026	0.3145–0.3188	0.3136–0.3142
'81–'84 (dies.)	L	45③	44.5	56②	1.547	0.0008–0.0022	0.0016–0.0030	0.3336–0.3342	0.3328–0.3335

▲Valve guides are removable
① Minimum pressure for used spring—54 lbs.
② 1984: 64 lbs.
③ Blend the seat with 30° and 60° cutters to center the 45° portion on the valve face.

TOYOTA

CAMSHAFT SPECIFICATIONS
(All measurements in inches)

Engine	Journal Diameter	Bearing Clearance	Maximum Journal Runout	Lobe Height▲ Intake	Lobe Height▲ Exhaust	Maximum Thrust Clearance (End-Play)
20R & 22R	1.2982–1.2984⑦	0.0004–0.0020	0.0080	1.6783–1.6819	1.6806–1.6842	0.0010①
2F	②	0.0010–0.0030	0.0059	1.4960–1.5142	1.4920–1.5098	0.0080③
L (Diesel)	1.3767–1.3774	0.0009–0.0029	0.0020	1.6810–1.6948⑤	1.6900–1.7020⑥	0.0120④

▲Measured from the bottom of the base
circle to the top of the lobe (with the cam
lobe pointing upward)

① Preferred—0.003–0.007
② Front—1.8880–1.8888
    Second—1.8289–1.8297
    Third—1.7699–1.7707
    Rear—1.7108–1.7116
③ Preferred—0.0035–0.0060
④ Preferred—0.0022–0.0061
⑤ 1984: 1.6809–1.6812
⑥ 1984: 1.6880–1.6900
⑦ 1983–84: 1.2984–1.2992

CRANKSHAFT AND CONNECTING ROD SPECIFICATIONS
(All measurements in inches)

Year	Engine Type	Crankshaft Main Brg Journal Dia	Crankshaft Main Brg Oil Clearance	Crankshaft Shaft End-Play	Crankshaft Thrust on No.	Connecting Rod Journal Diameter	Connecting Rod Oil Clearance	Connecting Rod Side Clearance
'77–'84	2F	①	0.0008–0.0017	0.0024–0.0063	3	2.1252–2.1260	0.0008–0.0024	0.0043–0.0091
'77–'80	20R	2.3614–2.3622	0.0010–0.0022	0.0007–0.0079	3	2.0862–2.0866	0.0010–0.0022	0.0063–0.0102
'81–'84	22R	2.3614–2.3622	0.0006–0.0020	0.0008–0.0089	3	2.0862–2.0866	0.0008–0.0020	0.0008–0.0087
'81–'84 (dies.)	L	2.4402–2.4409	0.0012–0.0028	0.0016–0.0098	3	2.0858–2.0866	0.0012–0.0028	0.0031–0.0079

① No. 1—2.6367–2.6376; No. 2—2.6957–2.6967; No. 3—2.7548–2.7557; No. 4—2.8139–2.8148

TORQUE SPECIFICATIONS
(All readings in ft. lbs.)

Year	Engine Type	Cylinder Head Bolts	Rod Bearing Bolts	Main Bearing Bolts	Crankshaft Pulley Bolt	Flywheel-to-Crankshaft Bolts	Manifolds Intake	Manifolds Exhaust
'77–'84	2F	83–98	35–55	90–108①	116–145	59–62	28–37②	28–37②
'75–'79	20R	52.1–63.7	39.1–47.7	68.7–83.2	79.6–94.0	61.5–68.7	10.6	28.9–36.2
'80	20R	53–63	40–47	69–83	120–130	73–86	13–19	29–36②
'81–'84	22R	53–63	40–47	69–83	120–130	73–86	13–19	29–36
'81–'84 (dies.)	L	84–90	37–43	71–81	69–75③	84–90	8–11④	11–15⑤

① Rear bearing—76–94 ft. lbs.
② California vehicles—37–51 ft. lbs.
③ 1984: 101
④ 1984: 17
⑤ 1984: 29

T612

PISTON AND RING SPECIFICATIONS
(All measurements in inches)

| Year | Engine Type | Piston Clearance 68°F | Ring Gap | | | Ring Side Clearance (Ring to Land) | | |
			Top Compression	Bottom Compression	Oil Control	Top Compression	Bottom Compression	Oil Control
'77–'84	2F	0.0012–0.0020	0.0080–0.0160	0.0080–0.0160	snug	0.0012–0.0024	0.0008–0.0024	snug
'77–'80	20R	0.0012–0.0020	0.0040–0.0120	0.0040–0.0120	0.0040–0.0120	0.0012–0.0028	0.0012–0.0028	snug
'81–'84	22R	0.0020–0.0028	0.0094–0.0142	0.0071–0.0154	snug	0.0080	0.0080	snug
'81–'83	L	0.0014–0.0022	0.0780–0.0157	0.0118–0.0197	0.0118–0.0197	0.0024–0.0039	0.0016–0.0031	0.0012–0.0028
'84	L	0.0020–0.0028	0.0138–0.0232	0.0079–0.0213	0.0079–0.0193	0.0008–0.0026	0.0016–0.0039	0.0012–0.0028

ALTERNATOR AND REGULATOR SPECIFICATIONS

| Year | Engine | Alternator | | | Regulator | | | | | |
| | | | | | Field Relay | | | Regulator | | |
		Manufacturer	Output (amps)	Type	Contact Spring Deflection (in.)	Point Gap (in.)	Volts to Close (in.)	Air Gap (in.)	Point Gap (in.)	Volts
'77–'82	Exc. Diesel	Nippondenso	40	External	0.008–0.0018	0.016–0.047	4.5–5.8	0.008	0.010–0.018	13.8–14.8
'79–'84	Exc. Diesel	Nippondenso	①	Built-in	②	②	②	②	②	14.0–14.7
'81–'84	Diesel	Nippondenso	55	Built-in	②	②	②	②	②	13.8–14.8

① 40–45 Amp Standard, 55 Amp Optional
② Not Adjustable

STARTER SPECIFICATIONS

| Engine Type | Starter Type/ Rated Voltage | No Load Test | | Minimum rpm | Brush Spring Tension | Minimum Brush Length |
		Maximum Amps	Volts			
20R	Reduction Gear/12 V	50	11.5	5000	21②	0.47
22R	Reduction Gear/12 V	90	12.0	3500	64②	0.39
L (dies.)	Reduction Gear/12 V	180	11.0	3500	7.1–8.8③	0.47
2F	Direct Drive/12 V	50	11.5	5000	①	0.39

① Not specified by manufacturer
② Ounces
③ Pounds

BRAKE SPECIFICATIONS
(All measurements in inches)

| Year | Model | Lug Nut Torque (ft. lbs.) | Front Brake Disc | | Maximum Drum Diameter | | Minimum Lining Thickness | |
			Minimum Thickness	Maximum Run-Out	Front	Rear	Front	Rear
'77	Pick-up	65–86	0.450	0.006	10.10	10.10	0.04	0.04
'78	Pick-up	65–86	0.450①	0.006	10.08	10.08	0.04	0.04

BRAKE SPECIFICATIONS
(All measurements in inches)

| Year | Model | Lug Nut Torque (ft. lbs.) | Front Brake Disc | | Maximum Drum Diameter | | Minimum Lining Thickness | |
			Minimum Thickness	Maximum Run-Out	Front	Rear	Front	Rear
'79–'80	Pick-up	65–86	②	0.006	—	10.08	—	0.04
'81–'83	Pick-up	65–86	②	0.006	—	10.08	—	0.04
'84	Pick-up	65–86	④	0.006	—	10.08	0.04	0.04
'77–'79	Land Cruiser	65–86	0.740	0.005	11.70	11.70	③	0.06
'80–'84	Land Cruiser	66–86	0.750	0.005	—	11.70	—	0.06

① "K" type disc brake—0.750
② Except cab and chassis—0.453; cab and chassis—0.748
③ Drum brakes—0.06; disc brakes—0.04

TUNE-UP PROCEDURES

NOTE: The procedures outlined below are the specific procedures for Toyota vehicles; general tune-up procedures may be found in the section at the end of this book.

Spark Plugs

REPLACEMENT

Check, clean, and adjust the spark plugs every 6,000 miles. Replace them every 12,000 miles.

Clean any foreign material from around the spark plugs before removing them. Use the spark plug wrench supplied in the tool kit.

Clean any plugs which appear to be dirty and file their electrodes flat. Adjust the gap to the figure given in the "Tune-up Specifications" chart, above, using a wire feeler gauge.

NOTE: Do not use a flat gauge; an inaccurate reading will result.

Inspect the spark plug hole threads for rust and, if necessary, use a 14 mm plug tap to clean them.

Lightly oil the threads and torque the plugs to 11–14 ft. lbs. Use caution when tightening the plugs, as most Toyota models use aluminum heads.

Breaker Points and Condenser

REPLACEMENT

Loosen the clips which attach the distributor cap to the distributor body and lift the cap straight up. Leave the leads connected to the cap. Remove the rotor and dust cover.

Clean the distributor cap and rotor with alcohol. Inspect them for cracks and other signs of wear or damage. Polish the points with a point file.

NOTE: Do not use emery cloth or sandpaper; these may leave particles on the points, causing them to arc.

If the points are badly pitted or worn, replace them as follows:

1. Unfasten the point lead connector.

The arrow indicates the feeler gauge used to set the point gap. Make certain that the rubbing block rests on the high spot of the cam, as shown.

2. Remove the point retaining clip and remove the point hold-down screw.
3. Remove the point set.
4. Installation is the reverse of removal.

After replacing the points, or as routine maintenance, adjust the points to the specifications given in the tune-up chart at the beginning of this section as follows:

1. Rotate the engine by hand or by using a remote starter switch, so that the rubbing block is on the high point of the cam lobe.
2. Insert a 0.018 in. feeler gauge between the points; a slight drag should be felt.

NOTE: Some 20R engines with breaker points have a plastic cap over the contact points, making it necessary to adjust the point gap at the rubbing block. Set the rubbing block between two cam lobes and adjust the clearance to 0.018 in. (See illustration). Always check the dwell angle after setting the points.

3. If no drag is felt or if the feeler gauge cannot be inserted at all, loosen, but do not remove, the point hold-down screw.
4. Insert a screwdriver into the adjustment slot. Rotate the screwdriver until the proper point gap is attained. The point gap is increased by rotating the screwdriver counterclockwise and decreased by rotating it clockwise.
5. Tighten the point hold-down screw. Lubricate the cam lobes, breaker arm, rubbing block, arm pivot, and distributor shaft with special high-temperature distributor grease.

Check the operation of the centrifugal advance mechanism by moving the rotor

Some 20R engines are adjusted at the rubbing block rather than the contact points—see text

clockwise. Release the rotor; it should return to its original position. If it does not, check it for binding.

Check the vacuum advance unit by removing the cap and pressing in on the octane selector. Release the octane selector. It should snap back to its original position. Check for binding if it fails to do so.

Replace the condenser if it is suspect or as routine maintenance during the point replacement operation, in the following manner:

1. Remove the nut and washer from the condenser lead terminal.

2. Remove the condenser mounting screw and withdraw the condenser.

3. Installation is the reverse of removal.

NOTE: The condenser is mounted on the outside of the distributor body on all models, except the Land Cruiser, which has it mounted inside the body.

Install the dust cover, rotor and the distributor cap on the distributor. Adjust the dwell and timing, as outlined below.

ADJUSTMENT

Connect a dwell/tachometer, in accordance with its manufacturer's instructions, between the distributor primary lead and a ground.

—————— CAUTION ——————
On models with electronic ignition, hook the dwell meter or tachometer to the negative (−) side of the coil, not to the distributor primary lead; damage to the ignition control unit will result.

With the engine warmed up and running at the specified idle speed (see the tune-up chart), take a dwell reading. If the point dwell is not within specifications, shut the engine off and adjust the point gap, as outlined above.

NOTE: Increasing the point gap decreases the dwell angle and vice versa.

Install the dust cover, rotor, and cap. Check the dwell reading again.

Electronic Ignition

NOTE: **Two types of electronic ignition systems are used. The first is a semi-transistorized unit (1977) which uses conventional breaker points along with a transistorized igniter in lieu of the condensor. The igniter, which contains two transistors and an assortment of resistors, serves as a switching device to control the primary coil circuit. This system reduces the amount of current passing through the breaker points, thereby increasing breaker point life. Breaker points are replaced in the conventional manner. The second type of electronic ignition (1978 and later) is fully transistorized. A stationary magnetic pick-up coil (mounted in the distributor) and a toothed timing rotor (mounted on the distributor shaft) entirely replace the conventional breaker points and condensor. Because no mechanical contact exists between the pick-up coil and the timing rotor, the system is considered to be maintenance-free.**

PRECAUTIONS—FULLY TRANSISTORIZED SYSTEM

1. If the engine will not start, do not leave the ignition switch "ON" for more than 10 minutes.

2. Make sure that your test equipment (tachometer, dwell meter, etc.) is compatible to this system before making any connections.

3. Do not connect the tachometer positive lead to the distributor. Connect this lead only to the service connector (yellow) provided in the system.

4. Do not disconnect the battery with the engine running.

5. Do not allow the ignition coil terminals or service connector terminal to touch ground: Damage to the igniter or ignition coil could result.

AIR GAP ADJUSTMENT

1. Remove the distributor cap, ignition rotor and dust cover from the distributor.

2. "Tap" the ignition key to the start

Check the air gap between the timing rotor and the pick-up coil

position until one of the timing rotor teeth aligns with the pick-up coil. Turn the ignition switch "OFF".

3. Using a flat, brass feeler gauge, check the gap between the timing rotor tooth and the pick-up coil. If adjustment is needed, loosen (but do not remove) the pick-up coil attaching screws and move the pick-up coil as necessary to attain the specified clearance. Tighten the pick-up coil attaching screws and recheck the clearance.

4. Reinstall the dust cover, ignition rotor and distributor cap.

IGNITER TROUBLESHOOTING

1977

If the igniter in the 1977 semi-transistorized ignition is suspected as faulty, it may be checked as follows.

1. Check the coil beforehand, using the methods outlined in the "Troubleshooting" section at the end of this Chapter.

2. Check to see if there is battery voltage at the resistor terminal. Connect a test light between igniter side ballast resistor terminal and the ground bolt at the igniter, or any suitable ground. With the ignition on, the test light should indicate a complete circuit there.

Troubleshooting the igniter: later models have a snap connector in the wire between the igniter and the distributor; on trucks with separate coil and igniter, you will not need the extra wire shown here.

3. Remove the coil primary wire from the distributor and hold it next to a ground. Disconnect the thin secondary wire from the side of the distributor. Make intermittent contacts with a suitable ground point with the secondary distributor wire. You may need an extra length of wire to do this on later models with piggyback coil and igniter assemblies. With the ignition on, sparks should be produced from the coil primary wire.

4. If no spark is produced the igniter is probably bad and should be replaced. If a spark is produced, the problem is in the points. Make certain that they are clean and properly adjusted.

FULLY TRANSISTORIZED IGNITION TROUBLESHOOTING

1978 and later

Troubleshooting this system is easy; but you must have an accurate ohmmeter and voltmeter. The numbers in the diagram correspond to the numbers of the following troubleshooting steps. Be sure to perform each step in order.

1. Check for a spark at the spark plugs by hooking up a timing light in the usual manner. If the light flashes, it can be assumed that voltage is reaching the plugs, which should then be inspected, along with the fuel system. If no flash is generated, go on to the following ignition checks.

2. Check all wiring and plastic connectors for tight and proper connections.

3. With an ohmmeter, check between the positive (+) and negative (−) primary terminals of the ignition coil. The resistance (cold) should be 1.3–1.7 ohms. Between the (+) primary terminal and the high tension terminal, the resistance (cold) should be 12–16 kilo-ohms. The insulation resistance between the (+) primary terminal and the ignition coil case should be infinite.

4. The resistor wire (brown and yellow) resistance should be 1.2 ohms (cold). To measure, disconnect the plastic connector at the igniter and connect one wire of the ohmmeter to the yellow wire and one to the brown.

5. Remove the distributor cap and ig-

Measure the signal generator (pick-up coil) resistance at the pink and white wires

Use the ohmmeter as resistance at the igniter end of the distributor connector

nition rotor. Check the air gap between the timing rotor spoke and the pick-up coil. When aligned, the air gap should be 0.008–0.016 in. You will probably have to bump the engine around with the starter to line up the timing rotor.

6. Unplug the distributor connector at the distributor. Connect one wire of the

ohmmeter to the white wire, and one wire to the pink wire. The resistance of the signal generator should be 130–190 ohms.

7. Checking the igniter last, connect the (−) voltmeter wire to the (−) ignition coil primary terminal, and the (+) voltmeter wire to the yellow resistor wire at the connector unplugged in step 4. With the ignition switch turned to "On" (not "Start") the voltage should measure 12 volts.

8. Check the voltage between the (−) ignition coil primary terminal and the yellow resistor wire again, but this time use the ohmmeter as resistance. Using the igniter end of the distributor connector unplugged in step 5, connect the positive (+) ohmmeter wire to the pink distributor wire, and the negative (−) ohmmeter wire to the white wire.

CAUTION

Do not intermix the (+) and (−) terminals of the ohmmeter.

Select either the 1 ohm or 10 ohm range of the ohmmeter. With the voltmeter connected as in step 7, and the ignition switch turned on "On" (not "Start"), the voltage should measure nearly zero.

Ignition Timing

NOTE: Timing mark locations differ between the engines used in the Pick-up (20R and 22R) and the Landcruiser (2F). The 20R and 22R timing marks are located on the crankshaft pulley (painted notch) and the timing cover (pointer). The 2F timing marks are located on the flywheel (ball) and the bellhousing (pointer).

1. Clean off the timing marks. You may want to retouch them if they are dark, using chalk or paint. You might have to bump the engine around with the starter to find the marks.

2. Warm the engine to operating temperature. Connect a tachometer and check the engine idle speed to see that it is within the range found in the "Tune-Up Specifications" chart. Adjust it, if necessary, according to the procedure found in the Carburetor section.

CAUTION

On 20R and 22R engines, connect the positive (+) tachometer terminal either to the negative (−) ignition coil terminal or to the yellow service connector, if provided. Do NOT connect it to the distributor side. Improper connections will damage the transistorized igniter.

---

3. Shut off the engine and connect a timing light according to the manufacturer's directions.

4. Disconnect and plug the vacuum hose from the distributor vacuum unit.

NOTE: On 1977 and later 20R and 22R engines with HAC (High Altitude

Fully transistorized ignition system troubleshooting

1979 and earlier 20R engine timing marks. The 8° notch is the larger and deeper of the two notches cut into the pulley. The 13° indication is only for 1977–79 trucks with High Altitude Compensation.

Mark on flywheel = 7° BTC

2F engine timing mark

1980 and later 20R and 22R engine timing marks—typical. The "8" mark is 8° before top dead center. Some engines will also have a "5" mark which denotes 5° before top dead center.

Compensation system) there are two vacuum hoses which connect to the distributor. Both must be disconnected and plugged. These systems require an extra step in the timing procedure, found at the end of this section.

5. Be sure that the timing light wires are clear of the fan and pulleys, and start the engine.

─────── CAUTION ───────

Keep fingers, clothes, hair, tools, and wires clear of the fan and fan belts. Run the engine only in a well-ventilated area.

6. Allow the engine to run at the specified idle speed with the gearshift in Neutral, or Drive with automatics as the case may be. Be certain that the parking brake

is set, the front wheels are blocked, and don't stand in front of the truck when making adjustments with the engine running.

7. Point the timing light at the marks. With the engine at the specified idle, the marks should line up.

8. If the timing is incorrect, loosen the bolt at the base of the distributor just enough so that the distributor can be turned. Hold the distributor by its base and turn it slightly to advance or retard the timing as required. Once the marks are seen to align properly, tighten the bolt. If only minor corrections in timing are necessary, adjustment can be made with the octane selector, rather than by moving the distributor. See the Octane Selector section following for information.

9. After tightening the bolt, or moving the octane selector, recheck the timing. It is not unusual for it to change during the tightening process. It may take two or three tries to get it perfect. Shut off the engine, disconnect the timing light, and connect the vacuum line at the distributor, except on engines with HAC.

10. On 1977 and later engines with HAC (identified in the Note earlier) after setting the initial timing, reconnect the vacuum hoses at the distributor. Recheck the timing. It should now be about 13° BTC. There is no mark on the pulley to indicate this 13° advance in 1977. It must be estimated according to the illustration found here.

11. If the advance is still about 8° pinch the hose between the HAC valve and the three way connector. It should now be about 13°. If not, the HAC valve should be checked for proper operation.

OCTANE SELECTOR ADJUSTMENT

The octane selector is used as a fine adjustment to match the ignition timing to the grade of gasoline being used. It is located opposite the distributor vacuum advance unit, under a plastic cover. Normally the octane selector should not require adjustment, however, adjustment is as follows:

1. Align the setting line with the threaded end of the housing and then align the center line with the setting mark on the housing.

2. Drive the truck at 16–22 miles per hour in High gear on a level road.

3. Depress the accelerator pedal all the way to the floor. A slight pinging sound should be heard. As the vehicle accelerates, the sound should go away.

ONE GRADUATION

CENTER LINE · SET LINE · MARK

Octane selector setting

4. If the pinging sound is loud, or if it fails to disappear as the vehicle accelerates, retard the timing by turning the knob toward "R" (retard).

5. If there is no pinging sound at all, advance the timing by turning the knob toward "A" (advance).

6. When the adjustment is completed, replace the dust cover.

NOTE: One graduation of the octane selector is equal to about 10° of crankshaft angle.

Valve Adjustment

20R AND 22R ENGINES

1. Start the engine and allow it to reach normal operating temperature (above 175°F).

2. Stop the engine. Remove the air cleaner assembly, its hoses, and bracket. Remove any other cables, hoses, wires, etc. which are attached to the valve cover. Remove the valve cover.

3. Check the torque of the valve rocker shaft bolts and the camshaft bearing bolts; they should be torqued to 12–17 ft. lbs.

4. Check the torque of the bearing cap union bolts; they should be torqued to 11–16 ft. lbs.

5. Set the no. 1 cylinder to TDC on its compression stroke. To do this, remove the spark plugs and turn the engine with a wrench applied to the crankshaft bolt. Place a finger on the no. 1 spark plug hole. When pressure is felt on your finger and the TDC line on the crankshaft pulley is aligned with the timing pointer (or line), the engine is at TDC. The rocker arms on cylinder no. 1

Valve clearance adjustment sequence—20R and 22R engines

should be loose, and the rocker arms on cylinder no. 4 should be tight if the engine is at TDC. Note that the timing mark you are watching is not the same one used for engine timing. That notch indicates a certain number of degrees before TDC.

NOTE: Do not start the engine. Valve clearances are checked with the engine stopped to prevent hot oil from being splashed out by the timing chain.

6. Check the clearances (see the "Tune-Up Specifications" chart) and adjust the first set of valves to the proper specifica-

tions, if necessary. See the illustrations for the proper adjusting sequence.

NOTE: The clearance is measured with a feeler gauge between the valve stem and the adjusting screw.

7. To adjust the valve clearance, loosen the locknut and turn the adjusting screw until the specified clearance is obtained. Tighten the locknut and check the clearance again.

8. Crank the engine one revolution (360°) and perform steps 6 and 7 for the second set of valves in the illustration. Crank the engine in a clockwise direction (to the right as you face the engine), passing the timing mark just before reaching the TDC mark.

9. Install the spark plug in the no. 1 cylinder. Install the valve cover, air cleaner assembly, and any other components which were removed.

NOTE: If you are assembling the engine after it has been dismantled, the valves must be adjusted with the engine cold. Obtain the valve clearance specification from the beginning of this section and add a minimum of .002″ to these values. Remember: Excess clearance will not damage the engine whereas too little clearance could. After the initial engine start-up, allow the engine to reach normal operating temperature and adjust the valves as previously described to the "Hot" clearances listed in the specification chart.

2F ENGINES

1. Start the engine and allow it to reach normal operating temperature (above 165°F).

2. Stop the engine. Remove the air cleaner assembly with related components. Remove any cables, hoses, wires, etc., which are attached to the valve cover and remove the valve cover.

3. Following the Torque Sequence and Torque Specification charts at the beginning of this section, re-torque the cylinder head bolts. On 2F engines, also torque the manifold attaching nuts (exc. Calif.—28–37 ft. lbs., Calif.—37–51 ft. lbs.) and the rocker support fasteners (8mm bolt—15–21 ft. lbs., 10mm bolt—22–32 ft. lbs.).

4. Start the engine and adjust the idle speed as described in the following procedure.

5. Check the clearance between each of the rocker arms and valve stems using a feeler gauge of the proper size (See the Tune-up Specification chart).

6. If the clearance is incorrect, loosen the locknut and turn the adjusting screw as required. Tighten the locknut and recheck the clearance.

7. After adjusting all of the valves, install the valve cover and any other components which were removed during step 2.

8. Recheck the engine idle speed and adjust if necessary.

DIESEL ENGINE

The valves are adjusted in basically the same manner as the 20R and 22R engines, in that the engine must be off during the adjustment and that the clearance is checked with a feeler gauge between the rocker arm and the valve stem end.

NOTE: The engine must be at normal operating temperature to obtain the proper valve clearances.

1. Remove the valve cover and rotate the crankshaft to align the TDC mark on the crankshaft pulley with the corresponding pointer. The valves of the number one cylinder should be closed (rocker arms should feel loose). If the rocker arms of the number one cylinder are tight, rotate the engine another 360° and again align the TDC marks.

2. Adjust the clearances of the following valves:
Number one cylinder: intake and exhaust
Number two cylinder: intake
Number three cylinder: exhaust

3. Rotate the crankshaft 360° and adjust the remaining valves:
Number two cylinder: exhaust
Number three cylinder: intake
Number four cylinder: intake and exhaust
Remember that the cylinder numbering from the front of the engine to the rear is

Valve clearance adjustment sequence—diesel engine

Carburetor adjusting screws—20R engines

#1 through #4, and that the valve arrangement from the front of the engine is E-I-E-I-E-I-E-I, with E designating each exhaust valve and I designating each intake valve. Choose your specifications from the Diesel Tune-Up Chart accordingly.
Reinstall the valve cover.

> ——— **CAUTION** ———
> *Never operate the engine with the valve cover removed.*

Carburetor

IDLE SPEED AND MIXTURE—20R AND 2F ENGINES

NOTE: Idle mixture adjustments cannot be performed on 1981 and later carburetors; these adjustments are pre-set at the factory.

The idle speed and mixture should be adjusted under the following conditions: the air cleaner must be installed, the choke fully opened, the transmission should be in Neutral (N), all accessories should be turned off, all vacuum lines should be connected, and the ignition timing should be set to specification.

1. Start the engine and allow it to reach normal operating temperature (180°F).

2. Check the float setting; the fuel level should be just about even with the spot on the sight glass. If the fuel level is too high or low, adjust the float level. (See the Fuel System section)

3. Connect a tachometer in accordance with its manufacturer's instructions. However, connect the tachometer positive (+) lead to the coil Negative (−) terminal or to the yellow service connector, if provided. Do NOT hook it up to the distributor side; damage to the transistorized ignition could result.

4. Turn the idle speed adjusting screw to obtain one of the following initial idle speeds:
20R—900 rpm
2F—690 rpm

5. Turn the idle mixture adjusting screw to increase the idle speed as much as is possible.

6. Next, turn the idle speed screw to again obtain the same idle speed figure given in step 4.

7. If possible, turn the idle mixture screw to increase the idle speed again.

8. Keep repeating steps 6 and 7 until the idle mixture adjusting screw will no longer increase the idle speed above the figure specified in step 4.

9. Slowly turn the idle mixture screw *clockwise*, until the idle speed specified in the "Tune-Up Specifications" chart is reached. (This makes the mixture leaner.)

10. Disconnect the tachometer.

Throttle Positioner Link

Throttle Positioner Diaphragm

Throttle Positioner Link Lever

Throttle Positioner Adjusting Screw

Mixture Adjusting Screw

Fast Idle Adjusting Screw   Idle Adjusting Screw

Carburetor adjusting screws—2F engine

Fuel Injection (Gasoline)

IDLE SPEED ADJUSTMENT

The 1984 22R-E engine is equipped with a computer activated, electronic fuel injection system. Prior to adjusting the idle speed, make sure that:

    a. The air cleaner is installed
    b. All vacuum hoses are connected
    c. All pipes and hoses in the air intake system are connected and in good condition

Idle Speed Adjusting Screw

EFI idle speed adjustment

    d. All fuel injection system wiring is connected and in good condition
    e. The engine is at normal operating temperature
    f. All accessories are OFF
    g. Transmission in NEUTRAL

— CAUTION —
Not all tachometers are compatible with the fuel injection system on your truck. Consult the tachometer manufacturer's recommendations before installing the tachometer. NEVER ALLOW THE TACHOMETER TERMINAL TO TOUCH GROUND AS THIS WILL CAUSE DAMAGE TO THE IGNITOR SYSTEM!

    1. Connect the tachometer, observing the above cautions.
    2. Run the engine at 2,500 rpm for 2 minutes.
    3. Run the engine at idle and turn the idle speed adjusting screw to obtain a speed of 750 rpm.

Fuel Injection (Diesel)

IDLE AND MAXIMUM SPEED ADJUSTMENTS

NOTE: The following adjustments are made with the transmission in neutral and the parking brake applied fully.

    1. Warm the engine to normal operating temperature and allow it to idle.
    2. Turn the idle adjustor knob counterclockwise; the knob should return to its unlocked position.
    3. Turn the engine off and remove the accelerator connection rod.
    4. Connect a tachometer to the engine

according to the tachometer manufacturers instructions.
    5. Start the engine and check the engine rpm at idle. The idle rpm should be 700 rpm.
    6. If adjustment is necessary, turn the idle adjusting screw on the fuel injection pump as required to obtain the 700 rpm idle speed.
    7. Fully depress the injection pump lever, note the maximum engine speed and release the accelerator pedal immediately. The maximum rpm should be 4900.

Diesel engine idle speed adjustment— disconnect the accelerator rod at the injection pump lever as shown, prior to adjustment

Diesel engine idle speed adjustment screw location

8. If adjustment is necessary:

a. Remove the wire seal of the maximum speed adjusting screw, if so equipped.

b. Using Toyota special service tool #09275-54020 or its equivalent, loosen the locknut of the maximum speed adjusting screw.

c. Turn the maximum speed adjusting screw until the proper maximum rpm is obtained.

9. Install the accelerator connecting rod and adjust its length so that there is no slack in the accelerator cable.

10. Check that the idle speed increases as the idle adjustor knob is pulled outward. Then turn the knob counterclockwise so that the rpm returns to the idle specification.

11. Turn the engine off and disconnect the tachometer from the engine.

Diesel engine maximum speed adjustment—push the lever until it contacts the maximum speed adjusting screw

Diesel engine maximum speed adjustment—using the Toyota special service tool to loosen the maximum speed adjusting screw locknut

After setting the idle and maximum speeds on diesel engines, reinstall the accelerator cable and adjust the cable so that there is no slack

ENGINE ELECTRICAL

Distributor

REMOVAL

1. Unfasten the cables from the spark plugs, after marking the wiring order. Remove the high tension cable from the coil.

2. Remove the primary wire and the vacuum line from the distributor. Remove the distributor cap.

3. Match-mark the distributor housing and the engine block; mark the rotor position in the distributor as well. This will

1. Grease stopper	11. O-ring	20. Distributor cap
2. Cam	12. Drive gear	21. Rotor
3. Governor spring	13. Washer	22. Dust cover
4. E-ring	14. Spring	23. Points cover
5. Governor weight	15. Washer	24. Breaker points and
6. Terminal insulator	16. Bearing	ground wire
7. Rubber plug	17. Washer	25. Breaker plate
8. Hold-down clip for cap	18. Distributor shaft	26. Damping spring
9. Octane selector cap	19. Vacuum unit and octane	
10. Distributor housing	selector assembly	

20R engine point type distributor

aid in correct positioning of the distributor during installation.

4. Remove the clamp from the distributor. Withdraw the distributor from the block.

NOTE: It is easier to install the distributor if the engine timing is not disturbed while it is removed. If the timing has been lost, see "Installation—Timing Disturbed".

INSTALLATION—TIMING NOT DISTURBED

1. Insert the distributor in the block and align the matchmarks made during removal.

2. Engage the distributor drive with the oil pump drive shaft.

3. Install the distributor clamp, cap, high tension wire, primary wire, and vacuum line.

4. Install the wires on the spark plugs.

5. Start the engine, Check the timing and adjust the octane selector.

INSTALLATION—TIMING DISTURBED

If the engine has been cranked, dismantled, or the timing otherwise lost, proceed as follows:

1. Determine the top dead center (TDC) of the number one (no. 1) cylinder's compression stroke by removing the spark plug from the no. 1 cylinder and placing a finger or a compression gauge over the spark plug hole.

Crank the engine until compression pressure starts to build up. Continue cranking the engine until the timing marks indicate TDC (or 0°).

2. Next, align the timing marks to the specifications given in the "Ignition Timing" column of the tune-up chart at the beginning of the Toyota section.

3. Temporarily install the rotor in the distributor shaft so that the rotor is pointing toward the number one terminal in the distributor cap.

4. Use a small screwdriver to align the slot on the distributor drive (oil pump driveshaft) with the key on the bottom of the distributor shaft.

5. Install the distributor in the block by rotating it slightly (no more than one gear tooth in either direction) until the driven gear meshes with the drive.

NOTE: Oil the distributor spiral gear and the oil pump driveshaft end before distributor installation.

6. Temporarily tighten the pinch bolt.

7. Remove the rotor and install the dust cover. Replace the rotor and the distributor cap.

8. Install the primary wire and the vacuum line.

9. Install the no. 1 cylinder spark plug. Connect the cables to the spark plugs in the proper order by using the marks made during removal. Install the high tension wire on the coil.

10. Start the engine. Adjust the ignition timing and the octane selector as previously outlined.

1. Distributor cap
2. Rotor
3. Cover
4. Breaker points and cover
5. Damping spring
6. Breaker plate
7. Advance weight and spring
8. Cam assembly
9. Terminal
10. Vacuum unit

2F engine point type distributor

Alternator

PRECAUTIONS

1. Always observe proper polarity of the battery connections; be especially careful when jump-starting the car.

2. Never ground or short out any alternator or alternator regulator terminals.

3. Never operate the alternator with any of its or the battery's leads disconnected.

4. Always remove the battery or disconnect its output lead while charging it.

5. Always disconnect the ground cable when replacing any electrical components.

6. Never subject the alternator to excessive heat or dampness if the engine is being steam-cleaned.

7. Never use arc-welding equipment with the alternator connected.

1. Cam grease stopper	10. Dustproof packing	19. Cord clamp
2. Signal rotor	11. Steel plate washer	20. Breaker plate
3. Governor spring	12. Rubber washer	21. Signal generator
4. Governor weight	13. Octane selector cap	22. Dustproof cover
5. Governor shaft	14. Housing	23. Distributor rotor
6. Plate washer	15. O-ring	24. Distributor cap
7. Compression coil spring	16. Spiral gear	25. Rubber cap
8. Thrust bearing	17. Pin	
9. Washer	18. Vacuum unit	

Electronic ignition distributor used on 20R engines

1. Alternator pulley	8. Bearing retainer plate	15. Rectifier end frame
2. Alternator fan	9. Space ring	assembly
3. Space collar	10. Snap-ring	16. Rear end cover
4. Drive end frame	11. Alternator rotor assembly	17. B terminal insulator
assembly	12. Bearing	18. Insulator
5. Felt	13. Alternator stator assembly	19. Brush spring
6. Felt cover	14. Holder with rectifiers	20. Alternator brush
7. Bearing		

Typical 1977–80 alternator

REMOVAL & INSTALLATION

NOTE: On some models the alternator is mounted very low on the engine. On these models it may be necessary to remove the gravel shield and work from underneath the car in order to gain access to the alternator.

1. Unfasten the starter-to-battery cable at the battery end.
2. Remove the air cleaner, if necessary, to gain access to the alternator.
3. Unfasten the bolts which attach the adjusting link to the alternator. Remove the alternator drive belt.
4. Unfasten and tag the alternator wiring connection.
5. Remove the alternator attaching bolt and then withdraw the alternator from its bracket.
6. Installation is the reverse order of removal. After installing the alternator, adjust the belt tension.

BELT TENSION ADJUSTMENT

Inspection and adjustment to the alternator drive belt should be performed every 3,000 miles or if the alternator has been removed.

1. Inspect the drive belt to see that it is not cracked or worn. Be sure that its surfaces are free of grease or oil.
2. Push down on the belt halfway between the fan and the alternator pulleys, (or crankshaft pulley) with thumb pressure. Belt deflection should be ⅜–½ in.
3. If the belt tension requires adjustment, loosen the adjusting link bolt and move the alternator until the proper belt tension is obtained.

--- CAUTION ---
Do not overtighten the belt; damage to the alternator bearings could result.

4. Tighten the adjusting link bolt.

Voltage Regulator

REMOVAL & INSTALLATION

1. Disconnect the negative battery cable.
2. Disconnect the wiring harness.

NOTE: On Land Cruisers disconnect the leads from their screw terminals after noting their position for installation.

3. Remove the retaining hardware and remove the regulator.
4. To install, attach the new regulator to the compartment panel, replace the wiring harness, and connect the battery cable.

Fan (IC Regulator Type)

Space Collar

Space Collar

Front Bearing

Space Collar
(IC Regulator Type)

Rear Bearing

Rotor

Stator Assembly

Space Collar
(TIRRILL Regulator Type)

Pulley

Drive End Frame

Fan (TIRRILL Regulator Type)

Insulator

Noise Supression

IC Regulator Type

Spring

Insulator

Rear End Frame

Brush

Rectifier

TIRRILL Regulator Type

Spring

Insulator

Insulator

Brush

Rectifier

Rear End Frame

1981–84 alternators

VOLTAGE ADJUSTMENT

NOTE: Only external regulators used with gasoline engines are adjustable.

1. Connect a voltmeter to the battery terminals.
2. Start the engine and gradually increase the engine speed to about 1,500 rpm. (2000 rpm for Land Cruisers).
3. At this speed, the voltage reading should be 13.8–14.8 volts.
4. If the voltage does not fall within this range, a minor adjustment may be made to the adjusting arm. Disconnect the ground cable of the battery and remove the regu-

lator cover. Bend the adjusting arm very slightly with a pair of needle nose pliers. Replace the cover and battery cable.

FIELD RELAY ADJUSTMENT

NOTE: Only external regulators used with gasoline engines are adjustable.

NOTE: This adjustment does not apply to Land Cruisers.

1. Remove the cover from the regulator assembly.
2. Use a feeler gauge to check the

amount that the contact spring is deflected while the armature is being depressed.
3. If the measurement is not 0.008″–0.018″, adjust the regulator by bending point holder P (See illustration).

CONTACT SPRING DEFLECTION

ADJUSTING ARM

POINT HOLDER (P₁)

POINT HOLDER (P₂)

POINT GAP

Field relay internal parts—external regulator

Pulley

Fan

Drive End Frame

Felt

Bearing

Retainer

Felt Cover

IC Regulator

Insulator

Rubber Washer

Felt Washer Cover

Felt

Spring

Brush Holder

Brush

Brush Holder Cover

Space Ring

Rotor

Stator Assembly

Insulator

Snap Ring

Rectifier Holder

Collar

Rear End Frame

Insulator

Rubber Cap

Diesel engine alternator

Magnetic Switch Assembly

Return Spring

Steel Ball

Starter Clutch Assembly

Idle Gear

Bearing

Starter Housing

Plate Washer

Lock Washer

Brush Spring

Brush

End Cover

O-Ring

Bearing

Bearing

Armature

Bearing

Felt Seal

Brush Holder

Field Frame

Diesel engine starter

T624

4. Check the point gap with a feeler gauge. The gap should be 0.016"–0.047".

5. Adjust the point gap, as required, by bending the point holder P (See illustration.)

6. Clean off the points with emery cloth if they are dirty and wash them with solvent.

VOLTAGE REGULATOR ADJUSTMENT

NOTE: Only external regulators used with gasoline engines are adjustable.

1. The air (armature) gap must measure 0.008 in. If it does not, adjust by bending the low speed point holder.

2. Measure the point gap with a feeler gauge. It should be 0.010–0.018 in. If it is not, bend the high speed point holder to correct the adjustment. Clean the points with emery paper and use a solvent to remove the dust.

Voltage regulator components—external regulator

3. Check the contact spring deflection with the armature depressed. It should measure between 0.008–0.018 in. as it does on the field relay. If it does not, REPLACE the regulator.

4. Perform the voltage test again. If the voltage reading cannot be brought to specification, replace the voltage regulator. If this fails to correct the situation, the alternator then must be suspected as the defective unit.

Starter

REMOVAL & INSTALLATION

1. Disconnect the cable which runs from the starter to the battery, at the battery end.

2. Remove the air cleaner assembly, if necessary, to gain access to the starter.

NOTE: On some models with automatic transmissions, it may be necessary to disconnect the throttle linkage connecting rod.

3. Disconnect all the wiring at the starter.

4. Remove the starter toward the front of the vehicle.

5. Installation is the reverse order of removal.

1. Solenoid
2. Engagement lever
3. Armature
4. Overrunning clutch
5. Clutch stop
6. Snap-ring
7. Drive housing
8. Bushing

9. Bearing cover
10. Bearing cover
11. Commutator end frame
12. Rubber bushing

13. Rubber grommet
14. Plate
15. Lock plate
16. Washer

17. Brake spring
18. Gasket
19. Brush
20. Brush spring
21. Brush holder
22. Field coil
23. Pole shoes
24. Field yoke

Direct drive starter components

SOLENOID AND BRUSH REPLACEMENT

Direct Drive Type

NOTE: The starter must be removed from the vehicle in order to perform this operation.

1. Remove the field coil lead from the solenoid terminal.

2. Unfasten the solenoid retaining screws. Remove the solenoid by tilting it upward and withdrawing it.

3. Remove the end frame bearing cover screws and remove the cover.

4. Remove the thru-bolts. Remove the commutator end-frame.

1. Field frame assembly
2. Armature
3. Felt seal
4. Brush spring

5. Brush holder
6. O-ring
7. Pinion gear
8. Idler gear

9. Magnetic switch assembly
10. Steel ball
11. Clutch assembly
12. Starter housing

Typical 1977–80 starter

1.0 kW Type

Through Bolt

Brush Spring

Field Frame

Bearing

Armature

Bearing

Felt Seal

Bearing

Bearing

Idle Gear

Magnetic Switch Assembly

Brush Holder

End Cover

Spring

Steel Ball

Starter Housing

Starter Clutch Assembly

1.4 kW Type

O-Ring

End Cover

O-Ring

O-Ring

Brush Spring

Field Frame

Armature

Bearing

O-Ring

Bearing

Brush Holder

Through Bolt

Idle Gear

Steel Ball

Pinion Gear

Starter Clutch Assembly

Bearing

Spring

Starter Housing

Magnetic Switch Assembly

1981–84 22R starter

5. Withdraw the brushes from their holder if they are to be replaced.

6. Check the brush length against the specification in the Battery and Starter Specifications chart. Replace the brushes with new ones if required.

7. Dress the new brushes with emery cloth so that they will make proper contact.

8. Use a spring scale to check the brush spring tension against the specification in the chart. Replace the springs if they do not meet specification.

Assembly is the reverse of disassembly. Pack the end bearing cover with multipurpose grease before installing it.

Reduction Type

NOTE: The starter must be removed from the vehicle, in order to perform this operation.

1. Disconnect the solenoid lead.

2. Loosen the two bolts on the starter housing and separate the field frame from the solenoid. Remove the O-ring and felt dust seal.

3. Remove the two screws and separate the starter drive from the solenoid.

4. Withdraw the clutch and gears. Remove the ball from the clutch shaft bore or solenoid.

5. Remove the brushes from the holder.

6. Measure brush length and compare it to the specification given in the Battery and Starter Specifications chart. Replace the brushes if they are too short.

7. Check the gears for wear or damage. Replace as required.

Assembly is the reverse of disassembly. Lubricate all bearings and gears with high temperature grease. Grease the ball before inserting it in the clutch shaft bore. Align the tab on the brush holder with the notch on the field frame. Check the positive (+) brush leads to see that they aren't grounded. Align the mark on the solenoid with the bolt anchors on the field frame.

ENGINE MECHANICAL

Engine

REMOVAL & INSTALLATION

Two Wheel Drive Pickups
GASOLINE ENGINES

1. Drain the radiator, cooling system, transmission, and engine oil.

2. Disconnect the battery-to-starter cable at the positive battery terminal.

3. Scribe marks on the hood and its hinges to aid in alignment during installation.

4. Remove the hood supports from the body. Remove the hood.

NOTE: Do not remove the supports from the hood.

5. Remove the headlight bezel and the radiator grille.

6. Remove the fan shroud, the hood lock base and the base support.

7. Detach both the upper and lower hoses from the radiator. On cars with automatic transmissions, disconnect the lines from the oil cooler. Remove the radiator.

8. Unfasten the clamps and remove the heater and bypass hoses from the engine. Remove the heater control cable from the water valve.

9. Remove the wiring from the coolant temperature and oil pressure sending units.

10. Remove the air cleaner from its bracket, complete with its attendant hoses.

11. Unfasten the accelerator torque rod from the carburetor. On models equipped with automatic transmissions, remove the transmission linkage as well.

12. Remove the emission control system hoses and wiring, as necessary.

13. Remove the clutch hydraulic line support bracket.

14. Unfasten the high-tension and primary wires from the coil.

15. Mark the spark plug cables and remove them from the distributor.

16. Detach the right-hand front engine mount.

17. Remove the fuel line at the pump.

18. Detach the downpipe from the exhaust manifold.

19. Detach the left-hand front engine mount.

20. Disconnect all the wiring harness multiconnectors.

Perform the following steps on models with manual transmissions:

21. Remove the center console if so equipped.

22. Remove the shift lever boot(s).

23. Unfasten the four shift lever cap retaining screws. Remove the cap and withdraw the shift lever assembly.

Perform the following steps on models equipped with automatic transmission:

24. Remove the transmission selector linkage:

   a. On models equipped with a floor-mounted selector, disconnect the control rod from the transmission.

   b. On column-mounted gear selector models, remove the shifter rod.

25. Disconnect the neutral safety switch wiring connector.

Perform the following steps on all models:

26. Raise the rear of the vehicle with jacks and support it on jackstands.

27. Remove the retaining screws and remove the parking brake equalizer support bracket. Disconnect the cable which runs between the lever and the equalizer.

28. Remove the speedometer cable from the transmission. Disconnect the back-up wiring.

29. Detach the driveshaft from the rear of the transmission.

NOTE: If oil runs out of the transmission, an old U-joint yoke sleeve makes an excellent plug.

30. Detach the clutch release cylinder assembly, complete with hydraulic lines. Do not disconnect the lines.

31. Unbolt the rear support member mounting insulators.

32. Support the transmission and detach the rear support member retaining bolts. Withdraw the support member from under the car.

33. Install lifting hooks on the engine lifting brackets. Attach a suitable hoist to the engine.

34. Remove the jack from under the transmission.

35. Raise the engine and move it toward the front of the car. Use care to avoid damaging the components which remain on the car.

36. Support the engine on a workstand. Install the engine in the reverse order of removal. Adjust all of the linkages as detailed in the appropriate section. Install the hood and adjust it. Replenish the fluid levels in the engine, radiator, and transmission.

DIESEL ENGINE

1. Make accurate marks on the body to indicate the relationship between the hood supports and the body. Unbolt the hood supports at the body and remove the hood.

2. Disconnect and remove both batteries from the vehicle.

3. Drain the cooling system and remove the radiator, shroud, and radiator hoses.

4. If the vehicle is equipped with air conditioning, remove the compressor drive belt, unbolt the compressor and tie the compressor out of the way. Do not disconnect the refrigerant lines from the compressor.

5. Remove the engine cooling fan, pulley, and drive belt.

6. Disconnect the two heater hoses from the left side of the engine.

7. Disconnect the vacuum reservoir hose from the rear of the alternator.

8. Disconnect the vacuum hose from the "idle-up" unit, if the vehicle is equipped with air conditioning.

9. Disconnect the fuel hoses from the fuel pump return connection and the sedimenter inlet connection.

10. Disconnect the wiring from the following components:

   a. Alternator
   b. Thermo-switch
   c. Oil pressure switch
   d. No. 1 glow plug relay (terminal +B)
   e. Starter

Mark these wires and tie them out of the way.

11. Disconnect the wiring from the left fender and the injection pump (accelerator wire). Also mark and tie these wires out of the way.

12. Using Toyota special service tool #09305-20012 or its equivalent, remove

the transmission shift lever from inside the vehicle.

13. Raise the vehicle and support it safely.

14. Drain the engine oil.

15. Remove the engine under-cover and remove the backup light switch wire.

16. Remove the engine shock absorber.

17. Remove the propeller (drive) shaft from the vehicle. Mark the propeller shaft and the companion flange so that the shaft may be reinstalled in its original position.

18. Disconnect the speedometer cable from the transmission.

19. Disconnect the exhaust pipe clamp from the transmission housing and the exhaust pipe mounting nuts from the exhaust manifold.

20. Unbolt the clutch release cylinder and lay the cylinder alongside the frame.

21. Remove the engine mounting bolts from each side of the engine.

22. Place a jack under the transmission so that it just touches the transmission.

23. Unbolt the transmission mounting bracket from the transmission and the crossmember. Remove the bracket.

24. Attach the engine lifting equipment to the engine.

25. Check that all wiring and hoses are clear of the engine and transmission.

26. Carefully raise the engine and transmission assembly out of the engine compartment, being especially careful not to damage the air conditioning compressor, if so equipped.

27. Remove the starter, and with the help of an assistant, disconnect the transmission from the engine. Mount the engine securely in a workstand and service the engine as necessary, according to the appropriate sections of this book.

28. Reverse the previous steps to install the engine. Replenish the fluids in the engine, cooling system, and transmission, if required.

Four Wheel Drive Pickups

─────── CAUTION ───────

Be sure to support the rear of the engine with a jack to avoid damage to the front motor mounts while performing engine removal procedures!

1. Set the engine to top dead center according to the marks on the vibration damper and timing cover pointer.

2. Remove the transmission and transfer case according to the procedures found in the appropriate sections.

3. Make accurate marks on the body to indicate the relationship between the hood supports and the body. Unbolt the hood supports at the body and remove the hood.

4. Remove the battery and the air cleaner assembly. Mark the hoses from the air cleaner to simplify installation.

5. Drain the cooling system and remove the radiator hoses.

6. Remove the radiator fan shroud and disconnect the heater outlet hose at the radiator.

7. Remove the radiator.

8. If the vehicle is equipped with air conditioning, remove the compressor drive belt, unbolt the compressor and tie it out of the way. It is not necessary to disconnect the refrigerant lines.

9. Remove the water pump drive belt, pulley and cooling fan.

10. Disconnect the heater inlet hose, brake booster hose and emission control hoses. Move the hoses out of the way and tie if necessary. Mark the hose locations to simplify installation.

11. Disconnect the two fuel hoses from the pipes beneath the intake manifold.

12. Disconnect all wiring attached to the engine. Mark the wire locations to simplify installation.

13. Remove the high voltage wiring from the spark plugs, distributor and ignition coil. Be sure to mark the spark plug wire locations.

14. Disconnect the accelerator linkage at the carburetor.

15. Attach an engine hoist to the engine but do not raise the hoist.

16. Remove the two engine mount-to-frame bolts from each side of the engine.

17. Be sure that all wires and hoses are clear of the engine.

18. Carefully raise the engine out of the engine compartment, being especially careful not to damage the air conditioning condensor, if so equipped.

19. Securely mount the engine on a workstand.

20. Perform the necessary service(s) to the engine according to the appropriate sections of the book.

21. Reverse the previous steps to install the engine. Replenish the fluids in the engine, cooling system, and transmission.

Land Cruiser and Wagon

1. Scribe marks on the hood and hinges to aid in alignment during installation. Remove the hinge bolts from the hood and then remove the hood.

2. Drain the cooling system and engine oil.

3. Unfasten the radiator grille mounting bolts and remove the grille.

NOTE: On station wagon models, remove the parking light assembly and wiring first.

4. Remove the hood latch support rod. Detach the hood latch assembly from the radiator upper bracket. Remove the bracket.

5. Disconnect the heater hose from the radiator.

6. Detach the upper radiator hose at the water outlet housing and the lower hose at water pump.

7. Remove the six bolts which secure the radiator and lift the radiator out of the vehicle.

8. Remove the heater hoses from the water valve and heater box. Disconnect the temperature control cable from the water valve.

9. Detach both the the battery cables and remove the battery.

10. Remove the wires from the starter solenoid terminal.

11. Detach the fuel lines from the pump and remove the fuel filter assembly.

12. Disconnect the primary wire from the ignition coil.

13. Detach both of the intermediate rods from the shifter shafts (columnshift models only).

14. Remove the air cleaner assembly complete with hoses, from its bracket.

15. Remove the emission control system cables and hoses as necessary.

16. Disconnect the alternator multiconnector.

17. Disconnect the hand throttle, accelerator, and choke linkages from the carburetor.

18. On models equipped with vacuum assisted 4WD engagement, remove the control unit vacuum hose from its manifold fitting.

19. Disconnect the oil pressure and water temperature gauge sender's wiring.

20. Unfasten the downpipe from the exhaust manifold.

21. Detach the parking brake cable from the intermediate lever.

22. Unbolt the front driveshaft from the flange on the transfer case output shaft.

23. Remove both the left and right engine stone shields. Remove the transmission skid-plate.

24. Remove the cotter pin and disconnect both the high- and low-range shifter rods from their respective inner levers.

25. Remove the high/low range shifter link lever and the high/low shift rod.

26. Disconnect the clutch release fork spring. Remove the clutch release cylinder from its mounting bracket at the rear of the engine.

27. Unfasten the clamp screws and withdraw the vacuum lines from the transfer case control unit vacuum chamber (only on models with vacuum-assisted 4WD engagement).

28. Remove the 4WD indicator switch assembly.

29. Unfasten the speedometer cable from the transmission.

30. Disconnect the rear driveshaft from the transmission.

31. Detach the gearshift rod and gear selector rod from the shift outer lever and the gear selector outer lever, respectively.

32. Unbolt the rear engine mounts from the frame.

33. Perform Step 32 to the front engine mounts.

34. Install lifting hooks on the engine lift-points and connect a hoist.

35. Lift the engine slightly and toward the front, so the engine/transmission assembly clears the front of the vehicle.

Engine removal is performed in the reverse order of its installation. Refill the engine with coolant and lubricant. Check and adjust all linkages, as outlined in the appropriate section. Install the hood and align the matchmarks.

Cylinder Head

——— CAUTION ———

Do not perform this operation on a warm engine. Remove the head bolts in the reverse of the tightening sequence. Loosen the head bolts evenly, not one at a time. Keep the pushrods in their original order. Do not attempt to slide the cylinder head off of the block, as it is located with dowel pins. Lift the head straight up and off the block.

REMOVAL & INSTALLATION

20R, 22R, and 22R-E Engines

1. Disconnect the battery, negative cable first.

2. Remove the three exhaust pipe flange nuts and separate the pipe from the manifold.

3. Drain the cooling system, both the radiator and the block. The engine block drain is on the driver's side of the engine. The coolant, if good, may be reused.

4. Remove the air cleaner assembly complete with hoses.

NOTE: Cover the carburetor or throttle body with a clean cloth so that nothing can fall into it.

5. Tag all the various vacuum and emission hoses for reassembly and disconnect them at the engine throttle body or carburetor. Remove all linkages, fuel lines, coolant lines, etc., from the throttle body carburetor, cylinder head, and manifolds. Remove the wire supports.

6. Mark the spark plug leads and disconnect them from the plugs.

7. Matchmark the distributor housing and the engine block. Disconnect the high tension wire and the primary lead and remove the distributor. Installation will be easier if you leave the cap and spark plug wires in place.

8. Remove the four nuts which secure the valve cover. On fuel injected engines, remove the throttle body and air valve from the intake manifold.

20R and 22R engines—rotate the camshaft so that the pin is at the top. Also note that the arrow on the camshaft bearing cap points to the front of the engine.

1. Rocker arm	9. Cam sprocket
2. Spring	10. Camshaft
3. Spacer	11. Camshaft bearing cap
4. Rocker shaft (intake)	12. Valve keeper
5. Head bolt	13. Spring retainer
6. Rocker stand	14. Valve spring
7. Rocker shaft (exhaust)	15. Valve seal
8. Distributor drive gear	16. Spring seat

17. Valve guide
18. Half circle cam seal
19. Cylinder head
20. Intake valve
21. Exhaust valve
22. Rear cover (EGR cooler)

Supply part

Cylinder head components—20R and 22R engines

9. Remove the rubber half circle cam seals. Remove the camshaft sprocket bolt. Slide the distributor drive gear off the camshaft and wire the cam sprocket in place to the timing chain.

10. Remove the timing chain cover bolt at the front of the head. This must be done before the head bolts are loosened.

11. Remove the cylinder head bolts. Loosen the bolts in two or three stages.

NOTE: Improper removal of the cylinder head bolts can cause head warpage.

12. Using pry bars applied evenly at the front and rear of the valve rocker assembly, pry the assembly off its mounting dowels.

13. Lift the head straight up off its dowels. Do NOT pry it off, or attempt to slide it off.

14. Drain the engine oil from the crankcase after the head has been removed, because the oil will become contaminated with coolant when the head is removed.

NOTE: Service procedures are covered in the Unit Repair Section.

Installation is as follows:

1. Clean off the top of the cylinder block and the head, using a scraper or a razor blade. Be careful not to gouge the aluminum head. You may also want to clean off the tops of the pistons, but as this requires rotation of the crankshaft, you must be careful to keep sufficient tension on the cam

chain to prevent it from slipping a tooth. Vacuum out any bits which have fallen into the cylinders, being careful not to nick the cylinder walls.

2. Apply a liquid sealer to the front corners of the block and install a new head gasket.

3. Lower the head over the locating dowels. Do not attempt to slide it into place.

4. Rotate the camshaft so that the sprocket aligning pin is at the top. Remove the wire and hold the cam sprocket tight against the chain. Manually rotate the engine so that the cam sprocket hole is also at the top. Wire the sprocket in place again.

5. Install the rocker arm assembly over its positioning dowels.

6. Clean the threads of the cylinder head bolts thoroughly and give them a light coat of oil. Install them and tighten evenly, in three stages, in the sequence shown. Torque

Cylinder head bolt tightening sequence—20R and 22R engines

the bolts to the values located in the Torque Specification Chart.

7. Install the timing chain cover bolt and tighten it to 7–12 ft. lbs.

8. Remove the wire and fit the sprocket over the camshaft dowel. If the chain won't allow the sprocket to reach, rotate the crankshaft back and forth, while lifting up on the chain and sprocket.

9. Install the distributor drive gear and tighten the sprocket bolt to 51–65 ft. lbs.

10. Adjust the valves as outlined earlier. After completing the adjustment, rotate the crankshaft 352°, so that the 8° BTDC mark on the pulley aligns with the timing mark on the block.

11. Install the distributor, as outlined earlier.

12. Install the spark plugs and leads.

13. Make sure the oil drain plug is in-stalled. Install the rubber half circle cam seals and fill the engine with oil. Pour the oil over the top of the head, onto the distributor drive gear and the valve rockers.

14. Install the rocker cover and tighten the nuts to 7–12 ft. lbs.

15. Connect all the vacuum hoses and electrical leads which were removed during disassembly. Reconnect the fuel line. Install the spark plug lead clips onto the rocker cover. Fill the cooling system. Install the air cleaner.

16. Tighten the exhaust pipe manifold nuts to 25–33 ft. lbs.

17. Reconnect the battery, negative ca-ble last. Start the engine and allow it to reach normal operating temperature. Check the timing and adjust the idle speed and mixture. Shut off the engine and reset the valves.

Diesel Engine

1. Disconnect the cables from both batteries.

2. Remove the air cleaner assembly.

3. Drain the cooling system and re-move the radiator, shroud, and radiator hoses.

4. If the vehicle is equipped with air conditioning, remove the compressor drive belt and unbolt the compressor from its mounting brackets. Tie the compressor out of the way. Do not remove the refrigerant lines.

5. Remove the engine cooling fan, pul-ley, and drive belt.

6. Disconnect the heater hoses at the engine and move the hoses aside.

7. Disconnect the cables which are po-sitioned above the valve cover and move the cables aside.

1. Glow plug
2. Injection pipe and fuel pipe
3. Injection nozzle holder and linkage pipe
4. Intake manifold
5. Exhaust manifold
6. Fan, fan pulley and crankshaft pulley
7. Timing gear cover and belt guide
8. Cylinder head cover
9. Idle pulley and timing belt
10. Crankshaft timing pulley
11. Pump drive pulley
12. Camshaft timing pulley
13. No. 2 oil seal retainer
14. Valve rocker shaft assembly
15. Camshaft
16. Cylinder head
17. Valve and compression spring
18. Combustion chamber subassembly

Cylinder head and related components—diesel engine

8. Remove the valve cover and upper front engine cover.

9. Disconnect and remove the glow plugs.

10. Disconnect the fuel injection lines at the injectors and the injection pump. Remove the lines.

11. Remove the fuel injectors. Arrange the injectors so that they may be reinstalled in their original locations.

12. Unbolt and remove the intake manifold assembly. Also remove the water outlet housing from the cylinder head.

13. Unbolt the exhaust manifold from the cylinder head. Secure the manifold in a position away from the cylinder head.

14. Disconnect the fuel feed line at the injection pump and plug the line.

15. Using a wrench on the center crankshaft pulley bolt, rotate the engine (clockwise only) until the TDC mark on the pulley is aligned with the pointer. Check that the valves on the number one cylinder are closed (rocker arms loose). If the valves are not closed, rotate the engine 360° and again align the TDC mark with the pointer.

16. Remove the crankshaft pulley using a puller.

17. Remove the timing belt cover from the front of the engine and the timing belt guide from the front of the crankshaft timing gear.

18. Remove the timing belt idler pulley. If the timing belt is to be reused, mark the belt and all timing gears to indicate their relationships. Remove the timing belt.

19. Remove the timing gear from the camshaft, using a puller.

20. Remove the camshaft oil seal retainer.

21. Gradually loosen the rocker shaft support nuts, working from the ends towards the center. Remove the rocker shaft and arms as an assembly.

22. Gradually remove the cylinder head bolts in the reverse order of the installation torque sequence.

23. Remove the cylinder head from the engine. Refer to the Unit Repair section for cylinder head service information.

Installation of the cylinder head is basically the reverse of the previous steps. Note the following points:

a. Clean the mating surfaces of the cylinder block and head, and use a NEW head gasket during installation.

1. Rocker arm and shaft assembly
2. Pushrods
3. Cylinder head
4. Intake and exhaust manifold gasket
5. Valve keepers
6. Valve spring retainer
7. Valve seal
8. Valve spring
9. Valve spring seat
10. Exhaust valve
11. Intake valve

Cylinder head components—2F engine

b. DO NOT rotate the engine while the cylinder head is removed.

c. Torque the cylinder head bolts gradually, following the head bolt tightening sequence.

d. Align the timing marks according to the illustration accompanying the Timing Belt Removal and Installation procedure.

e. Replenish the cooling system with the proper type and quantity of coolant.

f. Check for leaks after the engine has been started.

2F Engine

1. Disconnect the battery and drain the cooling system.

2. Remove the air cleaner assembly from its bracket, complete with its attendant hoses.

3. Detach the accelerator cable from its support on the cylinder head cover and also from the carburetor throttle arm.

4. Remove the choke cable and fuel lines from the carburetor.

5. Remove the water hose bracket from the cylinder head cover.

6. Unfasten the water hose clamps and remove the hoses from the water pump and the water valve. Detach the heater temperature control cable from the water valve.

7. Disconnect the PCV line from the cylinder head cover.

8. Disconnect the vacuum lines, which run from the vacuum switching valve, at the various components of the emission control system.

9. Drain the engine oil. Unfasten the

oil lines from the oil filter and remove the filter assembly from the manifold.

10. Detach the vacuum valve solenoid wire from the coil.

11. Disconnect any remaining lines from the carburetor and remove the carburetor from the manifold.

12. Unfasten the alternator adjusting link and then remove the drivebelt and the alternator.

13. Disconnect the distributor vacuum line from the distributor. Remove the wire from its supports on the head.

14. Disconnect the carburetor fuel line from the fuel pump. Remove the line.

15. Disconnect the spark plug and coil cables, after marking their respective locations.

16. Unfasten the primary wire from the distributor. Remove the distributor clamp bolts and withdraw the distributor.

17. Remove the oil gauge sending unit.

18. Remove the coil from its bracket on the cylinder head.

19. Remove the fuel pump.

20. Remove the oil filter tube clamping bolt from the valve lifter (side) cover. Drive the oil filler tube out of the cylinder block.

21. Remove the combination intake/exhaust manifold from the cylinder block.

22. Take off the cylinder head cover and its gasket.

23. Unfasten the oil delivery union, spring, and sleeve from the valve rocker shafts.

24. Unfasten the securing nuts and bolts

Cylinder head bolt tightening sequence— diesel engine

from the valve rocker shaft supports. Withdraw the rocker assembly.

25. Withdraw the pushrods from their bores. Be sure to keep them in the same order in which they were removed.

26. Remove the valve lifter (side) cover and gasket.

27. Withdraw the valve lifters from the block.

NOTE: The valve lifters should be kept, with their respective pushrods, in the sequence in which they were removed.

28. Unfasten the oil delivery union from the oil feed pipe.

29. Loosen the cylinder head bolts in two or three stages and in the order illustrated above.

30. Lift off the cylinder head and the gasket.

NOTE: Service procedures are covered in the Unit Repair Section.

Installation of the cylinder head is performed in the following order:

1. Clean the gasket mounting surfaces of both the cylinder head and block.

2. Place a *new* head gasket over the dowels on the block.

3. Lower the cylinder head on to the block with the air cleaner mounting bracket attached.

4. Tighten the bolts, in stages, and in the sequence illustrated, to the specified torque.

5. Install the oil feed pipe.

6. Place each valve lifter in the original position from which it came.

NOTE: Do not interchange valve lifters.

7. Perform step 6 for the pushrods, being careful to mate each pushrod with its original lifter.

8. Install the valve rocker assembly, oil delivery union, spring, and connecting sleeve in the head. Tighten the rocker assembly support nuts and bolts to the following torque specifications, in several stages:

10mm nuts and bolts—25–30 ft. lbs.
8mm bolts—14–22 ft. lbs.

9. Adjust the valves, as outlined above, to the following *cold* specifications (each piston TDC of its compression stroke):

Intake—0.008 in.
Exhaust—0.014 in.

NOTE: Adjust the valve clearance again after the engine is assembled and warmed up.

10. The rest of cylinder head installation is performed in the reverse order of the removal procedure.

Cylinder head bolt tightening sequence—2F engines

T632

Valve Rocker Shafts

REMOVAL & INSTALLATION

Gasoline Engines

Valve rocker shaft removal and installation is given as part of the cylinder head removal and installation procedure. Perform only the steps of the appropriate procedure necessary to remove or install the rocker shafts.

Note that on the 20R and 22R engines all of the rocker arms are the same, but all of the rocker shafts are different. Keep all parts in order so that they may be installed correctly. Lubricate all parts with engine oil prior to assembly.

Diesel Engine

1. Disconnect the cables which are positioned above the valve cover and move the cables aside.

2. Remove the valve cover.

3. Gradually loosen the rocker shaft support fasteners, working from the ends towards the center. Remove the rocker shaft and arms as an assembly. It is not necessary to remove the timing belt or related components.

4. To install the rocker shaft assembly, gradually tighten the support bolts, working from the center towards the ends. Finally tighten the bolts to 11–15 ft. lbs.

5. Adjust the valves as previously outlined and install the valve cover. Reposition and connect the cables which were moved during step 1.

Intake Manifold

REMOVAL & INSTALLATION

20R, 22R and 22R-E Engines

1. Disconnect the battery, negative cable first.

2. Drain the cooling system.

3. Remove the air cleaner assembly, complete with hoses.

4. Disconnect the vacuum lines from the manifold, EFI system or carburetor. Tag them for assembly.

5. Remove the fuel line, accelerator linkage, electrical leads, and coolant hose from the carburetor or EFI system.

6. Remove the coolant bypass hose from the manifold.

1. Vacuum fitting   4. Gasket
2. Intake manifold   5. Cover
3. Gasket

20R and 22R engine intake manifold components

7. On the 22 R-E, remove the throttle body and air valve from the manifold.

8. Unbolt and remove the intake manifold, complete with carburetor and EGR valve, or delivery pipe and nozzles.

9. Cover the cylinder head intake ports with a clean cloth.

Installation is the reverse of the removal. Use a new gasket, and torque the mounting nuts to the torque specified in the Torque Specifications Chart. Tighten the bolts in several stages, working from the inside bolts outward. Refill the cooling system.

Combination Manifold

REMOVAL & INSTALLATION

2F Engines

1. Remove the air cleaner assembly, complete with hoses.

2. Disconnect the accelerator and choke linkages from the carburetor, as well as the fuel and vacuum lines. Remove the hand throttle linkage.

3. Remove, or move aside, any of the emission control system components which are in the way.

4. Disconnect the oil filter lines and remove the oil filter assembly from the intake manifold. Unfasten the solenoid valve wire from the ignition coil terminal. Remove the EGR pipes from the exhaust gas cooler, if so equipped.

5. Unfasten the retaining bolts and remove the carburetor from the manifold.

6. Loosen the manifold retaining nuts, working from the inside out, in two or three stages.

Rocker shaft assembly of the diesel engine

7. Remove the intake/exhaust manifold assembly from the cylinder head as a complete unit.

Installation is performed in the reverse order of removal. Always use *new* gaskets. Tighten the bolts, working from the inside out.

NOTE: Tighten the bolts in two or three stages.

Exhaust Manifold

REMOVAL & INSTALLATION
20R, 22R and 22R-E Engines

1. Remove the three exhaust pipe flange bolts and disconnect the exhaust pipe from the manifold.

2. Disconnect the spark plug leads.

3. Matchmark the distributor rotor, housing and the engine block. Remove the distributor.

4. Remove the air cleaner tube from the heat stove. Remove the outer part of the heat stove.

a. Heat control valve bimetal case	d. Retaining spring
b. Valve coil	e. Heat control valve
c. Bolt	f. Heat control valve shaft
	g. Dowel

h. Manifold gasket
i. Counter weight stop
j. Exhaust manifold
k. Screw plug

2F engine combination manifold components

1. Inner heat stove
2. Exhaust manifold
3. Gasket
4. Gasket
5. Outer heat stove

20R and 22R engine exhaust manifold components

5. Remove the manifold (14 mm nuts), complete with air injection tubes and the inner portion of the heat stove.

6. Separate the inner portion of the heat stove from the manifold.

Installation is the reverse of removal. Tighten the retaining nuts to 29–36 ft. lbs., working from the inside out. Install the distributor and set the timing. Tighten the exhaust pipe flange nuts to 25–32 ft. lbs.

Diesel Manifolding

Removal of the intake manifold of the diesel engine requires removal of the air cleaner assembly, injection lines, and related hoses and bracketry. If you are in doubt during the disconnection of any item, be sure to mark the item so that it may be properly reinstalled. Before installing the manifold, be sure to clean the cylinder head and manifold mating surfaces of the old gasket material, and use a new gasket when installing the manifold.

The exhaust manifold is retained to the cylinder head with eight fasteners. Disconnect the exhaust pipe from the manifold and remove these fasteners to remove the exhaust manifold. On models with air conditioning, it may be necessary to remove the air conditioning compressor from the mounting brackets (without disconnecting the refrigerant lines) and tie the compressor out of the way. Also remove the compressor mounting bracket(s) if interference is encountered. Be sure that the manifold and cylinder head mating surfaces are clean, and install a new exhaust manifold gasket during manifold installation.

Refer to the torque specifications listed at the beginning of this secion to determine the required tightening torque of the fasteners.

Front Cover

REMOVAL & INSTALLATION
20R, 22R and 22R-E Engines

1. Remove the cylinder head as previously outlined.

20R and 22R engines—only the six bolts indicated need to be removed to remove the timing cover

2. After draining oil, remove the oil pan and its gasket.

3. Remove the radiator.

4. Remove the fan and drive belts.

5. Remove the air pump, hoses, and bracket, if so equipped.

6. Remove the alternator adjuster bracket and move it towards the alternator.

7. Remove the center bolt on the crankshaft pulley. Using a gear puller, remove the crankshaft pulley.

— **CAUTION** —
Do not remove the 10 mm bolt from the hole in the pulley, if present. It has been installed to correctly balance the engine.

8. Remove the 2 water bypass tube bolts, the one bolt at the rear of the cover on the left side (behind the coolant inlet pipe), and the six bolts on the front of the timing cover. Gently tap the timing cover off with a plastic faced hammer. If removal is difficult, there is probably a bolt still in place.

9. When installing, use a new gasket on the timing cover and oil pan. Use sealer at the corners of the oil pan. Tighten the timing cover bolts to 7–12 ft. lbs. Tighten the oil pan bolts to 35–70 in. lbs.

10. Install the crankshaft pulley. Tighten the bolt to 80–94 ft. lbs.

— **CAUTION** —
Do not allow the pulley to rotate when tightening the pulley bolt.

11. Further installation is the reverse of removal.

Diesel Engine

Refer to steps 1–8, then 15–17 of the Cylinder Head Removal and Installation procedure. Torque the timing belt cover fasteners to 3–5 ft. lbs., and the crankshaft pulley center bolt to 69–75 ft. lbs.

2F Engines

1. Drain the cooling system and the crankcase.

2. Disconnect the battery.

3. Remove the air cleaner assembly, complete with hoses, from its bracket.

4. Remove the hood latch as well as its brace and support.

5. Remove the headlight bezels and grille assembly.

6. Unfasten the upper and lower radiator hose clamps and remove both of the hoses from the engine.

7. Unfasten the radiator securing bolts and remove the radiator.

NOTE: Take off the shroud first, if so equipped.

8. Loosen the drive belt adjusting link and remove the drive belt. Unfasten the alternator multiconnector, withdraw the retaining bolts, and remove the alternator.

9. Perform step 8 to the air injection pump, if so equipped. Disconnect the hoses from the pump before removing it.

10. Remove the fan and water pump as an assembly.

11. Remove the crankshaft pulley with a gear puller.

12. Remove the gravel shield from underneath the engine.

13. Remove the front driveshaft.

14. Remove the front oil pan bolts, to gain access to the bottom of the timing chain cover.

NOTE: It may be necessary to insert a thin knife between the pan and the gasket in order to break the pan loose. Use care not to damage the gasket.

Installation is the reverse of removal. Be sure to adjust the drive belts.

Front Cover Oil Seal

REMOVAL & INSTALLATION

All Engines

1. Remove the timing chain or belt cover, as previously outlined.

2. Inspect the oil seal for signs of wear, leakage, or damage.

3. If worn, pry the old oil seal out, using a large flat-bladed screwdriver. Remove it toward the *front* of the cover.

NOTE: Once the oil seal has been removed, it must be replaced.

4. Use a socket, pipe, or block of wood and a hammer to drive the oil seal into place. Work from the *front* of the cover.

—— **CAUTION** ——
Be extremely careful not to damage the seal.

5. Install the timing chain or belt cover as outlined above.

Timing Chain and Tensioner

REMOVAL & INSTALLATION

20R, 22R and 22R-E Engines

1. Remove the cylinder head and timing chain cover as previously outlined.

20R and 22R engines—align the crankshaft gear mark with the single bright link of the timing chain

20R and 22R engines—align the camshaft sprocket mark between the two bright links of the timing chain

2. Remove the chain from the dampers and remove the chain and cam sprocket together.

3. If the chain and sprocket are worn, they will have to be replaced, along with the crankshaft sprocket. Pull the crankshaft sprocket and pump drive spline as a unit, using a gear puller.

4. Measure the chain tensioner for wear. If it is worn below 0.43 in., replace it as a unit.

5. Measure the chain dampers for wear. If either is visibly worn or measures below the limit, replace as a unit.
Damper #1   0.20 in.
Damper #2   0.18 in.
To install:

1. After installing any necessary dampers or a new tensioner, turn the crankshaft by hand until the key is at TDC. If removed, slide the crankshaft sprocket over the key. Place the chain on the sprocket so that the single bright link is over the mark on the sprocket.

2. Position the cam sprocket in the chain so that the timing mark on the sprocket is located between the two bright links of the chain.

3. Install the oil pump drive spline over the crankshaft key, if removed.

4. After cleaning the old gasket surface thoroughly, install a new cover gasket over the locating dowels.

5. Turn the camshaft sprocket counterclockwise to take any slack out of the chain.

6. Install the timing chain cover and cylinder head as previously outlined.

l. Distributor drive gear	5. Chain damper #1
2. Cam sprocket	6. Crankshaft pulley
3. Timing chain cover	7. Pump drive spline
4. Chain damper #2	8. Crankshaft sprocket
	9. Chain tensioner
	10. Timing chain

Timing cover and related components—20R and 22R engines

Timing Belt

REMOVAL & INSTALLATION

Diesel Engine

The diesel timing belt may be removed by following steps 1–8, then 15–18 of the Cylinder Head Removal and Installation procedure. To install the belt:

1. Temporarily install the idler pulley and check that the pulley bracket can be moved to the left and right by hand.

2. Align each timing gear according to the accompanying illustration. Note that the injection pump gear is positioned in a slightly retarded manner.

3. Install the timing belt without altering the position of any timing gear.

4. Install the idler pulley spring.

5. Temporarily install the crankshaft timing gear center bolt and turn the crankshaft exactly two revolutions (clockwise). As you turn the crankshaft, you should notice movement of the idler pulley bracket.

6. Each timing gear should now align as shown in the accompanying illustration. Note that the injection pump gear marking should now be aligned with the corresponding "diamond" mark on the engine.

7. Tighten the idler pulley bolts to 11–15 ft. lbs.

Final view of the timing marks after the crankshaft is turned twice—see text (diesel engine)

Preliminary timing gear positioning—see text (diesel engine)

> ——— **CAUTION** ———
> *DO NOT move the idler pulley bracket while tightening the bolts.*

8. Install the timing cover and tighten the cover fasteners to 3–5 ft. lbs.

9. Install the crankshaft belt drive pulley. Dip the pulley retaining bolt in engine oil, install the bolt and tighten to 69–75 ft. lbs. WITHOUT turning the engine.

10. Assemble the remaining engine components by reversing the disassembly steps.

Timing Gears

REMOVAL & INSTALLATION

2F Engines

NOTE: This procedure contains camshaft removal and installation.

1. Perform the cylinder head and timing cover removal procedures, as previously outlined.

2. Slip the oil slinger off the crankshaft.

3. Remove the camshaft thrust plate retaining bolts by working through the holes provided in the camshaft timing gear.

4. Remove the camshaft through the front of the cylinder block. Support the camshaft while removing it, so as not to damage its bearings or lobes.

NOTE: The timing gear is a press-fit and cannot be removed without removing the camshaft.

5. Inspect the crankshaft timing gear. Replace it if it has worn or damaged teeth.

6. To remove it, remove the sliding key from the crankshaft. Withdraw the timing gear with a gear puller.

Installation is performed in the following order:

1. Use a large piece of pipe to press the timing gear onto the crankshaft. Lightly and evenly tap the end of the pipe until the gear is in its original position.

2. Apply a coat of engine oil to the camshaft journals and bearings.

3. Insert the camshaft into the block.

> ——— **CAUTION** ———
> *Use care not to damage the camshaft lobes, bearings, or journals.*

1. Crankshaft pulley	4. Timing cover	7. Crankshaft key
2. Balancer	5. Oil slinger	8. Crankshaft gear
3. Timing cover seal	6. Crankshaft	9. Camshaft

Timing gears, cover and related components—2F engines

2F engines—align the camshaft and crankshaft gear marks

4. Align the mating marks on each of the gears as illustrated.

5. Slip the camshaft into position. Tighten the camshaft thrust plate bolts to 14.5 ft. lbs.

6. Check the gear backlash with a feeler gauge, inserted between the crankshaft and the camshaft timing gears. The backlash should be no more than 0.002–0.005 in.; if it exceeds this, replace one or both of the gears, as required.

7. Check the gear run-out with a dial indicator. Run-out, for both gears, should not exceed 0.008 in.; if it does, replace the gear.

8. Install the oil nozzle, if it was removed, by screwing it in place with a screwdriver and punching it in two places, to secure it.

NOTE: Be sure that the oil hole in the nozzle is pointed toward the timing gear before securing it.

9. Install the oil slinger on the crankshaft.

10. Install the timing gear cover and cylinder head, as outlined above.

Camshaft

NOTE: To service the 2F engine camshaft, refer to the previous Timing Gear Removal and Installation procedure.

REMOVAL & INSTALLATION

20R, 22R and 22R-E Engines

1. Disconnect the negative battery cable at the battery.

2. Remove the air cleaner assembly. Mark all of the hose locations to simplify installation.

3. Drain the radiator and remove the upper radiator hose.

4. Disconnect the flexible hoses at the fuel pump and remove the fuel pump. Replace the fuel pump gasket during installation, if necessary.

5. Remove the valve cover. Mark all of the attaching parts to simplify installation.

6. Mark and disconnect the spark plug wires at the spark plugs. Remove the spark plugs.

7. Rotate the engine while holding your finger over the number one spark plug hole. As pressure builds in the number one cylinder, watch the timing marks at the crankshaft damper and align the marks at top dead center.

8. Paint reference marks on both the cam sprocket and the timing chain to indicate their relationship for installation.

9. Remove the distributor cap (with wires intact) and move it out of the way.

10. Mark the position of the distributor rotor on the distributor housing.

11. Mark the position of the distributor housing and the cylinder head, indicating the relationship between these two components.

12. Disconnect the distributor primary wire and remove the distributor.

13. Remove the half circle seal from the cylinder head.

14. Remove the cam sprocket bolt, the distributor drive gear and the fuel pump eccentric.

15. Remove the rocker shafts as previously outlined.

16. Measure the camshaft thrust clearance using a feeler gauge inserted between the thrust bearing and the cylinder head. If the clearance is greater than 0.0098 in., the cylinder head must be replaced.

17. Remove the camshaft journal caps.

NOTE: The camshaft may now be lifted out of the cylinder head but it is recommended that you continue with the following checking procedures.

18. Check the camshaft journal caps for damage. Clean all of the bearing surfaces, including the caps, cam journal, and the cylinder head.

19. With the camshaft in place on the cylinder head, lay small strips of plastigage on each of the camshaft journals (at the tops of the journals, facing front-to-rear).

20. Reinstall the journal caps in their original locations (arrows facing forward), and torque the caps to 13–16 ft. lbs.

21. Remove the journal caps and gauge the width of the plastigage against the chart on the plastigage package. Maximum journal clearance is 0.004 in. If the journal clearance is greater than specified, measure the cam journal diameters with a micrometer (or have a professional machine shop do so). If the diameter of any cam journal is less than specified, obtain a new camshaft and recheck the journal clearance. If the clearance is still excessive, the cylinder head must be replaced.

To install the camshaft, position it in the cylinder head, install the journal caps (torque to specification), and reverse steps 1–15. Be sure to align all the reference marks made during removal. Replenish the cooling system. If a new cam is installed, use

an assembly lube (available at most auto stores) on the cam lobes and engine oil on the journals. If the old cam is damaged excessively (lobes worn round, etc.) change the engine oil and filter.

NOTE: If any of the reference marks made during removal will not align during assembly, remove the timing chain and re-time the engine as previously outlined.

Diesel Engine

Refer to step 1–8, then 15–21 of the Cylinder Head Removal and Installation procedure. The journal clearances are checked in the same manner as the 20R, 22R and 22R-E engines.

During Installation, note the following fastener torque values: rocker shaft supports—11–15 ft. lbs.; camshaft timing gear set bolt—69–75 ft. lbs.; oil seal retainer—8–12 ft. lbs. Refer to the Timing Belt Removal and Installation procedure to properly install the timing belt.

Pistons and Connecting Rods

REMOVAL & INSTALLATION

1. Remove the following components as outlined in the appropriate sections of this chapter:
   a. Cylinder head
   b. Oil pan
   c. Oil pump (not necessary on 20R, 22R and 22R-E engines)
   d. Oil strainer

NOTE: Details of the following steps can be found in the Engine Rebuilding section.

2. Remove the cylinder ridges with a ridge reamer.

3. Measure the connecting rod side clearance.

4. Mark the connecting rods and caps.

5. Remove the connecting rod cap of the number one cylinder and check the oil clearance with plastigage. Record the clearance and compare with the specification chart. Repeat this step for each connecting rod.

6. With the number one connecting rod cap removed, install a short piece of rubber

Ring gap staggering on 20R & 22R engines

2F engines—after installing the piston rings, rotate each ring so that the ring gaps are positioned as shown. Failure to stagger the ring gaps will result in excessive oil consumption.

Piston ring gap staggering—diesel engine

Oil ring installation on the diesel piston—position the ends of the expander opposite the ring gap

Piston and connecting rod installation—diesel engine

hose onto each connecting rod bolt (the hose must completely cover the bolt).

7. Using a wooden or plastic handle (an old hammer handle works well), carefully tap the piston/connecting rod assembly out of the cylinder. Do not use excessive force as this could damage the connecting rods. Repeat this step for each cylinder.

8. Refer to the Engine Rebuilding Section for checking the piston/connecting rod assembly and for installing these parts in the cylinder block.

9. Reinstall the oil strainer, oil pump, oil pan and cylinder head following the appropriate procedures.

Crankshaft

REMOVAL & INSTALLATION

NOTE: Main bearings may be replaced without removing the crankshaft. If the crankshaft must be removed, it is recommended that the engine be removed from the vehicle and mounted in a work stand. Refer to "Engine Rebuilding" in the Unit Repair section.

ENGINE LUBRICATION

Oil Pan

REMOVAL & INSTALLATION

Pick-ups (Incl. 4×2 and 4×4)

1. Raise the hood and leave it open for the duration of this repair.
2. Drain the engine oil.
3. Raise the front end of the truck and support it on jackstands.
4. On 2WD, through 1983, remove the steering relay rod and the tie-rods from the idler arm, pitman arm, and steering knuckles as outlined in the Front Suspension section.
5. On diesel engines, remove the engine stiffening plates.
6. Remove the splash pans from under the engine.
7. Support the front of the engine with a jack and remove the front motor mount attaching bolts.

1. Input shaft bearing
2. Flywheel and rear end plate
3. Oil pan
4. Rear oil seal
5. Oil strainer
6. Oil filter bracket
7. Injection pump
8. Water pump
9. Timing belt case
10. Piston and connecting rod
11. Crankshaft

Exploded view of the diesel cylinder block

8. Raise the front of the engine slightly with the jack.

9. Remove the oil pan bolts and remove the oil pan.

10. Installation is the reverse of removal. Apply gasket sealer to the oil pan when installing a new gasket. The oil pan bolts should be tightened to 33–70 in. lbs. Tighten the bolts in a circular pattern, starting in the middle of the pan and working out toward the ends.

Land Cruiser

1. Remove the engine skid plates.

2. Remove the flywheel side cover and skid plate.

3. Disconnect the front driveshaft from the engine.

4. Drain the engine oil.

5. Remove the bolts which secure the oil pan; remove the pan and its gasket.

6. Installation is performed in the reverse order from removal. Always use a new pan gasket.

Oil Pump

REMOVAL & INSTALLATION

20R, 22R and 22R-E Engines

1. Drain the oil, and remove the oil pan and the oil strainer and pick-up tube.

1. Relief valve spring
2. Relief valve
3. Pump body
4. Drive gear
5. Driven gear
6. O-ring
7. Drive spline

Exploded view of the 20R and 22R engine oil pump

Mounting of the 20R and 22R engine oil pump—apply sealer to the upper mounting bolt as shown

2. Remove the drive belts from the crankshaft pulley.

3. Remove the crankshaft bolt, and remove the pulley with a gear puller, as outlined in the timing chain cover section.

4. Remove the five bolts from the oil pump and remove the oil pump assembly. Refer to the oil pump specification chart to check the oil pump clearances.

Check the timing chain cover for excessive wear or damage. If necessary, replace the gears or pump body or cover. Unbolt the relief valve (the vertical bolt on the pump body when attached to the engine) and check the piston, oil passages, and sliding surfaces for burrs or scoring. Inspect the crankshaft front oil seal and replace if worn or damaged.

When installing, use a new O-ring if necessary. Apply sealer to the upper bolt and install the five bolts. Install the crankshaft pulley as outlined in the timing cover section, and use a new gasket on the oil strainer and oil pan. Be sure to apply sealer to the corners of the oil pan gasket before installing the pan. Also, apply sealer to the uppermost oil pump bolt threads before installing this bolt.

Diesel Engine

1. Disconnect the cables which are positioned above the valve cover and move the cables aside. Remove the valve cover.

2. Disconnect the cables from both batteries.

3. Using a wrench on the center crankshaft pulley bolt, rotate the engine (clockwise only) until the TDC mark on the pulley is aligned with the pointer. Check that the valves of the number one cylinder are closed (rocker arms loose). If the valves are not closed, rotate the engine 360° and again align the TDC mark with the pointer.

4. Remove the following components as previously outlined:

    a. Oil pan and pump strainer assembly

    b. Timing cover and belt

5. Disconnect the wiring from the alternator. Remove the alternator and the mounting brackets.

6. If equipped with air conditioning, unbolt the air conditioning compressor and tie it out of the way (without disconnecting the refrigerant hoses). Also remove the compressor bracketry.

7. Refer to the Diesel Fuel System section and remove the fuel injection pump.

8. Remove the crankshaft timing gear, using a puller.

9. Unbolt and remove the water pump.

10. Unbolt and remove the timing case assembly.

11. Remove the oil pump cover plate from the rear of the timing case assembly to gain access to the oil pump. Clearances are checked in the same manner as the pump used in the 20R and 22R engines.

12. Remove the pump gears and check the gears and timing case gear surfaces for damage or excessive wear.

13. Install the gears with the triangular markings of each gear facing the pump plate side of the timing case. Install the pump cover plate.

14. Reverse steps 1–10 to complete the installation. Note that all gasket surfaces must be cleaned, and that damaged gaskets must be replaced. Be sure to follow the specific procedures concerning timing belt installation and fuel injection pump installation, as outlined previously and in the Diesel Fuel System section.

2F Engines

1. Remove the oil pan as previously outlined.

2. Remove the oil strainer and unfasten the union nuts on the oil pump pipe.

3. Remove the lock wire and the oil pump retaining bolt and pipe from the engine.

4. Remove the oil pump cover and inspect the following parts for nicks, scoring, grooving, etc.:

    a. pump cover

1. Oil pump plate
2. Driven gear
3. Drive gear
4. Timing case

Exploded view of the diesel oil pump

b. drive and driven gears
c. pump body.
5. Replace either the damaged parts or the complete pump if damage is excessive. See the Oil Pump Specification chart to check the oil pump clearances.
6. Installation is the reverse of steps 1–3.

NOTE: Be sure to check all of the gaskets and replace if necessary.

Rear Main Seal

REMOVAL & INSTALLATION

All Engines

1. Remove the following components as outlined in the appropriate sections of this chapter:
   a. Transmission
   b. Torque convertor (auto. trans.)
   c. Clutch cover and disc (manual trans.)
   d. Flywheel
   e. Oil pan
2. Remove the oil seal retaining plate and seal assembly.
3. Carefully pry or drive the old seal from the retaining plate. Be careful not to damage the retaining plate.
4. Install a new seal using either a block of wood or a seal driver (preferred) to firmly seat the new seal.
5. Lubricate the lips of the seal with multipurpose grease.
6. Install the retaining plate and seal assembly.
7. Install the components removed during step 1 in reverse order.
8. If the vehicle is equipped with a manual transmission, adjust the clutch.

1. Strainer
2. Pump cover
3. Pressure relief valve
4. Drive gear
5. Driven gear

Exploded view of the 2F engine oil pump

OIL PUMP CLEARANCE SPECIFICATIONS

(All measurements in inches)

Engine	Maximum Gear Tip Clearance①	Maximum Gear Backlash②	Maximum Side Clearance③	Maximum Cover Wear④	Maximum Body Clearance⑤
2F	0.008	0.037	0.006	0.006	—
20R,22R,22R-E,L	0.012	—	0.006	—	0.008

① 2F Engines: Measured between the gear teeth of each gear and the pump body.
   20R,22R and L Engines: Measured between the gear teeth of each gear and the crescent.
② Measured between the gear teeth with the gears meshed together.
③ Measured between a straightedge positioned across the oil pump body and the gear faces.
④ Measured between a straightedge positioned across the cover and the cover wear (gear contact) surface.
⑤ Measured between the oil pump driven gear and the pump body.

ENGINE COOLING

Radiator

REMOVAL & INSTALLATION

All Models

1. Drain the cooling system.
2. Unfasten the clamps and remove the radiator upper and lower hoses. If equipped with an automatic transmission, remove the oil cooler lines.
3. Detach the hood lock cable and remove the hood lock from the radiator upper support.

NOTE: It may be necessary to remove the grille in order to gain access to the hood lock/radiator support assembly.

4. Remove the fan shroud, if so equipped.
5. On models equipped with a closed cooling system, disconnect the hose from the thermal expansion tank and remove the tank from its bracket.
6. Unbolt and remove the radiator upper support.
7. Unfasten and remove the radiator.

Installation is performed in the reverse order of removal. Remember to check the transmission fluid level on cars with automatic transmissions.

Fill the radiator to the specified level.

Water Pump

REMOVAL & INSTALLATION

All Engines

1. Drain the cooling system.
2. Unfasten the fan shroud securing bolts and remove the fan shroud, if so equipped.
3. Loosen the alternator adjusting link bolt and remove the drive belt.
4. Repeat step 3 for the air pump, air conditioning compressor, or power steering pump drive belts, if so equipped.
5. On diesels, remove the timing gear cover and timing belt tension spring.
6. Detach the bypass and radiator hoses from the water pump.
7. Unfasten the water pump retaining bolts and remove the water pump and fan assembly, using care not to damage the radiator with the fan.

—— **CAUTION** ——
If the fan is equipped with a fluid coupling, do not tip the fan/pump assembly on its side, as the fluid will run out.

8. Installation is the reverse of removal. Always use a new gasket between the pump body and its mounting. Check for leaks after installation is completed.

Thermostat

REMOVAL & INSTALLATION

All Engines

1. Partially drain the cooling system.
2. Unless the upper radiator hose is positioned over one of the thermostat housing (water outlet) bolts, it is not necessary to detach the hose.
3. Remove the bolts and remove the water outlet.
4. When installing a new thermostat always use a new gasket. Be sure that the thermostat is positioned with the spring down.

EMISSION CONTROLS

Positive Crankcase Ventilation System

A positive crankcase ventilation (PCV) system is used on all engines. Blow-by gases are routed from the crankcase to the carburetor or throttle body where they are combined with the air/fuel mixture and burned in the cylinders.

A valve is used to prevent the gases in the crankcase from being ignited in the event of a backfire. The quantity of blow-by gases is also regulated by the PCV valve which is spring-loaded and has a variable orifice. The valve is mounted on the valve cover of the engine and should be replaced every 24,000 miles, on 1977–78 trucks, and 30,000 miles on 1979 and later trucks.

REMOVAL & INSTALLATION

To remove the valve simply disconnect the hose from the top of the valve and remove the valve from the rubber grommet in the valve cover.

TESTING

Check the PCV system hoses and connections to determine that there are no leaks, then tighten or replace as necessary.

To check the operation of the valve, remove it and blow through both of its ends. When blowing through the end which goes toward the intake manifold, very little air should pass through the valve. When blowing from the valve cover side, the air should pass freely.

If the valve does not perform in this manner, replace it with a new valve.

NOTE: Toyota does not recommend cleaning of the PCV valve or any adjustments.

Evaporative Emission Control System

Toyota trucks are equipped with evaporative emission control (EEC) systems which prevent hydrocarbon emissions (fuel vapors) originating at the carburetor or throttle body and the fuel tank from entering the atmosphere. All models use a charcoal canister vapor storage system.

While the engine is off, fuel vapors from the carburetor or throttle body fuel bowl and the fuel tank are absorbed into the charcoal canister. On some later engines, this occurs even during idling and very low vehicle speeds. When the engine is started, and on some later engines when certain conditions are met (engine temperature, en-

Typical charcoal cannister vapor storage system

gine speed, vehicle speed), the vapors from the charcoal canister are drawn through the intake manifold to the combustion chambers to be burned with the air/fuel mixture. As the vapors are drawn from the canister, a slight vacuum is created in the canister. This vacuum draws fresh air into the canister through the canister filter. The fresh air purifies the charcoal so that it may be re-used.

Required maintenance for 1977–78 vehicles includes replacement of the charcoal canister at 50,000 mile intervals. On 1979 and later models the charcoal canister should be checked at 30,000 and 60,000 miles. Replacement of the charcoal canister is not necessary for these models.

Throttle Positioner (TP)

CARBURETED ENGINES

During rapid deceleration large volumes of fuel/air mixture are drawn into the cylinders due to high manifold vacuum. If the throttle plates close completely there is not sufficient oxygen to permit complete combustion. Therefore a throttle positioner is installed to keep the throttle plates slightly open during deceleration. Vacuum is reduced under the throttle valve which, in turn, acts on the retard chamber of the distributor vacuum unit. This ignition retard compensates for the loss of engine braking caused by the partially-opened throttle.

Once the vehicle drops below a predetermined speed, the vacuum switching valve provides vacuum to the throttle positioner diaphragm. The throttle positioner then retracts allowing the throttle valve to close completely. The distributor also returns to normal operation.

ADJUSTMENT

1. Start the engine and allow it to reach normal operating temperature.
2. Adjust the engine idle speed as previously outlined.
3. Detach the vacuum line from the throttle positioner diaphragm and plug the line.
4. Accelerate the engine slightly to set the throttle positioner.
5. Check the engine speed with a tachometer when the positioner is in place.
6. Check that the engine rpm reads as follows:

20R engine:	
manual transmission	1400
automatic transmission	1050
22R engine:	
all	1050
2F engine	
except '77–'80 Calif	1200
'77–'80 Calif	1400

Typical Throttle Positioner (TP) system

7. If necessary, adjust the engine rpm to the values listed in step 6 by turning the throttle positioner screw.
8. Connect the vacuum hose to the positioner diaphragm. The engine idle should return to normal as soon as the vacuum line is connected.
9. If the throttle positioner fails to perform properly, check the linkage and diaphragm unit. If there are no defects in these components, the problem probably lies in the vacuum switching valve or in the speed sensor unit.

Vacuum Retard— Advance Distributor

Most Toyota trucks are equipped with a distributor which employs a vacuum spark retard system. Such distributors may be identified by the presence of two vacuum lines connected to the distributor vacuum unit.

Retarding the ignition timing under certain conditions reduces exhaust emissions and helps to compensate for the lack of engine braking due to the activation of the throttle positioner.

TESTING

NOTE: Check all vacuum hoses for leaks, kinks, or improper connections before making any tests. Replace the hose(s) if necessary.

1. Connect a timing light to the engine as previously outlined.
2. Mark and disconnect the vacuum hoses at the distributor vacuum unit.
3. Start the engine and apply vacuum to one of the vacuum unit connections. Note the effect on the ignition timing with the timing light. Release the vacuum at this connection and apply vacuum to the other

vacuum unit connection. Note the effect on the ignition timing with the timing light.

4. If the ignition timing advanced and retarded during step 3, the vacuum unit is functioning properly. If the timing did not react in this manner, the distributor vacuum unit is defective.
5. Turn the engine off. Disconnect the timing light and reconnect the vacuum lines to the distributor.

EXHAUST GAS RECIRCULATION SYSTEM

The exhaust gas recirculation (EGR) system is used to reduce the oxides of nitrogen emissions from the engine. Oxides of nitrogen emission levels are highest during periods of high cylinder pressure and high cylinder temperature. The EGR system allows a small amount of engine exhaust gas to be recirculated back to the engine intake system. Since the exhaust gas is unable to be re-burned, its introduction to the combustion chambers results in a cooling effect on the combustion temperature. Consequently, oxides of nitrogen emissions are reduced. An added advantage to this cooling effect is that the engines tendency towards detonation (pinging) is reduced.

The EGR valve is controlled by the same computer and vacuum switching valve which is used to operate other emission control system components. There are several conditions which must be sensed by the computer in order for the computer to permit exhaust gas recirculation:
   a. Ignition switch position
   b. Vehicle speed
   c. Engine speed
   d. Engine coolant temperature

Due to the complexity of computer controlled emissions systems and the special equipment needed to properly service these systems, only the basic EGR valve tests will be covered here.

Carbureted engine EGR system

EGR VALVE TEST

1977 (Except 2F Engines)

1. Allow the engine to reach normal operating temperature and remove the air cleaner lid.

2. Disconnect the hose (coded with white tape) which runs from the vacuum switching valve to the EGR valve at the EGR valve end.

3. Remove the intake manifold hose (coded red) from the vacuum switching valve and connect it to the EGR valve.

4. With the engine idling, a "bubbling" sound should be heard from the carburetor. Disconnect the hose from the EGR valve. The "bubbling" sound should disappear.

5. If the sound does not vary, the EGR valve is defective and should be replaced.

6. Reconnect the vacuum hoses as originally connected and install the air cleaner lid.

1978 and Later (Incl. All 2F Engines)

1. Start the engine and allow it to idle.

2. Apply vacuum directly to the EGR valve. The engine should stall; on 2F engines, the rpm should drop about 50 rpm. If it does, the EGR valve is working properly. If not, the EGR valve is defective and must be replaced.

3. Reconnect the EGR valve vacuum line as originally connected.

Air Injection System

A belt-driven air pump supplies air to an injection manifold which has nozzles in each exhaust port. Injection of air at this point causes combustion of unburned hydrocarbons in the exhaust manifold rather than allowing them to escape into the atmosphere. An anti-backfire valve controls the flow of air from the pump to prevent back-firing which results from an overly rich mixture under closed throttle conditions.

A check valve prevents hot exhaust gas backflow into the pump and hoses, in case of a pump failure, or when the antibackfire valve is working.

In addition newer engines have an air switching valve (ASV). On engines without catalytic converters, the ASV is used to stop air injection under a constant heavy engine load.

On engines with catalytic converters the ASV is used to protect the catalyst from overheating, by blocking the air necessary for the reaction.

On all engines, except the early 2F, the relief valve is built into the ASV.

REMOVAL & INSTALLATION

Air Pump

1. Disconnect the air hoses from the pump.

2. Loosen the bolt on the adjusting link and remove the drive belt.

3. Remove the pump.

——— CAUTION ———
Do not pry on the pump housing; it may become distorted.

Installation is in the reverse order of removal. Adjust the drive belt tension to ½–¾ in. under thumb pressure.

Antibackfire Valve and Air Switching Valve

1. Detach the air hoses from the valve.

2. Remove the valve securing bolt.

3. Withdraw the valve.

Installation is performed in the reverse order of removal.

Check Valve

1. Detach the intake hose from the valve.

2. Use an open-end wrench to remove the valve from its mounting.

Installation is the reverse of removal.

Relief Valve (Pump Mounted Type)

1. Remove the air pump from the vehicle.

2. Support the pump so that it cannot rotate.

——— CAUTION ———
Never clamp the pump in a vise; the aluminum case will be distorted.

3. Use a jaw-type puller to remove the relief valve from the top of the pump.

4. Position the new relief valve over the opening in the pump.

NOTE: The air outlet should be pointing toward the left.

5. Gently tap the relief valve into place using a block of wood and a hammer.

6. Install the pump on the engine, as outlined above.

Air Injection Manifold

1. Remove the check valve, as outlined above.

2. Loosen the air injection manifold attachment nuts and withdraw the manifold.

NOTE: On 20R and 22R engines, it will first be necessary to remove the exhaust manifold as previously outlined.

Installation is the reverse order of removal.

TESTING

——— CAUTION ———
Do not hammer, pry, or bend the pump housing while tightening the drive belt or testing the pump.

Belt Tension and Air Leaks

1. Before proceeding with the tests, check the pump drive belt tension to see if it is within specifications.

2. Turn the pump by hand. If it has seized, the belt will slip, making a noise. Disregard any chirping, squealing, or rolling sounds from inside the pump; these are normal when it is turned by hand.

3. Check the hoses and connections for leaks. Hissing or a blast of air is indicative of a leak. Soapy water, applied lightly around the area in question, is a good method for detecting leaks.

Air Output

1. Disconnect the air supply hose at the antibackfire valve.

2. Connect a pressure gauge, using a suitable adaptor, to the air supply hose.

NOTE: If there are two hoses, plug the second one.

3. With the engine at normal operating

Checking the air pump output

temperature, increase the idle speed to 1,000–1,500 rpm and watch the vacuum gauge.

4. The air flow from the pump should be steady and fall between 2 and 6 psi. If it is unsteady or falls below this, the pump is defective and must be replaced.

Pump Noise Diagnosis

The air pump is normally noisy; as engine speed increases, the noise of the pump will rise in pitch. The rolling sound the pump bearings make is normal. But if this sound becomes objectionable at certain speeds, the pump is defective and will have to be replaced.

A continual hissing sound from the air pump pressure relief valve at idle, indicates a defective valve. Replace the relief valves.

If the pump rear bearing fails, a continual knocking sound will be heard.

Bypass Valve

1. Detach the hose which runs from the bypass valve to the check valve, at the bypass valve hose connection.

2. Connect a tachometer to the engine. With the engine running at normal idle speed, check to see that air is flowing from the bypass valve hose connection.

3. Speed up the engine so it is running at 1,500–2,000 rpm. Allow the throttle to snap shut. The flow of air from the bypass valve at the check valve hose connection should stop momentarily and air should then flow from the exhaust port on the valve body or the silencer assembly.

4. Repeat step 3 several times. If the flow of air is not diverted into the atmosphere from the valve exhaust port or if it fails to stop flowing from the hose connection, check the vacuum lines and connections. If these are tight, the valve is defective and requires replacement.

5. A leaking diaphragm will cause the air to flow out both the hose connection and the exhaust port at the same time. If this happens, replace the valve.

Air Switching Valve (ASV) Tests

1. Start the engine and allow it to reach normal operating temperature.

2. At curb idle, the air from the bypass valve should be discharged through the hose which runs to the ASV (output side of air pump).

3. When the vacuum line to the ASV is disconnected, the air from the bypass valve should be diverted out through the ASV-to-air cleaner hose. Reconnect the vacuum line.

4. Disconnect the ASV-to-check valve hose and connect a pressure gauge to it.

5. Increase the engine speed. The relief valve should open when the pressure gauge registers 2.7–6.5 psi.

6. If the ASV fails any of the above tests, replace it. Reconnect all hoses.

Vacuum Delay Valve

The vacuum delay valve is located in the line which runs from the intake manifold to the vacuum surge tank. To check it, proceed as follows:

1. Remove the vacuum delay valve from the vacuum line. Be sure to note which end points toward the intake manifold.

2. When air is blown in from the ASV (surge tank) side, it should pass through the valve freely.

3. When air is blown in from the intake manifold side, a resistance should be felt.

4. Replace the valve if it fails either of the above tests.

5. Install the valve in the vacuum line, being careful not to install it backwards.

Check Valve

1. Before starting the test, check all of the hoses and connections for leaks.

2. Detach the air supply hose from the check valve.

3. Insert a suitable probe into the check valve and depress the plate. Release it; the plate should return to its original position against the valve seat. If binding is evident, replace the valve.

4. With the engine running at normal operating temperature, gradually increase its speed to 1,500 rpm. Check for exhaust gas leakage. If any is present, replace the valve assembly.

NOTE: Vibration and flutter of the check valve at idle speed is at normal condition and does not mean that the valve should be replaced.

Catalytic Converter System

The catalytic converter is a muffler-shaped device, located in the exhaust system between the manifold and the muffler. Its purpose is to oxidize hydrocarbons (HC) and carbon monoxide (CO).

The catalyst is made of noble metals (platinum and palladium) bonded to pellets of granular alumina. These catalysts cause the HC and CO to break down into water and carbon dioxide (CO_2) without taking part in the reaction; thus, it is reasonable to expect a catalyst life of 50,000 miles in normal use. The air pump used in the air injection system also supplies fresh air to the catalyst via the exhaust pipe; this fresh air is used to supply oxygen for the reaction. A thermosensor, inserted into the body of the converter, shuts off the air supply if catalyst temperatures become excessive.

The same sensor circuit also causes an instrument panel warning light labeled "EXH TEMP" to come on when the temperature rises beyond the predetermined level.

NOTE: It is normal for the light to come on temporarily if the truck is driven downhill for long periods of time (such as when descending a mountain).

The light will come on and stay on if the air injection system is malfunctioning or if the engine is misfiring, both of which will cause the catalyst temperature to rise.

PRECAUTIONS

1. Use only unleaded fuel.

2. Avoid prolonged idling; the engine should run no longer than 20 minutes at curb idle, nor longer than 10 minutes at fast idle.

3. Reduce fast idle speed, by quickly depressing and releasing the accelerator pedal, as soon as the coolant temperature reaches 120°F.

4. Do not disconnect any spark plug leads while the engine is running.

5. Make engine compression checks as quickly as possible.

6. Do not dispose of the catalyst in a place where anything coated with grease, gas, or oil is present.

CATALYST TESTING

At the present time there is no known way to reliably test catalytic converter operation in the field. The only reliable test is a 12 hour and 40 minute "soak test" (CVS) which must be done in a laboratory.

An infrared HC/CO tester is not sensitive enough to measure the higher tailpipe emissions from a partially-failed converter. Thus, a bad converter may allow enough HC and CO emissions to escape, so that the truck is not in compliance with Federal (or state) standards, but still will not cause the needle on the HC/CO tester to move off zero.

A *completely* failed converter should cause the tester to show a slight reading. As a result, it should be possible to spot one of these.

As long as you avoid severe overheating or use of leaded fuels and the truck has less than 50,000 miles on it, it is safe to assume that the converter is working.

If you are in doubt about the converter, take your truck to the diagnostic center which has an infrared tester.

TOYOTA

WARNING LIGHT TESTING

NOTE: The warning light will come on when the ignition switch is turned to the Start position, as a means of checking its operation.

1. If the warning light illuminates and remains on, check the components of the air injection system. If these are not defective, check the ignition system for faulty leads, plugs, points, or igniter.

2. If no problems can be found in Step 1, check the warning light wiring for short or open circuits.

3. If nothing can be found in Steps 1 or 2, check the operation of the emission control system vacuum switching valve or the computer, either by substitution of a new unit, or by taking the truck to a service facility which has Toyota's diagnostic emission control system checker.

CONVERTER REMOVAL AND INSTALLATION

——— CAUTION ———
Do not perform this operation on a hot (or even warm) engine. Catalyst temperatures may go as high as 1,700°F, so that any contact with the catalyst could cause severe burns.

1. Disconnect the lead from the converter thermosensor.

2. Remove the wiring shield.

3. Unfasten the pipe clamp securing bolts at either end of the converter. Remove the clamps.

4. Push the tailpipe rearward and remove the converter, complete with thermosensor.

5. Carry the converter with the thermosensor upward to prevent the catalyst from falling out.

6. Unfasten the screws and take out the thermosensor and gasket.

Installation is as follows:

1. Place a new gasket on the thermosensor. Push the thermosensor into the converter and secure it with its two bolts. Be careful not to drop the thermosensor.

NOTE: Service replacement converters are provided with a plastic thermosensor guide. Slide the sensor into the guide to install it. Do not remove the guide.

2. Install new gaskets on the converter mounting flanges.

3. Secure the converter with its mounting clamps.

4. If the converter is attached to the body with rubber O-rings, install the O-rings over the body and converter mounting hooks.

5. Install the wire protector and connect the lead to the thermosensor.

Mixture Control System

The mixture control (MC) system is used on 1980 and later pickup trucks equipped with manual transmissions. The purpose of the MC system is to reduce hydrocarbon and carbon monoxide emissions during sudden engine deceleration. When the throttle is suddenly closed, the intake manifold vacuum increases rapidly. This vacuum, acting on the mixture control valve, causes the valve to open. When the mixture control valve opens, fresh air is admitted into the intake tract of the engine, which effectively lowers the emissions output.

TESTING

1. Start the engine.

2. Disconnect the upper vacuum (sensing) hose from the MC valve.

3. Place your hand over the air inlet of the MC valve. No suction should be felt.

4. Reconnect the upper vacuum (sensing) hose to the MC valve. Suction should be felt at the MC valve air inlet for a moment.

NOTE: At this time, the engine should either idle roughly or stall. This is normal.

5. Replace the valve if either the valve or the engine did not act as previously stated.

Transmission Controlled Spark System

The transmission controlled spark (TCS) is used on vehicles made prior to 1977. The TCS system alters the distributor advance curve under certain operating conditions, thereby reducing emissions of oxides of nitrogen (NO$_x$).

When the system is operational, the computer closes the vacuum switching valve (VSV) ground circuit. The valve in the VSV closes the passage between the distributor advance side and the carburetor advancer port. In this manner, advance of the engine timing is stopped.

The computer receives its messages from the speed sensor unit and the thermo sensor which only operates when the coolant temperature is between 140–210°F.

Spark Control System

A modified TCS system called spark control (SC) is used on all later trucks. The principle of delayed vacuum advance to minimize HC and NO$_x$ emissions remains the same, but the system is simplified by elimination of the computer control, VSV, and TVSV. Instead, a vacuum transmitting valve (VTV) is placed in the vacuum hose between the distributor diaphragm and the carburetor. Vacuum is delayed to the diaphragm by the closing of a check valve within the VTV. When intake vacuum drops (at wide throttle openings) the check valve opens and faster transmission of vacuum is allowed, thus advancing the distributor timing. The VTV is coded in a dark blue color in automatic transmission trucks, and brown in all manual transmission equipped trucks.

Auxiliary Acceleration Pump System

To reduce emissions, carburetor air/fuel mixtures are calibrated to be as lean as possible. Although a lean mixture will burn readily at hotter temperatures, it is reluctant to ignite when cold—not because of the mixture as such, but because fuel vaporizes less readily when cold. Thus, increasing the amount of fuel in a cold air/fuel mixture increases the amount of vaporized fuel available.

The problem of a poor air/vaporized fuel

Typical mixture control (MC) system

UPPER VACUUM (SENSING) HOSE
MC VALVE
MC VALVE AIR INLET

mixture in a cold engine is accentuated when accelerating. Although the carburetor is equipped with an acceleration pump for normal accelerating engine demands, its capacity is insufficient for a cold engine. The auxiliary acceleration pump (AAP) is designed to send additional fuel into the acceleration nozzle in the carburetor independent of the regular acceleration pump. All trucks are equipped with the AAP system.

The AAP itself is an integral part of the carburetor. It consists of two check valves controlled by springs, and a diaphragm controlled by both a spring and engine vacuum obtained from the intake manifold. At constant speeds, intake manifold vacuum draws the AAP diaphragm back, enlarging the AAP chamber and thus allowing gasoline to enter. When the engine is accelerated, intake manifold vacuum drops, allowing the AAP diaphragm to be pushed back by the spring. The resultant reduction in chamber volume forces the gasoline out through the other check valve, into the acceleration nozzle. Thus, the engine gets a needed squirt of gasoline.

AAP operation is governed by the same TVSV described in the AI section earlier. At cold coolant temperatures, the TVSV allows intake manifold vacuum to reach the AAP diaphragm. At approximately 122°F, the TVSV closes off the passage to vacuum, thus shutting off the AAP.

INSPECTION

The vacuum hose should be checked for leaks, kinks, or improper connections.

   1. With the engine cold (below 75°F) and idling (front wheels blocked, parking brake on, transmission in neutral) remove the air cleaner cap and look into the carburetor. At the instant the vacuum hose is removed from the AAP, gasoline should squirt from the nozzle.

   2. If it does not, check for vacuum in the hose. If present, the AAP diaphragm may be defective, the nozzle may be blocked, the check valves may be stuck, or gasoline may not be flowing into the chamber.

   3. If there is no vacuum in the line, either the line has an air leak or the TVSV is defective.

   4. After warming the engine to operating temperature, perform the same test as in Step 1. If gasoline spurts out, the TVSV is defective.

Choke Breaker System

All carbureted 20R and 22R engines use an automatic choke, consisting of a thermostatic bimetal spring which expands and contracts in response to cold and heat. This spring is connected by mechanical linkage to the choke plate, and heated by the engine coolant. When the engine is cold, the spring expands and closes the choke. As the engine heats, the spring contracts opening the choke.

Typical Auxiliary Acceleration Pump (AAP) system

The Choke Breaker (CB) system uses a diaphragm which is mechanically connected to the choke linkage and is actuated by intake manifold vacuum. The vacuum causes the diaphragm to pull back on the linkage, opening the choke plate slightly against the force of the automatic choke spring.

The purpose of the CB system is to prevent the cold engine from receiving an over-rich mixture, caused by the closed choke plate, because rich mixtures are higher in HC and CO emissions.

INSPECTION

Check the vacuum hose first for leaks, kinks, and improper connections.

   1. With the engine cold and idling (parking brake set, front wheels blocked, and transmission in neutral), remove the lid from the air cleaner. Disconnect the vacuum hose from the CB diaphragm, while watching to see if the link is pulled out of the diaphragm by the force of the automatic choke spring.

   2. When the hose is reconnected, the diaphragm should pull the link back inward itself.

If CB does not operate properly, either the linkage is binding or the diaphragm is faulty. The linkage should be cleaned thoroughly with a carburetor cleaning spray and a clean cloth, but it should not be lubricated with any substance whatsoever. If this does not restore proper CB operation, the diaphragm should be replaced.

Automatic Hot Air Intake System

The automatic hot air intake (HAI) system consists of a heat stove around the exhaust

manifold, a thermostatically controlled door (air control valve) in the air cleaner horn, and a length of insulated flexible pipe connecting the two. The purpose of the system is to keep the temperature of the air drawn into the carburetor as constant as possible. It directs a hot air supply to the carburetor in cold weather to provide faster engine warming and to reduce the possibility of carburetor icing. By providing the cold engine with warmer air, the choke stays on for a shorter length of time, thus reducing fuel consumption and the rich mixture condition. Leaner combustion mixtures are inherently lower in HC and CO emissions.

The air control valve in the air cleaner horn is controlled by a vacuum diaphragm. The vacuum hose is connected at one end to the diaphragm, and to both a thermo valve and intake manifold at the other. Initially, when cold, the thermo valve is closed. Intake manifold vacuum therefore causes the diaphragm to rise, opening the door in the air horn to admit preheated air drawn from the heat stove around the exhaust manifold. As the engine temperature rises, the thermo valve opens, thus reducing the level of intake manifold vacuum at the diaphragm. This allows the diaphragm to lower, which in turn closes the door in the air horn to admit cool outside air.

INSPECTION

With the engine idling and warm, connect the diaphragm hose directly to the intake manifold, and plug the thermo valve hose end. The air control valve should rise to admit hot air.

As with all vacuum-operated systems, the hoses should be checked for any kinks, breaks, or improper connections. If none are found and the air valve does not work properly, the diaphragm and the thermo valve must be checked. Suction applied to the vacuum hose should cause the diaphragm to raise the door. If it does, the thermo valve can be considered faulty. If not, the diaphragm should be replaced.

Deceleration Fuel Cut System

The purpose of this system is to prevent over-heating and afterburning in the exhaust system during deceleration. The system accomplishes this action by limiting the amount of fuel which is admitted to the slow circuit of the carburetor. During deceleration, intake manifold vacuum increases. This increase is sensed by the vacuum sensing switch which then sends this information electronically to the computer. If the vacuum is 14 in. Hg. or higher, and the engine rpm is above 2600 (1800 for 2F engines), the computer triggers the operation of the fuel cut solenoid valve. The fuel cut solenoid valve then limits the fuel flow to the carburetor slow circuit.

TESTING

General System Check

1. Connect a tachometer to the engine.
2. Start the engine and check that it runs normally.
3. Pinch the vacuum hose to the vacuum switch.
4. Gradually increase the engine rpm to 3000 rpm (2000 for 2F engines). The engine should misfire slightly between 2400 and 3000 rpm (1200 and 2000 for 2F engines).

─────── CAUTION ───────
Perform this procedure quickly to avoid overheating the catalytic converter.
────────────────────────

5. Release the hose and gradually increase the engine speed to 3000 rpm (2000 for 2F engines). Check that the engine operation is normal.

PRIMARY MAIN ALTITUDE COMPENSATOR PORT

PRIMARY SLOW ALTITUDE COMPENSATOR PORT

CHECK VALVE

DISTRIBUTOR VACUUM UNIT

SECONDARY MAIN ALTITUDE COMPENSATOR PORT

FUEL CUT PORT

HAC VALVE

Typical High Altitude Compensation (HAC) system

6. With the engine at idle unplug the solenoid valve. Check that the engine misfires or stalls.
7. If a problem is found check the switch and solenoid. If everything is normal connect the vacuum line and wiring.

FUEL CUT SOLENOID

1. Disconnect and remove the solenoid.
2. Connect one of the solenoid wires to the positive battery terminal; the other to the negative battery terminal. The solenoid should make a distinct clicking sound. If the solenoid does not click when energized, it is defective and should be replaced.
3. Check the solenoid O-ring for damage and replace if necessary.
4. Install and reconnect the solenoid.

VACUUM SWITCH

1. Disconnect the wire from the vacuum switch.

2. Using an ohmmeter, touch one ohmmeter probe to the body of the switch; the other ohmmeter probe to the terminal of the switch. Continuity should exist between these two points at this time.
3. Start the engine and check the continuity between the same two points (as in step 2). Continuity should NOT exist with the engine running.
4. If the switch performed correctly during steps 2 and 3, turn the engine off and reconnect the switch. If the switch did not perform correctly, replace the switch with a new unit.

High Altitude Compensation System

The piston downstroke (intake) of any engine is fixed, therefore the engine can only ingest a given volume of air in any altitude. There is progressively less oxygen available in air as the altitude changes, but basically, the carburetor will still meter the same amount of fuel. Because of this less oxygen/same amount of fuel condition, the air/fuel mixture available to the engine tends to richen.

The high altitude compensation (HAC) system is designed to perform the following functions as the altitude changes:

a. Adjust the air/fuel mixture available to the engine

b. (On some engines) Advance the ignition timing to improve the engines driveability characteristics.

INSPECTION

NOTE: Before checking the HAC system at altitudes near 4000 feet, determine the position of the HAC valve. This can be done by blowing into any one of the three ports on top of the HAC valve when the engine is idling. If the passage

Fuel Cut Solenoid Valve

Fuel Cut Port

Vacuum Switch

Typical Deceleration Fuel Cut system

is open, the valve is in the high altitude position. If it is closed, the valve is in the low altitude position. Proceed with the appropriate inspection procedure after the position of the valve is determined.

────── **CAUTION** ──────

Before performing any of the following tests, check the vacuum hoses for damage or leaks. Incorrect test results could occur if the vacuum hoses leak or are damaged.

High Altitude Mode—Except 2F Engines

1. Start the engine and allow it to reach normal operating temperature. Check the ignition timing as previously outlined. If it is about 13° BTC, go on with the procedure. If it is only slightly out of adjustment, adjust the timing. If the hose between the HAC valve and the three way connector is pinched, does the ignition timing become about 13° BTC? If so, the HAC valve should be replaced. If not, the check valve must be inspected. It should be possible to blow air through it from the HAC side, and not from the intake manifold side. If faulty, replace. If not, the distributor vacuum advance is faulty and must be repaired or replaced.

2. If the hose between the white side of the check valve and the three way connector is pinched, the ignition timing should stay at 13° BTC for a minute or more. If not, replace the HAC valve.

3. If the hose is disconnected from the black side of the check valve and the hose end blocked, the ignition timing should stay at 13° BTC for one minute or more. If not, replace the check valve.

4. Disconnect the two HAC hoses from the carburetor. If air is blown into each hose, it should flow into the HAC valve. If not, replace the HAC valve.

5. Reconnect the two hoses to the carburetor and disconnect the same hoses from the HAC valve. If air is blown into each hose, it should flow into the carburetor. If not, the carburetor air passages are blocked.

6. If the air does flow into the carburetor, reconnect the hoses. The HAC system is operating correctly.

High Altitude Mode—2F Engines

1. Start the engine and allow it to reach normal operating temperature.

2. Disconnect the outermost hose (furthest from the distributor cap) from the distributor vacuum unit and plug the hose end.

3. Check the ignition timing at the flywheel as previously outlined. The timing should be 7° BTDC.

4. Unplug and reconnect the distributor vacuum unit hose. The ignition timing should advance. If the timing advances, the system is functioning properly. If the timing does not advance, proceed with the following steps.

5. Disconnect the vacuum hose from the black side of the check valve and plug the hose end. The ignition timing should remain stationary for a minimum of one minute. If the timing varies at this time, the check valve is defective and must be replaced. If the timing remained stationary, the check valve is functioning properly.

6. Reconnect the check valve vacuum hose.

7. Disconnect the three hoses from the top of the high altitude compensation valve.

8. Blow air into each hose and check that air flows into the carburetor. If air does not flow into the carburetor, the high altitude compensation ports in the carburetor are blocked.

9. Reconnect the hoses as originally connected.

Low Altitude Mode—Except 2F Engines

1. Start the engine and disconnect the two HAC hoses from the carburetor.

2. If air is blown into each hose, it should not flow in into the HAC valve. If it does, replace the valve.

3. Reconnect the two hoses. Check the ignition timing outlined. It should be:

8° BTC @ 800 rpm with manual transmission
8° BTC @ 850 rpm with automatic transmission

The transmission should be in Neutral. If the timing is correct, the HAC system is okay.

4. If the timing is incorrect, disconnect the vacuum hose from the distributor sub-diaphragm. If the timing does not change, adjust the ignition timing. If the timing changes, replace the HAC valve.

Low Altitude Mode—2F Engines

1. Start the engine and allow it to reach normal operating temperature.

2. Check the ignition timing at the flywheel as previously outlined. The timing should be 7° BTDC for engines equipped with HAC.

3. Disconnect the vacuum hose from the bottom of the HAC valve and plug the hose end. The ignition timing should advance approximately 6°. If the timing advances, the system is functioning properly. If the timing does not advance, refer to steps 5–9 of the previous ''High Altitude Mode—2F Engines'' procedure.

HAC VALVE SERVICE

The only serviceable part of the HAC valve is the filter located in the bottom of the valve. If the filter is clogged, it can be either cleaned or (preferably) replaced.

CHECK VALVE TESTING

The check valve can be tested independent of the system by blowing air into the check valve ports. Air flow should be unrestricted when blowing from the white side to the black side of the valve. When blowing from the black side to the white side of the valve, there should be a noticeable resistance in air flow.

GASOLINE FUEL SYSTEM

Mechanical Fuel Pump

A mechanical fuel pump is used on all engines except the 1978 and earlier 20R engines and 1984 22R-E engines. These engines use an electric pump. The mechanical fuel pump is actuated by an eccentric which is integral with the engine camshaft on 2F engines, and bolted in front of the camshaft drive sprocket on 20R and 22R engines.

TESTING

Fuel pumps should always be tested on the vehicle. The larger line between the pump and tank is the suction side of the system and the smaller line, between the pump and carburetor or fuel injection pump is the pressure side. A leak in the pressure side would be apparent because of dripping fuel. A leak in the suction side is usually only apparent because of a reduced volume of fuel delivered to the pressure side.

1. Tighten any loose line connections and look for any kinks or restrictions.

2. Disconnect the fuel line at the carburetor or fuel injection pump. Disconnect the distributor-to-coil primary wire. Place a container at the end of the fuel line and crank the engine a few revolutions. If little or no fuel flows from the line, either the fuel pump is inoperative or the line is plugged. Blow through the lines with compressed air and try the test again. Reconnect the line.

3. If fuel flows in good volume, check the fuel pump pressure to be sure (pressure tests are possible only on gasoline engines).

4. Attach a pressure gauge to the pressure side of the fuel line. On cars equipped with a vapor return system, squeeze off the return hose.

5. Run the engine at idle and note the reading on the gauge. Stop the engine and compare the reading with the specifications listed in the ''Tune-Up Specifications'' chart. If the pump is operating properly, the pressure will be as specified and will be constant at idle speed. If pressure varies sporadically or is too high or low, the pump should be repaired or replaced, depending upon the pump type.

6. Remove the pressure gauge.

The following flow test can also be performed:

1. Disconnect the fuel line from the carburetor. Run the fuel line into a suitable measuring container.

2. Run the engine at idle until there is

one pint of fuel in the container. One pint should be pumped in 30 seconds or less.

3. If the flow is below minimum, check for a restriction in the line.

The only way to check fuel pump pressure is by connecting an accurate pressure gauge to the fuel line at the carburetor level. Never replace a fuel pump without performing this simple test. If the engine seems to be starving out, check the ignition system first. Also check for a plugged fuel filter or a restricted fuel line before replacing the pump. In rare cases, the fuel pump eccentric will wear to the point of preventing a full fuel pump stroke which will lower the fuel pump output. Keep this in mind, especially on high mileage engines.

REMOVAL & INSTALLATION

20R and 22R Engines—1979 and Later

1. Disconnect the negative battery terminal.

--- CAUTION ---
When working on the fuel system, do not smoke or work near any fire hazard. Keep gasoline off rubber or leather parts.

2. Drain the radiator.
3. Remove the upper radiator hose.
4. Remove all three lines from the fuel pump.
5. Remove the two bolts, the fuel pump, and gasket.

NOTE: The fuel pump is not repairable. It must be replaced as a complete unit.

6. Installation is the reverse of removal. On these engines, the fuel pump is serviced as an assembly. If the pump is defective, the entire pump must be replaced.

2F Engines

To remove the fuel pump simply disconnect and plug the fuel lines and remove the two bolts which hold the pump to the block.

When installing a new pump always use a new gasket between the pump and the block to prevent oil leakage. If any new rubber hose must be used to repair the fuel line, be sure that it is gasoline-resistant.

The 2F engine mechanical fuel pump is rebuildable, depending upon parts avail-

1. Diaphragm and spring
2. Cover and diaphragm
3. Upper body
4. Lower body

Mechanical fuel pump used on the 2F engine

ability. If you decide to rebuild the fuel pump rather than replace it, follow the instructions supplied with the rebuilding kit.

Electric Fuel Pump

An electric fuel pump is used on all 1978 and earlier 20R engined pickup trucks and 1984 22R-E engines. The fuel pump is wired into the ignition switch and oil pressure switch circuits. In the event of an oil pressure loss, the fuel pump is turned off so that the engine will stall, thus preventing engine damage due to the oil pressure loss. The fuel pump will operate only when the ignition switch is turned to the START position and when the oil pressure is normal.

TESTING

1. Disconnect the electrical clip from the oil pressure switch.
2. Turn the ignition switch to On.
3. Check for a smooth flow of gasoline from the fuel filter outlet. If the pump is noisy, it is probably defective. If the pump does not run, check the pump resistor and relay.

Turn the key off, and connect a pressure gauge to the filter outlet. Turn the ignition switch to On and measure to fuel pump pressure. It should be between 2.1 and 4.3 psi on 1978 and earlier, and 36–38 psi on 1984 engines.

As with the mechanical pump, all tests should be performed, and all lines and the filter should be checked, before replacing the pump.

REMOVAL & INSTALLATION

1. Remove the negative (−) cable from the battery.
2. Remove the fuel tank according to the appropriate procedure.
3. Remove the bolts which secure the access plate to the tank. Remove the plate and its gasket, and remove the pump.

--- CAUTION ---
Do not operate the fuel pump unless it is immersed in gasoline and connected to its resistor.

4. Installation is the reverse of removal. Use a new gasket on the access plate, and check for leaks after installation.

Cold Start Injector

EFI engines, 1984 22R-E, have a cold start injector located in the intake air chamber which aids in cold weather starting.

Cold start valve removal

REMOVAL & INSTALLATION

1. Disconnect the fuel pipe from the injector.
2. Disconnect the wire from the injector.
3. Unscrew and remove the injector.
4. Installation is the reverse of removal. Always use a new gasket.

Mechanical fuel pumps used on 20R and 22R engines—arrows indicate the fuel flow in and out of the pump

Fuel Pressure Regulator

This device, located in the air chamber of the EFI system, maintains a constant fuel pressure in the injection system.

Pressure regulator removal

REMOVAL & INSTALLATION

1. Disconnect the vacuum sensing hose from the regulator.
2. Place an absorbant towel under the fuel hose connection and disconnect the hose from the regulator.
3. Remove the locknut and remove the regulator from the air chamber.
4. Installation is the reverse of removal. Torque the locknut to 20–25 ft. lb.

Fuel Injector

TESTING

Each injector may be tested for operation while on the engine, in two ways. One, is to obtain an inexpensive mechanic's stethescope and listen for a clicking at the injector. The other way is by checking continuity at each injector terminal with a ohmmeter. Resistence should be 1.5–3.0 ohms.

Injector
Sound Scope
Listening to injector with a mechanic's stethescope

Testing the injector with an ohmmeter

REMOVAL & INSTALLATION

1. Remove the air chamber and throttle body as described earlier.
2. Disconnect the wires from the injector.
3. Disconnect the fuel hose from the delivery pipe.
4. Remove the two hold down bolts and remove the injector along with the delivery pipe. Take care in handling the injectors. DO NOT DROP THEM! KEEP THEM AS CLEAN AS POSSIBLE! Injector performance tests are possible, but expensive special tools are required. If these tools are unavailable, use the test procedures above. If the tools are available, they come with a set of instructions for their use.

Injector removal

5. Installation is the reverse of removal. Use a new O-ring on each injector. Note that each injector should have four insulators. Prior to installation, coat the O-rings with clean gasoline. Prior to tightening the hold down bolts, make sure that the injector rotates smoothly in its bore. If not, the O-rings are twisted. Torque the hold down bolts to 12–16 ft. lb. Check for fuel leakage.

Carburetors

REMOVAL & INSTALLATION

1. Disconnect the battery ground cable.
2. Remove the air cleaner assembly. Label the disconnected hoses so that they may be correctly reinstalled.
3. On 20R, drain the engine coolant and disconnect the heater hose from the choke unit.
4. Disconnect the fuel line at the carburetor.
5. Label and disconnect the vacuum hoses from the carburetor. Disconnect the choke pipe, if so equipped.
6. Disconnect the accelerator linkage and the automatic transmission throttle rod, if so equipped.
7. On 2F engines, disconnect the magnetic valve wire from the coil terminal and the choke cable from the carburetor.
8. Remove the carburetor-to-manifold attaching nuts and lift the carburetor off of the manifold.

9. Cover the open manifold with a clean cloth to prevent dirt and small objects from entering into the engine.

Installation is performed in the reverse order of removal. After the engine has been started, check for fuel and vacuum leaks.

OVERHAUL

Efficient carburetion depends greatly on careful cleaning and inspection during overhaul since dirt, gum, water, or varnish in or on the carburetor parts are often responsible for poor performance.

Overhaul your carburetor in a clean, dust-free area. Carefully disassemble the carburetor, referring often to the exploded views. Keep all similar and lookalike parts segregated during disassembly and cleaning to avoid accidental interchange during assembly. Make a note of all jet sizes.

When the carburetor is disassembled, wash all parts (except diaphragms, electric choke units, pump plunger, and any other plastic, leather, fiber, or rubber parts) in clean carburetor solvent. Do not leave parts in the solvent any longer than is necessary to sufficiently loosen the deposits. Excessive cleaning may remove the special finish from the float bowl and choke valve bodies, leaving these parts unfit for service. Rinse all parts in clean solvent and blow them dry with compressed air or allow them to air dry. Wipe clean all cork, plastic, leather, and fiber parts with a clean lintfree cloth.

Blow out all passages and jets with compressed air and be sure that there are no restrictions or blockages. Never use wire or similar tools to clean jets, fuel passages, or air bleeds. Clean all jets and valves separately to avoid accidental interchange.

Check all parts for wear or damage. If wear or damage is found, replace the defective parts. Especially check the following:
1. Check the float needle and seat for wear. If wear is found, replace the complete assembly.
2. Check the float hinge pin for wear and the float(s) for dents or distortion. Replace the float if fuel has leaked into it.
3. Check the throttle and choke shaft bores for wear or an out-of-round condition. Damage or wear to the throttle arm, shaft, or shaft bore will often require replacement of the throttle body. These parts require a close tolerance of fit; wear may allow air leakage, which could affect starting and idling.

NOTE: Throttle shafts and bushings are not included in overhaul kits. They can be purchased separately.

4. Inspect the idle mixture adjusting needles for burrs or grooves. Any such condition requires replacement of the needle, since you will not be able to obtain a satisfactory idle.
5. Test the accelerator pump check valves. They should pass air one way but not the other. Test for proper seating by blowing and sucking on the valve. Replace

1. Pump jet
2. Spring
3. Outlet check ball
4. Secondary venturi
5. Primary venturi
6. Pump plunger
7. Spring
8. Ball retainer
9. Inlet check ball
10. Plug
11. Spring
12. AAP outlet check ball
13. Plug

the valve if necessary. If the valve is satisfactory, wash the valve again to remove breath moisture.

6. Check the bowl cover for warped surfaces with a straightedge.

7. Closely inspect the valves and seats for wear and damage, replacing as necessary.

8. After the carburetor is assembled, check the choke valve for freedom of operation.

Carburetor overhaul kits are recommended for each overhaul. These kits contain all gaskets and new parts to replace those that deteriorate most rapidly. Failure to replace all parts supplied with the kit (especially gaskets) can result in poor performance later.

After cleaning and checking all components, reassemble the carburetor, using new parts and referring to the exploded view. When reassembling, make sure that all screws and jets are tight in their seats, but do not overtighten, as the tips will be distorted. Tighten all screws gradually, in rotation. Do not tighten needle valves into their seats; uneven jetting will result. Always use new gaskets. Be sure to adjust the float level when reassembling.

14. AAP inlet check ball	21. Sight glass	28. Solenoid valve
15. Throttle positioner	22. Glass retainer	29. Carburetor body
16. Thermostatic valve cover	23. Diaphragm housing cap	30. Diaphragm
17. Thermostatic valve	24. Spring	31. Spring
18. Primary slow jet	25. Diaphragm	32. AAP housing
19. Power valve	26. Housing	33. Secondary main jet
20. Power jet	27. Fast idle cam	34. Primary main jet

Carburetor main body parts—20R engine

FLOAT LEVEL ADJUSTMENT

20R, 22R

With the engine idling, check the fuel level in the carburetor sight glass. If the fuel level is even with the line, no adjustment is necessary. If it is not, adjust the float as follows:

1. Remove and invert the air horn so that the float hangs by its own weight towards the air horn. With the air horn gasket removed, measure the distance between the tip of the float and the air horn. The distance should be 0.197 for 1977 engines, 0.276 for 1978 engines, and 0.413 for 1981–82 (22R) engines and .386 for 1983–84 en-

1. Choke coil water housing	7. Choke shaft	13. Pump arm
2. Choke housing plate	8. Connecting lever	14. Spring
3. Choke lever	9. Choke valve	15. Power piston
4. Choke housing body	10. Air horn	16. Piston retainer
5. Choke breaker	11. Choke opener	17. Needle valve set
6. Relief lever	12. Union	18. Float

Carburetor air horn parts—20R engine

Float adjustment points—20R and 22R engines

Measuring the float level (raised position)—20R and 22R engines

Fuel Union

Air Horn

Metering Needle Guide

Secondary Main Jet

AAP

Slow Jet

Thermostatic Valve

Choke Opener

Fast Idle Cam

Carburetor Body

Solenoid Valve

Throttle Positioner

Fast Idle Adjusting Screw

Idle Mixture Adjusting Screw (Canada RN 4x4)

Metering Needle

Outer Vent Control Valve

Power Piston, Valve and Jet

Needle Valve

Float

Primary Main Jet

Acceleration Pump

Idle Speed Adjusting Screw

Carburetor Flange

Idle Mixture Adjusting Screw and Plug (Ex. Canada RN 4x4)

Throttle Positioner Adjusting Screw

1981 22R carburetor

gines. If the distance is incorrect, adjust the float by bending the center tab (marked "A" in the illustration) on all models except 1978. On 1978 models, adjust the float by bending the metal tab across the two slots and one hole right next to where it enters the float.

2. **20R Engines:** Raise the float away from the air horn and measure the distance between the needle valve push pin and the float lip. The distance should be 0.040 in.

If adjustment is necessary on 1977 and earlier floats, bend the portion of the float marked "B" in the illustration. If adjustment is necessary on 1978 and later floats, bend the single center tab which resembles the tab marked "A" in the illustration.

3. **22R Engines:** Raise the float away from the air horn and measure the distance between the air horn and the tips of the float furthest away from the air horn. The distance should be 1.89 in. If adjustment is

necessary, remove the float from the air horn and bend the tab which is furthest away from the floats (centered between the hinge points). Recheck the setting after the adjustment has been made.

2F Engines

1. Remove the carburetor air horn. Invert the air horn and allow the float to hang towards the air horn.

Fuel Union

Outer Vent Control Valve

Metering Needle

Air Horn

Metering Needle Guide

Secondary Main Jet

AAP

Power Piston Jet and Valve

Needle Valve

Primary Main Jet

Hot Idle Compensation

Slow Jet

Float

Choke Opener

Fast Idle Cam

Carburetor Body

Acceleration Pump

Idle Speed Adjusting Screw

Carburetor Flange

Plug (Except Canada RN4x4)
Idle Mixture Adjusting Screw

Idle-up Adjusting Screw

Solenoid Valve   Idle-up Diaphragm   Fast Idle Adjusting Screw

1982 22R carburetor

2. With the air horn gasket removed, measure the distance between the float and the air horn, at the end of the float opposite the needle valve. The distance should be 0.295 in. If adjustment is necessary, remove the float and bend the tab which is centered between the hinge pivot points. After the adjustment is completed, reinstall the float and recheck the setting.

3. Lift upward on the float and measure the distance between the needle valve push pin and the lip of the float. The distance should be 0.043 in. If adjustment is necessary, remove the float and bend the tabs located just inside of the hinge points. After the adjustment is completed, reinstall the float and recheck the setting.

FAST IDLE ADJUSTMENT— OFF VEHICLE

20R Engines (1979 and Earlier) and 2F Engines

1. Remove the carburetor as previously outlined.

Fuel Union

Metering Needle

Outer Vent Control Valve

Metering Needle Guide

Choke Breaker

Secondary Main Jet

AAP

Choke Opener

Power Piston, Jet and Valve

Needle Valve

Slow Jet

Primary Main Jet

Float

Carburetor Body

Acceleration Pump

Fast Idle Cam

Idle-Up Diaphragm

Carburetor Flange

Idle Mixture Adjusting Screw

Plug

Solenoid Valve

Idle-Up Adjusting Screw

Fast Idle Adjusting Screw

1983–84 22R carburetor

2. Close the choke valve completely and invert the carburetor.

3. Using a wire-type feeler gauge, check the clearance between the upper half of the primary throttle blade and the throttle bore. The clearance should be 0.047 for 20R engines; 0.051 for 2F engines. If necessary, adjust the clearance by turning the fast idle screw.

4. Install the carburetor as previously outlined.

Measuring the float level (lowered position)—20R engine

20R Engines (1980) and 22R Engines (1981 and Later)

NOTE: A special blade angle tool must be obtained to properly make this adjustment.

1. Remove the carburetor as previously outlined.

2. Close the choke valve completely and set the throttle shaft lever to the first step of the fast idle cam.

CARBURETOR SPECIFICATIONS

Year	Engine	Float Level Adjustment	Fast Idle Adjustment	Choke Unloader	Choke Breaker	Kick Up Adjustment	Accelerator Pump Adjustment
'77–'84	2F	0.295 in. ④	—	50°	38°	28° ⑦	0.374 in.
'77–'78	20R	0.197 in. ①	0.047 in.	50°	40°	0.008 in.	0.177 in.
'79–'80	20R	0.280 in.	0.047 in. ⑤	50°	38°	0.008 in.	0.177 in. ②
'81–'82	22R	0.413 in. ③	24°	45° ⑥	38°	—	—
'83–'84	22R	0.386 ③	22°	50°	42°	16.5°	—

① '78 20R 0.276 in.
② '80 20R 0.154 in.
③ Raised position; 1.89 lowered position
④ Raised position; 0.043 lowered position
⑤ '79 only. '80: 24°—see text
⑥ Except Canada. Canada: 50°
⑦ Except California. California: 25°

Special blade angle tool used for various carburetor adjustments—shown attached to choke valve

3. Attach the blade angle tool to the primary throttle blade. Adjust the primary throttle blade angle to the correct angle from horizontal by turning the fast idle screw.

4. Remove the angle tool from the carburetor and install the carburetor as previously outlined.

FAST IDLE ADJUSTMENT— ON VEHICLE

20R Engines (1979 and Earlier)

1. Start the engine and allow it to reach normal operating temperature.

2. Stop the engine and disconnect the vacuum hose from the EGR valve. Connect a tachometer to the engine as previously outlined.

3. Open the throttle valve slightly and close the choke plate, which will set the fast idle cam.

4. Disconnect the vacuum hose(s) from the distributor vacuum unit. Plug the vacuum hose end(s).

5. Without touching the accelerator pedal, start the engine and read the tachometer. If necessary, adjust the fast idle speed to 2400 rpm by turning the fast idle screw.

6. Reconnect the vacuum hoses to both the EGR valve and the distributor vacuum unit. Disconnect the tachometer from the engine.

20R Engines (1980) and 22R Engines (1981 and Later)

1. Start the engine and allow it to reach normal operating temperature.

2. Stop the engine and connect a tachometer to the engine as previously outlined.

3. Remove the air cleaner assembly.

4. Disconnect the vacuum hose at the fast idle cam breaker (if so equipped) and plug the hose end.

5. Disconnect the vacuum hose(s) from the distributor vacuum unit.

6. Disconnect the vacuum hose from the EGR valve.

7. Open the throttle valve slightly and fully pull up on the fast idle linkage. Release the throttle.

8. Without touching the accelerator pedal, start the engine and read the tachometer. If necessary, adjust the fast idle speed to 2400 rpm thru 1982 and 2600 rpm, 1983–84, by turning the fast idle screw.

9. Reconnect the vacuum hoses, disconnect the tachometer and reinstall the air cleaner.

2F Engines

1. Start the engine and allow it to reach normal operating temperature.

2. Stop the engine and connect a tachometer to the engine as previously outlined.

3. Remove the air cleaner assembly.

4. Disconnect the vacuum hoses from both the EGR valve and the distributor vacuum unit.

5. Pull the dash mounted choke control knob fully outward.

6. Open the choke plate and prevent it from closing using a screwdriver. Do not jam the screwdriver into place.

7. Start the engine and read the tachometer. If necessary, adjust the fast idle speed to 1800 rpm by turning the fast idle screw.

8. Remove the screwdriver from the choke, disconnect the tachometer and reconnect the vacuum hoses.

9. Install the air cleaner assembly.

IDLE MIXTURE PRESET ADJUSTMENT

NOTE: **Perform this adjustment on any rebuilt carburetor prior to installation of the carburetor.**

1. Carefully turn the idle mixture adjusting screw clockwise (in) until the screw seats lightly.

——————— CAUTION ———————
Do not force the screw! The tip of the screw is easily damaged.

2. Turn the screw counterclockwise (out) 1½ turns for 20R and 2F engines; 2½ turns for 1981 22R and 4½ turns, '82–'84 engines.

3. Reset the idle mixture adjustment after the engine is running, according to the procedure listed in the tune-up section.

AUTOMATIC CHOKE INSPECTION AND ADJUSTMENT

NOTE: **Steps 1–4 must be performed with the engine cold and turned OFF.**

1. Remove the air cleaner lid.

2. Depress the accelerator pedal. The choke plate should close. If the choke plate closes, proceed to step 5.

3. If the choke plate does not close, loosen the three screws around the thermostat case.

Do not loosen the center housing screw; coolant leakage will occur.

4. Rotate the case just until the choke plate closes and tighten the case screws.

5. Start the engine and allow it to reach normal operating temperature. If the choke plate opens fully, the choke adjustment is correct. If it does not, loosen the three case screws and rotate the case just until the choke plate is fully open. Tighten the case screws.

CHOKE UNLOADER ADJUSTMENT

NOTE: Perform the following adjustment on a cold engine. A special blade angle gauge is needed for this adjustment.

1. Remove the air cleaner lid.

2. Depress the accelerator pedal to set the choke plate in the fully closed position.

3. Attach the blade angle gauge to the choke plate.

4. Open the primary throttle valve completely. The unloader should open the choke plate to the figure shown in the carburetor specification chart. On 2F and 20R engines, bend the fast idle lever to adjust the angle. On 22R engines, bend the first throttle arm to adjust the angle.

5. Remove the blade angle gauge and reinstall the air cleaner lid.

CHOKE BREAKER ADJUSTMENT

NOTE: A special blade angle gauge is needed for this adjustment.

1. Remove the air cleaner assembly.

2. Attach the blade angle gauge to the choke plate.

3. With the choke blade closed, push the choke breaker link towards the choke breaker until resistance is felt. The choke plate should open to the angle shown in the carburetor specification chart. Bend the choke breaker link to adjust the opening.

4. Detach the blade angle gauge and install the air cleaner assembly.

SECONDARY KICK-UP ADJUSTMENT

This adjustment is not necessary on 22R engines.

20R Engines

1. Remove the carburetor as previously outlined.

2. With the carburetor inverted, open the primary throttle blade fully. Measure the distance between the uppermost portion of the secondary throttle blade and the secondary throttle bore, using a wire-type feeler gauge. The clearance should be 0.008 in. If adjustment is necessary, bend the sec-

ondary throttle lever as required to attain the proper clearance.

3. Install the carburetor as previously outlined.

2F Engines

NOTE: A special blade angle gauge is needed for this adjustment.

1. Remove the carburetor as previously outlined.

2. Attach the blade angle gauge to the secondary throttle blade.

3. Open the primary throttle blade fully and read the blade angle gauge. The secondary throttle blade should open slightly to an angle of 28° (except California) or 25° (California). If adjustment is necessary, bend the secondary throttle lever as required to attain the proper angle.

4. Detach the blade angle gauge and install the carburetor as previously outlined.

ACCELERATOR PUMP ADJUSTMENT

NOTE: This adjustment is not required on 22R engines.

1. Remove the air cleaner assembly.

2. With the choke plate fully open, measure the accelerator pump stroke at the top of the accelerator pump rod by fully opening the throttle from the closed position.

3. The total pump stroke should be 0.177 in. for 1979 and earlier 20R engines; 0.154 in. for 1980 20R engines; and 0.374 in. for 2F engines. Adjust the stroke by bending the linkage ("A") which is attached to the accelerator pump arm opposite the accelerator pump.

4. Install the air cleaner assembly.

DIESEL FUEL SYSTEM

Injection Pump

REMOVAL & INSTALLATION

1. Disconnect the cables which are positioned above the valve cover and move the cables aside. Remove the valve cover.

2. Disconnect the cables from both batteries.

3. Using a wrench on the center crankshaft pulley bolt, rotate the engine (clockwise only) until the TDC mark on the pulley is aligned with the pointer. Check that the valves of the number one cylinder are closed (rocker arms loose). If the valves are not closed, rotate the engine 360° and again align the TDC mark with the pointer.

4. Disconnect the fuel injection lines at the injection pump and the injectors. Remove the injection lines.

Measuring the accelerator pump stroke at the top of the accelerator pump rod—20R engine shown, others similar

5. Disconnect the fuel feed line at the injection pump and plug the line.

6. Remove the engine cooling fan, belts, and water pump pulley.

7. Remove the crankshaft pulley, using an appropriate puller.

8. Remove the timing belt cover.

9. Using a piece of chalk or a crayon, mark the relationships between each of the timing gears and the timing belt.

10. Remove the timing belt idler pulley, then remove the timing belt.

11. Remove the injection pump drive gear, using an appropriate puller.

12. Note the factory-made alignment mark next to the outer pump fastener. This mark signifies the required relationship between the pump and the timing case assembly. Align this mark during installation.

13. Unbolt and remove the injection pump.

DO NOT disassemble the injection pump; only factory-authorized repair centers have the facilities to do so. No adjustments to the pump are possible.

14. Installation of the pump is the reverse of the removal procedure. Observe the following torques: injection pump-to-oil pump, 15 ft. lb.; pump stay bolts, 13 ft. lb. See the Engine Mechanical section for specifics concerning timing belt installation. Make sure all gasket surfaces are clean, and replace any damaged gaskets.

Fuel Injectors

REMOVAL

1. Remove the injection lines.

2. Remove the leakage pipe from the injectors and note the location of each sealing washer.

3. Remove the nozzle(s) from the cylinder head, noting the positions of the nozzle seats and seat gaskets.

DO NOT allow dirt to enter the engine through the nozzle holes.

NOTE: Remove accumulations of carbon from the nozzle holes.

4. Keep the injectors in order so that

1. Injection pipe
2. Fuel pipe
3. Fan and fan pulley
4. Crankshaft pulley
5. Timing belt cover
6. Idler pulley
7. Timing belt
8. Pump drive pulley
9. Injection pump

Diesel fuel injection pump and related components

they may be installed in their original positions.

5. If the engine exhibited any type of severe miss, excessive smoking, or drastic decrease in power, it is best to have the nozzles professionally tested for opening pressure, leakage, and spray pattern.

1. Nozzle holder retaining nut
2. Adjusting shim
3. Pressure spring
4. Pressure pin
5. Distance piece
6. Nozzle assembly
7. Nozzle holder body

Exploded view of the diesel fuel injection nozzle

CLEANING

1. Remove the nozzle holder retaining nut from the nozzle holder body.
2. Disassemble the injector, following the accompanying illustration.

------- **CAUTION** -------
DO NOT touch the nozzle mating surfaces with your fingers.

3. Wash the nozzles in clean diesel fuel.
4. Remove carbon from the nozzle needle tip with a small, wooden stick. Don't use any metallic object to clean the nozzle tip.
5. Remove carbon from the exterior of the nozzle body with a brass bristled brush. Don't use a brush having regular, steel bristles.
6. Inspect all parts for damage and/or corrosion. If either of these conditions exist, the entire injector assembly must be replaced.
7. Assemble the injector, using the illustration as a guide. Torque the nozzle holder retaining nut to 44–57 ft. lbs.

Upward

Correct installation of the injector nozzle seat—diesel engine

INSTALLATION

1. Install the injector assembly, noting that:
   a. the nozzle seat is installed between the injector and the seat gasket, and
   b. the nozzle seat must be positioned with the concave side of the seat towards the injector.

Location of the fuel system priming pump on the diesel engine—pump the handle 30–40 times after any fuel system service to purge air from the system

2. Position a wrench on the hex of the nozzle body (NOT the nozzle retaining nut) and torque to 51–65 ft. lbs.
3. Assemble the remaining lines to the injectors. Torque the injection pipe union nuts to 15–21 ft. lbs.

NOTE: After any service is performed to the diesel fuel system, pump the priming handle on the fuel sedimenter assembly 30–40 times to purge air from the system.

1. Fuel pipe follow screw
2. Fuel pipe follow screw
3. Fuel filter body
4. Level warning switch
5. Fuel sedimenter case and nut

Fuel sedimenter exploded view—diesel engine

1. Fuel pipe follow screw
2. Fuel filter and O-ring
3. Fuel filter upper body

Fuel filter and filter body exploded view—diesel engine

Fuel Tank

REMOVAL & INSTALLATION

1. Disconnect the negative battery cable(s) at the battery.
2. Raise the rear of the vehicle and support it with jackstands.
3. Remove the fuel tank drain plug and drain the fuel into a suitable container.

NOTE: **It is best to run the vehicle as low on fuel as possible before removing the tank.**

4. Disconnect the electrical plug from the sending unit.
5. Disconnect the fuel lines from the tank.
6. Disconnect the filler neck and the vent line, if so equipped.
7. Remove the fuel tank skid plate, if so equipped.
8. Remove the tank retaining fasteners and carefully lower the tank from the vehicle.
9. Installation is the reverse of the previous steps. This procedure is basically the same on all models.

CLUTCH

REMOVAL & INSTALLATION

1. Remove the transmission according to the procedure following the clutch section.
2. Stamp or chalk matchmarks on the clutch cover and flywheel, indicating their relationship.
3. Loosen the clutch cover-to-flywheel retaining bolts one turn at a time. The pressure on the clutch disc must be released GRADUALLY.
4. Remove the clutch cover-to-flywheel bolts. Remove the clutch cover and the clutch disc.
5. If the clutch release bearing is to be replaced, do so at this time as follows:
   a. Remove the bearing retaining clip(s) and remove the bearing and hub.
   b. Remove the release fork and the boot.
   c. The bearing is press fitted to the hub. In some cases, the bearing is available with the hub from automotive suppliers. If this is not the case with your model, contact a machine shop and have the bearing replaced using a hydraulic press. Using other means to replace the bearing could result in personal injury.
   d. Clean all parts and lightly grease the input shaft splines and all of the contact points.
   e. Install the bearing/hub assembly, fork, boot, and retaining clip(s) in their original locations.
6. Inspect the flywheel surface for cracks, heat scoring (blue marks), and warpage. If oil is present on the flywheel surface, this indicates that either the engine rear oil seal or the transmission front oil seal is leaking. If necessary, refer to the appropriate section for seal replacement. If in doubt concerning the condition of the flywheel, consult an automotive machine shop.
7. Before installing any new parts, make sure that they are clean. During installation, do not get grease or oil on any of the components, as this will shorten clutch life considerably.

8. Position the clutch disc against the flywheel. (Pickups: The short side of the splined section faces the flywheel; Landcruisers—The long side of the splined section faces the flywheel.)
9. Install the clutch cover over the disc and install the bolts loosely. Align the matchmarks made during step 2. If a new or rebuilt clutch cover assembly is installed, use the matchmark on the old cover assembly as a reference.
10. Align the clutch disc with the flywheel using a clutch aligning tool, which is available in most auto stores at a reasonable price.
11. With the clutch aligning tool installed, tighten the clutch cover bolts gradually in a star pattern, as is done with lug nuts. Finally torque the bolts to 11–16 ft. lbs.
12. Install the transmission using the procedure following the clutch section.

CLUTCH PEDAL HEIGHT ADJUSTMENT

The pedal height measurement is gauged from the angled section of the floorboard to the center of the clutch pedal pad. Refer to the accompanying specification chart to determine the recommended pedal height.

If necessary, adjust the pedal height by loosening the locknut and turning the pedal stop bolt which is located above the pedal towards the drivers seat. Tighten the locknut after the adjustment.

1. Lock nut
2. Stop bolt
3. Lock nut
4. Push rod

Clutch pedal adjustment points—typical. The distance between the ends of the long arrow is the pedal height. The distance between the two short arrows is the pedal free-play. Push rod play is only a small movement of the pedal—see text.

CLUTCH PEDAL PUSH ROD PLAY ADJUSTMENT

The pedal push rod play is the distance between the clutch master cylinder piston and the pedal pushrod located above the pedal towards the firewall. Since it is nearly impossible to measure this distance at the source, it must be measured at the pedal pad, preferably with a dial indicator gauge. Refer to the accompanying specification chart to determine the recommended play.

1. Reservoir filler cap assembly
2. Master cylinder reservoir float
3. Master cylinder reservoir bolt
4. Reservoir bolt washer
5. Master cylinder reservoir
10. Compression spring
11. Master cylinder body
12. Master cylinder piston
13. Cylinder cup
14. Plate washer
15. Hole snap-ring
16. Master cylinder boot
17. Master cylinder pushrod
18. Nut
19. Master cylinder pushrod clevis

Clutch master cylinder exploded view—typical

Measuring the fork tip end-play—typical

If necessary, adjust the pedal play by loosening the pedal pushrod locknut and turning the pushrod. Tighten the locknut after the adjustment.

CLUTCH FORK TIP PLAY ADJUSTMENT

The fork tip play is the total amount of travel evident at the outer end of the clutch release fork where the fork comes in contact with the release cylinder pushrod. Refer to the accompanying specification chart to determine the recommended fork tip play.

The fork tip play is adjusted by loosening the release cylinder pushrod locknut and effectively increasing or decreasing the pushrod length as required.

NOTE: Some models do not have adjustable release cylinder pushrods. These models are identified by having no adjustment nuts on the pushrod.

CLUTCH PEDAL FREE-PLAY ADJUSTMENT

The free-play measurement is the total travel of the clutch pedal from the fully released position to where resistance is felt as the pedal is pushed downward. Refer to the accompanying specification chart to determine the recommended pedal free play.

If the clutch pedal free play is incorrect, perform the previous clutch adjustments then bleed the system accoridng to the procedure which follows. If a pedal free-play dimension is not listed for your model, perform the previous clutch adjustments and disregard the pedal free-play measurement.

Clutch Master Cylinder
REMOVAL

1. Disconnect the master cylinder pushrod from the clutch pedal.
2. Remove the hydraulic line from the master cylinder being careful not to damage the compression fitting.
3. Remove the nut(s) holding the master cylinder to the engine compartment.

----------- **CAUTION** -----------
Brake fluid dissolves paint. Do not allow it to drip onto the body when removing the master cylinder.

CLUTCH ADJUSTMENT SPECIFICATIONS
(All measurements in inches)

Year	Model	Pedal Height	Pedal Push Rod Play	Pedal Free-Play	Fork Tip Play
'79 and earlier	Pickup	6.0–6.4	0.020–0.200	0.200–0.600	—
'80 and later	Pickup	6.0–6.4	0.040–0.200	0.200–0.600①	②
'79 and earlier	Land Cruiser 2 dr. w/P.B.③	8.5	0.020–0.120	—	0.120–0.160
	wo/P.B.④	7.9	0.020–0.120	—	0.120–0.160
'80 and later	Land Cruiser 2 dr.	8.5	0.040–0.200	—	0.157–0.197
'79 and earlier	Land Cruiser Wagon w/P.B.③	7.3	0.020–0.200	—	0.120–0.160
	wo/P.B.④	6.8	0.020–0.200	—	0.120–0.160
'80 and later	Land Cruiser Wagon	7.7	0.040–0.200	—	0.160–0.197

① '80 4WD models—0.980–1.770
② '80 4WD models—0.079–0.118
③ With power brakes
④ Without power brakes

OVERHAUL AND INSTALLATION

1. Disassemble the master cylinder by unscrewing the clutch pedal clevis from the pushrod. Also remove the locknut.

2. Pull off the rubber boot to expose an internal snap-ring. Remove the snap-ring and withdraw the piston and compression spring.

3. Take a clean rag and wipe out the inside of the cylinder. Inspect the inside of the cylinder for scoring and deposits. Use crocus cloth or a small hone to refinish the inside of the cylinder. If light honing will not remove score marks replace the cylinder.

--- CAUTION ---

Be careful not to remove too much from the cylinder walls as the cups will not be able to seal the cylinder if the diameter is enlarged excessively.

4. Wash all metal parts in solvent.

5. Further disassembly should be avoided unless the reservoir is leaking. If the reservoir needs to be replaced, remove the cap and remove the master cylinder reservoir bolt located at the bottom of the reservoir. Tighten the bolt upon reassembly.

6. With new parts from a rebuilding kit assemble the master cylinder. Coat the cylinder wall with brake fluid so that the edges of the new cups will not be damaged.

7. Reinstall the master cylinder. Partially tighten the hydraulic line before tightening the master cylinder mounting nut(s). Torque the nut(s) to 25 ft. lb. Adjust the push rod play clearance as outlined earlier, after bleeding the system.

Clutch Release Cylinder

REMOVAL

1. Jack up the front of the truck and support it on jackstands.

2. Remove the tension spring on the clutch fork.

3. Remove the hydraulic line from the release cylinder. Be careful not to damage the fitting.

4. Turn the release cylinder pushrod in sufficiently to gain clearance from the fork.

5. Remove the mounting bolts and withdraw the cylinder.

OVERHAUL

1. Remove the pushrod, rubber boot, piston and cups from the cylinder.

2. Clean the inside of the cylinder with a rag and inspect for scoring. If there is no serious damage, hone the cylinder just enough to remove deposits. Replace the cylinder if light honing does not remove the score marks. Wash all the parts in brake fluid before assembly.

3. Coat the new rubber parts in brake fluid and reassemble.

INSTALLATION

1. Install the hydraulic line from the master cylinder.

2. Position the cylinder on the clutch housing and install the clamp and retaining screws.

3. Adjust the fork tip clearance as previously outlined.

NOTE: The system must be bled after the cylinder is reinstalled.

Hydraulic System Bleeding

NOTE: This procedure may be utilized when either the clutch master or release cylinder has been removed or if any of the hydraulic lines have been disturbed.

--- CAUTION ---

Do not spill brake fluid on the body of the vehicle as it will destroy the paint.

1. Fill the master cylinder reservoir with brake fluid.

2. Remove the cap and loosen the bleeder screw on the clutch release cylinder. Cover the hole with your finger.

3. Have an assistant pump the clutch pedal several times. Take your finger off the hole while the pedal is being depressed so that the air in the system can be released.

Put your finger back on the hole and release the pedal.

4. After fluid pressure can be felt (with your finger) tighten the bleeder screw.

5. Put a short length of hose over the bleeder screw and place the other end into a jar half full of clean brake fluid.

6. Depress the clutch pedal and loosen the bleeder screw. Allow the fluid to flow into the jar.

7. Tighten the plug and then release the clutch pedal.

8. Repeat steps 6 and 7 until no air bubbles are visible in the bleeder tube.

9. When there are no more air bubbles in the system, tighten the plug fully with the pedal depressed. Replace the plastic cap.

10. Fill the master cylinder to the correct level with brake fluid.

11. Check the system for leaks.

MANUAL TRANSMISSION AND TRANSFER CASE

REMOVAL & INSTALLATION

2WD Pickup

NOTE: A special service tool is needed for removal of the transmission shift lever on floorshift models: Toyota #09305-20011 is used on 1979 and earlier models; #09305-20012 is used on 1980–83 models. Equivalents of these special tools may also be used. No special tool is needed for 1984 models.

1. Disconnect the battery cables at the battery.

NOTE: Steps 2–4 apply to floorshift equipped models.

2. Remove the center floor console, if so equipped.

3. Remove the shift lever handle. Remove the floor mat or carpet along with the shift lever boot in order to gain access to the shift lever.

4. Using the proper shift lever removal tool mentioned previously, remove the shift lever.

5. Raise the vehicle and support it safely with jack stands.

6. Drain the transmission fluid.

7. Chalk matchmarks on the driveshaft flange and the differential pinion flange to indicate their relationships. These marks must be aligned during installation.

8. Remove the driveshaft flange bolts and the center support bearing-to-frame bolts (if equipped with a 2-piece driveshaft). Lower the driveshaft out of the vehicle.

9. Disconnect the wiring at the back-up lamp switch.

1. Bleeder plug cap
2. Bleeder plug
3. Slave cylinder body
4. Cylinder cup
5. Cylinder cup
6. Slave cylinder piston
7. Slave cylinder boot
8. Slave cylinder pushrod No. 1
9. Nut
10. Slave cylinder pushrod No. 2

Clutch slave cylinder exploded view—typical

10. Disconnect the speedometer cable at the transmission and tie the cable out of the way.

11. Disconnect the wiring at the starter. Remove the starter mounting bolts and lower the starter out of the vehicle.

12. If the hydraulic line from the clutch release cylinder is clamped to the frame, remove the clamp retaining bolt. Remove the release cylinder mounting bolts and the fork spring (if so equipped). Tie the release cylinder out of the way.

NOTE: It is not necessary to disconnect the hydraulic line from the release cylinder.

13. On column shift vehicles, disconnect the shift selector linkage at the transmission.

14. On column shift vehicles, remove the transmission cross shafts.

15. Support the rear of the transmission with a jack and remove the transmission-to-crossmember mounting bolts.

16. Raise the rear of the transmission SLIGHTLY; just enough to take the weight off of the crossmember.

17. Remove the crossmember-to-frame attaching bolts and remove the crossmember from the vehicle.

18. Place a support under the engine with a wooden block between the support and the engine.

———— **CAUTION** ————

The wooden block and support should be no more than about ¼ away from the engine so that when the engine is lowered, damage will not occur to any underhood components. If possible, shim the support so that the wooden block touches the engine.

19. Lower the jack until the engine rests on the support and block.

NOTE: For the next step, it is recommended that you have an assistant help you guide the transmission out of the vehicle.

20. Remove the transmission-to-engine attaching bolts and draw the transmission rearward and down away from the engine.

21. Refer to the Unit Repair Section for overhaul procedures.

Installation is the reverse of removal. Observe the following points:

1. If the clutch has been replaced, make sure that the clutch disc is aligned properly. Refer to the clutch section.

2. Lightly lubricate the following parts with multi-purpose grease:
   a. End of the input shaft
   b. Splines of the input shaft
   c. Inner surface of the release bearing
   d. Release fork contact points
   e. Driveshaft splines

3. Replenish the transmission (and transfer case) fluid levels.

4. If the clutch has been replaced, make the necessary adjustments as previously outlined in the clutch section.

5. Align the matchmarks made during disassembly.

6. Check the back-up lamp operation.

4WD Pickup (Including Transfer Case)

NOTE: A special service tool, Toyota #09305-20012 or its equivalent, is needed to remove the transmission shift lever.

1. Disconnect the battery cables at the battery.

2. Remove the shift lever handles. Remove the front floor mat or carpet along with both shift lever boots to gain access to the shift levers.

3. Using the special shift lever removal tool mentioned previously, remove the transmission shift lever.

4. Using needle nose pliers, remove the transfer case shift lever retainer, then remove the shift lever.

5. Raise the vehicle and support it securely with jackstands.

NOTE: Because of space limitations, it may be necessary to raise both the front and rear of the vehicle. If this is done, place jackstands under both axles as follows: On the outside of the U-bolts at the front axle; on the inside of the U-bolts at the rear axle.

6. Drain the lubricant from both the transmission and the transfer case.

7. Chalk matchmarks on the driveshaft flanges and the differential pinion flanges to indicate their relationships. These marks must be aligned during installation.

8. Remove the four bolts from each end of the front driveshaft and remove the driveshaft assembly.

NOTE: Do not disassemble the front driveshaft to remove it.

9. Chalk matchmarks on the rear driveshaft and the slip yoke to indicate their relationships. These marks must be aligned during installation.

10. Remove the four bolts from the rearward flange of the rear driveshaft. Lower the driveshaft out of the vehicle. Remove the four bolts from the slip yoke flange then remove the flange and yoke assembly.

11. Unbolt the clutch release cylinder and tie it out of the way.

NOTE: It is not necessary to disconnect the hydraulic line from the clutch release cylinder.

12. Disconnect the positive battery cable at the starter motor switch.

13. Disconnect the remaining wire at the starter.

14. Remove the two starter retaining bolts and lower the starter out of the vehicle.

15. Disconnect the speedometer cable at the transfer case and tie it out of the way.

16. Disconnect the exhaust pipe clamp at the transmission housing.

17. Disconnect the wiring for the back-up lamp switch and the 4WD indicator switch.

18. Remove the crossmember-to-transfer case adaptor mounting bolts. Using a jack, raise the transmission and transfer case assembly SLIGHTLY off of the crossmember; just enough to take the weight off of the crossmember.

19. Remove the crossmember-to-frame attaching bolts and remove the crossmember.

20. Place a support under the engine with a wooden block between the support and the engine.

———— **CAUTION** ————

The wooden block and support should be no more than about ¼" away from the engine so that when the engine is lowered, damage will not occur to any underhood components. If possible, shim the support so that the wooden block touches the engine.

21. Lower the jack until the engine rests on the support.

NOTE: For the next step, it is recommended that you have an assistant help you guide the transmission and transfer case assembly out of the vehicle.

22. Remove the transmission-to-engine attaching bolts and draw the transmission and transfer case assembly rearward and down away from the engine.

23. To separate the transmission and transfer case, stand the transmission on its front face with the tailshaft pointing upward. Remove the transfer case-to-adapter mounting bolts and lift the transfer case off of the transmission assembly.

24. Refer to the Unit Repair Section for overhaul procedures.

To install the transmission, reverse the previous steps. Refer to the end of the 2WD procedure for installation points.

Land Cruiser
1979 AND EARLIER MODELS

NOTE: Steps 2–4 pertain to 2 door models.

1. Disconnect the battery cables at the battery.

2. Remove the front seats, seat tracks, and the console box, if so equipped.

3. Remove the heater pipe clamp which is located on the transmission tunnel to the right of the transfer case shift lever.

4. If the fuel tank is mounted beneath the passenger seat, drain the fuel, remove the fuel tank cover, disconnect the lines, etc., and remove the fuel tank.

5. Remove the shift lever knobs and the shift lever boots.

6. Using Toyota special service tool #09305-60010 or its equivalent, remove the transmission shift lever.

7. Remove the transmission tunnel cover.

8. Raise the vehicle and support it safely with jack stands.

9. Drain the lubricant from both the transmission and the transfer case.

10. Remove the undercover located beneath the front driveshaft.

11. Chalk matchmarks on the driveshaft flanges and the differential pinion flanges to indicate their relationships. These marks must be aligned during installation.

12. Unbolt the driveshaft flanges and remove both the front and rear driveshafts.

13. Disconnect the speedometer cable from the transfer case and tie it out of the way.

14. Disconnect the parking brake cable at the parking brake lever. Leave the cable attached at the drum end; the cable will be removed with the transmission and transfer case assembly.

15. If the vehicle is equipped with a vacuum 4WD engagement system, mark and disconnect the following items at the transfer case:

    a. Wiring for the indicator

    b. Wiring for the transfer switch

    c. Vacuum hoses

16. Disconnect the wiring for the back-up lamp switch. Unbolt the back-up lamp wiring harness clamp from the transfer case, if so equipped.

17. On column shift models, disconnect the shift linkage at the transmission.

18. Remove the power take-off (PTO) lever, if so equipped.

19. Follow steps 18–22 of the 4WD Pickup procedure to remove the transmission and transfer case assembly.

20. To separate the transmission from the transfer case:

    a. Remove the 4WD engagement lever guide.

    b. Remove the 4WD lever and rod as an assembly.

    c. Remove the back-up lamp switch.

    d. If the vehicle is equipped with a PTO, remove the PTO unit from the transmission. If the vehicle does not have a PTO, remove the cover from the left side of the transfer case.

    e. Remove the rear transfer case cover (six bolts) from the transfer case. Remove the shaft nut located behind the cover.

NOTE: This nut is staked at the factory; to remove it, you must tap the staked portions outward to clear the shaft. Restake the nut after installation.

    f. Remove the five transfer case-to-transmission bolts.

NOTE: Two of these bolts are located inside the left side of the transfer case, where the PTO or cover was previously removed.

    g. Using a puller assembled to the transfer case and the transmission output shaft, separate the transfer case from the transmission.

21. Refer to the Unit Repair Section for overhaul procedures.

22. Installation is the reverse of the previous steps. Refer to the installation points at the end of the 2WD Pickup procedure.

1980 AND LATER

1. Disconnect the battery cables at the battery.

2. Remove the entrance scuff plates from the floor of the interior.

3. Remove both side trim panels from beneath the instrument panel.

4. Remove the center heater duct.

5. Remove the front floor mat or carpet.

6. Remove the handles from both shift levers.

7. Remove the transmission tunnel cover along with the shift lever boots.

8. Disconnect the wiring from both the back-up lamp switch and the 4WD indicator (if so equipped).

9. Using Toyota special service tool #09305-55010 or its equivalent, remove the transmission shift lever.

10. Raise the vehicle and support it safely with jack stands.

11. Remove the transfer case skid plate.

12. Disconnect the speedometer cable at the transfer case and tie it out of the way.

13. Chalk matchmarks on the driveshaft flanges and the differential pinion flanges to indicate their relationships. These marks must be aligned during installation.

14. Remove the mounting bolts from the driveshaft flanges and remove the driveshaft assemblies.

15. Disconnect the starter wiring. Remove the starter mounting bolts and remove the starter from the vehicle.

16. Unbolt the clutch release cylinder and move it out of the way.

NOTE: It is not necessary to disconnect the hydraulic line from the release cylinder.

17. Drain the lubricant from both the transmission and the transfer case.

18. Remove the tachometer sensor, if so equipped.

19. Follow steps 18–22 of the 4WD Pickup procedure to remove the transmission and transfer case assembly.

20. To separate the transfer case from the transmission, remove the transfer case mounting bolts and slide the transfer case off of the transmission.

21. Refer to the Unit Repair Section for overhaul procedures.

22. Installation is the reverse of the previous steps. Refer to the installation points at the end of the 2WD Pickup procedure.

OVERHAUL

For all overhaul procedures, please refer to "Manual Transmission Overhaul" in the Unit Repair section.

SHIFT LINKAGE ADJUSTMENT

Column Shifter

Shift lever adjustment:

The only adjustments which may be performed on the column shift linkages are for the length of the column-to-transmission rods. Adjust these so that the transmission operates smoothly.

Floor Shifter

All Toyota models equipped with a floor shifter have internally-mounted shift linkages. On older models, the linkage is contained in the side cover which is bolted on the transmission case.

No external adjustment is needed or possible.

AUTOMATIC TRANSMISSION

Description

The A-30 Toyoglide transmission is used in all 1977 and earlier models. The A-30 is a fully automatic three-speed transmission using a combination of multiple disc clutches and front and rear bands to accomplish gear ratio changes. Internal adjustments necessary on this transmission include only the front and rear bands.

The A-40 transmission is used in 1978–79 models. The A-40 is also a fully automatic three-speed, but it does not use bands for gear changes, thus internal adjustments are not possible.

In 1980, the A-40 was replaced by the A-43 three-speed, which is used through the current model year. Internal adjustments are not required on this transmission.

The A-43D is a fully automatic four-speed transmission first offered as an option on 1981 models and is available through the current model year. The fourth speed of this transmission is an overdrive ratio of 0.688 to 1, which offers improved gasoline mileage by lowering the engine rpm at highway speeds. The hydraulic circuit of the overdrive mode is electrically controlled. The main electrical components include the following:

1. A dash mounted overdrive control switch

2. A dash mounted "OVERDRIVE-OFF" indicator lamp

3. A transmission mounted solenoid

4. An engine mounted thermo-switch which prevents overdrive engagement until the engine coolant temperature reaches 131°F.

REMOVAL

A-30 and A-40 Transmissions

1. Disconnect the battery cables at the battery.

2. Disconnect the transmission throttle linkage at the carburetor.

3. Raise the vehicle and support it with jack stands.

4. Drain the transmission fluid.

5. Disconnect the wiring from the starter.

6. Unbolt the starter and lower it out of the vehicle.

7. Disconnect the exhaust pipe from the exhaust manifold. Remove the exhaust clamp from the exhaust pipe.

8. Disconnect the linkage from the drivers side of the transmission.

9. Disconnect the speedometer cable and tie it out of the way.

10. Disconnect the parking brake cable from the parking brake control lever.

11. Chalk matchmarks on the rear driveshaft flange and the differential pinion flange. These marks must be aligned during installation.

12. Unbolt the rear driveshaft flange. If the vehicle has a two-piece driveshaft, remove the center bearing bracket-to-frame bolts. Remove the driveshaft from the vehicle.

13. Support the transmission using a jack with a wooden block placed between the jack and the transmission pan. Do not raise the transmission—just raise the jack until the wooden block touches the transmission pan.

14. Place a support under the engine with a wooden block between the support and the engine.

— CAUTION —

The wooden block and support should be no more than about ¼″ away from the engine so that when the engine is lowered, damage will not occur to any underhood components.

15. Remove the transmission mount-to-crossmember bolts.

16. Raise the transmission SLIGHTLY, just enough to take the weight of the transmission off of the crossmember. Remove the crossmember-to-frame mounting bolts and remove the crossmember from the vehicle.

17. Slowly lower the transmission until the engine rests on the support placed during step 14.

18. Disconnect the two fluid cooler lines at the transmission. Plug the lines and the holes in the transmission to prevent the entry of dirt.

— CAUTION —

Before performing step 19, place a drain pan under the torque convertor area of the transmission. Fluid leakage will occur as the transmission is uncoupled.

19. Remove the transmission-to-engine mounting bolts. Carefully pull the transmission to the rear and after the transmission uncouples from the engine, lower the transmission out of the vehicle.

20. Remove the torque convertor from the flywheel.

A-43 and A-43D Transmissions

1. Disconnect the battery cables at the battery.

2. Remove the air cleaner assembly.

3. Disconnect the transmission throttle cable at the carburetor.

4. Raise the vehicle and support it safely with jack stands.

5. Disconnect the wiring connectors (near the starter) for the neutral start switch and the back-up light switch. Also, on A-43D transmission equipped models, disconnect the solenoid switch wiring at the same location.

6. Disconnect the starter wiring at the starter. Unbolt the starter and remove it from the vehicle.

7. Drain the transmission fluid.

8. Chalk matchmarks on the rear driveshaft flange and the differential pinion flange. These marks must be aligned during installation.

9. Unbolt the rear driveshaft flange. If the vehicle has a two-piece driveshaft, remove the center bearing bracket-to-frame bolts. Remove the driveshaft from the vehicle.

10. Disconnect the speedometer cable from the transmission and tie it out of the way.

11. Disconnect the shift linkage at the transmission.

12. Disconnect the exhaust pipe clamp at the bellhousing and remove the oil filler tube.

13. Disconnect the transmission oil cooler lines at the transmission.

14. Support the transmission using a jack with a wooden block placed between the jack and the transmission pan. Do not raise the transmission—just raise the jack until the wooden block touches the transmission pan.

15. Place a wooden block (or blocks) between the engine oil pan and the front frame crossmember.

— CAUTION —

The wooden block(s) should be no more than about ¼″ away from the engine so that when the engine is lowered, damage will not occur to any underhood components.

16. Remove the transmission mount-to-crossmember bolts.

17. Raise the transmission SLIGHTLY— just enough to take the weight of the transmission off of the crossmember. Remove the crossmember-to-frame mounting bolts and remove the crossmember from the vehicle.

18. Slowly lower the transmission until

the engine rests on the wooden block placed during step 15.

19. Remove the engine undercover in order to gain access to the engine crankshaft pulley.

20. Remove the two rubber plugs from the service holes located at the rear of the engine in order to gain access to the torque convertor bolts.

21. Rotate the crankshaft as necessary to remove the torque convertor bolts (6). Access to these bolts is through the service holes mentioned in step 20.

22. Obtain a bolt of the same dimensions as the torque convertor bolts. Cut the head off of the bolt and hacksaw a screwdriver slot in the bolt opposite the threaded end.

NOTE: This modified bolt is used as a guidepin. Two guides pins are needed to properly install the transmission.

23. Thread the guide pin into one of the torque convertor bolt holes. The guide pin will help keep the convertor with the transmission.

24. Remove the transmission-to-engine mounting bolts.

25. Carefully move the transmission rearward by prying on the guide pin through the service hole.

— CAUTION —

As soon as the transmission is away from the engine about ⅛″, feed wire through the front of the transmission and secure the wire in order to keep the convertor attached to the transmission. Also, try to keep the nose of the transmission pointed upward SLIGHTLY to help keep the convertor in place.

26. Pull the transmission rearward and lower it out of the vehicle.

— CAUTION —

Do not allow the attached cables to catch on any components during removal.

27. With the transmission out of the vehicle, remove the torque convertor as follows:

    a. Place a drain pan under the front of the transmission.

    b. Pull the convertor straight off of the transmission and allow the fluid to drain.

TORQUE CONVERTOR AND FLYWHEEL RUN-OUT

Testing

Prior to installation of the transmission, Toyota recommends to check the torque convertor and flywheel run-out dimensions. If either of these run-out limits are beyond the maximum allowable limits, excessive wear of the front transmission seal will occur.

Refer to the accompanying chart to assist in performing and interpreting this procedure. A dial indicator gauge is needed to perform the run-out checks.

TORQUE CONVERTOR AND FLYWHEEL
RUN-OUT TESTING

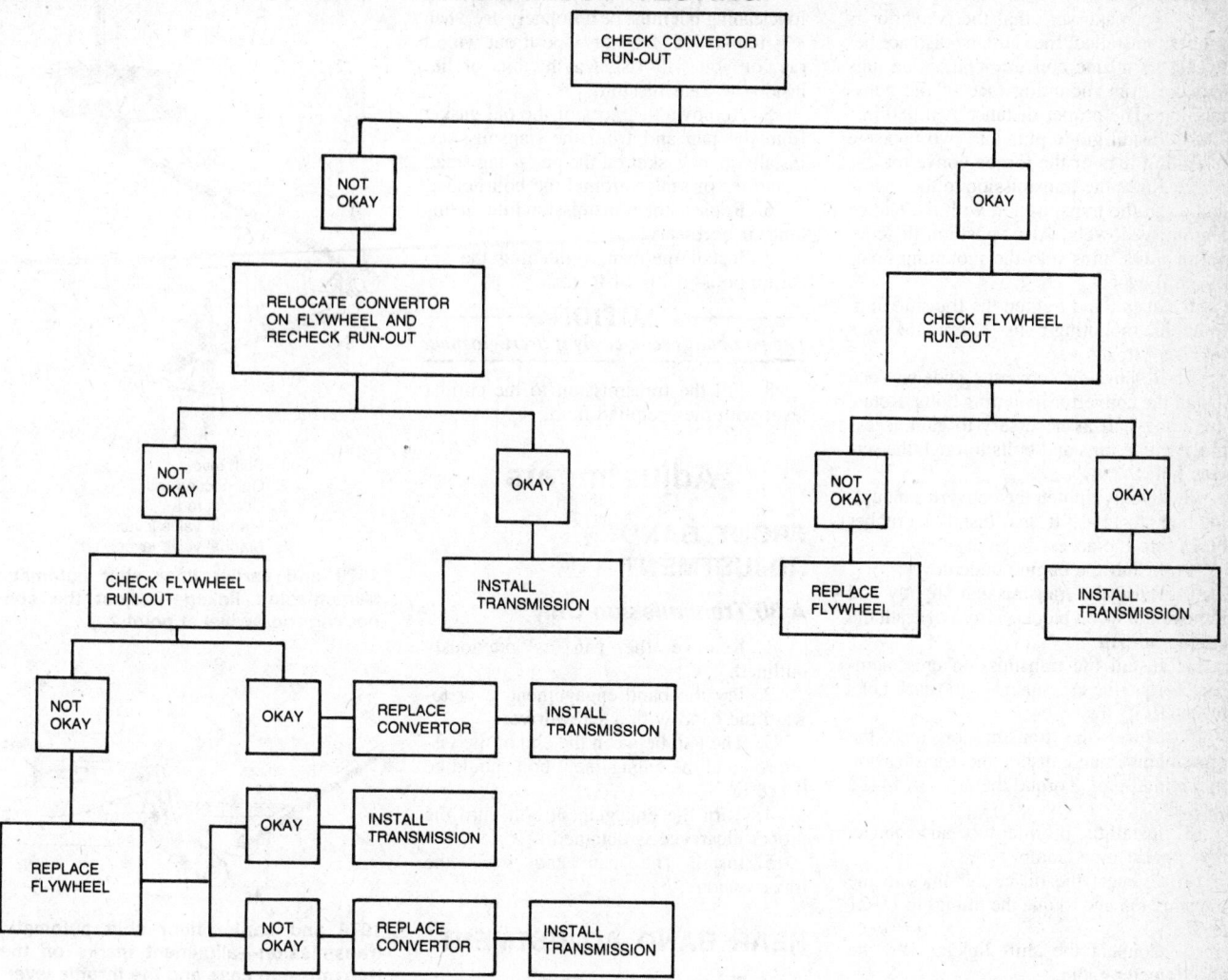

1. Mount the torque convertor on the flywheel and torque the convertor bolts to 11–16 ft. lbs.

2. Mount the dial indicator so that the indicator probe touches the outer surface of the convertor extension sleeve (90° to the convertor centerline).

3. Adjust the dial indicator to zero.

4. Slowly rotate the convertor and read the dial indicator. The indicator needle should not deviate more than the following amounts:

1980 and earlier transmissions—0.008 in.
1981 and later transmissions—0.012 in.

5. Remove the torque convertor from the flywheel.

6. Except A-43 and A-43D transmissions: Mount the dial indicator so that the indicator probe touches the flywheel drive plate (convertor mounting) surface. A-43 and A-43D transmissions: Mount the dial indicator so that the indicator probe touches the flywheel ring gear just inside of the gear teeth (surface faces the rear of the vehicle).

7. Zero the indicator needle and slowly rotate the flywheel. The indicator needle should not deviate more than the following amounts:

A-30 transmissions: 0.005 in.
A-40 transmissions: 0.012 in.
A-43 and A-43D trans: 0.008 in.

INSTALLATION

A-30 and A-40 Transmissions

1. Apply a coat of multipurpose grease to the torque converter stub shaft and the pilot hole of the flywheel.

2. Assemble the torque converter into the transmission, so that its output shaft and the transmission input shaft are aligned. Rotate the torque converter until the dowel pin is at the bottom.

3. Install a guide pin into the bottom bolt hole next to the dowel pin. Align the flywheel and the torque converter.

4. Tighten the torque converter bolts to 11–16 ft. lbs. Rotate the crankshaft half a turn to reach all the bolts, and tighten them evenly.

5. Bolt the transmission to the engine.

Tighten the bolts to 37–51 ft. lbs.

6. Replace the frame crossmember and the driveshaft. Attach the parking brake cable.

7. Replace the starter and its wiring. Attach the transmission cooler lines. Attach the speedometer cable.

8. Replace the exhaust pipe clamp and bolt the exhaust pipe to the manifold.

9. Install and adjust the throttle linkage rod. Attach the connecting rod to the transmission and adjust the shift lever linkage.

10. Fill the transmission with the specified type fluid. If the torque converter was completely drained, the transmission will need about 7 quarts of fluid.

11. Connect the battery cables. Road test and check for leaks.

A-43 and A-43D Transmissions

1. Apply a coat of multi-purpose grease to the torque convertor stub shaft and the corresponding pilot hole in the flywheel.

2. Install the torque convertor into the front of the transmission. Push inward on

the torque convertor while rotating it to completely couple the torque convertor to the transmission.

3. To make sure that the convertor is properly installed, measure the distance between the torque convertor mounting lugs and the front mounting face of the transmission. The proper distance is 0.080 in.

4. Install guide pins into two opposite mounting lugs of the torque convertor.

5. Raise the transmission to the engine and align the transmission with the engine alignment dowels. Also, position the convertor guide pins into the mounting holes of the flywheel.

6. Install and tighten the transmission-to-engine mounting bolts. Torque the bolts to 37–57 ft. lbs.

7. Remove the convertor guide pins and install the convertor mounting bolts. Rotate the crankshaft as necessary to gain access to the guide pins and bolts through the service holes.

8. Evenly tighten the convertor mounting bolts to 11–15 ft. lbs. Install the rubber plugs into the access holes.

9. Install the engine undercover.

10. Raise the transmission slightly and remove the wood block(s) from beneath the engine oil pan.

11. Install the transmission crossmember. Torque the crossmember-to-frame bolts to 26–36 ft. lbs.

12. Lower the transmission onto the crossmember and install the transmission mounting bolts. Torque the bolts to 14–22 ft. lbs.

13. Install the oil filler tube and connect the exhaust pipe clamp.

14. Connect the oil cooler lines to the transmission and torque the fittings to 15–21 ft. lbs.

15. Connect the shift linkage and the speedometer cable.

16. Install the driveshaft and the starter.

17. Connect the wiring which was disconnected during removal of the transmission.

18. Connect and adjust the transmission throttle cable (adjustment covered in a later procedure).

19. Install the air cleaner assembly and connect the battery cables.

20. Fill the transmission with the specified type of fluid. If the torque convertor was completely drained, the transmission will need about 7 quarts of fluid.

21. Road test the vehicle and check for leaks.

Transmission Pan and Filter

REMOVAL & INSTALLATION

1. Jack up the front end of the vehicle and support it on jackstands.

2. Place a container under the transmission drain plug and drain the transmission fluid.

3. Remove the pan securing bolts and remove the pan and gasket.

4. The pan may be washed in solvent for cleaning but must be absolutely dry when it is reinstalled. Do not wipe it out with a rag, or you will risk leaving bits of lint inside the transmission.

5. Remove all traces of the old gasket from the pan and from the transmission. Install a new gasket on the pan using small quantities of sealer around the bolt holes.

6. Replace the transmission filter at this time, if necessary.

7. Install the pan, tightening the securing bolts to 11–14 ft. lbs.

------- CAUTION -------
The pan bolts break easily if overtightened.

8. Fill the transmission to the correct level with the specified fluid.

Adjustments

FRONT BAND ADJUSTMENT

A-30 Transmission Only

1. Remove the pan as previously outlined.

2. Pry the band engagement lever toward the band with a screwdriver.

3. The gap between the end of the piston rod and the engagement bolt should be 0.118 in.

4. Turn the engagement bolt until the proper clearance is obtained.

5. Install the pan and refill the transmission.

REAR BAND ADJUSTMENT

A-30 Transmission Only

The rear band adjusting bolt is located on the outside of the transmission case so that it is not necessary to remove the pan in order to perform the adjustment.

1. Loosen the adjusting bolt locknut and turn the screw all the way in.

2. Back off the adjusting screw one full turn.

3. Lock the adjustment by tightening the adjusting screw locknut.

SHIFT LINKAGE ADJUSTMENT

1979 AND EARLIER TRANSMISSION

1. Check all of the shift linkage bushings for wear. Replace any that are excessively worn.

2. Set the manual valve lever on the transmission in the Neutral position.

3. Lock the connecting rod swivel with the locknut so that the pointer, selector, and manual valve lever are all in the Neutral position.

1. Shift lever
2. Connecting rod
3. Control rod
4. Manual valve lever
5. Manual valve lever shaft

1979 and earlier floor shift automatic transmission linkage—adjust the connecting rod swivel at point 2.

1979 and earlier floor shift automatic transmission—alignment marks on the transmission case and the throttle lever

4. Check the operation by moving the selector through all the gears.

1980 AND LATER TRANSMISSIONS

1. Loosen the adjustment nut on the transmission connecting rod.

2. Push the manual lever of the transmission fully forward.

3. Move the manual lever back three notches, which is the NEUTRAL position.

On 1980 and later automatics, loosen this nut to adjust the shift linkage

4. Set the gearshift selector lever in its NEUTRAL position.

5. Apply a slight amount of forward pressure on the selector lever (towards the reverse position) and tighten the connecting rod adjustment nut.

Transmission Throttle Control

LINKAGE ADJUSTMENT (1977 AND EARLIER)

When the carburetor throttle is wide open, the throttle linkage pointer should line up with the mark stamped on the transmission case. To adjust:

1. Loosen the locknuts on either end of the linkage adjusting turnbuckle located midway between the carburetor and the transmission.

2. Detach the throttle linkage connecting rod from the carburetor.

3. Align the pointer on the throttle valve lever with the mark stamped on the transmission case.

4. Rotate the turnbuckle so that the end of the throttle linkage rod and the carburetor throttle lever are aligned.

Throttle control linkage adjustment—1977 and earlier automatic transmissions

NOTE: The throttle valve of the carburetor must be fully open during this adjustment.

5. Tighten the turnbuckle locknuts and connect the throttle rod to the carburetor.

6. Open the throttle valve and check to see that the pointer and the mark are aligned on the transmission.

7. Road-test the truck. If the transmission keeps shifting rapidly back and forth between gears at certain speeds or if it fails to down-shift properly when going up hills, repeat the throttle linkage adjustment.

CABLE ADJUSTMENT (1978 AND LATER)

1. Remove the air cleaner assembly.

2. Push the accelerator to the floor and check that the throttle opens fully. If not, adjust the accelerator link so that it does.

3. Push back the rubber boot from the throttle cable which runs down to the trans-

mission. Loosen the throttle cable adjustment nuts so that the cable housing can be adjusted.

4. Fully open the carburetor throttle by having an assistant press the accelerator all the way to the floor.

5. Adjust the cable housing so that, with the throttle wide open, the distance between the outer cable end rubber cap to the inner cable stopper is 2.05 in. for 1977–78; 0–0.04 in. for 1979–84.

6. Tighten the nuts and double check the adjustment. Install the rubber boot and the air cleaner.

Throttle control cable adjustment—1978 and later automatic transmissions

Neutral Safety Switch

The neutral safety switch prevents the vehicle from starting unless the gearshift selector is in either the PARK or NEUTRAL positions. If the vehicle will start in these positions, adjustment of the switch is required.

ADJUSTMENT

1979 and Earlier

1. Remove the screws which hold the center console in place.

2. Remove the electrical connector and remove the console from the vehicle.

3. Loosen the switch securing bolts.

4. Set the selector in the Drive position.

5. Move the switch so that the arm just contacts the control shaft lever.

6. Tighten the switch retaining bolts.

7. Check the operation of the switch; the truck should start only in Neutral or in Park. The back-up lamps should only operate in the Reverse position.

8. If the switch cannot be adjusted so that it functions properly, replace it with a new one.

9. Reinstall the console.

1980–83

1. Loosen the neutral start switch bolt.

2. Place the gearshift selector lever in the Neutral position.

3. Align the shaft groove of the switch with the neutral Basic line. Hold the switch in this position and tighten the switch bolt to 35–60 in. lbs.

1980–83 neutral safety switch adjustment

1984

1. Loosen the neutral start switch bolt.

2. Place the selector lever in N.

3. Disconnect the wires from the neutral start switch.

4. Connect an ohmmeter between the terminals of the switch.

5. Adjust the switch until there is continuity between the N and B terminals.

Checking neutral start switch continuity

6. Reconnect the wires.

7. Torque the bolt to 48 in. lb.

DRIVE TRAIN

Driveshaft

REMOVAL & INSTALLATION

2WD Standard Bed Pickup

1. Jack up the rear of the truck and support the rear axle housing with jack stands.

2. Paint a mating mark on the two halves of the rear universal joint flange.

3. Remove the bolts which hold the rear flange together.

4. Remove the splined end of the driveshaft from the transmission.

NOTE: Plug the end of the transmission with a rag or dummy flange to avoid losing transmission oil.

5. Remove the driveshaft from under the truck.

Installation is the reverse of removal. Grease the splined end of the shaft before installing. Tighten bolts to 11–16 ft. lbs.

Exploded view of a one-piece driveshaft assembly—typical

1. Sliding shaft dust cover
2. Universal joint yoke sleeve
3. Universal joint spider
4. Spider bearing seal
5. Snap-ring
6. Spider bearing
7. Driveshaft
8. Universal joint yoke falnge

2WD Long Bed Pickup

1. Jack up the rear of the truck and support the rear axle housing with jackstands.
2. Paint mating marks on all six flange halves.
3. Remove the bolts attaching the rear universal joint flange to the drive pinion flange.
4. Drop the rear section of the shaft slightly and pull the unit out of the center bearing sleeve yoke.
5. Remove the center bearing support from the crossmember.
6. Unbolt the driveshaft flange from the rear of the transmission and remove driveshaft along with center bearing support.
To install:
1. Connect the output flange of the transmission to the flange on the front half of the shaft.
2. Install the center bearing support to the crossmember, but do not fully tighten the bolts.
3. Install the rear section of the shaft making sure that all mating marks are aligned. Make sure line on bearing in the center support mount is in the middle of the hole at the bottom of center mount.

4. Tighten the flange bolts to 11–16 ft. lbs.

4WD Pickup—All

1. Jack the truck off the ground and place support stands under both the front and rear axles.
2. Match-mark all driveshaft flanges BEFORE removing the bolts.
3. Unbolt the rear driveshaft flange from the rear pinion flange.
4. Unbolt the rear driveshaft flange from the rear transfer case flange and remove driveshaft.
5. Repeat steps 3 and 4 on front driveshaft.
6. Reverse order for reassembly. Tighten flange bolts to 29–43 ft. lbs.

NOTE: For 4 × 4 Long Bed Pickups, see above for rear driveshaft removal and installation.

Land Cruiser

1. Raise the vehicle and support it with jackstands.
2. Match-mark all driveshaft flanges BEFORE removing the bolts.

3. Unfasten the bolts which secure the universal joint flange to the differential pinion flange.
4. Perform step 2 for the U-joint-to-transfer case flange bolts.
5. Withdraw the driveshaft from beneath the vehicle.
6. Repeat steps 3–5 on the front driveshaft.
Installation is performed in the reverse order of removal.

NOTE: Lubricate the U-joints and sliding joints with multipurpose grease before installation.

Universal Joints

OVERHAUL

Universal joints are marked at the factory if oversize parts have been used during assembly. Before buying a rebuilding kit for your truck, note any "V" punch marks on the sleeve yoke, drilled marks, or red painted marks on the bearing caps. These marks will correspond to the oversize parts you will have to get from your dealer. The rebuilding kit or parts you buy should include new bearing seals, snap-rings, spiders, and spider bearings.

Although there are special tools available for rebuilding universal joints, you should be able to do the job easily with the assortment of sockets noted in this procedure. Be certain to paint or scratch mating marks on the driveshaft(s) and universal joint flange yoke(s) before disassembling the joints.

Removing the universal joint spider from the driveshaft flange—note the size and positions of the service tools

1. Select two sockets. One should be small enough to pass through the universal joint yoke hole. The other should be large enough so that the spider bearing cap fits easily inside it.
2. Remove the snap-rings from the bearing holes of the yoke.
3. Position the yoke in a vise so that one socket is centered against a bearing cap and the other socket aligned so that the bearing cap may pass inside of it.

NOTE: Refer to the positions of the service tools in the illustration.

4. Tighten the vise just enough to hold the sockets and yoke in position. Check to see that they are positioned correctly.

Exploded view of a two-piece driveshaft assembly—typical

1. Intermediate driveshaft
2. Dust deflector No. I
3. Dust deflector No. 2
4. Hole snap-ring
5. Dust deflector No. 3
6. Radial ball bearing
7. Dust deflector No. 4
8. Center support bearing cushion
9. Set ring
10. Hole snap-ring
11. Dust deflector No. 2
12. Center support bearing housing No. 1
13. Center support bearing housing No. 2
14. Dust deflector No. 1
15. Universal joint flange
16. Plate washer
17. Castle nut
18. Cotter pin
19. Universal joint flange yoke
20. Universal joint spider
21. Universal joint spider bearing seal
22. Universal joint spider bearing
23. Hole snap-ring
24. Grease fitting
25. Universal joint sleeve yoke
26. Sliding shaft dust cover
27. Balance piece
28. Driveshaft

5. As you tighten the vise, one bearing cap will be pressed against the cross of the U-joint forcing the other cap out of the yoke.

6. Proceed in this manner to remove all caps and then remove the cross.

To assemble:

1. Note any markings and use oversize parts as necessary.

2. Repack the spider bearing cups with grease, and assemble the needle bearing rollers into the cups.

3. Position the spider in the driveshaft yoke. Place the bearing cups inside the lip of the yoke, so that they are held in place by the ends of the spider.

4. Position two sockets of equal size on either side of the bearings, and slip this assembly between the jaws of the vise.

5. As you close the vise, the sockets should force the bearing caps into the holes of the yoke and onto the arms of the spider.

6. After assembling the joints, check the spider thrust play. Select and install new snap-rings which will allow a maximum of 0.002 in. of play. The snap-rings must be of equal size on opposite arms of the spider.

7. Check the joints for smooth movement and install the driveshaft.

Center Driveshaft Bearing

REPLACEMENT

The center support bearing is a sealed unit which requires no periodic maintenance. The following procedure should be used if it should become necessary to replace the bearing.

1. Remove the intermediate driveshaft and the center support bearing assembly.

2. Paint mating marks on the universal joint flange and the intermediate driveshaft.

3. Remove the cotter pin and castle nut from the intermediate driveshaft. Remove the universal joint flange from the driveshaft using a press.

4. Remove the center support bearing assembly from the driveshaft.

5. Remove the two bolts from the bearing housing and remove the housing.

6. Remove the dust deflectors (type #2) from both sides of the bearing cushion. Remove the dust deflectors type #3 and #4 from either side of the bearing.

7. Remove the snap-rings from each side of the bearing. This is easy to do if you have a snap-ring tool which fits the holes in the ring, and very difficult otherwise. Remove the bearing.

To assemble:

1. Install the new bearing into the cushion and fit a snap-ring on each side.

2. Apply a coat of multipurpose grease to the dust deflectors type #3 and #4, and put them in their respective places on each side of the bearing. Type #4, which has a slightly larger outside diameter, goes on the rear of the bearing.

3. Press the type #2 dust deflectors onto each side of the cushion. The water drain holes in the deflectors should be in the same position on each side of the cushion.

4. Assemble the two halves of the housing around the cushion. The water drain holes should face the bottom of the housing.

5. Press the support bearing assembly firmly onto the intermediate driveshaft, with the #3 type seal facing the front.

6. Match the mating marks painted earlier, and install the universal joint flange to the driveshaft. Tighten the castle nut to about 130 ft. lbs., and use a new cotter pin to lock it in place. Tighten the nut to align the holes for the cotter pin, but do not loosen it. It is okay to tighten it up to 150 ft. lbs.

NOTE: Check to see if the center support bearing assembly will rotate smoothly around the driveshaft.

7. When reinstalling the driveshaft, be certain to match up the marks on both the front transmission flange and the flange on the sleeve yoke of the rear driveshaft.

FRONT DRIVE AXLE

Axle Shaft

REMOVAL & INSTALLATION

4WD Pickup

1. Set the control handle in the free position.

2. Remove the bolts in the hub and remove the hub and gasket.

3. Remove the nuts, spring washers and cone washers.

NOTE: Cone washers can be removed by using a tapered punch.

4. Remove hub body and gasket.

5. Remove snap-ring from free wheel hub body.

6. Remove hub ring, spacer and inner hub.

1. Oil seal
2. Oil seal set
3. Bearings
4. Steering knuckle
5. Bearing cup and shim
6. Nut, washer dowel
7. Oil seal retainer
8. Front axle shaft
9. Knuckle spindle and gasket
10. Dust cover
11. Dust seal and gasket
12. Front axle hub with disc
13. Brake caliper
14. Brake line

Front axle and steering knuckle (4WD)—pick-up illustrated, Land Cruiser similar

7. Remove compression spring, follower, tension spring, and clutch.

8. Remove snap-ring, free wheel hub cover ball and spring, seal, and control handle.

NOTE: Check inner hub and free wheel hub ring oil clearance. Clearance should be 0.012 in.

9. Disconnect the brake line and the two bolts holding the brake caliper.

10. Remove the dust cap and snap-ring.

11. Remove the cone washers with a tapered punch.

12. Remove the flange by installing two bolts in the special holes for flange removal. Tighten these bolts until the flange comes loose. Remove the bolts by loosening them and remove the flange.

13. Remove the locknut, washer, and adjusting nut. Pull the rotor assembly off the spindle. The outer and inner bearings and seal will come apart as a unit.

14. Set the rotor on two blocks of wood. Using a drift pin drive the seal out. The inner bearing will drop out at this time. Using this pin drive the front and rear race from the rotor.

15. Place the rotor in a vice and remove the front axle hub.

16. Inspect the rotor, spindle, and hub for damage.

17. Remove the dust seal, gasket, and dust cover.

18. Remove the spindle and gasket.

19. Position the flat part of the outer shaft up and pull out the shaft.

20. Remove the oil seal retainer.

21. Remove the cone type washers from the drag link with a tapered punch.

22. Remove the drag link and tie rod.

23. Remove the bottom bearing cap and shim.

24. Remove the upper and lower bearings with the proper tool.

NOTE: The steering knuckle bearing remover is available from your Toyota dealer. Part #09606-60010. Remember to mark the bearings in order to reassemble them in their proper place:

25. Remove the upper and lower races with a brass drift pin.

26. Remove the steering knuckle and inspect for damage or wear.

27. Place the inner shaft in a vice. Using a drift pin drive the outer shaft apart and remove six ball bearings.

NOTE: Tilt the inner race and cage. Take the balls out one at a time.

28. Remove the cage and race from the shaft.

NOTE: Turn the large opening in the cage against the protruding portion of the shaft, pull the race and cage out.

29. Remove the inner race from the cage through the large opening.

30. Remove the inner oil seal.
Thoroughly wash and inspect all parts for wear or damage.

31. Installation is the reversal of removal with the following suggestions:
   a. Replace all oil and grease seals.
   b. Pack the hub interior, inner and outer bearings with a multipurpose grease.

Land Cruiser

1. Raise and support the vehicle securely and remove the wheel/tire assembly.

2. Plug the brake master cylinder reservoir to prevent brake fluid leakage from the disconnected brake flexible hose.

3. Remove the outer axle shaft flange cap, and then remove the shaft snap-ring on the outer shaft. If equipped with free wheel locking hubs, complete steps 1–4 under 4WD Pick-up axle shaft removal.

4. Remove the bolts retaining the outer axle shaft flange onto the front axle hub, and then, screw in two service bolts into the shaft flange alternately, and remove the shaft flange with its gasket.

5. Remove the brake drum set screws and remove the brake drum. If equipped with disc brakes, remove the caliper and disc.

6. Straighten the lockwasher, and remove the front wheel bearing adjusting nuts with front wheel adjusting nut wrench or similar tool.

7. Remove the front axle hub together with its claw washer, bearings, and oil seal.

8. Remove the clip and disconnect the brake flexible hose from the brake tube.

9. Cut and remove the lock wire and remove the bolts retaining the brake backing plate onto the steering knuckle. Remove the brake backing plate together with brake shoes, tension springs, and the wheel cylinder still assembled to the backing plate.

10. Tap the steering knuckle spindle lightly with a soft mallet, and remove the spindle with its gasket.

NOTE: When removing the steering knuckle spindle on a vehicle equipped with the ball joint type axle shaft joint, be prepared for the disconnection of the outer axle shaft from the joint. The joint ball will fall from the joint. Try to cushion its fall or catch it if you can.

11. On those models equipped with the ball type axle shaft joint, slide the inner front axle shaft out of the axle housing. On those models equipped with the Birfield constant velocity joint type of axle joint, remove the entire axle shaft assembly from the axle housing.

12. Remove bushing from inside of knuckle spindle with a bearing puller. Install new bushing using a metal tube as a seating tool.

13. Remove axle housing oil seal with a bearing puller. To install, use a metal tube as a seating tool.
Install the axle shaft in the reverse order of removal.

14. On those models equipped with the ball joint type axle joint, install the inner axle with its proper spacer in position until the splines are fully meshed with the differential side gear splines. Next, fill the steering knuckle three quarters full with grease and place the joint ball on the inner shaft end. Install the outer shaft and the front axle shaft spacer into the steering knuckle spindle and install the spindle with its gasket onto the steering knuckle.

15. On those models equipped with the Birfield constant velocity joint axle joint, install the axle into the housing and rotate the axle shaft until its splines mesh with the splines in the differential. Fill the steering knuckle housing three quarters full with grease and install the steering knuckle spindle.

16. Install and assemble the remaining components in the reverse order of removal. Adjust the wheel bearing preload.

NOTE: See brake drum or disc removal section for wheel bearing preload instructions.

Locking Hubs

REMOVAL & INSTALLATION

1. Set the hub control handle to the FREE position.

2. Remove the hub bolts which retain the front cover and handle assembly and remove the assembly.

3. Remove the snap-ring from the axle shaft using snap-ring pliers.

4. Remove the hub body mounting nuts.

5. Remove the cone washers from the hub body mounting studs by tapping on the washer slits with a tapered punch.

6. Remove the hub body from the axle hub.

7. Installation is the reverse of the previous steps. Use a new gasket when installing the hub.

DISASSEMBLY

1. Remove the snap-ring which attaches the control handle to the hub cover. Remove the control handle.

2. Remove the ball and spring from the control handle.

3. Remove the snap-ring which holds the free wheel hub ring and the inner hub into the hub body.

4. Remove the inner hub and the free wheel hub ring from the hub body.

5. Remove the snap-ring from the inner hub and remove the free wheel hub and spacer from the inner hub.

INSPECTION

1. Check all parts for damage or excessive wear.

2. Temporarily install the control handle into the hub cover and make sure the handle operates freely.

3. Check that the clutch slides freely within the hub body.

1. Snap-ring
2. Free wheel hub body
3. Snap-ring
4. Free wheel hub ring
5. Spacer
6. Inner hub
7. Spring
8. Pawl
9. Spring
10. Clutch
11. Snap-ring
12. Free wheel hub cover
13. Steel ball and spring
14. Seal
15. Control handle

Exploded view of a free-wheeling hub assembly

4. Measure the inner diameter of the hub ring and the outer diameter (smooth surface) of the inner hub. The difference between these measurements should be no greater than 0.012 in.

ASSEMBLY

1. Apply a coat of multipurpose grease to the sliding service of each part.
2. Install the seal, spring, and ball into the control handle.
3. Install the control handle and snap-ring.

Aligning the end of the tension spring with the initial groove of the clutch—see text

4. Install the tension spring into the clutch with the end of the spring aligned with the initial groove of the clutch.
5. Install the follower pawl as follows:
   a. Place the pawl on the tension spring with one of the large tabs (of the pawl) against the bent end of the tension spring.
   b. Place the top ring of the tension spring on the small tabs of the pawl.
6. Position the hub cover into the large end of the tension spring. Compress the spring and install the clutch with the pawl tab of the clutch fit to the control handle.
7. Install the inner hub and hub ring into the hub body. Install the snap-ring.
8. Temporarily install the cover and handle assembly into the hub body. Adjust the control handle to the FREE position and check that the inner hub turns smoothly.
9. Remove the cover and handle assembly from the hub body and install these components as previously outlined.

Differential

Overhaul of the differential carrier is a complex operation requiring special tools and technical knowledge. If either of these is not available, it may be wise (economically) to remove the carrier yourself and

have a professional perform the overhaul, rather then purchase special (and expensive) tools or take the vehicle to a shop.

REMOVAL & INSTALLATION

1. Drain the lubricant from the differential.
2. Remove the axle shafts as previously outlined.
3. Remove the driveshaft as previously outlined.
4. Remove the carrier retaining nuts and pull the carrier assembly out of the differential housing.
5. Installation is performed in the reverse of the previous steps. Apply a thin coat of liquid or silicone sealer to the new carrier to housing gasket before installing the carrier. Also apply sealer to the carrier side face of each carrier retaining nut before installing these nuts.

OVERHAUL

1. Thoroughly wash and rinse the carrier and blow dry with compressed air.
2. Securely clamp the carrier in a vise or suitable stand.
3. Apply a light coating of mechanic's blue to the teeth of the ring gear.
4. Applying a slight drag on the ring gear to avoid backlash, rotate the pinion in a smooth and continuous manner to obtain a good tooth pattern on the ring gear.
5. Next, attach a dial indicator gauge to the carrier base and check the ring gear backlash.
6. Also check ring gear runout at this time. If the tooth pattern obtained is correct, and the backlash and runout are within limits, any gear noise must come from the side gear.
7. With the dial indicator gauge set up on the carrier, check the backlash between the pinion gears and side gears. Excessive backlash usually is due to either worn thrust washers or a worn pinion shaft.
8. Check side gear thrust clearance with a feeler gauge.
9. If everything is within specifications, test the preload on the differential drive pinion nut. Punch mark both pinion and nut in their original positions, then loosen the pinion nut about ½ turn and torque to specifications. If the punch marks line up again (within 60°) the pinion preload was correct.
10. Punch mark both the carrier and the side bearing caps for identification, remove the lock-nuts and take off the caps.
11. Remove the differential case assembly from the carrier. Do not mix the bearing cups; paint mark them for identification.
12. Remove the differential pinion nut (do not let the pinion drop out), then remove the pinion spacer, yoke and oil seal.
13. With a brass punch, drive out the pinion bearing cups.

a. Housing assembly
b. Filler plug
c. Gasket
d. Bolt
e. Lock washer
f. Hexagon bolt
g. Bearing adjusting nut lock
h. Lockwasher
i. Stud
j. Bearing adjusting nut
k. Bearing
l. Breather plug
m. Lockwasher

n. Ring gear and drive pinion 1 and 2
o. Case
p. Lockplate
q. Bolt
r. Lockpin
s. Pinion shaft
t. Side gear
u. Thrust washer
v. Pinion
w. Thrust washer
x. Drain plug
y. Oil reservoir

aa. Shim
ab. Bearing
ac. Spacer
ad. Shim
ae. Bearing
af. Oil slinger
ag. Gasket
ah. Carrier
ai. Nut
aj. Oil seal
ak. Dust deflector
al. Universal joint flange
am. Flat washer

Differential components

NOTE: This should be done only when the bearings are to be replaced.

14. Press or pull off the drive pinion rear bearing. Avoid damaging the flat spacer behind the bearing.

15. Measure the spacer thickness and note the measurement for future use. Remove both side bearings from the differential case

and mark them "L" and "R" for identification.

NOTE: Remove side bearings only if they must be replaced.

16. Punch mark the differential case and cover, then remove the cover bolts and the cover (where fitted).

17. Remove the shaft and pinions, the side gears and all thrust washers.

NOTE: Some differential types have four spider pinion gears; punch mark the gears before removal so they can be correctly reinstalled.

Check all bearing cones and cups for wear. Inspect the tooth surfaces of all gears carefully and inspect all thrust washers for wear and signs of slipping in their seats. Check all gear shafts for scoring, wear or distortion. Finally, inspect the case and carrier housing for cracks or other damage. Also check the case for signs of wear at the side gear bores, bearing cap and mounting hubs.

Assembly is performed in the following order:

1. Wash and clean all parts before installation.

2. Lightly oil all bearings and gear shafts, except the ring gear and drive pinion teeth.

3. Place the side gears and the pinion gears, with their thrust washers, into the differential case.

4. Insert the shaft and align the lock pin holes in the case and shaft.

5. Install the case cover in place and install the lock pin (bolt) and tighten the cover bolts to specification; check the play.

6. If the side bearings were removed, install them now. If the ring gear was removed, install it now. Tighten the bolts in symmetrical sequence to avoid distortion and runout.

7. Install the drive pinion bearing cups into the carrier housing, using a suitable installing tool. Make sure the cups are seated solidly.

8. Assemble the drive pinion rear bearing to the drive pinion and insert it into the carrier housing. Install the spacer and front

DIFFERENTIAL SPECIFICATIONS

Model	Backlash (in.)		Runout (in.) Ring Gear	Torque (ft. lbs.)		Pinion Bearing Preload④ (in. lbs.)	
	Ring Gear and Pinion	Side Gears		Side Bearing Cap	Differential Pinion Nut	New	Used
Pick-up (all)	0.005–0.007	0.002–0.008	①	51–65	②	③	③
Land Cruiser (all)	0.006–0.008	0.001–0.008	0.004	65–80	145–175	16–23	8–11

① '77—0.004 in.
'78–84:
w/7½" ring gear—0.003 in.
w/8" ring gear—0.004 in.

② 1977–82
w/7.5" ring gear—80–173 ft. lbs.
w/8.0" ring gear—123–151 ft. lbs.
1983–84
½ & ¾ ton, exc short wheel base
w/22 R: 80–173
chassis/cab & 4WD, incl. short wheel base
w/22R: 145–253

③ '77–82 except '81–'82
2WD w/7.5" ring gear:
16.5–22.5 new
7.8–11.3 used
'81–'82
2WD w/7.5" ring gear:
10.4–16.5 new
5.2–8.7 used
'83–'84
½ ton & ¾ ton, exc. short wheel
base w/22R: 5.2–8.7
chassis/cab & 4WD, incl. short wheel base
w/22R: 7.8–11.3

④ Without oil seal or differential gears installed

bearing to the drive pinion; install the yoke and tighten the nut to specifications.

— **CAUTION** —

The drive pinion oil seal is NOT installed at this point.

9. The drive pinion preload is measured in in. lbs. (not ft. lbs.). Adjust the preload by changing the length of the bearing spacer (between the front and rear bearings) until the required preload is obtained.

10. Place the previously assembled differential case into position in the bearing hubs and put the caps into position as marked (L and R).

11. Set the case so that there will be the least amount of backlash between the ring gear and pinion (in order to save time adjusting).

12. Install the adjusting nuts (also marked L and R) and take care not to cross-thread them.

13. Finger-tighten the bearing caps until the threads are lined up correctly, then tighten slowly.

14. Back off the right-hand adjusting nut (ring gear teeth side) and screw in the other nut until almost no backlash is felt.

15. Attach a dial indicator gauge so that it reads at right angles to the back of the ring gear, then screw in the righthand adjusting nut until the gauge indicates that all side play has been eliminated.

16. Tighten the adjusting nut another 1 or 1½ notches (depending on the fit of the lock tabs).

17. Recheck the preload on the drive pinion as before; this time the specifications are different.

18. If too loose, readjust the side bearing preload; if too tight, adjust the ring gear backlash.

19. Install the dial indicator gauge so that it contacts the ring gear teeth at right angles. Adjust the backlash to specifications.

20. If too great, adjust by loosening the bearing cap bolts slightly and screwing the right-hand adjusting nut (ring gear teeth side) out about two notches.

21. Tighten the left-hand adjusting nut the same amount.

NOTE: One notch of the adjusting nut equals about 0.002 in. of backlash.

22. Recheck the backlash, then tighten the bearing cap nuts.

23. Using a dial indicator recheck all runout dimensions (ring gear back, ring gear outer circumference and differential case).

24. Apply a thin coat of mechanic's blue, red lead or even lipstick to the ring gear teeth. Rotate the gear several times, applying a light drag to the ring gear. Rotate the gear in both directions.

25. Inspect the tooth pattern. There are four basic tooth patterns: heel, toe, flank and face. Most often the tooth pattern obtained will be a combination of two of these patterns and the adjustments must be made accordingly.

Ring gear tooth contact patterns

Heel contact Move the drive pinion, in by increasing the thickness of the spacer (between the pinion head and rear bearing). Readjust backlash by moving the ring gear away from the pinion.

Face contact Adjust same as above.

Toe contact Adjust by moving the drive pinion out by reducing the thickness of the spacer. Readjust backlash.

Flank contact Adjust same as toe contact. Continue assembling as follows:

26. Remove the drive pinion nut and install the seal into the differential carrier housing, then install the oil slinger, dust shield and yoke and retorque the pinion nut as specified.

27. Install the differential carrier assembly into the axle housing.

Steering Knuckle

REMOVAL & INSTALLATION

2WD Pick-up

NOTE: On Pickups with coil springs, it will be necessary to obtain a spring compressor for installation.

1. Jack up front of vehicle and support on stands.

2. Remove wheel.

3. If vehicle has front disc brakes, remove brake caliper.

4. Remove axle hub dust cap. Remove cotter key, lock, front nut and front nut washer from axle hub. Remove front bearing and remove brake disk or drum.

5. On drum brakes, remove brake line and plug.

6. Remove cotter keys and four bolts holding the brake backing plate and brake shoes on drum and the rotor dust cover on disk brakes. Remove the plate or cover.

7. Remove steering link from back of knuckle.

8. Support the lower arm with a jack and raise to put pressure on spring.

— **CAUTION** —

Be careful not to unbalance vehicle support stands when jacking up lower arm!

9. Remove cotter key and large lower ball joint nut and separate the ball joint from the steering knuckle with a gear puller

10. Repeat step 9 on upper ball joint.

NOTE: Do not let the steering knuckle fall after removing upper ball joint.

Installation is the reverse of removal.

11. On Pickups with coil springs, use a spring compressor when reassembling. Observe the following torques:

Large nut on upper ball joint: 66–94 ft. lbs.

Large nut on lower ball joint: 87–123 ft. lbs.

Rotor dust cover or drum backing plate to steering knuckle: 66–94 ft. lbs.

NOTE: See brake section for hub nut installation procedures.

— **CAUTION** —

Be sure to bleed brakes.

4WD Pickup and Land Cruiser

1. Complete front axle shaft removal procedures in drive axle section, above.

2. Unbolt and remove the tie rod from the knuckle arm with a gear puller. On the Pickup, if removing the driver's side knuckle see section on steering adjustment below for removal of the steering drag link.

3. Remove the oil seal retainer at the back of the steering knuckle.

4. Remove the four nuts on the top steering knuckle cap along with the cone washers. See section on axle shaft removal for procedures in removing cone washers.

5. Remove the four nuts on the bottom steering knuckle cap along with cone washers.

6. Using a small drift and hammer, tap the knuckle bearing caps out from inside the steering knuckle.

— **CAUTION** —

Do not tap on the bearings!

NOTE: Do not mix or lose the upper and lower bearing cap shims.

Installation is the reverse of removal.

To test the knuckle bearing preload, attach a spring scale to the end hole in the steering knuckle at a right angle to the arm. The force required to move the knuckle from side to side should be 4–8 lbs. 4WD Pickup; 4–5 lbs. (Land Cruiser). If the preload is not correct, adjust by replacing shims.

REAR DRIVE AXLE

Axle Shaft

REMOVAL & INSTALLATION

Pick-Ups

1. Loosen the lug nuts on the wheel, then raise the truck and support it on jackstands.
2. Drain the axle housing.
3. Remove the lug nuts and remove the wheel.
4. Remove the brake drum securing screw and remove the drum.
5. Remove the brake springs and the retracting spring clamp bolt. Remove the lower springs and shoe strut. Remove the brake shoes, screws, and the parking brake lever. Disengage the parking brake cable from the lever and the backing plate.
6. Plug the master cylinder reservoir inlet to prevent the fluid from running out. Disconnect the brake line from the wheel cylinder, being careful not to damage the fitting. Plug the brake line.
7. Remove the four nuts retaining the brake backing plate to the axle housing.
8. Pull the backing plate and axle from the axle housing.

Install the Axle in the Following Manner:

1. Install a new O-ring onto the axle housing.
2. Install the axle shaft and brake backing plate assembly into the axle housing. Be careful not to damage the oil seal with the axle splines. Rotate the axle back and forth until the shaft splines mesh with the differential gear splines.
3. Install the brake backing plate nuts and tighten to 44–58 ft. lbs.
4. Install the brake shoes and lever assembly. Connect the parking brake cable and the brake shoe springs. Connect the brake line to the wheel cylinder.
5. After installing the brake drum, bleed the brakes and adjust the brake shoe clearance. Refill the axle housing with SAE 90W GL5 gear oil.

Land Cruiser
SEMI-FLOATING TYPE DIFFERENTIAL

1. Remove the hub cap and loosen the wheel nuts.
2. Raise the rear axle housing with a jack and support the rear of the vehicle with jackstands.
3. Drain the oil from the differential.
4. Remove the wheel nuts and take off the wheels.
5. Remove the brake drum and related parts, as detailed below.
6. Remove the cover from the back of the differential housing.

7. Remove the pin from the differential pinion shaft.
8. Withdraw the pinion shaft and its spacer from the case.
9. Use a mallet to tap the rear axle shaft toward the differential, to aid in removal of the axle shaft C-lock.
10. Remove the C-lock.
11. Withdraw the axle shaft from the housing.
12. Repeat the removal procedure for the opposite side.
13. To remove oil seal and bearing, use a bearing puller and remove axle bearing and oil seal together. To replace, use a metal tube to drive bearing and seal into seat.

CAUTION

Do not mix the parts of the left and right axle shaft assemblies.

Installation is performed in the reverse order of removal. After installing the axle shaft, C-lock, spacer, and pinion shaft, measure the clearance between the axle shaft and the pinion shaft spacer with a feeler gauge. The clearance should fall between 0.0024–0.0181 in. If the clearance is not within specifications, use one of the following spacers to adjust it:

1.172–1.173 in.
1.188–1.189 in.
1.204–1.205 in.

The rest of the axle shaft installation is the reverse of removal. Remember to fill the axle with lubricant.

FULL FLOATING TYPE DIFFERENTIAL

1. Remove the nuts from the rear axle shaft plate.
2. Remove the cone washers from the mounting studs by tapping the slits of the washers with a tapered punch.
3. Install bolts into the two unused holes of the axle shaft plate.
4. Tighten the bolts to draw the axle shaft assembly out of the housing.
5. Installation is the reverse of the previous steps. Install the axle using a new gasket and torque the axle shaft nuts to 21–25 ft. lbs.

Rear Axle Hub

REMOVAL & INSTALLATION

Land Cruiser
FULL FLOATING TYPE DIFFERENTIAL

1. Raise the vehicle and support it safely with jack stands.
2. Remove the rear wheels.
3. Remove the rear axle shaft as previously outlined.
4. Loosen the lock screws and remove the adjusting nut from inside the hub using Toyota special tool #09509-25011 or its equivalent.

5. Remove the hub from the axle housing. Inspect all parts for damage or excessive wear. If the seal needs to be replaced, pry the seal out of the hub with an appropriate tool. The seal is installed by tapping it into the hub until it is firmly seated. If the bearing race(s) needs replacement, drive the race(s) from the hub using a brass drift. Use the brass drift to install the new race(s). Drive the new race(s) into the hub until firmly seated.

Install the hub in the following manner:

1. Place the hub on the axle housing and install the outer bearing.
2. Install the lock plate with the lock plate tab positioned into the groove of the axle housing.
3. Install and tighten the adjusting nut with the special tool used during removal.
4. Torque the nut to 43 ft. lbs. Rotate the hub a few times and retorque the adjusting nut to 43 ft. lbs.
5. Loosen the adjusting nut until the hub can be turned by hand.
6. Tighten the nut a small amount and check the amount of pressure required to rotate the hub using a spring tension gauge.
7. The recommended rotational torque is 5.7–12.6 ft. lbs. Tighten or loosen the adjusting nut as required to obtain this reading.
8. Align one of the axle housing slots with one of the adjusting nut slots. Install the lock screws into the holes of the adjusting nut which are at right angles to the aligned slots. Torque the lock screws to 35–60 in. lbs.
9. Recheck the rotational torque and install the axle shaft using a new gasket. Tighten the axle shaft nuts to 21–25 ft. lbs.
10. Install the wheels and lower the vehicle.

Differential

REMOVAL, INSTALLATION, AND OVERHAUL

Refer to the procedures listed with the Front Drive Axle section.

STEERING

Steering Wheel

REMOVAL & INSTALLATION

Three-Spoke

CAUTION

Do not attempt to remove or install the steering wheel by hammering on it. Damage to the energy-absorbing steering column could result.

---

1. Unfasten the horn and turn signal multiconnector(s) at the base of the steering column shroud.

2. Loosen the trim pad retaining screws from the back side of the steering wheel.

3. Lift the trim pad and horn button assembly(ies) from the wheel.

4. Remove the steering wheel hub retaining nut.

5. Scratch matchmarks on the hub and shaft to aid in correct installation.

6. Use a steering wheel puller to remove the steering wheel.

Installation is the reverse of removal. Tighten the wheel retaining nut to 22–29 ft. lbs.

Two-Spoke

The two-spoke steering wheel is removed in the same manner as the three-spoke, except that the trim pad should be pried off with a screwdriver. Remove the pad by lifting it toward the top of the wheel.

Four-Spoke

———— CAUTION ————

Do not attempt to remove or install the steering wheel by hammering on it. Damage to the energy absorbing steering column could result.

1. Unfasten the horn and turn signal connectors at the base of the steering column shroud, underneath the instrument panel.

2. Gently pry the center emblem off the front of the steering wheel.

3. Insert a wrench through the hole and remove the steering wheel retaining nut.

4. Scratch matchmarks on the hub and shaft to aid installation.

5. Use a steering wheel puller to remove the steering wheel.

Installation is the reverse of removal. Tighten the steering wheel retaining nut to 15–22 ft. lbs.

Turn Signal Switch

REMOVAL & INSTALLATION

1. Disconnect negative (−) battery cable at the battery.

2. Remove the steering wheel, as outlined in the appropriate section above.

3. Unfasten the screws which secure the upper and lower steering column shroud halves.

4. Unfasten the screws which retain the turn signal switch and remove the switch from the column. On 1979 and later Pickups, the windshield wiper switch is part of the assembly, and will be removed as well.

Installation is performed in the reverse order of removal.

Ignition Lock/Switch

REMOVAL & INSTALLATION

1. Disconnect the negative (−) battery cable.

2. Unfasten the ignition switch connector underneath the instrument panel.

3. Remove the screws which secure the upper and lower halves of the steering column cover.

4. Turn the lock cylinder to the "ACC" position with the ignition key.

5. Push the lock cylinder stop in with a small, round object (cotter pin, punch, etc.)

NOTE: On some models it may be necessary to remove the steering wheel and turn signal switch first.

6. Withdraw the lock cylinder from the lock housing while depressing the stop tab.

7. To remove the ignition switch, unfasten its securing screws and withdraw the switch from the lock housing.

Installation is performed in the following order:

1. Align the locking cam with the hole in the ignition switch and insert the switch in the lock housing.

2. Secure the switch with its screw(s).

3. Make sure that both the lock cylinder and the column lock are in the "ACC" position. Slide the cylinder into the lock housing until the stop tab engages the hole in the lock.

4. The rest of installation is performed in the reverse order of removal.

Power Steering Pump

REMOVAL & INSTALLATION

1. Remove the fan shroud.

2. Unfasten the nut from the center of the pump pulley.

NOTE: Use the drive belt as a brake to keep the pulley from rotating.

3. Withdraw the drive belt.

4. Remove the pulley and the Woodruff key from the pump shaft.

5. Detach the intake and outlet hoses from the pump reservoir.

NOTE: Tie the hose ends up high so the fluid cannot flow out of them. Drain or plug the pump to prevent fluid leakage.

6. Remove the bolt from the rear mounting brace.

7. Remove the front bracket bolts and withdraw the pump.

Installation is performed in the reverse order of removal. Note the following, however:

1. Tighten the pump pulley mounting bolt to 25–39 ft. lbs.

2. Adjust the pump drive belt tension. The belt should deflect 0.31–0.39 in. under thumb pressure applied midway between the air pump and the power steering pump.

3. Fill the reservoir with "Dexron" automatic transmission fluid. Bleed the air from the system.

BLEEDING

1. Raise the front of the car and support it securely with jackstands.

2. Fill the pump reservoir with "Dexron" automatic transmission fluid.

3. Rotate the steering wheel from lock to lock several times. Add fluid as necessary.

4. With the steering wheel turned fully to one lock, crank the starter while watching the fluid level in the reservoir.

NOTE: Do not start the engine. Operate the starter with a remove starter switch or have an assistant do it from inside of the car. Do not run the starter for prolonged periods.

5. Repeat step 4 with the steering wheel turned to the opposite lock.

6. Start the engine. With the engine idling, turn the steering wheel from lock to lock two or three times.

7. Lower the front of the car and repeat step 6.

8. Center the wheel at the midpoint of its travel. Stop the engine.

9. The fluid level should not have risen more than 0.2 in. If it does, repeat step 7.

10. Check for fluid leakage.

Manual Steering Gear

REMOVAL & INSTALLATION

2WD Pick-Up

1. Remove the pitman arm from the sector shaft with a puller.

2. Match mark the flexible coupling and worm-shaft and remove the lock bolt.

3. Unbolt and remove the steering gear housing.

4. Install in reverse of removal. Torque the housing bolts to 26–36 ft. lbs., and the pitman arm to 80–90 ft. lbs. Tighten the coupling yoke to 15–20 ft. lbs.

4WD Pick-up

1. Remove the stone shield from the gear housing, if equipped.

2. Match-mark the intermediate shaft and yoke, and disconnect them.

3. Remove the cotter pin and plug from the drag link.

4. Disconnect the drag link from the pitman arm.

5. Remove the pitman arm nut and, with a puller, remove the pitman arm from the sector shaft.

6. Unbolt and remove the gear housing from the frame.

7. Installation is the reverse of removal. Torque the gear housing mounting

2WD pick-up manual steering gear

4WD pick-up manual steering gear

bolts to 42 ft. lb.; the intermediate shaft bolts to 29 ft. lb.; the pitman arm-to-sector shaft nut to 127 ft. lb.

Land Cruiser
55 SERIES

1. Remove the worm yokes from the worm and main shaft.
2. Remove the intermediate shaft assembly.
3. Remove the Pitman arm from the sector shaft.
4. Unbolt and remove the gear housing.
5. Install in reverse of removal. Torque the Pitman arm to 119–141 ft. lb.

NOTE: The intermediate shaft must be installed with the wheels in a straight ahead position and the steering wheel straight ahead.

40 SERIES

1. Remove the horn button assembly and, using a puller, remove the steering wheel.
2. Remove the steering column jacket lower clamp.
3. Remove the turn signal switch assembly.
4. Remove the steering column access plate.
5. Remove the carburetor and oil filter. (not necessary on 1975–76)
6. Disconnect the # 1 shift rod and select rod at the ends of the shift control and select levers.
7. Remove the lower shift control bracket clamp.
8. Remove the shift control lever, select lever, control shaft lower bracket, control shaft low speed lever, and control shaft lower bracket.
9. Pull the control shaft out toward the driver's side.
10. Remove the pitman arm with a puller.
11. Remove the steering gear box bracket cap and lift out the gear box.
12. Installation is the reverse of removal. Torque the gear box bracket cap to 75–90 ft. lbs. (30–40 for 1975–76); the pitman arm to 120–140 ft. lbs., the steering wheel nut to 30–50 ft. lbs.

ADJUSTMENTS

Adjustments to the manual steering gear are not necessary during normal service. Adjustments are performed only as part of overhaul, which is covered in the General Repair Section.

Power Steering Gear

REMOVAL & INSTALLATION

1977–80 Pick-Ups

1. Disconnect the hydraulic lines from the steering gear.
2. Mark the relationship between the

intermediate shaft U-joint yoke and the steering gear worm shaft.

3. Loosen the set bolt of the intermediate shaft U-joint yoke and disconnect the intermediate shaft from the steering gear worm shaft.

4. Using a puller, remove the Pitman arm from the steering gear.

5. Remove the steering gear mounting bolts and remove the steering gear through the engine compartment.

6. Installation is the reverse of the previous steps. Be sure to align the marks made during step 2. Torque the steering gear mounting bolts to 37–47 ft. lbs., the pitman arm nut to 116–137 ft. lbs.; the U-joint yoke bolt to 22–32 ft. lbs.; the pressure hose fitting to 29–36 ft. lbs.; and the return line fitting to 24–30 ft. lbs.

NOTE: During installation of the hydraulic lines, position each line clear of any surrounding components then tighten the fittings.

1981–84 2WD Pick-Ups

1. Remove the pressure line clamp bolts, and using special tool SST 09631-22020, or its equivalent, disconnect the pressure lines.

2. Remove the intermediate shaft coupling bolt, match-mark the shaft and yoke and remove the shaft from the yoke.

3. Remove the pitman arm-to-sector shaft nut.

4. Disconnect the pitman arm from the relay rod.

5. Using a puller, remove the pitman arm from the sector shaft.

6. Remove the gear housing mounting bolts and lift out the gear.

7. Installation is the reverse of removal. Torque the gear mounting bolts to 48 ft. lb.; the pitman arm-to-sector shaft nut to 90 ft. lb.; the pitman arm-to-relay rod nut to 67 ft. lb.; the intermediate shaft coupling bolt to 19 ft. lb.; the pressure line nuts to 33 ft. lb. Bleed the system.

1981–84 4WD Pick-Ups

1. Remove the battery.

2. Remove the engine lower gravel shield.

3. Remove the pressure line clamp bolts, and, using special tool SST 09631-022020, or its equivalent, remove the pressure lines.

4. Remove the steering gear stone shield.

5. Remove the intermediate shaft coupling bolt, match-mark the intermediate shaft and yoke and disconnect the intermediate shaft from the yoke.

6. Remove the pitman arm-to-sector shaft nut, and, using a puller, remove the pitman arm from the shaft.

7. Unbolt and remove the gear housing.

8. Installation is the reverse of removal. Torque the gear mounting bolts to 42 ft. lb.; the pitman arm-to-sector shaft nut to 127 ft. lb.; the intermediate shaft

2WD pick-up power steering gear

coupling bolt to 29 ft. lb.; the pressure line union nuts to 33 ft. lb. Bleed the system.

Land Cruiser

1. Disconnect the hydraulic lines from the steering gear.

2. Remove the steering shaft coupling set bolt.

3. Remove the steering column-to-firewall bolts.

4. Loosen the steering column-to-dash bolts.

5. Using a puller, disconnect the relay rod from the Pitman shaft.

6. Using a puller, remove the Pitman arm from the steering gear.

7. Pull the steering column towards the passenger compartment to uncouple the steering shaft from the steering gear.

8. Remove the steering gear mounting fasteners and remove the steering gear from the vehicle.

9. Installation is the reverse of the previous steps. Be sure to align the marks on

the pitman arm with the corresponding marks on the pitman shaft. Torque the steering gear mounting fasteners to 40–63 ft. lbs.; the Pitman arm nut to 120–141 ft. lbs.; the coupling set bolt to 22–32 ft. lbs.; the pressure hose fitting to 29–36 ft. lbs.; and the return hose fitting to 24–30 ft. lbs.

NOTE: During installation of the hydraulic lines, position each line clear of any surrounding components then tighten the fittings.

Steering Linkage

REMOVAL & INSTALLATION

2WD Pick-up

1. Raise the front of the vehicle and support it with jack stands.

2. Remove the front wheels.

3. Remove the nut on the pitman arm and using a puller remove it from the steering sector shaft.

4WD pick-up power steering gear

2WD Pick-up steering linkage—1979 and later shown, earlier models similar

4. Unfasten the idler arm support securing bolts and remove the support from the frame.

5. Remove the castle nuts and cotter pins from the tie-rod ends and separate them from the steering knuckle arms with a puller.

6. Remove the relay rod complete with the tie-rods, Pitman arm and idler arm.

Installation is the reverse of removal with the following notes.

7. Align the marks on the Pitman arm and sector shaft before installing the Pitman arm.

8. Torque all of the following to 55–79 ft. lbs.: tie-rod ends to steering knuckles and relay rod; relay rod to Pitman arm. Torque the relay rod to the idler arm at 37–50 ft. lbs. Torque the Pitman arm to the sector shaft at 80–90 ft. lbs.

4WD Pick-up

1. Jack up the vehicle and support it on stands.

2. Remove the front wheels.

3. Remove cotter pin and nut from the shimmy damper at the tie-rod and remove shimmy damper from the tie-rod with a puller. Remove the lock nut from other end of the damper. Be sure to note the order of the rubber spacers and washers, and remove damper.

4. Repeat the above procedure where the tie-rod ends connect to the steering knuckles. Remove the tie-rod.

5. To remove the drag link, remove the cotter pin from the steering knuckle end of the drag, and, using a screw driver, unscrew the cap at the end of the drag link.

NOTE: The cap may be tight, so you may have to use a wrench or pliers to turn the screw driver.

6. When the cap is removed, you should be able to dislodge the spring seat, spring and outer socket holder inside the drag link by working the steering knuckle back and forth. The steering knuckle socket in the drag link can now be removed.

NOTE: Be sure to note the order in which the spring seat, spring and outer socket come out of the drag link. Their order will be reversed on the side of the drag link that attaches to the Pitman arm.

7. Repeat steps 5 and 6 on the Pitman arm side of the drag link.

Installation is the reverse of removal. Be sure to insert assemblies in drag link in their correct orders. On drag link, screw in caps completely then loosen 1–⅓ turns.

Observe the following torques:

Shimmy damper to axle housing mount: 8–11 ft. lbs.

Tie-rod end to steering knuckle arm: 55–79 ft. lbs.

Shimmy damper to tie-rod end: 37–50 ft. lbs.

NOTE: Be sure to grease drag link ends at their grease nipples, and, when installing drag link end caps, you tighten them completely and then loosen them 1⅓ turns.

Land Cruiser

1. Remove the hubcaps and loosen the lug nuts.

2. Jack up the front of the vehicle and support it on stands. Remove the wheels.

3. Unfasten the Pitman arm retaining nut.

4. Punch matchmarks on the Pitman arm and the sector shaft to aid reinstallation.

5. Remove the Pitman arm from the sector shaft with a puller.

6. Detach the drag link from the center arm with a tie-rod puller. Remove the link together with the Pitman arm.

7. Detach the tie rod ends from the steering knuckle arm with a puller.

8. Detach the relay rod ends from the center arm. Remove the tie rod/relay rod assembly.

9. Disconnect the end of the steering damper from its bracket on the front crossmember.

10. Remove the center arm attaching nut and use a puller to remove the arm, complete with damper.

11. Remove the skid plate and then remove the center arm bracket from the frame.

Installation is the reverse of removal.

12. Be sure to align the matchmarks, which were made during removal, on the Pitman arm and the sector shaft. Tighten the mounting bolt to 120–140 ft. lbs.

13. Lubricate all of the rod ends and damper ends with multipurpose grease.

14. After the linkage is installed, adjust the toe-in to the proper specifications.

4WD Pick-up steering linkage

1. Bolt
2. Lockwasher
3. Center arm shaft nut
4. Center arm nut lock plate
5. Compression spring
6. Center arm shaft
7 Shaft bushing
8. Center arm bracket
9. Grease fitting
10. Bolt
11. Steering drag link assembly
12. Set ring

13. Joint dust seal
14. Lock nut
15. Cotter pin
16. Tie-rod assembly
17. Steering tie-rod
18. Lock nut
19. Tie-rod end clamp
20. Bolt
21. Tie-rod end assembly
22. Steering knuckle arm
23. Steering knuckle arm
24. Dust seal

25. Center arm dust lower seal
26. Steering center arm
27. Lock washer
28. Nut
29. Steering damper
30. Damper bracket
31. Steering relay rod assembly
32. Steering relay rod
33. Bolt
34. Tie-rod end clamp
35. Relay rod end assembly

Land Cruiser steering linkage

FRONT SUSPENSION

Springs

REMOVAL & INSTALLATION

2WD Pick-up

1977–78

1. Remove the hubcap and loosen the lug nuts.

2. Raise the front end of the truck and support the front suspension crossmember with jackstands.

3. Remove the lug nuts and the wheel.

4. Remove the stabilizer bar connecting bolts and remove the bracket parts, being careful to note their removal sequence in order to aid in installation.

5. Remove the tie rod cotter pin and nut. Use a puller to remove the end of the tie rod from the knuckle arm.

6. Remove the shock absorber, as detailed in the appropriate section. Detach the brake hose.

7. Raise the lower control arm, using a jack, so that the arm is free of the steering knuckle.

8. Loosen the ball joint attachment nut and remove the ball joint puller.

9. Slowly lower the jack underneath the control arm.

CAUTION

If the jack is lowered too fast, the spring could suddenly release, causing damage or injury.
---

10. Remove the coil spring and its insulator from underneath the truck.

Inspect the coil spring, its insulator; and bumper for cracks, wear, or damage. Replace parts as necessary.

Installation is basically performed in the reverse order of removal. However, a coil spring compressor should be used to install the spring, rather than the method used for removing it.

Torque the suspension components to the following specifications:

Lower control arm—51–65 ft. lbs. (1976–78 33–43 ft. lbs.)

Ball joint—87–123 ft. lbs.

1979 AND LATER

1979 and later models are equipped with torsion bar front springs.

CAUTION

Great care must be taken to make sure springs are not mixed after removal. It is strongly suggested that before removal, each spring be marked with paint, showing front and rear of spring and from which side of the truck it was taken. If springs are installed backwards or on the wrong sides of the truck, they could fracture. If replacing springs, it is not necessary to mark them.
---

1. Jack up truck and support the frame on stands. Remove the wheel.

2. Slide the boot from the rear of torsion bar spring and paint an exact mark from spring housing onto spring.

1. Arm pivot bushing
2. Arm pivot dust seal
3. Upper suspension arm shaft
4. Front spring bumper No. 2
5. Upper ball joint assembly
6. Suspension upper arm subassembly
7. Steering knuckle
8. Steering knuckle grease retainer
9. Lower suspension arm shaft
10. Lower arm bumper stop plate
11. Suspension lower arm subassembly
12. Lower ball joint
13. Lower ball joint dust cover
14. Set ring
15. Lower ball joint dust cover plate
16. Cushion retainer
17. Shock absorber cushion
18. Cushion retainer
19. Front spring bumper No. 1
20. Front shock absorber
21. Stablizer bushing
22. Stablizer link cover
23. Stablizer link
24. Front coil spring
25. Front coil spring insulator
26. Cushion retainer
27. Collar
28. Stablizer cushion
29. Stablizer bar

Front suspension components—1978 and earlier 2WD pick-up

1979–83 2WD front suspension components

3. Follow the same procedure on the front of the spring.

— **CAUTION** —
Be sure to make a mark showing front of spring from back of spring.

4. On the rear torsion bar spring holder, there is a long bolt that passes through the arm of the holder and up through the frame crossmember. REMOVE THE LOCKING NUT ONLY FROM THIS BOLT.

5. Using a small ruler, measure the length from the bottom of the remaining nut to the threaded tip of the bolt and record this measurement.

— **CAUTION** —
Be sure to complete step five accurately.

6. Place a jack under the rear torsion bar spring holder arm and jack up the arm to remove the spring pressure from the long bolt. Remove the adjusting nut from the long bolt.

7. SLOWLY lower jack.

8. Remove long bolt and its spacers and remove rear holder. You should be able to pull the torsion bar out of the front and rear holders.

Inspect all parts for wear damage or cracks. Check the boots for rips and wear. Inspect the splined ends of the torsion bar spring and the splined holes in the rear holder and the front torque arm for damage. Replace as necessary.

Upper Arm

Upper Arm Bushing

Upper Ball Joint

Steering Knuckle

Stabilizar Bar

Anchor Arm

Lower Arm Bushing

Lower Arm Shaft

Torque Arm

Shock Absorber

Torsion Bar Spring

Lower Arm

Lower Ball Joint

Strut Bar

1984 2WD pick-up front suspension components

On the rear ends of the torsion bar springs, there are markings to show which is right and which is the left bar. Do not confuse them.

To install:

9. Coat the splined ends of the torsion bar with multipurpose grease.

10. If refitting old torsion bars:

a. Slide the front of the bar into the opening on the torque arm, making sure you line up the marks you made earlier on the torsion bar spring and the torque arm.

b. Repeat the above step with the rear spring holder and replace the long bolt and its spacers.

c. Place a pipe that will fit in the notch on the rear holder arm on a jack and jack up the arm.

d. Tighten the adjusting nut so that it is the same length as it was before removal.

NOTE: Do not replace the lock nut yet.

11. When installing a new torsion bar spring:

a. Slide the front of the torsion bar into the opening on the torque arm.

b. Fit the rear holder in place and install the rear of the torsion in it so that when the long bolt and spacers are installed, the distance from the top of the upper spacer to the tip of the threaded end of bolt is 0.7–1.0 in.

NOTE: Make sure the bolt and bottom spacer are snuggly in the holder arm while measuring.

c. When the correct measurement is achieved, fit a pipe or round bar in the notch on the rear holder arm. Jack up arm on pipe.

d. Replace the adjusting nut and tighten until the distance from the bottom of the nut to the tip of the threaded end of the bolt is 71–89 mm (2.8–3.5 in.).

NOTE: Do not install the lock nut yet.

12. Apply multipurpose grease to the boot lips and refit the boots over splines.

13. Replace the wheel and lower the truck.

14. With the wheels on the ground, measure the distance from the ground to the center of the lower arm shaft (See chart). Adjust vehicle height with the adjusting nut on the rear spring holder.

NOTE: If, after achieving the correct vehicle height, the distance from the bottom of the adjusting nut to the top of the threaded end of the long bolt is more than 3.8 in., change the position of the rear spring holder arm spline and reassemble.

15. Replace and tighten the lock nut on the long bolt.

— CAUTION —

Make sure the adjusting nut does not move when tightening lock nut.

4WD Pick-up

1. Jack up the front of vehicle and place support stands under the chassis frame.

NOTE: Do not place supports under front axle housing.

2. Remove wheel.
3. Remove the bolt from the bottom of the shock absorber and raise shock up out of the way.
4. If removing driver's side front leaf spring, remove the cotter pin from the end of the steering drag link at the axle housing. Unscrew the slitted bolt in the end of the drag link and remove the bolt, spring holder, spring, and outer socket holder. Remove drag link from steering knuckle arm.

NOTE: Be careful not to lose inner socket holder.

5. Remove stabilizer bar bolt and spacer and washer assembly.
6. Disconnect brake line at the holder behind the brake assembly. Drive out shim holding brake line to holder and withdraw brake line. Plug end of brake line running to master cylinder to prevent fluid loss.

7. Place a jack under the front axle housing and raise to put pressure on the leaf spring. Remove the four nuts holding the two U-bolts to the axle housing and remove the U-bolts.
8. Lower the jack enough to take the pressure off the leaf spring but so it still supports the axle housing.
9. Remove the bolts holding the leaf spring to its hangers and carefully pry the spring from its holders.

NOTE: It may be necessary to lower the jack under the axle housing to remove spring.

Installation is the reverse of removal.

— CAUTION —

Be sure to refill brake master cylinder reservoir and bleed brakes!

NOTE: Finger tighten the front and rear leaf spring hanger pin nuts. After the spring is attached to the axle housing and chassis, jack up the axle housing until the vehicle clears its support stands and then torque pin nuts.

Observe the following torques:
U-bolt nuts: 73–108 ft. lbs.
Front hanger pin placer bolts: 8–11 ft. lbs.
Front hanger pin nut: 55–79 ft. lbs.
Rear shackle pin nuts: 55–79 ft. lbs.

Land Cruiser

Land Cruiser models are equipped with leaf springs in the front and rear. Thus, front spring removal is performed in almost the same manner as rear spring removal. Follow the procedure outlined in the rear suspension section, below.

— CAUTION —

Be careful when raising or lowering the front suspension with a jack so as not to damage any of the steering system components.

Shock Absorber
REMOVAL & INSTALLATION
2WD Pick-up

1. Remove the hubcap and loosen the lug nuts.
2. Raise the front of the truck and support it with jack stands.
3. Remove the lug nuts and the wheel.
4. Unfasten the double nuts at the top end of the shock absorber. Remove the cushions and cushion retainers.
5. Remove the two bolts which secure the lower end of the shock absorber to lower control arm.
6. Remove the shock absorber. Installation is the reverse of removal.

4WD Pick-up

Removal and installation is the same as the 2WD Pick-up, except there is only one through-bolt holding the bottom of the shock in place.

Land Cruiser

Complete steps 1–3 of the 2WD Pick-up shock absorber removal.

— CAUTION —

Be careful not to damage steering assembly when jacking up front of vehicle.

Remove bolts holding the top and bottom of the shock in place and remove shock. Installation is the reverse of removal.

Stabilizer Bar
REMOVAL & INSTALLATION
2WD Pick-up

1. Remove one torsion bar spring according to the previous spring removal and installation procedure.
2. Remove the stabilizer bar attachment hardware from the ends of the stabilizer bar. During installation, be sure to arrange the spacers, bushings, and washers as originally installed.
3. Remove the stabilizer bar-to-frame brackets and bushings and lower the stabilizer bar from the vehicle.
4. Installation is the reverse of the previous steps. Be sure to carefully inspect each bushing for damage and replace the bushing(s) if necessary. Torque all stabilizer bar fasteners to 8–11 ft. lbs.

4WD Pick-up and Land Cruiser

Follow steps 2–4 of the previous 2WD Pick-up procedure. Removal of a spring is not necessary on these models.

1. Shock absorber
2. Stablizer bar
3. Torque rod
4. Leaf spring

Front suspension components (4WD)—pick-up shown, Land Cruiser similar

Upper Control Arm

REMOVAL & INSTALLATION

2WD Pick-up

1. Raise and support the truck under the frame.
2. Remove the wheel. Remove the caliper and suspend it from the frame.
3. Raise the lower control arm with a jack.
4. Remove the nut from the upper ball joint stud.
5. Separate the ball joint from the steering knuckle.
6. Unbolt and remove the upper arm at the two bolts holding the inner shaft to the frame, taking note of the number and size of the aligning shims.
7. Installation is the reverse of removal. Replace the shims as found. Tighten fasteners, but do not torque them until the truck is on the ground.
8. Lower the truck and torque the upper arm mounting bolts to 95–153 ft. lbs. on 1977–83 trucks; 90–95 ft. lb. on 1984 trucks.

Lower Control Arm

REMOVAL & INSTALLATION

2WD Pick-up

1. Raise and support the front end.
2. On 1977–78 Pick-ups, remove the coil spring as previously outlined. On 1979 and later Pick-ups, remove the torsion bar spring as previously outlined.
3. Remove the stablizer bar and the strut bar from the lower arm, if so equipped.
4. On 1979 and later Pick-ups, remove the bottom of the shock absorber from the lower arm.
5. Unbolt and remove lower ball joint.

NOTE: If the lower ball joint is not to be replaced, simply unbolt it from the lower control arm. It is not necessary to separate the ball joint from the steering knuckle.

6. On 1977–78 Pick-ups, unbolt and remove the lower control arm at the four bolts mounting the lower control arm on the frame. On 1979 and later Pick-ups, unbolt and remove the nut from the lower arm shaft. Remove the spring torque arm from the other side of the lower control arm and remove the lower arm shaft bolt and the lower arm.
Installation is the reverse of removal. Tighten the bolt(s) holding the lower control arm to the frame but do not torque them until the vehicle is on the ground.
Observe the following torques during installation:
Ball joint stud nut: 105 ft. lb.
Shock absorber lower: 13 ft. lb.
upper: 18 ft. lb.
Lower arm mounting nuts:
1977–78 43 ft. lb.
1979–84 199 ft. lb.

———— CAUTION ————
Do not tighten the control arm bolts fully until the vehicle is lowered; if the bolts are tightened with the control arm(s) hanging, excessive bushing wear will result.

Ball Joints

INSPECTION

To check the lower ball joint for wear, jack up the lower suspension arm, after removing all excess play from the other suspension parts (wheel bearings, tie-rods, etc.). The bottom of the tire should not move more than 0.2 in. when the tire is pushed and pulled inward and outward. The tire should not move more than 0.09 in. up and down. If the play is greater than these figures, replace the ball joint. The upper ball joint should be replaced if a distinct looseness is felt when turning the ball joint stud with the steering knuckle removed.

REMOVAL & INSTALLATION

1977–78

1. Remove the wheel and tire.
2. Support the front suspension crossmember with jackstands.
3. Place a jack under the lower control arm and raise the control arm until the spring bumper is off the frame.
4. Disconnect the flexible brake hose.
5. Disconnect the tie-rod end from the steering knuckle using a puller.
6. Using a suitable puller remove the ball joint from the steering knuckle.
7. Remove the ball joint from the lower arm.
8. From this position the upper ball joint may also be removed in a similar manner. Removal and installation will be easier if the lower is removed first.
9. Install the new ball joints and reassemble the steering components. Due to the fact that the shock absorber is not removed in this procedure the coil spring may be positioned with the jack and no compressor is necessary.

NOTE: Be sure to grease the new ball joints before using the vehicle.

10. Tighten the upper ball joint nuts to 15–22 ft. lbs., the lower to 22–29 ft. lbs. Tighten the steering knuckle to the upper joint to 65–94 ft. lbs.; the knuckle to the lower joint to 87–123 ft. lbs. Bleed the brakes before driving the truck.

1979 AND LATER

1. Jack up the vehicle and support it with jackstands.
2. Remove the front wheel.
3. Support the lower control arm with a jack.
4. Remove the brake caliper and tie it out of the way, as outlined later in this section.

---

5. Remove the tie rod end.
6. Remove the ball joint from the steering knuckle.

NOTE: You can also remove the upper ball joint now if needed. Removal and installation will be easier if the bottom joint is removed first.

7. Installation is the reverse of removal.

NOTE: Be sure to grease the ball joints before moving the vehicle.

The following torque figures are needed. Upper mounting bolts 15–21 ft. lbs. Upper ball joint 66–94 ft. lbs. lower mounting bolts 15–39 ft. lbs. lower ball joint 87–122 ft. lbs.

Front-End Alignment

Front-end alignment measurements require the use of special equipment. Before measuring alignment or attempting to adjust it, always check the following points:
1. Be sure that the tires are properly inflated.
2. See that the wheels are properly balanced.
3. Check the ball joints to determine if they are worn or loose.
4. Check front wheel bearing adjustment.
5. Be sure that the car is on a level surface.
6. Check all suspension parts for tightness.

CASTER AND CAMBER ADJUSTMENTS

Measure the caster and camber angles. If they are not within specifications, adjust them by adding or subtracting the shims on the mounting bolts between the upper control arm and the suspension member:
1. To increase camber, remove shims equally from both of the control shaft mounting bolts. Do the reverse to decrease camber.
2. To increase caster, add camber adjusting shims to the rear mounting bolt, or remove them from the front mounting bolt. Do the reverses to decrease caster.

NOTE: Caster and camber adjustments should always be performed in a single operation.

TOE-IN ADJUSTMENT

Measure the toe-in. Adjust it, if necessary, by loosening the tie rod end clamping bolts and rotating the tie rod adjusting tubes. Tighten the clamping bolts when finished.

NOTE: Both tie rod ends should be the same length. If they are not, perform the adjustment until the toe-in is within specifications and the tie rod ends are equal in length.

REAR SUSPENSION

Springs
REMOVAL & INSTALLATION

1. Loosen the rear wheel lug nuts.
2. Raise the rear of the vehicle. Support the frame and rear axle housing with stands.
3. Remove the lug nuts and the wheel.
4. Remove the cotter pin, nut, and washer from the lower end of the shock absorber.
5. On Land Cruiser models, perform the following:
   a. Remove the cotter pins and nuts from the lower end of the stabilizer link.
   b. Detach the link from the axle housing.
6. Detach the shock absorber from the spring seat pivot pin.
7. Remove the parking brake cable clamp (except Land Cruiser).
NOTE: Remove the parking brake equalizer, if necessary.
8. Unfasten the U-bolt nuts and remove the spring seat assemblies.
9. Adjust the height of the rear axle housing so that the weight of the rear axle is removed from the rear springs.
10. Unfasten the spring shackle retaining nuts. Withdraw the spring shackle inner plate. Carefully pry out the spring shackle with a bar.
11. Remove the spring bracket pin from the front end of the spring hanger and remove the rubber bushings.
12. Remove the spring.

------ CAUTION ------
Use care not to damage the hydraulic brake line or the parking brake cable.

Installation is performed in the following order:
1. Install the rubber bushings in the eye of the spring.
2. Align the eye of the spring with the spring hanger bracket and drive the pin through the bracket holes and rubber bushings.
NOTE: Use soapy water as lubricant, if necessary, to aid in pin installation. Never use oil or grease.
3. Finger-tighten the spring hanger nuts and/or bolts.
4. Install the rubber bushings in the spring eye at the opposite end of the spring.
5. Raise the free end of the spring. Install the spring shackle through the bushings and the bracket.
6. Install the shackle inner plate and finger-tighten the retaining nuts.
7. Center the bolt head in the hole which is provided in the spring seat on the axle housing.

8. Fit the U-bolts over the axle housing. Install the lower spring seat.
9. Tighten the U-bolt nuts.
2WD: 72 ft. lb.
4WD: 90 ft. lb.
NOTE: Some models have two sets of nuts, while others have a nut and lockwasher.
10. Install the parking brake cable clamp. Install the equalizer, if it was removed.
11. 4WD Pick-up and Land cruiser:
   a. Raise the rear axle with the jack so that the stands no longer support the frame.
   b. Tighten the hanger pin and shackle nuts.
   c. Install the shock absorber bushings and washers. Tighten and install the cotter pins. Torque the hanger pin nuts to 80 ft. lb.; the shackle pin nuts to 67 ft. lb.
   d. Install the stabilizer link and hand-tighten its retaining nuts (Land Cruiser).
   e. Install the wheels, remove the stands, and lower the vehicle to the ground.
   f. Tighten the stabilizer link bolts, bounce the vehicle, and tighten them again (Land Cruiser).

Shock Absorbers
REMOVAL & INSTALLATION

1. Jack up the rear of the vehicle.
2. Support the rear axle housing with jackstands.
3. Unfasten the upper shock absorber retaining nuts and/or bolts from the upper frame member.
4. Depending upon the type of rear springs used, either disconnect the lower end of the shock absorber from the spring seat, or the rear axle housing, by removing its cotter pins, nuts, and/or bolts.
5. Remove the shock absorber.
Inspect the shock for wear, leaks, or other signs of damage.
Installation is performed in the reverse order from removal. Torque as follows:
Upper bolt, 2WD 19 ft. lb.; 4WD 47 ft. lb.
Lower bolt, 2 WD 19 ft. lb; 4WD 47 ft. lb.

BRAKE SYSTEM

NOTE: For brake component service, see the Unit Repair section.

Adjustments

REAR DRUM BRAKE

Land Cruiser

These models are equipped with rear drum brakes which require manual adjustment.

Perform the adjustment in the following order.
1. Chock the front wheels and fully release the parking brake.
2. Raise the rear of the vehicle and support it with jackstands.
3. Remove the adjusting hole plug from the backing plate.
4. Expand the brake shoes by turning the adjusting wheel with a star-wheel adjuster or a thin-bladed screw driver.
5. Pump the brake pedal several times, while expanding the shoes, so that the shoe contacts the drum evenly.
NOTE: If the wheel still turns when your foot is removed from the brake pedal, continue expanding the shoes until the wheel locks.
6. Back off on the adjuster, just enough so that the wheel rotates without dragging.
7. After this point is reached, continue backing off for five additional notches.
NOTE: On models which have two wheel cylinders at each wheel, adjust each set of brakes separately; never adjust both at once.
8. If the wheel still does not turn freely, back off one or two more notches. If after this, it still drags, check for worn or defective parts.
9. Pump the brake pedal again, and check wheel rotation.
10. Reverse steps 1–3.

Pick-up, 4WD Pick-up

These models are equipped with self-adjusting rear drum brakes. No adjustment is necessary.

FRONT DRUM BRAKE

Perform the adjustments in the same manner as detailed for the rear drum brakes.

FRONT DISC BRAKE

Front disc brakes require no adjustment. Hydraulic pressure maintains the proper brake pad-to-disc contact at all times.

NOTE: Because of this, the brake fluid level should be checked regularly.

Master Cylinder

REMOVAL & INSTALLATION

Be careful not to spill brake fluid on the painted surfaces of the vehicle; it will damage the paint.
1. Unfasten the hydraulic line from the master cylinder.
2. Detach the hydraulic fluid pressure differential switch wiring connectors.
3. Loosen the master cylinder reservoir mounting bolt.
4. Then do one of the following:
   a. On models with manual brakes, re-

move the master cylinder securing bolts and the clevis pin from the brake pedal. Remove the master cylinder.

b. On other models with power brakes, unfasten the nuts and remove the master cylinder assembly from the power brake unit.

Installation is performed in the reverse order of removal. Note the following however:

1. Before tightening the master cylinder mounting nuts or bolts, screw the hydraulic line into the cylinder body, a few turns.

2. After installation is completed, bleed the master cylinder and the brake system.

Proportioning Valve

A proportioning valve is used on all models to reduce the hydraulic pressure to the rear brakes because of weight transfer during high speed stops. This helps to keep the rear brakes from locking up by improving front to rear brake balance.

REMOVAL & INSTALLATION

1. Disconnect the brake lines from the valve unions.

2. Remove the valve mounting bolt, if used, and remove the valve.

NOTE: If the proportioning valve is defective, it must be replaced as an assembly; it cannot be rebuilt.

Installation is the reverse of removal. Bleed the brake system after it is completed.

Power Brake Booster

REMOVAL & INSTALLATION

1. Remove brake master cylinder. See above for instructions.

2. Remove the air line running from the brake booster to the manifold.

3. Working inside the driver's compartment, remove the clevis pin that connects the brake pedal to the booster rod. Remove the four nuts holding the booster assembly to the fire wall and remove the assembly.

Installation is the reverse of removal.

NOTE: When installing a new booster, make sure there is a little clearance between the push rod end and the master cylinder piston.

Wheel Cylinders

REMOVAL & INSTALLATION

Front

1. Perform the brake drum and brake shoe removal procedures.

2. Plug the master cylinder reservoir inlet, to prevent fluid from leaking out.

3. Remove the hydraulic lines from the wheel cylinders by unfastening the union bolt.

4. Remove the wheel cylinder attachment screws and withdraw the wheel cylinders.

--------- CAUTION ---------
Do not mix the right and left wheel cylinders.

To install the wheel cylinders, proceed in the following manner:

1. Use the attaching screws to install the wheel cylinder to the backing plate.

NOTE: The wheel cylinder adjusting nut and bolt on the right side of the brake have left-hand threads; while those on the left side have right-hand threads. Be careful not to mix them.

2. Connect the hydraulic line to the wheel cylinders.

--------- CAUTION ---------
Use care to see that the hydraulic line is not twisted.

3. Install the brake drum and shoes. Bleed the brake system.

General Overhaul

Remove the boots, pistons and the cups and closely inspect the bores for signs of wear, scoring and/or scuffing. When in doubt, replace or hone the wheel cylinders with a special brake hone, using clean brake fluid as lubricant. Wash residue from the bores using clean fluid; never use oil or any other solvent on any brake components. Blow dry with air and install with fresh brake fluid. The general limit for a honed cylinder is 0.005 in. oversize (Do not try to save money by reusing brake components such as cylinders and cups.) The self-adjuster screws should be taken apart and all dirt and rust removed with a wire brush. Lightly coat with Lubriplate before assembly; components should turn freely.

Rear

PICK-UP AND 4WD PICK-UP

1. Plug the master cylinder inlet to prevent hydraulic fluid from leaking.

2. Remove the brake drums and shoes as detailed in the appropriate section above.

3. Working from behind the backing plate, disconnect the hydraulic line from the wheel cylinder.

4. Unfasten the screws retaining the wheel cylinder and withdraw the cylinder.

Installation is performed in the reverse order of removal.

Remember to bleed the brake system after completing wheel cylinder, brake shoe and drum installation.

LAND CRUISER

The front brake wheel cylinder removal procedure is performed in the same manner as the procedure for the Pick-up and Land Cruiser rear brakes. For details see the section dealing with these vehicles.

Overhaul

See "General Overhaul" for a description of wheel cylinder overhaul procedures.

Parking Brake

ADJUSTMENT

Pick-up, 4WD Pick-up
1977–80

NOTE: Adjust the rear brake shoes, as detailed at the beginning of this chapter, before attempting to adjust the parking brake.

1. Loosen the parking brake warning light switch bracket.

2. Push the parking brake lever in until it is stopped by the pawl.

3. Move the switch so that it will be "off" at this position but "on" when the handle is pulled out.

4. Tighten the switch bracket and push the brake lever in again.

5. Working from underneath the vehicle, loosen the locknut on the parking brake cable equalizer.

6. Screw the adjusting nut *in*, just enough so that the brake cables have no slack.

7. Hold the adjusting nut in this position while tightening the locknut.

8. Check the rotation of the rear wheels to make sure that the brakes are not dragging.

9. Pull out on the parking brake lever, and count the number of notches needed to apply the parking brake. 7–10 notches is preferred.

1981–84

1. Make sure that the rear brakes are properly adjusted.

2. Pull the parking brake lever out as far as it will go, counting the number of notches heard in the travel. On 2WD models, 10–16 notches should be heard; on 4WD models, 7–15 notches is the norm.

3. If these standards are not met, procede as follows:

2WD Models

a. From under the truck, tighten the adjusting nut at the equalizer until the travel is within limits, and there is no drag at the rear shoes.

b. Apply the parking brake several times and again check that there is no drag with the brake released.

4WD

a. From under the truck, tighten the equalizer nut until the play at the rear brake links is gone, then loosen the nut one full turn. Tighten the locknut.

b. Tighten one of the adjusting nuts on the intermediate lever while loosening the other, until the travel is correct. Tighten the two locknuts.

c. Confirm that the equalizer nut is in contact with the backing plate.

LAND CRUISER

Land Cruiser models use a separate drum brake assembly, operating on the driveshaft, to serve as a parking brake. Adjust it as follows:

1. Push the parking brake lever all the way in, so that the brake is released.
2. Raise the rear of the vehicle and support it with jackstands.
3. Turn the parking brake adjustment shaft, which is located at the bottom of the parking brake backing plate, counterclockwise until the shoes seat against the drum.
4. Back the adjuster off one notch.
5. Apply the parking brake; the drum should be locked. Release the brake; the drum should rotate freely.

NOTE: If the drum does not rotate freely with the brake off, loosen the adjuster one more notch.

6. Adjust the turnbuckles on the parking brake intermediate levers and the adjusting nuts on the end of the parking brake cables, so that 7–12 notches are required to apply the parking brake.

CHASSIS ELECTRICAL

Heater

NOTE: On models equipped with air conditioning, the heater and air conditioner are completely separate units. The heater removal procedure is the same as outlined here. However, be certain when working under the dashboard that only the heater hoses are disconnected. The air conditioning hoses are under pressure; if disconnected, the escaping refrigerant will freeze any surface with which it comes in contact, including your skin and eyes.

REMOVAL & INSTALLATION

Pick-up
1977–78

The heater core and blower motor are assembled into one unit which is centrally located in the passenger compartment. To effect repairs on either the core or blower motor, remove the entire assembly from the truck and separate the components with the unit removed.

1. Drain the cooling system completely.
2. Remove the package tray from under the dashboard.
3. Unfasten the hose clamps holding the heater hoses to the core.

NOTE: Hold a shallow pan under the hoses so that any water left in them will not run on the floor of the truck.

4. Remove the defroster hoses from the heater case.
5. Disconnect the heater control cables from the heater case.
6. Remove the fresh air intake duct.
7. Remove the electrical connector feeding the heater blower motor.
8. There are four bolts holding the assembly in the inside of the cowl. Remove the bolts and withdraw the heater assembly from the passenger compartment.
9. To remove the blower motor, tap the fan retaining nut slightly and then remove the nut from the shaft. Withdraw the fan. Remove the blower motor-to-heater case attaching screws and remove the motor.
10. To remove the core, remove the heater control panel and heater lower case cover as a unit. The core may then be taken out of the heater case.
11. Upon reassembly of the unit be sure to tighten all clamps to prevent leaks. Fill the cooling system with the correct mixture of coolant. With the heater off, run the engine to operating temperature. Open the heater control valve and see if the system is functioning properly.

1979–84

1. Disconnect the battery ground.
2. Drain the cooling system.
3. Remove the glove box, defroster hoses, air damper, air duct and two side defroster ducts.
4. Remove the control unit from the instrument panel.
5. Disconnect the heater hoses from the core tubes.
6. Remove the retaining bolts and lift out the heater unit. At this point, the core may be pulled from the case.
7. Installation is the reverse of removal.

Front Heater Core

NOTE: To service the heater core of Pick-up models, refer to the previous Heater Removal and Installation procedure.

REMOVAL & INSTALLATION

Land Cruiser
1977–79

1. Turn off the water valve.
2. Detach both hoses from the heater core.
3. Unfasten the air duct clamp.
4. Detach the defroster hoses from the heater box.
5. Unfasten its attachment bolts and withdraw the core.
Installation is the reverse of removal.

1980 AND LATER

NOTE: The entire heater unit must be removed to gain access to the heater core. This procedure requires almost complete disassembly of the instrument panel and lowering of the steering column. If you decide to perform this operation, note the following points before proceeding:

a. Be sure to tag any wiring which must be disconnected so that it may be correctly installed.
b. As fasteners are removed, arrange them so that they may be installed in their original locations.
c. Do not force any parts to remove them; if a part cannot easily be removed, remove any additional fasteners which may have been initially overlooked.
d. When disconnecting coolant hoses, be careful not to damage the heater core tubes. Place a drain pan under the coolant hose connections before disconnecting the hoses.

1. Disconnect the negative battery cable at the battery.
2. Remove the glove box and the glove box door.
3. Remove the lower heater ducts (#2 in the accompanying illustration).
4. Remove the large heater duct from the passenger side of the heater unit (#3 in the accompanying illustration).
5. Remove the ductwork from behind the instrument panel (#4 in the accompanying illustration).
6. Remove the radio, if so equipped.
7. Disconnect the wiring connector from the right side inner portion of the glove opening.
8. Remove the instrument panel pad (8 fasteners).
9. Remove the hood release lever.
10. Disconnect the hand throttle control cable.
11. Remove the retaining screw from the left side of the fuse block.
12. Remove the steering column-to-instrument panel attaching nuts and carefully lower the steering column. Tag and disconnect the wiring as necessary in order to lower the column assembly.
13. Disconnect the electrical connector from the rheostat located to the left of the steering column opening.
14. Remove the center dual outlet duct which is attached to the upper portion of the heater unit (#11 in the accompanying illustration).
15. Remove the lower instrument panel. The fasteners are located in the following places:

a. Left side of the instrument panel: two at the left side end and two at the left lower end.
b. Above the steering column: two.
c. To the right of the steering column opening: two.
d. Left upper corner of the glove box opening: two.

1. Glove compartment
2. Duct
3. Duct
4. Duct
5. Safety pad
6. Hood release lever
7. Throttle cable
8. Fuse block setting screw
9. Rheostat connector
10. Steering column mounting nut
11. Center duct
12. Lower instrument panel
13. Heater unit

Heater unit—1980 and later Land Cruiser

e. Left lower corner of the glove box opening: one.

f. Right side of the instrument panel: two at the right side end and two at the right lower end.

16. Tag and disconnect the hoses from the heater unit.

17. Remove the heater unit-to-firewall fasteners and remove the heater unit.

18. Remove the heater core pipe clamps from the heater unit. Also remove the heater core retaining clamp.

19. Withdraw the heater core from the heater unit.

Installation of the heater core and heater unit is the reverse of the previous steps. Torque the steering column-to-instrument panel fasteners to 14–15 ft. lbs. Replenish the cooling system and check for leaks.

Rear Heater Core

REMOVAL & INSTALLATION

Land Cruiser

1. Shut the water valve.
2. Detach both of the hoses from the rear heater core.
3. Detach the wiring from the rear heater.

4. Unfasten the bolts and lift out the core.

Installation is the reverse of removal.

Heater Blower Motor

REMOVAL & INSTALLATION

Pick-Ups
1977–79

See Heater Removal and Installation.

1980–84

1. Disconnect the electrical connector at the motor.
2. Remove the three screws securing the motor and lift the motor from the case.
3. Installation is the reverse of removal. Make sure that the seal around the motor flange is in good condition.

Land Cruiser
1977–79

1. Loosen the air duct clamping screws and remove the ducts.
2. Remove the air duct screen.
3. Unfasten the mounting bolts and remove the blower motor complete with fan.

Installation is the reverse of removal.

1980 AND LATER

1. Disconnect the electrical connector from the blower motor.
2. Disconnect the flexible tube from the side of the blower motor.
3. Remove the blower motor fasteners and lower the blower motor out of the air inlet duct.

Installation is the reverse of the previous steps. During installation, be sure to position the motor so that the flexible tube can be attached to the motor.

Radio

---- **CAUTION** ----

Never operate the radio without a speaker; severe damage to the output transistors will result. If the speaker must be replaced, use a speaker of the correct impedance (ohms) or else the output transistors will be damaged and require replacement.

REMOVAL & INSTALLATION

Pick-up
1977–78

1. Remove the knobs from the radio.

2. Remove the nuts from the radio control shafts.

3. Detach the antenna lead from the jack on the radio case.

4. Detach the power and speaker leads.

5. Remove the radio support nuts and bolts.

6. Remove the radio from beneath the dashboard.

Installation is the reverse of removal.

1979 AND LATER

1. Disconnect the negative battery cable from the battery.

2. Remove steering column upper and lower covers.

3. Remove the five screws holding the instrument cluster trim panel and remove trim panel.

4. Remove the knobs from the radio and remove the securing nuts from the control shafts.

5. Remove the heater/air conditioner knobs from their control arms. Do not remove the blower fan control knob.

6. Remove the two screws holding the heater control dash light. Remove the ashtray and remove all of the screws holding the center dash facade onto the dash.

7. Pull the facade out, and carefully disconnect the cigarette lighter and the blower fan control at their plugs.

8. Unscrew any remaining screws holding the radio and pull it out part way. Disconnect the power source, speaker coupling and antenna from the radio and remove through the dash.

Installation is the reverse of removal.

Windshield Wipers

MOTOR REMOVAL AND INSTALLATION

Pick-up

1. Disconnect the wiring from the wiper motor and unbolt it from the fire wall.

2. On 1977–78 and earlier models, remove the arm nut and crank arm from the wiper motor. On 1979 and later models, remove the nut, then pry the wiper link from the crank arm.

3. Remove the motor.

Installation is the reverse of removal.

Land Cruiser

EXCEPT 1980 AND LATER STATION WAGON

1. Detach the wiper link from the motor with a screwdriver.

2. Unfasten the two bracket bolts at the rear of the motor.

3. Disconnect the wiper motor wiring.

4. Unfasten the wiper motor screws and withdraw the motor.

Installation is the reverse of removal.

1980 AND LATER STATION WAGON

NOTE: On these models, the wiper motor is removed with the linkage assembly.

1. Remove the wiper arm retaining nuts and remove the wiper arm and blade assemblies.

2. Remove both wiper arm pivot covers.

3. Remove the pivot-to-cowl attaching screws.

4. Remove the two service hole covers from the cowl area of the engine compartment.

5. Disconnect the wiring from the wiper motor.

6. From the engine compartment, remove the wiper motor plate-to-cowl retaining screws.

7. Withdraw the wiper motor and linkage from the cowl panel as an assembly.

8. Pry the linkage off of the wiper motor and disconnect the linkage from the motor.

Installation is the reverse of the previous steps.

LINKAGE REMOVAL AND INSTALLATION

Pick-up

1. Remove the wiper motor as described above.

2. Remove the wiper arms by removing their retaining nuts and working them off their shafts.

3. Remove the nuts and spacers holding the wiper shafts and push the shafts down into the body cavity. Pull the linkage out of the cavity through the wiper motor hole.

Installation is the reverse of removal.

Land Cruiser—2 Door

1. Remove the wiper arm assemblies.

2. Remove the end plate from the pivot housing.

3. Remove the wiper motor complete with the linkage cable.

4. Separate the wiper motor and transmission.

5. Remove the linkage cable.

Installation is performed in the reverse order of removal.

Land Cruiser—Station Wagon
1977–79

1. Perform the wiper motor removal procedures above.

2. Remove the wiper arm assemblies.

3. Remove the instrument cluster, as detailed below.

4. Loosen the throttle cable to improve access to the wiper linkage.

5. Remove the linkage attachment bolts and withdraw the linkage.

Installation is the reverse of removal.

1980 AND LATER

Refer to the Motor Removal and Installation procedure.

Instrument Cluster

REMOVAL & INSTALLATION

Pick-up
1977–78

1. Loosen the steering column clamp bolts at the base of the instrument panel. This will allow the steering column to drop slightly.

2. Remove the three retaining screws on the instrument group and pull out gently on the hood of the cluster.

3. Disconnect the speedometer cable and the wiring connector and withdraw the cluster.

Installation is the reverse of removal.

1980 AND LATER

1. Disconnect the negative battery cable at the battery.

2. Remove the upper and lower steering column covers.

3. Remove the five screws holding the instrument trim panel and remove the panel.

4. Disconnect the speedometer cable from the back of the speedometer.

5. Remove the four screws holding the instrument panel in place and pull the panel forward. Unplug the two connectors from the back of the panel and remove the panel.

Installation is the reverse of removal.

Land Cruiser

1. Disconnect the speedometer cable.

2. Remove the instrument panel attaching screws.

3. Loosen the steering column clamp by removing the attaching bolts.

4. Pull out the instrument panel and the speedometer, disconnect the wiring connectors, and remove the panel.

Install the panel in the reverse order from removal.

Fuses and Fusible Links

The fuse box is located on the lefthand side, underneath the dashboard, on all models. All models are equipped with fusible links on the battery cables running from the positive (+) battery terminal.

Volkswagen

INTRODUCTION

The Volkswagen pick-up was introduced in 1980. It is the first VW ever to be both designed and built by Volkswagen of America.

The pick-up is based on the Rabbit, and like the Rabbit is available with either a fuel injected gasoline or a diesel engine. The available transmissions are a four or five-speed manual, or a three-speed automatic (1980).

The engines are all water cooled, transversely mounted units. The truck has an independent front suspension, rack and pinion steering and power assisted brakes (disc in the front, self-adjusting drums in the rear).

MODEL IDENTIFICATION

Vehicle Identification Plate

On the Rabbit pick-up, the plate is on top of the body crossmember above the grille. On the plate are the date of manufacture and the chassis number.

Chassis Number

The chassis number is located on the left front corner of the instrument panel on the Rabbit pick-up, and is visible through the windshield. The chassis number is also on top of the right suspension strut mounting. It also appears on the vehicle identification plate.

Engine Number

The Engine number is stamped on the front of the engine block between the fuel pump and the distributor.

Vehicle identification plate

Chassis number

Engine number

GENERAL ENGINE SPECIFICATIONS

Year	Engine Displacement cu in. (cc)	Carburetor Type	Horsepower @ rpm (SAE)	Torque @ rpm (ft lbs) (SAE)	Bore × Stroke (in.)	Compression Ratio	Oil Pressure @ rpm (psi)
'80	88.9 (1457)	Fuel inj.	71 @ 5800	73 @ 3500	3.13 × 2.89	8:1	28 @ 2000
	89.7 (1471)	Diesel	48 @ 5000	56.5 @ 3000	3.01 × 3.15	23.5:1	27 @ 2000
'81–'82	105.0 (1715)	Fuel inj.	78 @ 5500①	88.2 @ 3100②	3.13 × 3.40	8.2:1	28 @ 2000
	97.1 (1588)	Diesel	52 @ 4800	71.5 @ 3000	3.01 × 3.40	23:1	28 @ 2000

① 74 @ 5000—California
② 89.6 @ 3000—California

GASOLINE TUNE-UP SPECIFICATIONS

Year	Engine Displacement cm³	Spark Plugs Type	Spark Plugs Gap (in.)	Distributor Point Dwell (deg)	Distributor Point Gap (in.)	Ignition Timing (deg)	Intake Valve Opens (deg)	Compression Pressure (psi)	Idle Speed (rpm)	Valve Clearance (in.) In	Valve Clearance (in.) Ex
'80	1457	W7D N8Y	.024–.028	44–50	.016	3A @ idle	4B	142–184	850–1000	.008–.012	.016–.020
'81–'82	1715	W7D N8Y	.028	Electronic	—	3A @ idle	4B	142–184	850–1000①	.008–.012	.016–.020

NOTE: The underhood specifications sticker often reflects tune-up specification changes made in production. Sticker figures must be used if they disagree with those in this chart.
A—After Top Dead Center
B—Before Top Dead Center
① w/o idle stabilizer

DIESEL TUNE-UP SPECIFICATIONS

Year	Valve Clearance (cold) Intake (in.)	Valve Clearance (cold) Exhaust (in.)	Intake Valve Opens (deg)	Injection Pump Setting (deg)	Injection Nozzle Pressure (psi) New	Injection Nozzle Pressure (psi) Used	Idle Speed (rpm)	Cranking Compression Pressure (psi)
'80	.008–.012	.016–.020	NA	Align marks	1849	1706	770–870	398 minimum
'81–'82	.008–.0012	.016–.020	NA	Align marks	1849	1706	800–850	398 minimum

NOTE: Valve clearance need not be adjusted unless it varies more than 0.002 in. from specification.
NA: Information not available

FIRING ORDER

Firing order; 1-3-4-2

CAPACITIES

Year	Engine Displacement cu in. (cc)	Engine Crankcase (qts) With Filter	Engine Crankcase (qts) Without Filter	Transmission (pts) Manual	Transmission (pts) Automatic	Drive Axle (pts)	Gasoline Tank (gals)	Cooling System (pts)
'80	Gasoline	3.7	3.2	3.2①	6.4	1.6	15	9.8
	Diesel	3.7	3.2	2.6	—	1.6	15	12.6
'81–'82	Gasoline Diesel	4.7	4.2	3.2①	—	1.6	15	14.6

① 5-speed—4.2

CRANKSHAFT AND CONNECTING ROD SPECIFICATIONS

(All measurements are given in inches)

Year	Crankshaft Main Brg. Journal Dia.	Crankshaft Main Brg. Oil Clearance	Crankshaft Shaft End-Play	Thrust on No.	Connecting Rod Journal Diameter	Connecting Rod Oil Clearance	Connecting Rod Side Clearance (max.)
'80–'82	2.126	0.001–0.003	0.003–0.007	3	1.811	0.001–0.003	0.015

NOTE: Main and connecting rod bearings are available in three undersizes.

VALVE SPECIFICATIONS

Year	Seat Angle (deg)	Spring Test Pressure (lbs. @ in.)	Stem to Guide Clearance (in.)		Stem Diameter (in.)	
			Intake	Exhaust	Intake	Exhaust
'80–'82	45	96–106① @ 0.92 in.	0.001–0.002	0.001–0.002	0.314	0.314

NOTE: Exhaust valves must be grounded by hand.
① Outer spring, inner spring test pressure is 46–51 lbs. @ 0.72 in.

PISTON AND RING SPECIFICATIONS

(All measurements in inches)

Year, Model	Piston Clear-ance	Ring Gap			Ring Side Clearance		
		Top Compression	Bottom Compression	Oil Control	Top Compression	Bottom Compression	Oil Control
Gasoline Engine	0.001–0.003	0.012–0.018	0.012–0.018	0.010–0.016	0.001–0.002	0.001–0.002	0.001–0.002
Diesel Engine	0.001–0.003	0.012–0.020	0.012–0.020	0.010–0.016	0.002–0.400	0.002–0.003	0.001–0.002

NOTE: Three piston sizes are available to accommodate overbores up to 0.040 in.

TORQUE SPECIFICATIONS

(All readings in ft. lbs.)

Year	Cylinder Head Bolts	Rod Bearing Bolts	Main Bearing Bolts	Crankshaft Pulley Bolt	Flywheel To Crankshaft Bolts	Manifold	
						Intake	Exhaust
'80–'82	61①	33	47	56	54②	18	18

① 69 ft. lbs. warm
② Pressure plate to crankshaft bolts

Cylinder head torque sequence

BATTERY AND STARTER SPECIFICATIONS

(All models use 12 volt, negative ground system)

Year	Battery Amp Hour Capacity	Lock Test			No Load Test			Brush Spring Tension (oz.)	Minimum Brush Length (in.)
		Amps	Volts	Torque (ft. lbs.)	Amps	Volts	RPM		
'80–'82	45/54①	280–370	7.5	2.42	33–55	11.5	6000–8000	35.5	0.5

① w/AC

WHEEL ALIGNMENT

Year	CASTER		CAMBER		Toe-in (in.)	Steering Axis Inclination (deg)
	Range (deg)	Pref Setting (deg)	Range (deg)	Pref Setting (deg)		
'80–'82	+1°20'–2°20'	+1°50'	–10'–+50'	+20'	0.08	10°30'

TUNE-UP PROCEDURES

VW recommends a tune-up, including new points and plugs, at 15,000 mile intervals. The only procedure required for diesel engines in this section is the valve lash adjustment and minimum/maximum engine speed checking and adjustment.

Spark Plugs

The firing order is 1-3-4-2, with no. 1 cylinder at the right of the engine.

1. Grasp the spark plug boot and pull it straight out. Don't pull on the wire. Either number the wires or remove them one at a time to avoid mixups.
2. Place the spark plug socket firmly on the plug and screw the spark plug out.

NOTE: The cylinder head is aluminum alloy, which is easily stripped of threads. Remove the plugs only when the engine is cold.

If removal is difficult, loosen the plug only slightly and drip penetrating oil onto the threads.

3. Inspect the plugs and clean or discard them. The recommended spark plug gap is listed in the "Tune-Up Specifications" chart. Use a round wire feeler gauge to check the gap between the plug electrodes. If the gap is incorrect, gently bend the side electrode to correct. Do not bend the center electrode.
4. Torque the new spark plugs to 22 ft. lbs. Install the ignition wire boots firmly.

Breaker Points and Condenser

Snap off the two retaining clips on the dis-

Breaker points and condenser. Lubricate at (1) with a drop of engine oil and at (2) with high melting point grease

tributor cap. Remove the cap and examine it for cracks, deterioration, or carbon tracking. Replace the cap, if necessary, by transferring one wire at a time from the old cap to the new one. Examine the rotor for corrosion or wear and replace it if questionable. Remove the dust shield. Check the points for pitting and burning. Slight imperfections on the contact surface may be filed off with a point file. It is best to replace the breaker point set. Always replace the condenser when you replace the point set.

To replace the breaker points:

1. Remove the rotor.
2. Unsnap the point connector from the terminal at the side of the distributor. Remove the retaining screw, and lift out the point set.
3. Install the new point set, making sure that the pin on the bottom engages the hole in the breaker plate.
4. Install the wire connector and the retaining screws (hand-tight).
5. Turn the engine with a wrench on the crankshaft pulley until the breaker arm rubbing block is in the high point of one of the cam lobes. Turn the engine only in the direction of normal rotation to avoid damage to the timing belt.

Adjusting the point gap

6. A 0.016 in. feeler gauge should just slip through the points. If the gap is incorrect, pivot a screwdriver in the point set notch and the two projections on the breaker plate to bring it within specifications.
7. When the gap is correct, tighten the retaining screw. Recheck the adjustment.
8. Lubricate the distributor cam with silicone grease.
9. Install the dust cover, rotor and distributor cap.
10. Check the dwell angle and the ignition timing.
11. The condenser is mounted on the outside of the distributor. Undo the mounting screw and the terminal block to replace.

Dwell Angle (Breaker-Point Gasoline Engines Only)

The dwell angle or cam angle is the number of degrees that the distributor cam rotates while the points are closed. There is an inverse relationship between dwell angle and point gap. Increasing the point gap will

Timing window

Timing mark aligned at 3° ATDC

decrease the dwell angle and vice versa. Checking the dwell angle with a meter is a far more accurate method of measuring point opening than the feller gauge method.

After setting the point gap to specification with a feeler gauge, check the dwell angle. Attach the dwell meter. The negative lead is grounded and the positive lead is connected to the primary wire, Terminal No. 1 that runs from the coil to the distributor. Start the engine, let it idle and reach operating temperature, and observe the dwell on the meter. The reading should fall within the allowable range. If it does not, the gap will have to be reset. Dwell can also be checked with the engine cranking. In this case, dwell will vary between 0° and the dwell figure for that setting.

Hall Effect Electronic Ignition System

1981 and later trucks are equipped with the Hall effect electronic ignition system.

The distributor contains the Hall Effect pickup assembly which replaces the breaker points assembly in conventional systems.

The "Hall Effect" is a shift in magnetic field caused when one of the rotors on the distributor shaft passes the sensors mounted in the distributor. This shift performs the same function as breaker points, which is to allow the current (coil field) stored in the coil to collapse, causing a spark to run from the coil to the distributor and down to the spark plugs which make the current jump a gap between the two spark plug electrodes, causing a spark which ignites the air-fuel mixture in the combustion chamber. Since there are no breaker points and condenser to replace, the system should be maintenance free.

ELECTRONIC IGNITION PRECAUTIONS

When working on the Hall ignition, observe the following precautions to prevent damage to the ignition system.

1. Connect and disconnect test equipment only when the ignition switch is OFF.

2. Do not crank the engine with the starter for compression tests, etc., until the high tension coil wire is grounded.

3. Do not replace the original equipment coil with a conventional coil.

4. Do not install any kind of condenser to coil terminal.

5. Do not use a battery booster for longer than 1 (one) minute.

6. Do not tow cars with defective ignitions systems without disconnecting the plugs on the idle stabilizer (if equipped) at the ignition control unit.

IGNITION COIL TEST

A defective Hall ignition coil cannot be checked with standard coil testing equipment. If there is no high tension current and all other components of the ignition system check out, see if you're getting a spark from the coil wire to the distributor cap by unplugging the coil wire at the distributor, holding the end of it with insulated pliers about ½ in. from ground (engine block, etc.) and turning over the engine. If a weak or no spark is obtained, try replacing the coil.

HALL PICKUP UNIT TEST

1. Check for voltage on positive terminal (15) of the ignition coil. There should be voltage with the ignition ON.

2. Ground a high tension coil wire.

3. Connect a test light (4 to 24 volts) between positive terminal (15) and negative terminal (1).

4. Crank the engine with the starter for approximately 5 seconds. The test light should flicker. If not, replace the ignition distributor.

IGNITION CONTROL UNIT TEST

1. Disconnect the plugs at the control unit and connect the plugs to each other.

2. Turn the ignition switch on and make sure there is current at positive terminal (15) of the ignition coil. Turn the ignition OFF.

3. Disconnect the high tension wire between the ignition coil and the distributor at the distributor.

4. Disconnect the wire (plug) between the control unit and the distributor at the distributor.

5. Connect the positive (+) terminal of the voltmeter to negative terminal (1) of the ignition coil and the negative (−) ter-

minal to ground.

6. Turn the ignition ON. There must be a voltage reading of at least 12 volts. If voltage drops below 12 volts in one second, turn off the ignition. The control unit is defective and will have to be replaced.

7. Disconnect the green wire where it connects to the distributor and ground the wire. Turn the ignition switch ON. The voltmeter should read about 12 volts. Disconnect the ground wire. The voltage should drop to 6 volts. If not, replace the control unit. Turn off the ignition.

8. Connect the terminals of the voltmeter to the outer connector of the control unit. Connect the positive (+) lead to the red wire and the negative (−) lead to the brown wire. Switch on the ignition. The voltmeter should read about 10 volts. If not, replace the control unit.

IDLE STABILIZER

The idle stabilizer is located on top of the ignition control unit. The idle stabilizer controls idle speed by either advancing or retarding the distributor timing in accordance with engine load (air conditioner on, lights on, etc.) If idle speed is erratic or if the engine fails to start, try bypassing the idle stabilizer by disconnecting the two plugs at the idle stabilizer and plugging them together. If idle improves, the idle stabilizer should probably be replaced.

Ignition Timing

BREAKER-POINT IGNITION SYSTEMS

1. Attach the timing light according to the manufacturer's instructions. Hook-up a dwell/tachometer since you'll need an rpm indication for correct timing.

2. Locate the timing mark opening in the clutch or torque converter housing at the rear of the engine directly behind the distributor. The OT mark stands for TDC or 0° advance. The other mark(s) identify advance and correct timing position. Mark them with chalk so that they will be more visible. Don't disconnect the vacuum line(s).

3. Start the engine and allow it to reach the normal operating temperature. The engine should be running at normal idle speed.

4. Shine the timing light at the marks.

5. The light should now be flashing when the timing mark and the V-shaped pointer are aligned.

6. If not, loosen the distributor hold-down bolt and rotate the distributor very slowly to align the marks.

7. Tighten the mounting nut when the ignition timing is correct.

8. Recheck the timing when the distributor is secured.

With ignition timing correctly adjusted, the spark plugs will fire at the exact instant in which the piston is nearing the top of the compression stroke, thus providing maximum power and economy.

ELECTRONIC IGNITION SYSTEMS

1. Run the engine to operating temperature. Connect tachometer. See Electronic Ignition Precautions.

2. Stop the engine. Disconnect the plugs on the idle stabilizer (if equipped) at the control unit and plug them together.

3. Check the idle speed. It should be between 800 and 1000 rpm.

4. Attach the timing light according to its manufacturer's instruction. Shine the light at the timing marks (located on the flywheel; see step 2 of Point Ignition Systems). The pointer in the hole must line up with the timing mark on the flywheel. To adjust the timing, loosen the distributor at its base and turn it until the marks are aligned.

5. Stop the engine and reconnect the plugs at the control unit.

Valve Lash

Check the valve clearance every 20,000 miles, with the engine at normal operating temperature.

1. Remove the camshaft cover and the distributor cap.

2. Set the engine at TDC on no. 1 cylinder by aligning the 0° T mark on the flywheel with the pointer and aligning the distributor rotor with the no. 1 cylinder mark on the rim of the distributor body.

NOTE: Always turn the crankshaft in the normal direction of rotation. Do not turn the engine by means of the timing belt (or camshaft bolt), because the belt will stretch or lose teeth.

3. The valve clearances of cylinder no. 1 should be checked when the valves of no. 4 cylinder overlap, i.e., when both no. 4 cylinder valves move in opposite directions simultaneously. It may be necessary to move the crankshaft slightly to find this position. When this happens, the exhaust valve is closing and the intake opening. Check and note the clearance of both the intake and exhaust valves for no. 1 cylinder.

4. Turn the crankshaft 180° (90° at the distributor rotor) in the normal direction of rotation. Check and note the valve clearances of cylinder no. 3 at the overlap position of cylinder no. 2.

5. Turn the crankshaft 180°. Check and note the valve clearances of cylinder no. 4 at the overlap position of cylinder no. 1.

6. Turn the crankshaft 180°. Check and note the valve clearances of cylinder no. 2 at the overlap position of cylinder no. 3.

7. Compare the noted clearances with those listed in the Tune-Up Specifications. Adjustment is made by replacing the tappet clearance disc in the top of each tappet. These are available in 26 sizes ranging from

ELECTRONIC IGNITION TESTING SPECIFICATIONS

Component Tested	Specification
Rotor resistance	5000 ohms
Plug wire resistance	
With radio	800–1200 ohms
W/O radio	0 ohms
Spark Plug Connector resistance	
Suppressed	4000–6000 ohms
Not suppressed	800–1200 ohms
Air gap ①	0.25 mm (0.010 in.)
Inductive signal resistance ②	890–1285 ohms
Resistance from the coil tower to the negative coil terminal	5500–8000 ohms
Resistance from the coil positive terminal to the coil negative terminal	0.95–1.50 ohms
Vacuum retard	8°–10°
Vacuum advance	4°–8°
Centrifugal advance	6°–12°

① Air gap is adjustable by bending the teeth on the stator (reluctor)

② Measure resistance between the connectors to the control unit on the distributor (connects to the green and white wires)

3.0 mm (0.119 in.) to 4.25 mm (0.166 in.) in increments of 0.05 mm (0.002 in.). The thickness of each disc is marked on the bottom.

NOTE: If a valve clearance deviates 0.002 in. or less from the specified clearance, it need not be adjusted.

8. To remove a tappet clearance disc, turn the cylinder to TDC and press down the tappet so that the disc can be lifted out.

NOTE: When adjusting clearances on a diesel, the pistons must not be at TDC. Turn the crankshaft ¼ turn past TDC, so that the valves do not contact the pistons when the tappets are depressed.

A special tool is available from VW for this operation. Once the disc is removed, check its size and determine what size will be needed to produce the required adjustment.

9. Install the required disc. When all the clearances have been corrected, recheck valve clearances.

CIS Fuel Injection

IDLE AND CO ADJUSTMENT

All Except 1980 California And 1981–82 Models

The following adjustments can be made *only*

Checking valve clearance with a feeler guage

with a CO meter and the CO adjusting tool (VW-P377).

1. Run the engine until it reaches normal operating temperature.

2. Adjust the ignition timing to specification with the vacuum hoses connected and the engine at idle.

3. Adjust the idle speed to specification.

4. Remove the charcoal filter hose from the air cleaner except on Canadian models.

5. Turn on the headlight high beams.

6. Remove the plug from the CO adjusting hole and insert adjustment tool VW-P377. Turn the adjustment screw clockwise

Using special tools to depress the tappet and remove the tappet clearance disc

Fuel injection idle adjustment screw

CO-adjusting tool installed—CIS fuel injection

Rotor adjustment with notch for cylinder no. 1

Special adapter VW 1324 is necessary to use an external techometer on diesel engines

Diesel engine idle speed (upper) and maximum speed (lower) adjustment screws

to raise the percentage of CO and counterclockwise to lower the percentage of CO.

--- CAUTION ---

Do not push the adjustment tool down or accelerate the engine with the tool in place.

7. Remove the tool after each adjustment and accelerate the engine briefly before reading the percentage of CO. The correct CO values are as follows:
49 States: 1.5% M/T; 0.1% A/T
0.6 + 0.4%

1980 California, 1981–82 Models

1. The engine must be at operating temperature.
2. Disconnect crankcase breather hose at the cylinder head and plug the hose.
3. Disconnect the two plugs on the idle stabilizer at the control unit and plug them together.
4. Do not have any electrical accessories (air conditioner, lights, etc.) on.
5. Connect a tachometer and timing light. Check the timing. Adjust if necessary.

6. Check the idle speed against the specifications chart or your underhood sticker. Adjust the idle at the idle adjustment screw on the throttle chamber (880–1000 rpm).

NOTE: Only adjust the idle when the radiator fan is not on.

The only way CO levels can be adjusted on these models is with special dealer tools (frequency counter, CO tester, etc.) which are usually not available to the general public.

Diesel Fuel Injection

IDLE SPEED/MAXIMUM SPEED ADJUSTMENTS

Volkswagen diesel engines have both an idle speed and a maximum speed adjustment. The maximum engine speed adjustment prevents the engine from over-revving and swallowing itself whole. The adjusters are located side by side on top of the injection pump. The screw closest to the engine is the idle speed adjuster, while the outer screw is the maximum speed adjuster.

The idle and maximum speed must be adjusted with the engine warm (normal operating temperature). Because the diesel engine has no conventional ignition, you will need a special adaptor (VW 1324) to connect your tachometer, or use the tachometer in the instrument panel, if equipped. You should check with the manufacturer of your tachometer to see if it will work with diesel engines. Adjust all engines to 770–870 rpm (through 1980) or 800–850 rpm (from 1981).

When adjustment is correct, lock the locknut on the screw and apply a dab of paint of non-hardening thread sealer to prevent the screw from vibrating loose.

The maximum speed for all engines is between 5500 and 5600 rpm (through 1980) or 5300–5400 rpm (from 1981). If it is not in this range, loosen the screw and correct the speed (turning the screw clockwise decreases rpm). Lock the nut on the adjusting screw and apply a dab of paint in the same manner as you did on the idle screw.

--- CAUTION ---

Do not attempt to squeeze more power out of your engine by raising the maximum speed. If you do, you'll probably be in for a major overhaul in the not too distant future.

ENGINE ELECTRICAL

Distributor

The distributor is a single breaker point unit

on some 1980 models. Electronic ignition is used on all models since 1981. It has both centrifugal and vacuum advance mechanisms. A vacuum retard system works only at idle.

The distributor is gear driven by an intermediate shaft which also drives the fuel pump. The distributor shaft also turns the oil pump.

REMOVAL AND INSTALLATION

1. Disconnect the coil high tension wire.
2. Detach the primary wire.
3. Remove the distributor cap.
4. Turn the engine until the rotor aligns with the index mark on the outer edge of the distributor. This is the No. 1 position. Mark the bottom of the distributor housing and its mounting flange on the engine.
5. Remove the bolt and lift off the retaining flange. Lift the distributor straight out of the engine.

If the engine has not been disturbed while the distributor was out, i.e., the crankshaft was not turned, then reinstall the distributor in the reverse order of removal. Carefully align the marks.

If the engine has been rotated while the distributor was out, then proceed as follows:

1. Turn the crankshaft so that no. 1 piston is on its compression stroke and the O°T timing mark is aligned with the V-shaped pointer.
2. Turn the distributor so that the rotor points approximately 15° before the No. 1 cylinder position on the distributor.
3. Insert the distributor into the engine block. If the oil pump drive doesn't engage, remove the distributor and, using a long screwdriver turn the pump shaft so that it is parallel to the centerline of the crankshaft.
4. Install the distributor, aligning the marks. Tighten the retaining nut.
5. Install the cap. Adjust the ignition timing.

Alternator

ALTERNATOR PRECAUTIONS

An alternating current (AC) generator (alternator) is used. Unlike the direct current (DC) generators, there are several precautions which must be strictly observed in order to avoid damaging the unit.

1. Reversing the battery connections will result in damage to the diodes.
2. Booster batteries should be connected from negative to ground, and positive to positive.
3. Never use a fast charger as a booster to start cars with AC circuits.
4. When servicing the battery with a fast charger, always disconnect the car battery cables.

5. Never attempt to polarize an AC generator.
6. Avoid long soldering times when replacing diodes or transistors. Prolonged heat is damaging to AC generators.
7. Do not use test lamps of more than 12 volts (V) for checking diode continuity.
8. Do not short across or ground any of the terminals on the AC generator.
9. The polarity of the battery, generator, and regulator must be matched and considered before making any electrical connections within the system.
10. Never operate the AC generator on an open circuit. Make sure that all connections within the circuit are clean and tight.
11. Disconnect the battery terminals when performing any service on the electrical system. This will eliminate the possibility of accidental reversal of polarity.
12. Disconnect the battery ground cable if arc welding is to be done on any part of the car.

REMOVAL AND INSTALLATION

The alternator and voltage regulator are combined in one housing. No voltage adjustment can be made with this unit. The regulator can be replaced without removing the alternator. Unbolt the regulator and remove from the rear.

1. Disconnect the battery cables.
2. Remove the multi-connector retaining bracket and unplug the connector from the rear of the alternator.
3. Loosen and remove the top mounting nut and bolt.
4. Using a socket inserted through the timing belt cover (it is not necessary to remove the cover), loosen the lower mounting bolt.
5. Swing the alternator over and remove the alternator belt.
6. Remove the lower nut and bolt.
7. Remove the alternator.
8. Install the alternator with the lower bolt. *Do not* tighten it at this point.
9. Install the alternator belt over the pulleys.
10. Loosely install the top mounting bolt and pivot the alternator until the belt is correctly tensioned.
11. Tighten the top and bottom bolts to 14 ft. lbs.
12. Connect the alternator and battery wires.

BELT REPLACEMENT AND TENSIONING

1. Loosen the top alternator mounting bolt.
2. Using a socket inserted through the timing belt cover loosen the lower mounting bolt.
3. Use a wooden hammer handle or a broomstick to lever the alternator over and

The oil pump drive should be parallel to the crankshaft

Removing the lower alternator bolt through the timing cover

Starter electrical connections: (1) solenoid, (2) coil, (3) positive battery cable

remove the belt.
4. Slip the new belt over the pulleys.
5. Pry the alternator over until the belt deflection midway between the crankshaft pulley and the alternator pulley is ⅜–⁹⁄₁₆ in. (10–15 mm).
6. Securely tighten the mounting bolts.

Starter

A new type of starter has been installed on some models that are equipped with a manual transmission. The new style starter is not interchangeable with the old design. The new starter does not need a rear support bracket.

Exploded view of new type starter

1.	Mounting bracket	9.	Solenoid
2.	End cap screws	10.	Disc
3.	Housing screws	11.	Mounting housing
4.	Cupped washer	12.	Drive pinion
5.	End plate bushing	13.	Stop ring
6.	Brushes	14.	Solenoid bolt
7.	Field coil housing	15.	Starter bolt and nut
8.	Armature	16.	Circlip

NEW TYPE   OLD TYPE

New and old type starters are not interchangeable

REMOVAL AND INSTALLATION

Old Style

1. Disconnect the battery ground cable.
2. Raise the front of the car.
3. Mark with tape and then disconnect the wires from the starter solenoid.
4. Disconnect the large cable.
5. Remove the starter retaining nuts.
6. Unscrew the bolt. Remove the starter.
7. Installation of the starter is carried out in reverse order of removal.

New Style

1. Disconnect the battery ground cable.
2. Support the weight of the engine with either Volkswagen special tool 10-222 or use a jack with a block of wood under the oil pan. Don't jack the engine too high, just take the weight off the motor mounts. Be careful not to bend the oil pan.
3. Remove the engine/transmission cover plate.
4. Unbolt and remove the starter side motor mount and carrier.
5. Disconnect and mark the starter wiring.
6. Remove the bolts holding the starter and remove the starter.
7. Install the starter and tighten the nuts and bolts to 14 ft. lbs.
8. Install the engine mount and carrier.
9. Install and attach remaining components. Don't forget to reconnect the battery cable.

OVERHAUL

Use the following procedure to replace brushes or starter drive.

1. Remove the solenoid.
2. Remove the end bearing cap.
3. Loosen both of the long housing screws.
4. Remove the lockwasher and spacer washers.
5. Remove the long housing screws and remove the end cover.
6. Pull the two field coil brushes out of the brush housing.
7. Remove the brush housing assembly.
8. Loosen the nut on the solenoid housing, remove the sealing disc, and remove the solenoid operating lever.
9. Loosen the large screws on the side of the starter body and remove the field coil along with the brushes.

NOTE: If the brushes require replacement, the field coil and brushes and/or the brush housing and its brushes must be replaced as a unit.

10. If the starter drive is being replaced on the new type starter, push the stop-ring down and remove the circlip on the end of the shaft. Remove the stop-ring and remove

the drive.

11. To remove the starter drive on old type starters, remove the armature and pull the drive unit off the end.

12. Assembly of the starter is carried out in the reverse order of disassembly. Use a gear puller to install the stop-ring in its groove (on models so equipped). Use a new circlip on the shaft.

SOLENOID REPLACEMENT

1. Remove the starter.

2. Remove the nut which secures the connector strip on the end of the solenoid.

3. Take out the two retaining screws on the mounting bracket and pull out the solenoid after it has been unhooked from the operating lever.

4. Installation is the reverse of removal. In order to facilitate engagement of the lever, the pinion should be pulled out as far as possible when inserting the solenoid.

ENGINE MECHANICAL

The engine is an inline four cylinder unit with single overhead camshaft. It is inclined 30° to the rear. The crankshaft runs in five bearings with thrust taken on the center bearing. The cylinder block is cast iron. A steel reinforced rubber belt drives the intermediate shaft and camshaft. The intermediate shaft drives the oil pump, distributor and fuel pump.

The cylinder head is lightweight aluminum alloy. The intake and exhaust manifolds are mounted on the same side of the cylinder head. The valves are opened and closed by camshaft lobes operating on cupped cam followers which fit over the valves and springs. This design results in lighter valve train weight and fewer moving parts.

The key difference between the gasoline and diesel engine is that the diesel has no carburetor and no electrical ignition system. There are no plugs, points or coil to replace. Combustion occurs when a fine mist of diesel fuel is sprayed into hot compressed air (1650°F) under high pressure (850 psi). The air is heated by the compression as the piston moves up on the compression stroke. The diesel engine has a compression ratio of 23.5:1 compared to the gasoline engine's compression ratio of 8.2:1.

VW's diesel block, flywheel, bearings and crankshaft are identical to those in the Rabbit gasoline engine. The connecting rod wrist pins were strengthened and new pistons and cylinder head, made of aluminum for lightness, were designed.

Exploded view of the old type starter

Removal and Installation

MANUAL TRANSMISSION

Gasoline Engines

The engine and transmission are removed as an assembly.

1. Disconnect the battery ground cable.

2. Drain the coolant by unbolting the lower water pump flange or by removing the hoses.

——— CAUTION ———
Do not disconnect or loosen any refrigerant hose connections during engine removal on cars equipped with air conditioning.

3. On cars equipped with air conditioning:

a. Loosen the compressor support bolts and remove the compressor.

b. Remove the radiator cooling fan, air ducts and radiator.

c. Remove the condenser.

d. Place the air conditioning compressor and condenser out of the way without disconnecting any refrigerant lines.

4. Remove the radiator with the air ducts and fan.

5. Detach and label all the electrical wires connecting the engine to the body.

6. Disconnect and plug the fuel line at the fuel pump. Detach the coolant hoses at the left end of the engine. Disconnect the accelerator cable and remove the air cleaner.

7. Disconnect the speedometer cable from the transmission. Detach the clutch cable.

8. Remove the engine support to the right of the starter.

9. Remove the headlight caps inside the engine compartment.

10. Unbolt the driveshafts from the transmission and wire them up.

11. Unbolt the exhaust pipe from the manifold and unbolt the exhaust pipe brace.

12. Unbolt the transmission rear mount from the body (alongside the tunnel).

13. Detach the ground strap from the transmission and body.

14. Remove the shift linkage.

15. Attach a chain sling to the alternator bracket and the lifting eye at the left end of the engine. Lift the engine and transmission slightly.

Aligning the flywheel for manual transmission and engine separation

16. Detach the engine carrier from the body and remove the left transmission carrier.

17. Lift the engine/transmission assembly carefully out of the car.

18. To separate the engine and transmission, turn the flywheel to align the lug on the flywheel (to the left of TDC) with the pointer in the opening. The engine and transmission can only be separated in this position. Remove the cover plate over the driveshaft flange and remove the engine to transmission bolts and the transmission housing cover plate.

To install the engine:

19. To attach the transmission to the engine, the recess in the flywheel edge must be at 3:00 o'clock (facing the left end of the engine). Torque the engine to transmission bolts to 40 ft. lbs. Lift the engine/transmission assembly into place. Loosen the bolts for the engine and transmission mounts. Move the engine assembly from side to side until the rear transmission mount is straight. Center the left and right transmission mounts and tighten all transmission bolts. Push the front mount upward to center the rubber cone, then tighten the mount. Loosen the exhaust pipe clamps, release any strain, then tighten the clamps. Torque the 10 mm bolts to 29 ft. lbs. Torque the driveshaft flange bolts to 32 ft. lbs. Refill the cooling system.

AUTOMATIC TRANSMISSION

Gasoline Engines

The engine and transmission are removed as an assembly.

1. Shift the transmission into "Park." Disconnect both battery cables.

2. Drain the coolant by unbolting the lower water pump flange or by removing the hoses.

------- **CAUTION** -------

Do not disconnect or loosen any refrigerant hose connections during engine removal on cars equipped with air conditioning.

3. On cars equipped with air conditioning, proceed as follows:

a. Loosen the compressor support bolts and remove the compressor.

b. Remove the radiator cooling fan, air ducts, and radiator.

c. Remove the condenser.

d. Place the air conditioning components out of the way without disconnecting any refrigerant lines.

4. Remove the radiator with the air ducts and fan.

5. Remove the air cleaner.

6. Detach the speedometer cable from the transmission.

7. Detach and label all electrical wires connecting the engine to the body. Detach the coolant hoses.

8. Remove the screws holding the accelerator cable bracket to the carburetor float bowl (do not disassemble linkage), detach the end of the gearshaft selector cable from the transmission, detach the accelerator cable and pedal cable at the transmission, and remove the two bracket bolts behind this linkage on the transmission.

9. Unbolt the exhaust pipe from the manifold.

10. Remove the rear transmission mount. Unbolt the driveshafts and wire them up out of the way.

11. Remove the converter cover plate and remove the three torque converter to drive plate bolts.

12. Attach a chain sling to the alternator bracket and the lifting eye at the left end of the engine. It may be necessary to remove the alternator. Lift the engine and transmission slightly.

13. Detach the engine front mounting support; remove the left transmission carrier and the right engine carrier.

14. Lift the engine/transmission assembly carefully out of the car.

15. The transmission can now be detached from the engine.

To install the engine:

16. The engine to transmission bolts should be torqued to 40 ft. lbs. Lift the engine/transmission assembly into place and install the left transmission carrier, tightening first the body, then the transmission bolts. Lower the assembly to attach the engine carrier to the body, tightening the bolts to 40 ft. lbs. Install the engine mounting support. Check that all mounts and clamps are free of strain. Torque converter bolts should be torqued to 21 ft. lbs. and driveshaft bolts to 32 ft. lbs. Refill the cooling system. Check the adjustment of transmission and carburetor linkages.

DIESEL ENGINES

The diesel engine is removed with the transmission attached.

1. Disconnect the battery.

2. Disconnect the radiator hoses and drain the coolant. It can be saved for reuse, if it's not too old.

3. Remove the radiator complete with fan.

4. Remove the alternator.

5. Disconnect the fuel filter and set it aside near the windshield washer reservoir.

6. Detach the supply and return lines from the injection pump.

7. Disconnect the accelerator cable from the lever on the injection pump and remove the injection pump complete with bracket.

8. Disconnect the cold start cable from the pump.

9. Disconnect and label all electrical wires and leads.

10. Remove the front transmission mount.

11. Disconnect the clutch cable.

12. Remove the relay rod and connecting rod from the transmission and turn the relay lever shaft to the rear.

13. Disconnect the selector rod.

14. Unbolt the driveshafts and wire them up out of the way. Remove the rear support.

15. Disconnect the exhaust pipe at the manifold and remove the rear transmission mount.

16. Attach a lifting sling to the engine and take the weight from the engine mounts. Remove the left and right transmission mounts.

17. Carefully guide the engine out of the car while turning it slightly.

18. To separate the engine from the transmission, unscrew the plug from the TDC sensor opening and turn the flywheel to align the mark on the flywheel with the pointer. The engine/transmission can only be separated in this position.

19. Remove the cover plate over the driveshaft flange and remove the engine-to-transmission bolts.

20. Press the engine off the transmission.

21. Installation is the reverse of removal. Turn the flywheel so that the recess in the flywheel is level with the driveshaft flange. Lower the engine into the car and attach the left transmission mount to the transmission first. Align the rear transmission mount, center the engine/transmission and center the front transmission mount. Adjust the accelerator and cold start cables and bleed the injection system.

Cylinder Head

REMOVAL AND INSTALLATION

The engine should be cold before the cylinder head can be removed. The head is retained by 10 socket head bolts. It can be removed without removing the intake and exhaust manifolds.

NOTE: 12 point socket head bolts are used. These should be used in complete sets only and need not be retorqued.

Gas Engines

1. Disconnect the battery ground cable.
2. Drain the cooling system.
3. Disconnect the air duct from the throttle valve assembly.
4. Disconnect the throttle valve assembly.
5. Remove the injectors and disconnect the line from the cold start valve.
6. Disconnect the radiator and heater hoses.
7. Disconnect the vacuum and PCV lines (label lines for installation).
8. Remove the auxiliary air regulator from the intake manifold.
9. Disconnect all electrical lines and remove the spark plugs (label all lines and wires for installation).
10. Separate the exhaust pipe from the exhaust manifold.
11. Remove the EGR line from the exhaust manifold.
12. Remove the intake manifold.
13. Remove the timing belt cover and belt.
14. Loosen the cylinder head bolts in the reverse of the tightening sequence.
15. Remove the bolts and lift the head straight off.
16. Check the flatness of the cylinder block.
17. Install the new cylinder head gasket with the word TOP or OBEN facing upward.
18. Install bolts no. 10 and 8 first; these holes are smaller and will properly locate the gasket and cylinder head.
19. Install the remaining bolts. Tighten them in three stages using the sequence shown in the illustration. Cylinder head bolts must be torqued cold to 55 ft. lbs., then tightened ¼ turn more.
20. Install the remaining components in the reverse order of removal.

Diesel Engines

The head is retained by Allen bolts. The engine should be cold when the head is removed. The word TOP or OBEN on the new gasket should face up.

1. Disconnect the battery ground cable.
2. Drain the cooling system.
3. Remove the air cleaner.
4. Disconnect the fuel lines. Disconnect and tag all electrical wires and leads.
5. Separate the exhaust pipe from the manifold. Disconnect the radiator and heater hoses.
6. Remove the timing cover and belt (See timing belt replacement).
7. Loosen the cylinder head bolts in the reverse order of the tightening sequence.
8. Remove the head. Do not lay the head on the gasket surface with the injectors installed. Support it at the ends on strips of wood.
9. Install the cylinder head with a new gasket. Be sure the new gasket has the same

Exploded view of the cylinder showing valve train components

number of notches and the same identifying number as the old one, unless the pistons were also replaced.

Install bolts 8 and 10 first and torque the bolts to the specification in the proper sequence.

OVERHAUL

Valve guides are a shrink fit. Always install new valve seals when doing a valve job. Valve seats are not replaceable; the cylinder head should be replaced if the seat width and face angle cannot be maintained.

Refer to the general information section under Engine Overhaul.

Intake Manifold

REMOVAL AND INSTALLATION

1. Disconnect the air duct from the throttle valve body. Drain the cooling system.
2. Disconnect the accelerator cable.
3. Remove the injectors and disconnect the line from the cold start valve.
4. Disconnect all coolant hoses.
5. Disconnect all vacuum and emission control hoses (label all hoses for installation).
6. Remove the auxiliary air regulator.
7. Disconnect all electrical lines (label all wires for installation).
8. Disconnect the EGR line from the exhaust manifold.
9. Loosen and remove the retaining bolts and lift off the manifold.
10. Install a new gasket. Install the manifold and tighten the bolts to 18 ft. lbs.
11. Install the remaining components in the reverse order of removal.

Exhaust Manifold

REMOVAL AND INSTALLATION

1. Disconnect the EGR tube from the exhaust manifold.
2. Remove the interfering air pump components if so equipped.
3. Remove the air cleaner hose from the exhaust manifold.
4. Disconnect the intake manifold support.

Camshaft sprocket alignment

Crankshaft pulley and intermediate shaft alignment

5. Separate the exhaust pipe from the manifold.

6. Remove the retaining nuts and remove the manifold.

7. Clean the cylinder head and manifold mating surfaces.

8. Install the exhaust manifold using a new gasket.

9. Tighten the nuts to 18 ft. lbs. Work from the inside out.

10. Install the remaining components in the reverse order of removal. Use a new manifold flange gasket.

Timing Belt Cover

REMOVAL AND INSTALLATION

1. Loosen the alternator mounting bolts.

2. Pivot the alternator and slip the drive belt off the sprockets.

3. Unscrew the cover retaining nuts and remove the cover.

4. Reposition the spacers on the studs and then install the washers and nuts.

5. Install the alternator belt and adjust its tension.

Timing Belt

NOTE: The timing belt is designed to last for more than 60,000 miles and does not normally require tension adjustments. If the belt is removed or replaced, the basic valve timing must be checked and the belt retensioned.

REMOVAL, INSTALLATION, AND TENSIONING

Gasoline Engines

Timing belt installation will be easier if the engine is set to TDC prior to belt removal. The 0°T mark will be aligned with the pointer on the bell housing, and the mark on the rear face of the camshaft pulley will align with the camshaft cover gasket on the left. Also, the V-notch in the crankshaft pulley should align with the dot mark on the intermediate shaft, and the distributor rotor should be pointing toward the mark on the rim of the housing.

If the belt has broken and timing is off, remove the belt cover and belt, then set the engine to TDC before installing the belt, as outlined in steps 5, 6 and 7.

1. Remove the timing belt cover.

2. While holding the large hex on the tension sprocket, loosen the pulley locknut.

3. Release the tensioner from the timing belt.

4. Slide the belt off the three toothed sprockets and remove it.

5. Turn the crankshaft until no. 1 cylinder is at TDC. At this point, the 0°T mark will be aligned with the pointer on the bell housing.

6. Align the timing mark on the rear face of the camshaft pulley with the camshaft cover gasket on the left.

7. Align the V-notch in the crankshaft pulley with the dot mark on the intermediate shaft. The distributor rotor should be pointing to the no. 1 cylinder mark on the rim of the distributor.

—————— CAUTION ——————
If the timing marks are not correctly aligned, valve timing will be incorrect. Poor performance and serious engine damage can result from improper valve timing. Steps 5, 6 and 7 should not be necessary if the engine was in time and set to TDC prior to belt removal.

8. Install the belt on the sprockets.

9. Adjust the tensioner by turning the large tensioner hex to the right. Tension is correct when you can just twist the belt 90° with two fingers at the midpoint. Tighten the locknut to 32 ft. lbs.

10. Install the timing belt cover and check the ignition timing.

Diesel Engine

The drive belt on the diesel also drives the injection pump. It is necessary that this procedure be followed exactly to ensure proper valve timing and injection pump timing. You will also need special tool VW 210 to properly tension the belt.

1. Remove the alternator belt.

2. Remove the timing belt cover and rocker cover.

3. Set the engine at TDC on no. 1 cylinder. In this position both valves of no. 1 cylinder will be closed and the OT mark on the flywheel will be aligned with the pointer on the bell housing.

4. Use a pin (VW special tool 2064) or suitable bolt to hold the injection pump sprocket and camshaft sprocket in position. The pin or bolt must be exactly the size of the hole. There can be no ''slop'' in the gears.

5. Loosen the tensioner. Remove the fan belt pulley from the crankshaft.

6. Remove the belt and belt shield from the drive gears.

To install the belt:

7. Check that the TDC mark is aligned with the flywheel mark.

8. Loosen the camshaft sprocket bolt ½ turn and tap the gear loose from the camshaft with a rubber mallet.

9. Install the drive belt and remove the pin from the camshaft and injection pump gears.

10. Tension the belt by turning the tensioner to the right.

11. Check the belt tension between the camshaft and injection pump sprockets. On VW 210 special tool, the scale should read 12–13.

12. Tighten the camshaft sprocket bolt to 32 ft. lbs.

13. Turn the crankshaft 2 complete turns in the direction of normal rotation and check the belt tension again.

Timing Sprockets

REMOVAL AND INSTALLATION

The camshaft, intermediate shaft, and crankshaft sprockets are located by keys on their respective shafts and each is retained by a bolt. To remove any or all of the pulleys, first remove the timing belt cover and belt.

NOTE: When removing the crankshaft pulley, don't remove the four allen head bolts which hold the outer belt pulley to the timing belt sprocket.

1. Remove the center bolt.

2. Gently pry the sprocket off the shaft. If the gear does not come off easily, use a gear puller. Don't hammer on the sprocket.

3. Remove the sprocket and key.

4. Install in the reverse order of removal.

5. Tighten the center bolt to 58 ft. lbs.

6. Install the timing belt, check the valve timing, tension the belt, and install the cover.

Camshaft

REMOVAL AND INSTALLATION

1. Remove the timing belt.
2. Remove the camshaft sprocket.
3. Remove the air cleaner.
4. Remove the camshaft cover.
5. Unscrew and remove the no. 1, 3 and 5 bearing caps.
6. Unscrew the no. 2 and 4 bearing caps, diagonally and in increments.
7. Lift the camshaft out of the cylinder head.
8. Lubricate the camshaft journals and lobes with assembly lube or gear oil before installing it in the cylinder head.
9. Replace the camshaft oil seal with a new one whenever the cam is removed.
10. Install the no. 1, 3 and 5 bearing caps and tighten the nuts to 14 ft. lbs. Note that the bores are offset, and the numbers are not always on the same side.
11. Install the no. 2 and 4 bearing caps and diagonally tighten the nuts to 14 ft. lbs.

NOTE: If checking end-play, install a dial indicator so that the feeler touches the camshaft snout. End-play should be no more than 0.006 in. (0.15 mm)

12. Replace the seal in the no. 1 bearing cap. If necessary, replace the end plug in the cylinder head.
13. Install the camshaft cover.

1. Alternator belt
2. Belt pulleys
3. Timing gear cover
4. Crankshaft sprocket
5. Intermediate sprocket
6. Drive belt
7. Tensioner
8. Camshaft sprocket

Exploded view of camshaft drive arrangement

The connecting rod and cap alignment casting grooves must face the intermediate shaft

Piston height measurement, diesel engine

Diesel pistons are identified by the number "9" next to the arrow denoting installation direction

Turn the tensioner (3) toward (1) to tighten belt and toward (2) to loosen. Check tension at (4)

14. Install the camshaft pulley and the timing belt.

15. Check the valve clearance.

Piston and Connecting Rods

GASOLINE ENGINES

The pistons must be installed in the block with the arrow at the edge of the crown facing toward the right front wheel. The connecting rod and cap alignment casting grooves must face the intermediate shaft. New connecting rod bolts must always be used. The pistons must be heated to 140°F in an oven before the piston pins can be pressed in. Three piston oversizes are available to accommodate overbores up to 0.040 in.

There is a piston size code stamped on the cylinder block above the water pump.

DIESEL ENGINES

The same installation procedures apply to the diesel as to the gas engine. However, whenever new pistons or a short block are installed, the piston projection must be checked.

A spacer (VW 385/17) and bar with a micrometer are necessary, and must be set up to measure the maximum amount of piston projection above the deck height.

ENGINE LUBRICATION

The lubrication system is a conventional wet-sump design. The gear type oil pump is driven by the intermediate shaft. A pressure relief valve limits pressure and prevents extreme pressure from developing in the system. All oil is filtered by a full flow replaceable filter. A bypass valve assures lubrication in the event the filter becomes plugged. The oil pressure switch is located at the end of the cylinder head gallery (the end of the system) to assure accurate pressure readings.

Oil Pan

REMOVAL AND INSTALLATION

1. Drain the engine oil.
2. Loosen and remove the bolts retaining the oil pan.
3. Lower the pan from the car.
4. Install the pan using a new oil pan gasket.

Rear main oil seal assembly

5. Tighten the retaining bolts in a crisscross pattern. Tighten hex head bolts to 14 ft. lbs., or Allen head bolts to 7 ft. lbs.

6. Refill the engine with oil. Start the engine and examine the pan for leaks.

Rear Main Oil Seal

REPLACEMENT

The engine should be removed from the car. See Transmission Removal and Installation.

1. Remove the transmission and flywheel.
2. Using a small prybar, very carefully pry the old seal out of the support ring.
3. Remove the seal.
4. Lightly oil the replacement seal and then press it into place using a circular piece of flat metal. Be careful not to damage the seal or score the crankshaft.
5. Install the flywheel and transmission. Flywheel-to-engine bolts are tightened to 36 ft. lbs.

Oil Pump

REMOVAL AND INSTALLATION

1. Remove the oil pan.
2. Remove the two mounting bolts.
3. Pull the oil pump down and out of the engine.
4. Unscrew the two bolts and separate the pump halves.

5. Remove the driveshaft and gear from the upper body.

6. Clean the bottom half in solvent. Pry up the metal edges to remove the filter screen for cleaning.

7. Examine the gears and driveshaft for wear or damage. Replace them if necessary.

8. Reassemble the pump halves.

9. Prime the pump with oil and install in the reverse order of removal.

ENGINE COOLING

The cooling system consists of a belt driven, external water pump, thermostat, radiator, and thermostatically controlled electric cooling fan. When the engine is cold the thermostat is closed and blocks the water from the radiator so the coolant is circulated only through the engine. When the engine warms up, the thermostat opens and the radiator is included in the coolant circuit. The thermostatic switch is in the bottom of the radiator and turns the electrical fan on at 199°F, off at 186°F. This reduces power loss and engine noise.

--- CAUTION ---

The fan may run with the engine shut off. Keep fingers out of the way when the engine is warm.

Radiator and Fan

REMOVAL AND INSTALLATION

1. Drain the cooling system.
2. Remove the inner shroud mounting bolts.
3. Disconnect the lower radiator hose.
4. Disconnect the thermostatic switch lead.
5. Remove the lower radiator shroud.
6. Remove the lower radiator mounting units.
7. Disconnect the upper radiator hose.
8. Detach the upper radiator shroud.
9. Disconnect the heater and intake manifold hoses.
10. Remove the side mounting bolts and lift the radiator and fan out as an assembly.
11. Installation is the reverse of removal.

Thermostat

REMOVAL AND INSTALLATION

The thermostat is located in the bottom radiator hose neck on the water pump.
1. Drain the cooling system.
2. Remove the two retaining bolts from the lower water pump neck.

NOTE: It isn't necessary to disconnect the hose.

3. Move the neck, with the hoses attached, out of the way.
4. Remove the thermostat.
5. Install a new seal on the water pump neck.
6. Install the thermostat with the spring end up.
7. Replace the water pump neck and tighten the two retaining bolts.

Water Pump

REMOVAL AND INSTALLATION

1. Drain the cooling system.
2. Remove the alternator and drive belt.
3. Remove the timing belt cover.
4. Disconnect the lower radiator hose, engine hose, and heater hose from the water pump.
5. Remove the four pump retaining bolts. Notice where the different length bolts are located.
6. Turn the pump slightly and lift it out of the engine block.
7. Installation is the reverse of removal. Use a new seal on the mating surface with the engine.

EMISSION CONTROLS

Crankcase Ventilation

The crankcase ventilation system keeps harmful vapor byproducts of combustion from escaping into the atmosphere and prevents the building of crankcase pressure which can lead to oil leaking. Crankcase vapors are recirculated from the camshaft cover through a hose to the air cleaner. Here they are mixed with the air/fuel mixture and burned in the combustion chamber.

SERVICE

The only maintenance required on the crankcase ventilation system is a periodic check. At every tune up, examine the hoses for clogging or deterioration. Clean or replace the hoses as necessary.

Evaporation Emission Control System

This system prevents the escape of raw fuel vapors (unburned hydrocarbons or HC) into the atmosphere. The system consists of a sealed carburetor, unvented fuel tank filler cap, fuel tank expansion chamber, an activated charcoal filter canister and connector hoses. Fuel vapors which reach the filter deposit hydrocarbons on the surface of the charcoal filter element. Fresh air enters the filter when the engine is running and forces the hydrocarbons to the air cleaner where they join the air/fuel mixture and are burned.

Many models are equipped with a charcoal filter valve which prevents vapors from escaping from the canister when the engine is not running.

SERVICE

Maintenance of the system requires checking the condition of the various connector hoses and the charcoal filter at 10,000 mile intervals. The charcoal filter should be replaced at 50,000 mile intervals.

Dual Diaphragm Distributors

The purpose of the dual diaphragm distributor is to improve exhaust emissions during one of the engine's dirtier operating modes—idling. The distributor has a vacuum retard diaphragm, in addition to a vacuum advance diaphragm. A temperature valve shuts off vacuum from the carburetor when coolant temperatures are below 130°F.

TESTING

Advance Diaphragm

1. Connect a timing light to the engine. Check the ignition timing.
2. Remove the retard hose from the distributor and plug it. Increase the engine speed. The ignition timing should advance. If it doesn't, then the vacuum unit is faulty and must be replaced.

Temperature Valve

1. Remove the temperature valve and place the threaded portion in hot water.
2. Create a vacuum by sucking on the angled connection.
3. The valve must be open above approximately 130°F.

Exhaust Gas Recirculation (EGR)

To reduce NOx (oxides of nitrogen) emissions, metered amounts of exhaust gases are added to the air/fuel mixture. The recirculated exhaust gas lowers the peak flame temperature during combustion. Exhaust gas from the manifold passes through a filter where it is cleaned. The vacuum operated EGR valve controls the volume of this exhaust gas which is allowed into the intake manifold. There is no EGR at idle, partial at slight throttle and full EGR at mid-throttle.

The EGR valve on fuel injected models is controlled by a temperature valve and a vacuum amplifier. The valve is located at the front of the intake manifold.

TESTING

EGR Valve—Fuel Injected Models

Be sure the vacuum lines are not leaking. Replace any that are leaking or cracked.
1. Warm the engine to normal operating temperature.
2. Run the engine at idle.
3. Remove the vacuum hose from the EGR valve.
4. Connect the line from the brake booster to the EGR valve (this can be done

EGR system schematic

by installing a Tee in the vacuum line to the retard side of the distributor diaphragm and running a separate hose from there to the EGR valve).

5. If the engine speed does not change, the EGR valve is clogged or damaged.

EGR Temperature Valve

Warm the engine to normal operating temperature.

1. With the engine at idle, attach a vacuum gauge between the EGR temperature control valve and the EGR valve. The valve should be replaced if the gauge shows less than 2 in. Hg.

EGR Deceleration Valve

1. Remove the hose from the deceleration valve. Plug the hose.
2. Run the engine for a few seconds at 3000 rpm.
3. Snap the throttle valve closed.
4. With your finger, check for suction at the hose connection.
5. Remove the hose from the connector.
6. Run the engine at about 3000 rpm. No suction should be felt.

EGR Vacuum Amplifier

1. Run the engine at idle.
2. Connect a vacuum gauge between the vacuum amplifier and the throttle valve port.
3. The gauge should read 0.2–0.3 in. Hg. If not, check the throttle plate for correct position or check the port for obstruction.
4. Connect a vacuum gauge between the vacuum amplifier and the temperature valve.
5. Replace the vacuum amplifier if the gauge reads less than 2 in. Hg.

MAINTENANCE

The only maintenance to is reset the EGR elapsed mileage switch.

Resetting the EGR elapsed mileage odometer

Resetting the Elapsed Mileage Switch

The EGR reminder light in the speedometer should light up every 15,000 miles as a reminder for maintenance.

To reset the light switch, press the white button. The speedometer light should go out.

REMOVAL AND INSTALLATION

EGR Valve

1. Disconnect the vacuum hose from the EGR valve.
2. Unbolt the EGR line fitting on the opposite side of the valve.
3. Remove the two remaining bolts and lift the EGR valve from the intake manifold.
4. Install the EGR valve in the reverse order of removal. Use a new gasket at the intake manifold.

Catalytic Converter

MAINTENANCE

Required maintenance on the catalytic converter involves checking the condition of the ceramic insert every 30,000 miles. As this interval is reached, an indicator light on the dash will glow. Once service to the converter is performed, the odometer must be reset.

TESTING AND SERVICE

——— **CAUTION** ———

Do not drop or strike the converter assembly or damage to the ceramic insert will result.

Damage and overheating of the catalytic converter, indicated by the flickering of the "CAT" warning light, can be caused by the following:

1. Engine misfire caused by faulty spark plug, ignition wires and so on.
2. Improper ignition timing.
3. CO valve set too high.
4. Faulty air pump diverter valve.
5. Faulty temperature sensor.
6. Engine under strain caused by trailer hauling high speed driving in hot weather, etc.

A faulty converter is indicated by one of the following symptoms:

1. Poor engine performance.
2. The engine stalls.
3. Rattling in the exhaust system.
4. A CO reading greater than 0.4% at the tail pipe.

Check or replace the converter as follows:

1. Disconnect the temperature sensor.
2. Loosen and remove the bolts holding the converter to the exhaust system and

the chassis.

3. Remove the converter.
4. Hold the converter up to a strong light and look through both ends, checking for blockages. If the converter is blocked, replace it.
5. Install the converter in the reverse order of removal.
6. Reset the elapsed mileage odometer by pushing the white button marked "CAT".

Oxygen Sensor System

Many models are equipped with an oxygen sensor system which lowers toxic exhaust emissions while increasing fuel economy. In effect, the sensor system monitors the oxygen content in the exhaust system and, through a control unit and frequency valve, makes adjustments to the air/fuel mixture to achieve maximum fuel efficiency over a wide range of operating conditions. The system consists of the following:

1. **Oxygen Sensor:** located in the exhaust manifold. Unscrew to replace.

Resetting the catalytic converter elapsed mileage odometer

Checking the catalytic converter—the arrow indicates the temperature sensor

2. **Control Unit:** located behind the glove compartment cover.
   Frequency Valve: located next to the fuel distributor.

3. Thermoswitch: located in the coolant system.

4. **Oxygen Sensor System Relay:** white colored relay located in the fuse/relay panel.

5. **Elapsed Mileage Switch:** located on the firewall.

6. **Warning Light:** marked OXS and located in the instrument panel. Comes on when the oxygen sensor must be replaced (every 30,000 miles).

RESETTING THE ELAPSED MILEAGE SWITCH

After replacing the oxygen sensor, reset the elapsed mileage switch by pushing the white button on the front of the switch.

FUEL SYSTEM

Fuel Pump

TESTING—ELECTRICAL

1. Have a helper operate the starter. Listen at the rear wheel to determine if the pump is running.

2. If the pump is not running, check the fuse on the front of the fuel pump relay.

3. If the fuse is good, replace the fuel pump relay.

4. If the fuel pump still does not operate, the fuel pump is faulty and must be replaced.

TESTING—FUEL PUMP DELIVERY

1. Check the condition of the fuel filter, make sure it is clean.

2. Connect a jumper wire between the #1 terminal on the ignition coil and ground.

3. Disconnect the return fuel line and hold it in a measuring container with a capacity of 1 quart or 1000 cc.

4. Have a helper run the starter for 30 seconds while watching the quantity of fuel delivered.

The minimum allowable flow is 900 cc (⁹/₁₀ of a quart) in 30 seconds.

NOTE: For the above test, the battery must be fully charged. Also, make sure you have plenty of fuel in the tank.

If the pump fails its specific test, check for a dirty fuel filter, blocked lines or blocked fuel tank strainer (if so equipped). If all of these are in good condition, replace the pump.

1. Fuel distributor
2. Fuel filter
3. Air flow sensor
4. EGR temperature control valve (not shown)
5. Control pressure regulator
6. Thermo-time switch
7. Cold start valve
8. EGR valve
9. Idle adjust
10. Deceleration valve
11. Plug for CO adjustment
12. Auxiliary air regulator (not shown)
13. Fuel injector

CIS fuel injection components

REMOVAL AND INSTALLATION

1. Raise the vehicle and support it on jack stands. Disconnect the battery ground cable.

2. Remove the right rear wheel on all cars.

3. Remove the gas tank filler cap to release the fuel pressure.

4. Clamp off the line between the fuel pump and the fuel tank with a pair of soft jawed vise grips or other suitable lock pliers. Don't clamp the line too tightly or you may damage it.

5. Disconnect the clamped line from the fuel pump. There's bound to be a little gas in the line, so be careful.

6. If your vehicle has an accumulator mounted next to the fuel pump, disconnect the fuel lines from the accumulator. Disconnect the wiring from the fuel pump and remove all other lines after marking them for assembly.

7. Remove the nuts on the lower bracket, loosen the nut on the upper slotted bracket where it connects to the body and slide the pump out.

8. Install the new fuel pump in the reverse order of removal. Make sure that the new seal washers are installed on the fuel discharge line.

CIS Fuel Injection

AIR FLOW SENSOR-TESTING AND ADJUSTMENT

Sensor Plate Lever and Control Plunger

1. Run the engine for a short time at idle.

2. Remove the air duct from the air flow sensor assembly.

3. Using a magnet, lift the sensor plate. A light even resistance must be felt over the sensor plate entire travel.

NOTE: Make certain that the air sensor plate is centered in the air cone. If adjustment is necessary, proceed as follows:

a. Loosen the centering bolt slightly.

b. Run a 0.004 in. (0.10 mm) feeler gauge around the perimeter of the air gap.

c. Tighten the centering bolt.

4. No resistance must be felt when the sensor plate is moved rapidly up and down. If resistance is felt, the air sensor must be replaced.

5. If the sensor plate is hard to move

Adjusting the air flow sensor spring stop

upward but moves freely down, the control plunger is sticking. Remove the fuel distributor and clean the control plunger in solvent. If after installation the plunger is still sticking, the fuel distributor must be replaced.

Sensor Plate Height Adjustment

The height adjustment of the sensor plate must be checked under fuel pressure. You will also need a bridging adaptor (US 4480/3).

1. Install a pressure gauge in the line between the fuel distributor and control pressure regulator.
2. Remove the rubber elbow from the air flow sensor housing.
3. Remove the fuel pump relay from the fuse panel and install a bridging adapter (US 4480/3).
4. Switch the adapter ON and wait until pressure reads 49–54 psi.
5. Switch the bridging adapter OFF; the pressure should fall to 28–37 psi.
6. The upper edge of the sensor plate must be even with the bottom of the air cone taper or no more than 0.020 in. below the bottom of the taper.
7. Bend the clip to adjust the height.
8. Recheck the pressure readings after adjusting.
9. Remove the pressure gauge, reconnect the fuel lines and install the fuel pump relay.

Thermo-Time Switch—Testing

NOTE: To properly perform the following tests, the engine must be cold with the water temperature below 95°F (35°C).

1. Disconnect the electrical connector from the cold start valve on the end of the intake manifold.
2. Connect a test light across the cold start valve terminals.
3. Connect a jumper wire from the #1 terminal on the ignition coil to a good ground.
4. Have an assistant operate the starter. If the test light fails to light after 8 seconds, the thermo-time switch is defective and should be replaced.

Cold Start Valve—Testing

1. Remove the electrical connector from the cold start valve.

NOTE: Do not remove the fuel line from the cold start valve.

2. Remove the cold start valve from the manifold and point the nozzle into a measuring container.
3. Connect a jumper wire from one terminal of the cold start valve to terminal #15 on the ignition coil.
4. Connect a second jumper wire from the other cold start valve terminal to ground.
5. Remove the fuel pump relay and bridge the relay plate terminals #L13 and #L14 with a fused (8 amp) jumper wire.
6. Have an assistant turn the ignition switch on while observing the fuel spray pattern from the cold start valve. The spray pattern from the nozzle must be cone-shaped and steady, if not replace the valve.
7. Turn the ignition switch off.
8. Wipe the nozzle dry with a clean rag and check for leakage. If drops form within one minute, the valve is defective and must be replaced.

Auxiliary Air Regulator—Testing

NOTE: The engine must be cold to perform this test.

1. Unplug the electrical connector from the auxiliary air regulator.
2. Start the engine and check the idle.
3. Pinch the hose between the auxiliary air regulator and the intake manifold. The engine idle should drop. Reconnect the electrical connector.
4. Repeat the test on the engine at operating temperature. The idle speed should remain constant when the hose is pinched. If not, replace the auxiliary air regulator.

Control Pressure Regulator—Testing

The system is under considerable constant pressure. The only practical test that should be attempted by the owner is one using an ohmmeter.

Be sure the engine is at normal operating temperature. There should be no loose fuel fittings or other fire hazards when the electrical connections are disengaged.

1. Remove the electrical connector from the control pressure regulator and auxiliary air regulator.
2. Start the engine and run it at idle.
3. Check the terminals of the control pressure regulator wiring harness for voltage. It should be at least 11.5 volts.
4. Connect an ohmmeter across the terminals of the control pressure regulator socket. Resistance should be between 16 and 22 ohms. If there is no resistance, replace the control pressure regulator.

Fuel Injectors—Testing

1. Remove the injector but leave it connected to the fuel line.

2. Point the injector into a measuring container.
3. Remove the fuel pump relay and bridge the relay plate terminals #L13 and L14 with a fused (8 amp) jumper wire.
4. Remove the air duct from the air flow sensor.
5. Have an assistant turn the ignition switch on.
6. Lift the air flow sensor plate with a magnet and observe the injector nozzle spray pattern. The spray pattern must be cone-shaped and even, if not replace the injector.
7. Turn the ignition off and hold the injector horizontally. It should not drip.

NOTE: One or more injectors may be checked at the same time.

8. Moisten the rubber seals on the injectors with fuel before installing.
9. Press the injectors firmly into place.

Fuel Distributor—Removal and Installation

1. Release the pressure in the system by loosening the fuel line on the control pressure regulator (large connector). Have a rag ready to catch the fuel that escapes.
2. Mark the fuel lines in the top of the distributor so that you will be able to put them back in their correct positions.

NOTE: Using different colored paints is usually a good marking device. When you mark each line, be sure to mark the spot where it connects to the distributor.

3. Clean the fuel lines, then remove them from the distributor. Remove the little looped wire plug (the CO adjusting screw plug). Remove the two retaining screws in the top of the distributor.

NOTE: When removing the fuel distributor be sure the control plunger does not fall out from underneath.

4. If the control plunger has been removed, moisten it with gasoline before installing. The small shoulder on the plunger is inserted first.

NOTE: Always use new gaskets and O-ring when removing and installing fuel distributor. Lock all retaining screws with Loctite or its equivalent.

System Pressure Adjustments

The fuel system pressure is present at the factory and is adjusted by either adding or subtracting shims to or from the back of the pressure relief valve spring located in the fuel distributor.

Since special pressure and measuring gauges are needed to adjust system pressure, this job should be left to your Volkswagen dealer.

Substitute for Bridging Adapter 4480/3

The bridging adapter simply connects two terminals of the fuel pump relay socket. To fashion a homemade adapter, attach an 8 amp in-line fuse (the kind commonly used in radios; make sure it's 8 amp, though) between term1nals L13 and L14 of the fuel pump relay socket in the fuse/relay panel.

Diesel Fuel Injection

The diesel fuel system is an extremely complex and sensitive system. Very few repairs or adjustments are possible by the owner. Any service other than that listed here should be referred to an authorized VW dealer or diesel specialist. The injection pump itself is not repairable, it can only be replaced.

Any work done to the diesel fuel injection should be done with absolute cleanliness. Even the smallest specks of dirt will have a disastrous effect on the injection system.

Do not attempt to remove the fuel injectors. They are very delicate and must be removed with a special tool to prevent damage. The fuel in the system is also under tremendous pressure (1700–1850 psi), so it's not wise to loosen any lines with the engine running. Exposing your skin to the spray from the injector at working pressure can cause fuel to penetrate the skin.

CHECKING INJECTION PUMP TIMING

Checking the injection pump timing also involves checking the valve timing. To alter the injection pump timing, the camshaft gear must be removed and repositioned. This also changes the valve timing. Special tool (VW 210) is necessary to properly tension the injection pump drive belt on the diesel engine.

1. Set the engine at TDC on no. 1 cylinder. In this position, the TDC mark on the flywheel should be aligned with boss on the bell housing and both valves of no. 1 cylinder should be closed.
2. The marks on the pump and mounting plate should also be aligned.
3. If the valve timing is incorrect, set the valve timing as detailed in the engine section.

ACCELERATOR CABLE ADJUSTMENT

The ball pin on the pump lever should be pointing up and be aligned with the mark in the slot. The accelerator cable should be attached at the upper hole in the bracket. With the pedal in the full throttle position, adjust the cable so that the pump lever contacts the stop with no binding or strain.

COLD START CABLE ADJUSTMENT

When the cold start knob on the dash is pulled out, the fuel injection pump timing is advanced 2.5°. This improves cold start-ing and running until the engine warms up.
1. Insert the washer on the cable.
2. Insert the cable in the bracket with the rubber housing. Install the cable in the pin.
3. Install the lockwasher.
4. Move the lever to the zero position (direction of arrow). Pull the inner cable tight and tighten the clamp screw.

CHECKING GLOW PLUGS CURRENT SUPPLY

1. Connect a test light between No. 4 cylinder glow plug and ground.
2. Turn the key to the heat position. The test light should light up.
3. If not, check the glow plug relay, ignition switch, or fuse box relay plate.

CHECKING GLOW PLUGS

Make this check after establishing that there is current to the glow plugs.
1. Remove the wire and glow plug bus bar.
2. Connect the test light between the battery positive terminal and each glow plug in turn.
3. If the light lights, the glow plug is OK. If not, the glow plug is defective and must be replaced.

MANUAL TRANSMISSION

Transaxle

REMOVAL AND INSTALLATION

The engine and transaxle may be removed together as explained under Engine Removal and Installation or the transaxle may be removed alone, as explained here.
1. Disconnect the battery ground cable.
2. Support the left end of the engine at the lifting eye.
3. Remove the left transmission mount (between the transmission and the firewall).
4. Turn the engine until the lug on the flywheel (to the left of the TDC mark) aligns with the flywheel timing pointer.
5. Detach the speedometer drive cable, backup light wire, and clutch cable.
6. Remove the engine to transmission bolts.
7. Disconnect the shift linkage.
8. Detach the transmission ground strap.
9. Remove the starter.
10. Remove the engine mounting support near the starter.
11. Remove the rear transmission mount.
12. Unbolt and wire up the driveshafts.
13. From underneath, remove the bolts for the large cover plate, but don't remove it. Unbolt the small cover plate on the firewall side of the engine. Remove the engine to transmission nut immediately below the small plate.
14. Press the transmission off the dowels and remove it from below the car.

To install the transaxle:
15. The recess in the flywheel edge must be at 3:00 o'clock. Tighten the engine to transmission bolts to 47 ft. lbs. Tighten the engine mounting support bolts to 47 ft. lbs. Tighten the driveshaft bolts to 32 ft. lbs.
16. Check the adjustment of the shift linkage.

SHIFT LINKAGE ADJUSTMENT

1. Align the holes of the lever housing plate with the holes of the lever bearing plate.
2. Loosen the shift rod clamp. Pull the boot off the lever housing and push it out of the way. It may be necessary to loosen the screws in the cover plate to free the boot.
3. Check that the shift finger is in the center of the stopping plate.
4. Adjust the shift rod end so that it is ¾ in. (⁹⁄₃₂ in. for five speed transmissions) from the right side of the lever housing. Tighten the shift rod clamp and check the shifter operation.

SELECTOR SHAFT LOCKBOLT ADJUSTMENT

Make this adjustment after linkage adjustment, if the linkage still feels spongy or jams.
1. Disconnect the shift linkage and put the transmission in Neutral.
2. Loosen the locknut and turn the adjusting sleeve in until the lockring lifts off the sleeve.
3. Turn the adjusting sleeve back until the lockring just contacts the sleeve. Tighten the locknut.
4. Turn the shaft slightly. The lockring should lift as soon as the shaft is turned.
5. Reconnect the linkage.

FIFTH GEAR LOCKBOLT ADJUSTMENT

This adjustment is made with the transmission in neutral. The fifth gear lockbolt is located on top of the transmission next to the selector shaft lockbolt. It has a large protective cap over it.
1. Remove the protective cap.
2. Loosen the locknut and tighten the adjusting sleeve until the detent plunger in the center of the sleeve just begins to move up.
3. Loosen the adjusting sleeve ⅓ of a

Clutch assembly: the pressure plate is bolted to the crankshaft and the clutch is actuated by a pushrod working on the release plate

turn and tighten the locknut. Make sure the transmission shifts in and out of fifth gear easily. Replace the protective cap.

Clutch

PEDAL FREE PLAY ADJUSTMENT

The clutch should have 9/16 in. free play at the pedal. Pedal free play is the distance the pedal can be depressed before the linkage starts to act on the throwout bearing.

1. Adjust the clutch pedal free play by loosening the two nuts on the cable near the front of the transmission.
2. After obtaining the correct free play, tighten the adjusting nuts.

REMOVAL AND INSTALLATION

1. Remove the transmission.
2. Attach a toothed flywheel holder and gradually loosen the flywheel to pressure plate bolts one or two turns at a time in a crisscross pattern to prevent distortion.
3. Remove the flywheel and the clutch disc.
4. Use a screwdriver to remove the release plate retaining ring. Remove the release plate.
5. Lock the pressure plate in place and unbolt it from the crankshaft. Loosen the bolts one or two turns at a time in a crisscross pattern to prevent distortion.
6. On installation, use new bolts to attach the pressure plate to the crankshaft. Use a thread locking compound and torque the bolts in a diagonal pattern to 54 ft. lbs.

7. Lubricate the clutch disc splines with multi-purpose grease. Lubricate the release plate contact surface and pushrod socket with multi-purpose grease. Install the release plate, retaining ring, and clutch disc.
8. Install a dummy shaft to align the clutch disc.
9. Install the flywheel, tightening the bolts one or two turns at a time in a crisscross pattern to prevent distortion. Torque the bolts to 14 ft. lbs.
10. Replace the transmission.

AUTOMATIC TRANSMISSION

Transaxle

REMOVAL AND INSTALLATION

The engine and transaxle may be removed together as explained under Engine Removal and Installation or the transaxle may be removed alone, as explained here.

1. Disconnect both battery cables.
2. Disconnect the speedometer cable at the transmission.
3. Support the left end of the engine at the lifting eye. Attach a hoist to the transaxle.
4. Unbolt the rear transmission carrier from the body then from the transaxle. Unbolt the left side carrier from the body.
5. Unbolt the driveshafts and wire them up.

6. Remove the starter.
7. Remove the three converter to drive plate bolts.
8. Shift into P and disconnect the floorshift linkage at the transmission.
9. Remove the accelerator and carburetor cable bracket at the transmission.
10. Unbolt the left side transmission carrier from the transmission.
11. Unbolt the front transmission mount from the transmission.
12. Unbolt the bottom of the engine from the transmission. Lift the transaxle slightly, remove the rest of the bolts, pull the transmission off the mounting dowels, and lower the transaxle out of the car. Secure the converter so it doesn't fall out.

—————— **CAUTION** ——————
Don't tilt the torque converter.

To install:
1. Be sure the torque converter is fully seated on the one-way clutch support. Push the transmission onto the mounting dowels and install two bolts. Lift the unit until the left driveshaft can be installed and install the rest of the bolts. Torque them to 39 ft. lbs.
2. Tighten the front transmission mount bolts to 39 ft. lbs. Install the left side transmission carrier to the transmission.
3. Connect the accelerator and carburetor cable bracket. Connect the floorshift linkage.
4. Tighten the torque converter to drive plate bolts to 22 ft. lbs. Torque the driveshaft bolts to 32 ft. lbs.
5. Install the rear transmission carrier and make sure that the left side carrier is aligned in the center of the body mount. Bolt the left side carrier to the body.
6. Connect the speedometer cable and the battery cables.

PAN REMOVAL AND INSTALLATION, STRAINER SERVICE

1. Remove the drain plug and let the fluid drain into a pan. If the pan has no drain plug, loosen the pan bolts until a corner of the pan can be lowered to drain the fluid.
2. Remove the pan bolts and take off the pan.
3. Discard the old gasket and clean the pan out. Be very careful not to get any threads or lint from rags into the pan.
4. The filter needn't be replaced unless the fluid is dirty or smells burnt. The specified torque for the strainer screws is 2 ft. lbs.
5. Replace the pan with a new gasket and tighten the bolts, in a crisscross pattern, to 14 ft. lbs.
6. Using a long-necked funnel, pour in 2½ qts. of Dextron automatic transmission fluid through the dipstick tube. Start the engine and shift through all the transmis-

sion ranges with the car stationary. Check the level on the dipstick with the lever in Neutral. It should be up to the lower end of the dipstick. Drive the car until it is warmed up and recheck the level.

LINKAGE ADJUSTMENT

Check the cable adjustment as follows:

1. Run the engine at 1000—1200 rpm with the parking brake on.

2. Select Reverse. A drop in engine speed should be noticed.

3. Select Park. Engine speed should increase. Pull the shift lever against Reverse, the engine speed shouldn't drop (because reverse gear has not been engaged).

4. Move the shift lever to engage Reverse. Engine speed should drop as the gear engages.

5. Move the shift lever to Neutral. An increase in engine speed should be noticed.

6. Shift the lever into Drive. A noticeable drop in engine speed should result.

7. Shift into 1. The lever must engage without having to overcome any resistance.

8. To adjust the cable, shift into Park. Loosen the cable clamp at the transmission end of the cable, press the transmission lever all the way to the left and tighten the cable clamp.

TRANSMISSION CABLE ADJUSTMENT

Make sure the throttle is closed, and the choke and fast idle cam are off (carbureted models).

1. Detach the cable end at the transmission.

2. Press the lever at the transmission into its closed throttle position.

3. You should be able to attach the cable end onto the transmission lever without moving the lever.

4. Adjust the cable length to the correct setting.

SECOND GEAR (REAR) BAND ADJUSTMENT

NOTE: The transmission must be horizontal when band adjustments are performed.

1. Loosen the locknut on the adjusting screw, which is located on the front of the transmission.

2. Tighten the adjusting screw to 7 ft. lbs.

3. Loosen the screw and tighten it again to 4 ft. lbs.

4. Turn the screw out exactly 2½ turns and then tighten the locknut.

NEUTRAL START/BACKUP LIGHT SWITCH

The combination neutral start and backup light switch is mounted inside the shifter

Axle shaft—exploded view

housing. The starter should operate in Park or Neutral only. Adjust the switch by moving it on its mounts. The backup lights should only come on when the shift selector is in the Reverse position.

Drive Axles

HALFSHAFT REMOVAL AND INSTALLATION

1. With the car on the ground, remove the front axle nut.
2. Raise and support the front of the vehicle.
3. Remove the socket head bolts retaining the axle shaft to the transaxle.
4. Remove the bolt holding the ball joint to the steering knuckle and separate the knuckle from the ball joint.
5. Removing the ball joint from the knuckle should give enough clearance to remove the axle shaft. It pulls right out of the steering hub.
6. Installation is the reverse of removal. Tighten the axle shaft to transaxle bolts to 32 ft. lbs., the ball joint bolt to 21 ft. lbs. and the axle nut to 173 ft. lbs. Be sure to check the alignment after work is completed.

REAR SUSPENSION

Leaf Springs

REMOVAL AND INSTALLATION

———— **CAUTION** ————
The springs are under a considerable amount of tension. Be very careful when removing or installing them; they can exert enough force to cause serious injuries.

1. Jack up the rear of the truck and support it with jackstands placed under the frame.
2. Disconnect the shock absorbers at their lower end.
3. Remove the nuts securing the U-bolts around the axle housing.
4. Place a jack under the rear axle housing and raise the housing to remove the weight off the springs.
5. Remove the nuts from the spring shackles, drive out the shackle pins and remove the spring from the vehicle.
6. Install the spring in the reverse order of removal. The weight of the truck must be on the rear wheels before tightening the front pin, shackle, and shock absorber attaching nuts. Tighten the front pin and shackle nuts, the U-bolt nuts and the shock absorber lower end nut.

Shock Absorbers

REMOVAL AND INSTALLATION

The rear shock absorbers are removed simply by removing the upper and lower attaching nuts, and removing the component from the vehicle. They are installed in the reverse order. The weight of the vehicle must be on the rear wheels before tightening the shock absorber attaching nuts.

FRONT SUSPENSION

The front suspension is a simple strut design. It consists of a lower control arm, ball joint, and suspension strut. In a MacPherson strut design, such as this, the shock absorber strut serves as a locating member of the suspension as well as a damper. A shock absorber insert is located inside the strut. A coil spring is used.

Ball Joint

REMOVAL AND INSTALLATION

1. Jack up the front of the truck and support it on stands.
2. Remove the retaining bolt and nut.
3. Pry the lower control arm and ball joint down and out of the strut.
4. Drill out the rivets; enlarge the holes to 21/64 in.
5. Remove the ball joint assembly.
6. Bolt the new ball joint in place. Torque the bolts to 18 ft. lbs. Tighten the retaining bolt for the ball joint stud to 21 ft. lbs.

Shock Absorber

REMOVAL AND INSTALLATION

Since the shock absorber cartridge is con-

A pinch bolt holds the ball joint to the combination strut and steering knuckle

Rear suspension

tained within the strut assembly, it is necessary to remove the strut and then compress the coil spring in order to remove the shock.

Strut

REMOVAL AND INSTALLATION

1. Remove the brake hose from the strut clip.
2. Mark the position of the camber adjustment bolts before removing them from the hub (wheel bearing housing).
3. Remove the upper mounting nuts and remove the strut from the car.
4. Installation is the reverse. The upper nuts are tightened to 14 ft. lbs., and the lower strut-to-hub bolts to 58 ft. lbs. Use new washers on the lower bolts. If the shock absorber was replaced, camber will have to be adjusted.

Coil Spring

REMOVAL AND INSTALLATION

To remove the spring, the strut must be mounted in a large vise, the spring compressed, the retaining nut and cover removed, and the spring slowly released. A special tool is needed to remove the shock absorber retainer, after which the shock absorber is easily removed. Assembly is the reverse of removal.

Front End Alignment

CAMBER ADJUSTMENT

Camber is adjusted by loosening the nuts of the two bolts holding the top of the wheel bearing housing to the bottom of the strut, and turning the top eccentric bolt. The range of adjustment is 2°.

CASTER

Other than the replacement of damaged suspension components, caster is not adjustable.

TOE-IN ADJUSTMENT

Toe-in is checked with the wheels straight ahead. Only the right tie-rod is adjustable, but replacement left tie-rods are adjustable. Replacement left tie-rods should be set to the same length as the original. Toe-in should be adjusted only with the right tie-rod. If the steering wheel is crooked, remove and align it.

Exploded view of the front suspension

2 mkg (14 ft lb)
Suspension strut
8 mkg (58 ft lb)
Washer, always replace
Eccentric washer
Camber adjustment bolt before removing mark position
6 mkg (43 ft lb)
Wheel bearing housing
Circlip check for proper seating
3 mkg (21 ft lb)
Ball joint
Drive shaft
Bonded rubber bushing press off
3 mkg (21 ft lb) always replace cotter pin
4.5 mkg (32 ft lb)
4.5 mkg (32 ft lb)
Bonded rubber bushing
Wishbone
6 mkg (43 ft lb)

STEERING

The Rabbit pick-up has rack and pinion steering with end-mounted tie-rods. No periodic maintenance is required on either rack and pinion steering system.

Steering Wheel

REMOVAL AND INSTALLATION

1. Grasp the center cover pad and pull it from the wheel.
2. Loosen and remove the steering shaft nut.
3. Pull the wheel off the shaft. A puller isn't normally needed.
4. Disconnect the horn wire.
5. Replace the wheel in the reverse order of removal. Tighten the nut to 36 ft. lbs.

Dimensions for drilling the ignition lock cylinder hole (if not equipped)

Turn Signal and Headlight Dimmer Switch

REPLACEMENT

1. Disconnect the battery ground cable.
2. Remove the steering wheel.

3. Remove the switch retaining screws.

4. Pry the switch housing off the column.

5. Disconnect the electrical plugs at the back of the switch.

6. Remove the switch housing.

7. Replace in the reverse order of removal.

Right side tie rod adjustment

Ignition Switch and Steering Lock

REMOVAL AND INSTALLATION

NOTE: The access hole for removing the lock cylinder may be missing. Before the lock cylinder can be removed, drill a hole according to following dimensions:
a = 12 mm (0.472 in.)
b = 10 mm (0.393 in.)

Drill the hole ⅛ in. deep.

1. Remove the steering wheel and turn signal switch. Remove the steering column shaft covers.

2. The lock is clamped to the steering column with special bolts whose heads shear off on installation. These must be drilled out in order to remove the switch.

3. On replacement, make sure that the lock tang is aligned with the slot in the steering column.

Note
In production a non-adjustable tie rod is installed on left side. Adjust toe on right side only. For replacement only adjustable tie rod No. 171 419 804 is available

30 Nm (22 ft lb)

30 Nm (22 ft lb)

Universal joint shaft
removing/installing page 48.5
identifying page 48.5

Tie rod (left)
replacing/adjusting Fig. 1 to Fig. 4

30 Nm (22 ft lb)

Steering drive
adjusting, Fig. 1 and Fig. 2
installing, Fig. 5
Note
When installing: insert pinion in universal joint first

Rubber boot
slide off and on over tie rod

Steering gear adjusting screw
adjusting Fig. 6

30 Nm (22 ft lb)

Lock nut

Lock ring

30 Nm (22 ft lb)

Tie rod (right)
replacing/adjusting Fig. 1 to Fig. 2

Spring clamp
always replace
remove to adjust toe
installing: ends of clamp point upward

Rubber boot
slide off and on over tie rod

30 Nm (22 ft lb)

Steering gear components

Steering Gear

REMOVAL AND INSTALLATION

1. Disconnect the steering shaft universal joint and wire up out of the way.

2. Disconnect the tie rods at the steering rack and wire up and out of the way.

3. Remove the steering rack and drive.

4. Install the steering rack and drive and torque the attaching hardware to 14 ft. lbs.

5. Set the steering rack with equal distances between the housing on the right side and left side.

6. Install the tie rods and screw both sides in until an equal distance is reached on both rods.

7. Tighten the steering gear adjusting screw until it touches the thrust washer. Tighten the lock nut.

8. Install the steering shaft.

9. Check the front end alignment.

Steering Linkage

TIE-ROD REMOVAL AND INSTALLATION

1. Center the steering rack.

2. Remove the cotter pin and nut from the tie rod end.

3. Disconnect the tie rod from the steering rack.

4. If the left side tie rod is being replaced, adjust it to 14.92 in. (379 mm).

5. Adjust the steering rack and tie rods as outlined in steps 5 and 6 of the "Steering Gear Removal and Installation".

6. Tighten the tie rod end retaining nut to 21 ft. lbs. and install a new cotter pin.

BRAKE SYSTEMS

The hydraulic system is a dual circuit type that has the advantage of retaining 50% braking effectiveness in the event of failure in one system. The circuits are arranged so that you always have one front and one rear brake for a more controlled emergency stop.

Dimension	a	b
manual	69 mm (2.717 in.)	69 mm (2.717 in.)
automatic	67 mm (2.638 in.)	69 mm (2.717 in.)

Adjusting the tie rod position

The right front and left rear are in one circuit; the left front and right rear are in the second circuit.

There is also a brake failure switch and a proportioning valve.

The brake failure unit is a hydraulic valve/electrical switch which warns of brake problems by the warning light on the instrument panel. A piston inside the switch is kept centered by one brake system pressure on one side and the other system pressure on the opposite side. Should a failure occur in one system, the piston would go to the "failed" side and complete an electrical circuit to the warning lamp. This switch also functions as a parking brake reminder light and will go out when the parking brake is released. The proportioning valve provides balanced front-to-rear braking during hard stops.

Extreme brake line pressure will overcome the spring pressure on the piston within the valve causing it to proportionally restrict pressure to the rear brakes. In this manner, the rear brakes are kept from locking. The proportioner doesn't operate under normal braking conditions.

ADJUSTMENT

The front disc brakes require no adjustment, as disc brakes automatically adjust themselves to compensate for pad wear. The VW pick-up has self-adjusting rear drum brakes.

Master Cylinder

REMOVAL AND INSTALLATION

1. Disconnect and plug the brake lines.
2. Disconnect the electrical plug from the sending unit for the brake failure switch.
3. Remove the two master cylinder mounting nuts.
4. Lift the master cylinder and reservoir out of the engine compartment being careful not to spill any fluid on the fender. Empty out and discard the brake fluid.

— CAUTION —
Do not depress the brake pedal while the master cylinder is removed.

5. Position the master cylinder and reservoir assembly onto the studs for the booster and install the washers and nuts. Tighten the nuts to no more than 9 ft. lbs.
6. Remove the plugs and connect the brake lines.
7. Bleed the entire brake system.

OVERHAUL

1. Remove the master cylinder from the booster.
2. Firmly mount the master cylinder in a vise. Use clean rags to protect the cylinder from the vise jaws.

3. Grasp the plastic reservoir and pull it out of the rubber plugs. Remove the plugs.
4. In the center of the cylinder there is a stop screw; remove it. Discard the stop screw seal; there should be a new one in the rebuilding kit.
5. At the end of the master cylinder is a snap-ring (circlip). Remove it, using snap-ring pliers.
6. Shake out the secondary piston assembly. If the primary piston remains lodged in the bore, it can be forced by applying compressed air to the open line fitting.
7. Disassemble the secondary piston. The two secondary springs will be replaced with those in the rebuilding kit. Save the washers and spacers.
8. Carefully clamp the secondary piston. Slightly compress the spring and screw out the stroke limiting bolt.
9. Remove the secondary piston stop sleeve bolt, spring, spring seat, and support washer.
10. Replace all the parts with those supplied in the overhaul kit. Be careful not to interchange the piston cups and the piston seals.
11. Clean all metal parts in alcohol and dry them with compressed air.
12. Check every part you are reusing. Pay close attention to the cylinder bores. If there is any scoring or rust, have the master cylinder honed or replace it.
13. Lightly coat the bores and cups with brake fluid. Assemble the cylinder com-

ponents in the exact sequence shown in the illustration.

14. Install the primary piston assembly; notice that the primary spring is conically shaped. Be sure that you aren't using the secondary spring.

15. Using a plastic rod or other non-metallic tool, push the primary piston assembly into the housing until the stop bolt (with a new seal), can be screwed in and tightened.

16. Assemble the secondary piston. Fasten the spring, spring seat, primary cup, and stop sleeve to the piston with the stroke limiting bolt.

17. Assemble the remaining master cylinder components in the reverse order of disassembly. Ensure that the snap-ring is properly positioned. Install the secondary piston with master cylinder opening facing down.

18. Install and tighten the brake failure warning sending unit.

BLEEDING

Anytime a brake line has been disconnected the hydraulic system should be bled. The brakes should also be bled when the pedal travel becomes unusually long ("soft pedal") or the car pulls to one side during braking. The proper bleeding sequence is: right rear wheel, left rear wheel, right front caliper, and left front caliper. You'll need a helper to pump the brake pedal while you open the bleeder valves.

NOTE: If the system has been drained, first refill it with fresh brake fluid. Following the above sequence, open each bleeder valve by ½ to ¾ of a turn and pump the brake pedal until fluid runs out of the valve. Proceed with the bleeding as outlined below.

1. Remove the bleeder valve dust cover and install a clear rubber bleeder hose.

2. Insert the other end of the hose into a container about ⅓ full of brake fluid.

3. Have an assistant pump the brake pedal several times until the pedal pressure increases.

4. Hold the pedal under pressure and then start to open the bleeder valve about ½ to ¾ of a turn. At this point, have your assistant depress the pedal all the way and then quickly close the valve. The helper should allow the pedal to return slowly.

NOTE: Keep a close check on the brake fluid in the reservoir and top it up as necessary throughout the bleeding process.

5. Keep repeating this procedure until no more air bubbles can be seen coming from the hose in the brake fluid.

6. Remove the bleeder hose and install the dust cover.

7. Continue the bleeding at each wheel in sequence.

NOTE: Don't splash any brake fluid on the paintwork. Brake fluid is very corrosive and will eat paint away. Any fluid accidentally spilled on the body should be immediately flushed off with water.

Front Disc Brakes

Single piston floating caliper disc brakes are used. In this design, the single piston forces one pad against the rotating disc brake.

1. Reservoir cap
2. Washer
3. Filter screen
4. Reservoir
5. Master cylinder plugs
6. Stop screw
7. Stop screw seal
8. Master cylinder seal
9. Residual pressure valves
10. Warning light sender unit
11. Brake master cylinder housing

Master cylinder body and reservoir

1. Conical spring
2. Spring seat
3. Primary cup
4. Washer
5. Secondary cups
6. Primary piston assembly
7. Stroke limiting screw
8. Cylindrical spring
9. Spring seat
10. Primary cup
11. Washer
12. Secondary cups
13. Circlip
14. Secondary piston assembly

Exploded view of the master cylinder components

Counter pressure forces against the floating frame and the frame then pushes the second pad into the disc. The advantages of the floating caliper are better heat dissipation, simpler repair, fewer leaks, and less sensitivity to variance in disc thickness and parallelism.

Brake Pads

REMOVAL AND INSTALLATION

Brake pads should be replaced when there is no visible clearance between the pads and the cross-spring or when they are worn to a thickness of ¼ in.

1. Jack up the front of the truck and support it on stands. Remove the wheels.
2. Pry the clip out of both retaining pins.
3. While pressing down on the cross-spring, push the pad retaining pins out with a drift or small screwdriver.
4. Reference mark positions of the brake pads if they are being reused.
5. Remove the cross-spring from the caliper.
6. Remove the inner brake pad. VW has a special tool for this purpose, but by using a small drift or punch you can pry the pad out of the caliper until it can be gripped by a pair of pliers and removed.
7. The outer brake pad is positioned in a notch. Use a flat, smooth piece of hardwood or metal to press the floating caliper frame and piston cylinder outward.
8. Grip the outer pad and remove it.
9. Siphon out about half of the brake fluid in the reservoir to prevent it from overflowing when the piston is pushed in and new thicker pads are inserted. Press the piston back into the cylinder with the flat piece of wood or metal. *Do not apply the brakes with the pads removed.*
10. Check that piston is at the proper 20° angle. You can make a gauge out of stiff cardboard.
11. Install the brake pads into the caliper.

NOTE: Replace used pads in the side of the caliper from which they were removed. When installing new pads always replace the pads on the opposite wheel at the same time.

12. Position the cross-spring in the caliper and then carefully tap the pad retaining pins into place with a small hammer. Install the pin clip.

Calipers

REMOVAL AND INSTALLATION

1. Jack up and support the front of the truck.
2. Remove the brake pads.

3. If you are removing the caliper for overhaul, disconnect and plug the brake line at the caliper. If not, do not remove the hose—hang the caliper by a wire.
4. Remove the two caliper-to-strut retaining bolts and remove the caliper.
5. Install the caliper using the reverse of the removal procedure. Tighten the two retaining bolts to 43 ft. lbs.
6. Bleed the brakes.

OVERHAUL

1. Remove the caliper.
2. Mount the caliper in a soft-jawed vise or place cloths over the jaws to protect the caliper.

Checking that the piston is at the correct 20° angle

1. Brake disc
2. Retaining pins
3. Brake caliper
4. Brake pads
5. Splash shield

Caliper and disc mounting

1. Brake disc
2. Caliper mounting frame
3. Pads
4. Cross spring
5. Retaining pin
6. Clamp ring
7. Boot
8. Piston
9. Seal
10. Cylinder
11. Bleeder nipple
12. Guide spring

Exploded view of the caliper

3. Pry the fixed mounting frame off the floating frame.

4. Separate the caliper cylinder from the floating frame by prying it and the guide spring off the frame. Use a brass drift to lightly tap on the cylinder and place a piece of wood under the piston to protect it.

5. Using pliers remove the piston clamp ring. Remove and discard the rubber dust cover, a new one should be supplied with the rebuilding kit.

6. Remove the piston from the cylinder. If it is stubborn, remove the bleeder screw and blow it out with compressed air.

──────── CAUTION ────────

Hold the piston over a block of wood when doing this as the piston will fly out with considerable force.

7. When the piston pops out of the caliper, remove the rubber seal with a wood or plastic pin to avoid damaging the seal groove.

8. Clean all metal parts in alcohol. Inspect the pistons and their bores, they must be free of scoring and pitting. Replace the cylinder if there is any damage.

9. Discard all rubber parts. The caliper rebuilding kit includes new boots and seals which should be used as the caliper is reassembled.

10. Lightly coat the cylinder bore, piston, and seal with brake assembly paste or fresh brake fluid.

11. Using a vise, install the piston into the cylinder.

12. Piston the guide spring in the groove of the brake cylinder and using a brass drift install the cylinder on the floating frame.

13. Place the mounting frame in the guide spring and slip it onto the floating frame. The fixed frame has two grooves which position it over the raised ribs of the floating frame.

14. Install the caliper and bleed the brakes.

Brake Disc

INSPECTION

Brake discs may be checked for lateral runout while on the car. This check will require a dial indicator and stand to mount it on the caliper. VW has a special tool for this purpose which mounts the dial indicator to the caliper, but it can also be mounted on the shaft of a C-clamp attached to the outside of the caliper.

1. Remove the wheel and reinstall the wheel bolts to retain the disc to the hub.

2. Mount the dial indicator securely to the caliper. The feeler should touch the disc about ½-in. below the outer edge.

3. Rotate the disc and observe the gauge. Radial run-out (wobble) must not exceed 0.004 in. A disc which exceeds this specification must be replaced or refinished.

4. Brake discs which have excessive radial runout, sharp ridges, or scoring can be refinished. Finish grinding must be done on both sides of disc to prevent squeaking and vibrating. Discs which have only light grooves and are otherwise acceptable can be used without refinishing.

The standard disc is 0.47 in. thick. It should not be ground to less than 0.41 in.

REMOVAL AND INSTALLATION

1. Loosen the wheel bolts. Remove the hub cap.

2. Jack up the front of the truck and place it on stands. Remove the wheel(s).

3. Remove the caliper.

4. Remove the disc-to-hub retaining screw.

5. Remove the disc with a sharp pull by hand or use a puller.

6. The disc is installed in the reverse order of removal. Install the caliper and bleed the brakes.

7. Install the wheel and lower the truck. Tighten the wheel bolts diagonally to 65 ft. lbs.

Front Wheel Bearings

There is no front wheel bearing adjustment. The bearing is pressed into the steering knuckle. Axle nut torque is 175 ft. lbs. The axle nut should be tightened only with the wheels resting on the ground.

Drum Brakes

BRAKE DRUMS

Removal

1. Remove one wheel bolt.

2. Insert a screwdriver through the wheel bolt hole and push the adjusting wedge upward.

3. Reinstall the wheel bolt and tighten to 65 ft. lbs.

4. Remove the grease cap, axle nut, and cotter pin, and remove the drum. See the inspection procedure.

Inspection

Check the brake drum for any cracks, scores, grooves, or an out-of-round condition. Replace a drum that shows cracking. Smooth out light scoring with fine emery cloth. If scoring is extensive have the drum turned. Never have a drum turned more than 0.020 in.

The stub axle bearings in the rear brake drum must be pressed out for replacement. Always use new seals on reassembly.

After greasing the bearings and installing them in the drum with new seals, place the drum onto the stub axle.

Installation

1. Install the washer and the hex nut. Tighten the nut and then loosen it. Retighten the nut slightly so that the washer between the nut and the bearing can just be moved with a screwdriver. Correct bearing play is 0.001–.003 in.

2. Install the castellated nut and insert a new cotter pin. Fill the hub cap with grease and install it.

3. Install the wheel and adjust the brakes.

Brake Shoes

REMOVAL AND INSTALLATION

1. Remove the drum.

2. Remove the spring retainers by pressing in and turning ¼ turn.

3. Remove the brake shoes from the supports and the lower return spring.

4. Unhook the parking brake cable on the lever.

5. Use pliers to unhook the spring for the adjusting wedge and the upper return spring.

6. Remove the brake shoes.

7. To remove the self-adjuster push rod, place the push rod in a vise and unhook the tensioning spring.

8. To install, place the push rod in a vise, attach the brake shoe to the push rod to install the tension spring on the rod and shoe.

9. Install the adjusting wedge with the lug toward the backing plate.

10. Attach the brake shoe with the lever to the push rod. Install the upper return spring.

11. Hook the parking brake cable on the lever. Place the shoes on the cylinder pistons and hook the lower return spring into the shoes.

12. Mount the brake shoes on the support and hook the spring for the adjusting wedge into the wedge and shoe.

13. Install the retaining springs and retainers. Install the drum and adjust the wheel bearings. Apply the brakes firmly to set the self-adjuster.

Wheel Cylinders

REMOVAL AND INSTALLATION

1. Remove the brake shoes.

2. Loosen the brake line on the rear of the cylinder, but do not pull the line away from the cylinder or it may bend.

3. Remove the bolts and lockwashers that attach the wheel cylinder to the backing plate and remove the cylinder.

4. Position the new wheel cylinder on

the backing plate and install the cylinder attaching bolts and lockwashers.

5. Attach the brake line.

6. Install the brakes and bleed the system.

OVERHAUL

1. Remove the brakes.

2. Place the bucket or some newspapers under the brake backing plate to catch the brake fluid that will run out to the wheel cylinder.

3. Remove the boots from the ends of the wheel cylinders.

4. Push one piston toward the center of the cylinder to force the opposite piston and cup out the other end of the cylinder. Reach in the open end of the cylinder and push the spring, cup, and piston out of the cylinder.

5. Remove the bleeder screw from the rear of the cylinder, on the back of the backing plate.

6. Inspect the inside of the wheel cylinder. If it is scored in any way, the cylinder must be honed with a wheel cylinder hone or fine emery paper, and finished with crocus cloth if emery paper is used. If the inside of the cylinder is excessively worn the cylinder will have to be replaced, as only 0.003 in. of material can be removed from the cylinder walls. Whenever honing or cleaning wheel cylinders, keep a small amount of brake fluid in the cylinder to serve as a lubricant.

7. Clean any foreign matter from the pistons. The sides of the pistons must be smooth for the wheel cylinders to operate properly.

8. Clean the cylinder bore with alcohol and a lint-free rag. Pull the rag through the bore several times to remove all foreign matter and dry the cylinder.

9. Install the bleeder screw and the return spring in the cylinder.

10. Coat new cylinder cups with new brake fluid and install them in the cylinder. Make sure they are square in the bore or they will leak.

11. Install the pistons in the cylinder after coating them with new brake fluid.

12. Coat the insides of the boots with new brake fluid and install them on the cylinder. Install and bleed the brakes.

REAR WHEEL BEARINGS

Rear wheel bearing adjustment is covered under Brake Drum Removal and Installation.

Parking Brake

CABLE

Adjustment

On the Rabbit pick-up, adjustment is made at the cable end nuts on top of the handbrake lever.

1. Block the front wheels. Raise the rear of the car.

2. Apply the parking brake so that the lever is on the second notch.

3. Tighten the compensator nut or adjusting nuts until both rear wheels cannot be turned by hand.

4. Release the parking brake lever and check that both wheels can be easily turned.

Heater

The heater core and blower are contained in the heater assembly which is located in

1. Wheel cylinder boot
2. Piston
3. Cup
4. Wheel cylinder spring
5. Wheel cylinder housing

Exploded view of the brake wheel cylinder

LOCKING NUT

PARKING BRAKE ADJUSTING NUT

PIN (LIGHTLY LUBRICATE)

Parking brakes: only one of the two cables is shown

the passenger compartment under the center of the dash.

REMOVAL AND INSTALLATION

1. Disconnect the battery ground cable.

2. Drain the cooling system.

3. Remove the windshield washer container from its mounts. Remove the ignition coil.

4. Disconnect the two hoses from the heater core connections at the firewall.

5. Unplug the electrical connector.

6. Remove the heater control knobs on the dash.

7. Remove the two retaining screws and remove the controls from the dash complete with brackets.

8. Pull the cable connection off the electric motor.

9. Disconnect the cable from the lever on the round knob.

10. Using a screwdriver, pry the retaining clip off the fresh air housing (the front portion of the heater).

11. Remove the fresh air housing complete with the controls.

12. Detach the left and right air hoses.

13. Remove the heater-to-dash panel mounting screws and lower the heater assembly.

14. Pull out the two pins and remove the heater cover. Unscrew and remove the fan motor.

15. Separate the heater halves to remove the heater core.

16. Installation is the reverse of removal. Refill the cooling system.

Exploded view of wiper linkage

Labels: Wiper blade, Wiper arm, Nut, Relay for intermittent wiper action, Wiper motor, lubricate with MoS

Windshield Wiper Motor

REMOVAL AND INSTALLATION

When removing the wiper motor, leave the mounting frame in place. Do not remove the wiper drive crank from the motor shaft—if it must be removed for any reason, matchmark the shaft, motor, and crank for reinstallation.

1. Access is with the hood open. Disconnect the battery ground cable.

2. Detach the connecting rods from the motor crank arm.

3. Pull off the wiring plug.

4. Remove the 4 mounting bolts. You may have to energize the motor for access to the top bolt.

5. Remove the motor. Reverse the procedure for installation.

Instrument Cluster

REMOVAL AND INSTALLATION

1. Disconnect the battery ground cable.

2. Remove the fresh air controls trim plate.

3. Remove the radio or glove box.

4. Unscrew the speedometer drive cable from the back of the speedometer. Detach the electrical plug.

5. Remove the attaching screw inside the radio/glove box opening.

6. Remove the instrument cluster. Reverse the procedure for installation.

Unit Repair Section

Tools and Equipment

The service procedures in this book presuppose a familiarity with hand tools and their proper use. However, it is possible that you may have a limited amount of experience with the sort of equipment needed to work on an automobile. This section is designed to help you assemble a basic set of tools that will handle the majority of jobs you may undertake.

In addition to the normal assortment of screwdrivers and pliers, automotive service work requires an investment in wrenches, sockets and the handles needed to drive them, and various measuring tools such as torque wrenches and feeler gauges.

The best approach to gathering the required equipment is to proceed slowly, buying high-quality tools as they are needed. An initial investment should be made in a set of quality wrenches, ranging in size from ¼ inch to one inch, if your car has standard bolts, or from 5 mm to 19 mm if your car has metric fasteners. High quality forged wrenches are available in three styles: open end, box end, and combination open/box end. The combination tools are generally the most desirable as a starter set; the wrenches shown in the illustration are of the combination type.

The other set of tools inevitably required is a ratchet handle and socket set. This set should have the same size range as your wrench set. The ratchet, extension, and flex drives for the sockets are available in many sizes; it is advisable to choose a ⅜ inch drive set initially. One break in the inch/metric sizing war is that metric-sized sockets sold in the U.S. have inch-sized drive (¼, ⅜, ½, etc.). Sockets are available in six and twelve point versions; six point types are generally cheaper and are a good choice for a first set. The choice of a drive handle for the sockets should be made with some care. If this is your first set, take the plunge and invest in a flex-head ratchet; it will get into many places otherwise accessible only through a long chain of universal joints,

extensions and adapters. An alternative is a flex handle; such a tool is shown in the illustration, below the ratchet handle. In addition to the range of sockets mentioned, a rubber-lined spark plug socket should be purchased. Spark plugs have either a ¹³⁄₁₆ or a ⅝ inch hex; get the correct socket for the plugs in your car.

The most important thing to consider when purchasing hand tools is quality. Don't be misled by the low cost of "bargain" tools. Forged wrenches, tempered screwdriver blades, and fine tooth ratchets are a much better investment than their less expensive counterparts. The skinned knuckles and frustration inflicted by poor quality tools make any job an unhappy chore. Another consideration is that quality tools sold by reputable firms come with an on-the-spot replacement guarantee—if the tool breaks, you get a new one, no questions asked.

The tools needed for basic maintenance jobs, in addition to those just mentioned, include:

1. Jackstands, for support
2. Oil filter wrench
3. Oil filler spout or funnel
4. Grease gun
5. Battery hydrometer
6. Battery post and clamp cleaner
7. Container for draining oil
8. Lots of rags for the inevitable spills

In addition to these items there are several others which are not absolutely necessary, but handy to have around. These include a transmission funnel and filler tube, a drop (trouble) light on a long cord, an adjustable wrench (crescent wrench), and slip joint pliers.

A more extensive list of tools, suitable for tune-up work, can be drawn up easily. While the tools involved are slightly more sophisticated, they need not be outrageously expensive. For example, there are several inexpensive tach/dwell meters on the market that are every bit as good for the average mechanic as a $100.00 profes-

sional model. The key to these purchases is to make them with an eye towards adaptability and wide range. Using the tach/dwell meter example again, if the model you buy runs up to at least 1,500 rpm on the tachometer scale, the dwell meter works on 4, 6, or 8 cylinder engines, and the tachometer unit is adaptable to both conventional and electronic ignitions, it will serve for a long time on a variety of automobiles. A basic list of tune-up tools could include:

1. A tach/dwell meter
2. Spark plug gauge and gapping tool
3. Feeler blades
4. Timing light

In this list, the choice of a timing light should be made carefully. A light which works on the DC current supplied by the car battery is the best choice; it should have a xenon tube for brightness. If your car has electronic ignition, the light should have an inductive pick-up (the timing light illustrated has one of these), and since nearly all cars will have electronic ignition in the future, this feature is a reasonable one to look for.

In addition to these basic tools, there are several other tools and gauges you may find useful. These include:

1. A compression gauge. The screw-in type is slower to use, but eliminates the possibility of a faulty reading due to escaping pressure.
2. A manifold vacuum gauge
3. A test light
4. An induction meter. This is used to determine whether or not there is current flowing in a wire, and thus is extremely helpful in electrical troubleshooting.

Finally, you will probably find a torque wrench necessary for all but the most basic of work. The beam–type models are perfectly adequate, although the newer click (breakaway) type are more precise. Whichever type you choose, plan on having it recalibrated every once in a while.

WIRE TYPE FEELER GAUGES

FLAT TYPE FEELER GAUGES

TORQUE WRENCH (BEAM TYPE)

JACKSTAND

TIMING LIGHT (WITH INDUCTIVE PICKUP)

VACUUM GAUGE

COMPRESSION GAUGE

DWELL TACHOMETER

A basic tool collection will handle almost any automotive repair work

SERVICING YOUR CAR SAFELY

It is virtually impossible to anticipate all of the hazards involved with automotive maintenance and service, but care and common sense will prevent most accidents.

The rules of safety for mechanics range from ''don't smoke around gasoline,'' to ''use the proper tool for the job.'' The trick to avoiding injuries is to develop safe work habits and take every possible precaution.

DO'S

● DO keep a fire extinguisher and first aid kit within easy reach.

● DO wear safety glasses or goggles when cutting, drilling, grinding, or prying, even if you have 20-20 vision. If you wear glasses for the sake of vision, they should be made of hardened glass that can serve also as safety glasses, or wear safety goggles over your regular glasses.

● DO shield your eyes whenever you work around the battery. Batteries contain sulphuric acid. In case of contact with the eyes or skin, flush the area with water or a mixture of water and baking soda and get medical attention immediately.

● DO use safety stands for any undercar service. Jacks are for raising vehicles; safety stands are for making sure the vehicle stays raised until you want it to come down. Whenever the car is raised, block the wheels

Always support the car securely with jackstands; never use cinder blocks, tire changing jacks or the like

remaining on the ground and set the parking brake.

● DO use adequate ventilation when working with any chemicals or hazardous materials. Follow the manufacturer's directions for usage. Brake fluid, anti-freeze, solvents, paints, etc. are all deadly poisons if taken internally. Seal the containers tightly after use and store them safely, out of the reach of children.

● DO use caution when working on clutches or brakes. The asbestos used in the friction material will cause lung cancer if inhaled. Wipe the component with a damp rag to remove dust, and dispose of the rag after use.

● DO disconnect the negative battery cable when working on the electrical system. The secondary ignition system can contain up to 40,000 volts.

● DO properly maintain your tools. Loose hammerheads, mushroomed punches and chisels, frayed or poorly grounded electrical cords, excessively worn screwdrivers, spread open-end wrenches, cracked sockets, slipping ratchets, or faulty droplight sockets can cause accidents.

● DO use the proper size and type of tool for the job being done.

● DO when possible, pull on a wrench handle rather than push on it, and adjust your stance to prevent a fall.

● DO be sure that adjustable wrenches are tightly closed on the nut or bolt and pulled so that the face is on the side of the fixed jaw.

● DO select a wrench or socket that fits the nut or bolt. The wrench or socket should sit straight, not cocked.

● DO strike squarely with a hammer; avoid glancing blows.

● DO set the parking brake and block the drive wheels if the work requires the engine running.

DONT'S

● DON'T run an engine in a garage or anywhere else without proper ventilation—

EVER! Carbon monoxide is poisonous; it takes a long time to leave the human body and you can build up a deadly supply of it in your system by simply breathing in a little every day. You may not realize you are slowly poisoning yourself. Always use power vents, windows, fans or open the garage doors.

● DON'T work around moving parts while wearing a necktie or other loose clothing. Short sleeves are much safer than long, loose sleeves; hard-toed shoes with neoprene soles protect your toes and give a better grip on slippery surfaces. Jewelry such as watches, fancy belt buckles, beads or body adornment of any kind is not safe working around a car. Long hair should be hidden under a hat or cap.

● DON'T use pockets for toolboxes. A fall or bump can drive a screwdriver deep into your body. Even a wiping cloth hanging from the back pocket can wrap around a spinning shaft or fan.

● DON'T smoke when working around gasoline, cleaning solvent or other flammable material.

● DON'T smoke when working around the battery. When the battery is being charged, it gives off explosive hydrogen gas.

● DON'T use gasoline to wash your hands; there are excellent soaps available. Gasoline may contain lead, and lead can enter the body through a cut, accumulating in the body until you are very ill. Gasoline also removes all the natural oils from the skin so that bone dry hands will suck up oil and grease.

● DON'T service the air conditioning system unless you are equipped with the necessary tools and training. The refrigerant, R-12, is extremely cold when compressed, and when released into the air will instantly freeze any surface it contacts, including your eyes. Although the refrigerant is normally non-toxic, R-12 becomes a deadly poisonous gas in the presence of an open flame. One good whiff of the vapors from burning refrigerant can be fatal.

Basic Maintenance

INTRODUCTION

Routine maintenance is probably the most important part of automobile care and the easiest to neglect. A regular program aimed at monitoring essential systems ensures that all components are in good and safe working order, and can prevent small problems from developing into major headaches. Routine maintenance also pays big dividends in keeping major repair costs at a minimum and extending the life of the car.

The owner's manual that came with your car includes a maintenance schedule, indicating service intervals in numbers of months or thousand of miles. This schedule should always be followed. We have provided, in each section, a guide to service intervals based on an averaging of manufacturer's recommendations. In most cases, the suggested interval offered here will be close to that given by the manufacturer of your car, but the manufacturer's schedule should always take precedence.

We have divided the maintenance work to be done into three categories: Under Hood, Under Car, and Exterior. The checks in each section require only a few minutes of attention every few weeks; the services to be performed can be easily accomplished in a morning. The most important part of any maintenance program is regularity. The few minutes or occasional morning spent on these seemingly trivial tasks will forestall or eliminate major problems later.

UNDER HOOD
Automatic Transmission, Automatic Transaxle

The fluid level in the automatic transmission or transaxle should be checked every three months or 6000 miles. All automatic transmissions have a dipstick for fluid level checks.

1. Drive the car until it is at normal operating temperature. The level should not be checked immediately after the car has been driven for a long time at high speed, or in city traffic in hot weather; in those cases, the transmission should be given a half hour to cool down.

2. Stop the car, apply the parking brake, then shift slowly through all gear positions, ending in Park. Leave the engine running.

3. Remove the dipstick, wipe it clean, then reinsert it, pushing it fully home.

4. Pull the dipstick again and, holding it horizontally, read the fluid level.

5. Cautiously feel the end of the dipstick to determine the temperature. Most dipsticks are marked with both cool and hot levels. If the fluid is not up to the correct level, more will have to be added.

6. Fluid is added through the dipstick tube. You will probably need the aid of a spout or a long-necked funnel. Be sure that whatever you pour through is perfectly clean and dry. Fluid recommendations can be found in the owner's manual.

Add fluid slowly, and in small amounts, checking the level frequently between additions. Do not overfill, which will cause foaming, fluid loss, slippage, and possible transmission damage.

Check the automatic transmission fluid level with the dipstick provided

Fill the automatic transmission through the dipstick tube

Battery

FLUID LEVEL (EXCEPT "MAINTENANCE FREE" BATTERIES)

Check the battery electrolyte level at least once a month, or more often in hot weather or during periods of extended car operation. The level can be checked through the case on translucent polypropylene batteries; the cell caps must be removed on other models. The electrolyte level in each cell should be kept filled to the split ring inside, or the line marked on the outside of the case.

If the level is low, add only distilled water, or colorless, odorless drinking water, through

Fill the battery cell to the bottom of the split ring

the opening until the level is correct. Each cell is completely separate from the others, so each must be checked and filled individually.

If water is added in freezing weather, the car should be driven several miles to allow the water to mix with the electrolyte. Otherwise, the battery could freeze.

SPECIFIC GRAVITY (EXCEPT "MAINTENANCE FREE" BATTERIES)

While not technically exact, a practical measurement of the chemical condition of the battery is indicated by measuring the specific gravity of the acid (electrolyte) contained in each cell. The electrolyte in a fully charged battery is usually between 1.260 and 1.280 times as heavy as pure water at the same temperature (80°F). Variations in the specific gravity readings for a fully charged battery may differ. Therefore, it is most important that all battery cells produce an equal reading.

As a battery discharges, a chemical change takes place within each cell. The sulfate factor of the electrolyte combines chemically with the battery plates, reducing the weight of the electrolyte. A reading of the specific gravity of the acid, or electrolyte, of any partially charged battery, will therefore be less than that taken in a fully charged one.

The hydrometer is the instrument used for determining the specific gravity of liquids. The battery hydrometer is readily available from many sources, including local auto replacement parts stores. The following chart gives an indication of specific gravity value, related to battery charge condition. If, after charging, the specific gravity between any two cells varies more than 50 points (.050), the battery is probably bad.

Specific Gravity Reading	Charged Condition
1.260–1.280	Fully charged
1.230–1.250	Three-quarter charged
1.200–1.220	One-half charged
1.170–1.190	One-quarter charged
1.140–1.160	Just about flat
1.110–1.130	All the way down

CABLES AND CLAMPS

Once a year, the battery terminals and the cable clamps should be cleaned. Loosen the clamps and remove the cables, negative cable first. On batteries with posts on top, the use of a puller specially made for the purpose is recommended. These are inexpensive, and available in auto parts stores. Side terminal battery cables are secured with a bolt.

Clean the cable clamps and the battery terminal with a wire brush until all corrosion, grease, etc. is removed and the metal is shiny. It is especially important to clean the inside of the clamp thoroughly, since a small deposit of foreign material or oxidation there will prevent a sound electrical connection and inhibit either starting or charging. Special tools are available for cleaning these parts, one type for conventional batteries and another type for side terminal batteries.

Before installing the cables, loosen the battery hold-down clamp or strap, remove the battery and check the battery tray. Clear it of any debris, and check it for soundness. Rust should be wire brushed away, and the metal given a coat of anti-rust paint. Replace the battery and tighten the hold-down clamp or strap securely, but be careful not to overtighten, which will crack the battery case.

Clean the clamp with a wire brush

After the clamps and terminals are clean, reinstall the cables, negative cable last; do not hammer on the clamps to install. Tighten the clamps securely, but do not distort them. Give the clamps and terminals a thin external coat of grease after installation, to retard corrosion.

Check the cables at the same time that the terminals are cleaned. If the cable insulation is cracked or broken, or if the ends are frayed, the cable should be replaced with a new cable of the same length and gauge.

NOTE: Keep flame or sparks away from the battery; it gives off explosive hydrogen gas. Battery electrolyte contains sulphuric acid. If you should splash any on your skin or in your eyes, flush the affected area with plenty of clear water; if it lands in your eyes, get medical help immediately.

Testing battery specific gravity

Use a puller to remove the clamp on post-type batteries

The posts are easily cleaned with a wire brush, or the battery post tool shown

A special tool is required to clean the terminals and clamps on side terminal batteries

Brake Fluid

Once a month, the fluid level in the brake master cylinder should be checked.

1. Park the car on a level surface.

2. Clean off the master cylinder cover before removal. Some covers are retained by a bolt. Some of the newer master cylinders with plastic reservoirs have screw caps. Remove the cover, being careful not to drop or tear the rubber diaphragm which will probably be underneath. Be careful also not to drip any brake fluid on painted surfaces, as it eats paint.

NOTE: Brake fluid absorbs moisture from the air, which reduces effectiveness and will corrode brake parts once in the system. Never leave the master cylinder or the brake fluid container uncovered for any longer than necessary.

3. The fluid level should be about ¼ inch below the lip of the master cylinder well.

4. If fluid addition is necessary, use only extra heavy duty disc brake fluid meeting DOT 3 or DOT 4 specifications. The fluid should be reasonably fresh, because brake fluid deteriorates with age.

5. Replace the cover, making sure that the diaphragm is correctly seated.

If the brake fluid is constantly low, the system should be checked for leaks. However, it is normal for the fluid level to fall gradually as the disc brake pads wear; expect the fluid level to drop about ⅛ inch for every 10,000 miles of wear.

Belt Tension

Every six months or 12,000 miles, check

Check the belts for wear

the water pump, alternator, power steering pump, air pump, and air conditioning compressor drive belts for proper tension. Also look for signs of wear, fraying, separation, glazing and so on, and replace the belts as required.

Belt tension should be checked with a gauge made for the purpose. If a gauge is not available, tension can be checked with moderate thumb pressure applied to the belt at its longest span midway between pulleys. If the belt has a free span less than twelve inches, it should deflect approximately ⅛–¼ inch. If the span is longer than twelve inches, deflection can range between ⅛ and ⅜ inches.

Check the belt tension at the middle of the longest span between pulleys

To adjust or replace belts:

1. Loosen the driven accessory's pivot and mounting bolts. Some air conditioning compressor belts are tensioned by an idler pulley; in this case, loosen the idler pulley and use a ½ in. drive ratchet in the square hole provided to lever the idler pulley up or down.

2. Move the accessory toward or away from the engine until the tension is correct. You can use a wooden hammer handle or broomstick as a lever, but do not use anything metallic.

3. Tighten the bolts and recheck the tension. If new bolts have been installed, run the engine for a few minutes, then recheck and readjust as necessary.

To either adjust or remove a belt, loosen the driven component's adjusting bolt

Push the component toward the engine to remove the belt

Pull outwards on the component to tension the belt, then tighten the bolts; recheck the belt tension after tightening

Slip the replacement belt over the pulley

NOTE: If the driven component has two drive belts, the belts should be replaced in pairs to maintain proper tension.

It is better to have belts too loose than too tight, because overtight belts will lead to bearing failure, particularly in the water pump and alternator. However, loose belts place an extremely high impact load on the driven components due to the whipping action of the belt.

Carburetor and Choke Linkage

Every 12 months or 6000 miles, examine the carburetor linkage and choke plate for free movement. The choke plate action can generally be freed, if necessary, with the application of a solvent made for the purpose to the ends of the choke shaft. This solvent will also clean grease and dirt from the throttle linkage.

Use a spray solvent on the choke shaft, but do not apply any lubricants

Cooling System

Once a month, the engine coolant level should be checked. On cars without a coolant recovery system, this should only be done when the engine is cold. Remove the radiator cap; the coolant level should be about one inch below the radiator filler neck.

— CAUTION —
To avoid injury when working with a hot engine, cover the radiator cap with a thick cloth. Wear a heavy glove to protect your hand. Turn the radiator cap slowly to the first stop, and allow all the pressure to vent (indicated when the hissing noise stops). When the pressure has been released, remove the cap the rest of the way.

Fill level mark on crossflow radiator.

Hot and cold level fill marks, constant-full system.

Proper coolant level is about one inch below the radiator neck, or between the lines on the recovery tank

On cars with a coolant recovery tank, coolant should be visible within the tank; as long as the coolant is between the markings on the tank, the level is correct.

If coolant is needed, a 50/50 mix of ethylene glycol-based antifreeze and water should always be used, both winter and summer. This is imperative on cars with air conditioning; without the antifreeze, the heater core could freeze when the air conditioning is used. Add coolant to the radiator if the car does not have a coolant recovery system. Add coolant to the recovery tank on cars so equipped.

The radiator hoses and clamps and the radiator cap should be checked at the same time as the coolant level. Hoses which are brittle, cracked, or swollen should be replaced. Clamps should be checked for tightness (screwdriver tight only—do not allow the clamp to cut into the hose or crush the fitting). The radiator cap gasket should

Check the radiator cap gasket and sealing surface

be checked for any obvious tears, cracks or swelling, or any signs of incorrect seating in the radiator neck.

The cooling system should be drained, flushed and refilled after the first 24 months or 24,000 miles, and every year thereafter.

1. Drain the radiator by opening the drain cock at the bottom. Some radiators do not have these; the lower radiator hose must be disconnected at the radiator instead. If the engine block has drain plugs, they should be opened to speed draining.

2. Close the drain cocks and fill the system with clear water. A cooling system flushing additive can be used, if desired.

3. Run the engine until it is hot. The heater should be turned on to its maximum heat position so that the core is flushed out.

4. Drain the system, then flush with water until it runs clear.

5. Clean out the coolant recovery tank, if equipped.

6. Fill the system with a 50/50 mix of ethylene glycol-based antifreeze and water. Fill the coolant recovery tank midway between the marks with this mixture also.

7. Run the engine until it is hot, then let it cool and top up the radiator or coolant recovery tank as necessary with the antifreeze/water mixture.

Heat Riser

The heat riser is a thermostatically or vacuum operated valve in the exhaust manifold (not all cars have one). It closes when the engine is warming up, in order to preheat the incoming fuel/air mixture. If it sticks open, the result will be frequent stalling during warmup, especially in cold and damp weather. If it sticks shut, the result will be a rough idle after the engine is warm.

Exploded view of a vacuum-operated heat riser

The heat riser should move freely. It can be checked easily when the engine is cold by giving the counterweight on the valve shaft a twirl, or pulling the vacuum rod to open and shut the valve. If the valve is sticking or binding, a quick shot of solvent made for the purpose will free it up. This solvent should be applied every six months or 6000 miles to keep the valve free. If the valve is still stuck after application of the solvent, sometimes rapping the end of the

Thermostatically-operated heat control valve

shaft lightly with a hammer will break it loose. Otherwise, the components will have to be removed for further repairs.

Ignition Cables

The ignition system (points, condenser, rotor, spark plugs, etc.) receives regular attention in the form of a tune-up, and thus is not covered here. But one of the most commonly overlooked components is the ignition cable, or spark plug wire.

Inspect the ignition cables for cracks or breaks in the insulation

Although they rarely show any visible signs of deterioration, the ignition cables should be checked at every tune-up, and replaced at least every 50,000 miles. Cracking and embrittlement are of course obvious signs of wear, but most newer ca-

Test the ignition cables with an ohmmeter. Conventional ignition cables should be removed from the distributor cap, but electronic ignition wires should first be tested through the cap

bles have silicone insulation and thus are not prone to display these conditions.

The most reliable way to check the cables is with an ohmmeter. On conventional ignitions, the resistance should be less than 7,000 ohms per foot (wire removed). On cars with electronic ignitions, it is generally recommended to leave the wire attached to the distributor cap; test with one lead from the ohmmeter connected to the corresponding terminal in the distributor cap, the other lead touched to the disconnected end of the cable at the spark plug. Then, if resistance seems close to the limit, remove the wire from the cap and retest. In general, the spark plug wires on electronic ignitions should be replaced if the total resistance is over 36,000 ohms.

Always replace the cables with new ones of the same type. Replace the wires one at a time, working from the longest to the shortest.

Oil Level

The engine oil should be checked on a regular basis, ideally at each fuel stop, or once a week. It is best to check when the engine is at operating temperature, but checking the level immediately after shutting off the engine will give a false reading, because all of the oil will not yet have drained back into the crankcase. The car should be parked on a level surface to obtain an accurate reading.

Check the engine oil level with the dipstick

1. Remove the oil dipstick. Wipe it clean, then replace it, seating it firmly.
2. Remove the dipstick again and hold it horizontally to prevent the oil from running. The level should be between the "Add" and "Full" marks on the dipstick. The dipstick may be marked "Add" and "Full," "Add" and "Safe," or may have lines scribed on it; in any case, the oil level should be above the lower marking.
3. If the oil is below the lower mark, enough oil should be added to the engine to raise the level to the upper mark. The markings are usually spaced so that one quart of oil will raise the level from the "Add" mark to the "Full" mark. Oil is added through the capped opening in the valve cover. Only oils labeled SF (gasoline engines) or CC (diesel engines) should be

Add oil through the valve cover

used; select a viscosity that will be compatible with the temperatures expected until the next drain interval.

4. Replace the dipstick, then check the level again after any additions of oil. Be careful not to overfill, which will lead to leakage and seal damage.

Power Steering

The power steering fluid level is usually checked with a dipstick inserted into the pump reservoir. The dipstick may be attached to the reservoir cap, or inserted into a tube on the pump body. The level should be checked at every oil change. On some models, the power steering reservoir is translucent, allowing the level to be checked through the sides of the container without removing the cap. On others, the reservoir is a metal canister with a wingnut-attached

The power steering fluid level on many models is checked by means of a dipstick installed in the reservoir

cap. After the cap is removed, the level is checked with the scribed lines on the inside of the container.

On most models, the fluid level may be checked with the fluid either warm or cold. If checked with the fluid cold, the level will be slightly lower than with the fluid warm. If doubts arise about the specific procedures

Typical power steering dipstick markings

"HOT" MARK
"COLD" MARK
"ADD"

for the car being checked, consult the owner's manual.

1. On all models, with the engine off, remove the dipstick, remove the cap or check the level through the side of the reservoir. If warm, the level should be between the "Hot" and "Cold" marks or even with the scribed line in the reservoir. If the fluid is cold, the level should be slightly lower.

2. If the level is low, add power steering fluid until the correct level is reached. Do not overfill the reservoir.

Windshield Washer Fluid

Check the fluid level in the windshield washer tank at every oil level check. The fluid can be mixed in a 50% solution with water, if desired, as long as temperatures remain above freezing. Below freezing, the fluid should be used full strength. Never add engine coolant antifreeze to the washer fluid, because it will damage the car's paint.

UNDER CAR

Axle

The fluid level in the rear axle should be checked every 12 months or 12,000 miles.

1. With the car parked on a level surface, remove the filler plug. The plug can be found either in the rear cover of the differential, or on the front of the pinion housing.

2. If lubricant trickles out when the plug is removed, the level is correct. If not, stick your finger in the hole (watch out for sharp threads); the fluid level should be even with edge of the filler hole.

3. If lubricant is needed, use SAE 80W-90 GL-5 gear oil (SAE 80W GL-5 in very cold climates) to fill standard axles. Limited

FILLER PLUG

Rear axle filler plug locations

slip axles require a special lubricant, available in auto parts stores.

4. When the level is correct, install the plug and tighten until snug. Do not over-tighten.

Standard axles should be drained and refilled with fresh lubricant every 15,000 miles when the car is used to pull a trailer. Limited slip axles should be drained and refilled at the first 7500 miles; the limited slip lubricant should be changed every 7500 miles when the car is used for trailer pulling. The axle may be drained by removing the drain plug at the bottom of the differential housing, if present. Otherwise, the rear cover must be removed, or a suction gun used through the filler hole. When installing a rear cover which does not use a gasket, apply a thin bead of silicone sealer to the cover, running the bead around the inside of the bolt holes. Install the cover, then tighten the bolts a few turns at a time in a crisscross pattern.

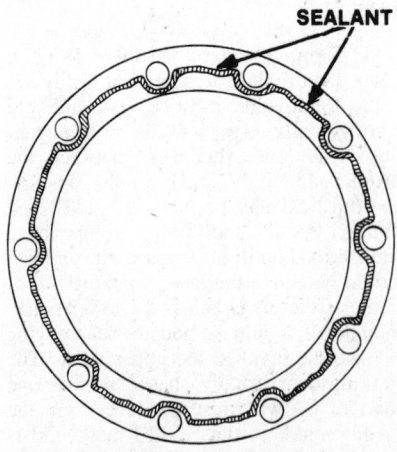

SEALANT

Apply a bead of silicone sealer to the rear cover if no gasket is used

NOTE: On many later models, the rear axle is filled for life and fluid does not have to be replaced.

Exhaust System

The exhaust system should be checked twice a year for general soundness. Inspect the pipes for holes, broken welds, leaking seams, or loose connections. Leaks at connections can sometimes be successfully repaired with the use of a commercial exhaust pipe sealer, but holes or breaks warrant replacement of the part. The exhaust pipe hangers and straps should be examined for any breaks or cracks; replace these as necessary. Some slight cracking of rubber hangers is normal, but deep cracks or cuts are cause for replacement.

—————— **CAUTION** ——————

Check the exhaust system only when it is cold. The temperature on an exhaust system using a catalytic converter can reach 1000°F after only a short period of engine operation.

Manual Transmission, Manual Transaxle

The fluid level in the manual transmission (or transaxle on front wheel drive cars) should be checked twice a year, or every 6000 miles.

1. Park the car on a level surface. The transmission should be cool to the touch.

2. Remove the filler plug from the side of the transmission or transaxle. If lubricant trickles out as the plug is removed, the fluid level is correct. If not, stick your finger into the hole (watch out for sharp threads); the lubricant should be right up to the edge of the filler hole.

3. If lubricant is needed, consult the owner's manual for the correct weight and type of fluid.

FILL PLUG

MANUAL TRANSMISSION
FILL TO BOTTOM OF FILLER HOLE WITH VEHICLE ON LEVEL GROUND.

Typical manual transmission filler plug location

Lubricate the parking brake cable with white waterproof grease

PARKING BRAKE LEVER

LUBRICATE ALL PIVOT AND SLIDING CONTACT AREAS

EQUALIZER

INTERMEDIATE CABLE

NOTE: Some manual transmission/transaxle assemblies are filled with automatic transmission fluid rather than gear oil. Consult the owner's manual for lubricant information.

4. When the level is correct, install the filler plug and tighten until snug.

Parking Brake Linkage

The parking brake cable assembly should be inspected twice a year for fraying, kinks, and binding. A smooth white waterproof lubricant should be applied at the same time to all pivot points and areas in sliding contact.

Suspension Lubrication

Depending on the year of manufacture, there may be as many as twelve grease fittings on the suspension parts, or as few as two. Typical locations for grease nipples are on the ball joints, control arm pivot points, steering linkage, and the tie rod ends.

Lubricate these fittings with a small hand operated grease gun filled with EP chassis lubricant. Pump grease into the fitting slowly, until it begins to ooze out around the joint, or until the grease begins to expand the rubber boot around the fitting. Be extremely careful not to rupture any seals or boots, as this will lead to lubricant loss and contamination of the parts involved.

Occasionally, the grease nipples may become clogged with dirt or hardened grease. If so, unscrew them with a wrench of the proper size and clean them out with solvent. When reinstalled, they may be covered with plastic caps made for the purpose, or a piece of aluminum foil.

The chassis and suspension parts should be lubricated once a year, or every 7500 miles, whichever comes first.

Transfer Case

The transfer case on the four wheel drive Subaru shares a common lubricant supply with the transmission, therefore the transfer case lubricant supply does not have to be checked separately.

EXTERIOR

Drain Holes and Underbody

Most cars have drain holes spaced along the lower edge of the rocker panels and doors. These holes should be cleared of any debris or rust twice a year. A small screwdriver can be used to open plugged drain holes.

CHECK STRAP — LUBRICATE

HINGE LUBRICATE

Use engine oil to lubricate the door, hood, and trunk hinges

Every spring, the underbody should be flushed with clear water to remove deposits of mud, road salt, and debris. It is advisable to loosen any packed-in sediment before flushing to assure a more thorough cleaning.

Hinges and Locks

Once a year, the door, hood, and trunk hinges, and all locks should be lubricated to ensure smooth operation. The hinge points should be lightly oiled. Lock cylinders may be easily lubricated with a shot of silicone spray directed into the keyhole. Silicone lubricant also works well on the door latch mechanisms, and keeps the door, trunk, and window weatherseals pliable when applied in a light film.

Tires

Tires should be checked weekly for proper air pressure. A chart, located either in the glove compartment or on the driver's or passenger's door, gives the recommended inflation pressures. Maximum fuel economy and tire life will result if the pressure is maintained at the highest figure given on the chart. Pressures should be checked before driving since pressure can increase as

Tire tread depth can be checked with a penny. If the top of Lincoln's head is visible, the tires are due for replacement

much as six pounds per square inch (psi) due to heat buildup. It is a good idea to have your own accurate pressure gauge, because not all gauges on service station air pumps can be trusted. When checking pressures, do not neglect the spare tire. Note that some spare tires require pressures considerably higher than those used in the other tires.

While you are about the task of checking air pressure, inspect the tire treads for cuts, bruises and other damage. Check the air valves to be sure that they are tight. Replace any missing valve caps.

Check the tires for uneven wear that might indicate the need for front end alignment or tire rotation. Tires should be replaced when a tread wear indicator appears as a solid band across the tread.

Tread wear indicators will appear as a band across the tire when the tread has worn out.

When buying new tires, give some thought to the following points, especially if you are considering a switch to larger tires or a different profile series:

1. All four tires must be of the same construction type. This rule cannot be violated. Radial, bias, and bias-belted tires must not be mixed.

2. The wheels should be the correct width for the tire. Tire dealers have charts of tire and rim compatibility. A mismatch will cause sloppy handling and rapid tire wear. The tread width should match the rim width (inside bead to inside bead) within an inch. For radial tires, the rim width should

be 80% or less of the tire (not tread) width.

3. The height (mounted diameter) of the new tires can change speedometer accuracy, engine speed at a given road speed, fuel mileage, acceleration, and ground clearance. Tire manufacturers furnish full measurement specifications.

4. The spare tire should be usable, at least for short distance and low speed operation, with the new tires.

5. There shouldn't be any body interference when loaded, on bumps, or in turns.

TIRE ROTATION

Tire rotation is recommended every 6000 miles or so, to obtain maximum tire wear. The pattern you use depends on whether or not your car has a usable spare. Radial tires should not be cross-switched (from one side of the car to the other); they last longer if their direction of rotation is not changed. Snow tires sometimes have directional arrows molded onto the side of their carcass; the arrow shows the direction of rotation. They will wear very rapidly if the rotation is reversed. Studded tires will lose their studs if their rotational direction is reversed.

NOTE: Mark the wheel position or direction of rotation on radial tires or studded snow tires before removing them.

STORAGE

Store the tires at proper inflation pressure

if they are mounted on wheels. Keep them in a cool dry place, laid on their sides. If the tires are stored in the garage or basement, do not let them stand on a concrete floor; set them on strips of wood.

Windshield Wipers and Washers

For maximum effectiveness, and longest element life, the windshield and wiper blades should be kept clean. Dirt, tree sap, road tar and so on will cause streaking, smearing and blade deterioration if left on the glass. It is advisable to wash the windshield carefully with a commercial glass cleaner at least once a month. Wipe off the rubber blades with the wet rag afterwards. For access to the blades on wiper systems which park below the hood line, turn the ignition key to "On" and run the wipers to the center of the windshield. Shut the wipers off with the ignition key, not the wiper switch. Do not attempt to move the wipers by hand; damage to the motor and drive mechanism will result.

If the blades are found to be cracked, broken or torn, they should be replaced immediately. Replacement intervals will vary with usage, although ozone deterioration usually limits blade life to about one year. If the wiper pattern is smeared or streaked, or if the blade chatters across the glass, the elements should be replaced. It is easiest and most sensible to replace the elements

BIAS PLY TIRE 4-WHEEL ROTATION   BIAS PLY TIRE 5-WHEEL ROTATION   RADIAL PLY TIRES 4-WHEEL ROTATION   RADIAL PLY TIRES 5-WHEEL ROTATION

Tire rotation diagrams; note that radials should not be cross-switched

TRICO

ANCO

POLYCARBONATE

TRIDON

THE LENGTH OF THE 16" AND 16.5" TRIDON BLADES ARE MOLDED IN EACH END. REPLACE ONLY WITH IDENTICAL BLADES OR REFILLS.

Windshield wiper blade replacement methods

in pairs.

There are basically three different types of refills, which differ in their method of replacement. One type has two release buttons, approximately one-third of the way up from the ends of the blade frame. Pushing the buttons down releases a lock and allows the rubber filler to be removed from the frame. The new filler slides back into the frame and locks in place.

The second type of refill has two metal tabs which are unlocked by squeezing them together. The rubber filler can then be withdrawn from the frame jaws. A new refill is installed by inserting the refill into the front frame jaws and sliding it rearward to engage the remaining frame jaws. There are usually four jaws; be certain when installing that the refill is engaged in all of them. At the end of its travel, the tabs will lock into place on the front jaws of the wiper blade frame.

The third type is a refill made from polycarbonate. The refill has a simple locking device at one end which flexes downward out of the groove into which the jaws of the holder fit, allowing easy release. By sliding the new refill through all the jaws and pushing through the slight resistance when it reaches the end of its travel, the refill will lock into position.

Regardless of the type of refill used, make sure that all of the frame jaws are engaged as the refill is pushed into place and locked. The metal blade holder and frame will scratch the glass if allowed to touch it.

WASHER NOZZLE ADJUSTMENT

Centered Single Post–Non-Adjustable Nozzles

This type is usually located on the rear center of the hood panel, directly in front of the windshield. By loosening the body retaining nut from under the hood, the nozzle body can be turned to provide the best spray discharge to cover the windshield. Tighten the retaining nut while holding the nozzle in position.

Centered Single Post–Adjustable Nozzles

This nozzle is adjusted with a wrench, screwdriver, or pliers. If the nozzle has no gripping area, the adjustment is made by inserting a stiff wire into the nozzle opening and moving the nozzle in the direction desired. When using the wire as an adjuster tool, do not force the nozzle; the wire can be broken within the nozzle opening.

Individual Nozzles

A tab is usually fastened to the nozzle stem to assist in turning the nozzle in the desired direction. If a tab is not present, use a pair of pliers to gently move the nozzle.

Wiper Arm Nozzles

No adjustment is necessary on this type of nozzle, because the opening is centered on the wiper arm and moves along with the arm.

Diesel Service

NOTE: Most procedures associated with diesel engined cars are similar to gas engined cars, although many parts of the diesel engine are unique compared to their gas engine counterparts. Standard maintenance and service procedures are given here while component removal, installation and adjustment procedures unique to diesel engines can be found in the appropriate section.

HOW THE DIESEL ENGINE WORKS

Four-stroke diesels require four piston strokes for the complete cycle of actions, exactly like a gasoline engine. The difference lies in how the fuel mixture is ignited. A diesel engine does not rely on a conventional spark ignition to ignite the fuel mixture for the power stroke. Instead, a diesel relies on the heat produced by compressing air in the combustion chamber to ignite the fuel and produce a power stroke. This is known as a compression-ignition engine. No fuel enters the cylinder on the intake stroke, only air. At the end of the compression stroke, fuel is sprayed into the precombustion chamber (prechamber). The mixture ignites and spreads out into the main combustion chamber, forcing the piston downward (power stroke). The fuel/air mixture ignites because of the very high combustion chamber temperatures generated by the extraordinarily high compression ratios used in diesel engines. Typically, the compression ratios used in automotive diesels run any-where from 16:1 to 23:1. A typical spark-ignition engine has a ratio of about 8:1. This is why a spark-ignition engine which continues to run after you have shut off the engine is said to be "dieseling". It is running on combustion chamber heat alone.

Designing an engine to ignite on its own combustion chamber heat poses certain problems. For instance, although a diesel engine has no need for a coil, spark plugs, or a distributor, it does need what are known as "glow plugs". These superficially resemble spark plugs, but are only used to warm the combustion chambers when the engine is cold. Without these plugs, cold starting would be impossible, due to the enormously high compression ratios and the characteristics of the diesel fuel itself.

All diesel engines use fuel injection, be-

4-stroke diesel engine cycle. At *air intake* (1), rotation of the crankshaft drives a toothed belt that turns the camshaft, opening the intake valve. As the piston moves down, a vacuum is created, sucking fresh air into the cylinder, past the open intake valve. *Air compression* (2): As the piston moves up, both valves are closed, and the air is compressed about 23 times smaller than its original volume. The compressed air reaches a temperature of about 1,650°F., far above the temperature needed to ignite diesel fuel. *Fuel injection and compression* (3): As the piston reaches the top of the stroke, the air temperature is at its maximum. A fine mist of fuel is sprayed into the prechamber, where it ignites, and the flame front spreads rapidly into the combustion chamber. The piston is forced downward by the pressure (about 500 psi) of expanding gases. *Exhaust* (4): As the energy of combustion is spent and the piston begins to move upward again, the exhaust valve opens, and burnt gases are forced out past the open valve. As the piston starts down, the exhaust valve closes, the intake valve opens, and the air intake stroke begins again.

Increasingly, modern diesel engines are being equipped with turbochargers, exhaust gas–driven devices that force more air into the engine to increase power output

Maintenance and Service Procedures

Maintenance procedures for the diesel engine generally fall into three categories:

1. Fuel system
2. Starting system
3. Engine mechanical systems

Of these, the fuel system is usually the most likely source of engine troubles, and should be high on the list for regular maintenance attention.

FUEL SYSTEM

The typical diesel engine fuel system consists of fuel tank, fuel feed and return lines, mechanical fuel injection pump, fuel injectors and lines, and a large capacity fuel filter. On some models, the engine may also be equipped with a small, low pressure fuel pump which feeds the injection pump.

In addition to these, the air intake system (air cleaner, inlet manifold) should be checked over regularly to insure unrestricted air flow into the cylinders.

In operation, fuel is sucked out of the fuel tank by the injection pump (or its feed pump) and fed by the injection pump to the injectors in the cylinder head at a very high pressure. Before the fuel is allowed to enter the main injection pump, it passes through a specially built fuel filter which traps solid particles (and water on some models) in the fuel. Fuel that is not used is pumped back to the fuel tank through the fuel return lines. This recirculated fuel helps cool the injection pump.

Cutaway view of typical 4-cylinder diesel engine.

cause unlike spark-ignited engines, the fuel cannot be drawn through the intake tract and into the cylinders. The introduction of fuel into a diesel engine must be precisely timed so that each cylinder "fires" at the proper moment. Also, the fuel injection pressure (at the cylinder) must be great enough to overcome the high compression pressures, and properly atomize the fuel without the aid of a moving air mass (as in a carbureted gas engine). It is not uncommon for diesel engine fuel injection pressures to be set at 1500–1700 psi.

Diesel engines share many of their basic mechanical components with gasoline engines, though the cylinder block, head(s), crankshaft, connecting rods, pistons, etc., are manufactured to be much stronger for use in diesel engines. The additional strength of the components is necessary due to the very high cylinder pressure generated within the diesel engine.

Air Cleaner

On a gasoline engine, the volume of air taken in by the engine is controlled by throttle valves. When the throttle valves are closed (engine idling), air intake is restricted. When the throttle valves are wide open (accelerator pedal to the floor), the engine draws

Typical diesel engine fuel system schematic.

Because a greater quantity of air passes through the diesel engine, air filter maintenance is particularly important. Most diesel air filters on passenger cars are similar to their counterparts on gasoline engines.

in the maximum amount of air it possibly can. This applies to both carbureted and fuel injected gasoline engines.

The speed (rpm) of a diesel engine is controlled by the quantity of fuel which is injected into the engine; no air metering restrictions (throttle valves) are used. Because of this, diesel engines ingest as much air as they possibly can under all conditions. A much greater volume of air passes through the air cleaner of a diesel per mile, therefore, diesel air filters must either be larger or the filter replacement intervals more frequent than those of a similarly sized gasoline engine.

One word of caution: never remove the air cleaner on a diesel with the engine running, and never run the engine with the air cleaner removed. The volume of air drawn through the inlet manifold is very great, and, because the inlet manifold is unobstructed, anything drawn into the inlet manifold (air cleaner wing nut, etc.) goes straight to the combustion chambers, where it can cause major engine damage.

Fuel Filter

The diesel engine fuel filter is usually larger than the filter used on gasoline engines. The extra capacity is needed to trap the suspended particles in diesel fuel, which is generally ''dirtier'' than gasoline.

Many diesel engines use a spin-on type primary fuel filter.

On some engines, the fuel filter looks like a second engine oil filter, and is removed and installed in the same manner as the canister-type oil filter.

The fuel filter must be changed according to the manufacturer's suggested interval. See the owner's manual for information.

After installing the fuel filter start the engine and check for leaks. Run the engine for about two minutes, then stop the engine for the same amount of time to allow any air trapped in the injection system to bleed off.

Many diesels also have a small, in-tank filter which is usually maintenance-free.

A smaller, in-line secondary filter is used on many engines.

Check the tightness of the clamps securing the injector lines. Note that the injector lines are all the same length.

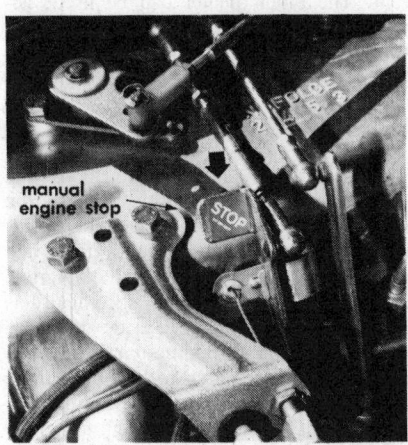

manual engine stop

Mercedes-Benz diesel engines use this stop switch, which shuts off fuel delivery

Water In Fuel

Diesel fuel is a hydrophilic fluid, that is, it naturally attracts water. Since diesel fuel and water do not mix, the water remains floating beneath the fuel at the bottom of the tank. This water must be removed every now and then, or it will be sucked into the fuel circuit and pass through the injection system, causing corrosion and possible component failure (injection pumps can cost up to $1,000). Water in the fuel system will also cause the engine to run poorly, if at all.

Most diesel fuel tanks are equipped with

a separator which can isolate from 1 to 3 gallons of water from the fuel.

Many diesels are also equipped with ''Water in Fuel'' lights in the dashboard which warn of the presence of water in the fuel tank. These warning systems can be installed on models not so equipped.

On some diesels, there is a water catcher in the bottom of the fuel filter which can easily be bled off. In addition, there are several bolt-on water filters on the market which attach to the fuel line under the hood and separate water from the fuel. Depending on which kind you buy, draining water from the system is simply a matter of opening the petcock at the bottom of the filter and letting the water drain out, or, if money is no object, a separator is available on which water is drained from the filter simply by activating a switch on the dashboard.

Removing Water from the Fuel Tank

Treat diesel fuel with the same respect you would gasoline, and after the procedure, properly dispose of the fuel.

1. Remove the fuel tank cap.
2. Connect a pump or siphon hose to the 1/4 in. fuel return hose (smaller of the two fuel hoses) above the rear axle, or under the hood near the fuel pump (on the passenger's side of the engine, near the front).
3. Siphon until all water is removed from the tank. Do not use your mouth to create siphon vacuum, EVER! The best method is to siphon the water into a large capacity see-through container. The water will collect at the bottom of the container.
4. When all water has been removed from the tank, be sure to reinstall the fuel return hose and fuel cap.

NOTE: If the entire fuel system (not just the tank) is contaminated by water, the vehicle must be stopped immediately and the fuel system must be purged. This includes draining and removing the fuel tank, blowing low pressure compressed air backwards through the fuel feed and return lines, and bleeding the water out of all injection components. This job should be referred to a qualified technician.

Cold Weather Fuel System Maintenance

————— **CAUTION** —————
NEVER use ''starting aids'' (e.g.—ether) to help start a diesel engine—serious engine damage will result.

As will be explained later under ''Fuel Recommendations'', diesel fuel tends to become ''cloudy'', or thicker, as the temperature drops. The thicker the diesel fuel becomes, the slower it flows through the fuel system, until finally it stops flowing altogether somewhere near the bottom of the thermometer.

One way to fight sluggish fuel flow is to use winterized blends of diesel fuel, straight No. 1 diesel fuel or add cold weather additives to the fuel to improve flow in cold weather.

NOTE: Consult your owners manual for recommendations and be sure to use a fuel conditioner compatible with water separators.

Another way is to install an aftermarket fuel system pre-heater. These are generally canisters which connect into the fuel line and use coolant from the engine cooling system to heat the fuel before it reaches the injection pump. The one drawback with this system is the engine must be started before the pre-heater begins to work. Also available are electric fuel warmers. These preheat the fuel going into the filter and can be used in conjunction with the coolant-type fuel heater.

Cold weather additives and fuel conditioners can help improve cold weather flow of diesel fuel.

Some manufacturers offer an optional electric diesel fuel heater and engine block heaters. The fuel heater is thermostatically controlled to heat the fuel before it enters the fuel filter when fuel temperature is 20°F or lower. The fuel heater works only when the ignition key is in the RUN position. On these models, the fuel tank filter has a by-pass valve which allows fuel to flow to the heater when the tank filter is covered with fuel wax. The engine block heater is equipped with an electrical cord wrapped up in the engine compartment. The cord

Some diesel engines come equipped with a built-in heating system to keep the engine warm in cold temperatures.

Most OEM heaters work from 110-volt house current.

Some aftermarket diesel fuel warmers are thermostatically controlled heat exchangers that use engine coolant to keep diesel fuel above its "cloud point," the temperature at which it gels and forms wax that can clog a fuel system.

plugs into regular 110 volt household current. The block heater can be used, according to the type of oil in the crankcase, up to eight hours or overnight to warm up the block.

STARTING SYSTEM

The diesel starting system includes one (sometimes two) heavy duty batteries, the starter, and the glow plug circuit. In addition to the heavy duty battery(ies), the majority of diesel engines also have starters and battery cables designed specifically as heavy duty items for diesel usage only. Because of the high compression of any diesel, the torque required to turn the engine is much greater than a gasoline engine. The starter must be powerful enough to handle the increased load; the battery cables must be thick enough to withstand the heat generated by the starter load.

For battery maintenance, see the regular "Maintenance" section. Jump starting procedures for a dual battery car are given below. Starter maintenance is included in the appropriate car section.

The glow plug circuit is used on the diesel to initially start the engine. When the ignition switch is turned to the ON position, a light will come on in the instrument panel signalling that the glow plugs are preheating the combustion chambers. After a certain interval (depending on how cold the engine is), the light will go off. This signals that the starter may be engaged and the engine started. If the glow plug circuit mal-

functions, especially in cold weather, the engine will be almost impossible to start.

------ **CAUTION** ------
NEVER use "starting aids" (e.g.—ether) to help start a diesel engine—serious engine damage will result.

Glow Plug Testing

To test each individual glow plug, disconnect the busbar and/or wire connector from the glow plug and connect a test light between the glow plug terminal and the positive battery terminal. If the test light lights, the glow plug is working. Replace individual glow plugs which do not work.

NOTE: Some diesel engines are equipped with either "slow glow" or "fast glow" glow plugs. Do not attempt to interchange any parts of these two glow plug systems.

To test the glow plug circuit, connect a test light to the terminal of one of the glow plugs (glow plug wiring still attached) and turn the ignition to the heating position. The test light should light for a short while. If not, the glow plug circuit is malfunctioning and must be diagnosed and repaired.

NOTE: Perform this operation on a cold engine only.

Jump-Starting a Dual Battery Diesel

Some diesels are equipped with two 12 volt batteries. The batteries are connected in parallel circuit (positive terminal to positive terminal, negative terminal to negative terminal). Hooking the batteries up in parallel circuit increases battery cranking power without increasing total battery voltage output (12 volts). On the other hand, hooking two 12 volt batteries up in a series circuit (positive terminal to negative terminal, positive terminal to negative terminal) increases total battery output to 24 volts (12 volts + 12 volts).

------ **CAUTION** ------
NEVER hook the batteries up in a series circuit; SEVERE electrical system damage will result.

In the event that a dual battery diesel must be jumped started, use the following procedure.

1. Open the hood and locate the batteries.

2. Position the donor car so that the jumper cables will reach from its battery (must be 12 volt, negative ground) to the appropriate battery in the diesel. Do not allow the cars to touch.

3. Shut off all electrical equipment on both vehicles. Turn off the engine of the donor car, set the parking brakes on both vehicles and block the wheels. Also, make sure both vehicles are in Neutral (manual

transmission models) or Park (automatic transmission models).

4. Using the jumper cables, connect the positive (+) terminal of the donor car battery to the positive terminal of one (not both) of the diesel batteries.

5. Using the second jumper cable, connect the negative (−) terminal of the donor battery to a solid, stationary, metallic point on the diesel (alternator bracket, engine block, etc.). Be very careful to keep the jumper cables away from moving parts (cooling fan, alternator belt, etc.) on both vehicles.

6. Start the engine of the donor car and run it at moderate speed.

7. Start the engine of the diesel.

8. When the diesel starts, disconnect the battery cables in the reverse order of attachment.

ENGINE MECHANICAL SYSTEMS

Included are engine lubrication and engine compression.

Although diesel engines are very low in carbon monoxide (CO) and hydrocarbon (HC) emissions, ''particulate'' emission output is very high from diesel engines. This is evident from the black smoke emitted by diesels, which is most noticeable during hard acceleration or high engine loads. The particulates are made up of mostly soot (carbon) and sulpher particles. The majority of these particulates are released into the atmosphere. However, some of the particulate matter, because it is produced within the engines cylinders, is left inside the engine and gradually contaminates the engine oil. This contamination makes the oil corrosive, due to the sulpher, and abrasive, due to the carbon. Serious engine damage will result if these contaminants continue to accumulate in the oil. Engine oil and filters of diesel engines must be changed more frequently than those of gasoline engines, due to the increased rate at which the contaminants form in the diesel. Consult the ''Maintenance'' section for oil and filter change procedures. The manufacturer's recommended oil change interval will be given in the owner's manual. An explanation of diesel engine oils is given at the end of this section.

As explained earlier, very high cylinder compression is the key to the operation of the diesel engine. The normal compression of most gasoline engines will rarely exceed 180 psi; whereas with diesel engines, compression pressures of 350–400 psi are commonplace.

——— CAUTION ———

DO NOT attempt to check the compression of a diesel engine with a standard compression gauge—personal injury could result. A special, high pressure compression gauge is needed to safely check the compression of any diesel.

A diesel compression tester kit with adaptors (Courtesy S & G Tools)

Compression Test

1. Remove the air cleaner.

2. Disconnect the wire from the fuel shutoff solenoid terminal of the injection pump.

3. Disconnect the wires from the glow plugs and remove all glow plugs.

4. Screw compression gauge into the glow plug hole in the cylinder being checked.

5. Crank the engine, allowing six ''puffs'' for each cylinder.

The lowest reading cylinder should not be less than 70% of the highest, and no cylinder should be less than 275 pounds.

Idle Speed Adjustments

Idle speed adjustment procedures for individual diesel engines are given in the car section. Consult the following section for procedures to measure idle speed

Connecting a Tachometer to a Diesel Engine

As mentioned earlier, the diesel engine does not require an electrical ignition system. Because of this, problems arise when attempts are made to connect a tachometer to the engine for the purpose of idle adjustments, etc. The average gasoline engine tachometer senses the ignition spark pulses and converts them into a readable engine rpm signal. This type of tachometer is use-

less on the diesel engine, because of the diesel's compression ignition system.

There are several magnetic and photoelectric tachometers available from various tool manufacturers which were designed specifically for use with the diesel engine. These units can run into a little more money than the average do-it-yourselfer may be willing to spend, in which case any adjustments requiring the monitoring of engine rpm should be performed by a competent service technician.

The newest equipment for measuring idle speed on a diesel engine includes (clockwise from lower left) a digital diesel tach display, photomagnetic pick-up with display input, magnetic swivel base (holder), DC power source for the display unit and a roll of magnetic tape.

The magnetic tape is attached to any moving part (such as the balancer). The pieces of tape must be at least 6 inches apart. Aim the photomagnetic pick-up at the moving object and adjust the position of the pick-up until the "on-target" light is lit. Flip the switch to TACH and read the rpm.

Diesel Engine Precautions

• Never run the engine with the air cleaner removed: if anything is sucked into the inlet manifold it will go straight to the combustion chambers, or jam behind a valve.

• Never wash a diesel engine: the reaction of a warm fuel injection pump to cold (or even warm) water can ruin the pump.

• Never operate a diesel engine with one or more fuel injectors removed unless fully familiar with injector testing procedures: some diesel injection pumps spray fuel at up to 1400 psi—enough pressure to allow the fuel to penetrate your skin.

• Do not skip engine oil and filter changes.

• Strictly follow the manufacturer's oil and fuel recommendations as given in the owner's manual.

• Do not use home heating oil as fuel for your diesel.

• Do not use "starting aids" (e.g.—ether) in the automotive diesel engine, as these "aids" can cause severe internal engine damage.

• Do not run a diesel engine with the "Water in Fuel" warning light on in the dashboard.

• If removing water from the fuel tank yourself, use the same caution you would use when working around gasoline engine fuel components.

• Do not allow diesel fuel to come in contact with rubber hoses or components on the engine, as it can damage them.

Fuel and Oil Recommendations

FUEL

Fuel makers produce two grades of diesel fuel, No. 1 and No. 2, for use in automotive diesel engines. Generally speaking, No. 2 fuel is recommended over No. 1 for driving

in temperatures above 20°F. In fact, in many areas, No. 2 diesel is the only fuel available. By comparison, No. 2 diesel fuel is less volatile than No. 1 fuel, and gives better fuel economy. No. 2 fuel is also a better injection pump lubricant.

Two important characteristics of diesel fuel are its cetane number and its viscosity.

The cetane number of a diesel fuel refers to the ease with which a diesel fuel ignites. High cetane numbers mean that the fuel will ignite with relative ease or that it ignites well at low temperatures. Naturally, the lower the cetane number, the higher the temperature must be to ignite the fuel. Most commercial fuels have cetane numbers that range from 35 to 65. No. 1 diesel fuel generally has a higher cetane rating than No. 2 fuel.

Cetane (diesel engine) versus octane (gasoline engine) ratings. The higher the cetane number, the faster the fuel burns

Viscosity is the ability of a liquid, in this case diesel fuel, to flow. Using straight No. 2 diesel fuel below 20°F can cause problems, because this fuel tends to become cloudy, meaning wax crystals begin forming in the fuel. In extreme cold weather, No. 2 fuel can stop flowing altogether. In either case, fuel flow is restricted, which can result in a "no start" condition or poor engine performance. Fuel manufacturers often "winterize" No. 2 diesel fuel by using various fuel additives and blends (No. 1 diesel fuel, kerosene, etc.) to lower its winter-time viscosity. Generally speaking, though, No. 1 diesel fuel is more satisfactory in extremely cold weather.

NOTE: No. 1 and No. 2 diesel fuels will mix and burn with no ill effects, although the engine manufacturer will undoubtedly recommend one or the other. Consult the owner's manual for information.

Depending on local climate, most fuel manufacturers make winterized No. 2 fuel available seasonally.

Many automobile manufacturers publish pamphlets giving the locations of diesel fuel stations nationwide. Contact the local dealer for information.

Do not substitute home heating oil for automotive diesel fuel. While in some cases, home heating oil refinement levels equal those of diesel fuel, many times they are far below diesel engine requirements. The result of using "dirty" home heating oil will be a clogged fuel system, in which case the entire system may have to be dismantled and cleaned.

One more word on diesel fuels. Don't thin diesel fuel with gasoline in cold weather. The lighter gasoline, which is more explosive, will cause rough running at the very least, and may cause extensive engine damage if enough is used.

OIL

Diesel engines require different engine oil from those used in gasoline engines. Besides doing the things gasoline engine oil does, diesel oil must also deal with increased engine heat and the diesel blow-by gases, which create sulphuric acid, a high corrosive.

Under the American Petroleum Institute (API) classifications, gasoline engine oil codes begin with an "S", and diesel engine oil codes begin with a "C". This first letter designation is followed by a second letter code which explains what type of service (heavy, moderate, light) the oil is meant for. For example, the top of a typical oil can will include: "API SERVICES SC, SD, SE, CA, CB, CC". This means the oil in the can is a good, moderate duty engine oil when used in a diesel engine.

It should be noted here that the further

COMPARISON OF #1 AND #2 DIESEL FUEL

Requirement	1-D	2-D
Flash Point, °F minimum	100	125
Cetane Number, minimum	40	40
Viscosity at 100°F, Centistokes		
Minimum	1.4	2.0
Maximum	2.5	4.3
Water and Sediment, % by volume maximum	Trace	0.05
Sulfur, % by weight maximum	0.5	0.5
Ash, % by weight maximum	0.01	0.01

Flash Point: The temperature at which diesel fuel ignites when exposed to a flame *in the open air.*

Cetane Number: See text

down the alphabet the second letter of the API classification is, the greater the oil's protective qualities are (CD is the severest duty diesel engine oil, CA is the lightest duty oil, etc.). The same is true for gasoline engine oil classifications (SF is the severest duty gasoline engine oil, SA is the lightest duty oil, etc.).

Many diesel manufacturers recommend an oil with both gasoline and diesel engine API classifications. Consult the owner's manual for specifications.

The top of the oil can will also contain an SAE (Society of Automotive Engineers) designation, which gives the oil's viscosity. A typical designation will be: SAE 10W-30, which means the oil is a "winter" viscosity oil, meaning it will flow and give protection at low temperatures.

On the diesel engine, oil viscosity is critical, because the diesel is much harder to start (due to its higher compression) than a gasoline engine. Obviously, if you fill the crankcase with a very heavy oil during winter (SAE 20W-50, for example), the starter is going to require a lot of current from the battery to turn the engine. And, since batteries don't function well in cold weather in the first place, you may find yourself stranded some morning. Consult the owner's manual for recommended oil specifications for the climate you live in.

LUBE OIL ANALYSIS

From an oil sample a laboratory can diagnose many potential engine problems—from piston wear to impending bearing failure. What's more, the laboratory can spot them quicker, and with greater accuracy. Just as easily, the lab can give the diesel a clean bill of health, saving the car owner unnecessary servicing and other routine preventive maintenance, costly in time and money.

There's nothing new about engine lube oil analysis. Thousands of the nation's trucks and buses regularly have their engine's lube oil analyzed by laboratories specializing in this type of work. What is new is the availability of lube oil analysis to individual vehicle owners rather than, as before, almost exclusively to companies operating fleets of diesel equipment.

Lube oil analysis can be a valuable indicator of internal engine condition.

Here's how lube oil analysis works. You write one of the several laboratories that offer individual diesel vehicle owners lube analysis service. By return mail you'll receive an oil sampling kit. It will probably contain a two-ounce plastic oil sampling container with a screw-on plastic top. Instructions tell you how to take the sample. Usually, a lab-bound sample of diesel lube oil may be taken in any of three ways, but always right after the engine has been shut off, so that the sampled oil is as close as possible to normal engine operating temperature. That's important to assure that the lab's test will be accurate. Oil samples can be taken during normal oil changes, when lube oil is drained anyway. Between oil changes, a sample can be drawn from the engine through the dipstick tube (where you normally check the oil's level). In drawing an oil sample from the dipstick tube, a small suction bulb fitted with a length of disposable tubing is used. The tubing is merely inserted into the dipstick tube, the suction bulb depressed, and the oil sample drawn. The third method of sampling is by loosening the drain plug on the engine's bypass oil filter (if your diesel has one). A little oil is caught in the lube sampling container. In all cases, extreme cleanliness is a must, so as not to contaminate the sample with dirt, grease, or other substances not actually found inside the engine. For example, using a rag that contains solvents, metal filings, or other impurities can contaminate the oil sample, leading to false and even alarming lab reports. A bit of technique is required: In taking a sample of lube oil during a routine oil drain, about half of the crankcase's lube oil should be allowed to drain out before the sample is taken. The sample taken, the date, make and model of the engine, its mileage, mileage since last oil change, and sometimes oil type are noted on the container's label, and the container is mailed to the laboratory.

Shortly, you'll receive the lab's report, which, based on a number of tests, including spectrochemical analysis (using a spectrometer, which can detect the presence of virtually all basic elements and contaminants), tells what's in the oil in what quantities and analyzes both the probable source of what was found and whether it indicates trouble. For one example, the finding of more than trace amounts of copper in an oil sample may strongly point to excessive bearing wear in a particular diesel whose bearings contain copper. Some analyses report on as many as eighteen basic elements that may be found in a diesel's lube oil sample, and in the report's "recommendation" may pinpoint their probable source—as, "indicates piston ring wear." Also indicated is the presence of such contaminants as water, solids (the products of oxidation and engine blow-by), and fuel dilution. Noted, too, is the lubricity of the sample—whether, or not, in the lab's opinion, it is still doing its internal engine lubricating job.

NOTE: Never use lube analysis and a lab's report of "good oil" to extend, beyond the manufacturer's recommendation, the mileage period between oil changes. Follow the manufacturers recommendations.

The more frequently an engine is lube-sampled, the more accurate and meaningful the lab's reports. Infrequent samplings, although they can spot sudden, unusual changes in internal engine condition, may fail to show the gradual deterioration of engine parts. Ideally, you should have the laboratory analyze a lube sample every other oil change. For most automobile diesels, that's every 6,000 miles. Analysis costs from $7 to $11 per sample. Drive an average 18,000 miles a year and you'd change your diesel's oil three times. In that time, you'd submit three samples to the lab at an annual lube analysis cost of $21 to $33.

Aftermarket Fuel System Accessories

Due to reasons described previously, most diesel engine problems can be attributed to either fuel contamination or cold weather fuel performance characteristics. Diesel-engined vehicle manufacturers have designed and installed various systems to combat these problems, but ultimately, their best efforts are limited by cost.

Inconvenience is a major concern to diesel owners. If water accumulates (in substantial quantities) in the diesel fuel system, the fuel and water must be siphoned from the fuel tank and purged from the remainder of the fuel system. It goes without saying that this operation is a messy, time-consuming process. Even if the vehicle is equipped with a water/fuel separator having a drain valve, the owner must manually open the valve from either under the hood or beneath the vehicle.

Although the fuel filter installed by the manufacturer offers adequate performance when maintained properly, the addition of another, separate diesel fuel filter is a wise improvement.

If you live in an extremely cold climate, you've probably experienced cold starting problems due to fuel "waxing", plugged filters, "gelled" fuel, etc. If your vehicle is not factory-equipped with the optional fuel line or cylinder block heaters, these

Aftermarket fuel filter/water separator and fuel line heater

heaters can be purchased from the after-market (retail auto parts manufacturers). The installation of either of these items can improve cold-starting dramatically.

WATER/FUEL SEPARATORS

Centrifugal Action

Sometimes referred to as a "cyclonic" water/fuel separator, this device uses baffles which spin the fuel as it comes through the separator inlet. Since water is heavier than diesel fuel, the water will spin away from the fuel, sink to the bottom of the separator, and collect in the sediment bowl.

This type of separator is most efficient in dealing with large water droplets. If the water is in emulsion with the fuel, that is, if the water is equally dispersed through the fuel in very small droplets, some of the water will remain with the fuel to travel through the fuel system.

Coalescing Action

In this type of separator, the fuel must pass through a coalescent filtering media before proceeding through the fuel system. The idea behind the coalescent media is to trap even the smallest droplets of water on the media. As the small droplets combine into larger, heavier droplets, gravity acts on the droplets to pull them downward, off of the media and into the sediment bowl.

FUEL FILTER/SEPARATOR COMBINATION UNITS

Most separators of either the centrifugal or coalescent types are available with disposeable fuel filtering elements which are built into the separator unit. If your car already has a large, disposeable filter, it would probably be more cost-effective to stay with a separator only, and to change the factory-equipped filter at the recommended intervals. Should your vehicle have a fairly small filter, and/or an inconveniently located water drain (or none at all), choose the filter/separator combination. The filter/separator offers both increased fuel filtering ability and efficient water separation.

Convenience Add-Ons

Available with many separators and filter/separators are items such as dash-mounted water-in-fuel indicator lamps, audible water-in-fuel alarms, and dash-controlled water ejection systems. A properly chosen system would warn you of water in the fuel, and allow you to eject the water by simply "flipping" a dash-mounted switch.

Installing a Separator

Clear installation instructions and the necessary installation parts will be provided with the separator kit. Follow those instructions exactly. A general list of suggestions follows:

1. Fuel additives should not be used unless approved by the separator manufacturer.

2. Do not install a separator within 4″ of any exhaust system component.

3. If plastic fittings are supplied with the kit, do not replace them with metal fittings. Also, use extreme caution when tightening the fittings, especially those made of plastic.

4. Use a fuel-proof sealer on all fitting threads, only if the threads are not factory-coated with sealer.

5. Use only fuel-proof hoses for the installation.

6. Do not eliminate the original equipment fuel filter, even if a filter/separator is installed.

7. For new car warranty purposes, a filter/separator should be located BEFORE the original equipment filter. The fuel must pass through the original filter last, before entering the fuel injection pump.

8. If any type of fuel line heater is installed, it is best to position the heater between the fuel tank and the separator inlet.

9. To ease the job of the separator, the separator should be installed between the fuel transfer pump and the tank (unless the separator manufacturer specifies otherwise). Fuel and water which have been churned through the fuel transfer pump will be more difficult to separate.

10. Be sure that any wiring (for warning lamps, water ejection, etc.) is routed and connected properly. If the wiring must pass through a drilled hole, be sure to use a rubber grommet between the drilled component(s) and the wire to prevent damage to the wire.

FUEL LINE HEATERS

Two popular types of fuel line heaters are available for diesel passenger cars. Both types raise the temperature of the fuel to prevent "waxing" and "gelling" of the fuel in the lines during cold weather operation. One type uses engine coolant as a heating source. In order for this type to heat the fuel, the engine must first be started and allowed to run until the coolant temperature increases. Though this type of heater will usually increase fuel mileage, it offers no aid in starting ability.

The other type of heater uses a 12V DC electric heating element. This type is recommended, due to its ability to warm the fuel BEFORE the engine is started. This type of heater will also usually increase the overall fuel mileage.

Installation

Follow the manufacturer's instructions exactly. Also, see suggestions 5, 8, and 9 under "Separator Installation".

CYLINDER BLOCK HEATERS

A cylinder block heater electrically (usually 110V house current) heats the engine coolant, which in turn warms the cylinder block, heads, and engine oil. In this case, the warmth is not used to alter the characteristics of the fuel. Block heaters offer two main advantages when starting a diesel in cold weather:

1. The reduced viscosity (thinning) of the engine oil from the warmth allows the engine to be "turned over" easier (and faster) by the starter. Less strain is imposed on the starting system.

2. Because the diesel relies on the heat of compression to ignite the fuel, the increase in the base combustion chamber temperature results in a higher tempearture during compression. This allows the fuel to ignite easier than if just the glow plugs were used.

Installation

Most cylinder block heaters replace one of the existing freeze (or expansion) plugs of the cylinder block. Follow the manufacturers installation instructions exactly. Also, refer to the manufacturers recommendations for usage.

Air Conditioning

AIR CONDITIONING SYSTEMS

Automotive air conditioning systems are basic in design and operation, but many different components are used by the vehicle manufacturers to operate and control the systems to their specifications.

Basic System

The basic air conditioning system utilizes the compressor, condenser, evaporator, receiver-drier, expansion valve and a thermostatic or ambient type switch to control evaporator freeze-up. The controls are manually operated and the unit is basic in design. This system is usually installed as an add-on or after-market unit. A sight glass may be used in the system.

P.O.A. System

The P.O.A. (pilot operated absolute) suction throttling valve system contains the compressor, condenser, evaporator, receiver-drier, expansion valve and a suction throttling valve. The suction throttling valve is used to keep the refrigerant gas in the evaporator at a pressure which will not allow the temperature of the evaporator core surface to go below 32 degrees F., thus preventing evaporator freeze-up. For the system to operate effectively, an equalizer line is connected between the suction side of the suction throttling valve and the expansion valve diaphragm. This modifies the operation of the expansion valve which now is controlled by the evaporator outlet temperature and compression suction pressure.

When a crank type compressor is used with the P.O.A. system, an accumulator is placed between the evaporator and the compressor. The accumulator operates as its name implies, accumulating any liquid refrigerant that may have passed from the evaporator and to prevent its moving to the compressor as a liquid, which may, in its form, cause internal compressor damage. A sight glass is normally used in this system.

V.I.R. System

The V.I.R. system contains the compressor, evaporator, condenser, muffler and a unit containing the P.O.A. valve, expansion valve and the receiver-drier. This unit is called the V.I.R. (valves in receiver) assembly. A muffler is normally used with this system and is located between the com-

Basic air conditioning system

Pilot Operated Absolute (POA) system

LOW PRESSURE GAS

LOW PRESSURE LIQUID

HIGH PRESSURE LIQUID

HIGH PRESSURE GAS

SUPERHEATED GAS

HIGH PRESSURE VAPOR

HIGH PRESSURE LIQUID

LOW PRESSURE LIQUID

LOW PRESSURE VAPOR

Valves In Receiver (VIR) system

pressor and the condenser, to absorb the compressor pulsations.

The V.I.R. assembly eliminates the outside equalizer line between the outlet of the P.O.A. valve and the expansion valve. The equalizer is now a drilled orifice in the wall between the P.O.A. valve and the expansion valve cavities of the V.I.R. housing. Should the valve prove defective during tests, the unit should be replaced, as it is not repairable or adjustable. A sight glass is normally used with this system.

E.P.R. System

The E.P.R. (evaporator pressure regulator)

system includes the condenser, muffler, low pressure shut off valve, receiver-drier, expansion valve, evaporator and a V-block, reciprocating crank type compressor. The E.P.R. valve is mounted on the suction side of the compressor and operates in conjunction with the expansion valve assembly, to regulate the flow of refrigerant from the evaporator to the compressor, under light air conditioning loads. By regulating the refrigerant flow, the evaporator temperature is controlled and freezing of the evaporator is prevented.

In contrast to other systems, the E.P.R. system uses the reheat procedure to control the temperature of the air, after it is cooled by passing through the evaporator fins. A

manually controlled operating lever is connected to the heater water flow control valve and to a blend air door and the opening of the blend door proportions the amount of air around and through the heater core to control the mix of the cool and hot air for the desired inside temperature. A sight glass is used with this system.

Two types of expansion valves are used with this system. The first type has a capillary tube, mounted in a well on the suction line. The second type has no capillary tube, but senses the need to meter refrigerant into the evaporator by an internal sensing tube. This type of expansion valve is called the "H" type.

"H" Valve System

As was described in the E.P.R. system, the "H" expansion valve can be used with the E.P.R. valve, located in the V-block, reciprocating crank type compressor, to control the amount of refrigerant metered into the evaporator and to control the temperature of the evaporator coils to prevent freeze-up of the condensed moisture. However, when the "H" valve is used with the three piston, axial compressor, a cycling switch is used to control the temperature of the evaporator to prevent freeze-up, rather than the E.P.R. valve, as used with the reciprocating crank type compressor. This can be called the "H" valve system for explanation purposes only and should be recognized as such. The "H" system uses the same components as the other systems, basically the compressor (axial type), condenser, evaporator, expansion valve without a capillary tub ("H" type), receiver-drier, muffler and a low pressure shut off valve. The cycling clutch switch uses a capillary tube, attached to the surface of the suction line, to sense the need for refrigerant movement and compressor operation, therefore, causing the electrical clutch pulley and coil to operate the compressor on demand from the cycling switch and to open the circuit to the coil when the demand is not needed. A sight glass is used with this system.

CCOT System

The CCOT (cycling clutch orifice tube) system includes the compressor, condenser, evaporator, an accumulator-drier, a clutch cycling switch with a capillary tube, and a fixed orifice tube, mounted to the evaporator, replacing the expansion valve.

The clutch cycling switch with a temperature probing capillary tube, cycles the compressor clutch off and on as required to maintain a selected comfortable temperature within the vehicle, while preventing evaporator freeze-up. Full control of the system is maintained through the use of a selector control, mounted in the dash assembly. The selector control makes use of

Evaporator Pressure Regulator (EPR) system

H type expansion valve system

Evaporator pressure can only be measured on this system and a special type connector must be used to attach the high pressure gauge line to the service gauge port.

When either of the external type expansion valves are used, separate suction throttling valves are used. The operation of each is basically the same as the components of the combination valve assembly.

The type of external expansion valve used with the system will dictate either low suction or evaporator pressure measurements from the gauge service ports. To determine the pressure measurement that may be obtained from the system, examine the external expansion valve for one of the following conditions:

a. Should the expansion valve have one capillary tube and one equalizer line, it is of the conventional externally equalizer type and low pressure suction would be measured at the service port, normally located on the suction line. A second gauge port may be located on the POA valve body and an evaporator pressure reading can be obtained from this port.

b. If the expansion valve has only one capillary tube, it is the by-pass orifice (BPO) type and only evaporator pressure will be measured at the service port valve, located on the STV assembly.

GENERAL SERVICING PROCEDURES

The most important aspect of air conditioning service is the maintenance of a pure and adequate charge of refrigerant in the system. A refrigeration system cannot function properly if a significant percentage of the charge is lost. Leaks are common because the severe vibration encountered in an automobile can easily cause a sufficient cracking or loosening of the air conditioning fittings; as a result, the extreme operating pressures of the system force refrigerant out.

The problem can be understood by considering what happens to the system as it is operated with a continuous leak. Because the expansion valve regulates the flow of refrigerant to the evaporator, the level of refrigerant there is fairly constant. The receiver-drier stores any excess of refrigerant, and so a loss will first appear there as a reduction in the level of liquid. As this level nears the bottom of the vessel, some refrigerant vapor bubbles will begin to appear in the stream of liquid supplied to the expansion valve. This vapor decreases the capacity of the expansion valve very little as the valve opens to compensate for its presence. As the quantity of liquid in the

a vacuum supply and electrical switches to operate mode doors and the blower motor. A sight glass is not used in this system and one should not be installed. When charging the system, the correct quantity of refrigerant must be installed by measurement.

STV/BPO System

The STV/BPO (suction throttling valve/by-pass orifice) system uses either two types of external expansion valves or a mini-combination valve assembly. The mini-combination valve assembly contains an expansion valve, suction throttling valve and a service port. The expansion valve is of the "H" block design and is used to regulate the flow of refrigerant into the evap-

orator core. It is also the dividing point for the high and low pressure within the system. The suction throttling valve is used to control the evaporator pressure and to prevent coil freeze-up. The suction throttling starts when the compressor suction pressure decreases below the valve setting. The compressor suction pressure can continue to drop, but the evaporator pressure is held steady by the controlling or throttling action of the STV. A pressure differential valve is used within the combination valve assembly, to allow oil laden refrigerant to by-pass the restriction formed when the STV assembly is closed, to assure oil return to the compressor during times of reduced heat loads on the system. The by-pass valve remains closed under high heat loads since ample oil is moving through the system and compressor.

Cycling Clutch Orifice Tube (CCOT) system

Suction Throttling Valve/By-Pass Orifice (STV/BPO) system

system and mix with the R-12 and the oil. Trace amounts of moisture will cause sludging of the oil, and corrosion of the system. Saturation and clogging of the filter-drier, and freezing of the expansion valve orifice will eventually result. As air fills the system to a greater and greater extent, it will interfere more and more with the normal flows of refrigerant and heat.

From this description, it should be obvious that much of the repairman's time will be spent detecting leaks, repairing them, and then restoring the purity and quantity of the refrigerant charge. A list of general precautions that should be observed while doing this follows:

1. Keep all tools as clean and dry as possible.

2. Thoroughly purge the service gauges and hoses of air and moisture before connecting them to the system. Keep them capped when not in use.

3. Thoroughly clean any refrigerant fitting before disconnecting it, in order to minimize the entrance of dirt into the system.

4. Plan any operation that requires opening the system beforehand, in order to minimize the length of time it will be exposed to open air. Cap or seal the open ends to minimize the entrance of foreign material.

5. When adding oil, pour it through an extremely clean and dry tube or funnel. Keep the oil capped whenever possible. Do not use oil that has not been kept tightly sealed.

6. Use only refrigerant 12. Purchase refrigerant intended for use in only automatic air conditioning systems. Avoid the use of refrigerant-12 that may be packaged for another use, such as cleaning, or powering a horn, as it is impure.

7. Completely evacuate any system that has been opened to replace a component, or that has leaked sufficiently to draw in moisture and air. This requires evacuating air and moisture with a good vacuum pump for at least one hour.

If a system has been open for a considerable length of time it may be advisable to evacuate the system for up to 12 hours (overnight).

8. Use a wrench on both halves of a fitting that is to be disconnected, so as to avoid placing torque on any of the refrigerant lines.

9. When overhauling a compressor, pour some of the oil into a clean glass and inspect it. If there is evidence of dirt or metal particles, or both, flush all refrigerant components with clean refrigerant before evacuating and recharging the system. In addition, if metal particles are present, the compressor should be replaced.

10. Schrader valves may leak only when under full operating pressure. Therefore, if leakage is suspected but cannot be located, operate the system with a full charge of refrigerant and look for leaks from all Schrader valves. Replace any faulty valves.

condenser decreases, the operating pressure will drop there and throughout the high side of the system. As the R-12 continues to be expelled, the pressure available to force the liquid through the expansion valve will continue to decrease, and, eventually, the valve's orifice will prove to be too much of a restriction for adequate flow even with the needle fully withdrawn.

At this point, low side pressure will start to drop, and severe reduction in cooling capacity, marked by freeze-up of the evaporator coil, will result. Eventually, the operating pressure of the evaporator will be lower than the pressure of the atmosphere surrounding it, and air will be drawn into the system wherever there are leaks in the low side.

Because all atmospheric air contains at least some moisture, water will enter the

Additional Preventive Maintenance Checks

ANTIFREEZE

In order to prevent heater core freeze-up during A/C operation, it is necessary to maintain permanent type antifreeze protection of + 15 degrees F. or lower. A reading of − 15 degrees F. is ideal since this protection also supplies sufficient corrosion inhibitors for the protection of the engine cooling system.

NOTE: The same antifreeze should not be used longer than the manufacturer specifies.

RADIATOR CAP

For efficient operation of an air conditioned car's cooling system, the radiator cap should have a holding pressure which meets manufacturer's specifications. A cap which fails to hold these pressures should be replaced.

CONDENSER

Any obstruction of or damage to the condenser configuration will restrict the air flow which is essential to its efficient operation. It is therefore a good rule to keep this unit clean and in proper physical shape.

NOTE: Bug screens are regarded as obstructions.

CONDENSATION DRAIN TUBE

This single molded drain tube expels the condensation, which accumulates on the bottom of the evaporator housing, into the engine compartment.

If this tube is obstructed, the air conditioning performance can be restricted and condensation buildup can spill over onto the vehicle's floor.

Safety Precautions

Because of the importance of the necessary safety precautions that must be exercised when working with air conditioning sytems and R-12 refrigerant, a recap of the safety precautions are outlined.

1. Avoid contact with a charged refrigeration system, even when working on another part of the air conditioning system or vehicle. If a heavy tool comes into contact with a section of copper tubing or a heat exchanger, it can easily cause the relatively soft material to rupture.

2. When it is necessary to apply force to a fitting which contains refrigerant, as when checking that all system couplings are securely tightened, use a wrench on both parts of the fitting involved, if possible.

This will avoid putting torque on refrigerant tubing.

(It is advisable, when possible, to use tube or line wrenches when tightening these flare nut fittings.)

3. Do not attempt to discharge the system by merely loosening a fitting, or removing the service valve caps and cracking these valves. Precise control is possible only when using the service gauges. Place a rag under the open end of the center charging hose while discharging the system to catch any drops of liquid that might escape. Wear protective gloves when connecting or disconnecting service gauge hoses.

4. Discharge the system only in a well ventilated area, as high concentrations of the gas can exclude oxygen and act as an anaesthetic. When leak testing or soldering, this is particularly important, as toxic gas is formed when R-12 contacts any flame.

5. Never start a system without first verifying that both service valves are back-seated, if equipped, and that all fittings throughout the system are snugly connected.

6. Avoid applying heat to any refrigerant line or storage vessel. Charging may be aided by using water heated to less than 125° to warm the refrigerant container. Never allow a refrigerant storage container to sit out in the sun, or near any other source of heat, such as a radiator.

7. Always wear goggles when working on a system to protect the eyes. If refrigerant contacts the eyes, it is advisable in all cases to see a physician as soon as possible.

8. Frostbite from liquid refrigerant should be treated by first gradually warming the area with cool water, and then gently applying petroleum jelly. A physician should be consulted.

9. Always keep refrigerant drum fittings capped when not in use. Avoid sudden shock to the drum, which might occur from dropping it, or from banging a heavy tool against it. Never carry a drum in the passenger compartment of a car.

10. Always completely discharge the system before painting the vehicle (if the paint is to be baked on), or before welding anywhere near refrigerant lines.

AIR CONDITIONING TOOLS AND GAUGES

Test Gauges

Most of the service work performed in air conditioning requires the use of a set of two gauges, one for the high (head) pressure side of the system, the other for the low (suction) side.

The low side gauge records both pressure and vacuum. Vacuum readings are calibrated from 0 to 30 inches and the pressure graduations read from 0 to no less than 60 psi.

The high side gauge measures pressure from 0 to at least 600 psi.

Both gauges are threaded into a manifold that contains two hand shut-off valves. Proper manipulation of these valves and the use of the attached test hoses allow the user to perform the following services:

1. Test high and low side pressures.
2. Remove air, moisture, and contaminated refrigerant.
3. Purge the system (of refrigerant).
4. Charge the system (with refrigerant).

NOTE: Chrysler Corp. requires the use of a third gauge on those units that have an evaporator pressure regulator (EPR) valve mounted on the suction side of the compressor.

Typical manifold gauge set

GAUGE PORT
VALVE OPEN

SUCTION OR
PRESSURE
LINE

MANIFOLD
GAUGE HOSE
ASSEMBLY

Manifold gauge hose connected to a Schraeder type service port

The manifold valves are designed so they have no direct effect on gauge readings, but serve only to provide for, or cut off, flow of refrigerant through the manifold. During all testing and hook-up operations, the valves are kept in a closed position to avoid disturbing the refrigeration system. The valves are opened only to purge the system of refrigerant or to charge it.

When purging the system, the center hose is uncapped at the lower end, and both valves are cracked open slightly. This allows refrigerant pressure to force the entire contents of the system out through the center hose. During charging, the valve on the high side of the manifold is closed, and the valve on the low side is cracked open. Under these conditions, the low pressure in the evaporator will draw refrigerant from the relatively warm refrigerant storage container into the system.

SYSTEMS WITH A SIGHT GLASS

The air conditioning systems that use a sight glass as a means to check the refrigerant level, should be carefully checked to avoid under or over charging. The gauge set should be attached to the system for verification of pressures.

To check the system with the sight glass, clean the glass and start the vehicle engine. Operate the air conditioning controls on maximum for approximately five minutes to stabilize the system. The room temperature should be above 70 degrees. Check the sight glass for one of the following conditions:

1. If the sight glass is clear, the compressor clutch is engaged, the compressor

discharge line is warm and the compressor inlet line is cool, the system has a full charge of refrigerant.

2. If the sight glass is clear, the compressor clutch is engaged and there is no significant temperature difference between the compressor inlet and discharge lines, the system is empty or nearly empty. By having the gauge set attached to the system, a measurement can be taken. If the gauge reads less than 25 psi, the low pressure cutoff protection switch has failed.

3. If the sight glass is clear and the compressor clutch is disengaged, the clutch is defective, or the clutch circuit is open, or the system is out of refrigerant. By-pass the low pressure cut-off switch momentarily to determine the cause.

4. If the sight glass shows foam or bubbles, the system can be low on refrigerant. Occasional foam or bubbles is normal when the air temperature is above 110 degrees or below 70 degrees. To verify, increase the engine speed to approximately 1500 rpm and block the airflow through the condenser to increase the compressor discharge pressure to between 225 to 250 psi. If the sight glass still shows bubbles or foam, the refrigerant level is low.

─────── CAUTION ───────

Do not operate the vehicle engine any longer than necessary with the condenser airflow blocked. This blocking action also blocks the cooling system radiator and will cause the system to overheat rapidly.

When the system is low on refrigerant, a leak is present or the system was not properly charged. Use a leak detector and locate the problem area and repair. If no leakage is found, charge the system to its capacity. (Refer to the refrigerant capacity chart at the end of this section).

─────── CAUTION ───────

It is not advisable to add refrigerant to a system utilizing the suction throttling valve and a sight glass, because the amount of refrigerant required to remove the foam or bubbles will result in an overcharge and potentially damage system components.

CCOT SYSTEM

When charging the CCOT system, attach only the low pressure line to the low pressure gauge port, located on the accumulator. Do not attach the high pressure line to any service port or allow it to remain attached to the vacuum pump after evacuation. Be sure both the high and low pressure control valves are closed on the gauge set. To complete the charging of the system, follow the outline supplied.

1. Start the engine and allow to run at idle, with the cooling system at normal operating temperature.

2. Attach the center gauge hose to a multi-can dispenser.

3. Allow one pound or the contents of

one or two 14 oz. cans to enter the system through the low pressure side by opening the gauge low pressure control valve.

4. Close the low pressure gauge control valve and turn the A/C system on to engage the compressor. Place the blower motor in its high mode.

5. Open the low pressure gauge control valve and draw the remaining charge into the system. Refer to the capacity chart at the end of this section for the individual vehicle or system capacity.

6. Close the low pressure gauge control valve and the refrigerant source valve on the multi-can dispenser. Remove the low pressure hose from the accumulator quickly to avoid loss of refrigerant through the Schrader valve.

7. Install the protective cap on the gauge port and check the system for leakage.

8. Test the system for proper operation.

Leak Testing the System

There are several methods of detecting leaks in an air conditioning system; among them, the two most popular are (1) halide leak-detection or the "open flame method," and (2) electronic leak-detection.

The halide leak detection is a torch like device which produces a yellow-green color when refrigerant is introduced into the flame at the burner. A brilliant blue or violet color indicates the presence of large amounts of refrigerant at the burner. A small leak will cause the flame to turn a yellow-green color.

An electronic leak detector is a small portable electronic device with an extended probe. With the unit activated the probe is passed along those components of the system which contain refrigerant. If a leak is detected, the unit will sound an alarm signal or activate a display signal depending on the manufacturer's design. It is advisable to follow the manufacturer's instructions as the design and function of the detection may vary significantly.

NOTE: Caution should be taken to operate either type of detector in well ventilated areas, so as to reduce the chance of personal injury, which may result from coming in contact with poisonous gases produced when R-12 is exposed to flame or electric spark.

Service Valves

For the user to diagnose an air conditioning system he or she must gain "entrance" to the system in order to observe the pressures. There are two types of terminals for this purpose, the hand shut off type and the familiar Schrader valve.

The Schrader valve is similar to a tire valve stem and the process of connecting the test hoses is the same as threading a

Manual service valve positions

hand pump outlet hose to a bicycle tire. As the test hose is threaded to the service port the valve core is depressed, allowing the refrigerant to enter the test hose outlet. Removal of the test hose automatically closes the system.

Extreme caution must be observed when removing test hoses from the Schrader valves as some refrigerant will normally escape, usually under high pressure. (Observe safety precautions.)

Some systems have hand shut-off valves (the stem can be rotated with a special ratcheting box wrench) that can be positioned in the following three ways:

1. FRONT SEATED—Rotated to full clockwise position.

a. Refrigerant will not flow to compressor, but will reach test gauge port. COMPRESSOR WILL BE DAMAGED IF SYSTEM IS TURNED ON IN THIS POSITION.

b. The compressor is now isolated and ready for service. However, care must be exercised when removing service valves from the compressor as a residue of refrigerant may still be present within the compressor. Therefore, remove service valves slowly observing all safety precautions.

2. BACK SEATED—Rotated to full counter clockwise position. Normal position for system while in operation. Refrigerant flows to compressor but not to test gauge.

3. MID-POSITION (CRACKED)—Refrigerant flows to entire system. Gauge port (with hose connected) open for testing.

USING THE MANIFOLD GAUGES

The following are step-by-step procedures to guide the user to correct gauge usage.

1. WEAR GOGGLES OR FACE SHIELD DURING ALL TESTING OPERATIONS. BACKSEAT HAND SHUT-OFF TYPE SERVICE VALVES.

2. Remove caps from high and low side service ports. Make sure both gauge valves are closed.

3. Connect low side test hose to service valve that leads to the evaporator (located between the evaporator outlet and the compressor).

4. Attach high side test hose to service valve that leads to the condenser.

5. Mid-position hand shutoff type service valves.

6. Start engine and allow for warm-up. All testing and charging of the system should be done after engine and system have reached normal operation temperatures (except when using certain charging stations).

7. Adjust air conditioner controls to maximum cold.

8. Observe gauge readings.

When the gauges are not being used it is a good idea to:

a. Keep both hand valves in the closed position.

b. Attach both ends of the high and low service hoses to the manifold, if extra outlets are present on the manifold, or plug them if not. Also, keep the center charging hose attached to an empty re-

frigerant can. This extra precaution will reduce the possibility of moisture entering the gauges. If air and moisture have gotten into the gauges, purge the hoses by supplying refrigerant under pressure to the center hose with both gauge valves open and all openings unplugged.

DISCHARGING, EVACUATING AND CHARGING

Discharging the System

-------- CAUTION --------
Perform operation in a well-ventilated area.

When it is necessary to remove (purge) the refrigerant pressurized in the system, follow this procedure:

1. Operate air conditioner for at least 10 minutes.

2. Attach gauges, shut off engine and air conditioner.

3. Place a container or rag at the outlet of the center charging hose on the gauge. The refrigerant will be discharged there and this precaution will avoid its uncontrolled exposure.

4. Open low side hand valve on gauge slightly.

5. Open high side hand valve slightly.

NOTE: Too rapid a purging process will be identified by the appearance of an oily foam. If this occurs, close the hand valves a little more until this condition stops.

6. Close both hand valves on the gauge set when the pressures read 0 and all the refrigerant has left the system.

Evacuating the System

Before charging any system it is necessary to purge the refrigerant and draw out the trapped moisture with a suitable vacuum pump. Failure to do so will result in ineffective charging and possible damage to the system.

BAR GAUGE MANIFOLD AND COMPRESSOR SERVICE VALVE SETTINGS

Condition	Manifold Valves	Compressor Valves
Testing System	Both fully closed	Both cracked off backseat
Depressurizing System	Both cracked open	Both at mid position
Evacuating the system	Both wide open	Both at mid position
Charging in gas form with compressor running	High pressure valve closed	High pressure valve cracked off backseat
	Low pressure valve cracked	Low pressure valve at mid position
Charging in liquid form with compressor off	Low pressure valve closed	Both valves mid positioned
	High pressure valve wide open	

Note: A very small leak, causing system discharge about every two weeks, can be caused by a leaky Schrader type service valve. Check these valves with extra care when testing for a small leak.

Typical gauge connections for discharge, evacuation and charging the system

Schematic for evacuating the system

Use this hook-up for the proper evacuation procedure:

1. Connect both service gauge hoses to the high and low service outlets.

2. Open high and low side hand valves on gauge manifold.

3. Open both service valves a slight amount (from back seated position), allow refrigerant to discharge from system.

4. Install center charging hose of gauge set to vacuum pump.

5. Operate vacuum pump for at least one hour. (If the system has been subjected to open conditions for a prolonged period of time it may be necessary to "pump the system down" overnight. Refer to "System Sweep" procedure.)

NOTE: If low pressure gauge does not show at least 28″ hg. within 5 minutes, check the system for a leak or loose gauge connectors.

6. Close hand valves on gauge manifold.

7. Shut off pump.

8. Observe low pressure gauge to determine if vacuum is holding. A vacuum drop may indicate a leak.

System Sweep

An efficient vacuum pump can remove all the air contained in a contaminated air conditioning system very quickly, because of its vapor state. Moisture, however, is far more difficult to remove because the vacuum must force the liquid to evaporate before it will be able to remove it from the system. If a system has become severely contaminated, as, for example, it might become after all the charge was lost in conjunction with vehicle accident damage, moisture removal is extremely time consuming. A vacuum pump could remove all of the moisture only if it were operated for 12 hours or more.

Under these conditions, sweeping the system with refrigerant will speed the process of moisture removal considerably. To sweep, follow the following procedure:

1. Connect vacuum pump to gauges, operate it until vacuum ceases to increase, then continue operation for ten more minutes.

2. Charge system with 50% of its rated refrigerant capacity.

3. Operate system at fast idle for ten minutes.

4. Discharge the system.

5. Repeat twice the process of charging to 50% capacity, running the system for ten minutes, and discharging it, for a total of three sweeps.

6. Replace drier.

7. Pump system down as in step 1.

8. Charge system.

Charging the System

— **CAUTION** —
Never attempt to charge the system by opening the high pressure gauge control while the compressor is operating. The compressor accumulating pressure can burst the refrigerant container, causing severe personal injuries.

BASIC SYSTEM

In this procedure the refrigerant enters the suction side of the system as a vapor while the compressor is running. Before proceeding, the system should be in a partial vacuum after adequate evacuation. Both hand valves on the gauge manifold should be closed.

1. Attach both test hoses to their respective service valve ports. Mid-position manually operated service valves, if present.

2. Install dispensing valve (closed position) on the refrigerant container. (Single and multiple refrigerant manifolds are available to accommodate one to four 15 oz. cans.)

3. Attach center charging hose to the refrigerant container valve.

4. Open dispensing valve on the refrigerant can.

5. Loosen the center charging hose coupler where it connects to the gauge manifold to allow the escaping refrigerant to purge the hose of contaminants.

6. Tighten center charging hose connection.

7. Purge the low pressure test hose at the gauge manifold.

8. Start car engine, roll down the car windows and adjust the air conditioner to maximum cooling. The car engine should be at normal operating temperature before proceeding. The heated environment helps the liquid vaporize more efficiently.

9. Crack open the low side hand valve on the manifold. Manipulate the valve so that the refrigerant that enters the system does not cause the low side pressure to exceed 40 psi. Too sudden a surge may permit the entrance of unwanted liquid to the compressor. Since liquids cannot be compressed, the compressor will suffer damage if compelled to attempt it. If the suction side of the system remains in a vacuum the system is blocked. Locate and correct the condition before proceeding any further.

NOTE: Placing the refrigerant can in a container of warm water (no hotter than 125° F) will speed the charging process. Slight agitation of the can is helpful too, but be careful not to turn the can upside down.

Some manufacturers allow for a partial charging of the A/C system in the form of a liquid (can inverted and compressor off) by opening the high side gauge valve only, and putting the high side compressor service valve in the middle position (if so equipped). The remainder of the refrigerant is then added in the form of a gas in the normal manner, through the suction side only.

SYSTEMS WITHOUT SIGHT GLASS, EXCEPT CCOT SYSTEM

The following procedure can be used to quickly determine whether or not an air conditioning system has the proper charge of refrigerant (providing ambient temperature is above 70° F. or 21° C.). This check can be made in a manner of minutes, thus facilitating system diagnosis by pinpointing the problem to the amount of charge in the system or by eliminating this possibility from the overall checkout.

1. Engine must be warm (thermostat open).

2. Hood and body doors open.

3. Selector lever set at NORM.

4. Temperature lever at COLD.

5. Blower on HI.

6. Normal engine idle.

7. Hand-feel temperature of evaporator inlet and outlet pipes with compressor engaged.

a. Both same temperature or some degree cooler than ambient—proper condition: check for other problems.

b. Inlet pipe cooler than outlet pipe—low refrigerant charge.

• Add a slight amount of refrigerant until both pipes feel the same.

• Then add 15 oz. (1 can) additional refrigerant.

c. Inlet pipe has frost accumulation—outlet pipe warmer: proceed as in Step b above.

If during the charging process the head pressure exceeds 200 psi, place an electric fan in front of the car and direct the turbulent air to the condenser. If no fan is available, repeatedly pour cool water over the top of the condenser. These cooling actions may be necessary on an extremely warm day to help dissipate the heat emitted by the engine during idle.

If this fails and pressure on the discharge side continues to rise, the system may be overcharged or the engine might be overheating. *Never* allow head pressure to go beyond 240 psi. during charging. If this condition occurs, stop engine, find and correct the problem.

8. Continue dispensing refrigerant until container is no longer cool to the touch. On a humid day, the outside of the container will frost. When the frost disappears the can is usually empty. To detach dispensing can:

a. close low pressure test gauge hand valve.

b. crack open low pressure test hose at manifold until remaining pressure escapes.

c. tighten hose coupler.

d. loosen hose coupler connected to refrigerant can.

e. discard empty can and repeat steps 2 to 8.

9. Continue to add refrigerant to the required capacity of the system. (Usually marked on the compressor).

CAUTION

DO NOT OVERCHARGE. This condition is usually indicated by an abnormally high side pressure reading and a noisy compressor resulting in ineffective cooling and damage to the system.

SYSTEMS WITH A SIGHT GLASS

The air conditioning systems that use a sight glass as a means to check the refrigerant level, should be carefully checked to avoid under or over charging. The gauge set should be attached to the system for verification of pressures.

To check the system with the sight glass,

Check item \ Amount of refrigerant	Almost no refrigerant	Insufficient	Suitable	Too much refrigerant
Temperature of high pressure and low pressure lines.	Almost no difference between high pressure and low pressure side temperature.	High pressure side is warm and low pressure side is fairly cold.	High pressure side is hot and low pressure side is cold.	High pressure side is abnormally hot.
State in sight glass.	Bubbles flow continuously. **Bubbles will disappear and something like mist will flow when refrigerant is nearly gone.**	The bubbles are seen at intervals of 1 - 2 seconds.	Almost transparent. Bubbles may appear when engine speed is raised and lowered. **No clear difference exists betwen these two conditions.**	No bubbles can be seen.
Pressure of system.	High pressure side is abnormally low.	Both pressure on high and low pressure sides are slightly low.	Both pressures on high and low pressure sides are normal.	Both pressures on high and low pressure sides are abnormally high.
Repair.	**Stop compressor immediately** and conduct an overall check.	Check for gas leakage, repair as required, replenish and charge system.		Discharge refrigerant from service valve of low pressure side.

Using a sight glass to determine the relative refrigerant charge

clean the glass and start the vehicle engine. Operate the air conditioning controls on maximum for approximately five minutes to stabilize the system. The room temperature should be above 70 degrees. Check the sight glass for one of the following conditions:

1. If the sight glass is clear, the compressor clutch is engaged, the compressor discharge line is warm and the compressor inlet line is cool, the system has a full charge of refrigerant.

2. If the sight glass is clear, the compressor clutch is engaged and there is no significant temperature difference between the compressor inlet and discharge lines, the system is empty or nearly empty. By having the gauge set attached to the system, a measurement can be taken. If the gauge reads less than 25 psi, the low pressure cut-off protection switch has failed.

3. If the sight glass is clear and the compressor clutch is disengaged, the clutch is defective, or the clutch circuit is open, or the system is out of refrigerant. By-pass the low pressure cut-off switch momentarily to determine the cause.

4. If the sight glass shows foam or bubbles, the system can be low on refrigerant. Occasional foam or bubbles is normal when the room temperature is above 110 degrees or below 70 degrees. To verify, increase the engine speed to approximately 1500 rpm and block the airflow through the condenser to increase the compressor discharge pressure to between 225 to 250 psi. If the sight glass still shows bubbles or foam, the refrigerant level is low.

—— CAUTION ——

Do not operate the vehicle engine any longer than necessary with the condenser airflow blocked. This blocking action also blocks the cooling system radiator and will cause the system to overheat rapidly.

When the system is low on refrigerant, a leak is present or the system was not properly charged. Use a leak detector and locate the problem area and repair. If no leakage is found, charge the system to its capacity. (Refer to the refrigerant capacity chart at the end of this section).

—— CAUTION ——

It is not advisable to add refrigerant to a system utilizing the suction throttling valve and a sight glass, because the amount of refrigerant required to remove the foam or bubbles will result in an overcharge and potentially damaged system components.

CCOT SYSTEM

When charging the CCOT system, attach only the low pressure line to the low pressure gauge port, located on the accumulator. Do not attach the high pressure line to any service port or allow it to remain attached to the vacuum pump after evacuation. Be sure both the high and the low pressure control valves are closed on the gauge set. To complete the charging of the system, follow the outline supplied.

1. Start the engine and allow to run at idle, with the cooling system at normal operating temperature.

2. Attach the center gauge hose to a single or multi-can dispenser.

3. With the multi-can dispenser inverted, allow one pound or the contents of one or two 14 oz. cans to enter the system through the low pressure side by opening the gauge low pressure control valve.

4. Close the low pressure gauge control valve and turn the A/C system on to engage the compressor. Place the blower motor in its high mode.

5. Open the low pressure gauge control valve and draw the remaining charge into the system. Refer to the capacity chart at the end of this section for the individual vehicle or system capacity.

6. Close the low pressure gauge control valve and the refrigerant source valve, on the multi-can dispenser. Remove the low pressure hose from the accumulator quickly to avoid loss of refrigerant through the Schrader valve.

7. Install the protective cap on the gauge port and check the system for leakage.

8. Test the system for proper operation.

Leak Testing the System

There are several methods of detecting leaks in an air conditioning system; among them, the two most popular are (1) halide leak-detection or the "open flame method," and (2) electronic leak-detection.

The halide leak detection is a torch like device which produces a yellow-green color when refrigerant is introduced into the flame at the burner. A purple or violet color indicates the presence of large amounts of refrigerant at the burner.

An electronic leak detector is a small portable electronic device with an extended probe. With the unit activated the probe is passed along those components of the system which contain refrigerant. If a leak is detected, the unit will sound an alarm signal or activate a display signal depending on the manufacturer's design. It is advisable to follow the manufacturer's instructions as the design and function of the detection may vary significantly.

—— CAUTION ——

Caution should be taken to operate either type of detector in well ventilated areas, so as to reduce the chance of personal injury, which may result from coming in contact with poisonous gases produced when R-12 is exposed to flame or electric spark.

Electronic leak detector

Electrical

INDEX

ELECTRICAL DIAGNOSIS

To satisfy the growing trend toward organized engine diagnosis and tune-up, the following gauge and meter hook-ups, as well as diagnosis procedures are covered. The most sophisticated tune-up and diagnostic facilities are no more than a complex of the basic gauges and meters in common, everyday use. Therefore, to understand gauge and meter hook-ups, their applications and procedures, is to be equipped with the knowhow to perform the most exacting diagnosis.

Basic electrical circuits

KNOW YOUR INSTRUMENTS

Ohmmeter

An ohmmeter is used to measure electrical resistance in a unit or circuit. The ohmmeter has a self-contained power supply. In use, it is connected across (or in parallel with) the terminals of the unit being tested.

Ammeter

An ammeter is used to measure current (amount of electricity) flowing through a unit, or circuit. Ammeters are always connected in the line (in series) with the unit or circuit being tested.

Voltmeter

A voltmeter is used to measure voltage

Voltmeter connected in parallel circuit

Ammeter connected to test wire

(electrical pressure) pushing the current through a unit, or circuit. The meter is connected across the terminals of the unit being tested.

Testing the Starting Motor

TESTING THE STARTER CIRCUIT

The starter circuit should be divided and tested in four separate phases:
1. Cranking voltage check
2. Amperage draw
3. Voltage drop—grounded side
4. Voltage drop—battery side

NOTE: The battery must be in good condition for this test to have significance. To accurately check battery condition, use equipment designed to measure its capacity under a load. Instructions accompanying the equipment should be followed.

Cranking Voltage

Connect voltmeter leads to prods tapped into the battery posts (observe polarity and reverse meter leads if necessary). Remove the high tension wire from the distributor cap and ground it to prevent starting. With electronic ignition, disconnect the control box harness from the distributor. Now, turn the key. Observe both voltmeter reading and cranking speed. The cranking speed should be even, and at a satisfactory rate of speed, with a voltmeter reading of at least 9.6 volts for 12-volt systems.

Amperage Draw

The amount of current the starter motor draws is usually (but not always) associated with the mechanical problems involved in cranking the engine. (Mechanical trouble in the engine, frozen or worn starter parts, misaligned starter or starter components, etc.) Because starter motor amperage draw is directly influenced by anything restricting the free turning of the engine, or starter, it is important that the engine and all components be at operating temperatures.

To measure starter current draw, remove the high tension wire from the center of the distributor cap and ground it. With electronic ignition, disconnect the control box harness from the distributor. A very simple and inexpensive starter current indicator is available at auto stores. This indicator is an induction type gauge and shows, without disconnecting any wires, starter current draw.

Place the yoke of the meter directly over the insulated starter supply cable (cable must be straight for a minimum of 2 in.). Close the starter switch for about 20 seconds, watch the meter dial and record the average reading. If the indicator swings in the wrong direction, reverse the position of the meter.

The cranking amperage draw can vary from 150 to 400 amperes, depending on the engine size, engine compression, and starter type.

NOTE: When starter specifications are not available, average starter draw amperage can be derived from testing a like starter unit, known to be operating satisfactorily.

More accurate but complex equipment is available from many manufacturers. This equipment consists of a combination voltmeter, ammeter, and carbon pile rheostat. When using this equipment, follow the equipment manufacturer's procedures and recommendations.

High amperage and lazy performance would suggest an excessively tight engine, friction in the starter or starter drive, grounded starter field or armature.

Normal amperage and lazy performance suggest high resistance, or possibly poor connections somewhere in the starter circuit.

Low amperage and lazy or no performance suggest battery condition poor, bad cables or connections along the line.

Voltage Drop—Grounded Side

With a voltmeter on the 3-volt scale, without disconnecting any wires, connect negative test lead of the voltmeter to a prod secured in the grounded battery post. The positive test lead is connected to a cleaned, bare metal portion of the starter motor housing. Close the starter switch and note the voltmeter reading. If the reading is the same as battery reading, the ground circuit is open

Ohmmeter connected to test wire resistance

somewhere between the battery and the starter. In many cases the reading will be very small. The reading shown will indicate voltage drop (loss) between battery ground post and starter housing. The drop should not exceed 0.2 volt. If the voltage drop is above the specified amount, the next step is to isolate and correct the cause. It can be a bad cable or connection anywhere in the battery-to-starter ground circuit. A check of this type should progress along the various points of possible trouble, between the battery ground post and the starter motor housing, until the trouble spot has been located.

Voltmeter connected to battery for cranking voltage test

Voltage Drop—Battery Side

Bad starter cranking may result from poor connections or faulty components of the battery or hot phase of the starter motor circuit. To check this phase of the circuit, without disconnecting any wires, connect one lead of a voltmeter to a prod secured in the hot post of the battery and the other voltmeter lead to the field terminal of the starting motor. The meter should be set to the 16–20 volt scale. Before closing the starter switch, the voltmeter reading will be that of the battery. After closing the starter switch, change the selector on the voltmeter to the 3-volt scale. With a jumper wire between the relay battery terminal and the relay starter switch terminal, crank the engine. If the starting motor cranks the engine, the relay (solenoid) is operating.

While the engine is being cranked, watch the voltmeter. It should not register more than 0.5 volt. If more than this, check each part of the circuit for voltage drop to isolate the trouble. (high resistance).

Without disturbing the voltmeter-to-battery hook-up, move the free voltmeter lead to the battery terminal of the relay (solenoid), and crank the engine. The voltmeter should show no more than 0.1 volt.

If this reading is correct, move the same voltmeter lead to the starting motor terminal of the relay (solenoid). While the engine is being cranked, the voltmeter should show no more than 0.3 volt. If it does, the trouble lies in the relay.

If the reading is correct, the trouble is in the cable or connections between the relay and the starting motor.

Diagnosis

Starter Won't Crank the Engine

1. Dead battery.

Positive engagement starter circuits

2. Open starter circuit, such as:
   a. Broken or loose battery cables.
   b. Inoperative starter motor solenoid.
   c. Broken or loose wire from starter switch to solenoid.
   d. Poor solenoid or starter ground.
   e. Bad starter switch.
3. Defective starter internal circuit, such as:
   a. Dirty or burnt commutator.
   b. Stuck, worn or broken brushes.
   c. Open or shorted armature.

Starter cable resistance tests

Starter current indicator

Checking charging system resistance

Alternator system with ammeter in the circuit

d. Open or grounded fields.

4. Starter motor mechanical faults, such as:

a. Jammed armature end bearings.

b. Bad bearing, allowing armature to rub fields.

c. Bent shaft.

d. Broken starter housing.

e. Bad starter worm or drive mechanism.

f. Bad starter drive or flywheel driven gear.

5. Engine hard or impossible to crank such as:

a. Hydrostatic lock, water in combustion chamber.

b. Crankshaft seizing in bearings.

c. Piston or ring seizing.

d. Bent or broken connecting rod.

e. Seizing of connecting rod bearing.

f. Flywheel jammed or broken.

STARTER SPINS FREE, WON'T ENGAGE

1. Sticking or broken drive mechanism.

ALTERNATORS AND REGULATORS

IS IT THE ALTERNATOR OR THE VOLTAGE REGULATOR?

The first step in diagnosing troubles of the charging system, is to identify the source of failure. Does the fault lie in the alternator or the regulator? The next move depends upon preference or necessity; either repair or replace the offending unit.

It is just as easy to separate an alternator, electrically, from the AC regulator as it is to separate its counterpart, the DC generator from its regulator.

AC generator output is controlled by the amount of current supplied to the field circuit of the system.

Unlike the DC generator, an AC generator is capable of producing substantial current at idle speed. Higher maximum output is also a possibility. This presents a potential danger when testing. As a precaution, a field rheostat should be used in the field circuit when making the following isolation test. The field rheostat permits positive control of the amount of current allowed to pass through the field circuit during the isolation test. Unregulated alternator capacity could ruin the unit.

NOTE: Most manufacturers of precision gauges offer special test connectors, in sets, that will adapt to the leads and connections of any AC charging system.

ALTERNATOR TEST PLANS

The following is a procedure pattern for testing the various alternators and their control systems.

There are certain precautionary measures that apply to alternator tests in general. These items are listed in detail to avoid repetition when testing each make of alternator, and to encourage a habit of good test procedure.

1. Check alternator drive belt for condition and tension.

2. Disconnect battery cables, check physical, chemical, and electrical condition of battery.

3. Be absolutely sure of polarity before connecting any battery in the circuit. Reversed polarity will ruin the diodes.

4. Never use a battery charger to start the engine.

5. Disconnect both battery cables when making a battery recharge hook-up.

6. Be sure of polarity hook-up when using a booster battery for starting.

7. Never ground the alternator output or battery terminal.

8. Never ground the field circuit between alternator and regulator.

9. Never run any alternator on an open circuit with the field energized.

10. Never try to polarize an alternator.

11. Do not attempt to motor an alternator.

12. The regulator cover must be in place when taking voltage limiter readings.

13. The ignition switch must be in off position when removing or installing the regulator cover.

14. Use insulated tools only to make adjustments to the regulator.

15. When making engine idle speed adjustments, always consider potential load factors that influence engine rpm. To compensate for electrical load, switch on the lights, radio, heater, air conditioner, etc.

Diagnosis

LOW OR NO CHARGING

1. Blown fuse.
2. Broken or loose fan belt.
3. Voltage regulator not working.
4. Brushes sticking.
5. Slip ring dirty.
6. Open circuit.
7. Bad wiring connections.
8. Bad diode rectifier.

9. High resistance in charging circuit.
10. Voltage regulator needs adjusting.
11. Grounded stator.
12. May be open rectifiers (check all three phases).
13. If rectifiers are found blown or open, check capacitor.

NOISY UNIT

1. Damaged rotor bearings.
2. Poor alignment of unit.
3. Broken or loose belt.
4. Open diode rectifiers.

REGULATOR POINTS BURNT OR STUCK

1. Regulator set too high.
2. Poor ground connections.
3. Shorted generator field.
4. Regulator air gap incorrect.

Chrysler Isolated Field Alternator (Electronic Regulator)

The Chrysler isolated field alternator derives its name from its construction. Both of the brushes are insulated from ground and there is no heat sink connection, thereby isolating the internal field.

TROUBLESHOOTING

Fusible Links

Chrysler Corporation trucks have a single fusible link which is connected between the starter relay and the junction block. Failure of this link will cause all electrical systems to stop functioning.

Charging System Operation

NOTE: If the current indicator is to give an accurate reading, the battery cables must be of the same gauge and length as the original equipment.

1. With the engine running and all electrical systems off, place a current indicator over the positive battery cable.
2. If a charge of about 5 amps is recorded, the charging system is working. If a draw of about 5 amps is recorded the system is not working. The needle moves toward the battery when a charge condition is indicated and away from the battery when a draw condition is indicated. If a draw is indicated, proceed to the next testing procedure. If an overcharge of 10–15 amps is indicated, check for a faulty regulator.

Ignition Switch-to-Regulator Circuit Check

1. Disconnect the regulator wires at the regulator.

2. Turn the key on but do not start the engine.
3. Using a voltmeter or test light, check for voltage across the I and F terminals. If there is current present, the circuit is good. If there is no current, check for bad connections, a bad ballast resistor, a bad ammeter, broken wires, or bad ground at the alternator or voltage regulator. Also, check for voltage from the I wire to ground; current should be present. Check for voltage from the F terminal to ground; current should not be present.

Isolation Test

This test determines whether the regulator or alternator is bad if everything else in the circuit was OK.

1. Disconnect, at the alternator, the wire that runs between one of the alternator field connections and the voltage regulator.
2. Run a jumper wire from the disconnected alternator terminal to ground.
3. Connect a voltmeter to the battery. The positive voltmeter lead connects to the positive battery terminal, and the negative lead goes to the negative terminal. Record the reading.
4. Make sure that all electrical systems are turned off. Start the engine. Do not race the engine.
5. Gradually raise engine speed to 1500–2000 rpm. There should be an increase of one to two volts on the voltmeter. If this is true, the alternator is good and the voltage regulator should be repaired. If there is no voltage increase, the alternator is faulty.

Charging Circuit Resistance Test

The purpose of this test is to determine the amount of "voltage drop" between the alternator output terminal wire and the battery.

1. Disconnect the battery ground cable and the "BAT" lead at the alternator output terminal.
2. Connect an ammeter with a scale to 100 amps in series between the alternator "BAT" terminal and the disconnected "BAT" wire.
3. Connect the positive lead of a voltmeter to the disconnected "BAT" wire. Connect the negative lead of the voltmeter to the negative post of the battery.
4. Disconnect the green colored regulator field wire from the alternator. Connect a jumper lead from the alternator field terminal to ground.
5. Connect a tachometer to the engine and reconnect the battery ground cable.
6. Connect a variable carbon pile rheostat to the battery cables.

— CAUTION —
Be sure the carbon pile is in the "OPEN" or "OFF" position before connecting the leads to the battery terminals.

7. Start the engine and operate at an idle.
8. Adjust the engine speed and carbon pile to maintain a flow of 20 amperes in the circuit. Observe the voltmeter reading which should not exceed .7 volts.

Checking current output of the charging system

Checking field current draw

NEGATIVE RECTIFIERS   POSITIVE RECTIFIERS

NEGATIVE
RECTIFIER
ASSEMBLY

POSITIVE
RECTIFIER
ASSEMBLY

BEARING

OUTPUT
TERMINAL

FIELD BRUSHES

View of the rear housing of the 100 amp Chrysler alternator

BATTERY OUTPUT
TERMINAL

GROUND
TERMINAL

FIELD TERMINAL

View of the rear housing on all but 100 amp Chrysler alternator

and reconnect the battery ground wire.

6. Connect a variable carbon pile rheostat between the positive and negative battery cables.

—————— **CAUTION** ——————

Be sure the rheostat control is in the "OPEN" or "OFF" position before connecting the leads to the battery cables.

7. Start the engine and operate at idle. Adjust the carbon pile rheostat control and the engine speed in increments until the voltmeter reading is 15 volts (13 volts for the 100 and 117 amp alternators) and the engine speed is 1250 rpm (900 rpm for the 100 and 117 amp alternators).

—————— **CAUTION** ——————

Do not allow the voltage to rise above 16 volts.

8. The ammeter readings must be within the following specifications.

Current Rating	Identification	Current Output
41 amp	Red or violet tag	40 amps min.
60 amp	Blue, natural or yellow	57 amps min.
100, 117 amp	Yellow	72 amps min.

NOTE: If measured at the battery, current output will be approximately 5 amperes lower than specified.

9. If the readings are less than specified, the alternator should be removed and checked during a bench test.

10. After the current output test is completed, reduce the engine speed, turn the carbon pile rheostat off and then stop the engine.

11. Disconnect the battery ground cable, remove the ammeter, voltmeter and carbon pile. Remove the jumper wire from the field terminal and reconnect the green colored wire to the alternator field terminal.

12. Reconnect the battery cable, if no further testing is to be done to the charging circuit.

Rotor Field Coil Draw Test

The rotor field coil can be tested on or off the vehicle.

1. If on the vehicle, remove the drive belt and wiring connections from the alternator.

2. Connect a jumper wire from the negative terminal of the battery to one of the field terminals of the alternator.

3. Connect the test ammeter positive lead to the other field terminal of the alternator and the negative ammeter lead to the positive battery terminal.

4. Connect a jumper wire between the alternator end shield and the battery negative terminal.

5. Slowly rotate the alternator pulley

9. If a higher voltage reading is indicated, inspect, clean and tighten all connections in the charging system.

10. If necessary, a voltage drop test can be done at each connection until the excessive resistance is located.

11. If the charging system resistance is within specifications, reduce the engine speed, turn off the carbon pile rheostat and stop the engine. Remove battery ground cable.

12. Remove the test instruments from the electrical system and reconnect the charging system wiring. Reconnect the battery ground cable.

Current Output Test

This test determines if the alternator is capable of delivering its rated current output.

1. Disconnect the battery ground cable and the "BAT" lead wire at the alternator output terminal.

2. Connect an ammeter in series between the alternator output terminal and the disconnected "BAT" lead wire.

NOTE: The ammeter must have a scale of 100 amps.

3. Connect the positive lead of a voltmeter to the output terminal of the alternator and the negative lead to a good ground.

4. Disconnect the green colored wire at the voltage regulator and connect a jumper wire from the alternator field terminal to ground.

5. Connect a tachometer to the engine

Typical Chrysler alternator

by hand and observe the ammeter reading.

6. The field coil draw should be 4.5 to 6.5 amperes at 12 volts. (4.75 to 6.0 amperes at 12 volts—100 and 117 amp alternators).

7. A low rotor coil draw is an indication of high resistance in the field coil circuit (brushes, slip rings or rotor coil). A higher rotor coil draw indicates possible shorted rotor coil or grounded rotor. No reading indicates an open rotor or defective brushes.

8. Remove the test equipment and jumper leads.

Rotor field coil current draw test

Electronic Voltage Regulator Test

1. Make sure battery terminals are clean and battery is charged.

2. Connect the positive lead of a test voltmeter to ignition Terminal No. 1 of the ballast resistor.

3. Connect the negative voltmeter lead to a good *body* ground.

4. Start engine and allow it to idle at 1250 rpm, all lights and accessories turned off. Voltage should be as follows:

Ambient Temp. ¼ in. from Regulator	Voltage
20°F.	14.9 to 15.9
80°F.	13.9 to 14.6
140°F.	13.3 to 13.9
Above 140°F.	Less Than 13.6

5. If the voltage is *below* specifications, check the following:

a. Voltage regulator ground—check voltage drop between regulator cover and ground.

b. Harness wiring—disconnect regulator plug (ign. switch off), then turn on

ign. switch and check for battery voltage at the terminals having the red and green leads. *Wiring harness must be disconnected from the regulator when checking individual leads*. If no voltage is present in either lead, the problem is in the truck wiring or alternator field.

6. If Step 5 tests showed no malfunctions, install a new regulator and repeat Step 4.

7. If voltage is *above* specifications (Step 4), or fluctuates, check the following:

a. Ground between regulator and body, and between body and engine.

b. Ignition switch circuit between switch and regulator.

8. If voltage is still more than ½ volt above specifications, install a new regulator and repeat Step 4.

Stator test for ground on Chrysler systems

Chrysler Overhaul and Internal Testing

Alternator disassembly, repair and assembly procedures are basically the same for all Chrysler alternators. Certain variations in design, or production modifications, could require slightly different procedures that should be obvious upon inspection of the unit being serviced.

Disassembly

To prevent damage to the brush assemblies (100 and 117 amp), they should be removed before proceeding with the disassembly of the alternator. The brushes are mounted in a plastic holder that positions the brushes vertically against the slip rings.

1. Remove the retaining screw, flat washer, nylon washer and field terminal and carefully lift the plastic holder containing the spring and brush assembly from the end housing.

2. The ground brush (40 and 60 amp) is positioned horizontally against the slip ring and is retained in the holder that is integral with the end housing. Remove the retaining screw and lift the clip, spring and brush assembly from the end housing.

CAUTION

The stator is laminated, don't burr the stator or end housings.

---

3. Remove the through bolts and pry between the stator and drive end housing with a thin blade screwdriver. Carefully separate the drive end housing, pulley and rotor assembly from the stator and rectifier housing assembly.

4. The pulley is an interference fit on the rotor shaft. Remove with a puller and special adapters.

5. Remove the three nuts and washers and, while supporting the end frame, tap the rotor shaft with a plastic hammer and separate the rotor and end housing.

6. The drive end ball bearing is an interference fit with the rotor shaft. Remove the bearing with puller and adapters.

NOTE: Further dismantling of the rotor is not advisable, as the remainder of the rotor assembly is not serviced separately.

7. Remove the DC output terminal nuts and washers and remove terminal screw and inside capacitor (on units so equipped).

8. Remove the insulator.

NOTE: Positive rectifiers are pressed into the heat sink and negative rectifiers in the end housing. When removing the rectifiers, it is necessary to support the end housing and/or heat sink to prevent damage to these castings. Another caution is in order relative to the diode rectifiers. Don't subject them to unnecessary jolting. Heavy vibration or shock may ruin them.

a. Cut rectifier wire at point of crimp.
b. Support rectifier housing.

NOTE: The factory tool is cut away and slotted to fit over the wires and around the bosses in the housing. Be sure that the bore of the tool completely surrounds the rectifier, then press the rectifier out of the housing.

NOTE: The roller bearing in the rectifier end frame is a press fit. To protect the end housing it is necessary to support the housing with a tool when pressing out the bearing.

BENCH TESTS

Testing Silicon Diode Rectifiers With Ohmmeter

Preferred method—rectifiers open in all three phases.

Disassemble the alternator and separate the wires at the Y-connection of the stator.

There are six diode rectifiers mounted in the back of the alternator (40 and 60 amp). Three of them are marked with a plus (+), and three are marked with a minus (−). These marks indicate diode case polarity.

NOTE: The 100 and 117 amp alternator has twelve silicone diodes. Six positive and six negative.

To test, set ohmmeter to its lowest range. If case is marked positive (+), place positive meter probe to case and negative probe to the diode lead. Meter should read between 4 and 10 ohms. Now, reverse leads of ohmmeter, connecting negative meter probe to positive case and positive meter probe to wire of rectifier. Set meter on a high range. Meter needle should move very little, if any (infinite reading). Do this to all positive diode rectifiers.

The diode rectifiers with minus (−) marks on their cases are checked the same way as above. Only now the negative ohmmeter probe is connected to the case for a reading of 4 to 10 ohms. Reverse leads as above for the other part to test.

If a reading of 4 to 10 ohms is obtained in one direction and no reading (infinity) is read on the ohmmeter in the other direction, diode rectifiers are good. If either infinity or a low resistance is obtained in both directions on a rectifier, it must be replaced.

If meter reads more than 10 ohms when ohmmeter positive probe is connected to positive on diode, and negative probe to negative, replace diode rectifier.

NOTE: With this test, it is necessary to determine the polarity of the ohmmeter probes. This can be done by connecting the ohmmeter to a DC voltmeter. The voltmeter will read up-scale when the positive probe of the ohmmeter is connected to the positive side of the voltmeter and the negative probe of the ohmmeter is connected to the negative side of the voltmeter.

Alternate method—test light.

USE JUMPER WIRE TO CONNECT "A" AND "F" TERMINALS AT REGULATOR PLUG

USE OF JUMPER WIRE AT REGULATOR PLUG TO TEST ALTERNATOR FOR NORMAL OUTPUT AMPS AND FOR FIELD CIRCUIT WIRING CONTINUITY

Isolation test jumper wire

Be sure that the lead from the center of the diode rectifiers is disconnected.

To test rectifiers with plus (+) case, touch positive probe of tester to case and minus (−) probe to lead wire of rectifier. Bulb should light if rectifier is good. If bulb does not light, replace rectifier.

Now reverse tester probe connections to rectifier. Bulb should not light. If bulb does light, replace rectifier.

For testing minus (−) marked cases, follow above procedure, except that now bulb should light with negative probe of tester touching rectifier case and positive probe touching lead wire.

Rectifier is good if the bulb lights when tester probes are connected one way, and does not light when tester connections are reversed.

Rectifier must be replaced if the bulb does not light either way. Also, replace rectifier if bulb lights both ways.

NOTE: The usual cause of an open or blown diode or rectifier is a defective capacitor or a battery that has been installed in reverse polarity. If the battery is installed properly and the diodes are open, test the capacitor.

Capacitor capacities:
Int. installed . . . . 158 microfarad. min.
Ext. installed . . . . 5 microfarad. min.

VOLTMETER TEST TYPICAL VOLTAGE BANDS SHOWN

Voltmeter reading during isolation test

Rotor tests for short or open circuits on Chrysler systems

ALTERNATOR BENCH TESTS

FIELD COIL DRAW

1. Connect a jumper between one FLD terminal and the positive terminal of a fully charged 12 volt battery.

2. Connect the positive lead of a test ammeter to the other field (FLD) terminal and the negative test lead to the negative battery terminal.

3. Slowly rotate the rotor by hand and observe the ammeter. The proper field coil draw is 2.3–2.7 amps at 12 volts.

NOTE: Field coil draw for the 100 and 117 ampere alternators should be 4.75 amperes to 6.0 amperes at 12 volts.

Field Circuit Ground Test

1. Touch one test lead of a 110 volt AC test bulb to one of the alternator brush (field) terminals and the other test lead to the end shield.
2. If the lamp lights, remove the field brush assemblies and separate the end housing by removing the three through-bolts.
3. Place one test lead on a slip ring and the other on the end shield.
4. If the lamp lights, the rotor assembly is grounded internally and must be replaced.
5. If the lamp does not light, the cause of the problem was a grounded brush.

Grounded Stator

1. Disconnect the diode rectifiers from the stator leads.
2. Test from stator leads to stator core, using a 110-volt test lamp. Test lamp should not light. If it does, stator is grounded and must be replaced.

Low Output

(About 50% output accompanied with a growl-hum caused by a shorted phase or a shorted rectifier.)

Perform steps 1, 2 and 3 (rectifier open in all three phases). If the rectifiers are found to be within specifications, replace the stator assembly.

Rotor tests for ground on Chrysler systems

Current Output Too High (No Control) Caused by Open Rectifier or Open Phase

Perform steps 1, 2 and 3 (rectifier open in all three phases). If the rectifier tests satisfactorily, inspect the stator connections before replacing the stator.

Assembly

1. Support the heat sink or rectifier end

housing on circular plate.
2. Check rectifier identification to be sure the correct rectifier is being used. The part numbers are stamped on the case of the rectifier. They are also marked, red for positive and black for negative.
3. Start the new rectifier into the casting and press it in squarely.

CAUTION
Do not start rectifier with a hammer or it will be ruined.

---

4. Crimp the new rectifier wire to the wires disconnected at removal, or solder (using a heat sink with rosin core solder).
5. Support the end housing on tool so that the notch in the support tool will clear the raised section of the heat sink, then press the bearing into position with tool SP-3381, or equivalent.

NOTE: New bearings are pre-lubricated, additional lubrication is not required.

6. Insert the drive end bearing in the drive end housing and install the bearing plate, washers and nuts to hold the bearing in place.
7. Position the bearing and drive end housing on the rotor shaft and, while supporting the base of the rotor shaft, press the bearing and housing in position on the rotor shaft with an arbor press and arbor tool.

CAUTION
Be careful that there is no cocking of the bearing at installation; or damage will result. Press the bearing on the rotor shaft until the bearing contacts the shoulder on the rotor shaft.

---

8. Install pulley on rotor shaft. Shaft of rotor must be supported so that all pressing force is on the pulley hub and rotor shaft.

NOTE: Do not exceed 6,800 lbs. pressure. Pulley hub should just contact bearing inner race.

9. Some alternators will be found to have the capacitor mounted internally. Be sure the heat sink insulator is in place.
10. Install the output terminal screw with the capacitor attached through the heat sink and end housing.
11. Install insulating washers, lockwashers and locknuts.
12. Make sure the heat sink and insulator are in place and tighten the locknut.
13. Position the stator on the rectifier end housing. Be sure that all of the rectifier connectors and phase leads are free of interference with the rotor fan blades and that the capacitor (internally mounted) lead has clearance.
14. Position the rotor assembly in the rectifier end housing. Align the through bolt holes in the stator with both end housings.
15. Enter stator shaft in the rectifier end housing bearing, compress stator and both end housings manually and install through bolts, washers and nuts.
16. Install the insulated brush and terminal attaching screw.
17. Install the ground screw and attaching screw.
18. Rotate pulley slowly to be sure the rotor fan blades do not hit the rectifier and stator connectors.

Delcotron 10-SI, 15-SI and 27-SI, Type 100 (General Motors Corp.)

NOTE: The internal alternator wiring is identical between the 10-SI, 15-SI and the 27-SI units, except the 10-SI uses a

Delcotron end-frame view

Wye stator winding while a Delta stator winding is used in the 15-SI and 27-SI alternators. The disassembly and assembly of the units remain basically the same.

Delcotron 10-SI and 15-SI

This system is an integrated AC generating system containing a built-in voltage regulator. Removal and replacement is essentially the same as for the standard AC generator.

The regulator is mounted inside the slip ring end frame. All regulator components are enclosed in an epoxy molding, and the regulator cannot be adjusted.

Troubleshooting

NOTE: See the "Alternator Test Plans" section before proceeding further. Make sure that the continuous running blower, if equipped, is disconnected. This blower will run with the key on even if the blower control is off, unless disconnected.

CHARGING SYSTEM TEST

Low Charging Rate

1. After battery condition, drive belt tension, and wiring terminals and connections have been checked, charge the battery fully and perform the following test:
2. Connect a test voltmeter between the alternator BAT. terminal and ground, ignition switch on. Connect the voltmeter in turn to alternator terminals No. 1 and No. 2, the other voltmeter lead being grounded as before. A zero reading indicates an open circuit between the battery and each connection at the alternator. If this test discloses no faults in the wiring, proceed to Step 3.
3. Connect the test voltmeter to the alternator BAT. terminal (the other test lead to ground), start the engine and run at 1,500–2,000 rpm with all lights and electrical accessories turned on. If the voltmeter reads 12.8 volts or greater, the alternator is good and no further checks need be made. If the voltmeter reads less than 12.8 volts, ground the field winding by inserting a screwdriver into the test hole in the end frame.

CAUTION
Do not force tab more than ¾ in. into end frame.

---

a. If voltage increases to 13 volts or more, the regulator unit is defective.
b. If voltage does not increase significantly, alternator is defective.

Alternator Output Test

1. Connect a test voltmeter, ammeter and a 10 ohm, 6 watt resistor into the charging circuit. Do not connect the carbon pile to the battery posts at this time.
2. Increase alternator speed and ob-

serve voltmeter—if voltage is uncontrolled with speed and increases to 15.5 volts or more, check for a grounded brush lead clip as covered previously. If brush lead clip is not grounded, the voltage regulator is faulty and must be replaced.
3. Connect the carbon pile load to the battery terminals.
4. Operate the alternator at moderate speed and adjust the carbon pile to obtain maximum alternator output as indicated on the ammeter. If output is within 10 amperes of rated output as stamped on the alternator frame, alternator is O.K. If output is not within specifications, ground the alternator field by inserting a screwdriver into the test hole in the end frame. If output now is within 10 amperes of rating, replace the voltage regulator; if still not within specifications, check field winding, diode trio, rectifier bridge and stator, as described later.

Disassembly and Assembly

1. Hold generator in a vice, clamping the mounting flange lengthwise.
2. Make a scribe mark to help locate frame end parts in the same position during assembly.
3. Remove 4 through-bolts and separate the slip ring end frame from the drive end frame and rotor assembly.

NOTE: Prying with a screwdriver at stator slot will aid disassembly.

4. Remove 3 stator lead attaching nuts and separate stator from end frame.
5. Remove insulated screws and ground screw from brush holder.
Remove diode trio, resistor, brush holder, and regulator from end frame.
6. Remove screws attaching capacitor to end frame and diode bridge; remove capacitor.
7. **10-SI Series**
Remove ground screw and battery terminal stud nut from rectifier bridge. Remove rectifier bridge, terminal stud, and

insulating washer from end frame.
27-SI Series
Remove 2 ground screws, a connector strap screw, and the battery terminal stud nut. Remove rectifier bridge, connector, terminal stud, and insulating washers from end frame.
8. Press bearing from end frame using a tube slightly smaller OD than the bearing. Support the end frame from inside and press bearing from outside toward the inside.

NOTE: Some models may have a seal separate and in front of bearing. Discard the seal when replacing the bearing as the new bearing has an integral seal.

9. Separate drive end frame from rotor as follows:
a. Place rotor in a vise and tighten only enough to permit pulley nut removal.

10-SI Delcotron

10-SI output test

NOTE: Rotor may be distorted if vise is over tightened.

b. Remove pulley nut, washer, pulley, fan, and collar from rotor shaft.

c. Remove drive end frame from rotor shaft and remove rotor from vise.

10. Press bearing from drive end frame after removing bearing retainer plate:

a. Remove screws attaching bearing seal and retainer assembly to housing.

b. Support end frame from inside the housing on a metal tube with a slightly larger ID than the OD of the bearing.

c. Press bearing and grease slinger (or flat washer used on some models) from end frame using a metal tube or collar against the grease slinger.

11. To assemble, reverse the order of the disassembly procedure. Torque the pulley nut to 50 ft. lbs.

— CAUTION —

During the assembly, do not interchange the ground screw (without insulator) for an insulated screw as this would cause uncontrolled or no alternator output.

Cleaning and Inspection

1. Clean all metal parts, except stator and rotor assemblies, in solvent.

2. Wipe off bearings and inspect them for pitting or roughness.

3. Inspect rotor slip-rings for scoring. They may be cleaned with 400 grit sandpaper (not emery), rotating the rotor to make the rings concentric. Maximum out-of-true is 0.001 in. If slip-rings are deeply scored, the entire rotor must be replaced as a unit.

4. Inspect brushes for wear; minimum length is ¼ in.

TESTING ROTOR

(CHECK FOR GROUNDS) (OHMMETER)

OHMMETER

Checking Delcotron rotor for grounds or open circuits

CHARGING SYSTEM TEST

High Charging Rate

1. With the battery fully charged, connect a voltmeter between alternator terminal no. 2 and ground. If the reading is zero, no. 2 circuit from the battery is open.

2. If no. 2 circuit is OK, but an obvious overcharging condition still exists, proceed as follows:

a. Remove the alternator and separate the end frames.

b. Connect a low-range ohmmeter between the brush lead clip and the end frame, as illustrated (test no. 1), then reverse the lead connections. If both readings are zero, either the brush lead clip is grounded or the regulator is defective. A grounded brush lead clip can be due to a damaged insulating sleeve or omission of the insulating washer.

TESTING TRIO

OHMMETER

SINGLE CONNECTOR

THREE CONNECTORS

Testing the 10-SI diode trio

DIODE TRIO

Initial Testing

1. Before removing this unit, connect an ohmmeter between the brush lead clip and the end frame. The lowest reading scale should be used for this test.

2. After taking a reading, reverse the lead connections. If the meter reads zero, the brush lead clip is probably grounded, due to omission of the insulating sleeve or insulating washer.

Removal

1. Remove the three nuts which secure the stator.

2. Remove stator.

3. Remove the screw which secures the diode trio lead clip, then remove diode trio.

NOTE: The position of the insulating washer on the screw is critical; make sure it is returned to the same position on reassembly.

Testing

1. Connect an ohmmeter, on lowest range, between the single brush connector and one stator lead connector.

2. Observe the reading, then reverse the meter leads. Repeat this test with each of the other two stator lead connectors. The readings on each of these tests should NOT be identical, there should be one low and one high reading for each test. If this is not the case, replace the diode trio.

— CAUTION —

Do not use high voltage on the diode trio.

RECTIFIER BRIDGE

Testing

1. Connect an ohmmeter between the heat sink (ground) and the base of one of the three terminals. Then, reverse the meter leads and take a reading. If both readings are identical, the bridge is defective and

END FRAME VIEW

INSULATING WASHERS

RESISTOR (USED ON SOME MODELS)

RECTIFIER BRIDGE

CAPACITOR

ATTACHING NUTS

DIODE TRIO

10-SI brush lead clip ground test

must be replaced.

2. Repeat this test with the remaining two terminals, then between the INSULATED heat sink (as opposed to the GROUNDED heat sink in previous test) and each of the three terminals. As before, if any two readings are identical, on reversing the meter leads, the rectifier bridge must be replaced.

Removal

1. Remove the attaching screw and the BAT. terminal screw.
2. Disconnect the condenser lead.
3. Remove the rectifier bridge.

NOTE: The insulator between the insulated heat sink and the end frame is extremely important to the operation of the unit. It must be replaced in exactly the same position on reassembly.

BRUSH AND/OR VOLTAGE REGULATOR R & R

1. Remove two brush holder screws and stator lead to strap nut and washer, brush holder screws and one of the diode trio lead strap attaching screws.

NOTE: The insulating washers must be replaced in the same position on reassembly.

2. Remove brush holder and brushes. The voltage regulator may also be removed at this time, if desired.
3. Brushes and brush spring must be free of corrosion and must be undamaged and completely free of oil or grease.

BRUSHES RETAINED IN HOLDER

BRUSH RETAINER

BRUSHES

10-SI brush holder

4. Insert spring and brushes into holder, noting whether they slide freely without binding. Insert wooden or plastic toothpick into bottom hole in holder to retain brushes.

NOTE: The brush holder is serviced as a unit; individual parts are not available.

5. Reassemble in reverse order of disassembly.

Delcotron 27-SI Series, Type 200

The 27-SI Series, type 200 alternator features a solid state voltage regulator that is mounted inside the slip ring end frame. The regulated voltage can be adjusted externally by repositioning a voltage adjustment cap, located on the slip ring end frame. Two brushes carry current through the two slip rings to the field coil, mounted on the rotor.

The stator windings are assembled on the inside of a laminated core that forms part of the frame. A rectifier bridge connected to the stator windings contains six diodes, their main function is to change the stator A.C. current to a D.C. current which is present at the output terminal. Field current is supplied through residual magnetism and a diode trio, which is also connected to the stator windings. A capacitor (or condensor) is mounted in the end frame to protect the rectifier bridge and diode trio from high voltages and also suppresses radio noise. An "R" terminal is provided to operate auxiliary equipment in some circuits.

Alternator bench test connections

Alternator Output Test

To test the output of the alternator in a bench test stand, have a fully charged battery and connect an ammeter between the battery positive post (on negative grounded units) and the battery terminal of the alternator. Connect a voltmeter to the positive and negative posts of the battery. Ground the battery negative post to the alternator frame or to a common ground.

─── **IMPORTANT** ───

Rotor magnetism must be present in this alternator to perform properly. If the alternator has been disassembled for service, it may be necessary to induce magnetism back into the rotor to provide voltage build-up when the engine is started. To magnetize the rotor, connect the Integral Charging System to the battery in a normal manner, then momentarily connect

Testing the 10-SI rectifier bridge

a jumper lead from the battery positive post to the Integral Charging System relay terminal. This procedure will restore normal residual magnetism in the rotor.

After making the required meter connections between the alternator and the battery on the test stand, proceed as follows:

1. Slowly increase the alternator speed and observe the voltage.

2. If the voltage is uncontrolled with speed and increases over 15.5 volts on a 12 volt system, test the regulator.

NOTE: The regulator can be tested on a commercial tester. If a tester is not available, replace the voltage regulator.

3. If the voltage is below 15.5 volts on a 12 volt system, connect a carbon pile rheostat to the battery.

4. Operate the alternator at a moderate speed and adjust the rheostat as required to obtain the maximum current output.

5. If the output is within 10 amperes of the rated output as stamped on the alternator frame, the alternator is good.

6. If the output is not within 10 amperes of the rated output, keep the battery loaded with the carbon pile and ground the tab in the end frame hole.

────── CAUTION ──────
The tab is within ¾ inch of the casting surface. Do not force the probe tool deeper than one inch into the end frame.
─────────────────────

7. Operate the alternator at moderate speed and adjust the carbon pile rheostat as required to obtain maximum output, with the tab pushed in to ground.

8. If the output is within 10 amperes of the rated output, check field winding and regulator.

9. If the output is not within 10 amperes of the rated output, check the field winding, diode trio, rectifier bridge and stator.

10. Stop the unit and disconnect the various test meters from the alternator and make necessary repairs or tests.

ELECTRICAL TESTS

The electrical tests are made in the same manner as the tests for the 10-SI and 27-SI, type 100 alternators with the exception of the following:

1. The Delta windings of the stator cannot be checked for open circuits.

2. The regulator can be checked with a commercial tester and the connector cap can be checked with an ohmmeter. Check the connector body with the ohmmeter in the middle range scale. Connect the ohmmeter to each adjacent pair of terminals, making four checks in all. If any one check is infinite, replace the connector body.

Voltage Adjustment

A four positioned cap (connector body), is used to regulate the desired increase or decrease of voltage by removing the cap from its seat and rotating in 90 degree increments. Reposition the cap in its seat and align the proper marking on the cap with the indicator arrow on the alternator housing. The cap is marked "LO", "2", "3" and "HI".

Disassembly and Assembly

1. Hold generator in a vice, clamping the mounting flange lengthwise.

2. Make a scribe mark to help locate frame end parts in the same position during assembly.

3. Remove 4 through-bolts and separate the slip ring end frame from the drive end frame and rotor assembly.

NOTE: Prying with a screwdriver at stator slot will aid disassembly.

4. Remove 3 stator lead attaching nuts and separate stator from end frame.

5. Remove 3 screws from brush holder and disconnect regulator lead from regulator. Remove diode trio and brush holder. Then lift regulator and unplug it from the voltage adjustment connector body.

6. Remove screw and clip attaching the

connector body to the end frame. Pull connector body from end frame.

7. Remove screws attaching capacitor to end frame and diode rectifier bridge.

8. Remove 2 ground screws attaching diode bridge to end frame. Then disconnect the "R" terminal and battery terminal connectors from the bridge and end frame. Remove rectifier bridge from end frame.

9. Press bearing from end frame using a tube with a slightly smaller OD than the bearing. Support the end frame from inside and press bearing from outside toward the inside.

15-SI test connectors

NOTE: Some models have a seal separate and in front of bearing. Discard the seal when replacing the bearing as the new bearing has an integral seal.

10. Separate drive end frame from rotor as follows:

  a. Place rotor in a vise and tighten only enough to permit pulley nut removal.

NOTE: Rotor may be distorted if vise is over tightened.

  b. Remove pulley nut, washer, pulley, fan, and slinger collar from rotor shaft.

  c. Remove drive end frame and rear

Charging system schematic with electro-mechanical regulator and charging light

collar from rotor shaft and remove rotor from vise.

11. Press bearing from drive end frame after removing bearing retainer plate:

a. Remove screws attaching bearing seal and retainer assembly to housing.

b. Support end frame from inside the housing on a metal tube slightly larger ID than the OD of the bearing.

c. Press bearing from end frame using a metal tube or collar against the bearing inner race.

12. The assembly is in the reverse order of the disassembly. Tighten the pulley nut to 75 ft. lbs.

── **CAUTION** ──

Do not interchange the ground screw (without insulator) for an insulated screw as this may cause uncontrolled or no alternator output.

Delcotron 27-SI Series, Type 205

The type 205, 27-SI series is basically the same as the type 200, but with internal wiring changes. A recognizable feature of this alternator from the outside is the splined rotor shaft extending from the rear of the end housing. The regulator voltage setting is not adjustable and the rotor field windings do not rely on residual magnetism to excite the field circuit to begin the charging cycle. The initial field current is supplied through an indicator light circuit with connectors engaging their respective terminals at the end frame housing.

27SI-205 generators are used with the

Deutz air-cooled diesel. Both 65A and 80A models are similar to those used on gas engine vehicles except for the inclusion of a vacuum pump.

TEST SPECIFICATIONS

	Field Current	Output Amps @ rpm
65A	4.4–4.9	55 @ 2000
		68 @ 7000
80A	4.4–4.9	52 @ 2000
		72 @ 5000

ELECTRICAL TESTS

The electrical tests of the internal components are basically the same as the tests performed on the type 200 components.

Disassembly and Assembly

The disassembly and assembly is typical of the 27-SI series.

Ford-Autolite (Ford Motor Co.)

The Ford-Autolite charging system is a negative ground system. It includes an alternator, an electro-mechanical regulator or an electronic regulator, a charge indicator or an ammeter and a storage battery.

NOTE: Late model Ford systems have replaced the electro-mechanical regulator with either a non-adjustable transistorized regulator or an adjustable transistorized regulator. The adjustable transistorized unit used with high output

systems has a single, voltage limit adjusting screw under the cover. Do not use a metal screwdriver for adjustment.

TROUBLESHOOTING

NOTE: See the "Alternator Test Plans" section before proceeding further.

Fusible Links

1. Check the fusible link located between the starter relay and the alternator. Replace the link if it is burned or open.

CHARGING SYSTEM OPERATION

NOTE: If the current indicator is to give an accurate reading, the battery cables must be of the same gauge and length as the original equipment.

1. With the engine running, and all electrical systems turned off, place a current indicator over the positive battery cable.

2. If a charge of about 5 amps is recorded, the charging system is working. If a draw of about 5 amps is recorded, the system is not working. The needle moves toward the battery when a charge condition is indicated, and away from the battery when a draw condition is indicated. If a draw is indicated, continue to the next testing procedure. If an overcharge of 10–15 amps is indicated, check for a faulty regulator or a bad ground at the regulator or the alternator.

Testing the Ignition Switch to Regulator Circuit

1. Disconnect the regulator wiring harness from the regulator.

2. Turn on the key. Using a test light or voltmeter, check for voltage between the I wire and ground. Check for voltage between the A wire and ground. If voltage is

27-SI schematic

Alternator charging system with indicator lamp

Alternator charging system with ammeter

present at this part of the system, the circuit is OK. If there is no voltage at the I wire, check for a burned-out charge indicator bulb, a burned-out resistor, or a break or short in the wiring. If there is no voltage present at the A wire, check for a bad connection at the starter relay or a break or short in the wire.

Isolation Test

This test determines whether the regulator or the alternator is faulty, after the rest of the circuit is found to be in good working order.

1. Disconnect the regulator wiring harness from the regulator.
2. Connect a jumper wire from the A wire to the F wire in the wiring harness plug.
3. Connect a voltmeter to the battery. The positive voltmeter lead goes to the positive terminal and the negative lead to the negative terminal. Record the reading on the voltmeter.
4. Turn off all of the electrical systems and start the engine. Do not race the engine.
5. Gradually increase engine speed to 1500–2000 rpm. The voltmeter reading should increase above the previously recorded battery voltage reading by at least one to two volts. If there is no increase, the alternator is not working correctly. If there is an increase, the voltage regulator needs to be replaced.

OVERHAUL

Disassembly—1977–80 Rear Terminal Alternator

1. Mark both end housings with a scribe mark for assembly.
2. Remove the three housing through-bolts.
3. Separate the front housing and rotor

from the stator and rear housing.
4. Remove the nuts from the rectifier to rear housing mounting studs, and remove the rear housing.
5. Remove the brush holder mounting screws and the holder, brushes, springs, insulator, and terminal.
6. If replacement is necessary, press the bearing from the rear end housing, support housing on inner boss.
7. If rectifiers are to be replaced, carefully unsolder the leads from the terminals.

—————— **CAUTION** ——————
Use only a 100-watt soldering iron. Leave the soldering iron in contact with the diode terminals only long enough to remove the wires. Use pliers as temporary heat sinks in order to protect the diodes.

8. There are various types of rectifier assembly circuit boards installed in production. One type has the circuit board spaced away from the diode plates and the diodes are exposed. Another type consists of a single circuit board with integral diodes; and still another has integral diodes with an additional booster diode plate containing two diodes. This last type is used only on the eight-diode, 61-amp. Autolite alternator. To disassemble, use the following procedures:
   a. Exposed Diodes—remove the screws from the rectifier by rotating bolt heads ¼ turn clockwise to unlock, then unscrewing.
   b. Integral Diodes—press out the stator terminal screw, making sure not to twist it while doing this. Do not remove grounded screw.
   c. Booster Diodes—press out the stator terminal screw about ¼ in., then remove the nut from the end of the screw and lift screw from circuit board, making sure not to twist it as it comes out.
9. Remove the drive pulley and fan. On alternator pulleys with threaded holes in the outer end of the pulley, use a standard puller for removal.
10. Remove the three screws that hold the front bearing retainer, and remove the front housing.
11. If the bearing is to be replaced, press from housing.

Cleaning and Inspection

1. The rotor, stator, diode rectifier assemblies, and bearings are not to be cleaned with solvent. These parts are to be wiped off with a clean cloth. Cleaning solvent may cause damage to the electrical parts or contaminate the bearing internal lubricant. Wash all other parts in solvent and dry them.
2. Rotate the front bearing on the driveshaft. Check for any scraping noise, looseness or roughness that indicates that the bearing is excessively worn. As the bearing is being rotated, look for excessive lubricant leakage. If any of these conditions exist, replace the bearing. Check rear bearing and rotor shaft.

JUMPER WIRE CONNECTED TO ALTERNATOR "BAT" AND "FLD" TERMINALS

JUMPER WIRE CONNECTED TO ALTERNATOR "BAT" AND "FLD" TERMINALS

REGULATOR PLUG REMOVED FROM REGULATOR

Location of jumper wire for circuit tests on rear and side terminal alternators

3. Place the rear end housing on the slip ring end of the shaft and rotate the bearing on the shaft. Make a similar check for noise, looseness or roughness. Inspect the rollers and cage for damage. Replace the bearing if these conditions exist, or if the lubricant is missing or contaminated.

4. Check both the front and rear housings for cracks.

5. Check all wire leads on both the stator and rotor assemblies for loose soldered connections, and for burned insulation. Solder all poor connections. Replace parts that show burned insulation.

6. Check the slip rings for damaged insulation and runout. If the slip rings are more than 0.0005 in. out of round, take a light cut (minimum diameter limit 1.22 in.) from the face of the rings to true them. If the slip rings are badly damaged, the entire rotor will have to be replaced, as they are serviced as a complete assembly.

7. Replace any parts that are burned or cracked. Replace brushes that are worn to less than 5/16 in. in length. Replace the brush spring if it had less than 7–12 oz. tension.

Field Current Draw Test

NOTE: Alternator must be removed

Testing the diodes on a 65 amp alternator

from the truck.

1. Connect a test ammeter between the alternator frame and the positive post of a 12-volt test battery.

2. Connect a jumper wire between the negative test battery post and the alternator field terminal.

3. Observe the ammeter:
   a. Little or no current flow indicates

high brush resistance, open field windings, or high winding resistance.

b. Current in excess of specifications (approximately 2.9 amps. for most models) indicates shorted or grounded field windings, or brush leads touching.

NOTE: Sometimes the alternator produces current output at low engine speeds, but ceases to put out at higher speeds. This can be caused by centrifugal force expanding the rotor windings to the point where they short to ground. Place in a test stand and check field current draw while spinning alternator.

Diode Tests

Disassemble the alternator. Disconnect diode assembly from stator and make tests. To test one set of diodes, contact one ohmmeter probe to the diode plate and contact each of the three stator lead terminals with the other probe. Reverse the probes and repeat the test. All six tests (eight for 61 amp. Autolite eight-diode models) should show a reading of about 60 ohms in one direction and infinite ohms in the other. If two high readings, or two low readings, are obtained after reversing probes the diode is faulty and must be replaced.

Stator Tests

Disassemble the stator from the alternator assembly and rectifiers. Connect test ohmmeter probes between each pair of stator leads. If the ohmmeter does not indicate equally between each pair of leads, the stator coil is open and must be replaced.

Testing the diodes on all but 65 amp alternators

Charging system schematic with transistor regulator and ammeter

General charging system tests with ohmmeter and voltmeter

used on the molded circuit boards only. Using these washers on a fiber board will result in a serious short circuit, as only a flat insulating washer between the stator terminal and the board is used on fiber circuit boards.

   c. Booster Diodes—position the stator wire terminal on the stator terminal screw, then position screw on rectifier. Position square insulator over the screw and into the square hole in the rectifier, rotate terminal screw until it locks, then press it in fingertight. Position the stator wire, then press the terminal screw into the rectifier and insulator with a vise.

11. Place the radio noise suppression condenser on the rectifier terminals. With molded circuit board, install the STA and BAT terminal insulators. With fiber circuit board, place the square stator terminal insulator in the square hole in the rectifier assembly, then position BAT terminal insulator.

Position the stator and rectifier assembly in the rear housing, making sure that all terminal insulators are seated properly in the recesses. Position STA, BAT and FLD insulators on terminal bolts; install nuts.

12. Clean the rear bearing surface of the rotor shaft with a rag, then position rear housing and stator assembly over rotor. Align matchmarks made during disassembly and install through-bolts. *Remove brush retracting wire and place a dab of silicone sealer over the hole.*

Disassembly—1981 and Later Rear Terminal Alternators

1. Scribe the end housings and stator frame for alignment during reassembly, and then remove the three housing through bolts.

2. Separate the front housing and rotor assembly from the stator and rear housing. If there is resistance in pulling the front housing free, tap the front housing lightly with a plastic tipped hammer to break it loose.

3. Remove the brush springs from the brush holder, located in the rear housing.

4. Note the colors and locations of nuts, washers, and insulators on the back of the rear housing for reconnection. Then, remove all of them.

5. Remove the stator and rectifier assembly from the rear housing.

6. Remove the screws attaching the brush holder to the rear housing; then remove the brush holder, brushes, and brush terminal insulator.

7. Press the bearing out of the rear housing with an arbor press. Make sure the housing is supported as close as possible to the bearing boss to prevent damage to it.

8. Clamp the front housing in a vise equipped with protective jaws. Remove the drive pulley retaining nut. This requires a 5⁄16 in. socket and ¾ in. wrench to drive it, and a special tool that passes through the center of the socket wrench, and locks onto the rotor shaft, and prevents it from turning

Connect test ohmmeter probes between one of the stator leads and the stator core. The ohmmeter should not show any reading. If it does show continuity, the stator winding is grounded and must be replaced.

Assembly—1977–80 Rear Terminal Alternator

1. Press the front bearing into the front housing boss, putting pressure on outer race only. Install bearing retainer.

2. If the stop ring on the driveshaft was damaged, install a new stop ring. Push the new ring onto the shaft and into the groove.

3. Position the front bearing spacer on the driveshaft against the stop ring.

4. Place the front housing over the shaft, with the bearing positioned in the front housing cavity.

5. Install fan spacer, fan, pulley, lockwasher and retaining nut and tighten nut to 60–100 ft. lbs. holding the drive shaft with an Allen key.

6. If rear bearing was removed, press a new one into rear housing.

7. Assemble brushes, springs, terminal and insulator in the brush holder, retract the brushes and insert a short length of ⅛ in. rod or stiff wire through the hole in the holder to hold the brushes in the retracted position.

8. Position the brush holder assembly in the rear housing and install mounting screws. Position brush leads to prevent shorting.

9. Wrap the three stator winding leads around the circuit board terminals and solder them using only rosin core solder and a 100-watt iron. Position the stator neutral lead eyelet on the stator terminal screw and install the screw in the rectifier assembly.

10a. Exposed Diodes—insert the special screws through the wire lug, dished washers and circuit board. Turn ¼ turn counterclockwise to lock in place.

   b. Integral Diodes—insert the screws straight through the holes.

NOTE: The dished washers are to be

Side terminal alternator

Stator and rectifier assemblies

Exploded view of typical late model rear terminal alternator (© Ford Motor Co.)

FLAT TYPE (INTEGRATED) RECTIFIER

RECTIFIER (DISCRETE) WITH EXPOSED DIODES

Rectifier assembly exploded view

On late model rear terminal alternators and all side model alternators, use this special tool to remove the pulley retaining nut (© Ford Motor Co.)

as the nut is removed. Then, remove the lockwasher, drive pulley, fan, and fan spacer.

9. Remove the rotor from the front housing and remove the housing from the vise.

10. Remove the front bearing spacer from the rotor shaft, but leave the stop ring in place unless it is damaged.

11. Remove the screws that attach the front bearing retainer to the front housing and remove the retainer. Then remove the bearing from the housing by sliding it out, or, if there is resistance, using an arbor press. If a press is needed, make sure to support the housing close to the bearing boss to prevent damage.

12. Remove the battery terminal insulator and radio suppression capacitor from the rectifier assembly.

13. Use a 100-watt soldering iron to unsolder the stator leads where they connect to the rectifier. Make sure the iron is hot before starting and work quickly to avoid damaging the rectifier. Do this by using needle nose pliers to pull upwards on the stator lead terminals where they connect to

the rectifier assembly. Once each connector comes loose, shake the molten solder from it.

14. Disconnect the stator neutral lead from the rectifier of each type as follows:

Flat, integrated type rectifier—Press the stator terminal screw straight out of the rectifier. *Do not turn the screw during removal* or the serrations holding it in place will be damaged.

Exposed diode, separate type rectifier—turn the stator terminal screw ¼ turn to unlock it and remove it.

15. If it is necessary to remove the ground terminal, follow the appropriate procedure above.

Cleaning and Inspection

NOTE: These alternators come equipped with either standard or high temperature rectifier assemblies and bearings. High temperature alternators must use high temperature parts or failure will occur.

1. Wipe the rotor, stator and bearings with a clean cloth. *Do not use solvent.*

2. Rotate the front bearing on the drive end of the rotor shaft, checking for noise, looseness, roughness, or lubricant leakage. Replace the bearing if any of these defects are noted.

3. Inspect the rear bearing surface of the rotor shaft for roughness or severe chatter marks; replace the rotor assembly if the shaft is not smooth. Then, place the rear bearing onto the slip ring end of the shaft and rotate it. Inspect as for the front bearing, checking additionally for damaged rollers or cage. Replace the bearing if there are any of these conditions present or if the lubricant has been lost or contaminated.

4. Check the pulley and fan for looseness on the rotor shaft and distortion, and replace if either condition exists.

5. Inspect both halves of the housing

for cracks, especially in webbed areas, and replace as necessary.

6. Check all leads on the stator and rotor for loose or broken soldered connections and for burned insulation. Resolder poor connections and replace parts with burned insulation.

7. Check the slip rings for nicks and surface roughness. Turn the rings to as small as 1.22 in. diameter, if necessary. If they are badly damaged, the rotor must be replaced.

8. Inspect the brushes for wear beyond ¼ in. and replace as necessary.

Assembly—1981 and Later Rear Terminal Alternators

1. Install the front bearing in its housing, pressing on the outer race only. Then, position the bearing retainer on the front housing and install the attaching screws, torquing to 25-40 in. lbs.

2. If the stop ring was removed from the rotor shaft, install a new one. Slide it over the end of the shaft and into the groove *without opening it with snap ring pliers,* or permanent deformation will result.

3. Install the bearing spacer onto the rotor shaft with the recessed side against the stop ring.

4. Install the rotor into the front housing. Clamp the housing in a vise.

5. Install the fan spacer, fan, drive pulley, lockwasher, and nut onto the rotor shaft. Torque the nut to 60-100 ft. lbs. using the special tool used in removal.

6. Install the rear bearing with an arbor press and supporting the housing close to the bearing boss. Make sure the bearing is flush with the surface of the housing.

7. Position the brush wiring eyelet over the brush terminal and install the terminal insulator.

8. Install the springs and brushes into the brush holder and then insert a piece of stiff wire through the brush holder to hold

them in position against spring tension. Then position the brush holder in the rear housing. Install the brush holder mounting screws, making sure the ground brush wiring eyelet is positioned under the left hand mounting screw. Then, holding the brush holder firmly against the housing, torque the screws to 17-25 in. lbs.

9. Connect the stator neutral lead to the rectifier of each type as follows:

Flat, integrated type rectifier—Position the stator terminal insulator and the stator neutral lead on the rectifier assembly. Insert the terminal screw and press it into position. Make sure it is pressed in far enough to keep the neutral lead terminal from moving.

Exposed diode, separate type rectifier—Position the stator neutral lead and dished washer on the rectifier assembly. Insert the terminal screw and lock it into place by rotating it ¼ turn.

10. If the ground terminal was removed from the rectifier assembly, install it pressing or turning it as outlined above for the appropriate type of rectifier.

11. Make sure the insulator sleeves are in place. Then, wrap the stator winding leads around the terminals of the rectifier assembly and solder them with a 100 watt iron and rosin core electrical solder. Work quickly to make sure you do not overheat the rectifier.

12. Install the radio suppression capacitor and battery terminal insulator to the rectifier assembly. Then, install the insulator onto the stator terminal screw. Finally, align the terminal screws on the rectifier assembly with the holes on the back of the rear housing and install the stator rectifier assembly in to the rear housing. Make sure the terminal insulators are seated in their recesses.

13. Install the external insulators, washers, and nuts onto the terminals, following this color coding:

Black on "STA" terminal
Red on "BAT" terminal
Orange on "FLD" terminal

Torque the nut for the red lead to 30-55 in. lbs., and the other two to 25-35 in. lbs.

14. Wipe the rear end bearing surface of the rotor shaft with a clean, lint-free rag. Then, remove the rotor and front housing assembly from the vise. Finally, position the rear housing and stator assembly over the rotor and align the scribe marks made during disassembly. Make sure the machined portion of the stator core is seated in the stop in both end housings. Install the through bolts and torque to 35-60 ft. lbs.

15. Remove the wire holding the brushes in a retracted position.

Disassembly—1977 and Later Side Terminal Alternator

1. Mark the front and rear housings and the stator for reassembly in the same positions. Then, remove the four housing through bolts. Without separating the rear

housing and stator, pull the front housing and rotor from the assembly. Slots are provided in the front housing to help you pry it away from the stator.

2. Remove the drive pulley nut with a 5/16 in. socket and ¾ in. wrench to drive it and a special tool that passes through the center of the socket to hold the shaft in place. Remove the lockwasher, pulley, fan, and fan spacer from the rotor shaft. Finally, pull the rotor and shaft from the front housing and remove the rotor shaft spacer.

3. Remove the three screws retaining the bearing to the front housing. If the bearing shows either wear or loss of lubricant, press it out of the housing, being sure to support the housing close to the bearing boss to prevent damage to it.

4. Unsolder and disengage the three stator leads from the rectifier. Use a hot iron and work quickly to avoid overheating it. Then, lift the stator from the rear housing.

5. Quickly unsolder and disengage the brush holder lead from the rectifier.

6. Remove the screw attaching the capacitor lead to the rectifier. Then, remove the four screws attaching the rectifier to the rear housing. Finally, remove the two terminal nuts and insulator from the outside of the housing and remove the rectifier.

7. Remove the two screws attaching the brush holder to the housing and remove the brushes and holder. Remove the two rectifier insulators from the housing bosses.

8. Remove any sealing compound from the rear housing and brush holder.

9. Remove the screw attaching the capacitor to the rear housing and remove the capacitor.

10. Inspect the rear bearing for excessive wear, damage, or loss of lubricant and, if necessary press it out, supporting the housing close to the bearing boss to prevent damage to it.

Cleaning and Inspection

See the procedures for cleaning and inspection of the 1981 and later rear terminal alternator above, which are identical.

Assembly—1977 and Later Side Terminal Alternators

1. If the front bearing is being replaced, first press the new bearing into the housing, putting pressure on the outer race only. Then, install the bearing retaining screws and torque them to 25-40 in.-lbs.

2. Place the inner spacer on to the rotor shaft and insert the rotor shaft into the center of the front bearing.

3. Install the fan spacer, fan, pulley, lockwasher, and nut onto the rotor shaft, in that order. Then, tighten the nut using the socket, open end wrench, and special tool used in removal.

4. If the rear bearing is being replaced, press a new one in by the outer race only until the rear face is flush with the outer surface of the bearing boss.

5. Position the brush terminal on the

brush holder. Then, install the springs and brushes in the holder, and insert a piece of stiff wire across in front of the brushes to retain them in a retracted position for assembly.

6. Position the brush holder in the rear housing and start the attaching screws. Make sure the wire retaining the brushes sticks out far enough for you to pull it from the housing after the alternator is assembled. Poke any sealer that may be present out of the pin hole in the housing. Then, hold the brush holder firmly toward the brush enclosure opening while tightening the attaching screws. Finally, reseal the crack between the brush holder and the brush cavity in the rear housing with a body sealer. *Don't* use a silicone sealant.

7. Position the capacitor in the rear housing and start install the attaching screw.

8. Place the two rectifier bosses in the housing.

9. Place the insulator on the larger ("BAT") terminal of the rectifier and position the rectifier in the rear housing. Place the outside insulator on the "BAT" terminal install the nuts on both "BAT" and "GRD" terminals finger tight.

10. Start the four rectifier attaching screws. Then, tighten the "BAT" terminal nut to 35-50 in.-lbs. and the "GRD" nut to 25-30 in.-lbs. These nuts are located on the outside of the housing. Finally, tighten the four rectifier attaching screws to 40-50 in. lbs.

11. Connect the capacitor lead to the rectifier with the attaching screw.

12. Press the brush holder lead onto the rectifier pin and solder it securely. Use a hot iron and work quickly so the rectifier does not overheat.

13. Position the stator in the rear housing, aligning the scribe marks made at the beginning of disassembly. Press the three stator leads onto the rectifier pins and solder securely. Again, work quickly to protect components.

14. Position the rotor and front housing into/onto the stator and rear housing. Align the marks made in disassembly, and then install the through bolts. Tighten two opposing bolts first; then, tighten the other two opposing bolts.

15. Test the unit for binding by spinning the fan. Remove the wire retracting the brushes and seal the hole with waterproof cement. *Do not* use a silicone sealer.

Autolite Alternator with Integral Regulator

Some vehicles are equipped with an Autolite alternator having an integral regulator mounted to the rear end housing. The regulator is a hybrid unit featuring use of solid state integrated circuits. These circuits may consist of transistors, diodes and resistors. The unusual feature of this type of micro-electronic circuit is that the entire circuit is within a silicone crystal approximately ⅛ in. square. Because of the small size of the circuit, it is not repairable or adjustable and must be replaced as a unit if found to be defective. It should be noted that the size of the regulator housing is dictated only by the fact that some means of connecting the regulator to the alternator is necessary. Overhaul is the same as for other Autolite alternators.

TROUBLESHOOTING

NOTE: See the "Alternator Test Plans" section before proceeding further.

Fusible Links

1. Check the fusible link located between the starter relay and the alternator. Replace the link if it is burned or open.

Output Test

1. Place transmission in Neutral or Park.
2. Remove the positive battery cable and install a battery adapter switch in the line.
3. Attach one lead of a test voltmeter to the negative battery post and the other

Charging system schematic with integral regulator

test lead to the circuit side of the adapter switch.

4. Connect a test ammeter to each side of the adapter switch, so that charging current will go through the ammeter when the switch is opened.

5. Connect a jumper wire between the alternator frame and the integral regulator

field terminal (cover plug removed).

6. Close adapter switch, start engine and open adapter switch.

7. Running engine at 2,000 rpm, observe voltmeter and ammeter. At 15 volts indicated, the ammeter should read 50–57 amps. If so, and there is still a no-charge condition, the regulator is probably faulty

34803-S (X-60)
★351256-S
10329
10328
★10370
%♦10347
10349
10351
10329
10335
10A355
10A303
10333
★10330
10A396 (3)
10A344
10A310
34053-S (M-156)
♦%10347
★10350
10344
40917-S (U-257)
10B372
%10B368
10A304
10334
351496-S (XX-306)
♦10B367
★379201-S
★374549-S
■10A377
†10A383
★10378 (3)
★10374 (3)
34055-S (M-158)
■10310
34805-S (X-62)
10329
■10A358 (6)
†10A383
375483-S (XX-85-A)
†10B371
†10B330
34053-S (M-156)
10336
356488-S (XX-226)
34803-S (X-60)
10329
351124-S (MM-42)
★351256-S
■(4)
■10310
†10A383 (2) ■(2)
■10397 (6)
■(4)
†10373 (3)
★10A350

†ALSO SUPPLIED IN 10304 RECTIFIER ASSEMBLY
■SUPPLIED ONLY IN 10304 RECTIFIER ASSEMBLY
%ALSO SUPPLIED IN 10347 BRUSH REPAIR KIT
♦ALSO SUPPLIED IN 10B363 COVER & BRUSH ASSEMBLY

70 and 90 amp rear terminal alternators

Output test

VOLTAGE LIMITER TEST

Voltage limiter test

and must be replaced. An output 2–8 amps. below 50 amps. usually indicates an open diode rectifier, while an output 10–15 amps. below minimum specifications usually indicates a shorted diode. An alternator with a shorted diode usually will whine at idle speed.

Field Test (Voltmeter)

1. Turn ignition switch to OFF position.
2. Remove wire from regulator supply terminal.
3. Remove cover plug from regulator field terminal and connect one test voltmeter lead to this terminal. A ¼ ohm resistor should be in the circuit.
4. Connect the other test voltmeter lead to a good engine ground.
5. The voltmeter should read 12 volts. If *no* voltage is present, the field circuit is open or grounded.
6. If voltmeter reads more than I volt, but still less than battery voltage, there is probably a partial ground in the alternator field circuit and the circuit should be checked with an ohmmeter.

Field Test (Ohmmeter)

1. Disconnect battery ground cable; remove alternator from truck.
2. Remove the regulator from the alternator (covered later).
3. Make the ohmmeter tests as illustrated. If any of the tests indicates a field circuit problem, disassemble the alternator to further isolate the trouble.
   a. Contact each ohmmeter probe to a slip ring. Resistance should be 4–5 ohms. A higher reading indicates a damaged slip ring soldered connection or a broken wire. A lower reading indicates a shorted wire or slip ring assembly.
   b. Contact one ohmmeter probe to a slip ring and the other probe to the rotor

shaft. Any reading other than infinite ohms indicates a short to ground. If neither of these tests (A and B) isolates the trouble, the brushes or brush assembly are the probable cause.

Voltage Limiter Test

1. Check the battery specific gravity. If it is not at least 1.230, charge the battery or install a charged battery for the test.
2. Make sure all lights and accessories are turned off, including such items as dome lights.
3. Make the test connections as illustrated.
4. Place transmission in Neutral or Park, close battery adapter switch and start the engine.

Field test

5. Open the battery adapter switch and operate engine at 2,000 rpm for 5 minutes. The voltmeter should read 13.3–15.3 volts.
6. If voltage does not rise above 12 volts, perform a regulator supply voltage test to determine whether or not the regulator is getting voltage from the battery. Before replacing a regulator, check the wiring of the entire charging system for shorts, opens, or high resistance connections.

Regulator Supply Voltage Test

The regulator is "turned on" by the application of battery voltage through a 10 ohm resistor wire. If the supply circuit is defective, the regulator will not function and the alternator will not put out current.

1. Connect a 12-volt test light or voltmeter between the regulator supply lead and ground.

Supply voltage test

2. Turn on the ignition switch. The test light should glow or the voltmeter indicate. If not, the supply circuit should be checked back to the battery, especially the resistance wire.

Overhaul

The overhaul procedures for the alternator are the same as for the Ford Autolite electro-mechanical alternator.

Motorola System

The Motorola alternator is an electro-mechanical device producing alternating current, which is changed to direct current by the rectifier diodes, accomplished by the characteristics of the diodes to allow current to flow in one direction only.

A three phase stator winding is used, a "Wye" type for the 37 ampere rated alternator, and a "Delta" type for the 51 and 55 ampere rated alternators.

A field diode assembly is used to provide the excitation current to the rotor (field) windings when the alternator is operating and is sensed and regulated by the voltage regulator to control the output of the alternator.

The field diode assembly is either mounted on a circuit board or encased within a epoxy "pot" with the leads attached in parallel to the positive rectifier diodes. If one or more of the field diodes become open, shorted, or downgraded, the alternator output will be affected.

NOTE: Do not use the regulator terminal for a source of current for any reason. To do so would adversely affect the operation of the voltage regulator.

— CAUTION —

Some alternators are equipped with a 7 volt terminal for the supply of current to the electric automatic choke. This terminal is located on the negative rectifier assembly. Do not interchange the wires between the regulator terminal and this terminal.

The voltage regulator is a sealed unit and requires no adjustment. Replacement of the unit is required if the regulator becomes defective.

TROUBLESHOOTING

NOTE: See the "Alternator Test Plans" section before proceeding further.

Fusible Link Test

There are many fuse links in the truck however the fuse link located in the wiring between the battery terminal of the horn relay to the main wire harness is the only one that concerns the charging system. This link protects the entire wiring harness. If it fails, all the electrical systems will fail to function.

Testing the Ignition Switch to Regulator Circuit

1. Disconnect the regulator wires from the regulator.
2. Turn on the key. Using a test light or voltmeter, check for current between the voltage supply wire and ground. This wire is usually orange and has another wire connected to it, usually blue or orange with a tracer.
3. If current is present, this part of the system is OK. If no voltage is present, check for broken or shorted wiring, a bad indicator bulb, a bad fuse in the fuse panel, or a bad connection at the ignition switch or on the battery side of the starter relay.

ALTERNATOR TESTS (IN VEHICLE)

NOTE: Various types of charging system testers are available to perform the tests necessary to determine if the system or components are defective. Follow the manufactures instructions for the tester being used, as the following charging system tests are generalized.

— CAUTION —

Do not disconnect the output lead or the voltage regulator, other than as directed, while the alternator is being operated. Do not ground the field terminal. Severe charging system damage could result.

Alternator Output Test

1. Connect voltmeter to battery, observing proper polarity.
2. Start the engine and operate at 1000 RPMs for two minutes with the headlamps on low beam.
3. Observe the voltage reading. If the voltage remains above 13 volts and below 15 volts, the alternator and the regulator are working satisfactorily.
4. If the voltage is registering out of the above range, further testing will have to be done.

Field Draw Test

1. Loosen the alternator belt so that the rotor can be turned by hand.
2. Connect ammeter leads between the positive battery post and the positive brush post on the alternator.
3. The ammeter should register a reading within a range of 1½ to 3 amperes and if by turning the rotor by hand, the reading varies within the scale, the brushes and the slip rings require cleaning or repairs.
4. If the readings are too high or too

Field circuit test with ohmmeter

Motorola alternator

low, the alternator should be removed and disassembled for further tests and repairs.

Regulator Bypass Test

1. Connect a voltmeter to the battery, observing the proper polarity. Disconnect the voltage regulator.

2. Start the engine and allow to idle.

3. Connect an ammeter lead between the positive battery post to the alternator positive brush terminal.

4. Increase the engine speed while observing the voltage reading. A reading of 16 volts should be obtained, if the alternator is not defective.

NOTE: Do not allow the voltage to increase over 16 volts, as damage to the charging system can result.

Field Diode Assembly Test

NOTE: A shorted or open field diode assembly will cause reduced alternator output and require unit disassembly and removal of the diode assembly for testing. A downgrading of one or more of the diodes will cause the dash indicator bulb to glow dimly, but will normally not effect the alternator output.

1. Start the engine and operate at idle speed.

2. With the voltmeter adjusted to the low scale, connect the leads to the alternator output terminal and the negative lead to the regulator terminal.

3. Turn the blower motor to the high position and turn the headlamps to the high beam position for approximately two minutes of operation. This causes the diode assembly to heat up due to the electrical load.

4. Observe the reading on the voltmeter. A range of 0 to 0.2 volts indicates the diode assembly is good. A reading above 0.2 volts indicates the downgrading of the diode assembly although it is not necessary to replace the assembly unless the reading is over 0.6 volts.

5. A pulsating reading on the meter indicates a positive diode of the rectifier or a soldered connection is breaking down under heat, and the alternator will have to be disassembled for testing repairs.

6. If the reading is over 0.6 volts and the alternator output was deemed satisfactory in the earlier tests, a bench test of the diode assembly will have to be made.

7. If the dash indicator bulb remains on dimly after a satisfactory diode assembly test has been made, inspect the following locations for loose or corroded connections.

51 and 55 amp Motorola alternator internal circuit

Motorola field diode test

Motorola terminal locations

Motorola brush assembly

a. Alternator output terminal
b. Starter relay battery terminal
c. Ignition switch
d. Fuse panel
e. Instrument harness connections
f. Instrument cluster printed circuits
g. Indicator bulb socket
h. Main wiring harness connectors

ALTERNATOR

Disassembly

1. Remove the two self-tapping screws and the cover. Pull the brush assembly straight up to clear the locating pins, then lift out the brush assembly.

2. Scribe a matchmark across the front housing, stator, and rear housing. Remove the four through bolts and nuts, then carefully separate the rear housing and stator from the front housing using two screwdrivers in the slots provided.

NOTE: Do not insert screwdrivers deeper than 1/16 in., to avoid damaging stator winding.

3. Remove the four locknuts and insulating washers that hold the stator and diode assembly, then separate the assembly from the rear housing. Avoid bending the stator wires—do not unsolder the wires without using pliers as a heat sink.

4. There is no reason to remove the rotor from the front housing unless there is a defect in the field coil or front bearing. Front and rear bearings are lubricated for life and sealed, and as a rule, do not go

bad unless the drive belt has been adjusted with too much tension. If the rotor must be removed, use a puller to remove the front drive pulley, then unseat the split-ring washer using long-nose pliers through the front housing to compress the washer while pulling on the rotor. Tap the rotor shaft lightly to remove the rotor and front bearing, then reach in and remove the split-ring washer. Bearings must be removed using a puller and new bearings must be pressed into place.

Assembly

1. Clean the bearing and the inside of the bearing hub in the front housing, then gently seat the bearing using a socket of appropriate size and a small hammer.

2. Insert the split-ring washer into the hub of the front housing and seat the washer in its groove. Be extremely careful doing this, because the bearing seal is easily damaged.

3. The front bearing now must be seated against the shoulder on the rotor shaft. Install the fan and pulley spacer, then the Woodruff key, fan and pulley. Using a 7/16 in. socket or equivalent tool to fit inside the rear bearing race, apply pressure to drive the bearing against the shoulder of the rotor shaft.

4. Assemble the front and rear housing assemblies by hand, making certain that the rear bearing is properly seated in the rear housing hub and that the diode wires are not touching the rotor at any point.

5. Align the matchmarks made during disassembly, then spin the rotor to make

sure sufficient clearance exists between it and the diode wires. Install the through-bolts and tighten them evenly, using only a hand wrench. Continue assembly in reverse of disassembly.

STATOR

In-Circuit Test

NOTE: When making the in-circuit test, consideration must be given to the rectifier diodes, which are connected to the stator windings. When properly polarized, the diode will conduct current in one direction only. A shorted diode would make the stator appear to be shorted also, so if during this test, a defect is noted, the stator windings and the rectifier diodes must be tested individually. Do not use a 120 volt test lamp as the diodes will be damaged.

1. With the use of a diode continuity light tool or a dc test lamp, connect one test lead to a diode terminal and the second lead to ground. Observe the test lamp and reverse the test leads.

2. The test lamp should light in one direction and not in the other with the leads reversed.

   a. If the test lamp lights in both directions, the stator windings are shorted or one of the negative diodes are shorted. Disassemble, unsolder, and test.

   b. If the test lamp does not light in either direction, all three rectifiers in the negative assembly are indicated to be open. Disassemble, unsolder, and test.

Out of Circuit Tests

To prepare for out of the circuit tests, the stator and diode assembly must be removed from the rear housing. Unsolder the stator leads from the diode stems. Upon reassembly, be certain that the same leads are soldered to the diodes in the same location as removed.

Stator Short Test

1. With the use of a test lamp or ohmmeter, test the windings of the stator by attaching one lead to the stator core and

Motorola charging system

Motorola circuit in-stator test

Motorola stator winding short test

51 and 55 amp Motorola stator load test

ALTERNATOR	LOAD	MAXIMUM VOLTAGE DROP	MAXIMUM VARIANCE BETWEEN WINDINGS
37	20A	7.2 – 8.2	.7
51	20A	5.5 – 6.5	.6

Rectifier diode test producing a 15 amp load

probing the stator leads with the other test lead.

2. The test lamp will light and the ohmmeter will register if a short circuit exists between the windings and the core. The short circuit must be found or the stator unit be replaced.

Stator Load Test

To test the stator coil windings for short circuits or high resistance, the following tools are needed. A fully charged 12 volt battery, a voltmeter, an ammeter, and a variable load control.

1. Connect the negative battery lead to any one of the three stator leads.

2. Connect the positive battery lead to one lead of the variable load control.

NOTE: If the load control has a built-in ammeter, the other load control lead would be connected to either of the two remaining stator leads. If the ammeter is a separate unit, the remaining load control lead would be connected to the positive ammeter lead and the negative ammeter lead would be connected to one of the two remaining stator leads. (series connection)

3. Connect the voltmeter leads between the two stator leads being tested, (parallel connection) and adjust the variable load control to draw 20 amperes. Allow the windings to warm up for 15 seconds and note the reading on the voltmeter scale. The reading should not exceed 8.2 volts for a 37 ampere rated alternator, or exceed 6.5 volts for the 51 and 55 ampere rated alternators.

4. Stop the current flow to the coil and disconnect the test leads from the stator leads and reconnect them to the remaining stator leads and test the circuits as outlined in paragraph 3. Continue with the test for the third set of windings.

5. Note the variance between the windings. It should not exceed 0.7 volt for the 37 ampere alternator or 0.6 volt for the 51 and 55 ampere alternator.

Rectifier Diode Test

1. With diodes unsoldered, use a commercial type tester and follow the manufacturer's test procedure or make up a heavy load tester as illustrated.

NOTE: A 15 ampere load is necessary to properly test the rectifier diodes for heat related defects.

2. With the use of the heavy load tester probes, connect them to the diode so the test bulb is lighted.

3. Maintain the test load on the diode for 1 to 3 minutes. If the light flickers or goes out, the diode is defective.

4. If the light remains on after three minutes, immediately reverse the test leads. If the test bulb lights, the diode is defective.

5. Test the remaining diodes in the same manner.

NOTE: The diodes are normally not replaced separately, but are replaced as a positive or negative rectifier bridge assembly.

——————— CAUTION ———————
When soldering the stator wires to the diodes, it is advisable to use a set of needle nose pliers attached to the diode stem, to act as a heat sink to avoid heat damage to the diodes.

Field Diode Assembly (Diode Trio)

Two types of diode assemblies are used. The board and the potted type and both are tested with the same procedure.

1. With the diode assembly removed, use a commercial type tester and follow the manufacturer's test procedures or make a load tester as illustrated.

2. Connect the test leads to one of the diodes so that the test bulb is lighted.

NOTE: A one ampere load is needed to properly test the field diode assembly for heat related defects.

3. Maintain a load on the diode for approximately one minute to detect any heat failure.

4. Reverse the test leads and if the test bulb would light, the diode is defective. Test the remaining diodes as outlined.

Rotor Winding Tests

With the rotor removed, use a test probe connected in series with a 110 volt test lamp. Place one probe on a slip ring and the other

probe on the rotor core. The rotor is shorted if the test bulb lights.

To test for shorted windings, use a fully charged 12 volt battery, an ammeter, a voltmeter, a variable rheostat, and test probes.

With the use of the test probe leads, place the rheostat and ammeter in series with the battery. Connect one test probe to one slip ring and the other test probe to the other slip ring. Place the voltmeter in parallel with the slip rings.

Slowly reduce the resistance of the rheostat to zero and with full battery voltage, $(12.6 \pm 0.2 \text{ volt})$, applied to the rotor coil, the field current should register between 1.8 to 2.5 amperes. Excessive ampere draw would indicate shorted windings and low ampere draw would indicate open windings of the rotor.

The Prestolite System

Prestolite alternators incorporate an *isolation diode,* mounted as a component part of the internal positive heat sink assembly. Such alternators are almost identical to late model Motorola units in operation. Test procedures for the Motorola alternator also apply to the diode-equipped Prestolite.

TROUBLESHOOTING

NOTE: See the "Alternator Test Plans" section before proceeding further.

Fusible Link Test

See the Motorola system section for the fuse link test.

Motorola rotor winding test

Charging System Operation

See the Motorola system section for the "Charging System Operation" tests.

Testing the Ignition Switch-to-Regulator Circuit

1. Disconnect the regulator wires from the regulator.

2. Turn on the key. Using a test light or voltmeter, check for current between the I terminal and ground and the L terminal ground. If voltage is present, this part of the system is OK. If no voltage is present, check for broken or shorted wires, a bad indicator bulb, a bad ammeter (if so equipped), or bad connections.

Alternator Disassembly

1. Remove the two brush mounting screws and cover, then tip the brush assembly away from the alternator and remove.

2. Matchmark the rear housing, stator and drive end housing, then remove the four retaining screws. The stator and rear housing are removed as a unit by tapping lightly with a fiber hammer to separate them from the front housing.

3. The rotor should not be removed unless it or the front bearing is defective. To remove the rotor under these conditions, first remove the pulley nut and pulley (using a two-jaw puller), then remove the fan, Woodruff key and spacer. The rotor is removed from the front housing using a three-paw puller.

4. The front bearing is easily removed, after taking out the retaining ring, by pressing it out in a large vise using sockets to support the housing from the rear.

Stator Coil Test—Diode Type

1. Using a No. 57 bulb, connected in series with a 12-volt battery, as a test light, touch one test lead to the connection of the three stator windings and the other test lead to each stator lead that is connected to the diodes. If the bulb does not light, the winding is open.

2. To test for a grounded stator, use a 110-volt test lamp. First disconnect the diodes from the stator leads, then touch one test lead to the stator core and the other test lead to each of the three stator leads. If the test lamp lights, the winding is grounded.

Field diode test producing a 1 amp load

Prestolite alternator

NOTE: If all other components are O.K. and alternator still does not work, it can be assumed that the stator windings are internally shorted. This type of short is impossible to detect by using the previous test. Diode tests are the same as for the Motorola alternator.

Alternator Assembly

1. Press the front bearing into the front housing, making sure the dust seal faces the rotor. Install the bearing retaining snap-ring, then press the shoulder of the shaft against the inner bearing race using a tool that fits over the shaft and against the race. Install the spacer, Woodruff key, fan and pulley, then install lockwasher and pulley nut.

2. Install the diode heat sink, negative diodes and stator. Solder any stator to diode connections that were unsoldered, using pliers as a heat sink to prevent overheating.

3. Install the rotor and front drive housing to stator and rear housing, aligning matchmarks made during disassembly. Install the four retaining screws, then the brush holder assembly and retaining screws.

4. Make sure the stator leads and brush holder assembly clear the rotor and that the rotor can be spun by hand without binding.

ELECTRONIC IGNITION SYSTEM

Ford-Motorcraft Solid-State Ignition System (SSI)

The Ford-Motorcraft Solid-State Ignition System is a pulse triggered, breakerless, transistor controlled ignition system. The system utilizes most of the standard ignition components, but substitutes an amplifier module and magnetic pickup assembly for the conventional ignition contact points.

OPERATION

With the ignition switch "on", the primary circuit is on and the ignition coil is energized. When the armature "spokes" approach the magnetic pick-up coil assembly, they induce a voltage which tells the amplifier to turn the coil primary current off. A timing circuit in the amplifier module will turn the current on again after the coil field has collapsed. When the current is "on", it flows from the battery through the ignition switch, the primary windings of the ignition coil, and through the amplifier

module circuits to ground. When the current is off, the magnetic field built up in the ignition coil is allowed to collapse, inducing a high voltage into the secondary windings of the coil. High voltage is produced each time the field is thus built up and collapsed.

The high voltage flows through the coil high tension lead to the distributor cap where the rotor distributes it to one of the spark plug terminals in the distributor cap. This process is repeated for every power stroke of the engine.

Ignition system troubles are caused by a failure in the primary and/or the secondary circuit; incorrect ignition timing; or incorrect distributor advance. Circuit failures may be caused by shorts, corroded or dirty terminals, loose connections, defective wire insulation, cracked distributor cap or rotor, defective pick-up coil assembly or amplifier module, defective distributor points, fouled spark plugs, or by improper dwell angle.

If an engine starting or operating trouble is attributed to the ignition system, start the engine and verify the complaint. On engines that will not start, be sure that there is gasoline in the fuel tank and that fuel is reaching the carburetor. Then locate the ignition system problem by an oscilloscope test or by a spark intensity test.

PRIMARY CIRCUIT TESTING

A breakdown or energy loss in the primary circuit can be caused by: defective primary wiring, loose or corroded connections, inoperative or defective magnetic pick-up coil assembly, or defective amplifier module.

A complete test of the primary circuit consists of checking the circuits in the ignition coil, the magnetic pick-up coil assembly and the amplifier module. Wiring

harness checks will be included as a part of basic component circuit tests.

Always inspect connectors for dirt, corrosion or poor fit before assuming you have spotted a possible problem.

Dura Spark II Ignition System

The Dura Spark II is a solid state ignition system incorporating high energy secondary components. The distributor, coil and module are the same as the units used in the regular Solid State Ignition system (SSI). The system incorporates an adapter on the distributor to accomodate the larger cap and larger rotor used with the higher voltage. The high voltage and wide spark plug gap increases the spark plug life and overall engine performance. The higher voltage is accomplished through the use of a 1.10 ohm ballast resistor, integral with the primary wire harness, which increases the energy input to the coil and in turn, the secondary energy level. The system is easily identified by the large blue adapter and distributor cap.

8-cylinder breakerless distributor

DUAL MODE TIMING IGNITION MODULE

On some applications, a special Dura Spark II ignition module is used with altitude compensation. This special module plus the barometric pressure switch, allows the base engine timing to be modified to suit altitude conditions. All other elements and performance characteristics of this module are identical in both modes of operation to the basic Dura Spark II system. All Dura Spark II modules equipped with altitude features, have three connectors instead of the normal two. A barometric switch provides an automatic retard signal to the module at different altitudes, giving appropriate advanced timing at higher altitude and retard mode for spark knock control at lower altitudes.

DISTRIBUTOR

The distributors are equipped with both vacuum and centrifugal spark advances which operate the same regardless of the type of ignition system used. A dual vacuum advance is used on certain engines to provide ignition retard during engine closed throttle operation, to help control engine exhaust emissions.

CIRCUIT OPERATION

All systems consist of a primary (low voltage) and a secondary (high voltage) circuit.
The Primary Circuit—The components involved in the primary circuit are:
    1. Battery
    2. Ignition switch
    3. Primary circuit resistance wire (integral wire in the SSI and Dura Spark II systems)
    4. Primary windings of the ignition coil
    5. Magnetic pickup coil assembly in the distributor
    6. Ignition module.
The Secondary Circuit—The components of the secondary circuit are:
    1. Secondary windings of the ignition coil
    2. Distributor rotor
    3. Distributor cap and adapter (Dura Spark II)
    4. Secondary spark plug wires
    5. Spark plugs

Operation

With the ignition switch in the "ON" position, the primary circuit is energized and the magnetic field is built up by the current flowing through the primary windings of the ignition coil. When the armature spokes align with the center of the magnetic pickup coil, the module turns off the coil primary current and the high voltage is produced in the secondary circuit by the collapsing magnetic field. High voltage is produced each time the magnetic field is caused to

collapse due to a timing circuit in the module, which starts and stops the primary circuit through the coil. The high voltage flows

through the coil secondary lead to the distributor cap, where the rotor distributes the spark to the proper spark plug terminal in

Breakerless ignition circuit routings

6-cylinder breakerless distributor

the distributor cap. The secondary current then flows through the secondary wire to the spark plug.

Armature alignment

System Adjustments

No adjustments are made to the Dura Spark II ignition system except the initial timing and spark plug gap.

SECONDARY WIRE USAGE

Dura Spark II

Spark plug wires that are used with the Dura Spark II system are 8mm in size, to contain the higher output voltage. Two types of wires are used in this system and some engines will have both types. It is important to identify the type of wire to a cylinder before a replacement is obtained and installed. Both types are blue in color and have silicone jacketing. The insulation material underneath the jacketing can be a EPDM or have another silicone layer, separated by glass braid. EPDM wires are used where the engine temperatures are cooler and are identified by the letters "SE". The

silicone jacket type are used where the engine temperatures are high and are identified by the letters "SS".

NOTE: Whenever a Dura Spark II high tension wire is removed for any purpose from a spark plug, coil or distributor cap, silicone grease must be applied to the boot before it is reconnected.

The spark plug wires are marked with the cylinder number, model year and date of cable manufacture (quarter and year). Service replacement wires do not have this information.

Solid State Ignition System (SSI)

The SSI system uses 7mm secondary wires and should not be interchanged with the Dura Spark II secondary wires.

Dura Spark III Ignition System

This system is used in conjunction with EEC III—an Electronic Engine Control system that controls spark advance in response to various engine sensors. On 3.8 litre V–6 engines, the distributor is only slightly modified from the Dura Spark II model. The distributor stator provides the signal that, on Dura Spark II systems, caused the ignition module to interrupt the primary circuit; on this system, however, the EEC microprocessor determines the actual instant at which spark occurs. This means that the centrifugal and vacuum advance systems on the distributor are disabled and the microprocessor determines vacuum and centrifugal advance curves.

On V–8 engines, the distributor stator assembly is replaced by a crankshaft position sensor; thus, the distributor consists only of the mechanical shaft and housing and the high tension parts—cap and rotor. On these engines, the distributor has a fixed position in relation to the engine and it is the rotor position, rather than distributor position that is adjustable. In all other respects, the system resembles the Dura Spark II.

Rotor Alignment—V–8 Engines with Dura Spark III

1. Remove the distributor cap, noting the approximate location of the high tension wire going to No. 1 cylinder. Rotate the engine until No. 1 cylinder firing position is being approached by the rotor and the engine nears 0 degrees TDC. Remove the rotor and position a distributor alignment tool so that when the alignment slots reach an aligned position, the tool will slip into place.

2. Turn the engine very slowly until the tool just slips into the alignment slots, and then stop rotating the engine. Read the position of the timing mark on the vibration damper. If it is between 4 degrees Before Top Center and 4 degrees After Top Center, the rotor alignment meets specification. In this case, remove the tool, and reposition the rotor and cap. If the timing mark is outside these limits, proceed with the steps that follow.

3. Remove the alignment tool. Rotate the engine until the timing marks align at 0 degrees, TDC.

4. Loosen the two sleeve assembly adjustment screws. Then, rotate the sleeve

DURASPARK III

Wiring diagram of basic Dura Spark III ignition system

Rotor alignment—Dura Spark III

assembly until the alignment tool can be inserted. With the tool in position, tighten the adjusting screws. Then, remove the tool, and install the rotor and cap.

Troubleshooting

DURA SPARK II—1977

TROUBLESHOOTING

Make sure that the battery is fully charged before beginning tests. Perform a Spark Intensity Test. If no spark is observed, make sure that the high tension coil wire is good. Disconnect the three-way and four-way connectors at the electronic module.

The first trouble isolation test will be conducted on the harness terminals, with the electronic module disconnected from the circuit. The pin numbers shown in the schematic correspond to those shown in the trouble isolation test table.

Make the following tests using a sensitive volt-ohmmeter. These tests will direct you to the proper follow-up test to determine the actual problem.

If the circuit checks good at all these test points, connect a known good electronic module in place of the vehicle module and again perform the spark intensity test. If the substitution corrects the malfunction again reconnect the vehicle module and perform the spark intensity test. If the malfunction still exists, the problem is in the module and it must be replaced. If the problem is gone, it may be in the wiring connectors.

If the substitute module does not correct the problem, reconnect the original module and make repairs elsewhere in the system.

Module Bias Test, '75–'77

Measure the voltage at Pin 3 to engine ground with the ignition key "on". If the voltage observed is less than battery voltage, repair the voltage feed wiring to the module for running conditions (re-wire).

Battery Source Test

1. Connect the voltmeter leads from the battery terminal at the coil to engine ground, without disconnecting the coil from the circuit.
2. Install a jumper wire from the DEC terminal of the coil to a good engine ground.
3. Turn the lights and all accessories off.
4. Turn the ignition switch "on".
5. If the voltmeter reading is between 4.9 and 7.9 volts, the primary circuit from the battery is satisfactory.

6. If the voltmeter reading is less than 4.9 volts, check the following:
   a. The primary wiring for worn insulation, broken strands, and loose or corroded terminals.
   b. The resistance wiring for defects.
7. If the voltmeter reading is greater than 7.9 volts, the resistance wire should be replaced after verifying a defect.

Cranking Test

Measure the voltage at Pin 1 to engine ground with the engine cranking. If the voltage observed is not 8 to 12 volts, repair the voltage feed to the module for starting conditions (white wire).

Starting Circuit Test

If the reading is not more than 6 volts, the ignition by-pass circuit is open or grounded from either the starter solenoid or the ignition switch to Pin 5. Check the primary connections at the coil.

Dura-Spark schematic

Distributor Hardware Test

1. Disconnect the three-wire weatherproof connector at the distributor pigtail.

2. Connect a D.C. voltmeter on a 2.5 volt scale to the two parallel blades. With the engine cranking, the meter needle should oscillate.

3. Remove the distributor cap and check for visual damage or misassembly.

   a. Sintered iron armature (6 or 8 toothed wheel) must be tight on the sleeve, and the roll pin aligning the armature must be in position.

   b. Sintered iron stator must not be broken.

   c. Armature must rotate when the engine is cranked.

4. If the hardware is alright, but the meter doesn't oscillate, replace the magnetic pick-up assembly.

Magnetic Pick-up Tests

1. Resistance of pick-up coil measured between two parallel pins in the distributor connector must be 400–800 ohms.

2. Resistance between the third blade (ground) and the distributor bowl must be zero ohms.

3. Resistance between either parallel blade and engine ground must be greater than 70,000 ohms.

4. If any test fails, the distributor stator assembly is defective and must be replaced.

5. If the above readings are not the same as measured in the original test, check for a defective harness. If the readings are the same, proceed.

6. If these tests check alright, the signal generator portion of the distributor is working properly.

Ignition Coil Test

The breakerless ignition coil must be diagnosed separately from the rest of the ignition system.

1. Primary resistance must be 1.0–2.0 ohms, measured from the BAT to the DEC terminals.

2. Secondary resistance must be 7,000–13,000 ohms, measured from the BAT or DEC terminal to the center tower of the coil.

3. If resistance tests are alright, but the coil is still suspected, test the coil on a coil tester by following the test equipment manufacturer's instructions for a standard coil. If the reading differs from the original test, check for a defective harness.

Module Test

1. Unplug the electronic module connector, but don't remove the existing module from the car.

2. Connect a module which is known to be good to the connector. There is no need to attach the module to the car in order to have it work.

3. Start the engine; if it starts and operates correctly go on to the next step. If it

won't start and run, the trouble is somewhere else. Check and repair the wiring and other systems, as required.

4. If the engine started in step 3, reconnect the original module and try to start the engine again. If the engine won't start, replace the module.

5. If the engine starts in step 4, the original module is not defective. Check all the wiring and connections in the ignition system.

Short Test

If the resistance from Pin 5 to ground is less than 4 ohms, check for a short to ground at the DEC terminal of the ignition coil or in the connection wiring to that terminal.

HIGH VOLTAGE TESTS— ELECTRONIC IGNITION SYSTEMS

When performing the high voltage tests on the ignition systems, the proper test equipment should be used and the manufacturer's recommended procedures followed in order to obtain correct results.

1. Connecting the test equipment to the ignition system in the proper order, measure the coil reserve voltage, which should be 28 KV minimum.

2. Measure the spark plug required voltage of each spark plug. The required voltage is 8-20 KV.

——— **CAUTION** ———

Do not remove the following spark plug wires when performing these tests.

No. 1 or No. 8 wires on V-8 engines.
No. 3 or No. 5 wires on I-6 engines.
No. 1 or No. 4 wires on V-6 engines.
No. 1 or No. 3 wires on 4 cylinder engines.

3. Check the coil to distributor cap, distributor cap to spark plug wires with an ohmmeter. The reading should be 5 K ohms per inch maximum.

——— **CAUTION** ———

Unless specified, all high voltage measurements are to be made with a "clamp-on" probe. Never attempt to puncture the high voltage insulation to perform tests. A spark plug wire should never be removed for longer than 30 seconds on catalytic converter equipped vehicles.

NOTE: When removing any Dura Spark II high tension lead, the interior of the terminal boot must be greased with a silicone grease, meeting Ford Motor Co. specifications.

Adjustments

The air gap between the armature and magnetic pick-up coil in the distributor is not adjustable, nor are there any adjustments for the amplifier module. Inoperative components are simply replaced. Any attempt to connect components outside the vehicle may result in component failure.

Dura Spark II Solid State Ignition (SSI)

1978 and Later

To properly diagnose the ignition system, a starting place must be established and an order of inspection followed until the fault is found and repaired. A recheck should be made, again in its order of inspection, to verify the repairs and to assure trouble-free operation.

Run Mode Test

1. If no spark is available at the spark plug, remove the coil high tension lead at the distributor and either place it ¼ inch from the engine block or place a modified spark plug into the coil wire and ground the spark plug body.

2. Turn the ignition switch to the "RUN" position and tap the distributor body with a screwdriver type tool handle. Check for spark while tapping.

3. If spark is available, crank the engine with the starter and check for spark. If spark occurs, the primary ignition system is OK.

4. If no spark occurs, turn the key to the "OFF" position and crank the engine to align the engine timing pointer with the initial timing degree line on the damper pulley. Turn the key to the "RUN" position and again tap the distributor and check for spark.

5. If no spark occurs, measure battery voltage and measure the battery voltage on the module's red wire without disconnecting any connectors. The voltage in the red wire should equal battery voltage.

6. If battery voltage is not present in the module red wire, repair the circuit between the battery and the module connector. Recheck the voltage supply.

7. With the voltage present in the module's red wire, cycle the ignition switch between the "RUN" and "OFF" position. A spark should be seen each time the switch is turned to the "OFF" position.

8. If no spark occurs, measure the voltage on the battery side of the coil.

   a. Less than 6 volts—Repair the wire carrying current to the battery terminal of the coil and repeat test.

   b. If voltage is 6–8 volts—Substitute, but do not install, a known good module and repeat the test. If spark then occurs, reconnect the original module to verify its being defective. Replace as required. Refer to step 10 if the battery voltage is present.

9. If a spark occurs from step 7, substitute, but do not install, and ground a good distributor of any calibration 4, 6 or 8 cylinder. Spin the distributor shaft and check for high tension spark.

   a. If a spark occurs, reconnect the old distributor and verify its being defective.

Replace as required.

b. If no spark occurs, disconnect the distributor connector and 4 post connector at the module. Check the harness wires that mate with the module and distributor orange and purple wires for continuity between the module and distributor end of the harness. Check to be sure there is no short between the two wires and there is an open circuit to ground. If not OK, repair the wiring and repeat the test to verify repairs.

c. If no spark occurs after completing step 9b, reconnect the distributor connector and substitute, but do not install, a known good module and repeat the test. If a spark occurs, reconnect the original module and verify it is defective. Repair as required.

10. If battery voltage is present at the battery terminal of the coil,

a. Disconnect the 4 wire connector at the module. Insert a paper clip between the green and black wires of the module and remeasure the voltage at the battery terminal of the coil.

b. If the voltage is between 6 to 8 volts, substitute, but do not install, a known good module and repeat the tests. If spark occurs, reconnect the old module and verify its being defective. Replace as required.

c. If battery voltage is still present at the battery terminal of the coil, be sure the coil connector remains in place on the coil and ground the negative terminal of the coil. Remeasure the voltage on the coil battery terminal. If battery voltage still is present, remove the paper clip from the 4 wire connector and reconnect the module. Substitute, but do not install, a known good coil and repeat the test. If a spark does not occur, connect the original coil and substitute a known good module, but do not install, and repeat the test. If a spark occurs, replace the module as required. If 4 to 7 volts is measured at the coil positive terminal, remove the ground from the coil negative terminal and ground the paper clip connector in the 4 wire connector. Remeasure the voltage at the coil battery terminal. The voltage should be 4 to 7 volts. If the 4 to 7 volts are present, repair the ground circuit mating with the module black wire. Remove the paper clip from the 4 wire connector and reconnect the module. Repeat the test. If no voltage is present, repair the module to coil wire that mates with the module green wire. Remove the paper clip from the connector and reconnect the module. Repeat the test.

Cranking Test

1. Measure the voltage at the battery terminal of the ignition coil while cranking the engine. The reading should be within 1.0 volt of battery voltage. If not with-in specifications, repair the wire or circuit to the coil terminal.

2. While cranking the engine, check for spark from the high tension leads.

3. If no spark occurs, check the battery voltage on the white wire, while cranking the engine without disconnecting the module's two wire connectors. The voltage should be within 1.0 volt of battery voltage. If not, repair the white feed wire to the module.

4. Substitute, but do not install, a known good module and repeat the test. If a spark occurs, reconnect the original module and verify its being defective. Replace as required.

INTERMITTENT OPERATION DIAGNOSIS

Should the ignition system become operative during the tests and a repair has not been made to the system, it is likely an intermittent connection or component has become functional. Try to duplicate the problem with the engine running, by wiggling the wires at the coil, module, distributor and other harness connections, preferrably the connections that have been disturbed during the test proceedings. Check all ground connections, especially with-in the distributor. Disconnecting and connecting connectors may also help.

Heating Components for Tests
PICK-UP COIL

Using a 250 watt heat lamp, approximately 1 to 2 inches from the pick-up coil, apply heat for 4 to 6 minutes while monitoring the pick-up coil continuity between the parallel blades of the disconnected distributor connector. The resistance should be 400 to 1000 ohms. Tapping with a screwdriver type handle may also be helpful to locate problem. If specifications cannot be met or held, replace the pick-up coil.

IGNITION MODULE

With the engine running, heat the module by placing a 250 watt heat lamp bulb approximately 1 to 2 inches from the module top surface.

——— CAUTION ———
This procedure should not heat the module over 212 degrees F. After the first 10 minutes of heating, check the temperature by applying a few drops of water on the module housing. Repeat the check every one to two minutes until the water droplets boil.

Tapping the module may be helpful, but do not tap hard enough to damage or distort the housing. If this procedure results in an ignition malfunction, substitute, but do not install, a known good module. If the ignition malfunction is corrected by the substitution, reinstall the original module and recheck. Replace the module as required.

Dura Spark III Ignition System

PRELIMINARY CHECKOUT

NOTE: When making these tests, make sure to follow wiring back to the module for color coding purposes. All instrument checks for wiring integrity should be accompanied by visual inspection and by wiggling of connectors to check for either bad insulation or loose connections.

Begin troubleshooting by inspecting all vacuum hoses and both high tension and wiring harness wiring for proper routing and secure connections. Check also for damaged insulation and burned connectors.

Make sure the battery is fully charged and turn off all accessories before starting tests. The procedure requires the following equipment:

1. A precise volt—ohmmeter, preferably with digital readout.

2. A commercially available spark tester that can replace a spark plug in the circuit and provide visible evidence of a hot spark.

3. A diagnostic test adapter designed for the Dura Spark III system. This must plug into the three-wire connector going to the ignition module and apply voltage to the right module circuit for testing it directly from the battery.

Connecting the Dura Spark III test adapter.

4. A 12 volt test light and a supply of straight pins for testing for voltage and resistance in the wiring.

TEST 1

1. Disconnect the three–wire ignition module connector. Inspect the connector for damage, dirt, or corrosion. If none are present, proceed with Step 2. Otherwise, make repairs as necessary.

2. Install the test adapter between the two halves of the connector. Pull the coil high tension lead out of the distributor, install and ground the spark tester. Turn the ignition switch to the "RUN" position.

3. Touch the lead to the test adapter to the battery positive terminal while observing the spark tester. There should be a spark as the lead touches the terminal. Test repeatedly. If spark occurs consistently, go to Test 2. Otherwise, see Test 4.

TEST 2

1. Remove the diagnostic test adapter from the ignition module circuit, and reconnect the connector. Leave the spark tester in place, and observe it while cranking the engine. If there is no spark, go on to test three. If there is spark, follow the rest of the steps in this test.

2. Inspect the distributor cap, rotor, and adapter for cracks or carbon tracking and replace parts as necessary. Make sure there is silicone compound to protect the tip of the rotor.

3. If the inspections above do not reveal and cure the problem, check the distributor rotor alignment and correct as necessary.

TEST 3

1. If the starter relay has an "I" terminal, disconnect the cable from the starter relay to the starter motor. If it has no "I" terminal, disconnect the wire to the "S" terminal of the relay.

2. Insert a straight pin through the center of the white wire leading to the ignition module. Make sure it **does not** contact any ground.

3. Measure the voltage existing between the positive and negative battery terminals.

4. Connect the VOM negative lead to a good engine ground. Use a pin to get a connection to the white wire going to the ignition module (without grounding the pin). Connect the positive lead to the VOM to the pin. Finally, turn the ignition switch to the START position and read the voltage while wiggling the wiring.

5. Connect the positive lead of the VOM to the "Batt" terminal of the ignition coil and with the ignition switch in the START position, repeat the test.

6. If either reading was less than 90 percent of battery voltage, refer to a wiring

diagram and repair wiring and connectors in the faulty circuit. Otherwise, replace the ignition switch.

7. Remove the straight pin and reconnect the wiring to the starter relay. If the required repairs do not resolve the problem, or if both circuits passed the test, proceed to Test 4.

TEST 4

1. Connect a test lamp between the TACH terminal of the ignition coil and a ground on the engine. Connect the diagnostic test adapter into the ignition system as in the first test. Turn the ignition switch to the "RUN" position.

2. Touch the test lead for the adapter to the battery positive terminal repeatedly while observing the test light.

3. Remove the diagnostic connector and test light and reconnect the three–prong connector. If the light flashes consistently, go to Test 5; if not, go to Test 6.

TEST 5

1. Disconnect the coil high tension wire and connector. Inspect the wire and connector for a burned appearance and replace parts as necessary. Inspect the coil for cracks or carbon tracking in the high tension connector, and replace it if necessary.

2. Test the high tension lead with an ohmmeter by removing it and connecting the meter to either end. Resistance should be 5,000 ohms per inch or less. If resistance is too high, replace the wire.

3. Measure the coil secondary circuit resistance by connecting the ohmmeter between the coil BATT terminal and the high voltage connector. Resistance must be between 7,700 ohms and 10,500 ohms. If resistance is either above or below this range, replace the coil.

4. Replace or reconnect parts as necessary.

TEST 6

1. If the starter relay has an "I" terminal, disconnect the cable from the relay to the starter motor. If there is no "I" terminal on the relay, disconnect the wire to the "S" terminal of the relay. Insert straight pins into the centers of the red and white module wires. DO NOT GROUND. Measure the exact voltage by connecting the voltmeter between the positive and negative battery terminals.

2. Connect the voltmeter negative lead between the base of the distributor and the pin passing through the red lead. Turn the ignition switch to the "RUN" position. Measure the voltage while wiggling the wiring.

3. Connect the voltmeter positive lead over to the pin running through the white wire. Turn the ignition switch to the START position and read the voltage while wiggling the wiring.

4. Repeat the step above, but with the positive lead attached to the BATT terminal on the ignition coil to test the ballast resistor bypass. Turn the ignition switch off, remove the straight pins, and reconnect the starter wiring.

5. If the voltage was more than 90 percent of battery voltage in every case, go on to the next test. If voltage was lower than 90 percent of battery voltage, inspect the wiring harness for faulty circuits and repair as necessary. Replace the ignition switch, or replace the radio interference capacitor on the coil as necessary until the system can pass the test.

TEST 7

1. Attach the negative lead of the voltmeter to an engine ground, and the positive lead to the BATT terminal on the coil.

2. With the ignition switch in the RUN position, measure the voltage.

3. Turn the ignition switch off and remove the voltmeter leads. If the voltage is 6 to 8 volts, proceed to Test 8; if it is less than 6 volts or greater than 8 volts, proceed to Test 9.

TEST 8

1. Disconnect the ignition module three wire connector and the connector at the coil for the wire from the ignition module. Repair or replace bad connectors as necessary.

2. Connect an ohmmeter between an engine ground (–) and the TACH terminal of the coil. Reconnect module and coil connectors. If resistance is greater than one ohm, replace the module. If it is one ohm or less, just inspect the wiring harness between the module and coil to make sure there are no wiring problems.

TEST 9

1. Disconnect the ignition coil primary connectors. Measure coil primary resistance by connecting an ohmmeter between the BATT and TACH terminals. Disconnect the ohmmeter and reconnect connectors.

2. If resistance is between .8 and 1.6 ohms, proceed to Test 10. If resistance is less than or greater than specification, replace the coil.

TEST 10

1. Insert a straight pin into the green wire at the module *without grounding it*.

2. Attach the negative lead of the voltmeter to an engine ground. Then, turn the ignition switch on and measure the voltage, first at the straight pin in the green wire and then at the TACH terminal of the ignition coil. If the difference in voltage is more than .5 volts, inspect and repair the green module-to-coil wire as necessary. If it is less than .5 volts, but more than 1.5, proceed to Test 12. If it is 1.5 volts or less,

proceed to the test of the ballast resistor—Test 11.

3. Turn the ignition off and remove the leads and straight pin.

TEST 11

1. Disconnect the two-wire connector to the ignition module. Repair any defects in the connectors. Disconnect the coil primary connector.

2. Use an ohmmeter to measure resistance of the circuit between the BATT terminal of the ignition coil connector and the wiring harness connector mating with the red wire from the module. In both cases, measure on the wiring harness side—not at the coil or at the wire leading to the module.

3. If the resistance is .8–1.6 ohms, replace the ignition module. If it is less than .8 or greater than 1.6 ohms, replace the ballast resistor.

4. Remove the ohmmeter and reconnect connectors as necessary.

TEST 12

1. Insert a straight pin into the black wire at the ignition module *without grounding it*.

2. Connect a voltmeter between the pin and an engine ground, with the positive lead at the pin. Turn the ignition switch to RUN position.

3. If the voltage read is less than .5 volt, replace the ignition module. If it is greater than .5 volts, proceed to the final test for further diagnosis of problems in the ground circuit.

4. Turn the ignition switch off, remove the voltmeter connectors and remove the straight pin.

TEST 13

1. Disconnect the three-wire connector to the module. Connect an ohmmeter between an engine ground and the *harness side* terminal mating with the black wire from the module. Read the resistance while wiggling the harness.

2. If resistance is less than one ohm, look for a problem in the wiring harness connectors and the module black wire. The problem is either intermittent or not in the ignition system. If resistance is greater than one ohm, inspect the harness and connectors between the module and ground connection. Repair wiring as necessary, disconnect the ohmmeter, and reconnect the connector.

Delco-Remy High Energy Ignition (HEI) System

COMPONENTS

The Delco-Remy High Energy Ignition (HEI)

HEI schematic

System is a breakerless, pulse triggered, transistor controlled, inductive discharge ignition system.

There are only nine external electrical connections; the ignition switch feed wire, and the eight spark plug leads. On V8 engines, the ignition coil is located within the distributor cap, connecting directly to the rotor.

OPERATION

The magnetic pick-up assembly located inside the distributor contains a permanent magnet, a pole piece with internal teeth, and a pick-up coil. When the teeth of the rotating timer core and pole piece align, an induced voltage in the pick-up coil signals the electronic module to open the coil primary circuit. As the primary current decreases, a high voltage is induced in the secondary windings of the ignition coil, directing a spark through the rotor and high voltage leads to fire the spark plugs. The dwell period is automatically controlled by the electronic module and is increased with increasing engine rpm. The HEI System features a longer spark duration which is instrumental in firing lean and EGR diluted fuel/air mixtures. The condenser (capacitor) located within the HEI distributor is provided for noise (static) suppression purposes only and is not a regularly replaced ignition system component.

Some 1983 and later engines use an Electronic Spark Timing (EST) distributor. This unit replaces vacuum and centrifugal advance units with an electronic actuator. A vacuum sensor provides manifold vacuum information, and a reference pulse is generated by a pulse generator located near the engine vibration damper. These signals are fed to an Electronic Control Module which, in turn, sends a signal to the EST distributor for ignition timing determination.

Some 1983 and later 5.0 liter V-8s also use an Electronic Spark Control (ESC) which responds to engine detonation with retardation of ignition timing. An engine-block-mounted sensor detects the presence of vibration generated by detonation and signals the ESC controller to process the signal and adjust the timing via the actuator on the distributor. The system gradually retards the spark until detonation has disappeared. A failed sensor would produce occasional detonation.

1. Screw
2. Bracket
3. Capacitor
4. Thin C-washer (retainer)
5. Pole piece and plate assembly (pick up coil)
6. Screw
7. Module assembly
8. Felt washer
9. Plastic grease retainer seal
10. Screw
11. Vacuum control assembly
12. Retainer (wire harness)
13. Wire harness assembly
14. Housing assembly
15. Gear
16. Roll pin
17. Ignition coil
18. Cover
19. Distributor shaft assembly
20. Rotor
21. Screw
22. Distributor cap

6-cylinder HEI distributor

These ESC equipped engines also have a "tip in" vacuum switch. When the throttle is suddenly opened and manifold vacuum is suddenly decreased, the switch contacts close to send a signal to the ESC controller to arbitrarily retard the spark to prevent knock. Thus, if the engine knocks for a very short time after a rapid opening of the throttle, this switch may be at fault.

MAJOR REPAIR OPERATIONS (DISTRIBUTOR IN ENGINE)

Ignition Coil Replacement V8 Engines

1. Disconnect the feed and module wire terminal connectors from the distributor cap.

2. Remove the ignition set retainer.

3. Remove the 4 coil cover-to-distributor cap screws and the coil cover.

4. Remove the 4 coil-to-distributor cap screws.

5. Using a blunt drift, press the coil wire spade terminals up out of distributor cap.

6. Lift the coil up out of the distributor cap.

7. Remove and clean the coil spring, rubber seal washer and coil cavity of the distributor cap.

8. Reverse the above procedures to install.

Six Cylinder Engines

On 6 cylinder engines, a separate ignition coil is used. To remove and install it, proceed as follows:

1. Remove the ignition switch-to-coil lead from the coil.

2. Unfasten the distributor leads from the coil.

3. Remove the screws which secure the coil to the engine and lift it off.

Installation is the reverse of removal.

Distributor Cap Replacement

1. Remove the feed and module wire terminal connectors from the distributor cap.

2. Remove the retainer and spark plug wires from the cap.

3. Depress and release the 4 distributor cap-to-housing retainers and lift off the cap assembly.

4. Remove the 4 coil cover screws and cover (V8 only).

5. Using a finger or a blunt drift, push the spade terminals up out of the distributor cap (V8 only).

6. Remove all 4 coil screws and lift the coil, coil spring and rubber seal washer out of the cap coil cavity (V8 only).

7. Using a new distributor cap, reverse the above procedures to assemble.

Rotor Replacement

1. Disconnect the feed and module wire connectors from the distributor.

2. Depress and release the 4 distributor cap-to-housing retainers and lift off the cap assembly.

3. Remove the two rotor attaching screws and rotor.

4. Reverse the above procedure to install.

Vacuum Advance Unit Replacement

1. Remove the distributor cap and rotor as previously described.

2. Disconnect the vacuum hose from the vacuum advance unit. Remove the module.

3. Remove the two vacuum advance retaining screws, pull the advance unit outward, rotate and disengage the operating rod from its tang.

4. Reverse the above procedure to install.

Module Replacement

1. Remove the distributor cap and rotor as previously described.

2. Disconnect the harness connector and pick-up coil spade connectors from the module (note their positions).

3. Remove the two screws and module from the distributor housing.

4. Coat the bottom of the new module with dielectric lubricant. Reverse the above procedure to install. Be sure that the leads are installed correctly.

Distributor Removal

1. Disconnect the ground cable from the battery.

2. Disconnect the feed and module terminal connectors from the distributor cap. (Don't use a screwdriver).

3. Disconnect the hose at the vacuum advance.

4. Depress and release the 4 distributor cap-to-housing retainers and lift off the cap assembly.

5. Using crayon or chalk, make locating marks on the rotor and module and on the distributor housing and engine for installation purposes.

6. Loosen and remove the distributor clamp bolt and clamp, and lift distributor out of the engine. Noting the relative position of the rotor and module alignment marks, make a second mark on the rotor to align it with the one mark on the module.

Distributor Installation

1. With a new O-ring on the distributor housing and the second mark on the rotor aligned with the mark on the module, install the distributor, taking care to align the mark on the housing with the one on the engine. It may be necessary to lift the distributor and turn the rotor slightly to align the gears and the oil pump driveshaft.

2. With the respective marks aligned, install the clamp and bolt finger tight.

3. Install and secure the distributor cap.

4. Connect the feed and module connectors to the distributor cap.

5. Connect a timing light to the engine and plug the vacuum hose.

1. Screw
2. Bracket
3. Capacitor
4. Screw
5. Wiring harness assembly
6. Module assembly
7. Thin C-washer (retainer)
8. Pole piece and plate assembly (pick up coil)
9. Screw
10. Plastic retainer
11. Felt washer
12. Plastic grease retainer seal
13. Housing assembly
14. Thrust washer
15. Shim
16. Gear
17. Roll pin
18. Distributor shaft assembly
19. Rotor
20. Screw
21. Distributor cap
22. Resistor brush and spring
23. Seal
24. Ignition coil
25. Screw
26. Ground lead
27. Cover
28. Screw

V8 HEI distributor

6. Connect the ground cable to the battery.

7. Start the engine and set the timing.

8. Turn the engine off and tighten the distributor clamp bolt. Disconnect the timing light and unplug and connect the hose to the vacuum advance.

SERVICE PROCEDURES (DISTRIBUTOR REMOVED)

Driven Gear Replacement

1. With the distributor removed, use a ⅛ in. pin punch and tap out the driven gear roll pin.

2. Hold the rotor end of shaft and rotate the driven gear to shear any burrs in the roll pin hole.

3. Remove the driven gear from the shaft.

4. Reverse the above procedure to install.

ENGINE CRANKS, BUT WILL NOT START

NOTE: IF A TACHOMETER IS CONNECTED TO THE TACHOMETER TERMINAL, DISCONNECT IT BEFORE PROCEEDING WITH THE TEST.

NOTE: VIEWS ARE IN PART 2.

Mainshaft Replacement

1. With the driven gear and rotor removed, gently pull the mainshaft out of the housing.

2. Remove the advance springs, weights and slide the weight base plate off the mainshaft.

3. Reverse the above procedure to install.

Pole Piece, Magnet or Pick-up Coil Replacement

1. With the mainshaft out of its housing, remove the 3 retaining screws, pole

INTERMITTENT OPERATION OR MISS

CHECK SPARK AT TWO PLUG WIRES
WITH ST-125

SPARK ON ONE OR BOTH

NO SPARK

CHECK FOR DWELL INCREASE FROM LOW TO HIGH RPM

SEE NO START PROCEDURE

CHECK PICK-UP COIL WITH OHMMETER

BAD

REPLACE

DWELL INCREASED

GOOD

DWELL DIDN'T INCREASE

TROUBLE NOT FOUND

REPLACE MODULE

CHECK FUEL, PLUG WIRES, CAP AND PLUGS.

CUT A SPARK PLUG BOOT AS SHOWN

DISCARD

7/16" (11mm) FROM TIP OF SPARK PLUG

INSERT BOOT OVER PORCELAIN END OF ST-125

REMOVE GREEN AND WHITE LEADS FROM MODULE

(TO BAT +)

TEST LIGHT

CONNECT VOLTMETER, "TACH" TERMINAL TO GROUND

VIEW B

CONNECT TO GROUND

LEAVE HARNESS CONNECTED

VIEW A

piece and magnet and/or pick-up coil.

2. Reverse the removal procedure to install making sure that the pole piece teeth do not contact the timer core teeth by installing and rotating the mainshaft. Loosen the 3 screws and realign the pole piece as necessary.

ESC SERVICE PROCEDURES

Diagnosis

Before attempting to find an electrical or electronic problem with the Electronic Spark Control or Computer Command Control System, check that all electrical and vacuum connectors are securely connected. Otherwise, needless diagnostic or repair time may be expended.

If no bad electrical or vacuum connections are found, refer to the accompanying charts.

Chrysler electronic ignition schematic

ESC SYSTEMS DIAGNOSIS

ENGINE DETONATION ①

BEFORE ATTEMPTING ANY DIAGNOSIS, CHECK CONNECTION AT SENSOR AND INSURE THAT ALL CONNECTIONS ARE CLEAN AND TIGHT

WITH ENGINE RUNNING AT FAST IDLE SPEED & TRANS. IN N OR P (ENGINE SPEED ABOVE 1000 RPM), TAP EXHAUST MANIFOLD LIGHTLY & REPEATEDLY & CHECK FOR SPARK TIMING RETARD (WITH TIMING LIGHT).

RETARD → CHECK OTHER "ENGINE DETONATION" CAUSES

NO RETARD

DISCONNECT 10-PIN CONNECTOR FROM ESC CONTROLLER. MEASURE VOLTAGE FROM PIN B TO PIN K IN CONNECTOR WITH ENGINE OPERATING AT APPROX. 2000 RPM. VOLTAGE SHOULD BE GREATER THAN 80 MILLIVOLTS, (.08 VOLTS)

LOW → DISCONNECT SENSOR WIRE FROM SENSOR. MEASURE VOLTAGE FROM SENSOR TERMINAL TO GROUND. SHOULD BE GREATER THAN 80 MILLIVOLTS (.08 VOLTS) WITH ENGINE OPERATING AT APPROX 2000 RPM.

OK

TRY TO START ENGINE (WITH 10-PIN CONNECTOR DISCONNECTED).

OK → CHECK WIRES FROM PINS A, B, & K (IN 10-PIN CONNECTOR) FOR OPEN & SHORT CIRCUITS.

HIGH OR LOW → REPLACE SENSOR.

NO START

START → REPLACE DISTRIBUTOR MODULE.

OK → REPAIR SENSOR CONNECTOR.

NOT OK → REPAIR HARNESS.

RECONNECT 10-PIN CONNECTOR TO CONTROLLER. DISCONNECT SENSOR WIRE FROM SENSOR & INSERT A JUMPER WIRE INTO SENSOR WIRE CONNECTOR. WITH ENGINE RUNNING AT FAST IDLE SPEED, LAY WIRE ON TOP OF DISTRIBUTOR OVER IGNITION COIL & CHECK FOR SPARK TIMING RETARD.

RETARD → REPLACE SENSOR.

NO RETARD

MEASURE VOLTAGE FROM PIN H TO PIN K WITH IGNITION SWITCH ON. SHOULD BE MORE THAN 0.2 VOLT.

OK → REPLACE ESC CONTROLLER.

NOT OK → REPAIR OPEN CIRCUIT IN WIRE FROM PIN H IN ESC HARNESS.

① SOME OCCASIONAL TRACE-TO-LIGHT DETONATION IS ACCEPTABLE.

HEI DIAGNOSIS CHART 1983–84
Engine Cranks, But Will Not Start
1983 CCC
ENGINE CRANKS, BUT WILL NOT RUN
(WITH INTEGRAL IGNITION COIL)

PRELIMINARY

NOTE: Perform Diagnostic Circuit Check before using this procedure.
If a tachometer is connected to the tachometer terminal, disconnect it before proceeding with the test.
Intermittent no start may be caused by wrong pick-up or ignition coil.

* A few sparks and then nothing, is considered no spark.

HEI DIAGNOSIS CHART 1983–84
Continued

TROUBLE CODE 42
BYPASS OR EST PROBLEM

If vehicle will not start and run, check for grounded EST wire to ECM terminal "12." (Grounded and open EST circuit on 5.0L VIN "Y".)

A 1981 HEI module can cause a Code 42.

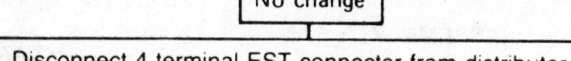

With engine at fast idle, note timing. Ground "test" terminal and note timing; it should change.

↓

No change — **OK**

→ No trouble found

- Disconnect 4 terminal EST connector from distributor.
- With engine stopped, connect jumper from "A" to "B" in distributor side of EST connector.
- Start engine, ground "test" terminal and connect test light from Battery + to term. "C" of same conn.

Engine stops | **Engine runs**

Check for open EST wire to terminal "E" of HEI module. If wire is OK, it is faulty HEI module connection or module. | With test light still connected, remove jumper between terminals "A" and "B."

Engine runs | **Engine stops**

Check distributor wires for:
- Open or ground to module terminal "B".
- Short between module terminals "R" and "E". If wires are OK, it is faulty HEI module connection or module.

| - Check for correct HEI module.
- Check for open wire from EST Connector terminal "A" to ECM terminal "12"
- Check for open or ground wire from EST Connector terminal "C" to ECM terminal "11".

If not grounded or open, check for voltage from terminal "21" to ground. | **If grounded or open**

→ Repair

Under 4.5 volts | **Over 4.5 volts**

Check for grounded wire to ECM term. "21" | It is faulty ECM connection or ECM.

ECM | 11 — C | — B | HEI
| 12 — A | — E |
| 21 — TPS
— MAP SENSOR
— BARO. OR VAC. SENSOR

Detonation Sensor Replacement

The detonation sensor is located on the lower portion of the block on the right side—just in front of the starter. To replace it, first unlatch and then pull off the connector. Apply a wrench to the flats and unscrew the sensor. Screw the new sensor in place and tighten with the wrench. Reconnect the connector and try to gently pull the connector from the sensor (with a force of about three lb.) to make sure it is latched in place. Finally, push it back on with about 10 lb. of force to make sure it's seated.

ESC Controller Replacement

The ESC Controller is located on the mounting bracket for the brake pedal, just to the right of the steering column. To replace it, first release and disconnect the wiring connector from underneath. Remove the screw fastening the top of the brace which runs from the brake pedal bracket to the lower controller mounting bracket. This is the screw nearest the firewall accessible from inside the brake pedal bracket.

Remove the two screws holding the lower controller mounting bracket and lower brace

in place, and remove the lower bracket, brace and controller.

To install, first position the controller with the connection at the bottom and tabs facing away from the steering column. Slide the controller unit up under the tab at the top of its mounting bracket. Put the lower controller mounting bracket in position and install its rear screw. Position the brace so that its lower screw hole lines up with the open screw hole in the lower mounting bracket and its upper screw hole lines up with that in the brake pedal bracket. Install the screw which fastens the lower controller bracket and brace. Install the screw fastening the upper brace to the pedal mounting bracket. Finally, connect the electrical connector, checking that it locks securely.

DISTRIBUTOR 4 CYL. OHC ENGINE, CHEVY S–15

Overhaul
DISASSEMBLY

1. Remove the cap, rotor, and the packing which seals the cap at the bottom.
2. Remove the reluctor cover by squeezing together the fastening tangs and pulling it out.
3. Remove the vacuum advance unit's mounting screws and remove the unit from the distributor.
4. Remove the screw which attaches the wiring harness clip to the side of the distributor and remove the clip. Disconnect the two connectors from the breaker plate. Slide the harness sealing grommet up and out of the side of the distributor and remove the harness.
5. Using screwdrivers to pry on both sides simultaneously, remove the reluctor from the rotor shaft.
6. Remove the breaker plate mounting screws, and remove the breaker plate assembly.
7. Remove the screws fastening the module to the breaker plate, and remove module from the breaker plate.
8. Drive the roll pin out of the shaft

with a hammer and punch. (This refers to the roll pin in the collar keeping the shaft in the housing.)
9. Remove the distributor shaft from the housing.
10. Slide the O-ring off the shaft. Then, remove the screw from the top of the shaft (this screw retains the governor shaft).
11. Scribe the relationship between the governor shaft and rotor shaft to maintain the offset in the governor shaft after reassembly. Then, remove the governor shaft.
12. Remove the governor weights and springs from the governor shaft assembly.

ASSEMBLY

1. Assemble in reverse order, noting the following points:

When installing the governor springs, make sure the hooks of smaller springs are positioned below those of the larger springs on the posts.

Make sure the offset of the end of the governor shaft is correct by aligning scribe marks.

Use a new rollpin to fasten the collar which retains the mainshaft.

Twist and release the governor shaft to check that centrifugal advance will respond to changes in engine speed. The mechanism should return fully when released.

Measure the air gap between the pole piece and the stator with a feeler gauge. Adjust if necessary until it is 0.12-0.020 in.

Chrysler Electronic Ignition

COMPONENTS

This system consists of a special pulse-sending distributor, an electronic control unit, a two-element ballast resistor, and a special ignition coil.

The distributor does not contain breaker points or a condenser, these parts being replaced by a distributor reluctor and a pick-up unit.

OPERATION

The ignition primary circuit is connected from the battery, through the ignition switch, through the primary side of the ignition coil, to the control unit where it is grounded. The secondary circuit is the same as in conventional ignition systems: the secondary side of the coil, the coil wire to the distributor, the rotor, the spark plug wires, and the spark plugs.

The magnetic pulse distributor is also connected to the control unit. As the distributor shaft rotates, the distributor reluctor turns past the pick-up unit. As the reluctor turns past the pick-up unit, each of the eight teeth on the reluctor pass near the pick-up unit once during each distributor revolution (two crankshaft revolutions since

1. Cap
2. Carbon
3. Rotor
4. Seal
5. Rotor Assembly
6. Screw
7. Vacuum Control Unit
8. Screw
9. Harness
10. Reluctor
11. Roll Pin
12. Screw
13. Governor Base
14. Screw
15. Pickup Unit
16. Bushing
17. Screw
18. Plate
19. Spacers
20. Key
21. Washer and Bearing
22. Shaft Assembly
23. Cam
24. Felt
25. Screw
26. Governor Weight
27. Governor Springs

Exploded view of distributor

the distributor runs at one-half crankshaft speed). As the reluctor teeth move close to the pick-up unit, the magnetic rotating reluctor induces voltage into the magnetic pick-up unit. This voltage pulse is sent to the ignition control unit from the magnetic pick-up unit. When the pulse enters the control unit, it signals the control unit to interrupt the ignition primary circuit. This causes the primary circuit to collapse and begins the induction of the magnetic lines of force from the primary side of the coil into the secondary side of the coil. This induction provides the required voltage to fire the spark plugs.

The advantages of this system are that the transistors in the control unit can make and break the primary ignition circuit much faster than conventional ignition points can, and higher primary voltage can be utilized, since this system can be made to handle higher voltage without adverse effects, whereas ignition breaker points cannot. The quicker switching time of this system allows longer coil primary circuit saturation time and longer induction time when the primary circuit collapses. This increased time allows the primary circuit to build up more current and the secondary circuit to discharge more current.

PICK-UP COIL REPLACEMENT

1. Remove the distributor from the engine.
2. Using two small pry-bars or screwdrivers (maximum 7/16 in. wide), pry the reluctor off the shaft from the bottom.

--------- CAUTION ---------
Do not damage the teeth on the reluctor.

3. Unfasten the vacuum advance-to-distributor housing screws. Remove the vacuum unit, after disconnecting the arm from the upper plate.
4. Unfasten the pick-up coil wires from the distributor housing.
5. Unfasten the two screws which secure the lower plate to the distributor housing. Lift out the lower plate together with the upper plate and pick-up coil.
6. Separate the upper and lower plates by depressing the retaining clip on the underside of the plate and slide it away from the stud. The pick-up coil will come off with the upper plate; they cannot be separated; they must be serviced as an assembly.
Installation is the reverse of removal. Place a small amount of distributor grease on the support pins on the lower plate.

Air Gap Adjustment

1. Align one reluctor tooth with the pick-up coil tooth.
2. Loosen the pick-up coil hold-down screw.
3. Insert a 0.008 in. nonmagnetic feeler gauge between the reluctor tooth and the

Chrysler electronic ignition underhood layout

pick-up coil tooth.
4. Adjust the air gap so that contact is made between the reluctor tooth, the feeler gauge, and the pick-up coil tooth.
5. Tighten the hold-down screw.
6. Remove the feeler gauge.

NOTE: No force should be required in removing the feeler gauge.

7. Check the air gap with a 0.008 in. feeler gauge. A 0.008 in. feeler gauge should not fit into the air gap.

--------- CAUTION ---------
A 0.008 in. feeler gauge can be forced into the air gap. Do not force the gauge into the air gap.

8. Apply vacuum to the vacuum unit and rotate the governor shaft. The pick-up pole should not hit the reluctor teeth. The gap was not properly adjusted if any hitting occurs. If hitting occurs on only one side of the reluctor, the distributor shaft is probably bent, and the governor and shaft assembly should be replaced.

TROUBLESHOOTING ELECTRONIC IGNITION SYSTEM

Chrysler Corporation has an Electronic Ignition System Tester to be used when checking the system. However, many shops are not able to obtain this equipment, so an alternate method has been developed. The system may be tested using a voltmeter with a scale of 20 volts and an ohmmeter with a scale of 20,000 ohms.

When the ignition system is suspected of malfunctions, the following procedure should be used.
1. Inspect the secondary wires for cracks and tightness.
2. Check all primary wires and connections at the components for tightness.
3. Check and note the battery voltage.
4. Be sure the ignition switch is in the "OFF" position and remove the multi-wiring connector from the control unit.
5. Turn the ignition switch to the "ON"

V8 distributor

position and connect the negative lead of the voltmeter to a good ground.
6. Connect the positive lead of the voltmeter to the number 1 terminal of the wiring harness connector. The voltage should be within 1 volt of battery voltage. If more than 1 volt, the circuit must be checked for high resistance.

TROUBLESHOOTING CHRYSLER ELECTRONIC IGNITION

Condition	Possible Cause	Correction
ENGINE WILL NOT START (Fuel and carburetion known to be OK)	a) Dual Ballast	Check resistance of each section: Compensating resistance: .50-.60 ohms @ 70°-80°F Auxiliary Ballast: 4.75-5.75 ohms Replace if faulty. Check wire positions.
	b) Faulty Ignition Coil	Check for carbonized tower. Check primary and secondary resistances: Primary: 1.41-1.79 ohms @ 70°-80°F Secondary: 9,200-11,700 ohms @ 70°-80°F Check in coil tester.
	c) Faulty Pickup or Improper Pickup Air Gap	Check pickup coil resistance: 400-600 ohms Check pickup gap: .010 in. feeler gauge should not slip between pickup coil core and an aligned reluctor blade. No evidence of pickup core striking reluctor blades should be visible. To reset gap, tighten pickup adjustment screw with a .008 in. feeler gauge held between pickup core and an aligned reluctor blade. After resetting gap, run distributor on test stand and apply vacuum advance, making sure that the pickup core does not strike the reluctor blades.
	d) Faulty Wiring	Visually inspect wiring for brittle insulation. Inspect connectors. Molded connectors should be inspected for rubber inside female terminals.
	e) Faulty Control Unit	Replace if all of the above checks are negative. Whenever the control unit or dual ballast is replaced, make sure the dual ballast wires are correctly inserted in the keyed molded connector.
ENGINE SURGES SEVERELY (Not Lean Carburetor)	a) Wiring	Inspect for loose connection and/or broken conductors in harness.
	b) Faulty Pickup Leads	Disconnect vacuum advance. If surging stops, replace pickup.
	c) Ignition Coil	Check for intermittent primary.
ENGINE MISSES (Carburetion OK)	a) Spark Plugs	Check plugs. Clean and regap if necessary.
	b) Secondary Cable	Check cables with an ohmmeter, or observe secondary circuit performance with an oscilloscope.
	c) Ignition Coil	Check for cabonized tower. Check in coil tester.
	d) Wiring	Check for loose or dirty connections.
	e) Faulty Pickup Lead	Disconnect vacuum advance. If miss stops, replace pickup.
	f) Control Unit	Replace if the above checks are negative.

7. Connect the positive lead of the voltmeter to the wiring harness connector number 2 terminal. Available voltage should be within 1 volt of battery voltage. If more than 1 volt, the circuit should be checked for high resistance.

8. Connect the positive lead of the voltmeter to the wiring harness connector terminal number 3. Available voltage should be within 1 volt of battery voltage. If more than 1 volt, the circuit must be checked for high resistance.

9. Turn the ignition switch to the "OFF" position.

10. Connect an ohmmeter to the wiring harness connector terminal numbers 4 and 5. This checks the distributor pick-up coil. The ohmmeter resistance reading should be between 150 and 900 ohms. If the readings are higher or lower than specified, disconnect the dual lead connector coming from the distributor. Using the ohmmeter leads, check the resistance at the dual lead connector. If the reading is not between 150 and 900 ohms, replace the pick-up coil assembly in the distributor. If the reading is within specifications at the dual lead connector, check the wiring harness between the control unit and the dual lead connector.

11. Connect one ohmmeter lead to a good

ground and the other lead to either connector of the distributor. The ohmmeter should show an open circuit. If the ohmmeter shows a reading, the pickup coil in the distributor must be replaced.

12. When checking the electronic control unit, connect one ohmmeter lead to a good ground and the other lead to the control unit connector pin number 5. The ohmmeter should show continuity between the ground and the connector pin. If continuity does not exist, tighten the bolts holding the control unit to the vehicle panel and recheck. If continuity does not exist, the control unit must be replaced.

13. Reconnect the wiring harness at the control unit and distributor.

--- CAUTION ---
Whenever removing or replacing the wiring harness connector to the control unit or the distributor, the ignition switch must be in the "OFF" position.

14. Check the reluctor tooth and pickup coil air gaps, specifications of 0.008 inch.

15. To check the secondary ignition system, remove the high voltage cable from the center tower of the distributor cap and

hold approximately 3/16 inch from the engine block and crank the engine with the ignition switch in the "START" position.

16. If arcing does not occur, replace the control unit. Recheck by cranking the engine. If arcing still does not occur, replace the ignition coil.

AMC Breakerless Inductive Discharge (BID) Ignition

COMPONENTS

The AMC breakerless inductive discharge (BID) ignition system consists of five components:
1. Control unit
2. Coil
3. Breakerless distributor
4. Ignition cables
5. Spark plugs

The control unit is a solid-state, epoxy-sealed module with waterproof connectors. The control unit has a built-in current regulator, so no separate ballast resistor or resistance wire is needed in the primary circuit. Battery voltage is supplied to the ignition coil positive (+) terminal when the ignition key is turned to the "ON" or "START" position; low voltage is also supplied by the control unit.

The coil used with the BID system requires no special service. It works just like the coil in a conventional ignition system.

The distributor is conventional, except for the lack of points, condenser and cam. Advance is supplied by both a vacuum unit and a centrifugal advance mechanism. A standard cap, rotor, and dust shield are used.

In place of the points, cam, and condenser, the distributor has a sensor and trigger wheel. The sensor is a small coil which generates an electromagnetic field when excited by the oscillator in the control unit.

Standard spark plugs and ignition cables are used.

OPERATION

When the ignition switch is turned on, the control unit is activated. The control unit then sends an oscillating signal to the sensor which causes the sensor to generate a magnetic field. When one of the trigger wheel teeth enters this field, the strength of the oscillation in the sensor is reduced. Once the strength drops to a predetermined level, a demodulator circuit operates the control unit's switching transistor. The switching transistor is wired in series with the coil primary circuit; it switches the circuit off when it gets the demodulator signal.

From this point on, the BID ignition system works in the same manner as a conventional ignition system.

TROUBLESHOOTING

1. Check all of the BID ignition system electrical connections.

2. Disconnect the coil-to-distributor high tension lead.

3. Hold the end of the lead ½ in. away from a ground. Crank the engine. If there is a spark, the trouble is not in the ignition system.

4. If there was no spark in step 3, connect a test light with a No. 57 bulb between the positive coil terminal (+) and a good ground. Have an assistant turn the ignition switch to "ON" and "START" (Do not start the engine). The bulb should light in both positions; if it doesn't, the fault lies in the battery-to-coil circuit. Check the ignition switch and related wiring.

5. If the test light lit in step 4, disconnect the coil-to-distributor leads at the connector and connect the test light between the positive (+) and negative (−) coil terminals.

6. Turn the ignition switch on. If the test light doesn't come on, check the control unit's ground lead. If the ground lead is in good condition, replace the control unit.

7. If the bulb lights in step 6, leave the test light in place and short the terminals on the coil-to-distributor connector together with a jumper lead, (connector separated) at the coil side of the connector. If the light stays on, replace the control unit.

8. If the test light goes out, remove it. Check for a spark, as in step 2, each time that the coil-to-distributor connector terminals are shorted together with the jumper lead. If there is a spark, replace the control unit; if there is no spark, replace the coil.

Coil Testing

Test the coil with a conventional coil checker or an ohmmeter. Primary resistance should be 1–2 ohms and secondary resistance should be 8–12 kilohms. The open output circuit should be more than 20 kilovolts. Replace the coil if it doesn't meet specifications.

Using a special gauge to align the BID sensor coil

POSITION GAUGE AGAINST FLAT SIDE OF YOKE

SENSOR CORE

BID schematic

Sensor Testing

Check the sensor resistance by connecting an ohmmeter to its leads. Resistance should be 1.8 ohms (± 10%) at 77° F. Replace the sensor if it doesn't meet these specifications.

DISTRIBUTOR OVERHAUL

NOTE: If you must remove the sensor from the distributor for any reason, it will be necessary to have the special sensor positioning gauge in order to align it properly during installation.

1. Scribe matchmarks on the distributor housing, rotor, and engine block. Disconnect the leads and vacuum lines from the distributor. Remove the distributor. Unless the cap is to be replaced, leave it connected to the spark plug cables and position it out of the way.

2. Remove the rotor and dust cap.

3. Place a small gear puller over the trigger wheel, so that its jaws grip the inner shoulders of the wheel and not its arms. Place a thick washer between the gear puller and the distributor shaft to act as a spacer; do not press against the smaller inner shaft.

4. Loosen the sensor hold-down screw with a small pair of needle-nosed pliers; it has a tamperproof head. Pull the sensor lead grommet out of the distributor body and

Fabricating a BID wheel clearance gauge

GAUGE   TRIGGER WHEEL

SENSOR BASE

pull out the leads from around the spring pivot pin.

5. Release the sensor securing spring by lifting it. Make sure that it clears the leads. Slide the sensor off the bracket.

NOTE: A special gauge is required for sensor installation.

6. Remove the vacuum advance unit securing screw. Slide the vacuum unit out of the distributor. Remove it only if it is to be replaced.

7. Clean and dry the vacuum unit and sensor brackets. Lubrication of these parts is not necessary.

BID distributor assembly is as follows:

IHC electronic ignition system

Voltmeter connected to coil negative terminal

1. Install the vacuum unit, if it was removed.

2. Assemble the sensor, sensor guide, flat washer, and retaining screw. Tighten the screw only far enough to keep the assembly together; don't allow the screw to project below the bottom of the sensor.

NOTE: Replacement sensors come with a slotted-head screw to aid in assembly. If the original sensor is being used, replace the tamper-proof screw with a conventional one. Use the original washer.

3. Secure the sensor on the vacuum advance unit bracket, making sure that the tip of the sensor is placed in the notch on the summing bar.

4. Position the spring on the sensor and route the leads around the spring pivot pin. Fit the sensor lead grommet into the slot on the distributor body. Be sure that the lead can't get caught in the trigger wheel.

5. Place the special sensor positioning gauge over the distributor shaft, so that the flat on the shaft is against the large notch on the gauge. Move the sensor until the sensor core fits into the small notch on the gauge. Tighten the sensor securing screw with the gauge in place (through the round hole in the gauge).

6. It should be possible to remove and install the gauge without any side movement of the sensor. Check this and remove the gauge.

7. Position the trigger wheel on the shaft. Check to see that the sensor core is centered between the trigger wheel legs and that the

Sensor-to-trigger wheel gap

legs don't touch the core.

8. Bend a piece of 0.050 in. gauge wire, so that it has a 90° angle and one leg ½ in. long. Use the gauge to measure the clearance between the trigger wheel legs and the sensor boss. Press the trigger wheel on the shaft until it just touches the gauge. Support the shaft during this operation.

9. Place 3 to 5 drops of SAE 20 oil on the felt lubricator wick.

10. Install the dust shield and rotor on the shaft.

11. Install the distributor on the engine using the matchmarks made during removal and adjust the timing. Use a new distributor mounting gasket.

IH Electronic Ignition

HOLLEY MODEL 1530 '78 (EARLY PRODUCTION)

The system uses a standard ignition coil with no ballast resistor or resistance wire, since the control box regulates the primary, low-voltage, current. The distributor part of the system consists of a metal detecting sensor and a toothed trigger wheel in place of the distributor cam. The only adjustment is for sensor to trigger wheel air gap. The control box components are permanently sealed in a waterproof and vibration resistant compound. Most of these systems use vacuum spark advance in addition to mechanical advance.

Disassembly and overhaul of the distributor is very similar to that for International V8 point-type distributors.

Sensor to Trigger Wheel Air Gap Adjustment

1. Align the trigger wheel so that one tooth is aligned with the centerline of the sensor. The tooth should be at right angles to the flat side of the sensor.

2. The gap should be .008 in. for 1978 and later models.

3. A distributor machine or a dwell/tachometer calibrated for electronic ignition systems can be used to measure dwell.

NOTE: Most ordinary dwell/tachometers will give a reading, but this will not be accurate.

On 1978 and later models, dwell should be 26–32 degrees at curb idle and also at 300 distributor rpm with 12–13 volts primary input.

4. Adjust the gap and dwell by moving the sensor. Move the sensor toward the trigger wheel to decrease dwell or away to increase dwell. .001 in. of sensor movement equals about ½ degree of dwell change.

TROUBLESHOOTING

1. Make sure that the battery is fully charged, delivering 12–13 volts. Make sure that all wiring, connections, and mounting bolts are in good condition.

2. Disconnect one spark plug wire and insert an extension of some sort into the boot. Hold the wire with insulated pliers and a heavy glove so that there is a gap of about ¼–½ in. between the extension and a ground. If the spark jumps the gap when the engine is cranked with the starter, the system is in good condition. If not, replace the wire and go on.

3. Detach the coil wire from the center of the distributor cap. Attach one end of a jumper wire to a ground and the other around the coil wire (don't pierce the insulation) ¼–½ in. from the metal tip. If there is a spark when the engine is cranked, the distributor cap, rotor, or spark plug and coil wires may be faulty. If not, keep the jumper in place and go on.

4. Disconnect the primary wiring plug near the distributor and plug a tester switch, part no. SE-2503, into the wiring harness. The switch replaces the distributor sensor in the circuit. Turn the ignition switch on and press the tester switch button. If there is a spark at the jumper, the sensor is defective and must be replaced. If not, go on.

5. Disconnect the primary wiring plug near the control box and install the tester switch. Turn the ignition switch on and press the tester switch button. If there is a spark at the jumper now, the primary wiring harness is defective. If not, go on.

6. Connect a voltmeter between the coil negative terminal and a ground. Voltage

Spark gap test

should be 12–13 volts. A low reading indicates high resistance between the battery and the coil, probably due to defective wires or ignition switch.

7. Connect the voltmeter between the coil negative terminal and a ground. With the ignition switch on, voltage should be 5–8 volts. A lower or higher reading indicates a bad coil. Press the tester switch button; voltage should go up to 12–13 volts and go back down when the button is released. If the voltage doesn't go up and down, the control box is faulty and must be replaced. If the voltage goes up and down but there is no spark at the jumper, the coil is defective.

8. Reconnect the system and make a final check for spark at the plug wire, as in Step 2.

Breakerless Integral Electronic Ignition System

PRESTOLITE IDN-4000 SERIES 1978 AND LATER

The Breakerless Integral Electronic Ignition system is available for both the four cylinder and V-8 engines. The system consists of two major components, the ignition coil and the distributor. The electronic control unit, consisting of a circuit board and sensor, is located within the distributor and is replaced as a complete unit, should service be required. Either a four or eight toothed trigger wheel is located on the distributor shaft, depending upon the engine in which it is to be used.

The distributor is easily identified by the male type terminal on the distributor cap secondary system. The distributor incorporates a mechanical (centrifugal) spark advance system. Most distributors will have a vacuum operated advance system to automatically provide the correct spark advance timing for the various engine speed and load conditions.

The sensor mounting plate configuration and vacuum advance unit location varies

between distributors with clockwise and counterclockwise rotation.

Disassembly and Overhaul

The disassembly and overhaul of the distributor is similar to that of the conventional point type distributor. Certain specifications should be adhered to during the overhaul of the distributor. The distributor shaft side play should be between 0.002 and 0.004 inch with a maximum of 0.006 inch. The distributor shaft end play should be 0.035 to 0.040 inch, except distributors with left hand (counterclockwise) rotation, which should be 0.004 to 0.018 inch. The distributor dwell should be 26 to 32 degrees, except distributors numbered IDN-4001B, IDN-4002R, IDN-4001, IDN-4010 and IDN-4001A, which have a dwell of 28 to 34 degrees.

All distributors should have an air gap between the end of the trigger wheel tooth and the sensor of 0.008 inch.

Sensor to Trigger Wheel Air Gap Adjustment

1. Rotate the distributor shaft until one tooth of the trigger wheel is aligned with the center of the sensor.

NOTE: The trigger wheel tooth should be perpendicular to the flat surface of the sensor when properly aligned.

2. Using an appropriate feeler gauge,

measure the air gap between the sensor and the end of the trigger wheel tooth.

3. Loosen and move the sensor as needed to obtain the specified air gap. Tighten the sensor mounting screw and recheck the air gap.

4. The dwell can be checked by installing the distributor in a test stand or in the vehicle engine. Use the appropriate dwell meter to check the dwell.

5. Should the dwell need to be changed, move the sensor towards the trigger wheel to decrease dwell or away from the trigger wheel to increase dwell. Dwell is affected approximately ½ degree per 0.001 inch of sensor movement.

TROUBLESHOOTING

Engine Not Starting

1. Battery voltage should be 12–13 volts before starting the tests.

2. Disconnect spark plug wire at the spark plug and hold the end terminal with an adapter, approximately ½ inch from a ground on the engine. Have an assistant crank the engine and observe for a spark from the wire and adapter to ground. Test at least two wires.

3. If a spark occurs, the electrical system is functioning and the no-start problem is elsewhere.

4. If no spark occurs, check for spark

1. From ignition switch
2. Ignition coil
3. Red wire
4. To decelerate throttle modulator (where used)
5. Brown wire
6. To governor control unit (where used)
7. Distributor

Distributor primary wiring

1. Cap
2. Rotor
3. Dust shield
4. Trigger wheel
5. Felt lubricator
6. Sensor assembly
7. Distributor body
8. Vacuum unit screw
9. Vacuum advance unit
10. Shim
11. Drive gear
12. Pin

BID distributor

Air gap adjustments

at the coil lead by disconnecting it from the distributor cap and holding it approximately ½ inch from a ground and again, have an assistant crank the engine.

5. If a spark occurs, the problem is in the distributor cap, rotor or spark plug cables.

6. If no spark occurs, check the distributor trigger wheel tooth to sensor air gap as previously outlined.

7. If the air gap is out of specifications, adjust and retest for spark. If still no spark occurs, "bump" the starter to position two trigger wheel teeth to straddle the sensor.

8. Connect a voltmeter between the coil positive (+) terminal and ground. Turn the ignition on and the voltage should read battery voltage (12–13 volts).

9. Should the voltage be noticeably lower than battery voltage, a high resistance exists between the battery and the coil. This resistance must be found and repaired before proceeding.

NOTE: Refer to the Primary Voltage Drop Test at the end of this trouble-shooting outline.

10. If battery voltage is present at the coil positive (+) terminal, move the clip of the voltmeter lead to the negative (−) coil terminal and check the voltage present with the ignition switch on. The voltage obtained will be one of the following:
   a. 5–8 volts—Normal
   b. 12–13 volts—Problem
   c. 0–5 volts—Problem

If Voltage Is 5 To 8 Volts—(A)

1. With the voltmeter still connected to the negative (−) terminal of the coil, turn the ignition switch on and place the blade of a flat screwdriver against the face of the sensor while observing the voltmeter.

2. The voltage should increase to 12–13 volts.

3. Remove the screwdriver and the voltage should drop to 5–8 volts.

4. The voltage should switch up and down when the screwdriver blade is placed against and then removed from the sensor surface.

5. If the voltage does not switch up or down, the electronic control unit is defective and must be replaced.

6. To verify the secondary spark from the coil to ground as the voltage moves up or down, re-establish the ½ inch gap between the coil lead and engine ground.

7. With the ignition switch on, place the screwdriver blade against the face of the sensor and a spark should occur across the gap. If no spark occurs, the coil is defective and must be replaced.

8. After replacing the defective component(s), reassemble the shield, rotor, distributor cap and wiring. Recheck for spark at the spark plugs.

9. Check the dwell and the ignition timing. Adjust as required in this order. When the distributor is equipped with a vacuum advance, disconnect the vacuum hose before adjusting the timing.

If Voltage Reading Is 12–13 Volts (B)

1. Connect a jumper wire between the distributor housing and the battery negative (−) terminal.

2. Observe the voltage reading. If the voltage remains at 12–13 volts, the electronic control unit is defective and must be replaced.

3. Should the voltage change to 5–8 volts with the jumper wire connected, a poor ground circuit exists between the distributor and the battery. All grounding straps should be examined, cleaned and tightened as required.

If The Voltage Is Between 0–5 Volts (C)

1. Disconnect the voltmeter lead from the coil and disconnect the brown wire from the coil negative (−) terminal.

2. Reconnect the voltmeter lead to the coil negative (−) terminal, with the other voltmeter lead still connected to a ground.

3. With the ignition switch on, observe the voltage reading. If the voltage is still 0–5 volts, the coil is faulty and must be replaced.

1. Battery
2. Ignition switch
3. Ignition coil
4. Voltmeter
5. Screwdriver

Testing the electronic control unit

4. If the voltage increases to 12–13 volts, the electronic control unit is defective and must be replaced.

5. After the necessary repairs are made, be sure to reconnect the brown wire to the coil negative (−) terminal.

PRIMARY VOLTAGE DROP TEST

1. Remove the distributor cap, rotor and shield. "Bump" the starter to position two teeth of the trigger wheel, straddling the sensor.

2. Connect the voltmeter positive (+) lead to the battery positive (+) post and connect the voltmeter negative (−) lead to the coil positive (+) terminal.

3. Turn the ignition on and observe the voltmeter reading. A reading of less than one volt should be obtained.

4. If a voltage reading higher than one volt exists, move the following components while observing the voltmeter scale.
   a. Battery cables
   b. Starter solenoid battery terminal
   c. Dash panel connector at the firewall (if used)
   d. Ammeter terminals
   e. Ignition switch connectors

5. If a fluctuation or upswing of the voltmeter is noted while flexing the connectors and cables, a poor connection or defective cable exists and must be corrected.

SWITCHES AND SOLENOIDS

Magnetic Switches

Magnetic switches serve only to make contact for the starter motor. Usually, such switches are located on the inner fender panel, although they are found mounted on the starter in a few cases.

Magnetic Switches with Two Control Terminals

On this type of magnetic switch current is supplied from the ignition switch or transmission neutral button to one of the magnetic switch control terminals. The other control terminal is connected to the transmission neutral safety switch (on the transmission) where it is grounded.

Starter solenoid mounted on starter motor

Magnetic Switches with Ignition Resistor By-Pass Terminals

All normally use a magnetic switch with a single control terminal. The second terminal is an ignition resistor by-pass terminal.

SOLENOIDS WITHOUT RELAYS

This type of starter solenoid is always mounted on the starter. Makes electrical contact for the starter and pulls the starter and drive clutch into mesh with the flywheel. The Chrysler reduction gear starter has this solenoid embodied in the starter housing.

There is only one control terminal on the solenoid.

The ignition by-pass terminal is usually marked R or IGN, if it is used.

SOLENOIDS WITH SEPARATE RELAYS

The solenoid itself is always mounted on the starter. In addition to making contact for the starter, it also pulls the starter drive clutch gear into mesh with the flywheel. A single control terminal is used on the solenoid itself. The relay is usually found mounted to the inner fender panel or on the firewall.

SOLENOIDS WITH BUILT-IN RELAYS

These units are always mounted on the starter and are connected, through linkage, to the starter drive clutch. The relay portion is a square box built into and integral with the front end of the solenoid assembly.

NEUTRAL SAFETY SWITCHES

The purpose of the neutral safety switch is to prevent the starter from cranking the engine except when the transmission is in neutral or park.

On some trucks the neutral safety switch is located on the transmission. It serves to ground the solenoid or magnetic switch, whichever is used.

On other trucks the neutral safety switch is located either at the bottom of the steering column, where it contacts the shift mechanism, on the steering column, underneath the dash, or on the shift linkage (console).

Some manual transmission models have a clutch linkage safety switch to prevent starter operation unless the clutch pedal is depressed.

On most trucks the neutral safety switch and the backup light switch are combined into a single switch mechanism.

Troubleshooting Neutral Safety Switches—Quick Test

If the starter fails to function and the neutral safety switch is to be checked, a jumper can be placed across its terminals. If the starter then functions the safety switch is defective.

In the case of neutral safety switches with one wire, this wire must be grounded for testing purposes. If the starter works with the wire grounded, the switch is defective.

Reduction gear starter motor

Removing the drive gear snap-ring on reduction gear starter motors

Removing the terminal screw on reduction gear starter motors

Neutral Safety Switch—Back-Up Light Switch

When the neutral safety switch is built in combination with the back-up light switch, the easiest way to tell which terminals are for the back-up lights is to take a jumper and cross every pair of wires. The pair of wires which light the back-up lamps should be ignored when testing the neutral safety switch. Once the back-up light wires have been located, jump the other pair of wires to test the neutral safety switch. If the starter functions only when the jumper is placed across these two wires, the neutral safety switch is defective or requires adjustment.

Reduction gear starter

STARTING SYSTEMS

Reduction-Gear Starter Motor

CHRYSLER CORPORATION

The housing is die-cast aluminum. A 3.5 to 1 reduction, combined with the starter to ring gear ratio, results in a total gear reduction of about 45 to 1.

NOTE: The high-pitched sound is caused by the higher starter speed.

The positive shift solenoid is enclosed in the starter housing and is energized through the ignition switch. When ignition switch is turned to start, the solenoid plunger engages drive gear through a shifting fork. At the completion of travel, the plunger closes a switch to revolve the starter.

The tension of the spring-type shifting prevents a butt-tooth lock up and motor will not start before total shift.

An overrunning clutch prevents motor damage if key is held on after engine starts.

No lubrication is required due to Oilite bearings.

Disassembly

1. Support assembly in a vise equipped with soft jaws. Do not clamp. Care must be used not to distort or damage the die cast aluminum.
2. Remove the through-bolts and the end housing.
3. Carefully pull the armature up and out of the gear housing, and the starter frame and field assembly. Remove the steel and fiber thrust washer.

NOTE: On eight cylinder engines the starting motors have the wire of the shunt field coil soldered to the brush terminal. Six cylinder engines have the four coils in series and do not have a wire soldered to the brush terminal. One pair of brushes is connected to this terminal. The other pair of brushes is attached to the series field coils by means of a terminal screw. Carefully pull the frame and field assembly up just enough to expose the terminal screw and the solder connection of the shunt field at the brush terminal. Place two wood blocks between the starter frame and starter gear housing to facilitate removal of the terminal screw and unsoldering of the shunt field wire at the brush terminal.

4. Support the brush terminal with a finger behind terminal and remove screw.
5. On eight cylinder engine starters unsolder the shunt field coil lead from the brush terminal and housing.
6. The brush holder plate with terminal, contact and brushes is serviced as an assembly.
7. Clean all old sealer from around plate and housing.
8. Remove the brush holder attaching screw.
9. On the shunt type, unsolder the solenoid winding from the brush terminal.
10. Remove $^{11}/_{32}$ in. nut, washer and insulator from solenoid terminal.
11. Remove brush holder plate with brushes as an assembly.
12. Remove gear housing ground screw.
13. The solenoid assembly can be removed from the well.
14. Remove nut, washer and seal from

Removing the clutch assembly from a reduction gear starter

Shift fork and clutch arrangement on a reduction gear starter

starter battery terminal and remove terminal from plate.

15. Remove solenoid contact and plunger from solenoid and remove the coil sleeve.

16. Remove the solenoid return spring, coil retaining washer, retainer and the dust cover from the gear housing.

17. Release the snap-ring that locates the driven gear on pinion shaft.

18. Release front retaining ring.

19. Push pinion shaft toward the rear and remove snap-ring, thrust washers, clutch and pinion, and two shift fork nylon actuators.

20. Remove driven gear and friction washer.

21. Pull shifting fork forward and remove moving core.

22. Remove fork retainer pin and shifting fork assembly. The gear housing with bushings is serviced as an assembly.

Replacement of Brushes

1. Brushes that are worn more than one-half the length of new brushes, or are oil-soaked, should be replaced.

2. When resoldering the shunt field and solenoid lead, make a strong, low-resistance connection using a high-temperature solder and resin flux. Do not use acid or acid-core solder. Do not break the shunt field wire units when removing and installing the brushes.

Starter Clutch and Pinion Gear Inspection

1. Do not immerse the starter clutch unit in a cleaning solvent. The outside of the clutch and pinion must be cleaned with a cloth so as not to wash the lubricant from the inside of the clutch.

2. Rotate the pinion. The pinion gear should rotate smoothly and in one direction only. If the starter clutch unit does not function properly, or if the pinion is worn, chipped, or burred, replace the starter clutch unit.

Commutator Inspection

1. Inspect the commutator and the surface contacted by the brushes when the starter is assembled, for flat spots, out-of-roundness, or excessive wear.

2. Reface the commutator if necessary, removing only a sufficient amount of metal to provide a smooth, even surface.

3. Using light pressure, clean the grooves of the face of the commutator with a pointed tool. Neither remove any metal or widen the grooves.

Assembly

1. The shifter fork consists of two spring steel plates held together by two rivets. Before assembling the starter, check the plates for side movement. After lubricating between the plates with a small amount of SAE 10 engine oil, they should have about

Removing the retaining ring from a reduction gear starter

$1/16$ in. side movement to insure proper pinion gear engagement.

2. Position the shift fork in the drive housing and install the shifting fork retainer pin. One tip of the pin should be straight and the other bent at a 15 degree angle away from the housing. The fork and retainer pin should operate freely after bending the tip of the pin.

3. Install the solenoid moving core and engage the shifting fork.

4. Place the pinion shaft into the drive housing and install the friction washer and drive gear.

5. Install the clutch and pinion assembly, thrust washer, and retaining washer.

6. Engage the shifting fork with the clutch actuators.

—————— **CAUTION** ——————

The friction washer must be positioned on the shoulder of the splines of the pinion shaft before the driven gear is positioned.

7. Install the driven gear snap-ring.

8. Install the pinion shaft retaining ring.

9. The starter solenoid return spring can now be inserted in the moveable core.

10. Install the solenoid contact plunger assembly into the solenoid and reform the double wires so they can be curved around the contactor. This will allow the terminal stud to enter the brush holder properly.

—————— **CAUTION** ——————

The contactor must not touch these double wires after assembly is complete.

11. Assemble the battery terminal stud in the brush holder.

12. Position the seal on the brush holder plate.

13. Run the solenoid lead wire through the hole in the brush holder and attach the solenoid stud, insulating washers, flat washer, and nut.

14. Wrap the solenoid lead wire tightly around the brush terminal post and solder it.

15. Fix the brush holder to the solenoid attaching screws.

16. Gently lower the solenoid coil and brush plate into the gear housing.

17. Position the brush plate assembly into the starter gear housing, install the nuts, and tighten.

18. Solder the shunt coil lead wire to the starter brush terminal.

19. Install the brush terminal screw.

20. Position the field frame on the gear housing and start the armature into the housing, carefully engaging the splines on the shaft with the reduction gear by rotating the armature.

21. Install the fiber thrust washer and the steel washer on the armature shaft.

22. Replace the starter end housing and starter through-bolts; tighten securely.

Direct Drive Starter Motor

CHRYSLER CORPORATION

This starter can be identified by the externally mounted solenoid bolted to the case.

Disassembly

1. Remove through-bolts and tap commutator end head from frame.

2. Remove thrust washers from armature shaft.

3. Lift brush holder springs and remove brushes from holders.

4. Remove brush holder plate.

5. Disconnect the field coil wires at the solenoid connector, and remove the solenoid screws.

6. Remove solenoid and boot.

7. Drive out shift fork pivot pin.

8. Remove drive end pinion housing and spacer washer.

9. Remove shift fork from starter drive.

10. Slide overrunning clutch pinion gear toward commutator, drive stop retainer toward clutch pinion gear and remove the now-exposed snap-ring.

11. Remove overrunning clutch drive from armature shaft.

12. If field coils are good, stop disassembly at this point. If field coils must be replaced, remove ground brushes terminal screw and remove brushes, terminal and shunt wire. Remove pole shoe screws, using a ratchet-type impact driver and special wide screwdriver blade, then remove field coils.

13. Replacement of the brushes, inspection of the starter clutch and pinion, and inspection of the commutator procedures are the same as the reduction-gear starter procedures.

Assembly

1. Install field coils into frame, if removed.

2. Lubricate armature shaft and splines with engine oil.

3. Install starter drive, stop retainer, lock ring and spacer washer.

4. Install shift fork, with *narrow* leg of fork toward commutator.

5. Install pinion housing onto armature shaft, indexing shift fork with slot in housing.

6. Install shift fork pivot pin.

7. With clutch drive, shift fork, and pinion housing assembled onto the armature, slide armature into frame until pinion housing indexes with slot.

SHIFTER FORK PIN

MOVING CORE

CLUTCH ASSEMBLY

SHIFTER FORK

Removing the shift fork from a direct drive starter

8. Install solenoid and boot, tightening bolts to 60–70 in. lbs.

9. Connect field coil wires to solenoid connector, making sure they do not touch frame.

10. Install brush holder plate, indexing tang in frame hole.

11. Place brushes in holders, making sure field coil wires do not interfere.

12. Install thrust washers on commutator end of armature shaft to obtain a maximum of 0.010 in. end-play.

13. Install commutator end head and through-bolts. Tighten bolts to 40–50 in. lbs.

14. Measure drive gear pinion clearance; it should be ⅛ in. Adjust by moving solenoid fore and aft as required.

Motorcraft Positive Engagement Starter Motor

FORD MOTOR CO.

This starting motor is a series-parallel wound, four pole, four brush unit. It is equipped with an overrunning clutch drive pinion, which is engaged with the flywheel ring gear by an actuating lever, operated by a movable pole piece. This pole piece is hinged to the starter frame and can drop into position through an opening in the frame.

Three conventional field coils are located at three pole piece positions. The fourth field coil is designed to serve also as an engaging coil and a hold-in coil for the operation of the drive pinion.

When the ignition switch is turned to the start position, the starter relay is energized and current flows from the battery to the starter motor terminal. This prime surge of current first flows through the starter engaging coil, creating a very strong magnetic field. This magnetism draws the movable pole piece down toward the starter frame, which then causes the lever attached to it

to move the starter pinion into engagement with the flywheel ring gear.

When the movable pole shoe is fully seated, it opens the field coil, grounding contacts, and the starter is then in normal operation. A holding coil is used to hold the movable pole shoe in the fully seated position during the engine cranking operation.

Trucks, equipped with automatic transmissions have a starter neutral switch circuit control. This is to prevent operation of the starter if the selector lever is not in Neutral or Park.

Disassembly

1. Remove brush cover band and starter drive gear actuating lever cover. Observe the brush lead locations for reassembly, then remove the brushes from their holders.

NOTE: Factory brush length is ½ in.; wear limit is ¼ in.

2. Remove the through-bolts, starter drive gear housing and the drive gear actuating lever return spring.

3. Remove the pivot pin retaining the starter gear actuating lever and remove the lever and the armature.

4. Remove the stop ring retainer. Remove and discard the stop ring holding the drive gear to the armature shaft; then remove the drive gear assembly.

5. Remove the brush end plate.

6. Remove the two screws holding the ground brushes to the frame.

7. On the field coil that operates the starter drive gear actuating lever, bend the tab up on the field retainer and remove the field coil retainer.

8. Remove the three coil retaining screws. Unsolder the field coil leads from the terminal screw, then remove the pole shoes and coils from the frame (use a 300 watt iron).

9. Remove the starter terminal nut, washer, insulator and terminal from the starter frame.

10. Check the commutator for runnout. If the commutator is rough, has flat spots, or is more than 0.005 in. out of round, reface the commutator. Clean the grooves in the commutator face.

11. Inspect the armature shaft and the two bearings for scoring and excessive wear. Replace if necessary.

12. Inspect the starter drive. If the gear teeth are pitted, broken, or excessively worn, replace the starter drive.

Assembly

1. Install starter terminal, insulator, washers and retaining nut in the frame. (Be sure to position the slot in the screw perpendicular to the frame end surface.)

2. Position coils and pole pieces, with the coil leads in the terminal screw slot, then install the retaining screws. As the pole screws are tightened, strike the frame several sharp hammer blows to align the

Ford starter

pole shoes. Tighten, then stake the screws.

3. Install solenoid coil and retainer and bend the tabs to hold the coils to the frame.

4. Solder the field coils and solenoid wire to the starter terminal, using rosin-core solder and a 300 watt iron.

5. Check for continuity and ground connections in the assembled coils.

6. Position the solenoid coil ground terminal over the nearest ground screw hole.

7. Position the ground brushes to the starter frame and install retaining screws.

8. Position the brush end plate to the frame, with the end plate boss in the frame slot.

9. Lightly lubricate the armature shaft splines and install the starter drive gear assembly in the shaft. Install a new retaining stop ring and stop ring retainer.

10. Position the fiber thrust washer on the commutator end of the armature shaft, then position the armature in the starter frame.

11. Position the starter drive gear actuating lever to the frame and starter drive assembly, and install the pivot pin.

NOTE: Fill drive gear housing bore ¼ full of grease.

12. Position the drive actuating lever return spring and the drive gear housing to the frame, then install and tighten the through-bolts. Do not pinch brush leads between brush plate and frame. Be sure that the stop ring retainer is properly seated in the drive housing.

13. Install the brushes in the brush holders and center the brush springs on the brushes.

14. Position the drive gear actuating lever cover on the starter and install the brush cover band with a new gasket.

15. Check starter no-load amperage draw.

Motorcraft Solenoid Actuated Starter Motor

FORD MOTOR CO.

This starter motor is a four-brush, four-field, four-pole wound unit. The frame encloses a wound armature, which is supported at the drive end by caged needle bearings and at the commutator end by a sintered copper bushing. The four pole shoes are retained to the frame by one pole screw apiece, and on each pole shoe is wound a ribbon-type field coil connected in series-parallel.

Field coil assembly

11072
33924-S (M-28)
34052-S (M-155)
44710-S (X-10)
382136-S (MM-295-AG)
44727-S (X-24)
34079-S (M-163)
44713-S (X-13)
11390
*50940-S
11049
11068
11091
34806-S (X-64)
11059
11126
27185-S (U-177-A)
11052
34141-S (M-147)
11A122
11103
11393
50409-S (U-126)
11036
*43485-S
*11A120
11415
†11102
†11083
*305054-S
11139
11067
11005
†11083
11003
11350
11222
11223
11036
11130
11135
11057
†11085
†11083

†ALSO SUPPLIED IN 11082 COMPLETE FIELD COIL ASSEMBLY
♦SUPPLIED ONLY IN 11002 STARTER ASSEMBLY

Ford solenoid type starter

The solenoid is mounted to a flange on the starter drive housing, which encloses the entire shift mechanism and solenoid plunger. The solenoid utilizes two windings—a pull-in winding and a hold-in winding.

Disassembly

1. Disconnect the copper strap from the solenoid starter terminal, remove the remaining screws and remove the solenoid.

2. Loosen the retaining screw and slide the brush cover band back far enough to gain access to the brushes.

3. Remove the brushes from their holders, then remove the through-bolts and separate the drive end housing from the frame and brush end plate.

NOTE: Factory brush length is ½ in., wear limit ¼ in.

4. Remove the solenoid plunger and shift fork. These two items can be separated from each other by removing the roll pin.

5. Remove the armature and drive assembly from the frame. Remove the drive stop ring and slide the drive off the armature shaft.

6. Remove the drive stop ring retainer from the drive housing.

7. Inspection of the commutator, armature and bearings, and pinion gear procedures is the same as the positive engagement starter procedures.

Assembly

1. Lubricate the armature shaft splines with Lubriplate, then install drive assembly and a new stop ring.

2. Lubricate shift lever pivot pin with Lubriplate, then position solenoid plunger and shift lever assembly in the drive housing.

3. Place a new retainer in the drive housing. Apply a small amount of Lubriplate to the drive end of the armature shaft, then place armature and drive assembly into the drive housing, indexing the shift lever tangs with the drive assembly.

4. Apply a small amount of Lubriplate to the commutator end of the armature shaft, then position the frame and field assembly to the drive housing.

5. Position the brush plate assembly to the frame, making sure it properly indexes. Install through-bolts and tighten to 45–85 in. lbs.

6. Install brushes into their holders and make sure leads are not touching any interior starter components.

7. Place the rubber gasket between the solenoid mount and the frame surface.

8. Place the starter solenoid in position with metal gasket and spring, install heat shield (if so equipped) and install solenoid screws.

9. Connect copper strap and install cover band.

Delco-Remy Starter Motor

There are many different versions of the Delco-Remy starter, depending upon application. In general, six-cylinder engines use a unit having four field coils in series between the terminal and armature. Standard V8 engines use, depending on displacement, one of three types: one has two field coils in series with the armature and parallel to each other; another has two field coils in parallel between the field terminal and ground, and another has three field coils in series with the armature and one field

Solenoid windings

Delco starter

connected between the motor terminal and ground. Heavy-duty starter motors, such as used on some of the largest G.M. high-output engines (over 400 cu. in.) have series compound windings. The relatively recent 20MT, 25MT, and 27MT starters are used with diesels only. They differ from the others mainly in the use of a center bearing. Most repair procedures are generally similar for them, too. Where additional procedures are required for the center bearing, they will be noted.

In spite of these differences, all Delco-Remy starters are disassembled and assembled in essentially the same manner.

Disassembly

1. Disconnect the field coil connectors from the motor solenoid terminal. Remove the solenoid mounting screws. Rotate the solenoid 90 degrees and remove it along with the plunger return spring.

NOTE: On models so equipped, remove solenoid mounting screws.

2. Remove the through bolts.
3. Remove the commutator end frame. On diesel starters only, remove the insulator. On all starters, remove the washer,

field frame assembly, and armature assembly from the drive housing. On diesel starters, the armature remains in the drive end frame.

4. On diesel starters only, remove the shift lever pivot bolt. On the 25MT only, remove the center bearing screws and remove the drive gear housing from the armature shaft. The shift lever/plunger assembly can now be separated from the starter clutch.

5. Remove the overrunning clutch from the armature shaft as follows:

a. Slide the two-piece thrust collar off the end of the armature shaft.

b. Slide a standard ½ in. pipe coupling or other spacer onto the shaft so that the end of the coupling butts against the edge of the retainer.

c. Tap the end of the coupling with a

REPLACE BRUSH HOLDER

(STANDARD STARTER)

(SMALL 5MT STARTER)

If necessary to replace brush holder parts, proceed as follows:

a. Remove brush holder pivot pin which positions one insulated and one grounded brush.

b. Remove brush spring.

c. Replace brushes as necessary.

a. Remove brush holder from brush support.

b. Remove screw from brush holder and separate brush and holder.

c. Inspect brush holder for wear or damage.

d. Replace brushes and/or holders as necessary.

Brush holder removal—1981 and later Delco-Remy starters (© General Motors Corp.)

hammer, driving retainer towards armature end of snap-ring.

d. Remove snap-ring from its groove in the shaft using pliers. Slide retainer and clutch from armature shaft. On diesel starters, also remove the fiber washer and center bearing.

6. On 1980 and earlier starters, disconnect the brush assembly from the field frame by releasing the V-spring and removing the support pin. Pull the brush holders, brushes, and springs out as a unit and disconnect leads.

On 1981 and later starters (except 5MT), remove the pivot pin which holds the brush holder and one insulated and one grounded brush in place. Remove the brush spring. On the 5MT starter, remove the brush holder from the brush support. Remove the screw from the brush holder and separate the brush and holder.

7. On models so equipped, separate solenoid from lever housing.

Cleaning and Inspection

1. Clean parts with a rag, but do not immerse the parts in a solvent. Immersion in a solvent will dissolve the grease that is packed in the clutch mechanism and damage the armature and field coil insulation.

2. Test overrunning clutch action. The pinion should turn freely in the overrunning direction and must not slip in the cranking direction. Check pinion teeth to see that they have not been chipped, cracked, or excessively worn. Replace the unit if necessary.

3. Inspect the armature commutator. If the commutator is rough or out of round, it should be turned down.

Some starter motor models use a molded armature commutator design and no attempt to undercut the insulation should be made or serious damage may result to the commutator.

Assembly

1. Install brushes into holders. Install solenoid, if so equipped.

2. Assemble insulated and grounded brush holder together using the V-spring and position the assembled unit on the support pin. Push holders and spring to bottom of support and rotate spring to engage the slot in support. Attach ground wire to grounded brush and field lead wire to insulated brush, then repeat for other brush sets.

Forcing the snap-ring into the retainer

3. Assemble overrunning clutch to armature shaft as follows:

a. Lubricate drive end of shaft with silicone lubricant.

b. On diesel starters, install the center bearing assembly with the bearing facing the armature winding. Then, slide the clutch assembly onto the armature shaft with the pinion facing outward.

c. Slide retainer onto shaft with cupped surface facing away from pinion.

d. Stand armature up on a wood surface, commutator downwards. Position snap-ring on upper end of shaft and drive it onto shaft with a small block of wood and a hammer. Slide snap-ring into groove.

e. Install thrust collar onto shaft with shoulder next to snap-ring.

f. With retainer on one side of snap-ring and thrust collar on the other side, squeeze together with two sets of pliers until ring seats in retainer. On models without thrust collar, use a washer. Remember to remove washer before continuing.

4. Lubricate drive end bushing with silicone lubricant, then slide armature and clutch assembly into place, at the same time engaging shift lever with clutch. On 1981 and later non-diesel starters, the shift lever may be installed in the drive gear housing first. On the 25MT diesel starter only, install the center bearing screws and the shift lever pivot bolt. Tighten all securely.

5. Position field frame over armature and apply sealer (silicone) between frame and solenoid case. Position frame against drive housing, making sure brushes are not damaged in the process.

6. Lubricate the commutator end bushing with silicone lubricant. Place a leather

brake washer on the armature shaft of gas engine starters. Place an insulator on the shaft of diesel engine starters. Slide the commutator end frame onto the shaft. Install the through bolts, making sure they pass through the bolt holes in the insulator on diesel starters. Install the through bolts and tighten to 65 in. lbs.

7. Reconnect field coil connector(s) to the solenoid motor terminal. Install solenoid mounting screws, if so equipped.

8. Check pinion clearance; it should be 0.010–0.140 in. on all models.

Prestolite Starter Motor

Disassembly

1. Remove the cover band and remove the brushes from their holders.

2. Remove the brush end plate mounting screws and the two through-bolts.

3. Remove the drive housing, end brush plate, and armature from the starter frame.

4. Compress the starter drive spring on the armature side of the shaft and remove the lock screw and remove the starter drive, center bearing plate and thrust washers.

5. Remove the four field pole shoes and remove the field coils from the frame.

NOTE: The positive brushes can be replaced on the field coils by soldering, and the negative brushes replaced on the brush end plate by riveting.

Assembly

1. Assemble the field coils and pole shoes into the frame and secure with screws.

2. Assemble the center bearing plate, thrust washers, and starter drive on the armature shaft and secure with the locking screw.

3. Place the armature assembly into the drive housing aligning the slot in the shaft center bearing support with the pin in the drive housing.

4. Install the end frame to the frame housing and install the six mounting screws.

5. Position the armature assembly into the frame housing and engage the frame dowel with the bolt of the drive frame. Install the two through-bolts and secure.

6. Install the brushes into the holders. Center the brush springs on the brushes and locate the insulated brush leads clear of the armature. Install the cover band.

SPECIFICATIONS

PRESTOLITE STARTER

Vendor	Current Draw Under Normal Load (Amperes)	Minimum Stall Torque		Maximum Load (Amperes)	No-Load (Amperes)	Brushes				Through Bolt Torque (In-Lbs)	Mounting Bolt Torque (Ft-Lbs)
						Mfg. Length (Inches)	Wear Limit (Inches)	Brush Spring Tension (Ounces)			
		(Ft-Lbs)	Volts								
Prestolite	200	17.2	5	525	60	0.46–0.48	0.25	45–53		72–96	23–28

Maximum commutator runout in inches is 0.005. Maximum starting circuit voltage drop (battery + terminal to starter terminal) at normal engine temperature 0.5 volt.

Emissions

INDEX

GASOLINE ENGINE EMISSION CONTROL

Introduction

The emission control devices required by law on trucks are determined by weight classification and were considered either "light duty" or "heavy duty" applications, with the Gross Vehicle Weight (GVW) of 6000 lbs. as the dividing line. State and

Federal Government regulations have now mandated a new weight standard from the 6000 lbs. GVW to a new GVW of 8500 lbs. or less as "light duty" and a GVW of 8500 lbs. or more as "heavy duty" applications.

The light duty emission devices are normally the same as used on the passenger cars.

During certain model years, passenger carrying vehicles, such as window vans with greater GVW of 6000 lbs. were also considered to be light duty models and must comply with the light duty emission control requirements.

Heavy duty truck models use fewer emission control devices than the light duty models, although more emission controls are being required in each succeeding year

to comply with the changing emission control regulations and requirements.

The State of California remains stringent in their emission control standards and through out this section, reference will be made to either the California, High Altitude or to the Federal engines. (Federal referring to the remaining 49 states, High Altitude referring to areas above 4000 ft. (1,219 meters)).

Engine Modifications

Internal engine modifications have been made from year to year by redesigning the following:

1. Lowering the compression ratios to allow the use of low or nonleaded fuels.

2. Combustion chambers and piston modifications for a more efficient air/fuel flow rate and burning time.

3. Camshaft modification to improve valve timing and to increase valve overlap periods.

4. Higher engine operating temperatures and increased cooling areas.

5. Balanced fuel induction manifolds to properly balance the air/fuel flow to the cylinders.

6. Other modifications include changes in metals used in the construction of the engines and components to allow the operation of the engine with non-leaded, non-lubricating fuels.

External engine modifications have been made to the carburetors and distributors to provide the proper air/fuel mixture and to provide the proper timing of the ignition spark to insure the engine emission levels remain within the legislated limits, while providing the best engine performance and fuel economy at varying speeds and loads.

Emission Control Systems

In order to control the engine crankcase, fuel and exhaust emissions, three major systems have been designated.

1. Crankcase controls are used to provide a more complete scavenging of the crankcase vapors and to route the vapors to the engine fuel induction system for burning with the air/fuel mixture.

2. Evaporation controls are used to prevent the emission of gasoline vapors from the fuel tank and carburetor, into the atmosphere. Charcoal canisters are used to store the gasoline vapors during periods of engine shutdown and during periods of engine operation, the gasoline vapors are drawn into the fuel induction system and burned with the air/fuel mixture.

3. Exhaust controls are used to limit the emission of Carbon Monoxide (CO), Hydrocarbons (HC) and Oxides of Nitrogen (NOx) from the engine exhaust. Numerous controls are used on the engines and the exhaust systems to perform this removal of pollutants.

MAINTENANCE

In order for the emission controls to function properly, maintenance must be performed at regular intervals, either by time or mileage increments. Owner manuals will normally contain a maintenance schedule for services to be done and should be followed for longer emission systems and vehicle life.

Emission Certification Label

An Emission Certification label is attached to either the engine or engine compartment sheet metal and should be consulted before any adjustments are made to the engine.

DISTRIBUTOR
- Electronic Ignition
- Reduced Tolerances
- Permanently Lubricated

CARBURETOR
- Improved Distribution
- Faster Acting Choke, Electric Assist
- External Idle Mixture Limiter
- Solenoid Throttle Stop
- Gasoline Vapor Control
- Idle Enrichment
- Throttle Positioner

ORIFICE SPARK ADVANCE CONTROL VALVE (OSAC)

VAPOR VENT TUBE TO FUEL TANK

INTAKE MANIFOLD
- Improved Hot Spot

COOLANT CONTROL ENGINE VACUUM SWITCH

CTS TIMER

EGR VACUUM SOLENOID

OXIDATION CATALYTIC CONVERTER

CHARCOAL CANISTER

CHARGE TEMPERATURE SWITCH

MANIFOLD VACUUM

CLOSED CRANKCASE VENTILATION

HEATED AIR INTAKE

INCREASED CAM OVERLAP

EXHAUST GAS RECIRCULATION
- EGR Control Valve
- EGR Vacuum Amplifier
- Charge Temperature Switch
- CTS Timer

AIR PUMP

MODIFIED COMBUSTION CHAMBER AND REDUCED COMPRESSION RATIO

Typical Emission Control System

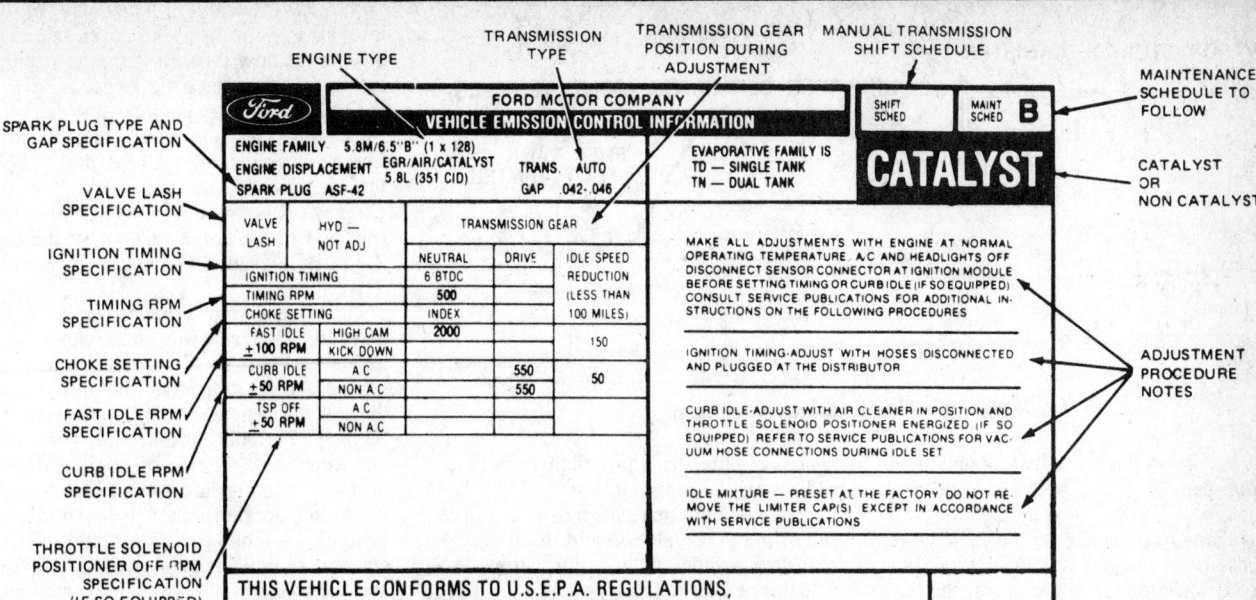

Emission Certification Label (typical)

NOTE: It is a good practice to copy the information from the Emission Certification label and keep with the owners manual, in case the label becomes mutilated or lost.

Crankcase Control System

POSITIVE CRANKCASE VENTILATION (PCV)

With the engine operating, crankcase ventilation air is drawn through an air cleaner mounted filter assembly, through a hose to the crankcase air inlet, down into the crankcase and up to the rocker arm chamber, out through a flow control valve and into a hose connected to the base of the carburetor or to the intake manifold. The crankcase vapors are then mixed with the air/fuel mixture and burned through the normal combustion process. The purpose of the flow control valve is to restrict the flow of crankcase vapors when the intake manifold vacuum is high (such as idle or coast modes), to avoid upsetting the air/fuel mixture at idle and causing roughness of the engine at low speeds or while idling.

With the flow control valve open at times of low engine vacuum and high air flow through the carburetor (such as having the throttle valves open as in the drive mode), the added crankcase vapor flow has no noticable effect on the engine operation.

CRANKCASE CONTROL TESTING

Checking crankcase vacuum is the most effective way to test any PCV system. If there

PCV valve at low engine speed or during idle

is vacuum in the crankcase, then the major part of the system has to be working.

On many models, you can effectively test the system with either a vacuum gauge designed for testing the PCV system or with a piece of paper. It is best to test the system at the fresh air intake—that is, where a large, open tube enters the air cleaner, often at a filter. Leave the PCV valve and its hose, and the oil filler cap, in place. Disconnect the fresh air hose at the air cleaner and test at the end of the hose.

If this is awkward, you can also test at the oil filler hole. In this case, disconnect the fresh air hose at the air cleaner and use

PCV valve operation with engine off or during backfire

PCV valve operation at high engine speed

some positive means to plug it such as a cork or clean rag. Start the engine and leave it idling in Park or Neutral in either case.

It may take a few seconds for the vacuum to build up enough to suck the paper against the opening. Make sure you allow time for the full force of the vacuum to take effect. If you don't get any vacuum, pull the PCV valve from the valve cover and hold your finger over the open end. You should soon feel full manifold vacuum. If you feel vacuum here, but did not get an indication of vacuum at the oil filler hole or fresh air intake, check for a clogged fresh air intake hose, or leaks at the grommets, valve cov-

Closed crankcase ventilation system

Typical gasoline evaporation system

ers, or oil pan gasket. Often, simply tightening pan or cover bolts will cure the problem.

If there's no vacuum at the PCV valve, check for a clogged valved or hose, or a poor connection. In some cases, the hose is attached to a fitting that's screwed into the intake manifold. Tightening the fitting, or, better yet, removing it, coating the threads with sealer, and reinstalling it snugly will cure the problem.

If you're still uncertain about the condition of the PCV valve or system, you can make some additional checks. You can remove the valve and shake it—if it rattles, this is an indication that it's probably working although in rare cases the valve may still malfunction sometimes. If the valve

does not rattle, the inner plunger is stuck and it must be replaced.

Jeep specifies that closing off the open end of the PCV valve should result in a 50 rpm drop at idle. If the engine drops less than this or does not change speed the valve is clogged.

With any vehicle, if the engine idles roughly and you can restore a smooth idle by closing off the open end of the PCV valve, this is a sure sign that the valve must be replaced.

On Datsuns, Toyotas, and Luvs, you can use a blow-through test. Remove the valve and blow through in the direction of normal flow—from the carburetor or intake manifold side. There should be a resistance to flow. Turn the valve around and blow

through it from the valve cover side. The air should flow through it freely; if either test is failed, replace the valve.

On Mazda rotary engines, test the valve by Teeing a vacuum gauge into the PCV line between the valve a filler tube. Check the air cleaner and make sure it is not clogged. Run the engine at 2,500–3,000 rpm and measure the vacuum. It must be 2.4 in HG or more. Otherwise, replace the valve.

On some foreign vehicles such as Isuzu and Luv, Dodge Arrow and D-50, as well as VW, there is no PCV valve. Instead, an orifice serves to restrict the flow of air through the system under high vacuum conditions. Periodic maintenance includes checking the condition of hoses and connections, making sure hoses and especially the orifice are clean and, if the air cleaner contains a crankcase ventilation filter, cleaning or replacing it as necessary. Hoses and the steel wool filter on the Arrow and D-50 can be cleaned with solvent and air dried.

Evaporation Control System

To prevent the emission of gasoline vapors into the atmosphere from the gasoline tank and carburetor vents, vapors are routed by hoses to one or more charcoal filled canisters for storage while the engine is stopped and are routed from and/or through the canister(s) to the engine fuel induction system, when the engine is operating.

On single canister arrangements, the throttle valve is normally used as purge valve, with the vapor hoses routed to the intake manifold or to the carburetor base. On some vehicle models, the purging of the canister is accomplished by air movement through the air cleaner snorkel and into the engine, by having the purge hose connected from the canister to the snorkel.

On dual canister arrangements, the purging action of the secondary canister is triggered by a vacuum signal from the distributor vacuum hose to open the canister purge switch, which allows the vapors to purge through the PCV system and into the engine.

On some vehicles, a solenoid valve activated by the ignition switch allows intake vacuum to purge the cannister. When the ignition is turned off, the solenoid valve closes to retain the vapors in the system. Valve failure occurs in the closed position and can result in lean running due to the existence of a vacuum in the float bowl.

Fuel filler caps that are used with the vapor Emission Control System, normally have a pressure-vacuum valve assembly as part of the cap, to allow air to enter the tank as the fuel is consumed to avoid fuel tank collapse, when the vacuum is between 15 to 25 in. Hg. When the fuel tank internal pressure builds up from .75 to 2.0 psi (nominal) over atmospheric pressure, the pres-

Typical vapor canister storage

Vapor storage with twin fuel tanks (typical)

sure valve opens to relieve the excess internal pressures.

Larger trucks will normally have fuel caps with anti-surge mechanisms built into the caps to prevent fuel spillage during truck operation or will have non-vented caps with the fuel tanks vented through vapor storage canisters.

Vapor separators and anti-rollover valves are used with the vapor control systems, to avoid having raw fuel collect in the charcoal canister or to have fuel leakage in case of a vehicle rollover.

EVAPORATION CONTROL SYSTEM INSPECTION

The system inspection consists of examining the fuel resistance hoses, connections, metal lines, nylon lines, valves, separators and canisters. The only needed replacement is the canister air filter.

Thermostatic Air Cleaner

Fresh air supplied to the air cleaner comes either from the normal snorkel, or from a tube connected to an exhaust manifold stove. A door in the snorkel regulates the source of incoming air so that a warm engine always takes in warm air, approximately 100°F. The door may be controlled by a thermostatic spring or expansion bulb, or it may be vacuum operated. The vacuum operated designs use a thermostatic bimetal

Thermostatic controlled air cleaner operation

switch inside the air cleaner that bleeds off vacuum as the engine warms up, and regulates the position of the air door. On all late models, the snorkel is connected to a long tube so it takes in cooler air from outside the engine compartment. In hot climates the cool air tube is necessary because underhood air can easily reach 200°F.

Vacuum operated air doors are all designed so that the air cleaner takes in cold air when there is no vacuum. This means that an air door in the hot air position will switch to the cold position at wide open

Dual vapor storage with twin tanks (typical)

throttle because of the loss of manifold vacuum. The sudden switching of the door from hot to cold may cause a stumble or misfire in the engine, so some designs include a modulator valve mounted on the side of the air cleaner to block the vacuum and hold the door in the hot air position. A small thermostat inside the modulator opens it when the underhood temperatures reach normal. Other designs use a delay valve that allows the air door to move to the cold position slowly, to prevent stumble.

TESTING AIR CLEANERS, NON-VACUUM TYPE

To test the non-vacuum type of heated air cleaner, start with an engine that is cold enough to have the air door in the hot air position. Remove the top of the air cleaner and put a thermometer inside the cleaner, then replace the cover without the nuts. Start the engine and watch the air door through the end of the air cleaner. You may have to remove some air ducting to be able to see the air door. As soon as the air door starts to move from the hot air position, lift the top off the air cleaner and read the temperature. If the temperature is between 130 and 150°F, the thermostat is working correctly. If not, replace the thermostat.

—— CAUTION ——
Do not replace the thermostat if the temperature is off by only a few degrees. It must be considerably out of specification, or perhaps not opening at all, to affect the running of the vehicle.

TESTING AIR CLEANERS, VACUUM TYPE

To test the vacuum type of heated air cleaner, inspect the air door with the engine off. It should be in the cold air position. Start the engine. If the engine is cold, the air door should move to the hot air position. As the engine warms up, the air door should move to a mid position, depending on the outside air temperature.

If the outside air is extremely cold, the air door may stay in the hot air position indefinitely. On a warm day, after the engine warms up the air door should move to the cold air position. If it doesn't, the temperature sensor inside the air cleaner might be faulty, or the air door itself might be

Vacuum operated air cleaner operation

Pressure-vacuum type fuel filler type cap operation

EVAPORATION CONTROL SYSTEM DIAGNOSIS CHART

Problem	Cause	Remedy
Persistent odor of fuel vapors	Canister saturated due to extend parking of vehicle.	Operate (idle) engine for several minutes to purge canister.
	Fuel tank cap not sealing.	Replace cap.
	Canister not purging:	
	a. Vacuum hose to intake manifold or tee obstructed or leaking.	Check for vacuum at canister end of hose. Blow through hose with compressed air. Replace hose if cracked, deteriorated or obstruction cannot be removed.
	b. Vacuum orifice in manifold fitting or tee obstructed.	Remove manifold fitting or tee and blow orally through fitting to check for obstruction. If orifice is plugged, soak fitting in solvent and blow out with compressed air.
	Loose vent hose connections or loose filler neck connections.	Pressure test vapor vent system for leakage. If leakage is indicated, visually inspect for damaged hoses or tubes, loose, damaged or missing clamps. Repair is needed.
Fuel leakage:		
a. From fuel tank cap	Fuel tank cap seal faulty.	Replace cap.
	Pressure relief valve in fuel tank cap faulty.	Test operation of pressure relief valve. If valve is faulty, replace cap.
	Valve vent hoses obstructed.	Remove fuel tank cap and blow hoses with compressed air. Replaced hoses if necessary.
b. From fuel tank liquid vapor separator or connecting tubes and hoses	Loose connections, cracked or broke tube or hose.	Pressure test vapor vent system for leakage. If leakage is indicated, repair as needed.
	Cracked or damaged fuel tank or liquid/vapor separator	Replace damaged components.
c. From vapor storage canister (through air flow filter)	Pressure relief valve in fuel tank cap faulty.	Test operation of valve. If faulty, replace cap.
Noisy fuel tank— wall fluctuation ("oilcanning")	Vacuum buildup in tank:	
	Vacuum relief valve in fuel tank cap faulty.	Test operation of valve. If faulty, replace cap.
	Pressure buildup in tank:	
	a. Pressure relief valve in fuel tank cap faulty.	Test operation of valve. If faulty, replace cap.
	b. Vapor vent hoses obstructed.	Remove fuel tank cap and blow out hoses with compressed air. Replace hoses if necessary.

hanging up. Check the air door by running a hose from manifold vacuum to the vacuum motor. Connect and disconnect the hose to see if the air door moves freely. If the air door is free, check out the hoses for leaks or blockage. If the hoses are okay, the trouble must be in the temperature sensor, and it should be replaced.

Modulators are used in the air cleaner vacuum line on some engines. The modulator mounts on the side of the air cleaner and has two hose connections, one to the air cleaner temperature sensor, and the other to the vacuum motor. Below 50–80°F. the modulator is a one-way check valve, which allows vacuum to move the air door to the hot air position, but traps the vacuum so the door will not jump back to the cold air position during acceleration. This prevents a stumble.

After the modulator warms up, the check valve unseats so that the vacuum can pass freely in either direction, and the air door then operates normally. The connections for the modulator are important. The connection in the center goes to the vacuum motor, and the connection on the edge goes to the vacuum source, which is the temperature sensor.

To test the modulator on a cold engine, apply enough vacuum to the edge port to move the air door to the hot position. Then remove the hose from the port, and the air door should stay in the hot position. Make the same test when the engine is warmed up, and the air door should move to the cold position when you pull off the hose.

FROM OUTER (E) PORT OF CTO TO EGR VALVE

EGR VALVE

COOLANT TEMPERATURE OVERRIDE SWITCH

FROM INNER (S) PORT OF CTO TO CARBURETOR EGR PORT

Typical 6 cylinder engine EGR system

DIAPHRAGM COVER

SPRING

VACUUM TUBE CONNECTED TO THERMAL VACUUM SWITCH

VALVE SHAFT

SEAL

ACTUATING DIAPHRAGM

VALVE SEAT

VALVE OPEN

VALVE CHAMBER

TO INTAKE MANIFOLD

EXHAUST GAS INLET PORT

Cross section—ported vacuum signal EGR valve (typical)

Deceleration Control Devices

Deceleration—especially sudden release of the throttle—produces more hydrocarbon and CO emissions than any other gas engine operating mode. Because of high manifold vacuum, both compression and turbulence in the cylinder are at a minimum. At the same time, fuel laying in the manifold under cruise or acceleration conditions may suddenly be evaporated and pass through the engine practically unburned.

As a result of these combustion/emissions problems, many vehicles—especially those using high rpm engines and manual transmissions—are equipped with devices which slow or limit closing of the throttle when the vehicle is at speed, or admit extra mixture. In some cases, ignition timing may be advanced.

When improperly adjusted or malfunctioning, these systems may cause: engine racing and difficult shifting; inconsistent behavior of the engine when the throttle is released, also causing difficult shifting; or backfiring.

Since such a system can radically raise engine idle speed, you should make sure adjustments are to specification and that all elements of the system are snugly connected and working smoothly. Careless work could contribute to an accident!

CHEVROLET AND GMC THROTTLE RETURN CONTROL SYSTEM

1978–82

A throttle return control system (TRC) is used on some California truck engines. When the truck is coasting against the engine, the control valve is open to allow vacuum to operate the throttle lever actuator. The throttle lever actuator then pushes the throt-

tle lever slightly open reducing the HC (hydrocarbon) emission level during coasting. When manifold vacuum drops below a predetermined level, the control valve closes, the throttle lever retracts, and the throttle lever closes to the idle position.

Control Valve Check and Adjustment

1. Disconnect the valve-to-carburetor hose and connect it to an external vacuum source and a vacuum gauge.
2. Disconnect the valve-to-actuator hose at the connector and connect it to a vacuum gauge.
3. Place a finger firmly over the end of the bleed fitting.
4. Apply a minimum of 23 in. Hg vac-

uum to the control valve and seal off the vacuum source. The gauge on the actuator side should read the same as the gauge on the source side. If not, the valve needs adjustment. If vacuum drops off on either side (with the finger still on the bleed fitting), the valve is defective and should be replaced.

5. With a minimum of 23 in. Hg vacuum in the valve, remove the finger from the bleed fitting. The vacuum level in the actuator side will drop to zero and the reading on the source side will drop to a value that will be the valve set point of 21.5 in. Hg. If the valve is not within ½ in. Hg vacuum of the specified valve set point, adjust the valve.

6. Gently pry off the conical plastic cover.

DIAPHRAGM IS SEATED WHEN ENGINE IS NOT RUNNING

VACUUM SIGNAL TUBE

DIAPHRAGM PLATE

TRANSDUCER

ORIFICE OPENING .030 (SEE OPTIONAL CONSTRUCTION)

ORIFICE OPENING .020 in.

SEAT

INTAKE MANIFOLD VACUUM

EXHAUST

OPTIONAL CONSTRUCTION

Cross section—typical negative back pressure EGR valve

7. Turn the adjusting screw in (clockwise) to raise the set point or out (counterclockwise) to lower the set point.

8. Recheck the valve set point.

9. If necessary, repeat the adjustment.

Throttle Valve Check and Adjustment

1. Disconnect the valve-to-actuator hose at the valve and connect it to an external vacuum source.

2. Apply 20 in. Hg vacuum to the actuator and seal the vacuum source. If the vacuum gauge reading drops, the valve is leaking and should be replaced.

3. Check the throttle lever, shaft, and linkage for freedom of operation.

4. Start the engine and warm it to operating temperature.

5. Note the idle rpm.

6. Apply 20 in. Hg vacuum to the actuator and manually operate the throttle. Allow it to close against the extended actuator plunger. Note the engine rpm.

7. Release and reapply 20 in. Hg vacuum to the actuator and note the rpm at which the engine speed increases (do not assist the actuator).

8. If the engine speed obtained in step 7 is not within 150 rpm of that obtained in step 6, then the actuator may be binding. If the binding cannot be corrected, replace the actuator.

9. Release the vacuum from the actuator and the engine speed should return to within 50 rpm of the speed noted in steps 4 and 5.

To adjust the actuator:

10. Turn the screw on the actuator plunger until the specified TRC speed range (1475–1525 rpm) is obtained.

1983–84

This system is used on 1983–84 trucks with heavy duty emission controls. It consists of a vacuum operated throttle lever actuator, an electronic speed sensor, and a solenoid vacuum control valve, which converts the sensor's electronic signal to vacuum to actuate the system. The system opens the throttle slightly beyond its curb idle position to reduce hydrocarbons when the engine is overrunning.

Problems with the system would be indicated by inconsistent idle speed or unaccustomed engine braking or backfiring. Troubleshoot the system as described below.

1. Inspect all vacuum hoses for cracks or bad connections and replace as necessary. Make sure wiring connectors are firmly attached at the distributor, speed switch, and vacuum solenoid.

2. Connect a tachometer sensitive enough to measure a change of 10 rpm to the distributor TACH terminal. Then, start the engine and run it at exactly 1890 rpm. Observe the throttle lever actuator. It should be extended.

3. Close the throttle until engine speed is exactly 1700 rpm. The throttle lever actuator should be retracted at this speed.

4. If either of these tests is failed, accelerate the engine within a wider range. If the actuator works this way, but not within the specs above, replace the electronic speed switch. Otherwise, proceed with the tests below.

5. Connect the negative probe of a voltmeter to an engine ground, and the positive probe to the hot connector of the wire to the vacuum solenoid. You do not have to disconnect the electrical connector to do this—the probe can be inserted into the connector body on the wire side to contact the metal terminal. Check for 12–14 volts here and, in a similar manner, at the speed switch. If voltage is present at only one of the two devices, repair the wiring harness as necessary. If there is no voltage at either device, repair connections at the distributor and bulkhead.

6. If proper voltage exists both places, ground the solenoid-to-switch connecting wire at the solenoid connector with a jumper. The throttle lever actuator should extend with the engine running.

7. If it does not extend, disconnect the hose at the side port of the solenoid that connects to the actuator. Check the orifice inside the port for plugging and clear it if necessary. If there is no plugging, replace the solenoid. Otherwise, retest it as in Step 6.

8. If the solenoid extended in Step 6, ground the solenoid-to-switch wire terminal at the speed switch. If it did not extend, repair the wire connecting the speed switch and solenoid. If it does extend, check the effectiveness of the speed switch ground connection. With the engine running, the voltmeter should read zero volts at the ground wire connection. If ground voltage is high, make repairs to the wiring.

9. Check the speed switch-to-distrib-utor wire for proper connection. Make repairs as necessary. Then, repeat the test in which the engine is accelerated to 1890 rpm and the actuator is observed. If the actuator does not extend, replace the speed switch.

10. If the actuator remains extended at all speeds, remove the connector from the vacuum solenoid. If the actuator remains extended, check the orifice in the side port of the solenoid for plugging and, if necessary, clear it out. Reconnect the vacuum line and run the test again. If the actuator now does not retract, disconnect the solenoid electrical connector. If the actuator still does not retract, replace the vacuum solenoid.

11. If the actuator retracts with the solenoid connector off, reconnect and then remove the speed switch connector. If the actuator now retracts, replace the speed switch. If the actuator does not retract, the solenoid-to switch wire is shorted to ground in the wiring harness. Make required repairs.

DODGE/PLYMOUTH VACUUM THROTTLE POSITIONER

Some 1978 and later models have a throttle positioner to hold the throttle slightly open on deceleration above 2000 rpm. This prevents excessive emission of unburned hydrocarbons. The system consists of an electronic speed switch, a vacuum solenoid valve, and a vacuum actuated throttle positioner. Adjust this device as follows:

1. Run the engine at about 2500 rpm.

2. Loosen the vacuum unit locknut and turn it until it just contacts the throttle lever.

3. Release the throttle. Adjust the unit to decrease engine speed until speed suddenly drops 1000 rpm or more. Back off the adjuster ¼ turn more and tighten the locknut.

THROTTLE RETURN CONTROL SYSTEM

CARBURETOR (TYPICAL)

EXTENDED POSITION (WHEN VACUUM IS APPLIED)

PRIMARY THROTTLE LEVER

THROTTLE LEVER ACTUATOR

MANIFOLD VACUUM

MANIFOLD VACUUM (VALVE OPEN ONLY)

ELECTRONIC SPEED SENSOR

VENT TO ATMOSPHERE

SOLENOID VACUUM CONTROL VALVE

ENGINE SPEED SIGNAL FROM DISTRIBUTOR

GMC/Chevrolet throttle return control system

4. Check the adjustment by accelerating the engine to about 2500 rpm and releasing the throttle. The engine should return to normal idle speed.

COURIER DECELERATION CONTROL SYSTEM

The deceleration control system is designed to maintain a balanced air/fuel mixture during periods of engine deceleration. Although the components used vary in some years, the basic theory remains the same. To more thoroughly burn or dilute the initial rich mixture formed when the throttle is suddenly closed, and to smooth out the transition to a lean mixture by enriching the mixture slightly after the throttle has closed. Although the processes may seem contradictory, they act in sequence to provide an overall ideal mixture.

1977–78 Couriers with 1.8 engines use an air by-pass valve, a carburetor dashpot, and a throttle opener system comprised of a servo diaphragm connected to the throttle and a vacuum control valve. The air bypass valve prevents afterburn in the exhaust by shutting off air to the exhaust manifold from the air pump during deceleration. The dashpot holds the throttle open slightly for an instant during sudden deceleration.

1977–78 2.3 engine 49 states and Canada trucks use an air by-pass valve, a dashpot (on trucks with manual transmissions only), and a coasting richer valve controlled by speed and accelerator switches. The air by-pass valve and dashpot are the same as those used on the 1977–78 1.8 and the coasting richer valve is the same as that on 1975–76 Couriers. 1977–78 California Couriers use the air by-pass valve, and the dashpot if the truck has a manual transmission.

1979–82 2.0 liter 49 states models use an anti-afterburn valve and a throttle positioner. California models have an air by-pass valve and a throttle positioner. Canadian models have an air by-pass valve, a dashpot, and a throttle positioner.

1979–82 2.3 liter 49 states models have a coasting richer solenoid valve activated by a speed switch and an accelerator switch; this system is the same as that used on earlier models. California and Canada models have an air by-pass valve, and a coasting richer solenoid valve activated by a speed switch and an accelerator switch; manual transmission models add a dashpot to these systems.

Anti-Afterburn Valve Test

1. Remove the outlet hose from the anti-afterburn valve.
2. Hold a hand over the outlet fitting and raise the engine rpm. Quickly release the accelerator. Air should flow for approximately three seconds. If the valve passes air for more than three seconds, or does not pass air at all, it should be replaced.

Coasting Richer Valve Test (Deceleration Valve)

1. Remove the coasting richer valve from the carburetor.
2. Connect the coasting richer valve to the battery.
3. As power is applied to the valve, the solenoid plunger should be pulled into the valve body.
4. Reinstall the coasting richer valve. Connect a test light.
5. Raise the rear wheels and support the truck on stands. Block the front wheels.
6. Start the engine and raise the engine speed above 30 mph. Release the accelerator pedal. The test light should come ON and remain ON until the speed falls below 17–23 mph.
7. If the system is operating properly, no further tests are required. If not, proceed with the other tests.
8. Remove the stands and lower the truck. Disconnect the test light.

Accelerator Switch Test

The accelerator switch is actuated by a throttle lever link on the carburetor through 1978; the switch is located on the accelerator pedal on 1979–80 models. When checking the switch with a circuit tester, the test light should be ON when the accelerator pedal is fully released and should be OFF when the pedal is depressed.

Speed Switch Test

1. Remove the instrument cluster and attach a test light to the speedometer switch.
2. Reconnect the speedometer cable and ground wire.
3. Raise both wheels off the ground and support the truck on stands. Block the front wheels.
4. Start the engine.
5. Depress the accelerator pedal to accelerate the engine and confirm that the speed switch is ON at speeds of 17–23 mph and OFF at speeds below 17–23 mph.
6. If not, replace the switch.
7. Lower the truck and remove the test light. Reinstall the instrument cluster.

Speed Switch Relay Test

Check the speed switch relay with a test light to be sure that it is operating at 17–23 mph.

Three Way Solenoid Valve Test
1979–82 2.0 ENGINES ONLY

1. Start the engine and allow it to reach normal operating temperature. Check the idle speed and adjust as necessary.
2. Disconnect the wire at the three way solenoid valve. This wire is coded either black with a white stripe or brown with a red stripe on some models.
3. When the wire is disconnected, the engine speed should increase to 1000 rpm for 49 States trucks, or 1100 rpm for California models.

4. If the engine speed does not increase, the three way solenoid valve or the servo diaphragm is not operating correctly. Check the servo diaphragm using the following procedure; if the servo diaphragm is operating correctly, the three way valve is faulty and should be replaced.

Servo Diaphragm Test

1. Start the engine and set the idle speed to specification.
2. Stop the engine and disconnect the vacuum line between the vacuum control valve and the diaphragm at the diaphragm.
3. Disconnect the vacuum line between the intake manifold and the vacuum control valve at the manifold on models through 1978. On 1979–82 models, disconnect the vacuum hose at the vacuum amplifier and the vacuum hose at the three way solenoid valve. Connect the vacuum hose from the servo diaphragm to the vacuum amplifier so that the intake manifold vacuum is applied directly to the servo diaphragm.
4. Disconnect and plug the vacuum line between the carburetor and the distributor.
5. Connect a vacuum line from the intake manifold to the servo diaphragm on models through 1978.
6. Connect a tachometer and start the engine. The engine should idle at 1300–1500 rpm for models through 1978, or 900–1100 rpm, 1979 and later (1000–1200 rpm for 1979 and later California models). If the engine speed is not correct, adjust by means of the servo diaphragm adjusting screw. If the correct speed is not obtainable, replace the diaphragm.

Vacuum Control Valve Test

1. Disconnect the vacuum hose between the vacuum control valve and the intake manifold at the manifold.
2. Attach a vacuum gauge in the line using a T-fitting.
3. Connect a tachometer to the engine. Start the engine and raise the speed to 300 rpm, then suddenly release the throttle. The vacuum reading should rise above 21.3 in., drop to that figure and hesitate there for one or two seconds, then drop to the normal idle vacuum of 16–18 in. Note that these readings are for sea level, and should be corrected accordingly.
4. If the vacuum reading is not within specification, adjust the vacuum control valve by turning the adjusting screw in the top of the valve. If the correct reading is unobtainable, replace the valve.

Vacuum Switch Test

1. Disconnect the vacuum hose between the vacuum switch and the vacuum control valve.
2. Using a T-fitting, connect a vacuum gauge between the vacuum switch and an external vacuum source.
3. Raise the vacuum reading above 8 in., then allow the vacuum to drop. The

switch should click at approximately 6 in. If it does not, or if it clicks at a higher reading, replace the switch.

Air By-Pass Valve Test

1. Disconnect the air hose from the side of the air by-pass valve.
2. Connect a tachometer to the engine. Start the engine and raise the speed above 2000 rpm.
3. Release the throttle and check for air flow from the port on the side of the air by-pass valve. If there is no airflow, replace the valve.

Dashpot Adjustment

1. Check the engine idle speed and mixture, and adjust as necessary.
2. Remove the air cleaner.
3. With the tachometer still connected to the engine, loosen the dashpot locknut. Move the throttle lever and hold to maintain the engine speed at 2400–2600 rpm (2100–2300 rpm for California trucks).
4. Turn the dashpot until its rod contacts the throttle lever. Release the throttle lever and tighten the locknut.
5. Move the throttle lever until it contacts the dashpot rod and recheck the engine speed. Repeat the adjustment if necessary.

Accelerator Switch Adjustment
1978

1. Be sure that the throttle valve is fully closed.
2. Loosen the switch adjusting screw and turn the switch off.
3. Gradually tighten the adjusting screw until the switch produces a clicking sound and is turned on.
4. Tighten the adjusting screw another 1½ turns.

1979 AND LATER

The accelerator switch is mounted on the arm of the accelerator pedal.
1. Check the accelerator pedal to make sure that it moves freely.
2. Loosen the accelerator switch locknut.

3. Gradually turn the adjusting screw until the accelerator switch clicks.
4. Tighten the locknut.

Component Replacement

With the exception of the speed switch, replacement of the various components is simply a matter of disconnecting hoses, wires, etc., and dismounting the component. Mark all disconnected items so that they may be properly reconnected.

The speed switch is integrated with the speedometer assembly. To replace the speed switch, remove the speedometer as outlined later in the Courier section.

D-50/ARROW DECELERATION DEVICE

Closing of the throttle valve on deceleration is delayed in order to burn the air/fuel mixture more thoroughly. A vacuum controlled dashpot, attached to the carburetor linkage is used.

A servo valve detects intake manifold vacuum and closes if vacuum exceeds a preset value. Since the air in the dashpot diaphragm chamber can not escape, the throttle linkage opening is temporarily retained. If the vacuum is below the preset value, the servo valve opens and the dashpot works normally.

Maintenance

Inspect the hoses for breaks and damage, and the valve body for cracks.

Adjustment

1. Have the engine running, brakes locked, and a tachometer attached.
2. Push the dashpot rod, connected to the carburetor arm, upward and into the dashpot until it stops.
3. Note the rpm of the engine under these conditions and, if necessary, adjust it to these specifications: U-engine—2100–2300; W-engine—1600–1800. Note the time that elapses between suddenly releasing the dashpot rod and return to normal idle speed.

It should be 3–6 seconds; if not, replace the unit.

D-50/ARROW DECELERATION VALVE

This valve is used to supply additional air to the intake manifold to decrease vacuum and help burn up accumulated gasoline that evaporates when the throttle is released. It is activated by a sudden increase in manifold vacuum.

Testing

1. Run the engine at idle speed. The valve should be in a closed position. If the valve is stuck partway open, a lean idle mixture and poor idle will result. If the valve is sticking open, replace it.
2. Race the engine to 2,500 rpm and release the throttle suddenly. Watch the valve. It should open wide and then gradually close. If the valve does not operate smoothly and open quickly every time the engine is raced, replace it.

D-50/ARROW FUEL CUTOFF SYSTEM

Some vehicles have an air switching valve activated above 1700 rpm and at closed throttle. Under these conditions, carburetor ported vacuum opens the air switching valve and that valve, in turn, admits air to the idle and transition passages of the carburetor. The air pressure stops the flow of fuel, to improve fuel economy and eliminate emissions when the engine is overrunning.

Below 1700 rpm, a solenoid valve, activated through an engine speed senser, deprives the system of vacuum so the engine will idle and operate at low speeds in the normal manner.

Testing

Start the engine and run it at idle. Then, disconnect the electrical connector to the solenoid valve. The engine should stall or nearly stall due to lean mixture. If not, check the vacuum passage for clogging. If the passage is clear, check the solenoid valve by disconnecting the vacuum line running to it. If disconnecting the vacuum line with the electrical connector disconnected makes the engine stall, replace the solenoid valve.

If the vehicle has a stalling problem, make the following checks:
1. Test the voltage at the solenoid connector with the engine idling. If there is no voltage, check for wiring problems and replace or repair parts as necessary.
2. If there is voltage at the connector at idle, increase the engine speed to 1500 rpm. If voltage is lost before the engine reaches 1500 or at 1500, replace the engine speed sensor.
3. Increase the engine speed to 2500 rpm. If the voltage is not lost, replace the engine speed sensor.

Schematic of D-50/Arrow deceleration fuel cutoff system

DATSUN BOOST CONTROL DECELERATION DEVICE

The BCDD reduces hydrocarbon emissions during coasting conditions.

High manifold vacuum during coasting prevents the complete combustion of the air/fuel mixture because of the reduced amount of air. This condition will result in large HC emissions. Enriching the air/fuel mixture for a short time (during the high vacuum condition) will reduce the emission of HC in conjunction with the AIR system.

However, enriching the air/fuel mixture with only the mixture adjusting screw will cause poor engine idle, or invite an increase in the carbon monoxide (CO) content of the exhaust gases.

The BCDD consists of an independently operated auxiliary fuel system. This system functions when the engine is coasting to enrich the air-fuel mixture which minimizes the hydrocarbon content of the exhaust gases through more efficient combustion. This is accomplished without adversely affecting engine idle and the carbon monoxide content of the exhaust gases.

When intake manifold vacuum exceeds a predetermined value, a vacuum-actuated diaphragm opens an air passage allowing additional air to enter the intake manifold. When the additional air passage is opened, vacuum is brought to bear on another diaphragm which opens a fuel passage allowing additional fuel to enter the intake manifold.

When the engine changes from a coasting condition to that of idling, the transmission speed sensor closes an electrical circuit, energizing the vacuum control solenoid valve. When energized, the vacuum control solenoid valve vents the intake manifold vacuum to the atmosphere, thus causing the two diaphragms to return to their normal positions, closing off the additional air and fuel mixture. The transmission switch is not used on 1978–79 models.

LUV MIXTURE CONTROL VALVE

1978 and Later California and High Altitude Models

Disconnect the rubber hose connecting the mixture control valve with the intake manifold and plug the intake manifold side of the valve. If the mixture control valve is operating correctly, air will continue to blow out the mixture control valve for a few seconds after the accelerator pedal is fully depressed (engine running) and released quickly. If air continues to blow out for more than five seconds, replace the mixture control valve.

LUV COASTING ENRICHMENT SYSTEM

This system functions when the engine is coasting, to enrich the air/fuel mixture, which

Schematic of LUV Coasting enrichment System—49 states

minimizes hydrocarbon content of the exhaust gases through efficient combustion.

A solenoid operated valve in the carburetor allows extra fuel to be drawn into the intake manifold during coasting. The solenoid is energized by the following switches:

1978 and later Federal with manual transmission:
1. Accelerator switch
2. Clutch switch
3. 3rd-4th gear switch

1978 and later California with manual transmission:
1. Accelerator switch
2. Clutch switch
3. Transmission neutral switch
4. Engine speed sensor

1978 and later California with automatic transmission:
1. Accelerator switch
2. Inhibitor switch
3. Engine speed sensor

When all of these switches turn on and the engine is coasting, the solenoid valve on the secondary side of the carburetor energizes and causes the valve to open. When the valve opens, the fuel is drawn out of the float chamber by engine vacuum and metered by the coasting jet below the secondary throttle valve. On acceleration the coasting richer circuit is opened causing the coasting richer valve to close, shutting off the supply of extra fuel.

Solenoid Valve Test

The valve should be open when the circuit is energized. A clicking noise should be heard when the valve operates.

Accelerator Switch Test

The accelerator switch should be closed when the pedal is not depressed and open when the pedal is depressed. Check with a test lamp.

Clutch Switch Test
1975 AND LATER

When the clutch pedal is depressed, the switch contacts are opened and the coasting

richer system is de-energized. Test all years' clutch switches with a test lamp.

Transmission Switch Test
FEDERAL MANUAL TRANSMISSION MODELS

The transmission switch turns on when the transmission is shifted into 3rd or 4th gear and energizes the coasting richer system. It de-energizes the system when the transmission is shifted into any other position.

CALIFORNIA MANUAL TRANSMISSION MODELS

The transmission switch turns on when the transmission is shifted into any gear and turns off when it is shifted into neutral position. The solenoid is energized when the switch is in the On position. Test with a test lamp.

Inhibitor Switch
CALIFORNIA AUTOMATIC TRANSMISSION MODELS

The inhibitor switch is installed on the shift linkage lever and energizes the coasting richer system in drive, low or second gear positions. Test the inhibitor switch with a test lamp.

MAZDA ROTARY ENGINE DECELERATION CONTROL SYSTEM

The deceleration control system used an anti-afterburn valve, a coasting valve, and an air supply valve. In addition, an idle sensing switch is fitted to the carburetor. The No. 1 control box is shared with the air flow control system.

The anti-afterburn valve, which is located on the intake manifold, is used to supply fresh air to the manifold during deceleration or when the engine is shut off, in order to prevent afterburning.

A coasting valve, which functions in a similar manner, is used to prevent an overly rich mixture during deceleration. The

Combination anti-afterburn and coasting valve connections

coasting valve also vents the vacuum chamber of the air control valve during deceleration. The valve is operated by a solenoid which is controlled by the No. 1 control box and the idle sensing switch.

An idle sensing switch is attached to the carburetor. When the throttle closes, its linkage contacts a plunger on the switch which completes the circuit from the No. 1 control box to the coasting valve thus causing the coasting valve to operate. On automatic transmission equipped models, it also determines trailing distributor operation.

A solenoid-operated air supply valve opens when the ignition is shut off to prevent the engine from dieseling (running on).

In addition to the above components, the truck is equipped with an altitude compensator which provides air to lean out the overly rich mixture that accrues at high altitudes.

On models with an automatic transmission, a kick-down control system is used. Regardless of the gear selected, the transmission will not go above second gear when the choke knob is pulled out.

Component Testing
ANTI-AFTERBURN VALVE

1. Remove the air cleaner assembly.
2. Remove the hose from the air intake on the anti-afterburn valve.
3. With the engine idling, place your hand over the air intake of the valve. If a strong suction is felt, the valve is defective and should be replaced.
4. Increase the engine speed to 3,500–3,800 rpm. Release the throttle and allow it to snap shut. Air should be drawn in

Testing the Coasting Valve

through the valve air intake for no longer than one second.

5. Keep the engine idling and disconnect the anti-afterburn valve solenoid wiring. Air should flow into the air intake while the solenoid is disconnected.

If the anti-afterburn valve fails to function properly, replace it with a new one. Remember to connect the air supply hose and the solenoid wiring after completing the test.

COMBINATION ANTI-AFTERBURN AND COASTING VALVE

1. Disconnect the hose which runs from the air cleaner to the combination valve at the air cleaner end.
2. Start the engine and run it at curb idle.
3. There should be no vacuum present at the end of the hose which you disconnected in step 1.
4. Turn the engine off.
5. Disconnect the hose which runs from the coasting valve portion of the combination valve to the intake manifold from the coasting valve end and plug up the port.
6. Operate the engine at idle.
7. Disconnect the anti-afterburn valve solenoid connector.
8. Check for vacuum at the end of the hose which you disconnected in step 1; there should be vacuum present. If not, the anti-afterburn valve is defective.
9. Turn the engine off. Reconnect the anti-afterburn valve electrical leads and the hose to the coasting valve.
10. Disconnect the intake manifold-to-anti-afterburn valve vacuum line at the valve end, and plug the vacuum fitting on the valve.
11. Start the engine and allow it to idle.
12. Disconnect the coasting valve solenoid at the multiconnector.
13. Hold your hand over the end of the vacuum line which you disconnected in step 10. Vacuum should be felt; if not, replace the defective coasting valve.
14. Turn the engine off and reconnect the leads and hoses that were disconnected above.

IDLE SWITCH

1. Unfasten the idle switch leads.
2. Connect a test meter to the switch terminals.
3. With the engine at idle, the meter should indicate a completed circuit.
4. Depress the plunger on the idle switch; the circuit should be broken (no meter reading).

If the idle switch is not functioning properly, replace it with a new one.

COOLANT TEMPERATURE SWITCH

Start this test with the coolant temperature below 68°F.

1. Disconnect the electrical lead from the temperature switch.

2. Connect a test electrical lead from the temperature switch.
3. Connect a test light between one terminal of the switch and a 12 volt battery. Ground the other terminal.
4. The test light should light.
5. Start the engine and allow it to warm up. Once the engine reaches normal operating temperature, the test light should go out.
6. Replace the switch if it doesn't work as outlined.

CHOKE SWITCH (SEMI-AUTOMATIC CHOKE)

1. Working underneath the instrument panel, disconnect the lead at the back of the choke switch.
2. Connect a ohmmeter to the terminals on the choke switch side of the connector.
3. With the choke knob in (off), the meter should show continuity (resistance reading).
4. Pull the choke knob out, about ½ in. for manual transmission cars or 1 in. for automatics. The meter should show no continuity (read zero).
5. Replace the switch if defective.

Arrow indicates the position of the afterburn valve

Component Removal and Installation
ANTI-AFTERBURN VALVE

1. Remove the air cleaner assembly.
2. Disconnect the air hoses and vacuum lines from the valve.
3. Unfasten the solenoid wiring.
4. Remove the securing nuts and withdraw the valve.

Installation is performed in the reverse order of removal.

COASTING VALVE

The coasting valve is removed and installed in the same manner as the anti-afterburn valve.

IDLE SWITCH

1. Remove the coasting valve.
2. Remove the carburetor as detailed in the truck section.
3. Disconnect the wiring from the switch.
4. Unfasten the securing screws and remove the switch.

Installation is performed in the reverse order of removal. After installing the switch, adjust it as outlined under "Adjustments", below.

AIR SUPPLY VALVE

1. Remove the air cleaner and the hot air duct.
2. Disconnect the air hose, the vacuum lines, and the solenoid wiring from the valve.
3. Unfasten the screws which secure the valve and remove it.

Air supply valve installation is performed in the reverse order of removal.

ALTITUDE COMPENSATOR

1. Disconnect both hoses from the altitude compensator. Be sure to note their positions for correct hook-up.
2. Unfasten the altitude compensator securing bolts.
3. Remove the compensator from its bracket.

Installation is the reverse of removal.

COOLANT TEMPERATURE SWITCH

1. Drain the coolant from the radiator enough to bring the coolant level below the temperature switch.
2. Remove the alternator and drive belt if they are in the way.
3. Disconnect the switch multiconnector.
4. Use an open-end wrench to remove the switch.
5. Installation is the reverse of removal.

Adjustments
IDLE SWITCH

1. Warm up the engine until the water temperature is at least 159°F.
2. Make sure that the mixture and idle speed are properly adjusted.
3. Adjust the idle speed to 975–1,100 rpm (1,200–1,300 rpm-automatic transmission) by rotating the throttle adjusting screw.
4. Rotate the idle switch adjusting screw until the switch changes from OFF to ON position.
5. Slowly turn the idle switch adjusting screw back to the point where the switch just changes from ON to OFF.
6. Turn the throttle screw back so that the engine returns to idle.

NOTE: Be sure that the idle switch goes on when the idle speed is still above 1,000 rpm.

MAZDA PISTON ENGINE THROTTLE OPENER

The throttle opener system consists of a servo-diaphragm connected to the throttle lever and a vacuum control valve which controls intake manifold vacuum through the servo-diaphragm.

Testing the System
SERVO-DIAPHRAGM

1. Start the engine and set the idle speed to 800 rpm. Stop the engine.
2. Disconnect the vacuum sensing tube between the servo-diaphragm and the vacuum control valve at the diaphragm.
3. Remove the intake manifold suction hole plug.
4. Connect the intake manifold and the servo-diaphragm with a tube so that the intake manifold vacuum goes directly to the servo-diaphragm.
5. Connect a tachometer and remove the vacuum sensing tube between the carburetor and distributor.
6. Start the engine and read the speed. If the engine is running 1300–1500 rpm, the servo-diaphragm is operating normally. If the engine speed is 800–1300, adjust the speed with the throttle opening screw. If the engine speed remains normal, about 800 rpm, the servo-diaphragm is defective and should be replaced.
7. Remove the test equipment and reconnect all the lines.

Servo-Diaphragm
Removal and Installation

1. Remove the air cleaner.
2. Disconnect the vacuum sensing tube from the diaphragm.
3. Remove the cotter pin and link.
4. Loosen the locknut and remove the servo-diaphragm.
5. Installation is the reverse of removal. Adjust the servo-diaphragm.

Vacuum Control Valve
Removal and Installation

1. Remove the air cleaner.
2. Disconnect the vacuum sending tubes from the vacuum control valve.
3. Unbolt and remove the vacuum control valve.
4. Installation is the reverse of removal.

TOYOTA THROTTLE POSITIONER (TP) SYSTEM

During rapid deceleration large volumes of fuel/air mixture are drawn into the cylinders due to high manifold vacuum. If the throttle plates close completely there is not sufficient oxygen to permit complete combustion. Therefore a throttle positioner is installed to keep the throttle plates slightly open during deceleration. Vacuum is reduced under the throttle valve which, in turn, acts on the retard chamber of the distributor vacuum unit. This ignition retard compensates for the loss of engine braking caused by the partially-opened throttle.

Once the vehicle drops below a predetermined speed, the vacuum switching valve provides vacuum to the throttle positioner diaphragm. The throttle positioner then retracts allowing the throttle valve to close completely. The distributor also returns to normal operation.

ADJUSTMENT

1. Start the engine and allow it to reach normal operating temperature.
2. Adjust the engine idle speed as previously outlined.
3. Detach the vacuum line from the throttle positioner diaphragm and plug the line.
4. Accelerate the engine slightly to set the throttle positioner.
5. Check the engine speed with a tachometer when the positioner is in place.
6. Check that the engine rpm reads as follows:

20R engine:	
manual transmission	1400
automatic transmission	1050
22R engine:	
all	1050

Schematic of a typical Toyota throttle positioner system

2F engine
except '78–'80 Calif	1200
'78–'80 Calif	1400

7. If necessary, adjust the engine rpm to the values listed in step 6 by turning the throttle positioner screw.

8. Connect the vacuum hose to the positioner diaphragm. The engine idle should return to normal as soon as the vacuum line is connected.

9. If the throttle positioner fails to perform properly, check the linkage and diaphragm unit. If there are no defects in these components, the problem probably lies in the vacuum switching valve or in the speed sensor unit.

EGR valve with external, non-integral back pressure sensor

Cross section—typical positive back pressure EGR valve

Typical time delay circuitry—EGR valve

EXHAUST GAS RECIRCULATION

NOx (oxides of nitrogen) is a tailpipe emission caused by the oxidation of nitrogen in the combustion chamber. When the peak combustion temperatures go over 2500°F. NOx is formed in excessive amounts. To keep the combustion temperatures down, exhaust gas is recirculated.

Recirculation of the exhaust gases is accomplished by having a movable valve between the exhaust and intake manifolds, and upon a predetermined demand, route engine vacuum to the valve and open the connecting port to allow the exhaust gases to flow into the intake manifold and mix with the air/fuel mixture.

Three types of EGR valves are used, with the major differences in the method used to control the valve opening. The three types are as follows:

1. An EGR valve with no back pressure sensor and is controlled by ported vacuum.

2. An EGR valve with an integral back pressure sensor and is controlled by ported vacuum and exhaust gas back pressure. Both positive and negative type transducers are used to react to either high or low exhaust gas back pressures.

3. An EGR valve with an external, non-integral back pressure sensor and is controlled by ported vacuum and exhaust gas back pressure.

NOTE: Venturi vacuum is used as a triggering agent when a vacuum amplifier is used in the EGR system.

Several different types of controls are used to turn the vacuum to the EGR valve on and off. Most of them have to do with engine temperature, as described later.

When the EGR valve hose is connected to the base of the carburetor, without a separate amplifier, the system is operated by ported vacuum. The hose may not run directly from the EGR valve to the carburetor, but may go through a temperature control valve of some sort. In a ported vacuum system, the vacuum to operate the EGR valve is taken from a port that is above the throttle plate at idle, and thus not subject to vacuum. Because there is no vacuum, the spring in the EGR valve closes it, and the exhaust gas does not recirculate. As the throttle is opened, the port is exposed to vacuum, and the EGR valve opens.

Vacuum systems, with an amplifier, are the most complicated, because of the number of hoses. Manifold vacuum is connected to the amplifier by a hose, and then connects to the EGR valve. The amplifier also connects to venturi vacuum. At idle there is no venturi vacuum, but above idle the air moves through the carburetor venturi fast enough to create a vacuum. This slight amount of vacuum opens the amplifier, which then allows manifold vacuum to open the EGR valve.

Temperature controls for EGR systems

come in many different designs. They are all made so that the EGR valve stays closed when the engine or the outside air is cold. After the engine or the outside air warms up, the temperature control allows the EGR valve to operate normally. Before March 15, 1973, many EGR systems used a temperature control that was sensitive to outside air temperature. Even with a fully warmed up engine, the EGR system would stay off if the outside temperature was cold enough. On vehicles made after March 15, 1973, the temperature controls were all sensitive to engine coolant temperature, or engine compartment temperature.

Cutaway of a monolith converter

TESTING EGR SYSTEMS

Testing of the EGR systems should verify that the EGR valve is closed at idle, open above idle, and that the exhaust gas is actually recirculating. If the EGR valve sticks open at idle, the engine will run very rough, or may not even start. If this happens the valve should be removed and cleaned, or replaced. To check for valve opening above idle, check with a mirror or your fingers to see if the diaphragm or stem moves when the engine is at a fast idle in Park or Neutral. If the diaphragm does not move when the throttle is opened, there is either a problem with vacuum, or the valve is stuck closed. With a vacuum gauge connected to the EGR port, you should see vacuum on the gauge when the throttle is opened. EGR valves should not leak when tested with a hand vacuum pump. If they do they must be replaced.

To find out if the exhaust gas is actually

recirculating, use a hand vacuum pump or mouth suction through a hose to open the EGR valve with the engine idling. If the engine runs rough or dies, you know the exhaust gas is recirculating. If the engine does not run rough, make a second test at 2500 rpm. Opening the EGR valve at that rpm should cause a change in engine speed. If it does, you know the exhaust gas is recirculating. To make the 2500 rpm test, remove and plug the hose from the EGR port. Attach your suction hose to the EGR valve before running the engine at 2500 rpm. Simply pulling off the EGR hose at 2500 rpm is not a valid test, because the extra air entering the engine through the hose could cause a speed change all by itself. On most engines you won't have to go this far, because opening the EGR valve at idle will prove that the exhaust is recirculating.

Underfloor converter—showing replaceable pellets

If the exhaust is not recirculating, it means that a passageway or the valve itself is clogged up. The only way to fix it is to scrape out the clogging as best you can, or replace the valve.

The back-pressure sensor is a pressure-operated bleed that disables the EGR valve and keeps it closed when there is no exhaust pressure. This type of valve cannot be tested with a hand vacuum pump with the engine off because the bleed is open. The only practical way to test these new valves is by substitution of a known good valve. If a valve is not available, the suspected valve

can be removed, and the holes temporarily taped shut. If this corrects the problem, then a new valve should be installed.

EGR delay systems are used on some vehicles to prevent the recirculation of the exhaust gases for approximately 60 seconds after the ignition switch is turned on by an electrical timer, connected to an engine mounted solenoid switch. The solenoid is connected in the vacuum line between the carburetor venturi nipple and the vacuum amplifier.

A charge temperature switch is used on some models by being installed in the intake manifold on the number 6 branch, 6 cyl., and on the number 8 branch on the V8 engine. No EGR timer on EGR valve operation is permitted when the air/fuel mixture temperature is below 60°F. (16°C).

UNIQUE EGR SYSTEM FEATURES

Certain vehicles use EGR system features other than the standard ones previously described. These are covered below by vehicle brand and year.

Ford

The high speed EGR modulator subsystem consists of a speed sensor, an electronic module and a solenoid vacuum valve. The speed sensor, driven by the speedometer cable, provides an AC signal in relation to engine speed, to the electronic module. The electronic module processes the information from the speed sensor and sends a signal to the high speed modulator (vacuum solenoid) valve. When the vehicle speed exceeds the module trigger speed, the solenoid vacuum valve closes which, in turn, causes the EGR valve to close.

Jeep

The EGR system consists of a diaphragm actuated flow control valve (EGR valve), coolant temperature override switch (EGR CTO) and connecting hoses. In 1980, a Thermal Vacuum Switch, located in the air cleaner, was added to control the vacuum signal between the EGR and CTO.

The purpose of the EGR system is to limit the formation of oxides of nitrogen by

EXHAUST GAS RECIRCULATION SYSTEM DIAGNOSIS CHART

Condition	Possible Cause	Correction
Engine idles abnormally rough and/or stalls.	EGR valve vacuum hoses misrouted.	Check EGR valve vacuum hose routing. Correct as required.
	Leaking EGR valve.	Check EGR valve for correct operation.
	EGR valve gasket failed or loose EGR attaching bolts.	Check EGR attaching bolts for tightness. Tighten as required. If not loose, remove EGR valve and inspect gasket. Replace as required.
	EGR thermal control valve and/or EGR-TVS.	Check vacuum into valve from carburetor EGR port with engine at normal operating

EXHAUST GAS RECIRCULATION SYSTEM DIAGNOSIS CHART

Condition	Possible Cause	Correction
Engine idles abnormally rough and/or stalls.		temperature and at curb idle speed. Then check the vacuum out of the EGR thermal control valve to EGR valve. If the two vacuum readings are not equal within ± ½ in. Hg. (1.7 kPa), then proceed to EGR vacuum control diagnosis.
	Improper vacuum to EGR valve at idle.	Check vaccum from carburetor EGR port with engine at stabilized operating temperature and at curb idle speed. If vacuum is more than 1.0 in. Hg., refer to carburetor idle diagnosis.
Engine runs rough on light throttle acceleration, poor part load performance and poor fuel economy.	EGR valve vacuum hose misrouted.	Check EGR valve vacuum hose routing. Correct as required.
	Failed EGR vacuum control valve.	Same as listing in "Engine Idles Rough" condition.
	EGR flow unbalanced due to deposit accumulation in EGR passages or under carburetor.	Clean EGR passages of all deposits.
	Sticky or binding EGR valve.	Remove EGR valve and inspect. Clean or replace as required.
	Wrong or no EGR gaskets.	Check and correct as required.
Vehicle with back pressure EGR valve.	Control valve blocked or air flow restricted.	Check internal control valve function per service procedure.
Engine stalls on decelerations.	Restriction in EGR vacuum line.	Check EGR vacuum lines for kinks, bends, etc. Remove or replace hoses as required. Check EGR vacuum control valve function.
		Check EGR valve for excessive deposits causing sticky or binding operation. Clean or repair as required.
	Sticking or binding EGR valve.	Remove EGR valve and inspect, clean or repair as required.
Vehicle with a back pressure EGR valve.	Control valve blocked or air flow restricted.	Check internal control valve function per service procedure.
Part throttle engine detonation.	Insufficient exhaust gas recirculation flow during part throttle accelerations.	Check EGR valve hose routing. Check EGR valve operation. Repair or replace as required. Check EGR thermal control valve and/or EGR-TVS as listed in "Engine Idles Rough" section. Replace valve as required. Check EGR passage and valve for excessive deposit. Clean as required.
Vehicle with a back pressure EGR valve.	Control valve blocked or air flow restricted.	Check internal control valve function per service procedure.
Engine starts but immediately stalls when cold.	EGR valve hoses misrouted.	Check EGR valve hose routing.
	EGR system malfunctioning when engine is cold.	Perform check to determine if the EGR thermal control valve and/or EGR-TVS are operational. Replace as required.
Vehicle with a back pressure EGR valve.	Control valve blocked or air flow restricted.	Check internal control valve function per service procedure.

①Detonation can be caused by several other engine variables. Perform ignition and carburetor related diagnosis.

diluting the fresh air intake charge with a metered amount of exhaust gas, thereby reducing the peak temperatures of the burning gases in the combustion chambers.

EGR VALVE

The EGR valve is mounted on a machined surface at the rear of the intake manifold on V8 engines and on the side of the intake manifold on the Sixes. When a backpressure sensor is used, the EGR valve is mounted on a spacer which is an integral part of the backpressure sensor.

The valve is held in a normally closed position by a coil spring located above the diaphragm. A special fitting is provided at the carburetor to route ported (above the throttle plates) vacuum through the CTO and a TVS or BPS (when used) and hose connections to a fitting located above the diaphragm on the valve. A passage in the intake manifold directs exhaust gas from the exhaust crossover passage on V8s and from near the heat riser on the Sixes, to the EGR valve. When the diaphragm is actuated by vacuum, the valve opens and meters exhaust gas through special passages into the intake manifold below the carburetor.

COOLANT TEMPERATURE OVERRIDE SWITCH

This switch is located in the intake manifold at the coolant passage adjacent to the oil filler tube on V8s and on the left side of the cylinder block on the Sixes. The outer port of the switch is connected to either the EGR valve or BPS (when used). The inner port is connected by a hose to the EGR fitting at the carburetor. When the coolant temperature reaches 115°F the inner port of the switch opens and a vacuum signal is applied to the EGR valve. This vacuum signal is subject to regulation by the BPS when used.

THERMAL VACUUM SWITCH (TVS)

The TVS is located in the air cleaner on all 1980 and later engines, and functions as an on/off switch controlled by air cleaner air temperature. The TVS controls the vacuum passage between the EGR CTO valve and the EGR valve. Air temperature in the 40–50°F range cause the TVS to limit the vacuum applied to the EGR valve, thus improving cold engine driveability.

EXHAUST BACKPRESSURE SENSOR (BPS)

This device is used on some 1978–81 models in conjunction with the EGR system.

The BPS monitors exhaust backpressure and permits EGR operation only when engine operating conditions are favorable. The BPR units are variously calibrated, are not serviceable, and must be replaced with the identical part as a unit when necessary.

The BPS consists of a diaphragm valve and a spacer connected by a metal tube projecting into an exhaust port in the spacer

Typical throttle return control system used on G.M. vehicles

Typical throttle modulator operation used on IHC vehicles

EGR system typical of 4-151

EGR system typical of 6-258

Typical V8 EGR system

body. The EGR valve mounts directly on the spacer. On some 1978–81 sixes, the sensor is integral with the EGR valve.

In operation, the metal tube connecting the diaphragm valve to the spacer routes exhaust backpressure from the particular exhaust port to the sensor. When the backpressure reaches a certain level the diaphragm valve spring pressure is overcome, permitting a vacuum signal to the EGR valve, providing that the CTO switch is open.

Thus, EGR operations is only permitted when the engine is warmed up sufficiently and exhaust backpressure relatively high, such as during acceleration and at some

cruising speeds. When temperature or backpressure conditions are not met, the vacuum signal is vented to the atmosphere from a vent at the diaphragm valve.

Courier
THREE-WAY SOLENOID VALVE

The Courier EGR system incorporates an EGR valve, vacuum amplifier, and water temperature thermal switch, all components typical of such systems. However, the signal produced by the thermal switch is communicated to the vacuum portion of the system by a three-way solenoid valve which is somewhat unique.

To test the valve, proceed as follows:

1. Disconnect the electrical connectors from the thermo switch. Connect a jumper wire between the connectors to simulate a complete circuit.

2. Turn the ignition switch to ON.

3. Disconnect the vacuum hose from the EGR valve and blow into the hose. Air should be discharged from the three-way solenoid valve relief port. If it is not, replace the three-way valve.

4. Turn the ignition switch off, and remove the jumper wire from the thermo switch connectors. Disconnect the vacuum amplifier vacuum line from the three-way solenoid. Turn the ignition switch back to ON.

5. Blow into the vacuum line disconnected from the EGR valve, and check for air discharge from the vacuum amplifier port on the three-way solenoid valve. If there is no discharge, replace the solenoid valve.

6. After completion of all tests, reconnect the hoses to their original locations.

Datsun
B.P.T. VALVE

1978–79 models have a B.P.T. valve installed between the EGR and the thermal

vacuum valve. The B.P.T. valve has a diaphragm raised or lowered by exhaust back pressure. The diaphragm opens or closes an air bleed, which is connected into the EGR vacuum line. High pressure results in higher levels of EGR, because the diaphragm is raised, closing off the air bleed, which allows more vacuum to reach and open the EGR valve. Thus, the amount of recirculated exhaust gas varies with exhaust pressure.

VACUUM DELAY VALVE

1978–79 California models have a vacuum delay valve installed in the line between the thermal vacuum valve and the EGR valve. This valve delays rapid drops in vacuum in the EGR line, thus effecting a longer EGR time.

Mazda
EGR CONTROL VALVE TEST

1. Remove the air cleaner.
2. Run the engine at idle.
3. Disconnect the vacuum sensing tube from the EGR control valve.
4. Disconnect the vacuum sensing tube from the intake manifold vacuum control valve.
5. Connect this vacuum tube to the EGR control valve. The engine should stop. If not, clean or replace the EGR control valve.

REPLACING EGR CONTROL VALVE

1. Remove air cleaner.
2. Disconnect the vacuum sensing tube from the EGR control valve.
3. Disconnect the EGR control valve to exhaust manifold pipe.
4. Disconnect the pipe between the EGR control valve and the intake manifold.
5. Unbolt and remove the EGR control valve.

1. Thermal vacuum valve
2. Vacuum delay valve (California only)
3. B.P.T. valve
4. EGR valve

Datsun 1978 and later EGR system components. The hose at the top runs to the carburetor; the hose at the bottom runs to the exhaust manifold

6. If old valve is to be reused, it should be cleaned with a wire brush before installation.

7. To install, reverse the above procedure.

TESTING THE THREE-WAY SOLENOID VALVE

The valve is located at the top center of the firewall in the engine compartment.

1. Disconnect the wiring to the water thermo switch and connect a jumper wire to the two connectors of the switch.

2. Disconnect the vacuum sensing tube from the EGR valve.

3. Disconnect the vacuum sensing tube which runs to the vacuum amplifier from the three way solenoid valve.

4. Turn the ignition switch on.

5. Blow through the solenoid valve from the tube disconnected from the EGR valve. Air should pass through the valve to the valve air filter.

6. Disconnect the jumper wire from the thermo switch.

7. Blow through the tube disconnected from the EGR valve and make sure the air passes through the opening to the vacuum amplifier tube.

8. If the solenoid valve does not operate properly, replace.

Volkswagen
EGR DECELERATION VALVE TEST

1. Remove the hose from the deceleration valve. Plug the hose.

2. Run the engine for a few seconds at 3000 rpm.

3. Snap the throttle valve closed.

4. With your finger, check for suction at the hose connection.

5. Remove the hose from the connector.

6. Run the engine at about 3000 rpm. No suction should be felt.

RESETTING THE ELAPSED MILEAGE SWITCH

The EGR reminder light in the speedometer should light up every 15,000 miles as a reminder for maintenance.

To reset the light switch, press the white button. The speedometer light should go out.

Catalytic Converter

A catalytic converter is a chamber in the exhaust system that contains a catalyst. When hydrocarbons or carbon monoxide pass over the catalyst they react with the oxygen in the exhaust and are converted into harmless water and carbon dioxide. The catalyst inside the converter is made in two forms. General Motors and Jeep use the pellet form, in which loose pellets are packaged into the converter and can be emptied out and changed, if necessary. Ford, International and Chrysler use the honeycomb cat-

alyst, which is built into the converter shell and is not replaceable. On Ford, International and Chrysler products the entire converter must be replaced if it goes bad.

There is no way to test a converter in the field to see if it is actually working. Tailpipe readings may be used to set carburetor idle mixtures, when the car maker requires it, but taking a tailpipe reading to determine if the converter is working is not possible.

The one field check that is recommended in all cases is to inspect for mechanical damage. If a converter gets overheated, the catalyst can melt and block the exhaust. Pellets or pieces of the catalyst may even come flying out the tailpipe while the engine is running. If this happens, the pellets or the entire converter must be changed.

Checking for a melted converter that restricts the exhaust can be done with a vacuum gauge connected to the engine. Run the engine at about 2500 rpm in Park or Neutral. If the vacuum reading is steady, the exhaust is okay. If the vacuum reading slowly drops, it indicates a buildup of pressure in the exhaust.

The use of leaded fuel will slowly destroy the efficiency of the catalyst until finally, after several tanks full, it won't do its job any more. If used long enough, leaded fuel can even cause catalyst plugging to the point that the engine will not run. If you know that a vehicle has been run on several tanks of leaded fuel, then you can be sure that the catalyst has lost its ability to convert. But there is no way to test for this condition in the field.

Do not change the catalyst if the vehicle has been run on only one tank or less of leaded fuel. Switching back to lead free fuel will allow the catalyst to recover and be almost as efficient as it was.

CONVERTER OVERHEAT PROTECTION

Engine controls are used to prevent the converter from being damaged by overheating

due to overly rich fuel mixtures during periods of deceleration.

The controls are named differently by the manufacturers, but are all designed to accomplish the same purpose and to operate basically in the same manner. To prevent the engine from operating at a rich mode when the throttle plates are closed during deceleration, electrical and/or mechanical means are provided to hold the throttle plates open at predetermined engine speeds, in order to lean the air/fuel mixture as necessary to control the exhaust emissions. The engine control should be inoperative under engine speeds of 1800 to 2000 RPMs to avoid engine overrun or vehicle overspeed in slow traffic.

The various parts are as follows:

1. The throttle level actuator is mounted as part of the carburetor assembly and operates when vacuum is applied to it from a separate solenoid vacuum control valve.

2. The solenoid vacuum control valve is controlled by a signal from the electronic speed sensor or a throttle modulator deceleration valve vacuum signal to allow vacuum to be routed to the throttle lever actuator.

3. Electronic speed sensor is mounted near or included with the distributor and senses the engine speed and sends a signal to the solenoid vacuum control valve as long as the preset speed is exceeded.

TESTING THE SYSTEM

To test the electrical speed sensor system, place the transmission in neutral or park and set the hand brake. With a tachometer attached to the engine, increase the engine speed to approximately 2000 RPM. The solenoid or modulator stem should extend to hold the carburetor throttle lever off curb idle setting. As the engine speed is reduced to below 1800 RPM, the solenoid or modulator stem should retract to the off position. A hand held vacuum pump and test lamp can be used to test the individual components of the system.

Typical throttle positioner system used on Chrysler Corp. vehicles having California Emission requirements

Testing an electric speed sensor switch

Typical vacuum modulator testing

Testing an electric solenoid valve with the engine running

To test the vacuum operated system, without an electrical sensor, 21 to 22 in. Hg. must be directed to the decel valve to open the port to direct vacuum to the throttle modulating diaphragm, located on the carburetor base. With the vacuum present, the stem of the modulating diaphragm will be extended. Release of the vacuum should allow the stem of the modulating diaphragm to retract.

Vacuum Operated Exhaust Heat Riser Valves

Exhaust heat riser valves have been used for many years to force part of the engine exhaust through a passageway under the intake manifold and preheat the fuel mixture. The heat valve was spring loaded into the closed position, but heat would make the spring relax so that during high speed operation or after warmup the exhaust would push it open.

Now, many engines use vacuum operated heat valves, controlled by a vacuum switch that is sensitive to engine temperature.

On these systems, manifold vacuum is used to close the valve, and force the exhaust gases through the crossover passage in the intake manifold. All the systems have a temperature valve that shuts the vacuum off when the engine warms up.

A simple coolant temperature-sensitive vacuum switch is mounted on the intake manifold coolant passage and has two hose connections. It actually does triple duty because it also controls the vacuum supply to the idle enrichment system and the air switching valve.

A second type vacuum switch has three hose connections, but one of them is a vent with a filter to keep the dirt out.

A third control uses either a coolant vacuum switch, or a vacuum solenoid connected to an oil temperature switch. The coolant vacuum switch has two hose connections and a vent when it controls the heat valve only. When it is tied into other emission control systems, it can have as many as five hose connections, and a vent. Some models also have a check valve in the hose so that vacuum will be trapped in the heat valve actuator when the engine is accelerated. This keeps the heat valve in the closed position and prevents a rattle.

TESTING VACUUM OPERATED EXHAUST HEAT RISER VALVES

Testing the vacuum operated heat riser valve is a matter of making sure it closes and opens freely. You can move it to see if it works, on a warm engine. On a cold engine, the valve should be closed, and disconnecting the hose should allow it to open. On a cold engine, there should be vacuum at the vacuum actuator, and on a warm engine the vacuum should be shut off.

Typical throttle positioner electrical circuitry used on Chrysler Corp. vehicles

Typical vacuum throttle modulating system

Typical vacuum operated exhaust heat control valve

Chevrolet/GMC Early Fuel Evaporation System

This system is used on all light duty models. The six cylinder system consists of an EFE valve mounted at the flange of the exhaust manifold, an actuator, a thermal vacuum switch (TVS), and a vacuum solenoid. The TVS is on the right side of the engine forward of the oil pressure switch. The TVS is normally closed and sensitive to oil temperature.

The V8 EFE system consists of an EFE valve at the flange of the exhaust manifold, an actuator, and a thermal vacuum switch. The TVS is located in the coolant outlet housing and directly controls vacuum.

In both systems, manifold vacuum is applied to the actuator, which in turn, closes the EFE valve. This routes hot exhaust gases to the base of the carburetor. When coolant (V8) or oil (six cylinder) temperatures reach a set limit, vacuum is denied to the actuator allowing an internal spring to return the actuator to its normal position, opening the EFE valve.

1983–84 4.8 L V8s use a manifold mounted thermostatic spring to actuate the EFE valve, much as was done with the traditional heat riser valve.

DIAGNOSIS

1. Allow the engine to cool until it is below 105°F. On some V8 engines, the EFE valve actuator arm is protected by a two-piece metal cover. Remove the cover if so equipped.

2. Start the engine while watching the EFE valve. The actuator link should be pulled into the diaphragm housing. If so, continue to run the engine to check that the valve opens before the engine is warmed up—see the last two steps.

3. If the valve fails to close, disconnect the vacuum line running to it and apply a vacuum of at least 10 in. HG with a hand pump or by tapping directly to engine manifold vacuum with the engine idling. If the valve still does not close, it could be seized. Lubricate it with a manifold heat valve lubricant, and then retest it. If it does close, test it further by removing the source of vacuum and sealing off the vacuum line. The valve should remain closed for at least 20 seconds—if not, replace it. A valve which is not seized and still does not close has a bad vacuum diaphragm and must be replaced.

4. If the valve closes when external vacuum is applied, check the rest of the system for loose, kinked, pinched, plugged or cracked hoses and repair or replace parts as required. Also make sure vacuum is get-ting through the TVS or EFE vacuum solenoid (with engine still below 105°F.). Replace the thermostatic control device if necessary.

5. Warm up the engine to operating temperature. If the valve does not open, check the engine thermostat to ensure the engine reaches operating temperature; check the TVS or EFE solenoid to ensure vacuum is cut off before the engine reaches operating temperature; and check the valve to

Chevrolet/GMC EFE systems use either a TVS or EFE vacuum solenoid to shut off the EFE valve when the engine warms up

Diverter valve operation

Typical exhaust heated control valve vacuum circuit using a ported vacuum coolant switch

Diverter valve with internal muffler

ensure it is not mechanically bound in the cold position. If these checks do not reveal the reason the valve won't open, there is no air bleed effect in the diaphragm and the valve must be replaced.

Air Injection Systems

A belt-driven air pump supplies air to small tubes positioned in the exhaust port near each exhaust valve. The air mixes with un-

Three types of diverter valves: A. Air by-pass valve; B. Closed air by-pass valve; C. Timed air by-pass valve with vacuum vent

burned hydrocarbons in the exhaust and the hydrocarbons actually burn up in the exhaust system. Air injection systems are used on engines with catalytic converters, so that the converter gets enough air to keep the reaction going.

Plumbing on air injection systems varies considerably.

A check valve is used between the pump and the exhaust port nozzle to keep hot exhaust gases from traveling up the plumbing and destroying the pump. V8s use two check valves.

An anti-backfire valve, also called bypass valve or diverter valve, is used between the pump and the check valve. Usually, the diverter valve is mounted on the pump or near it. A small sensing hose connects the diverter valve to intake manifold vacuum. When the vacuum rises during deceleration, the diverter valve opens, and sends the pump air into the atmosphere. This prevents the overrich deceleration mixture in the exhaust system from exploding or backfiring out the tailpipe.

Some models started using a diverter valve that has the small hose connection on the end instead of the side. The older diverter valve was normally in the running position, but the new one is normally in the dump position. In other words, the old valve allowed the air to pass through the engine exhaust ports regardless of whether the small sensing line was hooked up. The new valve, being normally in the dump position, must have the small sensing line hooked up to manifold vacuum, which pulls the valve mechanism from the dump position into the normal running position.

Unfortunately, the new style valve will not go into the dump position automatically during deceleration. To get the valve to dump, a vacuum differential valve (VDV) is connected in the sensing line. Manifold vacuum goes through the VDV and then to the diverter valve. When the manifold vacuum increases during deceleration, the VDV

closes the sensing line. This shuts off the vacuum to the diverter valve, and the valve goes into the dump position.

A further refinement of this, is to connect the sensing line to ported (above the throttle plates) vacuum instead of manifold vacuum and eliminate the VDV. In this situation, the diverter valve only receives vacuum above idle, because the vacuum port in the carburetor throat is above the throttle plate at idle. So whenever the engine idles, the diverter valve goes to the dump position. It also dumps during deceleration, because the throttle at that time is in the idle position.

Some systems have a delay valve, similar to a spark delay valve, in the sensing hose. This delays for a few seconds the drop in vacuum when the throttle closes, so that the air is not dumped every time the driver takes his foot off the throttle in traffic.

Temperature controls are also used in the sensing hose hookup. Usually, the temperature valve shuts the vacuum off when the engine is cold, so that the pump air doesn't go to the engine exhaust ports until the engine warms up.

An idle vacuum valve is used to operate in conjunction with the vacuum delay valve, to provide backfire control, full time idle dumping of secondary air during cold engine operation, deceleration or extended idle periods of ½ to 2 minutes or more. The valve also provides cold temperature protection for the catalyst and a cold EGR valve lockout.

AIR PUMP TESTS

CAUTION

Do not hammer on, pry or bend the pump housing while tightening the drive belt or testing the pump.

Before proceeding with the tests, check the pump drive belt tension.

If the belt squeals when the engine is running, the pump may be dragging or

Typical air injection system

seized. Remove the belt and turn the pump by hand to check for seizure. Disregard any chirping, squealing, or rolling sounds from inside the pump when turning it by hand, as these are normal.

Check the hoses and connections for leaks. Hissing or a blast of air is indicative of a leak. Soapy water, applied lightly around the area in question, is a good method for detecting leaks.

To test air output, disconnect the air hose from the pump wherever it is convenient. If you disconnect it from one check valve on a V8, the other hose should also be disconnected and plugged for the test. Run the engine at idle and feel the blast of air from the hose with your hand. Increase the engine speed to 1500 rpm and feel the blast of air again. If the blast increases, and is steady, the pump is okay.

PUMP NOISE DIAGNOSIS

The air pump is normally noisy; as engine speed increases, the noise of the pump will rise in pitch. The rolling sound the pump bearings make is normal. However, if this sound becomes objectionable at certain speeds, the pump may be defective and will have to be replaced.

A continual hissing sound from the air pump pressure relief valve at idle indicates a defective valve. Replace the relief valve.

If the pump rear bearing fails, a continual knocking sound will be heard. Since the rear bearing is not separately replaceable, the pump will have to be replaced as an assembly.

ANTI-BACKFIRE VALVE TESTS

Detach the hose, which runs from the by-pass valve to the check valve.

AIR INJECTION REACTOR SYSTEM DIAGNOSIS CHART

Condition	Possible Cause	Correction
No air supply—accelerate engine to 1500 rpm and observe air flow from hoses. If the flow increases as the rpm's increase, the pump is functioning normally. If not, check possible cause.	Loose drive belt.	Tighten to specifications.
	Leaks in supply hose.	Locate leak and repair.
	Leak at fittings.	Tighten or replace clamps.
	Air expelled through by-pass valve:	
	a. Connect a vacuum line directly from engine manifold vacuum to by-pass valve	If this corrects the problem, go to step b. If not, replace air by-pass valve.
	b. Connect vacuum line from engine manifold vacuum source to by-pass valve through vacuum diffential valve directly, by passing the differential vacuum delay and separator valve.	If this corrects the problem, check differential vacuum, delay and separator valve and vacuum source line for plugging. Replace as required. If it doesn't, replace vacuum differential valve.
	Check valve inoperative.	Disconnect hose and blow through hose toward check valve. If air passes, function is normal. If air can be sucked from check valve, replace check valve.
	Pump failure.	Replace pump.
Excessive pump noise, chirping, rumbling, knocking, loss of engine performance.	Leak in hose.	Locate source of leak using soap solution and correct.
	Loose hose	Reassemble and replace or tighten hose clamp.
	Hose touching other engine parts.	Adjust hose position.
	Vacuum differential valve inoperative.	Replace vacuum differential valve.
	By-pass valve inoperative.	Replace by-pass valve.
	Pump mounting fasteners loose.	Tighten mounting screws as specified.
	Pump failure.	Replace pump.
	Check valve inoperative.	Replace check valve.
Excessive belt noise.	Loose belt.	Tighten to spec.
	Seized pump.	Replace pump.
Excessive pump noise. Chirping.	Insufficient break-in.	Run vehicle 10–15 miles at interstate speeds. Recheck.
Centrifugal filter fan damaged or broken.	Mechanical damage.	Replace centrifugal filter fan.
Exhaust tube bent or damaged.	Mechanical damage.	Replace exhaust tube.
Poor idle or driveability.	A defective A.I.R. system cannot cause poor idle or driveability.	Do not replace A.I.R. system.

Connect a tachometer to the engine. With the engine running at normal idle speed, check to see that air is flowing from the bypass valve hose connection.

Speed the engine up, so that it is running at 1,500–2,000 rpm. Allow the throttle to snap shut. The flow of air from the bypass valve at the check valve hose connection should stop momentarily and air should then flow from the exhaust port on the valve body or the silencer assembly.

Let the throttle snap shut several times. If the flow of air is not diverted into the atmosphere from the valve exhaust port or if it fails to stop flowing from the hose connection, check the vacuum lines and connections. If these are tight, either the bypass valve or one of the accessory valves in the small sensing hose is defective and must be replaced.

A leaking diaphragm will cause the air to flow out both the hose connection and the exhaust port at the same valve.

Late model systems should stop flowing at idle, as described earlier. If not, the by-pass valve or accessory valve is defective.

CHECK VALVE TEST

Remove the hose from the check valve. With the engine running at 1,500 rpm in Park or Neutral, hold the back of your hand near the check valve to test for exhaust gas leakage. If the valve leaks, it must be replaced.

NOTE: Vibration and flutter of the valve at idle is a normal condition caused by exhaust pulsations. It does not mean that the valve is defective.

VACUUM DIFFERENTIAL VALVE TEST

Disconnect the small sensing hose at the bypass valve and connect a vacuum gauge to the hose. With the engine idling in Park or Neutral, the gauge should read full manifold vacuum.

Run the engine at a steady 2500 rpm in Park or Neutral and release the throttle. As the engine decelerates, the vacuum gauge should drop close to zero, then return to full manifold vacuum as the engine speed drops to idle. If not, the VDV is defective and must be replaced.

NOTE: The small hose nozzle should be connected to manifold vacuum.

AIR PUMP FILTER REPLACEMENT

Several American truck brands employ a standard type of air pump filter that requires periodic replacement. Proceed as follows:

1. Disconnect the air and vacuum hoses from the diverter valve.

2. Loosen the pump pivot and adjusting bolts and remove the drive belt.

3. Remove the pivot and adjusting bolts from the pump. Remove the pump and the diverter valve as an assembly.

— CAUTION —

Do not clamp the pump in a vise or use a hammer or pry bar on the pump housing.

4. To change the filter, break the plastic fan from the hub. It is seldom possible to remove the fan without breaking it.

5. Remove the remaining portion of the fan filter from the pump hub. Be careful that filter fragments do not enter the air intake hole.

6. Position the new centrifugal fan filter on the pump hub. Place the pump pulley against the fan filter and install the securing screws. Torque the screws alternately to 95 in. lbs. and the fan filter will be pressed onto the pump hub.

7. Install the pump on the engine and adjust its drive belt.

ISUZU AIR SWITCHING VALVE

This valve is designed to switch air flow from the air pump. It is operated by vacuum and air pump pressure which are switched by a vacuum switching valve.

While air pump pressure acts in the diaphragm chamber "B" (see illustration) through the vacuum switching valve, this

Typical air injection tubes

Typical air injection system operation

Typical air injection system with an idle vacuum valve used to control converter overheating

Typical air diverter valve operation

valve flows the air from the air pump to the check valve. When manifold vacuum switched by the vacuum switching valve acts in the diaphragm chamber "B" the valve closes the air passage to the check valve, and at the same time opens the port to the atmosphere, so the air from the pump is diverted to the atmosphere.

MAZDA ROTARY AIR INJECTION SYSTEM

The air injection system used on the Mazda rotary engine differs from one used on a conventional piston engine in two respects:

1. Air is supplied not only to burn the gases in the exhaust ports, it is also used to cool the thermal reactor.

2. A three-way "air control valve" is used in place of the conventional antibackfire and diverter valves. It contains an air cut-out valve, a relief valve, and a safety valve.

Air is supplied to the system by a normal vane-type air pump. The air flows from the pump to the air control valve where it is routed to the air injection nozzles, to cool the thermal reactor or, in case of a system malfunction, to the air cleaner. A check valve, located beneath the air control valve seat, prevents the back-flow of hot exhaust gases into the air injection system, in case of loss of air pressure.

Air injection nozzles are used to feed air into the exhaust ports, just as in a conventional piston engine.

Air Control Valve Test

CAUTION

When testing the air control valve, avoid touching the thermal reactor as severe burns will result.

Typical rotary engine emission control system

1. Test the air control valve solenoid as follows:

a. Turn the ignition switch off and on. A click should be heard coming from the solenoid. If no sound is audible, check the solenoid wiring.

b. If no defect is found in the solenoid wiring, connect the solenoid directly to the truck's battery. If the solenoid still does not click, it is defective and must be replaced. If the solenoid is functioning, then check the components of the air flow control system, below.

2. Start the engine and run it at idle speed. The pressure gauge should read 0.37–0.75 psi. No air should leak from the two outlets which were unplugged.

3. Increase the engine speed to 3,500 rpm (3,000—automatic transmission). The pressure gauge should now read 1.2–2.8 psi and the two outlets still should not be leaking air.

4. Return the engine to idle.

5. Disconnect the solenoid wiring. Air should not flow from the outlet marked "A", but not from the outlet marked "B". The pressure gauge reading should remain the same as in step 2.

6. Reconnect the solenoid.

MAZDA AIR INJECTION SYSTEM DIAGNOSIS CHART

Problem	Cause	Solution
Noisy drive belt	Loose belt	Tighten belt
	Seized pump	Replace
Noisy pump	Leaking hose	Trace and fix leak
	Loose hose	Tighten hose clamp
	Hose contacting other parts	Reposition hose
	Air control or check valve failure	Replace
	Pump mounting loose	Tighten securing bolts
	Defective pump	Replace
No air supply	Loose belt	Tighten belt
	Leak in hose or at fitting	Trace and fix leak
	Defective air control valve	Replace
	Defective check valve	Replace
	Defective pump	Replace
Exhaust backfire	Vacuum or air leaks	Trace and fix leak
	Defective air control valve	Replace
	Sticking choke	Service choke
	Choke setting rich	Adjust choke

Isuzu air switching valve

Rotary engine thermal reactor cooling circuit

7. If the relief valve is faulty, air sent from the air pump will flow into the cooling passages of the thermal reactor when the engine is at idle speed.

8. If the safety valve is faulty, air will flow into the air cleaner when the engine is idling.

9. Replace the air control valve if it fails to pass any one of the above tests. Remember to disconnect the pressure gauge.

Check Valve Test

1. Run engine at operating temperature.
2. Disconnect air hose at air control valve.
3. Run engine at 1500 rpm. No exhaust leakage should be felt at the air inlet fitting of the air control valve.

Check Valve Replacement

1. Perform the air control valve removal procedure. Be sure to pay attention to the CAUTION.
2. Remove the check valve seat.
3. Withdraw the valve plate and spring. Install the check valve in the reverse order of removal.

Air Injection Nozzle Replacement

1. Remove the gravel shield from underneath the truck.
2. Perform the oil pan removal procedure as detailed in Engine Lubrication.
3. Unbolt the air injection nozzles from both of the rotor housings.

Nozzle installation is performed in the reverse order of removal.

MAZDA THERMAL REACTOR

A thermal reactor is used in place of a conventional exhaust manifold. It is used to oxidize unburned hydrocarbons and carbon monoxide before they can be released into the atmosphere.

If the engine speed exceeds 4,000 rpm, or if the car is decelerating, the air control valve diverts air into passages in the thermal reactor housing in order to cool the reactor.

A one-way valve prevents hot exhaust gases from flowing back into the air injection system. The valve is located at the reactor air intake.

Inspection

--------- CAUTION ---------
Perform thermal reactor inspection only after the reactor has cooled sufficiently to prevent severe burns.

1. Examine the reactor housing for cracks or other signs of damage.
2. Remove the air supply hose from the one-way valve. Insert a screwdriver into the valve and test the butterfly for smooth operation. Replace the valve if necessary.

3. If the valve is functioning properly, connect the hose to it again.

NOTE: Remember to check the components of the air injection system which are related to the thermal reactor.

Removal and Installation

Thermal reactor removal and installation procedures are given in the Engine Mechanical section of the truck section.

MAZDA AIR FLOW CONTROL SYSTEM

The control box is located beneath the dash, next to the fuse box and the thermodetector is behind the radiator grille.

Component Testing

NO. 1 THERMOSENSOR

NOTE: Begin this test procedure with the engine cold.

1. Remove the air cleaner.
2. Examine the no. 1 thermosensor, which is located next to the thermostat housing, for leakage around the boot and for signs of wax leakage.
3. Disconnect the multiconnector from the thermosensor and place the prods of an ohmmeter on the thermosensor terminals.

The ohmmeter should read over 7 k-ohms with the engine cold and less than 2.3 k-ohms after the engine has been warmed up.

4. Replace the thermosensor with a new one, if the reading on the ohmmeter is not within specifications.
5. If the no. 1 thermosensor is functioning properly, proceed with the appropriate test for the thermodetector below.

THERMODETECTOR

1. Unfasten the thermodetector connections.
2. Connect the test prods of an ohmmeter to the leads coming out of the thermodetector.
3. If the ohmmeter reading is below 200 k-ohms, the thermodetector is functioning satisfactorily.
4. Replace the thermodetector if it is defective and proceed with the vacuum switch if it is not.

THERMODETECTOR RESISTANCE SPECIFICATIONS

Ambient Temperature (°F)	Resistance (k-ohms ± 5%)
−4	10.0
+32	3.0
+68	1.2
+105	0.5

Component Removal and Installation

NO. 1 THERMOSENSOR

1. Remove the air cleaner assembly.
2. If necessary, remove the starter motor as detailed under "Engine Electrical" or the deceleration control valve (see below).
3. Unplug the thermosensor multiconnector.
4. Withdraw the boot from the thermosensor.
5. Unfasten its securing nuts and remove the thermosensor.

Installation is performed in the reverse order of removal.

CONTROL BOX

--------- CAUTION ---------
Be sure that the ignition switch is turned off to prevent damage to the control box.

1. Working from underneath the instrument panel, locate and disconnect the control box multiconnector.
2. Remove the screws which secure the control box.
3. Remove the control box.

Installation is performed in the reverse order of removal.

NO. 2 THERMOSENSOR

1. Drain the engine oil into a large, clean container for reuse.
2. Unfasten the connector from the No. 2 thermosensor.
3. Unscrew the thermosensor from the oil pan.

Installation is performed in the reverse order of removal.

NO. 2 CONTROL BOX

The No. 2 control box is located in the luggage compartment next to the No. 1 control box. Its removal and installation are performed in the same manner as the no. 1 control box.

Pulse Air Injection Reactor Systems

GM PAIR

The Pulse Air Injection Reactor (PAIR) system is installed on the small inline 6 cylinder engine, used in General Motors light duty trucks, beginning in 1979. The PAIR system uses no air pump, but relies on the negative and positive exhaust gas impulses to draw fresh air into the exhaust manifold to assist in the further burning of the hydrocarbons (HC) before leaving the tailpipe.

Four individual check valves are used to prevent the exhaust gases from entering the fresh air intake chamber plenums. Two sets of pipes are used, one set in the front section of the exhaust manifold and the second set in the rear section of the exhaust manifold.

Two sets of plenum chambers are used and connected to the carburetor air cleaner by a common hose, for the fresh air intake.

During periods of high engine rpm, the check valves will remain closed to prevent the flow of exhaust gases to the engine air cleaner.

FAILURE DIAGNOSIS

1. Inspect the pulse air valve and pipes for leakage or defective operation, if a hissing noise is heard.

2. If one or more of the check valves are defective, exhaust gases will enter the carburetor area and cause poor drive-ability such as stalling, surge, or poor performance.

INSPECTION OF PULSE AIR INJECTION REACTOR SYSTEM

1. Burned off paint on the rocker arm plenum chambers indicates a defective pulse air valve. Rubber grommets and hoses will deteriorate and can cause a hissing noise.

2. Inspect the carburetor for pieces of rubber hoses or grommets, indicating an overheating of the components.

3. Inspect the operation of the pulse air valve by applying at least 17 in. Hg at the grommet end of the valve. A drop of 6 in. Hg in two seconds is allowed.

COURIER SECONDARY AIR INJECTION SYSTEM

Reed Valve and Air Pipe Assembly

This assembly is the main component of what is termed the secondary air injection system. Vehicles having this system are not equipped with air pumps.

The second system operates by sensing exhaust gas pulsations which in turn causes the reed valve to draw fresh air from the air cleaner and inject the fresh air into the exhaust system. The main advantage of this system is that it eliminates the parasitic horse-

power drain associated with systems using belt driven pumps.

Removal of the reed valve is simply a matter of disconnecting the hose at the valve and unbolting the valve from its mounting bracket.

REED VALVE TESTING

1. Warm the engine to normal operating temperature.

2. Disconnect the inlet hose from the reed valve.

3. Start the engine and allow it to idle.

4. Place your finger over the reed valve inlet. It should be felt that air is being drawn into the valve. Replace the valve if suction is not apparent.

5. Raise the engine rpm to 1500. Exhaust gas should not leak from the reed valve inlet; if it does, replace the valve.

Vacuum Delay Valve(s)

The description of this item is self-explanatory. The vacuum delay valve(s) "fine tunes" the vacuum operation of the Thermactor system for vehicles which are to be used in areas with stringent emission control regulations (e.g.—Calif.). Failure of a vacuum delay valve is extremely rare.

DATSUN AIR INDUCTION SYSTEM

Description

The air induction system is designed to send secondary air to the exhaust manifold, utilizing a vacuum caused by exhaust pulsation in the exhaust manifold.

Datsun air induction valve

The exhaust pressure in the exhaust manifold usually pulsates in response to the opening and closing of the exhaust valve and it decreases below atmospheric pressure periodically.

If a secondary air intake pipe is opened to the atmosphere under vacuum conditions, secondary air can be drawn into the exhaust manifold in proportion to the vacuum.

Therefore, the air induction system reduces CO and HC emissions in exhaust gases. The system consists of two air induction valves, a filter, hoses and E.A.I. tube(s).

Air Induction Valve Case

The air induction valve case consists of two reed valves, a rubber seal and a filter and is attached to the air cleaner. There are two types of air induction valve cases. Type-A is equipped with two hose connectors and is installed on California models, while Type-B is equipped with one connector and is installed on non-California models.

49 states air induction case

California air induction case

Air induction filter

Anti-Backfire Valve

Courier secondary air injection system

Air Induction Valve

Two reed valve type check valves are installed in the air cleaner. When the exhaust pressure is below atmospheric pressure (negative pressure), secondary air is sent to the exhaust manifold.

When the exhaust pressure is above atmospheric pressure, the reed valves prevent secondary air from being sent back to the air cleaner.

Air Induction Valve Filter

The air induction valve filter is installed at the dust side of the air cleaner. It purifies secondary air to be sent to the exhaust manifold.

Air Induction Pipe

The secondary air fed from the air induction valve goes through the E.A.I. pipe to the exhaust manifold.

Anti-Backfire (A.B.) Valve

This valve is actuated by intake manifold vacuum to prevent backfire in the exhaust system at the initial period of deceleration.

At this period, the mixture in the intake manifold becomes too rich to ignite and burn in the combustion chamber and burns easily in the exhaust system with injected air in the exhaust manifold.

The A.B. valve provides air to the intake manifold to make the air-fuel mixture leaner and prevents backfire.

The correct function of this valve reduces hydrocarbon emission during deceleration.

Electronic Ignition System

A change has been made through the model years from the conventional distributors to the electronic ignition systems for more precise ignition control.

Different types are available from the manufacturers, but the operation of the systems are basically the same. Greater dependability, higher secondary voltages and less need for adjustments are the important factors considered in using this system for emission control.

Refer to the individual truck sections and to the Electrical section for expanded information.

DISTRIBUTOR CONTROLS

All distributor controls act in some way to change or eliminate vacuum advance during certain operating conditions. Usually, the control cuts down on the amount of vacuum advance, in effect retarding the spark, so that the exhaust will get hotter and burn up hydrocarbon and carbon monoxide emissions before they go out the tailpipe.

The distributor vacuum advance unit might be connected, according to factory design, to either manifold vacuum or ported (above the throttle plates) carburetor vacuum. Either way, the vacuum spark advance curve is approximately the same for all running conditions above idle. At idle, however, the manifold vacuum hookup results in full advance, while the ported hookup gives zero advance. If the hoses are hooked up the wrong way, the addition or lack of advance will affect idle speed, requiring a readjustment of the throttle position to bring the idle speed back to specifications. When this is done, emissions will usually be high, so it is important to keep the hoses hooked up correctly.

DUAL DIAPHRAGM DISTRIBUTORS

These distributors have two hose connections, one in the normal position, and the other closer to the distributor body. The hose fitting next to the body is for the retard diaphragm, and is connected to manifold vacuum. The retard diaphragm affects the spark only at idle, when there is no vacuum on the advance diaphragm. In effect, the retard diaphragm provides a movable resting place for the advance diaphragm. When ported vacuum is not acting on the advance

diaphragm, it returns to the neutral or no-advance position against the retard diaphragm. At idle, manifold vacuum pulls the retard diaphragm to the retard position, and the advance diaphragm follows along to retard the spark.

Testing Dual Diaphragm Distributors

To test a dual diaphragm distributor, connect a timing light to the engine. Remove the retard hose from the distributor and plug the hose. With the engine running, increase the speed to a fast idle and watch the timing marks. The timing should advance. If not, either the vacuum unit is faulty, the vacuum port is plugged, or there is a temperature control device that is shutting off the vacuum. Apply hand pump or mouth suction vacuum to the advance diaphragm and the timing should advance. If not, the distributor or advance unit must be repaired or replaced. Failure to advance could be caused by a faulty diaphragm or a sticky advance plate.

Remove the advance hose from the vacuum unit and read the timing at normal idle speed. Remove the plug that was inserted in the retard hose, and check for full manifold vacuum at the end of it. If there is no vacuum, temperature controls may be shutting it off.

Connect the hose to the retard diaphragm, or apply vacuum from another source. The timing should immediately retard several degrees. If not, the diaphragm is not working, and the unit must be replaced. Reconnect all hoses as they were originally.

DISTRIBUTOR VACUUM DECELERATION VALVE

Its purpose is to advance the spark during deceleration, by sending full manifold vacuum to the vacuum advance unit. At all other times the vacuum advance unit receives ported (above the throttle plates) carburetor vacuum.

Three checks should be made on the valve: the amount of vacuum at the distributor, any valve leaks, and the adjustment. To check the amount of vacuum at the distributor, use a T-fitting and a short length of vacuum hose to connect a vacuum gauge into the distributor vacuum line near the distributor. At idle, with the engine fully warmed up, the vacuum on the gauge should be less than 1 Hg. If the gauge shows more than 1 Hg. the idle speed is too fast, or the valve is leaking. To check for a leak, remove the large manifold vacuum hose on the side of the valve. If the vacuum drops, the valve is leaking and must be replaced. If the vacuum stays high, reduce the engine idle speed so that the port in the carburetor is covered.

To check the valve adjustment, connect the manifold vacuum hose and run the engine at 2000 rpm for 5 seconds. Then re-

Cross section of an idle vacuum valve

Pulse Air Injection System (PAIR)

Dual diaphragm vacuum control

lease the throttle. The distributor vacuum should go over 16 in. Hg. and stay there for about one second. Within about three seconds after you release the throttle, the distributor vacuum should drop to below 6 in. Hg. If the carburetor is equipped with a dashpot to make the throttle close slowly, the time may be about one second longer. If the time is too long, remove the cover on the valve and turn the screw clockwise to reduce the time. To increase the time, turn the screw counterclockwise. If the valve will not adjust properly, it must be replaced, and the new valve adjusted to specifications.

SPARK DELAY VALVE

This small valve is connected between the carburetor and the distributor vacuum advance, so that the ported (above the throttle plates) vacuum to the distributor must pass through the valve. A restriction in the valve delays the vacuum applied to the vacuum advance unit so that the advance comes in slowly. When there is no vacuum at the carburetor port, as during idle or wide open throttle a check valve inside the spark delay valve opens and dumps the vacuum so that the vacuum advance unit returns to the no-advance position without any delay.

Spark delay valves can be tested for correct operation and leaks with a source of vacuum such as a hand vacuum pump or a running engine, and a vacuum gauge. Connect the vacuum gauge to the distributor side of the valve, and the vacuum source to the other side. The gauge should rise slowly until it reads the amount of vacuum available. The time to rise to the maximum reading should be from one to 28 seconds. If the vacuum gauge does not read anything, the valve is plugged. If the vacuum reads instantly, without any delay, the valve is open. In either case, the spark delay valve must be replaced. To test the check valve part of the spark delay valve, remove the vacuum source and the vacuum gauge should drop instantly to zero without any delay. If there is any delay, the spark delay valve is defective and must be replaced.

TRANSMISSION CONTROLLED SPARK

The purpose of the transmission controlled spark is to eliminate vacuum spark advance in the lower gears. When the transmission is in high gear, vacuum spark advance is allowed for better gasoline milage and part throttle response. This system was used during the 1975–1976 model years on most light duty models and continued on some California and High Altitude vehicles in later years.

Testing TCS Systems

Testing the system is done by connecting a vacuum gauge to the distributor vacuum line with a long hose so you can put it through the window into the front seat and see it while driving. There should be no vacuum in the lower gears on a warm engine, but after the transmission shifts into a gear that allows vacuum advance, you should see vacuum on the gauge. Engines that run their distributors on manifold vacuum will show vacuum at all times when in the proper gear. Engines that use ported

Carburetor-control valve-distributor relationship

Typical transmission controlled spark system

(above the throttle plates) vacuum will show vacuum in the proper gear only when the throttle is open. If you don't get vacuum when you should, test the individual units in the system.

Vacuum solenoids can be tested by disconnecting all wiring and connecting hot and ground wires to the solenoid terminals, to make it open or close. You should be able to blow through the solenoid when it is open, but not when it's closed. Because solenoids exist in both normally open and normally closed designs, it is important to use the right solenoid. If the wrong solenoid is used, the system will work backwards, giving advance in the lower gears but not in high. The same goes for the transmission switch, which exists in both normally open and normally closed designs. The term "normally open" means that the solenoid or switch is open when it is not energized or activated. In the case of a vacuum solenoid, normally open means that if you were holding the solenoid in your hand without any wires connected to it, the vacuum passages would be open, allowing vacuum to pass. In the case of a transmission switch, the term "normally open" refers to the electrical path, which is "open" or "off" so that it will not conduct electricity. Normally closed, of course, means that the electric contacts are closed so that the current can pass. But normally closed on a vacuum solenoid means that the vacuum passage is blocked so the vacuum can't get through.

TEMPERATURE ACTIVATED VACUUM (TAV) AND COLD TEMPERATURE ACTIVATED VACUUM (CTAV) SYSTEMS

This system switches the vacuum source back and forth between the carburetor spark port and EGR port, according to the air temperature. A 3-nozzle vacuum solenoid is used. Below approximately 55°F. outside air temperature, the temperature switch is

open, and the solenoid is not energized. In this position, the solenoid connects the spark port to the vacuum advance unit. Above 55°F. the temperature switch closes, and energizes the solenoid. In this position, the solenoid connects the EGR port to the vacuum advance unit.

The temperature switch is located in the air cleaner, and a latching relay is on the firewall. Once the temperature switch has closed, the relay latches so that any sudden rush of cold air through the air cleaner will not cycle the solenoid on and off. The latching relay keeps the solenoid energized as long as the ignition switch is on. When the ignition switch is turned off, the relay unlatches and the system is ready for the next start, whether the air temperature is hot or cold. If the air at the temperature switch is over 55°F. the latching relay will come on when the ignition switch is turned on.

Testing

Test the system with a vacuum gauge connected to the vacuum advance hose at the distributor. With the temperature above 65°F. (to be sure the temperature switch has closed) you should be getting vacuum from the EGR port. If you disconnect the EGR port hose and the vacuum drops, you know the system is working. When making a cold test, the vacuum should come from the spark port hose, so disconnecting that hose should make the vacuum drop. Because both ports are above the throttle plate, the throttle must be opened slightly to get vacuum at the hose.

Identifying the spark port and EGR ports on the carburetor is easy if they are marked. If there is no marking on the carburetor, connect two vacuum gauges, one to each port. At idle you should not have any vacuum. If you do have vacuum, it usually means the engine is idling too fast. Close the throttle slightly to slow down the idle and the vacuum should drop to almost zero.

When you open the throttle, you will see vacuum on one gauge before the other. The gauge that gets vacuum first is connected to the spark port.

ORIFICE SPARK ADVANCE CONTROL (OSAC)

It is a mechanism that delays the application of vacuum to the distributor vacuum advance unit. When the throttle is opened, the carburetor port is exposed to vacuum. This vacuum goes through a hose to the OSAC valve, and then to the distributor vacuum advance. The OSAC valve is sometimes mounted on the firewall, and sometimes on the air cleaner. Inside the OSAC valve is a calibrated orifice that delays the vacuum as much as 27 seconds, depending on the calibration of the valve.

Some OSAC valves have temperature control that senses the temperature inside the air cleaner or inside the plenum chamber behind the firewall, depending on where the valve is mounted. If the valve contains temperature control, it will be wide open below 60°F. bypassing the orifice and allowing vacuum advance without any delay. Above 60°F. the bypass closes and the delay takes over.

Testing

To test the valve, connect a vacuum gauge to the DIST connection on the valve. With the engine idling, you should have no reading on the gauge. If there is a reading, the engine is idling too fast. With the engine idling, open the throttle to a fast idle, and hold it steady. The vacuum on the gauge will rise slowly until it reaches a maximum reading. If not, there is something wrong with the system, and you should check out the hoses and the carburetor port, or replace the valve is necessary.

VACUUM REDUCER VALVE

Inserted between the manifold vacuum source and the distributor, this valve reduces the vacuum acting on the advance diaphragm by about 3 in. Hg. This valve is always used on a system that includes a distributor thermal vacuum switch. The vacuum advance unit operates on ported (above the throttle plates) vacuum, except when the engine overheats above 225°F. This opens the thermal vacuum switch and sends full manifold vacuum through the vacuum reducer valve to the advance unit. Thus, the vacuum reducer valve is only operating when the engine is overheated.

To test the valve, connect a vacuum gauge to the TVS nozzle, and a hand vacuum pump to the MAN nozzle. When you pump up 15 in. Hg. vacuum on the hand pump, the vacuum on the separate gauge should be 3 to 4 in. Hg. lower. Both gauges should hold the vacuum without leakdown. If not, the valve is defective and must be replaced.

RETARD DELAY VALVE

When the throttle is suddenly opened, engine vacuum drops immediately, and this causes the vacuum advance to move quickly

Cold temperature activated vacuum system

from the advance position to the neutral or no advance position. A retard delay valve is a restriction with a one-way check valve. It allows the vacuum to act on the vacuum advance unit normally, but when the vacuum drops, the delay valve traps the vacuum in the advance unit and lets it out slowly. It takes several seconds for the advance unit to return to the neutral position.

Some models have the retard delay valve hooked up so that it only operates when the engine is cold. At normal operating temperature the delay is bypassed.

Testing of the delay valve can be done with a hand vacuum pump. Connect the pump to the MAN side of the valve, or the side that connects to the vacuum source on the engine. Connect a separate vacuum gauge to the other side of the valve. When the hand pump is operated, the vacuum will rise on both the pump gauge and the separate gauge equally. When the release is pulled, the pump gauge will drop to zero immediately, but the separate gauge will take several seconds to drop to zero. If it doesn't work that way, the delay valve is defective, and must be replaced.

COLD START SPARK ADVANCE

A coolant sensitive vacuum switch (PVS) is combined with a delay valve (distributor retard control valve) to provide retard delay when the engine coolant is below 128°F. The hose routing is set up so that the vacuum advance unit operates on manifold vacuum through the retard delay valve when the engine is cold, and on ported vacuum through a spark delay valve when the engine is warm. The system also has an overheat PVS that switches the vacuum advance over to manifold vacuum (through the spark delay valve) when the engine coolant gets over 235°F.

Testing the spark delay valve is covered in this section under Spark Delay Valve. Testing for the distributor retard control valve is the same as for the retard delay valve in this section.

When the 128° PVS is cold, connection No. 2 is blocked and D and 1 are connected. When it is over 128°F No. 1 is blocked and D and 2 are connected.

Carburetor Choke Controls

NON-ELECTRIC CHOKE

A non-electric choke uses a "stove" on the exhaust manifold or a well on the intake manifold to provide heat. When the well is used, the choke coil is surrounded by the warm intake manifold, heated by the exhaust crossover passage. When the stove is used, the choke housing is connected to engine vacuum, and a long tube pulls the heated air from the stove into the choke housing to heat up the choke coil and cause the choke to open as the engine warms up. When an electric choke is used, it can be in addition to all the above, or it can be the only source of choke heat, depending on the design.

ELECTRIC CHOKE

The electric choke has a small heater next to the choke coil. This heater receives its current from different sources, depending on the car maker.

Ford Motor Company and Jeep chokes are powered from the alternator "center tap," which produces about 7 volts. As the alternator is only putting out voltage when the engine is running, the electric choke is automatically shut off when the engine is off. It is important that the choke is connected only to the special "center tap" provided on the alternator. The description "center tap" refers to the construction of the alternator wiring, and not to the location of the connection.

Inside is a thermostatic switch that turns on the heating element at approximately 80°F. Above that, the element stays on as long as the engine is running. The 80°F. figure was selected because the engine is warm enough at that temperature to keep running without the choke. When the heater comes on, the choke opens very quickly. When the engine is shut off and cools down, the choke switch may stay on to as low as 65°F. at the choke housing. On a warm restart, where the choke switch was still on, the heating element would heat up the choke and open it shortly after the engine started.

Chrysler Corporation vehicles with an electric choke use a well type choke, which receives heat both from the intake manifold and the electric choke heater. A separate choke control unit is mounted on top of the

Electric choke assembly—Used with a choke stove

Non-electric choke assembly using a manifold heated choke stove

Manifold heat type choke assembly

intake manifold and connected to the heater with a wire. This wire disconnects at the choke control unit only, not at the heater.

Choke control units may be single and double stage. The double stage is recognized by the external resistor alongside the unit. The single stage unit turns on the choke heater at approximately 60°F. and off at 110°F. The double stage unit keeps the heater on below 60°F. but the current runs through the resistor. At approximately 60°F. the resistor is taken out of the circuit and the heater gets full current. At 110°F. the control unit turns the heater off.

Testing can be done with a non-powered test light on the choke terminal to find out if the heater is on or off. The ignition switch must be on. If the light glows, you know the control unit is on. On two-stage units, the light will glow dimly when the resistor is in the circuit, and brightly when the resistor is out. The current to the control unit

comes from the ignition switch, and there is no fuse.

Chevrolet and GMC use an electric choke that is mounted on the carburetor. The choke has a dual element behind the coil spring. Whenever the engine is running, the choke heater is in operation. Below 50–70°F. a bimetal snap disc in the choke cover turns off the large section of the heating element so that only the small section gives off heat. Above 50–70°F. the disc switches on the large heating element for faster choke opening.

Current to the choke is controlled by a three-terminal oil pressure switch. One of the terminals is a ground for the red oil pressure light on the instrument panel. The other two terminals are a switch in series between the ignition switch and the choke heater. Oil pressure operates the switch so that the choke gets current only when the engine is running. The circuit is fused

through the backup light or transmission fuse in the fuse block.

NOTE: Failure of the choke heater circuit will cause the oil pressure light to go on.

IDLE ENRICHMENT SYSTEM

In order to reduce the cold engine stalling, a metering system is used to relate to the carburetor, rather than to the choke. The system enriches the carburetor mixtures in the curb idle and fast idle modes. The carburetor will have the complete idle system enriched during periods of cold to semi-cold operating conditions. The idle enrichment valve is manifold vacuum controlled and opens or closes a passageway that admits extra air to the idle circuit.

Some models have a coolant temperature control valve, mounted on a coolant pas-

Typical feedback carburetor and electronic control system

sage and connected by hose between the manifold vacuum source and the idle enrichment valve. When the engine is cold, the valve is open and allows vacuum to operate the idle enrichment valve to richen the idle fuel mixture. When the engine warms up, the valve closes and cuts off the vacuum to the coolant temperature valve.

A vacuum solenoid may be included in the vacuum hose arrangement to provide EGR valve delay while the engine is cold.

Testing

Testing the system can be done on a cold engine by disconnecting the hose at the carburetor and connecting a vacuum gauge to the hose. Start the engine and note the length of time that vacuum appears on the gauge. At the end of the timed period, the gauge should drop to zero. Allow the engine to warm up to operating temperature and make the test again. This time you should not see any vacuum on the gauge, because the CCIE (coolant control idle enrichment), valve should be closed. If there is no timer, you will see vacuum for several minutes after a cold start, until the engine warms up.

To check the effect of the idle enrichment use a hand vacuum pump on the idle enrichment valve on the carburetor. With vacuum applied, the valve will be closed, richening the idle, and changing the idle speed. Release the vacuum and the speed should go back where it was. If there is no speed change, either the valve is not working, or a carburetor passage is blocked with dirt. The valve should also hold vacuum without leaking down.

Electronic Fuel Mixture Control Systems

The prime purpose of this system is to permit the use of a three-way catalyst, which improves driveability while maintaining emissions levels. The heart of the system is a catalyst composed of metals which not only oxidize unburnt hydrocarbons and CO, but reduce NO—nitrogen oxide emissions.

While the ordinary catalyst simply speeds the burning or combining with oxygen of CO and hydrocarbons, this system actually uses CO, a compound which has a strong affinity for oxygen to draw the oxygen from NO—the basic nitrogen oxide found in auto exhaust. Each molecule of CO becomes CO_2, by drawing one atom of oxygen from an NO molecule—a combination of one oxygen and one nitrogen. The system uses a catalyst to make this reaction occur much faster than it would under ordinary conditions.

The exact amount of oxygen necessary to oxidize all the CO produced in the combustion chambers must be present—and no more. Less will leave CO in the tailpipe, while more will leave NO. That's why the system must use an oxygen sensor. This is located in the tailpipe and, via a stepper motor, adds fresh air to the main circuit of the carburetor, reducing or increasing the added air as necessary to maintain perfect mixture. While most of these systems use an EGR valve, less exhaust gas must be recirculated because of what happens in the tailpipe. And, because the system uses both the oxygen present in nitrogen-oxides and oxygen from air added via an air pump to finish off the combustion process in the catalyst, the mixture conditions are pretty rich in the combustion chambers. The result is

EGR VALVE

AIR CHARGE TEMPERATURE (ACT) SENSOR

EGR VALVE POSITION (EVP) SENSOR

THROTTLE KICKER SOLENOID

EGR VENT/ EGR CONTROL (EGRC/EGRV) SOLENOID VALVES ASSEMBLY

THROTTLE KICKER ACTUATOR

IGNITION MODULE (IM)

THROTTLE POSITION (TP) SENSOR

EXHAUST GAS OXYGEN (EGO) SENSOR

ENGINE COOLANT TEMPERATURE (ECT) SENSOR

THERMACTOR AIR BYPASS AND DIVERTER (TAB/TAD) SOLENOID VALVES ASSEMBLY

BAROMETRIC/MANIFOLD ABSOLUTE PRESSURE (B/MAP) SENSOR

THROTTLE BODY

CANISTER PURGE (CANP) SOLENOID VALVE

CRANKSHAFT POSITION (CP) SENSOR

EFI wiring and vacuum diagram

smooth running and top performance if everything is working right.

While rough running may make you suspect that this system is performing erratically, you should not condemn it until a thorough check of all the car's basic running systems has been made. This is because the stepper motor control of mixture has only a very small leeway—it can only adjust mixture within a very small range. Dirt in the fuel filter or a carburetor passage, improperly set ignition timing or a bad plug or wire would be more than enough to create conditions for which the system could not possibly correct. In fact, if the symptoms are severe at all, it's almost a sure indication that the electronic mixture control system can't be at fault. Severe hesitation, misfire or hard starting don't come from mixture that's no more than 10% off optimum settings. And, under cold engine conditions or heavy throttle, the system often does not control mixture anyway.

If you're satisfied that all the basic systems are working right, what symptoms might indicate that this system is at fault?

1. Excessive CO reading at the tailpipe.
2. Excessive NO.
3. Catalyst odor (slightly rich mixture).
4. Moderately poor fuel economy (slightly rich mixture).
5. Moderate surge or hesitation (slightly lean mixture).

GM suggests that the first thing to do with their California Computer Command Control System is to very carefully go over every electrical and vacuum connection in the system. A loose connection of either kind can readily duplicate the symptoms of a bad sensor or other component. This is excellent procedure for all such emission controls.

Electrical connectors should be disconnected and inspected for improper installation, bent, broken, or dirty terminals or mating tabs. Clean or straighten terminals or replace connectors as required. Note that such a system may typically contain the following sensors:

1. Throttle position sensor.
2. Barometric/manifold absolute pressure (vacuum) sensor.
3. Exhaust gas oxygen sensor.
4. Crankshaft position (timing) sensor.
5. Engine coolant temperature sensor.
6. Air intake temperature sensor.
7. EGR valve position sensor.

SYSTEM SERVICE

Most of these systems cannot be serviced or even diagnosed without extremely specialized testing equipment; often, only one brand or type of system can be diagnosed with a given tester. We suggest that you confine yourself to making routine checks of basic engine and emissions systems, and then proceed as described above.

REPLACING THE GM PROM—COMPUTER COMMAND CONTROL SYSTEM (CALIFORNIA ONLY)

While many system problems cannot be diagnosed without a complex procedure, you can fairly quickly determine that this system's Programmable Read Only Memory unit is malfunctioning.

First, locate the Assembly Line Diagnostic Link, located under the left side of the dash. Turn the ignition on. Then, jumper B to A (see illustration) which grounds the TEST lead. This will cause trouble code 12

1. JUMPER "B" TO "A" TO DISPLAY DIAGNOSTIC CODES
2. TEST TERMINAL
3. GROUND TERMINAL

VIEW A

Grounding the "TEST" lead of the Assembly Line Diagnostic link

and any other stored codes to flash on the dashboard. A code "51" indicates the PROM is defective.

If there is no code "51", there are also two other indications of a defective PROM. One is a 0 degree dwell reading with the engine hot and running. Another is the engine "HOT" light and "Check Engine" lights coming on simultaneously.

Replace the PROM with the following steps:

1. Locate the ECM under the dash, disconnect the two electrical connectors and remove it.

2. Unscrew and remove the access cover from the ECM. Check that the locator marks for the PROM are aligned. Then, pull the PROM out carefully, so as to avoid bending the connector pins.

3. If pins are bent, the Code 51 may have appeared simply because of a bad connection. Straighten bent pins, reinstall the PROM with locator marks aligned, install the access cover and ECM, reconnect the ECM connectors, and operate the engine to determine whether or not Code 51 reappears.

4. If pins are in good condition and the locator marks for the PROM were properly aligned, install a new PROM. Connect it carefully, making sure locating marks align and inserting it straight to avoid bending the pins.

5. Install the access cover, install the ECM, and reconnect the ECM connectors.

ENGINE CALIBRATION UNIT (PROM) MOUNTED IN CARRIER — SCREW — ACCESS COVER — ECM

The GM ECM contains a PROM unit mounted as shown

The 1983 Isuzu Closed Loop Emission Control System for California, incorporating a typical electronic mixture control system

DIESEL ENGINE EMISSION CONTROLS

Crankcase Depression Regulator

Diesels use a crankcase ventilation system that provides for positive removal and re-burning of blowby gases, much as a PCV system does. The system is different, however, because of the very low vacuum that is present in the unthrottled diesel intake system. Because of the minimal vacuum, no fresh air is drawn in to scavenge the crankcase gases. The gases are drawn out of the crankcase via a line to the oil filler or a valve cover and drawn through the crankcase depression regulator and into the intake manifold. The regulator maintains a constant vacuum—on GM 6.2 liter engines it's 3–4 in. of water. Under conditions of high manifold vacuum, such as high rpm operation, the regulator closes to keep crankcase vacuum from getting too high. Under ideal conditions, it opens to maintain it. The unit will also attempt to compensate for varying intake restriction, for example from a clogged air cleaner.

CDR VALVE

TO INTAKE MANIFOLD

SEAL RING

BACK-UP RING

O-RING

CRANKCASE VENT TUBE

VALLEY COVER GROMMET

TO VALLEY COVER

Exploded view of Ford and IH 6.9 liter CDR valve

A clogged CDR valve, or a valve stuck in the closed position would produce high crankcase pressure and oil leaks or even a blown front seal. A valve stuck in the open position could draw air and dust into the crankcase, especially if there are leaks in valve cover or crankcase gaskets.

To test the system, adapt a suitable gauge to the oil filler tube in place of the cap, making certain there are no air leaks. Make sure the air cleaner is in reasonable condition and that there are no restrictions in the intake system. Idle and accelerate the engine while watching the gauge. A constant low vacuum that varies very little with engine rpm indicates the system is working.

CRANKCASE DEPRESSION REGULATOR

INTAKE MANIFOLD

HOSE TO INTAKE

BLOW BY GASES FROM THE CRANKCASE

OIL FILL PIPE

MOD PIPE HARN ASM

Schematic of GM 6.2 liter CDR system

Replacement is simply a matter of removing the air cleaner and unbolting the valve, and then bolting on a new one. Make sure, however, that you replace all seals and gaskets and that they are properly seated.

EGR Systems

GM 6.2 L DIESEL

This diesel engine uses an EGR valve located under the air cleaner cover to recirculate exhaust gas and reduce peak combustion temperatures. This reduces NO_x much as in a gas engine.

There are several differences in the way the EGR valve is energized, however. And, because there is little intake system vacuum in a diesel, a special EPR valve increases exhaust backpressure to aid EGR flow at idle. This valve, too requires a unique actuation system.

One unique feature of the system is that a throttle position switch on the injection pump actuate the EGR valve and EPR valve at different throttle positions.

IDLE OPERATION

Both valves are energized by vacuum produced via the engine's vacuum pump. Vacuum to each valve is controlled via a solenoid—so there's an EGR solenoid valve and an EPR solenoid valve.

At idle, both are open passing vacuum through and opening both the EGR and EPR valves. Just off idle, the EPR solenoid is de-energized, and the EPR valve closes. EGR is maintained under these conditions because of an increase in intake vacuum and exhaust backpressure.

At high throttle openings, diesels do not require EGR as the fuel mixture becomes richer, leaving less excess oxygen for NO_x formation. Under these conditions, at a fairly advanced throttle opening, the Throttle Position Switch sends current to the EGR solenoid closing the valve, vacuum to the EGR valve is cut off, and the EGR valve closes.

This minimizes diesel smoke at full or near-full throttle conditions.

TROUBLESHOOTING THE SYSTEM

If the engine gives heavy exhaust smoke under full throttle conditions only, suspect the EGR system, and proceed as follows:

1. Operate the engine until the thermostat opens. Then, remove the air cleaner cover and watch the operation of the EGR valve with the engine idling. The valve should be open. This is indicated if the valve head is in the up position and there is noticeable exhaust noise in the intake. If the valve is not open, check for loose electrical or vacuum connections. Confirm that the EGR valve is actually open by pulling off the vacuum hose to the top of the valve. The valve stem should drop and there should be a noticeable reduction in noise. Reconnect the hose. If the valve is working, skip to Step 4.

2. Check the vacuum to the EGR valve with a vacuum gauge. It should be 20 in. of water. If not, check for this vacuum at the outlet of the vacuum pump, and replace the pump or replace repair vacuum lines as necessary.

3. If the EGR valve is actually receiving vacuum but does not open and close as the hose is connected and disconnected, replace the EGR valve.

4. Operate the throttle lever through 20 degrees of travel. The EGR valve should close when the throttle position switch reaches the calibration point. If not, proceed with the following steps.

5. Check the pink wire leading to the Throttle Position Switch. If there is no voltage at the connector, check for loose connections, damaged wiring, or a blown 20 amp gauge circuit fuse.

6. Once voltage is supplied to the TPS, check that the blue wire from the TPS (leading to the EPR solenoid) also has voltage. If the contact at the TPS has no voltage at idle with the pink wire hot, replace the TPS.

7. With the engine off, key on operate the throttle through 20 degrees of travel. Measure voltage at the blue wire. It should cut out at approximately 15 degrees of throttle opening. Then measure voltage at the yellow wire. It should cut in at 20 degrees of throttle opening.

8. Check that all electrical connections are good and correctly wired, and that all vacuum connections are good and properly routed. If wiring and vacuum lines are good, and operation of the throttle through 20 degrees does not first close the EPR valve and then close the EGR valve, replace the appropriate solenoid.

ISUZU/LUV DIESEL EGR (CALIFORNIA ONLY)

This system incorporates an ordinary EGR valve mounted on the intake manifold. The valve is vacuum actuated, the vacuum being produced by the engine's vacuum pump and sent to the valve through a vacuum switching valve. The solenoid operated vacuum switching valve interrupts the vacuum to the EGR valve under conditions determined by an EGR controller. This device, in turn, receives signals indicating engine rpm and throttle lever position. At light throttle, the EGR valve receives vacuum between 1600 and 2200 rpm. Under heavy throttle, it receives vacuum only above 2200 rpm.

A thermal vacuum switch measures coolant temperature and is connected in series in the vacuum line between the vacuum pump and the EGR valve. It prevents EGR from occurring at coolant temperatures below 122 degrees F.

TROUBLESHOOTING THE SYSTEM

1. Apply about 14 in. HG vacuum to the EGR valve with a vacuum pump. The valve should open all the way and should not leak down. Otherwise, replace it.

2. Remove the Thermal Vacuum Valve from the cooling system (drain coolant first, as necessary). Try to blow through the valve (make sure it has cooled if removed from a hot engine). No air should pass. Then, immerse the wet portion of the valve in water and heat it to about 130 degrees F. Now, air should pass through the valve. If either test is failed, replace the valve.

3. Disconnect the connectors to the Vacuum Switching Valve, and run jumper wires so battery voltage can be applied directly. If you can hear the plunger operating when current is applied, the valve is good. Otherwise, replace it.

4. Connect a voltmeter positive lead to the light green/black terminal of the EGR controller, and the negative lead to black/yellow terminal. Run the engine at over 1600 rpm. There should be just under 12 volts across the leads. Otherwise, replace the unit.

5. Connect a voltmeter positive lead to

the blue/yellow terminal of the control lever position sensor, and connect the negative lead to the blue/red terminal. Do not disconnect the connector. Move the control

lever until there is a clearance of .275 in. between the lever and the idle adjusting screw. The voltage reading should be 3.3–4.4 volts. Otherwise, replace the sensor.

Isuzu/LUV EGR system

Carburetors

INDEX

CARBURETORS

Carburetor Identification

All carburetors are identified by code numbers, either stamped on the attaching flange side, the main body or on a metal tag, retained by a bowl cover screw. This identifying number is most important to the repairman in order to obtain the correct carburetor replacement or parts and to properly adjust the carburetor when matched to a specific engine.

Carter carburetors for Jeep usage—typical (© Jeep Corp.)

Rochester two barrel models—typical (© General Motors Corp.)

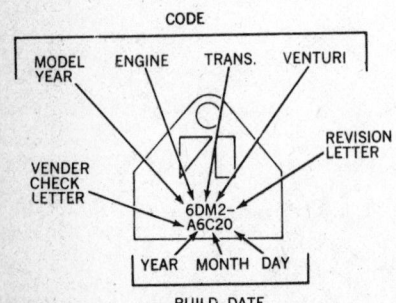

Motorcraft carburetors for Jeep usage—typical (© Jeep Corp.)

Rochester one barrel models—typical (© General Motors Corp.)

Motorcraft carburetors for Ford usage—typical (© Ford Motor Co.)

Angle Degree Tool

An angle degree tool is recommended by Rochester Products Division, for use to confirm adjustments to the choke valve and related linkages on their late model two and four barrel carburetors, in place of the plug type gauges.

Degree angle tool—typical (© Kent-Moore Tools)

Decimal and degree conversion charts are provided for use by technicians who have access to an angle gauge and not plug gauges. It must be remembered that the relationship between the decimal and the angle readings are not exact, due to manufacturers tolerances.

To use the angle gauge, rotate the degree scale until zero (0) is opposite the pointer. With the choke valve completely closed, place the gauge magnet squarely on top of the choke valve and rotate the bubble until it is centered. Make the necessary adjustments to have the choke valve at the specified degree angle opening as read from the degree angle tool.

NOTE: The carburetor may be off the engine for adjustments. Be sure the carburetor is held firmly during the use of the angle gauge.

Rochester four barrel models—typical (© General Motors Corp.)

U126

MODEL BBD
Dodge/Plymouth
(All measurements in inches)

Year	Carburetor List Number	Float Level	Choke Unloader	Fast Idle Cam Setting	Choke Valve Initial Opening w/Vacuum Kick	Fast Idle Speed (RPM)	Choke Setting	Accelerator Pump Setting	Step-up Piston Gap
'77	8081S	.250	.280	.070	.150	1500	Fixed	.500	—
	8082S	.250	.280	.070	.130	1500	Fixed	.500	—
	8085S	.250	.280	.070	.130	1500	Fixed	.500	—
	8147S	.250	.310	.070	.070	1500	Fixed	.500	—
	8146S	.250	.280	.070	.070	1600	Fixed	.500	—
	8113S	.250	.310	.070	.130	1500	Fixed	.500	—
	8110S	.250	.280	.070	.095	1500	Fixed	.500	—
'78	8149S	.250	.280	.070	.130	1500	Fixed	.500	.035
	8151S	.250	.280	.070	.130	1500	Fixed	.500	.035
	8180S	.250	.280	.070	.150	1600	Fixed	.500	.035
	8152S	.250	.280	.070	.130	1500	Fixed	.500	.035
	8147S	.250	.310	.070	.070	1500	Fixed	.500	.035
	8154S	.250	.310	.070	.130	1500	Fixed	.500	.035
	8156S	.250	.310	.070	.110	1500	Fixed	.500	.035
	8146S	.250	.280	.070	.070	1500	Fixed	.500	.035
'79	8214S	.250	.280	.070	.110	1400	Fixed	.500	—
	8215S	.250	.280	.070	.110	1600	Fixed	.500	—
	8249S	.250	.280	.070	.110	1400	Fixed	.500	—
	8232S	.250	.280	.070	.110	1500	Fixed	.500	—
	8210S	.250	.280	.070	.110	1400	Fixed	.500	—
	8211S	.250	.280	.070	.110	1500	Fixed	.500	—
'80–'82	8146S	.250	.310	.070	.070	1500	Fixed	.500	.035
	8147S	.250	.310	.110	.150	1500	Fixed	.500	.035
'82	8348S	.250	.310	.070	.130	1600	Fixed	.500	.035
	8352S	.250	.310	.070	.130	1600	Fixed	.500	.035
'83	4041580	.250	.310	.070	.070	1500	Fixed	.470	.035
	4041583	.250	.310	.110	.150	1500	Fixed	.470	.035
	4287029	.250	.280	.070	.130	1600	Fixed	.470	.035
	4287055	.250	.280	.070	.130	1400	Fixed	.470	.035
	4287018	.250	.280	.070	.130	1400	Fixed	.470	.035
	4287017	.250	.280	.070	.130	1400	Fixed	.470	.035

MODEL TQ
Dodge/Plymouth

(All measurements in inches)

Year	Carburetor List Number	Float Level	Fast Idle Speed (RPM)	Auto Choke Setting	Fuel Bowl Vent Adjustment	Accelerator Pump Stroke Adjustment①	Secondary Throttle Lock-Out Adjustment	Metering Rod Adjustment	Vacuum Kick Adjustment	Choke Diaphragm Rod Adjustment	Fast Idle Cam and Linkage Adjustment③	Choke Unloader Adjustment②
'77	6545S	27/32	1700	Fixed	—	½ (5/16)	.060–.090	—	.160	.040	.100	.310
	9096S	27/32	1700	Fixed	—	½ (5/16)	.060–.090	—	.160	.040	.100	.310
'78	9118S	27/32	1700	Fixed	—	½ (5/16)	.060–.090	—	.160	.040	.100	.310
	9151S	27/32	1700	Fixed	—	½ (5/16)	.060–.090	—	.160	.040	.100	.310
	9116S	29/32	1600	Fixed	—	11/32 (9/64)	.060–.090	—	.100	.040	.100	½
	9149S	29/32	1600	Fixed	—	11/32 (9/64)	.060–.090	—	.100	.040	.100	½
	9117S	27/32	1700	Fixed	—	½ (5/16)	.060–.090	—	.100	.040	.100	.310
	9150S	27/32	1700	Fixed	—	½ (5/16)	.060–.090	—	.100	.040	.100	.310
	9173S	29/32	1500	Fixed	—	5/16 (3/16)	.060–.090	—	.150	.040	.100	.310
	9123S	29/32	1600	Fixed	—	33/64 (5/16)	.060–.090	—	.150	.040	.100	½
	9124S	29/32	1600	Fixed	—	33/64 (5/16)	.060–.090	—	.100	.040	.100	½
	9152S	29/32	1600	Fixed	—	33/64 (5/16)	.060–.090	—	.100	.040	.100	½
	9175S	29/32	1700	Fixed	—	33/64 (5/16)	.060–.090	—	.150	.040	.100	½
	9126S	29/32	1600	Fixed	—	33/64 (5/16)	.060–.090	—	.100	.040	.100	½
	9151S	29/32	1400	Fixed	—	33/64 (5/16)	.060–.090	—	.160	.040	.100	½
	9150S	29/32	1400	Fixed	—	33/64 (5/16)	.060–.090	—	.100	.040	.100	½
'79	9228S	29/32	1600	Fixed	—	11/32 (9/64)	.060–.090	—	.100	.040	.100	.500
	9229S	29/32	1600	Fixed	—	11/32 (9/64)	.060–.090	—	.100	.040	.100	.500
	9223S	29/32	1600	Fixed	—	11/32 (9/64)	.060–.090	—	.100	.040	.100	.500
	9227S	29/32	1600	Fixed	—	11/32 (9/64)	.060–.090	—	.100	.040	.100	.500
	9224S	29/32	1600	Fixed	—	5/16 (3/16)	.060–.090	—	.100	.040	.100	.500
	9225S	29/32	1600	Fixed	—	5/16 (3/16)	.060–.090	—	.100	.040	.100	.500
	9207S	29/32	1600	Fixed	—	31/64 (23/64)	.060–.090	—	.150	.040	.100	.310
	9208S	29/32	1600	Fixed	—	31/64 (23/64)	.060–.090	—	.150	.040	.100	.310
	9209S	29/32	1600	Fixed	—	31/64 (23/64)	.060–.090	—	.150	.040	.100	.310
	9210S	29/32	1600	Fixed	—	31/64 (23/64)	.060–.090	—	.150	.040	.100	.310
	9211S	29/32	1400	Fixed	—	31/64 (23/64)	.060–.090	—	.100	.040	.100	.500
	9212S	29/32	1400	Fixed	—	31/64 (23/64)	.060–.090	—	.100	.040	.100	.500
	9247S	29/32	1400	Fixed	—	31/64 (23/64)	.060–.090	—	.100	.040	.100	.500
	9248S	29/32	1400	Fixed	—	31/64 (23/64)	.060–.090	—	.100	.040	.100	.500
'80	9279S	29/32	1600	Fixed	—	.340(.190)	.060–.090	—	.130	.040	.130	.310
	9288S	29/32	1600	Fixed	—	.340(.190)	.060–.090	—	.120	.040	.120	.310
	9296S	29/32	1500	Fixed	—	.340(.140)	.060–.090	—	.100	.040	.100	.310
	9254S	29/32	1500	Fixed	—	.340(.190)	.060–.090	—	.130	.040	.100	.310
	9265S	29/32	1600	Fixed	—	.340(.140)	.060–.090	—	.150	.040	.100	.310
	9255S	29/32	1600	Fixed	—	.340(.190)	.060–.090	—	.120	.040	.100	.310

MODEL TQ
Dodge/Plymouth
(All measurements in inches)

Year	Carburetor List Number	Float Level	Fast Idle Speed (RPM)	Auto Choke Setting	Fuel Bowl Vent Adjustment	Accelerator Pump Stroke Adjustment①	Secondary Throttle Lock-Out Adjustment	Metering Rod Adjustment	Vacuum Kick Adjustment	Choke Diaphragm Rod Adjustment	Fast Idle Cam and Linkage Adjustment③	Choke Unloader Adjustment②
'80	9252S	29/32	1600	Fixed	—	.340(.190)	.060–.090	—	.120	.040	.120	.310
	9251S	29/32	1600	Fixed	—	.340(.190)	.060–.090	—	.120	.040	.120	.310
	9292S	29/32	1600	Fixed	—	.340(.190)	.060–.090	—	.150	.040	.130	.310
	9298S	29/32	1600	Fixed	—	.340(.140)	.060–.090	—	.150	.040	.100	.310
	9299S	29/32	1600	Fixed	—	.340(.140)	.060–.090	—	.150	.040	.100	.310
	9281S	29/32	1600	Fixed	—	.340(.190)	.060–.090	—	.180	.040	.130	.310
	9261S	29/32	1600	Fixed	—	.340(.190)	.060–.090	—	.130	.040	.130	.310
'81	9311S	29/32	1500	Fixed	—	.340	.060–.090	—	.150	.040	.100	.310
	9314S	29/32	1500	Fixed	—	.340	.060–.090	—	.150	.040	.100	.310
	9325S	29/32	1500	Fixed	—	.340	.060–.090	—	.120	.040	.100	.310
	9329S	29/32	1600	Fixed	—	.340	.060–.090	—	.130	.040	.100	.310
	9330S	29/32	1500	Fixed	—	.340	.060–.090	—	.130	.040	.100	.310
	9331S	29/32	1700	Fixed	—	.340	.060–.090	—	.110	.040	.100	.310
	9332S	29/32	1700	Fixed	—	.340	.060–.090	—	.110	.040	.100	.310
	9357S	29/32	1800	Fixed	—	.340	.060–.090	—	.130	.040	.100	.310
	9358S	29/32	1700	Fixed	—	.340	.060–.090	—	.180	.040	.100	.310
	9359S	29/32	1500	Fixed	—	.340	.060–.090	—	.130	.040	.100	.310
'82	TQ-9342S	29/32	1600	Fixed	—	.340	.060–.090	—	.130	.040	.100②	.310
	TQ-9375S	29/32	1800	Fixed	—	.340	.060–.090	—	.130	.040	.130②	.310
	TQ-9376S	29/32	1700	Fixed	—	.340	.060–.090	—	.130	.040	.130②	.310
	TQ-9379S	29/32	1500	Fixed	—	.340	.060–.090	—	.130	.040	.130②	.310
'83	4287013	29/32	1600	Fixed	—	.340(.390)	.060	—	.130	.040	.100②	.310
	4241752	29/32	1800	Fixed	—	.340(.390)	.060	—	.130	.040	.130②	.310
	4287016	29/32	1500	Fixed	—	.340(.390)	.060	—	.130	.040	.130②	.310
	4241753	29/32	1700	Fixed	—	.340(.390)	.060	—	.180	.040	.100②	.310

① Stage I (Stage II). No Stage II adjustment on 1981–82 models   ② Measure at the lowest edge of the choke valve on the throttle lever side   ③ Set the linkage with idle on the second highest step of the cam

MODELS YF/YFA
Ford
(All measurements in inches)

Year	Carburetor List Number	Float Level	Float Drop	Choke Unloader Setting	Choke Setting	Dash Pot Plunger	Initial Choke Opening
'77	D5TE						
	AGA	3/8	—	.280	1 Rich	—	.230
	AGB	23/32	—	.280	1 Rich	—	.230
	AJA	3/8	—	—	Manual	—	—
	AJB	3/8	—	—	Manual	—	—

MODELS YF/YFA
Ford
(All measurements in inches)

Year	Carburetor List Number	Float Level	Float Drop	Choke Unloader Setting	Choke Setting	Dash Pot Plunger	Initial Choke Opening
'77	AFA	3/8	—	—	Manual	—	—
	AFB	3/8	—	—	Manual	—	—
	D5PF						
	ANA	3/8	—	.280	—	—	—
	D7PE						
	LA	3/8	—	—	—	—	—
	KA	3/8	—	—	—	—	—
	SA	3/8	—	—	—	—	—
	RA	3/8	—	—	—	—	—
	NA	3/8	—	—	—	—	—
	D7TE						
	CAA	25/32	—	—	—	—	—
	CBA	25/32	—	—	—	—	—
	CCA	25/32	—	—	—	—	—
	PA	25/32	—	.280	Index	—	.290
	CFA	25/32	—	—	—	—	—
	CFB	25/32	—	—	—	—	—
	MA	25/32	—	.280	Index	—	.290
	CDA	25/32	—	—	—	—	—
	CEA	25/32	—	—	—	—	—
	D6TE						
	ZA	23/32	—	.280	Index	—	.290
	HA	23/32	—	.280	Index	—	.290
	D6UE						
	MA	23/32	—	.280	Index	—	.290
'78	D8TE						
	BVA	25/32	1 19/32	.280	Index	—	.230
	CKB	25/32	1 19/32	.280	Index	.070	.230
	BWA	25/32	1 19/32	.280	Index	.070	.230
	BUA	25/32	1 19/32	.280	Index	.070	.230
	BUB	25/32	—	—	—	—	—
	CNA	25/32	1 19/32	.280	Index	.070	.230
	AAA	25/32	1 19/32	.280	Index	.070	.230
	UA	23/32	1 1/2	—	Manual	—	—
	CDA	23/32	1 1/2	—	Manual	—	—
	D8UE						
	AAA	—	—	—	—	—	—
	ZA	25/32	1 19/32	.280	Index	.070	.230

MODELS YF/YFA
Ford
(All measurements in inches)

Year	Carburetor List Number	Float Level	Float Drop	Choke Unloader Setting	Choke Setting	Dash Pot Plunger	Initial Choke Opening
'78	D6TE ZA	23/32	—	.280	Index	—	.290
	D6UE MA	23/32	—	.280	Index	—	.290
	D2UE EA	25/32	1 19/32	—	—	—	—
'80	E0TE-9510 ABA,FA, LA,KA	.69	1.53	.28	①	—	.290
	ACA,ARA	.69	1.53	.28	①	—	.320
	AEA,AFA, ALA,AKA, ATA,CA, GA	.69	1.53	.28	①	—	.230
'81	E0TE-9510 AMA,FA	.69	—	.28	Index	—	.290
	D5TE-9510 CA,VA	.69	—	.28	Index	—	.290
	AGB	3/8	—	.28	1 Rich	—	.230
	E1TE-9510 UA,ARA, ARB	.78	—	.28	Index	—	.230
	AUA,VA	.78	—	.28	2 Rich	—	.300
	AZA,GA	.78	—	.330	2 Rich	—	.320
'82	E2TE-AMA E2UE-EA	.78	—	.28	Index	—	.230
	E2TE BZA,BVA	.78	—	.28	Index	—	.270
	CEA,JA	.78	—	.320	2 Rich	—	.330
	YA,AAA	.78	—	.280	Index	—	.300
	MA,ANA	.78	—	.280	2 Rich	—	.300
	KA	.78	—	.330	2 Rich	—	.320
	AAA	.78	—	.280	Index	—	.300
	E2UE-DA	.78	—	.330	2 Rich	—	.320
'83–'84	E37E-9510 LB,NB, RB,TB	.65	—	.270	Gray ②	—	.320
	E37E-9510 BB	.65	—	.270	Yellow ②	—	.320

① See Ford calibration specifications
② Choke cap index plate color

MODEL TQ
International
(All measurements in inches)

Year	Carburetor List Number	Float Level	Fast Idle Speed (RPM)	Auto Choke Setting	Fuel Bowl Vent Clearance	Accelerator Pump Stroke Adjustment	Secondary Throttle Lock-Out Adjustment	Metering Rod Adjustment	Vacuum Kick Adjustment	Vacuum Pull-off Choke Adjustment	Fast Idle Cam and Linkage Adjustment	Choke Unloader Adjustment
'79	TQ91285	.91 ± .030 (Old Needles) .88 ± .030 (New Needles)	1600	¼ Rod	.800–.830	Primary① .328–.358 Secondary① .120–.260	.060–.090	.468 ± .031	Vac. High .440–.460 Vac. Low .235–.255	.840–.880	.089–.109	.280–.320
	TQ6591S, 6550S	1.06	1550–1600	1 Rich	.800–.830	Primary .328–.358 Secondary .120–.260	.060–.090	¹⁵/₃₂	Vac. High .335–.355 Vac. Low .250–.270	.840–.880 (6550S only)	.089–.109	.280–.320
	TQ6590S, 6552S, 6551S	1.06	1550–1600	1 Rich	.800–.830	Primary .328–.358	.060–.090	¹⁵/₃₂	Vac. High .335–.355 Vac. Low .250–.270	.840–.880 (6551S only)	.089–.109	.280–.320

① Rod in inner hole

MODEL BBD–2
Jeep
(All measurements in inches)

Year	Carburetor Number	Float Level (in.)	Step-up Piston Gap (in.)	Initial Choke Clearance (in.)	Fast Idle Cam Setting (in.)	Choke Cover Setting	Choke Unloader (Min.) (in.)	Fast Idle Speed (RPM)①
'77	8107	.250	.040	.128	.095	2 Rich	.280	1700
'78	8107	.250	.040	.128	.095	2 Rich	.280	1700
'79	8185	.250	.035	.140	.110	1 Rich	.280	1600
	8186	.250	.035	.150	.110	1 Rich	.280	1500
	8187	.250	.035	.140	.110	1 Rich	.280	1600
	8188	.250	.035	.150	.110	1 Rich	.280	1500
	8195	.250	.035	.140	.110	1 Rich	.280	1500(M) 1600(A)
	8229	.250	.035	.128	.095	1 Rich	.280	1500
'80	8256	.250	.035	.128	.093	2 Rich	.280	1850
	8257	.250	.035	.128	.095	2 Rich	.280	1700
	8253	.250	.035	.128	.095	2 Rich	.280	1850
	8254	.250	.035	.120	.086	2 Rich	.280	1700
	8255	.250	.035	.140	.093	2 Rich	.280	②
	8277	.250	.035	.116	.081	1 Rich	.280	1700
'81	8302	.250	.035	.140	.095	1 Rich	.280	1850
	8303	.250	.035	.140	.095	1 Rich	.280	1700
	8311	.250	.035	.120	.085	1 Rich	.280	1700
	8306	.250	.035	.140	.095	1 Rich	.280	1700
	8312	.250	.035	.140	.095	1 Rich	.280	②
	8307	.250	.035	.140	.095	1 Rich	.280	1700

MODEL BBD–2
Jeep
(All measurements in inches)

Year	Carburetor Number	Float Level (in.)	Step-up Piston Gap (in.)	Initial Choke Clearance (in.)	Fast Idle Cam Setting (in.)	Choke Cover Setting	Choke Unloader (Min.) (in.)	Fast Idle Speed (RPM)①
'82	8338	.250	.035	.140	.095	1 Rich	.280	1850
	8339	.250	.035	.140	.095	1 Rich	.280	1700
	8340	.250	.035	.150	.110	1 Rich	.280	1700
	8341	.250	.035	.150	.150	1 Rich	.280	1700
	8349	.250	.035	.128	.095	2 Rich	.280	②
	8351	.250	.035	.130	.095	Index	.280	1700

①On second step of fast idle cam with TCS solenoid and EGR disconnected.
②Manual transmission 1700 rpm and automatic transmission 1850 rpm

MODEL YF
Jeep
(All measurements in inches)

Year	Carburetor Number	Float Level	Float Drop	Initial Choke Clearance	Fast Idle Cam Setting	Choke Cover Setting	Choke Unloader (Min.)	Fast Idle Speed (RPM)	Dash Pot
'77	7154	.476	1⅜	.215	.195	1 Rich	.275	1600①	—
	7151	.476	1⅜	.215	.195	1 Rich	.275	1600①	—
	7153	.476	1⅜	.215	.195	1 Rich	.275	1600①	—
	7110, 7111 (Alt.)	.476	1⅜	.221	.201	2 Rich	.275	1800①	—
'78	7201	.476	1⅜	.215	.195	Index	.275	1600②	—
	7228	.476	1⅜	.215	.195	1 Rich	.275	1600②	—
	7230	.476	1⅜	.215	.195	1 Rich	.275	1600②	—
	7231 (Alt.)	.476	1⅜	.221	.201	2 Rich	.275	1500②	—

①On 2nd step of fast idle cam with TCS solenoid and EGR disconnected
②Engine hot, EGR valve disconnected

MODEL YFA
Jeep
(All measurements in inches)

Year	Carburetor Number	Float Level	Fast Idle Cam Setting Index	Initial Choke Clearance	Choke Cover Setting	Choke Unloader (Min.)	Fast Idle Speed (RPM)①	Bowl Vent Opens
'83	7452	.600	.175	.280	Fixed	.280	2300	2 Step
	7453	.600	.175	.280	Fixed	.280	2000	2 Step
	7454	.600	.175	.280	Fixed	.280	2300	2 Step
	7455	.600	.175	.280	Fixed	.280	2000	2 Step

①Engine hot, EGR valve disconnected

Measurement of float drop—YF/YFA carburetor (© Ford Motor Co.)

Adjustment of initial opening (vacuum kick)—BBD carburetor (© Chrysler Corp.)

Adjusting choke unloader — BBD carburetor

Carter TQ float height measurement (© Chrysler Corp.)

Measurement of float drop—YF carburetor (© Jeep Corp.)

Carter TQ choke unloader adjustment (© Chrysler Corp.)

FAST IDLE CAM LINK

FAST IDLE CAM

HIGH STEP

FAST IDLE CAM

CURB IDLE ADJUSTING SCREW

KICK DOWN STEP

FAST IDLE SPEED ADJUSTING SCREW

Typical adjustment points—YF carburetor with electric choke
(© Ford Motor Co.)

SCALE

SEE SPEC

SCREW BACKED OUT TO CLOSE THROTTLE

BEND HERE TO ADJUST

BBS pump adjustment

INSERT GAUGE

BEND HERE TO ADJUST

CHOKE VALVE CLOSED

THROTTLE CLOSED

BBS fast idle adjustment

ADJUSTING SCREW

PRESS DOWN ON PUMP SHAFT

METERING ROD

Metering rod adjustment—YF carburetor with electric choke
(© Jeep Corp.)

DRILL GAUGE

DASH POT

THROTTLE LEVER (OPEN POSITION)

MAKE DECHOKE ADJUSTMENT HERE

Choke plate unloader (dechoke) adjustment—typical YFA carburetor (© Ford Motor Co.)

CHOKE ROD UPPER ANGLE

FAST IDLE CAM

FAST IDLE SPEED ADJUSTING SCREW

Fast idle cam and linkage adjustment—YF carburetor (© Jeep Corp.)

Exploded view of YF carburetor—typical (© Jeep Corp.)

1. Air horn screw (short)
2. Air horn screw (long)
3. Dashpot and bracket
4. Solenoid and bracket
5. Coil housing screw
6. Coil housing retainer
7. Choke cover
8. Coil housing gasket
9. Coil housing baffle plate
10. Upper pump spring retainer
11. Upper pump spring

12. Metering rod arm
13. Diaphragm lifter link
14. Washer
15. Diaphragm spring
16. Diaphragm housing screw (4)
17. Diaphragm housing
18. Washer
19. Spacer
20. Diaphragm
21. Idle screw limiter cap
22. Idle mixture screw

23. Spring
24. Throttle body
25. Body flange screw (3)
26. Throttle shaft arm
27. Pump connector link
28. Body gasket
29. Fast idle cam
30. Fast idle cam screw
31. Main body
32. Discharge ball
33. Discharge ball weight
34. Metering jet

35. Low speed jet
36. Float
37. Float pin
38. Needle pin
39. Needle spring
40. Needle, needle seat, gasket
41. Choke connector rod
42. Choke connector rod retainer
43. Metering rod
44. Air horn gasket
45. Air horn

WITH AUTOMATIC TRANSMISSION

Carter BBD two barrel carburetor—typical (© Chrysler Corp.)

1. Diaphragm connector link
2. Screw
3. Choke vacuum diaphragm
4. Hose
5. Valve
6. Metering rod
7. S-Link
8. Pump arm
9. Gasket
10. Rollover check valve
11. Screw
12. Lock
13. Rod lifter
14. Bracket
15. Nut
16. Solenoid
17. Screw
18. Air horn retaining screw (short)
19. Air horn retaining screw (long)
20. Pump lever
21. Venturi cluster screw
22. Idle fuel pick-up tube
23. Gasket
24. Venturi cluster
25. Gasket
26. Check ball (small)
27. Float
28. Fulcrum pin
29. Baffle
30. Clip
31. Choke link
32. Screw
33. Fast idle cam
34. Gasket
35. Thermostatic choke shaft
36. Spring
37. Screw
38. Pump link
39. Clip
40. Gasket
41. Limiter cap
42. Screw
43. Throttle body
44. Choke housing
45. Baffle
46. Gasket
47. Retainer
48. Choke coil
49. Lever
50. Choke rod
51. Clip
52. Needle and seat assembly
53. Main body
54. Main metering jet
55. Check ball (large)
56. Accelerator pump plunger
57. Fulcrum pin retainer
58. Gasket
59. Spring
60. Air horn
61. Lever

Adjusting float level with bowl inverted—BBD carburetor (© Chrysler Corp.)

Carter Thermo-Quad® float height measurement (© Chrysler Corp.)

Step-up piston clearance adjustment—BBD carburetor (© Chrysler Corp.)

Step-up piston qualification—BBD carburetor (© Chrysler Corp.)

Adjustment of fast idle cam setting—Thermo-Quad® carburetor (© Chrysler Corp.)

1. Fuel inlet nut and gasket
2. Idle compensator screw
3. Idle compensator
4. Idle compensator gasket
5. "E" retainer
6. Primary diaphragm choke pull-off rod washer
7. Primary diaphragm choke pull-off rod
8. Auxiliary diaphragm choke pull-off rod (if equipped)
9. Choke lever screw
10. Choke lever
11. Choke connector rod
12. Countershaft lever screw
13. Countershaft, lever, outer
14. Countershaft lever spring
15. Countershaft lever, inner
16. Fast idle cam rod
17. Throttle connector rod
18. Cover plate screw
19. Metering rod cover plate (opposite pump)
20. Metering rod cover plate (pump side)
21. Step-up piston cover plate
22. Step-up piston and hanger assembly
23. Metering rod
24. Step-up piston spring
25. Bowl cover screw
26. IH part number location
27. Bowl cover assembly
28. Float pin
29. Float assembly
30. Needle, seat, and gasket
31. Pump passage tube
32. Bowl cover gasket
33. Secondary metering jet
34. Primary metering jet
35. Quad rings

36. Pin spring retainer
37. Bowl vent valve lever, upper
38. Bowl vent valve lever spring
39. Bowl vent valve arm
40. Bowl vent valve grommet
41. Rivet plug
42. Pump housing screw
43. Pump housing
44. Pump housing gasket
45. Discharge check needle
46. Pump arm screw
47. Pump arm

48. Pump "S" link
49. Air valve lock plug
50. Air valve adjustment plug
51. Air valve spring
52. Pump intake check assembly
53. Plunger assembly
54. Plunger spring
55. Main body
56. Main body gasket
57. Step-up piston lifter
58. Step-up piston lifter lever pin
59. Solenoid and diaphragm choke pull-off bracket screw
60. Solenoid
61. Solenoid operating lever screw
62. Curb idle speed screw and lever
63. Bowl vent lever, lower
64. Throttle shaft washer
65. Hose
66. Primary diaphragm choke pull-off bracket
67. Auxiliary choke pull-off and dashpot
68. Auxiliary choke pull-off and bracket (if equipped)
69. Dashpot and bracket
70. Limiter cap
71. Idle mixture screw
72. Idle mixture screw spring
73. Throttle body assembly
74. Carter part number location
75. Low idle speed screw

Exploded view of a typical late-model Thermo-Quad® (© Chrysler Corp.)

Carter Thermo-Quad® fast idle speed adjustment cam position (© Chrysler Corp.)

Adjustment of the primary and secondary accelerator pump— Thermo-Quad® carburetor (© Chrysler Corp.)

Choke unloader adjustment—Thermo-Quad® carburetor (© Chrysler Corp.)

BEND LINK
TO ADJUST

IDLE
SCREW BACKED OFF.
THROTTLE VALVE
FULLY CLOSED

Accelerator pump stroke adjustment—Thermo-Quad® carburetor
(© Chrysler Corp.)

MODEL 2150
Ford
(All measurements in inches)

Year	Carburetor List Number	Float Level (Dry)	Choke Unloader Setting	Choke Setting	Accelerator Pump Rod Location	Fuel Level (Wet)	Choke Pulldown Setting (Min)
'77	D7TE						
	AHA	$31/64$	—	Index	3	$7/8$	.160
	ALA	$31/64$	—	Index	3	$7/8$	.160
	AKA	$31/64$	—	Index	3	$7/8$	.160
	BEA	$31/64$	—	Index	3	$7/8$	.160
	BZA	$31/64$	—	Index	3	$7/8$	.160
	BZB	$31/64$	—	Index	3	$7/8$	.160
	ANA	$31/64$	—	3 Rich	4	$7/8$	.160
	CJA	$31/64$	—	3 Rich	4	$7/8$	.160
	CZA	$31/64$	—	3 Rich	4	$7/8$	.160
	AMA	$31/64$	—	3 Rich	4	$7/8$	.160
	DBA	$31/64$	—	3 Rich	4	$7/8$	.160
	ARA	$31/64$	—	3 Rich	4	$7/8$	.160
	AUA, CKA	$31/64$	—	3 Rich	4	$7/8$	.160
	AYA, DAA	$31/64$	—	3 Rich	4	$7/8$	.160
	AZA, APA	$31/64$	—	3 Rich	4	$7/8$	.160
	CUA	$31/64$	—	3 Rich	4	$7/8$	.160
	D7PE						
	AGA	$31/64$	—	2 Rich	3	$7/8$	.145

MODEL 2150
Ford
(All measurements in inches)

Year	Carburetor List Number	Float Level (Dry)	Choke Unloader Setting	Choke Setting	Accelerator Pump Rod Location	Fuel Level (Wet)	Choke Pulldown Setting (Min)
'77	D7UE						
	ADA	31/64	—	2 Rich	4	7/8	.170
	TA	7/16	—	3 Rich	3	13/16	.170
	ZC	7/16	—	Index	3	13/16	.170
	YA	7/16	—	3 Rich	2	13/16	.170
	AAA	31/64	—	1 Rich	2	13/16	.170
	ACA	31/64	—	1 Rich	3	7/8	.170
	AEA	31/64	—	1 Rich	4	7/8	.170
	ABA	31/64	—	1 Rich	4	7/8	.170
	ARB	31/64	—	1 Rich	4	7/8	.170
	ANA	31/64	—	2 Rich	3	7/8	.170
	APA	31/64	—	2 Rich	3	7/8	.170
'78	D8TE						
	LA	31/64	—	Index	3	7/8	.130
	ARA	31/64	—	Index	3	7/8	.145
	DA	31/64	—	Index	4	7/8	.130
	CTA	31/64	—	Index	4	7/8	.130
	DBA	31/64	—	2 Rich	4	7/8	.130
	BLA	31/64	—	2 Rich	4	7/8	.130
	CRA	31/64	—	2 Rich	4	7/8	.130
	BJA	31/64	—	3 Rich	3	7/8	.175
	ATA	31/64	—	2 Rich	3	7/8	.145
	BEA	31/64	—	3 Rich	2	7/8	.200
	BA	31/64	—	Index	3	7/8	.140
	DP7E						
	AGA	31/64	—	2 Rich	3	7/8	.145
	D7UE						
	APA	31/64	—	2 Rich	3	7/8	.170
	D8UE						
	VA	31/64	—	Index	4	7/8	.145
	DA	31/64	—	3 Rich	3	7/8	.185
	KA	7/16	—	Index	3	13/16	.185
	GA	31/64	—	1 Rich	2	7/8	.205
	HA	31/64	—	Index	2	7/8	.215
	MA	31/64	—	Index	2	7/8	.215
	MB	31/64	—	Index	2	7/8	.215
	SA	31/64	—	3 Rich	3	7/8	.180

MODEL 2150
Ford
(All measurements in inches)

Year	Carburetor List Number	Float Level (Dry)	Choke Unloader Setting	Choke Setting	Accelerator Pump Rod Location	Fuel Level (Wet)	Choke Pulldown Setting (Min)
'80	E0TE-9510 BGA, CYA, GZA, ABA, BEA	.810	—	.20	—	—	.140
	BHA	.810	—	.20	—	—	.135
	BRA, DDA	.810	—	.20	—	—	.128
	CFA, EAA	.810	—	.25	—	—	.128
	CVA, NA	.875	—	.20	—	—	.105
	BYA	.875	—	.115	—	—	.140
	BSA Calibration Number: 0-59J-R0 0-59G-R10	.875	—	.115	—	—	.140
	0-59J-R10 0-59H-R10	.875	—	.20	—	—	.140
	DCA	.875	—	.25	—	—	.140
	AAA, PA, SA, TA, VA	.810	—	.25	—	—	.185
	AA	.810	—	.25	—	—	.105
	CLA	.875	—	.20	—	—	.140
	BLA, BFA, BZA	.875	—	.25	—	—	.148
	CCA, CBA	.875	—	.25	—	—	.159
	EDA, DGA	.875	—	.25	—	—	.155
	EEA, EFA	.875	—	.20	—	—	.160
	DEA, ECA	.875	—	.25	—	—	.175
	DFA	.875	—	.25	—	—	.185
'81	E1TE-9510 BJA, CHA, BCA	$^{31}/_{64}$	—	.250	V notch	—	.148
	BTA	$^{31}/_{64}$	—	.250	V notch	—	.130
	BVA	$^{7}/_{16}$	—	.200	V notch	—	.130
	CEA, CFA	$^{31}/_{64}$	—	.200	V notch	—	.160
	CAA, BYA	$^{31}/_{64}$	—	.250	V notch	—	.175
	BSA	$^{31}/_{64}$	—	.250	V notch	—	.130
	CCA	$^{31}/_{64}$	—	.250	V notch	—	.155
	BZA, CBA	$^{31}/_{64}$	—	.250	V notch	—	.180

MODEL 2150
Ford
(All measurements in inches)

Year	Carburetor List Number	Float Level (Dry)	Choke Unloader Setting	Choke Setting	Accelerator Pump Rod Location	Fuel Level (Wet)	Initial Choke Valve Setting (Min)
'81	CNA, CMA, CPA, CRA, CSA, CKA, CLA	7/16	—	.200	V notch	—	.125
	E1UE-9510 KA	31/64	—	.250	V notch	—	.180
	GA	7/16	—	.200	V notch	—	.130
	HA	31/64	—	.200	V notch	—	.125
'82	E2TE- BNA, CGA	7/16	.200	V notch	2	.810	.125
	BMA, CFA	7/16	.250	V notch	2	.810	.125
	DAA, CYA	7/16	.250	V notch	2	.810	.115–.135
	BEA	7/16	.200	V notch	2	.810	.130
	BLA	7/16	.200	V notch	2	.810	.125
	AYA, BEA, CJA, BFA	7/16	.200	V notch	2	.810	.130
	E2UE-JA	31/64	.200	V notch	2	.875	.130
	E2TE-BAA, BBA	7/16	.200	V notch	2	.810	.130
	CKA	7/16	.200	V notch	2	.810	.120
	E2UE-FA E1UE-JA	31/64	.200	V notch	3	.875	.120
	E2UE-KA	31/64	.200	V notch	2	.875	.120
	E2TE-BPA,BRA	31/64	.200	V notch	2	.875	.120
	E2UE-ANA AAA AKA E2UE-RA	31/64	.250	V notch	3	.875	.170–.190
	E2UE-SA	31/64	.250	V notch	3	.875	.182
	E2UE-HA ABA E1UE-KA	31/64	.250	V notch	3	.875	.170–.190
	E2TE-BHA BGA	31/64	.250	V notch	4	.875	.180
	E2TE-DCA E2TE-DBA	31/64	.250	V notch	3	.875	.170–.190
	E2TE-BKA BJA	31/64	.250	V notch	4	.875	.175
	E2TE-DDA DEA	31/64	.250	V notch	3	.875	.170–.190

MODEL 2150
Ford
(All measurements in inches)

Year	Carburetor List Number	Float Level (Dry)	Choke Unloader Setting	Choke Setting	Accelerator Pump Rod Location	Fuel Level (Wet)	Initial Choke Valve Setting (Min)
'83	E3TE-9510 BCA BFA BBA BGA	—	.25	V notch	3	.810	.115–.135
	AUA	$7/16$	.20	V notch	3	.810	.142
	BHA	$7/16$	.20	V notch	3	.810	.152
	AYA	$7/16$	.25	V notch	4	.810	.137
	AVA	$7/16$	.25	V notch	3	.810	.149
	BJA	$7/16$	.20	V notch	4	.810	.157
	BLA	$7/16$	.20	V notch	3	.810	.157
	BEA	$7/16$	.20	V notch	3	.810	.149
	BMA	$7/16$	.20	V notch	4	.810	.150
	E3UE-9510 CA,FA	$31/64$	.20	V notch	3	.875	.120
	BA,KA	$31/64$	.20	V notch	2	.875	.120
	E3TE-9510 BAA,BPA	$31/64$	.25	V notch	3	.875	.130
	E2UE-9510 DA EA ANA AKA	$31/64$	.25	V notch	3	.875	.180
	E37E-9510 LB	.650	.27	—	—	—	.320
	E37E-9510 ABA AAA ADA	$7/16$	.250	V notch	4	.810	.126–.146

① Wet float setting 1980 only   ② For choke settings see the Ford Calibration Specifications 1980 only   ③ For 1979 carburetor specifications see Ford Calibration Specifications

MODEL 7200
Ford
(All measurements in inches)

Year	Carburetor List Number	Float Level (Dry)	Float Drop	Choke Unloader Setting	Choke Setting	Dash Pot Plunger	Initial Choke Setting
'81	E1TE-9510 YA,AHA	1.455①	—	—	Index	—	—
	ZA	1.040①	—	—	Index	—	—

① ± .025 inches

MODEL 7200
Ford
(All measurements in inches)

Year	Carburetor List Number	Float Setting	Float Drop	Control Vacuum Regulator	Pulldown Timing	Pump lever Lash
'82	E1TE-2A, AHA E2TE-CDA, CCA	1.070–1.010	1.490–1.430	.245–.255	2–5 sec.	.010①
'83	E3TE-9510– BVA, BYA	1.070–1.010	1.490–1.430	.245–.255	2–5 sec.	.010①

① Plus one turn counter-clockwise.

MODEL 4350
Ford
(All measurements in inches)

Year	Carburetor List Number	Float Level (Dry)	Choke Unloader Setting	Choke Setting	Accelerator Pump Rod Location	Fuel Level (Wet)	Initial Choke Valve Setting (Min)
'77	D7TE						
	BLA	1.0	.300	Index	3	—	.160
	BJA	1.0	.300	Index	3	—	.160
	D7UE						
	AGA	1.0	.300	Index	3	—	.160
	AFA	1.0	.300	Index	3	—	.160
'78	D8TE						
	AKA	1.0	.300	Index	3	①	.160
	AMA	1.0	.300	Index	3	①	.160
	D7UE						
	ASA	1.0	.300	Index	3	①	.160
	D8UE						
	AA	1.0	.300	Index	3	①	.160
	CA	1.0	.300	Index	3	①	.160

① Fuel level between 4 and 6 on special gauge

MODEL 2100
Jeep
(All measurements in inches)

Year	Carburetor List Number	Float Level (Dry)	Fuel Level (Wet)	Initial Choke Valve Clearance	Fast Idle Cam Setting ②	Choke Cover Setting	Choke Unloader Valve Clearance	Fast Idle Speed ①	Dash Pot Clearance	Bowl Vent Clearance	Rod Pump Location Hole
'77	6RHM2	.555	.930	.136	.115	2 Rich	.250	1600	—	—	3
	6RHA2	.555	.930	.136	.115	2 Rich	.250	1600	—	—	3
	6DM2	.555	.930	.132	.120	2 Rich	.250	1600	.093	—	3
	6DA2J	.555	.930	.136	.120	1 Rich	.250	1600	—	—	3
	6DM2J	.555	.930	.132	.126	1 Rich	.250	1600	.093	—	3

MODEL 2100
Jeep
(All measurements in inches)

Year	Carburetor List Number	Float Level (Dry)	Fuel Level (Wet)	Initial Choke Valve Clearance	Fast Idle Cam Setting ②	Choke Cover Setting	Choke Unloader Valve Clearance	Fast Idle Speed ①	Dash Pot Clearance	Bowl Vent Clearance	Rod Pump Location Hole
'78	8DM2	.555	.930	.132	.120	2 Rich	.250	1500	—	.120	3
	8DM2C	.555	.930	.132	.120	1 Rich	.250	1500	—	.120	3
	8DA2J	.555	.930	.136	.126	1 Rich	.250	1600	—	.120	3
	8DA2JC	.555	.930	.136	.126	1 Rich	.250	1600	—	.120	3
	6RHA2	.555	.930	.136	.115	2 Rich	.250	1600	—	.120	3
	6RHM2	.555	.930	.136	.115	2 Rich	.250	1600	—	.120	3
'79	9DM2	.555	.930	.125	.120	2 Rich	.250	1500	—	.120	—
	9DM2C	.555	.930	.132	.120	1 Rich	.250	1500	—	.120	—
	9DA2J	.555	.930	.128	.113	1 Rich	.250	1600	—	.120	—
	9DM2H	.555	.930	.140	.125	Index	.250	1500	—	.120	—
'80	ODMJ12	.375	.093	.125	.113	2 Rich	.300	1500	—	.120	3
	ODM2JC	.375	.093	.120	.106	2 Rich	.300	1500	—	.120	3
	ODA2J2	.375	.093	.120	.106	2 Rich	.300	1600	—	.120	3
	ODA2J	.375	.093	.128	.113	2 Rich	.300	1600	—	.120	3
	ODM2A	.375	.093	.128	.113	2 Rich	.360	1500	—	.120	3

① TCS solenoid and EGR disconnected, fast idle screw on 2nd cam step.
② Measured between choke valve and air horn, fast idle screw on 2nd cam step.

MODEL 2150
Jeep
(All measurements in inches)

Year	Carburetor List Number	Float Level (Dry)	Fuel Level (Wet)	Initial Choke Valve Clearance	Fast Idle Cam Setting ②	Choke Cover Setting	Choke Unloader Valve Clearance	Fast Idle Speed ①	Dash Pot Clearance	Bowl Vent Clearance	Rod Pump Location Hole
'77	7DM2A	.555	.930	.110	.089	2 Rich	.290	1600	—	—	3
	7DA2A	.555	.930	.104	.089	1 Rich	.290	1600	—	—	3
'78	8DA2A	.555	.930	.089	.078	2 Rich	.290	1600	—	—	3
	8DM2A	.555	.930	.093	.078	2 Rich	.290	1600	—	—	3
'79	9RHM2	.555	.930	.104	.086	2 Rich	.348	1500	—	—	3
	9RHA2	.555	.930	.113	.093	2 Rich	.350	1600	—	—	3
'80	ORHM2	.575	.930	.104	.081	2 Rich	.348	1500	—	.120	3
	ORHA2	.575	.930	.104	.081	2 Rich	.350	1600	—	.120	3
'81	DMJ2	.375	.930	.125	.113	2 Rich	.300	1500	—	.120	3
	DA2J	.375	.930	.128	.113	1 Rich	.300	1600	—	.120	3
	DM2A	.375	.930	.128	.113	1 Rich	.360	1500	—	.120	3
	RHM2	.575	.930	.104	.081	2 Rich	.348	1500	—	.120	3
	RHA2	.575	.930	.113	.086	2 Rich	.350	1600	—	.120	3

MODEL 2150
Jeep
(All measurements in inches)

Year	Carburetor List Number	Float Level (Dry)	Fuel Level (Wet)	Initial Choke Valve Clearance	Fast Idle Cam Setting ②	Choke Cover Setting	Choke Unloader Valve Clearance	Fast Idle Speed ①	Dash Pot Clearance	Bowl Vent Clearance	Rod Pump Location Hole
'82	2RHM2	19/64–23/64 ③	.930	.116	.076	1 Rich	.350	1500	—	.120	—
	2RHA2	19/64–23/64 ③	.930	.116	.076	1 Rich	.350	1600	—	.120	—

① TCS solenoid and EGR disconnected, fast idle screw on 2nd cam step

② Measured between choke valve and air horn fast idle screw on 2nd cam step

③ Measured from machined bowl surface to a point ⅛ inch from float tip with the needle seated

MODEL 4350
Jeep
(All measurements in inches)

Year	Carburetor List Number	Float Level (Dry)	Fuel Level (Wet)	Initial Choke Valve Clearance	Fast Idle Cam Setting ②	Choke Cover Setting	Choke Unloader Valve Clearance	Fast Idle Speed ①	Dash Pot Clearance	Bowl Vent Clearance	Rod Pump Location Hole
'77	6THA4	.900	—	.135	.135	2 Rich	.325	1600	—	—	—
	6THM4	.900	—	.135	.135	2 Rich	.325	1600	—	—	—
	6THA4C	.900	—	.135	.135	2 Rich	.325	1600	—	—	—
'78	6THA4	.900	—	.135	.135	2 Rich	.325	1600	—	—	—
	6THM4	.900	—	.135	.135	2 Rich	.325	1600	—	—	—

① TCS solenoid and EGR disconnected, fast idle screw on 2nd cam step.

② Measured between choke valve and air horn, fast idle screw on 2nd cam step.

Fuel level adjustment (wet)—models 2100 and 2150 carburetors (© Ford Motor Co.)

THERMOSTATIC SPRING HOUSING INDEX MARK

CHOKE HOUSING INDEX MARK

Indexing marks for automatic choke thermostatic spring housing and choke housing—typical models 2100 and 2150 carburetors (© Ford Motor Co.)

Accelerator pump stroke hole location—typical models 2100 and 2150 carburetors (© Ford Motor Co.)

UPPER BODY SCREWS (6 REQ'D)

CHOKE PLATE SCREWS (4 REQ'D)

BYPASS CHOKE PLATE

CHOKE PLATE

CHOKE PLATE LEVER

LEVER SCREW

CHOKE PLATE ROD

RETAINER

DUST COVER

BYPASS CHOKE SHAFT AND LEVER ASSEMBLY

CHOKE SHAFT LINK

BOOSTER VENTURI SCREW

CHOKE SHAFT AND LEVER ASSEMBLY

YOKE

METERING RODS

AIR HORN

YOKE SCREW

GASKET

SCREEN

SUPPORT AND BOOSTER ASSEMBLY

GASKET

SCREW (3 REQ'D)

ADJUSTMENT SCREW

ANEROID

GASKET

SCREW (4 REQ'D)

METERING VALVE ASSEMBLY

RETAINER

GASKET

WEIGHT

PUMP CHECK BALL

FLOAT

FLOAT SHAFT

FLOAT SHAFT RETAINER

FUEL INLET NEEDLE

THROTTLE SHAFT AND LEVER ASSEMBLY

CHOKE ARM ADJUSTING SCREW

IDLE SPEED ADJUSTING SCREW (2)

INLET NEEDLE SEAT

SHIELD

SCREW (2 REQ'D)

RESTRICTOR

VACUUM HOSE

SPRING

FILTER SCREEN RETAINER SPRING

CHOKE PULLDOWN DIAPHRAGM ASSEMBLY

MAIN BODY

MAIN JETS

ELASTOMER VALVE

POSITIVE CLOSURE SPRING

RETAINER

LOCKING CAP

RETURN SPRING

ACCELERATOR PUMP ROD

NYLON CHOKE ARM

LINKAGE LEVER

DIAPHRAGM LINK

FAST IDLE CAM LINK

SHAFT RETAINER

PUMP DIAPHRAGM ACCELERATOR PUMP COVER

LOCKING TAB

LOCKING PLUG

CHOKE HOUSING SHAFT

CHOKE HOUSING

CHOKE LEVER

GASKET

RETAINER

GASKET

FAST IDLE CAM

SPRING

FAST IDLE LEVER

THROTTLE PLATES

SPRING

ENRICHMENT VALVE

GASKET

MIXTURE SCREW

PIN

COVER SCREW (4 REQ'D)

LEVER SCREW

HOUSING SCREW (3 REQ'D)

HIGH SPEED BLEED CAM

FAST IDLE ADJUSTMENT SCREW

COVER

PUMP OPERATING LEVER

VENT VALVE ACTUATING LEVER

SCREW (3 REQ'D)

HOT AIR INLET

SHIELD

COVER SCREW

SHIELD SCREW (2 REQ'D)

VENT VALVE BRACKET

THERMOSTATIC SPRING HOUSING

Typical late model 2150 carburetor (© Ford Motor Co.)

Exploded view of model 2100 carburetor (with manual choke, manual throttle, and automatic choke mechanisms shown) (© Ford Motor Co.)

Automatic choke assembly (typical)—model 2100 carburetor

Float level adjustment (dry)—models 2100 and 2150 carburetors (© Ford Motor Co.)

Setting accelerator pump stroke—Motorcraft 4350 carburetor

Metering rod vacuum piston adjustment to a clearance of .120 inches (© Jeep Corp.)

Fabrication of the float gauge—models 4300 and 4350 carburetors

AIR VALVE LINK

C-CLIP

DAMPER LINK

VENT VALVE ADJUSTING SCREW

SCREW

RETAINER

OPERATING ARM

SCREW

CHOKE PLATE

AIR VALVE PLATE

SCREW

LEVER

SCREW

CHOKE PLATE SHAFT

AIR VALVE SHAFT

UPPER BODY

VACUUM PISTON LIMITER LEVER

SPACER

ACCELERATOR PUMP ARM

METERING ROD

SHAFT

ACCELERATOR PUMP SPRING RETAINER

ACCELERATOR PUMP LEVER AND ROD

GASKET

PUMP SPRING

ACCELERATOR PUMP LINK

SPRING

BOWL VENT VALVE

PUMP SHAFT

PIN RETAINER

PUMP PISTON

AIR VALVE DAMPER PISTON AND ROD

PIN

RETAINER

METERING RODS & YOKE

FUEL INLET VALVE AND SEAT

FLOAT AND LEVER ASSEMBLY

MAIN JETS

VACUUM PISTON

GASKET

SPRING

BALL CHECK RETAINER

VALVE

MAIN BODY

WEIGHT

INLET BALL CHECK

VACUUM PISTON CYLINDER

PRIMARY THROTTLE PLATE

GASKET

PRIMARY THROTTLE SHAFT AND LEVER ASSEMBLY

SCREW

GASKET

THROTTLE AUXILIARY LEVER

LINK

SCREW

AUTOMATIC CHOKE SHAFT AND LEVER

RETAINER

CAM ADJUSTING SCREW

FAST IDLE CAM

SECONDARY THROTTLE SHAFT AND LEVER (L.H.)

RETAINER

CAP

BUSHING

CHOKE CONTROL ROD

SECONDARY THROTTLE FLATES

RETURN SPRING

IDLE SPEED SCREW

SCREW

SPRING

PISTON AND LEVER ASSEMBLY

GASKET

CHOKE THERMOSTATIC CAP

THROTTLE BODY AND CHOKE HOUSING

CHOKE HEAT CONNECTION

RETAINER

SCREW

THROTTLE STOP LEVER

PULLOFF LINKAGE

SCREW

FAST IDLE LEVER

CHOKE DELAYED PULLDOWN AND FAST IDLE TOP STEP PULLOFF DIAPHRAGM ASSEMBLY

LINK

RETURN SPRING

FAST IDLE SPEED ADJUSTING SCREW

FILTER CAP

SECONDARY THROTTLE SHAFT AND LEVER (R.H.)

Exploded view of Motorcraft 4350—typical of 4300 series carburetors

DRILL GAUGE OF SPECIFIED CLEARANCE SIZE

CHOKE PLATE

TAPER-LOCK CHOKE SHAFT SCREW (LEFT HAND THREAD)

FAST IDLE CAM ADJUSTING SCREW

0.036-INCH WIRE GAUGE

FAST IDLE ADJUSTING SCREW

APPLY LIGHT PRESSURE TO CHOKE LEVER

Choke plate initial setting (pull-down) and fast idle cam adjustment—models 4300 and 4350 carburetors (© Ford Motor Co.)

BEND TAB TO RAISE OR LOWER FLOAT

FLOATS SHOULD JUST CONTACT GAUGE

SET GAUGE TO SPECIFICATIONS

INSTALL FLOAT PIN FROM THIS SIDE

Checking the float level with a fabricated gauge—models 4300 and 4350 carburetors (© Ford Motor Co.)

FLAT SURFACE OF FLOAT PONTOON (BOTH SIDES)

FLOAT LEVEL ADJUSTING TAB

SMOOTH AREA OF CASTING

Adjustment of the float level with a "T" scale—models 4300 and 4350 carburetors (© Jeep Corp.)

MODEL 4150G
Chevrolet/GMC
(All measurements in inches)

Year	Carburetor List No.	Float Level (Dry)	Fuel Level (Wet)	Accelerator Pump (Min.)	Fast Idle (RPM)	Air Vent Clearance	Fast Idle Mechanical Clearance
'77	R7703A	②	—	.015	2200	.045–.075	.038
	R7704A	②	—	.015	2200	.045–.075	.031

② Primary bowl—.194
Secondary bowl—.213

MODEL 4150EG
Chevrolet/GMC
(All measurements in inches)

Year	Carburetor List No.	Float Level (Dry)	Fuel Level (Wet)	Accelerator Pump (Min.)	Fast Idle (RPM)	Air Vent Clearance	Fast Idle Mechanical Clearance
'78	R7923A	②	—	.015	2200	.045–.075	.031
	R7927A	②	—	.015	2200	.045–.075	.031
	R7925A	②	—	.015	2200	—	.031
	R7928A	②	—	.015	2200	—	.031
	R7924A	②	—	.015	2200	.045–.075	.031
	R7926A	②	—	.015	2200	—	.031
'79	R8278A	②	—	.015	2200	.045–.075	.031
	R8280A	②	—	.015	2200	.045–.075	.031
	R8282A	②	—	.015	2200	.045–.075	.031
	R8283A	②	—	.015	2200	.045–.075	.031
	R8444A	②	—	.015	2200	.045–.075	.031
	R8279A	②	—	.015	2200	.045–.075	.031
	R8281A	②	—	.015	2200	.045–.075	.031
'80	R8848A	②	—	.015	2200	.045–.075	.031
	R8849A	②	—	.015	2200	.045–.075	.031
	R8852A	②	—	.015	2200	.045–.075	.031
	R8853A	②	—	.015	2200	.045–.075	.031
	R8856A	②	—	.015	2200	.045–.075	.031
	R8850A	②	—	.015	2200	—	.031
	R8851A	②	—	.015	2200	—	.031
	R8854A	②	—	.015	2200	—	.031
	R8855A	②	—	.015	2200	—	.031
	R8857A	②	—	.015	2200	—	.031

② Primary bowl—.194
Secondary bowl—.213

MODEL 1945 1–bbl
Dodge/Plymouth
(All measurements in inches)

Year	Carburetor List No.	Float Level (Dry)	Vacuum Kick Choke (Unloader)	Choke Setting	Pump Rod Adjustment (Hole)	Fast Idle Cam Position	Fast Idle Speed	Vacuum Kick (Initial Choke Opening)
'77	R7815A	①	.250	②	$2^{21}/_{64}(3)$	.080	1600	.110
	R7816A	①	.250	②	$2^{21}/_{64}(3)$	.080	1700	.110
	R7847A	①	.250	②	$2^{7}/_{32}(2)$	.080	1600	.110
	R7848A	①	.250	②	$2^{21}/_{64}(3)$	.080	1700	.110
'78	—	—	—	—	—	—	—	—
'79	R8593A	①	.250	②	$2^{7}/_{32}(1)$	.080	1600	.100
	R8594A	①	.250	②	$2^{21}/_{64}(2)$	.080	1600	.100
	R8799A	①	.250	②	$2^{7}/_{32}(1)$	.080	1600	.100
	R8800A	①	.250	②	$2^{21}/_{64}(2)$	.080	1600	.100
'80	R8978A	①	.250	②	1.70(1)	.080	1600	.130
	R8720A	①	.250	②	1.61(2)	.090	1600	.130
	R9107A	①	.250	②	1.70(1)	.080	1600	.100
	R9106A	①	.250	②	1.61(2)	.080	1600	.100
	R8979A	①	.250	②	1.70(1)	.080	1600	.130
	R8721A	①	.250	②	1.61(2)	.080	1600	.130
'81	R9131A	①	.250	②	1.615(2)	.090	1600	.130
	R9132A	①	.250	②	1.615(2)	.090	1600	.130
	R9134A	①	.250	②	1.615(2)	.090	1600	.130
	R9152A	①	.250	②	1.615(2)	.080	1800	.130
	R9153A	①	.250	②	1.615(2)	.080	1800	.130
	R9399A	①	.250	②	1.615(2)	.080	1800	.130
'82	R9132A	①	.250	②	#2	.090	1600	.130
	R9134A	①	.250	②	#2	.090	1600	.130
	R9153A	①	.250	②	#2	.080	1800	.130
	R9399A	①	.250	②	#2	.080	1800	.130
	R9762A	①	.250	②	#2	.090	1600	.130
	R9765A	①	.250	②	#2	.080	1800	.130
'83	R40055A	①	.250	②	#2	.080	1600	.130
	R40056A	①	.250	②	#2	.080	1600	.130
	R9399-1A	①	.250	②	#2	.080	1800	.130
	R9134-1A	①	.250	②	#2	.090	1800	.130

① Flush with top of bowl cover gasket, carb inverted
② Fixed setting

MODEL 2210 2–bbl
Dodge/Plymouth
(All measurements in inches)

Year	Carburetor List No.	Float Level (Dry)	Vacuum Kick Choke (Unloader)	Choke Setting	Pump Rod Location	Fast Idle Cam Position	Fast Idle Speed	Vacuum Kick (Initial Choke Opening)
'77	R7676A	3/16 ③	.170	①	⑤	.110	1700	.150
	R7870A	3/16 ③	.170	①	④	.110	1800	.150
	R6886–1A	3/16 ③	.170	①	④	.110	1600	.90

① Fixed setting
③ Bottom of float to be parallel with air horn bottom
④ At curb idle—slot #1—.310 in.
⑤ At curb idle—slot #2—.320 in.

MODEL 2245
Dodge/Plymouth
(All measurements in inches)

Year	Carburetor List No.	Float Level (Dry)	Choke Unloader	Choke Setting	Pump Rod Location (Hole)	Fast Idle Cam Position	Fast Idle Speed (RPM)	Vacuum Kick (Initial Choke Opening)
'77	R7697A	3/16 ③	.170	①	④	.110	1600	.150
	R7871A	3/16 ③	.170	①	⑤	.110	1600	.150
	R8036A	3/16 ③	.170	①	④	.110	1600	.150
	R8182A	3/16 ③	.170	①	④	.110	1600	.150
'78	R8453A	.180	.170	①	⑥	.110	1600	.150
	R8135A	.180	.170	①	⑦	.110	1600	.90
	R6886A	.180	.170	①	⑦	.110	1600	.150
	R7756A	.180	.170	①	⑦	.110	1600	.150
	R8484A	.180	.170	①	⑥	.110	1600	.150
	R7088A	.180	.170	①	⑦	.110	1600	.150
	R8028A	.180	.170	①	⑥	.110	1600	.150
	R7871A	.180	.170	①	⑥	.110	1600	.130
	R8026A	.180	.170	①	⑥	.110	1600	.150
'79	R8597A	.200 ③	.170	①	.290(1)	.110	1600	.110
	R8598A	.200 ③	.170	①	.290(1)	.110	1600	.110
	R8925A	.200 ③	.170	①	.290(1)	.110	1600	.110
'80–'81	R7871A	3/16	.170	Fixed	Slot #1	.110	1700	.150
'82	R9816A	3/16	.170	Fixed	Slot #3	.110	1700	.150
'83	R9816A	5/32–7/32	.170	Fixed	Slot #2	.110	1700	.150

NOTE: Number in Parenthesis is number of slot
① Fixed setting
② Accelerator pump setting:
  Curb idle—.260 in.
  Closed throttle—.310 in.
  #1 Slot
③ Float drop—bottom of float to be parallel with air horn bottom
④ At idle—slot #1—.310 in.
⑤ At idle—slot #2—.320 in.
⑥ At idle—slot #2—.260 in.
⑦ At idle—slot #2—.260 in.

MODEL 2280G
Dodge/Plymouth
(All measurements in inches)

Year	Carburetor List Number	Float Level	Choke Vacuum Kick	Fast Idle Cam	Fast Idle (rpm)	Choke Unloader	Bowl Vent Valve
'80	R8999A	5/16	.130	.070	1600	.310	.030
	R9000A	5/16	.130	.070	1600	.310	.030
	R9001A	5/16	.150	.070	1600	.310	.030
	R9209A	5/16	.150	.070	1600	.310	.030
	R9224A	5/16	.150	.070	1600	.310	.030

MODEL 2280
Dodge/Plymouth
(All measurements in inches)

Year	Carburetor List Number	Float Level	Choke Vacuum Kick	Fast Idle Cam	Fast Idle (rpm)	Choke Unloader	Vent Valve
'81	R9135A	9/32	.110	.070	1500	.310	—
	R9136A	9/32	.130	.070	1500	.310	—
	R9151A	9/32	.110	.070	1500	.310	—
	R9437A	9/32	.130	.070	1500	.310	—
'82	R9491A	7/32–10/32	.140	.052	1500	.200	—
	R9493A	7/32–10/32	.140	.052	1500	.200	—
	R9572A	7/32–10/32	.140	.052	1500	.200	—
'83	R9949A R9951A	4/16–5/16	.140	.052	1500	.200	—

MODEL 6145
Dodge/Plymouth
(All measurements in inches)

Year	Carburetor List Number	Float Setting	Choke Vacuum Kick	Choke Unloader Adjustment	Fast Idle Cam Position	Fast Idle RPM	Pump Piston Stroke
'83	R40029A	①	.150	.250	.090	1600	1.70
	R40030A	①	.150	.250	.090	1600	1.61

① With bowl inverted, float lungs just touch a straightedge run along gasket surface.

MODEL 2300G
Dodge/Plymouth
(All measurements in inches)

Year	Carburetor List Number	Float Level	Choke Unloader	Pump Rod Location	Fast Idle Cam Position	Fast Idle (rpm)	Vacuum Kick Initial Choke Opening
'77	R6769–1A	①	—	—	.035	—	—
	R7137A	①	—	—	.035	—	—

① Check the float level to the bottom of the sight plug on the carburetor

MODELS 2300, 2300G
Ford
(All measurements in inches)

Year	Carburetor List No.	Float Level	Choke Unloader Setting	Choke Setting	Accelerator Pump Rod Location	Fuel Level (Wet)	Initial Choke Valve Setting
'77–'78	D4TE						
	AJA	②	—	Manual	#2 hole	①	—
'78	D8TE						
	BPA	②	—	Manual	#2 hole	①	—
	CEA	②	—	Manual	#2 hole	①	—
	AJA	②	—	Manual	#2 hole	①	—

① At lower edge of sight plug opening
② Float parallel to bowl, bowl top inverted

MODEL 2300C
Ford
(All measurements in inches)

Year	Carburetor List Number	Fuel Level (Wet)	Pump Cam Location	Pulldown Setting	Choke Setting	Choke Unloader
'83	E2TE-9510-DPA	①	1	.210–.230	3 Rich	.300

MODEL 4150G
Ford
(All measurements in inches)

Year	Carburetor List No.	Float Level	Choke Unloader Setting	Choke Setting	Accelerator Pump Rod Location	Fuel Level (Wet)	Initial Choke Valve Setting
'77–'78	D5TE						
	CB	②	—	Manual	#2 hole	①	—
	CA	②	—	Manual	#1 hole	①	—
	CB	②	—	Manual	#2 hole	①	—
'77	D5TE						
	BA	②	—	Manual	#2 hole	①	—
	AA	②	—	Manual	#2 hole	①	—
'77–'78	D5TE						
	BRA	②	—	Manual	#2 hole	①	—
'78	D8TE						
	AHA	②	—	Manual	—	①	—
	BZA	②	—	Manual	—	①	—
	AGA	②	—	Manual	—	①	—
	BRA	②	—	Manual	—	①	—
	CBA	②	—	Manual	—	①	—
	BSA	②	—	Manual	—	①	—

MODEL 4150EG
Ford
(All measurements in inches)

Year	Carburetor List Number	Float Level (Dry)	Float Drop	Choke Unloader Setting	Choke Setting	Dash Pot Plunger	Initial Choke Setting
'80	D9HE–9510 CA, DA, EA, FA	①	—	—	—	—	—
	E0HE–9510 CA,EA	①	—	—	—	—	—
'81	D9HE–9510 CA,EA	①	—	—	Manual	—	—

① Check float level to the bottom of the sight plug in the carburetor

MODEL 4150MG
Ford

Year	Carburetor List Number	Float Level	Choke Unloader Setting	Choke Setting	Accelerator Pump Rod Location	Fuel Level (Wet)	Initial Choke Valve Setting
'77	D7HE AA	②	—	Manual	#1 hole	①	—
	CA	②	—	Manual	#1 hole	①	—
'78	D8HE AA	②	—	Manual	#1 hole	①	—
	EA	②	—	Manual	#1 hole	①	—
	CA	②	—	Manual	#1 hole	①	—
	BA	②	—	Manual	#1 hole	①	—
	FA	②	—	Manual	#1 hole	①	—
	DA	②	—	Manual	#1 hole	①	—

MODEL 4180EG
Ford
(All measurements in inches)

Year	Carburetor List Number	Float Level (Dry)	Float Drop	Choke Unloader Setting	Choke Setting	Dash Pot Plunger	Initial Choke Setting
'80	E0TE-9510 ETA, JB, JA, RA, EUA, RB, ERA, MB, SB, SA, ESA, MA	①	—	—	—	—	.210
	D9TE-9510 AHE, EBA, ETA, EUA	①	—	—	—	—	.210
'81	D9TE-9510 EBA, AHE, ETA, EUA	①	—	—	Manual	—	.185–.235
	E0TE-9510 RA, JA, MA, SA	①	—	—	Manual	—	.185–.235

① Check float level to the bottom of the sight plug in the carburetor

MODEL 4180EG
Ford
(All measurements in inches)

Year	Carburetor List Number	Fuel Level (Wet)	Choke Pulldown Setting	Pump Lever Location	Power Valve Timing
'82	E2TE- CSA AJA CUA CTA AKA CVA E0TE- SA495 D9TE- EVA495	①	.180–.440	#1	9.5-7.0/3.0-.5

① At bottom of sight plug

MODEL 4180C
Ford
(All measurements in inches)

Year	Carburetor List Number	Float Level (Dry)	Float Drop	Choke Unloader Setting	Choke Setting	Dash Pot Plunger	Initial Choke Setting
'80	D9TE-9510 DKA	①	—	.315②	—	—	.210
'81	D9TE-9510 BKA	①	—	—	5 Rich	—	.195–.225

① Check float level to the bottom of the sight plug in the carburetor   ② ±.015 inch

MODEL 4180C
Ford
(All measurements in inches)

Year	Carburetor List Number	Fuel Level (wet)	Choke Pulldown Setting	Choke Unloader Setting	Choke Setting	Pump Lever Location	Power Valve Timing
'82	E1UE- RA	①	.200–.220	.295–.335	2 Rich	#1	9.5-7.0/3.0-.5

① At bottom of sight plug

MODEL 4180C
Ford
(All measurements in inches)

Year	Carburetor List Number	Fuel Level (Wet)	Choke Pulldown Setting	Choke Unloader Setting	Choke Setting	Pump Cam Location	Enrichment Valve Ident.
'83	E3TE- 9510-PC 9510-PC	①	.210–.230	.300–.330	3 Rich	#1	11
	E3TE- 9510-SB 9510-TB	①	.210–.230	.300–.330	3 Rich	#1	8

① At bottom of sight plug

MODEL 1920
International
(All measurements in inches)

Year	Carburetor List No. (49 States)	Carburetor List No. (Calif.)	Float Level	Fuel Level	Fast Idle Speed (RPM)	Auto Choke Setting	Dash-Post Setting	Fuel Bowl Vent Clearance	Pump Piston Stroke Adjustment	Fast Idle Cam Pos. Adjustment (Top Step—Hot)	Choke Vac. Pulldown (Kick) Adjustment	Choke Unloader Adjustment	Choke qualification Adjustment
'77–'78	7161, 7161–1	7576 8238	①	11/16 ± 1/32	2000	1 Rich	—	—	25/32	—	—	.235– .295	.100– .130
'79–'80	7771	7771	①	11/16 ± 1/32	2200	1 Lean	—	—	25/32	—	—	.235– .295	.150– .180

①Flush with top edge of bowl and with fuel inlet valve held closed

MODEL 1940C
International
(All measurements in inches)

Year	Carburetor List Number	Float Level	Fuel Level	Automatic Choke	Dash Pot Setting	Choke Unloader	Fast Idle (rpm)	Curb Idle (rpm)	Pump Stroke	Idle CO %
'77–'78	7161 7161–1 7576	①	11/16 ± 1/32	1 Rich	.100–.130	.235–.295	2000	525–575	25/32	0.5–2.0
'79	7771	①	11/16 ± 1/32	1 Rich	.100–.130	.235–.295	2200	675–725	25/32	0.3–1.5

①Flush with top edge of bowl, with fuel inlet valve held closed

MODEL 2210C
International
(All measurements in inches)

Year	Carb. List No. (48 States)	Carb. List No. (Calif.)	Float Level	Fuel Level	Fast Idle Speed	Auto Choke Setting	Dash Pot Setting	Fuel Bowl Vent Clearance	Pump Piston Stroke Adjustment	Fast Idle Cam Position Adjustment (Top Step—Hot)	Choke Vac. Pulldown (Kick) Adjustment	Choke Unloader Adjustment	Choke Qualification Adjustment
'77–'80	6620–1 7309	—	.180	1/2①	2000	②	—	—	—	—	—	.198– .258	.040– .070
	7214, 7214–1	—	.180	1/2①	1800	Preset	—	—	—	—	—	.228 ± .030	.135 ± .015
	—	7309, 6620–2, 7133, 7940 8241	.180	1/2①	2200	②	—	—	—	—	—	.198– .258	.040– .070
	—	7657, 7217, 8244	.180	1/2①	1800	Preset	—	—	—	—	—	.198– .258	.120– .150

①@ 5.5 PSI

②Choke with index marks—1 notch lean (restrained)
Choke without index marks—preset (unrestrained)

MODEL 2245C
International
(All measurements in inches)

Year	Carburetor Number	Float Level	Fuel① Level	Automatic Choke	Dash Pot Setting	Choke Unloader	Fast Idle (rpm)	Curb② Idle (rpm)	Idle CO %
'79	7773	.180	1/2	Pre-set	.105–.135	.198–.258	2200	675–725	0.1–0.8

①5.5 psi of fuel pressure ②Transmission in neutral and air conditioning off

MODEL 2300, 2300C, 2300G, 2300EG
International
(All measurements in inches)

Year	Carburetor List Number	Fuel Level	Fast Idle (rpm)	Automatic Choke Setting	Dash Pot Setting	Governor No load (rpm)	Governor Full load (rpm)	High Idle (rpm)	Curb Idle (rpm)	Idle CO %
'77–'78	6801-1	3/8	2200	—	—	4000	3800	1350 ± 50	650–700	2.0
	8232	3/8	2200	—	—	4000	3800	1350 ± 50	650–700	1.5
	7213	3/8	2400	—	—	3800	3600	1350 ± 50	525–575	0.5–2.5
	8235	3/8	2400	—	—	3800	3600	1350 ± 50	525–575	0.5–2.5
	6908	3/8	2000	—	—	3400	3200	1350 ± 50	500–550	1.5–3.0
	8238	3/8	2000	—	—	3400	3200	1350 ± 50	500–550	1.5–3.0
	7656	3/8	2000	—	—	4000	3800	1450 ± 50	625–675	1.0–3.0
	8242	3/8	2000	—	—	4000	3800	1450 ± 50	625–675	1.0–3.0
	7580	3/8	2400	—	—	3800	3600	1350 ± 50	525–575	0.5–2.0
	7922	3/8	2400	—	—	3800	3600	1350 ± 50	525–575	0.5–2.0
	8245	3/8	2400	—	—	3800	3600	1350 ± 50	525–575	0.5–2.0
	7198	3/8	2000	—	—	3400	3400	1350 ± 50	500–550	1.0–2.0
	8248	3/8	2000	—	—	3400	3400	1350 ± 50	500–550	1.0–2.0
'79–'81	8736	3/8	2200	—	—	4000	3800	1450 ± 50	625–675	1.0–3.0
	7922	3/8	2400	—	—	3800	3600	1350 ± 50	525–575	0.5–2.5
	8741	3/8	2000	—	—	3400	3200	1350 ± 50	500–550	1.0–2.0
	9072	3/8	2000	—	—	3800	3600	1350 ± 50	625–675	1.0–3.0
	8242	3/8	2000	—	—	4000	3800	1450 ± 50	625–675	1.0–3.0
	9076	3/8	2400	—	—	3800	3600	1350 ± 50	525–575	0.5–2.0
	8245	3/8	2400	—	—	3800	3600	1350 ± 50	525–575	0.5–2.0
	8248	3/8	2000	—	—	3400	3200	1350 ± 50	500–550	1.0–2.0
	8232	3/8	2200	—	—	4000	3800	1350 ± 50	650–700	2.0
	8180	3/8	2200	—	—	4000	3800	1300 ± 50	650–700	1.5
	8236	3/8	2400	—	—	3800	3600	1350 ± 50	525–575	0.5–2.5
	8235	3/8	2400	—	—	3800	3600	1350 ± 50	525–575	0.5–2.5
	8238	3/8	2000	—	—	3400	3200	1350 ± 50	500–550	1.5–3.0

MODELS 4150G, 4150EG
International
(All measurements in inches)

Year	Carburetor List No.	Fuel Valve Seal	Fuel Level	Fast Idle Setting (in. or RPM)	Governor Speed No-Load (RPM)	Governor Speed Full-Load (RPM)	Curb Idle Speed (RPM)	Idle Mixture Setting % CO
'77–'80 (Federal)	6803-3	—	①	2000	3800	3600	650–700	2.0 Max
	7215	—	①	2400	3800	3600	525–575	0.5–2.5
	7251	—	①	2400	3800	3600	525–575	0.5–2.5
	6911	—	①	2000	3400	3200	500–550	1.5–3.0

MODELS 4150G, 4150EG
International
(All measurements in inches)

Year	Carburetor List No.	Fuel Valve Seal	Fuel Level	Fast Idle Setting (in. or RPM)	Governor Speed No-Load (RPM)	Governor Speed Full-Load (RPM)	Curb Idle Speed (RPM)	Idle Mixture Setting % CO
'77–'80 (Calif.)	7028, 7529	—	①	.015–.020	3800	3600	625–675	0.5–1.5
	7218, 7218-1	—	①	2400	3800	3600	525–575	0.5–2.5
	7581	—	①	2400	3800	3600	525–575	0.5–2.5
	7921	—	①	2400	3800 ± 50	—	525–575	0.5–2.5
'77–'80 (50 States)	7029, 7029-1	—	①	2400	3800	3600	525–575	0.5–2.5
	6974	—	①	2000	3400	3200	500–550	1.0–2.0

① Primary ⅜ in., Secondary ⅝ in.

Fast idle cam position adjustment—models 2210, 2210C, and 2245 carburetors (© Chrysler Corp.)

Adjusting the fuel level with the fuel bowl inverted—model 1945 carburetor (© Chrysler Corp.)

Checking float setting—model 1920 one barrel (© Chrysler Corp.)

GAUGE

CHECK VALVE

15 INCHES OF VACUUM MINIMUM TO FULLY RETRACT DIAPHRAGM STEM

LIGHT CLOSING PRESSURE ON CHOKE LEVER

TO VACUUM SOURCE

BEND LINK HERE TO ADJUST

Choke valve initial setting (vacuum kick)—model 1945 carburetor (© Chrysler Corp.)

THROTTLE LEVER IN CURB IDLE POSITION

SCALE

BEND LINK HERE FOR ADJUSTMENT

Accelerator pump piston stroke adjustment—model 1945 carburetor (© Chrysler Corp.)

FLOAT

GAUGE OR DRILL

AIR HORN INVERTED

FLOAT STOP

Adjusting the float level—models 2210, 2210C and 2245 carburetors (© Chrysler Corp.)

GAUGE

BEND UNLOADER TANG HERE FOR ADJUSTMENT

THROTTLE LEVER IN WIDE OPEN POSITION

Choke valve unloader adjustment—model 1945 carburetor (© Chrysler Corp.)

RETAINING SCREWS

SAFETY WIRE-9990

GOVERNOR HOUSING-9B570

CHOKE PLATE-9549

GOVERNOR LEVER ASSEMBLY-9B575

COVER GASKET-9982

FUEL ENRICHMENT PISTON-9975

SCREW-50420-S

SEAL 9989

SCREW 43251-S

GOVERNOR SPRING-9980

GASKET-9945

GASKET 9580

DISCHARGE NOZZLE-9577

SCREW-373625-S

RETAINER-351825-S

NUT 34709-S

PLUG-9C510

SCREW 370551-S

SPRING-9976

GASKET-9580

ACCELERATING PUMP DISCHARGE NEEDLE-9A516

DISTRIBUTOR VACUUM FITTING-87971-S

COVER-9981

GASKET 351207-S

CHOKE ROD RETAINER-9B501

FUEL ENRICHMENT ADJUSTING SCREW-353570-S

CHOKE SHAFT-9546

IDLE SPEED SCREW-359539-S AND SPRING - 9578

SAFETY WIRE 9990

SCREW-370552-S

THROTTLE OPERATING LEVER

FAST IDLE PIN-9B503

9989 SCREW 357136-S

JETS-9973

GASKET 9853

NUT

BRACKET-9595

CLIP-506

THROTTLE OPERATING SHAFT HOUSING-9B505

COVER-9507

WASHER-34803-S

SEAL-9948

FRESH AIR FITTING

GASKET 9B510

SCREW-31061-S

DIAPHRAGM ASSEMBLY-9503

POWER VALVE-9A565

SCREW-43248-S

SCREW-43248-S

VACUUM ADVANCE FITTING

GASKET-9A588

MAIN BODY 9512

ACCELERATING PUMP CAM-9526

BAFFLE

GASKET-9516

SCREW-31061-S

SCREW-37611-S

THROTTLE LEVER

LOCK SCREW 373246-S

RETAINER 358675-S

SCREW-31037-S

RETAINER-358675

GASKET-9A522

C

IDLE ADJUSTING NEEDLES-9541

9A514

SCREW-370554-S

ADJUSTING NUT-372426-S

SPRING 9636

CHOKE CONTROL SHAFT

SCREW-33174-S

9564

GASKET-9A522

FLOAT 9550

CLAMP-9792

NUT-34052-S

FUEL INLET NEEDLE AND SEAT

MAIN JETS 9533

BUSHINGS-9B508

FAST IDLE CAM-9597

O-RING-9609

METERING BLOCK-9A511

WASHER-

NUT-355829-S

FUEL LEVEL SIGHT PLUG-9562

GASKET-9561

SCREW-359736-S

GASKET 9B507

SCREW 9586

RETAINER-356249-S

BACK-UP PLATE-9B506

GASKET-9592

FLOAT SPRING-9A519

THROTTLE BODY-9447

NUT-373235-S

BAFFLE PLATE-9A517

GASKET-9229

THROTTLE PLATES-9585

RETAINER 9568

GASKET-9A588

FUEL INLET FITTING-9A520

RETAINER-354331-S

FILTER SCREEN-9938

THROTTLE CLUTCH AND SHAFT ASSEMBLY-9581

FUEL BOWL-9A507

SPRING-9636

SPRING-9571

PUMP OPERATING LEVER

SCREW-359747-S

DIAPHRAGM-9B559

ACCELERATING PUMP COVER

9528

SCREW-43255-S

Holley two barrel—typical

UNDERSIDE SURFACE OF AIR HORN

BOTTOM EDGE OF FLOAT SHOULD BE PARALLEL

Adjusting the float drop—models 2210, 2210C and 2245 carburetors (© Chrysler Corp.)

MINIMUM 15 INCHES VACUUM ON DIAPHRAGM

GAUGE

TO VACUUM SOURCE

LIGHT CLOSING PRESSURE ON CHOKE LEVER

Adjusting the initial choke valve setting—models 2210, 2210C and 2245 carburetors (© Chrysler Corp.)

Checking the accelerator pump lever clearance—Holley 4150 typical (© Ford Motor Co.)

Fast idle cam-to-choke valve adjustment—model 1945 carburetor (© Chrysler Corp.)

Choke unloader adjustment—models 2210, 2210C and 2245 carburetors (© Chrysler Corp.)

Adjustment locations—model 2300 carburetor (© Chrysler Corp.)

LIGHT CLOSING
PRESSURE

GAUGE

FAST IDLE SPEED
ADJUSTING SCREW ON
SECOND HIGHEST
STEP OF CAM

Fast idle cam position—models 2210, 2210C and 2245 carburetors
(© Chrysler Corp.)

SPECIAL WRENCH

SPECIAL WRENCH

FAST IDLE CAM

ADJUSTING SCREW
FAST IDLE

CHOKE VALVE OPEN

FAST IDLE CAM

Fast idle speed adjustment—Holley 4150 typical (© Chrysler Corp.)

LOCKSCREW

LOCKSCREW

ADJUSTING NUT

SIGHT PLUG
(SECONDARY)

ADJUSTING
NUT

SIGHT PLUG (PRIMARY)

Fuel level sight plug location—Holley 4150 typical (© Chrysler
Corp.)

SCREWDRIVER

WRENCH

GASKET

SIGHT PLUG

Adjusting the fuel level—Holley 4150 typical (© Chrysler Corp.)

Holley 2300 carburetor—typical (© Ford Motor Co.)

FUEL BOWL VENT

CHOKE PLATE

FUEL LEVEL ADJUSTMENT

GOVERNOR HOUSING

CHOKE CABLE CLAMP

FUEL BOWL

ACCELERATING PUMP

FUEL INLET

IDLE SPEED ADJUSTING SCREW

THROTTLE LEVER

TURN ADJUSTING NUT UNTIL FLOAT IS PARALLEL WITH TOP OF BOWL (HOLDING BOWL UPSIDE DOWN)

Adjusting the float level (dry)—Holley 4150 typical (© Ford Motor Co.)

LOCK SCREW

ADJUSTING NUT

FUEL LEVEL SIGHT PLUG OPENING

Adjusting the fuel level (wet)—Holley 4150 typical (© Ford Motor Co.)

SECONDARY FUEL BOWL

MAIN BODY

SECONDARY THROTTLE OPERATING DIAPHRAGM

PRIMARY FUEL BOWL

GOVERNOR ASSEMBLY

THROTTLE BODY

ACCELERATING PUMP ASSEMBLY

Holley 4150 carburetor—typical (© Ford Motor Co.)

DIAPHRAGM ASSEMBLY
COVER
AIR CLEANER ANCHOR SCREW
SECONDARY HOUSING
ACCELERATING PUMP DISCHARGE NOZZLE
DIAPHRAGM SPRING
ACCELERATING PUMP DISCHARGE NEEDLE
SECONDARY VACUUM CHECK BALL
CHOKE SHAFT
CHOKE ROD PICK-UP LEVER AND BUSHING
FUEL LEVEL SIGHT PLUG AND GASKET
FAST IDLE CAM PLUNGER
FAST IDLE PIN
CHOKE ROD
GOVERNOR BY-PASS JETS
GOVERNOR SPRING PIN
CHOKE ROD SEAL
SECONDARY FUEL BOWL
GOVERNOR HOUSING
CHOKE CONTROL LEVER
SECONDARY FUEL BOWL GASKET
GOVERNOR HOUSING COVER
SPRING
CHOKE PLATE
SECONDARY METERING BLOCK
GOVERNOR SPRING
GOVERNOR LEVER
FUEL TRANSFER TUBE
GOVERNOR VACUUM FITTING
BALANCE TUBE
GOVERNOR DIAPHRAGM COVER
O-RING SEAL
WASHER
METERING BLOCK GASKET
GOVERNOR DIAPHRAGM
CLEAN AIR FITTING
PLUNGER SPRING
MAIN BODY
FAST IDLE CAM AND SHAFT ASSEMBLY
PRIMARY METERING BLOCK
GOVERNOR HOUSING SEAL
DISTRIBUTOR VACUUM FITTING
POWER VALVE
LOCK SCREW
THROTTLE BODY-TO-MAIN BODY GASKET
IDLE LIMITER
BAFFLE
POWER VALVE GASKET
THROTTLE OPERATING HOUSING PLATE
GASKET
FUEL LEVEL ADJUSTING NUT
FUEL INLET NEEDLE AND SEAT
SHAFT BUSHINGS
SECONDARY THROTTLE PLATES
GASKET
IDLE ADJUSTING NEEDLE
WASHER
FUEL LEVEL SIGHT PLUG AND GASKET
FLOAT
SECONDARY THROTTLE SHAFT
O-RING
BAFFLE PLATE
MAIN JETS
IDLE LIMITER
SPACER
THROTTLE CONNECTING ROD
FLOAT SPRING
THROTTLE SHAFT DRIVER
FILTER SCREEN
THROTTLE BODY
THROTTLE OPERATING LEVER
FUEL INLET FITTING
PRIMARY THROTTLE PLATES
PRIMARY FUEL BOWL
ACCELERATING PUMP OPERATING LEVER
PRIMARY THROTTLE SHAFT
HOT ENGINE IDLE SCREW
DIAPHRAGM SPRING
DIAPHRAGM ASSEMBLY
THROTTLE OPERATING HOUSING
THROTTLE PICK-UP LEVER
ACCELERATING PUMP CAM
ACCELERATING PUMP COVER

Holley four barrel—typical

PRIMARY STAGE THROTTLE PLATES
POWER VALVE VACUUM PICK UP
PRIMARY FUEL BOWL
AUTOMATIC CHOKE
FAST IDLE SPEED
HOT ENGINE IDLE SPEED
SECONDARY THROTTLE STOP SCREW
CHOKE HOUSING VACUUM PICK UP
SECONDARY FUEL BOWL
SECONDARY STAGE THROTTLE PLATES

Bottom view—Holley 4160C carburetor (© Ford Motor Co.)

Bottom view—Holley 4180C carburetor (© Ford Motor Co.)

MODEL 2GV/2GC/2GE
Chevrolet/GMC
(All measurements in inches)

Year	Carburetor Number	Float Level	Float Drop	Choke Unloader Setting	Choke Setting	Pump Rod Location	Fast Idle Speed (RPM)	Metering Rod Setting	Fast Idle Cam 2nd Step	Choke Vacuum Break
'77	7044133	$^{19}/_{32}$	$1^9/_{32}$	.325	Index	$1^{21}/_{32}$	—	—	.260	.130
	7044134	$^{19}/_{32}$	$1^9/_{32}$	.325	Index	$1^{21}/_{32}$	—	—	.260	.130
	17056433	$^{19}/_{32}$	$1^9/_{32}$	.325	Index	$1^{21}/_{32}$	—	—	.260	.130
	17056434	$^{19}/_{32}$	$1^9/_{32}$	.325	Index	$1^{21}/_{32}$	—	—	.260	.130
	17056137	$^{19}/_{32}$	$1^9/_{32}$	.325	Index	$1^{21}/_{32}$	—	—	.260	.190
'78	7044133	$^{19}/_{32}$	$1^9/_{32}$	—	Manual	$1^9/_{16}$	—	—	—	—
	7044134	$^{19}/_{32}$	$1^9/_{32}$	—	Manual	$1^7/_{16}$	—	—	—	—
	17058423	$^{19}/_{32}$	$1^9/_{32}$	—	Manual	$1^9/_{16}$	—	—	—	—
	17058424	$^{19}/_{32}$	$1^9/_{32}$	—	Manual	$1^7/_{16}$	—	—	—	—
	17058104	$^{15}/_{32}$	$1^9/_{32}$	.325	Index	$1^{21}/_{32}$	—	—	.260	.130
	17058105	$^{15}/_{32}$	$1^9/_{32}$	.325	Index	$1^{21}/_{32}$	—	—	.260	.130
	17058107	$^{15}/_{32}$	$1^9/_{32}$	.325	Index	$1^{17}/_{32}$	—	—	.260	.130
	17058109	$^{15}/_{32}$	$1^9/_{32}$	.325	Index	$1^{17}/_{32}$	—	—	.260	.130
	17058102	$^{15}/_{32}$	$1^9/_{32}$	.325	Index	$1^{17}/_{32}$	—	—	.260	.130
	17058103	$^{15}/_{32}$	$1^9/_{32}$	.325	Index	$1^{17}/_{32}$	—	—	.260	.130

MODEL 2GV/2GC/2GE
Chevrolet/GMC
(All measurements in inches)

Year	Carburetor Number	Float Level	Float Drop	Choke Unloader Setting	Choke Setting	Pump Rod Location	Fast Idle Speed (RPM)	Metering Rod Setting	Fast Idle Cam 2nd Step	Choke Vacuum Break
'78	17058405	½	1⁹⁄₃₂	.325	½ Lean	1²¹⁄₃₂	—	—	.260	.140
	17058405	½	1⁹⁄₃₂	.325	½ Lean	1²¹⁄₃₂	—	—	.260	.140
	17058447	⁷⁄₁₆	1⁵⁄₃₂	.140	1 Rich	1⁵⁄₈	—	—	.080	.110
	17058143	⁷⁄₁₆	1⁵⁄₃₂	.140	1 Rich	1⁵⁄₈	—	—	.080	.040
	17058147	⁷⁄₁₆	1⁵⁄₃₂	.140	1 Rich	1⁵⁄₈	—	—	.080	.100
	17058144	⁷⁄₁₆	1⁵⁄₃₂	.140	1 Rich	1⁵⁄₈	—	—	.080	.060
'79	7044133	1⁹⁄₃₂	1⁹⁄₃₂	—	Index	1⁹⁄₁₆	—	—	—	—
	7044134	1⁹⁄₃₂	1⁹⁄₃₂	—	Index	1⁷⁄₁₆	—	—	—	—
	17059126	⅝	1⁹⁄₃₂	—	Index	1¹⁵⁄₃₂	—	—	—	—
	17059127	1⁷⁄₃₂	1⁹⁄₃₂		Index	1¹⁵⁄₃₂	—	—	—	—
	17059423	⅝	1⁹⁄₃₂	—	Index	1²¹⁄₃₂	—	—	—	—
	17059424	1⁷⁄₃₂	1⁹⁄₃₂	—	Index	1¹⁵⁄₃₂	—	—	—	—
	17059420	1⁷⁄₃₂	1⁹⁄₃₂	—	Index	1¹⁵⁄₃₂	—	—	—	—

MODEL 2G/2GV
Chevrolet/GMC
(All measurements in inches)

Year	Carburetor Number	Float Level	Float Drop	Choke Unloader	Choke Setting	Pump Rod Adj.	Fast Idle (rpm)	Metering Rod Setting	Fast Idle Cam 2nd step	Choke Vacuum Break
'80	7044133	1¹⁄₁₆	1⁹⁄₃₂	—	Manual	1⁹⁄₁₆	—	—	—	—
	7044134	1¹⁄₁₆	1⁹⁄₃₂	—	Manual	1⁷⁄₁₆	—	—	—	—
	17058120	1¹⁄₁₆	1⁹⁄₃₂	—	Manual	1²¹⁄₃₂	—	—	—	—
	17080120	⅝	1⁹⁄₃₂	—	Manual	1²¹⁄₃₂	—	—	—	—
	17080126	⅝	1⁹⁄₃₂	—	Manual	1²¹⁄₃₂	—	—	—	—
	17080127	⅝	1⁹⁄₃₂	—	Manual	1²¹⁄₃₂	—	—	—	—
	17080129	⅝	1⁹⁄₃₂	—	Index	1²¹⁄₃₂	—	—	—	.130
	17080420	⅝	1⁹⁄₃₂	—	Manual	1²¹⁄₃₂	—	—	—	—
	17080423	⅝	1⁹⁄₃₂	—	Manual	1²¹⁄₃₂	—	—	—	—
	17080424	⅝	1⁹⁄₃₂	—	Manual	1²¹⁄₃₂	—	—	—	—

MODEL M2MC/M2ME
Chevrolet/GMC
(All measurements in inches)

Year	Carburetor Number	Float Level	Float Drop	Choke Unloader	Choke Setting	Pump① Rod Adj.	Fast② Idle (rpm)	Metering Rod Setting	Fast Idle Cam Setting	Choke Vacuum Break
'79	17059100	15/32	—	—	1 Lean	13/32	1600	—	38°	29°
	17059101	15/32	—	—	1 Lean	13/32	1600	—	38°	29°
	17059102	15/32	—	—	1 Lean	13/32	1600	—	38°	29°
	17059103	15/32	—	—	1 Lean	13/32	1600	—	38°	29°
	17059142	15/32	—	—	1 Lean	13/32	1600	—	38°	29°
	17059143	15/32	—	—	1 Lean	13/32	1600	—	38°	29°
	17059144	15/32	—	—	1 Lean	13/32	1600	—	38°	29°
	17059145	15/32	—	—	1 Lean	13/32	1600	—	38°	29°
'80	17080100	7/16	—	38°	—	9/32	③	—	38°	29°
	17080102	7/16	—	38°	—	9/32	③	—	38°	29°
	17080142	7/16	—	38°	—	9/32	③	—	38°	29°
	17080143	7/16	—	38°	—	9/32	③	—	38°	29°
	17080145	7/16	—	38°	—	9/32	③	—	38°	29°
'81	17081101	13/32	—	38°	—	5/16	③	—	38°	29°
	17081103	13/32	—	38°	—	5/16	③	—	38°	29°
	17081142	13/32	—	38°	—	5/16	③	—	38°	29°
	17081143	13/32	—	38°	—	5/16	③	—	38°	29°
	17081144	13/32	—	38°	—	5/16	③	—	38°	29°
	17081145	13/32	—	38°	—	5/16	③	—	38°	29°

① Rod installed in the inner hole of the pump
   lever (nearest the carburetor)
② Manual transmission—1300 rpm in neutral
③ See underhood emissions label for idle
   speed specifications

MODEL IME/IM
Chevrolet/GMC
(All measurements in inches)

Year	Carburetor Number	Float Level	Float Drop	Choke Unloader Setting	Choke Setting	Pump Rod Location	Fast Idle Speed (RPM)	Metering Rod Setting	Fast Idle Cam 2nd Step	Choke Vacuum Break
'77	17057001	3/8	—	.325	Index	—	2100	.080	.125	.150
	17057002	3/8	—	.325	Index	—	2100	.080	.110	.135
	17057004	3/8	—	.325	Index	—	2100	.080	.110	.135
	17057005	3/8	—	.325	Index	—	2100	.080	.125	.180

MODEL IME/IM
Chevrolet/GMC

(All measurements in inches)

Year	Carburetor Number	Float Level	Float Drop	Choke Unloader Setting	Choke Setting	Pump Rod Location	Fast Idle Speed (RPM)	Metering Rod Setting	Fast Idle Cam 2nd Step	Choke Vacuum Break
	17057010	3/8	—	.325	Index	—	2100	.080	.110	.180
	17057302	3/8	—	.325	Index	—	2100	.080	.150	.135
	17057303	3/8	—	.325	Index	—	2100	.090	.125	.150
	17057006	5/16	—	.275	Index	—	2400	.070	.150	.180
	17057007	5/16	—	.275	Index	—	2400	.070	.150	.180
	17057008	5/16	—	.275	Index	—	2400	.065	.150	.180
	17057009	5/16	—	.275	Index	—	2400	②.065	.150	.180
	17057308	5/16	—	.275	Index	—	2400	.065	.150	.180
	17057309	5/16	—	.275	Index	—	2400	.065	.150	.180
'78	17058009	1/4	—	—	Index	—	2400①	.065	—	—
	17058011	1/4	—	—	Index	—	2400①	.065	—	—
	17058423	19/32	19/32	—	Index	19/16	—	—	—	—
	17058434	19/32	19/32	—	Index	17/16	—	—	—	—
	7044133	19/32	19/32	—	Index	19/16	—	—	—	—
	7044134	19/32	19/32	—	Index	17/16	—	—	—	—
	17058013	3/8	—	.500	Index	—	2000①	.080	.180	.200
	17058014	5/16	—	.500	Index	—	2100①	.100	.180	.200
	17058020	5/16	—	.500	Index	—	2100①	.100	.180	.200
	17058314	3/8	—	.400	Index	—	2000①	.100	.190	.245
'79	17058009	1/4	—	—	Index	—	2400	.065	—	—
	17058011	1/4	—	—	Index	—	2400	.065	—	—
	17059009	5/16	—	.520	2 Rich	—	2400	.065②	.275	.400
	17059309	5/16	—	.521	2 Rich	—	2400	.065	.275	.400
	17059359	5/16	—	.521	2 Rich	—	2400	.065	.275	.400
'80	17080009	11/32	—	.520	③	—	2400	.090	.275	.400
	17080309	11/32	—	.520	③	—	2400	.090	.275	.400
	17080359	11/32	—	.520	③	—	2400	.090	.275	.400
'81	17081009	11/32	—	.520	③	—	④	.090	.275	.400
	17081309	11/32	—	.520	③	—	④	.090	.275	.400
	17081329	11/32	—	.520	③	—	④	.090	.275	.400

① In neutral
② .090 inches on medium duty truck applications
③ Not adjustable
④ See emission label under hood of vehicle

MODEL 2SE
Chevrolet/GMC

(All measurements in inches)

Year	Carburetor Number	Float Level	Float Drop	Choke① Unloader	Choke Setting	Pump③ Rod Adj.	Fast Idle (rpm)	Metering Rod Setting	Fast Idle① Cam 2nd step	Choke① Vacuum Break
'79	17059640	1/8	—	49°	②	9/16	2000	—	—	20°
	17059641	1/8	—	49°	②	9/16	1800	—	—	23.5°
	17059643	1/8	—	49°	②	9/16	1800	—	—	23.5°
	17059740	1/8	—	49°	②	9/16	2000	—	—	20°
	17059741	1/8	—	49°	②	9/16	2100	—	—	20°
	17059764	1/8	—	49°	②	9/16	2100	—	—	20°
	17059765	1/8	—	49°	②	9/16	2100	—	—	23.5°
	17059767	1/8	—	49°	②	9/16	2100	—	—	23.5°
'80	17080621	1/8	—	41°	⑤	9/16	④	—	17°	22°
	17080622	1/8	—	41°	⑤	9/16	④	—	17°	22°
	17080623	1/8	—	41°	⑤	9/16	④	—	17°	22°
	17080626	1/8	—	41°	⑤	9/16	④	—	17°	22°
	17080720	1/8	—	41°	⑤	9/16	④	—	17°	22°
	17080721	1/8	—	41°	⑤	9/16	④	—	17°	23.5°
	17080722	1/8	—	41°	⑤	9/16	④	—	17°	20°
	17080723	1/8	—	41°	⑤	9/16	④	—	17°	23.5°
'81	17081621	3/16	—	38°	⑤	5/8	④	—	15°	38°
	17081622	3/16	—	38°	⑤	5/8	④	—	15°	38°
	17081623	3/16	—	38°	⑤	5/8	④	—	15°	38°
	17081624	3/16	—	38°	⑤	5/8	④	—	15°	38°
	17081625	3/16	—	38°	⑤	5/8	④	—	15°	38°
	17081626	3/16	—	38°	⑤	5/8	④	—	15°	38°
	17081627	3/16	—	38°	⑤	5/8	④	—	15°	38°
	17081629	3/16	—	41°	⑤	5/8	④	—	15°	38°
	17081630	3/16	—	38°	⑤	5/8	④	—	15°	38°
	17081633	3/16	—	38°	⑤	5/8	④	—	15°	38°
	17081720	3/16	—	41°	⑤	5/8	④	—	15°	38°
	17081721	3/16	—	41°	⑤	5/8	④	—	15°	38°
	17081725	3/16	—	41°	⑤	5/8	④	—	15°	38°
	17081726	3/16	—	41°	⑤	5/8	④	—	15°	38°
	17081727	3/16	—	41°	⑤	5/8	④	—	15°	38°

① Use angle degree tool or change over to decimal equivalent on the conversion chart at the end of this section
② 1 notch counterclockwise
③ Measure distance from air horn casting
④ See emissions label underhood for exact rpm specification
⑤ Riveted choke cap is not adjustable under normal circumstances

MODEL 2SE
Chevrolet/GMC
(All measurements in inches or degrees)

Year	Carburetor Number	Float Level	Air① Valve Rod	Choke① ② Rod	Primary Vacuum Break①	Secondary Vacuum Break①	Choke Unloader①
'82	17082334	3/16	1°	15°	26°	38°	42°
	17082335	3/16	1°	15°	26°	38°	42°
	17082336	3/16	1°	15°	26°	38°	42°
	17082337	3/16	1°	15°	26°	38°	42°
	17082338	3/16	1°	15°	26°	38°	42°
	17082339	3/16	1°	15°	26°	38°	42°
	17082341	3/16	1°	15°	30°	37°	42°
	17082342	3/16	1°	15°	30°	37°	42°
	17082344	3/16	1°	15°	30°	37°	42°
	17082345	3/16	1°	15°	30°	37°	42°
	17082431	3/16	1°	15°	24°	38°	42°
	17082433	3/16	1°	15°	24°	38°	42°
	17082480	3/16	1°	15°	26°	38°	42°
	17082481	3/16	1°	15°	26°	38°	42°
	17082482	3/16	1°	15°	23°	38°	42°
	17082483	3/16	1°	15°	26°	38°	42°
	17082484	3/16	1°	15°	26°	38°	42°
	17082485	3/16	1°	15°	26°	38°	42°
	17082486	3/16	1°	15°	28°	38°	42°
	17082487	3/16	1°	15°	28°	38°	42°
	17082488	3/16	1°	15°	28°	38°	42°
	17082489	3/16	1°	15°	28°	38°	42°
	17082348	7/16	1°	22°	26°	32°	40°
	17082349	7/16	1°	22°	28°	32°	40°
	17082350	7/16	1°	22°	26°	32°	40°
	17082351	7/16	1°	22°	28°	32°	40°
	17082353	7/16	1°	22°	28°	35°	30°
	17082355	7/16	1°	22°	28°	35°	30°

① Specified angle for use with angle degree tool.
② Adjust with fast idle cam on 2nd step.

MODEL 2SE
Chevrolet/GMC
(All measurements in inches or degrees)

Year	Carburetor Number	Float Level	Choke Coil Lever	Choke① ② Rod	Primary Vacuum① Break	Secondary Vacuum① Break	Air① Valve Rod	Choke① Unloader
'83	17083410	3/16	.085	15°	23°	38°	1°	42°
	17083411	3/16	.085	15°	26°	38°	1°	42°
	17083412	3/16	.085	15°	23°	38°	1°	42°
	17083413	3/16	.085	15°	26°	38°	1°	42°
	17083414	3/16	.085	15°	23°	38°	1°	42°
	17083415	3/16	.085	15°	26°	38°	1°	42°
	17083416	3/16	.085	15°	23°	38°	1°	42°
	17083417	3/16	.085	15°	26°	38°	1°	42°
	17083419	3/16	.085	15°	28°	38°	1°	42°
	17083421	3/16	.085	15°	26°	38°	1°	42°
	17083423	3/16	.085	15°	28°	38°	1°	42°
	17083425	3/16	.085	15°	26°	38°	1°	42°
	17083427	3/16	.085	15°	26°	38°	1°	42°
	17083429	3/16	.085	15°	28°	38°	1°	42°
	17083560	3/16	.085	15°	28°	38°	1°	42°
	17083562	3/16	.085	15°	28°	38°	1°	42°
	17083565	3/16	.085	15°	28°	38°	1°	42°
	17083569	3/16	.085	15°	28°	38°	1°	42°

① Specified angle for use with angle degree tool.
② Adjust with fast idle cam on 2nd step against high step.

MODEL M4MC/4MV
QUADRAJET FOUR BARREL
Chevrolet/GMC
(All measurements in inches)

Year	Model or Type	Float Level	Air Valve Dashpot	Pump Rod Adj.	Pump Rod Hole	Initial Choke Valve Opening	Vacuum Break	Choke Unloader	Air Valve Spring Wind-up
'77	17057202	15/32	.015	9/32	Inner	.325	.160	.280	7/8
	17057204	15/32	.015	9/32	Inner	.325	.160	.280	7/8
	17057502	15/32	.015	9/32	Inner	.325	.165	.280	7/8
	17057582	15/32	.015	3/8	Outer	.325	.182	.280	7/8
	17057584	15/32	.015	3/8	Outer	.325	.180	.280	7/8
	17057503	15/32	.015	9/32	Inner	.325	.165	.280	7/8
	17057504	15/32	.015	9/32	Inner	.325	.165	.280	7/8
	17057209	7/16	.015	9/32	Inner	.325	—	.325	7/8
	17057218	7/16	.015	9/32	Inner	.325	.160	.280	7/8
	17057222	7/16	.015	9/32	Inner	.325	.160	.280	7/8

MODEL M4MC/4MV
QUADRAJET FOUR BARREL
Chevrolet/GMC

(All measurements in inches)

Year	Model or Type	Float Level	Air Valve Dashpot	Pump Rod Adj.	Pump Rod Hole	Initial Choke Valve Opening	Vacuum Break	Choke Unloader	Air Valve Spring Wind-up
'77	17057518	7/16	.015	9/32	Inner	.325	.165	.280	7/8
	17057522	7/16	.015	9/32	Inner	.325	.165	.280	7/8
	17057586	7/16	.015	3/8	Outer	.325	.180	.295	7/8
	17057588	7/16	.015	3/8	Outer	.325	.180	.280	7/8
	17057219	7/16	.015	9/32	Inner	.325	.165	.280	7/8
	17057519	7/16	.015	9/32	Inner	.325	.165	.280	7/8
	17057512	7/16	.015	9/32	Inner	.325	.165	.240	7/8
	17057517	7/16	.015	9/32	Inner	.325	.165	.240	7/16
	17056212	3/8	.015	9/32	Inner	.290	.120	.295	7/16
	17057221	3/8	.015	9/32	Inner	.325	.160	.325	7/8
	17056217	3/8	.015	9/32	Inner	.290	.120	.295	7/16
	17057213	11/32	.015	9/32	Inner	.285	.115	.205	7/8
	17057215	11/32	.015	9/32	Inner	.285	.115	.205	7/8
	17057216	11/32	.015	9/32	Inner	.285	.115	.205	7/8
	17057525	11/32	.015	9/32	Inner	.285	.120	.225	3/4
	17057514	11/32	.015	9/32	Inner	.285	.120	.280	7/8
	17507529	11/32	.015	9/32	Inner	.285	.110	.205	7/8
	17057229	11/32	.015	9/32	Inner	.285	.110	.205	7/8
	7045583	11/32	.015	9/32	Inner	.285	.120	.295	7/8
	7045585	11/32	.015	9/32	Inner	.285	.120	.295	7/8
	7045586	11/32	.015	3/8	Outer	.285	.120	.295	7/8
'78	17058201	15/32	.015	9/32	Inner	.314	.168	.277	7/8
	17058213	15/32	.015	9/32	Inner	.217	.095	.204	7/8
	17058215	15/32	.015	9/32	Inner	.217	.095	.204	7/8
	17058229	15/32	.015	9/32	Inner	.217	.095	.204	7/8
	17058503	15/32	.015	9/32	Inner	.217	.179	.277	7/8
	17058506	15/32	.015	9/32	Inner	.314	.179	.277	7/8
	17058508	15/32	.015	9/32	Inner	.314	.179	.277	7/8
	17058509	15/32	.015	11/32	Outer	.314	.179	.277	7/8
	17058510	15/32	.015	11/32	Outer	.314	.179	.277	7/8
	17058513	15/32	.015	9/32	Inner	.314	.120	.225	7/8
	17058514	15/32	.015	9/32	Inner	.217	.120	.225	7/8
	17058515	15/32	.015	9/32	Inner	.217	.120	.225	7/8
	17058518	15/32	.015	9/32	Inner	.217	.179	.277	7/8
	17058519	15/32	.015	9/32	Inner	.314	.179	.277	7/8
	17058522	15/32	.015	9/32	Inner	.314	.179	.277	7/8

MODEL M4MC/4MV
QUADRAJET FOUR BARREL
Chevrolet/GMC

(All measurements in inches)

Year	Model or Type	Float Level	Air Valve Dashpot	Pump Rod Adj.	Pump Rod Hole	Initial Choke Valve Opening	Vacuum Break	Choke Unloader	Air Valve Spring Wind-up
'78	17058523	15/32	.015	9/32	Inner	.314	.179	.277	7/8
	17058524	15/32	.015	9/32	Inner	.314	.179	.277	7/8
	17058527	15/32	.015	9/32	Inner	.314	.179	.277	7/8
	17058528	15/32	.015	9/32	Inner	.314	.179	.277	7/8
	17058529	15/32	.015	9/32	Inner	.314	.112	.277	7/8
	17058586	15/32	.015	11/32	Outer	.314	.179	.277	7/8
	17058588	15/32	.015	11/32	Outer	.314	.179	.277	7/8
	17058212	7/16	.015	9/32	Inner	.217	.120	.225	7/8
	17058218	7/16	.015	9/32	Inner	.314	.157	.277	7/8
	17058219	7/16	.015	9/32	Inner	.314	.168	.277	7/8
	17058222	7/16	.015	9/32	Inner	.314	.157	.277	7/8
	17058525	7/16	.015	9/32	Inner	.314	.120	.277	3/4
	17058501	3/8	.015	9/32	Inner	.314	.164	.277	7/8
	17058520	3/8	.015	9/32	Inner	.314	.164	.277	7/8
	17058521	3/8	.015	9/32	Inner	.314	.164	.277	7/8
	17058512	13/32	.015	9/32	Index	.314	.168	.260	7/8
'79	17059212	7/16	.015	9/32	Inner	.314	.136	.260	3/4
	17059512	13/32	.015	9/32	Inner	.314	.136	.260	3/4
	17059061	15/32	.015	13/32	Inner	.314	.129	.277	7/8
	17059201	15/32	.015	13/32	Inner	.314	.129	.277	7/8
	17059065	15/32	.015	13/32	Inner	.314	.129	.277	7/8
	17059205	15/32	.015	13/32	Inner	.314	.129	.277	7/8
	17059066	15/32	.015	13/32	Inner	.314	.129	.277	7/8
	17059206	15/32	.015	13/32	Inner	.314	.129	.277	7/8
	17059068	15/32	.015	13/32	Inner	.314	.129	.277	7/8
	17059208	15/32	.015	13/32	Inner	.314	.129	.277	7/8
	17059069	15/32	.015	13/32	Inner	.314	.129	.277	7/8
	17059209	15/32	.015	13/32	Inner	.314	.129	.277	7/8
	17059076	15/32	.015	13/32	Inner	.314	.129	.277	7/8
	17059226	15/32	.015	13/32	Inner	.314	.129	.277	7/8
	17059077	15/32	.015	13/32	Inner	.314	.129	.277	7/8
	17059227	15/32	.015	13/32	Inner	.314	.129	.277	7/8
	17059213	15/32	.015	9/32	Inner	.234	.129	.260	1
	17059215	15/32	.015	9/32	Inner	.234	.129	.260	1
	17059363	15/32	.015	13/32	Inner	.314	.149	.277	7/8
	17059503	15/32	.015	13/32	Inner	.314	.149	.277	7/8

MODEL M4MC/4MV
QUADRAJET FOUR BARREL
Chevrolet/GMC

(All measurements in inches)

Year	Model or Type	Float Level	Air Valve Dashpot	Pump Rod Adj.	Pump Rod Hole	Initial Choke Valve Opening	Vacuum Break	Choke Unloader	Air Valve Spring Wind-up
'79	17059506	15/32	.015	13/32	Inner	.314	.149	.277	7/8
	17059368	15/32	.015	13/32	Inner	.314	.149	.277	7/8
	17059508	15/32	.015	13/32	Inner	.314	.149	.277	7/8
	17059377	15/32	.015	9/32	Outer	.314	.149	.277	7/8
	17059527	15/32	.015	9/32	Outer	.314	.149	.277	7/8
	17059378	15/32	.015	9/32	Outer	.314	.149	.277	7/8
	17059528	15/32	.015	9/32	Outer	.314	.149	.277	7/8
	17059509	15/32	.015	13/32	Inner	.314	.179	.277	7/8
	17059515	15/32	.015	9/32	Inner	.234	.129	.260	1
	17059510	15/32	.015	9/32	Inner	.314	.179	.277	7/8
	17059529	15/32	.015	9/32	Inner	.234	.129	.260	1
	17059513	15/32	.015	9/32	Inner	.234	.129	.260	1
	17059586	15/32	.015	13/32	Inner	.314	.179	.277	7/8
	17059588	15/32	.015	13/32	Inner	.314	.179	.277	7/8
	17059229	15/32	.015	9/32	Inner	.234	.129	.260	1
	17059520	3/8	.015	9/32	Inner	.324	.164	.277	7/8
	17059521	3/8	.015	9/32	Inner	.314	.164	.277	7/8

MODEL M4MC/4MV
Chevrolet/GMC

(All measurements in inches)

Year	Carburetor Number	Float Level	Float Drop	Choke Unloader	Choke Setting	Pump① Rod Adj.	Fast Idle (rpm)	Metering Rod Setting	Fast Idle Cam 2nd Step	Choke Vacuum Break
'80	17080201	15/32	—	42°	②	9/32	—	—	46°	23°
	17080205	15/32	—	42°	②	9/32	—	—	46°	23°
	17080206	15/32	—	42°	②	9/32	—	—	46°	23°
	17080224	15/32	—	42°	②	9/32	—	—	46°	23°
	17080290	15/32	—	42°	②	9/32	—	—	46°	26°
	17080291	15/32	—	42°	②	9/32	—	—	46°	26°
	17080292	15/32	—	42°	②	9/32	—	—	46°	26°
	17080295	15/32	—	42°	②	9/32	—	—	46°	23°
	17080297	15/32	—	42°	②	9/32	——	—	46°	23°
	17080503	15/32	—	42°	②	9/32	—	—	46°	26°
	17080506	15/32	—	42°	②	9/32	—	—	46°	26°
	17080508	15/32	—	42°	②	9/32	—	—	46°	26°

MODEL M4MC/4MV
Chevrolet/GMC
(All measurements in inches)

Year	Carburetor Number	Float Level	Float Drop	Choke Unloader	Choke Setting	Pump① Rod Adj.	Fast Idle (rpm)	Metering Rod Setting	Fast Idle Cam 2nd Step	Choke Vacuum Break
'80	17080523	15/32	—	42°	②	9/32	—	—	26°	23°
	17080524	15/32	—	42°	②	9/32	—	—	46°	23°
	17080525	15/32	—	42°	②	9/32	—	—	46°	23°
	17080526	15/32	—	42°	②	9/32	—	—	46°	23°
	17080226	15/32	—	42°	②	9/32	—	—	46°	23°
	17080227	15/32	—	42°	②	9/32	—	—	46°	23°
	17080527	15/32	—	42°	②	9/32	—	—	46°	23°
	17080528	15/32	—	42°	②	9/32	—	—	46°	23°
	17080213	3/8	—	40°	②	9/32	—	—	37°	30°
	17080215	3/8	—	40°	②	9/32	—	—	37°	30°
	17080513	3/8	—	40°	②	9/32	—	—	37°	30°
	17080515	3/8	—	40°	②	9/32	—	—	37°	30°
	17080229	3/8	—	40°	②	9/32	—	—	37°	30°
	17080529	3/8	—	40°	②	9/32	—	—	37°	30°
	17080225	15/32	—	42°	②	9/32	—	—	46°	23°
	17080212	3/8	—	40°	②	9/32	—	—	30°	24°
	17080512	3/8	—	40°	②	9/32	—	—	30°	24°
'81	17080212	3/8	—	40°	②	9/32	—	—	30°	24°
	17080213	3/8	—	40°	②	9/32	—	—	30°	23°
	17080215	3/8	—	40°	②	9/32	—	—	30°	23°
	17080298	3/8	—	40°	②	9/32	—	—	30°	23°
	17080507	3/8	—	40°	②	9/32	—	—	30°	23°
	17080512	3/8	—	40°	②	9/32	—	—	30°	24°
	17080513	3/8	—	40°	②	9/32	—	—	30°	23°
	17081200	15/32	—	42°	②	9/32	—	—	23°	24°
	17081201	15/32	—	42°	②	9/32	—	—	23°	23°
	17081205	15/32	—	42°	②	9/32	—	—	23°	23°
	17081206	15/32	—	42°	②	9/32	—	—	23°	23°
	17081220	15/32	—	42°	②	9/32	—	—	23°	23°
	17081226	15/32	—	42°	②	9/32	—	—	23°	24°
	17081227	15/32	—	42°	②	9/32	—	—	—	24°
	17081290	13/32	—	42°	②	9/32	—	—	24°	23°
	17081291	13/32	—	42°	②	9/32	—	—	24°	23°
	17081292	13/32	—	42°	②	9/32	—	—	24°	23°
	17081506	13/32	—	36°	②	9/32	—	—	36°	23°
	17081508	13/32	—	36°	②	9/32	—	—	36°	23°

MODEL M4MC/4MV
Chevrolet/GMC
(All measurements in inches)

Year	Carburetor Number	Float Level	Float Drop	Choke Unloader	Choke Setting	Pump① Rod Adj.	Fast Idle (rpm)	Metering Rod Setting	Fast Idle Cam 2nd Step	Choke Vacuum Break
	17081524	13/32	—	36°	②	5/16③	—	—	36°	25°
	17081526	13/32	—	36°	②	5/16③	—	—	36°	25°

① Place the pump arm linkage in the inner hole of the arm, except on carburetors with a 5/16 pump rod height (see ③)

② 1980 and 1981 choke cover are riveted in position and are not adjustable under normal conditions

③ On carburetors with 5/16 pump rod height, place the pump arm linkage in the outer hole of the arm

MODEL M4MC/M4ME
Chevrolet GMC
(All measurements in inches or degrees)

Year	Carburetor Number	Float Level	Pump Rod Location	Pump Rod Setting	Choke Rod① Setting	Air Valve Rod	Vacuum Break Front	Vacuum Break Rear	Air Valve Windup	Unloader
'82	17080212	3/8	inner	9/32	46°	.025	24°	30°	3/4	40°
	17080213	3/8	inner	9/32	37°	.025	23°	30°	1	40°
	17080215	3/8	inner	9/32	37°	.025	23°	30°	1	40°
	17080298	3/8	inner	9/32	37°	.025	23°	30°	1	40°
	17080507	3/8	inner	9/32	37°	.025	23°	30°	1	40°
	17080512	3/8	inner	9/32	46°	.025	24°	30°	3/4	40°
	17080513	3/8	inner	9/32	37°	.025	23°	30°	3/4	40°
	17082213	3/8	inner	9/32	37°	.025	23°	30°	1	40°
	17082220	13/32	inner	9/32	46°	.025	24°	34°	7/8	39°
	17082221	13/32	inner	9/32	46°	.025	24°	34°	7/8	39°
	17082222	13/32	inner	9/32	46°	.025	24°	34°	7/8	39°
	17082223	13/32	inner	9/32	46°	.025	24°	34°	7/8	39°
	17082224	13/32	inner	9/32	46°	.025	24°	34°	7/8	39°
	17082225	13/32	inner	9/32	46°	.025	24°	34°	7/8	39°
	17082226	13/32	inner	9/32	46°	.025	24°	34°	7/8	39°
	17082227	13/32	inner	9/32	46°	.025	24°	34°	7/8	39°
	17082230	13/32	inner	9/32	46°	.025	26°	36°	7/8	39°
	17082231	13/32	inner	9/32	46°	.025	26°	36°	7/8	39°
	17082234	13/32	inner	9/32	46°	.025	26°	36°	7/8	39°
	17082235	13/32	inner	9/32	46°	.025	26°	36°	7/8	39°
	17082290	13/32	inner	9/32	46°	.025	24°	34°	7/8	39°

MODEL M4MC/M4ME
Chevrolet GMC
(All measurements in inches or degrees)

Year	Carburetor Number	Float Level	Pump Rod Location	Pump Rod Setting	Choke Rod① Setting	Air Valve Rod	Vacuum Break Front	Vacuum Break Rear	Air Valve Windup	Unloader
'82	17082291	13/32	inner	9/32	46°	.025	24°	34°	7/8	39°
	17082292	13/32	inner	9/32	46°	.025	24°	34°	7/8	39°
	17082293	13/32	inner	9/32	46°	.025	24°	34°	7/8	39°
	17082506	13/32	inner	9/32	46°	.025	23°	36°	7/8	39°
	17082508	3/8	inner	9/32	46°	.025	23°	36°	7/8	39°
	17082513	13/32	inner	9/32	46°	.025	23°	30°	3/4	40°
	17082524	13/32	outer	5/16	46°	.025	25°	36°	7/8	39°
	17082526	13/32	outer	5/16	46°	.025	25°	36°	7/8	39°
'83	17080201	15/32	inner	9/32	46°	.025		23°	7/8	42°
	17080205	15/32	inner	9/32	46°	.025		23°	7/8	42°
	17080206	15/32	inner	9/32	46°	.025		23°	7/8	42°
	17080213	3/8	inner	9/32	37°	.025	23°	30°	1	40°
	17080290	15/32	inner	9/32	46°	.025		26°	7/8	42°
	17080291	15/32	inner	9/32	46°	.025		26°	7/8	42°
	17080292	15/32	inner	9/32	46°	.025		26°	7/8	42°
	17080298	3/8	inner	9/32	37°	.025	23°	30°	1	40°
	17080507	3/8	inner	9/32	37°	.025	23°	30°	1	40°
	17080513	3/8	inner	9/32	37°	.025	23°	30°	1	40°
	17082213	9/32	inner	9/32	37°	.025	23°	30°	1	40°
	17083234	13/32	inner	9/32	46°	.025		26°	7/8	39°
	17083235	13/32	inner	9/32	46°	.025		26°	7/8	39°
	17083290	13/32	inner	9/32	46°	.025		24°	7/8	39°
	17083291	13/32	inner	9/32	46°	.025		24°	7/8	39°
	17083292	13/32	inner	9/32	46°	.025		24°	7/8	39°
	17083293	13/32	inner	9/32	46°	.025		24°	7/8	39°
	17083298	3/8	inner	9/32	37°	.025	23°	30°	1	40°
	17083507	3/8	inner	9/32	37°	.025	23°	30°	1	40°
	17080212	3/8	inner	9/32	46°	.025	24°	30°	3/4	40°
	17080512	3/8	inner	9/32	46°	.025	24°	30°	3/4	40°
	17083220	13/32	inner	9/32	46°	.025		24°	7/8	39°
	17083221	13/32	inner	9/32	46°	.025		24°	7/8	39°
	17083222	13/32	inner	9/32	46°	.025		24°	7/8	39°
	17083223	13/32	inner	9/32	46°	.025		24°	7/8	39°
	17083224	13/32	inner	9/32	46°	.025		24°	7/8	39°
	17083225	13/32	inner	9/32	46°	.025		24°	7/8	39°
	17083226	13/32	inner	9/32	46°	.025		24°	7/8	39°

MODEL M4MC/M4ME
Chevrolet GMC
(All measurements in inches or degrees)

Year	Carburetor Number	Float Level	Pump Rod Location	Pump Rod Setting	Choke Rod① Setting	Air Valve Rod	Vacuum Break Front	Vacuum Break Rear	Air Valve Windup	Unloader
'82	17083227	13/32	inner	9/32	46°	.025		24°	7/8	39°
	17083230	13/32	inner	9/32	46°	.025		26°	7/8	39°
	17083231	13/32	inner	9/32	46°	.025		26°	7/8	39°

① Place cam follower on second step of
cam, against the rise of high step.

MODEL 2SE
Jeep
(All measurements in inches)

Year	Carburetor Number	Float Level	Pump Stem Height	Fast② Idle Cam	Fast Idle (rpm)	Air① Valve Link	Primary Vacuum Break	Choke Unloader	Choke Setting
'81	17081790	.208	.128	25°	2400	2°	19°	32°	③
	17081791	.256	.128	25°	2600	2°	19°	32°	③
'82	17082380	.169	1.28	18°	2400	2°	21°	34°	③
	17082381	.169	1.28	18°	2400	2°	21°	34°	③

①Maximum degree setting
②2nd step on cam
③Tamper resistant—riveted cover

MODEL 2SE
(All measurements in inches)

Year	Carburetor Number	Float Level	Air Valve Windup	Choke Coil Lever	Fast Idle Cam 2nd Step	Primary Vacuum Break	Secondary Vacuum Break	Air Valve Rod	Choke Unloader
'83	17084581	5/32	1	.085	22°	26°	32°	1°	40°
	17084580	5/32	1	.085	22°	26°	32°	1°	40°
	17084582	5/32	1	.085	22°	26°	32°	1°	40°
	17084583	5/32	1	.085	22°	26°	32°	1°	40°

MODEL E2SE
Jeep
(All measurements in inches)

Year	Carburetor Number	Float Level	Pump Stem Height	Fast Idle Cam 2nd step	Fast Idle (rpm)	Air① Valve Link	Choke Unloader	Choke Setting
'81	170811796	.208	.128	25°	2400	2°	19°	②
	170811797	.208	.128	25°	2600	2°	19°	②
'82	17082389③	.169	.128	18°	2400	2°	34°	②

①Maximum degree setting
②Tamper resistant—Riveted choke cover
③Primary vacuum break setting is 19°.

MODEL E2SE
(All measurements in inches)

Year	Carburetor Number	Float Level	Air Valve Windup	Choke Coil Lever	Fast Idle Cam 2nd Step	Primary Vacuum Break	Secondary Vacuum Break	Air Valve Rod	Choke Unloader
'83	17084384	⅛	1	.085	22°	25°	30°	1°	40°

DCH3HO
(All measurements in inches)

Float Needle Valve Stroke	Primary Throttle Valve Adjustment	Secondary Throttle Opening Point	Kick Lever Adjustment
.059	.050–.059 ①	.24–30	②

① Applies to manual trans. automatic trans- .059–.069

② Zero clearance between kick lever screw and return plate—throttle fully closed.

DCH340 needle valve stroke adjustment

Secondary throttle opening point clearance—DCH340

END OF SCREW MUST BE RESTING AGAINST RETURN PLATE

101605

Kick lever adjustment—DCH340

① HOLD RETAINER FIRMLY IN PLACE

② PUSH FLOAT DOWN LIGHTLY AGAINST NEEDLE

③ GAUGE AT LARGE TOE OF FLOAT AT POINT FURTHEST AWAY FROM FLOAT HINGE PIN (SEE INSET)

④ REMOVE FLOAT AND BEND FLOAT ARM UP OR DOWN TO ADJUST

⑤ VISUALLY CHECK FLOAT ALIGNMENT AFTER ADJUSTING

Setting float level—model 2SE carburetor— (© G.M. Corp.)

Primary throttle valve adjustment— DCH340

Float drop adjustment—Rochester model 2G (© General Motors Corp.)

Float level adjustment—Rochester model 2G (© General Motors Corp.)

Accelerator pump rod adjustment—Rochester model 2G (© General Motors Corp.)

Rochester Monojet® carburetor—typical (© General Motors Corp.)

Fast idle adjustment—Monojet® carburetor (© General Motors Corp.)

IDLE VENT VALVE

CHOKE KICK LEVER

CHOKE LEVER

TCS CLEAN AIR TUBE

FUEL INLET AND FILTER

PUMP LEVER

PUMP ROD

CHOKE ROD

CHOKE VACUUM BREAK

FAST IDLE CAM

IDLE SPEED SCREW

DISTRIBUTOR VACUUM TUBE

THROTTLE LEVER

THERMAC TUBE

IDLE MIXTURE SCREW

Rochester model 2GV—typical (© General Motors Corp.)

DISTRIBUTOR VACUUM TUBE

PUMP PLUNGER

CHOKE ROD

IDLE VENT

FAST IDLE CAM

FUEL INLET AND FILTER

TCS CLEAN AIR TUBE

AIR VALVE DASHPOT LEVER

FUEL INLET AND FILTER

PUMP ROD AND LEVER

PCV VALVE TUBE

IDLE MIXTURE SCREW

CHOKE ASSIST SPRING

CHOKE VACUUM BREAK

CHOKE LEVER

CANISTER PURGE SIGNAL TUBE

IDLE SPEED SCREW

THROTTLE LEVER

SECONDARY THROTTLE LOCKOUT LEVER

THERMAC TUBE

Rochester Quadrajet® carburetor (4MV shown)—typical (© General Motors Corp.)

Idle vent adjustment—Monojet® carburetor (© General Motors Corp.)

Float level adjustment—Monojet® carburetor (© General Motors Corp.)

Secondary opening adjustment—typical Quadrajet® carburetor (© General Motors Corp.)

Fast idle adjustment—typical Quadrajet® carburetor (© General Motors Corp.)

Float level adjustment—typical Quadrajet® carburetor (© General Motors Corp.)

Pump rod adjustment—typical Quadrajet® carburetor (© General Motors Corp.)

Choke rod adjustment—typical Quadrajet® carburetor (© General Motors Corp.)

Secondary closing adjustment—typical Quadrajet® carburetor (© General Motors Corp.)

M4MC/M4ME carburetor exploded view— (© G.M. Corp.)

ELECTRIC
CHOKE MODELS

1. Air Horn Assy.
2. Gasket—Air Horn
3. Lever—Pump Actuating
4. Roll Pin—Pump Lever Hinge
5. Screw—Air Horn Long (2)
6. Screw—Air Horn Short ( )
7. Screw — Air Horn Countersunk (2)
8. Metering Rod—Secondary (2)
9. Holder and Screw—Secondary Metering Rod
10. Baffle—Secondary Air
11. Seal—Pump Plunger
12. Retainer—Pump Seal
13. Vac. Break Control & Bracket—Front
14. Screw—Control Attaching (2)
15. Hose—Vacuum
16. Rod—Air Valve
16A. Rod—Air Valve (Truck)
17. Lever—Choke Rod (Upper)
18. Screw—Choke Lever
19. Rod—Choke
20. Lever—Choke Rod (Lower)

21. Seal—Intermediate Choke Shaft
22. Lever—Secondary Lockout
23. Link—Rear Vacuum Break
24. Int. Choke Shaft & Lever
25. Cam—Fast Idle
26. Seal—Choke Housing to Bowl (Hot Air Choke)
27. Kit—Choke Housing
28. Screw—Choke Housing to Bowl
29. Seal—Intermediate Choke Shaft (Hot Air Choke)
30. Lever—Choke Coil
31. Screw—Choke Coil Lever
32. Gasket—Stat Cover (Hot Air Choke)
33. Stat Cover & Coil Assy. (Hot Air Choke)
34. Stat Cover & Coil Assy. (Electric Choke)
35. Kit — Stat Cover Attaching
36. Rear Vacuum Break Assembly
37. Screw—Vacuum Break Attaching (2)
40. Ball—Pump Discharge

41. Retainer—Pump Discharge Ball
42. Baffle—Pump Well
43. Needle & Seat Assembly
44. Float Assembly
45. Hinge Pin — Float Assembly
46. Power Piston Assembly
47. Spring—Power Piston
48. Rod—Primary Metering (2)
49. Spring—Metering Rod Retainer
50. Insert—Float Bowl
51. Insert—Bowl Cavity
52. Spring—Pump Return
53. Pump Assembly
54. Rod—Pump
55. Baffle—Secondary Bores
56. Idle Compensator Assembly
57. Seal—Idle Compensator
58. Cover—Idle Compensator
59. Screw—Idle Compensator Cover (2)
60. Filter Nut—Fuel Inlet
61. Gasket—Filter Nut
62. Filter—Fuel Inlet
63. Spring—Fuel Filter

64. Screw—Idle Stop
65. Spring — Idle Stop Screw
66. Idle Speed Solenoid & Bracket Assembly
67. Idle Load Compensator & Bracket Assembly
68. Bracket—Throttle Return Spring
69. Actuator—Throttle Lever (Truck Only)
70. Bracket—Throttle Lever Actuator (Truck Only)
71. Washer—Actuator Nut (Truck Only)
72. Nut—Actuator Attaching (Truck Only)
73. Screw—Bracket Attaching (2)
74. Throttle Body Assembly
75. Gasket—Throttle Body
76. Screw—Throttle Body (3)
77. Idle Mixture Needle & Spring Assy. (2)
78. Screw — Fast Idle Adjusting
79. Spring — Fast Idle Adjusting
80. Tee—Vacuum Hose
81. Gasket—Flange

WITH LOCK SCREW LOOSENED AND WITH AIR VALVE CLOSED, TURN ADJUSTING SCREW SPECIFIED NUMBER OF TURNS AFTER SPRING CONTACTS PIN TIGHTEN LOCK SCREW

LOCK SCREW

ADJUSTING SCREW

Air valve spring adjustment—typical Quadrajet® carburetor (© General Motors Corp.)

AIR VALVE COMPLETELY CLOSED

BEND HERE FOR SPECIFIED CLEARANCE BETWEEN ROD AND END OF SLOT

DIAPHRAGM SEATED

Air valve dashpot adjustment—typical Quadrajet® carburetor (© General Motors Corp.)

MEASURE FROM CASTING SURFACE NEXT TO AIR CLEANER STUD HOLE TO TOP OF METERING ROD

BEND HANGER AT THIS POINT TO ADJUST

Secondary metering adjustment—typical Quadrajet® carburetor (© General Motors Corp.)

HOLD CHOKE VALVE WIDE OPEN BY ROTATING VACUUM BREAK LEVER TOWARDS OPEN CHOKE (CLOCKWISE)

.015 INCH CLEARANCE

BEND LEVER TO ADJUST

CHOKE VALVE CLOSED

BEND PIN TO ADJUST

.015 INCH MAX. CLEARANCE

① SECONDARY LOCKOUT OPENING CLEARANCE

② SECONDARY LOCKOUT LEVER SIDE CLEARANCE

Secondary lockout adjustment—typical Quadrajet® carburetor (© General Motors Corp.)

U187

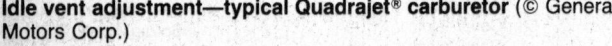

Idle vent adjustment—typical Quadrajet® carburetor (© General Motors Corp.)

Vacuum break adjustment—typical Quadrajet® carburetor (© General Motors Corp.)

ANGLE DEGREE TO DECIMAL CONVERSION
Model M2MC, M2ME and M4MC Carburetor

Angle Degrees	Decimal Equiv. Top of Valve	Angle Degrees	Decimal Equiv. Top of Valve
5	.023	33	.203
6	.028	34	.211
7	.033	35	.220
8	.038	36	.227
9	.043	37	.234
10	.049	38	.243
11	.054	39	.251
12	.060	40	.260
13	.066	41	.269
14	.071	42	.277
15	.077	43	.287
16	.083	44	.295
17	.090	45	.304
18	.096	46	.314
19	.103	47	.322
20	.110	48	.332
21	.117	49	.341
22	.123	50	.350
23	.129	51	.360
24	.136	52	.370
25	.142	53	.379
26	.149	54	.388
27	.157	55	.400
28	.164	56	.408
29	.171	57	.418
30	.179	58	.428
31	.187	59	.439
32	.195	60	.449

ANGLE DEGREE TO DECIMAL CONVERSION
Model 4MV Carburetor

Angle Degrees	Decimal Equiv. Top of Valve	Angle Degrees	Decimal Equiv. Top of Valve
5	.019	33	.158
6	.022	34	.164
7	.026	35	.171
8	.030	36	.178
9	.034	37	.184
10	.038	38	.190
11	.042	39	.197
12	.047	40	.204
13	.051	41	.211
14	.056	42	.217
15	.060	43	.225
16	.065	44	.231
17	.070	45	.239
18	.075	46	.246
19	.080	47	.253
20	.085	48	.260
21	.090	49	.268
22	.095	50	.275
23	.101	51	.283
24	.106	52	.291
25	.112	53	.299
26	.117	54	.306
27	.123	55	.314
28	.128	56	.322
29	.134	57	.329
30	.140	58	.337
31	.146	59	.345
32	.152	60	.353

FORD CALIBRATION NUMBERS LIGHT TRUCK ONLY

Year	Emission Calibration Number	Choke Setting	Fast Idle (RPM) High Cam	Kick Down①	Choke Valve Pull Down
'77	7-53G-RO	3 Rich	2000	—	—
	7-53H-RO	3 Rich	2000	—	—
	7-53S-RO	3 Rich	2000	—	—
	7-54K-RO	3 Rich	2100	—	—
	7-54S-RO	3 Rich	2100	—	—
	7-54T-RO	3 Rich	2100	—	—
	7-59G-RO	Index	1900	—	—
	7-60G-RO	Index	1900	—	—
	7-62G-RO	Index	1900	—	—
	7-64U-RO	3 Rich	—	1500	—

FORD CALIBRATION NUMBERS LIGHT TRUCK ONLY

Year	Emission Calibration Number	Choke Setting	Fast Idle (RPM) High Cam	Kick Down①	Choke Valve Pull Down
	7-65G-RO	3 Rich	—	1500	—
	7-65H-RO	3 Rich	—	1500	—
	7-65U-RO	Index	—	1500	—
	7-71-RO	3 Rich	—	1250	—
	7-71J-RO	3 Rich	—	1250	—
	7-72-RO	3 Rich	—	1500	—
	7-72J-RO	3 Rich	—	1500	—
	7-73-RO	3 Rich	—	1200	—
	7-74-RO	3 Rich	—	1500	—

①Kickdown—2nd step of fast idle cam

CARBURETORS

FORD CALIBRATION NUMBERS LIGHT AND HEAVY TRUCKS

Year	Emission Calibration Number	Choke Setting	Fast Idle (RPM) High Cam	Fast Idle (RPM) Kick Down①	Choke Valve Pull Down
'78	5-81A-RO	None	—	—	—
	5-81B-RO	None	2200	—	—
	5-82-RO	None	2200	—	—
	5-82A-RO	None	2200	—	—
	5-85A-R1	None	2200	—	—
	5-85J-R6	None	—	—	—
	5-86A-RO	None	2200	—	—
	5-86J-R3	None	2500	—	—
	5-89-R2	None	2000	—	—
	5-89J-R3	None	2200	—	—
	5-90A-R1	None	2200	—	—
	5-90B-R1	None	2200	—	—
	5-90J-R3	None	2200	—	—
	6-51A-RO	Index	—	1600	—
	6-51E-RO	Index	—	1600	—
	6-93-R7	None	2500	—	—
	6-94-R4	None	2500	—	—
	6-95-R6	None	2500	—	—
	6-95-95	None	2500	—	—
	7-60E-R11	Index	1900	—	—
	7-71-R10	2 Rich	—	1250	—
	7-71J-R10	2 Rich	—	1450	—
	7-72-R11	3 Rich	—	1500	—
	7-72J-R11	3 Rich	—	1500	—
	7-73-R10	2 Rich	—	1250	—
	7-74-R10	3 Rich	—	1500	—
	7-74J-R11	3 Rich	—	1500	—
	7-75A-R16	1 Rich	—	1250	—
	7-76A-R10	2 Rich	—	1500	—
	7-76J-R11	3 Rich	—	1700	—
	7-77-R10	1 Rich	—	1500	—
	7-77A-R10	None	—	1500	—
	7-77J-R10	1 Rich	—	1500	—
	7-77M-R10	None	—	1500	—
	7-78-R10	1 Rich	—	1500	—
	7-78J-R10	1 Rich	—	1500	—
	7-79-R1	3 Rich	—	1250	—
	7-80-RO	3 Rich	—	1500	—
	7-81K-RO	None	1400	—	—
	7-93J-RO	None	2500	—	—
	7-95J-RO	None	2500	—	—

FORD CALIBRATION NUMBERS LIGHT AND HEAVY TRUCKS

Year	Emission Calibration Number	Choke Setting	Fast Idle (RPM) High Cam	Fast Idle (RPM) Kick Down①	Choke Valve Pull Down
	7-96J-90	None	2500	—	—
	8-51J-RO	Index	—	1600	—
	8-51K-RO	Index	—	1600	—
	8-51L-RO	Index	—	1600	—
	8-51M-RO	Index	—	1600	—
	8-51S-RO	Index	—	1600	—
	8-51T-RO	Index	—	1600	—
	8-52K-RO	Index	—	1600	—
	8-52L-R10	Index	—	1600	—
	8-52U-RO	Index	—	1600	—
	8-53A-RO	1 Rich	2000	—	—
	8-53G-RO	3 Rich	2000	—	—
	8-53S-RO	3 Rich	2000	—	—
	8-54A-RO	3 Rich	2000	—	—
	8-54G-RO	3 Rich	2000	—	—
	8-54S-RO	3 Rich	2100	—	—
	8-54T-R10	3 Rich	2100	—	—
	8-59G-RO	Index	2100	—	—
	8-59T-R2	Index	2100	—	—
	8-60A-RO	2 Rich	2200	—	—
	8-60J-RO	Index	2100	—	—
	8-60S-R11	Index	1900	—	—
	8-60S-R12	Index	1900	—	—
	8-62T-RO	—	—	—	—
	8-62J-RO	Index	2100	—	—
	8-64G-RO	3 Rich	—	1750	—
	8-64S-RO	Index	—	1500	—
	8-65A-RO	Index	2100	—	—
	8-65G-RO	1 Rich	2000	—	—
	8-65S-RO	Index	—	1500	—
	8-65U-RO	Index	—	1500	—
	R-66U-RO	Index	—	1500	—
	8-97-RO	Index	—	1200	—
	7-97J-RO	Index	—	1200	—
'79	9-51G-RO	Index	—	1600	.230
	9-51J-RO	Index	—	1600	.230
	9-51K-RO	Index	—	1600	.230
	9-51L-RO	Index	—	1600	.230
	9-51M-RO	Index	—	1600	.230
	9-51S-RO	Index	—	1600	.230
	9-51T-RO	Index	—	1600	.230

FORD CALIBRATION NUMBERS LIGHT AND HEAVY TRUCKS

Year	Emission Calibration Number	Choke Setting	Fast Idle (RPM) High Cam	Kick Down①	Choke Valve Pull Down
	9-52G-RO	Index	—	1600	.230
	9-52J-RO	Index	—	1600	.230
	9-52L-RO	Index	—	1600	.230
	9-52M-RO	Index	—	1600	.230
	9-53G-RO	3 Rich	2000	—	.140
	9-53H-RO	3 Rich	2000	—	.140
	9-54A-RO	—	—	—	.145
	9-54G-RO	3 Rich	2000	—	.145
	9-54H-RO	3 Rich	2000	—	.145
	9-54J-RO	2 Rich	2000	—	.145
	9-54R-RO	3 Rich	2000	—	.145
	9-54S-RO	1 Rich	2400	—	.136
	9-54T-RO	3 Rich	2000	—	.145
	9-54U-RO	1 Rich	2400	—	.136
	9-59H-RO	Index	2000	—	.135
	9-59J-RO	Index	2000	—	.145
	9-59K-RO	Index	2000	—	.145
	9-59S-RO	Index	2000	—	.135
	9-60T-RO	—	—	—	.150
	9-60G-RO	Index	2000	—	.145
	9-60H-RO	Index	2000	—	.150
	9-60J-RO	Index	2000	—	.140
	9-60L-RO	Index	2000	—	.150
	9-60M-RO	Index	2000	—	.150
	9-60S-RO	3 Rich	2100	—	.150
	9-61G-RO	Index	2000	—	.145
	9-61H-RO	Index	2000	—	.135
	9-62A-RO	—	—	—	.145
	9-62B-RO	—	—	—	.145
	9-62J-RO	Index	1900	—	.145
	9-62M-RO	Index	1900	—	.145
	9-63H-RO	Index	—	1500	.190
	9-64G-RO	Index	2200	—	.200
	9-64H-RO	Index	2200	—	.200
	9-64S-RO	Index	2200	—	.200
	9-66G-RO	5 Rich	—	1600	.210
	9-72J-RO	3 Rich	2000	—	.150
	9-77J-RO	Index	—	1600	.290
	9-77M-RO	Manual	2550	—	—
	9-78J-RO	Index	—	1600	.290
	9-83G-RO	Manual	2200	—	—

FORD CALIBRATION NUMBERS LIGHT AND HEAVY TRUCKS

Year	Emission Calibration Number	Choke Setting	Fast Idle (RPM) High Cam	Kick Down①	Choke Valve Pull Down
	9-83H-RO2	Manual	2500	—	—
	9-87G-RO	Manual	2700	—	—
	9-97J-RO	5 Rich	—	1600	.210
	7-76J-R11	3 Rich	—	1700	.180
	7-93J-RO	Manual	2500	—	—
	7-95J-RO	Manual	2500	—	—
	9-71J-RO	3 Rich	1750	—	—
	9-73J-RO	2 Rich	1750	—	—
	9-74J-RO	3 Rich	2000	—	—
	9-97J-R11	5 Rich	—	1600	—
'80	0-51F-RO	Index	—	1600	—
	0-51G-RO	2 Rich	—	1400	—
	0-51H-RO	2 Rich	—	1400	—
	0-51L-RO	Index	—	1400	—
	0-51M-RO	Index	—	1400	—
	0-51S-RO	Index	—	1600	—
	0-51T-RO	Index	—	1600	—
	0-52H-RO	2 Rich	—	1400	—
	0-52J-RO	2 Rich	—	1400	—
	0-52L-RO	2 Rich	—	1400	—
	0-52M-RO	2 Rich	—	1400	—
	0-52S-RO	Index	—	1600	—
	0-53D-RO	3 Rich	2000	—	—
	0-53G-RO	3 Rich	2000	—	—
	0-53H-RO	3 Rich	2000	—	—
	0-53K-RO	3 Rich	2000	—	—
	0-53L-RO	3 Rich	2000	—	—
	0-53N-RO	3 Rich	2500	—	—
	0-53Q-RO	3 Rich	2500	—	—
	0-53S-RO	3 Rich	2500	—	—
	0-54D-RO	3 Rich	2000	—	—
	0-54F-RO	3 Rich	2000	—	—
	0-54G-RO	Index	2000	—	—
	0-54H-RO	3 Rich	2000	—	—
	0-54K-RO	Index	2000	—	—
	0-54L-RO	3 Rich	2000	—	—
	0-54M-RO	3 Rich	2100	—	—
	0-54N-RO	1 Rich	2400	—	—
	0-54P-RO	3 Rich	2000	—	—
	0-54Q-RO	1 Rich	2400	—	—
	0-54R-RO	3 Rich	2100	—	—

CARBURETORS

FORD CALIBRATION NUMBERS LIGHT AND HEAVY TRUCKS

Year	Emission Calibration Number	Choke Setting	Fast Idle (RPM) High Cam	Kick Down①	Choke Valve Pull Down
	0-54T-RO	3 Rich	2000	—	—
	0-54V-RO	3 Rich	2100	—	—
	0-60A-RO	3 Rich	2000	—	—
	0-59C-RO	3 Rich	2000	—	—
	0-59G-RO	3 Rich	2000	—	—
	0-59G-R10	3 Rich	2000	—	—
	0-59H-RO	3 Rich	2000	—	—
	0-59H-R10	3 Rich	2000	—	—
	0-59J-RO	3 Rich	2000	—	—
	0-59J-R10	3 Rich	2000	—	—
	0-59S-RO	3 Rich	2000	—	—
	0-60B-RO	3 Rich	2000	—	—
'81	1-57G-R1	—	2200	—	—
	1-58G-RO	—	2000	—	—
	1-51D-RO	—	—	1400	—
	1-51D-R10	—	—	1400	—
	1-51E-RO	—	—	1400	—
	1-51F-RO	—	—	1400	—
	1-51G-RO	—	—	1400	—
	1-51H-RO	—	—	1400	—
	1-51K-RO	—	—	1400	—
	1-51L-RO	—	—	1400	—
	1-51E-R10	—	—	1400	—
	1-51F-R10	—	—	1400	—
	1-51G-R10	—	—	1400	—
	1-51H-R10	—	—	1400	—
	1-51K-R10	—	—	1400	—
	1-51L-R10	—	—	1400	—
	1-51S-RO	—	—	1400	—
	1-51S-R10	—	—	1400	—
	1-51T-RO	—	—	1400	—
	1-52G-RO	—	—	1400	—
	1-52H-RO	—	—	1400	—
	1-52K-RO	—	—	1400	—
	1-52L-RO	—	—	1400	—
	1-52G-R10	—	—	1400	—
	1-52H-R10	—	—	1400	—
	1-52K-R10	—	—	1400	—
	1-52L-R10	—	—	1400	—
	1-52S-RO	—	—	1400	—
	1-52T-RO	—	—	1400	—

FORD CALIBRATION NUMBERS LIGHT AND HEAVY TRUCKS

Year	Emission Calibration Number	Choke Setting	Fast Idle (RPM) High Cam	Kick Down①	Choke Valve Pull Down
	1-53D-RO	—	2200	—	—
	1-53F-RO	—	2200	—	—
	1-53G-RO	—	2200	—	—
	1-53H-RO	—	2200	—	—
	1-53K-RO	—	2200	—	—
	1-53D-R10	—	2200	—	—
	1-53G-R10	—	2200	—	—
	1-53K-R10	—	2200	—	—
	1-59A-RO	—	2000	—	—
	1-59B-RO	—	2000	—	—
	1-59H-RO	—	2000	—	—
	1-59K-RO	—	2000	—	—
	1-60A-RO	—	2200	—	—
	1-60B-RO	—	2200	—	—
	1-60H-R1	—	2000	—	—
	1-60J-RO	—	2000	—	—
	1-60K-RO	—	2000	—	—
	1-63T-RO	—	1700	—	—
	1-64A-RO	—	2000	—	—
	1-64G-R1	—	2000	—	—
	1-64H-R2	—	2000	—	—
	1-64R-R1	—	1650	—	—
	1-64S-RO	—	1650	—	—
	1-64T-RO	—	1650	—	—

① Kickdown—2nd step of fast idle cam

FORD CALIBRATION NUMBERS LIGHT TRUCK ONLY

Year	Emission Calibration Number	Choke Pulldown Setting	Choke Unloader Setting	Choke Cap Setting	Float Setting (Dry)	Float Level (Wet)	Pump Lever Location
'82	2-55D-R0	.125	.200	V-Notch	7/16	.810	#2
	2-56D-R0	.125	.250	V-Notch	7/16	.810	#2
	2-56D-R10	.115–.135	.250	V-Notch	7/16	.810	#2
	2-57G-R0	.130	.200	V-Notch	7/16	.810	#2
	2-58H-R0	.125	.200	V-Notch	7/16	.810	#2
	2-51D-R0	.270	.28	Index	.78	—	—
	2-51E-R0	.270	.28	Index	.78	—	—
	2-51F-R0	.270	.28	Index	.78	—	—
	2-51G-R0	.270	.28	Index	.78	—	—
	2-51K-R0	.230	.28	Index	.78	—	—
	2-51L-R0	.230	.28	Index	.78	—	—
	2-51P-R0	.320	.330	2 Rich	.78	—	—

FORD CALIBRATION NUMBERS LIGHT TRUCK ONLY

Year	Emission Calibration Number	Choke Pulldown Setting	Choke Unloader Setting	Choke Cap Setting	Float Setting (Dry)	Float Level (Wet)	Pump Lever Location
	2-51P-R10	.320	.330	2 Rich	.78	—	—
	2-51S-R0	.320	.330	2 Rich	.78	—	—
	2-51T-R0	.320	.330	2 Rich	.78	—	—
	2-51X-R0	.300	.28	Index	.78	—	—
	2-51Y-R0	.300	.28	Index	.78	—	—
	2-52G-R0	.300	.28	2 Rich	.78	—	—
	2-52H-R0	.300	.28	2 Rich	.78	—	—
	2-52K-R0	.300	.28	2 Rich	.78	—	—
	2-52L-R0	.300	.28	2 Rich	.78	—	—
	2-52S-R0	.320	.330	2 Rich	.78	—	—
	2-52T-R0	.320	.330	2 Rich	.78	—	—
	2-52Y-R0	.300	.28	Index	.78	—	—
	2-53D-R0	.130	.200	V-Notch	7/16	.810	#2
	2-53F-R0	.130	.200	V-Notch	7/16	.810	#2
	2-53G-R0	.130	.200	V-Notch	7/16	.810	#2
	2-53H-R0	.130	.200	V-Notch	7/16	.810	#2
	2-53K-R0	.130	.200	V-Notch	7/16	.810	#2
	2-53X-R1	.130	.200	V-Notch	7/16	.810	#2
	2-54D-R0	.125	.200	V-Notch	7/16	.810	#2
	2-54F-R0	.130	.200	V-Notch	31/64	.875	#2
	2-54G-R0	.125	.200	V-Notch	7/16	.810	#2
	2-54H-R0	.130	.200	V-Notch	31/64	.875	#2
	2-54K-R0	.125	.200	V-Notch	7/16	.810	#2
	2-54L-R0	.125	.200	V-Notch	7/16	.810	#2
	2-54P-R0	—	—	Index	1.070–1.010	—	—
	2-54R-R0	—	—	Index	1.070–1.010	—	—
	2-54X-R1	.120	.200	V-Notch	7/16	.810	#2
	1-63T-R0	—	—	Index	1.070–1.010	—	—
	1-63T-R10B	—	—	Index	1.070–1.010	—	—
	1-64H-R2	.120	.200	V-Notch	31/64	.875	#3
	1-64R-R1	—	—	—	1.070–1.010	—	—
	1-64S-R0	—	—	—	1.070–1.010	—	—
	1-64T-R0	—	—	—	1.070–1.010	—	—
	1-64T-R10	—	—	—	1.070–1.010	—	—
	2-63Y-R10B	—	—	Index	1.070–1.010	—	—
	2-64X-R0	.120	.200	V-Notch	31/64	.875	#2
	2-64Y-R10B	—	—	Index	1.070–1.010	—	—

FORD CALIBRATION NUMBERS LIGHT TRUCK ONLY

Year	Emission Calibration Number	Choke Pulldown Setting	Choke Bi-Metal I.D.	Cam Index Setting	Choke Unloader	Float Level (Dry)
'83	3-41D-R01	.320	REL	.140	.22	.650
	3-41D-R10	.320	REL	.140	.22	.650
	3-41P-R02	.320	REL	.140	.22	.650
	3-41P-R11	.320	REL	.140	.22	.650

FORD CALIBRATION NUMBERS LIGHT TRUCK ONLY

Year	Emission Calibration Number	Choke Pulldown Setting	Choke Bi-Metal I.D.	Cam Index Setting	Choke Unloader	Float Level (Dry)
	3-41P-R12	.320	REL	.140	.22	.650
	3-49S-R01	.320	REL	.140	.22	.650
	3-49S-R10	.320	REL	.140	.22	.650
	3-49S-R11	.320	REL	.140	.22	.650
	3-49X-R01	.320	REL	.140	.22	.650
	3-49X-R11	.320	REL	.140	.22	.650
	3-50S-R01	.320	REL	.140	.22	.650
	3-50S-R11	.320	REL	.140	.22	.650
	3-50X-R10	.320	REL	.140	.22	.650
	3-50X-R11	.320	REL	.140	.22	.650
	3-55D-R00	.115–.135	2080ME350	V-Notch	.25	.810①
	3-56D-R00	.115–.135	2080ME350	V-Notch	.25	.810①
	3-51D-R00	.270	EC	.140	.28	.780
	3-51E-R01	.270	EB	.140	.28	.780
	3-51F-R00	.270	EC	.140	.28	.780
	3-51G-R00	.270	EC	.140	.28	.780
	3-51H-R00	.270	EB	.140	.28	.780
	3-51K-R00	.270	EB	.140	.28	.780
	3-51L-R00	.270	EB	.140	.28	.780
	3-51P-R00	.320	EC	.140	.330	.780
	3-51R-R00	.320	EC	.140	.330	.780
	3-51R-R10	.320	EC	.140	.330	.780
	3-51S-R00	.320	EC	.140	.330	.780
	3-51S-R10	.320	EC	.140	.330	.780
	3-51T-R00	.320	EC	.140	.330	.780
	3-51T-R10	.320	EC	.140	.330	.780
	3-51V-R00	.300	EB	.140	.28	.780
	3-51X-R00	.300	EB	.140	.28	.780
	3-51Z-R00	.300	EB	.140	.28	.780
	3-52E-R00	.270	EC	.140	.28	.780
	3-52F-R00	.300	EC	.140	.28	.780
	3-52G-R00	.300	EC	.140	.28	.780
	3-52K-R00	.300	EC	.140	.28	.780
	3-52R-R00	.320	EC	.140	.330	.780
	3-52R-R10	.320	EC	.140	.330	.780
	3-52S-R00	.320	EC	.140	.330	.780
	3-52S-R10	.320	EC	.140	.330	.780
	3-52T-R00	.320	EC	.140	.330	.780
	3-52T-R10	.320	EC	.140	.330	.780
	3-52V-R00	.300	EB	.140	.28	.780
	3-52Y-R00	.300	EB	.140	.28	.780
	3-52Z-R00	.300	EB	.140	.28	.780
	3-53F-R00	.142	2100MF	V-Notch	.20	7/16
	3-53G-R00	.142	2100MF	V-Notch	.20	7/16
	3-53K-R00	.142	2100MF	V-Notch	.20	7/16
	3-53L-R00	.142	2100MF	V-Notch	.20	7/16
	3-53W-R00	.152	2100MF400	V-Notch	.20	7/16

CARBURETORS

FORD CALIBRATION NUMBERS LIGHT TRUCK ONLY

Year	Emission Calibration Number	Choke Pulldown Setting	Choke Bi-Metal I.D.	Cam Index Setting	Choke Unloader	Float Level (Dry)
'83	3-53Y-R00	.152	2100MF400	V-Notch	.20	7/16
	3-53Z-R00	.152	2100MF400	V-Notch	.20	7/16
	3-54E-R00	.137	2100MF	V-Notch	.25	7/16
	3-54F-R00	.149	2100KH	V-Notch	.25	7/16
	3-54J-R00	.137	2100MF	V-Notch	.25	7/16
	3-54L-R00	.149	2100KH	V-Notch	.25	7/16
	3-54P-R00	.157	2080ME400	V-Notch	.20	7/16
	3-54R-R00	.157	2080ME400	V-Notch	.20	7/16
	3-54T-R00	.157	2100ME400	V-Notch	.20	7/16
	3-54W-R00	.149	2120KH400	V-Notch	.20	7/16
	3-54Y-R00	.150	2100MF400	V-Notch	.20	7/16

FORD CALIBRATION NUMBERS LIGHT TRUCK ONLY

Year	Emission Calibration Number	Choke Pulldown Setting	Choke Bi-Metal I.D.	Cam Index Setting	Choke Unloader	Float Level (Dry)
	3-54Z-R00	.150	2100MF400	V-Notch	.20	7/16
	1-63T-R12	②	③	.355–.365④	.245–.255⑤	1.010–1.070
	1-63T-R13	②	③	.355–.365④	.245–.255⑤	1.010–1.070
	1-64H-R02	.120	2150ME	V-Notch	.20	31/64
	1-64T-R12	②	③	.355–.365	.245–.255⑤	1.010–1.070
	1-64T-R13	②	③	.355–.365	.245–.255⑤	—
	2-63Y-R11	②	③	.355–.365④	.245–.255⑤	1.010–1.070
	2-63Y-R12	②	③	.355–.365④	.245–.255⑤	1.010–1.070
	3-64X-R00	.120	2100ME	V-Notch	.20	31/64
	2-64Y-R11	②	③	.355–.365	.245–.255⑤	1.010–1.070
	2-64Y-R12	②	③	.355–.365	.245–.255⑤	1.010–1.070

Engine Rebuilding

This section describes, in detail, the procedures involved in rebuilding a typical engine. The procedures are basically identical to those used in rebuilding engines of nearly all design and configurations.

The section is divided into two parts. The first, Cylinder Head Reconditioning, assumes that the cylinder head is removed from the engine, all manifolds are removed, and the cylinder head is on a workbench. The camshaft should be removed from overhead cam cylinder heads. The second section, Cylinder Block Reconditioning, covers the block, pistons, connecting rods and crankshaft. It is assumed that the engine is mounted on a work stand, and the cylinder head and all accessories are removed.

Procedures are identified as follows:

Unmarked—Basic procedures that must be performed in order to successfully complete the rebuilding process.

Starred (*)—Procedures that should be performed to ensure maximum performance and engine life.

Double starred (**)—Procedures that may be performed to increase engine performance and reliability.

In many cases, a choice of methods is also provided. Methods are identified in the same manner as procedures. The choice of method for a procedure is at the discretion of the user.

The tools required for the basic rebuilding procedure should, with minor exceptions, be those included in a mechanic's tool kit. An accurate torque wrench, and a dial indicator (reading in thousandths) mounted on a universal base should be available. Special tools, where required, all are readily available from the major tool suppliers. The services of a competent automotive machine shop must also be readily available.

When assembling the engine, any parts that will be in frictional contact must be pre-lubricated, to provide protection on initial start-up. Any product specifically formulated for this purpose may be used. NOTE: *Do not use engine oil.* Where semi-permanent (locked but removable) installation of bolts or nuts is desired, threads should be cleaned and coated with Loctite® or a similar product (non-hardening).

Aluminum has become increasingly popular for use in engines, due to its low weight and excellent heat transfer characteristics. The following precautions must be observed when handling aluminum engine parts:

—Never hot-tank aluminum parts.

—Remove all aluminum parts (identification tags, etc.) from engine parts before hot-tanking (otherwise they will be removed during the process).

—Always coat threads lightly with engine oil or anti-seize compounds before installation, to prevent seizure.

—Never over-torque bolts or spark plugs in aluminum threads. Should stripping occur, threads can be restored using any of a number of thread repair kits available (see next section).

Magnaflux and Zyglo are inspection techniques used to locate material flaws, such as stress cracks. Magnafluxing coats the part with fine magnetic particles, and subjects the part to a magnetic field. Cracks cause breaks in the magnetic field, which are outlined by the particles. Since Magnaflux is a magnetic process, it is applicable only to ferrous materials. The Zyglo process coats the material with a fluorescent dye penetrant, and then subjects it to blacklight inspection, under which cracks glow brightly. Parts made of any material may be tested using Zyglo. While Magnaflux and Zyglo are excellent for general inspection, and locating hidden defects, specific checks of suspected cracks may be made at lower cost and more readily using spot check dye. The dye is sprayed onto the suspected area, wiped off, and the area is then sprayed with a developer. Cracks then will show up brightly. Spot check dyes will only indicate surface cracks; therefore, structural cracks below the surface may escape detection. When questionable, the part should be tested using Magnaflux or Zyglo.

REPAIRING DAMAGED THREADS

Several methods of repairing damaged threads are available. Heli-Coil® (shown here), Keenserts® and Microdot® are among the most widely used. All involve basically

the same principle—drilling out stripped threads, tapping the hole and installing a prewound insert— making welding, plugging and oversize fasteners unnecessary.

Two types of thread repair inserts are usually supplied—a standard type for most Inch Coarse, Inch Fine, Metric Coarse and Metric Fine thread sizes and a spark plug type to fit most spark plug port sizes. Consult the individual manufacturer's catalog to determine exact applications. Typical thread repair kits will contain a selection of prewound threaded inserts, a tap (corresponding to the outside diameter threads of the insert) and an installation tool. Most manufacturers also supply blister-packed thread repair inserts separately and a master kit with a variety of taps and inserts plus installation tools.

Before effecting a repair to a threaded hole, remove any snapped, broken or damaged bolts or studs. Penetrating oil can be used to free frozen threads; the offending item can be removed with locking pliers or with a screw or stud extractor. After the hole is clear, the thread can be repaired as follows.

A. Drill out the damaged threads with the specified drill. Drill completely through the hole or to the bottom of a blind hole.

B. With the tap supplied tap the hole to receive the threaded insert. Keep the tap well oiled and back it out frequently to avoid clogging the threads.

C. Screw the threaded insert onto the installation tool until the tang engages the slot. Screw the insert into the tapped hole until it is ¼–½ turn below the top surface. After installation, break the tang off with a hammer and punch.

STANDARD TORQUE SPECIFICATIONS AND CAPSCREW MARKINGS

Newton-Meter has been designated as the world standard for measuring torque and will gradually replace the foot-pound and kilogram-meter torque measuring standard. Torquing tools are still being manufactured with foot-pounds and kilogram-meter scales, along with the new Newton-Meter standard. To assist the repairman, foot-pounds, kilogram-meter and Newton-Meter are listed in the following charts, and should be followed as applicable.

U.S. BOLTS

SAE Grade Number	1 or 2			5			6 or 7			8		
Capscrew Head Markings — Manufacturer's marks may vary. Three-line markings on heads below indicate SAE Grade 5.												
Usage	Used Frequently			Used Frequently			Used at Times			Used at Times		
Quality of Material	Indeterminate			Minimum Commercial			Medium Commercial			Best Commercial		
Capacity Body Size	Torque			Torque			Torque			Torque		
(inches)–(thread)	Ft-Lb	kgm	Nm	Ft-Lb	kgm	Nm	Ft-Lb	kgm	Nm	Ft-Lb	kgm	Nm
1/4–20	5	0.6915	6.7791	8	1.1064	10.8465	10	1.3630	13.5582	12	1.6596	16.2698
–28	6	0.8298	8.1349	10	1.3830	13.5582				14	1.9362	18.9815
5/16–18	11	1.5213	14.9140	17	2.3511	23.0489	19	2.6277	25.7605	24	3.3192	32.5396
–24	13	1.7979	17.6256	19	2.6277	25.7605				27	3.7341	36.6071
3/8–16	18	2.4894	24.4047	31	4.2873	42.0304	34	4.7022	46.0978	44	6.0852	59.6560
–24	20	2.7660	27.1164	35	4.8405	47.4536				49	6.7767	66.4351
7/16–14	28	3.8132	37.9629	49	6.7767	66.4351	55	7.6065	74.5700	70	9.6810	94.9073
–20	30	4.1490	40.6745	55	7.6065	74.5700				78	10.7874	105.7538
1/2–13	39	5.3937	52.8769	75	10.3725	101.6863	85	11.7555	115.2445	105	14.5215	142.3609
–20	41	5.6703	55.5885	85	11.7555	115.2445				120	16.5860	162.6960
9/16–12	51	7.0533	69.1467	110	15.2130	149.1380	120	16.5960	162.6960	155	21.4365	210.1490
–18	55	7.6065	74.5700	120	16.5960	162.6960				170	23.5110	230.4860
5/8–11	83	11.4789	112.5329	150	20.7450	203.3700	167	23.0961	226.4186	210	29.0430	284.7180
–18	95	13.1385	128.8027	170	23.5110	230.4860				240	33.1920	325.3920
3/4–10	105	14.5215	142.3609	270	37.3410	366.0660	280	38.7240	379.6240	375	51.8625	508.4250
–16	115	15.9045	155.9170	295	40.7985	399.9610				420	58.0860	568.4360
7/8–9	160	22.1280	216.9280	395	54.6285	535.5410	440	60.8520	596.5520	605	83.6715	820.2590
–14	175	24.2025	237.2650	435	60.1605	589.7730				675	93.3525	915.1650
1–8	236	32.5005	318.6130	590	81.5970	799.9220	660	91.2780	894.8280	910	125.8530	1233.7780
–14	250	34.5750	338.9500	660	91.2780	849.8280				990	136.9170	1342.2420

METRIC BOLTS

Torque ft-lbs. (Nm)

Description Thread for general purposes (size x pitch (mm))	Head Mark 4		Head Mark 7	
6 x 1.0	2.2 to 2.9	(3.0 to 3.9)	3.6 to 5.8	(4.9 to 7.8)
8 x 1.25	5.8 to 8.7	(7.9 to 12)	9.4 to 14	(13 to 19)
10 x 1.25	12 to 17	(16 to 23)	20 to 29	(27 to 39)
12 x 1.25	21 to 32	(29 to 43)	35 to 53	(47 to 72)
14 x 1.5	35 to 52	(48 to 70)	57 to 85	(77 to 110)
16 x 1.5	51 to 77	(67 to 100)	90 to 120	(130 to 160)
18 x 1.5	74 tc 110	(100 to 150)	130 to 170	(180 to 230)
20 x 1.5	110 to 140	(150 to 190)	190 to 240	(160 to 320)
22 x 1.5	150 to 190	(200 to 260)	250 to 320	(340 to 430)
24 x 1.5	190 to 240	(260 to 320)	310 to 410	(420 to 550)

CAUTION: Bolts threaded into aluminum require much less torque

NOTE: This engine rebuilding section is a guide to accepted rebuilding procedures. Typical examples of standard rebuilding procedures are illustrated.

CYLINDER HEAD RECONDITIONING

Procedure	Method
Identify the valves:	Invert the cylinder head, and number the valve faces front to rear, using a permanent felt-tip marker.
Remove the rocker arms (OHV engines only):	Remove the rocker arms with shaft(s) or balls and nuts. Wire the sets of rockers, balls and nuts together, and identify according to the corresponding valve.
Remove the camshaft (OHC engines only):	See the engine service procedures earlier in this book for details concerning specific engines.
Remove the valves and springs:	Using an appropriate valve spring compressor (depending on the configuration of the cylinder head), compress the valve springs. Lift out the keepers with needlenose pliers, release the compressor, and remove the valve, spring, and spring retainer.
Remove glow plugs and fuel injectors (Diesel engines only):	Label and remove all fuel injectors and glow plugs from the head. Glow plugs unscrew. See the appropriate car section for injector removal. Inspect glow plugs for bulges, cracks or signs of melting. Clean injector tips with a steel brush, then inspect for evidence of melting.
**Remove pre-combustion chamber inserts (Diesel engines only): Removing pre-combustion chamber with a drift (© G.M. Corp.)	**Remove the pre-combustion chambers using a hammer and a thin, blunt brass drift, inserted through the injector hole (or glow plug hole, whichever is more convenient). If chamber is to be reused, carefully remove all carbon from it. NOTE: *Remove chamber only if being replaced, if a glow plug tip has broken off and must be removed, or if chamber is obviously damaged or loose.*
Check the valve stem-to-guide clearance: Checking the valve stem-to-guide clearance	Clean the valve stem with lacquer thinner or a similar solvent to remove all gum and varnish. Clean the valve guides using solvent and an expanding wire-type valve guide cleaner. Mount a dial indicator so that the stem is at 90° to the valve stem, as close to the valve guide as possible. Move the valve off its seat, and measure the valve guide-to-stem clearance by rocking the stem back and forth to actuate the dial indicator. Measure the valve stems using a micrometer, and compare to specifications, to determine whether stem or guide wear is responsible for excessive clearance.

CYLINDER HEAD RECONDITIONING

Procedure	Method

De-carbon the cylinder head and valves:

Chip carbon away from the valve heads, combustion chambers, and ports, using a chisel made of hardwood. Remove the remaining deposits with a stiff wire brush.
NOTE: *Ensure that the deposits are actually removed, rather than burnished.*

WIRE BRUSH

Removing carbon from the cylinder head

Hot-tank the cylinder head (cast iron heads only):
CAUTION: *Do not hot-tank aluminum parts.*

Have the cylinder head hot-tanked to remove grease, corrosion, and scale from the water passages.
NOTE: *In the case of overhead cam cylinder heads, consult the operator to determine whether the camshaft bearings will be damaged by the caustic solution.*

Degrease the remaining cylinder head parts:

Using solvent (i.e., Gunk), clean the rockers, rocker shaft(s) (where applicable), rocker balls and nuts, springs, spring retainers, and keepers. Do not remove the protective coating from the springs.

Check the cylinder head for warpage:

Place a straight-edge across the gasket surface of the cylinder head. Using feeler gauges, determine the clearance at the center of the straight-edge. Measure across both diagonals, along the longitudinal centerline, and across the cylinder head at several points. If warpage exceeds .003′ in a 6′ span, or .006′ over the total length, the cylinder head must be resurfaced.
NOTE: *If warpage exceeds the manufacturer's maximum tolerance for material removal, the cylinder head must be replaced.*
When milling the cylinder heads of V-type engines, the intake manifold mounting position is altered, and must be corrected by milling the manifold flange a proportionate amount.

1 & 3 CHECK DIAGONALLY
2 CHECK ACROSS CENTER

Checking cylinder head for warpage

**Porting and gasket matching:

**Coat the manifold flanges of the cylinder head with Prussian blue dye. Glue intake and exhaust gaskets to the cylinder head in their installed position using rubber cement and scribe the outline of the ports on the manifold flanges. Remove the gaskets. Using a small cutter in a hand-held power tool gradually taper the walls of the port out to the scribed outline of the gasket. Further enlargement of the ports should include the removal of sharp edges and radiusing of sharp corners. Do not alter the valve guides.
NOTE: *The most efficient port configuration is determined only by extensive testing. Therefore, it is best to consult someone experienced with the head in question to determine the optimum alterations.*

CYLINDER HEAD RECONDITIONING

Procedure	Method

*Knurling the valve guides:

Cut-away view of a knurled valve guide

*Valve guides which are not excessively worn or distorted may, in some cases, be knurled rather than replaced. Knurling is a process in which metal is displaced and raised, thereby reducing clearance. Knurling also provides excellent oil control. The possibility of knurling rather than replacing valve guides should be discussed with a machinist.

Replacing the valve guides:
NOTE: *Valve guides should only be replaced if damaged or if an oversize valve stem is not available.*

A—VALVE GUIDE I.D.   B—LARGER THAN THE VALVE GUIDE O.D.
Valve guide removal tool

WASHERS

A—VALVE GUIDE I.D.   B—LARGER THAN THE VALVE GUIDE O.D.
Valve guide installation tool (with washers used for installation)

Depending on the type of cylinder head, valve guides may be pressed, hammered, or shrunk in. In cases where the guides are shrunk into the head, replacement should be left to an equipped machine shop. In other cases, the guides are replaced as follows: Press or tap the valve guides out of the head using a stepped drift (see illustration). Determine the height above the boss that the guide must extend, and obtain a stack of washers, their I.D. similar to the guide's O.D., of that height. Place the stack of washers on the guide, and insert the guide into the boss.
NOTE: *Valve guides are often tapered or beveled for installation.*
Using the stepped installation tool (see illustration), press or tap the guides into position. Ream the guides according to the size of the valve stem.

Replacing valve seat inserts:

Replacement of valve seat inserts which are worn beyond resurfacing or broken, if feasible, must be done by a machine shop.

Resurfacing the valve seats using reamers:

45°   VALVE MARGIN
SEAT WIDTH
CORRECT
NO MARGIN
INCORRECT
Valve seat width and centering

Reaming the valve seat

Select a reamer of the correct seat angle, slightly larger than the diameter of the valve seat, and assemble it with a pilot of the correct size. Install the pilot into the valve guide, and using steady pressure, turn the reamer clockwise.
CAUTION: *Do not turn the reamer counterclockwise.*
Remove only as much material as necessary to clean the seat. Check the concentricity of the seat (see below). If the dye method is not used, coat the valve face with Prussian blue dye, install and rotate it on the valve seat. Using the dye marked area as a centering guide, center and narrow the valve seat to specifications with correction cutters.
NOTE: *When no specifications are available, minimum seat width for exhaust valves should be 5/64", intake valves 1/16".*
After making correction cuts, check the position of the valve seat on the valve face using Prussian blue dye.
NOTE: *Do not cut induction hardened seats; they must be ground.*

CYLINDER HEAD RECONDITIONING

Procedure	Method

*Resurfacing the valve seats using a grinder:

*Select a pilot of the correct size, and a coarse stone of the correct seat angle. Lubricate the pilot if necessary, and install the tool in the valve guide. Move the stone on and off the seat at approximately two cycles per second, until all flaws are removed from the seat. Install a fine stone, and finish the seat. Center and narrow the seat using correction stones, as described above.

CYLINDER

VALVE SEAT

Grinding a valve seat

Resurfacing (grinding) the valve face:

Using a valve grinder, resurface the valves according to specifications.
CAUTION: *Valve face angle is not always identical to valve seat angle.*
A minimum margin of 1/32" should remain after grinding the valve. The valve stem top should also be squared and resurfaced, by placing the stem in the V-block of the grinder, and turning it while pressing lightly against the grinding wheel.
NOTE: *Do not grind sodium filled exhaust valves on a machine. These should be hand lapped.*

FOR DIMENSIONS,
REFER TO
SPECIFICATIONS

CHECK FOR
BENT STEM

DIAMETER

VALVE FACE ANGLE

1/32" MINIMUM

THIS LINE
PARALLEL WITH
VALVE HEAD

Critical valve dimensions

Valve grinding by machine

CYLINDER HEAD RECONDITIONING

Procedure	Method

Checking the valve seat concentricity:

Checking valve seat concentricity using a dial gauge

Coat the valve face with Prussian blue dye, install the valve, and rotate it on the valve seat. If the entire seat becomes coated, and the valve is known to be concentric, the seat is concentric.
*Install the dial gauge pilot into the guide, and rest the arm on the valve seat. Zero the gauge, and rotate the arm around the seat. Run-out should not exceed .002".

*Lapping the valves:
NOTE: *Valve lapping is done to ensure efficient sealing of resurfaced valves and seats.*

HAND DRILL

ROD

SUCTION CUP

Hand lapping the valves

Home made mechanical valve lapping tool

*Invert the cylinder head, lightly lubricate the valve stems, and install the valves in the head as numbered. Coat valve seats with fine grinding compound, and attach the lapping tool suction cup to a valve head.
NOTE: *Moisten the suction cup.*
Rotate the tool between the palms, changing position and lifting the tool often to prevent grooving. Lap the valve until a smooth, polished seat is evident. Remove the valve and tool, and rinse away all traces of grinding compound.
**Fasten a suction cup to a piece of drill rod, and mount the rod in a hand drill. Proceed as above, using the hand drill as a lapping tool.
CAUTION: *Due to the higher speeds involved when using the hand drill, care must be exercised to avoid grooving the seat.* Lift the tool and change direction of rotation often.

Check the valve springs:

NOT MORE THAN 5/64"

CLOSED COIL END DOWNWARD

Checking valve spring free length and squareness   Measuring valve spring test pressure

Place the spring on a flat surface next to a square. Measure the height of the spring, and rotate it against the edge of the square to measure distortion. If spring height varies (by comparison) by more than 1/16" or if distortion exceeds 1/16", replace the spring.
**In addition to evaluating the spring as above, test the spring pressure at the installed and compressed (installed height minus valve lift) height using a valve spring tester. Springs used on small displacement engines (up to 3 liters) should be ∓ 1 lb. of all other springs in either position. A tolerance of ∓ 5 lbs. is permissible on larger engines.

CYLINDER HEAD RECONDITIONING

Procedure	Method

Install pre-combustion chambers (Diesel engines only)

Pre-combustion chambers are press-fit into the head. The chambers will fit only one way: on G.M. V8, align the notches in the chamber and head; on 1.8L 4 cyl., install lock ball into groove in chamber, then align lock ball in chamber with groove in cylinder head. Press the chamber into the head. Fit a piece of metal against the chamber face for protection. On 1.8L, after installation, grind the face of the chamber flush with the face of the cylinder head. On G.M. V8, use a 1¼ in. socket to install the chamber (the chamber should be flush ± .003 in. to the face of the head).

DRIVE ON OUTER AREA OF PRE-CHAMBER ONLY

PRE-CHAMBER

NOTCH

Align the notches to install the pre-combustion chamber (© G.M. Corp.)

Install fuel injectors and glow plugs (Diesel engines)

Before installing glow plugs, check for continuity across plug terminals and body. If no continuity exists, the heater wire is broken and the plug should be replaced.

*Install valve stem seals:

*Due to the pressure differential that exists at the ends of the intake valve guides (atmospheric pressure above, manifold vacuum below), oil is drawn through the valve guides into the intake port. This has been alleviated somewhat since the addition of positive crankcase ventilation, which lowers the pressure above the guides. Several types of valve stem seals are available to reduce blow-by. Certain seals simply slip over the stem and guide boss, while others require that the boss be machined. Recently, Teflon guide seals have become popular. Consult a parts supplier or machinist concerning availability and suggested usages.

NOTE: *When installing seals, ensure that a small amount of oil is able to pass the seal to lubricate the valve guides; otherwise, excessive wear may result.*

RETAINER

SPRING

VALVE

SEAL

Valve stem seal installation

Install the valves:

Lubricate the valve stems, and install the valves in the cylinder head as numbered. Lubricate and position the seals (if used, see above) and the valve springs. Install the spring retainers, compress the springs, and insert the keys using needlenose pliers or a tool designed for this purpose.

NOTE: *Retain the keys with wheel bearing grease during installation.*

CYLINDER HEAD RECONDITIONING

Procedure	Method

Check valve spring installed height:

GRIND OUT THIS PORTION

Valve spring installed
height dimension

Measuring valve spring
installed height

Measure the distance between the spring pad and the lower edge of the spring retainer, and compare to specifications. If the installed height is incorrect, add shim washers between the spring pad and the spring.
CAUTION: *Use only washers designed for this purpose.*

Install the camshaft (OHC engines only) and check end play:

See the engine service procedures earlier in this book for details concerning specific engines.

Inspect the rocker arms, balls, studs, and nuts (OHV engines only):

SMALL FRACTURES

Stress cracks in the rocker nuts

Visually inspect the rocker arms, balls, studs, and nuts for cracks, galling, burning, scoring or wear. If all parts are intact, liberally lubricate the rocker arms and balls, and install them on the cylinder head. If wear is noted on a rocker arm at the point of valve contact, grind it smooth and square, removing as little material as possible. Replace the rocker arm if excessively worn. If a rocker stud shows signs of wear, it must be replaced (see below). If a rocker nut shows stress cracks, replace it. If an exhaust ball is galled or burned, substitute the intake ball from the same cylinder (if it is intact), and install a new intake ball.
NOTE: *Avoid using new rocker balls on exhaust valves.*

Replacing rocker studs (OHV engines only):

AS STUB BEGINS TO PULL UP,
IT WILL BE NECESSARY TO REMOVE
THE NUT AND ADD MORE WASHERS

⅜″ NUT

FLAT WASHERS

Extracting a pressed-in rocker stud

In order to remove a threaded stud, lock two nuts on the stud, and unscrew the stud using the lower nut. Coat the lower threads of the new stud with Loctite®, and install.

Two alternative methods are available for replacing pressed in studs. Remove the damaged stud using a stack of washers and a nut (see illustration). In the first, the boss is reamed .005–.006″ oversize, and an oversize stud pressed in. Control the stud extension over the boss using washers, in the same manner as valve guides. Before installing the stud, coat it with white lead and grease. To retain the stud more positively drill a hole through the stud and boss, and install a roll pin. In the second method, the boss is tapped, and a threaded stud installed. Retain the stud using Loctite® Stud and Bearing Mount.

Reaming the stud bore for oversize rocker studs

CYLINDER HEAD RECONDITIONING

Procedure	Method

Inspect the rocker shaft(s) and rocker arms (OHV engines only):

Disassemble the rocker shaft for inspection

Remove rocker arms, springs and washers from rocker shaft. NOTE: *Lay out parts in the order as they are removed.*
Inspect rocker arms for pitting or wear on the valve contact point, or excessive bushing wear. Bushings need only be replaced if wear is excessive, because the rocker arm normally contacts the shaft at one point only. Grind the valve contact point of rocker arm smooth if necessary, removing as little material as possible. If excessive material must be removed to smooth and square the arm, it should be replaced. Clean out all oil holes and passages in rocker shaft. If shaft is grooved or worn, replace it. Lubricate and assemble the rocker shaft.

Rocker arm-to-rocker shaft contact area

Inspect the camshaft bushings and the camshaft (OHC engines):

See next section.

Inspect the pushrods (OHV engines only):

Remove the pushrods, and, if hollow, clean out the oil passages using fine wire. Roll each pushrod over a piece of clean glass. If a distinct clicking sound is heard as the pushrod rolls, the rod is bent, and must be replaced.

*The length of all pushrods must be equal. Measure the length of the pushrods, compare to specifications, and replace as necessary.

Inspect the valve lifters (OHV engines only):

CHECK FOR CONCAVE WEAR ON FACE OF TAPPET USING TAPPET FOR STRAIGHT EDGE

Checking the lifter face

Remove lifters from their bores, and remove gum and varnish, using solvent. Clean walls of lifter bores. Check lifters for concave wear as illustrated. If face is worn concave, replace lifter, and carefully inspect the camshaft. Lightly lubricate lifter and insert it into its bore. If play is excessive, an oversize lifter must be installed (where possible). Consult a machinist concerning feasibility. If play is satisfactory, remove, lubricate, and reinstall the lifter.
NOTE: *1981 and later G.M. diesel V8 valve lifters have roller cam followers. Check these for smooth operation and wear. The roller should rotate freely, but without excessive play. Check the rollers for missing or broken needle bearings. If the roller is pitted or rough, check the camshaft lobe for wear.*

*Testing hydraulic lifter leak down (OHV gasoline engines only):

Typical exploded view of hydraulic valve lifter

Submerge lifter in a container of kerosene. Chuck a used pushrod or its equivalent into a drill press. Position container of kerosene so pushrod acts on the lifter plunger. Pump lifter with the drill press, until resistance increases. Pump several more times to bleed any air out of lifter. Apply very firm, constant pressure to the lifter, and observe rate at which fluid bleeds out of lifter. If the fluid bleeds very quickly (less than 15 seconds), lifter is defective. If the time exceeds 60 seconds, lifter is sticking. In either case, recondition or replace lifter. If lifter is operating properly (leak down time 15–60 seconds), lubricate and install it.

CYLINDER HEAD RECONDITIONING

Procedure	Method
Bleed the hydraulic lifters (diesel engines only):	After the cylinder heads are installed on G.M. V8 diesels, the valve lifters must be bled down before the crankshaft is turned. Failure to bleed down the lifters will cause damage to the valve train. See diesel engine rocker arm replacement procedure in Oldsmobile 88, 98, etc. car section for procedures. NOTE: *When installing new lifters, prime by working the lifter plunger while submerged in clean kerosene or diesel fuel.*

CYLINDER BLOCK RECONDITIONING

Procedure	Method
Checking the main bearing clearance: Plastigage® installed on the lower bearing shell Measuring Plastigage® to determine bearing clearance	Invert engine, and remove cap from the bearing to be checked. Using a clean, dry rag, thoroughly clean all oil from crankshaft journal and bearing insert. NOTE: *Plastigage is soluble in oil; therefore, oil on the journal or bearing could result in erroneous readings.* Place a piece of Plastigage along the full length of journal, reinstall cap, and torque to specifications. Remove bearing cap, and determine bearing clearance by comparing width of Plastigage to the scale on Plastigage envelope. Journal taper is determined by comparing width of the Plastigage strip near its ends. Rotate crankshaft 90° and retest, to determine journal eccentricity. NOTE: *Do not rotate crankshaft with Plastigage installed.* If bearing insert and journal appear intact, and are within tolerances, no further main bearing service is required. If bearing or journal appear defective, cause of failure should be determined before replacement. *Remove crankshaft from block (see below). Measure the main bearing journals at each end twice (90° apart) using a micrometer, to determine diameter, journal taper and eccentricity. If journals are within tolerances, reinstall bearing caps at their specified torque. Using a telescope gauge and micrometer, measure bearing I.D. parallel to piston axis and at 30° on each side of piston axis. Subtract journal O.D. from bearing I.D. to determine oil clearance. If crankshaft journals appear defective, or do no meet tolerances, there is no need to measure bearings; for the crankshaft will require grinding and/or undersize bearings will be required. If bearing appears defective, cause for failure should be determined prior to replacement.
Checking the connecting rod bearing clearance:	Connecting rod bearing clearance is checked in the same manner as main bearing clearance, using Plastigage. Before removing the crankshaft, connecting rod side clearance also should be measured and recorded. *Checking connecting rod bearing clearance, using a micrometer, is identical to checking main bearing clearance. If no other service is required, the piston and rod assemblies need not be removed.

CYLINDER BLOCK RECONDITIONING

Procedure

Method

Removing the crankshaft:

Using a punch, mark the corresponding main bearing caps and saddles according to position (i.e., one punch on the front main cap and saddle, two on the second, three on the third, etc.). Using number stamps, identify the corresponding connecting rods and caps, according to cylinder (if no numbers are present). Remove the main and connecting rod caps, and place sleeves of plastic tubing over the connecting rod bolts, to protect the journals as the crankshaft is removed. Lift the crankshaft out of the block.

Connecting rod matched to cylinder with a number stamp

Scribe connecting rod matchmarks

Remove the ridge from the top of the cylinder:

In order to facilitate removal of the piston and connecting rod, the ridge at the top of the cylinder (unworn area; see illustration) must be removed. Place the piston at the bottom of the bore, and cover it with a rag. Cut the ridge away using a ridge reamer, exercising extreme care to avoid cutting to deeply. Remove the rag, and remove cuttings that remain on the piston.

CAUTION: *If the ridge is not removed, and new rings are installed, damage to rings will result.*

RIDGE CAUSED BY CYLINDER WEAR

CYLINDER WALL
TOP OF PISTON

Cylinder bore ridge

Removing the piston and connecting rod:

Invert the engine, and push the pistons and connecting rods out of the cylinders. If necessary, tap the connecting rod boss with a wooden hammer handle, to force the piston out.

CAUTION: *Do not attempt to force the piston past the cylinder ridge (see above).*

Removing the piston

CYLINDER BLOCK RECONDITIONING

Procedure	Method
Service the crankshaft:	Ensure that all oil holes and passages in the crankshaft are open and free of sludge. If necessary, have the crankshaft ground to the largest possible undersize. **Have the crankshaft Magnafluxed, to locate stress cracks. Consult a machinist concerning additional service procedures, such as surface hardening (e.g., nitriding, Tuftriding) to improve wear characteristics, cross drilling and chamfering the oil holes to improve lubrication, and balancing.
Removing freeze plugs:	Drill a small hole in the middle of the freeze plugs. Thread a large sheet metal screw into the hole and remove the plug with a slide hammer.
Remove the oil gallery plugs:	Threaded plugs should be removed using an appropriate (usually square) wrench. To remove soft, pressed in plugs, drill a hole in the plug, and thread in a sheet metal screw. Pull the plug out by the screw using pliers.
Hot-tank the block: NOTE: *Do not hot-tank aluminum parts.*	Have the block hot-tanked to remove grease, corrosion, and scale from the water jackets. NOTE: *Consult the operator to determine whether the camshaft bearings will be damaged during the hot-tank process.*

Check the block for cracks:	Visually inspect the block for cracks or chips. The most common locations are as follows:
	    Adjacent to freeze plugs.
	    Between the cylinders and water jackets.
	    Adjacent to the main bearing saddles.
	    At the extreme bottom of the cylinders.
	Check only suspected cracks using spot check dye (see introduction). If a crack is located, consult a machinist concerning possible repairs.
	
	**Magnaflux the block to locate hidden cracks. If cracks are located, consult a machinist about feasibility of repair.

Install the oil gallery plugs and freeze plugs:	Coat freeze plugs with sealer and tap into position using a piece of pipe, slightly smaller than the plug, as a driver. To ensure retention, stake the edges of the plugs. Coat threaded oil gallery plugs with sealer and install. Drive replacement soft plugs into block using a large drift as a driver. *Rather than reinstalling lead plugs, drill and tap the holes, and install threaded plugs.
*Check the deck height:	*The deck height is the distance from the crankshaft centerline to the block deck. To measure, invert the engine, and install the crankshaft, retaining it with the center main cap. Measure the distance from the crankshaft journal to the block deck, parallel to the cylinder centerline. Measure the diameter of the end (front and rear) main journals, parallel to the centerline of the cylinders, divide the diameter in half, and subtract it from the previous measurement. The results of the front and rear measurements should be identical. If the difference exceeds .005″, the deck height should be corrected. NOTE: *Block deck height and warpage should be corrected at the same time.*

CYLINDER BLOCK RECONDITIONING

Procedure	Method

Check the block deck for warpage:

Using a straightedge and feeler gauges, check the block deck for warpage in the same manner that the cylinder head is checked (see Cylinder Head Reconditioning). If warpage exceeds specifications, have the deck resurfaced.
NOTE: *In certain cases a specification for total material removal (Cylinder head and block deck) is provided. This specification must not be exceeded.*

Check the bore diameter and surface:

Measuring the cylinder bore with a dial gauge

Visually inspect the cylinder bores for roughness, scoring, or scuffing. If evident, the cylinder bore must be bored or honed oversize to eliminate imperfections, and the smallest possible oversize piston used. The new pistons should be given to the machinist with the block, so that the cylinders can be bored or honed exactly to the piston size (plus clearance). If no flaws are evident, measure the bore diameter using a telescope gauge and micrometer, or dial guage, parallel and perpendicular to the engine centerline, at the top (below the ridge) and bottom of the bore. Subtract the bottom measurements from the top to determine taper, and the parallel to the centerline measurements from the perpendicular measurements to determine eccentricity. If the measurements are not within specifications, the cylinder must be bored or honed, and an oversize piston installed. If the measurements are within specifications the cylinder may be used as is, with only finish honing (see below).
NOTE: *Prior to boring, check the block deck warpage, height and bearing alignment.*
CAUTION: *The 4 cyl. 140 G.M. engine cylinder walls are impregnated with silicone. Boring or honing can be done only by a shop with the proper equipment.*

TELESCOPE GAUGE 90°
FROM PISTON PIN

Measuring cylinder bore with a
telescope gauge

◄— CENTERLINE OF ENGINE —►

A—AT RIGHT ANGLE TO
CENTERLINE OF ENGINE
B—PARALLEL TO
CENTERLINE OF ENGINE
Cylinder bore measuring points

TELESCOPE GAUGE

MICROMETER

Determining cylinder bore by measuring
telescope gauge with a micrometer

Check the cylinder block bearing alignment:

Checking main bearing saddle alignment

Remove the upper bearing inserts. Place a straightedge in the bearing saddles along the centerline of the crankshaft. If clearance exists between the straightedge and the center saddle, the block must be alignbored.

CYLINDER BLOCK RECONDITIONING

Procedure	Method

Clean and inspect the pistons and connecting rods:

RING EXPANDER

Removing the piston rings

RING GROOVE CLEANER

Cleaning the piston ring grooves

Using a ring expander, remove the rings from the piston. Remove the retaining rings (if so equipped) and remove piston pin.

NOTE: *If the piston pin must be pressed out, determine the proper method and use the proper tools; otherwise the piston will distort.*

Clean the ring grooves using an appropriate tool, exercising care to avoid cutting too deeply. Thoroughly clean all carbon and varnish from the piston with solvent.

CAUTION: *Do not use a wire brush or caustic solvent on pistons.*

Inspect the pistons for scuffing, scoring, cracks, pitting, or excessive ring groove wear. If wear is evident, the piston must be replaced. Check the connecting rod length by measuring the rod from the inside of the large end to the inside of the small end using calipers (see illustration). All connecting rods should be equal length. Replace any rod that differs from the others in the engine.

*Have the connecting rod alignment checked in an alignment fixture by a machinist. Replace any twisted or bent rods.

*Magnaflux the connecting rods to locate stress cracks. If cracks are found, replace the connecting rod.

Check the connecting rod length (arrow)

Fit the pistons to the cylinders:

90°

Measuring the piston prior to fitting

Using a telescope gauge and micrometer, or a dial gauge, measure the cylinder bore diameter perpendicular to the piston pin, 2½° below the deck. Measure the piston perpendicular to its pin on the skirt. The difference between the two measurements is the piston clearance. If the clearance is within specifications or slightly below (after boring or honing), finish honing is all that is required. If the clearance is excessive, try to obtain a slightly larger piston to bring clearance within specifications. Where this is not possible, obtain the first oversize piston, and hone (or if necessary, bore) the cylinder to size.

Assemble the pistons and connecting rods:

Inspect piston pin, connecting rod small end bushing, and piston bore for galling, scoring, or excessive wear. If evident, replace defective part(s). Measure the I.D. of the piston boss and connecting rod small end, and the O.D. of the piston pin. If within specifications, assemble piston pin and rod.

CAUTION: *If piston pin must be pressed in, determine the proper method and use the proper tools; otherwise the piston will distort.*

CYLINDER BLOCK RECONDITIONING

Procedure	Method

Installing piston pin lock rings

Install the lock rings; ensure that they seat properly. If the parts are not within specifications, determine the service method for the type of engine. In some cases, piston and pin are serviced as an assembly when either is defective. Others specify reaming the piston and connecting rods for an oversize pin. If the connecting rod bushing is worn, it may in many cases be replaced. Reaming the piston and replacing the rod bushing are machine shop operations.

Clean and inspect the camshaft:

Checking the camshaft for straightness

Degrease the camshaft, using solvent, and clean out all oil holes. Visually inspect cam lobes and bearing journals for excessive wear. If a lobe is questionable, check all lobes as indicated below. If a journal or lobe is worn, the camshaft must be reground or replaced.

NOTE: *If a journal is worn, there is a good chance that the bushings are worn.*

If lobes and journals appear intact, place the front and rear journals in V-blocks, and rest a dial indicator on the center journal. Rotate the camshaft to check straightness. If deviation exceeds .001°, replace the camshaft.

*Check the camshaft lobes with a micrometer, by measuring the lobes from the nose to base and again at 90° (see illustration). The lift is determined by subtracting the second measurement from the first. If all exhaust lobes and all intake lobes are not identical, the camshaft must be reground or replaced.

Camshaft lobe measurement

Replace the camshaft bearings (OHV engines only):

Camshaft removal and installation tool (typical)

If excessive wear is indicated, or if the engine is being completely rebuilt, camshaft bearings should be replaced as follows: Drive the camshaft rear plug from the block. Assemble the removal puller with its shoulder on the bearing to be removed. Gradually tighten the puller nut until bearing is removed. Remove remaining bearings, leaving the front and rear for last. To remove front and rear bearings, reverse position of the tool, so as to pull the bearings in toward the center of the block. Leave the tool in this position, pilot the new front and rear bearings on the installer, and pull them into position: Return the tool to its original position and pull remaining bearings into postion.

NOTE: *Ensure that oil holes align when installing bearings.*

Replace camshaft rear plug, and stake it into position to aid retention.

CYLINDER BLOCK RECONDITIONING

Procedure	Method

Finish hone the cylinders:

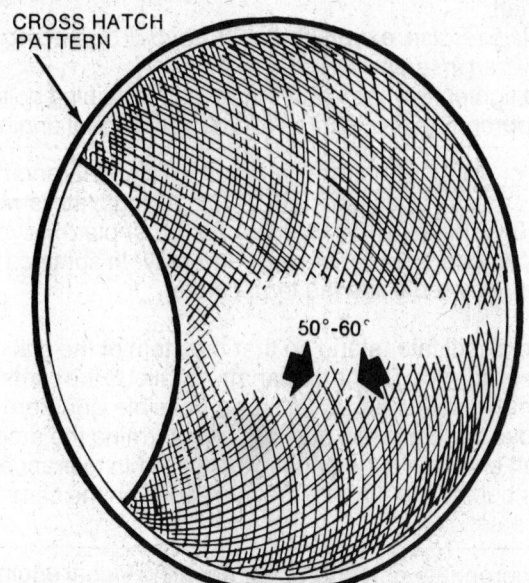

CROSS HATCH PATTERN

50°-60°

Chuck a flexible drive hone into a power drill, and insert it into the cylinder. Start the hone, and move it up and down the cylinder at a rate which will produce approximately a 60° cross-hatch pattern (see illustration).
NOTE: *Do not extend the hone below the cylinder bore.*
After developing the pattern, remove the hone and recheck piston fit. Wash the cylinders with a detergent and water solution to remove abrasive dust, dry, and wipe several times with a rag soaked in engine oil.

Check piston ring end-gap:

Checking ring end-gap

Compress the piston rings to be used in a cylinder, one at a time, into that cylinder, and press them approximately 1″ below the deck with an inverted piston. Using feeler gauges, measure the ring end-gap, and compare to specifications. Pull the ring out of the cylinder and file the ends with a fine file to obtain proper clearance.
CAUTION: *If inadequate ring end-gap is utilized, ring breakage will result.*

Install the piston rings:

PISTON RING

FEELER GAUGE

RING GROOVE

Checking ring side clearance

Inspect the ring grooves in the piston for excessive wear or taper. If necessary, recut the groove(s) for use with an overwidth ring or a standard ring and spacer. If the groove is worn uniformly, overwidth rings, or standard rings and spacers may be installed without recutting. Roll the outside of the ring around the groove to check for burrs or deposits. If any are found, remove with a fine file. Hold the ring in the groove, and measure side clearance. If necessary, correct as indicated above.
NOTE: *Always install any additional spacers above the piston ring.*
The ring groove must be deep enough to allow the ring to seat below the lands (see illustration). In many cases, a "go-no-go" depth gauge will be provided with the piston rings. Shallow grooves may be corrected by recutting, while deep grooves require some type of filler or expander behind the piston. Consult the piston ring supplier concerning the suggested method. Install the rings on the piston, lowest ring first, using a ring expander.
NOTE: *Position the ring markings as specified by the manufacturer (see car section).*

CYLINDER BLOCK RECONDITIONING

Procedure	Method
Install the camshaft (OHV engines only):	Liberally lubricate the camshaft lobes and journals, and install the camshaft. CAUTION: *Exercise extreme care to avoid damaging the bearings when inserting the camshaft.* Install and tighten the camshaft thrust plate retaining bolts. See the appropriate procedures for each individual engine.
Check camshaft end-play (OHV engines only): Checking camshaft end-play with a feeler gauge Checking camshaft end-play with a dial indicator	Using feeler gauges, determine whether the clearance between the camshaft boss (or gear) and backing plate is within specifications. Install shims behind the thrust plate, or reposition the camshaft gear and retest end-play. In some cases, adjustment is by replacing the thrust plate. *Mount a dial indicator stand so that the stem of the dial indicator rests on the nose of the camshaft, parallel to the camshaft axis. Push the camshaft as far in as possible and zero the gauge. Move the camshaft outward to determine the amount of camshaft endplay. If the endplay is not within tolerance, install shims behind the thrust plate, or reposition the camshaft gear and retest.
Install the rear main seal (where applicable):	See the appropriate procedures for each individual engine.
Install the crankshaft: Removal and installation of upper bearing insert using a roll-out pin Home-made bearing roll-out pin	Thoroughly clean the main bearing saddles and caps. Place the upper halves of the bearing inserts on the saddles and press into position. NOTE: *Ensure that the oil holes align.* Press the corresponding bearing inserts into the main bearing caps. Lubricate the upper main bearings, and lay the crankshaft in position. Place a strip of Plastigage on each of the crankshaft journals, install the main caps, and torque to specifications. Remove the main caps, and compare the Plastigage to the scale on the Plastigage envelope. If clearances are within tolerances, remove the Plastigage, turn the crankshaft 90°, wipe off all oil and retest. If all clearances are correct, remove all Plastigage, thoroughly lubricate the main caps and bearing journals, and install the main caps. If clearances are not within tolerance, the upper bearing inserts may be removed, without removing the crankshaft, using a bearing roll out pin (see illustration). Roll in a bearing that will provide proper clearance, and retest. Torque all main caps, excluding the thrust bearing cap, to specifications. Tighten the thrust bearing cap finger tight. To properly align the thrust bearing, pry the crankshaft the extent of its axial travel several times, the last movement held toward the front of the engine, and torque the thrust bearing cap to specifications. Determine the crankshaft end-play (see below), and bring within tolerance with thrust washers.

Aligning the thrust bearing

CYLINDER BLOCK RECONDITIONING

Procedure	Method

Measure crankshaft end-play:

Checking crankshaft end-play with a dial indicator

Checking crankshaft end-play with a feeler gauge

Mount a dial indicator stand on the front of the block, with the dial indicator stem resting on the nose of the crankshaft, parallel to the crankshaft axis. Pry the crankshaft the extent of its travel rearward, and zero the indicator. Pry the crankshaft forward and record crankshaft end-play.
NOTE: *Crankshaft end-play also may be measured at the thrust bearing, using feeler gauges* (see illustration).

Install the pistons:

Tubing used to protect crankshaft journals and cylinder walls during piston installation

Press the upper connecting rod bearing halves into the connecting rods, and the lower halves into the connecting rod caps. Position the piston ring gaps according to specifications (see car section), and lubricate the pistons. Install a ring compressor on a piston, and press two long (8") pieces of plastic tubing over the rod bolts. Using the tubes as a guide, press the pistons into the bores and onto the crankshaft with a wooden hammer handle. After seating the rod on the crankshaft journal, remove the tubes and install the cap finger tight. Install the remaining pistons in the same manner. Invert the engine and check the bearing clearance at two points (90° apart) on each journal with Plastigage.
NOTE: *Do not turn the crankshaft with Plastigage installed.*
If clearance is within tolerances, remove *all* Plastigage, thoroughly lubricate the journals, and torque the rod caps to specifications. If clearance is not within specifications, install different thickness bearing inserts and recheck.
CAUTION: *Never shim or file the connecting rods or caps.*
Always install plastic tube sleeves over the rod bolts when the caps are not installed, to protect the crankshaft journals.

Installing a piston

CYLINDER BLOCK RECONDITIONING

Procedure	Method
Check connecting rod side clearance: Checking connecting rod side clearance	Determine the clearance between the sides of the connecting rods and the crankshaft, using feeler gauges. If clearance is below the minimum tolerance, the rod may be machined to provide adequate clearance. If clearance is excessive, substitute an unworn rod, and recheck. If clearance is still outside specifications, the crankshaft must be welded and reground, or replaced.
Inspect the timing chain (or belt):	Visually inspect the timing chain for broken or loose links, and replace the chain if any are found. If the chain will flex sideways, it must be replaced. Install the timing chain as specified. Be sure the timing belt is not stretched, frayed or broken. NOTE: *If the original timing chain is to be reused, install it in its original position.*
Check timing gear backlash and runout (OHV engines): Checking camshaft gear backlash	Mount a dial indicator with its stem resting on a tooth of the camshaft gear (as illustrated). Rotate the gear until all slack is removed, and zero the indicator. Rotate the gear in the opposite direction until slack is removed, and record gear backlash. Mount the indicator with its stem resting on the edge of the camshaft gear, parallel to the axis of the camshaft. Zero the indicator, and turn the camshaft gear one full turn, recording the runout. If either backlash or runout exceed specifications, replace the worn gear(s). Checking camshaft gear runout

Completing the Rebuilding Process

Following the above procedures, complete the rebuilding process as follows:

Fill the oil pump with oil, to prevent cavitating (sucking air) on initial engine start up. Install the oil pump and the pickup tube on the engine. Coat the oil pan gasket as necessary, and install the gasket and the oil pan. Mount the flywheel and the crankshaft vibration damper or pulley on the crankshaft. NOTE: *Always use new bolts when installing the flywheel.*

Inspect the clutch shaft pilot bushing in the crankshaft. If the bushing is excessively worn, remove it with an expanding puller and a slide hammer, and tap a new bushing into place.

Position the engine, cylinder head side up. Lubricate the lifters, and install them into their bores. Install the cylinder head, and torque it as specified. Insert the pushrods (where applicable), and install the rocker shaft(s) (if so equipped) or position the rocker arms on the pushrods. Adjust the valves.

Install the intake and exhaust manifolds, the carburetor(s), the distributor and spark plugs. Adjust the point gap and the static ignition timing. Mount all accessories and install the engine in the car. Fill the radiator with coolant, and the crankcase with high quality engine oil.

Break-in Procedure

Start the engine, and allow it to run at low speed for a few minutes, while checking for leaks. Stop the engine, check the oil level, and fill as necessary. Restart the engine, and fill the cooling system to capacity. Check the point dwell angle and adjust the ignition timing and the valves. Run the engine at low to medium speed (800–2500 rpm) for approximately ½ hour, and retorque the cylinder head bolts. Road test the car, and check again for leaks.

Follow the manufacturer's recommended engine break-in procedure and maintenance schedule for new engines.

Steering Gear

INDEX

STEERING GEAR ALIGNMENT

Before any steering gear adjustments are made, it is recommended that the front end of the truck be raised and a thorough in-spection be made for stiffness or lost mo-tion in the steering gear, steering linkage and front suspension. Worn or damaged parts should be replaced, since a satisfac-tory adjustment of the steering gear cannot be obtained if bent or badly worn parts exist.

It is also very important that the steering gear be properly aligned in the truck. Mis-alignment of the gear places a stress on the steering worm shaft, therefore a proper ad-justment is impossible. To align the steer-ing gear, loosen the steering gear-to-frame mounting bolts to permit the gear to align itself. Check the steering gear to frame

STEERING TROUBLE DIAGNOSIS

Condition	Possible Cause	Correction
Excessive Play or Looseness in the Steering	1. Steering gear shaft adjusted too loose or shaft and/or bushing badly worn.	1. Replace worn parts and adjust according to instructions.
	2. Excessive steering gear worm end play due to bearing adjustment.	2. Adjust according to instructions.
	3. Steering linkage loose or worn.	3. Replace worn parts.
	4. Front wheel bearings improperly adjusted.	4. Adjust wheel bearings.
	5. Steering arm loose on steering gear shaft.	5. Inspect for damage to the gear shaft and steering arm, replace parts as necessary.
	6. Steering gear housing attaching bolts loose.	6. Tighten the attaching bolts to specifications.
	7. Steering arms loose at steering knuckles.	7. Tighten according to specifications.
	8. Working pins or bushings.	8. Replace king pins and bushings.
	9. Loose spring shackles.	9. Adjust or replace parts as necessary.
Hard Steering	1. Low or uneven tire pressure.	1. Inflate the tires to recommended pressures.
	2. Insufficient lubricant in the steering gear housing or in steering linkage.	2. Lubricate as necessary.
	3. Steering gear shaft adjusted too tight.	3. Adjust according to instructions.
	4. Improper caster or toe-in.	4. Align the wheels.
	5. Steering column misaligned.	5. See "Steering Gear Alignment."
Wheel Tramp (Excessive Vertical Motion of Wheels)	1. Incorrect tire pressure.	1. Inflate the tires to recommended pressures.
	2. Improper balance of wheels, tires and brake drums.	2. Balance as necessary.
	3. Loose tie rod ends or steering connections.	3. Inspect and repair as necessary.
	4. Worn or inoperative shock absorbers.	4. Replace the shock absorbers.
	5. Excessive run-out of brake drums, wheels or tires.	5. Repair or replace as required.
Shimmy	1. Badly worn and/or unevenly worn tires.	1. Rotate tires or replace if necessary.
	2. Wheels and tires out of balance.	2. Balance wheel and tire assemblies.
	3. Worn or loose steering linkage parts.	3. Replace parts are required.
	4. Worn king pins and bushings.	4. Replace king pins and bushings.
	5. Loose steering gear adjustments.	5. Adjust steering gear as necessary.
	6. Loose wheel bearings.	6. Adjust wheel bearings.
	7. Improper caster setting.	7. Adjust caster to specifications.
	8. Weak or broken springs.	8. Replace as required.
	9. Incorrect tire pressure or tire sizes not uniform.	9. Check tire sizes and inflate tires to recommended pressure
	10. Faulty shock absorbers.	10. Replace as necessary.
Pull to One Side (Tendency of the Vehicle to Veer in one Direction Only)	1. Incorrect tire pressure or tires not uniform.	1. Check tire sizes and inflate the tires to recommended pressures.
	2. Wheel bearings improperly adjusted.	2. Adjust wheel bearings.
	3. Dragging brakes.	3. Inspect for weak, or broken brake shoe spring, binding pedal.
	4. Improper caster, camber or toe-in.	4. Adjust to specifications.
	5. Grease, dirt, oil or brake fluid on brake linings.	5. Inspect, replace and adjust as necessary.
	6. Broken or sagging rear springs.	6. Replace the rear springs.
	7. Bent front axle, linkage or steering knuckle.	7. Replace the parts as necessary.
	8. Worn or tight king pin bushings.	8. Lubricate or replace as necessary.
Wander or Weave	1. Improper caster, camber or toe-in.	1. Adjust to specifications.
	2. Worn king pin and bushings.	2. Replace parts as required.
	3. Worn or improperly adjusted front wheel bearings.	3. Adjust or replace parts as necessary.
	4. Loose spring shackles.	4. Adjust or replace parts as necessary.
	5. Incorrect tire pressure or tire sizes not uniform.	5. Check tire sizes and inflate tires to recommended pressure.
	6. Loose steering gear mounting bolts.	6. Tight to specifications.
	7. Tight king pin bushings.	7. Lubricate or ream to proper fit.
	8. Tight king pin thrust bearings.	8. Adjust to .001 to .005 inch cleareance.

LOCK NUT FILLER PLUG SECTOR SHAFT WORM BEARING ADJUSTER WORM SHAFT

Steering gear adjustments

UPPER BEARING CUP UPPER BEARING STEERING SHAFT AND WORM ASSEMBLY STEERING GEAR HOUSING ASSEMBLY STEERING COLUMN TUBE AND BEARING ASSEMBLY END PLATE GASKET (SHIM) STEERING COLUMN CLAMP STEERING SECTOR SHAFT END PLATE AND TUBE ASSEMBLY LOWER BEARING LOWER BEARING CUP SECTOR SHAFT ARM (PITMAN ARM)

Worm and roller type steering gear

end-play by shaking the front wheel sideways and noting if there is any end movement that may be felt between the steering wheel hub and the steering jacket tube. (Be sure any movement noted is not looseness in the steering jacket tube.)

3. If end play is present, adjust the worm bearings by loosening the four cover cap screws about ⅛". Separate the top shim, using a knife blade, and remove it. Do not damage the remaining shims or gaskets.

4. Replace the cover and recheck the end-play again. If necessary, repeat steps 2 and 3 until the end-play movement is as small as possible without tightening the steering gear too much.

NOTE: **Adjustment may be done with the Pitman arm disconnected. With the steering wheel turned about one full turn from straight ahead and using a spring scale tool, adjust with the shims as given above until the spring scale pull is between ¼ and ⅝ ft. lbs.**

CROSS SHAFT ROLLER AND WORM MESH ADJUSTMENT

1. Turn the steering wheel to the middle of its turning limits with the Pitman arm disconnected. The steering gear roller should be on the worm high spot.

2. Shake the Pitman arm sideways to determine the amount of clearance between the worm cross shaft roller. Movement of more than ½₂" indicates that the roller and worm mesh must be adjusted.

3. Loosen the adjusting screw lock nut and tighten the external cross shaft adjusting screw a small amount. Recheck the clearance by shaking the Pitman arm. Repeat until the clearance is correct. (Do not overtighten.)

NOTE: **The cross shaft roller and worm mesh adjustment may be done, using a spring scale tool, by measuring the amount of wheel pull as the external cross shaft adjusting screw is tightened. When the spring scale pull is between ⅞ and 1⅛ ft. lbs., the adjustment is correct.**

4. Tighten the Pitman arm attaching nut to 100–125 ft. lbs. The steering wheel nut (if loosened) should be tightened to 15–20 ft. lbs. torque.

Disassembly

1. Remove steering gear oil seal, using a suitable puller.

2. Remove cross shaft, using an arbor to prevent bearings from dropping out.

3. Remove cover, shims and cover gasket.

4. Remove worm gear, thrust bearings and bearing cups.

mounting seat. If there is a gap at any of the mounting bolts, proper alignment may be obtained by placing shims where excessive gap appears. Tighten the steering gear-to-frame bolts. Alignment of the gear in the truck is very important and should be done carefully so that a satisfactory, trouble-free gear adjustment may be obtained.

Gemmer Worm and Double Roller Tooth Type

With Screw Adjusted Mesh

The steering gear is of the worm and roller

type with a 24 to 1 gear ratio. The cross shaft is straddle mounted with a bearing surface at the top and bottom points of the shaft mounting areas. The three tooth cross shaft roller is mounted in ball bearings. The proper lubricant used in the gear box is S.A.E. 90 Extreme Pressure Lubricant.

The external adjustments given below will properly adjust the steering gear.

WORM BEARING ADJUSTMENT

1. Turn the steering wheel about one full turn from straight ahead and secure it so it doesn't move.

2. Determine if there is any worm gear

Assembly

1. Clean and inspect all parts, replace as necessary.

NOTE: If either thrust bearing is excessively worn, replace them both.

2. Reassemble steering gear, using new oil seal.

3. Perform worm bearing and cross shaft roller and worm mesh adjustments.

4. Lubricate to specifications.

Ford Steering Gear— Recirculating Ball Type

STEERING WORM AND SECTOR GEAR ADJUSTMENTS

The ball nut assembly and the sector gear must be adjusted properly to maintain a minimum amount of steering shaft end play and a minimum amount of backlash between the sector gear and the ball nut. There are only two adjustments that may be done on this steering gear and they should be done as given below:

1. Remove the steering gear from the vehicle.

2. Loosen the locknut on the sector shaft adjustment screw and turn the adjusting screw counterclockwise about three turns.

3. Measure the worm bearing preload by attaching an in. lbs. torque wrench to the input shaft. Note the reading required to rotate input shaft about 1½ turns either side of center. If the torque reading is not about 4–5 in. lbs., adjust the gear as given in the next step.

4. Loosen the steering shaft bearing adjuster lock nut and tighten or back off the bearing adjusting screw until the preload is within the specified limits.

5. Tighten the steering shaft bearing adjuster lock nut, and recheck the preload torque.

6. Turn the input shaft slowly to either stop. Turn gently against the stop to avoid possible damage to the ball return guides. Then rotate the shaft three turns to center the ball nut.

7. Turn the sector adjusting screw clockwise until the proper torque (9–10 in. lbs.) is obtained that is necessary to rotate the worm gear past its center (high spot).

8. With the input shaft centered, hold the sector shaft and check the lash between the ball nuts, balls, and worm shaft by applying 15 lbs. torque to the steering input shaft in both right and left turn directions. The total travel of the wrench should not exceed 1¼".

9. Tighten the sector adjusting screw locknut, and recheck the backlash. Install the steering gear.

Disassembly

1. Rotate the steering shaft three turns from either stop.

2. Remove the sector shaft adjusting screw locknut and loosen the screw one turn. Remove the steering shaft bearing adjuster, and the housing cover bolts and remove the sector shaft. Remove the shaft by turning the screw clockwise. Keep the shim with the screw.

3. Remove the sector shaft from the housing.

4. Carefully pull the steering shaft and ball nut from the housing, and remove the steering shaft lower bearing. Do not run the ball nut to either end of the worm gear to prevent damaging the ball return guides. Disassemble the ball nut only if there are signs of binding or tightness.

5. To disassemble the ball nut, remove the ball return guide clamp and the ball return guides from the ball nut. Keep ball

Removing bearing retainer from the adjuster plug

nut clamp side up until ready to remove the ball bearings.

6. Turn the ball nut over and rotate the worm shaft from side to side until all 50 balls have dropped out into a clean pan. With all balls removed, the nut will slide off the wormshaft.

7. Remove the upper bearing cup from the bearing adjuster and the lower cup from the housing. It may be necessary to tap the housing or the adjuster on a wooden block to jar the bearing cups loose.

Inspection

1. Carefully clean and inspect all parts. If the inspection shows bearing damage, the sector shaft bearing and the oil seal should be pressed out.

2. If the sector shaft bearing and oil seals were removed, press new bearings and oil seals into the housing. Do not clean, wash, or soak seals in cleaning solvent.

3. Apply the recommended steering gear lubricant to the housing and seals, filling the pocket between sector shaft bearings.

Assembly

1. Install the bearing cup in the lower end of the housing and a bearing cup in the adjuster nut. Install a new seal in the bearing adjuster if the old seal was removed.

2. Apply gear lube to the outside of the worm shaft and the inside of the ball nut. Lay the steering shaft down, and position the ball nut on the shaft with the guide holes

upward and the shallow end of the teeth to the left of the steering wheel position. Align the grooves in worm and ball nut by sighting through the guide holes.

3. Insert the ball guides into the holes in the ball nut, lightly tapping them, if necessary, to seat them.

4. Insert 25 balls into the hole in the top of each ball guide. If necessary, rotate the shaft slightly to distribute the balls evenly in the circuit.

5. Install the ball guide clamp, tightening the screws to the proper torque. Check that the worm shaft rotates freely.

6. Coat the threads of the steering shaft bearing adjuster, the housing cover bolts, and the sector adjusting screw with a suitable oil-resistant sealing compound. Do not apply sealer to female threads and do not get sealer on the steering shaft bearings.

7. Coat the worm bearings, sector shaft bearings, and gear teeth with steering gear lubricant.

8. Clamp the housing in a vise, with the sector shaft axis horizontal, and place the steering shaft lower bearing in its cup. Place the steering shaft and ball nut assemblies in the housing.

9. Position the steering shaft upper bearing on top of the worm gear and install the steering shaft bearing adjuster, adjuster nut, and the bearing cup. Leave the nut loose.

10. Adjust the worm bearing preload according to the instructions given earlier.

11. Position the sector adjusting screw and adjuster shim, and check for a clearance of not more than 0.002" between the screw head and the end of the sector shaft. If the clearance exceeds 0.002", add enough shims to reduce the clearance to under 0.002" clearance.

12. Start the sector shaft adjusting screw into the housing cover. Install a new gasket on the cover.

13. Rotate the steering shaft until the ball nut teeth mesh with the sector gear teeth, tilting the housing so the ball will tip toward the housing cover opening.

14. Lubricate the sector shaft journal and install the sector shaft and cover. With the cover moved to one side, fill the gear with lubricant (about 0.97 lb.). Push the cover and the sector shaft into place, and install the two top housing bolts. Do not tighten the bolts until checking to see that there is some lash between the ball nut and the sector gear teeth. Hold or push the cover away from the ball nut and tighten the bolts to the proper torque (30–40 ft. lbs.).

15. Loosely install the sector shaft adjusting screw lock nut and adjust the sector shaft mesh load as given earlier. Tighten the adjusting screw lock nut.

Saginaw Recirculating Ball Type

The steering gear is of the recirculating ball nut type. the ball nut, mounted on the worm

WORMSHAFT BALLS AND GUIDES WORMSHAFT ADJUSTER PLUG LOCK NUT

SEAL

WORM BEARING (UPPER) WORM BEARING (LOWER)

BALL NUT SECTOR

Cross section of Saginaw recirculating ball model

gear, is driven by means of steel balls which circulate in helical grooves in both the worm and nut. Ball return guides attached to the nut serve to recirculate the two sets of balls in the grooves. As the steering wheel is turned to the right, the ball nut moves upward. When the wheel is turned to the left, the ball nut moves downward.

The sector teeth on the pinion shaft and the ball nut are designed so that they fit the tightest when the steering wheel is straight ahead. This mesh action is adjusted by an adjusting screw which moves the pinion shaft endwise until the teeth mesh properly. The worm bearing adjuster provides proper preloading of the upper and lower bearings.

Before doing the adjustment procedures given below, ensure that the steering problem is not caused by faulty suspension components, bad front end alignment, etc. Then, proceed with the following adjustments.

STEERING WORM AND SECTOR ADJUSTMENT

1. Tighten the worm bearing adjuster plug until all end play has been removed, then loosen ¼ turn.

2. Use an $^{11}/_{16}$ in. 12 point socket to carefully turn the wormshaft all the way into the right corner then turn back about ½ turn.

3. Tighten the adjuster plug until the proper thrust bearing preload is obtained (5–8 in. lbs.). Tighten the adjuster plug locknut to 85 ft. lbs.

4. Turn the wormshaft from one stop to the other counting the number of turns. Then turn the shaft back exactly half the number of turns to the center position.

5. Turn the lash (sector shaft) adjuster screw clockwise to remove all lash between the ball nut and sector teeth. Tighten the locknut to 25 ft. lbs.

6. Using an $^{11}/_{16}$ in. 12 point socket and an in. lb. torque wrench, observe the highest reading while the gear is turned through

BALL NUT

WORMSHAFT

SECTOR

Removing sector shaft assembly —Saginaw recirculating ball model

the center position. It should be 16 in. lbs. or less.

7. If necessary repeat steps 5 and 6.

Disassembly

1. Place the steering gear in a vise, clamping onto one of the mounting tabs. The wormshaft should be in a horizontal position.

2. Rotate the wormshaft from stop to stop and count the total number of turns. Turn back exactly halfway, placing the gear on center.

3. Remove the three self locking bolts which attach the sector cover to the housing.

4. Using a plastic hammer, tap lightly on the end of the sector shaft and lift the sector cover and sector shaft assembly from the gear housing.

NOTE: It may be necessary to turn the wormshaft by hand until the sector will pass through the opening in the housing.

5. Remove the locknut from the adjuster plug and remove the adjuster plug assembly.

6. Pull the wormshaft and ball nut assembly from the housing.

NOTE: Damage may be done to the ends of the ball guides if the ball nut is allowed to rotate to the end of the worm.

7. Remove the worm shaft upper bearing from inside the gear housing.

8. Pry the wormshaft lower bearing retainer from the adjuster plug housing and remove the bearing.

Removing the bearing retainer from the worm bearing adjuster—Saginaw recirculating ball model

TOOL

BUSHING

Removing sector shaft bushing—Saginaw recirculating ball model

Removing worm shaft lower bearing cup from the adjuster plug—Saginaw recirculating ball model

Filling the ball circuits—Saginaw recirculating ball model

9. Remove the locknut from the lash adjuster screw in the sector cover. Turn the lash adjuster screw clockwise and remove it from the sector cover. Slide the adjuster screw and shim out of the slot in the end of the sector shaft.

10. Pry out and discard both the sector shaft and wormshaft seals.

Inspection

1. Wash all parts in cleaning solvent and blow dry with an air hose.

2. Use a magnifying glass and inspect the bearings and bearing caps for signs of indentation, or chipping. Replace any parts that show signs of damage.

3. Check the fit of the sector shaft in the bushings in the sector cover and housing. If these bushings are worn, a new sector cover and bushing assembly or housing bushing should be installed.

4. Check steering gear wormshaft assembly for being bent or damaged.

SHAFT SEAL REPLACEMENT

1. Remove the old seal from the pump body.

2. Install the new seal by pressing the outer diameter of the seal with a suitable size socket.

NOTE: Make sure the socket is large enough to avoid damaging the external lip of the seal.

SECTOR SHAFT BUSHING REPLACEMENT

1. Place the steering gear housing in an arbor press.

2. Press the sector shaft bushing from the housing.

NOTE: Service bushings are bored to size and require no further reaming.

SECTOR COVER BUSHING REPLACEMENT

1. The sector cover bushing is not serviced separately. The entire sector cover assembly including the bushing must be replaced as a unit.

BALL NUT SERVICE

If there is any indication of binding or tightness when the ball nut is rotated on the worm the unit should be disassembled, cleaned and inspected as follows:

Ball Nut Disassembly

1. Remove the screws and clamp retaining the ball guides in the ball nut. Pull the guides out of the ball nut.

2. Turn the ball nut upside down and rotate the wormshaft back and forth until all the balls have dropped out of the ball nut. The ball nut can now be pulled endwise off the worm.

3. Wash all parts in solvent and dry them with air. Use a magnifying glass and inspect the worm and nut grooves and the surface of all balls for signs of indentation. Check all ball guides for damage at the ends. Replace any damaged parts.

Ball Nut Assembly

1. Slip the ball nut over the worm with the ball guide holes up and the shallow end of the ball nut teeth to the left from the steering wheel position. Sight through the ball guide to align the grooves in the worm.

2. Place two ball guide halves together and insert them in the upper circuit in the ball nut. Place the two remaining guides together and insert them in the lower circuit.

3. Count out 25 balls and place them in a suitable container. This is the proper number of balls for one circuit.

4. Load the 25 balls into one of the guide holes while turning the wormshaft gradually away from that hole.

5. Fill the remaining ball circuit in the same manner.

6. Assemble the ball guide clamp to the ball nut and tighten the screws to 18–24 in. lbs.

Checking lash adjuster end clearance —Saginaw recirculating ball model

7. Check the assembly by rotating the ball nut on the worm to see that it moves freely.

NOTE: Do not rotate the ball nut to the end of the worm threads as this may damage the ball guides.

Assembly

1. Coat the threads of the adjuster plug, sector cover bolts and lash adjuster with a non-drying oil resistant sealing compound.

NOTE: Do not apply compound to the female threads. Use extreme care when applying compound to the bearing adjuster so that it does not come in contact with the wormshaft bearing.

2. Place the steering gear housing in a vise with the wormshaft bore horizontal and the sector cover opening up.

3. Make sure that all seals, bushings and bearing cups are installed in the gear housing and that the ball nut is installed on the wormshaft.

4. Slip the wormshaft upper bearing assembly over the wormshaft and insert the wormshaft and ball nut assembly into the housing, feeding the end of the shaft through the upper ball bearing cup and seal.

5. Place the wormshaft lower bearing assembly in the adjuster plug bearing cup and press the stamped retainer into place with a suitable size socket.

6. Install the adjuster plug and locknut into the lower end of the housing while carefully guiding the end of the wormshaft into the bearing until nearly all end play has been removed from the wormshaft.

7. Position the lash adjuster including the shim in the slotted end of the sector shaft.

NOTE: End clearance should not be greater than .002. If the end clearance is greater than .002 a shim package is available with thicknesses of .063, .065, .067, .069.

8. Lubricate the steering gear with 11 oz. of steering gear grease. Rotate the wormshaft until the ball nut is at the other end of its travel and then pack as much new lubricant into the housing as possible without losing out the sector shaft opening. Rotate the wormshaft until the ball nut is at the other end of its travel and pack as much lubricant into the opposite end as possible.

9. Rotate the wormshaft until the ball nut is in the center of travel. This is to make sure that the sector shaft and ball nut will engage properly with the center tooth of the sector entering the center tooth space in the ball nut.

10. Insert the sector shaft assembly including lash adjuster screw and shim into the housing so that the center tooth of the sector enters the center tooth space in the ball nut.

11. Pack the remaining portion of the lubricant into the housing and also place some in the sector cover bushing hole.

12. Place the sector cover gasket on the housing.

13. Install the sector cover onto the sector shaft by reaching through the sector cover with a screwdriver and turning the lash adjuster screw counterclockwise until the screw bottoms, then back the screw off one-half turn. Loosely install a new lock nut onto the adjuster screw.

14. Install and tighten the sector cover bolt to 30 ft. lbs.

Chrysler Recirculating Ball Type

The steering gear is of the recirculating ball nut type. The ball nut, mounted on the worm gear, is driven by means of steel balls which circulate in helical grooves in both the worm and nut. Ball return guides attached to the nut serve to recirculate the two sets of balls in the grooves. As the steering wheel is turned to the right, the ball nut moves upward. When the wheel is turned to the left, the ball nut moves downward.

The sector teeth on the pinion shaft and the ball nut are designed so that they fit the tightest when the steering wheel is straight ahead. This mesh action is adjusted by an adjusting screw which moves the pinion shaft endwise until the teeth mesh properly. The worm bearing adjuster provides proper preloading of the upper and lower bearings.

WORM BEARING PRE-LOAD ADJUSTMENT

1. Remove the steering gear arm and lockwasher from the sector shaft, using a suitable gear puller.

2. Remove the horn button or horn ring.

3. Loosen the sector-shaft adjusting screw locknut, and back out the adjusting screw about two turns.

4. Turn the steering wheel two complete turns from the straight ahead position, and place an in. lb. torque wrench on the steering shaft nut.

5. Rotate the steering shaft at least one turn toward the straight ahead position while measuring the torque on the torque wrench. The torque should be between 1⅛ and 4½ in. lbs. to move the steering wheel. If torque

Removing sector shaft assembly—typical

Chrysler recirculating ball type steering gear

is not within these limits, loosen the worm shaft bearing adjuster locknut and turn the adjuster clockwise to increase the preload or counterclockwise to decrease the preload. When the preload is correct, hold the adjuster screw steady and tighten the locknut. Recheck preload.

BALL NUT RACK AND SECTOR MESH ADJUSTMENT

NOTE: This adjustment can be accurately made only after proper preloading of worm bearing.

1. Turn steering wheel gently from one stop to the other, counting the number of turns. Turn the steering wheel back exactly half way, to the center position.

2. Turn the sector-shaft adjusting screw clockwise to remove all lash between ball nut rack and the sector gear teeth, then tighten adjusting screw locknut to 35 ft. lbs.

Steering gear adjustment locations

3. Turn the steering wheel about ¼ turn away from the center or high spot position. With the torque wrench on the steering wheel nut measure the torque required to turn the steering wheel through the high spot at the center position. The reading should be between 8 and 11 in. lbs. This is the total of the worm shaft bearing preload and the ball nut rack and sector gear mesh load. Readjust the sector-shaft adjustment screw if necessary to obtain a correct torque reading.

4. After completing the adjustments, place the front wheels in a straight ahead position, and with the steering wheel and steering gear centered, install the steering arm on sector-shaft. Tighten the steering arm retaining nut to 180 ft. lbs.

STEERING GEAR

Disassembly and Assembly

1. Attach the steering gear assembly to a holding fixture and put the holding fixture in a bench vise. Thoroughly clean the outside surface before disassembly.

2. Loosen the sector-shaft adjusting screw locknut, and back out the adjusting screw about two turns to relieve the mesh load between the ball nut rack and the sector gear teeth.

3. Position the steering gear worm shaft in a straight ahead position.

4. Remove the attaching bolts from the sector-shaft cover and slowly remove the sector-shaft while sliding an arbor tool into the housing. Remove the locknut from the adjusting screw and remove the screw from the cover by turning it clockwise. Slide the adjustment screw and its shim out of the slot in the end of the sector-shaft.

5. Loosen the worm shaft bearing adjuster locknut with a brass drift (punch) and remove the locknut. Hold the worm shaft steady while unscrewing the adjuster. Slide

Removing the wormshaft and ballnut assembly

the worm adjuster off the shaft.

CAUTION

Handle the adjuster carefully to avoid damaging the aluminum threads. Also, do not run the ball nut down to either end of the worm shaft to avoid damaging the ball guides.

6. Carefully remove the worm and ball nut assembly. This assembly is serviced as a complete assembly only and is not to be disassembled or the ball return guides removed or disturbed.

7. Remove the sector-shaft needle bearing by placing the gear housing in an arbor press; insert a tool in the lower end of the housing and press both bearings through the housing.
The sector-shaft cover assembly, including a needle bearing or bushing, is serviced as an assembly.

8. Remove the worm shaft oil seal from the worm shaft bearing adjuster by inserting a blunt punch behind the seal and tapping alternately on each side of the seal until it is driven out of the adjuster.

9. Remove the worm shaft in the same manner as that given in step 8. *Be careful not to cock the bearing cup and distort the adjuster counter bore.*

10. Remove the lower cup if necessary.

Pull the bearing cup out.

11. Wash all parts in clean solvent and dry thoroughly. Inspect all parts for wear, scoring, pitting, etc. Test operation of the worm shaft and ball nut assembly. If ball nut does not travel smoothly and freely on the worm shaft or if there is binding, replace the assembly.

NOTE: Extreme care must be taken when handling the aluminum worm bearing adjuster to avoid thread damage. Also, be careful not to damage the threads in the gear housing. Always lubricate the worm bearing adjuster before screwing it into the housing.

Removing sector shaft bushing

12. Inspect the sector-shaft for wear and check the fit of the shaft in the housing bearings. Inspect the fit of the shaft pilot bearing in the housing. Be sure the worm shaft is not bent or damaged.

13. Install the sector-shaft lower needle bearing. Press the bearing into the housing about $\frac{7}{16}$ in. below the end of the bore to leave space for the new oil seal.

14. Install the upper needle bearing in the same manner and press it into the inside end of the housing bore flush with the inside end of the bore surface.

15. Install the worm shaft bearing cups (upper and lower) by placing them and their spacers in the adjuster nut and press them into place.

16. Install the worm shaft oil seal by placing the seal in the worm shaft adjuster with the metal seal retainer up. Drive the seal into place with a suitable sleeve until it is just below the end of the bore in the adjuster.

Installing the wormshaft upper bearing cup

NOTE: Apply a coating of steering gear lubricant to all moving parts during assembly. Also, put lubricant on and around oil seal lips.

17. Clamp the holding fixture and housing in a bench vise with the bearing adjuster opening upward. Place a thrust bearing in the lower cup in the housing.

18. Hold the ball nut from turning and insert the worm shaft and ball nut assembly into the housing with the end of the worm shaft resting in the thrust bearing. Place the upper thrust bearing on the worm shaft. Thoroughly lubricate the threads on the adjuster and the threads in the housing.

19. Place a protective sleeve of tape over the splines on the worm shaft to avoid damaging the seal. Slide the adjuster assembly over the shaft.

20. Thread the adjuster into the housing

Removing wormshaft lower bearing cup using special tool

SHIM SECTOR SHAFT

ADJUSTING SCREW

Measuring the sector shaft adjusting screw end clearance

and tighten the adjuster to 50 ft. lbs. while rotating the worm shaft to seat the bearings.

21. Loosen the adjuster so no bearing preload exists. Tighten the adjuster for a worm shaft bearing preload of 1⅛ to 4½ in. lbs. Tighten the bearing adjuster locknut and recheck the preload.

22. Before installing the sector-shaft, pack the worm shaft cavities in the housing above and below the ball nut with steering gear lubricant. A good grade of multi-purpose lubricant may be used if steering gear lubricant is not available. *Do not use gear oil.* Pack enough lubricant into the worm cavities to cover the worm.

23. Slide the sector-shaft adjusting screw and shim into the slot in the end of the shaft. Check the end clearance for no more than 0.004 in. clearance. If the clearance is not within the limit, remove old shim and install a new shim, available in three different thicknesses, to get the proper clearance.

24. Start the sector-shaft and adjuster screw into the bearing in the housing cover. Using a screwdriver through the hole in the cover, turn the screw counterclockwise to pull the shaft into the cover. Install the adjusting screw locknut, but do not tighten at this time.

25. Rotate the worm shaft to center the ball nut.

26. Place a new gasket on the housing cover and install the sector-shaft and cover aasembly into the steering gear housing. Be sure to coat the sector-shaft and sector teeth with steering gear lubricant before installing the sector-shaft in the housing. Allow some lash between the sector-shaft sector teeth and the ball nut rack. Install and tighten the cover bolts to 25 ft. lbs.

27. Place the sector-shaft seal on the cross-shaft with the lip of the seal facing the housing. Press the seal in place.

28. Turn the worm shaft about ¼ turn away from the center of the high spot position. Using a torque wrench and a ¾ in. socket on the worm shaft spline, check the torque needed to rotate the shaft through the high spot. The reading should be between 8 and 11 in. lbs. Readjust the sector-shaft adjusting screw until the proper reading is obtained. Tighten the locknut to 35 ft. lbs. and recheck sector-shaft torque.

SECTOR-SHAFT OIL SEAL
Replacement

1. Remove the steering gear arm retaining nut and lockwasher.

2. Remove seal with a seal puller or other appropriate tool.

3. Place a new oil seal onto the splines of the sector-shaft with the lip of the seal facing the housing.

4. Remove the tool, and install the steering gear arm, lockwasher, and retaining nut. Tighten the nut to 180 ft. lbs. torque.

Ross Worm and Roller Steering Gear

The steering gear is of the worm and roller type, with shim adjustments provided for the worm gear bearings and an adjusting screw for the sector shaft adjustment.

This steering gear assembly is manufactured in different housing configurations, but the disassembly, assembly and adjustments are basically the same. The different models are identified by the size of the sector shaft.

Models	Sector Shaft Diameter
254, 301	1¼ inch
376, 378	1⅜ inch
408	1½ inch
504	1¾ inch

BEARING PRELOAD ADJUSTMENT

1. Loosen the four capscrews which fasten the end cover to the steering gear housing.

2. Alternately tighten the capscrews evenly and rotate the worm gear shaft. Tighten the screws to 18 to 22 ft. lbs.

3. If necessary, remove the end cover and either add or subtract from the number of shims, and repeat steps 1 and 2 to obtain the correct bearing preload.

WORM GEAR AND ROLLER GEAR BACKLASH ADJUSTMENT

1. Loosen the locknut and turn the adjustment at the side cover counterclockwise until the worm gear shaft turns freely through its entire range of travel.

2. Count the number of turns necessary to rotate the worm gear shaft through its

SEAL PLUG HOUSING BUSHING SEAL
GEAR SECTOR SHAFT THRUST BEARING
SCREW WASHER THRUST BEARING
ADJUSTING SCREW CUP ADJUSTMENT SHIMS
SNAP RING TUBE WITH WORM
NUT GASKET
COVER CUP SCREW
WORM COVER

Ross worm and roller steering gear

entire range of travel.

3. Turn the shaft back exactly half the number of turns to the center position.

4. Turn the shaft back and forth through its center of travel and tighten the adjustment screw to obtain a rolling torque requirement of 7 to 12 inch lbs.

5. Hold the adjustment screw in position and torque the locknut to 16–20 ft. lbs.

6. Recheck the rolling torque and repeat the above procedure if necessary.

Disassembly

1. Drain the lubricant from the gear.

2. Make index marks on the roller gear and shaft assembly and on the steering arm to assure correct alignment during reassembly.

3. Remove the nut and lockwasher from the shaft.

4. Using a puller remove the arm from the shaft.

NOTE: Do not use a hammer or wedge to remove the steering arm or damage to the gear and shaft assembly may result.

5. Remove the four side cover attaching screws and remove the cover and roller gear and shaft assembly as a unit.

6. Remove the locknut from the adjustment screw and turn the screw clockwise until it is completely unthreaded from the side cover, then remove the roller gear and shaft assembly from the cover.

7. Remove the four end cover attaching screws and remove the cover from the housing.

8. Withdraw the worm gear and shaft assembly from the housing.

9. Remove the lower and upper bearing cups and ball bearings from the shaft.

10. Remove and discard both the worm gear shaft and roller gear shaft housing oil seals.

Inspection

1. Clean all parts with a suitable cleaning solvent and blow dry with an air hose.

2. Check the steering gear housing for cracks, leaks or breaks and replace if damaged.

3. Examine the roller gear to assure that it has proper freedom of movement and does not have excessive lash or roughness. Replace if necessary.

4. Check the adjustment screw of the roller gear and shaft assembly for excessive end play. If end play exceeds 0.015 inch, remove the retaining ring, thrust washer and screw from the gear and shaft assembly and replace with new parts.

5. Inspect the roller gear and shaft needle bearings for wear or damage. Insert a shaft through each bearing and check for clearance. If clearance exceeds 0.010 inch, replace the bearings. Either needle bearing may be removed by pressing out with a piloted mandrel. When pressing in a new bearing make sure that the face of the bearing is flush with the bearing boss of the cover or housing.

6. Inspect the worm gear and shaft assembly for wear, scoring or pitting. Polish the assembly with a fine abrasive cloth or replace if necessary.

7. Check the upper and lower ball bearings and cups of the worm gear and shaft assembly for wear and damage. Replace the ball bearings as a full set if worn or damaged.

Assembly

1. Press new oil seals into the worm gear shaft and roller gear shaft oil seal bores of the housing with the longer lip of each seal facing into the housing.

2. Lubricate the worm gear and shaft assembly and upper ball bearing and cup with SAE 80 gear lubricant.

3. Install the bearing and cup on the shaft.

4. Carefully install the shaft assembly into the steering gear housing.

5. Lubricate the lower end of the worm gear and shaft assembly and lower ball bearing and cup with SAE 80 gear lubricant.

6. Install the bearing, cups and spacer on the shaft.

7. Position the shims and end cover on the steering gear housing and install the four capscrews loosely.

8. Adjust the bearing preload.

9. Position the tapped hole of the side cover to the adjustment screw of the roller gear and shaft assembly and thread the adjustment screw counterclockwise into the cover until the end of the shaft just touches the inner face of the cover.

10. Install a locknut loosely on the adjustment screw.

11. Install a new side cover gasket.

12. Lubricate the roller gear with SAE 80 gear lubricant.

13. Carefully insert the gear and shaft assembly into the steering gear housing. The roller gear and worm gear must mesh to seat the side cover to the housing.

14. Tighten the side cover capscrews to 18–22 ft. lbs.

15. Make a worm gear and roller gear backlash adjustment.

16. Clamp the exposed section of the roller gear and shaft assembly firmly into a soft jaw vise.

17. Align the index marks made during disassembly and position the steering arm to the splined end of the shaft.

18. Install the lockwasher and nut on the shaft threads and tighten the nut to draw the arm into position on the splines.

19. Fill the steering gear housing to the required level with SAE 80 gear lubricant.

STEERING TROUBLE DIAGNOSIS
Power Steering

Condition	Possible Cause	Correction
Hard Steering	1. Low or uneven tire pressure.	1. Inflate the tires to recommended pressures.
	2. Insufficient lubricant in the steering gear housing or in steering linkage.	2. Lubricate as necessary.
	3. Steering gear shaft adjusted too tight.	3. Adjust according to instructions.
	4. Improper caster or toe-in.	4. Align the wheels.
	5. Steering column misaligned.	5. See "Steering Gear Alignment."
	6. Loose, worn or broken pump belt.	6. Adjust or replace belt.
	7. Air in system.	7. Bleed air from system.
	8. Low fluid level in the pump reservoir.	8. Fill to correct level.
	9. Pump output pressure low.	9. See "Pressure Test."
	10. Leakage at power cylinder piston rings. (Linkage type).	10. Replace piston rings and repair as required.
	11. Binding or bent cylinder linkage. (Linkage type).	11. Replace or repair as required.
	12. Valve spool and/or sleeve sticking. (Linkage type).	12. Free-up or replace as required.

STEERING TROUBLE DIAGNOSIS
Power Steering

Condition	Possible Cause	Correction
Intermittent or No Power Assist	1. Belt slipping and/or low fluid level.	1. Adjust or replace belt. Add fluid as necessary.
	2. Piston or rod binding in power cylinder. (Linkage type).	2. Repair or replace piston and rod.
	3. Sliding sleeve stuck in control valve. (Linkage type).	3. Free-up or replace sleeve.
	4. Improper pump operation.	4. Refer to "Power Steering Pump."
Poor or No Recovery from Turns	1. Improper caster setting.	1. Adjust to specifications.
	2. Steering gear adjustments too tight.	2. Adjust according to instructions.
	3. Improper spool nut adjustment. (Linkage type).	3. Adjust according to instructions.
	4. Valve spool installed backwards. (Linkage type).	4. Install valve spool correctly.
	5. Low tire pressure.	5. Inflate tires to recommended pressure.
	6. Tight steering linkage.	6. Lubricate as necessary.
	7. King pins frozen.	7. Lubricate as necessary.
Lack of Effort (Both Turns)	1. Improper sector shaft adjustment.	1. Adjust Sector Shaft.
	2. Pressure plates on wrong side of reactions rings.	2. Gear Recondition.
Lack of Effort (Left Turn Only)	1. Left turn reaction seal "O" ring worn, damaged or missing.	1. Gear Recondition.
	2. Left turn reaction oil passageway not drilled in housing or cylinder head.	2. Replace parts as required.
	3. Left turn reaction ring sticking in cylinder head.	3. Replace parts as required.
Lack of Effort (Right Turn Only)	1. Right turn U-shaped reaction seal worn, damaged, or missing.	1. Gear Recondition.
	2. Right turn reaction oil passageway not drilled in housing head, or ferrule pin.	2. Replace parts as required.
	3. Right turn reaction ring sticking in housing head.	3. Replace parts as required.
Lack of Assist (Left Turn Only)	1. Left turn reaction seal "O" ring worn, damaged, or missing.	1. Gear Recondition.
Lack of Assist (Right Turn Only)	1. Right turn U-shaped reaction seal worn, damaged, or missing.	1. Gear Recondition.
	2. Worm sealing ring (teflon) worm sleeve seal, ferrule pin "O" ring damaged or worn.	2. Gear Recondition.
	3. Excessive internal leakage thru piston end plug and/or side plugs.	3. Replace worm-piston assembly.
Lack of Assist (Both Turns)	1. Low oil level in pump reservoir (usually accompanied by pump noise).	1. Fill to proper level.
	2. Loose pump belt.	2. Adjust belts.
	3. Pump output low.	3. Pressure test pump.
	4. Engine idle too low.	4. Adjust engine idle.
	5. Excessive internal leakage thru piston end plug and/or side plugs.	5. Replace worm-piston assembly.

STEERING TROUBLE DIAGNOSIS
Power Steering Noise

Condition	Possible Cause	Correction
Objectionable "Hiss"	1. Noisy valve	1. Do not replace valve unless "hiss" is extremely objectionable. A replacement valve will also exhibit sight noise and is not always a cure for the objection.
Rattle or Chuckle Noise in Steering Gear	1. Gear loose on frame. 2. Steering linkages looseness. 3. Pressure hose touching other parts of truck. 4. Loose Pitman shaft over center adjustment. **NOTE:** A slight rattle may occur on turns because of increased clearance off the "high point". This is normal and clearance must not be reduced below specified limits to eliminate this slight rattle. 5. Loose Pitman arm.	1. Check gear mounting bolts. Torque bolts to specifications. 2. Check linkage pivot points for wear. Replace if necessary. 3. Adjust hose position. Do not bend tubing by hand. 4. Adjust 5. Torque Pitman arm pinch bolt.
Squawk Noise in Steering Gear When Turning or Recovering From a Turn	1. Dampener O-ring on valve spool cut. 2. Loose or worn valve.	1. Replace dampener O-Ring. 2. Replace valve.
Chirp Noise in Steering Gear	1. Gear relief valve.	1. Replace relief valve.
Chirp Noise in Steering Pump	1. Loose belt.	1. Adjust belt tension.
Belt Squeal (Particularly Noticeable at Full Wheel Travel and Standstill Parking)	1. Loose belt.	1. Adjust belt tension.
Growl Noise in Steering Pump	1. Excessive back pressure in hoses or steering gear caused by restriction.	1. Locate restriction and correct. Replace part if necessary.
Growl Noise in Steering Pump (Particularly Noticeable at Standstill Parking)	1. Scored pressure plates, thrust plate or rotor. 2. Extreme wear of cam ring.	1. Replace parts and flush system. 2. Replace parts.
Groan Noise in Steering Pump	1. Low oil level. 2. Air in the oil. Poor pressure hose connection.	1. Fill reservoir to proper level. 2. Torque connector. Bleed system.
Rattle or Knock Noise in Steering Pump	1. Loose pump pulley nut.	1. Torque nut.
Rattle Noise in Steering Pump	1. Vanes not installed properly. 2. Vanes sticking in rotor slots.	1. Install properly. 2. Repair or replace.
Swish Noise in Steering Pump	1. Defective flow control valve.	1. Replace part.
Whine Noise in Steering Pump	1. Pump Shaft bearing scored.	1. Replace housing and shaft. Flush and bleed system.

STEERING TROUBLE DIAGNOSIS
Power Steering Pump

Condition	Possible Cause	Correction
Intermittent Assist	1. Flow control valve sticking. 2. Slipping belt. 3. Low fluid level. 4. Low pump efficiency.	1. Pressure test pump and service as necessary. 2. Adjust belt. 3. Inspect and correct fluid level. 4. Pressure test pump and service as necessary.
No Assist	1. Pump seizure. 2. Broken slipper spring(s). 3. Flow control bore plug ring not in place. 4. Flow control valve sticking.	1. Replace pump. 2. Recondition pump or replace as necessary. 3. Replace snap ring. Inspect groove for depth. 4. Pressure test pump and service as necessary.
No Assist When Parking Only	1. Wrong pressure relief valve. 2. Broken "O" ring on flow control bore plug. 3. Loose pressure relief valve. 4. Low pump efficiency	1. Install proper relief valve. 2. Replace "O" ring. 3. Tighten valve. DO NOT ADJUST. 4. Pressure test pump and service as necessary.
Noisy Pump	1. Low fluid level. 2. Belt noise. 3. Foreign material blocking pump housing oil inlet hole.	1. Inspect and correct fluid level. 2. Inspect for pulley alignment, paint or grease on pulley and correct. Adjust belt. 3. Remove reservoir, visually check inlet oil hole and service as necessary.
Pump Vibration	1. Pump hose interference with sheet metal or brake lines. 2. Belt loose. 3. Pulley loose or out of round. 4. Crankshaft pulley loose or damaged. 5. Bracket pivot bolts loose.	1. Reroute hoses. 2. Adjust belt. 3. Replace pulley. 4. Replace crankshaft pulley. 5. If unable to tighten, replace bracket.
Pump Leaks	1. Cap or filler neck leaks. 2. Reservoir solder joints leak. 3. Reservoir "O" ring leaking. 4. Shaft seal leaking. 5. Loose rear bracket bolts. 6. Loose or faulty high pressure ferrule. 7. Rear bolt holes stripped or casting cracked.	1. Correct fluid level. 2. Resolder or replace reservoir as necessary. 3. Inspect sealing area of reservoir. Replace "O" ring or reservoir as necessary. 4. Replace seal. 5. Tighten bolts. 6. Tighten fitting to 24 foot-pounds or replace as necessary. 7. Repair, if possible, or replace pump.

POWER STEERING

GENERAL INFORMATION

The procedures for maintaining, adjusting, and repairing the power steering systems and components discussed in this chapter are to be done only after determining that the steering linkages and front suspension systems are correctly aligned and in good condition. All worn or damaged parts should be replaced before attempting to service the power steering system. After correcting any condition that could affect the power steering, do the preliminary tests of the steering system components.

PRELIMINARY TESTS

Lubrication

Proper lubrication of the steering linkage and the front suspension components is very important for the proper operation of the steering systems of trucks equipped with power steering. Most all power steering systems use the same lubricant in the steering gear box as in the power steering pump reservoir, and the fluid level is maintained at the pump reservoir.

With power cylinder-assist power steering, the steering gear is of the standard mechanical type and the lubricating oil is self contained within the gear box and the level is maintained by the removal of a filler plug on the gear box housing. The control valve assembly is mounted on the gear box and is lubricated by power steering oil from the power steering pump reservoir, where the level is maintained.

Air Bleeding

Air bubbles in the power steering system

must be removed from the fluid. Be sure the reservoir is filled to the proper level and the fluid is warmed up to operating temperature. Then, turn the steering wheel through its full travel three or four times until all the air bubbles are removed. Do not hold the steering wheel against its stops. Recheck the fluid level.

Fluid Level Check

1. Run the engine until the fluid is at the normal operating temperature. Then, turn the steering wheel through its full travel three or four times, and shut off the engine.

2. Check the fluid level in the steering reservoir. If the fluid level is low, add enough fluid to raise the level to the Full mark on the dipstick or filler tube.

Power steering pump test circuit diagram

Testing power steering hydraulic system for internal leakage using a pressure gauge, shut off valve and flow meter —typical

Pump Belt Check

1. Inspect the pump belt for cracks, glazing, or worn places. Using a belt tension gauge, check the belt tension for the proper range of adjustment. The amount of tension varies with the make of truck and the condition of the belt. New belts (those belts used less than 15 minutes) require a higher figure. The belt deflection method

of adjustment may be used only if a belt tension gauge is not available. The belt should be adjusted for a deflection of ¼" to ⅜".

Fluid Leaks

Check all possible leakage points (hoses, power steering pump, or steering gear) for loss of fluid. Turn engine on and rotate the steering wheel from stop to stop several times. Tighten all loose fittings and replace any defective lines or valve seats.

Turning Effort

Check the turning effort required to turn the steering wheel after aligning the front wheels and inflating the tires to the proper pressure.

1. With the vehicle on dry pavement and the front wheel straight ahead, set the parking brake and turn the engine on.

2. After a short warm-up period for the engine, turn the steering wheel back and forth several times to warm the steering fluid.

3. Attach a spring scale to the steering wheel rim and measure the pull required to turn the steering wheel one complete revolution in each direction. The effort needed to turn the steering wheel should not exceed the limits specified.

NOTE: This test may be done with the steering wheel removed and a torque wrench applied on the steering wheel nut.

Power Steering Pump Flow

Since the power steering pump provides all the power assist in a power steering system,

the pump must operate properly at all times for the system to work. After performing all the checks given above, the power steering pump may be tested for proper flow by the following procedures:

Two Gauges and Flow Meter

1. Disconnect the pressure and return lines at the power steering pump and connect the test pressure and return lines. The test lines are connected to a pressure gauge and two manual valves.

2. Open the two manual valves, connect a tachometer to the engine, and start the engine. Run the engine at idle speed until the reservoir fluid temperature reaches about 165–175 degrees Fahrenheit. This temperature must be maintained during the test. Manual valve B may be partially opened to create a back pressure of no more than 350 psi to aid the temperature rise. Reservoir fluid must be at the proper level.

3. After the engine and the reservoir fluid are sufficiently warmed up, close the manual valve B. Note the pressure gauge reading. It must be a minimum of 620 psi.

4. If the pressure reading is below the minimum acceptable pressure, the pump is defective and must be repaired. If the pressure reading is at or above the minimum value, the pump is normal. Open manual valve B and proceed to the pump fluid pressure test.

Power Steering Pump Fluid Pressure Test

1. Keep the lines and pressure gauge connected as in the Pump Flow Test.

Identification of power steering pumps used on General Motors Trucks—typical

2. With manual valve A and B opened fully, run the engine at the proper idle speed. Then, close manual valve A and manual valve B, in that order.

─────────── **CAUTION** ───────────

Do not keep both valves closed for more than 5 seconds since the fluid temperature will increase abnormally and cause unnecessary wear to the pump.

3. With both manual valves closed, the pressure reading should be as given in the specifications. If the pressure is below the minimum reading, the pump is defective and must be repaired. If the pressure reading is at or above the minimum reading, the pump is normal and the power steering gear or power assist control valve must be checked.

Checking the Oil Flow and Pressure Relief Valve in the Pump Assembly

When the wheels are turned hard right, or hard left, against the stops, the oil flow and pressure relief valves come into action. If these valves are working and are not stuck there should be a slight buzzing noise.

─────────── **CAUTION** ───────────

Do not hold the wheels in the extreme position for over three or four seconds because, if the pressure relief valve is not working, the pressure could get high enough to damage the system.

Single Gauge

1. Install the test presure gauge (O-2000 psi) between the power steering pump and the control valve.

2. With the fluid at a temperature of 170 to 190°F, the engine running above idle and the shut-off valve open, observe the pressure reading while moving the wheels to the end of their right and left travel.

3. If the gauge registers the correct relief valve pressure, the hydraulic system should be satisfactory. If pressure cannot be built up on either side of the gear, internal pump or gear problems exist.

NOTE: A shuttle valve equipped power cylinder may register a sharp drop-off in pressure at the end of the wheel travel and is considered normal.

4. To check the pump, close the shut-off valve and observe the pressure gauge. The pressure reading should be at relief valve pressure.

NOTE: Do not keep the shut-off valve closed longer than 15 seconds as damage to the pump could occur.

5. Repeat the closing of the shut-off valve twice more and record the highest pressure reading each time.

6. If the pressure readings are within 50 lbs. of each other and with-in the pump relief valve specifications, the pump operation is normal.

Example: Pump specifications—900 to 1500 psi.

    Readings: 1st—1310 psi
              2nd—1290 psi
              3rd—1320 psi

7. If the readings are high but do not repeat within-in 50 lbs. of each other, the flow control valve can be sticking. If 100 lbs. difference is noted below the low listed specification, replace the flow valve and recheck the system.

Relief Valve Pressure

Relief valve pressures normally range between 800 to 2000 psi, depending upon the requirements of the power steering system and the axle application used on the vehicle. The lighter the truck, the less pressure is needed to operate the steering system, while the opposite is true of the heavier vehicles.

The minimum pressures with the wheels straight ahead and at engine idle should be in the 80 to 120 psi range.

Power Steering Hose Inspection

1. Inspect both the input and output hoses of the power steering pump for worn spots, cracks, or signs of leakage. Replace hose if defective, being sure to reconnect the replacement hose properly. Many power steering hoses are identified as to where they are to be connected by special means, such as fittings that will only fit on the correct pump fitting, or hoses of special lengths.

Test Driving Truck to Check the Power Steering

When test driving to check power steering, drive at a speed between 15 and 20 mph. Make several turns in each direction. When a turn is completed, the front wheels should return to the straight ahead position with very little help from the driver.

If the front wheels fail to return as they should and yet the steering linkage is free, well oiled and properly adjusted, the trouble is probably due to misalignment of the power cylinder or improper adjustment of the spool valve.

The power steering pump supplies all the power assist used in power steering systems of all designs. There are various designs of pumps used by the truck manufacturers but all pumps supply power to operate the steering systems with the least effort. All power steering pumps have a reservoir tank built onto the oil pump. These pumps are driven by belt turned by pulleys on the engine, normally on the front of the crankshaft.

During operation of the engine at idle speed, there is provision for the power steering pump to supply more fluid pressure. During driving speeds or when the truck is moving straight ahead, less pressure is needed and the excess is relieved through a pressure relief and flow control valve. The pressure relief part of the valve

is inside the flow control and is basically the same for all pumps. The flow control valve regulates, or controls, the constant flow of fluid from the pump as it varies with the demands of the steering gear. The pressure relief valve limits the hydraulic pressure built up when the steering gear is turned against its stops.

During pump disassembly, make sure all work is done on a clean surface. Clean the outside of the pump thoroughly and do not allow dirt of any kind to get inside. Do not immerse the shaft oil seal in solvent.

If replacing the rotor shaft seal, be extremely careful not to scratch sealing surfaces with tools.

Pump Overhaul

VANE TYPE POWER STEERING PUMP

The vane type power steering pump is used in Saginaw steering systems. The operation is basically the same as that of the roller type pumps. Centrifugal force moves a number of vanes outward against the pump ring, causing a pumping action of the fluid to the control valve.

Removal

1. Disconnect hoses at the pump, securing them in a raised position to prevent oil drainage. Cap or cover the ends of the hoses to keep dirt out.

2. Install two caps on the pump fittings to prevent oil drainage.

3. Loosen the bracket-to-pump mounting nuts, move pump toward engine slightly, and remove the pump drive belt.

4. Remove the bracket-to-pump bolts and remove the pump from the truck.

5. While holding the drive pulley steady, loosen and remove the pulley attaching nut. Slide the pulley off the shaft.

NOTE: Do not hammer the pulley off the shaft.

Installation

1. To install the pump on the truck, reverse the removal procedure. Always use a new pulley nut, tightening it to 35–45 ft. lbs. torque.

2. After reconnecting the hoses to the pump, fill the reservoir with fluid and bleed the pump of air by turning the drive pulley counterclockwise (as viewed from the front) until air bubbles do not appear.

3. Install the pump drive belt over the pulley, move the pump against the belt until tight enough, then tighten the mounting bolts and nuts.

4. Bleed the air from the system.

Disassembly

1. Clean the outside of the pump in a non-toxic solvent before disassembling.

2. Mount the pump in a vise, being

Exploded view of vane type pump

Removing end cover retaining ring

careful not to squeeze the front hub too tight.

3. Remove the union and seal.

4. Remove the reservoir retaining studs and separate the reservoir from the housing.

5. Remove the mounting bolt and union O-rings.

6. Remove the filter and filter cage; discard the element.

7. Remove the end plate retaining ring by compressing the retaining ring and then prying it out with a removal tool. The retaining ring may be compressed by inserting a small punch in the ⅛" diameter hole

in the housing and pushing in until the ring clears the groove.

8. Remove the end plate. The end plate is spring-loaded and should rise above the housing level. If it is stuck inside the housing, a slight rocking or gentle tapping should free the plate.

9. Remove the shaft woodruff key and tap the end of the shaft gently to free the pressure plate, pump ring, rotor assembly, and thrust plate. Remove these parts as one unit.

10. Remove the end plate O-ring. Separate the pressure plate, pump ring, rotor

assembly, and thrust plate.

Inspection

Clean all metal parts in a non-toxic solvent and inspect them as given below:

1. Check the flow control valve for free movement in the housing bore. If the valve is sticking, see if there is dirt or a rough spot in the bore.

2. Check the cap screw in the end of the flow control valve for looseness. Tighten if necessary being careful not to damage the machined surfaces.

3. Inspect the pressure plate and the pump plate surfaces for flatness and check that there are no cracks or scores in the parts. Do not mistake the normal wear marks for scoring.

4. Check the vanes in the rotor assembly for free movement and that they were installed with the radiused edge toward the pump ring.

5. If the flow control valve plunger is defective, install a new part. The valve is factory calibrated and supplied as a unit.

6. Check the drive shaft for worn-splines, breaks, bushing material pick-up, etc.

7. Replace all rubber seals and O-rings removed from the pump.

8. Check the reservoir, studs, casting, etc. for burrs and other defects that would impair operation.

Assembly

1. Install a new shaft seal in the housing and insert the shaft at the hub end of

housing, splined end entering mounting face side.

2. Install the thrust plate on the dowel pins with the ported side facing the rear of the pump housing.

3. Install the rotor on the pump shaft over the splined end. Be sure the rotor moves freely on the splines. Countersunk side must be toward the shaft.

4. Install the shaft retaining ring. Install the pump ring on the dowel pins with the rotation arrow toward the rear of the pump housing. Rotation is clockwise as seen from the pulley.

5. Install the vanes in the rotor slots with the radius edge towards the outside.

6. Lubricate the outside diameter and chamfer of the pressure plate with petroleum jelly so as not to damage the O-ring and install the plate on the dowel pins with the ported face toward the pump ring. Seat the pressure plate by placing a large socket on top of the plate and pushing down with the hand.

7. Install the pressure plate spring in the center groove of the plate.

8. Install the end plate O-ring. Lubricate the outside diameter and chamfer of the end plate with petroleum jelly so as not to damage the O-ring and install the end plate in the housing, using an arbor press. Install the end plate retaining ring while pump is in the arbor press. Be sure the ring is in the groove and the ring gap is positioned properly.

9. Install the flow control spring and plunger, hex head screw end in bore first. Install the filter cage, new filter stud seals and union seal.

10. Place the reservoir in the normal position and press down until the reservoir seats on the housing. Check the position of the stud seals and the union seal.

11. Install the studs, union, and drive shaft woodruff key. Support the shaft on the opposite side of the key when tapping the key into place.

ROLLER TYPE POWER STEERING PUMP

The roller type power steering pump is designed similar to other constant flow centrifugal force pumps. A star-shaped rotor forces 12 steel rollers against the inside surface of a cam ring. As the rollers follow the eccentric pattern of the cam ring, oil is drawn into the inlet ports and exhausted through the discharge ports while the rollers are moved into vee shaped cavities of the

Installing end cover plate and retainer ring

Roller type power steering pump

Flow control valve, vane type pump

Removing shaft seal

rotor, forcing oil into the high pressure circuit. A flow control valve permits a regulated amount of fluid to return to the intake side of the pump when excess output is produced during high speed operation. This reduces the power needs to drive the pump and minimizes temperature build-up.

The flow control valve used in one make of pump is a two-stage valve. Fluid under high pressure passes through two holes into a metering circuit located in a sealed passage. At low speed, about 2.7 gpm. passes to the gear. As speed increases and the valve moves, excess fluid is bypassed to the inlet and the valve blocks flow through one hole. This drops the flow to about 1.6 gpm. at high speeds.

When steering conditions produce excessive pressure needs (such as turning the wheels against the stops), the pressure built up in the steering gear exerts force on the spring end of the flow control valve.

This end of the valve contains the pressure relief valve. High pressure lifts the relief valve ball from its seat, allowing fluid to flow through a trigger orifice located in the front land of the flow control valve. This reduces pressure on the spring end of the valve which then opens and allows the fluid to return to the intake side of the pump. This action limits the maximum pressure output of the pump to a safe level. Normally, the pressure needs of the pump are

below the maximum limits, causing the pressure relief ball and the flow control valve to remain closed.

Removal

1. Loosen the pump mounting and locking bolts and remove the belt.
2. Disconnect both hoses at the pump. Cap and tie the hoses out of the way. Cap the hose fittings on the pump.
3. Remove the mounting and locking bolts, the pump and brackets from the truck.

Installation

1. Position the pump and brackets on the engine and install the mounting and locking bolts.
2. Install the drive belt and adjust for the proper tension.
3. Connect the pressure and return hoses, using a new pressure hose O-ring.
4. Fill the pump reservoir to the top of the filler neck with power steering fluid.
5. Start the engine and turn the steering wheel several times from stop to stop to bleed the pump of air. Check the level and add fluid if necessary.

NOTE: When checking the level, see that the level is as follows: engine cold—bottom of filler tube; engine hot—half way up filler tube.

Disassembly

1. Remove pump from engine, drain reservoir, and clean outside of pump. Clamp the pump in a vise at the mounting bracket.
2. Remove the drive pulley.
3. Remove the shaft seal by installing the seal remover adapter over the end of the drive shaft with the large end toward the pump. Place the seal remover tool over the shaft and through the adapter. Then, screw the tapered thread well into the metal portion of the seal. Tighten the large drive nut and remove the seal.
4. Remove the pump from the vise and remove the bracket mounting bolts. Remove the bracket.
5. Remove the reservoir and place the pump in a soft-faced vise with the shaft down. Discard the mounting bolt and the reservoir O-rings.
6. Move the end cover retaining ring around until one end of the ring lines up with the hole in the pump body. Insert a small punch in the hole and push it in far enough to bend the ring so a screwdriver can be inserted between the ring and the housing. Remove the ring.
7. Remove the end cover and spring from the housing. It may be necessary to tap the cover gently to loosen it in the housing.
8. Remove the pump from the vise and turn the pump over so the rotating pump may come out of the housing. Tap the end of the drive shaft to loosen these parts. Lift the pump body off the rotating group. Check that the seal plate is removed from the bottom of the housing bore.
9. Discard the O-rings from the pressure plate and end cover.
10. Remove the snap-ring, bore plug, flow control valve and spring from the housing. Discard the O-ring. If necessary to dismantle the flow control valve for cleaning, see the procedure for disassembly.

Installing pressure plate

Inspection

1. Remove the clean out plug with an Allen wrench.

2. Wash all metal parts in clean, non-toxic solvent. Blow out all passages with compressed air and air dry all cleaned parts.

3. Inspect the drive shaft for excessive wear and the seal area for nicks or scoring. Replace if necessary.

4. Inspect the end plates, rollers, rotor and cam ring for nicks, burrs, or scratches. If any of the components are damaged enough to cause poor operation of the pump, all the interior parts may have to be replaced to prevent later failures.

5. Inspect the pump body drive shaft bushing for excessive wear. Replace the pump body and bushing as one assembly.

Assembly

1. Install the 1/8" pipe clean out plug, tightening it to 80 in. lbs. torque.

2. Place the pump body on a clean flat surface and install a new shaft seal into the bore.

3. Install a new end cover O-ring into the groove in the pump bore. Be sure to lubricate the O-ring with power steering fluid before installing it.

4. Lubricate and install a new O-ring in the groove on the pump body where the reservoir fits snugly.

5. Install the brass seal plate to the bottom of the housing bore. Align the notch in the seal plate with the dowel pin hole in the housing.

6. Carefully install the front plate with the chamfered edge down in the pump bore. Align the index notch in the plate with the dowel pin hole in the housing.

CAUTION

Be extremely careful to align the dowel pin hole properly. Pump can be completely assembled with the dowel pin not seated properly in the hole.

7. Place the dowel pin in the cam ring and position the cam ring inside the pump bore. Notch in the cam ring must be facing up (away from the pulley end of pump housing). If the cam ring has two notches, one machined and one cast, install the cam ring with the machined notch up. Check the amount of dowel pin extending above the cam ring surface. If more than 3/16" is showing, the dowel pin is not seated in the index hole in the housing.

8. Install the rotor and shaft in the cam ring and carefully install the 12 steel rollers in the cavities of the rotor. Lubricate the rotor, rollers, and the inside surface of the cam ring with power steering fluid. Rotate the shaft by hand to be sure all the rollers are seated parallel with the shaft and are not sticking or binding.

9. Position the pressure plate by carefully aligning the index notch on the plate with the dowel pin and inserting a clean drill (number 13 to 16) in the cam ring oil hole next to the dowel pin notch until it bottoms on the housing floor.

10. Lubricate and install a new O-ring on the pressure plate. Position the pressure plate in the pump bore so that the dowel pin is in the index notch on the plate and the drill extends through the oil passage in the pressure plate. Seat the pressure plate on the cam ring using a clean 1 1/8" socket and a soft-faced hammer to tap it gently. Remove the drill and inspect the plate at both oil passage slots to be sure that the plate is squarely seated on the cam ring.

11. Place the large coil spring over the raised portion of the installed pressure plate.

12. Place the end cover, lip edge facing up, over the spring. Press the end cover down below the retaining ring groove. Install the retaining ring in the groove. Be sure the end cover chamfer is squarely seated against the snap-ring.

13. Replace the reservoir mounting bolt seal.

14. Lubricate the flow control valve assembly with power steering fluid and insert the valve spring and valve in the bore. Install a new O-ring on the bore plug, lubricate with fluid, and carefully install in the bore. Install the snap-ring with the sharp edge up. Do not depress the bore plug more than 1/16" below the snap-ring groove.

15. Place the reservoir on the pump body and visually align the mounting bolt hole. Tap the reservoir down on the pump with a plastic-faced hammer.

16. Remove the pump from the vise and install the mounting brackets with the mounting bolts on the pump. Tighten the bolts to 18 ft. lbs. torque.

17. Install the drive pulley by using the installer tool as follows: place the pulley on the end of the shaft and thread the installer tool into the 3/8" threaded hole in the end of the shaft. Put the installer shaft in a vise and tighten the drive nut against the thrust bearing, pressing the pulley on the shaft until it is flush. Do not try to press the pulley on the shaft without the special installer tool since the pump interior will be damaged by any other installation procedure. A small amount of drive shaft end play will be seen when the pulley is installed. This end play is necessary and will be minimized by a thin coat of oil between the rotor and the end plates when the pump is operating.

18. Install the pump assembly on the engine, install the drive belt and hoses (use new O-ring on pressure hose), and check for leaks.

FLOW CONTROL VALVE

Disassembly

1. After removing the pump from the engine and the reservoir from the pump, remove the snap-ring and plug from the flow bore. Discard the O-ring.

2. Depress the control valve against the spring pressure and allow the valve to spring out of the bore. If the valve is stuck in the bore or it did not come out of the bore far enough, it may be necessary to tap the housing lightly to remove it.

3. If the valve has dirt or foreign particles on it or in its bore, the rest of the pump needs cleaning. The hoses should be flushed and the steering gear valve body reconditioned. If the valve bore is badly scored, replace the pump body and the flow control valve.

4. Remove any nicks or burrs by gently rubbing the valve with crocus cloth. Clamp the valve land in a vise with soft-jaws and remove the hex head ball seat and shims. Note the number and gauge (thickness) of the shims on the ball seat. They must be re-installed for the same shim thickness to keep the same value of relief pressure.

5. Remove the valve from the vise and remove the pressure relief ball, guide, and spring.

Assembly

1. Insert the spring, guide and pressure relief ball in the end of the flow control valve.

2. Install the hex head plug using the exact number and thickness shims that were

PRESSURE PLATE
OIL PASSAGE SLOT

1 1/8 IN. SOCKET

NUMBER DRILL

OIL PASSAGE SLOT

Seating pressure plate

DRIVE PULLEY

DIPSTICK

SLIPPER AND SPRING

FILLER TUBE

FLOW CONTROL VALVE

RELIEF VALVE

PUMP ROTOR

RESERVOIR

ORIFICE PLUG

Ford Thompson power steering pump—sectional view

SEAL

PUMP HOUSING PLATE

CAM AND ROTOR ASSEMBLY

BELLEVILLE SPRING

RETAINER

SHAFT

LOWER PLATE

SHAFT SEAL   DOWEL PINS

CAP

SEAL

RESERVOIR

VALVE COVER

OUTLET FITTING

VALVE BODY

SEAL

RETAINING RING

UPPER PLATE   SPRING   SEAL

Exploded view of model C-11 slipper type pump

removed. Tighten the plug to 80 in. lbs. torque.

3. Lubricate the valve with power steering fluid and insert the flow control valve spring and valve in the housing bore. Install a new O-ring on the bore plug, lubricate with fluid and carefully install into the bore. Install the snap-ring. Do not depress the bore plug more than $1/16''$ beyond the snap-ring groove.

Slipper Type Power Steering Pump

The slipper type power steering pump is a belt-driven constant displacement assembly that uses a number of spring-loaded slippers in the pump rotor to force fluid from the inlet side to the flow control valve. Openings in the metering pin allow a flow of about two gpm. of fluid to the steering gear before the flow control valve directs the excess fluid to the inlet side of the pump again. Maximum pressure in the pump is limited by the pressure relief valve which opens when the pressure exceeds the maximum limits.

The slipper type power steering pump discussed in this section is used on Ford trucks and is called the Ford-Thompson power steering pump.

Removal

1. Drain the fluid from the pump reservoir by disconnecting the fluid return hose at the pump. Then, disconnect the pressure hose from the pump.

2. Remove the mounting bolts from the front of the pump. On eight cylinder engines, there is a nut on the rear of the pump that must be removed. After removing all the mounting bolts and nuts from the pump, move the unit inward to loosen the belt tension and remove the belt from the pulley. Then remove the pump from the engine.

Installation

1. Position the pump on the mounting bracket and loosely install the mounting bolts and nuts. Put the drive belt over the pulley and move the pump outward against the belt until the proper belt tension is obtained. Measure the belt tension with a gauge for the proper adjustment. Only in cases where a belt tension gauge is not available should the belt deflection method be used. If the belt deflection method is used, be sure to check the belt with a tension gauge at the earliest time since the deflection method is not accurate.

2. Tighten the mounting bolts and nuts to the specified torque limits.

3. Tighten the pressure hose fitting hex nut to the proper torque. Then connect the pressure hose to the pump and tighten the hose nut to the proper torque.

4. Connect the fluid return hose to the pump and tighten the clamp.

Installing cam ring

5. Fill the pump reservoir with power steering fluid and bleed the air bubbles from the system.

6. Check for leaks and recheck the fluid level. If necessary, add fluid to raise the level properly.

Correct slipper installation—Ford models

Disassembly

1. Drain as much fluid from the pump as possible after removing the pump from the truck.

2. Install a ⅜–16″ capscrew in the end of the pump shaft to avoid damaging the shaft end with the pulley remover tool. Install the pulley remover tool on the pulley hub and place the pump and remover tool in a vise. Hold the pump steady and turn the tool nut counterclockwise to draw the pulley off the shaft. The pulley must be removed without in and out pressure on the pump shaft to avoid damaging the internal thrust washers.

3. Remove the pump reservoir by installing the pump in a holding fixture with an adapter plate in a vise with the reservoir facing up.

4. Remove the outlet fitting hex nut and any other attaching parts from the reservoir case.

5. Invert the pump so the reservoir is now facing down. Using a wooden block, remove the reservoir by tapping around the flange until the reservoir is loose. Remove the reservoir O-ring seal and the outlet fitting gasket from the pump.

6. Again invert the pump assembly in the vise, remove the pump housing holding bolts and the pump housing.

7. Remove the housing cover, the O-ring seal and the pressure springs from inside the pump housing. Remove the pump cover gasket and discard it.

8. Remove the retainer end plate and upper pressure plate. In some pumps, the end plate and the upper pressure plate are made as one unit.

9. Remove the loose fitting dowel pin. Be careful not to bend the fixed dowel pin which remains in the housing plate assembly.

10. Remove the rotor assembly being careful not to let the slippers and springs fall out of the rotor. It may not be necessary to disassemble the rotor assembly unless the lower pressure plate, housing plate, rotor shaft and/or seal is to be replaced. However, the rotor assembly may be disassembled by removing the slippers and springs from the cam ring.

11. Remove any rust, dirt, burrs, or scoring from the pulley end of the rotor shaft before removing the shaft from the housing plate. The shaft must come out without restrictions to avoid scoring or damaging the bushing. Remove the pump rotor shaft.

12. Remove the lower pressure plate.

13. Remove the rotor shaft seal after first wrapping a piece of 0.005″ shim stock around the shaft and pushing it into the inside of the seal until it touches the bushing. With a sharp tool, pierce the seal body and pry the seal out. Do not damage the bushing, housing, or the shaft. Install a new seal

Ford Thompson power steering pump—sectional view

using a soft-faced hammer.

14. If the pump has a flow control valve, disassemble according to instructions given in the section on the roller type power steering pump.

Inspection

1. Wash all metal parts in clean, non-toxic solvent. Blow out all oil passages with compressed air and air dry all cleaned parts.

2. Inspect the drive shaft for excessive wear and seal area for nicks or scoring. Replace if necessary.

3. Inspect the pressure plates, slippers, rotor, and cam ring for nicks, burrs, or scratches. If any of the parts are damaged enough to cause poor operation or binding of the pump, replace the defective part.

4. Inspect the pump body drive shaft bushing for excessive wear. Replace if necessary.

Correct slipper installation—Chrysler models

Upper pressure plate installation

Assembly

1. With the pump assembly positioned on the adapter plate in the holding fixture, install the lower pressure plate on the anchor pin with the chamfered slots at the center hole facing up.

2. Lubricate the rotor shaft with power steering fluid and insert the shaft into the lower pressure and housing plates.

3. Assemble the rotor, slippers, and springs by wrapping a piece of wire around the rotor, installing the springs, and sliding a slipper in each groove of the rotor over the springs. Then, insert the assembly into the cam ring. Be sure the flat side of the slippers are toward the left side. Be sure that the springs are installed straight and are not cocked to one side under the slippers.

4. Install the cam ring and rotor assembly on the drive shaft with the fixed dowel passing through the first hole to the left of the cam notch when the arrow on the cam outside diameter is pointing toward the lower pressure plate. If the cam and rotor assembly does not seat properly, turn the rotor shaft slightly until the spline teeth mesh, allowing the cam and rotor to drop into position.

5. Insert the loose fitting dowel through the cam insert and lower pressure plate into the hole in the housing plate assembly. When

Cam and rotor installation

both dowels are installed properly, they will be the same height.

6. Install the upper pressure plate so the tapered notch is facing down against the cam insert. The fixed dowel should pass through the round dowel hole and the loose dowel through the long hole. The slot between the ears on the outside of the pressure plate should match the notch on the cam insert.

7. Install the retainer end plate so the slot on the end plate matches the notches on the upper pressure plate and the cam insert.

Lower pressure plate installed

8. Install the pump valve assembly O-ring seal on the pump valve assembly. Do not twist the seal.

9. Place the pump valve assembly on top of the retainer end plate with the large exhaust slot on the pump valve in line with the outside notches of the cam, upper pressure plate, and retainer end plate. All parts must be fully seated. If correctly installed, the relief valve stem will be in line with the lube return hole in the pump housing plate.

10. Put small amounts of vaseline on the pump housing plate to hold the cover gasket in place. Install the cover gasket in place.

11. Insert the pressure plate springs into the pockets in the pump valve assembly.

12. Plug the intake hole in the housing.

13. Lubricate the inside of the housing and the housing cover seal with power steering fluid. Install two studs for use as positioning guides, one in the bolt hole nearest the drain hole and the other in the bolt hole on the opposite side of the housing plate.

14. Align the small lube hole in the housing rim and the lube hole in the housing plate. Install the housing, using a steady, even, downward pressure. Do not jar the pressure spring out of position. Remove the

Retainer end plate installation

guide studs and loosely install the housing retaining bolts finger tight.

15. Tighten the retaining bolts evenly to 28–32 ft. lbs. until the housing flange contacts the gasket.

16. Install a ⅜–16 hex head screw into the end of the rotor shaft and put a torque wrench on it. Check the amount of torque needed to rotate the rotor shaft. If the torque is more than 15 in. lbs., loosen the retaining bolts slightly and rotate the rotor shaft. Then, retighten the retaining bolts evenly. Do not use the pump if the shaft torque exceeds 15 in. lbs.

17. Release the pin in the bench holding fixture and shake the pump assembly back and forth. If there is a rattle, the pressure springs have fallen out of their seats and must be reinstalled.

18. Install the reservoir O-ring seal on the housing plate without twisting it. Lubricate the seal and install the reservoir, aligning the notch in the reservoir flange with the notch in the outside edge of the pump housing plate and bushing assembly. Using only a soft-faced hammer, tap at the rear outer corners of the reservoir. Inspect the assembly to be sure the reservoir is fully seated on the housing plate.

19. Install the identification tag (if one was removed) on the outlet valve fitting. Install the outlet valve fitting nut and tighten to 48–45 ft. lbs. torque.

20. Turn the pump assembly over and install the pulley using the tool used to remove the pulley. Turn the tool nut clockwise to draw the pulley on the shaft until it is flush with the shaft end. Do not exert inward and outward pressures on the shaft to avoid damaging the internal thrust areas. Remove the tool.

Bendix Linkage—Type Power Steering System

The Bendix linkage-type power steering is

Valve and pressure spring installation

(labels on image: O-RING SEAL, LUBE RETURN HOLE, EXHAUST SLOT, EARS)

Linkage type power steering installation—typical

(labels on image: RETURN LINE, PRESSURE LINE, STOP BRACKET, LEFT TURN HOSE, PITMAN ARM, CONTROL VALVE, DRAG LINK, POWER CYLINDER, PUMP AND RESERVOIR, CYLINDER BRACKET, RIGHT TURN HOSE)

a hydraulically controlled system composed of an integral pump and fluid reservoir, a control valve, a power cylinder, connecting fluid lines, and the steering linkage. The hydraulic pump, which is driven by a belt turned by the engine, draws fluid from the reservoir and provides pressure through hoses to the control valve and the power cylinder. There is a pressure relief valve to limit the pressures within the steering system to a safe level. After the fluid has passed from the pump to the control valve and the power cylinder, it returns to the reservoir.

CONTROL VALVE CENTERING SPRING

Adjustment

1. Raise the truck and remove the spring cap attaching screws and remove the spring cap.

———— **CAUTION** ————

Be very careful not to position the hoist adapters of two post hoists under the suspension and/or steering components. Place the hoist adapters under the front suspension lower arms.

2. Tighten the adjusting nut snug (about 90–100 in. lbs.); then, loosen the nut ¼ turn (90 degrees). Do not turn the adjusting nut too tight.

3. Place the spring cap on the valve housing. Lubricate and install the attaching screws and washers. Tighten the screws to 72–100 in. lbs. torque.

4. Lower the truck and start the engine. Check the steering effort using a spring scale attached to the steering wheel rim for a pull of no more than 12 lbs.

POWER STEERING CONTROL VALVE

Removal

1. Raise the truck. If a two post hoist is used, be sure to place the hoist adapters under the front suspension steering arms.

Do not allow the hoist adapters to contact the steering linkage.

2. Disconnect the four fluid line fittings at the control valve and drain the fluid from the lines. Turn the front wheels back and forth to force all the fluid from the system.

3. Loosen the clamping nut and bolt at the right end of the sleeve.

4. Remove the roll pin from the steering arm-to-idler arm rod through the slot in the sleeve.

5. Remove the control valve ball stud nut.

6. Remove the ball stud from the sector shaft arm.

7. After turning the front wheels fully to the left, unthread the control valve from the center link steering arm-to-idler arm rod.

Installation

1. Thread the valve on the center link until about four threads are still visible.

2. Position the ball stud in the sector shaft arm.

3. Measure the distance between the grease plug in the sleeve and the stud at the inner end of the left spindle connecting rod. If the distance is not correct, disconnect the ball stud from the sector shaft arm and turn the valve on the center link until the correct distance is obtained.

4. When the distance is correct and the ball stud is positioned in the sector shaft arm, align the hole in the steering arm-to-idler arm rod with the slot near the end of the valve sleeve. Install the roll pin in the rod hole to lock the valve in place on the rod.

5. Tighten the valve sleeve clamp bolt to the proper torque.

6. Install the ball stud nut and tighten to the proper torque. Install a new cotter pin.

7. Connect all fluid lines to the control valve and tighten all fittings securely. Do not over-tighten.

8. Fill the fluid reservoir with power steering fluid to the full mark on the dipstick.

9. Start the engine and run it for a few minutes to warm the fluid in the power steering system. Turn the steering wheel

back and forth to the stops and check the system for leaks.

10. Increase the engine idle speed to about 1000 rpm. Turn the steering wheel back and forth several times, then stop the engine. Check the control valve and hose connections for leaks.

11. Recheck the fluid level and add fluid if necessary.

12. Start the engine again, and check the position of the steering wheel when the front wheels are straight ahead. Do not make any adjustments until toe-in is checked.

13. With engine running, check front wheel toe-in.

14. Check steering wheel turning effort which should be equal in both directions.

POWER STEERING POWER CYLINDER

Removal and Installation

1. Disconnect the two fluid lines from the power cylinder and drain the fluid.

2. Remove the pal nut, attaching nut, washer and the insulator from the end of the power cylinder rod. Remove the cotter pin and castellated nut holding the power cylinder stud to the center link.

3. Disconnect the power cylinder stud from the center link.

4. Remove the insulator sleeve and washer from the end of the power cylinder.

5. Inspect the tube fittings and seats in the power cylinder for nicks, burrs, or other

Phantom view of power cylinder—typical

damage. Replace the seats or tubes if damaged.

6. Install the washer, sleeve and the insulator on the end of the power cylinder rod.

7. While extending the rod as far as possible, insert the rod in the bracket on the frame and then, compress the rod so the stud may be inserted in the center link. Secure the stud with the castellated nut and a new cotter pin.

8. Install the insulator, washer, nut, and a pal nut on the power cylinder rod.

9. Connect the two fluid lines to their proper ports on the power cylinder.

10. Fill the reservoir with power steering fluid to the full mark on the dipstick. Start the engine and run for a few minutes to warm the fluid. Turn the steering wheel back and forth to the stops to fill the system. Stop the engine.

11. Recheck the fluid level and add fluid if necessary. Check for fluid leaks.

12. Start the engine again, turn the steering wheel back and forth, and check for leaks while the engine is running.

CONTROL VALVE
Disassembly

1. Clean the outside of the control valve of dirt and fluid.

2. Remove the centering spring cap from the valve housing. The control valve should be put in a soft-faced bench vise during disassembly. Clamp the control valve around the sleeve flange only to avoid damaging the valve housing, spool, or sleeve.

3. Remove the nut from the end of the valve spool bolt. Remove the washers, spacer, centering spring, adapter, and the bushing from the bolt and valve housing.

Control valve cross section—typical

4. Remove the two bolts holding the valve housing and the sleeve together. Separate the valve housing and the sleeve.

5. Remove the plug from the sleeve. Push the valve spool out of the centering spring end of the valve housing, and remove the seal from the spool.

6. Remove the spacer, bushing and valve housing.

7. Drive the pin out of the travel regulator stop with a punch and hammer. Pull the head of the valve spool bolt tightly against the travel regulator stop before driving the pin out of the stop.

8. Turn the travel regulator stop counterclockwise in the valve sleeve to remove the stop from the sleeve.

9. Remove the valve spool bolt, spacer, and rubber washer from the travel regulator stop.

10. Remove the rubber boot and clamp from the valve sleeve. Slide the bumper, spring, and ball stud seat out of the valve sleeve and remove the ball stud socket from the sleeve.

11. Remove the return port hose seat and the return port relief valve.

12. Remove the spring plug and O-ring. Then remove the reaction limiting valve.

13. Replace all worn or damaged hose seats by using an Easy-Out screw extractor or a bolt of proper size as a puller. Tap the existing hole in the hose seat, using a starting tap of the correct size. Remove all metal chips from the hose seat after tapping. Place a nut and washer on a bolt of the same size as the tapped hole. The washer must be large enough to cover the hose seat port. Insert the bolt in the tapped hole and remove the hose seat by turning the nut clockwise and drawing the bolt out. Install a new hose seal in the port, and thread a bolt of the correct size in the port. Tighten the bolt enough to bottom the seal in the port.

Assembly

1. Coat all parts of the control valve assembly with power steering fluid. Seals should be coated with lubricant before installation.

2. Install the reaction limiting valve, spring and plug. Install the return port relief valve and the hose seat.

3. Insert one of the ball stud seats (flat end first) into the ball stud socket, and insert the threaded end of the ball stud into the socket.

4. Place the socket in the control valve sleeve so that the threaded end of the ball stud can be pulled out through the slot.

5. Place the other ball stud seat, spring, and bumper in the socket. Install and securely tighten the travel regulator stop.

6. Loosen the stop just enough to align the nearest hole in the stop with the slot in the ball stud socket and install the stop pin in the ball stud socket, travel regulator stop, and valve spool bolt.

7. Install the rubber boot, clamp, and the plug on the control valve sleeve. Be sure the lubrication fitting is turned on tightly and does not bind on the ball stud socket.

8. Insert the valve spool in the valve housing, rotating it while installing it.

9. Move the spool toward the centering spring end of the housing, and place the small seal bushing and spacer in the sleeve end of the housing.

10. Press the valve spool against the inner lip of the seal and, at the same time, guide the lip of the seal over the spool with a small screwdriver. Do not nick or scratch the seal or the spool during installation.

11. Place the sleeve end of the housing on a flat surface so that the seal, bushing and spacer are at the bottom end; then push down the valve spool until it stops.

12. Carefully install the spool seal and bushing in the centering spring end of the housing. Press the seal against the end of the spool, guiding the seal over the spool with a small flat tool. Do not nick or scratch the seal or the spool during installation.

13. Pick up the housing, and slide the spool back and forth in the housing to check for free movement.

14. Place the valve sleeve on the housing so that the ball stud is on the same side of the housing as the ports for the two power cylinder lines. Install the two bolts in the sleeve, and torque them to the proper torque.

15. Place the adapter on the centering spring end of the housing, and install the bushing, washers, spacers and centering spring on the valve spool bolt.

16. Compress the centering spring and install the nut on the bolt. Tighten the nut snug (about 90–100 in. lbs.); then, loosen it not more than ¼ turn. Do not over-tighten to avoid breaking the stop pin at the travel regulator stop.

17. Move the ball stud back and forth to check for free movement.

18. Lubricate the two cap attaching bolts. Install the centering spring cap on the valve housing, and tighten the two cap bolts to the proper torque.

19. Install the nut on the ball stud so that the valve can be put in a vise. Then, push forward on the cap end of the valve to check the valve spool for free movement.

20. Turn the valve around in the vise, and push forward on the sleeve end to check for free movement.

POWER CYLINDER SEAL

Removal

1. Clamp the power cylinder in a vise and remove the snap-ring from the end of the cylinder. Do not distort or crack the cylinder in the vise.

2. Pull the piston rod out all the way to remove the scraper, bushing, and seals. If the seals cannot be removed in this manner, remove them by carefully prying them out of the cylinder with a sharp pick. Do not damage the shaft or seal seat.

Installation

1. Coat the new seals with power steering fluid and place the parts on the piston rod. Coat with grease or lubricant.

2. Push the rod in all the way, and install the parts in the cylinder with a deep socket slightly smaller than the cylinder opening.

POWER STEERING PUMP

Removal and Replacement

To remove or install the power steering pump, see the section on the slipper type pump.

Saginaw Linkage-Type Power Cylinder

Removal

1. Remove the two hoses which are connected to the cylinder and drain fluid into a container.

2. Remove power cylinder from frame bracket.

3. Remove cotter pin and nut and pull stud out of relay rod.

4. Remove cylinder from vehicle.

Inspection

1. Check seals for leaks around cylinder rod. If leaks are found, replace seals.

2. Check hose connection seats for damage and replace if necessary.

3. For service other than seat or seal replacement, it is necessary to replace the power cylinder.

4. The ball stud may be replaced by removing snap-ring.

Disassembly and Assembly

1. To remove piston rod seal, remove snap-ring and pull out on rod. Remove back-up washer, piston rod scraper and piston rod seal from rod.

2. To remove the ball stud, depress the end plug and remove the snap-ring. Push on the end of the ball stud and the end plug, spring, spring seat, ball stud and seal may be removed. If the ball seat is to be replaced, it must be pressed out.

3. Reverse disassembly procedure. Be sure snap-ring is properly seated.

Installation

1. Install power cylinder on vehicle in reverse of removal procedure.

2. Reconnect the hydraulic lines, fill system and bleed out air as described in the installation and balancing section of control valve servicing.

POWER STEERING HOSES

Carefully inspect the hoses. When installing, be sure to place in such a position as

PITMAN SHAFT SECTOR

RACK PISTON

CONSTANT RATIO VARIABLE RATIO

Comparison of constant ratio and variable ratio steering shaft teeth

to avoid all chafing or other abuse when making sharp turns.

Saginaw Rotary-Type Power Steering

The rotary-type power steering gear is designed with all components in one housing.

The power cylinder is an integral part of the gear housing. A double-acting type piston allows oil pressure to be applied to either side of the piston. The one-piece piston and power rack is meshed to the sector shaft.

The hydraulic control valve is composed of a sleeve and valve spool. The spool is held in the neutral position by the torsion bar and spool actuator. Twisting of the torsion bar moves the valve spool, allowing oil pressure to be directed to either side of the power piston, depending upon the directional rotation of the steering wheel, to give power assist.

On many trucks of the General Motors Corporation, a modified version of the rotary valve power steering system provides variable ratio steering to assist the driver to steer the truck easier and safer. The steering gear ratio will vary from a high ratio of about 16:1 while steering straight ahead to a lower gear ratio of about 12.1:1 while making a full turn to either side.

ROLLER PUMP

Removal

Remove the reservoir cover and use a suction gun to empty the reservoir. Disconnect the hoses from the pump and tie them in a raised position to prevent oil drainage. Loosen the pump adjusting screw and remove the pump belt, then take out the retaining bolts and remove the pump and reservoir.

Installation

Position the pump assembly and install the retaining bolts. Be sure there is clearance between the pump bracket and the engine front support bracket. Install the hoses and place the pump belt on the pulley. Adjust the belt to ½" deflection, then tighten the adjusting screw.

Connect the hoses to the pump assembly.

Fill the reservoir to within ½" of the top with Dexron II® automatic transmission fluid.

Start the engine and rotate the steering wheel several times to the right and left to expel air from the system, then recheck the oil level and install the reservoir cover.

POWER STEERING UNIT

Fluid Used

This unit uses Dexron II® automatic transmission fluid. The fluid capacity is 4½ pints.

Bleeding the System

Fill the pump reservoir to within ½" of the top. Start and run the engine to attain normal operating temperatures. Now, turn the steering wheel through its entire travel three or four times to expel air from the system, then recheck the fluid level.

Checking Steering Effort

Run the engine to attain normal operating temperatures. With the wheels on a dry floor, hook a pull scale to the spoke of the steering wheel at the outer edge. The effort required to turn the steering wheel should be 3½–5 lbs. If the pull is not within these limits, check the hydraulic pressure.

NUT

COVER 3580

GASKET 3581

ADJUSTER

SECTOR SHAFT 3575

CLAMP 3544

BALL RETURN GUIDE 3D727

BALLS 3647

RACK PISTON 3524

HOUSING 3548

O-RING 87144-S

OIL SEALS

TEFLON RING 3805

RACK-PISTON END PLUG 3D530

O-RING

HOUSING END PLUG 3A745

RETAINING RING 3A746

INLET PORT SEAT CHECK VALVE

RETURN PORT SEAT

SPRING

WORM RACES THRUST BEARING 3D730

BEARING 3576

SPACER WASHERS

RETAINING RING

3D732

3812

TEFLON RINGS (3)

VALVE SPOOL

O-RING SPOOL DAMPER SEAL

STUB SHAFT ASSEMBLY

VALVE BODY

O-RING SEAL

O-RING (3)

RACES

FLEXIBLE COUPLING

BEARING LOCK NUT 3707

GROUND STRAP

RETAINING RING

DUST SEAL

OIL SEAL

ADJUSTER PLUG

O-RING SEAL

THRUST BEARING

SPACER

BEARING RETAINER

3B700

Exploded view of Saginaw power steering gear used on light trucks

SPANNER WRENCH
TOOL—T65P-3A537-A

Removing adjuster plug

BEARING RETAINER

SPACER

Removing thrust bearing retainer

Pressure Test

To check the hydraulic pressure, disconnect the pressure hose from the gear. Now connect the pressure gauge between the pressure hose from the pump and the steering gear housing. Run the engine to attain normal operating temperatures, then turn the wheel to a full right and a full left turn to the wheel stops.

Hold the wheel in this position only long enough to obtain an accurate reading.

The pressure gauge reading should be within the limits specified. If the pressure reading is less than the minimum needed for proper operation, close the valve at the gauge and see if the reading increases. If the pressure is still low, the pump is defective and needs repair. If the pressure reading is at or near the minimum reading, the pump is normal and needs only an adjustment of the power steering gear or power

assist control valve.

Worm Bearing Preload and Sector Mesh Adjustments

Disconnect the pitman arm from the sector shaft, then back off on the sector shaft adjusting screw on the sector shaft cover.

Center the steering on the high point, then attach a pull scale to the spoke of the steering wheel at the outer edge. The pull required to keep the wheel moving for one complete turn should be ½–⅔ lbs.

If the pull is not within these limits, loosen the thrust bearing locknut and tighten or back off on the valve sleeve adjuster locknut to bring the preload within limits. Tighten the thrust bearing locknut and recheck the preload.

Slowly rotate the steering wheel several times, then center the steering on the high point. Now, turn the sector shaft adjusting

screw until a steering wheel pull of 1–1½ lbs. is required to move the worm through the center point. Tighten the sector shaft adjusting screw locknut and recheck the sector mesh adjustment.

Install the pitman arm and draw the arm in position with the nut.

Service Operations

ADJUSTER PLUG AND ROTARY VALVE

Removal

1. Thoroughly clean exterior of gear assembly. Drain by holding valve ports down and rotating worm back and forth through entire travel.
2. Place gear in vise.
3. Loosen adjuster plug locknut with punch. Remove adjuster plug with spanner.
4. Remove rotary valve assembly by grasping stub shaft and pulling it out.

ADJUSTER PLUG

Disassembly & Assembly

1. Remove upper thrust bearing retainer with screwdriver. Be careful not to damage bearing bore. Discard retainer. Remove spacer, upper bearing and races.
2. Remove and discard adjuster plug O-ring.
3. Remove stub shaft seal retaining ring (Truarc pliers will help) and remove and discard dust seal.
4. Remove stub shaft seal by prying out and discard.
5. Examine needle bearing and, if required, remove same by pressing from thrust bearing end.
6. Inspect thrust bearing spacer, bearing rollers and races.
7. Reassemble in reverse of above.

ROTARY VALVE

Disassembly

Repairs are seldom needed. Do not disassemble unless absolutely necessary. If the O-ring seal on valve spool dampener needs replacement, perform this portion of operation only.

BEARING RETAINER — SPACER — THRUST BEARING — O-RING — ROLLER BEARING — DUST SEAL

INNER RACE — OUTER RACE — ADJUSTER PLUG — OIL SEAL — RETAINING RING

Adjuster plug disassembled

1. Remove cap-to-worm O-ring seal and discard.

2. Remove valve spool spring by prying on small coil with a small tool to work spring onto bearing surface of stub shaft. Slide spring off shaft. Be careful not to damage shaft surface.

3. Remove valve spool by holding the valve assembly in one hand with the stub shaft pointing down. Insert the end of pencil or wood rod through opening in valve body cap and push spool until it is out far enough to be removed. In this procedure, rotate to prevent jamming. If spool becomes jammed it may be necessary to remove stub shaft, torsion bar and cap assembly.

RETAINING RING

ADJUSTER PLUG

SNAP RING PLIERS

Removing adjuster plug retaining seal ring

"O" RING

VALVE ASSEMBLY

STUB SHAFT ASSEMBLY

Separating valve spool (center) from valve body

Assembly

> ### CAUTION
>
> *All parts must be free and clear of dirt, chips, etc., before assembly and must be protected after.*

1. Lubricate three new back-up O-ring seals with automatic transmission oil and reassemble in the ring grooves of valve body. Assemble three new valve body rings in the grooves over the O-ring seals by carefully slipping over the valve body.

NOTE: If the valve body rings seem loose or twisted in the grooves, the heat of the oil during operation will cause them to straighten.

2. Lubricate a new dampener O-ring with automatic transmission fluid and install in valve spool groove.

3. Assemble stub shaft torsion bar and cap assembly in the valve body, aligning the groove in the valve cap with the pin in the valve body. Tap lightly with soft remainder of assembly. Valve body pin must be in the cap groove. Hold parts together during the remainder of assembly.

4. Lubricate spool. With notch in spool toward valve body, slide the spool over the stub shaft. Align the notch on the spool with the spool drive pin on stub shaft and carefully engage spool in valve body bore. Push spool evenly and with slight rotating motion until it reaches the drive pin. Rotate slowly, with some pressure, until notch engages pin. Be sure dampener O-ring seal is evenly distributed in the spool groove.

> ### CAUTION
>
> *Use extreme care because spool to valve body clearance is very small. Damage is easily caused.*

5. With seal protector over stub shaft, slide valve spool spring over shaft, with small diameter of spring going over shaft last. Work spring onto shaft until small coil is located in stub shaft groove.

6. Lubricate a new cap to O-ring seal and install in valve body.

ADJUSTER PLUG AND ROTARY VALVE

Installation

1. Align narrow pin slot on valve body with valve body drive pin on the worm. Insert the valve assembly into gear housing by pressing against valve body with finger tips. Do not press on stub shaft or torsion bar. The return hole in the gear housing should be fully visible when properly assembled.

> ### CAUTION
>
> *Do not press on stub shaft as this may cause shaft and cap to pull out of valve body, allowing the spool dampener O-ring seal to slip into valve body oil grooves.*

2. With seal protector over end of stub shaft, install adjuster plug assembly into gear housing snugly with spanner, then back plug off approximately one-eighth turn. Install plug locknut but do not tighten. Adjust preload as described in the adjustment section.

3. After adjustment, tighten locknut.

PITMAN SHAFT

Removal and Installation

1. Completely drain the gear assembly and thoroughly clean the outside.

2. Place gear in vise.

3. Rotate stub shaft until pitman shaft gear is in center position. Remove side cover

retaining bolts.

4. Tap end of pitman shaft with soft hammer and slide shaft out of housing.

5. Remove and discard side cover O-ring seal.

6. The seals, washers, retainers and bearings may now be removed and examined.

7. Examine all parts for wear or damage and replace as required.

8. Install in reverse of above. Make proper adjustment as described in adjustment section.

RACK-PISTON NUT AND WORM ASSEMBLY

Removal

1. Completely drain the gear assembly and thoroughly clean the outside.

2. Remove pitman shaft assembly as previously described.

3. Rotate housing end plug retaining ring so that one end of ring is over hole in gear housing. Spring one end of ring so pin punch can be inserted to lift it out.

4. Rotate stub shaft to full left turn position to force end plug out of housing.

5. Remove and discard housing end plug O-ring seal.

6. Remove rack-piston nut end plug with ½" square drive.

7. Insert special tool in end of worm. Turn stub shaft so that rack-piston nut will go into tool and then remove rack-piston nut from gear housing.

8. Remove adjuster plug and rotary valve assemblies as previously described.

9. Remove worm and lower thrust bearing and races.

10. Remove cap O-ring seal and discard.

RACK-PISTON NUT AND WORM

Disassembly and Assembly

1. Remove and discard piston ring and back-up O-ring on rack piston nut.

2. Remove ball guide clamp and return guide.

3. Place nut on clean cloth and remove ball retaining tool. Make sure all balls are removed.

4. Inspect all parts for wear, nicks, scoring or burrs. If worm or rack-pinion nut need replacing, both must be replaced as a matched pair.

5. In reassembling reverse the above.

NOTE: When assembling, alternate black and white balls, and install guide and clamp. Packing with grease helps in holding during assembly. When new balls are used, various sizes are available and a selection must be made to secure proper torque when making the high point adjustment.

Installing balls in rack piston

Removing valve body assembly

Removing pilot lever

RACK-PISTON NUT AND WORM ASSEMBLY

Installation

1. Install in reverse of removal procedure.

2. In all cases use new O-ring seals.

3. Make adjustments as previously described.

Retaining bearing rollers with arbor tool

Removing reaction seal from wormshaft support

Removing worm shaft oil seal

Chrysler Full-Time Power Steering (Constant Control Type)

The Chrysler Corporation Constant Control Type Power Steering Gear System consists of a hydraulic pressure pump, a power steering gear and connecting hoses.

The power steering gear housing contains a gear shaft and sector gear, a power piston with gear teeth milled into the side of the piston which is in constant mesh with the gear shaft sector teeth, a worm shaft which connects the steering wheel to the power piston through a coupling. The worm shaft is geared to the piston through recirculating ball contact.

A pivot lever is fitted into the spool valve at the upper end and into a drilled hole in the center thrust bearing race at the lower end. The center thrust bearing race is held firmly against the shoulder of the worm shaft by two thrust bearings, bearing races and an adjusting nut. The pivot lever pivots in the spacer which is held in place by the pressure plate.

When the steering wheel is turned to the left the worm shaft moves out of the power piston a few thousandths of an inch, the center thrust bearing race moves the same distance since it is clamped to the worm shaft. The race thus tips the pivot lever and moves the spool valve down, allowing oil under pressure to flow into the left-turn power chamber and force the power piston down. As the power piston moves, it rotates the cross-shaft sector gear and, through the steering linkage, turns the front wheels.

On a right turn the worm shaft moves into the power piston, the center thrust bearing race thus tips the pivot lever and moves the spool valve up, allowing oil under pressure to flow into the right power chamber and force the power piston up.

Pressure Test

Connect the pressure test hoses with the pressure gauge installed between the pump and steering gear.

Now, fill the reservoir to the level mark, then start the engine and bleed the system. Allow the engine to idle until the fluid in the reservoir is between 150° F. and 170° F. Now turn the steering wheel to the extreme right and check the pressure reading, then turn to the extreme left and check the reading again. The gauge reading should be equal in each direction. If not, it indicates excessive internal leakage in the unit.

The pressure should agree with the specifications in Pump section for satisfactory power steering operation.

Reconditioning

1. Drain gear by turning worm shaft from limit to limit with oil connections held downward. Thoroughly clean outside.

2. Remove valve body attaching screws, body and three O-rings.

3. Remove pivot lever and spring. Pry under spherical head with a small bar.

NOTE: Use care not to collapse slotted end of valve lever as this will destroy bearing tolerances of the spherical head.

4. Remove steering gear arm from sector shaft.

Removing cylinder head oil seal

Removing reaction seal from cylinder head

5. Remove snap-ring and seal back-up washer.

6. Remove seal, using proper tool to prevent damage to relative parts.

7. Loosen gear shaft adjusting screw locknut and remove gear shaft cover nut.

8. Rotate wormshaft to position sector teeth at center of piston travel. Loosen power train retaining nut.

9. Insert tools into housing until both tool and shaft are engaged with bearings.

10. Turn worm shaft either to full left or full right (depending on car application) to compress power train parts. Then remove power train retaining nut as mentioned above.

11. Remove housing head tang washer.

12. While holding power train completely compressed, pry on piston teeth with a small bar, using shaft as a fulcrum, and remove complete power train.

NOTE: Maintain close contact between cylinder head, center race and spacer assembly and the housing head. This will eliminate the possibility of reactor rings becoming disengaged from their grooves in cylinder and housing head. It will prohibit center spacer from separating from center race and cocking in the housing. This could make it impossible to remove the power train without damaging involved parts.

13. Place power train in soft-jawed vise in vertical position. The worm bearing rollers will fall out. Use of arbor tool will hold roller when the housing is removed.

14. Raising housing head until wormshaft oil shaft just clears the top of wormshaft and position arbor tool on top of shaft and into seal. With arbor in position, pull up on housing head until arbor is positioned in bearing. Remove when the housing is removed.

15. Remove large O-ring from housing head groove.

16. Remove reaction seal from groove in face of head with air pressure directed into ferrule chamber.

17. Remove reactor spring, reactor ring, worm balancing ring and spacer.

18. While holding wormshaft from turning, turn nut with enough force to release staked portions from knurled section and remove nut.

NOTE: Pay strict attention to cleanliness.

19. Remove upper thrust bearing race (thin) and upper thrust bearing.

20. Remove center bearing race.

21. Remove lower thrust bearing and lower thrust bearing race (thick).

22. Remove lower reaction ring and reaction spring.

23. Remove cylinder head assembly.

24. Remove O-rings from outer grooves in head.

25. Remove reaction O-ring from groove in face of cylinder head. Use air pressure in oil hole located between O-ring grooves.

26. Remove snap-ring, sleeve and rectangular oil seal from cylinder head counterbore.

27. Test wormshaft operation. Not more than 2 in. lbs. should be required to turn it through its entire travel, and with a 15 ft. lb. side load.

NOTE: The worm and piston is serviced as a complete assembly and should not be disassembled.

28. Shaft side play should not exceed 0.008 in. under light pull applied $2\frac{5}{16}$ in. from piston flange.

29. Assemble in reverse of above, noting proper adjustments and preload requirements following.

30. When cover nut is installed, tighten to 20 ft. lbs. torque.

31. Valve mounting screws should be tightened to 200 in. lbs. torque.

32. With hoses connected, system bled, and engine idling roughly, center valve unit until not self-steering. Tap on head of valve body attaching screws to move valve body

Ball nut and valve housing

REMOVING WORM BEARING RACE NUT

TOOL T66P-3553-C

TOOL T66P-3553-B

T57L-500-B

Removing worm bearing race nut

VALVE HOUSING 3A587

BEARING-3D526

OIL SEAL-3D526

SNAP RING -352109-S

DUST SEAL 3D527

INLET TUBE SEAT-374309-S

OUTLET TUBE SEAT-374480-S

Valve housing disassembled

up, and tap on end plug to move valve body down.

33. With steering gear on center, tighten gear shaft adjusting screw until lash just disappears.

34. Continue to tighten ⅜ to ½ turn and tighten locknut to 50 ft. lbs.

Ford Integral Power Steering Gear

The Ford integral power steering unit is a torsion-bar type.

The torsion bar power steering unit includes a worm and one-piece rack piston, which is meshed to the gear teeth on the steering sector shaft. The unit also includes a hydraulic valve, valve actuator, input shaft and torsion bar assembly which are mounted on the end of the worm shaft and operated by the twisting action of the torsion bar.

The torsion-bar type of power steering gear is designed with the one piece rack-piston, worm and sector shaft in one housing and the valve spool in an attaching housing. This makes possible internal fluid passages between the valve and cylinder, thus eliminating all external lines and hoses, except the pressure and return hoses between the pump and gear assembly.

The power cylinder is an integral part of the gear housing. The piston is double acting, in that fluid pressure may be applied

STEERING GEAR HOUSING

UPPER SEAL

LOWER SEAL

SPACER WASHER

SNAP RING

Removing bearing and oil seal

to either side of the piston.

A selective metal shim, located in the valve housing of the gear is for the purpose of tailoring steering gear efforts. If efforts are not within specifications they can be changed by increasing or decreasing shim thickness as follows:

1. Efforts heavy to the left—increase shim thickness.
2. Efforts light to the left—decrease shim thickness.

Adjustments

The only adjustment which can be performed is the total over center position load, to eliminate excessive lash between the sector and rack teeth.

1. Disconnect the Pitman arm from the sector shaft.
2. Disconnect the fluid return line at the reservoir, at the same time cap the reservoir return line pipe.
3. Place the end of the return line in a clean container and cycle the steering wheel in both directions as required, to discharge the fluid from the gear.
4. Turn the steering wheel to 45 degrees from the left stop.
5. Using an in. lb. torque wrench on the steering wheel nut, determine the torque required to rotate the shaft slowly through an approximately ⅛ turn from the 45 degree position.
6. Turn the steering gear back to center, then determine the torque required to rotate the shaft back and forth across the center position. Loosen the adjuster nut, and turn the adjuster screw until the reading is 11–12 in. lbs. greater than the torque 45

degrees from the stop. Tighten the lock nut while holding the screw in place.

7. Recheck the readings and replace the Pitman arm and the steering wheel hub cover.
8. Correct the fluid return line to the reservoir and fill the reservoir with specified lubricant to the proper level.

VALVE CENTERING SHIM

Removal and Installation

1. Hold the steering gear over a drain pan in an inverted position and cycle the input shaft several times to drain the remaining fluid from the gear.
2. Mount the gear in a soft-jawed vise.
3. Turn the input shaft to either stop then, turn it back approximately 1¾ turns to center the gear.
4. Remove the two sector shaft cover attaching screws, the brake line bracket and the identification tag.
5. Tap the lower end of the sector shaft with a soft-faced hammer to loosen it, then lift the cover and shaft from the housing as an assembly. Discard the O-ring.
6. Remove the four valve housing attaching bolts. Lift the valve housing from the steering gear housing while holding the piston to prevent it from rotating off the worm shaft.
7. Remove the valve housing and the lube passage O-rings and discard them.
8. Place the valve housing, worm and piston assembly in the bench mounted holding fixture with the piston on the top.
9. Rotate the piston upward (back off) 3½ turns.
10. Insert tool T66P-3553-C or equivalent (with the arm facing away from the piston) into a bolt hole in the valve housing. Rotate the arm into position under the piston.
11. Loosen the Allen head race nut set screw from the valve housing.
12. Using tool T66P-3553-B or equivalent, loosen the worm bearing race nut.
13. Lift the piston-worm assembly from the valve housing. During removal hold the piston to prevent it from spinning off at the shaft.
14. Change the power steering valve centering shim.

15. Install the piston-worm assembly into the valve housing. Hold the piston worm to prevent it from spinning off of the shaft.

16. Install the worm bearing race nut and torque to 2–8 in. lbs. using tool T66P-3553-B or equivalent.

17. Install the race nut set screw (Allen head) through the valve housing.

18. Rotate the piston upward (back off) ½ turn and remove tool T66P-3553-C or equivalent.

19. Remove the valve housing, worm, and piston assembly from the holding fixture.

20. Position a new lube passage O-ring in the counterbore of the gear housing.

21. Apply vaseline to the teflon seal on the piston.

22. Place a new O-ring on the valve housing.

23. Slide the piston and valve into the gear housing being careful not to damage the teflon seal.

24. Align the lube passage in the valve housing with the one in the gear housing, and install but do not tighten the attaching bolts.

25. Rotate the ball nut so that the teeth are in the same place as the sector teeth. Tighten the four valve housing attaching bolts to 35–45 ft. lbs.

26. Position the sector shaft cover O-ring in the steering gear housing. Turn the input shaft as required to center the piston.

27. Apply vaseline to the sector shaft journal; then, position the sector shaft and cover assembly in the gear housing. Install the brake line bracket, steering gear identification tag and the two sector shaft cover attaching studs.

28. Position an in. lb. torque wrench on the gear input shaft and adjust the meshload to approximately 4 in. lbs. Then, torque the sector shaft cover attaching studs to 55–70 ft. lbs.

29. After the cover attaching bolts have been tightened to specification, adjust the mesh load to 17 in. lbs. with an in. lb. torque wrench.

STEERING GEAR DISASSEMBLY

1. Hold the steering gear over a drain pan in an inverted position and cycle the input shaft several times to drain the remaining fluid from the gear.

2. Mount the gear in a soft-jawed vise.

3. Remove the lock nut from the adjusting screw.

4. Turn the input shaft to either stop then, turn it back approximately 1¾ turns to center the gear.

5. Remove the two sector shaft cover attaching studs, the brake line bracket and the identification tag.

6. Tap the lower end of the sector shaft with a soft-hammer to loosen it, then lift the cover and shaft from the housing as an assembly. Discard the O-ring.

7. Turn the sector shaft cover counter-clockwise off the adjuster screw.

8. Remove the four valve housing attaching bolts. Lift the valve housing from the steering gear housing while holding the piston to prevent it from rotating off the worm shaft. Remove the valve housing and the lube passage O-rings and discard them.

9. Stand the valve body and piston on end with the piston end down. Rotate the input shaft counterclockwise out of the piston allowing the ball bearings to drop into the piston.

10. Place a cloth over the open end of the piston and turn it upside down to remove the balls.

11. Remove the two screws that attach the ball guide clamp to the ball nut and remove the clamp and the guides.

12. Install the valve body assembly in the holding fixture (do not clamp in a vise) and loosen the race nut screw (Allen head) from the valve housing and remove the worm bearing race nut.

13. Carefully slide the input shaft, worm and valve assembly out of the valve housing. Due to the close diametrical clearance between the spool and housing, the slightest cocking of the spool may cause it to jam in the housing.

14. Remove the shim from the valve housing bore.

Valve Housing

1. Remove the dust seal from the rear of the valve housing and discard the seal.

2. Remove the snap-ring from the valve housing.

3. Turn the fixture to place the valve housing in an inverted position.

4. Insert special tool in the valve body assembly opposite the seal end and gently tap the bearing and seal out of the housing. Discard the seal. Caution must be exercised when inserting and removing the tool to prevent damage to the valve bore in the housing.

5. Remove the fluid inlet and outlet tube seats with an EZ-out if they are damaged.

6. Coat the fluid inlet and outlet tube seats with vaseline and position them in the housing. Install and tighten the tube nuts to press the seats to the proper location.

7. Coat the bearing and seal surface of the housing with a film of vaseline.

8. Seat the bearing in the valve housing. Make sure that the bearing is free to rotate.

9. Dip the new oil seal in gear lubricant; then, place it in the housing with the metal side of the seal facing outward. Drive the seal into the housing until the outer edge of seal does not quite clear the snap-ring groove.

10. Place the snap-ring in the housing; then, drive on the ring until the snap-ring seats in its groove to properly locate the seal.

11. Place the dust seal in the housing with the dished side (rubber side) facing out. Drive the dust seal into place. The seal must be located behind the undercut in the input shaft when it is installed.

Worm and Valve

1. Remove the snap-ring from the end of the actuator.

2. Slide the control valve spool off the actuator.

3. Install the valve spool evenly and slowly with a slight oscillating motion into the flanged end of valve housing with the valve identification groove between the valve spool lands outward, checking for freedom of valve movement within the housing working area. The valve spool should enter

Steering gear housing and sector shaft seal assembly

the housing bore freely and fall by its own weight.

4. If the valve spool is not free, check for burrs at the outward edges of the working lands in the housing and remove with a hard stone.

5. Check the valve for burrs and if burrs are found, stone the valve in a radial direction only. Check for freedom of the valve again.

6. Remove the valve spool from the housing.

7. Slide the spool onto the actuator making sure that the groove in the spool annulus is toward the worm.

8. Install the snap-ring to retain the spool. The beveled ID of the snap-ring must be assembled toward the spool.

9. Check the clearance between the spool and the snap-ring. The clearance should be between .0005–.035 inch. If the clearance is not within these limits, select a snap-ring that will allow a clearance of .002 inch.

Piston and Ball Nut

1. Remove the teflon ring and the O-ring from the piston and ball nut.

2. Dip a new O-ring in gear lubricant and install it on the piston and ball nut.

3. Install a new teflon ring on the piston and ball nut being careful not to stretch it any more than necessary.

Steering Gear Housing

1. Remove the snap-ring and the spacer washer from the lower end of the steering gear housing.

2. Remove the lower seal from the housing. Lift the spacer washer from the housing.

3. Remove the upper seal in the same manner as the lower seal. Some housings require only one seal and one spacer.

4. Dip both sector shaft seals in gear lubricant.

5. Apply lubricant to the sector shaft seal bore of the housing and position the sector shaft inner seal into the housing with the lip facing inward. Press the seal into place. Place a spacer washer (0.090 inch) on top of the seal and apply more lubricant to the housing bore.

6. Place the outer seal in the housing with the lip facing inward and press it into place. Then, place a 0.090 inch spacer washer on top of the seal.

7. Position the snap-ring in the housing. Press the snap-ring into the housing to properly locate the seals and engage the snap-ring in the groove.

STEERING GEAR ASSEMBLY

Do not clean, wash, or soak seals in cleaning solvent.

1. Mount the valve housing in the holding fixture with the flanged end up.

2. Place the required thickness valve spool centering shim in the housing.

3. Carefully install the worm and valve in the housing.

4. Install the race nut in the housing and torque it to 42 ft. lbs.

5. Install the race nut set screw (Allen head) through the valve housing and torque to 20–25 in. lbs.

6. Place the piston on the bench with the ball guide holes facing up. Insert the worm shaft into the piston so that the first groove is in alignment with the hole nearest to the center of the piston.

7. Place the ball guide in the piston. Place the 27 to 29 balls, depending on the piston design, in the ball guide turning the worm in a clockwise direction as viewed from the input end of the shaft. If all of the balls have not been fed into the guide upon reaching the right stop, rotate the input shaft in one direction and then in the other while installing the balls. After the balls have been installed, do not rotate the input shaft or the piston more than 3½ turns off the right stop to prevent the balls from falling out of the circuit.

8. Secure the guides in the ball nut with the clamp.

9. Position a new lub passage O-ring in the counterbore of the gear housing.

10. Apply petroleum jelly to the teflon seal on the piston.

11. Place a new O-ring on the valve housing.

12. Slide the piston and valve into the gear housing being careful not to damage the teflon seal.

13. Align the lube passage in the valve housing with the one in the gear housing and install but do not tighten the attaching bolts.

14. Rotate the ball nut so that the teeth are in the same plane as the sector teeth. Tighten the four valve housing attaching bolts to 35–45 ft. lbs.

15. Position the sector shaft cover O-ring in the steering gear housing. Turn the input shaft as required to center the piston.

16. Apply vaseline to the sector shaft journal then position the sector shaft and cover assembly in the gear housing. Install the brake line bracket, the steering identification tag and two sector shaft cover attaching bolts. Torque the bolts to 55–70 ft. lbs.

17. Attach an in. lb. torque wrench to the input shaft. Adjust the mesh load to 17 in. lbs.

T/C Series Power Steering Pump

The TC Series Power Steering Pump is a vane type, constant displacement pump. This pump will use a remote fluid reservoir. A pressure relief valve inside the flow control valve limits pump pressure. The TC series pump will be used on the Isuzu Diesel Engine.

RETURN TUBE REMOVAL

1. Plug return tube to prevent chips from entering pump.

2. Use a tap, washers, and nut to remove damaged return tube.

INSTALLATION

1. Using Loctite® Solvent 75559 and Loctite® 290 adhesive, coat the end of new return tube.

2. Using a press, press tube into housing until bottomed.

BALL GUIDE —

FIRST GROOVE OF WORM SHOULD BE IN ALIGNMENT WITH THIS HOLE

Loading balls into the ball guide

1-HOUSING ASM., HYD. PUMP
2-SLEEVE, ASM.
3-PIN, DOWEL
4-SEAL, O-RING
5-SPRING, PRESSURE PLATE
6-SEAL, O-RING
7-PLATE, PRESSURE
8-PIN, PUMP RING DOWEL (2)
9-VANE (10)
10-ROTOR, PUMP
11-RING, PUMP
12-SEAL, O-RING
13-PLATE ASM. THRUST

14-RING, THRUST PLATE RETAINING
15-TUBE, RETURN
16-SEAL, DRIVE SHAFT
17-SHAFT, DRIVE
18-BEARING ASM., BALL
19-RING, RETAINING
20-SPRING, FLOW CONTROL

21-VALVE ASM., CONTROL
22-SEAL, O-RING
FITTING, O-RING UNION

TC Series—Power Steering Pump

Rotating Group removal

Control valve removal and installation

FITTING
Tighten to 75 N·m

ROTATING GROUP REMOVAL

1. Using a small punch in the access hole, remove the retaining ring.

2. Using a ⅝″ piece of bar stock or suitable brass drift, press on pressure plate hub from drive shaft side of housing until thrust plate can be removed.

3. The O-ring seal in housing must be removed next. It is now possible to remove the remaining parts of the rotating group from housing. It may still be necessary to use a press to remove the pressure plate.

4. Remove O-ring seal from the sleeve assembly and dispose.

INSTALLATION

1. Lubricate new O-ring seal and install into sleeve assembly.

2. Insert dowel pin in housing.

3. Install spring over sleeve assembly in housing.

4. Lubricate O-ring seal and install on pressure plate.

5. Mark top of pressure plate directly over dowel pin hole in plate. This will help line up hole with dowel pin.

6. Install pressure plate in housing. Be sure dowel pin and hole in pressure plate engage properly.

7. Install two (2) pump ring dowel pins in holes in pressure plate. Slide pump ring over these two pins. Be sure identification marks on pump ring are facing upward.

8. Install rotor with counter bore side toward drive shaft end of housing. Add ten vanes.

9. Lubricate O-ring seal and install in housing.

10. Install thrust plate in housing, making sure that dimples in thrust plate line up with bolt holes in housing and that thrust plate engages pump ring dowel pins.

11. Using a press, press on thrust plate far enough to install retaining ring.

12. Install retaining ring with opening of ring centered with bolt hole in housing nearest to access hole.

DRIVE SHAFT & BEARING REMOVAL

1. Remove retaining ring with snap ring pliers.
2. Remove drive shaft and bearing assembly.
3. Remove the bearing using a press.

INSTALLATION

1. Using a press, install the bearing on the driveshaft.
2. Slide bearing assembly into housing while rotating drive shaft so shaft serrations engage with rotor.
3. Bottom bearing in housing.

4. Install retaining ring with beveled side outward.

CONTROL VALVE REMOVAL & INSTALLATION

1. Remove the fitting and O-ring.
2. Remove the control valve assembly.
3. Remove the flow control spring.
4. Replace damaged or defective parts.
5. Installation is the reverse of removal.

DRIVE SHAFT SEAL REMOVAL & INSTALLATION

1. Using a seal puller carefully remove the seal from the housing.

2. Check housing for damage.
3. Install the new seal using a suitable socket. Drive the seal into the housing until it bottoms.

SLEEVE ASSEMBLY REMOVAL & INSTALLATION

1. Remove the driveshaft and bearing assembly as previously outlined.
2. From the driveshaft side of the housing remove sleeve assembly using a punch.
3. Using a suitable socket, press sleeve assembly into housing from pressure plate side.
4. Be sure sleeve assembly is fully seated in housing.

Return Tube removal and installation

Seal Removal

Wheel Alignment

SUSPENSION & ALIGNMENT TROUBLE DIAGNOSIS

UNEVEN TIRE WEAR

1. Tire pressures low
2. Excessive camber
3. Tires out of balance
4. Tires overloaded
5. Out of round tires and rims
6. Caster incorrect
7. Toe-in incorrect
8. High speed driving into turns
9. Unequal tire size
10. Improper tracking
11. Bent or worn steering and suspension components

STEERING WHEEL SPOKE POSITION NOT PROPERLY CENTERED

1. Steering gear set off "high-spot"
2. Improper toe-in
3. Relationship between lengths of tie-rods not equal
4. Bent steering components
5. Steering wheel improperly placed on steering shaft

HARD STEERING

1. Tire pressure low
2. Wheel spindle bent
3. Steering assembly binding or maladjusted
4. Tie rod ends tight
5. Caster excessive
6. Kingpins or ball joints too tight
7. Lack of lubrication to steering and suspension units

SHIMMY

1. Tire pressure incorrect
2. Tires of unequal size
3. Loose wheel bearings
4. Loose steering arms or steering gear adjustment
5. Steering gear loose on frame
6. Loose or broken steering linkage rods or internal adjustment parts
7. Spring shackles loose
8. Ball joints or kingpins and bushings worn
9. Front end alignment out of specifications
10. Wheels and tires out of balance
11. Wheels and tires out of round or loose on hub
12. Shock absorbers worn out
13. U-bolts loose on axle to spring
14. Worn or out-of-round brake drum or rotor (shimmy felt upon brake application)

WANDER OR WEAVE

1. Tire pressure incorrect
2. Tires of unequal size
3. Bent spindle
4. Wheel bearings loose or worn
5. Kingpins worn or bent
6. Kingpins tight in steering knuckle or bushings
7. Steering gear assembly too tight or too loose
8. Too little caster
9. Too much or too little camber
10. Too much or too little toe-in
11. Front axle bent or shifted
12. Springs broken

13. Frame diamond shaped
14. Rear axle housing shifted or bent
15. Steering linkage tight or binding
16. Lack of lubrication to front suspension or steering linkage
17. Defective power steering assembly

FRONT END RIDES HARD

1. Improper tire pressure
2. Springs broken or too stiff
3. Shock absorbers too stiff or malfunctioning
4. Front end alignment incorrect
5. Loose suspension components

VEHICLE STEERS TO ONE SIDE AT ALL TIMES

1. Incorrect caster setting
2. Incorrect camber setting
3. Incorrect kingpin inclination or wheel support angle
4. Unequal tire pressure or tire size
5. One side brake drag
6. Unequal shock absorber control
7. Bent or damaged steering and suspension components
8. Uneven or weak spring condition, front or rear
9. Broken center or shackle bolts
10. Frame bent causing improper tracking

NOISY FRONT END

1. Lack of, or improper lubrication
2. Loose steering linkage
3. Loose suspension parts
4. Loose brake parts
5. Worn universal (FWD)
6. Worn differential (FWD)
7. Loose sheet metal

LUBRICATION LEAKING INTO DRUM OR ON ROTOR

1. Excessive differential lubricant (FWD)
2. Clogged axle housing vent (FWD)
3. Damaged or worn universal drive-shaft oil seal (FWD)
4. Loose steering knuckle flange bearings (FWD)
5. Defective outer seal
6. Rough spindle to oil seal surface
7. Wheel bearings overpacked or use of wrong lubricate
8. Clogged oil slinger drain
9. Cracked steering knuckle outer flange

EXCESSIVE TIRE WEAR

1. Incorrect wheel alignment
2. Failure to rotate tires
3. Improper tire inflation
4. Overload or improperly loaded vehicle
5. High tire temperature operation
6. Excessive speed, quick starts and quick stops
7. Bent suspension, frame or wheel parts
8. Tires out of balance
9. Uneven brake application

Wheel Alignment

For a truck to have safe steering control with a minimum of tire wear, certain established rules must be followed. These rules fix the values of planes, angles and radii relative to each other and to truck and tire dimensions. Some factors are built in, with no provision for adjustment; others are adjustable within limits. The entire system depends upon all value factors, separately and combined. It is therefore difficult to change some of the established settings without influencing others.

This system is called steering geometry or wheel alignment and requires a complete check of all the factors involved. Definitions of these factors and the effect each one has on the truck are given in the following paragraphs.

STEERING WHEEL POSITION

Always check steering wheel alignment in conjunction with and at the same time as toe-in. In fact, the steering wheel spoke position, with the truck on a straight section of highway, may be the first indication of front end misalignment.

If the truck has been wrecked, or indicates any evidence of steering gear or linkage disturbance, the Pitman arm should be disconnected from the sector shaft. The steering wheel (or gear) should be turned from extreme right to extreme left to determine the halfway point in its turning scope.

This will be the spot on the gear that is in action during straight ahead driving and in which position the steering gear should be adjusted. With the steering wheel in the straight-ahead position and the steering gear adjusted to zero lash status, reconnect the Pitman arm.

Steering Geometry

CAMBER ANGLE

Camber is the amount that the front wheels are inclined outward or inward at the top. Camber is spoken of, and measured, in degrees from the perpendicular.

The purpose of the camber angle is to take some of the load off the spindle outboard bearing.

CASTER ANGLE

Caster is the amount that the kingpin (or in the case of trucks without king-pins, the knuckle support pivots) is tilted towards the back or front of the truck. Caster is usually spoken of, and measured, in degrees. Positive caster means that the top of the kingpin is tilted toward the back of the truck. Positive caster is indicated by the sign +.

Negative caster is exactly the opposite; the top of the kingpin is tilted toward the front of the truck. This is generally indicated by the sign −. Negative caster is sometimes referred to as reverse caster.

The effect of positive caster is to cause the truck to steer in the direction in which it tends to go. Positive caster in the front wheels may cause the truck to steer down off a crowned road or steer in the direction of a cross wind. For this reason, a number of our modern trucks are arranged with negative caster so that the opposite is true; the truck tends to steer up a crowned road and into a cross wind.

CASTER ANGLE CORRECTION

Caster angle specifications are based on the vehicle load limits, which will usually result in a level frame.

Since load requirements may vary, the frame does not always remain level and must be considered when determining the correct caster angle.

To measure the frame angle, the vehicle should be on a smooth and level surface. Place a bubble protractor on the frame rail and measure the degree of frame tilt and in what direction, either front or rear.

Two methods of determining caster angles are used. The first method is to determine the caster angle from the wheel with alignment equipment, and the second method is to obtain the desired caster angle from the specification charts. The frame angle is then added to or subtracted from the caster angles as necessary. The two methods are outlined.

First Method

1. Determine the frame angle
   a. Frame high at rear—frame angle is negative.
   b. Frame low at rear—frame angle is positive.
2. Determine the caster angle at the wheel with the alignment checking equipment.
3. Add or subtract frame angle from or to the determined caster angle.
   a. Negative frame angle is added to positive caster angle.
   b. Positive frame angle is subtracted from positive caster angle.
   c. Negative frame angle is subtracted from negative caster angle.
   d. Positive frame angle is added to negative caster angle.
4. Determine the corrected caster angle and the specified caster angle and correct on the vehicle. Use the following examples as guides.

EXAMPLE NO. 1 (FRAME LOWER AT REAR—POSITIVE)

Measured wheel caster angle	+2°
Frame angle	3°
Actual caster angle (Frame at zero degrees)	−1°
Specifications (desired)	+2°
Necessary degrees to change	+3°

EXAMPLE NO. 2 (FRAME HIGHER AT REAR—NEGATIVE)

Measured wheel caster angle	+2°
Frame angle	2°
Actual caster angle (Frame at zero degrees)	+4°
Specifications (desired)	+3°
Necessary degrees to change	−1°

Second Method

1. Measure the frame angle.
   a. Front of frame down—frame angle positive.
   b. Front of frame up—frame angle negative.
2. From the specifications, determine the specified or desired caster setting.
3. Add or subtract the frame angle from the specified caster setting.
   a. Positive frame angle is subtracted from the specified setting.
   b. Negative frame angle is added to the specified caster setting.
4. Using wheel alignment equipment, obtain the measured caster angle from the wheel and determine the corrected specified setting, using the following examples as guides.

EXAMPLE NO. 3 (FRONT OF FRAME LOWER—POSITIVE)

Specified setting	+1°
Frame angle (positive—subtract)	−1°
Corrected specified setting	0°
Reading obtained from wheel	−1°
Adjust wheel to corrected specified setting of—	0°

EXAMPLE NO. 4 (FRONT OF FRAME HIGHER—NEGATIVE)

Specified setting	+2°
Frame angle (negative—add)	1°
Corrected specified setting	+3°
Reading obtained from wheel	+2°
Adjust to corrected specified setting of—	+3°

Angle of Kingpin Inclination

In addition to the caster angle, the kingpins (or knuckle support pivots) are also inclined toward each other at the top. This angle is known as kingpin inclination and is usually spoken of, and measured, in degrees.

The effect of kingpin inclination is to cause the wheels to steer in a straight line regardless of outside forces such as crowned roads, cross winds, etc., which may tend to make it steer at a tangent. As the spindle is moved from extreme right to extreme left it apparently rises and falls. Notice that it reaches its highest position when the wheels are in the straight-ahead position. In actual operation, the spindle cannot rise and fall because the wheel is in constant contact with the ground.

Therefore, the truck itself will rise at the extreme right turn and come to its lowest point at the straight-ahead position, and again rise for an extreme left turn. The weight of the truck will tend to cause the wheels to come to the straight-ahead position, which is the lowest position of the truck itself.

INCLUDED ANGLE

Included angle is the name given to that angle which includes kingpin inclination and camber. It is the relationship between the centerline of the wheel and the centerline of the kingpin (or the knuckle support pivots). This angle is built into the knuckle (spindle) forging and will remain constant throughout the life of the truck, unless the spindle itself is damaged.

When checking a truck on the front end stand, always measure kingpin inclination as well as camber unless some provision is made on the stand for checking condition of the spindle. Where no such provision is made, add the kingpin inclination to the camber for each side of the truck. These totals should be exactly the same, regard-less of how far from the norm the readings may be.

For example the left side of the truck checks 5½° kingpin inclination and 1° positive camber—total 6½°. Since both sides check exactly the same for the included angle, it is unlikely that both spindles, in this instance, are bent. Adjusting to correct for camber will automatically set correct kingpin inclination.

A bent spindle would show up like this: left side of the truck has ¾° positive camber. 5¼° kingpin inclination—total 6° included angle. Right side of truck has 1¼° positive camber, 6° kingpin inclination—total 7¼° included angle. One of these spindles is bent and if adjustments are made to correct camber, the kingpin inclination will be incorrect due to the bent spindle.

Since the most common cause of a bent spindle is striking the curb when parking, which causes the spindle to bend upward, the side having the greater included angle usually has the bent spindle. It will be found impossible to achieve good alignment and minimum tire wear unless the bent spindle is replaced.

Toe-in

Toe-in is the amount that the front wheels are closer together at the front than they are at the back. This dimension is usually spoken of, and measured, in inches or fractions of inches.

Generally speaking, the wheels are toed-in because they are cambered. When a truck operates with 0° camber it will be found to operate with zero toe-in. As the required camber increases, so does the toe-in. The reason for this is that the cambered wheel tends to steer in the direction in which it is cambered. Therefore it is necessary to overcome this tendency of the wheel by compensating very slightly in the direction opposite to that in which it tends to roll. Caster and camber both have an effect on toe-in. Therefore toe-in is the last thing on the front end which should be corrected.

TOE-OUT STEERING RADIUS

When a truck is steered into a turn, the outside wheel of the vehicle scribes a much larger circle than the inside wheel. Therefore, the outside wheel must be steered to a somewhat less angle than the inside wheel. This difference in angle is often called toe-out.

The change in angle from toe-in in the straight-ahead position to toe-out in the turn is caused by the relative position of the steering arms to the kingpin and to each other.

If a line were drawn from the center of the kingpin through the center of the steering arm-tie rod attaching hole at each wheel, these lines would be found to cross almost exactly in the center of the rear axle.

If the front end angles, including toe-in, are set correctly, and the toe-out is found to be incorrect, one or both of the steering arms are bent.

Tracking

While tracking is more a function of the rear axle and frame, it is difficult to align the front suspension when the truck does not track straight. Tracking means that the centerline of the rear axle follows exactly the path of the centerline of the front axle when the truck is moving in a straight line.

On trucks that have equal tread, front and rear, the rear tires will follow in exactly the tread of the front tires, when moving in a straight line. However, there are many trucks whose rear tread is wider than the front tread. On such trucks, the rear axle tread will straddle the front axle tread an equal amount on both sides, when moving in a straight line.

Perhaps the easiest way to check a truck for tracking is to stand directly in back of it and watch it move in a straight line down the street. If the observer will stand as near to the center of the truck as possible, he can readily observe, even with the difference in perspective between the front and rear wheels, whether or not they are tracking properly. If the truck is found to track incorrectly, the difficulty will be found in either the frame or in the rear axle alignment.

Another more accurate method to check tracking is to park the truck on a level floor and drop a plumb-line from the extreme outer edge of the front suspension lower A-frame. Use the same drop point on each side of the truck. Make a chalk line where the plumb-line strikes the floor. Do the same with the rear axle, selecting a point on the rear axle housing for the plumb-line.

Measure diagonally from the left rear mark to the right front mark and from the right rear mark to the left front mark. These two diagonal measurements should be exactly the same. A ¼" variation is acceptable.

If the diagonal measurements taken are different, measure from the right rear mark to the right front mark and from the left rear to the left front. These two measurements should also be the same within ¼".

If the diagonal measurements are different, but the longitudinal measurements are the same, the frame is swayed (diamond shaped).

However, in the event that the diagonal measurements are unequal and the longitudinal measurements are also unequal, and the truck is tracking incorrectly, the rear axle is misaligned.

If the diagonal and longitudinal measurements are both unequal, but the truck appears to track correctly on the street, a kneeback is indicated.

NOTE: A kneeback means that one complete side of the front suspension is bent back. This is often caused by crimping the front wheels against the curb when parking the vehicle, then starting up without straightening the wheels out.

DOMESTIC TRUCKS
Chevrolet and GMC

Year / Chevrolet Model (A)	GMC Model (A)	Adj. Ill. No.	Caster @ Height Measurement (Degrees) — Suspension Height Measurement (M) 1½	2	2½	3	3½	3¾	4	Camber (Degrees) Min	Pref.	Max.	Toe-in (Inches)	Toe-in (Millimeters)
1982–84 S-10 (4 × 2)	S-15 (4 × 2)	(1)	①	①	①	①	①	①	①	0	13/16	1⅝	⅛	3.2
S-10 (4 × 4)	S-15 (4 × 4)	(2)	①	①	①	①	①	①	①	0	13/16	1⅝	⅛	3.2
1982–84 C-10	C-1500	(3)	—	—	3⅝	3⅛	2⅝	2⅜	2	0	11/16	1⅜	3/16 ± ⅛	4.8 ± 3.2
C-20,30	C-2500,3500	(3)	—	—	1½	15/16	5/16	⅛	0	−½	3/16	⅞	3/16 ± ⅛	4.8 ± 3.2
1982–84 K-10,20	K-1500,2500	N/A	—	—	8	8	8	8	8	5/16	1	1 11/16	3/16 ± ⅛	4.8 ± 3.2
K-30	K-3500	N/A	—	—	8	8	8	8	8	−3/16	½	1 3/16	3/16 ± ⅛	4.8 ± 3.2
1982–84 G-10,20	G-1500,2500	(3)	3½	3⅛	2 11/16	2⅜	2⅛	1 15/16	1⅞	−3/16	½	1 3/16	3/16 ± ⅛	4.8 ± 3.2
G-30	G-3500	(3)	2⅞	2 3/16	1⅝	1	½	3/16	0	−½	3/16	⅞	3/16 ± ⅛	4.8 ± 3.2
1982–84 P-10	P-1500	(3)	—	—	2 5/16	1 11/16	1 3/16	15/16	⅝	−½	3/16	⅞	3/16 ± ⅛	4.8 ± 3.2
P-20,30	P-2500,3500	(3)	—	—	2 5/16	1 11/16	1 3/16	15/16	⅝	−½	3/16	⅞	3/16 ± ⅛	4.8 ± 3.2
1982–84 P30 Motor Home	P-3500 Motor Home	(3)	—	—	5½	5	4⅜	4⅛	3⅞	−½	3/16	⅞	5/16 ± ⅛	7.9 ± 3.2
1980–81 G-10,20	G-1500,2500	(3)	3½	3⅛	2 11/16	2 13/32	2⅛	1 13/16	—	−3/16	½	1 3/16	3/16 ± ⅛	4.8 ± 3.2
G-30	G-3500	(3)	2 3/16	2 3/16	1⅝	1	½	0	—	−½	3/16	⅞	3/16 ± ⅛	4.8 ± 3.2
1979–81 C-10	C-1500	(3)	—	—	2 13/32	1 13/32	1 3/16	11/16	3/16	−½	3/16	1⅞	3/16 ± ⅛	4.8 ± 3.2
C-20,30	C-2500,3500	(3)	—	—	1½	29/32	5/16	0	−11/16	−½	3/16	⅞	3/16 ± ⅛	4.8 ± 3.2
K-10,20	K-1500,2500	N/A	—	—	8	8	8	8	8	5/16	1	1 11/16	0 ± ⅛	0 ± 3.2
K-30	K-3500	N/A	—	—	8	8	8	8	8	−3/16	½	1 3/16	0 ± ⅛	0 ± 3.2
P-10	P-1500	(3)	—	—	2 5/16	1 11/16	1 3/16	⅝	⅛	−½	3/16	⅞	3/16 ± ⅛	4.8 ± 3.2
P-20,30 (B)	P-2500,3500 (B)	(3)	—	2 29/32	2 11/16	1 11/16	1 3/16	⅝	3/16	−½	3/16	⅞	3/16 ± ⅛	4.8 ± 3.2
P-30 Motor Home (B)	P-3500 Motor Home (B)		—	—	5½	5	4 13/32	3 13/16	3 5/16	−½	3/16	⅞	5/16 ± ⅛	7.9 ± 3.2
1979 G-10,20	G-1500,2500	(3)	2 29/32	2 5/16	2	1⅝	1 5/16	29/32	—		N/A		3/16 ± ⅛	4.8 ± 3.2
G-30	G-3500	(3)	3 13/32	2 11/16	2⅛	1½	1	13/32	—		N/A		3/16 ± ⅛	4.8 ± 3.2
1977–78 C-10	C-1500	(3)		2	1¼	¾	¼	0	−½		¼		3/16 ± ⅛	4.8 ± 3.2
1977–78 C-20,30	C-2500,3500	(3)	1½	1	½	0	−½	¾	−1		¼		3/16 ± ⅛	4.8 ± 3.2
1977–78 K-10,20	K-1500,2500, 3500	N/A	8	8	8	8	8	8	8		¼		0 ± ⅛	0 ± 3.2
1978 G-10,20	G-1500,2500	(3)	3¼	2¾	2½	2	1¾	1½	1½		¼		3/16 ± ⅛	4.8 ± 3.2
G-30	G-3500	(3)	2¼	1½	1	½	0	−¼	−½		¼		3/16 ± ⅛	4.8 ± 3.2
1977–78 P-10	P-1500	(3)	2½	2	1½	¾	¼	0	−¼		See Camber/ Height Chart		3/16 ± ⅛	4.8 ± 3.2
P-20,30	P-2500,3500	(3)	2½	2	1½	¾	¼	0	−¼		See Camber/ Height Chart		3/16 ± ⅛	4.8 ± 3.2
1977 G-10,20,30	G-1500,2500, 3500	(3)	2¼	1½	1	½	0	−¼	−½		¼		3/16 ± ⅛	4.8 ± 3.2

With vehicle level, measure frame angle with a bubble protractor. Record the suspension height measurement.

a. Subtract an up-in-rear frame angle from a positive caster specification.

b. Subtract a down-in-rear frame angle from a negative caster specification.

c. Add an up-in-rear frame angle to a negative caster specification.

d. Add a down-in-rear frame angle to a positive caster specification.

(A) Vehicle height must be checked and corrected before alignment is performed.

① 1° Min. 2° Pref. 3° Max.

Chevrolet and GMC

Vehicle Identification			Adj. Ill. No.	Chamber @ Height Measurement (Degrees) Suspension Height Measurement (MM)										
Chevrolet Year Model		GMC Model		2½	2½	2¾	3½	3¾	4	4¼	4½	4¾	5	5¼
1977–78 P-10		P-1500	(3)	0	0	¼	¼	¼	¼	0	0	0	– ¼	– ½
P-20, 30		P-2500, 3500	(3)	0	0	¼	¼	¼	¼	¼	0	0	– ¼	– ½

FRONT SUSPENSION HEIGHT S10/S15 (4 × 4)

CROSS MEMBER

4.8″

LOWER BALL JOINT

FRONT SUSPENSION HEIGHT 1983 S10/S15 (4 × 2)

4.8″

CROSS MEMBER

FRONT

BUMPER

SUSPENSION HEIGHT MEASUREMENT (M)

Chevrolet/GMC measuring points

Dodge and Plymouth

Vehicle Identification Year Model	Adj. Ill. No.	Caster (B) (Degrees)			Camber (Degrees)			Toe-In (A) (Inches)			Toe-In (A) (Millimeters)			Toe-Out On Turns (Degrees) Outside Inside		Strg. Axis Incl. (Deg.)
		Min.	Pref.	Max.	Min.	Pref.	Max.	Min.	Pref.	Max.	Min.	Pref.	Max.	Wheel	Wheel	
1981–84 B100, 200 300; PB100, 200, 300; MB300, 400 CB300, 400	(4)	1¼	2¼	3¼	0	½	1	0	⅛	¼	0.0	3.2	6.0	NA	NA	NA
1983–84 Ramcharger 4 × 2, D-150, D-250, D350	(2)	– ½	½	1½	0	½	1	1/16	⅛	3/16	0.0	3.2	4.8	33	33	NA
1979–82 Ramcharger 4 × 2 Trail Duster 4 × 2, D100, 150, 200, 250, 300, 350	(2)	– ½	½	1½	0	¼	1	0	⅛	¼	0	3.2	6.4	33	33	8½

Dodge and Plymouth

Vehicle Identification Year Model	Adj. Ill. No.	Caster (B) (Degrees) Min.	Pref.	Max.	Camber (Degrees) Min.	Pref.	Max.	Toe-In (A) (Inches) Min.	Pref.	Max.	Toe-In (A) (Millimeters) Min.	Pref.	Max.	Toe-Out On Turns (Degrees) Outside Wheel	Inside Wheel	Strg. Axis Incl. (Deg.)
1983–84 Ramcharger 4 × 4, W-150, W-250, W-350	(5)	½	2	3½	½	1	1½	⅛	¼	⅜	3.2	6.4	9.5	①	①	8.5
1979–82 W150, 200, Ramcharger 4 × 4, Trail Duster 4 × 4	(5)		3			1½		⅛ (out)		⅛ (in)	3.2 (out)		3.2 (in)	NA	NA	8½
1979–82 W200, W250 w/extra equip., W300, W350, W400	(5)		3			½		⅛ (out)		⅛ (in)	3.2 (out)		3.2 (in)	NA	NA	8½
1977–80 B100, 200, 300, PB100, 200, 300; MB300, 400; CB300, CB400	(4)	1¼	2¼	3¼	0	½	1	0	⅛	¼	0	3.2	6.4	NA	NA	NA
w/Heavy Front Axle Load	(4)	¼		2¾	– ¼	⅜	1	⅛ (out)	0	⅛ (in)	3.2 (out)	0.0	3.2 (in)	NA	NA	NA
1978 D100, 200, 300	(2)	– ½	½	1½		¼		⅛ (out)	0	⅛ (in)	3.2 (out)	0	3.2 (in)	NA	NA	NA
1977–78 Ramcharger 4 × 2, Trail Duster 4 × 2	(2)	– ½	½	1½	0	¼	1	0	⅛	¼	0	3.2	6.4	NA	NA	NA
Ramcharger 4 × 4, Trail Duster 4 × 4 W100, 200	(5)	1½	3	4½	1	1½	2	⅛ (out)	0	⅛ (in)	3.2 (out)	0	3.2 (in)	NA	NA	8½
1977–78 W200 w/extra equip., W300, W400	(5)	1½	3	4½	0	½	1	⅛ (out)	0	⅛ (in)	3.2 (out)	0	3.2 (in)	NA	NA	8½
1977 D100, 200, 300	(2)	– ½	½	1½	0	¼	1	0	⅛	¼	0	3.2	6.4	NA	NA	NA

(A) Engines must be running on vehicles equipped with power steering when centering the steering wheel and setting toe.
(B) Caster shown is for unladen vehicles. Caster will vary with increased load. If loaded vehicle wanders, increase caster. If loaded vehicle is hard to steer in corners, decrease caster.
① Varies with ride height.

Ford

Year, Model and Axle Part Number Ride Height Min.	Max.	Adj. Ill. No.	Caster (Degrees) Min.	Max.	Camber (Degrees) Min.	Max.	Toe-In (Inches)	Toe-In (Millimeters)
1983–84 Ranger, 4 × 2 (1)(3)(6)		(6)	(4)	(4)				
2¾	3¼		4½	7	– 1	1	1/32	0.8
3¼	3½		4	6½	– ½	1¾	1/32	0.8
3½	4		3⅜	5⅞	0	2⅜	1/32	0.8
4	4¼		2⅝	5⅛	¾	3	1/32	0.8
4¼	4¾		2	4½	1½	3¾	1/32	0.8

Ford

Year, Model and Axle Part Number Ride Height		Adj. Ill. No.	Caster (Degrees)		Camber (Degrees)		Toe-In (Inches)	Toe-In (Millimeters)
Min.	Max.		Min.	Max.	Min.	Max.		
1983–84								
Ranger, Bronco II								
4 × 4(1)(3)(6)		NA	(4)	(4)	(4)	(4)		
2¾	3¼		5	8	− 1	½	1/32	0.8
3¼	3½		4	7	0	1½	1/32	0.8
3½	4		3	6	½	2	1/32	0.8
4	4¼		2½	5½	1¼	2¾	1/32	0.8
4¼	4¾		1¾	5	2	3¾	1/32	0.8
1983–84								
F250, 350, 4 × 2(1)(3)(A)			(4)	(4)				
2½	2¾		5½	7	− ½	½	1/32	0.8
2¾	3¼		5	6	− ½	1½	1/32	0.8
3¼	3½		4	5	¼	2¼	1/32	0.8
3½	4		3	4	1	3	1/32	0.8
4	4¼		(7)	(7)	2	3½	1/32	0.8
1981–82 F-250, 350,								
4 × 2(1)(3)		N/A	(4)	(4)	(4)	(4)		
2	2¼		5¾	9	− 2½	0	1/32	0.8
2¼	2¾		4¾	8	− 1½	1	1/32	0.8
2¼	3¼		3¾	7	− ¼	1¾	1/32	0.8
3¼	3¾		2¾	6	¼	2¾	1/32	0.8
3½	4		1¾	5	1	3½	1/32	0.8
4	4¼		¾	4	2	4½	1/32	0.8
1983–84								
F-250, 350, 4 × 4								
(1)(3)(A)			(4)	(4)	(4)	(4)		
5	5½		31/16	5⅛	− 1¾	¾	1/32	0.8
5½	6		3⅛	5¼	− ¾	1¾	1/32	0.8
6	6¼		3¼	5⅜	¼	3	1/32	0.8
6¼	6¾		3⅜	5½	1½	4	1/32	0.8
6¾	7		3½	5½	2½	4¼	1/32	0.8
1981–82								
F-250, 350 4 × 4								
(1)(3)		N/A	(4)	(4)				
4¾	5		3	5	4¾	5	1/32	0.8
5	5½		3⅛	5⅛	− 1¾	¾	1/32	0.8
5½	6		3⅛	5⅛	− ¾	1¾	1/32	0.8
6	6¼		3¼	5¼	¼	2¾	1/32	0.8
6¼	6¾		3⅜	5⅜	1¼	4	1/32	0.8
6¾	7		3½	5½	2½	5	1/32	0.8
1983–84 E-100,								
150(1)(3)		(6)						
3¾	4		—	—	− ¾	¾	1/32	0.8
4	4½		4½	5¼	− ⅝	1⅝	1/32	0.8
4½	5		3¼	4	⅜	2⅝	1/32	0.8
5	5½		2	2¾	1¼	3⅝	1/32	0.8
5½	5¾		¾	2¼	2¼	4⅛	1/32	0.8
1981–82 E-100,								
150(1)(3)		N/A						
3¼	3½		6¼	8	− 1¾	− ¼	1/32	0.8
3½	3¾		5¾	7¼	− 1½	¼	1/32	0.8
3¾	4		5	6¾	− 1	¾	1/32	0.8
4	4¼		4½	5¾	− ½	1¼	1/32	0.8
4¼	4½		4	5¼	0	1¾	1/32	0.8
4½	4¾		3¼	4½	½	2¼	1/32	0.8
4¾	5		2½	4	1	2¾	1/32	0.8
5	5¼		2	3¼	1½	3¼	1/32	0.8
5¼	5½		1½	2¾	2	3¾	1/32	0.8
1983–84								
F-100, 150,								
4 × 2(1)(3)(A)		(6)	(4)	(4)				
2¾	3¼		5½	7½	− 1½	¾	1/32	0.8
3¼	3½		5	6	− ¾	1½	1/32	0.8
3½	4		4¼	5¼	¼	2½	1/32	0.8
4	4¼		3¼	4¼	1	3½	1/32	0.8
4¼	4¾		2½	3½	2	4½	1/32	0.8

WHEEL ALIGNMENT

Ford

Year, Model and Axle Part Number Ride Height Min.	Max.	Adj. Ill. No.	Caster (Degrees) Min.	Max.	Camber (Degrees) Min.	Max.	Toe-In (Inches)	Toe-In (Millimeters)
1981–82								
F-100, F-150 4 × 2(1)(3)		N/A	(4)	(4)	(4)	(4)		
2¼	2¾		6	10	−3	− ½	1/32	0.8
2¾	3¼		5	9	−2	½	1/32	0.8
3¼	3½		4	8	−1¼	1¼	1/32	0.8
3½	4		3	7	− ¼	2¼	1/32	0.8
4	4¼		2	6	½	3	1/32	0.8
4¼	4¾		1	5	1½	4	1/32	0.8
1980								
F-100, 150 4 × 2(1)(2)		N/A	(4)	(4)	(4)	(4)		
2¼	2¾		6	10	−3	− ½	3/32	2.4
2¾	3¼		5	9	−2	½	3/32	2.4
3¼	3½		4	8	−1¼	1¼	3/32	2.4
3½	4		3	7	− ¼	2¼	3/32	2.4
4	4¼		2	6	½	3	3/32	2.4
4¼	4¾		1	5	1½	4	3/32	2.4
1981–82								
F-150, Bronco 4 × 4(1)(3)			(4)	(4)				
2¾	3¼		6	9	−2½	− ¼	1/32	0.8
3¼	3½		5	8	−1¾	½	1/32	0.8
3½	4		4	7	− ¾	1½	1/32	0.8
4	4¼		3	6	0	2¼	1/32	0.8
4¼	4¾		2	5	1	3¼	1/32	0.8
4¾	5		1	4	1¾	4	1/32	0.8
1983–84								
F-150, Bronco 4 × 4								
4 × 4(1)(3)		(6)	(4)	(4)				
3¼	3½		6	7	−1½	¾	1/32	0.8
3½	4		5	6	− ¾	1¾	1/32	0.8
4	4¼		4	5	¼	2¾	1/32	0.8
4¼	4¾		3	4	1¼	3½	1/32	0.8
1980								
F-150, Bronco 4 × 4(1)(2)			(4)	(4)				
2¾	3¼		6	9	−2½	− ¼	3/32	2.4
3¼	3½		5	8	−1¾	½	3/32	2.4
3½	4		4	7	− ¾	1½	3/32	2.4
4	4¼		3	6	0	2¼	3/32	2.4
4¼	4¾		2	5	1	3¼	3/32	2.4
4¾	5		1	4	1¾	4	3/32	2.4
1983–84								
E-250, 350(1)(3)		N/A						
3¾	4		—	—	− ⅝	⅞	1/32	0.8
4	4½		7¼	8	− ½	1⅞	1/32	0.8
4½	5		6	6¾	½	2⅞	1/32	0.8
5	5½		4¾	5½	1½	3⅞	1/32	0.8
5½	5¾		3¼	4	2½	4⅜	1/32	0.8
1980–82								
E-250, 350(1)(3)		N/A						
3¼	3½		9	10½	−1¾	− ¼	1/32	0.8
3½	3¾		8½	9¾	−1½	¼	1/32	0.8
3¾	4		7⅞	9	−1	¾	1/32	0.8
4	4¼		7⅛	8½	− ½	1¼	1/32	0.8
4¼	4½		6½	7¾	0	1¾	1/32	0.8
4½	4¾		5¾	7	½	2¼	1/32	0.8
4¾	5		5¼	6½	1	2¾	1/32	0.8
5	5¼		4⅝	6	1½	3¼	1/32	0.8
5¼	5½		4	5½	2	3¾	1/32	0.8
1980								
F-250, 350 4 × 2(1)(3)		N/A	(4)	(4)	(4)	(4)		
2	2¼		5¼	9	−2½	0	1/32	0.8
2¼	2¾		4¾	8	−1½	1	1/32	0.8
2¾	2¼		3¾	7	− ¾	1¾	1/32	0.8
3¼	3½		2¾	6	¼	2¾	1/32	0.8
3½	4		1¾	5	1	3½	1/32	0.8
4	4¼		¾	4	2	4½	1/32	0.8
1980								
F-250, 350 4 × 4(1)(2)		(6)	(4)	(4)				
4¼	4¾		3½	5¾	−4	−1¼	3/32	2.4
4¾	5		3¼	5½	−2¾	0	3/32	2.4
5	5½		3	5¼	−1½	1¼	3/32	2.4
5½	6		2¾	5	− ¼	2½	3/32	2.4
6	6¼		2½	4¾	1	3¾	3/32	2.4
6¼	6¾		2¼	4½	2¼	5	3/32	2.4

Ford

Year, Model and Axle Part Number Ride Height Min.	Max.	Adj. Ill. No.	Caster (Degrees) Min.	Max.	Camber (Degrees) Min.	Max.	Toe-In (Inches)	Toe-In (Millimeters)
1980								
E-100, 150(1)(5)		N/A						
$3\frac{1}{4}$	$3\frac{1}{2}$		$6\frac{1}{4}$	8	$-1\frac{3}{4}$	$-\frac{1}{4}$	$\frac{1}{4}$	6.4
$3\frac{1}{2}$	$3\frac{3}{4}$		$5\frac{3}{4}$	$7\frac{1}{4}$	$-1\frac{1}{2}$	$\frac{1}{4}$	$\frac{1}{4}$	6.4
$3\frac{3}{4}$	4		5	$6\frac{3}{4}$	-1	$\frac{3}{4}$	$\frac{1}{4}$	6.4
4	$4\frac{1}{4}$		$4\frac{1}{2}$	$5\frac{3}{4}$	$-\frac{1}{2}$	$1\frac{1}{4}$	$\frac{1}{4}$	6.4
$4\frac{1}{4}$	$4\frac{1}{2}$		4	$5\frac{1}{4}$	0	$1\frac{3}{4}$	$\frac{1}{4}$	6.4
$4\frac{1}{2}$	$4\frac{3}{4}$		$3\frac{1}{4}$	$4\frac{1}{2}$	$\frac{1}{2}$	$2\frac{1}{4}$	$\frac{1}{4}$	6.4
$4\frac{3}{4}$	5		$2\frac{1}{2}$	4	1	$2\frac{3}{4}$	$\frac{1}{4}$	6.4
5	$5\frac{1}{4}$		2	$3\frac{1}{4}$	$1\frac{1}{2}$	$3\frac{1}{4}$	$\frac{1}{4}$	6.4
$5\frac{1}{4}$	$5\frac{1}{2}$		$1\frac{1}{2}$	$2\frac{3}{4}$	2	$3\frac{3}{4}$	$\frac{1}{4}$	6.4
1979								
F-100, F-150, F-250 (D) (6200-6800 GVW) (4 × 2)		N/A						
$2\frac{3}{4}$	3		$8\frac{3}{8}$	$9\frac{5}{8}$	-2	$-\frac{1}{4}$	$\frac{3}{32}$	2.4
3	$3\frac{1}{4}$		$7\frac{3}{4}$	9	$-1\frac{1}{2}$	$\frac{1}{8}$	$\frac{3}{32}$	2.4
$3\frac{1}{4}$	$3\frac{1}{2}$		7	$8\frac{3}{8}$	$-1\frac{1}{8}$	$\frac{1}{2}$	$\frac{3}{32}$	2.4
$3\frac{1}{2}$	$3\frac{3}{4}$		$6\frac{1}{4}$	$7\frac{5}{8}$	$-\frac{3}{4}$	1	$\frac{3}{32}$	2.4
$3\frac{3}{4}$	4		$5\frac{7}{8}$	$7\frac{1}{8}$	$-\frac{3}{8}$	$1\frac{1}{4}$	$\frac{3}{32}$	2.4
4	$4\frac{1}{4}$		$5\frac{1}{8}$	$6\frac{1}{2}$	0	$1\frac{5}{8}$	$\frac{3}{32}$	2.4
$4\frac{1}{4}$	$4\frac{1}{2}$		$4\frac{1}{2}$	$5\frac{7}{8}$	$\frac{3}{8}$	2	$\frac{3}{32}$	2.4
$4\frac{1}{2}$	$4\frac{3}{4}$		$3\frac{3}{4}$	$5\frac{1}{4}$	$\frac{3}{4}$	$2\frac{3}{8}$	$\frac{3}{32}$	2.4
$4\frac{3}{4}$	5		$3\frac{1}{4}$	$4\frac{5}{8}$	$1\frac{1}{4}$	$1\frac{3}{4}$	$\frac{3}{32}$	2.4
5	$5\frac{1}{4}$		$2\frac{1}{2}$	4	$1\frac{7}{8}$	$3\frac{1}{8}$	$\frac{3}{32}$	2.4
1979								
F-250 R/C (7700-7900) (4 × 2) (D) F-250 S/C (6300-7800) (D8TA-BA) (D)		N/A						
$2\frac{3}{4}$	3		$7\frac{3}{4}$	9	$-1\frac{7}{8}$	$-\frac{1}{4}$	$\frac{3}{32}$	2.4
3	$3\frac{1}{4}$		7	$7\frac{3}{8}$	$-1\frac{1}{2}$	$\frac{1}{8}$	$\frac{3}{32}$	2.4
$3\frac{1}{4}$	$3\frac{1}{2}$		$6\frac{3}{8}$	$7\frac{3}{4}$	$-1\frac{1}{8}$	$\frac{1}{2}$	$\frac{3}{32}$	2.4
$3\frac{1}{2}$	$3\frac{3}{4}$		$5\frac{7}{8}$	$7\frac{1}{8}$	$-\frac{3}{4}$	$\frac{7}{8}$	$\frac{3}{32}$	2.4
$3\frac{3}{4}$	4		$5\frac{1}{8}$	$6\frac{1}{2}$	$-\frac{3}{8}$	$1\frac{1}{4}$	$\frac{3}{32}$	2.4
4	$4\frac{1}{4}$		$4\frac{1}{2}$	$5\frac{7}{8}$	0	$1\frac{5}{8}$	$\frac{3}{32}$	2.4
$4\frac{1}{4}$	$4\frac{1}{2}$		$3\frac{7}{8}$	$5\frac{1}{4}$	$\frac{3}{8}$	2	$\frac{3}{32}$	2.4
$4\frac{1}{2}$	$4\frac{3}{4}$		$3\frac{1}{4}$	$4\frac{5}{8}$	$\frac{7}{8}$	$2\frac{1}{2}$	$\frac{3}{32}$	2.4
$4\frac{3}{4}$	5		$2\frac{5}{8}$	4	$1\frac{1}{4}$	$2\frac{3}{4}$	$\frac{3}{32}$	2.4
5	$5\frac{1}{4}$		2	$3\frac{3}{8}$	$1\frac{5}{8}$	$3\frac{1}{8}$	$\frac{3}{32}$	2.4
1979								
F-350, F-250 S/C (3100) (D) (4 × 2) F-250 S/C RPO Suspension (D8TA-DA)(D)		N/A						
$2\frac{3}{4}$	3		$9\frac{5}{8}$	11	$-2\frac{1}{8}$	$-\frac{5}{8}$	$\frac{3}{32}$	2.4
3	$3\frac{1}{4}$		$8\frac{7}{8}$	$10\frac{3}{8}$	$-1\frac{3}{4}$	$-\frac{1}{4}$	$\frac{3}{32}$	2.4
$3\frac{1}{4}$	$3\frac{1}{2}$		$8\frac{3}{8}$	$9\frac{3}{4}$	$-1\frac{3}{8}$	$\frac{1}{8}$	$\frac{3}{32}$	2.4
$3\frac{1}{2}$	$3\frac{3}{4}$		$7\frac{3}{4}$	9	$-1\frac{1}{8}$	$\frac{1}{2}$	$\frac{3}{32}$	2.4
$3\frac{3}{4}$	4		7	$8\frac{3}{8}$	$-\frac{3}{4}$	$\frac{3}{4}$	$\frac{3}{32}$	2.4
4	$4\frac{1}{4}$		$6\frac{3}{8}$	$7\frac{3}{4}$	$-1\frac{1}{4}$	$1\frac{1}{4}$	$\frac{3}{32}$	2.4
$4\frac{1}{4}$	$4\frac{1}{2}$		$5\frac{3}{4}$	$7\frac{1}{8}$	0	$1\frac{5}{8}$	$\frac{3}{32}$	2.4
$4\frac{1}{2}$	$4\frac{3}{4}$		$5\frac{1}{8}$	$6\frac{1}{2}$	$\frac{3}{8}$	2	$\frac{3}{32}$	2.4
$4\frac{3}{4}$	5		$5\frac{1}{8}$	$6\frac{1}{2}$	$\frac{3}{4}$	$2\frac{3}{8}$	$\frac{3}{32}$	2.4
5	$5\frac{1}{4}$		$3\frac{7}{8}$	$5\frac{1}{4}$	$1\frac{1}{4}$	$2\frac{1}{4}$	$\frac{3}{32}$	2.4
1979								
E-100/150 (D7UA-BB) (C) (4 × 2)		N/A						
$3\frac{1}{4}$	$3\frac{1}{2}$		$6\frac{1}{4}$	8	$-1\frac{3}{4}$	$-\frac{1}{4}$	$\frac{1}{32}$	0.8
$3\frac{1}{2}$	$3\frac{3}{4}$		$5\frac{3}{4}$	$7\frac{1}{4}$	$-1\frac{1}{2}$	$\frac{1}{4}$	$\frac{1}{32}$	0.8
$3\frac{3}{4}$	4		5	$6\frac{3}{4}$	-1	$\frac{3}{4}$	$\frac{1}{32}$	0.8
4	$4\frac{1}{4}$		$4\frac{1}{2}$	$5\frac{3}{4}$	$-\frac{1}{2}$	$1\frac{1}{4}$	$\frac{1}{32}$	0.8
$4\frac{1}{4}$	$4\frac{1}{2}$		4	$5\frac{1}{4}$	0	$1\frac{3}{4}$	$\frac{1}{32}$	0.8
$4\frac{1}{2}$	$4\frac{3}{4}$		$3\frac{1}{4}$	$4\frac{1}{2}$	$\frac{1}{2}$	$2\frac{1}{4}$	$\frac{1}{32}$	0.8
$4\frac{3}{4}$	5		$2\frac{1}{2}$	4	1	$2\frac{3}{4}$	$\frac{1}{32}$	0.8
5	$5\frac{1}{4}$		2	$3\frac{1}{4}$	$1\frac{1}{2}$	$3\frac{1}{4}$	$\frac{1}{32}$	0.8
$5\frac{1}{4}$	$5\frac{1}{2}$		$1\frac{1}{2}$	$2\frac{3}{4}$	2	$3\frac{3}{4}$	$\frac{1}{32}$	0.8

WHEEL ALIGNMENT

Ford

1979 E-250/350 (D5UA-AB) (C) (4 × 2)

Ride Height Min.	Max.	Adj. Ill. No.	Caster Min.	Caster Max.	Camber Min.	Camber Max.	Toe-In (Inches)	Toe-In (Millimeters)
		N/A						
3¼	3½		9	10½	−1¾	−¼	1/32	0.8
3½	3¾		8½	9¾	−1½	¼	1/32	0.8
3¾	4		7⅞	9	−1	¾	1/32	0.8
4	4¼		7⅛	8½	−½	1¼	1/32	0.8
4¼	4½		6½	7¾	0	1¾	1/32	0.8
4½	4¾		5¾	7	½	2¼	1/32	0.8
4¾	5		5¼	6½	1	2¾	1/32	0.8
5	5¼		4⅝	6	1½	3¼	1/32	0.8
5¼	5½		4	5½	2	3¾	1/32	0.8

1978 F-100, 150, 250 (4 × 2) 6200-6900 GVW Regular Cab

Ride Height Min.	Max.	Adj. Ill. No.	Caster Min.	Caster Max.	Camber Min.	Camber Max.	Toe-In (Inches)			Toe-In (Millimeters)		
		N/A										
2¾	3		8¼	9⅝	−1	½	1/32 (out)	3/32 (in)	7/32 (in)	0.8 (out)	2.4 (in)	5.6 (in)
3	3¼		7¾	9	−½	1	1/32 (out)	3/32 (in)	7/32 (in)	0.8 (out)	2.4 (in)	5.6 (in)
3¼	3½		7	8⅜	−¼	1½	1/32 (out)	3/32 (in)	7/32 (in)	0.8 (out)	2.4 (in)	5.6 (in)
3½	3¾		6¼	7⅜	0	1¾	1/32 (out)	3/32 (in)	7/32 (in)	0.8 (out)	2.4 (in)	5.6 (in)
3¾	4		5¾	7	½	2¼	1/32 (out)	3/32 (in)	7/32 (in)	0.8 (out)	2.4 (in)	5.6 (in)
4	4¼		5	6½	¾	2½	1/32 (out)	3/32 (in)	7/32 (in)	0.8 (out)	2.4 (in)	5.6 (in)
4¼	4½		4½	5⅞	1¼	3	1/32 (out)	3/32 (in)	7/32 (in)	0.8 (out)	2.4 (in)	5.6 (in)
4½	4¾		3¾	5	1⅝	3¼	1/32 (out)	3/32 (in)	7/32 (in)	0.8 (out)	2.4 (in)	5.6 (in)
4¾	5		3⅛	4½	2	3¾	1/32 (out)	3/32 (in)	7/32 (in)	0.8 (out)	2.4 (in)	5.6 (in)
5	5¼		2½	4	3⅜	4⅛	1/32 (out)	3/32 (in)	7/32 (in)	0.8 (out)	2.4 (in)	5.6 (in)

1978 F-250 7800-8000 GVW Regular Cab 6350-7800 Super Cab (4 × 2)

Ride Height Min.	Max.	Adj. Ill. No.	Caster Min.	Caster Max.	Camber Min.	Camber Max.	Toe-In (Inches)			Toe-In (Millimeters)		
		N/A										
2¾	3		7⅞	8⅞	−½	1	1/32 (out)	3/32 (in)	7/32 (in)	0.8 (out)	2.4 (in)	5.6 (in)
3	3¼		6⅞	8⅜	−1¼	1½	1/32 (out)	3/32 (in)	7/32 (in)	0.8 (out)	2.4 (in)	5.6 (in)
3¼	3½		5⅜	7¾	0	1¾	1/32 (out)	3/32 (in)	7/32 (in)	0.8 (out)	2.4 (in)	5.6 (in)
3¾	4		5	6½	¾	2½	1/32 (out)	3/32 (in)	7/32 (in)	0.8 (out)	2.4 (in)	5.6 (in)
4	4¼		4½	5⅞	1¼	3	1/32 (out)	3/32 (in)	7/32 (in)	0.8 (out)	2.4 (in)	5.6 (in)
4¼	4½		3⅜	5⅛	1¾	3¼	1/32 (out)	3/32 (in)	7/32 (in)	0.8 (out)	2.4 (in)	5.6 (in)
4½	4¾		3⅛	4½	2	3½	1/32 (out)	3/32 (in)	7/32 (in)	0.8 (out)	2.4 (in)	5.6 (in)
4¾	5		2½	4	2⅜	4⅛	1/32 (out)	3/32 (in)	7/32 (in)	0.8 (out)	2.4 (in)	5.6 (in)
5	5¼		2	3¼	2¾	4½	1/32 (out)	3/32 (in)	7/32 (in)	0.8 (out)	2.4 (in)	5.6 (in)

Ford

Year, Model and Axle Part Number Ride Height Min.	Max.	Adj. Ill. No.	Caster (Degrees) Min.	Max.	Camber (Degrees) Min.	Max.	Toe-In (Inches)			Toe-In (Millimeters)		
1978												
F-350 All F-250 8100 GVW Super Cab F-250 Super Cab W/RPO Suspension (4 × 2)		N/A										
2¾	3		9¾	10⅞	−⅜	−¼	1/32 (out)	3/32 (in)	7/32 (in)	0.8 (out)	2.4 (in)	5.6 (in)
3	3¼		9	10¼	−1	−⅝	1/32 (out)	3/32 (in)	7/32 (in)	0.8 (out)	2.4 (in)	5.6 (in)
3¼	3½		8¼	9⅝	−½	1	1/32 (out)	3/32 (in)	7/32 (in)	0.8 (out)	2.4 (in)	5.6 (in)
3½	3¾		7⅝	8⅝	−¼	1½	1/32 (out)	3/32 (in)	7/32 (in)	0.8 (out)	2.4 (in)	5.6 (in)
3¾	4		6⅞	8⅛	0	1¾	1/32 (out)	3/32 (in)	7/32 (in)	0.8 (out)	2.4 (in)	5.6 (in)
4	4¼		6⅜	7¼	½	2¼	1/32 (out)	3/32 (in)	7/32 (in)	0.8 (out)	2.4 (in)	5.6 (in)
4¼	4½		5¾	7	¾	2½	1/32 (out)	3/32 (in)	7/32 (in)	0.8 (out)	2.4 (in)	5.6 (in)
4½	4¾		5⅛	6½	1¼	3	1/32 (out)	3/32 (in)	7/32 (in)	0.8 (out)	2.4 (in)	5.6 (in)
4¾	5		4½	5⅞	1¾	3¼	1/32 (out)	3/32 (in)	7/32 (in)	0.8 (out)	2.4 (in)	5.6 (in)
5	5¼		3⅞	5⅛	2	3¼	1/32 (out)	3/32 (in)	7/32 (in)	0.8 (out)	2.4 (out)	5.6 (in)
1978												
E-100, 150 (4 × 2)		N/A										
4	4¼		3¾	6½	−¾	½	0		¼	0		6.4
4¼	4½		3¼	5¾	−½	¾	0		¼	0		6.4
4½	4¾		2½	5¼	0	1¼	0		¼	0		6.4
4¾	5		2	4½	½	1¾	0		¼	0		6.4
5	5¼		1¼	4	1¼	2½	0		¼	0		6.4
5¼	5½		¾	3¼	1¾	3¼	0		¼	0		6.4
5½	5¾		0	2¾	1½	3¾	0		¼	0		6.4
1978												
E-250, 350 (4 × 2)		N/A										
4	4¼		6¼	9	−1	¾	3/32 (out)	1/32 (in)	5/32 (in)	2.4 (out)	0.8 (in)	4.0 (in)
4¼	4½		5¾	8¼	−½	1¼	3/32 (out)	1/32 (in)	5/32 (in)	2.4 (out)	0.8 (in)	4.0 (in)
4½	4¾		5¼	7¾	0	1¾	3/32 (out)	1/32 (in)	5/32 (in)	2.4 (out)	0.8 (out)	4.0 (in)
4¾	5		4½	7¼	½	2¼	3/32 (out)	1/32 (in)	5/32 (in)	2.4 (out	0.8 (in)	4.0 (in)
5	5¼		4	6½	1	2¾	3/32 (out)	1/32 (in)	5/32 (in)	2.4 (out)	0.8 (in)	4.0 (in)
5¼	5½		3¼	6	1½	3¼	3/32 (out)	1/32 (in)	5/32 (in)	2.4 (out)	0.8 (in)	4.0 (in)
1977												
F-100, 150, 250, 6200-6900 GVW Regular Cab (4 × 2)		N/A										
2¾	3		7½	10	−1	½	1/32 (out)	3/32 (in)	7/32 (in)	0.8 (out)	2.4 (in)	5.6 (in)
3	3¼		7	9½	−½	1	1/32 (out)	3/32 (in)	7/32 (in)	0.8 (out)	2.4 (in)	5.6 (in)
3¼	3½		6½	9	−¼	1½	1/32 (out)	3/32 (in)	7/32 (in)	0.8 (out)	2.4 (in)	5.6 (in)
3½	3¾		5¾	8½	0	1¾	1/32 (out)	3/32 (in)	7/32 (in)	0.8 (out)	2.4 (in)	5.6 (in)
3¾	4		5¼	7¾	½	2¼	1/32 (out)	3/32 (in)	7/32 (in)	0.8 (out)	2.4 (in)	5.6 (in)
4	4¼		4½	7	¾	2½	1/32 (out)	3/32 (in)	7/32 (in)	0.8 (out)	2.4 (in)	5.6 (in)
4¼	4½		4	6½	1¼	3	1/32 (out)	3/32 (in)	7/32 (in)	0.8 (out)	2.4 (in)	5.6 (in)

Ford

Year, Model and Axle Part Number Ride Height Min.	Max.	Adj. Ill. No.	Caster (Degrees) Min.	Max.	Camber (Degrees) Min.	Max.	Toe-In (Inches)			Toe-In (Millimeters)		
1977 F-250 7800-8000 GVW Regular Cab; 6350-7800 Super Cab (4 × 2)		N/A										
2¾	3											
3	3¼		6½	9	− ¼	1½	1/32 (out)	3/32 (in)	7/32 (in)	0.8 (out)	2.4 (in)	5.6 (in)
3¼	3½		5¾	8½	0	1¾	1/32 (out)	3/32 (in)	7/32 (in)	0.8 (out)	2.4 (in)	5.6 (in)
3½	3¾		5¼	7¾	½	2¼	1/32 (out)	3/32 (in)	7/32 (in)	0.8 (out)	2.4 (in)	5.6 (in)
3¾	4		4½	7	¾	2½	1/32 (out)	3/32 (in)	7/32 (in)	0.8 (out)	2.4 (in)	5.6 (in)
4	4¼		4	6½	1¼	3	1/32 (out)	3/32 (in)	7/32 (in)	0.8 (out)	2.4 (in)	5.6 (in)
4¼	4½		3¼	6	1¾	3¼	1/32 (in)	3/32 (in)	7/32 (in)	0.8 (in)	2.4 (in)	5.6 (in)
4½	4¾		2¾	5½	2	3½	1/32 (out)	3/32 (in)	7/32 (in)	0.8 (out)	2.4 (in)	5.6 (in)
1977 E-100, 150 (4 × 2)		N/A										
4¼	4½		3¼	5¾	− ¾	¾	1/32 (out)	3/32 (in)	7/32 (in)	0.8 (out)	2.4 (in)	5.6 (in)
4½	4¾		2½	5¼	− ½	1¼	1/32 (out)	3/32 (in)	7/32 (in)	0.8 (out)	2.4 (in)	5.6 (in)
4¾	5		2	4½	0	1¾	1/32 (out)	3/32 (in)	7/32 (in)	0.8 (out)	2.4 (in)	5.6 (in)
5	5¼		1¼	4	½	2½	1/32 (out)	3/32 (in)	7/32 (in)	0.8 (out)	2.4 (in)	5.6 (in)
1977 E-100, 150 (4 × 2)		N/A										
5¼	5½		¾	3¼	1½	3¼	1/32 (out)	3/32 (in)	7/32 (in)	0.8 (out)	2.4 (in)	5.6 (in)
5½	5¾		0	2¾	2	3¾	1/32 (out)	3/32 (in)	7/32 (in)	0.8 (out)	2.4 (in)	5.6 (in)
1977 E-250, 350 (4 × 2)		N/A										
4	4¼		6¼	9	− 1	¾	3/32 (out)	1/32 (in)	5/32 (in)	2.4 (out)	0.8 (in)	4.0 (in)
4¼	4½		5¾	8¼	− ½	1¼	3/32 (out)	1/32 (in)	5/32 (in)	2.4 (out)	0.8 (in)	4.0 (in)
4½	4¾		5¼	7¾	0	1¾	3/32 (out)	1/32 (in)	5/32 (in)	2.4 (out)	0.8 (in)	4.0 (in)
4¾	5		4½	7¼	½	2¼	3/32 (out)	1/32 (in)	5/32 (in)	2.4 (out)	0.8 (in)	4.0 (in)
5	5¼		4	6½	1	2¾	3/32 (out)	1/32 (in)	5/32 (in)	2.4 (out)	0.8 (n)	4.0 (in)
5¼	5½		3¼	6	1½	3¼	3/32 (out)	1/32 (in)	5/32 (in)	2.4 (out)	0.8 (in)	4.0 (in)
1977 F-350 All F-250 8100 GVW Super Cab (4 × 2) F-250 Super Cab w/RPO		N/A										
3½	3¾		7	9½	− ¼	1½	1/32 (out)	3/32 (in)	7/32 (in)	0.8 (out)	2.4 (in)	5.6 (in)
3¾	4		6½	9	0	1¾	1/32 (in)	3/32 (in)	7/32 (in)	0.8 (out)	2.4 (in)	5.6 (in)
4	4¼		5¾	8½	½	2¼	1/32 (out)	3/32 (in)	7/32 (in)	0.8 (out)	2.4 (in)	5.6 (in)
4¼	4½		5¼	7¾	¾	2½	1/32 (out)	3/32 (in)	7/32 (in)	0.8 (out)	2.4 (in)	5.6 (in)
4½	4¾		4½	7	1¼	3	1/32 (out)	3/32 (in)	7/32 (in)	0.8 (out)	2.4 (in)	5.6 (in)
4¾	5		4	6½	1¾	3¼	1/32 (out)	3/32 (in)	7/32 (in)	0.8 (out)	2.4 (in)	5.6 (in)
5	5¼		3¼	6	2	3¾	1/32 (out)	3/32 (in)	7/32 (in)	0.8 (out)	2.4 (in)	5.6 (in)

(A)Right side height measurement shown; left side height should be 0″ to 7/16″ higher on any one vehicle.
(1)All vehicles with normal operating attitude.
(2)Nominal toe setting is 2.5 mm (3/32 inch). Range is 0.8 mm (3/32 inch) out to 5.6 mm (7/32 inch) in.
(3)Nominal toe setting is 8 mm (1/32 inch). Range is 2.5 mm (3/32 inch) out to 4 mm (5/32 inch) in.
(4)Not Adjustable.
(5)Toe range is 0″ to ¼″, ⅛″ nominal.
(6)Side-to-side variation: Caster 1½°, Camber 23/32°.
(7)Vehicle height is too high.

Ford

Vehicle Identification Year Model	Caster (Degrees) Min.	Pref.	Max.	Camber (Degrees) Min.	Pref.	Max.	Toe-In (Inches) Min.	Pref.	Max.	Toe-In (Millimeters) Min.	Pref.	Max.	Toe-Out On Turns (Degrees) Outside Wheel	Inside Wheel	Strg. Axis Incl. (Deg.)
79F-250(4 × 4), F-150 (4 × 4) SC, F-350(4 × 4)	2½	4	5½	0	1½	3		3/32			2.4		NA	NA	NA
79F-150(4 × 4), Bronco	6½	8	9½	1	1½	3		3/32			2.4		NA	NA	NA
78F-250(4 × 4)	2⅛	4	5	½	1	1½	1/16	5/32	¼	1.6	4.0	6.4	NA	NA	NA
78F-150,(4 × 4), Bronco	2¾	3½	4¼	1	1½	2	1/16	5/32	5/16	1.6	2.4	8.0	NA	NA	NA
77F-250(4 × 4)	3	4	5	½	1	1½	1/16	5/32	¼	1.6	4.0	6.4	NA	NA	NA
77F-150(4 × 4) Bronco	2¾	3½	4¼	1	1½	2	1/16	5/32	5/16	1.6	4.0	8.0	NA	NA	NA

If caster or camber are not with specifications, find the true ride height by installing wooden blocks as pictured below. This will aid in determining which wheel is out of specification.

To find ride height on vehicles equipped with front leaf springs:
Measure from bottom of frame to top of front axle.

Ford measuring points

International Harvester

Vehicle Identification Year Model	Adj. Ill. No.	Caster (Degrees) Min.	Pref.	Max.	Camber (Degrees) Min.	Pref.	Max.	Toe-In (Inches) Min.	Pref.	Max.	Toe-In (Millimeters) Min.	Pref.	Max.	Toe-Out On Turns (Degrees) Outside Wheel	Inside Wheel
80 Scout, All Models	(5)		2½			½		3/32		5/16	1.6		7.9	NA	NA
79 Scout, All Models	(5)		0			1		0		3/16	0		5.1	NA	NA
77-78 Scout, All Models	(5)	−1	0	1	½	1	1½	0	1/16	⅛	0	1.6	3.2	NA	NA

JEEP

Vehicle Identification Year Model	Adj. Ill. No.	Caster (Degrees) Min.	Pref.	Max.	Camber (Degrees) Min.	Pref.	Max.	Toe-In (Inches) Min.	Max.	Toe-In (Millimeters) Min.	Max.	Toe-Out On Turns (Degrees) Outside Wheel	Inside Wheel	Strg. Axis Incl. (Deg.)
'82-'84 Pickup	5	4	4	5	0	0	½	3/64	3/32	1.2	2.4	36	37	8½
'80-'81 Pickup	5		4			0		3/64	3/32	1.2	2.4	(A)	37	8½
'77-'79 Pickup	5		4			1½		3/64	3/32	1.2	2.4		37½	8½

IMPORTED TRUCKS

Vehicle Identification Year Model	Adj. Ill. No.	Caster (Degrees) Min.	Pref.	Max.	Camber (Degrees) Min.	Pref.	Max.	Toe-In (Inches) Min.	Pref.	Max.	Toe-In (Millimeters) Min.	Pref.	Max.	Toe-Out on Turns (Degrees) Outside Wheel	Inside Wheel
CHEVROLET LUV															
82-81 Series 12, 11(4 × 2)	(1)	0	1/2	1	0	1/2	1	0	1/16	1/8	0.0	2.0	4.0	33	37
82-81 Series 12, 11(4 × 4)	(7)	− 3/16	5/16	13/16	1/16	9/16	11/16	1/16 (out)	0	1/16 (in)	2.0 (out)	0	2.0 (in)	33	35
80-79 Series 10, 9(4 × 4)	(7)	− 11/16	5/16	15/16	− 3/16	9/16	15/16	1/8 (out)	0	1/8 (in)	3.2 (out)	0	3.2 (in)	30	39
80-77 Series 10,9,8,6(4 × 2)	(1)	− 13/16	− 3/16	13/16	− 1/4	1/2	1 1/4	1/8 (out)	0	1/8 (in)	3.2 (out)	0	3.2 (in)	30	39
DATSUN/NISSAN															
84-82 Pickup Truck (4 × 2)	(7)	13/16		1 13/16	0		1	7/32		9/32	5.1		7.1	18	20
84-81 Pickup Truck (4 × 4)	(7)	13/16		2 3/16	0		1	13/64		9/32	5.6		7.1	18	18 1/2
81-80 Pickup Truck	(7)	13/16		1 13/16	0		1	13/64		9/32	5.6		7.1	18	20
79 Pick up Truck	(7)	1/2		2	− 1/4		1 1/4	7/32		9/32	5.6		7.1	30 1/2	35 +
78 Pick up Truck	(7)	9/16		2 1/16	− 1/4		1 1/4	0		9/32	0		7.1	30 1/2	35 +
77 Pick up Truck	(7)	1 1/16	1 13/16	2 9/16	1/4	1 1/4	2 1/4	3/32		1/8	2.4		3.2	31	36
+ Plus or minus 1° is considered acceptable.															
DODGE D50, PLYMOUTH ARROW, MITSUBISHI (A)(B)															
84-83 D-50 Pickup Truck (4 × 4)	(1)	1	2	3	1/2	1	1 1/2	3/32		11/32	2.4		8.7	28	30 3/4
84-80 D-50 Pickup Truck (4 × 2)	(1)	1 1/2	2 1/2	3 1/2	1/2	1	1 1/2	3/32		11/32	2.4		8.7	30 1/2	37
79 D-50 Pickup Truck	(1)	2	3	4	1/2	1	1 1/2	3/32		11/32	2.4		8.7	30 1/2	37
82-80 Arrow Pickup Truck	(1)	1 1/2	2 1/2	3 1/2	1/2	1	1 1/2	3/32		11/32	2.4		8.7	30 1/2	37
79 Arrow Pickup Truck	(1)	2	3	4	1/2	1	1 1/2	3/32		11/32	2.4		8.7	30 1/2	37
84-83 Mitsubishi(4 × 2)	(1)	1 1/2	2 1/2	3 1/2	1/2	1	1 1/2	3/32		11/32	2.0		9.0	30 1/2	37
84-83 Mitsubishi(4 × 4)	(1)	1	2	3	1/2	1	1 1/2	3/32		11/32	2.0		9.0	28	30 3/4
ISUZU															
81-84 Pick up Truck(4 × 2)	(8)(9)	0	1/2	1	0	1/2	1	0	5/64	5/32	0.0	2.0	4.0	33	37
81-84 Pick up Truck(4 × 4)	(7)	− 3/16	5/16	13/16	1/16	9/16	11/16	5/64 (out)	0	5/64 (in)	2.0 (out)	0.0	2.0 (in)	33	35
MAZDA															
79-84 B2000, B2200	(3)	11/16	1	1 5/16	7/16	3/4	1 1/4	0	1/8	1/4	0	3.0	6.0	30 11/16	32 1/2
77-78 B1800	(3)	11/16	1	1 5/16	7/16	3/4	1 1/4	0	1/8	1/4	0	3.2	6.4	30 11/16	32 1/2
77 Rotary Pickup	(3)	1 5/8	1 15/16	2 1/4	− 1/16	1/4	9/16	0	1/8	1/4	0	3.2	6.4	32 9/16	33 5/16
Maximum variation between wheel, caster 1 1/16°, camber 1/2°															
TOYOTA															
84-80 Hilux(4 × 4)	N/A	2 3/4	3 1/2	4 1/4	1/4	1	1 3/4							29	30 1/2
w/Radial Tires								0	3/64	5/64	0	1.0	2.0		
w/Bias Tires								1/8	5/32	13/64	3.0	4.0	5.0		
84-82 Hilux(4 × 2) Pick up RN 1/2 Ton	(1)	1/2	1	1 1/2	9/16	1 1/16	1 9/16							29	36
w/Bias Tires								5/32	13/64	15/64	4.0	5.0	6.0		
w/Radial Tires								3/64	5/64	1/8	1.0	2.0	3.0		
RN 3/4 Ton, Cab & Chassis	(1)	0	1/2	1	9/16	1 1/16	1 9/16							29	36
w/Bias Tires								5/32	13/64	15/64	4.0	5.2	6.0		
w/Radial Tires								3/64	5/64	1/8	1.2	2.0	3.1		
81-80 Hilux(4 × 2)	(1)	0	1/2	1	9/16	1 1/16	1 9/16							29	36
w/Radial Tires								3/64	5/64	1/8	1.2	2.0	3.2		
w/Bias Tires								5/32	13/64	1/4	4.0	5.2	6.4		
79 Hilux(4 × 2)	(1)	0	1/2	1	9/16	1 1/16	1 9/16	5/32	13/64	15/64	4.0	5.2	6.0	29	36
79 Hilux(4 × 4)	N/A		3 1/2			1									
w/HR78 × 15B								0	3/64	5/64	0	1.2	2.0	29	36
w/H78 × 15B								7/64	5/32	15/64	2.8	4.0	6.0	29	30 1/2
78-77 Hilux(4 × 2)	(1)	0	1/2	1	1/2	1	1 1/2	15/64		9/32	6.0		7.1		
w/Radial Tires														26 1/4	31
w/Bias Tires														27 1/2	33 1/4

IMPORTED TRUCKS

Vehicle Identification Year Model	Adj. Ill. No.	Caster (Degrees) Min.	Pref.	Max.	Camber (Degrees) Min.	Pref.	Max.	Toe-In (Inches) Min.	Pref.	Max.	Toe-In (Millimeters) Min.	Pref.	Max.	Toe-Out on Turns (Degrees) Outside Wheel	Inside Wheel
VOLKSWAGEN															
83-81 Rabbit Pick-up Front	(10)	13/16	15/16	1 13/16	− 3/16	5/16	13/16	7/32 (out)	1/8 (out)	1/32 (out)	5.6 (out)	3.2 (out)	0.8 (out)	18 1/2	20
Rear	N/A				− 1	0	1	1/2 (out)	0	1/2 (in)	12.7 (out)	0.0	12.7 (in)		
80 Rabbit Pickup: Front	(10)	15/16	1 13/16	2 5/16	− 3/16	5/16	13/16	7/32 (out)	1/8 (out)	1/32 (out)	5.6 (out)	3.2 (out)	0.8 (out)	18 1/2	20
Rear	N/A				− 9/16	0	9/16	0	5/32 (out)	5/16 (out)	0	4.0	7.9		

(A) Variation between wheel 1/2°.
(B) Side to side variation 1/2° or less.

LUV SUSPENSION HEIGHT TABLES

Model & Year	Measurement at	Front Suspension Inches	MM	Rear Suspension Inches	MM
82-81 (4 × 4)		5	127	7 11/16	195
82-81 (4 × 2)	Base Model, Soft Ride	4	102	6 1/8	155
	Base Model, Cab & Chassis Comp.	4	102	7 1/2	190
	Cab & Chassis	4	102	8 5/16	210
	Long Wheel Base Model	4	102	7 1/2	190
80-79 4 × 4		4 13/16	122	7 11/16	195
80-78 4 × 2	Base Model, Soft Ride	4 5/8	116.8	6 1/8	155
	Base Model, Cab & Chassis Comp.	4 5/8	116.8	7 1/2	190
	Cab & Chassis	4 5/8	116.8	8 5/16	210
	Long Wheel Base Model	4 5/8	116.8	7 1/2	190
77-76 4 × 2	at Curb	4 5/8	116.8	6	152.4
	at G.V.W.	3 5/8	92.0	5 1/32	127.8
75-74 4 × 2	at Curb	4 5/8	116.8	7 13/32	188.0
	at G.V.W.	3 5/8	92.0	5 1/32	127.8

CROSSMEMBER

A

LOWER BALL JOINT

1982-73 FRONT

EDGE OF FRAME

TOP OF AXLE

REAR

TRIM HEIGHTS

Upper Arm Bracket

Caster/Camber Shims

Type 1

CASTER/CAMBER CAMS

Type 2

Type 3

Type 4

Caster Adjustment

Type 5

Type 6

Type 7

Type 8

Type 9

Type 10

Manual Transmission Overhaul

INDEX

Jumping Out of High Gear

1. Misalignment of transmission case or clutch housing.
2. Worn pilot bearing in crankshaft.
3. Bent transmission shaft.
4. Worn high speed sliding gear.
5. Worn teeth in clutch shaft.
6. Insufficient spring tension on shifter rail plunger.
7. Bent or loose shifter fork.
8. End-play in clutch shaft.
9. Gears not engaging completely.
10. Loose or worn bearings on clutch shaft or mainshaft.

Sticking in High Gear

1. Clutch not releasing fully.
2. Burred or battered teeth on clutch shaft.
3. Burred or battered transmission mainshaft.
4. Frozen synchronizing clutch.
5. Stuck shifter rail plunger.
6. Gearshift lever twisting and binding shifter rail.
7. Battered teeth on high speed sliding gear or on sleeve.
8. Lack of lubrication.
9. Improper lubrication.

10. Corroded transmission parts.
11. Defective mainshaft pilot bearing.

Jumping out of Second Gear

1. Insufficient spring tension on shifter rail plunger.
2. Bent or loose shifter fork.
3. Gears not engaging completely.
4. End-play in transmission mainshaft.
5. Loose transmission gear bearing.
6. Defective mainshaft pilot bearing.
7. Bent transmission shaft.
8. Worn teeth on second speed sliding gear or sleeve.

9. Loose or worn bearings on transmission mainshaft.

10. End-play in countershaft.

Sticking in Second Gear

1. Clutch not releasing fully.

DIAGNOSIS

2. Burred or battered teeth on sliding sleeve.

3. Burred or battered transmission mainshaft.

4. Frozen synchronizing clutch.

5. Stuck shifter rail plunger.

6. Gearshift lever twisting and binding shifter rail.

7. Lack of lubrication.

8. Second speed transmission gear bearings locked will give same effect as gears stuck in second.

9. Improper lubrication.

10. Corroded transmission parts.

Jumping out of Low Gear

1. Gears not engaging completely.

2. Bent or loose shifter fork.

3. End-play in transmission mainshaft.

4. End-play countershaft.

5. Loose or worn bearings on transmission mainshaft.

6. Loose or worn bearings in countershaft.

7. Defective mainshaft pilot bearing.

Sticking in Low Gear

1. Clutch not releasing fully.

2. Burred or battered transmission mainshaft.

3. Stuck shifter rail plunger.

4. Gearshift lever twisting and binding shifter rail.

5. Lack of lubrication.

6. Improper lubrication.

7. Corroded transmission parts.

Jumping out of Reverse Gear

1. Insufficient spring tension on shifter rail plunger.

2. Bent or loose shifter fork.

3. Badly worn gear teeth.

4. Gears not engaging completely.

5. End-play in transmission mainshaft.

6. Idler gear bushings loose or worn.

7. Loose or worn bearings on transmission mainshaft.

8. Defective mainshaft pilot bearing.

Sticking in Reverse Gear

1. Clutch not releasing fully.

2. Burred or battered transmission mainshaft.

3. Stuck shifter rail plunger.

4. Gearshift lever twisting and binding shifter rail.

5. Lack of lubrication.

6. Improper lubrication.

7. Corroded transmission parts.

Failure of Gears to Synchronize

1. Binding pilot bearing on mainshaft, will synchronize in high gear only.

2. Clutch not releasing fully.

3. Detent springs weak or broken.

4. Weak or broken springs under balls in sliding gear sleeve.

5. Binding bearing on clutch shaft.

6. Binding countershaft.

7. Binding pilot bearing in crankshaft.

8. Badly worn gear teeth.

9. Scored or worn cones.

10. Improper lubrication.

11. Constant mesh gear not turning freely on transmission mainshaft. Will synchronize in that gear only.

Gears Spinning When Shifting into Gear from Neutral

1. Clutch not releasing fully.

2. In some cases an extremely light lubricant in transmission will cause gears to continue to spin for a short time after clutch is released.

3. Binding pilot bearing in crankshaft.

— CAUTION —

Care must be exercised during the disassembly and assembly of manual transmission due to the usage of metric nuts and bolts. The proper wrenches and sockets should be used to avoid damage to the transmission and fasteners. Do not attempt to interchange metric threaded fasteners with U.S. Fine or Standard fasteners as damage can result.

CLEANING OF TRANSMISSION COMPONENTS

Cleanliness of parts, tools, and work area is of the utmost importance. All transmission components (except bearing assemblies) should be cleaned in cleaning solvent and dried with compressed air before any inspection or work is begun. Great care should be taken when cleaning bearings. Bearings should always be cleaned separately from other parts in clean cleaning solvent and not gasoline. They must never be cleaned in a hot solution tank. It is advisable that they be soaked in cleaning fluid and then tapped against a block of wood in order to free any solidified lubricant that may be trapped inside. Rinse bearings thoroughly in clean solvent and then dry them with moisture-free compressed air being careful not to spin the bearings with the air stream. Rotate each bearing slowly and inspect rollers or balls for any signs of excessive wear, roughness, or damage. Those bearings not in excellent condition must be replaced. If they pass this inspection, they should be dipped in clean oil and wrapped in clean lintless cloth to protect them until installation.

INSPECTION OF TRANSMISSION COMPONENTS

All parts must be completely and carefully inspected and replaced for any signs of wear, stress, discoloration or warpage due to excessive heat. Whenever available, the magna flux process should be used on all parts except roller and ball bearings, to detect small cracks unseen by the eye. Inspect the breather assembly to see that it is not clogged or damaged and check all threaded parts for stripped or cross threads. Oil passages must be cleared of obstructions by the use of air pressure or brass rods and all gaskets, oil seals, lock wires, cotter pins, and snaprings are to be replaced. Small nicks or burrs in gears or splines can be removed with a fine abrasive stone. It is important that any housings or covers having cracks or other damage should be replaced and not welded. Synchronizers, not in excellent condition, must be replaced. The bronze synchronizer cone should be checked for wear or for any steel chips that may have become imbedded in it. Springs must be inspected for free length, compressed length, distortion, or collapsed coils.

NOTE: The splines on many clutch gears, mainshafts, etc., are equipped with a machined relief called a ''hopping guard.'' With the clutch gear engaged, the mating gear is free to slip into this notch, preventing the two gears from separating or ''walking out of gear'' under various load conditions. This is not a worn or chipped gear. Do not grind or discard the gear.

Check all shafts for spline wear or damage. If the mainshaft 1st and reverse sliding gear or clutch hub have worn into the sides of the splines, the shaft should be replaced. Shift forks, shift rods, interlock balls and pins must be replaced if scored, worn, distorted or damaged.

AMC—Jeep

Model AX 4 is a 4-speed manual transmission while AX 5 is a 5-speed manual transmission. Both transmissions have synchromesh engagement in all forward gears controlled by a floor shift mechanism integrated into the transmission top cover.

NOTE: The following components and materials must be replaced whenever the transmission is overhauled.

- Lip-type oil seals
- Lock nuts
- All roll pins
- All snap-rings
- Loctite Thread Lock or Loctite 242 Sealer

Disassembly

1. Remove the clutch housing.

2. Remove the straight screw plug,

1. Shift Lever
2. Shift Lever Retainer
3. Restrict Pins
4. Front Bearing Retainer
5. Clutch Housing
6. Snap Ring
7. Back-up Light Switch
8. Intermediate Plate
9. Adapter Housing
10. Adapter Screw Plug

SEE I.S. NOTES

11. Output Shaft
12. Reverse Idler Gear
13. Input Shaft
14. Counter Gear
15. Straight Screw Plug
16. Spring
17. Locking Ball

Jeep 4-5 speed

spring and ball using a Torx bit to remove the screw plug, and a magnet to remove spring and ball.

3. Remove five adapter housing bolts and one nut.

4. Remove the shift lever housing set bolt and lock plate.

5. Remove the plug at the rear of the shift fork shaft.

6. Remove the large magnet to pull the shaft out.

7. Remove the select lever from the top while rotating.

8. Remove the five adapter housing bolts two studs and one nut.

9. Using a plastic hammer, tap and remove the extension housing.

NOTE: Leave the gasket attached to the intermediate plate.

10. Remove the front bearing retainer and outer snap-rings from the two front bearings.

11. Separate the intermediate plate from the transmission case using a small plastic hammer and remove the case.

12. Mount the intermediate plate in a vise. Be careful not to damage the plate.

NOTE: Before placing the intermediate plate in a vise, insert bolts, washers, and nuts in the open holes at the bottom of plate. Tighten vise against these bolts to prevent damage to the plate.

13. Remove the straight screw plug,

locking balls and springs using a Torx bit and magnet.

14. Remove the five slotted spring pins using a hammer and punch and then remove the two E-rings from the shift rails.

— **CAUTION** —
The locking ball from the reverse shift head and locking ball and pin from the intermediate housing will fall from the holes so be sure to catch them. If they do not come out, remove them with a magnet.

15. Pull out the shift fork shaft No. 4 from the intermediate plate and catch the locking ball.

16. Remove shift fork shaft No. 4 and the 5th gear fork.

17. Pull out shift fork shaft No. 5 from the intermediate plate, and remove it with the reverse shift head.

— **CAUTION** —
The interlock pins will fall from their hole. If they do not come out, remove them with a magnet.

18. Remove the shift fork shaft No. 3 from the intermediate plate and catch the interlock pins.

— **CAUTION** —
The interlock pin will fall from the hole so be sure to catch it. If it does not come out, remove it with a magnet.

19. Remove shift fork shaft No. 1 from the intermediate plate being careful not to drop the interlock pin.

20. Remove shift fork shaft No. 2, shift fork No. 2 and shift fork No. 1.

21. Remove the reverse idle gear shaft stopper, reverse idler gear and shaft.

22. Remove the reverse shift arm from the reverse shift arm bracket.

23. Using a feeler gauge, measure the counter 5th gear thrust clearance. Standard Clearance: 0.10–0.30 mm (0.004–0.012 in.).

24. Engage two gears to lock the output shaft. Using a hammer and chisel, loosen the staked part of the nut on the counter shaft.

25. Remove the lock nut. Disengage the gears.

26. Remove the gear spline piece No. 5, synchronizer ring, needle roller bearing and counter fifth gear using tool J-22888 or equivalent.

27. Remove the spacer and use a magnet to remove the ball.

28. Remove the reverse shift arm bracket.

29. Remove the rear bearing retainer bolts with a Torx bit and the snap-ring using snap-ring pliers.

30. Remove the output shaft, counter gear and input shaft as a unit from the intermediate plate by pulling on the counter gear and tapping on the intermediate plate with a plastic hammer.

31. Remove the input shaft with fourteen needle roller bearings from the output shaft.

32. Remove the counter rear bearing from the intermediate plate.

33. Measure the thrust clearance of each gear. Standard Clearance: 0.10–0.25 mm (0.004–0.010 in.).

34. Using two awls and a hammer, tap out the snap-ring.

35. Using a press, remove the fifth gear, rear bearing, first gear and the inner race.

36. Remove the needle roller bearing.

37. Remove the synchronizer ring and locking ball.

38. Using a press, remove hub sleeve No. 1 Assembly, synchronizer ring, second gear.

39. Remove the needle roller bearing.

40. Remove the snap-ring from hub sleeve No. 2.

41. Using a press, remove the hub sleeve, synchronizer ring, and third gear.

42. Remove the needle roller bearing.

Component Inspection

OUTPUT SHAFT & INNER RACE

1. Check the output shaft and inner race for wear or damage.

2. Using calipers, measure the output shaft flange thickness. Minimum Thickness: 4.80 mm (0.189 in.).

3. Using calipers, measure the inner face

flange thickness. Minimum Thickness: 3.99 mm (0.157 in.).

4. Using a micrometer, measure the outer diameter of the output shaft journal surface. 2nd Gear Minimum: 37.964 mm (1.495 in.). 3rd Gear Minimum: 34.984 mm (1.377 in.).

5. Using a micrometer, measure the outer diameter of the inner race. Minimum Diameter: 38.985 mm (1.535 in.).

6. Using a dial indicator, measure the shaft runout. Maximum Runout: 0.05 mm (0.002 in.).

FIRST GEAR OIL CLEARANCE

1. Using a dial indicator, measure the oil clearance between the gear and inner race with the needle roller bearing installed. Standard Clearance: 0.009–0.032 mm (0.0004–0.0013 in.).

2. Using a dial indicator, measure the oil clearance between the gear and shaft with the needle roller bearing installed. Standard Clearance: 2nd and 3rd Gears: 0.009–0.033 mm (0.0004–0.0013 in.). Counter 5th Gear: 0.009–0.032 mm (0.0004–0.0013 in.).

Synchronizer Ring Inspection

1. Check for wear or damage. Turn the ring and push it in to check the braking action.

2. Measure the clearance between the synchronizer ring back and the gear spline end. Standard Clearance: 1.0–2.0 mm (0.040–0.078 in.). Minimum Clearance: 0.8 mm (0.031 in.).

Shift Fork and Hub Sleeve Clearance

1. Using a feeler gauge, measure the clearance between the hub sleeve and shift fork. Maximum Clearance: 1.0 mm (0.039 in.).

Input Shaft and Bearing Inspection and Removal

1. Check for wear or damage. If necessary, remove the bearing snap-ring using snap-ring pliers and remove the bearing.

2. Using a press, remove the bearing.

3. Using a press and tool J-34603 or equivalent, install the new bearing.

4. Select a snap-ring that will allow minimum axial play and install it on the shaft.

Thickness mm (in.)	
2.05–2.10	(0.0807–0.0827)
2.10–2.15	(0.0827–0.0846)
2.15–2.20	(0.0846–0.0866)
2.20–2.25	(0.0866–0.0886)
2.25–2.30	(0.0886–0.0906)
2.30–2.35	(0.0906–0.0925)

Counter Gear and Bearing Inspection

1. Check the gear teeth for wear or damage.

2. Check the bearing for wear or damage.

Counter Gear Front Bearing Replacement

1. Using snap-ring pliers, remove the snap-ring.

2. Press out the bearing using tool J-22912-01 or equivalent.

3. Replace the side race.

4. Using tool J-28406 or equivalent, press in the bearing and inner race.

5. Select a snap-ring that will allow minimum axial play and install it on the shaft.

Thickness mm (in.)	
2.05–2.10	(0.0807–0.0827)
2.10–2.15	(0.0827–0.0846)
2.15–2.20	(0.0846–0.0866)
2.20–2.25	(0.0866–0.0886)
2.25–2.30	(0.0886–0.0906)
2.30–2.35	(0.0906–0.0925)

Front Bearing Retainer Inspection

1. Check retainer for damage.

2. Check the oil seal lip for wear or damage.

Oil Seal Replacement

1. Using a awl, pry the old seal out of the housing.

2. Press in the new oil seal using tool J-34602 or equivalent.

3. The oil seal depth is 11.2 mm (0.441–0.480 in.) from the housing-to-transmission surface to the top edge of the seal.

Reverse Restrict Pin Replacement

1. Check for wear or damage.

2. Using a Torx bit, remove the screw plug.

3. Using a hammer and pin punch, drive out the slotted spring pin.

4. Pull off the lever housing and slide out the shaft.

5. Install the lever housing.

6. Using a hammer and pin punch, drive out the slotted spring pin.

7. Using a Torx bit, install and torque the screw plug to 37 N·m (27 ft. lbs.) torque.

Adapter Housing & Oil Seal Inspection & Replacement

1. Check the adapter housing for wear or damage.

2. Replace the oil seal with tool J-29184 or equivalent.

OUTPUT SHAFT

Assembly

1. Install the clutch hub No. 1 and No. 2 into hub sleeves along with the shifting keys.

——— CAUTION ———

Install the key springs so their gaps are not in line.

2. Install the shifting springs under the shifting keys.

3. Apply gear oil on the output shaft and 3rd gear needle roller bearing.

4. Place the 3rd gear synchronizer ring on the gear and align the ring slots with the shifting keys.

5. Install the needle roller bearing in the 3rd gear and hub sleeve No. 2.

6. Select a new snap-ring (2) that will allow minimum axial play and install it on the shaft.

Thickness mm (in.)	
1.75–1.80	(0.0689–0.0709)
1.80–1.85	(0.0709–0.0728)
1.85–1.90	(0.0728–0.0748)
1.90–1.95	(0.0748–0.0768)
1.95–2.00	(0.0768–0.0787)
2.00–2.05	(0.0788–0.0807)
2.05–2.10	(0.0807–0.0827)

7. Using a feeler gauge, measure the 3rd gear thrust clearance. Standard Clearance: 0.10–0.25 mm (0.004–0.010 in.).

8. Apply gear oil on the output shaft and 2nd gear needle bearing.

9. Place the 2nd gear synchronizer ring on the 2nd gear and align the ring slots with the shifting keys.

10. Install the needle roller bearing in the 2nd gear.

11. Using a press install the 2nd gear and hub sleeve No. 1.

12. Install the first gear locking ball in the output shaft.

13. Apply gear oil to the needle roller bearing.

14. Assemble the first gear, synchronizer ring, needle roller bearing and bearing inner race.

15. Install the assembly on the output shaft, with the synchronizer ring slots aligned with the shifting keys.

16. Turn the inner race to align it with the locking ball.

17. Install the output shaft rear bearing using tool J-34603 or equivalent and a press.

18. Install the bearing on the output shaft with the outer race snap-ring groove toward the rear.

NOTE: Hold the 1st gear inner race to prevent it from falling.

19. Measure the 1st and 2nd gear thrust clearance with a feeler gauge. Standard Clearance: 0.10–0.25 mm (0.004–0.010 in.).

20. Install 5th gear on the output shaft using tool J-34603 or equivalent and a press.

21. Select a snap-ring that will allow minimum axial play.

22. Using a screwdriver and a hammer, tap the snap into position.

Thickness mm (in.)	
2.67–2.72	(0.1051–0.1071)
2.73–2.78	(0.1075–0.1094)
2.79–2.84	(0.1098–0.1118)
2.85–2.90	(0.1122–0.1142)
2.91–2.96	(0.1146–0.1165)
2.97–3.02	(0.1169–0.1189)
3.03–3.08	(0.1193–0.1213)
3.09–3.14	(0.1217–0.1236)
3.15–3.20	(0.1240–0.1260)
3.21–3.26	(0.1264–0.1283)
3.27–3.32	(0.1287–0.1307)

23. Apply multi-purpose grease to the fourteen needle roller bearings and install them in the input shaft.

24. Install the output shaft into the intermediate plate by pulling on the output shaft and tapping on the intermediate plate.

25. Install the input shaft to the output shaft with the synchronizer ring slots aligned with the shifting keys.

26. Install the counter gear into the intermediate plate while holding the counter gear, and install the counter rear bearing with a suitable driver.

27. Install the bearing snap-ring using snap-ring pliers.

NOTE: Be sure the snap-ring is flush with the intermediate plate surface.

28. Using a Torx bit, install and tighten the screws to 18 N·m (13 ft. lbs.) torque.

29. Install the reverse shift arm bracket and tighten the bolts to 18 N·m (13 ft. lbs.) torque.

30. Install the ball and spacer.

31. Install the shifting keys and hub sleeve No. 3 onto the counter 5th gear.

------ **CAUTION** ------
Install the key springs positioned so the end gaps are not in line.

32. Install shifting key springs under the shifting keys.

33. Apply gear oil to the needle roller bearing and install the counter 5th gear with hub sleeve No. 3 and needle roller bearings.

34. Install the synchronizer ring on gear spline piece.

35. Using tool J-28406 or equivalent drive in gear spline piece No. 5 with the synchronizer ring slots aligned with the shifting keys.

NOTE: When installing gear spline piece No. 5, support the counter gear in front with a 3–5 lb. hammer or equivalent.

36. Engage two gears to lock the output shaft.

37. Install and tighten the lock nut to 122 N·m (90 ft. lbs.) torque on the counter shaft.

38. Stake the lock nut.

39. Disengage the gears.

40. Measure the counter fifth gear thrust clearance using a feeler gauge. Standard Clearance: 0.10–0.30 mm (0.004–0.012 in.).

41. Install the reverse shift arm to the pivot of the reverse shift arm bracket.

42. Install the reverse idler gear on the shaft.

43. Align the reverse shift arm shoe to the reverse idler gear groove and insert the reverse idler gear shift to the intermediate plate.

44. Install the reverse idler gear shaft stopper and tighten the bolt to 18 N·m (13 ft. lbs.) torque.

45. Place shift forks No. 1 and No. 2 into groove of hub sleeves No. 1 and No. 2 and install fork shaft No. 2 to the shift forks No. 1 and No. 2 through the intermediate plate.

46. Apply multi-purpose grease to the interlock pins.

47. Using a magnet and screwdriver, install the interlock pin into the intermediate plate.

48. Install the interlock pin into the shaft hole.

49. Install fork shaft No. 1 to shift fork No. 1 through the intermediate plate.

50. Using a magnet and screwdriver, install the interlock pin into the intermediate plate.

51. Install the interlock pin into the shaft hole.

52. Install fork shaft No. 3 to the reverse shift arm through the intermediate plate.

53. Install the reverse shift head into fork shaft No. 5.

54. Insert fork shaft No. 5 to the intermediate plate and put in the reverse shift head to the shift fork No. 3.

55. Using a magnetic finger and screwdriver, install the locking ball into the reverse shift head hole.

56. Shift hub sleeve No. 3 to the 5th speed position.

57. Place shift fork No. 3 into the groove of hub sleeve No. 3 and install fork shaft No. 4 to shift fork No. 3 and reverse shift arm.

58. Using a magnet and screwdriver, install the locking ball into the intermediate plate and insert fork shaft No. 4 to the intermediate plate.

59. Check the interlock by positioning the shift fork shaft No. 1 to the 1st speed position.

60. Fork shafts No. 2, No. 3, No. 4 and No. 5 should not move.

61. Using a pin punch and a hammer, drive in new slotted spring pins in each shift fork, reverse shift arm and reverse shift head.

62. Install two fork shaft E-rings.

63. Apply liquid sealer to the screw plugs.

64. Install the locking balls, springs and screw plugs with a Torx bit and tighten to 19 N·m (14 ft. lbs.) torque.

NOTE: Install the short spring into the tower of the intermediate plate.

65. Remove the intermediate plate from the vise.

66. Remove the bolts, nuts, washers and gasket.

Transmission Case Installation

1. Align each bearing outer race, each fork shaft end and reverse idler gear with the holes in the case and install the case on the intermediate plate. If necessary, tap on the case with a plastic hammer.

2. Install two new bearing snap-rings.

3. Install front bearing retainer with a new gasket.

4. Apply liquid sealer to the bolts.

5. Install and tighten the bolts to 16 N·m (12 ft. lbs.) torque.

6. Install the new gasket to the intermediate plate.

7. Install the adapter housing.

8. Install and tighten the adapter bolts to 37 N·m (27 ft. lbs.) torque.

9. Install the shift lever housing.

10. Insert the shift lever into the adapter and shift lever housing.

11. Install and tighten shift lever housing bolt with a lock plate to 38 N·m (28 ft. lbs.) torque. Lock the lock plate.

12. Install and tighten the adapter screw plug to 18 N·m (13 ft. lbs.) torque.

13. Apply liquid sealer to the plug.

14. Install the locking ball, spring and screw plug and tighten the plug to 19 N·m (14 ft. lbs.) torque.

15. Check to see that the input shaft and output shafts rotate smoothly.

16. Check to see that shifting can be done smoothly to all positions.

17. Install the black restrict pin on the reverse gear/5th gear side.

18. Install the remaining pin and tighten the pins to 27 N·m (20 ft. lbs.) torque.

19. Install the shift lever retainer with a new gasket and tighten the bolts to 18 N·m (13 ft. lbs.) torque.

20. Install the back-up light switch and tighten to 37 N·m (27 ft. lbs.) torque.

21. Install the clutch housing and tighten the bolts to 37 N·m (27 ft. lbs.) torque.

Arrow/D–50/Mitsubishi 4–Speed Transmission

Disassembly

1. Remove the undercover.

2. Remove the back-up light switch. Be careful not to lose the steel ball.

3. Remove the speedometer gear sleeve clamp and remove the speedometer driven gear and sleeve assembly from the extension housing assembly.

4. Remove the extension housing bolts. Turn the shift lever to the left and pull off the extension housing.

5. Loosen the three poppet plugs, then remove the three poppet springs and the three steel balls.

6. Place the 1st/2nd speed shift rod in Neutral position.

7. Remove the reverse shift rail and fork assembly together with the reverse idler gear.

8. Using a ³⁄₁₆ in. punch, drive off the 3rd/4th and 1st/2nd speed shift fork spring pins. Push each shift rod toward the rear of the transmission case and remove the shift forks. Remember to remove the interlock plunger.

9. Remove the snap-ring from the rear end of the counter gear and then remove the reverse counter gear.

10. Unlock the mainshaft locknut and remove the locknut. The locknut can be loosened by double-engaging the 3rd speed gear and the 1st speed gear.

11. Remove the reverse gear from the mainshaft.

12. Remove the five attaching screws and then remove the rear bearing retainer.

13. Remove the front bearing retainer.

14. With the counter gear pressed to the rear, remove the rear bearing snap-ring. Then using a bearing puller remove the rear counter bearing.

15. Remove the snap-ring from the front counter bearing. Pull off the bearing with a bearing puller.

16. Pull the counter gear out of the case.

17. Remove the main drive pinion from the front of the case. To remove the bearing from the main drive pinion, remove the two snap-rings and then remove the bearing with a bearing puller.

18. Remove the mainshaft bearing snap-ring and remove the bearing using a dual post bearing puller (D-50/Plymouth Arrow special tool MD998056-10 and MD998056).

19. Remove the mainshaft assembly by lifting it up through the case.

20. Disassemble the mainshaft assembly in the following order.

   a. Pull off the 1st speed gear, the 1st/2nd speed synchronizer and the 2nd speed gear toward the rear of the mainshaft.

   b. Remove the snap-ring from the forward end of the mainshaft, then remove the 3rd/4th speed synchronizer and the 3rd speed gear.

21. If removing the shift control shaft assembly, remove the pin locking the gear shifter using a ³⁄₁₆ in. punch. To remove the lock pin, press the gear shifter forward and drive the lock pin off, being careful not to bend the control shaft.

Inspect the parts after cleaning. Replace any worn, damaged or defective.

Assembly

1. If the main drive pinion bearing has been removed, replace it using a pipe fit over the end of the pinion shaft.

─── CAUTION ───
Make sure the pipe does not apply pressure on the ball bearings but only on the bearing race, or bearing damage could result.

2. Fit a snap-ring which gives a clearance of no more than 0–0.002 in. and install it on the drive pinion.

3. Assemble the mainshaft in the following order.

   a. Assemble the 3rd/4th speed and the 1st/2nd speed synchronizers.

   b. Install the needle bearing, 3rd speed gear, synchronizer ring and the 3rd/4th speed synchronizer assembly onto the mainshaft from the front end. Be careful not to confuse the front and the rear of the synchronizer assembly.

4. Select and install a snap-ring that will give the 3rd/4th speed synchronizer hub an end-play from 0.0 to 0.003 in.

5. Third speed gear end-play should be from 0.002 to 0.008 in.

6. Install the needle bearing, the 2nd speed gear, the synchronizer assembly, the bearing sleeve, the needle bearing, the 1st speed gear, and the bearing spacer onto the mainshaft from the rear end.

7. Push the bearing spacer forward and check the 1st and 2nd speed gear end-play. Clearance should be within 0.002–0.008 in.

8. Insert the mainshaft assembly into the transmission case and fit the mainshaft center bearing using a bearing driver. Hold the forward end of the mainshaft by hand at the front of the case.

9. Install the needle bearing and the synchronizer ring, then insert the main drive pinion assembly into the case from the front.

10. Insert the countershaft gear into the case. With a snap-ring fitted to the countershaft front needle bearing, drive the bearing into the case by hammering on the outer race of the bearing.

11. Fit a snap-ring to the countershaft rear ball bearing and then install the bearing with a bearing installer.

12. Install the front bearing retainer. When installing the retainer, install a spacer that will give a clearance (C) of 0.0–0.004 in. Apply sealant to both sides of the front bearing retainer packing and apply gear oil to the oil seal lip. Install packing and oil seal.

13. Install the rear bearing retainer and its five screws. It is suggested that each screw head be staked with a pointed punch to prevent them from coming loose.

14. Install the reverse gear on the mainshaft and tighten the locknut to 73–94 ft. lbs. Lock the nut at the notch of the mainshaft.

15. Install the spacer and counter reverse gear to the counter gear rear end.

16. Install a snap-ring of the proper size so that the reverse counter gear and play will be from 0.0 to 0.003 in.

17. Install the 3rd/4th and 1st/2nd speed shift forks into their respective synchronizer sleeves. Insert each shift rod from the rear of the case. Lock the shift forks and rod with spring pins, install the interlock plunger between the shift rods.

NOTE: The spring pins should be installed with the slits parallel to the shift rod.

18. Install the reverse shift rod and fork assembly together with the reverse idler gear.

19. Insert the ball and poppet spring with the small end on the ball side into each shift rod. Tighten the plugs to the specified positions. After installation, seal each plug head with sealant.

20. Apply sealant to both sides of the extension housing packing and fit the packing into the housing.

21. Turn the gear shift control down to the left and install the extension to the transmission case.

22. Make sure the forward end of the control finger is snug in the slot of the shift lug and fit the extension housing bolts after coating their threads with sealant.

23. Apply gear oil to the speedometer driven gear and install the gear and sleeve assembly in the extension housing. Make sure the sleeve flange and its mating areas on the extension housing are free of dirt, or it will cause the gears to be misaligned and could damage them.

24. Rotate the speedometer driven gear and sleeve assembly so that the number on the sleeve, which is the same as the number of teeth on the gear, is in the "U" mark position as the assembly is installed.

25. Install the speedometer gear clamp with its tongs in the sleeve positioning slots.

26. Install the backup light switch with its steel ball.

27. Refit the under cover and torque the bolts to 6–7 ft. lbs.

28. Install the transmission control lever assembly and fill the gear shifter area with grease. Fill the transmission with lubricant.

Arrow/D–50/Mitsubishi 5–Speed Transmission

Disassembly

1. Remove the clutch release bearing and carrier.

2. Remove the spring pin and the clutch control shaft. Remove the felt, return spring and clutch shift arm.

3. Remove the case cover.

4. Remove the back-up light switch.

5. Remove the extension housing.

6. Remove the speedometer drive gear.

7. Remove the ball bearing from the mainshaft rear end.

8. Loosen three poppet spring plugs, then remove three poppet springs and three balls.

9. Remove the 3-4 and 1-2 speed shift fork spring pins. Pull off each shift rail toward the rear of the transmission case, then remove the shift fork. Remove the interlock plunger.

10. Remove the overtop and reverse shift forks spring pins, shift rails and forks.

11. Loosen the locknuts (mainshaft and countershaft rear ends).

1. Transmission case
2. Main drive pinion
3. Synchronizer assy (3-4 speed)
4. 3rd speed gear
5. 2nd speed gear
6. Synchronizer assy (1-2 speed)
7. 1st speed gear
8. Rear bearing retainer
9. Synchronizer assy (overtop)
10. Overtop gear
11. Control finger
12. Neutral return finger
13. Control shaft
14. Control lever cover
15. Control lever assy
16. Stopper plate
17. Control housing
18. Change shifter
19. Mainshaft
20. Speedometer drive gear
21. Extension housing
22. Counter overtop gear
23. Counter reverse gear
24. Reverse idler gear
25. Reverse idler gear shaft
26. Case cover
27. Counter gear
28. Front bearing retainer
29. Clutch shift arm
30. Release bearing carrier
31. Clutch control shaft
32. Return spring

Cross section of 5-speed transmission, model KM 132

12. Pull off the counter overtop gear and the ball bearing at the same time using a puller. Remove the spacer and the counter reverse gear.

13. Remove the overtop gear and sleeve from the mainshaft. Remove the overtop synchronizer assembly and spacer.

14. Remove the reverse idler gear.

15. Remove the rear bearing retainer.

16. Drive the reverse idler gear shaft from inside the case.

17. Remove the front bearing retainer.

18. With the counter gear pressed to the rear, remove the rear bearing snap-ring. Remove the counter rear bearing.

19. Remove the counter front bearing.

20. Remove the counter gear from the inside of the case.

21. Remove the main drive pinion from the front of the case. Remove the main drive pinion bearing.

22. Remove the mainshaft bearing snap-ring. Remove the ball bearing.

23. Pull the mainshaft assembly from the case.

24. Disassemble the mainshaft in the following order:

   a. Remove the 1st gear, the 1-2 speed synchronizer and the 2nd speed gear toward the rear of the mainshaft.

   b. Remove the snap-ring from the forward end of the mainshaft. Remove the 3-4 speed synchronizer and the 3rd gear.

25. Disassemble the extension housing.

   a. Remove the lock plate and the speedometer driven gear.

   b. Remove the plug, spring and neutral return plunger.

   c. When removing the control shaft assembly, pull off the lock pin locking the gear shifter. To remove the lock pin, press the gear shifter forward and pull it off.

Assembly

1. Install the ball bearing on the main drive pinion. Install a selective snap-ring so that there will be 0–0.002 in. clearance between the snap-ring and the bearing.

Thickness of snap-ring
   .0906 in.
   .0925 in.
   .0945 in.
   .0965 in.
   .0984 in.

Identification color
   White
   None
   Red
   Blue
   Yellow

2. Install the mainshaft in the following order:

   a. Assemble the 3-4 speed and 1-2 speed synchronizers. The front and rear ends of the synchronizer sleeve and hub can be identified as shown. The synchronizer spring can be installed as shown.

   b. Install the needle bearing, the 3rd speed gear, the synchronizer ring, and the 3-4 speed synchronizer assembly on to the mainshaft from the front end. Select and install a snap-ring of proper size so that the 3-4 speed synchronizer hub end-play will be 0–0.003 in.

Thickness of snap-ring
   .0846 in.
   .0874 in.
   .0902 in.
   .0929 in.

Identification color
   None
   Yellow

Green
White

c. Check the 3rd gear end-play (.0016–.0079 in.).

d. Install the needle bearing, the 2nd speed gear, the synchronizer assembly, the bearing sleeve, the needle bearing, the 1st speed gear, and the bearing spacer on the mainshaft from the rear. With the bearing spacer pressed forward, check the 2nd and 1st gear end-play (0.0016–0.0079 in.).

3. Install the mainshaft into the transmission case and drive in the mainshaft center bearing.

4. Install the needle bearing and the synchronizer ring. Install the main drive pinion assembly into the case from the front.

5. Install the countershaft gear into the case. Drive the front bearing into the case.

6. Install the snap-ring on the countershaft rear bearing.

7. Install the front bearing retainer. Select and install a spacer of proper size so that the clearance will be 0–0.0039 in.

Thickness of spacer
.0030 in.
.0366 in.
.0402 in.
.0437 in.
.0472 in.
.0508 in.
.0543 in.

Identification color
Black
None
Red
White
Yellow
Blue
Green

Replace the front bearing retainer oil seal.

8. Install the rear bearing retainer.

9. Install the reverse idler gear shaft.

10. Install the needle bearing, the reverse idler gear and the thrust washer. Check the reverse idler gear end-play (.0047–.0110 in.). Install the thrust washer with the ground side toward the gear side.

11. Assemble the overtop synchronizer.

12. Install the spacer, the stop plate, the overtop synchronizer assembly, the overtop gear bearing sleeve, the needle bearing, the synchronizer ring and the overtop gear in the written order on to the mainshaft from the rear end. Check the overtop gear end-play.

13. Install the spacer, the counter reverse gear, the spacer, the counter overtop gear and the ball bearing on to the countershaft gear from the rear end.

14. Insert the 3-4 and 1-2 speed shift forks into respective synchronizer sleeves. Insert each shift rail from the rear of the case. Lock the shift forks and rails with spring pins. Install an interlock plunger between shift rails. The pin should be installed with the slit in the axial direction of the shift rail.

15. Insert the ball and poppet spring into each shift rail. Install the poppet spring with the small end on the ball side.

16. Install the ball bearing on to the rear end of the mainshaft.

17. Install the speedometer drive gear.

18. Install the extension housing. Turn the change shifter fully down to the left. Make sure the forward end of the control finger is snugly fitted in the slot of the shift lug.

19. Install the neutral return plungers (A) and (B), the spring, and resistance spring and ball. Tighten each plug till its top is flush with the boss top surface.

20. Install the speedometer driven gear sleeve into the extension housing and into mesh with the drive gear.

21. Install the back-up light switch. Remember the steel ball.

22. Install the under cover.

23. Insert the clutch control shaft. Install the packing (felt), the return spring and the clutch shift arm. The spring pin should be installed in such a manner that the slip will be at right angles with the axis of the control shaft.

24. Install the transmission control lever assembly. Fill the gear shifter area with grease.

25. After reassembly, rotate the drive pinion to see if it rotates smoothly.

Chevrolet/GMC S Series

77m 4–SPEED TRANSMISSION

Disassembly

1. Remove drain plug and drain lubricant from transmission.

2. Thoroughly clean the exterior of the transmission assembly.

3. Using a hammer and punch, remove the roll pin that attaches the offset lever to shift rail.

4. Remove extension housing attaching bolts. Separate the extension housing from the transmission case and remove housing and offset lever as an assembly.

5. Remove detent ball and spring from offset lever and remove roll pin from extension housing or offset lever.

6. Remove transmission shift cover attaching bolts. Using a screwdriver, pry shift cover loose and remove cover from transmission case.

7. Remove clip that retains reverse lever to reverse lever pivot bolt.

8. Remove reverse lever pivot bolt and remove reverse lever and fork as an assembly.

9. Using a hammer and punch, mark position of front bearing cap to transmission case. Remove front bearing cap bolts and remove bearing cap.

10. Remove small retaining and large locating snap rings from front drive gear bearing.

11. Install bearing puller J-22912-01 on front bearing and puller J-8433-1 with two bolts on end of drive gear and remove and discard bearing. A new bearing must be used when assembling the transmission.

12. Remove retaining and locating snap rings from rear bearing and mainshaft. Install puller J-22912-01 on bearing and puller J-8433-1 with two bolts (J-33171) on end of mainshaft and remove and discard used bearing. A new bearing must be used when assembling transmission.

13. Remove drive gear from mainshaft and transmission case as shown.

14. Remove mainshaft from transmission case by tipping mainshaft down at the rear and lifting shaft out through shift cover opening.

15. Using a hammer and punch, remove roll pin retaining reverse idler gear shaft in transmission case. Remove idler gear and shaft from case.

16. Remove countershaft from rear of case using loading tool J-26624. Remove countershaft gear and loading tool as an assembly from case along with thrust washers.

Mainshaft Disassembly

1. Scribe alignment mark on third-fourth synchronizer hub and sleeve for reassembly. Remove retaining snap ring and remove third-fourth synchronizer assembly from mainshaft.

2. Slide third gear off mainshaft.

3. Remove second gear retaining snap ring. Remove tabbed thrust washer, second gear and blocker ring from mainshaft.

4. Remove first gear thrust washer and roll pin from mainshaft. Use pliers to remove roll pin.

5. Remove first gear and blocker ring from mainshaft.

6. Scribe alignment mark on first-second synchronizer hub and sleeve for reassembly.

7. Remove synchronizer springs and keys from first-second sleeve and remove sleeve from shaft.

NOTE: Do not attempt to remove the first-second hub from the mainshaft. The hub and mainshaft are assembled and machined as a unit.

8. Remove loading Tool J-26624, roller bearings, spacers and thrust washers from the countershaft gear.

Drive Gear Disassembly

1. Remove roller bearings from cavity of drive gear.

2. Wash parts in a cleaning solvent.

3. Inspect gear teeth for wear.

4. Inspect drive shaft pilot for wear.

Cover Disassembly

1. Place selector arm plates and shift rail in neutral position (centered).

2. Rotate shift rail until selector arm disengages from selector arm plates and roll pin is accessible.

3. Remove selector arm roll pin using a pin punch and hammer.

4. Remove shift rail, shift forks, selector arm plates, selector arm, interlock plate and roll pin.

5. Remove shift cover to extension housing "O" ring seal using a screwdriver.

6. Remove nylon inserts and selector arm plates from shift forks. Note position of inserts and plates for assembly reference.

Assembly

1. Install nylon inserts and selector arm plates in shift forks.

2. If removed, install shift rail plug. Coat edges of plug with sealer before installing.

3. Coat shift rail and rail bores with light weight grease and insert shift rail in cover. Install rail until flush with inside edge of cover.

4. Place first-second shift fork in cover with fork offset facing rear of cover and push shift rail through fork. The first-second shift fork is the larger of the two forks.

5. Position selector arm and C-shaped interlock plate in cover and insert shift rail through arm. Widest part of interlock plate must face away from cover, and selector arm roll pin hole must face downward and toward rear of cover.

6. Position third-fourth shift fork in cover with fork offset facing rear of cover. Third-fourth shift fork selector arm plate must be under first-second shift fork selector arm plate.

7. Push shift rail through third-fourth shift fork and into front bore in cover.

8. Rotate shift rail until selector arm plate at forward end of rail faces away from, but is parallel to cover.

9. Align roll pin holes in selector arm and shift rail and install roll pin. Roll pin must be flush with surface of selector arm to prevent pin from contacting selector arm plates during shifts.

10. Install a new shift cover to extension housing "O" ring seal. Coat "O" ring seal with transmission lubricant.

Drive Gear Assembly

1. Coat roller bearings and drive gear bearing bore with light weight grease. Install roller bearings into bore of drive gear.

Mainshaft Assembly

1. Coat mainshaft and gear bores with transmission lubricant.

2. Install first-second synchronizer sleeve on mainshaft, aligning marks previously made.

3. Install synchronizer keys and springs into the first-second synchronizer sleeve. Engage tang end of springs into the same synchronizer key but position open ends of springs so they face away from one another.

4. Place blocking ring on first gear and

install gear and ring on mainshaft. Be sure synchronizer keys engage notches in first gear blocking ring.

5. Install first gear roll pin in mainshaft.

6. Place blocking ring on second gear and install gear and ring on mainshaft. Be sure synchronizer keys engage notches in second gear blocking ring. Install second gear thrust washer and snap ring on mainshaft. Be sure thrust washer tab is engaged in mainshaft notch.

7. Measure second gear end play using feeler gauge. Insert gauge between gear and thrust washer. End play should be 0.10 to 0.35 mm (0.004 to 0.014). If end play is over 0.35 mm (0.014), replace thrust washer and snap ring and inspect synchronizer hub for excessive wear.

8. Place blocking ring on third gear and install gear and ring on mainshaft.

9. Install third-fourth synchronizer sleeve on hub, aligning marks previously made.

10. Install synchronizer keys and springs in third-fourth synchronizer sleeve. Engage tang end of each spring in same key but position open ends of springs so they face away from one another.

11. Install third-fourth synchronizer assembly on the mainshaft with machined groove in hub facing forward. Install snap ring on mainshaft. Be sure synchronizer keys are engaged in notches in third gear blocker ring.

12. Install Tool J-26624 into countershaft gear. Using a light weight grease, lubricate roller bearings and install into bores at front and rear of countershaft gear. Install roller bearing retainers on Tool J-26624.

Transmission Assembly

1. Coat countershaft gear thrust washers with grease and position washer in case.

2. Position countershaft gear in case and install countershaft from rear of case. Be sure that thrust washers stay in place during installation of countershaft and gear.

3. Position reverse idler gear in case with shift lever groove facing rear of case and install reverse idler shaft from rear of case. Install roll pin in shaft and center pin in shaft.

4. Install mainshaft assembly into the case. Do not disturb position of synchronizer assemblies during installation.

5. Install fourth gear blocking ring in third-fourth synchronizer sleeve. Be sure synchronizer keys engage in notches in blocker ring.

6. Install drive gear into case and engage with mainshaft.

7. Position mainshaft first gear against rear of case. Using a new bearing, start front bearing onto drive gear. Align bearing with bearing bore in case and drive bearing onto drive gear and into case using Tool J-25234.

8. Install front bearing retaining and locating snap rings.

9. Apply a 3mm diameter (⅛ inch) bead of RTV sealant, #732 or equivalent, on

case mating surface of front bearing cap. Install bearing cap aligning marks previously made. Apply nonhardening sealer on attaching bolts and install bolts. Torque bolts to specifications.

10. Install first gear thrust washer with oil groove facing first gear on mainshaft, aligning slot in washer with first gear roll pin.

11. Using a new bearing, position rear bearing on mainshaft. Align bearing with bearing bore in case and drive bearing into case using Tool J-25234.

12. Install locating and retaining snap rings on rear bearing.

13. Install speedometer gear and retaining clip on mainshaft.

14. Apply nonhardening sealer to threads of reverse lever pivot bolt and start bolt into case. Engage reverse lever fork in the reverse idler gear and reverse lever on pivot bolt. Tighten bolt to specifications and install retaining clip.

15. Rotate drivegear and mainshaft gears. If blocker rings tend to stick on gears, release the rings by gently prying them off the cones.

16. Apply a 3mm diameter (⅛ inch) bead of RTV Sealant, #732 or equivalent, on the cover mating surface of transmission. Place reverse lever in neutral, and position cover on case.

17. Install 2 dowel type bolts first to align cover on case. Install remaining cover bolts and torque to specifications. The offset lever to shift rail roll pin hole must be in the vertical position after cover installation.

18. Apply a 3mm diameter (⅛ inch) bead of RTV Sealant, #732 or equivalent, on the extension housing to transmission case mating surface.

19. Place extension housing over mainshaft to a position where shift rail is in shift cover opening.

20. Install detent spring in offset lever. Place ball in neutral guide plate detent position. Apply pressure on the offset lever, slide offset lever onto shift rail and seat extension housing to transmission case.

21. Install extension housing retaining bolts. Torque bolts to specifications.

22. Align hole in offset lever and shift rail and install roll pin.

23. Fill transmission to its proper level with recommended lubricant.

5–Speed Transmission

Disassembly

1. Remove drain bolt on transmission case and drain lubricant.

2. Thoroughly clean the exterior of the transmission assembly.

3. Using pin punch and hammer, remove roll pin attaching offset lever to shift rail.

4. Remove extension housing-to-transmission case bolts and remove housing and offset lever as an assembly.

33. GEAR, 2nd Speed
34. KEY, 1 & 2 Syn
35. PIN, 1st Spd Gr Thr Wa Ret
36. BEARING, Cntr Gr Frt
37. WASHER, Cntr Gr Frt Thr
38. GEAR, Counter
39. SPACER, Counter Gr Brg Frt
40. BEARING, Cntr Gr Rr
41. SPACER, Counter Gr Brg Rr
42. RING, Snap
43. GEAR, 5th Spd Drive
44. RING, 5th Syn
45. KEY, 5th Syn
46. HUB, 5th Syn
47. SPRING, 5th Syn
48. SLEEVE, 5th Syn
49. RETAINER, 5th Syn Key
50. RACE, 5th Syn Thr Brg Frt
51. BEARING, 5th Syn Ndl Thr
52. RACE, 5th Syn Thr Brg Rr
53. RING, Snap
54. FUNNEL, Trans Oiling
55. NUT, Magnet
56. MAGNET
57. CASE, Trans
58. PLUG, Fill & Drain
59. SPRING, Rev Lock
60. FORK, Rev Shift
61. ROLLER, Fork
62. PIN, Rev Fork
63. PIN, Shift Rail
64. ROLLER, Rail pin
65. RAIL, 5th & Rev Shft
66. INSERT, Shift Fork
67. PIN, Roll
68. FORK, 5th Shift
69. LEVER, 5th & Rev Relay
70. RING, Rev. Relay Lever Ret
71. SHAFT, Rev Idler Gr
72. GEAR, Rev Idler (Incl Bshg)
73. PIN, 5th Spd Shft Lvr Piv
74. VENTILATOR, Ext
75. BALL, Steel
76. SPRING, Detent
77. RETAINER, Cont Lvr Boot
78. BOOT, Cont Lvr
79. RETAINER, Cont Lvr Boot Lwr
80. CONTROL, Trans Lvr & Hsg
81. SLEEVE, Shft Lvr Dmpr
82. LEVER, Offset Shift
83. PLATE, Detent & Guide
84. SEAL, Ext Rr Oil
85. BUSHING, Extension Housing
86. HOUSING, Extension
87. GEAR, Main Drive
88. BEARING, Front
89. SHIM, Brg Adj
90. RETAINER, Drive Gr Brg
91. SEAL, Drive Gr Brg Oil

1. COVER, Trans
2. SEAL, "O" Ring, Cvr to Ext.
3. SHAFT, Shift
4. FORK, 3rd & 4th Shift
5. PLATE, Shift Fork
6. ARM, Control Selector
7. PLATE, Gear Sel Intlk
8. FORK, 1st & 2nd Shift
9. INSERT, Shift Fork
10. PIN, Roll
11. SPRING, Syn
12. GEAR, Rev Sldg
13. SHAFT, Output, W/1 & 2 Syn
14. RING, 1 & 2 Syn Blkg
15. GEAR, 1st Speed
16. WASHER, 1st Spd Gr Thrust

17. BEARING, Rear
18. GEAR, 5th Spd Drvn
19. RING, Snap
20. GEAR, Speedo Dr
21. CLIP, Speedo Dr Gr
22. BEARING, Main Shf Rir
23. BEARING, Main Dr Gr Thr Ndl
24. RACE, Main Dr Gr Ghr Brg
25. RING, 3 & 4 Syn
26. SPRING, 3 & 4 Syn
27. HUB, 3 & 4 Syn
28. KEY, 3 & 4 Syn
29. SLEEVE, 3 & 4 Syn
30. GEAR, 3rd Speed
31. RING, Snap
32. WASHER, 2nd Spd Gr Thr

77mm 5-speed exploded view

NOTE: Do not attempt to remove the offset lever while the extension housing is still bolted in place. The lever has a positioning lug engaged in the housing detent plate which prevents moving the lever far enough for removal.

5. Remove detent ball and spring from offset lever and remove roll pin from extension housing or offset lever.

6. Remove plastic funnel, thrust bearing race and thrust bearing from rear of countershaft.

NOTE: The countershaft rear thrust bearing, bearing washer and plastic fun- nel may be found inside the extension housing.

7. Remove bolts attaching transmission cover and shift fork assembly and remove cover.

NOTE: Two of the transmission cover

attaching bolts are alignment-type dowel bolts. Note the location of these bolts for assembly reference.

8. Using a punch and hammer, drive the roll pin from the fifth gearshift fork while supporting the end of the shaft with a block of wood.

9. Remove fifth synchronizer gear snap ring, shift fork, fifth gear synchronizer sleeve, blocking ring and fifth speed drive gear from rear of countershaft.

10. Remove snap ring from fifth speed driven gear.

11. Using a hammer and punch, mark both bearing cap and case for assembly reference.

12. Remove front bearing cap bolts and remove front bearing cap. Remove front bearing race and end play shims from front bearing cap.

13. Rotate drive gear until flat surface faces countershaft and remove drive gear from transmission case.

14. Remove reverse lever C-clip and pivot bolt.

15. Remove mainshaft rear bearing race and then tilt mainshaft assembly upward and remove assembly from transmission case.

16. Unhook overcenter link spring from front of transmission case.

17. Rotate fifth gear-reverse shift rail to disengage rail from reverse lever assembly. Remove shift rail from rear of transmission case.

18. Remove reverse lever and fork assembly from transmission case.

19. Using hammer and punch, drive roll pin from forward end of reverse idler shaft and remove reverse idler shaft, rubber "O" ring and gear from the transmission case.

20. Remove rear countershaft snap ring and spacer.

21. Insert a brass drift through drive gear opening in front of transmission case and, using an arbor press, carefully press countershaft rearward to remove rear countershaft bearing.

22. Move countershaft assembly rearward, tilt countershaft upward and remove from case. Remove countershaft front thrust washer and rear bearing spacer.

23. Remove countershaft front bearing from transmission case using an arbor press.

Mainshaft Disassembly

1. Remove thrust bearing washer from front end of mainshaft.

2. Scribe reference mark on third-fourth synchronizer hub and sleeve for reassembly.

3. Remove third-fourth synchronizer blocking ring, sleeve, hub and third gear as an assembly from mainshaft.

4. Remove snap ring, tabbed thrust washer, and second gear from mainshaft.

5. Remove fifth gear with Tool J-22912-01 or its equal and arbor press. Slide rear bearing off mainshaft.

6. Remove first gear thrust washer, roll pin, first gear and synchronizer ring from mainshaft.

7. Scribe reference mark on first-second synchronizer hub and sleeve for reassembly.

8. Remove synchronizer spring and keys from first-reverse sliding gear and remove gear from mainshaft hub. Do not attempt to remove the first-second-reverse hub from mainshaft. The hub and shaft are assembled and machined as a matched set.

Drive Gear Disassembly

1. Remove bearing race, thrust bearing, and roller bearings from cavity of drive gear.

2. Using Tool J-22912-01 or its equal and arbor press, remove bearing from drive gear.

3. Wash parts in a cleaning solvent.

4. Inspect gear teeth and drive shaft pilot for wear.

Drive Gear Assembly

1. Using Tool J-22912-01 or its equal with an arbor press, install bearing on drive gear.

2. Coat roller bearings and drive gear bearing bore with grease. Install roller bearings into bore of drive gear.

3. Install thrust bearing and race in drive gear.

Mainshaft Assembly

1. Coat mainshaft and gear bores with transmission lubricant.

2. Install first-second synchronizer sleeve on mainshaft hub aligning marks made at disassembly.

3. Install first-second synchronizer keys and springs. Engage tang end of each spring in same synchronizer key but position open end of springs opposite of each other.

4. Install blocker ring and second gear on mainshaft. Install tabbed thrust washer and second gear retaining snap ring on mainshaft. Be sure washer tab is properly seated in mainshaft notch.

5. Install blocker ring and first gear on mainshaft. Install first gear roll pin and then first gear thrust washer.

6. Slide rear bearing on mainshaft.

7. Install fifth speed gear on mainshaft using Tool J-22912-01 and arbor press. Install snap ring on mainshaft.

8. Install third gear, third-fourth synchronizer assembly and thrust bearing on mainshaft. Synchronizer hub offset must face forward.

Assembly

1. Coat countershaft front bearing bore with Loctite 601, or equivalent, and install front countershaft bearing flush with facing of case using an arbor press.

2. Coat countershaft tabbed thrust washer with grease and install washer so tab engages depression in case.

3. Tip transmission case on end and install countershaft in front bearing bore.

4. Install countershaft rear bearing spacer. Coat countershaft rear bearing with grease and install bearing using Tool J-29895 and sleeve J-33032, or its equivalent. The bearing when correctly installed will extend beyond the case surface .125 inch (3mm).

5. Position reverse idler gear in case with shift lever groove facing rear of case and install reverse idler shaft from rear of case. Install roll pin in idler shaft.

6. Install assembled mainshaft in transmission case. Install rear mainshaft bearing race in case.

7. Install drive gear in case, and engage in third-fourth synchronizer sleeve and blocker ring.

8. Install front bearing race in front bearing cap. Do not install shims in front bearing cap at this time.

9. Temporarily install front bearing cap.

10. Install fifth speed-reverse lever, pivot bolt and retaining clip. Coat pivot bolt threads with nonhardening sealer. Be sure to engage reverse lever fork in reverse idler gear.

11. Install countershaft rear bearing spacer and retaining snap ring.

12. Install fifth speed gear on countershaft.

13. Insert fifth speed-reverse rail in rear of case and install in to reverse fifth speed lever. Rotate rail during installation to simplify engagement with lever. Connect spring to front of case.

14. Position fifth gear shift fork on fifth gear synchronizer assembly and install synchronizer on countershaft and shift fork on shift rail. Make sure roll pin hole in shift fork and shift rail are aligned.

15. Support fifth gear shift rail and fork on a block of wood and install roll pin.

16. Install thrust race against fifth speed synchronizer hub and install snap ring. Install thrust bearing against race on countershaft. Coat both bearing and race with petroleum jelly.

17. Install lipped thrust race over needle-type thrust bearing and install plastic funnel into hole in end of countershaft gear.

18. Temporarily install extension housing and attaching bolts. Turn transmission case on end, and mount a dial indicator on extension housing with indicator on the end of mainshaft.

19. Rotate mainshaft and zero dial indicator. Pull upward on mainshaft until end play is removed and record reading. Mainshaft bearings require a preload of .001 to .005 (0.03 to 0.13 mm). To set preload, select a shim pack measuring .001 to .005 (0.03 to 0.13 mm) greater than the dial indicator reading recorded.

20. Remove front bearing cap and front bearing race. Install necessary shims to obtain preload and reinstall bearing race.

21. Apply a 3mm diameter (⅛ inch) bead of RTV sealant, #732 or equivalent, on case mating surface of front bearing cap.

Install bearing cap aligning marks made during disassembly and torque bolts to specification.

22. Remove extension housing.

23. Move shift forks on transmission cover and synchronizer sleeves inside transmission to the neutral position.

24. Apply a 3mm diameter (⅛ inch) bead of RTV sealant, #732 or equivalent, on cover mating surface of transmission.

25. Lower cover onto case while aligning shift forks and synchronizer sleeves. Center cover and install the 2 dowel bolts. Install remaining bolts and torque to specification. The offset lever to shift rail roll pin hole must be in the vertical position after cover installation.

26. Apply a 3mm diameter (⅛ inch) bead of RTV Sealant, #732 or equivalent, on extension housing to transmission case mating surface.

27. Install extension housing over mainshaft and shift rail to a position where shift rail just enters shift cover opening.

28. Install detent spring into offset lever and place steel ball in neutral guide plate detent. Position offset lever on steel ball and apply pressure on offset lever and at the time seat extension housing against transmission case.

29. Install extension housing bolts and torque to specification.

30. Align and install roll pin in offset lever and shift rail.

31. Fill transmission to its proper level with lubricant.

Chevrolet LUV/Isuzu 4–Speed Transmission

Disassembly

1. Remove the boot, clutch fork and throwout bearing.

2. Remove bearing retainer, gasket and spring washer.

3. Remove the speedometer gear and bushing.

4. Remove the shifter cover and gasket.

5. Remove the back-up switch on California vehicles and both back-up and CRS switches on all others.

6. Remove the rear extension and gasket.

7. Remove the thrust washers and reverse idler gear.

8. Remove the snap-rings, speedometer drive gear and key from the mainshaft.

9. Remove the spring pin from the reverse shifter fork and reverse gear.

10. Remove the snap-ring from the outer circumference of the clutch gear shaft ball bearing.

11. Remove the center support assembly from the transmission case.

12. Drive out the spring pins from the third and fourth and first and second shift forks.

NOTE: When removing the spring pin,

hold a round bar against the end of the shifter rods to prevent damage.

13. Remove the detent spring plate from the center support, then remove the detent springs and balls.

14. Remove the first and second and the third and fourth shifter rods from the center support, then remove the shifter forks.

15. Remove the reverse shifter rod forward as it is fitted with a stopper pin.

NOTE: Be careful not to lose the detent interlock plugs located between the shifter rods in the center support.

16. Move both synchronizers rearward to prevent turning of the mainshaft.

NOTE: It may be necessary to tap the synchronizers with the hammer handle to get them engaged.

17. Remove the locknut and washer from the mainshaft.

18. Remove the nut, washer countershaft reverse gear and collar from the rear of the countergear.

19. Remove the center support countergear bearing snap-ring.

20. Remove the center support.

21. Separate the clutch gear, needle bearings and blocker ring from the mainshaft assembly.

22. Press the rear bearing from the mainshaft.

23. Remove the thrust washer, 1st speed gear, needle roller bearing, a collar and blocker ring.

24. Remove the 1st and 2nd gear synchronizer assembly.

25. Remove the 2nd gear, blocker ring and needle roller bearing from the mainshaft.

26. Remove the snap-ring, 3rd and 4th synchronizer assembly and blocker ring from the mainshaft.

27. Remove the 3rd gear and needle bearings.

28. Remove the snap-ring and press off the clutch bearing and countergear bearing from the shaft.

Assembly

1. Stand the front of the mainshaft upward and install the 3rd speed gear and needle roller bearing with the tapered side of the gear facing the front of the mainshaft.

2. Install a blocker ring with the clutching teeth upward over the synchronizing surface of the 3rd speed gear.

3. If it is necessary to reassemble the synchronizer assembly, turn the face of the synchronizer hub with the heavy boss to the face of the sleeve with the light chamfering on the outer rim.

4. Fit the keys into the key groove and position the synchronizer springs into the hole in the side face of the hub.

5. Install the 3rd and 4th synchronizer assembly on the mainshaft with the face of the sleeve with the light chamfer rearward.

6. Turn the rear of the mainshaft upward and install the 2nd speed gear and needle roller bearing on the mainshaft with

the tapered surface of the gear facing the rear of the mainshaft.

7. Install a blocker ring with the clutching teeth downward over the synchronizing surface of the 2nd speed gear.

8. Install the 1st and 2nd synchronizer assembly with the chamfer on the sleeve facing the front of the mainshaft.

9. Install a blocker ring with the clutching teeth rearward.

10. Install the collar, needle roller bearing and 1st speed gear on the mainshaft.

NOTE: The tapered side of the gear should be facing the front of the mainshaft.

11. Install the 1st speed gear thrust washer on the mainshaft with the grooved side facing 1st gear.

12. Press the rear bearing on the mainshaft with the snap-ring groove facing front of the mainshaft.

13. If removed, press the ball bearing on the clutch gearshaft with the snap-ring groove on the bearing facing the front of the transmission. Install the snap-ring on the clutch gear shaft.

14. Assemble the needle roller bearing, blocker ring and clutch gear to the front of the mainshaft.

15. If removed, press on the countergear ball bearing with the snap-ring groove facing the rear of the transmission.

16. If removed, install the snap-rings in the inner circumference of the mainshaft and countergear holes of the center support.

17. If removed, insert the idler gear shaft with the lock plate groove side into the center support from the rear, then install the lock plate.

18. Mesh the countergear with the mainshaft assembly and install a holding tool on the mainshaft and countergear.

19. Install the center support.

20. Press the center support onto the shaft until the countergear bearing is brought into contact with its snap-ring.

21. Expand the countergear bearing snapring and press the center support further until the mainshaft and countergear snaprings are fitted into their grooves.

22. Remove the holding tool from the mainshaft and countergear.

23. Move both synchronizers rearward to prevent turning of the mainshaft.

24. Install the collar, countershaft reverse gear, washer and nut on the rear of the countergear.

NOTE: Install the locknut so that the chamfered side is facing the lock washer.

25. Install the locknut and lock washer on the mainshaft.

NOTE: Install the locknut so that the chamfered side is facing the lockwasher.

26. Apply grease to the two detent plugs and insert them into their detent holes from the middle hole of the center support.

27. Install the 1st and 2nd shifter forks and the 3rd and 4th into their grooves in the synchronizer assembly.

28. Install 3rd and 4th shifter rod from the rear of the center support through the middle hole and into the 1st and 2nd, 3rd and 4th shifter forks. Align the spring pin hole in the shifter fork with the hole in the shifter rod.

NOTE: Identify the 3rd and 4th shifter rod by the two detent grooves on the side of the rod.

29. Install the 1st and 2nd shifter rod from the rear of the center support through the 1st and 2nd shifter fork and align the hole in the rod to the hole in the shifter fork.

30. If removed, install the stopper pin in the reverse shifter rod and the front of the center support.

31. Install the two spring pins in the 1st/2nd and 3rd/4th shifter forks.

32. Install the detent balls, spring, gasket and retainer on the center support.

33. Install the center support assembly and gasket.

34. Assemble the reverse shifter fork to the reverse gear and install these parts into position from the rear side of the mainshaft, then connect them to the reverse shifter rod.

35. Install the spring pin in the reverse shifter fork.

36. Install the thrust washer and reverse idler gear on the idler shaft.

NOTE: The reverse idler gear should be installed with undercut teeth forward.

37. Install the speedometer drive gear snap-ring and key on the mainshaft.

38. Install a new oil seal in the rear extension.

39. Apply grease to the outer thrust washer of the reverse idler shaft and insert it in the rear extensions.

40. Install the rear extension and gasket.

41. Install the back-up lamp switch and CRS switch.

42. Install the shifter cover and gasket.

43. Install the oil O-ring to the speedometer drive gear and install the gear.

44. Install the front bearing retainer seal.

45. Install a snap-ring in the outer circumference of the clutch gear bearing.

46. Apply grease to the bearing retainer spring washer and place it in the bearing retainer with the dished face turned to the bearing outer race.

47. Install the bearing retainer to the front of the transmission case.

NOTE: The shorter bolts are used on countergear front bearing side of the bearing retainer.

48. Install the ball stud to the bearing retainer.

49. Install the boot clutch fork and throwout bearing, then install the retaining spring.

Chrysler A-412 Manual Transaxle

Gear reduction, ratio selection and differ-

Chrysler A-412 transaxle

ential functions are combined in a single unit. The transaxle assembly is housed in a two piece magnesium case. One piece is the transmission housing and the other piece is the clutch and differential assembly housing.

Disassembly

1. Remove the clutch push rod.
2. Remove the drive flange dust plug, snap-ring, cone washer drive flange and drive flange oil seal.
3. Remove the selector shaft cover, push out the selector shaft and remove the selector shaft oil seal.
4. Remove the mainshaft bearing retaining nut rubber plugs, and remove the clutch release bearing end cover. While removing, hold the clutch release lever in upward position to avoid loading end cover and damaging case threads.
5. Remove the release bearing and the sleeve.
6. Remove the circlips from the torque shaft, and remove the clutch torque shaft, return spring and release lever.
7. Remove the mainshaft bearing retainer nuts. The three studs and clips will drop into the case.
8. Remove the case attaching bolts, the reverse idler shaft set screw and the back-up light switch. Remove the transmission case, and mark the shims for installation reference.
9. Remove the reverse shift fork supports and remove the reverse shift fork.

10. Remove the mainshaft assembly and pinion shaft fourth speed gear.
11. Disassemble the mainshaft by removing the bearing and fourth speed gear, the third-fourth synchronizer and third speed gear and needle bearing.

NOTE: Synchronizers are serviced as an assembly.

12. Remove the shift rail "E" clips, and remove the shift forks assembly.
13. Remove the clutch push rod seal and bushing assembly.
14. On the pinion shaft, remove the snap-ring, third speed gear, second speed gear and needle bearing.
15. Remove the reverse gear idler shaft.
16. Complete pinion shaft disassembly by removing the first-second gears synchronizer, the second speed gear sleeve, the first gear stop ring and the first speed gear. The inner sleeve for second speed gear and the first speed gear are removed together.

NOTE: Before installing the puller to remove the synchronizer, remove the plastic thrust bottom, and install Tool L-4443-4 or equivalent in the pinion shaft. The pinion shaft bearing retainer is notched in two places for puller jaws.

17. Remove the pinion shaft retainer and first gear thrust washer, and remove the pinion shaft.

Differential Repair

1. Remove the axle shaft circlips.

2. Remove differential bearing cone and cup.

NOTE: Bearing cones and cups are matched sets and must be replaced as assemblies.

3. Remove the side gears.
4. Remove the pinion shaft snap-ring, and drive out the pinion shaft. Pinion shaft gears and plastic thrust washer can now be removed from differential case. When installing pinion shaft be sure to align plastic thrust washer with case to avoid damage to thrust washer holes.
5. Drill out the ring gear rivets. The new ring gear is installed with bolts and nuts.

Differential Bearing Preload Adjusting

NOTE: Differential Bearing Preload adjustment is necessary after replacement of the transmission case, clutch housing, differential case or differential bearings.

1. Install cup of bearing (opposite ring gear) with shim S2 in clutch/differential housing. Shim S2 is always 1 mm. (.039 inch) thick.
2. Install outer race on ring gear side without shim S1 in transmission housing.
3. Install differential in its housing.
4. Place transmission housing in position with gasket and tighten five bolts to 14 ft. lbs.
5. Install a dial indicator, and move the differential up and down for measurement reading.

NOTE: Do not turn differential when measuring because bearings will settle and give incorrect reading.

6. Correct bearing preload is obtained by adding a constant figure (0.40 mm)(.015 inch) to measured reading. For example:

	mm.	inch
Measured reading	0.90	.035
Plus preload (constant figure)	0.40	.015
Shim Thickness (S1) =	1.30	.050

7. Remove the transmission case, and drive out the outer bearing cup.
8. Insert selected shim S1; the thickest shim first. Shims are available in sizes ranging from 0.15 mm (.006 inch) to 0.80 mm (.031 inch).
9. Drive in bearing cup and install transmission housing with gasket and tighten. Before installing transmission housing, remove one axle shaft to check turning torques.

Checking Turning Torque

1. Lubricate bearings with transmission oil, and check for the following turning torque:
New bearings—10.4 to 21.7 inch-pounds
Used bearings—minimum 2.7 inch-pounds

Pinion Shaft Bearing Preload Adjustment

1. If clutch housing, ring and pinion gears or differential bearing are changed, it is necessary to adjust preload on pinion shaft bearing.
2. Place a 0.65 mm shim in bearing housing, and press in the small bearing cup.
3. Install pinion shaft and tighten cover nuts to 14 foot-pounds.
4. Mount a dial gauge and move pinion shaft up and down for measurement reading. Do not turn pinion shaft when measuring because bearings will settle and give incorrect measurement.
5. Specified bearing preload is obtained by adding a constant figure (0.20 mm) to measured reading and shim thickness (0.65 mm).

For example:

Shim installed	0.65 mm	(.025 inch)
Measured reading	0.30 mm	(.012 inch)
Preload (constant figure)	0.20 mm	(.008 inch)
Shim	= 1.15 mm	

Shims are available in sizes from 0.65 mm (.025 inch) to 1.40 mm (.055 inch).

6. Remove ball bearing retainer, pinion shaft and small bearing cup and 0.65 mm shim. Install correct shim.

Transaxle Assembly

1. Install the pinion shaft.
2. Install first gear thrust washer flat side up, and install pinion shaft retainer.
3. Install first gear and stop ring and first/second gears synchronizer. The lowest thrust collar on the hub must go toward second gear. Install the sleeve with reverse teeth nearest fifth gear. Slots in synchronizer ring must be aligned with struts in first/second gears synchronizer assembly to avoid damage to stop ring on assembly.

4. Install second gear bearing race.
5. Install and correctly align reverse idler gear shaft.
6. Install needle bearing and second speed gear.
7. Install third speed gear. Select and install a retaining snap-ring which will provide 0.00 to less than 0.1 mm (.000 to less than .004 inch) end-play.
8. Install the mainshaft and third/fourth gears synchronizer assembly.
9. Install fourth speed gear mainshaft needle bearing and mainshaft fourth speed gear.
10. Install fourth speed gear and snap-ring on pinion shaft.
11. Use Tool L-4442 to correctly adjust mainshaft position to specifications.
12. Adjust mainshaft end-play only if transmission case, clutch housing or mainshaft has been changed.
13. Install shift forks and "E" clips.
14. Install reverse shift fork and support brackets.
15. Use guide pins to install transmission case on clutch housing. Be sure pinion shaft is aligned with pinion shaft needle bearing in transmission case.
16. Install mainshaft bearing snap-ring.
17. Install reverse idler shaft bolt and install selector shaft assembly.
18. Install mainshaft bearing retainer and washer.
19. Install clutch torque shaft, return spring, release lever and circlips.
20. Install release bearing and sleeve.
21. Install the clutch release bearing end cover and mainshaft bearing retainer nut rubber plug.
22. Install selector shaft cover.
23. Install back-up light switch.
24. Install and adjust detent plunger:
   a. Loosen lock nut.

A-412 MANUAL TRANSAXLE TORQUE SPECIFICATIONS

Clutch Housing Case Bolt	250 in/lbs
Clutch Housing Case Stud	250 in/lbs
Release Bearing End Cover Screw	105 in/lbs
Back-up Light Switch	144 in/lbs
Electronic Timing Probe Retainer	80 in/lbs
Gearshift Selector Shaft Cover	35 ft/lbs
Gearshift Detent Body Lock Nut	175 in/lbs
Drain Plug	175 in/lbs
Fill Plug	175 in/lbs
Pinion Shaft Bearing Retainer Bolt	29 ft/lbs
Mainshaft Ball Bearing Retaining Nut	155 in/lbs
Reverse Idler Shaft Set Screw	175 in/lbs
Reverse Idler Fork Bracket—Clutch Housing Screw	105 in/lbs

b. Tighten adjusting sleeve until gap can be seen between lock ring and adjusting sleeve.

c. Loosen adjusting sleeve ¼ turn.

d. Hold adjusting sleeve in this position and tighten lock nut.

25. Install the clutch push rod and the selector shaft boot seal.

Chrysler A–460 Manual Transaxle

Intermediate Shaft Assembly

The 1-2 and 3-4 shift forks and synchronizer stop rings are interchangeable. However, if parts are to be reused, reassemble them in their original position. When assembling the intermediate shaft, make sure all gears turn freely and have a minimum of .076 mm (.003 inch) end-play.

INPUT SHAFT

Shim thickness calculation need only be done if any of the following parts are replaced:
1. Transaxle case
2. Input shaft seal retainer
3. Bearing retainer plate
4. Rear end cover
5. Input shaft
6. Input shaft bearings

Refer to Bearing Adjustment Procedure to determine the proper shim thickness for correct bearing preload and proper bearing turning torque.

DIFFERENTIAL

Shim thickness calculation need only be done if any of the following parts are replaced:
1. Transaxle case
2. Differential bearing retainer
3. Extension housing
4. Differential case
5. Differential bearings

Refer to Bearing Adjustment Procedure to determine the proper shim thickness for correct bearing preload and proper bearing turning torque.

BEARING ADJUSTMENT PROCEDURE

1. Take extreme care when removing and installing bearing cups and cones. Use only an arbor press for installation, as a hammer may not properly align the bearing cup or cone. Burrs or nicks on the bearing seat will give a false end play reading while gauging for proper shims. Improperly seated bearing cups and cones are subject to low mileage failure.

2. Bearing cups and cones should be replaced if they show signs of pitting or heat distress. If distress is seen on either the cup or bearing rollers, both cup and cone must be replaced.

3. Bearing end play and drag torque specifications *must be maintained* to avoid premature bearing failures.

Used (original) bearing may lose up to 50% of the original drag torque after break-in.

NOTE: All bearing adjustments must be made with no other component interference or gear inter-mesh.

4. Replace bearings as a pair. For example, if one differential bearing is defective, replace both differential bearings. If one input shaft bearing is defective, replace both input shaft bearings.

5. Bearing cones *must* be reused if removed.

6. Turning torque readings should be obtained while smoothly rotating in either direction (breakaway reading is not indicative of the true turning torque).

7. Replace the oil baffle, if damaged.

Datsun 4–Speed Transmission

Disassembly

This transmission is constructed in three sections: clutch housing, transmission housing and extension housing. There are no case cover plates. There is a cast iron adapter plate between the transmission and extension housings.

1. Remove the clutch housing dust cover. Remove the retaining spring, release bearing sleeve, and withdrawal lever.

2. Remove the backup light/neutral safety switch.

3. Unbolt and remove the clutch housing, rapping with a soft hammer if necessary. Remove the gasket, mainshaft bearing shim, and countershaft bearing shim.

4. Remove the speedometer pinion sleeve.

5. Remove the striker rod pin from the rod. Separate the striker rod from the shift lever bracket.

6. Unbolt and remove the rear extension. It may be necessary to rap the housing with a soft hammer.

7. Remove the mainshaft bearing snap-ring.

8. Remove the adapter plate and gear assembly from the transmission case.

9. Punch out the shift fork retaining pins. Remove the shift rod snap-rings. Remove the detent plugs, springs and balls from the adapter plate. Remove the shift rods, being careful not to lose the interlock balls.

10. Remove the snap-ring, speedometer drive gear and locating ball.

11. Remove the nut, lockwasher, thrust washer, reverse hub and reverse gear.

12. Remove the snap-ring and countershaft reverse gear. Remove the snap-ring, reverse idler gear, thrust washer and needle bearing.

13. Support the gear assembly while rapping on the rear of the mainshaft with a soft hammer.

14. Remove the setscrew from the adapter plate. Remove the shaft nut, spring washer, plain washer and reverse idler shaft.

15. Remove the bearing retainer and the mainshaft rear bushing.

16. To disassemble the mainshaft (rear section), remove the front snap-ring, third/fourth synchronizer assembly, third gear and needle bearing. From the rear, remove the thrust washer, locating ball, first gear, needle bearing, first gear bushing, first/second synchronizer assembly, second gear, and needle bearing.

17. To disassemble the clutch shaft, remove the snap-ring and bearing spacer and press off the bearing.

18. To disassemble the countershaft, press off the front bearing. Press off the rear bearing, press off the gears and remove the keys.

19. Remove the retaining pin, control arm pin and shift control arm from the rear of the extension housing.

Assembly

1. Place the O-ring in the front cover. Install the front cover to the clutch housing with a press. Put in the front cover oil seal.

2. Install the rear extension oil seal.

3. Assemble the first/second and third/fourth synchronizer assemblies. Make sure that the ring gaps are not both on the same side of the unit.

4. On the rear end of the mainshaft, install the needle bearing, second gear, baulk ring, first/second synchronizer assembly, baulk ring, first gear bushing, needle bearing, first gear, locating ball and thrust washer.

5. Drive or press on the mainshaft rear bearing.

6. Install the countershaft rear bearing to the adapter plate. Drive or press the mainshaft rear bearing into the adapter plate until the bearing snap-ring groove comes through the rear side of the plate. Install the snap-ring. If it is not tight against the plate, press the bearing back in slightly.

7. Insert the countershaft bearing ring between the countershaft rear bearing and bearing retainer. Install the bearing retainer to the adapter plate. Stake both ends of the screws.

8. Insert the reverse idler shaft from the rear of the adapter plate. Install the spring washer and plain washer to the idler shaft.

9. Place the two keys on the countershaft and oil the shaft lightly. Press on third gear and install a snap-ring.

10. Install the countershaft into its rear bearing.

11. From the front of the mainshaft, install the needle bearing, third gear, baulk ring, third/fourth synchronizer assembly and snap-ring. Snap-rings are available in thick-

nesses from 0.0561 in. to 0.0640 in. to adjust gear end-play.

12. Press the main drive bearing onto the clutch shaft. Install the main drive gear spacer and a snap-ring. Snap-rings are available in thicknesses from 0.0710 in. to 0.0820 in. to adjust gear end-play.

13. Insert a key into the countershaft drive gear with fourth gear and drive on the countershaft fourth gear with a drift. The rear end of the countershaft should be held steady while driving on the gear, to prevent rear bearing damage.

14. Install the reverse hub, reverse gear, thrust washer, and lock tab on the rear of the mainshaft. Install the shaft nut temporarily.

15. Install the needle bearing, reverse idler gear, thrust washer, and snap-ring.

16. Place the countershaft reverse gear and snap-ring on the rear of the countershaft. Snap-rings are available in thicknesses from 0.0433 in. to 0.0590 in. to adjust gear end-play.

17. Engage both first and second gears to lock the shaft.

18. On the rear of the mainshaft, install the snap-ring, locating ball, speedometer drive gear, and snap-ring. Snap-rings are available in thicknesses from 0.0433 in. to 0.0590 in.

19. Recheck end-play and backlash of all gears.

20. Place the reverse shift fork on the reverse gear and install the reverse shift rod. Install the detent ball, spring and plug. Install the fork retaining pin. Place two interlock balls between the reverse shift rod and the third/fourth shift rod location. Install the third/fourth shift fork and rod. Install the detent ball, spring and plug. This plug is shorter than the other two. Install the fork retaining pin. Place two interlock balls between the first/second shift rod location and the third/fourth shift rod. Install the first/second shift fork and rod. Install the detent ball, spring and plug.

21. Install the shift rod snap-rings.

22. Apply sealant sparingly to the adapter plate and transmission housing. Install the transmission housing to the adapter plate and bolt it down temporarily.

23. Drive in the countershaft front bearing with a drift. Place the snap-ring in the mainshaft front bearing.

24. Apply sealant sparingly to the adapter plate and extension housing. Align the shift rods in the neutral positions. Position the striker rod to the shift rods and bolt down the extension housing.

25. Insert the striker rod pin, connect the rod to the shift lever bracket and install the striker rod pin retaining ring. Replace the shift control arm.

26. To select the proper mainshaft bearing shim, first measure the amount the bearing protrudes from the front of the transmission case. This is measurement (B). Then measure the depth of the bearing recess in the rear of the clutch housing. This is measurement (A). Required shim thickness is found by subtracting (B) from (A). Shims are available in thicknesses of 0.0551 in. and 0.0630 in.

27. To select the proper countershaft front bearing shim, measure the amount that the bearing is recessed into the transmission case. Shim thickness should equal this measurement. Shims are available in thicknesses from 0.0157 in. (.4 mm) to 0.0394 in. (1.0 mm).

28. Apply sealant sparingly to the clutch and transmission housing mating surfaces.

29. Replace the clutch operating mechanism.

30. Install the shift lever temporarily and check shifting action.

5–Speed Transmission

This transmission is similar to the 4 speed transmission, model F4W71B and the overhaul can be accomplished by following the outline for the disassembly and assembly of the model F4W71B transmission.

Servo type synchromesh is used, instead of the Borg Warner type in the four speed. Shift linkage and interlock arrangements are the same, except the reverse shift rod also operates fifth gear. Most service procedures are identical to those for the four speed unit.

Those unique to the five-speed follow.

Disassembly

To disassemble the synchronizers, remove the circlip, synchronizer ring, thrust block, brake band, and anchor block. Be careful not to mix parts of the different synchronizer assemblies.

Assembly

1. The synchronizer assemblies for second, third, and fourth are identical. When assembling the first gear synchronizer, be sure to install the 0.0866 in. thick brake band at the bottom.

2. When assembling the mainshaft, select a third gear synchronizer hub snap-ring to minimize hub end-play. Snap-rings are available in thicknesses of 0.061–0.630 in., 0.0591–0.0610 in. and 0.0571–0.0591 in. The synchronizer hub must be installed with the longer boss to the rear.

3. When reassembling the gear train, install the mainshaft, countershaft, and gears to the adapter plate. Hold the rear nut and force the front nut against it to a torque of 217 ft. lbs., 123 ft. lbs. '80–'84. Select a snap-ring to minimize end-play of the fifth gear bearing at the rear of the mainshaft. Snap-rings are available in thicknesses from 0.0433 in. to 0.0551 in.

Dodge/Plymouth A-230 3–Speed

The Dodge A-230 is a three-speed transmission equipped with two synchronizer units to assist in the engagement of all forward gears. Lubricant capacity is 5 pints.

Disassembly
SHIFT HOUSING AND MECHANISM

1. Shift to second gear.
2. Remove side cover. If shaft O-ring seals need replacement:
   a. Pull shift-forks out of shafts.
   b. Remove nuts and operating levers from shafts.
   c. Deburr shafts. Remove shafts.

DRIVE PINION RETAINER AND EXTENSION HOUSING

1. Remove pinion bearing retainer from front of transmission case. Pry off retainer oil seal. For clearance:
   a. With a brass drift, tap drive pinion as far forward as possible. Rotate cut away part of second gear next to countershaft gear. Shift second–third synchronizer sleeve forward.
   b. Remove speedometer pinion adapter retainer. Work adapter and pinion out of extension housing.
   c. Unbolt extension housing. Break housing loose with plastic hammer and carefully remove.

IDLER GEAR AND MAINSHAFT

1. Insert dummy shaft in case to push reverse idler shaft and key out of case.
2. Remove dummy shaft and idler rollers.
3. Remove both tanged idler gear thrust washers.
4. Remove mainshaft assembly through rear of case.

COUNTERSHAFT GEAR AND DRIVE PINION

1. Using a mallet and dummy shaft, tap the countershaft rearward enough to remove key. Drive countershaft out of case, being careful not to drop the washers.
2. Lower countershaft gear to bottom of case.
3. Remove snap-ring from pinion bearing outer race (outside front of case).
4. Drive pinion shaft into case with plastic hammer. Remove assembly through rear of case.
5. If bearing is to be replaced, remove snap-ring and press off bearing.
6. Lift counter shaft gear and dummy shaft out through rear of case.

MAINSHAFT

1. Remove snap-ring from front end of mainshaft along with second gear stop ring and second gear.
2. Spread snap-ring in mainshaft bearing retainer. Slide retainer back off the bearing race.
3. Remove snap-ring at rear of mainshaft. Support front side of reverse gear. Press bearing off mainshaft.

1. 1st speed gear	36. Retainer gasket
2. Ring	37. Bearing retainer
3. Spring	38. Plug
4. Sleeve	39. Countershaft bearing washer
5. Struts	40. Countershaft
6. Clutch gear	41. Roller
7. Spring	42. Thrust washer
8. Snap-ring	43. Rev. idler gear shaft
9. Reverse gear bushing	44. Key
10. Reverse gear	45. Rev. idler gear shaft
11. Output shaft bearing	46. Reverse idler gear
12. Snap-ring	47. Rev. roller
13. Snap-ring	48. Countershaft gear
14. Bearing retainer	49. Low and rev. lever
15. Extension housing gasket	50. Interlock lever
16. Extension seal	51. Housing
17. Seal	52. Bolt
18. Extension bushing	53. Gasket
19. Snap-ring	54. Back-up light switch
20. Synchronizer ring	55. Locking nut
21. Spring	56. Lever
22. Sleeve	57. Lever
23. Clutch gear	58. Seal
24. Struts	59. Retainer
25. Spring	60. Housing gasket
26. Ring	61. Interlock spring
27. 2nd speed gear	62. Snap-ring
28. Output shaft	63. Lever w/shaft
29. Snap-ring	64. Gearshift fork
30. Roller	65. Plug
31. Main drive gear (pinion)	66. Case
32. Drive pinion bearing	67. Expansion plug
33. Snap-ring	68. Countershaft key
34. Snap-ring	69. Clip
35. Drive pinion seal	70. Magnet
	71. Extension vent

A-230 3-speed

4. Remove from press. Remove main-shaft bearing and reverse gear from shaft.

5. Remove snap-ring and first-reverse synchronizer assembly from shaft. Remove stop ring and first gear rearward.

Cleaning and Inspection

See Cleaning and Inspection instructions at the beginning of the Transmission section.

Assembly

COUNTERSHAFT GEAR

1. Slide dummy shaft into countershaft gear.

2. Slide one roller thrust washer over dummy shaft and into gear, followed by 22 greased rollers.

3. Repeat Step 2, adding one roller thrust washer on end.

4. Repeat steps 2 and 3 at other end of countershaft gear. There is a total of 88 rollers and 6 thrust washers.

5. Place greased front thrust washer on dummy shaft against gear with tangs forward.

6. Grease rear thrust washer and stick it in place in the case, with tangs rearward. Place countershaft gear assembly in bottom

of transmission case until drive pinion is installed.

PINION GEAR

1. Press new bearing on pinion shaft with snap-ring groove forward. Install new snap-ring.

2. Install 15 rollers and retaining ring in drive pinion gear.

3. Install drive pinion and bearing assembly into case.

4. Position countershaft gear assembly by positioning it and thrust washers so countershaft can be tapped into position. Be careful to keep the countershaft against the dummy shaft to keep parts from falling between them. Install key in countershaft.

5. Tap drive pinion forward for clearance.

MAINSHAFT

1. Place a stop ring flat on the bench. Place a clutch gear and a sleeve on top. Drop the struts in their slots and insert a strut spring with the tang inside on strut. Turn the assembly over and install second strut spring, tang in a different strut.

2. Slide first gear and stop ring over rear of mainshaft and against thrust flange between assembly over rear of mainshaft, first and second gears on shaft.

3. Slide first–reverse synchronizer indexing hub slots to first gear stop ring lugs.

4. Install first–reverse synchronizer clutch gear snap-ring on mainshaft.

5. Slide reverse gear and mainshaft bearing on shaft, supporting inner race of bearing. Be sure snap-ring groove on outer race is forward.

6. Install bearing retaining snap-ring on mainshaft. Slide snap-ring over the bearing and seat it in groove.

7. Place second gear over front of mainshaft with thrust surface against flange.

8. Install stop ring and second–third synchronizer assembly against second gear. Install second–third synchronizer clutch gear snap-ring on shaft.

9. Move second–third synchronizer sleeve forward as far as possible. Install front stop ring inside sleeve with lugs indexed to struts.

10. Rotate cut out on second gear toward countershaft gear for clearance.

11. Insert mainshaft assembly into case. Tilt assembly to clear cluster gears and insert pilot rollers in drive pinion gear. If assembly is correct, the bearing retainer will bottom to the case without force. If not, check for a misplaced strut, pinion roller, or stop ring.

REVERSE IDLER GEAR

1. Place dummy shaft into idler gear. Insert 22 greased rollers.

2. Position reverse idler thrust washers in case with grease.

3. Position idler gear and dummy shaft in case. Install idler shaft and key.

TORQUE SPECIFICATIONS

Manual A-203 3-Speed	ft. lbs.
Back up light switch	15
Extension housing bolts	50
Drive pinion bearing retainer bolts	30
Gearshift operating lever nuts	18
Transmission to clutch housing bolts	50
Transmission cover retaining bolts	12
Transmission drain plug	25

EXTENSION HOUSING

1. Remove extension housing yoke seal. Drive bushing out from inside housing.

2. Align oil hole in bushing with oil slot in housing. Drive bushing into place. Drive new seal into housing.

3. Install extension housing and gasket to hold mainshaft and bearing retainer in place.

DRIVE PINION BEARING RETAINER

1. Install outer snap-ring on drive pinion bearing. Tap assembly back until snap-ring contacts case.

2. Using seal installer tool or equivalent, install a new seal in retainer bore.

3. Position main drive pinion bearing retainer and gasket on front of case. Coat threads with sealing compound, install bolts, torque to 30 ft. lbs.

GEARSHAFT MECHANISM AND HOUSING

1. If removed, place two interlock levers in pivot pin with spring hangers offset toward each other, so that spring installs in a straight line. Place E-clip on pivot pin.

2. Grease and install new O-ring seals on both shift shafts. Grease housing bores and insert shafts.

3. Install spring on interlock lever hangers.

4. Rotate each shift shaft fork bore to straight up position. Install shift forks through bores and under both interlock levers.

5. Position second–third synchronizer sleeve to rear, in second gear position. Position first–reverse synchronizer sleeve to middle of travel, in neutral position. Place shift forks in the same positions.

6. Install gasket and gearshift mechanism. The bolt with the extra long shoulder must be installed at the center rear of the case. Torque bolts to 15 ft. lbs.

7. Install speedometer drive pinion gear and adapter. Range number on adapter, which represents the number of teeth on the gear, should be in 6 o'clock position.

Dodge/Plymouth A-390 3–Speed

The A-390 is a three speed synchromesh transmission. Lubricant capacity is 4½ pints.

Disassembly

1. Remove the bolts that attach the cover to the case. Remove the cover and gasket.

2. Remove the long spring that retains the detent plug in the case. Remove the detent plug with a small magnet.

3. Remove the bolt and retainer securing the speedometer pinion adapter to the transmission case. Carefully work the adapter and pinion out of the extension housing.

4. Remove the bolts that attach the extension housing to the transmission case. Slide the extension housing off the output shaft.

5. Remove the bolts that attach the input shaft bearing retainer to the case. Slide the retainer off the shaft. Using a suitable tool, pry the seal out of the retainer. Be careful not to nick or scratch the bore in which the seal is pressed or the surface on which the seal is bottomed.

6. Remove the lubricant fill plug from the right side of the case. Working through the fill plug opening, drive the roll pin out of the countershaft with a ¼ inch punch.

7. Working with the countershaft bearing arbor and a soft faced hammer, tap the countershaft toward the front of the case with the arbor tool to remove the expansion plug from the countershaft bore at the front of the case. The countershaft is a loose fit in the case and will slide easily.

8. Insert the arbor tool through the front of the case and push the countershaft out of the rear of the case so the roll pin hole in the countershaft does not travel through the roller bearings. The countershaft gear will drop to the bottom of the case. Remove the countershaft from the rear of the case.

9. Place both shift levers in neutral (center) position.

10. Remove the input shaft assembly and stop ring from the front of the case.

11. Remove the set screw that secures the first–reverse shift fork to the shift rail. Slide the first–reverse shift rail out through the rear of the case.

12. Move the second–third shift fork rearward for access to the set screw. Remove the set screw from the fork. Using a suitable tool, rotate the shift rail one quarter (¼) turn.

13. Lift the interlock plug from the case with a magnet.

14. Tap on the inner end of the second–third shift rail to remove the expansion plug from the front of the case. Remove

A-390 3-speed

20. Gasket, back-up lamp switch
21. Screw, extension lockwasher, extension screw
22. Retainer, output shaft brg.
23. Gasket, extension
24. Rail, gearshift first and reverse
25. Screw, fork set
26. Fork, gearshift first and reverse
27. Seal, gearshift lever shaft oil
28. Lever, gearshift
29. Case
30. Plug
31. Rail, gearshift second and third
32. Spring, gearshift detent pin
33. Fork, gearshift second and third
34. Pin, gearshift detent
35. Spring, gearshift detent pin
36. Plug
37. Plug, case filler
38. Gear, countershaft
39. Synchronizer assy., second and third
40. Ring, synchronizer second and third stop
41. Gear, second speed
42. Snap-ring, low speed gear thrust washer
43. Washer, low speed gear thrust
44. Gear, Low Speed
45. Ring, synchronizer low stop
46. Snap-ring, synchronizer low and reverse clutch gear
47. Synchronizer assy., low and reverse
48. Shaft, output
49. Roller, output shaft pilot
50. Shaft, input
51. Bearing, input shaft
52. Snap-ring, bearing, outer
53. Snap-ring, bearing, inner
54. Seal, bearing retainer oil
55. Gasket, bearing retainer
56. Retainer, bearing
57. Screw, bearing retainer

1. Cover, case
2. Screw, case cover
3. Gasket, case cover
4. Roller, countershaft brg.
5. Washer, countershaft brg.
6. Washer, countershaft thrust
7. Washer, reverse idler thrust
8. Bushing, reverse idler
9. Countershaft
10. Pin, countershaft roll
11. Gear, reverse idler
12. Bearing, output shaft
13. Shaft, reverse idler
14. Pin, reverse idler stop
15. Snap-ring, output shaft brg. outer
16. Snap-ring, output shaft, inner
17. Extension
18. Seal, extension
19. Switch, back-up lamp

the shift rail through the front of the case.

15. Remove the second–third shift rail detent plug and spring from the detent bore with a magnet.

16. Tap the output shaft assembly rearward until the output shaft bearing clears the case. Remove both shift forks. Remove the snap-ring that retains the output shaft bearing to the output shaft.

17. Assemble the output shaft bearing removal tool over the output shaft and bearing. Remove the output shaft bearing.

18. Remove the output shaft assembly through top of the case.

19. Using a suitable drift, drive the reverse idler gear shaft toward the rear, and out of the transmission case.

20. Lift the reverse idler gear and thrust washer out of the case.

21. Remove the countershaft gear, arbor assembly, and thrust washers from the bottom of the case.

22. Remove the countershaft roll pin from the bottom of the case.

23. Remove the snap-ring that retains the second–third synchronizer clutch gear and sleeve assembly on the output shaft.

Slide the second–third synchronizer assembly off the end of the output shaft.

NOTE: Do not separate the second-third synchronizer clutch gear, sleeve, struts, or spring unless inspection reveals that a replacement is necessary.

24. Slide the second gear and stop ring off the output shaft.

25. Remove the snap-ring and thrust washer retaining the first gear. Slide the first gear and stop ring off the output shaft.

26. Remove the snap-ring that retains

the first–reverse synchronizer hub on the output shaft. The first–reverse synchronizer hub is a press fit on the output shaft. To avoid damage to the synchronizer, remove the synchronizer hub using an arbor press. Do not attempt to remove or install the hub by hammering or prying.

Overhaul

SHIFT LEVERS AND SEALS

1. Remove the operating levers from their respective shafts. Remove any burrs from the shafts to avoid damage to the case.

2. Push the shift levers out of the transmission case. Remove and discard the O-ring seal from each shaft.

3. Lubricate the new seals with transmission oil and install them on the shafts.

4. Install the shift levers in the case.

5. Install the operating levers and tighten the retaining nuts to 18 ft. lbs.

INPUT SHAFT BEARING AND ROLLERS

1. Remove the snap-ring securing the bearing on the input shaft. Carefully press the input shaft out of the bearing with an arbor press.

2. Remove the fifteen bearing rollers from the cavity in the end of the input shaft.

3. Install the 15 bearing rollers in the cavity of the input shaft. Coat the rollers with a thin film of grease to retain them during installation.

4. Slide the input shaft bearing over the input shaft, snap-ring groove away from the gear end. Seat the bearing assembly on the input shaft with an arbor press.

5. Secure the bearing with the snap-ring. Be sure the snap-ring is properly seated. If a large snap-ring around the bearing was removed, be sure to install it at this time.

SYNCHRONIZERS

NOTE: If either synchronizer is to be disassembled, mark all parts so that they will be reassembled in the same position. Do not mix parts from the two synchronizers.

1. Push the synchronizer hub off each synchronizer sleeve.

2. Separate the struts and springs from the hubs.

3. Install the spring on the front side of the first–reverse synchronizer hub, making sure that all three strut slots are fully covered. Hang the three struts on the spring and in the slots with the wide end of the strut inside the hub.

4. With the alignment marks on the hub and sleeve aligned, push the sleeve down on the hub until the struts are in the neutral detent. Place the stop ring on top of the synchronizer assembly.

5. With the alignment marks on the second–third synchronizer sleeve and hub aligned, slide the sleeve on the hub. Drop in the three struts in the strut slots. Install the spring with the hump in the center, into the hollow of the strut. Turn the assembly

over and install the other spring so that the hump in the center of the spring is inserted in the same strut. Place the stop ring on each end of the synchronizer assembly.

COUNTERSHAFT GEAR AND BEARING

1. Remove the countershaft bearing arbor, the roller bearings and the two bearing retainers from the countershaft gear.

2. Coat the bore in each end of the countershaft gear with grease.

3. Insert the countershaft arbor and install twenty five roller bearings and the retainer washer in each end of the countershaft gear.

4. Position the countershaft gear and arbor assembly in the transmission case. Align the gear bore and the thrust washers with the bores in the case and install the countershaft.

5. Using a feeler gauge, check the countershaft gear end play. The end play should be within 0.004–0.018 inch. If the clearance is not within limits, replace the thrust washers.

6. After establishing the correct end play, install the arbor tool in the countershaft gear and lower the gear and tool out of the bottom of the transmission case.

Assembly

1. Coat the countershaft gear thrust surfaces in the case with a thin film of grease and position the two thrust washers in place. Place the countershaft gear and arbor assembly in the proper position in the bottom of the transmission case. The countershaft gear will remain in the bottom of the case until the output and input shafts are installed.

2. Coat the reverse idler gear thrust surfaces in the case with a thin film of grease and position the two thrust washers in place. Install the reverse idler gear in the case and align the gear bore with the thrust washers in the case bore. Install the reverse idler shaft.

3. Measure the reverse idler gear end play with a feeler gauge. End play should be 0.004–0.018 inch. If the clearance is not within limits, replace the thrust washers. If the end-play is correct, leave the reverse idler gear in place.

4. Lubricate the output shaft splines and the machined surfaces with transmission oil.

5. Slide the first reverse synchronizer onto the output shaft with the fork groove toward the front. The first–reverse synchronizer hub is a press fit on the output shaft. To eliminate the possibility of damage to the hub, install the hub using an arbor press.

NOTE: Do not attempt to install the hub by hammering or driving.

Secure the hub on the output shaft with the snap-ring.

6. Slide the first gear and stop ring onto the output shaft, aligning the slots in the stop ring with the struts. Install the thrust washer and snap-ring.

7. Slide the second gear and stop ring on the output shaft.

8. Install the second–third synchronizer assembly on the output shaft. Rotate the second gear to index the struts with the slots in the stop ring. Secure the synchronizer with a snap-ring.

9. Position the output shaft assembly in the transmission case. Place the transmission in a vertical position with the front of the case flat on the work bench. Place a 1¼ inch block of wood under the end of the output shaft. The block of wood will hold the output shaft assembly up during installation of the output shaft bearing.

10. Install the large snap-ring on the output shaft bearing. Place the bearing on the output shaft with the large snap-ring up. Drive the bearing on the shaft until it is seated on the shaft. Secure the bearing on the output shaft with the snap-ring. Return the transmission to a horizontal position.

11. Insert both shift forks in the case and in their proper sleeves. Push the output shaft assembly into position and tap it forward until the output shaft bearing is seated in the transmission case.

12. Install the *shortest* detent spring followed by a detent plug into the case. Place the second–third synchronizer assembly in the second gear position.

13. Align the second–third shift fork and install the second–third shift rail. The second–third shift rail is the shortest of the two shift rails. It will be necessary to depress the detent plug to enter the shift rail in the bore. Move the rail inward until the detent plug engages the forward notch (second gear position).

14. Secure the fork to the rail with the set screw. Move the synchronizer to the neutral position.

15. Install a new expansion plug in the transmission case.

16. Install the interlock plug in the transmission case with a magnet. If the second–third shift rail is in the neutral position, the top of the interlock plug will be slightly lower than the surface of the first–reverse shift rail bore.

17. Align the first–reverse fork and install the first–reverse shift rail. Move the rail inward until the center notch (neutral) is aligned with the detent bore. Secure the fork to the rail with the set screw.

18. Using a suitable tool, install a new oil seal in the input shaft bearing retainer bore.

19. Coat the bore of the input shaft gear with a thin film of grease.

NOTE: A thick, heavy grease will plug the lubricant holes and prevent lubrication of the roller bearings.

Install the fifteen roller bearings in the bore.

20. Place the stop ring, slots aligned with the struts, into the second–third synchronizer. Tap the input shaft assembly into place in the case while holding the output shaft to prevent the roller bearings from dropping.

21. Roll the transmission over so that it rests on both the top edge and the shift levers. The countershaft gear will drop into place. Using a screwdriver, align the countershaft gear and thrust washers with the bore in the transmission case.

22. Working from the rear of the case, slide the countershaft into position being careful to keep the countershaft in contact with the arbor to avoid dropping parts out of position. Be sure that the roll pin hole in the countershaft aligns with the roll pin hole in the case.

23. Install the roll pin. Install a new expansion plug in the countershaft bore at the front of the case. Install the plug flush or below the face of the case to prevent interference with the clutch housing.

24. Slide the extension housing, with a new gasket, over the output shaft and against the case. Coat the attaching bolt threads with a sealing compound. Install and tighten the attaching bolts to 50 ft. lbs.

25. Install the input shaft bearing retainer and a new gasket. Make sure that the oil return slot is at the bottom. Coat the threads with a sealing compound, install the attaching bolts and tighten to 30 ft. lbs.

26. Install the remaining detent plug into the case followed by the detent spring.

27. Install the filler plug and the back-up light switch. Pour lubricant over the entire gear train while rotating the input shaft and the output shaft.

28. Place the cover and a new gasket on the transmission. Coat the attaching screw threads with a sealing compound. Install and tighten the attaching screws to 22 ft. lbs.

Dodge/Plymouth Overdrive-4

The overdrive-4 transmission is a four speed unit with all forward gears synchronized. Third gear is direct, while the fourth gear is the overdrive ratio. Lubricant capacity is 7 pints.

Disassembly

GEARSHIFT HOUSING AND MECHANISM

1. If available, mount transmission in a repair stand.

2. Disconnect gearshift control rods from the shift control levers and the transmission operating levers.

3. Remove the two gearshift control housing mounting bolts.

4. Remove gearshift control housing from the transmission extension housing or mounting bracket (if so equipped).

5. Remove the gearshift control housing mounting bracket bolts, then remove the bracket (if so equipped).

6. Remove back-up light switch (if so equipped).

7. Remove output companion flange nut

TORQUE SPECIFICATIONS

	ft. lbs.
Cover to case screws	22
Back-up light switch	15
Extension housing to case bolts	
50	
Extension housing to cross member bolts	50
Gearshift lever nuts	18
Input shaft bearing retainer bolts	30
Shift fork to shift rail set screw	10
Transmission to clutch housing bolts	50
Transmission drain plug	25
Transmission filler plug	15

and washer, if used, then pull the flange from the mainshaft (output shaft).

8. Remove gearshift housing-to-transmission case attaching bolts.

9. With all levers in the neutral detent position, pull housing out and away from the case.

NOTE: If first and second, or third and fourth shift forks remain in engagement with the synchronizer sleeves, move the sleeves and remove forks from the case.

10. Remove nuts, lock washers and flat washers that hold first–second, and third–fourth speed shift operating levers to the shafts.

11. Disengage shift levers from the flats on the shafts and remove levers. Remove the E-ring on the overdrive four speed.

EXTENSION HOUSING, MAINSHAFT AND MAIN DRIVE PINION

1. Remove the bolt and retainer holding the speedometer pinion adapter in the extension housing, then remove the pinion adapter.

2. Remove the bolts attaching the extension housing to the transmission case.

3. Rotate the extension housing on the output shaft to expose the rear of the countershaft. Install one bolt to hold the extension in place.

4. Drill a hole in the countershaft extension plug at the front of the case.

5. Reaching through this hole, push the countershaft to the rear to expose the Woodruff key; when exposed, remove it. Push the countershaft forward against the expansion plug, and using a brass drift, tap the countershaft forward until the expansion plug is removed.

6. Using a countershaft arbor, push the countershaft out the rear of the case, but don't let the countershaft washers fall out of position. Lower the cluster gear to the bottom of the transmission case.

7. Remove the bolt and rotate the extension back to the normal position.

8. Remove the drive pinion attaching bolts and slide the retainer and gasket from

the pinion shaft, then pry the pinion or seal from the retainer. When installing the new seal, don't nick or scratch the seal bore in the retainer or the surface on which the seal bottoms.

9. Using a brass drift, tap the pinion and bearing assembly forward and remove through the front of the case.

10. Slide the third and overdrive synchronizer sleeve slightly forward, slide the reverse idler gear to the center of its shaft, and tap the extension housing rearward. Slide the housing and mainshaft assembly out and away from the case.

11. Remove the snap-ring holding the third and overdrive synchronizer clutch gear and sleeve assembly to the mainshaft, then remove the synchronizer assembly.

12. Slide the overdrive gear and stop ring off the mainshaft. Using pair of long nose pliers, compress the snap ring holding the mainshaft bearing in the extension housing. With it compressed, pull the mainshaft assembly and bearing out of the extension housing.

13. Remove the snap-ring holding the mainshaft on the shaft. The bearing is removed by inserting steel plates on the front side of the first speed gear, then pressing the mainshaft through the bearing being careful not to damage the gear teeth.

14. Remove the bearing, retainer ring, first speed gear and stop ring from the shaft.

15. Remove the snap-ring. Remove the first and second clutch gear and sleeve assembly from the mainshaft.

16. Remove the drive pinion bearing inner snap-ring, then using an arbor press, remove the bearing. Remove the snap-ring and bearing rollers from the cavity in the drive pinion.

17. Remove the countershaft gear from the bottom of the case, then remove the arbor, needle bearings, thrust washers and spacers from the center of the countershaft gear.

18. Remove the reverse gearshift lever detent spring retainer, gasket, plug, and detent ball spring from the rear of the case.

19. The reverse idler gear shaft is a tight fit in the case and will have to be pressed out.

A-833 4-speed

8. Reverse fork
9. 1st and 2nd fork
10. Drain plug
11. Retainer
12. Screw
13. Retainer gasket
14. Drive pinion seal
15. Snap-ring
16. Snap-ring
17. Drive pinion bearing
18. Plug
19. Housing gasket
20. Transmission case
21. Filler plug
22. Rev. detent ball spring
23. Gasket
24. Retainer
25. Plug
25a. Gasket
26. Main drive gear (pinion)
27. Roller
28. Snap-ring
29. Back-up light switch
30. Gasket
31. Rev. Lever detent ball
32. Rev. idler shaft key
33. Rev. idler gear shaft
34. Magnet clip
35. Magnet
36. Bushing
37. Reverse idler gear
38. Reverse lever w/shaft
39. Seal
40. Reverse lever
41. Nut
42. 1st and 2nd lever w/shaft
43. Seal
44. Housing
45. 1st and 2nd lever
46. Nut
47. Rollers
48. Countershaft gear
49. Countershaft washer
50. Countershaft key
51. Countershaft
52. Washer
53. Spacer
54. Stop ring
55. Snap-ring
56. Spring
57. Sleeve
58. Overdrive gear
59. Main or output shaft
60. Struts
61. 3rd and direct gear
62. Spring
63. Snap-ring
64. Front bearing
65. Extension bolt
66. Extension vent
67. Output shaft seal
68. Extension bushing
69. Extension
70. Extension gasket
71. Vent baffle
72. Snap-ring
73. Snap-ring
74. 1st speed gear
75. 1st and 2nd clutch sleeve gear
76. Synchronizer struts
77. Clutch gear
78. 2nd speed gear
79. Case housing bolt

1. Interlock pin
2. Direct and overdrive lever (3rd/4th)
3. Interlock lever
4. Snap-ring
5. Interlock spring
6. 3rd and overdrive (4th) lever
7. 3rd and overdrive (4th) fork

20. If there is oil leakage visible around the reverse gearshift lever shaft, push the lever shaft in and remove it from the case. Remove the detent ball from the bottom of the transmission case and remove the shift fork from the shaft and detent plate.

Assembly
REVERSE SHAFT

Follow the first four steps only if you removed the reverse shaft in the disassembly procedure.

1. Install a new oil seal O-ring on the lever shaft and coat the shaft with grease; insert it into its bore and install the reverse fork in the lever.

2. Install the reverse detent spring and gasket; insert the ball and spring and install the plug and gasket.

3. Place the reverse idler gear shaft in position in the end of the case and drive it in far enough to position the reverse idler gear on the protruding end of the shaft with the fork slot toward the rear. While doing this, engage the slot with the reverse shift fork.

4. With the reverse idler gear correctly positioned, drive the reverse gear shaft into the case far enough to install the Woodruff key. Drive the shaft in flush with the end of the transmission case. Install the back-up light switch and gasket.

COUNTERSHAFT GEAR AND DRIVE PINION

1. Coat the inside bore of the countershaft gear with a thin film of grease and install the roller bearing spacer with an arbor, into the gear; center the spacer and arbor.

2. Install the roller bearings and a spacer ring on each end.

3. Replace worn thrust washers; coat the new ones with grease and install them over the arbor with the tang side toward the case boss.

4. Install the countershaft assembly into the case and allow the gear assembly to sit on the bottom of the case so that the thrust washers won't come out of position.

5. Press the drive pinion bearing on the pinion shaft. Make sure the outer snap ring groove is toward the front end and the bearing is seated against the shoulder on the gear.

6. Install a new snap-ring on the shaft to hold the bearing in place; make sure the snap-ring is seated and that there is minimum end play. There are several snap-ring thicknesses available for adjustment.

7. Place the pinion shaft in a soft-jawed vise and install the roller bearings in the cavity of the shaft. Coat them with grease and install the bearing retaining snap-ring.

8. Install a new oil seal in the bore.

EXTENSION HOUSING BUSHING

1. Remove the yoke seal from the extension housing.

2. Drive out the old bushing and drive in a new one, aligning the oil hole in the bushing with the slot in the housing.

3. Place a new seal in the opening of the extension housing and then drive it into place.

MAINSHAFT

Assemble the synchronizer as follows:

1. Place a stop ring flat on a bench followed by the clutch gear and sleeve; drop the struts in their slots and snap in a strut spring placing the tang inside one strut. Install the second strut spring tang in a different strut after turning the assembly over.

2. Slide the second speed gear over the mainshaft with the synchronizer cone toward the rear and down against the shoulder on the shaft.

3. Slide the first and second gear synchronizer assembly including stop rings with lugs indexed in the hub slots, over the mainshaft down against the second gear cone and hold it there with a new snap-ring. Slide the next snap-ring over the shaft and index the lugs into the clutch hub slots.

4. Slide the first speed gear with the synchronizer cone toward the clutch sleeve just installed over the mainshaft and into position against the clutch sleeve gear.

5. Install the mainshaft bearing retaining ring followed by the mainshaft rear bearing; press the bearing down into position and install a new snap ring to secure it. There are several snap-ring thicknesses available for minimum end play.

6. Install the partially assembled mainshaft into the extension housing far enough to engage the bearing retaining ring in the slot in the extension housing. Compress the ring with pliers so that the mainshaft ball bearing can move in and bottom against its thrust shoulder in the extension housing. Release the ring and make sure that it is seated.

7. Slide the overdrive gear over the mainshaft with the synchronizer cone toward the front followed by the gear's snapring.

8. Install the third-overdrive gear synchronizer clutch gear assembly on the mainshaft against the overdrive gear. Make sure to index the rear stop ring with the clutch gear struts.

9. Install the snap-ring and position the front stop ring over the clutch gear again lining up the ring lugs with the struts; coat a new extension gasket with grease and place it in position.

10. Slide the reverse idler gear to the center of its shaft and move the third-overdrive synchronizer as far forward as possible without losing the struts.

11. Insert the mainshaft assembly in the case tilting it as necessary. Place the third-overdrive sleeve in the neutral detent.

12. Rotate the extension on the mainshaft to expose the rear of the countershaft and install one bolt to hold it in position.

13. Install the drive pinion and bearing assembly through the front of the case and position it in the front bore. Install the outer snap-ring in the bearing groove and tap lightly into place. If it doesn't bottom easily, check to see if a strut, pinion roller or stop ring is out of position.

14. Turn the transmission upside down while holding the countershaft gear to prevent damage. Then lower the countershaft gear assembly into position making sure that the teeth mesh with the drive pinion gear.

15. Start the countershaft into the bore at the rear of the case and push until it is in about halfway; then install the Woodruff key and push it in until it is flush with the rear of the case.

16. Rotate the extension back to normal position and install the bolts; turn the transmission upright and install the drive pinion bearing retainer and gasket. Coat the threads with sealing compound and tighten the attaching bolts to 30 ft. lbs.

17. Install a new expansion plug in its bore.

GEARSHIFT HOUSING AND MECHANISM

1. Install the interlock levers on the pivot pin and secure with the E-ring. Install the spring with a pair of pliers.

2. Grease and install new O-ring seals on both shift shafts; grease the housing bores and push the shafts through.

3. Install the operating levers and tighten the retaining nuts to 18 ft. lbs.; make sure the third-overdrive lever points down.

4. Rotate each shift shaft fork bore straight up and install the third-overdrive shift fork in its bore and under both interlock levers.

5. Position both synchronizer sleeves in neutral and place the first and second gear shift fork in the groove of the first and second gear synchronizer sleeve. Slide the reverse idler gear to neutral. Turn the transmission on its right side and place the gearshift housing gasket in place holding it there with grease. Install the reverse detent ball and spring into the case bore.

6. As the shift housing is lowered in place, guide the third-overdrive shift fork into its synchronizer groove then lead the shaft of the first and second shift lever.

7. Raise the interlock lever with a screwdriver to allow the first and second shift fork to slip under the levers. The shift housing will now seat against the case.

8. Install the bolts lightly and shift through all the gears to check for proper operation.

9. The reverse shift lever and the first and second gear shift lever have cam surfaces which mate in reverse position to lock the first and second lever, the fork and synchronizer in the neutral position.

10. To check for proper operation, put the transmission in reverse, and, while turning the input shaft, move the first and second lever in each direction. If it locks up or becomes harder to turn, select a new shift lever size with more or less clearance.

If there is too little cam clearance, it will be difficult or impossible to shift into reverse.

11. Grease the reverse shaft, install the operating lever and nut, and install the speedometer drive pinion gear and adapter, making sure the range number is in the straight down position.

Ford 3.03 3–Speed

The Ford 3.03 is a fully synchronized three speed transmission. All gears except reverse are in constant mesh. Forward speed gear changes are accomplished with synchronizer sleeves.

Disassembly

1. Drain the lubricant by removing the lower extension housing bolt.
2. Remove the case cover and gasket.
3. Remove the long spring that holds the detent plug in the case and remove the detent plug with a small magnet.
4. Remove the extension housing and gasket.
5. Remove the front bearing retainer and gasket.
6. Remove the filler plug on the right side of the transmission case. Working through the plug opening, drive the roll pin out of the case and countershaft with a ¼ inch punch.
7. Hold the countershaft gear with a hook. Install dummy shaft and push the countershaft out of the rear of the case. As the countershaft comes out, lower the gear cluster to the bottom of the case. Remove the countershaft.
8. Remove the snap-ring that holds the speedometer drive gear on the output shaft.

Slip the gear off the shaft and remove the gear lock ball.

9. Remove the snap-ring that holds the output shaft bearing. Using a special bearing puller, remove the output shaft bearing.
10. Place both shift levers in the neutral (center) position.
11. Remove the set screw that holds the first–reverse shift fork to the shift rail. Slip the first–reverse shift rail out through the rear of the case.
12. Move the first–reverse synchronizer forward as far as possible. Rotate the first–reverse shift fork upwards and lift it out of the case.
13. Place the second–third shift fork in the second position. Remove the set screw. Rotate the shift rail 90 degrees.
14. Lift the interlock plug out of the case with a magnet.
15. Remove the expansion plug from the second–third shift rail by lightly tapping the end of the rail. Remove the second–third shift rail.

16. Remove the second–third shift rail detent plug and spring from detent bore.
17. Remove the input gear and shaft from the case.
18. Rotate the second–third shift fork upwards and remove from case.
19. Using caution, lift the output shaft assembly out through top of case.
20. Lift the reverse idler gear and thrust washers out of case. Remove the countershaft gear, thrust washer and dummy shaft from case.
21. Remove the snap-ring from the front of the output shaft. Slip the synchronizer and second gear off shaft.
22. Remove the second snap-ring from output shaft and remove the thrust washer, first gear and blocking ring.
23. Remove the third snap-ring from the output shaft. The first–reverse synchronizer hub is a press fit on the output shaft. Remove the synchronizer hub with an arbor press.

TORQUE SPECIFICATIONS

	ft. lbs.
Back up light switch	15
Drive pinion bearing, retainer bolts	30
Extension housing to case bolts	50
Gearshift to mounting plate	24
Gearshift mounting plate to extension	12
Shift lever nuts	18
Transmission to clutch housing bolts	50
Transmission drain plug	25

Ford 3.03 3-speed

Disassembly and Assembly of Sub-Assemblies

SHIFT LEVERS AND SEALS

1. Remove shift levers from the shafts. Slip the levers out of case. Discard shaft sealing O-rings.
2. Lubricate and install new O-rings on shift shafts.
3. Install the shift shafts in the case and secure shift levers.

INPUT SHAFT BEARINGS

1. Remove the snap-ring securing the input shaft bearing. Using an arbor press, remove the bearing.
2. Press the input shaft bearing onto shaft using correct tool.

SYNCHRONIZERS

1. Scribe alignment marks on synchronizer hubs before disassembly. Remove each synchronizer hub from the synchronizer sleeves.
2. Separate the inserts and insert springs from the hubs.

3. Install the insert spring in the hub of the first–reverse synchronizer. Be sure that the spring covers all the insert grooves. Start the hub on the sleeve making certain that the scribed marks are properly aligned. Place the three inserts in the hub, small ends on the inside. Slide the sleeve and reverse gear onto hub.
4. Install one insert spring into a groove on the second–third synchronizer hub. Be sure that all three insert slots are covered. Align the scribed marks on the hub and sleeve and start the hub into the sleeve. Position the three inserts on the top of the retaining spring and push the assembly together. Install the remaining retainer spring so that the spring ends cover the same slots as the first spring. Do not stagger the springs. Place a synchronizer blocking ring on the ends of the synchronizer sleeve.

COUNTERSHAFT GEAR BEARINGS

1. Remove the dummy shaft, needle bearings and bearing retainers from the countershaft gear.
2. Coat the bore in each end of the countershaft gear with grease.
3. Hold the dummy shaft in the gear and install the needle bearings in the case.
4. Place the countershaft gear, dummy shaft, and needle bearings in the case.
5. Place the case in a vertical position. Align the gear bore and the thrust washers with the bores in the case and install the countershaft.

6. Place the case in a horizontal position. Check the countershaft gear end play with a feeler gauge. Clearance should be between 0.004–0.018 inch. If clearance does not come within specifications, replace the thrust washers.
7. Install the dummy shaft in the countershaft gear and leave the gear at the bottom of the transmission case.

Assembly

1. Cover the reverse idler gear thrust surfaces in the case with a thin film of lubricant, and install the two thrust washers in the case.
2. Install the reverse idler gear and shaft in the case. Align the case bore and thrust washers with gear bore and install the reverse idler shaft.
3. Measure the reverse idler gear end play with a feeler gauge; clearance should be between 0.004–0.018 inch. If end play is not within specifications, replace the thrust washers. If clearance is correct, leave the reverse idler gear in case.
4. Lubricate the output shaft splines and machined surfaces with transmission oil.
5. The first–reverse synchronizer hub is a press fit on the output shaft. Hub must be installed in an arbor press. Install the synchronizer hub with the teeth-end of the gear facing towards the rear of the shaft.

6. Place the blocking ring on the tapered surface of the first gear.
7. Slide the first gear on the output shaft with the blocking ring toward the rear of the shaft. Rotate the gear as necessary to engage the three notches in the blocking ring with the synchronizer inserts. Install the thrust washer and snap-ring.
8. Slide the blocking ring onto the tapered surface of the second gear. Slide the second gear with blocking ring and the second–third synchronizer on the mainshaft. Be sure that the tapered surface of second gear is facing the front of the shaft and that the notches in the blocking ring engage the synchronizer inserts. Install the snap-ring and secure assembly.
9. Cover the core of the input shaft with a thin coat of grease.

Install bearings.
10. Install the input shaft through the front of the case and insert snap-ring in the bearing groove.
11. Install the output shaft assembly in the case. Position the second–third shift fork on the second–third synchronizer.
12. Place a detent plug spring and a plug in the case. Place the second–third synchronizer in the second gear position (to-

ward the rear of the case). Align the fork and install the second–third shift rail. It will be necessary to depress the detent plug to install the shift rail in the bore. Move the rail forward until the detent plug enters the forward notch (second gear).
13. Secure the fork to the shift rail with a set screw and place the synchronizer in neutral.
14. Install the interlock plug in the case.
15. Place the first–reverse synchronizer in the first gear position (towards the front of the case). Place the shift fork in the groove of the synchronizer. Rotate the fork into position and install the shift rail. Move the shift rail inward until the center notch (neutral) is aligned with the detent bore. Secure shift fork with set screw.
16. Install a new shift rail expansion plug in the front of the case.
17. Hold the input shaft and blocking ring in position and move the output shaft forward to seat the pilot in the roller bearings on the input gear.
18. Tap the input gear bearing into place while holding the output shaft. Install the front bearing retainer and gasket. Torque attaching bolts to specifications.
19. Install the large snap-ring on the rear bearing. Place the bearing on the output shaft with the snap-ring end toward the rear of the shaft. Press the bearing into place using a special tool. Secure the bearing to the shaft with the snap-ring.
20. Hold the speedometer drive gear lock ball in the detent and slide the speedometer drive gear into position. Secure with snap-ring.
21. Place the transmission in the vertical position. Working with a screwdriver through the drain hole in the bottom of the case, align the bore of the countershaft gear and the thrust washer with the bore in the case.
22. Working from the rear of the case, push the dummy shaft out of the countershaft gear with the countershaft. Align the roll pin hole in the countershaft with the matching hole in the case. Drive the shaft into place and install the roll pin.
23. Position the new extension housing gasket on the case with sealer. Install the extension housing and torque to specification.
24. Place the transmission in gear and pour gear oil over entire gear train while rotating the input shaft.
25. Install the remaining detent plug and long spring in case.
26. Position cover gasket on case with sealer and install cover. Torque cover bolts to specifications.
27. Check operation of transmission in all gear positions.

Lubricant Refill Capacity

	U.S. Pints	Imp. Pints
Ford Type 3.03	3.5	3.0

TORQUE SPECIFICATIONS

	ft. lbs.
Input shaft gear bearing retainer to transmission case	30–36
Transmission to flywheel housing	37–42
Transmission cover to transmission case	14–19
Speedometer cable retainer to transmission extension	3–4.5
Transmission extension to transmission case	42–50
Flywheel housing to engine	40–50
Gear shift lever to cam and shaft assembly lock nuts	18–23
U-Joint flange to output shaft	60–80
Filler plug	10–20
Shifter fork set screws	10–18
T.R.S. switch to case	15–20

Ford 4-Speed Overdrive Transmission

The Ford 4-speed overdrive transmission is fully synchronized in all forward gears. The 4-speed shift control is serviced as a unit and should not be disassembled. The lubricant capacity is 4.5 pints.

Disassembly

1. Remove retaining clips and flat washers from the shift rods at the levers.
2. Remove shift linkage control bracket attaching screws and remove shift linkage and control brackets.
3. Remove cover attaching screws. Then lift cover and gasket from the case. Remove the long spring that holds the detent plug in the case. Remove the plug with a magnet.

4. Remove extension housing attaching screws. Then, remove extension housing and gasket.
5. Remove input shaft bearing retainer attaching screws. Then, slide retainer from the input shaft.
6. Working a dummy shaft in from the front of the case, drive the countershaft out the rear of the case. Let the countergear assembly lie in the bottom of the case. Remove the set screw from the first–second shift fork. Slide the first–second shift rail out of the rear of the case. Use a magnet to remove the interlock detent from between the first–second and third–fourth shift rails.
7. Locate first–second speed gear shift lever in neutral. Locate third–fourth speed gear shift lever in third speed position.

NOTE: On overdrive transmissions, locate third–fourth speed gear shift-lever in the fourth speed position.

8. Remove the lockbolt that holds the third–fourth speed shift rail detent spring and plug in the left side of the case. Remove spring and plug with a magnet.
9. Remove the detent mechanism set screw from top of case. Then, remove the detent spring and plug with a small magnet.
10. Remove attaching screw from the third–fourth speed shift fork. Tap lightly on the inner end of the shift rail to remove the expansion plug from front of case. Then, withdraw the third–fourth speed shift rail from the front. Do not lose the interlock pin from rail.
11. Remove attaching screw from the first and second speed shift fork. Slide the first–second shift rail from the rear of case.
12. Remove the interlock and detent plugs from the top of the case with a magnet.
13. Remove the snap-ring or disengage retainer that holds the speedometer drive gear to the output shaft, then remove speedometer gear drive ball.
14. Remove the snap-ring used to hold the output shaft bearing to the shaft. Pull out the output shaft bearing.
15. Remove the input shaft bearing snap-rings. Use a press to remove the input shaft bearing. Remove the input shaft and blocking ring from the front of the case.
16. Move output shaft to the right side of the case. Then, maneuver the forks to permit lifting them from the case.
17. Support the thrust washer and first-speed gear to prevent sliding from the shaft, then lift output shaft from the case.
18. Remove reverse gear shift fork attaching screw. Rotate the reverse shift rail 90°, then, slide the shift rail out the rear of the case. Lift out the reverse shift fork.
19. Remove the reverse detent plug and spring from the case with a magnet.
20. Using a dummy shaft, remove the reverse idler shaft from the case.
21. Lift reverse idler gear and thrust washers from the case. Be careful not to drop the bearing rollers or the dummy shaft from the gear.
22. Lift the countergear, thrust washers, rollers and dummy shaft assembly from the case.
23. Remove the next snap-ring from the front of the output shaft. Then, slide the

Removing output shaft bearing

Removing shift fork from case

SPEEDOMETER DRIVE GEAR 17285

BEARING 7065

SNAP RING

SNAP RING 7026

THRUST WASHER 7A385

FIRST SPEED GEAR-7A029

OUTPUT SHAFT-7061

SPEEDOMETER GEAR DRIVE BALL-353351-S

SNAP RING 7109

THRUST WASHER-7071

BLOCKING RING-7107

FIRST AND SECOND SPEED SYNCHRONIZER-7124

OVERDRIVE GEAR-7B340

BLOCKING RING-7107

STEPPED SURFACE TOWARD FRONT OF TRANSMISSION

BLOCKING RING-7107

SECOND SPEED GEAR-7109

SNAP RING 7109

SNAP RING 7109

THIRD AND FOURTH SPEED SYNCHRONIZER-7124

NARROW THRUST SURFACE OF HUB TOWARD FRONT—WIDE THRUST SURFACE TOWARD REAR.

Output shaft

third–fourth synchronizer blocking ring and the third speed gear from the shaft.

24. Remove the next snap-ring and the second speed gear thrust washer from the shaft. Slide the second speed gear and the blocking ring from the shaft.

25. Remove the snap-ring, then slide the first–second synchronizer, blocking ring and the first speed gear from the shaft.

26. Remove the thrust washer from rear of the shaft.

Unit Repairs

CAM AND SHAFT SEALS

1. Remove attaching nut and washers from each shift lever, then remove the three levers.

2. Remove the three cams and shafts from inside the case.

3. Replace the old O-rings with new ones that have been well-lubricated.

4. Slide each cam and shaft into its respective bore in the transmission.

5. Install the levers and secure them with their respective washers and nuts.

SYNCHRONIZERS

1. Push the synchronizer hub from each synchronizer sleeve.

2. Separate the inserts and springs from the hubs. Do not mix parts of the first–second with parts of third–fourth synchronizers.

3. To assemble, position the hub in the sleeve. Be sure the alignment marks are properly indexed.

4. Place the three inserts into place on the hub. Install the insert springs so that the irregular surface (hump) is seated in one of the inserts. Do not stagger the springs.

COUNTERSHAFT GEAR

1. Dismantle the countershaft gear assembly.

2. Assemble the gear by coating each end of the countershaft gear bore with grease.

3. Install dummy shaft in the gear. Then install 21 bearing rollers and a retainer washer in each end of the gear.

REVERSE IDLER GEAR

1. Dismantle reverse idler gear.

2. Assemble reverse idler gear by coating the bore in each end of reverse idler gear with grease.

3. Hold the dummy shaft in the gear and install the 22 bearing rollers and the retainer washer into each end of the gear.

4. Install the reverse idler sliding gear on the splines of the reverse idler gear. Be sure the shift fork groove is toward the front.

INPUT SHAFT SEAL

1. Remove the seal from the input shaft bearing retainer.

2. Coat the sealing surface of a new seal with lubricant, then press the new seal into the input shaft bearing retainer.

SHAFT COLLAR

SHAFT SLEEVE REPLACING T75L-7025-K

REMOVER/REPLACER TUBE (LONG) T75L-7025-C

FORCING NUT

Installing output shaft bearing

THIRD AND OVERDRIVE CAM AND SHAFT (SHORT) 7C124

REVERSE GEAR CAM AND SHAFT SHORT 7C124

FIRST AND SECOND SPEED CAM AND SHAFT LONG 7C124

O-RING - 7288

O-RING 7288

CASE 7005

FIRST AND SECOND SPEED SHIFT LEVER 7290

44727-S
34807-S
33800-S

44727-S
34807-S

REVERSE SHIFT LEVER 7290

33300 S

THIRD AND OVERDRIVE SHIFT LEVER 7285

44727-S
34807 S
33800-S

Cams, shafts and shift levers

Assembly

1. Grease the countershaft gear thrust surfaces in the case. Then, position a thrust washer at each end of the case.

2. Position the countershaft gear, dummy shaft, and roller bearings in the case.

3. Align the gear bore and thrust washers with the bores in the case. Install the countershaft.

4. With the case in a horizontal position, countershaft gear end-play should be from .004–.018 in. Use thrust washers to obtain play within these limits.

5. After establishing correct endplay, place the dummy shaft in the countershaft gear and allow the gear assembly to remain on the bottom of the case.

6. Grease the reverse idler gear thrust surfaces in the case, and position the two thrust washers.

7. Position the reverse idler gear, sliding gear, dummy, etc., in place. Make sure that the shift fork groove in the sliding gear is toward the front.

8. Align the gear bore and thrust washers with the case bores and install the reverse idler shaft.

9. Reverse idler gear end-play should be 0.004–0.018 in. Use selective thrust washers to obtain play within these limits.

10. Position reverse gear shift rail detent spring and detent plug in the case. Hold the reverse shift fork in place on the reverse idler sliding gear and install the shift rail from the rear of the case. Lock the fork to the rail with the Allen head set screws.

11. Install the first-second synchronizer onto the output shaft. The first and reverse synchronizer hub are a press fit and should be installed with gear teeth facing the rear of the shaft.

NOTE: On overdrive transmissions, first and reverse synchronizer hub is a slip fit.

12. Place the blocking ring on second gear. Slide second speed gear onto the front of the shaft with the synchronizer coned surface toward the rear.

13. Install the second speed gear thrust washer and snap-ring.

14. Slide the fourth gear onto the shaft with the synchronizer coned surface front.

15. Place a blocking ring on the fourth gear.

16. Slide the third–fourth speed gear synchronizer onto the shaft. Be sure that the inserts in the synchronizer engage the notches in the blocking ring. Install the snap-ring onto the front of the output shaft.

17. Put the blocking ring on the first gear.

18. Slide the first gear onto the rear of the output shaft. Be sure that the inserts engage the notches in the blocking ring and that the shift fork groove is toward the rear.

19. Install heavy thrust washer onto the rear of the output shaft.

20. Lower the output shaft assembly into the case.

21. Position the first–second speed shift fork and the third–fourth speed shift fork in place on their respective gears. Rotate them into place.

22. Place a spring and detent plug in the detent bore. Place the reverse shift rail into neutral position.

23. Coat the third–fourth speed shift rail interlock pin (tapered ends) with grease, then position it in the shift rail.

24. Align the third–fourth speed shift fork with the shift rail bores and slide the shift rail into place. Be sure that the three detents are facing the outside of the case. Place the front synchronizer into fourth-speed position and install the set screw into the third–fourth speed shift fork. Move the synchronizer to neutral position. Install the third–fourth speed shift rail detent plug, spring and bolt into the left side of the trans-

INSERT

SLEEVE

ETCH MARKS

INSERT SPRING

INSERT SPRING

INSERT

HUB

NARROW THRUST SURFACE TOWARD FRONT WIDE THRUST SURFACE TOWARD REAR

INSERT

FIRST AND SECOND SPEED SYNCHRONIZER

ETCH MARKS

SLEEVE

INSERT SPRING

INSERT

INSERT

HUB

STEPPED SURFACE TOWARD FRONT OF TRANSMISSION

HUMP

INSERT SPRING

THIRD AND OVERDRIVE SYNCHRONIZER

Synchronizers disassembled

ROLL PIN

1st AND 2nd FORK

TURRET

BACKUP LAMP SWITCH

ROLL PIN

SHIFT SHAFT SEAL

TURRET COVER

TURRET SNAP RING

GEARSHIFT LEVER REVERSE STOP

SHIFTER SHAFT

COVER

BUSHING

SEAL

GASKET

CASE ASSEMBLY

EXTENSION

LEVER ASSEMBLY

HOUSING

PLUG CAP NUT BOLT

3RD & 4TH RAIL

ROLL PIN

INPUT SHAFT BEARING RETAINER

REVERSE IDLER GEAR

SPRING

SCREW

3RD & 4TH FORK

COUNTERSHAFT

DETENT PLUG

3RD & 4TH SYNCHRONIZER ASSEMBLY

SPACER TRANS REVERSE FORK

THRUST WASHER

ROLL PIN

REVERSE GEAR RAIL

REVERSE IDLER GEAR SHAFT

SLEEVE

RING

OVERDRIVE GEAR

REVERSE IDLER SLIDING GEAR

ROLLER BEARINGS

HUB 3RD & 4TH

BLOCKING RING

SPEEDOMETER DRIVE GEAR

ROLLER BEARING

SNAP RING

INPUT SHAFT

OUTPUT SHAFT BEARING

INPUT SHAFT BEARING

1ST GEAR

OUTPUT SHAFT

RING

RING

SNAP RING

ROLLER BEARINGS

1ST & 2ND HUB

RING

SPEEDOMETER GEAR DRIVE BALL

2ND GEAR

REVERSE SLIDING GEAR

1ST & 2ND SYNCHRONIZER ASSEMBLY

COUNTERSHAFT GEAR

Single rail overdrive transmission

mission case. Place the detent plug (tapered ends) in the detent bore.

25. Align first–second speed shift fork with the case bores and slide the shift rail into place. Lock the fork with the set screw.

26. Coat the input gear bore with a small amount of grease. Then install the 15 bearing rollers.

27. Put the blocking ring in the third–fourth synchronizer. Place the input shaft gear in the case. Be sure that the output shaft pilot enters the roller bearing of the input shaft gear.

28. With a new gasket on the input bearing retainer, dip attaching bolts in sealer, install bolts and torque to 30–36 ft. lbs.

29. Press on the output shaft bearing, then install the snap-ring to hold the bearing.

30. Position the speedometer gear drive ball in the output shaft and slide the speedometer drive gear into place. Secure gear with snap-ring.

31. Align the countershaft gear bore and thrust washers with the bore in the case. Install the countershaft.

32. With a new gasket in place, install and secure the extension housing. Dip the extension housing screws in sealer, then torque screws to 42–50 ft. lbs.

33. Install the filler plug and the drain plug.

34. Pour E.P. gear oil over the entire gear train while rotating the input shaft.

35. Place each shift fork in all positions to make sure they function properly. Install the remaining detent plug in the case, followed by the spring.

36. With a new cover gasket in place, install the cover. Dip attaching screws in sealer, then torque screws to 14–19 ft. lbs.

37. Coat the third–fourth speed shift rail plug bore with sealer. Install a new plug.

38. Secure each shift rod to its respective lever with a spring washer, flat washer and retaining pin.

39. Position the shift linkage control bracket to the extension housing. Install and torque the attaching screws to 12–15 ft. lbs.

Ford Single Rail 4-Speed, Overdrive Transmission

The Single Rail Overdrive (SROD) transmission is a 4-speed unit that has all forward speeds synchronized. A single control rod (rail) connects the shift lever to the transmission shift lever rails. The lubricant capacity is 4.5 pints.

Disassembly

1. Remove the lower extension housing bolt to drain the transmission.

2. Remove the cover screws; remove the cover and discard the gasket.

3. Remove the screw, detent spring and plug from the case; a magnetized rod will aid in removal.

4. Drive the roll pin from the shifter shaft.

5. Remove the backup lamp switch, snap-ring, and the dust cover from the rear of the extension housing.

6. Remove the shifter shaft from the turret assembly.

7. Remove the extension housing bolts and housing; discard the gasket.

8. Remove the speedometer gear snap-ring; slide the gear from the shaft and remove the drive ball.

9. Remove the output shaft bearing snap-ring. Remove the bearing.

10. Use a dummy shaft to push the countershaft out of the rear of the case. Lower the countershaft gear to the bottom of the case.

11. Remove the input shaft bearing retainer attaching bolts and slide the retainer and gasket from the input shaft; discard the gasket.

12. Remove the input shaft bearing snap-ring; remove the bearing.

13. Remove the input shaft and blocking ring (including roller bearings) from the case.

14. Remove the overdrive shift pawl, gear selector and interlock plate. Remove the 1–2 gearshift selector arm plate. Remove the roll pin from the 3rd–overdrive shift fork.

15. Drive the 3rd–overdrive shift rail and expansion plug from the rear of the case. Remove the mainshaft.

16. Remove the 1st and 2nd gear shift fork; remove the 3rd–overdrive shift fork.

17. Remove the countershaft gear and thrust washers from the case.

18. Remove the snap-ring from the front of the output shaft. Slide the 3rd gear and O.D. synchronizer, blocking ring, and gear from the shaft.

19. Remove the next snap-ring and washer; remove second gear. Remove next snap-ring and remove the 1st–2nd synchronizer. Slide the 1st gear and blocking ring from the rear of the shaft.

20. Remove the roll pin from the reverse fork, slide the reverse shifter rail through the rear of the case, and remove the reverse gearshift fork and spacer.

21. Drive the reverse gear shaft out the rear of the case.

22. Remove the reverse idler gear, thrust washers and roller bearings.

23. Remove the retaining clip, reverse gearshift relay lever and reverse gear se-

lector fork pivot pin. Remove the O.D. shift control link assembly. Remove the shift shaft seal from the rear of the case; remove the expansion plug from the front of the case.

Assembly

Assembly is the reverse. Tighten the extension housing bolts in a criss-cross pattern to 42–50 ft. lbs. The bearing rollers, extension housing bushing, shifter shaft and gear shift damper bushing are to be lubricated with grease before assembly (Ford #ESW-M1C109-A or the equivalent). The gear shift shaft sleeve and the turret cover assembly should be coated with sealer prior to installation. The intermediate and high rail welch plug must be seated firmly; it must not protrude above the front face of the case, nor seat below 0.6 in. below the front face.

With the 1st gear thrust washer clamped tightly against the output shaft shoulder, 1st gear endplay must be 0.005–0.024 in. 2nd gear endplay must be 0.003–0.021 in. O.D. endplay must be 0.009–0.023 in. Countershaft gear endplay, checked after installation between the thrust washers, must be 0.004–0.018 in.

When the gearshift selector arm plate is seated in the 1st–2nd shift fork plate slot, the shifter shaft must pass freely through the bore without binding.

Ford 5–Speed Overdrive (Gasoline Engines)

Disassembly

1. Remove the nuts attaching the bell housing to the transmission case. Remove the bell housing gasket.

2. Remove the drain plug and drain lubricant from the transmission into a suitable container. Clean the metal filings from the magnet of the drain plug, if necessary. Install the drain plug.

3. (Optional) Position the Bench Mount Holding Fixture (T57L-500-B) or its equal to the studs on the right side of the transmission housing. Secure in place with the Bench Holding Fixture Adapter (T77J-7025-D) or its equal to prevent damage to the metric stud threads.

Ranger 5-speed overdrive

4. Place the transmission in neutral.

5. Remove the speedometer sleeve and driven gear assembly from the extension housing.

6. Remove the three bolts (14mm) and four nuts (14mm) attaching the extension housing to the transmission case. There are two longer outer bolts and one short center (bottom) bolt used.

7. Raise the control lever to the left and slide toward the rear of the transmission. Slide the extension housing off the mainshaft, being careful not to damage the oil seal.

8. Pull the control lever and rod out the front end of the extension housing.

9. If required, remove the back-up lamp switch from the extension housing.

10. Remove the anti-spill seal from the mainshaft and discard. (A seal is not necessary for assembly.)

11. Remove the snap-ring that secures the speedometer drive gear to the mainshaft. Slide the drive gear off the mainshaft, and remove the lock ball.

12. Evenly loosen the fourteen 10mm bolts securing the transmission case cover to the transmission case. Remove the cover and gasket.

13. Mark the shift rails and forks to aid during transmission assembly. Remove the roll pins attaching the shift rod ends to the shift rod and remove the shift rod ends.

14. Gently pry the bearing housing away from the transmission case with a screwdriver, being careful not to damage the housing or case. Slide the bearing housing off the mainshaft.

15. Remove the snap-ring and washer retaining the mainshaft rear bearing to the mainshaft.

16. Assemble the Bearing Puller Ring Tool (T77J-7025-J), Bearing Puller Tool (T77J-7025-H), and Forcing Screw (T75L-7025-J) on the Remover and Replacer Tube Tool (T75L-7025-B) or their equal. Slide the tool assembly over the mainshaft and engage the puller jaws behind the rear bearing. Tighten the jaws evenly onto the bearing with a wrench, then turn the forcing screw to remove the mainshaft rear bearing.

17. Remove the snap-ring from the rear end of the countershaft. Assemble the Bearing Puller Tool (T77J-7025-H), Bearing Puller Ring (T77J-7025-J) and Forcing Screw (T75L-7025-J) onto the Remover Tube (T77J-7025-B) or their equal. Slide the tool assembly over the countershaft and engage the puller jaws behind the countershaft rear bearing. Tighten the jaws evenly onto the bearing with a wrench, then turn the forcing screw to remove the bearing.

18. Remove the counter fifth gear and spacer from the rear of the countershaft.

19. Tap the housing with a plastic hammer, if necessary, and remove center housing. Remove the reverse idler gear and two spacers with housing.

20. Remove the cap screw (12mm) from center housing and remove idler gear shaft.

21. Remove the three spring cap bolts.

The two bolts on the case upper portion are 17mm and the bolt on the case side is 14mm. Remove the detent springs and the detent balls with a magnet from the transmission case.

22. Remove the four 10mm bolts attaching the blind covers to the transmission case and remove the blind covers and gaskets.

23. Remove the roll pin from the fifth-and-reverse shift fork. Slide the fifth-and-reverse shift fork shaft out of the transmission case.

24. Shift the transmission into fourth gear. This will provide adequate space to drive out the roll pin. With a small drift, drive the roll pin from third-and-fourth shift fork. Slide the third-and-fourth shift fork shaft out of the rear of the transmission case.

25. Remove the roll pin from the first-and-second shift fork. Slide the first-and-second shift fork shaft assembly out the rear of the transmission case. Remove both inter-lock pins.

26. Remove the snap-ring that secures the fifth gear to the mainshaft.

27. Remove the thrust washer and lock ball, fifth gear and synchronizer ring from the rear of the mainshaft.

28. Install the Synchronizer Ring Holder and Countershaft Spacer (T77J-7025-E) or its equal between the fourth-speed synchronizer ring and synchromesh gear on the mainshaft. Shift the transmission into second gear to lock the mainshaft and prevent the assembly from rotating.

29. Straighten the staked portion of the mainshaft bearing locknut with the Staking Tool (T77J-7025-F) or its equal. Using the Locknut Wrench (T77J-7025-C) or its equal remove the mainshaft bearing locknut.

30. Slide the reverse gear and clutch hub assembly off the mainshaft.

31. Remove the counter reverse gear from the countershaft.

32. If installed, remove the transmission from the holding fixture and set on a workbench.

33. Remove the bolts (12mm) attaching the mainshaft center bearing cover to the transmission and remove the bearing cover.

34. To remove the countershaft center bearing, install Puller T77J-7025-H, Puller Rings T77J-7025-J, Remover Tube T77J-7025-B, and Forcing Screw T75L-7025-J or their equal. Squarely insert the jaws of the puller behind the center bearing retainer ring in the two recessed areas of the case.

NOTE: The retainer ring may need to be turned to position the split in the retainer ring midway between the recessed areas before the puller is installed. This will reduce the possibility of the retainer ring becoming distorted as the bearing is removed.

35. Turn the forcing screw to remove the bearing.

36. To remove the mainshaft center bearing, install Puller T77J-7025-H, Puller Rings T77J-7025-J, Long Remover Tube

T75L-7025-C and Forcing Screw T75L-7025-J or their equal. Squarely insert the jaws of the puller behind the rear mainshaft bearing retainer ring in the two recessed areas of the case.

37. Turn the forcing screw clockwise to remove the bearing.

38. Remove the shim and spacer from behind the mainshaft rear bearing along with the bearing.

39. Remove the front cover by first removing the four studs attaching the cover to case. Remove the studs by installing two nuts (10mm × 1.5) on the stud and drawing the stud out of the case. Remove the four 14mm bolts and remove the cover. Save the shim found on the inside of the cover.

40. Remove the snap-ring from the input shaft.

41. Remove the input shaft bearing by installing Puller T77J-7025-H, Puller Rings T77J-7025-J, Remover Tube T75L-7025-B, and Forcing Screw T75L-7025-J or their equal. Squarely insert the jaws of the puller behind the input shaft bearing retainer ring in the two recessed areas of the case.

NOTE: The retainer ring may need to be turned to position the split in the ring midway between the recessed areas before the puller is installed.

42. Turn the forcing screw clockwise to remove the bearing.

43. Rotate both shift forks so that the main gear train will fall to the bottom of the case. Remove the shift forks. Rotate the input shaft so that one of the two flats on the input shaft faces upward.

44. Remove the snap-ring from the front of the countershaft.

45. Remove Synchronizer Ring Holder T77J-7025-E or its equal from the front of the case and insert between the first gear on the countershaft and the rear of the case.

46. Install Forcing Screw T75L-7025-J, Press Frame T77J-7025-N, and Press Frame Adapter T82T-7003-BH or their equal against the countershaft assembly.

47. Turn the forcing screw clockwise to press the countershaft rearward. Press the countershaft (3/16 inch movement) until it contacts the Synchronizer Ring Holder and Countershaft Spacer.

48. To remove the countershaft front bearing, first remove the press frame. Then, install Puller T77J-7025-H, Puller Rings T77J-7025-J, Remover Tube T77J-7025-B, and Forcing Screw T75L-7025-J or their equal. Squarely insert the jaws of the puller behind the front bearing retainer ring in the two recessed areas of the case.

NOTE: The retainer ring may need to be turned to position the split in the ring midway between the recessed areas before the puller is installed.

49. Turn the forcing screw clockwise to remove the bearing.

50. Remove the shim from behind the countershaft front bearing.

51. Remove the countershaft from the transmission case.

52. Remove the input shaft from the transmission case. Remove the synchronizer ring and caged bearing from the mainshaft.

53. Remove the mainshaft and gear assembly from the transmission case.

54. Remove the inner race of the countershaft center bearing from the countershaft in a press frame using Axle Bearing Seal Plate T75L-1165-B and Pinion Bearing Cone Remover D79L-4621-A or their equal.

55. Remove first gear and first-and-second synchronizer ring. Remove snap-ring retainer from mainshaft.

NOTE: Do not mix synchronizer rings.

56. Install Bearing Remover Tool T71P-4621-B or its equal between second and third gear.

57. Press the mainshaft out of third gear and third-and-fourth clutch hub sleeve.

58. Press the first-and-second clutch hub and sleeve assembly, and first gear sleeve from the mainshaft.

59. Clean and inspect the case, gears, bearings and shafts.

Assembly

NOTE: As each part is assembled, coat the part with manual transmission oil D8DZ-19C547-A (ESP-M2C83-C) or equivalent.

Before beginning the assembly procedure, three measurements must be performed: Mainshaft Thrust Play, Countershaft Thrust Play and Mainshaft Bearing Clearance.

Mainshaft Thrust Play

Check the mainshaft thrust play by measuring the depth of the mainshaft bearing bore in the transmission rear cage by using a depth micrometer (D80P-4201-A). Then measure the mainshaft rear bearing height. The difference between the two measurements indicates the required thickness of the adjusting shim. The standard thrust play is 0 to 0.0039 inch (0 to 0.1mm). Adjusting shims are available in 0.0039 inch (0.1mm) and 0.0118 inch (0.3mm) sizes.

Countershaft Thrust Play

Check the countershaft thrust play by measuring the depth of the countershaft front bearing bore in the transmission case by using a depth micrometer (D80P-4201-A). Then measure the countershaft front bearing height. The difference between the two measurements indicates the required thickness of the adjusting shims. The standard thrust play is 0 to 0.0039 inch (0 to 0.1mm).

Adjusting shims are available in 0.0039 inch (0.1mm) and 0.0118 inch (0.3mm) sizes.

Mainshaft Bearing Clearance

Check the mainshaft bearing clearance by measuring the depth of the bearing bore in the clutch adapter plate with a depth micrometer, D80P-4201-A. Make sure the micrometer is on the second step of the plate. Measure the bearing height. The difference between the two measurements indicates the required adjusting shim thickness. The standard clearance is 0 to 0.0039 inch (0 to 0.1mm). If an adjusting shim is required, select one to bring the clearance to within specifications.

1. Assemble the first-and-second synchromesh mechanism and the third-and-fourth synchromesh mechanism by installing the clutch hub to the sleeve. Place the three synchronizer keys into the clutch hub key slots and install the key springs to the clutch hub.

NOTE: When installing the key springs, the open end tab of the springs should be inserted into hub holes with springs turned in the same direction. This will keep the spring tension on each key uniform.

2. Place the synchronizer ring on the second gear and position the second gear to the mainshaft with the synchronizer ring toward the rear of the shaft.

3. Slide the first-and-second clutch hub and sleeve assembly to the mainshaft with the oil grooves of the clutch hub toward the front of the mainshaft. Make sure that the three synchronizer keys in the synchromesh mechanism engage the notches in the second synchronizer ring.

4. Press into position using press and suitable replacer tool.

5. Insert the first gear sleeve on the mainshaft.

6. Place the synchronizer ring on the third gear along with the caged roller bearing and slide the third gear to the front of the mainshaft with the synchronizer ring toward the front.

7. Press the third-and-fourth clutch hub and sleeve assembly to the front of the mainshaft. Make sure that the three synchronizer keys in the synchromesh mechanism engage the notches in the synchronizer ring.

NOTE: The direction of the third-and-fourth clutch hub and sleeve assembly should be as shown in Fig. 68.

8. Install the snap-ring to the front of the mainshaft.

9. Slide the needle bearing for the first gear to the mainshaft.

10. Place the synchronizer ring on the first gear. Slide the first gear onto the mainshaft with the synchronizer ring facing the front of the shaft. Rotate the first gear, as necessary, to engage the three notches in the synchronizer ring with the synchronizer keys.

11. Install the original thrust washer to the mainshaft.

12. Position the mainshaft and gear assembly in the case.

13. Position the first-and-second shift fork and third-and-fourth shift fork in the groove of the clutch hub and sleeve assembly.

14. Position the caged bearing in the front end of the mainshaft.

15. Place the synchronizer ring on the input shaft (fourth gear) and install the input shaft to the front end of the mainshaft. Make sure that the three synchronizer keys in the third-and-fourth synchromesh mechanism engage the notches in the synchronizer ring.

16. Press the inner race of the countershaft rear bearing onto the countershaft using Center Bearing Replacer T77J-7025-K or its equal.

17. Position the countershaft gear in the case, making sure that the countershaft gear engages each gear of the mainshaft assembly.

18. Install the correct shim on the mainshaft center bearing as determined in the Mainshaft Thrust Play Measurement in this Section.

19. Position the input shaft bearing and the mainshaft center bearing to the proper bearing bores. Be sure the synchronizer and shifter forks have not been moved out of position.

20. Install the Synchronizer Ring Holder Tool T77J-7025-E or its equal between the

Clutch hub assembly direction

fourth synchronizer ring and the synchromesh gear on the mainshaft.

21. Install the Dummy Bearing Replacer T75L-7025-Q, Input Shaft Bearing Replacer T82T-7003-DH, Replacer Tube T77J-7025-M, and Press Frame T77J-7025-N or their equal on the case. Turn the forcing screw on the press frame until both bearings are properly seated.

22. Install the input shaft bearing snapring.

NOTE: Be sure that the synchronizer and shift forks are properly positioned during seating of bearings. After bearings are seated, make certain that both synchronizers operate freely.

23. Place the correct shim in the countershaft front bearing bore.

24. Position the countershaft front and center bearings in the bores and install the tools. Turn the forcing screw until the bearing is properly seated. Use the center bearing as a pilot.

25. Install the snap-ring to secure the countershaft front bearing.

26. Remove the synchronizer ring holder.

27. Install the bearing cover to the transmission case and tighten the four attaching bolts. Tighten to 56–79 N·m (41–59 ft. lbs.).

28. Install the reverse idler gear and shaft with a spacer on each side of shaft.

29. Slide the counter reverse gear (chamfer side forward) and spacer onto the countershaft.

30. Slide the thrust washer, reverse gear, caged roller bearings and clutch hub assembly onto the mainshaft. Install a new locknut (hand tight).

31. Shift into second gear and reverse gear to lock the rotation of the mainshaft. Tighten the locknut to 156–233 N·m (115 to 172 ft. lbs.) using the Locknut Wrench T77J-7025-C or its equal.

32. Stake the locknut into the mainshaft keyway using the staking tool.

33. Place the fourth-and-third clutch sleeve in third gear using Synchronizer Ring Holder and Countershaft Spacer T77J-7025-E.

34. If new synchronizers have been installed, check the clearance between the synchronizer key and the exposed edge of the synchronizer ring with a feeler gauge. If the measurement is greater than 2.0mm (0.079 inch), the synchronizer key can pop out of position. To correct this, change the thrust washer (selective fit) between the mainshaft center bearing and the first gear. Available thrust washer sizes are .098, .118 and .138.

35. If new synchronizers were installed, check the clearance again with a feeler gauge. If the clearance is within specifications, bend the tab of the lockwasher.

36. Position the fifth synchronizer ring on the fifth gear. Slide the fifth gear onto the mainshaft with the synchronizer ring toward the front of the shaft. Rotate the fifth gear, as necessary, to engage the three

notches in the synchronizer ring with the synchronizer keys in the reverse and clutch hub assembly.

37. Install the lock ball and thrust washer on the rear of the fifth gear.

38. Install the snap-ring on the rear of the thrust washer. Check the clearance between the thrust washer and the snap-ring. If the clearance is not within 0.1mm to 0.3mm (0.0039 to 0.0118 inch), select the proper size thrust washer to bring the clearance within specifications.

39. Slide the first-and-second shift fork shaft assembly into the case (front rear of case). Secure the first-and-second shift fork to the fork shaft with the roll pin.

NOTE: Be sure to use a new roll pin.

40. Insert the inter-lock pin into the transmission using the lockout pin replacer tool.

41. Shift transmission into fourth gear. Slide the third-and-fourth shift fork shaft into the case, from rear of case. Secure the third-and-fourth shift fork to the fork shaft with the roll pin. Insert inter-lock pin.

NOTE: Be sure to use a new roll pin.

42. Shift synchronizer hub into fifth gear. Position reverse and fifth fork on the clutch hub and slide the reverse-and-fifth fork shaft into the case (from rear of case). Secure the reverse-and-fifth shift fork to the fork shaft with the roll pin.

NOTE: Be sure to use a new roll pin.

43. Install the two blind covers and gaskets. Tighten the attaching bolts (10mm) to 32–45 N·m (23–34 ft. lbs.).

44. Position the three detent balls and three springs into the case and install the spring cap bolts (12mm and 17mm).

45. Apply a thin coat of Gasket Maker E2AZ-19562-A (ESE-M4G234-A2) or equivalent to the contacting surfaces of the center housing and transmission case.

46. Position the center housing on the case. Align the reverse idler gear shaft boss with the center housing attaching bolt boss. Install and tighten the idler shaft capscrew (12mm) and tighten to 56–79 N·m (41–59 ft. lbs.).

47. Slide the counter fifth gear to the countershaft.

48. Position the countershaft rear bearing on the countershaft. Press into position using the Adjustable Press Frame T77J-7025-N and Forcing Screw T75L-7025-J or their equal.

49. Install the thrust washer and snapring to the rear of the countershaft rear bearing. Check the clearance between the thrust washer and the snap-ring using a feeler gauge.

50. If the clearance is not within 0.00 to 0.15mm (0.0000 to 0.0059 inch), select the proper size thrust washer to bring the clearance within specifications, .0748, .0787, .0827, or .0866.

51. If installed, remove filler plugs. Position the mainshaft rear bearing on the

mainshaft. Press into place using the Adjustable Press Frame T77J-7025-N, Dummy Bearing T75L-7025-Q1 and Forcing Screw T75L-7025-J or their equal.

52. Install the thrust washer and snapring to the rear of the mainshaft rear bearing. Check the clearance between the thrust washer and the snap-ring. The clearance should be 0.00 to 0.10mm (0.0000 to 0.0039 inch). If the clearance is not within specifications, replace the thrust washer to bring the clearance within specifications, .0787, .0846, or .0906.

53. Apply a thin coat of Gasket Maker E2AZ-19562-A (ESE-M4G234-A2) or equivalent to the contacting surfaces of the bearing housing and center housing.

54. Position the bearing housing on the center housing.

55. Install each shift fork shaft end onto the proper shift fork shaft. (Note the scribe marks made during disassembly) and secure with roll pins.

56. Install the lock ball, speedometer drive gear, and snap-ring onto the mainshaft.

57. If removed, install control lever and rod in extension housing.

58. Apply a thin coat of Gasket Maker E2AZ-19562-A (ESE-M4G234-A2) or equivalent to the contacting surfaces of the bearing housing and extension housing.

59. Position the extension housing in the bearing housing with the gearshift control lever end laid down to the left as far as it will go. Tighten the attaching bolts and nuts (14mm) to 82–108 N·m (60–80 ft. lbs.). There are two longer outer bolts and one shorter center (bottom) bolt used.

60. If removed, insert the speedometer driven gear assembly to the extension housing and secure it with the bolt.

61. Check to ensure the gearshift control lever operates properly.

62. Install the transmission case cover gasket and cover with drain plug to the rear. Install and tighten the fourteen 10mm attaching bolts to 32–45 N·m (23–34 ft. lbs.).

63. Install the correct size shim on the second step of the front cover as determined by the mainshaft bearing clearance measurement.

64. Coat the front cover with Gasket Maker E2AZ-19562-A (ESE-M4G234-A2) or equivalent. Install the front cover to the transmission case and tighten the four bolts and four studs.

65. Install 1.4 liters (3.0 pints) of Ford Manual Transmission Lube D8DZ-19C547-A (ESP-M2C83-C) or equivalent. Re-install the filler plugs and tighten to 25–39 N·m (18–29 ft. lbs.).

5–Speed Overdrive (Diesel Engines)

Disassembly

1. If not already drained, remove the drain plug and drain the transmission fluid

TRANSMISSION CASE BEARING HOUSING

INTERMEDIATE HOUSING EXTENSION HOUSING

5-speed manual overdrive (diesel engines)

into a suitable container. Remove the fork and release bearing from the transmission case.

2. Install the transmission in Bench Mounted Holding Fixture, T57L-500-B or its equal. Remove the six bolts (12mm) attaching the front cover to the transmission case and remove the front cover, shim (located in cover) and gasket.

3. Remove the front cover oil seal using Inner Seal Removal Tool, T75P-3504-G and Impact Slide Hammer, T50T-100-A or their equal.

4. Remove the input shaft snap-ring.

5. If installed, remove the gearshift lever. Remove the four bolts (12mm) and remove the retainer and gasket from the extension housing.

6. Remove the outer retaining ring on the input shaft bearing. Install Bearing Collet Tool, T75L-7025-E on the input shaft bearing, and Remover Tube, T75L-7025-B and Forcing Screw T75L-7025-J or their equal. Slide Bearing Collet Sleeve, T75L-7025-G or its equal over the Remover Tube and Bearing Collet, and turn the forcing screw to remove the input shaft bearing.

7. Remove the bolt (12mm) that attaches the control lever end to the control rod and remove the control lever end and rod from the extension housing.

8. Remove the eight (12mm) bolts attaching the extension housing to the intermediate housing and transmission housing. Slide the extension housing off the output shaft with the control lever end laid down and to the left as far as it will go.

9. Remove the speedometer driven gear assembly from the extension housing.

10. Remove the back-up lamp switch and the neutral safety switch.

11. Remove the grommet from the end of the output shaft. Remove the snap-ring that secures the speedometer drive gear on the output shaft. Slide the speedometer drive gear off the output shaft and remove the lock ball.

12. Install Bearing Pusher Tool, T83T-7111-A or its equal over the countershaft front bearing. Turn the forcing screw to force the countershaft (together with the countershaft front bearing) from the transmission case. Remove the pusher tool assembly.

NOTE: The countershaft front bearing may remain in the transmission case. Remove the bearing with a suitable driver.

13. Remove and discard the roll pin from the 1-2 shift fork. Remove the cir-clip from the rail. Remove the upper cap bolt and with a magnet, remove the spring and detent ball from the bore. Remove the 1-2 shift rail and 1-2 shift fork.

NOTE: Note the position of the 1-2 shift fork in relation to the 3-4 shift fork for positioning during reassembly. The shift forks and rails are not interchangeable. Also note the position of the shift rail and the relationship of the detent slots to the bore for positioning during reassembly. The three detent slots in the shift rails face towards the cap bolts.

14. Remove the roll pin from the 3-4 shift fork. Remove the cir-clip from the rail. Remove the middle cap bolt and with a magnet, remove the spring and detent ball from the bore. Remove the 3-4 shift fork and rail. An interlock pin will drop out of the bore when the 3-4 shift rail is removed.

NOTE: Note the position of the shift rail and the relationship of the detent slots to the bore for positioning during reassembly.

15. Remove the cir-clip and washer from the 5-R (Reverse) shift rail. Remove the bottom cap bolt and with a magnet, remove the shorter length spring and detent ball.

16. Drive the roll pin from the 5-R shift lever and remove the lever from the rail. With a magnet remove the other detent ball and shorter length spring from the bottom (5-R) bore.

17. Gently pry the intermediate housing away from the bearing housing. Remove the gear and bearing assembly out of the intermediate housing.

18. Install the gear train and bearing housing assembly in a fabricated holding tool positioned in a vise. A soft-jawed vise may be used in place of the holding tool.

19. Remove the bottom cap bolt and with a magnet, remove the shorter length spring and detent ball from the bore. Drive the roll pin out of the 5-R shift fork and discard. Remove the 5-R shift rail. An inter-lock pin will drop out of the bore when the 5-R shift rail is removed.

NOTE: Note the position of the 5-R shift fork in relation to the bearing housing for positioning during reassembly. Also note the position of the shift rail and the relationship of the detent slots to the bore for positioning during reassembly. The three detent slots in the shift rail face towards the cap bolt.

20. Remove the retaining ring from the output shaft ball bearing. Remove the thrust washer.

21. To remove the output shaft rear bearing, place Shaft Protectors, D80L-625-2 and D80L-625-3 or their equal on the end of the output shaft. It may be necessary to hold the shaft protectors in place with putty. Install Puller, T77J-7025-H, Collet (2), T77J-7025-J or their equal against the bearing so the jaws of the puller are against the rear of the bearing. Place Tube (Long), T75L-7025-C or its equal over the output shaft. Install Forcing Screw, T75L-7025-J or its equal into the tube and turn the forcing screw clockwise to remove the bearing. Discard the bearing and install a new one during reassembly.

22. Remove the snap-ring from the countershaft rear bearing. Install Puller, T77J-7025-H, Collet (2), T77J-7025-J, Tube (Short, T77J-7025-B) and Forcing Screw, T75L-7025-J or their equal. Turn the forcing screw clockwise and remove the bearing. Discard the bearing and install a new one during reassembly.

23. Remove the retaining ring, thrust washer and lock ball from the output shaft.

24. Remove the fifth gear and sleeve from the countershaft.

NOTE: The collar of the fifth gear faces towards the bearing housing.

25. Remove the reverse gear from the countershaft.

NOTE: The collar of the counter-reverse gear faces towards the bearing housing.

26. Remove the fifth gear from the output shaft and remove the 5-R synchronizer ring.

27. Straighten the peen on the locknut with Staking Tool, T77J-7025-F or its equal. Lock the transmission gears in Reverse and any forward gear. Install Lock Nut Wrench T77J-7025-C or its equal on the locknut and remove the locknut and discard.

28. Remove the 5-R synchronizer assembly from the output shaft.

29. Pry the reverse gear, caged needle bearing, sleeve and thrust washer from the output shaft.

30. Remove the snap-ring and remove the reverse idler gear from the idler shaft. Remove the keyed thrust washer from the shaft.

31. Remove the five (12mm) bolts that attach the bearing cover to the bearing housing and remove the cover.

32. If required, remove the bolt retaining the idler shaft to the bearing housing and drive the plate and shaft assembly out of the housing.

33. With a soft hammer, tap the rear end of the output shaft and countershaft in turn, being careful not to damage the shafts. Remove the shafts from the bearing housing.

34. Carefully separate the input shaft, caged needle bearing and synchronizer ring from the output shaft.

35. Press the rear countershaft bearing from the bearing housing using Remover Tube Tool, T77J-7025-B or its equal.

36. Press the rear output shaft bearing from the bearing housing using Bearing Remover Tool, T77F-4222-A and Remover Tube Tool, T77J-7025-B or their equal.

37. Remove the thrust washer, first gear, sleeve and synchronizer ring from the rear of the output shaft.

38. Using snap-ring pliers, remove the snap-ring from the front of the output shaft.

39. Using a press and Remover Tool, T71P-4621-B or its equal, remove the third-and-fourth hub, sleeve, synchronizer ring and third gear from the front of the output shaft.

40. Using a press and Remover Tool, T71P-4621-B or its equal, remove the first-and-second hub and sleeve assembly synchronizer ring, and second gear from the rear of the output shaft in the same manner as described in the previous step.

41. Press the front bearing from the countershaft using Remover Tool D79L-4621-A or T71P-4621-B and suitable press stock.

42. Inspect all parts.

Assembly

1. Assemble the 3-4 synchronizer assembly by installing the keys in the hub and sliding the sleeve over the hub and keys. Install the springs onto the hub.

NOTE: When installing the springs, the open end tab of the springs should be inserted into the hub holes. This will keep the spring tension on each key uniform.

2. Assemble the 1-2 synchronizer assembly in the same manner as described in Step 1. Assemble the 5-R synchronizer assembly as also described in Step 1 and install the retaining ring in the 5-R assembly.

3. Install the third gear and synchronizer ring onto the front section of the output shaft.

4. Install the 3-4 synchronizer assembly onto the output shaft by using a press. Hold the assembly together and slowly press in place. Make sure the three recesses in

Synchronizer hub installation

the synchronizer ring are aligned with the three keys in the synchronizer hub.

NOTE: The direction of the hub is as shown. The recesses in each synchronizer sleeve must face each other.

5. Fit the snap-ring on the output shaft.

6. Install the second gear, synchronizer ring onto the rear section of the output shaft.

7. Install the 1-2 synchronizer assembly onto the output shaft by using a press. Hold the assembly together and slowly press in place. Make sure the three keys recesses in the synchronizer ring are aligned with the three keys in the synchronizer hub.

NOTE: The direction of the hub is as shown. The recesses in the synchronizer sleeve must face each other.

8. Install the synchronizer ring, first gear with sleeve, and thrust washer onto the output shaft.

9. Install the input shaft and the needle roller bearing to the output shaft.

10. Check the countershaft rear bearing clearance. Measure the depth of the countershaft bearing bore in the bearing housing with a depth micrometer (D80P-4201-A or equivalent). Install the retaining ring on the bearing and with a depth micrometer measure the distance between the inside edge of the ring and the end of the bearing. The difference between the two measurements indicates the required thickness of the adjusting shim. The clearance should be less than 0.1mm (0.0039 inch). The adjusting shims are available in 0.1mm (0.0039 inch) and 0.3mm (0.0118 inch) sizes.

11. Check the output shaft bearing clearance. Measure the depth of the bearing bore with a depth micrometer. Measure the width of the bearing with a micrometer. The difference between the two measurements indicates the required thickness of the adjusting shim. The clearance should be less than 0.1mm (0.0039 inch). Adjusting shims are available in 0.1mm (0.0039 inch) and 0.3mm (0.0118 inch) sizes.

12. Position the proper shim on the countershaft rear bearing and press into the bearing housing using Installer Tool, T77J-7025-B or its equal.

13. Position the proper shim on the output shaft bearing and press the bearing into

the bearing housing using Installer Tool, T77J-7025-K or its equal.

14. Position the front bearing on the countershaft and press the bearing into place using Bearing Replacer Tool, T71P-7025-A or its equal.

15. Mesh the countershaft and the output shaft assembly and position the two in the bearing housing. Make sure that the thrust washer is installed on the mainshaft assembly at the rear of the first gear. Make sure the three recesses in the synchronizer ring are aligned with the three keys in the synchronizer hub.

16. While holding the mainshaft assembly in place, press the countershaft assembly into the bearing housing using Replacer Tool T71P-7025-A or its equal to hold the rear countershaft bearing in the housing.

17. Position the bearing cover on the bearing housing. Install the five (12mm) bolts and tighten.

18. If removed, drive the reverse idler shaft into the bearing housing. Install the bolt and tighten.

19. Install the thrust washer, sleeve, caged needle bearing and reverse gear on the output shaft.

20. Install the reverse gear on the countershaft. The offset on the gear must face the bearing housing.

21. Place the keyed thrust washer so the tab is in the groove in the bearing housing. Install the reverse idler gear so the squared portion of the gear faces the bearing housing. Make sure the reverse idler gear and reverse gear are in mesh. Install the spacer and snap-ring on the idler shaft.

22. Install the 5-R synchronizer assembly on the output shaft.

23. Lock the transmission in Reverse and any forward gear. Install a new locknut on the output shaft and tighten to 130–210 N·m (94–152 ft. lbs.) using Locknut Wrench, T77J-7025-C or its equal.

24. Bend the tab on the locknut with Staking Tool, T77J-7025-F or its equal.

25. Install the 5-R synchronizer ring and gear on the output shaft. Make sure the three recesses in the synchronizer ring are aligned with the three keys in the synchronizer hub.

26. Install the sleeve and the counter-fifth gear on the countershaft.

27. Install the lock ball in the output shaft and position the thrust washer so the slot in the washer is over the lock ball. Install the retaining ring.

28. Position the output shaft assembly in a press and press the output shaft bearing on the shaft using Dummy Bearing Replacer, T75L-7025-Q or its equal and an appropriate length of press stock. Install the thrust washer and retaining ring.

29. Position the countershaft in a press and press the countershaft rear bearing on the shaft using Dummy Bearing Replacer, T75L-7025-Q or its equal and an appropriate length of press stock. Install the thrust washer and retaining ring.

30. Position all synchronizers in the

neutral position. Install the shorter length spring and detent ball in the bottom (5-R) bore. Compress the ball and spring with Dummy Shift Rail Tools, T72J-7280 or its equal and install the dummy shift rail in the bore. Install the 5-R shift rail in the bottom bore and make sure the three detent slots in the rail face the cap bolt and the inter-lock slot in the 5-R rail faces towards the 1-2 bore. Install the inter-lock pin through the top bore so it is positioned in the channel between the 5-R rail bore and 3-4 rail bore. Install the 3-4 rail in the housing and make sure the three detent slots in the rail face the middle bore. Insert the inter-lock pin in the channel the 3-4 rail and the 1-2 rail bore. Install the 1-2 shift rail in the housing so the three detent slots in the rail face the top bore.

NOTE: The inter-lock pins are identical and all four detent balls are identical. The springs for the 5-R or bottom bore are of a shorter length than the other two springs.

31. Install the first-and-second shift fork and the third-and-fourth shift forks to their respective sleeves.

32. Align the roll pin holes of each shift fork and rod. Install new roll pins.

NOTE: When installing the shift fork and control end, a new roll pin should be installed with a pin slit positioned in the direction of the shift rod axis.

NOTE: If not removed, remove the shift levers from the shift rails. Remember from which rail each lever was removed for correct installation upon assembly.

33. Install the detent balls and springs into their respective bores and install the three cap bolts.

NOTE: The shorter length spring is installed in the bottom (reverse) bore.

34. Install the cir-clips on the 1-2 and 3-4 shift rails. Install the cir-clip and washer on the 5-R shift rail.

35. Apply a thin coating of Silicone Sealer, D6AZ-19562-B or equivalent to the mating surfaces of the transmission case and the bearing housing. Install the transmission case on the bearing housing.

36. Apply a thin coating of Silicone Sealer, D6AZ-19562-B or equivalent to the mating surfaces of the bearing housing and intermediate housing. Install the intermediate housing to the bearing housing.

37. Position the shift lever gates on the appropriate shift rails. Install new roll pins.

38. Place the lock ball in the output shaft and position the speedometer drive gear over the ball. Install the snap-ring. Install the grommet on the end of the output shaft.

39. Apply a thin coating of Silicone sealer, D6AZ-19562-B or equivalent to the extension housing and the intermediate housing. Slide the extension housing over the output shaft (the control lever must be moved to the far left) and onto the extension housing. Install the bolts and tighten.

NOTE: If necessary, remove the plugs from the transmission case shift rod bores to align the shift rods. After the installation of the bearing housing assembly, reinstall the plugs using Silicone Sealer, D6AZ-19562-B or equivalent.

40. With the outer snap-ring in place on the input shaft front bearing, place the bearing, shim and Adapter Tool, T75L-7025-N or its equal over the input shaft.

41. Thread the Replacer Shaft, T75L-7025-K or its equal onto the Adapter Tool. Install the Replacer Tube, T75L-7025-B or its equal over the Replacer Shaft and install the nut and washer on the forcing screw.

42. Slowly tighten the nut until the adapter is securely on the input shaft. Make sure the tools are aligned.

43. Tighten the nut on the forcing screw until the bearing outer snap-ring is seated. Remove the installation tools.

NOTE: The input shaft bearing retaining ring must be flush with the transmission case. If not flush, it will be necessary to tap on the end of the input shaft with a soft hammer until the bearing is seated.

44. Install the input shaft snap-ring.

45. Measure the distance between the end of the installed input bearing in the transmission case with a depth micrometer. Measure the distance between the bearing cover gasket and the bottom of the bearing bore in the cover. The difference between the two measurements is the clearance between the outer bearing race and the front cover. The clearance should be less than 0.1mm (0.0039 inch). Clearance can be adjusted by installing an adjusting shim. Shims are available in sizes of 0.15mm (0.006 inch) and 0.30mm (0.012 inch).

46. Install a new oil seal in the front cover using Installer Tool, T71P-7050-A. Install the shim in the recess in the front cover.

47. Apply gear lubricant to the lip of the oil seal inside the front cover and install the front cover to the transmission case. Install the six (12mm) bolts and tighten.

48. Install the control lever end to the control lever and tighten the attaching bolt (10mm) to 28–34 N·m (20–25 ft. lbs.).

49. Install the back-up lamp switch and the neutral safety switch to the extension housing and tighten the switches to 28–34 N·m (20–25 ft. lbs.).

50. Install the gearshift lever retainer and gasket to the extension housing. Install the four (12mm) bolts and tighten to 28–36 N·m (20–27 ft. lbs.). If required, install the gearshift lever.

51. Install the release bearing and fork.

4–Speed Transmission (Diesel Engines)

Disassembly

1. If not already drained, remove the drain plug and drain the transmission fluid into a suitable container. Remove the fork and release bearing from the clutch housing.

2. Install transmission in Holding Fixture T57L-500-B. Remove six bolts (12mm) attaching the front cover to the transmission case and remove the front cover shim and gasket.

3. Remove front cover oil seal.

4. Remove the input shaft snap-ring.

5. Remove outer snap-ring on input shaft bearing. Install Bearing Collet Tool T75L-7025-E or its equal on main input shaft front bearing, Remover Tube T75L-7025-B and Forcing Screw T75L-7025-J or their equal. Slide Bearing Collet Sleeve T75L-7025-G or its equal over remover tube and bearing collet, and turn forcing screw to remove input shaft bearing.

6. Remove the eight bolts (12mm) attaching the extension housing to the transmission case. Slide the extension housing off the mainshaft, with the control lever end laid down and to the left as far as it will go.

7. Remove the bolt (10mm) attaching the control lever end to the control rod and

Four speed manual (diesel engines)

remove the control lever end and rod from the extension housing.

8. Remove the speedometer driven gear assembly from the extension housing.

9. Remove the back-up lamp switch and neutral sensing switch.

10. Remove the snap-ring that secures the speedometer drive gear on the mainshaft. Slide the speedometer drive gear off the mainshaft and remove the lock ball.

11. Install Bearing Pusher Tool T83T-7111-A or its equal over countershaft front bearing. Turn forcing screw to force countershaft, together with the countershaft front bearing, from the transmission housing.

12. Slide Bearing Holder and Gear Shaft Assembly from the transmission housing.

13. Remove three spring cap bolts, three springs and shift locking balls.

NOTE: Reverse spring is shortest.

--- CAUTION ---
SPRING-LOADED LOWER BALL WILL POP OUT.

14. Remove the reverse shift rod and shift fork assembly and reverse gear from the bearing housing.

15. Remove roll pins fixing shift forks to the rods. Push each of the shift rods rearward through the fork and bearing housing and remove the shift rods and forks.

NOTE: Mark 3rd-4th and 1st-2nd shift forks before removal to simplify installation.

16. Remove the lower reverse shift rod locking ball and spring, and the interlock pins from the bearing housing.

17. Straighten the tab of the lockwasher. Lock transmission synchronizers into any two gears and remove the mainshaft lock nut using Adapter Tool T83T-7025-A and Tool Shaft T77J-7025-C or its equal.

18. Remove the snap-ring from the rear end of the countershaft and slide off the counter reverse gear.

19. Remove the five bearing cover bolts (12mm) and cover, and the reverse idler gear shaft from the bearing housing.

20. With a soft hammer, tap the rear end of the mainshaft and countershaft in turn, being careful not to damage the shafts, and remove these shafts from the bearing housing.

21. Carefully separate the input shaft and caged needle roller bearing from the mainshaft.

22. Remove rear countershaft bearing from the bearing housing using Remover Tube Tool T77J-7025-B or its equal.

23. Remove rear mainshaft bearing from the bearing housing using Bearing Remover Tool T77F-4222-A and Remover Tube Tool T77J-7025-B or its equal.

24. Remove the thrust washer, first gear, sleeve and synchronizer ring from the rear of the mainshaft.

25. Using snap-ring pliers, remove the snap-ring from the front of the mainshaft.

26. Using a press and Remover Tool T71P-4621-B or its equal, remove the third-

and-fourth clutch hub, sleeve, synchronizer ring and third gear from the front of the mainshaft.

27. Using a press and Remover Tool T71P-4621-B or its equal, remove the first-and-second clutch hub and sleeve assembly synchronizer ring, and second gear from the rear of the mainshaft in the same manner as described in the previous step.

28. Press front bearing from countershaft using Remover Tool D79L-4621-A or T71P-4621-B or its equal and a suitable stock piece.

29. Perform cleaning and inspection procedures described in a separate section of this manual.

Assembly

1. Assemble the third-and-fourth clutch by installing the clutch hub and synchronizer into the sleeve, placing the three keys into the clutch hub slots and installing the springs onto the hub.

NOTE: When installing the key springs, the open end tab of the springs should be inserted into the hub holes. This will keep the spring tension on each key uniform.

2. Assemble the first-and-second clutch hub and sleeve in the same manner as described in Step 1 above.

3. Install the third gear and synchronizer ring onto the front section of the mainshaft.

4. Install the third-and-fourth clutch hub assembly onto the mainshaft by using a press. Hold assembly together and slowly press into place.

5. Fit the snap-ring on the mainshaft.

6. Install the second gear, synchronizer ring onto the rear section of the mainshaft.

7. Install the first-and-second clutch hub assembly onto the mainshaft by using a press.

8. Install the synchronizer ring, first gear with sleeve, and thrust washer onto the mainshaft.

9. Install the input shaft and the needle roller bearing to the mainshaft.

10. Check the countershaft rear bearing clearance. Measure the depth of the countershaft bearing bore in the bearing housing using a depth micrometer (D80P-4201-A or equivalent). Then, measure the countershaft bearing height. The difference between the two measurements indicates the required thickness of the adjusting shim. The clearance should be less than 0.1mm (0.0039 in.). The adjusting shims are available in the following thickness:
Adjusting shims:
0.1mm (0.0039 in.)
0.3mm (0.0118 in.)

11. Check the mainshaft bearing clearance in the same manner as for the countershaft rear bearing clearance. The clearance should be less than 0.1mm (0.0039 in.). The adjusting shims are available in the following thickness:
0.1mm (0.0039 in.)
0.3mm (0.0118 in.)

12. Position proper shim on countershaft rear bearing and press into bearing housing using Installer Tool T77J-7025-B.

13. Position proper shim on mainshaft bearing and press into bearing housing using Installer Tool T77J-7025-K or its equal.

14. Position front bearing on countershaft and press into place using Bearing Replacer Tool T71P-7025-A or its equal.

15. Mesh countershaft and mainshaft assembly and position the two on the bearing housing. Make certain that thrust washer is installed on mainshaft assembly at the rear of the first gear.

16. While holding mainshaft assembly in place, press countershaft assembly into bearing housing using Replacer Tool T71P-7025-A or its equal to hold rear countershaft bearing in housing.

17. Install the bearing cover and reverse idle gear shaft to the bearing housing. The cover must be seated in the groove on the idle gear shaft.

18. Install the reverse gear with the key onto the mainshaft. Install the lock nut on the mainshaft and hand tighten.

NOTE: When installing the mainshaft reverse gear and the countershaft reverse gear, both gears should be fitted so that the chamfer on the teeth faces rearward.

19. Install the countershaft reverse gear and secure it with the snap-ring.

NOTE: After installing reverse gears, lock transmission in any two gears.

20. Insert the short spring and locking ball into the reverse bore of the bearing housing.

21. While holding down the ball with a punch or other suitable tool, install the reverse shift rod and shift lever assembly with the reverse idle gear at the same time.

22. Using the dummy shift rails (Tool Number T72J-7280 or its equal), install each shift fork rod and interlock pins.

23. Install the first-and-second shift fork and third-and-fourth shift fork to their respective clutch sleeves.

24. Align the roll pin holes of each shift fork and rod. Install the new roll pins.

NOTE: When assembling the shift fork and control end, a new roll pin should be installed with a pin slit positioned in the direction of the shift rod axis.

25. Install the shift locking balls and springs into their respective positions and install the spring cap bolt.

NOTE: The short spring and ball are installed in the reverse bore.

26. Apply a thin coat of Silicone Sealer D6AZ-19562-B, or equivalent, on both contacting surfaces of the bearing housing.

27. Install the bearing housing assembly to the transmission case.

28. Temporarily attach the bearing housing to the transmission with two top and two bottom bolts and tightened exten-

sion housing mounting bolts to position the countershaft front bearing in the bore.

NOTE: If necessary, remove plugs from bell housing shift rod bores to align shift rods. After installation of bearing housing assembly is complete, reinstall plugs using a silicone sealer (D6AZ-19562-B or equivalent).

29. Tighten the mainshaft locknut to 160–240 N·m (116–174 ft. lbs.) using Adapter T83T-7025-A and Tool Shaft T77J-7025-C or equivalent.

30. Bend a tab on the lockwasher using Staking Tool T77J-7025-F or equivalent.

31. Install the speedometer drive gear with the lock ball onto the mainshaft and secure it with a snap-ring.

32. With the outer snap-ring in place on the main driveshaft front bearing, place bearing, shim 389117-2S, and Adapter Tool T75L-7025-N or equivalent over the input shaft.

33. Thread the Replacer Shaft T75L-7025-K or equal onto the Adapter Tool. Install the Replacer Tube T75L-7025-B or equal over the Replacer Shaft and install the nut and washer on the forcing screw.

34. Slowly tighten the nut until the adapter is secure on the input shaft. Make certain that all tools are aligned.

35. Tighten the nut on the forcing screw until the bearing outer snap-ring is seating against the housing. Remove the installation tools.

36. Install the input shaft snap-ring.

37. Install the speedometer driven gear assembly to the extension housing and attach with the bolt and lock plate.

38. Insert the shift control lever through the holes from the front side of the extension housing.

39. Install the control lever end to the control lever and tighten the attaching bolt (10mm) to 28–34 N·m (20–25 ft. lbs.).

40. Install the back-up lamp switch and neutral sensing switch to the extension housing and tighten the switches to 28–34 N·m (20–25 ft. lbs.).

41. Remove the bolts installed previously to temporarily hold the bearing housing.

42. Apply a thin coat of Silicone Sealer D6AZ-19562-B or equivalent on the contacting surface of the bearing housing and extension housing.

43. Install the extension housing to the bearing housing with the control lever and laid down to the left as far as it will go. Tighten the eight attaching bolts (12mm). Check to ensure that the control rod operates properly.

4–Speed Transmission (Gasoline Engines)

Disassembly

1. Remove the nuts attaching the bell

Four speed manual (gasoline engines)

housing to the transmission case. Remove the bell housing and gasket.

2. Remove the drain plug and drain lubricant from the transmission. Clean the metal filings from the magnet of the drain plug (if necessary). Install the drain plug.

3. Place transmission in neutral.

4. Remove the four 12mm bolts attaching the gearshift lever retainer to the extension housing. Remove the gearshift lever retainer and gasket.

5. Remove the six 14mm bolts attaching the extension housing to the transmission case.

6. Raise the control lever to the left and slide toward the rear of the transmission. Slide the extension housing off the mainshaft, being careful not to damage the oil seal.

7. If required, remove the bolt attaching the gearshift control lever end to the gearshift control lever, and remove the control lever end and control lever.

8. If required, remove the back-up lamp switch from the extension housing.

9. Remove the anti-spill seal from the output shaft and discard (a seal is not necessary for assembly).

10. Remove the snap-ring that secures the speedometer drive gear to the mainshaft. Slide the drive gear off the mainshaft, and remove the lock ball.

11. Evenly loosen the fourteen 10mm bolts securing the transmission case cover to the transmission case and remove the cover and gasket.

12. Remove the three spring cap bolts (the two bolts on the case upper portion are 17mm and the bolt on the case side is 14mm), the detent springs and the detent balls with a magnet from the transmission case.

13. Remove the four 10mm bolts attaching the blind covers to the transmission case and remove the blind covers and gaskets.

14. Slide the reverse shift fork shaft assembly and reverse idler gear out of the transmission case.

15. Shift the transmission into fourth gear. This will provide adequate space to drive out the roll pin. With a small drift, drive the roll pin from third-and-fourth fork assembly. Slide the third-and-fourth shift fork shaft out of the rear of the transmission case.

16. Remove the roll pin from the first-and-second shift fork. Slide the first-and-second shift fork shaft assembly out the rear

of the transmission case. Remove both inter-lock pins.

17. Reinstall the reverse idler gear to lock the gears. Install the Synchronizer Ring Holder and Countershaft Spacer (T77J-7025-E) or its equal between the fourth speed synchronizer ring and synchromesh gear on the mainshaft. Shift the transmission gear into second gear to lock the mainshaft and prevent the assembly from rotating.

18. Straighten the bent portion of the lockwasher with a chisel.

19. Remove the locknut and washer using Locknut Wrench Adapter T82T-7003-CH and Locknut Wrench, T77J-7025-C or their equal. Slide the reverse-idler gear off the mainshaft.

20. Remove the key from the mainshaft.

21. Remove the reverse idler gear.

22. Remove the snap-ring from the rear end of the countershaft. Slide the countershaft reverse gear off the countershaft.

23. Remove the four 12mm bearing retainer attaching bolts.

24. Remove the bearing retainer together with the reverse idler gear shaft.

25. To remove the countershaft rear bearing, install Puller, T77J-7025-H; Puller Rings, T77J-7025-J; Remover Tube, T77J-7025-B; and Forcing Screw, T75L-7025-J or their equal. Squarely insert the jaws of the puller behind the front bearing retainer ring in the two recessed areas of the case.

NOTE: The retainer ring may need to be turned to position the split in the retainer ring midway between the recessed areas, before the puller is installed. This will reduce the possibility of the retainer ring becoming distorted as the bearing is removed.

26. Turn the forcing screw clockwise to remove the bearing.

27. To remove the mainshaft rear bearing, install Puller, T77J-7025-H; Puller Rings, T77J-7025-J; Remover and Replacer Tube—Long Tube, T75L-7025-C and Forcing Screw, T75L-7025-J or their equal. Squarely insert the jaws of the puller behind the rear mainshaft bearing retainer ring in the two recessed areas of the case.

NOTE: The retainer ring may need to be turned to position the split in the ring midway between the recessed areas before the puller is installed. This will reduce the possibility of the retainer ring becoming distorted as the bearing is removed.

28. Turn the forcing screw clockwise to remove the bearing.

29. Remove the shim and spacer from behind the mainshaft rear bearing.

30. Remove the front cover by removing the four studs attaching the cover to case. Remove the studs by installing two nuts (10mm × 1.5) on the stud and drawing the stud out of the case. Remove the four 14mm bolts and remove cover. Save the shim found on the inside of the cover.

31. Remove the snap-ring from the input shaft.

32. Remove the mainshaft drive gear bearing by installing Puller, T77J-7025-H; Puller Rings, T77J-7025-J; Remover and Replacer Tube—Short Tube, T75L-7025-B; and Forcing Screw, T75L-7025-J or their equal. Squarely insert the jaws of the puller behind the mainshaft drive gear bearing retainer ring in the two recessed areas of the case.

NOTE: The retainer ring may need to be turned to position the split in the ring midway between the recessed areas before the puller is installed. This will reduce the possibility of the retainer ring becoming distorted as the bearing is removed.

33. Turn the forcing screw clockwise to remove the bearing.

34. Rotate both shift forks so that the main geartrain will fall to the bottom of the case. Remove the shift forks. Rotate the input shaft so that one of the two flats on the input shaft face upward.

35. Insert Synchronizer Ring Holder and Countershaft Spacer, T77J-7025-E or its equal between the first gear on the countershaft and the rear of the case.

36. Remove the snap-ring from the front of the countershaft.

37. Install Forcing Screw, T75L-7025-J; Press Frame, T77J-7025-N; and Press Frame Adapter, T82T-7003-BH or their equal against the countershaft assembly.

38. Turn the forcing screw clockwise to press the countershaft rearward. Press the countershaft (3/16 inch movement) until it contacts the Synchronizer Ring Holder and Countershaft Spacer.

39. To remove the countershaft front bearing, install Puller, T77J-7025-H; Puller Rings, T77J-7025-J; Remover Tube, T77J-7025-B; and Forcing Screw, T75L-7025-J or their equal. Squarely insert the jaws of the puller behind the front bearing retainer ring in the two recessed areas of the case.

NOTE: The retainer ring may need to be turned to position the split in the ring midway between the recessed areas, before the puller is installed. This will reduce the possibility of the retainer ring becoming distorted as the bearing is removed.

40. Turn the forcing screw clockwise to remove the bearing.

41. Remove the shim from behind the countershaft front bearing.

42. Remove the input shaft from the transmission case. Remove the synchronizer ring and caged bearing from the main driveshaft.

43. Remove the countershaft from the transmission case.

44. Remove the inner race of the countershaft center bearing from the countershaft in a press frame using Axle Bearing Seal Plate, T75L-1165-B and Pinion Bearing Cone Remover, D79L-4621-A or their equal.

45. Remove the mainshaft and gear assembly from the transmission case.

46. Remove the snap-rings from the front of the mainshaft.

47. Slide the third-fourth clutch hub and sleeve assembly, the third synchronizer ring, and third gear off of the front of the mainshaft.

NOTE: Do not mix the synchronizer rings.

48. Slide the thrust washer, first gear, and gear sleeve off the rear mainshaft. Press the bushing from the first gear using a press and suitable pressing stock.

49. Remove the first-and-second clutch hub and sleeve assembly from the mainshaft.

50. Clean and inspect transmission case, gears, bearings, and shafts.

Assembly

Before beginning the assembly procedure, three measurements must be performed: Mainshaft Thrust Play, Countershaft Thrust Play and Mainshaft Bearing Clearance.

Mainshaft Thrust Play

Check the mainshaft thrust play by measuring the depth of the mainshaft bearing bore in the transmission rear cage by using a depth micrometer (D80P-4201-A) or its equal. Then measure the mainshaft rear bearing height. The difference between the two measurements indicates the required thickness of the adjusting shim. The standard thrust play is 0 to 0.0039 inch (0 to 0.1mm). Adjusting shims are available in 0.0039 inch (0.1mm) and 0.0118 inch (0.3mm) sizes.

Countershaft Thrust Play

Check the countershaft thrust play by measuring the depth of the countershaft front bearing bore in the transmission case by using a depth micrometer (D80P-4201-A) or its equal. Then measure the countershaft front bearing height. The difference between the two measurements indicates the required thickness of the adjusting shims. The standard thrust play is 0 to 0.0039 inch (0–0.1mm). Adjusting shims are available in 0.0039 inch (0.1mm) and 0.0118 inch (0.3mm) sizes.

Mainshaft Bearing Clearance

Check the main driveshaft bearing clearance by measuring the depth of the bearing bore in the clutch adapter plate with a depth micrometer, D80P-4201-A or its equal.

Make sure the micrometer is on the second step of the plate. Measure the bearing height. The difference between the two measurements indicates the required adjusting shim thickness. The standard clearance is 0 to 0.0039 inch (0 to 0.1mm). If an adjusting shim is required, select one to bring the clearance to within specifications.

1. Assemble the first-and-second synchromesh mechanism by installing the clutch hub to the sleeve, placing the three synchronizer keys into the clutch hub key slots and installing the key springs to the clutch hub.

NOTE: When installing the key springs, the open end tab of the springs should be inserted into the hub holes with the springs turned in the same direction. This will keep the spring tension on each key uniform.

2. Assemble the third-and-fourth synchromesh mechanisms in the same manner as first-and-second synchromesh mechanism.

3. Place the synchronizer ring on the third gear and slide the third gear to the front of the mainshaft with the synchronizer ring toward the front.

4. Slide the third-and-fourth clutch hub and sleeve assembly to the front of the mainshaft, making sure that the three synchronizer keys in the synchromesh mechanism engage the notches in the synchronizer ring.

3RD & 4TH CLUTCH   1ST & 2ND CLUTCH

FRONT

Clutch hub assembly direction

NOTE: The direction of the third-and-fourth clutch hub and sleeve assembly should be as shown.

5. Install the snap-ring to the front of the mainshaft.

6. Place the synchronizer ring on the second gear and slide the second gear to the mainshaft with the synchronizer ring toward the rear of the shaft.

7. Slide the first-and-second clutch hub and sleeve assembly to the mainshaft with the oil grooves of the clutch hub toward the front of the mainshaft. Make sure that the three synchronizer keys in the synchromesh mechanism engage the notches in the second synchronizer ring.

8. Insert the first gear sleeve in the mainshaft.

9. Press the bushing in the first gear using a press and suitable press stock.

10. Place the synchronizer ring on the first gear and slide the first gear onto the mainshaft with the synchronizer ring facing the front of the shaft. Rotate the first gear as necessary to engage the three notches in the synchronizer ring with the synchronizer keys.

11. Install the original thrust washer on the mainshaft.

12. Position the mainshaft and gears assembly in the case.

13. Position the caged bearing in the front end of the mainshaft.

14. Place the synchronizer ring on the input shaft (fourth gear), and install the input shaft to the front end of the mainshaft, making sure that the three synchronizer keys in the third-and-fourth synchromesh mechanism engage the notches in the synchronizer ring.

15. Position the first-and-second shift fork and third-and-fourth shift fork in the groove of the clutch hub and sleeve assembly.

16. Press the inner race of the countershaft rear bearing onto the countershaft using Center Bearing Replacer, T77J-7025-K or its equal.

17. Position the countershaft gear in the case, making sure that the countershaft gear engages each gear of the mainshaft assembly.

18. Install the correct shim in the mainshaft rear bearing bore as determined in the Mainshaft Thrust Play Measurement.

19. Position the main drive gear bearing and the mainshaft rear bearing into the proper bearing bores. Be sure the synchronizer and shifter forks have not been moved out of position.

20. Install the Dummy Bearing Replacer, T75L-7025-Q; Mainshaft Front Bearing Replacer, T82T-7003-DH; Replacer Tube, T77J-7025-M; Press Frame Adapter, T82T-7003-BH; and Press Frame, T77J-7025-N or their equal on the case. Position the Synchronizer Ring Holder and Countershaft Spacer, T77J-7025-E or their equal between the mainshaft drive gear and synchronizer ring. Turn the forcing screw on the press frame until both bearings are properly seated.

21. Install the main drive gear bearing snap-ring.

22. Place the correct shim in the countershaft front bearing bore as determined by the Countershaft Thrust Play Measurement.

23. Position the countershaft front and rear bearings in the bores and install the tools. Turn the forcing screw until the bearing is properly seated. Use the rear bearing as a pilot.

24. Install the snap-ring to secure the countershaft front bearing.

25. Install the bearing retainer together with the reverse idler gear shaft to the transmission case and tighten the four 12mm attaching bolts.

26. Slide the counter reverse gear onto the countershaft with the chamfer to the rear. Install the snap-ring to secure the counter reverse gear.

27. Install the key on the mainshaft.

28. Slide the reverse gear and lockwasher (tab facing outward) onto the mainshaft (chamfer on teeth should be to rear). Install a new locknut and hand tighten.

29. Shift into second gear and reverse gear to lock rotation of the mainshaft. Tighten the locknut to 197–275 N·m (145–203 ft. lbs.)(16–24m-Kg) torque using the Locknut Wrench (T77J-7025-C) and Locknut Adapter, T82T-7003-CH or their equal.

30. Place the fourth-and-third clutch sleeve in third gear using Synchronizer Ring Holder and Countershaft Spacer, T77J-7025-E or its equal.

31. Check the clearance between the synchronizer key and the exposed edge of the synchronizer ring with a feeler gauge. If the measurement is greater than 0.079 inch (2.0mm), the synchronizer key can pop out of position. To correct this, change the thrust washer (selective fit) between the mainshaft rear bearing and the first gear. Available thrust washer sizes are .098, .118, and .138.

32. Check the clearance again with a feeler gauge. If the clearance is within specifications, bend the tab of the lockwasher.

33. Slide the first-and-second shift fork shaft assembly into the case (from rear of case). Install the roll pin. Secure the first-and-second shift fork to the fork shaft by staking the roll pin.

NOTE: Be sure to use a new roll pin.

34. Insert the inter-lock pin into the transmission using the lockout pin replacer tool.

35. Slide the third-and-fourth shift fork shaft assembly into the case (from rear of case). Secure the third-and-fourth shift fork to the fork shaft by staking the roll pin. Place transmission in neutral.

NOTE: Be sure to use a new roll pin.

36. Insert the inter-lock pin into the transmission.

37. Slide the reverse fork shaft assembly and reverse idler gear into the transmission case from the rear of the case with the gear chamfer forward. Secure the reverse shift fork to the fork shaft by staking the roll pin.

NOTE: Be sure to use a new roll pin.

38. Position the three detent balls and three springs into the case. Place copper washers on the top two bolts and install the three spring cap bolts.

39. Install the two blind covers and gaskets. Tighten the 10mm attaching bolts.

40. Install the lock ball, speedometer drive gear, and snap-ring onto the mainshaft.

41. Apply a thin coat of sealing agent, Gasket Maker, E2AZ-19562-A (ESE-M4G234-A2) or equivalent to the contacting surfaces of the transmission case and extension housing.

42. Position the extension housing with the gearshift control lever end laid down to the left as far as it will go. Tighten the four 14mm attaching bolts.

NOTE: The lower two bolts must be coated with Loctite or equivalent.

43. If removed, insert the speedometer driven gear assembly to the extension housing and secure it with the bolt.

44. Check to ensure the gearshift control lever operates properly.

45. Install the transmission case cover gasket and cover with drain plug to rear. Install and tighten the fourteen 10mm attaching bolts.

46. Position the gasket and gearshift lever retainer to the extension housing, and tighten the four attaching bolts.

47. Install the correct size shim on the second step of the clutch adapter plate as determined by the Mainshaft Bearing Clearance Measurement.

48. Coat the clutch adapter plate with sealer, Gasket Maker, E2AZ-19562-A (ESE-M4G234-A2) or equivalent. Install the clutch adapter plate to the transmission case and tighten the four bolts and four studs.

49. Remove the filler plug and install 1.4 liters (3.0 pints) of Ford Manual Transmission Lube, D8DZ-19C547-A (ESP-M2C83-C) or equivalent. Reinstall filler plug and tighten to 25–39 N·m (18–29 ft. lbs.).

Mazda/Courier 4 and 5–Speed Transmission—Models T40–T50

Disassembly

──────── CAUTION ────────
The clutch housing, split transmission case, and extension housing are all made of aluminum.

1. Drain the oil.

2. Remove the clutch housing, bearing retainer, release bearing, and release fork.

3. Remove the speedometer shaft sleeve and driven gear.

4. Remove the extension housing.

5. Remove the back-up light switch.

6. Separate the case halves. Do not pry apart.

7. Measure gear backlash. The backlash for all gears should be 0.004–0.008 in.

8. Remove the countergear set from the right-hand half of the case.

9. Use a magnet to remove the ball from the second countergear bearing.

10. Withdraw the input and the output shafts as a unit.

11. Use a punch to drive the three slotted spring pins out of the shift forks and shift fork shafts.

NOTE: The slotted pin cannot always be fully removed from the first/second

4-Speed (T40)

5-Speed (T50)

Cross section of models T4- and T50

shift fork; however, the shift fork can still be withdrawn. Do not try to force the pin out, as damage to the transmission case could result.

12. Remove the case cover and the three detent balls and springs.

13. Remove the shift fork shafts in the following order:

    a. First/second shaft
    b. Pin
    c. Reverse shift fork shaft
    d. Third/fourth shaft
    e. Pin

14. Measure the thrust clearance of the reverse idler gear. The specified clearance is 0.002–0.020 in.

15. Remove the idler shaft. Remove the gear and washer.

16. Measure the thrust clearance of the gears on the output shaft.

1st, 2nd, 5th	0.006–0.010 in.
3rd	0.006–0.012 in.
Reverse	0.008–0.012 in.

5th gear is optional

17. Disassemble the components of the output shaft. Five-speed transmissions have an extra gearset and related parts.

Replace the front bearing, if it is rough or noisy. Use a drift and a press. Remove the snap-ring first.

For bearing installation, replacement snap-rings are available in a range of sizes (0.0925–0.1024 in.) to obtain *minimum* axial play between the input shaft and the bearing.

Assembly

1. Assemble the components of the synchronizer hubs, and the output shaft.

2. Install the rear bushing on the output shaft, being careful to install it in the proper direction.

3. Install the ball into the groove of the bushing and slide the bushing over the shaft.

4. Install the needle roller bearing, reverse gear, the ball and the reverse gear synchronizer hub.

5. Install the following items on the output shaft of the four-speed transmission, in the order indicated:

    a. Large-diameter reverse gear spacer
    b. Long spacer
    c. Shims

6. Install the following items on the output shaft of the five-speed transmission in the order indicated:

    a. Ball
    b. Fifth gear synchronizer ring
    c. Fifth gear
    d. Needle roller bearing
    e. Bushing
    f. Rear support ball bearing.

7. Install the shims and the nut on the end of the output shaft.

NOTE: If the original nut is being used, change the number of shims to alter the locking portion of the nut.

8. Check the thrust clearance of each gear.

9. Working from the rear of the output shaft, install 3rd gear, synchronizer, spacer, and 3rd/4th synchronizer hub (should face forward).

10. Select a snap-ring to obtain a thrust clearance of less than 0.002 in. for the 3rd/4th synchronizer hub.

11. Assemble the following from the rear of the output shaft:

    a. Snap-ring
    b. Key
    c. Speedometer drive gear
    d. Snap-ring

12. Check thrust clearance of gears.

13. Install the fork and shaft assembly in the transmission case.

14. Insert the straight pins in the grooves on either side of the third/fourth shift shaft.

15. Assemble the first/second gear shaft and fork.

16. Perform Step 11 for the reverse shift fork shaft.

17. Insert the three detent balls, followed by their springs.

18. Place the cover gasket on the case and install the cover.

19. Use a punch to drive a slotted spring pin into each shift fork to secure it.

20. Assemble the input and output shafts.

21. Install the shift forks into their respective grooves on the input/output shaft assembly.

22. Install the shaft assembly in the right-hand half of the transmission case, so that the snap-ring is positioned firmly against the front surface of the transmission case.

23. Apply grease to the countergear rear bearing lockball. Insert the ball into the hole in the rear bearing outer race.

24. Place the countergear assembly into the right-hand half of the transmission case. Mate the lockball with the hole in the transmission case. Place the bearing snap-ring firmly against the front surface of the transmission case.

25. Install the reverse idler gear.

26. Install the washers, so that their protrusions align with the grooves in the transmission case.

27. Install the shaft into the case and through the gears and washers.

28. Align the grooves in the idler shaft with the hole in the shaft boss. Install the retaining bolt and washer into the boss.

29. Apply a light coating of liquid sealer over the joint surfaces of the transmission case halves.

—————— CAUTION ——————

Do not apply sealer to the ½ in. hole for the back-up light switch.

30. Align the transmission case locating pins with their holes and assemble the halves of the case.

NOTE: There are four different bolt lengths, do not install the wrong bolt in the wrong hole.

31. Insert the ball, spring, and washer in the back-up light switch hole. Screw in the switch assembly.

32. Install the gasket and bolt the extension housing to the rear of the transmission.

33. Install the speedometer shaft sleeve and drive gear.

34. Apply grease to the conical springs. Install one spring over the input shaft bearing and the other over the countershaft bearing. Install the spacer over the countershaft bearing spring, after coating the spacer with grease.

35. Install the gasket and the clutch housing.

Mazda/Courier 4–Speed Transmission

Disassembly

1. Install the transmission in a workstand.

2. Drain the oil.

3. Remove the fork and throwout bearing out of the housing.

4. Remove the bellhousing.

5. Remove the adjusting shim from the bellhousing bearing bore.

6. Remove the shift lever tower and gasket.

7. Remove the extension housing. Set the control lever end in the neutral position, press the control lever end as far left as possible, and slide the extension housing off the transmission.

8. Remove the neutral switch from the transmission (models with seat belt interlock).

9. Remove the gearshift yoke from the central lever.

10. Remove the speedometer sleeve and driven gear. Remove the back-up light switch.

11. Unfasten the speedometer drive gear

1. Adjusting shim	13. First-and-second clutch hub
2. Main driveshaft bearing	14. Clutch sleeve
3. Main driveshaft and gear	15. First gear
4. Needle bearing	16. First gear sleeve
5. Synchronizer ring	17. Thrust washer
6. Third-and-fourth clutch hub	18. Mainshaft bearing
7. Synchronizer key	19. Adjusting shim
8. Clutch sleeve	20. Bearing cover plate
9. Third gear	21. Key
10. Second gear	22. Gearshift lever retainer
11. Synchronizer ring	23. Cover
12. Synchronizer key	24. Shim

25. Boot	37. Drain plug
26. Gearshift lever	38. Gasket
27. Gearshift lever knob	39. Countershaft rear bearing
28. Bush	40. Counter reverse gear
29. Control lever end	41. Reverse gear
30. Gearshift control lever	42. Lock washer
31. Adjusting shim	43. Locknut
32. Transmission case	44. Mainshaft
33. Countershaft front bearing	45. Speedometer drive gear
34. Gasket	46. Lock ball
35. Transmission under cover	47. Extension housing
36. Countershaft	48. Mainshaft oil seal

Cross section of Mazda/Courier 4-speed without intermediate housing

snap-ring, slide the drive gear off of the output shaft, and remove the lockball.

12. Remove the bottom cover and gasket.

13. Remove the cap bolts, the detent springs, and detent balls.

14. Remove the blind covers and gaskets from the transmission case.

15. Remove the reverse shift rod and idler gear from the rear of the transmission case. Remove the reverse shift fork.

16. Unfasten third/fourth shift fork securing bolt and remove the third/fourth shift rod from the rear of the case.

17. Repeat Step 16 for the first/second shift rod.

18. Straighten out the output shaft lockwasher. Hold the output shaft to keep it from turning, and loosen the locknut. Slide the reverse gear and key off the end of the output shaft.

19. Remove the countershaft snap-ring (rear) and remove the reverse countergear.

20. Remove the bearing cover.

21. Remove the reverse idler gear.

22. Hold the fourth synchronizer ring and gear on the output shaft.

23. Remove the countershaft front bearing snap-ring. Remove the front bearing.

Remove the adjusting shim from the case bearing bore.

24. Remove the countershaft rear bearing. Remove the adjusting shim from the case bearing bore.

25. Remove the input shaft bearing snap-ring and remove the bearing with the puller.

26. Lift the countershaft out.

27. Separate the input and output shafts. Remove the input shaft. Remove the fourth synchronizer ring and needle bearing from the input shaft.

28. Remove the output shaft gear assembly.

29. Remove first/second and third/fourth shift forks from the case. Withdraw the shift interlock pins.

30. Remove the third/fourth clutch hub snap-ring, then slide the clutch hub sleeve, third synchronizer ring and third gear off the front of the output shaft. Be careful not to mix up the synchronizer rings.

31. Slide the first gear and synchronizer ring off the rear of the output shaft.

32. Slide the first gear sleeve, second gear, second synchronizer ring and first/second clutch hub/sleeve assembly off the output shaft.

Assembly

1. Install the first/second clutch hub on its sleeve, place the three shift keys in the clutch hub key slots, and install the key springs. Be sure to keep the open ends of the key springs 120° apart.

2. Perform Step 33 for the third/fourth synchronizer assembly.

3. Place the synchronizer ring on second gear and then slide second gear on the output shaft, so that the synchronizer ring faces the rear of the shaft.

4. Slide the first/second clutch hub and sleeve on the output shaft so that the clutch oil grooves face forward. Be sure that the three synchronizer keys engage the notches on the second gear synchronizer ring.

5. Install the first gear sleeve in the output shaft.

6. Install the synchronizer ring in the first gear and install the gear on the output shaft so that the ring faces the front of the shaft.

7. Install the same thrust washer on the output shaft that was removed.

8. Perform Step 38 for third gear.

9. Install the third/fourth clutch hub and

sleeve on the output shaft, being sure to engage the three synchronizer keys with the notches in the ring.

NOTE: The larger boss on the third/fourth clutch hub goes toward the front.

10. Install the snap-ring on the front of the output shaft. Install the output shaft/gear set assembly in the case. Fit the needle bearing on the front of the output shaft.

11. Place the synchronizer ring on the input shaft gear (fourth) and install the gear on the front of the output shaft. Be sure that the synchronizer keys engage the notches in the synchronizer ring.

12. Position the first/second and third/fourth shift forks in groove on the clutch hub/sleeve assembly.

13. Install the countergear assembly in the case, being careful to engage each countergear with its respective output shift gear.

14. Check the output shaft bearing end-play as follows:

   a. Measure the depth of the transmission case output shaft bearing bore.

   b. Measure the height of the bearing.

   c. The difference of these two measurements indicates the correct thickness of the adjusting shim to be used. The amount of end-play permitted is 0–0.0039 in.

   d. Shims are available in thicknesses of 0.0039 or 0.0118 in.

15. Hold the fourth synchronizer ring off the input shaft synchronizer gear.

16. Install the input and output shaft bearings in their respective bores with a press.

17. Install the input shaft bearing snap-ring.

18. Check the countershaft bearing end-play, as outlined in Step 46 for the input shaft. The amount of end-play allowed and available shim size are the same for both bearings.

19. Perform Step 47 again.

20. Press the countershaft front and rear bearings into their respective bores. Install the snap-ring on the front bearing.

21. Install the reverse countergear on the rear of the countershaft.

22. Install the reverse gear idler shaft in the transmission case.

23. Install the bearing cover on the case.

24. Secure the reverse gear on the output shaft with its key.

25. Hold the output shaft to keep it from turning and tighten to 150–180 ft. lbs.

26. Install the first/second shift rod into the case and secure it to the shift fork with the lockbolt. Place the shift rod in Neutral. Drive the interlock pin into its bore.

27. Perform Step 58 for the third/fourth shift rod.

28. Slide the reverse shift rod, complete with the reverse idler gear, in from the rear of the case. Secure the shift rod to the reverse fork with its lockbolt.

29. Install the detent balls and springs

in their bores and secure them with their cap bolts.

30. Check the synchronizer key-to-exposed edge of the synchronizer ring clearance with a feeler gauge; it should be 0.026–0.079 in. If the clearance is greater, the synchronizer key could pop out. If clearance is greater than specified, replace the selective-fit thrust washer with one of the three available sizes.

31. Install the blind covers over their gaskets.

32. Install the lockball, speedometer drive gear, and snap-ring, in that order, on the rear of the output shaft.

33. Install the gearshift control lever through the holes in the front of the extension housing. Install the Woodruff key on the control lever and install the yoke over it. Secure the yoke with its setbolt.

34. Thread the Neutral switch (for seat belt interlock) into the extension housing.

35. Fit the spring and plunger in the extension housing and secure them with the capbolt.

36. Install the back-up light switch.

37. Secure the speedometer driven gear in its extension housing bore with the lockplate and bolt.

38. Push the gearshift control lever over to the left as far as possible. Place a gasket on the rear of the transmission case and install the extension housing over it.

39. Install the bottom cover.

40. Insert the select lockpin and spring

in the shift tower. Align the slot in the pin with the lockball bore. Drop the lockball and spring into the bore; secure with the capbolt.

41. Install the shift tower on the extension housing and secure it with its bolts.

42. Perform Step 46 for the input shaft bearing and clutchhousing bore. The endplay and shim thickness are the same as in Step 46.

43. Lubricate the lip of the bellhousing oil seal.

44. Put a gasket on the front of the transmission case, and install the bell housing.

45. Install the throwout bearing, release fork and boot in the bellhousing.

Mazda/Courier 4 and 5–Speed Transmission

The 4 and 5 speed transmissions are basically the same, with an added housing located between the adapter plate and the rear extension housing, to carry the 5th and reverse gears. Added roller bearings are used in the housing to prevent shaft misalignment.

Disassembly

1. Remove the throwout bearing return spring, throwout bearing, and the release fork.

1. Spring cap bolt/packing/ spring/locking ball	6. Spring/locking ball
2. Spring cap bolt/packing/ spring/locking ball	7. Bolt/washer
3. Spring cap bolt/packing/ spring/locking ball	8. Shift rod (3rd & 4th)
	9. Shift rod (1st & 2nd)
4. Bolt/washer	10. Interlock pin
5. Shift fork (Reverse)/rod/ reverse idler gear	11. Shift fork (3rd & 4th)
	12. Shift fork (1st & 2nd)

Exploded view of shift selector rods and forks, 4-speed with intermediate housing

2. Remove the bearing housing.

3. Remove the input shaft and countershaft snap-rings.

4. Remove the floorshift lever retainer, complete with gasket.

5. Unfasten the cap bolt and withdraw the spring, steel ball, select lock pin and spring from the retainer.

6. Remove the extension housing. Turn the control lever as far left as it will go and slide the extension housing off the output shaft.

7. Remove the spring seat and spring from the end of the shift control lever.

8. Loosen the spring cap and withdraw the spring and plunger from their bore.

9. Remove the control rod and boss from the extension housing.

10. Remove the speedometer driven gear. Remove the back-up light switch.

11. Remove the speedometer drive gear.

12. Tap the front ends of the input shaft and countershaft with a plastic hammer; then remove the intermediate housing assembly from the transmission case.

13. Remove the three cap bolts; then withdraw the springs and lockballs.

14. Remove the reverse shift rod, reverse idler gear, and shift lever.

15. Remove the setscrews from all the shift forks and push the shift rods rearward to remove them. Remove the shift forks.

16. Withdraw the reverse shift rod lockball, spring, and interlock pins from the intermediate housing.

17. Remove reverse gear and key from the output shaft.

18. Remove the reverse countergear.

19. Remove the countershaft and output shaft from the intermediate housing.

20. Remove the bearings from the intermediate housing and transmission case.

21. Remove the snap-ring from the output shaft.

22. Slide the third/fourth clutch hub, sleeve, synchronizer ring, and third gear off the output shaft.

23. Remove the thrust washer, first gear, sleeve, synchronizer ring, and second gear from the rear of the output shaft.

Assembly

1. Install the third/fourth synchronizer clutch hub on the sleeve. Place the three synchronizer keys in the clutch hub key slots. Install the key springs with their open ends 120° apart.

2. Install third gear and the synchronizer ring on the front of the output shaft. Install the third/fourth clutch hub assembly on the output shaft. Be sure that the larger boss faces the front of the shaft.

3. Secure the gear and synchronizer with the snap-ring.

4. Perform Step 1 to the first/second synchronizer assembly.

5. Position the synchronizer ring on second gear. Slide second gear on the output shaft so that the synchronizer ring faces the rear of the shaft.

6. Install the first/second clutch hub assembly on the output shaft so that its oil grooves face the front of the shaft. Engage the keys in the notches on the second gear synchronizer ring.

7. Slide the first gear sleeve onto the output shaft. Position the synchronizer ring on first gear. Install the first gear on the output shaft so that the synchronizer ring faces frontward. Rotate the first gear as required to engage the notches in the synchronizer ring with the keys in the clutch hub.

8. Slip the thrust washer on the rear of the output shaft. Install the needle bearing on the front of the output shaft.

9. Install the synchronizer ring on fourth gear and install the input shaft on the front of the output shaft.

10. Press the countershaft rear bearing and shim into the intermediate housing, then press the countershaft into the rear bearing.

11. Keep the thrust washer and first gear from falling off the output shaft by supporting the shaft. Install the output shaft on the intermediate housing. Be sure that each output shaft gear engages with its opposite number on the countershaft.

12. Tap the output shaft bearing and shim into the intermediate housing with a plastic hammer. Install the cover.

13. Install reverse gear on the output shaft and secure it with its key.

NOTE: The chamfer on the teeth of both the reverse gear and the reverse countergear should face rearward.

14. Install the reverse countergear.

15. Install the lockball and spring into the bore in the intermediate housing. Depress the ball with a screwdriver.

16. Install the reverse shift rod, lever, and idler gear at the same time. Place the reverse shift rod in the neutral position.

17. Align the bores and insert the shift interlock pin.

18. Install the third/fourth shift rod into the intermediate housing and shift bores. Place the shift rod in Neutral.

19. Install the next interlock pin in the bore.

20. Install the first/second shift rod.

21. Install the lockballs and springs in their bores. Install the cap bolt.

22. Install the speedometer drive gear and lockball on the output shaft, and install its snap-ring.

23. Apply sealer to the mating surfaces of the intermediate housing. Install the intermediate housing in the transmission case.

24. Install the input shaft and countershaft front bearings in the transmission case.

25. Secure the speedometer driven gear.

26. Install the control rod through the holes in the front of the extension housing.

27. Align the key with the keyway and install the yoke on the end of the control rod. Install the yoke lockbolt.

28. Fit the plunger and spring into the extension housing bore and secure with the spring cap.

29. Turn the control rod all the way to the left and install the extension housing on the intermediate housing.

30. Insert the spring and select lockpin inside the gearshift retainer. Align the steel ball and spring with the lockpin slot, and secure it with the spring cap.

31. Install the spring and spring seat in the control rod yoke.

32. Install the gearshift lever retainer over its gasket on the extension housing.

33. Lubricate the lip of the front bearing cover oil seal and secure the cover on the transmission case.

34. Check the clearance between the front bearing cover and bearing. It should be less than 0.006 in. If it is not within specifications insert additional adjusting shims. The shims are available in 0.006 in. or 0.012 in. sizes.

35. Install the throwout bearing, return spring and release fork.

5-Speed

The disassembly and assembly of the rear extension housing, selector levers and forks are completed in the same manner as the 4 speed transmission. After this has been done, the added housing can be removed by taking out the retaining bolts. The housing will have to be lightly tapped with a soft-faced hammer. The removal of the housing exposes the 5th/reverse synchronizer assembly, the reverse countergear, the countershaft and mainshaft bearings. The bearings are pulled from the shafts and then the gears can be removed. The assembly is in the reverse of the removal procedure.

Mazda/Courier 5-Speed Transmission

Disassembly

1. Pull the release fork outward until the spring clip of the fork releases from the ball pivot.

2. Remove the fork and release bearing.

3. Remove the clutch housing shim and gasket.

4. Remove the gearshift lever retainer and gasket.

5. Remove the spring and steel ball, select lock spindle and spring from the gearshift lever retainer.

6. Remove the extension housing with the control lever end down to the left as far as it will go.

7. Remove the control lever end, key and control rod.

8. Remove the lock plate and speedometer gear.

9. Remove the back-up light switch.

10. Remove the snap-ring and slide the speedometer drive gear from the mainshaft.

11. Remove the bottom cover and gasket.

12. Remove the shift rod ends.

13. Remove the rear bearing housing.

1. Adjusting shim
2. Main driveshaft bearing
3. Main driveshaft gear
4. Needle bearing
5. Synchronizer ring
6. Synchronizer key
7. 3rd-and-4th clutch hub
8. Clutch sleeve
9. 3rd gear
10. 2nd gear
11. Synchronizer ring
12. Synchronizer key
13. 1st-and-2nd clutch hub
14. Clutch sleeve
15. 1st gear
16. Needle bearing
17. Needle bearing inner race
18. Thrust washer
19. Mainshaft front bearing
20. Adjusting shim
21. Bearing cover plate
22. Spacer

23. Reverse gear and clutch
    sleeve assembly
24. Synchronizer key
25. Synchronizer ring
26. Lock washer
27. Locknut
28. 5th gear
29. Needle bearing
30. Thrust washer
31. Gearshift lever
    retainer
32. Cover
33. Gasket
34. Boot
35. Gearshift lever
36. Gearshift lever
    knob
37. Bush
38. Gearshift control
    lever end
39. Gearshift control
    lever

40. Adjusting shim
41. Transmission case
42. Countershaft front bearing
43. Countershaft
44. Transmission under cover
45. Gasket
46. Drain plug
47. Gasket
48. Countershaft center bearing
49. Counter reverse gear
50. Drain plug
51. Spacer
52. Counter 5th gear
53. Countershaft rear bearing
54. Thrust washer
55. Mainshaft rear bearing
56. Thrust washer
57. Speedometer drive gear
58. Lock ball
59. Mainshaft
60. Extension housng
61. Mainshaft oil seal

Cross section Mazda/Courier 5-speed

14. Remove the snap-ring and remove the mainshaft rear bearing, thrust washer and race.

15. Using the puller, remove the washer and countershaft rear bearing.

16. Remove the counter fifth gear.

17. Remove the intermediate housing.

18. Remove the springs and shift locking balls.

19. Remove the two blind covers and gaskets from the case.

20. Remove the reverse/fifth shift rod, fork and interlock pin.

21. Remove the first/second and third/fourth shift forks, rods and interlock pins.

22. Remove the snap-ring and slide the washer, fifth gear and synchronizer ring from the mainshaft. Also, remove the steel ball and needle bearing.

23. Lock the rotation of the mainshaft with second and reverse.

24. Remove the locknut and slide the reverse/fifth clutch hub and sleeve assembly, synchronizer ring, reverse gear and needle bearing from the mainshaft.

25. Remove the spacer and counter reverse gear from the countershaft.

26. Remove the reverse idler gear, thrust washers and shaft from the transmission case.

27. Remove the bearing rear cover plate.

28. Remove the snap-ring from the front end of the countershaft and install Mazda tool number 49 0839 445 synchronizer ring holder or its equivalent between the fourth synchronizer ring and the synchromesh gear on the main driveshaft.

29. Remove the countershaft front bearing.

30. Remove the adjusting shim from the countershaft front bearing bore.

31. Remove the countershaft center bearing outer race.

32. With a special puller and attachment, remove the mainshaft front bearing, thrust washer and inner race along with the adjusting shim from the mainshaft front bearing bore.

33. Remove the snap-ring, and remove the main driveshaft bearing.

34. Remove the countershaft center bearing inner race with the puller.

35. Separate the input shaft from the mainshaft and remove the input shaft.

36. Remove the synchronizer ring and needle bearing from the input shaft.

37. Remove the mainshaft assembly.

38. Remove the first/second and third/fourth shift forks from the case.

39. Remove the snap-ring and slide the third/fourth clutch hub and sleeve assembly, synchronizer ring and third gear from the mainshaft.

40. Remove the thrust washer, first gear and needle bearing from the rear of the mainshaft.

41. Press out the needle bearing inner race, synchronizer ring, first and second clutch hub, sleeve assembly, synchronizer ring and second gear from the mainshaft.

Assembly

1. Install the third/fourth clutch hub into the sleeve, place the three keys into the clutch hub slots and install the springs onto the hub.

2. Assemble the first/second and reverse/fifth clutch hub and sleeve as described in Step 42.

3. Install the needle bearing, second gear, synchronizer ring, and first/second clutch assembly on the rear section of the mainshaft.

4. Press on the first gear needle bearing inner race.

5. Install the third gear and synchronizer ring onto the front section of the mainshaft.

6. Install the third/fourth clutch assembly onto the mainshaft.

7. Install the snap-ring on the mainshaft.

8. Install the needle bearing, synchronizer ring, first gear and thrust washer on the mainshaft.

9. Install the mainshaft assembly.

10. Install the needle bearing on the front end of the mainshaft.

11. Install the first/second and third/fourth shift forks in their respective clutch sleeves.

12. Check the mainshaft bearing end-play. Check the depth of the mainshaft bearing bore in the case. Measure the mainshaft bearing height. The difference indicates the required adjusting shim to give a total end-play of less than 0.0039 in.

13. Install the synchronizer ring holder tool between the fourth synchronizer ring and the synchromesh gear on the input shaft.

14. Position the shims and mainshaft bearing in the bore and install with a press.

15. Install the input shaft bearing in the same way.

16. Check the countershaft front bearing end-play in the same way as the mainshaft bearing end-play.

17. Install the front bearing snap-ring.

18. Press the countershaft center bearing into position.

19. Install the bearing cover plate.

20. Install the reverse idler gearshaft, thrust washers and reverse idler gear.

21. Install the counter reverse gear and spacer on the rear end on the countershaft.

22. Install the thrust washer and press the needle bearing inner race of the reverse gear on the mainshaft.

23. Install the needle bearing, reverse gear, synchronizer ring, reverse/fifth clutch assembly and new mainshaft locknut on the mainshaft.

24. Lock the mainshaft with the second and reverse gears. Tighten the locknut.

25. Install the needle bearing, synchronizer ring and fifth gear on the mainshaft.

26. Install the thrust washer, steel ball and snap-ring on the mainshaft.

27. Check the thrust washer-to-snap-ring clearance. It should be 0.0039–0.0118 in.

28. Install the first/second shift rod through the holes in the case and fork.

29. Install the interlock pin with a special installer and guide.

30. Install the third/fourth shift rod through the holes in the case and fork.

31. Align the holes and install the lockbolts of each shift fork and rod.

32. Install the interlock pin as above.

33. Position the reverse/fifth shift fork on the clutch sleeve and install the shift rod.

34. Tighten the lockbolt.

35. Install the three shift locking balls, springs and cap bolts.

36. Place the third/fourth clutch sleeve in third gear.

37. Check the clearance between the synchronizer key and the exposed edge of the synchronizer ring with a feeler gauge. The gap should be 0.026–0.079 in. Adjust by varying thrust washers.

38. Install the two blind covers and gaskets.

39. Install the undercover and gasket.

40. Apply a thin coat of sealer to the mating edges and install the intermediate housing on the transmission case. Align the lockbolt holes of the housing and reverse idler gearshaft, install and tighten the lockbolt.

41. Position the counter fifth gear and bearing to the rear end of the countershaft and install with a press.

42. Install the thrust washer and snap-ring.

43. Check the clearance between the washer and snap-ring. Clearance should be less than 0.0039 in.

44. Install the mainshaft rear bearing.

45. Install the thrust washer and snap-ring.

46. Check the thrust washer-to-snap-ring clearance. Clearance should be less than 0.0059 in.

47. Apply a thin coat of sealing agent to the mating surfaces and install the bearing housing on the intermediate housing.

48. Install the shift rod ends on their respective rods.

49. Install the speedometer drive gear and steel ball on the mainshaft. Secure it with a snap-ring.

50. Install a speedometer driven gear assembly on the extension housing and secure it with the bolt and lock plate.

51. Insert the control rod through the holes from the front side of the extension housing.

52. Align the key and insert the control lever end in the control rod.

53. Install the bolt and tighten it to 20–30 ft. lbs.

54. Install the back-up light switch.

55. Place the gasket on the case and install the extension housing with the control lever end down and as far to the left as it will go.

56. Insert the select lock spindle and spring from the underside of the shift lever retainer.

57. Install the steel ball and spring in alignment with the spindle groove and install the spring cap bolt.

58. Install the gearshift lever retainer and gasket on the extension housing.

59. Check the bearing end-play. Measure the depth of the bearing bore in the housing. Measure the height of the bearing protrusion. The difference indicates the thickness of the shim needed. The end-play should be less than 0.0039 in.

60. Place the gasket on the front side of the case. Apply lubricant to the lip of the oil seal and install the clutch housing on the case.

61. Install the release bearing and fork on the clutch housing.

Muncie Model SM330 3–Speed (83MM)

The G.M. Corporation Model SM 330 (83MM) (Muncie) is a three-speed transmission using helical constant mesh gears. The engagement of all gears except reverse is assisted by synchronizers.

GENERAL DATA

Type	3-Speed
Synchromesh gears	1st, 2nd, and 3rd
Model	SM330 (83MM)
Gear ratios	
1st speed	3.03:1
2nd speed	1.75:1
3rd speed	1.00:1
Reverse	3.02:1

TRANSMISSION UNIT

Disassembly

1. Remove side cover and shift forks.

2. Unbolt extension and rotate to line up groove in extension flange with reverse idler shaft. Drive reverse idler shaft and key out of case with a brass drift.

3. Move second-third synchronizer sleeve forward. Remove extension housing and mainshaft assembly.

4. Remove reverse idler gear from case.

5. Remove third speed blocker ring from clutch gear.

6. Expand snap-ring which holds mainshaft rear bearing. Tap gently on end of mainshaft to remove extension.

7. Remove clutch gear bearing retainer and gasket.

8. Remove snap-ring. Remove clutch gear from inside case by gently tapping on end of clutch gear.

1. Bearing retainer	14. Oil seal	28. Reverse idler gear	40. Pilot bearings
2. Bolt and lock washer	15. Thrust washer	29. Reverse idler bushing	41. 3rd speed blocker ring
3. Gasket	16. Bearing washer	30. Reverse idler shaft	42. 2nd and 3rd
4. Oil seal	17. Needle bearings	31. Woodruff key	synchronizer collar
5. Snap-ring (bearing-to-	18. Countergear	32. 1st speed gear	43. Snap-ring
main drive gear)	19. Countershaft	33. 1st speed blocker ring	44. Synchronizer key
6. Main drive gear	20. Woodruff key	34. Synchronizer key	spring
bearing	21. Bolt (extension-to-	spring	45. Synchronizer keys
7. Snap-ring bearing	case)	35. Synchronizer keys	46. 2nd and 3rd
8. Oil slinger	22. Reverse gear	36. 1st and reverse	synchronizer hub
9. Case	23. Thrust washer	synchronizer hub	47. 2nd speed blocker
10. Gasket	24. Rear bearing	assembly	ring
11. Snap-ring (rear	25. Snap-ring	37. Snap-ring	48. 2nd speed gear
bearing-to-extension)	26. Speedometer drive	38. 1st and reverse	49. Mainshaft
12. Extension	gear	synchronizer collar	50. Gasket
13. Extension bushing	27. Retainer clip	39. Main drive gear	51. 2nd and 3rd shifter

fork
52. 1st and reverse shifter fork
53. 2-3 shifter shaft assembly
54. 1st and reverse shifter shaft assembly
55. Spring
56. O-ring seal
57. 1st and reverse detent cam
58. 2nd and 3rd detent cam
59. Side cover
60. Bolt and lock washer

Muncie 83 mm 3-speed

9. Remove oil slinger and 16 mainshaft pilot bearings from clutch gear cavity.

10. Slip clutch gear bearing out front of case. Aid removal with a screwdriver between case and bearing outer snap-ring.

11. Drive countershaft and key out to rear.

12. Remove countergear and two tanged thrust washers.

MAINSHAFT

Disassembly

1. Remove speedometer drive gear. Some speedometer drive gears, made of metal, must be pulled off.

2. Remove rear bearing snap-ring.

3. Support reverse gear. Press on rear of mainshaft to remove reverse gear, thrust washer, and rear bearing. Be careful not to cock the bearing on the shaft.

4. Remove first and reverse sliding clutch hub snap-ring.

5. Support first gear. Press on rear of mainshaft to remove clutch assembly, blocker ring, and first gear.

6. Remove second and third speed sliding clutch hub snap-ring.

7. Support second gear. Press on front of mainshaft to remove clutch assembly, second speed blocker ring, and second gear from shaft.

CLEANING AND INSPECTION

For more detailed information, see the "Cleaning and Inspection" instructions at front of transmission section.

1. Wash all parts in solvent.

2. Air dry.

CLUTCH KEYS AND SPRINGS

Replacement

Keys and springs may be replaced if worn or broken, but the hubs and sleeves must be kept together as originally assembled.

1. Mark hub and sleeve for reassembly.

2. Push hub from sleeve. Remove keys and springs.

3. Place three keys and two springs, one on each side of hub, so all three keys are engaged by both springs. The tanged end of the springs should not be installed into the same key.

4. Slide the sleeve onto the hub, aligning the marks.

EXTENSION OIL SEAL AND BUSHING

Replacement

1. Remove seal.

2. Using bushing remover and installer, or other suitable tool, drive bushing into extension housing.

3. Drive new bushing in from rear. Lubricate inside of bushing and seal. Install new oil seal with extension seal installer or suitable tool.

CLUTCH BEARING RETAINER OIL SEAL

Replacement

1. Pry old seal out.
2. Install new seal using seal installer or suitable tool. Seat seal in bore.

MAINSHAFT

Assembly

1. Lift front of mainshaft.
2. Install second gear with clutching teeth up; the rear face of the gear butts against the mainshaft flange.
3. Install a blocking ring with clutching teeth downward. All three blocking rings are the same.
4. Install second and third synchronizer assembly with fork slot down. Press it onto mainshaft splines. Both synchronizer assemblies are identical but are assembled differently. The second-third speed hub and sleeve is assembled with the sleeve fork slot toward the thrust face of the hub; the first-reverse hub and sleeve, with the fork slot opposite the thrust face. Be sure that the blocker ring notches align with the synchronizer assembly keys.
5. Install synchronizer snap-ring. Both synchronizer snap-rings are the same.
6. Turn rear of shaft up.
7. Install first gear with clutching teeth upward; the front face of the gear butts against the flange on the mainshaft.
8. Install a blocking ring with clutching teeth down.
9. Install first and reverse synchronizer assembly with fork slot down. Press it onto mainshaft splines. Be sure blocker ring notches align with synchronizer assembly keys and synchronizer sleeves face front of mainshaft.
10. Install snap-ring.
11. Install reverse gear with clutching teeth down.
12. Install steel reverse gear thrust washer with flats aligned.
13. Press rear ball bearing onto shaft with snap-ring slot down.
14. Install snap-ring.
15. Install speedometer drive gear and retaining clip.

TRANSMISSION UNIT

Assembly

1. Place a row of 29 roller bearings, a bearing washer, a second row of 29 bearings, and a second bearing washer at each end of the countergear. Hold in place with grease.
2. Place countergear assembly through rear case opening with a tanged thrust washer, tang away from gear, at each end. Install countershaft and key from rear of case. Be sure that thrust washer tangs are aligned with notches in case.

TORQUE SPECIFICATIONS
Muncie-83MM

	ft. lbs.
Extension to case attaching	45
Drain plug	30
Filler plug	15
Side cover attaching bolts	22
Main drive gear retainer bolts	22
Transmission case to clutch housing bolts	45

3. Place reverse idler gear in case. Do not install reverse idler shaft yet.

NOTE: The reverse idler gear bushing may not be replaced separately—only as a unit.

4. Expand snap-ring in extension. Assemble extension over mainshaft and onto rear bearing. Seat snap-ring.
5. Load 16 mainshaft pilot bearings into clutch gear cavity. Assemble third speed blocker ring onto clutch gear clutching surface with teeth toward gear.
6. Place clutch gear assembly, without front bearing, over front of mainshaft. Make sure that blocker ring notches align with keys in second-third synchronizer assembly.
7. Stick gasket onto extension housing with grease. Assemble clutch gear, mainshaft, and extension to case together. Make sure that clutch gear teeth engage teeth of countergear anti-lash plate.
8. Rotate extension housing. Install reverse idler shaft and key.
9. Torque extension bolts to 45 ft. lbs.
10. Install oil slinger with inner lip facing forward. Install front bearing outer snap-ring and slide bearing into case bore.
11. Install snap-ring to clutch gear stem. Install bearing retainer and gasket and torque to 20 ft. lbs. Retainer oil return hole must be at 6 o'clock.
12. Shift both synchronizer sleeves to neutral positions. Install side cover, inserting shifter forks in synchronizer sleeve grooves.
13. Torque side cover bolts to 20 ft. lbs.

Muncie Model SM465 4–Speed (117mm)

Muncie model CH-465-SM-465 transmission is a four speed transmission using helical gears. The action of all gears except reverse is aided by synchronizers.

TRANSMISSION UNIT

Disassembly

1. Remove transmission cover assembly.

NOTE: Move reverse shifter fork so that reverse idler gear is partially engaged before attempting to remove cover.

Forks must be positioned so rear edge of the slot in the reverse fork is in line with the front edge of the slot in the forward forks as viewed through tower opening.

2. Lock transmission into two gears. Remove the universal joint flange nut, universal joint front flange and brake drum assembly.

NOTE: On 4-wheel drive models, use a special tool to remove mainshaft rear lock nut.

3. Remove parking brake and brake flange plate assembly on those vehicles having a drive-shaft parking brake.
4. Remove rear bearing retainer and gasket.
5. Slide speedometer drive gear off mainshaft.
6. Remove clutch gear bearing retainers and gasket.
7. Remove countergear front bearing cap and gasket.
8. Using a prybar, pry off countershaft front bearing.
9. Remove countergear rear bearing snap-rings from shaft and bearing. Using special tool, remove countergear rear bearings.
10. Remove clutch gear bearing outer race to case retaining ring.
11. Remove clutch gear and bearing by tapping gently on bottom side of clutch gear shaft and prying directly opposite against the case and bearing snap-ring groove at the same time. Remove fourth gear synchronizer ring.

------ CAUTION ------
Index cut out section of clutch gear in down position with countergear to obtain clearance for removing clutch gear.

12. Remove rear mainshaft bearing snap-ring and, using special tools, remove bearing from case. Slide 1st speed gear thrust washer off mainshaft.
13. Lift mainshaft assembly from case. Remove synchronizer cone from shaft.
14. Slide reverse idler gear rearward and move countergear rearward, then lift to remove from case.
15. To remove reverse idler gear, drive reverse idler gear shaft out of case from front to rear using a drift. Remove reverse idler gear from case.

1. 1st speed gear
2. Reverse driven gear
3. 1st gear bushing
4. 1st-2nd gear synchronizer hub assembly
5. 2nd speed blocker ring
6. 2nd speed gear
7. Thrust washer
8. 3rd speed bushing
9. 3rd speed gear
10. 3rd speed blocker ring
11. 3rd-4th speed synchronizer hub assembly
12. 3rd-4th speed synchronizer sleeve
13. 4th speed blocker ring
14. Snap-ring
15. Mainshaft
16. 2nd speed gear bushing

Muncie 117 mm 4-speed mainshaft

SUBASSEMBLIES
TRANSMISSION COVER

Disassembly

1. Remove shifter fork retaining pins and drive out expansion plugs.

NOTE: The third and fourth shifter fork must be removed before the reverse shifter head pin can be removed.

2. With shifter shafts in neutral position, remove shafts.

——————— CAUTION ———————
Care should be taken when removing the detent balls and springs since removal of the shifter shafts will cause these parts to be forcibly ejected.

3. Remove retaining pin and drive out reverse shifter shaft.

Assembly

1. In reassembling the cover, care should be taken to install the shifter shafts in order—reverse, 3rd–4th, and 1st–2nd.

2. Place fork detent ball springs and balls in cover.

3. Start shifter shafts into cover and, while depressing the detent balls, push the shafts over the balls. Push reverse shaft through the yoke.

4. With the 3rd–4th shaft in neutral, line up the retaining holes in the fork and shaft.

NOTE: Detent balls should line up with detents in shaft.

5. After 1st and 2nd fork is installed, place two inner-lock balls between the low speed shifter shaft and the high speed shifter shaft in the crossbore of the front support boss. Grease the interlock pin and insert it in the 3rd–4th shifter shaft hole. Continue pushing this shaft through cover bore and fork until retainer hole in fork lines up with hole in shaft.

6. Place two interlock balls in crossbore in front support boss between reverse, and 3rd and 4th shifter shaft. Then push remaining shaft through fork and cover bore, keeping both balls in position between shafts until retaining holes line up in fork and shaft. Install retaining pin.

7. Install 1st/2nd fork and reverse fork retaining pins. Install new shifter shaft hole expansion plugs.

CLUTCH GEAR AND SHAFT

Disassembly

1. Remove mainshaft pilot bearing rollers from clutch gear if not already removed, and remove roller retainer. Do not remove snap-ring on inside of clutch gear.

2. Remove snap-ring securing bearing on steam of clutch gear.

3. To remove bearing, position a special tool to the bearing and, with an arbor press, press gear and shaft out of bearing.

Assembly

1. Press bearing and new oil slinger onto clutch gear shaft using a special tool. Slinger should be located flush with bearing shoulder on clutch gear.

——————— CAUTION ———————
Be careful not to distort oil slinger.

2. Install bearing snap-ring on clutch gear shaft.

3. Install bearing retainer ring in groove on O.D. of bearing.

——————— CAUTION ———————
The bearing must turn freely on the shaft.

4. Install snap-ring on I.D. of mainshaft pilot bearing bore in clutch gear.

5. Lightly grease bearing surface in shaft recess, install transmission mainshaft pilot roller bearings and install roller bearing retainer.

NOTE: This roller bearing retainer holds bearings in position, and, in final transmission assembly, is pushed forward into recess by mainshaft pilot.

BEARING RETAINER OIL SEAL

Replacement

1. Remove retainer and oil seal assembly and gasket.

2. Pry out oil seal.

3. Install new seal with lip of seal toward flange of tool.

4. Support front surface of retainer in press and drive seal into retainer.

5. Install retainer and gasket on case.

MAINSHAFT

Disassembly

1. Remove first speed gear.

2. Remove reverse driven gear.

3. Press behind second speed gear to remove 3rd–4th synchronizer assembly, 3rd speed gear and 2nd speed gear along with 3rd speed gear bushing and thrust washer.

4. Remove 2nd speed synchronizer ring and keys.

5. Using a press, remove 1st speed gear bushing and 2nd speed synchronizer hub.

6. Without damaging the mainshaft, chisel out the 2nd speed gear bushing.

Inspection

Wash all parts in cleaning solvent and inspect them for excessive wear or scoring.

NOTE: Third and fourth speed clutch sleeve should slide freely on clutch hub but clutch hub should fit snugly on shaft splines.

Third speed gear must be running fit on mainshaft bushing and mainshaft bushing should be press fit on shaft.

First and reverse sliding gear must be sliding fit on synchronizer hub and must not have excessive radial or circumferential play. If sliding gear is not free on hub, inspect for burrs which may have rolled up on front end of half-tooth internal splines and remove by honing as necessary.

Assembly

1. Lubricate with E.P. oil and press onto mainshaft.

——————— CAUTION ———————
1st, 2nd and 3rd speed gear bushings are sintered iron, exercise care when installing.

2. Press 1st and 2nd speed synchronizer hub onto mainshaft with annulus toward rear of shaft.

3. Install 1st and 2nd synchronizer keys and springs.

4. Press 1st speed gear bushing onto mainshaft until it bottoms against hub.

NOTE: Lubricate all bushings with E.P. oil before installation of gears.

5. Install synchronizer blocker ring and 2nd speed gear onto mainshaft and against synchronize hub. Align synchronizer key slots with keys in synchronizer hub.

6. Install 3rd speed gear thrust washer onto mainshaft inserting washer tang in slotted shaft. Then press 3rd speed gear bushing onto mainshaft against thrust washer.

7. Install 3rd speed gear and synchronizer blocker ring against 3rd speed gear thrust washer.

8. Align synchronizer key ring slots with synchronizer assembly keys and drive 3rd and 4th synchronizer assembly onto mainshaft. Secure assembly with snap-ring.

9. Install reverse driven gear with fork groove toward rear.

10. Install 1st speed gear against 1st and 2nd synchronizer hub. Install 1st speed gear thrust washer.

COUNTERSHAFT

Disassembly

1. Remove front countergear retaining ring and thrust washer. Do not re-use this snap-ring or any others.

2. Press countershaft out of clutch countergear assembly.

3. Remove clutch countergear and 3rd speed countergear retaining rings.

4. Press shift from 3rd speed countergear.

Assembly

1. Press the 3rd speed countergear onto the shaft.

NOTE: Install gear with marked surface toward front of shaft.

2. Using snap-ring pliers, install new 3rd speed countergear retaining ring.

3. Install new clutch countergear rear retaining ring.

——— CAUTION ———
Do not over stress snap-ring. Ring should fit tightly in groove with no side play.

4. Press countergear onto shaft against snap-ring.

5. Install clutch countergear thrust washer and front retaining ring.

TRANSMISSION UNIT

Assembly

1. Lower the countergear into the case.
2. Place reverse idler gear in transmission case with gear teeth toward the front.

1. Transmission cover	6. Detent ball
2. Interlock balls	7. Detent spring
3. 3rd-4th shifter shaft	8. 3rd-4th shifter fork
4. Reverse shifter shaft	9. C-ring lock clip
5. Fork retaining pin	10. Reverse shifter fork
11. Shifter shaft hole plugs	14. Reverse interlock plunger
12. 1st-2nd shifter fork	15. 1st-2nd shifter shaft
13. Interlock plunger spring	16. Interlock pin
	17. Cover gasket

Muncie 117 mm 4-speed cover assembly

Install idler gear shaft from rear to front, being careful to have slot in end of shaft facing down and flush with case.

3. Install mainshaft assembly into case with rear of shaft protruding out rear bearing hole in case. Rotate case onto front end.

NOTE: Install 1st speed gear thrust washer on shaft, if not previously installed.

4. Install snap-ring on bearing O.D. and place rear mainshaft bearing on shaft. Drive bearing onto shaft and into case.

5. Install synchronizer cone on mainshaft and slide rearward to clutch hub.

——— CAUTION ———
Make sure three cut-out sections of 4th speed synchronizer cone align with three clutch keys in clutch assembly.

6. Install snap-ring on clutch gear bearing O.D. Index cut out portion of clutch gear teeth to obtain clearance over countershaft drive gear teeth, and install into case.

7. Install clutch gear bearing retainer and gasket and torque to 15–18 ft. lbs.

8. Rotate case onto front end.

9. Install snap-ring on countergear rear bearing O.D., and drive bearing into place. Install snap-ring on countershaft at rear bearing.

10. Tap countergear front bearing assembly into case.

11. Install countergear front bearing cap and new gasket and torque to 20–30 in. lbs.

12. Slide speedometer drive gear over mainshaft to bearing.

13. Install rear bearing retainer with new gasket. Be sure snap-ring ends are in lube slot and cut out in bearing retainer. Install bolts and tighten to 15–18 ft. lbs. Install brake backing plate assembly on those models having driveshaft brake.

NOTE: On models equipped with 4-wheel drive, install rear lock nut and washer and torque to 120 ft. lbs. and bend washer tangs to fit slots in nut.

TORQUE SPECIFICATIONS
Muncie-117MM

	ft. lbs.
Rear bearing retainer	18
Cover bolts	25
Filler plug	35
Drain plug	35
Clutch gear bearing retainer bolts	18
Universal joint front flange nut	95
Power take off cover bolts	18
Parking brake	22
Countergear front cover screws	25
Rear mainshaft lock nut (4 wheel drive models)	95

14. Install parking brake drum and/or universal joint flange.

NOTE: Lightly oil seal surface.

15. Lock transmission in two gears at once. Install universal joint flange locknut and tighten to 90–120 ft. lbs.

16. Move all transmission gears to neutral except the reverse idler gear which should be engaged approximately ⅜ of an inch (leading edge of reverse idler gear taper lines up with the front edge of the 1st speed gear). Install cover assembly and gasket. Shifting forks must slide into their proper positions on clutch sleeves and reverse idler gear. Forks must be positioned as in removal.

17. Install cover attaching bolts and gearshift lever and check operation of transmission.

New Process 435 4–Speed Transmission

TRANSMISSION UNIT

Disassembly

1. Mount the transmission in a holding fixture. Remove the parking brake assembly, if one is installed.

2. Shift the gears into neutral by replacing the gear shift lever temporarily, or by using a bar or screw driver.

3. Remove the cover screws, the second screw from the front on each side is shouldered with a split washer for installation alignment.

4. While lifting the cover, rotate slightly counterclockwise to provide clearance for the shift levers. Remove the cover.

5. Lock the transmission in two gears and remove the output flange nut, the yoke, and the parking brake drum as a unit assembly.

NOTE: The drum and yoke are balanced and unless replacement of parts are required, it is recommended that the drum and yoke be removed as a assembly.

6. Remove the speedometer drive gear pinion and the mainshaft rear bearing retainer.

7. Before removal and disassembly of the drive pinion and mainshaft, measure the end play between the synchronizer stop ring and the third gear.

NOTE: Record this reading for reference during assembly.

Clearance should be within 0.050–0.070 inch. If necessary, add corrective shims during assembly.

8. Remove the drive pinion bearing retainer.

9. Rotate the drive pinion gear to align the space in the pinion gear clutch teeth with the countershaft drive gear teeth. Remove the drive pinion gear and the tapered

roller bearing from the transmission by pulling on the pinion shaft, and rapping the face of the case lightly with a brass hammer.

10. Remove the snap-ring, washer, and the pilot roller bearings from the recess in the drive pinion gear.

11. Place a brass drift in the front center of the mainshaft and drive the shaft rearward.

12. When the mainshaft rear bearing has cleared the case, remove the rear bearing and the speedometer drive gear with a suitable gear puller.

13. Move the mainshaft assembly to the rear of the case and tilt the front of the mainshaft upward.

14. Remove the roller type thrust washer.

15. Remove the synchronizer and stop rings separately.

16. Remove the mainshaft assembly.

17. Remove the reverse idler lock screw and lock plate.

18. Using a brass drift held at an angle, drive the idler shaft to the rear while pulling.

19. Lift the reverse idler gear out of the case.

NOTE: If the countershaft gear does not show signs of excessive side play or end play and the teeth are not badly worn or chipped, it may not be necessary to replace the countershaft gear.

20. Remove the bearing retainer at the rear end of the countershaft. The bearing assembly will remain with the retainer.

21. Tilt the cluster gear assembly and work it out of the transmission case.

22. Remove the front bearings from the case with a suitable driver.

SUBASSEMBLIES MAINSHAFT

Disassembly

1. Remove the clutch gear snap-ring.

2. Remove the clutch gear, the synchronizer outer stop ring to third gear shim, and the third gear.

3. Remove the special split lock ring with two screw drivers. Remove the second gear and synchronizer.

4. Remove the first-reverse sliding gear.

5. Drive the old seal out of the bearing retainer.

Assembly

1. Place the mainshaft in a soft-jawed vise with the rear end up.

2. Install the first-reverse gear. Be sure the two spline springs, if used, are in place inside the gear as the gear is installed on the shaft.

3. Place the mainshaft in a soft-jawed vise with the front end up.

4. Assemble the second speed synchronizer spring and synchronizer brake on the second gear. Secure the brake with a snap-ring making sure that the snap-ring tangs are away from the gear.

5. Slide the second gear on the front of the mainshaft. Make sure that the syn-

chronizer brake is toward the rear. Secure the gear to the shaft with the two piece lock ring. Install the third gear.

6. Install the shim between the third gear and the third-fourth synchronizer stop ring. Refer to the measurements of end play made during disassembly to determine if additional shims are needed.

NOTE: The exact determination of end-play must be made after the complete assembly of the mainshaft and the main drive pinion is installed in the transmission case.

REVERSE IDLER GEAR

———— CAUTION ————

Do not disassemble the reverse idler gear. If it is no longer serviceable, replace the assembly complete with the integral bearings.

COVER AND SHIFT FORK UNIT

NOTE: The cover and shift fork assembly should be disassembled only if inspection shows worn or damaged parts, or if the assembly is not working properly.

Disassembly

1. Remove the roll pin from the first-second shift fork and the shift gate with an "easy out".

NOTE: A square type or a closely wound spiral "easy out" mounted in a tap is preferable for this operation.

2. Move the first-second shift rail forward and force the expansion plug out of the cover. Cover the detent ball access hole in the cover with a cloth to prevent it from flying out. Remove the rail, fork, and gate from the cover.

3. Remove the third-fourth shift rail, then the reverse rail in the manner outlined in steps 1 and 2 above.

4. Compress the reverse gear plunger and remove the retaining clip. Remove the plunger and spring from the gate.

Assembly

1. Install the spring on the reverse gear plunger and hold it in the reverse shift gate. Compress the spring in the shift gate and install the retaining clip.

2. Insert the reverse shift rail in the cover and place the detent ball and spring in position. Depress the ball and slide the shift rail over it.

3. Install the shift gate and fork on the reverse shift rail. Install a new roll pin in the gate and the fork.

4. Place the reverse fork in the neutral position.

5. Install the two interlock plungers in their bores.

6. Insert the interlock pin in the third-

COVER GASKET
7223

SPEEDOMETER
DRIVE
GEAR
17285

GASKET
7086

SPEEDOMETER
DRIVEN GEAR
17322

FILLER PLUG

SNAP
RING—7059

YOKE

DRAIN PLUG

SEAL—7052

REVERSE IDLER
SHAFT 7140

OUTPUT SHAFT BEARING
RETAINER—7085

INPUT SHAFT
BEARING RETAINER
7050

POWER TAKE-OFF
COVER

GUIDE
STUD

REVERSE
IDLER
GEAR
7142

SECOND-SPEED
GEAR-7176

GASKET—7051

CASE
7005

7181

7195

COUNTERSHAFT REAR
BEARING CAP

SEAL

SYNCHRONIZER
RETAINER

COUNTERSHAFT FRONT
BEARING CAGE

SNAP RING
7109

THIRD-SPEED
GEAR 7196

PILOT
ROLLER
BEARINGS
7120

SNAP RING
7059

SYNCHRONIZER SHIM
(AS REQUIRED)
7060

THIRD AND FOURTH SPEED
SYNCHRONIZER
ASSEMBLY—7124

INPUT
SHAFT
7017

ROLLER
THRUST
BEARING
7C096

SCYNCHRONIZER
CLUTCHING
GEAR—7183

WASHER
7063

RACE
4628

BEARING
4630

SPRING

SNAP RING
7070

FIRST-SPEED
GEAR STOP
7072

OUTPUT SHAFT
BEARING
7065

OUTPUT SHAFT
7061

FIRST-SPEED
GEAR—7100

7174

7B137

SPRING

NEEDLE BEARING
7127

NEEDLE
BEARINGS

SECOND SPEED
SYNCHRONIZER
BRAKE AND SPRING

7119

7C096

NEEDLE THRUST
BEARING AND RACE

REVERSE IDLER GEAR

COUNTERSHAFT GEAR

THRUST WASHER

New Process 435 4-speed

NP 435 gearshift housing

fourth shift rail. Install the shift rail in the same manner as the reverse shift rail.

7. Install the first-second shift rail in the same manner as outlined above. Make sure the interlock plunger is in place.

8. Check the interlocks by shifting the reverse shift rail into the Reverse position. It should be impossible to shift the other rails with the reverse rail in this position.

9. If the shift lever is to be installed at this point, lubricate the spherical ball seat and place the cap in place.

10. Install the back-up light switch.

11. Install new expansion plugs in the bores of the shift rail holes in the cover. Install the rail interlock hole plug.

DRIVE PINION AND BEARING RETAINER

Disassembly

1. Remove the tapered roller bearing from the pinion shaft with a suitable tool.

2. Remove the snap-ring, washer, and the pilot rollers from the gear bore, if they have not been previously removed.

3. Pull the bearing race from the front bearing retainer with a suitable puller.

4. Remove the pinion shaft seal with a suitable tool.

Assembly

1. Position the drive pinion in an arbor press.

2. Place a wood block on the pinion gear and press it into the bearing until it contacts the bearing inner race.

3. Coat the roller bearings with a light film of grease to hold the bearings in place, and insert them in the pocket of the drive pinion gear.

4. Install the washer and snap-ring.

5. Press a new seal into the bearing retainer. Make sure that the lip of the seal is toward the mounting surface.

6. Press the bearing race into the retainer.

TRANSMISSION UNIT

Assembly

1. Press the front countershaft roller bearings into the case until the cage is flush with the front of the transmission case. Coat the bearings with a light film of grease.

2. Place the transmission with the front of the case facing down. If uncaged bearings are used, hold the loose rollers in place in the cap with a light film of grease.

3. Lower the countershaft assembly into the case placing the thrust washer tangs in the slots in the case, and inserting the front end of the shaft into the bearing.

4. Place the roller thrust bearing and race on the rear end of the countershaft. Hold the bearing in place with a light film of grease.

5. While holding the gear assembly in alignment, install the rear bearing retainer gasket, retainer, and bearing assembly. Install and tighten the cap screws.

6. Position the reverse idler gear and bearing assembly in the case.

7. Align the idler shaft so that the lock plate groove in the shaft is in position to install the lock plate.

8. Install the lock plate, washer, and cap screw.

9. Make sure the reverse idler gear turns freely.

10. Lower the rear end of the mainshaft assembly into the case, holding the first gear on the shaft. Maneuver the shaft through the rear bearing opening.

NOTE: With the mainshaft assembly moved to the rear of the case, be sure the third-fourth synchronizer and shims remain in position.

11. Install the roller type thrust bearing.

12. Place a wood block between the front of the case and the front of the mainshaft.

13. Install the rear bearing on the mainshaft by carefully driving the bearing onto the shaft and into the case, snap-ring flush against the case.

14. Install the drive pinion shaft and bearing assembly. Make sure that the pilot rollers remain in place.

15. Install the spacer and speedometer drive gear.

16. Install the rear bearing retainer and gasket.

17. Place the drive pinion bearing retainer over the pinion shaft, without the gasket.

18. Hold the retainer tight aginst the bearing and measure the clearance between the retainer and the case with a feeler gauge.

NOTE: End play in steps 19 and 20 below allows for normal expansion of parts during operation, preventing seizure and damage to bearings, gears, synchronizers, and shafts.

19. Install a gasket shim pack 0.010–0.015 inch thicker than measured clearance between the retainer and case to obtain the required 0.007–0.017 inch pinion shaft end play. Tighten the front retainer bolts and recheck the end play.

20. Check the synchronizer end play clearance (0.050–0.070 inch) after all

mainshaft components are in position and properly tightened. Two sets of feeler gauges are used to measure the clearance. Care should be used to keep both gauges as close as possible to both sides of the mainshaft for best results.

NOTE: In some cases, it may be necessary to disassemble the mainshaft and change the thickness of the shims to keep the end play clearance within the specified limits, 0.050–0.070 inch. Shims are available in two thicknesses.

21. Install the speedometer drive pinion.
22. Install the yoke flange, drum, and drum assembly.
23. Place the transmission in two gears at once, and tighten the yoke flange nut.
24. Shift the gears and/or synchronizers into all gear positions and check for free rotation.
25. Cover all transmissions components with a film of transmission oil to prevent damage during start up after initial lubricant fill-up.
26. Move the gears to the neutral position.
27. Place a new cover gasket on the transmission case, and lower the cover over the transmission.
28. Carefully engage the shift forks into their proper gears. Align the cover.
29. Install a shouldered alignment screw with split washer in the screw hole second from the front of the cover. Try out gear operation by shifting through all ranges. Make sure everything moves freely.
30. Install the remaining cover screws.

New Process 445 4–Speed Transmission

TRANSMISSION UNIT

Disassembly

1. Place the transmission in a holding fixture and drain the lubricant.
2. Shift the transmission gears into neutral. Remove the gearshift cover attaching bolts. Note that the two bolts opposite the tower are shouldered to properly position the cover. Lift the cover straight up and remove.
3. Lock the transmission in two gears at once and remove the mainshaft nut and yoke.
4. Loosen and remove the extension housing bolts. Remove the mainshaft extension housing and the speedometer drive pinion.
5. Remove the bolts from the drive pinion front bearing retainer and pull the bearing retainer and gasket off.
6. Rotate the drive pinion gear to align the pinion gear flat with the countershaft drive gear teeth. Remove the drive pinion gear and the tapered roller bearing from the transmission.

TORQUE SPECIFICATIONS
New Process 435

	ft. lbs.
Cover screws	20–40
Drive gear retaining screw	15–25
Front countershaft retainer screw	15–25
Front countershaft bearing washer screw	12–22
Flange nut	125
Mainshaft rear retainer screw	15–25
Rear countershaft retainer screw	15–25
PTO cover screws	8–12
Filler and drain plugs	25–45
Reverse idler shaft lock screw	20–40
Brake link shoulder screw	20–40

LUBRICANT CAPACITY

New Process 435	7 pt.

7. Remove the mainshaft thrust bearing.
8. Push the mainshaft assembly to the rear of the transmission and tilt the front of the mainshaft up.
9. Remove the mainshaft assembly from the transmission case.
10. Remove the reverse idler lock screw and lock plate.
11. Using a suitable size brass drift, carefully drive the reverse idler shaft out the REAR of the case.

— CAUTION —
Do not attempt to drive the reverse idler shaft forward! This will damage the transmission case and the reverse idler shaft.

12. Remove the countershaft rear bearing retainer.
13. Slide the countershaft to the rear, then up and out of the case.
14. Drive the countershaft forward, out of the bearing and the case.

SUBASSEMBLIES
MAINSHAFT

Disassembly

1. Place the mainshaft in a soft-jawed vise with the front end up.
2. Lift the third-fourth synchronizer and high speed clutch off the mainshaft.
3. Remove the third gear.
4. Remove the second gear snap-ring. Lift off the thrust washer.
5. Remove the second gear.
6. Remove the first-reverse synchronizer and clutch gear.
7. Install the mainshaft in the vise rear end up.
8. Remove the tapered bearing from the shaft with a suitable gear puller.
9. Remove the first gear snap-ring and thrust washer.
10. Remove the first gear.

Assembly

1. Lubricate all parts with transmission lubricant prior to assembly.
2. Place the mainshaft in a soft-jawed vise with the rear end up.
3. Slide the first gear over the mainshaft, with the clutch gear facing down. Install the thrust washer and snap-ring.
4. Install the revese gear over the end of the mainshaft with the fork groove facing down.
5. Install the mainshaft rear bearing on the mainshaft with a sleeve of suitable size. Press the bearing on its inner race.
6. Install the mainshaft in the vise with the front end facing up.
7. Install the first-reverse synchronizer.
8. Install the second gear on the mainshaft.
9. Install the keyed thrust washer, ground side toward the second gear and secure with the snap-ring.
10. Install the third gear and one shim on the mainshaft.
11. Install the third fourth synchronizer over the mainshaft. Make sure that the slotted end of the clutch gear is positioned toward the third gear.

COVER AND SHIFT FORK UNIT

Disassembly

NOTE: The cover and shift fork assembly should be disassembled only if inspection shows worn or damaged parts, or if the assembly is not working properly.

1. Remove the roll pin from the first-second shift fork and the shift gate. Use a square-type or spirial wound "easy-out" mounted in a tap handle for these operations.
2. Move the first-second shift rail rearward and force the expansion plug out of the cover. Cover the detent ball access hole in the cover with a cloth to prevent it from flying out. Remove the rail fork, and gate from the cover.
3. Remove the third-fourth shift rail,

BEARING RETAINER

GASKET

SEAL

3RD-4TH SPEED SYNCHRONIZER

BEARING RACE

3RD SPEED GEAR

THRUST WASHER

PINION BEARING

SNAP RING

CLUTCH GEAR

DRIVE PINION AND SHAFT ASSEMBLY

2ND SPEED GEAR

1ST-2ND SPEED SYNCHRONIZER ASSEMBLY

REVERSE IDLER THRUST WASHER

COUNTERSHAFT THRUST WASHER

GASKET

NEEDLE BEARINGS

WASHER

MAINSHAFT NEEDLE THRUST BEARING

LOCK RING

COUNTERSHAFT FRONT BEARING

REVERSE IDLER NEEDLE BEARING

MAIN SHAFT

CASE

GASKET

P.T.O. COVER

BUSHING

LOW SPEED GEAR

REVERSE IDLER SHAFT

LOCK

THRUST WASHER

REVERSE IDLER GEAR

COUNTERSHAFT

BEARING

STUD

DRAIN PLUG

FILLER PLUG

THRUST WASHER

SNAP RING

REVERSE GEAR

BEARING CASE

COUNTERSHAFT REAR BEARING RETAINER

GASKET

COUNTERSHAFT REAR BEARING

New Process 445

then the reverse rail in the manner outlined in steps 1 and 2 above.

4. Compress the reverse gear plunger and remove the retaining clip. Remove the plunger and spring from the gate.

Assembly

1. Apply a thin film of grease on the interlock slugs and slide them into the openings in the shift rail supports.

2. Install the reverse shift rail through the reverse shift fork plate and the reverse shift fork.

3. Secure the reverse shift plate and the shift fork with the roll pins. Install the interlock pin in the third-fourth shift rail. Hold in place with a thin film of grease.

4. Slide the third-fourth shift rail into the rail support from the rear of the cover. Slide the rail through the third-fourth shift fork and poppet ball and spring. Secure the third-fourth shift fork with the roll pin.

5. Install the interlock pin in the first-second shift rail and secure with a light coat of grease. Slide the first-second shift rail into the case, through the shift fork and shift gate. Hold the poppet ball and spring down until the shaft rail passes.

6. Secure the first-second shift rail and gate with the roll pins.

TRANSMISSION UNIT

Assembly

1. Install the countershaft front bearing in the case using a 1⅜ inch socket as a driver. Grease the needle bearings prior to installation. Hold the bearings in place with a socket of suitable size while seating the bearing retainer. Drive the retainer in until it is flush with the case.

2. Install the tanged thrust washer on the countershaft with the tangs facing out. Install the countershaft in the transmission case.

3. Install the countershaft rear bearing retainer over the rear bearing. Use a new washer and position the retainer with the curved segment toward the bottom of the case.

4. Install the reverse idler gear into the case with the chamfered section facing the rear. Hold the thrust washer and needle bearings in position.

5. Slide the reverse idler shaft into the case, from the rear, and through the reverse idler gear. Make sure that the lock notch is down and at the rear of the case.

6. Install the reverse idler shaft lock and bolt.

7. Place the mainshaft in a soft-jawed vise with the front end facing up.

8. Install the drive gear on top of the mainshaft.

9. Measure the clearance between the high-speed synchronizer and the drive gear with two feeler gauges.

If the clearance is greater than 0.043–0.053 inch, install synchronizer shims between the third gear and the synchronizer

brake drum. After the required shims have been installed, remove the drive gear from the mainshaft.

10. Install the mainshaft into the transmission case. Place the thrust washer over the pilot end of the mainshaft.

11. Position the drive gear so that the cutaway portion of the gear is facing down. Slide the drive gear into the front of the case and engage the mainshaft pilot in the pocket of the drive gear.

12. Slip the drive gear front bearing retainer over the shaft on gasket, and do not secure with bolts.

13. Install the mainshaft rear bearing retainer. Tighten the screws to specifications.

14. Hold the retainer against the front of the transmission case and measure the clearance between the front bearing retainer and the front of the case with a feeler gauge. Record the measurement and remove the bearing retainer.

15. Install a gasket pack on the front bearing retainer which is 0.010–0.015 inch thicker than the clearance measured in step 14. Install the front bearing retainer and torque attaching screws to specification.

16. The end play float of the front synchronizer must be checked before installation of the transmission cover assembly. Measure the end play "float" by inserting two feeler gauges opposite one another between the third gear and the synchronizer stop ring. Accurate measurement can be made only after all mainshaft parts are in place and torqued to specification.

17. If the front synchronizer end play "float" does not fall between 0.050–0.070 inch, shims should be added or removed as required, from between the third gear and the synchronizer stop ring.

18. Install the yoke retaining nut on the rear of the mainshaft. Shift the transmission into two gears at the same time and torque the yoke nut to 125 ft. lbs.

19. Shift the transmission into neutral.

20. Install the cover gasket.

21. Shift the transmission into second gear. Shift the cover into second.

22. Carefully lower the cover into position. It may be necessary to position the

TORQUE SPECIFICATIONS
New Process 445

	ft. lbs.
Cover screws	20–40
Drive gear retaining screw	15–25
Front countershaft retaining screw	15–25
Front countershaft bearing washer screw	12–22
Flange nut	125
Mainshaft rear retainer screw	15–25
Rear countershaft retainer screw	15–25
PTO cover screws	8–12
Filler and drain plugs	25–45
Reverse idler shaft lock screw	20–40
Brake link shoulder screw	20–40

LUBRICANT CAPACITY

New Process 445	7½ pts.

reverse gear to permit the fork to engage its groove.

23. Install the cover aligning screws (shouldered) and tighten with fingers only.

24. Install the remaining cover screws and tighten to specifications.

Saginaw 3–Speed (GM–SM326–76mm)

The G.M. Corporation Model SM326 (Saginaw) is a synchromesh three-speed transmission using helical constant mesh gears. The engagement of all gears except reverse is assisted by synchronizers.

GENERAL DATA

Type	3-Speed
Synchromesh gears	1st, 2nd, and 3rd

Models SM326 and SM326 w/Overdrive
Gear ratios
1st speed	2.85:1
2nd speed	1.68:1
3rd speed	1.00:1
Reverse	2.95:1

TRANSMISSION UNIT

Disassembly

1. Remove side cover assembly and shift forks.

2. Remove clutch gear bearing retainer.

3. Remove clutch gear bearing to gear stem snap-ring. Pull clutch gear outward until a screwdriver can be inserted between bearing and case. Remove clutch gear bearing.

4. Remove speedometer driven gear and extension bolts.

5. Remove reverse idler shaft snap-ring. Slide reverse idler gear forward on shaft.

Saginaw transmission

1. Synchronizer retainer ring
2. Synchronizer blocking ring
3. Synchronizer assembly
4. Second speed gear
5. Main shaft
6. Synchronizer assembly
7. Gear assembly
8. Thrust washer
9. Retainer clip
10. Speedometer drive gear
11. Ring
12. Mainshaft bearing
13. Washer
14. Seal
15. Extension housing
16. Bolt
17. Washer
18. Rear bearing location ring
19. Gasket
20. Case
21. Bearing assembly
22. Ring
23. Clutch gear
24. Gasket
25. Bolt and lockwasher
26. Retainer assembly
27. Ring
28. Clutch gear bearing locating ring
29. Cover gasket
30. Cover assembly
31. Bolt and lockwasher
32. Woodruff keys
33. Gear assembly
34. Retaining ring
35. Shaft
36. Roller
37. Washer
38. Washer
39. Gear assembly
40. Counter gear shaft
41. Mainshaft bearing roller

6. Remove mainshaft and extension assembly.

7. Remove clutch gear and third-speed blocker ring from inside case. Remove 14 roller bearings from clutch gear.

8. Expand the snap-ring which retains the mainshaft rear bearing. Remove the extension.

9. Using a dummy shaft, drive the countershaft and key out the rear of the case. Remove the gear, two tanged thrust washers, and dummy shaft. Remove bearing washer and 27 roller bearings from each end of countergear.

10. Use a long drift to drive the reverse idler shaft and key through the rear of the case.

11. Remove reverse idler gear and tanged steel thrust washer.

MAINSHAFT

Disassembly

1. Remove second and third speed sliding clutch hug snap-ring from mainshaft. Remove clutch assembly, second speed blocker ring, and second speed gear from front of mainshaft.

2. Depress speedometer drive gear retaining clip. Remove gear. Some units have a metal speedometer drive gear which must be pulled off.

3. Remove rear bearing snap-ring.

4. Support reverse gear. Press on rear of mainshaft. Remove reverse gear, thrust washer, spring washer, rear bearing, and snap-ring. When pressing off the rear bearing, be careful not to cock the bearing on the shaft.

5. Remove first and reverse sliding clutch hub snap-ring. Remove clutch assembly, first speed blocker ring, and first gear.

Cleaning and Inspection

See Cleaning and Inspection instructions at the beginning of Transmission section.

CLUTCH KEYS AND SPRINGS

Replacement

Keys and springs may be replaced if worn or broken, but the hubs and sleeves are matched pairs and must be kept together.

1. Mark hub and sleeve for reassembly.

2. Push hub from sleeve. Remove keys and springs.

3. Place three keys and two springs, one on each side of hub, in position, so all three keys are engaged by both springs. The tanged end of the springs should not be installed into the same key.

4. Slide the sleeve onto the hub, aligning the marks.

NOTE: A groove around the outside of the synchronizer hub marks the end that must be opposite the fork slot in the sleeve when assembled.

EXTENSION OIL SEAL AND BUSHING

Replacement

1. Remove seal.
2. Using bushing remover and installer tool, or other suitable tool, drive bushing into extension housing.
3. Drive new bushing in from the rear. Lubricate inside of bushing and seal. Install new oil seal with extension seal installer tool or other suitable tool.

CLUTCH BEARING RETAINER OIL SEAL

Replacement

1. Pry old seal out.
2. Install new seal using seal installer or suitable tool. Seat seal in bore.

MAINSHAFT

Assembly

1. Turn front of mainshaft up.
2. Install second gear with clutching teeth up; the rear face of the gear butts against the flange on the mainshaft.
3. Install a blocker ring with clutching teeth down. All three blocker rings are the same.
4. Install second and third speed synchronizer assembly with fork slot down. Press it onto mainshaft splines. Both synchronizer assemblies are the same. Be sure that blocker ring notches align with synchronizer assembly keys.
5. Install synchronizer snap-ring. Both synchronizer snap-rings are the same.
6. Turn rear of shaft up.
7. Install first gear with clutching teeth up; the front face of the gear butts against the flange on the mainshaft.
8. Install a blocker ring with clutching teeth down.
9. Install first and reverse synchronizer assembly with fork slot down. Press it onto mainshaft splines. Be sure blocker ring notches align with synchronizer assembly keys.
10. Install snap-ring.
11. Install reverse gear with clutching teeth down.

12. Install steel reverse gear thrust washer and spring washer.
13. Press rear ball bearing onto shaft with snap-ring slot down.
14. Install snap-ring.
15. Install speedometer drive gear and retaining clip. Press on metal speedometer drive gear.

TRANSMISSION UNIT

Assembly

1. Using dummy shaft load a row of 27 roller bearings and a thrust washer at each end of countergear. Hold in place with grease.
2. Place countergear assembly into case through rear. Place a tanged thrust washer, tang away from gear at each end. Install countershaft and key, making sure that tangs align with notches in case.
3. Install reverse idler gear thrust washer, gear, and shaft with key from rear of case. Be sure thrust washer is between gear and rear of case with tang toward notch in case.

NOTE: The reverse idler gear bushing may not be replaced separately—only as a unit with the gear.

4. Expand snap-ring in extension. Assemble extension over rear of mainshaft and onto rear bearing. Seat snap-ring in rear bearing groove.
5. Install 14 mainshaft pilot bearings into clutch gear cavity. Assemble third speed blocker ring onto clutch gear clutching surface with teeth toward gear.
6. Place clutch gear, pilot bearings, and third speed blocker ring assembly over front of mainshaft assembly. Be sure blocker rings align with keys in second-third synchronizer assembly.
7. Stick extension gasket to case with grease. Install clutch gear, mainshaft, and extension together. Be sure clutch gear engages teeth of countergear anti-lash plate. Torque extension bolts to 45 ft. lbs.
8. Place bearing over stem of clutch gear and into front case bore. Install front bearing to clutch gear snap-ring.
9. Install clutch gear bearing retainer and gasket. The retainer oil return hole must be at the bottom. Torque to 10 ft. lbs.
10. Install reverse idler gear shaft E-ring.
11. Shift synchronizer sleeves to neutral positions. Install cover, gasket, and forks,

aligning forks with synchronizer sleeve grooves. Torque side cover bolts to 10 ft. lbs.

12. Install speedometer driven gear.

Toyota 4-Speed Transmission

Disassembly

NOTE: The shifting controls are mounted in a side cover on the transmission case. The remote controls are either column or floor mounted.

1. Remove speedometer drive unit in the extension housing (Except 4 × 4 Pickup).
2. Some models have a driveshaft flange and crimped nut at the end of the extension housing. Remove them. Unbolt and remove the extension housing.
3. Unbolt and remove the case cover assembly.
4. Remove the release fork and bearing. Remove the front bearing retainer inside the bell housing.
5. Unbolt and remove the clutch bell housing.
6. Using a brass rod, gently tap the reverse idler gear shaft toward the rear and remove it. Remove the reverse idler gear.
7. Check the countergear thrust clearance with a feeler gauge, record the reading, then pick the proper adjusting gear side thrust washer to obtain the specified clearance of 0.004–0.010 in.
8. Using a dummy shaft, drive out the countershaft and the Woodruff key to the rear. Allow the countergear to drop into the case.
9. Shift the hub sleeve toward the top speed and draw out the output shaft. Be careful not to lose the synchronizer ring.
10. Turn the input shaft assembly so that one of the flat sides of the synchronizer engagement teeth on the input shaft clears the countergear and remove the input shaft.
11. Remove the countergear along with its thrust washers.
12. Secure the output shaft in a soft-jawed vise. Remove the spacer and snap-ring at the rear end of the output shaft if so equipped. Remove the snap-ring behind the speedometer drive gear and remove the gear along with its Woodruff key and second snap-ring.

TORQUE SPECIFICATIONS
Saginaw-76mm

	ft. lbs.
Extension to case attaching bolts	35–55
Drain and filler plugs	10–15
Side cover attaching bolts	18–24
Clutch gear retainer bolts	18–24

13. Check and record the following clearances: first gear thrust clearance, second gear thrust clearance, third gear thrust clearance and clearance between snap-ring and clutch hub.

14. Remove the snap-ring holding the clutch hub in place and remove clutch hub and third speed gear.

15. Remove the snap-ring behind the rear bearing and press the bearing off the shaft with the first speed gear.

NOTE: Be careful not to lose the small locking ball.

—————— CAUTION ——————

Do not attempt to force the bearing and first speed gear off by striking on the end of the output shaft, or you may damage the shaft.

16. Remove the synchronizer rings and clutch hub along with reverse and second gears.

17. Loosen and remove the back-up light switch. Move the third and fourth shift fork into the fourth speed position (to the front).

18. Using a long drift punch, drive out the slotted spring pin which connects the shift fork to the shift fork shaft.

19. Slide the shift fork shaft out of the rear of the case cover gradually, preventing the lockball from popping out under spring tension. Remove the lockball, spring and two interlock pins from the case cover.

20. Drive the slotted spring pin out of the first and second shift fork and the shift fork shaft in the same manner. Remove the shift fork shaft and the shift fork, then remove the lockball and the spring from the case cover.

21. Remove the shift arm pivot locknut. Remove the shift arm from the case cover. Drive out the slotted spring pin, and remove the reverse shift head and the shift fork shaft. Remove the lockball and the spring. Remove the selector outer lever and the selector lever shaft.

22. Remove the shift lever shaft lockbolt, slide out the shift lever shaft from the case cover. Be careful to prevent the lockball from popping out under spring tension.

23. Remove the sliding shift lever, lockball and spring. Remove the wire and shift lever lockbolt.

24. Remove the shift and selector lever shaft toward the rear side of the case.

Wash all disassembled parts thoroughly. Check the transmission case, case cover and the extension housing for cracks; check the bearing fitting portions and gasket surfaces for burrs and nicks.

Check the output shaft splines, snap-ring grooves, bearing contact surfaces, bearing fitting portions and oil seal lip contact surface for wear, scores, or damage. Check the output shaft for run-out. If the run-out exceeds 0.0024 in. replace the shaft. To measure run-out, place a dial indicator on the center point of the shaft and rotate the shaft slowly to read the maximum and minimum values. The run-out equals the maximum value minus the minimum value divided by two.

Check the bearings for roughness and wear. Check for noise or damage by rotating the bearing after applying a few drops of oil. To remove the input shaft bearing, remove the shaft snap-ring with a snap-ring expander, then remove the bearing from the input shaft with a puller. Check the bushings and the bearing rollers for abnormal wear. If the wear is excessive, replace the busings or the bearing rollers.

Inspect the extension housing bushing for wear or scoring. To replace the bushing, press the bushing out of the extension housing to the front side. To install, align the oil grooves of the bushing and the extension housing, and press the bushing into the housing. After installing the bushing, ream the bushing to fit the outer diameter of the universal joint sleeve yoke.

SPECIFIED GEAR BACKLASH

Input shaft gear to countergear: 0.004 in.
Third gear to countergear: 0.004–0.008 in.
Second gear to countergear: 0.004–0.008 in.
First gear to countergear: 0.004–0.008 in.
Reverse idler gear to countergear: 0.004–0.008 in.
Reverse idler gear to reverse gear: 0.004–0.008 in.

Assembly

Assembly is performed in the following order:

NOTE: Always install new gaskets, apply liquid sealer or gasket cement when assembling. Apply a thin coating of transmission lubricant on all parts before installation. Thrust clearances of gears and bearings are important factors for smooth shifting. Therefore, select and assemble thrust washers, snap-rings and spacers of proper thickness.

1. If the shifting hubs have been disassembled, reassemble them by:

a. Install the two shifting springs in the inner hub with the spring ends 120° apart, so that the spring tension on each shifting key will be uniform.

b. Place the three shifting keys into the clutch hub key slots and onto the shifting springs.

NOTE: The shifting keys for each hub are of different sizes. The keys with the shorter straddle length should be installed on the third and fourth gear synchronizer unit.

c. Slide the hub sleeve onto the clutch hub. The clutch hubs and the hub sleeves of the gear are matched, and should be kept together as an assembly for smooth operation.

NOTE: The hubs fit into the clutch sleeves directionally, that is, they must fit into the clutch sleeves facing a certain way. Check the illustration to make sure you fit them correctly.

2. Install the second gear and its synchronizer ring on the output shaft. Install the first and second gear clutch hub behind second gear. Be sure to align the grooves in the synchronizer ring with the shift keys in the clutch hub. Place the small steel lockball in its slot on the output shaft.

3. Oil and place the roller bearings on the bushing. Slide the bushing into the first speed gear with the collared end of the bushing butting the flat side of the gear. Fit the synchronizer ring on the other side of the gear and insert the gear on the output shaft. Take care to fit the notch in the bushing over the steel lockball and align the notches in the synchronizer ring with those in the clutch hub.

4. Press the bearing retainer assembly on the output shaft. Check the gears for smooth rotation. Select a snap-ring that will give 0–0.006 in. clearance on the output shaft and install. Five different snap-ring thicknesses are available.

5. Check the second and first gear thrust clearances. The allowable limits are 0.004–0.010 in.

6. Install first speedometer snap-ring and Woodruff key on the output shaft and install speedometer gear and second snap-ring.

7. Oil and install the third speed gear on the front of the output shaft. Fit its synchronizer ring and install the clutch hub, making sure to align the grooves in the synchronizer with the keys in the clutch hub.

8. Select a snap-ring that will give an allowable thrust clearance of 0–0.006 in. between the hub end and the snap-ring. Fit the snap-ring.

9. Measure the thrust clearance of the third speed gear. Allowable limit for clearance is 0.004–0.010 in.

10. Assemble the countergear by placing the spacers and greased roller bearings in both ends and fitting a tube or rod that is the exact length of the countergear with the thrust washers on its ends and fit it into the countergear.

11. Referring to the thrust measurement on the countergear when disassembling, select thrust washers that give an allowable clearance of 0.004–0.010 in. Adjust clearance by replacing the rear thrust washer.

12. Install the thrust washers on the ends of the countergear. Rear thrust washers are identified by Number 1, 2, 3 or 4 stamped on their outside face. Be sure to install the washers with their protruding groove facing out.

13. Place the countergear assembly into the case with the notches in the thrust washers facing up and align the notches with the case grooves.

14. Allow the countergear to drop down into the case. Do not replace the countergear shaft at this point!

15. Install the input shaft in the same manner of removal, aligning one of the flat sides of the clutch hub with the large countershaft gear and, using a brass drift, drive the input shaft bearing into the case, tapping it around the outer ball race.

16. Fit the synchronizer ring on the input shaft. Shift the clutch hub on the end of the output shaft forward.

17. Fit the output shaft into the case, making sure the slotted spring pin in the bearing retainer aligns with its groove in the case, and align the grooves in the synchronizer ring with the clutch hub keys.

18. Oil the countershaft. Raise the countergear assembly so that it aligns with the case holes and, making sure the thrust washers are in place, insert the countergear shaft from the rear of the case with the Woodruff key slot at the rear. The countergear shaft will push the tube out of the case. Install the Woodruff key and fit it into its slot in the case.

19. Install the reverse idler gear with its toothed end facing forward. Slide the reverse idler gear shaft in with its Woodruff key slot end facing the rear. Install the Woodruff key and tap the shaft in so that the key is in its seat in the case.

20. Install the front bearing retainer. Be sure to align the oil seal slot in the retainer with the oil hole in the case. Coat the bolt threads with sealer and tighten to 2.9–5.1 ft. lbs. (1977–78); 5–6 ft. lbs. (1979 and later).

21. Install the clutch bell housing. Coat the bolt threads with sealer and tighten to 37–50 ft. lbs.

22. Install clutch release fork assembly.

23. Apply grease to the extension housing rear oil seal and install the extension housing.

NOTE: Be careful not to damage the oil seal on the output shaft when assembling.

24. Coat the extension housing bolts with sealer and tighten to 22–32 ft. lbs.

25. Oil the speedometer gear assembly and fasten to the extension housing.

26. To assemble the transmission case cover, install the shift arm pivot onto the reverse shift arm, and insert into the case.

27. Assemble the shift and selector lever shaft together with the shift and selector lever, and secure the bolt with a wire.

28. Insert the reverse shift fork shaft compression spring and lockball into the case, and insert the fork shaft from the rear side, then secure the shift head with a new slotted spring pin.

29. Align the fork shaft positioning groove with the shift interlock pin groove.

30. Align the reverse shift arm knob with the reverse shift fork shaft, and install the O-ring, washer and nut onto the shift arm pivot. Insert the shift interlock pin into the rear side of the case cover and the compression spring and lockball into the front side, and assemble the shift fork together with

the first and second shift fork shaft. Secure the shift fork with a new slotted spring pin.

31. Align the shift fork shaft positioning groove with the shift interlock pin groove. Insert the two shift interlock pins into the front side of the case cover.

32. Insert the compression spring and the lockball, and assemble the shift fork together with the third and fourth shift fork shaft, then secure the shift fork with a new slotted spring pin.

33. Install the lockball, compression spring and reverse restricting ball holder.

34. Check all shift forks for smooth movement. Tighten to 27–32 ft. lbs.

35. Install the back-up light switch on the case cover.

36. Align each shift fork and the reverse shift arm with the respective gears, and install the transmission case cover, within the gasket, onto the transmission. Torque the case cover retaining bolts to 11–16 ft. lbs.

37. To adjust the shift arm pivot, loosen the locknut on the shift arm pivot, turn the shift arm pivot clockwise until friction is felt, when the reverse idler gear contacts with the first gear and/or the countergear.

38. Next from this position, turn the shift arm pivot counterclockwise approximately 90 degrees. Tighten the pivot locknut securely.

39. With the input shaft rotating, make sure that there is no noise and that the reverse idler gear does not contact other gears in the transmission.

40. If no friction is felt when the shift arm pivot is turned clockwise, set the pivot line mark at 60 degrees rearward from its horizontal position to the case cover surface.

41. If necessary, replace the oil seal in the extension housing after assembling the transmission using the oil seal puller, and pull out the oil seal together with the dust seal.

Toyota
5–Speed Transmission

Disassembly

1. Drain the oil.
2. Remove the clutch housing, with the release fork, bearing and hub still attached.
3. Remove the back-up light switch.
4. Remove the gearshift lever retainer.
5. Rotate the shift rod housing counterclockwise (viewed from behind) and then disconnect the rod from the shift fork shafts.
6. Unbolt and remove the extension housing.
7. Drive out the slotted pin and separate the shift rod, housing and spring.
8. Remove the front bearing retainer.
9. Take off both of the front countershaft covers, and the spacer.
10. Remove the snap-rings from the input and countershaft bearings.
11. Remove the intermediate plate.
12. When removing the intermediate

plate, leave all the gears and other parts attached.

13. Remove the speedometer driven gear.

NOTE: There are two reverse restrictor pins. The pins are located underneath plugs on the extension housing.

14. Remove the straight screw plugs from the shift forks and withdraw the springs.

15. Drive the slotted spring pins out of each shift fork.

16. Slide the gear shift fork shafts back and remove the forks.

17. Remove the speedometer drive gear snap-ring and remove the drive gear.

18. Remove the output shaft bearing.

19. Remove the countershaft bearing.

20. Remove the fifth and reverse gears from the countershaft.

21. Remove the snap-ring, fifth gear, its synchronizer ring, needle roller bearing, and fifth gear bearing inner race from the output shaft.

22. Remove the reverse gear and clutch hub from the output shaft.

23. Loosen the bolt and remove the reverse idler gear stop from the rear cover. Withdraw the reverse idler shaft from the rear; remove the reverse idler gear and spacer.

24. Remove the output shaft rear bearing retainer. Remove the rear bearing snap-ring.

25. Push the countergear bearing outer race rearward, and remove the bearing. Separate the countergear from the intermediate plate.

26. Separate the input shaft and synchronizer ring from the output shaft.

27. Remove the output shaft from the intermediate plate.

28. Remove the hub and synchronizer ring, followed by third gear.

29. Press off the rear bearing.

30. Remove the following items from the output shaft, in the order listed:

  a. First gear
  b. Roller bearing with inner race
  c. Synchronizer ring
  d. Reverse gear
  e. Clutch hub
  f. Second gear
  g. Synchronizer ring

Assembly

1. Install the sleeve over the third gear synchronizer hub. Insert the three shift keys into the hub and sleeve keyways. Install the hub two springs.

2. Assemble the synchronizer ring to third gear, and fit both of them on the output shaft.

3. Insert the third/fourth synchronizer hub on the output shaft, until it contacts the shoulder of the shaft.

4. Select a snap-ring to provide 0.002 in. axial play for the synchronizer hub and fit it onto the shaft. Snap-rings are available in a range of sizes.

5. Measure third gear thrust clearance with a feeler gauge. The clearance should

be 0.004–0.010 in. Replace third gear if the clearance exceeds the limit of 0.010 in.

6. Install the synchronizer ring for second gear to the gear and install the assembly on the output shaft.

7. Install the reverse gear over its clutch hub.

8. Install the reverse gear and hub on the output shaft so that they contact the shoulder.

9. Measure second gear thrust clearance; it should be between 0.004–0.010 in. Replace the gear if the clearance is more than 0.010 in.

10. Coat the locking ball with grease. Insert it, and the roller bearing inner race, on the output shaft.

11. Assemble first gear with its synchronizer ring, bearing and bearing inner race. Install them on the output shaft, so that the end of the inner race contacts the clutch hub and the groove on the inner race aligns with the locking ball.

12. Press the rear bearing onto the output shaft.

13. Measure first gear thrust clearance.

NOTE: The thrust clearance of all gears in the 5-speed transmission should be between 0.006–0.010 in.; the thrust clearance limit for all gears is 0.012 in.

14. Use a press to insert the straight pin into the intermediate plate, until it protrudes ¼–⁵⁄₁₆ in. from the cover front side.

15. Install the output shaft on the intermediate plate.

16. Coat the roller bearing with grease and install it over the input shaft.

17. Apply gear oil to the front synchronizer ring on the output shaft.

18. Assemble the output shaft and the input shaft.

19. Install the countergear on the intermediate plate.

20. Install the cylindrical roller bearing into the intermediate plate, and then install the spacer.

21. Assemble the output shaft and countergear, then fit them through the holes in the intermediate plate. Push them in until the snap-ring sticks out beyond the intermediate plate. Install the snap-ring and then push the shafts back until the snap-ring is flush with the intermediate plate surface.

22. Install the shaft through the reverse idler gear. Insert the end of the shaft into the end of the intermediate plate.

23. Install the spacer on the idler shaft and secure it with a snap-ring.

24. Lock the reverse idler shaft on the intermediate plate with its stop. Check the reverse idler gear thrust clearance, it should be 0.006–0.010 in.

25. Install the reverse clutch hub on the reverse gear.

26. Install the three shift keys into the hub keyways and secure them with the two springs and a snap-ring.

27. Slide the reverse gear hub over the output shaft until it registers against the inner race of the intermediate plate bearing.

28. Insert the inner race lockball into the output shaft bore, after greasing it so that it can't fall out.

29. Assemble fifth gear, its synchronizer ring, needle roller bearing, and race. Slide the assembly onto the output shaft until the inner bear face rests against the reverse clutch hub. Be sure that the inner race groove is aligned with the lockball.

30. Secure fifth gear with a snap-ring.

31. Measure fifth gear thrust clearance; it should be 0.004 to 0.010 in. The thrust clearance limit is 0.012 in.

32. Install the countershaft reverse gear so that it just rests against the bearing inner race. Install the countershaft fifth gear and then install the countershaft bearing with a brass drift.

33. Install a snap-ring on the countershaft; select a snap-ring from one of the four available sizes.

34. Install a snap-ring on the output shaft, and drive its bearing into place with a brass drift. Coat the bearing with grease first.

35. Install the spacer, ball, and speedometer drive gear on the output shaft.

36. Install the three shift forks in their hub sleeve grooves. Install the first and third shift fork shafts and secure them with their interlock pins. Install the second shift fork shaft next.

NOTE: Place each shift fork shaft in Neutral during assembly.

37. Secure the shift fork shafts to the end cover by inserting the lockballs into their bores, followed by the lockball springs.

38. Use a new gasket between the transmission case and the intermediate plate. Slide the case into place.

39. Fit snap-rings on the input shaft and countershaft front bearings.

40. Install the shift lever housing on the end of the shifter shaft. Slide the shifter shaft into the extension housing and secure it with a slotted spring pin.

41. Install a new gasket and slide the extension housing into place, until there is about an inch of clearance between it and the intermediate plate.

42. Rotate the shift lever housing clockwise (as viewed from the rear) to engage the shifter shaft with the selector lever and the shift fork shaft.

43. Slide the extension housing the rest of the way.

44. Install the spacer and then the countershaft end covers.

45. Align the front bearing retainer gasket with the oil holes. Install the bearing retainer over the gasket.

46. Bolt the clutch housing onto the front of the transmission case.

47. Fit the restrictor pins and springs into their extension housing bores.

48. Install the shift lever retainer over the oil baffle on the extension housing.

49. Install the shift lever conical spring, large side down, and install the ball seat in the shift lever retainer.

50. Attach the shift lever retainer to the extension housing.

51. Install the speedometer driven gear.

52. Install the back-up light switch.

53. Check to see that the input shaft has no more than 0.020 in. end-play. Put the transmission in Neutral and see if the output shaft can be rotated freely by hand.

Toyota Land Cruiser 3–Speed Transmission

Disassembly

1. Remove the transfer case shift lever guide, cotter pin, and lockbolt. Remove the shift lever and linkage; do not lose the link lever shoe.

2. Remove the back-up light switch and gasket from the transmission cover.

3. Remove the transfer case cover, complete with gasket. Remove the power take-off cover and gasket.

4. Straighten out the tabs on the input shaft nut lockwasher and remove the nut. Slide the spacer off.

NOTE: Lock the power take-off drive gear with a wooden block or brass drift to keep the shaft from turning while the nut is being removed.

5. Loosen the five bolts which secure the transfer case to the transmission case and separate the cases with a puller. Hold the power take-off drive gear, spacer, and input gear, so that they don't drop out.

6. Unfasten the bolt and remove the gear selector outer lever.

7. Unfasten the bolts and remove the transmission case cover, complete with gasket.

8. Loosen the bolts and remove the front bearing retainer, with gasket, from the transmission case.

9. Drive the shift fork shaft out toward the front of the case with a hammer and a brass drift. Use care not to lose the fork balls, springs and pin.

10. Withdraw the first/reverse shift fork and the second/third shift fork from the transmission case. Remove the lockballs and springs.

11. Drive the countershaft rearward with a brass drift. Remove the countershaft Woodruff key.

NOTE: The countergear should remain in the case.

12. Remove the input shaft and bearing with a puller. Install the puller on the front of the input shaft.

13. Use a hammer and a brass drift to drive the output shaft rearward until the output shaft bearing clears the case. Do not pound on the output shaft; tap it lightly.

14. Separate the bearing from the output shaft with a puller.

15. Remove the output shaft and the related components from the transmission case.

16. Use a snap-ring expander to remove

1. Case cover
2. Front bearing retainer
3. Shift forks & shaft
4. Countershaft & key
5. Input shaft assy. & synchronizer ring
6. Bearing
7. Output shaft assy.
8. Reverse idler gear assy.
9. Countergear assy.

Exploded view of model J-30

the snap-ring from the front of the output shaft. Slide the synchronizer clutch hub, sleeve, synchronizer ring, second gear, and the first/reverse gearset off of the shaft.

17. Remove the countershaft drive gear, spacer, roller bearing, and washers. Note the placement of the gear thrust washers. Use care not to lose the rollers.

18. Drive the reverse idler gear shaft rearward and remove its Woodruff key.

19. Remove the reverse idler gear, rollers and thrust washers from the case.

GEAR BACKLASH

Input shaft gear-to-countershaft drive gear—0.004 in.
Second-to-countergear—0.004 in.
First/reverse gear-to-countergear—0.008 in.
Countergear-to-reverse idler gear—0.008 in.
Reverse gear-to-reverse idler gear—0.008 in.
Synchronizer ring-to-gear—0.039 in.

Assembly

NOTE: Use new gaskets, oil seals, and dust seals. Coat the gaskets with sealer.

1. Apply a light coating of gear oil to all components, prior to assembly.

2. Grease the bore of the reverse idler gear. Insert the bearing rollers and washer in the bore.

3. Install the reverse idler gear and the two thrust washers into the case. Drive the reverse idler gear shaft through the case, by gently tapping it into place from behind. Lock the shaft into place with the Woodruff key.

4. Grease the bore of the countershaft drive gear and fit its spacer. Install the rollers in the bore and hold them in place with a heavy coating of grease. Install the washers in the bore.

5. Place the countershaft drive gear, thrust washer, and side thrust washers in the case.

6. If the bearing was removed from the input shaft, press it into place on the shaft.

7. Select a snap-ring that will give the input shaft minimum end-play, and install it on the shaft.

8. Grease bore of the input shaft, install the rollers, and then fit the snap-ring.

9. Carefully drive the input shaft assembly and bearing into the transmission case.

10. Lift the countershaft drive gear up and install the countershaft from the rear of the case. Secure the countershaft with its Woodruff key.

11. Use a feeler gauge to measure the countershaft thrust clearance; it should be 0.002–0.008 in. Select a countergear side thrust washer of the proper size to obtain the specified thrust clearance.

12. Install the two synchronizer shifting key springs into the clutch hub, so that the open ends are 120° apart. Place the three shifting keys into the clutch hub key slots.

13. Slide the clutch hub sleeve into the clutch hub.

14. Fit second gear, its synchronizer ring, and the synchronizer assembly on the output shaft. Check second gear thrust clearance with a feeler gauge. It should be 0.003–0.009 in.

15. Working from the rear, slide the first/reverse gearset on the output shaft.

16. Install the output shaft assembly in the transmission case. Using a suitable brass drift, install the rear bearing over the output shaft and into the case.

17. Install both shift forks and retain them with their balls and lockpins.

18. Depress the shift fork lockballs with a screwdriver, then drive the shift fork shaft through the case, and into shift forks.

19. Install a new O-ring on the shift fork shaft and lock it in place with its pin.

20. Coat the front bearing retainer with liquid sealer and install the bearing retainer over it.

21. Install a suitable size pipe over the transmission output shaft. Place the transfer case input gear, power take-off drive gear, and the spacers over the pipe, which should be projecting through the transfer case.

22. Coat a new gasket with liquid sealer and install.

23. Install the transfer case on the transmission case. Be sure to install the two short bolts from the *inside* of the transfer case.

24. Install the bearing over the end of the transmission output shaft and into the transfer case with a drift.

25. Install the transfer case input shaft spacer.

26. Install the transfer case cover over its gasket.

27. Coat the gasket with liquid sealer and install the power take-off cover.

28. Install the back-up light switch and gasket.

29. Install the transfer front drive fork and its gasket on the transfer case extension housing.

4-Speed Transmission

Disassembly

1. Remove the transfer case shift lever guide, cotter pin, and lockbolt. Remove the shift lever and linkage, do not lose the link lever shoe.

2. Remove the back-up light switch and gasket from the transmission cover.

3. Remove the transfer case cover, complete with gasket. Remove the power take-off cover and gasket.

4. Straighten out the tabs on the input shaft nut lockwasher and remove the nut. Slide the spacer off.

NOTE: Lock the power take-off drive gear with a wooden block or brass drift to keep the shaft from turning while the nut is being removed.

5. Loosen the five bolts which secure the transfer case to the transmission case and separate the cases with a puller. Hold the power take-off drive gear, spacer, and input gear, so that they don't drop out.

6. Remove the transfer case input shaft gear stop from the transmission rear bearing retainer.

7. Remove the rear bearing retainer and gasket.

8. Remove the front bearing retainer and gasket.

9. Remove the input shaft and front bearing from the case with a puller.

NOTE: Prior to removing the input shaft, align the slot in the input shaft with the countershaft drive gear.

10. Remove the synchronizer ring.

11. Use an expander to remove the snapping on the output shaft rear bearing. Remove the bearing with a puller.

12. Withdraw the output shaft and gearset from the transmission case.

13. Straighten out the tabs on the countershaft front bearing retainer and remove the bolts; then remove the retainer and lockwasher.

14. Remove the front countershaft bearing. Remove the bearing spacer. Remove the rear countershaft bearing.

15. Remove the countershaft.

16. Remove the reverse shift arm pivot and shift arm.

17. Install a puller on the reverse idler shaft, and pull the gear shaft and key from the transmission case. Remove the reverse idler gear from the case.

18. Slide the first gear and its thrust washer off the back end of the output shaft.

19. Remove the snap-ring from the front of the output shaft; then remove the clutch hub, sleeve, synchronizer ring, and third gear from the shaft.

20. Remove the snap-ring and slide second gear and thrust washer off the shaft.

21. Slide the reverse gear synchronizer ring off the output shaft.

22. Press the countershaft drive gear off of the countershaft. Remove the Woodruff key and spacer from the shaft.

23. Repeat Step 22 for the third gear and Woodruff key.

24. Move the shift forks into neutral. Drive the slotted spring pin out of the third/fourth shift fork with a long drift.

25. Without using excessive force, drive the third/fourth shift fork shaft and plug forward with a brass drift. Remove the shift fork, lockball, and spring.

26. Drive the spring pins out of the reverse shift fork and boss with a long pin punch.

27. Remove the plug from the rear of the transmission case. Drive the first/second shift fork shaft forward with a brass drift. Remove the shift fork, boss, lockball, and spring.

28. Drive the spring pins out of the reverse shift fork and boss. Loosen and remove the tapered screw plugs from the transmission cover; then push the interlock rollers out with a long drift.

29. Remove the cotter pin, spring, and lockball from the shift fork boss.

30. Remove the C-washer, then withdraw the reverse return spring and plunger from the boss.

GEAR BACKLASH

Input gear-to-countershaft drivegear—0.004 in.
Third gear-to-countershaft gear—0.004 in.
Second gear-to-countershaft gear—0.004 in.
First gear-to-countershaft gear—0.004 in.
Reverse gear-to-reverse idler gear—0.005 in.

Assembly

1. Apply a light coating of gear oil to all components, prior to assembly.

2. Place the reverse idler gear in the case with its fork groove facing forward.

3. Align the Woodruff key, groove, and slot. Carefully drive the reverse idler shaft through the holes in the case, and into the gear.

NOTE: If you install new bushings in the idler gear, be sure that their openings are at least 90° apart.

4. Adjust the reverse idler gear position by trunging the shaft arm pivot to obtain a distance of 4.49 in. between the outer rear of the transmission case and the reverse idler gear. Move the gear to neutral, the distance between the front end of the gear and outer rear of the transmission case should now be 2.71 in. Adjust by rotating the shift arm pivot.

5. Install the Woodruff key into the groove of the countershaft and align its keyway with the countershaft third gear. Place the gear on the shaft with the long hub facing forward.

6. Slide the spacer on the countershaft and press its drivegear on, in a similar manner to third gear (Step 5), with its long hub facing rearward.

7. Place the countershaft assembly into the transmission case and install the countershaft rear bearing with a press. Install the snap-ring over the end of the countershaft.

8. Install the front bearing spacer, protruded end forward, on the countershaft. Press the front bearing on, until its snapring registers firmly against the transmission case.

─── **CAUTION** ───
Apply pressure to the outer bearing race only, to prevent damage to the bearing.

9. Place the bearing retainer and lockwasher on the front of the countershaft.

10. Slide second gear on the output shaft so that its synchronizer outer ring faces rearward. Select a snap-ring so that second gear has a thrust clearance of 0.004–0.012 in.

11. Slide third gear on the output shaft, so that its synchronizer cone faces forward.

12. Install the two synchronizer shifting key springs into the clutch hub, so that the open ends are 120° apart. Place the three shifting keys into the clutch hub key slots.

13. Slide the clutch hub sleeve into the clutch hub.

14. Install the synchronizer ring and slide the synchronizer assembly over the output shaft. The grooves should face the rear.

15. Select a snap-ring to provide 0.008 in. thrust clearance for the clutch hub.

16. Slide the reverse gear synchronizer ring over the output shaft. Check the ring for smooth movement.

17. Slide first gear on the output shaft.

18. Place the output shaft assembly in the transmission case.

19. Fit the first gear thrust washer on the output shaft. Align the slot in the thrust washer with the output shaft pin.

20. Install the output shaft rear bearing with a press. Be sure to apply pressure on the bearing *outer* race only. Install the rear bearing and its gasket.

21. Press-fit the bearing on the input shaft. Grease the bearing rollers and install all 18 in the input shaft.

22. Place the input shaft in the transmission case, so that the synchronizer ring keyways align with the shift keys. Install the output shaft bearing spacer in the output shaft.

─── **CAUTION** ───
Be sure the bearing rollers or the spacer do not fall into the transmission case during installation.

23. Install the input shaft bearing retainer and gasket.

NOTE: Make sure that all shift fork shafts are in neutral during the shift fork shaft assembly steps, below.

24. Install the spring and return plunger in the reverse shift boss. Secure them with the C-washer. Install the ball and spring then secure them with a cotter pin.

25. Place the reverse shift fork and boss in the transmission cover, its bore, shift fork and into its boss, while depressing the lockball with a screwdriver.

26. Slide the reverse shift fork shaft through the front of the cover. Install the fork lock-spring and ball in the cover.

27. Align the holes and drive the slotted spring pin through the reverse shift fork and boss to secure them to the shaft.

28. Coat the roller with grease and install it into the interlock hole in the cover.

29. Place the first/second shift boss and fork into the cover. Install the first/second shift fork shaft and spacer from the front of the cover, after fitting its pin, and while depressing the lockball with a screwdriver.

30. Secure the first/second shift fork and boss with their slotted spring pins. Install another roller into the hole in the cover.

31. Install the third/fourth shift fork lock-spring and ball in the shift fork. Install the shift fork and shaft in the cover and secure them with a slotted spring pin.

32. Check the shift fork assembly for smooth operation. Install the plugs.

33. Install a suitable size pipe over the transmission output shaft. Place the transfer case input gear, power take-off drive gear,

and the spacers over the pipe, which should be projecting through the transfer case.

34. Coat a new gasket with liquid sealer and install.

35. Install the transfer case on the transmission case. Be sure to install the two short bolts from the *inside* of the transfer case.

36. Remove the pipe from the output shaft and transfer case.

37. Install the bearing over the end of the transmission output shaft and into the transfer case with a drift.

38. Install the transfer case input shaft spacer.

39. Install the transfer case cover over its gasket.

40. Coat the gasket with liquid sealer and install the power take-off cover.

41. Install the back-up light switch and gasket.

42. Install the transfer front drive fork and its gasket on the transfer case extension housing.

Tremec T-150
3–Speed
Transmission (77 mm)

The Tremec T-150 (77 mm) transmission is used in varied vehicle applications, with or without transfer cases. The gear selection is controlled by either a top shift housing or by a remote control shift lever assembly. Although some of the gears and case applications are not interchangeable, the gear arrangement is basically the same.

Disassembly

1. Remove the bolts securing the transfer case to the transmission. Remove the transfer case.

2. Remove the transfer case drive gear locknut, flat washer, and drive gear. Remove the large fiber washer from the rear bearing adapter. Move the second-third clutch sleeve forward and the first-reverse sleeve to the rear before removing the locknut.

3. Remove the transmission oil plug and drive the countershaft out of the case with a suitable size drift. Do not lose the countershaft access plug when removing the countershaft. With the countershaft removed the countershaft gear will lie at the bottom of the case, leave it there until the mainshaft is removed.

4. Punch alignment marks in the front bearing cap and the transmission case for assembly reference.

5. Remove the front bearing cap and gasket.

6. Remove the large lock ring from the front bearing.

7. Remove the clutch shaft, front bearing, and the second-third synchronizer assembly. A special tool is required for this operation.

1. Mainshaft retaining snap-ring
2. Synchronizer blocking rings (3)
3. Second-third synchronizer sleeve
4. Second-third synchronizer insert spring (2)
5. Second-third hub
6. Second-third synchronizer insert (3)
7. Second gear
8. First gear retaining snap-ring
9. First gear tabbed thrust washer
10. First gear
11. First-reverse synchronizer insert spring
12. First-reverse sleeve
13. First-reverse hub retaining snap-ring
14. First-reverse synchronizer insert (3)
15. First-reverse hub
16. Countershaft access plug
17. Mainshaft
18. Mainshaft spacer
19. Rear bearing adapter lock ring
20. Rear bearing and adapter assembly
21. Fiber washer
22. Flat washer
23. Locknut
24. Roll pin
25. Reverse idler gear shaft
26. Thrust washer
27. Bushing (part of idler and gear)
28. Reverse idler gear
29. Transmission case
30. Thrust washer (2)
31. Bearing retainer (2)
32. Countershaft needle bearings (50)
33. Countershaft gear
34. Front bearing cap
35. Bolt (4)
36. Front bearing cap oil seal
37. Gasket
38. Front bearing retainer snap-ring
39. Front bearing lockring
40. Front bearing
41. Clutch shaft
42. Mainshaft pilot roller bearings
43. Roll pin
44. Countershaft

Warner T-150

8. Remove the rear bearing and adapter assembly with a brass drift and hammer. Drive the adapter out the rear of the case with light blows from the hammer.

9. Remove the mainshaft assembly. Tilt the spline end of the shaft downward and lift the front end up and out of the case.

10. Remove the countershaft tool and arbor as an assembly. Remove the countershaft thrust washers, countershaft roll pin, and any pilot roller bearings that may have fallen into the case.

11. Remove the reverse idler shaft. Insert a brass drift through the clutch shaft bore in the front of the case and tap the shaft until the end with the roll pin clears the counter bore in the rear of the case. Remove the shaft.

12. Remove the reverse idler gear and thrust washers from the case.

13. Remove the retaining snap-ring from the front of the mainshaft. Remove the second-third synchronizer assembly and second gear. Mark the hub and sleeve for reference during assembly.

NOTE: Observe the position of the insert springs and the inserts during removal for correct assembly.

14. Remove the insert springs from the second-third synchronizer, remove the three inserts, and separate the sleeve from the synchronizer hub retaining snap-ring.

15. Remove the snap-ring and the tabbed thrust washer from the mainshaft and remove the first gear blocking ring.

16. Remove the first-reverse synchronizer hub snap-ring.

NOTE: Observe the position of the in-

sert springs and the inserts during removal for correct assembly.

17. Remove the first-reverse sleeve, insert spring and the three insert from the hub. Remove the spacer from the rear of the mainshaft.

CAUTION

Do not attempt to remove the press fit hub by hammering. Hammer blows will damage the hub and mainshaft.

---

18. Remove the front bearing retaining snap-ring and any remaining roller bearings from the clutch shaft.
19. Press the front bearing off the clutch shaft with an arbor press.

CAUTION

Do not attempt to remove the bearing by hammering. Hammer blows will damage the bearing and the clutch shaft.

---

20. Clamp the rear bearing adapter in a soft-jawed vise. Do not over-tighten.
21. Remove the rear bearing retaining snap-ring. Remove the bearing adapter from the vise.
22. Press the rear bearing out of the adapter with an arbor press.

Cleaning and Inspection

1. Thoroughly wash all parts in clean solvent and dry with compressed air.

NOTE: Do not dry the bearings with compressed air, use a clean shop cloth.

2. Clean the needle and clutch shaft bearings by placing them in a shallow parts cleaning tray and covering them with solvent. Allow the bearings to air dry on a clean shop cloth.
3. Check the case for the following:
   a. Cracks in the bores, bosses, or bolt holes.
   b. Stripped threads in bolt holes.
   c. Nicks, burrs, rough surfaces in the shaft bores or on the gasket surfaces.
4. Check the gear and synchronizer assemblies for the following:
   a. Broken, chipped, or worn gear teeth.
   b. Damaged splines on the synchronizer hubs or sleeves.
   c. Bent or damaged inserts.
   d. Damaged needle bearings or bearing bores in the countershaft gear.
   e. Broken or worn teeth or excessive wear of the blocking rings.
   f. Wear of galling of the countershaft, clutch shaft, or reverse idler shaft.
   g. Worn thrust washers.
   h. Nicked, broken, or worn mainshaft or clutch shaft splines.
   i. Bent, distorted, or weak snap-rings.
   j. Worn bushings in the reverse idler gear. Replace the gear if the bushings are worn.
   k. Rough, galled, or broken front or rear bearings.

Assembly

1. Lubricate the reverse idler shaft bore and bushings with transmission oil.
2. Coat the transmission case reverse idler gear thrust washer surfaces with petroleum jelly and install the thrust washers in the case.

NOTE: Make sure the locating tangs on the thrust washers are aligned in the slots in the case.

3. Install the reverse idler gear. Align the gear bore, thrust washers, and case bore. Install the reverse idler shaft from the rear of the transmission case. Be sure to align and seat the roll pin in the shaft into the counter bore in the rear of the case.
4. Measure the reverse idler gear end-play by inserting a feeler gauge between the thrust washer and the gear. End-play should be 0.004–0.018 inch. If end play exceeds 0.018 inch, remove the reverse idler gear and replace the thrust washers.
5. Coat the needle bearing bores in the countershaft gear with petroleum jelly. Insert the arbor tool in the bore of the gear and install the (25) needle bearings and the retainer washers at each end of the countershaft gear.
6. Coat the countershaft gear thrust washer surface with petroleum jelly and position the thrust washers in the case.

NOTE: Make sure the locating tangs on the thrust washers are aligned in the slots in the case.

7. Insert the countershaft into the bore at the rear of the case just far enough to hold the thrust washer in place.
8. Install the countershaft gear in the case. Do not install the roll pin at this time. Align the gear bore, thrust washers, the bores in the case, and install the countershaft.

NOTE: Do not remove the arbor tool completely.

9. Measure the countershaft gear end-play by inserting a feeler gauge between the washer and the countershaft gear. End-play should be 0.004–0.018 inch. If the end-play exceeds 0.018 inch, remove the gear and replace the thrust washer.
10. When the correct countershaft gear end-play has been obtained, install the countershaft arbor and remove the countershaft. Allow the countershaft gear to remain at the bottom of the case, leave the countershaft in the case enough to hold the thrust washer in place.
11. Coat the splines and machined surfaces on the mainshaft with transmission oil. Install the first-reverse synchronizer on the output shaft splines by hand. The end of the hub with the slots should face the front of the shaft. Use an arbor press to complete the hub installation. Install the retaining snap-ring in the groove farthest to the rear.

CAUTION

Do not attempt to drive the hub on the shaft with a hammer.

---

12. Coat the splines of the first-reverse hub with transmission oil and install the first reverse sleeve and gear halfway onto the hub, with the gear end of the sleeve facing the rear of the shaft. Align the marks made during disassembly.
13. Install the insert spring in the first-reverse hub. Make sure the spring bottoms in the hub and covers all three insert slots. Position the three "T" shaped inserts in the hub with the small ends in the hub slots and the large ends inside the hub. Push the inserts fully into the hub so they seat on the insert spring, slide the first-reverse sleeve and gear over the inserts until the inserts engage in the sleeve.
14. Coat the bore and the blocking ring surface of first gear with transmission oil and place blocking ring on the tapered surface of the gear.
15. Install the first gear on the output shaft. Rotate the gear until the notches in the blocking ring engage the inserts in the first-reverse synchronizer assembly. Install the tanged thrust washer, sharp end facing out, and retaining snap-ring on the mainshaft.
16. Coat the bore and blocking ring surface of the second gear with transmission oil. Place the second gear blocking ring on the tapered surface of second gear.
17. Install the second gear on the output shaft with the tapered surface of the gear facing the front of the mainshaft.
18. Install one insert spring into the second-third synchronizer hub. Be sure that the spring covers all three insert slots in the hub. Align the second-third sleeve with the hub using the marks made during disassembly. Start the sleeve onto the hub.
19. Place the three inserts into the hub slots and on top of the insert spring. Push the sleeve fully onto the hub to engage the inserts in the sleeve. Install the remaining insert spring in the exact position as the first spring. The ends of both springs must cover the same slot in the hub and not be staggered.

NOTE: The inserts have a small lip on each end. When they are correctly installed, this lip will fit over the insert spring.

20. Install the second-third synchronizer assembly on the mainshaft. Rotate the second gear until the notches in the blocking ring engage the inserts in the second-third synchronizer assembly.
21. Install the retaining snap-ring on the mainshaft and measure the end-play between the snap-ring and the second-third synchronizer hub. The end-play should be 0.040–0.014 inch. If the end-play exceeds the limit, replace the thrust washer and all the snap-rings on the mainshaft assembly. Install the spacer on the rear of the mainshaft.
22. Install the mainshaft assembly in the case. Be sure that the first-reverse sleeve

and gear is in the neutral (centered) position.

23. Press the rear bearing into the rear bearing adapter with an arbor press. Install the rear bearing retaining ring and the bearing adapter lockring.

24. Support the mainshaft assembly and install the rear bearing and adapter assembly in the case. Use a soft faced hammer to seat the adapter in the case.

25. Install the large fiber washer in the rear bearing adapter. Install the transfer drive gear, flat washer, and locknut. Tighten the locknut to 150 ft. lbs. torque.

26. Press the front bearing onto the clutch shaft. Install the bearing retaining snap-ring on the clutch shaft and the lockring into its groove.

27. Coat the bore of the clutch shaft assembly with petroleum jelly and install the (15) roller bearings in the clutch shaft bore.

— CAUTION —

Do not use chassis grease or a similar heavy grease in the clutch shaft bore. Heavy grease will plug the lubricant holes in the shaft and prevent proper lubrication of the roller bearings.

28. Coat the blocking ring surface of the clutch shaft with transmission oil. Position the blocking ring on the clutch shaft.

29. Support the mainshaft assembly and insert the clutch shaft through the front bearing bore in the case. Seat the mainshaft pilot in the clutch shaft roller bearings. Tap the bearings into place with a soft faced hammer.

30. Apply a thin film of sealer to the front bearing cap gasket and position the gasket on the case. Be sure the cutout in the gasket is aligned with the oil return hole in the case.

31. Remove the front bearing cap oil seal with a suitable tool. Install a new seal with a suitable driver.

32. Install the front bearing cap and tighten the bolts to 33 ft. lbs. Be sure that the marks on the cap and the transmission case are aligned and the oil return slot in the cap lines up with the oil return hole in the case.

33. Make a wire loop about 18–20 inches long and pass the wire under the countershaft gear assembly. The wire loop should raise and support the countershaft gear assembly when it is pulled upward.

34. Raise the countershaft gear with the wire. Align the bore in the countershaft gear with the front thrust washer and the countershaft. Start the countershaft into the gear with a soft faced hammer.

35. Align the roll pin hole in the countershaft with the roll pin holes in the case and complete the installation of the countershaft. Install the countershaft access plug in the rear of the case and seat with a soft faced hammer.

36. Install the countershaft roll pin in the case. Use a magnet or needle nose pliers to insert and start the pin in the case. Use

a ½ inch punch to seat the pin. Install the transmission filler plug.

37. Shift the synchronizer sleeves through all gear ranges and check their operation. If the clutch shaft and mainshaft appear to bind in the neutral position, check for blocking rings sticking on the first or second gear tapers.

38. Install the transfer case on the transmission. Tighten the attaching bolts to 30 ft. lbs.

TORQUE SPECIFICATIONS
Tremec T-150

	ft. lbs.
Back-up light switch	15–20
Fill and drain plugs	10–20
Front bearing cap bolt	30–36
Shift control housing bolts	20–25
Transfer case drive gear locknut	150
Transfer case to transmission bolts	30
TCS switch	18

LUBRICANT CAPACITY

SAE 80–90 gear lube	3 pts.

SHIFT CONTROL HOUSING

Disassembly

1. Remove the back-up light switch and the transmission controlled spark switch (TCS) if so equipped.

2. Remove the shift control housing cap, gasket, spring retainer, and the shift lever spring as an assembly.

3. Invert the housing and mount in a soft-jawed vise.

4. Move the second-third shift rail to the rear of the housing, rotate the shift fork toward the first-reverse rail until the roll pin is accessible. Drive the roll pin out of the fork and rail with a pin punch. Remove the shift fork and the roll pin.

NOTE: The roll pin hole in the shift fork is offset. Mark the position of the shift fork for assembly reference.

5. Remove the second-third shift rail using a brass drift or hammer. Catch the shift rail plug as the rail drives it out of the housing. Cover the shift and poppet ball holes in the cover to prevent the poppet ball from flying out. Mark the location of the shift rail for assembly reference.

6. Rotate the first-reverse shift fork away from the notch in the housing until the roll pin is accessible. Drive the roll pin out of the fork and rail using a pin punch. Remove the shift fork and roll pin.

NOTE: The roll pin hole in the shift fork is offset. Mark the position of the shift fork for assembly reference.

7. Remove the first-reverse shift rail using a brass drift or hammer. Catch the shift rail plug as the rail drives it out of the housing. Cover the shift and poppet ball holes in the cover to prevent the poppet ball from flying out. Mark the location of the shift rail for assembly reference.

8. Remove the poppet balls, springs, and the interlock plunger from the housing.

Assembly

1. Install the poppet springs and the detent plug in the housing.

2. Insert the first-reverse shift rail into the housing, and install the shift fork on the shift rail.

3. Install the poppet ball on the top of the spring in the first-reverse rail.

4. Using a punch or wooden dowel, push the poppet ball and spring downward into the housing bore and install the first-reverse shift rail.

5. Align the roll pin holes in the first-reverse shift fork and install the roll pin. Move the shift rail to the neutral (center) detent.

6. Insert the second-third shift rail into the housing and install the poppet ball on top of the spring in the shift rail bore.

7. Using a punch or wooden dowel, push the poppet ball and spring downward into the housing bore and install the second-third shift rail.

8. Align the roll pin holes in the second-third shift rail and the shift fork and install the roll pin. Move the shift rail to the neutral (center) position.

9. Install the shift rail plugs in the housing, and remove the shift control cover from the vise.

10. Install the shift lever, shift lever spring, spring retainer, gasket, and the shift control housing cap as an assembly. Tighten the cap securely.

11. Install the back-up light switch and the TCS switch if so equipped.

Volkswagen Transaxle

Disassembly

NOTE: A five speed transaxle is available for use in later vehicles. The disassembly and assembly procedures remain basically the same and the same precautions and care should be exercised during the overhaul procedure as is done in the overhaul of the four speed unit.

1. Mount the transaxle assembly in a holding fixture.

2. Remove the end cover and gasket.

3. Remove the circlips from the clutch release shaft. Slide the shaft out of the gear carrier and remove the clutch lever and return spring.

4. Remove the clutch release bearing and clutch pushrod.

5. Mount a bar with a locknut and spacer across the final drive housing to support the mainshaft.

6. Remove the selector shaft cover. Remove the interlock plunger springs, and the selector shaft.

7. Remove the circlip from the gear carrier side drive flange. Install the special tool with two bolts on the drive flange. Remove the drive flange.

8. Remove the plastic caps covering the clamping screws. Remove the clamping screw nuts.

9. Remove the reverse shaft retaining bolt.

10. Mount the special tool on the gear carrier assembly and lift the gear carrier off the final drive assembly while threading the special tool bolt in.

11. Drive the drive flange oil seal out of the gear carrier housing.

12. Pry the clutch operating shaft oil seal out of the carrier housing.

13. Pull the pinion shaft needle bearing out of the gear carrier.

14. Remove the shift fork assembly and the mainshaft from the final drive housing.

15. Remove the remaining drive flange as outlined in Step 7.

16. Remove the needle bearing stop and the first circlip from the pinion shaft. Lift fourth gear off the shaft.

17. Remove the second circlip from the pinion shaft. Lift third gear, second gear, second gear inner race and needle bearing off the shaft.

18. Remove the reverse shaft and gear.

19. Using a gear puller, remove the synchronizer hub and first/second gear from the pinion shaft.

20. Remove the pinion bearing cover and outer bearing race. Remove the pinion shaft.

21. Remove the differential assembly.

22. Pry the mainshaft oil seal out of the final drive housing.

23. Drive the drive flange oil seal out of the final drive housing.

24. Pull the starter bushing out of the final drive housing.

25. Pull the pinion outer bearing race out of the final drive housing.

26. Drive the differential outer bearing race out of the final drive housing.

27. Pull the mainshaft needle bearing out of the final drive housing.

28. Remove the two circlips from the shift fork shaft and slide the components off the shaft.

29. Remove the first circlip from the mainshaft and discard. Press the bearing off the shaft.

30. Mount the separator assembly on fourth gear and press the gear off the mainshaft. Remove the needle bearings.

31. Remove the second circlip from the mainshaft and discard. Press third gear and the synchronizer assembly off the shaft. Remove the needle bearings.

32. Slide a ⅜ in. rod in the mainshaft and drive the clutch pushrod out.

33. Press the two tapered roller bearings off the pinion shaft.

Pinion shaft gears must be removed to take out pinion shaft

2.0 mkg (14 ft lb)

Main shaft

Shift fork set disassemble only to replace individual parts

Ring gear when removing, pinion shaft must be removed

2 Circlips removing with screwdriver

Drive flange

Circlip for drive shaft always replace

Gear train assembly and final drive housing

34. Remove the circlips from the differential pinion shaft and drive out.

35. Remove the differential pinion gears and thrust washers.

36. Remove the circlips from the drive flange shafts. Remove the side gears and thrust washers.

37. Press the tapered roller bearing off the housing side of the differential.

38. Remove the tapered roller bearing from the ring gear side of the differential.

39. Remove the ring gear. On 1977 models, the ring gear is riveted in place. Drill out rivets and replace with special bolts.

Assembly

NOTE: The ring gear and pinion shaft can be replaced only as a matched set.

1. Heat the pinion shaft small tapered bearing to 212°F. and press onto the shaft.

2. Heat the pinion shaft large tapered bearing to 212° F. and press onto the shaft.

3. Place a 0.75 mm shim in the pinion bore in the final drive housing and press the small bearing outer position.

4. Install the pinion shaft and cover.

5. Assemble the pinion adjustment fixture tools. Place the end plate on the pinion shaft. Attach the dial indicator and zero with a 1 mm preload.

────── CAUTION ──────

Do not turn the pinion shaft while measuring because the bearings will settle and give incorrect reading.

6. Move the pinion shaft up and down and note the reading.

7. Specified bearing preload is obtained by adding the constant figure of 0.20 mm to the measured reading and the shim thickness (0.75 mm).
Example:

Shim installed	0.75 mm
reading	0.30 mm
preload (constant figure)	+ 0.20 mm
shim size	1.25 mm

8. Remove the pinion shaft cover and the pinion shaft. Pull the pinion shaft small bearing outer race of the final drive housing.

9. Install the correct shim and press the pinion shaft small bearing outer race into the final drive housing.

NOTE: If new bearings have been installed on the pinion shaft, check the pinion shaft turning torque. Reading should be 4.4–13.1 in. lbs.

10. Install the side gears and thrust washers in the differential housing.

11. Install the pinion gears and thrust washers. Drive the pinion shaft into the differential housing.

12. Install centering pins on the differential housing. Heat the ring gear to 212° F. and press onto the differential housing.

13. Heat the housing side differential bearing to 212°F. and press the bearing into place.

14. Heat the ring gear side bearing to 212°F. and press the bearing into place.

NOTE: If new bearings have been installed, the differential must be adjusted.

15. Slide the drive flange shafts into the side gears. Determine the thickness of the circlip by pressing the drive flange shaft against the pinion gearshaft, while pressing the side gears against the housing. Insert the thickest possible circlip. The circlip should not be jammed sideways.

────── CAUTION ──────

The differential inner and outer bearing races are matched to their bearings and cannot be interchanged.

16. If new differential bearings have been installed, proceed as follows:

   a. Install the race in the final drive housing with a 1 mm shim.

   b. Install the race in the gear carrier without a shim.

   c. Place the differential assembly in the final drive housing. Install the gear carrier on the final drive housing, with the gasket.

   d. Install the dial indicator fixture on the gear carrier tool and place the end plate on the drive flange. Install the dial indicator with a 1 mm preload.

────── CAUTION ──────

Do not turn the differential when making the measurements because the bearings will settle and give incorrect readings.

   e. Move the differential up and down and note the reading.

   f. The correct bearing preload is determined by adding a constant figure or .40 mm to the measured reading.
Example:

measured reading	0.90 mm
preload (constant figure)	+ 0.40 mm
shim (for gear carrier side)	1.30 mm

   g. Remove the gear carrier from the final drive housing.

   h. Pull the bearing race out of the gear carrier housing with a suitable extractor.

   i. Install the shims (determined in Step f) in the gear carrier starting with the thickest. Install the bearing race.

17. With the differential in the final drive housing, install the pinion shaft and tighten the nuts on the cover plate to 14 ft. lbs.

NOTE: Synchronizers can be replaced only as a matched unit.

18. Position the keys in the slots in the synchronizer hub. Place the synchronizer sleeve over the hub and align the marks. Install the springs 120° offset with the angled ends engaged in the hollow of a key.

19. Press the synchronizer rings onto the first and second gears. Check the gap between the ring and gear with a feeler gauge. The gap on new parts should be between 0.042–0.066 in. and no less than 0.019 in. on used parts.

20. Install the thrust washer and needle bearing for first gear on the pinion shaft. The recess in the thrust washer faces the roller bearing.

21. Align the grooves in the first gear synchronizer ring with the synchronizer shift keys. Position the shift fork slot in the operating sleeve toward second gear. The groove on the synchronizer hub should face toward first gear.

22. Heat the first gear and synchronizer as an assembly to 250°F. and press onto the pinion shaft.

23. Drive the second gear needle bearing race onto the pinion shaft.

24. Install the second gear needle bearings and second gear.

25. Install third gear on the pinion shaft with the collar facing toward second gear. Secure third gear with the selective circlip which will give an axial play between 0.00–0.20 mm. Measure the play with a feeler gauge between the circlip and third gear.

26. Warm the reverse gear bushing and press it on the reverse shaft until the top of the bushing is 41 mm (1.614 in.) from the bottom of the shaft.

27. Install the reverse gear shaft retaining bolt in the shaft. Center the shaft and drive it in until the collar makes contact with the final drive housing. Remove the retaining bolt.

28. Assemble the third/fourth synchronizer in the same way outlined in Step 57.

29. Press the synchronizer rings onto third and fourth gear. The gap between the gear and synchronizer ring should be as follows.

New Part in. (mm)	Wear Limit in. (mm)
Third 0.045–0.068	0.019
(1.15–1.75)	(0.5)
Fourth 0.051–0.074	0.19
(1.3–1.9)	(0.5)

30. Press the clutch pushrod bushing into the mainshaft until it is flush.

31. Install third gear needle bearings on the mainshaft.

32. Turn the synchronizer ring on third gear until the grooves align with the shift keys in the synchronizer hub. The chamfer on the synchronizer hub inner splines must face toward third gear.

33. Press the third gear and synchronizer onto the mainshaft as a unit. Install the circlip.

NOTE: If the mainshaft thrust washer is replaced, the mainshaft position must be readjusted.

34. Install the fourth gear needle bearings on the mainshaft. Install fourth gear.

35. Press the mainshaft thrust washer on until it contacts fourth gear.

36. Drive the mainshaft oil seal into the final drive housing. Drive the mainshaft needle bearings into the final drive housing.

37. Make sure that the mainshaft support bar, locknut and spacer are in place. Insert the mainshaft. Install the shift fork assembly and secure with the circlips. Make sure that the gears are in Neutral.

38. Lift the shaft with the spindle until the play between second gear on the pinion shaft and third gear on the mainshaft can be checked. Measure the end-play with a feeler gauge. Measurement should be 0.039 in. (1.0 mm). Lock the spindle at the support bar and check the measurement to make sure it has not changed.

39. Install the measuring sleeve tool on the mainshaft. Place a new gasket on the final drive housing and install the gear carrier. Tighten the bolts to 14 ft. lbs.

40. Mount a dial indicator in a holding assembly and zero the indicator with a 3 mm preload. Move the measuring sleeve up and down, and record the indicator reading.

Mainshaft Play	Shim Size
mm	mm
0.00–0.46	No Shim Used
0.47–0.75	0.30
0.76–1.04	0.60
1.05–1.45	0.90

41. Remove the gear carrier from the final drive housing.

42. Install the shim (determined in Step 40) in the mainshaft bearing bore. Press the mainshaft bearing into the gear carrier, and secure with the clamping screws and nuts. Tighten the nuts to 11 ft. lbs.

43. Drive the drive flange oil seal into the final drive housing until it bottoms against the bearing race.

44. Install the drive flange on the final drive housing side, with the special tool (VW391), secure with a new circlip.

45. Drive the starter bushing into the final drive housing.

46. Drive the selector shaft oil seal into the gear carrier.

47. Drive the clutch operating lever oil seal into the gear carrier.

48. Drive the pinion shaft needle bearings into the gear carrier.

49. Drive the drive flange oil seal into the gear carrier cover until it bottoms on the differential bearing race.

50. Position the gasket on the final drive housing. Install the gear carrier housing on the final drive housing. Make sure that the reverse gear shaft is aligned with the hole in the gear carrier, install the reverse shaft retaining screw.

51. Install the gear carrier to final drive housing bolts and tighten to 14 ft. lbs.

52. Install the mainshaft circlip through the clutch release bearing opening in the gear carrier.

53. Install the remaining driveshaft flange and circlip using special tools.

54. Remove the mainshaft support bar. Insert the clutch pushrod.

55. Insert the clutch release bearing assembly. Insert the clutch operating lever through the spring and clutch bearing lever. The bent end of the spring must contact the gear carrier. The center part of the spring is hooked over the end of the clutch bearing lever. Install the two circlips. Install the gasket and cover.

56. Insert the selector shaft and springs into the selector opening in the gear carrier assembly. Lubricate the selector with a multipurpose grease before assembly. Install the selector shaft cover.

57. Install the interlock plunger assembly in the gear carrier assembly. Adjust the interlock plunger as follows:

    a. Turn the slotted screw (interlock plunger) in until the nut starts to move out (bottoms).
    b. Back the slotted screw out ¼ turn.
    c. Install the plastic cap.

58. Install the plastic caps over the bearing clamping screws.

Warner T-14A, T-15A 3–Speed Transmission

The Warner T-14A, T-15A are fully synchronized three-speed transmissions having helical drive gears throughout. Lubricant capacity is 2½ pints.

TRANSMISSION UNIT

Disassembly

1. Separate transfer case from transmission by removing five capscrews.

2. Remove gearshift housing and disassembly by removing shift rails, poppet balls, springs, and shift forks.

3. Remove nut, flat washer, transfer case drive gear, adapter, and spacer.

4. Remove main drive gear bearing retainer gasket.

5. Remove main drive gear and mainshaft bearing snap-rings and bearings.

6. Remove main drive gear and mainshaft assembly.

NOTE: The T-15A transmission must be shifted into second gear to allow removal of the mainshaft and gear assembly.

7. On remote shift models, remove roll pins from lever shafts and housing. From inside case, slide levers and interlock assembly out. Remove forks and lever assemblies.

8. Remove lock plate from reverse idler shaft and countershaft.

9. Drive countershaft out to rear with dummy shaft. Remove countergear and two thrust washers. Remove spacer washers, rollers, and spacer from gear.

10. Drive reverse idler shaft out to rear. Remove gear, washers, and roller bearings.

11. Remove clutch hub snap-ring and second-third synchronizer assembly.

12. Remove second and reverse gears.

13. Remove clutch hub snap-ring and low synchronizer assembly.

14. Remove low gear.

SYNCHRONIZER

Disassembly and Assembly

1. Remove springs. Low synchronizer has only one spring; second-third, two.

2. Mark sleeve and hub before separating.

3. Remove hub.

4. Remove three shifter plates from hub.

5. Inspect all parts for wear.

6. Assembly in reverse order of disassembly. On second-third unit, make sure that spring openings are 120 degrees from each other, with spring tension opposed.

NOTE: If a synchronized assembly is replaced on a floor shift unit, the shift fork operating the synchronizer being replaced must have the letter A just under the shaft hole on the side opposite the pin.

Inspection

1. Wash all parts in solvent.

2. Air dry but do not spin bearings with air pressure.

3. Check case bearing and shaft bores for cracks or burrs.

4. Check all gears and bronze blocking rings for cracks, and chipped, worn, or cracked teeth. If any gears are replaced, also replace the meshing gears.

5. Check all bearings and bushings for wear or damage.

6. Check that synchronizer sleeves slide freely on clutch hubs.

TRANSMISSION UNIT

Assembly

1. Place reverse idler gear with dummy shaft, roller bearing, and thrust washers in case. Install reverse idler shaft.

2. Assemble countershaft center spacer, four bearing spacers, and bearing rollers in countershaft gear.

3. Install large countergear thrust washer in front of case. Position small thrust washer on countergear hub with lip facing groove in case. Holding countergear in position, push in countershaft from rear.

4. Install lock plate in slots of reverse idler shaft and countershaft.

5. Install to mainshaft:
    a. Low gear
    b. Bronze blocking ring
    c. Low synchronizer assembly
    d. Largest snap-ring that fits in groove
    e. Second gear
    f. Bronze blocking ring
    g. Second-third synchronizer assembly
    h. Largest snap-ring that fits in groove
    i. Reverse gear

6. Install mainshaft assembly through top of case.

7. Install bronze blocking ring to second-third synchronizer assembly.

8. On remote shift units, install shifter shafts, with new O-rings, into case.

NOTE: T-15 interlock levers are marked as to location. T-14 levers have no marks and are interchangeable.

9. Depress interlock lever while installing shift fork into shift lever and synchronizer clutch sleeve. Install poppet spring. Install tapered pins securing shafts in case.

10. Install main drive gear roller bearings.

11. Install main drive gear and oil slin-

1. Spline shaft
2. Gasket
3. Case cover
4. Bolt
5. First gear
6. Clutch friction ring set
7. Shaft plate retaining spring
8. Clutch shaft first and reverse plate
9. First and reverse clutch assembly
10. Shifter second and high fork
11. Clutch first and reverse gear snapring
12. Reverse gear
13. Shifter first and reverse R fork
14. Shifter interlock first and reverse lever
15. Speed finder interlock poppet spring
16. Shifter interlock second and third lever
17. Shifter fork first and reverse shaft
18. Shifter fork second and third shaft
19. Shifter fork interlock lever pivot pin
20. Shifter fork shaft seal
21. Rear bearing cap oil seal
22. Rear bearing cap bushing
23. Rear bearing cap
24. Bolt
25. Lock washer
26. Idler gear shaft
27. Rear bearing cap gasket
28. Speedometer drive gear ring
29. Speedometer drive gear
30. Speedometer drive gear ball
31. Rear ball bearing lockring
32. Rear ball bearing lockring
33. Rear ball bearing
34. Countershaft
35. Shifter fork retaining pin
36. Solenoid control switch
37. Bolt
38. Lock washer
39. Case
40. Spline shaft pilot bearing roller
41. Clutch shaft
42. Front ball bearing washer
43. Front ball bearing
44. Front ball bearing lockring
45. Front ball bearing snap-ring
46. Gasket
47. Front bearing cap
48. Bolt
49. Drain plug
50. Filler pipe plug
51. Front countershaft gear thrust washer
52. Countershaft gear
53. Countershaft gear bearing roller
54. Countershaft gear roller bearing spacer
55. Countershaft gear
56. Reverse idler gear bearing roller washer
57. Reverse idler gear bearing roller
58. Reverse idler gear
59. Rear countershaft thrust washer (less lip)
60. Clutch second and third snap-ring
61. Clutch shaft second and third plate
62. Second and third clutch assembly
63. Second gear

Warner T-14 or T-15

ger into case with cutaway portion of gear toward countergear. Install main drive gear to mainshaft.

12. Using bearing installer and thrust yoke tool, install main drive gear and mainshaft bearings and drive into position. The thrust yoke is needed to prevent damage to the synchronizer clutch.

13. Install main drive gear and mainshaft bearing snap-rings. The mainshaft bearing snap-ring is 0.010 thicker than main drive gear bearing snap-ring.

TORQUE SPECIFICATIONS

Location	N.m.	ft. lbs.
Front bearing retainer to case	14–20	10–15
Cover to case	14–24	10–18
Control levers to lever shafts	20–34	15–25
Rear bearing retainer to case	31–37	23–27
Companion flange to mainshaft	122–163	90–120
Control lever housing bolt	14–20	10–15

14. Install mainshaft rear bearing adapter, spacer, transfer case drive gear, flat washer, and nut. Torque nut to 130–170 ft. lbs.

15. Install main drive gear bearing retainer (with new oil seal) and gasket. Align oil drain holes in retainer and gasket.

16. Install case cover gasket. On remote shift units, install cover gasket with vent holes to left side.

17. Position gear train and floor-shift assembly in neutral. Insert shifter forks into clutch sleeves and torque to 8–15 ft. lbs.

Warner T-18, T-18A and T-19 Series 4–Speed

The Warner T-18, T-18A and T-19 transmissions have four forward speeds and one reverse. A power take-off opening is provided on certain transmissions, depending upon the models and applications and can be located on either the right or left sides of the case. The T-18 and T-18A transmissions are synchronized in second, third and fourth speeds only, while the T-19 transmission is synchronized in all forward gears. The disassembly and assembly remains basically the same for the transmission models.

TRANSMISSION UNIT

Disassembly

1. After draining the transmission and removing the parking brake drum (or shoe assembly), lock the transmission in two gears and remove the U-joint flange, oil seal, speedometer driven gear and bearing assembly. Lubricant capacity is 6½ pints.

2. Remove the output shaft bearing retainer and the speedometer drive gear and spacer.

3. Remove the output shaft bearing snap-ring, and remove the bearing.

4. Remove the countershaft and idler shaft retainer and the power take-off cover.

5. After removing the input shaft bearing retainer, remove the snap-rings from the bearing and the shaft.

6. Remove the input shaft bearing and oil baffle.

7. Drive out the countershaft (from the front). Keep the dummy shaft in contact with the countershaft to avoid dropping any rollers.

8. After removing the input shaft and the synchronizer blocking ring, pull the idler shaft.

9. Remove the reverse gear shifter arm, the output shaft assembly, the idler gear, and the cluster gear. When removing the cluster, do not lose any of the rollers.

SUBASSEMBLIES

Disassemblies
OUTPUT SHAFT

1. Remove the third- and high-speed synchronizer hub snap-ring from the output shaft, and slide the third- and high-speed synchronizer assembly and the third-speed gear off the shaft. Remove the synchronizer sleeve and the inserts from the hub. Before removing the two snap-rings from the ends of the hub, check the end play of the second-speed gear (0.005–0.024 inch).

2. Remove the second-speed synchro-nizer snap-ring. Slide the second-speed synchronizer hub gear off the hub. Do not lose any of the balls, springs, or plates. Pull the hub off the shaft, and remove the second-speed synchronizer from the second-speed gear. Remove the snap-ring from the rear of the second-speed gear, and remove the gear, spacer, roller bearings, and thrust washer from the output shaft. Remove the remaining snap-ring from the shaft.

CLUSTER GEAR

Remove the dummy shaft, pilot bearing rollers, bearing spacers, and center spacer from the cluster gear.

REVERSE IDLER GEAR

Rotate the reverse idler gear on the shaft, and if it turns freely and smoothly, disassembly of the unit is not necessary. If any roughness is noticed, disassemble the unit.

GEAR SHIFT HOUSING

1. Remove the housing cap and lever. Be sure all shafts are in neutral before disassembly.

2. Tap the shifter shafts out of the housing while holding one hand over the holes in the housing to prevent loss of the springs and balls. Remove the two shaft lock plungers from the housing.

SUBASSEMBLIES

Assembly
CLUSTER GEAR ASSEMBLY

Slide the long bearing spacer into the cluster gear bore, and insert the dummy shaft in the spacer. Hold the cluster gear in a vertical position, and install one of the bear-

Warner T-18

Warner T-19

ing spacers. Position the 22 pilot bearing rollers in the cluster gear bore. Place a spacer on the rollers, and install 22 more rollers and another spacer. Hold a large thrust washer against the end of cluster gear and turn the assembly over. Install the rollers and spacers in the other end of the gear.

REVERSE IDLER GEAR ASSEMBLY

1. Install a snap-ring in one end of the idler gear, and set the gear on end, with the snap-ring at the bottom.

2. Position a thrust washer in the gear on top of the snap-ring. Install the bushing on top of the washer, insert the 37 bearing rollers, and then a spacer followed by 37 more rollers. Place the remaining thrust washer on the rollers, and install the other snap-ring.

OUTPUT SHAFT ASSEMBLY

1. Install the second speed gear thrust washer and snap-ring on the output shaft. Hold the shaft vertically, and slide on the second speed gear. Insert the bearing rollers in the second-speed gear, and slide the spacer into the gear. (The T-18 model does not contain second speed gear rollers or spacer). Install the snap-ring on the output shaft at the rear of the second-speed gear. Position the blocking ring on the second-speed gear. Do not invert the shaft because the bearing rollers will slide out of the gear.

2. Press the second-speed synchronizer hub onto the shaft, and install the snap-ring. Position the shaft vertically in a soft-jawed vise. Position the springs and plates in the second-speed synchronizer hub, and place the hub gear on the hub.

3. With the T-19 model, press the first and second speed synchronizer onto the shaft and install the snap-ring. Install the first speed gear and snap-ring on the shaft and press on the reverse gear. For the T-19, ignore steps 2 and 4.

4. Hold the gear above the hub spring and ball holes, and position one ball at a time in the hub, and slide the hub gear downward to hold the ball in place. Push the plate upward, and insert a small block to hold the plate in position, thereby holding the ball in the hub. Follow these procedures for the remaining balls.

5. Install the third speed gear and synchronizer blocking ring on the shaft.

6. Install the snap-rings at both ends of the third and high-speed synchronizer hub. Stagger the openings of the snap-rings so that they are not aligned. Place the inserts in the synchronizer sleeve, and position the sleeve on the hub.

7. Slide the synchronizer assembly onto the output shaft. The slots in the blocking ring must be in line with the synchronizer inserts. Install the snap-ring at the front of the synchronizer assembly.

GEAR SHIFT HOUSING

1. Place the spring on the reverse gear shifter shaft gate plunger, and install the spring and plunger in the reverse gate. Press the plunger through the gate, and fasten it with the clip. Place the spring and ball in the reverse gate poppet hole. Compress the spring and install the cotter pin.

2. Place the spring and ball in the reverse shifter shaft hole in the gear shift housing. Press down on the ball, and position the reverse shifter shaft so that the reverse shifter arm notch does not slide over the ball. Insert the shaft part way into the housing.

3. Slide the reverse gate onto the shaft, and drive the shaft into the housing until the ball snaps into the groove of the shaft. Install the lock screw lock wire to the gate.

4. Insert the two interlocking plungers in the pockets between the shifter shaft holes. Place the spring and ball in the low and second shifter shaft hole. Press down on the ball, and insert the shifter shaft part way into the housing.

5. Slide the low and second shifter shaft gate onto the shaft, and install the corresponding shifter fork on the shaft so that the offset of the fork is toward the rear of the housing. Push the shaft all the way into the housing until the ball engages the shaft groove. Install the lock screw and wire that fastens the fork to the shaft. Install the third and high shifter shaft in the same manner. Check the interlocking system. Install new expansion plugs in the shaft bores.

TRANSMISSION UNIT

Assembly

1. Coat all parts, especially the bearings, with transmission lubricant to prevent scoring during initial operation.

2. Position the cluster gear assembly in the case. Do not lose any rollers.

3. Place the idler gear assembly in the case, and install the idler shaft. Position the slot in the rear of the shaft so that it can engage the retainer. Install the reverse shifter arm.

4. Drive out the cluster gear dummy shaft by installing the countershaft from the

rear. Position the slot in the rear of the shaft so that it can engage the retainer. Use thrust washers as required to get 0.006 to 0.020 inch cluster gear end play. Install the countershaft and idler shaft retainer.

5. Position the input shaft pilot rollers and the oil baffle, so that the baffle will not rub the bearing race. Install the input shaft and the blocking ring in the case.

6. Install the output shaft assembly in the case, and use a special tool to prevent jamming the blocking ring when the input shaft bearing is installed.

7. Drive the input shaft bearing onto the shaft. Install the thickest select-fit snap-ring that will fit on the bearing. Install the input shaft snap-ring.

8. Install the output shaft bearing.

9. Install the input shaft bearing without a gasket, and tighten the bolts only enough to bottom the retainer on the bearing snap-ring. Measure the clearance between the retainer and the case, and select a gasket (or gaskets) that will seal in the oil and prevent end play between the retainer and the snap-ring. Torque the bolts to specification.

10. Position the speedometer drive gear and spacer, and install a new output shaft bearing retainer seal.

11. Install the output shaft bearing retainer. Torque the bolts to specification, and install safety wire.

12. Install the brake shoe (or drum), and torque the bolts to specification. Install the U-joint flange. Lock the transmission in two gears and torque the nut to specification.

13. Install the power take-off cover plates with new gaskets. Fill the transmission according to specifications.

Warner T-15-D 3–Speed Transmission

The Warner T-15-D transmission has three synchronized forward speeds and one reverse. The transmission has either a remote controlled shift lever on the steering column or a top cover shift lever assembly. This transmission can be used with or without a transfer case in the drive line with the use of different extension housing or bearing retainer designs.

MAINSHAFT

Removal

1. Drain the transmission of its lubricant and remove either the top cover or the shift lever assembly from the top of the transmission. Remove the front bearing retainer.

2. Remove the front main drive gear bearing snap-rings and remove the bearing from the shaft and transmission case with the aid of a bearing puller or its equivalent.

3. Remove the main drive gear from

the transmission case by having the cutaway portion of the gear teeth positioned downward towards the cluster gear. As the gear is removed from the mainshaft, do not lose the needle roller bearing from the bearing pocket.

4. Remove the rear extension housing or the bearing retainer from the rear of the transmission case.

5. Remove the mainshaft rear bearing snap-rings and remove the bearing from the mainshaft and transmission case with a bearing puller or its equivalent.

6. *Column shift:* Position the gears in second speed, move the mainshaft to the left and remove the shift forks.

7. Remove the mainshaft by tilting the front of the assembly upward and lifting it through the top of the case.

IDLER GEAR, CLUSTER GEAR AND SHAFTS

Removal

1. Tap the reverse idler gear shaft and the countershaft rearward to allow the removal of the lockplate from the slots in both shafts.

2. Using a brass drift, drive the reverse idler gear shaft towards the rear and out of the transmission case. Avoid losing the needle roller bearings from the gear bore.

3. Using a dummy countershaft or its equivalent, drive the countershaft from the rear of the transmission case. Lift the cluster gear assembly from the transmission case. Mark the thrust washer locations.

MAINSHAFT

Disassembly

1. Remove the second/third speed synchronizer snap-ring from the front of the mainshaft. Remove the synchronizer from the mainshaft, after matchmarking the sleeve and hub.

2. Remove the second speed gear from the mainshaft.

3. Remove the reverse gear from the rear of the mainshaft. Remove the rear synchronizer (first/reverse) hub snap-ring.

4. Remove the first/reverse synchronizer unit from the rear of the mainshaft.

NOTE: Only one blocker ring is used with the first/reverse synchronizer assembly as the reverse speed gear is not a synchromesh unit.

5. Remove the first speed gear from the mainshaft.

Cleaning and Inspection

1. Clean the transmission case with solvent and inspect for cracks, worn bearing bores or other damages.

2. Clean and inspect all gears and bronze blocking rings for cracks, chipped or cracked teeth or excessive wear on the teeth. Should

a gear require replacement, the meshing gear should be replaced also.

3. Inspect all bearings and bushings for wear or damage. The thrust washers should be renewed upon transmission assembly, if grooved or distorted.

4. Inspect the synchronizer clutch sleeves for abnormal wear and ease of operation.

5. Lubricate all internal transmission components before installation.

MAINSHAFT

Assembly

1. The assembly of the mainshaft gears is in the reverse of the removal procedure. During the assembly, the snap-rings are of the selective thickness type and should be selected to obtain the following end play measurements.

   a. Second/third speed synchronizer—0.004 to 0.020 inch (0.10 to 0.51 mm) measured between the snap-ring and the second speed synchronizer hub.

   b. First/reverse synchronizer—0.005 to 0.020 inch (0.13 to 0.51 mm) measured between the first speed gear and the collar on the mainshaft.

IDLER GEAR AND COUNTERSHAFT

Installation

1. Using the dummy countershaft or its equivalent, install the needle roller bearings, spacers and thrust washers in the cluster gear bore.

NOTE: Use vaseline type lubricant to hold the needle, roller bearings in place.

2. Place the cluster gear assembly into the transmission case and install the countershaft from the rear to the front of the case, through the cluster gear, forcing the dummy shaft out the front shaft bore of the case.

3. During the installation of the countershaft, be sure to maintain alignment of the spacers and thrust washers.

4. Install the needle roller bearings into the bore of the reverse idler gear and hold in place with a vaseline type lubricant.

5. Position the thrust washers on the gear and place the assembly between the transmission case web and the rear inner surface of the case.

6. Carefully drive the reverse idler gear shaft through the case bore and into the reverse idler gear assembly. Be sure to keep the thrust washers aligned to avoid damage to them.

7. With both the countershaft and the reverse idler gear shaft in Place, install the lock plate with the tabs on the top side, into the slots of each shaft. Drive the shafts forward until the lock plate is flush against the case surface.

MAINSHAFT

Installation

1. Tilt the mainshaft assembly and install the rear of the shaft assembly into the case. Lower the mainshaft assembly into the case. If the transmission is controlled by a steering column shift lever, move the mainshaft and install the shifting forks into place on the clutch sleeves and shift mechanism.

2. Using a mainshaft support or equivalent, block and support the front of the mainshaft. Install the rear mainshaft bearing with a bearing installer tool or equivalent.

3. Install the large and small snap-rings on the rear bearing and mainshaft. Remove the front shaft support.

4. Install the main drive gear with the oil baffle, into the case. Position the cutaway portion of the gear downward towards the countershaft/cluster gear assembly, to aid in the installation of the drive gear. Use caution to avoid dropping the needle roller bearings as the mainshaft front stub enters the main drive gear bearing pocket.

5. Install the main drive gear bearing and the retaining snap-rings. Be sure the oil baffle is in place.

6. Install the front bearing retainer with a new gasket.

7. Install the rear bearing retainer or extension housing, using a new gasket. Install the oil seal as required.

8. **Floor Shift:** Place the gears in a neutral position and the shift lever housing components in neutral. Place the shifting levers in their respective sliding sleeve grooves and bolt the cover to the transmission case.

Column Shift: Install the top cover with a new gasket and bolt into place on the transmission.

9. Fill the transmission with lubricant to its proper level (3 pints) and move the gear shifting mechanism by hand to be assured of proper gear selection before installation of the transmission into the vehicle.

Warner SR-4 4–Speed Transmission

The Warner SR-4 transmission is a four speed, constant mesh unit, providing synchromesh engagement in all forward gears.

TRANSMISSION UNIT

Disassembly

1. Separate the transmission from the transfer case, if attached.

2. Drain the lubricant from the transmission by removing the lower adapter housing bolt.

3. If the shift lever housing has not been removed, place the shift lever in the neutral position, remove the retaining bolts and lift the shift lever housing from the transmission.

4. Remove the flanged nut holding the offset lever to the shift rail. Remove the offset lever.

5. Remove the adapter housing retaining bolts and the housing from the transmission case.

6. Remove the shift control housing retaining bolts and remove the cover and gasket. Mark the location of the two dowel bolts to reinstall in their original position.

7. Remove the spring clip holding the reverse lever to the reverse lever pivot bolt. Remove the reverse lever pivot bolt, allowing the removal of the reverse lever and reverse lever fork as an assembly.

8. Match mark the front bearing retainer to the transmission case and remove the bearing retainer and gasket.

9. Remove the large and small snap-rings from the front and rear ball bearings on the input and output shafts.

10. With the aid of a bearing puller tool or equivalent, remove the input shaft ball bearing and remove the input shaft from the case.

11. Remove the rear (output shaft) bearing from the shaft with the aid of a bearing puller tool or equivalent.

12. Remove the output shaft assembly as a unit from the transmission case. Do not allow the synchronizer sleeves to separate from the hubs during the removal.

13. Push the reverse idler gear shaft rearward and remove the shaft and gear from the case.

14. Using a dummy countershaft, push the countershaft to the rear of the case. Remove the cluster gear assembly and dummy countershaft as a unit, from the transmission case.

15. Separate the dummy countershaft and remove the 50 needle roller bearings, spacers and thrust washers from the cluster gear.

NOTE: The cluster gear front thrust washer is of a plastic material, while the rear thrust washer is metal.

COUNTERSHAFT GEAR BEARING

Replacement

1. Remove the dummy shaft, bearing retainer washers and needle bearings from the countershaft gear. Clean and inspect the parts.

2. Coat the bore at each end of the countershaft gear with grease to retain the needle bearings.

3. While holding the dummy shaft in the gear, install the needle bearings and retainer washers in each end of the gear.

4. Slide first gear off the output shaft, and remove the first speed blocker ring. Take care not to lose the sliding gear from the first and second speed synchronizer assembly.

5. Clean and inspect all parts.

Assembly

1. Place a blocker ring on the cone of first gear, and slide the gear and ring assembly onto the output shaft. Make sure that the inserts in the synchronizer engage in the blocker ring notches.

2. Install the spring pin retaining first gear to the output shaft.

3. Install a blocker ring on the cone of second gear, and slide the gear and ring assembly onto the output shaft. Make sure that the inserts in the synchronizer engage in the blocker ring notches.

4. Install the second gear thrust washer and new snap-ring on the shaft.

5. Install a blocker ring on the cone of third gear, and slide the gear and ring assembly onto the output shaft. Install the third and fourth speed synchronizer. Make sure that the inserts in the synchronizer engage in the blocker ring notches.

6. Install a new third and fourth gear synchronizer snap-ring.

7. Place the first gear thrust washer (oil slinger) on the shaft and on the spring pin retaining first gear.

8. Assembly end play measurements are as follows:

a. Second gear—0.004 to 0.014 inch (0.10 to 0.35 mm), measured between the second speed gear and the thrust washer.

b. Third/fourth synchronizer hub—0.004 to 0.014 inch (0.10 to 0.35 mm), measured between the output shaft snapring and the third speed synchronizer hub.

COVER ASSEMBLY

Disassembly

1. Remove the detent screw, spring and plunger.

2. Pull the shifter shaft rod rearward, rotating it counterclockwise.

3. Remove the spring pin retaining the manual selector and interlock to the shifter shaft.

4. Remove the shifter shaft from the cover taking care not to damage the seal.

5. Remove the manual selector and interlock plate.

6. Remove the first and second speed shifter fork. Remove the third and fourth speed shifter fork.

7. Clean and inspect all parts. Replace the shifter shaft seal and welch plug, if damaged.

Assembly

1. Assemble the two plastic inserts to each shift fork; the two projections on the inside of the inserts fit into the blind holes in the ends of the shift forks. Insert the selector arm plates into the shift forks.

2. Install the third and fourth speed shifter fork into the cover.

3. Install the first and second speed shifter fork into the cover. Lubricate the shifter shaft bore with grease.

1. Case assembly—transmission
2. Case—transmission
3. Magnet—transmission case chip
4. Nut spring $^9/_{64}$
5. Pin—$^3/_{16}$ diameter × $^{13}/_{16}$ rolled spring
6. Lever assembly—transmission gearshift shaft offset
7. Lever transmission gearshift shaft offset
8. Pin—transmission gearshift shaft offset lever
9. Shaft—transmission shifter
10. Seal—O-ring
11. Gear and bush assembly—transmission reverse idler sliding
12. Gear—transmission reverse idler sliding
13. Bushing—transmission reverse idler gear
14. Pin—transmission reverse gear selector fork pivot
15. Ring—$^7/_{16}$ retaining
16. Pin—$^1/_4$ x 1 spring
17. Shaft—transmission reverse idler gear
18. Gear—transmission countershaft
19. Roller—transmission countershaft bearing
20. Washer—208/.918 flat
21. Washer—transmission countershaft gear thrust
22. Countershaft—transmission
23. Shaft assembly—transmission output
24. Shaft—transmission

output
25. Hub—transmission synchronizer 1st and 2nd gear cluster
26. Shaft and gear assembly—transmission output
27. Gear—transmission reverse sliding
28. Insert—transmission synchronizer hub
29. Spring—transmission synchronizer retaining
30. Ring—transmission synchronizer blocking
31. Ring—transmission 2nd speed gear retaining snap
32. Gear—transmission 2nd speed
33. Washer—transmission 2nd speed gear thrust
34. Pin—$^1/_8$ × $^1/_4$ rolled spring
35. Gear—transmission 3rd speed
36. Synchronizer assembly—3rd and 4th speed
37. Hub—transmission synchronizer
38. Insert—transmission synchronizer hub
39. Sleeve—transmission 3rd and 4th gear clutch hub
40. Spring—transmission synchronizer retaining
41. Ring—transmission synchronizer blocking
42. Ring—transmission m/d gear bearing shaft snap
43. Fork—transmission 1st & 2nd gear shift
44. Fork—transmission 3rd & 4th gear shift
45. Lever assembly—transmission reverse gear shaft relay

46. Retaining—transmission reverse gear shaft relay lever
47. Lever—transmission reverse gear shaft relay
48. Fork—transmission reverse gear shift
49. Spring—transmission shifter interlock
50. Plunger—transmission meshlock
51. Screw—m12 x 10 round head flat
52. Plate—transmission gear selector interlock
53. Screw & washer assembly—m10 x 30 hex head
54. Plug—$^3/_4$ diameter welch type
55. Shaft—transmission input
56. Roller—transmission mainshaft bearing
57. Bearing assembly—transmission m/d gear ball
58. Ring—m/d gear bearing retaining snap
59. Ring—1.00 retaining
60. Seal—transmission shift shaft
61. Gear—transmission 1st speed
62. Clip—spark control switch wire retaining
63. Gear—speedometer drive
64. Extension assembly—transmission
65. Extension—transmission
66. Bushing—transmission extension
67. Stop—transmission gear shift lever reverse
68. Gasket—transmission

extension
69. Seal assembly—transmission extension oil
70. Plug—transmission extension
71. Retainer—transmission input shaft gear bearing
72. Seal assembly—transmission input shaft oil
73. Gasket—transmission input shaft bearing retainer
74. Bolt—M8 x 20 hex head-lock
75. Gasket—transmission case cover
76. Cover—transmission case
77. Screw—m6 x 20 hex head
78. Bolt—m6 x 32 hex washer HD shoulder
79. Plug—$^1/_2$-14 pipe (filler)
80. Bushing—transmission gear shift damper
81. Washer—spring lock
82. Nut—hexagon
83. Switch assembly—back-up lamp
84. Switch assembly—transmission seat belt warning sensor
85. Tag—transmission service identification
86. Washer—transmission 1st gear thrust
87. Ball—.25 diameter
88. Screw and lockwasher assembly—m12 x 40
89. Arm assembly—transmission control selector
90. Arm—transmission control selector
91. Pin—transmission gear shift

Warner SR-4

4. Install the manual selector arm through the interlock plate, and position the two pieces into the cover, with the wide leg of the interlock plate towards the inside of the transmission case.

5. Align the shifter shaft in the cover, and insert the shaft through the shifter forks and manual selector. Coat the shifter shaft with a light coating of grease. Make sure the detent grooves face the plunger side of the cover.

6. Align the pin holes in the manual selector arm and shifter shaft. Install the spring pin flush with the surface of the selector arm.

7. Install the detent plunger, spring, and plug. Tighten the plug to 8–12 ft. lbs.

8. Check the operation of the shift forks in each gear position.

OUTPUT SHAFT

Disassembly

1. Scribe alignment marks on the synchronizer and blocker rings. Remove the snap-ring from the front of the output shaft. Slide the third and fourth speed synchronizer assembly, blocker rings and third gear off the shaft.

2. Remove the next snap-ring and the second gear thrust washer from the shaft. Slide second gear and the blocker ring off the shaft, taking care not to lose the sliding gear from the first and second speed synchronizer assembly. The first and second speed synchronizer hub cannot be removed from the output shaft.

3. Remove the first gear thrust washer (oil slinger) from the rear of the output shaft. Remove the spring pin retaining first gear onto the shaft.

SYNCHRONIZER

Disassembly and Assembly

1. Scribe reference marks on the hub and sleeve of the synchronizer.

2. Push the sleeve from the hub of each synchronizer.

3. Separate the inserts and insert springs from the hubs. Do not mix the parts between the first/second speed synchronizer and the third/fourth speed synchronizer. Clean and inspect all parts.

NOTE: The first/second speed synchronizer hub is not to be removed from the shaft. They have been assembled and machined as a matched unit during manufacturing to assure concentricity.

4. To assemble, position the sleeve on the hub, aligning the previously marked reference points.

5. Position the three inserts per hub and install the insert springs, being sure that the bent end of the springs are seated in one of the inserts. The springs on each side of the hubs must face in opposite directions and the openings be 180 degrees apart.

TRANSMISSION UNIT

Assembly

1. Coat the countershaft thrust washers with a vaseline type lubricant and position the plastic type washer at the front of the case and the metal washer at the rear of the case.

2. With the 50 needle roller bearings in place in the cluster gear and the dummy countershaft in place, install the countershaft/cluster gear assembly into the case.

------ CAUTION ------
Be sure the thrust washers are not displaced during the gear installation.

3. Align the cluster gear bore with the case bores and install the countershaft from the rear to the front of the case, pushing the dummy countershaft from the gear and case.

4. Position the reverse idler gear with the shift lever groove facing to the front and install the shaft from the rear of the case.

5. Being careful not to disturb the synchronizers, install the output shaft assembly into the transmission case. Install the fourth gear blocking ring in the third speed synchronizer sleeve, engaging the inserts on the hub with the grooves of the blocking ring.

6. Install the 15 roller bearings in the input shaft pocket and retain with a vaseline type lubricant. Install the input shaft into the case and engage the shaft in the third/fourth synchronizer, while the stub of the output shaft is installed in the pocket of the input shaft.

------ CAUTION ------
Do not jam or drop the 15 roller bearings during the input shaft installation.

7. Install the input shaft front bearing. Block the first speed gear against the rear of the case, align the bearing with the bearing bore in the case and drive the bearing completely onto the input shaft and into the transmission case.

NOTE: To identify the front and rear bearings, look for a notch in the front bearing race. The rear bearing has no notch.

8. Install the front bearing retaining and locating snap-rings.

9. Install the front bearing cap oil seal and install the cap (bearing retainer) with a new gasket to the transmission case. Install the retaining bolts.

10. Install the first speed thrust washer on the output shaft with the oil grooves facing the first speed gear. Install the rear bearing onto the output shaft and into the case bearing bore.

NOTE: Be sure the first gear thrust washer is engaged on the first gear roll pin before installing the rear bearing.

11. Install the retaining and locating snap-rings on the rear bearing and output shaft.

12. Position the reverse lever in the case, on the pivot bolt and install the retaining clip. Tighten the pivot bolt. Be sure the reverse lever fork is engaged in the reverse idler gear.

13. Rotate the input shaft and output shaft gears and blocking rings to insure freeness of movement. Blocking ring to gear clutch tooth face should have a clearance of 0.030 inch (0.001 mm).

14. Place the reverse lever in the neutral position and install the cover assembly on the transmission case. Place the two dowel bolts in their original positions and install the remaining retaining bolts.

15. Install a new oil seal in the adapter housing and, using a new gasket, install the adapter housing to the transmission case.

16. Install 3 pints of lubricant into the transmission.

17. Install the offset lever and retain with the flanged nut.

18. Depending upon the installation of the transmission into a vehicle, the shift lever housing can be installed and the transmission attached to the transfer case.

TORQUE SPECIFICATIONS①

	ft. lbs.	N.m.
Backup lamp switch	10	14
Adapter housing bolt	23	31
Detent plug (in housing)	10	14
Fill plug	20	27
Front bearing cap bolt	13	18
Offset lever nut	10	14
Reverse lever pivot bolt	20	27
Shift control housing bolt	10	14
Transmission-to-clutch housing bolt	55	75
Universal joint clamp strap bolt	14	19

①All torque values given in foot-pounds and newton-meters with dry fits unless otherwise specified.

Warner T-176 4–Speed Transmission

The Warner T-176 transmission is a constant mesh unit, synchronized in all forward gears and with one reverse gear.

TRANSMISSION UNIT

Disassembly

1. Remove the transfer case from the rear of the transmission.
2. Remove the shift control housing. Mark the location of the two dowel bolts in the housing.
3. Drain the lubricant from the transmission, if not previously done. Remove the rear adapter housing.
4. With a dummy countershaft tool, remove the countershaft from the transmission, front to rear. Allow the cluster gear to lay on the bottom of the case.
5. Remove the rear bearing locating and retaining snap-rings. Remove the rear bearing with a bearing remover tool or equivalent.
6. Match mark the front bearing retainer to the case for easier installation, remove the retaining bolts and the retainer.
7. Remove the locating and retaining snap-rings from the front bearing. Remove the front bearing and the input shaft using a puller tool or equivalent.
8. Remove the mainshaft pilot bearing rollers from the input shaft pocket. Engage the third speed synchronizer.
9. Remove the mainshaft assembly by lifting the front of the shaft upward and out.
10. Remove the cluster gear assembly from the case. Locate and remove any thrust washers and needle roller bearings from the case.
11. Tap the reverse idler gear shaft from the case and remove the reverse idler gear and thrust washers.
12. Separate the reverse idler gear from the sliding gear. Do not lose the needle roller bearings.

MAINSHAFT

Disassembly

1. Remove the third/fourth speed synchronizer snap-ring from the front of the mainshaft.
2. Remove the third/fourth synchronizer from the mainshaft and slide the hub from the sleeve. Remove the inserts and springs. Inspect the blocking rings for wear and damage.
3. Remove the third speed gear and the second speed gear snap-ring. Remove the second speed gear and the blocking ring. Remove the tabbed thrust washer.
4. Remove the snap-ring from the first/second synchronizer hub. Remove the hub and the reverse gear with sleeve as an assembly. Match mark the hub and sleeve for

1. Third-fourth gear snap-ring
2. Fourth gear synchronizer ring
3. Third-fourth gear clutch assembly
4. Third-fourth gear plate
5. Third gear synchronizer ring
6. Third speed gear
7. Second gear snap-ring
8. Second gear thrust washer
9. Second speed gear
10. Second gear synchronizer ring
11. Main shaft snap-ring
12. First-second synchronizer spring
13. Low-second plate
14. First gear synchronizer ring
15. First gear
16. Third-fourth synchronizer spring
17. First-second gear clutch assembly
18. Front bearing cap
19. Oil seal
20. Gasket
21. Snap-ring
22. Lock ring
23. Front ball bearing
24. Clutch shaft
25. Roller bearing
26. Drain plug
27. Fill plug
28. Case
29. Gasket
30. Spline shaft
31. First gear thrust washer
32. Rear ball bearing
33. Snap-ring
34. Adapter plate
35. Adapter seal
36. Front countershaft gear thrust washer
37. Roller washer
38. Rear roller bearing
39. Countershaft gear
40. Rear countershaft thrust washer
41. Countershaft
42. Pin
43. Idler gear shaft
44. Pin
45. Idler gear roller bearing
46. Reverse idler sliding gear
47. Reverse idler gear
48. Idler gear washer
49. Idler gear thrust washer

Warner T-176

assembly references. Remove the inserts and springs as the sleeve is removed.

5. Remove the first speed gear thrust washer from the rear of the shaft and remove the first speed gear and the blocking ring.

Inspection of Transmission Components

CASE

1. Cracks in the bores, sides, bosses or at bolt holes.
2. Stripped bolt hole threads.
3. Nicks, burrs, roughness on gasket or shaft bore surfaces.

GEARS, SHAFTS AND SYNCHRONIZER UNITS

1. Chipped, broken or worn gear teeth.
2. Damaged splines.
3. Worn or broken teeth or blocking rings.

4. Bent or broken synchronizer inserts or springs.
5. Damaged needle bearings or operating surfaces.
6. Wear or galling of the mainshaft, countershaft, clutch shaft or idler gear shaft.
7. Worn or broken thrust washers.
8. Bent, distorted, broken or weak snap-rings.
9. Rough, galled, worn or broken front or rear bearing.

MAINSHAFT

Assembly

1. Assemble the first/second synchronizer hub, inserts and springs. Install the clutch sleeve. Be sure to position the spring ends 180 degrees apart.
2. Install the assembled first/second speed synchronizer hub and the reverse gear

with sleeve, on the mainshaft. Secure with a new snap-ring.

3. Install the first speed gear and blocking ring on the rear of the mainshaft and install the first gear thrust washer.

4. Install a new tabbed thrust washer on the mainshaft with the tab seated in the mainshaft tab bore.

5. Install the second speed gear and the blocking ring on the mainshaft and secure with a new snap-ring.

6. Install the third speed gear and blocking ring on the mainshaft.

7. Assemble the third/fourth speed synchronizer hub, inserts, and springs. Be sure the spring ends are 180 degrees apart.

8. Install the assembled third/fourth speed synchronizer on the mainshaft and secure with a new snap-ring.

9. The measured end play between the snap-ring and the third/fourth speed synchronizer should be 0.004 to 0.014 inch (0.10 to 0.35 mm).

TRANSMISSION UNIT

Assembly

1. Load the reverse idler gear with the 44 needle roller bearings and a bearing retainer on each end of the gear. Install the sliding gear on the reverse idler gear. Install lubricated thrust washers into the case.

2. Install the reverse idler assembly into the case and install the reverse idler gear shaft.

3. Be sure to engage the thrust washer locating tabs in the case locating slots.

4. Seat the reverse idler gear shaft roll pin into the counterbore in the case. The reverse idler gear end play should be 0.004 to 0.018 inch (0.10 to 0.45 mm).

5. Install the 42 needle roller bearings in the cluster gear, using the dummy countershaft as a bearing holder. Use of a vaseline type lubricant is suggested to hold the bearings in place.

6. Position the lubricated thrust washers in place on the inside of the transmission case. Position the thrust washer tabs in the tab slots of the case.

7. Insert the countershaft into the rear case bore, just far enough to hold the rear thrust washer. Lower the cluster gear assembly into the case and align the gear bore with the case bore. Push the countershaft into the cluster gear, displacing the dummy countershaft out the front case bore hole. Do not completely remove the dummy countershaft.

8. Measure the cluster gear end play which should be 0.004 to 0.018 inch (0.10 to 0.45 mm). Correct as required and reinstall the dummy countershaft into the cluster gear, pushing the countershaft from the gear.

9. Allow the cluster gear to remain at the bottom of the case until the input and mainshaft has been installed to provide the necessary assembly clearance.

10. With the synchronizers in the neutral position, install the mainshaft assembly into the case.

11. Install the front bearing part way on the input shaft and install the 15 roller bearing in the shaft pocket.

NOTE: Do not use a heavy grease to hold the bearings in the pocket as the grease can plug the lubrication holes. Use only a vaseline type lubricant.

12. Position the blocking ring on the third/fourth synchronizer. Support the mainshaft assembly and insert the input shaft through the front bearing bore of the case. Seat the mainshaft pilot hub into the bearing pocket of the input shaft and tap the front bearing and input shaft into the case, using a soft faced hammer.

13. When the bearing is fully seated, install the bearing retainer housing, but not the snap-rings at this time.

14. Install the rear bearing on the main-shaft and the bearing bore of the case. It will be necessary to seat the rear bearing further than the locating snap-ring would allow, so do not install the locating snap-ring until after the retaining snap-ring is installed.

15. Remove the front bearing retainer housing and fully seat the front bearing on the input shaft. Install the retaining and locating snap-rings. Install a new oil seal in the retainer housing and install on the transmission case.

16. Install the locating snap-ring on the rear bearing, if not previously done.

17. To install the cluster gear and countershaft, turn the transmission case on end with the input shaft down. Align the cluster gear bore and thrust washers with the case bores. Tap the countershaft into place and displace the dummy countershaft out the front of the case. Do not allow the dummy shaft to drop to the floor.

18. Level the transmission case and install the extension adapter housing with a new gasket.

19. Shift the synchronizer sleeves by hand to insure correct operation. Install 3.5 pints of lubricant into the case and install a new gasket on the shift housing flange. With the gears in the neutral position and the shift lever forks in their neutral position, install the shift lever housing in place on the transmission case.

TORQUE SPECIFICATIONS①

	ft. lbs.	N.m.
Backup lamp switch	15	20
Drain and fill plugs	15	20
Front bearing cap bolts	13	18
Shift housing-to-transmission case bolts	13	18
Support plate bolts	18	24

①All torque values given in foot-pounds and newton-meters with dry fits unless otherwise specified.

T-176 SPECIFICATIONS
Lubricant Capacity and End-Play Tolerances

End-Play Tolerances:
Countershaft Gear to Case .... 0.004 to 0.018 inch (0.10 to 0.45 mm)
Reverse Idler Gear to Case .... 0.004 to 0.018 inch (0.10 to 0.45 mm)
Mainshaft Gear Train .... 0.004 to 0.018 inch (0.10 to 0.45 mm)
Lubricant Capacity .... 3.5 pints (1.7 liters)
Lubricant Type .... SAE 85W-90, APJ GL5

Transfer Cases

TRANSFER CASE APPLICATION CHART

	Chev./GMC	Dodge/Plymouth	Ford	International	Jeep
Borg Warner 13-50			X		
Dana 20			X	X	X
Dana 21			X		
Dana 24			X		
Dana 300				X	X
International TC-143				X	
Jeep Selec-Trac 229					X
New Process 201		X			
New Process 202				X	
New Process 203	X	X	X		
New Process 205	X		X	X	
New Process 207	X				
New Process 208	X	X	X		X
New Process 219					X
Rockwell T223		X	X	X	
Spicer 20				X	X
Warner Quadra-Trac					X
Warner 1345			X		

TRANSFER CASE

Trouble Analysis

SLIPS OUT OF GEAR (HIGH–LOW)

1. Shifting poppet spring weak.
2. Bearing broken or worn.
3. Shifting fork bent.
4. Improper control rod adjustment.

SLIPS OUT OF FRONT WHEEL DRIVE

1. Shifting poppet spring weak or broken.
2. Bearing worn or broken.
3. Excessive shaft end-play.
4. Shifting fork bent.

HARD SHIFTING

1. Lack of lubricant.
2. Shift lever binding on shaft.
3. Shifting poppet ball scored.
4. Shifting fork bent.
5. Low tire pressure.

BACKLASH

1. Companion yoke loose.
2. Transfer case loose on mounts.
3. Internal parts excessively worn.

NOISY

1. Low lubricant level.
2. Bearings improperly adjusted or excessively worn.
3. Gears worn or damaged.
4. Improper alignment of driveshafts or U-joints.

OIL LEAKAGE

1. Excessive amount of lubricant in case.
2. Vent clogged.
3. Gaskets or seals leaking.

4. Bearings loose or damaged.
5. Driveshaft yoke mating surfaces scored.

OVERHEATING

1. Excessive or insufficient amount of lubricant.
2. Bearing adjustment too tight.

CLEANING & INSPECTION

CLEANING

During overhaul, all components of the transfer case (except bearing assemblies) should be thoroughly cleaned with solvent and dried with air pressure prior to inspection and reassembly.

1. Clean the bearing assemblies as follows.

NOTE: Proper cleaning of bearings is of utmost importance. Bearings should always be cleaned separately from other parts.

a. Soak all bearing assemblies in clean solvent or fuel oil. Bearings should never be cleaned in a hot solution tank.

b. Slush bearings in solvent until all old lubricant is loosened. Hold races so that bearings will not rotate; then clean bearings with a soft bristled brush until all dirt has been removed. Remove loose particles of dirt by tapping bearing flat against a block of wood.

c. Rinse bearings in clean solvent; then blow bearings dry with air pressure.

CAUTION
Do not spin bearings while drying.

---

d. After drying, rotate each bearing slowly while examining balls or rollers for roughness, damage, or excessive wear. Replace all bearings that are not in first class condition.

NOTE: After cleaning and inspecting bearings lubricate generously with recommended lubricant, then wrap each bearing in clean paper until ready for reassembly.

2. Remove all portions of old gaskets from parts, using a stiff brush or scraper.

INSPECTION

1. Inspect all parts for discoloration or warpage.
2. Examine all gears and splines for chipped, worn, broken or nicked teeth. Small nicks or burrs may be removed with a fine abrasive stone.
3. Inspect the breather assembly to make sure that it is open and not damaged.
4. Check all threaded parts for damaged, stripped, or crossed threads.
5. Replace all gaskets, oil seals and snap-rings.
6. Inspect housings, retainers and covers for cracks or other damage. Replace the damaged parts.
7. Inspect keys and keyways for condition and fit.
8. Inspect shift forks for wear, distortion or any other damage.
9. Check detent ball springs for free length, compressed length, distortion or collapsed coils.
10. Check bearing fit on their respective shafts and in their bores or cups. Inspect bearings, shafts and cups for wear.

NOTE: If either bearings or cups are worn or damaged, it is advisable to replace both parts.

11. Inspect all bearing rollers or balls for pitting or galling.
12. Examine detent balls for corrosion or brinneling. If shift bar detents show wear, replace them.
13. Replace all worn or damaged parts. When assembling the transfer case, coat all moving parts with recommended lubricant.

Borg Warner 13–50 Transfer Case

The Borg Warner 13–50 is a three-piece aluminum part time transfer case. It transfers power from the transmission to the rear axle and when actuated, also to the front drive axle. The unit is lubricated by a positive displacement oil pump that channels oil flow through drilled holes in the rear output shaft. The pump turns with the rear output shaft and allows towing of the vehicle at maximum legal road speeds for extended distances without disconnecting the front and/or rear driveshaft.

Removal

1. Raise the vehicle on a hoist.
2. If so equipped, remove the skid plate from frame.
3. Place a drain pan under transfer case, remove the drain plug and drain fluid from the transfer case.
4. Disconnect the four-wheel drive indicator switch wire connector at the transfer case.
5. Disconnect the front driveshaft from the axle input yoke.
6. Loosen the clamp retaining the front driveshaft boot to the transfer case, and pull the driveshaft and front boot assembly out of the transfer case front output shaft.
7. Disconnect the rear driveshaft from the transfer case output shaft yoke.
8. Disconnect the speedometer driven gear from the transfer case rear cover.
9. Disconnect the vent hose from the control lever.
10. Loosen or remove the large bolt and the small bolt retaining the shifter to the extension housing. Pull on the control lever until the bushing slides off the transfer case shift lever pin. If necessary, unscrew the shift lever from the control lever.
11. Remove the heat shield from the transfer case.

Borg-Warner 13-50 transfer case

12. Support the transfer case with a transmission jack.

13. Remove the five bolts retaining the transfer case to the transmission and the extension housing.

14. Slide the transfer case rearward off the transmission output shaft and lower the transfer case from the vehicle. Remove the gasket from between the transfer case and extension housing.

SHIFT LEVER

Removal

NOTE: Remove the shift ball only if the shift ball, boot or lever is to be replaced. If the ball, boot or lever is not being replaced, remove the ball, boot and lever as an assembly.

1. Remove the plastic insert from the shift ball. Warm the ball with a heat gun to 60°–87°C (140°–180°F) and knock the ball off the lever with a block of wood and a hammer. Be careful not to damage the finish on the shift lever.

2. Remove the rubber boot and floor pan cover.

3. Disconnect the vent hose from the control lever.

4. Unscrew the shift lever from the control lever.

5. Remove the bolts retaining the shifter to the extension housing. Remove the control lever and bushings.

Disassembly

1. Remove the transfer case from the vehicle.

2. Remove the transfer case drain plug with a ⅜ inch drive ratchet and drain the fluid.

3. Remove the four-wheel drive indicator switch and the breather vent.

4. Remove the rear output shaft yoke by removing the 30mm nut, steel washer and rubber seal from the output shaft.

5. Remove the nine 15mm bolts which retain the front case to the rear cover. Insert a ½ inch drive breaker bar between the three pry bosses and separate the front case from the rear cover. Remove all traces of RTV gasket sealant from the mating surfaces of the front case and rear cover.

6. If the speedometer drive gear or ball bearing assembly is to be replaced, first, drive out the output shaft oil seal from either the inside of the rear cover with a brass drift and hammer or from the outside by bending and pulling on the curved-up lip of the oil seal. Remove and discard the oil seal. Remove the speedometer drive gear assembly (gear, clip and spacer). Note that the round end of the speedometer gear clip faces the inside of the rear cover.

7. Remove the internal snap-ring that retains the rear output shaft ball bearing in the bore. From the outside of the case, drive out the ball bearing with Output Shaft Bearing Replacer, T83T-7025-B and Drive Handle, T80T-4000-W or equivalent.

8. If required, remove the front output shaft caged needle bearing from the rear cover with Puller Collet, D80L-100-S and Impact Slide Hammer, T50T-100-A or equivalent.

9. Remove the 2W-4W shift fork spring from the boss in the rear cover.

10. Remove the shift collar hub from the output shaft. Remove the 2W-4W lock-up assembly and the 2W-4W shift fork together as an assembly. Remove the 2W-4W fork from the 2W-4W lock-up assembly. If required, remove the external clip and remove the roller bushing assembly (bushing, shaft and external clip) from the 2W-4W shift fork.

11. If required to disassemble the 2W-4W lock-up assembly, remove the internal snap-ring and pull the lock-up hub and spring from the lock-up collar.

12. Remove the external snap-ring and thrust washer that retains the driven sprocket to the front output shaft.

13. Remove the chain, driven sprocket and drive sprocket as an assembly.

14. Remove the collector magnet from the notch in the front case bottom.

15. Remove the output shaft and oil pump as an assembly.

16. If required to disassemble the oil pump, remove the four 8mm bolts from the body. Note the position and markings of the front cover, body, pins, spring, rear cover, and pump retainer as removed.

17. Pull out the shift rail.

18. Slip the high-low range shift fork out of the inside track of the shift cam. If required, remove the external clip and remove the roller bushing assembly (bushing, shaft and external clip) from the high-low range shift fork.

19. Remove the high-low shift hub from out of the planetary gearset in the front case.

20. Push and pull out the anchor end of the torsion spring from the locking post in the front case half. Remove the torsion spring and roller out of the shift cam (if so equipped).

21. Turn the front case over and remove the six 15mm bolts retaining the mounting adapter to the front case. Remove the mounting adapter, input shaft and planetary gearset as an assembly.

22. If required, remove the ring gear from the front case using a press. Note the relationship of the serrations to the chamfered pilot diameter during removal.

23. Expand the tangs of the large snap-ring in the mounting adapter and pry under the planetary gearset and separate the input shaft and planetary gearset from the mounting adapter.

24. If required, remove the oil from the mounting adapter with Seal Remover, Tool-1175-AC and Impact Slide Hammer, T50T-100-A or equivalent.

25. Remove the internal snap-ring from the planetary carrier and separate the planetary gearset from the input shaft assembly.

26. Remove the external snap-ring from the input shaft. Place the input shaft assembly in a press and remove the ball bearing from the input shaft using Bearing Splitter, D79L-4621-A or equivalent. Remove the thrust washer, thrust plate and sun gear off the input shaft.

27. Move the shift lever by hand until the shift cam is in the FOUR WHEEL HIGH detent position (4WH) and mark a line on the outside of the front case using the side of the shift lever and a grease pencil.

28. Remove the two phillips head set screws from the front case and from the shift cam.

29. Turn the front case over and remove the external clip. Pry the shift lever out of the front case and shift cam.

NOTE: Removal of four-wheel drive indicator switch will ease removal of the shift lever and shift cam assembly.

30. Remove the O-ring from the second groove in the shift lever shaft.

31. Remove the detent plunger and compression spring from the inside of the front case.

32. Remove the internal snap-ring and remove the ball bearing retainer from the front case by tapping on the face of the front output shaft and U-joint assembly with a plastic hammer. Remove the internal snap-ring and drive the ball bearing out of the bearing retainer using Output Shaft Bearing Replacer, T83T-7025-B and Driver Handle, T80T-4000-W or equivalent.

NOTE: The clip is required to prevent the bearing retainer from rotating. Do not discard the clip.

33. Remove the front output shaft and U-joint assembly from the front case. If required, remove the oil seal with Seal Remover, Tool-1175-AC and Impact Slide Hammer, T50T-100-A or equivalent. If required, remove the internal snap-ring and drive the ball bearing out of the front case bore using Output Shaft Replacer, T83T-7025-B and Driver Handle, T80T-4000-W or equivalent.

34. If required, place the front output shaft and U-joint assembly in a vise, being careful not to damage the assembly. Use copper or wood vise jaws.

35. Remove the internal snap-rings that retain the bearings in the shaft.

36. Position the U-Joint Tool, T74P-4635-C or equivalent, over the shaft ears and press the bearing out. If the bearing cannot be pressed all the way out, remove it with vise grip or channel lock pliers.

37. Re-position the U-joint tool on the spider in order to remove the opposite bearing.

38. Repeat the above procedure until all bearings are removed.

Assembly

Before assembly, lubricate all parts with DEXRON® II, Automatic Transmission Fluid.

1. If removed, start a new bearing into an end of the shaft ear. Support the output shaft in a vise equipped with copper or wood jaws, in order not to damage the shaft.

2. Position the spider into the bearing and press the bearing below the snap-ring groove using U-joint Tool, T74P-4635-C or equivalent.

3. Remove the tool and install a new internal snap-ring on the groove.

4. Start a new bearing into the opposite side of the shaft ear and using the tool, press the bearing until the opposite bearing contacts the snap-ring.

5. Remove the tool and install a new internal snap-ring in the groove.

6. Re-position the front output shaft assembly and install the other two bearings in the same manner.

7. Check the U-joint for freedom of movement. If a binding condition occurs due to misalignment during the installation procedure, tap the ears of both shafts sharply to relieve the bind. Do not install the front output shaft assembly if the U-joint shows any sign of binding.

8. If removed, drive the ball bearing into the front output case bore using Output Shaft Bearing Replacer, T83T-7025-B and Drive Handle, T80T-4000-W or equivalent. Drive the ball bearing in straight, making sure that it is not cocked in the bore. Install the internal snap-ring that retains the ball bearing to the front case.

9. If removed, install the front output oil seal in the front case bore using Output Shaft Seal Installer, T83T-7065-B and Driver Handle, T80T-4000-W or equivalent.

10. If removed, install the ring gear in the front case. Align the serrations on the outside diameter of the ring gear to the serrations previously cut in the front case bore. Using a press, start the piloted chamferred end of the ring gear first and press in until it is fully seated. Make sure the ring gear is not cocked in the bore.

11. If removed, install the ball bearing in the bearing retainer bore. Drive the bearing into the retainer using Output Shaft

Bearing Replacer, T83T-7025-B and Driver Handle, T80T-4000-W or equivalent. Make sure the ball bearing is not cocked in the bore. Install the internal snap-ring that retains the ball bearing to the retainer.

12. Install the front output shaft and U-joint assembly through the front case seal. Position the ball bearing and retainer assembly over the front output shaft and install in the front case bore. Make sure the clip on the bearing retainer aligns with the slot in the front case. Tap the bearing retainer into place with a plastic hammer. Install the internal snap-ring that retains the ball bearing and retainer assembly to the front case.

13. Install the compression spring and the detent plunger into the bore from the inside of the front case.

14. Install a new O-ring in the second groove of the shift lever shaft. Coat the shaft and O-ring with Multi-Purpose Long-Life Lubricant.

NOTE: Use a rubber band to fill the first groove so as not to cut the O-ring. Discard the rubber band.

15. Position the shift cam inside the front case with the 4WH detent position over the detent plunger. Holding the shift cam by hand, push the shift lever shaft into the front case to engage the shift cam aligning the side of the shift lever with the mark previously scribed on the front case. Install the external clip on the end of the shift lever shaft.

16. Install the two phillips head set screws in the front case and in the shift cam. Tighten the screws to 6.8–9.5 N·m (5–7 ft. lbs.). Make sure the set screw in the front case is in the first groove of the shift lever shaft and not bottomed against the shaft itself. The shift lever should be able to move freely to all detent positions.

17. Slide the sun gear, thrust plate, thrust washer, and press the ball bearing over the input shaft. Install the external snap-ring to the input shaft.

NOTE: The sun gear recessed face and ball bearing snap-ring groove should be toward the rear of the transfer case. The stepped face of the thrust washer should face towards the ball bearing.

18. Install the planetary gear set to the sun gear and input shaft assembly. Install the internal snap-ring to the planetary carrier.

19. Drive the oil seal into the bore of the mounting adapter with Input Shaft Seal Installer, T83T-7065-A and Driver Handle, T80T-4000-W or equivalent.

20. Place the tanged snap-ring in the mounting adapter groove. Position the input shaft and planetary gearset in the mounting adapter and push inward until the planetary assembly and input shaft assembly are seated in the adapter. When properly seated, the tanged snap-ring will snap into place. Check installation by holding the mounting adapter by hand and tapping the face of the input shaft against a wooden

block to ensure that the snap-ring is engaged.

21. Remove all traces of RTV gasket sealant from the mating surfaces of the front case and mounting adapter. Install a bead of RTV gasket sealant on the surface of the front case.

22. Position the mounting adapter on the front case. Install six bolts and tighten to 31–41 N·m (23–30 ft. lbs.).

23. Position the roller on the 90° bent tang of the torsion spring. The larger diameter end of the spring must be installed first.

24. Install the roller into the torsion spring roller track of the shift cam while locating the center of the spring in the pivot groove in the front case. Push the anchor end of the torsion spring behind the locking post adjacent to the ring gear face.

25. Position the High-Low shift hub into the planetary gearset. Slip the High-Low shift fork bushing into the High-Low roller track of the shift cam and the groove of the High-Low shift hub.

NOTE: Make sure the nylon wear pads are installed on the shift fork. Make sure the dot on the pad is installed in the fork hole.

26. Install the shift rail through the high-low fork and make sure the shift rail is seated in the bore in the front case.

27. Place the oil pump cover with the word TOP facing the front of the front case. Install the two pump pins (flats facing upwards) with the spring between the pins and place the assembly in the oil pump bore in the output shaft. Place the oil pump body and pickup tube over the shaft and make sure the pins are riding against the inside of the pump body. Place the oil pump rear cover with the words TOP REAR facing the rear of the front case. The word TOP on the front cover and the rear cover should be on the same side. Install the pump retainer, the four bolts and rotate the output shaft while tightening the bolts to prevent the pump from binding. Tighten the bolts to 4.0–4.5 N·m (36–40 in. lbs.).

NOTE: The output shaft must turn freely within the oil pump. If binding occurs, loosen the four bolts and retighten again.

28. Install the output shaft and oil pump assembly in the input shaft. Make sure the external splines of the output shaft engage the internal splines of the high-low shift hub. Make sure the oil pump retainer and oil filter leg are in the groove and notch of the front case.

29. Install the collector magnet in the notch in the front case.

30. Install the chain, drive sprocket and driven sprocket as an assembly over the shafts. Install the thrust washer on the front output shaft and install the external snap-ring over the thrust washer to retain the driven sprocket.

31. If disassembled, assemble the 2W-

4W lockup assembly. Install the spring in the lockup collar. Place the lockup hub over the spring and engage the lockup hub in the notches in the lockup collar. Retain the lockup hub to the lockup collar with an internal snap-ring.

32. Install the 2W-4W shift fork to the 2W-4W lockup assembly. If removed, make sure the nylon wear pads are installed on the fork. The dot on the pad must be installed in the hole in the fork. Install the 2W-4W lockup collar and hub assembly over the output shaft and onto the shift rail. If removed, install the shaft, bushing and external clip to the 2W-4W lockup fork.

33. Install the shift collar hub to the output shaft.

34. If removed, drive the caged needle bearing into the rear cover bore with Needle Bearing Replacer, T83T-7127-A and Driver Handle, T80T-4000-W or equivalent.

35. If removed, install the ball bearing in the rear cover bore. Drive the bearing into the rear cover bore with Output Shaft Bearing Replacer, T83T-7025-B and Driver Handle, T80-4000-W or equivalent. Make sure the ball bearing is not cocked in the bore. Install the internal snap-ring that retains the ball bearing to the rear cover.

36. Install the speedometer drive gear assembly into the rear cover bore with the round end of the speedometer gear clip facing towards the inside of the rear cover. Drive the oil seal into the rear cover bore with Output Shaft Seal Installer, T83T-7065-B and Driver Handle, T80T-4000-W or equivalent.

37. Install the 2W-4W shift fork spring on the inside boss of the rear cover.

38. Prior to final assembly of rear cover to front case half, the transfer case shift lever assembly should be shifted into the "4H" detent position to assure positioning of the shift rail to the rear cover.

39. Coat the mating surface of the front case with a bead of Silicone Rubber.

40. Position the rear cover on the front case, making sure that the 2W-4W shift fork spring engages the shift rail and does not fall off the rear cover boss. Install the nine bolts (starting with the bolts on the rear cover) and tighten to 31–41 N·m (23–30 ft. lbs.).

NOTE: If the rear cover assembly does not seat properly, move the rear cover up and down slightly to permit the end of the shift rail to enter the shift rail hole in the rear cover boss.

41. Install the rear yoke on the output shaft. Install the rubber seal, washer and nut. Tighten the nut to 163–203 N·m (120–150 ft. lbs.).

42. Install the four-wheel drive indicator switch and tighten to 34–47 N·m (25–35 ft. lbs.).

43. Install the breather plug and tighten to 8–19 N·m (6–14 ft. lbs.).

44. Install the drain plug and tighten to 19–30 N·m (14–22 ft. lbs.).

45. Place a ⅜ inch drive ratchet in the

TORQUE SPECIFICATIONS
Borg-Warner 13-50 Transfer Case

Description	Torque	
	N·m	Ft. Lb.
Breather Vent	8–19	6–14
Case to Cover Bolts	31–41	23–30
Drain and Fill Plug	19–30	14–22
Four-Wheel Drive Indicator Switch	34–47	25–35
Front and Rear Driveshaft Bolts	16–20	12–15
Shift Control Bolts—Large	95–122	70–90
Shift Control Bolts—Small	42–57	31–42
Shift Shaft and Shift Cam Set Screw	6.8–9.5	5–7
Skid Plate to Frame Bolt	30–41	22–30
Transfer Case to Transmission Adapter	34–47	25–35
Upper Shift Control Lever and Heat Shield Bolts	37–50	27–37
Yoke Nut	163–203	120–150
	N·m	In. Lb.
Oil Pump Bolts	4.0–4.5	36–40
Speedometer Screw	2.3–2.8	20–25

fill plug and remove the plug. Fill the transfer case with 1.4 liters (3.0 U.S. pints) of DEXRON® II, Automatic Transmission Fluid. Install the fill plug and tighten to fill and drain plugs to 19–30 N·m (14–22 ft. lbs.).

46. Reinstall the transfer case.

Dana Model 20

The Dana Model 20 is a two-speed gearbox that controls the power from the transmission to the front and rear driving axles. Positions of the transfer case are: four-wheel-drive low (4L), neutral (N), two-wheel-drive high (2H) and four-wheel-drive high (4H).

Disassembly
TRANSFER CASE

1. Clean any dirt from the transfer case and remove the bottom cover plate.

2. Remove the retaining plug, flat washer, detent spring and ball which engages the front drive shift rail detent rod. Then, remove plug from front drive detent rod access hole.

3. Remove the retaining plug, detent spring and ball which engages the rear drive shift rail detent rod.

4. Remove the idler shaft lockplate.

5. Using a hammer and soft drift, drive the idler shaft rearward and out of the case;

then lift out the thrust washers and idler gear.

NOTE: When removing the idler gear, do not lose any of the rollers.

6. Remove the flange retaining nuts from the front and rear output shafts.

7. Remove the flange from the front and rear output shafts. Discard the O-ring.

8. Remove the bolts securing the adapter housing to the case; then remove the adapter as an assembly.

9. Remove the bolts which attach the rear output shaft bearing retainer to the case; then remove the retainer and output shaft as an assembly.

NOTE: Be sure not to lose any of the rollers.

10. Disconnect the shift rail link from the two shift rails.

11. Lift out the rear output shaft sliding gear.

12. Remove the setscrew securing the rear fork to the shift rail; then remove the rear drive shift rail and fork.

13. Remove the front output shaft rear cover and shims. Fasten the shims together.

14. Remove the front output shaft bearing retainer and gasket.

15. Tap the threaded end of the front output shaft; then remove the rear cup.

16. Angle the front output shaft front bearing away from the main drive gear to allow removal of the snap-ring; then tap the shaft and rear bearing out of the case.

17. Lift out the sliding gear, main drive gear, front bearing, spacer and snap-ring.

1 Input shaft
2 Transfer case
3 Input gear
4 Snap ring
5 Sliding clutch gear
6 Rear input shaft
  needle bearing
7 Rear output shaft
  front bearing

8 Rear Output shaft
  front bearing cup
9 Rear output shaft
  housing gasket
10 Rear output shaft
  housing breather
11 Speedometer driven
  gear
12 Rear output shaft
  housing
13 Rear output shaft
  rear bearing cup
14 Rear output shaft
  rear bearing
15 Rear output shaft
  yoke
16 Rear output shaft
  locknut
17 Washer
18 Rear output shaft
19 Rear output shaft
  seal
20 Shims
21 Speedometer drive
  gear
22 Intermediate shaft
  lock plate bolt
23 Intermediate shaft
  lock plate
24 Intermediate shaft
  bearing spacer
25 Intermediate shaft
26 Intermediate shaft
  needle bearings
27 Intermediate shaft
  tanged thrust
  washer

28 Intermediate gear
29 Front output shaft
  rear cover
30 Front output shaft
  rear bearing
31 Front output shaft
  rear cover shim
  pack
32 Front output shaft
  rear bearing cup
33 Front output shaft
  sliding clutch gear
34 Drain Plug
35 Front output shaft
  drive gear
36 Spacer
37 Front output shaft
  front bearing
38 Front output shaft
  front bearing cup
39 Spacer
40 Front output shaft
  seal
41 Front output shaft
  bearing
42 Front output shaft
  yoke
43 Rubber "O" ring
44 Washer
45 Front Output shaft
  locknut

FRONT

Cross section of Dana model 20 transfer case (© General Motors Corp.)

18. Remove the front cup.
19. Remove the setscrew securing the front shift fork to the shift rail; then remove the rail and fork.
20. Remove the detent rods.
21. Remove shift rail oil seal.

INPUT SHAFT

1. Remove the snap-ring from the front of the shaft.
2. Place the adapter housing and input shaft on a press and force the shaft out of the main drive gear and housing.
3. Remove the bearing retaining snap-ring; then remove bearing.
4. Remove the seal in the adapter housing.

Exploded view of the input shaft of a Dana 20 transfer case (© Ford Motor Co.)

REAR OUTPUT SHAFT

1. Remove needle bearings from bore of shaft.
2. Remove speedometer driven gear.
3. Place bearing retainer and shaft assembly in a press; then force shaft out of retainer.
4. Lift off speedometer drive gear and shims. Tag shims for reassembly.
5. Press out the outer cup, bearing and seal.
6. Remove the inner cup.
7. Remove the inner bearing.

FRONT OUTPUT SHAFT

Using the sliding gear as a base, press rear bearing off shaft.

Assembly

INPUT SHAFT

1. Install a new seal in the adapter housing.
2. Install bearing in the housing and secure with snap-ring.
3. Using the main drive gear as a base, force the input shaft through the housing, seal, bearings and main drive gear. Secure with snap-ring on front of shaft.

REAR OUTPUT SHAFT

1. Press the shaft into the inner bearing.
2. Install outer cup in the bearing retainer.
3. Install the inner cup.
4. Position the outer bearing in the retainer; then place the shims and speedometer drive gear on the shaft. Install shaft in the bearing retainer housing.
5. Place the bearing retainer and shaft in a vise. Install the output shaft flange and torque the retaining nut to specifications.
6. With a dial indicator on the flange end of the shaft, measure end-play. Adjust shim pack between the speedometer drive gear and outer bearing to achieve correct clearance.
7. After setting correct end-play, remove flange and press bearing retainer seal into housing.
8. Install the flange, washer and nut. Tighten the nut to specifications.

FRONT OUTPUT SHAFT

Using a press, force front output rear bearing on shaft.

Exploded view of the rear output shaft of a Dana 20 transfer case (© Ford Motor Co.)

SHIFT RAIL OIL SEALS

Install the two shift rail oil seals with appropriate tools.

TRANSFER CASE

1. Install the front detent rod in the case.
2. Slide the front drive shift rail all the way into the case and place the shift fork on the rail as it enters the case. Secure the fork to the rail with the setscrew.
3. Position the front output shaft sliding gear in the shift fork.
4. Install the rear detent rod.
5. Slide the rear drive shift rail into the case and position the shift fork on the rail as the rail enters the case. Secure the fork to the rail with the setscrew.

NOTE: The shift rails should be inserted so that the detents are positioned as shown in illustration.

6. While holding the sliding gear and main drive gear in position, install the front output shaft and rear bearing assembly through the two gears.
7. Install the main drive gear spacer and secure with the snap-ring.
8. Install the front output shaft rear bearing cup.
9. Place the front output shaft rear cover and shims on the case and install the attaching bolts.
10. Install the front output shaft front bearing on the shaft. Install the front bearing cup.
11. If the front bearing retainer oil seal was removed, install a new seal. Position

the bearing retainer and gasket to the case and install the attaching bolts.

12. Place the rear output shaft rear bearing retainer on a work bench and install 13 needle bearings in the splined hub of the output shaft, using vaseline or grease.
13. Position the rear output shaft rear bearing retainer assembly to the case and install the attaching bolts.
14. Install the rear output shaft sliding gear in the shifting fork and on the splines of the output shaft.
15. Position the adapter housing assembly on the rear output shaft and case. Install the attaching bolts.
16. Install the roller bearings in the bore of the idler shaft gear with vaseline or grease.
17. Position the idler gear and thrust washers in the case; then drive the idler shaft into the rear of the case through the idler gear and thrust washers.

NOTE: After installing the idler shaft, tap the sides of the case to relieve any possible binding.

18. Install the idler shaft lock plate.
19. Secure the shift rail link to the two shift rails.

SPECIFICATIONS

END PLAY (IN.)

Front output shaft	0.001–0.005
Rear output shaft	0.001–0.005

TORQUE LIMITS (FT. LBS.)

Transfer case to transmission extension bolts	20–30
Transfer case to transmission output shaft nut	60–80
Front output shaft rear cover bolts	25–32
Front output shaft bearing retainer bolts	25–32
Idler shaft cover bolts	25–32
Front and rear output flanges	80–85

Exploded view of the front output shaft of a Dana 20 transfer case (© Ford Motor Co.)

20. Install the front and rear drive shift rail detent balls, springs and retaining plugs.

NOTE: Be sure that the heavier loaded spring and flat washer are installed in the front drive shift rail.

21. Install the rod access hole plug.

22. Install the flange, washer and retaining nut on each of the output shafts. Be sure to install a new O-ring in the front output shaft flange. Torque the attaching nuts to specifications.

23. With a dial indicator on the front drive output shaft, check the end-play. If not within specifications, adjust the shim pack at the front output shaft rear cover.

24. Place the cover plate on the case and install the attaching bolts.

Dana Model 21

The Dana Model 21 is a single-speed gearbox that transmits power to the front driving axle. There are two positions of the transfer case; front drive axle engaged and front drive axle disengaged.

Disassembly
TRANSFER CASE

1. Clean all dirt from transfer case and drain lubricant.

2. Remove bolts that attach the cover to the top of the case; then remove the cover.

3. Remove the setscrew securing the shift fork to the rail. Tap the shift rail rearward; then remove the rail cap from the rear of the case.

4. Remove the shift rail and fork.

5. Remove the detent spring and ball which engages the front drive shift rail.

6. Remove the flange attaching nuts, flat washer and O-ring from the front and rear output shafts. Discard the O-rings.

7. Remove the flange from the front and rear output shafts.

8. Remove the bolts that attach the rear output shaft bearing retainer to the case; then remove the retainer and output shaft as an assembly.

9. Remove the front and rear idler shaft covers.

10. Using a hammer and soft drift, drive the idler shaft and rear idler bearing rearward out of the case; then lift out the front bearing and idler gear.

11. Remove the front output shaft bearing retainer and gasket. Remove the retainer seal if it is worn or damaged.

12. Remove the front output shaft rear cover and shims. Tie the shims together for reassembly.

13. Tap the end of the front output shaft toward the front of the case; then remove the front bearing cup. Remove the rear bearing cup by tapping the shaft rearward.

14. Angle the front output shaft front bearing away from the main drive gear to remove the snap-ring from its groove in the shaft. Drive the output shaft and rear bearing out of the case.

Exploded view of the case housing and shift mechanism of a Dana 21 transfer case (© Ford Motor Co.)

15. Remove the sliding gear, main drive gear, front bearing, thrust washer and snap-ring from the case.

16. Remove the shift rail seal.

FRONT OUTPUT SHAFT BEARING

To remove the front output shaft rear bearing, use the sliding gear as a base and press off the bearing.

IDLER SHAFT

1. Remove the snap-ring from the idler shaft.

2. Using the idler gear as a base, press the idler shaft out of the rear bearing.

REAR OUTPUT SHAFT

1. To remove the output shaft from the bearing retainer tap shaft rearward. Remove the shims and spacer.

2. Remove the inner bearing from the output shaft.

3. Place the bearing retainer on a press and force out the outer cup, outer bearing and oil seal.

4. Using a soft drift, drive out the inner bearing cup.

Assembly
FRONT OUTPUT SHAFT

Using an arbor press, force rear bearing on front output shaft.

IDLER SHAFT

1. Using a press, install rear idler bearing on the shaft.

Exploded view of the idler shaft of a Dana 21 transfer case (© Ford Motor Co.)

Exploded view of the rear output shaft of a Dana 21 transfer case (© Ford Motor Co.)

Exploded view of the front output shaft of a Dana 21 transfer case (© Ford Motor Co.)

END PLAY (IN.)	
Front output shaft	0.001–0.005
Rear output shaft	0.001–0.005

TORQUE LIMITS (FT. LBS.)	
Transfer case to transmission extension bolts	20–30
Transfer case to transmission output shaft nut	125–150
Front output shaft rear cover bolts	25–32
Front output shaft bearing retainer bolts	25–32
Idler shaft cover bolts	25–32

2. Install snap-ring.

REAR OUTPUT SHAFT

1. Press the inner bearing on the output shaft.

2. Using a soft-faced hammer, tap the inner bearing cup into the retainer.

3. Install the outer cup.

4. Place spacer and shims on the output shaft; then install the shaft in the bearing retainer housing.

5. Install the outer bearing on the shaft.

6. Place the bearing retainer and output shaft in a vise. Measure end-play with a dial indicator on end of the shaft. If not within specifications, adjust shim pack between the spacer and the front and rear bearing cones.

7. After setting correct end-play, install the bearing retainer seal.

TRANSFER CASE

1. While holding the drive gear, sliding gear and thrust washer in the case, install the front output shaft, from the rear, through the gears and washer. Install the snap-ring.

2. Install the front output shaft rear bearing cup.

3. Place the front output shaft rear cover and shims on the case. After removing old sealant from all mating surfaces with thinner, apply gasket sealer to the attaching bolts and torque to specifications. With the cover installed, apply sealer to the outside edge of the adjusting shims, case and cover joints.

4. Install the front output shaft rear bearing on the shaft. Install the front bearing.

5. If the front bearing retainer oil seal was removed, install a new seal. Position the bearing retainer and gasket to the case and install attaching bolts.

6. Install the flange, new O-ring, washer and attaching nut on the front output shaft.

7. With a dial indicator on the front drive output shaft, check the end-play. If not within specified limits, increase or decrease the shim pack thickness at the front output shaft rear cover.

8. Place the idler gear in the case; then install the idler shaft through the gear. Install the front bearing.

9. Place the front and rear idler covers and gaskets on the case; then install attaching bolts.

10. Install a new shift rail seal.

11. Install the shift rail detent ball and spring in the top of the case.

12. Slide the shift rail into the case and position the fork on the rail as the rail enters the case. Depressing the detent ball and spring will allow the rail to pass. Secure the fork to the rail with the setscrew. Install the shift rail cap.

13. Position the rear output shaft and bearing retainer assembly to the case, then install the attaching bolts.

14. Install the flange, new O-ring, washer and attaching nut on the rear output shaft.

15. Place the top cover and gasket on the case, then install attaching bolts.

16. Fill the transfer case to the proper level with the recommended lubricant.

Dana Model 24

The Dana Model 24 is a two-speed gearbox that is manually controlled by a shift lever in the cab. The transfer case positions are: four-wheel-drive low (4L), neutral (N), two-wheel-drive high (2H) and four-wheel-drive high (4H).

Dana Model 24 gear train—neutral position illustrated (© Ford Motor Co.)

Disassembly

1. Clean any dirt from the transfer case and remove the power take-off cover plate.

2. Remove both idler shaft bearing retainers.

3. Using a soft-faced hammer, tap the idler shaft and bearing to the rear until the bearing is free of the case.

4. Remove the idler shaft, two gears and spacer.

5. Remove the idler shaft front bearing.

6. Remove the flange retaining nuts from the front output shaft, the input shaft and the rear output shaft.

7. Remove the flanges and washers.

8. Remove the front output shaft front and rear bearing retainers.

9. Tap the front output shaft and rear bearing through the gears and case. Remove the high speed gear.

10. Remove the front output shaft front bearing and washer.

11. Remove the setscrew that retains the front drive shaft fork to the shift rail.

12. Remove the front output shaft sliding gear.

13. If the input shaft oil seal is to be replaced, remove it with a four-jaw puller and slide hammer.

14. Remove the input shaft bearing retainer.

15. If the output shaft bearing retainer oil seal is to be replaced, remove it with a puller and slide hammer.

16. Remove the rear output shaft bearing retainer; then remove the speedometer drive assembly.

17. Loosen the rear output shaft assembly from the case by driving on the front end of the input shaft with a soft-faced hammer.

18. Remove the rear output shaft and bearing retainer as an assembly.

19. Tap the input shaft through the front bearing, through the main drive gear, through the sliding gear and out of the case.

20. Lift the main drive gear out of the case and then drive out the input shaft front bearing.

Removing/installing the front output shaft of a Dana 24 transfer case (© Ford Motor Co.)

21. Remove the setscrew that retains the rear drive shift fork to the shift rail.

22. Remove the rear output shaft sliding gear.

23. Remove the shift rail link from the two shift rails.

24. Remove the retaining plug, detent spring and ball which engage the front drive shift rail detent rod.

25. Remove the retaining plug detent spring and ball which engages the rear drive shift rail detent rod. Remove the front drive detent rod access hole plug.

26. Pull the front drive shift rail to the furthest outward position.

27. Pull the rear drive shift rail far enough to allow the two detent rods to slide out.

28. Remove the rear drive shift rail and fork.

29. Remove the shift rail seals.

Removing/installing the rear output shaft of a Dana 24 transfer case (© Ford Motor Co.)

Removing/installing the input shaft of a Dana 24 transfer case (© Ford Motor Co.)

Assembly

1. Slide the front drive shift rail all the way into the case and position the shift fork on the rail as the rail enters the case.

2. Install the two detent rods in the case.

3. Install the rear drive shift fork and hold the detent rods and the fork in place as the rear drive shift rail is pushed in as far as possible.

NOTE: In steps 2 and 3, the shift rails should be inserted so that the detents are positioned as shown in illustration.

4. Pull the front drive shift rail out to its next detent. This will permit the rear

The rear drive shift fork and sliding gear of the Dana 24 transfer case (© Ford Motor Co.)

drive shift rail to be pushed in to the full extent of its travel. After pushing the rear drive shift rail all the way in, push the front drive shift rail back to its extreme inward position.

5. Install the rear drive shift detent ball, spring and retaining plug; then install the access hole plug.

6. Install the front drive shift rail detent ball, spring and retaining plug.

7. Secure the shift rail link in the two shift rails.

8. Place the rear output sliding gear in the shift fork and secure the fork to the rear drive shift rail with the setscrew.

9. Install the input shaft front bearing and retainer assembly. Coat retainer and bolts with sealer.

10. Place the main drive gear in the case; then slide the input shaft into the rear of the case through the main drive gear and through the front bearing and retainer.

11. Install the roller bearings in the splined hub of the rear output shaft assembly with petrolatum jelly or grease. Then install the shaft and bearing retainer assembly, making sure that the output shaft is aligned correctly with the input shaft. Coat the case, bearing retainer and bolts with sealer.

12. Position the front output sliding gear in the shift fork and secure the fork to the front drive shift rail with the setscrew.

13. While holding the sliding gear and high speed gear in position, install the front output shaft and rear bearing assembly through the two gears from the rear of the case.

14. After coating with sealer, install the front output shaft rear bearing retainer and gasket.

15. Install the washer and bearing over the front output shaft at the front of the case and then install the front bearing retainer and gasket. Coat retainer with sealer.

16. Install the flange, washer, flange retaining nut and cotter key on each of the three shafts. Torque to specifications.

17. Place the idler shaft gears in the case and install the shaft and rear bearing assembly from the rear. After applying sealer to the plate and bolts, install the rear bearing retainer.

18. Position the spacer on the front end

of the idler shaft and install the front bearing. Tap the bearing lightly with a mallet or soft-faced hammer.

19. Install the washer, retaining nut and cotter pin on the front end of the idler shaft.

20. After applying sealer to the plates and bolts, install the idler shaft front bearing retainer and the power take-off cover plate.

The shift mechanism of a Dana 24 transfer case (© Ford Motor Co.)

SPECIFICATIONS

END PLAY (IN.)	
Front Output Shaft	0.003–0.007
Rear Output Shaft	0.003–0.007

TORQUE LIMITS (FT. LBS.)	
Transfer case to transmission extension bolts	20–30
Transfer case to transmission output shaft nut	60–80
Front output shaft rear cover bolts	25–32
Front output shaft bearing retainer bolts	25–32
Idler shaft cover bolts	25–32

Dana 300

The 300 is used in Jeep® CJ models only. It has a cast iron case, four gear positions and employs an external floor mounted gearshift linkage for range control. It is a part time, 2 speed unit with undifferentiated high and low ranges. It is used with both manual and automatic transmission. Low range reduction is 2.6:1.

Disassembly

1. Drain the unit and remove the shift lever assembly.

2. Remove the bottom cover.

NOTE: The bottom cover has been coated with a sealant. Use a putty knife to break the seal and work the knife around the bottom of the cover to break it loose. Don't try to wedge the cover off.

3. With a puller, remove the front and rear yokes.

4. Unbolt and remove the input shaft support from the case. The rear output shaft gear and input shaft will come with it as an assembly.

NOTE: The support has been coated with sealant, remove it as you did the bottom cover.

5. Remove the rear output shaft clutch sleeve from the case.

6. Remove and discard the snap ring retaining the rear output shaft gear on the input shaft and remove the gear.

7. Remove and discard the input bearing snapring.

8. Remove the input shaft bearing from the support. Tap the end of the shaft with a soft mallet to aid removal.

9. Remove the input shaft bearing and end-play shims from the shaft with an arbor press.

10. Remove the input shaft oil seal from the support.

11. Unbolt and remove the intermediate shaft lockplate.

12. Remove the intermediate shaft. Tap the shaft out of the case using a brass punch and plastic mallet.

13. Remove and discard the intermediate shaft O-ring seal.

14. Remove the intermediate gear assembly and thrust washers.

NOTE: The thrust washers have locating tabs which must fit into notches in the case at assembly.

15. Remove the needle bearings and spacers from the intermediate gear. There are 48 needle bearings and three spacers.

16. Remove the rear bearing cap attaching bolts and remove the cap. A plastic mallet will aid in removal.

NOTE: The rear bearing cap has been coated with sealant.

17. Remove the end play shims and speedometer drive gear from the rear output shaft.

18. Remove and discard the rear output shaft oil seal. Remove the bearings and races from the rear cap.

19. Unbolt and remove the front and rear output shaft shift forks from the shift rods.

20. Remove the shift rods. Insert a punch through the clevis pin holes in the rods and

Dana 300 power flow

1	Interlock plugs and interlocks	
2	Shift rod—rear output shaft fork	
3	Poppet balls and springs	
4	Shift rod—front output shaft fork	
5	Front output shaft shift fork	
6	Rear output shaft shift fork	
7	Transfer case	
8	Thimble covers	
9	Clutch sleeve—front output shaft	
10	Clutch gear—front output shaft	
11	Bearing—front output shaft rear	
12	Race—front output shaft bearing	
13	End play shims—front output shaft	
14	Cover plate	
15	Lock plate, bolt and washer	
16	Intermediate gear shaft	
17	Thrust washer	
18	Bearing spacer (thin)	

19	Intermediate gear shaft needle bearings
20	Bearing spacer (thick)
21	Intermediate gear
22	Bottom cover
23	Stud (case-to-trans.)
24	Front output shaft
25	Front ouptut shaft gear
26	Front output shaft bearing (front)
27	Front output shaft bearing race
28	Oil seal
29	Front yoke
30	Seal
31	Support—input shaft
32	Input shaft
33	Shims
34	Input shaft bearing
35	Input shaft bearing snap ring

36	Rear output shaft gear
37	Snap ring
38	Clutch sleeve—rear output shaft
39	Input shaft rear bearing (needle) (or pilot bearing)
40	Rear output shaft
41	Vent
42	Clutch gear—rear output shaft
43	Thrustwasher
44	Bearing—rear output shaft front
45	Race—rear output shaft bearing
46	Speedometer drive gear
47	End play shims
48	Rear yoke
49	Rear output shaft oil seal
50	Bearing—rear output shaft rear
51	Bearing race
52	Rear bearing cap
53	Front bearing cap

Exploded view of Dana 300

rotate the rods while pulling them out of the case.

NOTE: When the shift rods are free of the case, take care to avoid losing the shift rod poppet balls and springs.

21. Remove the shift forks from the case.

22. Remove the bolts attaching the front cap to the case and remove the cap.

NOTE: The front cap has been coated with sealant.

23. Remove the front output shaft and shift rod oil seals from the front cap.

24. Remove the bearing race from the front cap.

25. Remove the cover plate bolts and remove the plate and end play shims from the case. Keep the shims together for assembly.

26. Move the front output shaft toward the front of the case.

27. Remove the front output shaft rear bearing race.

Front support, input shaft and rear output shaft gear removal

Front output shaft rear bearing removal

Shift fork set screw removal

Cover plate, shims and front output shaft rear bearing race

28. Remove the rear output shaft front bearing. Position the case on wood blocks. Seat the clutch gear on the case interior surface and tap the shaft out of the bearing with a soft mallet.

NOTE: If the bearing is difficult to remove, an arbor press may have to be used.

29. Remove the rear output shaft front bearing, thrust washer, clutch gear and output shaft from the case.

30. Remove the front output shaft rear bearing with an arbor press.

——————— CAUTION ———————

Be sure to support the case with wood blocks positioned on either side of the case bore.

31. Remove the case from the press and remove the output shaft, clutch gear and sleeve and the shaft rear bearing.

32. Remove the front output shaft front bearing with an arbor press and tool J-22912-01 or its equivalent.

Shift rod oil seal removal

33. Remove the front output shaft from the gear.

34. Remove the input shaft rear needle bearing from the rear output shaft using tool J-29369-1 or its equivalent. Support the shaft in a vise during removal.

35. Using a ⅜" drive, ⁷/₁₆" socket, remove the shift rod thimbles from the case.

Assembly

Coat all parts with SAE 85W-90 oil before assembly.

1. Apply Loctite® 220 or its equivalent to the thimbles and install them in the case.

2. Install the front output shaft gear on the front output shaft. Be sure that the clutch teeth on the gear face the shaft gear teeth.

3. Install the front bearing on the front output shaft using an arbor press. Be sure that the bearing is seated against the gear.

4. Install the front output shaft in the case and install the clutch sleeve and gear on the shaft.

5. Install the front output shaft rear bearing using an arbor press.

NOTE: Install an old yoke nut on the shaft to avoid damage to the threads.

Front output shaft rear bearing positioning

Checking rear output shaft end-play

6. Install the input shaft needle bearings in the rear output shaft with tool J-29179 or its equivalent.

7. Position the rear output shaft clutch gear in the case and insert the rear output shaft into the gear.

8. Install the thrust washer and front bearing on the rear output shaft using an arbor press.

9. Install the shims and bearing on the input shaft using an arbor press.

10. Install a new input shaft seal.

11. Using a new snap-ring, install the input shaft and bearing in the support.

12. Install the rear output shaft gear on the input gear and install a new gear retaining ring.

13. Measure the clearance between the input gear and the gear retaining snap-ring using a feeler gauge. Clearance should not exceed .003 in. If clearance is beyond tolerance, add shims between the input shaft and bearing.

14. Install the clutch sleeve on the rear output shaft.

15. Apply Loctite® 515 or equivalent to the mating surfaces of the input shaft support and install the support assembly, shaft and gear in the case. Use two support bolts to align the support on the case and tap the support into position with a soft mallet. Torque the support bolts to 10 ft. lbs.

16. Install the rear bearing cap front bearing race.

17. Install the rear bearing cap rear bearing race.

18. Position the rear output shaft rear bearing in the rear bearing cap.

19. Install the rear output shaft yoke oil seal.

20. Install the speedometer gear and end-play shims on the rear output shaft.

21. Apply Loctite® 515 or equivalent to the mating surfaces of the cap and install the rear bearing cap. Use two cap bolts to

align the cap and tap it into place with a soft mallet.

22. Tighten the cap bolts to 35 ft. lbs.

23. Install the rear output shaft yoke. Torque a new locknut to 120 ft. lbs.

24. Clamp a dial indicator on the rear output shaft bearing cap. Position the indicator stylus so that it contacts the end of the shaft.

25. Pry the shaft back and forth to check end-play. End-play should be .001–.005 in. If play is not correct, remove or add shims between the speedometer drive gear and the output shaft rear bearing.

26. Install the front output shaft rear bearing race.

27. Install the front output shaft end play shims and cover plate. Tighten the cover plate bolts to 35 ft. lbs.

NOTE: Apply Loctite® 220 to the bolts before installation.

28. Install the front output shaft front bearing race.

29. Install the front output shaft yoke oil seal.

30. Install the shift rod oil seals.

31. Install the front bearing cap, using Loctite® 515 on the mating surfaces. Use two bolts to align the cap and tap it into position with a soft mallet.

32. Install and tighten the bearings cap bolts to 35 ft. lbs.

33. Seat the rear bearing cup against the cover plate by tapping the end of the front output shaft with a plastic mallet. Mount a dial indicator on the front bearing cap and position the stylus against the end of the output shaft. Pry the shaft back and forth to check end-play. End-play should be .001–.005 in. If the play is not correct, add or remove shims between the cover plate and case. If shims are added seat the rear bearing cup again before checking.

34. Install the front output shaft yoke.

Tighten the new locknut to 120 ft. lbs.

35. Install the front and rear output shaft shift forks.

36. Install the front output shaft shift rod poppet ball and spring in the front bearing cap.

37. Compress the poppet ball and spring and install the front output shaft shift rod part way in the case.

38. Insert the front output shaft shift rod through the shift fork.

39. Align the setscrew hole in the shift fork and rod. Install and tighten the setscrew to 14 ft. lbs.

40. Install the rear output shaft shift rod poppet ball and spring in the front bearing cap.

41. Compress the ball and spring and install the rear output shaft shift rail part way. The front output shaft shift rod should be in neutral and the interlocks seated in the front bearing cap bore.

42. Insert the rear output shaft shift rod through the shift fork.

43. Align the setscrew holes in the fork and rod. Torque the setscrew to 14 ft. lbs.

44. Insert tool J-25142 in the intermediate gear and install the needle bearings and spacer.

45. Install the intermediate gear thrust washers in the case. Make sure that the tangs are aligned with the grooves in the case. The thrust washers may be held in place with petroleum jelly.

46. Install a new O-ring seal on the intermediate shaft.

47. Position the intermediate gear in the case.

48. Install the intermediate shaft in the case bore. Tap the shaft into the gear until the shaft forces the tool out of the case.

49. Install the intermediate shaft lock plate and bolt. Torque the bolt to 23 ft. lbs.

50. Install the bottom cover, applying Loctite® 515 or equivalent to the mating

surfaces. Install and torque the bolts to 15 ft. lbs.

51. Fill the case with 4 pints of SAE 85W-90 gear oil.

FRONT OUTPUT SHAFT SHIFT FORK

REAR OUTPUT SHAFT SHIFT FORK

Shift fork installation

International Harvester Model TC-143

The IH Model TC-143 "Silent Drive" transfer case is a chain driven single speed unit. Unlike conventional gear driven transfer cases, this unit has a high-strength link-belt type loop of chain driving two broad-faced sprockets. There is no neutral position. There are two variations of this transfer case; one is frame mounted with a short intermediate drive shaft between the input shaft of the transfer case and the transmission output shaft and the other type is mounted directly to the rear of the transmission.

Disassembly

1. After removing the transfer case from the vehicle and draining all of the lubricant out, clean the outside of the case.
2. Remove the shift cover.
3. Unscrew and remove the indicator light switch from the case.
4. With the rear output shaft flange clamped in a soft jawed vise, remove the flange retaining nut. Remove the flange from the vise and remove the flange from the rear output shaft. Use a puller, if necessary.
5. Turn the case so it rests on the flanges and remove the bolts securing the two halves of the case. Lift the top (rear) half of the case from the assembly and discard the gasket.
6. If present, remove the short spacer from the rear side of the input shaft. Also, if the thrust washer did not stay with the cover when removed, remove it now from the front output shaft.
7. With the case again secured in a soft jawed vise, place your thumbs on the ends of the shafts with your fingers under the sprockets. Pull the sprockets together with the chain off the shafts and out of the case as an assembly.
8. Unhook and remove the shift spring.
9. Remove the shift assembly mounting bolt and spring stud from the case.
10. Pull the shift cranks from the bosses inside the case.
11. If present, remove the long spacer from the input shaft and the washer from the front output shaft.

12. Lift the sliding clutch and its shift shoe from the front output shaft.
13. The two shafts are removed from the case with a press or by tapping them out with a soft hammer.

NOTE: If the transfer case is a transmission mounted unit, a snap ring on the input shaft must be removed before the shaft can be removed from the case.

14. After the shafts are removed, remove the oil seals and the bearing snap rings, and press or tap out the two ball bearings.
15. Pry and remove the thrust washer from the boss for the front output shaft roller bearing in the other half of the case.
16. Press the roller bearing cage from the inside and out of the cover.
17. Press the ball bearing on the outer race from the outside and out of the cover.

Cleaning and Inspection

1. Clean all parts in solvent, removing all traces of old gaskets, sealants and lubricants, and dry the parts with compressed air.
2. Examine all the ball and roller bearings for wear or damage and replace as necessary.
3. Inspect the sprocket teeth and bores for damage and wear. Check the internal splines and clutch teeth for chipped surfaces. Small nicks or burrs can be removed with a file.
4. Check the smooth and splined surfaces of the shafts for wear or damage. The sliding clutch must move freely on the output shaft, but excessive clearance is remedied by replacement of parts.
5. Examine the chain for bent or broken lines. If either condition exists, replace the chain.

1. Input shaft end nut
2. Washer
3. Seal
4. Flange bolt
5. Frame-mounted type case
6. Gasket
7. Shift cover
8. Bearing snap ring
9. Ball bearing
10. Long spacer
11. Upper sprocket (Old style)

12. Chain
13. Input shaft
14. Short spacer
15. Dowel ring
16. Cover
17. Flange nut
18. Roller bearing
19. Drain plug
20. Thrust washer
21. Output shaft
22. Lower sprocket
23. Thrust washer
24. Sliding clutch
25. Ball bearing
26. Seal
27. Washer
28. Output shaft end nut
29. Shift shoe
30. Assembly shifter
31. Spring stud
32. Shift spring
33. Shift clevis
34. Clevis pin
35. Shift cover gasket
36. Upper sprocket (new style)

Exploded view of a frame mounted type International Harvester TC-143 transfer case (© International Harvester Co.)

1. Transmission shaft coupling
2. Washer
3. Transmission shaft end nut
4. Input shaft coupling
5. Speedometer gear
6. Gasket
7. Transmission mounted type case
8. Flange bolt
9. Gasket
10. Snap input shaft ring
11. Bearing snap ring
12. Ball bearing
13. Long spacer
14. Upper sprocket (Old style)
15. Chain
16. Input shaft
17. Short spacer
18. Dowel ring
19. Cover
20. Flange nut
21. Seal
22. Washer
23. End nut
24. Roller bearing
25. Drain plug
26. Thrust washer
27. Output shaft
28. Lower sprocket
29. Thrust washer
30. Sliding clutch
31. Ball bearing
32. Seal
33. Washer
34. Output shaft end nut
35. Shift shoe
36. Assembly shifter
37. Spring stud
38. Shift spring
39. Shift clevis
40. Clevis pin
41. Shift cover gasket
42. Shift cover
43. Upper sprocket (new style)

Exploded view of a transmission mounted type International Harvester TC-143 transfer case (© International Harvester Co.)

Removing the shifter mechanism from the TC-143 transfer case (© International Harvester Co.)

Installation of the thrust washer and long spacer, if so equipped, on the TC-143 transfer case (© International Harvester Co.)

Removing the shifter cover on a TC-143 transfer case (© International Harvester Co.)

Removing the rear half of the case (cover) from the TC-143 transfer case (© International Harvester Co.)

Assembly

1. Install the two snap rings in the outer grooves of both bearing bores in the front half of the case.

2. Coat both bearing bores with lubricant and press or tap with a soft hammer both ball bearing assemblies into the case.

3. Install the two snap rings in the inner grooves of the two bearing bores in the front case half.

4. Install the shaft oil seals from the outside of the front case half. They are best installed with a press.

5. On a frame mounted transfer case, position the lightly lubricated shafts in the bearings, then, pull the shafts into the bearings by tightening the flange attaching nuts with the flanges installed. The input shaft is installed with the identification groove toward the rear of the transfer case. Tighten the flange attaching nut on the front output shaft to 200–250 ft. lbs., and the flange attaching nut on the input shaft until it bottoms, then back off two turns and retighten to 140–150 ft. lbs.

6. The output shaft in transmission mounted transfer case is installed in the same manner as outlined for frame mounted units in step 5.

7. The input shaft in transmission mounted transfer cases has a snap-ring to be installed on the front end of the shaft prior to installation in the bearing. The shaft is then pressed or tapped into the bearing with a soft hammer until the snap-ring is bottomed against the bearing.

8. Assemble the shift shoe to the sliding clutch and install the sliding clutch to the front output shaft.

9. Insert the shifter assembly into the transfer case so the shift cranks of the shifter pass through the shift shoe before being guided into the shift bosses. Make sure the shifter operates the sliding clutch and then secure the assembly with the bolt and spring stud.

NOTE: The flange bolt must be installed before the spring stud because the position of the spring stud when installed prevents the installation of the flange bolts.

10. Install the thrust washer to the front output shaft and the long spacer to the input shaft, if so equipped with a long spacer.

NOTE: Be sure the thrust washer tangs fit down into the splines on the shaft.

11. Lightly lubricate the bores of both sprockets and secure the case in a soft jawed vise by the end of the input shaft.

12. Install the upper sprocket to the outer end of the input shaft. Do not slide the sprocket completely into the case.

13. Position the chain over the sprocket and place the lower sprocket inside the chain.

14. Pull down on the lower sprocket enough to slide the lower sprocket onto the output shaft.

15. Slide both sprockets and chain onto the sprockets as far as they will go.

16. Install the short spacer on the input shaft (not required on later models).

17. Install the shift spring between the spring post and the shifter assembly.

18. Press the ball bearing into the input shaft bore of the rear cover from the inside surface.

19. Press the roller bearing into the output shaft bore of the rear cover from the outside surface until it is flush with the bearing bore.

20. Press the seal for the rear of the input shaft (rear output) into the cover until it is flush.

21. Place the cover on a bench, inside facing up. Coat the back side of the thrust washer with a thin coat of sealant and position it on the roller bearing boss with the tang on the washer mated with the oil passage in the boss.

NOTE: Use the sealant sparingly and make sure none of it enters the bearing or blocks the two oil passages.

22. Position a new gasket and two dowel rings on the mating surface of the case.

23. Position the cover onto the case, guiding the two shafts into their respective bearings. Secure the cover to the case with the attaching nuts and bolts, tightening them to 29–38 ft. lbs.

24. Install the indicator light switch to the case and check its operation with a test light.

25. Install the shift cover gasket and cover on the case and secure it with bolts and lockwashers tightened to 4–6 ft. lbs. *Do not overtighten.*

26. Install the rear output flange on the rear of the input shaft so both the input flange and the output flange are on the same plane. The flanges must be assembled in this manner to prevent vibration.

27. Install the washer and a nylon insert locknut on the shaft tightened to 140–150 ft. lbs. to secure the flange.

Jeep Selec–Trac Model 229

Removal

1. Raise and support the vehicle.

2. Drain the lubricant from the transfer case.

3. Disconnect the speedometer cable and vent hose. Disconnect the transfer case shift lever link at the operating lever.

4. Place a support stand under the transmission and remove the rear crossmember.

5. Mark the transfer case front and rear output shafts at the transfer case yokes and propeller shafts for installation alignment reference.

6. Disconnect the front and rear propeller shafts at the transfer case yokes. Secure the shafts.

7. Disconnect the shift motor vacuum hoses.

8. Disconnect the transfer case shift linkage.

9. Remove the transfer case-to-transmission bolts.

10. Move the transfer case assembly rearward until clear of the transmission output shaft and remove the assembly.

11. Remove all gasket material from the rear of the transmission adapter housing.

RANGE CONTROL LINKAGE

Adjustment

1. Place the range control lever in high range.

2. Insert a 1/8 inch spacer between gate and lever.

3. Hold the lever in this position.

4. Place range control lever in high range position.

5. Adjust as needed.

Disassembly

1. Remove the drain plug and drain the lubricant from the transfer case.

2. Remove the front and rear yoke nuts and seal washers. Discard the washers.

3. Mark the front and rear yokes for installation alignment reference.

4. Remove the front and rear yokes. Use Tool J-8614-01 or equivalent to remove the yokes if necessary.

5. Place the transfer case on wooden blocks. Cut V-notches in the blocks for clearance for the front case mounting studs.

6. Mark the rear retainer and rear case for assembly reference.

7. Remove the rear retainer bolts and remove the retainer. Use two prybars to pry the retainer off the transfer case. Position the prybars in slots in the retainer and case to pry the retainer loose.

8. Remove the differential shim(s) and speedometer drive gear from the rear output shaft.

9. Remove the bolts attaching the rear transfer case half to the front case half. Note that the bolts used at each end of the transfer case require flat washers.

--- **CAUTION** ---

Insert two prybars in the slots at each end of the rear transfer case half to loosen it. Do not attempt to wedge the transfer case halves apart or the case mating surfaces will be damaged.

10. Remove the rear transfer case half from the front case half using two prybars.

11. Remove the thrust bearing and races from the front output shaft. Note the position of the bearing and races for assembly reference.

12. Remove the oil pump from the rear output shaft. Note the position of the pump for assembly reference. The recessed side of the pump faces the case interior.

13. Remove the rear output shaft from the viscous coupling.

14. Remove the 15 mainshaft pilot bear-

1. Spacer	
2. Side Gear	34. Front Output Shaft Bearing Assembly Race (Thick)
3. Viscous Coupling	35. Front Output Shaft Bearing Assembly Thrust
4. Pilot Bearing Rollers	36. Front Output Shaft Bearing Assembly Race (Thin)
5. O-Ring Seal	37. Retaining Ring
6. Rear Output Shaft	38. Chain
7. Oil Pump	39. Driven Sprocket
8. Speedometer Drive Gear	40. Front Output Shaft
9. Shim Kit	41. Front Output Front Bearing
10. Mainshaft	42. Nut
11. Mainshaft Thrust Washer	43. Washer
12. Spline Gear	44. Mode Lever
13. Retaining Ring	45. Snap Ring
14. Sprocket	46. Range Lever
15. Spacer	47. O-Ring Retainer
16. Sprocket Thrust Washer	48. O-Ring Seal
17. Viscous Clutch Gear	49. Front Half Case
18. Side Gear Roller (82)	50. Front Output Yoke
19. Spacer (Short)	51. Low Range Plate Bolt
20. Spacer (Long)	52. Input Shaft Oil Seal
21. Rear Yoke	53. Input Shaft Bearing
22. Nut and Seal Washer	54. Stud
23. Seal	55. Ball
24. Rear Retainer	56. Plunger
25. Plug Assembly	57. Plunger Spring
26. Bolt	58. Screw
27. Identification Tag	59. Input Race
28. Plug Assembly	60. Input Thrust Bearing
29. Dowel Bolt	61. Input Race (Thick)
30. Dowel Bolt Washer	62. Input Shaft
31. Case Half Dowel	63. Input Bearing
32. Rear Half Case	64. Planetary Gear Assembly
33. Magnet	65. Input Gear Thrust Washer

66. Annulus Gear Assembly
67. Annulus Bushing
68. Thrust Washer
69. Retaining Ring
70. Thrust Bearing
71. High Range Sliding Clutch Sleeve
72. Mode Sliding Clutch Sleeve
73. Carrier
74. Carrier Rollers (120)
75. Rear Retainer Bolt
76. Vent
77. Vent Seal
78. Output Bearing
79. Bolt
80. Seal
81. Front Output Rear Bearing
82. Output Shaft Inner Bearing
83. Range Sector
84. Range Bracket (Outer) and Spring
85. Range Bracket (Inner)
86. Mode Sector
87. O-Ring Seal
88. Range Rail
89. Low Range Lockout Plate
90. Mode Fork, Rail and Pin
91. Mode Fork Pad
92. Range Fork
93. Range Fork Pads
94. Range Bracket Spring (Inner)
95. Locking Fork Bushing
96. Locking Fork Pads
97. Locking Fork

Jeep Selec. Trac 229

ing rollers from the shaft or coupling (if the rollers dropped off during removal of the rear output shaft).

15. Remove the mainshaft O-ring from the end of the shaft.

16. Remove the viscous coupling from the mainshaft and side gear.

17. Remove the front output shaft, driven sprocket and drive chain assembly. Lift the front shaft, sprocket and chain upward. Tilt the front shaft toward the mainshaft. Slide the chain off the drive sprocket and remove the assembly.

18. Remove the mainshaft, side gear, clutch gear, drive sprocket and spline gear as an assembly. Place the assembly on a clean shop towel and set aside until the front case disassembly is completed.

19. Remove the front output shaft front thrust bearing assembly from the front case, or from the shaft (if the bearing and races remained on the shaft during removal).

20. Remove the drive chain from the front output shaft and sprocket.

21. Remove the snap-ring that retains the driven sprocket on the front output shaft. Mark the sprocket and shaft for assembly reference and remove the sprocket from the shaft.

22. Remove the mode fork, shift rail, and mode sliding clutch sleeve as an assembly. Mark the sleeve and fork for assembly reference and remove the sleeve from the fork.

NOTE: The mode fork and rail are pinned together so that they will operate as a unit. Remove the pin to separate the two components if necessary.

23. Remove the locking fork, high range sliding clutch sleeve, fork brackets and fork springs as an assembly. Note the position of the components for assembly reference and disassemble the components for cleaning and inspection.

24. Remove the range sector detent screw and remove the detent spring, plunger and ball.

25. Move the range operating lever downward to the last detent position.

26. Disengage the low range fork lug from the range sector slot.

27. Remove the retaining snap-ring from the annulus gear and remove the thrust washer.

28. Remove the annulus gear, range fork and rail as an assembly. Separate the components for cleaning and inspection.

29. Remove the planetary thrust washer from the planetary assembly hub.

30. Remove the planetary assembly. Grasp the planetary hub and lift the assembly upward to remove it.

31. Remove the mainshaft thrust bearing from the input shaft.

32. Remove the input shaft and remove the input shaft thrust bearing and race.

33. Remove the range sector and operating lever attaching nut and lockwasher. Remove the lever.

34. Remove the range sector and shaft from the front case.

35. Remove the range sector O-ring and retainer.

MAINSHAFT

Disassembly

1. Grasp the drive sprocket and lift the sprocket clutch gear and side gear upward and off the mainshaft.

2. Remove the mainshaft needle bearings and two bearing spacers from the mainshaft; a total of 82 bearings are used; note the spacer position for assembly reference.

3. Remove the spline gear and thrust washer from the mainshaft.

4. Remove the side gear, clutch gear, and clutch gear thrust washer from the sprocket carrier and sprocket.

5. Remove the clutch gear and thrust washer from the side gear.

6. Remove one sprocket carrier snap-ring and remove the drive sprocket from the carrier; mark for assembly reference.

─── CAUTION ───

The sprocket carrier and mainshaft needle bearings are different in size. Take care to avoid intermixing them.

7. Remove the three bearing spacers and all sprocket carrier needle bearings from the carrier; a total of 120 needle bearings are used.

8. Remove the rear output bearing and rear yoke seal from the rear retainer; the bearing is shielded on one side; note the bearing position for assembly reference.

9. Remove the input gear and front yoke seals from the front case; use a screwdriver to pry the seals out of the case.

Cleaning & Inspection

1. Wash all components thoroughly in clean solvent. Ensure that all lubricant, metallic particles, dirt, and foreign material are removed from the surfaces of every component.

2. Apply compressed air to each oil supply port and channel in each transfer case half to remove any obstructions or cleaning solvent residue.

3. Inspect all gear teeth for excessive wear or damage. Inspect all gear splines for burrs, nicks, wear or damage.

4. Remove minor nicks or scratches using an oilstone. Replace any component exhibiting excessive wear or damage.

5. Inspect all snap-rings and thrust washers for excessive wear, distortion and damage. Replace any component exhibiting these conditions.

6. Inspect the transfer case halves and rear retainer for cracks, porosity, damaged mating surfaces, stripped bolt threads and distortion. Replace any component exhibiting these conditions.

7. Inspect the viscous coupling and dif-ferential pinions. If the pinions or carrier are damaged or worn excessively, replace the coupling as an assembly only. If the coupling is cracked, leaking, or damaged, replace the coupling as an assembly only.

8. Inspect the condition of all needle, roller, ball and thrust bearings in the front and rear transfer case halves. Also inspect to determine the condition of the bearing bores in both transfer case halves and in the input gear, rear output shaft, side gear, and rear retainer.

9. Replace any component that is excessively worn or damaged. If any shaft, case half or input gear bearing requires replacement, refer to Bushing/Bearing Replacement.

NOTE: The front output shaft thrust bearing race surfaces are heat treated during manufacture. Heat treatment causes a brown or blue discoloration of these surfaces. Do not replace a front output shaft because of this type of discoloration.

BEARING & BUSHING

─── CAUTION ───

All of the bearings used in the transfer case must be correctly positioned to avoid blocking the bearing oil supply holes. After replacing any bearing, check the bearing position and ensure that the supply hole is not obstructed by the bearing.

REAR OUTPUT SHAFT BEARING

Removal and Installation

1. Remove the bearing using Remover Tool J-26941 and Slide Hammer J-2619-01 or equivalent. Remove the rear output lip seal using a small awl.

2. Install a replacement lip seal.

3. Install a replacement bearing using Driver Handle J-8092 and Installer Tool J-29166 or equivalent.

4. Remove the tools and inspect the oil supply hole. The bearing must not obstruct the supply hole.

FRONT OUTPUT SHAFT FRONT BEARING

Removal and Installation

1. Remove the bearing using Tools J-8092 and J-29168 or equivalent.

2. Remove the tools and inspect the oil supply hole. The bearing must not obstruct the supply hole.

FRONT OUTPUT SHAFT REAR BEARING

Removal and Installation

1. Remove the bearing using Remover

Tool J-26941 and Slide Hammer J-2619-01 or equivalent.

2. Install a replacement bearing using Driver Handle J-8092 and Installer Tool J-29163 or equivalent.

3. Remove the installer tools and inspect the bearing position to ensure the oil supply hole is not obstructed. Also ensure that the bearing is seated flush with the edge of the bore in the case to allow clearance for the thrust bearing assembly.

INPUT GEAR FRONT & REAR BEARINGS

Removal and Installation

1. Remove both bearings simultaneously using Driver Handle J-8092 and Remover Tool J-29170 or equivalent.

2. Install the new bearings one at a time. Install the rear bearing first; then install the front bearing. Use Driver Handle J-8092 and Installer Tool J-29169 or equivalent.

3. Remove the installer tools and inspect the bearing position to ensure the oil supply holes are not obstructed. Also ensure that the bearings are flush with the transfer case bore surfaces.

4. Install a replacement oil seal using seal Installer Tool J-29162 or equivalent.

MAINSHAFT PILOT BUSHING

Removal and Installation

1. Remove the bushing using Slide Hammer J-2619-01 and Remover Tool J-29369-1 or equivalent.

2. Install a replacement bearing using Driver Handle J-8092 and Installer Tool J-29174 or equivalent.

3. Inspect bushing position to ensure that the oil supply hole is not obstructed.

ANNULUS GEAR BUSHING

Removal and Installation

1. Remove the bushing using Driver Handle J-8092 and Remover/Installer Tool J-29185 or equivalent.

2. Install a replacement bushing using Tools J-8092 and J-29185-2 or equivalent.

3. Remove any chips generated by the bushing removal and/or installation.

REAR OUTPUT BEARING AND REAR YOKE SEAL

Removal and Installation

1. Remove the bearing using a brass drift and hammer.

2. Remove the seal from the retainer using a brass drift and hammer.

──── CAUTION ────
The rear output bearing is shielded on one side. Ensure that the shielded side faces the transfer case interior after installation.

3. Install a replacement bearing using Driver Handle J-8092 and Installer Tool J-7818 or equivalent.

4. Install a replacement seal in the retainer using Tool J-29162 or equivalent.

Assembly

NOTE: During assembly, lubricate all transfer case internal components with Dexron II® or petroleum jelly as indicated in the procedure. Do not use chassis lubricant or similar thick lubricants.

1. Install a replacement input shaft and rear output shaft bearing oil seals. Seat the seals flush with the edge of the seal bore or in the seal groove in the transfer case. Coat the seal lips with petroleum jelly after installation.

2. Install the input shaft thrust bearing race in the transfer case counterbore.

3. Install the input gear thrust bearing on the input shaft and install the shaft and bearing in the transfer case.

4. Install the mainshaft thrust bearing in the bearing recess in the input shaft.

5. Install the planetary assembly on the input shaft. Ensure that the planetary pinion teeth mesh fully with the input shaft.

6. Install the planetary thrust washer on the planetary hub.

7. Install a replacement sector shaft O-ring and install the retainer in the shaft bore in the transfer case.

8. Install the O-ring on the mode sector shaft and insert the mode sector through the range sector.

9. Install the range sector in the front transfer case half. Install the operating lever and the snap-ring on the range sector shaft.

10. Install the lever, attaching washer, and locknut on the mode sector shaft. Tighten the locknut with 23 N·m (17 ft. lbs.) torque.

11. Assemble the annulus gear, range fork and rail.

12. Install the assembled fork on and over the planetary assembly.

13. Ensure that the annulus gear is fully meshed with the planetary pinions.

14. Engage the range sector lug into the range sector.

15. Install the annulus thrust washer and the annulus retaining ring on the annulus gear hub.

16. Install the detent ball, plunger, spring and retaining screw in the front transfer case half detent bore.

17. Tighten the bolt with 30 N·m (22 ft. lbs.) torque.

──── CAUTION ────
The locking mode clutch sleeve and the high range clutch sleeve are not interchangeable. The sleeve splines are different. Ensure that the correct sleeve is installed in the corresponding shift fork.

18. Assemble and install the locking fork, fork bracket, fork springs, and high range clutch sleeves.

19. Ensure that the lug on the fork is seated in the range sector detent slot.

20. Install the range fork lug in the range sector detent notch.

21. Move the range sector to the high range position.

22. Assemble and install the range fork, shift rail and mode clutch sleeve.

23. Install the thrust washer and a replacement O-ring on the mainshaft.

24. Install the needle bearings and bearing spacers on the mainshaft.

25. Coat the shaft bearing surface and all needle bearings with petroleum jelly.

26. Install the first 41 needle bearings.

27. Install the long bearing spacer, the remaining 41 needle bearings and the remaining short spacer.

28. Be careful to avoid displacing the bearings when the spacers are installed.

29. Use additional petroleum jelly to hold the bearings in place if necessary.

30. Install the spline gear on the mainshaft.

31. Take care to avoid displacing the bearings while installing the gear.

32. Install the sprocket carrier in the drive sprocket and install the sprocket carrier snap-rings.

33. Ensure that the carrier and sprocket are aligned according to the reference marks made during disassembly.

NOTE: The sprocket carrier teeth are tapered on one side and the drive sprocket has a deep recess on one side. Ensure that these components are assembled so that the carrier tapered teeth and sprocket recess are on the same side.

34. Install the sprocket carrier bearings and spacers.

35. Coat the carrier bore and all 120 carrier needle bearings with petroleum jelly.

36. Install the center spacer.

37. Install 60 bearings in each end of the carrier and install the remaining two spacers, one at each side of the carrier.

38. Use additional petroleum jelly to hold the bearings in place if necessary.

39. Install the assembled sprocket carrier and drive sprocket on the mainshaft. Do not displace the mainshaft bearings during installation.

40. Ensure that the recessed side of the drive sprocket is facing downward.

41. Install the clutch gear thrust washer in the mainshaft.

42. Position the washer on the sprocket carrier.

43. Install the clutch gear on the side gear.

44. Ensure that the tapered edge of the clutch gear faces the side gear teeth.

45. Install the assembled side gear and clutch gear on the mainshaft. Ensure that the side gear is fully seated in the sprocket carrier.

46. Take care to avoid displacing any of the carrier or mainshaft needle bearings.

47. Install the mainshaft and gear assembly in the case.

48. Ensure that the mainshaft is fully seated in the input gear.

49. Install the driven sprocket on the front output shaft and install the sprocket retaining snap-ring. Ensure that the sprocket is installed according to reference marks made during disassembly.

50. Install the front output shaft front thrust bearing assembly in the transfer case front half.

51. Install the thick race in the transfer case and then install the bearing and the thin race.

52. Install the drive chain, front output shaft and driven sprocket.

53. Install the chain on the driven sprocket.

54. Raise and tilt the driven sprocket and chain and install the opposite end of the chain on the drive sprocket.

55. Align the front output shaft with the shaft bore in the transfer case front half and install the shaft in the transfer case.

56. Ensure that the front shaft thrust bearing assembly is seated in the transfer case.

57. Install the front output shaft rear thrust bearing assembly on the front output shaft.

58. Install the thin race first, then install the bearing and thick race.

59. Install the viscous coupling on the side gear and clutch gear.

60. Ensure that the coupling is fully seated on the clutch gear. The clutch gear should be flush with the coupling and the gear teeth should be visible.

61. Coat the mainshaft pilot bearing surface and all 15 pilot roller bearings with petroleum jelly and install the bearings on the shaft.

62. Use additional petroleum jelly to hold the bearings in place if necessary.

63. Install the rear output shaft on the mainshaft and into the viscous coupling. Ensure that the shaft is completely seated in the coupling.

64. Tap the shaft with a plastic mallet or brass punch to seat it if necessary.

65. Do not displace the pilot bearings during installation of the shaft.

66. Install a replacement rear output shaft bearing seal in the rear transfer case half.

67. Apply a bead of Loctite 515, or equivalent sealer, to the mating surface of the rear transfer case half.

68. Install the magnet in the case, if removed.

69. Attach the rear transfer case half to the front transfer case half. Ensure that the alignment dowels at the front case half ends are aligned with the bolt holes in the rear case half and mate the rear case half with the front case half.

NOTE: If the rear transfer case half will not mate completely with the front case, inspect for the following: oil in the range fork rail bore, the front output shaft rear thrust bearing assembly is not aligned with the rear case half, the mainshaft is not completely seated, the rear case half is not aligned with the oil pump.

70. Install the rear case half to the front case half bolts. Tighten the bolts with 31 N·m (23 ft. lbs.) torque. Ensure that the flat washers are used on the bolts at the case end where the alignment dowels are located.

71. Install the speedometer drive gear on the rear output shaft.

72. Measure the thickness of the shim pack and record.

73. Install a 0.762-mm (0.030-in) shim (approximately) on the rear output shaft.

74. Align the rear retainer on the rear transfer case half and install the retainer. Install the retainer bolts. Tighten the bolts securely but not with the specified torque.

75. Install the front rear output shaft yokes and the original yoke nuts. Tighten the nuts finger-tight only. Check the differential end play.

76. Set the shift lever in the 4-High range position.

77. Position Dial Indicator J-8001 on the rear retainer and position the indicator stylus so it contacts the rear yoke nut.

78. Support the transfer case to prevent the front output yoke from turning.

79. Slowly turn the rear output shaft while maintaining moderate inward pressure on the rear yoke. Turn the rear output shaft at least two full turns to determine the maximum run-out of the shaft.

NOTE: A wrench should be used to turn the yoke to provide the leverage needed to turn the viscous coupling in the transfer case.

80. Set the shaft at its maximum run-out point and zero the dial indicator.

81. Pull upward on the rear output yoke, note the dial indicator pointer position and record it.

82. Remove the retainer. Add or subtract differential shims as necessary to correct the end play. The end play should be between 0.05 and 0.25 mm (0.002 to 0.010 in.). The recommended end play is 0.15 mm (0.006 in.).

83. After adjusting the end play, remove the front and rear yokes. Discard the original yoke nuts.

84. Apply a bead of Loctite 515, or equivalent sealer, to the retainer mating surface and install the retainer.

85. Apply sealer to the retainer bolts and install the bolts. Tighten the bolts with 31 N·m (23 ft. lbs.) torque.

86. Position the front and rear yokes. Install replacement yoke seal washers and nuts.

87. Tighten the yoke nuts with 163 N·m (120 ft. lbs.) torque. Use Tool J-8614-01 or equivalent to hold the yokes in place while tightening the nuts.

88. Install the detent ball, spring and bolt if these were not installed previously. Apply sealer to the bolt before installing it. Tighten the bolt with 31 N·m (23 ft. lbs.) torque.

89. Install the drain plug and washer.

90. Fill the transfer case with 2.82 liters (6 pints) of Dexron II® Automatic Transmission Fluid (ATF) and install the fill plug and washer.

91. Tighten the drain and fill plugs with 24 N·m (18 ft. lbs.) torque.

92. Install the plug and washer in the front transfer case half, if removed. Tighten the plug with 24 N·m (18 ft. lbs.) torque.

93. Reinstall transfer case in vehicle.

TORQUE SPECIFICATIONS
Model 229

Component	Service Set-To Torque
Detent Retainer Bolt	31 N·m (23 ft-lbs)
Drain and Fill Plugs	24 N·m (18 ft-lbs)
Front/Rear Yoke Nuts	163 N·m (120 ft-lbs)
Operating Lever Locknut	24 N·m (18 ft-lbs)
Rear Case-to-Front Case Bolts (All)	31 N·m (23 ft-lbs)
Rear Retainer Bolts	31 N·m (23 ft-lbs)
Transfer Case-to-Transmission Adapter Nuts	35 N·m (26 ft-lbs)
Universal Joint Strap Bolt-to-Transfer Case	19 N·m (170 in-lbs)

New Process Model T201

The New Process Model 201 transfer case is a 2-speed gearbox which provides speed reduction and couples power to the front and rear driving axles.

——————— **CAUTION** ———————
Do not engage front driving axle when operating truck on hard surfaced roads at high speeds.

DE-CLUTCH AND SHIFT ROD

Adjustment

NOTE: All adjustments must be made with the front axle engaged and the transfer case in low range.

1. Disconnect de-clutch and shift rods at shift levers.

2. Adjust de-clutch rod length until lever clears rear end of slot in cab underbody by ⅝ in. Secure adjusting yoke with locknut.

3. Adjust shift rod length until distance between protusions on shift and de-clutch levers is ¼ in. Secure adjusting yoke with locknut.

4. Connect de-clutch and shift rods at shift levers and then road test vehicle.

1 Ball, shift bar poppet
2 Spring, shift bar poppet ball
3 Bar, front output shaft
4 Fork, shift
5 Screw, set
6 Clutch, front output sliding
7 Fork, shift
8 Gear, front output drive
9 Bearing, roller (70 req'd)
10 Spacer, bearing
11 Shaft, front output front gear
12 Washer, thrust
13 Bearing, ball
14 Retainer, lock
15 Nut, bearing retaining
16 Shaft, idler gear
17 Cone, idler gear bearing
18 Cup, idler gear bearing
19 Shim, set
20 Spacer, bearing
21 Shaft input
22 Ring, snap
23 Bearing, roller (15 req'd)
24 Gear, rear output drive w/shaft
25 Gear, speedometer drive
26 Spacer, speedometer drive gear
27 Clutch, two-speed sliding
28 Plug, pipe
29 Gasket, set
30 Bolt, hex head, w/lock washer
31 Retainer, front output shaft rear bearing
32 Bolt, hex head, w/lock washer
33 Washer, lock
34 Nut, hex
35 Breather
36 Cup, rear output shaft outer bearing
37 Cone, rear output shaft outer bearing
38 Support, hand brake
39 Seal, rear output shaft outer bearing oil
40 Stud
41 Retainer, rear output drive gear bearing
42 Plate, idler shaft cover
43 Cup, rear output shaft inner bearing
44 Cone, rear output shaft inner bearing
45 Case, transfer
46 Bolt. w/washer
47 Bolt, hex head
48 Washer, lock
49 Cover, power take-off opening

50 Gasket, power take-off cover
51 Stud
52 Bearing, input and front output ball
53 retainer, input and front output bearing
54 Washer, lock
55. Nut, hex

56 Seal, input and front output bearing retainer oil
57 Gasket
58 Seal, front and rear output shift bar oil
59 Screw, poppet ball retainer
60 Washer, thrust
61 Bearing, roller (70 req'd)

62 Spacer, bearing
63 Gear, input drive
64 Gear, power take-off
65 Bar, two-speed shift
66 Washer
67 Nut, hex
68 Pin, cotter
69 Gear, idler

Exploded view of the New Process T-201 transfer case (© Chrysler Corp.)

Disassembly

REAR OUTPUT SHAFT

1. Remove cotter pin and flange nut at rear output shaft.

2. Remove attaching bolts and nuts, then remove bearing retainer and gasket. Discard gasket.

3. Remove output shaft assembly from case.

4. Remove nut and washer at rear of shaft.

5. Remove brake drum by tapping on it lightly (if necessary).

6. Remove shaft and gear from bearing retainer.

7. Remove shims, spacer and speed-

Removing/installing the rear output shaft on a New Process T-201 transfer case (© Chrysler Corp.)

ometer drive gear. Tie shims together for reassembly.

8. Remove inner bearing cone, using a suitable puller.

9. Remove snap-ring and roller bearings from shaft gear bore.

NOTE: The rear output shaft and gear is serviced as an assembly. Do not remove gear from shaft.

10. Remove attaching nuts, brake support, bearing and oil seal. Discard seal.

FRONT OUTPUT SHAFT

1. Remove attaching bolts and nuts, then remove rear bearing retainer and gasket. Discard gasket.

2. Remove cotter pin and nut at front output shaft.

3. Remove attaching nut, washer and companion flange.

4. Remove the front output shaft assembly through the rear of the case.

5. Remove sliding clutch gear.

6. Position front output shaft assembly in a soft-jawed vise.

7. Remove lock retainer and bearing nut.

8. Using a suitable puller, remove bearing.

9. Remove front output shaft drive gear by lifting upward and holding the thrust washers against the hub to retain bearing rollers.

10. Carefully set aside thrust washers, then remove the two rows of bearing rollers (70 rollers) and the spacer separating them.

11. Remove attaching nuts and bearing retainer with gaskets. Note number of gaskets used.

IDLER GEAR, SHIFT BAR AND FORK

1. Remove safety wire and setscrews securing shift forks to shift bars.

2. Remove poppet ball retaining plugs, gaskets and poppet ball springs.

3. Pull shift bars out of the case, then remove shift forks and poppet balls.

4. Remove cotter pin, nut and washer from front end of idler shaft.

5. Remove attaching bolts, gasket and idler gear shaft cover plate.

FRONT OUTPUT SHAFT ASSEMBLY
Removing/installing the front output shaft on a New Process T-201 transfer case (© Chrysler Corp.)

6. Remove idler gear assembly.

NOTE: When removing the idler gear assembly, use an arbor as shown in illustration and perform the following:

a. Install arbor on threaded end of shaft so that it seats against the shaft shoulder.

b. Drive arbor until shaft is free at rear of case.

c. Separate shaft and arbor.

d. Remove gear with arbor through front output shaft opening.

e. Remove arbor, shims, spacer and bearing cones. Tie shims together for reassembly.

INPUT SHAFT

1. Remove cotter pin and input shaft flange nut.

2. Remove nut, flat washer and companion flange.

3. Remove input shaft assembly through rear output shaft opening in case.

NOTE: Make certain to retain power take-off and drive gear on the shaft.

4. Mount input shaft in a soft-jawed vise.

5. Remove power take-off gear.

6. Remove input drive gear while holding thrust washers tightly against hub.

7. Carefully remove the two rows of bearing rollers (70 rollers) and the separating spacer.

8. Remove attaching nuts, bearing retainer, gaskets and oil seal. Note the number of gaskets used and discard the oil seal.

Assembly

The transfer case is assembled in the reverse order of disassembly. The following procedures concerning preloading bearings and bearing adjustment however, must all be completed before (or in some cases, during) installation of shaft and gear assemblies.

INPUT SHAFT

1. The input shaft drive gear bearing consists of 70 rollers divided into two rows by a spacer.

2. Coat gear bore with grease, then position rollers and spacer.

3. Hold thrust washers against hub to retain rollers, then install gear on shaft.

4. Input shaft end-play is controlled by gasket thickness between case and bearing retainer.

5. Position retainer on case, then measure clearance with a feeler gauge.

6. Select gasket(s) with a thickness .005 in. more than measured clearance.

7. Remove retainer and install selected gasket(s), then reinstall retainer.

Removing/installing the idler gear shaft on a New Process T-201 transfer case (© Chrysler Corp.)

REMOVING AND INSTALLING ARBOR

INPUT SHAFT ASSEMBLY

Removing/installing the input shaft assembly on a New Process T-201 transfer case (© Chrysler Corp.)

REAR OUTPUT SHAFT

1. Rear output shaft bearing preload is set by shim set size selection.

2. Using an arbor press and suitable sleeve, install inner bearing cone on shaft. The cone should be firmly seated against gear.

3. Install speedometer drive gear, spacer and original bearing shim set.

4. Install rear output shaft in bearing retainer, then position outer bearing cone on shaft.

5. Install parking brake drum, flat washer and slotted nut. Torque nut to 125 ft. lbs.

6. Mount shaft and retainer assembly in a vise so that shaft is free to rotate.

7. Turn shaft until bearing rolls smoothly. Then, using an inch-pound torque wrench, measure bearing preload with the wrench in motion. Subtract or add shims as necessary to meet specifications.

NOTE: Shims for adjusting bearing preload are available in four thicknesses.

8. After the final adjustment, remove slotted nut, washer and brake drum.

9. Install parking brake support and new support oil seal.

10. Reinstall brake drum, washer and slotted nut. Torque nut to specifications.

IDLER GEAR

1. Idler gear bearing end-play is controlled by shim set size selection.

2. Clamp the idler gear shaft (large end) in a soft-jawed vise.

3. Install bearing cone against shoulder on shaft.

4. Install bearing spacer and original shim set.

5. Install idler gear (small end down) on shaft, then install other bearing cone.

6. Position spacer tool as shown in illustration, then install flat washer and nut. Torque nut to specifications.

7. Rotate gear until bearing rolls smoothly. Then using a dial indicator, measure idler gear bearing end-play. Add or subtract shims as necessary to meet specifications.

8. Disassemble idler gear shaft assembly. Tie newly selected shims together.

9. To install gear assembly in the case, position bearing cone in in the large end of the gear, then place gear (small end up) on a bench.

10. Install the same arbor used to remove idler gear shaft, a spacer, new shims and other bearing cone in the idler gear.

11. Hold the idler gear assembly in the case with the small diameter gear facing rearward, then insert the shaft through the case (from rear) and thread it into the previously installed arbor.

12. Tap on the shaft until arbor extends through opposite side of case.

13. Remove arbor.

TWO-SPEED CLUTCH

When installing the two-speed clutch on the input shaft, make certain that the recessed side of the gear is toward the front of the case.

FRONT OUTPUT SHAFT

1. The front output shaft drive gear bearing consists of 70 bearing rollers divided into two rows by a spacer.

2. Coat gear bore with grease, then position rollers and spacer.

3. Hold thrust washers against each hub to retain rollers, then install gear on shaft.

4. Shaft end-play is controlled by gasket thickness between case and bearing retainer.

5. Position retainer on case, then measure clearance with a feeler gauge.

6. Select gasket(s) with a thickness .005 in. more than measured clearance.

7. Remove retainer and install selected gasket(s), then reinstall retainer.

8. When installing the front output shaft assembly in the case, locate front output shift bar as far toward rear of case as possible. This will make it possible to position shift fork in clutch gear collar and to align clutch gear splines on front output shaft.

SPECIFICATIONS

END PLAY (IN.)

Input shaft	0.005
Front output shaft	0.005
Idler gear	0.000–0.002

BEARING PRELOAD (IN. LBS.)

Rear output shaft bearings	15–30

TORQUE LIMITS (FT. LBS.)

Front retainer nut	35–55
Poppet screw	15–25
Idler cover screw	15–25
Drain and filler plugs	25–45
Top cover	38–42
All bearing caps	38–42
Flange and idler shaft nut	125
Input shaft	300–400
Front output shaft	300–400
Rear output shaft	300–400
Idler shaft nut	140–160
Front output shaft flange nut	140–160
Input shaft flange nut	140–160
Driveshaft mating flange nuts	35
Breather	8–12
Brake support nut	25–45
Brake retaining screw	20–40
Brake retainer nut	25–45
Brake drum	60–66
Brake mounting	60–66
Brake drum nut	140–160
P.T.O. screw	8–12
P.T.O. to case	38–42
P.T.O. bearing cap	38–42
P.T.O. top cover	38–42
P.T.O. shaft	300–400

FRONT OUTPUT SHAFT
Checking clearance between case and bearing retainer

Checking idler gear bearing adjustment

New Process Model 202

The New Process Model 202 transfer case is a two-speed gear box which is used to transmit power from the main transmission to a front driving axle, as well as to a conventional rear axle. Sliding clutch gears in the transfer case are controlled by a single lever to select various driving ranges. A separate control lever is provided for operating the power take-off assembly on units so equipped.

The transfer case should not be operated in four-wheel high range on dry, hard surface roads, as rapid tire wear will result.

——————— **CAUTION** ———————

Do not operate transfer case in neutral range for extended periods of time when power take-off assembly is disengaged.

Disassembly

NOTE: The following procedure covers a disassembly of the transfer case removed from the chassis and mounted in a suitable stand.

REAR (UPPER) OUTPUT SHAFT

1. Remove cotter pin from flange nut located at end of rear output shaft. Apply hand brake to prevent shaft from rotating; then break the torque on nut.

2. Remove hex head bolts and two nuts securing bearing retainer to case. Remove the rear output shaft assembly. Remove and discard gasket.

3. Place the output shaft assembly on a bench.

4. Remove the nut and flat washer at rear of shaft. Tap brake drum lightly and remove drum from shaft. Slide off brake drum flange spacer.

5. Remove output shaft with drive gear from upper rear bearing retainer. Slide off speedometer drive gear, spacer and drive gear inner bearing. Remove snap-ring and fifteen roller bearings.

6. Remove hex nuts and lock washers securing hand brake support to upper rear bearing retainer. Remove brake support and drive gear outer bearing. Remove oil seal and discard.

INPUT SHAFT

1. Remove ten capscrews and lock

washers attaching power take-off cover or assembly (if so equipped). Remove and discard gasket.

2. Remove shift bar poppet screw, spring and ball. Through the rear output shaft opening in case, remove roll pin securing two-speed shift fork on bar. Use a $5/32$ in. diameter steel rod to drive out roll pin.

NOTE: Where case interference prevents complete removal of roll pin, drive the pin until shift bar can be removed. Shift fork can then be moved toward input shaft clutch gear to provide clearance for removal of roll pin.

3. Position idler shift bar in four-wheel high drive position (shift bar to extreme rear in case). Simultaneously remove input shaft clutch gear and two-speed shift fork.

4. Remove cotter pin from nut at outer end of input shaft. Use a suitable flange holder to prevent shaft from turning; then break torque on nut. Remove the nut, flat washer and companion flange.

5. Move the input shaft and gear assembly toward rear of case by lightly tapping on the outer end of shaft. This will

1 Link, shift lever	8 Plunger, shift bar interlock
2 Lever, shift	9 Bar, shift idler
3 Pin, rod	10 Fork, shift, two-speed
4 Spring, shift bar poppet	11 Fork, shift, idler
5 Ball, shift bar poppet	12 Pin, idler shaft
6 Bar, shift, two-speed	13 Bearing, thrust, race
7 Pin, rod	14 Bearing, thrust, needle

15 Ring, snap, idler
16 Gear, idler drive
17 Gear, sliding, idler
18 Bearing, roller, idler, shaft
19 Gear, lower shaft (front output)
20 Spacer, rotating shaft
21 Shaft, idler gear, rotating
22 Shaft, idler gear, stationary
23 Gear, PTO, input shaft, upper
24 Spring, friction washer, input shaft
25 Washer, friction, input shaft
26 Gear, drive, input shaft, upper
27 Bearing, roller, input shaft, front
28 Spacer, input shaft drive gear bearing
29 Washer, input shaft sliding clutch
30 Gear, clutch, input shaft, upper
31 Shaft, input
32 Ring, snap
33 Bearing, roller, drive gear
34 Gear, shaft, output drive
35 Seal, oil, input and output shaft, front

36 Retainer, bearing, input and output shaft, front
37 Gasket, bearing retainer
38 Bearing, input and output shaft, front
39 Seal, oil, shift bar
40 Gasket, shift bar poppet screw
41 Screw, shift bar poppet
42 Gasket, PTO cover
43 Cover, PTO opening
44 Plug, pipe
45 Case, transfer
46 Bearing, gear, output shaft, inner
47 Gasket, rear bearing retainer, upper
48 Plug, pipe
49 Gasket, rear bearing retainer, lower
50 Retainer, lower rear bearing (front output shaft)
51 Bearing, lower shaft, rear
52 Retainer, upper rear (output shaft) bearing
53 Gear, speedometer drive gear
54 Spacer, speedometer drive gear
55 Bearing, output shaft drive gear, outer
56 Spacer, brake drum flange
57 Gasket, brake drum support
58 Support, hand brake
59 Seal, oil, output shaft bearing, rear

Exploded view of the New Process T-202 transfer case (© International Harvester Co.)

free shaft from bearing and permit shaft and power take-off gear to be removed.

> **CAUTION**
>
> *Hold input drive gear firmly against shoulder on shaft to retain roller bearings in bore of gear.*

6. Place input shaft on a bench and remove drive gear, roller bearings, spacer and sliding clutch gear washer. Remove friction washer and washer spring from hub of power take-off gear.

7. Remove input shaft bearing retainer, gasket and bearing. If necessary, remove and discard oil seal from bearing retainer.

FRONT (LOWER) OUTPUT SHAFT

1. Remove cotter pin from nut at outer end of front output shaft. Use a suitable flange holder to prevent shaft from turning; then break torque on nut. Remove nut, flat washer and flange.

2. Remove hex head bolts and nuts attaching input shaft rear bearing retainer to case. Lightly tap on end of shaft, moving it toward rear of case to displace shoulder on rear bearing retainer. Remove drive gear and shaft.

3. Press drive gear rear bearing from retainer. Remove front bearing retainer and bearing. If lubricant leakage is evident at the retainer, remove oil seal and discard.

IDLER SHIFT BAR AND GEAR

1. Remove roll pin securing fork to idler shift bar. Use a 5⁄32" diameter steel rod to drive out pin. Withdraw shift bar and fork.

NOTE: Spring tension on poppet ball will displace ball from case upon removing shift bar.

2. Remove shift bar interlock plunger and spring.

3. Remove roll pin from outer end of idler gear stationary shaft. Using a brass

Removing the front output shaft assembly from a New Process T-202 transfer case (© International Harvester Co.)

drift, drive the idler shaft toward rear of case. Remove shaft.

4. Remove idler gear rotating shaft assembly through the opening from which the rear output shaft assembly was removed. Place the gear assembly on a bench.

5. Remove thrust bearing and thrust bearing race at each end of rotating shaft. Remove individual roller bearing and spacer.

6. Remove snap-ring; then separate idler drive gear and shaft. Remove sliding clutch gear.

Assembly

Lubricate all bearings, bushings, spline shafts and shift bar forks at their contact surfaces during assembly. This will provide initial lubrication and avoid possible damage when the transfer case is first operated.

IDLER SHIFT BAR AND GEAR

1. Place the idler gear rotating shaft in a vertical position with the large splined gear end resting on bench.

2. Position sliding clutch gear on shaft with the groove which receives idler shift fork, facing upward.

3. Position drive gear on shaft so that gear internal splines engage splines on shaft.

> **CAUTION**
>
> *The long shoulder side of drive gear must face slid-clutch gear to provide clearance with the inside face of case.*

4. Install snap-ring and check for proper side clearance with drive gear. This is accomplished by inserting a feeler gauge between the ring and gear. Three different thicknesses of snap-rings are available for obtaining proper clearance. Select and install proper size. Refer to Specifications for recommended snap-ring side clearance.

NOTE: Snap-ring side clearance must be maintained to prevent possible ring breakage.

5. Coat the bore of idler gear rotating shaft with Lubriplate No. 110; then assemble roller bearings and spacer. Apply Lu-

Removing the input shaft and P.T.O. gear from a New Process T-202 transfer case (© International Harvester Co.)

Checking the side clearance between the idler drive gear and retaining snap-ring—New Process T-202 transfer case (© International Harvester Co.)

briplate to thrust bearing and bearing race; then assemble at each end of idler rotating shaft. Carefully place rotating shaft assembly in case. Align shaft with opening in front and rear of case for installing the stationary shaft. Install stationary shaft, making certain not to disturb roller bearing arrangement in bore of rotating shaft. Tap the shaft lightly until seated. Install roll pin in shaft at front of case.

6. Position poppet spring and ball in case. Hold the spring and ball in a compressed position and insert idler shift bar at front side of case. Place idler shift fork in position on sliding gear (shoulder on fork toward front of case) and install on shift bar. Secure fork to shift bar with roll pin.

NOTE: Side of shift bar employing only one detent must be facing upwards.

INPUT SHAFT

1. Place the input drive gear on a bench and assemble roller bearings and spacer. Coat the gear bore with Lubriplate No. 110 to retain bearing rollers.

2. Install sliding clutch washer; then carefully position drive gear with bearings on shaft. Place friction washer on shaft next to drive gear, with the tang opposite gear.

3. Assemble friction washer spring on hub of power take-off gear.

NOTE: Install spring on recess side of gear.

4. Assemble input shaft with drive gear and power take-off gear in case. Hold the drive gear firmly to clutch gear washer to keep roller bearings in place.

NOTE: Rotate friction washer until tang engages blind hole in power take-off gear.

5. With the idler shift bar in four-wheel high drive position (shift bar to extreme rear of case), insert interlock plunger in case.

6. Install two-speed shift bar in case so that side of bar with the single detent is facing the idler shift bar. Install sliding clutch gear and two-speed shift bar fork. Install rod pin to secure fork to shift bar.

7. Install input shaft bearing.

———— **CAUTION** ————

Movement of input shaft toward rear of case while installing bearing will permit rollers to become displaced from bore of drive gear.

8. Position bearing retainer to case and install hex head bolts finger tight. Do not torque bolts at this time since gasket thickness must be determined following installation of rear output shaft assembly.

FRONT (LOWER) OUTPUT SHAFT

1. Install front output shaft bearing in face of case.

2. Install front output shaft and drive gear.

3. Press drive gear rear bearing in retainer. Install bearing with stamped end of bearing resting on press. Position gasket and retainer at rear face of case. Install hex head bolts with lock washers and tighten securely.

4. Install new oil seal in bearing retainer. Assemble retainer to front face of case and install hex head bolts finger tight. Do not torque bolts at this time.

REAR (UPPER) OUTPUT SHAFT

1. Support rear output shaft bearing retainer in a press; then install shaft inner bearing flush with outer surface of retainer.

2. Place bearing retainer on a bench and assemble drive gear and shaft. Position speedometer drive gear and spacer on shaft. Assemble outer bearing on shaft and install in upper rear bearing retainer. Install hand brake drum spacer.

3. Install new oil seal in hand brake support. Install gasket and brake support to upper rear bearing retainer.

4. Position gasket to bearing retainer and install the rear output assembly on case.

INPUT AND FRONT OUTPUT SHAFT

Bearing Adjustment

The fit of the input and front output shaft bearing retainer to their respective bearings is controlled by gasket thickness. To determine the correct thickness or number of gaskets required, measure the clearance between retainer and case with a feeler gauge. Select gasket(s) which will give a bearing retainer fit within specified limits. See Specifications. Remove the retainer; then install selected gasket(s) and retainer.

SPECIFICATIONS

BEARING CLEARANCE (IN.)	
Input and front output shaft bearings	0.003–0.006
Gasket thickness available	0.009–0.011
	0.0135–0.0165

SNAP RING (IN.)	
Side clearance	0.007–0.013
Thickness available	0.092–0.094
	0.095–0.097
	0.098–0.100

POPPET BALL SPRING	
Free length	1.0 in.
Pressure @ $^{21}/_{32}$"	30 lbs.

TORQUE LIMITS (FT. LBS.)	
Flange nut	Minimum 125

New Process Model 203 (Full Time Four Wheel Drive)

The New Process Model 203 transfer case is a full-time 4WD unit that operates in 4WD at all times. The unit incorporates a differential similar to axle differentials; compensating for different speeds of the front and rear axles resulting from varying speeds while turning and operating over different surfaces.

There are five shift positions with this transfer case; Neutral, High and High Lock, and Low and Low Lock. The Lock positions are used under low traction conditions. In the Lock position, the differential action of the transfer case is eliminated, by locking the front and rear output shafts together. In this mode, neither the front or rear axle can rotate independently of the other.

Disassembly

1. Loosen rear output shaft flange retaining nut and remove front output shaft flange and washer.

2. Tap the front output shaft dust seal away from case assembly. Remove front output shaft bearing retainer and gasket.

3. Position transfer case assembly on blocks with input shaft facing downward.

4. Remove rear output shaft assembly from transfer case. Slide the differential carrier off the shaft.

5. Place a 1½ in. to 2 in. band type hose clamp on input shaft to retain bearings.

6. Lift shift rail and driveout pin retaining shift fork.

7. Remove shift rail poppet ball plug, gasket and ball from case. Use a magnet to remove poppet ball.

8. Push shift rail down, lift up on lockout clutch and remove shift fork from clutch assembly.

9. Remove front output shaft rear bearing retainer. It may be necessary to gently tap front of shaft or cautiously pry retainer from case. Make certain that no roller bearings are lost from rear cover.

10. When necessary, remove rear bearing by pressing.

11. Pry front output shaft front bearing from lower side of case.

Removing the pin retaining the shift fork to the shift rail in a New Process 203 transfer case (© Ford Motor Co.)

1 Adapter
2 Input Gear Bearing Retainer
3 Input Gear Bearing Retainer Gasket
4 Input Gear Bearing Retainer Seals
5 Bearing Outer Ring
6 Bearing to Shaft Retaining Ring
7 Input Gear Bearing
8 Adapter to Selector Housing Gasket
9 Range Selector Housing (Range Box)
10 P.T.O. Cover Gasket
11 P.T.O. Cover
12 Selector Housing to Chain Housing Gasket
13 Main Drive Input Gear
14 Range Selector Sliding Clutch
15 Shift Lever Lock Nut
16 Range Selector Shift Lever
17 Shift Lever Retaining Ring
18 Lockout Shift Lever
19 Detent Plate Spring Plug
20 Detent Plate Spring Plug Gasket
21 Detent Plate Spring
22 Detent Plate
23 Lockout Shifter Shaft
24 "O" Ring Seal
25 Lockout Shaft Connector Link
26 "O" Ring Seal
27 Range Selector Shifter Shaft
28 Range Selector Shift Fork
29 Detent Plate Pivot Pin
30 Thrust Washer
31 Spacer (short)
32 Range Selector Counter Gear
33 Counter Roller Bearings and Spacers (72 Bearings Req'd.)
34 Countergear Shaft
35 Thrust Washer
36 Input Shaft Roller Bearings (15 Req'd.)
37 Thrust Washer Pins (2 Req'd.)
38 Input Shaft
39 "O" Ring Seal
40 Low Speed and Bushing
41 Thrust Washer
42 Input Shaft Bearing Retainer
43 Input Shaft Bearing
44 Input Shaft Bearing Retaining Ring (Large)
45 Input Shaft Bearing Retaining Ring
46 Chain Drive Housing
47 Lockout Shift Rail Poppet Plug, Gasket, Spring and Ball
48 Thrust Washer
49 Lubricating Thrust Washer
50 Retaining Ring
51 Flange Lock Nut
52 Washer
53 Seal
54 Front Output Yoke
55 Dust Shield
56 Front Output Shaft Bearing Retainer Seal
57 Front Output Shaft Bearing Retainer
58 Front Output Shaft Bearing
59 Bearing Outer Ring
60 Bearing Retainer Gasket
61 Front Output Shaft
62 Front Output Shaft Rear Bearing
63 Front Output Rear Bearing Retainer Cover Gasket
64 Front Output Rear Bearing Retainer
65 Drive Shaft Sprocket
66 Drive Chain
67 Retaining Ring
68 Sliding Lock Clutch
69 Lockout Shift Rail
70 Shift Fork Retaining Pin
71 Lockout Shift Fork
72 Lockout Clutch Spring
73 Spring Washer Cup
74 Front Side Gear
75 Front Side Gear Bearing and Spaces (123 Bearings Req'd.)
76 Differential Carrier Assembly (132 Bearings Req'd.)
77 Rear Output Shaft Roller Bearings (15 Req'd.)

78 Rear Output Shaft
79 Speedometer Drive Gear
80 Rear Output Shaft Front Roller Bearing
81 Oil Pump "O" Ring Seal
82 Rear Output Housing Gasket
83 Rear Output Housing
84 Shim Pack

85 Rear Output Rear Bearing
86 Bearing Retainer
87 Rear Output Shaft Seal
88 Rear Output Flange
89 Rear Output Shaft Rubber Seal
90 Washer
91 Flange Nut

Exploded view of a New Process 203 full time transfer case (© General Motors Corp.)

12. Remove front output shaft assembly from case.

13. Lift intermediate housing from range box, after removing bolts.

14. Remove chain from intermediate housing.

15. Remove lockout clutch, drive gear and input shaft from range box.

16. Install a 1½" to 2" band type hose clamp on end of input shaft to retain roller bearings.

17. Pull up on shift rail and remove rail from link.

18. Lift input shaft assembly from range box.

Removing the rear output shaft. The differential carrier assembly is removed next—New Process 203 transfer case (© Ford Motor Co.)

Assembly

1. Position range box with input gear side down, on wood blocks.

2. Place gasket on input housing.

3. Install lockout clutch and drive sprocket on input shaft assembly. Install a 2" band type hose clamp on end of input shaft to prevent loss of bearings during installation.

4. Place input shaft, lockout clutch and drive sprocket in range box. Align tab on bearing retainer with notch in gasket.

5. Engage lockout clutch shift rail to the connector link. Position rail in housing bore and turn shifter shaft lowering rail into the housing. This will prevent the link and rail from becoming disconnected.

6. Place the drive chain in housing with the chain around the outer wall.

7. Secure the chain housing to the range box. Be sure that the shift rail engages the channel of the housing. Place the chain on the input drive sprocket.

8. Place the front output sprocket in transfer case. Turn the clutch drive gear to assist in positioning chain on sprocket.

9. Position the shift fork and rail on the clutch assembly. Install the clutch assembly completely into the drive sprocket. Insert retaining pin in shift fork and rail.

10. Install front output bearing, gasket, retainer, bolts, flange, gasket, seal, washer and retaining nut.

11. If rear bearing was removed from front output shaft, press a new bearing into the outside face of cover until bearing is flush with opening.

12. Install front output shaft, rear bearing, retainer, gasket and bolts.

13. Slip differential carrier assembly on the input shaft. Bolts on carrier must face rear of shaft.

14. Load bearings in pinion shaft, install rear output housing assembly, gasket and bolts.

15. Install a dial indicator on the rear housing. The indicator must contact the end of the output shaft. While holding the rear flange, rotate the front output shaft and find the highest point of gear hop. Reset indicator and with rear output shaft at high point, pull up on the end of the shaft to determine end-play. Remove indicator and install shim pack to control end-play to between 0 and .005". The shim pack is positioned on the shaft in front of the rear bearing. Check for binding of rear output shaft.

16. Insert lockout clutch shift rail poppet ball, spring and screw plug in transfer case.

17. Install poppet plate spring, gasket and plug, if they were not previously installed.

18. Install shift levers on the range box, if these were not left on vehicle.

19. Torque all bolts, locknuts and plugs to specifications.

20. Fill transfer case with specified lubricant until the proper level is reached. Secure filler plug.

Transfer Case Subassemblies Overhaul

LOCKOUT CLUTCH ASSEMBLY

Disassembly

1. Remove front side gear from input shaft assembly.

2. Remove thrust washer, roller bearings and spacers from front side gear bore. The position of the spacers must be noted.

3. Remove the snap-ring which holds the drive sprocket to clutch assembly. Slip the drive sprocket from the front side gear.

4. Remove the lower snap-ring.

5. Remove sliding gear, spring and spring cup washer from the front side gear.

6. Thoroughly clean and inspect all component parts. Replace any component that is worn or defective.

Assembly

1. Place spring cup washer, spring and sliding clutch gear on front side gear.

Place a hose clamp around the end of the input shaft to prevent losing the 123 roller bearings out of the clutch assembly—New Process 203 transfer case (© Ford Motor Co.)

2. Secure sliding clutch to front side gear with a snap-ring.

3. Spread petroleum jelly on front side gear and install roller bearings and spacers.

4. Place thrust washer in gear end of front side gear.

5. Slide drive sprocket on clutch splines and secure with snap-ring.

DIFFERENTIAL CARRIER ASSEMBLY

Disassembly

1. Separate differential carrier sections and lift out pinion gear and spider assembly.

2. Note that undercut side of pinion gear spider faces toward front of side gear.

Disengaging the shift rail from the locknut connecting link in a New Process 203 transfer case (© Ford Motor Co.)

3. Remove pinion thrust washers, pinion roller washer gears and roller bearings from spider unit.

4. Thoroughly clean and inspect all component parts. Replace any component that is worn or damaged.

Assembly

1. Spread petroleum jelly on pinion gears and install roller bearings.

2. Position on the leg of each spider, pinion roller washer, pinion gear and thrust washer.

3. Position the spider assembly in front half of the carrier. The undercut surface of the spider thrust surface face downward or toward teeth.

4. Secure carrier halves together. Make certain the marks are aligned. Torque all bolts to specifications.

INPUT SHAFT ASSEMBLY

Disassembly

1. Remove thrust washer and spacer from shaft.

2. Remove bearing retainer assembly from input shaft.

3. Hold low speed gear and lightly tap shaft from gear. Note the position of the thrust washer pins in input shaft.

4. Remove snap-ring holding input bearing in retainer using a screw driver. Lightly tap rear bearing out of retainer.

5. Remove pilot roller bearing and O-ring from end of input shaft.

6. Thoroughly clean and inspect all component parts. Replace any component that is worn or damaged.

Assembly

1. Tap or press input bearing into retainer. Be sure that ball loading slots are toward concave side of retainer. Install securing snap ring. Make certain that selective snap-ring of proper thickness is used to provide tightest fit.

2. Position low speed gear on shaft, clutch end facing gear end of input shaft.

3. Place thrust washers on input shaft, align slot in washer with pin in shaft. Slide or tap washers into position.

4. Place input bearing retainer on shaft and secure with snap-ring. Snap-rings are selective. Use snap-ring that provides tightest fit.

5. Slip spacer and thrust washer on shaft and align with locating pin.

6. Spread heavy grease on end of shaft and install roller bearings.

7. Install rubber O-ring at end of shaft.

RANGE BOX

Disassembly

1. Remove poppet plate spring, plug and gasket.

2. Remove clutch fork and sliding gear by disengaging sliding clutch gear from input gear.

3. Remove upper shift lever from shifter shaft.

4. Remove snap-ring and lower shift lever.

5. Push shifter shaft assembly down and remove lockout clutch connector link. The long end of connector link engages poppet plate.

6. Remove shifter shaft assembly and separate shafts. Remove O-rings.

7. When necessary to remove poppet plate, drive pivot shaft out and remove plate and spring from bottom of case.

8. Remove input gear bearing retainer and seal assembly. Release snap-ring from retainer and tap bearing out of assembly.

9. Release snap-ring holding input shaft bearing to shaft and remove bearing.

10. Remove countershaft from cluster gear and case assembly from intermediate case side. Remove cluster gear assembly from range box.

11. Remove cluster gear thrust washers from case.

12. Thoroughly clean and inspect all component parts. Replace any component that is worn or damaged.

Assembly

1. Spread heavy grease in cluster bore and using proper tool install roller bearings and spacers.

2. Spread heavy grease on case and install thrust washers. Engage tab on thrust washers with slot in case.

3. Place cluster gear assembly in case and install countershaft through front of range box and into gear assembly. Flat face of countershaft must be aligned with case gasket.

4. Place bearing on input gear shaft with snap-ring groove facing out, install a new retaining ring. Insert input gear and bearing in housing. The retaining ring used in this operation is a select fit. Use ring that provides the tightest fit.

5. Secure input gear and bearing with a snap-ring.

6. Match up oil slot in retainer with drain hole in case and insert input gear bearing retainer and gaskets. Install bolts and torque to specifications.

7. Spread sealant on pin and install poppet pin and pivot pin in housing.

8. Lubricate and install new O-rings on inner and outer shifter shafts.

9. Insert shifter shafts in housing and engage long end of lockout clutch connector link with outer shifter shaft. Complete this operation before assembly bottoms out.

10. Install lower shift lever and retaining ring.

11. Install upper shift lever and shaft retaining nut.

12. Install shift fork and sliding clutch gear. Push fork up into shifter shaft and engage poppet plate. Move sliding clutch gear onto input shaft gear.

13. Insert poppet plate spring, gasket and plug in housing top. Make certain that spring engages poppet plate.

INPUT GEAR BEARING

Replacement

1. Remove bearing retainer and gasket from housing.

2. Remove and discard snap-ring holding bearing in retainer.

3. Pry bearing from case and remove from shaft.

4. Inspect input gear and bearing retainer for damage or wear. Replace if necessary.

5. Place new bearing and snap-ring on input gear. Using a soft hammer, tap bearing into position. Secure snap-ring.

6. Insert bearing retainer into housing and secure with attaching bolts. Tighten bolts to specifications.

INPUT GEAR RETAINER SEAL

Replacement

1. Remove bearing retainer from housing.

2. Remove seal from retainer by prying.

3. Place new seal on retainer and install with proper seal driver.

4. Install bearing retainer in housing and secure with attaching bolts. Tighten bolts to specifications.

REAR OUTPUT SHAFT HOUSING ASSEMBLY

Disassembly

1. Remove speedometer driven gear from housing.

2. Remove rear output flange and washer, if they have not been removed previously.

3. Using a soft hammer tap on flange end of pinion and remove the pinion. If speedometer drive gear does not come off with pinion reach into case and remove.

4. Remove old seal from bore with suitable prying tool.

5. Remove snap ring retaining rear output rear bearing.

6. Tap bearing out of housing.

7. Install a long drift into rear opening of housing and drive out front output bearing. Remove seal and discard.

Assembly

1. Spread grease on front bearing seal and place in bore. Place bearing in bore and press until it bottoms in housing.

2. Using a soft hammer tap rear bearing into place. Secure with proper snap-ring. Snap-rings are selective, use the one that provides the tightest fit.

3. Place rear seal in bore and drive into position with suitable tool. When seal is in position it should be approximately $1/8''$ to $3/16''$ below housing face.

4. Place speedometer drive gear on output shaft with shims of approximately .050'' thickness. Insert output shaft into carrier through housing front opening.

5. Install flange and washer on output shaft. Leave retaining nut loose until shim requirements are known.

6. Install speedometer driven gear.

FRONT OUTPUT SHAFT BEARING RETAINER SEAL

Replacement

1. Remove old seal from retainer bore.
2. Inspect and clean retainer.
3. Spread sealer on outer edge of new seal.
4. Place new seal in retainer bore and drive into position with proper tool.

FRONT OUTPUT BEARING

Replacement

1. Remove rear cover from case assembly and discard gasket.
2. Press old bearing from cover.
3. Place new bearing on outside face of cover. Cover bearing with a wood block and press into cover until bearing is flush with opening.
4. Place gasket on transfer case and tap cover into position using a soft hammer. Secure cover with attaching bolts and tighten to specifications.

SPECIFICATIONS

TORQUE (FT. LBS.)

Adapter to transfer case bolts	38
Adapter to transmission bolts	40
Transfer case to frame nuts (upper)	50
Transfer case to frame nuts (lower)	65
Shift lever attaching nuts	25
Shift lever rod swivel locknuts	50
Shift lever locking arm nut	150 in. lbs.
Skid plate bolt retaining nuts	45
Crossmember bolt retaining nuts	45
Adapter mount bolts	25
Intermediate case to range box bolts	30
Front output bearing retainer bolts	30
Output shaft yoke nuts	150
Front output rear bearing retainer bolts	30
Differential assembly screws	45
Rear output shaft housing	30
Poppet ball retainer nut	15
PTO cover bolts	15
Front input bearing retainer bolts	20
Filler plug	25

New Process Model 205

The New Process Model 205 transfer case is a two-speed gearbox mounted between the main transmission and the rear axle. The gearbox transmits power from the transmission and engine to the front and rear driving axles.

Disassembly

TRANSFER CASE

1. Clean the exterior of the case.
2. Remove the nuts from the universal joint flanges.
3. Remove the front output shaft rear bearing retainer, front bearing retainer and drive flange.
4. Tap the front output shaft assembly from the case with a soft hammer. Remove the sliding clutch, front output high gear, washer and bearing from the case.
5. Remove the rear output shaft housing attaching bolts and remove the housing, output shaft, bearing retainer and speedometer gear.
6. Slide the rear output shaft from the housing.

NOTE: Be careful not to lose the 15 needle bearings that will be loose when the rear output shaft is removed.

7. Drive the two ¼ in. shift rail pin access hole plugs into the transfer case with a punch and hammer.
8. Remove the two shift rail detent nuts and springs from the case. Use a magnet to remove the two detent balls.
9. Position both shift rails in neutral and remove the shift fork retaining roll pins with a long punch.
10. Remove the clevis pin from one shift rail and rail link.
11. Remove the range shift rail first, then the 4WD shift rail.
12. Remove the shift forks and sliding clutch from the case. Remove the input shaft bearing retainer, bearing and shaft.

13. Remove the cup plugs and rail pins, if they were driven out, from the case.
14. Remove the locknut from the idler gear shaft.
15. Remove the idler gear shaft rear cover.
16. Remove the idler gear shaft, using a soft hammer and a drift.
17. Roll the idler gear assembly to the front output shaft hole and remove the assembly from the case.

REAR OUTPUT SHAFT AND YOKE

1. Loosen rear output shaft yoke nut.
2. Remove shaft housing bolts, then remove the housing and retainer assembly.
3. Remove retaining nut and yoke from the shaft, then remove the shaft assembly.
4. Remove the discard snap ring.
5. Remove thrust washer and pin.
6. Remove tanged bronze washer. Remove gear needle bearings, spacer and second row of needle bearings.
7. Remove tanged bronze thrust washer.
8. Remove pilot rollers, retainer ring and washer.
9. Remove oil seal retainer, ball bearing, speedometer gear and spacer. Discard gaskets.
10. Press out bearing.
11. Remove oil seal from the retainer.

Rear output shaft assembly removed: removal of the bearing, spacer and speedometer gear—New Process 205 transfer case (© International Harvester Co.)

Rear view of a New Process 205 transfer case (© General Motors Corp.)

1. Shift lever link	9. Ball	17. Washer	25. Spacer	33. Cup	41. Shaft	49. Spacer
2. Bar	10. Plug	18. Gear	26. Gear	34. Shim set	42. Ring	50. Retainer
3. Bar	11. Nut	19. Shaft	27. Washer	35. Gear	43. Washer	51. Breather
4. Plunger	12. Washer	20. Pin	28. Ring	36. Spacer	44. Bearing	52. Gasket
5. Seal	13. Seal	21. Clutch	29. Bearing	37. Shaft	45. Gear	53. Retainer
6. Screw	14. Retainer	22. Fork	30. Gasket	38. Gasket	46. Washer	54. Seal
7. Gasket	15. Gasket	23. Pin	31. Retainer	39. Cover	47. Bearing	55. Case
8. Spring	16. Bearing	24. Bearing	32. Cone	40. Bearing	48. Gear	56. Gasket

Exploded view of a New Process 205 transfer case (© International Harvester Co.)

FRONT OUTPUT SHAFT

1. Remove lock nut, washer and yoke.
2. Remove attaching bolts and front bearing retainer.
3. Remove rear bearing retainer attaching bolts.
4. Tap output shaft with a soft-faced hammer and remove shaft, gear assembly and rear bearing retainer.
5. Remove sliding clutch, gear, washer and bearing from high output gear.
6. Remove sliding clutch from the high output gear; then remove gear, washer and bearing.
7. Remove gear retaining snap-ring from the shaft, using large snap-ring picks. Discard ring.
8. Remove thrust washer and pin.
9. Remove gear, needle bearings and spacer.
10. Replace rear bearing, if necessary.

——————— **CAUTION** ———————

Always replace the bearing and retainer as an assembly. Do not try to press a new bearing into an old retainer.

SHIFT RAILS AND FORKS

1. Remove the two poppet nuts, springs, and using a magnet, the poppet balls.
2. Remove cup plugs on top of case, using a ¼" punch.
3. Position both shift rails in neutral, then remove fork pins with a long handled screw extractor.

4. Remove clevis pins and shift rail link.
5. Lower shift rails; upper rail first and then lower.
6. Remove shift forks and sliding clutch.
7. Remove the front output high gear, washer and bearing. Remove the shift rail cup plugs.

INPUT SHAFT

1. Remove snap-ring in front of bearing. Tap shaft out rear of case and bearing out front of case, using a soft-faced hammer or mallet.
2. Tilt case up on power take-off and remove the two interlock pins from inside.

IDLER GEAR

1. Remove idler gear shaft nut.
2. Remove rear cover.
3. Tap out idler gear shaft, using a soft-faced hammer and a drift approximately the same diameter as the shaft.
4. Remove idler gear through the front output shaft hole.
5. Remove two bearing cups from the idler gear.

Assembly

TRANSFER CASE

1. Assemble the idler shaft gears, bearings, spacer and shims, and bearings on a dummy shaft tool and install the assembly into the case through the front output shaft bore, large end first.

2. Install the idler shaft from the large bore side, using a soft hammer to drive it through the bearings, spacer, gears, and shims.
3. Install a washer and new locknut on the end of the idler shaft. Check to make sure the idler gear rotates freely. Tighten the locknut to specification.
4. Install the idler shaft cover with a new gasket so the flat side faces the rear bearing retainer of the front output shaft. Install and tighten the two retaining screws to the proper torque.
5. Install the interlock pins into the interlock bore through the front of the output shaft opening.
6. Start the 4WD shift rail into the front of the case, solid end of the rail first, with the detent notches facing up.
7. Position the shift fork onto the shift rail with the long end facing inward. Push the rail through the fork and into the Neutral position.
8. Position the input shaft and bearing in the case.
9. Start the range shift rail into the case from the front, with the detent notches facing up.
10. Position the sliding clutch to the shift fork. Place the sliding clutch on the input shaft and align the fork with the shift rail. Push the rail through the fork into the Neutral position.
11. Install the roll pins that lock the shift forks to the shift rails with a long punch.

12. Position the front wheel drive high gear and its thrust washer in the case. Position the sliding clutch in the shift fork. Shift the rail and fork into the front wheel drive (4WD-Hi) position, while at the same time, meashing the clutch with the mating teeth on the front wheel drive high gear.

13. Align the thrust washer, high gear and sliding clutch with the bearing bore in the case and insert the front output shaft and low gear into the high gear assembly.

14. Install a new seal in the front bearing retainer of the front output shaft, and install the bearing and retainer and new gasket in the case. Tighten the bearing retainer cap screws to the proper torque.

15. Lubricate the roller bearing in the front output shaft rear bearing retainer, which is the aluminum cover, and install it over the front output shaft and to the case. Install and tighten the retaining screws to the proper torque.

16. Move the range shift rail to the High position and install the rear output shaft and retainer assembly to the housing and input shaft. Use one or two new gaskets, as required, to adjust the clearance on the input shaft pilot. Install the rear output shaft housing retaining bolts and tighten them to specification.

17. Using a punch and sealing compound, install the shift rail pin access plugs.

18. Install the fill and drain plugs and the cross-link clevis pin.

IDLER GEAR

1. Press the two bearing cups in the idler gear.

2. Assemble the two bearing cones, spacer, shims and idler gear on a dummy shaft, with bore facing up. Check end-play.

3. Install idler gear assembly (with dummy shaft) into the case, large end first, through the front output shaft bore.

4. Install idler shaft from large bore side, driving it through with a soft-faced hammer or mallet.

5. Install washer and new locknut. Check for free rotation and meausre end-play. Torque locknut to specifications.

6. Install idler shaft cover and new gasket. Torque cover bolts to specifications.

NOTE: Flat side of cover must be positioned towards front output shaft rear cover.

SHIFT RAILS AND FORKS

1. Press the two rail seals into the case.

NOTE: Install seals with metal lip outward.

2. Install interlock pins from inside case.

3. Insert slotted end of front output drive shift rail (with poppet notches up) into back of case.

4. While pushing rail through to neutral position, install shift fork (long end inward).

5. Install input shaft and bearing into case.

6. Install end of range rail (with poppet notches up) into front of case.

7. Install sliding clutch on fork, then place over input shaft in case.

8. Push range rail, while engaging sliding clutch and fork, through to neutral position.

9. Drive new lockpins into forks through holes at top of case.

NOTE: Tilt case on power take-off opening to install range rail lockpin.

FRONT OUTPUT SHAFT AND GEAR

1. Install two rows of needle bearings in the front low output gear and retain with grease.

NOTE: Each row consists of 32 needle bearings and the two rows are separated by a spacer.

2. Position front output shaft in a soft-jaw vise, with spline end down. Place front low gear over shaft with clutch gear facing down; then install thrust washer pin, thrust washer and new snap-ring.

NOTE: Position snap ring gap opposite the thrust washer pin.

3. Place front drive high gear and washer in case. Install sliding clutch in the shift fork, then put fork and rail into 4-High position, meshing front drive high gear and clutch teeth.

4. Align washer, high gear and sliding clutch and bearing bore. Insert front output shaft and low gear assembly through the high gear assembly.

5. Install front output bearing and retainer with a new seal in the case.

6. Clean and grease rollers in front output rear bearing retainer. Install on case with one gasket and bolts coated with sealant. Torque bolts to specifications.

7. Install front output shaft yoke, washer and locknut. Torque locknut to specifications.

REAR OUTPUT SHAFT

1. Install two rows of needle bearings into the output low gear, retaining them with grease.

NOTE: Each row consists of 32 needle bearings and the two rows are separated by a spacer.

2. Install thrust washer (with tang down in clutch gear groove) onto the rear output shaft.

3. Install output low gear onto shaft with clutch teeth facing downward.

4. Install thrust washer over gear with tab pointing up and away. Install washer pin.

5. Install large thrust washer over shaft and pin. Turn washer until tab fits into slot located approximately 90° away from pin.

6. Install snap-ring and measure shaft end-play.

7. Grease pilot bore and install needle bearings.

NOTE: There are 15 pilot needle bearings.

8. Install thrust washer and new snap-ring in pilot bore.

9. Press new bearing into retainer housing.

10. Install housing on output shaft assembly.

11. Install spacer and speedometer gear. Install rear bearing.

12. Install rear bearing retainer seal.

13. Install bearing retainer assembly on housing, using one or two gaskets to achieve specified clearance. Torque attaching bolts to specifications.

14. Install yoke, washer and locknut on output shaft.

15. Position range rail in high, then install output shaft and retainer assembly on case. Torque housing bolts to specifications.

CASE

1. Install power take-off cover and gasket. Torque attaching bolts to specifications.

2. Install cup plugs at rail pin holes.

NOTE: After installing, seal the cup plugs.

3. Install drain and filler plugs. Torque to specifications.

4. Install shift rail cross link, clevis pins and lock pins.

SPECIFICATIONS

END PLAY (IN.)

Idler gear	0.000–0.002
Rear output shaft	0.002–0.027

TORQUE LIMITS (FT. LBS.)

Idler shaft locknut	150
Idler shaft cover	20
Front output shaft front bearing retainer	30–35
Front output shaft yoke locknut	130–150
Rear output shaft bearing retainer and housing	30–35
Rear output shaft yoke locknut	130–150
P.T.O. cover	15
Front output shaft rear bearing retainer	30–35
Filler and drain plugs	30
Case to frame	130
Case to adapter	25
Adapter mount	75
Case bracket to frame	
Upper	30
Lower	65
Adapter to transmission	
Manual transmission	30–35
Automatic transmission	30–35

New Process Model 207

The 207 transfer case is an aluminum case, chain drive, four position unit providing four-wheel drive high and low ranges, a two-wheel high range, and a neutral position. It is a part-time four-wheel drive unit. Torque input in four-wheel high and low ranges is undifferentiated. The range positions on the 207 transfer case are selected by a floor mounted gearshift lever.

The 207 case is a two-piece aluminum case containing front and rear output shafts, two drive sprockets, a shift mechanism and a planetary gear assembly. The drive sprockets are connected and operated by the drive chain. The planetary assembly which consists of a three pinion carrier and an annulus gear provide the four-wheel drive low range when engaged.

TRANSFER CASE

Removal

1. Shift transfer case into 4 Hi.
2. Disconnect negative cable at battery.
3. Raise vehicle and remove skid plate.
4. Drain lubricant from transfer case.
5. Mark transfer case front output shaft yoke and propeller shaft for assembly reference. Disconnect front propeller shaft from transfer case.
6. Mark rear axle yoke and propeller shaft for assembly reference. Remove rear propeller shaft.
7. Disconnect speedometer cable and vacuum harness at transfer case. Remove shift lever from transfer case.
8. Remove catalytic converter hanger bolts at converter.
9. Raise transmission and transfer case and remove transmission mount attaching bolts. Remove mount and catalytic converter hanger and lower transmission and transfer case.
10. Support transfer case and remove transfer case attaching bolts. On vehicles equipped with an automatic transmission, it will be necessary to remove the shift lever bracket mounting bolts from the transfer case adapter in order to remove the upper left transfer case attaching bolt.
11. Separate transfer case from adapter (auto) or extension housing (man.) and remove from vehicle.

Disassembly

1. Remove fill and drain plugs.
2. Remove front yoke. Discard yoke seal washer and yoke nut.
3. Turn transfer case on end and position front case on wood blocks.
4. Shift transfer case to 4 Lo.
5. Remove extension housing attaching bolts. Using a hammer, tap the shoulder on the extension housing to break sealer loose.

1. SHAFT, Main Drive
2. HOUSING, Case
3. SEAL, Oil Pump Hsg.
4. HOUSING, Oil Pump
5. PUMP, Oil
6. GEAR, Speedo Drive
7. RETAINER, Main Shf. Rr. Brg.
8. CONNECTOR, Case Vent
9. BOLT
10. BEARING, Main Shf. Rr.
11. RING, Main Shf. Rr. Brg. Ret.
12. EXTENSION, Main Shf.
13. BOLT, Hex
14. BUSHING, Case Main Shf. Ext.
15. SEAL, Main Shf. Ext.
16. PLUG, Case Oil
17. BOLT, Hex (M10 × 1.5 × 35)(2 req'd)
18. WASHER, Hsg. Alignment Dowel
19. DOWEL, Hsg. Alignment
20. BEARING, Frt. Optpt. Shf. Pilot
21. SHAFT, Frt. Otpt.
22. CARRIER ASM, Planet Gear
23. WASHER, Planet Gr. Carr. Ret. Rg. Thrust
24. RING, Planet Gr. Carr. Ret.
25. GEAR, Planet Gr. Carr. Annulus
26. RING, Main Dr. Shf. Syn.

27. SYNCHRONIZER ASM, Main Dr. Shf.
28. STRUT, Syn.
29. SPRING, Syn. Strut
30. RING, Syn. Stop
31. BEARING, Dr. Chain Sprocket
32. SPROCKET, Dr. Chain
33. WASHER, Dr. Chain Sprocket Thrust
34. WASHER, Input Main Dr. Gr. Thrust
35. BEARING, Input Dr. Gr. Pilot
36. PLUG, Cup
37. GEAR ASM, Input Main Dr.
38. BEARING, Input Dr. Gr. Thrust
39. WASHER, Input Dr. Gr. Thrust Brg.
40. PLATE, Low Range Lock
41. SWITCH, Four Whl. Dr. Ind. Light
42. SEAL, Four Whl. Dr. Ind. Light Switch
43. PLUG, Oil Access Hole
44. HOUSING, Case (Frt. Half)
45. BEARING, Input Dr.
46. SEAL, Input Dr. Gr.
47. BOLT, Hex
48. YOKE, Frt. Otpt. Prop. Shf.
49. NUT, Frt. Otpt. Prop. Shf. Yoke
50. WASHER, Frt. Otpt. Prop.

Shf. Yoke (Rubber)
51. DEFLECTOR, Frt. Otpt. Prop. Shf. Yoke
52. SEAL, Frt. Otpt. Shf.
53. RING, Frt. Otpt. Shf. Brg. Ret.
54. BEARING, Frt. Otpt. Shf.
55. SCREW, Shift Sector Spr.
56. SCREW
57. SEAL, Shift Sector & Shf. Oil
58. RETAINER, Shift Sector & Shf.
59. LEVER, Shifter Shf.
60. NUT, Shift Shf. Lvr.
61. SPRING ASM, Shift Sector
62. BUSHING, Range Fork
63. PAD, Fork End
64. PIN, Range Shift Fork
65. PAD, Range Shift Fork Center
66. FORK ASM, Range Shift
67. PIN, Mode Shift Fork Brkt.
68. PAD, Mode Shift Fork Center
69. FORK ASM, Mode Shift
70. CUP, Mode Shift Fork Spr.
71. SPRING, Mode Shift Fork
72. BRACKET ASM, Mode Shift Fork
73. SHAFT, Shift Fork
74. SECTOR, W/Shf., Shift
75. SPACER, Shift Sector Shf.
76. CHAIN, Drive

Exploded view new process 207

6. Remove the snap-ring for the rear bearing from the mainshaft and discard.

7. Remove the rear retainer attaching bolts. Using a hammer, tap the shoulder on the retainer to break sealer loose.

8. Remove the rear retainer and pump housing from the transfer case.

9. Remove the pump seal from the pump housing and discard.

10. Remove the speedometer drive gear from the mainshaft.

11. Remove the pump gear from the mainshaft.

12. Remove the bolts attaching the rear case to the front case and remove rear case. To separate the case, insert a prybar into the slots casted in the case ends and pry upward. DO NOT attempt to wedge the case halves apart at any point on the mating surfaces.

13. Remove the front output shaft and drive chain as an assembly. It may be necessary to raise the mainshaft slightly for the output shaft to clear the case.

14. Pull up on the mode fork rail until rail clears range fork and rotate mode fork and rail and remove from transfer case.

15. Pull up on the mainshaft until it separates from the planetary assembly. Remove the mainshaft from the transfer case.

16. Remove the planetary assembly with the range fork from the transfer case.

17. Remove the planetary thrust washer, input gear thrust bearing and front thrust washer from the transfer case.

18. Remove the shift sector detent spring and retaining bolt.

19. Remove the shift sector, shaft and spacer from the transfer case.

20. Remove the locking plate retaining bolts and lock plate from the transfer case.

21. Remove the input gear pilot bearing using J-29369-1 or equivalent with a slide hammer.

22. Remove the front output shaft seal, input shaft seal and the rear extension seal using a brass drift.

23. Using J-33841 with J-8092 or equivalent, press the 2 caged roller bearings for the front input shaft gear from the transfer case.

24. Using J-29369-2 with J-33367 or a slide hammer, remove the rear bearing for the front output shaft.

25. Using a hammer and drift, remove the rear mainshaft bearing from the rear retainer.

26. Using an awl, remove the snap-ring retaining the front output shaft bearing. Using a hammer and drift, remove the bearing from the case.

27. Remove the bushing from the extension housing using J-33839 with J-8092 or equivalent. Press bushing from the extension housing.

MAINSHAFT

Disassembly

1. Remove the speedometer gear.

2. Using an awl, pry off the pump gear from the mainshaft.

3. Remove the snap-ring retaining the synchronizer hub from the mainshaft.

4. Using a brass hammer, tap the synchronizer hub from mainshaft.

5. Remove the drive sprocket.

6. Using J-33826 and J-8092 or equivalent, press 2 caged roller bearings from the drive sprocket.

7. Remove synchronizer keys and retaining rings from the synchronizer hub.

8. Clean and inspect all parts. Replace any parts if they show evidence of excessive wear, distortion or damage.

PLANETARY GEAR

Disassembly

1. Remove the snap-ring retaining the planetary gear in the annulus gear.

2. Remove outer thrust ring and discard.

3. Remove planetary assembly from the annulus gear.

4. Remove inner thrust ring from the planetary assembly and discard.

5. Clean and inspect parts. Replace any parts if they show evidence of excessive wear, distortion or damage.

Cleaning & Inspection

Wash all parts thoroughly in clean solvent. Be sure all old lubricant, metallic particles, dirt, or foreign material are removed from the surfaces of every part. Apply compressed air to each oil feed port and channel in each case half to remove any obstructions or cleaning solvent residue.

Inspect all gear teeth for signs of excessive wear or damage and check all gear splines for burrs, nicks, wear or damage. Remove minor nicks or scratches with an oil stone. Replace any part exhibiting excessive wear or damage.

Inspect all snap-rings and thrust washers for evidence of excessive wear, distortion or damage. Replace any of these parts if they exhibit these conditions.

Inspect the two case halves for cracks, porosity damaged mating surfaces, stripped bolt threads, or distortion. Replace any part that exhibits these conditions. Inspect the low range lock plate in the front case. If the lock plate teeth or the plate hub is cracked, broken, chipped, or excessively worn, replace the lock plate and the lock plate attaching bolts.

Inspect the condition of all needle, roller and thrust bearings in the front and rear case halves and the input gear. Also, check the condition of the bearing bores in both cases and in the input gear, rear output shaft and rear retainer. Replace any part that exhibits signs of excessive wear or damage.

PLANETARY GEAR

Assembly

1. Install the inner thrust ring on planetary assembly.

2. Install the planetary assembly into the annulus gear.

3. Install the outer thrust ring and then the snap-ring.

MAINSHAFT

Assembly

1. Using J-33828 and J-8092 or equivalent, install the front drive sprocket bearing. Press bearing until tool bottoms out. Bearing should be flush with front surface. Reverse tool on J-8092 or equivalent and press rear bearing into sprocket until tool bottoms out. The rear bearing should be recessed after installation.

2. Install thrust washer on the mainshaft.

3. Install drive sprocket on the mainshaft.

4. Install blocker ring and synchronizer hub on the mainshaft. Seat hub on mainshaft and install a new snap-ring to retain.

5. Install pump gear on the mainshaft. Tap the gear with a hammer to seat on mainshaft.

6. Install speedometer gear on the mainshaft.

TRANSFER CASE

Assembly

All of the bearings used in the transfer case must be correctly positioned to avoid covering the bearing oil feed holes. After installation of bearings, check the bearing position to be sure the feed hole is not obstructed or blocked by a bearing.

1. Install the lock plate in the transfer case. Coat case and lock plate surfaces around bolt holes with Loctite 515 or equivalent.

2. Position the lock plate to the case and align bolt holes in lock plat with case. Install attaching bolts and torque to specification.

3. Install the roller bearings for the input shaft into the transfer case using J-33830 and J-8092 or equivalent. Press bearings until tool bottoms in bore.

4. Install the front output shaft rear bearing, using J-33832 and J-8092 or equivalent. Press bearing until tool bottoms in case.

5. Install the front output shaft front bearing using J-33833 and J-8092 or equivalent. Press bearing until tool bottoms in bore.

6. Install the snap-ring that retains the front output shaft bearing in case.

7. Install the front output shaft seal using J-33834 or equivalent.

8. Install the input shaft seal using J-33831 or equivalent.

9. Install spacer on shift sector shaft and install sector in transfer case. Install shift lever and retaining nut. Torque to specification.

10. Install shift sector detent spring and retaining bolt.

11. Install the pilot bearing into the input

gear using J-33829 and J-8092 or equivalent. Press bearing until tool bottoms out.

12. Install the input gear front thrust bearing and input gear in transfer case.

13. Install the planetary gear thrust washer on the input gear. Position range fork on planetary assembly and install planetary assembly into the transfer case.

14. Install the mainshaft into the transfer case. Make sure the thrust washer is aligned with the input gear and planetary assembly before installing mainshaft.

15. Install mode fork on synchronizer sleeve and rotate until mode fork is aligned with range fork. Slide mode fork rail down through range fork until rail is seated in bore of transfer case.

16. Position drive chain on front output shaft and install chain on drive sprocket. Install front output shaft in the transfer case. It may be necessary to slightly raise the mainshaft to seat the output shaft in the case.

17. Install the magnet into pocket of transfer case.

18. Apply ⅛″ bead of Loctite 515 or equivalent to the mating surface of the front case. Install rear case on the front case aligning dowel pins. Install bolts and torque to 20–25 ft. lbs. Install the two bolts with washers into the dowel pin holes.

19. Install the output bearing into the rear retainer using J-33833 and J-8092 or equivalent. Press bearing until seated in bore.

20. Install pump seal in pump housing using J-33835 or equivalent. Apply petroleum jelly to pump housing tabs and install housing in rear retainer.

21. Apply ⅛″ bead of Loctite 515 or equivalent to mating surface of rear retainer. Align retainer to case and install retaining bolts. Torque bolts to specification 15–20 ft. lbs.

22. Using a new snap-ring, install snap-ring on mainshaft. Pull up on mainshaft and seat snap-ring in its groove.

23. Install bushing in extension housing using J-33826 and J-8092 or equivalent. Press bushing until tool bottoms in bore.

24. Install a new seal in the extension housing using J-33843 or equivalent.

25. Apply ⅛″ bead of Loctite 515 or equivalent to mating surface of extension housing. Align extension housing to the rear retainer and install attaching bolts. Torque bolts to specification 20–25 ft. lbs.

26. Install front yoke on output shaft. Install a new yoke seal washer with a new nut and torque to specification.

27. Install drain plug and torque to specification. Install fill plug.

New Process 208

The 208 is a part-time unit with a two piece aluminum housing. On the front case half, the front output shaft, front input shaft, four wheel drive indicator switch and shift lever assembly are located. On the rear case half,

TORQUE SPECIFICATIONS
Model 207

Description	N•m	Ft. lbs.
Bolt Locking Plate to Transfer Case	27–40	20–30
Nut-Front Output Yoke	122–176	90–130
Switch Vacuum	20–34	15–25
Nut-Shift Lever	20–27	15–20
Bolt-Transfer Case	27–34	20–25
Bolt-Rear Retainer	20–27	15–20
Bolt-Extension Housing	27–34	20–25
Bolt-Drain-Fill	40–54	30–40
Bolt-Adapter to Transfer Case	26–40	19–29
Bolt-Shift Bracket	65–85	47–62
Bolt-Shift Lever Pivot	120–140	88–103
Bolt-Shift Lever Adjusting	34–48	25–35

the rear output shaft, bearing retainer and drain and fill plugs are located.

Disassembly

1. Drain the fluid from the case.
2. Remove the attaching nuts from the front and rear output yokes. Remove the yokes and sealing washers.

3. Remove the four bolts and separate the rear bearing retainer from the rear case half.

4. Remove the retaining ring, speedometer drive gear nylon oil pump housing, and oil pump gear from the rear output shaft.

5. Remove the eleven bolts and separate the case halves by inserting a screwdriver in the pry slots on the case.

208 power flow

1 Input gear thrust washer
2 Input gear thrust bearing
3 Input gear
4 Mainshaft pilot bearing
5 Planetary assembly
6 Planetary thrust washer
7 Annulus gear
8 Annulus gear thrust washer
9 Needle bearing spacers
10 Mainshaft needle bearings (120)
11 Needle bearing spacer
12 Thrust washer
13 Oil pump
14 Speedometer gear
15 Drive sprocket retaining ring
16 Drive sprocket
17 Sprocket carrier stop ring
18 Sprocket carrier
19 Clutch spring
20 Sliding clutch
21 Thrust washer
22 Mainshaft
23 Mainshaft thrust bearing
24 Annulus gear retaining ring
25 Mode fork

26 Mode fork spring
27 Range fork inserts
28 Range fork
29 Range sector
30 Mode fork bracket
31 Rear case
32 Seal
33 Pump housing
34 Rear retainer
35 Rear output bearing
36 Bearing snap ring
37 Vent tube
38 Rear seal
39 Rear yoke
40 Yoke seal washer
41 Yoke nut
42 Drain and fill plugs
43 Front output shaft rear bearing
44 Front output shaft rear thrust bearing
   race (thick)
45 Case magnet
46 Front output shaft rear thrust bearing
47 Front output shaft rear thrust bearing
   race (thin)
48 Driven sprocket retaining ring

49 Drive chain
50 Driven sprocket
51 Front output shaft
52 Front output shaft front thrust bearing
   race (thin)
53 Front output shaft front thrust bearing
   race (thick)
54 Front output shaft front bearing
55 Front output shaft front thrust bearing
56 Operating lever
57 Washer and locknut
58 Range sector shaft seal retainer
59 Range sector shaft seal
60 Detent ball, spring and retainer bolt
61 Front seal
62 Front yoke
63 Yoke seal washer
64 Yoke nut
65 Input gear oil seal
66 Input gear front bearing
67 Front case
68 Lock mode indicator switch
   and washer
69 Input gear rear bearing
70 Lockplate
71 Lockplate bolts
72 Case alignment dowels

Exploded view of 208

6. Remove the magnetic chip collector from the bottom of the rear case half.

7. Remove the thick thrust washer, thrust bearing and thin thrust washer from the front output shaft assembly.

8. Remove the drive chain by pushing the front input shaft inward and by angling the gear slightly to obtain adequate clearance to remove the chain.

9. Remove the output shaft from the front case half and slide the thick thrust washer, thrust bearing and thin thrust washer off the output side of the front output shaft.

10. Remove the screw, poppet spring and check ball from the front case half.

11. Remove the four wheel drive indicator switch and washer from the front case half.

12. Position the front case half on its face and lift out the rear output shaft, sliding clutch and clutch shift fork and spring.

13. Place a shop towel on the shift rail. Clamp the rail with a vise grip pliers so that they lay between the rail and the case edge. Position a pry bar under the pliers and pry out the shift rail.

14. Remove the snap ring and thrust

Driven sprocket retaining snap-ring removal

Drive sprocket thrust washer and spacer removal

washer from the planetary gear set assembly in the front case half.

15. Remove the annulus gear assembly and thrust washer from the front case half.

16. Lift the planetary gear assembly from the front case half.

17. Lift out the thrust bearing, sun gear, thrust bearing and thrust washer.

18. Remove the six bolts and lift the gear locking plate from the front case half.

19. Remove the nut retaining the external shift lever and washer. Press the shift

Sprocket and chain removal

Front output shaft and front thrust bearing assembly removal

control shaft inward and remove the shift selector plate and washer from the case.

20. From the rear output shaft, remove the snap-ring and thrust washer retaining the chain drive sprocket and slide the sprocket from the drive gear.

21. Remove the retaining ring from the sprocket carrier gear.

22. Carefully slide the sprocket carrier gear from the rear output shaft. Remove the two rows of 60 loose needle bearings. Remove the three separator rings from the output shaft.

Assembly

1. Slide the thrust washer against the gear on the rear output shaft.

2. Place the three space rings in position on the rear output shaft. Liberally coat the shaft with petroleum jelly and install the two rows (60 each) of needle bearings in position on the rear output shaft.

Rear retainer removal

Front output shaft rear thrust bearing removal

OIL PUMP

MAINSHAFT

Oil pump removal

3. Carefully slide the sprocket gear carrier over the needle bearings. Be careful not to dislodge any of the needles.

4. Install the retaining ring on the sprocket gear.

5. Slide the chain drive sprocket onto the sprocket carrier gear.

6. Install the thrust washer and snap ring on the rear output shaft.

7. Install the shift selector plate and washer through the front of the case.

8. Place the shift lever assembly on the shift control shaft and torque the nut to 14–20 ft. lbs.

9. Place the locking plate in the front case half and torque the bolts to 25–35 ft. lbs.

10. Place the thrust bearing and washer over the input shaft of the sun gear. Insert the input shaft through the front case half from the inside and insert the thrust bearing.

11. Install the planetary gear assembly so the fixed plate and planetary gears engage the sun gear.

12. Slide the annulus gear and clutch

assembly with the shift fork assembly engaged, over the hub of the planetary gear assembly. The shift fork pin must engage the slot in the shift selector plate. Install the thrust washer and snap ring.

13. Position the shift rail through the shift fork hub in the front case. Tap lightly with a soft hammer to seat the rail in the hole.

14. Position the sliding clutch shift fork on the shift rail and place the sliding clutch and clutch shift spring into the front case half. Slide the rear output shaft into the case.

15. On the output side of the front output shaft, assemble the thin thrust washer, thrust bearing, and thick thrust washer and partially insert the front output shaft into the case.

16. Place the drive chain on the rear output shaft drive gear. Insert the rear output shaft into the front case half and engage the drive chain on the front output shaft drive gear. Push the front output shaft into position in the case.

17. Assemble the thin thrust washer,

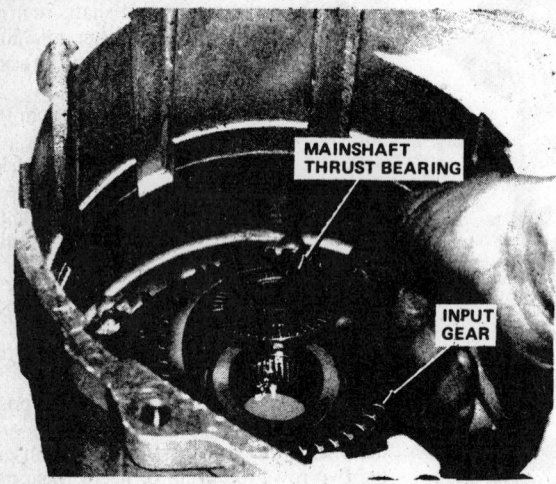

MAINSHAFT THRUST BEARING

INPUT GEAR

Mainshaft thrust bearing and input gear

PLANETARY THRUST WASHER

PLANETARY ASSEMBLY

Planetary thrust washer and planetary assembly

SPROCKET CARRIER STOP RING

CLUTCH SHIFT SPRING

Sprocket carrier clutch ring and spring removal

INPUT GEAR THRUST BEARING

THRUST BEARING RACE

LOCKPLATE

Input gear thrust bearing and race removal

Annulus gear and shift rail installation

Assembling sprocket carrier components

thrust bearing and thick thrust washer on the inside of the front output shaft drive gear.

18. Position the magnetic chip collector into position in the front case half.

19. Place a bead of RTV sealant completely around the face of the front case half and assemble the case halves being careful that the shift rail and forward output shafts are properly retained.

20. Alternately tighten the bolts to 20–25 ft. lbs.

21. Slide the oil pump gear over the input shaft and slide the spacer collar into position.

22. Engage the speedometer drive gear onto the rear output shaft and slide the retaining ring into position.

23. Use petroleum jelly to hold the nylon oil pump housing in position at the rear bearing retainer. Apply a bead of RTV sealant around the mounting surface of the retainer and carefully position the retainer assembly over the output shaft and onto the rear case half. The retainer must be installed so that the vent hole is vertical when the case is installed.

24. Torque the retainer bolts alternately to 20–25 ft. lbs.

25. Place a new thrust washer under each yoke and install the yokes on their respective shafts. Place the oil slinger under the front yoke. Torque the nuts to 90–130 ft. lbs.

26. Install the poppet ball, spring and screw in the front case half. Torque the screw to 20–25 ft. lbs.

27. Install the 4WD indicator switch and washer and tighten to 15–20 ft. lbs.

28. Fill the unit with 6 pints of Ford CJ fluid or Dexron® II.

New Process 219

Introduced in the 1980 model year of Jeep vehicles as the Quadra-Trac®, this is a full-time unit. The 4WD mode is fully differentiated in 4H only. The 4L and Lock ranges are undifferentiated. The 4H differentiation is accomplished by a torque biasing viscous coupling and an open differential connected to the coupling. Two drive sprockets and an interconnecting drive chain are used to distribute input torque.

Disassembly

1. Drain the lubricant from the case.

2. Remove the front and rear output shaft yokes and discard the yoke seal washers and yoke nuts.

3. Mark the rear retainer and rear case for an alignment reference.

4. Unbolt and remove the rear retainer. If necessary, use a soft mallet to loosen the retainer. Under no circumstances should the retainer be pried off.

5. Remove the differential shims and

N.P. 219 Quadra-Trac® power flow

1 Mainshaft rear bearing spacer—short (2)	31 Input gear front bearing	63 Drain plug and gasket
2 Side gear	32 Front case mounting stud (6)	64 Rear case bolt
3 Viscous coupling and differential assembly	33 Front case	65 Washer (2)
4 Mainshaft rear pilot roller bearings (15)	34 Lock mode indicator switch gasket	66 Case alignment dowel
5 Mainshaft O-ring	35 Lock mode indicator switch	67 Front output shaft rear bearing
6 Rear output shaft	36 Input gear rear bearing	68 Magnet
7 Oil pump	37 Low range lockplate	69 Front output shaft rear thrust bearing race (thick)
8 Speedometer gear	38 Shift rail	70 Front output shaft rear thrust bearing
9 Differential end play shims (selective)	39 Range sector	71 Front output shaft rear thrust bearing race (thin)
10 Mainshaft needle bearings (82)	40 Range fork	72 Driven sprocket retaining snap ring
11 Mainshaft rear bearing spacer	41 Range fork insert	73 Drive chain
12 Clutch gear	42 Range fork pads	74 Driven sprocket
13 Clutch gear locating ring	43 Mode fork spring	75 Front output shaft
14 Drive sprocket locating ring	44 Mode fork pads	76 Front output shaft front thrust bearing race (thin)
15 Drive sprocket	45 Mode fork insert	77 Front output shaft front thrust bearing
16 Side gear clutch	46 Mode fork	78 Front output shaft front thrust bearing race (thick)
17 Mainshaft thrust washer	47 Shift rail spring	79 Front output shaft front bearing
18 Mainshaft	48 Mode fork bracket	80 Washer
19 Clutch sleeve	49 Rear output shaft bearing	81 Locknut
20 Mainshaft thrust bearing	50 Rear output shaft bearing seal	82 Operating lever
21 Annulus gear retaining ring	51 Rear case	83 Range sector shaft seal retainer
22 Annulus gear thrust washer	52 Wiring clip	84 Range sector shaft seal
23 Annulus gear	53 Spline bolt	85 Detent ball
24 Planetary thrust washer	54 Rear output bearing	86 Detent spring
25 Planetary assembly	55 Rear retainer	87 Detent retaining bolt
26 Mainshaft front pilot bearing	56 Vent	88 Front output shaft seal
27 Input gear	57 Output shaft oil seal	89 Front yoke
28 Input gear thrust bearing	58 Rear Yoke	90 Lockplate bolts
29 Input gear thrust bearing race	59 Yoke seal washer	
30 Input gear oil seal	60 Yoke locknut	
	61 Vent chamber seal	
	62 Fill plug and gasket	

Exploded view of N.P. 219

Differential shim, speedometer gear and oil pump

Rear case half removal

Mainshaft and thrust washer

Annulus gear snap-ring and thrust washer

Annulus gear and range fork removal

Planetary thrust washer removal

Planetary assembly removal

speedometer drive gear from the rear output shaft. Mark the shims for reference.

6. Remove the rear output bearing snap-ring and remove the bearing from the retainer using a soft mallet.

NOTE: The rear output bearing has one side shielded. Note this for reassembly.

7. Remove the rear output shaft seal from the retainer using a screwdriver or punch.

8. Position the front case assembly on wood blocks. The blocks should have V cuts made in them for more positive support of the case.

9. Remove the case halve bolts. The case halves may be pried apart using a screwdriver in the notches provided at the case ends.

NOTE: The two case end bolts have flat washers and alignment dowels. Note their location for assembly.

10. Remove the rear output shaft and viscous coupling as an assembly. Tap the shaft with a plastic mallet if necessary.

11. Remove the O-ring seal and pilot roller bearings from the mainshaft.

12. Remove the rear output shaft from the viscous coupling.

13. Remove the shift rail spring from the rail.

14. Remove the plastic oil pump from the shaft bore in the rear case. Note the pump position for assembly reference. The end with the recess must face the shaft bore when installed.

15. Remove the rear output shaft bearing seal from the case. A screwdriver may be used to pry it out.

16. Remove the front output shaft thrust bearing assembly. Remove the thick washer, bearing and thin washer.

17. Remove the driven sprocket retaining snap-ring.

18. Remove the drive sprocket, drive chain, driven sprocket, side gear clutch and clutch gear as an assembly. Place the assembly on a workbench and mark the components for assembly.

19. Remove the needle bearings and spacers from the mainshaft and side gear bore. A total of 82 bearings and three spacers is used.

20. Remove the side gear/clutch gear assembly from the drive sprocket. Remove two snap-rings and remove the clutch gear from the side gear.

21. Remove the side gear clutch, mainshaft thrust washer and remaining mainshaft needle bearing spacer.

22. Remove the front output shaft and shaft thrust bearing assembly. Note the installation sequence of the bearing assembly.

23. Remove the front output shaft seal from the front case using a screwdriver or punch.

24. Remove the shift rail spring from the shift rail.

25. Remove the clutch sleeve, mode fork and spring as an assembly.

26. Remove the mainshaft thrust washer and mainshaft. Grasp the shaft and pull it straight up and out.

27. Move the range operating lever downward to the last detent position.

28. Disengage the range fork lug from the range sector slot.

29. Remove the annulus gear retaining snap-ring and thrust washer.

30. Remove the annulus gear and range fork.

31. Remove the planetary thrust washer from the hub.

32. Remove the planetary assembly.

33. Remove the mainshaft thrust bearing from the input gear.

34. Remove the input gear and remove the input gear thrust bearing and race.

35. Remove the range selector detent ball and spring retaining bolt and remove the detent ball and spring.

36. Remove the range selector and operating lever attaching nut and lockwasher, and remove the lever.

37. Remove the range selector.

38. Remove the range selector O-ring and retainer.

39. Remove the input gear oil seal from the front case with a screwdriver.

Assembly

Lubricate all parts before assembly with 10W-30 motor oil. Petroleum jelly will be indicated for some assemblies. Do not use chassis lube or other heavy lubricants.

1. Install new input gear and rear output shaft bearing oil seals. Seat the seals flush with the edge of the seal bore or with the seal groove in the case. Coat the seal lips with petroleum jelly after installation.

2. Install the input gear thrust bearing race in the case counterbore.

3. Install the input gear thrust bearing on the input gear and install the gear and bearing in the case.

4. Install the mainshaft thrust bearing in the bearing recess in the input gear.

5. Install the planetary assembly on the

Clutch sleeve and mode fork removal

input gear. Make sure that the planetary pinion teeth mesh fully with the input gear.

6. Install the planetary thrust washer on the planetary hub.

7. Install a new sector shaft O-ring and retainer in the shaft bore in the case.

8. Install the range selector in the front case. Install the operating lever on the sector shaft and install the lever attaching washer and locknut on the shaft. Tighten the locknut to 17 ft. lbs.

9. Install the detent spring, ball and retaining bolt in the front case detent bore. Tighten the bolt to 22 ft. lbs.

10. Move the range selector to the last detent position.

11. Assemble the annulus gear and range fork. Install the assembled fork and gear over the planetary assembly. Be sure that the annulus gear is fully meshed with the planetary pinions.

12. Insert the range fork lug in the range detent slot.

13. Install the annulus thrust washer and retaining ring on the annulus gear hub.

14. Align the mainshaft thrust washer in the input gear, if necessary.

15. Install the mainshaft. Be sure the shaft is fully seated in the input gear.

16. Install the mainshaft thrust washer on the mainshaft.

17. Install the short mainshaft needle bearing spacer on the shaft.

18. Apply a liberal coating of petroleum jelly to the mainshaft needle bearing surface and install 41 of the 82 needle bearings on the shaft. Be sure the bearings seat on the short spacer.

19. Install the long needle bearing spacer on the shaft. Lower the spacer onto the previously installed needle bearings carefully to avoid displacing them.

20. Align the shift rail bore in the case with the bore in the range fork and install the shift rail.

NOTE: Remove all traces of oil from the case shift rail bore before installing the rail. Oil in the case bore may prevent the rail from seating completely and prevent rear case installation.

Input gear and thrust bearing removal and installation

Mainshaft and thrust washer installation

21. Assemble the mode fork, mode fork spring and mode fork bracket.

22. Install the clutch sleeve in the mode fork. Be sure the sleeve is positioned so that the ID numbers on the sleeve face upward when the sleeve is installed.

23. Align the clutch sleeve and mode fork assembly with the shift rail and install the assembly on the shift rail and mainshaft. Be sure that the clutch sleeve is meshed with the mainshaft gear.

24. Lubricate the remaining 41 needle bearings and place them on the mainshaft.

25. Install the side gear clutch on the mainshaft with the teeth facing downward. Be sure the gear teeth mesh with the clutch sleeve.

26. Install the remaining short mainshaft needle bearing spacer. Install the spacer carefully to avoid displacing previously installed bearings.

27. Install the front output shaft front thrust bearing in the front case. Correct sequence is thick race, bearing, thin race.

28. Install the front output shaft in the front case.

29. Install the clutch gear on the side gear. The tapered side of the clutch gear teeth must face the side gear teeth.

30. Install the clutch gear and drive sprocket locating snap-rings on the side gear. Install the snap-rings so that they face each other.

31. Position the drive and driven sprockets in the drive chain and install the assembled side and clutch gears in the drive sprocket.

32. Install the assembled drive chain, sprockets and side gear on the mainshaft and front output shaft. Align the sprockets with the shaft, keeping the assembly level and carefully lower the assembly onto both shafts simultaneously. Do not displace any of the needle bearings.

33. Install the driven sprocket retaining snap-ring.

34. Install the front output shaft rear thrust bearing assembly on the front output shaft. Correct installation sequence is thin race, thrust bearing, thick race.

35. Install the shift rail spring on the shift rail.

36. Install a new O-ring on the mainshaft pilot bearing hub.

37. Coat the mainshaft pilot roller bearing hub and bearings with a liberal amount of petroleum jelly and install the rollers on the shaft.

38. Install the rear output shaft in the viscous coupling. Be sure it is fully seated.

39. Install the assembled viscous coupling and rear output shaft on the mainshaft. Align the mainshaft pilot hub with the pilot bearing bore in the rear output shaft and carefully lower the assembly onto the mainshaft. Take care to avoid displacing the roller bearings.

40. Align the clutch gear teeth with the viscous coupling teeth and seat the coupling fully onto the clutch gear.

NOTE: When correctly installed, the clutch gear teeth will not be visible or extend out of the coupling.

41. Install the magnet in the front case, if removed.

42. Clean the mating surfaces of the case halves thoroughly.

43. Apply Loctite® 515 or equivalent to the mating surfaces and all attaching bolts.

44. Join the case halves, aligning the dowels and install the bolts. Torque the bolts to 22 ft. lbs.

NOTE: The two end bolts require flat washers.

45. Install the oil pump on the rear output shaft and seat it in the case. The side with the recess should face the inside of the case.

46. Install the speedometer drive gear and differential shift, on the output shaft.

47. Install the vent chamber seal in the rear retainer.

48. Align and install the rear retainer on the case. Make the retainer finger tight only.

49. Install the yoke on the rear output shaft. Make the yoke finger tight only.

50. Mount a dial indicator on the rear retainer. Position the indicator stylus so that it contacts the top of the yoke nut.

51. Install the yoke on the front output shaft and rotate the shaft ten complete revolutions.

52. Rotate the front output shaft again and note the play indicated on the dial. End play should be .002–.010 inch. If the end play must be adjusted, remove the rear retainer and add or subtract shims as required.

53. Remove both output shaft yokes and discard the nuts.

54. Install the front and rear yoke seals.

55. Remove the rear retainer bolts, apply Loctite® 515 or equivalent to the mating surface of the retainer and to the bolts and install the bolts. Torque them to 22 ft. lbs.

56. Install new yoke seal washers on the output shafts, install yokes on the shafts and install new yoke nuts. Tighten the nuts to 110 ft. lbs.

57. Install the drain plug and tighten to 18 ft. lbs.

58. Pour 4 pints of 10W-30 motor oil into the case and install the fill plug. Tighten it to 18 ft. lbs.

Warner Quadra-Trac®

The Quadra-Trac® transfer case provides full-time, four-wheel drive under all driving conditions. The front and rear drive-

Exploded view of the optional reduction unit (© Jeep Corp.)

Exploded view of the Warner Quadra-Trac® without the optional reduction unit (© Jeep Corp.)

shafts are driven by a limited slip differential in the transfer case. The limited slip differential is connected to the input shaft by a link-belt type chain. In operation, if the rear axle loses traction, then the engine torque will be transfered through the transfer case differential to the front axle.

The transfer case contains a manually actuated lockout system that locks the front and rear driveshafts together, cancelling the differential action. This feature is used under extreme marginal traction situations.

NOTE: In order to spare the transfer case differential side gears and brake cones from excessive and possibly damaging wear, do not spin the wheels excessively when the vehicle is stuck or bogged down.

An optional gear reduction unit mounted at the rear of the input shaft is available for the Quadra-Trac® unit, making it a two-speed transfer case.

PERFORMANCE CHECKS TRANSFER CASE DIFFERENTIAL TORQUE BIAS CHECK

1. With the lock-out feature *not* engaged and the transmission in Park, raise the vehicle until the front wheels are free of the ground.
2. Disconnect the rear driveshaft from the transfer case.

3. Turn the rear yoke retaining nut with a torque wrench and socket, taking note of how much torque is required to force the cone clutches to slip. They should slip when 110 to 270 ft. lbs. are applied.

Slippage below 10 ft. lbs. indicates replacement of the differential is needed. If no slippage occurs at 270 ft. lbs., improper lubrication is indicated. Drain and refill the transfer case and reduction unit, if so equippped, with the proper lubricant mixture.

DRIVE CHAIN TENSION CHECK

1. Drain the lubricant from the transfer case.
2. Remove the chain inspection plug and insert a steel rule into the hole.
3. A new chain will be 1.575 in. from the outer edge of the plug hole. When the slack in the chain reaches ½–¾ in., the chain should be replaced. No adjustment is possible.
4. Reinstall the drain and chain inspection plugs, and refill the unit with the proper lubricant mixture.

REAR CASE COVER

Removal

Most Quadra-Trac® components can be serviced without removing the complete unit from the vehicle. To gain access to the rear output shaft, drive sprocket and thrust

washer, chain, differential and needle bearing, or the diaphragm control system, just the rear cover has to be removed.

1. Lift and support the vehicle.
2. If the vehicle is equipped with a reduction unit, continue on to the next step for the reduction unit removal procedure. If the vehicle is not equipped with a reduction unit, proceed to step 7.
3. Loosen all the bolts that attach the reduction unit to the transfer case cover.
4. Move the reduction unit backward just enough to allow the oil to drain from the unit.
5. Loosen the cable retaining bolt at the shift control lever. Loosen the cable clamp bolt and remove the control cable from the clamp bracket and control lever.
6. When the oil has drained, remove the bolts which hold the reduction unit to the transfer case cover. Move the reduction unit rearward to clear the transmission output shaft and pinion cage which is attached to the transfer case drive sprocket. The pinion cage will remain with the transfer case assembly.

NOTE: The pinion cage should not be removed if the transfer case cover assembly is to be removed, but may be removed for inspection or replacement if the transfer case cover assembly is to remain in the vehicle. Removal of the pinion cage involves only removing the snapring which holds the cage to the sprocket and sliding the cage backward.

7. Remove the transfer case drain plug and allow the unit to drain.

8. Mark the rear output shaft yoke and universal joint to provide an alignment reference during reassembly. Disconnect the rear drive shaft front universal joint from the transfer case rear yoke.

9. Mark the diaphragm control vacuum hoses for identification during reassembly, then disconnect them. Also remove the lock-up indicator switch wire and the speedometer cable. Remove the indicator switch.

WOOD BLOCK

The Quadra-Trac® transfer case positioned for disassembly (© Jeep Corp.)

Mark the end caps and case sprocket of the differential assembly before disassembling the differential—Warner Quadra-Trac® (© Jeep Corp.)

WOOD BLOCK

The differential and drive sprocket positioned for installation of the drive chain—Warner Quadra-Trac® (© Jeep Corp.)

10. Disconnect the parking brake cable guide from the pivot on the right frame side.

11. Remove the bolts which attach the case cover assembly to the case (front housing). Carefully slide the cover assembly backward off the front output shaft and the transmission output shaft.

Disassembly

1. To disassemble the unit, remove the rear output shaft yoke.

2. If the unit is *not* equipped with a reduction unit, remove the power take-off cover from the rear of the transfer case cover. Remove the sealing ring from the transfer case cover.

3. Using a piece of wood 2 in. × 4 in. and 6 in. long, support the cover and drive sprocket.

4. If *not* equipped with a reduction unit, remove the drive hub and sleeve from the drive sprocket rear splines by expanding the internal snap-ring. The ring expanding tabs are accessible through a slot in the outside edge of the drive sleeve.

5. If equipped with a reduction unit, remove the pinion cage snap-ring and carrier.

6. Lift the case cover from the drive sprocket and differential. The cover, rear output shaft, bearings and seal, drive sprocket rear needle bearing, and lock-up

LONG SIDE OF FORK TO REAR

FRONT

Install the lock-up hub assembly shift fork with the long side of the fork facing toward the rear—Warner Quadra-Trac® (© Jeep Corp.)

hub can now be serviced without any further disassembly of other components.

7. Slide the drive sprocket toward the differential unit and remove the chain. The differential unit may now be serviced without any further disassembly of other components.

Assembly

1. Position the drive sprocket on a block of wood 2 in. × 4 in. and 6 in. long.

2. Place the differential assembly about 2 in. from the drive sprocket and with the front end of the differential on the bench.

3. Position the drive chain around the drive sprocket and the differential assembly. Be sure that the chain is properly engaged with the sprocket and differential teeth and that the slack is removed from the chain.

4. Insert the rear output shaft into the differential.

5. Shift the lock-up hub rearward in the case cover. Lubricate the drive sprocket thrust washer and insert it in position on the case cover.

6. Carefully align the case cover and position it onto the drive sprocket and differential. The output shaft may have to be slightly rotated to align it with the lock-up hub. Be sure that the drive sprocket thrust washer stays positioned correctly.

7. If equipped with a reduction unit, install the pinion cage onto the drive sprocket rear splines. Install the snap-ring. Be sure that the snap-ring seats properly in the groove.

8. If the vehicle is *not* equipped with a reduction unit, assemble the drive hub,

MATCHED FRONT SET   CASE SPROCKET   MATCHED REAR SET

FRONT END CAP   SMALL THRUST WASHER   PRELOAD SPRINGS   LARGE THRUST WASHER   BRAKE CONE   SIDE GEAR   SIDE GEAR   BRAKE CONE   LARGE THRUST WASHER   PRELOAD SPRINGS   SMALL THRUST WASHER   REAR END CAP

Exploded view of the differential assembly—Warner Quadra-Trac® (© Jeep Corp.)

drive sleeve, and snap-ring, then install them onto the drive sprocket rear splines. Be sure the snap-ring seats properly.

9. Turn the drive sleeve or pinion cage to make sure the drive sprocket thrust washer did not come out of position. No binding should be present.

10. If *not* equipped with a reduction unit, install the power take-off sealing ring and cover and tighten the attaching screws.

11. Install the speedometer gear on the rear output shaft.

12. Install the rear output shaft oil seal and the rear yoke and nut. Tighten the nut to specification.

Installation

13. Clean the groove which the front oil seal gasket fits into and install the seal.

14. Install two 3/8 in. 16 × 2 in. long pilot studs into the transfer case front cover housing.

15. Move the cover assembly forward to mesh with the front output shaft and transmission output shaft. It may be necessary to rotate the rear output shaft slightly to allow the two sets of splines to engage.

16. After the cover assembly has been moved forward and is evenly touching the front half of the case, remove the pilot studs and install the rear cover attaching bolts. Tighten the bolts alternately and evenly to specifications.

17. Install the lock out indicator switch and connect the lock out switch wire, diaphragm control vacuum hoses, and the speedometer cable.

18. Install the rear drive shaft.

19. Install the parking brake cable guide to the pivot on the right frame side.

20. Install the reduction unit, if so equipped, as follows:

21. Position the reduction unit to the transfer case and mesh the caged pinions with the sun gear and ring gear, and align the sun gear inner splines with the transmission output shaft splines.

22. Move the reduction unit forward until it touches the sealing ring.

23. Install the attaching screws loosely, then tighten them alternately to specification.

24. Connect the shift control cable and

adjust it by first removing the swivel block from the control lever. Move the control lever to the most forward position. Thread the swivel block in or out on the cable end to obtain the correct length to fit the swivel block in the control lever.

25. Install the proper type and amount of lubricant and lower the vehicle.

NOTE: Use 8 oz. of Jeep Lubricant Concentrate Part No. 8123004 or 5356068 or Lubrizol® 762 (there is no substitute) mixed with SAE 30 non-detergent motor oil. 3.5 pints of the mixture is required to fill the transfer case without a reduction unit, 4.5 pints with a reduction unit.

DIFFERENTIAL ASSEMBLY

Disassembly

1. Mark end caps and case sprocket with paint. Marks must be used to identify front end cap, rear end cap and proper orientation of caps to case sprocket.

2. Remove front end cap. If necessary, tap gently with a soft hammer.

3. Remove thrust washer, preload springs, brake cone and side gears from case sprocket. Care must be taken to keep the various pieces together as they must be installed as a unit.

4. Invert the case sprocket and remove rear cap. If necessary, tap gently with a soft hammer.

5. Remove the thrust washers, preload springs, brake cone and side gears. Care must be taken to keep the various pieces together as they must be installed as a unit.

6. Raise the case sprocket. The pinion shaft lock pin should fall out. If the pin does not fall, drive the pin out with a 1/4 in. pin punch.

7. Drive the pinion mate shaft out of case sprocket, using a brass drift and hammer. Care must be taken to avoid damaging the pinion mate thrust washers.

8. Thoroughly clean and inspect all component parts. Replace any damaged or worn parts with a complete matched set.

Assembly

Prelubricate all bearings and thrust surfaces

with Jeep Lubricant Concentrate Part No. 8123004 or 5356068 or Lubrizol® 762 (there is no substitute) prior to installation.

1. Slide the pinion mate shaft in the case sprocket three inches.

2. Install the pinion mate thrust washers and gears on shaft in the proper order.

3. Align the pinion mate shaft lockpin hole with hole in case sprocket. Lightly drive the pinion mate shaft into case sprocket until lockpin holes are exactly aligned.

4. Move the pinion mate gears apart until the gears are pressing the washers against the case sprocket.

5. Engage the pinion mate gear with the front side gears. Insert the brake cone over the gear and in case sprocket. Install the large thrust washer and preload springs, concave side of springs facing toward brake cone.

6. Lubricate the small thrust washer and place it on the front end cap. Install the front end cap, secure with attaching screws and alternately tighten to proper torque. Make certain that alignment marks are in order.

7. Invert the case sprocket and end cap and install the pinion shaft lock pin.

8. Mesh remaining side gear with pinion mate gears.

9. Insert the remaining brake cone over the side gear. Install the large thrust washer and preload spring, concave side of springs facing toward brake cone.

10. Lubricate the small thrust washer and place it on the rear end cap. Install the rear cap, tighten attaching screws finger tight.

11. Insert the front and rear output shafts in the differential and rotate until both shafts have aligned with the splines on the brake cones and side gears. Alternately tighten the retaining screws to proper torque.

DIAPHRAGM CONTROL, SHIFT FORK AND LOCK-UP HUB

Disassembly

1. Remove the vent cover and seal ring.

2. Remove the retaining rings positioning the shift fork on diaphragm. Care-

fully pry the shift fork forward to gain access to the retaining rings. Remove the spring with a magnet.

3. Caution must be exercised in removal of the diaphragm control rod as it is retained by a spring loaded detent ball. Insert a magnet into the hole to hold the detent ball. Slip the diaphragm control rod out of case. Remove detent ball and spring.

4. Remove shifting fork, plastic shifting shoes and lock-up hub.

Assembly

1. Lubricate the shifting shoes and place them in the shift fork.

2. Install the shift fork and lock-up hub assembly in the case cover, long end of shift fork first (toward rear). Make certain that the shift fork does not separate from the lock-up hub by reaching through the needle bearings.

3. Insert the diaphragm control rod in the case and shifting fork, stopping before the detent ball hole is reached.

4. Install the detent ball and spring. Depress the detent ball with a ¼ in. pin punch and slide the diaphragm control rod into place.

5. Install the shift fork retaining pin, (clips) and the diaphragm retaining spring, the spring should be below the surface of the bore.

6. Install the vent cover and seal ring.

REDUCTION UNIT

Disassembly

1. Remove PTO cover and gasket.

2. Remove snap-ring from reduction main shaft rear end, slide the reduction main shaft and sun gear assembly forward and out. Remove needle bearings.

3. Remove as an assembly, the ring gear, reduction collar plate, pinion cage lock plate, shift collar hub and reduction collar hub. Using a soft hammer, remove the shift collar hub from the pinion cage lock plate.

4. Remove the pinion cage lock plate, needle bearing, ring gear, reduction collar plate and shift collar hub. Separate the reduction collar hub and needle bearing from shift collar hub.

5. When necessary, separate the reduction collar plate and ring gear by removing retaining snap-ring.

6. Remove needle bearing and direct drive sleeve from the reduction shift collar.

7. Shift the reduction shift collar to the neutral (center) detent with the control lever. Disengage the shift fork. Place the shift in the direct drive detent position (rear), align the collar outer teeth with the inner teeth in the reduction holding plate. Place the fork and collar in the reduction position (front) detent, and remove the reduction shift collar.

8. Remove the annular bearing rear snap-ring and bearing.

9. Remove the shift fork locating spring

pin, large expansion plug, shift rail taper plug, and control lever.

10. Drive the spring pin out of the shift fork and rail with a ³⁄₁₆ in. pin punch. Slide the shift rail forward out of the shift fork, and remove the shift fork. Remove the spring shift fork poppet ball. Drive the poppet taper plug into the shift rail bore and remove the plug and spring.

11. Remove the shift lever retaining pin and the shift lever assembly.

12. Remove the reduction holding plate snap-ring and reduction holding plate.

Assembly

1. Align the shift fork locating spring holes in the reduction holding plate and housing. Install the reduction holding plate. Locating pins should index the plate in the case. Secure the plate with a snap-ring, tabs facing forward.

2. Install the shift lever assembly into the housing, lever towards the rear. Position seal ring on groove in shift lever shaft.

3. Move the shift lever assembly inward and install taper pin.

4. Install the shift rail in the shift rail rear bore, grooved end first. Position the shift rail with flat side towards the poppet spring. Engage the shift rail with the shift lever assembly and position the rail so it is flush with the edge of the poppet bore. Place the poppet ball on the end of spring and insert the assembly in the poppet bore, using a spring pin as an installation tool. Depress the poppet ball and slide the shift rail over the poppet ball as far as the spring pin will allow. Remove the spring pin and place the shift rail in the first detent position.

5. Position the shift rail so the flat side is facing the shift lever assembly and the spring pin bore is aligned with the spring pin bore in the shift fork. Once the spring pin holes are aligned, install the spring pin so that it is flush with the outside surface of the shift fork.

6. Install the shift rail taper plug, poppet bore taper plug, shift rail cover expansion plug, shift fork spring locating pin and the control lever.

7. Place the shift fork in the neutral position (center) detent. Install the reduction shift collar so that the outer teeth engage with the reduction holding plate inner teeth, and the shift collar fork groove forward of the shift fork. Place the shift fork in the direct drive (rear) detent. Move the shift collar away and to the rear of the shift fork until the groove aligns with the shift fork. Engage the collar groove with the shift fork.

8. Place the direct drive sleeve in the reduction shift collar, needle bearing surface facing toward the front. Lubricate and install the needle bearing, against the direct drive sleeve.

9. Assemble the reduction collar plate hub and ring gear. Make certain that snaprings are seated in their grooves.

10. Install the needle bearing and reduction collar hub on the shift collar hub.

11. Install the ring gear, reduction collar plate and hub on the shift collar hub.

12. Place a needle bearing on the shift collar hub and the reduction collar hub.

13. Tap the pinion cage lock into place on the shift collar hub with a soft hammer and install assembly in housing. Place needle bearings on the shift collar hub and the pinion cage lock plate.

14. Install the reduction main shaft and sun gear into shift collar hub and through the direct drive sleeve and annular bearing. With a brass drift gently tap the assembly as far to the rear as possible. Place the rear spacer on the main shaft and secure with the selective snap-ring which gives the tightest fit, between .004 in. and .009 in. clearance. Snap rings are available in thicknesses ranging from 0.089 in. to 0.105 in.

15. Install PTO cover and gasket, tighten attaching bolts to proper torque.

SPECIFICATIONS

TORQUE (FT. LBS.)

Transfer case breather	6–10
Chain measuring access hole plug	6–14
Drain plug	15–25
Fill plug	15–25
Lock-up cover to transfer case	8–10
Lock-out indicator switch	10–15
Output Shaft Nut	90–150
PTO cover to transfer case bolts: ⅜ in.-16	15–25
⁵⁄₁₆ in.-18	10–20
Speedometer adapter	20–30
Transfer case cover to transfer case	15–25
Transfer case to transmission extension bolt	30–50
Reduction unit cable housing clamp nut	7–12
Fill plug	15–25
Shift lever cable clamp nut	10–20
Shift lever to shift nut	15–25
Reduction PTO cover to case	15–25
Reduction unit to transfer case bolts: ⅜ in.-16	15–25
⁵⁄₁₆ in.-18	8–10

Rockwell T-223

The Rockwell T-223 transfer case is a two speed unit used to transmit power to both the front and rear driving axles. The transfer case is mounted behind the transmission and is driven by a short drive shaft. A parking brake drum is mounted to the case on the opposite side of the front output shaft.

It is intended and recommended by the manufacture that only through severe operating conditions or poor traction, should the four wheel drive unit be engaged.

Disassembly

TRANSFER CASE

1. Clean the exterior of the case and remove the three driving yokes from the input and output shafts, using a slide hammer.

2. Remove the retaining screws and lift the top cover and gasket. Discard the gasket and clean the mating surfaces.

SHIFT COMPONENTS

1. Remove the detent springs and remove the detent balls with a magnet.

2. Pull both of the shift shafts out through the front of the case. If the shafts cannot be removed this way, drive the shafts and expansion plugs out through the rear of the case.

3. Remove the shift shaft oil seals from the front of the case.

4. Lift the range and declutch shift forks from the case.

FRONT OUTPUT SHAFT

1. Remove the front output shaft bearing cap and gasket and pull the shaft and declutch collar from the case.

2. Slide a long bar through the front output shaft gear and tap out the small and large expansion plugs in the brake hub.

PARKING BRAKE

1. Cut the wire lock and remove the retaining screws from the brake drum, and remove the brake drum from the hub.

2. Remove the brake hub retaining snap ring and remove the brake hub from the front output shaft, using a large gear puller.

3. Disconnect the brake shoe return springs and remove the brake shoes and lever.

4. Remove the brake backing plate mounting bolts and remove the backing plate, washer, deflector plate and washer.

NOTE: Do not try to remove the front output shaft at this time. The idler shaft must be removed first, due to the interference of the gears.

IDLER SHAFT

1. Remove the idler shaft front and rear bearing caps. Wire the forward bearing cap shims together for reassembly.

2. Remove the screws and retainer plate from the front end of the idler shaft and press the idler shaft out through the rear of the case.

3. Lift the Low gear, spacer and front bearing from the case.

4. Remove the High gear and tap the idler shaft front bearing cup from the case.

5. Remove the retaining snap-ring and press the bearing from the idler shaft.

FRONT OUTPUT GEAR

1. After removing the idler shaft assembly, remove the front output shaft rear bearing cap and gasket.

2. Remove the bearing retaining snap-ring and tap the front output gear and bearing into the case. Reach through the cover opening and lift the gear and bearing out of the case.

1. Cotter key
2. Nut
3. Washer
4. Oil seal
5. Rear output shaft rear bearing cap
6. Cap screw
7. Lock washer
8. Cap screw
9. Lock washer
10. Speedometer driven gear bushing
11. Speedometer driven gear and shaft
12. Gasket
13. Speedometer drive gear
14. Spacer
15. Rear output shaft rear bearing cup
16. Rear output shaft rear bearing
17. Brake backing plate
18. Cap screw
19. Lock washer
20. Input shaft rear bearing cage
21. Gasket
22. Idler shaft rear bearing
23. Input shaft rear bearing
24. Gasket
25. Spacer
26. Shift shaft hole plug
27. Cap screw
28. Lock washer
29. Snap ring
30. Idler shaft rear bearing cup
31. Idler shaft rear bearing
32. **Front output shaft**
33. Idler shaft hi gear
34. Gear spacer
35. Direct drive gear
36. Direct drive gear bushing
37. Low speed sliding gear
38. Range shift fork
39. Detent ball
40. Detent spring
41. Beather
42. Cap screw
43. Washer
44. Housing cover
45. Detent spring
46. Detent ball
47. Shift fork set screw
48. Shift fork set screw
49. Front axle declutch shift fork
50. Idler shaft lo gear
51. Rear output shaft gear
52. Shift shaft oil seal
53. Direct drive gear spacing washer
54. Range shift shaft
55. Input shaft
56. Input shaft front bearing
57. Shims
58. Input shaft front bearing cap
59. Lock washer
60. Screw
61. Oil seal
62. Washer
63. Nut
64. Idler shaft
65. Idler shaft front bearing
66. Idler shaft front bearing cup
67. Bearing retainer plate
68. Cap screw
69. Idler shaft front bearing cap
70. Lock washer
71. Cap screw
72. Cotter key
73. Declutch shift shaft
74. Rear output shaft
75. Rear output shaft front bearing
76. Rear output shaft front bearing cup
77. Shims
78. Rear output shaft front bearing cap
79. Cap screw
80. Locker washer
81. Nut
82. Cotter key
83. Washer
84. Oil seal
85. Cap screw
86. Lock washer
87. Front output shaft front bearing cap
88. Gasket
89. Shims
90. Front output shaft front bearing (with snap ring)
91. Front output shaft
92. Declutch collar
93. Shift shaft oil seal
94. Oil filler plug (some units employ elbow arrangement)
95. Drain plug
96. Cover to housing gasket
97. Transfer case housing
98. Front output shaft rear bearing (with snap ring)
99. Shift shaft hole plug
100. Oil seal
101. Gasket
102. Front output shaft rear bearing cap
103. Washer
104. Cap screw
105. Brake shoe return spring
106. Brake shoe
107. Gasket
108. Oil deflector
109. Washer
110. Brake lever
111. Oil baffle
112. Brake hub
113. Snap ring
114. Small expansion plug
115. Brake drum
116. Lock washer
117. Large expansion plug
118. Cap screw
119. Lock wire

A-INPUT
B-IDLER

Exploded view of the Rockwell T-223 transfer case (© Chrysler Corp.)

Idler shaft assembly—Rockwell T-223 transfer case (© Ford Motor Co.)

Front output shaft assembly—Rockwell T-223 transfer case (© Ford Motor Co.)

3. The bearing has to be pressed off the front output shaft.

REAR OUTPUT SHAFT

1. Remove the retaining screws and lift the rear output shaft front and rear bearing caps off the case. Wire the shims together for reassembly.

2. Remove the speedometer drive gear and spacer.

3. Block the rear output gear with a piece of wood and press the rear output shaft and front bearing out of the case. The rear output gear and rear bearing can be lifted out through the cover opening.

INPUT SHAFT

1. Remove the input shaft front and rear bearing covers and wire the shims together for reassembly.

2. Place a block of wood between the sliding gear and the case and press out the input shaft and front bearing.

NOTE: If the gear should cock and become bound on the shaft, try to block it evenly with an additional piece of wood. Do not pound on the shaft.

3. Lift the sliding gear, drive gear, and spacer from the case.

4. Remove the front bearing from the input shaft.

Assembly
INPUT SHAFT

1. Slide the input shaft front bearing onto the input shaft with the shielded side against the shaft shoulder.

2. Start the input shaft into the case. Mount the sliding gear, spacer and drive gear with its bushing onto the input shaft, working through the cover opening.

3. Tap the input shaft into position using a suitable sleeve placed against the in-ner race of the front bearing and a soft hammer.

4. Position the input shaft front cover and the original shim pack plus an additional 0.010 in. shim on the case. Tighten the retaining screws to the proper torque.

5. Install the rear thrust washer on the shaft and install the rear bearing with the shielded side toward the inside of the case.

6. Position a new gasket on the rear bearing cover and install the cover. Tighten the retaining screws to the proper torque.

7. Mount a dial indicator to the transfer case with the stem against the front end of the input shaft and check the amount of end play present. Remove enough shims from under the front bearing cover to provide 0.003 to 0.005 in. end play. Tighten the front bearing cover retaining screws to specification.

REAR OUTPUT SHAFT

1. Press the front bearing onto the rear output shaft.

2. Hold the rear output gear in position inside the case and slide the shaft through it.

3. Install the front bearing cup and the original shim pack plus an additional 0.010 in. shim, together with the front bearing cover. Install the retaining screws and tighten them to specifications.

4. Press the rear bearing onto the rear output shaft and tap the bearing cup into place.

5. Install the speedometer drive gear and spacer on the shaft.

6. Position a new gasket and the bearing cap and oil seal over the shaft. Install the retaining screws and tighten them to the proper torque.

7. Rotate the shaft to seat the bearings, then install a dial indicator against the rear end of the shaft to check the end play. Remove enough shims from under the front bearing cap to provide zero end-play and zero preload.

FRONT OUTPUT GEAR

NOTE: The front output gear must be installed in the case before the idler shaft assembly is installed.

1. Install the ball bearing on the front output gear hub.

2. Position the gear and bearing in the case and install the retaining snap ring on the bearing.

3. Install the rear bearing cap over a new gasket and tighten the retaining screws to the proper torque.

IDLER SHAFT

1. Press the rear bearing onto the idler shaft and install the retaining snap-ring.

2. Hold the high gear in position inside

Input shaft assembly—Rockwell T-223 transfer case (© Ford Motor Co.)

Rear output shaft assembly—Rockwell T-223 transfer case (© Ford Motor Co.)

the case and tap the idler shaft through it with a soft hammer. The short hub side of the gear faces toward the rear of the case.

3. Install the gear spacer on the idler shaft, then install the low gear with the long hub toward the front of the case.

4. Install the rear bearing cup in the case and install the rear bearing cap with a new gasket, tightening the retaining screws to the proper torque.

5. Drive the front bearing onto the idler shaft while holding the shaft rigid to avoid damaging the rear bearing and cup. Install the bearing retainer plate, torque the retaining screws and lock wire them.

6. Tap the front bearing cup into place in the case.

7. Install the front bearing cap with the original shim pack and some extras in order to set up the shaft end play. Torque the front bearing cap retaining screw to specification.

8. Mount a dial indicator on the case with the stem set against the inside face of the lower gear. Check the amount of end play by working the assembly back and forth with a pry bar. Remove enough shims to arrive at 0.003 to 0.005 in. end-play.

FRONT OUTPUT SHAFT

1. Install the ball bearing onto the front output shaft with the retaining snap-ring toward the front.

2. Install the sliding declutch collar onto the shaft and install the shaft into the case.

3. With the shaft in position, install the bearing cap with a new gasket and torque the retaining screws to specification.

PARKING BRAKE

1. Mount the brake backing plate to the case, together with the deflector and stamped washer, with a new gasket between the backing plate and the case. Tighten the retaining screws with star washers to the proper torque.

2. Position the brake lever on the backing plate.

3. Position the brake shoes on the backing plate with the actuating pawl in the web slot.

4. Install the brake shoe return springs.

5. Slide the brake hub onto the splines of the front output shaft and install the retaining snap ring.

6. Install the brake drum with the attaching lockwashers and screws. Tighten the screws to specification and insert lock wires.

7. Install the expansion plugs. The smaller plug goes in the bore of the front output gear.

SHAFT COMPONENTS

1. Install the new shift shaft oil seals in the case.

2. Position the declutch fork in the shift collar.

3. Lubricate the declutch shift shaft and slide it into the case and through the shift fork bore.

4. With the shift shaft in position insert the set screw. Tighten the screw and lock wire it to the fork.

5. Position the range shift fork in the sliding gear.

6. Slide the range shift shaft through the bore of the fork and install the set screw. Tighten the set screw and lock wire it to the shift fork.

7. Install the expansion plugs at the rear of the case and flatten them to expand them.

8. Place the detent balls and springs in position in the case bores and install the case cover with a new gasket, tightening them to the specified torque.

9. Install the driving yokes on the shafts with their lockwashers and retaining nuts and tighten them to the proper torque.

SPECIFICATIONS

TORQUE (FT. LBS.)

Top cover-to-case bolts	38–49
Bearing cap retaining bolts	38–49
Brake drum-to-hub bolts	60–77
Brake mounting plate bolts	60–77
Input shaft yoke nut	300–400
Output shaft yoke nuts	300–400

Spicer Model 20

The Spicer Model 20 transfer case is essentially a two-speed gear box located at the rear of the standard transmission, which provides low and direct gear ranges. It also provides a means of connecting the power to the front axle.

Disassembly

1. Remove cover and gasket from bottom of transfer case.

2. Remove the front drive shift bar poppet spring access hole plugs from front output shaft bearing retainer. If necessary to remove shift bar lock plungers, remove the two expansion plugs from the housing.

3. Remove the idler gear shaft lock plate bolt and lock plate from rear of transfer case.

4. Using a hammer and brass drift, remove idler gear shaft, driving from the front end of the transfer case (opposite slotted end of shaft). As shaft passes thrust washers, remove washers. Remove idler gear with bearings and spacers as a sub-assembly. Remove bearings and spacer from bore of idler gear.

5. Remove end yoke retaining lock nuts from the front and rear output shafts. Using a suitable puller, remove the end yokes from both shafts.

6. Remove steady springs from shift levers. Remove setscrew securing shift lever pivot pin. Remove pin and lift out each lever as it is freed.

7. Remove socket-head setscrew from underdrive shift fork.

8. Move underdrive shift fork and rear output shaft sliding gear forward far enough for gear to clear splines on rear output shaft. Swing fork and gear toward cover opening and lift out gear.

9. Remove rear output shaft bearing retainer and output shaft as an assembly.

10. Remove front output shaft rear cover and shims. Tag shims for reassembly.

11. Remove socket-head setscrew from front wheel drive shift fork.

12. Remove front output shaft bearing retainer with shift bars and gasket.

13. Pull forward on front output shaft as far as possible to permit removal of bearing cup. Remove bearing cone from front output shaft, using suitable puller.

14. Remove front output shaft bearing snap-ring. Using a soft-faced hammer, tap on front end of output shaft and remove it from the rear side of housing. Take out driven gear and sliding gear with shift fork as shaft is withdrawn.

15. Remove shift bars from retainer.

— CAUTION —
Be sure the poppet balls and springs are secured when withdrawing shift bars. This will prevent possible personal injury.

16. Remove shift bar oil seals.

17. Remove speedometer driven gear.

18. Support inner face of bearing retainer on an arbor press and press output shaft from retainer.

19. Remove oil seal from retainer bore.

20. Remove tapered bearing cone and cup from rear bore of retainer. Remove tapered bearing cup from front bore. Remove O-ring seal.

21. Using a suitable puller, remove bearing cone from output shaft. Remove shims from shaft and tie together before laying aside. Remove speedometer drive gear.

22. Using a puller, remove bearing cone from front output shaft.

Assembly

1. Press bearing cone on rear end of front output shaft.

2. Install speedometer drive gear, shims and bearing cone on output shaft.

3. Position new O-ring seal in bore of rear output shaft bearing retainer. Install tapered bearing cup in front bore of retainer. Install other tapered bearing cup in rear bore of bearing retainer.

4. Place rear output shaft into bearing retainer and support shaft in an arbor press. Position bearing cone over end of shaft and using an adapter slightly larger in diameter than the shaft, press bearing cone on shaft. Locate rear output shaft bearing retainer assembly in a fixed position. Set up a dial

indicator and check shaft endplay. Add or remove shims between speedometer drive gear and rear bearing cone to bring end-play within specifications.

NOTE: It is very important to set endplay correctly, since it controls the seating of the tapered bearings. Incorrect endplay will shorten the lift of bearings.

5. Install new oil seal in rear bore of bearing retainer, using proper adapter.

6. Install speedometer driven gear.

7. Using an adapter of correct size, install shift bar oil seals in front output shaft bearing retainer.

8. Install poppet springs and balls into bearing retainer.

NOTE: Make certain that the heavier loaded spring is installed for the front drive shift bar.

9. Depress poppet balls and insert shift bars into front output shaft bearing retainer.

NOTE: Be sure when installing shift bars that the seal lips are not damaged.

10. Start front output shaft into transfer case from rear. As shaft emerges inside of case, sliding gear with shift fork and front output driven gear can be installed. Hold shaft in position and install bearing cup in rear bore of case. Install front output shaft bearing snap-ring.

11. Support rear end of front output shaft and using an adapter of correct diameter, tap bearing cone onto front end of shaft. With shaft held in position, install bearing cup in front bore of case.

12. Using a new gasket, install front output shaft bearing retainer with shift bars on front of transfer case.

13. Install socket-head setscrew in front wheel drive shaft fork.

SPECIFICATIONS

END PLAY

Rear Output Shaft	0.003–0.005 in.
Front Output Shaft	0.000–0.001 in.

BALL POPPET SPRING

Free Length

Red	1.028 in.
Yellow	1.078 in.

Pressure @ Test Length

Red @ 59/64 in.	16 lbs.
Yellow @ 49/64 in.	12 lbs.

TORQUE LIMITS (ft. lbs.)

Rear Output Shaft Bearing Retainer	25–32
Front Output Shaft Rear Bearing Cover	25–32
Front Output Shaft Front Bearing Retainer	25–32
Bottom Cover	10–15
Idler Shaft Lock Bolt	12–17
Companion Flange Nut	225–300

14. Install shims and front output shaft rear cover on case. Secure with bolts and torque to specifications. Set up a dial indicator at front end of front output shaft and check end-play. Add or remove shims under rear cover to meet specifications.

NOTE: It is essential to set end-play within specifications, since it controls seating of the tapered bearings. Improper end-play can shorten life of bearings.

15. Install rear output shaft bearing retainer and output shaft as an assembly. Secure with bolts and tighten to specifications.

16. Place rear output shaft sliding gear in underdrive shift fork. Swing fork and gear into case until gear can be positioned on rear output shaft.

17. Install socket-head setscrew in underdrive shift fork.

18. Position shift levers in front output shaft bearing retainer and install shift lever pivot pin. Install pivot pin retaining bolt. Install steady springs on shift levers.

19. Install end yokes on front and rear output shafts and secure with retaining lock nuts.

20. Install spacers and bearings in bore of idler gear. Position idler gear and thrust washers in transfer case. Insert idler shaft into rear of case until slot is flush with case face. Install lock plate and secure with retaining bolt. Tighten to specifications.

21. Install shift bar lock plungers and expansion plugs. Install shift bar poppet spring access hole plugs.

22. Position new gasket on bottom of transfer case and install cover. Secure with bolts and tighten to specifications.

Warner 1345

The 1345 is a two piece all aluminum part time unit, lubricated by a positive displacement oil pump that channels oil through drilled holes in the rear output shaft. The pump turns with the output shaft and allows towing of the vehicle for extended distances.

Disassembly

1. Drain the fluid from the case.
2. Remove both output shaft yokes.
3. Remove the 4WD indicator switch.
4. Unbolt and remove the case cover.

Exploded view of Warner 1345

The cover may be pried off using a screwdriver in the pry bosses.

5. Remove the magnetic chip collector from the bottom of the case.

6. Slide the shift collar hub off the rear output shaft.

7. Compress the shift fork spring and remove the upper and lower spring retainers from the shaft.

8. Lift the four wheel drive lockup fork and lockup shift collar assembly from the case.

9. Remove the thrust washer being careful not to lose the nylon wear pads on the lockup fork.

10. Remove the snap ring and thrust washer from the front output shaft.

11. Grip the chain and both sprockets and lift them straight up to remove the drive sprocket, driven sprocket and chain from the output shafts.

12. Lift the front output shaft from the case.

13. Remove the four oil pump attaching screws and remove the oil pump rear cover, pickup tube, filter and pump body, two pump pins, pump spring and oil pump front cover from the rear output shaft.

14. Remove the snap ring that holds the bearing retainer inside the case. Lift the rear output shaft while tapping on the bearing retainer with a plastic hammer.

NOTE: Two dowel pins will fall into the case when the retainer is removed.

Lift the rear output shaft and bearing retainer from the case.

15. Remove the rear output shaft from the bearing retainer. If necessary, press the needle bearing assembly out of the retainer.

16. Remove the C-clip that holds the shift cam to the actuating lever inside the case.

17. Remove the retaining screw and lift the shift lever from the case.

NOTE: When removing the lever, the shift cam will disengage from the shift lever shaft and may release the detent ball and spring from the case.

18. Remove the planetary gear set, shift rail, shift cam, input shaft and shift forks, as an assembly, from the case. Be careful not to lose the two nylon wear pads on the shift fork.

Removing the input shaft from the planetary gear set

19. Remove the spacer washer from the bottom of the case.

20. Drive the plug from the detent spring bore.

Assembly

Before assembly, lubricate all parts with clean automatic transmission fluid; either Ford CJ or Dexron® II.

1. Assemble the planetary gear set, shift rail, shift cam, input shaft and shift fork together as a unit. Make sure that the boss on the shift cam is installed toward the case. Install the spacer washer on the input shaft.

2. Place the rear output shaft in the planetary gear set, making sure that the shift cam engages the shift fork actuating pin.

3. Lay the case on its side. Insert the rear output shaft and planetary gear set into the case. Make sure the spacer washer remains on the input shaft.

4. Install the shift rail into the hole in the case. Install the outer roller bushing into the guide in the case.

5. Remove the rear output shaft and position the shift fork in neutral.

6. Place the shift control lever shaft through the cam, and install the clip ring. Make sure that the shift control lever is pointed downward and is parallel to the front face of the case.

7. Check the shift fork and planetary gear engagement.

8. If removed, press a new needle bearing assembly into the bearing retainer.

9. Insert the output shaft through the bearing retainer from the bottom outward.

10. Insert the rear output shaft pilot into

Connect shift cam engagement

the input shaft bushing. Align the dowel holes and the lower bearing.

11. Install the dowel pins. Install the snap ring that retains the bearing retainer in the case.

12. Insert the detent ball and spring in the detent bore in the case. Coat the seal plug with RTV sealant or its equivalent. Drive the plug into the case until the lip of the plug is $1/32$ in. below the surface of the case. Peen the case over the plug in two places.

13. Install the pump front cover over the output shaft with the flanged side down. The word "TOP" must be facing the top of the transfer case.

14. Install the oil pump spring and two pump pins with the flat side outward in the hole in the output shaft. Push both pins in to install the oil pump body, pickup tube and filter.

15. Place the oil pump rear cover on the output shaft with the flanged side outward. The word "TOP" must be positioned toward the top of the case. Apply Loctite®

Front view of Warner 1345 transfer case

Rear view of Warner 1345 transfer case

Installing the planetary gear set and shifter mechanism

Installing the detent ball

or its equivalent to the oil pump bolts and torque them to 36–40 in. lbs.

16. Install the thrust washer on the rear output shaft nest to the oil pump.

17. Place the drive sprocket on the front output shaft. Install the snap ring and thrust washer.

18. Install the chain on the drive sprocket and driven sprocket. Lower the chain into position in the case. The driven sprocket is installed through the front output shaft bearing and the drive sprocket is installed in the rear output shaft.

19. Engage the 4WD shift fork on the shift collar. Slide the shift fork over the shift shaft and the shift collar over the rear output shaft. Make sure the nylon wear pads are installed on the shift fork tips and the necked-down part of the shift collar is facing downward.

20. Push the 4WD shift spring downward and install the upper spring retainer. Push the spring upward and install the lower retainer.

21. Install the shift collar hub on the rear output shaft.

22. Apply a bead of RTV sealant on the case mounting surface. Lower the cover over the rear output shaft. Align the shift rail with its blind hole in the cover. Make sure the front output shaft is fully seated in its support bearing. Install and tighten the bolts to 40–45 ft. lbs. Allow one hour curing time for the RTV sealant prior to using the case.

23. Install the 4WD indicator switch. Torque to 8–12 ft. lbs.

24. Press the oil slinger on the front yoke. Install the front and rear output shaft yokes. Coat the nuts with Loctite® or equivalent and torque to 100–130 ft. lbs.

25. Fill the unit with 6 pints of Ford CJ or Dexron® II ATF. Tighten the fill plug to 18 ft. lbs.

26. Install the unit in the vehicle and start the engine. Remove the level plug. If the fluid is flowing from the hole in a stream, the pump is not operating properly. The fluid should drip slowly from the hole.

Drive Axles

INDEX

The rear axle must transmit power through 90°. To accomplish this, straight cut bevel gears or spiral bevel gears were used. This type of gear is satisfactory for differential side gears, but since the centerline of the gears must intersect, they rapidly became unsuited for ring and pinion gears. The lowering of the driveshaft brought about a variation of the bevel gear, which is called the hypoid gear. This type of gear does not require a meeting of the gear centerlines and can therefore be underslung, relative to the centerline of the ring gear.

Gear Ratios

The drive axle of a vehicle is said to have a certain axle ratio. This number (usually a whole number and a decimal fraction) is actually a comparison of the number of gear teeth on the ring gear and the pinion gear. For example, a 4.11 rear means that theoretically, there are 4.11 teeth on the ring gear and one tooth on the pinion. Actually, on a 4.11 rear, there are 37 teeth on the ring gear and nine teeth on the pinion gear. By dividing the number of teeth on the pinion gear into the number of teeth on the ring gear, the numerical axle ratio (4.11) is obtained. This also provides a good method of ascertaining exactly which axle ratio one is dealing with.

Differential Operation

The differential is an arrangement of gears that permits the rear wheels to turn at different speeds when cornering and divides the torque between the axle shafts. The differential gears are mounted on a pinion shaft and the gears are free to rotate on this shaft. The pinion shaft is fitted in a bore in the differential case and is at right angles to the axle shafts.

Power flow through the differential is as follows. The drive pinion, which is turned by the driveshaft, turns the ring gear. The ring gear, which is bolted to the differential case, rotates the case. The differential pinion forces the pinion gears against the side gears. In cases where both wheels have equal traction, the pinion gears do not rotate on the pinion shaft, because the input force of the pinion gear is divided equally between the two side gears. Consequently the pinion gears revolve with the pinion shaft, although they do not revolve on the pinion shaft itself. The side gears, which are splined

Hypoid gear application
(© Chevrolet Div., G.M. Corp)

Bevel gear application
(© Chevrolet Div., G.M. Corp)

to the axle shafts, and meshed with the pinion gears, rotate the axle shafts.

When it becomes necessary to turn a corner, the differential becomes effective and allows the axle shafts to rotate at different speeds. As the inner wheel slows down, the side gear splined to the inner wheel axle shaft also slows down. The pinion gears act as balancing levers by maintaining equal tooth loads to both gears while allowing unequal speeds of rotation at the axle shafts. If the vehicle speed remains constant, and the inner wheel slows down to 90 percent of vehicle speeds, the outer wheel will speed up to 110 percent.

Differential action during cornering
(© Chevrolet Div., G.M. Corp)

Limited-Slip Differential Operation

Limited-slip differentials provide driving force to the wheel with the best traction before the other wheel begins to spin. This is accomplished through clutch plates or cones. The clutch plates or cones are located between the side gears and inner wall of the differential case. When they are squeezed together through spring tension and outward force from the side gears, three reactions occur. Resistance on the side gears causes more torque to be exerted on the clutch packs or clutch cones. Rapid one-wheel spin cannot occur, because the side gear is forced to turn at the same speed as the case. Most important, with the side gear and the differential case turning at the same speed, the other wheel is forced to rotate in the same direction and at the same speed as the differential case. Thus driving force is applied to the wheel with the better traction.

DIFFERENTIAL DIAGNOSIS

The most essential part of rear axle service is proper diagnosis of the problem. Bent or broken axle shafts or broken gears pose little problem, but isolating an axle noise and correctly interpreting the problem can be extremely difficult, even for an experienced mechanic.

Any gear driven unit will produce a certain amount of noise, therefore, a specific diagnosis for each individual unit is the best practice. Acceptable or normal noise can be classified as a slight noise heard only at certain speeds or under unusual conditions. This noise tends to reach a peak at 40–60 mph depending on the road condition, load, gear ratio and tire size. Frequently, other noises are mistakenly diagnosed as coming from the rear axle. Vehicle noises from tires, transmission, driveshaft, U-joints and front and rear wheel bearings will often be mistaken as emanating from the rear axle. Raising the tire pressure to eliminate tire noise (although this will not silence mud or snow treads), listening for noise at varying speeds and road conditions and listening for noise at drive and coast conditions will aid in diagnosing alleged rear axle noises.

External Noise Elimination

It is advisable to make a thorough road test to determine whether the noise originates in the rear axle or whether it originates from the tires, engine transmission, wheel bearings or road surface. Noise originating from other places cannot be corrected by overhauling the rear axle.

Road Noise

Brick roads or rough surfaced concrete, may cause a noise which can be mistaken as coming from the rear axle. Driving on a different type of road (smooth asphalt or dirt) will determine whether the road is the cause of the noise. Road noise is usually the same on drive or coast conditions.

Tire Noise

Tire noise can be mistaken as rear axle noises, even though the tires on the front are at fault. Snow tread and mud tread tires or tires worn unevenly will frequently cause vibrations which seem to originate elsewhere; *temporarily, and for test purposes only,* inflate the tires to 40–50 lbs. This will significantly alter the noise produced by the tires, but will not alter noise from the rear axle. Noises from the rear axle will normally cease at speeds below 30 mph on coast, while tire noise will continue at lower tone as car speed is decreased. The rear axle noise will usually change from drive conditions to coast conditions, while tire noise will not. Do not forget to lower the tire pressure to normal after the test is complete.

Engine and Transmission Noise

Engine and transmission noises also seem to originate in the rear axle. Road test the vehicle and determine at which speeds the noise is most pronounced. Stop the car in a quiet place to avoid interfering noises. With the transmission in neutral, run the engine slowly through the engine speeds corresponding to the car speed at which the noise was most noticeable. If a similar noise was produced with the car standing still, the noise is not in the rear axle, but somewhere in the engine or transmission.

Front Wheel Bearing Noise

Front wheel bearing noises, sometimes confused with rear axle noises, will not change when comparing drive and coast conditions. While holding the car speed steady, lightly apply the footbrake. This will often cause wheel bearing noise to lessen, as some of the weight is taken off the bearing. Front wheel bearings are easily checked by jacking up the wheels and spinning the wheels. Shaking the wheels will also determine if the wheel bearings are excessively loose.

Rear Axle Noises

If a logical test of the vehicle shows that the noise is not caused by external items, it can be assumed that the noise originates from the rear axle. The rear axle should be tested on a smooth level road to avoid road noise. It is not advisable to test the axle by jacking up the rear wheels and running the car.

True rear axle noises generally fall into two classes—gear noise and bearing noises, and can be caused by a faulty driveshaft, faulty wheel bearings, worn differential or pinion shaft bearings, U-joint misalignment, worn differential side gears and pinions, or mismatched, improperly adjusted, or scored ring and pinion gears.

Rear Wheel Bearing Noise

A rough rear wheel bearing causes a vibration or growl which will continue with the car coasting or in neutral. A brinelled rear wheel bearing will also cause a knock or click approximately every two revolutions of the rear wheel, due to the fact that the bearing rollers do not travel at the same speed as the rear wheel and axle. Jack up the rear wheels and spin the wheel slowly, listening for signs of a rough or brinelled wheel bearing.

DIFFERENTIAL SIDE GEAR AND PINION NOISE

Differential side gears and pinions seldom cause noise since their movement is relatively slight on straight ahead driving. Noise produced by these gears will be more noticeable on turns.

PINION BEARING NOISE

Pinion bearing failures can be distinguished by their speed of rotation, which is higher than side bearings or axle bearings. Rough or brinelled pinion bearings cause a continuous low pitch whirring or scraping noise beginning at low speeds.

SIDE BEARING NOISE

Side bearings produce a constant rough noise, which is slower than the pinion bearing noise. Side bearing noise may also fluctuate in the above rear wheel bearing test.

GEAR NOISE

Two basic types of gear noise exist. First is the type produced by bent or broken gear teeth which have been forcibly damaged. The noise from this type of damage is audible over the entire speed range. Scoring or damage to the hypoid gear teeth generally results from insufficient lubricant, improper lubricant, improper breaking, insufficient gear backlash, improper ring and pinion gear alignment or loss of torque on the drive pinion nut. If not corrected, the scoring will lead to eventual erosion or fracture of the gear tooth. Hypoid gear tooth fracture can also be caused by extended overloading of the gear set (fatigue fracture) or by shock overloading (sudden failure). Differential and side gears rarely give trouble, but common causes of differential failure are shock loading, extended overloading and differential pinion seizure at the cross-shaft, resulting from excessive wheel spin and consequent lubricant breakdown.

The second type of gear noise pertains to the mesh pattern between the ring and pinion gears. This type of abnormal gear noise can be recognized as a cycling pitch or whine audible in either drive, float or coast conditions. Gear noises can be recognized as they tend to peak out in a narrow speed range and remain constant in pitch, whereas bearing noises tend to vary in pitch with vehicle speeds. Noises produced by the ring and pinion gears will generally follow the pattern below.

A. Drive Noise: Produced under vehicle acceleration.

B. Coast Noise: Produced while the car coasts with a closed throttle.

C. Float Noise: Occurs while maintaining constant car speed (just enough to keep speed constant) on a level road.

D. Drive, Coast and Float Noise: These noises will vary in tone with speed and be very rough or irregular if the differential or pinion shaft bearings are worn.

Bearing Diagnosis

This section will help in the diagnosis of bearing failure and the causes. Bearing di-

Two types of damage which cause gear noise
(© Chevrolet Div., G.M. Corp)

agnosis can be very helpful in determining the cause of rear axle failure.

When disassembling a rear axle, the general condition of all bearings should be noted and classified where possible. Proper recognition of the cause will help in correcting the problem and avoiding a repetition of the failure.

Some of the common causes of bearing failure are:

    a. Abuse during assembly or disassembly.

    b. Improper assembly methods.

    c. Improper or inadequate lubrication.

    d. Bearing contact with dirt or water.

    e. Wear caused by dirt or metal chips.

    f. Corrosion or rust.

    g. Seizing due to overloading.

    h. Overheating.

    i. Frettage of the bearing seats.

    j. Brinelling from impact or shock loading.

    k. Manufacturing defects.

    l. Pitting due to fatigue.

To avoid damage to the bearing from improper handling, it is best to treat a used bearing the same as a new bearing. Always work in a clean area with clean tools. Remove all outside dirt from the housing before exposing a bearing and clean all bearing seats before installing a bearing.

——————— CAUTION ———————

Never spin a bearing, either by hand or with compressed air, as this will lead to almost certain bearing failure.

LIMITED-SLIP DIFFERENTIAL DIAGNOSIS

Lubrication

The use of proper lubricant is very important in limited-slip type drive axles. The forces applied when cornering tend to apply the clutch pack or clutch cones. The use of the wrong lubricant can cause the clutch surfaces to grab and chatter while turning. Always follow the manufacturer's recommendations regarding drive axle lubrica-

tion. When chatter is encountered, the differential lubricant should be drained and refilled with the specified lubricant.

Testing

The clutch operation on all limited-slip type axles can be tested as follows. Refer to the manufacturer in question.

AMERICAN MOTORS "TWIN-GRIP"

1. With the engine off and the transmission in neutral, jack up one rear wheel.

2. Block the other wheel to prevent it from moving.

3. With a socket and torque wrench on the axle shaft nut, turn the raised wheel forward.

4. The torque required to move the wheel should be 70–100 ft lbs for 8⅞ in. axles or 80–120 ft lbs for 7⁹⁄₁₆ in. axles.

5. A breakaway torque which is less than the specified figure, indicates a need for repair or replacement.

CADILLAC CONTROLLED DIFFERENTIAL

This unit should not be serviced. If a malfunction exists that cannot be cured by changing the fluid, remove the unit and install a new one.

CHRYSLER CORP. SURE-GRIP

1. Place the vehicle on a hoist with the engine off and the automatic transmission in Park (manual transmission in low gear).

2. Attempt to rotate the wheel by hand, by gripping the tire.

3. If it is extremely difficult, if not impossible, to rotate either wheel the Sure-Grip differential can be assumed to be performing satisfactorily.

4. If it is relatively easy to continuously turn either rear wheel, the unit should be removed and replaced.

——————— CAUTION ———————

The Sure-Grip differential is serviced as a unit only. Under no circumstances should the unit be disassembled and reinstalled.

FORD MOTOR COMPANY EQUA-LOK

1. Jack up one rear wheel and remove the wheel cover.

2. Block the other wheel front and rear to prevent the car from moving.

3. Using a 200 ft lbs capacity torque wrench on one of the wheel lug nuts, measure the torque required to continuously rotate the wheel. The breakaway torque reading can be disregarded. The minimum torque to continuously rotate the wheel should be as follows.

All axles except integral carrier type: 75 ft lbs.

Integral carrier type axles: 50 ft lbs.

4. If the minimum torque is not as specified, the differential should be checked for improper assembly.

FORD MOTOR COMPANY
TRACTION-LOK

1. Follow the procedure for the Ford Motor Company Equa-Lok rear. The minimum torque to continuously rotate the wheel (disregarding the breakaway torque) should be at least 40 ft lbs through 1979 and 30 ft lbs for 1980 and later.

GENERAL MOTORS CORP.
(EXCEPT CADILLAC)
POSITRACTION

1. Place the transmission in neutral.

2. Raise one rear wheel off the floor and block the other rear wheel (front and rear) to prevent the car from moving.

3. Install a torque wrench and extension on the lug nut and note the torque required to continuously rotate one rear wheel. Disregard the breakaway torque figure, as this may be a great deal higher.

4. The minimum torque to continuously rotate the rear wheel should be at least 35 ft lbs. If it is not, the rear axle is in need of service.

General Diagnosis

Improper operation of a limited-slip type rear axle is generally indicated by clutch slippage or grabbing, which will sometimes produce a whirring or chatter sound. Occasionally, this condition is induced by improper lubrication. Check the unit for the wrong type of lubricant or lubricant which has broken down or become contaminated. Replace the lubricant with the type specified by the manufacturer.

During normal operation, i.e., straight-ahead driving, both wheels are rotating at equal speeds, and the driving force is distributed equally between both wheels. When cornering, the inside wheel delivers extra driving force, causing slippage in both clutch packs. Therefore, if the wheel rotation of both rear wheels is not equal, the unit will constantly be functioning as if the car were cornering. This will cause constant slippage

Gear tooth contact pattern showing load centered on gear tooth

and lead to eventual failure of the unit. It is important that there be no excessive differences in wheel and tire size, wear pattern, or tire pressures between both rear wheels. Swerving on acceleration is an indication of one or more of the above conditions. Before attempting an overhaul or replacement operation, check both rear wheels for identical tire sizes, tire pressure, tire tread depth, and wear pattern.

DRIVE AXLE DISASSEMBLY ANALYSIS

Testing the Gear Tooth Contact Pattern

Once it has been established that the differential is indeed in need of service, the worst procedure is to simply plunge ahead and remove the differential and disassemble the parts. Prior to disassembly, a tooth contact pattern test should be made. However, it is worthwhile to first know the nomenclature associated with hypoid gear teeth.

The thick end of the tooth is called the heel and the thin end of the tooth is called the toe. The base half of the tooth is called the flank and the other end of the tooth is known as the face. The imaginary line at the halfway point between the face and flank is known as the pitch line. The space between the meshed pinion and ring gear tooth is known as backlash.

A gear tooth contact pattern can be made with the carrier in or out of the housing depending on the type of carrier. On integral carrier models, the lubricant must be drained and the rear cover removed. The ring gear will now be exposed and the test can be made with the carrier still in the housing. On removable carrier models, drain the lubricant and remove the carrier from the housing. The test can be made on the bench.

Unlike simple spur gears, hypoid gear teeth leave a complex pattern on the ring gear. When hypoid gears turn, the line contact between pinion and ring gear teeth has the same wiping motion as with spur gear teeth. Because of the complicated movement of hypoid gear teeth, the contact area takes an oval shape as opposed to the rectangular shape left by spur gear teeth. Ac-

Gear tooth face and flank showing oval gear tooth contact pattern

Gear tooth contact pattern showing load centered on gear tooth

tually, the tooth contact test shows where each gear tooth has been wiped by the movement of the contact line, so that you can tell whether the gears are set correctly. With a properly adjusted ring and pinion (with properly adjusted pinion depth and backlash) the tooth contact will be close to center. In this case, the load is borne by the strongest part of the tooth. If the gear setting is off, the contact line may reach any part of the edge of a tooth, and the metal will be overloaded at that point. When overload occurs, rapid deterioration of the gears will follow.

PREPARING THE TEST

Coat the drive gear teeth with a metallic base artists' oil color such as zinc white or titanium white. The tooth coating material must be smooth and firm enough to spread without running. A consistency somewhat like toothpaste works well. If it is necessary to thicken the material, add a small amount of cup grease.

NOTE: Prussian blue dye does not work well, since the blue tends to smear the pattern.

Thoroughly clean the ring gear and pinion before applying the testing material. Any gear lube left on the teeth will make the pattern quite unreadable. Coat the drive and coast sides of all the ring gear teeth, but leave the pinion gear teeth clean. Do not apply the coating too thickly as the pattern will be smeared.

Because the axle gears are normally easy to rotate, turning resistance must be applied to produce pressure between the pinion and ring gear teeth to make a legible pattern. On a removable carrier type axle, insert a large screwdriver between the carrier housing and the differential case rim. Apply the load squarely against the case rim while prying out against the upper or lower section of the carrier housing. On integral carrier models, apply the parking brake to a point where it requires approximately 50 ft lbs to turn the pinion with a torque wrench. Since the shape and position of the contact pattern will vary, depending on the load,

THICKER SPACER NEEDED

TOE END

HEEL END-DRIVE SIDE (CONVEX) HEEL END-COAST SIDE (CONCAVE)

Tooth contact patterns high on the tooth side

try to use the same load for each test or the results can be misleading. This is especially true when testing after an overhaul.

Once the gears have a load applied, obtain a tooth contact pattern by rotating the ring gear and pinion one complete turn in each direction. This will produce a constant pattern on the coast and drive side of each tooth. Do not rotate the ring gear more than one revolution in each direction as this will tend to obscure the pattern.

NOTE: If the pattern does not look right on the first try, try again.

Making a good gear tooth test takes a little practice; so if it is not right, try again.

INTERPRETING GEAR TOOTH CONTACT PATTERNS

The tooth contact pattern should be the same on every tooth. If the pattern shows heavy and light areas on different teeth, check the ring gear and differential case for excessive run-out.

NOTE: Run-out can be cured in many cases by removing the ring gear from the case, rotating it 90° or 180°, and remounting it.

Since you can only apply test load pressure to the gears, the contact pattern will be less distinct toward the tooth ends. But,

when the ring gear and pinion are under operating loads in the vehicle, the tooth contact area spreads out, especially towards the heel end of the tooth. For this reason, do not try to "get by" with a tooth contact pattern that is centered, but favors the heel end of the teeth. This will only lead to overloading at the heel ends of the gear teeth. On the other hand, a contact pattern which is reasonably centered, but favors the toe end of the teeth, is acceptable.

Assuming that the tooth contact pattern is even on all teeth, the main problems is to get the most distinct part of the pattern centered on both the teeth. The contact patterns should be nearly opposite each other on both sides of each tooth. In some cases, the pattern will be centered on the drive side and off center on the coast side, or vice versa. The off center pattern can be moved to a more acceptable position by slightly altering the backlash. This procedure will not seriously affect the other pattern. More often, however, the pattern will be off center on both sides of the teeth. The basic cause of this condition is an improperly adjusted pinion.

ADJUSTING PINION DEPTH

It is necessary to understand that an incorrect pinion depth setting moves the contact

PRY BETWEEN CARRIER AND DIFFERENTIAL CASE

Applying a load to the differential case

HEAVY AND LIGHT AREAS

Excessive run-out will cause an uneven pattern

pattern away from the center on both sides of the tooth in opposite directions. This means that when you install a thicker or thinner washer under the pinion head you bring the pattern into the center of the tooth from opposite ends.

When the contact pattern is high on the heel end of the drive side and low on the toe end of the coast side, a thicker washer is needed to bring the pinion in, toward the center of the drive gear. Increasing the thickness of the spacer washer will bring the pattern in, toward the center of the drive gear teeth, and also will move the pattern down from the tooth face. However, this movement is less than the in-or-out movement.

When tooth contact is low on the toe end of the drive side and high on the heel end of the coast side, the pinion must be moved out, by installing a thinner washer under the pinion head. This will move the pattern inward toward the center, and will also result in slight movement of the pattern up from the tooth flank.

A factory service facility will use special tools and gauge blocks to determine the thickness of the spacer under the pinion head. In the absence of such specialized equipment, the following procedure may be used. Bear in mind that with the "hit-or-miss" method, each time you are wrong with the pinion depth, the unit must be disassembled, the spacer thickness changed, and the unit must be completely set up again.

Selecting drive pinion height adjusting shims

Gather a handful of spacers to cover any thickness and several collapsible pinion spacers (if the unit uses them). Assemble the unit. If the original gear set is being reused, and the tooth contact pattern is reasonably correct, install a new spacer of the same thickness as the old one. This will provide a reasonable starting point. If the gear contact pattern test indicates a need for movement of the pinion, use a new spacer 0.001–0.002 in. thicker or thinner, depending on the direction the pinion must go. If a new gear set is being used, the thickness of the spacer will have to be determined in the following manner. Compare the markings on the old and new pinion. It will usually be marked with a number preceded by a plus (+) or minus (−) sign. This number indicates the production deviation from the nominal pinion, which are

THINNER SPACER NEEDED

HEEL END-DRIVE SIDE (CONVEX) HEEL END-COAST SIDE (CONCAVE)

Gear contact pattern low on tooth side

PATTERN MOVES TOWARD CENTER AND DOWN

HEEL END-DRIVE SIDE (CONVEX) HEEL END-COAST SIDE (CONCAVE)

A thicker spacer moves the pattern in and down

PATTERN MOVES INWARD AND UP

HEEL END-DRIVE SIDE (CONVEX) HEEL END-COAST SIDE (CONCAVE)

A thinner spacer will move the pattern up and inward

One example of pinion markings

CHECK FOR END PLAY

Checking differential bearing end-play

TOTAL END PLAY
MEASURED BY
FEELER BLADES

Checking total differential end-play

known as "zero pinions." In service, zero pinions are rare. Assume that the old pinion is marked with a plus two ($+2$). Assume that the new pinion is marked with a $+3$. By comparing the pinion markings, find the numerical difference between the two pinions, in this case $+1$. With a micrometer, measure the thickness of the original spacer. We will assume that the older spacer is 0.030 in. thick. If the numerical difference between pinions is a positive number ($+1$) the spacer should be 0.001 in. thinner than the original spacer, or 0.029 in. total. If the numerical difference is a negative number (say, -1) then the spacer should be increased by 0.001 in., to 0.031 in. total. This will only provide a reasonable beginning point.

It is rare that this method works out the first time. Assemble the pinion, differential, and ring gear with the spacer of calculated thickness. The side bearing preload, backlash, pinion nut torque, and pinion rotating torque must all be set correctly.

Obtain a gear tooth pattern on the ring gear teeth and analyze the results. Small deviations from the acceptable pattern can usually be made by varying the backlash within the limits of specifications. If the gear tooth contact pattern is off, the unit must be disassembled and another spacer installed. This spacer must be of suitable thickness to compensate for the contact pattern test.

NOTE: Without special tools, there is absolutely no way of determining exactly how much to increase or decrease the thickness of the pinion shim; it must be estimated.

After estimating the thickness of the new shim, assemble the unit again, setting all preloads and backlash. Check the contact pattern again and act accordingly. If the unit uses a collapsible spacer, be sure a new one is installed each time it is disassembled. Crushed spacers can not be used again. It is well to note that the unit may have to be assembled and disassembled several times

before an acceptable contact pattern is obtained.

Adjusting Backlash

The tooth contact pattern can be altered slightly, by varying the backlash adjustment within the limits of the specifications. The backlash adjustment can be used to alter a pattern which is slightly off center on either side of the tooth, but should not be used as a substitute for pinion depth adjustment. This adjustment must always be made after the pinion depth has been adjusted.

Courier/Mazda Differential

INSPECTION

An inspection of the adjustments and parts as the carrier is disassembled can assist in

Front Wheel Drive Halfshaft Troubleshooting

Clicking Noise in Turns	Vibration at Highway Speeds	Shudder or Vibration During Acceleration	
Damaged outboard CV joint. Check for cut or damaged CV joint boots	Out of balance front wheels or tires; out of round front tires*	Excessively worn or damaged inboard or outboard CV joint	Sticking inboard CV joint

*Halfshafts do not usually contribute to rotational vibrations.

learning the cause of the trouble and in determining what corrections are needed.

Mount the carrier in a holding fixture. Wipe the lubricant from the internal working parts and visually inspect them for damage. Rotate the gears to see if there is any roughness which could indicate worn or damaged bearings or chipped gears. Look carefully at the surface of the gear teeth for any scoring, flaking, or signs of abnormal wear.

Mark the ring gear at four points at approx. 90° intervals and mount a dial indicator to the carrier flange. Check to see that the backlash at one of the marked points is 0.19–0.21mm (0.0075–0.0083 in). Also check the backlashes at other three marked points and make sure that the difference between the maximum and minimum backlashes is less than 0.07mm (0.0028 in).

If no obvious misadjustment or damage is noted, inspect the gear tooth contact. Coat the gear teeth with special compound available, or red lead. Too fluid a mixture will run and smear. Too dry a mixture cannot be squeezed out from between the teeth. Rotate the ring gear back and forth (use a box wrench on the ring gear attaching bolts for a lever), until a clean tooth contact pattern is obtained.

Certain types of gear tooth contact patterns on the ring gear indicate incorrect adjustment. A noise condition caused by incorrect adjustment can often be corrected by readjusting the gears. Gear tooth runout can be detected by an erratic pattern on the teeth. If ring gear runout is suspected, mount a dial indicator to measure the runout of the back face of the ring gear.

Disassembly

1. Remove the carrier as outlined in this section.
2. Mount the carrier in a holding fixture.
3. Apply identification punch marks on the carrier, the differential bearing cap and the adjusters for accurate reassembly.
4. Remove the adjuster lock plates. If a problem exists in the axle where preload could be a factor, observe what the preload is before relieving it.
5. Loosen the bolts securing the bearing cap and slowly back off the adjuster slightly with spanner tool T72J-4067 or equivalent to relieve the preload. As this is being done, watch the dial to see what preload existed.
6. Remove the nuts, bearing caps and adjusters. Keep each bearing cap with its own adjuster.
7. Lift out the differential assembly and keep each bearing outer race with its own bearing.
8. If the differential bearings are to be replaced, remove them using a puller.
9. Remove the bolts and washers retaining the ring gear to the case.
10. Remove the ring gear.
11. Position the assembly in a vise and remove the lock pin with a suitable punch.

1. Lock nut/washer
2. Companion flange
3. Oil seal
4. Front bearing
5. Collapsible spacer
6. Carrier
7. Bearing cap
8. Lock plate
9. Adjuster
10. Side bearing
11. Thrust washer
12. Side gear
13. Rear bearing
14. Spacer
15. Drive pinion
16. Ring gear
17. Pinion gear
18. Pinion shaft
19. Pinion shaft pin
20. Thrust block
21. Gear case

Mazda rear axle assembly

12. Remove the pinion shaft and the thrust block.
13. Rotate the differential pinion gears 90 degrees and remove.
14. Remove the differential side gears and thrust washers.
15. Using a holding tool, steady the companion flange and remove the nut.
16. Remove the companion flange.
17. Remove the drive pinion and rear bearing from the carrier, which may require tapping with a plastic or rubber mallet. Guide the pinion to avoid damage to the teeth.
18. Remove the oil seal and the front bearing.
19. The pinion bearing outer races (cups) can be removed from the carrier by using a drift in the slots provided for the purpose.
20. Remove the bearing from the pinion using Tool T72J-4630 or equivalent.

With the carrier completely apart, check the drive pinion for damaged or worn teeth, damaged bearing journals or splines. Inspect the ring gear again for worn or chipped teeth. If any of the above conditions are found, replace both drive pinion and ring gear as these are only available in sets.

Before reassembly of the carrier, inspect

bearing cones and cups and replace any showing wear, flaking or damage. Replace only in sets.

NOTE: Do not use an old cup with a new bearing or an old bearing with a new cup. If this is done, damage will result.

Check the companion flange carefully for cracks or worn splines. If either exist, the part should be replaced. Check for rough or scratched oil seal contact surface. If only slight scratches appear, it may be possible to repair with crocus cloth. Otherwise, replace it. Be sure to use a new oil seal when reassembling the carrier.

Assembly
PINION DEPTH

If you use the same pinion and ring gear, the shim combination found on the pinion may prove satisfactory provided other things are equal.

Individual differences in machining the carrier casting and the gear set require a shim or shims between the pinion rear bearing and the pinion gear to locate the pinion for correct tooth contact with the ring gear.

NOTE: When replacing a ring gear and pinion, it should be noted that the original factory installed spacers are of the correct thickness to adjust for individual variations in both the carrier casting dimension and in the original gear set dimension; therefore, to select the correct spacer thickness for the new gear set to be installed, follow these steps:

1. Examine the new pinion gear. Look on the face of the tapered end. There may be a number with an "A" in front of it with or without a minus mark. There also may be a number without an "A" in front of it. This mark is a pair mark and should not be confused. If there is not a mark with an "A" in front of it, the pinion is mid-range or nominal size. If it carries a mark such as A-1, A-2 or A-3, it is undersize.

To understand the meaning of these markings, see chart. This shows the amount in thousandths over or under nominal.

Gear Mark	mm	Inches
A1	0.01	0.0004
A-1	−0.01	−0.0004
A2	0.02	0.0008
A-2	−0.02	−0.0008
A3	0.03	0.0012
A-3	−0.03	−0.0012

2. Examine the old pinion gear. If it does not have a mark with an "A" in front (which would indicate that it is a nominal gear) and the new pinion gear does not have a mark with an "A" in front, then the spacer which came in the carrier should give good results, as the gears would be the same.

3. If, however, the new gear was marked A-3, then the total spacer thickness should be increased 0.0012 because the gear is that much undersize.

If the new gear is marked A3, then the total spacer thickness should be reduced by 0.0012 inch to allow for oversize.

In the event, however, that the old pinion had a mark of A2 and the new pinion was marked A3, then the new pinion is only one mark over that provided for in the spacer which came in the carrier. In that case, reduce the spacer thickness only by one mark or 0.0004.

This should give the correct pinion depth position.

NOTE: In no case should more than four shims be used.

4. Position the correct spacer pack and bearing on the pinion and position the bearing cups. Complete the installation using T72J-4616 or equivalent.

Pinion Bearing Preload

1. Install the pinion and bearing in the carrier.
2. Install the collapsible spacer.

3. Install the front bearing oil seal and companion flange.
4. Install the pinion washer and nut. Before tightening the nut, check the drag of the oil seal.
5. Adjust the preload drag to 11.3–15.6 in. lbs., and oil seal drag while tightening the nut to 145–250 ft. lbs.

Differential Assembly

1. Install the thrust washer on each differential side gear and install these in the case.
2. Through the openings of the case, insert each of two pinion gears exactly 180 degrees opposite each other.
3. Rotate the gears 90 degrees so the pinion shaft holes of the case align with the holes in the two pinion gears.
4. Insert the pinion shaft through the case and pinion gears.
5. Check the backlash of the side gear and pinion gear. The backlash should not exceed 0.008. If it exceeds this, adjustment can be made with the side gear thrust washers.
6. After adjustment, remove the pinion shaft and install the thrust block so the hole is centered between the differential pinion gears. Reinstall the pinion shaft into the case until the lock pin hole in the pinion shaft is in exact alignment with the hole in the case.
7. Install the lock pin to secure the pinion shaft. Stake the lock pin into position with a punch to prevent it from working out.
8. Install the ring gear on the case and tighten the bolts to the specification listed at the end of this Part.
9. Install each differential bearing to the case using T72J-4221 or equivalent by press or with a hammer. Install the outer races to their respective bearing.
10. Place the differential gear assembly in the carrier.
11. Note the identification marks on the adjusters and install each to its respective side.
12. Install the bearing caps making sure that the identification marks on the caps correspond with those on the carrier and install the bolts.
13. Turn the adjusters with the spanner tool T72J-4067 or equivalent until the bearings are properly positioned in their respective outer race and the end play is eliminated with some amount of backlash existing between the ring gear and drive pinion.
14. Slightly tighten one of the bearing cap bolts on each side and adjust the backlash.
15. Mark the ring gear at four points at approx. 90° intervals and mount a dial indicator to the carrier flange so that the feeler comes in contact at right angles with one of the ring gear teeth. Turn both bearing adjusters equally until the backlash becomes 0.19–0.21mm (0.0075–0.0083 in). Check the backlashes at the other three marked points and make sure that the dif-

ference between the maximum and minimum backlashes is less than 0.07mm (0.0028 in).

16. Adjust the preload taking care not to disturb the backlash. Use a dial indicator and carefully set the preload at 0.0045.
17. The bearing cap bolts should be tightened to 45 ft. lbs.
18. Install the adjuster lock plates.

Dana Corporation

9¾ AND 10½ INCH RING GEAR AXLE ASSEMBLIES

The Dana Corporation's 9¾ and 10½ inch ring gear axle assemblies are basically the same, but with certain exceptions. The differential side bearing shims are located between the side bearing cup assembly and the differential case on the 9¾ inch ring gear axle assembly, while on the 10½ inch ring gear axle assembly, the side bearing shims are located between the side bearing cup and the axle housing. Both axles use inner and outer shims on the pinion gear. The inner shims are used to control the pinion depth in the housing, while the outer shims are used to preload the pinion bearings. The 9¾ inch ring gear axle uses a solid differential carrier with a removable side and pinion gear shaft. The 10½ inch ring gear axle uses a split differential carrier with the side and pinion gears mounted on a cross shaft.

DIFFERENTIAL CASE

Removal
9¾ AND 10½ INCH

1. The axle assembly can be overhauled either in or out of the vehicle, depending on the repairman's discretion. Either way, the free-floating axles and wheel assemblies must be removed.
2. Drain the lubricant and remove the rear cover and gasket.
3. Matchmark the bearing caps and the housing for reassembly in the same position. Remove the bearing caps and bolts.
4. Using a spreader tool mounted to the carrier housing, spread the housing a maximum of 0.015 inch.

——— CAUTION ———
Do not exceed this measurement. The housing could be permanently damaged. The use of a dial indicator is recommended to prevent over-stretching the housing.

5. Using a pry bar, remove the differential case from the housing. Separate the shims and record the dimensions and location on the 10½ inch ring gear axle. Remove the spreader tool from the housing.

Dana 9¾ inch ring gear axle

1. Nut
2. Washer
3. Companion flange
4. Pinion oil seal
5. Gasket
6. Outer pinion oil slinger
7 and 8. Cone and roller (outer pinion bearing)
9. Shims (outer pinion bearing)
10. Inner pinion oil slinger
11. Shims (inner pinion bearing)
12. Cup (inner pinion bearing)

13. Cone and roller (inner pinion)
14. Ring and pinion
15. Gasket (housing cover)
16. Screw and washer (cover)
17. Cover and plug
18. Lock pin (pinion shaft)
19. Differential case

20. Shims (differential adjusting)
21. Cone and roller (differential bearing)
22. Cup (differential bearing)
23. Cap (differential bearing)
24. Bolt (differential bearing cap)
25. Bolt (ring gear)
26. Pinion shaft
27. Thrust washer (pinion)
28. Pinion
29. Side gear
30. Thrust washer (side gear)

Dana 10½ inch ring gear axle

1. Pinion nut
2. Washer
3. Companion flange
4. Oil seal
5. Oil slinger

6. Pinion front bearing
7. Front bearing cup
8. Preload shim pack
9. Pinion depth shim pack
10. Rear bearing cup

11. Pinion rear bearing
12. Drive pinion
13. Ring gear
14. Differential case
15. Ring gear bolt

16. Differential side bearing
17. Side bearing cup
18. Side bearing adjusting shims
19. Bearing cap
20. Bearing cap bolt
21. Differential spider
22. Differential side gear
23. Washer
24. Pinion gear
25. Washer
26. Gasket
27. Cover
28. Cover screw
29. Drain plug

Disassembly

10½ INCH

1. Remove the differential side bearings from the case, using the necessary puller tools.

2. Remove the ring gear bolts and tap the ring gear from the case with a soft-faced hammer.

3. Scribe the case halves for reassembly and remove the retaining bolts.

4. Tap the top half of the case to separate it from the bottom half. Remove the internal gears, washers and cross.

Inspection

9¾ AND 10½ INCH

1. Clean the gears, bearings and component parts with solvent and inspect for scoring, chipping or excessive wear.

2. Replace the necessary parts as required.

Assembly

10½ INCH

1. Install new thrust washers to the side gears and lubricate the contact surfaces.

2. Assemble the side gears, pinion bears, washers and cross shaft into the flanged half of the case.

3. Install the top half of the case to the bottom half, making sure the scribe marks are lined up.

4. Install the retaining bolts finger tight. Then tighten the bolts alternately to the proper torque specifications.

5. If a new ring gear is to be installed or the old one used, install it to the differential case and align the bolt holes. Tighten the bolts aternately to the proper torque specifications.

6. Install the side carrier bearings by using the proper installation tools.

7. Cover the assembled unit and set aside until ready for the installation into the housing.

Disassembly

9¾ INCH

1. Remove the differential side bearing cups and tag to identify the side, if they are to be used again.

Removing the companion flange

2. Remove the differential gear pinion shaft lock pin and remove the shaft. Rotate the side and pinion gears to remove them from the carrier. Remove the thrust bearings.

3. Remove the bearing cones and rollers from the carrier, marking and noting the shim locations.

4. Remove the ring gear retaining bolts and tap the ring gear from the carrier housing.

5. Inspect the components as outlined earlier.

Assembly

9¾ INCH

1. Install the differential side gears, the differential pinion gears and new thrust washers into the differential carrier.

2. Align the pinion gear shaft holes and install the pinion shaft into the carrier. Align the lock pin hole in the shaft and carrier. Install the lock pin and peen the hole to avoid having the pin drop from the carrier.

3. Install the differential case side bearings with the proper installation tools. Do not install the shims at this time.

4. Place the carrier assembly into the axle housing with the bearing cups on the bearing cones. Install the bearing caps in their original position and tighten the bearing cap bolts enough to keep the bearing caps in place.

5. Install a dial indicator on the housing so that the indicator button contacts the car-

Installing the side bearing

rier flange. Press the differential carrier to prevent side play and center the dial indicator. Rotate the carrier and check the flange for run-out. If the run-out is greater than 0.002 inch, the defect is probably due to the bearings or to the carrier and should be corrected.

6. Remove the assembly and install the ring gear. Torque the retaining bolts to specifications and reinstall the assembly into the housing and again install the bearing caps in their original position and tighten

Prying out against the case with prybars

Internal parts inspection

the cap bolts enough to keep the bearings caps in place.

7. Again, install the dial indicator and position the indicator button to contact the ring gear back surface. Rotate the assembly and the run-out should be less than 0.002 inch. If over 0.002 inch, remove the assembly and relocate the ring gear 180 degrees. Reinstall the assembly and recheck. If the run-out remains over the 0.002 inch tolerance, the ring gear is defective. If the measurement is within tolerances, continue on with the assembly.

8. Position two pry bars between the bearing cap and the housing on the side opposite the ring gear. Pull on the pry bars and force the differential carrier as far as possible towards the dial indicator. Rock the assembly to seat the bearings and reset the dial indicator to "O".

9. Reposition the prybars to the opposite side of the carrier and force the carrier assembly as far towards the center of the housing. Read the dial indicator scale. This will be the total amount of shims required for setting the backlash during the reassembly, less the bearing preload. Record the measurement.

10. Remove the differential carrier from the housing and set aside.

SIDE BEARING SHIM SELECTION FOR THE 10½ INCH

1. With the pinion gear not in the axle housing, place the bearing cups over the side bearings and install the differential carrier into the axle housing.

2. Place the shim that was originally installed on the ring gear side back into its original position.

3. Install the bearing caps in their proper positions and tighten the bolts enough to keep the bearings in place.

4. Mount a dial indicator on the axle housing with the indicator button contacting the back of the ring gear.

5. Position two prybars between the bearing shim and the housing on the ring gear side of the differential carrier. Force the differential carrier away from the dial indicator and set the indicator to "0".

6. Reposition the prybars to the opposite side of the differential carrier and force the carrier back towards the dial indicator. Repeat several times until the same reading is obtained each time.

7. To the dial indicator reading, add the thickness of the shim and record the results to be used later in the assembly.

DRIVE PINION

Removal

9¾ AND 10½ INCH

1. Remove the pinion nut and flange from the pinion gear, using the proper removing tools.

Pinion code location

2. Remove the pinion gear assembly from the housing. It may be necessary to tap the pinion from the housing with a soft faced hammer. Catch the pinion so as not to allow it to drop on the floor.

3. With a long drift, remove the inner bearing cup, pinion seal, slinger, gasket, outer pinion bearing and the shim pack. Tag the shim pack for reassembly.

4. Remove the rear pinion bearing cup and shim pack from the housing. Tag the shims for reassembly.

5. Remove the rear pinion bearing from the pinion gear with an arbor press and special plates.

Inspection of the Components

1. Clean all components in a solvent and inspect the bearings, cups and rollers for scoring, chipping or excessive wear. Inspect the flanges and splines for excessive wear. Inspect all gear surfaces for excessive wear or chipping.

2. Replace the necessary bearing assemblies, gears and thrustwashers as required.

PINION SHIM SELECTION

Ring gears and pinions are supplied in matched sets only. The matched numbers are etched on both gears for verification. On the rear face of the pinion, a + (plus) or a − (minus) number will be etched,

indicating the best running position for each particular gear set. This dimension is controlled by the shimming behind the inner bearing cup. Whenever baffles or oil slingers are used, they become part of the adjusting shim pack. An example: If a pinion is etched +3, this pinion would require 0.003 inch less shims than a pinion etched 0. This means by removing shims, the mounting distance of the pinion is increased by 0.003 inch, which is just what a + (plus) etching indicates. If a pinion is etched −3, it would be necessary to add 0.003 inch more shims than would be required if the pinion was etched 0. By adding the 0.003 inch shims, the mounting distance of the pinion is decreased 0.003 inch, which is just what the − (minus) etching indicates. Pinion adjusting shims are available in thicknesses of 0.003, 0.005 and 0.010 inch. An example: If a new gear set is used and the old pinion reads +2 and the new pinion reads −2, add 0.004 inch shims to the original shim pack.

Assembly

9¾ AND 10½ INCH

1. Select the correct pinion depth shims and install in the rear pinion bearing cup bore.

2. Install the rear bearing cup in the axle housing with the proper tool.

3. Add or subtract an equal amount of shim thickness to or from the preload or

Old Pinion Marking	New Pinion Marking								
	− 4	− 3	− 2	− 1	0	+ 1	+ 2	+ 3	+ 4
+ 4	+ 0.008	+ 0.007	+ 0.006	+ 0.005	+ 0.004	+ 0.003	+ 0.002	+ 0.001	0
+ 3	+ 0.007	+ 0.006	+ 0.005	+ 0.004	+ 0.003	+ 0.002	+ 0.001	0	− 0.001
+ 2	+ 0.006	+ 0.005	+ 0.004	+ 0.003	+ 0.002	+ 0.001	0	− 0.001	− 0.002
+ 1	+ 0.005	+ 0.004	+ 0.003	+ 0.002	+ 0.001	0	− 0.001	− 0.002	− 0.003
0	+ 0.004	+ 0.003	+ 0.002	+ 0.001	0	− 0.001	− 0.002	− 0.003	− 0.004
− 1	+ 0.003	+ 0.002	+ 0.001	0	− 0.001	− 0.002	− 0.003	− 0.004	− 0.005
− 2	+ 0.002	+ 0.001	0	− 0.001	− 0.002	− 0.003	− 0.004	− 0.005	− 0.006
− 3	+ 0.001	0	− 0.001	− 0.002	− 0.003	− 0.004	− 0.005	− 0.006	− 0.007
− 4	0	− 0.001	− 0.002	− 0.003	− 0.004	− 0.005	− 0.006	− 0.007	− 0.008

Pinion code chart

outer shim pack, as was added or subtracted from the inner shim pack.

4. Install the front pinion bearing cup into its bore in the axle housing.

5. Press the rear pinion bearing onto the pinion gear shaft and install the pinion gear with bearing into the axle housing.

6. Install the preload shims and the front pinion bearing. Do not install the oil seal at this time.

7. Install the flange with the holding bar tool attached, the washer and the nut on the pinion shaft end. Torque the nut to 250 ft. lbs. for the 10½ inch and 255 ft. lbs. for the 9¾ inch.

8. Remove the holding bar from the flange and with an inch pound torque wrench, measure the rotating torque of the pinion gear. The rotating torque should be 10 to 20 in. lbs. with the original bearings and 20 to 40 in. lbs. with new bearings. Disregard the torque reading necessary to start the shaft to turn.

9. If the preload torque is not in specifications, adjust the shim pack as required.

a. To increase preload, decrease the thickness of the preload shim pack.

b. To decrease preload, increase the thickness of the preload shim pack.

10. When the proper preload is obtained, remove the nut, washer and flange from the pinion shaft.

11. Install a new pinion seal into the housing and reinstall the flange, washer and nut. Using the holder tool, torque the nut to 250 ft. lbs. for the 10½ inch and 255 ft. lbs. for the 9¾ inch.

Assembly of Differential Carrier Into Axle Housing

9¾ INCH

1. As outlined in the Differential Carrier Assembly procedure, the amount of shims required for setting the backlash less bearing preload had been selected and the measurement recorded.

2. With the pinion gear installed and properly set, position the differential carrier assembly into the axle housing and install the bearing caps in their proper positions. Tighten the cap bolts just enough to hold the bearing caps in place.

3. Install a dial indicator on the axle housing with the indicator button contacting the back of the ring gear.

4. Position two prybars between the bearing cup and the axle housing on the ring gear side of the case and pry the ring gear into mesh with the pinion gear teeth, as far as possible. Rock the ring gear to allow the teeth to mesh and the bearings to seat. With the pressure still applied by the prybars, set the dial indicator to "0".

5. Reposition the prybars on the opposite side of ring gear and pry the gear as far as it will go. Take the dial indicator reading. Repeat this procedure until the same reading is obtained each time. This reading represents the necessary amount of shims

between the differential carrier and the bearing on the ring gear side.

6. Remove the bearing from the differential carrier on the ring gear side and install the proper amount of shims. Reinstall the bearing.

7. Remove the differential carrier bearing from the opposite side of the ring gear. To determine the amount of shims needed, use the following method.

a. Subtract the size of the shim pack just installed on the ring gear side of the carrier from the reading obtained and recorded when measurement was taken without the pinion gear in place during the Differential Carrier Assembly procedure. To this figure, add an additional 0.015 inch to compensate for preload and backlash. An example: If the first reading was 0.085 inch and the shims installed on the ring gear side of the carrier were 0.055 inch, the correct amount of shims whould be 0.085 − 0.055 + 0.015 = 0.045 inch.

8. Install the required shims as determined under step 7 and install the differential side bearing. The installation of the shims should give the proper preload to the bearings and the proper backlash to the ring and pinion gears.

10½ INCH

1. Install the differential carrier, with the side bearings and cups installed, in place in the axle housing.

2. Select the smallest of the original shims as a gauging shim and place it between the bearing cup and the housing on the ring gear side.

3. Install the bearing caps and tighten the bolts enough to hold the cups in place.

4. Mount a dial indicator on the ring gear side of the axle housing and position the indicator button on the rear side of the ring gear.

5. Position two prybars between the bearing cup and the housing on the side opposite the ring gear. With the prybars, force the differential carrier towards the dial indicator and set the indicator dial to "0".

6. Reposition the prybars on the ring gear side of the carrier and force the ring gear into mesh with the pinion gear while observing the dial indicator reading. Repeat this operation until the same reading is obtained each time.

7. Add this indicator reading to the gauging shim thickness to determine the correct shim dimension for installation on the ring gear side of the differential carrier.

8. An example: If the gauging shim was 0.115 inch and the indicator reading was 0.017 inch, the correct shim would be 0.115 + 0.017 = 0.172 inch.

9. Remove the gauging shim and install the correct shim into position between the bearing cup and the axle housing on the ring gear side of the housing.

10. To determine the correct dimension for the remaining shim, refer to the Side Bearing Shim Selection for the 10½ inch

and obtain the recorded shim size. From that figure, subtract the size of the shim installed in step 9 and then add 0.006 inch for the bearing preload and backlash.

11. An example: If the reading of the shim just installed on the ring gear side of the carrier was 0.172 inch and the reading obtained during the checking of clearance without the pinion installed was 0.329, the correct shim dimension would be as follows: 0.329 − 0.172 = 0.157 + 0.006 = 0.163 inch.

Installation of Differential Carrier Into Axle Housing

9¾ INCH

1. Spread the axle housing with the spreader tool no more than 0.015 inch. Install the differential bearing outer cups in their correct locations and install the cups in their respective locations.

2. Install the bolts and tighten finger-tight. Rotate the differential carrier and ring gear and tap with a soft-faced hammer to insure proper seating of the assembly in the axle housing.

3. Remove the spreader tool and torque the cap bolts to specifications.

4. Install a dial indicator and check the ring gear backlash at four equally spaced points of the ring gear circle. The backlash must be within a range of 0.004 to 0.009 inch and must not vary more than 0.002 inch between the points checked.

5. If the backlash is not within specifications, the shim packs must be corrected to bring the backlash within limits.

6. Check the tooth contact pattern and verify.

7. Complete the assembly, fill to proper level with lubricant and operate to verify proper assembly.

10½ INCH

1. Spread the axle housing with a spreader tool, no more than 0.015 inch. The carrier assembly is in place in the housing.

2. Assemble the shim, as determined previously, into place between the bearing cup and the housing. Remove the spreader tool.

3. Install the bearing caps in their marked positions and torque the bolts to specifications.

4. Install a dial indicator and check the ring gear backlash at four equally spaced points around the ring gear.

5. The backlash must be within 0.004 to 0.009 inch and must not vary more than 0.002 inch between the positions checked.

6. Whenever the backlash is not within the allowable limits, it must be corrected. Changing of the shim packs is required.

a. Low backlash is corrected by decreasing the shim on the ring gear side and increasing the opposite side shim an equal amount.

b. High backlash is corrected by increasing the shim on the ring gear side

Bearing cap identification

Spreading rear axle housing

and decreasing the opposite side shim an equal amount.

7. Check the tooth contact pattern and correct as required.

8. Complete the assembly, fill to the correct level and operate to verify correct repairs.

Dana-Spicer Single Reduction Models 30, 44, 44-1, 60-1,2, 70

DIFFERENTIAL

Removal

1. Drain lubricant.
2. Remove cover and gasket.

NOTE: Attached to a cover bolt is a metal tag which shows the number of teeth on pinion and ring (drive) gear.

3. Remove bearing cap screws. Note the matching marks on cap and carrier and make sure caps are reassembled to correct markings.

4. Using a spreader tool, spread carrier

a maximum of 0.020 inch and measure amount of spread with a dial indicator.

— CAUTION —

Carrier may be permanently damaged if spread more than 0.020 inch. Do not attempt differential removal without using a spreader.

5. Carefully lift differential assembly out of carrier.

6. Remove the spreader assembly after removing the differential assembly from the housing.

DRIVE PINION

Disassembly

1. Pull flange (yoke) from shaft splines of drive pinion.

2. Using a press or soft hammer, drive pinion and inner bearing cone assembly out of carrier.

3. Remove and tag shim pack from splined end of pinion.

NOTE: If either ring (drive) gear or pinion are to be replaced, write down markings (+), (−), or (0) located at face end of pinion for reassembly reference.

4. Remove oil seal assembly from carrier bore. This frees oil seal gasket, oil slinger, and bearing cone.

5. If replacement of the pinion tapered bearings is necessary, the bearing cups should be removed from carrier as follows:

   a. Use remover with a driver or slide hammer to remove inner bearing cup from carrier. This frees shim pack. Remove and tag shims for reassembly.

   b. Remove outer bearing cup.

6. Use remover set to separate bearing cone from drive pinion.

7. Separate oil slinger from pinion.

NOTE: This oil slinger is only found on some axle models.

DIFFERENTIAL

Disassembly

1. Remove and label the two bearing cups.

2. Use a suitable type puller to remove the bearing cones. Remove and label adjusting shims.

3. Drive out pinion shaft lock pin.

Measuring differential case drive gear mounting flange runout

Removing differential pinion shaft lock pin

Removing differential bearings

Pinion rear bearing removal

NOTE: On the Spicer Model 70 rear axle, punch-mark the differential case halves (for reassembly reference) and separate. Remove the differential spider, pinion gears, side gears and thrust washers.

4. Separate ring gear from case.

5. Remove pinion shaft, two pinions, two side gears, and four thrust washers from case.

Assembly

1. Place side gears with new thrust washers in position inside case.

2. Place pinions and thrust washers in position in case.

3. Install the differential pinion shaft in position in case between two pinions. Align shaft lock pin hole with lock pin hole in case and install pinion shaft lock pin. Peen hole to prevent pin from falling out.

NOTE: On the Spicer Model 70 rear axle, install the differential spider along with its pinion gears, side gears and thrust washers into the differential case halves. Bolt the two halves together making sure the punch-marks line up.

4. Place ring (drive) gear in proper po-

sition against flange of case and bolt ring gear to case. Alternately tighten these bolts until all bolts are tightened to proper torque.

NOTE: Do not install differential cones or shim packs until pinion depth and bearing preload have been checked out. Differential bearing adjustment is a part of axle assembly procedure.

DIFFERENTIAL BEARING

Adjustment

1. Press fit bearing cones tightly against shoulders on case.

NOTE: Do not install shims at this time.

2. Install bearing cups.

3. Install spreader tool and dial indicator, and spread carrier as described in Differential Removal.

4. Place differential assembly into carrier.

5. Install bearing caps using their respective cap screws. Make sure caps are assembled to their correct markings. Hand tighten bearing cap screws.

6. Install dial indicator at carrier with indicator button contacting back of ring (drive) gear. Rotate ring gear and check run-out.

7. If run-out exceeds 0.002-inch, remove the differential assembly and remove the ring gear from the case.

8. Reinstall differential assembly without ring gear and check run-out of differential case flange. If run-out still exceeds 0.002-inch, the defect is probably due to bearings or case, and should be corrected before proceeding.

9. Remove differential from carrier.

NOTE: Do not install shims behind the bearings until final installation.

DRIVE PINION

Installation

1. If either drive pinion or ring (drive) gear must be replaced, they must be in-

stalled as a set. (These parts are matched and lapped at time of manufacture to obtain the correct gear tooth contact.)

2. Whenever it is necessary to install a new drive pinion, the plus (+) or minus (−) marking on face of rear end of pinion must be considered. Select a new pinion and ring gear set with markings as near as possible to those on old pinion. If marking on both old and new pinion is the same, do not change thickness of shim pack.

3. The approximate difference between markings on old and new drive pinion is the adjustment that will have to be made in the shim packs.

4. In the first listing below note that the new pinion is a plus eight (+8) while the old pinion is a plus five (+5). Making a difference of plus three (+3). This means that the thickness of each shim pack must be decreased by 0.003-inch. Other examples are:

5. Once proper adjustment in shim packs has been made, place oil slinger, if so equipped, over pinion shaft. Install pinion inner bearing cone over shaft, and use bearing installer and an arbor press to press bearing onto pinion shaft. Bearing must be seated tightly against shoulder or oil slinger.

6. Use pinion front bearing cup installer to install outer bearing cup into carrier bore.

7. Install the selected inner shim pack in carrier. Then use pinion rear bearing cup installer to install inner bearing cup.

8. Insert pinion, oil slinger (when used) and inner bearing cone assembly into carrier and place the selected shim pack into position on outer end of pinion shaft.

9. Place outer bearing cone over pinion shaft, then use installer to seat bearing tight against shim pack.

10. Install pinion flange (yoke), washer and nut. Hold flange while tightening the nut to proper torque.

NOTE: Install oil slinger and oil seal only after pinion depth and pinion bearing preload have been checked out.

Checking Pinion Depth Adjustment

1. A pinion depth gauge and correct adapter, which gives a micrometer reading, should be used to determine pinion depth. The actual pinion depth setting can be determined by adding gauge reading to thickness of step plate and comparing result with the nominal dimension of 2.625-inch (models 44/60) or 3.125-inch (model 60), or 3.500 inch (model 70).

2. If the pinion setting is within minus (−) 0.001-inch to plus (+) 0.003-inch of this nominal dimension, the pinion position can be considered satisfactory.

3. If pinion setting exceeds these limits, it must be corrected by adjusting thickness of shim pack behind the pinion inner bearing cup.

PINION SETTING CHARTS (U.S. AND METRIC)
By utilizing these specifications, proper gear contact should be established.

Old Pinion Marking	New Pinion Marking (U.S. Standards)								
	−4	−3	−2	−1	0	+1	+2	+3	+4
+4	+0.008	+0.007	+0.006	+0.005	+0.004	+0.003	+0.002	+0.001	0
+3	+0.007	+0.006	+0.005	+0.004	+0.003	+0.002	+0.001	0	−0.001
+2	+0.006	+0.005	+0.004	+0.003	+0.002	+0.001	0	−0.001	−0.002
+1	+0.005	+0.004	+0.003	+0.002	+0.001	0	−0.001	−0.002	−0.002
0	+0.004	+0.003	+0.002	+0.001	0	−0.001	−0.002	−0.003	−0.004
−1	+0.003	+0.002	+0.001	0	−0.001	−0.002	−0.003	−0.004	−0.005
−2	+0.002	+0.001	0	−0.001	−0.003	−0.003	−0.004	−0.005	−0.005
−3	+0.001	0	−0.001	−0.002	−0.003	−0.004	−0.005	−0.006	−0.007
−4	0	−0.001	−0.002	−0.003	−0.004	−0.005	−0.006	−0.007	−0.008

Old Pinion Marking	New Pinion Marking (Metric)								
	−10	−8	−5	−3	0	+3	+5	+8	+10
+10	+.20	+.18	+.15	+.13	+.10	+.08	+.05	+.03	0
+8	+.18	+.15	+.13	+.10	+.08	+.05	+.03	0	−.03
+5	+.15	+.13	+.10	+.08	+.05	+.03	0	−.03	−.05
+3	+.13	+.10	+.08	+.05	+.03	0	−.03	−.05	−.08
0	+.10	+.08	+.05	+.03	0	−.03	−.05	−.08	−.10
−3	+.08	+.05	+.03	0	−.03	−.05	−.08	−.10	−.13
−5	+.05	+.03	0	−.03	−.05	−.08	−.10	−.13	−.15
−8	+.03	0	−.03	−.05	−.08	−.10	−.13	−.15	−.18
−10	0	−.03	−.05	−.08	−.10	−.13	−.15	−.18	−.20

PRODUCTION NUMBERS NO SIGNIFICANCE

PINION DEPTH ADJUSTMENT FIGURE

+2

F   0

754

GEAR MATING MARK (SAME AS ON DRIVE GEAR)

Drive pinion markings

AXLE MODEL	PINION SETTING
60	3.125 (79.37 mm)
70	3.500 (88.9 mm)

CENTER LINE OF AXLE

Pinion setting dimensions

Pinion Bearing Preload Adjustment

1. Use a torque wrench to check pinion bearing preload.

2. Rotating torque of pinion should be from 15 to 30 in. lbs.

3. Add or remove shims from pack just behind outer bearing cone to bring preload within these torque limits.

Master pinion block installed in the pinion bore

C-4171 HANDLE

D-163 PINION SEAL INSTALLER

Installing pinion seal

PINION BLOCK

ARBOR

ARBOR DISC

Arbor discs and arbor in position

C-3718 YOKE INSTALLER

C-3281 YOKE HOLDING TOOL

Installing pinion and yoke

NOMINAL ASSEMBLY DIMENSION AND ADAPTOR DISC CHART

Axle Model	Nominal Assembly Dimension	Adapter Disc Tool Number
44	2.625″	SE-1065-9-SS
60	3.125″	SE-1065-9-Y
70①	3.500″	SE-1065-9-Y

① Model 70—Use a 0.375 shim under dial pointer

DIFFERENTIAL

Installation

1. Use dial indicator and spreader tool as described in Differential Removal, to spread carrier a maximum of 0.020-inch.

2. Install bearing cups and place differential assembly in carrier. Rotate differential and, with a soft hammer, tap ring (drive) gear to assure a proper bearing seating.

3. Reinstall bearing caps in their proper locations as indicated by marks made during the removal procedure. Finger tighten cap screws. Relieve the spreader tool pressure, and tighten cap screws to 70–90 ft. lbs.

4. Move differential assembly tightly against drive pinion.

5. Install dial indicator securely to carrier, then set button at zero and against back of drive gear.

6. Move the differential toward the dial indicator and note the reading. For accuracy, repeat this operation several times.

7. Remove the differential assembly from carrier. Install a shim pack behind differential bearing cone at drive gear side, equal to the dimension indicated by dial indicator.

8. Subtract the indicator reading from the reading previously obtained in paragraph Differential Bearing Adjustment.

9. To the above result should be added 0.015 to 0.020-inch in shims to provide bearing preload.

10. Install the above shim pack behind differential bearing cone at side opposite to drive gear.

11. Spread differential carrier, using spreader tool.

12. Install differential bearing cups then locate differential assembly in carrier.

13. Rotate differential assembly, tapping gear to seat bearings.

14. Install differential bearing caps in their correct location as indicated by marks made upon disassembly. Finger tighten cap screws.

15. Remove differential carrier spreader tool. Tighten differential bearing cap screws to proper torque.

16. Install dial indicator and check drive gear to drive pinion backlash at four equally spaced points around the drive gear. Backlash must be held to 0.003 to 0.006-inch and must not vary more than 0.002-inch between positions checked.

17. Whenever backlash is not within limits, differential bearing shim pack should be corrected.

Datsun Rear Differential Model H190—ML, H190A

PRE-DISASSEMBLY INSPECTION

1. Check backlash of ring gear with a dial indicator at several points. If it is not within specification, .0059–.0079 in., adjust as needed.

2. Check runout of ring gear with a dial indicator. If it is over specification (.0031 in.), hypoid gear set or differential case should be replaced.

NOTE: When backlash varies excessively in different places, the variance may have resulted from foreign matter caught between ring gear and differential case.

3. Check tooth contact.

4. Check backlash of side gear. Using a thickness gauge, measure clearance between side gear and differential case.

If it is not within specification, adjust it by selecting side gear thrust washer .0305–.0364 in.

TOOTH CONTACT

Gear tooth contact pattern check is necessary to verify correct relationship between ring gear and drive pinion.

Hypoid gear set which are not positioned properly may be noisy, or have short life or both. With a pattern check, the most desirable contact for low noise level and long life can be assured.

1. Thoroughly clean ring gear and drive pinion teeth.

2. Sparingly apply a mixture of pow-

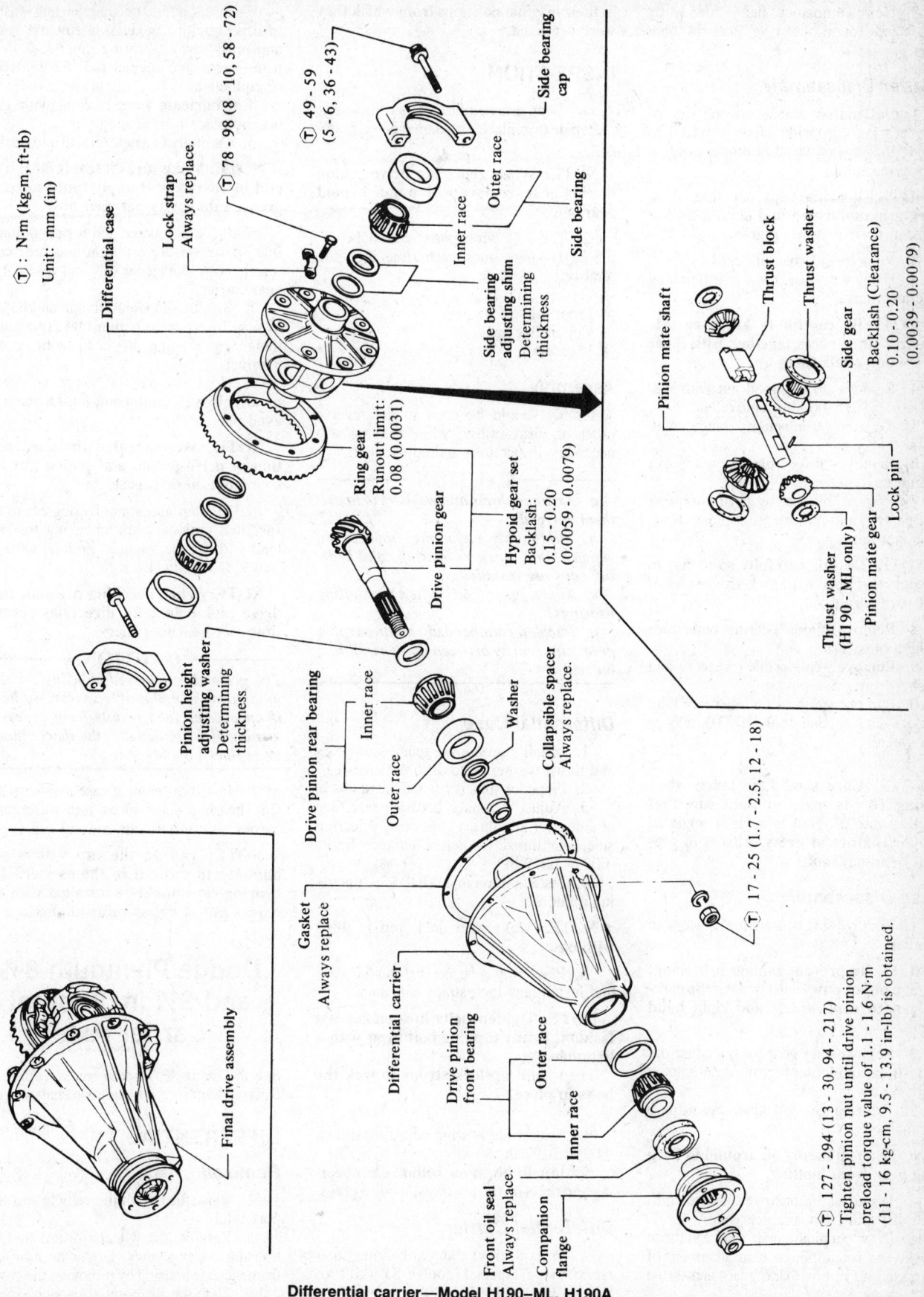

(T) : N·m (kg-m, ft-lb)

Unit: mm (in)

Differential case

Lock strap
Always replace.

(T) 78 - 98 (8 - 10, 58 - 72)

(T) 49 - 59
(5 - 6, 36 - 43)

Side bearing cap

Outer race

Inner race

Side bearing

Side bearing adjusting shim
Determining thickness

Pinion mate shaft

Thrust block

Thrust washer

Side gear

Backlash (Clearance)
0.10 - 0.20
(0.0039 - 0.0079)

Ring gear
Runout limit:
0.08 (0.0031)

Drive pinion gear

Hypoid gear set
Backlash:
0.15 - 0.20
(0.0059 - 0.0079)

Thrust washer
(H190 - ML only)

Pinion mate gear

Lock pin

Pinion height adjusting washer
Determining thickness

Inner race

Outer race

Drive pinion rear bearing

Washer

Collapsible spacer
Always replace.

(T) 17 - 25 (1.7 - 2.5, 12 - 18)

Gasket
Always replace.

Differential carrier

Drive pinion front bearing

Outer race

Inner race

Final drive assembly

Front oil seal
Always replace.

Companion flange

(T) 127 - 294 (13 - 30, 94 - 217)
Tighten pinion nut until drive pinion
preload torque value of 1.1 - 1.6 N·m
(11 - 16 kg-cm, 9.5 - 13.9 in-lb) is obtained.

Differential carrier—Model H190–ML, H190A

dered ferric oxide and oil or equivalent to 3 or 4 teeth of ring gear **drive side**.

3. Hold companion flange steady by hand and rotate the ring gear in both directions.

Carrier Disassembly

1. **Put match marks** on one side of side bearing cap with paint or punch to ensure that it is replaced in proper position during reassembly.

NOTE: Bearing caps are line-bored during manufacture and should be put back in their original places.

2. Remove side bearing caps.

3. Using a pry bar, remove differential case assembly.

NOTE: Be careful to keep the side bearing outer races together with inner race—don't mix them up.

4. Remove drive pinion nut with special tool ST31530000 or equivalent.

5. Remove companion flange with puller.

6. Remove drive pinion with soft hammer.

7. Remove oil seal by prying up with a large awl, and remove front pinion bearing inner race.

NOTE: Do this carefully so as not to scratch seal bore with awl. Cover end of awl with a rag.

8. Remove pinion bearing outer race using a brass drift.

9. Remove collapsible spacer and washer from drive pinion.

10. Pull out rear bearing inner race with a press and special tool ST30031000 or equivalent.

NOTE: Care should be taken when setting Tool in press to make sure that parting line of Tool is a right angle to support fixture of press. This is to prevent bending Tool.

Case Disassembly

1. Remove side bearing inner race with a puller.

NOTE: To prevent damage to bearing, engage puller paws with groove. Be careful not to confuse left and right hand parts.

2. Remove ring gear by spreading out lock straps and loosening ring gear bolts in a criss-cross fashion.

3. Tap ring gear off gear case using a soft hammer.

NOTE: Tap evenly all around to keep ring gear from binding.

4. Drive out pinion mate shaft lock pin, with drift pin from ring gear side.

5. Draw out pinion mate shaft and thrust block, and rotate pinion mate gears out of the case and remove side gears and thrust washers.

NOTE: Put marks on gears and thrust washers so that they can be reinstalled in their original positions from which they were removed.

INSPECTION

1. Clean disassembled parts completely. Repair or replace any damaged or faulty parts.

NOTE: When replacing drive pinion or ring gear, replace with a new hypoid gear set.

2. The following parts should be replaced by new ones each time they are removed.
① Gasket
② Front oil seal
③ Collapsible spacer
④ Lock strap

Assembly

Assembly should be done in the reverse order of disassembly, while making any necessary inspections and adjustments.

──────── CAUTION ────────
a. Arrange shims and washers to install them correctly.
b. Thoroughly clean the surfaces on which shims, washers bearings and bearing caps are installed.
c. Apply gear oil when installing bearings.
d. Pack recommended multi-purpose grease into cavity between lips when fitting oil seal.

Differential Case

1. Install pinion mate gears, side gears and thrust washers into differential case.

2. Fit pinion mate shaft and thrust block.

3. Adjust clearance between rear face of side gear and thrust washer by selecting side gear thrust washer. Clearance limits .0039–.0079 in.

4. Install pinion mate shaft lock pin using a punch.

NOTE: Make sure lock pin is flush with case.

5. Place ring gear on differential case and install new lock straps and bolts.

NOTE: Tighten bolts in a criss-cross fashion, lightly tapping bolt head with a hammer.
Then bend up lock straps to lock the bolts in place.

6. Select side bearing adjusting shims, .0020–.0197 in.

7. Install the shims behind each bearing and press on the bearings, using a press.

Differential Carrier

1. Press fit front and rear bearing outer races using special tools ST3061100, ST30613000, ST30621000 or equivalent.

2. Select pinion height adjusting washer, .1016–.1252 in.

3. Install pinion height adjusting washer in drive pinion, **bevel side toward gear**, and press fit rear bearing inner race in it, using press and special tool ST30901000 or equivalent.

4. **Lubricate** front bearing with gear oil and place it in gear carrier.

5. Carefully fit a **new** oil seal into carrier.

NOTE: Make sure oil seal is flush with end of carrier and apply multi-purpose grease into cavity between lips.

6. Place a **washer** and a **new** collapsible spacer on drive pinion and **lubricate** rear bearing with gear oil, and insert it in gear carrier.

7. Install companion flange and hold it firmly. Insert drive pinion into companion flange by tapping its head with a soft hammer.

8. Hold companion flange and temporarily tighten pinion nut, until there is no axial play.

NOTE: Ascertain that threaded portion of drive pinion and pinion nut are free from oil or grease.

9. Tighten pinion nut by degrees to the specified preload while checking the preload with torque wrench. Preload with oil seal 9.5–13.9 in. lbs.

NOTE: When checking preload, turn drive pinion in both directions several times set bearing rollers.

──────── CAUTION ────────
The preload is achieved by using the permanent set of collapsible spacer. So here, if an over-preload results from excessive turning of the pinion nut, the spacer should be replaced by new one.

10. Install differential case assembly and side bearing outer races into differential carrier, and install side bearing cap.

NOTE: Tap on the cap with a soft hammer to settle it in the carrier. The bearing cap should be installed with the marks put at disassembly aligned.

Dodge/Plymouth 8⅜ and 9¼ in. Integral Carrier Axle

See the Dodge/Plymouth truck section for external identification and axle shaft service.

DIFFERENTIAL

Removal

1. Raise the rear of the vehicle and support safely.

2. Remove the wheels, drums and the housing cover screws. Drain the lubricant from the axle housing by removing the cover.

3. Turn the differential carrier case to

make the differential pinion shaft lock screw accessible and remove it from the case. Slide the pinion shaft from the case.

4. Push both axle shafts towards the center of the axle assembly and remove the C-washer clips from the recessed grooves of the axle shafts. Withdraw the axle shafts carefully to avoid damaging the axle shaft bearings in the axle tubes.

5. Clean the inside of the differential case with solvent and blow dry with compressed air.

6. Check for differential side-play by inserting a prybar between the left side of the axle housing and the differential case flange. Using a prying motion, determine whether side-play exists. There should be no side-play.

7. Paint the ring gear teeth and make a gear tooth contact pattern. Determine if proper depth of mesh can be obtained.

8. If side-play was found in step six, proceed to step nine. If no side-play was found in step six, check the drive gear run-out. Mount a dial indicator and index the indicator stem at right angles in the rear face of the ring gear. Rotate the ring gear and mark the ring gear and case at the point of greatest run-out. Total indicator reading should not exceed 0.005 in. If it does, the possibility exists that the case must be replaced.

9. Measure and record the pinion bearing preload. Use an in. lb. torque wrench to measure the preload.

10. Remove the pinion nut, washer and pinion flange.

11. Remove and discard the pinion oil seal.

12. Match-mark the axle housing and the differential bearing caps.

13. Remove the threaded adjusters and the differential bearing caps. There is a special wrench to do this through the axle tube.

14. Remove the differential case from the housing. The differential bearing cups and threaded adjuster must be kept together so they can be installed in their original position.

Disassembly

1. To remove the drive pinion or front bearing cone, drive the pinion rearward out of the bearing. This will result in damage to the bearing and cup. The bearing cone and cup must be replaced with new parts. Discard the collapsible spacer.

2. Drive the front and rear bearing cups from the housing with a brass drift. Remove the shim from behind the rear bearing cup and record the thickness.

3. Remove the rear bearing cone from the pinion stem with a puller.

4. Clamp the differential case and ring gear in a vise with soft jaws.

5. Remove the ring gear bolts (left-hand thread). Tap the ring gear loose with a soft-faced mallet.

6. If the ring gear run-out exceeded 0.005 in., recheck the case as follows. Install the differential case, cups, caps, and

Using shims to adjust gear tooth contact

Removing differential pinion shaft lock pin

Removing axle shaft C-locks

Removing axle shaft bearing and seal

Installing axle shaft oil seal

Checking differential side play

Measuring drive gear runout

adjusters in the housing. Turn the adjusters to eliminate all side-play and tighten the differential cap bolts snugly. Measure the run-out at the ring gear flange face. Total indicator reading should not exceed 0.003 in. It is often possible to reduce run-out by removing the ring gear and remounting 180° from its original position. Remove the differential case from the housing.

7. Remove the pinion shaft lock-screw and remove the pinion shaft.

8. Rotate the differential side gears until the differential pinion shafts can be removed through the opening in the case.

9. Remove the differential side gears and thrust washers.

10. Using a puller or a press and press plates, remove the differential side bearings.

Assembly

1. Lubricate all parts, before assembly, with rear axle lubricant.

2. Install the thrust washers on the differential side gears and install the side gears into the case.

3. Place thrust washers on both differential pinions and, working through the opening in the case, mesh the pinion gears with the side gears. The pinions should be exactly 180° apart.

4. Rotate the side gears 90° to align the pinions and thrust washers with the pinion shaft holes.

5. From the pinion shaft lockpin hole side of the case, insert the slotted end of the pinion shaft through the case, conical thrust washer and just through one of the pinion gears.

6. Install a thrust block through the side gear hub, so that the slot is centered between the side gears.

7. Hold all these parts in alignment, and align the lockpin holes in the pinion shaft and case. Install the lockpin from the pinion shaft side of the ring gear flange, temporarily.

8. With a stone, relieve the edge of the chamfer on the inside diameter of the ring gear.

9. Heat the ring gear (fluid bath or heat lamp) to a temperature not exceeding 300°F.

NOTE: Do not heat ring gear with a torch.

10. Align the ring gear with the case. Insert the ring gear screws through the case flange and into the ring gear.

11. Alternately tighten each cap screw to 70 ft. lbs.

12. Position each differential bearing cone on the hub of the differential case (taper away from ring gear) and install the bearing cones. An arbor press may be helpful.

Pinion Depth of Mesh

1. The proper pinion setting (relative to the ring gear) is determined by a shim which has been selected before the pinion is to be installed in the carrier. Pinion bearing shims are available in 0.001 in. increments.

Putting identification marks on bearing caps and housing

Determining drive pinion depth mesh shim pack thickness

2. The head of the pinion is marked with a "plus" (+) or a "minus" (−) mark that is followed by a number ranging from zero to four. If the old and new pinions have the same marking and the old bearing is being installed, use a shim of the original thickness. If the old pinion is marked zero (0), however, and the new pinion is marked plus two (+ 2), try a shim that is 0.002 in. thinner. If the new pinion is marked axle housing cup bore and install minus two (− 2), try a shim that is 0.002 in. thicker.

3. Position the selected shim in the bore of the rear bearing cup. Install the cup.

NOTE: Special pinion depth measuring tools are available for both the 8⅜ and 9⅜ inch axles. When using the special tools, follow the manufacturer's recommended procedures. Without the special tools, complete the following procedure and check the pinion depth by examining the pinion to ring gear tooth contact pattern. Correct as required by adding or subtracting shims controlling the pinion depth.

4. Place the rear pinion bearing cone on the pinion stem (small side away from pinion head).

5. Lubricate the front and rear bearing cones and install the rear pinion bearing cone onto the pinion stem with an arbor press.

6. Insert the pinion bearing and collapsible spacer assembly through the carrier and install the front bearing cone. Install the companion flange.

NOTE: During installation of the pinion bearing do not collapse the spacer.

7. Install the drive pinion oil seal into the carrier. Be sure to properly seat the seal.

8. Support the pinion in the carrier.

9. Install the Belleville washer (convex side up) and pinion nut.

10. Hold the companion flange and tighten the pinion nut to remove all endplay, while rotating the pinion to ensure proper bearing seating. Remove the tools and rotate the pinion several revolutions.

11. Torque the pinion nut to 210 ft. lbs. With an in. lbs. torque wrench, measure the pinion bearing preload, which would be

Installing drive pinion rear bearing cone

Loosening or tightening hex adjuster

Removing drive pinion companion flange

Checking drive gear mounting flange face

TOOL

TOOL ADAPTERS

Removing differential bearing cone

Seating bearing caps in axle housing

Installing differential bearing cone

20–35 in. lbs. for new bearings or 10 in. lbs. over the original figure if the old pinion bearing is used.

NOTE: The correct preload reading can only be obtained with the carrier nose upright. The final assembly is incorrect if the final pinion nut torque is below 210 ft. lbs. or if the pinion bearing preload is not within specifications. Under no circumstances should the pinion nut be backed off to reduce the pinion bearing preload; if this is done, a new collapsible spacer will have to be installed and the unit adjusted again until proper preload is obtained.

DIFFERENTIAL BEARING PRELOAD AND RING GEAR-TO-PINION BACKLASH

The threaded adjuster uses a hex drive hole, and requires special tool C-4164 to adjust the side bearing preload through the axle tube. An adjuster lock with two pointed teeth which engage in the exposed adjuster thread when the lock is tightened is provided. The shims will range from 0.020–0.038 in. and will be equipped with internal centering tabs. The shims, marked with a number which represents its thickness in thousandths of an inch, can be installed with either side against the pinion head.

1. Index the gears so that the same gear teeth are in contact throughout the adjustment.

2. The differential bearing cups will not always move with the adjusters. It is important to seat the bearings by rotating them

REAR PINION BEARING

FRONT PINION BEARING

8⅜ inch rear axle setting gauge tool

TOOL

TOOL

Installing drive pinion companion flange

5–10 times in each direction, each time the adjusters are moved.

3. With the pinion bearings installed and the preload set, install the differential with adjusters, caps and bearings. Lubricate the bearings and adjuster threads. Check to be sure that there are no crossed threads. Tighten the top cap screws on the right and left to 10 ft. lbs. Tighten the bottom cap screws fingertight until the head is just seated on the bearing cap.

TOOL

Installing drive pinion oil seal

4. Using the tool, check to be sure that the adjuster rotates freely. Turn both adjusters in until bearing play is eliminated with some drive gear backlash (0.010 in.). Seat the bearing rollers.

5. Install and register a dial indicator against the drive side of a gear tooth. Check the backlash at four positions to find the point of minimum backlash. Rotate the gear to the position of least backlash and mark the tooth so that all readings will be taken at the same point.

6. Loosen the right adjuster and turn the right adjuster until the backlash is 0.003–0.004 in. with each adjuster tightened to 10 ft. lbs. Seat the bearings rollers.

7. Tighten the differential bearing cap screws to 100 ft. lbs.

8. Tighten the right adjuster to 70 ft. lbs. and seat the rollers, until the torque remains constant at 70 ft. lbs. Measure the backlash. If the backlash is not 0.006–0.008 in. increase the torque on the right adjusters and seat the rollers until the correct back-

lash is obtained. Tighten the left adjuster to 70 ft. lbs. and seat the bearings until the torque remains constant.

9. If the assembly is properly done, the initial reading on the left adjuster will be approximately 70 ft. lbs. If it is substantially less, the entire procedure should be repeated.

10. After adjustments are complete, install the adjuster locks. Be sure the teeth are engaged in the adjuster threads. Torque the lockscrews to 90 in. lbs.

Final Assembly

1. Install the axle shafts, C-clips, reinstall the pinion shaft and lock screw and tighten securely.

2. Install the cover on the differential housing, using a new gasket.

3. Refill the rear axle housing with lubricant.

Removing rear wheel bearing retaining ring

PLATE–T75L-1165-B

AXLE SHAFT ASSEMBLY

TUBE ASSEMBLY T 5L-1165-C

AXLE SHAFT BEARING

TUBE ASSEMBLY T75L-1165-C

OUTER RETAINER (OR BRAKE ADAPTOR)

REMOVER–T75L-1165-A

REMOVER–T75L-1165-A

Bearing remover installed

Pressing bearing from the shaft

Drilling retaining ring

Ford–Bronco II/Ranger 6¾ Inch Ring Gear

Disassembly

1. Raise the vehicle and support it on the underbody, so that the rear axle drops down as far as the springs and shock absorbers permit.

2. Remove the cover from the carrier casting rear face, and drain the lubricant. Perform the inspection before disassembly of carrier as directed under the Cleaning and Inspection Section.

3. Remove both rear wheels. Remove the brake drums.

4. Working through the hole provided in the axle shaft flange, remove the nuts that attach the wheel bearing retainers to the axle housing. Pull the axle shafts.

5. Remove the brake backing plate and wire it to the frame rail. Remove both seals with the tool shown.

6. Make scribe marks on the driveshaft end yoke and the axle U-joint flange to ensure proper position of the driveshaft at assembly. Disconnect the driveshaft from the axle U-joint flange. Remove the driveshaft from the transmission extension housing. Install an oil seal replacer tool in the transmission extension housing to prevent transmission leakage.

7. Check and record the ring gear runout and the ring gear backlash.

8. Mark one differential bearing cap and the case to help ensure proper position of the parts during assembly.

9. Loosen the differential bearing cap bolts and bearing caps. Pry the differential case, bearing cups and shims out until they are loose in the bearing caps. Remove the bearing caps and the differential assembly from the carrier.

NOTE: The direction of arrows on bearing caps must be noted. When reassembled, the arrows must be pointing outward.

10. Mark the companion flange in relation to the pinion shaft. Hold the rear axle companion flange with the proper tool and remove the pinion nut. If a new gear set (4209) is being installed, the companion flange need not be marked.

11. Remove the companion flange.

12. With a soft-faced hammer, drive the pinion out of the front bearing cone and remove it through the rear of the carrier casting.

13. Remove the pinion seal and front bearing cone from the front of the carrier casting.

DRIVE PINION

Disassembly

1. Remove the drive pinion, front bearing cone, spacer, and seal.

2. Remove the pinion rear bearing cone. Measure the shim found under the bearing cone with a micrometer. Record the thickness of the shim.

NOTE: Before assembling the rear bearing cone to the pinion, it will be necessary to adjust Pinion Depth.

DRIVE PINION DEPTH ADJUSTMENT

Individual differences in machining the carrier casting and the gear set and variation in bearing widths require a shim between the pinion rear bearing and pinion head, in order to locate the pinion for correct tooth contact with the ring gear. When replacing a ring and pinion gear, the correct shim thickness for the new gear set to be installed is determined by following procedure using Tool T79P-4020-A or equivalent.

1. Place the rear pinion bearing (new or used if in good condition) over the aligning disc and insert it into the pinion bearing cup of the carrier. Place the front bearing into the front bearing cup and assemble the tool handle into the screw and tighten to 27 N·m (20 ft. lbs.).

NOTE: The gauge block must be offset to obtain an accurate reading.

2. Center the gauge tube into the differential bearing bore. Install the bearing caps and torque the bolts to specification. (Caps to be installed with the arrows pointing outboard).

- Make sure that the gauge handle adapter screw, aligning adapter, gauge disc and gauge block assembly are securely mounted between front and rear bearing. Recheck tool handle torque prior to gauging to ensure that bearings are properly seated. This can affect final shim selection when improperly assembled. Clean bearing cups and differential pedestal surfaces thoroughly. Apply only light oil film on bearing assemblies prior to gauging.

- Gauge block should then be rotated several half turns to ensure rollers are properly seated in bearing cups. Rotational torque on the gauge assembly should be 20 in. lbs with new bearings. Final position should be approximately 45° across gauge tube to ensure that gauge block is in line with gauge tube high point. This area should be utilized for pinion shim selection. Selection of pinion shim with gauge block not lined up with tube high point will cause improper shim selection and may result in axle noise.

- Utilize pinion shims as the gauge for shim selection. This will minimize errors in attempting to stack feeler gauge stock together or simple addition errors in calculating correct shim thickness.

NOTE: Shims must be flat. Do not use dirty, bent, nicked or mutilated shims as a gauge.

- **It is important to utilize a light drag on the shim for the correct selection.** Do not attempt to force the shim between the gauge block and gauge tube. This will minimize selection of a shim thicker than required, which results in a deep tooth contact in final assembly for integral axles.

Exploded view 6¾ inch axle assembly

If the pinion has a plus (+) marking, subtract this amount from the feeler gauge measurement.

If the pinion has a minus (−) marking, add this amount to the feeler gauge measurement.

DRIVE PINION REAR BEARING

NOTE: The same rear pinion bearing used in this procedure must be used in final assembly of the axle.

1. Place the selected shim(s) on the pinion shaft and press the pinion bearing until firmly seated on the shaft.

PINION BEARING CUPS

Disassembly and Assembly

Do not remove the pinion bearing cups from the carrier casting unless the cups are to be replaced; drive them out of the carrier casting with a drift. Install the new cups with tool T71P-4616-A or equivalent. Make sure the cups are properly seated in their bores. If a 0.0015 inch feeler gauge can be inserted between a cup and the bottom of its bore at any point around the cup, the cup is not properly seated. Whenever the cups are replaced, the cone and roller assemblies should also be replaced.

DIFFERENTIAL CASE

Disassembly

1. If the differential bearings are to be removed, use tool T77F-4220-B or equivalent. Mark the differential case, cover and ring gear for assembly in the original position.

2. Remove the bolts that attach the ring gear to the differential case and discard them. Press the ring gear from the case or tap it off with a soft-faced hammer.

3. Remove the left side of the differential case.

4. With a drift, drive out the differential pinion shaft lock pin.

5. Drive out the pinion shaft with a brass drift. Remove the gears and thrust washers. Clean and inspect all the parts. Repair or replace all parts as indicated by the inspection.

Assembly

1. Install the differential side gears and thrust washers in their bores.

2. Install the pinion shaft aligning the pinion gears and thrust washers.

3. Install the left case on the right and tap them together.

4. Install the pinion shaft lockpin.

5. Install the differential bearing.

AXLE

Assembly

The drive pinion should be set to the correct depth before final assembly setting is proper. Drive pinion preload requires that a new spacer be used when the pinion is removed. Drive pinion bearing preload is set with the drive pinion assembly installed and the pinion nut tightened to specification. Correct preload is indicated when the rotational torque is 0.9–1.6 N·m (8–14 in. lbs.) with original bearings or 1.8–3.2 N·m (16–29 in. lbs.) for new bearings.

Differential Bearing Preload and Ring Gear Backlash is adjusted with the drive pinion and differential case installed. Adjustment is performed by the installation of shims between the differential bearing cup and axle housing.

DRIVE PINION AND DRIVE PINION BEARING PRELOAD ADJUSTMENT

1. Install the pinion front bearing.

2. Install the pinion seal.

3. Insert the companion flange into the seal and hold it firmly against the pinion front bearing cone. From the rear of the carrier casting, insert the pinion shaft with a new spacer into the flange.

4. Start a new pinion nut. Hold the flange and tighten the pinion shaft nut. As the nut is tightened, the pinion shaft is pulled into the front bearing cone and into the flange.

As the pinion shaft is pulled into the front bearing cone, pinion shaft end play is reduced. While there is still end play in the pinion shaft, the flange and bearing cone will be felt to bottom on the collapsible spacer.

From this point, a much greater torque must be applied to turn the pinion nut, since the spacer must be collapsed. Very slowly, tighten the nut, but check the pinion shaft end play often, to see that the pinion bearing preload does not exceed the limits.

If the pinion nut is tightened to the point that pinion bearing preload exceeds the limits, the pinion shaft must be removed and a new collapsible spacer installed. **Do not decrease the preload by loosening the pinion nut.** This will remove the compression between the pinion front and rear bearing cones and the collapsible spacer and may permit the front bearing cone to turn on the pinion shaft.

5. As soon as there is a preload on the bearings, **turn the pinion shaft in both directions several times to set the bearing rollers.**

6. Adjust the bearing preload to specification. Measure the preload with a torque wrench.

DIFFERENTIAL ASSEMBLY

For shim selection after a complete replacement of the rear axle housing, the differential assembly or differential side bearings, use the following instructions. For a ring and pinion replacement only or a backlash adjustment, follow Steps 9 through 13 and Step 15, using the side bearing shims that were originally in the axle.

1. With pinion depth set and pinion installed, place differential case and gear assembly with bearings and cups in carrier.

2. Install a 6.73mm (0.265 inch) shim on left side.

3. Install left bearing cap and tighten bolts finger tight.

4. Install progressively larger shims on the right side until the largest shim selected can be assembled with a slight drag feel.

NOTE: Apply pressure towards left side to ensure bearing cup is seated.

5. Install right side bearing cap and tighten bearing cup bolts to 95–115 N·m (70–85 ft. lbs.).

6. Rotate assembly to ensure free rotation.

7. Check ring gear and pinion backlash (Fig. 31). If the backlash is 0.20–0.38mm (0.008–0.015 inch) with 0.30–0.38mm (0.012–0.015 inch) preferred, proceed to Step 14. If backlash is not within specifications, go to Step 10, unless zero backlash is measured, then go to Step 8.

8. If a zero backlash condition occurs, add .020 inch to the right side and subtract .020 inch from the left side to allow backlash indication.

9. Recheck backlash.

10. If backlash is not to specification, correct backlash by increasing thickness of one shim and decreasing thickness on the other shim the same amount. Refer to chart for approximate shim change.

11. Install shim and bearing caps. Tighten cap bolts to 95–115 N·m (70–85 ft. lbs.).

12. Rotate assembly several times.

13. Recheck backlash. If backlash is within specification, go to Step 14. If backlash is not within specification, repeat Step 10. Backlash specification is 0.20–0.38mm (0.008–0.015 inch). Preferred range is 0.30–0.38mm (0.012–0.015 inch).

14. Increase both left and right shim sizes by .006 and install for correct differential bearing preload. Make sure shims are fully seated and assembly turns freely.

BACKLASH CHANGE REQUIRED (INCH)	THICKNESS CHANGE REQUIRED (INCH)	BACKLASH CHANGE REQUIRED (INCH)	THICKNESS CHANGE REQUIRED (INCH)
.001	.002	.009	.012
.002	.002	.010	.014
.003	.004	.011	.014
.004	.006	.012	.016
.005	.006	.013	.018
.006	.008	.014	.018
.007	.010	.015	.020
.008	.010		

MORE BACKLASH
LESS BACKLASH

DECREASE— FOR MORE BACKLASH LEFT SIDE   INCREASE+ FOR LESS BACKLASH   DECREASE— FOR LESS BACKLASH   INCREASE+ FOR MORE BACKLASH RIGHT SIDE

Shim changes for ring gear and pinion backlash

15. Utilize white marking compound to obtain a tooth mesh contact pattern in your assembly.

Reincorporation of pattern inspection is intended to allow technicians the ability to detect gross errors in set up prior to complete reassembly. Pattern contact should be within the primary area of the ring gear tooth surface, avoiding any "narrow" or "hard" contact with outer perimeter of tooth (top fo root, toe to heel). Pattern inspection should be on the drive (pull) side. Correct assembly of drive pattern will result in satisfactory coast performance. If gross pattern error is detected, with preferred backlash 0.30–0.38mm (0.012–0.015 inch), recheck pinion shim selection.

16. Install bearing caps and tighten cap bolts to 95–115 N·m (70–85 ft. lbs.).

17. Inspect the machined surfaces of the axle shaft and the axle housing for rough spots or other irregularities which would affect the sealing action of the oil seal. Check the axle shaft splines for burrs, wear or damage. Carefully remove any burrs or rough spots. Replace worn or damaged parts. Install a new gasket on the housing flange and install the brake backing plate.

18. Carefully slide the axle shaft into the housing so that the rough forging of the shaft will not damage the oil seal. Start the axle splines into the side gear, and push the shaft in until the bearing bottoms in the housing. Install the bearing retainer plate on the mounting bolts at the axle housing, and install the attaching nuts. Tighten the nuts to 27–54 N·m (20–40 ft. lbs.).

19. Remove the oil seal replacer from the transmission extension housing. Install the driveshaft in the extension housing. Align the scribe marks on the flange and driveshaft and connect the driveshaft at the drive pinion flange. Apply Loctite (E0AZ-19554-B) or equivalent to the threads of the attaching bolts and tighten to 95–128 N·m (70–95 ft. lbs.).

20. Install the brake drum and attaching shakeproof retainers. Install the wheel and tire on the brake drum. Install the wheel covers.

21. Clean the gasket mating surface of the rear axle housing and cover. Apply a new continuous bead of silicone rubber sealant (D6AZ-19562-B or equivalent) to the carrier casting face.

CAUTION

Make sure machined surfaces on both cover and carrier are clean before installing the new silicone sealant. Inside of axle must be covered when cleaning the machined surface to prevent axle contamination.

22. Install cover and tighten cover bolts to 34–47 N·m (25–35 ft. lbs.), except the ratio tag bolt, which is tightened to 20–34 N·m (15–25 ft. lbs.).

NOTE: Cover assembly must be installed within 15 minutes of application of the silicone or new sealant must be applied.

23. Add E0AZ-19580-A (ESP-M2C154-A) lubricant or equivalent through the filler hole until the lubricant level reaches the bottom of the filler hole with the axle in the running position. Install filler plug and tighten to 21–40 N·m (15–30 ft. lbs.).

24. Lower vehicle and road test.

Ford–Bronco II/Ranger 7½ Inch Ring Gear Axle Assembly

Disassembly

All service operations on the differential case assembly and the drive pinion can be performed with the axle housing installed in the vehicle.

1. Raise the vehicle and place jack stands under the rear frame crossmember. Lower the hoist so that the axle drops down far enough for working ease.

Exploded view 7½ inch axle assembly

2. Remove the cover from the carrier casting rear face and drain the lubricant. Inspect the case assembly and drive pinion before removal.

3. Remove the rear wheels and brake drums.

4. Remove the axle shafts.

5. Make scribe marks on the driveshaft and yoke and the rear axle companion flange to ensure proper alignment at assembly. Disconnect the driveshaft from the rear axle companion flange. Remove the driveshaft assembly from the vehicle. Insert an oil seal replacement tool in the transmission extension housing to prevent leakage.

6. Check and record the ring gear runout.

Check and record the ring gear backlash.

7. Mark on differential bearing cap to help position the caps properly during assembly.

8. Loosen the differential bearing cap bolts and bearing caps.

NOTE: The direction of arrows on bearing caps must be noted. When reassembled, the arrows must be pointing in the same direction as before removal.

9. Pry the differential case, bearing cups and shims out until they are loose in the bearing caps. Remove the bearing caps and remove the differential assembly out of the carrier. On conventional differentials, if the ring is removed, discard the bolts. Install new bolts, coated with Loctite or equivalent. Tighten to 95–115 N·m (70–85 ft. lbs.).

10. Mark the companion flange in relation to the pinion shaft. Hold the rear axle companion flange with the proper tool and remove the pinion nut. If a new gear set is being installed, the companion flange need not be marked.

11. Remove the companion flange. With a soft-faced hammer, drive the pinion out of the front bearing cone and remove it through the rear of the carrier casting.

12. Remove the drive pinion oil seal with Tool-1125-AC and T50T-100-A or their equivalent. Remove the front pinion bearing cone and roller and slinger from the carrier casting.

DRIVE PINION

Disassembly

1. Remove the drive pinion, front bearing cone, spacer, and seal.

2. To remove the pinion rear bearing cone, use tool T71P-4621-B or equivalent. Measure the shim found under the bearing cone with a micrometer. Record the thickness of the shim.

NOTE: Before assembling the rear bearing cone to the pinion, it will be necessary to adjust pinion depth.

DRIVE PINION DEPTH ADJUSTMENT

Individual differences in machining the carrier casting and the gear set and variation in bearing widths require a shim between the pinion rear bearing and pinion head, in order to locate the pinion for correct tooth contact with the ring gear. When replacing a ring and pinion gear, the correct shim thickness for the new gear set to be installed, is determined by following procedure using tool T79P-4020-A or equivalent.

PINION DEPTH TOOL SET

1. Place the rear pinion bearing (new or used if in good condition) over the aligning disc and insert it into the pinion bearing cup of the carrier. Place the front bearing into the front bearing cup and assemble the tool handle into the screw and tighten to 27 N·m (20 ft. lbs.).

NOTE: The gauge block must be offset to obtain an accurate reading.

2. Center the gauge tube into the differential bearing bore. Install the bearing caps and torque the bolts to specification. (Caps to be installed with the arrows pointing outboard.)

- Make sure that the gauge handle adapter screw, aligning adapter, gauge disc and gauge block assembly are securely mounted between front and rear bearing. Recheck tool handle torque prior to gauging to ensure that bearings are properly seated. This can affect final shim selection when improperly assembled. Clean bearing cups and differential pedestal surfaces thoroughly. Apply only **light** oil film on bearing assemblies prior to gauging.

- Gauge block should then be rotated several half turns to ensure rollers are properly seated in bearing cups. Rotational torque on the gauge assembly should be 20 in. lbs. with new bearings. Final position should be approximately 45° across gauge tube to ensure that gauge block is in line with gauge tube high point. This area should be utilized for pinion shim selection. Selection of pinion shim with gauge block not lined up with tube high point will cause improper shim selection and may result in axle noise.

- Utilize pinion shims as the gauge for shim selection. This will minimize errors in attempting to stack feeler gauge stock together or simple addition errors in calculating correct shim thickness.

NOTE: Shims must be flat.

Do not use dirty, bent, nicked or mutilated shims as a gauge.

- **It is important to utilize a light drag on the shim for the correct selection.** Do not attempt to force the shim between the gauge block and gauge tube. This will minimize selection of a shim thicker than required which results in a deep tooth contact in final assembly for integral axles.

If the pinion has a plus (+) marking, subtract this amount from the feeler gauge measurement.

If the pinion has a minus (−) marking, add this amount to the feeler gauge measurement.

ASSEMBLY OF DRIVE PINION REAR BEARING CONE

NOTE: The same rear pinion bearing used in this procedure must be used in final assembly of the axle.

1. Place the selected shim(s) on the pinion shaft and press the pinion bearing until firmly seated on the shaft.

DRIVE PINION BEARING CUPS

Disassembly & Assembly

Do not remove the pinion bearing cups from the carrier casting unless the cups are worn or damaged. If the pinion bearing cups are to be replaced, drive them out of the carrier casting with a drift. Install the new cups. Make sure the cups are properly seated in their bores. If a 0.0015 inch feeler gauge can be inserted between a cup and the bottom of its bore at any point around the cup, the cup is not properly seated. Whenever the cups are replaced, the cone and roller assemblies should also be replaced.

Assembly

The drive pinion must be set to the correct depth before final assembly. Drive pinion preload requires that a new spacer be used when the pinion is removed. Drive pinion bearing preload is set with the drive pinion assembly installed and the pinion nut tightened to specification. Correct preload is indicated when the rotational torque is 0.9–1.6 N·m (8–14 in. lbs.) with the original bearings or 1.8–3.2 N·m (16–29 in. lbs.) for used bearings.

Differential Bearing Preload and Ring Gear Backlash is adjusted with the drive pinion and differential case installed. Adjustment is performed by the installation of shims between the differential bearing cup and axle housing.

DRIVE PINION AND DRIVE PINION BEARING PRELOAD ADJUSTMENT

1. Install the pinion front bearing and slinger.

2. Apply grease, C1AZ-19590-B or equivalent between the lips of the pinion seal and install the pinion seal.

3. Insert the companion flange into the seal and hold it firmly against the pinion front bearing cone. From the rear of the carrier casting, insert the pinion shaft, with a new spacer, into the flange.

4. Start a new pinion nut. Hold the flange with special tool T78P-4851-A or equivalent and tighten the pinion nut. As the nut is tightened, the pinion shaft is pulled into the front bearing cone and into the flange.

As the pinion shaft is pulled into the front bearing cone, pinion shaft end play is reduced. While there is still end play in the pinion shaft, the flange and bearing cone will be felt to bottom on the collapsible spacer.

From this point, a much greater torque must be applied to turn the pinion nut, since the spacer must be collapsed. Very slowly, tighten the nut, but check the pinion shaft end play often to see that the pinion bearing preload does not exceed the limits.

If the pinion nut is tightened to the point that pinion bearing preload exceeds the limits, the pinion shaft must be removed and a new collapsible spacer installed.

NOTE: Do not decrease the preload by loosening the pinion nut.

This will remove the compression between the pinion front and rear bearing cones and the collapsible spacer, and may permit the front bearing cone to turn on the pinion shaft.

5. As soon as there is a preload on the bearings, **turn the pinion shaft in both directions several times to set the bearing rollers.**

6. Adjust the bearing preload to specification. Measure the preload.

Differential Assembly

For shim selection after a complete replacement of the rear axle housing, the differential assembly or differential side bearings use the following instructions. For a ring and pinion replacement only or a backlash adjustment, follow Steps 9 through 13 and Step 15, using the side bearing shims that were originally in the axle.

1. With pinion depth set and pinion installed, place differential case gear assembly with bearings and cups in carrier.

2. Install a 6.73mm (0.265 inch) shim on left side.

3. Install left bearing cap and tighten bolts finger tight.

4. Install progressively larger shims on the right side until the largest shim selected can be assembled with a slight drag feel.

NOTE: Apply pressure towards left side to ensure bearing cup is seated.

5. Install right side bearing cap and tighten bearing cup bolts to 95–115 N·m (70–85 ft. lbs.).

6. Rotate assembly to ensure free rotation.

7. Check ring gear and pinion backlash. If the backlash is 0.20–0.38mm (0.008–0.015 inch) with 0.304–0.381mm (0.012–0.015 inch) preferred, proceed to Step 14. If backlash is not within specifications, go to Step 10, unless zero backlash is measured, then go to Step 8.

8. If a zero backlash condition occurs, add .020 inch to the right side and subtract .020 inch from the left side to allow backlash indication.

9. Recheck backlash.

10. If backlash is not to specification, correct backlash by increasing thickness of one shim and decreasing thickness on the other shim the same amount. Refer to chart for approximate shim change.

11. Install shim and bearing caps. Tighten cap bolts to 95–115 N·m (70–85 ft. lbs.).

12. Rotate assembly several times.

13. Recheck backlash. If backlash is within specification, go to Step 14. If backlash is not within specification, repeat Step 10. Backlash specification is 0.20–.038mm (0.008–0.015 inch). Preferred range is 0.304–0.381mm (0.012–0.015 inch).

14. Increase both left and right shim sizes by .006 inch and install for correct differential bearing preload. Make sure shims are fully seated and assembly turns freely.

15. Utilize white marking compound to obtain a tooth mesh contact pattern in your assembly.

Reincorporation of pattern inspection is intended to allow technicians the ability to detect gross errors in set up prior to complete reassembly. Pattern contact should be within the primary area of the ring gear tooth surface avoiding any "narrow" or "hard" contact with outer perimeter of tooth (top to root, toe to heel). Pattern inspection should be on the drive (pull) side. Correct assembly of drive pattern will result in satisfactory coast performance. If gross pattern error is detected, with preferred backlash of 0.30–0.38mm (0.012–0.015 inch), recheck pinion shim selection.

16. Install bearing caps and tighten cap bolts to 95–115 N·m (70–85 ft. lbs.).

17. Install the axle shafts.

18. Remove the oil seal replacer from the transmission extension housing. Install the driveshaft in the extension housing. Align the scribe marks on the flange and driveshaft and connect the driveshaft at the drive pinion flange. Apply Loctite (E0AZ-19554-B) or equivalent to the threads of the attaching bolts. Tighten attaching bolts to 90–128 N·m (70–95 ft. lbs.).

19. Install the brake drum and attaching shakeproof retainers. Install the wheel and tire on the brake drum. Install the wheel covers.

20. Clean the gasket mating surface of the rear axle housing and cover.

Apply a new continuous bead of silicone rubber sealant (D6AZ-19562-B or equivalent) to the carrier casting face.

— CAUTION —
Make sure machined surfaces on both cover and carrier are clean before installing the

SHIM CODE CHART

NUMBER OF STRIPES AND COLOR CODE	DIM.
2 — C-COAL	.3070–.3075
1 — C-COAL	.3050–.3055
5 — BLU	.3030–.3035
4 — BLU	.3010–.3015
3 — BLU	.2990–.2995
2 — BLU	.2970–.2975
5 — PINK	.2930–.2935
4 — PINK	.2910–.2915
3 — PINK	.2890–.2895
2 — PINK	.2870–.2875
1 — PINK	.2850–.2855
5 — GRN	.2830–.2835
4 — GRN	.2810–.2815
3 — GRN	.2790–.2795
2 — GRN	.2770–.2775
1 — GRN	.2750–.2755
5 — WH	.2730–.2735
4 — WH	.2710–.2715
3 — WH	.2690–.2695
2 — WH	.2670–.2675
1 — WH	.2650–.2655
5 — YEL	.2630–.2635
4 — YEL	.2610–.2615
3 — YEL	.2590–.2595
2 — YEL	.2570–.2575
1 — YEL	.2550–.2555
5 — ORNG	.2530–.2535
4 — ORNG	.2510–.2515
3 — ORNG	.2490–.2495
2 — ORNG	.2470–.2475
1 — ORNG	.2450–.2455
2 — RED	.2430–.2435
1 — RED	.2410–.2415

BACKLASH ADJUSTMENTS

BACKLASH SPECIFICATIONS

BACKLASH CHANGE REQUIRED (INCH)	THICKNESS CHANGE REQUIRED (INCH)	BACKLASH CHANGE REQUIRED (INCH)	THICKNESS CHANGE REQUIRED (INCH)
.001	.002	.009	.012
.002	.002	.010	.014
.003	.004	.011	.014
.004	.006	.012	.016
.005	.006	.013	.018
.006	.008	.014	.018
.007	.010	.015	.020
.008	.010		

Shim changes for ring gear and pinion backlash

new silicone sealant. Inside of axle must be covered when cleaning the machined surface to prevent axle contamination.

21. Install cover and tighten cover bolts to 34–47 N·m (25–35 ft. lbs.), except the ratio tag bolt, which is tightened to 20–34 N·m (15–25 ft. lbs.).

NOTE: Cover assembly must be installed within 15 minutes of application of the silicone or new sealant must be reapplied.

22. Add E0AZ-19580-A (ESP-M2C154-A) or equivalent through the filler hole until the lubricant level is 9.5mm (⅜ inch) below the filler hole with the axle in the running position.

23. Lower vehicle and road test.

Ford Semi-Floating Single Speed Axle, Removable Carrier Type

This is a conventional type axle used on light duty Ford trucks. The axle design uses a removable carrier with the assembly bolted to the axle housing. The axle uses hypoid type gears and has the pinion gear mounted below the center line on the ring gear. The pinion gear is supported by two bearings in front of the gear and one behind. It is important to refer to the tag showing the axle and model number which is secured to the housing to obtain proper replacement parts.

CARRIER ASSEMBLY

Removal

1. With the vehicle raised on a lift, remove the axle shafts from the housing.

Installing the pinion seal

2. Remove the drive shaft from the carrier assembly.

3. With a drain pan under the axle, remove the retaining bolts from the carrier and drain the gear lube.

4. Remove the carrier assembly from the axle.

Installation

1. Clean the surfaces of the carrier and the axle housing. Install a new gasket.

2. Position the carrier assembly on the studs in the housing and install the retaining nuts. Torque the nuts to 30–40 ft. lbs.

Removing the pinion seal

Removing the companion flange

Removing the pinion shaft nut

3. Install the drive shaft and torque the bolts to 13–17 ft. lbs.

4. Install the axles in the housing and secure.

5. Fill the axle housing to the proper level with gear lube and road test for proper operation.

DIFFERENTIAL CASE

Removal & Disassembly

1. Remove the carrier assembly from the axle housing and mount the carrier in a holding fixture.

2. Mark the bearing caps and adjusting nuts so they may be installed in their original positions when assembling.

3. Remove the adjusting nut locks, bearing caps and adjusting nuts.

4. Lift the differential assembly out of the carrier. Using a bearing puller, remove the side bearings from the differential case.

5. Mark the side of the case, the ring gear and the cover so they can be installed in their original positions.

6. Remove the bolts that retain the ring gear to the case and using a soft hammer, tap the ring gear from the case.

7. Using a drift, drive the lock pin from the pinion shaft and separate the halves of the differential case.

8. Drive the pinion shaft out of the case using a brass drift and remove the thrust washers and gears.

DRIVE PINION AND BEARING RETAINER

Removal & Disassembly

1. With a holding fixture installed on the flange, remove the pinion nut and washer. Leave the holding fixture on the flange and using a puller, remove the flange from the pinion shaft.

2. Using a seal puller, remove the pinion seal from the retainer assembly.

3. Remove the bolts from the retainer assembly and lift the retainer from the carrier. Measure the thickness of the shim that was between the retainer and the carrier assembly. Record the result.

4. Install a piece of hose on the pinion pilot bearing surface in front of the pinion gear. Mount the retainer assembly in a press and press the pinion gear out of the retainer.

5. Mount the pinion shaft in a press and press the rear bearing from the pinion shaft.

PINION BEARING CUP

Replacement

1. With the retainer assembly mounted in a press, using the proper tool, press the front and rear bearing cups from the assembly.

Removing the differential bearing

2. Check the inside surfaces of the retainer for any nicks, dirt or distortion.

3. Install the new cups by pressing them into place with the proper tool. When the cups are installed, make sure they are seated in the retainer by trying to fit a .0015 in. feeler gauge, between the cup and the bottom of the bore.

PILOT BEARING

Replacement

1. Using a bearing driver, drive the bearing and retainer out of the carrier assembly.

2. Using the same tool, drive the new bearing into place until the driver bottoms against the case.

3. Drive a new retainer into place with the concave side up.

Installing the pinion front bearing cup

Removing the differential pinion shaft lock pin

Removing the pinion rear bearing cup

Removing the pinion front bearing cone

DRIVE PINION AND BEARING RETAINER

Assembly & Installation

1. Mount the pinion gear in a press and press the rear bearing into place.

2. Install the bearing spacer, bearing retainer and front bearing on the pinion shaft and press them into place. Be careful not to crush the bearing spacer.

3. Install a new O-ring in the groove in the retainer assembly. Do not twist the O-ring when fitting it into place.

4. Lubricate both pinion bearings.

5. Check the thickness of the original shim that was recorded earlier. Located on the head of the pinion gear is the shim adjustment number. Compare the number on the old pinion with the one on the new pinion. Refer to the table which indicates the amount of change to the original shim thickness for proper operation.

6. Install the new shim on the housing and install the pinion and retainer assembly, being careful not to damage the O-ring.

7. Install the bearing retainer bolts and torque them to 30–40 ft. lbs.

8. Using a seal driver, install a new pinion seal in the retainer assembly.

9. Position a holding tool on the flange and install the flange on the pinion shaft. With the holding tool still in place, install the washer and nut on the pinion shaft and torque the nut to 175 ft. lbs. Check the pinion bearing preload. The preload should be 8–14 in. lbs. for used bearings and 22–32 in. lbs. for new bearings. *Do not* overtighten the nut. *Do not* back off the nut to obtain the proper preload. If the 175 ft. lbs. initial torque was too much, the collapsible spacer must be replaced. Tighten the pinion only enough to obtain the right preload torque.

Removing the pinion retainer assembly

Installing the pinion rear bearing cup

Removing the pinion rear bearing cone

DIFFERENTIAL CASE

Assembly & Installation

1. Lubricate all of the differential parts with gear lube before assembling.

2. Install a side gear and thrust washer in the case bore. Using a soft hammer, drive the pinion shaft into the case far enough to hold a pinion thrust washer and gear. Place the second pinion thrust washer and gear in position and carefully tap the pinion shaft into place. Be sure to line up the holes for the lock pin in the pinion shaft.

3. With the second side gear and thrust washer in place, install the cover on the differential case. Drive the pinion lock pin into place. Insert an axle shaft spline into the side gear and check for free rotation of the gears.

4. Install two, two inch long $7/16$ (N.F.) bolts through the differential case and thread them a little way into the ring gear. These will act as a guide when installing the ring gear on the case. Tap the ring gear into place.

5. Remove the guide pins and install the ring gear bolts. Tighten the bolts evenly to 65–85 ft. lbs.

6. If the differential bearings were removed, install the assembly in a press and press the new bearings into place.

7. Coat the bearing bores in the carrier with gear lube and install the bearing cups on the bearings. Place the differential assembly in the carrier.

8. Slide the differential case in the carrier bore until there is a slight amount of backlash between the gears.

9. Install the adjusting nuts in the carrier so that they just contact the bearing cups. The nuts should be engaged about the same number of threads on each side.

10. Position the bearing caps in the carrier. Be careful to line up the marks. Install the cap bolts and torque them to 70–80 ft. lbs. Make sure the adjusting nuts turn freely as the bolts are being tightened.

11. Adjust the backlash and bearing preload as follows:

a. Loosen the bearing cap bolts then retighten them to 35 ft. lbs.

b. Loosen the adjusting nut on the pinion side so that it is away from the bearing cup. Tighten the nut on the opposite side so that the ring gear is forced into the pinion with no backlash.

c. Recheck the nut on the pinion side to make sure it is still loose. Now tighten this nut until it contacts the bearing cup. After it contacts the cup, turn it two more notches.

d. Rotate the ring gear several times in each direction. This helps to seat the bearings in the cups.

e. Again loosen the nut on the pinion side. If there is any backlash between the gears, tighten the nut on the ring gear side until the backlash is removed.

f. Install a dial indicator on the carrier assembly. Tighten the nut on the pinion side until it just contacts the cup. With

Installing the pinion front bearing

PAINT MARKING INDICATES POSITION IN WHICH GEARS WERE LAPPED
Pinion and ring mesh timing

Driving out the differential pinion shaft

the dial indicator set at zero, tighten the pinion side nut until the case is spread 0.008–0.012 in. with new bearings and 0.005–0.008 in. with old bearings. As this preload is applied the ring gear is forced away from the pinion and usually results in the correct backlash.

g. Mount the dial indicator on the ring gear and check the gear for backlash. Make sure the bearing caps are torqued to 75–85 ft. lbs.

h. The backlash should be between 0.008–0.012 in. If the backlash is not correct, loosen one nut and tighten the other an equal amount to move the ring gear in or out to correct the measurement. When making final adjustments, always move the adjusting nuts in a tightening direction. To do this, if a nut had to be loosened one notch, loosen it two notches and tighten it one. This makes certain the nut is in contact with the cup and will not shift when the vehicle is in operation.

i. Coat the ring gear teeth with a marking compound and check the tooth pattern. If the pattern is not correct make the necessary changes to bring it into adjustment.

12. Install the carrier assembly in the vehicle and road test for proper operation.

Chevrolet and GMC Rear Axle Assemblies

The single speed rear axles used on the Chevrolet and GMC light and medium trucks are categorized by the ring gear diameter and are identified as follows:
7½, 8½, 8⅞ inch (corporation)   semi-floating axles
9¾, 10½ inch (Dana)   full floating axles
10½ inch (Corporation) full floating axles
12¼ inch (Corporation) full floating axles

Two speed axles are used by both Chevrolet and GMC trucks that are manufactured

by General Motors Corporation or by Eaton Corporation. The Eaton Corporation models can be identified by their use of a spiral bevel pinion gear arrangement, while the remaining axles are of the hypoid gear arrangement.

General Motors Corp. 7½ Inch Ring Gear Axle Assembly

REAR AXLE CASE

Removal

1. Before removing the rear axle case from the housing, ring gear to drive pinion backlash should be checked. This will indicate gear or bearing wear or an error in backlash or preload setting which will help in determining cause of axle noise.

2. Remove rear axle bearing cap bolts. Bearing caps should be marked "R" and "L" to make sure they will be reassembled in their original location.

Checking pinion preload

3. Remove rear axle case. Exercise caution in prying on carrier so that gasket sealing surface is not damaged. Place right and left bearing outer races and shims in sets with marked bearing caps so that they can be reinstalled in their original positions.

Disassembly

1. If rear axle side bearings are to be replaced, they must be removed using a puller.

2. Remove rear axle pinions, side gears and thrust washers from case. Mark side gears and case so they can be installed in their original location.

3. If ring gear is to be replaced and it is tight on case after removing bolts (L.H. Threads), drive it off using a brass drift and hammer. Do not pry between ring gear and case.

DRIVE PINION, BEARING AND RACES

Removal

1. Check drive pinion bearing pre-load. If there is no preload reading, check for looseness of pinion assembly by shaking. Looseness could be caused by defective bearings or worn pinion flange. If rear axle was operated for an extended period with very loose bearings, the ring gear and drive pinion will also require replacement.

2. Remove pinion flange nut and washer.

3. Remove pinion flange.

4. Install drive Pinion Remover J-22536 or its equal and drive out pinion. Apply heavy hand pressure on pinion remover toward rear axle housing to keep front bearing seated to avoid damage to outer race.

BEARING REPLACEMENT

Disassembly

The rear pinion bearing must be removed when it becomes necessary to change the pinion depth adjustment.

1. With drive pinion removed from carrier, press bearing from the pinion gear.

2. Drive pinion oil seal from carrier and remove front pinion bearing. If this

Installing the differential bearing

Backlash adjustment

bearing is to be replaced, remove outer race from carrier.

3. If rear pinion bearing is to be replaced, remove outer race from carrier using a punch in slots provided for this purpose.

CLEANING & INSPECTION

1. Clean all rear axle bearings thoroughly in clean solvent (do not use a brush). Examine bearings visually and by feel. All bearings should feel smooth when oiled and rotated while applying as much hand pressure as possible. Minute scratches and pits that appear on rollers and races at low mileage are due to the initial pre-load, and bearings having these marks should not be rejected.

2. Examine sealing surface of pinion flange for nicks, burrs, or rough tool marks which would cause damage to the seal and result in an oil leak. Replace if damaged.

3. Examine carrier bore and remove any burrs that might cause leaks around the O.D. of the pinion seal.

4. Examine the ring gear and drive pinion teeth for excessive wear and scoring. If any of these conditions exist, replacement of the gear set will be required.

5. Inspect the pinion gear shaft for unusual wear; also check the pinion and side gears and thrust washers.

6. Check the press fit of the side bearing inner race on the rear axle case hub by prying against the shoulder at the puller recess in the case. Side bearings must be a tight press fit on the hub.

7. Diagnosis of a rear axle failure such as: chipped bearings, loose (lapped-in) bearings, chipped gears, etc., is a warning that some foreign material is present; therefore, the axle housing must be cleaned.

DRIVE PINION

Assembly

1. If a new rear pinion bearing is to be installed, install new outer race.

2. If a new front pinion bearing is to be installed, install new outer race.

SETTING PINION DEPTH

Pinion depth is set with Pinion Setting Gauge J-21777-01. The pinion setting gauge provides in effect, a "Normal" or "zero" pinion as a gauging reference. Instructions are included in gauge set.

1. Make certain all of the gauge parts are clean.

2. Lubricate front and rear pinion bearings liberally with rear axle lubricant.

3. While holding pinion bearings in position, install depth setting gauge assembly.

4. Hold stud stationary with a wrench positioned over the flats on the ends of stud and tighten nut to 2.2 N·m (20 in. lbs.) torque. Rotate gauge plate assembly several complete revolutions to seat the bearings. Then tighten nut until a torque between 1.6

and 2.2 N·m (15 and 25 in. lbs.) is obtained to keep the gauge plate in rotation.

5. Rotate the gauge plate until the gauging areas are parallel with the discs.

6. Make certain rear axle side bearing support bores are clean and free of burrs.

7. Install the correct discs on the gauge shaft.

8. Position the gauge shaft assembly in the carrier so that the dial indicator rod is centered on the gauging area of the gauge block, and the discs seated fully in the side bearing bores. Install side bearing caps and torque bolts to 75 N·m (55 ft. lbs.). Use dial indicator J-8001 or an equivalent indicator reading from 0 to 2.5mm (0″ to 100″).

9. Set dial indicator at ZERO. Then position on mounting post of the gauge shaft with the contact button touching the indicator pad. Push dial indicator downward until the needle rotates approximately ¾ turn clockwise. Tighten the dial indicator in this position and recheck.

10. Rotate gauge shaft slowly back and forth until the dial indicator reads the greatest deflection. At the point of greatest deflection, set the dial indicator to ZERO. Repeat rocking action of gauge shaft to verify the ZERO Setting.

11. After the ZERO setting is obtained, rotate gauge shaft until the dial indicator rod does not touch the gauge block.

12. Record dial reading at pointer position. Example: If pointer moved counterclockwise 1.70mm (.067″) to a dial reading of .84mm (.033″), this indicates a shim thickness of .84mm (.033″) except as follows: Dial indicator reading should be within the range of .50 to 1.27mm (.020″ to .050″).

13. Loosen Stud J-21777-43 and remove gauge plate, washer and both bearings from carrier.

14. Position correct shim on drive pinion and install the drive pinion rear bearings.

REAR AXLE CASE

Assembly

Before assembling the rear axle case, lubricate all parts with rear axle lubricant.

1. Place side gear thrust washers over side gear hubs and install side gears in case. If same parts are reused, install in original sides.

2. Position one pinion (without washer) between side gears and rotate gears until pinion is directly opposite from loading opening in case. Place other pinion between side gears so that pinion shaft holes are in line; then rotate gears to make sure holes in pinions will line up with holes in case.

3. If holes line up, rotate pinions back toward loading opening just enough to permit sliding in pinion thrust washers.

4. After making certain that mating surfaces of case and ring gear are clean and free of burrs, thread two bolts into opposite sides of ring gear; then install ring gear on case. Install NEW ring gear attaching bolts just snug. NEVER REUSE OLD BOLTS. Torque bolts alternately in progressive stages to 120 N·m (90 ft. lbs.).

5. If case side bearings were removed, re-install bearings.

SIDE BEARING PRE-LOAD ADJUSTMENT

The side bearing pre-load adjustment is to be made before installing the pinion. If the pinion is installed, remove ring gear.

Case side bearing pre-load is adjusted by changing the thickness of both the right and left shims by an equal amount. By changing

Checking pinion depth

Installing case side bearings

the thickness of both shims equally, the original backlash will be maintained.

Production shims are cast iron and vary in thickness from 5.33 to 6.91 mm (.210″ to .272″) in increments of .05mm (.002″).

Standard service spacers are 4.32mm (.170″) thick and steel service shims are available from 1.02 to 2.08mm (.040″ to .082″) in increments of .05mm (.002″).

Do not attempt to reinstall the production shims as they may break when tapped into place. If service shims were previously installed, they can be reused, but (whether using new or old bearings) adhere to the following procedure in all cases.

1. Before installation of the case assembly, make sure that side bearing surfaces in the carrier are clean and free of burrs. If the same bearings are being reused, they must have the original outer races in place.

2. Determine the approximate thickness of shims needed by measuring each production shim or each service spacer and shim pack.

3. In addition to the service spacer, a service shim will be needed. To select a starting point in service shim thickness, use the following chart:

4. Place case with bearing outer races in position in carrier. Slip the service spacer between each bearing race and carrier housing with chamfered edge against housing.

Install the left bearing cap loose so that the case may be moved while checking adjustments. Another bearing cap bolt can be added in the lower right bearing cap hole. This will prevent case from dropping while making shim adjustments.

Select one or two shims totaling the amount shown in the right-hand column and position between the right bearing race and the service spacer. Be sure left bearing race and spacer are against left side of housing.

5. Insert progressively larger feeler gauge sizes .25mm, .30mm, .36mm, etc. (.010″, .012″, .014″, etc.) between the right shim and service spacer until there is noticeable increased drag. Push the feeler gauge downward until the end of the gauge makes

4.32mm (.170″) SERVICE SPACER

Total Thickness of Both Prod. Shims Removed	Total Thickness of Service Shims to be Used as a Starting Point
10.57mm .420″	1.52mm .060″
10.92mm .430″	1.78mm .070″
11.18mm .440″	2.03mm .080″
11.43mm .450″	2.29mm .090″
11.68mm .460″	2.54mm .100″
11.94mm .470″	2.79mm .110″
12.19mm .480″	3.05mm .120″
12.45mm .490″	3.30mm .130″
12.70mm .500″	3.56mm .140″
12.95mm .510″	3.81mm .150″
13.21mm .520″	4.06mm .160″
13.46mm .530″	4.32mm .170″
13.97mm .550″	4.83mm .190″

contact with the carrier bore so as to obtain a correct reading. The point just before additional drag begins is correct feeler gauge thickness. Rotate case while using feeler gauge to assure an even reading.

The original light drag is caused by weight of the case against the carrier while additional drag is caused by side bearing pre-load. By starting with a thin feeler gauge, a sense of "feel" is obtained so that the beginning of pre-load can be recognized to obtain Zero clearance. It will be necessary to work case in and out and to the left in order to insert the feeler gauge.

6. Remove left bearing cap and shim from carrier. The total shim pack needed (with no pre-load on side bearings) is the feeler gauge reading found in Step 5 plugs thickness of shims installed in Step 4.

7. Select two shims of approximately equal size whose total thickness is equal to the value obtained in Step 5. These shims will be installed between each side bearing race and service spacer when the case is installed in the carrier. The object of Step 7 is to obtain the equivalent of a "slip fit" of the case in the carrier. For convenience in setting backlash, the preload will not be added until the final step.

8. If the pinion is in position, install the ring gear, then proceed to REAR AXLE BACKLASH ADJUSTMENT.

DRIVE PINION, BEARING AND RACES

Installation

1. Install NEW collapsible spacer on pinion and position assembly in carrier. Lubricate pinion bearings with Rear Axle Lubricant before installing pinion.

2. Hold forward on pinion into case assembly.

3. Install front bearing on pinion and drive bearing on pinion shaft until sealed in race.

4. Position pinion oil seal in carrier. Install seal.

5. Coat lips of pinion oil seal and seal surface of pinion flange with Lubricant, No. 1050169 or equivalent. Install pinion flange on pinion by tapping with a soft hammer until a few pinion threads project through flange.

6. Install pinion washer and nut. Hold pinion flange. While intermittently rotating pinion to seat pinion bearings, tighten pinion flange nut until end play begins to be taken up. When no further end play is detectable and when holder will no longer pivot freely as pinion is rotated, pre-load specifications are being approached. No further tightening should be attempted until the pre-load has been checked.

7. Check pre-load by using an inch pound torque wrench. After pre-load has been checked, final tightening should be done very carefully. For example, if when checking, pre-load was found to be 0.6 N·m (5 in. lbs.), any additional tightening of the pinion nut can add many additional inch pounds of torque. Therefore, the pinion nut should be further tightened only a little at a time and the pre-load should be checked after each slight amount of tightening. Exceeding pre-load specifications will compress the collapsible spacer too far and require the installation of a new collapsible spacer.

While observing the preceding note, carefully set pre-load at 2.7 to 3.6 N·m (24 to 32 in. lbs.) on new bearings or 1.0 to 1.4 N·m (8 to 12 in. lbs.) on used bearings.

8. Rotate pinion several times to assure that bearings have been seated. Check pre-load again. If pre-load has been reduced by rotating pinion, reset pre-load to specifications.

REAR AXLE BACKLASH ADJUSTMENT

1. Install rear axle case into carrier, using shims as determined by the side bearing pre-load adjustment.

2. Rotate rear axle case several times to seat bearings, then mount dial indicator. Use a small button on the indicator stem so that contact can be made near heel end of tooth. Set dial indicator so that stem is in line as nearly as possible with gear rotation and perpendicular to tooth angle for accurate backlash reading.

3. Check backlash at three or four points around ring gear. Lash must not vary over .05mm (.00″) around ring gear. Pinion must be held stationary when checking backlash. If variation is over .05mm (.002″) check for burrs, uneven bolting conditions or distorted case flange and make corrections as necessary.

4. Backlash at the point of minimum lash should be between .13 and .23mm (.005″ and .009″) for all new gears.

5. If backlash is not within specifications, correct by increasing thickness of one shim and decreasing thickness of other shim the same amount. This will maintain correct

rear axle side bearing pre-load. For each .03mm (.001″) change in backlash desired, transfer .05mm (.002″) in shim thickness. To decrease backlash .03mm (.001″), decrease thickness of right shim .05mm (.002″) and increase thickness of left shim 0.5mm (.002″). To increase backlash .05mm (.002″), increase thickness of right shim .10mm (.004″) and decrease thickness of left shim .10mm (.004″).

6. When backlash is correctly adjusted, remove both bearing caps and both shim packs. Keep packs in their respective position, right or left side.

Select a shim .10mm (.004″) thicker than one removed from left side, then insert left side shim pack between the spacer and the left bearing race. Loosely install bearing cap.

7. Select a shim .10mm (.004″) thicker than the one removed from right side and insert between the spacer and the right bearing race. It will be necessary to drive the right shim into position.

8. Torque to 75 N·m (55 ft. lbs.).

9. Recheck backlash and correct if necessary.

10. Install axles.

11. Install new cover gasket. Install cover and torque cover bolts to 27 N·m (20 ft. lbs.).

12. Fill rear axle to proper level.

General Motors Corp. 10½ Inch Ring Gear Axle Assembly

This axle is a full floating type that uses special hypoid type drive and pinion gears. The pinion gear is supported by three bearings, two in front of the pinion gear and one behind. The differential assembly has either two or four pinions depending on the application of the axle. This axle assembly must be removed from the vehicle to remove and service the differential.

DIFFERENTIAL

Removal

1. With the axle assembly removed from the vehicle, place the axle assembly in a vise or holding fixture.

2. Remove the bolts that retain the cover assembly and remove the cover, allowing the gear lubricant to drain into a pan.

3. Remove the axle shafts from the axle assembly.

NOTE: Before going any further, check the pinion backlash and record the measurement so that if the same gears are reused they may be installed at the same backlash to avoid changing the gear tooth pattern.

4. From the bearing caps, remove the adjusting nut lock retainers.

5. Mark the bearing caps so they may

Loosening the adjusting nuts

be reinstalled in the same position and remove the bearing caps.

6. Loosen the side bearing adjusting nut and remove the differential carrier from the axle housing.

PINION ASSEMBLY

Removal

1. Remove the differential assembly from the axle.

2. Check the pinion bearing for the proper preload. The force required to turn the pinion should be 25–35 in. lbs. for used bearings. If there is no reading, shake the companion flange to check for any looseness in the bearing. If there is any looseness present the bearing should be replaced.

3. Remove the retaining bolts for the pinion bearing from the axle housing.

4. Remove the bearing retainer and pinion assembly from the axle housing. It may be necessary to tap the pilot end of the pinion shaft to help remove the pinion assembly from the carrier.

5. Record the thickness of the shims that are removed from between the carrier assembly and the bearing retainer assembly.

Differential bearing removal

Differential bearing installation

DRIVE PINION

Disassembly

1. With the pinion assembly clamped in a vise, install a holder assembly on the flange.

2. Using the proper size socket, remove the pinion nut and washer from the pinion. When reassembling the pinion use a new nut and washer assembly.

3. With the holder assembly still in place, use a puller to remove the flange from the pinion.

4. With the bearing retainer supported in a press, press the pinion out of the retainer assembly. Be careful not to allow the pinion gear to fall onto the floor because this can damage the gear.

5. Separate the pinion flange, oil seal, front bearing and the bearing retainer. If the oil seal needs to be replaced it may have to be driven from the retainer.

6. Using a drift, drive the front and rear bearing cups from the bearing retainer.

7. Support the pinion assembly in a

Removing retainer bolts

Removing pinion nut

press, with the bearing supported. Press the bearing from the pinion gear.

8. Using a drift, drive the straddle bearing from the carrier assembly.

Cleaning & Inspection

1. Clean off all the parts in solvent and blow dry.

2. Check the pinion gear for signs of wear, chips, cracks or any other imperfections. Check the splines for signs of wear or distortion.

3. Check the bearings for signs of wear or pitting on the rollers and races and check the bearing cage for dents and bends. Check the bearing retainer for any cracks, pits, grooves or corrosion.

4. Check the pinion flange splines for any signs of wear or distortion.

5. Replace parts that show any of the signs mentioned above.

DIFFERENTIAL CASE

Disassembly

1. Scribe a line across the two halves of the differential case so they may be reas-

sembled in the same position, and with the ring gear removed, separate the two halves. To remove the ring gear, remove the ring gear bolts and washers, and using a soft hammer tap the ring gear from the case.

2. Remove the internal parts from the inside of the case and set them aside in order that they may be reassembled in the same position.

Cleaning & Inspection

1. Check the differential gears, pinions, thrust washers and spider for any signs of unusual wear, chips, cracks or pitting.

2. Check all mating surfaces for signs of wear.

3. Replace parts that show any of the signs mentioned above.

DIFFERENTIAL CASE

Assembly

1. Using a good quality gear lubricant coat all of the parts.

2. Assemble the differential pinions and thrust washers onto the spider and install the assembly into the differential case.

3. Line up the scribe marks on the two halves of the differential case and install the ring gear. Install the ring gear washers and bolts and torque the bolts to approx. 10 ft. lbs.

SIDE BEARING

Replacement

1. Install a bearing puller on the bearing and remove the bearing assembly from the differential case.

2. Check the bearings for any signs of wear on distortion.

3. Install the new bearing by setting it in place on the differential case and, using a bearing driver, drive the bearing onto the case assembly until it seats against the shoulder on the case.

DRIVE PINION

Assembly & Adjustment

1. Coat all of the parts with a good quality gear lubricant.

2. With the pinion gear in a press, press the rear bearings onto the pinion assembly.

3. In the bearing retainer, install the front and rear bearing cups using a driver of the proper size.

4. In the axle housing, install the straddle bearing assembly using the proper size driver.

5. Install the bearing retainer with the bearing cups in place on the pinion gear and install a new collapsible spacer.

6. Press the front bearing onto the pinion gear.

7. Lubricate the oil seal with a good quality high pressure grease and install the seal into the retainer bore. Be sure to press the seal down until it rests against the internal shoulder.

8. Install the pinion flange and oil deflector onto the splines of the pinion gear and install a new lock washer and pinion nut.

9. With the pinion flange clamped in a vise and a holder assembly installed on the flange, tighten the nut to obtain the proper preload. Measure the amount of torque required to turn the pinion gear. For a new bearing the torque required is 25–35 in. lbs. and for an old bearing it is 5–15 in. lbs. To preload the bearing, tighten the pinion nut to approx. 350 ft. lbs. and take a reading of the torque required to turn the pinion. Continue tightening the nut until the proper preload is obtained.

--- **CAUTION** ---

Do not tighten the nut too tightly because it will collapse the spacer too much. This will make replacement necessary.

DRIVE PINION ASSEMBLY

Installation

1. If installing a new pinion gear, check the top of the new gear for the depth code number.

2. Compare the new number with the old number on top of the old pinion and check the pinion depth chart for preliminary setting of the pinion depth.

3. Check the thickness of the original shims removed from the pinion and either add or subtract from the shims according to the chart.

4. Place the shim on the carrier assembly and line the holes up with those in the axle housing. Make sure the surfaces are clean of all dirt and grease.

5. Install the retainer and pinion assembly in the housing making sure the holes line up and install the retaining bolts. Torque the bolts to approx. 45 ft. lbs.

DIFFERENTIAL CASE

Installation & Adjustments

1. Place the bearing cups over the side bearings on the differential assembly and place the unit into the carrier in the axle housing.

2. Install the bearing caps making sure the marks are lined up and install the bolts. Tighten the bearing retaining bolts.

3. Loosen the right side nut and tighten the left side nut until the ring gear comes in contact with the pinion gear. Do not force the gears together. This brings the gears to zero lash.

4. Back off the left side adjusting nut about two slots and install the lock fingers into the nut.

5. In this order tighten the right side adjusting nut firmly to force the case assembly into tight contact with the left side adjusting nut and then loosen the right side nut until it is free from the bearing.

6. Again retighten the right side adjusting nut until it comes in contact with the bearing. Tighten the right adjusting nut about two slots if it is an old bearing or three slots if it is a new bearing.

7. Install the lock retainers into the slots and torque the bearing cap bolts to 100 ft. lbs. This procedure now insures that the bearings are preloaded properly. If more adjustments are made, make sure the preload stays the same. To do this, one adjusting nut must be loosened the same amount the other nuts is tightened.

8. Install a dial indicator on the housing and measure the amount of backlash between the ring and pinion gear. The backlash should measure between 0.003 to 0.012 of an inch with the best figure being between 0.005 to 0.008 of an inch.

9. If the backlash is more than 0.012 of an inch, loosen the right side adjusting nut one slot and tighten the left side one slot. If the backlash is less than 0.003 of an inch, loosen the left side nut one slot and tighten the right side one slot. These adjustments should bring the backlash measurement into an acceptable range.

Measuring backlash

Pattern Check

1. Clean all the oil off the ring gear and using a gear marking compound, coat all of the teeth of the ring gear.

2. Make sure the bearing caps are torqued to 110 ft. lbs. and apply load to the gears while rotating the pinion. Rotate the ring gear one full turn in both directions.

Removing pinion rear bearing

Installing pinion rear bearing

NOTE: Load must be applied to the assembly while rotating or the pattern will not show completely.

3. Check the pattern on the ring gear and following the chart, adjust the assembly to get the contact pattern located centrally on the face of the ring gear teeth.

Removing flange

Removing straddle bearing

Pressing drive pinion from bearing retainer

		\+2	\+1	0	−1	−2
				CODE NUMBER ON ORIGINAL PINION		
CODE NUMBER ON SERVICE PINION	\+2	—	ADD .001	ADD .002	ADD .003	ADD .004
	\+1	SUBT. .001	—	ADD .001	ADD .002	ADD .003
	0	SUBT. .002	SUBT. .001	—	ADD .001	ADD .002
	−1	SUBT. .003	SUBT. .002	SUBT. .001	—	ADD .001
	−2	SUBT. .004	SUBT. .003	SUBT. .002	SUBT. .001	—

Pinion depth codes

Installing straddle bearing

General Motors Corp. 8½ and 8⅞ Inch Ring Gear Axle Assembly

This axle assembly is the semi-floating type with Hypoid type drive pinion and ring gears. The drive pinion gear is supported by two bearings. The differential case contains two pinion gears. The carrier assembly is not removable since it is part of the axle assembly but the design allows for the differential assembly to be serviced while the axle is still in the vehicle. The ring gear is bolted to a one piece differential case that is supported by two preloaded roller bearings.

DIFFERENTIAL CASE

Removal

1. Remove the inspection cover from the axle housing and drain the gear lubricant into a pan.

2. Remove the screw or pin that holds the pinion shaft in place and remove the shaft.

3. Push the axle shaft(s) in a little and remove the "C" locks from the ends of the shafts. Remove the axle shafts from the housing.

4. Before going any further, the backlash should be measured and recorded. This will allow the old gears to be reassembled at the same amount of lash to avoid changing the gear tooth pattern. It also helps to indicate if there is gear or bearing wear, and if there is any error in the original backlash setting.

5. Roll the differential pinions and thrust washers out of the case and also remove the side gears and thrust washers. Make sure to mark the pinions and side gears so they can be reassembled in their original position.

6. Mark the bearing caps and housing and loosen the retaining bolts. Tap the caps lightly to loosen them. When the caps are loose, take the bolts all the way out and then reinstall the bolts just a few turns. This will keep the case from falling out of the housing when it is pried loose.

Differential pinion shaft removal

7. With a pry bar, very carefully pry the case assembly loose. Be careful not to damage the gasket surface on the housing when prying. The case assembly may suddenly come free if the bearings were preloaded, so pry very slowly.

8. When the case assembly is loose, remove the bolts for the bearing caps and remove the caps. Place the caps so they may be reinstalled in the same position. Place any shims that are removed with the cap they were removed from.

Measuring rotating torque

DRIVE PINION

Removal

1. With the differential removed, check the pinion preload. Do this by checking the amount of torque needed to turn the pinion gear. For a new bearing, it should be 20–25 in. lbs., and for a used bearing it should be 10–15 in. lbs. If there is no preload reading check the pinion for looseness. If there is any looseness the bearing should be replaced.

2. With a holder assembly installed on the flange, use a socket of the proper size and remove the flange nut and washer.

3. Remove the flange by using a puller assembly and drawing the flange off the pinion splines.

4. Thread the pinion nut a few turns onto the pinion shaft. Using a brass drift and hammer, lightly tap the end of the pinion shaft to remove the pinion from the carrier. Be careful not to allow the pinion to fall out of the carrier after it breaks loose.

5. With the pinion removed from the carrier, discard the old seal pinion nut and collapsible spacer and install new ones when reassembling.

Cleaning & Inspection

1. Clean all parts in solvent and blow dry.

2. Check all of the parts for any signs of wear, chips, cracks or distortion. Replace any parts that are defective.

3. Check the fit of the differential side gears in the case and the fit of the side gear and axle shaft splines.

DIFFERENTIAL BEARING

Replacement

1. With a bearing puller attached to the bearing, pull the bearing from the case.

2. Place the new bearing on the case hub with the thick side of the inner race toward the case. Using a bearing driver, drive the bearing onto the case until it seats against the shoulder on the case.

Pushing the axle shaft inward

Drive pinion flange removal

DRIVE PINION BEARING

Replacement & Adjustment

1. Depending on the bearing that is being replaced, remove the front or rear bearing cup from the carrier assembly.

2. With the pinion gear mounted in a press, press the rear bearing from the pinion shaft. Be sure to record the thickness of the shims that are removed from between the bearing and the gear.

3. Using a bearing driver of the proper size, install a new bearing cup for each one that was removed. Make sure the cups are seated fully against the shoulder in the housing.

4. The pinion depth must now be checked to determine the nominal setting. This allows for machining variations in the housing and enables you to select the proper shim so that the pinion depth can be set for the best bear tooth contact.

5. Clean the housing and carrier assemblies to insure accurate measurement of the pinion depth.

6. Lubricate the front and rear pinion bearings with gear lubricant and install them in their races in the carrier assembly.

7. Using a pinion setting gauge, select the proper clover leaf plate, and install it on the preload stud.

8. Insert the stud through the rear bearing, with the proper size pilot on the stud, and through the front bearing using the proper pilot. Install the hex nut and tighten it until it is just snug.

9. Holding the preload stud with a wrench, tighten the hex nut until 20 in. lbs. of torque are required to rotate the bearings.

Positioning case for best clearance

Removing lock screw

A - SERVICE SPACER
B - SERVICE SHIM
C - FEELER GAUGE

PINION

BEARING

BEARING

CASE

CARRIER

A
B C

CARRIER

Tool J-22779

RING GEAR

EXAMPLE

	RING GEAR SIDE			OPPOSITE SIDE
.250"	Thickness of Tool J-22779 required to force ring gear into contact with pinion		Combined total of: Service Spacer (A) Service Shim (B) Feeler Gauge (C)	.265"
- .010" .240"	TO MAINTAIN PROPER BACKLASH (.005" - .008"), ring gear is moved away from pinion by subtracting .010" shims from ring gear side and adding .010" shims to other side			+ .010" .275"
+ .004"	TO OBTAIN PROPER PRELOAD on side bearings, add .004" shims to each side.			+ .004"
.244"	Shim dimension required for ring gear side		Shim dimension required for opposite side	.279"

Determining side bearing shim requirements

C-LOCK
THRUST BLOCK

C-LOCK

CORRECT   INCORRECT

C-LOCK

PINION SHAFT

THRUST BLOCK

Correct C-lock position

10. Install the side bearing discs on the ends of the arbor assembly, using the step of the disc that fits the bore of the carrier.

11. Install the arbor and plunger assembly into the carrier. Make sure the side bearing discs fit properly.

12. Install the bearing caps in the carrier assembly finger tight to make sure the discs do not move.

13. Mount a dial indicator on the mounting post of the arbor. Have the contact button resting on the top surface of the plunger.

14. Preload the dial indicator by turning it one-half revolution and tightening it in this position.

15. Use the button on the gauge plate that corresponds to the ring gear size and turn the plate so the plunger rests on top of it.

16. Rock the plunger rod back and forth across the top of the button until the dial indicator reads the greatest amount of variation. Set the dial indicator to zero at the point of most variation. Repeat the rocking of the plunger several times to check the setting.

17. Turn the plunger until it is removed from the gauging plate button. The dial indicator will now read the pinion shim thickness required to set the nominal pinion depth. Make a note of the reading.

18. Check for the pinion code number on the rear face of the pinion gear being used. This number will indicate the necessary change to the pinion shim thickness. If the pinion is marked with a plus (+) and a number, add that much to the reading you got from the dial indicator. If the pinion

Drive pinion nut removal

DRIFT

Removing drive axlion

TOOL

TOOL

TOOL

Wheel bearing removal

has no mark, use the reading from the dial indicator as the correct shim thickness. If the pinion is marked with a minus (−) and a number, subtract that much from the reading on the dial indicator.

19. Remove the depth gauging tools from the carrier assembly and install the proper size shim on the pinion gear.

20. Lubricate the bearing with gear lubricant and using a press, press the bearing into place on the pinion shaft.

Removing drive pinion rear bearing

PINION GEAR

Installation & Adjustment

1. Lubricate the front bearing with gear lubricant and install it in the front cup.

2. Install the pinion seal in the bore. Using a seal driver and the proper size gauge plate, drive the seal in until the gauge plate is flush with the shoulder of the carrier.

3. Coat the seal lips with gear lubricant and install a new bearing spacer on the pinion gear.

4. Install the pinion gear in the carrier assembly and using a large washer and nut, draw the pinion gear in through the front bearing far enough to get companion flange in place.

5. With the companion flange installed on the pinion shaft, use a holder assembly and tighten the pinion nut until all of the end play is removed from the drive pinion.

6. When there is no more end play the preload of the bearing should be checked. The preload of the bearing is the amount of torque required to turn the pinion gear. The preload should be 20–25 in. lbs. on new bearings and 10–15 in. lbs. on reused bearings. Tighten the pinion nut until these figures are reached. Do Not over tighten the pinion. This will collapse the spacer too much and make it necessary to replace it.

7. Turn the pinion gear several times to make sure the bearings are seated and recheck the preload.

Checking ring gear runout

RING GEAR

Replacement

1. Remove all of the bolts that hold the ring gear to the differential case and with a soft hammer, tap the ring gear off the case.

NOTE: Do not try to pry the ring gear off the case. This will damage the machined surfaces.

2. Clean all dirt from the case assembly and lubricate the case with gear lube. Align the ring gear bolt holes with the holes in the carrier and lightly press the ring gear onto the case assembly. Install all of the bolts and tighten them all evenly, using a criss-cross pattern to avoid cocking the ring gear.

3. When the ring gear is firmly seated against the case, tighten the bolts to 60 ft. lbs.

DIFFERENTIAL CASE ASSEMBLY

Installation & Adjustment

1. Install the thrust washers and side gears into the case assembly. If the original parts are being used, be sure to place them in their original position.

2. Place the pinions in the case so they are 180 degrees apart as they engage the side gears.

3. Turn the pinion gears so the hole in the case lines up with the holes in the gears.

Differential bearing installation

Measuring gauge plate thickness

Checking ring gear backlash

Installing pinion rear bearing cup

Gauging tools installed in carrier

Ring gear-to-case installation

Installing differential shims

When the holes are aligned, install the pinion shaft and lock screw. Do not tighten the lock screw too tightly at this time.

4. Check the bearings, bearing cups, cup seat and carrier caps to make sure they are in good condition.

5. Lubricate the bearings with gear lube. Install the cups on the proper bearings and install the differential assembly in the car-

Installing rear bearing

rier. Support the carrier assembly to keep it from falling.

6. Install a support strap on the left side bearing and tighten the bearing bolts to an even, snug fit.

7. With the ring gear tight against the pinion gear, insert a gauging tool between the left side bearing cup and the carrier housing.

8. While lightly shaking the tool back and forth, turn the adjusting wheel until a slight drag is felt. Tighten the lock nut.

9. Between the right side bearing and carrier, install a service spacer, 0.170 of an inch thick, a service shim and a feeler gauge. The feeler gauge must be thick enough so a light drag is felt when it is moved between the carrier and the shim.

10. Add the total of the service spacer, service shim and the feeler gauge. Remove the gauging tool from the left side of the carrier and using a micrometer, measure the thickness in at least three places. Average the readings and record the result.

11. Refer to the chart to determine the proper thickness of the shim packs.

12. Install the left side shim first, then install the right side shim between the bearing cup and spacer. Position the shim so the chamfered side is outward or next to the spacer. If there is not enough chamfer around the outside of the shim, file or grind the chamfer a little to allow for easy installation.

13. If there is difficulty in installing the shim, partially remove the case from the carrier and slide both the shim and case back into place.

14. Install the bearing caps and torque them to 60 ft. lbs. Tighten the pinion shaft lock screw.

NOTE: The differential side bearings are now preloaded. If any adjustments are made in later procedures, make sure not to change the preload. Do Not change the total thickness of the shim packs.

15. Mount a dial indicator on the carrier assembly with the indicator button perpendicular to the tooth angle and in line with the gear rotation.

16. Measure the amount of backlash between the ring and pinion gears. The backlash should be between 0.005–0.008 of an inch. Take readings at four different spots on the gear. There should not be variations greater than 0.002 of an inch.

17. If there are variations greater than 0.002 of an inch between the readings, check the runout between the case and ring gear. The gear runout should not be greater than 0.003 in. If the runout does exceed 0.003 in. check the case and ring gear for the deformation or dirt between the case and gear.

18. If the gear backlash exceeds 0.008 in., increase the thickness of the shims on the ring gear side and decrease the thickness of the shims on the opposite side, an equal amount.

19. If the backlash is less than 0.005 in., decrease the shim thickness on the ring gear side and increase the shim thickness on the opposite side an equal amount.

Gear Pattern Check

Before final assembly of the differential, a pattern check of the gear teeth must be made. This determines if the teeth of the ring and pinion gears are meshing properly, for low noise level and long life of the gear teeth.

The most important thing to note is if the pattern is located centrally up and down on the face of the ring gear.

1. Wipe any oil out of the carrier and wipe all dirt and oil from the teeth of the ring gear.

2. Coat the teeth of the ring gear with a gear marking compound.

3. With the bearing caps torqued to 55 ft. lbs., expand the brake shoes until it takes 20–30 ft. lbs. of torque to turn the pinion gear.

4. Turn the companion flange so the ring gear makes one full rotation in one direction, then turn it one full rotation in the opposite direction.

5. Check the pattern on the teeth and refer to the chart for any adjustments necessary.

6. With the gear tooth pattern checked and properly adjusted, install the axle housing cover gasket and cover and tighten securely. Fill the axle with gear lube to the correct level.

7. Road test the vehicle to check for any noise and proper operation of the rear.

Gauge plate installed

Installing pinion front bearing cup

Installing pinion oil seal

Pinion rear bearing removal

General Motors Corp. 12¼ Inch Rear Axle Models H110, H135, H150 and H170

DISASSEMBLY OF SUBASSEMBLIES

Differential Disassembly

1. Remove lock nut, adjusting screw, and thrust block.

2. Remove two adjuster lock cap screws and locks.

3. Punch-mark bearing caps and carrier to help in locating caps for assembly. Remove bearing adjusters and bearing caps.

NOTE: Do not pry caps free with a screwdriver or distort locating dowels.

4. Carefully remove differential assembly from carrier.

5. Use differential side bearing remover to pull bearing cones off each side of case.

Measuring rotating torque

6. Make sure that differential case halves are punch-marked so that they can be reassembled in same position.

7. Remove drive gear, and separate case halves.

8. Remove two side gears; differential spider, and four differential pinions.

9. Remove pinion and side gear thrust washers to complete differential disassembly.

Drive Pinion Disassembly

1. Remove seal retainer and gasket from carrier.

Pinion oil seal installation

Drive pinion front bearing removal

Pinion rear bearing lock ring installation

2. Use brass drift against inner end of pinion to drive out pinion and bearings assembly.

3. Remove shim pack from carrier from those models having tapered roller outer bearings.

4. According to the model, it may be necessary to use a drift to remove the pinion rear bearing.

5. Clamp yoke in soft-jawed vise. Remove yoke nut and washer and separate drive pinion from yoke.

6. Separate yoke from oil seal retainer.

7. Place retainer in a soft-jawed vise and, using a hammer and chisel, remove oil seal and then the felt oil seal.

8. On models with tapered roller outer bearing, remove bearing cup, outer tapered bearing cone, and bearing spacer from drive pinion.

9. Using bearing remover press plate with press, separate bearing cone (some models) or roller bearing (on all other models) from drive pinion.

10. On models H110 and H135, remove bearing lock ring, and use press plates with arbor press to remove roller bearing from inner end of drive pinion. This completes drive pinion disassembly.

ASSEMBLY OF SUBASSEMBLIES

NOTE: Thoroughly clean and lubricate all components with axle lubricant before reassembling.

Drive Pinion Assembly

1. Clean counterbore of oil seal retainer. Saturate felt seal in oil and install evenly in retainer. Soak oil seal in light engine oil for about one hour before installing. Coat outer surface of seal lightly with sealing compound to prevent oil leaks between seal and retainer.

2. Install oil seal into retainer with lip of seal toward inner side of retainer. Using a seal installer, press oil seal into retainer with face of seal flush with retainer face.

3. Retainer surface must be clean and smooth to prevent oil leaks between retainer and carrier.

4. On models H150 and H170, press bearing into place into carrier bore.

5. On models H110 and H135, press roller bearing into position on drive pinion with chamfered side of inner race facing toward pinion shoulder. Position bearing lock ring to secure bearing on drive pinion.

NOTE: Opposed tapered roller bearing cones, two bearing cups, and spacer used on some models are serviced and replaced as a unit. The spacer is a preselected one to provide proper bearing adjustment.

6. Models with tapered roller bearings:

a. Press inner bearing cone into place with largest side of cone facing pinion gear end.

b. Install original shim pack in carrier. If original ring gear and pinion are reinstalled, use shims that were removed. Shims are available in five thicknesses: 0.012, 0.015, 0.018, 0.021 and 0.024 inch. When using new gears, start with one 0.021 inch shim and refer to General Axle Service section for details on checking pinion depth.

c. Insert pinion assembly into carrier (on models H150 and H170), align roller bearing with carrier boss. Install bearing spacer, bearing cup and bearing cone with wide side facing pinion splines.

7. Models with double-row ball bearing: Using a 2-inch pipe or tubing, drive bearing unit into proper seating position.

8. With pinion assembly properly positioned in carrier, install new gasket. Install seal retainer onto yoke, and assemble yoke and retainer assembly onto splined end of drive pinion.

9. Secure retainer to carrier with lock washers and cap screws and torque to specifications.

10. Secure pinion assembly with yoke washer and nut and torque to 220 ft. lbs. This completes drive pinion assembly.

Differential Assembly

1. To facilitate installation of drive gear, install two guide pins (cut ½″–20 × 2″ bolts) in gear. Start guide pins through case flange holes and tap drive gear onto case. If one differential gear is bad, the complete set should be replaced.

2. Lubricate differential case inner walls and all component parts with axle lubricant. Place differential pinions and thrust washers on spider.

3. Assemble side gears, pinions and side gear and pinion thrust washers to left half of differential.

4. Assemble drive gear half (right half of differential, being sure to line up marks on the two halves.

5. Install differential-to-drive gear cap screw and lock washers and tighten evenly until drive gear is flush with case flange. Remove guide pins and install cap screws and torque to specifications.

Differential bearing removal

Differential bearing installation

Differential case alignment marks

6. Differential side bearing cones can be installed with special installer tool.

INSTALLATION OF SUBASSEMBLIES

Differential Installation

1. Install bearing cap locating dowels in caps. Lubricate side bearings and place bearing cups on bearings.

2. Install differential assembly into carrier. Carefully install bearing adjusters into carrier.

3. Install bearing caps, aligning punch marks previously made. Be sure that bearing adjuster threads are engaged with carrier and caps. Tighten adjusters alternately and evenly. Tighten bearing cap screws until lock washers are flat.

Drive Gear and Pinion Adjustment

1. Loosen bearing cap screws just enough to loosen right-hand bearing adjuster (pinion side) and tighten left-hand bearing adjuster (opposite pinion side.) Using adjuster, remove all backlash between drive gear and pinion.

2. Back off left-hand bearing adjuster about two notches to point where notch in adjuster is aligned with lock. Tighten right-hand bearing adjuster solidly to seat bearing. Again loosen right-hand adjuster enough to free bearing; then retighten snugly against bearing. Draw up right-hand adjuster one or two more notches until adjuster notch aligns with lock.

3. With dial indicator on carrier adjuster, slowly oscillate drive gear and take backlash reading. Backlash should be 0.005 to 0.008–inch.

4. If backlash exceeds 0.008–inch, loosen right-hand adjuster one notch; then tighten left-hand adjuster one notch. If less than 0.005 inch, loosen left-hand adjuster one notch and tighten right-hand adjuster one notch.

Checking backlash

Backlash and preload adjustment

5. After backlash has been adjusted, again tighten bearing cap screws until their respective lock washers flatten out.

6. Check drive gear run-out.

7. Install side bearing adjusting nut lock and secure with cap screws and lock washers.

Checking Pinion Depth (Models with Tapered Roller Bearings Only)

NOTE: Refer to tooth contact chart in the General Axle Service section.

1. Coat drive gear with red lead. Turn pinion shaft several revolutions in both directions while applying considerable drag on drive gear.

2. Pinion depth is determined by shim pack selection. Shim packs are available in thicknesses of: 0.012, 0.015, 0.018, 0.021, and 0.024-inch.

3. Changing pinion depth will again require adjusting backlash. After pinion depth and backlash have been adjusted, torque bearing caps to specifications.

Thrust Block Installation

1. Install thrust block and lock nut to adjusting screw. Thread screw and block into carrier until block contacts drive gear. Rotate gear and note change of drag. Adjust these parts until point of greatest drag is reached. Back screw off about a 30 degree turn to provide 0.005 to 0.007-inch clearance between block and gear. Make certain screw does not turn at all when tightening lock nut to 135 foot-pounds torque.

12¼ INCH REAR AXLE SPECIFICATIONS
Models H110, H135, H150 and H170

TYPE:	Hypoid
ADJUSTMENTS AND CLEARANCES:	
Backlash—Ring Gear To Pinion	0.005"–0.008"
Adjustment Method	See text
Pinion Depth Adjustment:	
Models With Tapered Bearings: Adjustment Method	Shims
Shim Pack Thickness:	
Initial	0.021"
Available	0.012", 0.015", 0.018", 0.021", 0.024"
Models With Ball Bearings: Adjustment Method	None
Backlash-Side Gear to Pinion Gear	0.007"–0.009"
Thrust Block To Gear Clearance	0.005"–0.007"
TOLERANCES:	
Ring Gear Run-out (Max. when mounted to case)	
H110	0.005"
H135, H150, H170	0.0065"
Differential Case Run-out At Flange (Max.): All Models	0.002"
Axle Shaft Run-out At Center of Shaft (Max.): All Models	0.016"
DIMENSIONS:	
Differential Case Diameter At Side Gear	
H110	2.193"–2.195"
H135, H150, H170	2.409"–2.411"
Side Gear Hub Diameter	
H110	2.189"–2.191"
H135, H150, H170	2.405"–2.407"
Pinion Gear (Inside Diameter)	
H110	0.879"–0.882"
H135, H150, H170	0.9415"–0.9445"
Thrust Washer Thickness: All Models	0.058"–0.062"
Diameter Of Spider Arms	
H110	0.874"–0.875"
H135, H150, H170	0.9365"–0.9375"
Thrust Block Thickness: All Models	0.1845"–0.1885"
Diameter of Axle Shaft Splines	
H110	0.874"–0.875"
H135, H150, H170	0.9365"–0.9375"

12¼ INCH REAR AXLE SPECIFICATIONS
Models H110, H135, H150 and H170

TYPE:	Hypoid
TORQUE VALUES:	
Ring Gear Bolts	
H110	118 ft. lbs.
H135, H150, H170	165 ft. lbs.
Differential Bearing Cap Bolts: All Models	205 ft. lbs.
Pinion Yoke Nut: All Models	220 ft. lbs.
Differential Bearing Adjuster Nut Lock Bolt: All Models	15 ft. lbs.
Differential Carrier To Housing Bolts: All Models	83 ft. lbs.
Thrust Block Lock Nut: All Models	128 ft. lbs.
Pinion Bearing Retainer Bolts	
H110	95 ft. lbs.
H135	98 ft. lbs.
H150	93 ft. lbs.
H170	165 ft. lbs.

Separating the case halves

International Harvester Co. Single Speed

The rear axles may vary as to the design and the construction, but the components of the axles perform similarly regardless of the type. The components of the rear axle that the serviceman will be concerned with are the drive gears, the differential assembly and the axle housing. The removal and installation of the carrier assembly is accomplished in the conventional manner, regardless of a single or tandem axle.

CARRIER ASSEMBLY

Disassembly

1. Mount the carrier assembly in a suitable fixture.

2. Remove the cotter pins from the bearing adjuster locks and remove the locks from the bearing caps.

3. Match mark the carrier legs to the bearing caps to identify properly upon reassembly.

4. Remove the ring gear thrust block and adjusting screw from the carrier housing.

5. Cut and remove the lock wire. Remove the bearing cap stud nuts or cap screws. Remove the bearing cap stud nuts or cap screws. Remove the bearing caps and adjusting nuts.

NOTE: Bearing cap pilot rings may be used on some axle models. Do not lose or damage.

6. Tip the differential assembly away from the pinion and lift the assembly from the housing.

Ring gear thrust pad adjustment

Spreading the gear carrier

Removing the rivets

Correct and incorrect backlash using worn gears

NOTE: Due to the weight of the differential assembly, a lifting device may be used to assist in the removal.

DIFFERENTIAL CASE AND GEAR ASSEMBLY

Disassembly

1. Match mark the differential case halves for the proper reassembly.
2. Cut the lock wire and remove the cap screws or stud nuts and separate the case halves.
3. Remove the spider, pinions, side gears and thrust washers from the case halves.

Rivet Size	Pressure Tons
7/16	18–20
1/2	20–25
9/16	36
5/8	45–50
3/4	50

4. Remove the ring gear rivets by center punching each rivet head and using a drill, 1/32 inch smaller than the rivet body, drill through the rivet head. Use a punch to press out the remaining part of the rivet.

——— CAUTION ———
Never use a chisel to cut off the head of the rivets or damage to the differential case can result.

PINION AND CAGE ASSEMBLY

Removal

1. Remove the pinion cage cap screws and remove the pinion cage assembly from the differential carrier.

NOTE: Puller screw holes are provided on some pinion cages, to assist in the removal of the cage from the housing. If no puller screw holes are present, a brass drift can be used on the inner end of the pinion to force the pinion and cage assembly from the carrier housing.

——— CAUTION ———
Do not use a drift on pinion shafts that have the straddle bearing retained by a snap-ring. The snap-ring groove may collapse.

2. Retain the shim pack for use during the reassembly.
3. Remove the companion flange from the pinion shaft, after the removal of the cotter pin and nut.

NOTE: The companion flange may have to be tapped off the pinion shaft with a soft hammer.

4. Remove the outer bearing from the cage by holding the cage in a vise and tapping on the pinion shaft end, and forcing the shaft through the cage.

——— CAUTION ———
Do not allow the component parts to fall.

5. Remove the spacer or spacer combination from the pinion shaft.
6. Remove the rear tapered thrust bearing from the pinion with the aid of a suitable puller.
7. Remove the straddle bearing retainer, if equipped, and remove the bearing with the aid of a suitable puller.

NOTE: The straddle bearing may be retained by staking of the pinion shaft end, by a snap-ring, or by a cap screw and washer.

8. Remove the cork seal, and oil seal from the pinion cage.

DIFFERENTIAL CARRIER ASSEMBLY

Precautions to be Observed During the Reassembly

1. Before assembly, lubricate the bearings and cups and rewrap to maintain cleanliness.
2. Use correct rivet pressure when installing the ring gear to the differential case, or if bolts are available, be assured that the proper torque is applied in tightening.
3. Be sure that the bearing caps and adjusting nuts are correctly aligned and that the bearing cups fit properly. Irreparable damage can result to the differential carrier or bearing caps if the alignment is off.
4. Observe the proper torque settings when tightening any nuts or bolts.

Five Steps in the Reassembly of the Differential Assembly

1. **Pinion bearing preload:** This is determined by the thickness of the spacer between the two pinion thrust bearings, when tightened in the pinion cage.
2. **Establish pinion nominal dimension:** Use the manufacturers pinion setting gauge (SE-1065), or use an equivalent tool. Changes to this dimension can be made by adding or removing shims to move the pinion in or out of the carrier housing.
3. **Set the ring gear lash:** Move the ring gear to or from the pinion by means of the differential bearing adjusters.
4. **Preload the differential bearings:** This is accomplished by tightening the bearing adjusting nuts after zero end play has been obtained on the bearings.
5. **Check the gear tooth contact:** Use the paint impression method for this operation.

Typical gear tooth contact patterns

DIFFERENTIAL CARRIER

Assembly

1. Install the ring gear on the differential case with either the rivet method or by bolts.

2. When installing rivets, observe the pressures needed to upset the rivets.

NOTE: Hold the pressure force for one minute to assure that the rivet will fill the hole.

3. Install the side gear and thrust washer in the ring gear half of the differential case.

4. Place the spider, the pinion gears and thrust washers in position and install the component side gear and thrust washer.

5. Align the previously made match marks and position the component case half to the ring gear case half.

6. Install the cap screws or stud nuts and torque to specifications.

7. Check the gears for freedom of movement and install the lock wire.

8. Install the differential bearings on the differential case.

PINION AND CAGE ASSEMBLY

Installation

1. Install the rear thrust tapered bearing and the straddle bearing on the pinion shaft.

2. Install the straddle bearing retainer.

NOTE: If the straddle bearing is of the type to be staked, use a blunt pin punch and stake in at least four to six equidistant places, approximately ⅛ inch in from the pinion circumference. The size of the pinion will dictate the number of staked points on the pinion end.

3. Renew the bearing cups in the pinion cage, as necessary.

4. Lubricate the bearings and cups and install the pinion shaft through the pinion cage.

5. Install the spacer or spacer combination on the pinion shaft, followed by the outer pinion tapered bearing.

6. Temporarily assemble the companion flange and the washer and nut onto the pinion shaft, tightening the nut to specifications while holding the flange in a vise.

7. To measure the pinion bearing preload, wrap a strong cord or soft wire around the pinion cage and attach the other end to a inch-pound scale. Rotate the pinion cage by pulling on the spring scale and reading the scale while the cage is rotating. Refer to the specifications listed within this chapter.

8. If the preload does not agree with the specifications, a thicker or thinner spacer or spacer combination must be used.

9. When the proper preload is obtained, assemble the pinion bearing cage by removing the companion flange, install the oil seal, cork gasket, reinstall the com-

panion flange, washer and nut. Torque the nut to specifications and install the cotter pin.

PINION NOMINAL DIMENSION

To locate the pinion nominal dimension, refer to the specifications listed within this chapter. Some pinions will have the dimension stamped or etched on the gear end of the shaft. Refer and compare to the specifications. The pinion variation, noted in thousands of an inch, will be etched on the gear end of the pinion shaft. This figure will be used in determining the amount of shims needed to locate the pinion gear in the proper relationship to the ring gear centerline.

NOTE: Refer to the beginning of the Rear Axle Drive section for the procedure to follow in the use of the pinion setting gauge tool. If the pinion setting gauge tools are not available, the pinion depth will have to be adjusted by assembling the carrier assembly, installing the pinion cage assembly and the differential assembly into the carrier housing, and observing the tooth contact pattern on the ring gear. This is a trial and error method and very time consuming.

DIFFERENTIAL ASSEMBLY

Installation, Preload, Backlash

1. Install the differential assembly with the bearing cups on the differential bearings into the legs of the carrier housing.

2. Install the bearing adjusting nuts and the bearing caps. Install the cap screws or stud nuts and turn the adjusting nuts while tightening the bearing caps to assure freedom of movement of the adjusting nuts.

——————— CAUTION ———————

If the bearing caps are not positioned properly, the adjusting nuts may be crossthreaded, and irreparable damage to the carrier housing or to the bearing cups may result.

3. With the side bearing caps loosened to permit the bearing cup movement, loosen the adjusting nuts only enough to notice end play on a dial indicator, mounted on the carrier assembly with the button contacting the back side of the ring gear.

4. Tighten the adjusting nuts to obtain zero end-play on the indicator.

5. Move the dial indicator to the coast side of the ring gear teeth, and determine the amount of back lash present between the pinion and the ring gear.

6. To adjust the back lash, move the ring gear towards or away from the pinion by means of the differential bearing adjusting nuts. Move the adjusting nuts the same distance, either in or out to maintain the differential bearing zero end-play.

7. When the correct backlash clearance is established, tighten each adjusting nut one or two notches (depending upon the axle model), to preload the differential bearings. Tighten the bearing cap screws or stud nuts to the proper torque and recheck the gear backlash. Install the adjusting nut locks and cotter pins.

8. Coat approximately twelve teeth of the ring gear with oiled red lead paint and rotate the pinion in its normal rotation and check the drive side of the ring gear teeth for the tooth contact impression.

NOTE: A sharper tooth contact impression may be obtained by applying a small amount of resistance to the gear with a flat steel bar and using a wrench to turn the pinion.

9. If the area of contact starts near the toe end of the ring gear and extends about ⅔ of the tooth length, the tooth contact is satisfactory.

10. Install the ring gear thrust block, if equipped. Adjust the block firmly against the back face of the ring gear and back off the screw ¼ turn and lock the jam nut.

11. Install the carrier assembly into the housing, following the reverse procedure of the removal operation.

LUV/Isuzu Differential

Removal

1. Raise vehicle on hoist.

2. Remove both wheel covers, wheel and tire assemblies, and brake drums.

3. Disconnect brake pipes at both rear wheel cylinders. Cover ends of pipes to prevent entry of foreign material into system.

4. Remove four through bolts from each end-flange.

5. Disengage axle shafts from carrier assembly and partially withdraw shafts from axle tube. It is not necessary to completely remove axle shafts. Move only enough to allow the differential to be removed.

6. Disconnect the propeller shaft at the companion flange and remove propeller shaft.

7. Remove eight nuts and two bolts mounting the differential carrier and case assembly to the axle housing.

8. Remove the carrier and case assembly and take to bench. On some bench operations, it may be advantageous to use a holding fixture. Tool J-21533 or equivalent is an available tool that works well for this purpose.

Disassembly

NOTE: Before disassembling, make a pattern check of the ring gear and pinion.

1. Mark the side bearing caps for reinstallation in the same position.

2. Remove the nuts and bearing caps, then remove the differential case and ring gear assembly. Keep the right and left side

1. Pinion Nut
2. Washer
3. Companion Flange
4. Oil Seal
5. Outer Bearing
6. Collapsible Spacer
7. Bearing Cap Stud
8. Differential Carrier
9. Bearing Cap
10. Inner Bearing
11. Depth Shim
12. Ring and Pinion
13. Side Bearing Shims
14. Side Bearing
15. Ring Gear to Case Bolt
16. Differential Case
17. Pinion Shaft Lock Pin
18. Thrust Washer
19. Differential Gear
20. Pinion Gear
21. Thrust Block
22. Pinion Shaft

LUV/Isuzu rear axle assembly

bearing races in separate groups for reinstallation in same positions.

3. Remove the differential side bearings from the case by using puller J-22888 and plug J-8107-2 or equivalent. Carefully record the thickness of each side bearing and each shim pack removed for later use in reassembly and keep separated.

NOTE: Puller arms must not pull against roller cage. Use care to position legs against inner race. As bearing is being removed, check for free rotation of bearing. If bearing does not rotate freely, check position of puller legs.

4. Remove the ring gear bolts and separate the ring gear from the differential case.

NOTE: Use care when removing ring gear to prevent damage to differential case or ring gear. Do not force a chisel or other tools between the joining faces.

5. Drive out the pinion shaft lock pin with a long drift. It may be necessary to first remove caulking in the lock pin with a 5mm drill.

6. Remove the pinion shaft with a drift and take out the thrust block, pinion gears,

side gears and thrust washers from the differential case.

7. Remove the pinion nut by use of Holder, J-8614-11 or equivalent. Save the pinion nut for pinion bearing preload adjustment procedure.

8. Remove companion flange by use of Nut J-8614-2, and Screw J-8614-3 or equivalent. Install nut onto screw; position nut into J-8614-11 or equivalent and rotate 45 degrees to locking position. Turn screw to draw companion flange off of the drive pinion splines.

9. Hold a soft metal rod against the end of the drive pinion. Drive the pinion from the carrier by using a hammer against the metal rod. The outer (front) bearing will fall loose in the carrier, while the inner (rear) bearing will remain pressed on the drive pinion. Both races will remain in the carrier bores.

10. Remove a rear bearing from the drive pinion by use of a press and tool J-22912-01 or equivalent.

11. Remove the oil seal and then drive the two outer races from the carrier by use of a drift.

Inspection

1. Wash the bearings in a suitable solvent. Then examine bearings carefully for wear, separation, cracks, seizure and other abnormal conditions. Replace bearings as necessary.

2. Check the ring gear and drive pinion teeth for wear, chipping, cracks, pitting, and abnormal contact. Check the drive pinion splines for cracks, distortion and step wear. Replace parts if needed. Ring gears and pinions come only in matched sets. If either item is defective, both parts must be replaced.

3. Check the pinion gears and side gears for wear, chipped teeth and separation, and replace if needed.

4. Check and replace the thrust blocks and thrust washers, if worn.

5. Check the lock pin for bending, dents and other abnormal conditions. Replace if necessary.

6. Check the side gear-to-axle shaft fit. Also check the fit of the pinion shaft to pinion gears.

7. Examine the contact surfaces between side gears and differential case, and between ring gear and case.

NOTE: It is important to clean and assemble parts with care and to follow adjustment procedures. Axles which are contaminated with dirt or other foreign material, or which are incorrectly adjusted may be noisy and have short life. Be sure to use new seals, gaskets and flange nuts when reassembling axle.

Setting Pinion Depth

1. Install the drive pinion front and rear bearing outer races into carrier bores. Use Drive Handle J-8092 with J-24256 for front bearing race and J-24252 or equivalent for rear bearing race.

2. Lubricate and position the front and rear bearings to be used for final assembly into their respective races.

3. Install gauging plate J-23597-7 and preload stud and pilot J-23597-9 or their equivalent through front and rear bearings and tighten nut snugly.

4. Rotate the bearings to insure proper seating and tighten lock nut until 2.2 N·m (20 lb. in.) of torque are required to rotate new bearings, and 1.0–1.2 N·m (8–10 lb. in.) for used bearings.

5. Place discs J-23597-8 onto arbor J-23597-1 or equivalent, and place tool into position in side bearing bores.

6. Install bearing caps snugly.

7. Mount dial indicator J-8001 or equivalent on arbor post, and preload dial one-half revolution. Tighten indicator in this position.

8. Position the indicator plunger on the gauge plate, and slowly swing across until the highest reading is obtained. "Zero" the indicator on the highest reading of the gauge plate.

9. Carefully swing the plunger off the gauge plate. Note the indicator reading. Re-

check to verify the reading. The reading on the dial is the correct dimension for the rear pinion depth shim, on a nominal pinion. Shims are available in sizes ranging from 2.18–2.56mm (.086 to .101"). An indicator reading of .000 or 0.03mm (.001") requires shims of 2.54 and 2.57mm (.100" and .101"), respectively.

a. Examine the head of the drive pinion. The pinion depth code is stamped by chemical ink and is in the lower position of the three numbers.

b. The number indicates a necessary change in the pinion mounting distance. A plus number indicates the need for a greater mounting distance (which can be achieved by decreasing the shim thickness). A minus number indicates the need for a smaller mounting distance (which can be achieved by increasing the shim thickness). If examination reveals no pinion depth code, the pinion is "nominal."

c. Use the chart to determine the proper shim variation to compensate for plus or minus markings.

Pinion Depth Code Number	Alter the Shim Thickness as Determined by Dial Indicator Reading, as Follows:
+ 10	Subtract 0.13 mm (.005")
+ 8	Subtract 0.10 mm (.004")
+ 6	Subtract 0.08 mm (.003")
+ 4	Subtract 0.05 mm (.002")
+ 2	Subtract 0.03 mm (.001")
0	Use Indicator Reading
− 2	Add 0.03 mm (.001")
− 4	Add 0.05 mm (.002")
− 6	Add 0.08 mm (.003")
− 8	Add 0.10 mm (.004")
−10	Add 0.13 mm (.005")

10. Place the shim on the drive pinion, then install the rear bearing, using J-6133-01 or equivalent.

NOTE: Do not press on roller cage. Press only on inner race.

PINION BEARING PRELOAD

1. Place the drive pinion and spacer into the carrier.

2. Lubricate, then position the front bearing to be used in final assembly into the carrier. Install new oil seal.

3. Mount companion flange to drive pinion. Apply hypoid lubricant to pinion threads. Install new pinion nut and torque to 115 N·m (85 lb. ft.), using J-8614-11 or equivalent to hold companion flange.

4. Remove J-8614-11 and rotate drive pinion to insure that bearings are seated.

5. Wind a small amount of string (approximately 4–6 windings) around the pinion flange. Connect scale to string. Note the scale reading required to rotate the flange.

6. Continue tightening pinion nut in small increments, using J-8614-11 or equivalent, until the pull required to rotate the flange becomes 7.7 kg (17 lbs.) for new bearings, 3.2–4.1 kg (7–9 lbs.) for used bearings.

NOTE: The pinion nut should be tightened only in small increments, and the pull scale should be used after each small amount of tightening. Exceeding preload specifications may compress the collapsible spacer too far and require its replacement.

Case Reassembly

1. Install the side gears and thrust washers in the differential case.

2. Position the pinion gears 180 degrees apart. Roll gears into position, making sure they are in alignment, to allow installation of the pinion shaft.

3. Place the thrust block between the pinion gears, and drive the pinion shaft into position. Make sure that the lock pin hole in cross shaft aligns with the hole in the case.

4. Measure the amount of backlash between the differential gears and the pinion gears. If the backlash is greater than 0.8mm (.003"), make the necessary adjustment with the thrust washers, available in thicknesses of 1.04, 1.14, 1.24 and 1.35mm (.041, .045, .049 and .053").

a. Increasing washer thickness will decrease backlash.

b. Decreasing washer thickness will increase backlash.

5. Install lock pin into cross shaft and caulk its end to prevent loosening.

6. Clean and apply primer to the bolts. Apply Loctite or equivalent to the threaded portion of the bolts. Install the ring gear in position on the differential case. Tighten the bolts in diagonal sequence to 110–120 N·m (80–87 lb. ft.).

SIDE BEARING PRELOAD/INITIAL BACKLASH SETTING

If the original side bearings, differential case, ring and pinion, and differential carrier are being reused, and if the pattern check taken before removal showed proper tooth contact, the original shims (or new shims of the same dimension) may be reinstalled in their respective positions.

If new side bearings only are being installed, and if the pattern check taken before removal showed proper tooth contact, this alternate procedure of shim selection may be used:

a. Measure the new bearing with a micrometer, and compare its thickness with the original bearing.

b. If the new bearing is thicker, subtract the numerical difference between new and old bearing from the original shim pack.

c. If the new bearing is thinner, add the numerical difference between old and new bearing to the original shim pack.

If new bearings and/or differential case, ring and pinion, or differential carrier are being installed, new shims will have to be selected for installation behind side bearings.

1. Install the side bearings to be used in final assembly onto the differential case. Do not install shims at this time. Use J-24244 or equivalent for the first bearing installation.

2. Support case on plug J-8107-2 or equivalent for opposite bearing installation.

3. Mount the case into carrier bores.

4. Move the ring gear tightly against the carrier on the ring gear side, away from the drive pinion, and hold in this position. Using a feeler gauge just thick enough to produce a slight drag, carefully measure the clearance between the bearing and differential carrier on the side opposite the ring gear. Record the result.

5. To determine the proper shims for installation, use the following procedure:

a. A predetermined dimension of 0.05mm (.002") is always needed to establish proper preload. Therefore, add 0.05mm (.002") (for proper preload) to the clearance measured in step 4. This will give the necessary combined total thickness of both shim packs.

For example, if the measure clearance was 1.12mm (.044"), the combined shims packs would be 1.12 + 0.05 = 1.17mm (.044 + .002 = .046").

b. Divide the total dimension into two shim packs, so that the numerical difference between the packs equals the numerical difference between the original shim packs.

For example, if the original packs measured 1.02 and 0.41mm (.040" and .016"), the difference between them was 1.02 − 0.41 = 0.61mm (.040 − .016 = .024"). If the new combined shim packs are to total 1.17mm (.046"), the individual shim packs would measure 0.89 and 0.28mm (.035" and .011"). The difference between 0.89 and 0.28mm (.035" and .011"), is 0.61mm (.024"); the same numerical difference as between the original packs.

6. Remove the case from the carrier. Carefully remove both side bearings. Install shims as determined in step 5 behind each bearing, install bearings onto case.

7. Install case onto carrier, tapping carefully into place. Install side bearing caps in original position. Tighten to 100 N·m (75 lb. ft.).

8. Measure the run-out of the ring gear. If the run-out exceeds 0.05mm (.002"), correct by cleaning or replacement of parts.

9. Mount a dial indicator against the ring gear teeth. Make sure indicator button is perpendicular to tooth travel. Measure backlash in three locations. Backlash should be 0.13–0.18mm (.005–.007").

10. If backlash is not within limits, the shims behind each side bearing will have to be adjusted. In order to maintain proper preload, whenever the backlash is adjusted, the total thickness of both shim packs must not be changed. Therefore, if it is necessary to increase one shim pack, the opposite shim pack must be decreased the same amount.

11. To increase backlash, the right side bearing shim must be increased, and the left side decreased.

12. To decrease backlash, the right side shim must be decreased, while the left side is increased. Backlash changes approximately 0.05mm (.002") for each 0.08mm (.003") shim change.

Gear Tooth Pattern Check

Prior to final assembly of the differential, a Gear Tooth Contact Pattern Check is necessary to verify the correct relationship between ring gear and drive pinion. Gear sets which are not positioned properly may be noisy, or have short life, or both. With a pattern check, the most desirable contact between ring gear and drive pinion for low noise level and long life can be assured.

The side of the ring gear tooth which curves outward, or is convex, is referred to as the "drive" side. The concave side is the "coast" side. The end of the tooth nearest center of ring gear is referred to as the "toe" end. The end of the tooth farthest away from center is the "heel" end. Toe end of tooth is smaller than heel end.

Test

1. Wipe oil out of carrier and carefully clean each tooth of ring gear.

2. Use gear marking compound and apply this mixture sparingly to all ring gear teeth using a medium stiff brush. When properly used, the area of pinion tooth contact will be visible when hand load is applied.

3. Hand load the companion flange and rotate the ring gear one revolution in each direction. Excessive turning of ring gear is not recommended.

4. Observe the pattern made on ring gear teeth. The contact pattern should be centrally located up and down on the face of the ring gear teeth.

Adjustments

Two adjustments can be made which will affect tooth contact pattern: (1) backlash, and (2) position of drive pinion in differential carrier. The effects of bearing preloads are not readily apparent on (hand loaded) tooth pattern tests; however, these adjustments should be within specifications before proceeding with backlash and drive pinion adjustments. It may be necessary to adjust both pinion depth and backlash to obtain the correct pattern.

The position of the drive pinion is adjusted by increasing or decreasing the shim thickness between the pinion head and inner race of rear bearing. The shim is used in the differential to compensate for manu-

facturing tolerances. Increasing shim thickness will move the pinion closer to centerline of the ring gear. Decreasing shim thickness will move pinion farther away from centerline of the ring gear.

Backlash is adjusted by means of the side bearing adjusting shims which moves the entire case and ring gear assembly closer to, or farther from the drive pinion. (The adjusting shims are also used to set side bearing preload.) To increase backlash, increase right shim and decrease left shim an equal amount. To decrease backlash, decrease right shim and increase left shim an equal amount.

Installation

1. Clean the faces of the rear axle case and differential carrier and apply a thin coat of liquid gasket and install the gasket.

2. Mount the differential case and carrier assembly to the rear axle case and tighten the nuts to 24 N·m (18 lb. ft.).

3. Install the axle shaft assemblies.

4. Connect the companion flange with the propeller shaft and tighten the bolts to 24 N·m (18 lb. ft.).

NOTE: This propeller shaft to pinion flange fastener is an important attaching part in that it could affect the performance of vital components and systems, and/or could result in major repair expense. It must be replaced with one of the same part number or with an equivalent part if replacement becomes necessary. Do not use a replacement part of lesser quality or substitute design. Torque values must be used as specified during reassembly to assure proper retention of this part.

5. Fill the rear axle case with hypoid gear lubricant, to just below the filler hole.

Mitsubishi/Arrow/D–50

Case Disassembly

1. Remove the lock plate, and then remove the side bearing nut using special tool (MB990201) or equivalent.

2. Remove the carrier cap. Then remove the differential case assembly using the wooden handle of a hammer or similar object so that gears and other parts will not be damaged.

3. Using a bearing puller pull off the side bearing.

NOTE: Keep the side bearings and side bearing nuts separate, so that they do not become mixed at the time of reassembly.

4. Make the mating marks to the differential case and the drive gear.

5. Loosen the drive gear mounting bolts in diagonal sequence, and then remove.

6. Remove the lock pin from the drive gear back side using a long punch. Then pull out the pinion shaft and the pinion gears.

The side gears with the side gear thrust spacers can then be removed.

NOTE: The removed side gears and side gear thrust spacers, left and right, should be retained for reassembly.

DRIVE PINION

1. Hold the end yoke with special tool (MB990850) or equivalent and after removing the self-locking nut, remove the end yoke.

2. Make the mating marks to the drive pinion and end yoke.

3. Tap the drive pinion end with a plastic hammer or a wheel puller and force out the drive pinion with the drive pinion height adjusting shim, drive pinion bearing (rear) inner race, drive pinion spacer and the drive pinion preload adjusting shim still installed on the drive pinion.

4. Using special tools (MB990339 and MB990648 or their equal) remove the drive pinion bearing (rear) inner race from the drive pinion. Remove the drive pinion height adjusting shim at the same time.

NOTE: The drive pinion height adjusting shim should be retained for reassembly.

5. Remove the drive pinion bearing (front and rear) outer race. When removing drive pinion bearing (front) outer race, remove oil seal and drive pinion bearing (front) inner race at the same time.

NOTE: The removed oil seal should not be reused.

INSPECTION

1. Check differential gear tooth contact. Replace any gear that is worn or damaged.

2. Check the bearing race curvature for discoloration caused by seizure, and rough surface. Replace any bearing that is defective.

3. Install the side gear onto the splined end of the axle shaft. Check for looseness of the axle shaft spline using a dial indicator on the side gear.

Description	Service Limit mm (in.)
Axle shaft spline looseness	0.6 (.024)

4. Check the differential pinion and pinion shaft for wear or seizure.

ASSEMBLY & ADJUSTMENT DIFFERENTIAL CASE

1. Install the side gear thrust spacers in their original positions behind the side gears. Then assemble the side gears (left and right) in the differential case.

2. With pinion washers attached to the

(1) End yoke (companion flange)
(2) Oil seal
(3) Drive pinion bearing, front
(4) Drive pinion preload adjusting shim
(5) Gear carrier
(6) Carrier cap
(7) Drive pinion spacer
(8) Drive pinion bearing, rear
(9) Drive pinion height adjusting shim
(10) Drive pinion
(11) Drive gear
(12) Differential case
(13) Lock plate
(14) Side bearing nut
(15) Side bearing
(16) Side gear thrust spacer
(17) Side gear
(18) Center block
(19) Pinion shaft
(20) Pinion gear
(21) Pinion washer
(22) Lock pin
(23) Packing

54 to 63 (40 to 47)

187 to 245
(138 to 180)

15 to 21
(11 to 15)

79 to 88
(58 to 65)

25 to 29 (19 to 21)

Tightening torque: Nm(ft-lbs.)

Exploded view Mitsubishi/Arrow/D-50 rear axle assembly

pinion gears, insert the both pinion gears at the same time and mesh with the side gears by rotating the pinion gears.

3. Complete the temporary assembly of the differential gears by inserting the pinion shaft.

4. Check the pinion gear and side gear backlash. If the backlash exceeds the repair limit, adjust it by selecting a side gear thrust spacer of proper thickness. The backlash, left and right, should be adjusted to an equal value.

Description	Standard Value mm (in.)
Pinion gear and side gear backlash	0.051 to 0.127 (.002 to .005)

TYPES OF SIDE GEAR THRUST SPACER

Part No.	Thickness of Spacer mm (in.)	
MB092034	0.8—0.08 —0.17	(.0315—.0031 —.0067)
MB092035	0.8—0.18 —0.27	(.0315—.0071 —.0106)
MB092036	0.8—0 —0.07	(.0315—0 —.0028)

5. Align the pinion shaft with the lock pin hole in the differential case, and drive the lock pin into the hole from the back side of the drive gear. Securely stake the lock pin at two places with a punch to prevent it from moving.

6. Remove old adhesive from the drive gear mounting bolts using a wire brush and from the internal thread using hand tap. Apply "LOCTITE 271" or equivalent anaerobic adhesive. Temporarily tighten each bolt evenly, and then tighten to the specified torque in a criss-cross fashion.

NOTE: Keep the differential stationary to harden the anaerobic adhesive for half an hour to one hour.

Adjusting Drive Pinion Height

1. Press the drive pinion bearing (front and rear) outer races into the gear carrier using special tools (MB990934, MB990936 and MB990938) or their equal. Use great care so that the outer race does not tilt and be sure the race bottoms in its bore in the gear carrier.

2. Install the drive pinion bearings and special tool (MB990819) or equivalent. Gradually tighten with the nut until the drive pinion preload becomes within the 0.7 to 1.0 N·m (6 to 9 in. lbs.).

— CAUTION —
When installing the washer, apply a thin coat of grease on the washer.

3. Mount the special tool (MB990552) or equivalent in the side bearing seat of the gear carrier, and then select a drive pinion height adjusting shim of a thickness which corresponds to the gap between the special tools (MB990552 and MB990819) or their equal.

NOTE: Be sure to clean the side bearing seat thoroughly. When mounting the special tool (MB990552) or equivalent, be sure that the cut-out sections are in the position shown in the illustration, and also confirm that the tool is in close contact with the side bearing seat.

4. Install the selected drive pinion height adjusting shim between the drive pinion and the drive pinion bearing (rear). Using special tool (MB990802) or equivalent, press the drive pinion bearing (rear) onto the drive pinion.

5. If the gear set is to be replaced, install new shims of the same thickness as the shims previously used on the drive pinion.

— CAUTION —
In determining the thickness of the shim pack, the amount of compression of the shim pack and wear of the bearing (when the old bearing is reused) should be taken into account.

Adjusting Drive Pinion Preload

1. Insert drive pinion preload adjusting shim between drive pinion spacer and drive pinion bearing (front). Tighten end yoke to specified torque, to obtain standard preload 9–11 in. lbs. with seal, 6–9 in. lbs. no seal.

If preload is wrong, install a preload adjusting shim of a different thickness until preload is in the standard value.

NOTE: Beside the drive pinion preload adjusting shims, the drive pinion spacers may be used for adjustment.

2. After completion of the drive pinion preload adjustment, remove the end yoke. Apply a thin coat of grease to the periphery of the oil seal, and drive it into the gear carrier using special tool (MB990031) or equivalent.

3. Next apply grease (cotaining 50% or more of molybdenum disulfide) to the oil seal lip contact surface of the end yoke shaft, insert the end yoke, and tighten the self-locking nut to the specified torque.

Side Bearing

1. Press in the side bearing inner race to the differential case using special tool (MB990802) or equivalent.

2. Place differential case assembly into gear carrier. Line up the mating mark on gear carrier with that on carrier cap, and tighten set bolts for tightening bearing cap to gear carrier with fingers. Then install side bearing nut, and tighten it on carrier cap to the specified torque 40–47 ft. lbs.

3. Screw in the side bearing nut on each side of drive gear using the special tool (MB990201) or equivalent to adjust the standard backlash value. Make sure the side bearing nuts are tightened to 50 N (11 lbs.) at end of special tool. Turn the bearing nuts in and out several times until they operate smoothly, then tighten them to the proper torque.

4. Apply a dial indicator to the drive gear tooth, and make certain that backlash is within the standard value.

NOTE: If the backlash is smaller than the standard value, loosen the side bearing nut on the back side of the drive gear and tighten the side bearing nut on the teeth side by the same amount.

5. After adjustment, tighten side bearing nut on both sides by a half pitch to give preload on side bearings. One pitch means space between two adjacent holes on the side of the side bearing nuts.

6. Measure the backlash again to ensure that it is within the standard value. Choose a lock plate of proper type, and tighten it to the specified torque 11–15 ft. lbs.

Drive Gear

1. Apply a dial indicator to the back of the drive gear and measure the amount of runout. Maximum Runout .002 in.

------ **CAUTION** ------
Measure the runout at 4 or more points.

MATCHED GEAR SET
IDENTIFICATION

Pinion and ring markings

2. If the runout exceeds the repair limit, change the mounting position of drive gear to differential case and measure the runout again. If the runout is still excessive, replace drive gear or the differential case as necessary.

Installation

During installation, observe the following items:

1. Apply gear oil to bearing and gear slide surfaces.

2. Apply a semi-drying sealer to axle housing and gasket.

3. Install carrier into axle assembly. Torque to 19–21 ft. lbs.

4. Install axle shafts.

5. Fill differential with SAE 80W-90 gear oil.

Rockwell-Standard 12 Inch Ring Gear

This rear axle is a full-floating type with a hypoid drive gear and pinion, and uses a four-pinion differential assembly. The straddle mounted pinion has two tapered roller bearings in front of the pinion teeth and a straight roller bearing behind the pinion teeth. The differential carrier assembly can be removed while the axle remains in the truck.

DIFFERENTIAL CARRIER ASSEMBLY

Removal

1. Remove axle shafts.

2. Drain lubricant. Disconnect propeller shaft at pinion shaft yoke.

3. Remove carrier from axle housing and clean thoroughly.

Disassembly

1. Punch mark carrier leg, bearing cap, and bearing adjusting nut to assist in reassembly.

2. Remove screws, adjusting nut locks, bearing caps and adjusting nuts.

3. Loosen lock nut and back off drive gear thrust block adjusting screw.

4. Lift differential out of carrier and remove thrust block from end of adjusting screw inside of carrier.

5. Punch mark differential case halves for correct reassembly alignment and separate case halves.

6. Remove pinion shaft, pinions, side gears, thrust washers and differential bearing cones.

7. To remove drive gear, carefully center punch each rivet in center of rivet head. Use a drill 1/32 inch smaller than the body of rivet to drill through the rivet head. Press out rivets.

8. Remove pinion shaft nut, washer and yoke. Driving yoke off will cause runout.

9. Remove pinion bearing cover and oil seal assembly and, using puller screws, remove bearing cage. Using a pinch bar to remove cage will damage shims. Driving pinion from inner end with a drift will damage bearing lock ring groove.

10. Wire bearing cage shim pack to-

Checking backlash

Pinion bearing preload check

Differential case assembly

①

②

③

④

Feeler Gauge Reading		Shim Required		Feeler Gauge Reading		Shim Required		Feeler Gauge Reading		Shim Required	
(mm)	(in)	(mm)	(in)	(mm)	(in)	(mm)	(in)	(mm)	(in)	(mm)	(in)
.889	.035	.127	.005	.584	.023	.432	.017	.279	.011	.737	.029
.864	.034	.152	.006	.559	.022	.451	.018	.254	.010	.0762	.030
.838	.033	.178	.007	.533	.021	.483	.019	.229	.009	.787	.031
.813	.032	.203	.008	.508	.020	.508	.020	.203	.008	.813	.032
.787	.031	.229	.009	.483	.019	.533	.021	.178	.007	.838	.033
.762	.030	.254	.010	.457	.018	.559	.022	.152	.006	.864	.034
.737	.029	.279	.011	.432	.017	.584	.023	.127	.005	.889	.035
.711	.028	.305	.012	.406	.016	.610	.024	.102	.004	.914	.036
.686	.027	.330	.013	.381	.015	.635	.025	.076	.003	.940	.037
.660	.026	.356	.014	.356	.014	.660	.026	.051	.002	.965	.038
.635	.025	.381	.015	.330	.013	.686	.027				
.610	.024	.406	.016	.305	.012	.711	.028				

Using the pinion depth gauge tool

Side bearing preload adjustment

DIFFERENTIAL BEARING NUT WRENCH—T70P-4067-A

Carrier mounted in the repair stand

Inspect all machined surfaces for nicks, burrs or scratches.

Assembly

1. Press drive pinion inner bearing cone firmly against pinion shoulder.
2. Press rear pilot bearings firmly against pinion shoulder and install lock ring into pinion shaft groove.

Thrust adjusting screw

gether to facilitate adjustment when reassembling.

11. Tap pinion shaft out of cage with soft mallet or press shaft from cage. Remove bearing from cage.

12. Remove spacers and inner bearing from shaft.

13. Remove pinion shaft rear pilot bearing lock ring, and then bearing.

14. Remove oil seal assembly from bearing cover.

15. Clean all parts thoroughly in a suitable solvent and blow dry with compressed air. Do not spin bearings with air pressure as they might score due to absence of any lubrication.

Inspect all parts for wear or roughness and replace if necessary. (For details, see Cleaning and Inspection in General Axle Service section).

15/32 DRILL

RIGHT

WRONG

Removing the rivets

Punch-marking the carrier leg

PART OF BEARING ASSEMBLY

PRESS BEARING THIS SURFACE

Bearing installation

Carrier identification marks

Removing the bearing cage

Removing the inner bearing

STRADDLE MOUNTED PINION
(Shown with parallel sided splines)

Gear set identification

3. Press bearing cups firmly against bearing cage shoulders.

4. Lubricate pinion bearings with SAE 90 oil and insert pinion and bearing assembly into pinion cage.

5. Place original spacers on pinion shaft, and install front bearing and press firmly against spacers. Rotate cage several revolutions to assure normal bearing contact. If a press is not available, install pinion yoke and nut and torque to specifications.

6. While the assembly is in the press under pressure or pinion nut torques to specifications, check pinion bearing pre-load. The correct pressures and torque for checking pre-load are:

7. Wrap a soft wire around cage and pull on horizontal line with pound scale when determining pinion bearing pre-load, first measure diameter of the pinion cage. Assuming cage diameter is 6 inches, the pulling radius would be 3 inches; therefore, 5 pounds pull on the scale would equal 15 inch-pounds pre-load.

8. Use rotating torque, not starting torque. If rotating torque is not within 5 to 15 inch-pounds, use thinner spacer to increase pre-load or thicker spacer to decrease pre-load. Torque must be near low limit inch-pounds with original pinion bearings and near high limit when using new bearings. Remove yoke and install new oil seal.

9. Lubricate pinion shaft oil seal and lightly coat outer edge of seal body with non-hardening sealing compound. Press seal against cover shoulder. Install new gasket and bearing cover.

10. Install pinion yoke, washer and nut. Place pinion and cage assembly over carrier studs, hold hoke and tighten nut to specified torque. Install cotter key without backing off nut to align cotter key holes.

11. Place original shim pack on carrier studs with thin shims on both sides to create maximum sealing. Position pinion and cage assembly over studs and tap into position with soft mallet. Install lock washers and nuts. Tighten nuts to specified torque. If a new pinion is being installed, consult the General Axle Service section for correct procedure.

12. Rivet drive gear to differential case using new rivets. Rivets should not be heated, but always upset cold. When correct rivet is used, head being formed will be at least ⅛ inch larger in diameter than rivet hole and approximately the same height

Installing the seal

Installing the flange

as performed head. Avoid excessive pressure as it might distort case holes and cause gear eccentricity. Unless shops are equipped to do cold upsetting of rivets properly, replacement bolts should be used.

13. Lubricate differential case inner walls and all component parts with rear axle gear lubricant during assembly.

14. Install thrust washer and side gear in drive gear half of case. Assemble pinions and thrust washers on pinion shaft and position this assembly in the case. Place other side gear and thrust washer in position on the four pinions.

15. Install other case half with mating marks aligned. Draw case down evenly with

Measuring preload torque

Aligning the mating marks

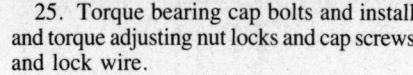

four bolts. Check for free rotation of differential gears and correct if necessary. Install and torque remining bolts and then lock wire.

16. Press differential bearings squarely and firmly on differential case halves. Differential bearing cup fit in the pedestal bores should be checked before installing assembly in carrier.

17. Temporarily install bearing cups, threaded adjusting nuts or split ring and bearing caps. Tighten cap bolts to specified torque. Bearing cups must be of a hand push fit in the bores; if not, the bores must be enlarged with a scraper or emery cloth. Use a blued bearing cup as a gauge to check each fit.

18. Lubricate differential bearings and cups with axle lubricant. Place cups over bearings and position assembly in carrier housing. Turn adjusting nuts hand tight against bearing cups.

19. Install bearing caps in correct location as marked, and tap lightly into position. Be sure caps fit over adjusting nuts properly and are not cross-threaded. Some backlash must be present between drive gear

and pinion. Install and torque bearing cap bolts.

20. Attach a dial indicator to the carrier with the pointer resting against back face of drive gear. Eliminate all end play by turning right adjusting nut clockwise. Rotate drive gear and check runout. If runout exceeds 0.008 inch, remove differential and check the cause.

21. Tighten adjusting nuts, one notch each, to pre-load differential bearings.

22. Position dial indicator so the pointer rests against face of one of the drive gear teeth. Check backlash between drive gear and pinion at 90 degree intervals of rotation.

23. Adjust backlash to 0.006–0.012 inch (0.006 preferred, especially on new gears). When adjusting backlash, back off one adjusting nut and advance opposite nut the same amount to maintain bearing pre-load.

24. If the Pinion Setting Procedures (depth gauge method) for adjusting pinion depth (see General Axle Service section) was not used, adjust gears using the tooth contact method. Then proceed to step 25. If depth gauge method was used, go directly to step 25.

25. Torque bearing cap bolts and install and torque adjusting nut locks and cap screws and lock wire.

26. Hold drive gear thrust block on rear face of gear with heavy grease, rotate gear until hole in thrust block aligns with adjusting screw hole in carrier. Install adjusting screw and lock nut, tighten screw enough to locate thrust block firmly against back face of gear. Back off adjusting screw ¼ turn to create 0.010–0.015 inch clearance and lock securely with nut. Recheck to assure minimum clearance of 0.010 inch during full rotation of drive gear.

Installation

1. Install a new gasket on axle housing flange. Start carrier into clean housing and hold in place with four equally spaced washers and nut. Tighten nuts alternately to draw carrier evenly into housing. Install and torque carrier flange lock washers and nuts.

2. Install axle drive shafts and connect universal joint at pinion flange.

3. Fill axle housing to proper level and road test vehicle.

Fitting the bearing caps

Checking the rotating torque

Adjusting the bearing preload

**PINION BEARING CAGE TO
CARRIER CAPSCREWS**

	GRADE 5 *	GRADE 7 *	GRADE 8 *
3/8''-16	25-35 LB. FT.	30-40 LB. FT.	35-50 LB. FT.

PINION SHAFT (INPUT) NUTS
1.0'' - 20   300-400 LB. FT.

**OIL FILLER PLUG
THREAD INTO CARRIER HOUSING
TO ALLOW ONE THREAD STAND OUT**

3/4''-14   35 LB. FT. MIN.

**GRADE IDENTIFICATION
FOR CAPSCREWS (HEAD MARKINGS)**

GRADE 5
GRADE 7
GRADE 8

**ADJUSTING RING LOCK
(SOME MODELS ONLY)**

**ADJUSTING RING LOCK TO DIFF.
BEARING CAP CAPSCREWS**

5/16''-18   20-30 LB. FT.

THRUST SCREW JAM NUT
3/4''-16   150-190 LB. FT.

DIFF. BEARING CAP TO CARRIER CAPSCREWS
9/16''-12   115-140 LB. FT.

**DIFF. CASE CAPSCREWS
(4 LONG & 8 SHORT)**
7/16''-14   60-75 LB. FT.

FOR ALL FASTENERS

- ALL TORQUES GIVEN APPLY TO PARTS LIGHTLY
  COATED WITH RUST PREVENTATIVE TYPE OIL

- FOR DRY PARTS - INCREASE TORQUES 10%

- FOR PARTS HEAVILY COATED WITH OIL
  - DECREASE TORQUES 10%

GEAR TO DIFF. CASE BOLT NUTS
1/2''-20   85-115 LB. FT.

Fastener torques

ROCKWELL–STANDARD BEARING PRELOAD

Axle Model	Pinion Shaft Nut–Thread Size and Torque Limits (ft. lbs.)		Press Ram Pressure for Preload Check (Tons)	Pinion and Cross Shaft Bearing Preload (in. lbs.)	Backlash Limits (in.)	Differential Bearing Preload Adjusting Nut Notches Tighten from Zero End Play (each Adjusting Nut)
Single–speed	1–20	300–400	6	5–15	0.005–0.015	1
Single reduction	1¼ × 18	700–900	11	5–15	0.005–0.015	1
	1¼ × 18	800–1100	14	5–15	0.005–0.015	1
	1½ × 12	800–1100	14	5–15	0.005–0.015	1
	1½ × 18	800–1100	14	5–15	0.005–0.015	1

Installing the bearing caps

Checking backlash

TORQUE SPECIFICATIONS

Carrier to housing screw or stud nut	½–20	94–102
	⅝–18	186–205
	¾–16	325–360
Differential case bolt	½–20	94–102
	9/16–18	132–145
	⅝–18	186–205
	¾–16	325–360
Differential bearing cap bolt	⅝–11–18	127–140
	¾–10–16	230–250
	⅞–9	345–370
	⅞–14	375–415
	1–12	555–615
Differential bearing adjuster lock bolt	5/16–18	15–17
	½–13	85–91
	9/16–12	120–129
	⅝–11	168–180
Pinion shaft yoke nut	1–20	300–400
	1–¼–18	700–900
	1–½–18	800–1100
	1–½–12	800–1100
	1–¾–12	800–1100
Shaft flange stud	7/16–20	52–58

Toyota Rear Differential

NOTE: If the differential is noisy, perform the following pre-inspection before disassembly to determine the cause of the noise.

1. Check ring gear runout. If the runout is greater than maximum, install a new ring gear.
Maximum runout:
½ ton and ¾ ton   0.07 mm (0.0028 in.)
C&C and 4 × 4   0.10 mm (0.0039 in.)
2. Check ring gear backlash. If the backlash is not within specification, adjust the side bearing preload or repair as nec-essary. Backlash: 0.13–0.18 mm (0.0051–0.0071 in.)
3. Check the tooth contact.
4. Using a torque meter, measure the total preload. Total preload (Starting): Drive pinion preload plus 4–6 kg-cm (3.5–5.2 in. lb.)

Disassembly

1. Remove differential case and ring gear. Put alignment marks on the bearing cap and differential carrier. Remove two adjusting nut locks.
2. Remove two bearing caps and two adjusting nuts. Remove the bearing outer races. Remove the differential case from the carrier.

3. Remove companion flange, oil seal and front bearing.
4. Remove drive pinion from differential carrier.
5. Remove drive pinion rear bearing using a universal puller.
6. Remove front and rear drive pinion bearing outer race, using a hammer and punch.
7. Remove ring gear from differential case.
8. Remove the ring gear set bolts and lock plates.
9. Using a brass bar and hammer, tap on the ring gear to separate it from the differential case.

——————— CAUTION ———————
Be careful not to damage the side bearing.

10. Remove the side bearings using a universal puller.
11. Disassemble differential case using a hammer and punch. Drive out the straight pin. Remove the pinion shaft, two pinion gears, two side gears and two thrust washers.
12. Inspect differential case parts.
13. Replace parts that are damaged or worn.

Inspection

1. Clean all parts with solvent.
2. Inspect drive pinion bearings and outer races. If the bearing or outer race are damaged or worn, replace them as a set.
3. Inspect ring gear and drive pinion. If the ring gear or drive pinion are damaged or worn, replace them as a set.

Toyota differential—exploded view

Toyota—4 × 4 and cab/chassis

4. Inspect pinion and side gears. If the pinion or side gears are damaged or worn, replace the gears.

5. Inspect side bearings and outer races. If the side bearings or outer races are damaged or worn, replace the bearing and race.

6. Check side gear backlash. Measure the side gear backlash while holding one pinion gear toward the case.
Standard backlash: 0.05–0.20 mm (0.0020–0.0079 in.)
If the backlash is out of specification, install the correct thrust washers.

Assembly

½ AND ¾ TON

1. Adjust drive pinion protrusion. Install the bearings and adjusting gauge (tool 09530-30012 and 09536-30030 or equivalent) in the differential carrier in the following order:
  (1) Rear bearing
  (2) Base rod
  (3) Drive pinion front bearing
  (4) Collar
  (5) Flange
  (6) Nut
  (7) Base rod head (SST 09536-30030) or equivalent
  (8) Bolt

NOTE: Tighten the bolt only to the point where the drive pinion gear has no play.

2. Place the master gauge on the differential carrier.

3. Align the marks and install the bearing caps. Torque the bearing cap bolts 51–65 ft. lbs.

4. Select a washer that can just be inserted into the clearance between the master gauge and the base rod.
Washer thickness .0878–1.075 in.
Remove the adjusting gauge.

5. Install rear bearing and washer on drive pinion using a press.

NOTE: The chamfered end of the washer should face toward the gear.

6. Coat the bearings with gear oil and install the drive pinion into the carrier.

7. Install new bearing spacer, front bearing and oil slinger.

8. Install new oil seal. Apply multipurpose grease to the oil seal.

9. Install companion seal.

10. Tighten drive pinion nut and adjust preload. Coat threads of a new nut with multipurpose grease. Torque nut to 80 ft. lbs. Turn the companion flange several times to snug down the bearing.

11. Using a torque meter, measure the preload of the backlash between the drive pinion and ring gear.
Preload:
New bearing: 12–19 kg-cm (10.4–16.5 in. lbs.)
Reused bearing: 6–10 kg-cm (5.2–8.7 in. lbs.)

Toyota—½ and ¾ ton

If preload is greater than specification, replace the bearing spacer.

If preload is less than specification, retighten the nut 5–10° at a time until the specified preload is reached.

If the maximum torque is exceeded while retightening the nut, replace the bearing spacer and repeat the preload procedure. Do not back off pinion nut to reduce the preload.
Maximum torque: 2,400 kg-cm (173 ft. lb.)

12. Using a dial indicator, measure the longitudinal and latitudinal deviation of the companion flange.
If the deviation is greater than the maximum, inspect the bearings.
Maximum
longitudinal deviation: 0.10 mm (0.0039 in.)
Maximum
latitudinal deviation: 0.10 mm (0.0039 in.)

CAB CHASSIS AND 4 × 4

1. Adjust drive pinion preload. Install the bearings, spacer, shim and adjusting gauge in the differential carrier in the order listed below:
  (1) Drive pinion rear bearing
  (2) Base rod
  (3) Spacer
  (4) Shim
  (5) Drive pinion front bearing
  (6) Collar
  (7) Flange
  (8) Nut
  (9) Base rod head (SST 09536-26010)
  (10) Bolt
SST 09530-30012 and 09536-26010 or equivalent

NOTE: Do not install the oil seal. Do not install the shim for drive pinion height.

2. Using a wrench to hold the collar, tighten the nut. Torque the nut 123–151 ft. lbs.

3. Using a torque meter, measure the preload.

Preload (starting):

New bearing: 19–26 kg-cm
(16.5–22.6 in. lb.)

Reused bearing: 9–13 kg-cm
(7.8–11.3 in. lb.)

If the preload is not within specification, correct by increasing or decreasing the number of shims.

4. Adjust drive pinion protrusion. Place the master gauge on the differential carrier. Align the marks and install the bearing caps. Torque the bearing cap bolts, 51–65 ft. lbs.

5. Select a washer than can just be inserted into the clearance between the master gauge and the base rod. Remove the adjusting gauge.

6. Using a press and special tool 09506-30011 or equivalent, press the washer and rear bearing on the drive pinion.

NOTE: The chamfered end of the washer should face the gear.

7. Install drive pinion, bearing spacer, shim, front bearing and washer in differential carrier. Coat the bearings with gear oil.

8. Install new oil seal.

9. Install companion flange.

10. Place the bearing outer races on their respective bearings. Make sure left and right races are not interchanged. Install the case in the carrier.

11. Install the adjusting nuts on their respective carrier. Make sure the nuts are threaded properly.

NOTE: Make sure that there is backlash between the gear and drive pinion.

12. Install the adjusting nuts. Align the marks on the cap and carrier. Screw in the two bearing cap bolts two or three turns and press down the bearing cap by hand.

NOTE: If the bearing cap does not fit tightly on the carrier, the adjusting nut threads are not threaded properly. Reinstall adjusting nuts if necessary.

13. To adjust side bearing preload tighten the bearing cap bolts until the spring washers are slightly compressed. Using an adjusting nut wrench special tool 09504-00010 or equivalent, tighten the adjusting nut on the ring gear side until the ring gear has a backlash of about 0.2 mm (0.008 in.).

14. Using an adjusting nut wrench, firmly tighten the adjusting nut on the drive pinion side.

15. Check the ring gear backlash. If tightening the adjusting nut creates ring gear backlash, loosen the nut so that backlash is eliminated.

16. Place a dial indicator on the top of the bearing cap on the ring gear side.

17. Adjust the side bearing for zero preload by tightening the other adjusting nut until the pointer on the indicator begins to move.

18. Tighten the adjusting nut 1 to 1½ notches from the zero preload position.

19. Using a dial indicator and adjusting nut wrench, adjust the ring gear backlash until the backlash is within specification. Backlash: 0.13–0.18 mm (0.0051–0.0071 in.)

NOTE: At this point the differential bearings are properly preloaded. If any additional adjustments are required, make sure that this proper preload remains. If one adjusting nut is loosened, the other nut must be tightened an equal amount to maintain this preload.

5. Mount a dial indicator on the housing and measure the backlash between the drive gear and pinion. Backlash should be from 0.003 to 0.012 inch with 0.005 to 0.008 inch preferred.

NOTE: If backlash is more than 0.012 inch, loosen the right adjusting nut one notch and tighten left adjusting nut one notch. If backlash is less than 0.003 inch, loosen the left adjusting nut one notch and tighten the right adjusting nut one notch.

Checking Pinion Depth

1. Thoroughly clean drive and pinion gear teeth.

2. Paint drive gear teeth lightly and evenly with a mixture of powdered red lead and oil.

3. Rotate pinion through several revolutions in both directions until a definite contact pattern is developed on drive gear. Apply pressure to drive gear while turning pinion. This will create load on gears to simulate a driving pattern.

4. Examine the pattern on drive gear teeth. If the pinion depth is correct, the tooth pattern will be centered on the pitch line and toward the toe of drive gear.

5. If the pattern is below the pitch line on drive gear teeth, the pinion is too deep and it will be necessary to remove the pinion assembly and increase the shim thickness between the pinion bearing retainer and the carrier.

6. If the pattern is above the pitch line on drive gear teeth, the pinion is too shallow and it will be necessary to remove the pinion assembly and decrease the shim thickness between the pinion bearing retainer and the carrier.

7. Changing the pinion depth will cause some change in backlash. Therefore adjust backlash to maintain correct specifications.

8. Torque bearing cap screws to specifications and recheck drive gear to pinion backlash. Install adjusting nut locks and torque to specifications.

9. Install oil trough to drive gear so that clearance is 0.03 to 0.09-inch. Torque retaining cap screws.

SHIFTER COMPONENTS

Installation

1. Position shift yoke in shift sleeve groove.

2. Slide yoke and sleeve assembly over sun gear. Splines of sleeve and sun gear should properly mesh.

3. Install shift lever through carrier housing into yoke mating splines together. Tap end of lever lightly to seat it in yoke.

4. Position the shifter unit and gasket over mounting pad, aligning lever in carrier with shift rod in shift unit.

NOTE: On axles equipped with electrical shift units, shift electrical leads must be connected to shift unit before installing unit to carrier.

5. Install and torque bolts.

6. Install differential assembly into axle housing.

NOTE: The backlash is adjusted by turning the left and right adjusting nuts equal amounts. For example, loosen the nut on the left side one notch and tighten the nut on the right side one notch.

20. Torque the bearing cap bolts 51–65 ft. lbs.

21. Recheck the ring gear backlash.

22. Measure the total preload. Total preload (Starting): Drive pinion preload plus 4–6 kg-cm (3.5–5.2 in. lb.)

24. Inspect tooth contact between ring gear and drive pinion. Adjust if needed.

25. Stake the drive pinion nut.

26. Install the adjusting nut locks.

27. Install differential carrier assembly in the axle housing.

28. Install axle shafts.

29. Connect the driveshaft.

30. Fill differential with SAE 80W-90 gear oil.

U-Joint/CV-Joint Overhaul

UNIVERSAL JOINTS

U-joint is mechanic's jargon for universal joint. U-joints should not be confused with U-bolts, which are U-shaped bolts used to connect U-joints to the differential pinion flange.

Universal joints provide flexibility between the driveshaft and axle housing to accommodate changes in the angle between them (changes of length are accommodated by the sliding splined yoke between the driveshaft and transmission). The engine and transmission are mounted rigidly on the car frame, while the driving wheels are free to move up and down in relation to the frame. The angles between the transmission, driveshaft and axle change constantly as the car responds to various road conditions.

To give flexibility and still transmit power as smoothly as possible, several types of universal joints are used.

The most common type of universal joint is the cross and yoke type. Yokes are used on the ends of the driveshaft with the yoke arms opposite each other. Another yoke is used opposite the driveshaft and when placed together, both yokes engage a center member, or cross, with four arms spaced 90° apart (the U-joint cross is alternately referred to as a spider, and the arms are called trunnions). A bearing cup (or cap) is used on each arm of the cross to accommodate movement as the driveshaft rotates. The bearings used are needle bearings.

A conventional universal joint will cause the driveshaft to speed up and slow down through each revolution and cause a corresponding change in the velocity of the driven shaft. This change in speed causes natural vibrations to occur through the driveline, necessitating a third type of universal joint: the constant velocity joint. A rolling ball moves in a curved groove, located between two yoke-and-cross universal joints, connected to each other by a coupling yoke. The result is a uniform motion as the driveshaft rotates, avoiding the fluctuations in driveshaft speed. This type of joint is found in cars with sharp driveline angles, or where the extra measure of isolation is desirable.

CROSS AND YOKE U-JOINT OVERHAUL

There are two types of cross and yoke U-joints. One type retains the cross within the yoke with C-shaped snap rings. The second type of joint is held together by injection molded plastic retainer rings. The second type cannot be reassembled with the same parts, once disassembled. However, repair kits are available.

Snap-Ring Type

1. Remove the driveshaft. For the correct procedure, see the car section for the model you are working on.

2. If the front yoke is to be disassembled, matchmark the driveshaft and sliding splined yoke (transmission yoke) so that driveline balance is preserved upon reassembly. Remove the snap rings which retain the bearing caps.

3. Select two sockets, one small enough

Typical driveshaft with cardan type U–joints

TRUNNION SEAL BEARINGS CAP SNAP RING

Snap ring type universal joint

to pass through the yoke holes for the bearing caps, the other large enough to receive the bearing cap.

4. Using a vise or a press, position the small and large sockets on either side of the U-joint. Press in on the smaller socket so that it presses the opposite bearing cap out of the yoke and into the larger socket. If the cap does not come all the way out, grasp it with a pair of pliers and work it out.

5. Reverse the position of the sockets so that the smaller socket presses on the cross. Press the other bearing cap out of the yoke.

6. Repeat the procedure on the other bearings.

7. To install, grease the bearing caps and needles thoroughly if they are not pre-greased. Start a new bearing cap into one side of the yoke. Position the cross in the yoke.

8. Select two sockets small enough to pass through the yoke holes. Put the sockets against the cross and the cap, and press the bearing cap ¼ inch below the surface of the yoke. If there is a sudden increase in the force needed to press the cap into place,

or if the cross starts to bind, the bearings are cocked. They must be removed and re-started in the yoke. Failure to do so will greatly reduce the life of the bearing.

9. Install a new snap ring.

10. Start a new bearing into the opposite side. Place a socket on it and press in until the opposite bearing contacts the snap ring.

11. Install a new snap ring. It may be necessary to grind the facing surface of the snap ring slightly to permit easier installation.

12. Install the other bearings in the same manner.

13. Check the joint for free movement. If binding exists, smack the yoke ears with a brass or plastic faced hammer to seat the bearing needles. Do not strike the bearings, and support the shaft firmly. Do not install the driveshaft until free movement exists at all joints.

Plastic Retainer Type

Remove and install the bearing caps and trunnion (cross) as described for the snap-ring type universal joints. On an original universal joint, however, the bearing caps will be secured in the yokes with injected

plastic. The plastic will shear when the bearing caps are pressed. Service snap-rings are installed in the groove on the inside (of yoke) of the installed caps.

BEARING FOR
SNAP RING RETAINER
NYLON RETAINER
SNAP RING
BEARING FOR NYLON RETAINER
GROOVE FOR SNAP RING

U-joint locking methods
(© Pontiac Div., G.M. Corp.)

Bearing removal

The driveshaft may be retained to the differential pinion by a flange (top) or by U-bolts or straps (bottom) (© Pontiac Div., G.M. Corp.)

Press a bearing cap into the yoke, then install the cross

BEARING RETAINER

BEARING CUP

ROUND PLASTIC WASHER

ROLLER BEARINGS

SEAL

FLAT PLASTIC WASHER

CROSS

Plastic retainer U-joint repair kit components

NOTE: The plastic which retains the bearing will be sheared when the bearing cup is pressed out. Be sure to remove the remains of the plastic retainer from the ears of the yoke. It is easier to remove the remains if a small pin or punch is first driven through the injection holes in the yoke. Failure to remove all of the plastic remains may prevent the bearing cups from being pressed into place and the bearing retainers from being properly seated.

CARDAN TYPE U-JOINT OVERHAUL

Some with Cardan type U-joints use snap rings to retain the bearing cups in the yokes. Other cars have plastic retainers. Be sure to obtain the correct rebuilding kit.

1. Use a punch to mark the coupling yoke and the adjoining yokes before disassembly, to ensure proper reassembly and driveline balance.

Service snap rings are installed inside the yoke

2. It is easiest to remove the bearings from the coupling yoke first. Follow the order indicated in the illustration.

3. Support the driveshaft horizontally on a press stand, or on the workbench if a vise is being used.

4. If snap rings are used to retain the bearing cups, remove them. Place the rear ear of the coupling yoke over a socket large enough to receive the cup. Place a smaller socket, or a cross press made for the purpose, over the opposite cup. Press the bearing cup out of the coupling yoke ear. If the cup is not completely removed, insert a spacer and complete the operation, or grasp the cup with a pair of slip joint pliers and work it out. If the cups are retained by plastic, this will shear the retainers. Remove any bits of plastic.

5. Rotate the driveshaft and repeat the operation on the opposite cup.

6. Disengage the trunnions of the spider, still attached to the flanged yoke, from the coupling yoke, and pull the flanged yoke and spider from the center ball on the ball support tube yoke.

NOTE: The joint between the shaft and coupling yoke can be serviced without disassembly of the joint between the coupling yoke and flanged yoke.

7. Pry the seal from the ball cavity, remove the washers, spring and three seats. Examine the ball stud seat and the ball stud for scores or wear. Worn parts can be replaced with a kit. Clean the ball seat cavity and fill it with grease. Install the spring, washer, ball seats, and spacer (washer) over the ball.

8. To assemble, insert one bearing cup

Cardan joint disassembly sequence

Cardan type joint

ALIGNMENT PUNCH MARKS

THIS NOTCH IDENTIFIES DRIVE SHAFT WITH REPLACEABLE BALL

LINK YOKE

BEARING

SOLID BALL

REPLACEABLE BALL

Match marks for double cardan joint

Solid and replaceable U-joint balls

part way into one ear of the ball support tube yoke and turn this cup to the bottom.

9. Insert the spider (cross) into the tube yoke so that the trunnion (arm) seats freely in the cup.

10. Install the opposite cup part way, making sure that both cups are straight.

11. Press the cups into position, making sure that both cups squarely engage the spider. Back off if there is a sudden increase in resistance, indicating that a cup is cocked or a needle bearing is out of place.

12. As soon as one bearing retainer groove clears the yoke, stop and install the retainer (plastic retainer models). On models with snap rings, press the cups into place, then install the snap rings over the cups.

13. If difficulty is encountered installing the plastic retainers or the snap rings, smack the yoke sharply with a hammer to spring the ears slightly.

14. Install one bearing cup part way into the ear of the coupling yoke. Make sure that the alignment marks are matched, then engage the coupling yoke over the spider and press in the cups, installing the retainers or snap rings as before.

15. Install the cups and spider into the flanged yoke as with the previous yoke.

NOTE: The flange yoke should snap over center to the right or left and up or down by the pressure of the ball seat spring.

CONSTANT VELOCITY JOINTS

Front wheel drive vehicles present several unique problems to engineers because the driveshaft must do three things, simultaneously. It must allow the wheels to turn for steering, telescope to compensate for road surface vibrations, and it must transmit torque continuously without vibration.

To compensate for these three factors a two-joint driveshaft allows the front wheels to perform these functions. This driveshaft mates disc type straight groove ball joint design with the bell type Rzeppa CV universal joint.

The Rzeppa joint on the outboard end of each driveshaft provides steering ability by allowing drive wheels to steer up to 43° while transmitting all available torque to the wheels. The inboard joint allows telescoping (up to 1½") through the rolling action of balls in straight grooves and operates at angles up to 20°. The combined action of these two ball type u-joints eliminates vibration.

The typical front wheel drive vehicle uses two driveshaft assemblies—one to each driving wheel. Each assembly has a CV–joint at the wheel end called the outboard joint. A second joint on each shaft located at the transaxle end is called the inboard joint. This joint may be either the ball or tripode type. It allows the slip motion required when the driveshaft must shorten or lengthen in response to suspension action when traveling over an irregular surface.

Constant velocity joints are precision machined parts that have difficult jobs to perform in a hostile environment. They are exposed to heat, shock, torque, and many thousands of miles of service. For this reason, the lubricants used are specially formulated to be compatible with the rubber boot and give proper lubrication. Most CV-joint repair kits have this special lubricant included.

NOTE: Wear pattern in a used ball or tripode CV-joint are impossible to match during reassembly. If there are any signs of wear, abnormal operating noise, corrosion, heat discoloration, the joint must be replaced.

TROUBLESHOOTING

Noises from the engine, drive axles, suspension and steering in the front drive cars can be misleading to the untrained ear. Ideally a smooth road serves best for detecting

Fixed CV joint

Ball style (Rzeppa) plunging CV joint

SHAFT REMOVAL

1. Remove the hub nut and discard it.
2. Drain the lubricant from the transaxle.

CAUTION
The lubricant may be hot.

operating condition(s) that cause noise.

• A humming noise could indicate that early stage of insufficient or incorrect lubricant.

• Worn driveshaft joints will cause a continuous knock at low speeds.

• A popping or clicking sound on sharp turns indicates trouble in the outer or wheel end joint.

• The clunk noise at acceleration from coasting or deceleration from a load pull indicates two possibilities—damaged inner or transaxle joint or differential problem(s).

• An inner joint will create a vibration during acceleration due to plunging action hanging up and releasing repeatedly. Probable cause would be foreign particles or lack of lubrication, or improper assembly.

• Remember that tires, suspension, engine, and exhaust system are all up front to add their noises.

• Make a check with front wheels elevated off ground. Spin the wheels by hand to determine if wheel bearing could be noisy or if out of round tires are causing vibration. Many wheel bearings are prelubed and sealed at the factory.

CAUTION
Personal injury can occur from spinning wheels by engine power. Spinning a wheel at excess speed may cause damage to CV-joints that could be operating at angles too steep when wheels are allowed to hang. Over speeding might also cause damage to tires and the differential.

3. The speedometer pinion gear assembly must be removed before the right drive shaft can be removed. (Automatic transaxles only).

4. Rotate the driveshaft to view the circlip.

5. Compress the circlip tangs with needle nose pliers as you pry into the side gear. This compresses the circlip in position for shaft removal later. Keep an awl between the differential pinion shaft and the end face of the shaft to prevent circlip reentry to the groove.

NOTE: This applies to Chrysler only.

6. Remove the ball joint clamp bolt. Drop the lower arm too allow clearance. This will permit the front wheel to swing free.

Typical CV driveshaft assembly

Closed tulip plunging CV joint   **Open tulip plunging CV joint**

7. Pull the outer splined shaft from the wheel hub, when swinging wheel hub away. Do not pull on the shaft. Grasp the joint housing.

8. Remove the inner joint by pulling outward on the inner joint housing. Do not pull the shaft.

NOTE: Do not allow the assembly to hang at either end. This can jam the CV-joint and cause vibration during operation. If necessary, support the shaft at either end by rope or wire.

INNER JOINT/BOOT

9. Place the assembly in a vise. Care must be taken not the crush the tubular shafts. Some shafts are solid steel.

10. If the inner joint needs replacement, cut the small rubber clamp, large metal clamp, and remove the rubber boot. These items must be discarded.

11. Inspect for internal wear and/or damage.

12. Clean the grease by hand from inside the joint housing and around the 3 ball trunnion assembly to inspect. Mark the tripod and housing for proper reassembly, if it is to be reinstalled.

13. To replace the boot, CV-joint, or both, remove the snap ring from the groove and tap the trunnion lightly with a brass drift pin. Leave the tripode bearings on the trunnion. Care must be taken to support the bearings as they may fall off.

14. Installation is the reverse of removal with the following recommendations: When reinstalling the tripode on the shaft place the chamfer face toward the retainer groove. The grease provided with the repair kit must be used. It can not be substituted with any other type grease.

OUTER JOINT/BOOT

1. Place the shaft in a vise. Be careful not to over tighten the vise thereby damaging the shaft.

2. Remove the boot and clamps. Discard these parts.

3. Using a soft hammer rap sharply on the housing. This forces the inner race over the internal circlip. Never remove the slinger from the housing.

4. Remove and discard the circlip. A new one is included with the boot kit. Leave the lock ring in place.

NOTE: Never disassemble the cage and balls from the housing. Reuse the joint assembly with a new boot kit, unless the grease is contaminated and prior diagnosis indicated trouble. In that case replace the joint and boot.

5. Installation is the reverse of removal.

Brakes

INDEX

HYDRAULIC BRAKE SYSTEM TROUBLE DIAGNOSIS

Condition	Possible Cause	Correction
Insufficient brakes	1. Improper brake adjustment. 2. Worn lining. 3. Sticking brakes. 4. Brake valve pressure low. 5. Slack adjuster to diaphragm rod not adjusted properly. 6. Master cylinder low on brake fluid.	1. Adjust brakes. 2. Replace brake lining and adjust brakes. 3. Lubricate brake pivots and support platforms. 4. Inspect for leaks and obstructed brake lines. 5. Adjust slack adjuster. 6. Fill master cylinder and inspect for leaks.
Brakes apply slowly	1. Improper brake adjustment or lack of lubrication. 2. Low air pressure. 3. Brake valve delivery pressure low. 4. Excessive leakage with brakes applied. 5. Restriction in brake line or hose.	1. Adjust brakes and lubricate linkage. 2. Check belt tension and compressor for output. Adjust as necessary. 3. Check valve pressure and clean or replace as necessary. 4. Inspect all fittings and lines for leaks and repair as necessary. 5. Clean or replace brake line or hose.
Spongy pedal	1. Air in hydraulic system. 2. Swollen rubber parts due to contaminated brake fluid. 3. Improper brake shoe adjustment. 4. Brake fluid with low boiling point. 5. Brake drums ground excessively.	1. Fill and bleed hydraulic system. 2. Clean hydraulic system and recondition wheel cylinders and master cylinder. 3. Adjust brakes. 4. Flush hydraulic system and refill with proper brake fluid. 5. Replace brake drums.
Erratic brakes	1. Linings soaked with grease or brake fluid. 2. Primary and secondary shoes mounted in wrong position.	1. Correct the leak and replace brake lining. 2. Match the primary and secondary shoes and mount in proper position.
Chattering brakes	1. Improper adjustment of brake shoes. 2. Loose front wheel bearings. 3. Hard spots in brake drums. 4. Out-of-round brake drums. 5. Grease or brake fluid on lining.	1. Adjust brakes. 2. Clean, pack and adjust wheel bearings. 3. Grind or replace brake drums. 4. Grind or replace brake drums. 5. Correct leak and replace brake lining.
Squealing brakes	1. Incorrect lining. 2. Distorted brakedrum. 3. Bent brake support plate. 4. Bent brake shoes. 5. Foreign material embedded in brake lining. 6. Dust or dirt in brake drum. 7. Shoes dragging on support plate. 8. Loose support plate. 9. Loose anchor bolts. 10. Loose lining on brake shoes or improperly ground lining.	1. Install correct lining. 2. Grind or replace brake drum. 3. Replace brake support plate. 4. Replace brake shoes. 5. Replace brake shoes. 6. Use compressed air and blow out drums and support plate and shoes. 7. Sand support plate platforms and lubricate. 8. Tighten support plate attaching nuts. 9. Tighten anchor bolts. 10. Replace brake shoes and cam-grind lining.
Brakes fading	1. Improper brake adjustment. 2. Improper brake lining. 3. Improper type of brake fluid. 4. Brake drums ground excessively.	1. Adjust brakes correctly. 2. Replace brake lining. 3. Drain, flush and refill hydraulic system. 4. Replace brake drums.
Dragging brakes	1. Improper brake adjustment. 2. Distorted cylinder cups. 3. Brake shoe seized on anchor bolt. 4. Broken brake shoe return spring. 5. Loose anchor bolt. 6. Distorted brake shoe. 7. Loose wheel bearings.	1. Correct adjust brakes. 2. Recondition or replace cylinder. 3. Clean and lubricate anchor bolt. 4. Replace brake shoe return spring. 5. Adjust and tighten anchor bolt. 6. Replace defective brake shoes. 7. Lubricate and adjust wheel bearings.

HYDRAULIC BRAKE SYSTEM TROUBLE DIAGNOSIS

Condition	Possible Cause	Correction
	8. Obstruction in brake line.	8. Clean or replace brake line.
	9. Swollen cups in wheel cylinder or master cylinder.	9. Recondition wheel or master cylinder.
	10. Master cylinder linkage improperly adjusted.	10. Correctly adjust master cylinder linkage.
Hard pedal	1. Incorrect brake lining.	1. Install matched brake lining.
	2. Incorrect brake adjustment.	2. Adjust brakes and check fluid.
	3. Frozen brake pedal linkage.	3. Free up and lubricate brake linkage.
	4. Restricted brake line or hose.	4. Clean out or replace brake line hose.
Wheel locks	1. Loose or torn brake lining.	1. Replace brake lining.
	2. Incorrect wheel bearing adjustment.	2. Clean, pack and adjust wheel bearings.
	3. Wheel cylinder cups sticking.	3. Recondition or replace the wheel cylinder.
	4. Saturated brake lining.	4. Reline front, rear or all four brakes.
Brakes fade (high speed)	1. Improper brake adjustment.	1. Adjust brakes and check fluid.
	2. Distorted or out of round brake drums.	2. Grind or replace the drums.
	3. Overheated brake drums.	3. Inspect for dragging brakes.
	4. Incorrect brake fluid (low boiling temperature).	4. Drain flush and refill and bleed the hydraulic brake system.
	5. Saturated brake lining.	5. Reline brakes as necessary.

HYDRAULIC BRAKES

NOTE: Procedures contained in this section apply to domestic and imported trucks.

Basic Hydraulic System

The hydraulic system controls the braking operation and consists of a master cylinder, hydraulic lines and hoses, control valves and calipers and/or wheel cylinders. When the brake pedal is depressed, the master cylinder forces brake fluid to the calipers and/or cylinders, via lines and hoses. Sliding rubber seals contain the fluid and prevent leakage.

Return springs in the master cylinder help the brake pedal return to the original unapplied position. Check valves (in most cases) regulate the return flow of the fluid to the master cylinder. Other valves, such as the metering valve, proportioning valve, or combination valve, regulate the flow of fluid to the caliper/wheel cylinder, to achieve efficient braking.

Single Braking Systems

On single brake systems, the master cylinder has only one piston which operates all of the wheel cylinders. The single brake system is confined to over-the-road trucks above 10,000 lbs. GVW, industrial and construction equipment.

Dual Braking Systems

The "dual" system differs from the "single" system by employing a "tandem" master cylinder, essentially two master cylinders (usually) formed by aligning two separate pistons and fluid reservoirs into one cylinder bore. Dual brake lines "split" the calipers and/or wheel cylinders into two groups, each actuated by a separate master cylinder piston. In event of failure of one of the "dual" systems, the other should provide enough braking power to safely stop the vehicle. The dual system usually includes a red warning light on the instrument panel which is activated by a pressure differential valve. The valve is sensitive to any loss of hydraulic pressure that might result from a braking failure on either side of the system.

Light trucks are equipped with either a front/rear wheel "split" or a diagonally "split" system. On front/rear systems, the front wheels are connected to one circuit while the rear wheels are connected to the other circuit. Diagonally split systems have diagonally opposite wheels connected to each circuit. Medium and heavy trucks may use the front/rear split or, if equipped with two wheel cylinders per wheel, each circuit will operate one cylinder per wheel.

Service Information

Servicing the hydraulic brake system is chiefly a matter of adjustments, replacement of worn or damaged parts and correcting the damage caused by grit, dirt or contaminated brake fluid. Always make sure the brake system is clean and tightly sealed when a brake job is completed and that only approved heavy duty brake fluid is used.

The approved heavy duty type brake fluid retains the correct consistency throughout the widest range of temperature variation, will not affect rubber cups, helps protect the metal parts of the brake system against failure and assures long trouble-free brake operation.

Never use brake fluid from a container that has been used for any other liquid. Mineral oil, alcohol, anti-freeze, or cleaning solvents, even in very small quantities, will contaminate brake fluid. Contaminated brake fluid will cause piston cups and the valve(s) in the master cylinder to swell or deteriorate.

Brake adjustment is required after installation of new or relined brake shoes. Adjustment is also necessary whenever excessive travel of pedal is needed to start braking action.

LOW PEDAL

Normal brake lining wear reduces pedal reserve. Low pedal reserve may also be caused by the lack of brake fluid in the master cylinder. The wear condition may be compensated for by a minor brake adjustment. Check fluid level in master cylinder and add as required.

FLUID LOSS

If the master cylinder requires constant addition of hydraulic fluid, fluid may be leaking past the piston cups in the master cylinder or brake cylinders, the hydraulic lines; hoses or connections may be loose or broken. Loose connections should be tightened, or other necessary repairs or parts replacement made and the hydraulic brake system bled.

FLUID CONTAMINATION

To determine if contamination exists in the brake fluid, as indicated by swollen, deteriorated rubber cups, the following tests can be made.

Place a small amount of the drained brake fluid into a small clear glass bottle. Separation of the fluid into distinct layers will indicate mineral oil content. Be safe and discard old brake fluid that has been bled from the system. Fluid drained from the bleeding operation may contain dirt particles or other contamination and should not be reused.

BRAKE ADJUSTMENT

Self adjusting brakes usually do not require manual adjustment but in the event of a brake reline it may be advisable to make the initial adjustment manually to speed up adjusting time.

AUTOMATIC ADJUSTER CHECK

Raise and safely support the vehicle, have a helper in the driver's seat to apply brakes. Remove the plug from the adjustment slot to observe adjuster star wheel. Then, to exclude possibility of maximum adjustment; that is, the adjuster refuses to operate because the closest possible adjustment has been reached; the star wheel should be backed off approximately 30 notches. It will be necessary to hold adjuster lever away from star wheel to allow backing off of the adjustment.

Spin the wheel and brake drum in reverse direction and apply brakes vigorously. This will provide the necessary inertia to cause the secondary brake shoe to leave the anchor. The wrap up effect will move the secondary shoe, and a cable or link will pull the adjuster lever away from the star-wheel teeth. Upon release of brake pedal, the lever should snap back in position, turning star wheel. Thus, a definite rotation of adjuster star wheel can be observed if automatic adjuster is working properly. If by the described procedure one or more automatic adjusters do not function properly, the respective drum must be removed for adjuster servicing.

HYDRAULIC LINE REPAIR

Steel tubing is used in the hydraulic lines between the master cylinder and the front brake tube connector, and between the rear brake tube connector and the rear brake cylinders. Flexible hoses connect the brake tube to the front brake cylinders or calipers and to the rear brake tube connector.

When replacing hydraulic brake tubing, hoses, or connectors, tighten all connections securely. After replacement, bleed the brake system at the wheel cylinders or calipers and at the booster, if equipped with a bleeder screw.

BRAKE TUBE

If a section of the brake tube becomes damaged, the entire section should be replaced with tubing of the same type, size, shape, and length. Copper tubing should not be used in the hydraulic system. When bending brake tubing to fit the frame or rearaxle contours, be careful not to kink or crack the tube.

All brake tubing should be double flared to provide good leak-proof connections. Always clean the inside of a new brake tube with clean isopropyl alcohol.

BRAKE HOSE

A flexible brake hose should be replaced if it shows signs of softening, cracking, or other damage.

When installing a new brake hose, position the hose to avoid contact with other truck parts.

Hydraulic Control Valves

PRESSURE DIFFERENTIAL VALVE

Also known as a "warning valve", "dash-lamp valve" or "system effectiveness indicator". The valve activates a panel warning lamp in event of pressure loss failure. As pressure fails in one "split" system, the other system's normal pressure causes a piston in the switch to compress a spring and move until an electrical circuit is completed lighting the dash lamp. On some vehicles the spring balanced piston automatically recenters when the brake pedal is released, thus flashing the warning lamp

Typical light duty pressure differential valve

Typical heavy duty pressure differential valve

only during brake application. On other vehicles the lamp will stay on until the cause of pressure loss is corrected.

Valves (pressure differential, metering or proportioning) may be located separately, but are usually part of a combination valve. On some brake systems the valve and switch are part of the master cylinder.

Re-setting Valves:

The pressure differential valve on many vehicles (equipped with a combination valve) will re-center automatically upon brake application after repairs to the system are completed. Other systems require manual resetting. Repair system as required, open a bleeder screw in the half of the system that did not fail. Turn on the ignition to light the warning lamp and slowly depress the brake pedal until the lamp goes out. If too much pressure is applied the piston will go to the other side and the procedure will have to be reversed by opening a bleeder screw in the opposite half of the system.

METERING VALVE

Often used on vehicles equipped with front disc and rear drum brakes, the metering valve improves braking balance during light brake applications by preventing application of the front disc brakes until pressure is built-up in the hydraulic system. The built-up hydraulic pressure overcomes the tension of the rear brake shoe return springs. Thus, when the front brake pads contact the rotor the rear brakes shoes move outward to contact the brake drum at the same time.

The metering valve should be inspected whenever the brakes are serviced. A slight amount of moisture inside the boot does not indicate a defective valve, however a great deal of fluid indicates a worn valve and replacement is indicated. Make sure to install the brake lines in the correct ports when installing a new valve, crossed lines will cause the rear brakes to drag.

If a pressure bleeder is used to bleed a hydraulic system that includes a metering valve, the valve stem (inside the boot on some valves) must either be pushed in or pulled out, depending upon the type of valve. Never apply excessive pressure that might damage the valve. Never use a solid block or clamp to force the valve open. If the valve must be blocked, rig the stem with a yieldable spring load and take care not to exert more than normal pressure.

If the brakes are to be bled manually using the brake pedal, the pressure developed is sufficient to overcome the metering valve and the stem need not be pushed in or pulled out.

PROPORTIONING VALVE

Used on vehicles equipped with front disc and rear drum brakes, the proportioning valve is installed in the line(s) to the rear drum brakes, and in a split system, below the pressure differential valve. By reducing pressure to the rear drum brakes, the valve helps to prevent premature lock-up during severe brake application and provides better braking balance.

Whenever the brakes are serviced, the valve should be inspected. To check valve operation, install hydraulic gauges ahead and behind the valve and determine that it has an operative transition point above which rear brake pressure is proportioned. If the valve is leaking replacement is required. Make sure the valve port marked "R" is connected to the rear brake line(s).

COMBINATION VALVE

A valve combining two or three functions (metering, proportioning, and/or brake warning) may be used. The combination valve is usually mounted under the hood close to the master cylinder, where the brake lines can be easily routed to the front and rear wheels. The combination valve is a non-serviceable unit, and if found to be malfunctioning, must be replaced as a unit.

Master Cylinder Service

NOTE: Servicing for "special types" are found after this section.

Removal & Disassembly

1. Clean the area around the master cylinder to prevent dirt and grease from contaminating the cylinder or the hydraulic lines. Disconnect the tubes, remove nuts or bolts that secure the master cylinder to fire wall or power brake, and remove the master cylinder.

On vehicles with manual brakes, the push rod must be disconnected from the brake pedal before removing the master cylinder.

2. Remove the reservoir cover, and drain the brake fluid from the reservoir. Then remove the piston stop bolt, if present, from the master cylinder. Remove boot and snap ring, then slide the primary piston assembly out of the master cylinder. Next, if dual system, remove the secondary piston assembly by tapping the master cylinder, or

RESERVOIR COVER

RESERVOIR DIAPHRAGM

RESERVOIR

RESERVOIR GROMMET

SPRING RETAINER

PRIMARY SEAL

SECONDARY PISTON

SECONDARY SEAL

MASTER CYLINDER BODY

SPRING

SECONDARY PISTON ASSEMBLY

PRIMARY PISTON ASSEMBLY

LOCK RING

Typical Delco master cylinder

Typical Chrysler master cylinder

by using needle nose pliers to pull from bore, or by carefully using compressed air. Disassemble the secondary piston assembly (unless a replacement is provided in the rebuilding kit).

3. Clamp the master cylinder in a vise with outlet ports facing up. Test for presence of check valve by probing with wire through hole in tube seats. Replace tube seat(s) and check valve(s) only if check valve is present and supplied in rebuild kit. Remove the tube seat inserts, if required,

by partially threading a self-tapping screw into each tube seat and using two small pry bars to pry each seat out of the master cylinder. Remove the residual check valve and the spring from the outlet(s) (if present).

Plastic Reservoir Cleaning and Removal

Plastic reservoirs need to be removed only for the following reasons:

A) Reservoir is damaged or the rubber

grommet(s) between the reservoir and bore is leaking.

B) Removal of stop pin from Chrysler style plastic reservoir master cylinder to allow removal of pistons. Pin is located underneath front reservoir nipple.

C) Service "Quick Take-up" valve on GM.

The reservoir should be removed by first clamping the flange in a vice. Next remove the reservoir for the Chrysler style. Grasp the reservoir base on one end and pull away from the body. GM reservoirs must be removed by prying between the reservoir and casting with a pry bar. Grommets can be reused if they are in good condition. Whether or not the reservoir is removed, it and the cover or caps should be thoroughly cleaned.

CLEANING AND INSPECTION

Thoroughly clean the master cylinder and any other parts to be reused in clean alcohol. DO NOT USE PETROLEUM PRODUCTS FOR CLEANING. If the bore is not badly scored, rusted or corroded, it is possible to rebuild the master cylinder in some cases. A slight bit of honing is permissible to clean up and smooth out the bore. A master cylinder rebuilding kit and fresh fluid should be used. If the cylinder bore is badly pitted or corroded, or if it has been rebuilt before, the master cylinder should be replaced with a new one.

Typical Ford master cylinder

─────── **CAUTION** ───────
Do not hone or repair a scratched or pitted bore of an aluminum master cylinder.

Replace the master cylinder. Be sure to note the relative positions of all the parts, paying particular attention to the way the rubber cups are facing. Lubricate all new rubber parts with brake fluid or brake system assembly lubricant.

Cast Iron Bore Clean-up

Crocus cloth or an approved cylinder hone should be used to remove lightly pitted, scored, or corroded areas from the bore. Brake fluid can be used as a lubricant while honing lightly. The master cylinder should be replaced if it cannot be cleaned up readily. After using the crocus cloth or a hone, the master cylinder should be thoroughly washed in clean alcohol or brake fluid to remove all dust and grit. If alcohol is used, dry parts thoroughly before reinstalling.

─────── **CAUTION** ───────
Other solvents should not be used.

Then the clearance between the bore wall and the piston (primary piston of a dual system master cylinder) should be checked. If a narrow (⅛" (3.2 mm) to ¼" (6.4 mm) wide) 0.006" (0.15 mm) feeler gauge can be inserted between the wall and a new piston, the clearance is excessive, and the master cylinder should be replaced. The maximum clearance allowed for units containing pistons without replenishing holes is .009" (0.23 mm).

Aluminum Bore Clean-up

Inspect the bore for scoring, corrosion and pitting. If the bore is scored or badly pitted and corroded the assembly should be replaced. Under no conditions should the bore be cleaned with an abrasive material. This will remove the wear and corrosion resistant anodized surface. Clean the bore with a clean piece of cloth around a wooden dowel and wash thoroughly with alcohol. Do not confuse bore discoloration or staining with corrosion.

Reassembly & Installation

1. Carefully install the new cups or seals in the same positions and in reverse order of removal.
2. Use brake fluid or assembly fluid very generously to keep from damaging the seals.
3. Placing the small end of the pressure spring into the secondary piston retainer, slide the assembly into the cylinder bore, taking care not to nick or gouge any rubber part.
4. Place the spring retainer of the primary piston assembly over the secondary piston shoulder and push both assemblies into the bore.
5. Install and tighten the piston retaining screw and gasket, while holding the

pistons in their seated positions. At the same time, reinstall any piston snap rings.
6. Install the residual check valve and spring in the proper master cylinder outlet (or both outlets, if originally present). If the tube seat inserts were removed, install new seats in both fluid outlets making sure that they are securely seated.

BLEEDING & CHECKING

NOTE: Be sure to bench bleed a rebuilt or new master cylinder before installation.

Check master cylinder vent port clearance by watching for a spurt of brake fluid in both reservoir vent holes when brake pedal is slightly depressed, indicating proper port clearance.

Quick Take Up—GMC

1. Depress the primary piston and remove the snap-ring.
2. Remove the primary and secondary pistons and return springs from the cylinder bore.
3. Disassemble the secondary piston.
4. Inspect the master cylinder bore. If it is corroded, replace the master cylinder. Never use abrasives on the bore.

NOTE: Always lubricate parts with clean, fresh brake fluid before assembly.

5. Install new seals on the secondary piston.
6. Install the spring and secondary piston into the cylinder.
7. Install the primary piston, depress and install the snap-ring.

Bendix Mini-Master

1. Remove the reservoir cover and diaphragm, and drain the fluid from the reservoir.
2. Remove the four bolts that secure the body to the reservoir using Chevrolet special socket number J-25085 or equivalent.

NOTE: Do not remove the two small filters from the inside of the reservoir unless they are damaged and are to be replaced.

3. Remove the small O-ring and the two compensating valve seals from the recessed areas on the bottom side of the reservoir.
4. Depress the primary piston using a tool with a smooth round end. Then remove the compensating valve poppets and the compensating valve springs from the compensating valve ports in the master cylinder body.
5. Remove the snap-ring at the end of the master cylinder bore. Then release the piston and remove the primary and secondary piston assemblies from the cylinder

bore. It may be necessary to plug the front compensating valve port to remove the secondary piston assembly.
6. Lubricate the secondary piston assembly and the master cylinder bore with clean brake fluid.
7. Assemble the secondary spring (shorter of the two springs) in the open end of the secondary piston actuator, and assemble the piston return spring (longer spring) on the projection at the rear of the secondary piston.
8. Insert the secondary piston assembly, actuator end first, into the master cylinder bore and press the assembly to the bottom of the bore.
9. Lubricate the primary piston assembly with clean brake fluid. Insert the primary piston assembly, actuator end first, into the bore.
10. Place the snap-ring over a smooth round ended tool and depress the pistons in the bore.
11. Assemble the retaining ring in the groove in the cylinder bore.
12. Assemble the compensating valve seals and the small O-ring seal in the recesses on the bottom of the reservoir. Be sure that all seals are fully seated.
13. While holding the pistons depressed, assemble the compensating valve springs and the compensating valve poppets in the compensating valve ports.
14. Holding the pistons compressed, position the reservoir on the master cylinder body and secure it with the four mounting bolts. Torque the bolts to 12–15 ft. lbs. (16–20 Nm).

Bleeding Brakes

BENCH BLEEDING PROCEDURES

Bench bleeding master cylinders before installation saves time and money. In order to expel *all* air trapped in the cylinder, tandem master cylinders must be bench bled before they are installed on the vehicle. Bench bleeding reduces the possibility of air getting in the brake lines. Follow this simple procedure for bench bleeding:

1. Route two shortened brake lines from the outlet connection(s) into the fluid reservoir(s), below the normal fluid level.
2. Fill the reservoir(s) with fresh brake fluid and pump the cylinder until air bubbles no longer appear in the reservoir. If the cylinder does not have a check valve at the outlet port, use a *clean* piece of rubber or plastic, or the end of your finger to close off the end of the tubing during the back stroke. Otherwise, the fluid will merely pump back and forth in the tubing.
3. When all air has been purged from the master cylinder, bend the tubes up out of the fluid, and remove them. Refill the cylinder and securely install the master cylinder cap.

4. Install the master cylinder on the vehicle. Attach the lines, but do not tighten the tube connection.

5. Force out any air that might have been trapped in the connection by *slowly* depressing the pedal several times. Tighten the nut slightly before releasing pedal, and loosen before depressing each time. Catch the fluid in a rag to avoid damaging car finish. DO NOT BOTTOM THE PISTON. Tighten the connections when air bubbles are no longer present in the fluid. Make sure the master cylinder is adequately filled with brake fluid.

MANUAL BLEEDING

NOTE: See below for GM "Quick Take-Up" cylinder bleeding sequence

Bleed the longest line first on the individual system (i.e. front/rear split or diagonally-front wheel, opposite side rear wheel split. If a single system, the right rear is usually the longest.) being serviced. *During the complete bleeding operation, do not allow the reservoir to run dry.* Keep the master cylinder reservoirs filled with the specified brake fluid. *Never use brake fluid that has been drained from the hydraulic system.*

1. Bleed the master cylinder at the outlet port side of the system being serviced.

NOTE: On a master cylinder without bleed screws, loosen the master cylinder to hydraulic line nut. Operate the brake pedal slowly until the brake fluid at the outlet connection is free of bubbles, then tighten the tube nut to the specified torque. Do not use the secondary piston stop screw located on the bottom of the master cylinder to bleed the brake system. Loosening or removing this screw could result in damage to the secondary piston or stop screw. Operate the brake pedal slowly until the brake fluid at the outlet connection is free of air bubbles, then tighten the bleed screw.

2. Position a suitable size (usually ⅜″) box wrench on the bleeder fitting on the cylinder or caliper to be bled. Attach a rubber drain tube to the bleeder fitting. The end of the tube should fit snugly around the bleeder fitting.

3. Submerge the free end of the tube in a container partially filled with clean brake fluid, and loosen the bleeder fitting approximately ¾ turn.

4. Push the brake pedal down slowly thru its full travel. Close the bleeder fitting, then return the pedal to the full-released position. Repeat this operation until air bubbles cease to appear at the submerged end of the bleeder tube.

5. When the fluid is completely free of air bubbles, close the bleeder fitting and remove the bleeder tube.

6. Repeat this procedure at the brake cylinder or caliper on the other side of the "split" system. Refill the master cylinder reservoir after each cylinder or caliper is bled.

When the bleeding is complete, the master cylinder fluid level should be filled to within ¼″ from the top of the reservoirs.

7. Centralize the pressure differential valve.

GM QUICK TAKE UP MASTER CYLINDER

General Motors specifies that these diagonally split dual systems be bled in this order: Right Rear, Left Front, Left Rear, Right Front.

Special procedures are required to manually bleed the quick take-up brake system used on some General Motors vehicles. Bleed the master cylinder first. Disconnect the left front brake line at the master cylinder, and fill the master cylinder until fluid flows from the port.

—— CAUTION ——
Catch fluid in a rag and don't allow fluid or rag to contact car finish.

Connect the line and tighten fitting.

Depress the brake pedal *one time slowly* and hold. Loosen same brake line fitting to purge air from the system. Retighten the fitting and release the brake pedal slowly. *Wait 15 seconds*. Then repeat the sequence, including the 15 second wait until all air is removed.

Next bleed the right front connection in the same way as the left front.

Bleed the wheel cylinders and calipers only after you are sure that all the air has been removed from the master cylinder. Follow the specified RR, LF, LR, RF sequence and depress the brake pedal slowly one time before opening bleeder screw to release air. Tighten screw, *slowly release pedal*, and *wait 15 seconds*. Repeat all steps, including the 15 second delay until all air has been removed from the system.

—— CAUTION ——
Rapid pumping of this system moves the secondary master cylinder piston down the bore in a manner that makes it difficult to

bleed the left front/right rear part of the system.

SURGE BLEEDING

This method includes both manual and pressure bleeding, and deliberately creates a churning (higher pressure) turbulence in wheel cylinders so that any remaining air can be drawn off in the form of aerated fluid. It is important to remove all possible air *before* surging; thus this method is never used unless the routine manual or pressure bleeding method proves inadequate.

Following simple procedure is recommended for surge bleeding:

1. Bleed the brakes at all wheels in a usual manner.

2. At each wheel cylinder, in turn, open the bleeder screw and press the brake pedal down sharply several times. Close the bleeder screw. The action creates a turbulence in each cylinder, forcing out practically all of the remaining trapped air.

—— CAUTION ——
After bleeding the brake system, road test to insure proper operation of the braking system.

BLEEDING THE POWER BRAKE UNIT

On power booster equipped vehicles, the engine should be turned off and the power system purged of vacuum or compressed air by depressing the brake pedal several times. After bleeding the master cylinder, bleed the power brake unit (if equipped with a bleeder screw).

Pressure-multiplying type power units often have bleeder screws to remove the air trapped within the unit. If the unit has more that one bleeder screw, bleed the one at the pressure (main) cylinder first; the control valve second. When bleeding, manually close the bleeder screw before the pedal is allowed to back-stroke each time.

BLEEDER SCREW

COMPRESSION SPRING AND EXPANDERS

WHEEL CYLINDER

PISTON CUP

PISTON

LINK

DUST BOOT

Typical wheel cylinder

Wheel Cylinders and Calipers

WHEEL CYLINDER OPERATION

The space between the cups in the cylinder bore must remain filled with fluid at all times. After depressing the brake pedal, additional brake fluid is forced into the cylinder bore. As a result of this, cups and pistons move outward in the cylinder bore pushing the shoe links and the brake shoes outward to contact the drum and apply the brakes. On some designs, the end of the shoe web bears directly against the pistons and therefore, shoe links are not used.

SERVICE PROCEDURES

Wheel cylinders may need reconditioning or replacement whenever the brake shoes are replaced or when required to correct a leak condition. On many designs, the wheel cylinders can be diassembled without removing them from the backing plate. On some designs, however, the cylinder is mounted in an indention in the backing plate or a cylinder piston stop is welded to the backing plate. When servicing brakes of this type, the cylinder must be removed from the backing plate before being disassembled.

Diagnostic Inspection and Cleaning

Leaks which coat the boot and the cylinder with fluid, or result in a dropped reservoir fluid level, or dampen and stain the brake linings are dangerous. Such leaks can cause the brakes to "grab" or fail and should be immediately corrected. A leakage, not immediately apparent, can be detected by pulling back the cylinder boot. A small amount of fluid seepage dampening the interior of the boot is normal; a dripping boot is not. Unless other conditions causing a brake to pull, grab, or drag becomes obvious, the wheel cylinder is a suspect and should be included in general reconditioning.

Cylinder binding may be caused by rust, deposits, grime, or swollen cups due to fluid contamination, or by a cup wedged into an excessive piston clearance. If the clearance between the pistons and the bore wall exceeds allowable values, a condition called "heel drag" may exist. It can result in rapid cup wear and can cause the pistons to retract very slowly when the brakes are released.

A ring of a hard, crystal-like substance is sometimes noticed in the cylinder bore where the piston stops after the brakes are released.

Some front wheel cylinders have a baffle located between the opposed pistons. The baffle contains a small hole which causes the cylinder to act as a fluid shock absorber damping servo brake shoes as they become energized. These cylinders cannot be honed and should be replaced if the bore is pitted or corroded.

CAUTION

Hydraulic system parts should not be allowed to come in contact with oil or grease, neither should those be handled with greasy hands. Even a trace of any petroleum based product is sufficient to cause damage to the rubber parts.

RECONDITIONING DRUM BRAKE WHEEL CYLINDERS

It is a common practice to recondition a drum brake wheel cylinder without dismounting it, however some brakes are equipped with external piston stops which prevent disassembly unless the cylinder is removed. In order to dismount, remove the shoe springs and spread the shoes apart, disconnect the brake line, remove the mounting bolts or retaining clips, and pull the cylinder free.

Most wheel cylinders are attached to the backing plate with bolts and are easily removed for service or replacement. In recent years, some GM vehicles use a retaining clip for this purpose. To remove this type cylinder, use a special service tool, or this alternate method: Insert ⅛" diameter or less awls or pins into the slots between wheel cylinder pilot and retainer locking tabs. Bend both tabs away at the same time until tabs spring over the shoulder, releasing cylinder. DISCARD the old retainer.

To replace cylinder, use a new retainer and the following procedure:

1. Hold wheel cylinder against backing plate by inserting a block between the wheel cylinder and axle shaft flange.

2. Position wheel cylinder retainer clip so the tabs will be away from and in horizontal position with the backing plate when installing.

3. Press new retaining clip over wheel cylinder abutment and into position using 1⅛ inch 12 point socket. Retainer is in place when the tabs are snapped under the retainer abutment. Examine closely to be sure both retainer tabs are properly engaged.

Another variation of retainer clip is used on some imported vehicles. The retainer usually consists of two or three separate pieces which when slid together will lock themselves and the wheel cylinder in place. The retainers can be carefully removed without incurring damage which allows them to be reused. If they are damaged or corroded, however, they must be replaced.

Pull the protective dust boots off the cylinder. Internal parts should slide out, or be picked out easily.   Parts can be driven out with a wooden dowel, or blown out at low pressure by applying compressed air to the fluid inlet port. Parts which cannot be removed easily indicate they are damaged beyond repair and the cylinder should be replaced.

Clean the cylinder and the parts in alcohol and/or brake fluid. (Do *NOT* use gasoline or other petroleum based products.) Use only lint-free wiping cloths. Crocus cloth can be used to clean minute scratches, signs of rust, corrosion or discoloration from the cylinder bore and pistons. Slide the cloth in a circular rather than a lengthwise motion. A clean-up hone may be used. After a cylinder has been honed, inspect it for excessive piston clearance and remove any burrs formed on the edge of fluid intake or bleeder screw ports.

CAUTION

Do not rebuild aluminum cylinders. A cylinder that does not clean up at .002" should be discarded and a new cylinder installed. (Black stains on the cylinder walls are caused by the piston cups and will do no harm.)

Assemble the cylinder with the internal parts, making sure that the cylinder wall is wet with brake fluid. Insert the cups and pistons from each end of a double-end cylinder; do not slide them through the cylinder. Cup lips should always face inward.

Disc Brake Caliper

An integral part of the caliper, the caliper bore(s) contains the piston(s) that direct thrust against the brake pads supported within the caliper. Since all braking forces (pad application force) are applied on each side of the rotor with no self energization, the cylinder and piston are large in comparison to a drum brake wheel cylinder.

FIXED CALIPER TYPE

A fixed type caliper is mounted solidly to the spindle bracket.

Pistons are located on both sides of the rotor, in inboard and outboard caliper halves. Fluid passes between caliper halves through an external crossover tube or through internal passages. A bleeder screw is located in the inboard caliper half. A dust boot protecting each cylinder fits in a circumferential groove on the piston.

FLOATING CALIPER TYPE

Floating or sliding calipers are free to move in a fixed bracket or support.

The piston is located only on the inboard side of the caliper housing, which straddles the rotor. The cylinder piston applies the inboard brake shoe directly, and simultaneously hydraulic pressure slides the caliper in a clamping action which forces the caliper to apply the outboard brake shoe.

The actual applying movement is small. The unit merely grips during application, relaxes upon release, and the shoes do not retract an appreciable distance from the rotor. The fluid inlet port and the bleeder screw are located on the inboard side of the

BRAKES

caliper. A dust boot is fitted into a circumferential groove on the piston and into a recess at or near the outer end of the cylinder bore.

HYDRAULIC SEAL ARRANGEMENTS

Seal arrangements at the caliper pistons vary depending upon the brake manufacturer. Three makes of fixed caliper brakes, Bendix, Budd, and Delco-Moraine, use a ring seal which fits in a circumferential groove on the piston.

A fixed seal is now commonly used in brake calipers. During the very small applying movement of the piston, the elasticity of the fixed seal permits some deflection in the cylinder groove. The seal deflects as the brakes are applied and relaxes as the brakes are released, retracting the piston a small amount. Some GM types have a rolling seal that retracts the piston slightly further to reduce pad rubbing friction.

A scratched piston, nicked seal, or a sludge or varnish deposit which lifts the sealing edge away from the piston will cause a fluid leak. A serious leak could develop if calipers are not reconditioned when new pads are installed. Then dust and road grime, gradually accumulating behind the dust boot, could be carried into the seal when the piston is shoved inward to accommodate new thick linings. Old seals may have taken a "set," thus preventing proper seating in the retainer groove and on the piston. Therefore, when reconditioning calipers, new seals should be installed.

Service Procedures

Before servicing, syphon or syringe about ⅔ of the fluid from the master cylinder reservoir; do not, however, lower the fluid level below the cylinder intake port. To prevent a gravity loss of fluid, plug the brake line after disconnecting from the caliper. To recondition, remove the caliper from the vehicle, allow the unit to drain, and remove the brake shoes. For benchwork, clamp the caliper housing in a soft jaw vice. On fixed-caliper types, remove the bridge bolts and separate the caliper into halves. Remove the sealing O-rings at crossover points, if the unit has internal fluid passages across the halves.

Whenever required, use special tools to remove pistons, dust boots, and seals. If compressed air is used, apply it gradually, gently ease the pistons from the cylinders, and trap them in a clean cloth; do not allow them to pop out. Take care to avoid pinching hands or fingers.

While removing stroking type seals and boots, work lip of boot from the groove in the caliper. After the boot is free, pull the piston, and strip the seal and boot from the piston.

While removing fixed position (rectan-

gular ring) seals and boots, pull the piston through the boot. Do not use a metal tool which would scratch the piston. Use a small pointed wooden or plastic tool to lift the boots and seals from the grooves in the cylinder bore.

Cleaning, Inspection, and Installation

Use only alcohol and/or brake fluid and a lint free wiping cloth to clean the caliper and parts.

———————— CAUTION ————————

Other solvents should not be used. Blow out passages with compressed air. Always wear eye protection when using compressed air or cleaning calipers.

To correct minor imperfections in the cylinder bore, polish with a fine grade of crocus cloth working in a circular rather than a lengthwise motion. Do not use any form of abrasive on a plated piston. Discard a piston which is pitted or has signs of plating wear.

Inspect the new seal. It should lie flat and be round. If it has suffered a distorted "set" during its shelf life, do not use it. Lubricate the cylinder wall and parts with brake fluid.

While installing stroking type seals and boots, stretch the boot and the seal over the piston and seat them in position.

Use special alignment tools for inserting lip cup seals. Be sure the seal does not twist or roll.

Where the boot lip is retained inside the cylinder bore the following method works well:

1. Lubricate bottom inside edge of piston and brake seal in caliper with brake fluid.

2. Pull boot over bottom end of piston so that boot is positioned on bottom of piston with lip about ¼ inch up from bottom end.

3. Hold piston suspended over bore.

4. Insert back boot lip into groove in caliper.

5. Then tuck the sides of boot into groove and work forward until only one bulge remains.

6. Tuck the final bulge into front of the groove.

7. Then push the piston carefully through the seal and boot to the bottom of the bore. The inside of the boot should slide on the piston and come to rest in the boot groove.

If the boot lip is retained outside the cylinder bore, first stretch boot over the piston and seat it in its groove, then press the piston through the seal. Fully depress the piston. You'll need 50 to 100 pounds force to fasten the boot lip in place. On some designs, it is necessary to use a wooden drift or a special tool to seat the metal boot in the caliper counterbore below the face of the caliper.

INSTALLING FIXED CALIPER BRIDGE BOLTS

If the caliper contains internal fluid crossover passages, be sure to install the new O-ring seals at joints. Install high tensile strength bridge bolts on the mated caliper halves. Never replace the bridge bolts with ordinary standard hardware bolts.

Rotor Runout

Manufacturers differ widely on permissible runout, but too much can sometimes be felt as a pulsation at the brake pedal. A wobble pump effect is created when a rotor is not perfectly smooth and the pad hits the high spots forcing fluid back into the master cylinder. This alternating pressure causes a pulsating feeling which can be felt at the pedal when the brakes are applied. This excessive runout also causes the brakes to be out of adjustment because disc brakes are self-adjusting; they are designed so that the pads drag on the rotor at all times and therefore automatically compensate for wear. To check the actual runout of the rotor, first tighten the wheel spindle nut to a snug bearing adjustment, end-play removed. Fasten a dial indicator on the suspension at a convenient place so that the indicator stylus contacts the rotor face approximately one inch from its outer edge. Set the dial at zero. Check the total indictor reading while turning the rotor one full revolution. If the rotor is warped beyond the runout specification, it is likely that it can be successfully remachined.

Lateral Runout: A wobbly movement of the rotor from side to side at it rotates. Excessive lateral runout causes the rotor faces to knock bac the disc pads and can result in chatter, excessive pedal travel, pumping or fighting pedal and vibration during the breaking action.

Parallelism (lack of): Refers to the amount of variation in the thickness of the rotor. Excessive variation can cause pedal vibration or fight, front end vibrations and possible "grab" during the braking action; a condition comparable to an "out-of-round brake drum." Check parallelism with a micrometer, "mike" the thickness at eight or more equally spaced points, equally distant from the outer edge of the rotor, preferrably at mid-points of the braking surface. Parallelism then is the amount of variation between maximum and minimum measurements.

Surface of Micro-inch finish, flatness, smoothness: Different from parallelism, these terms refer to the degree of perfection of the flat surface on each side of the rotor; that is, the minute hills, valleys and swirls inherent in machining the surface. In a visual inspection, the remachined surface should have a fine ground polish with, at most, only a faint trace of nondirectional swirls.

Drum Brakes

A typical drum brake assembly includes a backing or support plate, with one or two wheel cylinders attached to it. Mounted on the backing plate are two lined brake shoes with shoe return springs and hold-down parts, and a means of adjusting the shoes to compensate for lining wear. A brake drum encloses these parts. The drum brakes on the rear of most vehicles also normally include the parts required for parking brakes. All of the drum brakes used on modern vehicles have these components but there is a variety of configurations for each.

Drum brakes are designed to be either "servo" or "non-servo" acting.

SERVO TYPE BRAKES

In these brakes the shoes are assembled to form a compound, "primary" and "secondary" shoe unit joined at one end by an adjustable floating link. The drag of a normal (forward) drum rotation causes the primary shoe to leave its anchor and holds the secondary shoe anchored.

All of the forces applying and anchoring the primary shoe are transmitted through

Typical Bendix non-servo brake

the shoe link, in a servo action, and also apply the secondary shoe, thus compounding its braking effect. When the drum is rotated backward, this compounding action

of the shoes is reversed. When equipped with a double-end wheel cylinder (two opposed pistons), brake effectiveness can be substantially the same with either forward

Typical Bendix Duo-Servo brake

or reverse movement of the vehicle. With a single-end wheel cylinder (one piston), the brake is energized in only one direction. Since the secondary shoe performs more of the work in forward movement, it shows more lining wear. A longer or thicker lining is often used to offset this wear.

NON-SERVO TYPE BRAKES

In these brakes each shoe is separately anchored and their action is not compounded. On single cylinder brakes a "forward" or "leading" shoe is self-energized by the usual (forward) drum rotation while a "reverse" or "trailing" shoe is de-energized. When the drum is rotated backward, this action reverses, thus energizing the reverse shoe and de-energizing the forward shoe. The lining wear is unbalanced because the shoes perform different amounts of work; the wear is more rapid on the forward acting shoe during a forward stop.

Large two cylinder non-servo brakes, found on certain models, make use of two double-end wheel cylinders which enable the shoes to be anchored or actuated at either end. This arrangement is non-directional in effectiveness. With two-cylinder brakes, lining wear is balanced on both shoes.

MECHANICAL COMPONENTS

To be sure of restoring the brake components correctly after servicing, closely observe the arrangement of shoe hook-up parts as the brake is disassembled. These arrangements may vary on different models. Usually the brake shoes are held in a sliding fit by spring tensions, at rest upon their anchor by the return springs, and against support pads by spring or clip type holddowns. Opposite the anchor, a star wheel adjuster links the shoe webs and provides a threaded adjustment which permits the shoes to be expanded or contracted. Some rear brakes have adjustable links. The shoes are held against the adjuster by a spring.

Shoe Hold-Downs

Various shoe hold-downs are shown in the illustration.

To unlock or lock the straight pin holddowns, depress the locking cup and coil spring, or the spring clip, and rotate the pin or lock 90 degrees. On certain lever type adjusters, the inner (bottom) cup has a sleeve which aligns the adjuster lever.

Shoe Anchors

There are various types of anchors such as the fixed non-adjustable type, or self-centering shoe sliding type, or, on some earlier models, adjustable fixed type providing either an eccentric or a slotted adjustment. On some front brakes, fixed anchors are threaded into or are bolted through the steering knuckle and also support the wheel cylinder.

On adjustable anchors, when necessary to re-center the shoes in the drum or drum gauge, loosen the locknut enough to permit the anchor to slip out, but not so much that it can tilt.

On the eccentric type anchors, tighten the star wheel to heavy brake drag. Rotate the eccentric anchor in the direction which frees the brake until drag cannot be relieved. Tighten the anchor nut. Back off the star wheel to a normal manual adjustment.

On the slotted type anchor, tighten the star wheel to heavy drag. Tap the support plate until the anchor slips and frees the brake. Repeat this sequence until drag cannot be relieved. Tighten the locknut to the proper torque. Back off the star wheel to a normal manual adjustment.

Brake Shoes

In the same brake sizes, there can be differences in web thickness, shape of web cut-outs and positions of any reinforcements. Some vehicles require shoes made of higher tensile strength steels. Higher strength shoes usually are coded with a letter symbol stamped on the shoe web. Shoes with extra web holes or table nibs or tabs which do not cause interference generally are considered interchangeable with other shoes.

Stops

An eccentric stop under the primary or secondary shoe web on tilted front brakes prevents the shoes from bumping against the drum. Before adjusting the star wheel, loosen the lock nut on the support plate and rotate the eccentric in the forward direction until the shoe drags. Back-off until drag is relieved and tighten the lock nut.

Piston Stops

If the brake is equipped with piston stops, the wheel cylinder must be dismounted for reconditioning.

Basic Service

─────── CAUTION ───────

Do not blow the brake dust out of the drums with compressed air or lung power; always use a damp cloth and wipe it out. Brake linings contain asbestos, a known cancer causing substance. Dispose of the cloth after use.

NOTE: Never work on a vehicle supported only on a jack. Use a hydraulic lift or jack stands to support the vehicle while working.

Raising both front or rear wheels at once and supporting them on jackstands also allows comparison of the brake being serviced to the brake on the opposite side.

Check for Leaks

Press the brake pedal to ensure that there are no leaks in the hydraulic system. If the pedal does not remain hard, and drops to the floor, it is an indication of a leak in the master cylinder, hoses, wheel cylinders, or disc brake calipers. When performing this test, the engine should be running if equipped with power brakes. With power brakes it is normal for the pedal to drop slightly when the engine starts. If it continues to drop, start looking for a leak.

Drum Removal

Safely support the vehicle and release the parking brake if working on the rear axle. Remove the lug nuts, the wheel/tire assembly and then pull off the drums. If the brake shoes have expanded too tightly against the drum, or have cut into the friction surface of the brake drum, the drums may be too tight for removal. In such a case, adjust the shoes inward before the brake drum is removed. On vehicles with self-adjusting mechanisms, reach through the adjusting slot with a very small prybar (or similar tool) and carefully push the self-adjusting lever away from the star wheel by a maximum of $\frac{1}{16}$" (1.5 mm). While holding the lever back, insert a brake adjusting tool into the slot and turn the star wheel in the proper direction until the brake drum can be removed. On vehicles with manual adjusting mechanisms, try lightly tapping the drum with a rubber mallet. If this does not work, simply reverse the manual adjustment procedures given later in this section until the drum can be removed.

Drum Inspection

Check the drums for any cracks, scores, grooves, or an out-of-round condition. Replace if cracked. Slight scores can be removed with fine emery cloth while extensive scoring requires turning the drum on a lathe.

If the friction surface of the brake drum appears scored or otherwise damaged beyond repair, it will require reconditioning. After machining, the drum diameter must not exceed the diameter cast on the drum or 0.060" (1.5 mm) over the original nominal diameter. Carefully look for signs of grease or oil at the center of the assembly. If any leak is noticed, the seal should be replaced.

Rebuild the Cylinders

It is *always* a good idea to rebuild or replace the wheel cylinders when relining the brakes. This will help assure a properly operating brake system.

Remove Brake Shoes

It is convenient to disassemble one wheel at a time so the opposite side serves as a reference. Carefully note the colors and locations of different springs and parts. This is necessary to distinguish different springs that appear to be the same but have different tensions. If there are extra unused holes close to the ones in which the springs are located, use a dab of paint or other marking on the new shoes to identify the holes to be used. Replace any discolored springs and other parts found corroded or distorted. Use special tools whenever necessary. Examine the springs for signs of stretching or other defects and replace if their condition is at all questionable. Examine the flexible brake hoses and replace any that show signs of cracking or other damage.

Clean and Lubricate

With all the brake parts off, clean the backing plate with a damp cloth to avoid raising any asbestos dust, and dispose of the rag after use. Clean any rust with a wire brush. File smooth any ridges or rough edges on the contact points on the backing plate, and lubricate with approved brake lubricant. Clean and lightly lubricate the adjuster threads, and screw the adjuster all the way together to facilitate reassembly later on. Wash the wheel bearings with solvent and repack them with the proper grease. Check backing plate bolts to make sure they are tight.

Reassemble and Install Brake Shoes

Reassemble the brakes in the reverse order of disassembly. Make sure all parts are in their proper locations and that both brake shoes are properly positioned in either end of the adjuster. Also, both brake shoes should correctly engage the wheel cylinder push rods and parking brake links, and should be centered on the backing plate. Parking brake links and levers should be in place on the rear brakes. With all the parts in place, try the fit of the brake drum over the new shoes. If not slightly snug, pull it off and turn the star wheel until a slight drag is felt when sliding the drum on. The use of a brake preset gauge will make this job easy. This makes final brake adjustment simpler. Then install the brake drum, wheel bearings, spindle nuts, cotter pins, dust caps, and wheel/tire assemblies, and make final brake adjustments as specified. Torque the spindle and lug nuts to specifications.

Bleed and Road-Test

Bleed the brakes to make sure of a high, hard brake pedal, and road-test the car. Most self-adjusting mechanisms are activated only during the rearward motion of a car. So, whenever servicing self-adjusting brakes,

make sure that the road test includes enough stops, traveling in reverse, to allow the self-adjusters to perform the proper match-up of all wheels. Or, operate the parking brake several times if that activates the automatic adjuster.

CHILTON TIPS

- The primary brake shoe is the one toward the front of the vehicle, and its lining is usually shorter than that on the secondary (rearward) shoe.
- Self-adjusting mechanisms are usually mounted on the secondary shoe.
- The star wheel part of an adjuster usually (but not always) goes toward the rear of the vehicle.
- Different color springs belong in different locations.
- Self-adjusters and related parts are not interchangeable from one side to the other since the direction of adjuster rotation varies from one side to the other. Adjusters on one side usually have right hand threads, and the adjusters on the other side left hand threads.
- Never press the brake pedal when one or more brake drums are off, or a wheel cylinder will pop apart.

POWER BOOSTER TROUBLE DIAGNOSIS

Condition	Possible Cause	Correction
Vacuum leak (booster in released position)	1. End plate, center plate or control valve body gaskets leak.	1. Recondition booster unit.
	2. Distortion of end plate.	2. Replace end plate.
	3. Misalignment of control valve poppet.	3. Disassemble, clean and correctly reassemble.
	4. Loose vacuum cylinder bolts.	4. Coat vacuum cylinder bolts lightly with a suitable sealing compound and tighten to specified torque.
	5. Loose control valve body screws.	5. Tighten control valve body screws to specified torque.
	6. Large control valve poppet spring not centered in spring retainer.	6. Disassemble unit and correctly reassemble.
Vacuum leak (booster in applied position)	1. Leak at control valve poppet and seat.	1. Clean and inspect poppet and seat for damage and repair as necessary.
	2. Dry or faulty piston leather packing.	2. Clean and lubricate piston leather or replace.
	3. Faulty control valve disphragm assembly.	3. Replace faulty parts.
External hydraulic leaks	1. Gasket (O-ring) leaking at hydraulic end plate joint.	1. Disassemble clean and replace (O-ring) gasket and reassemble.
	2. Fluid leaking at copper gasket under hydraulic cylinder end cap.	2. Remove end cap and inspect copper gasket and seat install new copper gasket.
Internal hydraulic leak at low pressures	1. Control valve hydraulic piston cup failure.	1. Recondition control valve unit.
	2. Faulty push rod seal.	2. Replace push rod seal.

POWER BOOSTER TROUBLE DIAGNOSIS

Condition	Possible Cause	Correction
Internal leaks at high pressure	1. Fluid passing copper gasket under hydraulic fitting in control valve. 2. Inspect cups and seals of master cylinder for cuts and scores. 3. Inspect cups of the control valve hydraulic piston.	1. Clean and inspect gasket and fitting, replace if faulty. 2. Hone master cylinder and replace cups and seals. 3. Replace faulty cups.
Hydraulic pressure buildup (without added input)	1. Check hydraulic piston check valve and slot for foreign material under valve.	1. Clean or replace valve and seats as condition indicates.
Failure to release	1. Weak vacuum cylinder piston return spring. 2. Dry vacuum piston leather packing. 3. Swollen rubber cups due to inferior or contaminated brake fluid. 4. Damaged or dented vacuum cylinder shell. 5. Dirty or sticky control valve piston.	1. Replace vacuum cylinder piston return spring. 2. Lubricate vacuum piston leather packing. 3. Flush hydraulic system and recondition or replace all cylinders. 4. Replace vacuum cylinder shell. 5. Recondition control valve assembly.
Failure of booster to operate within specified pressures	1. Rusty, dirty or distorted vacuum cylinder shell. 2. Dry or worn vacuum cylinder leather packing. 3. Swollen rubber cups due to inferior brake fluid. 4. Worn or scored hydraulic cups. 5. Dirt, rust or foreign matter in any component of the system.	1. Clean or replace vacuum cylinder shell. 2. Recondition and lubricate the vacuum booster. 3. Recondition the master cylinder. Replace brake fluid. 4. Recondition the master cylinder. 5. Recondition and lubricate the brake booster assembly.
Loss of fluid	1. Fluid leaking past cup in master cylinder. 2. Brake wheel cylinders leaking. 3. Loose hydraulic hose connectors. 4. Leaking stop light switch.	1. Recondition master cylinder or replace. 2. Recondition or replace wheel cylinders. 3. Inspect and tighten all hydraulic connections. 4. Replace stop light switch.
Presence of brake fluid on hy-power vacuum cylinder	1. Piston cup or push rod seal leaking.	1. Recondition master cylinder.
Pedal kicks back against foot when brakes are applied	1. Vacuum leakage. 2. Dirt under control valve or damaged seat. 3. Weak or broken spring.	1. Inspect and correct vacuum leak. 2. Clean and recondition booster assembly. 3. Replace spring.
Brakes are slow to release ①	1. Incorrect pedal linkage adjustment. 2. Compensating port of master cylinder plugged. 3. Brake shoes sticking. 4. Weak brake shoe return spring. 5. Booster control valve piston sticking. 6. Booster air filter clogged. 7. Control valve diaphragm return spring missing. 8. Defective check valve in slave cylinder piston. 9. Dirt under atmospheric valve disc.	1. Adjust and lubricate pedal linkage. 2. Clean master cylinder with compressed air. 3. Free up and lubricate brake shoes. 4. Replace brake shoe return spring. 5. Clean booster control valve piston and lubricate. 6. Clean air filter in mineral spirits. 7. Install new control valve return spring. 8. Recondition slave cylinder pistons. 9. Clean atmospheric valve.
Engine runs unevenly at idle with brakes	1. Vacuum leakage. 2. Dirt under control valve disc or damaged seat.	1. Inspect and tighten all vacuum fittings. 2. Clean control valve or replace.

POWER BOOSTER TROUBLE DIAGNOSIS

Condition	Possible Cause	Correction
released	3. Defective spring.	3. Replace defective spring.
Engine runs evenly and pedal is hard with brakes applied	1. Control valve piston assembly not seating on vacuum disc. 2. Defective control valve plate and diaphragm. 3. Defective pressure plate and diaphragm.	1. Clean or replace control valve piston assembly. 2. Replace control valve plate and diaphragm. 3. Replace pressure plate and diaphragm.
Brake pedal is hard at different intervals	1. Defective manifold check valve. 2. Slave cylinder piston sticking due to dirt or inferior brake fluid. 3. Brake booster air cleaner clogged.	1. Clean or replace manifold check valve. 2. Clean and recondition slave cylinder. 3. Clean air cleaner in mineral spirits and blow dry with compressed air.

①Jack up truck and determine whether or not the brakes are dragging before further testing is done.

POWER BRAKE BOOSTER SERVICE

Brake System Preliminary Checks

Always check the fluid level in the brake master cylinder reservoir(s) before performing the test procedures. If the fluid level is not within ¼" of the top of the master cylinder reservoirs, add the specified brake fluid.

Push the brake pedal down as far as it will go. If the pedal travels more than halfway between the released position and the floor, adjust the brakes. If the vehicle is equipped with automatic brake adjusters, serveral sharp brake applications while backing up may be necessary to adjust the brakes.

Road test the vehicle and apply the brakes at a speed of about 20 mph to see if the vehicle stops evenly. If not, the brakes should be adjusted. Perform the road test only when the brakes will apply and the vehicle can be safely stopped.

DUAL BRAKE WARNING LIGHT SYSTEM TESTS

1. Turn the ignition switch to the ACC or ON position. If the light on the brake warning lamp remains on, the condition may be caused by a shorted or broken switch, grounded switch wires or the differential pressure valve is not centered. Centralize the differential pressure valve. If the warning light remains on, check the switch connector and wire for a grounded condition and repair or replace the wire assembly. If the condition of the wire is good, replace the brake warning lamp switch.

2. Turn the ignition switch to the start position. If the brake warning lamp does not light, check the light and wiring and replace or repair wiring as necessary. When both brake systems are functioning normally, the equal pressure at the pressure differential valve during brake pedal application keeps the valve centered. The brake warning light will be on only when the ignition key is in the start position.

3. If the brake warning lamp does not light when a pressure differential condition exists in the brake system, the warning lamp may be burned out, the warning lamp switch is inoperative or the switch to lamp wiring has an open circuit. Check the bulb and replace it, if required. Check the switch to lamp wires for an open circuit and repair or replace them, if required. If the warning lamp still does not light, replace the switch.

POWER BRAKE FUNCTION TEST

With the engine stopped, eliminate all vacuum from the system by pumping the brake pedal several times. Then push the pedal down as far as it will go, and note the effort required to hold it in this position. If the pedal gradually moves downward under this pressure, the hydraulic system is leaking and should be checked by a hydraulic pressure test.

With the brake pedal still pushed down, start the engine. If the vacuum system is operating properly, the pedal will move downward. If the pedal position does not change, the vacuum system is not operating properly and should be checked by a vacuum test.

VACUUM BOOSTER CHECK VALVE TEST

Disconnect the line from the bottom of the vacuum check valve, and connect a vacuum gauge to the valve. Start the engine, run it at idle speed, and check the reading on the vacuum gauge.

The gauge should register 17–19" with standard transmission and 14–15" in Drive range if equipped with an automatic transmission. Stop the engine and note the rate of vacuum drop. If the vacuum drops more than one inch in 15 seconds, the check valve is leaking. If the vacuum reading does not reach 18" or is unsteady, an engine tuneup is needed.

Remove the gauge and reconnect the vacuum line to the check valve.

VACUUM BOOSTER TEST

Bendix Piston Type

Disconnect the vacuum line from the booster end plate. Install a tee fitting in the end plate, and connect a vacuum gauge (no. 1) and vacuum line to the fitting. Install a second vacuum gauge (no. 2) in place of the pipe plug in the booster control valve body.

Start the engine, and note the vacuum reading on both gauges. If both gauges do not register manifold vacuum, air is leaking into the vacuum system. If both gauges register manifold vacuum, stop the engine and note the rate of vacuum drop on both gauges. If the drop exceeds one inch in 15 seconds on either gauge, air is leaking into the vacuum system. Tighten all vacuum connections and repeat the test. If leakage still exists, the leak may be localized as follows:

1. Disconnect the vacuum line and gauge no. 1 from the booster.

2. Connect vacuum gauge no. 1 directly to the vacuum line. Start the engine and note the gauge reading. Stop the engine and check the rate of vacuum drop. If gauge no. 1 does not register manifold vacuum, or if the vacuum drop exceeds 1" in 15 seconds, the leak is in the vacuum line or check valve connections.

3. Reconnect vacuum gauge no. 1 and

the vacuum line to the tee fitting. Start the engine, and run it at idle speed for one minute. Depress the brake pedal sufficiently to cause vacuum gauge no. 2 to read from zero to 1 inch of vacuum. Gauge no. 1 should register manifold vacuum of 17–19″ with standard transmission and 14–16″ in Drive range if equipped with an automatic transmission. If the drop of vacuum on gauge no. 2 is slow, the air cleaner, or air cleaner line, may be plugged. Inspect and if necessary, clean the air cleaner.

4. Release the brake pedal and observe the action of gauge no. 2. Upon releasing the pedal, the vacuum gauge must register increasing vacuum until manifold vacuum is reached. The rate of increase must be smooth, with no lag or slowness in the return to manifold vacuum. If the gauge readings are not as outlined, the booster is not operating properly and should be removed and overhauled.

VACUUM BOOSTER TEST

Diaphragm Type

This procedure can be used to test all diaphragm boosters which are equipped with a pipe thread outlet on the atmosphere portion of the diaphragm chamber.

Remove the pipe plug from the rear half of the booster chamber, and install a vacuum gauge. Start the engine and run it at idle speed. The gauge should register 18–21″ of vacuum.

1. With the engine running, depress the brake pedal with enough pressure to show a zero reading on the vacuum gauge. Hold the pedal in the applied position for one minute. Any downward movement of the pedal during this time indicates a brake fluid leak. Any kickback (upward movement) of the pedal indicates brake fluid is leaking past the hydraulic piston check valve.

2. With the engine running, push down on the brake pedal with sufficient pressure to show a zero reading on the vacuum gauge. Hold the pedal down, and shut the engine off. Maintain pedal position for one minute. A kickback of the pedal indicates a vacuum leak in the vacuum check valve, in the vacuum line connections, or in the booster.

BLEEDING VACUUM-HYDRAULIC BOOSTER SYSTEMS

1. Eliminate vacuum in the booster by depressing the brake pedal several times while the engine is not running.

2. On trucks not equipped with reservoir tanks, disconnect the manifold tube at the booster side of the manifold check valve (engine not running).

3. Alternately loosen the brake tube at each unit until all air is expelled. Booster slave-cylinder is bled first.

CAUTION

Where air pressure brake bleeding equipment is used to bleed brakes, do not use more than 25–30 psi.

NOTE: A piston stop is provided in the slave cylinder to eliminate the possibility of damaging the return spring while bleeding the system. This damage occurs only when bleeding the brakes with a vacuum present in the booster system.

Bendix Hydro-Boost

The Bendix Hydro-Boost uses the hydraulic pressure supplied by the power steering pump to provide a power assist to brake application.

Disassembly

1. Place the booster in a vise with the bracket end up. Using a hammer and chisel, cut the bracket nut that holds the linkage bracket to the booster assembly. The nut should be cut at the open slot in the booster cover threads. Care must be exercised to avoid damage to the threads. Spread the nut and remove the bracket.

2. Remove the pedal boot by pulling if off over the pedal rod eyelet.

3. Position pedal rod removing tool around the pedal rod. The tool should be resting on the booster cover. Insert a punch through the pedal rod from the lower side of the special tool. Push the punch through until it rests on the higher side of the tool.

Push up on the punch to shear the pedal rod retainer; remove the pedal rod.

4. Remove the grommet from the groove near the end of the pedal rod and from the groove in the input rod.

5. Disengage the tabs of the spring retainer from the ledge inside the opening near the master cylinder mounting flange of the booster. Remove the retainer and piston return spring from the opening.

6. Pull straight out on the output push rod to remove the push rod and push rod retainer from inside the booster piston.

7. Press in on the spool plug, and insert a small punch into the hole on top of the housing. This unseats one side of the spool plug snap-ring from the groove in the bore. Remove the snap-ring.

8. Remove the spool plug from the bore with a pair of pliers. Remove the O-ring

Removing the spool plug from the Hydro-Boost unit

1. Pedal push rod	11. Plunger seat	22. Push rod retainer
2. Pedal push rod grommet	12. O-ring	23. Spiral snapring
3. Pedal push rod boot	13. Spacer	24. Spool spring
4. Bracket nut	14. Spacer	25. Plug O-ring
5. Linkage bracket	15. Check valve ball	26. Spool plug
6. Booster cover	16. Accumulator check valve	27. Snapring
7. Cover to housing seal	17. O-ring	28. Piston return spring
8. Input rod seals	18. Piston seal	29. Spring retainer
9. Input rod and piston assy	19. Booster housing	30. Housing to cover bolts
10. Spool assembly	20. Tube seat inserts	
	21. Output push rod	

Bendix Hydro-Boost

from the plug and discard. Remove the spool spring from the bore.

9. Place the booster cover in a soft-faced vise and remove the cover retaining bolts. Remove the booster assembly from the vise and separate the booster cover from the housing. Remove the large seal ring and discard.

10. Press in on the end of the spool assembly, and use a spiral snap-ring removing tool to remove the snap-ring from the forward groove in the spool. Discard the snap-ring.

11. Remove the input rod and piston assembly, and the spool assembly from the booster housing.

12. Remove the input rod seals from the input rod end, and the piston seal from the piston bore in the housing. Discard the seals.

13. Remove the plunger, seat, spacer and ball from the accumulator valve bore in the flange of the booster housing. Remove the O-ring from the seat and discard.

14. Thread a screw extractor into the opening in the check valve in the bottom of the accumulator valve bore, and remove the check valve from the bottom of the bore. Discard the check valve and O-ring.

NOTE: Using a screw extractor damages the seat in the check valve. A new check valve, O-ring and valve must be installed whenever the check valve is removed from the accumulator valve bore.

15. Using a ¼" or a 5⁄16" spiral flute type screw extractor, remove the tube seats from the booster ports.

Cleaning & Inspection

1. Clean all parts in a suitable solvent.
2. Inspect the valve spool and the valve spool bore for any damage or ware. Discoloration of the spool or bore is normal, particulary in the grooves. If any damage is noted, replace the valve spool and housing.

NOTE: The clearance between the valve

Removing the booster pedal rod

Staking the steering linkage bracket nut

spool and the bore is very important. Because of this, the valve spool and housing are to be replaced only as an assembly.

3. Inspect the input rod and piston assembly for any damage or ware. Replace any defective components.

4. Inspect the piston bore in the housing for any damage or ware. If defective, replace the booster housing and spool valve assembly.

Assembly

─────── CAUTION ───────
Parts must be kept VERY clean. If there is any reason to doubt the cleanliness of the components, re-wash before assembly.

Lubricate all seals and metal friction points with power steering fluid before assembly. Whenever the booster is disassembled, be sure that seals, tube inserts, spiral snap-ring, check valve and ball are replaced.

1. Position a tube seat in each booster port and screw a spare tube nut in each port to press the seat down into the port. Do not tighten the tube nuts in the port as this may deface the seats. Remove the spare tube nuts and check for aluminium chips in the ports. Be sure that there is no foreign matter in the ports.

2. Coat the piston bore and piston seal with clean power steering fluid. Assemble the seal in the piston bore. The lip of the seal must be towards the rear (away from the master cylinder mounting flange). Be sure that the seal is fully seated in the housing.

3. Lubricate the input rod end, input rod seals and the seal installer tool with clean power steering fluid. Slide the seals on the tool with the lip of the cups towards the open end of the tool. Slide the tool over the input rod end end down to the second groove; then slide the forward seal off the tool and into the groove. Assemble the other seal in the first groove. Be sure, that both seals are fully seated.

4. Lubricate the piston and piston installing tool with clean power steering fluid. Insert the large end of the tool into the piston and the tool and piston into the piston

Removing the spiral snap-ring

Installing the pushrod seals

Installing the spiral snap-ring

Installing the input rod and piston assembly in the booster

Installing the linkage braket nut

bore, through the seal.

5. Position the O-ring on the accumulator check valve and coat the assembly with clean power steering fluid. Insert the check valve in the accumulator valve recess in the housing flange. Place the ball and spacer in the same recess.

6. Place the O-ring on the changing valve plunger seat and insert the plunger into the seat. Dip the assembly in clean power steering fluid and insert it into the changing valve recess.

7. Coat the spool assembly with clean power steering fluid and insert in the spool bore. Be sure that the pivot pins on the upper end of the input rod lever assembly are engaged in the groove in the sleeve. Remove piston installing tool.

8. Separate the two components of the snap-ring installation tool and place the spiral snap-ring on the tool. Insert the rounded end of the installer into the spool bore. While pressing on the rear of the spool, slide the snap-ring off the tool and into the groove near the forward end of the spool by pressing in on the tool sleeve. Check to be sure that the retaining ring is fully seated.

9. Place the housing seal in the groove in the housing cover. Join the booster housing and cover and secure with five attaching bolts. Tighten the bolts to 18–26 ft. lbs.

CAUTION

It is very important that the same cover attaching bolts are used as they are designed for the booster only. If they are damaged replace with the same part numbers.

---

10. Place an O-ring on the spool plug. Insert the spool spring and the spool plug in the forward end of the spool bore. Press in on the plug and position the snap-ring in its groove in the spool valve bore.

11. Place the linkage bracket on the booster assembly. The tab on the inside of the large hole in the bracket should fit into the slot in the threaded portion of the booster cover.

12. Install the bracket nut with a staking groove outward on the threaded portion to the booster cover. Use special tool and tighten to 95–120 ft. lbs.

13. Insert a small punch into the staking groove of the nut, at the slot in the booster cover, and with a hammer stake the nut in place. Be sure that the threads on the nut are deformed so the nut will not loosen.

14. Position a new boot and grommet on the pedal rod. Moisten the grommet and insert the grommet end of the pedal rod into the input rod of the booster. When the grommet is fully seated, the pedal rod will rotate freely.

15. Install the boot on the booster cover.

Bendix Master Vac

Removal

1. Disconnect clevis at brake pedal to

Bendix Master Vac

push rod.

2. Remove vacuum hoses from power cylinder.

3. Disconnect hydraulic line from master cylinder.

4. Remove the four attaching nuts and lock washers that hold the unit to the firewall. Remove the power brake unit.

Disassembly

1. Remove four master cylinder to vacuum cylinder attaching nuts and washers.

2. Separate master cylinder from vacuum cylinder, then remove the rubber seal from the outer groove at end of master cylinder.

3. Remove the push rod from the power section. (Do not disturb adjusting screw.)

4. Remove push rod boot and valve operating rod.

5. Scribe alignment marks across the rear shell and vacuum cylinder. Remove all but two of the end plate attaching screws (opposite each other). Hold down on the rear shell while removing the two remaining screws to prevent the piston return spring from expanding.

6. Scribe a mark across the face of the piston, to index the mark on the rear shell, and remove rear shell with vacuum piston and piston return spring.

7. Remove vacuum hose from vacuum piston and from vacuum tube on inside of rear shell. Separate rear shell from vacuum piston.

8. Remove air cleaner and vacuum tube assembly, and air filter from the rear shell.

9. Spring the felt retaining ring enough to disengage ring from grooves in bosses on rear piston plate.

10. Remove piston felt and expander ring from piston assembly.

11. Remove six piston plate attaching screws and separate front piston plate and

piston packing from piston plate.

12. Remove valve return spring, floating control valve and diaphragm assembly, valve spring and diaphragm plate. Separate floating control valve spring-retainer and control valve diaphragm from control valve.

13. Remove rubber reaction disc and shim (if present) from front piston plate.

NOTE: Do not remove the valve operating rod and valve plunger from the rear piston plate unless it is necessary to replace defective parts. Normally, the next two steps can be omitted.

14. When it is necessary to replace the valve operating rod or valve plunger, remove valve rod seal from groove in piston plate and pull seal over end of rod.

15. Hold piston with valve plunger side down and inject alcohol into valve plunger through opening around valve rod. This will wet the rubber lock in the plunger. Then drive or pry valve plunger off the valve rod.

NOTE: If master cylinder is not to be rebuilt, omit steps 16–19.

16. Remove snap-ring from groove in base at end of master cylinder.

17. Remove piston assembly, primary cup, retainer spring, and check-valve from master cylinder.

18. Remove filler cap and gasket from master cylinder body.

19. Remove secondary cup from master cylinder piston.

Cleaning Note

After disassembly, cleaning of all metal parts in satisfactory commercial cleaner solvent is recommended. Use only alcohol or Declene on rubber parts or parts containing rubber. After cleaning and drying, metal parts should be rewashed in clean alcohol or Declene before assembly.

Assembly

Steps 1–5 apply to a completely disassembled master cylinder. Otherwise, omit steps 1–5.

1. Coat bore of master cylinder with brake fluid.

2. Dip secondary cup in brake fluid and install on master cylinder piston.

3. Dip other piston parts in brake fluid and assemble the piston. Install piston.

4. Install snap-ring into groove of cylinder.

5. Use new gasket and install filler cap.

6. Assemble valve rod seal on rod and insert valve rod through the piston. Dip valve plunger in alcohol and assemble to ball end of valve rod. Be sure ball end of rod is locked in place in plunger.

7. Assemble floating control valve diaphragm over end of floating control valve. Be sure disphragm is in recess of floating control valve. Press control valve spring retainer over end of control valve and diaphragm.

8. Clamp valve operating rod in a vise with rear piston plate up. Lay leather piston packing on rear piston plate with lip of leather over edge of piston plate.

9. Install floating control valve return spring over end of valve plunger.

10. Assemble diaphragm plate to diaphragm and assemble floating control valve with diaphragm in recess of rear piston plate.

11. Install floating control valve spring over retainer. Align and assemble front piston plate with rear piston plate. Center the floating control valve spring on front piston plate and center valve plunger stem in hole of piston.

12. Holding front and rear piston plates together, loosely install six piston plate cap screws.

13. Install shim and rubber reaction disc in recess at center of front piston plate.

NOTE: A piston assembling ring is handy in assembling the piston.

14. Place the assembling tool over piston packing, turn piston assembly upside down and assemble the expander ring against inside lip of leather packing. Saturate felt with vacuum cylinder oil or shock absorber fluid—type A. Then assemble in expander ring. Assemble retainer ring over bosses on rear piston plate. Be sure retainer is anchored in grooves of piston plate.

15. Assemble air cleaner filter over vacuum tube of air cleaner and attach air cleaner shell in position with screws.

16. Slide vacuum hose onto vacuum inlet tube of piston and align hose to lay flat against piston.

17. Wipe a coat of vacuum cylinder oil on bore of cylinder. Remove assembling ring from vacuum piston and coat leather piston packing with vacuum cylinder oil.

18. Install rear shell over end of valve operating rod and attach vacuum hose to tube end on each side of end plate.

19. Center small diameter end of piston return spring in vacuum cylinder. Center large diameter of spring on piston. Check alignment mark on piston with marks on vacuum cylinder and rear shell, compress spring and install two attaching screws at opposite sides to hold rear shell and cylinder together. Now, install balance of screws and tighten evenly.

20. Dip small end of pushrod boot in alcohol and assemble guard over end of valve operating rod and over flange of shell.

21. Insert large end of pushrod through hole in end of vacuum cylinder and guide into hole of front piston plate.

NOTE: Before going on with assembly, check the distance from the outer end of the pushrod to the master cylinder mounting surface on the vacuum cylinder. This measurement should be 1.195–1.200″.

22. After pushrod adjustment is correct, replace rubber seal in groove on master cylinder body.

23. Assemble master cylinder to the vacuum cylinder at four studs. Replace lock washers and nut and securely tighten.

Bendix Single Diaphragm Booster

Disassembly

1. Scribe a line across the front and rear housings for reassembly.

2. Pull the piston rod from the front housing and remove the seal.

3. Attach a holding fixture to the front housing and clamp the base in a vise with the power section up.

4. Loosen the locknut and remove the pushrod device and locknut.

5. Remove the mounting bracket from the rear housing.

6. Remove the dust boot retainer, dust boot and silencer from the diaphragm plate extension.

7. The edge of the rear housing contains twelve lances. Four of these lances (one in each quadrant) are deeper than the other lances. The metal that forms the four deep lances must be partially straightened so that the lances will clear the cutouts in the front housing.

NOTE: If the metal tabs that form the deep lances crack or break during straightening, the housing must be replaced.

8. Place a spanner wrench over the studs on the rear housing and attach with nuts and washers.

9. Press down on the spanner wrench and rotate the rear housing clockwise to separate the two housings.

NOTE: It may be necessary to tap the rear housing lightly with a plastic hammer to loosen.

10. Lift the rear housing assembly from the unit.

11. Use a small screwdriver and carefully remove the air filter element from the diaphragm plate extension.

12. Separate the diaphragm plate assembly from the rear housing and disassemble the plate assembly.

13. Remove the rolling diaphragm from the groove in the diaphragm plate hub.

NOTE: Protect the diaphragm from oil, and nicks.

14. Hold the diaphragm plate in a horizontal position and depress the push rod approximately $1/16″$ and rotate the piston so the air valve lock will fall from its location. Remove the air valve pushrod assembly and the reaction disc.

15. If a new seal is needed, support the outer surface of the rear housing and drive out the seal with a suitable tool.

NOTE: Do not reuse old seal once it has been removed.

16. Remove the check valve and grommet from the front housing and discard.

17. Remove the front housing from the holding fixture.

Assembly

1. Use clean brake fluid and thoroughly clean all reusable brake parts.

2. Inspect all rubber parts and replace if nicked, cut or damaged.

3. When rebuilding, make sure that no grease or mineral oil comes in contact with any of the rubber parts.

4. Install a new check valve grommet in the front housing.

5. Position and secure the holding fixture to the front housing and place in a vise.

6. Place the rear housing on a block of wood, stud side down, and position the housing seal in the center hole. Using the special installing tool seat the seal in the recess of the rear housing.

7. Assemble the diaphragm plate assembly:

a. Apply a silicone lubricant to the outside diameter of the diaphragm plate and extension, to the bearing surfaces of the air valve and to the outer edge of the valve poppet. Insert the air valve and pushrod assembly in the extension of the diaphragm plate.

b. Depress the pushrod slightly and install the air valve. Make sure the lock indexes and retains the air valve.

c. Install the rolling diaphragm in the groove of the diaphragm plate.

d. Apply silicone lubricant to the surface of the reaction disc and position the disc in the center bore of the diaphragm plate. Use the piston rod to seat the disc in the bore.

NOTE: It is important that the disc be fully seated before removing the piston rod.

8. Apply silicone lubricant to the inside diameter of the rear housing seal and the diaphragm bead contact surface of the rear housing. Install the diaphragm plate assembly in the rear housing.

9. Position the air filter element over the pushrod and into the diaphragm plate extension. Install the air filter retainer.

10. Attach the base of the holding fixture to the front housing and clamp the base in a vise with the power section up.

11. Place a spanner wrench over the studs on the rear housing.

12. Place a diaphragm plate return spring in the front housing and position the rear housing assembly on the front housing with the small end of the spring downward. Align the scribe marks and lock in place.

13. Press down on the spanner wrench and rotate the rear housing counterclockwise to assemble the two housings.

NOTE: Bend the lances in on the rear housing. If the tangs crack or break, it will be necessary to replace that half of the housing.

14. Remove the spanner wrench from the rear shell.

15. Install the air silencer over the push rod end, then the boot retainer.

16. On vehicles with a clevis type push rod, install the locknut and clevis.

17. Install the mounting bracket to the rear shell, if so equipped.

18. Remove the cylinder from the vise and remove the holding fixture.

19. Apply silicone lubricant to the piston rod and guide the rod into the center bore of the diaphragm plate until it is fully seated.

NOTE: Keep the lubricant away from the rounded end of the rod.

20. Press the seal into the front housing until it is bottomed in the recess of the housing.

Kelsey-Hayes Diaphragm Type

IDENTIFICATION

The Kelsey-Hayes power brake unit can be identified by the twistlock method of locking the housing and cover together, plus the white-colored vacuum check valve assembly.

Removal

1. With engine off, apply brakes several times to equalize internal brake pressure.

2. Disconnect hydraulic line from master cylinder.

3. Disconnect vacuum hose from power brake check valve.

4. Disconnect power brake from brake pedal (under instrument panel).

5. Disconnect power brake unit from dash panel.

6. Remove power brake and master cylinder assembly from the vehicle.

Disassembly

1. Separate master cylinder from power brake unit.

2. Remove master cylinder pushrod and air cleaner plate.

3. Mount the power unit in a vise with the master cylinder attaching-studs up.

4. Scribe an index line across the housing and cover for reassembly reference.

5. Pry out the housing lock. Do not damage the lock, as it must be used at assembly.

6. Remove check valve from cover by prying out of rubber grommet.

7. Place parking brake flange holding tool over the master cylinder mounting studs.

8. Rotate the tool and cover in a counterclockwise direction. Then, separate the cover from the housing. This will expose the power piston return spring and diaphragm.

9. Lift out the power piston return spring. Remove the brake unit from the vise.

10. Remove power piston by slowly lifting the piston straight up.

11. Remove air cleaner, guide seal and seal retainer from the cover.

12. Remove the block seal from the center hole of the housing, using a blunt drift. (Don't scratch the bore of the housing, it could cause a vacuum leak.)

Power Piston Disassembly

1. Remove power piston diaphragm from the power piston. Keep it clean.

2. Remove screws that attach the plastic guide to the power piston. Remove guide and place to one side.

3. Remove the power piston square seal ring, reaction ring insert, reaction ring and reaction plate.

4. Depress operating rod slightly, then remove the Truarc snap-ring.

5. Remove control piston by pulling the operating rod.

6. Remove the O-ring seal from the end of the control piston.

7. Remove the filter elements and dust felt from the control piston rod.

Cleaning and Inspection

Thoroughly wash all metal parts in a suitable solvent and dry with compressed air. The power diaphragm, plastic power piston and guide should be washed in a mild soap and water solution. Blow dust and all cleaning material out of internal passages. All rubber parts should be replaced, regardless of condition. Install new air filters at assembly. Inspect all parts for scoring, pits, dents or nicks. Small imperfections can be smoothed out with crocus cloth. Replace all badly damaged parts.

Assembly

When assembling, be sure that all rubber parts, except the diaphragm and the reaction ring are lubricated with silicone grease.

1. Install control piston O-ring onto the piston.

2. Lubricate and install the control piston into the power piston. Install the Truarc snap-ring into its groove. Wipe all lubricant off the end of the control piston.

3. Install air filter elements and felt seal over the pushrod and down past the retaining shoulder on the rod. Install the power piston square seal ring into its groove.

4. Install the reaction plate in the power piston. Align the three holes with those in the power piston.

5. Install the rubber reaction ring in the reaction plate. Do not lubricate this ring.

6. Lubricate outer diameter of the reaction insert and install in the reaction ring.

7. Install reaction insert bumper into the guide.

8. Place guide on the power piston, align the holes with the aligning points on the power piston. Install retaining screws and torque to 80–100 in. lbs.

9. Install diaphragm on power piston; be sure that the diaphragm is correctly seated in the power piston groove.

10. With the housing blocked to prevent damage, install the block seal in the housing.

11. Install a new cover seal on the retainer and lubricate thoroughly, inside and out, with silicone grease, then install in the cover bore. Install new air filter.

12. Lubricate check valve grommet and install the vacuum check valve.

13. Mount the power unit in a vise, with master cylinder attaching studs up.

14. Apply a light coating of silicone grease to the bead, outer edge only, of the power piston diaphragm.

15. Install the power piston assembly in the housing with the operating rod down.

16. Install the power piston return spring into the flange of the guide.

17. Place the cover over the return spring and press down on the cover. At the same time, pilot the guide through the seal.

18. Rotate the cover to lock it to the housing. Be sure the scribe lines are in correct index and that the diaphragm is not pinched during assembly.

19. Install the housing lock on one of the long tangs of the housing.

20. Remove the power unit from the vise.

21. Install the master cylinder push-rod and air cleaner plate, then install the master cylinder on the studs. Install attaching nuts and washers. Torque to 200 in. lbs.

Installation

1. Install the power brake seal to the firewall.

2. Install power brake unit onto firewall and torque the attaching nuts to 200 in. lbs.

3. Install pushrod to brake pedal attaching bolt. Torque to 30 ft. lbs.

4. Install vacuum hose onto the power brake unit.

5. Attach the hydraulic tube and fill the master cylinder. Bleed hydraulic system.

6. Adjust stop-light switch if necessary.

Delco Single Diaphragm Booster

Disassembly

1. Scribe a mark on the bottom center of front and rear housings for reassembly.

2. Attach a base tool to the front housing and clamp the base in a vise with the power section up.

3. Separate the front and rear housings by securing a spanner wrench to the bracket. Press down on the wrench and rotate rear housing counterclockwise to the unlocked position. Loosen the housing carefully as it is spring loaded.

4. Remove the spanner wrench, then lift the rear housing and power piston assembly from the unit. Remove the return spring.

5. Remove the silencer by removing the retaining ring on the push rod.

6. Remove the seal, vacuum check valve and grommet from the front housing.

7. Remove the power piston assembly from the rear housing.

8. Remove the silencer from the neck of the power piston tube.

9. Remove the lock ring from the power piston.

10. Remove the reaction retainer, piston, plate, levers, bumper and spring.

11. Place a power piston wrench in a vise and position the assembly so that the three lugs on the tool fit into the three notches in the piston.

12. Press down on the support plate and rotate it counterclockwise until it separates from the power piston.

13. Remove the diaphragm from the support plate.

14. Position the power piston, tube down, in a tool fabricated from a piece of wood 2″ × 4″ × 8″ long with a 1⅜″ hole in the center clamped in a vise.

15. Remove the snap-ring on the air valve.

16. Using the power pump and press plate insert the power piston, tube down, in a press plate and remove the air valve assembly using a ⅜″ drive extension as a remover.

17. Remove the floating control valve assembly from the push rod. Use a new one when rebuilding.

18. Push the master cylinder push rod from the center of the reaction retainer.

19. Remove the O-ring from the groove in the master cylinder piston rod.

Assembly

1. Use clean brake fluid and thoroughly clean all resuable brake parts.

2. Inspect all rubber parts and replace

Delco single diaphragm booster

Power piston assembly

if nicked, cut or damaged.

3. When rebuilding make sure that no grease or mineral oil comes in contact with any of the rubber parts.

4. Install a new vacuum check valve using a new grommet.

Staking the housing locking tabs

5. Position a new front housing seal so that the flat surface of the cup lies against the bottom depression in the housing.

Housing locking tabs

6. Place a new O-ring in the groove on the master cylinder piston rod, wipe a thin film of silicone lubricant on the O-ring.

7. Insert the master cylinder piston rod through the reaction retainer so the round end protrudes from the end of the tube on the reaction retainer.

8. Place the power piston wrench in a vise and position the power piston on the wrench so that the three lugs fit into the notches.

9. Position a new O-ring on the air valve on the second groove from the push rod end.

10. Place a new floating control valve on the push rod-air valve assembly so that the flat face of the valve will seat against the valve seat on the air valve.

NOTE: The old floating control valve assembly must be replaced with a new one since the force required to remove it distorts component parts.

11. Wipe a thin film of silicone lubricant on the control valve and the O-ring on the air valve.

12. Push the air valve push rod assembly, air valve first, onto its seat in the tube of the power piston.

13. Place the control valve retainer over the push rod so that the flat side seats on the floating control valve.

14. Press the floating control valve and its retainer onto the power piston tube by use of an installer tool and pushing down by hand.

15. After the floating control valve is seated, position the push rod limiter washer over the push rod and down onto the valve.

16. Stretch the air filter element over the end of the push rod and press it into the power piston tube.

17. Assemble the power piston diaphragm to the support plate. The raised flange of the diaphragm is pressed through the hole in the center of the support plate.

NOTE: Be sure that the edge of the center hole fits into the groove in the flange of the diaphragm.

18. Pull the diaphragm away from the outside diameter of the support plate so that the support plate can be gripped with both hands.

19. With the power piston still positioned on the holding tool in a vise, coat the bead of the diaphragm that contacts the power piston with silicone lubricant.

20. Place the support plate and diaphragm assembly over the tube of the power piston with the locking tangs facing downward.

NOTE: The flange of the power piston will fit into the groove on the power piston.

21. Press down and rotate the support plate clockwise, until the lugs on the power piston come against the stops on the support plate.

22. Turn the assembly over and place tube down in a tool, fabricated from a piece of wood 2″ × 4″ × 8″ long with a 1⅜″ hole in the center, clamped into a vise.

23. Replace the snap-ring into the groove of the air valve.

24. Place the air valve spring retainer on the snap-ring and assemble the reaction bumper into the groove in the end of the air valve.

25. Position the air valve return spring, large end down, on the spring retainer.

26. Place the three reaction levers into position with the wide ends in the slots of the power piston and the narrow ends resting on top of the air valve return springs.

27. Position the reaction plate (with the numbered side up) on top of the reaction levers. Press down on the plate until the large ends of the reaction levers pop up so the plate rests flat on the levers and is centered.

28. With the round end of the master cylinder piston rod up, and with the reaction retainer held toward the top of the piston rod, place the small end of the piston rod in the hole in the center of the reaction plate. Line up the ears on the reaction retainer with the notches in the power piston and push the reaction retainer down until the ears seat in the notches.

29. With pressure on the reaction retainer, position the large lock ring down over the master cylinder push rod.

30. There is a lug on the power piston which has a raised divider in the center. One end of the lock ring goes under the lug and on one side of the divider.

31. As you work your way around the power piston, the lockring goes over the ear of the reaction retainer and under a lug on the power piston until the other end of the lock ring is seated under the lug with the raised divider.

NOTE: Make certain both ends of the lock ring are securely under the large lug.

32. Place a new power piston bearing in the center of the rear housing so the flange on the center hole of the housing fits into the groove of the power piston bearing. The large flange on the power piston bearing will be on the stud side of the housing. Coat the inside of the bearing with silicone lubricant.

33. Place the air silencer over the holes on the tube of the power piston. Wipe the tube with silicone lubricant.

34. Attach the holding fixture to the front housing and clamp the base in a vise.

35. Place the power piston return spring over the insert in the front housing.

36. Lubricate the inside diameter of the support plate seal, the reaction retainer tube, and the beaded edge of the diaphragm with silicone lubricant.

37. Place the rear housing assembly over the front housing assembly and align the scribe marks of the two housings so they will match when in the locked position.

38. Place a spanner wrench on the rear housing and tighten the nuts and washers to the bolts.

39. Press down on the spanner wrench and twist the rear housing clockwise until fully locked.

NOTE: Do not break the studs loose in the rear housing or put pressure on the power piston tube when locking the housings.

40. Remove the spanner wrench and the holding fixture from the front housing.

41. Push the felt silencer over the push-rod and seat it against the end of the power piston tube.

42. Push the plastic boot and seat it against the rear housing. The raised tabs on the side of the boot will locate in the holes in the center of the brackets.

43. Stake the front and rear housing in two places: 180° apart.

NOTE: The interlock tabs should not be used for staking a second time. When all tabs have been staked once, the housing must be replaced.

Delco tandem dual diaphragm booster

Delco Tandem Dual Diaphragm Type

Disassembly

1. Scribe a line across the front and rear housing for reassembly.

2. Attach the base of a special holding fixture or equivalent to the front housing with nuts and washers and draw down tight to eliminate damage to the studs. Clamp the base in a vise with the power section up.

3. On vehicles with a straight mounting bracket place a spanner wrench over the studs on the rear housing and attach with

Unlocking the front and rear housings

nuts and washers.

4. On vehicles with a tilted mounting bracket there is a special tool placed inside the mounting bracket with the spanner wrench placed on top.

5. Press down on the spanner wrench and rotate the rear housing counterclockwise to separate the two housings. Remove the special tools.

6. Remove the power piston return spring, and remove and discard the vacuum check valve and grommet from the front housing.

7. Remove the front housing seal.

8. Remove the boot retainer and boot from the rear housing and remove the felt silencer from inside the boot.

9. Remove the power piston group from the rear housing and remove the primary power piston bearing from the center opening of the rear housing.

10. Remove piston rod retainer and piston rod from the secondary piston.

11. Mount a special double ended tool with the large diameter end up in a vise. Position the secondary power piston so that the two radial slots in the piston fit over the ears of the tool.

NOTE: Due to an optional construction design on the primary and secondary power pistons the special tool used in step 11 will have to be reworked.

12. Fold back the primary diaphragm from the outside diameter of the primary support plate. Grip the edge of the support plate and rotate it counterclockwise to unscrew the primary power piston from the secondary power piston.

13. Remove the housing divider from the secondary power piston bearing from the housing divider.

14. The secondary power piston should still be positioned on the special double ended tool. Fold back the secondary diaphragm from the outside diameter of the secondary support plate. Rotate the support plate clockwise to unlock the secondary power piston.

15. Remove the secondary diaphragm from the secondary support plate.

16. Remove the reaction piston and disc from the center of the secondary power piston by pushing down on the end of the piston.

17. Remove the air valve spring from the end of the valve, if not removed earlier.

18. Remove the primary diaphragm and piston using the same procedure as the secondary with the exception of turning the support plate counterclockwise to unlock it.

19. Remove the air filter from the tubular section of the primary power piston.

20. Remove the power head silencer from the neck of the power piston tube.

21. Remove the rubber reaction bumper from the end of the air valve.

22. Using snap-ring pliers, remove the retaining ring from the air valve.

23. Remove the air valve push rod assembly.

a. The recommended method would be to place the primary power piston in an arbor press and press the air valve push rod assembly out the bottom of the power piston tube using a rod not larger than ½″ in diameter.

b. An alternate method would be to insert a heavy, round shanked screwdriver on both sides of the pushrod and pull the air valve-push rod assembly straight out.

24. Remove the O-ring seal from the air valve.

Assembly

1. Use clean brake fluid and thoroughly clean all reusable brake parts.

2. Inspect all rubber parts and replace if nicked, cut or damaged.

3. When rebuilding, make sure that no grease or mineral oil comes in contact with any of the rubber parts.

4. Install a new vacuum check valve and a new grommet in the front housing.

5. Place a new seal in the front housing so that the flat surface lies against the bottom of the depression in the housing.

6. Reassemble the power piston group.

7. Lubricate the inside and outside diameter of the O-ring seal with silicone lubricant and place on the air valve.

8. Wipe a thin film of silicone lubricant on the large and small outside diameter of the floating control valve. If the floating control valve needs replacement, it will be necessary to replace the complete air valve-push rod assembly.

9. Place the air valve end of the air valve push rod assembly into the tube of the primary power piston. Manually press the air valve push rod assembly so that the floating control valve bottoms on the tube section of the primary power piston.

10. Place the inside diameter of the floating control valve retainer on the outside diameter of the special installer. Place it over the pushrod so that the closed side of the retainer seats on the floating control valve. Using the installer manually press the retainer and floating control valve to seat in the tube.

11. Stretch the filter element over the pushrod and press it into the piston tube.

12. Place the retaining ring into the groove in the air valve using snap-ring pliers.

13. Position the rubber reaction bumper on the end of the air valve.

14. Determine the correct reaction piston and apply a light coat of silicone lubricant to the outside diameter of the rubber reaction disc.

15. Place the rubber reaction disc in the large cavity of the secondary power piston and push the disc down to seat on the reaction piston.

16. Unlock the secondary power piston from the primary power piston.

17. Assemble the primary diaphragm to the primary support plate opposite the locking tangs. Press the raised flange on the inside diameter of the diaphragm through

Reworking the tool for optional power piston design

Locking or unlocking the secondary support plate and secondary power piston

the center hole of the support plate. Be sure that the edge of the support plate center hole fits into the groove of the flange.

NOTE: Lubricate the inside diameter of the diaphragm and the raised surface of the flange with a light coat of silicone lubricant.

18. Mount the special tool used in step 11 of the disassembly procedures in a vise with the small end up. Position the primary power piston so that the two radial slots in the piston fit over the ears (tangs) of the tool.

19. Fold the primary diaphragm away from the outside diameter of the primary support plate.

20. Place the primary support plate and diaphragm assembly over the tube of the primary piston. Make sure the locking tangs are facing down.

21. Press down and rotate the support plate clockwise until the tabs on the piston

PRIMARY DIAPHRAGM — PRIMARY SUPPORT PLATE — SILENCER — RETAINER RING — REACTION BUMPER — AIR VALVE SPRING — 'O' RING SEAL — FLOATING CONTROL VALVE — FLOATING CONTROL VALVE RETAINER — FILTER — PRIMARY POWER PISTON — SECONDARY POWER PISTON — REACTION PISTON — REACTION DISC — SECONDARY POWER PISTON BEARING — HOUSING DIVIDER — SECONDARY SUPPORT PLATE — SECONDARY DIAPHRAGM — PISTON ROD RETAINER — PISTON ROD

Power piston group

Installing the floating control valve retainer

Seating the floating control valve assembly

contact the stops.

22. Place the power head silencer on the tube of the piston so that the holes at the base of the tube are covered.

23. Coat the outside of the tube with silicone lubricant.

24. Remove the primary piston assembly from the special tool and lay it aside.

25. Assemble the secondary diaphragm to the secondary support plate following the same steps for assembling the primary support plate except mount the special tool with the large diameter up, and press down and turn the plate counterclockwise until the piston contacts the stops.

26. Leave the secondary power piston on the tool and in the vise.

27. Apply a light coat of talcum powder or silicone lubricant to the bead on the outside diameter of the secondary diaphragm.

This will make it easier for reassembly of the front and rear housing.

28. Place the secondary bearing in the inside diameter of the housing divider so that the extended lip of the bearing faces up.

29. Lubricate the inside diameter of the bearing with silicone lubricant.

30. Using a special protector tool or equivalent, position the secondary bearing on the threaded end of the secondary power piston.

31. Hold the housing divider so that the six oblong protrusions on the middle of the divider are facing up. Press the divider down over the tool and onto the piston tube so it rests against the support ring. Remove the bearing protector tool.

32. Pick up the primary power piston assembly and fold the primary diaphragm

away from the outside diameter of the support plate.

33. Place the small end of the air valve return spring on the air valve so that it contacts the air valve retaining ring.

34. Position the primary power piston. Make sure that the air valve return spring seats down over the raised center section of the secondary piston.

35. Rotate the secondary power piston clockwise into the threaded portion of the primary piston. Tighten to 5–15 ft. lbs.

36. Fold the primary diaphragm back into position.

37. Cover the outside diameter of the piston rod retainer with a light coat of silicone lubricant.

38. Insert the master cylinder piston rod retainer into the secondary power piston so that the flat end bottoms against the rubber reaction disc.

39. Place the new primary piston bearing in the rear housing center hole. The thin lip of the bearing will protrude to the outside of the housing. Coat the inside diameter of the bearing with silicone lubricant.

40. Mount the holding fixture in a vise and position the front housing so that the housing studs fit in the holes provided in the tool.

41. Place the power piston return spring over the inset in the front housing.

42. Assemble the power piston assembly to the rear housing by pressing the tube of the primary piston through the rear housing bearing until the housing divider seats in the rear housing and the primary piston bottoms against the housing.

43. Hold the rear housing with the mounting studs and position it so that the tangs on the edge of the front housing are locked in the slots on the edge of the rear housing. The scribe marks on the top of the housings will be in line.

44. Lower the rear housing assembly onto the front housing.

NOTE: The power piston spring must seat in the depression in the face of the secondary power piston. Check that the bead on the outside diameter of the secondary diaphragm is positioned between the edges of the housing.

45. Assemble the front and rear housings with the spanner wrench.

46. Replace the silencer and boot.

DISC BRAKES—TROUBLE DIAGNOSIS

Cause	Correction
1. Master cylinder fluid level low.	1. Fill to proper level with approved fluid. (Fluid level drops as disc brake linings wear.)
2. Poor quality brake fluid (low boiling point) in system.	2. Drain hydraulic system and fill with approved.
3. Air in hydraulic system.	3. Bleed hydraulic system and refill with approved fluid.
4. Hoses soft or weak (expanding under pressure).	4. Replace defective hoses. Combination valve and all cups and seals in complete brakes.

DISC BRAKES—TROUBLE DIAGNOSIS

Cause	Correction
1. Power brake malfunctioning.	1. Check and repair power unit.
2. Linings soiled with brake fluid, oil or grease.	2. Replace shoes and linings.
3. Lines, hoses or connections dented, kinked, collapsed, clogged or disconnected.	3. Repair or replace defective parts.
4. Master cylinder cups swollen.	4. Drain hydraulic system, flush system with brake fluid and replace combination valve and all cups and seals in complete brake system.
5. Master cylinder bore corroded or rough.	5. Repair or replace master cylinder.
6. Caliper pistons frozen or seized.	6. Disassemble caliper and free pistons (replace if necessary).
7. Caliper cylinder bores corroded or rough.	7. Disassemble caliper and remove corrosion or roughness, or replace caliper.
8. Pedal push rod and linkage binding.	8. Free and lubricate.
9. Metering valve not working.	9. Replace combination valve.

GRABBING OR PULLING (Severe Reaction To Pedal Pressure and Out of Line Stops)

Cause	Correction
1. Linings soiled with brake fluid, oil or grease.	1. Replace shoes and linings.
2. Caliper loose.	2. Tighten caliper mounting bolts to specified torque.
3. Lines, hoses or connection dented, kinked, collapsed or clogged.	3. Repair or replace defective parts.
4. Master cylinder bore corroded or rough.	4. Repair or replace master cylinder.
5. Caliper pistons frozen or seized.	5. Disassemble caliper and free pistons (replace if necessary).
6. Caliper cylinder seals soft or swollen.	6. Drain hydraulic system, flush system with brake fluid and replace all cups and seals in complete brake system.
7. Caliper cylinder bores corroded or rough.	7. Disassemble caliper and remove corrosion or roughness, or replace caliper.
8. Pedal linkage binding (and suddenly releasing).	8. Free and lubricate linkage.
9. Metering valve not functioning properly.	9. Replace combination valve.

FADING PEDAL (Pedal Falling Away Under Steady Pressure)

Cause	Correction
1. Poor quality brake fluid (low boiling point) in system.	1. Drain hydraulic system and fill with approved fluid.
2. Hydraulic connections loose; lines or hoses ruptured (causing leakage).	2. Tighten or replace defective parts.
3. Master cylinder cup worn or damaged. (primary, secondary or both).	3. Repair master cylinder.
4. Master cylinder bore corroded, worn or scored.	4. Repair or replace master cylinder.
5. Caliper cylinder seals worn or damaged.	5. Replace seals.
6. Caliper cylinder bores corroded, worn or scored.	6. Disassemble caliper and remove corrosion or scoring, or replace caliper.
7. Bleed screw open.	7. Close bleed screw and bleed hydraulic system.

NOISE AND CHATTER (May Be Accompanied By Brake Roughness and Pedal Pumping)

Cause	Correction
1. Disc has excessive lateral runout.	1. Replace or machine disc.
2. Disc has excessive thickness variations (out of parallel).	2. Replace or machine disc.
3. Disc has casting imperfections.	3. Replace disc.
4. Car creeping or moving slowly with brakes applied (may produce groan or crunching noise).	4. Increase or decrease pedal effort slightly.
5. Squeal, during application.	5. A small amount of high-pitched squeal is inherent in disc brake design and must be considered normal. Some relief may be obtained with service package backing.

DRAGGING BRAKES (Slow or Incomplete Release of Brakes)

Cause	Correction
1. Lines, hoses or connections dented, kinked, collapsed or clogged.	1. Repair or replace defective parts.
2. Master cylinder compensating port restricted by swollen primary cup.	2. Drain hydraulic system, flush system with brake fluid and replace combination valve and all cups and seals in complete brake system.
3. Residual pressure check valve in lines to front wheels.	3. Remove check valve.
4. Caliper pistons frozen or seized.	4. Disassemble caliper and free pistons (replace if necessary).

BRAKES

Cause	Correction
DRAGGING BRAKES (Slow or Incomplete Release of Brakes)	
5. Caliper cylinder seals swollen.	5. Drain hydraulic system, flush system with clean brake fluid and replace combination valve and all cups and seals in complete brake system.
6. Caliper cylinder bores corroded or rough.	6. Disassemble caliper and remove corrosion or roughness, or replace caliper.
7. Hydraulic push rod on power brake out of adjustment or binding (causing primary cup to restrict master cylinder compensating port).	7. Adjust or free and lubricate.

DOMESTIC TRUCKS—DISC BRAKE SERVICE

Floating Caliper Disc Brakes

This disc brake is a floating caliper design with one or two pistons on one side of the rotor. It is a two piece unit consisting of the caliper and cylinder housing. The caliper is mounted to the anchor plate on two mounting pins which travel in bushings in the anchor plate. The bushings and pins are protected by toot type seals.

Two brake shoe and lining assemblies are used in each caliper, one on each side of the rotor. The shoes are identical and are attached to the caliper with two mounting pins.

The cylinder housing contains the two pistons. The pistons are fitted with an insulator on the front and a seal on the back lip. A friction ring is attached to the back of the piston with a shouldered cap screw. The pistons and cylinder bores are protected by boot seals which are fitted to a groove in the piston and attached to the cylinder housing with retainers. The cylinder assembly is attached to the caliper with two cap screws and washers.

The anchor plate is bolted directly to the spindle. It positions the caliper assembly over the rotor forward of the spindle.

DISC BRAKE SHOE ADJUSTMENT

The front disc brake assembly is designed so that it is inherently self-adjusting and requires no manual adjustment.

Automatic adjustment for lining wear is achieved by the piston and friction ring sliding outward in the cylinder bore. The piston assumes a new position in the cylinder and maintains the correct adjustment.

FRONT DISC BRAKE SHOE AND LINING

NOTE: Refer to following section for caliper and pad service for the Ford Ranger and Bronco II.

Replace shoe and lining assemblies when lining is worn to a minimum of $\frac{1}{16}''$ in thickness (combined thickness of shoe and lining $\frac{1}{4}''$ minimum).

Removal

1. Remove the shoe and lining mounting pins, anti-rattle springs and old shoe and lining assemblies.

Installation

1. Remove the master cylinder cover.
2. Loosen the piston housing-to-caliper mounting bolts sufficiently to permit the installation of new shoe and lining assemblies. Do not move pistons.
3. Install new shoe and lining assemblies. Install the brake shoe mounting pins

Typical floating caliper disc brake

and anti-rattle springs. Be sure that the spring tangs are located in the holes provided in the shoe plates.

4. Torque the brake shoe mounting pins to 17–23 ft. lbs.

5. Reset the pistons to the correct location in the cylinders by placing shims or feeler gauges of .023 to .035″ thickness between the shoe plate of the outboard shoe and lining assembly and the caliper; then, retighten the piston housing-to-caliper mounting bolts. Keep the cylinder housing square with the caliper.

6. Loosen the piston housing-to-caliper mounting bolts and remove the shims.

7. Torque the piston housing-to-caliper mounting bolts to 155 to 185 ft. lbs.

8. Check the master cylinder reservoirs.

9. Install the master cylinder cover.

DISC BRAKE CALIPER

Removal

1. Remove the wheel and tire assembly.

2. Remove the pins and nuts retaining the caliper assembly to the anchor plate.

3. Disconnect the brake hose from the caliper and remove the caliper.

Installation

1. Connect the brake hose to the caliper.

2. Position the caliper assembly to the anchor plate and install the retaining pins and nuts. Torque the nuts to specifications.

3. Install drum and wheel and bleed brake system.

If the caliper assembly is leaking, the piston assemblies must be removed from the piston housing and replaced. If the cylinder bores are scored, corroded or excessive wear is evident, the piston housing must be replaced. Do not hone the cylinder bores. Piston assemblies are not available for oversize bores. The piston housing must be removed from the caliper for replacement.

Disassembly

1. Remove the two pins and nuts retaining the caliper to the support. Disconnect the flexible brake hose and plug the end to prevent brake fluid leakage.

2. Remove the boot retainers and remove the dust boots from the pistons and cylinder housing.

3. Position the caliper assembly in a vise.

4. Place a block of wood between the caliper and the cylinders, and apply low pressure air to the brake hose inlet. One piston will be forced out.

5. Reverse the piston and install it by hand pressure back into the cylinder bore far enough to form a seal. Block the reversed piston from moving out of the bore and place the wooden block between the remaining piston and the caliper.

6. Force out the second piston with low pressure air. Care should be taken as the piston is forced out of the bore.

7. Remove the two bolts and separate the caliper from the cylinder housing.

Assembly

The piston assembly and dust boots are not to be reused. A new set is to be used each time the caliper is assembled.

1. Apply a film of clean brake fluid in the cylinder bores and on the piston assemblies. Do not apply brake fluid on the insulators.

2. Start the piston assemblies into the cylinder bores using firm hand pressure. Exercise care to avoid cocking the piston in the bore.

3. Lightly tapping with a rawhide mallet, seat each piston assembly until the friction ring bottoms out in the cylinder bore.

4. Install the piston dust boots and retainers.

5. Position the piston housing on the caliper and install the piston housing-to-caliper mounting bolts and washers. Torque the piston housing-to-caliper mounting bolts to 155 to 185 ft. lbs.

6. Install the flexible brake hose.

7. Bleed the brake system and centralize the pressure differential valve.

NOTE: Do not move the vehicle after working on the disc brakes until a firm brake pedal is obtained.

Sliding Caliper Disc Brakes—Single Piston

This caliper is a one piece type with a single piston on the inboard side. The piston is made of steel and is plated to resist wear and corrosion. The piston has a square cut seal which provides for a seal between the

piston and the caliper cylinder wall. A rubber dust boot located in a groove in the cylinder helps keep contamination from the piston and cylinder wall.

The caliper is mounted on an adapter which is mounted on the steering knuckle.

DISC BRAKE ADJUSTMENT

No adjustment is required on this unit other than applying the pedal several times after the unit has been worked on. This is to seat the shoes and after this is done the hydraulic pressure maintains the proper clearance between the brake shoes and the rotor.

BRAKE SHOES

Replace the brake shoes when the linings are worn within 1/16″ of the shoe or the rivets.

Removal

1. Remove the master cylinder cover and if the cylinder is more than 1/3 full remove the fluid necessary to make the cylinder only 1/3 full. This is done to prevent any overflow from the cylinder when the piston is pushed into the bore of the caliper.

2. Raise vehicle on hoist and remove the front wheels.

3. Compress the piston back into the bore by using a large C-clamp and compressing the unit until the piston bottoms in the bore.

4. Remove the two retaining bolts that hold the caliper into the support. If the caliper has retaining clips remove the retaining clips and anti-rattle springs. If the caliper has key type retainers, remove the key retaining screws, and using a hammer and drift, punch drive the key out of the caliper.

5. Slide the caliper off the rotor disc.

Typical single piston sliding caliper disc brake

Be careful not to damage the dust boot on the piston when removing the caliper.

NOTE: Do not let the caliper hang with the brake hose supporting the weight. This can cause damage to the hose which could result in a loss of brakes. Set the caliper on the front suspension arm or tie rod.

6. Remove the outer shoe from the caliper. It may be necessary to tap the shoe to loosen it from the caliper. Remove the inner shoe from the caliper or spindle assembly depending on where the shoe stays.

7. Remove the shoe support spring from the piston.

Cleaning and Inspection

Clean the sliding surfaces of the caliper and clean any dirt from the mounting bolts, clips or keys.

Inspect the boot on the piston for signs of cracks, cuts or other damage. Check to see if there is signs of fluid leaking around the seal on the piston. This will show up in the boot. If there is an indication of a fluid leak, the entire caliper has to be disassembled and the seal replaced.

Installation

1. Make sure that the piston is fully bottomed in the cylinder bore and install the outboard shoe in the recess of the caliper.

NOTE: On shoes with anti-rattle springs be sure to install the spring before installing the shoe in the caliper.

2. Place the outer shoe on the caliper and press it into place with finger pressure.

3. Position the caliper on the rotor and carefully slide it down into position over the rotor.

4. Install the caliper mounting bolts and torque them to 35 ft. lbs. On models with retaining clips install the anti-rattle springs and the retaining clips and torque the retaining screws to 200 in. lbs. On models with key type retainers press down the caliper and install the key in its slot and drive it in place with a hammer and drift. Install the retaining screw and torque to 12–18 ft. lbs.

5. Install the wheels and lower the vehicle. Check the master cylinder fluid level and add any fluid necessary to bring it up to the proper level.

6. Pump the brake pedal several times until a firm brake pedal is established. Road test the vehicle to check for proper operation.

DISC CALIPER
Removal

1. Remove the cover on the master cylinder and check if the fluid level is 1/3 full. If it is more than 1/3 full remove the necessary amount to bring the level down. This step is necessary to avoid overflow from the master cylinder when the piston is compressed into the cylinder bore.

2. Raise the vehicle and remove the wheel.

3. Compress the piston into the caliper bore and remove the brake hose from the caliper. Tape the end of the hose to prevent dirt from entering the line.

4. Remove the caliper retaining bolts, clips or wedges and remove the caliper from the vehicle.

Disassembly

1. Clean the outside of the caliper with clean brake fluid and drain any fluid from the caliper.

2. Remove the piston from the caliper by connecting the hydraulic line to the caliper and gently stroking the brake pedal. This will push the piston from the caliper bore.

3. With care remove the boot from the caliper piston bore.

4. Remove the piston seal from the caliper bore using a piece of wood or plastic.

NOTE: DO NOT use a metal tool to remove the seal. This can damage the bore or burr the edges of the seal groove.

5. Remove the bleeder valve.

Cleaning and Inspection

1. Clean all the parts with clean brake fluid and blow out all the passages in the caliper.

NOTE: When ever the caliper is disassembled discard the boot and piston seal. These parts must not be reused.

2. Inspect the outside of the piston for signs of wear, corrosion, scores or any other defects. If any defects are detected replace the piston.

3. Check the caliper bore for the same defects as the piston. However, the bore can be cleaned up to a point with crocus cloth. If there are any marks that will not clean up with the cloth the caliper must be replaced.

Assembly and Installation

1. Lube the caliper bore and the piston with clean brake fluid and position the seal for the piston in the cylinder bore groove.

2. Install the dust boot into the groove in the piston with the fold faces toward the open end of the piston.

3. Install the piston in the bore being careful not to unseat the piston seal in the bore.

4. With the piston bottomed in the cylinder position the boot in the groove in the caliper. Make sure that the retaining ring in the seal is pressed down evenly around the cylinder.

5. Install the bleeder screw in the caliper and install the caliper back on the vehicle.

6. Connect the brake hoses and bleed the calipers of air. When bleeding is done pump the pedal several times to develop a firm brake pedal.

Sliding Caliper Disc Brakes (Double Piston)

BRAKE SHOE AND CALIPER
Removal

1. Drain about 2/3 of the total brake fluid from the reservoir.

2. Jack up the vehicle and remove the front wheels.

3. Remove the four screws and remove the caliper hold-down assembly.

4. Lift the caliper off the hub and rotor. If the caliper is to be removed, disconnect the hydraulic line; if not, lay the caliper on the suspension or support with a length of wire.

5. Remove the inner and outer shoe and lining.

Disassembly

1. Drain the brake fluid from the caliper and clean the exterior with clean brake fluid.

2. Place a small block of wood under the caliper pistons and place a protective pad over the exterior. Remove the pistons by directing compressed air into the caliper fluid outlet.

3. Remove and discard piston boots.

4. Remove the piston seals from the groove in the caliper bore.

Assembly

1. Clean all parts in clean brake fluid and blow dry.

2. Dip the new piston seal in clean brake fluid and install it into the cylinder groove.

NOTE: Be sure that the seal is not rolled or twisted in the groove.

3. Install the dust boot in the cylinder groove.

4. Coat the outside diameter of the piston with clean brake fluid. Use something plastic or wood and gradually work the dust boot around the piston.

5. Press the piston straight into the caliper bore until it bottoms. Position the boot in the piston groove.

Installation

1. Install a new shoe and lining assembly into the anchor plate.

2. Push the pistons to the bottom of the piston bore. Place a small block of wood over both pistons and boots. Push the pistons to the bottom of the bores with a C-clamp.

3. Install the outer shoe and lining onto the caliper and install the shoe hold-down spring and pin.

4. Install the caliper assembly over the hub, rotor and inner shoe, and position into the inner grooves in the anchor plate.

5. Install the caliper hold-down parts and tighten to 40 ft. lbs.

NUT–34989-S2
WASHER–376916-S2
SUPPORT ASSEMBLY 2B304
BOLT–34989-S2
SHIELD 2K005
WASHER 376916
CALIPER ASSEMBLY 2B120-RH 2B121-LH
SPINDLE ASSEMBLY 3105
HUB AND ROTOR ASSEMBLY 1102
NUT 381542-S2
SPRING 2B486
KEY 2B487
BOLT 385194-S2
INNER CONE AND ROLLER 4221
GREASE SEAL 1190
OUTER CONE AND ROLLER 1216
WITH DUAL REAR WHEEL SAME AS MAIN VIEW EXCEPT AS SHOWN
COTTER PIN 72072-S36
WHEEL ADAPTER 1A090
HUBCAP 1130
NUT 1012
WASHER 1195
NUT 374504-S100
NUT RETAINER 374536-S
CAP 1131
WHEELCOVER

Typical dual piston sliding caliper disc brake

6. Add extra heavy duty brake fluid to bring the level to ¼″ from the top of the reservoir.

7. Bleed the system and add fluid as necessary.

Ford Ranger and Bronco II

INSPECTION

Replace the front pads when the pad thickness is at the minimum thickness recommended by Ford Motor Co. (1/32″), or at the minimum allowed by the applicable state or local motor vehicle inspection code. Pad thickness may be checked by removing the wheel and looking through the inspection port in the caliper assembly.

FRONT CALIPER AND DISC BRAKE PADS

Removal & Installation

NOTE: Always replace all disc pad assemblies on an axle. Never service one wheel only.

1. To avoid fluid overflow when the caliper piston is pressed into the caliper cylinder bores, siphon or dip part of the brake fluid out of the larger master cylinder reservoir (connected to the front disc brakes). Discard the removed fluid.

2. Raise the vehicle and install jack stands. Remove a front wheel and tire assembly.

3. Place an eight-inch C-clamp on the caliper and tighten the clamp to bottom the caliper piston in the cylinder bore. Remove the clamp.

NOTE: Do not use a screwdriver or similar tool to pry piston away from the rotor.

4. There are three types of caliper pins used: a single tang type, a double tang type and a split-shell type. The pin removal process is dependent upon how the pin is installed (bolt head direction). Remove the upper caliper pin first.

NOTE: On some applications, the pin may be retained by a nut and torx-head bolt (except the split-shell type).

If the bolt head is on the outside of the caliper, use the following procedure:

a. From the inner side of the caliper, tap the bolt within the caliper pin until the bolt head on the outer side of the caliper shows a separation between the bolt head and the caliper pin.

b. Using a hacksaw or bolt cutter, remove the bolt head from the bolt.

c. Depress the tab on the bolt head end of the upper caliper pin with a screwdriver, while tapping on the pin with a hammer. Continue tapping until the tab is depressed by the v-slot.

d. Place one end of a punch (½ inch or smaller) against the end of the caliper pin and drive the caliper pin out of the caliper toward the inside of the vehicle. Do not use a screwdriver or other edged tool to help drive out the caliper pin as the v-grooves may be damaged.

— **CAUTION** —
Never reuse caliper pins. Always install new pins whenever a caliper is removed.

If the nut end of the bolt is on the outside of the caliper, use the following procedure:

a. Remove the nut from the bolt.

b. Depress the lead tang on the end of the upper caliper pin with a screwdriver while tapping on the pin with a hammer. Continue tapping until the lead tang is depressed by the v-slot.

c. Place one end of a punch (½ inch or smaller) against the end of the caliper pin and drive the caliper pin out of the caliper toward the inside of the vehicle. Do not use a screwdriver or other edged tool to help drive out the caliper pin as the v-grooves may be damaged.

5. Repeat the procedure in Step 4 for the lower caliper pin.

6. Remove the caliper from the rotor. If the caliper is to be removed for service, remove the brake hose from the caliper.

7. Remove the outer pad. Remove the anti-rattle clips and remove the inner pad. To install:

8. Place a new anti-rattle clip on the lower end of the inner pad. Be sure the tabs

on the clip are positioned properly and the clip is fully seated.

9. Position the inner pad and anti-rattle clip in the pad abutment with the anti-rattle clip tab against the pad abutment and the loop-type spring away from the rotor. Compress the anti-rattle clip and slide the upper end of the pad in position.

10. Install the outer pad, making sure the torque buttons on the pad spring clip are seated solidly in the matching holes in the caliper.

11. Install the caliper on the spindle, making sure the mounting surfaces are free of dirt and lubricate the caliper grooves with Disc Brake Caliper Grease. Install new caliper pins, making sure the pins are installed with the tang in position as shown.

The pin must be installed with the lead tang in first, the bolt head facing outward (if equipped) and the pin positioned as shown. Position the lead tang in the v-slot mounting surface and drive in the caliper until the drive tang is flush with the caliper assembly. Install the nut (if equipped) and tighten to 32-47 in-lbs.

—— CAUTION ——
Never reuse caliper pins. Always install new pins whenever a caliper is removed.

12. If removed, install the brake hose to the caliper.

13. Bleed the brakes as described earlier in this chapter.

14. Install the wheel and tire assembly. Torque the lug nuts to 85-115 ft.-lbs.

15. Remove the jack stands and lower the vehicle. Check the brake fluid level and fill as necessary. Check the brakes for proper operation.

DOMESTIC TRUCK—DRUM BRAKE SERVICE

Non-Servo Type

This brake is a non-servo, floating shoe type brake. Upper ends of shoes extend through wheel cylinder boots and contact inserts in wheel cylinder pistons. Shoe ends are held firmly against pistons by the brake shoe return spring. Lower ends of shoes are held against a fixed anchor plate by the anchor spring. Hold-down spring at center of each shoe holds shoes in alignment. Lining-to-drum clearance adjustment is made through eccentric cam type adjusting studs.

Brake Shoe Removal

1. Back off brake adjustment, then remove brake drum.

2. Remove brake shoe return spring. Spread upper end of shoes until they are clear of wheel cylinders and hold-down springs, then disengage shoes from anchor plate at bottom. Remove anchor spring from shoes.

3. Do not depress brake pedal while shoes are removed.

Cleaning and Inspection

1. Clean all dirt out of brake drum. Inspect drum for roughness, scoring, or out-of-round. Replace or recondition drum as necessary.

2. Carefully pull lower edge of each wheel cylinder boot away from cylinder and note whether interior is excessively wet with brake fluid. Excessive fluid indicates leakage past piston cups, requiring overhaul of wheel cylinder.

NOTE: A slight amount of fluid is nearly always present and acts as a lubricant for pistons.

3. Check backing plate attaching bolts to make sure they are tight. Clean all rust and dirt from ledges on backing plate where shoe rims make contact using fine emery cloth.

4. Inspect the shoe return and anchor springs and hold-down springs. If broken, cracked, or weakened by rust or corrosion, replace springs.

5. If brake linings are worn to the extent that replacement is necessary, replace linings.

Brake Shoe Installation

1. Inspect brake shoe lining assemblies and make sure there are no nicks or burrs on edges of shoes which contact backing plate.

2. Apply a light film of grease at the following points: where shoe webs contact hold-down springs; where anchor ends of shoe webs contact anchor plate; and at six places where shoe rims contact ledges on backing plate.

3. Install hold-down springs on backing plate. Hook anchor spring into slot at bottom of each shoe. Swing upper ends of shoes apart and position at backing plate, with lower ends of shoe webs engaging anchor plate and with anchor spring behind extension on anchor plate.

NOTE: The shoe with the shorter lining must be to the rear of the vehicle.

4. Swing shoes up into position with center of shoe webs engaging hold-down springs, and with upper ends inserted through wheel cylinder boots.

5. Install brake shoe return spring, being sure short end is hooked into slotted hole in rear shoe and long end in round hole in front shoe.

6. Install brake drum and wheel. Adjust brakes.

To Adjust the Lining Clearance: On the forward shoe, rotate the drum and the adjuster cam in *forward direction* until the brake drags. Back-off until the drag is relieved. On reverse shoe, rotate the drum and the adjuster cam in *reverse direction* until the brake drags. Back-off until the drag is relieved.

Duo Servo Type

Removal & Installation

1. With the vehicle elevated on a hoist, jack or suitable stand, loosen parking brake equalizer nut, remove rear wheel, and drum retaining clips. Remove drum.

2. Remove brake shoe return springs. (Note how secondary spring overlaps primary spring.)

3. Remove brake shoe retainers, springs and nails.

4. Slide eye of automatic adjuster cable off anchor and then unhook from lever. Remove cable, cable guide and anchor plate.

5. Disconnect lever spring from lever and disengage from shoe web. Remove spring and lever.

6. Spread anchor ends of the primary and secondary shoes and remove parking brake strut and spring.

7. Disengage parking brake cable from parking brake lever and remove brake assembly.

8. Remove the primary and secondary brake shoe assemblies and adjusting star wheel from support. Install wheel cylinder to hold pistons in cylinders.

9. Inspect the platforms of support for nicks or burrs. Apply a thin coat of lubricant to support platforms.

10. Attach parking brake lever to the back side of the secondary shoe.

11. Place the secondary and primary shoe in their relative position on a work bench.

12. Lubricate threads of adjusting screw and install it between the primary and secondary shoes with star wheel next to secondary shoe. The star adjusting wheels are stamped "R" (right side) and "L" (left side), and indicate their location on vehicle.

13. Overlap anchor ends of the primary and secondary brake shoes and install adjusting spring and lever.

14. Hold the brake shoes in their relative position and engage parking brake cable into parking brake lever.

15. Install parking brake strut and spring between the parking brake lever and primary shoe.

16. Place brake shoes on the support and install retainer nails, springs and retainers.

17. Install anchor pin plate.

18. Install "eye" of adjusting cable over anchor pin and install return spring between primary shoe and anchor pin.

19. Install cable guide in secondary shoe then install secondary return spring. (Be sure secondary spring overlaps primary.)

20. Place adjusting cable in groove of cable guide and engage hook of cable into adjusting lever.

21. Install brake drum and retaining clips.

22. Adjust brakes.

Typical brake adjustment procedure

Measuring brake drum diameter

Measuring shoe mounted width

Kelsey Hayes

Removal & Installation

1. Raise the truck until the wheel clears the floor.

2. Remove the wheel, hub and drum assembly.

3. Clamp the brake cylinder boots against the ends of the cylinder with brake piston clamps.

4. The two different types of brake shoe retracting springs and remove the springs.

5. Remove the brake shoe hold down post cotter key, nut, and shoe hold down washer.

6. Loosen and remove the eccentric adjuster bolt, lock washer, eccentric and adjusting link.

7. Remove the shoe and lining assembly from the backing plate.

8. Remove the anchor block spring and slide the adjuster assembly from the shoe web.

9. Remove the adjuster star wheel and screw from the adjuster block. Unthread the star wheel from the adjuster screw.

10. Wipe all brake dust from the brake assembly parts with a clean dry rag. Coat all points of contact between brake shoes and other parts with high temperature grease.

11. Coat the adjuster screw and the inside of the adjuster block with high temperature grease.

12. Thread the adjuster screw onto the star wheel and insert the adjuster screw assembly into the adjuster block. Maintain a 2.12–2.18 inch dimension from the end of the adjuster block to the adjuster screw web slot.

13. Install the adjuster assembly onto the shoe web and attach the anchor block spring.

14. Place the brake shoe over the retracting spring toggle pin and insert the ends of the shoe in the wheel cylinder links.

15. Install the shoe hold down washer and nut. Do not install the cotter pin.

16. Install the four brake shoe retracting springs. Make sure the retracting springs are installed. On 15 × 5″ brakes the inner

Kelsey-Hayes heavy duty brake

hook ends face the wheel cylinders. On 15 × 4″ brakes the inner hook ends face the center of the axle.

17. Install the adjusting link, eccentric, lockwasher and adjuster bolt. Do not tighten.

18. Remove the brake piston clamps.

19. Tighten the shoe hold down nut until there is 0.015–0.025″ clearance between the shoe and hold down washer with the shoe held against the backing plate. Install the cotter pin.

20. Center the shoes on the backing plate. Using a ½″ wrench, rotate the adjuster eccentric until the adjusting lever is at the index mark. Tighten the eccentric adjuster bolt to specification.

21. Install the wheel, hub and drum assembly.

22. Adjust the brake to obtain a slight drag. Subsequent adjustments will be automatic.

Self Adjusting Brakes

The brake shoes are automatically adjusted when the vehicle is driven in reverse and the brakes applied. A manual adjustment is required only after the brake shoes have been relined or replaced.

The two-cylinder brake assembly brake shoes are adjusted by turning adjusting wheels reached through slots in the backing plate.

Two types of two-cylinder brake assemblies are used on truck rear wheels. The assemblies differ primarily in the retracting spring hookup, and in the design of the adjusting screws and locks. However, the service procedures are the same for both assemblies.

The brake adjustment is made with the vehicle raised. Check the brake drag by rotating the drum in the direction of forward rotation as the adjustment is made.

1. Remove the adjusting slot covers from the backing plate.

2. Turn the rear (secondary shoe) adjusting screw inside the hole to expand the brake shoe until a slight drag is felt against the brake drum.

3. Repeat the above procedure on the front (primary) brake shoe.

4. Replace the adjusting hole covers.

5. Complete the adjustment by applying the brakes several times while backing the vehicle.

6. After the brake shoes have been properly adjusted, check the operation of the brakes by making several stops while operating in a forward direction.

Bendix

TWO-PISTON SINGLE CYLINDER HYDRAULICALLY ACTUATED TYPE

Description

Both shoes pivot on anchor pins at the bottom of the support plate. The shoes are actuated by one wheel cylinder which is of the double piston type. Specification for heel and toe clearance of shoes should be strictly followed to obtain efficient brake operation.

Brake Shoe Removal

1. Back off the adjusting cam and remove wheel and drum assembly.
2. Remove brake shoe return spring.
3. Install wheel cylinder brake clamp to prevent pistons from being forced out of cylinder.
4. Remove C-washer, oil washer and retainer, guide spring retainer and guide spring from anchor bolts to remove brake shoes.

Brake Shoe Installation

1. Install brake shoes, oil washers and retainers on anchor bolts and secure with C-washers.
2. Install brake return spring.
3. Install wheel and drum assembly.

Adjustments

Since tapered brake lining is thicker at the center than at the ends, the adjustment procedures outlined in the paragraphs that follow must be performed in order to assure maximum braking efficiency.

Minor Adjustment

1. Jack up truck so that one wheel can be rotated freely.
2. Then, while rotating that wheel forward and backward, bring the shoe out to the drum with the adjusting cam until a light drag is obtained.
3. Back off the adjustment until the wheel is free to turn.
4. Repeat this procedure on the other shoe.

Major Adjustment

1. Inspect the fluid level in the master cylinder and add fluid if the level is ⅜″ to ½″ from the top of the reservoir or lower.
2. Loosen lock nuts and turn brake shoe anchor bolts to the fully released position.
3. Adjust the anchor bolt and cam and the minor adjustment cam at the top of the shoe to give equal clearance at the toe and heel. Make sure that sufficient center contact is maintained to produce a slight drag.
4. Lock anchor adjusting nut. After adjusting the clearance on one shoe, repeat the procedure on the other shoe. Then apply the brakes a couple of times to make sure adjustment is up to specifications.

NOTE: Whenever cams are adjusted, check brakes by applying pressure on the brake pedal a couple of times so as to make sure wheel drag has not increased, since the spring loaded cams may cause shoe adjustment to change by shifting position. Wheel should only have a slight drag at room temperature.

Parking Brakes

INTERNAL SHOE TYPE

Adjustment
Nine-Inch Diameter Drum

1. Release the parking brake lever in the cab.
2. From under the truck, remove the cotter pin from the parking brake linkage adjusting clevis pin. Remove the clevis pin.
3. Lengthen the parking brake adjusting link by turning the clevis. Continue to lengthen the adjusting link until the shoes seat against the drum when the clevis pin is installed.
4. Remove the clevis pin and shorten the linkage adjustment until there is 0.010″ clearance between the shoes and the drum. The measurement should be taken at all points around the drum with the clevis pin installed.
5. Install a new cotter pin in the clevis retaining pin and check the brake operation.

Twelve-Inch Diameter Drum

There is no internal adjustment on this brake. Adjustment is made on the linkage. Remove the clevis pin, loosen the nuts on the adjusting rod, and turn the clevis on the rod until a ¼–⅜″ free play is obtained at the brake lever. Tighten the nuts, and connect the clevis to the bellcrank with the clevis pin.

EXTERNAL BAND TYPE

Adjustment

1. On cable-controlled parking brakes, move the parking brake lever to the fully released position. On a vehicle with a rod-type linkage, set the lever at the first notch.
2. Check the position of the cam to make sure the flat portion is resting on the brake band bracket. If the cam is not flat with the bracket, remove the clevis pin from the upper part of the cam, and adjust the clevis rod to allow the flat portion of the cam to rest on the brake band bracket. Install the clevis pin and cotter pin.
3. Remove the lock wire from the anchor adjusting screw, and turn the adjusting screw clockwise until a clearance of 0.010″ is established between the brake lining and the brake drum at the anchor bracket. Install the lock wire in the anchor adjusting screw.

4. Loosen the lock nut on the adjusting screw for the lower half of the brake band, and adjust the screw to establish a 0.010″ clearance between the lining and the brake drum at the lower half of the brake band. Tighten the lock nut.
5. Turn the upper band adjusting rod nut until a 0.010 clearance is established between the upper half of the band and the drum.
6. Apply and release brake several times to insure full release.

REAR BRAKE SHOE

Before attempting parking brake adjustment, make sure that the rear brakes are fully adjusted by making several stops in reverse.

1. Raise and support the rear axle. Release the parking brake.
2. Apply the pedal or handle one to four clicks.
3. Adjust the cable equalizer nut under the truck until a moderate drag can be felt when the rear wheels are turned forward.
4. Release the parking brake and check that there is no drag when the wheels are turned forward.

NOTE: If the parking brake cable is replaced, prestretch it by applying the parking brake hard about three times before attempting adjustment.

IMPORTED TRUCKS—DISC BRAKE SERVICE

INDEX TO CALIPER TYPES

Courier/Mazda	Type 1
Datsun	Type 2
D50/Arrow/Mitsubishi	Type 3
LUV/Isuzu	Type 1,4
Toyota	Type 1,5
VW	Type 2,3

Type 1

AKEBONO, GIRLING, ETC. SLIDING CALIPER

This unit is a single piston, one-piece caliper that slides on a mounting bracket or frame which bolts to the steering knuckle. The caliper is retained in the mounting bracket by caliper guides (retaining keys) and support springs. Narrow support plates

1. Bleeder screw cap
2. Bleeder screw
3. Brake pads
4. Spring
5. Caliper fastener spring
6. Caliper support bracket
7. Caliper locking block
8. Cotter pin
9. Piston seal
10. Piston dust boot
11. Assembled caliper

Type 1 caliper (typical)

under each brake pad are utilized to eliminate rattle. One or two caliper guides may be used—it is imperative that they are replaced as originally found.

Pad Replacement

1. Raise and support the front of the vehicle on jackstands. Remove the front wheel.

2. Siphon a sufficient quantity of brake fluid from the master cylinder reservoir to prevent the brake fluid from overflowing the master cylinder when removing or installing pads. This is necessary as the piston must be forced into the cylinder bore to provide sufficient clearance to remove the pads.

3. Remove the clips or pins that hold the caliper guides in position.

4. Lightly tap out the guides—there may only be one, so remember the correct positioning.

5. Lift the caliper off of the mounting bracket.

It may be necessary to rock it back and forth a bit in order to seat the piston so it will clear the brake pads. Position the caliper out of the way and support it with wire so it doesn't hang by the brake lines.

6. Remove the brake pads from the mounting bracket. *Do not remove the support springs.*

7. A support plate is under each pad; they are not interchangeable and must be replaced correctly. Remove the support plates.

8. Inspect the brake disc (rotor) as detailed in the appropriate section.

9. Inspect the caliper and piston assembly for breaks, cracks or other damage. Overhaul or replace the caliper as necessary.

10. Replace the support plates in their *original* positions.

11. Place the new pads in the support bracket over the support springs.

12. Push the piston all the way back into its bore (a C–clamp may be necessary for this operation).

13. Position the caliper over the pads and onto the mounting bracket.

14. Install the caliper guides (retaining keys) and then install the guide retaining pins or clips.

15. Refill the master cylinder with fresh brake fluid.

16. Install the tire and wheel assembly and then pump the brake pedal several times to bring the pads into adjustment. Road test the vehicle.

NOTE: If a firm pedal cannot be obtained, bleed the system as detailed in "Bleeding the Brakes".

Type 2

GIRLING/ANNETTE SLIDING YOKE CALIPER

This unit is a double piston, one-piece caliper. The cylinder body contains two pistons, back-to-back, in a thru-bore. The cylinder body is bolted to the steering knuckle, with both pistons inboard of the rotor. A yoke, which slides on the cylinder body, is installed over the rotor and the caliper.

When the brakes are applied, hydraulic pressure forces the pistons apart in the double ended bore. The piston closest to the rotor applies force directly to the inboard pad. The other piston applies force to the yoke, which transmits the force to the outer pad, creating a friction force on each side of the rotor.

One variation has a yoke that floats on guide pins screwed into the cylinder body.

Some designs incorporate parking brake mechanisms which are actuated by a lever and cam working between the piston and the yoke.

The yokes do not have to be removed to replace the brake pads.

Type 2 caliper (typical)

Pad Replacement

1. Raise and support the front of the vehicle on jackstands. Remove the wheel.

2. Siphon a sufficient quantity of brake fluid from the master cylinder reservoir to prevent the brake fluid from overflowing the master cylinder when removing or installing new pads. This is necessary as the piston must be forced into the cylinder bore to provide sufficient clearance to remove the pads.

3. Disconnect the brake pad lining wear indicator if so equipped.

4. Remove the dust cover and/or anti-rattle (damper) clip if so equipped.

5. Lift off the wire clip(s) which hold the guide pins or retaining pin in place.

6. Remove the upper guide pin and the two hanger springs. Carefully tap out the lower guide pin.

────── CAUTION ──────

The lower guide pin usually contains an anti-rattle coil spring—be careful not to lose this spring. If a retaining pin is used, pull the pin out and remove the two hanger springs.

7. Slide the yoke outward and remove the outer brake pad and the anti-noise shim (if so equipped).

8. Slide the yoke inward and repeat Step 7.

9. Check the rotor as detailed in the appropriate section.

10. Inspect the caliper and piston assembly for breaks, cracks or other damage. Overhaul or replace the caliper as necessary.

11. Push the piston next to the rotor back into the cylinder bore until the end of the piston is flush with the boot retaining ring.

────── CAUTION ──────

If the piston is pushed further than this, the seal will be damaged and the caliper assembly will have to be overhauled.

12. Retract the piston farthest from the rotor by pulling the yoke toward the outside of the vehicle.

13. Install the outboard pad. Anti-noise shims (if so equipped) must be located on the plate side of the pad with the triangular cutout pointing toward the top of the caliper.

14. Install the inboard pad with the shims (if so equipped) in the correct position.

15. Replace the lower guide pin and the anti-rattle coil spring.

16. Hook the hanger springs under the pin and over the brake pads.

17. Install the upper guide pin over the ends of the hanger springs.

NOTE: If a single two-sided retaining pin is used, install the pin and then install the hanger springs as in Steps 16–17.

18. Insert the wire clip locks into the holes in the guide pins or retaining pin.

19. Refill the master cylinder with fresh brake fluid.

20. Install the tire and wheel assembly.

Pump the brake pedal several times to bring the pads into adjustment. Road test the vehicle. If a firm pedal cannot be obtained, refer to "Bleeding the Brakes".

Type 3

KELSEY-HAYES FLOATING CALIPER

This unit is a single piston, one-piece caliper which floats on two guide pins screwed into the adapter (anchor plate). The adaptor, in turn, is held to the steering knuckle with two bolts. As the brake pads wear, the caliper floats along the adapter and guide pins during braking.

Pad Replacement

1. Raise the front of the vehicle and support it with jackstands. Remove the wheel.

2. Siphon some brake fluid from the master cylinder reservoir to prevent its overflowing when the piston is retracted into the cylinder bore.

3. Disconnect the brake pad warning indicator if so equipped.

4. Using a pair of needlenose pliers or the like, remove the anti-rattle springs.

5. Using an Allen wrench, back out the two guide pins that attach the caliper to the anchor plate.

NOTE: When replacing pads only, it is not necessary to remove the guide pins completely from the rubber bushings, as they may be difficult to reinstall.

6. Lift off the caliper and position it out of the way with some wire—you need not remove the brake lines.

────── CAUTION ──────

Never allow the caliper to hang by its brake lines.

7. Slide the outer pad out of the anchor plate and then remove the inner pad. Check the rotor as detailed in the appropriate section. Check the caliper for fluid leaks or cracked boots. If any damage is found, the caliper will require overhauling or replacement.

8. Carefully clean the anchor plate with a wire brush or some other abrasive material. Install the new brake pads into position on the anchor plate. The inner pad usually has chamfered edges.

NOTE: When replacing brake pads, always replace both pads on both sides of the vehicle. Mixed pads will cause uneven braking.

9. Slowly and carefully push the piston into its bore until it's bottomed and then position the caliper onto the anchor plate. Install the guide pins and tighten them to 25–30 ft. lbs.

NOTE: The upper guide pin is usually longer than the lower one.

────── CAUTION ──────

Use extreme care so as not to cross–thread the guide pins when tightening.

10. Install the anti-rattle springs between the anchor plate and brake pads ears. The loops on the springs should be positioned inboard.

11. Fill the reservoir with brake fluid and pump the brake pedal several times to set the piston. It should not be necessary to bleed the system; however, if a firm pedal cannot be obtained, the system must be bled (see "Bleeding the Brakes" in this section).

12. Install the wheel and lower the vehicle.

Type 3 caliper (typical)

Type 4

ATE, GIRLING, ETC. FLOATING CALIPER

Although similar in many respects to a sliding caliper, this single piston unit floats on guide pins and bushings which are threaded into a mounting bracket. The mounting bracket is bolted to the steering knuckle.

Variations in pad retainers, shims, anti-rattle and retaining springs will be encountered but the service procedures are all basically the same. Note the position of all springs, clips or shims when removing the pads. Work on one side at a time and use the other for reference.

Pad Replacement

1. Raise and support the front of the vehicle on jackstands. Remove the wheel.

2. Siphon a sufficient quantity of brake fluid from the master cylinder reservoir to prevent the brake fluid from overflowing the master cylinder when removing or installing new pads. This is necessary as the piston must be forced into the cylinder bore to provide sufficient clearance to remove the pads.

3. Grasp the caliper from behind and pull it toward you. This will push the piston back into the cylinder bore.

4. Disconnect the brake pad lining wear indicator if so equipped. Remove any anti-rattle springs or clips if so equipped.

NOTE: Depending on the model and year of the particular caliper, you may not have to remove it entirely to get at the brake pads. If the caliper is the "swing" type, remove the lower guide bolt, pivot the caliper on the upper bolt and swing it upward exposing the brake pads. If this method is employed, skip to Step 7.

5. Remove the caliper guide pins.

Type 4 caliper (typical)

6. Remove the caliper from the rotor by slowly sliding it out and away from the rotor. Position the caliper out of the way and support it with wire so that it doesn't hang by the brake line.

7. Slide the outboard pad out of the adapter.

8. Remove the inboard pad. Remove any shims or shields behind the pads and note their positions.

9. Install the anti-rattle hardware and then the pads (in their proper positions!).

10. Install any pad shims or heat shields.

11. Reposition the caliper and install the guide pins.

NOTE: If the caliper is the "swing" type, you need only pivot it back into position and install the lower guide pin.

12. Refill the master cylinder with fresh brake fluid.

13. Install the tire and wheel assembly and then pump the brake pedal several times to bring the pads into adjustment. Road test the vehicle.

NOTE: If a firm pedal cannot be obtained, bleed the system as detailed in "Bleeding the Brakes".

Type 5 caliper (two-piston, typical)

CALIPER HOUSING BOLTS

BLEEDER SCREWS

BRAKE PADS

ANTI-RATTLE SPRINGS

INNER CALIPER HOUSING
PISTON SEAL
PISTON
DUST BOOT
DUST BOOT RETAINER
PAD RETAINING PIN
HAIRPIN TYPE CLIP
DUST BOOT RETAINER
DUST BOOT
PISTON
PISTON SEAL
CALIPER HOUSING SEAL
OUTER CALIPER HOUSING

Type 5 caliper (four-piston, typical)

IMPORTED TRUCKS—DRUM BRAKE SERVICE

INDEX TO DRUM BRAKE TYPES

Courier/Mazda	Type 1,2
Datsun	Type 3,4
D50/Arrow/ Mitsubishi	Type 5,6
LUV/Isuzu	Type 5,7
Toyota	Type 3,5,6
VW	Type 6,8

Type 5

ATE, GIRLING, SUMITOMO FIXED CALIPER

These units are either two or four piston, two-piece calipers that are fixed directly to the steering knuckle or spindle.

Brake pads may be changed without removing the caliper on all of these models. There may be some differences in retainers or anti-rattle springs from the illustrations, but all versions are basically the same. Before removing any parts, carefully note the position of any springs, retainers or clips. Change pads on one wheel at a time and use the other as a reference.

All pads on all models are held in position by either retaining pins or retainer plates. The retainer plates are bolted to the caliper housing and need only be loosened and rotated out of the way for pad removal.

Pad Replacement

1. Raise the front (or rear) of the vehicle and support it with jackstands. Remove the wheel.

2. Siphon a sufficient quantity of brake fluid from the master cylinder reservoir to prevent the brake fluid from overflowing the master cylinder when removing or installing new pads. This is necessary as the pistons must be forced into the cylinder bore to provide sufficient clearance to remove the pads.

3. Some models may use a cover plate over the access hole for the pads, if so, remove it. Disconnect the brake pad lining wear indicator wire on models so equipped.

4. Carefully clean the exterior of the caliper with a wire brush and note the position of any dampening shims or anti-rattle springs.

5. Remove the pad retaining pins and any retaining clips holding them. Remove the anti-rattle springs if so equipped. Some pads may be held in position by a plate with a retaining bolt. If so, loosen the bolt and swing the plate away. Lift out the spreader spring if so equipped.

NOTE: It is a good idea to remove one retaining spring or plate and then remove the anti-rattle springs or spreader spring. Remove the second retaining pin or plate last.

6. Force the old pads away from the rotor for easy withdrawal and remove the pads from the caliper.

7. If so equipped, remove the lower anti-rattle springs and dampening shims using needlenose pliers.

8. Check the brake disc (rotor) as detailed in the appropriate section.

9. Examine the dust boot for cracks or damage and push the pistons back into the cylinder bores. If the pistons are frozen or if the caliper is leaking hydraulic fluid, it must be overhauled.

10. Install the anti-rattle spring or damping shims and slip the new pads into the caliper. If damping shims are used, be sure that the directional arrow on the shims face the forward rotation of the rotor.

11. Install one pad retaining pin and hairpin clip. Position the anti-rattle springs and/or spreader spring and then install the other pad retaining pin and clip.

12. Refill the master cylinder to the correct level with the proper brake fluid.

13. Replace the wheel and lower the vehicle. Pump the brake pedal several times to bring the pads into correct adjustment. Road test the vehicle.

NOTE: If a firm pedal cannot be obtained, the system will require bleeding (see "Bleeding the Brakes" in this section).

Type 1

DUAL CYLINDERS—DUAL PISTONS—MANUAL ADJUSTERS

Two dual piston wheel cylinders are used in each rear wheel brake assembly. The dual pistons act together to expand both the shoes equally against the brake drum when hydraulic fluid pressure is applied through the brake pedal and master cylinder.

The shoes and linings are interchangeable as are the brake shoe retracting springs.

Removal & Installation

1. Raise the vehicle. Remove the wheel and tire assembly. Remove the brake drum. Remove the brake drum attaching screws and install them into the tapped holes in the brake drum. Turn these screws in evenly to force the brake drum away from the wheel hub and remove the brake drum. Back off adjustment, if necessary, for drum removal.

2. Remove the brake shoe retracting springs.

3. Remove the shoe retaining spring guide pins and retaining spring by holding the guide pin to the backing plate and compressing and turning the retaining spring 90 degrees to release it from the guide pin.

4. Remove the parking brake link.

5. Disengage the parking brake cable from the parking brake lever.

6. Lubricate the threads of the adjusting screws, mating surfaces of the shoe webs and the brake backing plate ledges with a small amount of Lubriplate.

7. Position the parking brake lever on the rear shoe and install its retaining clip. Hold the rear brake shoe assembly near the brake backing plate and install the eye of the parking brake cable on the parking brake operating lever.

8. Position both brake shoes to the

Type 1 (typical)

backing plate, install the parking brake link between the two shoes and then engage the brake shoes with the slots in the wheel cylinder pistons and adjusting screws.

9. Install the shoe retaining spring guide pins. Position the retaining springs over the guide pins. Depress the retaining springs and turn them 90 degrees to lock the retaining springs in place.

10. Install the brake shoe retracting springs, being careful not to bend the hooks or stretch the springs beyond the attaching points.

11. Install the brake drum.

12. Install the wheel and tire. Torque the wheel stud nuts to 58–65 ft-lbs.

13. Adjust the brakes.

14. Lower the vehicle and check the brakes for proper operation.

Adjustment

The brake drums should be at normal room temperature, when the brake shoes are adjusted. If the shoes are adjusted when the drums are hot and expanded, the shoes may drag as the drums cool and contract.

A brake adjustment re-establishes the brake lining-to-drum clearance and compensates for normal lining wear.

The two-cylinder brake assembly brake shoes are adjusted by turning adjusting wheels reached through slots in the backing plate.

The brake adjustment is made with the vehicle raised. Check the brake drag by rotating the drum in the direction of forward rotation as the adjustment is made. **Be sure that the parking brake is fully released by disconnecting the equalizer clevis pin.**

1. Remove the adjusting slot covers from the backing plate.

2. Turn the lower wheel cylinder adjusting wheel inside the hole to expand the brake shoe until it locks against the brake drum.

3. Back off the adjusting screw (5 notches) so that the drum rotates freely without drag.

4. Repeat the above procedure on the upper wheel cylinder. Connect the parking brake equalizer clevis pin and recheck parking brake adjustment.

5. Replace the adjusting hole covers.

6. After the brake shoes on each wheel have been adjusted, test drive the vehicle to check for equal brake action. Readjust, if necessary.

Type 2

SINGLE CYLINDER–DUAL PISTONS—AUTOMATIC ADJUSTER

A dual piston wheel cylinder is used in each rear wheel brake assembly. The dual pistons act together to expand both the shoes

Type 2 (typical)

equally against the brake drum when hydraulic fluid pressure is applied through the brake pedal and master cylinder.

The shoes and linings are interchangeable as are the brake shoe retracting springs.

Removal & Installation

1. Raise the vehicle. Remove the wheel and tire assembly. Remove the brake drum attaching screws and install them into the tapped holes in the brake drum. Turn these screws in evenly to force the brake drum away from the wheel hub and remove the brake drum.

2. Remove the brake shoe retracting springs.

3. Remove the shoe retaining spring guide pins and retaining spring by holding the guide pin to the backing plate and compressing and turning the retaining spring 90 degrees to release it from the guide pin.

4. Remove the parking brake link.

5. Disengage the parking brake cable from the parking brake lever.

6. Lubricate the threads of the adjusting screws, mating surfaces of the shoe webs and the brake backing plate ledges with a small amount of Lubriplate.

7. Position the parking brake lever on the rear shoe and install its retaining clip. Hold the rear brake shoe assembly near the brake backing plate and install the eye of the parking brake cable on the parking brake operating lever.

8. Position both brake shoes to the backing plate, install the operating strut between the two shoes and then engage the brake shoes with the slots in the wheel cylinder pistons and adjusting screws.

9. Install the shoe retaining spring guide pins. Position the retaining springs over the guide pins. Depress the retaining springs and turn them 90 degrees to lock the retaining springs in place.

10. Install the brake shoe retracting springs, being careful not to bend the hooks or stretch the springs beyond the attaching points.

11. Install the brake drum.

12. Adjust the brakes.

13. Install the wheel and tire. Torque the wheel stud nuts to 58–65 ft-lbs.

14. Lower the vehicle and check the brakes for proper operation.

Adjustment

The brake drums should be at normal room temperature, when the brake shoes are adjusted. If the shoes are adjusted when the drums are hot and expanded, the shoes may drag as the drums cool and contract.

The rear brakes are self-adjusting and require a manual adjustment only after the brake shoes have been replaced, or when the length of the adjusting rod has been changed while performing some other service operation. To adjust the rear brake shoes, proceed as follows:

NOTE: When the shoe retaining spring

is removed or installed, retract the push rod fully.

1. Jack up the rear end of the vehicle until the wheels are free to turn. Then, support with stands.

2. Make sure that the parking brake is fully released.

3. Remove the two shoe adjusting hole plugs from the back of the backing plate.

4. Insert a screwdriver into the star wheel of the adjuster through the hole and turn the star wheel toward the arrow direction marked on the backing plate until the wheel is locked.

5. Through the hole, hold the pole lever of the self-adjuster with a suitable drift and back off the adjusting wheel about 3 or 4 notches so that the drum rotates freely without drag.

6. Repeat the above adjustment on the other rear wheel. The adjustments must be the same on both rear wheels.

7. After the brake shoes on each wheel have been adjusted, test drive the vehicle to check for equal brake action. Readjust, if necessary.

Type 3

NON-SERVO—MANUAL ADJUSTER

This brake consists of non-servo forward and reverse shoes with a double-end type

wheel cylinder. The shoes anchor upon the slotted adjusting screws which permit them a sliding self centering action. Brakes are mounted with cylinder and adjuster horizontally, or with the cylinder at the top and the adjuster at the bottom.

Removal & Installation

1. Raise the front/rear of the vehicle and support it on jackstands. Remove the tire and wheel.

2. Remove the drums (some vehicles may require special pullers).

3. Detach both retracting springs.

4. Remove the hold-down springs and lift the brake shoes from the backing plate. On the rear wheels, unhook the parking brake cable from parking brake lever before shoe removal.

5. Clean and lubricate the backing plate as detailed earlier.

6. Check the wheel cylinder for frozen pistons or fluid leaks. If any are found, rebuild or replace the cylinder. Disassemble the adjusters and clean and lubricate them.

7. Install the parking brake lever on a new reverse shoe (only on rear wheel brakes).

8. Place new brake shoes on the backing plate and attach the hold-down springs.

NOTE: Slots in the adjusting screws must be slanted toward the center of the assembly.

The ends of the shoes should engage the wheel cylinder piston slots, and the adjuster

1. Brake backing plate	9. Spring seat	17. Toggle lever
2. Brake shoe	10. Adjuster assembly	18. Extension link
3. Wheel cylinder	11. Adjuster head	19. Return spring
4. Return upper spring	12. Adjuster head shim	20. Adjuster spring
5. Return lower spring	13. Lock-spring	21. Lockplate
6. After shoe return spring	14. Adjuster housing	22. Adjuster shim
7. Retainer	15. Adjuster wheel	23. Rubber boot
8. Anti-rattle spring	16. Adjuster screw	24. Anti-rattle pin

Type 3 (typical)

slots. If the adjuster screw ends have a slot with a bevel on one side, make sure the bevel lines up with the bevel on the shoe web.

The end of the shoe with a slot for the parking strut should be installed near the wheel cylinder.

9. For rear wheels, hook the parking brake lever on the parking brake cable and then install the parking brake strut.

10. Install the heavier retracting spring between the toe or cylinder ends of the brake shoes.

11. Attach the lighter retracting spring to the heel or anchor ends of the shoes.

12. Replace the drums, bleed and adjust the assembly and road test the car.

Adjustment

Insert an adjusting spoon or a small screwdriver through the adjusting hole in the backing plate and expand the shoe assembly by revolving the notched adjusting wheel in a clockwise direction when facing the end of the wheel cylinder. Adjust the shoe until a heavy drag is felt when turning the wheel and drum; then, back off the adjustment until the wheel spins freely. Adjust one shoe at a time and repeat this procedure at all brake shoes.

Type 4

SERVO—AUTOMATIC ADJUSTER

Removal & Installation

1. Raise and safely support the vehicle. Remove the brake drum.

2. Place the hollow end of a brake spring service tool (available at auto parts stores) on the brake shoe anchor pin and twist it to disengage one of the brake retracting springs. Repeat this operation to remove the other spring.

CAUTION

Be careful the springs do not slip off the tool during removal, as they could cause personal injury.

---

3. Reach behind the brake backing plate and place a finger on the end of one of the brake hold-down spring mounting pins. Using a pair of pliers, grasp the washer on the top of the hold-down spring which corresponds to the pin that you are holding. Push down on the pliers and turn them 90° to align the slot in the washer with the head on the spring mounting pin. Remove the spring and washer and repeat this operation on the hold-down spring on the other brake shoe.

4. Place the tip of a prybar on the top of the brake adjusting screw and move the brake adjusting lever. When there is enough slack in the automatic adjuster cable, disconnect the loop on the top of the cable from the anchor. Grasp the top of each brake shoe and move it outward to disengage it from the wheel cylinder (and parking brake link on rear wheels). When the brake shoes are clear, lift them from the backing plate. Twist the shoes slightly and the automatic adjuster assembly will disassemble itself.

5. If you are working on rear brakes, grasp the end of the brake cable spring with a pair of pliers and, using the brake lever as a fulcrum, pull the end of the spring away from the lever. Disengage the cable from the brake lever.

6. Transfer the parking brake lever from the old secondary shoe to the new one. This is accomplished by spreading the bottom of the horseshoe clip and disengaging the lever. Position the lever on the new secondary shoe and install the spring washer and the horseshoe clip. Close the bottom of the clip after installing it. Grasp the metal

tip of the parking brake cable with a pair of pliers. Position a pair of side cutter pliers on the end of the cable coil spring and, using the pliers as a fulcrum, pull the coil spring back with the side cutters. Position the cable in the parking brake lever.

7. Apply a *light* coating of high-temperature grease to the brake shoe contact points on the backing plate. Position the primary brake shoe on the front of the backing plate and install the hold-down spring and washer over the mounting pin. Install the secondary shoe on the rear of the backing plate.

8. Install the parking brake link between the notch in the primary brake shoe and the notch in the parking brake lever.

9. Install the automatic adjuster cable loop end on the anchor pin. Make sure that the crimped side of the loop faces the backing plate.

10. Install the return spring in the primary brake shoe and, using the tapered end of a brake spring service tool, slide the top of the spring onto the anchor pin.

CAUTION

Be careful to make sure that the spring does not slip off the tool during installation, as it could cause injury.

---

11. Install the automatic adjuster cable guide in the secondary brake shoe, making sure that the flared hole in the cable guide is inside the hole in the brake shoe. Fit the cable into the groove in the top of the cable guide.

12. Install the secondary shoe return spring through the hole in the cable guide and the brake shoe. Using the brake spring tool, slide the top of the spring onto the anchor pin.

13. Clean the threads on the adjusting screw and apply a light coating of high-temperature grease to the threads. Screw the adjuster closed, then open it one-half turn.

14. Install the adjusting screw between the brake shoes with the starwheel nearest to the secondary shoe. Make sure that the starwheel is in a position that is accessible from the adjusting slot in the backing plate.

15. Install the short hooked end of the automatic adjuster spring in the proper hole in the primary brake shoe.

16. Connect the hooked end of the automatic adjuster cable and the free end of the automatic adjuster spring in the slot in the top of the automatic adjuster lever.

17. Pull the automatic adjuster lever (the lever will pull the cable and spring with it) downward and to the left and engage the pivot hook of the lever in the hole in the secondary brake shoe.

18. Check the entire brake assembly to make sure that everything is installed properly. Make sure that the shoes engage the wheel cylinder properly and are flush on the anchor pin. Make sure that the automatic adjuster cable is flush on the anchor pin and in the slot on the back of the cable guide. Make sure that the adjusting lever

PARKING BRAKE LINK

PARKING BRAKE LINK SPRING

REAR BRAKE ASSEMBLY

PARKING LEVER PIVOT POINT

SECONDARY SHOE AND LINING ASSEMBLY

FRONT OF TRUCK

PRIMARY SHOE AND LINING ASSEMBLY

AUTOMATIC ADJUSTER SPRING

PARKING BRAKE LEVER

PIVOT HOOK

PARKING BRAKE CABLE

Type 4 (typical)

rests on the adjusting screw starwheel. Pull upward on the adjusting cable until the adjusting lever is free of the starwheel, then release the cable. The adjusting lever should snap back into place on the adjusting screw starwheel and turn the wheel one tooth.

19. Expand the brake adjusting screw until the brake drum will just fit over the brake shoes.

20. Install the wheel and drum and adjust the brakes.

Adjustment

1. Raise the car and support it with safety stands.

2. Remove the rubber plug from the adjusting slot on the backing plate.

3. Insert a brake adjusting spoon into the slot and engage the lowest possible tooth on the starwheel. Move the end of the brake spoon downward to move the starwheel upward and expand the adjusting screw. Repeat this operation until the brakes lock the wheel.

4. Insert a small prybar or piece of firm wire (coat-hanger wire) into the adjusting slot and push the automatic adjuster lever out and free of the starwheel on the adjusting screw.

5. Holding the adjusting lever out of the way, engage the topmost tooth possible on the starwheel with a brake adjusting spoon. Move the end of the adjusting spoon upward to move the adjusting screw starwheel downward and contract the adjusting screw. Back off the adjusting screw starwheel until the wheel spins freely with the minimum of drag. Keep track of the number of turns the starwheel is backed off.

6. Repeat this operation for the other side. When backing off the brakes on the other side, the adjusting lever must be backed off the same number of turns to prevent side-to-side brake pull.

7. Repeat this operation on the other set of brakes.

8. When the brakes are adjusted, make several stops, while backing up the vehicle, to equalize all of the wheels.

9. Road-test the vehicle.

Type 5

SERVO—AUTOMATIC ADJUSTER

Removal & Installation

1. Remove the wheel and the brake drum.

2. Using a standard brake return spring tool, remove the return spring.

3. Remove the adjusting spring and the adjusting lever.

4. Remove the brake shoes and the adjusting assembly then remove the cable from the parking brake lever.

Installation is the reverse of removal with the following notes.

5. After the primary shoes have been

1. Wheel cylinder	8. Shoe hold down spring
2. Cable guide	9. Primary shoe
3. Cable assembly	10. Parking brake strut
4. Lever hold down spring	11. Shoe pull—back spring
5. Adjuster lever	12. Guide plate
6. Self adjuster	13. Anchor pin
7. Shoe return spring	

Type 5 (typical)

installed, install the parking brake cable. Set the adjuster assembly, then secure the secondary shoes.

NOTE: Grease the threaded area on the adjuster assembly and make sure it turns smoothly.

6. Install the primary shoe return springs, adjusting cable and the secondary shoe return springs in the given order.

NOTE: The spring for the primary shoe and secondary shoe are different colors. Do not mix them, as they are different lengths.

7. To check the adjuster assembly operation: pull the adjuster cable toward you to see if the adjuster lever goes into mesh with the next tooth on the adjuster wheel. Make sure that when the cable is released, the adjuster lever returns to its original position after the adjuster wheel has moved a tooth ahead.

8. Bleed system as necessary.

Adjustment

1. During reassembly of the rear brake shoes, manually adjust the automatic adjuster so that shoe to drum clearance is no more than 2.5 mm (o.lin.). An excessive clearance will cause malfunction of the adjuster.

2. After installation is complete, operate the vehicle in reverse and apply the brakes so that the adjuster will equalize.

Type 6

LEADING-TRAILING— AUTOMATIC ADJUSTER

Removal & Installation

1. Raise and safely support the vehicle.

1. Backing plate	7. Shoe and lining assembly	13. Autoadjuster lever
2. Wheel cylinder boot	8. Shoe return spring	14. Shoe hold-down cup
3. Wheel cylinder piston	9. Brake shoe adjuster	15. Shoe hold-down spring
4. Wheel cylinder piston cup	10. Shoe and lever assembly	16. Shoe retaining spring
5. Wheel cylinder body	11. Adjusting spring	17. Brake drum
6. Shoe hold-down pin	12. Parking brake lever	18. Wheel cylinder repair kit

Type 6 (typical)

2. Remove the rear wheel and brake drum.

3. Remove the shoe return spring(s) from the two brake shoes. Remove the two brake shoe holddown springs.

4. Remove the shoes and adjuster as an assembly. Disconnect the parking brake cable from the lever.

5. The wheel cylinder may be removed for servicing if necessary.

6. Transfer the parking brake lever and adjuster lever to the new trailing shoe.

7. Clean and lubricate the adjuster. Assemble the shoes and adjuster as in removal.

8. Lubricate the backing plate shoe contact points.

9. Connect the parking brake cable. Install the brake shoes and adjuster to the backing plate with the holddown pins and springs. Install the return spring(s).

10. Turn adjuster until the brake drum can be installed and turned with a slight drag. Remove drum and back off adjuster until the drum can be turned with no drag.

11. Install wheel and bleed brakes, if necessary.

Adjustment

The brakes are self-adjusting. Operate the vehicle in reverse while applying brakes, stop the vehicle and apply parking brake. Repeat the procedure several times until the adjusters equalize.

Type 7

NON-SERVO—AUTOMATIC ADJUSTER

Removal & Installation

1. Raise and safely support the vehicle. Remove the brake drums.

2. Unhook the brake drum return springs from the anchor pin using a brake tool and remove the springs.

3. Remove the brake shoe hold-down springs using pliers. Depress the spring retainer while rotating it 90° to align the slot in the retainer with the flanged end of the pin.

4. Remove the self-adjuster cable assembly by disconnecting the spring at the adjuster lever and removing the cable end from the anchor pin. Remove the guide plate from the anchor pin.

5. Remove the adjuster lever and the lever hold-down wire from the shoe pivot.

6. Separate the shoes from the wheel cylinder pushrods.

7. Separate the primary and secondary brake shoes, adjuster, return spring, and parking brake strut assemblies.

NOTE: If the brake shoes are to be reinstalled, be sure to identify them so that they can be reinstalled in their original positions.

8. Separate the parking brake lever and the rear cable. Remove the clip and washer

Type 7 (typical)

and remove the parking brake lever from the secondary shoe.

9. Lubricate the parking brake cable with Lubriplate®.

10. Assemble the parking brake lever to the secondary shoe and then assemble the parking brake cable to the lever.

11. Before installation, make sure that the adjusting screw is clean, lubricated and operable.

12. Connect the brake shoes together with bottom return spring and then place the adjuster screw into position. The adjuster screw is installed with the starwheel nearest to the secondary shoe.

13. Assemble the parking brake strut with the spring on the primary shoe end, and assemble the shoes to the wheel cylinder pushrods.

14. Install the shoe hold-down springs using a pair of pliers. Compress the springs and rotate the retainers 90°.

15. Install the guide plate on the anchor pin. Assemble the self-adjuster lever and the lever hold-down wire to the secondary shoe pivot pin. Place the adjuster cable over the anchor pin, route the cable around the shoe shield and then attach the spring at the opposite end to the adjuster lever.

16. Install the return springs using a brake tool.

17. Pry the shoes away from the backing plate and lubricate the shoe contact areas with a thin coat of Lubriplate®.

18. Check the operation of the parking brake. *Do not step on the brake pedal.*

19. Using a piece of fine (400 grit) sandpaper, evenly rough the surface of the brake linings before installing the brake drums. Do this for the linings on both wheels.

20. Install the brake drum and adjust the brake shoes.

Adjustment

1. With the brake drum removed, remove actuator from the starwheel on the rear brakes.

2. Turn the starwheel until the brake drum slides over the brake shoes with a slight drag.

3. Turn the starwheel on the rear brakes 1¼ turns to retract the shoes.

4. Install the brake drums and wheels and lower the vehicle.

5. Perform the final adjustment by making a number of forward and reverse stops, applying the brakes with a firm pedal effort until a satisfactory brake pedal height and straight-line braking is achieved.

Type 8

NON-SERVO—MANUAL ADJUSTER

This brake consists of non-servo forward and reverse shoes with a double-ended wheel cylinder. The shoes are held in position by an anchor plate and are manually adjusted.

Removal & Installation

1. Raise the rear of the vehicle and support it with jackstands. Remove the tire and wheel assembly.

2. Remove the plug from the brake adjusting hole. Using a small prybar or other suitable tool, release the brake shoes by rotating the shoe adjuster downward on the right side of the vehicle and upward on the left side of the vehicle.

3. Remove the brake drum.

4. Remove the parking brake cable from

6. Brake shoe with parking brake lever
7. Return spring
8. Wheel cylinder
9. Hold-down spring
10. Adjuster
11. Brake shoe

Type 8 (typical)

the parking brake lever by compressing the cable return spring.

5. Remove the shoe-to-anchor springs located at the bottom.

6. Remove the brake shoe hold-down clips and pins.

7. Remove the adjuster screw assembly by spreading the shoes apart making sure that the adjuster screw is fully backed off.

8. Pull the reverse shoe away from the anchor plate to release the tension on the upper return spring. Disengage the shoe and remove the spring. To facilitate the reassembly operation, note how the upper return spring is positioned on the shoe and how it is connected to the hole in the anchor plate.

9. Remove the forward shoe in the same manner as above.

10. Inspect the wheel cylinder and recondition or replace if necessary.

11. Clean and inspect the adjuster screw assembly. Apply a thin coat of lubricant to the adjuster threads.

12. Inspect the old springs. If old springs are damaged or have been overheated, they should be replaced. Indications of overheated springs are paint discoloration or distortion.

13. Lubricate the bosses on the anchor plate which make contact with the brake shoe tabs.

To install:

1. Remove the parking brake lever and attach the parking brake lever to the web of a new reverse shoe.

2. Position the upper return spring on the forward shoe and hook the other end of the spring into the hole in the backing plate.

3. Rotate the shoe outward with the upper part of the shoe against the wheel cylinder piston and insert the bottom part of the shoe under the anchor plate.

4. Repeat the above procedure for the reverse shoe.

5. With the adjuster screw fully retracted, position the straight forked end of the adjuster screw assembly on the parking brake lever. Make sure that the spring lock on the adjuster screw is on the outside and away from the adjusting hole.

6. Rotate the bottom of the forward shoe off the anchor plate and insert the curved fork end of the adjuster screw assembly into the web on the forward shoe.

NOTE: Make sure that the curved portion of the forked end is facing downward and that the spring lock is on the outside and away from the adjusting hole.

7. Insert the pins for the hold-down clips through the backing plate and web of the shoes. Install the hold-down clips.

8. Install the shoe-to-anchor springs.

9. Compress the brake cable return spring and attach the cable to the bottom of the parking brake lever.

10. Install the brake drum.

11. Install the wheel and tire assembly.

12. Adjust the brakes.

13. Bleed the system and road test the car.

Adjustment

Adjust the brakes through the adjusting hole located in the backing plate. Adjustment is made manually by spreading the adjuster screw assembly which is located directly under the wheel cylinder. Insert a small prybar or other suitable tool through the hole in the backing plate and rotate the adjuster wheel clockwise until the brakes drag as you turn the wheel in a forward direction. Turn the adjuster in the opposite direction until you just pass the point of drag. Repeat the procedure on the other wheel.

Troubleshooting and Diagnosis

ENGINE

Gasoline Engine Troubleshooting

See applicable Car or Unit Repair section for specific service procedures

INDEX TO PROBLEMS

Problem Symptom	Begin at Specific Diagnosis, Number
Engine Won't Start	
Starter doesn't turn	1.1, 2.1
Starter turns, engine doesn't	2.1
Starter turns engine very slowly	1.1, 2.4
Starter turns engine normally	3.1, 4.1
Starter turns engine very quickly	6.1
Engine fires intermittently	4.1
Engine fires consistently	5.1, 6.1
Engine Runs Poorly	
Hard starting	3.1, 4.1, 5.1, 8.1
Rough idle	4.1, 5.1, 8.1
Stalling	3.1, 4.1, 5.1, 8.1
Engine dies at high speeds	4.1, 5.1
Hesitation (on acceleration from standing stop)	5.1, 8.1
Poor pickup	4.1, 5.1, 8.1
Lack of power	3.1, 4.1, 5.1, 8.1
Backfire through the carburetor	4.1, 8.1, 9.1
Backfire through the exhaust	4.1, 8.1, 9.1
Blue exhaust gases	6.1, 7.1
Black exhaust gases	5.1
Running on (after the ignition is shut off)	3.1, 8.1
Susceptible to moisture	4.1
Engine misfires under load	4.1, 7.1, 8.4, 9.1
Engine misfires at speed	4.1, 8.4
Engine misfires at idle	3.1, 4.1, 5.1, 7.1, 8.4

SAMPLE SECTION

Test and Procedure	Results and Indications	Proceed to
4.1 Check for spark: Hold each spark plug wire approximately $\frac{1}{4}''$ from ground with gloves or a heavy, dry rag. Crank the engine and observe the spark.	→ If no spark is evident —————	→ 4.2
	→ If spark is good in some cases —————	→ 4.3
	→ If spark is good in all cases —————	→ 4.6

SPECIFIC DIAGNOSIS

This section is arranged so that following each test, instructions are given to proceed to another, until a problem is diagnosed.

SECTION 1—BATTERY

Test and Procedure	Results and Indications	Proceed to
1.1 Inspect the battery visually for case condition (corrosion, cracks) and water level. DIRT ON TOP OF BATTERY PLUGGED VENT CORROSION LOOSE CABLE OR POSTS CRACKS LOW WATER LEVEL **Inspect the battery case**	If case is cracked, replace battery.	1.4
	If the case is intact, remove corrosion with a solution of baking soda and water. **(CAUTION: Do not get the solution into the battery).** Fill with water.	1.2
1.2 Check the battery cable connections: Insert a screwdriver between the battery post and the cable clamp. Turn the headlights on high beam, and observe them as the screwdriver is gently twisted to ensure good metal to metal contact. TESTING BATTERY CABLE CONNECTIONS USING A SCREWDRIVER	If the lights brighten, remove and clean the clamp and post; coat the post with petroleum jelly, install and tighten the clamp.	1.4
	If no improvement is noted	1.3
1.3 Test the state of charge of the battery using an individual cell tester or hydrometer.	If indicated, charge the battery. **NOTE: If no obvious reason exists for the low state of charge (i.e., battery age, prolonged storage), proceed to:**	1.4

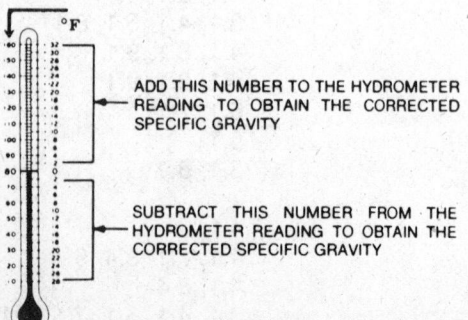

°F

ADD THIS NUMBER TO THE HYDROMETER READING TO OBTAIN THE CORRECTED SPECIFIC GRAVITY

SUBTRACT THIS NUMBER FROM THE HYDROMETER READING TO OBTAIN THE CORRECTED SPECIFIC GRAVITY

Specific Gravity (@ 80° F.)

Minimum	Battery Charge
1.260	100% Charged
1.230	75% Charged
1.200	50% Charged
1.170	25% Charged
1.140	Very Little Power Left
1.110	Completely Discharged

The effects of temperature on battery specific gravity (left) and amount of battery charge in relation to specific gravity (right)

Test and Procedure	Results and Indications	Proceed To
1.4 Visually inspect battery cables for cracking, bad connection to ground, or bad connection to starter.	If necessary, tighten connections or replace the cables.	2.1

SECTION 2—STARTING SYSTEM

Test and Procedure	Results and Indications	Proceed to

Note: Tests in Group 2 are performed with coil high tension lead disconnected to prevent accidental starting.

Test and Procedure	Results and Indications	Proceed to
2.1 Test the starter motor and solenoid: Connect a jumper from the battery post of the solenoid (or relay) to the starter post of the solenoid (or relay).	If starter turns the engine normally	2.2
	If the starter buzzes, or turns the engine very slowly	2.4
	If no response, replace the solenoid (or relay).	3.1
	If the starter turns, but the engine doesn't, ensure that the flywheel ring gear is intact. If the gear is undamaged, replace the starter drive.	3.1
2.2 Determine whether ignition override switches are functioning properly (clutch start switch, neutral safety switch), by connecting a jumper across the switch(es), and turning the ignition switch to "start".	If starter operates, adjust or replace switch.	3.1
	If the starter doesn't operate	2.3
2.3 Check the ignition switch "start" position: Connect a 12V test lamp or voltmeter between the starter post of the solenoid (or relay) and ground. Turn the ignition switch to the "start" position, and jiggle the key.	If the lamp doesn't light or the meter needle doesn't move when the switch is turned, check the ignition switch for loose connections, cracked insulation, or broken wires. Repair or replace as necessary.	3.1
	If the lamp flickers or needle moves when the key is jiggled, replace the ignition switch.	3.3

Checking the ignition switch "start" position

Test and Procedure	Results and Indications	Proceed to
2.4 Remove and bench test the starter, according to specifications in the car section.	If the starter does not meet specifications, repair or replace as needed	3.1
	If the starter is operating properly	2.5

Test and Procedure	Results and Indications	Proceed To
2.5 Determine whether the engine can turn freely: Remove the spark plugs, and check for water in the cylinders. Check for water on the dipstick, or oil in the radiator. Attempt to turn the engine using an 18" flex drive and socket on the crankshaft pulley nut or bolt.	If the engine will turn freely only with the spark plugs out, and hydrostatic lock (water in the cylinders) is ruled out, check valve timing.	9.2
	If engine will not turn freely, and it is known that the clutch and transmission are free, the engine must be disassembled for further evaluation.	See Car Section

SECTION 3—PRIMARY ELECTRICAL SYSTEM

Test and Procedure	Results and Indications	Proceed to
3.1 Check the ignition switch "on" position: Connect a jumper wire between the distributor side of the coil and ground, and a 12V test lamp between the switch side of the coil and ground. Remove the high tension lead from the coil. Turn the ignition switch on and jiggle the key.	If the lamp lights	3.2
	If the lamp flickers when the key is jiggled, replace the ignition switch.	3.3
	If the lamp doesn't light, check for loose or open connections. If none are found, remove the ignition switch and check for continuity. If the switch is faulty, replace it.	3.3

Checking the ignition switch "on" position

3.2 Check the ballast resistor or resistance wire for an open circuit, using an ohmmeter.	Replace the resistor or resistance wire if the resistance is zero. **NOTE: Some ignition systems have no ballast resistor.**	3.3

RESISTOR BLOCK

CALIBRATED RESISTANCE LEAD

Two types of resistors

3.3 On point-type ignition systems, visually inspect the breaker points for burning, pitting or excessive wear. Gray coloring of the point contact surfaces is normal. Rotate the crankshaft until the contact heel rests on a high point of the distributor cam and adjust the point gap to specifications. On electronic ignition models, remove the distributor cap and visually inspect the armature. Ensure that the armature pin is in place, and that the armature is on tight and rotates when the engine is cranked. Make sure there are no cracks, chips or rounded edges on the armature.	If the breaker points are intact, clean the contact surfaces with fine emery cloth, and adjust the point gap to specifications. If the points are worn, replace them. On electronic systems, replace any parts which appear defective. If condition persists	3.4

Test and Procedure	Results and Indications	Proceed To
3.4 On point-type ignition systems, connect a dwell-meter between the distributor primary lead and ground. Crank the engine and observe the point dwell angle. On electronic ignition systems, conduct a stator (magnetic pickup assembly) test. See Electronic Ignition Unit Repair Section.	On point-type systems, adjust the dwell angle if necessary. **NOTE: Increasing the point gap decreases the dwell angle and vice-versa.** If the dwell meter shows little or no reading On electronic ignition systems, if the stator is bad, replace the stator. If the stator is good, proceed to the other tests in The Electronic Ignition Unit Repair Section.	3.6 3.5

Dwell is a function of point gap

3.5 On the point-type ignition systems, check the condenser for short: connect an ohmeter across the condenser body and the pigtail lead.	If any reading other than infinite is noted, replace the condenser	3.6

Checking the condenser for short

3.6 Test the coil primary resistance: On point-type ignition systems, connect an ohmmeter across the coil primary terminals, and read the resistance on the low scale. Note whether an external ballast resistor or resistance wire is used. On electronic ignition systems, test the coil primary resistance.	Point-type ignition coils utilizing ballast resistors or resistance wires should have approximately 1.0 ohms resistance. Coils with internal resistors should have approximately 4.0 ohms resistance. If values far from the above are noted, replace the coil.	4.1

Checking the coil primary resistance

SECTION 4—SECONDARY ELECTRICAL SYSTEM

Test and Procedure	Results and Indications	Proceed to
4.1 Check for spark: Hold each spark plug wire approximately ¼" from ground with gloves or heavy, dry rag. Crank the engine, and observe the spark.	If no spark is evident	**4.2**
	If spark is good in some cylinders	**4.3**
	If spark is good in all cylinders	**4.6**

Check for spark at the plugs

4.2 Check for spark at the coil high tension lead: Remove the coil high tension lead from the distributor and position it approximately ¼" from ground. Crank the engine and observe spark. **CAUTION: This test should not be performed on engines equipped with electronic ignition.**	If the spark is good and consistent	**4.3**
	If the spark is good but intermittent, test the primary electrical system starting at 3.3.	**3.3**
	If the spark is weak or non-existent, replace the coil high tension lead, clean and tighten all connections and retest. If no improvement is noted	**4.4**

4.3 Visually inspect the distributor cap and rotor for burned or corroded contacts, cracks, carbon tracks, or moisture. Also check the fit of the rotor on the distributor shaft (where applicable).	If moisture is present, dry thoroughly, and retest per 4.1.	**4.1**
	If burned or excessively corroded contacts, cracks, or carbon tracks are noted, replace the defective part(s) and retest per 4.1.	**4.1**
	If the rotor and cap appear intact, or are only slightly corroded, clean the contacts thoroughly (including the cap towers and spark plug wire ends) and retest per 4.1.	
	If the spark is good in all cases	**4.6**
	If the spark is poor in all cases	**4.5**

CORRODED OR LOOSE WIRE
HIGH RESISTANCE CARBON
EXCESSIVE WEAR OF BUTTON
ROTOR TIP BURNED AWAY

Inspect the distributor cap and rotor

4.4 Check the coil secondary resistance: On point-type systems connect an ohmmeter across the distributor side of the coil and the coil tower. Read the resistance on the high scale of the ohmmeter. On electronic ignition systems, see The Electronic Ignition Unit Repair Section for specific tests.	The resistance of a satisfactory coil should be between 4,000 and 10,000 ohms. If resistance is considerably higher (i.e., 40,000 ohms) replace the coil and retest per 4.1. **NOTE: This does not apply to high performance coils.**

Testing the coil secondary resistance

Spark Plug Analysis

Normal

APPEARANCE
This plug is typical of one operating normally. The insulator nose varies from a light tan to grayish color with slight electrode wear. The presence of slight deposits is normal on used plugs and will have no adverse effect on engine performance. The spark plug heat range is correct for the engine and the engine is running normally.

CAUSE
Properly running engine

RECOMMENDATION
Before reinstalling this plug, the electrodes should be cleaned and filed square. Set the gap to specifications. If the plug has been in service for more than 10–12,000 miles, the entire set should probably be replaced with a fresh set of the same heat range.

Incorrect Heat Range

APPEARANCE
The effects of high temperature on a spark plug are indicated by clean white, often blistered insulator. This can also be accompanied by excessive wear of the electrode, and the absence of deposits.

CAUSE
Check for the correct spark plug heat range. A plug which is too hot for the engine can result in overheating. A car operated mostly at high speeds may require a colder plug. Also check ignition timing, cooling system level, fuel mixture and leaking intake manifold.

RECOMMENDATION
If all ignition and engine adjustments are known to be correct, and no other malfunction exists, install spark plugs one heat range colder.

Oil Deposits

APPEARANCE
The firing end of the plug is covered with a wet, oily coating.

CAUSE
The problem is poor oil control. On high mileage engines, oil is leaking past the rings or valve guides into the combustion chamber. A common cause is also a plugged PCV valve, and a ruptured fuel pump diaphragm can also cause this condition. Oil fouled plugs such as these are often found in new or recently overhauled engines, before normal oil control is achieved, and can be cleaned and reinstalled.

RECOMMENDATION
A hotter spark plug may temporarily relieve the problem, but the engine is probably in need of engine work.

Carbon Deposits

APPEARANCE
Carbon fouling is easily identified by the presence of dry, soft, black, sooty deposits.

CAUSE
Changing the heat range can often lead to carbon fouling, as can prolonged slow, stop-and-start driving. If the heat range is correct, carbon fouling can be attributed to a rich fuel mixture, sticking choke, clogged air cleaner, worn breaker points, retarded timing or low compression. If only one or two plugs are carbon fouled, check for corroded or cracked wires on the affected plugs. Also look for cracks in the distributor cap between the towers of affected cylinders.

RECOMMENDATION
After the problem is corrected, these plugs can be cleaned and reinstalled if not worn severely.

Ash Deposits

APPEARANCE
Ash deposits are characterized by light brown or white colored deposits crusted on the side or center electrodes. In some cases it may give the plug a rusty appearance.

CAUSE
Ash deposits are normally derived from oil or fuel additives burned during normal combustion. Normally they are harmless, though excessive amounts can cause misfiring. If deposits are excessive in short mileage, the valve guides may be worn. Reddish or rusty deposits are caused by manganese, an anti-knock compound replacing lead in unleaded gas. No engine malfunction is indicated.

RECOMMENDATION
Ash-fouled plugs can be cleaned, gapped and reinstalled.

Splash Deposits

APPEARANCE
Splash deposits occur in varying degrees as spotty deposits on the insulator.

CAUSE
These usually occur after a long delayed tune-up. By-products of combustion have accumulated on pistons and valves because of a delayed tune-up. Following tune-up or during hard acceleration, the deposits loosen and are thrown against the hot surface of the plug. If the deposits accumulate sufficiently, misfiring can occur.

RECOMMENDATION
These plugs can be cleaned, gapped and reinstalled.

High Speed Glazing

APPEARANCE
Glazing appears as shiny coating on the plug, either yellow or tan in color.

CAUSE
During hard, fast acceleration, plug temperatures rise suddenly. Deposits from normal combustion have no chance to fluff-off; instead, they melt on the insulator forming an electrically conductive coating which causes misfiring.

RECOMMENDATION
Glazed plugs are not easily cleaned. They should be replaced with a fresh set of plugs of the correct heat range. If the condition recurs, using plugs with a heat range one step colder may cure the problem.

Detonation

APPEARANCE
Detonation is usually characterized by a broken plug insulator.

CAUSE
A portion of the fuel charge will begin to burn spontaneously, from the increased heat following ignition. The explosion that results applies extreme pressure to engine components, frequently damaging spark plugs and pistons.

Detonation can result by over-advanced ignition timing, inferior gasoline (low octane) lean air fuel mixture, poor carburetion, engine lugging or an increase in compression ratio due to combustion chamber deposits or engine modification.

RECOMMENDATION
Replace the plugs after correcting the problem.

Test and Procedure	Results and Indications	Proceed To

4.5 Visually inspect the spark plug wires for cracking or brittleness. Ensure that no two wires are positioned so as to cause induction firing (adjacent and parallel). Remove each wire, one by one, and check resistance with an ohmmeter.

Replace any cracked or brittle wires. If any of the wires are defective, replace the entire set. Replace any wires with excessive resistance (over 8000 Ω per foot for suppression wire), and separate any wires that might cause induction firing.

4.6

Misfiring can be the result of spark plug leads to adjacent, consecutively firing cylinders running parallel and too close together

On point-type ignition systems, check the spark plug wires as shown. On electronic ignitions, do not remove the wire from the distributor cap terminal; instead, test through the cap

Spark plugs wires can be checked visually by bending them in a loop over your finger. This will reveal any cracks, burned or broken insulation. Any wire with cracked insulation should be replaced

---

4.6 Remove the spark plugs, noting the cylinders from which they were removed, and evaluate according to the chart in this section.

See chart.

See Chart

4.7 Reinstall the spark plugs.

NOTE: Modern electronic ignition systems generate extremely high voltages and high heats. The spark plug boots can soften and actually fuse to the ceramic insulator of the spark plugs after long exposures to high temperature and voltage. If this happens, the boot (and possibly the wire) must be replaced.

To help alleviate this condition, many manufacturers are recommending new silicone compounds to slow the deterioration. The compounds are generally nonconductive, protective lubricants that will not dry out, harden, or melt away. They form a weather-tight seal between rubber or plastic and metal and are found in several typical locations: Inside the insulating boots of spark plug wires, inside primary ignition circuit cable connectors, on distributor and rotor cap electrodes, and under the GM HEI control module.

4.8

Application Point	Silicone Compound
GENERAL MOTORS: Under HEI module	Supplied with new module, or use GE-642 or DC-340
FORD MOTOR COMPANY: Inside spark plug boots, on end of cable when installing new boot, and on rotor and cap electrodes	Ford part number D7AZ-19A331-A or use GE-627 or DC-111
CHRYSLER CORPORATION: ¼" deep within spark control computer connector cavity coating rotor electrode	Use Mopar part number 2932524 or NLGI Grade 2 EP (not a silicone) supplied with new rotor, or use GE-628 or DC-111
AMERICAN MOTORS (Prestolite system): Distributor primary connector—coat male terminal, fill female ¼ full	AMC part number 8127445 or GE-623

GE: General Electric
DC: Dow Corning

Test and Procedure	Results and Indications	Proceed To
4.8 Examine the location of all the plugs.	The following diagrams illustrate some of the conditions that the location of plugs will reveal.	4.9

Two adjacent plugs are fouled in a 6-cylinder engine, 4-cylinder engine or either bank of a V-8. This is probably due to a blown head gasket between the two cylinders.

An unbalanced carburetor is indicated. Following the fuel flow on this particular design shows that the cylinders fed by the right-hand barrel are fouled from overly rich mixture, while the cylinders fed by the left-hand barrel are normal.

Finding one plug overheated may indicate an intake manifold leak near the affected cylinder. If the overheated plug is the second of two adjacent, consecutively firing plugs, it could be the result of ignition cross-firing. Separating the leads to these two plugs will eliminate cross-fire.

The two center plugs in a 6-cylinder engine are fouled. Raw fuel may be "boiled" out of the carburetor into the intake manifold after the engine is shut-off. Stop-start driving can also foul the center plugs, due to overly rich mixture. Proper float level, a new float needle and seat or use of an insulating spacer may help this problem.

If the four rear plugs are overheated, a cooling system problem is suggested. A thorough cleaning of the cooling system may restore coolant circulation and cure the problem.

Occasionally, the two rear plugs in large, lightly used V-8's will become oil fouled. High oil consumption and smoky exhaust may also be noticed. It is probably due to plugged oil drain holes in the rear of the cylinder head, causing oil to be sucked in around the valve stems. This usually occurs in the rear cylinders first, because the engine slants that way.

Test and Procedure	Results and Indications	Proceed To
4.9 Determine the static ignition timing. Using the crankshaft pulley timing marks as a guide, locate top dead center on the compression stroke of the number one cylinder.	The rotor should be pointing toward the No. 1 tower in the distributor cap, and, on electronic ignitions, the armature spoke for that cylinder should be lined up with the stator.	**4.10**
4.10 Check coil polarity: Connect a voltmeter negative lead to the coil high tension lead, and the positive lead to ground. **NOTE: Reverse the hook-up for positive ground systems.** Crank the engine momentarily.	If the voltmeter reads up-scale, the polarity is correct.	**5.1**
	If the voltmeter reads down-scale, reverse the coil polarity (switch the primary leads).	**5.1**

Checking coil polarity

SECTION 5—FUEL SYSTEM

Test and Procedure	Results and Indications	Proceed to
5.1 Determine that the air filter is functioning efficiently: Hold paper elements up to a strong light, and attempt to see light through the filter.	Clean permanent air filters in solvent (or manufacturer's recommendation), and allow to dry. Replace paper elements through which light cannot be seen.	**5.2**
5.2 Determine whether a flooding condition exists: Flooding is identified by a strong gasoline odor, and excessive gasoline present in the throttle bore(s) of the carburetor.	If flooding is not evident	**5.3**
	If flooding is evident, permit the gasoline to dry for a few moments and restart.	
	If flooding doesn't recur	**5.7**
	If flooding is persistent	**5.5**

If the engine floods repeatedly, check the choke butterfly flap

Test and Procedure	Results and Indications	Proceed to
5.3 Check that fuel is reaching the carburetor: Detach the fuel line at the carburetor inlet. Hold the end of the line in a cup (not styrofoam), and crank the engine.	If fuel flows smoothly	**5.7**
	If fuel doesn't flow	**5.4**
	If fuel flows erratically.	
	NOTE: Make sure that there is fuel in the tank	

Check the fuel pump by disconnecting the output line (fuel pump-to-carburetor) at the carburetor and operating the starter briefly

Test and Procedure	Results and Indications	Proceed To
5.4 Test the fuel pump: Disconnect all fuel lines from the fuel pump. Hold a finger over the input fitting, crank the engine (with electric pump, turn the ignition or pump on); and feel for suction.	If suction is evident, blow out the fuel line to the tank with low pressure compressed air until bubbling is heard from the fuel filler neck. Also blow out the carburetor fuel line (both ends disconnected).	**5.7**
	If no suction is evident, replace or repair the fuel pump. **NOTE: Repeated oil fouling of the spark plugs, or a no-start condition, could be the result of a ruptured vacuum booster pump diaphragm, through which oil or gasoline is being drawn into the intake manifold (where applicable).**	**5.7**
5.5 Occasionally, small specks of dirt will clog the small jets and orifices in the carburetor. With the engine cold, hold a flat piece of wood or similar material over the carburetor, where possible, and crank the engine.	If the engine starts, but runs roughly the engine is probably not run enough.	
	If the engine won't start.	**5.9**
5.6 Check the needle and seat: Tap the carburetor in the area of the needle and seat.	If flooding stops, a gasoline additive (e.g., Gumout) will often cure the problem.	**5.7**
	If flooding continues, check the fuel pump for excessive pressure at the carburetor (according to specifications). If the pressure is normal, the needle and seat must be removed and checked, and/or the float level adjusted.	**5.7**
5.7 Test the accelerator pump by looking into the throttle bores while operating the throttle.	If the accelerator pump appears to be operating normally	**5.8**
	If the accelerator pump is not operating, the pump must be reconditioned. Where possible, service the pump with the carburetor(s) installed on the engine. If necessary, remove the carburetor. Prior to removal	**5.8**

Check for gas at the carburetor by looking down the carburetor throat while someone moves the accelerator

Test and Procedure	Results and Indications	Proceed To
5.8 Determine whether the carburetor main fuel system is functioning: Spray a commercial starting fluid into the carburetor while attempting to start the engine.	If the engine starts, runs for a few seconds, and dies	**5.9**
	If the engine doesn't start	**6.1**
5.9 Uncommon fuel system malfunctions: See below:	If the problem is solved	**6.1**
	If the problem remains, remove and recondition the carburetor.	

Condition	Indication	Test	Prevailing Weather Conditions	Remedy
Vapor lock	Engine will not re-start shortly after running.	Cool the components of the fuel system until the engine starts. Vapor lock can be cured faster by draping a wet cloth over a mechanical fuel pump.	Hot to very hot	Ensure that the exhaust manifold heat control valve is operating. Check with the vehicle manufacturer for the recommended solution to vapor lock on the model in question.
Carburetor icing	Engine will not idle, stalls at low speeds.	Visually inspect the throttle plate area of the throttle bores for frost.	High humidity, 32–40° F.	Ensure that the exhaust manifold heat control valve is operating, and that the intake manifold heat riser is not blocked.
Water in the fuel	Engine sputters and stalls; may not start.	Pump a small amount of fuel into a glass jar. Allow to stand, and inspect for droplets of a layer of water.	High humidity, extreme temperature changes.	For droplets, use one or two cans of commercial gas line anti-freeze. For a layer of water, the tank must be drained, and the fuel lines blown out with compressed air.

SECTION 6—ENGINE COMPRESSION

Test and Procedure	Results and Indications	Proceed to
6.1 Test engine compression: Remove all spark plugs. Block the throttle wide open. Insert a compression gauge into a spark plug port, crank the engine to obtain the maximum reading, and record.	If compression is within limits on all cylinders	7.1
	If gauge reading is extremely low on all cylinders	6.2
	If gauge reading is low on one or two cylinders: (If gauge readings are identical and low on two or more adjacent cylinders, the head gasket must be replaced.)	6.2

Checking compression

6.2 Test engine compression (wet): Squirt approximately 30 cc. of engine oil into each cylinder, and retest per 6.1.	If the readings improve, worn or cracked rings or broken pistons are indicated:	**See Car Section**
	If the readings do not improve, burned or excessively carboned valves or a jumped timing chain are indicated.	7.1
	NOTE: A jumped timing chain is often indicated by difficult cranking.	

SECTION 7—ENGINE VACUUM

Test and Procedure	Results and Indications	Proceed to
7.1 Attach a vacuum gauge to the intake manifold beyond the throttle plate. Start the engine, and observe the action of the needle over the range of engine speeds.	See below.	**See below**

INDICATION: Normal engine in good condition

Proceed to: 8.1

Normal engine

Gauge reading: Steady, from 17–22 in./Hg.

INDICATION: Sticking valves or ignition miss

Proceed to: 9.1, 8.3

Sticking valves

Gauge reading: Intermittent fluctuation at idle

INDICATION: Late ignition or valve timing, low compression, stuck throttle valve, leaking carburetor or manifold gasket

Proceed to: 6.1

Incorrect valve timing

Gauge reading: Low (10–15 in./Hg) but steady

INDICATION: Improper carburetor adjustment or minor intake leak.

Proceed to: 7.2

Carburetor requires adjustment

Gauge reading: Drifting needle

INDICATION: Ignition miss, blown cylinder head gasket, leaking valve or weak valve spring

Proceed to: 8.3, 6.1

Blown head gasket

Gauge reading: Needle fluctuates as engine speed increases

INDICATION: Burnt valve or faulty valve clearance: Needle will fall when defective valve operates

Proceed to: 9.1

Burnt or leaking valves

Gauge reading: Steady needle, but drops regularly

INDICATION: Choked muffler, excessive back pressure in system

Proceed to: 10.1

Clogged exhaust system

Gauge reading: Gradual drop in reading at idle

INDICATION: Worn valve guides

Proceed to: 9.1

Worn valve guides

Gauge reading: Needle vibrates excessively at idle, but steadies as engine speed increases

White pointer = steady gauge hand	Black pointer = fluctuating gauge hand

Test and Procedure	Results and Indications	Proceed To
7.2 Attach a vacuum gauge per 7.1, and test for an intake manifold leak. Squirt a small amount of oil around the intake manifold gaskets, carburetor gaskets, plugs and fittings. Observe the action of the vacuum gauge.	If the reading improves, replace the indicated gasket, or seal the indicated fitting or plug:	**8.1**
	If the reading remains low:	**7.3**
7.3 Test all vacuum hoses and accessories for leaks as described in 7.2. Also check the carburetor body (dashpots, automatic choke mechanism, throttle shafts) for leaks in the same manner.	If the reading improves, service or replace the offending part(s):	**8.1**
	If the reading remains low:	**6.1**

SECTION 8—SECONDARY ELECTRICAL SYSTEM

Test and Procedure	Results and Indications	Proceed to
8.1 Remove the distributor cap and check to make sure that the rotor turns when the engine is cranked. Visually inspect the distributor components.	Clean, tighten or replace any components which appear defective.	**8.2**
8.2 Connect a timing light (per manufacturer's recommendation) and check the dynamic ignition timing. Disconnect and plug the vacuum hose(s) to the distributor if specified, start the engine, and observe the timing marks at the specified engine speed.	If the timing is not correct, adjust to specifications by rotating the distributor in the engine: (Advance timing by rotating distributor opposite normal direction of rotor rotation, retard timing by rotating distributor in same direction as rotor rotation.)	**8.3**
8.3 Check the operation of the distributor advance mechanism(s): To test the mechanical advance, disconnect the vacuum lines from the distributor advance unit and observe the timing marks with a timing light as the engine speed is increased from idle. If the mark moves smoothly, without hesitation, it may be assumed that the mechanical advance is functioning properly. To test vacuum advance and/or retard systems, alternately crimp and release the vacuum line, and observe the timing mark for movement. If movement is noted, the system is operating.	If the systems are functioning	**8.4**
	If the systems are not functioning, remove the distributor, and test on a distributor tester.	**8.4**
8.4 Locate an ignition miss: With the engine running, remove each spark plug wire, one at a time, until one is found that doesn't cause the engine to roughen and slow down. **CAUTION: Do not pull on the wire to remove the boot from the plug. Be sure your hand is insulated from the wire.**	When the missing cylinder is identified	**4.1**

Test and Procedure	Results and Indications	Proceed To
11.5 Check the radiator pressure cap: Attach a radiator pressure tester to the radiator cap (wet the seal prior to installation). Quickly pump up the pressure, noting the point at which the cap releases.	If the cap releases within ±1 psi of the specified rating, it is operating properly.	**11.6**
	If the cap releases at more than ±1 psi of the specified rating, it should be replaced.	**11.6**

Checking radiator pressure cap

Test and Procedure	Results and Indications	Proceed To
11.6 Test the thermostat: Start the engine cold, remove the radiator cap, and insert a thermometer into the radiator. Allow the engine to idle. After a short while, there will be a sudden, rapid increase in coolant temperature. The temperature at which this sharp rise stops is the thermostat opening temperature.	If the thermostat opens at or about the specified temperature	**11.7**
	If the temperature doesn't increase (If the temperature increases slowly and gradually, replace the thermostat.)	**11.7**
11.7 Check the water pump: Remove the thermostat elbow and the thermostat, disconnect the coil high tension lead (to prevent starting), and crank the engine momentarily.	If coolant flows, replace the thermostat and retest per 11.6.	**11.6**
	If coolant doesn't flow, reverse flush the cooling system to alleviate any blockage that might exist. If system is not blocked, and coolant will not flow, replace the water pump.	**See Car Section**

SECTION 12—LUBRICATION

Test and Procedure	Results and Indications	Proceed to
12.1 Check the oil pressure gauge or warning light: If the gauge shows low pressure, or the light is on for no obvious reason, remove the oil pressure sender. Install an accurate oil pressure gauge and run the engine momentarily.	If oil pressure builds normally, run engine for a few moments to determine that it is functioning normally, and replace the sender.	—
	If the pressure remains low	**12.2**
	If the pressure surges	**12.3**
	If the oil pressure is zero	**12.3**
12.2 Visually inspect the oil: If the oil is watery or very thin, milky, or foamy, replace the oil and oil filter.	If the oil is normal	**12.3**
	If after replacing oil the pressure remains low	**12.3**
	If after replacing oil the pressure becomes normal	—
12.3 Inspect the oil pressure relief valve and spring, to ensure that it is not sticking or stuck. Remove and thoroughly clean the valve, spring, and the valve body.	If the oil pressure improves	—
	If no improvement is noted	**12.4**

Test and Procedure	Results and Indications	Proceed To
12.4 Check to ensure that the oil pump is not cavitating (sucking air instead of oil): See that the crankcase is neither over nor underfull, and that the pickup in the sump is in the proper position and free from sludge.	Fill or drain the crankcase to the proper capacity, and clean the pickup screen in solvent if necessary. If no improvement is noted	**12.5**
12.5 Inspect the oil pump drive and the oil pump:	If the pump drive or the oil pump appear to be defective, service as necessary and retest per 12.1. If the pump drive and pump appear to be operating normally, the engine should be disassembled to determine where blockage exists.	**12.1**
12.6 Purge the engine of ethylene glycol coolant: Competely drain the crankcase and the oil filter. Obtain a commercial butyl cellosolve base solvent, designated for this purpose, and follow the instructions precisely. Following this, install a new oil filter and refill the crankcase with the proper weight oil. The next oil and filter change should follow shortly thereafter (1000 miles).		

SECTION 9—VALVE TRAIN

Test and Procedure	Results and Indications	Proceed to
9.1 Evaluate the valve train: Remove the valve cover, and ensure that the valves are adjusted to specifications. A mechanic's stethoscope may be used to aid in the diagnosis of the valve train. By pushing the probe on or near push rods or rockers, valve noise often can be isolated. A timing light also may be used to diagnose valve problems. Connect the light according to manufacturer's recommendations, and start the engine. Vary the firing moment of the light by increasing the engine speed (and therefore the ignition advance), and moving the trigger from cylinder to cylinder. Observe the movement of each valve.	Sticking valves or erratic valve train motion can be observed with the timing light. The cylinder head must be disassembled for repairs.	**See Car Section**
9.2 Check the valve timing: Locate top dead center of the No. 1 piston, and install a degree wheel or tape on the crankshaft pulley or damper with zero corresponding to an index mark on the engine. Rotate the crankshaft in its direction of rotation, and observe the opening of the No. 1 cylinder intake valve. The opening should correspond with the correct mark on the degree wheel according to specifications.	If the timing is not correct, the timing cover must be removed for further investigation.	**See Car Section**

SECTION 10—EXHAUST SYSTEM

Test and Procedure	Results and Indications	Proceed to
10.1 Determine whether the exhaust manifold heat control valve is operating: Operate the valve by hand to determine whether it is free to move. If the valve is free, run the engine to operating temperature and observe the action of the valve, to ensure that it is opening.	If the valve sticks, spray it with a suitable solvent, open and close the valve to free it, and retest.	
	If the valve functions properly	10.2
	If the valve does not free, or does not operate, replace the valve.	10.2
10.2 Ensure that there are no exhaust restrictions: Visually inspect the exhaust system for kinks, dents, or crushing. Also note that gases are flowing freely from the tailpipe at all engine speeds, indicating no restriction in the muffler or resonator.	Replace any damaged portion of the system.	11.1

SECTION 11—COOLING SYSTEM

Test and Procedure	Results and Indications	Proceed to
11.1 Visually inspect the fan belt for glazing, cracks, and fraying, and replace if necessary. Tighten the belt so that the longest span has approximately ½″ play at its mid-point under thumb pressure (see Maintenance Section).	Replace or tighten the fan belt as necessary.	**11.2**

Checking belt tension

Test and Procedure	Results and Indications	Proceed to
11.2 Check the fluid level of the cooling system.	If full or slightly low, fill as necessary.	**11.5**
	If extremely low	**11.3**
11.3 Visually inspect the external portions of the cooling system (radiator, radiator hoses, thermostat elbow, water pump seals, heater hoses, etc.) for leaks. If none are found, pressurize the cooling system to 14–15 psi.	If cooling system holds the pressure	**11.5**
	If cooling system loses pressure rapidly, reinspect external parts of the system for leaks under pressure. If none are found, check dipstick for coolant in crankcase. If no coolant is present, but pressure loss continues	**11.4**
	If coolant is evident in crankcase, remove cylinder head(s), and check gasket(s). If gaskets are intact, block and cylinder head(s) should be checked for cracks or holes.	
	If the gasket(s) is blown, replace, and purge the crankcase of coolant.	**12.6**
	NOTE: Occasionally, due to atmospheric and driving conditions, condensation of water can occur in the crankcase. This causes the oil to appear milky white. To remedy, run the engine until hot, and change the oil and oil filter.	
11.4 Check for combustion leaks into the cooling system: Pressurize the cooling system as above. Start the engine, and observe the pressure gauge. If the needle fluctuates, remove each spark plug wire, one at a time, noting which cylinder(s) reduce or eliminate the fluctuation.	Cylinders which reduce or eliminate the fluctuation, when the spark plug wire is removed, are leaking into the cooling system. Replace the head gasket on the affected cylinder bank(s).	**See Car Section**

Pressurizing the cooling system

Diesel Engine Troubleshooting

NOTE: The following troubleshooting procedures cover problems usually associated with diesel engines. Those problems common to both gasoline and diesel engines are covered in the gasoline engine troubleshooting procedures.

INDEX TO PROBLEMS

Problem/Symptom	Begin at Specific Diagnosis, Number
Fuel System	Section 1
Engine Starting Difficulty:	
Feed pump does not feed fuel	1.1
Injection pump does not feed fuel	1.2
Incorrect injection timing	1.3
Defective injection nozzles	1.4
Engine Operating Instability:	
Engine shuts off immediately after starting	1.5
Uneven idling	1.6
Engine will not reach maximum rated speed	1.7
Engine exceeds maximum rated speed	1.8
Loss of power	1.9
Engine Knock:	
Associated with exhaust gas problems	1.10
Not associated with exhaust gas problems	1.11
Engine Mechanical	Section 2
Engine Starting Difficulty	2.1
Unusual Noises	2.2
Engine Operating Instability	2.3
Loss of Power	2.4
Exhaust gas Problem	2.5
Engine Shut-Off	2.6
Loss of Oil Pressure	2.7
Oil Leakage	2.8
Compression Pressure Leakage	2.9

SECTION 1—Fuel System

Test and Procedure	Results and Indication	Proceed To
1.1a Check for pressure at the outlet of the feed pump	If pressure exists, there is a clog in the supply line. Clean or replace it. If there is little or no pressure at the outlet, the filter is clogged. Clean or replace the filter. If the filter is clear, the feed pump piston is inoperative. Relace it.	1.1b
1.1b Check the feed pump valves	If the inlet and outlet valves do not operate, the check valve or spring is broken. Replace it.	1.2a
1.2a Check for fuel leakage at the overflow or return line	A clogged filter can result in high pressure causing leakage. Replace the filter.	1.2b
1.2b Check for fuel in the filter leaking at the overflow valve	If leakage is found, the overflow valve is damaged. Replace it.	1.2c
1.2c Check for leakage at the injection pump overflow valve	If leakage is found, it is caused by: damaged overflow valve, sticking plunger, or sticking delivery valve. Replace the defective part(s).	1.2d
1.2d Check the injection pump plunger feed pressures.	If pressure at the plungers is low, replace the plunger(s).	1.2e

Test and Procedure		Results and Indication	Proceed To
1.2e	Check to make sure the injection pump is operating	An inoperative pump is caused by: a damaged or missing shaft key, or a damaged drive gear train.	1.3a
1.3a	Check that the pump timing marks are correctly aligned in the gear train	Incorrect timing marks alignment must be corrected.	1.3b
1.3b	Check that the injection pump is properly mounted	Remove and install the pump correctly	1.4a
1.4a	Install an injection nozzle on a tester and make sure that fuel is continuously ejected	A broken or intermittent stream is caused by a damaged spring or a sticking nozzle needle	1.4b
1.4b	With the nozzle on the tester as in 1.4a, check that shutoff is clean with no dribble or afterdrip	Dribble is caused by a defective nozzle valve seat. Replace the nozzle.	1.4c
1.4c	Using a tester, check injection pressure	Low pressure is a result of a weak spring. Replace the spring or adjust the initial injection pressure.	1.5a
1.5a	See 1.2a	Proceed as in 1.2a	1.5b
1.5b	Check for water in the fuel	Drain and clean the tank	1.5c
1.5c	Check for air in the fuel lines	Air can be introduced through a damaged fuel inlet line, a loose inlet line connector or a damaged gasket	1.5d
1.5d	Check for insufficient fuel feed	Insufficient fuel feed is caused by: a damaged feed pump, a clogged tank vent, or a clogged filter. Replace or repair as necessary.	1.6a
1.6a	Check the control rack action for smooth operation	Uneven control rack operation is caused by: a sticking plunger, improper meshing of the rack and pinion, poor seating of the plunger spring, insufficient clearance between the plunger and lower spring seat, or an overly tight delivery valve holder. Replace or adjust as necessary.	1.6b
1.6b	Check that the injection pump discharge is uniform	If the output is uneven, adjust as necessary	1.6c
1.6c	Check that the injection pump discharge volume is adequate	An inadequate discharge volume is caused by a worn plunger or a broken spring	1.6d
1.6d	Check for even low speed engine performance	If the engine performs unevenly or erratically at low speed only, a worn feed pump piston or defective feed pump valve is the cause.	1.6e
1.6e	Check for smooth engine operation throughout the operating range	This problem is usually caused by mechanical governor defects such as: a defective low speed spring, defective damper spring, or excessive friction among moving parts. Replace the defective parts.	1.6f
1.6f	Check the injectors on a tester	Improper nozzle operation should be corrected accordingly	1.7a
1.7a	Check the operating governor	A broken or weak spring in the governor will prevent full speed operation.	1.7b
1.7b	Check the injectors on a tester for a drop in injector output	A drop in output is caused by a sticking needle or a dirty nozzle. Replace or clean as necessary.	1.8a

Test and Procedure		Results and Indications	Proceed To
1.8a	Check the injection pump for proper rack and pinion action	A catching or dirty rack and pinion will cause overspeeding.	1.8b
1.8b	Check the governor adjustment	An improperly adjusted governor will cause overspeeding. Adjust.	1.9a
1.9a	Check the injection pump output	Low output can be caused by: Incorrect adjustment—Adjust Loose delivery valve—Tighten Broken delivery valve seal—Replace Poor valve seat contact—Replace Broken/weak delivery valve spring—Replace	1.9b
1.9b	Check for unusual noise at the injection pump	A noisy pump is an indication of a broken plunger spring	1.9c
1.9c	Check plunger operation	A sticking injection pump plunger will cause power loss. Replace.	1.9d
1.9d	Check the injection timer	A lag in injection timing is caused by large clearances in the timer due to wear. Replace.	1.9e
1.9e	Check for air or water in the fuel	Bleed the air or drain the fuel and clean the tank and lines	1.9f
1.9f	Check the injection timing	Readjust timing if necessary	1.10a
1.10a	Check the initial injection timing	Adjust if necessary	1.10b
1.10b	Check the injection pressure	High pressure will cause knock. Adjust as necessary	1.10c
1.10c	Check the injector nozzle	A clogged nozzle causes knock. Clean or replace the nozzle.	1.11a
1.11a	Check the injection pump output and timing	Excessive output, coupled with incorrect timing causes knock. Adjust as necessary	1.11b
1.11b	Check the delivery valve seat	Replace a defective seat	1.11c
1.11c	Check the pump plungers	Replace badly worn plungers	1.11d
1.11d	Check injector opening pressure on a tester	Adjust as necessary	1.11e
1.11e	Check the injector	Replace a broken nozzle spring or sticking needle.	

SECTION 2—ENGINE MECHANICAL

Test and Procedure		Results and Indications	Proceed To
2.1a	Check for piston seizing	Seized pistons are caused by low oil pressure, oil breakdown, or overheating. Replace the pistons and liners.	2.1b
2.1b	Check for a damaged flywheel ring gear	A damaged ring gear will cause poor meshing with the starter. Replace the ring gear.	2.1c
2.1c	Make a compression check	Low compression can be caused by: sticking rings, worn rings, worn liners. Replace the rings or liners.	2.2a
2.2a	A knocking noise at idle or during acceleration can be caused by a variety of wear problems.	Use a stethoscope or similar listening device to try to pinpoint the source of the noise. Among other reasons for knocking are: piston pins, rod bearings, loose rod caps, crankshaft journals and/or bearings, crankshaft thrust washer. Replace any worn parts.	2.2b
2.2b	An infrequently encountered noise is a continuous growl during acceleration	This problem is usually caused by problems in the engine timing gears. Poor contact, excessive backlash or loose gears are usually at fault.	2.2c
2.2c	Intermittent noises are the hardest to find. They are usually caused by broken moving parts.	Check the gear train for a chipped or cracked gear; the oil pan for broken parts or foreign objects or the cylinder head for a broken valve or valve spring.	2.3
2.3	Check for oil in the combustion chambers	Oil entering the combustion chambers will cause the engine to overspeed if the amount of oil is too great, or run unevenly. Check for broken or sticking rings, bad head gasket(s) or worn valve guides.	2.4
2.4	Check the compression	Low compression is the main cause of power loss. The main causes for low compression are: worn rings or liners, cracked valves, warped head or block, and bad head gasket.	2.5
2.5	A large amount of black exhaust is caused by low compression	See 2.4 above	2.6
2.6	If the engine stops suddenly during operation, the cause is usually sudden damage	Check the pistons, main bearings or rod bearings for lack of lubrication. A seized camshaft is also a result of low or no lubrication. Check the timing gears for damage.	2.7
2.7	Check for excessive clearance between the bearings and journals on both the mains and rod bearings. Check the oil pressure.	Replace as necessary. Replace the pump as necessary.	2.8
2.8	Aside from the usual leaking gasket problems, check the condition of the combustion chamber O-rings.	Replace as necessary	2.9
2.9	Compression leakage is usually caused by a seal defect between the head and the block	Check the head gasket; check for loose head bolts; check for head or block warpage. Replace or repair as necessary.	

TROUBLESHOOTING AND DIAGNOSIS

Engine Overheating Troubleshooting

OVERHEAT SHOWN ON GAUGE, WITH BOILING, COOLANT LOSS OR STEAM

NOTE: THIS CHART IS DESIGNED TO AID IN THE DIAGNOSIS AND CORRECTION OF ENGINE OVERHEATING PROBLEMS. THE POSSIBILITY OF MULTIPLE MALFUNCTIONS SHOULD NOT BE OVERLOOKED.

OVERHEAT SHOWN ON GAUGE ONLY NO COOLANT LOSS

CHECK RADIATOR FAN MOTOR, RELAY AND FAN SWITCH

CHECK ALTERNATOR AND WATER PUMP BELT TENSION

ADJUST/REPLACE BELT AS NECESSARY

CHECK GAUGE AND SENDING UNIT

REPAIR AS NECESSARY

CHECK FOR RESTRICTED AIR FLOW THROUGH RADIATOR AND/OR AIR CONDITIONING CONDENSER

RESTRICTED AIR FLOW – BUGS, LEAVES, GRASS, BUG SCREEN, NONPRODUCTION BUMPER GUARDS. FOG LIGHTS

NO RESTRICTION

CHECK ENGINE OIL LEVEL – CHANGE OR ADD AS REQUIRED

CLEAN FINS OF RADIATOR AND/OR AIR CONDITIONING CONDENSER, REMOVE OR REPOSITION ACCESSORIES

CHECK LEVEL OF COOLANT IN RESERVE TANK AND RADIATOR TANK

COOLANT LEVEL LOW

CHECK FOR MISSING AND/OR OUT OF PLACE AIR SEALS

CHECK COOLANT FOR EVIDENCE OF FOAMING

COOLANT LEVEL NOT LOW

IN RADIATOR TOP TANK NOT IN RESERVE TANK

IN COOLANT RESERVE TANK

CHECK COOLANT ANTI-FREEZE PROTECTION

ALL AIR SEALS IN PLACE

AIR SEALS MISSING AND/OR OUT OF PLACE

CHECK RESERVE TANK SYSTEM FOR LEAKS

ADD COOLANT

PROTECTION O.K. TO AT LEAST –34°F

NO ANTI-FREEZE OR INADEQUATE ANTI-FREEZE PROTECTION

ADD ANTI-FREEZE OR FLUSH SYSTEM AND REFILL WITH 50/50 SOLUTION

REPLACE MISSING SEALS AND/OR ADJUST MISPLACED SEALS

Engine Overheating Troubleshooting

NO EVIDENCE OF EXCESSIVE FOAMING

CHECK SYSTEM FOR LEAKS, INCLUDING RADIATOR CAP, PRESSURE TEST COOLING SYSTEM

EXCESSIVE FOAMING EVIDENT

DRAIN AND FLUSH COOLING SYSTEM REFILL WITH NEW 50/50 SOLUTION

SYSTEM DOES NOT LEAK

SYSTEM LEAKS

REPAIR LEAKS AS NECESSARY

CIRCULATION POOR

CHECK FOR COLLAPSED LOWER RADIATOR HOSE

CHECK COOLANT CIRCULATION IN RADIATOR OR UPPER RADIATOR HOSE

HOSE NOT COLLAPSED

HOSE COLLAPSED

REPLACE HOSE

CIRCULATION GOOD

VISUALLY CHECK RADIATOR TUBES FOR EVIDENCE OF PLUGGED OR RESTRICTED RADIATOR

PLUGGED RADIATOR OR RESTRICTED TUBES EVIDENT

CORRECT OR REPAIR AS NECESSARY

CHECK IGNITION TIMING

NO EVIDENCE OF PLUGGED RADIATOR

REMOVE RADIATOR AND THOROUGHLY CLEAN BY RODDING. DIP IN 30/70 SOLDER

CHECK EXHAUST HEAT VALVE FOR FREE MOVEMENT

THERMOSTAT FAULTY

TEST THERMOSTAT

REPLACE THERMOSTAT

THERMOSTAT OK

CHECK WATER PUMP IMPELLER FOR LOOSENESS

IMPELLER LOOSE

IMPELLER NOT LOOSE

REPLACE WATER PUMP

REMOVE HEAD AND CLEAN OUT BLOCKED PASSAGES AS REQUIRED

CHECK HEAD AND/OR BLOCK FOR INTERNAL RESTRICTION

Low Engine Temperature Troubleshooting

ENGINE TEMPERATURE LOW- OR SLOW ENGINE WARM-UP

NORMAL TEMPERATURE SHOWN ON GAUGE. LOW HEATER AIR TEMPERATURE

LOW TEMPERATURE SHOWN ON GAUGE AND LOW HEATER AIR TEMPERATURE

LOW TEMPERATURE SHOWN ON GAUGE AND NO HEATER AIR TEMPERATURE COMPLAINTS

CHECK COOLANT LEVEL IN THE RADIATOR AND COOLANT RESERVE BOTTLE

COOLANT LEVEL LOW

CHECK COOLANT LEVEL IN THE RADIATOR AND COOLANT RESERVE BOTTLE

CHECK TEMPERATURE GAUGE AND SENDING UNIT

PROPER COOLANT LEVEL

INSPECT COOLING SYSTEM AND HEATER CIRCUIT FOR LEAKS

PROPER COOLANT LEVEL

REPAIR LEAKS AND/OR REFILL WITH COOLANT

POSSIBLE HEATER SYSTEM MALFUNCTIONS

HEATER SYSTEM WORKING PROPERLY

CHECK THERMOSTAT HOUSING BOLTS FOR PROPER TORQUE (POSSIBLE INTERNAL COOLANT LEAKAGE)

THERMOSTAT HOUSING BOLTS PROPERLY TORQUED

THERMOSTAT HOUSING BOLTS NOT PROPERLY TORQUED

CHECK THERMOSTAT OPERATION

TORQUE HOUSING BOLTS

THERMOSTAT TESTING PROCEDURE

1. REMOVE RADIATOR PRESSURE CAP.

   CAUTION: IF VEHICLE HAS BEEN RUN RECENTLY, WAIT 15 MINUTES BEFORE REMOVING CAP, THEN PLACE A RAG OVER THE CAP AND TURN IT TO THE FIRST STOP. ALLOW PRESSURE TO ESCAPE THROUGH THE OVERFLOW TUBE AND WHEN THE SYSTEM STABILIZES REMOVE THE CAP COMPLETELY.

2. DRAIN ONE QUART OF COOLANT FROM THE RADIATOR.

3. WARM THE ENGINE TO OPERATING TEMPERATURE BY IDLING FOR 20 MINUTES, WITH THE PRESSURE CAP OFF. IDLE LONGER IF WORKING OUTDOORS IN COLD TEMPERATURES.

4. WITH THE ENGINE IDLING, PLACE A THERMOMETER INTO THE COOLANT IN THE RADIATOR FILLER NECK.

5. COOLANT TEMPERATURE SHOULD STABILIZE AT NO LOWER THAN 187°F. (86°C) (OR 8° BELOW THERMOSTAT OPENING TEMPERATURE.)

IF TEMPERATURE OF COOLANT FAILS TO REACH OPERATING LEVEL, COVER FRONT OF RADIATOR CORE AND ALLOW COOLANT TEMPERATURE TO REACH 210°F. THEN REMOVE COVER, REPEAT STEPS 3 THRU 5 OF THERMOSTAT TEST PROCEDURE. (THE PURPOSE OF THIS OPERATION IS TO PURGE DIRT ACCUMULATION ON THERMOSTAT VALVE.)

IF TEMPERATURE STABILIZES ABOVE 187°F. (86°C) DO NOT REPLACE THE THERMOSTAT.

IF TEMPERATURE DOES NOT STABILIZE AT 187°F. (86°C) OR ABOVE, REPLACE THERMOSTAT.

DRIVELINE
Clutch System Troubleshooting

Condition	Possible Cause	Corrective Action
Clutch chatter	1. Grease on driven plate (disc) facing. 2. Binding clutch linkage. 3. Loose, damaged facings on driven plate (disc). 4. Engine mounts loose. 5. Incorrect height adjustment of pressure plate release levers. 6. Clutch housing or housing to transmission adapter misalignment. 7. Loose driven plate hub.	1. Replace plate. 2. Check for worn, bent, broken parts. Replace as required. Lube linkage. 3. Replace driven plate. 4. Tighten mounts. Replace if damaged. 5. Adjust release lever height. 6. Check bore and face run out. Correct as required. 7. Replace driven plate.
Clutch grabbing	1. Oil, grease on driven plate (disc) facing. 2. Broken pressure plate. 3. Warped or binding driven plate. Driven plate binding on clutch shaft.	1. Replace driven plate. 2. Replace pressure plate. 3. Replace warped driven plate. Replace clutch shaft if defective, scored, worn.
Clutch slips	1. Lack of lubrication in clutch linkage (linkage binds, causes incomplete engagement. 2. Incorrect pedal, or linkage adjustment. 3. Broken pressure plate springs. 4. Weak pressure plate springs. 5. Grease on driven plate facings (disc).	1. Lubricate linkage. 2. Adjust as required. 3. Replace pressure plate. 4. Replace pressure plate. 5. Replace driven plate.
Incomplete clutch release	1. Incorrect pedal or linkage adjustment or linkage binding. 2. Incorrect height adjustment on pressure plate release levers. 3. Loose, broken facings on driven plate (disc). 4. Bent, dished, warped driven plate caused by overheating.	1. Adjust as required. Lubricate linkage. 2. Adjust release lever height. 3. Replace driven plate. 4. Replace driven plate.
Grinding, whirring grating noise when pedal is depressed	1. Worn or defective throwout bearing. 2. Starter drive teeth contacting flywheel ring gear teeth.	1. Replace throwout bearing. 2. Look for milled or polished teeth on ring gear. Align clutch housing, replace starter drive or drive spring as required.
Squeal, howl, trumpeting noise when pedal is being released (occurs during first inch to inch and one-half of pedal travel)	1. Pilot bushing worn or lack of lubricant.	1. Replace worn bushing. If bushing appears OK, polish bushing with emery, soak lube wick in oil, lube bushing with oil, apply film of chassis grease to clutch shaft pilot hub, reassemble. **NOTE:** Bushing wear may be due to misalignment of clutch housing or housing to transmission adapter.
Vibration or clutch pedal pulsation with clutch disengaged (pedal fully depressed)	1. Worn or defective engine transmission mounts. 2. Flywheel run out, or damaged or defective clutch components.	1. Inspect and replace as required. 2. Replace components as required. (Flywheel run out at face not to exceed 0.005".)

Manual Transmission Troubleshooting

Condition	Probable Cause
Jumping out of high gear	1. Misalignment of transmission case or clutch housing. 2. Worn pilot bearing in crankshaft. 3. Bent transmission shaft. 4. Worn high speed sliding gear. 5. Worn teeth in clutch shaft. 6. Insufficient spring tension on shifter rail plunger. 7. Bent or loose shifter fork. 8. End-play in clutch shaft. 9. Gears not engaging completely. 10. Loose or worn bearings on clutch shaft or mainshaft.
Sticking in high gear	1. Clutch not releasing fully. 2. Burred or battered teeth on clutch shaft. 3. Burred or battered transmission mainshaft. 4. Frozen synchronizing clutch. 5. Stuck shifter rail plunger. 6. Gearshift lever twisting and binding shifter rail. 7. Battered teeth on high speed sliding gear or on sleeve. 8. Lack of lubrication. 9. Improper lubrication. 10. Corroded transmission parts. 11. Defective mainshaft pilot bearing.
Jumping out of second gear	1. Insufficient spring tension on shifter rail plunger. 2. Bent or loose shifter fork. 3. Gears not engaging completely. 4. End-play in transmission mainshaft. 5. Loose transmission gear bearing. 6. Defective mainshaft pilot bearing. 7. Bent transmission shaft. 8. Worn teeth on second speed sliding gear or sleeve. 9. Loose or worn bearings on transmission mainshaft. 10. End-play in countershaft.
Sticking in second gear	1. Clutch not releasing fully. 2. Burred or battered teeth on sliding sleeve. 3. Burred or battered transmission mainshaft. 4. Frozen synchronizing clutch. 5. Stuck shifter rail plunger. 6. Gearshift lever twisting and binding shifter rail. 7. Lack of lubrication. 8. Second speed transmission gear bearings locked will give same effect as gears stuck in second. 9. Improper lubrication. 10. Corroded transmission parts.
Jumping out of low gear	1. Gears not engaging completely. 2. Bent or loose shifter fork. 3. End-play in transmission mainshaft. 4. End-play in countershaft. 5. Loose or worn bearings on transmission mainshaft. 6. Loose or worn bearings in countershaft. 7. Defective mainshaft pilot bearing.
Sticking in low gear	1. Clutch not releasing fully. 2. Burred or battered transmission mainshaft. 3. Stuck shifter rail plunger. 4. Gearshift lever twisting and binding shifter rail. 5. Lack of lubrication. 6. Improper lubrication. 7. Corroded transmission parts.

Condition	Probable Cause
Jumping out of reverse gear	1. Insufficient spring tension on shifter rail plunger. 2. Bent or loose shifter fork. 3. Badly worn gear teeth. 4. Gears not engaging completely. 5. End-play in transmission mainshaft. 6. Idler gear bushings loose or worn. 7. Loose or worn bearings on transmission mainshaft. 8. Defective mainshaft pilot bearing.
Sticking in reverse gear	1. Clutch not releasing fully. 2. Burred or battered transmission mainshaft. 3. Stuck shifter rail plunger. 4. Gearshift lever twisting and binding shifter rail. 5. Lack of lubrication. 6. Improper lubrication. 7. Corroded transmission parts.
Failure of gears to synchronize	1. Binding pilot bearing on mainshaft, will synchronize in high gear only. 2. Clutch not releasing fully. 3. Detent spring weak or broken. 4. Weak or broken springs under balls in sliding gear sleeve. 5. Binding bearing on clutch shaft. 6. Binding countershaft. 7. Binding pilot bearing in crankshaft 8. Badly worn gear teeth. 9. Scored or worn cones. 10. Improper lubrication. 11. Constant mesh gear not turning freely on transmission mainshaft. Will synchronize in that gear only.
Gears spinning when shifting into gear from neutral	1. Clutch not releasing fully. 2. In some cases an extremely light lubricant in transmission will cause gears to continue to spin for a short time after clutch is released. 3. Binding pilot bearing in crankshaft.
Noisy in all gears	1. Insufficient lubricant. 2. Worn countergear bearings. 3. Worn or damaged main drive gear or countergear. 4. Damaged main drive gear or mainshaft bearings. 5. Worn or damaged countergear anti-lash plate.
Noisy in high gear	1. Damaged main drive gear bearing. 2. Damaged mainshaft bearing. 3. Damaged high speed gear synchronizer.
Noisy in neutral	1. Damaged main drive gear bearing. 2. Damaged or loose mainshaft pilot bearing. 3. Worn or damaged countergear anti-lash plate. 4. Worn countergear bearings.
Noisy in all reduction gears	1. Insufficient lubricant. 2. Worn or damaged drive gear or countergear.
Noisy in second only	1. Damaged or worn second gear constant mesh gears. 2. Worn or damaged countergear rear bearings. 3. Damaged or worn second gear synchronizer.
Noisy in second only	1. Damaged or worn second gear constant mesh gears. 2. Worn or damaged countergear rear bearings. 3. Damaged or worn second gear synchronizer.
Noisy in third only (four speed)	1. Damaged or worn third gear constant mesh gears. 2. Worn or damaged countergear bearings.

Condition	Probable Cause
Noisy in reverse only	1. Worn or damaged reverse idler gear or idler bushing. 2. Worn or damaged mainshaft reverse gear. 3. Worn or damaged reverse countergear. 4. Damaged shift mechanism.
Excessive backlash in all reduction gears	1. Worn countergear bearings. 2. Excessive end–play in countergear.

Automatic Transmission Troubleshooting

Keeping alert to changes in the operating characteristics of the transmission (changing shift points, noises, etc.) can prevent small problems from becoming large ones. If the problem cannot be traced to loose bolts, fluid level, misadjusted linkage, clogged filters or similar problems, you should probably seek professional service.

TRANSMISSION FLUID INDICATIONS

The appearance and odor of the transmission fluid can give valuable clues to the overall condition of the transmission. Always note the appearance of the fluid when you check the fluid level or change the fluid. Rub a small amount of fluid between your fingers to feel for grit and smell the fluid on the dipstick.

If The Fluid Appears	It Indicates
Clear and red colored	Normal operation
Discolored (extremely dark red or brownish) or smells burned	Band or clutch pack failure, usually caused by an overheated transmission. Hauling very heavy loads with insufficient power or failure to change the fluid often results in overheating. Do not confuse this appearance with newer fluids that have a darker red color and a strong odor (though not a burned odor).
Foamy or aerated (light in color and full of bubbles)	The level is too high (gear train is churning oil) An internal air leak (air is mixing with the fluid). Have the transmission checked professionally.
Solid residue in the fluid	Defective bands, clutch pack or bearings. Bits of band material or metal abrasives are clinging to the dipstick. Have the transmission checked professionally.
Varnish coating on the dipstick	The transmission fluid is overheating

Problem	Possible Cause	Correction
Slow initial engagement	1. Improper fluid level. 2. Damaged or improperly adjusted linkage. 3. Contaminated fluid. 4. Faulty clutch and band application, or oil control pressure system.	1. Add fluid as required. 2. Repair or adjust linkage. 3. Perform fluid level check. 4. Perform control pressure test.
Rough initial engagement in either forward or reverse	1. Improper fluid level. 2. High engine idle. 3. Looseness in the driveshaft, U-joints or engine mounts. 4. Incorrect linkage adjustment. 5. Faulty clutch or band application, or oil control pressure system. 6. Sticking or dirty valve body.	1. Perform fluid level check. 2. Adjust idle to specifications. 3. Repair as required. 4. Repair or adjust linkage. 5. Perform control pressure test. 6. Clean, repair or replace valve body.

Problem	Possible Cause	Correction
No drive, slips or chatters in first gear in D. All other gears normal.	1. Faulty one-way clutch.	1. Repair or replace one-way clutch.
No drive, slips or chatters in second gear.	1. Improper fluid level. 2. Damaged or improperly adjusted linkage. 3. Intermediate band out of adjustment. 4. Faulty band or clutch application, or oil pressure control system. 5. Faulty servo and/or internal leaks. 6. Dirty or sticking valve body. 7. Polished, glazed intermediate band or drum.	1. Perform fluid level check. 2. Repair or adjust linkage. 3. Adjust intermediate band. 4. Perform control pressure test. 5. Perform air pressure test. 6. Clean, repair or replace valve body. 7. Replace or repair as required.
No drive in any gear.	1. Improper fluid level. 2. Damaged or improperly adjusted linkage. 3. Faulty clutch or band application, or oil control pressure system. 4. Internal leakage. 5. Valve body loose. 6. Faulty clutches. 7. Sticking or dirty valve body.	1. Perform fluid level check. 2. Repair or adjust linkage. 3. Perform control pressure test. 4. Check and repair as required. 5. Tighten to specification. 6. Perform air pressure test. 7. Clean, repair or replace valve body.
No drive forward—reverse OK.	1. Improper fluid level 2. Damaged or improperly adjusted linkage. 3. Faulty clutch or band application, or oil pressure control system. 4. Faulty forward clutch or governor. 5. Valve body loose 6. Dirty or sticking valve body.	1. Perform fluid level check. 2. Repair or adjust linkage. 3. Perform control pressure test. 4. Perform air pressure test. 5. Tighten to specification. 6. Clean, repair or replace valve body.
No drive, slips or chatters in reverse—forward OK.	1. Improper fluid level 2. Damaged or improperly adjusted linkage. 3. Looseness in the drivehsaft, U-joints or engine mounts. 4. Bands or clutches out of adjustment. 5. Faulty oil pressure control system. 6. Faulty reverse clutch or servo. 7. Valve body loose. 8. Dirty or sticking valve body.	1. Perform fluid level check. 2. Repair or adjust linkage. 3. Repair as required. 4. Adjust as necessary. 5. Perform control pressure test. 6. Perform air pressure test. 7. Tighten to specifications. 8. Clean, repair or replace valve body.
Starts in high—in D drag or lockup at 1–2 shift point or in 2 or 1.	1. Improper fluid level. 2. Damaged or improperly adjusted linkage. 3. Faulty governor. 4. Faulty clutches and/or internal leaks. 5. Valve body loose. 6. Dirty, sticking valve body. 7. Poor mating of valve body to case mounting surfaces.	1. Perform fluid level check. 2. Repair or adjust linkage. 3. Repair or replace governor, clean screen. 4. Perform air pressure test. 5. Tighten to specifications. 6. Clean, repair or replace valve body. 7. Replace valve body or case.

Problem	Possible Cause	Correction
Starts up in 2nd or 3rd but no lockup at 1-2 shift points.	1. Improper fluid level. 2. Damaged or improperly adjusted linkage. 3. Improper band and/or clutch application, or oil pressure control system. 4. Faulty governor. 5. Valve body loose. 6. Dirty or sticking valve body. 7. Cross leaks between valve body and case mating surface.	1. Perform fluid level check. 2. Repair or adjust linkage. 3. Perform control pressure test. 4. Perform governor check. Replace or repair governor, clean screen. 5. Tighten to specification. 6. Clean, repair or replace valve body. 7. Replace valve body and/or case as required.
Shift points incorrect.	1. Improper fluid level. 2. Improper vacuum hose routing or leaks. 3. Improper operation of EGR system. 4. Linkage out of adjustment. 5. Improper speedometer gear installed. 6. Improper clutch or band application, or oil pressure control system. 7. Faulty governor. 8. Dirty or sticking valve body.	1. Perform fluid level check. 2. Correct hose routing. 3. Repair or replace as required. 4. Repair or adjust linkage. 5. Replace gear. 6. Perform shift test and control pressure test. 7. Repair or replace governor—clean screen. 8. Clean, repair or replace valve body.
No upshift at any speed in D.	1. Improper fluid level. 2. Vacuum leak to diaphragm unit. 3. Linkage out of adjustment. 4. Improper band or clutch application, or oil pressure control system. 5. Faulty governor. 6. Dirty or sticking valve bdy.	1. Perform fluid level check. 2. Repair vacuum line or hose. 3. Repair or adjust linkage. 4. Perform control pressure test. 5. Repair or replace governor, clean screen. 6. Clean, repair or replace valve body.
Shifts 1-3 in D.	1. Improper fluid level. 2. Intermediate band out of adjustment. 3. Faulty front servo and/or internal leaks. 4. Polished, glazed band or drum. 5. Improper band or clutch application, or oil pressure control system. 6. Dirty or sticking valve body.	1. Perform fluid level check. 2. Adjust band. 3. Perform air pressure test. Repair front servo and/or internal leaks. 4. Repair or replace band or drum. 5. Perform control pressure test. 6. Clean, repair or replace valve body.
Engine over-speeds on 2-3 shift.	1. Improper fluid level. 2. Linkage out of adjustment. 3. Improper band or clutch application, or oil pressure control system. 4. Faulty high clutch and/or intermediate servo. 5. Dirty or sticking valve body.	1. Perform fluid level check. 2. Repair or adjust linkage. 3. Perform control pressure test. 4. Perform air pressure test. Repair as required. 5. Clean repair or replace valve body.
Mushy 1-2 shift.	1. Improper fluid level 2. Incorrect engine idle and/or performance. 3. Improper linkage adjustment. 4. Intermediate band out of adjustment.	1. Perform fluid level check. 2. Tune, adjust engine idle as required. 3. Repair or adjust linkage. 4. Adjust intermediate band. 5. Perform control pressure test.

Problem	Possible Cause	Correction
Mushy 1-2 shift.	5. Improper band or clutch application, or oil pressure control system. 6. Faulty high clutch and/or intermediate servo release. 7. Polished, glazed band or drum. 8. Dirty or sticking valve body.	6. Perform air pressure test. Repair as required. 7. Repair or replace as required. 8. Clean, repair or replace valve body.
Rough 1-2 shift.	1. Improper fluid level. 2. Incorrect engine idle or performance. 3. Intermediate band out of adjustment. 4. Improper band or clutch application, or oil pressure control system. 5. Faulty intermediate servo. 6. Dirty or sticking valve body.	1. Perform fluid level check. 2. Tune, and adjust engine idle. 3. Adjust intermediate band. 4. Perform control pressure test. 5. Air pressure check intermediate servo. 6. Clean, repair or replace valve body.
Rough 2-3 shift	1. Improper fluid level. 2. Incorrect engine idle or performance. 3. Improper band or clutch application, or oil control pressure system. 4. Faulty intermediate servo apply and release and high clutch piston check ball. 5. Dirty or sticking valve body.	1. Perform fluid level check. 2. Tune and adjust engine idle. 3. Perform control pressure test. 4. Air pressure test the intermediate servo apply and release and the high clutch piston check ball. Repair as required. 5. Clean, repair or replace valve body.
Rough 3-1 shift at closed throttle in D.	1. Improper fluid level. 2. Incorrect engine idle or performance. 3. Improper linkage adjustment. 4. Improper clutch or band application or oil pressure control system. 5. Faulty governor operation. 6. Dirty or sticking valve body.	1. Perform fluid level check. 2. Tune, and adjust engine idle. 3. Repair or adjust linkage. 4. Perform control pressure test. 5. Perform governor test. Repair as required. 6. Clean, repair or replace valve body.
No forced downshifts.	1. Improper fluid level. 2. Linkage out of adjustment. 3. Improper clutch or band application, or oil pressure control system. 4. Faulty internal kickdown linkage. 5. Dirty or sticking valve body.	1. Perform fluid level check. 2. Repair or adjust linkage. 3. Perform control pressure test. 4. Repair internal kickdown linkage. 5. Clean, repair or replace valve body.
No 3-1 shift in D.	1. Improper fluid level. 2. Incorrect engine idle, or performance. 3. Faulty governor. 4. Dirty or sticking valve body.	1. Perform fluid level check. 2. Tune, and adjust engine idle. 3. Perform govenor check. Repair as required. 4. Clean, repair or replace valve body.
Runaway engine on 3-2 downshift.	1. Improper fluid level. 2. Linkage out of adjustment. 3. Intermediate band out of adjustment. 4. Improper band or clutch application, or oil pressure control system.	1. Perform fluid level check. 2. Repair or adjust linkage. 3. Adjust intermediate band. 4. Perform control pressure test. 5. Air pressure test check the intermediate servo. Repair servo and/or seals.

Problem	Possible Cause	Correction
Runaway engine on 3-2 downshift.	5. Faulty intermediate servo. 6. Polished, glazed band or drum. 7. Dirty or sticking valve body.	6. Repair or replace as required. 7. Clean, repair or replace valve body.
No engine braking in manual first gear.	1. Improper fluid level. 2. Linkage out of adjustment. 3. Bands or clutches out of adjustment. 4. Faulty oil pressure control system. 5. Faulty reverse servo. 6. Polished, glazed band or drum.	1. Perform fluid level check. 2. Repair or adjust linkage. 3. Adjust as necessary. 4. Perform control pressure test. 5. Perform air pressure test of reverse servo. Repair reverse clutch or rear servo as required. 6. Repair or replace as required.
No engine braking in manual second gear.	1. Improper fluid level. 2. Linkage out of adjustment. 3. Intermediate band out of adjustment. 4. Improper band or clutch application, or oil pressure control system. 5. Intermediate servo leaking. 6. Polished or glazed band or drum.	1. Perform fluid level check. 2. Repair or adjust linkage. 3. Adjust intermediate band. 4. Perform control pressure test. 5. Perform air pressure test of intermediate servo for leakage. Repair as required. 6. Repair or replace as required.
Transmission noisy—valve resonance.	1. Improper fluid level. 2. Linkage out of adjustment. 3. Improper band or clutch application, or oil pressure control system. 4. Cooler lines grounding. 5. Dirty sticking valve body. 6. Internal leakage or pump cavitation.	1. Perform fluid level check. 2. Repair or adjust linkage. 3. Perform control pressure test. 4. Free up cooler lines. 5. Clean, repair or replace valve body. 6. Repair as required.
Transmission overheats.	1. Improper fluid level. 2. Incorrect engine idle, or performance. 3. Improper clutch or band application, or oil pressure control system. 4. Restriction in cooler or lines. 5. Seized one-way clutch. 6. Dirty or sticking valve body.	1. Perform fluid level check. 2. Tune, or adjust engine idle. 3. Perform control pressure test. 4. Repair restriction. 5. Replace one-way clutch. 6. Clean, repair or replace valve body.
Transmission fluid leaks.	1. Improper fluid level. 2. Leakage at gasket, seals, etc. 3. Vacuum diaphragm unit leaking.	1. Perform fluid level check. 2. Remove all traces of lube on exposed surfaces of transmission. Check the vent for free breathing. Operate transmission at normal temperatures and inspect for leakage. Repair as required. 3. Replace diaphragm.

Automatic Transmission Troubleshooting

Driveshaft Troubleshooting
Vibration, Roughness, Rumble and/or Boom

RIDE CAR TO DETERMINE PROBLEM & SPEED (ACCELERATION-ROAD-ENGINE)

ACCELERATION SHUDDER AT 0-15 M.P.H. (0-24 K.M.H.)

INCORRECT FRONT JOINT ANGLE

SET JOINT ANGLE TO SPECIFICATIONS

ROAD SPEED SMOOTH ROAD

RIDE AND EVALUATE AT 275 kPa (40 P.S.I.) TIRE PRESSURE

PROBLEM NOT IMPROVED   **PROBLEM IMPROVED**

PLACE VEHICLE ON HOIST REMOVE REAR TIRES AND RECHECK PROBLEM SPEED

PROBLEM IMPROVED   **CHECK AND/OR BALANCE TIRES**

IMPACT BOOM ROUGH ROAD

CHECK TIRES, SUSPENSION AND/OR BODY COMPARTMENT

VISUAL EXAMINATION

DAMAGED SHAFT

REPLACE SHAFT

UNDERCOATING ON SHAFT

CLEAN SHAFT

MISSING BALANCE WEIGHT

BALANCE SHAFT

BURRS OR NICKS ON SUPPORT YOKE AND/OR PINION FLANGE

REWORK OR REPLACE

EXCESSIVE LOOSENESS AT SLIP YOKE SPLINE

REPLACE NECESSARY PARTS

EVALUATE ON HOIST

PROBLEM NOT IMPROVED   **PROBLEM IMPROVED**   **ROAD TEST**

55-75 M.P.H. (88-120 K.M.H.)

ROTATE SHAFT 180° AT PINION FLANGE

PROBLEM NOT IMPROVED ← EVALUATE → PROBLEM IMPROVED

WORN JOINT

REPLACE JOINT

OUT OF BALANCE DRIVELINE EXCESSIVE PINION FLANGE OR SHAFT RUNOUT

BALANCE SHAFT IN CAR

ROAD TEST

Universal Joint Troubleshooting

Problem	Possible Cause	Correction
Leak at front slip yoke. **NOTE:** An occasional drop of lubricant leaking from splined yoke is normal and requires no attention.	1. Rough outside surface on splined yoke. 2. Defective transmission rear oil seal.	1. Replace seal if cut by burrs on yoke. Minor burrs can be smoothed by careful use of crocus cloth or honing with a fine stone. Replace yoke if outside surface is rough or burred badly. 2. Replace transmission rear oil seal. 3. Bring transmission oil up to proper level after correction.
Knock in drive line, clunking noise when car is operated under floating condition at 10 mph in high gear or neutral.	1. Worn or damaged universal joints. 2. Side gear hub counterbore in differential worn oversize.	1. Disassemble universal joints, inspect and replace worn or damaged parts. 2. Replace differential case and/or side gears as required.
Ping, snap or click in drive line. **NOTE:** Usually occurs on initial load application after transmission has been put into gear, either forward or reverse.	1. Loose upper or lower control arm bushing bolts. 2. Loose companion flange.	1. Tighten bolts to specified torque. 2. Remove companion flange, turn 180° from its original position, apply white lead to splines and reinstall. Tighten pinion nut to specified torque.

Front Wheel Drive Halfshaft Troubleshooting

*Halfshafts do not usually contribute to rotational vibrations.

Drive Axle Troubleshooting

Condition	Possible Cause	Correction
Rear wheel noise	1. Loose wheel. 2. Spalled wheel bearing cup or cone. 3. Defective or brinelled wheel bearing. 4. Excessive axle shaft endplay. 5. Bent or sprng axle shaft flange.	1. Tighten loose wheel nuts. 2. Check rear wheel bearings. If spalled or worn, replace. 3. Defective or brinelled bearings must be replaced. Check rear axle shaft end play. 4. Readjust axle shaft end play. 5. Replace bent or sprung axle shaft.
Scoring of differential gears and pinions	1. Insufficient lubrication. 2. Improper grade of lubricant. 3. Excessive spinning of one wheel.	1. Replace scored gears. Scoring marks on the pressure face of gear teeth or in the bore are caused by instantaneous fusing of the mating surfaces. Scored gears should be replaced. Fill rear axle to required capacity with proper lubricant. 2. Replace scored gears. Inspect all gears and bearings for possible damage. Clean and refill axle to required capacity with proper lubricant. 3. Replace scored gears. Inspect all gears, pinion bores and shaft for scoring, or bearings for possible damage.
Tooth breakage (ring gear and pinion)	1. Overloading. 2. Erratic clutch operation. 3. Ice-spotted pavements. 4. Improper adjustments.	1. Replace gear. Examine other gears and bearings for possible damage. Avoid future overloading. 2. Replace gear, and examine remaining parts for possible damage. Avoid erratic clutch operation. 3. Replace gears. Examine remaining parts for possible damage. Replace parts as required. 4. Replace gears. Examine other parts for possible damage. Be sure ring gear and pinion backlash is correct.
Rear axle noise	1. Insufficient lubricant. 2. Improper ring gear and pinion adjustment. 3. Unmatched ring gear and pinion. 4. Worn teeth on ring gear or pinion. 5. End-play in drive pinion bearings. 6. Side play in differential bearings. 7. Incorrect drive gearlash. 8. Limited-slip differential—moan and chatter.	1. Refill rear axle with correct amount of the proper lubricant. Also check for leaks and correct as necessary. 2. Check ring gear and pinion tooth contact. 3. Remove unmatched ring gear and pinion. Replace with a new matched gear and pinion set. 4. Check teeth on ring gear and pinion for contact. If necessary, replace with new matched set. 5. Adjust drive pinion bearing preload.

Problem	Possible Cause	Correction
Rear axle noise		6. Adjust differential bearing preload. 7. Correct drive gear lash. 8. Drain and flush lubricant. Refill with proper lubricant.
Loss of lubricant	1. Lubricant level too high. 2. Worn axle shaft oil seals. 3. Cracked rear axle housing. 4. Worn drive pinion oil seal. 5. Scored and worn companion flange. 6. Clogged vent. 7. Loose carrier housing bolts or housing cover screws.	1. Drain excess lubricant. 2. Replace worn oil seals with new ones. Prepare new seals before replacement. 3. Repair or replace housing as required. 4. Replace worn drive pinion oil seal with a new one. 5. Replace worn or scored companion flange and oil seal. 6. Remove obstructions. 7. Tighten bolts or cover screws to specifications and fill to correct level with proper lubricant.
Overheating of unit	1. Lubricant level too low. 2. Incorrect grade of lubricant. 3. Bearing adjusted too tightly. 4. Excessive wear in gears. 5. Insufficient ring gear-to-pinion clearance.	1. Refill rear axle. 2. Drain, flush and refill rear axle with correct amount of the proper lubricant. 3. Readjust bearings. 4. Check gears for excessive wear or scoring. Replace as necessary. 5. Readjust ring gear and pinion backlash and check gears for possible scoring.

CHASSIS

Shock Absorber and Rear Spring Troubleshooting

Front Suspension and Steering Linkage
Troubleshooting—Rear Wheel Drive

FRONT END NOISE	EXCESSIVE PLAY IN STEERING	FRONT WHEEL SHIMMY	INSTABILITY	HARD STEERING	CAR PULLS TO ONE SIDE
LOOSE OR WORN FRONT WHEEL BEARINGS	LOOSE OR WORN FRONT WHEEL BEARINGS	LOOSE OR WORN WHEEL BEARINGS	LOW OR UNEVEN TIRE PRESSURE	LOW OR UNEVEN TIRE PRESSURE	BROKEN REAR SPRING
LOOSE OR WORN SHOCK ABSORBER MOUNTING OR SHOCK ABSORBER	LOOSE OR WORN STEERING SHAFT COUPLING	TIRE, WHEEL OUT OF BALANCE	LOOSE WHEEL BEARINGS	LACK OF ASSIST OF POWER STEERING SYSTEM	POWER STEERING CONTROL VALVE OUT OF ADJUSTMENT
LOOSE STEERING GEAR TO FRAME MOUNTING BOLTS	LOOSE STEERING GEAR TO FRAME MOUNTING BOLTS	UNEVEN TIRE WEAR, OR EXCESSIVELY WORN TIRES	BROKEN REAR SPRING	STEERING GEAR NOT ADJUSTED	LOOSE OR WORN STRUT BUSHINGS
STEERING KNUCKLE ARM CONTACTING THE LOWER CONTROL ARM WHEEL STOP	WORN TIE ROD ENDS	WORN TIE ROD ENDS	SHOCK ABSORBER INOPERATIVE	INCORRECT FRONT WHEEL ALIGNMENT (PARTICULARLY CASTER)	INCORRECT FRONT WHEEL ALIGNMENT (PARTICULARLY CASTER)
WORN UPPER CONTROL ARM BUSHINGS	WORN IDLER ARM BUSHING	LOOSE OR WORN STRUT BUSHINGS	IMPROPER STEERING CROSS SHAFT ADJUSTMENT		
WORN LOWER CONTROL ARM SHAFT BUSHINGS	WORN STEERING GEAR PARTS	LOOSE OR WORN UPPER CONTROL ARM BALL JOINTS	STEERING GEAR NOT CENTERED		
LOOSE OR WORN STRUT BUSHINGS	INCORRECT STEERING GEAR ADJUSTMENT	INCORRECT FRONT WHEEL ALIGNMENT (PARTICULARLY CASTER)	WORN IDLER ARM BUSHING		
LOOSE STRUTS OR LOWER CONTROL ARM		WORN SHOCK ABSORBER	LOOSE OR WORN STRUT BUSHINGS		
BALL JOINTS REQUIRE LUBRICATION			INCORRECT FRONT WHEEL ALIGNMENT		

Suspension and Steering Linkage
Troubleshooting— Front Wheel Drive

NOISE	INSTABILITY	EXCESSIVE PLAY IN STEERING	HARD STEERING	CAR PULLS TO ONE SIDE
(DRIVE OR COAST) ROAD/TIRE NOISE	LOW OR UNEVEN TIRE PRESSURE	LOOSE OR WORN HUB BEARINGS	LOW OR UNEVEN TIRE PRESSURE	LOW OR UNEVEN TIRE PRESSURE
(PRONOUNCED ON TURNS) FRONT HUB BEARINGS	LOOSE OR WORN HUB BEARINGS	LOOSE OR WORN STEERING SHAFT COUPLING	LACK OF ASSIST OF POWER STEERING SYSTEM	WHILE BRAKING BRAKE SERVICE
(ON ACCELERATION OR DECELERATION) FRONT WHEEL BEARINGS TRANSAXLE GEARS	BROKEN SPRING OR BENT REAR SUSPENSION	LOOSE STEERING GEAR MOUNTING BOLTS	STEERING GEAR LOW ON LUBRICANT	BROKEN FRONT OR REAR SPRING OR BENT REAR SUSPENSION
(CLUNK-ON ACCELERATION OR DECELERATION) TRANSAXLE BEARINGS OR GEARS	INOPERATIVE SHOCK ABSORBING (STRUTS)	WORN TIE ROD ENDS	INCORRECT WHEEL ALIGNMENT	LOOSE LOWER CONTROL ARM
(CLICKING NOISE ON TURNS) EXCESSIVE WEAR OR BROKEN C.V. JOINT	IMPROPER STEERING GEAR ADJUSTMENT			INCORRECT WHEEL ALIGNMENT
	LOOSE OR WORN STRUT			UNBALANCED STEERING GEAR VALVE (POWER)
	INCORRECT WHEEL ALIGNMENT FRONT OR REAR			

Tapered Wheel Bearing Troubleshooting

CONSIDER THE FOLLOWING FACTORS WHEN DIAGNOSING BEARING CONDITION:

1. GENERAL CONDITION OF ALL PARTS DURING DISASSEMBLY AND INSPECTION.

2. CLASSIFY THE FAILURE WITH THE AID OF THE ILLUSTRATIONS.

3. DETERMINE THE CAUSE.

4. MAKE ALL REPAIRS FOLLOWING RECOMMENDED PROCEDURES.

GOOD BEARING

BENT CAGE

CAGE DAMAGE DUE TO IMPROPER HANDLING OR TOOL USAGE.

REPLACE BEARING.

BENT CAGE

CAGE DAMAGE DUE TO IMPROPER HANDLING OR TOOL USAGE.

REPLACE BEARING.

GALLING

METAL SMEARS ON ROLLER ENDS DUE TO OVERHEAT, LUBRICANT FAILURE OR OVERLOAD.

REPLACE BEARING — CHECK SEALS AND CHECK FOR PROPER LUBRICATION.

ABRASIVE STEP WEAR

PATTERN ON ROLLER ENDS CAUSED BY FINE ABRASIVES.

CLEAN ALL PARTS AND HOUSINGS, CHECK SEALS AND BEARINGS AND REPLACE IF LEAKING, ROUGH OR NOISY.

ETCHING

BEARING SURFACES APPEAR GRAY OR GRAYISH BLACK IN COLOR WITH RELATED ETCHING AWAY OF MATERIAL USUALLY AT ROLLER SPACING.

REPLACE BEARINGS — CHECK SEALS AND CHECK FOR PROPER LUBRICATION.

MISALIGNMENT

OUTER RACE MISALIGNMENT DUE TO FOREIGN OBJECT.

CLEAN RELATED PARTS AND REPLACE BEARING. MAKE SURE RACES ARE PROPERLY SEATED.

INDENTATIONS

SURFACE DEPRESSIONS ON RACE AND ROLLERS CAUSED BY HARD PARTICLES OF FOREIGN MATERIAL.

CLEAN ALL PARTS AND HOUSINGS, CHECK SEALS AND REPLACE BEARINGS IF ROUGH OR NOISY.

FATIGUE SPALLING

FLAKING OF SURFACE METAL RESULTING FROM FATIGUE.

REPLACE BEARING — CLEAN ALL RELATED PARTS.

Tapered Wheel Bearing Troubleshooting

BRINELLING

SURFACE INDENTATIONS IN RACEWAY CAUSED BY ROLLERS EITHER UNDER IMPACT LOADING OR VIBRATION WHILE THE BEARING IS NOT ROTATING.

REPLACE BEARING IF ROUGH OR NOISY.

CAGE WEAR

WEAR AROUND OUTSIDE DIAMETER OF CAGE AND ROLLER POCKETS CAUSED BY ABRASIVE MATERIAL AND INEFFICIENT LUBRICATION. CHECK SEALS AND REPLACE BEARINGS.

ABRASIVE ROLLER WEAR

PATTERN ON RACES AND ROLLERS CAUSED BY FINE ABRASIVES.

CLEAN ALL PARTS AND HOUSINGS, CHECK SEALS AND BEARINGS AND REPLACE IF LEAKING, ROUGH OR NOISY.

CRACKED INNER RACE

RACE CRACKED DUE TO IMPROPER FIT, COCKING, OR POOR BEARING SEATS.

SMEARS

SMEARING OF METAL DUE TO SLIPPAGE, SLIPPAGE CAN BE CAUSED BY POOR FITS, LUBRICATION, OVERHEATING, OVERLOADS OR HANDLING DAMAGE.

REPLACE BEARINGS, CLEAN RELATED PARTS AND CHECK FOR PROPER FIT AND LUBRICATION.

REPLACE SHAFT IF DAMAGED.

FRETTAGE

CORROSION SET UP BY SMALL RELATIVE MOVEMENT OF PARTS WITH NO LUBRICATION.

REPLACE BEARING. CLEAN RELATED PARTS. CHECK SEALS AND CHECK FOR PROPER LUBRICATION.

HEAT DISCOLORATION

HEAT DISCOLORATION CAN RANGE FROM FAINT YELLOW TO DARK BLUE RESULTING FROM OVERLOAD OR INCORRECT LUBRICANT.

EXCESSIVE HEAT CAN CAUSE SOFTENING OF RACES OR ROLLERS.

TO CHECK FOR LOSS OF TEMPER ON RACES OR ROLLERS A SIMPLE FILE TEST MAY BE MADE. A FILE DRAWN OVER A TEMPERED PART WILL GRAB AND CUT META, WHEREAS, A FILE DRAWN OVER A HARD PART WILL GLIDE READILY WITH NO METAL CUTTING.

REPLACE BEARINGS IF OVER HEATING DAMAGE IS INDICATED. CHECK SEALS AND OTHER PARTS.

STAIN DISCOLORATION

DISCOLORATION CAN RANGE FROM LIGHT BROWN TO BLACK CAUSED BY INCORRECT LUBRICANT OR MOISTURE.

RE-USE BEARINGS IF STAINS CAN BE REMOVED BY LIGHT POLISHING OR IF NO EVIDENCE OF OVERHEATING IS OBSERVED.

CHECK SEALS AND RELATED PARTS FOR DAMAGE.

Manual Steering Troubleshooting

INSPECTION AND ALIGNMENT

Before any steering gear adjustments are made, it is recommended that the front end of the car be raised and a thorough inspection be made for stiffness or lost motion in steering gear, steering linkage and front suspension. Worn or damaged parts should be replaced, since a satisfactory adjustment of the steering gear cannot be obtained if bent or badly worn parts exist.

It is also very important that the steering gear be properly aligned in the car. Misalignment of the gear places a stress on the steering worm shaft, therefore a proper adjustment is impossible. To align the steering gear, loosen the mounting bolts to permit the gear to align itself. Check the steering gear mounting seat, and if there is a gap at any of the mounting bolts, proper alignment may be obtained by placing shims where excessive gap appears. Tighten the steering gear bolts. Alignment of the gear in the car is very important and should be done carefully so that a satisfactory, trouble-free gear adjustment may be obtained.

Condition	Possible Cause	Corrective Action
Hard steering	1. Low or uneven tire pressure. 2. Insufficient lubricant in the steering gear housing or in steering linkage. 3. Steering gear shaft adjusted too tight. 4. Front wheels out of line. 5. Steering column misaligned.	1. Inflate tires to recommended pressures. 2. Lubricate as necessary. 3. Adjust according to instructions. 4. Align the wheels. 5. See the appropriate Car Section for alignment procedures.
Excessive play or looseness in the steering wheel	1. Steering gear shaft adjust too loose or badly worn. 2. Steering linkage loose or worn. 3. Front wheel bearings improperly adjusted. 4. Steering arm loose on steering gear shaft. 5. Steering gear housing attaching bolts loose. 6. Steering arms loose at steering knuckles. 7. Worn ball joints. 8. Worm shaft bearing adjustment too loose.	1. Replace worn parts and adjust according to instructions. 2. Replace worn parts. 3. Adjust according to instructions. 4. Inspect for damage to the gear shaft and steering arm, replace parts as necessary. 5. Tighten attaching bolts to specifications. 6. Tighten according to specifications. 7. Replace the ball joints as necessary. 8. Adjust worm bearing preload according to instructions.

Power Steering Systems Troubleshooting

Condition	Possible Cause	Corrective Action
Hard steering	1. Improper tire pressure. 2. Loose pump drive belt. 3. Low or incorrect fluid. 4. Loose, bent or poorly lubricated front end parts. 5. Improper front end alignment. 6. Bind in steering column or linkage.	1. Inflate tires to recommended pressures. 2. Tighten or replace belt. 3. Refill reservoir with proper fluid; check for leaks; 4. Tighten or replace parts; lubricate at all fittings. 5. Align front end.

Condition	Possible Cause	Correction Action
Hard steering	7. Air in hydraulic system. 8. Low pump output or leaks in system. 9. Obstruction in lines. 10. Pump valves sticking or out of adjustment.	6. Disassemble and inspect component parts. Repair or replace as necessary. 7. Bleed system, refill and check for leaks. 8. Disassemble pump, check for worn or damaged parts. Check for leaks in the system. 9. Clean or replace lines. 10. Replace or adjust valves.
Loose steering	1. Loose wheel bearings 2. Faulty shocks. 3. Worn linkage components. 4. Loose steering gear mounting or linkage points. 5. Steering mechanism worn or improperly adjusted. 6. Valve spool improperly adjusted	1. Adjust wheel bearings. 2. Relace shocks. 3. Replace worn components. 4. Tighten mountings or linkage. 5. Replace and/or adjust mechanism. 6. Adjust valve spool.
Veer or wander	1. Improper tire pressure. 2. Improper front end alignment. 3. Dragging brakes. 4. Bent frame. 5. Improper rear end alignment. 6. Faulty shocks or springs. 7. Loose or bent front end components. 8. Play in Pitman arm. 9. Loose wheel bearings. 10. Binding Pitman arm. 11. Spool valve sticking or improperly adjusted.	1. Inflate tires to recommended pressures. 2. Align front end. 3. Inspect, replace and/or adjust brakes. 4. Straighten frame. 5. Inspect shocks and control arm torque. Replace and/or adjust as necessary. 6. Replace as necessary. 7. Replace as necessary. 8. Inspect bushings and arm. Replace as necessary. 9. Adjust to specifications. 10. Replace arm. 11. Adjust or replace as necessary.
Wheel oscillation	1. Improper tire pressure. 2. Loose wheel bearings. 3. Improper front end alignment. 4. Bent spindle. 5. Worn, bent or broken front end components. 6. Tires out of round or out of balance. 7. Excessive lateral runout in disc brake rotor.	1. Inflate tires to recommended pressures. 2. Adjust to specifications. 3. Align front end. 4. Replace spindle. 5. Inspect, repair or replace as necessary. 6. Replace or balance tires. 7. Reface or replace rotor.
Noises	1. Loose belts. 2. Low fluid, air in system. 3. Foreign matter in system. 4. Improper lubrication. 5. Interference or chafing in linkage. 6. Steering gear mountings loose. 7. Incorrect adjustment or wear in gear box. 8. Faulty valves or wear in pump.	1. Replace and/or adjust belts. 2. Refill and check for leaks. 3. Disassemble and clean system. 4. Lubricate all fittings. 5. Disassemble, inspect, replace or adjust components. 6. Tighten mountings. 7. Disassemble, inspect, repair, replace and/or adjust parts. 8. Replace parts as necessary.

How To Read Tire Wear

The way your tires wear is a good indicator of other parts of the suspension. Abnormal wear patterns are often caused by the need for simple tire maintenance, or for front end alignment.

Over-inflation

Excessive wear at the center of the tread indicates that the air pressure in the tire is consistently too high. The tire is riding on the center of the tread and wearing it prematurely. Occasionally, this wear pattern can result from outrageously wide tires on narrow rims. The cure for this is to replace either the tires or the wheels.

Under-inflation

This type of wear usually results from consistent under-inflation. When a tire is under-inflated, there is too much contact with the road by the outer treads, which wear prematurely. When this type of wear occurs, and the tire pressure is known to be consistently correct, a bent or worn steering component or the need for wheel alignment could be indicated.

Feathering

Feathering is a condition when the edge of each tread rib develops a slightly rounded edge on one side and a sharp edge on the other. By running your hand over the tire, you can usually feel the sharper edges before you'll be able to see them. The most common causes of feathering are incorrect toe-in setting or deteriorated bushings in the front suspension.

One side wear

When an inner or outer rib wears faster than the rest of the tire, the need for wheel alignment is indicated. There is excessive camber in the front suspension, causing the wheel to lean too much putting excessive load on one side of the tire. Misalignment could also be due to sagging springs, worn ball joints, or worn control arm bushings. Be sure the vehicle is loaded the way it's normally driven when you have the wheels aligned.

Cupping

Cups or scalloped dips appearing around the edge of the tread almost always indicate worn (sometimes bent) suspension parts. Adjustment of wheel alignment alone will seldom cure the problem. Any worn component that connects the wheel to the suspension can cause this type of wear. Occasionally, wheels that are out of balance will wear like this, but wheel imbalance usually shows up as bald spots between the outside edges and center of the tread.

Second-rib wear

Second-rib wear is usually found only in radial tires, and appears where the steel belts end in relation to the tread. It can be kept to a minimum by paying careful attention to tire pressure and frequently rotating the tires. This is often considered normal wear but excessive amounts indicate that the tires are too wide for the wheels.

Drum Brake Troubleshooting

Condition	Possible Cause	Correction Action
Pedal goes to floor	1. Fluid low in reservoir. 2. Air in hydraulic brake system. 3. Improperly adjusted brake. 4. Leaking wheel cylinders. 5. Loose or broken brake lines. 6. Leaking or worn master cylinder. 7. Excessively worn brake lining.	1. Fill and bleed master cylinder. 2. Fill and bleed hydraulic brake system. 3. Repair or replace self-adjuster as required. 4. Recondition or replace wheel cylinder and replace both brake shoes. 5. Tighten all brake fittings or replace brake line. 6. Recondition or replace master cylinder and bleed hydraulic system. 7. Reline and adjust brakes.
Spongy brake pedal	1. Air in hydraulic system. 2. Improper brake fluid (low boiling point). 3. Excessively worn or cracked brake drums. 4. Broken pedal pivot bushing.	1. Fill master cylinder and bleed hydraulic system. 2. Drain, flush and refill with brake fluid. 3. Replace all faulty brake drums. 4. Replace nylon pivot bushing.
Brakes pulling	1. Contaminated lining. 2. Front end out of alignment. 3. Incorrect brake adjustment. 4. Unmatched brake lining. 5. Brake drums out of round. 6. Brake shoes distorted. 7. Restricted brake hose or line. 8. Broken rear spring.	1. Replace contaminated brake lining. 2. Align front end. 3. Adjust brakes and check fluid. 4. Match primary, secondary with same type of lining on all wheels. 5. Grind or replace brake drums. 6. Replace faulty brake shoes. 7. Replace plugged hose or brake line. 8. Replace broken spring.
Squealing brakes	1. Glazed brake lining. 2. Saturated brake lining. 3. Weak or broken brake shoe retaining spring. 4. Broken or weak brake shoe return spring. 5. Incorrect brake lining. 6. Distorted brake shoes. 7. Bent support plate. 8. Dust in brakes or scored brake drums.	1. Cam grind or replace brake lining. 2. Replace saturated lining. 3. Replace retaining spring. 4. Replace return spring. 5. Install matched brake lining. 6. Replace brake shoes. 7. Replace support plate. 8. Blow out brake assembly with compressed air and grind brake drums.
Chirping brakes	1. Out of round drum or eccentric axle flange pilot.	1. Repair as necessary, and lubricate support plate contact areas (6 places).
Dragging brakes	1. Incorrect wheel or parking brake adjustment. 2. Parking brakes engaged. 3. Weak or broken brake shoe return spring. 4. Brake pedal binding. 5. Master cylinder cup sticking. 6. Obstructed master cylinder relief port. 7. Saturated brake lining. 8. Bent or out of round brake drum.	1. Adjust brake and check fluid. 2. Release parking brakes. 3. Replace brake shoe return spring. 4. Free up and lubricate brake pedal and linkage. 5. Recondition master cylinder. 6. Use compressed air and blow out relief port. 7. Replace brake lining. 8. Grind or replace faulty brake drum.

TROUBLESHOOTING AND DIAGNOSIS

Condition	Possible Cause	Corrective Action
Hard pedal	1. Brake booster inoperative. 2. Incorrect brake lining. 3. Restricted brake line or hose. 4. Frozen brake pedal linkage.	1. Replace brake booster. 2. Install matched brake lining. 3. Clean out or replace brake line or hose. 4. Free up and lubricate brake linkage.
Wheel locks	1. Contaminated brake lining. 2. Loose or torn brake lining. 3. Wheel cylinder cups sticking. 4. Incorrect wheel bearing adjustment.	1. Reline both front or rear of all four brakes. 2. Replace brake lining. 3. Recondition or replace wheel cylinder. 4. Clean, pack and adjust wheel bearings.
Brakes fade (high speed)	1. Incorrect lining. 2. Overheated brake drums. 3. Incorrect brake fluid (low boiling temperature) 4. Saturated brake lining.	1. Replace lining. 2. Inspect for dragging brakes. 3. Drain, flush, refill and bleed hydraulic brake system. 4. Reline both front or rear or all four brakes.
Pedal pulsates	1. Bent or out of round brake drum.	1. Grind or replace brake drums.
Brake chatter and shoe knock	1. Out of round brake drum. 2. Loose support plate. 3. Bent support plate. 4. Distorted brake shoes. 5. Machine grooves in contact face of brake drum. (Shoe Knock). 6. Contaminated brake lining.	1. Grind or replace brake drums. 2. Tighten support plate bolts to proper specifications. 3. Replace support plate. 4. Replace brake shoes. 5. Grind or replace brake drum. 6. Replace either front or rear or all four linings.
Brakes do not self adjust	1. Adjuster screw frozen in thread. 2. Adjuster screw corroded at thrust washer. 3. Adjuster level does not engage star wheel. 4. Adjuster installed on wrong wheel.	1. Clean and free-up all thread areas. 2. Clean threads and replace thrust washer if necessary. 3. Repair, free up or replace adjusters as required. 4. Install correct adjuster parts.

Disc Brake Troubleshooting

Condition	Possible Cause	Correction Action
Noise—Groan—Brake noise emanating when slowly releasing brakes (creep-groan).	1. Not detrimental to function of disc brakes—no corrective action required. (Indicate to operator this noise may be eliminated by slightly increasing or decreasing brake pedal efforts.)	
Rattle—Brake noise or rattle emanating at low speeds on rough roads, (front wheels only).	1. Shoe anti-rattle spring missing or not properly positioned. 2. Excessive clearance between shoe and caliper.	1. Install new anti-rattle spring or position properly. 2. Install new shoe and lining assemblies.

Condition	Possible Cause	Corrective Action
Scraping	1. Mounting bolts too long. 2. Loose wheel bearings.	1. Install mounting bolts of correct length. 2. Readjust wheel bearings to correct specifications.
Front brakes heat up during driving and fail to release	1. Operator riding brake pedal. 2. Stop light switch improperly adjusted. 3. Sticking pedal linkage. 4. Frozen or seized piston. 5. Residual pressure valve in master cylinder. 6. Power brake malfunction.	1. Instruct owner how to drive with disc brakes. 2. Adjust stop light to allow full return of pedal. 3. Free up sticking pedal linkage. 4. Disassemble caliper and free up piston. 5. Remove valve. 6. Replace.
Leaky wheel cylinder	1. Damaged or worn caliper piston seal. 2. Scores or corrosion on surface of cylinder bore.	1. Disassemble caliper and install new seal. 2. Disassemble caliper and hone cylinder bore. Install new seal.
Grabbing or uneven brake action	1. Causes listed under "Pull." 2. Power brake malfunction.	1. Corrections listed under "Pull". 2. Replace.
Brake pedal can be depressed without braking effect	1. Air in hydraulic system or improper bleeding procedure. 2. Leak past primary cup in master cylinder. 3. Leak in system. 4. Rear brakes out of adjustment. 5. Bleeder screw open.	1. Bleed system. 2. Recondition master cylinder. 3. Check for leak and repair as required. 4. Adjust rear brakes. 5. Close bleeder screw and bleed entire system.
Excessive pedal travel	1. Air, leak, or insufficient fluid in system or caliper. 2. Warped or excessively tapered shoe and lining assembly. 3. Excessive disc runout. 4. Rear brake adjustment required. 5. Loose wheel bearing adjustment. 6. Damaged caliper piston seal. 7. Improper brake fluid (boil). 8. Power brake malfunction.	1. Check system for leaks and bleed. 2. Install new shoe and linings. 3. Check disc for runout with dial indicator. Install new or refinished disc. 4. Check and adjust rear brakes. 5. Readjust wheel bearing to specified torque. 6. Install new piston seal. 7. Drain and install correct fluid. 8. Replace.
Brake roughness or chatter (pedal pumping)	1. Excessive thickness variation of braking disc. 2. Excessive lateral runout of braking disc. 3. Rear brake drums out-of-round. 4. Excessive front bearing clearance.	1. Check disc for thickness variation using a micrometer. 2. Check disc for lateral runout with dial indicator. Install new or refinished disc. 3. Reface rear drums and check for out-of-round. 4. Readjust wheel bearings to specified torque.
Excessive pedal effort	1. Brake fluid, oil or grease on linings. 2. Incorrect lining. 3. Frozen or seized pistons. 4. Power brake malfunction.	1. Install new shoe linings as required. 2. Remove lining and install correct lining. 3. Disassemble caliper and free up pistons. 4. Replace.

Condition	Possible Cause	Corrective Action
Pull	1. Brake fluid, oil or grease on linings. 2. Unmatched linings. 3. Distorted brake shoes. 4. Frozen or seized pistons. 5. Incorrect tire pressure. 6. Front end out of alignment. 7. Broken rear spring. 8. Rear brake pistons sticking. 9. Restricted hose or line. 10. Caliper not in proper alignment to braking disc.	1. Install new shoe and linings. 2. Install correct lining. 3. Install new brake shoes. 4. Disassemble caliper and free up pistons. 5. Inflate tires to recommended pressures. 6. Align front end and check. 7. Install new rear spring. 8. Free up rear brake pistons. 9. Check hoses and lines and correct as necessary. 10. Remove caliper and reinstall. Check alignment.

ELECTRICAL

Turn Signal and Flasher Troubleshooting

TURN SIGNALS AND HAZARD WARNING FLASHER SERVICE DIAGNOSIS

TURN SIGNAL MALFUNCTION

HAZARD WARNING MALFUNCTION

SYSTEM DOES NOT FLASH ON ONE SIDE
- FAULTY EXTERNAL BULB
- POOR GROUND AT LAMP
- OPEN CIRCUIT IN WIRING TO EXTERNAL LAMP
- FAULTY CONTACT IN SWITCH

EXTERNAL LAMPS OPERATE PROPERLY, NO INDICATOR LAMP OPERATION
- FAULTY INDICATOR BULB IN INSTRUMENT CLUSTER OR ON FENDER
- BROKEN OR LOOSE CANCELLING CAM

SYSTEM DOES NOT CANCEL AFTER COMPLETION OF TURN
- BROKEN CANCELLING FINGER ON SWITCH
- IMPROPERLY ALIGNED CANCELLING CAM

SYSTEM DOES NOT FLASH ON EITHER SIDE
- FAULTY FUSE
- FAULTY FLASHER UNIT
- LOOSE BULKHEAD CONNECTOR
- OPEN CIRCUIT TO FLASHER UNIT

OPEN CIRCUIT IN FEED WIRE TO TURN SIGNAL SWITCH
- FAULTY SWITCH CONNECTIONS
- FAULTY CONNECTION IN SWITCH
- OPEN OR GROUNDED CIRCUIT IN WIRING TO EXTERNAL LAMPS

INDICATOR LAMP ILLUMINATES BRIGHTLY, EXTERNAL LAMP GLOWS DIMLY WITH SLOW OR NO FLASH
- LOOSE OR CORRODED EXTERNAL LAMP CONNECTION
- POOR GROUND CIRCUIT AT EXTERNAL LAMP

INDICATOR LAMP ILLUMINATES BRIGHTLY, EXTERNAL LAMP DOES NOT LIGHT
- OPEN CIRCUIT IN WIRE TO EXTERNAL LAMP

SYSTEM DOES NOT FLASH
- FAULTY FUSE
- FAULTY FLASHER
- OPEN CIRCUIT IN FEED WIRE TO SWITCH
- FAULTY CONTACT IN SWITCH
- OPEN OR GROUNDED CIRCUIT IN WIRING TO EXTERNAL LAMPS

Windshield Wiper Troubleshooting

```
                              ┌──────────────┐
                              │  MOTOR RUNS  │
                              └──────────────┘
```

MOTOR WILL NOT RUN AT ANY SPEED

- SWITCH CIRCUIT BREAKER DOES NOT CYCLE
  - OPEN CIRCUIT IN WIRING
  - LOOSE BULKHEAD CONNECTOR
  - MOTOR NOT GROUNDED
  - FAULTY SWITCH
  - FAULTY MOTOR*

- SWITCH CIRCUIT BREAKER CYCLES
  - GROUNDED WIRING
  - BINDING LINKAGE
  - FAULTY MOTOR
  - FAULTY SWITCH

MOTOR RUNS

BLADES CHATTER
- TWISTED ARM HOLDS BLADE AT WRONG ANGLE TO GLASS
- BENT OR DAMAGED BLADES
- FOREIGN SUBSTANCES SUCH AS BODY POLISH ON GLASS OR BLADES

BLADES SLAP AGAINST WINDSHIELD MOULDINGS ON DRY GLASS
- IMPROPERLY ADJUSTED WIPER ARM
- LOOSENESS OF THE MOTOR CRANK OR OTHER DRIVE PARTS

WIPER KNOCKS AT EXTREME WIPE
- AXIAL OR WORN OUT FREEPLAY IN LINKAGE

WIPER BLADES OPERATING PROPERLY

MOTOR STOPS BLADES DO NOT PARK PROPERLY

- MOTOR STOPS IN ANY POSITION WHEN SWITCH IS TURNED "OFF"
  - MOTOR PARK SWITCH OPEN.
  - OPEN PARK WIRING CIRCUIT
  - FAULTY SWITCH

- MOTOR WILL NOT STOP WHEN SWITCH IS TURNED "OFF"
  - DEFECTIVE MOTOR PARK SWITCH

- MOTOR DOES NOT OVERHEAT
  - ARM SET AT INCORRECT POSITION
  - BROKEN CRANK MECHANISM

- MOTOR OVERHEATS
  - BINDING LINKAGE
  - MOTOR DRAWS EXCESSIVE CURRENT

MOTOR RUNS BUT OUTPUT CRANK DOES NOT TURN
- CRANK NOT FASTENED PROPERLY TO OUTPUT GEAR SHAFT
- STRIPPED OR BROKEN GEARS

TROUBLESHOOTING AND DIAGNOSIS

Headlamp Troubleshooting

HEADLIGHTS DIM ENGINE IDLING OR SHUT OFF
→ PARTLY DISCHARGED BATTERY
→ FAULTY BATTERY
→ HIGH RESISTANCE IN LIGHT CIRCUIT
→ FAULTY SEALED BEAM UNITS
→ CORRODED BATTERY TERMINALS → CRACKED LENS HALOGEN SEALED BEAM ONLY

LIGHTS BURN OUT FREQUENTLY
→ HIGH VOLTAGE REGULATOR SETTING
→ LOOSE CONNECTION IN LIGHT CIRCUIT

HEADLIGHTS DIM ENGINE RUNNING ABOVE IDLE
→ HIGH RESISTANCE IN LIGHTING CIRCUIT
→ FAULTY SEALED BEAM UNITS
→ FAULTY VOLTAGE REGULATOR

LIGHTS FLICKER
→ LOOSE CONNECTIONS OR DAMAGED WIRES IN LIGHTING CIRCUIT
→ LIGHT WIRING INSULATION DAMAGED PRODUCING MOMENTARY SHORT

LIGHTS WILL NOT LIGHT
→ DISCHARGED BATTERY
→ LOOSE CONNECTIONS IN LIGHTING CIRCUIT
→ BURNED OUT SEALED BEAMS
→ OPEN OR CORRODED CONTACTS IN HEADLIGHT SWITCH
→ OPEN OR CORRODED CONTACT IN DIMMER SWITCH

Brake System Warning Light Troubleshooting

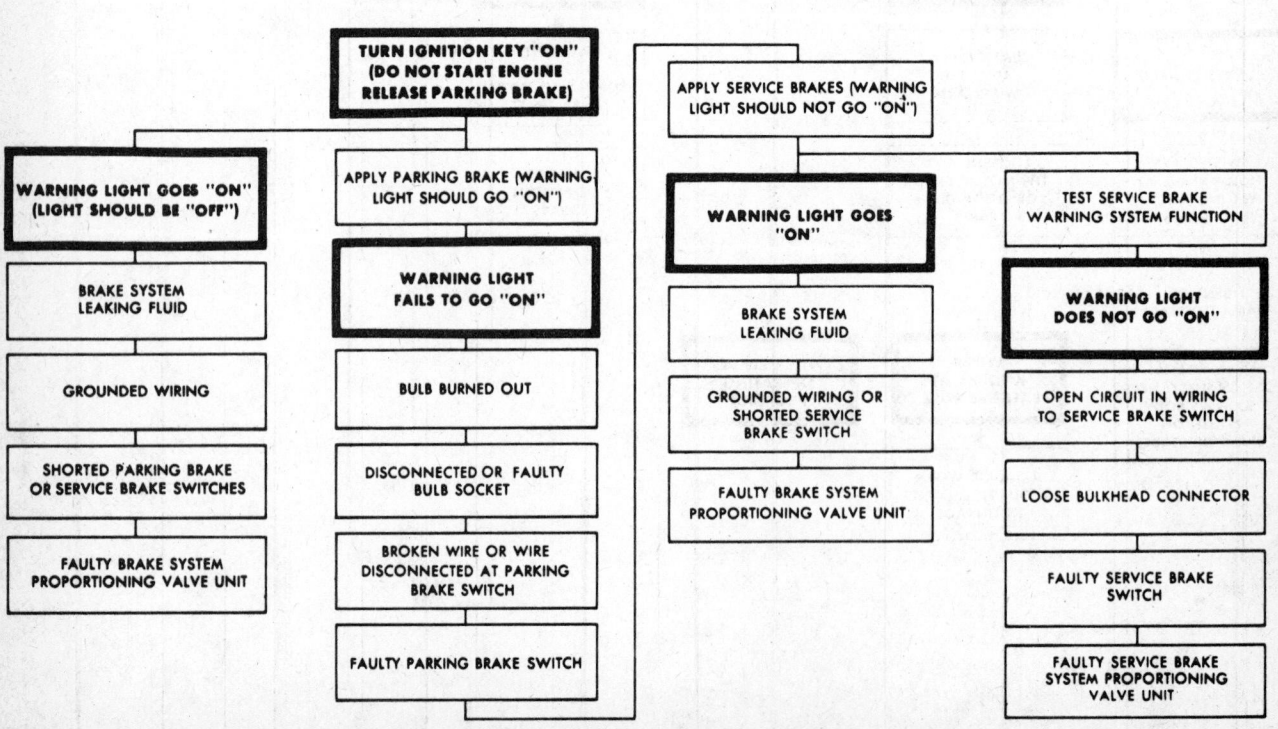

TURN IGNITION KEY "ON" (DO NOT START ENGINE RELEASE PARKING BRAKE)

WARNING LIGHT GOES "ON" (LIGHT SHOULD BE "OFF")
→ BRAKE SYSTEM LEAKING FLUID
→ GROUNDED WIRING
→ SHORTED PARKING BRAKE OR SERVICE BRAKE SWITCHES
→ FAULTY BRAKE SYSTEM PROPORTIONING VALVE UNIT

APPLY PARKING BRAKE (WARNING LIGHT SHOULD GO "ON")

WARNING LIGHT FAILS TO GO "ON"
→ BULB BURNED OUT
→ DISCONNECTED OR FAULTY BULB SOCKET
→ BROKEN WIRE OR WIRE DISCONNECTED AT PARKING BRAKE SWITCH
→ FAULTY PARKING BRAKE SWITCH

APPLY SERVICE BRAKES (WARNING LIGHT SHOULD NOT GO "ON")

WARNING LIGHT GOES "ON"
→ BRAKE SYSTEM LEAKING FLUID
→ GROUNDED WIRING OR SHORTED SERVICE BRAKE SWITCH
→ FAULTY BRAKE SYSTEM PROPORTIONING VALVE UNIT

TEST SERVICE BRAKE WARNING SYSTEM FUNCTION

WARNING LIGHT DOES NOT GO "ON"
→ OPEN CIRCUIT IN WIRING TO SERVICE BRAKE SWITCH
→ LOOSE BULKHEAD CONNECTOR
→ FAULTY SERVICE BRAKE SWITCH
→ FAULTY SERVICE BRAKE SYSTEM PROPORTIONING VALVE UNIT

Mechanics' Data

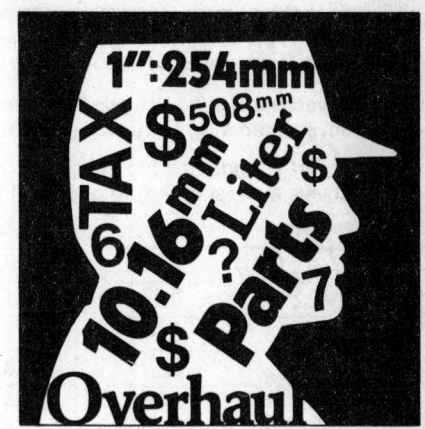

SI METRIC TABLES

The following tables are given in SI (International System) metric units. SI units replace both customary (English) and the older gavimetric units. The use of SI units as a new worldwide standard was set by the International Committee of Weights and Measures in 1960. SI has since been adopted by most countries as their national standard.

These tables are general conversion tables which will allow you to convert customary units, which appear in the text, into SI units.

The following are a list of SI units and the customary units, used in this book, which they replace:

To measure:	Use SI units:	Which replace (customary units):
mass	kilograms (kg)	pounds (lbs)
temperature	Celsius (°C)	Fahrenheit (°F)
length	millimeters (mm)	inches (in.)
force	newtons (N)	pounds force (lbs)
capacities	liters (l)	pints/quarts/gallons (pts/qts/gals)
torque	newton-meters (N·m)	foot pounds (ft lbs)
pressure	kilopascals (kPa)	pounds per square inch (psi)
volume	cubic centimeters (cm³)	cubic inches (cu in.)
power	kilowatts (kW)	horsepower (hp)

If you have had any prior experience with the metric system, you may have noticed units in this chart which are not familiar to you. This is because, in some cases, SI units differ from the older gravimetric units which they replace. For example, newtons (N) replace kilograms (kg) as a force unit, kilopascals (kPa) replace atmospheres or bars as a unit of pressure, and, although the units are the same, the name Celsius replaces centigrade for temperature measurement.

If you are not using the SI tables, have a look at them anyway; you will be seeing a lot more of them in the future.

ENGLISH TO METRIC CONVERSION: MASS (WEIGHT)

Current mass measurement is expressed in pounds and ounces (lbs. & ozs.). The metric unit of mass (or weight) is the kilogram (kg). Even although this table does not show conversion of masses (weights) larger than 15 lbs, it is easy to calculate larger units by following the data immediately below.

To convert ounces (oz.) to grams (g): multiply th number of ozs. by 28
To convert grams (g) to ounces (oz.): multiply the number of grams by .035

To convert pounds (lbs.) to kilograms (kg): multiply the number of lbs. by .45
To convert kilograms (kg) to pounds (lbs.): multiply the number of kilograms by 2.2

lbs	kg	lbs	kg	oz	kg	oz	kg
0.1	0.04	0.9	0.41	0.1	0.003	0.9	0.024
0.2	0.09	1	0.4	0.2	0.005	1	0.03
0.3	0.14	2	0.9	0.3	0.008	2	0.06
0.4	0.18	3	1.4	0.4	0.011	3	0.08
0.5	0.23	4	1.8	0.5	0.014	4	0.11
0.6	0.27	5	2.3	0.6	0.017	5	0.14
0.7	0.32	10	4.5	0.7	0.020	10	0.28
0.8	0.36	15	6.8	0.8	0.023	15	0.42

ENGLISH TO METRIC CONVERSION: TEMPERATURE

To convert Fahrenheit (°F) to Celsius (°C): take number of °F and subtract 32; multiply result by 5; divide result by 9

To convert Celsius (°C) to Fahrenheit (°F): take number of °C and multiply by 9; divide result by 5; add 32 to total

Fahrenheit (F)		Celsius (C)		Fahrenheit (F)		Celsius (C)		Fahrenheit (F)		Celsius (C)	
°F	°C	°C	°F	°F	°C	°C	°F	°F	°C	°C	°F
−40	−40	−38	−36.4	80	26.7	18	64.4	215	101.7	80	176
−35	−37.2	−36	−32.8	85	29.4	20	68	220	104.4	85	185
−30	−34.4	−34	−29.2	90	32.2	22	71.6	225	107.2	90	194
−25	−31.7	−32	−25.6	95	35.0	24	75.2	230	110.0	95	202
−20	−28.9	−30	−22	100	37.8	26	78.8	235	112.8	100	212
−15	−26.1	−28	−18.4	105	40.6	28	82.4	240	115.6	105	221
−10	−23.3	−26	−14.8	110	43.3	30	86	245	118.3	110	230
−5	−20.6	−24	−11.2	115	46.1	32	89.6	250	121.1	115	239
0	−17.8	−22	−7.6	120	48.9	34	93.2	255	123.9	120	248
1	−17.2	−20	−4	125	51.7	36	96.8	260	126.6	125	257
2	−16.7	−18	−0.4	130	54.4	38	100.4	265	129.4	130	266
3	−16.1	−16	3.2	135	57.2	40	104	270	132.2	135	275
4	−15.6	−14	6.8	140	60.0	42	107.6	275	135.0	140	284
5	−15.0	−12	10.4	145	62.8	44	112.2	280	137.8	145	293
10	−12.2	−10	14	150	65.6	46	114.8	285	140.6	150	302
15	−9.4	−8	17.6	155	68.3	48	118.4	290	143.3	155	311
20	−6.7	−6	21.2	160	71.1	50	122	295	146.1	160	320
25	−3.9	−4	24.8	165	73.9	52	125.6	300	148.9	165	329
30	−1.1	−2	28.4	170	76.7	54	129.2	305	151.7	170	338
35	1.7	0	32	175	79.4	56	132.8	310	154.4	175	347
40	4.4	2	35.6	180	82.2	58	136.4	315	157.2	180	356
45	7.2	4	39.2	185	85.0	60	140	320	160.0	185	365
50	10.0	6	42.8	190	87.8	62	143.6	325	162.8	190	374
55	12.8	8	46.4	195	90.6	64	147.2	330	165.6	195	383
60	15.6	10	50	200	93.3	66	150.8	335	168.3	200	392
65	18.3	12	53.6	205	96.1	68	154.4	340	171.1	205	401
70	21.1	14	57.2	210	98.9	70	158	345	173.9	210	410
75	23.9	16	60.8	212	100.0	75	167	350	176.7	215	414

MECHANIC'S DATA

ENGLISH TO METRIC CONVERSION: LENGTH

To convert inches (ins.) to millimeters (mm): multiply number of inches by 25.4

To convert millimeters (mm) to inches (ins.): multiply number of millimeters by .04

Inches	Decimals	Milli-meters	Inches to millimeters inches	mm	Inches	Decimals	Milli-meters	Inches to millimeters inches	mm
1/64	0.051625	0.3969	0.0001	0.00254	33/64	0.515625	13.0969	0.6	15.24
1/32	0.03125	0.7937	0.0002	0.00508	17/32	0.53125	13.4937	0.7	17.78
3/64	0.046875	1.1906	0.0003	0.00762	35/64	0.546875	13.8906	0.8	20.32
1/16	0.0625	1.5875	0.0004	0.01016	9/16	0.5625	14.2875	0.9	22.86
5/64	0.078125	1.9844	0.0005	0.01270	37/64	0.578125	14.6844	1	25.4
3/32	0.09375	2.3812	0.0006	0.01524	19/32	0.59375	15.0812	2	50.8
7/64	0.109375	2.7781	0.0007	0.01778	39/64	0.609375	15.4781	3	76.2
1/8	0.125	3.1750	0.0008	0.02032	5/8	0.625	15.8750	4	101.6
9/64	0.140625	3.5719	0.0009	0.02286	41/64	0.640625	16.2719	5	127.0
5/32	0.15625	3.9687	0.001	0.0254	21/32	0.65625	16.6687	6	152.4
11/64	0.171875	4.3656	0.002	0.0508	43/64	0.671875	17.0656	7	177.8
3/16	0.1875	4.7625	0.003	0.0762	11/16	0.6875	17.4625	8	203.2
13/64	0.203125	5.1594	0.004	0.1016	45/64	0.703125	17.8594	9	228.6
7/32	0.21875	5.5562	0.005	0.1270	23/32	0.71875	18.2562	10	254.0
15/64	0.234375	5.9531	0.006	0.1524	47/64	0.734375	18.6531	11	279.4
1/4	0.25	6.3500	0.007	0.1778	3/4	0.75	19.0500	12	304.8
17/64	0.265625	6.7469	0.008	0.2032	49/64	0.765625	19.4469	13	330.2
9/32	0.28125	7.1437	0.009	0.2286	25/32	0.78125	19.8437	14	355.6
19/64	0.296875	7.5406	0.01	0.254	51/64	0.796875	20.2406	15	381.0
5/16	0.3125	7.9375	0.02	0.508	13/16	0.8125	20.6375	16	406.4
21/64	0.328125	8.3344	0.03	0.762	53/64	0.828125	21.0344	17	431.8
11/32	0.34375	8.7312	0.04	1.016	27/32	0.84375	21.4312	18	457.2
23/64	0.359375	9.1281	0.05	1.270	55/64	0.859375	21.8281	19	482.6
3/8	0.375	9.5250	0.06	1.524	7/8	0.875	22.2250	20	508.0
25/64	0.390625	9.9219	0.07	1.778	57/64	0.890625	22.6219	21	533.4
13/32	0.40625	10.3187	0.08	2.032	29/32	0.90625	23.0187	22	558.8
27/64	0.421875	10.7156	0.09	2.286	59/64	0.921875	23.4156	23	584.2
7/16	0.4375	11.1125	0.1	2.54	15/16	0.9375	23.8125	24	609.6
29/64	0.453125	11.5094	0.2	5.08	61/64	0.953125	24.2094	25	635.0
15/32	0.46875	11.9062	0.3	7.62	31/32	0.96875	24.6062	26	660.4
31/64	0.484375	12.3031	0.4	10.16	63/64	0.984375	25.0031	27	690.6
1/2	0.5	12.7000	0.5	12.70					

ENGLISH TO METRIC CONVERSION: TORQUE

To convert foot-pounds (ft. lbs.) to Newton-meters: multiply the number of ft. lbs. by 1.3

To convert inch-pounds (in. lbs.) to Newton-meters: multiply the number of in. lbs. by .11

in lbs	N-m	in lbs	N-m	in lbs	N-m	in lbs	N-m	in lbs	N-m
0.1	0.01	1	0.11	10	1.13	19	2.15	28	3.16
0.2	0.02	2	0.23	11	1.24	20	2.26	29	3.28
0.3	0.03	3	0.34	12	1.36	21	2.37	30	3.39
0.4	0.04	4	0.45	13	1.47	22	2.49	31	3.50
0.5	0.06	5	0.56	14	1.58	23	2.60	32	3.62
0.6	0.07	6	0.68	15	1.70	24	2.71	33	3.73
0.7	0.08	7	0.78	16	1.81	25	2.82	34	3.84
0.8	0.09	8	0.90	17	1.92	26	2.94	35	3.95
0.9	0.10	9	1.02	18	2.03	27	3.05	36	4.07

ENGLISH TO METRIC CONVERSION: TORQUE

Torque is now expressed as either foot-pounds (ft./lbs.) or inch-pounds (in./lbs.). The metric measurement unit for torque is the Newton-meter (Nm). This unit—the Nm—will be used for all SI metric torque references, both the present ft./lbs. and in./lbs.

ft lbs	N-m	ft lbs	N-m	ft lbs	N-m	ft lbs	N-m
0.1	0.1	33	44.7	74	100.3	115	155.9
0.2	0.3	34	46.1	75	101.7	116	157.3
0.3	0.4	35	47.4	76	103.0	117	158.6
0.4	0.5	36	48.8	77	104.4	118	160.0
0.5	0.7	37	50.7	78	105.8	119	161.3
0.6	0.8	38	51.5	79	107.1	120	162.7
0.7	1.0	39	52.9	80	108.5	121	164.0
0.8	1.1	40	54.2	81	109.8	122	165.4
0.9	1.2	41	55.6	82	111.2	123	166.8
1	1.3	42	56.9	83	112.5	124	168.1
2	2.7	43	58.3	84	113.9	125	169.5
3	4.1	44	59.7	85	115.2	126	170.8
4	5.4	45	61.0	86	116.6	127	172.2
5	6.8	46	62.4	87	118.0	128	173.5
6	8.1	47	63.7	88	119.3	129	174.9
7	9.5	48	65.1	89	120.7	130	176.2
8	10.8	49	66.4	90	122.0	131	177.6
9	12.2	50	67.8	91	123.4	132	179.0
10	13.6	51	69.2	92	124.7	133	180.3
11	14.9	52	70.5	93	126.1	134	181.7
12	16.3	53	71.9	94	127.4	135	183.0
13	17.6	54	73.2	95	128.8	136	184.4
14	18.9	55	74.6	96	130.2	137	185.7
15	20.3	56	75.9	97	131.5	138	187.1
16	21.7	57	77.3	98	132.9	139	188.5
17	23.0	58	78.6	99	134.2	140	189.8
18	24.4	59	80.0	100	135.6	141	191.2
19	25.8	60	81.4	101	136.9	142	192.5
20	27.1	61	82.7	102	138.3	143	193.9
21	28.5	62	84.1	103	139.6	144	195.2
22	29.8	63	85.4	104	141.0	145	196.6
23	31.2	64	86.8	105	142.4	146	198.0
24	32.5	65	88.1	106	143.7	147	199.3
25	33.9	66	89.5	107	145.1	148	200.7
26	35.2	67	90.8	108	146.4	149	202.0
27	36.6	68	92.2	109	147.8	150	203.4
28	38.0	69	93.6	110	149.1	151	204.7
29	39.3	70	94.9	111	150.5	152	206.1
30	40.7	71	96.3	112	151.8	153	207.4
31	42.0	72	97.6	113	153.2	154	208.8
32	43.4	73	99.0	114	154.6	155	210.2

ENGLISH TO METRIC CONVERSION: FORCE

Force is presently measured in pounds (lbs.). This type of measurement is used to measure spring pressure, specifically how many pounds it takes to compress a spring. Our present force unit (the pound) will be replaced in SI metric measurements by the Newton (N). This term will eventually see use in specifications for electric motor brush spring pressures, valve spring pressures, etc.

To convert pounds (lbs.) to Newton (N): multiply the number of lbs. by 4.45

lbs	N	lbs	N	lbs	N	oz	N
0.01	0.04	21	93.4	59	262.4	1	0.3
0.02	0.09	22	97.9	60	266.9	2	0.6
0.03	0.13	23	102.3	61	271.3	3	0.8
0.04	0.18	24	106.8	62	275.8	4	1.1
0.05	0.22	25	111.2	63	280.2	5	1.4
0.06	0.27	26	115.6	64	284.6	6	1.7
0.07	0.31	27	120.1	65	289.1	7	2.0
0.08	0.36	28	124.6	66	293.6	8	2.2
0.09	0.40	29	129.0	67	298.0	9	2.5
0.1	0.4	30	133.4	68	302.5	10	2.8
0.2	0.9	31	137.9	69	306.9	11	3.1
0.3	1.3	32	142.3	70	311.4	12	3.3
0.4	1.8	33	146.8	71	315.8	13	3.6
0.5	2.2	34	151.2	72	320.3	14	3.9
0.6	2.7	35	155.7	73	324.7	15	4.2
0.7	3.1	36	160.1	74	329.2	16	4.4
0.8	3.6	37	164.6	75	333.6	17	4.7
0.9	4.0	38	169.0	76	338.1	18	5.0
1	4.4	39	173.5	77	342.5	19	5.3
2	8.9	40	177.9	78	347.0	20	5.6
3	13.4	41	182.4	79	351.4	21	5.8
4	17.8	42	186.8	80	355.9	22	6.1
5	22.2	43	191.3	81	360.3	23	6.4
6	26.7	44	195.7	82	364.8	24	6.7
7	31.1	45	200.2	83	369.2	25	7.0
8	35.6	46	204.6	84	373.6	26	7.2
9	40.0	47	209.1	85	378.1	27	7.5
10	44.5	48	213.5	86	382.6	28	7.8
11	48.9	49	218.0	87	387.0	29	8.1
12	53.4	50	224.4	88	391.4	30	8.3
13	57.8	51	226.9	89	395.9	31	8.6
14	62.3	52	231.3	90	400.3	32	8.9
15	66.7	53	235.8	91	404.8	33	9.2
16	71.2	54	240.2	92	409.2	34	9.4
17	75.6	55	244.6	93	413.7	35	9.7
18	80.1	56	249.1	94	418.1	36	10.0
19	84.5	57	253.6	95	422.6	37	10.3
20	89.0	58	258.0	96	427.0	38	10.6

MECHANIC'S DATA

ENGLISH TO METRIC CONVERSION: LIQUID CAPACITY

Liquid or fluid capacity is presently expressed as pints, quarts or gallons, or a combination of all of these. In the metric system the liter (l) will become the basic unit. Fractions of a liter would be expressed as deciliters, centiliters, or most frequently (and commonly) as milliliters.

To convert pints (pts.) to liters (l): multiply the number of pints by .47
To convert liters (l) to pints (pts.): multiply the number of liters by 2.1
To convert quarts (qts.) to liters (l): multiply the number of quarts by .95

To convert liters (l) to quarts (qts.): multiply the number of liters by 1.06
To convert gallons (gals.) to liters (l): multiply the number of gallons by 3.8
To convert liters (l) to gallons (gals.): multiply the number of liters by .26

gals	liters	qts	liters	pts	liters
0.1	0.38	0.1	0.10	0.1	0.05
0.2	0.76	0.2	0.19	0.2	0.10
0.3	1.1	0.3	0.28	0.3	0.14
0.4	1.5	0.4	0.38	0.4	0.19
0.5	1.9	0.5	0.47	0.5	0.24
0.6	2.3	0.6	0.57	0.6	0.28
0.7	2.6	0.7	0.66	0.7	0.33
0.8	3.0	0.8	0.76	0.8	0.38
0.9	3.4	0.9	0.85	0.9	0.43
1	3.8	1	1.0	1	0.5
2	7.6	2	1.9	2	1.0
3	11.4	3	2.8	3	1.4
4	15.1	4	3.8	4	1.9
5	18.9	5	4.7	5	2.4
6	22.7	6	5.7	6	2.8
7	26.5	7	6.6	7	3.3
8	30.3	8	7.6	8	3.8
9	34.1	9	8.5	9	4.3
10	37.8	10	9.5	10	4.7
11	41.6	11	10.4	11	5.2
12	45.4	12	11.4	12	5.7
13	49.2	13	12.3	13	6.2
14	53.0	14	13.2	14	6.6
15	56.8	15	14.2	15	7.1
16	60.6	16	15.1	16	7.6
17	64.3	17	16.1	17	8.0
18	68.1	18	17.0	18	8.5
19	71.9	19	18.0	19	9.0
20	75.7	20	18.9	20	9.5
21	79.5	21	19.9	21	9.9
22	83.2	22	20.8	22	10.4
23	87.0	23	21.8	23	10.9
24	90.8	24	22.7	24	11.4
25	94.6	25	23.6	25	11.8
26	98.4	26	24.6	26	12.3
27	102.2	27	25.5	27	12.8
28	106.0	28	26.5	28	13.2
29	110.0	29	27.4	29	13.7
30	113.5	30	28.4	30	14.2

ENGLISH TO METRIC CONVERSION: PRESSURE

The basic unit of pressure measurement used today is expressed as pounds per square inch (psi). The metric unit for psi will be the kilopascal (kPa). This will apply to either fluid pressure or air pressure, and will be frequently seen in tire pressure readings, oil pressure specifications, fuel pump pressure, etc.

To convert pounds per square inch (psi) to kilopascals (kPa): multiply the number of psi by 6.89

Psi	kPa	Psi	kPa	Psi	kPa	Psi	kPa
0.1	0.7	37	255.1	82	565.4	127	875.6
0.2	1.4	38	262.0	83	572.3	128	882.5
0.3	2.1	39	268.9	84	579.2	129	889.4
0.4	2.8	40	275.8	85	586.0	130	896.3
0.5	3.4	41	282.7	86	592.9	131	903.2
0.6	4.1	42	289.6	87	599.8	132	910.1
0.7	4.8	43	296.5	88	606.7	133	917.0
0.8	5.5	44	303.4	89	613.6	134	923.9
0.9	6.2	45	310.3	90	620.5	135	930.8
1	6.9	46	317.2	91	627.4	136	937.7
2	13.8	47	324.0	92	634.3	137	944.6
3	20.7	48	331.0	93	641.2	138	951.5
4	27.6	49	337.8	94	648.1	139	958.4
5	34.5	50	344.7	95	655.0	140	965.2
6	41.4	51	351.6	96	661.9	141	972.2
7	48.3	52	358.5	97	668.8	142	979.0
8	55.2	53	365.4	98	675.7	143	985.9
9	62.1	54	372.3	99	682.6	144	992.8
10	69.0	55	379.2	100	689.5	145	999.7
11	75.8	56	386.1	101	696.4	146	1006.6
12	82.7	57	393.0	102	703.3	147	1013.5
13	89.6	58	399.9	103	710.2	148	1020.4
14	96.5	59	406.8	104	717.0	149	1027.3
15	103.4	60	413.7	105	723.9	150	1034.2
16	110.3	61	420.6	106	730.8	151	1041.1
17	117.2	62	427.5	107	737.7	152	1048.0
18	124.1	63	434.4	108	744.6	153	1054.9
19	131.0	64	441.3	109	751.5	154	1061.8
20	137.9	65	448.2	110	758.4	155	1068.7
21	144.8	66	455.0	111	765.3	156	1075.6
22	151.7	67	461.9	112	772.2	157	1082.5
23	158.6	68	468.8	113	779.1	158	1089.4
24	165.5	69	475.7	114	786.0	159	1096.3
25	172.4	70	482.6	115	792.9	160	1103.2
26	179.3	71	489.5	116	799.8	161	1110.0
27	186.2	72	496.4	117	806.7	162	1116.9
28	193.0	73	503.3	118	813.6	163	1123.8
29	200.0	74	510.2	119	820.5	164	1130.7
30	206.8	75	517.1	120	827.4	165	1137.6
31	213.7	76	524.0	121	834.3	166	1144.5
32	220.6	77	530.9	122	841.2	167	1151.4
33	227.5	78	537.8	123	848.0	168	1158.3
34	234.4	79	544.7	124	854.9	169	1165.2
35	241.3	80	551.6	125	861.8	170	1172.1
36	248.2	81	558.5	126	868.7	171	1179.0

ENGLISH TO METRIC CONVERSION: PRESSURE

The basic unit of pressure measurement used today is expressed as pounds per square inch (psi). The metric unit for psi will be the kilopascal (kPa). This will apply to either fluid pressure or air pressure, and will be frequently seen in tire pressure readings, oil pressure specifications, fuel pump pressure, etc.

To convert pounds per square inch (psi) to kilopascals (kPa): multiply the number of psi by 6.89

Psi	kPa	Psi	kPa	Psi	kPa	Psi	kPa
172	1185.9	216	1489.3	260	1792.6	304	2096.0
173	1192.8	217	1496.2	261	1799.5	305	2102.9
174	1199.7	218	1503.1	262	1806.4	306	2109.8
175	1206.6	219	1510.0	263	1813.3	307	2116.7
176	1213.5	220	1516.8	264	1820.2	308	2123.6
177	1220.4	221	1523.7	265	1827.1	309	2130.5
178	1227.3	222	1530.6	266	1834.0	310	2137.4
179	1234.2	223	1537.5	267	1840.9	311	2144.3
180	1241.0	224	1544.4	268	1847.8	312	2151.2
181	1247.9	225	1551.3	269	1854.7	313	2158.1
182	1254.8	226	1558.2	270	1861.6	314	2164.9
183	1261.7	227	1565.1	271	1868.5	315	2171.8
184	1268.6	228	1572.0	272	1875.4	316	2178.7
185	1275.5	229	1578.9	273	1882.3	317	2185.6
186	1282.4	230	1585.8	274	1889.2	318	2192.5
187	1289.3	231	1592.7	275	1896.1	319	2199.4
188	1296.2	232	1599.6	276	1903.0	320	2206.3
189	1303.1	233	1606.5	277	1909.8	321	2213.2
190	1310.0	234	1613.4	278	1916.7	322	2220.1
191	1316.9	235	1620.3	279	1923.6	323	2227.0
192	1323.8	236	1627.2	280	1930.5	324	2233.9
193	1330.7	237	1634.1	281	1937.4	325	2240.8
194	1337.6	238	1641.0	282	1944.3	326	2247.7
195	1344.5	239	1647.8	283	1951.2	327	2254.6
196	1351.4	240	1654.7	284	1958.1	328	2261.5
197	1358.3	241	1661.6	285	1965.0	329	2268.4
198	1365.2	242	1668.5	286	1971.9	330	2275.3
199	1372.0	243	1675.4	287	1978.8	331	2282.2
200	1378.9	244	1682.3	288	1985.7	332	2289.1
201	1385.8	245	1689.2	289	1992.6	333	2295.9
202	1392.7	246	1696.1	290	1999.5	334	2302.8
203	1399.6	247	1703.0	291	2006.4	335	2309.7
204	1406.5	248	1709.9	292	2013.3	336	2316.6
205	1413.4	249	1716.8	293	2020.2	337	2323.5
206	1420.3	250	1723.7	294	2027.1	338	2330.4
207	1427.2	251	1730.6	295	2034.0	339	2337.3
208	1434.1	252	1737.5	296	2040.8	240	2344.2
209	1441.0	253	1744.4	297	2047.7	341	2351.1
210	1447.9	254	1751.3	298	2054.6	342	2358.0
211	1454.8	255	1758.2	299	2061.5	343	2364.9
212	1461.7	256	1765.1	300	2068.4	344	2371.8
213	1468.7	257	1772.0	301	2075.3	345	2378.7
214	1475.5	258	1778.8	302	2082.2	346	2385.6
215	1482.4	259	1785.7	303	2089.1	347	2392.5